National Directory of

Corporate Public Affairs

34th Edition

A profile of the
public and government affairs
programs and executives in America's
most influential corporations

Columbia Books, Inc.
Bethesda, MD

Managing Editor: Tara McCortney
Editorial Director: Duncan J. Bell
Project Managers: Adem Gokturk
Saleh Karaman

Thirty-Fourth Edition - 2016
Copyright © by Columbia Books, Inc.

ISBN: 978-1-938939-44-0
ISSN 0749-9736

Columbia Books, Inc.

4340 East-West Highway, Suite 300
Bethesda, MD 20814

Toll-Free: (888) 265-0600
Editorial Office: (202) 464-1662

National Directory of
Corporate Public Affairs
34th Edition

Table Of Contents

Organization and Use of This Directory

This book offers a profile of the corporate public affairs profession in the United States — identifying the key people in that important community and including the principal corporate offices from which the many forms of public affairs activities are conducted.

Companies selected for inclusion were identified as having an active public or government affairs program. Many are involved in federal lobbying, either through their in-house government affairs staff, or through an outside consultant. Others have active Political Action Committees (PACs) or support their communities through corporate philanthropic or volunteer programs. Over one-fifth of the companies listed maintain their own offices in Washington, DC. Almost all have at least one person charged with representing the company before the public and/or government.

Individuals included in this directory are those identified as having responsibilities in one of the following areas:

- Community Affairs
- Corporate Philanthropy
- Corporate Communications
- Government Affairs/Relations
- Human Resources
- Investor Relations
- Issues Management
- Legal Affairs
- Political Action
- Public Affairs/Corporate Affairs
- Public or Media Relations
- Regulatory Affairs/Compliance

The main index in this volume, The Companies, alphabetically catalogues 3,400 of the most influential companies in the United States and provides details on their public affairs-related activities and personnel. Listings include:

- Brief company description
- Size indicators (Annual Revenues and Number Employees)
- Key identifiers (NAICS and SIC codes, Ticker Symbol, Industries)
- Legislative issue priorities
- U.S.-based Chairmen and CEOs
- Headquarters and DC Office contact information (address, phone, fax, website)
- Active federal PACs and their FEC ID numbers, contact information, contribution summaries, and samplings of recent contribution recipients
- Corporate Foundations or Giving Programs and their contact information
- Roster of Public Affairs-related employees, arranged by the office where they reside, along with their individual phone, fax and emails. Individuals who are registered federal lobbyists are so identified.

PAC contribution summaries and sample recipients published in this edition were compiled from records obtained from the FEC in July, 2016 and pertain only to the 2015-2016 election cycle. Recipients from each government sector (President, Senate and House) who received $10,000 or more in total contributions from each PAC were selected for publication. PACs with no contribution summary in their listings are those whose contributions totaled less than $1 or whose contribution totals were not available at the time of publication.

Two additional indices, the Industry Index and Geographic Index, provide further assistance in finding company listings by subject or by headquarters office location.

For more details on each company's lobbying activities and spending, visit www.Lobbyists.info, the Washington Representatives directory online.

The Companies

The companies listed here include America's most influential corporations. Each has been identified as active in public or government affairs to some degree, whether through its lobbying, political action, philanthropic or community affairs activities or because it employs representatives charged with nurturing its relationship with the government or the general public.

1-800 Contacts

Distributes contact lenses via mail order and the internet.
www.1800contacts.com
Annual Revenues: $248.70 million
Employees: 1,100
SIC: 5961
Industry/ies: Health Care; Medicine/Health Care/Mental Health
Legislative Issues: CSP; HCR

Main Headquarters
Mailing: 51 W. Center St.
          Orem, UT 84057

Corporate Foundations and Giving Programs

1-800 Contacts Contributions Program

Public Affairs and Related Activities Personnel

At Other Offices

BINNS, Kristin   Tel: (801) 924-9800
Contact, Public Relations   Fax: (801) 924-9905
261 W. Data Dr., Third Floor
Draper, UT 84020

HUNTER, Robert G.   Tel: (801) 924-9800
Chief Financial Officer   Fax: (801) 924-9905
261 W. Data Dr., Third Floor
Draper, UT 84020

KLEINMAN, Michael   Tel: (801) 924-9800
Contact, Investor Relations   Fax: (801) 924-9905
261 W. Data Dr., Third Floor
Draper, UT 84020

NEVES, Max   Tel: (801) 924-9800
Vice President, Administration and Human Resources Fax: (801) 924-9905
261 W. Data Dr., Third Floor
Draper, UT 84020

ZEIDNER, R. Joe   Tel: (801) 924-9800
General Counsel and Secretary   Fax: (801) 924-9905
261 W. Data Dr., Third Floor
Draper, UT 84020
jonathan@1800contacts.com

101 Strategy Partners LLC

Public affairs and communications.
101sp.com
Legislative Issues: GOV

Chief Executive Officer   Tel: (202) 414-6169
JOHNSON, Lee   Fax: (202) 289-3923

Main Headquarters
Mailing: 101 Constitution Ave. NW   Tel: (202) 770-2055
          Suite L110   Fax: (202) 289-3923
          Washington, DC 20001

Public Affairs and Related Activities Personnel

At Headquarters

JOHNSON, Blake   Tel: (202) 414-6169
Project Director   Fax: (202) 289-3923

1st Global

See listing on page 327 under First Global Consulting & Management Corporation

1st Source Corporation

Provides commercial and consumer banking services through more than 60 branches in 15 northern Indiana and southwestern Michigan counties.
www.1stsource.com

Annual Revenues: $236.10 million
Employees: 1,100
Ticker: NASDAQ: SRCE
SIC: 6022
Industry/ies: Banking/Finance/Investments

Chairman of the Board and Chief Executive Officer   Tel: (574) 235-2000
MURPHY, Christopher J.   Fax: (574) 235-2882

Main Headquarters
Mailing: 100 N. Michigan St.   Tel: (574) 235-2000
          P.O. Box 1602   Fax: (574) 235-2882
          South Bend, IN 46634

Political Action Committees
1st Source Corporation PAC
FEC ID: C00181529
Contact: Andrea G. Short
P.O. Box 1602
South Bend, IN 46634

   Contributions to Candidates: $4,000 (2015-2016)
   Democrats: $1,000; Republicans: $3,000

Corporate Foundations and Giving Programs

1st Source Foundation
P. O. Box 1602
South Bend, IN 46634

Public Affairs and Related Activities Personnel

At Headquarters

DVORAK, Angie   Tel: (574) 235-2128
Assistant Vice President, Public Relations   Fax: (574) 235-2882

GRIFFITH, John B.   Tel: (574) 235-2000
Executive Vice President, General Counsel and Secretary Fax: (574) 235-2882

PERKINS, Tina   Tel: (574) 235-2000
Senior Vice President, Human Resources   Fax: (574) 235-2882

QUALEY, Allen R.   Tel: (574) 235-2000
President and Chief Operating Officer   Fax: (574) 235-2882

SHORT, Andrea G.   Tel: (574) 235-2000
PAC Treasurer, Treasurer and Chief Financial Officer Fax: (574) 235-2882

2-10 HBW

See listing on page 406 under Home Buyers Warranty

21st Century Systems, Inc.

A software development company.
21centurysystems.com
Annual Revenues: $17 million
Employees: 100
Industry/ies: Computer/Technology; Defense/Homeland Security; Government-Related; Military/Veterans; Science; Scientific Research

Chairman of the Board   Tel: (402) 505-7881
HICKS, Jeffrey D.
Jeffery.Hicks@21csi.com

President and Chief Executive Officer   Tel: (402) 505-7881
ANDERSEN, David
david.andersen@21csi.com

Main Headquarters
Mailing: 212 W. Spring Valley Rd.   Tel: (972) 235-7502
          Richardson, TX 75081   Fax: (972) 644-4911

Washington Office
Mailing: 2611 Jefferson Davis Hwy.   Tel: (703) 418-9333
          Suite 11100
          Arlington, VA 22202

Public Affairs and Related Activities Personnel

At Washington Office

JACKSON, Lawrence
Commanding Officer
larry.jackson@21csi.com
Tel: (703) 418-9333

At Other Offices

BERL, William E.
Executive Vice President, Corporate Development
6825 Pine St., Suite 141
Omaha, NE 68106
bill.berl@21csi.com
Tel: (402) 505-7881

THUMANN , Marcia
Director, Human Resources
6825 Pine St., Suite 141
Omaha, NE 68106
marcia.thumann@21csi.com
Tel: (402) 505-7881

3M

See listing on page 2 under 3M Cogent

3M Cogent

Provides biometric identification systems, products and services. Acquired by 3M in 2010.
www.cogentsystems.com
Annual Revenues: $129.58 million
Employees: 400
SIC: 3087; 3577; 7373; 3841
NAICS: 334119; 325991
Industry/ies: Chemicals & Chemical Industry; Mining Industry; Natural Resources; Pharmaceutical Industry; Plastics Industry; Science; Scientific Research
Legislative Issues: BUD; CHM; CPT; CSP; DEF; EDU; ENG; ENV; FIN; FOR; HCR; HOM; IMM; LBR; MMM; ROD; TAR; TAX; TRA; TRD; VET

Chairman of the Board, President and Chief Executive Officer
THULIN, Inge G.
Tel: (651) 733-1110
Fax: (651) 733-9973

Main Headquarters
Mailing: 3M Center
St. Paul, MN 55144-1000
Tel: (651) 733-1110
Fax: (651) 733-9973
TF: (888) 364-3577

Washington Office
Mailing: 1425 K St. NW
Suite 300
Washington, DC 20005
Tel: (202) 414-3000
Fax: (202) 414-3037

Political Action Committees
3M Company PAC
FEC ID: C00084475
Contact: Dan P. Sartori
Three M Center Bldg. 224-6S-03
St. Paul, MN 55144
Tel: (651) 733-1110
Fax: (651) 733-1110

Contributions to Candidates: $151,100 (2015-2016)
Democrats: $34,000; Republicans: $116,100; Other: $1,000

Principal Recipients

SENATE
SCHUMER, CHARLES E (DEM-NY)

Corporate Foundations and Giving Programs
3M Foundation
3M Corporate Headquarters, ThreeM Center
St. Paul, MN 55144
Tel: (651) 733-1110
Fax: (651) 733-1110

Public Affairs and Related Activities Personnel

At Headquarters

BIX, Erin
Contact, Public Relations and Corporate Communications
ebix@mmm.com
Tel: (651) 733-1110
Fax: (651) 733-9973

DELGADO, Joaquin
Executive Vice President, Health Care Business Group
Tel: (651) 733-1110
Fax: (651) 733-9973

FONG, Ivan
Senior Vice President, Legal Affairs and General Counsel
Tel: (651) 733-1110
Fax: (651) 733-9973

GANGESTAD, Nicholas C.
Senior Vice President and Chief Financial Officer
Tel: (651) 733-1110
Fax: (651) 733-9973

GINTER, Matt
Vice President, Investor Relations
Tel: (651) 733-8206
Fax: (651) 733-9973

HARDGROVE, Ian F.
Senior Vice President, Marketing, Sales and Communications
Tel: (651) 733-1110
Fax: (651) 733-9973

LUDGATE, Kristen M.
Vice President, Associate General Counsel and Chief Compliance Officer, Compliance and Business Conduct
Tel: (651) 733-1110
Fax: (651) 733-9973

MCGRATH, Marlene M.
Senior Vice President, Human Resources
Tel: (651) 733-1110
Fax: (651) 733-9973

SARTORI, Dan P.
PAC Treasurer
Tel: (651) 733-1110
Fax: (651) 733-9973

Mail Stop 224-6S-03
dpsartori@mmm.com

SINGH, Jesse G.
Senior Vice President, Marketing and Sales
Tel: (651) 733-1110
Fax: (651) 733-9973

THOMPSON, Connie
Communications Manager
cthompson1@mmm.com
Tel: (651) 733-8914
Fax: (651) 733-9973

At Washington Office

BOWLDEN, Taylor R.
Manager, Federal Government Affairs, Traffic Control Materials Division
Registered Federal Lobbyist
Tel: (202) 414-3001
Fax: (202) 414-3037

CARR, Megan Ivory
Government Affairs Manager
mmivory@mmm.com
Registered Federal Lobbyist
Tel: (202) 414-3001
Fax: (202) 414-3037

GARRY, Daniel
Contact, Issues Management
Tel: (202) 414-3000
Fax: (202) 414-3037

GEIER, Thomas
Federal Lobbyist
tgeier@mmm.com
Registered Federal Lobbyist
Tel: (202) 414-3001
Fax: (202) 414-3037

HICKEY, Daniel
Federal Lobbyist
Registered Federal Lobbyist
Tel: (202) 414-3001
Fax: (202) 414-3037

RAGETH, Jeffrey K.
Vice President, Government Affairs
jkrageth@mmm.com
Tel: (202) 414-3001
Fax: (202) 414-3037

At Other Offices

FONG, Ivan
Senior Vice President, Legal Affairs and General Counsel
639 N. Rosemead Blvd.
Pasadena, CA 91107
Tel: (626) 325-9600
Fax: (626) 325-9700

HANRAHAN, Ann Marie
Vice President and Associate General Counsel
639 N. Rosemead Blvd.
Pasadena, CA 91107
Tel: (626) 325-9600
Fax: (626) 325-9700

HARDGROVE, Ian F.
Senior Vice President, Marketing, Sales and Communications
639 N. Rosemead Blvd.
Pasadena, CA 91107
Tel: (626) 325-9600
Fax: (626) 325-9700

MCGRATH, Marlene M.
Senior Vice President, Human Resources
639 N. Rosemead Blvd.
Pasadena, CA 91107
Tel: (626) 325-9600
Fax: (626) 325-9700

MELINE, David W.
Senior Vice President and Chief Financial Officer
639 N. Rosemead Blvd.
Pasadena, CA 91107
Tel: (626) 325-9600
Fax: (626) 325-9700

SINGH, Jesse G.
Senior Vice President, Marketing and Sales
639 N. Rosemead Blvd.
Pasadena, CA 91107
Tel: (626) 325-9600
Fax: (626) 325-9700

WERPY, David G.
Vice President, Associate General Counsel and Chief Compliance Officer, Compliance and Business Conduct
639 N. Rosemead Blvd.
Pasadena, CA 91107
Tel: (626) 325-9600
Fax: (626) 325-9700

7-Eleven, Inc.

An operator of convenience stores. A subsidiary of 7-Eleven Japan.
corp.7-eleven.com
Employees: 31,500
SIC: 5412
Industry/ies: Food And Beverage Industry
Legislative Issues: FOO; TAX

President and Chief Executive Officer
DEPINTO, Joseph
Tel: (972) 828-0711
Fax: (972) 828-7848

Main Headquarters
Mailing: One Arts Plaza, 1722 Routh St.
Suite 1000
Dallas, TX 75201
Tel: (972) 828-7011
Fax: (972) 828-7848

Political Action Committees
7 - Eleven Inc. PAC
FEC ID: C00549717
Contact: Keith Jones
PO Box 711
Dallas, TX 75221

Corporate Foundations and Giving Programs
7-Eleven Contributions Program
One Arts Plaza, 1722 Routh St.
Tel: (972) 828-7011

Suite 1000
Dallas, TX 75201

Public Affairs and Related Activities Personnel

At Headquarters

CHABRIS, Margaret A.
Director, Public Relations
margaret.chabris@7-11.com
Tel: (214) 828-7285
Fax: (972) 828-7848

DELGADO-JENKINS, Jesus
Executive Vice President and Chief Merchandising Officer
Tel: (972) 828-7011
Fax: (972) 828-7848

DURST, Sherri
Vice President, Internal Audit
Tel: (972) 828-0711
Fax: (972) 828-7848

GASAWAY, Rankin
Senior Vice President, General Counsel and Secretary
Tel: (972) 828-7011
Fax: (972) 828-7848

HINTZ, Scott
Senior Vice President, Human Resources
Tel: (972) 828-0711
Fax: (972) 828-7848

REYNOLDS, Stanley
Executive Vice President and Chief Financial Officer
Tel: (972) 828-0711
Fax: (972) 828-7848

At Other Offices

JONES, Keith
PAC Treasurer
P.O. Box 711
Dallas, TX 75221-0711
Tel: (972) 828-7011
Fax: (972) 828-7848

835 Consulting, LLC

A private company categorized under Consultants-Business.
Legislative Issues: UTI

Main Headquarters

Mailing: P.O. Box 14364
Springfield, MO 65814

Public Affairs and Related Activities Personnel

At Headquarters

TWITTY, John
Registered Federal Lobbyist

99 Cents Only Stores

A deep-discount retailer of primarily name-brand consumable general merchandise.
www.99only.com
Annual Revenues: $1.55 Billions
Employees: 14,000
Ticker: NYSE: NDN
SIC: 5331
Industry/ies: Retail/Wholesale

Main Headquarters

Mailing: 4000 Union Pacific Ave.
City of Commerce, CA 90023
Tel: (323) 980-8145
Fax: (323) 980-8160
TF: (866) 384-4277

Corporate Foundations and Giving Programs

99 Cents Only Stores Contributions Program
4000 Union Pacific Ave.
City of Commerce, CA 90023
Tel: (323) 980-8145
Fax: (323) 980-8160

Public Affairs and Related Activities Personnel

At Headquarters

GAMEZ, Ana
Project Manager
anag@99only.com
Tel: (323) 881-1247
Fax: (323) 980-8160

IZETA, Maider
Marketing Specialist
maider.izeta@99only.com
Tel: (323) 595-9849
Fax: (323) 980-8160

THURSTAN, Angela
Contact, Investor Relations
athurstan@99only.com
Tel: (323) 881-1272
Fax: (323) 980-8160

A.H. Belo Corporation

A. H. Belo Corporation is a newspaper publishing and local news and information company that owns and operates four daily newspapers and a diverse group of websites. A. H. Belo publishes The Dallas Morning News, a Texas newspaper .
www.ahbelo.com
Annual Revenues: $273.83 million
Employees: 1,100
Ticker: NYSE: AHC
SIC: 2711
Industry/ies: Communications; Media/Mass Communication

Chairman of the Board, President, and Chief Executive Officer
MORONEY III, James M.
Tel: (214) 977-8200
Fax: (214) 977-8201

Main Headquarters

Mailing: P.O. Box 224866
Dallas, TX 75222-4866
Tel: (214) 977-8200
Fax: (214) 977-8201

Corporate Foundations and Giving Programs

The Belo Foundation
Contact: Amy M. Meadows
P.O. Box 655237
Dallas, TX 75265-5237
Tel: (214) 977-6661
Fax: (214) 977-6661

Public Affairs and Related Activities Personnel

At Headquarters

GROSS, David A.
Vice President, Investor Relations and Strategic Analysis
dgross@ahbelo.com
Tel: (214) 977-4810
Fax: (214) 977-8201

LARKIN, Christine E.
Senior Vice President, General Counsel
Tel: (214) 977-8200
Fax: (214) 977-8201

MURRAY, Katy
Senior Vice President and Chief Financial Officer
Tel: (214) 977-2248
Fax: (214) 977-8201

O'HARA, Michael J.
Senior Vice President and Chief Information Officer
Tel: (214) 977-8200
Fax: (214) 977-8201

At Other Offices

MEADOWS, Amy M.
Vice President and Executive Director, Foundation
P.O. Box 655237
Dallas, TX 75265-5237
ameadows@belo.com
Tel: (214) 977-6661
Fax: (214) 977-6620

A.G. Spanos Companies

A.G. Spanos Companies is a family-owned builder of multi-family housing and master planned communities with fifty years of operational experience. Our mission is to enhance the communities where we build and develop projects that endure.
www.agspanos.com
Employees: 100
Industry/ies: Real Estate

Chief Executive Officer and Chairman of the Board
SPANOS, Dean A.
Tel: (209) 478-7954
Fax: (209) 473-3703

Main Headquarters

Mailing: 10100 Trinity Pkwy.
Fifth Floor
Stockton, CA 95219
Tel: (209) 478-7954
Fax: (209) 473-3703

Corporate Foundations and Giving Programs

A.G. Spanos Companies Contributions Program
Contact: Alexis Spanos Ruhl
10100 Trinity Pkwy.
Fifth Floor
Stockton, CA 95219
Tel: (209) 478-7954

Public Affairs and Related Activities Personnel

At Headquarters

BERBERIAN, Dea Spanos
Secretary to the Board and Executive Vice President, Community relations
Tel: (209) 478-7954
Fax: (209) 473-3703

HARDY, Marc W.
General Counsel
Tel: (209) 478-7954
Fax: (209) 473-3703

ORFANOS, Natalia
Director, Public Relations and Communications
Tel: (209) 478-7954
Fax: (209) 473-3703

RUHL, Alexis Spanos
Founder, Board Member and Company liason for NGOs
Tel: (209) 478-7954
Fax: (209) 473-3703

SPANOS, Michael A.
President
Tel: (209) 478-7954
Fax: (209) 473-3703

A.O. Smith Corporation

Manufacturers of residential and commercial water heating equipment and electrical products. In November 2009, the company entered the global water treatment industry with the creation of a new venture, A. O. Smith (Shanghai) Water Treatment Products Co. Ltd.
www.aosmith.com
Annual Revenues: $2.55 billion
Employees: 13,400
Ticker: NYSE: AOS
SIC: 3621
Industry/ies: Utilities
Legislative Issues: ENG; ENV; TAX; TRD

Chairman and President and Chief Executive Officer
RAJENDRA, Ajita G.
Tel: (414) 359-4000
Fax: (414) 359-4115

Main Headquarters

Mailing: 11270 W. Park Pl.
Suite 170, P. O. Box 245008
Milwaukee, WI 53224
Tel: (414) 359-4000
Fax: (414) 359-4115

Political Action Committees

A.O. Smith Corporation PAC (AOSPAC)
FEC ID: C00104687
Contact: Daniel L. Kempken
11270 W. Park Pl.
P.O. Box 245008
Milwaukee, WI 53223
Tel: (414) 359-4000
Fax: (414) 359-4115

Contributions to Candidates: $5,000 (2015-2016)

Democrats: $2,500; Republicans: $2,500

Public Affairs and Related Activities Personnel

At Headquarters

ACKERMAN, Patricia K.	Tel:	(414) 359-4130
Vice President, Investor Relations and Treasurer	Fax:	(414) 359-4115
packerman@aosmith.com		
ADAMS, Charles	Tel:	(414) 359-4000
Chief Engineer and Director, Government Affairs	Fax:	(414) 359-4115
cadams@aosmith.com		
GREENE, Joshua	Tel:	(414) 359-4000
Registered Federal Lobbyist	Fax:	(414) 359-4115
KEMPKEN, Daniel L.	Tel:	(414) 359-4000
Vice President, Controller	Fax:	(414) 359-4115
KITA, John J.	Tel:	(414) 359-4000
Executive Vice President and Chief Financial Officer	Fax:	(414) 359-4115
LAUBER, Charles T.	Tel:	(414) 359-4000
Senior Vice President Strategy and Corporate Development	Fax:	(414) 359-4115
PETRARCA, Mark A.	Tel:	(414) 359-4000
Senior Vice President, Human Resources and Public Affairs	Fax:	(414) 359-4115
SMITH, Roger S.	Tel:	(414) 359-4000
Director, Community Affairs	Fax:	(414) 359-4064
Registered Federal Lobbyist		
STERN, James F.	Tel:	(414) 359-4000
Executive Vice President, General Counsel & Secretary	Fax:	(414) 359-4115

AAA

A federation of affiliated automobile clubs. Formerly known as the American Automobile Association.
www.aaa.com
Industry/ies: Automotive Industry; Transportation
Legislative Issues: BUD; CSP; TRA

Main Headquarters

Mailing:	1000 AAA Dr.	Tel: (407) 444-8000
	Heathrow, FL 32746-5063	

Washington Office

Mailing:	607 14th St. NW	Tel: (202) 942-2050
	Suite 200	Fax: (202) 783-4798
	Washington, DC 20005	

Corporate Foundations and Giving Programs

Foundation for Traffic Safety
607 14th St. NW
Suite 201
Washington, DC 20005

Public Affairs and Related Activities Personnel

At Washington Office

ANDERSON, Nadia	Tel:	(202) 942-2050
Manager, Federal Affairs	Fax:	(202) 783-4798
Registered Federal Lobbyist		
ASH, Avery A.	Tel:	(202) 942-2050
Manager, Regulatory Affairs	Fax:	(202) 783-4798
Registered Federal Lobbyist		
BOWER, Kathleen	Tel:	(202) 942-2050
Vice President, Public Affairs	Fax:	(202) 783-4798
Registered Federal Lobbyist		
DELMEGE, Andrew	Tel:	(202) 942-2050
Federal Lobbyist	Fax:	(202) 783-4798
INGRASSIA, Jill	Tel:	(202) 942-2050
Managing Director, Government Relations and Traffic Safety Advocacy	Fax:	(202) 783-4798
jingrassia@national.aaa.com		
Registered Federal Lobbyist		
MARVASO, Kathleen	Tel:	(202) 942-2050
Vice President, Public Affairs	Fax:	(202) 783-4798
Registered Federal Lobbyist		
NELSON, Jacob	Tel:	(202) 942-2050
Director, Traffic Safety Advocacy and Research	Fax:	(202) 783-4798
jnelson@national.aaa.com		
Registered Federal Lobbyist		
ORKISZ, Artur	Tel:	(202) 942-2050
	Fax:	(202) 783-4798
PARIS, Michelle	Tel:	(202) 942-2050
Manager	Fax:	(202) 783-4798
mparis@national.aaa.com		
PLAUSHIN, Chris	Tel:	(202) 942-2050
Director, Federal Relations	Fax:	(202) 783-4798
SWEARINGEN, Megan	Tel:	(202) 942-2050
Registered Federal Lobbyist	Fax:	(202) 783-4798
WATSON, John	Tel:	(202) 942-2050

	Fax:	(202) 783-4798
WHITE, Nancy	Tel:	(202) 942-2050
Director, Public Relations	Fax:	(202) 783-4798

AAI Corporation

Founded in 1950. AAI Corporation is an indirect wholly owned subsidiary of Textron Inc. Products and services include unmanned aircraft systems, training and simulation systems, automated aircraft test and maintenance equipment, armament systems, logistical and engineering services, and other leading-edge technology solutions for defense needs.
www.aaicorp.com
Annual Revenues: $161.7 million
Employees: 2,600
Industry/ies: Defense/Homeland Security; Electricity & Electronics; Electronics; Energy/Electricity; Government-Related

Main Headquarters

Mailing:	124 Industry Ln.	Tel: (410) 666-1400
	Hunt Valley, MD 21030-0126	Fax: (410) 628-3968

Public Affairs and Related Activities Personnel

At Headquarters

CRIST, Richard	Tel:	(410) 666-1400
PAC Treasurer and Federal Lobbyist	Fax:	(410) 628-3968
GREENE, Stephen	Tel:	(410) 666-1400
Contact, Communications	Fax:	(410) 628-3968
sgreene@systems.textron.com		
KUBIK, Thomas R.	Tel:	(410) 666-1400
Senior Vice President, Strategy and Planning	Fax:	(410) 628-3968

AAR Corporation

A supplier of parts and equipment for the aerospace and aviation industries.
www.aarcorp.com
Annual Revenues: $1.62 billion
Employees: 4,850
Ticker: NYSE: AIR
SIC: 5099; 5088
Industry/ies: Defense/Homeland Security; Government-Related
Legislative Issues: BUD

Chairman and Chief Executive Officer	Tel:	(630) 227-2000
STORCH, David P.	Fax:	(630) 227-2039

Main Headquarters

Mailing:	1100 N. Wood Dale Rd.	Tel: (630) 227-2000
	Wood Dale, IL 60191	Fax: (630) 227-2039
		TF: (800) 422-2213

Corporate Foundations and Giving Programs

AAR Corporation Charitable Foundation		
1100 N. Wood Dale Rd.	Tel:	(630) 227-2000
Wood Dale, IL 60191	Fax:	(630) 227-2039

Public Affairs and Related Activities Personnel

At Headquarters

CANTILLON, Kathleen M.	Tel:	(630) 227-2000
Vice President, Strategic Communications	Fax:	(630) 227-2039
JACKSON, Cheryle R.	Tel:	(630) 227-2000
Vice President, Government Affairs and Corporate Development	Fax:	(630) 227-2039
JADOTTE, Marcus	Tel:	(630) 227-2000
Vice President, Public Affairs	Fax:	(630) 227-2039
MARTINEZ, Randy J.	Tel:	(630) 227-2000
Vice President, Business Development	Fax:	(630) 227-2039
REGAN, Robert J.	Tel:	(630) 227-2000
Vice President, General Counsel and Secretary	Fax:	(630) 227-2039
ROMENESKO, Timothy J.	Tel:	(630) 227-2000
President and Chief Operating Officer	Fax:	(630) 227-2039
SHARP, Michael J.	Tel:	(630) 227-2000
Vice President, Chief Financial Officer	Fax:	(630) 227-2039
SKELLY, Timothy O.	Tel:	(630) 227-2000
Vice President and Chief Human Resources Officer	Fax:	(630) 227-2039
timothy.skelly@aarcorp.com		
WETEKAM, Donald J.	Tel:	(630) 227-2000
Senior Vice President, Government and Defense Business Development	Fax:	(630) 227-2039

ABB, INC.

Serves customers in power transmission and distribution; automation; oil, gas, and petrochemicals; industrial products and contracting; and financial services.
www.abb.us
Annual Revenues: $38.91 billion
Employees: 140,000
Ticker: NYSE: ABB
SIC: 3613
Industry/ies: Energy/Electricity; Engineering/Mathematics
Legislative Issues: ENG; TRD

Main Headquarters

Mailing:	12040 Regency Pkwy.	Tel:	(919) 856-2360
	Cary, NC 27518	Fax:	(919) 807-5022

Washington Office

Mailing:	1455 Pennsylvania Ave. NW	Tel:	(202) 638-1256
	# 670	Fax:	(202) 737-1311
	Washington, DC 20004		

Political Action Committees

Asea Brown Boveri (ABB) Policy Improvement Program PAC
FEC ID: C00041947
Contact: Mary M Tripp
1455 Pennsylvania Ave. NW
Willard Bldg. Suite 210
Washington, DC 20004

Tel: (202) 638-1256
Fax: (202) 737-1311

Contributions to Candidates: $11,000 (2015-2016)
Democrats: $1,000; Republicans: $10,000

Corporate Foundations and Giving Programs

ABB Foundation
501 Merritt Seven
P.O. Box 5308
Norwalk, CT 06851

Public Affairs and Related Activities Personnel

At Headquarters

FESMIRE, Bob
Manager, Strategic Communications
bob.fesmire@us.abb.com

Tel: (919) 856-2360
Fax: (919) 807-5022

ONUSCHECK, David
Senior Vice President, General Counsel

Tel: (919) 856-2360
Fax: (919) 807-5022

SAINT VICTOR, Diane de
Member, General counsel

Tel: (919) 856-2360
Fax: (919) 807-5022

YAP, Jimmy
Contact, Finance Processes

Tel: (919) 856-2360
Fax: (919) 807-5022

At Washington Office

CREEVY, Jim
Registered Federal Lobbyist

Tel: (202) 638-1256
Fax: (202) 737-1311

TALLEY, Bruce B.
Vice President, Government Affairs

Tel: (202) 639-4062
Fax: (202) 737-1311

TRIPP, Mary M
Treasurer
Registered Federal Lobbyist

Tel: (202) 638-1256
Fax: (202) 737-1311

Abbott Laboratories

A global, broad-based healthcare company working in the field of discovery, development, manufacture and marketing of pharmaceuticals and medical products, including nutritionals, devices and diagnostics. Abbott acquired Kos Pharmaceuticals in late 2006.
www.abbott.com
Annual Revenues: $20.39 billion
Employees: 77,000
Ticker: NYSE: ABT
SIC: 2834; 2819; 2869; 2879; 2899
Industry/ies: Nutrition; Pharmaceutical Industry
Legislative Issues: AGR; FIN; FOO; HCR; MED; MMM; NAT; SCI; TAX; TRD

Chairman of the Board and Chief Executive Officer
WHITE, Miles D.
miles.white@abbott.com

Tel: (847) 937-6100
Fax: (847) 937-9555

Main Headquarters

Mailing:	100 Abbott Park Rd.	Tel:	(847) 937-6100
	Abbott Park, IL 60064-3500	Fax:	(847) 937-9555

Washington Office

Mailing:	1399 New York Ave. NW	Tel:	(202) 378-2020
	Suite 200	Fax:	(202) 783-6631
	Washington, DC 20005		

Political Action Committees

Abbott Laboratories Employee PAC
FEC ID: C00040279
Contact: Joellen Medley
100 Abbott Park Rd.
D312 AP6D-2
Abbott Park, IL 60064

Tel: (847) 937-6100
Fax: (847) 937-9555

Contributions to Candidates: $545,625 (2015-2016)
Democrats: $247,000; Republicans: $298,625

Principal Recipients

SENATE
BLUNT, ROY (REP-MO)

HOUSE
BERA, AMERISH (DEM-CA)
BUSTOS, CHERI (DEM-IL)
CROWLEY, JOSEPH (DEM-NY)
DEGETTE, DIANA L. (DEM-CO)
DOLD, ROBERT JAMES JR (REP-IL)

GREEN, RAYMOND E. 'GENE' (DEM-TX)
HOYER, STENY HAMILTON (DEM-DC)
KIND, RONALD JAMES (DEM-WI)
MCCARTHY, KEVIN (REP-CA)
PAULSEN, ERIK (REP-MN)
PETERS, SCOTT (DEM-CA)
REED, THOMAS W II (REP-NY)
RYAN, PAUL D. (REP-WI)
SHIMKUS, JOHN M (REP-IL)
STIVERS, STEVE MR. (REP-OH)
SWALWELL, ERIC MICHAEL (DEM-CA)
TIBERI, PATRICK J. (REP-OH)
WALTERS, MIMI (REP-CA)

Corporate Foundations and Giving Programs

Abbott Fund
Contact: Catherine V. Babington
100 Abbott Park Rd.
Abbott Park, IL 60064

Tel: (847) 937-6100
Fax: (847) 937-9555

Abbott Laboratories Contributions Program
100 Abbott Park Rd.
Abbott Park, IL 60064

Tel: (847) 937-6100
Fax: (847) 937-9555

Public Affairs and Related Activities Personnel

At Headquarters

ALLEN, Hubert L.
Executive Vice President, General Counsel and Secretary

Tel: (847) 937-6100
Fax: (847) 937-9555

ASHLEY, Richard W.
Executive Vice President, Corporate Development

Tel: (847) 937-6100
Fax: (847) 937-9555

BABINGTON, Catherine V.
President, Abbott Fund

Tel: (847) 937-3931
Fax: (847) 937-9555

BROTZ, Melissa
Divisional Vice President and Public Affairs Head
Mellissa.brotz@abbott.com

Tel: (847) 937-6100
Fax: (847) 937-9555

BURCKY, Claude
Vice President, International Government Affairs
pclaude.burcky@abbott.com
Registered Federal Lobbyist

Tel: (847) 937-6100
Fax: (847) 937-9555

DRATZ, Catherine
Federal Lobbyist

Tel: (847) 937-6100
Fax: (847) 937-9555

EVERS, Thomas
Senior Vice President, U.S. Government Affairs
Registered Federal Lobbyist

Tel: (847) 937-6100
Fax: (847) 937-9555

FREYMAN, Thomas C.
Executive Vice President, Finance and Chief Financial Officer
thomas.freyman@abbott.com

Tel: (847) 937-6100
Fax: (847) 937-9555

FUSSELL, Stephen R.
Executive Vice President, Human Resources
stephen.fussell@abbott.com

Tel: (847) 937-6100
Fax: (847) 937-9555

GROVE, Jason
Head, Trade Policy
jason.grove@abbott.com
Registered Federal Lobbyist

Tel: (847) 937-6100
Fax: (847) 937-9555

HAAS, Rosemary T.
Divisional Vice President, Federal Government Affairs
rosemary.haas@abbott.com
Registered Federal Lobbyist

Tel: (847) 937-6100
Fax: (847) 937-9555

MAGILL, Paul K.
Senior Vice President, Chief Marketing Officer

Tel: (847) 937-6100
Fax: (847) 937-9555

MASON, Heather L.
Vice President, Global Commercial Operations

Tel: (847) 937-6100
Fax: (847) 937-9555

MEDLEY, Joellen
PAC Treasurer

Tel: (847) 937-6100
Fax: (847) 937-9555

MORRIS, Kristen
Deputy Vice President, Federal Government Affairs
kristen.morris@abbott.com
Registered Federal Lobbyist

Tel: (847) 937-6100
Fax: (847) 937-9555

SENSIBAUGH, Cynthia B.
Senior Director, Government Affairs
cynthia.sensibaugh@abbott.com
Registered Federal Lobbyist

Tel: (847) 937-6100
Fax: (847) 937-9555

THOMAS, John B.
Vice President, Investor Relations and Public Affairs

Tel: (847) 937-6100
Fax: (847) 937-9555

At Washington Office

BURNES, Austin
Federal Lobbyist
Registered Federal Lobbyist

Tel: (202) 378-2020
Fax: (202) 783-6631

DEVLIN, Anne
Federal Lobbyist
Registered Federal Lobbyist

Tel: (202) 378-2020
Fax: (202) 783-6631

FORD, John
Senior Director, Government Affairs and Policy

Tel: (202) 378-2020
Fax: (202) 783-6631

KELLY, Peter
Divisional Vice President, Reimbursement and Strategic
Initiatives
peter.kelly@abbott.com

Tel: (202) 378-2025
Fax: (202) 783-6631

LEAVENWORTH, Elaine
Senior Vice President, Chief Marketing and External Affairs
Officer
elaine.leavenworth@abbott.com

Tel: (202) 378-2020
Fax: (202) 783-6631

MOSKOWITZ, Andy
Senior Director, Federal Government Affairs
Registered Federal Lobbyist

Tel: (202) 378-2020
Fax: (202) 783-6631

Abbott Medical Optics

Formerly the Advanced Medical Optics, Inc. Changed name upon acquisition by Abbott Laboratories. Now a subsidiary of Abbott Laboratories. Focused on providing the full range of advanced refractive technologies and support to help eye care professionals.
www.amo-inc.com
Annual Revenues: $571.5 million
Employees: 4,100
SIC: 3841
Industry/ies: Medicine/Health Care/Mental Health; Pharmaceutical Industry
Legislative Issues: HCR

Chairman and Chief Executive Officer
WHITE, Miles D.

Tel: (714) 247-8200
Fax: (714) 247-8672

Main Headquarters
Mailing: 1700 E. St. Andrew Pl.
Santa Ana, CA 92705-4933

Tel: (714) 247-8200
Fax: (714) 247-8672
TF: (866) 427-8477

Public Affairs and Related Activities Personnel

At Headquarters

ALLEN, Hubert L.
Executive Vice President, General Counsel and Secretary

Tel: (714) 247-8200
Fax: (714) 247-8672

FREYMAN, Thomas C.
Executive Vice President, Finance and Chief Financial Officer

Tel: (714) 247-8200
Fax: (714) 247-8672

FUSSELL, Stephen R.
Executive Vice President, Human Resources
stephen.fussell@abbott.com

Tel: (847) 935-4878
Fax: (714) 247-8672

LEAVENWORTH, Elaine
Senior Vice President, Chief Marketing and External Affairs
Officer

Tel: (714) 247-8200
Fax: (714) 247-8672

RADY, Jane E.
Executive Vice President, Strategy and Corporate
Development

Tel: (714) 247-8200
Fax: (714) 247-8672

STOFFEL, Scott
Contact, Media Relations
scott.stoffel@abbott.com

Tel: (714) 247-8200
Fax: (714) 247-8672

At Other Offices

BENNETT, Edith
PAC Treasurer
100 Abbott Park Rd., D312 AP6D-2
Abbott Park, IL 60064
pacificon@earthlink.net

ABC Inc.

A subsidiary of Walt Disney. Operates the ABC Television Network, the ABC Radio Network, and various television and radio stations.
www.abc.go.com
Annual Revenues: $1.64 billion
Employees: 22,000
Industry/ies: Communications; Media/Mass Communication

Main Headquarters
Mailing: 77 W. 66th St.
Third Floor
New York City, NY 10023

Tel: (212) 456-7777
Fax: (212) 456-1424

Public Affairs and Related Activities Personnel

At Headquarters

ROSEN, Jeffrey S.
Senior Vice President, Human Resources

Tel: (212) 456-7777
Fax: (212) 456-1424

SEWELL, Susan
Vice President, Media Relations
sewells@abc.com

Tel: (212) 456-7777
Fax: (212) 456-7909

Abercrombie & Fitch

A retailer of casual apparel. Abercrombie & Fitch (A&F) sells upscale men's, women's, and kids' casual clothes and accessories.
www.abercrombie.com
Annual Revenues: $3.63 billion
Employees: 8,000
Ticker: NYSE: ANF
SIC: 5600; 5651; 5099; 5611; 5621; 5941

Industry/ies: Apparel/Textiles Industry; Retail/Wholesale

Main Headquarters
Mailing: 6301 Fitch Path
New Albany, OH 43054

Tel: (614) 283-6500
Fax: (614) 283-6710
TF: (888) 856-4480

Public Affairs and Related Activities Personnel

At Headquarters

CUPPS, David S.
Senior Vice President / General Counsel & Secretary

Tel: (614) 283-6500
Fax: (614) 283-6710

GRZYMKOWSKI, Ron
Senior Vice President, Human Resources
grzymkowski@abercrombie.com

Tel: (614) 283-6500
Fax: (614) 283-6710

RAMDSEN, Jonathon E.
Chief Operating Officer & Interim Principal Executive Officer

Tel: (614) 283-6500
Fax: (614) 283-6710

Abiomed

A provider of medical devices that provide circulatory support to acute heart failure patients. The company focuses in developing heart muscle recovery technologies to assist or replace the life-sustaining pumping function of the failing heart.
www.abiomed.com
Annual Revenues: $230.31 million
Employees: 400
Ticker: NASDAQ: ABMD
SIC: 3841
Industry/ies: Medicine/Health Care/Mental Health
Legislative Issues: HCR; MED; TAX

Chairman of the Board, President and Chief Executive Officer
MINOGUE, Michael R.

Tel: (978) 646-5410
Fax: (978) 777-8411

Main Headquarters
Mailing: 22 Cherry Hill Dr.
Danvers, MA 01923

Tel: (978) 646-1400
Fax: (978) 777-8411
TF: (800) 422-8666

Political Action Committees
Abiomed Inc. PAC (ABIOMED PAC)
FEC ID: C00426445
Contact: Daniel J. Sutherby
22 Cherry Hill Dr.
Danvers, MA 01923

Tel: (978) 777-5410
Fax: (978) 777-5410

Contributions to Candidates: $10,000 (2015-2016)
Democrats: $5,000; Republicans: $5,000

Corporate Foundations and Giving Programs
Abiomed, Inc. Contribution Program
22 Cherry Hill Dr.
Danvers, MA 01923

Tel: (978) 646-1400
Fax: (978) 777-8411

Public Affairs and Related Activities Personnel

At Headquarters

BOLT, William J.
Senior Vice President, Global Products Operations

Tel: (978) 646-5410
Fax: (978) 777-8411

BOWEN, Robert L.
Vice President and Chief Financial Officer

Tel: (978) 777-5410
Fax: (978) 777-8411

HOWLEY, Michael G.
Vice President and General Manager, Global Sales and
Marketing

Tel: (978) 777-5410
Fax: (978) 777-8411

MAILLETT, Aimee
Specialist, Public Relations and Manager, Corporate
Communications
amaillett@abiomed.com

Tel: (978) 646-1553
Fax: (978) 777-8411

MCEVOY, Stephen C.
Vice President and General Counsel

Tel: (978) 646-5410
Fax: (978) 777-8411

SUTHERBY, Daniel J.
PAC Contact

Tel: (978) 646-1400
Fax: (978) 777-8411

Ablitech

Creates platform technologies for medical purposes.
www.ablitech.com
Industry/ies: Medicine/Health Care/Mental Health; Science; Scientific Research

Chief Executive Officer and Chief Financial Officer
MALONE, PhD, Ken
ken.malone@ablitech.com

Fax: (601) 261-1319

Main Headquarters
Mailing: P.O. Box 9135
Lancaster, CA 93539-9135

Tel: (601) 466-7050
Fax: (601) 261-1319

Public Affairs and Related Activities Personnel

At Headquarters

CRAIG, Mary
Manager, Business Operations
mary.craig@ablitech.com

Tel: (601) 466-7050
Fax: (601) 261-1319

Academi LLC

Training and security solutions provider.
academi.com
Industry/ies: Defense/Homeland Security; Government-Related; Military/
Veterans

Chairman of the Board
MCCOMBS, Red
Tel: (252) 435-2488
Fax: (252) 435-6388

President
SORENSON, Chris

Main Headquarters
Mailing: 12018 Sunrise Valley Dr.
Suite 140
Reston, VA 20191

Public Affairs and Related Activities Personnel

At Headquarters

BELANGER , Gregory
General Counsel

LUCHTEFELD, Chris
Vice President, Business Development

At Other Offices

SPANGLER, Courtney McGrath
Director, Regulatory and Compliance Office and Associate
General Counsel
1001 19th St. N., 19th Floor
Arlington, VA 22209
Tel: (703) 312-6469
Fax: (252) 435-6388

Acadian Ambulance Service

Provides ground and air medical transportation services.
www.acadianambulance.com
Annual Revenues: $358.27 million
Employees: 3,000
Industry/ies: Medicine/Health Care/Mental Health
Legislative Issues: HCR

Chairman of the Board and Chief Executive Officer
ZUSCHLAG, Richard
Tel: (337) 291-3333
Fax: (337) 291-4465

Main Headquarters
Mailing: P.O. Box 98000
Lafayette, LA 70509-8000
Tel: (337) 291-3333
Fax: (337) 291-4465
TF: (800) 259-3333

Political Action Committees
Acadian Ambulance Service Inc. Employee PAC
FEC ID: C00335570
Contact: Timothy Burke
P. O. Box 98000
Lafayette, LA 70509
Tel: (337) 291-3333

Contributions to Candidates: $48,000 (2015-2016)
Democrats: $11,500; Republicans: $36,500

Corporate Foundations and Giving Programs
Acadian Ambulance Service Contributions Program
P. O. Box 98000
Lafayette, LA 70509-8000
Tel: (337) 291-3333
Fax: (337) 291-4465

Public Affairs and Related Activities Personnel

At Headquarters

BURKE, Timothy
PAC Treasurer and Vice President, Finance
Tel: (337) 291-3333
Fax: (337) 291-4465

KELLY, David
Executive Vice President and Chief Financial Officer
Tel: (337) 291-3333
Fax: (337) 291-4465

LIGHTFOOT, Joe
Vice President, Human Resources
Tel: (337) 291-3333
Fax: (337) 291-4465

PHARR, Allyson
Vice President and General Counsel
Tel: (337) 291-3333
Fax: (337) 291-4465

SIMON, W. Keith
Vice President, Public Relations and Marketing
ksimon@acadian.com
Tel: (337) 291-3347
Fax: (337) 291-4465

ZUSCHLAG, John
Executive Vice President, Chief Administrative Officer
Tel: (337) 291-3333
Fax: (337) 291-4465

Accenture

A global management and technology consulting firm.
www.accenture.com
Annual Revenues: $30.90 billion
Employees: 323,000
Ticker: NYSE: ACN
SIC: 7389
Industry/ies: Accounting; Banking/Finance/Investments; Management
Legislative Issues: BUD; CSP; DEF; EDU; FOR; GOV; HCR; HOM; IMM; IND;
LAW; LBR; TAX; TEC; TRA; TRD; VET

Chairman and Chief Executive Officer
NANTERME, Pierre
Tel: (917) 452-4400
Fax: (917) 527-9915

Main Headquarters
Mailing: 1345 Avenue of the Americas
New York City, NY 10105
Tel: (917) 452-4400
Fax: (917) 527-9915

Washington Office
Mailing: 800 CT Ave. NW
Suite 600
Washington, DC 20006
Tel: (202) 533-1100
Fax: (202) 533-1111

Political Action Committees
Accenture PAC
FEC ID: C00300707
Contact: Thomas W. Nagle
800 Connecticut Ave. NW
Suite 600
Washington, DC 20006
Tel: (202) 533-1100
Fax: (202) 533-1134

Contributions to Candidates: $213,500 (2015-2016)
Democrats: $86,000; Republicans: $127,500

Corporate Foundations and Giving Programs

Accenture Foundation
Contact: Stacey Jones
1345 Avenue of the Americas
New York City, NY 10105

Public Affairs and Related Activities Personnel

At Headquarters

JONES, Stacey
Contact, Corporate Citizenship
stacey.jones@accenture.com
Tel: (917) 452-6561
Fax: (917) 527-9915

SELL, Robert E.
Group Chief Executive, Communications, Media and
Technology
Tel: (917) 452-4400
Fax: (917) 527-9915

SHOOK, Ellyn J.
Chief Human Resources Officer
Tel: (917) 452-4400
Fax: (917) 527-9915

STRAUBE, David
Managing Director, Investor Relations
david.straube@accenture.com
Tel: (917) 452-2349
Fax: (917) 527-9915

SWEET, Julie Spellman
General Counsel, Secretary and Chief Compliance Officer
Tel: (917) 452-4400
Fax: (917) 527-9915

TAYLOR, Roxanne
Chief Marketing and Communications Officer
Tel: (917) 452-4400
Fax: (917) 527-9915

At Washington Office

AMBROSE, Angela
Registered Federal Lobbyist
Tel: (202) 533-1100
Fax: (202) 533-1111

ARKY, M. Elizabeth
Director, Government Relations
Tel: (202) 533-1100
Fax: (202) 533-1134

AZZAM, Samira K.
Federal Lobbyist
Tel: (202) 533-1174
Fax: (202) 533-1134

CARROLL, Jim
Managing Director, Government Relations US & Emerging
Markets
james.m.carroll@accenture.com
Registered Federal Lobbyist
Tel: (202) 533-1174
Fax: (202) 533-1134

DERGE, Mary Jennie
Federal Lobbyist
Registered Federal Lobbyist
Tel: (202) 533-1100
Fax: (202) 533-1134

MASSEY, Mary J.
Federal Lobbyist
Registered Federal Lobbyist
Tel: (202) 533-1100
Fax: (202) 533-1111

NAGLE, Thomas W.
PAC Treasurer
Registered Federal Lobbyist
Tel: (202) 533-1174
Fax: (202) 533-1134

NICHOLSON, Matthew
Federal Lobbyist
Registered Federal Lobbyist
Tel: (202) 533-1100
Fax: (202) 533-1111

NUNES, Elizabeth Tamariz
Federal Lobbyist
Registered Federal Lobbyist
Tel: (202) 533-1174
Fax: (202) 533-1134

O'CONNELL, Veronica
Registered Federal Lobbyist
Tel: (202) 533-1100
Fax: (202) 533-1111

ROBERSON, Latisha
Federal Lobbyist
Tel: (202) 533-1174
Fax: (202) 533-1134

STEPHENS, Nigel
Federal Lobbyist
Registered Federal Lobbyist
Tel: (202) 533-1174
Fax: (202) 533-1134

Access Community Health Network

Offers primary care health services from general check-ups to chronic disease management to
health education accessible to all in their own communities
www.accesscommunityhealth.net
Annual Revenues: $125.35 million
Employees: 1,000
Industry/ies: Medicine/Health Care/Mental Health; Social Service/Urban Affairs

Chairman of the Board	Tel:	(312) 526-2200
KITCHEN, Denise		
Chief Executive Officer	Tel:	(312) 526-2200
THOMPSON, RN, Donna		

Main Headquarters

Mailing:	222 N. Canal St.	Tel:	(312) 526-2200
	Chicago, IL 60606	TF:	(866) 882-2237

Corporate Foundations and Giving Programs

Access Community Health Network Contributions Program
1501 S. California Ave.   Tel: (312) 526-2109
Chicago, IL 60608

Public Affairs and Related Activities Personnel

At Headquarters

BOWEN, Elaine Hegwood	Tel:	(312) 526-2086
Specialist, Media Relations		
elaine.hegwoodbowen@accesscommunityhealth.net		
GAWRYS , RN, CPHQ, Janie	Tel:	(312) 526-2200
Chief Operating Officer		
GREGORY, Kathleen	Tel:	(312) 526-2200
Vice President of Strategy and Business Development		
HENDERSON, BA, MPH, Etta Ish	Tel:	(312) 526-2200
Chief Compliance Officer		
OUEDRAOGO, BS, CPA, Mahomed	Tel:	(312) 526-2200
Chief Financial Officer		
RILEY, Eleva	Tel:	(312) 526-2200
Vice President, Human Resources		
SOTELINO, Cristina	Tel:	(312) 526-2200
Vice President of Communications and Community Engagement		

Access Partnership LLC

Network operators, governments, and equipment manufacturers in developing and executing government affairs strategies.
www.accesspartnership.com
Legislative Issues: TRD

Main Headquarters

Mailing:	1730 Rhode Island Ave. NW	Tel:	(202) 503-1570
	Suite 803	Fax:	(202) 223-2009
	Washington, DC 20036		

Public Affairs and Related Activities Personnel

At Headquarters

FRANCIS, Gregory	Tel:	(202) 503-1570
Managing Director	Fax:	(202) 223-2009
SALLSTROM, Laura	Tel:	(202) 503-1570
Director, Public Policy	Fax:	(202) 223-2009
Laura.Sallstrom@AccessPartnership.com		
Registered Federal Lobbyist		

Access Services, Inc.

Access Services is responsible for the administration of Access, the Americans with Disabilities Act (ADA) mandated paratransit transportation program.
www.accessservices.org
Industry/ies: Transportation
Legislative Issues: CIV; TRA

President and Chief Executive Officer	Tel:	(215) 540-2150
REID, Rob W.	Fax:	(215) 540-2165

Main Headquarters

Mailing:	500 Office Center Dr.	Tel:	(215) 540-2150
	Suite 100	Fax:	(215) 540-2165
	Fort Washington, PA 19034		

Public Affairs and Related Activities Personnel

At Headquarters

MCMULLAN, Scott	Tel:	(215) 540-2150
Vice President, Finance	Fax:	(215) 540-2165
SMITH, Preston	Tel:	(215) 540-2150
Senior Vice President and Chief Operating Officer	Fax:	(215) 540-2165
SPENCER, Len	Tel:	(215) 540-2150
Human Resources Director	Fax:	(215) 540-2165

ACCESS Systems Americas, Inc.

Formerly PalmSource, Inc. Manufacturers Palm OS, an operating system that powers wireless devices.
www.access-company.com
Annual Revenues: $24.40 billion
Employees: 500
Industry/ies: Communications; Telecommunications/Internet/Cable

Senior Executive Officer, Director Board, and Chief Financial	Tel:	(408) 400-3000
Officer	Fax:	(408) 400-1500

MUROFUSHI, Nobuya

Main Headquarters

Mailing:	1188 E. Arques Ave.	Tel:	(408) 400-1900
	Sunnyvale, CA 94085	Fax:	(408) 400-1500

Washington Office

Mailing:	1050 Connecticut AVE. NW	
	Suite 1250	
	Washington, DC 20036	

Corporate Foundations and Giving Programs

Access Contributions Program
1188 E. Arques Ave.   Tel: (408) 400-3000
Sunnyvale, CA 94085   Fax: (408) 400-1500

Public Affairs and Related Activities Personnel

At Headquarters

TOGAMI, Takao	Tel:	(408) 400-1900
Executive Officer and Deputy Vice President of Sales	Fax:	(408) 400-1500

At Washington Office

COLGROVE, Ann
PAC Treasurer

ACCO Brands Corporation

The Company was formed through the spin-off of the ACCO World office products unit of Fortune Brands and its subsequent merger with General Binding Corporation. It is a manufacturer and supplier of office products.
www.accobrands.com
Annual Revenues: $1.65 billion
Employees: 5,240
Ticker: NYSE: ACCO
SIC: 2780; 3081; 2782
NAICS: 326113; 323118
Industry/ies: Machinery/Equipment

Executive Chairman	Tel:	(847) 541-9500
KELLER, Robert J.	Fax:	(847) 484-4492
President and Chief Executive Officer	Tel:	(847) 541-9500
ELISMAN, Boris	Fax:	(847) 484-4492

Main Headquarters

Mailing:	Four Corporate Dr.	Tel:	(800) 222-6462
	Lake Zurich, IL 60047		

Public Affairs and Related Activities Personnel

At Headquarters

KECK, Laurie	Tel:	(800) 222-6462
Vice President, Treasurer		
MCLACHLAN, Neil	Tel:	(800) 222-6462
Senior Vice President, Strategic Initiatives		
MITCHELL, James	Tel:	(800) 222-6462
Senior Vice President and President		
SCHNAEDTER, Kathleen D.	Tel:	(800) 222-6462
Senior Vice President, Corporate Controller		

At Other Offices

ANDERSON, CAE, FASAE, Mark C.	Tel:	(847) 541-9500
Senior Vice President, Corporate Development	Fax:	(847) 484-4492
300 Tower Pkwy.		
Lincolnshire, IL 60069		
mark.anderson@acco.com		
FENWICK, Neal V.	Tel:	(847) 541-9500
Executive Vice President and Chief Financial Officer	Fax:	(847) 484-4492
300 Tower Pkwy.		
Lincolnshire, IL 60069		
neal.fenwick@acco.com		
HARGROW, Ralph	Tel:	(847) 541-9500
Senior Vice President, Global Chief People Officer	Fax:	(847) 484-4492
300 Tower Pkwy.		
Lincolnshire, IL 60069		
NELSON, Richard	Tel:	(847) 484-3030
Vice President, Corporate Communications	Fax:	(847) 484-4492
300 Tower Pkwy.		
Lincolnshire, IL 60069		
rich.nelson@acco.com		
O'NEILL, Thomas P.	Tel:	(847) 541-9500
Senior Vice President, Finance and Accounting and Chief Accounting Officer	Fax:	(847) 484-4492
300 Tower Pkwy.		
Lincolnshire, IL 60069		
RICE, Jennifer	Tel:	(847) 484-3020
Vice President, Investor Relations	Fax:	(847) 484-4492
300 Tower Pkwy.		
Lincolnshire, IL 60069		
jennifer.rice@acco.com		
SCHNEIDER, Pamela R.	Tel:	(847) 541-9500

Senior Vice President, General Counsel and Corporate Secretary
300 Tower Pkwy.
Lincolnshire, IL 60069

Fax: (847) 484-4492

Accredited Surety and Casuality Company, Inc.

Accredited Surety and Casuality Company, Inc. specializes in underwriting bail and non-contract commercial surety bonds.
www.accredited-inc.com
Annual Revenues: $6 million
Employees: 30
Industry/ies: Banking/Finance/Investments

President and Chairman of the Board
SNOW, Deborah

Tel: (407) 629-2131
Fax: (407) 629-4571

Main Headquarters
Mailing: 4798 New Broad St., Suite 200
           P.O. Box 140855
           Orlando, FL 32814-0855

Tel: (407) 629-2131
Fax: (407) 629-4571
TF: (800) 432-2799

Public Affairs and Related Activities Personnel

At Headquarters

CAMPOFIORE, AJ
Chief Business Development Officer/President of Accredited Bond Agencies

Tel: (407) 629-2131
Fax: (407) 629-4571

EMEL, Marney
Chief Financial Officer
Marney.emel@accredited-inc.com

Tel: (407) 629-2131
Fax: (407) 629-4571

JALLAD, Sharon Snow
Chief Operating Officer and Director and Corporate Secretary
Sharon.jallad@accredited-inc.com

Tel: (407) 629-2131
Fax: (407) 629-4571

Accuray

Developer of medical device technologies. Accuray is the premier radiation oncology company. The company develops, manufactures and sells personalized, treatment solutions.
www.accuray.com
Annual Revenues: $380.05 million
Employees: 1,026
Ticker: NASDAQ: ARAY
SIC: 3841
Industry/ies: Medicine/Health Care/Mental Health
Legislative Issues: HCR

Chairman of the Board
LAVIGNE, Louis J.

Tel: (408) 716-4600
Fax: (408) 716-4601

President, Chief Executive Officer and Director of the Board
LEVINE, Joshua H.

Tel: (408) 716-4600
Fax: (408) 716-4601

Main Headquarters
Mailing: 1310 Chesapeake Ter.
           Sunnyvale, CA 94089

Tel: (408) 716-4600
Fax: (408) 716-4601
TF: (888) 522-3740

Public Affairs and Related Activities Personnel

At Headquarters

DADONE, Theresa L.
Senior Vice President, Human Resources

Tel: (408) 716-4600
Fax: (408) 716-4601

LICHTWARDT, Gregory E.
Executive Vice President, Operations and Chief Financial Officer

Tel: (408) 716-4600
Fax: (408) 716-4601

MORELAND, Darl S.
Senior Vice President, Regulatory, Quality and Compliance

Tel: (408) 716-4600
Fax: (408) 716-4601

NOURI, Alaleh
Senior Vice President, General Counsel and Corporate Secretary

Tel: (408) 716-4600
Fax: (408) 716-4601

PHILLIPS, Rebecca
Manager, Public Relations and Corporate Communications
rphillips@accuray.com

Tel: (408) 716-4773
Fax: (408) 716-4601

THOMPSON, Susan
Senior Director Patient Access

Tel: (408) 716-4600
Fax: (408) 716-4601

ACE Cash Express

Provides services to bankless customers.
www.acecashexpress.com
Annual Revenues: $202.20 million
Employees: 4,000
SIC: 6099
Industry/ies: Banking/Finance/Investments
Legislative Issues: BUD; FIN

President and Chief Executive Officer
SHIPOWITZ, Jay B.

Tel: (972) 550-5000
Fax: (972) 582-1406

Main Headquarters
Mailing: 1231 Greenway Dr.
           Suite 600
           Irving, TX 75038

Tel: (972) 550-5000
Fax: (972) 582-1406
TF: (866) 223-2274

Political Action Committees
ACE Cash Express Inc. PAC
FEC ID: C00392290
Contact: Jamey S Steffes-Parker
1231 Greenway Dr.
Suite 600
Irving, TX 75038

Contributions to Candidates: $65,200 (2015-2016)
Democrats: $13,500; Republicans: $51,700

Principal Recipients

HOUSE
HENSARLING, JEB HON. (REP-TX)

Corporate Foundations and Giving Programs

The ACE Community Fund
Contact: Annie Wood
1231 Greenway Dr.
Suite 600
Irving, TX 75038

Tel: (972) 550-5161

Public Affairs and Related Activities Personnel

At Headquarters

DIAZ, Jody
Senior Vice President, Human Resources

Tel: (972) 550-5000
Fax: (972) 582-1406

EADES, Ted M.
Senior Vice President and General Counsel
teades@acecashexpress.com

Tel: (972) 550-5000
Fax: (972) 582-1406

NORRINGTON, Eric C.
Senior Vice President, Public Affairs
enorrington@acecashexpress.com

Tel: (972) 550-5032
Fax: (972) 582-1406

STEFFES-PARKER, Jamey S
Treasurer

Tel: (972) 550-5000
Fax: (972) 582-1406

ACE Group

An insurance company. Formerly (2006) ACE INA Holdings, Inc.
www.acegroup.com
Annual Revenues: $19.38 billion
Employees: 20,000
Ticker: NYSE: ACE
SIC: 6331
Industry/ies: Insurance Industry
Legislative Issues: CSP; INS; TAX; TOR; TRD

Chairman of the Board and Chief Executive Officer
GREENBERG, Evan G.

Tel: (215) 640-1000
Fax: (215) 640-2489

Main Headquarters
Mailing: 436 Walnut St.
           P.O. Box 1000
           Philadelphia, PA 19106-3703

Tel: (215) 640-1000
Fax: (215) 640-2489

Washington Office
Mailing: 901 F St. NW
           Suite 550
           Washington, DC 20004

Tel: (202) 471-2911
Fax: (202) 347-9252

Political Action Committees
ACE Group Holding Inc. PAC
FEC ID: C00348938
Contact: Karen Valanzano
436 Walnut St.
WAO4P
Philadelphia, PA 19106

Tel: (202) 347-7440
Fax: (202) 347-9252

Contributions to Candidates: $152,000 (2015-2016)
Democrats: $58,500; Republicans: $93,500

Principal Recipients

HOUSE
MEEHAN, PATRICK L. MR. (REP-PA)

Corporate Foundations and Giving Programs

ACE Charitable Foundation
436 Walnut St.
P.O. Box 1000
Philadelphia, PA 19106

Tel: (215) 640-1000
Fax: (215) 640-2489

The Chubb Corporation Contributions Program
15 Mountain View Rd.
Warren, NJ 07059

Tel: (908) 903-2000
Fax: (908) 903-2027

Public Affairs and Related Activities Personnel

At Headquarters

BANCROFT, Philip V.
Executive Vice President and Chief Financial Officer

Tel: (215) 640-1000
Fax: (215) 640-2489

COLE, Phillip B.
Senior Vice President and Global Human Resources Officer

Tel: (215) 640-1000
Fax: (215) 640-2489

DOWD, Brian E.
Member of Office of the Chairman
brian.dowd@acegroup.com

Tel: (215) 640-1000
Fax: (215) 640-2489

FERRARA, Carla
Contact, Media Relations
carla.ferrara@acegroup.com
Tel: (215) 640-4744
Fax: (215) 640-2489

KEOGH, John
Vice Chairman and Chief Operating Officer
Tel: (215) 640-1000
Fax: (215) 640-2489

KIRCHGAESSNER, Rainer
Senior Vice President and Global Corporate Development Officer
Tel: (215) 640-1000
Fax: (215) 640-2489

LARSON, Eric
Chief Compliance Officer
Tel: (215) 640-1000
Fax: (215) 640-2489

MCGOVERN, Patrick
Senior Vice President and Chief Communications Officer
Tel: (215) 640-1000
Fax: (215) 640-2489

WAYLAND, Joseph
General Counsel
Tel: (215) 640-1000
Fax: (215) 640-2489

At Washington Office

HENRY, Patricia
Executive Vice President, Government & Industry Affairs
patricia.henry@acegroup.com
Registered Federal Lobbyist
Tel: (202) 347-7440
Fax: (202) 347-9252

MOLNAR, Yancy
Senior Vice President, International Government Affairs
Registered Federal Lobbyist
Tel: (202) 347-7395
Fax: (202) 347-9252

SCHRADIN, Sarah
Director, Government Affairs
sarah.schradin@acegroup.com
Registered Federal Lobbyist
Tel: (202) 347-8994
Fax: (202) 347-9252

VALANZANO, Karen
Senior Vice President, Federal Government Affairs
karen.valanzano@acegroup.com
Registered Federal Lobbyist
Tel: (202) 347-7393
Fax: (202) 347-9252

At Other Offices

CHANIN, Johanna
Vice President & Director, Federal Government Affairs
15 Mountain View Rd.
Warren, NJ 07061
Tel: (908) 903-2000
Fax: (908) 903-2027

CONWAY, Daniel J.
Senior Vice President
15 Mountain View Rd.
Warren, NJ 07061
Tel: (908) 903-2000
Fax: (908) 903-2027

KORKUCH, MaryLu
Vice President and Director, Government Affairs
15 Mountain View Rd.
Warren, NJ 07061
Tel: (908) 903-2000
Fax: (908) 903-2027

Ace Hardware Corporation

Richard Hesse founded Ace Hardware Corporation in Chicago in the early 1920s. A retailer-owned hardware cooperative. Ace offer a wide variety of hardware and fix-and-replace type products, as well as niche items and services.
www.acehardware.com
Annual Revenues: $3.53 billion
Employees: 6,000
SIC: 5251; 3429; 5072; 5099
NAICS: 44413; 332919; 42199
Industry/ies: Machinery/Equipment; Retail/Wholesale

Chairman of the Board
GLENN, J. Thomas
Tel: (630) 990-6600
Fax: (630) 990-6838

President and Chief Executive Officer
GRIFFITH, Ray A.
Tel: (630) 990-6600
Fax: (630) 990-6838

Main Headquarters
Mailing: 2200 Kensington Ct.
Oak Brook, IL 60523
Tel: (630) 990-6600
Fax: (630) 990-6838
TF: (866) 290-5334

Corporate Foundations and Giving Programs

Ace Hardware Foundation
Contact: Kane Calamari
2200 Kensington Ct.
Oak Brook, IL 60523
Tel: (630) 990-6738
Fax: (630) 990-6939

Public Affairs and Related Activities Personnel

At Headquarters

ALEXANDER, Jimmy
Vice President, Human Resources
jalex@acehardware.com
Tel: (630) 990-6620
Fax: (630) 990-1742

BODZEWSKI, Michael C.
Vice President Advertising, Marketing and Company Stores
Tel: (630) 990-6600
Fax: (630) 990-6838

BONIFACE, Christopher
Manager, Media Relations
cboni@acehardware.com
Tel: (630) 990-6600
Fax: (630) 990-6838

BOSSMANN, Lori L.
Vice President Merchandising, Marketing and Advertising
Tel: (630) 990-6600
Fax: (630) 990-6838

CALAMARI, Kane
Ace Foundation President
kcalam@acehardware.com
Tel: (630) 990-6791
Fax: (630) 990-6838

KNUTSON, Ronald J.
Vice President, Finance
Tel: (630) 990-6600
Fax: (630) 990-6838

MCGIVERN, Arthur J.
Senior Vice President, General Counsel and Secretary
Tel: (630) 990-6600
Fax: (630) 990-6838

Achaogen, Inc.

A biotechnology research company. It develops small molecule therapeutics to treat multi-drug resistant bacterial infections.
www.achaogen.com
Annual Revenues: $19.97 million
Employees: 44
SIC: 2834
Industry/ies: Science; Scientific Research
Legislative Issues: BUD; HCR

Chairman of the Board
ROBERTS, Bryan E.
Tel: (650) 266-1120
Fax: (650) 266-1130

Chief Executive Officer
HILLAN, Kenneth J.
Tel: (650) 266-1120
Fax: (650) 266-1130

Main Headquarters
Mailing: 7000 Shoreline Ct.
Suite 371
San Francisco, CA 94080
Tel: (650) 266-1120
Fax: (650) 266-1130

Corporate Foundations and Giving Programs

Achaogen, Inc. Contributions Program
7000 Shoreline Ct.
Suite 371
San Francisco, CA 94080
Tel: (650) 266-1120
Fax: (650) 266-1130

Public Affairs and Related Activities Personnel

At Headquarters

BERTOCCI, Derek A.
Senior Vice President and Chief Financial Officer
Tel: (650) 266-1120
Fax: (650) 266-1130

HOLLOWAY, John F.
Senior Vice President, Business Development
Tel: (650) 266-1120
Fax: (650) 266-1130

WELCH, Christine
Vice President, Regulatory Affairs
Tel: (650) 266-1120
Fax: (650) 266-1130

ACN, Inc.

An internet and digital phone service providing company.
www.acninc.com
Annual Revenues: $1.10 million
Employees: 20
Industry/ies: Communications; Telecommunications/Internet/Cable

Founder and Chairman of the Board
STEVANOVSKI, Robert
Tel: (704) 260-3000

President and Co-Founder
PROVENZANO, Greg
Tel: (704) 260-3000

Main Headquarters
Mailing: 1000 Progress Pl.
Concord, NC 28025-2449
Tel: (704) 260-3000
Fax: (704) 260-3640

Corporate Foundations and Giving Programs

ACN Contributions Program
1000 Progress Pl.
Concord, NC 28025-2449
Tel: (704) 260-3000

ACN Global Reach Charities
Contact: Katie Gracz
1000 Progress Pl.
Concord, NC 28025
Tel: (704) 260-3000
Fax: (704) 260-3640

Public Affairs and Related Activities Personnel

At Headquarters

GRACZ, Katie
Philanthropy Contact
grc@acninc.com
Tel: (704) 260-3000
Fax: (704) 260-3640

MULZAHY, Jim
Chief Financial Officer
Tel: (704) 260-3000

Acorn Growth Companies

A private equity firm focused on aerospace and defense opportunities.
www.acorngrowthcompanies.com
Industry/ies: Banking/Finance/Investments
Legislative Issues: DEF

Main Headquarters
Mailing: 316 N.W. 61st St.
Oklahoma, OK 73118
Tel: (405) 737-2676
Fax: (405) 732-4141

Public Affairs and Related Activities Personnel

At Headquarters

LUCAS, Erika
Vice President, Marketing
Tel: (405) 737-2676
Fax: (405) 732-4141

BARNETT, Todd
Vice President, Business Development
Tel: (405) 737-2676
Fax: (405) 732-4141

DAVIS, Jeff
Head, Operations and Investor Development
Tel: (405) 737-2676
Fax: (405) 732-4141

HINAMAN, Robert
Head, Mergers and Acquisitions and Corporate Finance functions
Tel: (405) 737-2676
Fax: (405) 732-4141

JORDAN, Dale
Vice President, Finance
Tel: (405) 737-2676
Fax: (405) 732-4141

At Other Offices

CLEMENTS, Kendra
Director, Human Resources
2701 Liberty Pkwy., Suite 311
Midwest City, OK 73110
Tel: (405) 737-2676
Fax: (405) 732-4141

MORTON, Jeff
Chief Financial Officer
2701 Liberty Pkwy., Suite 311
Midwest City, OK 73110
Tel: (405) 737-2676
Fax: (405) 732-4141

WILKERSON, Darryl
Vice President, Strategy
2701 Liberty Pkwy., Suite 311
Midwest City, OK 73110
Tel: (405) 737-2676
Fax: (405) 732-4141

ACT-I Personnel Services

Offers permanent placement and temporary staffing services.
www.act-1.com
Annual Revenues: $627 million
Employees: 1,400
Industry/ies: Employees & Employment

Founder, Chairman of the Board and Chief Executive Officer
HOWROYD, Janice Bryant
Tel: (310) 750-3400
Fax: (310) 750-1104

Main Headquarters
Mailing: 1999 W. 190th St.
Torrance, CA 90504-6202
Tel: (310) 750-3400
Fax: (310) 750-1104

Public Affairs and Related Activities Personnel

At Headquarters

KORNREICH, Jeff
Chief Financial Officer
Tel: (310) 750-3400
Fax: (310) 750-1104

ACT, Inc.

A non-profit organization dedicated to measurement and research primarily in support of individuals making decisions about education, training and careers starting in childhood and continuing throughout adulthood. ACT test instruments assist in college and university admission and placement and in school-to-work transitions. ACT maintains a large, historic database of educational performance records that is useful for research and evaluation of the American educational system.
www.act.org
Industry/ies: Education
Legislative Issues: EDU

Chief Executive Officer
WHITMORE, Jon
Tel: (319) 337-1000

Main Headquarters
Mailing: 500 Act Dr.
P.O. Box 168
Iowa City, IA 52243
Tel: (319) 337-1000

Washington Office
Mailing: One Dupont Cir. NW, Suite 340
Washington, DC 20036-1170
Tel: (202) 223-2318
Fax: (202) 293-2223

Public Affairs and Related Activities Personnel

At Headquarters

ERICKSON, Jon
President, Education and Career Solutions
Tel: (319) 337-1000

FREIN, Scott J.
Assistant Vice President, Policy, Advocacy, and Government Relations
scott.frein@act.org
Tel: (319) 337-1686

GODWIN, Janet
Chief Operating Officer
Tel: (319) 337-1000

GOEDKEN, Thomas J.
Chief Financial Officer
tom.goedken@act.org
Tel: (319) 337-1686

NETOLICKY, Sara
Vice President and General Counsel
Tel: (319) 337-1000

SKELTON, Jennie Unger
Attorney & Agent- Filer
Tel: (319) 337-1000

At Washington Office

CARTER, Katherine
Administrative Research Assistant
Tel: (202) 223-2318
Fax: (202) 293-2223

LINDSLEY, Thomas A.
Director, Federal Relations
Tom.Lindsley@ACT.org
Registered Federal Lobbyist
Tel: (202) 223-2318
Fax: (202) 293-2223

Actavis, Inc.

A pharmaceutical company. It develops, manufactures, and sells generic pharmaceuticals. The new Actavis, Inc. is a combination of the highly successful and previously separate Watson Pharmaceuticals and privately-held, Swiss-based Actavis Group.
www.actavis.com
Annual Revenues: $9.44 billion
Employees: 19,200
Ticker: NYSE: ACT
SIC: 2834; 5122
NAICS: 325412
Industry/ies: Medicine/Health Care/Mental Health; Pharmaceutical Industry
Legislative Issues: BUD; CPT; HCR; LBR; MED; MMM; PHA; TAX; TRD

Chairman and Chief Executive Officer
BISARO, Paul M.
Tel: (862) 261-7000

Main Headquarters
Mailing: Morris Corporate Center III, 400 Interpace Pkwy.
400 Interpace Pkwy.
Parsippany, NJ 07054
Tel: (862) 261-7000
TF: (800) 900-1644

Washington Office
Mailing: 1455 Pennsylvania Ave. NW, Suite 400
Washington, DC 20004

Political Action Committees
Actavis Inc Political Action Committee Aka ACT PAC
FEC ID: C00391086
Contact: Robert Joyce
Morris Corporate Center III
400 Interpace Pkwy.
Parsippany, NJ 07054
Tel: (862) 261-7000

Contributions to Candidates: $139,000 (2015-2016)
Democrats: $20,000; Republicans: $119,000

Principal Recipients

SENATE
CASSIDY, WILLIAM M (REP-LA)

HOUSE
ADERHOLT, ROBERT BROWN (REP-AL)
BRADY, KEVIN (REP-TX)
LANCE, LEONARD (REP-NJ)
SCHWEIKERT, DAVID (REP-AZ)

Corporate Foundations and Giving Programs
Actavis Contributions Program
60 Columbus Rd.
Building B
Morristown, NJ 07960
Tel: (973) 993-4500
Fax: (973) 993-4303

Public Affairs and Related Activities Personnel

At Headquarters

ARNADOTTIR, Hjordis
Director, External Communications
harnadottir@actavis.com
Tel: (862) 261-7000

BELIAN, David
Contact, Media
david.belian@actavis.com
Tel: (862) 261-8141

BUCHEN, David A.
Chief Legal Officer
David.Buchen@watson.com
Tel: (862) 261-7000

DEFRANCESCO, Lisa
Vice President, Investor Relations
investor.relations@actavis.com
Tel: (862) 261-7152

EAGAN, Patrick
Chief Human Resources Officer
Tel: (862) 261-7000

JOYCE, Todd R.
Chief Financial Officer
Tel: (862) 261-7000

JOYCE, Robert
PAC Treasurer
Tel: (862) 261-7000

MAYR, Charles M.
Chief Communications Officer
media.relations@actavis.com
Tel: (862) 261-8030

At Other Offices

DONOHUE, Kathleen
PAC Contact
60 Columbus Rd., Building B
Morristown, NJ 07960

FENTON, James
Tel: (202) 393-1220

Vice President, Government Affairs
500 N. Capitol St. NW
Washington, DC 20001

FISK, Brent — Tel: (202) 393-1220
500 N. Capitol St. NW
Washington, DC 20001
Registered Federal Lobbyist

LIVELY, Rob — Tel: (202) 393-1220
500 N. Capitol St. NW
Washington, DC 20001
Registered Federal Lobbyist

LONG, Tom — Tel: (202) 393-1220
Vice President, Government Affairs
500 N. Capitol St. NW
Washington, DC 20001

PIPER, Ted — Tel: (202) 393-1220
Associate, Govenment Relations
500 N. Capitol St. NW
Washington, DC 20001

RAGAN, Colman — Tel: (202) 393-1220
500 N. Capitol St. NW
Washington, DC 20001

VAN METER, Ashlie Van — Tel: (202) 393-1220
Director, Government Affairs
500 N. Capitol St. NW
Washington, DC 20001

Actinium Pharmaceuticals, Inc.

Focused on the development of therapeutics utilizing bismuth 213 and actinium 225. Combines key resources necessary for the development and commercialization of Alpha Particle Immunotherapy through its expertise.
www.actiniumpharmaceuticals.com
Annual Revenues: $5.10 million
Ticker: OTCBB: ATNM
SIC: 6770
Industry/ies: Pharmaceutical Industry; Science; Scientific Research

Executive Chairman
SETH, Sandesh

President and Chief Executive Officer
DAVE, Kaushik J.

Main Headquarters
Mailing: 546 Fifth Ave.
14th Floor
New York, NY 10036

Public Affairs and Related Activities Personnel

At Headquarters

CICIC, MD, MBA, Dragan
Chief Operating Officer and Chief Medical Officer
dcicic@actiniumpharmaceuticals.com

GOULD, David
Senior Vice President Finance and Corporate Development

SHERMAN, JD, J.D., Richard L.
Director

SOHMER, Corey
Vice President Finance and Business Development

At Other Offices

KING, Betsy C. — Tel: (646) 459-4201
Director, Regulatory Affairs — Fax: (973) 344-2539
501 Fifth Ave.
New York City, NY 10017

TRAVERSA, Sergio — Tel: (646) 459-4201
Director — Fax: (973) 344-2539
501 Fifth Ave.
New York City, NY 10017
straversa@actiniumpharmaceuticals.com

Activision Blizzard, Inc.

An independent interactive entertainment publishing company.
www.activisionblizzard.com
Annual Revenues: $4.58 billion
Employees: 6,690
Ticker: NASDAQ: ATVI
SIC: 7372
Industry/ies: Computer/Technology; Sports/Leisure/Entertainment

Chairman of the Board — Tel: (310) 255-2000
KELLY, Brian G. — Fax: (310) 255-2100

Chief Executive Officer — Tel: (310) 255-2000
KOTICK, Bobby A. — Fax: (310) 255-2100
R.Kotick@activision.com

Main Headquarters

Mailing: 3100 Ocean Park Blvd. — Tel: (310) 255-2000
Santa Monica, CA 90405 — Fax: (310) 255-2100

Corporate Foundations and Giving Programs

Activision Blizzard, Inc. Contributions Program
3100 Ocean Park Blvd. — Tel: (310) 255-2000
Santa Monica, CA 90405

Public Affairs and Related Activities Personnel

At Headquarters

DURKIN, Dennis — Tel: (310) 255-2000
Chief Financial Officer — Fax: (310) 255-2100

LÉVY, Jean-Bernard — Tel: (310) 255-2000
Director — Fax: (310) 255-2100

SAKHNINI, Humam — Tel: (310) 255-2000
Chief Strategy and Talent Officer — Fax: (310) 255-2100

SOUTHEY, Kristin Mulvihill — Tel: (310) 255-2635
Senior Vice President, Investor Relations and Treasurer — Fax: (310) 255-2100
ksouthey@activision.com

TIPPL, Thomas — Tel: (310) 255-2000
Chief Operating Officer — Fax: (310) 255-2100

WALTHER, Chris B. — Tel: (310) 255-2000
Chief Legal Officer — Fax: (310) 255-2100

Acxiom Corporation

Digital Impact has agreed to be acquired by data management and marketing giant Acxiom. A provider of data and software used for direct marketing and customer relationship management (CRM). Collects and maintains a storehouse of consumer information covering nearly every household in the US.
www.acxiom.com
Annual Revenues: $850.09 million
Employees: 3,475
Ticker: NASDAQ: ACXM
SIC: 7374
Industry/ies: Communications; Retail/Wholesale; Telecommunications/Internet/Cable
Legislative Issues: BUD; CPI; FIN

Non-Executive Chairman of the Board — Tel: (501) 342-8888
GRAMAGLIA, Jerry D.
directors@acxiom.com

President and Chief Executive Officer — Tel: (501) 342-1000
HOWE, Scott E. — Fax: (501) 342-3913

Main Headquarters
Mailing: 601 E. Third St. — Tel: (501) 342-1000
Little Rock, AR 72201 — Fax: (501) 342-3913
— TF: (888) 322-9466

Political Action Committees
Acxiom Corporation Associates PAC
FEC ID: C00350835
Contact: Sheila D. Colclasure
601 E. Third St.
P.O. Box 8180
Little Rock, AR 72201

Contributions to Candidates: $34,000 (2015-2016)
Democrats: $3,000; Republicans: $31,000

Principal Recipients

SENATE
BOOZMAN, JOHN (REP-AR)

Corporate Foundations and Giving Programs
Acxiom Corporation Contributions Program
One Information Way
P.O. Box 8180
Little Rock, AR 72203

Public Affairs and Related Activities Personnel

At Headquarters

BOYCE, Katharine — Tel: (501) 252-3545
Coordinator, Investor Relations — Fax: (501) 342-3913
investor.relations@acxiom.com

CINFIO, Janet — Tel: (501) 342-1000
Senior Vice President and Chief Information Officer — Fax: (501) 342-3913

EISENBERG, David — Tel: (501) 342-7799
Senior Vice President, Strategy and Corporate Development — Fax: (501) 342-3913

GLASGOW, Jennifer Barrett — Tel: (501) 342-1000
Chief Privacy Officer and PAC Treasurer — Fax: (501) 342-3913

JENSON, Warren C. — Tel: (501) 342-7799
Chief Financial Officer and Executive Vice President — Fax: (501) 342-3913

JONES, Jerry C. — Tel: (501) 342-7799
Chief Ethics and Legal Officer, Executive Vice President and — Fax: (501) 342-3913
Assistant Secretary

MONROE, Terilyn Juarez — Tel: (501) 342-7799

Chief People and Culture Officer, Senior Vice President,
Human Resources

Fax: (501) 342-3913

SELF, Dennis
President, Marketing Services

Tel: (501) 342-1000
Fax: (501) 342-3913

At Other Offices

COLCLASURE, Sheila D.
PAC Treasurer
P. O. Box 250266
Little Rock, AR 72225-0266

Tel: (501) 342-8888

Ad Astra Rocket Company

Ad Astra is an American company that specializes in rocket propulsion technologies.
Industry/ies: Aerospace/Aviation; Astronautics See Aerospace; Computer/
Technology; Transportation

Chairman and Chief Executive Officer
DIAZ , Franklin R. Chang

Tel: (281) 526-0500
Fax: (281) 526-0599

Main Headquarters
Mailing: 141 W. Bay Area Blvd.
                Webster, TX 77598

Tel: (281) 526-0500
Fax: (281) 526-0599

Public Affairs and Related Activities Personnel

At Headquarters

KRANZ, Jean Marie
Lobbyist

Tel: (281) 526-0500
Fax: (281) 526-0599

ADA Technologies, Inc.

A research, development and commercialization company.
www.adatech.com
Annual Revenues: $3.50 million
Employees: 31
Industry/ies: Energy/Electricity

Executive Vice President and Chairman of the Board
FARMER, Russell E.
russf@adatech.com

Tel: (303) 792-5615
Fax: (303) 792-5633

President and Chief Executive Officer
BUDIMLYA, James P.

Tel: (303) 792-5615
Fax: (303) 792-5633

Main Headquarters
Mailing: 8100 Shaffer Pkwy.
                Suite 130
                Littleton, CO 80127-4107

Tel: (303) 792-5615
Fax: (303) 792-5633
TF: (800) 232-0296

Public Affairs and Related Activities Personnel

At Headquarters

AUSTIN, Nada
Chief Financial Officer
nadaa@adatech.com

Tel: (303) 792-5615
Fax: (303) 792-5633

BAGNULO, Meredith
Contact, Public Relations

Tel: (303) 513-7494
Fax: (303) 792-5633

Adacel Systems, Inc.

A developer of advanced simulation and control systems for aviation and defense. Operates in
the Global Aerospace Systems market including Operational Air Traffic Management, Airport
and Air Traffic Control Training, and Airborne Vehicle Systems.
www.adacel.com
Annual Revenues: $18.14 million
Employees: 100
Industry/ies: Aerospace/Aviation; Airlines; Transportation

Chief Executive Officer
BROWN, Seth P.

Tel: (407) 581-1560
Fax: (407) 581-1581

Main Headquarters
Mailing: 9677 Tradeport Dr.
                Orlando, FL 32837-5318

Tel: (407) 581-1560
Fax: (407) 581-1581

Public Affairs and Related Activities Personnel

At Headquarters

EVERS, Tom
Director, Marketing and Communications
tom.evers@adacel.com

Tel: (407) 581-1560
Fax: (407) 567-2080

PEARSON, Gary
Chief Operating Officer

Tel: (407) 581-1560
Fax: (407) 581-1581

TYRCHA, Jeff
Vice President, Business Development and Marketing

Tel: (407) 581-1560
Fax: (407) 581-1581

Adage (AREVA/Duke Energy)

ADAGE, a joint venture between AREVA and Duke Energy, is focused on converting woody
biomass, a renewable resource.
www.adagebiopower.com
Industry/ies: Energy/Electricity; Environment And Conservation

Main Headquarters
Mailing;   7475 Wisconsin Ave.
                Suite 1100

Tel: (301) 841-2468

Bethesda, MD 20814

Public Affairs and Related Activities Personnel

At Headquarters

DEPONTY, Thomas
Director, Public Affairs
tom.deponty@areva.com

Tel: (301) 841-2468

Adams Outdoor Advertising, Inc.

Provides outdoor advertising services.
www.adamsoutdoor.com
Annual Revenues: $102 million
Employees: 400
SIC: 7310
Industry/ies: Advertising And Marketing

President and Chief Executive Officer
GLEASON, Kevin

Tel: (770) 333-0399
Fax: (770) 333-0599

Main Headquarters
Mailing: 500 Colonial Center Pkwy.
                Suite 120
                Roswell, GA 30076

Tel: (770) 333-0399
Fax: (770) 333-0599

Political Action Committees
Adams Outdoor Advertising Inc. PAC
FEC ID: C00413930
Contact: Nancy B. Cormican
500 Colonial Center Pkwy.
Suite 120
Roswell, GA 30076

Tel: (770) 333-0399
Fax: (770) 333-0399

Contributions to Candidates: $2,000 (2015-2016)
Republicans: $2,000

Corporate Foundations and Giving Programs
Adams Outdoor Advertising and Community
2802 Paces Ferry Rd.
Suite 200
Atlanta, GA 30339

Tel: (770) 333-0399
Fax: (770) 333-0969

Public Affairs and Related Activities Personnel

At Headquarters

CORMICAN, Nancy B.
Corporate Executive Adminstrator and PAC Treasurer

Tel: (770) 333-0399
Fax: (770) 333-0599

FRAWLEY, Pat
Co-Ordinator, Corporate Marketing

Tel: (770) 333-0399
Fax: (770) 333-0599

GRANT, Brian
Vice President, Human Resources
bgrant@adamsoutdoor.com

Tel: (770) 333-0399
Fax: (770) 333-0599

KECK, Michael
Director, National Sales

Tel: (770) 333-0399
Fax: (770) 333-0599

LEVINE, Abe
Chief Financial Officer
alevine@adamsoutdoor.com

Tel: (770) 333-0399
Fax: (770) 333-0599

ZECCHINO, Rich
General Counsel

Tel: (770) 333-0399
Fax: (770) 333-0599

ADC Telecommunications, Inc.

See listing on page 770 under TE Connectivity, Inc.

Adobe Systems Inc.

Provides digital marketing and digital media solutions.
www.adobe.com
Annual Revenues: $4.26 billion
Employees: 12,499
Ticker: NASDAQ: ADBE
SIC: 7372
Industry/ies: Computer/Technology
Legislative Issues: BUD; CPI; CPT; CSP; DEF; EDU; GOV; HOM; TAX; TRD

Chairman of the Board
GESCHKE, Charles M.

Tel: (408) 536-6000
Fax: (408) 537-6000

President and Chief Executive Officer
NARAYEN, Shantanu

Tel: (408) 536-6000
Fax: (408) 537-6000

Main Headquarters
Mailing: 345 Park Ave.
                San Jose, CA 95110-2704

Tel: (408) 536-6000
Fax: (408) 537-6000
TF: (800) 833-6687

Washington Office
Mailing: 7930 Jones Branch Dr.
                Fifth Floor
                McLean, VA 22102

Tel: (571) 765-5400
Fax: (571) 765-5450

Corporate Foundations and Giving Programs
Adobe Foundation
Contact: Michelle Yates
345 Park Ave.

Tel: (408) 536-3993

San Jose, CA 95110 — Fax: (408) 537-6313

Public Affairs and Related Activities Personnel

At Headquarters

DILLON, Michael A.
Senior Vice President, General Counsel and Corporate Secretary
Tel: (408) 536-6000
Fax: (408) 537-6000

GARRETT, Mark
Executive Vice President and Chief Financial Officer
Tel: (408) 536-6000
Fax: (408) 537-6000

LEWNES, Ann
Senior Vice President and Chief Marketing Officer
Tel: (408) 536-6000
Fax: (408) 537-6000

MORRIS, Donna
Senior Vice President, People and Places
Tel: (408) 536-6000
Fax: (408) 537-6000

OFFERMANN, Stefan
Group Manager, Public Relations
sofferma@adobe.com
Tel: (408) 536-4023
Fax: (408) 537-6000

ROZEN, Matt
Manager, Media Relations
mrozen@adobe.com
Tel: (408) 536-6000
Fax: (408) 537-6000

SAVIAGE, Mike
Vice President, Investor Relations
Tel: (408) 536-6000
Fax: (408) 537-6000

WEISKOPF, Paul
Senior Vice President, Corporate Development Executive and Strategic Business Advisor
Tel: (408) 536-6000
Fax: (408) 537-6000

YATES, Michelle
Executive Director, Adobe Foundation and Director, Corporate Social Responsibility
Tel: (408) 536-6000
Fax: (408) 537-6000

At Washington Office

HUGHES, Jr., Paul R.
Senior Director, Global Public Policy
Tel: (571) 765-5400
Fax: (571) 765-5450

JOHNSON, Jace
Vice President, Government Affairs and Public Policy
Registered Federal Lobbyist
Tel: (571) 765-5400
Fax: (571) 765-5450

At Other Offices

LINDGREN, Lisa H.
Manager, Government Relations
888 16th St. NW, Suite 800
Washington, DC 20006
Tel: (202) 709-5223

MILLER, Russell H.
Attorney & Agent for Filer
300 New Jersey Ave. NW, Suite 900
Washington, DC 20001

SCHRADER, Matthew
Federal Lobbyist
300 New Jersey Ave. NW, Suite 900
Washington, DC 20001
Registered Federal Lobbyist

ADP Brokerage Services Group

See listing on page 145 under Broadridge, Inc.

Advance America Cash Advance Center, Inc.

A financial services company. Provides non-bank cash advance services.
www.advanceamerica.net
Employees: 7,000
Ticker: NYSE: AEA
Industry/ies: Banking/Finance/Investments
Legislative Issues: FIN

Chairman of the Board and Director
WEBSTER, IV, William M.
Tel: (864) 342-5074
Fax: (864) 342-5612

President, Chief Executive Officer and Director
O'SHAUGHNESSY, J. Patrick
Tel: (864) 342-5074
Fax: (864) 342-5612

Main Headquarters
Mailing: 135 N. Church St.
Spartanburg, SC 29306
Tel: (864) 342-5600
Fax: (864) 342-5612
TF: (888) 310-4238

Political Action Committees
Advance America Cash Advance Centers, Inc. PAC
FEC ID: C00429001
Contact: Jamie Fulmer
135 N. Church St.
Spartanburg, SC 29306
Tel: (864) 342-5600
Fax: (864) 342-5612

Contributions to Candidates: $66,050 (2015-2016)
Democrats: $25,000; Republicans: $41,050

Principal Recipients

SENATE
SCOTT, TIMOTHY E (REP-SC)

Public Affairs and Related Activities Personnel

At Headquarters

FULMER, Jamie
Director, Public Affairs and PAC Treasurer
jfulmer@advanceamerica.net
Tel: (864) 342-5633
Fax: (864) 342-5612

OVENDEN, James A.
Executive Vice President and Chief Financial Officer
Tel: (864) 342-5074
Fax: (864) 342-5612

Advance Auto Parts

An automotive retailer. It operates as a specialty retailer of automotive replacement parts, accessories, batteries, and maintenance items.
corp.advanceautoparts.com
Annual Revenues: $9.68 billion
Employees: 40,000
Ticker: NYSE: AAP
SIC: 5531
Industry/ies: Automotive Industry; Transportation

Chairman
BERGSTROM, John F.
Tel: (540) 362-4911
Fax: (540) 561-1448

Chief Executive Officer
GRECO, Tom
Tel: (540) 362-4911
Fax: (540) 561-1448

Main Headquarters
Mailing: 5008 Airport Rd.
Roanoke, VA 24012
Tel: (540) 362-4911
Fax: (540) 561-1448
TF: (877) 238-2623

Corporate Foundations and Giving Programs
Advance Auto Parts Contribution Program
5008 Airport Rd.
Roanoke, VA 24012
Tel: (540) 362-4911
Fax: (540) 561-1448

Public Affairs and Related Activities Personnel

At Headquarters

FINLEY, Tammy
Executive Vice President, General Counsel and Corporate Secretary
Tel: (540) 362-4911
Fax: (540) 561-1448

MOORE, Joshua
Director, Planning and Performance Management
Joshua.moore@advanceautoparts.com
Tel: (952) 715-5076
Fax: (540) 561-1448

NORONA, Mike
Executive Vice President, Chief Financial Officer
Tel: (540) 362-4911
Fax: (540) 561-1448

ROTHMAN, Natalie
Senior Vice President, Human Resources
Tel: (540) 362-4911
Fax: (540) 561-1448

SCOTT , Walter
Senior Vice President, Chief Marketing Officer
Tel: (540) 362-4911
Fax: (540) 561-1448

SHERMAN, George
President
Tel: (540) 362-4911
Fax: (540) 561-1448

TYSON, Charles
Executive Vice President, Merchandising, Marketing and Supply Chain
Tel: (540) 362-4911
Fax: (540) 561-1448

Advance Polybag, Inc.

Advance Polybag specializes in the design and manufacture of plastic retail bags for supermarkets, convenience stores, fast food restaurants and other retailers nationwide.
www.apicorp.com
Annual Revenues: $70.80 million
Industry/ies: Plastics Industry

President
NGUYEN, Hank
Tel: (713) 580-4800
Fax: (281) 207-0565

Main Headquarters
Mailing: 12682 Cardinal Meadow Dr.
Sugar Land, TX 77478
Tel: (713) 580-4800

Public Affairs and Related Activities Personnel

At Headquarters

SHETH, Janak
Executive Vice President and Chief Financial Officer
Tel: (713) 580-4800

Advanced Acoustic Concepts LLC

AAC was formed in May of 1989. Advanced Acoustic Concepts (AAC) provides solutions for sonar detection and classification, torpedo defense, advanced distributed training, learning and knowledge management systems, software engineering and systems integration.
www.aactech.com
Annual Revenues: $20 million
Employees: 200
SIC: 3812
NAICS: 334511
Industry/ies: Defense/Homeland Security; Electricity & Electronics; Electronics; Energy/Electricity; Government-Related

President And Chief Executive Officer
CARNOVALE, Michael
Tel: (631) 273-5700
Fax: (631) 273-5809

Main Headquarters
Mailing: 425 Oser Ave.
Hauppauge, NY 11788
Tel: (631) 273-5700
Fax: (631) 273-5809

| | TF: | (877) 273-5701 |

Corporate Foundations and Giving Programs

Advanced Acoustic Concepts Contributions Program

| 425 Oser Ave. | Tel: | (631) 273-5700 |
| Hauppauge, NY 11788 | Fax: | (631) 273-5700 |

Advanced Biohealing Inc.

See listing on page 718 under Shire Pharmaceuticals Inc.

Advanced Cerametrics

Producers of ceramic fibers for sensors, actuators, energy harvesters and other electrical, mechanical, thermal and chemical applications

www.advancedcerametrics.com

Annual Revenues: $1.16 million

Industry/ies: Defense/Homeland Security; Government-Related; Machinery/Equipment

| **Chairman of the Board** | Tel: | (908) 797-9519 |
| SFONDRINI, John | Fax: | (609) 397-2708 |

Main Headquarters

Mailing:	245 N. Main St.	Tel:	(609) 397-2900
	P.O. Box 128	Fax:	(609) 397-2708
	Lambertville, NJ 08530-0128	TF:	(800) 261-1208

Public Affairs and Related Activities Personnel

At Headquarters

CATANZARETI, Tanya	Tel:	(609) 397-2900
Inside Sales and Customer Service Manager	Fax:	(609) 397-2708
tanya@acitek.com		

HENDRICKS, Michael R.	Tel:	(609) 397-2900
Vice President and Chief Operating Officer	Fax:	(609) 397-2708
mike.hendricks@acitek.com		

| STANIEWICZ, Mary | Tel: | (609) 397-2900 |
| *Accounting and Finance Contact* | Fax: | (609) 397-2708 |

Advanced Concepts & Technologies International LLC

Provides defense, water, and energy technical and life-cycle management solutions.

www.act-i.com

Annual Revenues: $2.20 million

Employees: 30

Industry/ies: Defense/Homeland Security; Government-Related

| **Chief Executive Officer** | Tel: | (254) 776-9511 |
| NIGGEL, Michael A. | Fax: | (254) 776-3813 |

Main Headquarters

Mailing:	1105 Wooded Acres	Tel:	(254) 776-9511
	Suite 500	Fax:	(254) 776-3813
	Waco, TX 76710		

Washington Office

Mailing:	200 12th St., S	Tel:	(703) 418-0636
	Suite 1101	Fax:	(703) 418-0638
	Arlington, VA 22202		

Political Action Committees

Advanced Concepts and Technologies International LLC PAC

FEC ID: C00448779

Contact: William N. Ward

1105 Wooded Acres	Tel:	(254) 776-9511
Suite 500	Fax:	(254) 776-3813
Waco, TX 76710		

Public Affairs and Related Activities Personnel

At Headquarters

MCCALEB, Mireille F.	Tel:	(254) 776-9511
Director, Human Resources	Fax:	(254) 776-3813
mmccaleb@act-i.com		

| RUIZ, David | Tel: | (254) 776-9511 |
| *Aurora Operations Manager* | Fax: | (254) 776-3813 |

WARD, William N.	Tel:	(254) 776-9511
PAC Treasurer, Vice President of Corporate Finance and Operations	Fax:	(254) 776-3813
wward@act-i.com		

Advanced Energy Economy

An advocacy organization for the cleantech and green business community.

www.cleaneconomy.net

Industry/ies: Energy/Electricity; Environment And Conservation; Manufacturers

Main Headquarters

Mailing:	1101 14th St. NW	Tel:	(415) 948-6365
	Suite 1200		
	Washington, DC 20001		

Public Affairs and Related Activities Personnel

At Headquarters

ANDERSON, Jeffrey	Tel:	(415) 948-6365
GANESAN, Arvin	Tel:	(415) 948-6365
KELLER, Todd	Tel:	(415) 948-6365
KING, Jeffrey	Tel:	(415) 948-6365

Advanced Medical Isotope Corporation

Produces and distributes the medical isotopes and medical isotope in advanced diagnostic and non-surgical therapeutic applications.

www.isotopeworld.com

Ticker: OTC: ADMD

SIC: 2810

Industry/ies: Medicine/Health Care/Mental Health

| **Founder, Chairman of the Board and Chief Executive Officer** | Tel: | (509) 736-4000 |
| KATZAROFF, James C. | Fax: | (509) 736-4007 |

Main Headquarters

| Mailing: | 1021 N. Kellogg St. | Tel: | (509) 736-4000 |
| | Kennewick, WA 99336 | Fax: | (509) 736-4007 |

Public Affairs and Related Activities Personnel

At Headquarters

JOLLIFF, Leonard Bruce	Tel:	(509) 736-4000
Chief Financial Officer	Fax:	(509) 736-4007
bjolliff@isotopeworld.com		

At Other Offices

COLONTRELLE, Laura	Tel:	(212) 825-3210
Contact, Media and Investor Relations	Fax:	(212) 825-3229
11 Stone St., Third Floor		
New York City, NY 10004		

HOLDSWORTH, Adam S.	Tel:	(212) 825-3210
Contact, Media and Investor Relations	Fax:	(212) 825-3229
11 Stone St., Third Floor		
New York City, NY 10004		

Advanced Micro Devices Inc.

A manufacturer of electronic computer components. Headquartered in California.

www.amd.com

Annual Revenues: $5.14 billion

Employees: 9,700

Ticker: NYSE: AMD

SIC: 3674

Industry/ies: Computer/Technology; Electricity & Electronics; Electronics; Energy/Electricity

Legislative Issues: GOV; INT; TEC

| **Chairman of the Board** | Tel: | (408) 749-4000 |
| CLAFLIN, Bruce | Fax: | (408) 749-4291 |

Main Headquarters

Mailing:	One AMD Way	Tel:	(408) 749-4000
	P.O. Box 3453	Fax:	(408) 749-4291
	Sunnyvale, CA 94087	TF:	(800) 538-8450

Political Action Committees

Advanced Micro Devices Inc. PAC

FEC ID: C00404483

Contact: Steven S. Lucas

2350 Kerner Blvd.

Suite 250

San Rafael, CA 94901

Corporate Foundations and Giving Programs

AMD Foundation

Contact: Kristi Fontenot

7171 Southwest Pkwy.

Austin, TX 78735

Public Affairs and Related Activities Personnel

At Headquarters

COTTER, Ruth	Tel:	(408) 749-4000
Corporate Vice President, Investor Relations	Fax:	(408) 749-4291
ruth.cotter@amd.com		

| FORD, Darrell L. | Tel: | (408) 749-4000 |
| *Senior Vice President and Chief Human Resources Officer* | Fax: | (408) 749-4291 |

| KUMAR, Devinder | Tel: | (408) 749-4000 |
| *Senior Vice President and Chief Financial Officer* | Fax: | (408) 749-4291 |

| LAFORCE, Colette | Tel: | (408) 749-4000 |
| *Senior Vice President and Chief Marketing Officer* | Fax: | (408) 749-4291 |

WOLIN , Harry	Tel:	(408) 749-4000
Senior Vice President, General Counsel and Secretary	Fax:	(408) 749-4291
harry.wolin@amd.com		

At Other Offices

FONTENOT, Kristi	Tel:	(512) 602-8963
Manager, Community Relations Program		
7171 Southwest Pkwy., Mail Stop 1003		
Austin, TX 78735		

PRAIRIE, Drew   Tel: (512) 602-1000
Director, Corporate Communications
7171 Southwest Pkwy., Mail Stop 1003
Austin, TX 78735
drew.prairie@amd.com

Advanced Navigation and Positioning Corporation
Provides airspace safety, efficiency, and capacity to users of aviation through tracking and guidance.
www.anpc.com
Employees: 30
Industry/ies: Aerospace/Aviation; Transportation

Main Headquarters
Mailing:	489 N. Eighth St.	Tel:	(541) 386-1747
	Suite 203	Fax:	(541) 386-2124
	Hood River, OR 97031-2007	TF:	(800) 228-1857

Public Affairs and Related Activities Personnel

At Headquarters

BOGGS, Casey   Tel: (503) 477-9215
Contact, Media Relations   Fax: (541) 386-2124
cboggs@ltpublicrelations.com

Advanced Solutions for Tomorrow, Inc.
Specializes in product integrity, system engineering, program support, and media development disciplines.
www.asftus.com
Employees: 100
Industry/ies: Business; Management; Small Business

President and Chief Executive Officer   Tel: (770) 641-8253
DUTTA-GUPTA, Anjan   Fax: (770) 641-8328

Main Headquarters
Mailing:	295 W. Crossville Rd.	Tel:	(770) 641-8253
	Building 200	Fax:	(770) 641-8328
	Roswell, GA 30075		

Public Affairs and Related Activities Personnel

At Headquarters

HIGGINS, Phillip   Tel: (770) 641-8253
Senior Vice President and Director, Government Services   Fax: (770) 641-8328

NAGLE, Patrick B.   Tel: (770) 641-8253
Senior Vice President, Contracts, Administration and PAC Treasurer   Fax: (770) 641-8328

Advanced Systems Development
Computer service firm specializing in life cycle information technology support.
www.asd-inc.com
Annual Revenues: $20.42 million
Industry/ies: Computer/Technology
Legislative Issues: GOV

Founder, President and Chief Executive Officer   Tel: (703) 998-3900
BENNETT, Richard L.   Fax: (703) 824-5699

Main Headquarters
Mailing:	4401 Ford Ave.	Tel:	(703) 998-3900
	Suite 500	Fax:	(703) 824-5699
	Alexandria, VA 22302		

Public Affairs and Related Activities Personnel

At Headquarters

PATEL, Mary Lou   Tel: (703) 998-3900
Chief Financial Officer   Fax: (703) 824-5699

THOMAS, Dwight F.   Tel: (703) 933-3464
Director, Business Development and Government Relations   Fax: (703) 824-5699
Dthomas@asd-inc.com

WASHINGTON, Samuel   Tel: (703) 998-3900
Director, Human Resources   Fax: (703) 824-5699
swashington@asd-inc.com

Advanced Systems Technology, Inc.
A systems and software engineering firm involved in the development of computer-based instruction and training.
www.astcorp.com
Annual Revenues: $23.77 million
Employees: 300
Industry/ies: Computer/Technology; Engineering/Mathematics

Vice President   Tel: (580) 248-0321
WARFIELD, Thomas   Fax: (888) 735-5395

Main Headquarters
Mailing:	4111 W. Gore Blvd.	Tel:	(580) 248-0321
	Lawton, OK 73505	Fax:	(580) 355-8929

Public Affairs and Related Activities Personnel

At Other Offices

JEMISON, Paul   Tel: (580) 248-0321
Contact, Business Development   Fax: (888) 735-5395
P.O. Box 2305
Lawton, OK 73502
pjemison@astcorp.com

LEIPPE, Karl   Tel: (580) 248-0321
Director, Finances   Fax: (888) 735-5395
P.O. Box 2305
Lawton, OK 73502

WEBLEY, Debbie   Tel: (580) 248-0321
Director, Human Resources   Fax: (888) 735-5395
P.O. Box 2305
Lawton, OK 73502
debbie@astcorp.com

Advanced Technology Services, Inc.
A provider of a combination of factory maintenance, industrial parts services, calibration and IT solutions.
www.advancedtech.com
Annual Revenues: $133.40 million
Employees: 2,000
SIC: 3599; 3625
NAICS: 333319; 335314
Industry/ies: Computer/Technology; Electricity & Electronics; Electronics; Energy/Electricity; Machinery/Equipment

Chairman of the Board and Chief Executive Officer   Tel: (309) 693-4000
BLAUDOW, Richard W.   Fax: (309) 693-4164

Main Headquarters
Mailing:	8201 N. University	Tel:	(309) 693-4000
	Peoria, IL 61615	Fax:	(309) 693-4164
		TF:	(800) 328-7287

Public Affairs and Related Activities Personnel

At Headquarters

DEBRUYN, John A.   Tel: (309) 693-4000
Controller   Fax: (309) 693-4164
jdebruyn@debruyn.com

HEFTI, James W.   Tel: (309) 693-4000
Vice President, Human Resources   Fax: (309) 693-4164

JOHNSON, Don   Tel: (309) 693-5959
Vice President, Marketing   Fax: (309) 693-4164
dkjohnso@advancedtech.com

KOSIOREK, Jeff   Tel: (309) 693-4000
Vice President and Chief Marketing Officer   Fax: (309) 693-4164

LUTZ, William M.   Tel: (309) 693-4000
Chief Financial Officer   Fax: (309) 693-4164

OWENS, Jeff   Tel: (309) 693-4000
President and Chief Operating Officer   Fax: (309) 693-4164

PYCZ, Joe   Tel: (309) 693-4000
Vice President, Operations   Fax: (309) 693-4164

Advantage Capital Partners
A group of venture capital partnerships that raises private funds to invest in states and communities that are underserved by traditional sources of risk capital.
www.advantagecap.com
Annual Revenues: $2 million
Industry/ies: Banking/Finance/Investments
Legislative Issues: TAX

Main Headquarters
Mailing:	909 Poydras St.	Tel:	(504) 522-4850
	Suite 2230	Fax:	(504) 522-4950
	New Orleans, LA 70112		

Washington Office
Mailing:	1028 33rd St. NW	Tel:	(202) 558-9940
	Suite 234	Fax:	(202) 457-4191
	Washington, DC 20007		

Corporate Foundations and Giving Programs

Advantage Capital Partners Contributions Program
7733 Forsyth Blvd.
Suite 1850
Austin, TX 78730

Public Affairs and Related Activities Personnel

At Headquarters

DE CASTRO, Samantha F.   Tel: (504) 522-4850
Communications Associate   Fax: (504) 522-4950

LORIO, Franchesca B.   Tel: (504) 522-4850
Vice President and Controller   Fax: (504) 522-4950

MAYGARDEN, Mary Beth   Tel: (504) 522-4850
Compliance Manager   Fax: (504) 522-4950

SCHIFFMAN, Cara M. Tel: (504) 522-4850
Vice President, Regulatory Affairs Fax: (504) 522-4950

SINGER II, Talmadge Tel: (504) 522-4850
Senior Vice President Fax: (504) 522-4950

At Other Offices

DELGADILLO, Danielle R. Tel: (512) 380-1168
Vice President Fax: (512) 241-1186
5000 Plaza, Suite 195
Austin, TX 78746

MURPHY, Scott
Managing Director and Chief Investment Officer
610 West End Ave.
New York, NY 10024

RAWIE, Damon L. Tel: (512) 380-1168
Managing Director Fax: (512) 241-1186
5000 Plaza, Suite 195
Austin, TX 78746

SUBERI, Adam M. Tel: (314) 725-0800
Vice President Fax: (314) 725-4265
190 Carondelet Plaza, Suite 1500
St. Louis, MO 63105-3442

Advantage PressurePro LLC

Tire pressure monitoring system developer. PressurePro distributes to several markets, including heavy duty (Mining, Logging, Construction, Agriculture), trucking, bus, RV, trailer and many specialized application markets. PressurePro introduced RS232 capabilities with all products allowing users the ability to communicate tire pressure readings to remote locations, offices, cell phones and more. Provides a full tire maintenance program to market.
www.advantagepressurepro.com
Annual Revenues: $1.50 million
Industry/ies: Consumers; Machinery/Equipment; Transportation

President and Chief Executive Officer Tel: (816) 887-3505
ZAROOR, Phillip G. Fax: (816) 887-3705
pzaroor@advantagepressurepro.com

Main Headquarters
Mailing: 205 W. Wall St. Tel: (816) 887-3505
Harrisonville, MO 64701-2356 Fax: (816) 887-3705
 TF: (800) 959-3505

Public Affairs and Related Activities Personnel

At Headquarters

MCMEEN, Douglas W. Tel: (816) 887-3505
Director, Operations Fax: (816) 887-3705
dmcmeen@pressurepro.us

SUTTON, Robin Tel: (816) 887-3505
Director, Finance Fax: (816) 887-3705
robin@pressurepro.us

ZAROOR, Jason Tel: (816) 887-3505
Chief Operating Officer and Director, Sales Fax: (816) 887-3705
jason@pressurepro.us

ZAROOR, Vanessa Tel: (816) 887-3505
Director, Marketing Fax: (816) 887-3705
vanessa@pressurepro.us

AECOM

AECOM is a provider of professional technical and management support services to a broad range of markets, including transportation, facilities, environmental, energy, water and government.
www.aecom.com
Annual Revenues: $13.25 billion
Employees: 95,000
Ticker: NYSE: ACM
Industry/ies: Architecture And Design; Construction/Construction Materials
Legislative Issues: GOV; TRA

Executive Chairman of the Board Tel: (213) 593-8000
DIONISIO, John M. Fax: (213) 593-8730
john.dionisio@aecom.co

President and Chief Financial Officer Tel: (213) 593-8000
KADENACY, Stephen M. Fax: (213) 593-8730

Main Headquarters
Mailing: 1999 Avenue of the Stars Tel: (213) 593-8100
Suite 2600 Fax: (213) 593-8178
Los Angeles, CA 90067

Washington Office
Mailing: 2101 Wilson Blvd. Tel: (703) 528-7444
Arlington, VA 22201 Fax: (703) 522-2329

Political Action Committees
AECOM PAC
FEC ID: C00374447
Contact: Ricardo Bernal
2450 Crystal Dr. Tel: (703) 418-3000

Suite 500 Fax: (703) 418-0248
Arlington, VA 22202-4812
 Contributions to Candidates: $42,200 (2015-2016)
 Democrats: $17,200; Republicans: $25,000

Corporate Foundations and Giving Programs
AECOM Contributions Program
555 S. Flower St.
Suite 3700
Los Angeles, CA 90071

Public Affairs and Related Activities Personnel

At Washington Office

POLECHRONIS, Stephen Tel: (703) 528-7444
Senior Vice President Fax: (703) 522-2329
stephen.polechronis@aecom.com

At Other Offices

CHING, Christina Tel: (213) 593-8000
Vice President, Corporate Secretary Fax: (213) 593-8730
555 S. Flower St., Suite 3700
Los Angeles, CA 90071-2300

LYNCH, Kevin Tel: (213) 593-8000
Executive Vice President Chief Strategy Officer Fax: (213) 593-8730
555 S. Flower St., Suite 3700
Los Angeles, CA 90071-2300

MACLEOD, Ian R. Tel: (213) 593-8000
Corporate Senior Vice President, Human Resources Fax: (213) 593-8730
555 S. Flower St., Suite 3700
Los Angeles, CA 90071-2300

Aegis Defense Services, LLC

A privately owned security and risk management company. Provides government and commercial clients with intelligence-led security solutions.
www.aegisworld.com
Annual Revenues: $10 million
Employees: 100
Industry/ies: Defense/Homeland Security; Government-Related

Chairman of the Board Tel: (571) 482-1260
CAVAIOLA, Lawrence J.

Chief Executive Officer Tel: (571) 482-1260
BINNS, Jr., Graham

Main Headquarters
Mailing: 1655 N. Fort Myer Dr. Tel: (571) 482-1260
Suite 360
Arlington, VA 22209

Corporate Foundations and Giving Programs
The Aegis Foundation
614 Dartmouth Terrace Ct. Tel: (636) 273-1011
Wildwood, MO 63011 Fax: (636) 273-1015

Aegon USA

See listing on page 794 under Transamerica

AEP

See listing on page 50 under American Electric Power Company

Aeroflex, Inc.

Aeroflex Incorporated is a global provider of high technology solutions to the aerospace, defense cellular and broadband communications markets. Aeroflex designs, develops, manufactures and markets a diverse range of microelectronic and test and measurement products.
www.aeroflex.com
Annual Revenues: $639.89 million
Employees: 2,600
Ticker: NYSE: ARX
SIC: 3679
NAICS: 334419
Industry/ies: Aerospace/Aviation; Transportation

Chairman of the Board Tel: (516) 694-6700
EVANS, Hugh Fax: (516) 694-0658

President, Chief Executive Officer and Director Tel: (516) 694-6700
BOROW, Leonard Fax: (516) 694-0658

Main Headquarters
Mailing: P.O. Box 6022 Tel: (516) 694-6700
35 S. Service Rd. Fax: (516) 694-0658
Plainview, NY 11803-0622 TF: (800) 843-1553

Washington Office
Mailing: 2800 Crystal Dr. Tel: (703) 412-1111
Suite 220 Fax: (703) 412-1005
Arlington, VA 22202

Political Action Committees
Aeroflex Inc. PAC

FEC ID: C00422824
Contact: Andrew Kaminsky
35 S. Service Rd.   Tel: (703) 412-1144
Suite 300   Fax: (703) 412-1105
Plainview, NY 11803

Public Affairs and Related Activities Personnel

At Headquarters

KAMINSKY, Andrew   Tel: (516) 752-6401
Senior Vice President, Corporate Development, Human   Fax: (516) 694-0658
Resources and Investor Relations and PAC Treasurer
andrew.kaminsky@aeroflex.com

WACTLAR, Ed   Tel: (516) 694-6700
Senior Vice President, General Counsel   Fax: (516) 694-0658

Aerojet

An aerospace and defense company.
www.aerojet.com
Employees: 3,000
Ticker: NYSE: GY
SIC: 3764; 3769
Industry/ies: Aerospace/Aviation; Defense/Homeland Security; Government-Related; Transportation
Legislative Issues: ACC; AER; BUD; CAW; DEF; ENV

Main Headquarters
Mailing: P.O. BOX 13222   Tel: (916) 355-4000
             Sacramento, CA 95813   Fax: (916) 351-8667

Washington Office
Mailing: 1300 Wilson Blvd.   Tel: (703) 650-0281
             Suite 1000
             Arlington, VA 22209

Political Action Committees
Aerojet & Gencorp PAC
FEC ID: C00129122
Contact: Brendan King
P.O. Box 13222   Tel: (916) 355-4000
Sacramento, CA 95813   Fax: (916) 351-8667

   Contributions to Candidates: $106,625 (2015-2016)
   Democrats: $30,500; Republicans: $76,125

Principal Recipients

HOUSE
ROGERS, MICHAEL DENNIS (REP-AL)

Public Affairs and Related Activities Personnel

At Headquarters

HENSLER, James D.   Tel: (916) 355-4000
Director, Congressional Relations   Fax: (916) 351-8667
Registered Federal Lobbyist

KING, Brendan   Tel: (916) 355-4000
PAC Treasurer   Fax: (916) 351-8667

LAVER, Susan   Tel: (916) 355-4000
Federal Lobbyists   Fax: (916) 351-8667
Registered Federal Lobbyist

MAHONE, Glenn   Tel: (202) 302-9941
Contact, Media Relations   Fax: (916) 351-8667
c.glenn.mahone@aerojet.com

MCCOLAUGH, Kevin   Tel: (916) 355-4000
Manager, Congressional Relations   Fax: (916) 351-8667
Registered Federal Lobbyist

MORGAN, Pat   Tel: (916) 355-4000
Associate Accountant   Fax: (916) 351-8667

PANOS, Kenneth   Tel: (916) 355-4000
Senior Director, Congressional Relations   Fax: (916) 351-8667
ken.panos@aerojet.com
Registered Federal Lobbyist

SCHUMACHER, John   Tel: (916) 355-4000
                                     Fax: (916) 351-8667

STERNER, Suzanne Chambers   Tel: (916) 355-4000
Federal Lobbyist   Fax: (916) 351-8667
Registered Federal Lobbyist

WALLACE, Diane   Tel: (916) 355-4000
Assistant Treasurer   Fax: (916) 351-8667

ZACHARIAS, Elizabeth   Tel: (916) 355-4000
Vice President, Human Resources   Fax: (916) 351-8667
Elizabeth.Zacharias@Aerojet.com

Aerojet Rocketdyne Holdings, Inc.

GenCorp, was formerly the General Tire and Rubber Company is presently known as Aerojet Rocketdyne Holdings, Inc. is a diversified company delivering innovative solutions that create value for its customers in the aerospace and defense, and real estate markets. It provides

propulsion and energetics to the space, missile defense and strategic systems, tactical systems and armaments areas, in support of domestic and international markets.
www.rocket.com
Annual Revenues: $1.58 billion
Employees: 5,071
Ticker: NYSE: AJRD
SIC: 3400
Industry/ies: Aerospace/Aviation; Defense/Homeland Security; Government-Related; Real Estate; Transportation
Legislative Issues: AER; BUD; DEF

Chairman of the Board   Tel: (916) 355-4000
HENDERSON, James R.   Fax: (916) 351-8668

Chief Executive Officer and President   Tel: (916) 355-4000
DRAKE, Eileen P.   Fax: (916) 351-8668

Main Headquarters
Mailing: P.O. Box 537012   Tel: (916) 355-4000
             Sacramento, CA 95853-7012   Fax: (916) 351-8668

Washington Office
Mailing: 1300 Wilson Blvd.   Tel: (703) 650-0281
             Suite 1000   Fax: (703) 562-4154
             Arlington, VA 22209

Political Action Committees
Aerojet & Gencorp PAC
FEC ID: C00129122
Contact: Brendan King
P.O. Box 13222   Tel: (916) 355-4000
Sacramento, CA 95813   Fax: (916) 351-8667

   Contributions to Candidates: $106,625 (2015-2016)
   Democrats: $30,500; Republicans: $76,125

Principal Recipients

HOUSE
ROGERS, MICHAEL DENNIS (REP-AL)

Corporate Foundations and Giving Programs

The Aerojet Rocketdyne Foundation (formerly the GenCorp Foundation)
Contact: Linda B. Cutler
P.O. Box 15619   Tel: (916) 355-3600
Sacramento, CA 95852   Fax: (916) 355-2515

Public Affairs and Related Activities Personnel

At Headquarters

CAMBRIA, Christopher C.   Tel: (916) 355-4000
Vice President, General Counsel and Secretary   Fax: (916) 351-8668

CUTLER, Linda B.   Tel: (916) 355-8650
Vice President, Corporate Responsibility   Fax: (916) 351-8667
linda.cutler@gencorp.com

MAHONE, Glenn   Tel: (916) 355-4000
Executive Director, Strategic Communications   Fax: (916) 351-8668
glenn.mahone@rocket.com

REDD, Kathleen E.   Tel: (916) 355-4000
Vice President, Chief Financial Officer and Secretary   Fax: (916) 351-8668

SCHUMACHER, John D.   Tel: (916) 355-4000
Vice President, Business Relations   Fax: (916) 351-8668

At Other Offices

KING, Brendan   Tel: (916) 355-4000
Vice President, Treasurer and PAC Treasurer   Fax: (916) 351-8668
P.O. Box 13222
Sacramento, CA 95813

AeroSat Corporation

Designs and manufactures antenna systems providing broadband Internet and satellite TV communications to in-flight aircraft.
www.aerosat.com
Industry/ies: Aerospace/Aviation; Transportation

Chairman of the Board   Tel: (603) 673-4014
EVATT, Nim

President   Tel: (603) 673-4014
FERGUSON, Dennis

Main Headquarters
Mailing: 60A Route 101A   Tel: (603) 879-0205
             Suite TwoB
             Amherst, NH 03031

Corporate Foundations and Giving Programs

AeroSat Corporation Contributions Program
62 Route 101A   Tel: (603) 672-0894
Suite 2B
Amherst, NH 03031

Public Affairs and Related Activities Personnel

At Headquarters

ALLEN, D. Grayson   Tel: (603) 672-0894

Vice President, Finance
FEHER, Skip Tel: (425) 677-5335
Vice President, Sales
sfeher@aerosat.com

MCNARY, William Tel: (603) 673-4014
Vice President, Business Development
wmcnary@aerosat.com

PAPALIA, Martha Tel: (603) 672-0894
Director, Marketing and Communications
mpapalia@aerosat.com

POPEK, Edward Tel: (603) 879-0205
Senior Director, Marketing

The Aerospace Corporation

A private company which provides engineering support for launch and satellite systems.
www.aerospace.org
Annual Revenues: $939.31 million
Employees: 4,000
Industry/ies: Aerospace/Aviation; Transportation

Chairman of the Board Tel: (310) 336-5000
BARRETT, Barbara M. Fax: (310) 336-7055

President and Chief Executive Officer Tel: (310) 336-5000
AUSTIN, Dr. Wanda M. Fax: (310) 336-7055
Wanda.m.austin@aero.org

Main Headquarters
Mailing: P.O. Box 92957 Tel: (310) 336-5000
Los Angeles, CA 90009-2957 Fax: (310) 336-7055

Corporate Foundations and Giving Programs

Aerospace Corporation Contributions Program
P.O. Box 92957
Los Angeles, CA 90009-2957

Public Affairs and Related Activities Personnel

At Headquarters

BEATTY, Ellen M. Tel: (310) 336-5000
Vice President, Chief Financial Officer and Treasurer Fax: (310) 336-7055
BRILL, Linda F. Tel: (310) 336-1192
Principal Director, Corporate Communications Fax: (310) 336-8249
linda.f.brill@aero.org

CLINTON, Malissia R. Tel: (310) 336-5000
Senior Vice President, General Counsel and Secretary Fax: (310) 336-7055
Malissia.Clinton@aero.org

LOCKE, Kimberly Tel: (310) 336-5000
Communications Specialist Fax: (310) 336-7055

Aerovironment, Inc.

Produces unmanned aircraft systems and efficient electric energy technologies.
www.avinc.com
Annual Revenues: $246.43 million
Employees: 625
Ticker: NASDAQ: AVAV
SIC: 3721
Industry/ies: Aerospace/Aviation; Energy/Electricity; Transportation
Legislative Issues: AVI; BUD; DEF; HOM

Chairman of the Board and Chief Executive Officer Tel: (626) 357-9983
CONVER, Timothy E. Fax: (626) 359-9628

Main Headquarters
Mailing: 181 W. Huntington Dr. Tel: (626) 357-9983
Suite 202 Fax: (626) 359-9628
Monrovia, CA 91016

Washington Office
Mailing: 241 18th St., South Tel: (703) 418-1001
Suite 415
Arlington, VA 22202

Public Affairs and Related Activities Personnel

At Headquarters

BOYER, Mark Tel: (310) 229-5956
Contact, Media Relations Fax: (626) 359-9628
mark@boyersyndicate.com

CLINE, Cathleen Tel: (626) 357-9983
Senior Vice President, Administration Fax: (626) 359-9628

COVINGTON, Teresa Tel: (626) 357-9983
Interim Chief Financial Officer Fax: (626) 359-9628

GITLIN, Steve Tel: (626) 357-9983
Contact, Media and Investor Relations Fax: (626) 359-9628
ir@avinc.com

NAWABI, Wahid Tel: (626) 357-9983
Senior Vice President and Chief Operating Officer Fax: (626) 359-9628

SCOTT, Doug Tel: (626) 357-9983
Senior Vice President and General Counsel Fax: (626) 359-9628

At Washington Office

HILL, Alex Tel: (703) 418-1001
Director, Washington Operations
Registered Federal Lobbyist

SHADE, Briggs M. Tel: (703) 418-1001
Director, Washington Operations
shade@avinc.com
Registered Federal Lobbyist

The AES Corporation

A global power company that owns and operates a diverse and growing portfolio of electricity generation and distribution businesses.
www.aes.com
Annual Revenues: $16.87 billion
Employees: 18,500
Ticker: NYSE: AES
SIC: 4991
Industry/ies: Energy/Electricity
Legislative Issues: CAW; ENG; ENV; FOR; HOM; TAX; TRA; TRD

Chairman Tel: (703) 522-1315
ROSSOTTI, Charles Fax: (703) 528-4510

President and Chief Executive Officer Tel: (703) 522-1315
GLUSKI, Andres Fax: (703) 528-4510
andres.gluski@aes.com

Main Headquarters
Mailing: 4300 Wilson Blvd. Tel: (703) 522-1315
11th Floor Fax: (703) 528-4510
Arlington, VA 22203

Political Action Committees
AES CORPORATION POLITICAL ACTION COMMITTEE
FEC ID: C00507962
Contact: Mark A Miller
4300 Wilson Blvd. Tel: (703) 522-1315
11th Floor Fax: (703) 528-4510
Arlington, VA 22203

  Contributions to Candidates: $147,350 (2015-2016)
  Democrats: $91,000; Republicans: $56,350
  Principal Recipients
    HOUSE
      LEVIN, SANDER M MR (DEM-MI)
      LUJAN, BEN R MR. (DEM-NM)
      MEEKS, GREGORY W. (DEM-NY)
      ROYCE, ED MR. (REP-CA)
      SHUSTER, WILLIAM MR. (REP-PA)

Corporate Foundations and Giving Programs

The AES Corporation Contributions Program
Contact: Peter Jaffe
4300 Wilson Blvd. Tel: (703) 522-1315
11th Floor Fax: (703) 528-4510
Arlington, VA 22203

Public Affairs and Related Activities Personnel

At Headquarters

ACKERMAN, Amy Tel: (703) 682-6399
Manager, Investor Relations Fax: (703) 528-4510
amy.ackerman@aes.com

DA SANTOS, Bernerd Tel: (703) 522-1315
Senior Vice President, Chief Operating Officer Fax: (703) 528-4510

HACKENSON, Elizabeth Tel: (703) 522-1315
Chief Information Officer and Senior Vice President, Global Fax: (703) 528-4510
Business Services
Registered Federal Lobbyist

JAFFE, Peter Tel: (703) 522-1315
Chief Ethics and Compliance Officer Fax: (703) 528-4510

MARK, Miller Tel: (703) 522-1315
Registered Federal Lobbyist Fax: (703) 528-4510

MILLER, Brian Tel: (703) 522-1315
Executive Vice President, General Counsel and Corporate Fax: (703) 528-4510
Secretary
Brian.Miller@aes.com
Registered Federal Lobbyist

MILLER, Mark A Tel: (703) 522-1315
Director, Policy Fax: (703) 528-4510
Registered Federal Lobbyist

O'FLYNN, Thomas Tel: (703) 522-1315
Executive Vice President, Chief Financial Officer Fax: (703) 528-4510

PASHA, Ahmed Tel: (703) 682-6451
Vice President, Investor Relations Fax: (703) 528-4510
ahmed.pasha@aes.com

At Other Offices

KIGER, Lundy

Vice President & Director, Government Relations
P. O. Box 1740
Panama, OK 74951

Aethon, Inc.

Developer of mobile robotic solutions for hospital supply chain logistics.
www.aethon.com
Annual Revenues: $8.20 million
Employees: 56
Industry/ies: Electricity & Electronics; Electronics; Energy/Electricity

President and Chief Executive Officer
ZINI, Aldo
azini@aethon.com
Tel: (412) 322-2975
Fax: (412) 322-3569

Main Headquarters
Mailing: 100 Business Center Dr.
            Pittsburgh, PA 15205
Tel: (412) 322-2975
Fax: (412) 322-3569
TF: (888) 201-9522

Public Affairs and Related Activities Personnel

At Headquarters

MELANSON, Tony
Vice President, Marketing
Tel: (412) 322-2975
Fax: (412) 322-3569

REILLY, Robert
Chief Financial Officer
Tel: (412) 322-2975
Fax: (412) 322-3569

SEIFF, Peter
Senior Vice President, Business Development
pseiff@aethon.com
Tel: (412) 322-2975
Fax: (412) 322-3569

Aetna Inc.

An insurance and health care benefits company. Its Health Care division offers HMO, PPO, point of service (POS), health savings account (HSA), and traditional indemnity coverage, along with dental, vision, behavioral health, and Medicare plans, to groups and individuals. Aetna's Group Insurance segment sells life and disability insurance nationwide. And its Large Case Pensions segment offers pensions, annuities, and other retirement savings products.
www.aetna.com
Annual Revenues: $59.10 billion
Employees: 48,800
Ticker: NYSE: AET
SIC: 6324
Industry/ies: Insurance Industry
Legislative Issues: BUD; HCR; INS; LBR; MMM; TAX

Chairman and Chief Executive Officer
BERTOLINI, Mark T.
BertoliniM@aetna.com
Tel: (860) 273-0123
Fax: (860) 975-3110

Main Headquarters
Mailing: 151 Farmington Ave.
            Hartford, CT 06156
Tel: (860) 273-0123
Fax: (860) 975-3110
TF: (800) 872-3862

Washington Office
Mailing: 1331 F St. NW
            Suite 450
            Washington, DC 20004

Political Action Committees
AETNA INC. POLITICAL ACTION COMMITTEE
FEC ID: C00181826
Contact: Peter L. Rubin
20 F St. NW
Suite 350
Washington, DC 20001

 Contributions to Candidates: $407,500 (2015-2016)
 Democrats: $145,500; Republicans: $262,000

Principal Recipients

SENATE
BLUNT, ROY (REP-MO)
BURR, RICHARD (REP-NC)
CRAPO, MICHAEL D (REP-ID)
MURRAY, PATTY (DEM-WA)
SCOTT, TIMOTHY E (REP-SC)

HOUSE
BLUMENAUER, EARL (DEM-OR)
CROWLEY, JOSEPH (DEM-NY)
HOYER, STENY HAMILTON (DEM-DC)
KIND, RONALD JAMES (DEM-WI)
REED, THOMAS W II (REP-NY)
RYAN, PAUL D. (REP-WI)
SCALISE, STEVE MR. (REP-LA)
TIBERI, PATRICK J. (REP-OH)
UPTON, FREDERICK STEPHEN (REP-MI)
WALDEN, GREGORY P MR. (REP-OR)

Corporate Foundations and Giving Programs
Aetna Foundation
Contact: Anne C. Beal MD, MPH

---

151 Farmington Ave.
Hartford, CT 06156
Tel: (860) 273-0123
Fax: (860) 273-3971
TF: (800) 872-3862

Public Affairs and Related Activities Personnel

At Headquarters

BEAL, MD, MPH, Anne C.
President, Aetna Foundation
Tel: (860) 273-0123
Fax: (860) 975-3110

CASAZZA, William J.
Executive Vice President and General Counsel
Tel: (860) 273-3658
Fax: (860) 273-3971

COWHEY, Tom
Vice President, Investor Relations
cowheyt@aetna.com
Tel: (860) 273-2402
Fax: (860) 975-3110

FIDLER, Deanna
Executive Vice President, Human Resources
Tel: (860) 273-0123
Fax: (860) 975-3110

FINKELSTEIN, Adam
Counsel
Tel: (860) 273-0123
Fax: (860) 975-3110

GUERTIN, Shawn
Senior Vice President, Chief Financial Officer and Chief Enterprise Risk Officer
Tel: (860) 273-0123
Fax: (860) 975-3110

IOVINO, Charlie
Vice President and Counsel
iovinoca@aetna.com
Registered Federal Lobbyist
Tel: (860) 273-0123
Fax: (860) 975-3110

JONES, Greg
Federal Lobbyist
Registered Federal Lobbyist
Tel: (860) 273-0123
Fax: (860) 975-3110

KELLY, Erin
Counsel
Tel: (860) 273-0123
Fax: (860) 975-3110

KELMAR, Steven B.
Executive Vice President, Corporate Affairs
Tel: (860) 273-0123
Fax: (860) 273-3971

KRAL, Abby
Senior Director, Strategy & Planning
Tel: (860) 273-0123
Fax: (860) 975-3110

LEWIS, Dijuana
Executive Vice President, Consumer Products and Enterprise Marketing
Tel: (860) 273-0123
Fax: (860) 975-3110

MCCARTHY, Meg
Executive Vice President, Operations and Technology
Tel: (860) 273-0123
Fax: (860) 975-3110

MURRAY, Robert Randall
Federal Lobbyist
Registered Federal Lobbyist
Tel: (860) 273-0123
Fax: (860) 975-3110

RICCIUTI, James
Federal Lobbyist
Registered Federal Lobbyist
Tel: (860) 273-0123
Fax: (860) 975-3110

SANDLER, Geoffrey
Senior Actuary, Health Policy
Tel: (860) 273-0123
Fax: (860) 975-3110

SOISTMAN, Fran S.
Executive Vice President, Government Services
Tel: (860) 273-0123
Fax: (860) 975-3110

ZOOK, Susan
Registered Federal Lobbyist
Tel: (860) 273-0123
Fax: (860) 975-3110

ZUBRETSKY, Joseph M.
Senior Executive Vice President, National Businesses
Tel: (860) 273-0123
Fax: (860) 975-3110

At Washington Office

ABEL, Kate
Director, Political Affairs
Tel: (202) 419-7041

SMITH, Jason
Chief Operating Officer
Tel: (202) 419-7041

At Other Offices

NYQUIST, Christina
Vice President, Head of Public Policy, and Government Affairs
20 F St. NW, Suite 350
Washington, DC 20001
Mail Stop Suite 350
NyquistC@aetna.com
Registered Federal Lobbyist

PATZMAN, Andrew
Counsel, Public Policy
20 F St. NW, Suite 350
Washington, DC 20001
Mail Stop Suite 350
Registered Federal Lobbyist

RUBIN, Peter L.
Federal Lobbyist & PAC Treasurer
20 F St. NW, Suite 350
Washington, DC 20001

AFC Enterprises

See listing on page 645 under Popeyes Louisiana Kitchen, Inc.

Affiliated Computer Services Inc.

A business process and technology outsourcing provider. As an outsourcer, ACS handles functions such as administration, including health care claims processing; finance and accounting; human resources; payment processing; sales, marketing, and customer care call centers; and supply chain management. In early 2010, ACS was acquired by printing equipment giant Xerox.

www.acs-inc.com
Annual Revenues: $22.24 billion
Employees: 143,200
Ticker: NYSE: ACS
SIC: 7374
NAICS: 42143
Industry/ies: Computer/Technology; Management
Legislative Issues: AGR; EDU; FIN; GOV; HCR; HOM; TAX

Chairman of the Board
DEASON, Darwin
darwin.deason@acs-inc.com

Tel: (214) 841-6111
Fax: (214) 821-8315

Chairman and Chief Executive Officer
BURNS, Ursula M.

Tel: (214) 841-6111
Fax: (214) 821-8315

Main Headquarters
Mailing: 2828 N. Haskell Ave.
Dallas, TX 75204

Tel: (214) 841-6111
Fax: (214) 821-8315

Washington Office
Mailing: 1800 M St. NW
Suite 700, North Tower
Washington, DC 20036

Political Action Committees
Xerox Corporation Political Action Committee (X-PAC)
FEC ID: C00207258
Contact: Michele L. Cahn
1800 M St. NW
North Tower, Suite 700
Washington, DC 20036

Tel: (202) 414-1200
Fax: (202) 414-1217

> **Contributions to Candidates:** $29,000 (2015-2016)
> Democrats: $12,000; Republicans: $17,000

Corporate Foundations and Giving Programs

ACS Philanthropic Foundation
Contact: Megan Swatek
2828 N. Haskell Ave.
Dallas, TX 75204

Tel: (214) 887-7678
Fax: (214) 821-8315

Public Affairs and Related Activities Personnel

At Headquarters

BESSIN, James
Vice President
James.bessin@acs-inc.com

Tel: (214) 841-6111
Fax: (214) 821-8315

BLODGETT, Lynn
Corporate Executive Vice President
lynn.blodgett@acs-inc.com

Tel: (214) 841-6111
Fax: (214) 821-8315

CARONE, Christa
Vice President & Chief Marketing Officer

Tel: (214) 841-6111
Fax: (214) 821-8315

ERICSON, Ken
Director, Corporate Communications
Kenneth.Ericson@xerox.com

Tel: (410) 571-0161
Fax: (214) 821-8315

LESKO, James H.
Corporate Vice President, Vice President Inverstor Relation

Tel: (214) 841-6111
Fax: (214) 821-8315

LIGHTFOOT, Kevin
Vice President, Corporate Communications
kevin.lightfoot@acs-inc.com

Tel: (214) 841-8191
Fax: (214) 821-8315

LIU, Don H.
Corporate Senior Vice President and General Counsel and Secretary

Tel: (214) 841-6111
Fax: (214) 821-8315

LONDON, John
Executive Vice President and Chief Financial Officer

Tel: (214) 841-6111
Fax: (214) 821-8315

MADDISON, Tom
Corporate Senior Vice President Chief Human Resource Officer

Tel: (214) 841-6111
Fax: (214) 821-8315

MIKELLS , Kathryn
Corporate Executive Vice President anf Chief Financial Officer

Tel: (214) 841-6111
Fax: (214) 821-8315

PUCKETT, Jon
Vice President, Investor Solutions
jon.puckett@acs-inc.com

Tel: (214) 841-8281
Fax: (214) 821-8315

REXFORD, John H.
Executive Vice President, Corporate Development
john.rexford@acs-inc.com

Fax: (214) 821-8315

SCHOLL, Rebecca
Senior Vice President, Corporate Marketing and Communications

Fax: (214) 821-8315

SWATEK, Megan

Tel: (214) 887-7678

Contact, Public and Community Affairs
megan.swatek@acs-inc.com

Fax: (214) 821-8315

At Washington Office

ADAMI, Ken
PAC Treasurer
ken.adami@acs-inc.com

Tel: (415) 486-2409

BEVILACQUA, Nicholas
Vice President and Senior Corporate Counsel
nicholas.bevilacqua@acs-inc.com

CAHN, Michele L.
PAC Treasurer

Tel: (415) 486-2409

COLEMAN, John A.
Senior Vice President, Legislative And Public Affairs

Tel: (415) 486-2409

Affymetrix Inc.

Manufacturer of DNA microarrays.
www.affymetrix.com
Annual Revenues: $354.77 million
Employees: 1,100
SIC: 3826
Industry/ies: Science; Scientific Research

President and Chief Executive Officer
WITNEY, PhD, Frank

Tel: (408) 731-5000
Fax: (408) 731-5380

Main Headquarters
Mailing: 3420 Central Expwy.
Santa Clara, CA 95051

Tel: (408) 731-5000
Fax: (408) 731-5380

Public Affairs and Related Activities Personnel

At Headquarters

CHIN, Siang
Senior Vice President, General Counsel and Secretary

Tel: (408) 731-5000
Fax: (408) 731-5380

FARRELL, Doug
Vice President, Investor Relations & Treasury

Tel: (408) 731-5285
Fax: (408) 731-5380

LAST, Andrew
Executive Vice President, Chief Operating Officer

Tel: (408) 731-5000
Fax: (408) 731-5380

TING, Tracy
Senior Vice President, Human Resources

Tel: (408) 731-5000
Fax: (408) 731-5380

WOOD, Gavin
Executive Vice President, Chief Financial Officer

Tel: (408) 731-5000
Fax: (408) 731-5380

At Other Offices

ROBERT C., Wells
Treasurer
3380 Central Expwy.
Santa Clara, CA 95051

AFLAC, Inc.

An accident and health insurance company.
www.aflac.com
Annual Revenues: $22.22 billion
Employees: 9,525
Ticker: NYSE: AFL
SIC: 6321
Industry/ies: Insurance Industry
Legislative Issues: CPI; FIN; INS; TAX; TRD

Chairman and Chief Executive Officer
AMOS, Daniel P.

Tel: (706) 323-3431
Fax: (706) 324-6330

Main Headquarters
Mailing: 1932 Wynnton Rd.
Columbus, GA 31999

Tel: (706) 323-3431
Fax: (706) 324-6330
TF: (800) 992-3522

Washington Office
Mailing: 1300 Pennsylvania Ave. NW
Washington, DC 20004

Political Action Committees
AFLAC Inc. PAC (AFLACPAC)
FEC ID: C00034157
Contact: Joey M. Loudermilk
1932 Wynnton Rd.
Columbus, GA 31999

> **Contributions to Candidates:** $1,015,000 (2015-2016)
> Democrats: $462,500; Republicans: $549,500; Other: $3,000

> **Principal Recipients**
>
> **SENATE**
> LEAHY, PATRICK J (DEM-VT)
> PORTMAN, ROB (REP-OH)
> SCOTT, TIMOTHY E (REP-SC)
>
> **HOUSE**
> BRADY, KEVIN (REP-TX)
> HENSARLING, JEB HON. (REP-TX)
> JOHNSON, HENRY C 'HANK' (DEM-GA)

MCCARTHY, KEVIN (REP-CA)
NEAL, RICHARD E MR. (DEM-MA)
PELOSI, NANCY (DEM-CA)
PRICE, THOMAS EDMUNDS (REP-GA)
ROGERS, MICHAEL DENNIS (REP-AL)
SCALISE, STEVE MR. (REP-LA)
SCOTT, DAVID ALBERT (DEM-GA)
SCOTT, JAMES AUSTIN (REP-GA)
TIBERI, PATRICK J. (REP-OH)
WATERS, MAXINE MS (DEM-CA)

Corporate Foundations and Giving Programs

AFLAC Contribution Program
1932 Wynnton Rd.   Tel: (706) 323-3431
Columbus, GA 31999   Fax: (706) 324-6330

Public Affairs and Related Activities Personnel

At Headquarters

ANDEL, Michael   Tel: (706) 323-3431
Registered Federal Lobbyist   Fax: (706) 324-6330

BLADES, Catherine H.   Tel: (706) 323-3431
Senior Vice President, Corporate Communications Fax: (706) 324-6330

CLARK, Mechell   Tel: (706) 323-3431
Manager, Media Relations   Fax: (706) 324-6330
meclark@aflac.com

CLONINGER, III, Kriss   Tel: (706) 323-3431
President, Chief Financial Officer and Treasurer Fax: (706) 324-6330

CRAWFORD, Fredrick J.   Tel: (706) 323-3431
Executive Vice President, Chief Financial Officer Fax: (706) 324-6330

DANIEL, Laree R.   Tel: (706) 323-3431
Senior Vice President, Internal Operations and Chief Fax: (706) 324-6330
Administrative Officer

DANIELS, J. Todd   Tel: (706) 323-3431
Senior Vice President, Global Chief Risk Officer Fax: (706) 324-6330

FOX, Elizabeth   Tel: (706) 323-3431
Federal Lobbyist   Fax: (706) 324-6330

FRIOU, Phillip J.   Tel: (706) 323-3431
Senior Vice President and Director, Governmental Relations Fax: (706) 324-6330

HISHIKAWA, Maki   Tel: (706) 323-3431
Senior Representative, International Affairs Fax: (706) 324-6330
Registered Federal Lobbyist

HOWARD, June P.   Tel: (706) 323-3431
Senior Vice President, Financial Services and Chief Fax: (706) 324-6330
Accounting Officer

KANE, Laura   Tel: (706) 323-3431
Vice President, Corporate Communications Fax: (706) 324-6330
lkane@aflac.com

KNOX, Bradley L.   Tel: (706) 323-3431
Registered Federal Lobbyist   Fax: (706) 324-6330

LEBISH, Daniel   Tel: (706) 323-3431
Executive Vice President; Chief Operating Officer Fax: (706) 324-6330

LOUDERMILK, Joey M.   Tel: (706) 323-3431
Executive Vice President, General Counsel, Corporate Fax: (706) 324-6330
Secretary and PAC Treasurer

MCKENNA, Thomas P.   Tel: (706) 323-3431
Senior Vice President, Deputy General Counsel Fax: (706) 324-6330

OWENBY, Matthew D.   Tel: (706) 323-3431
Senior Vice President, Chief Human Resources Officer Fax: (706) 324-6330

PRINGLE, David L.   Tel: (706) 323-3431
Senior Vice President, Federal Relations Fax: (706) 324-6330
dpringle@aflac.com

RIGBY, Gina J.   Tel: (706) 323-3431
Director, Federal Relations   Fax: (706) 324-6330
grigby@aflac.com
Registered Federal Lobbyist

ROGERS, Candice C.   Tel: (706) 323-3431
Federal Lobbyist   Fax: (706) 324-6330

TILLMAN, Audrey B.   Tel: (706) 323-3431
Executive Vice President, General Counsel Fax: (706) 324-6330

WILKEY, Robin Y.   Tel: (706) 323-3431
Senior Vice President, Investor and Rating Agency Relations Fax: (706) 324-6330

At Washington Office

DUGGER, Maurie
Director, Federal Relations

Afognak Native Corporation

Is committed to optimize financial benefits, land use and preserve cultural for the well-being of its shareholders. Afognak is an Alaska Native Corporation (ANC) formed under the 1971 Alaska Native Claims Settlement Act (ANCSA) and through the 1977 merger of two Alaska Native village corporations: Natives of Afognak, Inc. and Port Lions Native Corporation.

Native corporation shareholders are those Alaska Natives who were alive on December 18, 1971, and have proven their lineage to the respective region and village.
www.afognak.com
Employees: 5,000
Industry/ies: Economics And Economic Development; Minorities; Native American
Legislative Issues: BUD; DEF; IND

Chairwoman   Tel: (907) 222-9500
MAY, Denise   Fax: (907) 222-9501

President and Chief Executive Officer   Tel: (907) 222-9500
HAMBRIGHT, Gregory   Fax: (907) 222-9501

Main Headquarters
Mailing: 3909 Arctic Blvd.   Tel: (907) 222-9500
             Suite 400   Fax: (907) 222-9501
             Anchorage, AK 99503   TF: (888) 292-9580

Political Action Committees
Afognak Native Corporation-Alutiiq PAC
FEC ID: C00443937
Contact: Sarah L. Lukin
3909 Arctic Blvd.   Tel: (907) 222-9500
Suite 400   Fax: (907) 222-9501
Anchorage, AK 99503

   Contributions to Candidates: $15,700 (2015-2016)
   Democrats: $3,500; Republicans: $12,200

Corporate Foundations and Giving Programs
Afognak Settlement Trust
3909 Arctic Blvd.
Suite 400
Anchorage, AK 99503

Public Affairs and Related Activities Personnel

At Headquarters

GODFREY, Gerad   Tel: (907) 222-9500
Director, Corporate Affairs   Fax: (907) 222-9501

LUKIN, Sarah L.   Tel: (907) 222-9500
Senior Vice President, Corporate Affairs and PAC Treasurer Fax: (907) 222-9501

ORTH, Marci   Tel: (907) 762-9430
Vice President, Shareholder Services   Fax: (907) 222-9501
morth@afognak.com

At Other Offices

DRABEK, Alisha   Tel: (907) 486-6014
Senior Vice President, Community and Government Affair Fax: (907) 486-2514
300 Alimaq Dr.
Kodiak, AK 99615
alisha@afognak.com

AFS Trinity Power Corporation

An energy technology company.
afstrinity.com
Employees: 28
Industry/ies: Energy/Electricity

Chairman of the Board and Chief Executive Officer   Tel: (425) 454-1818
FURIA, Edward W.   Fax: (425) 455-9623

Main Headquarters
Mailing: P.O. Box 449   Tel: (425) 454-1818
             Medina, WA 98039   Fax: (425) 455-9623

Public Affairs and Related Activities Personnel

At Headquarters

KENT, Timothy C.   Tel: (425) 454-1818
Director and Advisor, Public Communications Fax: (425) 455-9623

LEVINTHAL, Joel   Tel: (425) 454-1818
President and Chief Operating Officer   Fax: (425) 455-9623

ROGERS, Peter N.   Tel: (425) 454-1818
Chief Financial Officer and Director   Fax: (425) 455-9623

AG Processing, Inc.

A farmer-owned cooperative, engaged in the procurement, processing, marketing, and transportation of grains and grain products.
www.agp.com
Employees: 1,100
SIC: 2041
Industry/ies: Agriculture/Agronomy
Legislative Issues: AGR; TAX

Chairman of the Board   Tel: (402) 396-7809
DAVIS, Bradley T.   Fax: (402) 498-2215

Chief Executive Officer and General Manager   Tel: (402) 396-7809
SPACKLER, J. Keith   Fax: (402) 498-2215

Main Headquarters
Mailing: P.O. Box 2047   Tel: (402) 496-7809
             Omaha, NE 68103-2047   Fax: (402) 498-2215

| | TF: | (800) 247-1345 |

Political Action Committees

AG Processing Inc. PAC (AGPAC)
FEC ID: C00207308
Contact: Dave Wilwerding
12700 W. Dodge Rd.
P.O. Box 2047
Omaha, NE 68154

| Tel: | (402) 496-7809 |
| Fax: | (402) 498-5548 |

> **Contributions to Candidates:** $29,250 (2015-2016)
> Democrats: $9,250; Republicans: $20,000

Public Affairs and Related Activities Personnel

At Headquarters

CASWELL, Matt
*Vice President, Member, Corporate Relations and
Government Affairs*

| Tel: | (402) 496-7809 |
| Fax: | (402) 498-2215 |

CRAIGMILE, Mark
Senior Vice President, Operations

| Tel: | (402) 496-7809 |
| Fax: | (402) 498-2215 |

RODENBURG, Jim
Manager, Communications
jrodenburg@agp.com

| Tel: | (402) 396-7809 |
| Fax: | (402) 498-2215 |

SIMMELINK, Scott
Group Vice President and Chief Financial Officer

| Tel: | (402) 496-7809 |
| Fax: | (402) 498-2215 |

WILWERDING, Dave
Senior Vice President, General Counsel and PAC Treasurer

| Tel: | (402) 496-7809 |
| Fax: | (402) 498-2215 |

At Other Offices

VAIR, Duke
Leader, Human Resources
P.O. Box 2047, 12700 W. Dodge Rd.
Omaha, NE 68154

AGCO Corporation

Leader focused on the design, manufacture and distribution of agricultural machinery.
www.agcocorp.com
Annual Revenues: $9.09 billion
Employees: 20,800
Ticker: NYSE: AGCO
SIC: 3523
Industry/ies: Agriculture/Agronomy

Chairman of the Board, President, and Chief Executive Officer
RICHENHAGEN, Martin H.
martin.richenhagen@agcocorp.com

| Tel: | (770) 813-9200 |
| Fax: | (770) 813-6118 |

Main Headquarters

Mailing:	4205 River Green Pkwy.	Tel:	(770) 813-9200
	Duluth, GA 30096	Fax:	(770) 813-6118
		TF:	(888) 989-8525

Public Affairs and Related Activities Personnel

At Headquarters

BATKIN, Roger N.
Vice President, General Counsel and Corporate Secretary

| Tel: | (770) 813-9200 |
| Fax: | (770) 813-6118 |

BECK, Andrew H.
Senior Vice President and Chief Financial Officer
andrew.beck@agcocorp.com

| Tel: | (770) 813-9200 |
| Fax: | (770) 813-6118 |

HOFFMAN, Randall G.
*Senior Vice President, Global Sales, Marketing and Product
Management*
randall.g.hoffman@agcocorp.com;randy.hoffman@agcocorp.com

| Tel: | (770) 813-9200 |
| Fax: | (770) 813-6118 |

PETERSON, Greg
Director, Investor Relations
greg.peterson@agcocorp.com

| Tel: | (770) 232-8229 |
| Fax: | (770) 813-6118 |

SMITH, Lucinda B.
Senior Vice President, Global Business Services
lucinda.smith@agcocorp.com

| Tel: | (770) 813-9200 |
| Fax: | (770) 813-6118 |

At Other Offices

FABIAN, Rebecca
Contact, Public Relations
1501 Broadway, Suite 12045
New York City, NY 10036
rf@stockheim-media.com

| Tel: | (646) 415-8518 |

AgFirst

See listing on page 23 under AgFirst Farm Credit Bank

AgFirst Farm Credit Bank

*Provides funding and financial services to 20 Agricultural Credit Associations (ACAs) in 15
eastern states and Puerto Rico.*
www.agfirst.com
Annual Revenues: $972.11 million
Employees: 320
Industry/ies: Agriculture/Agronomy; Banking/Finance/Investments

Chairman of the Board
SPIERS, Jr., Robert H.

| Tel: | (803) 799-5000 |
| Fax: | (803) 254-1776 |

President and Chief Executive Officer
AMERSON, Leon T. (Tim)

| Tel: | (803) 799-5000 |
| Fax: | (803) 254-1776 |

Main Headquarters

Mailing:	P.O. Box 1499	Tel:	(803) 799-5000
	Columbia, SC 29202	Fax:	(803) 254-1776
		TF:	(800) 874-7737

Corporate Foundations and Giving Programs

AgFirst Farm Credit Bank Contributions Program
Contact: Maribeth K. Corbett
1401 Hampton St.
Columbia, SC 29201

| Tel: | (803) 799-5000 |
| Fax: | (803) 874-7737 |

Public Affairs and Related Activities Personnel

At Headquarters

BUTLER, Charl L.
Chief Financial Officer & Senior Vice President

| Tel: | (803) 799-5000 |
| Fax: | (803) 254-1776 |

CORBETT, Maribeth K.
Corporate Secretary
mcorbett@agfirst.com

| Tel: | (803) 753-2418 |
| Fax: | (803) 254-1776 |

TUTEN, Ann---Lamar
Vice President, Marketing and Customer Support
atuten@agfirst.com

| Tel: | (803) 799-5000 |
| Fax: | (803) 753-2404 |

WILSON, Isvara
Senior Vice President and General Counsel

| Tel: | (803) 799-5000 |
| Fax: | (803) 254-1776 |

AGI

See listing on page 64 under Analytical Graphics Inc.

Agile Management Solutions

Project Managers, Business Analysts and Quality Assurance IT professionals.
www.agilemanagement.net
Industry/ies: Computer/Technology; Management

President
RIDNOUER, Dennis M.
dridnouer@mindspring.com

| Tel: | (704) 385-9613 |

Main Headquarters

| Mailing: | 6019 Polk Mountain Dr. | Tel: | (704) 385-9613 |
| | Marshville, NC 28103-9217 | | |

Public Affairs and Related Activities Personnel

At Headquarters

MOORE, Gary R.

| Tel: | (704) 385-9613 |

Agilent Technologies, Inc.

*Manufacturer of technical instruments, systems and solutions. It provides bio-analytical
solutions and services to the life sciences, diagnostics and genomics, chemical analysis,
communications, and electronics industries. Agilent was created when it spun off from
Hewlett-Packard Company in 1999.*
www.agilent.com
Annual Revenues: $6.97 billion
Employees: 12,000
Ticker: NYSE: A
SIC: 3825; 3679; 5084
NAICS: 334419; 334515; 42183
Industry/ies: Communications; Medicine/Health Care/Mental Health;
Telecommunications/Internet/Cable

Non-executive Chairman
CULLEN, James G.

| Tel: | (408) 345-8886 |
| Fax: | (408) 345-8474 |

President and Chief Executive Officer
MCMULLEN, Mike

| Tel: | (408) 345-8886 |
| Fax: | (408) 345-8474 |

Main Headquarters

Mailing:	5301 Stevens Creek Blvd.	Tel:	(408) 345-8886
	P.O. BOX 58059	Fax:	(408) 345-8474
	Santa Clara, CA 95051	TF:	(877) 424-4536

Washington Office

| Mailing: | 12351 Sunrise Valley Dr. | Tel: | (800) 248-8030 |
| | Reston, VA 20191 | Fax: | (703) 734-1803 |

Corporate Foundations and Giving Programs

Agilent Foundation
Contact: Terry Lincoln
5301 Stevens Creek Blvd.
Santa Clara, CA 95051

| Tel: | (408) 345-8886 |
| Fax: | (408) 345-8474 |

Public Affairs and Related Activities Personnel

At Headquarters

DRAKE, Michele
Manager, Communications
michele_drake@agilent.com

| Tel: | (408) 345-8396 |
| Fax: | (408) 345-8474 |

GRAU, Dominique

| Tel: | (408) 345-8886 |

Senior Vice President, Human Resources	Fax:	(408) 345-8474
HIRSCH, Didier	Tel:	(408) 345-8886
Senior Vice President and Chief Financial Officer	Fax:	(408) 345-8474
JOHNSON, Cynthia	Tel:	(408) 345-8229
Vice President, External Affairs & Global Policy	Fax:	(408) 345-8474
cynthia_johnson@agilent.com		
LINCOLN, Terry	Tel:	(408) 345-8886
Manager, Global Signature Programs at Agilent Foundation	Fax:	(408) 345-8474
terry_lincoln@agilent.com		
ORLANDELLA, Frank	Tel:	(408) 345-8886
Director, Federal Public Policy	Fax:	(408) 345-8474
ROBERTSON, Shiela Barr	Tel:	(408) 345-8886
Senior Vice President, Corporate Development and Strategy	Fax:	(408) 345-8474
shiela_robertson@agilent.com		
RODRIGUEZ, Alicia	Tel:	(408) 345-8948
Vice President, Investor Relations	Fax:	(408) 345-8474
alicia_rodriguez@agilent.com		
SULLIVAN, William P.	Tel:	(408) 345-8886
Senior Advisor	Fax:	(408) 345-8474

AgilityVideo

Formerly Vidient Systems. Video surveillance software.
www.vidient.com
Industry/ies: Computer/Technology

Main Headquarters

Mailing: 2830 Muscadine Dr.	Tel:	(865) 724-1230
Maryville, TN 37803		

Public Affairs and Related Activities Personnel

At Other Offices

HARSHMAN, Scott A.	Tel:	(650) 867-0066
Federal Lobbyist		
144 Uxbridge		
Cherry Hill, NJ 08034		
MCCANN, Patrick J.		
Federal Lobbyist		
144 Uxbridge		
Cherry Hill, NJ 08034		
MCCHESNEY, Peter Brooks		
PAC Treasurer		
640 W. California Ave., Suite 220		
Sunnyvale, CA 94086		

Agilysys, Inc.

Formerly known as Pioneer-Standard Electronics, Inc. A provider of enterprise computer technology solutions.
www.agilysys.com
Annual Revenues: $103.51 million
Employees: 504
Ticker: NASDAQ: AGYS
SIC: 7373
Industry/ies: Computer/Technology

Non-Executive Chairman — Tel: (770) 810-7800
KOLERUS, Keith M.

President and Chief Executive Officer — Tel: (770) 810-7800
DENNEDY, James

Main Headquarters

Mailing: 1000 Windward Concourse	Tel:	(770) 810-7800
Suite 250	TF:	(800) 241-8768
Alpharetta, GA 30005		

Public Affairs and Related Activities Personnel

At Headquarters

BADGER, Kyle C.	Tel:	(770) 810-7800
Senior Vice President, General Counsel and Secretary		
PUTNAL, Theresa	Tel:	(770) 810-7800
Director, Human Resources		
SEEBECK, Janine	Tel:	(770) 810-7800
Senior Vice President, Chief Financial Officer and Treasurer		
WALKER, Jim	Tel:	(770) 810-7800
Vice President, Sales and Marketing		

AGL Resources Inc.

A regional energy holding company whose core business is natural gas distribution and offers customers a wide range of energy services under one umbrella: seven regulated utilities as well as non-regulated businesses that offer retail, wholesale and storage services.
www.aglresources.com
Annual Revenues: $3.55 billion
Employees: 5,203
Ticker: NYSE: GAS
SIC: 4924
Industry/ies: Energy/Electricity

Legislative Issues: BUD; ENG; ENV; TAX

President and Chief Executive Officer — Tel: (404) 584-4000
EVANS, Andrew W. — Fax: (404) 584-3714

Main Headquarters

Mailing: P.O. Box 4569	Tel:	(404) 584-4000
Atlanta, GA 30302-4569	Fax:	(404) 584-3714
	TF:	(800) 468-9716

Political Action Committees

AGL Resources Inc. PAC
FEC ID: C00145037
Contact: Sister Ward

P.O. Box 4569	Tel:	(404) 584-4000
Location 1519	Fax:	(404) 584-3714
Atlanta, GA 30302		

Contributions to Candidates: $159,250 (2015-2016)
Democrats: $13,500; Republicans: $145,750

Principal Recipients

SENATE
BLUNT, ROY (REP-MO)
BURR, RICHARD (REP-NC)

HOUSE
BOUSTANY, CHARLES W. DR. JR. (REP-LA)
DAVIS, RODNEY L (REP-IL)
DOLD, ROBERT JAMES JR (REP-IL)
HULTGREN, RANDY (REP-IL)
KINZINGER, ADAM (REP-IL)
SHIMKUS, JOHN M (REP-IL)

Corporate Foundations and Giving Programs

AGL Resources Private Foundation
Contact: Annette Martinez

P.O. Box 4569	Tel:	(404) 584-4000
Atlanta, GA 30302	Fax:	(404) 584-3714

Public Affairs and Related Activities Personnel

At Headquarters

BATSON, Bryan	Tel:	(404) 584-4000
Senior Vice President, Southern Operations	Fax:	(404) 584-3714
BROWN, Jeffrey P.	Tel:	(404) 584-4000
Senior Vice President and Deputy General Counsel	Fax:	(404) 584-3714
CARTER, Scott	Tel:	(404) 584-4000
Senior Vice President, Commercial Operations and Chief	Fax:	(404) 584-3714
Regulatory Officer		
scarter@aglresources.com		
CAVE, Stephan	Tel:	(404) 584-3801
Senior Vice President and Treasurer	Fax:	(404) 584-3714
scave@aglresources.com		
GERKE, Tami	Tel:	(404) 584-3873
Director, External Communications	Fax:	(404) 584-3714
tgerke@aglresources.com		
KIBLER, Jim	Tel:	(404) 584-4000
Senior Vice President, External Affairs and Public Policy	Fax:	(404) 584-3714
LANG, Marshall	Tel:	(404) 584-4000
Senior Vice President, Marketing	Fax:	(404) 584-3714
PLATT, Melanie M.	Tel:	(404) 584-4000
Executive Vice President, Chief People Officer and President,	Fax:	(404) 584-3714
AGL Resources Foundation		
mplatt@aglresources.com		
REESE, Beth	Tel:	(404) 584-4000
Executive Vice President and Chief Financial Officer	Fax:	(404) 584-3714
SAWHILL, Matt	Tel:	(404) 584-4000
Managing Director, External Affairs	Fax:	(404) 584-3714
SEAS, Bryan	Tel:	(404) 584-4000
Senior Vice President and Chief Accounting Officer	Fax:	(404) 584-3714
SHLANTA, Paul R.	Tel:	(404) 584-4000
Executive Vice President, General Counsel and Chief Ethics	Fax:	(404) 584-3714
and Compliance Officer		
pshlanta@aglresources.com		
STASHAK, Sarah	Tel:	(404) 584-4577
Director, Investor Relations	Fax:	(404) 584-3714
sstashak@aglresources.com		
SUTTON, Jay	Tel:	(404) 584-4000
Senior Vice President, Operations Services	Fax:	(404) 584-3714
WARD, Sister	Tel:	(404) 584-4000
Treasurer	Fax:	(404) 584-3714

AGP

See listing on page 22 under AG Processing, Inc.

Agri-American Marketing, Inc.

Identifies products from Asian companies that desire to expand their products in the Western Hemisphere.
agri-americamarketing.com
Industry/ies: Agriculture/Agronomy

Chief Executive Officer
SAXON, Jr., Cole L.
saxon25@gru.net

Tel: (386) 462-0561
Fax: (386) 462-0432

Main Headquarters
Mailing: P.O. Box 817
            Alachua, FL 32616

Tel: (386) 462-0561
Fax: (386) 462-0432

AgriBank, FCB

A nationwide wholesale bank that provides funding to retail Farm Credit Associations that lends to farmers, ranchers, agribusiness owners, timber producers, and rural homeowners. AgriBank and AgAmerica merged in 2003 expanding the District's territory to 15 states.
www.agribank.com
Employees: 13,000
Industry/ies: Banking/Finance/Investments
Legislative Issues: AGR; BUD

Chairman
WALTHER, Matthew

Tel: (651) 282-8800
Fax: (651) 282-8666

Chief Executive Officer
YORK, L. William "Bill"

Tel: (651) 282-8800
Fax: (651) 282-8666

Main Headquarters
Mailing: 30 E. Seventh St.
            Suite 1600
            St. Paul, MN 55101

Tel: (651) 282-8800
Fax: (651) 282-8666

Corporate Foundations and Giving Programs
AgriBank, FCB Contributions Program
375 Jackson St.
St. Paul, MN 55101

Tel: (651) 282-8800
Fax: (651) 282-8666

Public Affairs and Related Activities Personnel

At Headquarters

ANDERSON, Megan Fairchild
Director, Communications
megan.fairchildanderson@agribank.com

Tel: (651) 282-8800
Fax: (651) 282-8666

GRANTHAM, Kirstin Brost
Contact, Marketing and Communications
Kirstin.Grantham@AgriBank.com

Tel: (612) 547-6397
Fax: (651) 282-8666

HICKS, Vicki J.
Vice President, Government Affairs
Registered Federal Lobbyist

Tel: (651) 282-8800
Fax: (651) 282-8666

JONES , Pat
Senior Vice President, Human Resources and
Communications

Tel: (651) 282-8800
Fax: (651) 282-8666

JONES, Jim
Senior Vice President, Chief Risk Officer

Tel: (651) 282-8800
Fax: (651) 282-8666

LADD, David
Manager, Government Affairs
Registered Federal Lobbyist

Tel: (651) 282-8529
Fax: (651) 282-8500

MOORE, Jeff
Senior Vice President, Finance

Tel: (651) 282-8800
Fax: (651) 282-8666

O'KEANE, Brian
Executive Vice President, Banking and Finance, and Chief
Financial Officer

Tel: (651) 282-8800
Fax: (651) 282-8666

O'KEANE, Brian J.
Executive Vice President, Banking and Finance, and Chief
Financial Officer

Tel: (651) 282-8800
Fax: (651) 282-8666

PREBIL, William J.
Associate General Counsel
bill.prebil@agribank.com

Tel: (651) 282-8528
Fax: (651) 282-8666

SMITH, Dana K.
Assistant General Counsel
dana.smith@agribank.com

Tel: (651) 282-8548
Fax: (651) 282-8666

STILLE, Barbara
Senior Vice President and General Counsel

Tel: (651) 282-8800
Fax: (651) 282-8666

THONE, Bill
Vice President and General Counsel

Tel: (651) 282-8800
Fax: (651) 282-8666

Agusta Westland, Inc.

A helicopter manufacturer.
www.agustawestland.com
Industry/ies: Aerospace/Aviation; Transportation

Main Headquarters
Mailing: 11700 Plaza America Dr.
            Suite 1000
            Reston, VA 20190

Tel: (703) 373-8000
Fax: (703) 243-0885

Public Affairs and Related Activities Personnel

At Headquarters

LUGO, Michael
Director, Marketing

Tel: (703) 373-8000
Fax: (703) 243-0885

AGY

Glass fiber and performance materials manufacturer.
www.agy.com
Annual Revenues: $183.65 million
Employees: 1,100
Ticker: NASDAQ TRACE: AGYH.GB
SIC: 3220
Industry/ies: Glass

Main Headquarters
Mailing: 2556 Wagener Rd.
            Aiken, SC 29801

Tel: (803) 648-8351
Fax: (803) 643-1180
TF: (888) 434-0945

Ahura Scientific, Inc.

See listing on page 783 under Thermo Fisher Scientific Inc.

AIG

See listing on page 54 under American International Group, Inc. (AIG)

AIG SunAmerica Inc.

A life insurance and financial services company. A subsidiary of American International Group, Inc. (see separate listing).
www.sunamerica.com
Annual Revenues: $2.65 billion
Employees: 26,000
Industry/ies: Banking/Finance/Investments; Insurance Industry

Main Headquarters
Mailing: 21650 Oxnard St.
            Suite 750
            Woodland Hills, CA 91367-4997

Tel: (310) 772-6533
Fax: (310) 772-6000
TF: (800) 445-7862

Public Affairs and Related Activities Personnel

At Headquarters

JONES, Edward
Contact, Sales

Tel: (310) 772-6533
Fax: (310) 772-6000

SKOLNICK, Linda
Manager, Corporate Communications

Tel: (310) 772-6533
Fax: (310) 772-6000

TREITLER, Betsy
Vice President, Marketing and Communications

Tel: (310) 772-6533
Fax: (310) 772-6000

Air Liquide America

The company supplies industrial gases (oxygen, nitrogen, CO2, argon, etc.) to companies in the automotive, chemicals, food and beverage, and health care industries.
www.us.airliquide.com
Annual Revenues: $15.33 million
Employees: 5,000
SIC: 2813; 5169
NAICS: 32512; 42269
Industry/ies: Chemicals & Chemical Industry
Legislative Issues: ENG; ENV; MED; TAX

Chairman of the Board and Chief Executive Officer
POTIER, Benoit

Tel: (713) 624-8000
Fax: (713) 624-8085

Main Headquarters
Mailing: 9811 Katy Fwy.
            Houston, TX 77024

Tel: (713) 624-8000
Fax: (713) 624-8085
TF: (877) 855-9533

Political Action Committees
American Air Liquide Holdings Inc. PAC
FEC ID: C00314054
Contact: Katherine M.S. Mcdonald
2700 Post Oak Blvd.
Suite 1800
Houston, TX 77056

Tel: (713) 624-8000
Fax: (713) 624-8000

Contributions to Candidates: $21,500 (2015-2016)
Democrats: $7,500; Republicans: $14,000

Public Affairs and Related Activities Personnel

At Headquarters

ABRIAL, François
Vice President, Human Resources

Tel: (713) 624-8000
Fax: (713) 624-8085

DUFOUR , Pierre
Senior Executive Vice President and Director

Tel: (713) 624-8000
Fax: (713) 624-8085

GRAFF, Michael J.
Senior Vice President

Tel: (713) 624-8000
Fax: (713) 624-8005

LECORVAISIF, Fabienne
Vice President and Chief Financial Officer

Tel: (713) 624-8000
Fax: (713) 624-8085

MCDONALD, Katherine M.S.

Tel: (713) 624-8000

PAC Contact	Fax:	(713) 624-8085
ROSEN, Michael	Tel:	(713) 624-8023
Vice President, Corporate Communications & Public Affairs	Fax:	(713) 624-8085
michael.rosen@airliquide.com		
Registered Federal Lobbyist		
TEMPLE, Andrew	Tel:	(713) 624-8000
Federal Lobbyist	Fax:	(713) 624-8085
Registered Federal Lobbyist		

Air Products and Chemicals, Inc.

Provider of atmospheric, process and specialty gases, performance materials, equipment and technology.
www.airproducts.com
Annual Revenues: $10.26 billion
Employees: 20,900
Ticker: NYSE: APD
SIC: 2813; 5169; 5172
NAICS: 42272; 32512; 42269
Industry/ies: Chemicals & Chemical Industry; Engineering/Mathematics; Environment And Conservation; Natural Resources; Pollution And Waste
Legislative Issues: ENG

Chairman, President and Chief Executive Officer	Tel:	(800) 654-4567
GHASEMI, Seifi	Fax:	(800) 880-5204

Main Headquarters

Mailing:	7201 Hamilton Blvd.	Tel:	(800) 654-4567
	Allentown, PA 18195-1501	Fax:	(800) 880-5204
		TF:	(800) 345-3107

Political Action Committees

Air Products and Chemicals Inc. Political Alliance PAC
FEC ID: C00127258
Contact: Linda Svoboda

P.O. Box 441	Tel:	(610) 481-4911
Trexlertown, PA 18087	Fax:	(610) 481-5900

Contributions to Candidates: $44,100 (2015-2016)
Democrats: $20,000; Republicans: $24,100

Principal Recipients

SENATE
BOOZMAN, JOHN (REP-AR)
CASEY, ROBERT P JR (DEM-PA)

HOUSE
DENT, CHARLES W. REP. (REP-PA)

Corporate Foundations and Giving Programs

Air Products and Chemicals Inc. Foundation
Contact: Laurie Gostley-Hackett

7201 Hamilton Blvd.	Tel:	(610) 481-4911
Allentown, PA 18195	Fax:	(610) 841-5900

Public Affairs and Related Activities Personnel

At Headquarters

AFFLERBACH , Mary T.	Tel:	(610) 481-4911
Corporate Secretary and Chief Governance Officer	Fax:	(610) 481-5900
CROCCO, Scott M.	Tel:	(610) 481-4911
Senior Vice President and Chief Financial Officer	Fax:	(610) 481-5900
GEORGE, Art	Tel:	(610) 481-1340
Contact, Media Relations	Fax:	(610) 481-5900
GOSTLEY-HACKETT, Laurie	Tel:	(610) 481-6118
Manager, Community Relations and Philanthropy	Fax:	(610) 481-5900
gostelj@airproducts.com		
GRANT, Jennifer L.	Tel:	(610) 481-4911
Vice President, Human Resources	Fax:	(610) 481-5900
HOLT, Timothy J.	Tel:	(610) 481-4453
Director, Corporate Relations	Fax:	(610) 481-5900
holttj@airproducts.com		
MOORE , Simon R.	Tel:	(610) 481-4911
Director, Investor Relations	Fax:	(610) 481-5900
mooresr@airproducts.com		
PAINTER , Corning F.	Tel:	(610) 481-4911
Senior Vice President and General Manager Merchant Gases	Fax:	(610) 481-5900
STANLEY, John D.	Tel:	(610) 481-7461
Senior Vice President and General Counsel and and Chief Administrative Officer	Fax:	(610) 481-2729
WALCK, Ken M.	Tel:	(610) 481-8315
Manager, Investor Relations	Fax:	(610) 481-2729
walckm@airproducts.com		

At Other Offices

SVOBODA, Linda	Tel:	(610) 481-4911
PAC Contact		
P.O. Box 441		
Trexlertown, PA 18087		

Air Transport Services Group, Inc.

A provider of air cargo transportation and related services to domestic and foreign air carriers and other companies that outsource their air cargo lift requirements.
www.atsginc.com
Annual Revenues: $580.34 million
Employees: 1,600
Ticker: NASDAQ: ATSG
SIC: 4513
Industry/ies: Aerospace/Aviation; Transportation

Chairman of the Board	Tel:	(937) 382-5591
RADEMACHER , Randy D.	Fax:	(937) 383-3838
President, Chief Executive Officer and PAC Treasurer	Tel:	(937) 382-5591
HETE, Joseph	Fax:	(937) 382-0896

Main Headquarters

Mailing:	145 Hunter Dr.	Tel:	(937) 382-5591
	Wilmington, OH 45177	Fax:	(937) 383-3838

Political Action Committees

Air Transport Services Group, Inc. PAC
FEC ID: C00238311
Contact: Joseph Hete

145 Hunter Dr.	Tel:	(937) 382-5591
Wilmington, OH 45177	Fax:	(937) 382-0896

Contributions to Candidates: $3,975 (2015-2016)
Republicans: $3,975

Public Affairs and Related Activities Personnel

At Headquarters

FEDDERS , Matt	Tel:	(937) 382-5591
Vice President, Corporate Controller	Fax:	(937) 383-3838
GOLDER, George	Tel:	(937) 382-5591
Vice President, General Counsel and Assistant Secretary	Fax:	(937) 383-3838
PAYNE, Joe	Tel:	(937) 382-5591
Senior Vice President, Corporate General Counsel and Secretary	Fax:	(937) 383-3838
joe.payne@atsginc.com		
TURNER, Quint	Tel:	(937) 382-5591
Chief Financial Officer	Fax:	(937) 383-3838

Airborne Tactical Advantage Company

Provides services to the U.S. military that include outsourced airborne tactical training, threat simulation, and research and development.
www.atacusa.com
Annual Revenues: $35 million
Employees: 32
Industry/ies: Aerospace/Aviation; Defense/Homeland Security; Government-Related; Transportation
Legislative Issues: DEF

Chief Executive Officer	Tel:	(757) 874-8100
PARKER, Jeffrey	Fax:	(757) 874-8810

Main Headquarters

Mailing:	1001 Providence Blvd.	Tel:	(757) 874-8100
	Suite 273	Fax:	(757) 874-8810
	Newport News, VA 23602-4413		

Public Affairs and Related Activities Personnel

At Headquarters

BANNON, Matt	Tel:	(757) 874-8100
Director, Strategy and Marketing	Fax:	(757) 874-8810
mbannon@atacusa.com		
MANNING, Kenya	Tel:	(757) 874-8100
Manager, Human Resources	Fax:	(757) 874-8810
STACY, Scott	Tel:	(757) 874-8100
President	Fax:	(757) 874-8810
sstacy@atacusa.com		
STEWART, Jeffery	Tel:	(757) 874-8100
Chief Finance Officer	Fax:	(757) 874-8810

Airbus Americas

Provides sales, marketing and service for Airbus aircraft in the U.S. and Canada. Formerly Airbus North America Holdings, Inc.
www.airbus.com/company/americas
Annual Revenues: $25.80 million
Employees: 200
Industry/ies: Aerospace/Aviation; Transportation
Legislative Issues: AER; AVI; DEF; TAX; TRD

Chairman of the Board	Tel:	(703) 834-3400
MCARTOR, T. Allan	Fax:	(703) 834-3593
Chief Executive Officer	Tel:	(703) 834-3400
ENDERS, Thomas	Fax:	(703) 834-3593

Main Headquarters

Mailing:	2550 Wasser Ter.	Tel:	(703) 834-3400

Suite 9100
Herndon, VA 20171

Fax: (703) 834-3593

Political Action Committees

Airbus Group, Inc. PAC
FEC ID: C00421230
Contact: Richard Beaudoin
2550 Wasser Ter.
Suite 9000
Herndon, VA 22209

Tel: (703) 236-3300
Fax: (703) 236-3301

Contributions to Candidates: $111,500 (2015-2016)
Democrats: $12,000; Republicans: $99,500

Corporate Foundations and Giving Programs

Airbus Corporate Foundation
Contact: Thomas Enders
198 Van Buren St.
Suite 300
Herndon, VA 20170

Tel: (703) 834-3400
Fax: (703) 834-3340

Public Affairs and Related Activities Personnel

At Headquarters

BEAUDOIN, Richard
PAC Treasurer

Tel: (703) 834-3400
Fax: (703) 834-3593

HICKS, Guy
Senior Vice President, Government Relations

Tel: (703) 834-3400
Fax: (703) 834-3593

WRIGLEY, Robert E.
Vice President, Government Relations

Tel: (703) 834-3400
Fax: (703) 834-3593

Airbus Group, Inc.

Aerospace, security, and defense systems company.
www.eadsnorthamerica.com
Industry/ies: Aerospace/Aviation; Defense/Homeland Security; Government-Related; Transportation
Legislative Issues: AER; AVI; BAN; BUD; CAW; DEF; ECN; HOM; MAN; TAX; TRA; TRD

Chairman and Chief Executive Officer
MCARTOR, Allan

Tel: (703) 466-5600

Main Headquarters
Mailing: 1616 N. Fort Myer Dr.
Suite 1600
Arlington, VA 22209

Tel: (703) 236-3300
Fax: (703) 236-3301

Washington Office
Mailing: 2550 Wasser Ter.
Suite 9000
Herndon, VA 20171

Tel: (703) 466-5600

Political Action Committees

Airbus Group, Inc. PAC
FEC ID: C00421230
Contact: Richard Beaudoin
2550 Wasser Ter.
Suite 9000
Herndon, VA 22209

Tel: (703) 236-3300
Fax: (703) 236-3301

Contributions to Candidates: $111,500 (2015-2016)
Democrats: $12,000; Republicans: $99,500

Public Affairs and Related Activities Personnel

At Headquarters

FINK, David
Chief Human Resources Officer

Tel: (703) 236-3300
Fax: (703) 236-3301

HICKS, Guy
Senior Vice President, Government Relations & Communications
Registered Federal Lobbyist

Tel: (703) 236-3300
Fax: (703) 236-3301

KIMBRELL, Aubert
Director, Government Relations
Registered Federal Lobbyist

Tel: (703) 236-3300
Fax: (703) 236-3301

MCGIVERN, Richard
Director, Government Relations
Registered Federal Lobbyist

Tel: (703) 236-3300
Fax: (703) 236-3301

PAROBY, Michael
Manager, Intergovernmental Affairs

Tel: (703) 236-3300
Fax: (703) 236-3301

TARDY, Xavier
Senior Vice President & Head, Finance and Controlling

Tel: (703) 236-3300
Fax: (703) 236-3301

At Washington Office

BEAUDOIN, Richard
PAC Treasurer

Tel: (703) 466-5600

BURKE, John P.
Vice President & Program Manager, Light Utility Helicopter

Tel: (703) 466-5655

HAMILTON, Jessica
Registered Federal Lobbyist

Tel: (703) 466-5600

HIXON, Courtney

Tel: (703) 466-5600

Lobbyist
Registered Federal Lobbyist

HIXON, Leigh

Tel: (703) 466-5600

KING, Jim
Defense Aerospace Government Relations and Business Development Professional

Tel: (703) 466-5600

MAZONKEY, Matthew
Registered Federal Lobbyist

Tel: (703) 466-5600

MICKEVICIUS, Ted
Vice President, Business Development
Registered Federal Lobbyist

Tel: (703) 466-5600

MOXLEY, Jodie
Director, Government Relations
Registered Federal Lobbyist

Tel: (703) 466-5600

MUNDT, Stephen
Senior Vice President, Government Strategy and Development

Tel: (703) 466-5600

PETTIS, Leigh
leighpettis@gmail.com
Registered Federal Lobbyist

Tel: (703) 466-5600

Airgas, Inc.

A distributor of industrial, medical, and specialty gases, as well as related equipment and safety supplies.
www.airgas.com
Annual Revenues: $5.30 billion
Employees: 17,000
Ticker: NYSE: ARG
SIC: 2813; 2819; 3841; 5084; 5099
Industry/ies: Chemicals & Chemical Industry
Legislative Issues: NAT

Executive Chairman of the Board
MCCAUSLAND, Peter

Tel: (610) 687-5253
Fax: (610) 687-1052

President and Chief Executive Officer
MOLININI, Michael L.

Tel: (610) 902-6270
Fax: (610) 687-1052

Main Headquarters
Mailing: 259 N. Radnor-Chester Rd.
Suite 100
Radnor, PA 19087-5283

Tel: (610) 687-5253
Fax: (610) 687-1052
TF: (800) 255-2165

Corporate Foundations and Giving Programs

Airgas, Inc. Contributions Program
259 N. Radnor-Chester Rd.
Suite 100
Radnor, PA 19087-5283

Tel: (610) 687-5253
Fax: (610) 687-1052

Public Affairs and Related Activities Personnel

At Headquarters

BATT, John
Director, Product Stewardship and Regulatory Advocacy
john.batt@airgas.com

Tel: (610) 902-6228
Fax: (610) 225-3271

CLAYPOOL, Pamela J.
Senior Vice President, Human Resources

Tel: (610) 687-5253
Fax: (610) 687-1052

GRAFF, Leslie J.
Senior Vice President, Corporate Development

Tel: (610) 687-5253
Fax: (610) 225-3271

MCLAUGHLIN, Robert M.
Senior Vice President and Chief Financial Officer

Tel: (610) 687-5253
Fax: (610) 687-1052

SHERMAN, Doug
Vice President, Communications
doug.sherman@airgas.com

Tel: (610) 902-6270
Fax: (610) 687-1052

STRZELEC, Barry
Director, Investor Relations and Corporate Communications
barry.strzelec@airgas.com

Tel: (866) 816-4618
Fax: (610) 687-1052

YOUNG, Jr., Robert H.
Senior Vice President and General Counsel

Tel: (610) 687-5253
Fax: (610) 225-3271

AirNet Systems, Inc.

An air transportation provider. AirNet also offers express delivery of such cargo as human organs and time-sensitive medications, as well as general freight and also provides both scheduled and charter cargo services. In 2008, AirNet was acquired by an affiliate of investment firm Bayside Capital.
www.airnet.com
Annual Revenues: $161.03 million
Employees: 600
SIC: 4512
Industry/ies: Aerospace/Aviation; Transportation

Main Headquarters
Mailing: 7250 Star Check Dr.
Columbus, OH 43217

Tel: (614) 409-4900
Fax: (614) 409-7852
TF: (888) 888-8463

Public Affairs and Related Activities Personnel

At Headquarters

DIMARIA, Frank
Senior Vice President, Sales and Marketing
frank.dimaria@airnet.com

Tel: (614) 409-4900
Fax: (614) 409-7852

SCHANER, Thomas
Vice President, Operations

Tel: (614) 409-4900
Fax: (614) 409-7852

TYLER, Clifton "Bud"
irector, Financial Planning and Analysis

Tel: (614) 409-4900
Fax: (614) 409-7852

AirTran Airways

An airline with Gogo Inflight Internet on every flight and offers coast-to-coast service on North America's all-Boeing fleet.
www.airtran.com
Annual Revenues: $2.62 billion
Employees: 5,000
Ticker: NYSE: AAI
SIC: 4512
Industry/ies: Aerospace/Aviation; Airlines; Transportation; Travel/Tourism/Lodging
Legislative Issues: AVI

Main Headquarters

Mailing: 9955 Airtran Blvd.
Orlando, FL 32827

Tel: (407) 318-5600
Fax: (407) 251-5567
TF: (800) 965-2107

Corporate Foundations and Giving Programs

AirTran Airways Contributions Program
9955 Airtran Blvd.
Orlando, FL 32827

Tel: (407) 318-5600
Fax: (407) 251-5567

Public Affairs and Related Activities Personnel

At Headquarters

HAAK, Arne G.
PAC Treasurer

Tel: (407) 318-5600
Fax: (407) 251-5567

AK Steel Holding Corporation

A producer of flat-rolled steel.
www.aksteel.com
Annual Revenues: $6.87 billion
Employees: 8,000
Ticker: NYSE: AKS
SIC: 3312
Industry/ies: Construction/Construction Materials
Legislative Issues: ENG; RET; TAX; TRD

Chairman of the Board, President and Chief Executive Officer
WAINSCOTT, James L.

Tel: (513) 425-5000
Fax: (513) 425-2676

Main Headquarters

Mailing: 9227 Centre Point Dr.
W. Chester, OH 45069

Tel: (513) 425-5000
Fax: (513) 425-2676
TF: (800) 331-5050

Political Action Committees

AK Steel Corporation PAC
FEC ID: C00290973
Contact: Roger K. Newport
9227 Centre Point Dr.
W. Chester, OH 45069

Tel: (513) 425-2888
Fax: (518) 425-2676

Contributions to Candidates: $64,100 (2015-2016)
Democrats: $9,900; Republicans: $54,200

Corporate Foundations and Giving Programs

AK Steel Foundation
9227 Centre Point Pkwy.
W. Chester, OH 45069

Tel: (513) 425-2826
Fax: (513) 425-2676

Public Affairs and Related Activities Personnel

At Headquarters

ALTER, Joseph C.
Vice President, General Counsel and Chief Compliance Officer

Tel: (513) 425-5000
Fax: (513) 425-2676

BISSELBERG, Stephanie S.
Vice President, Human Resources

Tel: (513) 425-5000
Fax: (513) 425-2676

FILIATRAUT, Renee S.
Vice President, Litigation, Labor and External Affairs

Tel: (513) 425-5000
Fax: (513) 425-2676

LAROCCO, Ben
Corporate Manager, Government Relations
Ben.LaRocco@aksteel.com
Registered Federal Lobbyist

Tel: (513) 425-5000
Fax: (513) 425-2676

NEWPORT, Roger K.
Senior Vice President, Finance and Chief Financial Officer and PAC Treasurer

Tel: (513) 425-5270
Fax: (513) 425-2676

RACEY, Barry L.
Director, Government and Public Relations
barry.racey@aksteel.com

Tel: (513) 425-2749
Fax: (513) 425-2676

ROSS, Christopher J.
General Manager, Strategic Planning and Financial Analysis

Tel: (513) 425-2249
Fax: (513) 425-2676

WALLNER, Michael P.
General Manager, Communications and Public Relations

Tel: (513) 425-2688
Fax: (513) 425-2676

Akamai Technologies

Leading backbone network provider.
Industry/ies: Computer/Technology; Computers & Databases
Legislative Issues: TEC

Chief Executive Officer
LEIGHTON, Dr. Tom

Tel: (877) 567-7167

Main Headquarters

Mailing: 90 Broadway
Cambridge, MA 02142

Tel: (877) 567-7167

Washington Office

Mailing: 601 Pennsylvania Ave. NW, Suite 900
Washington, DC 20004

Public Affairs and Related Activities Personnel

At Headquarters

BENSON, Jim
Executive Vice President and Chief Financial Officer

Tel: (877) 567-7167

GEMMELL, James
Executive Vice President and Chief Human Resources Officer

Tel: (877) 567-7167

HARATUNIAN, Melanie
Executive Vice President, General Counsel and Corporate Secretary

Tel: (877) 567-7167

HUGHES, Robert W.
President, Worldwide Operations

Tel: (877) 567-7167

RINKLIN, Brad
Senior Vice President and Chief Marketing Officer

Tel: (877) 567-7167

SURIYAPA, Seksom
Senior Vice President, Corporate and Business Development

Tel: (877) 567-7167

At Washington Office

VAN WAZER, Lauren
Vice President of Global Public Policy

Akeebo Corporation

A Lobbying Firm.
Industry/ies: Advertising And Marketing

Main Headquarters

Mailing: 9191 R.G. Skinner Pkwy.
Suite 401
Jacksonville Beach, FL 32256

Tel: (213) 341-0624

Public Affairs and Related Activities Personnel

At Headquarters

MISHRA, Aneeta

Tel: (213) 341-0624

MISHRA, Pushkal
Managing Partner

Tel: (213) 341-0624

Akermin, Inc.

A scientific technology company, Akermin is based in St. Louis, Mo. and was formed in 2004 to commercialize stabilized enzyme technology invented at St. Louis University.
www.akermin.com
Annual Revenues: $1.20 million
Industry/ies: Computer/Technology

President and Chief Executive Officer
BLACKWELL, Barry

Tel: (314) 669-2599
Fax: (314) 824-1960

Main Headquarters

Mailing: 1005 North Warson Rd.
Suite 101
St. Louis, MO 63132

Tel: (314) 669-2599
Fax: (314) 824-1960

Public Affairs and Related Activities Personnel

At Headquarters

SCHNIEDERS, CPA, Donna
Director, Finance

Tel: (314) 669-2599
Fax: (314) 824-1960

Alabama Aircraft Industries, Inc.

An industry leader in military aircraft maintenance.
www.alabamaaircraft.com
Annual Revenues: $53.50 million
Employees: 613
SIC: 3721
Industry/ies: Aerospace/Aviation; Transportation

President and Chief Executive Officer
ARAMINI, Ronald A.

Tel: (205) 592-0011
Fax: (205) 592-6306

Main Headquarters

Mailing: 1943 50th St., North

Tel: (205) 592-0011

Birmingham, AL 35212   Fax: (205) 592-6306

Political Action Committees
Alabama Aircraft Industries Inc. PAC
FEC ID: C00357723
Contact: Randall Shealy
1943 N. 50th St.   Tel: (205) 592-0011
Birmingham, AL 35212   Fax: (205) 592-6306

Corporate Foundations and Giving Programs
Alabama Aircraft Industries Inc. Contributions Program
1943 50th St., North   Tel: (205) 592-0011
Birmingham, AL 35212   Fax: (205) 592-6306

Public Affairs and Related Activities Personnel

At Headquarters

SEWELL, Doris K.   Tel: (205) 510-4935
Senior Vice President, Legal and Support Services   Fax: (205) 592-6306

SHEALY, Randall   Tel: (205) 510-4944
Senior Vice President, Chief Financial Officer and PAC   Fax: (205) 592-6306
Treasurer
randy.shealy@alabamaaircraft.com

Alabama Power Company
An electric utility subsidiary of Southern Company.
www.alabamapower.com
Employees: 6,800
Ticker: NYSE:ALP-N
SIC: 4911
Industry/ies: Energy/Electricity; Utilities

Chairman, President and Chief Executive Officer   Tel: (205) 257-1000
CROSSWHITE, Mark   Fax: (205) 257-2445

Main Headquarters
Mailing: P.O. Box 242   Tel: (205) 257-1000
Birmingham, AL 35292   Fax: (205) 257-2445

Political Action Committees
Alabama Power Company Employees Federal PAC (APC Employees Federal PAC)
FEC ID: C00077305
Contact: Joanna Bishop
600 N. 18th St.   Tel: (205) 257-1000
P.O.Box 2641   Fax: (205) 257-2445
Birmingham, AL 35219

    Contributions to Candidates: $63,500 (2015-2016)
    Democrats: $10,000; Republicans: $53,500

        Principal Recipients

           HOUSE
           BYRNE, BRADLEY ROBERTS (REP-AL)
           PALMER, GARY (REP-AL)
           ROBY, MARTHA (REP-AL)
           ROGERS, MICHAEL DENNIS (REP-AL)
           SEWELL, TERRYCINA ANDREA (DEM-AL)

Corporate Foundations and Giving Programs
Alabama Power Charitable Giving
Contact: John Hudson
600 N. 18th St.   Tel: (205) 257-2508
P.O. Box 2641   Fax: (205) 257-2445
Birmingham, AL 35291

Alabama Power Foundation, Inc.
Contact: John Hudson
600 N. 18th St.   Tel: (205) 257-1000
Birmingham, AL 35291   Fax: (205) 257-2445

Public Affairs and Related Activities Personnel

At Headquarters

BISHOP, Joanna   Tel: (205) 257-1000
PAC Treasurer   Fax: (205) 257-2445

HUDSON, John   Tel: (205) 257-1000
Vice President, Public Relations and Charitable Giving and   Fax: (205) 257-2445
President, Alabama Power Foundation
johudson@southernco.com

SZNAJDERMAN, Michael   Tel: (205) 257-1000
Coordinator, Media Relations   Fax: (205) 257-2445

Alanco Technologies, Inc.
The company once made pollution control systems, owned gold mines, and made unsuccessful forays into both the data storage and restaurant fryer businesses. It also made radio-frequency ID (RFID) tracking devices for correctional facilities.
www.alanco.com
Annual Revenues: $1.06 million
Employees: 40
Ticker: OTCBB: ALAN.OB
SIC: 3572
Industry/ies: Computer/Technology

Director, President and Chief Executive Officer   Tel: (480) 505-4869
CARLSON, John A.   Fax: (480) 607-1515

Main Headquarters
Mailing: 7950 E. Acoma Dr.   Tel: (480) 505-4869
Suite 111   Fax: (480) 607-1515
Scottsdale, AZ 85260

Public Affairs and Related Activities Personnel

At Headquarters

HANEY, Danielle   Tel: (480) 505-4869
Chief Financial Officer and Corporate Secretary   Fax: (480) 607-1515

OMAN, Steven P.   Tel: (480) 505-4869
Contact, Corporate Counsel   Fax: (480) 607-1515

POOL, Tom   Tel: (970) 596-7881
Contact, Communications   Fax: (480) 607-1515

Alaska Aerospace Development Corporation
The Alaska Aerospace Corporation was established by the State of Alaska to develop a high technology aerospace industry in the state.AAC serves the international aerospace industry providing comprehensive launch services. It owns and operates a commercial rocket launch facility for sub-orbital and orbital space launch vehicles by the name The Pacific Spaceport Complex-Alaska (formerly known as the Kodiak Launch Complex).
www.akaerospace.com
Annual Revenues: $6.86 million
Employees: 100
Industry/ies: Aerospace/Aviation; Transportation
Legislative Issues: AER; DEF

Chairman of the Board   Tel: (907) 561-3338
MCCOY, Robert P.   Fax: (907) 561-3339

President and Chief Executive Officer   Tel: (907) 561-3338
CAMPBELL, Craig E.   Fax: (907) 561-3339

Main Headquarters
Mailing: 4300 B St.   Tel: (907) 561-3338
Suite 101   Fax: (907) 561-3339
Anchorage, AK 99503

Corporate Foundations and Giving Programs
Alaska Aerospace Development Corporation Contributions Program
4300 B St.   Tel: (907) 561-3338
Suite 101   Fax: (907) 561-3339
Anchorage, AK 99503-5926

Public Affairs and Related Activities Personnel

At Headquarters

CRAMER, John W.   Tel: (907) 561-3338
Vice President and Chief Administrative Officer/ Chief   Fax: (907) 561-3339
Information Officer
john.cramer@akaerospace.com

GREBY, Mark J.   Tel: (907) 561-3338
Senior Vice President and Chief Operations Officer   Fax: (907) 561-3339

STEELE, Matt M.   Tel: (907) 561-3338
Vice President, Business Development   Fax: (907) 561-3339

Alaska Airlines
Provides scheduled air services. The parent carrier of its regional subsidiary, Horizon Air; both airlines are operated by the Alaska Air Group.
www.alaskaair.com
Employees: 12,000
SIC: 4512
Industry/ies: Aerospace/Aviation; Airlines; Transportation; Travel/Tourism/ Lodging
Legislative Issues: AVI; BUD; TRA

Chief Executive Officer and Chairman   Tel: (206) 392-5040
TILDEN, Bradley D.   Fax: (206) 392-2804
brad.tilden@alaskaair.com

Main Headquarters
Mailing: P.O. Box 68900   Tel: (206) 433-3200
Seattle, WA 98168   Fax: (206) 392-2804
     TF: (800) 252-7522

Washington Office
Mailing: 1200 19th St. NW   Tel: (206) 392-5805
Suite 300
Washington, DC 20036

Political Action Committees
Alaska Air Group Inc. PAC
FEC ID: C00024349
Contact: Brandon Pedersen
19300 Pacific Hwy., South   Tel: (206) 262-6781
Seattle, WA 98188   Fax: (206) 431-5558

    Contributions to Candidates: $70,000 (2015-2016)
    Democrats: $31,500; Republicans: $38,500

Corporate Foundations and Giving Programs

The Alaska Airlines Foundation
4750 Old International Airport Rd.   Tel: (907) 266-7230
Anchorage, AR 99502

Public Affairs and Related Activities Personnel

At Headquarters

ARDIZZONE, Ann   Tel: (206) 433-3200
Vice President, Strategic Sourcing and Supply Chain   Fax: (206) 392-2804
Management

HARTMAN, Donna   Tel: (206) 392-5040
Manager, Community Relations   Fax: (206) 392-2804
donna.hartman@alaskaair.com

JOHNSON, Barbara J.   Tel: (206) 392-5383
Manager, Community Relations - Corporate Giving   Fax: (206) 392-2804

LEVINE , Kyle   Tel: (206) 433-3200
Vice President Legal and General Counsel   Fax: (206) 392-2804

MINICUCCI , Ben   Tel: (206) 433-3200
President and Chief Operating Officer   Fax: (206) 392-2804

PEDERSEN, Brandon   Tel: (206) 392-5040
Chief Financial Officer and Executive Vice President, Finance   Fax: (206) 392-2804

SPRAGUE, Joseph   Tel: (206) 392-5040
Senior Vice President, Communications and External   Fax: (206) 392-2804
Relations
joe.sprague@alaskaair.com

WOERNER, Sangita   Tel: (206) 433-3200
Vice President, Marketing   Fax: (206) 392-2804

YOUNG, Tamara S.   Tel: (206) 433-3200
Vice President, Human Resources   Fax: (206) 392-2804

At Washington Office

CARRUTHERS, Ginny   Tel: (206) 392-5805
Director, Government Affairs
ginny.carruthers@alaskaair.com
Registered Federal Lobbyist

LAWRENCE, Megan   Tel: (206) 392-5805
Managing Director, Government and Community Relations
megan.lawrence@alaskaair.com
Registered Federal Lobbyist

OUELLETTE, Megan   Tel: (206) 392-5805
Federal Lobbyist
Registered Federal Lobbyist

At Other Offices

THOMPSON, Tim R.   Tel: (907) 266-7230
Manager, Public Affairs - Alaska
4750 Old International Airport Rd.
Anchorage, AR 99502

Alaska Pipeline Service Company
See listing on page 43 under Alyeska Pipeline Service Company

Alaska Power and Telephone Company
Promotes and develops long term reliable energy and communication solutions.
www.aptalaska.com
Annual Revenues: $27.81 million
Employees: 200
Industry/ies: Communications; Energy/Electricity; Telecommunications/
Internet/Cable
Legislative Issues: UTI

Chairman of the Board   Tel: (360) 385-1733
SQUIRES, JD, William A.   Fax: (360) 385-5177

President, Media Contact and Chief Executive Officer   Tel: (360) 385-1733
GRIMM, Robert S.   Fax: (360) 385-5177

Main Headquarters
Mailing: P.O. Box 3222   Tel: (360) 385-1733
   193 Otto St.   Fax: (360) 385-5177
   Port Townsend, WA 98368   TF: (800) 982-0136

Corporate Foundations and Giving Programs
Alaska Power and Telephone Contributions Program
193 Otto St.   Tel: (360) 385-1733
P.O. Box 3222   Fax: (360) 385-5177
Port Townsend, WA 98368

Public Affairs and Related Activities Personnel

At Headquarters

HAGGAR, CPA, Chad A.   Tel: (360) 385-1733
Vice President, Chief Financial Officer and Treasurer   Fax: (360) 385-5177

Alaska Railroad Corporation
A self-sustaining, full-service railroad serving ports and communities from the Gulf of Alaska to Fairbanks.
www.alaskarailroad.com
Annual Revenues: $189.7 million

Employees: 800
Industry/ies: Railroads; Transportation
Legislative Issues: BUD; RRR; TAX; TRA

President and Chief Executive Officer   Tel: (907) 265-2300
O'LEARY, William G.   Fax: (907) 265-2416

Main Headquarters
Mailing: P.O. Box 107500   Tel: (907) 265-2300
   327 W. Ship Creek Ave.   Fax: (907) 265-2416
   Anchorage, AK 99510-7500   TF: (800) 321-6518

Corporate Foundations and Giving Programs
Alaska Railroad Corporation Charitable Giving
Contact: Wendy Lindskoog
Corporate Affairs Department   Tel: (907) 265-2437
P. O. Box 107500   Fax: (907) 265-2437
Anchorage, AK 99510-7500

Public Affairs and Related Activities Personnel

At Headquarters

AMY, Barbara   Tel: (907) 265-2300
Chief Financial Officer   Fax: (907) 265-2416

HUPPRICH, William   Tel: (907) 265-2300
Vice President and General Counsel   Fax: (907) 265-2416

LINDEMUTH, Susan   Tel: (907) 265-2300
Director, Human Resources   Fax: (907) 265-2416
lindemuths@akrr.com

LINDSKOOG, Wendy   Tel: (907) 265-2300
Vice President, Business Management and Corporate Affairs   Fax: (907) 265-2416
lindskoogw@akrr.com

SULLIVAN, Tim   Tel: (907) 265-2357
Contact, Corporate Affairs   Fax: (907) 265-2416
sullivant@akrr.com

WADE, Dale   Tel: (907) 265-2300
Vice President, Business Development   Fax: (907) 265-2416

WHEELER, Stephenie   Tel: (907) 265-2671
Contact, Media   Fax: (907) 265-2416

Alaska Structures, Inc.
A defense contractor.
www.alaskastructures.com
Employees: 100
Industry/ies: Defense/Homeland Security; Government-Related
Legislative Issues: BUD; DEF; HOM; LBR

Chief Executive Officer   Tel: (425) 889-1205
HOTES, Richard A.   Fax: (425) 889-1206

Main Headquarters
Mailing: 9024 Vanguard Dr.   Tel: (907) 344-1565
   Suite 101   Fax: (425) 889-1206
   Anchorage, AK 99507-4659   TF: (888) 370-1800

Albany International Corporation
The company makes paper machine clothing (PMC, custom-made fabrics and belts that move paper stock through each phase of production).
www.albint.com
Annual Revenues: $746.36 million
Employees: 4,000
Ticker: NYSE: AIN
SIC: 3089; 2299
NAICS: 326199; 314999
Industry/ies: Paper And Wood Products Industry

Chairman of the Board   Tel: (518) 445-2200
KAILBOURNE, Erland E.   Fax: (518) 445-2250

President and Chief Executive Officer   Tel: (518) 445-2200
MORONE, Joseph G.   Fax: (518) 445-2250

Main Headquarters
Mailing: 216 Airport Dr.   Tel: (603) 330-5850
   Rochester, NH 03867   Fax: (603) 994-3835

Corporate Foundations and Giving Programs
Albany International Corporation Contributions Program
P.O. Box 1907   Tel: (518) 445-2200
Albany, NY 12201-1907

Public Affairs and Related Activities Personnel

At Headquarters

PAWLICK , David M.   Tel: (603) 330-5850
Vice President, Controller   Fax: (603) 994-3835

At Other Offices

COZZOLINO, John   Tel: (518) 445-2200
Chief Financial Officer and Treasurer   Fax: (518) 445-2250
P.O. Box 1907
Albany, NY 12201-1907

john.cozzolino@albint.com

SIEGEL, Susan
Director, Corporate Communications
P.O. Box 1907
Albany, NY 12201-1907
susan.siegel@albint.com
Tel: (603) 330-5866
Fax: (518) 445-2250

SILVA, Jr., Charles J.
Vice President, General Counsel and Secretary
P.O. Box 1907
Albany, NY 12201-1907
Tel: (518) 445-2200
Fax: (518) 445-2250

Albemarle Corporation

The company produces polymer additives, fine chemicals, and catalysts used by a variety of industries.
www.albemarle.com
Annual Revenues: $2.73 billion
Employees: 3,625
Ticker: NYSE: ALB
SIC: 2819; 2821
Industry/ies: Chemicals & Chemical Industry
Legislative Issues: CHM

President and Chief Executive Officer
KISSAM, IV, Luther C.
Tel: (225) 388-7402
Fax: (225) 388-7686

Main Headquarters
Mailing: 451 Florida St.
Baton Rouge Tower
Baton Rouge, LA 70801
Tel: (225) 388-7402
Fax: (225) 388-7686
TF: (800) 535-3030

Washington Office
Mailing: 700 Second St. NE
Suite 8200
Washington, DC 20002
Tel: (202) 223-1848

Political Action Committees
Albemarle Corporation PAC
FEC ID: C00377333
Contact: Scott A. Tozier
451 Florida St.
Baton Rouge, LA 70801
Tel: (804) 788-6000
Fax: (804) 788-5688

Contributions to Candidates: $16,500 (2015-2016)
Democrats: $7,500; Republicans: $9,000

Corporate Foundations and Giving Programs
Albemarle Foundation
Contact: Sandra Holub
451 Florida St.
Baton Rouge Tower
Baton Rouge, LA 70801
Tel: (225) 388-7402
Fax: (225) 388-7686

Public Affairs and Related Activities Personnel

At Headquarters

HOLUB, Sandra
Executive Director, Albemarle Foundation
Sandra.Holub@albemarle.com
Tel: (225) 388-7552
Fax: (225) 388-7686

JUNEAU, Matthew K.
Senior Vice President, Corporate Strategy and Investor Relations
invest@albemarle.com
Tel: (225) 388-7620
Fax: (225) 388-7686

KELLIHER, Susan M.
Senior Vice President, Human Resources
Tel: (225) 388-7402
Fax: (225) 388-7686

NARWOLD, Karen G.
Senior Vice President, General Counsel, Corporate and Government Affairs, Corporate Secretary
Tel: (225) 388-7402
Fax: (225) 388-7686

TOZIER, Scott A.
Senior Vice President and Chief Financial Officer and PAC Treasurer
Tel: (225) 388-7402
Fax: (225) 388-7686

At Washington Office

LITTLE, Barbara
Vice President, Government Relations
Little@albemarle.com
Registered Federal Lobbyist
Tel: (202) 223-1848

MENDOZA, Ashley
Director, Communications
Ashley.Mendoza@albemarle.com
Tel: (225) 388-8924

Alberto-Culver Company

The Alberto Culver Company is now a part of the Unilever Group. A manufacturer and distributor of hair, beauty-care and household consumer products.
www.alberto.com
Annual Revenues: $1.43 billion
Employees: 2,500
Ticker: NYSE: ACV
SIC: 2844; 5087
NAICS: 32562; 44612
Industry/ies: Personal Care/Hygiene

President, Chief Executive Officer
MARINO, V. James
Tel: (708) 450-3000
Fax: (708) 450-3409

Main Headquarters
Mailing: 2525 Armitage Ave.
Melrose Park, IL 60160
Tel: (708) 450-3000
Fax: (708) 450-3435

Corporate Foundations and Giving Programs
Alberto-Culver Corporate Contributions Program
2525 Armitage Ave.
Melrose Park, IL 60160
Tel: (708) 450-3000
Fax: (708) 450-3409

Alcoa Inc.

See listing on page 42 under Aluminum Company of America (Alcoa) Inc.

Alcon Laboratories

A manufacturer of ophthalmic pharmaceuticals, contact lens care solutions, ophthalmic surgical instruments and accessory products.
www.alcon.com
Annual Revenues: $564.10 million
Employees: 24,000
Ticker: NYSE: ACL
SIC: 3851; 2834
NAICS: 325412
Industry/ies: Medicine/Health Care/Mental Health

Division Head and Chief Executive Officer Alcon
BALL, Mike
Tel: (817) 293-0450
Fax: (817) 551-4030

Main Headquarters
Mailing: 6201 S. Fwy.
Fort Worth, TX 76134-2099
Tel: (817) 293-0450
Fax: (817) 551-4030
TF: (800) 862-5266

Corporate Foundations and Giving Programs
Alcon Cares, Inc.
6201 S. Fwy.
Fort Worth, TX 76134-2099
Tel: (800) 222-8103
Fax: (800) 554-2660

Alcon Foundation
6201 South Fwy.
Fort Worth, TX 76134
Tel: (817) 551-4973
Fax: (817) 568-7000

Public Affairs and Related Activities Personnel

At Headquarters

ACKERMAN, Christina
Senior Vice President, General Counsel
Tel: (817) 293-0450
Fax: (817) 551-4030

ATTIAS, Laurent
Head, Strategy, BD and L and Market Access
Tel: (817) 293-0450
Fax: (817) 551-4030

HARNESS, Elizabeth R.
Director, Global External Communications
Tel: (817) 551-8696
Fax: (817) 551-4030

MAUNZ, Bettina
Vice President, Global Head Communications
Tel: (817) 293-0450
Fax: (817) 551-4030

MCCLELLAN, Brette
Vice President, Health Policy Government Affairs
Tel: (817) 568-6349
Fax: (817) 551-4030

MCCRACKEN , Merrick
Senior Vice President, Human Resources
Tel: (817) 293-0450
Fax: (817) 551-4030

MCGOUGH, Ed
Senior Vice President, Global Manufacturing and Technical Operations
Tel: (817) 293-0450
Fax: (817) 551-4030

MURRAY, David
Chief Financial Officer
Tel: (817) 293-0450
Fax: (817) 551-4030

STOOKEY, Beverly Kay
Manager, Treasury Administration and Stock Programs
Tel: (817) 293-0450
Fax: (817) 551-4030

WHITBECK, Elaine E.
Senior Vice President, Chief Legal Officer, and General Counsel and Corporate Secretary
elaine.whitbeck@alconlabs.com
Tel: (817) 293-0450
Fax: (817) 551-4030

Alenia Aermacchi

Alenia Aeronautica is the largest Italian Aerospace company and a world wide leader in commercial and military aviation, unmanned aerial vehicles and aerostructures.
www.aleniana.com
Industry/ies: Aerospace/Aviation; Transportation

Chief Executive Officer
GIORDO, Giuseppe
Tel: (202) 292-2620
Fax: (202) 293-0677

Chief Executive Officer
BAGNATO, Filippo

Main Headquarters
Mailing: 1235 South Clark St.
Suite 700
Arlington, VA 22202

Washington Office
Mailing: 1625 Eye St. NW
Suite 1200
Washington, DC 20006
Tel: (202) 292-2620
Fax: (202) 293-0677

Public Affairs and Related Activities Personnel

At Headquarters

GHIONE, Massimo
Vice General Manager Sales

VINTI, Ugo
Chief Business Officer

At Washington Office

MELI, Larissa		Tel:	(202) 292-2620
Vice President, General Counsel		Fax:	(202) 293-0677
PENTASSUGLIA, Marta		Tel:	(202) 292-2620
Vice President, Human Resources and Ethics Officer		Fax:	(202) 293-0677
WILLARD, Karen		Tel:	(202) 293-3433
Government Affairs Manager		Fax:	(202) 293-0677
kwillard@aleniainc.com			

Alere Inc.

Manufactures and markets consumer and professional medical diagnostic products. Alere delivers reliable and actionable information through rapid diagnostic tests, resulting in better clinical and economic healthcare outcomes globally.
www.alere.com
Annual Revenues: $2.50 billion
Employees: 9,800
Ticker: NYSE: ALR
SIC: 2835
Industry/ies: Medicine/Health Care/Mental Health
Legislative Issues: HCR; MMM

Chairman of the Board		Tel:	(781) 647-3900
POWERS, Gregg J.		Fax:	(781) 647-3939
Chief Executive Officer and President		Tel:	(781) 647-3900
NAWANA, Namal		Fax:	(781) 647-3939

Main Headquarters

Mailing:	51 Sawyer Rd.	Tel:	(781) 647-3900
	Suite 200	Fax:	(781) 647-3939
	Waltham, MA 02453-3448		

Political Action Committees

Alere Inc Good Government Committee
FEC ID: C00567909
Contact: Peter Doyle

51 Sawyer Rd.		Tel:	(781) 647-3900
Suite 200		Fax:	(781) 647-3939
Waltham, MA 02453-3448			

> **Contributions to Candidates:** $4,500 (2015-2016)
> Democrats: $1,500; Republicans: $3,000

Corporate Foundations and Giving Programs

Alere Inc. Contributions Program

51 Sawyer Rd.		Tel:	(781) 647-3900
Suite 200		Fax:	(781) 647-3939
Waltham, MA 02453-3448			

Public Affairs and Related Activities Personnel

At Headquarters

BRIDGEN, PhD, John		Tel:	(781) 647-3900
Senior Vice President, Business Development		Fax:	(781) 647-3939
john.bridgen@alere.com			
CHINIARA, Ellen		Tel:	(781) 647-3900
Senior Vice President, General Counsel, Chief Ethics and Compliance Officer, and Secretary		Fax:	(781) 647-3939
ellen.chiniara@alere.com			
CUNNINGHAM, Juliet		Tel:	(858) 805-2232
Vice President, Alere Investor Relations		Fax:	(781) 647-3939
ir@alere.com			
DOYLE, Peter		Tel:	(781) 647-3900
PAC Treasurer		Fax:	(781) 647-3939
GUARINO, Doug		Tel:	(781) 647-3900
Director, Corporate Relations		Fax:	(781) 647-3939
doug.guarino@alere.com			
HARGADON, Robert		Tel:	(781) 647-3900
Senior Vice President, Global Human Resources		Fax:	(781) 647-3939
HINRICHS, James		Tel:	(781) 647-3900
Executive Vice President and Chief Financial Officer		Fax:	(781) 647-3939
LUSTIG, Jackie		Tel:	(781) 314-4009
Senior Director, Corporate Communications		Fax:	(781) 647-3939
Jackie.Lustig@alere.com			
RADUS, Seth		Tel:	(781) 647-3900
Vice President, Government Affairs		Fax:	(781) 647-3939
Registered Federal Lobbyist			
RUSSELL, Jon		Tel:	(781) 647-3900
Vice President, Finance		Fax:	(781) 647-3939
jon.russell@invmed.com			

Aleut Corporation

Aleut Corporation currently manages and sells sand, gravel, minerals and rock aggregates as part of its subsurface rights within the region. Primary areas of business are real estate, government operations and maintenance contracting, aggregate sales, and investments in oil and gas producing properties and marketable securities.
www.aleutcorp.com
Annual Revenues: $146.06 million
Employees: 900
Industry/ies: Minorities
Legislative Issues: DEF; IND; MAR; RES

Chairman of the Board		Tel:	(907) 561-4300
JACOBSEN, Dick		Fax:	(907) 563-4328
Chief Executive Officer		Tel:	(907) 561-4300
FAGNANI, Matthew		Fax:	(907) 563-4328

Main Headquarters

Mailing:	4000 Old Seward Hwy.	Tel:	(907) 561-4300
	Suite 300	Fax:	(907) 563-4328
	Anchorage, AK 99503	TF:	(800) 232-4882

Corporate Foundations and Giving Programs

The Aleut Foundation
Contact: Cynthia H. Lind

703 W. Tudor Rd.		Tel:	(907) 646-1929
Suite 102		Fax:	(907) 646-1949
Anchorage, AK 99503			

Public Affairs and Related Activities Personnel

At Headquarters

LIND, Sharon Guenther		Tel:	(907) 561-4300
Director		Fax:	(907) 563-4328
MACK, Thomas		Tel:	(907) 561-4300
President		Fax:	(907) 563-4328
tmackc@aleutcorp.com			
OSBORN, Toby		Tel:	(907) 561-4300
Chief Financial Officer		Fax:	(907) 563-4328

At Other Offices

LIND, Cynthia H.		Tel:	(907) 646-1929
Executive Director, Foundation		Fax:	(907) 646-1949
703 W. Tudor Rd., Suite 102			
Anchorage, AK 99503-6650			
cynthia.lind@thealeutfoundation.org			

Alex Lee, Inc.

A wholesale distributor of food and other products to retailers. The success of Alex Lee and all of its operating companies is predicated on the desire to provide superior service to each of its customers. This service has helped independent supermarkets and locally owned restaurants to compete effectively against national chains, fast food operators, and discount retailers.
www.alexlee.com
Annual Revenues: $3.1 billion
Employees: 9,000
SIC: 5141
Industry/ies: Food And Beverage Industry; Retail/Wholesale

Chairman of the Board and Chief Executive Officer		Tel:	(828) 725-4424
GEORGE, Boyd L.		Fax:	(828) 725-4435

Main Headquarters

Mailing:	P.O. Box 800	Tel:	(828) 725-4424
	120 Fourth St.	Fax:	(828) 725-4435
	Hickory, NC 28603		

Political Action Committees

Alex Lee Inc. PAC
FEC ID: C00371385
Contact: Michael J. Greene

120 Fourth St. SW		Tel:	(828) 725-4424
Hickory, NC 28602		Fax:	(828) 725-4435

> **Contributions to Candidates:** $40,000 (2015-2016)
> Republicans: $40,000

> #### Principal Recipients
>
> **SENATE**
> BURR, RICHARD (REP-NC)
>
> **HOUSE**
> FOXX, VIRGINIA ANN (REP-NC)
> RYAN, PAUL D. (REP-WI)

Corporate Foundations and Giving Programs

Alex Lee Contribution Program
P.O. Box 800
Hickory, NC 28603

Public Affairs and Related Activities Personnel

At Headquarters

GREENE, Michael J.		Tel:	(828) 725-4424
PAC Contact		Fax:	(828) 725-4435

KNEDLIK, Ronald W.
Executive Vice President, Chief Financial Officer and PAC Treasurer
Tel: (828) 725-4424
Fax: (828) 725-4435

Alexander & Baldwin, Inc.

A Hawaii-based diversified company in ocean transportation, food products (coffee and sugar) and real estate development and management.
www.alexanderbaldwin.com
Annual Revenues: $427.20 million
Employees: 1,446
Ticker: NYSE: AXEX
SIC: 4400
Industry/ies: Food And Beverage Industry

Chairman and Chief Executive Officer
KURIYAMA, Stanley M.
Tel: (808) 525-6611
Fax: (808) 525-6652

Main Headquarters
Mailing: 822 Bishop St.
Honolulu, HI 96813
Tel: (808) 525-6611
Fax: (808) 525-6652

Political Action Committees
Alexander & Baldwin Inc. FEDPAC
FEC ID: C00017681
Contact: Paul T. Oshiro
P.O. Box 3440
Honolulu, HI 96801
Tel: (808) 525-6611
Fax: (808) 525-6652

Contributions to Candidates: $47,900 (2015-2016)
Democrats: $38,900; Republicans: $9,000

Principal Recipients
SENATE
SCHATZ, BRIAN (DEM-HI)

Corporate Foundations and Giving Programs
Alexander & Baldwin Foundation
Contact: Meredith J. Ching
P.O. Box 3440
Honolulu, HI 96801
Tel: (808) 525-6669
Fax: (808) 525-6677

Public Affairs and Related Activities Personnel

At Headquarters

BENJAMIN, Christopher J.
President and Chief Operating Officer
Tel: (808) 525-6611
Fax: (808) 525-6652

CHING, Meredith J.
Senior Vice President, Government, Community Relations, Foundation Contact and Media Contact
mching@abinc.com
Tel: (808) 525-6611
Fax: (808) 525-6677

CHUN, Nelson N.S.
Senior Vice President and Chief Legal Officer
Tel: (808) 525-6611
Fax: (808) 525-6652

HOLLINGER, Suzy P.
Director, Investor Relations
shollinger@abinc.com
Tel: (808) 525-8422
Fax: (808) 525-6651

ITO, Paul K.
Senior Vice President, Chief Financial Officer, Treasurer and Controller
Tel: (808) 525-6611
Fax: (808) 525-6652

MORVIS, George M.
Vice President, Corporate Development
Tel: (808) 525-6611
Fax: (808) 525-6652

OSHIRO, Paul T.
Manager, Government Relations and PAC Treasurer
Tel: (808) 525-6611
Fax: (808) 525-6652

PAIK, Son-Jai
Vice President, Human Resources
Tel: (808) 525-6611
Fax: (808) 525-6677

Alexion Pharmaceuticals, Inc.

A global biopharmaceutical company that develops and delivers life-transforming therapies for patients with serious and life-threatening medical conditions.
www.alxn.com
Annual Revenues: $2.27 billion
Employees: 2,273
Ticker: NASDAQ: ALXN
SIC: 2834
Industry/ies: Pharmaceutical Industry
Legislative Issues: CPT; HCR; MMM; TAX; TRD

Chairman of the Board
BELL, MD, Dr. Leonard
Tel: (203) 272-2596
Fax: (203) 271-8198

Chief Executive Officer
HALLAL , David
Tel: (203) 272-2596
Fax: (203) 271-8198

Main Headquarters
Mailing: 352 Knotter Dr.
Cheshire, CT 06410
Tel: (203) 272-2596
Fax: (203) 271-8198
TF: (888) 765-4747

Political Action Committees
Alexion Pharmaceuticals Inc PAC
FEC ID: C00471169
Contact: Michael V. Greco
352 Knotter Dr.

Cheshire, CT 06410

Contributions to Candidates: $88,500 (2015-2016)
Democrats: $35,900; Republicans: $52,600

Principal Recipients
HOUSE
GUTHRIE, S. BRETT HON. (REP-KY)

Corporate Foundations and Giving Programs
Alexion Pharmaceuticals, Inc. Contribution Program
352 Knotter Dr.
Cheshire, CT 06410
Tel: (203) 272-2596
Fax: (203) 271-8198

Public Affairs and Related Activities Personnel

At Headquarters

ADLER, Irving
Vice President, Corporate Communications
adleri@alxn.com
Tel: (203) 271-8210
Fax: (203) 271-8198

CARMICHAEL, Clare
Senior Vice President and Chief Human Resources Officer
Tel: (203) 272-2596
Fax: (203) 271-8198

GRECO, Michael V.
Vice President, Law and Corporate Secretary
Tel: (203) 272-2596
Fax: (203) 271-8198

HOGAN, Mary
Senior Director, LAL-D US Marketing
Tel: (203) 272-2596
Fax: (203) 271-8198

ISLAM, Saqib
Senior Vice President, Chief Strategy and Portfolio Officer
Tel: (203) 272-2596
Fax: (203) 271-8198

KALBAUGH, Gregory
Executive Director, Global Government Affairs
Registered Federal Lobbyist
Tel: (203) 272-2596
Fax: (203) 271-8198

MACKAY, PhD, Martin
Executive Vice President, Global Head of Research & Development
Tel: (203) 272-2596
Fax: (203) 271-8198

MILLER, Edward
Senior Vice President, Global Chief Compliance Officer
Tel: (203) 272-2596
Fax: (203) 271-8198

MONNET, Dominique
Senior Vice President, Chief Marketing Officer
Tel: (203) 272-2596
Fax: (203) 271-8198

MORIARTY, John
Senior Vice President and General Counsel
Tel: (203) 272-2596
Fax: (203) 271-8198

OWANO, Leigh
Registered Federal Lobbyist
Tel: (203) 272-2596
Fax: (203) 271-8198

PROCTER, Vanessa
Senior Director, Global Government Affairs
Registered Federal Lobbyist
Tel: (203) 272-2596
Fax: (203) 271-8198

SINHA, Vikas
Senior Vice President and Chief Financial Officer
Tel: (203) 272-2596
Fax: (203) 271-8198

WAGNER, Esq., Heidi L.
Senior Vice President, Global Government Affairs
Registered Federal Lobbyist
Tel: (202) 737-0550
Fax: (203) 271-8198

Algenol Biofuels, Inc.

A biofuels company specializing in algae to ethanol technology. Headquartered in Bonita Springs, FL.
www.algenolbiofuels.com
Annual Revenues: $4.80 million
Employees: 160
Industry/ies: Energy/Electricity; Environment And Conservation; Fuels See Coal, Gas, Oil, Petroleum; Natural Resources; Petroleum Industry
Legislative Issues: CAW

Founder, Chairman of the Board, Chief Executive Officer and President
WOODS, Paul
Tel: (239) 498-2000

Main Headquarters
Mailing: 16121 Lee Rd.
Suite 110
Fort Myers, FL 33912
Tel: (239) 498-2000

Washington Office
Mailing: 12 S. Hudson St.
Arlington, VA 22204
Tel: (239) 405-5187

Public Affairs and Related Activities Personnel

At Headquarters

AHLM, Patrick
Assistant Director, Government and Regulatory Affairs and Business Development
Tel: (239) 498-2000

HA, Quang
General Counsel
Tel: (239) 498-2000

MCFADDEN, Kathleen
Chief Financial Officer
Tel: (239) 498-2000

ZENK, Timothy
Executive Vice President, Business Development
Tel: (239) 498-2000

At Washington Office

MCCARTHY, David J.　　　　　Tel:　(239) 405-5187
Vice President
dave.mccarthy@algenobiofuels.com

Alice Manufacturing Company, Inc.
Textile manufacturer of greige fabric and yarn.
www.alicemfgco.com
Annual Revenues: $37.40 million
Employees: 300
SIC: 2392; 2389
Industry/ies: Apparel/Textiles Industry

Chairman of the Board, Chief Executive Officer and President　Tel:　(864) 859-6323
MCKISSICK, Smyth E.　　　　Fax:　(864) 859-6328

Main Headquarters
Mailing:　208 E. First Ave.　　Tel:　(864) 859-6323
　　　　Easley, SC 29640-3039　Fax:　(864) 859-6328

Public Affairs and Related Activities Personnel

At Headquarters

BROOKS, Stan　　　　　　Tel:　(864) 859-6323
Director, Human Resources　　Fax:　(864) 859-6328

THOMAS, Robert　　　　　Tel:　(864) 859-6323
Chief Financial Officer　　　Fax:　(864) 859-6328

At Other Offices

ROLLINS, John A.　　　　　Tel:　(864) 306-2136
PAC Treasurer
P.O. Box 369
Easley, SC 29641

Alien Technology Corporation
Alien was founded in 1994 . Alien Technology provides UHF Radio Frequency Identification (RFID) products and services to customers in retail, consumer goods, manufacturing, defense, transportation and logistics, pharmaceuticals and other industries.
www.alientechnology.com
Annual Revenues: $28.40 million
Employees: 200
SIC: 3679
Industry/ies: Computer/Technology

Chairman of the Board　　　Tel:　(408) 782-3900
ZITZNER, Duane E.　　　　　Fax:　(408) 782-3910

Chief Executive Officer　　Tel:　(408) 782-3900
CHANG, Chris　　　　　　Fax:　(408) 782-3908

Main Headquarters
Mailing:　845 Embedded Way　Tel:　(408) 782-3900
　　　　San Jose, CA 95138-1030　Fax:　(408) 782-3908

Public Affairs and Related Activities Personnel

At Headquarters

ERVIN, Patrick　　　　　　Tel:　(408) 782-3900
Vice President, World Wide Marketing and Sales　Fax:　(408) 782-3908

FRANCISCO, Daniel　　　　Tel:　(408) 782-3900
Contact, Media, Marketing and Analyst, Investor Relations　Fax:　(408) 782-3908
dan@franciscogrp.com

HAEGELE, Glenn R.　　　　Tel:　(408) 782-3900
Chief Financial Officer　　　Fax:　(408) 782-3908

At Other Offices

AARON, David A.　　　　　Tel:　(408) 782-3900
PAC Contact, Chief Legal Officer and Vice President,　Fax:　(408) 782-3910
Business Development
18220 Butterfield Blvd.
Morgan Hill, CA 95037
daaron@alientechnology.com

Alion Science and Technology Corporation
Technology solutions company.
www.alionscience.com
Annual Revenues: $817.00 million
Employees: 3,000
SIC: 8711
Industry/ies: Science; Scientific Research

Chairman of the Board and Chief Executive Officer　Tel:　(703) 918-4480
ATEFI, Bahman　　　　　Fax:　(703) 714-6508

Main Headquarters
Mailing:　1750 Tysons Blvd.　　Tel:　(703) 918-4480
　　　　Suite 1300　　　　Fax:　(703) 714-6508
　　　　McLean, VA 22102

Political Action Committees
Alion Science and Technology Corporation PAC
FEC ID: C00431247
Contact: Tim Cook
1750 Tysons Blvd.　　　　　Tel:　(703) 918-4480

Suite 1300
McLean, VA 22102
　　Contributions to Candidates:　$41,285 (2015-2016)
　　Democrats: $15,285; Republicans: $26,000

Corporate Foundations and Giving Programs
Alion Science and Technology Contribution Program
1750 Tysons Blvd.　　　　　Tel:　(703) 918-4480
Suite 1300　　　　　　　Fax:　(703) 714-6508
McLean, VA 22102

Public Affairs and Related Activities Personnel

At Headquarters

BOYL, Kevin　　　　　　Tel:　(703) 918-4480
General Counsel　　　　　Fax:　(703) 714-6508

BROADUS, Barry　　　　　Tel:　(703) 918-4480
Chief Financial Officer　　　Fax:　(703) 714-6508

COOK, Tim　　　　　　Tel:　(703) 918-4480
　　　　　　　　　　Fax:　(703) 714-6508

IVES, Mark　　　　　　Tel:　(703) 918-4480
Chief Information Officer　　Fax:　(703) 714-6508

JACOBS, Peter　　　　　Tel:　(703) 269-3473
Director, Marketing and Communications　Fax:　(703) 506-1813
pjacobs@alionscience.com

KIMMEL, Steve　　　　　Tel:　(703) 918-4480
Director, Strategic Customers Relations　Fax:　(703) 714-6508
skimmel@aliontechnology.com

MADALENO, Kathy　　　　Tel:　(703) 918-4480
Director, Human Resources　　Fax:　(703) 714-6508

WEAVER, Patty　　　　　Tel:　(703) 918-4480
Chief Administrative Officer　Fax:　(703) 714-6508

Alkermes, Inc.
Global biopharmaceutical company specializing in innovative treatments.
www.alkermes.com
Annual Revenues: $649.79 million
Employees: 1,300
SIC: 2834
Industry/ies: Pharmaceutical Industry
Legislative Issues: ALC; HCR; LAW; MMM; PHA

Chairman and Chief Executive Officer　　Tel:　(781) 609-6000
POPS, Richard F.

Main Headquarters
Mailing:　852 Winter St.　　　Tel:　(781) 609-6000
　　　　Waltham, MA 02451

Washington Office
Mailing:　401 Ninth St. NW, Suite 710
　　　　Washington, DC 20004

Political Action Committees
Alkermes, Inc PAC
FEC ID: C00525063
Contact: James M. Frates
852 Winter St.
Waltham, MA 02451
　　Contributions to Candidates:　$109,200 (2015-2016)
　　Democrats: $23,700; Republicans: $85,500
　　　　　Principal Recipients
　　　　　　SENATE
　　　　　　PORTMAN, ROB (REP-OH)
　　　　　　HOUSE
　　　　　　WOMACK, STEVE (REP-AR)

Public Affairs and Related Activities Personnel

At Headquarters

BUCCERI , Dennis J.　　　　Tel:　(781) 609-6000
Vice President, Regulatory Affairs

COFFIN, Madeline D.　　　　Tel:　(781) 609-6000
Vice President, Human Resources

CRAWFORD, Brian　　　　　Tel:　(781) 609-6000
Head, Public Policy
brian.crawford@alkermes.com
Registered Federal Lobbyist

FORMAN, PhD, Rob　　　　Tel:　(781) 609-6000
Director, Professional Relations
robert.forman@alkermes.com
Registered Federal Lobbyist

FRATES, James M.　　　　Tel:　(781) 609-6000
Senior Vice President and Chief Financial Officer

LANDINE, Michael J.　　　　Tel:　(781) 609-6000
Senior Vice President, Corporate Development

PETERSON , Rebecca J.　　　Tel:　(781) 609-6000

Senior Vice President, Corporate Communications

PUGH, Gordon G.   Tel: (781) 609-6000
*Senior Vice President, Chief Operating Officer and Chief Risk
Officer*

TREWOLLA, David   Tel: (781) 609-6000
Registered Federal Lobbyist

At Washington Office

NORMAN, Peter
*Vice President, Government Affairs & Policy
Registered Federal Lobbyist*

All American Group

A manufacturer of recreational vehicles and modular homes.
www.allamericangroupinc.com
Annual Revenues: $60.62 million
Employees: 600
Ticker: NASDAQ: COHM
SIC: 1520
Industry/ies: Automotive Industry; Sports/Leisure/Entertainment;
Transportation

Chairman of the Board   Tel: (574) 266-2500
JOHNSON, William P.   Fax: (574) 266-2559

President and Chief Executive Officer   Tel: (574) 266-2500
LAVERS, Richard M.   Fax: (574) 266-2559

Main Headquarters
Mailing: 2831 Dexter Dr.   Tel: (574) 266-2500
    P.O. Box 3300   Fax: (574) 266-2559
    Elkhart, IN 46515

All-Circo, Inc.

A Lobbying Firm, monitoring legislative action on the state and local level.
www.allcirco.com
Industry/ies: Public Affairs And Public Relations

President   Tel: (312) 750-9262
KELLY, Jr., John J.
jmihm@allcirco.com

Main Headquarters
Mailing: 670 N. Clark St.   Tel: (312) 750-9262
    Fourth Floor
    Chicago, IL 60654

Public Affairs and Related Activities Personnel

At Headquarters

HOULIHAN, James M.   Tel: (312) 750-9262
Senior Advisor

ROGERS, Raechel   Tel: (312) 750-9262
Coordinator, Client Relations

Allegheny Energy Inc.

See listing on page 326 under First Energy Corporation

Allegheny Technologies, Inc.

A manufacturer of stainless steel and steel alloys.
www.atimetals.com
Annual Revenues: $3.35 billion
Employees: 9,200
Ticker: NYSE: ATI
SIC: 3546; 3494; 2819; 3499; 3317
NAICS: 332919; 325188; 333991; 332999
Industry/ies: Aerospace/Aviation; Defense/Homeland Security; Electricity
& Electronics; Electronics; Energy/Electricity; Engineering/Mathematics;
Environment And Conservation; Government-Related; Metals; Science; Scientific
Research; Transportation
Legislative Issues: BUD; DEF; MAN; TRD

Chairman of the Board, President and Chief Executive Officer   Tel: (412) 394-2800
HARSHMAN, Richard J.   Fax: (412) 394-3034
Rich.Harshman@ATImetals.com

Main Headquarters
Mailing: 1000 Six PPG Pl.   Tel: (412) 394-2800
    Pittsburgh, PA 15222   Fax: (412) 394-3034

Political Action Committees
Allegheny Technologies Corporation PAC
FEC ID: C00141697
Contact: Karl D. Schwartz
1000 Six PPG Pl.   Tel: (412) 394-2800
Pittsburgh, PA 15222   Fax: (412) 394-3034

    Contributions to Candidates: $30,500 (2015-2016)
    Democrats: $2,500; Republicans: $28,000

Corporate Foundations and Giving Programs
Allegheny Technologies Charitable Trust

1000 Six PPG Pl.   Tel: (412) 394-2800
Pittsburgh, PA 15222   Fax: (412) 394-3035

Public Affairs and Related Activities Personnel

At Headquarters

DAVIS, Elliot S.   Tel: (412) 394-2800
Senior Vice President, General Counsel, Chief Compliance   Fax: (412) 394-3034
Officer and Corporate Secretary
Elliot.Davis@ATImetals.com

DECOURCY, Patrick J.   Tel: (412) 394-2800
Senior Vice President, Finance and Chief Financial Officer   Fax: (412) 394-3034

GREENFIELD, Danny L.   Tel: (412) 394-3004
Vice President, Investor Relations and Corporate   Fax: (412) 394-3034
Communications
Dan.Greenfield@ATImetals.com

KRAMER, Kevin B.   Tel: (412) 394-2800
Senior Vice President, Chief Commercial and Marketing   Fax: (412) 394-3034
Officer

MANLEY, Rose Marie   Tel: (412) 394-2800
Vice President, Treasurer   Fax: (412) 394-3034

MCANDREWS, Lauren S.   Tel: (412) 394-2800
Vice President, Labor Relations and Assistant General   Fax: (412) 394-3034
Counsel

MOORE, Mary Beth   Tel: (412) 394-2800
Vice President, Human Resources   Fax: (412) 394-3034

POWERS, Elizabeth C.   Tel: (412) 394-2800
Senior Vice President, Chief Human Resources Officer   Fax: (412) 394-3034

SCHWARTZ, Karl D.   Tel: (412) 394-2800
Controller, Chief Accounting Officer and PAC Treasurer   Fax: (412) 394-3034

Allegheny Teledyne Incorporated

See listing on page 35 under Allegheny Technologies, Inc.

Allergan, Inc.

*A manufacturer of eye and skin care products, neuromuscular products and ophthalmic
surgical products.*
www.allergan.com
Annual Revenues: $7237.90 billion
Employees: 10,500
Ticker: NYSE: AGN
SIC: 2834
NAICS: 325412
Industry/ies: Medicine/Health Care/Mental Health; Pharmaceutical Industry
Legislative Issues: HCR; MMM

Chairman of the Board, President and Chief Executive Officer   Tel: (714) 246-4500
PYOTT, David E.I.   Fax: (714) 246-4971

Main Headquarters
Mailing: 2525 Dupont Dr.   Tel: (714) 246-4500
    P.O. Box 19534, Mail Code T1-4D   Fax: (714) 246-4971
    Irvine, CA 92612   TF: (800) 433-8871

Washington Office
Mailing: 100 M. St. SE, Suite 500
    Washington, DC 20003

Political Action Committees
Allergan Inc. PAC (APACE)
FEC ID: C00292102
Contact: Edith Bennett
2148 E. Organeview Ln.
Orange, CA 92867

    Contributions to Candidates: $37,596 (2015-2016)
    Democrats: $2,000; Republicans: $35,596

Corporate Foundations and Giving Programs
Allergan Foundation
Contact: Gwyn Grenrock
2525 Dupont Dr.
P.O. Box 19534, Mail Code T1-4D
Irvine, CA 92623

Public Affairs and Related Activities Personnel

At Headquarters

EDWARDS, Jeffrey L.   Tel: (714) 246-4500
Executive Vice President, Finance and Business Development   Fax: (714) 246-4971
and Chief Financial Officer

GRENROCK, Gwyn   Tel: (714) 246-2077
Executive Director, Allergan Foundation   Fax: (714) 246-4971

HINDMAN, Jim   Tel: (714) 246-4636
Chief Financial Officer   Fax: (714) 246-4971

INGRAM, Douglas S.   Tel: (714) 246-4500
President   Fax: (714) 246-4971

RENO, EDWARD   Tel: (714) 246-4500
National Director, Federal Government Affairs   Fax: (714) 246-4971

SKELTON, Jennie Unger	Tel:	(714) 246-5766
Attorney & Agent for filer	Fax:	(714) 246-4971
SWANSON, Rose Karen	Tel:	(714) 246-4500
Senior Vice President and Chief Compliance Officer	Fax:	(714) 246-4971
VAN HOVE, Caroline	Tel:	(714) 246-4500
Senior Director, Marketing	Fax:	(714) 246-4971
vanhove_caroline@allergan.com		

At Other Offices

BENNETT, Edith
PAC Treasurer
2148 E. Orangeview Ln.
Orange, CA 92867
pacificon@earthlink.net

Allete, Inc.

Provides energy services in the upper Midwest and has real estate holdings in Florida.
www.allete.com
Annual Revenues: $1.16 billion
Employees: 1,600
Ticker: NYSE: ALE
SIC: 4931
Industry/ies: Energy/Electricity
Legislative Issues: CAW; ENG; ENV; RRR; TAX; UTI

Chairman of the Board, President and Chief Executive Officer	Tel:	(218) 279-5000
HODNIK, Alan R.	Fax:	(218) 720-2502

Main Headquarters

Mailing:	30 W. Superior St.	Tel:	(218) 279-5000
	Duluth, MN 55802	Fax:	(218) 720-2502
		TF:	(800) 535-3056

Washington Office

Mailing:	122 C St. NW	Tel:	(202) 638-7707
	Suite 840		
	Washington, DC 20001		

Political Action Committees

ALLETE PAC
FEC ID: C00142489
Contact: Bernadette R. Nelson

30 W. Superior St.	Tel:	(218) 279-5000
Duluth, MN 55802		

    Contributions to Candidates: $36,000 (2015-2016)
    Democrats: $12,500; Republicans: $23,500

Public Affairs and Related Activities Personnel

At Headquarters

AMBERG, Deborah A.	Tel:	(218) 279-5000
Senior Vice President, General Counsel and Secretary	Fax:	(218) 720-2502
DEVINCK, Steven Q.	Tel:	(218) 279-5000
Senior Vice President and Chief Financial Officer	Fax:	(218) 720-2502
HANSON, Peggy	Tel:	(218) 720-2518
Community Relations and Foundation Director	Fax:	(218) 720-2502
mhanson@mnpower.com		
LIBRO, William J.	Tel:	(218) 279-5000
Director, Federal Affairs	Fax:	(218) 720-2502
blibro@allete.com		
Registered Federal Lobbyist		
MCMILLAN, David J.	Tel:	(218) 279-5000
Senior Vice President, External Affairs	Fax:	(218) 720-2502
MORRIS , Steven W.	Tel:	(218) 279-5000
Controller	Fax:	(218) 720-2502
NELSON, Bernadette R.	Tel:	(218) 279-5000
PAC Contact	Fax:	(218) 720-2502
NORBERG, Eric	Tel:	(218) 279-5000
President, ALLETE Clean Energy	Fax:	(218) 720-2502
THORP, Timothy J.	Tel:	(218) 723-3953
Vice President, Investor Relations	Fax:	(218) 720-2502
tthorp@allete.com		

Allina Hospitals and Clinics

Formerly known as Allina Health System. Allina Hospitals & Clinics is now Allina Health. An integrated provider of medical services.
www.allina.com
Employees: 26,292
Industry/ies: Insurance Industry; Medicine/Health Care/Mental Health

President and Chief Executive Officer	Tel:	(612) 262-5000
WHEELER, Penny	Fax:	(612) 863-5667

Main Headquarters

Mailing:	1656 S.E. Bay Blvd	Fax:	(801) 850-5001
	Suite 100	TF:	(800) 228-9851
	Provo, UT 84606		

Corporate Foundations and Giving Programs

Allina Hospitals and Clinics Contributions Program
Contact: Ellie Zuehlke
P.O. Box 43
Minneapolis, MN 55440-0043

Public Affairs and Related Activities Personnel

At Other Offices

GALLAGHER, Duncan P.	Tel:	(612) 262-5000
Executive Vice President, Chief Administrative Officer and Chief Financial Officer	Fax:	(612) 863-5667
2925 Chicago Ave.		
Minneapolis, MN 55407		
JORDAHL, Mark S.	Tel:	(612) 262-5000
Director	Fax:	(612) 863-5667
2925 Chicago Ave.		
Minneapolis, MN 55407		
KANIHAN, David	Tel:	(612) 262-4986
Director, Marketing and Communications	Fax:	(612) 863-5667
2925 Chicago Ave.		
Minneapolis, MN 55407		
david.kanihan@allina.com		
SMITH, Elizabeth Truesdell	Tel:	(612) 262-5000
Senior Vice President, General counsel and Secretary	Fax:	(612) 863-5667
2925 Chicago Ave.		
Minneapolis, MN 55407		

Alliance Gaming

See listing on page 706 under Scientific Games Corporation

Alliance Health Care Services

See listing on page 36 under Alliance Imaging - A Division of Alliance Health Services

Alliance Imaging - A Division of Alliance Health Services

Provider of advanced outpatient diagnostic imaging services. It also focuses on MRI, PET/CT, and CT technologies.
www.allianceimaging.com
Annual Revenues: $440.45 million
Employees: 1,582
Ticker: NYSE: AIQ
SIC: 8071
Industry/ies: Computer/Technology; Medicine/Health Care/Mental Health

Chairman of the Board	Tel:	(949) 242-5300
BUCKELEW, Larry C.		
Chief Executive Officer	Tel:	(949) 242-5300
TOMLINSON, Tom C.		

Main Headquarters

Mailing:	100 Bayview Cir.	Tel:	(949) 242-5300
	Suite 400	TF:	(800) 544-3215
	Newport Beach, CA 92660		

Corporate Foundations and Giving Programs

Alliance Imaging Contributions Program

100 Bayview Cir.	Tel:	(949) 242-5300
Suite 400		
Newport Beach, CA 92660		

Public Affairs and Related Activities Personnel

At Headquarters

AIHARA, Howard	Tel:	(949) 242-5300
Executive Vice President and Chief Financial Officer		
JOHNS, Richard W.	Tel:	(949) 242-5300
Executive Vice President, General Counsel and Secretary		
MILLER, Laurie	Tel:	(949) 242-5300
Senior Vice President, Human Resources		
SPRATT, Joseph	Tel:	(949) 242-5300
Senior Vice President, National Sales		
VIVIANO, Paul S.	Tel:	(949) 242-5300
Director		

Alliance One International Inc.

Formed by the merger of Dimon Incorporated and Standard Commercial Corp. in May 2005.
www.aointl.com
Annual Revenues: $1.90 billion
Employees: 3,281
Ticker: NYSE: AOI
SIC: 5150
Industry/ies: Machinery/Equipment
Legislative Issues: AGR; TRD

Chairman of the Board	Tel:	(919) 379-4300
KEHAYA, Mark W.	Fax:	(919) 379-4346
mkehaya@aointl.com		

President and Chief Executive Officer
SIKKEL, J Pieter

Tel: (919) 379-4300
Fax: (919) 379-4346

Main Headquarters
Mailing: 8001 Aerial Center Pkwy.
P.O. Box 2009
Morrisville, NC 27560-2009

Tel: (919) 379-4300
Fax: (919) 379-4346

Public Affairs and Related Activities Personnel

At Headquarters

COSTA GARCIA, Josè Maria
Executive Vice President, Global Operations and Supply Chain

Tel: (919) 379-4300
Fax: (919) 379-4346

FAIR, Jennifer
Corporate Communications and Compliance Manager

Tel: (919) 379-4300
Fax: (919) 379-4346

JONES, Laura D.
Vice President, Human Resources

Tel: (919) 379-4300
Fax: (919) 379-4346

KAYES, Graham J
Executive Vice President, Business Relationship Management and Leaf

Tel: (919) 379-4300
Fax: (919) 379-4346

O'QUINN, William L.
Senior Vice President, Chief Legal Officer and Secretary

Tel: (919) 379-4313
Fax: (919) 379-4346

THOMAS, Joel L.
Executive Vice President, Chief Financial Officer

Tel: (919) 379-4300
Fax: (919) 379-4346

Alliant Energy Corporation

Formed in 1998 from the merger of Interstate Power Co., Wisconsin Power & Light Co. and IES Industries, Inc. A regulated, investor-owned public utility holding company providing regulated electric and natural gas service to electric and natural gas customers in the states of Iowa, Wisconsin and Minnesota.
www.alliantenergy.com
Annual Revenues: $3.20 billion
Employees: 4,070
Ticker: NYSE: LNT
SIC: 4931
Industry/ies: Energy/Electricity; Utilities
Legislative Issues: BUD; ENV; TAX

Chairman of the Board, President and Chief Executive Officer
KAMPLING, Patricia Leonard

Tel: (608) 458-3311
Fax: (608) 458-0100

Main Headquarters
Mailing: 4902 N. Biltmore Ln.
Suite 1000
Madison, WI 53707

Tel: (608) 458-3311
Fax: (608) 458-0100
TF: (800) 255-4268

Washington Office
Mailing: 801 Pennsylvania Ave. NW
Suite 640, West Tower
Washington, DC 20004

Tel: (202) 347-8132
Fax: (202) 347-8136

Political Action Committees
Alliant Energy Corporation Employee's PAC
FEC ID: C00132092
Contact: Kathryn J. Barnett
801 Pennsylvania Ave. NW
Suite 640
Washington, DC 20004

Tel: (202) 347-8132
Fax: (202) 347-8136

> **Contributions to Candidates:** $55,500 (2015-2016)
> Democrats: $8,500; Republicans: $47,000

> ### Principal Recipients
> #### HOUSE
> RYAN, PAUL D. (REP-WI)

Corporate Foundations and Giving Programs
Alliant Energy Foundation
Contact: Julie Bauer
4902 N. Biltmore Ln.
P.O. Box 77007
Madison, WI 53707-1007

Fax: (608) 458-0100

Public Affairs and Related Activities Personnel

At Headquarters

BAUER, Julie
Executive Director

Tel: (608) 458-4483
Fax: (608) 458-0100

GALLEGOS, James H.
Senior Vice President, General Counsel and Corporate Secretary

Tel: (608) 458-3311
Fax: (608) 458-0100

GILLE, Susan Trapp
Manager, Investor Relations

Tel: (608) 458-3956
Fax: (608) 458-0132

HANSON, Thomas L.
Senior Vice President and Chief Financial Officer

Tel: (608) 458-3311
Fax: (608) 458-0100

RAINBOLT, III, John
Registered Federal Lobbyist

Tel: (608) 458-3311
Fax: (608) 458-0100

REIGSTAD, Scott
Contact, Corporate Communications and Spokesperson

Tel: (608) 458-3311
Fax: (608) 458-0100

RESCHKE, Wayne A.
Vice President, Human Resources

Tel: (608) 458-3311
Fax: (608) 458-0100

SCHMIDT, Joel J.
Vice President, Regulatory Affairs

Tel: (608) 458-3311
Fax: (608) 458-0100

At Washington Office

BARNETT, Kathryn J.
PAC Treasurer

Tel: (202) 347-8132
Fax: (202) 347-8136

HILL, Zack
Senior Manager, Strategic Planning
zackhill@alliantenergy.com

Tel: (202) 347-8133
Fax: (202) 347-8136

Allianz Life Insurance Company of North America

Provides fixed and variable annuities, life insurance policies, and long term care insurance products in the United States.
www.allianzlife.com
Annual Revenues: $136.20 million
Employees: 2,800
SIC: 6311
Industry/ies: Insurance Industry
Legislative Issues: TAX

President and Chief Executive Officer
WHITE, Walter

Tel: (763) 765-6500

Main Headquarters
Mailing: PO Box 1344
Minneapolis, MN 55416-1297

Corporate Foundations and Giving Programs
Allianz Life Corporate Giving
Contact: Laura Juergens
P.O. Box 1344
Minneapolis, MN 55416

Tel: (763) 582-6571

Public Affairs and Related Activities Personnel

At Headquarters

MAHONE, Cathy
Chief Administrative Officer

At Other Offices

CEPEK, Gretchen
General Counsel
5701 Golden Hills Dr.
Minneapolis, MN 55416-1297

Tel: (763) 765-6500

FAUST, Jeff
Senior Specialist, External Communications
5701 Golden Hills Dr.
Minneapolis, MN 55416-1297
jeff.faust@allianzlife.com

Tel: (763) 765-6500

JONES, Nancy
Chief Marketing Officer
5701 Golden Hills Dr.
Minneapolis, MN 55416-1297

Tel: (763) 765-6500

JUERGENS, Laura
Foundation Contact
5701 Golden Hills Dr.
Minneapolis, MN 55416-1297
Laura.Juergens@allianzlife.com

Tel: (763) 582-6571

QUITTER, Carsten
Chief Investment Officer
5701 Golden Hills Dr.
Minneapolis, MN 55416-1297

Tel: (763) 765-6500

STEVENS, Andrew
Director, Government & External Affairs
5701 Golden Hills Dr.
Minneapolis, MN 55416-1297

Tel: (763) 765-6500

TERZARIOL, Giulio
Chief Financial Officer
5701 Golden Hills Dr.
Minneapolis, MN 55416-1297

Tel: (763) 765-6500

ZELLER, Suzanne
Vice President and Chief Human Resources Officer
5701 Golden Hills Dr.
Minneapolis, MN 55416-1297

Tel: (763) 765-6500

Allianz of America Corporation Group (Fireman's Fund Insurance Company)

Fireman's Fund Insurance Company is a company of Allianz.
www.azoa.com
Industry/ies: Disaster; Insurance Industry
Legislative Issues: BAN; FIN; INS; RET; TAX; TOR

Main Headquarters
Mailing: 1101 Connecticut Ave. NW
Suite 950
Washington, DC 20036

Tel: (202) 785-3575

Political Action Committees

Allianz of America Corporation/Fireman's Fund Political Action Committee
FEC ID: C00095109
Contact: Sally Narey
1101 Connecticut Ave. NW
Suite 950
Washington, DC 20036

   Contributions to Candidates: $56,650 (2015-2016)
   Democrats: $15,800; Republicans: $40,850

Public Affairs and Related Activities Personnel

At Headquarters

HOLLY, William F.	Tel:	(202) 785-3575
Vice President, Government and Industry Affairs		
bholly@ffic.com		
LA VECK, Patrick	Tel:	(202) 785-3575
LEFKIN, Peter A.	Tel:	(202) 785-3575
Senior Vice President, Government & External Affairs		
peter.lefkin@azoac.com		
Registered Federal Lobbyist		
NAREY, Sally	Tel:	(202) 785-3575
PAC Contact		
STEVENS, Andrew	Tel:	(202) 785-3575
Registered Federal Lobbyist		
SUTTON, Rashmi	Tel:	(202) 785-3575
Director, Government Affairs		
rashmi.sutton@azoac.com		

Allied Capital Corporation

It provides corporate finance services to public and private companies, established growth companies, and companies with unusual financing requirements seeking private equity or mezzanine financing.
www.alliedcapital.com
Annual Revenues: $277.60 million
Employees: 107
Ticker: NYSE:AFC
Industry/ies: Banking/Finance/Investments

Chairman, Chief Executive Officer, and President	Tel:	(202) 721-6100
WALTON, William L.	Fax:	(202) 721-6101
President	Tel:	(416) 961-8907
SMALLEY, Katherine	Fax:	(416) 324-8253
ksmalley@alliedcap.ca		

Main Headquarters

Mailing:	368 Brunswick Ave.	Tel:	(416) 961-8907
	Toronto, ON M5R 2Y9	Fax:	(416) 324-8253

Washington Office

Mailing:	1919 Pennsylvania Ave. NW	Tel:	(202) 721-6100
	Suite 300	Fax:	(202) 721-6101
	Washington, DC 20006		

Allied Telesis

Electronics manufacturer and telecommunications provider.
www.alliedtelesis.com
Annual Revenues: $52.60 million
Employees: 200
Industry/ies: Communications; Computer/Technology; Telecommunications/Internet/Cable

Chairman of the Board and Chief Executive Officer	Tel:	(800) 424-4284
OSHIMA, Takayoshi	Fax:	(425) 481-3895

Main Headquarters

Mailing:	1530 Wilson Blvd	Tel:	(800) 424-4284
	Suite 170	Fax:	(425) 481-3895
	Arlington, VA 22209	TF:	(800) 424-4284

Public Affairs and Related Activities Personnel

At Headquarters

GRACE, Cort	Tel:	(800) 424-4284
VP Sales	Fax:	(425) 481-3895
JOHNSON, Ann	Tel:	(408) 519-8635
Senior Manager and Media Contact	Fax:	(425) 481-3895
ann_johnson@alliedtelesis.com		
KELLY, Michael T.	Tel:	(800) 424-4284
Director Government OEM & Channel	Fax:	(425) 481-3895
mike_kelly@alliedtelesis.com		

Allied Van Lines, North American Van Lines, Global Van Lines, SIRVA Relocation

See listing on page 723 under SIRVA, Inc.

Allied Waste Industries Inc.

See listing on page 680 under Republic Services, Inc.

Allina Hospitals and Clinics

See listing on page 36 under Allina Hospitals and Clinics

Allmerica Financial

See listing on page 384 under The Hanover Insurance Group

Allonhill

A mortgage services firm with experience in risk management and due diligence.
www.allonhill.com
Industry/ies: Banking/Finance/Investments

Chief Executive Officer	Tel:	(303) 305-4027
ALLON, Sue	Fax:	(303) 534-0741
sallon@allonhill.com		

Main Headquarters

Mailing:	1515 Arapahoe St.	Tel:	(303) 305-4025
	Tower Three Suite 400	Fax:	(303) 534-0741
	Denver, CO 80202	TF:	(866) 803-7897

Public Affairs and Related Activities Personnel

At Headquarters

BILLAT, Jeff	Tel:	(303) 305-4025
Chief Financial Officer	Fax:	(303) 534-0741
jbillat@allonhill.com		
GALLERY, Dan	Tel:	(303) 305-4024
Managing Director, Sales	Fax:	(303) 534-0741
dgallery@allonhill.com		
KAPLAN, David	Tel:	(303) 305-4041
President, General Counsel and Chief Compliance Officer	Fax:	(303) 534-0741
dkaplan@allonhill.com		
WORTHINGTON, Elizabeth	Tel:	(303) 305-4025
Managing Director, Human Resources	Fax:	(303) 534-0741
eworthington@allonhill.com		

Allscripts

See listing on page 38 under Allscripts Healthcare Solutions, Inc.

Allscripts Healthcare Solutions, Inc.

Formed through the merger of Allscripts (Nasdaq: MDRX) and Misys Healthcare LLC, a wholly-owned subsidiary of Misys Plc (FTSE: MSY.L) in 2008. Provides physician practices, hospitals, and other healthcare providers with practice management and electronic health record technology.
www.allscripts.com
Annual Revenues: $1.37 billion
Employees: 7,200
Ticker: NASDAQ (GS): MDRX
SIC: 7373
Industry/ies: Medicine/Health Care/Mental Health
Legislative Issues: HCR

Chairman of the Board	Tel:	(312) 506-1200
KLAYKO, Michael	Fax:	(312) 506-1201
Chief Executive Officer and President	Tel:	(312) 506-1200
BLACK, Paul M.	Fax:	(312) 506-1201

Main Headquarters

Mailing:	222 Merchandise Mart Plaza	Tel:	(312) 506-1200
	Suite 2024	Fax:	(312) 506-1201
	Chicago, IL 60654	TF:	(800) 334-8534

Corporate Foundations and Giving Programs

Allscripts-Misys Healthcare Solutions Contributions Program

222 Merchandise Mart Plaza	Tel:	(866) 358-6869
Suite 2024	Fax:	(866) 358-6869
Chicago, IL 60654		

Public Affairs and Related Activities Personnel

At Headquarters

DI FRANCO, Concetta	Tel:	(312) 447-2466
Public Relations Specialist	Fax:	(312) 506-1201
concetta.difranco@allscripts.com		
FARLEY, Brian P.	Tel:	(312) 506-1200
Senior Vice President and General Counsel	Fax:	(312) 506-1201
FRANK, Seth R.	Tel:	(312) 506-1213
Vice President, Investor Relations	Fax:	(312) 555-1205
seth.frank@allscripts.com		
POULTON, Richard J.	Tel:	(312) 506-1200
Chief Financial Officer	Fax:	(312) 506-1201
ROWELL, Diane	Tel:	(312) 506-1200
Vice President, Human Resources	Fax:	(312) 506-1201
STEIN, Todd	Tel:	(312) 506-1216
Senior Manager, Public Relations	Fax:	(312) 506-1201
todd.stein@allscripts.com		

Allstate Insurance Company

A provider of insurance and financial services.
www.allstate.com
Annual Revenues: $35.57 billion
Employees: 41,100
Ticker: NYSE: ALL
Industry/ies: Insurance Industry
Legislative Issues: AUT; BAN; BNK; CPT; CSP; DIS; HCR; HOM; INS; LBR; MMM; RET; TAX; TOR; TRA

Chairman of the Board and Chief Executive Officer Tel: (847) 402-5000
WILSON, II, Thomas J. Fax: (847) 326-7519

Main Headquarters
Mailing: 2775 Sanders Rd. Tel: (847) 402-5000
Suite A3 Fax: (866) 532-3029
Northbrook, IL 60062 TF: (800) 255-7828

Washington Office
Mailing: 444 N. Capitol St. NW Tel: (202) 382-2742
Suite 828 Fax: (202) 383-2740
Washington, DC 20001

Political Action Committees
Allstate Insurance Company PAC
FEC ID: C00040253
Contact: Mario Rizzo
2775 Sanders Rd.
Suite A2W
Northbrook, IL 60062

Contributions to Candidates: $169,000 (2015-2016)
Democrats: $44,500; Republicans: $124,500

Corporate Foundations and Giving Programs
The Allstate Foundation
Contact: Kyle Donash
2775 W. Sanders Rd. Tel: (847) 402-5000
Suite F4 Fax: (847) 326-7519
Northbrook, IL 60062

Public Affairs and Related Activities Personnel

At Headquarters

COLLINS, Edward T. Tel: (847) 402-5000
Vice President and Assistant General Counsel Fax: (847) 326-7519

GUPTA, Sanjay Tel: (847) 402-5000
Executive Vice President, Marketing, Innovation and Fax: (866) 532-3029
Corporate Relations

HARTY, Harriet Tel: (847) 402-5000
Executive Vice President, Human Resources Fax: (866) 532-3029

HOGAN, Bridget Tel: (847) 402-5000
Government Relations Analyst Fax: (866) 532-3029
Registered Federal Lobbyist

LEES, Susie L. Tel: (847) 402-5000
Executive Vice President and General Counsel Fax: (866) 532-3029
SLees@allstate.com

OLSON, Marianne Tel: (847) 402-5000
PAC Administrator Fax: (866) 532-3029

RIZZO, Mario Tel: (847) 402-5000
PAC Treasurer Fax: (866) 532-3029

SHEBIK, Steven E. Tel: (847) 402-5000
Executive Vice President, Chief Financial Officer and Chief Fax: (866) 532-3029
Information Officer

VAINISI, William Tel: (847) 402-5000
Senior Vice President and Deputy General Counsel Fax: (866) 532-3029

At Washington Office

WILLIAMS, Jeff Tel: (202) 382-2742
Director, Federal Legislative and Regulatory Affairs Fax: (202) 383-2740
jeff.williams@allstate.com
Registered Federal Lobbyist

Alon USA

A petroleum refiner and marketer.
www.alonusa.com
Annual Revenues: $6.12 billion
Employees: 2,745
Ticker: NYSE: ALJ
SIC: 5541; 5172; 4789; 4613; 2911
NAICS: 324110; 486910; 447110; 325120
Industry/ies: Energy/Electricity; Natural Resources
Legislative Issues: ENG; ENV

Executive Chairman of the Board Tel: (972) 367-3600
WIESSMAN, David Fax: (972) 367-3725

Chief Executive Officer and President Tel: (972) 367-3600
EISMAN, Paul Fax: (972) 367-3725

Main Headquarters
Mailing: 12700 Park Central Dr. Tel: (972) 367-3600
Suite 1600 Fax: (972) 367-3725

Dallas, TX 75251

Corporate Foundations and Giving Programs
Alon USA Energy Inc. Contributions Program
7616 LBJ Fwy.
Suite 300
Dallas, TX 75251

Public Affairs and Related Activities Personnel

At Headquarters

EVEN, Shai Tel: (972) 367-3600
Senior Vice President and Chief Financial Officer Fax: (972) 367-3725

HART, Claire A. Tel: (972) 367-3600
Senior Vice President Fax: (972) 367-3725
claire.hart@alonusa.com

HUDSON, Stacey Tel: (972) 367-3808
Manager, Investor Relations Fax: (972) 367-3725
stacey.hudson@alonusa.com

LEWIS, Blake Tel: (214) 635-3020
Contact, Media Relations Fax: (972) 367-3725
blewis@lewispublicrelations.com

MORET, Alan Tel: (972) 367-3600
Senior Vice President, Supply Fax: (972) 367-3725
alan.moret@alonusa.com

RANSPOT, James Tel: (972) 367-3600
Senior Vice President, General Counsel and Secretary Fax: (972) 367-3725

Alon USA

See listing on page 39 under Alon USA

Alpha Natural Resources, Inc.

Supplies coal to power plants operated by a group of electricity generators across the country. Acquired Massey Energy Company in 2011.
www.alphanr.com
Annual Revenues: $4.02 billion
Employees: 8,700
Ticker: NYSE: ANR
SIC: 1221
Industry/ies: Energy/Electricity; Mining Industry; Natural Resources
Legislative Issues: BUD; CAW; LBR; NAT; TAX

Chief Executive Officer and Chairman of the Board Tel: (276) 619-4410
CRUTCHFIELD, Kevin S.

Main Headquarters
Mailing: One Alpha Pl. Tel: (276) 619-4410
P.O. Box 16429
Bristol, VA 24209

Washington Office
Mailing: 1301 Pennsylvania Ave. NW Tel: (202) 626-6727
Suite 404
Washington, DC 20004

Political Action Committees
Alpha Natural Resources PAC
FEC ID: C00348524
Contact: Alan Jones
1301 Pennsylvania Ave. NW Tel: (202) 626-6727
Suite 404
Washington, DC 20004

Contributions to Candidates: $75,625 (2015-2016)
Democrats: $2,000; Republicans: $73,625

Corporate Foundations and Giving Programs
Alpha Natural Resources Contributions Program
One Alpha Pl. Tel: (276) 619-4410
P.O. Box 16429
Bristol, VA 24209

Public Affairs and Related Activities Personnel

At Headquarters

ANDERSON, Teresa Tel: (276) 619-4410

CAVATONI, Philip J. Tel: (276) 619-4410
Executive Vice President, Chief Strategy Officer and Chief
Financial Officer

GROVES, Vaughn R. Tel: (276) 619-4410
Executive Vice President, General Counsel and Secretary

HUTTON, Melanie
Senior Associate, Communications

PILE, Ted Tel: (276) 619-4410
Vice President, Corporate Communications

ROTONEN, CFA, Alex Tel: (276) 619-4410
Vice President, Investor Relations
arotonen@alphanr.com

VINING, Paul H. Tel: (276) 619-4410
President

At Washington Office

AXTHELM, Richard
Vice President, Corporate Communications
raxthelm@alphanr.com
Tel: (202) 626-6727

JONES, Alan
PAC Treasurer
Tel: (202) 626-6727

MARTIN, Jay
Director, Federal Government and External Affairs
Registered Federal Lobbyist
Tel: (202) 626-6727

ALSTOM, Inc.

ALSTOM, Inc. is the U.S. subsidiary of ALSTOM, headquartered in Levallois-Perret, France. A producer of transport and energy infrastructure.
www.alstom.com
SIC: 3621
Industry/ies: Energy/Electricity
Legislative Issues: BUD; TAX; TRA

Chairman and Chief Executive Officer
KRON, Patrick
Tel: (202) 495-4960
Fax: (202) 495-4961

Main Headquarters
Mailing: 100 M St. SE
Suite 600
Washington, DC 20003
Tel: (202) 495-4960
Fax: (202) 495-4961

Corporate Foundations and Giving Programs

Alstom Foundation
801 Pennsylvania Ave. NW
Suite 855
Washington, DC 20004
Tel: (202) 495-4960

Public Affairs and Related Activities Personnel

At Headquarters

AUCLAIR, Bob
Controller
robert.auclair@power.alstom.com
Tel: (202) 495-4960
Fax: (202) 495-4961

BROWN, Timothy S.
Director, Communications
timothy.s.brown@power.alstom.com
Tel: (860) 713-9530
Fax: (202) 495-4961

CARR, Keith
Group General Counsel
Tel: (202) 495-4960
Fax: (202) 495-4961

COHEN, John
Vice President, Government Affairs
john.cohen@power.alstom.com
Registered Federal Lobbyist
Tel: (202) 495-4960
Fax: (202) 495-4961

GUILLEMET, Bruno
Senior Vice-President, Human Resources
Tel: (202) 495-4960
Fax: (202) 495-4961

HILTON, Robert
Vice President , Power Technologies for Government Afffairs
robert.g.hilton@power.alstom.com
Tel: (202) 495-4978
Fax: (202) 495-4961

MORIN, Jean-Jacques
Chief Financial Officer
Tel: (202) 495-4960
Fax: (202) 495-4961

RITCHOTTE, James
Director, US Government Affairs
john.cohen@power.alstom.com
Tel: (202) 495-4960
Fax: (202) 495-4961

Altadis USA, Inc.

Altadis USA, based in Ft. Lauderdale, is the U.S. subsidiary of Altadis, S.A., headquartered in Madrid, Spain. Manufacturer of cigars, tobacco and accessories.
altadisusa.com
Annual Revenues: $99.20 million
Employees: 1,000
SIC: 2121; 2141; 5099
NAICS: 312229; 31221; 42199
Industry/ies: Tobacco Industry

President
ELLIS, Gary R.
Tel: (954) 772-9000
Fax: (954) 267-1198

Main Headquarters
Mailing: 5900 N. Andrews Ave.
Suite 1100
Ft. Lauderdale, FL 33309
Tel: (954) 772-9000
Fax: (954) 267-1198
TF: (800) 683-8800

Corporate Foundations and Giving Programs

The Montecristo Relief Organization
P.O. Box 407179
Ft. Lauderdale, FL 33340-7166

Public Affairs and Related Activities Personnel

At Headquarters

COLUCCI, James
Executive Vice President, Sales and Marketing
jcolucci@altadisusa.com
Tel: (954) 772-9000
Fax: (954) 267-1198

WORKMAN, Eric
Senior Vice Pesident, Marketing
Tel: (954) 772-9000
Fax: (954) 267-1198

Altair Nanotechnologies, Inc.

A provider of energy storage systems for clean, efficient power and energy management.
www.altairnano.com
Annual Revenues: $6.61 million
Employees: 90
Ticker: NASDAQ: ALTI
SIC: 2890
Industry/ies: Computer/Technology

Interim Chief Executive Officer
LEE, Alexander
Tel: (775) 856-2500
Fax: (775) 856-1619

Main Headquarters
Mailing: 204 Edison Way
Reno, NV 89502
Tel: (775) 856-2500
Fax: (775) 856-1619

Public Affairs and Related Activities Personnel

At Headquarters

LUO, Tony
Contact, Investor Relations
tluo@altairnano.com
Tel: (775) 858-3726
Fax: (775) 856-1619

STEGMAN, Casey
Media Contact
casey@stonegateinc.com
Tel: (214) 987-4121
Fax: (775) 856-1619

Altamed Health Services Corporation

Health services corporation.
www.altamed.org
Industry/ies: Medicine/Health Care/Mental Health

Chairperson Elect
GALLEGOS, Martin
Tel: (323) 725-8751

President and Chief Executive Officer
ROCHA, Cástulo de la
Tel: (323) 725-8751

Main Headquarters
Mailing: 2040 Camfield Ave.
Los Angeles, CA 90040
Tel: (323) 725-8751
TF: (877) 462-2582

Corporate Foundations and Giving Programs

AltaMed Foundation
Contact: Zoila D. Escobar
2040 Camfield Ave.
Los Angeles, CA 90040
Tel: (323) 725-8751

Public Affairs and Related Activities Personnel

At Headquarters

ASTOR, Lauren
Interim Director, Corporate Communications
Lastor@la.altamed.org
Tel: (323) 622-2408

DELGADO, Elvia
Vice President, Branding, Marketing and Sales
Tel: (323) 725-8751

ESCOBAR, Zoila D.
Vice President, Strategic Development and Community Support
Tel: (323) 725-8751

ESPARZA, José U.
Senior Vice President and Chief Financial Officer
Tel: (323) 725-8751

GOMEZ, Robert
Interim Vice President, Business Operations
Tel: (323) 725-8751

SPALDING, Jennifer
Vice President, Senior Care Operations
Tel: (323) 725-8751

TORRES, PhD, Marie S.
Senior Vice President, Government Relations and Community Research Initiative
Tel: (323) 725-8751

TURNER, Robert J.
Vice President, Human Resources
Tel: (323) 725-8751

Altec Industries Inc.

Manufacturer of lift trucks, digger derricks, and specialty equipment for use by linemen in the electric utility, telecommunications, and tree care industries.
www.altec.com
Annual Revenues: $151 million
Employees: 1,500
Industry/ies: Machinery/Equipment
Legislative Issues: AUT

Chairman, President and Chief Executive Officer
STYSLINGER, III, Lee J.
Tel: (205) 991-7733
Fax: (205) 991-7747

Main Headquarters
Mailing: 210 Inverness Center Dr.
Birmingham, AL 35242-4834
Tel: (205) 991-7733
Fax: (205) 408-8601

Public Affairs and Related Activities Personnel

At Headquarters

WEGEL, Mark
Manager, Corporate Communications
Tel: (205) 408-8048
Fax: (205) 991-7747

Altera Corporation

Altera Corporation is the programmable logic solutions Company. Altera offers FPGAs, CPLDs, and ASICs in combination with software tools, intellectual property, and customer support.
www.altera.com
Annual Revenues: $1.91 billion
Employees: 3,091
Ticker: NASDAQ: ALTR
SIC: 3674
Industry/ies: Computer/Technology

Chairman of the Board, President and Chief Executive Officer
DAANE, John P.

Tel: (408) 544-7000
Fax: (408) 544-6408

Main Headquarters
Mailing: 101 Innovation Dr.
San Jose, CA 95134

Tel: (408) 544-7000
Fax: (408) 544-6408

Corporate Foundations and Giving Programs

Altera Corporate Contributions Program
101 Innovation Dr.
San Jose, CA 95134

Public Affairs and Related Activities Personnel

At Headquarters

BIRAN, Danny
Senior Vice President, Corporate Strategy and Marketing

Tel: (408) 544-7000
Fax: (408) 544-6408

LYMAN, Kevin H.
Senior Vice President, Human Resources

Tel: (408) 544-7000
Fax: (408) 544-6408

PAPA , George A.
Senior Vice President, Sales

Tel: (408) 544-7000
Fax: (408) 544-6408

PASEK, Ronald J.
Senior Vice President, Finance and Chief Financial Officer

Tel: (408) 544-7000
Fax: (408) 544-6408

SCHUELKE, Katherine E.
Senior Vice President, General Counsel, and Corporate Secretary
kschuelk@altera.com

Tel: (408) 544-7000
Fax: (408) 544-6408

WYLIE, Scott
Vice President, Investor Relations
swylie@altera.com

Tel: (408) 544-6996
Fax: (408) 544-6408

Alticor, Inc.

Offers products, business opportunities, manufacturing and logistics services. Alticor is the parent company of Amway Corp., Amway Global, Access Business Group LLC, and Alticor Corporate Enterprises.
www.alticor.com
Employees: 14,000
Industry/ies: Personal Care/Hygiene; Retail/Wholesale
Legislative Issues: CPT; CSP; FOO; GOV; HCR; INS; TAX; TOR; TRA; TRD

Chairman of the Board
VAN ANDEL, Steve

Tel: (616) 787-1000
Fax: (616) 682-4000

President
DEVOS, Doug

Tel: (616) 787-1000
Fax: (616) 682-4000

Main Headquarters
Mailing: 7575 Fulton St., East
Ada, MI 49355-0001

Tel: (616) 787-1000
Fax: (616) 682-4000

Washington Office
Mailing: 419 New Jersey Ave. SE
Washington, DC 20003

Tel: (202) 547-5005
Fax: (202) 547-5008

Political Action Committees
Alticor PAC (ALTIPAC)
FEC ID: C00034884
Contact: Scott E. Smoes
7575 E. Fulton Rd.
Attn: Scott Smoes 56-3S
Ada, MI 49355

Tel: (202) 547-5005
Fax: (202) 547-5008

Contributions to Candidates: $89,500 (2015-2016)
Democrats: $5,000; Republicans: $82,500; Other: $2,000

Public Affairs and Related Activities Personnel

At Headquarters

HOLWILL, Richard N.
Vice President, Public Policy
Richard.Holwill@alticor.com
Registered Federal Lobbyist

Tel: (616) 787-1000
Fax: (616) 682-4000

SMOES, Scott E.
PAC Treasurer
Mail Stop 56-3S

Tel: (616) 787-1000
Fax: (616) 682-4000

At Washington Office

PENNINGER, Jennifer
Federal Lobbyist
Registered Federal Lobbyist

Tel: (202) 547-5005
Fax: (202) 547-5008

ZARRELLI, Michael J.

Tel: (202) 547-5005

Manager, Federal Affairs
mike.zarrelli@alticor.com
Registered Federal Lobbyist

Fax: (202) 547-5008

Altria Client Services, Inc.

Formerly known as Philip Morris Companies Inc. A diversified corporation active in the tobacco and food products industries. Subsidiaries include Kraft Foods Inc. and brands include Marlboro cigarettes, Tombstone Pizza, Oscar Mayer and Kraft Foods, among others.
www.altria.com
Annual Revenues: $18.21 billion
Employees: 9,000
Ticker: NYSE: MO
SIC: 2111
Industry/ies: Food And Beverage Industry; Tobacco Industry
Legislative Issues: AGR; BUD; CPT; DEF; FIN; FOO; FOR; HCR; HOM; MMM; NAT; RET; TAX; TOB; TOR; TRD

Chairman of the Board and Chief Executive Officer
BARRINGTON, Martin J.
Marty.Barrington@altria.com

Tel: (804) 484-8897
Fax: (804) 484-8231

Main Headquarters
Mailing: 6601 W. Broad St.
Richmond, VA 23230

Tel: (804) 484-8897
Fax: (804) 484-8231

Washington Office
Mailing: 101 Constitution Ave. NW
Suite 400 West
Washington, DC 20001

Tel: (202) 354-1500
Fax: (202) 354-1506

Political Action Committees
Altria Group, Inc PAC (ALTRIA-PAC)
FEC ID: C00089136
Contact: Phil W. Park
101 Constitution Ave. NW
Suite 400W
Washington, DC 20001

Tel: (202) 354-1500
Fax: (202) 354-1505

Contributions to Candidates: $552,000 (2015-2016)
Democrats: $98,000; Republicans: $451,000; Other: $3,000

Principal Recipients

SENATE
AYOTTE, KELLY A (REP-NH)
BLUNT, ROY (REP-MO)
BURR, RICHARD (REP-NC)
PAUL, RAND (REP-KY)

HOUSE
BOUSTANY, CHARLES W. DR. JR. (REP-LA)
COMSTOCK, BARBARA J HONORABLE (REP-VA)
HOYER, STENY HAMILTON (DEM-DC)
MCCARTHY, KEVIN (REP-CA)
SCALISE, STEVE MR. (REP-LA)

Corporate Foundations and Giving Programs

Altria Client Services, Inc. Contribution Program
P.O. Box 85088
Richmond, VA 23285

Public Affairs and Related Activities Personnel

At Headquarters

FERNANDEZ, Pascal A.
Senior Vice President, Market Information and Consumer Research

Tel: (804) 484-8897
Fax: (804) 484-8231

GIFFORD, JR., William F.
Chief Financial Officer

Tel: (804) 484-8897
Fax: (804) 484-8231

LUND, Nancy Brennan
Senior Vice President, Marketing

Tel: (804) 484-8897
Fax: (804) 484-8231

MANCUSO, Sal
Senior Vice President Strategy, Planning and Accounting

Tel: (804) 484-8897
Fax: (804) 484-8231

MURPHY, Daniel R.
Director, Investor Relations

Tel: (804) 484-8222
Fax: (804) 484-8231

WALKER, Todd
Vice President
Registered Federal Lobbyist

Tel: (804) 484-8897
Fax: (804) 484-8231

WALKER, Todd
Vice President
Registered Federal Lobbyist

Tel: (804) 484-8897
Fax: (804) 484-8231

WHITAKER, Charles N.
Senior Vice President, Human Resources and Chief Compliance Officer

Tel: (804) 484-8897
Fax: (804) 484-8231

At Washington Office

BIZZELL, Wesley D.
Assistant General Counsel
wesley.bizzell@altria.com

Tel: (202) 354-1500
Fax: (202) 354-1506

DIMAROB, Michelle
Director, Federal Affairs
Registered Federal Lobbyist

Tel: (202) 354-1500
Fax: (202) 354-1506

DRISCO, Gayle	Tel:	(202) 354-1500
Director, Government Affairs and PAC Treasurer	Fax:	(202) 354-1506
Gayle.Drisco@Altria.com		
FERNANDEZ, David	Tel:	(202) 354-1500
Federal Lobbyist	Fax:	(202) 354-1506
David.Fernandez@altria.com		
GATES, Bruce A.	Tel:	(202) 354-1500
Senior Vice President, External Affairs	Fax:	(202) 354-1506
bruce.gates@altria.com		
HAYDEN, Cindy L.	Tel:	(202) 354-1500
Director, Federal Government Affairs	Fax:	(202) 354-1506
Registered Federal Lobbyist		
HOEL, John	Tel:	(202) 354-1524
Vice President, Federal Government Affairs	Fax:	(202) 354-1506
john.hoel@altria.com		
Registered Federal Lobbyist		
KNAKMUHS, Sarah	Tel:	(202) 354-1500
Director, Federal Government Affairs	Fax:	(202) 354-1506
Sarah.Knakmuhs@Altria.com		
PARK, Phil W.	Tel:	(202) 354-1500
Federal Lobbyist	Fax:	(202) 354-1506
Registered Federal Lobbyist		
SUTTON, CAE, JD, David J.	Tel:	(202) 354-1500
Federal Lobbyist	Fax:	(202) 354-1506
TURNER, Henry	Tel:	(202) 354-1500
Vice President, State Government Affairs	Fax:	(202) 354-1506
henry.turner@altria.com		

At Other Offices

AMADO, Joseph S.
Senior Vice President and Chief Information Officer
P.O. Box 85088
Richmond, VA 23285
Joe.Amado@altria.com

DILLARD, III, James E.
Senior Vice President, Regulatory Affairs and Chief Innovation Officer
P.O. Box 85088
Richmond, VA 23285

HUNTER, Jennifer
Senior Vice President, Corporate Affairs
P.O. Box 85088
Richmond, VA 23285
Jennifer.L.Hunter@altria.com

KEANE, Denise F.
Executive Vice President, General Counsel
P.O. Box 85088
Richmond, VA 23285
Denise.Keane@altria.com

WILLARD, III, Howard A.
Chief Operating Officer
P.O. Box 85088
Richmond, VA 23285
Howard.A.Willard@altria.com

Aluminum Chambered Boats, Inc.

Boat manufacturer.
www.boats.com
Employees: 70
Industry/ies: Marine/Maritime/Shipping; Transportation

Main Headquarters

Mailing:	809 Harris Ave.	Tel: (360) 647-0345
	Bellingham, WA 98225-7030	Fax: (360) 647-6007

Public Affairs and Related Activities Personnel

At Headquarters

AUTON, Bryan	Tel:	(360) 647-0345
Chief Financial Officer	Fax:	(360) 647-6007
KAESTNER, Laura	Tel:	(360) 647-0345
Director, Marketing and Contact, Media Relations	Fax:	(360) 255-2295
laurak@acbboats.com		

Aluminum Company of America (Alcoa) Inc.

A producer of primary aluminum, fabricated aluminum, alumina and deliver value-add products made of titanium, nickel and aluminum, and produce best-in-class bauxite, alumina and primary aluminum products.
www.alcoa.com
Annual Revenues: $24.27 billion
Employees: 59,000
Ticker: NYSE: AA
SIC: 3350
Industry/ies: Metals
Legislative Issues: CAW; DEF; ENG; ENV; NAT; TAX; TRD

Chairman of the Board and Chief Executive Officer	Tel:	(212) 836-2600
KLEINFELD, Klaus	Fax:	(212) 836-2815

Main Headquarters

Mailing:	390 Park Ave.	Tel: (212) 836-2600
	New York City, NY 10022	Fax: (212) 836-2815

Washington Office

Mailing:	1050 K St. NW	Tel: (202) 956-5300
	Suite 1100	Fax: (202) 956-5305
	Washington, DC 20001	

Political Action Committees

Alcoa Inc. Employees Voluntary PAC
FEC ID: C00501106
Contact: Paul A Hayes
1050 K ST. NW
Suite 1100
Washington, DC 20001

> **Contributions to Candidates:** $10,500 (2015-2016)
> Democrats: $5,000; Republicans: $5,500

ALCOA INC. EMPLOYEES' VOLUNTARY STATE AND FEDERAL PAC
FEC ID: C00552679
Contact: Paul A Hayes

1050 K St. NW		
Suite 1100	Tel:	(202) 956-5300
Washington, DC 20001	Fax:	(202) 956-5305

> **Contributions to Candidates:** $116,500 (2015-2016)
> Democrats: $42,500; Republicans: $74,000

Corporate Foundations and Giving Programs

Alcoa Foundation
Contact: Scott Hudson
201 Isabella St.
Pittsburgh, PA 15212

Public Affairs and Related Activities Personnel

At Headquarters

ARCHELL, Libby	Tel:	(212) 836-2600
Vice President, Chief Communications Officer	Fax:	(212) 836-2815
BERGEN, John D.	Tel:	(212) 836-2600
Vice President, Corporate Projects	Fax:	(212) 836-2815
HARVEY, Roy	Tel:	(212) 836-2600
Executive Vice President Human Resources, Environment, Health and Safety and Sustainability	Fax:	(212) 836-2815
ORBE, Monica	Tel:	(212) 836-2600
Director, Corporate Affairs	Fax:	(212) 836-2815
STRAUSS, Audrey	Tel:	(212) 836-2600
Executive Vice President, Chief Legal and Compliance Officer, and Corporate Secretary	Fax:	(212) 836-2815

At Washington Office

BELWOOD, Michael	Tel:	(812) 604-0530
Vice President, U.S. Government Affairs	Fax:	(202) 956-5305
Registered Federal Lobbyist		
DAVID, Williams	Tel:	(202) 956-5300
Federal Lobbyist	Fax:	(202) 956-5305
Registered Federal Lobbyist		
HAYES, Paul A	Tel:	(202) 956-5300
PAC Treasurer	Fax:	(202) 956-5305
O'NEILL, Michelle	Tel:	(202) 956-5300
Vice President, Government Affairs & Trade Policy	Fax:	(202) 956-5305
OPLINGER, William F.	Tel:	(202) 956-5300
Executive Vice President and Chief Financial Officer	Fax:	(202) 956-5305
PRINCE , Beverly	Tel:	(202) 956-5300
Administrator, Departmental	Fax:	(202) 956-5305
WALTON , Keith	Tel:	(202) 956-5300
Vice President, Government Affairs	Fax:	(202) 956-5305

At Other Offices

HUDSON, Scott	Tel:	(412) 553-4545
Principal Manager	Fax:	(412) 553-4498
201 Isabella St.		
Pittsburgh, PA 15212-5858		
scott.hudson@alcoa.com		
LOWERY, Kevin G.	Tel:	(412) 553-1424
Director, Corporate Communications	Fax:	(412) 553-4498
201 Isabella St.		
Pittsburgh, PA 15212-5858		
kevin.lowery@alcoa.com		
SALTZMAN, Joyce	Tel:	(412) 553-4467
Manager, Corporate Communications	Fax:	(412) 553-4498
201 Isabella St.		
Pittsburgh, PA 15212-5858		
joyce.saltzman@alcoa.com		

Alutiiq Management Services, LLC
Alaska native corporation; government contracting.
www.alutiiq.com
Industry/ies: Business; Small Business

| **President and Chief Executive Officer** | Tel: (907) 222-9500 |
| HAMBRIGHT, Greg | Fax: (907) 222-9501 |

Main Headquarters
Mailing: 3909 Arctic Blvd.   Tel: (907) 222-9500
Suite 400   Fax: (907) 222-9501
Anchorage, AK 99503

Washington Office
Mailing: 8619 Westwood Center Dr.   Tel: (703) 992-7225
Suite 150   Fax: (703) 992-7355
Vienna, VA 22182

Public Affairs and Related Activities Personnel

At Headquarters

GODFREY, Gerad   Tel: (907) 222-9500
Corporate Affairs Manager   Fax: (907) 222-9501

Alyeska Pipeline Service Company
Operator of the trans-Alaskan pipeline.
www.alyeska-pipe.com
Annual Revenues: $51.90 million
Employees: 800
Industry/ies: Fuels See Coal, Gas, Oil, Petroleum; Natural Resources; Petroleum Industry

| **President** | Tel: (907) 787-8700 |
| BARRETT, Thomas | Fax: (907) 787-8240 |

Main Headquarters
Mailing: P.O. Box 196660   Tel: (907) 787-8700
Anchorage, AK 99519   Fax: (907) 787-8240

Washington Office
Mailing: 1667 K St.   Tel: (202) 466-3866
Suite 1230   Fax: (202) 466-3886
Washington, DC 20008

Corporate Foundations and Giving Programs

Alyeska Pipeline Service Company Contributions Program
P.O. Box 196660   Tel: (907) 787-8700
Anchorage, AK 99519   Fax: (907) 787-8240

Public Affairs and Related Activities Personnel

At Headquarters

EGAN, Michelle   Tel: (907) 787-8397
Director, Corporate Communications   Fax: (907) 787-8240

HENDRICKSON, Ed   Tel: (907) 787-8700
Senior Vice President and Chief Financial Officer   Fax: (907) 787-8240

MILLEN, Fred   Tel: (907) 787-8700
Director, Human Resources   Fax: (907) 787-8240

PARKES, Susan   Tel: (907) 787-8700
Vice President and General Counsel   Fax: (907) 787-8240
susan.parkes@alyeska-pipeline.com

AM & S Trade Services LLC
Deals in international trade, textiles and government relations.
www.amstradeservices.com
Employees: 100
Industry/ies: Trade (Foreign And Domestic)

| **President** | Tel: (202) 302-0754 |
| MOORE, Carlos F. J. | Fax: (202) 467-4732 |
cmoore@amstradeservices.com

Main Headquarters
Mailing: 1200 17th St. NW   Tel: (202) 302-0754
Fifth Floor   Fax: (202) 467-4732
Washington, DC 20036

AM General Corporation
A manufacturer of off-road vehicles.
www.amgeneral.com
Employees: 1,500
SIC: 3790
Industry/ies: Defense/Homeland Security; Government-Related
Legislative Issues: BUD; DEF

| **Chairman of the Board** | Tel: (574) 237-6222 |
| ARMOUR, James | Fax: (574) 284-2819 |

| **President and Chief Executive Officer** | Tel: (574) 237-6222 |
| HALL, Charles M. | Fax: (574) 284-2819 |

Main Headquarters
Mailing: 105 N. Niles Ave.   Tel: (574) 237-6222
P.O. Box 7025   Fax: (574) 284-2819
South Bend, IN 46617

Washington Office
Mailing: 950 N. Glebe Rd.   Tel: (703) 236-7026
Suite 850
Arlington, VA 22203

Political Action Committees
AM General Sales Corporation PAC
FEC ID: C00282210
Contact: Frank Berger
105 N. Niles Ave.
South Bend, IN 46617

Contributions to Candidates: $26,000 (2015-2016)
Democrats: $11,000; Republicans: $15,000

Public Affairs and Related Activities Personnel

At Headquarters

ADAMS, Jeffery   Tel: (574) 237-6222
Executive Director, Global Marketing and Communications   Fax: (574) 284-2819

BERGER, Frank   Tel: (574) 237-6222
PAC Treasurer   Fax: (574) 284-2819

CAFIERO, Paul J.   Tel: (574) 237-6222
Senior Vice President and Chief Financial Officer   Fax: (574) 284-2819

DELL'ORTO, Daniel J.   Tel: (574) 237-6222
Executive Vice President, Government Relations General Counsel   Fax: (574) 284-2819

ROSS, Celeste   Tel: (574) 284-2930
Contact, Media Relations   Fax: (574) 284-2819

SANTAMARIA, Mark E.   Tel: (574) 237-6222
Vice President, Chief Financial Officer   Fax: (574) 284-2819

SCHUCHMAN, Paul R.   Tel: (574) 237-6222
PAC Treasurer   Fax: (574) 284-2819

ULRICH, John   Tel: (574) 237-6222
Chief Operating Officer   Fax: (574) 284-2819

At Washington Office

DAOULAS, William A.   Tel: (703) 875-0041
Director, Government Affairs
william.daoulas@amgeneral.com

DOUGLAS, Thomas R.   Tel: (703) 236-7026
Senior Vice President, Business Development and Strategy

Amalgamated Bank
A banking and investment services company.
www.amalgamatedbank.com
Annual Revenues: $231.79 million
Employees: 400
Industry/ies: Banking/Finance/Investments

| **Chairman of the Board, President** | Tel: (212) 255-6200 |
| BEASLEY, Noel | Fax: (212) 895-4507 |

| **President and CEO** | Tel: (212) 255-6200 |
| MESTRICH, Keith | Fax: (212) 895-4507 |

Main Headquarters
Mailing: 275 Seventh Ave.   Tel: (212) 255-6200
New York City, NY 10001   Fax: (212) 895-4507
   TF: (800) 332-2693

Washington Office
Mailing: 1825 K St. NW   Tel: (202) 293-9800
Washington, DC 20006

Political Action Committees
Amalgamated Bank PAC
FEC ID: C00379693
275 Seventh Ave.
New York City, NY 10001

Contributions to Candidates: $28,500 (2015-2016)
Democrats: $28,500

Corporate Foundations and Giving Programs

Amalgamated Bank Contributions Program
275 Seventh Ave.   Tel: (212) 895-4833
New York City, NY 10001

Public Affairs and Related Activities Personnel

At Headquarters

SILODOR, Deborah   Tel: (212) 255-6200
Executive Vice President, General Counsel   Fax: (212) 895-4507

BROWN, Sam   Tel: (212) 255-6200
Executive Vice President, Business Development   Fax: (212) 895-4507

LABENNE, Drew   Tel: (212) 255-6200
Executive Vice President, Chief Financial Officer   Fax: (212) 895-4507

SFORZA, Toni-Ann   Tel: (212) 255-6200
Senior Vice President, Human Resources   Fax: (212) 895-4507

WILLS, Thomas
PAC Contact
Tel: (212) 255-6200
Fax: (212) 895-4507

ZDRAZIL, Scott
Director, Corporate Governance
ScottZdrazil@AmalgamatedBank.com
Tel: (347) 573-1278
Fax: (212) 895-4507

At Washington Office

GILBERTI, Philip
PAC Contact
Tel: (202) 293-9800

Amalgamated Life Insurance Company

An insurance company.
www.amalgamatedlife.com
Annual Revenues: $12.40 million
Employees: 50
Industry/ies: Insurance Industry

President and Chief Executive Officer
WALSH, David J.
Tel: (914) 367-5000
Fax: (212) 780-4104

Main Headquarters
Mailing: 333 Westchester Ave.
White Plains, NY 10604-2910
Tel: (914) 367-5000
Fax: (212) 780-4104

Corporate Foundations and Giving Programs
Amalgamated Life Insurance Community Contribution Program
333 Westchester Ave.
White Plains, NY 10604-2910
Tel: (914) 367-5000

Public Affairs and Related Activities Personnel

At Headquarters

DUNKIN, Ellen R.
Senior Vice prsident, General Counsel
Tel: (914) 367-5000
Fax: (212) 780-4104

HIRSCH, Michael
Executive Vice President
mhirsch@amalgamatedlife.com
Tel: (914) 367-5000
Fax: (212) 780-4104

MALLEN, Paul
Executive Vice President and Chief Financial Officer
Tel: (914) 367-5000
Fax: (212) 780-4104

SCHWARTZ, Mark
Senior Vice President and Chief Counsel
Tel: (914) 367-5000
Fax: (212) 780-4104

SPALDING, Kay
Director, Marketing
kspalding@amalgamatedlife.com
Tel: (914) 367-5826
Fax: (914) 367-2826

THORNTON, John A.
Executive Vice President, Sales and Marketing
Tel: (914) 367-5000
Fax: (212) 780-4104

Amazon.com Holdings, Inc.

An online sales company headquartered in Seattle, Wash.
www.amazon.com
Annual Revenues: $91.96 billion
Employees: 154,100
Ticker: NASDAQ: AMZN
SIC: 5961
Industry/ies: Communications; Retail/Wholesale; Telecommunications/Internet/Cable
Legislative Issues: AGR; AVI; BAN; CPI; CPT; CSP; DEF; EDU; ENG; FIN; HOM; IMM; INT; LBR; POS; SMB; TAX; TEC; TRA; TRD; WEL

Chairman of the Board, President and Chief Executive Officer
BEZOS, Jeffrey P.
Tel: (206) 266-2171
Fax: (206) 266-1355

Main Headquarters
Mailing: 601 New Jersey Ave. NW
Suite 900
Washington, DC 20001
Tel: (202) 347-7390
Fax: (206) 266-1821

Washington Office
Mailing: 126 C St., Suite Three
Washington, DC 20001

Political Action Committees
Amazon Corporate LLC Separate Segregated Fund (Amazon.com PAC)
FEC ID: C00360354
Contact: Brian Huseman
126 C St. NW, Suite 3
Washington, DC 20001
Tel: (202) 347-7390

Contributions to Candidates: $340,000 (2015-2016)
Democrats: $163,000; Republicans: $177,000

Principal Recipients

SENATE
SCHUMER, CHARLES E (DEM-NY)

HOUSE
CHAFFETZ, JASON (REP-UT)
RYAN, PAUL D. (REP-WI)
SMITH, D ADAM (DEM-WA)

Public Affairs and Related Activities Personnel

At Headquarters

BENTLEY, Vann
Registered Federal Lobbyist
Tel: (202) 347-7390
Fax: (206) 266-1821

BLOCK, Steven
Senior Manager, Public Policy
blocs@amazon.com
Registered Federal Lobbyist
Tel: (202) 347-7390
Fax: (206) 266-1821

DE LA TORRE, Ashleigh
Registered Federal Lobbyist
Tel: (202) 347-7390
Fax: (206) 266-1821

ELLINGTON, Laurie
Registered Federal Lobbyist
Tel: (202) 347-7390
Fax: (206) 266-1821

ELTING, Andrew
PAC Manager
elting@amazon.com
Tel: (202) 442-2953
Fax: (206) 266-1821

GIELOW, Ben
Registered Federal Lobbyist
Tel: (202) 347-7390
Fax: (206) 266-1821

HANDALY, Robin
Manager, Public Relations
Tel: (202) 347-7390
Fax: (206) 266-1821

HARRIS, Andrew
Registered Federal Lobbyist
Tel: (202) 347-7390
Fax: (206) 266-1821

HARTELL, STEPHEN
Registered Federal Lobbyist
Tel: (202) 347-7390
Fax: (206) 266-1821

HUDGINS, Sarah
Registered Federal Lobbyist
Tel: (202) 347-7390
Fax: (206) 266-1821

HUSEMAN, Brian
Vice President, Public policy
Registered Federal Lobbyist
Tel: (202) 347-7390
Fax: (206) 266-1821

KELLOGG, Shannon
Federal Lobbyist
Registered Federal Lobbyist
Tel: (202) 347-7390
Fax: (206) 266-1821

MISENER, Paul
Vice President, Global Public Policy
Registered Federal Lobbyist
Tel: (202) 347-7390
Fax: (206) 266-1821

VIAR, Kate
Registered Federal Lobbyist
Tel: (202) 347-7390
Fax: (206) 266-1821

At Washington Office

ACHORD, Darren A.
Senior Manager, Public Policy

BILLIMORIA, Jim
Public Relations Manager, Customer Delivery Programs

At Other Offices

BLACKBURN, Jeffrey M.
Senior Vice President, Business Development
P.O. Box 81226
Seattle, WA 98108
Tel: (206) 266-2171
Fax: (206) 266-1355

SZKUTAK, Thomas J.
Senior Vice President and Chief Financial Officer
P.O. Box 81226
Seattle, WA 98108
Tel: (206) 266-2171
Fax: (206) 266-1355

WILKE, Jeffrey A.
Senior Vice President, Consumer Business
P.O. Box 81226
Seattle, WA 98108
Tel: (206) 266-2171
Fax: (206) 266-1355

ZAPOLSKY, David A.
Senior Vice President, General Counsel and Secretary
P.O. Box 81226
Seattle, WA 98108
Tel: (206) 266-2171
Fax: (206) 266-1355

Ambac Financial Group, Inc.

A holding company that provides, through its subsidiaries, financial guarantee insurance and other financial services to both public and private clients worldwide. Its principal operating subsidiary, Ambac Assurance Corporation ("Ambac Assurance"), is a guarantor of public finance and structured finance obligations.
www.ambac.com
Annual Revenues: $621.7 million
Employees: 188
Ticker: NASDQ:AMBC
SIC: 6351
Industry/ies: Banking/Finance/Investments

Chairman of the Board
STEIN, Jeffrey S.
Tel: (212) 668-0340
Fax: (212) 509-9190

Interim President and Chief Executive Officer
TAVAKOLI, Nader
Tel: (212) 668-0340
Fax: (212) 509-9190

Main Headquarters
Mailing: One State St. Plaza
New York City, NY 10004
Tel: (212) 668-0340
Fax: (212) 509-9190
TF: (800) 221-1854

Public Affairs and Related Activities Personnel

At Headquarters

BARRANCO, David
Tel: (212) 668-0340

Senior Managing Director, Restructuring and Corporate Development	Fax:	(212) 509-9190
GOLDSTEIN, CFA, Abbe F.	Tel:	(212) 668-0340
Managing Director, Investor Relations and Corporate Communications	Fax:	(212) 509-9190
agoldstein@ambac.com		
KSENAK, Stephen M.	Tel:	(212) 668-0340
Senior Managing Director and General Counsel	Fax:	(212) 509-9190
REILLY, Michael	Tel:	(212) 668-0340
Senior Managing Director, Chief Information Officer and Chief Administrative Officer	Fax:	(212) 509-9190
TRICK, David	Tel:	(212) 668-0340
Senior Managing Director, Chief Financial Officer and Treasurer	Fax:	(212) 509-9190

AmberWave Systems

Specializes in the research, development and licensing of advanced technologies for semiconductor manufacturing.
www.amberwave.com
Annual Revenues: $3.20 million
Employees: 38
Industry/ies: Plastics Industry

Chairman, President and Chief Executive Officer	Tel:	(603) 870-8700
FAUBERT, Richard J.	Fax:	(603) 870-8607

Main Headquarters

Mailing:	13 Garahedian Dr.	Tel:	(603) 870-8700
	Salem, NH 03079	Fax:	(603) 870-8607

Public Affairs and Related Activities Personnel

At Headquarters

GASWIRTH, Stacy	Tel:	(972) 239-5119
Contact, Media Relations	Fax:	(603) 870-8607
sgaswirth@sheltongroup.com		

Ambre Energy North America Inc.

The U.S. subsidiary of Ambre Energy, headquartered in Brisbane, Australia. Develops and applies new technologies to the mining and processing of coal and other carbonaceous materials.
www.ambreenergy.com
Employees: 5
Industry/ies: Energy/Electricity

Chairman of the Board	Tel:	(801) 539-3788
O'REILLY, Terry	Fax:	(801) 531-5470
Executive Director President and Chief Executive Officer	Tel:	(801) 539-3788
KING, Everett	Fax:	(801) 539-3789

Main Headquarters

Mailing:	170 S. Main St.	Tel:	(801) 539-3788
	Suite 700	Fax:	(801) 531-5470
	Salt Lake City, UT 84101		

Public Affairs and Related Activities Personnel

At Headquarters

BAARLE, Michael van	Tel:	(801) 539-3788
Non Executive Director and Company Secretary	Fax:	(801) 539-3789

AMC Entertainment Inc.

Owns and operates cinemas in the U.S., Japan, Portugal and Spain.
www.amctheatres.com
Annual Revenues: $3.06 billion
Employees: 970
Ticker: NYSE: AMC
SIC: 7830
Industry/ies: Sports/Leisure/Entertainment

Chairman of the Board	Tel:	(816) 221-4000
ZHANG, Lin	Fax:	(816) 480-4617
Chief Executive Officer and President	Tel:	(816) 221-4000
ARON, Adam M.	Fax:	(816) 480-4617

Main Headquarters

Mailing:	P.O. Box 725489	Tel:	(816) 221-4000
	Atlanta, GA 31139-9923	Fax:	(816) 480-4617

Corporate Foundations and Giving Programs

AMC Corporate Contributions Program
Contact: Cindy Huffstickler
920 Main St.
Kansas City, MO 64105

Public Affairs and Related Activities Personnel

At Headquarters

FRANK, Elizabeth	Tel:	(816) 221-4000
Executive Vice President and Chief Content and Programming Officer	Fax:	(816) 480-4617

MERRIWETHER, John	Tel:	(866) 248-3872
Vice President, Investor Relations	Fax:	(816) 480-4617
InvestorRelations@amctheatres.com		
NOONAN, Ryan	Tel:	(816) 480-4724
Director, Public Relations	Fax:	(816) 480-4617
rnoonan@amctheatres.com		
SANDERS, Carla C.	Tel:	(816) 221-4000
Senior Vice President, Human Resources	Fax:	(816) 480-4617

At Other Offices

COLANERO, Stephen	Tel:	(816) 221-4000
Executive Vice President and Chief Marketing Officer	Fax:	(816) 480-4617
920 Main St.		
Kansas City, MO 64105		
CONNOR, Kevin M.	Tel:	(816) 221-4000
Senior Vice President, General Counsel and Secretary	Fax:	(816) 480-4617
920 Main St.		
Kansas City, MO 64105		
HUFFSTICKLER, Cindy	Tel:	(816) 480-4675
Assistant Manager, Office Services	Fax:	(816) 480-4617
920 Main St.		
Kansas City, MO 64105		
chuffstickler@amctheatres.com		
RAMSEY, Craig R.	Tel:	(816) 221-4000
Executive Vice President and Chief Financial Officer	Fax:	(816) 480-4617
920 Main St.		
Kansas City, MO 64105		
ZWONITZER, Mike	Tel:	(816) 221-4000
Senior Vice President, Finance	Fax:	(816) 480-4617
920 Main St.		
Kansas City, MO 64105		
mzwonitzer@amctheatres.com		

Amcot

Trade association representing the cotton industry.
www.amcot.org
Employees: 50
Industry/ies: Agriculture/Agronomy; Apparel/Textiles Industry
Legislative Issues: AGR; BUD; TRA

Chairman	Tel:	(806) 763-8011
DARNEILLE, Wally	Fax:	(806) 762-7335

Main Headquarters

Mailing:	P.O. Box 2827	Tel:	(806) 763-8011
	Lubbock, TX 79408	Fax:	(806) 762-7335

Amedisys

Provider of home health care and hospice services.
www.amedisys.com
Annual Revenues: $1.19 billion
Employees: 13,200
Ticker: NASDAQ: AMED
SIC: 8082
Industry/ies: Medicine/Health Care/Mental Health

Non-Executive Chairman of the Board	Tel:	(225) 292-2031
WASHBURN, Don	Fax:	(225) 292-8163
President and Chief Executive Officer	Tel:	(225) 292-2031
KUSSEROW, Paul	Fax:	(225) 292-8163

Main Headquarters

Mailing:	5959 S. Sherwood Forest Blvd.	Tel:	(225) 292-2031
	Baton Rouge, LA 70816	Fax:	(225) 292-8163
		TF:	(800) 467-2662

Political Action Committees

Amedisys Inc. PAC
FEC ID: C00436360
Contact: Dale E. Redman

5959 S. Sherwood Blvd.	Tel:	(225) 292-2031
Baton Rouge, LA 70816	Fax:	(225) 292-8163

> **Contributions to Candidates:** $7,500 (2015-2016)
> Democrats: $4,500; Republicans: $3,000

Corporate Foundations and Giving Programs

The Christen Foundation

5959 S. Sherwood Forest Blvd.	Tel:	(225) 292-2031
Baton Rouge, LA 70816		

Public Affairs and Related Activities Personnel

At Headquarters

BUCEY, David R.	Tel:	(225) 292-2031
Senior Vice President, General Counsel and Secretary	Fax:	(225) 292-8163
david.bucey@amedisys.com		
JETER, J.D., Jeffrey D.	Tel:	(225) 292-2031
Chief Compliance Officer	Fax:	(225) 292-8163
jeffrey.jeter@amedisys.com		

KEMMERLY, David	Tel:	(225) 292-2031
Senior Vice President, Government Affairs and Interim General Counsel	Fax:	(225) 292-8163
LABORDE, Ronald	Tel:	(225) 292-2031
Vice Chairman and Chief Financial Officer	Fax:	(225) 292-8163
MCCOY, Daniel P.	Tel:	(225) 292-2031
Chief Operating Officer	Fax:	(225) 292-8163
PERNOSKY, Larry R.	Tel:	(225) 292-2031
Chief Human Resources Officer	Fax:	(225) 292-8163
REDMAN, Dale E.	Tel:	(225) 292-2031
PAC Treasurer and Interim Chief Financial Officer	Fax:	(225) 292-8163
dredman@amedisys.com		
SEIM, Stephen	Tel:	(225) 292-2031
Chief Strategy Officer	Fax:	(225) 292-8163
VALENCIA, Jacqueline Chen	Tel:	(225) 295-9688
Senior Vice President, Marketing and Communications	Fax:	(225) 292-8163
jacqueline.chen@amedisys.com		
WILLIAMS, Martha Stuart	Tel:	(225) 292-2031
Chief Administrative Officer	Fax:	(225) 292-8163
YUNGK, Robert	Tel:	(225) 292-2031
Chief Development Officer	Fax:	(225) 292-8163

Amegy Bank NA

A banking services firm. It is a US bank operating in Texas that is a subsidiary of Zions Bancorporation.
www.amegybank.com
Annual Revenues: $14.00 billion
Employees: 1,618
Industry/ies: Banking/Finance/Investments

Senior Chairman	Tel:	(713) 235-8800
JOHNSON, Walter E.	Fax:	(713) 439-5949
Chairman	Tel:	(713) 235-8800
MCLEAN, Scott J.	Fax:	(713) 439-5949
President and Chief Executive Officer	Tel:	(713) 235-8810
STEPHENS, Steve D.	Fax:	(713) 439-5949

Main Headquarters

Mailing:	P.O. Box 4837	Tel:	(713) 235-8810
	Houston, TX 77210-4837	Fax:	(713) 439-5949
		TF:	(800) 287-0301

Political Action Committees

Amegy Bank National Association PAC
FEC ID: C00283069
Contact: Deborah S. Gibson
4400 Post Oak Pkwy.   Tel: (713) 235-8810
Houston, TX 77027

    Contributions to Candidates: $27,600 (2015-2016)
    Democrats: $2,000; Republicans: $25,600

Corporate Foundations and Giving Programs

Amegy Bank Contributions Program		
P.O. Box 4837	Tel:	(713) 235-8800
Houston, TX 77210-4837	Fax:	(713) 439-5949

Public Affairs and Related Activities Personnel

At Headquarters

AKIN, Leigh	Tel:	(713) 232-1433
Vice President, Corporate Communications	Fax:	(713) 439-5949
leigh.akin@amegybank.com		
GIBSON, Deborah S.	Tel:	(713) 232-1095
Executive Vice President, ManagerTrust Division and PAC Treasurer	Fax:	(713) 439-5949
MEYER, Randall E.	Tel:	(713) 235-8800
Executive Vice President and Chief Financial Officer	Fax:	(713) 439-5949
SCHAFFER, Jamie	Tel:	(713) 232-2397
Officer, Communications Representative	Fax:	(713) 439-5949
jamie.schaffer@amegybank.com		

AMERCO

A Holding company. Subsidiaries include U-Haul International Oxford Life Insurance Co., Republic Western Insurance Co. and Amerco Real Estate Co.
www.amerco.com
Annual Revenues: $3.28 billion
Employees: 11,880
Ticker: Nasdaq: UHAL
SIC: 7611
Industry/ies: Automotive Industry; Banking/Finance/Investments; Insurance Industry; Transportation

Chairman of the Board and President	Tel:	(775) 688-6300
SHOEN, Edward J.	Fax:	(775) 688-6338

Main Headquarters

Mailing:	5555 Kietzke Ln.	Tel:	(602) 263-6601

Suite 100
Reno, NV 89511

Public Affairs and Related Activities Personnel

At Other Offices

BERG, Jason A.	Tel:	(775) 688-6300
Principal Accounting Officer	Fax:	(775) 688-6338
1325 Airmotive Way, Suite 100		
Reno, NV 89502		
DE RESPINO, Laurence J.	Tel:	(775) 688-6300
General Counsel	Fax:	(775) 688-6338
1325 Airmotive Way, Suite 100		
Reno, NV 89502		
REYES, Sebastien	Tel:	(775) 688-6300
Director, Investor Relations	Fax:	(775) 688-6338
1325 Airmotive Way, Suite 100		
Reno, NV 89502		
investor_relations@amerco.com		

Ameren Services

An electric utility.
www.ameren.com
Annual Revenues: $5.77 billion
Employees: 8,527
Ticker: NYSE: AEE
SIC: 4931
Industry/ies: Energy/Electricity
Legislative Issues: BUD; CAW; COM; ENG; ENV; GOV; TAX; TEC; TRA; TRD; UTI

Chairman, President and Chief Executive Officer	Tel:	(314) 554-3502
BAXTER , Warner L.	Fax:	(314) 554-2401

Main Headquarters

Mailing:	P.O. Box 66887	Tel:	(314) 554-3502
	St. Louis, MO 63166-6887	Fax:	(314) 554-2401
		TF:	(800) 255-2237

Washington Office

Mailing:	1331 Pennsylvania Ave. NW	Tel:	(202) 783-7606
	Suite 550 South	Fax:	(202) 783-7602
	Washington, DC 20004		

Political Action Committees

Ameren Federal PAC (Ameren FedPAC)
FEC ID: C00206136
Contact: Mark Siedband
1331 Pennsylvania Ave. NW   Tel: (202) 783-7606
Suite 550S   Fax: (202) 783-7602
Washington, DC 20004

    Contributions to Candidates: $138,000 (2015-2016)
    Democrats: $29,000; Republicans: $103,000; Other: $6,000

Principal Recipients

HOUSE
SHIMKUS, JOHN M (REP-IL)

Corporate Foundations and Giving Programs

Ameren Corporate Giving Program
Contact: Mark C. Lindgren
1901 Chouteau Ave.
St. Louis, MO 63103

Public Affairs and Related Activities Personnel

At Headquarters

BIRK, Mark	Tel:	(314) 554-3502
Senior Vice President, Corporate Planning and Corporate Oversight	Fax:	(314) 554-2401
FISCHER, Doug	Tel:	(314) 554-4859
Director, Investor Relations	Fax:	(314) 554-2401
dfischer@ameren.com		
HUNT, David R.	Tel:	(314) 554-3502
Vice President, Corporate Communications	Fax:	(314) 554-2401
LINDGREN, Mark C.	Tel:	(314) 554-3502
Senior Vice President, Corporate Communications and Chief Human Resources Officer	Fax:	(314) 554-2401
LYONS, Martin J.	Tel:	(314) 554-3502
Executive Vice President and Chief Financial Officer	Fax:	(314) 554-2401
NELSON, Gregory L.	Tel:	(314) 554-3502
Senior Vice President, General Counsel and Secretary	Fax:	(314) 554-2401

At Washington Office

GARRISON, Shaun F.	Tel:	(202) 783-7606
Senior Specialist, Federal Legislative Affairs	Fax:	(202) 783-7602
sgarrison@ameren.com		
Registered Federal Lobbyist		
POWER, Joseph M.	Tel:	(202) 783-7604
Vice President, Federal Legislative and Regulatory Affairs	Fax:	(202) 783-7602
jpower@ameren.com		

Registered Federal Lobbyist

SIEDBAND, Mark Tel: (202) 783-7606
PAC Treasurer Fax: (202) 783-7602

Ameresco, Inc.

An energy solutions company.
www.ameresco.com
Annual Revenues: $607.94 million
Employees: 1,026
Ticker: NYSE: AMRC
SIC: 1700
Industry/ies: Energy/Electricity
Legislative Issues: ENG; ENV; TAX

Chairman, President and Chief Executive Officer Tel: (508) 661-2200
SAKELLARIS, PE, George P. Fax: (508) 661-2201

Main Headquarters
Mailing: 111 Speen St. Tel: (508) 661-2200
       Suite 410 Fax: (508) 661-2201
       Framingham, MA 01701 TF: (866) 263-7372

Washington Office
Mailing: 101 Constitution Ave. NW Tel: (202) 650-6200
       Suite 525 East
       Washington, DC 20001

Public Affairs and Related Activities Personnel

At Headquarters

CASTONGUAY, Michael R. Tel: (508) 661-2200
Vice President, Planning Fax: (508) 661-2201
CORRSIN, David J. Tel: (508) 661-2200
Executive Vice President, General Counsel and Corporate Fax: (508) 661-2201
Secretary, and Director
CUNNINGHAM, William J. Tel: (508) 661-2200
Senior Vice President, Corporate Government Relations Fax: (508) 661-2201
boyagian.consulting@verizon.net
Registered Federal Lobbyist
HIBBARD, CarolAnn M. Tel: (508) 661-2200
Vice President, Strategic Marketing and Communications Fax: (508) 661-2201
JACOBS, Ronald M. Tel: (202) 344-4000
Federal Lobbyist Fax: (508) 661-2201
Ameresco_LDA@venable.com
LONGBOTTOM, Eric Tel: (508) 661-2200
Vice President, Sales and Marketing Fax: (508) 661-2201
MESSERE, Suzanne Tel: (508) 598-3044
Director, Investor Relations Fax: (508) 661-2201
PATTERSON, Ashley Tel: (508) 661-2200
Director, Government Relations Fax: (508) 661-2201
Registered Federal Lobbyist
SPENCE, CPA, Andrew B. Tel: (508) 661-2200
Vice President and Chief Financial Officer Fax: (508) 661-2201

At Washington Office

DERRINGTON, PE, CEM, Keith A. Tel: (202) 650-6200
Executive Vice President and General Manager, Federal
Operations

The America Channel, LLC

A sports and lifestyle television programming network.
www.americachannel.us
Industry/ies: Sports/Leisure/Entertainment

PAC Contact, Chairman of the Board and Chief Executive Officer Tel: (407) 333-3031
GORSHEIN, Doron

Main Headquarters
Mailing: 801 International Pkwy. Tel: (407) 333-3031
       Fifth Floor
       Heathrow, FL 32746

Political Action Committees
America Channel LLC PAC
FEC ID: C00408070
Contact: Doron Gorshein
801 International Pkwy. Tel: (407) 333-3031
Fifth Floor
Heathrow, FL 32746

Public Affairs and Related Activities Personnel

At Headquarters

SHAW PITTMAN , Pillsbury Winthrop Tel: (407) 333-3031
Corporate Counsel

America Forward

Organization to promote social innovation and build cross-sector partnerships.
Industry/ies: Coalitions; Nonprofit
Legislative Issues: BUD; EDU

Executive Director Tel: (301) 263-3045
SMOLOVER. J.D, Deborah
Main Headquarters
Mailing: 1400 Eye St. Tel: (301) 263-3045
       Suite 400
       Washington, DC 20005

Public Affairs and Related Activities Personnel

At Headquarters

BARRETT, Lexi Tel: (301) 263-3045
Policy Director
CRAWFORD, Jessica Tel: (301) 263-3045
Director, Government Affairs
TRUHE, Nicole Tel: (301) 263-3045
Government Affairs Director

At Other Offices

KLUZ, Austen
Treasurer
321 Palomino, Ln APT 25
Madison, WI 53705

America Online Inc.

Web services brand company, offers a suite of online content, products, and services to
consumers, advertisers, publishers, and subscribers worldwide.
corp.aol.com
Annual Revenues: $2.57 billion
Employees: 4,500
Ticker: NYSE: AOL
SIC: 7812
Industry/ies: Computer/Technology

Chairman of the Board and Chief Executive Officer Tel: (212) 206-4400
ARMSTRONG, Tim

Main Headquarters
Mailing: 770 Broadway Tel: (212) 206-4400
       New York City, NY 10003 TF: (800) 827-6364

Washington Office
Mailing: 1050 K St. NW
       Suite 340
       Washington, DC 20001

Corporate Foundations and Giving Programs

America Online Contributions Program
770 Broadway Tel: (212) 206-4400
New York City, NY 10003

Public Affairs and Related Activities Personnel

At Headquarters

DYKSTRA, Karen Tel: (212) 206-4400
Executive Vice President, Chief Financial and Administrative
Officer
JACOBS, Julie Tel: (212) 206-4400
Executive Vice President, General Counsel and Corporate
Secretary
Julie.Jacobs@corp.aol.com
JEFFERSON, Tekedra Tel: (212) 206-4400
Senior Vice President, Public Policy, Esq.
KLINE, Allie Tel: (212) 206-4400
Chief Marketing Officer
RYAN, Eoin Tel: (212) 206-4400
Senior Vice President and Head, Corporate Communications
and Investor Relations
IR@teamaol.com
SULLIVAN, Maureen Tel: (212) 206-4400
President

America Votes, Inc.

Purpose is to increase voter participation through registration, education and mobilization and
to coordinate the efforts of organizations to increase voter awareness of electoral issues.
www.americavotes.org
Industry/ies: Politics/Political Science

President Tel: (202) 962-7240
SPEED, Greg Fax: (202) 962-7241

Main Headquarters
Mailing: 1155 Connecticut Ave. NW Tel: (202) 962-7240
       Suite 600 Fax: (202) 962-7241
       Washington, DC 20036

Washington Office
Mailing: 1401 New York Ave. NW
       Suite 720
       Washington, DC 20005

Political Action Committees
America Votes PAC

FEC ID: C90012097
1401 New York Ave. NW
Suite 720
Washington, DC 20005

Public Affairs and Related Activities Personnel

At Headquarters

ACCOLA, Liz	Tel:	(202) 962-7254
Manager, Communications	Fax:	(202) 962-7241
eaccola@americavotes.org		
FINKLE, Susan	Tel:	(202) 962-7240
Chief Financial Officer	Fax:	(202) 962-7241
sfinkle@americavotes.org		
NUNNERY, Scott	Tel:	(202) 962-7240
National Political Director	Fax:	(202) 962-7241
snunnery@americavotes.org		
SCHREIBER, Sara	Tel:	(202) 962-7240
Managing Director	Fax:	(202) 962-7241

America's Car-Mart

An automotive retailer.
www.car-mart.com
Annual Revenues: $530.32 million
Employees: 1,360
Ticker: NASDAQ: CRMT
Industry/ies: Automotive Industry; Retail/Wholesale; Transportation

President and Chief Executive Officer	Tel:	(479) 464-9944
HENDERSON, William H.	Fax:	(479) 273-7556

Main Headquarters

Mailing:	802 S.E. Plaza Ave.	Tel:	(479) 464-9944
	Suite 200	Fax:	(479) 273-7556
	Bentonville, AR 72712		

Public Affairs and Related Activities Personnel

At Headquarters

WILLIAMS, Jeffrey A.	Tel:	(479) 418-8021
Chief Financial Officer	Fax:	(479) 273-7556

At Other Offices

WILSON , Brad	Tel:	(479) 571-2277
Manager		
2724 W. Martin Luther King Blvd.		
Fayetteville, AR 72704		

American Airlines Group Inc.

AMR Corporation is the parent company to American Airlines.
www.aa.com
Annual Revenues: $42.48 billion
Employees: 116,800
Ticker: NYSE: AAL
SIC: 4512; 4581
NAICS: 621910; 481111; 488119
Industry/ies: Aerospace/Aviation; Airlines; Transportation; Travel/Tourism/Lodging
Legislative Issues: AVI; BUD; DEF; HOM; LAW; TAX; TRA; TRD

Chairman of the Board and Chief Executive Officer	Tel:	(480) 693-8360
PARKER, W. Douglas	Fax:	(480) 693-8371
douglas.parker@usairways.com		
Chairman of the Board	Tel:	(817) 963-1234
HORTON, Thomas W.	Fax:	(817) 967-2841
tom.horton@aa.com		
Chairman and Chief Executive Officer	Tel:	(817) 963-1234
PARKER , Douglas	Fax:	(817) 967-2841

Main Headquarters

Mailing:	P.O. Box 619616	Tel:	(817) 963-1234
	Dallas/Fort Worth, TX 75261-9616	Fax:	(817) 967-2841

Washington Office

Mailing:	1401 H St. NW	
	Washington, DC 20036	

Political Action Committees
American Airlines Political Action Committee
FEC ID: C00107300
Contact: Norma H. Kaehler

1101 17th St. NW Suite 600	Tel:	(202) 496-5654
Washington, DC 20036	Fax:	(202) 496-5671

Contributions to Candidates: $384,500 (2015-2016)
Democrats: $87,500; Republicans: $294,500; Other: $2,500

Principal Recipients

SENATE
MCCAIN, JOHN S (REP-VA)
MCCONNELL, MITCH (REP-KY)

HOUSE

SHUSTER, WILLIAM MR. (REP-PA)

AMR Corporation PAC
FEC ID: C70003157
Contact: Julie L. Nichols
1101 17th St. NW
Suite 600
Washington, DC 20036

US Airways Group, Inc. Federal PAC		
FEC ID: C00313650		
Contact: Thomas B. Chapman		
1401 H St. NW	Tel:	(480) 693-5729
Suite 1075		
Washington, DC 20005		

Corporate Foundations and Giving Programs

AMR/American Airlines Foundation		
433 Amon Carter Blvd.	Tel:	(817) 963-1234
Fort Worth, TX 76155	Fax:	(817) 967-4162
US Airways Community Foundation		
4000 E. Sky Harbor Blvd.	Tel:	(480) 693-5729
Phoenix, AZ 85034		
US Airways Do Crew		
111 W. Rio Salado Parkway	Tel:	(480) 693-0800
Tempe, AZ 85281		
US Airways Education Foundation		
4000 E. Sky Harbor Blvd.	Tel:	(480) 693-5729
Phoenix, AZ 85034		

Public Affairs and Related Activities Personnel

At Headquarters

KERR, Derek J.	Tel:	(817) 963-1234
Executive Vice President and Chief Financial Officer	Fax:	(817) 967-2841
EBERWEIN, Elise R.	Tel:	(817) 963-1234
Executive Vice President, People and Communications	Fax:	(817) 967-2841
JOHNSON, Stephen L.	Tel:	(817) 963-1234
Executive Vice President, Corporate Affairs and Assistant	Fax:	(817) 967-2841
Secretary		
KIRBY, Scott	Tel:	(817) 963-1234
President	Fax:	(817) 967-2841

At Other Offices

ANDERSON, Faith L	Tel:	(817) 963-1234
PAC Treasurer	Fax:	(817) 967-2841
4333 Amon Carter Blvd.		
Fort Worth, TX 76155		
CHAPMAN, Thomas B.	Tel:	(202) 326-5157
Vice President, Government Affairs		
1101 17st St. NW, Suite 600		
Washington, DC 20005		
CRAVENS, Daniel E.	Tel:	(480) 693-1227
Managing Director, Investor Relations	Fax:	(480) 693-8371
111 W. Rio Salado Pkwy.		
Tempe, AZ 85281		
investor.relations@usairways.com		
DONOVAN, Abigail	Tel:	(202) 496-5644
1200 17th St. NW, Suite 400		
Washington, DC 20036		
Registered Federal Lobbyist		
EBERWEIN, Elise R.	Tel:	(480) 693-8360
Executive Vice President, People, Communications and Public	Fax:	(480) 693-8371
Affairs		
111 W. Rio Salado Pkwy.		
Tempe, AZ 85281		
FISHER, Kevin	Tel:	(202) 496-5654
Federal Lobbyist	Fax:	(202) 496-5671
1200 17th St. NW, Suite 400		
Washington, DC 20036		
GOREN, Isabella D.		
Senior Vice President and Chief Financial Officer		
P.O. Box 619616		
Dallas/Ft. Worth, TX 75261-9616		
Isabella.Goren@aa.com		
HOWLETT, C.A.	Tel:	(480) 693-5729
Senior Vice President, Public Affairs	Fax:	(480) 693-5546
4000 E. Sky Harbor Blvd.		
Phoenix, AZ 85034		
ISOM, Robert	Tel:	(480) 693-8360
Executive Vice President and Chief Operating Officer	Fax:	(480) 693-8371
111 W. Rio Salado Pkwy.		
Tempe, AZ 85281		
JOHNSON, Stephen	Tel:	(480) 693-8360
Executive Vice President, Corporate and Government Affairs	Fax:	(480) 693-8371
111 W. Rio Salado Pkwy.		

Tempe, AZ 85281

JONES, Paul	Tel:	(480) 693-8360
Senior Vice President, General Counsel	Fax:	(480) 693-8371

III W. Rio Salado Pkwy.
Tempe, AZ 85281
paul.jones@usairways.com

KAEHLER, Norma H.	Tel:	(202) 496-5648
Federal Lobbyist & PAC Treasurer	Fax:	(202) 496-5660

1200 17th St. NW, Suite 400
Washington, DC 20036
norma.kaehler@aa.com
Registered Federal Lobbyist

KENNEDY, Gary F.
Senior Vice President, General Counsel and Compliance Officer
P.O. Box 619616
Dallas/Ft. Worth, TX 75261-9616
gary.kennedy@aa.com

KERR, Derek	Tel:	(480) 693-8360
Executive Vice President, Chief Financial Officer	Fax:	(480) 693-8371

III W. Rio Salado Pkwy.
Tempe, AZ 85281
derek.kerr@usairways.com

KIRBY, Scott	Tel:	(480) 693-8360
President	Fax:	(480) 693-8371

III W. Rio Salado Pkwy.
Tempe, AZ 85281

MORELL, CAPT Paul	Tel:	(480) 693-8360
Vice President, Safety and Regulatory Compliance	Fax:	(480) 693-8371

III W. Rio Salado Pkwy.
Tempe, AZ 85281
Paul.Morell@usairways.com

NELSON, Carl A.	Tel:	(202) 496-5644
Associate General Counsel		

1200 17th St. NW, Suite 400
Washington, DC 20036
Registered Federal Lobbyist

NICHOLS, Julie L.	Tel:	(202) 496-5644
PAC Treasurer		

1200 17th St. NW, Suite 400
Washington, DC 20036

NOCELLA, Andrew	Tel:	(480) 693-8360
Senior Vice President, Marketing and Planning	Fax:	(480) 693-8371

III W. Rio Salado Pkwy.
Tempe, AZ 85281

PRICE, Ryan	Tel:	(480) 693-8360
Vice President, Human Resources	Fax:	(480) 693-8371

III W. Rio Salado Pkwy.
Tempe, AZ 85281

RIS JR., Jr., William K.	Tel:	(202) 496-5644

1200 17th St. NW, Suite 400
Washington, DC 20036
will.ris@aa.com

WASOM, Michael D.	Tel:	(202) 496-5654
Managing Director, International and Government Affairs		

1200 17th St. NW, Suite 400
Washington, DC 20036
michael.wascom@aa.com

American Airlines Inc.
See listing on page 48 under American Airlines Group Inc.

American Axle and Manufacturing
Specializes in automotive parts and accessories.
www.aam.com
Annual Revenues: $3.90 billion
Employees: 13,050
Ticker: NYSE: AXL
SIC: 3714
NAICS: 336399
Industry/ies: Automotive Industry; Transportation

Chairman, President and Chief Executive Officer	Tel:	(313) 758-2000
DAUCH, David C.	Fax:	(313) 758-4257

Main Headquarters

Mailing: One Dauch Dr.	Tel:	(313) 758-2000
Detroit, MI 48211-1198	Fax:	(313) 758-4257
	TF:	(800) 299-2953

Public Affairs and Related Activities Personnel

At Headquarters

BOWES, Timothy E.	Tel:	(313) 758-2000
Senior Vice President, Strategic and Business Development	Fax:	(313) 758-4257

KEMP, Terri M.	Tel:	(313) 758-2000
Vice President, Human Resources	Fax:	(313) 758-4257
MAY, Christopher J.	Tel:	(313) 758-2000
Vice President and Chief Financial Officer	Fax:	(313) 758-4257
SATINE, Jr., Alberto L.	Tel:	(313) 758-2000
Senior Vice President, Global Driveline Operations	Fax:	(313) 758-3929
SIMONTE, Michael K.	Tel:	(313) 758-2000
President	Fax:	(313) 758-4257
SON, Christopher M.	Tel:	(313) 758-4814
Director, Investor Relations, Corporate Communications and Marketing	Fax:	(313) 758-4257

chris.son@aam.com

TWOREK, David	Tel:	(313) 758-4883
Manager, Communications	Fax:	(313) 758-4257

david.tworek@aam.com

American Century Companies, Inc.
A financial investment firm.
www.americancentury.com
Employees: 1,800
SIC: 8741
Industry/ies: Banking/Finance/Investments

President and Chief Executive Officer	Tel:	(816) 531-5575
THOMAS, Jonathan S.	Fax:	(816) 340-7962

Main Headquarters

Mailing: P.O. Box 419200	Tel:	(816) 531-5575
Kansas City, MT 64141-6200	Fax:	(816) 340-7962
	TF:	(800) 345-2021

Corporate Foundations and Giving Programs
American Century Company Foundation

4500 Main St.	Tel:	(816) 340-4200
Suite 1500	Fax:	(816) 340-9762
Kansas City, MO 64111		

Public Affairs and Related Activities Personnel

At Headquarters

BANNIGAN, Patrick	Tel:	(816) 531-5575
Executive Vice President and Chief Financial Officer	Fax:	(816) 340-7962
DOYLE, Chris	Tel:	(816) 340-4638
Contact, Media Relations	Fax:	(816) 340-7962

chris_doyle@americancentury.com

KOURI, Laura	Tel:	(816) 531-5575
Director, Media Relations	Fax:	(816) 340-7962

laura_kouri@americancentury.com

WOODHAMS, Gregory	Tel:	(816) 340-4638
Senior Vice President, Senior Portfolio Manager and Chief Investment Officer	Fax:	(816) 340-7962

American Commercial Lines
An integrated marine transportation and service company operating in the United States.
www.aclines.com
Employees: 2,200
Ticker: NASDAQ: ACLI
SIC: 4400
Industry/ies: Business; Marine/Maritime/Shipping; Small Business; Transportation

President and Chief Executive Officer	Tel:	(812) 288-0100
KNOY, Mark K.	Fax:	(812) 288-1766

Mark.Knoy@aclines.com

Main Headquarters

Mailing: 1701 E. Market St.	Tel:	(812) 288-0100
Jeffersonville, IN 47130	Fax:	(812) 288-1766
	TF:	(800) 457-6377

Political Action Committees
American Commercial Lines Inc. PAC
FEC ID: C00418269
Contact: Douglas Brown

1701 E. Market St.	Tel:	(812) 288-0100
Jeffersonville, IN 47130	Fax:	(812) 288-1766

Contributions to Candidates: $57,000 (2015-2016)
Democrats: $20,000; Republicans: $37,000

Public Affairs and Related Activities Personnel

At Headquarters

BLOCKER, Robert M.	Tel:	(812) 288-0100
Senior Vice President, Sales and Customer Service	Fax:	(812) 288-1766
BROWN, Douglas	Tel:	(812) 288-0100
PAC Treasurer	Fax:	(812) 288-1766
HULS, David J.	Tel:	(812) 288-0100
Senior Vice President and Chief Financial Officer	Fax:	(812) 288-1766
LANDRY, Dawn R.	Tel:	(812) 288-0100

Senior Vice President and General Counsel   Fax: (812) 288-1766
dawn.landry@aclines.com

TOBIN, Paul A.   Tel: (812) 288-0100
Senior Vice President and Chief Operating Officer   Fax: (812) 288-1766

American Crystal Sugar Company

An agricultural cooperative that specializes in sugar and sugar-based products and by-products.
www.crystalsugar.com
Annual Revenues: $1.48 billion
Employees: 1,400
SIC: 2061
Industry/ies: Food And Beverage Industry
Legislative Issues: AGR

Chairman of the Board   Tel: (218) 236-4400
GREEN, Robert M.   Fax: (218) 236-4422

President and Chief Executive Officer   Tel: (218) 236-4400
BERG, David   Fax: (218) 236-4422

Main Headquarters
Mailing: 101 N. Third St.   Tel: (218) 236-4400
         Moorhead, MN 56560   Fax: (218) 236-4422

Political Action Committees
American Crystal Sugar Company PAC
FEC ID: C00110338
Contact: Samuel S.M. Wai
101 N. Third St.   Tel: (218) 236-4400
Moorhead, MN 56560   Fax: (218) 236-4342

     Contributions to Candidates: $1,555,500 (2015-2016)
     Democrats: $768,500; Republicans: $777,000; Other: $10,000

Principal Recipients

SENATE
DAINES, STEVEN (REP-MT)
DUCKWORTH, L TAMMY (DEM-IL)
PEARCE, STEVE (REP-NM)
PETERS, GARY (DEM-MI)
STRICKLAND, TED (DEM-OH)

HOUSE
ADAMS, ALMA SHEALEY (DEM-NC)
ADERHOLT, ROBERT BROWN (REP-AL)
AGUILAR, PETE (DEM-CA)
ASHFORD, BRAD (DEM-NE)
BERA, AMERISH (DEM-CA)
BONAMICI, SUZANNE MS. (DEM-OR)
BROWNLEY, JULIA (DEM-CA)
BYRNE, BRADLEY ROBERTS (REP-AL)
CARTER, JOHN R. REP. (REP-DC)
CLARK, KATHERINE (DEM-MA)
COHEN, STEPHEN IRA (DEM-)
CONAWAY, MICHAEL HONORABLE (REP-TX)
CONNOLLY, GERALD EDWARD (DEM-VA)
COSTA, JIM MR. (DEM-CA)
CRAWFORD, ERIC ALAN RICK (REP-AR)
CROWLEY, JOSEPH (DEM-NY)
CUELLAR, HENRY (DEM-TX)
CURBELO, CARLOS (REP-FL)
DAVIS, RODNEY L (REP-IL)
DELAURO, ROSA L (DEM-CT)
DENHAM, JEFF (REP-CA)
DESAULNIER, MARK (DEM-CA)
DOYLE, MIKE (DEM-PA)
DUFFY, SEAN (REP-WI)
FARENTHOLD, RANDOLPH BLAKE (REP-TX)
FINCHER, STEVE MR. (REP-TN)
GRAVES, GARRET (REP-LA)
GRAVES, SAMUEL B JR 'SAM' (REP-MO)
HARTZLER, VICKY (REP-MO)
HUFFMAN, JARED (DEM-CA)
HURD, WILLIAM (REP-TX)
JENKINS, EVAN H (REP-WV)
JONES, WALTER B. (REP-NC)
KAPTUR, MARCY C HON. (DEM-OH)
KATKO, JOHN M (REP-NY)
KELLY, ROBIN L. (DEM-IL)
KINZINGER, ADAM (REP-IL)
KIRKPATRICK, ANN (DEM-AZ)
KRISHNAMOORTHI, S. RAJA (DEM-IL)
LARSON, JOHN B (DEM-CT)
LOFGREN, ZOE (DEM-CA)
LOWENTHAL, ALAN (DEM-CA)
LUCAS, FRANK D. (REP-OK)
LUJAN GRISHAM, MICHELLE (DEM-NM)
LUJAN, BEN R MR. (DEM-NM)
MATSUI, DORIS (DEM-CA)
MCCARTHY, KEVIN (REP-CA)

MOULTON, SETH (DEM-MA)
MULLIN, MARKWAYNE MR. (REP-OK)
NAPOLITANO, GRACE (DEM-CA)
NOLAN, RICHARD M. (DEM-MN)
PALAZZO, STEVEN MCCARTY (REP-MS)
PAULSEN, ERIK (REP-MN)
POE, TED (REP-TX)
RATCLIFFE, JOHN L (REP-TX)
REED, THOMAS W II (REP-NY)
RICE, KATHLEEN (DEM-NY)
ROBY, MARTHA (REP-AL)
ROONEY, TOM MR. (REP-FL)
RUIZ, RAUL DR. (DEM-CA)
SANCHEZ, LINDA (DEM-CA)
SCOTT, JAMES AUSTIN (REP-GA)
SEWELL, TERRYCINA ANDREA (DEM-AL)
SIMPSON, MICHAEL (REP-ID)
SLAUGHTER, LOUISE M (DEM-NY)
SMITH, ADRIAN (REP-NE)
SMITH, JASON T (OTHER-MO)
TAKAI, KYLE MARK (DEM-HI)
THOMPSON, BENNIE G. (DEM-MS)
THOMPSON, MIKE MR. (DEM-CA)
TORRES, NORMA (DEM-CA)
VALADAO, DAVID (REP-CA)
VELA, FILEMON MR. (DEM-TX)
WALZ, TIMOTHY J (DEM-MN)
WELCH, PETER (DEM-VT)
YARMUTH, JOHN A MR (DEM-KY)
YODER, KEVIN (REP-KS)
YOUNG, DAVID (REP-IA)

Public Affairs and Related Activities Personnel
At Headquarters

ASTRUP, Thomas   Tel: (218) 236-4400
Vice President, Operations   Fax: (218) 236-4422
thomas.astrup@crystalsugar.org

MOTT, Daniel C.   Tel: (218) 236-4400
Secretary and General Counsel   Fax: (218) 236-4422

PRICE, Kevin   Tel: (218) 236-4430
Vice President, Government Affairs   Fax: (218) 236-4422
kprice@crystalsugar.com
Registered Federal Lobbyist

SCHWEITZER, Jeff   Tel: (218) 236-4492
Manager, Public Relations   Fax: (218) 236-4422
jschweit@crystalsugar.com

WAI, Samuel S.M.   Tel: (218) 236-4430
PAC Treasurer and Federal Lobbyist   Fax: (218) 236-4422

WARNE, Teresa   Tel: (218) 236-4400
Vice President, Finance   Fax: (218) 236-4422

American Eagle Airlines, Inc.
See listing on page 48 under American Airlines Group Inc.

American Ecology Corporation
See listing on page 818 under US Ecology

American Electric Power Company
A multinational energy company. Mission is to bring comfort to customers, supporting business and commerce, and building strong communities.
www.aep.com
Annual Revenues: $17.08 billion
Employees: 18,529
Ticker: NYSE: AEP
SIC: 4911
NAICS: 221112
Industry/ies: Energy/Electricity; Utilities
Legislative Issues: BUD; CAW; ENG; ENV; LBR; MAR

President and Chief Executive Officer   Tel: (614) 716-1000
AKINS, Nicholas K.   Fax: (614) 223-1823

Main Headquarters
Mailing: One Riverside Plaza   Tel: (614) 716-1000
         Columbus, OH 43215-2372   Fax: (614) 716-1823

Washington Office
Mailing: 801 Pennsylvania Ave. NW   Tel: (202) 383-3430
         Suite 320   Fax: (202) 323-3459
         Washington, DC 20004   TF: (800) 277-2177

Political Action Committees
The American Electric Power Committee for Responsible Government PAC
FEC ID: C00096842
Contact: David L Moore
One Riverside Plaza, 26th Floor   Tel: (614) 223-1000
Columbus, OH 43215   Fax: (614) 223-1823

Contributions to Candidates: $233,325 (2015-2016)
Democrats: $26,500; Republicans: $205,825; Other: $1,000

Principal Recipients

HOUSE

BOEHNER, JOHN A. (REP-OH)
HOYER, STENY HAMILTON (DEM-DC)
MCCARTHY, KEVIN (REP-CA)
RYAN, PAUL D. (REP-WI)
TIBERI, PATRICK J. (REP-OH)
UPTON, FREDERICK STEPHEN (REP-MI)

Corporate Foundations and Giving Programs

The American Electric Power Foundation
Contact: Beth Smail
One Riverside Plaza   Tel: (614) 716-1000
Columbus, OH 43215   Fax: (614) 716-1823

Public Affairs and Related Activities Personnel

At Headquarters

FEINBERG, David	Tel:	(614) 716-1000
Executive Vice President, General Counsel and Secretary	Fax:	(614) 716-1823
FLORA, Terri	Tel:	(614) 883-7999
Director, Corporate Communications, AEP Ohio	Fax:	(614) 223-1823
HAGELIN, David	Tel:	(614) 716-1938
Contact, Corporate Media Relations	Fax:	(614) 223-1823
dmhagelin@aep.com		
HEMLEPP, Pat D.	Tel:	(614) 716-1620
Director, Corporate Media Relations	Fax:	(614) 223-1823
HILLEBRAND, Lana L.	Tel:	(614) 716-1000
Senior Vice President and Chief Administrative Officer	Fax:	(614) 716-1823
HOHL, Doreen W.	Tel:	(614) 716-2661
PAC Treasurer	Fax:	(614) 223-1823
dwhohl@aep.com		
KALTENBACH, Beth	Tel:	(614) 716-1000
Foundation Contact	Fax:	(614) 716-1823
bkaltenbach@aep.com		
MCHENRY, Melissa	Tel:	(614) 716-1120
Director, External Communications	Fax:	(614) 223-1823
mamchenry@aep.com		
MOORE, David L	Tel:	(614) 716-1000
PAC Contact	Fax:	(614) 716-1823
Mail Stop 26th Floor		
MUNCZINSKI, Richard E.	Tel:	(614) 716-1000
Senior Vice President, Regulatory Services	Fax:	(614) 716-1823
POWERS, Robert P.	Tel:	(614) 716-1000
Executive Vice President and Chief Operating Officer	Fax:	(614) 716-1823
RIDOUT, Tammy L.	Tel:	(614) 716-2347
Manager, Media Relations	Fax:	(614) 716-1823
ROZSA, Bette Jo	Tel:	(614) 716-2840
Managing Director, Investor Relations	Fax:	(614) 223-1823
bjrozsa@aep.com		
SHERWOOD, Julie	Tel:	(614) 716-2663
Director, Investor Relations	Fax:	(614) 716-1823
jasherwood@aep.com		
SMAIL, Beth	Tel:	(614) 716-1000
Foundation Contact	Fax:	(614) 716-1823
basmail@aep.com		
TIERNEY, Brian	Tel:	(614) 716-1000
Executive Vice President and Chief Financial Officer	Fax:	(614) 716-1823

At Washington Office

CAMPBELL, Sabrina V.	Tel:	(202) 383-3430
Director, Federal Agency Relations	Fax:	(202) 323-3459
svcampbell@aep.com		
CANNON, Alicia	Tel:	(202) 383-3430
Federal Lobbyist	Fax:	(202) 323-3459
aecannon@aep.com		
Registered Federal Lobbyist		
HARTSOE, Joseph R.	Tel:	(202) 383-3430
Vice President and Associate General Counsel, Federal Policy	Fax:	(202) 323-3459
Jrhartsoe@aep.com		
Registered Federal Lobbyist		
KAVANAGH, Anthony P.	Tel:	(202) 383-3430
Senior Vice President, Federal Affairs	Fax:	(202) 323-3459
apkavanagh@aep.com		
Registered Federal Lobbyist		
MCBROOM, Marty	Tel:	(202) 383-3430
Director, Federal Environmental Affairs	Fax:	(202) 323-3459
mamcbroom@aep.com		
Registered Federal Lobbyist		

At Other Offices

CREGGE, Lynette	Tel:	(614) 716-1000

Foundation Contact   Fax: (614) 716-1823
850 Tech Center Dr.
Gahanna, OH 43230
llcregge@aep.com

American Express Company

A global travel, financial and network services provider. It provides charge and credit payment card products and travel-related services to consumers and businesses.
www.americanexpress.com
Annual Revenues: $32.09 billion
Employees: 54,000
Ticker: NYSE: AXP
SIC: 4724; 6099; 6162; 6211; 6282; 6199
NAICS: 522292; 522390; 523120; 523930; 561510
Industry/ies: Banking/Finance/Investments
Legislative Issues: BAN; CPT; FIN; TAX

Chairman and Chief Executive Officer	Tel:	(212) 640-2000
CHENAULT, Kenneth I.	Fax:	(212) 619-9802

Main Headquarters

Mailing:	200 Vesey St.	Tel:	(212) 640-2000
	New York City, NY 10285	Fax:	(212) 640-0404
		TF:	(800) 528-4800

Washington Office

Mailing:	801 Pennsylvania Ave. NW	Tel:	(202) 624-0761
	Suite 650	Fax:	(202) 624-0775
	Washington, DC 20004		

Political Action Committees
American Express Company PAC
FEC ID: C00040535
Contact: David A. Morgan

801 Pennsylvania Ave.	Tel:	(202) 624-0761
Suite 650	Fax:	(202) 624-0775
Washington, DC 20004		

Contributions to Candidates: $373,125 (2015-2016)
Democrats: $128,500; Republicans: $240,125; Other: $4,500

Principal Recipients

SENATE

SCHUMER, CHARLES E (DEM-NY)

Corporate Foundations and Giving Programs

American Express Philanthropic Program and Foundation
Contact: Georgie P. Shields

World Financial Center	Tel:	(212) 640-0555
200 Vesey St.	Fax:	(212) 640-9238
New York City, NY 10285		

Public Affairs and Related Activities Personnel

At Headquarters

BERLAND (HARRISON), Leslie	Tel:	(212) 640-5142
Senior Vice President, Digital Partnerships and Development.	Fax:	(212) 640-9238
leslie.a.berland@aexp.com		
COX, L. Kevin	Tel:	(212) 640-2000
Chief Human Resources Officer	Fax:	(212) 640-0404
HAYES, John D.	Tel:	(212) 640-2000
Executive Vice President and Chief Marketing Officer	Fax:	(212) 640-0404
LAMBERT, Joanna	Tel:	(212) 640-9668
Senior Vice President, Strategy and Business Innovation	Fax:	(212) 640-9238
joanna.g.lambert@aexp.com		
NORVILLE, Marina	Tel:	(212) 640-2832
Vice President, Public Affairs and Communications –	Fax:	(212) 640-0404
Corporate, Financial & Risk		
marina.h.norville@aexp.com		
O'NEILL, Michael J.	Tel:	(212) 640-2000
Executive Vice President, Corporate Affairs and	Fax:	(212) 640-0404
Communications		
PAUKOWITS, Ken	Tel:	(212) 640-6348
Vice President, Investor Relations	Fax:	(212) 640-0404
ken.f.paukowits@aexp.com		
SEEGER, Laureen E.	Tel:	(212) 640-2000
Executive Vice President and General Counsel	Fax:	(212) 640-0404
SHIELDS, Georgie P.	Tel:	(212) 640-4649
Vice President, American Express Philanthropic Program	Fax:	(212) 640-0326
SQUERI, Stephen	Tel:	(212) 640-2000
Group President, Global Corporate Services	Fax:	(212) 619-9802

At Washington Office

BEST, Amy	Tel:	(202) 624-0761
Contact, Government Relations	Fax:	(202) 624-0775
Registered Federal Lobbyist		
LOPER, Brett S.	Tel:	(202) 624-0761
Senior Vice President, Government Affairs	Fax:	(202) 624-0775
Registered Federal Lobbyist		

MERIDA, Christian
Vice President, Federal Government Affairs
Registered Federal Lobbyist
Tel: (202) 624-0761
Fax: (202) 624-0775

MORGAN, David A.
Vice President, Government Affairs
david.a.morgan@aexp.com
Registered Federal Lobbyist
Tel: (202) 624-0761
Fax: (202) 624-0775

American Express Travel Related Services

See listing on page 51 under American Express Company

American Family Insurance Group

Specializes in property, casualty insurance, health, homeowners coverage, investment and retirement-planning products.
www.amfam.com
Annual Revenues: $6.36 billion
Employees: 8,000
Industry/ies: Insurance Industry
Legislative Issues: AVI; CPT; DIS; FIN; HOM; INS; MMM; RET; TAX

Chairman and Chief Executive Officer
SALZWEDEL, Jack C.
Tel: (608) 249-2111
Fax: (608) 243-4921

Main Headquarters
Mailing: 6000 American Pkwy.
Madison, WI 53783
Tel: (608) 249-2111
Fax: (608) 243-4921
TF: (800) 692-6326

Political Action Committees
American Family Mutual Insurance Company Federal PAC (AMFAM PAC)
FEC ID: C00354290
Contact: Heidi Krumenauer
6000 American Pkwy.
Madison, WI 53783
Tel: (608) 249-2111
Fax: (608) 243-4921

   Contributions to Candidates: $73,650 (2015-2016)
   Democrats: $23,500; Republicans: $50,150

Corporate Foundations and Giving Programs
American Family Insurance Group Contributions Program
6000 American Pkwy.
Madison, WI 53783
Tel: (608) 249-2111
Fax: (608) 243-4921

Public Affairs and Related Activities Personnel

At Headquarters

AFABLE, Mark V.
Chief Legal Officer
Tel: (608) 249-2111
Fax: (608) 243-4921

BENUSA, Gerry W.
Chief Sales Officer
Tel: (608) 249-2111
Fax: (608) 243-4921

FANSHAW, Lee
Director, Federal Government Affairs
lfanshaw@amfam.com
Registered Federal Lobbyist
Tel: (608) 249-2111
Fax: (608) 243-4921

FETHERSTON, Richard A.
Vice President, Public Relations
rfethers@amfam.com
Tel: (608) 249-2111
Fax: (608) 243-4921

HOLMAN, David C.
Chief Strategy Officer
Tel: (608) 249-2111
Fax: (608) 243-4921

KELLY, Daniel J.
Chief Financial Officer
Tel: (608) 249-2111
Fax: (608) 243-4921

KICK, Kelly
Manager, Strategic Communications
Tel: (608) 249-2111
Fax: (608) 243-4921

KRUMENAUER, Heidi
PAC Treasurer
Tel: (608) 249-2111
Fax: (608) 243-4921

MUTH, Ken
Director, Media Relations
Tel: (608) 242-4100
Fax: (608) 243-4921

SCHEMMEL, Judd
Federal Lobbyist
Tel: (608) 249-2111
Fax: (608) 243-4921

SCHULTZ, Daniel R.
President And Chief Operating Officer
Tel: (608) 249-2111
Fax: (608) 243-4921

SEYMOUR, Scott J.
Vice President, Government and Compliance Services
Tel: (608) 249-2111
Fax: (608) 243-4921

STEGER, Evonne M.
Associate Vice President, Business and Workplace Services
Tel: (608) 249-2111
Fax: (608) 243-4921

American Fidelity Assurance Company

A private, family-owned life insurance company.
americanfidelity.com
Annual Revenues: $877.97 million
Employees: 1,200
Industry/ies: Banking/Finance/Investments; Education; Insurance Industry

Chairman of the Board, President, and Chief Executive Officer
CAMERON, William M.
Tel: (405) 523-2000
Fax: (405) 523-5963

Main Headquarters
Mailing: 2000 N. Classen Blvd.
Suite Seven N
Tel: (405) 523-2000
Fax: (405) 523-5963

Oklahoma City, OK 73106-6013

Political Action Committees
American Fidelity Corporation PAC
FEC ID: C00210526
Contact: Robert D. Brearton
2000 N. Classen Blvd.
Suite 7N
Oklahoma City, OK 73106
Tel: (405) 523-2000
Fax: (405) 523-5421

   Contributions to Candidates: $33,000 (2015-2016)
   Democrats: $7,700; Republicans: $25,300

Corporate Foundations and Giving Programs
American Fidelity Foundation
P. O. Box 25523
Oklahoma City, OK 73125
Tel: (405) 523-2000
Fax: (405) 523-5421

Public Affairs and Related Activities Personnel

At Headquarters

BREARTON, Robert D.
PAC Treasurer
Tel: (405) 523-2000
Fax: (405) 523-5963

BURCHFIELD, Lisa
Senior Communications Specialist
Tel: (405) 523-2000
Fax: (405) 523-5963

CARPENTER, David R.
President and Chief Operating Officer
Tel: (405) 523-2000
Fax: (405) 523-5963

WILLIAMS, Shirley
Chief Financial Officer
Tel: (405) 523-2000
Fax: (405) 523-5963

WORTMANN, Melody
Assistant Vice President, Corporate Communications
Melody.Wortmann@af-group.com
Tel: (405) 523-2000
Fax: (405) 523-5963

American Financial Group Inc

An insurance and financial services company engaged primarily in property and casualty insurance ("P&C"), focusing on specialized commercial products for businesses, and in the sale of traditional fixed and fixed-indexed annuities.
www.afginc.com
Annual Revenues: $5.87 billion
Employees: 7,200
Ticker: NYSE:AFG
SIC: 2032; 2053; 5141; 6021; 6411
Industry/ies: Banking/Finance/Investments; Insurance Industry

Co-Chief Executive Officer, Co-President and Director
LINDNER, III, Carl H.
Tel: (513) 579-2121
Fax: (513) 412-0200

Co-Chief Executive Officer, President and Director
LINDNER, S. Craig
Tel: (513) 579-2121
Fax: (513) 412-0200

Main Headquarters
Mailing: 301 E. Fourth St.
Cincinnati, OH 45202
Tel: (513) 579-2121
Fax: (513) 412-0200
TF: (800) 545-4269

Public Affairs and Related Activities Personnel

At Headquarters

GILLIS, Michelle A.
Senior Vice President and Chief Administrative Officer
Tel: (513) 579-2121
Fax: (513) 412-0200

WEIDNER, Diane P.
Assistant Vice President, Investor Relations
Tel: (513) 369-5713
Fax: (513) 352-9230

At Other Offices

CONSOLINO, Joseph E.
Executive Vice President and Chief Financial Officer
One E. Fourth St.
Cincinnati, OH 45202-3715
Tel: (513) 579-2121
Fax: (513) 412-0200

GRAFE, Karl J.
Vice President, Assistant General Counsel and Secretary
One E. Fourth St.
Cincinnati, OH 45202-3715
Tel: (513) 579-2121
Fax: (513) 412-0200

American Freedom Innovations, LLC

A lobbying firm.
www.freedom-innovations.com
Industry/ies: Law/Law Firms

Chairman and Chief Executive Officer
CARKHUFF, Maynard
Tel: (949) 672-0032
Fax: (949) 672-0084

Main Headquarters
Mailing: Three Morgan
Irvine, CA 92618
Tel: (949) 672-0032
Fax: (949) 672-0084
TF: (888) 818-6777

Public Affairs and Related Activities Personnel

At Headquarters

CRIPE, Rob
Senior Vice President, Global Marketing
Tel: (949) 672-0032
Fax: (949) 672-0084

KIM, Lee
Chief Financial Officer
Tel: (949) 672-0032
Fax: (949) 672-0084

MARTIN, Joe W.	Tel:	(949) 672-0032
President and Chief Operating Officer	Fax:	(949) 672-0084
SAIPE, Joshua	Tel:	(949) 672-0032
Senior VicePresident, Corporate and Business Development	Fax:	(949) 672-0084

American General Life and Accident Insurance Company
See listing on page 54 under American International Group, Inc. (AIG)

American Greetings Corporation
American Greetings Corporation is a creator and manufacturer of innovative social expression products that assist consumers in making the world a more thoughtful and caring place.
www.americangreetings.com
Employees: 6,700
Ticker: NYSE: AM
SIC: 5112; 2731; 2759; 5099; 5947; 2771
Industry/ies: Furniture/Home Furnishings

Chairman of the Board	Tel:	(216) 252-7300
WEISS, Morry	Fax:	(216) 252-6778
Co-Chief Executive Officer	Tel:	(216) 252-7300
WEISS, Zev	Fax:	(216) 252-6778

Main Headquarters
| Mailing: | One American Rd. | Tel: | (216) 252-7300 |
| | Cleveland, OH 44144-2398 | Fax: | (216) 252-6778 |

Public Affairs and Related Activities Personnel
At Headquarters

BEEDER, John W.	Tel:	(216) 252-7300
President and Chief Operating Officer	Fax:	(216) 252-6778
HAFFKE, Christopher W.	Tel:	(216) 252-7300
General Counsel and Secretary	Fax:	(216) 252-6778
MCGRATH, Brian T.	Tel:	(216) 252-7300
Senior Vice President, Human Resources	Fax:	(216) 252-6778
OLMSTEAD, Meghan	Tel:	(216) 252-4938
Senior Manager, Social Media Marketing	Fax:	(216) 252-6778
meghan.olmstead@amgreetings.com		
PRIMOSCH, Maureen	Tel:	(216) 252-7300
Manager, National Meeting and Event	Fax:	(216) 252-6778
maureen.primosch@amgreetings.com		
ROMMEL, Douglas W.	Tel:	(216) 252-7300
Senior Vice President and Chief Information Officer	Fax:	(216) 252-6778
STEINBERG, Gregory M.	Tel:	(216) 252-4864
Chief Financial Officer	Fax:	(216) 252-6778
investor.relations@amgreetings.com		
TYLER, Robert D.	Tel:	(216) 252-7300
Corporate Controller and Chief Accounting Officer	Fax:	(216) 252-6778

American Health Care Professionals
Home health care & Hospice/Consultant/Telehealth Provider.
www.ahcpofva.com
Industry/ies: Health Care; Medicine/Health Care/Mental Health
Legislative Issues: HCR

President & Chief Executive Officer	Tel:	(703) 388-2813
TAYLOR, Dr. Clishia		
clishia.taylor@ahcpofva.com		

Main Headquarters
Mailing:	8500 Leesburg Pike	Tel:	(703) 388-2813
	Suite 202	TF:	(888) 515-2427
	Vienna, VA 22182		

Public Affairs and Related Activities Personnel
At Headquarters

ARROYAVE, Beatriz	Tel:	(703) 388-2813
Executive Vice President/Chief Financial Officer		
beatriz.arroyave@ahcpofva.com		
Registered Federal Lobbyist		
LISS, David	Tel:	(703) 388-2813
Director, Public Relations		
pr@ahcpofva.com		
TAYLOR, Cyle	Tel:	(703) 388-2813
Federal Lobbyist		

American Healthcare, LLC
Long term care provider.
www.americanhealthcarellc.com
Industry/ies: Health Care; Medicine/Health Care/Mental Health; Nursing

Main Headquarters
Mailing:	9540 Garland Rd.	Tel:	(972) 212-8780
	Suite 381-259		
	Dallas, TX 75218		

Public Affairs and Related Activities Personnel

At Headquarters
CRANWELL, Charles Richard	Tel:	(972) 212-8780
Director, Governmental Relations		
Registered Federal Lobbyist		

American Home Partners
Comprehensive home building company and it provides flexible construction loan financing.
Employees: 29
Industry/ies: Construction/Construction Materials; Housing

| **President, Chief Executive Officer and Director** | Tel: | (203) 699-3400 |
| HENDEL, Gregory J. | | |

Main Headquarters
| Mailing: | 1154 Highland Ave. | Tel: | (203) 699-3400 |
| | Cheshire, CT 06410-1624 | TF: | (800) 343-2884 |

Public Affairs and Related Activities Personnel

At Headquarters
| BUCCI, Salvatore A. | Tel: | (203) 699-3400 |
| *Executive Vice President and Chief Financial Officer* | | |

American Honda Motor Company, Inc.
See listing on page 53 under American Honda Motor Company, Inc.

American Honda Motor Company, Inc.
Subsidiary of American Honda Motor coordinating the operations in North America that manufacture, market, and distribute Accord, Civic, and Acura cars, as well as Gold Wing, Shadow, and Valkyrie motorcycles.
www.honda.com
Annual Revenues: $102.31 billion
Employees: 26,000
Ticker: NYSE HMC
SIC: 5012; 3524; 3714; 3751
Industry/ies: Automotive Industry; Transportation
Legislative Issues: AUT; AVI; BUD; CHM; CPT; CSP; EDU; ENV; FIN; TAX; TEC; TRA; TRD

Chairman and Chief Executive Officer	Tel:	(310) 783-3170
AMEMIYA, Koichi	Fax:	(310) 783-3622
President	Tel:	(310) 783-2000
YAMADA, Takuji	Fax:	(310) 783-2110

Main Headquarters
| Mailing: | 1919 Torrance Blvd. | Tel: | (310) 781-4000 |
| | Torrance, CA 90501 | Fax: | (310) 781-4142 |

Washington Office
Mailing:	1001 G St. NW	Fax:	(202) 661-4459
	Suite 950		
	Washington, DC 20001		

Corporate Foundations and Giving Programs
American Honda Foundation
Contact: Kathryn Carey
| 1919 Torrance Blvd. | Tel: | (310) 781-4090 |
| Torrance, CA 90501 | Fax: | (310) 781-4270 |
Honda of America Mfg. Foundation
1919 Torrance Blvd.
Torrance, CA 90501

Public Affairs and Related Activities Personnel
At Washington Office

BIENENFOLD, Robert	Fax:	(202) 661-4459
Senior Manager, Environment & Energy Strategy		
BRILLHART, Ember A.	Fax:	(202) 661-4459
Manager, State Relations		
DULANEY, Shannon	Fax:	(202) 661-4459
Analyst, Federal Affairs		
Registered Federal Lobbyist		
HAIRSTON, Tara	Fax:	(202) 661-4459
Analyst, Government Affairs		
Registered Federal Lobbyist		

At Other Offices
CAREY, Kathryn	Tel:	(310) 781-4090
Foundation Contact	Fax:	(310) 781-4270
1919 Torrance Blvd.		
Torrance, CA 90501		
kathryn_carey@ahm.honda.com		
COHEN, Edward B.		
Vice President, Government & Industry Affairs		
1001 G St. NW, Suite 950		
Washington, DC 20001		
edward_cohen@ahm.honda.com		
Registered Federal Lobbyist		
GERKE, Scott A.		
Manager		

1001 G St. NW, Suite 950
Washington, DC 20001
scott_gerke@ahm.honda.com
Registered Federal Lobbyist

HARRINGTON, Toni
Federal Lobbyist
1001 G St. NW, Suite 950
Washington, DC 20001
toni_harrington@ahm.honda.com
Registered Federal Lobbyist

MARIE, Sage	Tel:	(310) 783-2000
Senior Manager, Public Relations	Fax:	(310) 783-2110

1919 Torrance Blvd.
Torrance, CA 90501

SMITH, Jeffrey A.	Tel:	(310) 781-5062
Assistant Vice President, Corporate Affairs and	Fax:	(310) 787-4417

Communications
1919 Torrance Blvd.
Torrance, CA 90501
jeffrey_smith@ahm.honda.com

YOKOTA, Chitoshi	Tel:	(310) 783-2000
Senior executive vice president and Automobile Business	Fax:	(310) 783-2110

Managing Officer
1919 Torrance Blvd.
Torrance, CA 90501

American International Group, Inc. (AIG)

An insurance company serving commercial, institutional and individual customers.
www.aig.com
Annual Revenues: $63.40 billion
Employees: 65,000
Ticker: NYSE: AIG
SIC: 6331
Industry/ies: Insurance Industry; Medicine/Health Care/Mental Health
Legislative Issues: AVI; CSP; FIN; GOV; HCR; HOU; INS; RET; TAX

President and Chief Executive Officer	Tel:	(713) 522-1111
HANCOCK, Peter D.	Fax:	(713) 831-3028

Main Headquarters

Mailing:	P.O. Box 4373	Tel:	(713) 522-1111
	Houston, TX 77210-4373	Fax:	(713) 831-3028
		TF:	(888) 436-5256

Washington Office

Mailing:	901 K St. NW
	Suite 350
	Washington, DC 20001

Political Action Committees

American International Group, Inc. Employee PAC
FEC ID: C00097725
Contact: Jeffrey S. Lanning

180 Maiden Ln.	Tel:	(212) 770-7000
23rd Floor	Fax:	(212) 509-9705

New York City, NY 10038

> **Contributions to Candidates:** $63,500 (2015-2016)
> Democrats: $19,500; Republicans: $44,000

Corporate Foundations and Giving Programs

AIG American General Life Companies Contributions Program
Contact: Jennifer Waldner

P.O. Box 4373	Tel:	(888) 436-3028
Houston, TX 77210	Fax:	(713) 831-8687

American International Group Corporate Giving Program

70 Pine St.	Tel:	(212) 770-7000
New York City, NY 10270	Fax:	(212) 509-9705

Public Affairs and Related Activities Personnel

At Headquarters

CUMMINGS, Don	Tel:	(713) 522-1111
Senior Vice President, Controllers	Fax:	(713) 831-3028
HERZOG , David	Tel:	(713) 522-1111
Executive Vice President and Chief Financial Officer	Fax:	(713) 831-3028
HURD, Jeffrey	Tel:	(713) 522-1111
Senior Vice President, Human Resources and Administration	Fax:	(713) 831-3028
jeffrey.hurd@aig.com		
JENNINGS, Kyle	Tel:	(713) 522-1111
Executive Vice President and General Counsel	Fax:	(713) 831-3028
RUNGE, Debbie	Tel:	(713) 522-1111
Vice President, Human Resources	Fax:	(713) 831-3028
RUSSO, Thomas A.	Tel:	(713) 522-1111
Executive Vice President and General Counsel, Legal,	Fax:	(713) 831-3028
Compliance, Regulatory Affairs, and Government		
SCHREIBER, Brian	Tel:	(713) 522-1111
Executive Vice President and Chief Strategy Officer	Fax:	(713) 831-3028

At Washington Office

GALLAGHER, Shawn
Federal Lobbyist
Registered Federal Lobbyist

LOCONTE, Richard
Federal Lobbyist

MAJOR, Blake
Manager, Government Affairs
blakemajor@gmail.com
Registered Federal Lobbyist

TAYLOR, Daniel
Registered Federal Lobbyist

TILLOTSON, Frank
Registered Federal Lobbyist

TRIGONOPLOS, Darren
Federal Lobbyist
Registered Federal Lobbyist

At Other Offices

DIAT , Jon	Tel:	(212) 770-3505
Head, External Communications		

180 Maiden Ln.
New York, NY 10038
jon.diat@aig.com

HERZOG , David	Tel:	(212) 770-7000
Executive Vice President and Chief Financial Officer		

180 Maiden Ln.
New York, NY 10038

HURD, Jeffrey	Tel:	(212) 770-7000
Senior Vice President, Human Resources and Administration		

180 Maiden Ln.
New York, NY 10038
jeffrey.hurd@aig.com

JUHAS, Peter	Tel:	(212) 770-7000
Vice President and Head, Strategic Planning		

180 Maiden Ln.
New York, NY 10038

LANNING, Jeffrey S.	Tel:	(212) 770-7000
PAC Treasurer		

180 Maiden Ln.
New York, NY 10038
Mail Stop 29th Floor

NORAT, Cecelia	Tel:	(212) 770-7000
Director, State Relations	Fax:	(212) 770-7821

70 Pine St., 19th Floor
New York City, NY 10270

PRETTO, Christina	Tel:	(212) 770-7000
Senior Vice President, Corporate Communications		

180 Maiden Ln.
New York, NY 10038
christina.pretto@aig.com

RUSSO, Thomas A.	Tel:	(212) 770-7000
Executive Vice President and General Counsel, Legal,		

Compliance, Regulatory Affairs, and Government
180 Maiden Ln.
New York, NY 10038

WALDNER, Jennifer
Director, Community Relations
2929 Allen Pkwy., AT-40
Houston, TX 77019
Jennifer.Waldner@aglife.com

WERNER, Elizabeth A.	Tel:	(212) 770-7074
Vice President, Investor Relations		

180 Maiden Ln.
New York, NY 10038
elizabeth.werner@aig.com

American Management Services

Provides profit-improvement solutions to owners of small and mid-sized businesses.
www.amserv.com
Annual Revenues: $14.50 million
Employees: 100
Industry/ies: Business; Small Business

Founder, Chairman of the Board and Chief Executive Officer	Tel:	(407) 351-6545
CLOUTIER, George A.	Fax:	(407) 351-0552

Main Headquarters

Mailing:	7680 Universal Blvd.	Tel:	(407) 351-6545
	Suite 170	Fax:	(407) 345-5698
	Orlando, FL 32819-8900	TF:	(800) 743-0402

Public Affairs and Related Activities Personnel

At Headquarters

MOSCA, Louis M. Tel: (407) 351-6545
Executive Vice President and Chief Operating Officer Fax: (407) 345-5698

American Medical Security Group, Inc.
A health-care benefits provider.
www.eams.com
Annual Revenues: $51.60 million
SIC: 6324
Industry/ies: Medicine/Health Care/Mental Health

Chairman, President and Chief Executive Officer Tel: (920) 661-3681
MILLER, Samuel V. Fax: (920) 661-2222

Main Headquarters
Mailing: 3100 AMS Blvd. Tel: (920) 661-1111
P.O. Box 19032 Fax: (920) 661-2019
Green Bay, WI 54307-9032 TF: (800) 232-5432

Public Affairs and Related Activities Personnel

At Headquarters

PROCHNOW, James Tel: (920) 661-1111
PAC Contact Fax: (920) 661-2019

American National Insurance Company
A wholly-owned subsidiary of PacifiCare Health Systems. It offers products and services, which include life insurance, annuities, health insurance, credit insurance, pension plan services and property and casualty insurance for personal lines, agribusiness, and targeted commercial exposures.
www.anico.com
Annual Revenues: $3.03 billion
Employees: 4,736
Ticker: NASDAQ: ANAT
SIC: 6411; 4225
NAICS: 493110
Industry/ies: Insurance Industry

Chairman of the Board, President, Chief Executive Office Tel: (409) 763-4661
POZZI, James E. Fax: (409) 766-2912

Main Headquarters
Mailing: One Moody Plaza Tel: (409) 763-4661
Galveston, TX 77550-7947 Fax: (409) 766-2912
TF: (800) 899-6806

Corporate Foundations and Giving Programs

American National Insurance Company Contribution Program
One Moody Plaza Tel: (409) 763-4661
Galveston, TX 77550-7947 Fax: (409) 766-2912

Public Affairs and Related Activities Personnel

At Headquarters

AKINS, Dwain A. Tel: (409) 763-4661
Senior Vice President, Corporate Relations Fax: (409) 766-6663
AKINS@anico.com

DUNN, John J. Tel: (409) 763-4661
Corporate Chief Financial Officer Fax: (409) 766-2912
John.Dunn@anico.com

FLIPPIN, John Mark Tel: (409) 763-6537
PAC Treasurer Fax: (409) 766-6663
mark.flippin@anico.com

LEPARD, Bruce Tel: (409) 763-4661
Senior Vice President and Chief Human Resources Officer Fax: (409) 766-6663

REGINI, Judith L. Tel: (409) 763-4661
Assistant Vice President, Chief Compliance Officer Fax: (409) 766-6663
judy.regini@anico.com

American Pacific Corporation
A manufacturer of fine chemicals and specialty chemicals.
www.apfc.com
Annual Revenues: $215.09 million
Employees: 500
Ticker: NASDAQ: APFC
SIC: 2899; 6552; 2810
Industry/ies: Chemicals & Chemical Industry
Legislative Issues: ENV

Chairman of the Board, President and Chief Executive Officer Tel: (702) 735-2200
CARLEONE, Dr. Joseph Fax: (702) 735-4876

Main Headquarters
Mailing: 3883 Howard Hughes Pkwy. Tel: (702) 735-2200
Suite 700 Fax: (702) 735-4876
Las Vegas, NV 89169

Corporate Foundations and Giving Programs

American Pacific Corporation Contributions Program
3883 Howard Hughes Pkwy. Tel: (702) 735-2200
Suite 700 Fax: (702) 735-4876
Las Vegas, NV 89169

Public Affairs and Related Activities Personnel

At Headquarters
FERGUSON, Linda G. Tel: (702) 735-2200
Vice President, Administration and Corporate Secretary Fax: (702) 735-4876
KELLEY, Dana M. Tel: (702) 735-2200
Vice President, Chief Financial Officer and Treasurer Fax: (702) 735-4876
RICCARDI, Deanna P. Tel: (702) 735-2200
Manager, Investor Relations and Assistant Corporate Fax: (702) 735-4876
Secretary

American Patriot Alternative Fuels, LLC
Alternative energy and synthetic fuels development. Headquartered in Evansville, IN.
Industry/ies: Energy/Electricity

Main Headquarters
Mailing: 1111 19th St. NW Tel: (202) 729-4308
Suite 1100
Washington, DC 20036

American Science and Engineering, Inc.
A worldwide supplier of X-ray inspection systems. The company makes X-ray detection systems for inspection and security applications at airports, border protection sites, shipping ports, and special events. AS&E's complete range of products include cargo inspection systems for port and border security, baggage screening systems for facility and aviation security, and personnel and passenger screening systems.
www.as-e.com
Annual Revenues: $126.75 million
Employees: 400
Ticker: NASDAQ (GS): ASEI
SIC: 3829; 3844
NAICS: 334517; 334519
Industry/ies: Engineering/Mathematics; Science; Scientific Research
Legislative Issues: DEF; FOR; HOM

Chairman of the Board Tel: (978) 262-8700
BROWN, Denis R. Fax: (978) 262-0533

President and Chief Executive Officer Tel: (978) 262-8700
DOUGHERTY, Charles P. (Chuck) Fax: (978) 262-0533

Main Headquarters
Mailing: 829 Middlesex Tnpk. Tel: (978) 262-8700
Billerica, MA 01821 Fax: (978) 262-0533
TF: (800) 225-1608

Political Action Committees
American Science and Engineering Inc. PAC
FEC ID: C00343020
Contact: Kenneth J. Galaznik
829 Middlesex Tnpk. Tel: (978) 262-8700
Billerica, MA 01821 Fax: (978) 262-8812

  Contributions to Candidates: $7,500 (2015-2016)
  Democrats: $3,000; Republicans: $4,500

Public Affairs and Related Activities Personnel

At Headquarters

BERMAN, Laura Tel: (978) 262-8713
Director, Corporate Communications Fax: (978) 262-0533
lberman@as-e.com

GALAZNIK, Kenneth J. Tel: (978) 262-8700
Senior Vice President, Chief Financial Officer and PAC Fax: (978) 262-0533
Treasurer
ir@as-e.com

GRAZEWSKI, Paul H. Tel: (978) 262-8700
Senior Vice President, Product Management, Marketing and Fax: (978) 262-0533
Strategy
pgrazewski@as-e.com

LEVINE, Lanning L. Tel: (978) 262-8700
Senior Vice President, Human Resources Fax: (978) 262-0533

MUSCATELLO, Michael J. Tel: (978) 262-8700
Vice President, General Counsel, and Secretary Fax: (978) 262-0533

TROPEANO, Mike Tel: (978) 262-8700
Vice President, Customer Development and Support Fax: (978) 262-0533

American Signature, Inc.
Furniture and interior accessories for decorating the home.
www.americansignaturefurniture.com
Annual Revenues: $256.50 million
Employees: 5,000
Industry/ies: Furniture/Home Furnishings

Chairman of the Board and Chief Executive Officer Tel: (614) 221-9200
SCHOTTENSTEIN, Jay L.

Main Headquarters
Mailing: 4300 E. Fifth Ave. Tel: (614) 221-9200
Columbus, OH 43219 TF: (888) 751-8553

Public Affairs and Related Activities Personnel

At Headquarters

CORNELL, Edward	Tel:	(614) 221-9200

Executive Vice President and Chief Financial Officer

American Snuff Company, LLC

Engaged in the production of smokeless tobacco products.
www.americansnuff.com
Annual Revenues: $750 million
Employees: 900
SIC: 2111
Industry/ies: Tobacco Industry
Legislative Issues: INS

Main Headquarters

Mailing: P.O. Box 217	Tel:	(901) 761-2050
Memphis, TN 38101	Fax:	(901) 767-1302
	TF:	(800) 238-5990

Corporate Foundations and Giving Programs

American Snuff Co. Charitable Trust
Contact: Robert Banks

P.O. Box 217	Tel:	(901) 761-2050
Memphis, TN 38101	Fax:	(901) 767-1302

Public Affairs and Related Activities Personnel

At Headquarters

BANKS, Robert	Tel:	(901) 761-2050
Contact, Foundation	Fax:	(901) 767-1302
banksr@rjrt.com		
HATCHELL, Bryan	Tel:	(336) 741-0763
Contact, Federal Legislation, Taxation and Litigation	Fax:	(901) 767-1302
hatcheb@rjrt.com		
HOWARD, David	Tel:	(336) 741-3489
Contact, Media and Brand Marketing	Fax:	(901) 767-1302
HowardD1@AmericanSnuff.com		

American Standard

See listing on page 428 under Ingersoll-Rand Company

American Superconductor Corporation

Serves the utility, industrial and wind power markets with a energy technologies based on high temperature superconductor (HTS) wires and power electronic systems.
www.amsc.com
Annual Revenues: $61.69 million
Employees: 303
Ticker: NASDAQ: AMSC
SIC: 3621
Industry/ies: Electricity & Electronics; Electronics; Energy/Electricity; Metals; Science; Scientific Research
Legislative Issues: DEF; FIN; TAX

Chairman of the Board	Tel:	(978) 842-3000
WOOD, Jr., John W.	Fax:	(978) 842-3024
President and Chief Executive Officer	Tel:	(978) 842-3000
MCGAHN, Daniel	Fax:	(978) 842-3024
daniel.mcgahn@amsc.com		

Main Headquarters

Mailing: 64 Jackson Rd.	Tel:	(978) 842-3000
Devens, MA 01434-4020	Fax:	(978) 842-3024

Public Affairs and Related Activities Personnel

At Headquarters

FARRELL, Kerry	Tel:	(978) 842-3247
Contact, Investor Relations and Manager, Corporate Communications	Fax:	(978) 842-3024
kerry.farrell@amsc.com		
HENRY, David	Tel:	(978) 842-3000
Senior Vice President, Chief Financial Officer and Treasurer	Fax:	(978) 842-3024
david.henry@amsc.com		
MAGUIRE , James	Tel:	(978) 842-3000
Executive Vice President, Operations	Fax:	(978) 842-3024
SAMIA, John	Tel:	(978) 842-3000
General Counsel & Corporate Secretary	Fax:	(978) 842-3024
jsamia@amsc.com		
ULLIMAN, John	Tel:	(978) 842-3000
President, Business Development and Government Relations	Fax:	(978) 842-3024
julliman@amsc.com		
Registered Federal Lobbyist		

American Systems Corporation

A provider of technical and IT services to the following industries: financial services, healthcare, retail, travel, telecommunications and energy.
www.americansystems.com
Annual Revenues: $273.88 million
Employees: 1,200
Industry/ies: Computer/Technology
Legislative Issues: BUD

Chairman of the Board	Tel:	(703) 968-6300
HOOVER, William C.	Fax:	(703) 968-5151
President and Chief Executive Officer	Tel:	(703) 968-6300
SMITH, Peter L.	Fax:	(703) 968-5151

Main Headquarters

Mailing: 14151 Park Meadow Dr.	Tel:	(703) 968-6300
Suite 500	Fax:	(703) 968-5151
Chantilly, VA 20151	TF:	(800) 733-2721

Political Action Committees

American Systems Corporation PAC (ASC-PAC)
FEC ID: C00215590
Contact: Jack F. Baker

14151 Park Meadow Dr.	Tel:	(703) 968-6300
Suite 500	Fax:	(703) 968-5151
Chantilly, VA 20151		

   Contributions to Candidates: $10,000 (2015-2016)
   Democrats: $7,500; Republicans: $2,500

Corporate Foundations and Giving Programs

American Systems Corporation Con tributions Program
14151 Park Meadow Dr.
Suite 500
Chantilly, VA 20151

Public Affairs and Related Activities Personnel

At Headquarters

BAKER, Jack F.	Tel:	(703) 968-6300
PAC Treasurer	Fax:	(703) 968-5151
jack.baker@americansystems.com		
BRACCIO, Chris	Tel:	(703) 968-6300
Vice President, Human Resources	Fax:	(703) 968-5151
DOLTON, Mike	Tel:	(703) 968-5287
Director, Corporate Communications	Fax:	(703) 968-5151
Mike.Dolton@AmericanSystems.com		
KOPFMAN, Joe	Tel:	(703) 968-6300
Executive Vice President, Contracts and Administration and Chief Compliance Officer	Fax:	(703) 968-5151
WHITFIELD, Peter	Tel:	(703) 968-6300
Chief Financial Officer	Fax:	(703) 968-5151

American Tower Corporation

Operator of wireless and broadcast communications sites in North America.
www.americantower.com
Annual Revenues: $4.98 billion
Employees: 3,371
Ticker: NYSE: AMT
SIC: 6798
Industry/ies: Communications; Telecommunications/Internet/Cable
Legislative Issues: TAX; TEC; TRD

Chairman, President and Chief Executive Officer	Tel:	(617) 375-7500
TAICLET, Jr., James	Fax:	(617) 375-7575

Main Headquarters

Mailing: 116 Huntington Ave.	Tel:	(617) 375-7500
11th Floor	Fax:	(617) 375-7575
Boston, MA 02116		

Corporate Foundations and Giving Programs

American Tower Corporation Contributions Program

116 Huntington Ave.	Tel:	(617) 375-7500
11th Floor	Fax:	(617) 375-7575
Boston, MA 02116		

Public Affairs and Related Activities Personnel

At Headquarters

BARTLETT, Tom	Tel:	(617) 375-7500
Executive Vice President, Chief Financial Officer and Treasurer	Fax:	(617) 375-7575
thomas.bartlett@americantower.com		
DISANTO, Ed	Tel:	(617) 375-7500
Executive Vice President, Chief Administrative Officer and General Counsel	Fax:	(617) 375-7575
ed.disanto@americantower.com		
PETERSON, Matt	Tel:	(617) 375-7500
Vice President, Communications and Employee Development	Fax:	(617) 375-7575
media.relations@americantower.com		
STEARNS, Leah	Tel:	(617) 375-7500
Senior Vice President, Investor Relations and Treasurer	Fax:	(617) 375-7575

American United Life Insurance Company

Insurance company.

www.oneamerica.com/wps/wcm/connect/oa/AUL
Annual Revenues: $1.13 billion
Employees: 1,800
Industry/ies: Insurance Industry

Chairman of the Board, President, and Chief Executive Officer Tel: (317) 285-1370
MOLENDORP, Dayton H. Fax: (317) 285-1979

Main Headquarters
Mailing: One American Sq. Tel: (317) 285-2577
P.O. Box 6010 Fax: (317) 285-1979
Indianapolis, IN 46206-6010 TF: (800) 553-5318

Political Action Committees
OneAmerica Financial Partners Inc., PAC
FEC ID: C00143164
Contact: Douglas Wayne Collins
One American Sq.
P.O. Box 368
Indianapolis, IN 46206

Contributions to Candidates: $15,000 (2015-2016)
Democrats: $5,000; Republicans: $10,000

Public Affairs and Related Activities Personnel

At Headquarters

COLLINS, Douglas Wayne Tel: (317) 285-2577
Vice President Fax: (317) 285-1979

DAVISON, James Scott Tel: (317) 285-1370
Executive Vice President Fax: (317) 285-1979

American Water Works Service Company, Inc.
Provides water and wastewater services.
www.amwater.com
Annual Revenues: $3.03 billion
Employees: 6,400
Ticker: NYSE: AWK
SIC: 4941
Industry/ies: Environment And Conservation; Pollution And Waste; Utilities

Non-Executive Chairman of the Board Tel: (856) 346-8200
MACKENZIE, George Fax: (856) 346-8440

President & Chief Executive Officer Tel: (856) 346-8200
STORY, Susan N. Fax: (856) 346-8440

President and Chief Executive Officer Tel: (856) 346-8200
STERBA, Jeffry Fax: (856) 346-8440

Main Headquarters
Mailing: 1025 Laurel Oak Rd. Tel: (856) 346-8200
Voorhees, NJ 08043 Fax: (856) 346-8440
TF: (800) 565-7292

Washington Office
Mailing: 2223 Duke St.
Alexandria, VA 22314

Political Action Committees
merican Water Works Company, Inc. Federal PAC A/K/A American Water
Federal PAC
FEC ID: C00354548
Contact: William D. Rogers
1025 Laurel Oak Rd. Tel: (856) 346-8200
Voorhees, NJ 08043 Fax: (856) 346-8440

Contributions to Candidates: $12,700 (2015-2016)
Democrats: $4,700; Republicans: $8,000

Corporate Foundations and Giving Programs
American Water Works Service Company Contributions Program
1025 Laurel Oak Rd.
Voorhees, NJ 08043

Public Affairs and Related Activities Personnel

At Headquarters

DUFFY, Maureen Tel: (856) 309-4546
Vice President, Corporate Communications and External Fax: (856) 346-8440
Affairs
maureen.duffy@amwater.com

FREE, Denise Venuti Tel: (856) 309-4690
Manager, External Affairs Fax: (856) 346-8440
denise.free@amwater.com

ROGERS, William D. Tel: (856) 346-8200
PAC Treasurer Fax: (856) 346-8440
Mail Stop P.O. Box 1770

STRAUSS, Mark Tel: (856) 346-8200
Senior Vice President, Corporate Strategy and Business Fax: (856) 346-8440
Development

VALLEJO, Edward D. Tel: (856) 566-4005
Vice President, Investor Relations Fax: (856) 346-8440
edward.vallejo@amwater.com

WATSEY, Kevin Tel: (856) 782-2373
Manager, Government Affairs Fax: (856) 346-8440
kevin.watsey@amwater.com

AmeriCredit Financial Services
See listing on page 358 under General Motors Financial Company

AmeriGroup Corporation
A medical managed-care plan that aides financially vulnerable seniors and people with disabilities through publicly-funded programs. It is acquired by Wellpoint.
www.amerigroupcorp.com
Employees: 5,100
Ticker: NYSE: AGP
SIC: 6324
Industry/ies: Insurance Industry; Medicine/Health Care/Mental Health
Legislative Issues: HCR; MMM; TAX

Main Headquarters
Mailing: 4425 Corporation Ln. Tel: (757) 490-6900
Virginia Beach, VA 23462 Fax: (757) 222-2330

Washington Office
Mailing: 750 First St. NE Tel: (202) 218-4902
Suite 1120
Washington, DC 20002

Corporate Foundations and Giving Programs
Amerigroup Foundation
Contact: Leslie Porras
4425 Corporation Ln.
Virginia Beach, VA 23462

Public Affairs and Related Activities Personnel

At Headquarters

ANGLIN, Scott Tel: (757) 490-6900
Chief Financial Officer Fax: (757) 222-2330

BALDWIN, Stanley F. Tel: (757) 490-6900
Executive Vice President, General Counsel and Secretary Fax: (757) 222-2330

FOLEY, Georgia Dodds Tel: (757) 490-6900
Medicaid Compliance Officer Fax: (757) 222-2330

MCDONNELL, Maureen C. Tel: (757) 473-2731
Vice President, External Communications Fax: (757) 222-2330
mmcdonn@amerigroupcorp.com

PORRAS, Leslie Tel: (757) 490-6900
Contact, Media Relations Fax: (757) 222-2330
Leslie.Porras@WellPoint.com

YOUNG, Jack Tel: (757) 490-6900
Vice President and Counsel Fax: (757) 222-2330

At Washington Office

COYNE, Brian D. Tel: (202) 218-4902
Senior Vice President, Federal Government Relations

CRENSHAW, Jenn Tel: (202) 218-4902
Vice President, Human Resources

AmeriHealth Caritas Pennsylvania
Formerly (1982) known as the AmeriHealth Mercy Health Plan. A healthcare organization.
www.amerihealthcaritaspa.com
Annual Revenues: $20.50 Million
Employees: 200
Industry/ies: Medicine/Health Care/Mental Health
Legislative Issues: MMM

President and Chief Executive Officer Tel: (717) 651-3540
RASHID, Michael A. Fax: (717) 651-3555

Main Headquarters
Mailing: 8040 Carlson Rd. Tel: (717) 651-3540
Suite 500 Fax: (717) 651-3555
Harrisburg, PA 17112 TF: (888) 991-7200

Corporate Foundations and Giving Programs
AmeriHealth Caritas Partnership
200 Stevens Dr. Tel: (215) 937-8000
Philadelphia, PA 19113

AmeriHealth Mercy Health Plan Contributions Program
Contact: Rob Cooper
8040 Carlson Rd. Tel: (717) 651-3551
Suite 500
Harrisburg, PA 17112

Public Affairs and Related Activities Personnel

At Headquarters

ANGELLO, Marge Tel: (717) 651-3540
Executive Director Fax: (717) 651-3553

BOLINER, Steven H. Tel: (717) 651-3540
Chief Financial Officer and Senior Vice President, Finance Fax: (717) 651-3555

COOPER, Rob Tel: (717) 651-3551

Corporate Marketing Director	Fax:	(717) 651-3555
Robert.Cooper@amerihealthmercyhp.com		
DRUMM, Christopher	Tel:	(717) 651-3540
Senior Vice President, Government and External Affairs	Fax:	(717) 651-3555
GILMAN, Robert H.	Tel:	(717) 651-3540
Senior Vice President, Legal Affairs and General Counsel	Fax:	(717) 651-3555
JONES, Barbara G.	Tel:	(717) 651-3540
Vice President, Corporate Compliance and Privacy Officer	Fax:	(717) 651-3555
ORNDORFF , Steve	Tel:	(717) 651-3540
Associate Vice President, Provider and Community Affairs	Fax:	(717) 651-3555
PEARCE, Gale	Tel:	(717) 651-3540
Chief Marketing & Development Officer	Fax:	(717) 651-3555

At Other Offices

BERENATO, Andrew	Tel:	(215) 937-8089
Director, Office of Exchange Development and Strategy		
200 Stevens Dr.		
Philadelphia, PA 19113		
drew.berenato@amerihealthmercy.com		
BYRNES, Patricia D.	Tel:	(215) 937-8089
Director, Federal Government Relations		
200 Stevens Dr.		
Philadelphia, PA 19113		
Registered Federal Lobbyist		
KNAPP, Amy	Tel:	(215) 937-8000
Vice President, Corporate Communications		
200 Stevens Dr.		
Philadelphia, PA 19113		
WACHTMAN, Kelly	Tel:	(215) 937-8000
Vice President, Public Policy		
200 Stevens Dr.		
Philadelphia, PA 19113		

AmeriHealth Mercy Health Plan

See listing on page 57 under AmeriHealth Caritas Pennsylvania

Amerinet, Inc.

Established in June 1986, Amerinet is privately owned by Administrative Resources Inc., based in Warrendale, Pa.and Intermountain Healthcare of Salt Lake City and has four subsidiaries: Amerinet Choice®, Amerinet Diagnostix®, DataBay Resources® and Inquisit®. A national healthcare solutions organization.
www.amerinet-gpo.com
Employees: 200
Industry/ies: Medicine/Health Care/Mental Health
Legislative Issues: HCR

President and Chief Executive Officer	Tel:	(314) 878-2525
EBERT, Todd C.	Fax:	(314) 542-1999

Main Headquarters		
Mailing: 2060 Craigshire Rd.	Tel:	(314) 878-2525
St. Louis, MO 63146-4010	Fax:	(314) 542-1999
	TF:	(800) 388-2638

Political Action Committees
Amerinet, Inc. PAC (Amerinet PAC)
FEC ID: C00491555
Contact: Michael D Costabile
Two Cityplace Dr.
Suite 400
St. Louis, MO 63141

    Contributions to Candidates: $1,500 (2015-2016)
    Democrats: $1,500

Corporate Foundations and Giving Programs
Amerinet Contributions Program
2060 Craigshire Rd.
St. Louis, MO 63146-4010

Public Affairs and Related Activities Personnel

At Headquarters

DANIS, Evan	Tel:	(877) 711-5700
Director, Communications and Media	Fax:	(314) 542-1999
FIELDS, Amy G.	Tel:	(314) 878-2525
Chief Human Resources Officer	Fax:	(314) 542-1999

At Other Offices

COSTABILE, Michael D	Tel:	(877) 711-5700
Chief Financial Officer and PAC Treasurer		
Two Cityplace Dr., Suite 400		
St. Louis, MO 63141		
MCGRATH, Laurie	Tel:	(877) 711-5700
Chief Marketing Officer		
Two Cityplace Dr., Suite 400		
St. Louis, MO 63141		

Ameriprise Financial Inc.

A financial planning, asset management and insurance firm.
www.ameriprise.com
Annual Revenues: $12.35 billion
Employees: 12,209
Ticker: NYSE: AMP
SIC: 6282
Industry/ies: Banking/Finance/Investments
Legislative Issues: FIN; INS; LBR; RET; TAX

Chairman and Chief Executive Officer	Tel:	(612) 671-3131
CRACCHIOLO, James M.		

Main Headquarters		
Mailing: 707 Second Avenue South	Tel:	(612) 671-3131
Minneapolis, MN 55474		

Washington Office		
Mailing: 101 Constitution Ave. NW	Tel:	(202) 742-4496
Suite 912 West		
Washington, DC 20001		

Political Action Committees
Ameriprise Financial Inc. PAC (AmeriprisePAC)
FEC ID: C00414474
Contact: Elizabeth Varley

101 Constitution Ave. NW	Tel:	(202) 742-4495
Suite 912 West	Fax:	(202) 742-4497
Washington, DC 20001		

    Contributions to Candidates: $205,000 (2015-2016)
    Democrats: $89,500; Republicans: $115,500

Corporate Foundations and Giving Programs

Ameriprise Financial Inc. Contributions Program		
55 Ameriprise Financial Center	Tel:	(612) 671-3131
Minneapolis, MN 55474	Fax:	(612) 671-5112

Public Affairs and Related Activities Personnel

At Headquarters

BERMAN, Walter S.	Tel:	(612) 671-3131
Executive Vice President and Chief Financial Officer		
CHARITY , Alicia	Tel:	(612) 671-2080
Senior Vice President, Investor Relations		
alicia.a.charity@ampf.com		
HUNTER, Kelli A.	Tel:	(612) 671-3131
Executive Vice President, Human Resources		
JUNEK, John C.	Tel:	(612) 671-3131
Executive Vice President and General Counsel		
MCGRAW, Deirdre	Tel:	(612) 671-3131
Executive Vice President, Marketing, Corporate Communications and Community Relations		
MUELLER, Alison	Tel:	(612) 678-7183
Contact, Media Relations		
alison.g.mueller@ampf.com		
REESE, Chris	Tel:	(612) 671-3131
Senior Director, Public Communications		
chris.l.reese@ampf.com		
WOERNER, John R.	Tel:	(612) 671-3131
President, Insurance and Annuities and Chief Strategy Officer		

At Washington Office

VARLEY, Elizabeth	Tel:	(202) 742-4499
Vice President, Federal Government Affairs		
Registered Federal Lobbyist		
WRIGHT, Mary Ann	Tel:	(202) 742-4496
Manager, Government Affairs		
mary.ann.wright@ampf.com		

Ameriqual Group, LLC

Ameriqual Group, LLC specializes in the production, packaging, assembly and distribution of shelf-stable food products.
www.ameriqual.com
Employees: 700
SIC: 2099
Industry/ies: Food And Beverage Industry
Legislative Issues: BUD; DEF; DIS

Main Headquarters		
Mailing: 18200 Hwy. 41 North	Tel:	(812) 867-1444
Evansville, IN 47725	Fax:	(812) 867-0278

AmerisourceBergen Corporation

Pharmaceutical services company with a focus on the pharmaceutical supply chain.
www.amerisourcebergen.com
Annual Revenues: $142.11 billion
Employees: 16,500
Ticker: NYSE: ABC
SIC: 5122
Industry/ies: Pharmaceutical Industry

Legislative Issues: HCR; MMM; PHA; TAX

Chairman of the Board, President and Chief Executive Officer
COLLIS, Steven H.
Tel: (610) 727-7000
Fax: (610) 727-3600

Main Headquarters
Mailing: P.O. Box 959
Valley Forge, PA 19482
Tel: (610) 727-7000
Fax: (610) 727-3600

Washington Office
Mailing: 412 First St. SE
Suite 200
Washington, DC 20003
Tel: (202) 775-0135
Fax: (888) 211-1323

Political Action Committees
AmerisourceBergen Corporation PAC (ABC PAC)
FEC ID: C00400929
1300 Morris Dr.
Suite 100
Chesterbrook, PA 19355
Tel: (610) 727-7000
Fax: (610) 727-3600

  Contributions to Candidates: $502,200 (2015-2016)
  Democrats: $188,000; Republicans: $313,200; Other: $1,000

    Principal Recipients

    SENATE
    CRAPO, MICHAEL D (REP-ID)
    SCOTT, TIMOTHY E (REP-SC)

    HOUSE
    BRADY, KEVIN (REP-TX)
    BUCHANAN, VERNON (REP-FL)
    GUTHRIE, S. BRETT HON. (REP-KY)
    ISRAEL, STEVE J. (DEM-NY)
    MCCARTHY, KEVIN (REP-CA)

Public Affairs and Related Activities Personnel
At Headquarters

BARRY, June
Senior Vice President, Human Resources
Tel: (610) 727-7000
Fax: (610) 727-3600

BRUNGESS, Barbara A.
Vice President, Corporate and Investor Relations
bbrungess@amerisourcebergen.com
Tel: (610) 727-7199
Fax: (610) 727-3603

CLARK, Gina K.
Executive Vice President and Chief Marketing Officer
Tel: (610) 727-7000
Fax: (610) 727-3600

GADDES, Kathy H.
Executive Vice President and Chief Human Resources Officer
Tel: (610) 727-7000
Fax: (610) 727-3600

GUTTMAN, Tim G.
Executive Vice President and Chief Financial Officer
Tel: (610) 727-7000
Fax: (610) 727-3600

SENIOR, David M.
Senior Vice President, Finance
Tel: (610) 727-7000
Fax: (610) 727-3600

At Washington Office

ANDERSON, Mary
Associate, Government Affairs
meanderson2@crimson.ua.edu
Tel: (202) 775-0135
Fax: (888) 211-1323

MONEY, Jason R.
Registered Federal Lobbyist
Tel: (202) 775-0135
Fax: (888) 211-1323

NORTON, Rita E.
Senior Vice President, Government & Public Policy
rnorton@amerisourcebergen.com
Registered Federal Lobbyist
Tel: (202) 887-4942
Fax: (888) 211-1323

STAFFORD, Vivienne E.
Federal Lobbyist
Registered Federal Lobbyist
Tel: (202) 887-1469
Fax: (202) 466-3215

TALLAMY, Brad
Registered Federal Lobbyist
Tel: (202) 775-0135
Fax: (888) 211-1323

At Other Offices

CHOU, John G.
Executive Vice President and General Counsel and Secretary and PAC Treasurer
1300 Morris Dr., Suite 100
Valley Forge, PA 19087
Tel: (610) 727-7000
Fax: (610) 727-3600

EDDY, Julie
Director, State Government Affairs
1300 Morris Dr., Suite 100
Valley Forge, PA 19087
jeddy@amerisourcebergen.com
Tel: (610) 727-7361
Fax: (610) 727-3600

MARSH, Lawrence
Executive Vice President, New Market Development and Chief Strategy Officer
1300 Morris Dr., Suite 100
Valley Forge, PA 19087
Tel: (610) 727-7000
Fax: (610) 727-3600

Ameristar Casinos, Inc.

A hotel and casino operator.
www.ameristar.com
Annual Revenues: $1.19 billion

Employees: 4,680
Ticker: NASDAQ: ASCA
SIC: 7011
Industry/ies: Sports/Leisure/Entertainment

Chief Executive Officer
SANFILIPPO, Anthony
Tel: (702) 541-7777
Fax: (702) 755-2737

Main Headquarters
Mailing: 3980 Howard Hughes Pkwy.
Las Vegas, NV 89169
Tel: (702) 541-7777
Fax: (702) 755-2737

Political Action Committees
Ameristar Casinos, Inc Federal PAC
FEC ID: C00490466
Contact: Matthew Block
3200 N Ameristar Dr.
Kansas City, MO 64161

Corporate Foundations and Giving Programs
Ameristar Cares
3773 Howard Hughes Pkwy.
Suite 490 South
Las Vegas, NV 89169
Tel: (702) 567-7000
Fax: (702) 567-7000

Public Affairs and Related Activities Personnel
At Headquarters

KINKADE, Roxann
Director, Communications
Roxann.Kinkade@ameristar.com
Tel: (816) 414-7007
Fax: (702) 755-2737

STEINBAUER, Thomas M.
Senior Vice President and Chief Financial Officer
tom.steinbauer@ameristar.com
Tel: (702) 541-7777
Fax: (702) 755-2737

WALSH, Peter C.
Senior Vice President, General Counsel and Chief Administrative Officer
peter.walsh@ameristar.com
Tel: (702) 567-7000
Fax: (702) 369-8860

At Other Offices

BLOCK, Matthew
PAC Treasurer
3200 N. Ameristar Dr.
Kansas City, MO 64161
matthew.block@ameristar.com
Tel: (816) 414-7000

AmeriSteel Corporation

See listing on page 363 under Gerdau Long Steel North America

AMETEK - Advanced Measurement Technologies

A global manufacturer of electronic instruments and electromechanical devices. It provides advanced instruments for the process, aerospace, power, and industrial markets; process and analytical instruments for the oil, gas, petrochemical, pharmaceutical, semiconductor, and factory automation markets; and instruments for the laboratory equipment, ultra precision manufacturing, medical, and test and measurement markets.
www.ametek.com
Annual Revenues: $4.03 billion
Employees: 15,400
Ticker: NYSE: AME
SIC: 3621
Industry/ies: Science; Scientific Research

Chairman of the Board and Chief Executive Officer
HERMANCE, Frank S.
Tel: (610) 647-2121
Fax: (610) 323-9337

Main Headquarters
Mailing: 1100 Cassatt Rd.
P.O. Box 1764
Berwyn, PA 19312
Tel: (610) 647-2121
Fax: (610) 323-9337
TF: (800) 473-1286

Corporate Foundations and Giving Programs
The Ametek Foundation
Contact: Kathryn E. Sena
37 N. Valley Rd., Bldg. Four
P.O. Box 1764
Paoli, PA 19301
Tel: (610) 647-2121
Fax: (215) 323-9337

Public Affairs and Related Activities Personnel
At Headquarters

BURKE, William
Senior Vice President, Comptroller and Treasurer
bill.burke@ametek.com
Tel: (610) 889-5249
Fax: (610) 323-9337

COLEMAN, Kevin C.
Vice President, Investor Relations
Tel: (610) 889-5247
Fax: (610) 323-9337

DEENEY, Thomas A.
Vice President, Corporate Compliance and Auditing
Tel: (610) 647-2121
Fax: (215) 323-9337

EGINTON, William D.
Senior Vice President, Corporate Development
Tel: (610) 647-2121
Fax: (215) 323-9337

FEIT, Robert S.
Senior Vice President and General Counsel
Tel: (610) 647-2121
Fax: (215) 323-9337

KELBLE, George J.	Tel:	(610) 647-2121
Senior Vice President, Human Resources	Fax:	(215) 323-9337
MANDOS, Jr., Robert R.	Tel:	(610) 647-2121
Executive Vice President and Chief Financial Officer	Fax:	(610) 323-9337
MCKINLEY, James	Tel:	(610) 889-5234
Manager, Public Relations	Fax:	(610) 323-9337
pr.contact@ametek.com		
SENA, Kathryn E.	Tel:	(610) 647-2121
Director, Corporate Secretary	Fax:	(610) 323-9337
ZAPICO, David A.	Tel:	(610) 647-2121
Executive Vice President and Chief Operating Officer	Fax:	(610) 323-9337

Amgen Inc.

A therapeutics company in the biotechnology industry. Acquired Immunex Corporation in 2002. A human therapeutics company headquartered in Thousand Oaks, Calif.
www.amgen.com
Annual Revenues: $20.58 billion
Employees: 17,900
Ticker: NASDAQ: AMGN
SIC: 2834; 5122
NAICS: 325412; 42221
Industry/ies: Pharmaceutical Industry; Science; Scientific Research
Legislative Issues: BUD; CPT; HCR; MED; MMM; NAT; PHA; TAX; TRD

Chairman and Chief Executive Officer

BRADWAY, Robert A.	Tel:	(805) 447-1000
	Fax:	(805) 447-1010

Main Headquarters

Mailing:	One Amgen Center Dr.	Tel:	(805) 447-1000
	Thousand Oaks, CA 91230	Fax:	(805) 447-1010

Washington Office

Mailing:	601 13th St. NW, 12th Floor	Tel:	(202) 585-9500
	12th Floor	Fax:	(202) 585-9729
	Washington, DC 20005		

Political Action Committees
Amgen Inc. PAC
FEC ID: C00251876
Contact: Victoria H. Blatter

601 13th St. NW	Tel:	(202) 585-9500
12th Floor	Fax:	(202) 585-9728
Washington, DC 20005		

> **Contributions to Candidates:** $673,750 (2015-2016)
> Democrats: $250,500; Republicans: $420,250; Other: $3,000
>
> ### Principal Recipients
>
> #### SENATE
> BLUNT, ROY (REP-MO)
> CARPER, THOMAS R (DEM-DE)
>
> #### HOUSE
> BOUSTANY, CHARLES W. DR. JR. (REP-LA)
> BRADY, KEVIN (REP-TX)
> BUCHANAN, VERNON (REP-FL)
> GUTHRIE, S. BRETT HON. (REP-KY)
> MCCARTHY, KEVIN (REP-CA)
> TIBERI, PATRICK J. (REP-OH)
> UPTON, FREDERICK STEPHEN (REP-MI)

Corporate Foundations and Giving Programs
Amgen Foundation
Contact: Jean J. Lim

One Amgen Center Dr.	Tel:	(805) 447-1000
Thousand Oaks, CA 91320	Fax:	(805) 447-1010

Public Affairs and Related Activities Personnel

At Headquarters

BALACHANDRAN, Madhavan	Tel:	(805) 447-1000
Executive Vice President, Operations	Fax:	(805) 447-1010
BLAUG, Suzanne	Tel:	(805) 447-1000
Senior Vice President, Global Marketing and Commercial Development	Fax:	(805) 447-1010
GALSON, Steven K.	Tel:	(805) 447-1000
Senior Vice President, Global Regulatory Affairs and Safety	Fax:	(805) 447-1010
JORDAN, Raymond C.	Tel:	(805) 447-1000
Senior Vice President, Corporate Affairs	Fax:	(805) 447-1010
LIM, Jean J.	Tel:	(805) 447-1000
President, Amgen Foundation	Fax:	(805) 499-3507
MCNAMEE, Brian M.	Tel:	(805) 447-1000
Senior Vice President, Full Potential Initiatives	Fax:	(805) 447-1010
brianm@amgen.com		
MELINE, David W.	Tel:	(805) 447-1000
Executive Vice President and Chief Financial Officer	Fax:	(805) 447-1010
PATTON, Cynthia M.	Tel:	(805) 447-1000
Senior Vice President and Chief Compliance Officer	Fax:	(805) 447-1010
PIACQUAD, David A.	Tel:	(805) 447-1000

Senior Vice President, Business Development	Fax:	(805) 447-1010
REGAN, Christine	Tel:	(805) 447-5476
Director, Corporate Media Relations	Fax:	(805) 447-1010
cregan@amgen.com		
SCOTT, David J.	Tel:	(805) 447-1000
Senior Vice President, General Counsel and Secretary	Fax:	(805) 447-1010
SOOD, Arvind	Tel:	(805) 447-1060
Vice President, Investor Relations	Fax:	(805) 447-1010
STUART , Tross A.	Tel:	(805) 447-1000
Senior Vice President, Human Resources	Fax:	(805) 447-1010

At Washington Office

ANTORCHA, Nicole L.	Tel:	(202) 585-9500
Director, Government Affairs	Fax:	(202) 585-9729
nickiea@amgen.com		
Registered Federal Lobbyist		
BLATTER, Victoria H.	Tel:	(202) 585-9500
Senior Vice President, U.S. Government Affairs & PAC Treasurer	Fax:	(202) 585-9729
Registered Federal Lobbyist		
BURGESS, Chaka	Tel:	(202) 585-9500
Director, Global Government Affairs	Fax:	(202) 585-9729
COGBILL, Allison	Tel:	(202) 585-9500
Director, Government Affairs	Fax:	(202) 585-9729
CURRIE, L. Nicole	Tel:	(202) 585-9500
Federal Lobbyist	Fax:	(202) 585-9729
Registered Federal Lobbyist		
GUARDUCCI, Mara	Tel:	(202) 585-9500
Executive Director, Government Affairs	Fax:	(202) 585-9729
HOFFMAN, Ruth	Tel:	(202) 585-9500
Senior Vice President, U.S. Commercial Operations	Fax:	(202) 585-9729
Registered Federal Lobbyist		
KERNS, Jesse	Tel:	(202) 585-9500
Director, Global Government Affairs	Fax:	(202) 585-9729
Registered Federal Lobbyist		
MANCILL, Christopher	Tel:	(202) 585-9500
Executive Director, U.S. Health Policy and Reimbursement	Fax:	(202) 585-9729
Registered Federal Lobbyist		
MANDELL, Rebecca	Tel:	(202) 585-9500
Director, Global Government Affairs	Fax:	(202) 585-9729
rmandell@amgen.com		
Registered Federal Lobbyist		
MCCARTHY, Nancy Ellen	Tel:	(202) 585-9500
Federal Lobbyist	Fax:	(202) 585-9729
Registered Federal Lobbyist		
MOON, Howard	Tel:	(202) 585-9500
Director, Government Affairs	Fax:	(202) 585-9729
Registered Federal Lobbyist		
NEUREITER, Paul	Tel:	(202) 585-9500
Registered Federal Lobbyist	Fax:	(202) 585-9729
O'BRIEN, William	Tel:	(202) 585-9500
Senior Manager, Government Affairs	Fax:	(202) 585-9729
Registered Federal Lobbyist		
OFMAN, Joshua J.	Tel:	(202) 585-9500
Senior Vice President, Global Value and Access	Fax:	(202) 585-9729
OLSEN, Scott	Tel:	(202) 585-9500
Account Manager	Fax:	(202) 585-9729
Registered Federal Lobbyist		
PORTNER, MPA, Gregory A.	Tel:	(202) 585-9500
Executive Director, Government Affairs	Fax:	(202) 585-9729
Registered Federal Lobbyist		
RHEE, Helen	Tel:	(202) 585-9500
Executive Director, Government Affairs	Fax:	(202) 585-9729
Registered Federal Lobbyist		
SEHESTEDT, Rachel	Tel:	(202) 585-9500
Senior Manager, US Government Affairs	Fax:	(202) 585-9729
sherouse@amgen.com		
WELSH, Matthew	Tel:	(202) 585-9500
Manager	Fax:	(202) 585-9729
WILLIAM, O'Brien	Tel:	(202) 585-9500
Federal Lobbyist	Fax:	(202) 585-9729
Registered Federal Lobbyist		

Amica Mutual Insurance Company

An insurance and annuity products provider and is the oldest mutual insurer of automobiles in the country. We also offer home, marine, personal umbrella liability and life insurance products. Our employees are the key to providing exceptional service to our loyal policyholders.
www.amica.com
Annual Revenues: $1.41 billion
Employees: 3,200

Industry/ies: Insurance Industry

Chairman of the Board, President and Chief Executive Officer Tel: (401) 334-6000
DIMUCCIO, Robert A. Fax: (401) 334-4241

Main Headquarters
Mailing: P. O. Box 9128 Tel: (401) 334-6000
Providence, RI 02940-9128 Fax: (401) 334-4241

Political Action Committees
Amica Mutual Insurance Company/Fed-PAC
FEC ID: C00268987
Contact: Stephen F. Dolan
P. O. BOX 6008 Tel: (401) 334-6000
Providence, RI 02940-6008 Fax: (401) 334-6000

   Contributions to Candidates: $12,000 (2015-2016)
   Democrats: $6,500; Republicans: $5,500

Corporate Foundations and Giving Programs
Amica Companies Foundation
100 Amica Way Tel: (401) 334-6000
Lincoln, RI 02865 Fax: (401) 334-4241

Public Affairs and Related Activities Personnel

At Headquarters

DOLAN, Stephen F. Tel: (401) 334-6000
PAC Contact Fax: (401) 334-4241
Mail Stop P.O. Box 6008

WILLIAMSON, Mary Q. Tel: (401) 334-6000
Senior Vice President and PAC Treasurer Fax: (401) 334-4241

At Other Offices

BENSON, Robert Tel: (401) 334-6000
Senior Vice President and Chief Investment Officer Fax: (401) 334-4241
100 Amica Way
Lincoln, RI 02865-1167

BURKS, Vince Tel: (800) 652-6422
Director, Communications Fax: (401) 334-4241
100 Amica Way
Lincoln, RI 02865-1167
vburks@amica.com

LORING, CFA, CPA, James Tel: (401) 334-6000
Senior Vice President, Chief Financial Officer and Treasurer Fax: (401) 334-4241
100 Amica Way
Lincoln, RI 02865-1167

PHELPS, Craig Tel: (401) 334-6000
Senior Assistant Vice President and Director, Marketing Fax: (401) 334-4241
100 Amica Way
Lincoln, RI 02865-1167

Amkor Technology Inc.

A supplier of outsourced packaging and test semiconductor interconnect services.
www.amkor.com
Annual Revenues: $3.18 billion
Employees: 21,900
Ticker: NASDAQ: AMKR
SIC: 7389; 3674
NAICS: 56191; 334413
Industry/ies: Electricity & Electronics; Electronics; Energy/Electricity

Executive Chairman of the Board Tel: (480) 821-5000
KIM, James J. Fax: (480) 821-8276
jkim@amkor.com

President and Chief Executive Officer Tel: (480) 821-5000
KELLEY, Stephen D. Fax: (480) 821-8276

Main Headquarters
Mailing: 2045 E. Innovation Cir. Tel: (480) 821-5000
Tempe, AZ 85284 Fax: (480) 821-8276

Corporate Foundations and Giving Programs
Amkor Technology Contribution Program
Contact: Greg Johnson
1900 S. Price Rd. Tel: (480) 821-5000
Chandler, AZ 85286 Fax: (480) 821-8276

Public Affairs and Related Activities Personnel

At Headquarters

JOHNSON, Greg Tel: (480) 821-5000
Senior Director, Investor Relations, Corporate Fax: (480) 821-8276
Communications and Contact, Corporate Social Responsi
greg.johnson@amkor.com

SOLOMON, Joanne Tel: (480) 821-5000
Executive Vice President and Chief Financial Officer Fax: (480) 821-8276
joanne.solomon@amkor.com

STONE, John C. Tel: (480) 821-5000
Executive Vice President, Global Sales and Marketing Fax: (480) 821-8276

TILY, Gil C. Tel: (480) 821-5000
Fax: (480) 821-8276

Executive Vice President, Chief Administrative Officer and
General Counsel
gtily@amkor.com

AMO
See listing on page 6 under Abbott Medical Optics

Amoena USA Corporation
Manufacturer of post-mastectomy prosthetics and apparel.
www.amoena.us
Annual Revenues: $4.40 million
Employees: 100
Industry/ies: Apparel/Textiles Industry; Medicine/Health Care/Mental Health

Main Headquarters
Mailing: 1701 Barret Lakes Blvd. Tel: (770) 281-8300
Suite 410 Fax: (800) 723-3464
Kennesaw, GA 30144 TF: (800) 926-6362

Corporate Foundations and Giving Programs
Amoena Contributions Program
1701 Barret Lakes Blvd.
Suite 410
Kennesaw, GA 30144

Public Affairs and Related Activities Personnel

At Headquarters

LACEY, Chris Webb Tel: (770) 281-8300
Vice President, Finance and Operations Fax: (800) 723-3464

MAGYAR, Malissa Tel: (770) 281-8300
Global Head, Marketing Fax: (800) 723-3464
malissa.magyar@amoena.com

THRASH, Lee Tel: (770) 281-8225
E-Business and Coordinator, Public Relations Fax: (800) 723-3464
lee.thrash@amoena.com

amp
See listing on page 171 under CB&I

AMPCO-Pittsburgh Corporation
A manufacturer of air handling equipment and steel products.
www.ampcopgh.com
Annual Revenues: $275.03 million
Employees: 1,076
Ticker: NYSE: AP
SIC: 3561
Industry/ies: Metals

Chairman of the Board and Chief Executive Officer Tel: (412) 456-4453
PAUL, Robert A. Fax: (412) 456-4404

Main Headquarters
Mailing: 600 Grant St. Tel: (412) 456-4400
Suite 4600 Fax: (412) 456-4404
Pittsburgh, PA 15219

Public Affairs and Related Activities Personnel

At Headquarters

HOOVER, Rose Tel: (412) 456-4418
Executive Vice President and Chief Administrative Officer Fax: (412) 456-4404
rhoover@ampcopgh.com

Amphastar Pharmaceuticals
A pharmaceutical manufacturing company.
www.amphastar.com
Annual Revenues: $221.48 million
Employees: 1,361
Ticker: NASDAQ: AMPR
SIC: 2834
Industry/ies: Pharmaceutical Industry
Legislative Issues: HCR

Chairman and Chief Operating Officer Tel: (909) 980-9484
LUO, Mary Z. Fax: (909) 980-8296

President and Chief Executive Officer Tel: (909) 980-9484
ZHANG, Jack Y. Fax: (909) 980-8296

Main Headquarters
Mailing: 11570 Sixth St. Tel: (909) 980-9484
Rancho Cucamonga, CA 91730 Fax: (909) 980-8296
TF: (800) 423-4136

Political Action Committees
Amphastar Pharmaceuticals Inc. PAC
FEC ID: C00543835
Contact: Bill Peters
11570 Sixth St.,
Rancho Cucamonga, CA 91730

   Contributions to Candidates: $26,700 (2015-2016)

Democrats: $15,000; Republicans: $11,700

Public Affairs and Related Activities Personnel

At Headquarters

PETERS, Bill	Tel:	(909) 980-9484
PAC Contact	Fax:	(909) 980-8296
SKIBSTED, Russell	Tel:	(909) 980-9484
PAC Contact	Fax:	(909) 980-8296
WEBBER, John	Tel:	(909) 980-9484
Chief Financial Officer	Fax:	(909) 980-8296

Amports, Inc.

AMPORTS is a portside vehicle processing businesses company. AMPORTS offers real time vehicle tracking, state-of-the-art technology, custom software, and back up technology to ensure excellent quality service.
www.amports.com
Employees: 400
Industry/ies: Automotive Industry; Trade (Foreign And Domestic); Transportation

Main Headquarters

Mailing: 10201 Centurion Pkwy., North	Tel:	(904) 652-2962
Suite 401	Fax:	(904) 642-9167
Jacksonville Beach, FL 32256		

Public Affairs and Related Activities Personnel

At Other Offices

CALLIHAN, John F.	Tel:	(904) 751-4391
Chief Financial Officer	Fax:	(904) 751-1712
9240 Blount Island Blvd.		
Jacksonville Beach, FL 32226-4028		
SALVADOR, Gary	Tel:	(904) 751-4391
Vice President, Sales and Marketing	Fax:	(904) 751-1712
9240 Blount Island Blvd.		
Jacksonville Beach, FL 32226-4028		
gsalvador@amports.com		

Amsted Industries

A manufacturer of products for the railroad, construction, building markets and general industry.
www.amsted.com
Employees: 10,000
SIC: 3320
Industry/ies: Automotive Industry; Transportation

Chairman of the Board, President and Chief Executive Officer	Tel:	(312) 645-1700
REUM, W. Robert	Fax:	(312) 819-8494

Main Headquarters

Mailing: Two Prudential Plaza, 180 N. Stetson St.	Tel:	(312) 645-1700
Suite 1800	Fax:	(312) 819-8494
Chicago, IL 60601		

Political Action Committees

Amsted Industries Inc. PAC (AMSTED PAC)
FEC ID: C00438358
Contact: Glenn E. Chamberlin

Two Prudential Plaza	Tel:	(312) 645-1700
180 N. Stetson St., Suite 1800	Fax:	(312) 819-8994
Chicago, IL 60601		

Contributions to Candidates: $69,000 (2015-2016)
Democrats: $22,500; Republicans: $46,500

Principal Recipients

HOUSE
ROSKAM, PETER (REP-IL)

Corporate Foundations and Giving Programs

Amsted Industries Foundation		
Two Prudential Plaza	Tel:	(312) 645-1700
180 N. Stetson St., Suite 1800	Fax:	(312) 819-8494
Chicago, IL 60601		

Public Affairs and Related Activities Personnel

At Headquarters

CHAMBERLIN, Glenn E.	Tel:	(312) 645-1700
Vice President and PAC Treasurer	Fax:	(312) 819-8494
GREGORY, Stephen	Tel:	(312) 645-1700
Vice President, Finance Officer, and Chief Financial Officer	Fax:	(312) 819-8494
SMITH, Stephen R.	Tel:	(312) 645-1700
Vice President, General Counsel and Secretary	Fax:	(312) 819-8494
WHITESELL, Shirley J.	Tel:	(312) 645-1700
Vice President, People	Fax:	(312) 819-8494
swhitesell@amsted.com		

AMTRAK (National Railroad Passenger Corporation)

An intercity passenger rail company.
www.amtrak.com

Employees: 19,000
Industry/ies: Railroads; Transportation

Chairman of the Board and Chairman, Audit and Finance Committee	Tel:	(202) 906-3918
	Fax:	(202) 906-3865
COSCIA, Anthony R.		
President and Chief Executive Officer	Tel:	(202) 906-3918
BOARDMAN, Joseph H.	Fax:	(202) 906-3865

Main Headquarters

Mailing: 60 Massachusetts Ave. NE	Tel:	(202) 906-3918
Washington, DC 20002	Fax:	(202) 906-3865

Public Affairs and Related Activities Personnel

At Headquarters

ACHESON, Eleanor D.	Tel:	(202) 906-3000
Executive Vice President, Chief Legal Officer, General Counsel and Corporate Secretary	Fax:	(202) 906-3306
DECKER, Caroline	Tel:	(202) 906-3918
Vice President, Government Affairs	Fax:	(202) 906-3865
HARDISON, Matt	Tel:	(202) 906-3918
Executive Vice President, Chief Marketing and Sales Officer	Fax:	(202) 906-3865
LEONARD, Scott	Tel:	(202) 906-3918
Senior Manager	Fax:	(202) 906-3865
MCHUGH, Joseph H.	Tel:	(202) 906-3918
Senior Vice President, Government Affairs and Communications	Fax:	(202) 906-3865
MELNKOVIC, Barry	Tel:	(202) 906-3000
Executive Vice President, Chief Human Capital Officer	Fax:	(202) 906-3306
SOKOL, Jr., Gerald	Tel:	(202) 906-3918
Chief Financial Officer	Fax:	(202) 906-3865
STADTLER, D. J.	Tel:	(202) 906-3000
Executive Vice President, Chief Operations Officer	Fax:	(202) 906-3306
DJ.Stadtler@Amtrak.com		
WALSH, Eamon	Tel:	(202) 906-3918
Director, State Government Affairs	Fax:	(202) 906-3865

Amway Corporation

See listing on page 41 under Alticor, Inc.

Amylin Pharmaceuticals, Inc.

A biopharmaceutical company. Acquired by Bristol-Myers Squibb in 2012.
www.amylin.com
Annual Revenues: $650.68 million
Employees: 1,400
Ticker: NASDAQ: AMLN
SIC: 2834
Industry/ies: Pharmaceutical Industry
Legislative Issues: HCR; MED; MMM; PHA

Chairman
CORNELIUS, James M.

Main Headquarters

Mailing: 9360 Towne Centre Dr.	Tel:	(858) 552-2200
San Diego, CA 92121	Fax:	(858) 552-2212

Washington Office
Mailing: 1401 Eye St. NW, Suite 330
Washington, DC 20005

Corporate Foundations and Giving Programs

Amylin Pharmaceuticals Contributions Program		
9360 Towne Centre Dr.	Tel:	(858) 552-2200
San Diego, CA 92121	Fax:	(858) 552-2212

Amyris Biotechnologies, Inc.

Manufacturer of microbes capable of producing compounds to address major global health and energy challenges.
amyris.com
Annual Revenues: $45.10 million
Employees: 416
Ticker: NASDAQ: AMRS
SIC: 2860
Industry/ies: Science; Scientific Research

President and Chief Executive Officer	Tel:	(510) 450-0761
MELO, John G.	Fax:	(510) 225-2645

Main Headquarters

Mailing: 5885 Hollis St.	Tel:	(510) 450-0761
Suite 100	Fax:	(510) 225-2645
Emeryville, CA 94608		

Corporate Foundations and Giving Programs

Amyris Biotechnologies Contributions Program
5885 Hollis St.
Suite 100
Emeryville, CA 94608

Public Affairs and Related Activities Personnel

At Headquarters

ASADORIAN, Raffi	Tel:	(510) 450-0761
Chief Financial Officer	Fax:	(510) 225-2645
KHADDER, Nicholas	Tel:	(510) 450-0761
General Counsel and Corporate Secretary	Fax:	(510) 225-2645
MANNION, Erica	Tel:	(415) 471-2700
Contact, Investor Rewlations	Fax:	(510) 225-2645
investor@amyris.com		
ROHDE , Karen	Tel:	(510) 450-0761
Chief Human Resources Officer	Fax:	(510) 225-2645

Anacomp, Inc.

A provider of technology outsourcing services and document imaging solutions.
www.anacomp.com
Annual Revenues: $153.25 million
Employees: 1,200
Ticker: OTCBB: ANCPA/ANCPB
SIC: 5044; 3577; 3841
NAICS: 334119; 339112; 42142
Industry/ies: Electricity & Electronics; Electronics; Energy/Electricity

Chief Executive Officer	Tel:	(703) 234-3900
CUNNINGHAM, Thomas P.		
Tom.Cunningham@anacomp.com		

Main Headquarters

Mailing:	3675 Concorde Pkwy.	Tel:	(703) 234-3900
	Suite 1500		
	Chantilly, VA 20151-1135		

Public Affairs and Related Activities Personnel

At Headquarters

HICKEY, Marie	Tel:	(703) 234-3900
Vice President, Strategic Development		
JANOVICK, Isabella	Tel:	(703) 234-3900
Director, Marketing		
NOBLE, Carman	Tel:	(703) 234-3900
Director, Finance		
ROEH, Kimberly	Tel:	(703) 234-3900
Director, Human Resources		

Anadarko Petroleum Corporation

A petroleum exploration and production company. Acquired Kerr-McGee Corporation and Western Gas Resources in 2006.
www.anadarko.com
Annual Revenues: $14.62 billion
Employees: 6,100
Ticker: NYSE: APC
SIC: 1311
NAICS: 211111
Industry/ies: Fuels See Coal, Gas, Oil, Petroleum; Natural Resources; Petroleum Industry
Legislative Issues: BAN; ENG; ENV; TAX; TRD

Chairman of the Board, President and Chief Executive Officer	Tel:	(832) 636-1000
WALKER, R. A.	Fax:	(832) 636-8220

Main Headquarters

Mailing:	1201 Lake Robbins Dr.	Tel:	(832) 636-1000
	The Woodlands, TX 77380	Fax:	(832) 636-8220
		TF:	(800) 800-1101

Washington Office

Mailing:	800 Connecticut Ave. NW	Tel:	(202) 861-8064
	Suite 700	Fax:	(202) 861-8065
	Washington, DC 20006		

Political Action Committees

Anadarko Petroleum Corporation Political Action Committee
FEC ID: C00231951
Contact: Albert L. Richey

1201 Lake Robbins Dr.	Tel:	(832) 636-1000
The Woodlands, TX 77380	Fax:	(832) 636-8220

Contributions to Candidates: $91,500 (2015-2016)
Democrats: $11,000; Republicans: $80,500

Principal Recipients

HOUSE
BRADY, KEVIN (REP-TX)

Corporate Foundations and Giving Programs

Anadarko Petroleum Contributions Program

1201 Lake Robbins Dr.	Tel:	(832) 636-1000
The Woodlands, TX 77380	Fax:	(832) 636-8220

Public Affairs and Related Activities Personnel

At Headquarters

CAMPBLLL, CFA, Chris	Tel:	(832) 636-8434

Director, International Accounting
chris.campbell@anadarko.com

	Fax:	(832) 636-8220
CHRISTIANSEN, John	Tel:	(832) 636-8736
Director, External Communications	Fax:	(832) 636-8220
john.christiansen@anadarko.com		
COLGLAZIER, John M.	Tel:	(832) 636-2306
Senior Vice President, Investor Relations and Communications	Fax:	(832) 636-8220
john.colglazier@anadarko.com		
GWIN, Robert G.	Tel:	(832) 636-1000
Executive Vice President, Finance and Chief Financial Officer	Fax:	(832) 636-8220
MCMILLIAN, Amanda M.	Tel:	(832) 636-1000
Vice President, Deputy General Counsel, Corporate Secretary and Chief Compliance Officer	Fax:	(832) 636-8220
MOORE, A. Scott	Tel:	(832) 636-1000
Vice President, Marketing	Fax:	(832) 636-8220
scott.moore@anadarko.com		
REEVES, Robert K.	Tel:	(832) 636-1000
Executive Vice President, General Counsel and Chief Administrative Officer	Fax:	(832) 636-8220
robert.reeves@anadarko.com		
RICHEY, Albert L.	Tel:	(832) 636-1000
Senior Vice President, Finance and PAC Treasurer	Fax:	(832) 636-8220
STRUBLE, Julia A.	Tel:	(832) 636-1000
Vice President, Human Resources	Fax:	(832) 636-8220

At Washington Office

HANLEY, Mark	Tel:	(907) 273-6310
Manager, Public Affairs	Fax:	(202) 861-8065
Registered Federal Lobbyist		
PENSABENE, Gregory M.	Tel:	(202) 861-8064
Vice President, Government Relations	Fax:	(202) 861-8065
greg.pensabene@anadarko.com		
Registered Federal Lobbyist		

Anakam

Anakam enables the acceleration of eCommerce, eHealthcare and eGovernment by solving the problem of authenticating large and diverse web user bases.
www.anakam.com
Annual Revenues: $2.90 million
Employees: 25
Industry/ies: Disaster

Main Headquarters

Mailing:	1010 N Glebe Rd.	Tel:	(858) 622-9550
	# 500	Fax:	(858) 622-9584
	Arlington, VA 22201		

Public Affairs and Related Activities Personnel

At Headquarters

DIETERICH, David	Tel:	(858) 622-9550
Director, Government Policy Initiatives	Fax:	(858) 622-9584
SMITH, Krislyn	Tel:	(619) 233-7778
Contact, Media Relations	Fax:	(858) 622-9584
ksmith@anakam.com		

Analog Devices, Inc.

A manufacturer of precision, high-performance linear, digital and mixed signal integrated circuits used in analog and digital signal processing applications.
www.analog.com
Annual Revenues: $3.01 billion
Employees: 9,600
Ticker: NYSE: ADI
SIC: 3674
Industry/ies: Computer/Technology

Chairman of the Board	Tel:	(781) 329-4700
STATA, Ray	Fax:	(781) 326-8703

President and Chief Executive Officer	Tel:	(781) 329-4700
ROCHE, Vincent	Fax:	(781) 461-3113

Main Headquarters

Mailing:	One Technology Way	Tel:	(781) 329-4700
	Norwood, MA 02062	Fax:	(781) 461-3113
		TF:	(800) 262-5643

Corporate Foundations and Giving Programs

Analog Devices Contributions Program

Three Technology Way	Tel:	(781) 329-4700
Norwood, MA 02062	Fax:	(781) 461-3113

Public Affairs and Related Activities Personnel

At Headquarters

HESS, Rick	Tel:	(781) 329-4700
Senior Vice President, Communications and Automotive Business Group	Fax:	(781) 461-3113

MATSON, William
Senior Vice President, Human Resources
Tel: (781) 329-4700
Fax: (781) 461-4482

SEIF, Margaret K.
Senior Vice President, General Counsel and Secretary
margaret.seif@analog.com
Tel: (781) 329-4700
Fax: (781) 461-4482

TAGLIAFERRO, Maria
Director, Global Communications
Tel: (781) 461-3282
Fax: (781) 461-3491

WESSEL, Thomas
Senior Vice President, Worldwide Sales and Marketing
Tel: (781) 329-4700
Fax: (781) 461-3113

WYNNE, Eileen
Vice President and Chief Accounting Officer
Tel: (781) 329-4700
Fax: (781) 461-3113

ZINSNER, David A.
Vice President, Finance and Chief Financial Officer
david.zinsner@analog.com
Tel: (781) 329-4700
Fax: (781) 461-3113

Analogic Corporation

Analogic conceives, designs, and manufactures medical and security imaging systems and subsystems, primarily for Original Equipment Manufacturers (OEMs).
www.analogic.com
Annual Revenues: $527.82 million
Employees: 1,700
Ticker: NASDAQ: ALOG
SIC: 3841; 3823
NAICS: 339112; 334513
Industry/ies: Electricity & Electronics; Electronics; Energy/Electricity

President and Chief Executive Officer
GREEN, James W.
Tel: (978) 326-4000
Fax: (978) 977-6811

Main Headquarters
Mailing: Eight Centennial Dr.
Peabody, MA 01960
Tel: (978) 326-4000
Fax: (978) 977-6810

Public Affairs and Related Activities Personnel

At Headquarters

BOURQUE, Michael
Interim Chief Financial Officer
Tel: (978) 326-4000
Fax: (978) 977-6810

COOK, Amy
Media Contact
amycook@amcpublicrelations.com
Tel: (925) 552-7893
Fax: (978) 977-6810

COUMANS, Jacques
Vice President, Chief Marketing Officer and Chief Scientific Officer
Tel: (978) 326-4000
Fax: (978) 977-6810

FRY, John J.
Vice President, General Counsel and Corporation Secretary
jfry@analogic.com
Tel: (978) 326-4000
Fax: (978) 977-6811

KILROY, Joyce
Vice President, Global Quality Assurance, Regulatory Affairs, and Compliance
Tel: (978) 326-4000
Fax: (978) 977-6810

NAMAROFF, Mark
Director, Corporate Marketing and Investor Relations
Tel: (978) 326-4058
Fax: (978) 977-6810

ROSENFELD, Douglas B.
Vice President, Human Resources and Administration
Tel: (978) 326-4000
Fax: (978) 977-6810

SINGH, Yash
Vice President, Corporate Strategy and Development
Tel: (978) 326-4000
Fax: (978) 977-6810

Analytical Graphics Inc.

Provides commercial off-the-shelf software to national security and space professionals for integrated analysis of land, sea, air, and space assets.
www.agi.com
Annual Revenues: $28.50 million
Employees: 300
SIC: 7372
Industry/ies: Computer/Technology
Legislative Issues: DEF

Chief Executive Officer and Co-Founder
GRAZIANI, Paul
Tel: (610) 981-8000
Fax: (610) 981-8001

Main Headquarters
Mailing: 220 Valley Creek Blvd.
Exton, PA 19341
Tel: (610) 981-8000
Fax: (610) 981-8001
TF: (800) 220-4785

Washington Office
Mailing: 1725 I St. NW
Suite 300
Washington, DC 20006
Tel: (202) 530-3214
Fax: (202) 530-3215

Political Action Committees
Analytical Graphics Inc. PAC (AGI PAC)
FEC ID: C00370023
Contact: Eric Stallmer
220 Valley Creek Blvd.
Suite 300
Exton, PA 19341
Tel: (202) 530-3214
Fax: (202) 530-3215

Contributions to Candidates: $12,500 (2015-2016)

Democrats: $500; Republicans: $12,000

Public Affairs and Related Activities Personnel

At Headquarters

BRODERICK, William
Chief Financial Officer
Tel: (610) 981-8000
Fax: (610) 981-8001

EFTIMIADES, Stephanie
Contact, Public and Government Relations
seftimiades@agi.com
Tel: (610) 981-8167
Fax: (610) 981-8001

SHEEHAN, Joseph
President
Tel: (610) 981-8000
Fax: (610) 981-8001

STALLMER, Eric
PAC Treasurer
Tel: (610) 981-8000
Fax: (610) 981-8001

Andersen Corporation

Manufacturer of vinyl-clad wood window units and patio doors.
corporate.andersenwindows.com
Employees: 9,000
SIC: 2431; 3442
NAICS: 321918; 332321
Industry/ies: Construction/Construction Materials; Housing
Legislative Issues: ENG

Chairman of the Board and Chief Executive Officer
LUND, Jay
Tel: (651) 264-5150
Fax: (651) 264-5107

Main Headquarters
Mailing: 100 Fourth Ave., North
Bayport, MN 55003
Tel: (651) 264-5150
Fax: (651) 264-5107
TF: (888) 888-7020

Corporate Foundations and Giving Programs

Andersen Corporate Foundation
Contact: Susan Roeder
100 Fourth Ave. North
Bayport, MN 55003-1096
Tel: (651) 264-5150
Fax: (651) 264-5150

Public Affairs and Related Activities Personnel

At Headquarters

BERNICK, Alan E.
Senior Vice President, Chief Legal Officer and Corporate Secretary
Tel: (651) 264-5150
Fax: (651) 264-5107

DONALDSON, Philip
Executive Vice President and Chief Financial Officer
Tel: (651) 264-5150
Fax: (651) 264-5107

RICHARD, Karen
Senior Vice President and Chief Human Resources Officer
Tel: (651) 264-5150
Fax: (651) 264-5107

ROEDER, Susan
Director, Public Affairs and Vice President, Andersen Corporate Foundation
susan.roeder@andersencorp.com
Tel: (651) 264-7432
Fax: (651) 264-5107

The Anderson's Inc.

A diversified company with interests in the grain, ethanol and plant nutrient sectors of U.S. agriculture, as well as in railcar leasing and repair, industrial products formulation, turf products production, and general merchandise retailing.
www.andersonsinc.com
Annual Revenues: $4.49 billion
Employees: 2,214
Ticker: NASDAQ: ANDE
SIC: 2046; 3291
Industry/ies: Agriculture/Agronomy; Railroads; Transportation

President, Chairman and Chief Executive Officer
ANDERSON, Michael J.
mike.anderson@andersonsinc.com
Tel: (419) 893-5050
Fax: (419) 891-6670

Chairman, Anderson Foundation
ANDERSON, Thomas H.
Tel: (419) 891-6405
Fax: (419) 891-6695

Main Headquarters
Mailing: 480 W. Dussel Dr.
P. O. Box 119
Maumee, OH 43537
Tel: (419) 893-5050
Fax: (419) 891-6670
TF: (800) 537-3370

Corporate Foundations and Giving Programs

Anderson's Foundation
Contact: Michael J. Anderson
P.O. Box 119
480 W. Dussel Dr.
Maumee, OH 43537
Tel: (419) 893-5050
Fax: (419) 891-6670

Public Affairs and Related Activities Personnel

At Headquarters

BURCHINOW, Naran U.
Vice President, General Counsel and Corporate Secretary
Tel: (419) 893-5050
Fax: (419) 891-6670

BURMEISTER, Jim
Vice President, Finance and Treasurer
Tel: (419) 893-5050
Fax: (419) 891-6670

CROW, Debra A.
Tel: (419) 891-6483

Manager, Corporate Communications	Fax:	(419) 891-6670
debra_crow@andersonsinc.com		
DEPOMPEI, Arthur D.	Tel:	(419) 891-6368
Vice President, Human Resources	Fax:	(419) 891-6670
GRANATO, John J.	Tel:	(419) 893-5050
Chief Financial Officer	Fax:	(419) 891-6670
REED, Hal	Tel:	(419) 893-5050
Chief Operating Officer	Fax:	(419) 891-6670
SPARKS, Tamara S.	Tel:	(419) 893-5050
Vice President Corporate Relations and Business Analysis	Fax:	(419) 891-6670
WAGGONER, Tom	Tel:	(419) 893-5050
Vice President, Marketing and Operations Services	Fax:	(419) 891-6670

Andrews and Andrews, PLLC.

A law firm.
Legislative Issues: RET; TAX

Main Headquarters
Mailing: 1155 F St. NW
Suite 1050
Washington, DC 20004

Public Affairs and Related Activities Personnel

At Headquarters

ANDREWS, Lisa S.	Tel:	(202) 744-8361
Partner		
Registered Federal Lobbyist		
ANDREWS, Jr., Wright H.	Tel:	(202) 744-8361
Partner		

AndroBiosys, Inc.

Biotech company focused on prostate cancer treatment development.
www.androbiosys.com
Industry/ies: Medicine/Health Care/Mental Health; Science; Scientific Research

Main Headquarters

Mailing: 875 Ellicott St.	Tel:	(716) 845-8226
Buffalo, NY 14203	Fax:	(716) 849-6818

Public Affairs and Related Activities Personnel

At Headquarters

MOHLER, Dr. James L.	Tel:	(716) 845-8226
Chief Marketing Officer	Fax:	(716) 849-6818

Andrx Corporation

See listing on page 11 under Actavis, Inc.

Angelica Corporation

Provides textile services to healthcare institutions. It rents and cleans scrubs, bed sheets, towels, gowns, and surgical linens. Angelica also provides mops, mats, sterile surgical packs, and on-site linen room management. The firm operates about 30 laundry service centers across the US.
www.angelica.com
Annual Revenues: $378.90 million
Employees: 5,500
SIC: 7200
Industry/ies: Apparel/Textiles Industry; Medicine/Health Care/Mental Health

President and Chief Executive Officer

VAN VLIET, David A.	Tel:	(678) 823-4100
	Fax:	(678) 823-4165

Main Headquarters

Mailing: 1105 Lakewood Pkwy.	Tel:	(678) 823-4100
Suite 210	Fax:	(678) 823-4165
Alpharetta, GA 30009		

Public Affairs and Related Activities Personnel

At Headquarters

BELOTE, Lew	Tel:	(678) 823-4100
Chief Financial Officer	Fax:	(678) 823-4165
FENTZ, Barry	Tel:	(678) 823-4100
Senior Vice President, Operations	Fax:	(678) 823-4165
FIORILLO, Rich	Tel:	(678) 823-4100
Chief Administrative Officer	Fax:	(678) 823-4165
FREY, Steve	Tel:	(314) 854-3800
Vice President, General Counsel and Secretary	Fax:	(314) 854-3949
MCENANEY, Mike	Tel:	(678) 823-4100
Senior Vice President, Marketing and Strategy	Fax:	(678) 823-4165
SHELL, Bob	Tel:	(678) 823-4100
Vice President, Human Resources	Fax:	(678) 823-4165

Angiodynamics

Manufacturer of medical devices for the treatment of peripheral vascular disease.
www.angiodynamics.com
Annual Revenues: $356.16 million

Employees: 1,300
Ticker: NASDAQ (GS): ANGO
SIC: 3841
NAICS: 339112
Industry/ies: Medicine/Health Care/Mental Health

Chairman of the Board

BUCCI, Vincent	Tel:	(518) 798-1215
	Fax:	(518) 798-3625

President and Chief Executive Officer

DEVIVO, Joseph	Tel:	(518) 795-1400
	Fax:	(518) 795-1401

Main Headquarters

Mailing: 14 Plaza Dr.	Tel:	(518) 795-1400
Latham, NY 12110	Fax:	(518) 795-1401
	TF:	(800) 772-6446

Public Affairs and Related Activities Personnel

At Headquarters

CREGUT, Mary	Tel:	(518) 795-1400
Vice President, Human Resources	Fax:	(518) 795-1401
FROST, Mark	Tel:	(518) 795-1400
Executive Vice President and Chief Financial Officer	Fax:	(518) 795-1401
GALE, Chris	Tel:	(646) 201-5431
Contact, Communications	Fax:	(518) 795-1401
cgale@evcgroup.com		

AngloGold Ashanti North America, Inc.

Formerly known as Independence Mining Company, Inc. A gold producer.
www.anglogold.com
SIC: 1040
Industry/ies: Mining Industry; Natural Resources

Chief Executive Officer

VENKATAKRISHNAN, S	Tel:	(303) 889-0700
	Fax:	(303) 889-0707

Main Headquarters

Mailing: 6300 S. Syracuse Way	Tel:	(303) 889-0700
Suite 500	Fax:	(303) 889-0707
Centennial, CO 80111		

Corporate Foundations and Giving Programs

The AngloGold Ashanti Fund
7400 E. Orchard Rd.
Suite 350
Englewood, CO 80111-2529

	Tel:	(303) 889-0700
	Fax:	(303) 889-0707

Public Affairs and Related Activities Personnel

At Headquarters

BAILEY, Stewart	Tel:	(212) 836-4303
Senior Vice President, Investor Relations	Fax:	(303) 889-0707
sbailey@AngloGoldAshanti.com		
BONINELLI, I	Tel:	(303) 889-0700
Executive Vice President, People and Organizational Development	Fax:	(303) 889-0707
LARGENT, RW	Tel:	(303) 889-0700
Chief Operating Officer	Fax:	(303) 889-0707
PATTERSON, Marie	Tel:	(303) 889-0753
Manager, State Government Affairs	Fax:	(303) 889-0707
mpatterson@anglogoldashantiNA.com		
RAMON, KC	Tel:	(303) 889-0700
Chief Financial Officer, Executive Director	Fax:	(303) 889-0707

Anheuser-Busch InBev

Anheuser-Busch InBev, based in New York City, is the U.S. subsidiary of Anheuser-Busch InBev., headquartered in Leuven, Belgium. Producer of energy drinks and non-alcoholic malt beverages. Merged with InBev in late 2008.
www.ab-inbev.com
Annual Revenues: $46.91 billion
Employees: 155,000
Ticker: NYSE:BUD
SIC: 2082
Industry/ies: Food And Beverage Industry
Legislative Issues: AGR; BEV; BUD; CPT; FOO; LBR; MAN; TAX; TRA; TRD; TRU

Chief Executive Officer

BRITO, Carlos	Tel:	(212) 573-8800
	Fax:	(314) 577-2900

Main Headquarters

Mailing: 250 Park Ave.	Tel:	(212) 573-8800
New York City, NY 10177	Fax:	(314) 577-2900

Washington Office

Mailing: 1401 I St. NW	Tel:	(202) 293-9494
Suite 200		
Washington, DC 20005		

Political Action Committees

Anheuser-Busch Companies Inc. PAC
FEC ID: C00034488
Contact: Gary Tappanna

One Busch Pl.
202-7
St. Louis, MO 63118

Tel: (314) 577-2329
Fax: (314) 577-7622

Contributions to Candidates: $371,249 (2015-2016)
Democrats: $103,500; Republicans: $257,749; Other: $10,000

Principal Recipients

PRESIDENT
CLINTON, HILLARY RODHAM (DEM-NY)

SENATE
HOEVEN, JOHN (REP-ND)
ISAKSON, JOHN HARDY (REP-GA)
KIRK, MARK STEVEN (REP-IL)

HOUSE
BEATTY, JOYCE (DEM-OH)
BOEHNER, JOHN A. (REP-OH)
CLAY, WILLIAM LACY JR (DEM-MO)
CRENSHAW, ANDER (REP-FL)
HOYER, STENY HAMILTON (DEM-DC)
KATKO, JOHN M (REP-NY)
LABRADOR, RAUL R. HON. (REP-ID)
LOUDERMILK, BARRY (REP-GA)
MCCARTHY, KEVIN (REP-CA)
REED, THOMAS W II (REP-NY)
SMITH, JASON T (OTHER-MO)
TIBERI, PATRICK J. (REP-OH)
WAGNER, ANN L. (REP-MO)
WITTMAN, ROBERT J MR. (REP-VA)
ZINKE, RYAN K (REP-MT)

Corporate Foundations and Giving Programs

Anheuser-Busch Foundation
One Busch Pl.
St. Louis, MO 63118

Tel: (314) 577-2000
Fax: (314) 577-2900

Public Affairs and Related Activities Personnel

At Headquarters

CHALMERS, Sabine
Chief Officer, Legal and Coporate Affairs

Tel: (212) 573-8800
Fax: (314) 577-2900

CHENG, Y. R.
Vice President, Government Affairs
Registered Federal Lobbyist

Tel: (314) 577-2000
Fax: (314) 577-2900

DUTRA, Felipe
Chief Financial and Technology Officer

Tel: (212) 573-8800
Fax: (314) 577-2900

GARCIA, Claudio
Chief People Officer

Tel: (212) 573-8800
Fax: (314) 577-2900

PATRICIO, Miguel
Chief Marketing Officer

Tel: (212) 573-8800
Fax: (314) 577-2900

STALEY, Graham
Vice President, Global Investor Relations

Tel: (212) 573-4365
Fax: (314) 577-2900

VAN BIESBROECK , Jo
Chief Strategy Officer

Tel: (212) 573-8800
Fax: (314) 577-2900

VILLENEUVE, James
Vice President, Corporate Affairs and Communications
James.villeneuve@anheuser-busch.com

Tel: (314) 577-2000
Fax: (314) 577-2900

VOGT, Terri
Vice President, Communications
terri.vogt@anheuser-busch.com

Tel: (314) 577-7750
Fax: (314) 577-2900

At Washington Office

BAILEY, Douglas
Registered Federal Lobbyist

Tel: (202) 293-9494

BONILLA, Jennifer
Federal Lobbyist
Registered Federal Lobbyist

Tel: (202) 293-9494

CALLOWAY, JR., Donald
Federal Lobbyist

Tel: (202) 293-9494

HARTMAN, Zach
Federal Lobbyist
Registered Federal Lobbyist

Tel: (202) 293-9494

ROCHE, Michael F.
Vice President, National Affairs

Tel: (202) 293-9494

ROSS, Christopher P.
Federal Lobbyist

Tel: (202) 293-9494

At Other Offices

TAPPANNA, Gary
PAC Treasurer
One Busch Pl.
St. Louis, MO 63118
Mail Stop 202-7

Anixter International, Inc.

A distributor of communications components. Formerly called the Itel Corporation.
www.anixter.com

Annual Revenues: $6.62 billion
Employees: 8,700
Ticker: NYSE: AXE
SIC: 5063
Industry/ies: Computer/Technology; Electricity & Electronics; Electronics; Energy/Electricity

Director
ZELL, Samuel
samuel.zell@anixter.com

Tel: (224) 521-8000
Fax: (224) 521-8100

President and Chief Executive Officer
ECK, Robert J.

Tel: (224) 521-8000
Fax: (224) 521-8100

Main Headquarters
Mailing: 2301 Patriot Blvd.
Glenview, IL 60026-8020

Tel: (224) 521-8000
Fax: (224) 521-8100
TF: (800) 323-8167

Corporate Foundations and Giving Programs

Anixter International Inc. Contributions Program
2301 Patriot Blvd.
Glenview, IL 60026-8020

Tel: (224) 521-8000
Fax: (224) 521-8100

Public Affairs and Related Activities Personnel

At Headquarters

CHOI, Justin C.
Executive Vice President, General Counsel and Corporate Secretary

Tel: (224) 521-8000
Fax: (224) 521-8100

CLARKE, Ian R.
Executive Vice President - Global Sales and Marketing, Fasteners

Tel: (224) 521-8000
Fax: (224) 521-8100

DOSCH, Theodore A.
Executive Vice President, Finance and Chief Financial Officer
ted.dosch@anixter.com

Tel: (224) 521-8000
Fax: (224) 521-8100

FABER, Terrance A.
Senior Vice President Controller

Tel: (224) 521-8000
Fax: (224) 521-8100

MARKS, Dawn
Vice President, Global Marketing Communications
dawn.marks@anixter.com

Tel: (224) 521-8484
Fax: (224) 521-8100

MEERS, CFA, Lisa Micou
Vice President, Investor Relations

Tel: (224) 521-8895
Fax: (224) 521-8100

SHOEMAKER, Rodney A.
Senior Vice President, Treasurer

Tel: (224) 521-8000
Fax: (224) 521-8100

SMITH, Rodney A.
Executive Vice President, Human Resources

Tel: (224) 521-8000
Fax: (224) 521-8100

STANDISH, William A.
Executive Vice President Operations

Tel: (224) 521-8000
Fax: (224) 521-8100

The Anschutz Company

An investment company.
Industry/ies: Banking/Finance/Investments
Legislative Issues: TAX

Main Headquarters
Mailing: 1152 15th St. NW
Suite 250
Washington, DC 20005

Tel: (202) 393-0100
Fax: (202) 393-0102

Public Affairs and Related Activities Personnel

At Headquarters

JONES, Wiley N.
Vice President & Washington Counsel
wiley.jones@tac-dc.com
Registered Federal Lobbyist

Tel: (202) 393-0100
Fax: (202) 393-0102

Anthem Inc.

A health benefits company. Formed through the merger of WellPoint Health Networks Inc. and Anthem, Inc. in 2004.
www.wellpoint.com
Annual Revenues: $75.07 billion
Employees: 51,500
Ticker: NYSE: ANTM
SIC: 6324
Industry/ies: Insurance Industry; Medicine/Health Care/Mental Health
Legislative Issues: BUD; CSP; HCR; HOM; INS; LBR; MMM; TAX; VET

President and Chief Executive Officer
SWEDISH, Joseph R.

Tel: (317) 488-6000
Fax: (317) 488-6260

Main Headquarters
Mailing: 120 Monument Cir.
Indianapolis, IN 46204

Tel: (317) 488-6000
Fax: (317) 488-6028

Washington Office
Mailing: 1001 Pennsylvania Ave. NW
Suite 710
Washington, DC 20004

Tel: (202) 628-2113
Fax: (202) 638-1096

Political Action Committees

WELLPOINT, Inc.WELLPAC
FEC ID: C00197228
120 Monument Cir.
Indianapolis, IN 46204

Contributions to Candidates: $582,250 (2015-2016)
Democrats: $265,000; Republicans: $316,250; Other: $1,000

Principal Recipients

SENATE
BLUMENTHAL, RICHARD (DEM-CT)
BLUNT, ROY (REP-MO)
ISAKSON, JOHN HARDY (REP-GA)
MURPHY, PATRICK E (DEM-FL)
YOUNG, TODD CHRISTOPHER (REP-IN)

HOUSE
BERA, AMERISH (DEM-CA)
BROOKS, SUSAN MRS. (REP-IN)
GRAHAM, GWEN (DEM-FL)
HOYER, STENY HAMILTON (DEM-DC)
MCCARTHY, KEVIN (REP-CA)
SCALISE, STEVE MR. (REP-LA)
TIBERI, PATRICK J. (REP-OH)

Corporate Foundations and Giving Programs

WellPoint Foundation
120 Monument Cir.
Indianapolis, IN 46204 — Tel: (262) 523-4746

Public Affairs and Related Activities Personnel

At Headquarters

BECHER, Jill — Tel: (262) 523-4764 — Fax: (317) 488-6028
Vice President, Communications
jill.becher@wellpoint.

CANNON, John — Tel: (317) 532-6000 — Fax: (317) 488-6028
Executive Vice President, General Counsel and Chief Public Affairs Officer

DEVEYDT, Wayne — Tel: (317) 532-6000 — Fax: (317) 488-6028
Executive Vice President and Chief Financial Officer
wayne.deveydt@wellpoint.com

HAYTAIAN, Peter D. — Tel: (317) 488-6000 — Fax: (317) 488-6028
Executive Vice President, Government Business

KLEINMAN, Michael — Tel: (317) 488-6713 — Fax: (317) 488-6703
Vice President, Investor Relations
michael.kleinman@wellpoint.com

LARRIVEE, Scott — Tel: (262) 523-4746 — Fax: (317) 488-6260
Public Relations Director
scott.larrivee@wellpoint.com

MCCARTHY, Gloria — Tel: (317) 488-6000 — Fax: (317) 488-6028
Executive Vice President and Chief Administrative Officer

SILVERSTEIN, Martin — Tel: (317) 488-6000 — Fax: (317) 488-6028
Executive Vice President and Chief Strategy Officer

TOMAS, Jose — Tel: (317) 488-6000 — Fax: (317) 488-6028
Executive Vice President and Chief Human Resources Officer

WILLEY, John — Tel: (317) 532-6000 — Fax: (317) 488-6028
Senior Director, Public Affairs, Lobbyist and PAC Treasurer

ZIELINSKI, Thomas C. — Tel: (317) 488-6000 — Fax: (317) 488-6028
Executive Vice President and General Counsel

At Washington Office

COYNE, Brian — Tel: (202) 628-2113 — Fax: (202) 638-1096
Senior Vice President Federal Government Relations
Registered Federal Lobbyist

FAHRER, Gabriella — Tel: (202) 628-2113 — Fax: (202) 638-1096
Federal Lobbyist
Registered Federal Lobbyist

GOLDBERG, Adam — Tel: (202) 628-2113 — Fax: (202) 638-1096
Manager, Congressional Affairs
Registered Federal Lobbyist

HALANE, Warsan — Tel: (202) 628-2113 — Fax: (202) 638-1096

HALL, Elizabeth — Tel: (202) 628-2113 — Fax: (202) 638-1096
Vice President
elizabeth.hall@wellpoint.com
Registered Federal Lobbyist

LONG, Erika — Tel: (202) 628-2113 — Fax: (202) 638-1096

MARCHIO, Samuel — Tel: (317) 532-6000 — Fax: (202) 638-1096
Senior Director, Federal Affairs
Samuel.marchio@wellpoint.com
Registered Federal Lobbyist

ODOM, Amy O. — Tel: (202) 628-7840 — Fax: (202) 638-1096
Vice President, Federal Affairs
Registered Federal Lobbyist

VELLIKY, Patrick M. — Tel: (202) 628-2113 — Fax: (202) 638-1096
Registered Federal Lobbyist

VELLIKY, Patrick — Tel: (202) 628-2113 — Fax: (202) 638-1096
Registered Federal Lobbyist

ZIRKELBACH, Mary K. — Tel: (202) 628-2113 — Fax: (202) 638-1096
Federal Lobbyist

At Other Offices

SIMPSON, Doug — Tel: (212) 476-1473
Vice President, Investor Relations
165 Broadway (One Liberty Plaza)
New York City, NY 10006
Douglas.simpson@wellpoint.com

AOL

See listing on page 47 under America Online Inc.

Aon Corporation

An insurance holding company. Subsidiaries include Aon Risk Services, Inc.
www.aon.com
Annual Revenues: $11.92 billion
Employees: 68,633
Ticker: NYSE: AON
SIC: 6411
Industry/ies: Insurance Industry
Legislative Issues: FIN; INS; TAX

President and Chief Executive Officer — Tel: (312) 381-1000 — Fax: (312) 381-6032
CASE, Gregory C.

Main Headquarters
Mailing: 200 E. Randolph St. — Tel: (312) 381-1000
Chicago, IL 60601 — Fax: (312) 381-6032 — TF: (877) 384-4276

Political Action Committees

Aon Corporation PAC
FEC ID: C00211250
Contact: Paul Hagy
200 E. Randolph Dr. — Tel: (312) 381-1000
Chicago, IL 60601 — Fax: (312) 381-6032

Contributions to Candidates: $88,500 (2015-2016)
Democrats: $31,500; Republicans: $57,000

Corporate Foundations and Giving Programs

Aon Foundation
200 E. Randolph
Chicago, IL 60601

Public Affairs and Related Activities Personnel

At Headquarters

BESIO, Gregory J. — Tel: (312) 381-1000 — Fax: (312) 381-6032
Executive Vice President and Chief Human Resources Officer

CLEMENT, Philip B. — Tel: (312) 381-1000 — Fax: (312) 381-6032
Chief Marketing and Communications Officer
Phil.Clement@aon.com

DAVIES, Christa — Tel: (312) 381-1000 — Fax: (312) 381-6032
Executive Vice President and Chief Financial Officer

DRINKWINE, Kelly — Tel: (312) 381-2684 — Fax: (312) 381-6032
Contact, Media Relations
kelly_drinkwine@aon.com

GAINER, Bridget — Tel: (312) 381-3809 — Fax: (312) 381-6032
Director, Government Affairs
bridget_gainer@aon.com
Registered Federal Lobbyist

HAGY, Paul — Tel: (312) 381-1000 — Fax: (312) 381-6032
PAC Treasurer
pauLhagy@aon.com

HIMES, Kathryn S. — Tel: (312) 381-1000 — Fax: (312) 381-6032
Global Director, Public Affairs
Registered Federal Lobbyist

KARELLAS, Andreas — Tel: (312) 381-1000 — Fax: (312) 381-6032
Deputy Director, Government Affairs
Registered Federal Lobbyist

LIEB, Peter — Tel: (312) 381-1000 — Fax: (312) 381-6032
Executive Vice President and General Counsel

REILLY, Kathleen — Tel: (312) 381-1000 — Fax: (312) 381-6032
Global Director, Public Affairs
Registered Federal Lobbyist

REILLY, Kathryn — Tel: (312) 381-1000 — Fax: (312) 381-6032
Global Director, Public Affairs
Registered Federal Lobbyist

Aon Hewitt

A global human resources outsourcing and consulting firm.
www.hewittassociates.com

Employees: 23,000
Ticker: NYSE: HEW
SIC: 8742
Industry/ies: Business; Employees & Employment; Small Business
Legislative Issues: HCR; RET

Main Headquarters
Mailing: Four Overlook Point   Tel: (847) 295-5000
             Lincolnshire, IL 60069-4302

Corporate Foundations and Giving Programs
Hewitt Cares
100 Half Day Rd.
Lincolnshire, IL 60069

Public Affairs and Related Activities Personnel

At Headquarters

KANTER, Maurissa   Tel: (847) 295-5000
Contact, Media Relations
maurissa.kanter@hewitt.com

LEVIN, Matthew C.   Tel: (847) 295-5000
Executive Vice President and Head, Global Strategy

Aon Risk Services, Inc.

See listing on page 67 under Aon Corporation

Aova Technologies

An agricultural biotechnology company.
www.aovatech.com
Industry/ies: Agriculture/Agronomy; Animals; Science; Scientific Research

President and Chief Executive Officer   Tel: (608) 310-9595
MARTINEZ, Jesus   Fax: (608) 310-9596
jesus@aovatech.com

Main Headquarters
Mailing: 5976 Executive Dr.   Tel: (608) 661-8765
             Suite C   Fax: (608) 661-8766
             Madison, WI 53719   TF: (855) 870-9979

Public Affairs and Related Activities Personnel

At Headquarters

MONTGOMERY, Kyle   Tel: (608) 310-9595
Vice President, Sales and Marketing   Fax: (608) 310-9596
kyle@aovatech.com

Apache Corporation

An independent energy company engaged in exploration, development, production and marketing of natural gas, crude oil and natural gas liquids. It operates onshore and offshore assets primarily in the Permian Basin, the Anadarko basin in western Oklahoma, and the Texas Panhandle, Gulf Coast areas of the United States, as well as in Western Canada.
www.apachecorp.com
Annual Revenues: $11.66 billion
Employees: 4,950
Ticker: NYSE: APA
SIC: 1311
NAICS: 211111
Industry/ies: Energy/Electricity; Fuels See Coal, Gas, Oil, Petroleum; Natural Resources; Petroleum Industry
Legislative Issues: ENG

Chief Executive Officer and President   Tel: (713) 296-6000
CHRISTMANN, IV, John J.   Fax: (713) 296-6480

Main Headquarters
Mailing: 2000 Post Oak Blvd.   Tel: (713) 296-6000
             Suite 100   Fax: (713) 296-6480
             Houston, TX 77056-4400   TF: (800) 272-2434

Political Action Committees
Apache Corporation PAC (ApachePAC)
FEC ID: C00279224
2000 Post Oak Blvd.   Tel: (713) 296-6150
Suite 100   Fax: (713) 296-6480
Houston, TX 77056

   Contributions to Candidates: $21,000 (2015-2016)
   Democrats: $2,500; Republicans: $18,500

Corporate Foundations and Giving Programs
Apache Foundation
Contact: Debbie Carter
2000 Post Oak Blvd.   Tel: (713) 296-6150
Suite 100   Fax: (713) 296-6480
Houston, TX 77056

Public Affairs and Related Activities Personnel

At Headquarters

CARTER, Debbie   Tel: (713) 296-7038
Coordinator, Corporate Outreach Services   Fax: (713) 296-6496
debra.carter@apachecorp.com

CLARK, Gary T.   Tel: (713) 296-6000
Vice President, Investor Relations   Fax: (713) 296-6480

HARRIS, Margery M.   Tel: (713) 296-6000
Executive Vice President, Human Resources   Fax: (713) 296-6480

KENNEDY, Castlen   Tel: (713) 296-6150
Director, Public Affairs   Fax: (713) 296-6480
castlen.kennedy@apachecorp.com

LANNIE, P. Anthony   Tel: (713) 296-6000
Executive Vice President and General Counsel   Fax: (713) 296-6480

MINTZ, Bill   Tel: (713) 296-7276
Senior Vice President, Global Communications   Fax: (713) 296-6452
bill.mintz@apachecorp.com

O'BRIEN, Urban F.   Tel: (713) 296-6150
Vice President, Government Affairs   Fax: (713) 296-6480
obie.obrien@apachecorp.com

RINEY, Stephen J.   Tel: (713) 296-6000
Executive Vice President and Chief Financial Officer   Fax: (713) 296-6480

SULLIVAN , Timothy J.   Tel: (713) 296-6000
Senior Vice President, Operations Support   Fax: (713) 296-6480

TARANTA, Evan   Tel: (713) 296-6000
Federal Lobbyist   Fax: (713) 296-6496

TESLIK, Sarah B.   Tel: (713) 296-6000
Senior Vice President, Communications, Public Affairs and   Fax: (713) 296-6480
Governance

THOMPSON, Matthew   Tel: (713) 296-6000
Contact, Government Relations   Fax: (713) 296-6496

YELICH, Thomas E.   Tel: (713) 296-6000
Vice President, Business Development   Fax: (713) 296-6480

Apache Nitrogen Products Inc.

See listing on page 68 under Apache Corporation

APL Ltd.

An ocean shipping company.
www.apl.com
Annual Revenues: $343.40 million
Employees: 4,800
SIC: 4412
Industry/ies: Marine/Maritime/Shipping; Transportation
Legislative Issues: BUD; DEF; HOM; MAR; TAX

Chairman of the Board   Tel: (602) 586-4800
KEUNG, Cheng Wai   Fax: (602) 586-4861

Main Headquarters
Mailing: 1667 K St. NW   Tel: (202) 331-1424
             Suite 400   Fax: (202) 775-8427
             Washington, DC 20006

Political Action Committees
APL Ltd. PAC
FEC ID: C00137828
Contact: Scott T. Palmer
16220 N. Scottsdale Rd.   Tel: (602) 586-4800
Suite 300
Scottsdale, AZ 85254

   Contributions to Candidates: $40,000 (2015-2016)
   Democrats: $20,500; Republicans: $19,500

Corporate Foundations and Giving Programs
APL Limited Foundation
Contact: Mike Zampa
1579 Middle Harbor Rd.   Tel: (510) 272-7380
Oakland, CA 94607   Fax: (510) 272-7421

Public Affairs and Related Activities Personnel

At Headquarters

MENSING, Eric   Tel: (202) 331-1424
Senior Vice President, Government Trade and Affairs   Fax: (202) 775-8427
Registered Federal Lobbyist

PALMER, Scott T.   Tel: (202) 331-1424
PAC Contact   Fax: (202) 775-8427

PERRY, Tim   Tel: (202) 331-1424
Senior Manager, Regulatory & Government Affairs   Fax: (202) 775-8427
timothy_perry@apl.com
Registered Federal Lobbyist

SEEDS, Nathaniel   Tel: (202) 331-1424
Chief Operations Officer   Fax: (202) 775-8427

At Other Offices

WINDLE, Timothy J.   Tel: (602) 586-4800
General Counsel and PAC Treasurer   Fax: (303) 645-7679
16220 N. Scottsdale Rd., Suite 300
Scottsdale, AZ 85254

Apogee Enterprises, Inc.

Apogee Enterprises is a manufacturer of windows and glass. Apogee transforms plain glass to create distinctive solutions for architects, building owners, contractors, picture framers and others.
www.apog.com
Annual Revenues: $989.11 million
Employees: 4,614
Ticker: NASDAQ: APOG
SIC: 3231
Industry/ies: Glass

Chairman of the Board Tel: (952) 835-1874
ALDRICH, Bernard P. Fax: (952) 487-7565

Chief Executive Officer Tel: (952) 835-1874
PUISHYS, Joseph F. Fax: (952) 487-7565

Main Headquarters
Mailing: 4400 W. 78th St. Tel: (952) 835-1874
Suite 520 Fax: (952) 487-7565
Minneapolis, MN 55435 TF: (877) 752-3432

Corporate Foundations and Giving Programs

Apogee and Subsidiaries In-Service Team
7900 Xerxes Ave. South Tel: (952) 835-1874
Suite 1800 Fax: (952) 487-7565
Minneapolis, MN 55431

Public Affairs and Related Activities Personnel

At Headquarters

BEITHON, Patricia A. Tel: (952) 835-1874
General Counsel and Secretary Fax: (952) 487-7565
pbeithon@apog.com

JACKSON, Mary Ann Tel: (952) 487-7538
Director, Investor Relations Fax: (952) 487-7565
mjackson@apog.com

PORTER, James S. Tel: (952) 835-1874
Executive Vice President and Chief Financial Officer Fax: (952) 487-7565

Apollo Group, Inc.

Provides higher education programs for working adults.
www.apollogrp.edu
Annual Revenues: $2.33 billion
Employees: 34,000
Ticker: NASDAQ: APOL
SIC: 8200
Industry/ies: Education
Legislative Issues: BUD; EDU; VET

Chairman of the Board Tel: (480) 966-5394
SPERLING, Peter V. Fax: (480) 379-3503

Director and Chief Executive Officer Tel: (480) 966-5394
CAPPELLI, Gregory W. Fax: (480) 379-3503

Main Headquarters
Mailing: 4025 S. Riverpoint Pkwy. Tel: (480) 966-5394
Phoenix, AZ 85040 Fax: (480) 379-3503
TF: (800) 990-2765

Washington Office
Mailing: 1808 Eye St. NW
Suite 400
Washington, DC 20006

Political Action Committees
Apollo Group Inc. Political Organization for Legislative Leadership PAC
FEC ID: C00309781
Contact: Conwey James Casillas
4025 S. Riverpoint Pkwy. Tel: (480) 966-5394
MS CF-KX10 Fax: (480) 379-3503
Phoenix, AZ 85040

Contributions to Candidates: $73,000 (2015-2016)
Democrats: $26,000; Republicans: $47,000

Principal Recipients

SENATE
MCCAIN, JOHN S (REP-VA)
MURRAY, PATTY (DEM-WA)

Corporate Foundations and Giving Programs

University of Phoenix Foundation
4025 S. Riverpoint Pkwy. Tel: (480) 966-5394
Phoenix, AZ 85040

Public Affairs and Related Activities Personnel

At Headquarters

ACOCELLA, Joanna B. Tel: (480) 966-5394
Vice President, Regulatory & Federal Affairs Fax: (480) 379-3503
Registered Federal Lobbyist

BOWLING, Mitch Tel: (480) 966-5394
Chief Operating Officer Fax: (480) 379-3503

BRENNER, Mark Tel: (480) 966-5394

Senior Vice President, Corporate Communications and Fax: (480) 379-3503
External Affairs

CASILLAS, Conwey James Tel: (480) 966-5394
PAC Treasurer Fax: (480) 379-3503
Mail Stop MS CF-KX10
Registered Federal Lobbyist

CORONELLI, Beth Tel: (312) 660-2059
Chief of Staff and Senior Vice President, Investor Relations Fax: (480) 379-3503
beth.coronelli@apollogrp.edu

DAVIS, Jeremy Tel: (312) 660-2071
Director, Investor Relations Fax: (480) 379-3503
jeremy.davis@apollogrp.edu

IVERSON, Greg Tel: (480) 966-5394
Senior Vice President, Chief Financial Officer Fax: (480) 379-3503

LANGENBACH, Jeff Tel: (480) 966-5394
Senior Vice President, Strategy and Business Development Fax: (480) 379-3503

MARTIN, Sean B.W. Tel: (480) 966-5394
Senior Vice President, General Counsel and Secretary Fax: (480) 379-3503

NEWTON, Frederick J. Tel: (480) 966-5394
Senior Vice President, Chief Human Resources Officer Fax: (480) 379-3503

Apotex Corporation

Apotex Corporation, based in Weston City, is the U.S. subsidiary of Apotex Corporation, headquartered in Toronto, Canada. A pharmaceutical company. It is one of the world's most successful independent pharmaceutical companies in Research and Development, Quality, Manufacturing, Sales, and Customer Service.
www.apotex.com
Industry/ies: Pharmaceutical Industry
Legislative Issues: CPT; HCR; PHA

Chairman of the Board & Chief Executive Officer Tel: (954) 384-8007
SHERMAN, Bernard

Main Headquarters
Mailing: 2400 N. Commerce Pkwy. Tel: (954) 384-8007
Suite 400 TF: (800) 706-5575
Weston, FL 33326

Corporate Foundations and Giving Programs

Apotex Corporation Contributions Program
Contact: Bernard Sherman
2400 N. Commerce Pkwy. Tel: (954) 384-8007
Suite 400
Weston, FL 33326

Public Affairs and Related Activities Personnel

At Headquarters

BETITO, Elie Tel: (416) 749-9300
Director, Public and Government Affairs
ebetito@apotex.com

GIULI, Steve Tel: (301) 654-4964
Director, Government Affairs & Industry Relations
sgiuli@apotex.com
Registered Federal Lobbyist

Apple Computer, Inc.

See listing on page 69 under Apple Inc.

Apple Inc.

Designer and manufacturer of consumer electronics and software.
www.apple.com
Annual Revenues: $212.16 billion
Employees: 92,600
Ticker: NASDAQ: AAPL
SIC: 3571; 3577; 7372
Industry/ies: Computer/Technology
Legislative Issues: BAN; CPI; CPT; CSP; EDU; ENV; HCR; LAW; LBR; TAX; TEC; TRD

Chairman of the Board Tel: (408) 996-1010
LEVINSON, Arthur D. Fax: (408) 974-2113

Chief Executive Officer Tel: (408) 996-1010
COOK, Tim Fax: (408) 974-2113
tcook@apple.com

Main Headquarters
Mailing: 901 15th St. NW Tel: (202) 772-9500
Suite 1000
Washington, DC 20005

Public Affairs and Related Activities Personnel

At Headquarters

AMMANN, Nick Tel: (202) 772-9500
Federal Lobbyist

GOTTLI, Amber Tel: (202) 772-9500
Head, Government Affairs

ERRION, Lisa *Senior Manager, Global Trade Policy*	Tel:	(202) 772-9500
HOGAN, Cynthia *Registered Federal Lobbyist*	Tel:	(202) 772-9500
KUHN, Walt *Manager, Federal Government Affairs* *Registered Federal Lobbyist*	Tel:	(202) 772-9500
MARKS MOSHER, Alexis *Federal Lobbyist* *Registered Federal Lobbyist*	Tel:	(202) 772-9500
NOVELLI, Catherine A. *Vice President, Worldwide Government Affairs* glewis@apple.com *Registered Federal Lobbyist*	Tel:	(202) 772-9500
PEARLMAN, Lisa *Registered Federal Lobbyist*	Tel:	(202) 772-9500
POWDERLY, Timothy *Director, Federal Government Affairs* *Registered Federal Lobbyist*	Tel:	(202) 772-9500
RATNER, Jeffrey *Registered Federal Lobbyist*	Tel:	(202) 772-9500
ROLLINS, Ann *Federal Lobbyist*	Tel:	(202) 772-9500
TENUTA, Joshua P. *Director, Federal Government Affairs*	Tel:	(202) 772-9500
THOMAS, Chelsea *Federal Lobbyist*	Tel:	(202) 772-9500

At Other Offices

DOBROZSI, Jeff *Federal Lobbyist* 1200 G St. NW Washington, DC 20005 *Registered Federal Lobbyist*		
DOWLING, Steve *Vice President, Communications* One Infinite Loop Cupertino, CA 95014 dowling@apple.com	Tel: Fax:	(408) 974-1896 (408) 996-0275
MAESTRI, Luca *Senior Vice President and Chief Financial Officer* One Infinite Loop Cupertino, CA 95014	Tel: Fax:	(408) 996-1010 (408) 974-2483
OPPENHEIMER, Peter *Senior Vice President and Chief Financial Officer* One Infinite Loop Cupertino, CA 95014	Tel: Fax:	(408) 996-1010 (408) 974-2113
PAXTON, Nancy *Senior Director, Investor Relations* One Infinite Loop Cupertino, CA 95014 paxton1@apple.com	Tel: Fax:	(408) 974-5420 (408) 974-2113
SCHILLER , Philip W. *Senior Vice President, Worldwide Marketing* One Infinite Loop Cupertino, CA 95014	Tel: Fax:	(408) 996-1010 (408) 974-2483
SEWELL, Bruce *Senior Vice President and General Counsel* One Infinite Loop Cupertino, CA 95014	Tel: Fax:	(408) 996-1010 (408) 974-2483
SMITH, Denise Young *Vice President, Worldwide Human Resources* One Infinite Loop Cupertino, CA 95014	Tel: Fax:	(408) 996-1010 (408) 974-2483

Applied Biosystems

See listing on page 175 under Celara Genomics

Applied Energetics, Inc.

Formerly known as Ionatron, Inc. A weapon systems producer.
www.appliedenergetics.com
Employees: 25
Ticker: OTC: AERG
SIC: 3812
Industry/ies: Defense/Homeland Security; Government-Related

Chairman of the Board LISTER, Mark J.	Tel: Fax:	(520) 628-7415 (520) 917-3098
President and Principal Executive Officer HAYDEN, Joseph C.	Tel: Fax:	(520) 628-7415 (520) 917-3098
Main Headquarters Mailing: 4585 S. Palo Verde Rd. Suite 405	Tel: Fax:	(520) 917-3061 (520) 917-3098

Tucson, AZ 85714	TF:	(888) 278-0094

Public Affairs and Related Activities Personnel

At Headquarters

MCGRATH, Kevin *Contact, Investor Relations*	Tel: Fax:	(520) 628-7415 (520) 917-3098
WOMBLE, Alan M. *Vice President, Business Development* awomble@appliedenergetics.com	Tel: Fax:	(520) 628-7415 (520) 917-3098

Applied Industrial Technologies

Formerly known as Bearings, Inc., An industrial distributors of bearings, power transmission components, hydraulic components and systems, pneumatic components and systems, industrial rubber products, linear components, tools, safety products, general maintenance and a variety of material handling products.
www.applied.com
Annual Revenues: $2.56 billion
Employees: 5,635
Ticker: NYSE: AIT
SIC: 3562; 5063; 5085; 3561; 5080
NAICS: 332991; 333911
Industry/ies: Machinery/Equipment

Chairman of the Board WALLACE, Peter C.	Tel: Fax:	(216) 426-4000 (216) 426-4845
President and Chief Executive Officer SCHRIMSHER, Neil A.	Tel: Fax:	(216) 426-4000 (216) 426-4845
Main Headquarters Mailing: One Applied Plaza Cleveland, OH 44115	Tel: Fax: TF:	(216) 426-4000 (216) 426-4845 (877) 279-2799

Corporate Foundations and Giving Programs

Applied Industrial Technologies Contributions Program One Applied Plaza Cleveland, OH 44115	Tel: Fax:	(216) 426-4000 (216) 426-4000

Public Affairs and Related Activities Personnel

At Headquarters

ARMOLD, Thomas E. *Vice President, Sales*	Tel: Fax:	(216) 426-4000 (216) 426-4845
BAUER, Fred D. *Vice President, General Counsel and Secretary*	Tel: Fax:	(216) 426-4000 (216) 426-4845
EISELE, Mark O. *Vice President, Chief Financial Officer and Treasurer* meisele@applied.com	Tel: Fax:	(216) 426-4345 (216) 426-4845
KHO, Julie *Manager, Public Relations* jkho@applied.com	Tel: Fax:	(216) 426-4483 (216) 426-4845
LORING, Kurt W. *Vice President and Chief Human Resources Officer*	Tel: Fax:	(216) 426-4000 (216) 426-4845

Applied Materials, Inc.

A supplier of nanomanufacturing technology systems and services to the global semiconductor industry and other businesses.
www.appliedmaterials.com
Annual Revenues: $9.33 billion
Employees: 14,000
Ticker: NASDAQ: AMAT
SIC: 3559; 3674
NAICS: 334413
Industry/ies: Science; Scientific Research
Legislative Issues: BUD; CPT; ENG; IMM; SCI; TAX; TRD

Executive Chairman of the Board SPLINTER, Michael R.	Tel: Fax:	(408) 727-5555 (408) 748-9943
President and Chief Executive Officer DICKERSON, Gary E.	Tel: Fax:	(408) 727-5555 (408) 748-9943

Main Headquarters
Mailing: 3050 Bowers Ave.
        P.O. Box 58039
        Santa Clara, CA 95054-3299
	Tel:
	Fax:
		(408) 727-5555
		(408) 748-9943

Washington Office
Mailing: 1400 I St. NW
        Suite 540
        Washington, DC 20005
	Tel:	(202) 347-2753

Corporate Foundations and Giving Programs

Applied Materials Foundation 3050 Bowers Ave. P.O. Box 58039 Santa Clara, CA 95054-3299	Tel: Fax:	(408) 727-5555 (408) 748-9943

Public Affairs and Related Activities Personnel

At Headquarters

BOLANO, Madonna | Tel: (408) 727-5555
Group Vice President Human Resources | Fax: (408) 748-9943

DUNCAN, Connie | Tel: (408) 563-6209
Senior Manager, Public Relations | Fax: (408) 986-2855
connie_duncan@appliedmaterials.com

HALLIDAY, Bob | Tel: (408) 727-5555
Senior Vice President and Chief Financial Officer | Fax: (408) 748-9943

LARKINS , Thomas F. | Tel: (408) 727-5555
Senior Vice President, General Counsel and Corporate | Fax: (408) 748-9943
Secretary

VERA, Patricia Zepeda | Tel: (408) 563-8160
Manager, Social Media | Fax: (408) 986-7115
patricia_zepeda_vera@appliedmaterials.com

WIEGERT, Amaya | Tel: (408) 235-4795
Contact, Media Relations | Fax: (408) 986-7115
amaya_wiegert@appliedmaterials.com

At Washington Office

DABBS, Michael | Tel: (202) 638-4434
Director, Government Affairs

KANIA, John | Tel: (202) 638-4434
Director, Government Affairs
john_kania@amat.com
Registered Federal Lobbyist

MORIN, William G. | Tel: (202) 638-4434
Senior Director, Government Affairs
kirk.pessner@millerpoliticallaw.com
Registered Federal Lobbyist

At Other Offices

MILLER, Russell H.
Attorney & Agent for Filer
20 Park Rd., Suite E
Burlingame, CA 94010

Applied Measurement Professionals/ National Board for Respiratory Care

Provides certification organizations, government agencies, professional associations and private industry with innovative assessment and management solutions.
www.goamp.com
Industry/ies: Medicine/Health Care/Mental Health

President and Chief Executive Officer | Tel: (913) 895-4600
SMITH, Gary A. | Fax: (913) 895-4650

Main Headquarters
Mailing: 18000 W. 105th St. | Tel: (913) 895-4600
Olathe, KS 66061 | Fax: (913) 895-4650

Public Affairs and Related Activities Personnel

At Headquarters

DELK, Wade | Tel: (202) 253-7862
Director, Governmental Affairs | Fax: (913) 895-4650

FLANAGAN, CAE, CMP, Michael P. | Tel: (913) 895-4600
Association Manager | Fax: (913) 895-4650

GALLAGHER, Patrick | Tel: (913) 895-4600
Vice President , Sales and Marketing | Fax: (913) 895-4650

HERMANSEN, CPA, Scott M. | Tel: (913) 895-4600
Chief Financial Officer | Fax: (913) 895-4650

TINKLER, Lori M. | Tel: (913) 895-4600
Chief Operating Officer and Executive Vice President | Fax: (913) 895-4650

Appriss

Provider of criminal data information to law enforcement officials.
www.appriss.com
Annual Revenues: $11.20 million
Employees: 200
SIC: 8082
Industry/ies: Law Enforcement/Security

Chairman of the Board | Tel: (502) 561-8463
COBB, Douglas | Fax: (502) 561-1825

Co-Founder and Chief Executive Officer | Tel: (502) 561-8463
DAVIS, Michael | Fax: (502) 561-1825
mdavis@appriss.com

Main Headquarters
Mailing: 10401 Linn Stn. Rd. | Tel: (502) 561-8463
Louisville, KY 40223 | Fax: (502) 561-1825
| TF: (866) 277-7477

Political Action Committees
Appriss Inc. PAC
FEC ID: C00391532
Contact: Ted I. Williams CPA
10401 Linn Station Rd. | Tel: (502) 561-8463
Louisville, KY 40223 | Fax: (502) 561-1825

Contributions to Candidates: $2,500 (2015-2016)
Republicans: $2,500

Public Affairs and Related Activities Personnel

At Headquarters

DOUCETTE, Larissa | Tel: (847) 391-4405
Manager, Communications | Fax: (502) 561-1825
custserv@nabp.net

HOLTGRAVE, Bob | Tel: (502) 561-8463
Vice President, Government Sales | Fax: (502) 561-1825

SIMPSON, Rick | Tel: (502) 561-8463
Chief Financial Officer | Fax: (502) 561-1825

WILLIAMS, CPA, Ted I. | Tel: (502) 561-8463
PAC Treasurer | Fax: (502) 561-1825
twilliams@appriss.com

Appvion
See listing on page 72 under Apvion, Inc.

Apria Healthcare Group

A home medical equipment supplier.
www.apria.com
Annual Revenues: $2.08 billion
Employees: 12,000
Ticker: NASDAQ TRACE: AHG.GD
SIC: 8082
Industry/ies: Medicine/Health Care/Mental Health; Pharmaceutical Industry
Legislative Issues: MMM

Chairman of the Board | Tel: (949) 639-2000
FIGUEROA, John | Fax: (949) 587-9363

Chief Executive Officer | Tel: (949) 639-2000
STARCK, Dan | Fax: (949) 587-9363

Main Headquarters
Mailing: 26220 Enterprise Ct. | Tel: (949) 639-2000
Lake Forest, CA 92630 | Fax: (949) 587-9363
| TF: (800) 260-8808

Political Action Committees
Apria Healthcare Inc. PAC
FEC ID: C00240218
Contact: Raoul Smyth
26220 Enterprise Ct. | Tel: (949) 639-2000
Lake Forest, CA 92630 | Fax: (949) 587-9363

Contributions to Candidates: $158,000 (2015-2016)
Democrats: $76,000; Republicans: $82,000

Principal Recipients

SENATE
COCHRAN, THAD (REP-MS)

Public Affairs and Related Activities Personnel

At Headquarters

GETSON, Lisa M. | Tel: (949) 639-2000
Executive Vice President, Government Relations and | Fax: (949) 587-9363
Corporate Compliance

HOLCOMBE, Robert S. | Tel: (949) 639-2000
Executive Vice President, General Counsel and Secretary | Fax: (949) 587-9363

MORRIS, Debra L. | Tel: (949) 639-2000
Executive Vice President, Chief Financial Officer | Fax: (949) 587-9363

ROGERS-BOWERS, Kimberlie | Tel: (949) 639-2018
Federal Lobbyist | Fax: (949) 587-9363
Kimberlie.Rogers-Bowers@apria.com
Registered Federal Lobbyist

SCALLY, Celina M. | Tel: (949) 639-2000
Senior Vice President, Human Resources | Fax: (949) 587-9363

SMYTH, Raoul | Tel: (949) 639-2000
Senior Vice President | Fax: (949) 587-9363
raoul_smyth@apria.com

AptarGroup, Inc.

A manufacturer of personal care and household products.
www.aptar.com
Annual Revenues: $2.31 billion
Employees: 13,000
Ticker: NYSE: ATR
SIC: 3089
Industry/ies: Personal Care/Hygiene

Chairman of the Board | Tel: (815) 477-0424
HARRIS, King W. | Fax: (815) 477-0101

President and Chief Executive Officer | Tel: (815) 477-0424
HAGGE, Stephen I | Fax: (815) 477-0481

Main Headquarters

Mailing:	475 W. Terra Cotta	Tel:	(815) 477-0424
	Suite E	Fax:	(815) 477-0481
	Crystal Lake, IL 60014-9695		

Public Affairs and Related Activities Personnel

At Headquarters

DELLAMARIA, Matt	Tel:	(815) 477-0424
Vice President, Investor Relations	Fax:	(815) 477-0481
KUHN, Robert W.	Tel:	(815) 477-0424
Executive Vice President, Chief Financial Officer and Secretary	Fax:	(815) 477-0481
SAINT-LEGER, Ursula	Tel:	(815) 477-0424
Vice President, Human Resources	Fax:	(815) 477-0481

Apvion, Inc.

A producer of carbonless, thermal, coated free sheet and specialty coated papers.
www.appletonideas.com
Employees: 1,600
SIC: 2670
NAICS: 322121
Industry/ies: Paper And Wood Products Industry
Legislative Issues: HCR; TRD

Chairman of the Board	Tel:	(920) 734-9841
MURPHY, Terry M.	Fax:	(920) 991-7365

Chief Executive Officer	Tel:	(920) 734-9841
GILLIGAN, Kevin M.	Fax:	(920) 991-7365

Main Headquarters

Mailing:	825 E. Wisconsin Ave.	Tel:	(920) 734-9841
	P.O. Box 359	Fax:	(920) 991-7365
	Appleton, WI 54912-0359		

Corporate Foundations and Giving Programs

Apvion Contributions Program
825 E. Wisconsin Ave.   Tel: (920) 734-9841
P.O. Box 359
Appleton, WI 54912-0359

Public Affairs and Related Activities Personnel

At Headquarters

FERREE, Thomas J.	Tel:	(920) 734-9841
Senior Vice President, Finance and Chief Financial Officer	Fax:	(920) 991-7365
FLETCHER, Jeffrey J.	Tel:	(920) 734-9841
Vice President and Controller	Fax:	(920) 991-7365
GOODWIN, Ted E.	Tel:	(920) 734-9841
Vice President, Thermal Research and Development	Fax:	(920) 991-7365
VAN DEN BRANDT, Bill	Tel:	(920) 991-8613
Senior Manager, Corporate Communications	Fax:	(920) 991-7365
bvandenbrandt@appvion.com		
VAN STRATEN, Tami L.	Tel:	(920) 734-9841
Vice President, Secretary and General Counsel	Fax:	(920) 991-7365

APX, Inc.

APX facilitates transactions and information trading for the power and environmental markets.
www.apx.com
Employees: 100
Industry/ies: Computer/Technology

Chairman of the Board and Chief Executive Officer	Tel:	(408) 517-2100
STORMS, Brian M.	Fax:	(408) 517-2985

Main Headquarters

Mailing:	111 River St.	Tel:	(408) 899-3344
	Suite 1204		
	Hoboken, NJ 07030		

Public Affairs and Related Activities Personnel

At Other Offices

GALLEGOS, Cris	Tel:	(408) 517-2100
Sales and Sr. Account Manager	Fax:	(408) 517-2985
224 Airport Pkwy., Suite 600		
San Jose, CA 95110		
GRAHAM, Katherine	Tel:	(408) 517-2100
Managing Director and Chief Operating Officer	Fax:	(408) 517-2985
224 Airport Pkwy., Suite 600		
San Jose, CA 95110		

Aqua America, Inc.

A water and wastewater utility holding company.
www.aquaamerica.com
Annual Revenues: $787.56 million
Employees: 1,617
Ticker: NYSE: WTR
SIC: 4941
Industry/ies: Natural Resources; Utilities

Chairman of the Board, President and Chief Executive Officer	Tel:	(610) 527-8000
DEBENEDICTIS, Nicholas	Fax:	(610) 525-7658

Main Headquarters

Mailing:	762 W. Lancaster Ave.	Tel:	(610) 527-8000
	Bryn Mawr, PA 19010-3489	Fax:	(610) 525-7658
		TF:	(877) 987-2782

Political Action Committees

Aqua America Inc. H20 PAC
FEC ID: C00340455
Contact: Karen Carlson
762 W. Lancaster Ave.   Tel: (610) 527-8000
Bryn Mawr, PA 19010   Fax: (610) 525-7658

  Contributions to Candidates: $49,000 (2015-2016)
  Democrats: $8,000; Republicans: $41,000

Corporate Foundations and Giving Programs

Aqua America Contributions Program
762 W. Lancaster Ave.
Bryn Mawr, PA 19010-3489

Public Affairs and Related Activities Personnel

At Headquarters

ALSTON, Donna	Tel:	(610) 645-1095
Director, Communications	Fax:	(610) 525-7658
dpalston@aquaamerica.com		
BROUSSARD, Susan	Tel:	(610) 527-8000
Vice President, Human Resources	Fax:	(610) 525-7658
CARLSON, Karen	Tel:	(610) 527-8000
PAC Treasurer	Fax:	(610) 525-7658
DINGERDISSEN, Brian	Tel:	(610) 645-1191
Director, Investor Relations	Fax:	(610) 525-7658
investorrelations@aquaamerica.com		
FRANKLIN, Christopher H.	Tel:	(610) 527-8000
Executive Vice President and President and Chief Operating Officer, Regulated Operations	Fax:	(610) 525-7658
LUNING, Christopher P.	Tel:	(610) 527-8000
Senior Vice President, General Counsel and Secretary	Fax:	(610) 525-7658
RUBIN, Robert A.	Tel:	(610) 527-8000
Senior Vice President, Chief Accounting Officer and Controller	Fax:	(610) 525-7658
SMELTZER, David P.	Tel:	(610) 527-8000
Executive Vice President and Chief Financial Officer	Fax:	(610) 525-7658
STAHL, Esq., Roy H.	Tel:	(610) 527-8000
Of Counsel	Fax:	(610) 525-7658

ARAMARK Corporation

Provider of service management to institutions and the public in such areas as child care and education, food and support services, health care, and uniform and career apparel.
www.aramark.com
Annual Revenues: $14.32 billion
Employees: 167,500
Ticker: NASDAQ: ARMK
SIC: 4213; 5199; 5812; 5947; 5963
Industry/ies: Food And Beverage Industry; Travel/Tourism/Lodging
Legislative Issues: FOO; GOV; HCR; LBR; TAX; TOU

Chairman, President and Chief Executive Officer	Tel:	(215) 238-3000
FOSS, Eric J.	Fax:	(215) 238-3333

Main Headquarters

Mailing:	1101 Market St.	Tel:	(215) 238-3000
	Philadelphia, PA 19107	Fax:	(215) 238-3333
		TF:	(800) 999-8989

Political Action Committees

Aramark Services, Inc. PAC (Aramark PAC)
FEC ID: C00157677
Contact: Stephen R. Reynolds
1101 Market St.   Tel: (215) 238-3000
Philadelphia, PA 19107   Fax: (215) 238-3333

Corporate Foundations and Giving Programs

ARAMARK Corporate Contributions Program
Contact: Donna Irvin
1101 Market St.   Tel: (215) 238-3000
Philadelphia, PA 19107   Fax: (215) 238-3333

Public Affairs and Related Activities Personnel

At Headquarters

BAILEY, Ian	Tel:	(215) 409-7287
Vice President, Investor Relations	Fax:	(215) 238-3333
bailey-ian@aramark.com		
BRAMLAGE, Jr., Steve	Tel:	(215) 238-3000
Executive Vice President and Chief Financial Officer	Fax:	(215) 238-3333
FREIREICH, David	Tel:	(215) 238-4078
Contact, Media Relations	Fax:	(215) 238-3333

Freireich-david@aramark.com

IRVIN, Donna
Executive Director, Corporate Contributions

Tel:	(215) 238-3271
Fax:	(215) 238-3333

MCKEE, Lynn B.
Executive Vice President, Human Resources

Tel:	(215) 238-3000
Fax:	(215) 238-3333

REYNOLDS, Stephen R.
Executive Vice President, General Counsel, Secretary and PAC Treasurer

Tel:	(215) 238-3000
Fax:	(215) 238-3333

Arbitron, Inc.

Arbitron is a marketing research firm serving the media (radio, television, cable and out of-home) as well as advertisers and advertising agencies in the United States.
www.arbitron.com
Annual Revenues: $455.25 million
Employees: 1,292
Ticker: NYSE: ARB
SIC: 8700
Industry/ies: Communications; Media/Mass Communication

Chairman of the Board
GUARASCIO, Philip

Tel:	(410) 312-8000
Fax:	(410) 312-8650

Former President and Chief Executive Officer
KERR, William T.

Tel:	(410) 312-8000
Fax:	(410) 312-8650

Main Headquarters
Mailing: 9705 Patuxent Woods Dr.
Columbia, MD 21046

Tel:	(410) 312-8000
Fax:	(410) 312-8650
TF:	(800) 638-7091

Corporate Foundations and Giving Programs

Arbitron Corporate Contributions Program
Contact: Kim Myers
9705 Patuxent Woods Dr.
Columbia, MD 21046

Tel:	(410) 312-8000
Fax:	(410) 312-8607

Public Affairs and Related Activities Personnel

At Headquarters

MYERS, Kim
Senior Media Manager
Kim.Myers@arbitron.com

Tel:	(410) 312-8500
Fax:	(410) 312-8650

PIERZ, Henry
PAC Contact

Tel:	(410) 312-8000
Fax:	(410) 312-8650

SMITH, Timothy
Executive Vice President, Business Development and Strategy, Chief Legal Officer
tim.smith@arbitron.com

Tel:	(410) 312-8000
Fax:	(410) 312-8650

Arbor Vita Corporation

Biopharmaceutical company focused on the discovery, development and commercialization of novel drugs and diagnostics disease through PDZ proteins.
www.arborvita.com
Annual Revenues: $1.90 million
Industry/ies: Pharmaceutical Industry

Chairman of the Board
TRIMBLE, Charles

Tel:	(408) 585-3900
Fax:	(408) 585-3901

Founder and Chief Executive Officer
LU, MD, Peter S.
PETER.LU@ARBORVITA.COM

Tel:	(408) 585-3900
Fax:	(408) 585-3901

Main Headquarters
Mailing: 48371 Fremont Blvd.
Suite 101
Fremont, CA 94538

Tel:	(408) 585-3900
Fax:	(408) 585-3901

Public Affairs and Related Activities Personnel

At Headquarters

BANNISTER, Debra C.
Contact, Media Relations
debra.bannister@arborvita.com

Tel:	(530) 676-8001
Fax:	(408) 585-3901

FINUCANE, Ann
Manager, Human Resources
ann.finucane@arborvita.com

Tel:	(408) 585-3900
Fax:	(408) 585-3901

JACKSON, Justin
Contact, Media
jjackson@burnsmc.com

Tel:	(408) 585-3900
Fax:	(408) 585-3901

PETRAUSKENE, PhD, Olga
Director, Product Development, Marketing, and Business Development Operations

Tel:	(408) 585-3900
Fax:	(408) 585-3901

ArborGen

Provides research, development and commercialization of genetic solutions that improve forest sustainability and productivity.
www.arborgen.com
Employees: 200
Ticker: NASDAQ: ARBR
SIC: 0800

Industry/ies: Forestry

President and Chief Executive Officer
BAUM, Andrew

Tel:	(843) 851-4129
Fax:	(843) 851-4595

Main Headquarters
Mailing: 2011 Broadbank Ct.
Ridgeville, SC 29472

Tel:	(843) 851-4129
Fax:	(843) 851-4595

Corporate Foundations and Giving Programs

ArborGen Contribution Program
P.O. Box 840001
Summerville, SC 29483-4129

Tel:	(843) 851-4129
Fax:	(843) 832-2164

Public Affairs and Related Activities Personnel

At Headquarters

PAIT, John
Vice President, Sales, Marketing and Product Development

Tel:	(843) 851-4129
Fax:	(843) 851-4595

RADAK, John
Chief Financial Officer

Tel:	(843) 851-4129
Fax:	(843) 851-4595

At Other Offices

HOOD, Nancy M.
Director, Communications and Public Affairs
P.O. Box 840001
Summerville, SC 29483-4129

Tel:	(843) 851-5077
Fax:	(843) 832-2164

OWENS, Cathy L.
Manager, Communications
P.O. Box 840001
Summerville, SC 29483-4129
clowens@arborgen.com

Tel:	(843) 851-4143
Fax:	(843) 832-2164

PEARSON, Leslie
Director, Regulatory Affairs
P.O. Box 840001
Summerville, SC 29483-4129

Tel:	(843) 851-4129
Fax:	(843) 832-2164

QUINN, Cathy O.
Manager, Communications and Public Affairs
P.O. Box 840001
Summerville, SC 29483-4129
coquinn@arborgen.com

Tel:	(843) 851-4129
Fax:	(843) 851-4595

Arcadian Networks, Inc.

Arcadian Networks designs and delivers wireless broadband communication systems to the energy sector.
www.arcadianetworks.com
Industry/ies: Computer/Technology

Main Headquarters
Mailing: 400 Columbus Ave.
Suite 210E
Valhalla, NY 10595

Tel:	(914) 579-6300

Arcadis U.S., Inc.

An int'l company that provides consultancy, design, engineering and management services in the fields of infrastructure, water, environment and buildings.
www.arcadis-us.com
Industry/ies: Communications; Construction/Construction Materials; Environment And Conservation; Telecommunications/Internet/Cable
Legislative Issues: CAW; NAT; TRA

Chief Executive Officer
JASTREM , John

Tel:	(720) 344-3866

Main Headquarters
Mailing: 630 Plaza Dr.
Suite 200
Highlands Ranch, CO 80129

Tel:	(720) 344-3866

Public Affairs and Related Activities Personnel

At Headquarters

LANE, Patrick
Senior Consultant Traffic and Transportation
plane@arcadis-us.com

Tel:	(720) 344-3866

BOUTEN, Jan
Chief Financial Officer

Tel:	(720) 344-3866

COMSTOCK , Billie
Technical Publications
bcomstock@arcadis-us.com

Tel:	(720) 344-3866

DAY , Joy
Marketing and Proposal Specialist
jday@arcadis-us.com

Tel:	(720) 344-3866

EBERT , Joachim
Chief Operating Officer

Tel:	(720) 344-3866

TOBIASINSKY , Catherine
Chief Sales Officer

Tel:	(720) 344-3866

ARCCA, Inc.

A forensic engineering and litigation consulting firm.
www.arcca.com
Industry/ies: Defense/Homeland Security; Engineering/Mathematics;
Government-Related; Science; Scientific Research

Chief Executive Officer　　　　Tel:　(215) 598-9750
CANTOR, Alan　　　　　　　　　　Fax:　(215) 598-9751
acantor@arcca.com

Main Headquarters
Mailing:　2288 Second St. Pike　　Tel:　(215) 598-9750
　　　　　P.O. Box 78　　　　　　　Fax:　(215) 598-9751
　　　　　Penns Park, PA 18943-0078　TF:　(800) 700-4944

Public Affairs and Related Activities Personnel

At Headquarters

JENNINGS, Tom　　　　　　　　　Tel:　(866) 617-7690
Vice President & Principal　　　　Fax:　(215) 598-9751
tjennings@arcca.com

WHITMAN, Gary　　　　　　　　　Tel:　(215) 598-9750
Vice President, Research and Development　Fax:　(215) 598-9751
gwhitman@arcca.com

ArcelorMittal USA LLC

A subsidiary of Mittal Steel NV of The Netherlands. With the acquisition of International Steel Group, the company is merged with Mittal Steel's only US operation, Ispat Inland. This operation was renamed Mittal Steel USA. In March 2007, Mittal Steel USA opened a government affairs office in Washington, DC. Renamed Arcelor Mittal USA Inc.
www.arcelormittal.com
Employees: 20,000
Industry/ies: Metals
Legislative Issues: BAN; BUD; DEF; ENG; ENV; TAX; TRA; TRD

Chairman of the Board　　　　　Tel:　(312) 899-3400
MITTAL, Lakshimi N.　　　　　　　Fax:　(312) 899-3798

Executive Vice President and Chief Executive Officer　Tel:　(312) 899-3400
RIPPEY, Michael　　　　　　　　　Fax:　(312) 899-3798

Main Headquarters
Mailing:　One S. Dearborn St.　　　Tel:　(312) 899-3440
　　　　　13th Floor　　　　　　　 Fax:　(312) 899-3798
　　　　　Chicago, IL 60603-2302

Washington Office
Mailing:　1808 Eye St. NW　　　　 Tel:　(202) 835-3310
　　　　　Fifth Floor　　　　　　　 Fax:　(202) 835-3309
　　　　　Washington, DC 20006

Political Action Committees
ArcelorMittal USA Good Government Committee PAC
FEC ID: C00104109
Contact: Thomas A. McCue
1808 I St. NW　　　　　　　　　　Tel:　(202) 631-8576
Fifth Floor
Washington, DC 20006

　Contributions to Candidates: $53,500 (2015-2016)
　Democrats: $15,500; Republicans: $38,000

Corporate Foundations and Giving Programs
ArcelorMittal Foundation
Contact: William Steers
3210 Watling St.　　　　　　　　　Tel:　(312) 899-3400
E. Chicago, IL 46312

Public Affairs and Related Activities Personnel

At Headquarters

AGARWAL, Bhikam　　　　　　　　Tel:　(312) 899-3400
Executive Vice President and Head, Finance　Fax:　(312) 899-3798

BLAFFART, Henri　　　　　　　　　Tel:　(312) 899-3500
Executive Vice President, Head, Human Resources and　Fax:　(312) 899-3798
Corporate Services

CLARKE, David　　　　　　　　　　Tel:　(312) 899-3400
Executive Vice President and Head, Strategy　Fax:　(312) 899-3798

FAIRCLOUGH, Daniel　　　　　　　Tel:　(312) 899-3817
Vice President, Head, Investor Relations　Fax:　(312) 899-3798
daniel.fairclough@arcelormittal.com

STEERS, William　　　　　　　　　Tel:　(312) 899-3817
General Manager, Communications and Corporate　Fax:　(312) 899-3798
Responsibility
william.steers@mittalsteel.com

WEIGH, Paul　　　　　　　　　　　Tel:　(312) 899-3440
Head, media relations　　　　　　 Fax:　(312) 899-3798

At Washington Office

BURTSCHI, Mark R.　　　　　　　　Tel:　(202) 835-3310
Director, Government Relations　　　Fax:　(202) 835-3309
mark.burtschi@arcelormittal.com
Registered Federal Lobbyist

DOWER, Thomas R.　　　　　　　　Tel:　(202) 835-3310

Senior Director, Government Relations　Fax:　(202) 835-3309
Registered Federal Lobbyist

FORD, Amber　　　　　　　　　　　Tel:　(202) 835-3310
Representative, Government Relations　Fax:　(202) 835-3309
Registered Federal Lobbyist

MCCUE, Thomas A.　　　　　　　　Tel:　(312) 899-3927
Vice President, Investor Relations and PAC Treasurer　Fax:　(202) 835-3309
thomas.mccue@mittalsteel.com

MILLER, Marcia E.　　　　　　　　　Tel:　(202) 835-3310
Vice President, Government Relations　Fax:　(202) 835-3309
marcia.miller@arcelormittal.com
Registered Federal Lobbyist

Arch Chemicals, Inc.

Producer of microelectronic water and performance chemicals. Lonza Group Ltd. has aquired Arch Chemicals, Inc.
www.archchemicals.com
Annual Revenues: $1.38 billion
Employees: 2,900
Ticker: NYSE: ARJ
SIC: 2800
Industry/ies: Chemicals & Chemical Industry
Legislative Issues: CHM; TAR; TAX

Chairman of the Board, President and Chief Executive Officer　Tel:　(203) 229-2900
CAMPBELL, Michael E.　　　　　　Fax:　(203) 229-3652

Main Headquarters
Mailing:　P.O. Box 5204　　　　　　Tel:　(203) 229-2900
　　　　　501 Merritt Seven　　　　 Fax:　(203) 229-3652
　　　　　Norwalk, CT 06856-5204

Corporate Foundations and Giving Programs
Arch Chemicals Contributions Program
501 Merritt Seven　　　　　　　　 Tel:　(203) 229-2900
P.O. Box 5204　　　　　　　　　　Fax:　(203) 229-3652
Norwalk, CT 06856-5204

Public Affairs and Related Activities Personnel

At Headquarters

BODE, John R.　　　　　　　　　　Tel:　(203) 229-2900
PAC Contact　　　　　　　　　　Fax:　(203) 229-3652

BUSH, W Paul　　　　　　　　　　Tel:　(203) 229-2900
Vice President, PAC Contact and Treasurer　Fax:　(203) 229-3213

FAFORD, Mark E.　　　　　　　　　Tel:　(203) 229-2654
Vice President, Investor Relations and Communications　Fax:　(203) 229-3507
mefaford@archchemicals.com

GIULIANO, Steven C.　　　　　　　Tel:　(203) 229-2900
Senior Vice President and Chief Financial Officer　Fax:　(203) 229-3652

O'CONNOR, Sarah A.　　　　　　　Tel:　(203) 229-2900
Senior Vice President, Strategic Development and Chief Legal　Fax:　(203) 229-3652
Officer

SANDONATO, W. Anthony　　　　　Tel:　(203) 229-2900
Corporate Vice President, Human Resources　Fax:　(203) 229-3652

WALTER, Dale N.　　　　　　　　　Tel:　(203) 229-3033
Media Contact　　　　　　　　　 Fax:　(203) 229-3213
dnwalter@archchemicals.com

Arch Coal, Inc.

A coal producer headquarterd in St. Louis, Missouri.
www.archcoal.com
Annual Revenues: $2.81 billion
Employees: 5,000
Ticker: NYSE: ACI
SIC: 1221; 2999; 5052
NAICS: 324199; 212111; 42152
Industry/ies: Energy/Electricity; Mining Industry; Natural Resources
Legislative Issues: BUD; CAW; ENG; IND; LBR; NAT; TAX; TRD; WAS

President and Chief Executive Officer　Tel:　(314) 994-2700
EAVES, John W.　　　　　　　　　　Fax:　(314) 994-2878

Main Headquarters
Mailing:　One City Place Dr.　　　　Tel:　(314) 994-2700
　　　　　Suite 300　　　　　　　　Fax:　(314) 994-2878
　　　　　St. Louis, MO 63141　　　TF:　(800) 238-7398

Washington Office
Mailing:　2600 Virginia Ave. NW　　Tel:　(202) 333-5265
　　　　　Suite 505
　　　　　Washington, DC 20037

Political Action Committees
Arch Coal Inc. PAC (ARCHPAC)
FEC ID: C00167668
Contact: Deck S. Slone
Cityplace One　　　　　　　　　　Fax:　(314) 994-2878
St. Louis, MO 63141

Contributions to Candidates: $240,675 (2015-2016)
Democrats: $15,500; Republicans: $223,175; Other: $2,000

Principal Recipients

HOUSE

ROGERS, HAROLD DALLAS (REP-KY)

Corporate Foundations and Giving Programs

Arch Coal Foundation
One CityPlace Dr.   Tel: (314) 994-2700
Suite 300   Fax: (314) 994-2878
St. Louis, MO 63141

Public Affairs and Related Activities Personnel

At Headquarters

BESTEN, C. Henry   Tel: (314) 994-2700
Senior Vice President, Strategic Development   Fax: (314) 994-2878

COCHRAN, Kenneth D.   Tel: (314) 994-2700
Senior Vice President, Operations   Fax: (314) 994-2878

DREXLER, John T.   Tel: (314) 994-2700
Senior Vice President and Chief Financial Officer   Fax: (314) 994-2878

GILJUM , Matt C.   Tel: (314) 994-2700
Vice President, Finance and Treasurer   Fax: (314) 994-2878

JONES, Robert G.   Tel: (314) 994-2700
Senior Vice President, Law, General Counsel and Secretary   Fax: (314) 994-2878

KELLEY, Allen R.   Tel: (314) 994-2700
Vice President, Human Resources   Fax: (314) 994-2878

LANG, Paul A.   Tel: (314) 994-2700
President and Chief Operating Officer   Fax: (314) 994-2878

LORSON, John W.   Tel: (314) 994-2700
Vice President and Chief Accounting Officer   Fax: (314) 994-2878

SLONE, Deck S.   Tel: (314) 994-2700
Senior Vice President, Strategy and Public Affairs and PAC   Fax: (314) 994-2878
Treasurer

ZIEGLER, Jr., John   Tel: (314) 994-2700
Chief Commercial Officer   Fax: (314) 994-2878

At Washington Office

ALTMEYER, Thomas   Tel: (202) 333-5265
Vice President, Federal Government Affairs
taltmeyer@archcoal.com
Registered Federal Lobbyist

Archer Daniels Midland Company

Agri-business engaged in milling and other processing of food and feed products. ADM produces the food ingredients, animal feeds and feed ingredients, bio-fuels and other products that manufacturers around the world use to provide wholesome food and a better life to millions of people around the globe.
www.adm.com
Annual Revenues: $64.58 billion
Employees: 32,300
Ticker: NYSE: ADM
SIC: 2075; 2070
NAICS: 311222
Industry/ies: Agriculture/Agronomy; Food And Beverage Industry
Legislative Issues: AGR; ENG; ENV; FIN; FOO; TAX; TRA; TRD

Chairman of the Board and Chief Executive Officer   Tel: (312) 634-8100
LUCIANO, Juan R.   Fax: (217) 424-6196

Main Headquarters
Mailing: 77 W. Wacker Dr.   Tel: (312) 634-8100
           Suite 4600   Fax: (217) 424-6196
           Chicago, IL 60601   TF: (866) 637-5843

Washington Office
Mailing: 1212 New York Ave. NW   Tel: (202) 572-0580
           Suite 1275   Fax: (202) 572-0588
           Washington, DC 20005

Political Action Committees
Archer Daniels Midland Company-ADM PAC
FEC ID: C00093963
Contact: Christopher T. Riley
P.O. Box 1470
Decatur, IL 62525

Contributions to Candidates: $176,567 (2015-2016)
Democrats: $39,000; Republicans: $137,567

Principal Recipients

HOUSE

DAVIS, RODNEY L (REP-IL)
SHIMKUS, JOHN M (REP-IL)

Corporate Foundations and Giving Programs

Archer Daniels Midland Company Contributions Program
4666 Faires Pkwy.   Tel: (217) 424-5200
Decatur, IL 62526

Public Affairs and Related Activities Personnel

At Headquarters

BARD, Ben   Tel: (312) 634-8100
Vice President and Global Chief Compliance Officer   Fax: (217) 424-6196

D'AMBROSE, Michael   Tel: (312) 634-8100
Senior Vice President and Chief Human Resources Officer   Fax: (217) 424-6196

FINDLAY, D. Cameron   Tel: (312) 634-8100
Senior Vice President, General Counsel and Secretary   Fax: (217) 424-6196

LASTRA, Domingo A.   Tel: (312) 634-8100
Corporate Officer   Fax: (217) 424-6196

PODESTA, Victoria A.   Tel: (312) 634-8100
Vice President and Chief Communications Officer   Fax: (217) 424-6196

RILEY, Christopher T.   Tel: (217) 424-5200
PAC Treasurer   Fax: (217) 424-6196
chris.riley@adm.com

ROIG, Ismael   Tel: (312) 634-8100
Senior Vice President, Chief Strategy Officer   Fax: (217) 424-6196

YOUNG, Ray G.   Tel: (217) 451-7231
Executive Vice President and Chief Financial Officer   Fax: (217) 424-6196

At Washington Office

DIERLAM, Bryan   Tel: (202) 572-0580
Registered Federal Lobbyist   Fax: (202) 572-0588

HERZFELD, Shannon S.   Tel: (202) 572-0580
Vice President, Government Relations   Fax: (202) 572-0588
shannon_herzfeld@admworld.com
Registered Federal Lobbyist

HOLZMAN, Beth M.   Tel: (202) 572-0580
Federal Lobbyist   Fax: (202) 572-0588
beth.holzman@adm.com
Registered Federal Lobbyist

REED, Anthony   Tel: (202) 572-0580
Federal Lobbyist   Fax: (202) 572-0588
Anthony.Reed@adm.com
Registered Federal Lobbyist

Archinoetics

A high tech company that focuses on engineering and scientific research and development.
archinoetics.com
Annual Revenues: $3.80 million
Employees: 32
Industry/ies: Electricity & Electronics; Electronics; Energy/Electricity

Chief Executive Officer and Owner   Tel: (808) 585-7439
DOWNS, III, PhD, J. Hunter   Fax: (888) 279-0289
hunter@archinoetics.com

Main Headquarters
Mailing: 2800 Woodlawn Dr.   Tel: (808) 585-7439
           Suite 263   Fax: (888) 279-0289
           Honolulu, HI 96822

Public Affairs and Related Activities Personnel

At Headquarters

COOPER, CPA, MBA, Joe   Tel: (808) 585-7439
Chief Financial Officer   Fax: (888) 279-0289

DOWNS, PhD, Traci H.   Tel: (808) 585-7439
Chief Operating Officer   Fax: (888) 279-0289
traci@archinoetics.com

Arctic Slope Regional Corporation

A for-profit corporation.
www.asrc.com
Annual Revenues: $2.30 billion
Employees: 9,000
Industry/ies: Mining Industry; Natural Resources
Legislative Issues: ECN; ENG; ENV; GOV; IND; LBR; NAT; TAX; TEC

Chairman of the Board and Executive Vice President,   Tel: (907) 852-8633
Shareholder Community Programs   Fax: (907) 852-5733
PATKOTAK, Crawford

President and Chief Executive Officer   Tel: (907) 852-8633
ROCK, Sr., Rex A.   Fax: (907) 852-5733

Main Headquarters
Mailing: P.O. Box 129   Tel: (907) 852-8633
           Barrow, AK 99723   Fax: (907) 852-5733
                                          TF: (800) 770-2772

Political Action Committees
Arctic Slope Regional Corporation PAC (ASRC PAC)
FEC ID: C00511899
Contact: Rodney Butch Lincoln
3900 C St.   Tel: (907) 339-6000
Suite 801   Fax: (907) 339-6028
Anchorage, AK 99503-5963

Corporate Foundations and Giving Programs

Arctic Education Foundation
Contact: Teresa Imm
P.O. Box 129   Tel: (907) 852-9455
Barrow, AK 99723   Fax: (907) 852-2774

Public Affairs and Related Activities Personnel

At Headquarters

AKPIK, Debbie	Tel:	(907) 852-8633
Executive Vice President, Human Resources	Fax:	(907) 852-5733
GASPERLIN, Mary	Tel:	(907) 852-8633
Director, Communications	Fax:	(907) 852-5733
mgasperlin@asrc.com		
KEMPPEL, Denali	Tel:	(907) 852-8633
Executive Vice President, General Counsel	Fax:	(907) 852-5733
dkemppel@asrc.com		
KOZAK, Charlie	Tel:	(907) 852-8633
Executive Vice President and Chief Financial Officer	Fax:	(907) 852-5733
STINE, Cheryl	Tel:	(907) 852-8633
Executive Vice President, Chief Administrative Officer	Fax:	(907) 852-5733
SWEENEY, Tara Katuk	Tel:	(907) 852-8633
Executive Vice President, External Affairs	Fax:	(907) 852-5733
tsweeney@asrc.com		
WALDRON, Matt	Tel:	(907) 852-8633
Interim General Counsel	Fax:	(907) 852-5733

At Other Offices

HARDT, Ty	Tel:	(907) 339-6888
Director, Communications	Fax:	(907) 339-6028
3900 C St., Suite 801		
Anchorage, AK 99503-5963		
thardt@asrc.com		
IMM, Teresa	Tel:	(907) 339-6000
Director, Resource Development and Contact, Foundation	Fax:	(907) 339-6028
3900 C St., Suite 801		
Anchorage, AK 99503-5963		
timm@asrc.com		
LINCOLN, Rodney Butch	Tel:	(907) 339-6000
Executive Vice President, Chief Operating Officer and PAC	Fax:	(907) 339-6028
Treasurer		
3900 C St., Suite 801		
Anchorage, AK 99503-5963		

Arcturis

An architectural, planning and interior design firm.
www.arcturis.com
Annual Revenues: $9 million
Employees: 100
Industry/ies: Architecture And Design

President and Chief Executive Officer   Tel: (314) 206-7100
O'BRYAN, Traci   Fax: (314) 231-9801

Main Headquarters
Mailing: 720 Olive St.   Tel: (314) 206-7100
     Suite 200   Fax: (314) 231-9801
     St. Louis, MO 63101

Corporate Foundations and Giving Programs

Arcturis Contributions Program
720 Olive   Tel: (314) 206-7100
Suite 200   Fax: (314) 231-9801
St. Louis, MO 63101

Public Affairs and Related Activities Personnel

At Headquarters

JANUARY, Mary Kay	Tel:	(314) 206-7100
Chief Financial Officer	Fax:	(314) 231-9801
KEIL, Julie	Tel:	(314) 206-7100
Principal	Fax:	(314) 231-9801

Ardent Health Services, Inc.

A health care services provider.
www.ardenthealth.com
Annual Revenues: $683.80 million
Employees: 12,138
SIC: 8062
Industry/ies: Medicine/Health Care/Mental Health
Legislative Issues: MMM

President and Chief Executive Officer   Tel: (615) 296-3000
VANDEWATER, David T.   Fax: (615) 296-6351

Main Headquarters
Mailing: One Burton Hills Blvd.   Tel: (615) 296-3000
     Suite 250   Fax: (615) 296-6351
     Nashville, TN 37215

Political Action Committees

AHS Medical Holdings LLC Good Government Fund PAC
FEC ID: C00390963
Contact: Ashley M. Crabtree
One Burton Hills Blvd.   Tel: (615) 296-3000
Suite 250   Fax: (615) 296-6351
Nashville, TN 37215

     Contributions to Candidates: $15,000 (2015-2016)
     Democrats: $8,500; Republicans: $6,500

Public Affairs and Related Activities Personnel

At Headquarters

ADAMS, Clint	Tel:	(615) 296-3000
Chief Financial Officer	Fax:	(615) 296-6351
CRABTREE, Ashley M.	Tel:	(615) 296-3000
PAC Treasurer	Fax:	(615) 296-6351
GWINN, Kevin	Tel:	(615) 296-3146
Vice President, Communications	Fax:	(615) 296-6351
kevin.gwinn@ardenthealth.com		
HEMPHILL, Neil	Tel:	(615) 296-3000
Senior Vice President, Human Resources and Administration	Fax:	(615) 296-6351
neil.hemphill@ardenthealth.com		
PETROVICH, Steve	Tel:	(615) 296-3000
Senior Vice President and General Counsel	Fax:	(615) 296-6351

AREVA, Inc.

AREVA Inc. is the U.S. subsidiary of AREVA NP, headquartered in Paris, France. Engaged in supply and service of the nuclear fuel cycle.
www.us.areva.com
Employees: 5,000
Industry/ies: Energy/Electricity
Legislative Issues: BUD; DEF; ENG

President   Tel: (301) 841-1694
PERNOT, Laurence   Fax: (301) 841-1611
laurence.pernot@areva.com

Main Headquarters
Mailing: 4800 Hampden Ln   Tel: (301) 841-1600
     Suite 1100   Fax: (301) 841-1611
     Bethesda, MD 20814

Washington Office
Mailing: 1155 F St. NW
     Suite 800
     Washington, DC 20004

Political Action Committees

AREVA Inc. PAC
FEC ID: C00395285
Contact: Katherine Williams
1155 F St. NW   Tel: (301) 652-9197
Suite 800   Fax: (301) 652-5690
Washington, DC 20004

     Contributions to Candidates: $59,750 (2015-2016)
     Democrats: $13,750; Republicans: $46,000

Corporate Foundations and Giving Programs

AREVA Way
4800 Hampden Ln.
Suite 1100
Bethesda, MD 20814

Public Affairs and Related Activities Personnel

At Headquarters

ALEXANDER, Hoppes	Tel:	(301) 841-1600
Federal Lobbyist	Fax:	(301) 841-1611
Registered Federal Lobbyist		
DORSEY, Bryan	Tel:	(301) 841-1600
Vice President, Key Accounts	Fax:	(301) 841-1611
HARRISON, Laurie	Tel:	(301) 841-1600
Vice President, Government Affairs	Fax:	(301) 841-1611
laurie.harrison@areva.com		
Registered Federal Lobbyist		
HAYWARD , Mary Alice	Tel:	(301) 841-1600
Director, Congressional Affairs	Fax:	(301) 841-1611
HOPPES, Alec	Tel:	(301) 841-1600
Director, Congressional Affairs	Fax:	(301) 841-1611
Registered Federal Lobbyist		
MCMURPHY, Michael	Tel:	(301) 841-1600
Executive Vice President, Government Affairs and	Fax:	(301) 841-1611
Institutional Relations		
YU, James	Tel:	(301) 652-9197
Federal Lobbyist	Fax:	(301) 652-5691

At Washington Office

WILLIAMS, Katherine

PAC Treasurer

Argon ST, Inc.

Argon ST designs, develops, and produces systems and sensors for the command, control, communications, computers, combat systems, intelligence, surveillance, and reconnaissance (C5ISR) markets including SIGINT (Signals Intelligence), ESM (Electronic Support Measures), EW (Electronic Warfare), IO (Information Operations), imaging, and acoustic systems serving domestic and international markets. Acquired Radix Technologies, Inc.
www.argonst.com
Annual Revenues: $366.08 million
Employees: 1,100
Ticker: NASDAQ: STST
SIC: 3829
Industry/ies: Electricity & Electronics; Electronics; Energy/Electricity

Chairman of the Board and Chief Executive Officer
COLLINS, PhD, Dr. Terry L.
Tel: (703) 322-0881
Fax: (703) 322-0885

Main Headquarters
Mailing: 12701 Fair Lakes Cir.
            Suite 800
            Fairfax, VA 22033
Tel: (703) 322-0881
Fax: (703) 322-0885

Public Affairs and Related Activities Personnel

At Headquarters

DALY, III, Joseph T.
PAC Treasurer
Tel: (703) 322-0881
Fax: (703) 322-0885

YEAMANS, Becky
Senior Manager, International Communications
rebecca.c.yeamans@boeing.com
Tel: (703) 828-2250
Fax: (703) 322-0885

Argus International, Inc.

An apparel manufacturer.
www.aviationresearch.com
Industry/ies: Apparel/Textiles Industry

President and Chief Executive Officer
MOEGGENBERG, Joe
jjm@argus.aero
Tel: (513) 852-1010
Fax: (513) 672-0012

Main Headquarters
Mailing: 4240 Airport Rd.
            Suite 300
            Cincinnati, OH 45226
Tel: (513) 852-1010
Fax: (513) 672-0012
TF: (800) 361-2216

Public Affairs and Related Activities Personnel

At Headquarters

BAUMANN, Melissa
Contact, Human Resources and Contract Administrator
mbaumann@argus.aero
Tel: (513) 852-1022
Fax: (513) 672-0012

FELDMANN, Sally
Marketing Manager
sally.feldmann@argus.aero
Tel: (513) 852-1010
Fax: (513) 672-0012

MASON, Shirley
Senior Vice President, Market Intelligence
smason@argus.aero
Tel: (513) 852-1015
Fax: (513) 672-0012

PARRAN, David
Controller
david.parran@argus.aero
Tel: (513) 852-1013
Fax: (513) 672-0012

Argus Media Inc.

Argus Media Ltd (formerly known as Petroleum Argus Ltd) is a provider of price information, market data and business intelligence for the global petroleum, natural gas, electricity, emissions, biofuels, biomass, LPG and coal industries.
www.argusmedia.com
Employees: 500
Industry/ies: Communications; Media/Mass Communication
Legislative Issues: CDT; ENG; FIN; MIA

Chief Executive Officer
CRAIK, Euan
euan.craik@argusmedia.com
Tel: (202) 775-0240
Fax: (202) 872-8045

Main Headquarters
Mailing: 1012 14th St. NW
            Suite 1500
            Washington, DC 20005
Tel: (202) 775-0240
Fax: (202) 872-8045

Public Affairs and Related Activities Personnel

At Headquarters

FEER, Jason
Chief Operational Officer
jason.feer@argusmedia.com
Tel: (202) 775-0240
Fax: (202) 872-8045

GENTRY, Caroline
Manager, Business Development
caroline.gentry@argusmedia.com
Tel: (202) 775-0240
Fax: (202) 872-8045

MASSEY, Daniel
President and Head of Business Development
Tel: (202) 775-0240
Fax: (202) 872-8045

Registered Federal Lobbyist

MASSEY, Dan
President
daniel.massey@argusmedia.com
Registered Federal Lobbyist
Tel: (202) 775-0240
Fax: (202) 872-8045

WADDINGTON, Mark
Global Compliance Officer
Registered Federal Lobbyist
Tel: (202) 775-0240
Fax: (202) 872-8045

At Other Offices

ELKINS, Catherine
General Counsel
2929 Allen Pkwy., Suite 700
Houston, TX 77019
Tel: (716) 968-0000
Fax: (713) 622-2991

HOSCH, Rachel
Manager, Finance
2929 Allen Pkwy., Suite 700
Houston, TX 77019
Tel: (716) 968-0000
Fax: (713) 622-2991

ArianeSpace, Inc.

Headquartered in Evry, France, Arianespace Inc. promotes the marketing and sales of Ariane satellite launch services.
www.arianespace.com
Industry/ies: Aerospace/Aviation; Transportation
Legislative Issues: AER; BUD; DEF; GOV

Chairman of the Board and Chief Executive Officer
ISRAEL, Stephane
Tel: (202) 628-3936
Fax: (202) 628-3949

Main Headquarters
Mailing: 5335 Wisconsin Ave. NW
            Suite 520
            Washington, DC 20015
Tel: (202) 628-3936
Fax: (202) 628-3949

Public Affairs and Related Activities Personnel

At Headquarters

AARON, Lewis
Registered Federal Lobbyist
Tel: (202) 628-3936
Fax: (202) 628-3949

BRETON, Jacques
Senior Vice President, Sales and Customers
Tel: (202) 628-3936
Fax: (202) 628-3949

HUNDT, Thomas
Senior Vice President and Chief Financial Officer
Tel: (202) 628-3936
Fax: (202) 628-3949

LOWE, AAP, Aaron
Director, Media & Government Relations
aaron.lowe@aftermarket.org
Registered Federal Lobbyist
Tel: (202) 628-3936
Fax: (202) 628-3949

MOWRY, Clayton
President
Registered Federal Lobbyist
Tel: (202) 628-3936
Fax: (202) 628-3949

VEILLON, Isabelle
Vice President, Corporate Communication
Tel: (202) 628-3936
Fax: (202) 628-3949

ARINC, Inc.

The Information Management Services division of Rockwell Collins.
www.rockwellcollins.com
Annual Revenues: $1.08 billion
Employees: 2,000
SIC: 3728
Industry/ies: Aerospace/Aviation; Electricity & Electronics; Electronics; Energy/Electricity; Engineering/Mathematics; Transportation
Legislative Issues: AER; BAN; BUD; DEF; LBR; TAX

Main Headquarters
Mailing: 2551 Riva Rd.
            Annapolis, MD 21401-7435
Tel: (410) 266-4000
Fax: (410) 266-2020
TF: (800) 633-6882

Political Action Committees
Rockwell Collins Inc. Good Government Committee PAC
FEC ID: C00365684
Commonwealth Towers
1300 Wilson Blvd., Suite 200
Arlington, VA 22209
Tel: (703) 516-8228
Fax: (703) 516-8294

Contributions to Candidates: $109,500 (2015-2016)
Democrats: $23,000; Republicans: $84,500; Other: $2,000

Principal Recipients

HOUSE
HUNTER, DUNCAN D. (REP-CA)

Corporate Foundations and Giving Programs

ARINC Contributions Program
2551 Riva Rd.
Annapolis, MD 21401-7435
Tel: (410) 266-4000
Fax: (410) 266-1000

Rockwell Collins Charitable Corporation
Contact: Jenny Becker
400 Collins Rd. NE
Cedar Rapids, IA 52498
Tel: (319) 295-8122

Rockwell Collins Community Partnership Fund
Contact: Jenny Becker
400 Collins Rd. NE   Tel: (319) 295-8122
Cedar Rapids, IA 52498

Public Affairs and Related Activities Personnel

At Headquarters

MANIGOLD, Jr., Robert E.   Tel: (410) 266-4000
Vice President, Human Resources, Administration, Branding Fax: (410) 266-2020
and Corporate Communications

PETERSON, Timothy L.   Tel: (410) 266-4000
Senior Director, Government Relations   Fax: (410) 266-2020
tim.peterson@rockwellcollins.com
Registered Federal Lobbyist

ROSIA, Megan Rae   Tel: (410) 266-4000
Director, Government Relations, Washington Operations   Fax: (410) 266-2020
Registered Federal Lobbyist

STURGELL, Robert   Tel: (410) 266-4000
Senior Vice President, Washington Operations   Fax: (410) 266-2020
Registered Federal Lobbyist

SUSSMAN, Laurie   Tel: (410) 266-4000
laurie.sussman@rockwellcollins.com   Fax: (410) 266-2020

WAECHTER, Stephen L.   Tel: (410) 266-4000
Vice President, Business Operations and Chief Financial Fax: (410) 266-2020
Officer

WATKISS , Philip   Tel: (410) 266-4000
Director, Sales   Fax: (410) 266-2020

WELSH, Nancy   Tel: (410) 266-4652
Director, Communications   Fax: (410) 266-2020

The Arizona Electric Power Cooperative, Inc.

AEPCO owns and operates 600MW Apache generating station in AZ.
www.azgt.coop
Employees: 15
Industry/ies: Energy/Electricity; Utilities
Legislative Issues: NAT

Chief Executive Officer   Tel: (520) 586-5110
LEDGER, Patrick F.
pledger@ssw.coop

Main Headquarters
Mailing: P.O. Box 2165   Tel: (520) 586-5465
                Benson, AZ 85602

Public Affairs and Related Activities Personnel

At Headquarters

ALVES, Charles   Tel: (520) 586-5203
Senior Attorney & Compliance Officer
calves@ssw.coop

BRACKEEN, Tisha   Tel: (520) 586-5465
Member and Customer Services Liaison

OLDFATHER, Geoff   Tel: (520) 586-5465
Cooperative Communications & Public Relations Manager
goldfather@sww.coop

SCOTT, Pete   Tel: (520) 586-5319
Chief Financial Officer
pscott@ssw.coop

WALLACE, J. D.   Tel: (620) 586-5157
Cooperative Communications, Social Media & Marketing
Administrator
jdwallace@sww.coop

Arizona Public Service Company

A provider of energy.
www.aps.com
Annual Revenues: $3.24 billion
Employees: 7,000
SIC: 4931
Industry/ies: Energy/Electricity; Utilities

Chairman of the Board and Chief Executive Officer   Tel: (602) 371-7171
BRANDT, Donald   Fax: (602) 944-8208

Main Headquarters
Mailing: P.O. Box 2906   Tel: (602) 371-7171
                Phoenix, AZ 85062-2906   Fax: (602) 944-8208
                                                            TF: (800) 253-9405

Washington Office
Mailing: 801 Pennsylvania Ave. NW   Tel: (202) 293-2655
                Suite 214   Fax: (202) 293-2666
                Washington, DC 20004

Corporate Foundations and Giving Programs

APS Foundation
P.O. Box 2906

Phoenix, AZ 85062-2906

Public Affairs and Related Activities Personnel

At Headquarters

BEMENT, Bob   Tel: (602) 371-7171
Senior Vice President, Operations   Fax: (602) 944-8208

DANNER, Denise R.   Tel: (602) 371-7171
Vice President, Controller and Chief Accounting Officer   Fax: (602) 944-8208

FALCK, David P.   Tel: (602) 371-7171
Executive Vice President, General Counsel and Secretary   Fax: (602) 944-8208

GOMEZ, Barbara M.   Tel: (602) 371-7171
Vice President, Human Resources   Fax: (602) 944-8208

GOTFRIED, Steven   Tel: (602) 250-3040
Contact, External Communications   Fax: (602) 944-8208
Steven.Gotfried@APS.com

GULDNER, Jeffrey B.   Tel: (602) 371-7171
Senior Vice President, Public Policy   Fax: (602) 944-8208

GUZMAN , Chad   Tel: (602) 371-7171
Associate, Government Affairs   Fax: (602) 944-8208

HATFIELD, James R.   Tel: (602) 371-7171
Executive Vice President and Chief Financial Officer   Fax: (602) 944-8208

HATFIELD, John   Tel: (602) 371-7171
Vice President, Communications   Fax: (602) 944-8208
john.hatfield@aps.com

Arkansas Best Corporation

A diversified transportation holding company.
www.arcb.com
Annual Revenues: $2.15 billion
Employees: 10,000
Ticker: NASDAQ: ABFS
SIC: 4213
Industry/ies: Transportation
Legislative Issues: TAX; TRU

Chairman of the Board   Tel: (479) 785-6000
YOUNG, III, Robert A.   Fax: (479) 785-6004

President and Chief Executive Officer   Tel: (479) 785-6000
MCREYNOLDS, Judy R.   Fax: (479) 785-6004
jrmcreynolds@arkbest.com

Main Headquarters
Mailing: P.O. Box 10048   Tel: (479) 785-6000
                Ft. Smith, AR 72917-0048   Fax: (479) 785-6004

Political Action Committees
Arkansas Best Corporation PAC
FEC ID: C00193383
Contact: Michael R. Johns
3801 Old Greenwood Rd.   Tel: (479) 785-6000
P.O. Box 10048   Fax: (479) 785-6004
Ft. Smith, AR 72903

   Contributions to Candidates: $13,500 (2015-2016)
   Democrats: $4,500; Republicans: $9,000

Public Affairs and Related Activities Personnel

At Headquarters

ANDERSON, Dennis L.   Tel: (479) 785-6000
Vice President, Strategy   Fax: (479) 785-6004

COBB, David R.   Tel: (479) 785-6000
Vice President and Chief Financial Officer   Fax: (479) 785-6004

FIEWEGER, Kathy   Tel: (479) 785-6000
Vice President, Marketing and Corporate Communications, Fax: (479) 785-6004
Chief Marketing Officer

GATTIS, Erin K.   Tel: (479) 785-6000
Vice President, Human Resources   Fax: (479) 785-6004

HUMPHREY, R. David   Tel: (479) 785-6000
Vice President, Investor Relations and Corporate   Fax: (479) 785-6004
Communications
invrel@arkbest.com

NEWCITY, Michael E.   Tel: (479) 785-6000
Senior Vice President and Chief Information Officer   Fax: (479) 785-6004
mnewcity@arkbest.com

At Other Offices

JOHNS, Michael R.   Tel: (479) 785-6000
Vice President, General Counsel and Corporate Secretary and Fax: (479) 785-6004
PAC Treasurer
3801 Old Greenwood Rd.
Ft. Smith, AR 72903
mjohns@arkbest.com

Arkansas Blue Cross and Blue Shield

A health-care provider.
www.arkansasbluecross.com

Annual Revenues: $1.20 billion
Employees: 2,100
Industry/ies: Insurance Industry

Chairman of the Board and Director
SHOPTAW, Robert L.
Tel: (501) 378-2000
Fax: (501) 378-3258

President and Chief Executive Officer
WHITE, P. Mark
Tel: (501) 378-2000
Fax: (501) 378-3258

Main Headquarters
Mailing: 320 W. Capitol Ave., Suite 900
Little Rock, AR 72201-3556
Tel: (501) 378-2937
Fax: (501) 378-2855

Corporate Foundations and Giving Programs
Blue and You Foundation
Contact: Patrick Sullivan
320 W. Capitol
Suite 200
Little Rock, AR 72201
Tel: (501) 378-3300
Fax: (501) 378-2051

Public Affairs and Related Activities Personnel

At Other Offices

BAILEY, Jim
Senior Vice President and Chief Marketing Officer
P.O. Box 2181
Little Rock, AR 72203-2181
Tel: (501) 378-2010
Fax: (501) 378-3258

COOPER, Richard
Vice President, Human Resources, and Corporate Compliance Officer
P.O. Box 2181
Little Rock, AR 72203-2181
Tel: (501) 378-2000
Fax: (501) 378-3258

DILLARD, Gary
Senior Vice President, Financial Services, and Chief Financial Officer and Treasurer
P.O. Box 2181
Little Rock, AR 72203-2181
Tel: (501) 378-2000
Fax: (501) 378-3258

DOUGLASS, JD, Lee
Senior Vice President, Law and Government Relations, Corporate Secretary and Chief Legal Officer
P.O. Box 2181
Little Rock, AR 72203-2181
Tel: (501) 378-2000
Fax: (501) 378-3258

GREENWOOD, Max
Director, Governmental and Media Relations
P.O. Box 2181
Little Rock, AR 72203-2181
magreenwood@arkbluecross.com
Tel: (501) 378-2131
Fax: (501) 378-3258

KELLOGG, PhD, Calvin
Executive Vice President and Chief Strategy Officer
P.O. Box 2181
Little Rock, AR 72203-2181
Tel: (501) 378-2000
Fax: (501) 378-3258

Arkansas Capital Corporation Group (ACCG)
See listing on page 79 under Arkansas Capital Group

Arkansas Capital Group
Provides a mechanism for financing the state's transformation from an agricultural economy to an industrial economy. It is a privately held group of for-profit and non-profit corporations dedicated to improving the lives of Arkansans.
arcapital.com
Employees: 25
Industry/ies: Banking/Finance/Investments; Economics And Economic Development

Chairman and Acting Chief Executive Officer
DEACON, Rush
Tel: (501) 374-9247
Fax: (501) 374-9425

Main Headquarters
Mailing: 200 River Market Ave.
Suite 400
Little Rock, AR 72201
Tel: (501) 374-9247
Fax: (501) 374-9425
TF: (800) 216-7237

Corporate Foundations and Giving Programs
Arkansas Capital Group Contribution Program
200 River Market Ave.
Suite 400
Little Rock, AR 72201
Tel: (501) 374-9247
Fax: (501) 374-9425

Public Affairs and Related Activities Personnel

At Headquarters

CARSON, April
Contact Media
Tel: (501) 374-9247
Fax: (501) 374-9425

CLARK, Christa
Compliance Officer
cclark@arcapital.com
Tel: (501) 374-9247
Fax: (501) 374-9425

MOODY, Jamie
Director, Marketing
jmoody@arcapital.com
Tel: (501) 374-9247
Fax: (501) 374-9425

THOMAS, Sarah
Tel: (501) 374-9247

Media and Community Representative
WILSON, Judy
Manager, Finance
jwilson@arcapital.com
Fax: (501) 374-9425
Tel: (501) 374-9247
Fax: (501) 374-9425

Arkema, Inc.
A Diversified chemicals manufacturer.
www.arkema-inc.com
Employees: 2,400
SIC: 8880
Industry/ies: Chemicals & Chemical Industry
Legislative Issues: AGR; BUD; CAW; CHM; CPT; DEF; ENG; ENV; HOM; RRR; TAR; TAX; TRA; TRD

President and Chief Executive Officer
ROCHE, Bernard
Tel: (800) 331-7654
Fax: (215) 419-7413

Main Headquarters
Mailing: 900 First Ave.
King of Prussia, PA 19406
Tel: (610) 205-7000
Fax: (610) 878-6499
TF: (800) 225-7788

Corporate Foundations and Giving Programs
The Arkema Inc. Foundation
Contact: Diane Milici
2000 Market St.
Philadelphia, PA 19103
Fax: (215) 419-7591

Public Affairs and Related Activities Personnel

At Headquarters

BELL, Jim
Director, Communications Department
Tel: (610) 205-7293
Fax: (610) 878-6499

BLAZYNSKI, Larry
Federal Lobbyist
Registered Federal Lobbyist
Tel: (610) 205-7986
Fax: (215) 419-7413

DAVID, Kunz
Federal Lobbyist
Registered Federal Lobbyist
Tel: (610) 205-7000
Fax: (610) 878-6499

GIANGRASSO, Chris
Vice President, Human Resources and Communications
Tel: (610) 205-7000
Fax: (610) 878-6499

HAMEL, William
Senior Vice President and General Counsel
William.hamel@.arkema.com
Tel: (610) 205-7000
Fax: (610) 878-6499

KUNZ, David
Assistant General Counsel and Director
Registered Federal Lobbyist
Tel: (800) 331-7654
Fax: (215) 419-7413

MILICI, Diane
Executive Administrator
diane.milici@arkema.com
Tel: (610) 205-7000
Fax: (610) 878-6499

MUEHSAM, Monica
Paralegal
Tel: (610) 205-7000
Fax: (610) 878-6499

RITTER, Matthew
Federal Lobbyist
Registered Federal Lobbyist
Tel: (800) 331-7654
Fax: (215) 419-7413

ROBERTS, Daryl
Senior Director, Manufacturing and Regulatory Services
Registered Federal Lobbyist
Tel: (800) 331-7654
Fax: (215) 419-7413

SMITH , Marsha J.
Tel: (610) 205-7000
Fax: (610) 878-6499

At Other Offices

WERKEMA, Thomas
Vice President, Government Activities
2000 Market St.
Philadelphia, PA 19103
Tel: (215) 419-7615
Fax: (215) 419-5394

Armed Forces Benefit Association
Provides life insurance, health insurance and financial services to military personnel, federal employees, and civilians.
www.afba.com
Industry/ies: Defense/Homeland Security; Government-Related; Insurance Industry; Military/Veterans

Chairman of the Board and President
EBERHART, Ralph E."Ed"
Tel: (703) 549-4455
Fax: (703) 706-5961

President
BLANTON, USAF (Ret.), Lt. Gen. Charles C.
Tel: (703) 549-4455
Fax: (703) 706-5961

Main Headquarters
Mailing: 909 N. Washington St.
Alexandria, VA 22314
Tel: (703) 549-4455
Fax: (703) 706-5961
TF: (800) 776-2322

Public Affairs and Related Activities Personnel
At Headquarters
DELAHAN, Madeline
Chief Information Officer
Tel: (703) 549-4455
Fax: (703) 706-5961

SANDEFUR, Jeff   Tel: (703) 549-4455
Senior Vice President, Marketing   Fax: (703) 706-5961

Armstrong Holdings, Inc.

The parent company of Armstrong World Industries, Inc., a manufacturer and designer of floors, ceilings, and cabinets.
www.armstrong.com
Annual Revenues: $2.86 billion
Employees: 9,000
Ticker: NYSE: AWI
SIC: 2273; 2392; 2511; 2512; 2621; 3089
NAICS: 339994; 31411; 337121; 337122
Industry/ies: Furniture/Home Furnishings

Chief Executive Officer   Tel: (717) 397-0611
ESPE, Matthew J.   Fax: (717) 396-6133

Main Headquarters
Mailing: 2500 Columbia Ave.   Tel: (717) 397-0611
          Lancaster, PA 17603-4117   Fax: (717) 396-6133

Corporate Foundations and Giving Programs

Armstrong Foundation
2500 Columbia Ave.   Tel: (717) 397-0611
Lancaster, PA 17604   Fax: (717) 396-6133

Public Affairs and Related Activities Personnel

At Headquarters

HERSHEY, Mark   Tel: (717) 397-0611
General Counsel, Secretary and Chief Compliance Officer   Fax: (717) 396-6133
MAHershey@Armstrong.com

JOHNSON, Jennifer J.   Tel: (717) 397-0611
Corporate Communication   Fax: (717) 396-6133
jenniferjohnson@armstrong.com

MAIER, Don   Tel: (717) 397-0611
Senior Vice President, Operations

MANGAS, Thomas B.   Tel: (717) 397-0611
Senior Vice President and Chief Financial Officer   Fax: (717) 396-6133

OLSHAN, Kristy   Tel: (717) 397-0611
Investor Relations Manager

POOLE, Steve   Tel: (717) 397-0611
Vice President, Business Development and Corporate   Fax: (717) 396-6133
Communications

ROMANO, Ellen   Tel: (717) 397-0611
Senior Vice President, Human Resources   Fax: (717) 396-6133

SCHULZ, Dave   Tel: (717) 397-0611
Chief Financial Officer   Fax: (717) 396-6133

At Other Offices

MAIER, Don   Tel: (717) 396-6354
Senior Vice President, Operations
P.O. Box 3001
Lancaster, PA 17604

OLSHAN, Kristy   Tel: (717) 396-6354
Investor Relations Manager
P.O. Box 3001
Lancaster, PA 17604

WATERS, Thomas J.   Tel: (717) 396-6354
Vice President, Treasury, and Investor Relations
P.O. Box 3001
Lancaster, PA 17604
tjwaters@armstrong.com

Katharine Armstrong, Inc.

Governmental consulting, lobbying, public relations.
Industry/ies: Law/Law Firms

President   Tel: (512) 478-1003
ARMSTRONG, Katharine

Main Headquarters
Mailing: 807 Brazos St.   Tel: (512) 478-1003
          Suite 701
          Austin, TX 78701

Arotech Corporation

Products and Services for the Military and Security Markets.
www.arotech.com
Annual Revenues: $105.41 million
Employees: 531
Ticker: NASDAQ:ARTX
Industry/ies: Defense/Homeland Security; Government-Related; Law Enforcement/Security

Executive Chairman of the Board   Tel: (202) 438-0475
EHRLICH, Robert S.

President and Chief Executive Officer   Tel: (646) 415-8972
ESSES, Steven   Fax: (734) 761-5368

Main Headquarters
Mailing: 1229 Oak Valley Dr.   Tel: (646) 415-8972
          Ann Arbor, MI 48108   Fax: (734) 761-5368

Public Affairs and Related Activities Personnel

At Headquarters

COLE, Ray   Tel: (646) 415-8972
Registered Federal Lobbyist   Fax: (734) 761-5368

HAR-OZ, Yaakov   Tel: (646) 415-8972
Senior Vice President, General Counsel and Secretary   Fax: (734) 761-5368

PAUP, Thomas J.   Tel: (646) 415-8972
Senior Vice President, Finance and Chief Financial Officer   Fax: (734) 761-5368

At Other Offices

GRAHAM, Bill J.   Tel: (202) 438-0475
Vice President
7826 Royal Sydney Dr.
Gainesville, VA 20155

HALBERSTAM, Rivka   Tel: (202) 438-0475
7826 Royal Sydney Dr.
Gainesville, VA 20155

ARRIS Group, Inc.

ARRIS is a global communications technology company specializing in the design, engineering, and supply of broadband network services for residential and business subscribers around the world.
www.arrisi.com
Annual Revenues: $5.20 billion
Employees: 8,520
Ticker: NASDAQ: ARRS
SIC: 3663
Industry/ies: Computer/Technology

Chairman of the Board and Chief Executive Officer   Tel: (678) 473-2000
STANZIONE, Robert J.   Fax: (770) 622-8700

Main Headquarters
Mailing: 3871 Lakefield Dr.   Tel: (678) 473-2907
          Suwanee, GA 30024   Fax: (678) 473-8470

Public Affairs and Related Activities Personnel

At Headquarters

BREWSTER, Vicki   Tel: (678) 473-2907
Senior Vice President, Human Resources   Fax: (678) 473-8470

COPPOCK, Ronald M.   Tel: (678) 473-2907
President, International Sales and Global Marketing   Fax: (678) 473-8470

MACKEN, Patrick   Tel: (678) 473-2907
Senior Vice President, General Counsel and Secretary   Fax: (678) 473-8470

MARGOLIS, Lawrence A.   Tel: (673) 473-2000
Executive Vice President, Corporate Strategy and   Fax: (673) 473-8470
Administration
larry.margolis@arrisi.com

POTTS, David B.   Tel: (673) 473-2000
Executive Vice President, Chief Financial Officer and Chief   Fax: (673) 473-8470
Information Officer

PUCCINI, Bob   Tel: (720) 895-7787
Vice President, Investor Relations   Fax: (720) 895-7125
bob.puccini@arrisi.com

SWAN, Alex   Tel: (678) 473-8327
Lead, Events and Industry Relations   Fax: (770) 622-8700
alex.swan@arrisi.com

Arrow Electronics

A global provider of products, services, and solutions to industrial and commercial users of electronic components and computer products.
www.arrow.com
Annual Revenues: $22.69 billion
Employees: 17,000
Ticker: NYSE: ARW
SIC: 5065; 7373
NAICS: 421690; 541512
Industry/ies: Computer/Technology; Electricity & Electronics; Electronics; Energy/Electricity

Chairman of the Board, President and Chief Executive Officer   Tel: (631) 847-2000
LONG, Michael J.   Fax: (631) 847-2222

Main Headquarters
Mailing: 9201 E. Dry Creek Rd.   Tel: (303) 824-4000
          Centennial, CO 80112   Fax: (303) 824-4000

Corporate Foundations and Giving Programs

Arrow Electronics Inc. Corporate Contribution Program
50 Marcus Dr.   Tel: (631) 847-2000
Melville, NY 11747   Fax: (631) 847-2222

Public Affairs and Related Activities Personnel

At Headquarters

MAIO, Chris	Tel:	(303) 824-4000
Manager, Global Brand Management and Communications	Fax:	(303) 824-4000
cmaio@arrow.com		
MEGLING, Rita	Tel:	(303) 824-4000
Director, Supplier Marketing	Fax:	(303) 824-4000
rita.megling@nuhorizons.com		
TARPINIAN, Gregory	Tel:	(303) 824-4000
Senior Vice President, General Counsel and Secretary	Fax:	(303) 824-4000

At Other Offices

DOW, Tom	Tel:	(631) 396-5000
Vice President, Sales	Fax:	(631) 396-5050
7459 S. Lima St.		
Englewood, CO 80112-3879		
HOURIGAN, John H.	Tel:	(303) 824-4586
Vice President, Global Communications	Fax:	(631) 847-2222
7459 S. Lima St.		
Englewood, CO 80112-3879		
jhourigan@arrow.com		
MORRIS, M. Catherine	Tel:	(631) 847-2000
Senior Vice President and Chief Strategy Officer	Fax:	(631) 847-2222
7459 S. Lima St.		
Englewood, CO 80112-3879		
REILLY, Paul J.	Tel:	(631) 847-2000
Executive Vice President, Finance and Operations and Chief	Fax:	(631) 847-2222
Financial Officer		
7459 S. Lima St.		
Englewood, CO 80112-3879		
ZECH , Gretchen K.	Tel:	(631) 847-2000
Senior Vice President, Global Human Resources	Fax:	(631) 847-2222
7459 S. Lima St.		
Englewood, CO 80112-3879		

Arrowhead Group

A member of the Arrowhead Group. Provides insurance products nationwide.
www.arrowheadgrp.com
Annual Revenues: $90 million
Employees: 300
Industry/ies: Insurance Industry

Chief Executive Officer	Tel:	(619) 881-8600
WALKER, Chris L.		

Main Headquarters

Mailing:	701 B St.	Tel:	(619) 881-8600
	Suite 2100	Fax:	(619) 881-8694
	San Diego, CA 92101	TF:	(800) 669-1889

Corporate Foundations and Giving Programs

Arrowhead Group Contributions Program
701 B St.
Suite 2100
San Diego, CA 92101

Public Affairs and Related Activities Personnel

At Headquarters

BOUKER, Steve	Tel:	(619) 881-8600
Executive Vice President	Fax:	(619) 881-8694
BOYD, Steve	Tel:	(619) 881-8600
President and Chief Operating Officer	Fax:	(619) 881-8694
EAGLE, Christina	Tel:	(619) 881-8655
Vice President, Marketing and Communications	Fax:	(619) 881-8694
ceagle@arrowheadgrp.com		

Artel, Inc.

A telecom and information technology firm that provides network management, systems/ solutions integration, information assurance/ homeland security, and online government and commerce services and technologies.
www.artelinc.com
Annual Revenues: $21 million
Employees: 200
Industry/ies: Communications; Telecommunications/Internet/Cable

Main Headquarters

Mailing:	1893 Preston White Dr.	Tel:	(703) 620-1700
	Reston, VA 20191	Fax:	(703) 620-4262

Corporate Foundations and Giving Programs

Artel Contribution Programs
1893 Preston White Dr.
Reston, VA 20191

Public Affairs and Related Activities Personnel

At Headquarters

BERGER , Jackie	Tel:	(703) 620-1700

Vice President, Communications and Marketing	Fax:	(703) 620-4262
KADASI, Rosalind	Tel:	(703) 620-1700
Chief Financial Officer and Vice President, Administration	Fax:	(703) 620-4262
WHITMORE, David	Tel:	(703) 620-1700
Vice President, Human Resources	Fax:	(703) 620-4262

Arthur J. Gallagher & Company

The company delivers a full range of insurance and risk management products and services, including traditional and loss-sensitive coverages.
www.ajg.com
Annual Revenues: $5.37 billion
Employees: 21,537
Ticker: NYSE: AJG
SIC: 641112; 6411
NAICS: 51
Industry/ies: Insurance Industry
Legislative Issues: TAX

Chairman of the Board, President and Chief Executive Officer	Tel:	(630) 773-3800
GALLAGHER, Jr., Patrick	Fax:	(630) 285-4000

Main Headquarters

Mailing:	Two Pierce Pl.	Tel:	(630) 773-3800
	Itasca, IL 60143	Fax:	(630) 285-4000

Corporate Foundations and Giving Programs

Arthur J. Gallagher Foundation		
The Gallagher Center	Tel:	(630) 773-3800
Two Pierce Pl.		
Itasca, IL 60143		

Public Affairs and Related Activities Personnel

At Headquarters

AKIN, Marsha J.	Tel:	(630) 285-3501
Director, Investor Relations	Fax:	(630) 285-4000
marsha_akin@ajg.com		
BAY, Walter D.	Tel:	(630) 773-3800
Contact, General Counsel and Secretary	Fax:	(630) 285-4000
COLLINS, Linda	Tel:	(630) 285-4009
Vice President, Corporate Communications	Fax:	(630) 285-4000
linda_collins@ajg.com		
HOWELL, Douglas K.	Tel:	(630) 773-3800
Chief Financial Officer	Fax:	(630) 285-4000
PIETRUCHA, Susan E.	Tel:	(630) 773-3800
Chief Human Resources Officer	Fax:	(630) 285-4000
TALLO, Richard C.	Tel:	(630) 773-3800
Chief Marketing and Communications Officer	Fax:	(630) 285-4000

Arvesta Corporation

See listing on page 81 under Arysta LifeScience North America LLC

ArvinMeritor, Inc.

See listing on page 534 under Meritor, Inc.

Arysta LifeScience North America LLC

Arysta LifeScience is an agrochemical company which provides customer-driven products and service to crop protection customers, primarily in specialty crops and niche markets. In 2015, Arysta LifeScience was acquired by Platform Specialty Products Corporation.
www.arysta-na.com
Annual Revenues: $37.30 million
Employees: 200
Industry/ies: Chemicals & Chemical Industry

President and Chief Executive Officer	Tel:	(919) 678-4900
HEWITT, Wayne	Fax:	(415) 284-9884

Main Headquarters

Mailing:	15401 Weston Pkwy.	Tel:	(919) 678-4900
	Suite 150	Fax:	(901) 432-5021
	Cary, NC 27513-8640	TF:	(800) 642-7635

Corporate Foundations and Giving Programs

Arysta LifeScience North America, LLC Contributions Program
Contact: Linda Frerichs
15401 Weston Pkwy.
Suite 150
Cary, NC 27513-8640

Public Affairs and Related Activities Personnel

At Headquarters

ACREE, Charissa	Tel:	(502) 638-5981
Media Contact	Fax:	(901) 432-5021
cacree@perituspr.com		
FOULK, Ben	Tel:	(919) 678-4900
Head of Human Resources	Fax:	(901) 432-5021
FRERICHS, Linda	Tel:	(919) 678-4948
Manager, Global Communications	Fax:	(800) 358-7642
Linda.Frerichs@Arysta.com		

KOEPPL, Bryan	Tel:	(919) 678-4900
Chief Financial Officer	Fax:	(901) 432-5021
LENCE, Robert	Tel:	(919) 678-4900
General Counsel	Fax:	(901) 432-5021
PREZZI, Flavio E.	Tel:	(919) 678-4900
Chief Operating Officer	Fax:	(901) 432-5021

ASARCO

An integrated copper mining, smelting and refining company.
www.asarco.com
Employees: 2,600
Industry/ies: Mining Industry; Natural Resources
Legislative Issues: NAT

Main Headquarters

Mailing:	5285 E. Williams Cir.	Tel:	(520) 798-7749
	Suite 2000	Fax:	(520) 798-7780
	Tucson, AZ 85711		

Washington Office

Mailing:	2121 K. St. NW
	Suite 7000
	Washington, DC 20037

Political Action Committees

ASARCOPAC
FEC ID: C00034553
Contact: Emil A. Romagnoli
2121 K. St. NW
Suite 7000
Washington, DC 20037

Public Affairs and Related Activities Personnel

At Headquarters

ALDRICH, Thomas L.	Tel:	(520) 798-7749
Vice President, Environmental Affairs	Fax:	(520) 798-7780
BARRON, Oscar Gonzalez	Tel:	(520) 798-7749
Vice President, Chief Financial Officer	Fax:	(520) 798-7780
MCALLISTER, Douglas E.	Tel:	(520) 798-7749
Executive Vice President, General Counsel and Secretary	Fax:	(520) 798-7780
Registered Federal Lobbyist		
TREVINO, Agustin	Tel:	(520) 798-7749
General Manager, Human Resources	Fax:	(520) 798-7780
WATTS, Mike	Tel:	(520) 798-7749
Director, Purchasing	Fax:	(520) 798-7780

At Washington Office

ROMAGNOLI, Emil A.
PAC Treasurer

Asbury Automotive Group

An automotive retailer.
www.asburyauto.com
Annual Revenues: $6.60 billion
Employees: 8,600
Ticker: NYSE: ABG
SIC: 5500
Industry/ies: Automotive Industry; Transportation

President and Chief Executive Officer	Tel:	(770) 418-8200
MONAGHAN, Craig		
CMonaghan@asburyauto.com		

Main Headquarters

Mailing:	2905 Premiere Pkwy.	Tel:	(770) 418-8200
	Suite 300		
	Duluth, GA 30097		

Public Affairs and Related Activities Personnel

At Headquarters

COREY, Melissa	Tel:	(770) 418-8231
Manager, Public Relations and Communications		
mcorey@asburyauto.com		
DELOACH, Thomas	Tel:	(770) 418-8200
Director		
HULT, David W.	Tel:	(770) 418-8200
Executive Vice President and Chief Operating Officer		
JESUP, Barbara	Tel:	(770) 418-8200
Vice President Internal Audit and Risk		
KAROLIS, George C.	Tel:	(770) 418-8200
Vice President, Corporate Development and Real Estate		
gkarolis@asburyauto.com		
KEARNEY, Michael S.	Tel:	(770) 418-8200
Executive Vice President and Chief Operating Officer		
MARSH, Ryan	Tel:	(770) 418-8211
Vice President and Treasurer		

MCKENZIE, Renee	Tel:	(770) 418-8200
Vice President, Human Resources		
MULVOY, Sue	Tel:	(770) 418-8210
Executive Assistant to Senior Vice President and Chief Financial Officer		
ir@asburyauto.com		
PARHAM, Joe	Tel:	(770) 418-8200
Vice President and Chief Human Resources Officer		
PETTONI, Matt	Tel:	(770) 418-8200
Vice President and Treasurer		
STYLE, Keith	Tel:	(770) 418-8200
Senior Vice President and Chief Financial Officer		
VILLASANA, George A.	Tel:	(770) 418-8200
Vice President, General Counsel and Secretary		

Ascena Retail Group

See listing on page 184 under Charming Shoppes, Inc.

Ascena Retail Group, Inc.

A leading national specialty retailer of apparel for women and teen girls, operating, through its wholly-owned subsidiaries, the Dressbarn, Maurices, Justice, Lane Bryant and Catherines brands.
www.ascenaretail.com
Annual Revenues: $4.82 billion
Employees: 14,000
Ticker: NASDAQ:ASNA
SIC: 5600
Industry/ies: Retail/Wholesale; Retailers See Also Merchandising

Co-Founder and Non-Executive Chairman	Tel:	(551) 777-6700
JAFFE, Elliot S.		
Chief Executive Officer, President and Director	Tel:	(551) 777-6700
JAFFE, David R.		

Main Headquarters

Mailing:	933 MacArthur Blvd.	Tel:	(551) 777-6700
	Mahwah, NJ 07430		

Public Affairs and Related Activities Personnel

At Headquarters

GIAMMATTEO, Robb	Tel:	(551) 777-6700
Senior Vice President, Financial Planning and Investor Relations		
JAFFE, Roslyn S.	Tel:	(551) 777-6700
Co-Founder, Secretary, Treasurer and Director Emeritus		
LAPORTE, Ernest	Tel:	(551) 777-6700
Senior Vice President, Chief Accounting Officer		
SULLIVAN, John J.	Tel:	(551) 777-6700
Chief Operating Officer and Executive Vice President		
WEXLER, Gene	Tel:	(551) 777-6700
Senior Vice President, General Counsel		

Ascension Health

Ascension Health is a faith-based healthcare organization. It is a direct subsidiary of Ascension and operates a network of hospitals and related health facilities in the United States.
www.ascensionhealth.org
Annual Revenues: $1.8 billion
Employees: 150,000
Industry/ies: Medicine/Health Care/Mental Health
Legislative Issues: HCR; MMM

President and Chief Executive Officer	Tel:	(314) 733-8000
HENKEL, FACHE, Robert J.	Fax:	(314) 733-8013

Main Headquarters

Mailing:	101 South Hanley Rd., Suite 450	Tel:	(314) 733-8000
	St. Louis, MO 63105	Fax:	(314) 733-8013
		TF:	(877) 346-7284

Washington Office

Mailing:	111 K St. NE	Tel:	(202) 898-4680
	Ninth Floor	Fax:	(202) 628-1275
	Washington, DC 20002		

Corporate Foundations and Giving Programs

Congregation of St. Joseph		
4600 Edmundson Rd.	Tel:	(314) 733-8000
St. Louis, MO 63134		
Daughters of Charity National Health System (DCNHS)		
4600 Edmundson Rd.	Tel:	(314) 733-8000
St. Louis, MO 63134		
Sisters of St. Joseph of Carondelet		
4600 Edmundson Rd.	Tel:	(314) 733-8000
St. Louis, MO 63134		

Public Affairs and Related Activities Personnel

At Headquarters

ANDERSON, Rhonda C.
Senior Vice President and Chief Financial Officer
Tel: (314) 733-8000
Fax: (314) 733-8013

CARMAN, Kate
Executive Assistant
kate.carman@ascensionhealth.org
Tel: (314) 733-8000
Fax: (314) 733-8013

ENGLER, Eric S.
Senior Vice President and Chief Strategy Officer
Tel: (314) 733-8000
Fax: (314) 733-8013

LEIBOLD, Peter M.
Chief Advocacy Officer
Registered Federal Lobbyist
Tel: (314) 733-8000
Fax: (314) 733-8013

MARYLAND, Patricia A.
Chief Operating Officer
Tel: (314) 733-8000
Fax: (314) 733-8013

MCCOY, JD, Christine Kocot
Senior Vice President, Legal Services and General Counsel
Tel: (314) 733-8702
Fax: (314) 733-8013

RAGONE, Esq., Nick
Senior Vice President and Chief Communications Officer
Nick.Ragone@ascension.org
Tel: (314) 733-8941
Fax: (314) 733-8013

SHIELDS, JD, Juli
Vice President and Associate General Counsel
Tel: (314) 733-8000
Fax: (314) 733-8013

At Washington Office

COMMODORE, JD, Nicole
Senior Associate, Government Relations, Policy and Coalitions
Registered Federal Lobbyist
Tel: (202) 898-4680
Fax: (202) 628-1275

DUONG, Lee
Registered Federal Lobbyist
Tel: (202) 898-4680
Fax: (202) 628-1275

HAYES, Mark
Registered Federal Lobbyist
Tel: (202) 898-4680
Fax: (202) 628-1275

PAYNE, Mary Ella Ella
Senior Vice President, Policy & System Legislative Leadership
mepayne@ascensionhealth.org
Tel: (202) 898-4680
Fax: (202) 628-1275

VERES, Deborah
Federal Lobbyist
Registered Federal Lobbyist
Tel: (202) 898-4680
Fax: (202) 628-1275

ASET Corporation

Corporate security services. ASET has addressed corporate security concerns such as employee substance abuse, workplace violence, sabotage, product tampering, espionage, personal protection, sexual harassment, theft and fraud.
www.asetcorp.com
Annual Revenues: $5.10 million
Employees: 200
Industry/ies: Law Enforcement/Security

President and Chief Executive Officer
CARROLL, Charles R.
crcarroll@asetcorp.com
Tel: (937) 890-8881
Fax: (937) 890-2825

Main Headquarters
Mailing: One ASET Center
Dayton International Airport
Vandalia, OH 45377
Tel: (937) 890-8881
Fax: (937) 890-2825

Ash Grove Cement Company

A cement production and distribution company.
www.ashgrove.com
Employees: 2,600
Ticker: OTC: ASHG
SIC: 3241
NAICS: 32731
Industry/ies: Construction/Construction Materials
Legislative Issues: CAW; ENV; LBR; MAN; NAT; ROD; TAX; TRA

Chairman of the Board and Chief Executive Officer
SUNDERLAND, Charles T.
charlie.sunderland@ashgrove.com
Tel: (913) 451-8900
Fax: (913) 451-8324

Main Headquarters
Mailing: 11011 Cody St.
Overland Park, KS 66210
Tel: (913) 451-8900
Fax: (913) 451-8324
TF: (800) 545-1882

Political Action Committees
Ash Grove Cement PAC
FEC ID: C00102517
Contact: Kim R. Beachner
P.O. Box 25900
Overland Park, KS 66225

   Contributions to Candidates: $10,500 (2015-2016)
   Republicans: $10,500

Corporate Foundations and Giving Programs
Ash Grove Charitable Foundation
11011 Cody St.
Overland Park, KS 66210
Tel: (913) 451-8900
Fax: (913) 451-8324

Public Affairs and Related Activities Personnel

At Headquarters

CLARK, Jacqueline K.
Director, Communications and Public Affairs
Registered Federal Lobbyist
Tel: (913) 451-8900
Fax: (913) 451-8324

EZELL, David W.
Vice President, Human Resources
Tel: (913) 451-8900
Fax: (913) 451-8324

MEYER, David G.
Vice President and Chief Financial Officer
Tel: (913) 451-8900
Fax: (913) 451-8324

RYAN, Steve
Vice President, General Counsel and Secretary
Tel: (913) 451-8900
Fax: (913) 451-8324

VANCE, J. Randall
President and Chief Operating Officer
Tel: (913) 451-8900
Fax: (913) 451-8324

WELLS, George M.
Vice Chairman, Strategic Relationships
Tel: (913) 451-8900
Fax: (913) 451-8324

WOOD, Michael
Vice President, Sales
Tel: (913) 451-8900
Fax: (913) 451-8324

At Other Offices

BEACHNER, Kim R.
PAC Contact, Treasurer and West Division Controller
P.O. Box 25900
Overland Park, KS 66225
Tel: (913) 451-8900

Ashbritt Environmental Inc.

Operator of disaster recovery services, solid waste services, engineering services, and special environmental services.
www.ashbritt.com
Annual Revenues: $4.50 million
Employees: 40
Industry/ies: Environment And Conservation

Chief Executive Officer
PERKINS, Randal R.
Tel: (954) 725-6992
Fax: (954) 725-6991

Main Headquarters
Mailing: 565 E. Hillsboro Blvd.
Deerfield Beach, FL 33441
Tel: (954) 725-6992
Fax: (954) 725-6991
TF: (800) 244-5094

Corporate Foundations and Giving Programs

Ashbritt Environmental Inc. Contributions Program
Contact: Randal R. Perkins
480 S. Andrews Ave.
Suite 103
Pompano Beach, FL 33069-3538

Public Affairs and Related Activities Personnel

At Headquarters

JACKSON, Terry M.
Chief Marketing Officer
terry@ashbritt.com
Tel: (954) 725-6992
Fax: (954) 725-6991

NANCE, Rhyse
Director, Small Business Development
rhyse@ashbritt.com
Tel: (954) 545-3535
Fax: (954) 545-3585

NOBLE, John W.
Chief Operating Officer
Tel: (954) 725-6992
Fax: (954) 725-6991

RAY, Rob
Senior Vice President
rray@ashbritt.com
Tel: (954) 868-9502
Fax: (954) 545-3585

The Ashcroft Group, LLC

A consulting firm founded by former Attorney General John Ashcroft.
www.ashcroftgroupllc.com

Chairman
ASHCROFT, Hon. John D.
jashcroft@ashcroftgroupllc.com
Tel: (202) 942-0202
Fax: (202) 942-0216

Chief Executive Officer
AYRES, David T.
dayres@ashcroftgroupllc.com
Tel: (202) 942-0202
Fax: (202) 942-0216

Main Headquarters
Mailing: 950 N. Glebe Rd.
Suite 2400
Arlington, VA 22203
Tel: (703) 247-5454
Fax: (703) 247-5446

Public Affairs and Related Activities Personnel

At Headquarters

ALCORN, Tyler P.
Principal
Tel: (202) 942-0202
Fax: (202) 942-0216

BLUNT, Matt
Senior Advisor
mblunt@ashcroftgroupllc.com
Tel: (202) 942-0202
Fax: (202) 942-0216

BURLINGHAM, Britteny
Accounts Analyst
Tel: (703) 247-5454
Fax: (202) 942-0216

DAY, Lori Sharpe *Managing Partner* lday@ashcroftlawfirm.com	Tel: Fax:	(202) 942-0202 (202) 942-0216
NEDELKOFF, Richard *Federal Lobbyist*	Tel: Fax:	(202) 942-0202 (202) 942-0216
PROPST, Byron Edward *Federal Lobbyist*	Tel: Fax:	(202) 942-0202 (202) 942-0216
RATCLIFFE, John *Partner* jratcliffe@ashcroftlawfirm.com	Tel: Fax:	(202) 942-0202 (202) 942-0216
RICHMOND JOHNSON, Susan *Managing Principal*	Tel: Fax:	(202) 942-0202 (202) 942-0216
SCHAUDER, Andrew *Federal Lobbyist*	Tel: Fax:	(202) 942-0202 (202) 942-0216
SULLIVAN, Michael *Partner* msullivan@ashcroftlawfirm.com	Tel: Fax:	(202) 942-0202 (202) 942-0216
SUTTON, Johnny *Partner* jsutton@ashcroftlawfirm.com	Tel: Fax:	(202) 942-0202 (202) 942-0216
WEBB, Lauren *Controller* lwebb@ashcroftgroupllc.com	Tel: Fax:	(202) 942-0202 (202) 942-0216

Ashland Inc.

A chemical and transportation company. In 2008, Ashland acquired Hercules Inc.
www.ashland.com
Annual Revenues: $5.88 billion
Employees: 10,000
Ticker: NYSE: ASH
SIC: 5160
Industry/ies: Chemicals & Chemical Industry; Construction/Construction Materials; Energy/Electricity; Fuels See Coal, Gas, Oil, Petroleum; Natural Resources; Petroleum Industry
Legislative Issues: CHM; ENV; GOV; HCR; TAX

Chairman and Chief Executive Officer WULFSOHN, William A.	Tel: Fax:	(859) 815-3333 (859) 815-5053

Main Headquarters
Mailing:	50 E. River Center Blvd. P. O. Box 391 Covington, KY 41012-0391	Tel: Fax:	(859) 815-3333 (859) 815-5053

Political Action Committees
Ashland Inc. PAC for Employees (PACE)
FEC ID: C00075994
Contact: Mark S. Lindell
500 Hercules Rd.
Building 8145
Wilmington, DE 19808

> **Contributions to Candidates:** $37,500 (2015-2016)
> Democrats: $6,500; Republicans: $31,000

Public Affairs and Related Activities Personnel

At Headquarters
BONI, Eric N. *Vice President and Treasurer*	Tel: Fax:	(859) 815-3333 (859) 815-5053
ESLER, Susan B. *Vice President and Chief Human Resources and Communications Officer*	Tel: Fax:	(859) 815-3333 (859) 815-5053
GANZ, Peter *Senior Vice President, General Counsel, Secretary and and Chief Compliance Officer*	Tel: Fax:	(859) 815-3333 (859) 815-5053
HEITMAN, J. William *Vice President and Controller*	Tel: Fax:	(859) 815-3333 (859) 815-5053
JOY, John W. "Jack" *Vice President, Corporate Development*	Tel: Fax:	(859) 815-3333 (859) 815-5053
LOVE, Daryl K. *Manager Community Relations*	Tel: Fax:	(859) 815-3333 (859) 815-5053
RILEY, John *Director, Government Relations Registered Federal Lobbyist*	Tel: Fax:	(859) 815-3333 (859) 815-5053
SILVERMAN, PhD, Keith *Vice President, Environmental, Health and Safety, and Product Regulatory*	Tel: Fax:	(859) 815-3333 (859) 815-5053
THOMPSON, Jason *Director, Investor Relations*	Tel: Fax:	(859) 815-3527 (859) 815-5053
WILKINSON, Charles F. *Senior Corporate Counsel* cfwilkinson@ashland.com	Tel: Fax:	(859) 357-7510 (859) 815-5053
WILLIS, J. Kevin *Senior Vice President and Chief Financial Officer*	Tel: Fax:	(859) 815-3333 (859) 815-5053

At Other Offices
DUGAN, Katherine A.
Director, Accounting
500 Hercules Rd., Building 8145
Wilmington, DE 19808

LINDELL, Mark S.
PAC Treaurer
500 Hercules Rd., Building 8145
Wilmington, DE 19808

Ashland Oil
See listing on page 84 under Ashland Inc.

Ashta Chemicals, Inc.
Manufactures and markets chlorine, potassium hydroxide, and other basic chemicals.
www.ashtachemicals.com
Annual Revenues: $20.1 million
Employees: 90
SIC: 2812
NAICS: 325181
Industry/ies: Chemicals & Chemical Industry

Chairman of the Board, President, and Chief Executive Officer BAXTER, Reginald	Tel: Fax:	(440) 997-5221 (440) 992-0151

Main Headquarters
Mailing:	3509 Middle Rd. Ashtabula, OH 44004	Tel: Fax: TF:	(440) 997-5221 (440) 992-0151 (800) 344-8820

Political Action Committees
Ashta Chemicals Inc. PAC
FEC ID: C00335802
Contact: Thomas J. Adamo
3509 Middle Rd. Ashtabula, OH 44004	Tel: Fax:	(440) 997-5221 (440) 992-0151

> **Contributions to Candidates:** $2,700 (2015-2016)
> Republicans: $2,700

Corporate Foundations and Giving Programs
Ashta Chemicals Contributions Program
3509 Middle Rd. Ashtabula, OH 44004	Tel:	(440) 997-5221

Public Affairs and Related Activities Personnel

At Headquarters
ADAMO, Thomas J. *Vice President, Finance and Administration and Chief Financial Officer and PAC Treasurer*	Tel: Fax:	(440) 997-5221 (440) 992-0151

Aspect Energy, LLC
Aspect Holdings, LLC is a privately held independent exploration and energy investment company established in 1992 by Alex Cranberg. One major clean energy resource is natural gas, and approximately 80% of Aspect's current hydrocarbon production is natural gas.
www.aspectenergy.com
Annual Revenues: $14.70 million
Employees: 200
Industry/ies: Energy/Electricity

Chairman of the Board CRANBERG , Alex	Tel:	(303) 573-7011
President NEUGEBAUER, R. Todd	Tel:	(303) 573-7011

Main Headquarters
Mailing:	1775 Sherman Suite 2400 Denver, CO 80203	Tel:	(303) 573-7011

Corporate Foundations and Giving Programs
Alliance for CHOICE in Education 1775 Sherman Suite 2400 Denver, CO 80203	Tel:	(303) 573-7011

Foundation for Academic Innovation
1775 Sherman
Suite 2400
Denver, CO 80203

Public Affairs and Related Activities Personnel

At Headquarters
ERNYEY , Ibolya *Business Development Manager*	Tel:	(303) 573-7011
KURTENBACH, Richard *Vice President and Chief Accounting Officer*	Tel:	(303) 573-7011
MAYS, Lora *Vice President and General Counsel*	Tel:	(303) 573-7011

Asplundh Tree Expert Company

A vegetation management company.
www.asplundh.com
Annual Revenues: $2.62 billion
Employees: 30,000
SIC: 0782
Industry/ies: Horticulture And Landscaping

| **Chairman of the Board** | Tel: | (215) 784-4200 |
| ASPLUNDH, Christopher B. | Fax: | (215) 784-4493 |

| **Chief Executive Officer** | Tel: | (215) 784-4200 |
| ASPLUNDH, Scott M. | Fax: | (215) 784-4493 |

Main Headquarters
Mailing: 708 Blair Mill Rd.	Tel:	(215) 784-4200
Willow Grove, PA 19090	Fax:	(215) 784-4493
	TF:	(800) 248-8733

Political Action Committees
Asplundh Tree Expert Company PAC (ATE PAC)
FEC ID: C00177741
Contact: Joseph P. Dwyer
708 Blair Mill Rd.
| Willow Grove, PA 19090 | Tel: | (215) 784-4200 |
| | Fax: | (215) 784-4493 |

Contributions to Candidates: $110,000 (2015-2016)
Republicans: $110,000

Principal Recipients

SENATE
TOOMEY, PATRICK JOSEPH (REP-PA)

HOUSE
RYAN, PAUL D. (REP-WI)

Public Affairs and Related Activities Personnel

At Headquarters

CHIPMAN, Patricia	Tel:	(215) 784-4200
Manager, Corporate Communications	Fax:	(215) 784-4405
pchip@asplundh.com		

| DWYER, Joseph P. | Tel: | (215) 784-4200 |
| *Chief Financial Officer, Secretary and PAC Treasurer* | Fax: | (215) 784-4493 |

| WHEELER, Joe | Tel: | (246) 552-2348 |
| *Contact, Media Relations* | Fax: | (215) 784-4493 |

WILD, Kristin	Tel:	(800) 258-8733
Contact, Corporate Communications	Fax:	(215) 784-4493
kwild@asplundh.com		

Asset and Equity Corporation

A lobbying firm.
www.assetandequity.com
Legislative Issues: EDU; HCR; HOU

President	Tel:	(865) 544-4220
OWEN, William S.	Fax:	(865) 544-4225
wandgowen@aol.com		

Main Headquarters
Mailing: 601 W. Summit Hill Dr.	Tel:	(865) 544-4220
Suite B-300	Fax:	(865) 544-4225
Knoxville, TN 37902		

Public Affairs and Related Activities Personnel

At Headquarters

| RHODES, Richard | Tel: | (865) 544-4220 |
| *Contact, Government Relations* | Fax: | (865) 544-4225 |

Associa, Inc.

A community association management and developer services company.
www.associaonline.com
Industry/ies: Management

| **President and Chief Executive Officer** | Tel: | (800) 808-4882 |
| CARONA, John J. | Fax: | (214) 953-1886 |

Main Headquarters
Mailing: P.O. Box 600035	Tel:	(800) 808-4882
Dallas, TX 75360	Fax:	(214) 953-1886
	TF:	(800) 808-4882

Political Action Committees
Associations Inc. PAC/Associa PAC
FEC ID: C00413856
Contact: Nancy Cushman
5401 N. Central Expwy.
Suite 300
Dallas, TX 75205

Contributions to Candidates: $19,000 (2015-2016)
Democrats: $4,000; Republicans: $15,000

Public Affairs and Related Activities Personnel

At Headquarters

| NORTHUP, Lisa | Tel: | (800) 808-4882 |
| *Senior Vice President, Human Resources* | Fax: | (214) 953-1886 |

| REYES, Paul | Tel: | (800) 808-4882 |
| *Executive Vice President and Chief Legal Officer* | Fax: | (214) 953-1886 |

At Other Offices

BRENSINGER, Patrick	Tel:	(214) 239-4530
Executive Vice President and Chief Financial Officer	Fax:	(214) 953-1886
5401 N. Central Expwy., Suite 300		
Dallas, TX 75205		

BROCK, Andrew	Tel:	(214) 239-4530
Senior Vice President, Project Management and Operations	Fax:	(214) 953-1886
5401 N. Central Expwy., Suite 300		
Dallas, TX 75205		

CUSHMAN, Nancy	Tel:	(214) 239-4530
PAC treasurer	Fax:	(214) 953-1886
5401 N. Central Expwy., Suite 300		
Dallas, TX 75205		

FORTIN, Andrew S	Tel:	(214) 239-4530
Senior Vice President, External Affairs	Fax:	(214) 953-1886
5401 N. Central Expwy., Suite 300		
Dallas, TX 75205		

KRAFT, Matt	Tel:	(214) 239-4530
Senior Vice President, Sales and Corporate Development	Fax:	(214) 953-1886
5401 N. Central Expwy., Suite 300		
Dallas, TX 75205		

KRUPPA, Brian	Tel:	(214) 239-4530
Senior Vice President, Deputy General Counsel	Fax:	(214) 953-1886
5401 N. Central Expwy., Suite 300		
Dallas, TX 75205		

MALDONADO, Jose Bosco	Tel:	(214) 239-4530
Senior Vice President Finance and Accounting	Fax:	(214) 953-1886
5401 N. Central Expwy., Suite 300		
Dallas, TX 75205		

O'KEEFE, Chelle	Tel:	(214) 239-4530
Senior Vice President, Marketing and Communications	Fax:	(214) 953-1886
5401 N. Central Expwy., Suite 300		
Dallas, TX 75205		

Associated Banc-Corporation

A multibank holding company providing products that meet and exceed individual customer needs, to doing the "little things" that makes experience with Associated a special one.
www.associatedbank.com
Annual Revenues: $959.24 Million
Employees: 4,374
Ticker: NYSE : ASB
SIC: 6022
Industry/ies: Banking/Finance/Investments

| **Chairman of the Board** | Tel: | (920) 491-7000 |
| HUTCHINSON, William R. | Fax: | (920) 491-7090 |

| **President and Chief Executive Officer** | Tel: | (920) 491-7000 |
| FLYNN, Philip B. | Fax: | (920) 491-7090 |

Main Headquarters
Mailing: 433 Main St.	Tel:	(920) 491-7500
P.O. Box 13307	Fax:	(920) 433-3261
Green Bay, WI 54301	TF:	(800) 236-8866

Corporate Foundations and Giving Programs
Associated Banc-Corp Contributions Program
1200 Hansen Rd.	Tel:	(920) 491-7000
P.O. Box 13307	Fax:	(920) 491-7090
Green Bay, WI 54304		

Public Affairs and Related Activities Personnel

At Headquarters

| BODAGER, Brian R. | Tel: | (920) 491-7000 |
| *Executive Vice President, Chief Administrative Officer, General Counsel and Corporate Secretary* | Fax: | (920) 491-7090 |

| BOWERS, Cliff | Tel: | (920) 491-7542 |
| *Director, Public Relations* | Fax: | (920) 433-3261 |

| BUECHSE, Oliver | Tel: | (920) 491-7000 |
| *Executive Vice President and Chief Strategy Officer* | Fax: | (920) 491-7090 |

| DOCTER, Judith M. | Tel: | (920) 491-7000 |
| *Executive Vice President, Chief Human Resources Officer* | Fax: | (920) 491-7090 |

| ERICKSON, Randall J. | Tel: | (920) 491-7000 |
| *Executive Vice President, General Counsel and Corporate Secretary* | Fax: | (920) 433-3261 |

KAMINSKI, Jennifer	Tel:	(920) 491-7570
Manager, Public Relations	Fax:	(920) 491-7090
jennifer.kaminski@associatedbank.com		

| MORAL-NILES, Christopher Del | Tel: | (920) 491-7000 |
| *Executive Vice President, Chief Financial Officer* | Fax: | (920) 491-7090 |

PIOTROWSKI, Christopher
Executive Vice President, Chief Marketing Officer
Tel: (920) 491-7000
Fax: (920) 433-3261

YEE , Jim
Executive Vice President and Chief Information and Operation Officer
Tel: (920) 491-7000
Fax: (920) 433-3261

Associated Press

News gathering organization.
www.ap.org
Annual Revenues: $630.53 million
Employees: 3,200
Industry/ies: Communications; Media/Mass Communication

Chairman of the Board
JUNCK, Mary
Tel: (212) 621-1500
Fax: (212) 521-5447

President and Chief Executive Officer
PRUITT, Gary B.
Tel: (212) 621-1500
Fax: (212) 621-5447

Main Headquarters
Mailing: 450 W. 33rd St.
16th Floor
New York City, NY 10001
Tel: (212) 621-1500
Fax: (212) 621-1955

Corporate Foundations and Giving Programs
Associated Press Contributions Program
Contact: Ellen Hale
450 W. 33rd St.
16th Floor
New York City, NY 10001
Tel: (212) 621-1500
Fax: (212) 621-5447

Public Affairs and Related Activities Personnel

At Headquarters
BRUCE, Jessica
Senior Vice President and Director, Human Resources
Tel: (212) 621-1980
Fax: (212) 621-1955

COLFORD, Paul
Director, Media Relations
pcolford@ap.org
Tel: (212) 621-1895
Fax: (212) 521-5447

DALE, Ken
Senior Vice President,Chief Financial Officer
Tel: (212) 621-1980
Fax: (212) 621-1955

HALE, Ellen
Senior Vice President, Director, Corporate Communications
Tel: (212) 621-1500
Fax: (212) 521-5447

KAISER, Karen
Senior Vice President, General Counsel and Corporate Secretary
Tel: (212) 621-1500
Fax: (212) 621-5447

WHITE , Erin Madigan
Senior Media Relations Manager
Tel: (212) 621-7005
Fax: (212) 521-5447

Assurant, Inc.

Formerly Fortis, Inc. A provider of specialized insurance products, financial services and banking in North America and selected other markets. Parent of Assurant Health.
www.assurant.com
Annual Revenues: $9.84 billion
Employees: 16,700
Ticker: NYSE: AIZ
SIC: 6321
Industry/ies: Banking/Finance/Investments; Insurance Industry
Legislative Issues: COM; CSP; DIS; FIN; HOU; INS; TAX; TRA

Non-Executive Chair of the Board
ROSEN, Elaine D.

President and Chief Executive Officer
COLBERG, Alan B.
alan.cilberg@assurant.com
Tel: (212) 859-7000
Fax: (212) 859-7010

Main Headquarters
Mailing: One Chase Manhattan Plaza
New York City, NY 10005
Tel: (212) 859-7000
Fax: (212) 859-7010

Washington Office
Mailing: 601 13th St. NW
Suite 1010 North
Washington, DC 20005

Political Action Committees
Assurant Inc. PAC
FEC ID: C00185694
Contact: Robert Schwarz
501 W. Michigan St.
P.O. Box 3050
Milwaukee, WI 53203
Tel: (414) 299-7722
Fax: (414) 299-6168

Contributions to Candidates: $177,500 (2015-2016)
Democrats: $63,500; Republicans: $114,000

Principal Recipients

HOUSE
RYAN, PAUL D. (REP-WI)

Corporate Foundations and Giving Programs
Assurant Foundation

Contact: Michelle Rivard
One Chase Manhattan Plaza
41st Floor
New York City, NY 10005
Tel: (212) 859-7026
Fax: (212) 859-7010

Public Affairs and Related Activities Personnel

At Headquarters
ANDERSON, Michael D.
Interim President
Tel: (212) 859-7000
Fax: (212) 859-7010

CURATOLA, Marygrace
Director, Human Resources
MaryGrace.Curatola@assurant.com
Tel: (212) 859-7000
Fax: (212) 859-7010

KAHLE, Shawn
Vice President/ Senior Writer and Executive Director, Assurant Foundation
shawn.kahle@assurant.com
Tel: (212) 859-7000
Fax: (212) 859-7010

MERGELMEYER, Gene E.
Executive Vice President, Chief Administrative Officer
Tel: (212) 859-7000
Fax: (212) 859-7010

PAGANO, Christopher J.
Executive Vice President, Chief Financial Officer and Treasurer
Tel: (212) 859-7000
Fax: (212) 859-7010

STONEHILL, Robyn Price
Executive Vice President, Chief Human Resources Officer
Tel: (212) 859-7000
Fax: (212) 859-7010

At Other Offices
KANGAS, Paul
Vice President, Federal Policy and Government Relations
1101 Pennsylvania Ave. NW, Suite 600
Washington, DC 20004-2544
paul.kangas@assurant.com
Registered Federal Lobbyist

LANCASTER, Ronny B.
Senior Vice President
1101 Pennsylvania Ave. NW, Suite 600
Washington, DC 20004-2544
Registered Federal Lobbyist

LUTHI, Francesca
Executive Vice President, Chief Communication and Marketing Officer
1101 Pennsylvania Ave. NW, Suite 600
Washington, DC 20004-2544

RIVARD, Michelle
Senior Consultant, Communication
1101 Pennsylvania Ave. NW, Suite 600
Washington, DC 20004-2544
Michelle.Rivard@assurant.com

SCHWARTZ, Bart
Executive Vice President, Chief Legal Officer and Secretary
1101 Pennsylvania Ave. NW, Suite 600
Washington, DC 20004-2544
bart.schwartz@assurant.com

SCHWARZ, Robert
PAC Treasurer
501 W. Michigan St.
Milwaukee, WI 53203

SHEPHERD, Suzanne
Assistant Vice President, Investor Relations
1101 Pennsylvania Ave. NW, Suite 600
Washington, DC 20004-2544
Investor.Relations@assurant.com

WOODBERRY, Debra
Executive Assistant
1101 Pennsylvania Ave. NW, Suite 600
Washington, DC 20004-2544

Assure Tec

Creates ID authentication systems for identity documents such as passports, visas, drivers' licenses, military IDs, social security cards, alien registration cards, etc. The software operates on its own through a cloud-based offering and on a variety of third party ID scanners produced by leading document scanner manufacturers. AssureTec Technologies, Inc. is a privately-held, wholly-owned subsidiary of AssureTec Holdings, Inc.
www.assuretec.com
Annual Revenues: $18.00 million
Employees: 14
SIC: 7373; 7372
NAICS: 511210
Industry/ies: Law Enforcement/Security

Chairman, Chief Executive Officer and Director
REEVES, PhD, R. Bruce
Tel: (603) 641-8443
Fax: (603) 641-9535

Main Headquarters
Mailing: 200 Perimeter Rd.
Manchester, NH 03103
Tel: (603) 641-8443
Fax: (603) 641-9535

Public Affairs and Related Activities Personnel

At Headquarters

DEACON, Robert
Vice President of International Sales and Business Development
Tel: (603) 641-8443
Fax: (603) 641-9535

MALONEY, Stephen
President and Chief Operating Officer
Tel: (603) 641-8443
Fax: (603) 641-9535

MARTIN, PhD, CPP, Ron
Director, Strategic Programs and Alliances
Tel: (603) 641-8443
Fax: (603) 641-9535

REEVES, Robert
Vice President, Logistics and Operations
Tel: (603) 641-8443
Fax: (603) 641-9535

Assurity Life Insurance Company

Formed when Woodmen Accident, Assurity Life, and Lincoln Direct merged in 2003. Provides group and individual life insurance, disability income protection, and annuity products.
www.assurity.com
Annual Revenues: $14.30 million
Employees: 400
Industry/ies: Insurance Industry

Chairman of the Board, President and Chief Executive Officer
HENNING, CLU, ChFC, CFA, Thomas E.
thenning@assurity.com
Tel: (402) 476-6500
Fax: (402) 437-4395

Main Headquarters
Mailing: 2000 Q St.
P.O. Box 82533
Lincoln, NE 68501-2533
Tel: (402) 476-6500
Fax: (402) 437-4395
TF: (800) 869-0355

Corporate Foundations and Giving Programs

Assurity Life Insurance Company Contributions Program
1526 K St.
P.O. Box 82533
Lincoln, NE 68508
Tel: (402) 476-6500
Fax: (402) 437-4395

Public Affairs and Related Activities Personnel

At Headquarters

CHRISTENSEN, Roseann R
Vice President, Marketing Services
Tel: (402) 476-6500
Fax: (402) 437-4395

EHLY, Marvin P.
Vice President and Chief Financial Officer and Treasurer
Tel: (402) 476-6500
Fax: (402) 437-4395

FALTIN, Kevin G
Senior Director and Controller
Tel: (402) 476-6500
Fax: (402) 437-4395

GIDDINGS, Kathy L
Vice President, Business Sales
Tel: (402) 476-6500
Fax: (402) 437-4395

KEISLER-MUNRO, Susan L
Senior Vice President, Chief of Operations
Tel: (402) 476-6500
Fax: (402) 437-4395

REIMERS, CLU, LLIF, Todd W.
Senior Vice President and Chief Marketing Officer
Tel: (402) 476-6500
Fax: (402) 437-4395

SCHMEECKLE, William R
Vice President, Chief Investment Officer
Tel: (402) 476-6500
Fax: (402) 437-4395

WATSON, CLU, FLMI, J D, Carol S.
Vice President, General Counsel and Secretary
Tel: (402) 476-6500
Fax: (402) 437-4395

ZOUCHA, Janice A.
Vice President, Human Resources
Tel: (402) 476-6500
Fax: (402) 437-4395

Astar Air Cargo, Inc.

Formerly DHL Airways. Air freight service.
www.astaraircargo.com
Annual Revenues: $20.10 million
Employees: 300
Industry/ies: Aerospace/Aviation; Postal And Mail Services; Transportation

Chairman of the Board and Chief Executive Officer
DASBURG, John H.
Tel: (305) 982-0500
Fax: (305) 416-9564

President
DOYLE, Steve
Tel: (305) 982-0500
Fax: (305) 416-9564

Main Headquarters
Mailing: 1200 Brickell Ave.
16th Floor
Miami, FL 33131
Tel: (305) 982-0500
Fax: (305) 416-9564

Public Affairs and Related Activities Personnel

At Headquarters

DODD, Stephen
Vice President and Chief Financial Officer
stephen.dodd@astaraircargo.us
Tel: (305) 982-0500
Fax: (305) 416-9564

MILLER, Jennifer Borland
PAC Treasurer
Mail Stop Two S. Biscayne Blvd., Suite 3663
Tel: (305) 982-0500
Fax: (305) 416-9564

MILLER, Rob
Vice President, Employee Relations
Tel: (305) 982-0500
Fax: (305) 416-9564

Astellas Pharma US

Pharmaceutical manufacturer.

www.us.astellas.com
Annual Revenues: $94.60 million
Employees: 800
Industry/ies: Pharmaceutical Industry
Legislative Issues: CPT; HCR; MMM; TRD

Chief Executive Officer
YOSHIDA, Masao
Tel: (847) 317-8800
Fax: (847) 317-5977

Main Headquarters
Mailing: One Astellas Way
Northbrook, IL 60062
Tel: (847) 317-8800
Fax: (847) 317-5977
TF: (800) 888-7704

Political Action Committees
Astellas US LLC PAC (ASTELLAS PAC)
FEC ID: C00444885
Contact: Magdalena Lagowski
One Astellas Way
Northbrook, IL 60062
Tel: (847) 317-8800

Contributions to Candidates: $205,000 (2015-2016)
Democrats: $81,500; Republicans: $123,500

Principal Recipients
HOUSE
DOLD, ROBERT JAMES JR (REP-IL)

Corporate Foundations and Giving Programs

Astellas USA Foundation
Three Pkwy. North
Deerfield, IL 60015-5932

Public Affairs and Related Activities Personnel

At Headquarters

AMBROSE, Ryan
Specialist, Federal Affairs
Tel: (847) 317-8988
Fax: (847) 317-5977

BANASHAK, Melissa
Registered Federal Lobbyist
Tel: (847) 317-8800
Fax: (847) 317-5977

D'ORSIE, Sarah
Associate Director, Federal Affairs
Registered Federal Lobbyist
Tel: (847) 317-8800
Fax: (847) 317-5977

DEVANEY, Joseph
Vice President, Government Affairs & Policy
Tel: (847) 317-8800
Fax: (847) 317-5977

GOLDEN, Marty
Vice President, Government Affairs
Tel: (847) 317-8800
Fax: (847) 317-5977

LAGOWSKI, Magdalena
PAC Treasurer
Tel: (847) 317-8800
Fax: (847) 317-5977

LANDWEHR, Maribeth
Director, Corporate Communications
maribeth.landwehr@us.astellas.com
Tel: (847) 317-8988
Fax: (847) 317-5977

LENAHAN, Jennifer L
Assistant Director, Accounting and Financial Controls
Tel: (847) 317-8988
Fax: (847) 317-5977

LONG, Margaret
Tel: (847) 317-8800
Fax: (847) 317-5977

REUTHER, Mary Lacey
Director, Federal & External Affairs
Registered Federal Lobbyist
Tel: (847) 317-8800
Fax: (847) 317-5977

ROBINSON, Jim
President
Tel: (847) 317-8800
Fax: (847) 317-5977

Astoria Financial Corporation

A savings institution.
ir.astoriafederal.com
Annual Revenues: $405.53 million
Employees: 1,538
Ticker: NYSE: AF
SIC: 6035
Industry/ies: Banking/Finance/Investments

Chairman of the Board
PALLESCHI, Ralph F.
Tel: (516) 327-3000
Fax: (516) 327-7461

President and Chief Executive Officer
REDMAN, Monte N.
Tel: (516) 327-3000
Fax: (516) 327-7461

Main Headquarters
Mailing: One Astoria Federal Plaza
Lake Success, NY 11042-1085
Tel: (516) 327-3000
Fax: (516) 327-7461

Political Action Committees
Astoria Financial Corporation PAC
FEC ID: C00234245
Contact: Daniel Quirk
One Astoria Federal Plaza
Lake Success, NY 11042
Tel: (516) 327-3000

Contributions to Candidates: $1,000 (2015-2016)
Republicans: $1,000

Corporate Foundations and Giving Programs

Astoria Financial Corporation Contribution Program
One Astoria Federal Plaza
Lake Success, NY 11042

Tel: (516) 327-3000
Fax: (516) 327-7461

Public Affairs and Related Activities Personnel

At Headquarters

CUNNINGHAM, Peter J.
First Vice President and Director, Investor Relations

Tel: (516) 327-7877
Fax: (516) 327-7461

DESTEFANO, Robert J.
Executive Vice President and Chief Information Officer

Tel: (516) 327-3000
Fax: (516) 327-7461

EGGLESTON, Alan P.
Senior Executive Vice President, Secretary and Chief Risk Officer

Tel: (516) 327-3000
Fax: (516) 327-7461

FUSCO, Frank F.
Senior Executive Vice President and Chief Financial Officer

Tel: (516) 327-3000
Fax: (516) 327-7461

KEEGAN, Gerard C.
Vice Chairman, Senior Executive Vice President and Chief Operating Officer

Tel: (516) 327-3000
Fax: (516) 327-7461

QUIRK, Daniel
PAC Treasurer

Tel: (516) 327-3000
Fax: (516) 327-7461

AstraZeneca Pharmaceuticals, LP

A pharmaceutical company, subsidiary of global drugmaker AstraZeneca.
www.astrazeneca-us.com
Annual Revenues: $25.69 billion
Employees: 57,500
Ticker: NYSE: AZN
SIC: 2834; 3845; 5122; 8071
NAICS: 334510; 42221; 621511; 325412
Industry/ies: Pharmaceutical Industry
Legislative Issues: BUD; CPT; FOR; HCR; MMM; PHA; TAX

Chairman of the Board
JOHANSSON, Leif

Tel: (302) 886-3000
Fax: (302) 886-2972

Main Headquarters
Mailing: 1800 Concord Pike
         P.O. Box 15437
         Wilmington, DE 19850-5437

Tel: (302) 886-3000
Fax: (302) 886-2972
TF: (800) 456-3669

Washington Office
Mailing: 888 17th St. NW
         Suite 1000
         Washington, DC 20006

Tel: (202) 331-1120

Corporate Foundations and Giving Programs

AstraZeneca HealthCare Foundation
1800 Concord Pike
Wilmington, DE 19850

Tel: (302) 886-3000

AstraZeneca Pharmaceuticals Charitable Contributions Program
1800 Concord Pike
P.O. Box 15437
Wilmington, DE 19850

Tel: (302) 886-3000
Fax: (302) 886-2972

Public Affairs and Related Activities Personnel

At Headquarters

BLOOMQUIST, Christine
Federal Lobbyist
Registered Federal Lobbyist

Tel: (302) 886-3000
Fax: (302) 886-2972

BUCKLEY, Richard
Vice President, North America Corporate Affairs
Registered Federal Lobbyist

Tel: (302) 886-3000
Fax: (302) 886-2972

CASADAY , Laurie
Director, Brand Corporate Affairs

Tel: (302) 886-3000
Fax: (302) 886-2972

FELTON , Thomas F.
Senior Director, Program Agreements
thomas.felton@astrazeneca.com

Tel: (302) 886-3000
Fax: (302) 886-2972

FIRVIDA, Maria
Registered Federal Lobbyist

Tel: (302) 886-3000
Fax: (302) 886-2972

FLEMING, Jeffrey M.
Vice President, Compliance North America

Tel: (302) 886-3000
Fax: (302) 886-2972

GARNER, Julie
Registered Federal Lobbyist

Tel: (302) 886-3000
Fax: (302) 886-2972

HARNEY, Carrie
Federal Lobbyist
Registered Federal Lobbyist

Tel: (302) 886-3000
Fax: (302) 886-2972

HUDSON, Paul
President, AstraZeneca US and Executive Vice President, North America

Tel: (302) 886-3000
Fax: (302) 886-2972

JOLIVETTE, Theresa
Federal Lobbyist
Registered Federal Lobbyist

Tel: (302) 886-3000
Fax: (302) 886-2972

KIRBY, Jacqueline
Federal Lobbyist

Tel: (302) 886-3000
Fax: (302) 886-2972

LAUBNER, James

Tel: (302) 886-3000

Federal Lobbyist
Registered Federal Lobbyist

Fax: (302) 886-2972

LY, Danny
Federal Lobbyist

Tel: (302) 886-3000
Fax: (302) 886-2972

MABLY, Laura
Vice President, Human Resources, North America

Tel: (302) 886-3000
Fax: (302) 886-2972

MCKENNA, John
US Chief Financial Officer and Vice President, Finance, North America

Tel: (302) 886-3000
Fax: (302) 886-2972

MOHR, Stephen
Deputy General Counsel, North America and US General Counsel

Tel: (302) 886-3000
Fax: (302) 886-2972

MYERS, John
Federal Lobbyist
Registered Federal Lobbyist

Tel: (302) 886-3000
Fax: (302) 886-2972

ROLISON, Kelly J.
PAC Treasurer

Tel: (302) 886-3000
Fax: (302) 886-2972

ROSSIN, Bradley
Federal Lobbyist
Registered Federal Lobbyist

Tel: (302) 886-3000
Fax: (302) 886-2972

SNOW, Jennifer
Federal Lobbyist
Registered Federal Lobbyist

Tel: (302) 886-3000
Fax: (302) 886-2972

UHLE, Mark
Vice President and Chief Financial Officer, North America

Tel: (302) 886-3000
Fax: (302) 886-2972

At Washington Office

MARTIN-FIRVIDA, Cristina B.
Federal Lobbyist
Registered Federal Lobbyist

Tel: (202) 331-1120

MURAKAMI, Linda
Director, Political Affairs

Tel: (202) 331-1120

Asurion Corporation

Provides technology protection in the form of device replacement insurance for mobile phone carriers and Big-box stores.
www.asurion.com
Annual Revenues: $323.10 million
Employees: 6,000
Industry/ies: Insurance Industry
Legislative Issues: ENV; TRD

Chairman of the Board
COMOLLI, Bret

Tel: (615) 837-3000
Fax: (615) 837-3001

Chief Executive Officer
TAWEEL, Kevin

Tel: (615) 837-3000
Fax: (615) 837-3001

Main Headquarters
Mailing: 648 Grassmere Park
         Suite 300
         Nashville, TN 37211

Tel: (615) 837-3000
Fax: (615) 837-3001
TF: (888) 881-2622

Political Action Committees
Asurion LLC PAC (Asurion PAC)
FEC ID: C00450916
Contact: Paul Fassbender
648 Grassmere Park
Suite 300
Nashville, TN 37211

Tel: (615) 837-3000
Fax: (615) 837-3001

   Contributions to Candidates: $39,000 (2015-2016)
   Democrats: $8,000; Republicans: $31,000

Corporate Foundations and Giving Programs

Asurion Corporation Contributions Program
648 Grassmere Park
Suite 300
Nashville, TN 37211

Tel: (615) 837-3000
Fax: (615) 837-3001

Public Affairs and Related Activities Personnel

At Headquarters

AIN, Mike
Director, Government Affairs and Regulatory Counsel
main@asurion.com

Tel: (615) 837-7265
Fax: (615) 837-3001

COLOMBO, Bettie
Director, Marketing Communications
bcolombo@asurion.com

Tel: (615) 837-7283
Fax: (615) 837-3001

DAVIE, Jennifer
Federal Lobbyist

Tel: (615) 837-7265
Fax: (615) 837-3001

DEROSA, Christina
Senior Vice President, Product and Marketing

Tel: (615) 837-3000
Fax: (615) 837-3001

FASSBENDER, Paul
PAC Treasurer

Tel: (615) 837-3000
Fax: (615) 837-3001

GUNNING, Mark
Chief Financial Officer

Tel: (615) 837-3000
Fax: (615) 837-3001

PURYEAR, Gus

Tel: (615) 837-3000

General Counsel and Senior Vice President, Human
Resources
Fax: (615) 837-3001

SCHLOSSER, Rodney
Senior Vice President, Business Development and Strategic
Partnerships
Tel: (615) 837-3000
Fax: (615) 837-3001

AT&T Corporation

A provider of wireline voice communications services.
www.att.com
Employees: 250,790
Ticker: NYSE: T
SIC: 4812; 4841
NAICS: 515210
Industry/ies: Communications; Telecommunications/Internet/Cable

Chairman and Chief Executive Officer
STEPHENSON, Randall L.
Tel: (210) 821-4105

Main Headquarters
Mailing: P. O. Box 43078
Providence, RI 02940-3078
Tel: (210) 351-3327
TF: (800) 351-7221

Washington Office
Mailing: 1120 20th St. NW
Suite 800
Washington, DC 20036

Public Affairs and Related Activities Personnel

At Headquarters

GLAWE , Tracey
Executive Director
TG9645@SBC.COM
Tel: (210) 351-3327

BLASE, Jr., William A.
Senior Executive Vice President, Human Resources
Tel: (210) 351-3327

CICCONI, James W.
Senior Executive Vice President, External and Legislative
Affairs
Tel: (210) 351-3327

DONOVAN, John
Chief Strategy Officer and Group President
Tel: (210) 351-3327

HUNTLEY, David S.
Senior Executive Vice President and Chief Compliance Officer
Tel: (210) 351-3327

LEE, Lori
Senior Executive Vice President, Global Marketing Officer
Tel: (210) 351-3327

MCATEE II, David R.
Senior Executive Vice President and General Counsel
Tel: (210) 351-3327

NORDBERG, John
Business Marketing
john.nordberg@sbc.com
Tel: (210) 351-3327

STEPHENS, John
Senior Executive Vice President and Chief Financial Officer
Tel: (210) 351-3327

At Washington Office

REINSDORF, Andrew

ATC Management, Inc.

Provider of electricity transmission. Headquartered in Waukesha, WI.
www.atcllc.com
Employees: 525
Industry/ies: Energy/Electricity

Chairman of the Board
PROCARIO, John C.
Tel: (262) 506-6700
Fax: (262) 506-6710

President and Chief Executive Officer
ROWE, Mike
Tel: (262) 506-6700
Fax: (262) 506-6710

Main Headquarters
Mailing: P.O. Box 47
Waukesha, WI 53187-0047
Tel: (262) 506-6700
Fax: (262) 506-6710
TF: (866) 899-3204

Washington Office
Mailing: 300 New Jersey Ave.NW
Suite 601
Washington, DC 20001-2030
Tel: (202) 534-4930

Corporate Foundations and Giving Programs

ATC Management Contributions Program
P.O. Box 47
Waukesha, WI 53187

Public Affairs and Related Activities Personnel

At Headquarters

BANKS, Juanita
Vice President, Compliance and Risk Management
Tel: (262) 506-6700
Fax: (262) 506-6710

DAVIS, Mark
Executive Vice President and Chief Operating Officer
Tel: (262) 506-6700
Fax: (262) 506-6710

HOFBAUER, Mike
Tel: (262) 506-6700
Fax: (262) 506-6710

Executive Vice President, Chief Financial Officer and
Treasurer

JETT, Paul
Vice President, Business Development
Tel: (262) 506-6700
Fax: (262) 506-6710

LORENZ, Lori
Vice President, Human Capital
Tel: (262) 506-6700
Fax: (262) 506-6710

MARSAN, Bill
Executive Vice President, General Counsel and Corporate
Secretary
Tel: (262) 506-6700
Fax: (262) 506-6710

MILLER, Karen
Vice President, Business Administration Services
Tel: (262) 506-6700
Fax: (262) 506-6710

SATTERFIELD, Randy
Executive Vice President, Strategic Planning and Project
Development
Tel: (262) 506-6700
Fax: (262) 506-6710

SPALTHOLZ, Anne
Manager, Corporate Communications
aspaltholz@atcllc.com
Tel: (877) 506-6117
Fax: (262) 506-6710

At Washington Office

FINCO, Tom
Vice President, External Relations
Tel: (202) 534-4930

Atcor Medical, Inc.

The U.S. subsidiary of AtCor Medical Pty Ltd., which is headquartered in Australia. Develops
products for clinical use that can non-invasively assess the physiological status and the
functioning of the cardiovascular system in humans.
www.atcormedical.com
Annual Revenues: $1.40 million
Employees: 13
Industry/ies: Medicine/Health Care/Mental Health

Chairman of the Board
O'DWYER, Donald
Tel: (630) 228-8871
Fax: (630) 228-8872

Managing Director and Chief Executive Officer
ROSS, Duncan
Tel: (630) 228-8874
Fax: (630) 228-8872

Main Headquarters
Mailing: One Pierce Pl.
Suite 225 West
Itasca, IL 60143-2616
Tel: (630) 228-8871
Fax: (630) 228-8872

Public Affairs and Related Activities Personnel

At Headquarters

ABRAM, John
Manager, Regulatory Affairs
Tel: (630) 228-8871
Fax: (630) 228-8872

HARDING, Mark
Director, International Sales and Marketing
Tel: (630) 228-8871
Fax: (630) 228-8872

MANLEY, Peter
Chief Financial Officer and Secretary
p.manley@atcormedical.com
Tel: (630) 228-8871
Fax: (630) 228-8872

SCHULTZ, Lindsey
Manager, Operations
Tel: (630) 228-8871
Fax: (630) 228-8872

ATG

See listing on page 92 under Attorneys Title Guaranty Fund, Inc.

Athlone Global Security

An investment company that concentrates on the homeland security (HLS) venture market.
www.atlngroup.com
Industry/ies: Banking/Finance/Investments; Defense/Homeland Security;
Government-Related

Chairman of the Board
NEUBACH, Amnon

President and Chief Executive Officer
HAWKE, Gordon

Main Headquarters
Mailing: 175 Admiral Cochrane Dr.
Chesapeake Innovation Center
Annapolis, MD 21401

Washington Office
Mailing: 201 12th St., S
Suite 602
Arlington, VA 22202
Tel: (703) 942-9970

Public Affairs and Related Activities Personnel

At Headquarters

FAUGHT, George
Chief Financial Officer

ATK (Alliant Techsystems, Inc.)

Supplier of aerospace and defense products.
www.atk.com
Annual Revenues: $4.78 billion
Employees: 16,000

Ticker: NYSE: ATK
SIC: 3760
Industry/ies: Aerospace/Aviation; Defense/Homeland Security; Government-Related; Transportation
Legislative Issues: AER

Main Headquarters

Mailing:	7480 Flying Cloud Dr.	Tel:	(952) 351-3000
	Minneapolis, MN 55344	Fax:	(952) 351-3009

Washington Office

Mailing:	1300 Wilson Blvd.	Tel:	(703) 412-5960
	Suite 400	Fax:	(703) 412-5970
	Arlington, VA 22209		

Public Affairs and Related Activities Personnel

At Other Offices

BERL, William
45101 Warp Dr.
Dulles, VA 20166

BROOME, David
45101 Warp Dr.
Dulles, VA 20166

EMMETT, Robert
45101 Warp Dr.
Dulles, VA 20166

FORTUNATO, Edward
45101 Warp Dr.
Dulles, VA 20166

KANE, Kevin
45101 Warp Dr.
Dulles, VA 20166

KRONMILLER, Kathleen B.
45101 Warp Dr.
Dulles, VA 20166

Atlantic Diving Supply Inc.

Supply Chain Management & Distribution of Individual & Group Equipment.
Legislative Issues: DEF

Main Headquarters

Mailing:	621 Lynnhaven Pkwy.	
	Suite 400	
	Virginia Beach, VA 23452	

Public Affairs and Related Activities Personnel

At Headquarters

BOCK, Ellen
Corporate Communication Specialist and Contact, Media
ebock@adsinc.com

HICKEY, Kevin
Vice President, Product Management
Registered Federal Lobbyist

Atlantic Health Systems

Atlantic Health System is a non-profit health care systems in New Jersey and is committed to improving the health status of the communities it serves. It provides community benefit as part of a measured approach to meeting identified health needs in the community.
www.atlantichealth.org
Employees: 14,075
Industry/ies: Medicine/Health Care/Mental Health

Chairman of the Board	Tel: (973) 660-3261
TOOHEY, Robert A.	

President and Chief Executive Officer	Tel: (973) 660-3261
GRAGNOLATI, Brian A.	

Main Headquarters

Mailing:	325 Columbia Tpk.	Tel: (973) 660-3261
	Second Floor	
	Florham Park, NJ 07932	

Corporate Foundations and Giving Programs

Foundation for Morristown Medical Center	
475 South St.	Tel: (973) 593-2400
First Floor	Fax: (973) 290-7561
Morristown, NJ 07960	
Overlook Hospital Foundation	
36 Upper Overlook Rd.	Tel: (908) 522-2840
P.O. Box 220	Fax: (908) 273-3968
Summit, NJ 07902-0220	

Public Affairs and Related Activities Personnel

At Headquarters

FERRARO, Madeline	Tel: (973) 660-3261
Vice President, Government Affairs	
madeline.ferraro@ahsys.org	

KOVACH, Andrew L.	Tel: (973) 660-3261
Vice President, Human Resources and Chief Administrative Officer	

LENAHAN, Kevin	Tel: (973) 660-3261
Vice President, Finance and Chief Financial Officer	

NEIGHER, PhD, William D.	Tel: (973) 660-3261
Vice President, System Development and Chief Strategy Officer	

REGIER, Michael J.	Tel: (973) 660-3261
Vice President, Legal Affairs and Chief Legal Officer	

At Other Offices

SAMUELSON, Michael	Tel: (973) 593-2400
Director, Marketing and Public Relations	Fax: (973) 290-7561
475 South St., First Floor	
Morristown, NJ 07960	
michael.samuelson@atlantichealth.org	

Atlantic Marine Holding Company

See listing on page 102 under BAE Systems Southeast Shipyards AMHC Inc.

Atlantic Tele-Network, Inc.

A telecommunications company operating advanced wireless, wireline, and both terrestrial and submarine fiber optic networks in North America and the Caribbean.
www.atni.com
Annual Revenues: $346.51 million
Employees: 1,000
Ticker: NASDAQ: ATNI
SIC: 4813
Industry/ies: Communications; Telecommunications/Internet/Cable
Legislative Issues: TEC

Chairman of the Board	Tel: (978) 619-1300
PRIOR, Jr., Cornelius B.	

President and Chief Executive Officer	Tel: (978) 619-1300
PRIOR, Michael T.	

Main Headquarters

Mailing:	600 Cummings Center	Tel: (978) 619-1300
	Suite 268-Z	
	Beverly, MA 01915	

Washington Office

Mailing:	100 M St. SE	
	Suite 500	
	Washington, DC 20003	

Political Action Committees

Atlantic Tele-Network PAC
FEC ID: C00494526
Contact: Karl D. Noone

600 Cummings Center	Tel: (978) 619-1300
Suite 268-Z	
Beverly, MA 01915	

> **Contributions to Candidates:** $19,000 (2015-2016)
> Democrats: $8,000; Republicans: $11,000

Corporate Foundations and Giving Programs

Atlantic Tele-Network, Inc. Contributions Program	
600 Cummings Center	Tel: (978) 619-1300
Suite 268-Z	
Beverly, MA 01915	

Public Affairs and Related Activities Personnel

At Headquarters

BENINCASA, Justin D.	Tel: (978) 619-1300
Chief Financial Officer and Treasurer	

FOUGERE, Barry C	Tel: (978) 619-1300
Senior Vice President, Business Operations	

KREISHER, William F.	Tel: (978) 619-1300
Senior Vice President, Corporate Development	

NOONE, Karl D.	Tel: (978) 619-1300
PAC Treasurer	

SLAP, Leonard Q.	Tel: (978) 619-1300
Senior Vice President and General Counsel	

Atlanticus

See listing on page 90 under Atlanticus Holdings Corporation

Atlanticus Holdings Corporation

A financial holding company with investments primarily in companies focused on providing financial services.
www.atlanticus.com
Annual Revenues: $119.57 million
Employees: 314
Ticker: NASDAQ: ATLC
SIC: 6141

Industry/ies: Banking/Finance/Investments

Chairman of the Board and Chief Executive Officer   Tel: (770) 828-2000
HANNA, David G.

Main Headquarters
Mailing: Five Concourse Pkwy.   Tel: (770) 828-2000
           Suite 400
           Atlanta, GA 30328

Public Affairs and Related Activities Personnel

At Headquarters

GILBERT, Richard W.   Tel: (770) 828-2000
Chief Operating Officer

HARROD, Denise   Tel: (770) 828-2000
Contact, Corporate Affairs

MCCAMEY, William R.   Tel: (770) 828-2000
Chief Financial Officer

WALKER, Nicole O.   Tel: (770) 828-1576
Administrative Assistant

Atlas Energy Inc.

Develops and produces domestic natural gas and oil. Subsidiary companies are Atlas Pipeline Partners and Atlas Resource Partners.
www.atlasenergy.com
Annual Revenues: $682.36 million
Employees: 670
Ticker: NYSE: ATLS
SIC: 4922
Industry/ies: Energy/Electricity
Legislative Issues: TAX

Chairman of the Board   Tel: (877) 280-2857
COHEN, Jonathan Z.   Fax: (215) 405-2718

Chief Executive Officer and President   Tel: (877) 280-2857
COHEN, Edward E.   Fax: (215) 405-2718

Main Headquarters
Mailing: 1845 Walnut St.   Tel: (877) 280-2857
           Suite 1000   Fax: (215) 405-2718
           Philadelphia, PA 19103   TF: (877) 280-2857

Corporate Foundations and Giving Programs

Atlas Energy Contribution Program
1550 Coraopolis Heights Rd.   Tel: (412) 262-2830
Second Floor   Fax: (412) 262-7430
Moon Township, PA 15108

Public Affairs and Related Activities Personnel

At Headquarters

BEGLEY, Brian   Tel: (877) 280-2857
Vice President, Investor Relations   Fax: (215) 405-2718
bbegley@atlasenergy.com

SLOTTERBACK, Jeffrey M.   Tel: (877) 280-2857
Chief Accounting Officer   Fax: (215) 405-2718

At Other Offices

HERZ, Daniel   Tel: (412) 262-2830
Senior Vice President, Corporate Development and Strategy   Fax: (412) 262-7430
1550 Coraopolis Heights Rd., Second Floor
Moon Township, PA 15108

MCGRATH, Sean P.   Tel: (412) 262-2830
Chief Financial Officer   Fax: (412) 262-7430
1550 Coraopolis Heights Rd., Second Floor
Moon Township, PA 15108

WASHINGTON, Lisa   Tel: (412) 262-2830
Chief Legal Officer, Senior Vice President and Secretary   Fax: (412) 262-7430
1550 Coraopolis Heights Rd., Second Floor
Moon Township, PA 15108

Atmel Corporation

It is leader in the design and manufacture of microcontrollers, capacitive touch solutions, advanced logic, mixed-signal, nonvolatile memory and radio frequency (RF) components.
www.atmel.com
Annual Revenues: $3.43 billion
Employees: 4,700
Ticker: NASDAQ: ATML
SIC: 3674
Industry/ies: Defense/Homeland Security; Government-Related

Chairman of the Board   Tel: (408) 441-0311
SUGISHITA, David   Fax: (408) 441-4314

President and Chief Executive Officer   Tel: (408) 441-0311
LAUB, Steven A.   Fax: (408) 441-4314

Main Headquarters
Mailing: 1600 Technology Dr.   Tel: (408) 441-0311
           San Jose, CA 95110   Fax: (408) 436-1314

Public Affairs and Related Activities Personnel

At Headquarters

ARTS , Sander   Tel: (408) 441-0311
Vice President, Corporate Marketing   Fax: (408) 436-4314

SKAGGS , Steve   Tel: (408) 441-0311
Senior Vice President and Chief Financial Officer   Fax: (408) 436-4314

TOAN, Agnes   Tel: (408) 487-2963
Senior Manager, Global Communications   Fax: (408) 436-4314
agnes.toan@atmel.com

WORNOW , Scott   Tel: (408) 441-0311
Senior Vice President and Chief Legal Officer   Fax: (408) 436-4314
scott.wornow@atmel.com

ZOUMARAS , Suzanne   Tel: (408) 441-0311
Senior Vice President, Global Human Resources   Fax: (408) 436-4314

Atmos Energy Corporation

Engages in the distribution, transmission, and storage of natural gas.
www.atmosenergy.com
Annual Revenues: $4.53 billion
Employees: 4,761
Ticker: NYSE: ATO
SIC: 4924
NAICS: 221210
Industry/ies: Energy/Electricity

Executive Chairman of the Board   Tel: (972) 934-9227
BEST, Robert W.   Fax: (972) 855-3040
robert.best@atmosenergy.com

President and Chief Executive Officer   Tel: (972) 934-9227
COCKLIN, Kim R.   Fax: (972) 855-3040
kim.cocklin@atmosenergy.com

Main Headquarters
Mailing: P.O. Box 650205   Tel: (972) 934-9227
           Dallas, TX 75265-0205   Fax: (972) 855-3040
                                         TF: (888) 286-6700

Political Action Committees
Atmos Energy Corporation PAC
FEC ID: C00381954
Contact: David Mason
5430 LBJ Fwy.
Suite 160
Dallas, TX 75240

   Contributions to Candidates: $45,000 (2015-2016)
   Democrats: $9,000; Republicans: $36,000

Corporate Foundations and Giving Programs

Atmos Energy Corporation Contributions Program
P.O. Box 650205
Dallas, TX 75265-0205

Public Affairs and Related Activities Personnel

At Headquarters

ALTIERI, Jennifer   Tel: (972) 855-3797
Director, Media Relations   Fax: (972) 855-3040

ASTON, Jr., Verlon R.   Tel: (972) 934-9227
Vice President, Governmental and Public Affairs   Fax: (972) 855-3040

DAVIS, Charles M.   Tel: (972) 934-9227
Vice President, Corporate Development   Fax: (972) 855-3040

ECKERT, Bret   Tel: (972) 934-9227
Senior Vice President and Chief Financial Officer   Fax: (972) 855-3040

GILLES, Susan   Tel: (972) 855-3729
Vice President, Investor Relations   Fax: (972) 855-3040
susan.giles@atmosenergy.com

GREGORY, Louis P.   Tel: (972) 934-9227
Senior Vice President, General Counsel and Corporate   Fax: (972) 855-3075
Secretary
louis.gregory@atmosenergy.com

GRUBER, Conrad E.   Tel: (972) 934-9227
Vice President, Strategic Planning   Fax: (972) 855-3040
conrad.gruber@atmosenergy.com

HAEFNER, Michael E.   Tel: (972) 934-9227
Executive Vice President   Fax: (972) 855-3040
mike.haefner@atmosenergy.com

ROBBINS, Matt   Tel: (972) 934-9227
Vice President, Human Resources   Fax: (972) 855-3040

At Other Offices

GRANADO, Ray   Tel: (214) 206-2060
Manager, Public Affairs   Fax: (214) 206-2126
5420 LBJ Freeway, Suite 1800
Dallas, TX 75240
Mail Stop Suite 1800
ray.granado@atmosenergy.com

HUNTER, Gerald R.
Director, External Communications
5420 LBJ Freeway, Suite 1800
Dallas, TX 75240
gerald.hunter@atmosenergy.com
Tel: (972) 855-3797
Fax: (214) 206-2126

MASON, David
PAC Treasurer
5420 LBJ Freeway, Suite 1800
Dallas, TX 75240
Tel: (214) 206-2060
Fax: (214) 206-2126

ATN

See listing on page 90 under Atlantic Tele-Network, Inc.

Atna Resources Limited

Atna Resources Ltd. acquires, explores for, develops, and mines mineral properties in the United States and Canada. The company explores for precious metals, uranium, gold, silver, and other minerals.
www.atna.com
Annual Revenues: $41.44 Million
Employees: 116
Ticker: NASDAQ: ATNAQ
SIC: 1040
Industry/ies: Mining Industry; Natural Resources

Chairman of the Board
WATKINS, David H.
Tel: (303) 278-8464
Fax: (303) 279-3772

Chief Executive Officer, President and Director
HESKETH, James K.B.
Tel: (303) 278-8464
Fax: (303) 279-3772

Main Headquarters
Mailing: 14142 Denver W. Pkwy.
Suite 250
Golden, CO 80401
Tel: (303) 278-8464
Fax: (303) 279-3772
TF: (877) 692-8182

Public Affairs and Related Activities Personnel

At Headquarters

GLOSS, Rodney D.
Vice President and Chief Financial Officer
Tel: (303) 278-8464
Fax: (303) 279-3772

KIMBALL, Valerie
Investor Relations
vkimball@atna.com
Tel: (303) 278-8464
Fax: (303) 279-3772

Atofina Chemicals, Inc

See listing on page 79 under Arkema, Inc.

ATOFINA Petrochemicals

See listing on page 792 under Total Petrochemicals USA

Attorneys Title Guaranty Fund, Inc.

Provides legal assistance with real estate transactions, including real estate title insurance, estate planning, and related services. ATG is a lawyer service organization for the benefit of the profession and the public with practicing attorneys throughout Illinois, Indiana, Wisconsin, and Michigan.
www.atgf.com
Annual Revenues: $18 million
Employees: 200
Industry/ies: Real Estate

Chairman of the Board
AUSTIN, William W.
Tel: (217) 359-2000
Fax: (217) 359-2014

President and Chief Executive Officer
BIRNBAUM, Peter
pjb@atgf.com
Tel: (217) 359-2000
Fax: (217) 359-2014

Main Headquarters
Mailing: 2102 Windsor Pl.
Champaign, IL 61820-7758
Tel: (217) 359-2000
Fax: (217) 359-2014
TF: (800) 252-0402

Political Action Committees
Attorneys' Title Guaranty Fund, Inc. Federal PAC
FEC ID: C00301424
Contact: Michael K. Brandt
2408 Windsor Pl.
Champaign, IL 61820
Tel: (217) 359-2000
Fax: (217) 359-2014

    Contributions to Candidates: $7,000 (2015-2016)
    Democrats: $6,000; Republicans: $1,000

Corporate Foundations and Giving Programs
Attorneys Title Guaranty Fund, Inc. Contributions Program
2102 Windsor Pl.
Champaign, IL 61820-7758
Tel: (217) 359-2000

Public Affairs and Related Activities Personnel

At Headquarters

BRANDT, Michael K.
Land Trust Officer and PAC Treasurer
Tel: (217) 359-2000
Fax: (217) 359-2014

BUTERA, August R.
Tel: (217) 359-2000

Senior Vice President and General Counsel
Fax: (217) 359-2014

SHULRUFF, Henry L.
Senior Vice President, Business Development
Tel: (217) 359-2000
Fax: (217) 359-2014

STEVENS, Mona L.
Vice President, Human Resources
Tel: (217) 359-2000
Fax: (217) 359-2014

TRUBIANA, Ronald J.
Senior Vice President and Chief Financial Officer
Tel: (217) 359-2000
Fax: (217) 359-2014

ATX Group, Inc.

Formerly ATX Technologies. An automotive telematics company.
www.atxg.com
Annual Revenues: $27.30 million
Employees: 400
SIC: 4899
NAICS: 517410
Industry/ies: Computer/Technology

Chairman of the Board
VANDENBERG, Jr., Peter
Tel: (972) 753-6200
Fax: (972) 753-6226

Chief Executive Officer
FERRICK, Dave
Tel: (781) 393-9300
Fax: (781) 395-6706

Main Headquarters
Mailing: One Cabot Rd.
Medford, MA 02155
Tel: (781) 393-9300
Fax: (781) 395-6706

Public Affairs and Related Activities Personnel

At Headquarters

BLECHER, Jeffrey
Senior Vice President, Strategy
Tel: (781) 393-9300
Fax: (781) 395-6706

NECHELES, Peter
Senior Vice President, Corporate Development, Chief Legal Officer, Corporate Secretary
Tel: (781) 393-9300
Fax: (781) 395-6706

At Other Offices

SAXTON, Michael A.
Senior Advisor
8550 Freeport Pkwy.
Irving, TX 75063
Tel: (972) 753-6200
Fax: (972) 753-6226

WALLACE, Gary A.
Vice President, Corporate Relations and Chief Privacy Officer
8550 Freeport Pkwy.
Irving, TX 75063
gwallace@agero.com
Tel: (972) 753-6230
Fax: (972) 753-6226

WARD, Peggy
Executive Vice President and Chief Financial and Administrative Officer
8550 Freeport Pkwy.
Irving, TX 75063
Tel: (972) 753-6200
Fax: (972) 753-6226

Aura Renewable Energy Corporation

Biofuels company that maintains biogas plants in the U.S.
www.aurarenewableenergy.com
Industry/ies: Energy/Electricity

Main Headquarters
Mailing: 802 De Mun Ave.
Suite One
St. Louis, MO 63105-3197
Tel: (314) 787-5557
Fax: (314) 262-4869

Public Affairs and Related Activities Personnel

At Headquarters

LIMBAUGH, Andy
Executive Vice President, Government Relations
Tel: (314) 787-5557
Fax: (314) 262-4869

WONG, Tom
Chief Financial Officer
Tel: (314) 787-5557
Fax: (314) 262-4869

Aurora Flight Sciences Corporation

Designs and builds robotic aircraft and other advanced aerospace vehicles.
www.aurora.aero
Employees: 300
Industry/ies: Aerospace/Aviation; Transportation
Legislative Issues: BUD; DEF; HOM

Chairman of the Board and Chief Executive Officer
LANGFORD, John S.
Tel: (703) 369-3633
Fax: (703) 369-4514

Main Headquarters
Mailing: 9950 Wakeman Dr.
Manassas, VA 20110
Tel: (703) 369-3633
Fax: (703) 369-4514

Corporate Foundations and Giving Programs
Aurora Flight Sciences Corporation Contributions Program
Contact: Patricia Woodside
9950 Wakeman Dr.
Manassas, VA 20110
Tel: (703) 369-3633

Public Affairs and Related Activities Personnel

At Headquarters

CHERRY, Mark C.
President and Chief Operating Officer
Tel: (703) 369-3633
Fax: (703) 369-4223

CRONIN, Jack
Chief Strategy Officer
Tel: (703) 369-3633
Fax: (703) 369-4514

CROSSNO, Tim
Chief Financial Officer
Tel: (703) 369-3633
Fax: (703) 369-4514

TYLKO, John
Chief Innovation Officer
Tel: (703) 369-3633
Fax: (703) 369-4514

WOODSIDE, Patricia
Director, Public Relations
pwoodside@aurora.aero
Tel: (703) 396-6304
Fax: (703) 369-4514

Aurora Health Care, Inc.

Health care provider with Aurora hospitals, medical clinics, doctors and pharmacies. It is an integrated, not-for-profit, and all-for-people health care provider serving communities throughout eastern Wisconsin and northern Illinois.
www.aurorahealthcare.org
Employees: 25,087
Industry/ies: Medicine/Health Care/Mental Health

Chairman of the Board
DANIELS, John
Tel: (414) 647-6404
Fax: (414) 649-7982

President and Chief Executive Officer
TURKAL, MD, Nick
Tel: (414) 647-6404
Fax: (414) 649-7982

Main Headquarters
Mailing: 750 W. Virginia St.
P.O. Box 341880
Milwaukee, WI 53204
Tel: (414) 647-6404
Fax: (414) 649-7982
TF: (888) 863-5502

Corporate Foundations and Giving Programs

Aurora Health Care Foundation
Contact: Cristy Garcia-Thomas
950 N. 12th St.
Suite A511
Milwaukee, WI 53233

Public Affairs and Related Activities Personnel

At Headquarters

BABLITCH, Steve
Chief, Regulatory and Strategic Affairs, and Corporate Secretary
Tel: (414) 647-6404
Fax: (414) 649-7982

BROPHY, Michael
Chief of Staff and Chief Communications Officer
michael.brophy@aurora.org
Tel: (414) 647-6404
Fax: (414) 649-7982

COLMAN, Gerard
Chief Operating Officer
Tel: (414) 647-6404
Fax: (414) 649-7982

GARCIA-THOMAS, Cristy
Chief Diversity and Inclusion Officer and President, Aurora Health Care Foundation
cristy.garciathomas@aurora.org
Tel: (414) 647-6404
Fax: (414) 649-7982

HANSON, Gail
Chief Financial Officer
Tel: (414) 647-6404
Fax: (414) 649-7982

HART, Shelly
Senior Vice President and General Counsel
Tel: (414) 647-6404
Fax: (414) 649-7982

JANIS, Jerry
Senior Vice President, Strategic Planning
Tel: (414) 647-6404
Fax: (414) 649-7982

LAPPIN, Mike
Chief Administrative Officer, Corporate Secretary
Tel: (414) 647-6404
Fax: (414) 649-7982

MOON-MOGUSH, Cindy
Chief Marketing Officer
Tel: (414) 647-6404
Fax: (414) 649-7982

RABAS, Kristin
Senior Coordinator, Public Relations and Marketing Communications
kristin.rabas@aurora.org
Tel: (414) 647-6404
Fax: (414) 649-7982

RISLOV, Amy
Chief Human Resources Officer
Tel: (414) 647-6404
Fax: (414) 649-7982

ROLLER, Rachel
Senior Vice President, Government and Community Relations
Tel: (414) 647-6404
Fax: (414) 649-7982

Aurora Organic Dairy

A producer and processor of private-brand organic milk and butter, cream, and non-fat dry milk for large grocery retailers and natural food stores.
www.auroraorganic.com
Annual Revenues: $10.90 million
Employees: 530
Industry/ies: Dairy Industry; Food And Beverage Industry
Legislative Issues: AGR

Chairman of the Board
RETZLOFF, Mark A.
Tel: (720) 564-6296
Fax: (720) 564-0409

Chief Executive Officer
PEPERZAK, Marcus B.
Tel: (720) 564-6296
Fax: (720) 564-0409

Main Headquarters
Mailing: 1919 14th St.
Suite 300
Boulder, CO 80302
Tel: (720) 564-6296
Fax: (720) 564-0409

Corporate Foundations and Giving Programs

Aurora Organic Dairy foundation
1401 Walnut St.
Suite 500
Boulder, CO 80302
Tel: (720) 564-6296
Fax: (720) 564-0409

Public Affairs and Related Activities Personnel

At Headquarters

ABRAHAM, Jim
Vice President, Sales
Tel: (720) 564-6296
Fax: (720) 564-0409

GETMAN, Donna
Director, Human Resources and Corporate Secretary
Tel: (720) 564-6296
Fax: (720) 564-0409

MCGINTY, Scott
President
Tel: (720) 564-6296
Fax: (720) 564-0409

MULLER, Cammie
Chief Financial Officer
Tel: (720) 564-6296
Fax: (720) 564-0409

TUITELE, Sonja
Director, Communications & Sustainability
sonjat@aodmilk.com
Tel: (720) 564-6296
Fax: (720) 564-0409

Aushon Biosystems

A microarray system development firm. Aushon BioSystems provides protein biomarker measurement and analysis products and services.
www.aushon.com
Annual Revenues: $2.40 million
Industry/ies: Defense/Homeland Security; Government-Related

Chief Executive Officer
VOGT , Susan
Tel: (978) 436-6400
Fax: (978) 667-3970

Main Headquarters
Mailing: 43 Manning Rd.
Billerica, MA 01821-3925
Tel: (978) 436-6400
Fax: (978) 667-3970

Public Affairs and Related Activities Personnel

At Headquarters

HONKANEN, Peter
Founder and Chief Operations Officer
Tel: (978) 436-6400
Fax: (978) 667-3970

KEEFE , Susan
Vice President, Finance and Administration
Tel: (978) 436-6400
Fax: (978) 667-3970

MASTRANGELO, Lisa
Chief Financial Officer, Investor Relations Contact
lisa.mastrangelo@aushon.com
Tel: (978) 436-6400
Fax: (978) 667-3970

RADUAZO , Rocco
Vice President, World Wide Sales and Public Relations Contact
Rocco.Raduazo@aushon.com
Tel: (978) 436-6400
Fax: (978) 667-3970

The Austin Company

An international organization of consultants, designers, engineers and constructors specializing in industrial, governmental and commercial facilities.
www.theaustin.com
Annual Revenues: $61.24 million
Employees: 100
Industry/ies: Construction/Construction Materials; Engineering/Mathematics; Management

President
PIERCE, Michael G.
michael.pierce@theaustin.com
Tel: (440) 544-2607
Fax: (440) 544-2690

Main Headquarters
Mailing: 6095 Parkland Blvd.
Cleveland, OH 44124
Tel: (440) 544-2600
Fax: (440) 544-2690
TF: (800) 333-0780

Public Affairs and Related Activities Personnel

At Headquarters

DEEL, Jeff
Director, Human Resources
Tel: (440) 544-2600
Fax: (440) 544-2690

EDDLEMAN, Matt
Senior Vice President, Sales and Marketing
Tel: (440) 544-2600
Fax: (440) 544-2690

PHILLIPS, Mark
Senior Vice President, Finance
Tel: (440) 544-2600
Fax: (440) 544-2690

RIFFLE, Susan
Specialist, Communications and Contact, Media Relations
Tel: (440) 544-2600
Fax: (440) 544-2690

TODD, Phil
Senior Vice President, Operations and General Manager
Tel: (440) 544-2600
Fax: (440) 544-2690

Austin Industries

A construction company.

www.austin-ind.com
Annual Revenues: $2 billion
Employees: 6,000
NAICS: 236220
Industry/ies: Construction/Construction Materials

| **Chairman of the Board** | Tel: | (214) 443-5500 |
| BEST, Rhys | Fax: | (214) 443-5622 |

| **President and Chief Executive Officer** | Tel: | (214) 443-5500 |
| WALLS, David | Fax: | (214) 443-5622 |

Main Headquarters
| Mailing: P.O. Box 1590 | Tel: | (214) 443-5500 |
| Dallas, TX 75221-1590 | Fax: | (214) 443-5622 |

Political Action Committees
Austin Industries Companies PAC
FEC ID: C00093179
Contact: Justin Holt
| P.O. Box 1590 | Tel: | (214) 443-5500 |
| Dallas, TX 75221 | | |

   Contributions to Candidates: $32,000 (2015-2016)
   Democrats: $8,000; Republicans: $24,000

Public Affairs and Related Activities Personnel

At Headquarters

BISHOP, Kay	Tel:	(214) 443-5598
Manager, Corporate Communications	Fax:	(214) 443-5622
kbishop@austin-ind.com		

ELISE, Lori	Tel:	(214) 443-5544
Director, Corporate Communications	Fax:	(214) 443-5622
lori_elise@austin-ind.com		

| FISHER, J.T. | Tel: | (214) 443-5500 |
| *Chief Financial Officer* | Fax: | (214) 443-5622 |

FOLEY, John	Tel:	(214) 443-5500
Vice President, People	Fax:	(214) 443-5622
jfoley@austin-ind.com		

| HENRY, D. Steven | Tel: | (214) 443-5500 |
| *Senior Vice President and Chief Legal Officer* | Fax: | (214) 443-5622 |

| HOLT, Justin | Tel: | (214) 443-5500 |
| *Treasurer* | Fax: | (214) 443-5622 |

AuthenTec Inc.

AuthenTec provides fingerprint authentication sensors and solutions to the high-volume PC, wireless device, and access control markets.
www.authentec.com
Annual Revenues: $69.79 million
Employees: 217
Ticker: NASDAQ: AUTH
SIC: 3674
Industry/ies: Engineering/Mathematics

Chief Executive Officer	Tel:	(321) 308-1300
CIACCIA , Larry	Fax:	(321) 308-1430
Larry.ciaccia@authentec.com		

Main Headquarters
Mailing: 100 Rialto pl.	Tel:	(321) 308-1300
Suite 100	Fax:	(321) 308-1430
Melbourne, FL 32901		

Public Affairs and Related Activities Personnel

At Headquarters

| CALAMIA , Philip | Tel: | (321) 308-1300 |
| *Chief Financial Officer* | Fax: | (321) 308-1430 |

DIETZ, Brent	Tel:	(321) 308-1320
Director, Communications	Fax:	(321) 308-1430
brent.dietz@authentec.com		

Auto-Owners Insurance Group

A property, casualty and life insurance company.
www.auto-owners.com
Annual Revenues: $2.12 billion
Employees: 3,400
Industry/ies: Insurance Industry

| **Chairman of the Board and Chief Executive Officer** | Tel: | (517) 323-1200 |
| HARROLD, Jeffrey F. | Fax: | (517) 323-8796 |

Main Headquarters
Mailing: 6101 Anacapri Blvd.	Tel:	(517) 323-1200
Lansing, MI 48917	Fax:	(517) 323-8796
	TF:	(888) 869-2642

Autodesk, Inc.

A software manufacturer.
www.autodesk.com
Annual Revenues: $2.37 billion

Employees: 9,500
Ticker: NASDAQ: ADSK
SIC: 7372
Industry/ies: Computer/Technology
Legislative Issues: CPI; CPT; ENG; TRD

| **President and Chief Executive Officer** | Tel: | (415) 507-5000 |
| BASS, Carl | Fax: | (415) 507-5100 |

Main Headquarters
| Mailing: 111 McInnis Pkwy. | Tel: | (415) 507-5000 |
| San Rafael, CA 94903 | Fax: | (415) 507-5100 |

Corporate Foundations and Giving Programs
Autodesk Inc. Foundation
| 111 McInnis Pkwy. | Tel: | (415) 507-5000 |
| San Rafael, CA 94903 | Fax: | (415) 507-5100 |

Public Affairs and Related Activities Personnel

At Headquarters

| BECKER, Janice | Tel: | (415) 507-5000 |
| *Senior Vice President, Human Resources and Corp Real Estate* | Fax: | (415) 507-5100 |

| BRADSHAW, Chris | Tel: | (415) 507-5000 |
| *Chief Marketing Officer and Senior Vice President, Reputation, Consumer and Education and Media* | Fax: | (415) 507-5100 |

| CHIN, Moonhie | Tel: | (415) 507-5000 |
| *Senior Vice President, Global Customer Support and Operations* | Fax: | (415) 507-5100 |

CRANE, David C.	Tel:	(202) 207-3661
Vice Preisdent, Government Affairs	Fax:	(415) 507-5100
david.crane@autodesk.com		
Registered Federal Lobbyist		

DI FRONZO, Pascal	Tel:	(415) 507-5000
Senior Vice President, General Counsel and Secretary	Fax:	(415) 507-5100
pascal.di.fronzo@autodesk.com		

GENNARELLI, David	Tel:	(415) 507-6705
Director, Investor Relations	Fax:	(415) 507-6129
david.gennarelli@autodesk.com		

OHRENSTEIN, David J.	Tel:	(415) 507-5000
Federal Lobbyist	Fax:	(415) 507-5100
Registered Federal Lobbyist		

| SCOTT HERREN, R. | Tel: | (415) 507-5000 |
| *Senior Vice President and Chief Financial Officer* | Fax: | (415) 507-5100 |

Automatic Data Processing, Inc.

Provider of business outsourcing solutions. It is a provider of cloud-based Human Capital Management (HCM) solutions that unite HR, payroll, talent, time, tax and benefits administration, and a leader in business outsourcing services, analytics and compliance expertise.
www.adp.com
Annual Revenues: $12.79 billion
Employees: 61,000
Ticker: NASDAQ: ADP
SIC: 7374
Industry/ies: Employees & Employment; Management
Legislative Issues: HCR; TAX

| **Chairman of the Board** | Tel: | (973) 974-5000 |
| BRUN, Leslie | Fax: | (973) 974-3334 |

President and Chief Executive Officer	Tel:	(973) 974-5000
RODRIGUEZ, Carlos A.	Fax:	(973) 974-3334
Carlos.Rodriguez.csr@adp.com		

Main Headquarters
Mailing: One ADP Blvd.	Tel:	(973) 974-5000
Roseland, NJ 07068	Fax:	(973) 974-3334
	TF:	(800) 225-5237

Corporate Foundations and Giving Programs
Automatic Data Processing, Inc. Contributions Program
Contact: Carlos A. Rodriguez
One ADP Blvd.
Roseland, NJ 07068

Public Affairs and Related Activities Personnel

At Headquarters

| BONARTI, Michael A. | Tel: | (973) 974-5000 |
| *Corporate Vice President, General Counsel and Secretary* | Fax: | (973) 974-3334 |

CHARLES, Elena	Tel:	(973) 974-4077
Vice President, Investor Relations	Fax:	(973) 974-3334
elena.charles@ADP.com		

| DAGHER, Joseph | Tel: | (973) 974-5000 |
| *Senior Director, Government Relations* | Fax: | (973) 974-3334 |

DUFFY , James	Tel:	(973) 974-5000
Senior Director, Corporate Communications	Fax:	(973) 974-3334
Jim.Duffy@ADP.com		

FLYNN, Ed	Tel:	(973) 974-5000
Executive Vice President, Worldwide Sales and Marketing	Fax:	(973) 974-3334
MORRIS, Debbie	Tel:	(973) 974-7821
Senior Director, Finance	Fax:	(973) 974-3334
O'BRIEN, Dermot J.	Tel:	(973) 974-5000
Corporate Vice President and Chief Human Resources Officer	Fax:	(973) 974-3334
SHANLEY, Kelly	Tel:	(973) 974-7612
Senior Director, Global Events Marketing	Fax:	(973) 974-3334
SIEGMUND , Jan	Tel:	(973) 974-5000
Corporate Vice President and Chief Financial Officer	Fax:	(973) 974-3334
TIMKO, Joseph	Tel:	(973) 974-5000
Executive Vice President, Chief Strategy and Innovation Officer	Fax:	(973) 974-3334
WOLFE, Dick	Tel:	(973) 974-7034
Senior Director, Corporate Communications	Fax:	(973) 974-3334
dick.wolfe@adp.com		

AutoNation, Inc.

A waste collection, disposal and recycling company. They are also an Automotive Retailer and are the parent company of Alamo Rent-a-Car, an auto rental dealership.
www.autonation.com
Annual Revenues: $21.04 billion
Employees: 26,000
Ticker: NYSE: AN
SIC: 5500
Industry/ies: Automotive Industry; Environment And Conservation; Pollution And Waste; Retail/Wholesale; Transportation

Chairman of the Board and Chief Executive Officer	Tel:	(954) 769-6000
JACKSON, Michael J.	Fax:	(954) 769-6537
jacksonm@autonation.com		

Main Headquarters

Mailing: 200 S.W. First Ave.	Tel:	(954) 769-6000
Suite 1600	Fax:	(954) 769-6537
Ft. Lauderdale, FL 33301	TF:	(877) 204-1999

Political Action Committees

AutoNation Inc. PAC
FEC ID: C00330514
Contact: Coleman Edmunds

200 S.W. First Ave.		
14th Floor	Tel:	(954) 769-6000
Ft. Lauderdale, FL 33301	Fax:	(954) 769-6537

> **Contributions to Candidates:** $10,500 (2015-2016)
> Democrats: $5,000; Republicans: $5,500

Corporate Foundations and Giving Programs

AutoNation, Inc Contributions Program

200 S.W. First Ave.	Tel:	(954) 769-6000
Suite 1600	Fax:	(954) 769-6537
Ft. Lauderdale, FL 33301		

Public Affairs and Related Activities Personnel

At Headquarters

BERMAN, Bill Berman	Tel:	(954) 769-6000
Executive Vice President and Chief Operating Officer	Fax:	(954) 769-6537
CANNON, Marc	Tel:	(954) 769-3146
Senior Vice President, Corporate Communications and Public Policy	Fax:	(954) 769-6537
EDMUNDS, Coleman	Tel:	(954) 769-6000
Senior Vice President, Legal and PAC Treasurer	Fax:	(954) 769-6537
Mail Stop 14th Floor		
FERRANDO, Jonathan P.	Tel:	(954) 769-6000
Executive Vice President, General Counsel, Corporate Development and Human Resources	Fax:	(954) 769-6537
HUIZENGA, H. Wayne	Tel:	(954) 769-6000
Founder	Fax:	(954) 769-6537
MILLER, Cheryl	Tel:	(954) 769-7734
Executive Vice President and Chief Financial Officer	Fax:	(954) 769-6537
scullyc@autonation.com		
PARLAPIANO, Donna	Tel:	(954) 769-6000
Senior Vice President, Franchise Operations	Fax:	(954) 769-6537
QUARTARO, Robert	Tel:	(954) 769-7342
Director, Investor Relations	Fax:	(954) 769-6537
QuartaroR@autonation.com		

AutoZone, Inc.

An auto parts chain. AutoZone is the retailer and a leading distributor of automotive replacement parts and accessories
www.autozone.com
Annual Revenues: $9.95 billion
Employees: 43,320
Ticker: NYSE: AZO
SIC: 5531

Industry/ies: Automotive Industry; Transportation

Chairman of the Board, President and Chief Executive Officer	Tel:	(901) 495-6500
RHODES, III, William C.	Fax:	(901) 495-8300

Main Headquarters

Mailing: P.O. Box 2198	Tel:	(901) 495-6500
Memphis, TN 38101-2198	Fax:	(901) 495-8300
	TF:	(800) 288-6966

Political Action Committees

AutoZone Inc. Committee for Better Government PAC
FEC ID: C00233056
Contact: Ray Pohlman
123 S. Front St.
Memphis, TN 38103

> **Contributions to Candidates:** $16,500 (2015-2016)
> Democrats: $6,000; Republicans: $10,500

Corporate Foundations and Giving Programs

AutoZone Inc. Contributions Program

P.O. Box 2198	Tel:	(901) 495-6500
Memphis, TN 38101	Fax:	(901) 495-8300

Public Affairs and Related Activities Personnel

At Headquarters

CAMPBELL, Brian	Tel:	(901) 495-7005
Vice President	Fax:	(901) 495-8300
brian.campbell@autozone.com		
GILES, William T.	Tel:	(901) 495-6500
Chief Financial Officer and Executive Vice President, Finance and Information Technology	Fax:	(901) 495-8300
GOLDSMITH, Harry L.	Tel:	(901) 495-6500
Executive Vice President, Secretary and General Counsel	Fax:	(901) 495-8300
harry.l.goldsmith@autozone.com		
MCDONALD, Gail	Tel:	(901) 495-6500
Administrative Assistant	Fax:	(901) 495-8300
PALUMBO , Pam	Tel:	(901) 495-6500
Sign Manager	Fax:	(901) 495-8300
pam.palumbo@autozone.com		
RODRIGUEZ , Omar	Tel:	(901) 495-6500
Commercial Category Manager	Fax:	(901) 495-8300
omar.rodriguez@autozone.com		
SALTIEL, Albert "Al"	Tel:	(901) 495-6500
Senior Vice President, Marketing	Fax:	(901) 495-8300
SHANAMAN, Brett L	Tel:	(901) 495-6500
Vice President Marketing	Fax:	(901) 495-8300
brett_shanaman@autozone.com		
WRIGHT, Kristen Collier	Tel:	(901) 495-6500
Senior Vice President, General Counsel and Secretary	Fax:	(901) 495-8300

At Other Offices

POHLMAN, Ray	Tel:	(901) 495-8300
Vice President, Contact, Media and PAC Treasurer	Fax:	(901) 495-8300
123 S. Front St.		
Memphis, TN 38103		
ray.pohlman@autozone.com		

Availity, LLC

A healthcare transactions and professional services firm.
www.availity.com
Annual Revenues: $19.90 million
Employees: 200,000
Industry/ies: Banking/Finance/Investments; Law Enforcement/Security; Medicine/Health Care/Mental Health

Chief Executive Officer	Tel:	(904) 470-4900
THOMAS, Russ	Fax:	(904) 470-2190

Main Headquarters

Mailing: P.O. Box 550857	Tel:	(904) 470-4900
Jacksonville Beach, FL 32255-0857	Fax:	(904) 470-2190
	TF:	(800) 282-4548

Public Affairs and Related Activities Personnel

At Headquarters

EASTMAN, Nate	Tel:	(904) 470-4900
Chief Financial Officer	Fax:	(904) 470-2190
HERTZOG, Kathleen	Tel:	(904) 470-4910
Vice President, Marketing and Communications	Fax:	(904) 470-2190
khertzog@availity.com		
LINDGREN, Karin	Tel:	(904) 470-4900
Senior Vice President, Legal and Regulatory Affairs and General Counsel	Fax:	(904) 470-2190
MILLER, Ryan	Tel:	(904) 470-4900
Senior Vice President, Strategy and Corporate Development	Fax:	(904) 470-2190
REECE, Susan	Tel:	(904) 470-4900

Senior Vice President, Human Resources	Fax:	(904) 470-2190

Avalara

Transaction-tax software developer and provider.
www.avalara.com
Industry/ies: Computer/Technology

Founder and Chief Executive Officer
MCFARLANE, Scott

	Tel:	(206) 826-4900
	Fax:	(206) 780-5011

Main Headquarters

Mailing:	100 Ravine Ln. NE	Tel:	(206) 826-4900
	Suite 220	Fax:	(206) 780-5011
	Bainbridge Island, WA 98110	TF:	(877) 780-4848

Public Affairs and Related Activities Personnel

At Headquarters

DOOREN, Pascal Van	Tel:	(206) 826-4900
Revenue Officer	Fax:	(206) 780-5011
DUFFY, Shaunna	Tel:	(206) 826-4900
Vice President, Human Resources	Fax:	(206) 780-5011
KUSHNIRUK, Marshal	Tel:	(206) 826-4900
Business Development	Fax:	(206) 780-5011
PETERSON, Scott	Tel:	(206) 826-4900
Director, Government Affairs	Fax:	(206) 780-5011
PINNEY, Alesia	Tel:	(206) 826-4900
General Counsel	Fax:	(206) 780-5011
RIEGELSBERGER, Kevin	Tel:	(206) 826-4900
Strategic Initiatives	Fax:	(206) 780-5011
ROSTOV, David E.	Tel:	(206) 826-4900
Finance and Compliance	Fax:	(206) 780-5011
TURNER, Michael J	Tel:	(206) 826-4900
Marketing	Fax:	(206) 780-5011

Avaya Inc.

Communications equipment vendor.
www.avaya.com
Employees: 19,000
Ticker: NYSE: AV
SIC: 3661
Industry/ies: Communications; Telecommunications/Internet/Cable

President and Chief Executive Officer
KENNEDY, Kevin J.

	Tel:	(908) 953-6000
	Fax:	(908) 953-7609

Main Headquarters

Mailing:	211 Mt. Airy Rd.	Tel:	(908) 953-6000
	Basking Ridge, NJ 07920	Fax:	(908) 953-7609
		TF:	(866) 462-8292

Washington Office

Mailing:	80 M St. SE
	Suite 704
	Washington, DC 20003

Political Action Committees
Avaya Inc. PAC
FEC ID: C00363382
Contact: Steve Szeremeta
12730 Fair Lakes Cir. Fair Lakes
Suite 1212
Fairfax, VA 22033

Fax:	(202) 378-5798

Corporate Foundations and Giving Programs
Avaya Inc. Contributions Program
211 Mt. Airy Rd.
Basking Ridge, NJ 07920

Tel:	(908) 953-6000
Fax:	(908) 953-7609

Public Affairs and Related Activities Personnel

At Headquarters

ALLARD, Pierre-Paul	Tel:	(908) 953-6000
Senior Vice President Worldwide Sales and President, Global Field Operations	Fax:	(908) 953-7609
CHIRICO, Jim	Tel:	(908) 953-6000
Executive Vice President, Business Operations	Fax:	(908) 953-7609
CRAVEN, Pamela F.	Tel:	(908) 953-6000
Chief Administrative Officer	Fax:	(908) 953-7609
CUNNINGHAM, Andy	Tel:	(908) 953-6000
Chief Marketing Officer	Fax:	(908) 953-7609
GASTON, Roger C.	Tel:	(908) 953-6000
Senior Vice President, Human Resources	Fax:	(908) 953-7609
KLINE, Deb	Tel:	(908) 953-6179
Lead, Global Corporate and Technology & Public Relations	Fax:	(908) 953-7609
klined@avaya.com		
OLLI, Amy Fliegelman	Tel:	(908) 953-6000
Senior Vice President and General Counsel	Fax:	(908) 953-7609
PHILONENKO, Laurent	Tel:	(908) 953-6000

Senior Vice President, Corporate Strategy and Development	Fax:	(908) 953-7609
VELLEQUETTE, Dave	Tel:	(908) 953-6000
Senior Vice President and Chief Financial Officer	Fax:	(908) 953-7609

At Other Offices

ADAMS, Algenia	Tel:	(202) 378-5790
Associate, Management		
1212 New York Ave. NW, Suite 1212		
Washington, DC 20005		
SZEREMETA, Steve	Tel:	(703) 653-8000
Vice President, Legal and Contracts and PAC Treasurer	Fax:	(703) 653-8001
12730 Fair Lakes Cir.		
Fairfax, VA 22033		

Avego Corporation

A provider of software, hardware and real-time information systems for convenience of passenger transportation.
rtr.avego.com/rtr-desktop-web
Industry/ies: Computer/Technology

Main Headquarters

Mailing:	1050 17th St. NW	Tel:	(202) 318-0108
	Suite 810		
	Washington, DC 20036		

Public Affairs and Related Activities Personnel

At Headquarters

STEINBERG, Paul	Tel:	(202) 318-0108
Director, Sales and Operations		

Avenet LLC

Develops web solutions to meet the needs of targeted markets, including government, health care, education and nonprofit organizations.
www.avenet.net
Annual Revenues: $26.79 billion
Employees: 18,800
Ticker: NYSE:AVT
Industry/ies: Computer/Technology; Management

Chief Executive Officer
JOHNSON, Eric
ejohnson@avenet.net

Tel:	(612) 617-5700
Fax:	(612) 617-5701

Main Headquarters

Mailing:	2112 Broadway St. NE	Tel:	(612) 617-5700
	Suite 250	Fax:	(612) 617-5701
	Minneapolis, MN 55413		

Aventis Pasteur

See listing on page 700 under Sanofi-Pasteur, Inc.

Avery Dennison Corporation

Develops identification and decorative solutions for businesses and consumers.
www.averydennison.com
Annual Revenues: $5.92 billion
Employees: 25,000
Ticker: NYSE: AVY
SIC: 2670
Industry/ies: Retail/Wholesale

Executive Chairman
SCARBOROUGH, Dean A.
dean.scarborough@averydennison.com

Tel:	(626) 304-2000
Fax:	(626) 304-2192

President and Chief Executive Officer
BUTIER, Mitchell R.
mitchell.butier@averydennison.com

Tel:	(626) 304-2000
Fax:	(626) 304-2192

Main Headquarters

Mailing:	207 Goode Ave.	Tel:	(626) 304-2000
	Glendale, CA 91203-1222		

Political Action Committees
Avery Dennison Corporation Employee PAC (ADEPAC)
FEC ID: C00467340
Contact: Ashlee N. Titus
455 Capitol Mall
Suite 600
Sacramento, CA 95814

Corporate Foundations and Giving Programs

Avery Dennison Foundation
Contact: Alicia Maddox MPH
150 N. Orange Grove Blvd.
Pasadena, CA 91103

Tel:	(626) 304-2000

Public Affairs and Related Activities Personnel

At Headquarters

BRAMMAN, Anne L.	Tel:	(626) 304-2000
Senior Vice President and Chief Financial Officer		

At Other Offices

HILL, Anne
Senior Vice President and Chief Human Resources Officer
150 N. Orange Grove Blvd., Charles D. Miller Corporate
Center
Pasadena, CA 91103-3596

Tel: (626) 304-2000
Fax: (626) 304-2192

MADDOX, MPH, Alicia
President and Executive Director, Avery Dennison Foundation
150 N. Orange Grove Blvd., Charles D. Miller Corporate
Center
Pasadena, CA 91103-3596

Tel: (626) 304-2000
Fax: (626) 304-2192

MILLER, Susan C.
Senior Vice President, General Counsel and Secretary
150 N. Orange Grove Blvd., Charles D. Miller Corporate
Center
Pasadena, CA 91103-3596
susan.miller@averydennison.com

Tel: (626) 304-2000
Fax: (626) 304-2192

SILVA, Priscilla
Coordinator, Investor Relations
150 N. Orange Grove Blvd., Charles D. Miller Corporate
Center
Pasadena, CA 91103-3596
investorcom@averydennison.com

Tel: (626) 304-2165
Fax: (626) 304-2192

TITUS, Ashlee N.
PAC Treasurer
455 Capitol Mall, Suite 600
Sacramento, CA 95814

Aveta Inc.

Providers of managed healthcare services in the United States.
www.aveta.com
Annual Revenues: $505.30 million
Employees: 1,300
SIC: 8000
Industry/ies: Insurance Industry; Medicine/Health Care/Mental Health
Legislative Issues: HCR

President and Chief Executive Officer
SHINTO, MD, Richard

Tel: (201) 969-2300

Main Headquarters
Mailing: 173 Bridge Plaza., North
Ft. Lee, NJ 07024

Tel: (201) 969-2300

Public Affairs and Related Activities Personnel

At Headquarters

AYRES, Emily
Contact, Media Relations

Tel: (615) 254-0575

JOYCE, Christopher
General Counsel

Tel: (201) 969-2300

KLAUSNER, Paul J.
General Counsel and Corporate Secretary

Tel: (201) 969-2300

MALTON, Douglas
Chief Financial Officer
douglas@aveta.com

Tel: (201) 969-2300

O'ROURKE, Timothy
President, New Market Development

Tel: (201) 969-2300

WALTERMIRE, Nancy
Chief Compliance Officer

Tel: (201) 969-2300

WEYNE, Angela
Executive Vice President and Media Contact

Tel: (201) 969-2330

Avid Technology, Inc.

Avid Technology, Inc. is an American company specializing in video and audio production technology. It provides information on all-digital solutions for capturing, creating, editing and distributing digital media.
avid.com
Annual Revenues: $514.85 million
Employees: 1,413
Ticker: NASDAQ: AVID
SIC: 3861
Industry/ies: Communications; Media/Mass Communication

Chairman, President and Chief Executive Officer
HERNANDEZ, Jr., Louis

Tel: (978) 640-6789
Fax: (978) 640-3366

Main Headquarters
Mailing: 65-75, Network Dr.
Burlington, MA 01803

Tel: (978) 640-6789
Fax: (978) 640-3366

Public Affairs and Related Activities Personnel

At Headquarters

DESAI, Rashid
Senior Vice President and Chief Technology Officer

Tel: (978) 640-6789
Fax: (978) 640-3366

DUVA, Jason

Tel: (978) 640-6789
Fax: (978) 640-3366

Senior Vice President, General Counsel and Corporate Secretary
jason.duva@avid.com

FITZSIMMONS, Tom
Vice President, Financial Planning Analysis

Tel: (978) 640-3346
Fax: (978) 640-3116

GRIGGS, Sara
Senior Public Relations and Social Media Manager
sara.griggs@avid.com

Tel: (978) 640-6789
Fax: (978) 640-3366

JIMENEZ , Mariela
Meeting Manager

Tel: (978) 640-6789
Fax: (978) 640-3366

METTEL, Rhea
Manager, Government Solutions
rhea_mettel@avid.com

Tel: (978) 640-6789
Fax: (978) 640-3366

RAINE, Edward
Vice President, Human Resources
ed.raine@avid.com

Tel: (978) 640-6789
Fax: (978) 640-1366

ROOSE, Robert
Director, Corporate Development and Strategic Planning
robert.roose@avid.com

Tel: (978) 640-6789
Fax: (978) 640-3366

ROSICA, Jeff
Senior Vice President, Chief Sales and Marketing Officer

Tel: (978) 640-6789
Fax: (978) 640-3366

SIDI, Ilan
Vice President, Human Resources and Interim Chief Financial Officer

Tel: (978) 640-6789
Fax: (978) 640-3366

SWANSON, Suzanne
Meeting Planne
sswanson@avidcenter.org

Tel: (978) 640-6789
Fax: (978) 640-3366

Avis Budget Group

The vehicle rental division of Cendant Corporation previously known as Cendant Car Rental Group. Comprises Avis, Budget Rent A Car, and Budget Truck Rental. The Cendant name was dissolved in 2006 upon the divestiture of its remaining businesses.
www.avisbudgetgroup.com
Annual Revenues: $8.47 billion
Employees: 22,500
Ticker: NYSE: CAR
SIC: 7510
Industry/ies: Automotive Industry; Transportation
Legislative Issues: CSP; TAX; TRA

Chairman of the Board and Chief Executive Officer
NELSON, Ronald L.

Tel: (973) 496-3400
Fax: (888) 304-2315

Main Headquarters
Mailing: Six Sylvan Way
Parsippany, NJ 07054

Tel: (973) 496-3500
Fax: (302) 636-5454
TF: (888) 304-2315

Corporate Foundations and Giving Programs

Avis Budget Charitable Foundation
Contact: Alice Pereira
Six Sylvan Way
Parsippany, NJ 07054

Public Affairs and Related Activities Personnel

At Headquarters

BARROWS, John
Vice President, Communications
PR@avisbudget.com

Tel: (973) 496-7865
Fax: (888) 304-2315

DEAVER, Scott
Executive Vice President, Strategy

Tel: (973) 496-3500
Fax: (888) 304-2315

GARTLAND, Thomas M.
President
thomas.gartland@avisbudget.com

Tel: (973) 496-4700
Fax: (302) 636-5454

GOLDNER, Neal
Vice President, Investor Relations
IR@avisbudget.com

Tel: (973) 496-1040
Fax: (888) 304-2315

LINNEN, Ned
Senior Vice President and Chief Human Resources Officer

Tel: (973) 496-4700
Fax: (302) 636-5454

MARTINS, Izilda
Senior Vice President, Finance

Tel: (973) 496-4700
Fax: (302) 636-5454

PEREIRA, Alice
Contact, Communication

Tel: (973) 496-6113
Fax: (302) 636-5454

SERVODIDIO, Mark J.
Executive Vice President, Franchise and Corporate Services

Tel: (973) 496-3400
Fax: (302) 636-5454

TUCKER, Michael K.
Executive Vice President and General Counsel
Michael.tucker@avisbudget.com

Tel: (973) 496-3500
Fax: (888) 304-2315

WYSHNER, David B.
Senior Executive Vice President and Chief Financial Officer

Tel: (973) 496-3500
Fax: (888) 304-2315

Avista Corporation

An energy, information and technology company.
www.avistacorp.com

Annual Revenues: $1.46 billion
Employees: 1,938
Ticker: NYSE: AVA
SIC: 4931
Industry/ies: Energy/Electricity
Legislative Issues: ENG

Chairman of the Board, President and Chief Executive Officer　　Tel:　(800) 727-9170
MORRIS, Scott L.　　Fax:　(509) 495-8725

Main Headquarters
Mailing:　1411 E. Mission Ave.　　Tel:　(800) 727-9170
　　P.O. Box 3727　　Fax:　(509) 777-5075
　　Spokane, WA 99220-3727　　TF:　(800) 227-9187

Political Action Committees
Avista Employees for Effective Government PAC
FEC ID: C00041038
Contact: Patricia Tackes
1411 E. Mission Ave.
P.O. Box 3727
Spokane, WA 99220

　Contributions to Candidates: $20,380 (2015-2016)
　Democrats: $5,500; Republicans: $14,880

Corporate Foundations and Giving Programs
Avista Foundation
1411 E. Mission Ave.　　Tel:　(509) 495-4817
P.O. Box 3727
Spokane, WA 99220

Public Affairs and Related Activities Personnel

At Headquarters
DURKIN, Marian　　Tel:　(800) 727-9170
Senior Vice President, General Counsel and Chief　　Fax:　(509) 495-8725
Compliance Officer

FELTES, Karen S.　　Tel:　(800) 727-9170
Senior Vice President, Human Resources and Corporate　　Fax:　(509) 495-8725
Secretary

LANG, Jason　　Tel:　(509) 495-2930
Manager, Investor Relations　　Fax:　(509) 495-8725
jason.lang@avistacorp.com

MEYER, David J.　　Tel:　(509) 495-4817
Vice President and Chief Counsel, Regulatory and　　Fax:　(509) 495-8725
Government Affairs
david.meyer@avistacorp.com

SCHLECT, Ed　　Tel:　(800) 727-9170
Vice President and Chief Strategy Officer　　Fax:　(509) 777-5075

TACKES, Patricia　　Tel:　(800) 727-9170
PAC Treasurer　　Fax:　(509) 777-5075

THIES , Mark　　Tel:　(800) 727-9170
Senior Vice President and Chief Financial Officer　　Fax:　(509) 777-5075

WOODWORTH, Roger D.　　Tel:　(800) 727-9170
Vice President　　Fax:　(509) 777-5075

WUERST, Jessie　　Tel:　(509) 495-8578
Senior Manager, Communications　　Fax:　(509) 495-8725
jessie.wuerst@avistacorp.com

Aviva USA

Aviva USA is part of Aviva PLC and offers life insurance.
www.avivausa.com
Annual Revenues: $50.70 million
Industry/ies: Insurance Industry

President and Chief Executive Officer　　Tel:　(515) 362-3600
LITTLEFIELD, Christopher
clittlefield@avivausa.com

Main Headquarters
Mailing:　7700 Mills Civic Pkwy.　　Tel:　(515) 362-3600
　　W. Des Moines, IA 50266

Political Action Committees
Aviva USA Corporation PAC
FEC ID: C00180901
7700 Mills Civic Pkwy.
Suite 2000
Des Moines, IA 50266

Corporate Foundations and Giving Programs
Aviva Charitable Foundation
Contact: Karen Lynn
7700 Mills Civic Pkwy.　　Tel:　(515) 362-3600
Des Moines, IA 50266

Public Affairs and Related Activities Personnel

At Headquarters
COHAN, Jr., Richard C.　　Tel:　(515) 362-3600

Executive Vice President, General Counsel, PAC Treasurer
and Corporate Secretary
rich.cohan@avivausa.com

CUSHING, Brenda　　Tel:　(515) 362-3600
Executive Vice President and Chief Financial Officer

LYNN, Karen　　Tel:　(515) 342-3910
Head, Corporate Affairs
karen.lynn@avivausa.com

WAETKE, Kevin　　Tel:　(515) 342-3822
Director, Public Relations and Corporate Affairs
kevin.waetke@avivausa.com

AVL Powertrain Engineering, Inc.

Develops powertrain systems with internal combustion engines, simulation methodologies,
instrumentation, and test systems.
www.avl.com
Annual Revenues: $8.60 million
Employees: 120
Industry/ies: Machinery/Equipment

Chairman of the Board and Chief Executive Officer　　Tel:　(734) 414-9600
LIST, Helmut O.　　Fax:　(734) 414-9690
helmut.list@avl.com

Main Headquarters
Mailing:　47519 Halyard Dr.　　Tel:　(734) 414-9600
　　Plymouth, MI 48170-2438　　Fax:　(734) 414-9690
　　　　TF:　(877) 285-4278

Corporate Foundations and Giving Programs
AVL Cultural Foundation
Contact: Michael Ksela
47519 Halyard Dr.　　Tel:　(734) 414-9600
Plymouth, MI 48170-2438　　Fax:　(734) 414-9690

Public Affairs and Related Activities Personnel

At Headquarters
KSELA, Michael　　Tel:　(734) 414-9600
Spokesman　　Fax:　(734) 414-9690
michael.ksela@scoopandspoon.com

SCHUSTER, Werner　　Tel:　(734) 414-9600
Chief Financial Officer　　Fax:　(734) 414-9690

AVL-PEI, Inc.

See listing on page 98 under AVL Powertrain Engineering, Inc.

Avnet Inc.

A distributor of electronic components, computer products and services, and embedded
systems.
www.avnet.com
Annual Revenues: $28.18 billion
Employees: 19,000
Ticker: NYSE: AVT
SIC: 5065
NAICS: 421690
Industry/ies: Computer/Technology

Chairman of the Board　　Tel:　(480) 643-2000
SCHUMANN, III, William H.　　Fax:　(480) 643-7370

Chief Executive Officer　　Tel:　(480) 643-2000
HAMADA , Rick　　Fax:　(480) 643-7370

President　　Tel:　(480) 643-2000
BAWOL , Jeff　　Fax:　(480) 643-7370

Main Headquarters
Mailing:　2211 S. 47th St.　　Tel:　(480) 643-2000
　　Phoenix, AZ 85034　　Fax:　(480) 643-7370
　　　　TF:　(800) 332-8638

Corporate Foundations and Giving Programs
Avnet Inc. Contributions Program
Contact: Jessie Ferris
2211 S. 47th St.　　Tel:　(480) 643-2000
Phoenix, AZ 85034

Public Affairs and Related Activities Personnel

At Headquarters
BUSEMAN, Mike　　Tel:　(480) 643-2000
Senior Vice President and Chief Global Logistics and　　Fax:　(480) 643-7370
Operations Officer

CHURCH, Steve　　Tel:　(480) 643-2000
Chief Operational Excellence Officer　　Fax:　(480) 643-7370
steve.church@avnet.com

FERRIS, Jessie　　Tel:　(480) 643-4811
Contact, Corporate Philanthropy and Contributions and　　Fax:　(480) 643-7370
Administrative Assistant
Jessie.ferris@avnet.com

GOREL, Michelle	Tel:	(480) 643-7653
Vice President, Public Relations and Corporate	Fax:	(480) 643-7415
Communications		
michelle.gorel@avnet.com		
LEWIN, Erin	Tel:	(480) 643-2000
Senior Vice President, General Counsel and Assistant	Fax:	(480) 643-7370
Secretary		
MILLER, Mary Ann	Tel:	(480) 643-2000
Senior Vice President, Human Resources and Corporate	Fax:	(480) 643-7370
Communications		
maryann.miller@Avnet.com		
MORIARTY, Kevin	Tel:	(480) 643-2000
Senior Vice President, Chief Financial Officer, Controller and	Fax:	(480) 643-7370
Assistant		
RADOSEVICH, Teri	Tel:	(480) 643-2000
Vice President, Community Relations and Public Affairs	Fax:	(480) 643-7370
teri.radosevich@avnet.com		

Avon Products, Inc.

Manufacturer and distributor of cosmetics, fragrances, toiletries and costume jewelry.
www.avoncompany.com
Annual Revenues: $8.46 billion
Employees: 33,200
Ticker: NYSE: AVP
SIC: 2844; 3961
NAICS: 325620; 339914; 325611
Industry/ies: Animals; Jewelry & Gems; Personal Care/Hygiene; Retail/Wholesale

| **Chief Executive Officer** | Tel: | (212) 282-5000 |
| MCCOY, Sherilyn S. | Fax: | (212) 282-6049 |

Main Headquarters
| *Mailing:* 777 Third Ave. | Tel: | (212) 282-7000 |
| New York City, NY 10017 | | |

Political Action Committees
Avon Products Inc. Fund for Responsible Government PAC
FEC ID: C00112722
Contact: Josephine Mills
| 777 Third Ave. | Tel: | (212) 282-5609 |
| New York, NY 10017 | Fax: | (212) 282-6086 |

Avon Products Inc. Fund for Responsible Government PAC
FEC ID: C00112722
Contact: Josephine Mills
| 777 Third Ave. | Tel: | (212) 282-5609 |
| New York, NY 10017 | Fax: | (212) 282-6086 |

Corporate Foundations and Giving Programs

Avon Foundation
Contact: Carol Kurzig
1345 Ave. of the Amercas
New York City, NY 10105

Avon Foundation
Contact: Sherilyn S. McCoy
1345 Ave. of the Amercas
New York City, NY 10105

Public Affairs and Related Activities Personnel

At Headquarters

BENJAMIN, Jeff	Tel:	(212) 282-7000
Senior Vice President, General Counsel and Chief Ethics and		
Compliance Officer		
CHASEN, Amy	Tel:	(212) 282-5320
Contact, Investor Relations		
investor.relations@avon.com		
HEINONEN, Cheryl	Tel:	(212) 282-7000
Senior Vice President, Corporate Relations and Chief		
Communications Officer		
HEINONEN, Cheryl	Tel:	(212) 282-7000
Senior Vice President, Global Corporate Relations and Chief		
Communications Officer		
KURZIG, Carol	Tel:	(212) 282-5635
President, Avon Foundation		
Carol.Kurzig@avonfoundation.org		
MILLS, Josephine		
PAC Treasurer		
ORMISTON, Susan	Tel:	(212) 282-7000
Senior Vice President, Human Resources and Chief Human		
Resources Officer		
PEREZ-AYALA, Patricia	Tel:	(212) 282-7000
Senior Vice President and Chief Marketing Officer		
ROSS, Kimberly A.	Tel:	(212) 282-7000
Executive Vice President and Chief Financial Officer		
SCULLY, James 3.	Tel:	(212) 282-7000

Executive Vice President and Chief Financial Officer
At Other Offices
EERDMANS, Susan R.	Tel:	(212) 282-5000
Manager, Global Government Affairs	Fax:	(212) 282-6049
1345 Avenue of the Americas		
New York City, NY 10105		
susan.eerdmans@avon.com		
HEINONEN, Cheryl	Tel:	(212) 282-5000
Senior Vice President, Corporate Relations and Chief		
Communications Officer		
1345 Avenue of the Americas		
New York City, NY 10105		
JUNG, Andrea	Tel:	(212) 282-5000
Senior Advisor	Fax:	(212) 282-6049
1345 Avenue of the Americas		
New York City, NY 10105		
ORMISTON, Susan	Tel:	(212) 282-5000
Senior Vice President, Human Resources and Chief Human		
Resources Officer		
1345 Avenue of the Americas		
New York City, NY 10105		

Avue Technologies Corporation

Provides human resource technology services.
www.avuetech.com
Annual Revenues: $6.40 million
Employees: 100
Industry/ies: Employees & Employment

Chairman of the Board	Tel:	(253) 573-1877
PENNINE, D.R.	Fax:	(253) 573-1876
Chief Executive Officer	Tel:	(253) 573-1877
MILLER, James D.	Fax:	(253) 573-1876
Co Chief Executive Officer	Tel:	(253) 573-1877
RIX, Linda	Fax:	(253) 573-1876

Main Headquarters
Mailing: 1145 Broadway Plaza	Tel:	(253) 573-1877
Suite 800	Fax:	(253) 573-1876
Tacoma, WA 98402-3523		

Washington Office
Mailing: 1501 K. St. NW	Tel:	(202) 772-1007
Suite 300	Fax:	(202) 772-1022
Washington, DC 20005		

AWare Technologies

Provides software and services for the biometrics industry.
www.aware.com
Annual Revenues: $21.23 million
Employees: 70
Ticker: NASDAQ: AWRE
SIC: 7372
Industry/ies: Computer/Technology; Medicine/Health Care/Mental Health; Science; Scientific Research; Sports/Leisure/Entertainment

Chairman of the Board	Tel:	(617) 868-5868
STAFFORD, Jr., John S.		
Co-Chief Executive Officer, Co-President and Chief Financial	Tel:	(617) 868-5868
Officer		
MOBERG, Richard P.		
Co-Chief Executive Officer, Co-President and General Counsel	Tel:	(617) 868-5868
RUSSELL, Kevin T.		

Main Headquarters
| *Mailing:* 40 Middlesex Tnpk. | Tel: | (617) 868-5868 |
| Bedford, MA 01730 | | |

Public Affairs and Related Activities Personnel
At Headquarters
| LOCKWOOD, Becky | Tel: | (617) 868-5868 |
| *Contact, Sales and Marketing* | | |

AWS Convergence Technologies Inc.

See listing on page 274 under Earth Networks, Inc.

AXA Equitable Life Insurance Company

A financial services company with a purpose to help provide financial security for our clients and their families.
us.axa.com
Employees: 161,000
Ticker: NYSE: AXF
SIC: 6411
Industry/ies: Banking/Finance/Investments
Legislative Issues: FIN; INS; TAX

Director, President and Chief Executive Officer
PEARSON, Mark

Tel: (212) 534-1234
Fax: (212) 314-3954

Main Headquarters
Mailing: 1290 Avenue of the Americas
New York City, NY 10104

Tel: (212) 534-1234
Fax: (212) 314-3954
TF: (888) 292-4636

Political Action Committees
AXA Equitable Life Insurance Company Political Action Committee
FEC ID: C00161901
Contact: Josh Braverman
1290 Avenue of the Americas
New York City, NY 10104

Tel: (212) 534-1234

Contributions to Candidates: $29,500 (2015-2016)
Democrats: $7,500; Republicans: $22,000

Corporate Foundations and Giving Programs

AXA Foundation
1290 Avenue of the Americas
New York City, NY 10104

Tel: (212) 554-1234
Fax: (212) 314-4480

Public Affairs and Related Activities Personnel

At Headquarters

BRAVERMAN, Josh
Senior Executive Director, Treasurer and PAC Contact

Tel: (212) 534-1234
Fax: (212) 314-3954

HATTEM, Dave S.
Senior Executive Director and General Counsel

Tel: (212) 534-1234
Fax: (212) 314-3954

LOO, Carmen Y.
Lead Director, Internal Audit

Tel: (212) 534-1234
Fax: (212) 314-3954

MALMSTROM, Anders
Senior Executive Director and Chief Financial Officer

Tel: (212) 534-1234
Fax: (212) 314-3954

PIAZZOLLA, Rino
Senior Executive Director and the Chief Human Resources Officer

Tel: (212) 534-1234
Fax: (212) 314-3954

RITCHEY, Sharon
Senior Executive Director and the Chief Operating Officer

Tel: (212) 534-1234
Fax: (212) 314-3954

WINTER, Discretion
Media Contact
discretion.winter@axa-equitable.com

Tel: (212) 314-2968
Fax: (212) 314-3954

Axalto

See listing on page 351 under Gemalto, Inc.

Axiall Corporation

Formerly Georgia Gulf Corporation. Axiall Corporation is an integrated chemicals and building products company.
www.axiall.com
Annual Revenues: $4.52 billion
Employees: 6,000
Ticker: NYSE: AXLL
SIC: 2821
Industry/ies: Chemicals & Chemical Industry

Chairman of the Board
NOETZEL, Mark

Tel: (770) 395-4500
Fax: (770) 395-4529

President and Chief Executive Officer
CARRICO, Paul D.

Tel: (770) 395-4500
Fax: (770) 395-4529

Main Headquarters
Mailing: 1000 Abernathy Rd. NE
Suite 1200
Atlanta, GA 30328

Tel: (770) 395-4500
Fax: (770) 395-4529

Corporate Foundations and Giving Programs

Georgia Gulf Corporation Contributions Program
115 Perimeter Center Pl.
Suite 460
Atlanta, GA 30346

Tel: (770) 395-4500
Fax: (770) 395-4529

Public Affairs and Related Activities Personnel

At Headquarters

JR., Timothy Mann
Executive Vice President, Strategy, General Counsel and Corporate Secretary

Tel: (770) 395-4500
Fax: (770) 395-4529

At Other Offices

ADELMAN, Dean
Vice President, Human Resources
115 Perimeter Center Pl., Suite 460
Atlanta, GA 30346

Tel: (770) 395-4500
Fax: (770) 395-4529

CHAPPLE, Alan
Director, Corporate Communications and Public Relations
115 Perimeter Center Pl., Suite 460
Atlanta, GA 30346
chapplea@ggc.com

Tel: (770) 395-4538
Fax: (770) 395-4529

JAROSICK, Martin
Executive Director, Investor Relations

Tel: (770) 395-4524
Fax: (770) 395-4529

115 Perimeter Center Pl., Suite 460
Atlanta, GA 30346
jarosickm@ggc.com

THOMPSON, Gregory
Chief Financial Officer
115 Perimeter Center Pl., Suite 460
Atlanta, GA 30346

Tel: (770) 395-4500
Fax: (770) 395-4529

Axsys Technologies, Inc

Axsys Technologies manufactures applications, such as airborne thermal targeting, missile tracking.
www.axsystech.in
Annual Revenues: $245.50 million
Employees: 1,000
Ticker: NASDAQ (GS): AXYS
SIC: 3827
Industry/ies: Defense/Homeland Security; Government-Related
Legislative Issues: DEF

Main Headquarters
Mailing: 24 Simon St.
Nashua, NH 03060

Tel: (603) 864-6300
Fax: (603) 864-6250

Public Affairs and Related Activities Personnel

At Headquarters

RYAN, Lucy
Contact, Public Relations
PublicRelations@gd-ais.com

Tel: (703) 272-6010
Fax: (603) 864-6250

B. E. Meyers and Company

A supplier, manufacturer and systems integrator of electro-optical and other related products used for industrial, law enforcement and defense applications.
www.bemeyers.com
Annual Revenues: $29.70 million
Employees: 100
Industry/ies: Defense/Homeland Security; Government-Related
Legislative Issues: DEF; HOM; TRA

Founder and Chief Executive Officer
MEYERS, Brad E.
bradm@bemeyers.com

Tel: (425) 881-6648
Fax: (425) 867-1759

Main Headquarters
Mailing: 9461 Willows Rd. NE
Redmond, WA 98052

Tel: (425) 881-6648
Fax: (425) 867-1759
TF: (800) 327-5648

Public Affairs and Related Activities Personnel

At Headquarters

BAILEY, Jarrod
Manager, Business Development, US Government and Federal
jarrod.bailey@bemeyers.com

Tel: (425) 881-6648
Fax: (425) 867-1759

MEYERS , Nancy E.
Secretary and Treasurer
nancy.meyers@bemeyers.com

Tel: (425) 881-6648
Fax: (425) 867-1759

OLIVER, Stephen
Chief Operating Officer and Chief Financial Officer

Tel: (425) 881-6648
Fax: (425) 867-1759

TOTT, Chris
Senior Business Development Manager
chris.tott@bemeyers.com

Tel: (425) 881-6648
Fax: (425) 867-1759

The Babcock and Wilcox Company

Operates as a specialty constructor of nuclear components for customers in the power and other steam-using industries.
www.babcock.com
Annual Revenues: $2.99 billion
Employees: 11,000
Ticker: NYSE: BWC
SIC: 3510
Industry/ies: Energy/Electricity
Legislative Issues: AER; BUD; DEF; ENG; ENV; FOR; TAX

President and Chief Executive Officer
FERLAND, E. James

Main Headquarters
Mailing: 13024 Ballantyne Corporate Pl.
Suite 700
Charlotte, NC 28277

Tel: (704) 625-4900
Fax: (704) 625-4910

Washington Office
Mailing: 511 Second St. NE
Washington, DC 20002

Tel: (202) 756-7205
Fax: (202) 756-7204

Political Action Committees
Babcock and Wilcox Company PAC (B&W PAC)
FEC ID: C00365502
Contact: David S. Black

2016 Mt. Athos Rd.
Lynchburg, VA 24504

Contributions to Candidates: $138,500 (2015-2016)
Democrats: $19,000; Republicans: $119,500

Principal Recipients

HOUSE
MCCARTHY, KEVIN (REP-CA)
RENACCI, JAMES B. (REP-OH)

Corporate Foundations and Giving Programs

Babcock and Wilcox Contributions Program
800 Main St.   Tel: (434) 522-6800
Fourth Floor
Lynchburg, VA 24504

Bacardi USA, Inc.

Manufacturer and distributor of spirits.
www.bacardiusa.com
Employees: 500
Industry/ies: Food And Beverage Industry
Legislative Issues: ALC; CPT; FOR; TAX; TRD

Chief Executive Officer   Tel: (305) 573-8511
DOLAN, Michael J.   Fax: (305) 573-0756

Main Headquarters
Mailing: 2701 Le Jeune Rd.   Tel: (305) 573-8511
Coral Gables, FL 33134   Fax: (305) 573-0756

Washington Office
Mailing: 1101 Pennsylvania Ave. NW   Tel: (202) 756-4390
Suite 600
Washington, DC 20004

Political Action Committees

Bicardi USA Inc. PAC
FEC ID: C00160838
Contact: Roberto Del Rosal
2701 Le Jeune Rd.
Miami, FL 33134

Contributions to Candidates: $26,980 (2015-2016)
Democrats: $9,000; Republicans: $17,980

Corporate Foundations and Giving Programs

Bacardi U.S.A., Inc. Contributions Program
2701 Le Jeune Rd.   Tel: (305) 573-8511
Coral Gables, FL 33134   Fax: (305) 573-8511

Public Affairs and Related Activities Personnel

At Headquarters

FEDERMAN, Amy   Tel: (441) 294-1110
Contact, Media Relations   Fax: (305) 573-0756
afederman@bacardi.com

NEAL, Patricia M.   Tel: (441) 294-8317
Vice President, Corporate Communications   Fax: (305) 573-0756

NORTHCUTT, Scott M.   Tel: (305) 573-8511
Senior Vice President, Human Resources   Fax: (305) 573-0756

SÁNCHEZ, Eduardo   Tel: (305) 573-8511
Senior Vice President and General Counsel   Fax: (305) 573-0756

At Washington Office

BODENSTEDT, Kristin   Tel: (202) 756-4390
Assistant General Counsel & Director, Government Relations
kbodenstedt@bacardi.com
Registered Federal Lobbyist

ROSAL, Roberto Del   Tel: (202) 756-4390
PAC Contact

Bacardi-Martini U.S.A

See listing on page 101 under Bacardi USA, Inc.

BAE Systems Inc.

A manufacturer of armored combat vehicles and weapons delivery systems for American and allied armed forces. Registered in England and Wales as BAE Systems plc.
www.baesystems.com
Employees: 7,000
Industry/ies: Aerospace/Aviation; Communications; Defense/Homeland Security; Electricity & Electronics; Electronics; Energy/Electricity; Government-Related; Telecommunications/Internet/Cable; Transportation
Legislative Issues: BUD; CPI; DEF; ENV; TRA

Chairman   Tel: (703) 312-6100
CARR , Roger

President and Chief Executive Officer   Tel: (703) 907-8200
DEMURO, Gerard J. "Jerry"   Fax: (703) 907-8300

Main Headquarters
Mailing: 1101 Wilson Blvd.   Tel: (703) 312-6100
Suite 2000

Arlington, VA 22209

Political Action Committees

Bae Systems Inc. Political Action Committee
FEC ID: C00281212
Contact: Sydelle Lyon
1101 Wilson Blvd.   Tel: (703) 416-7800
Suite 2000   Fax: (703) 415-1459
Arlington, VA 22209

Contributions to Candidates: $10,734,015 (2015-2016)
Democrats: $161,500; Republicans: $280,500; Other: $10,292,015

Principal Recipients

SENATE
MCCAIN, JOHN S (REP-VA)
MURRAY, PATTY (DEM-WA)

HOUSE
CARTER, JOHN R. REP. (REP-DC)
CRENSHAW, ANDER (REP-FL)
FORBES, J. RANDY (REP-VA)
FRELINGHUYSEN, RODNEY P. (REP-NJ)
KUSTER, ANN MCLANE (DEM-NH)
THORNBERRY, MAC (REP-TX)
TURNER, MICHAEL R (REP-OH)
WALORSKI SWIHART, JACKIE (REP-IN)
WILSON, JOE THE HON. (REP-SC)
WITTMAN, ROBERT J MR. (REP-VA)

Corporate Foundations and Giving Programs

BAE Systems Charity Challenge
1601 Research Blvd.   Tel: (301) 738-4000
Rockville, MD 20850   Fax: (301) 738-4743

BAE Systems Corporate Responsibility
Contact: Dr. Deborah Allen
1601 Research Blvd.   Tel: (301) 838-6000
Rockville, MD 20850

Public Affairs and Related Activities Personnel

At Headquarters

ARSENEAULT, Tom   Tel: (703) 312-6100
Chief Operating Officer

BISHOP, Thomas A.   Tel: (703) 312-6100
Director, Legislative Affairs
Registered Federal Lobbyist

CAMPBELL, John   Tel: (703) 312-6100
Board of Director

DIVVER , Claire   Tel: (703) 312-6100
Director, Group Communications

GARWOOD, Alan   Tel: (703) 312-6100
Director, Group Business Development

GREENE, Morley   Tel: (703) 312-6100
Registered Federal Lobbyist

HOPKINS, Heather   Tel: (703) 312-6100
Contact, Government Relations

LYON, Sydelle   Tel: (703) 312-6100
PAC Treasurer
sydelle.lyon@baesystems.com

RUBRIGHT, Stephen   Tel: (703) 312-6100

RUGGIERO, Frank   Tel: (703) 312-6100
Senior Vice President, Government Relations
Registered Federal Lobbyist

SCHWENK, John   Tel: (703) 312-6100
Federal Lobbyist
Registered Federal Lobbyist

TAYLOR , Kevin   Tel: (703) 312-6100
Director, Group Strategy

TESTUT, Gary   Tel: (703) 312-6100
Federal Lobbyist

At Other Offices

BRAMWELL, Philip   Tel: (703) 907-8200
Group General Counsel   Fax: (703) 907-8300
1300 N. 17th St., Suite 1400
Arlington, VA 22209

GAGNE, Heather   Tel: (703) 907-8200
Director-Government Affairs, Federal Lobbyist   Fax: (703) 465-0329
1300 N. 17th St., Suite 1400
Arlington, VA 22209

HESCHELES, Heather   Tel: (703) 907-8200
Director, Sales and Marketing   Fax: (703) 465-0329
1300 N. 17th St., Suite 1400
Arlington, VA 22209
Registered Federal Lobbyist

LYNAS, Peter   Tel: (703) 907-8200

Group Finance Director	Fax:	(703) 907-8300
1300 N. 17th St., Suite 1400		
Arlington, VA 22209		
MCBRIDE, Col. Michael	Tel:	(703) 907-8200
Vice President, Legislative Affairs	Fax:	(703) 465-0329
1300 N. 17th St., Suite 1400		
Arlington, VA 22209		
Registered Federal Lobbyist		
MIKO, John	Tel:	(703) 907-8200
Vice President, Government Relations	Fax:	(703) 465-0329
1300 N. 17th St., Suite 1400		
Arlington, VA 22209		
Registered Federal Lobbyist		
MINELLA, Lynn C.	Tel:	(703) 907-8200
Director, Group Human Resources	Fax:	(703) 907-8300
1300 N. 17th St., Suite 1400		
Arlington, VA 22209		
ROEHRKASS, Brian	Tel:	(703) 312-6976
Vice President, External Communications	Fax:	(703) 907-8300
1300 N. 17th St., Suite 1400		
Arlington, VA 22209		
brian.roehrkasse@baesystems.com		
STEWART, Douglas D.	Tel:	(703) 907-8200
Vice President, Government Relations	Fax:	(703) 465-0329
1300 N. 17th St., Suite 1400		
Arlington, VA 22209		
douglas.d.stewart@baesystems.com		
STREET, Storme	Tel:	(703) 907-8200
Director, Government Relations and Policy Services	Fax:	(703) 465-0329
1300 N. 17th St., Suite 1400		
Arlington, VA 22209		
sstreet@eia.org		
WALLIN, Douglas R.	Tel:	(703) 907-8200
Director, Legislative Affairs	Fax:	(703) 465-0329
1300 N. 17th St., Suite 1400		
Arlington, VA 22209		
douglas.wallin@baesystems.com		
Registered Federal Lobbyist		

BAE Systems Southeast Shipyards AMHC Inc.

Provides full-service shipyards in the Gulf of Mexico and along the U.S. East Coast.
www.atlanticmarine.com
Annual Revenues: $268.80 million
Employees: 2,000
SIC: 3731
Industry/ies: Marine/Maritime/Shipping; Transportation

Acting Chief Executive Officer	Tel:	(904) 251-3164
FLEMMING, Ed	Fax:	(904) 251-3500

Main Headquarters		
Mailing: 8500 Hecksher Dr.	Tel:	(904) 251-1545
Jacksonville Beach, FL 32226	Fax:	(904) 251-3500

Public Affairs and Related Activities Personnel

At Headquarters

HICKEY, Larry	Tel:	(904) 251-1545
Director , Human Resources	Fax:	(904) 251-3500
JONES, David W.	Tel:	(904) 251-1545
PAC Treasurer	Fax:	(904) 251-3500
david@atlanticmarinesales.com		
QUINN, Bill	Tel:	(904) 251-1545
Vice President, Finance	Fax:	(904) 251-3500
VINYARD, Herschel T.	Tel:	(904) 251-1545
Vice President, Government Affairs and PAC Treasurer	Fax:	(904) 251-3500

Baker Hughes Inc.

A provider of products and services for the worldwide oil, gas and continuous process industries.
www.bakerhughes.com
Annual Revenues: $13.82 billion
Employees: 39,000
Ticker: NYSE: BHI
SIC: 3533
NAICS: 333132
Industry/ies: Fuels See Coal, Gas, Oil, Petroleum; Natural Resources; Petroleum Industry

Chairman of the Board and Chief Executive Officer	Tel:	(713) 439-8600
CRAIGHEAD, Martin	Fax:	(713) 439-8699

Main Headquarters		
Mailing: 2929 Allen Pkwy.	Tel:	(713) 439-8600
Suite 2100	Fax:	(713) 439-8699
Houston, TX 77019-2118	TF:	(800) 229-7447

Corporate Foundations and Giving Programs

Baker Hughes Foundation
2929 Allen Pkwy.
Suite 2100
Houston, TX 77019

	Tel:	(713) 439-8600
	Fax:	(713) 439-8699

Public Affairs and Related Activities Personnel

At Headquarters

CRAIN , Alan R.	Tel:	(713) 439-8600
Senior Vice President, Chief Legal and Governance Officer	Fax:	(713) 439-8699
KUPPUSWAMY, Murali	Tel:	(713) 439-8600
Chief Human Resources Officer	Fax:	(713) 439-8699
MARTIN, Jay G.	Tel:	(713) 439-8600
Vice President, Chief Compliance Officer and Senior Deputy Counsel	Fax:	(713) 439-8699
jay.martin@bakerhughes.com		
MATHIESON, Derek	Tel:	(713) 439-8600
Chief Commercial Officer	Fax:	(713) 439-8699
MILLER, Brian W.	Tel:	(713) 439-8600
Engineering Manger, Drill Bits US Land	Fax:	(713) 439-8699
ROSS, Kimberly	Tel:	(713) 439-8600
Senior Vice President and Chief Financial Officer	Fax:	(713) 439-8699
SHIRLEY, Kathy	Tel:	(800) 229-7447
Director, Marketing	Fax:	(713) 439-8699
kathy.shirley@bakerhughes.com		

Balfour Beatty Construction, LLC

Provider of heavy civil engineering and construction services for transportation and water infrastructure projects in the United States.
www.balfourbeattyus.com
Annual Revenues: $232.20 million
Employees: 2,200
Industry/ies: Architecture And Design; Railroads; Transportation
Legislative Issues: BUD

Chairman and Chief Executive Officer	Tel:	(214) 451-1000
LAYMAN, Mark	Fax:	(404) 607-7319

Main Headquarters		
Mailing: 3100 McKinnon St., 10th Floor	Tel:	(214) 451-1000
Tenth Floor	Fax:	(404) 607-7319
Dallas, TX 75201		

Corporate Foundations and Giving Programs

Balfour Beatty Construction Contributions Program
3100 Mckinnon St.
Tenth Floor
Dallas, TX 75201

Public Affairs and Related Activities Personnel

At Headquarters

BURNS, Glenn	Tel:	(214) 451-1000
Executive Vice President and Chief Legal Officer	Fax:	(404) 607-7319
CACERES, Liza	Tel:	(404) 253-6302
Manager, Communications and Strategy	Fax:	(404) 642-0823
lcaceres@bbinfrastructureinc.com		
JAGGERS, Richard	Tel:	(214) 451-1000
Senior Vice President and Chief Financial Officer	Fax:	(404) 607-7319
MAGRATH, Duncan	Tel:	(214) 451-1000
Chief Financial Officer	Fax:	(404) 607-7319
duncan.magrath@balfourbeatty.com		
RABY, Paul	Tel:	(404) 875-0356
Director, Human Resources	Fax:	(404) 607-7319
paul.raby@balfourbeatty.com		
TARPEY, John	Tel:	(214) 451-1000
Chief Operating Officer	Fax:	(404) 607-7319
VAUGHAN, Chris	Tel:	(214) 451-1000
Chief Corporate Officer	Fax:	(404) 607-7319

Ball Aerospace & Technologies Corporation

A producer of rigid packaging products for food and beverages, and a provider of aerospace and other technology products and services to government and commercial customers.
www.ballaerospace.com
Annual Revenues: $286.40 million
Employees: 3,000
Ticker: NYSE: BLL
SIC: 3571; 3812; 7371
NAICS: 332431
Industry/ies: Aerospace/Aviation; Defense/Homeland Security; Engineering/ Mathematics; Government-Related; Transportation
Legislative Issues: BUD; DEF; ENG; FOO; INT; LBR; MAN; SCI; TAX; TRD

President	Tel:	(303) 939-6100
STRAIN, Robert D.	Fax:	(303) 939-5100

Main Headquarters		
Mailing: 1600 Commerce St.	Tel:	(303) 939-6100
Boulder, CO 80301	Fax:	(303) 939-5100

Washington Office

Mailing:	2111 Wilson Blvd.	Tel:	(703) 284-5440
	Suite 1120	Fax:	(703) 284-5449
	Arlington, VA 22201		

Corporate Foundations and Giving Programs

Ball Aerospace and Technologies Corporation Contributions Program
1600 Commerce St.   Tel: (303) 939-6332
Bldg. RA-8
Boulder, CO 80301

Public Affairs and Related Activities Personnel

At Headquarters

BROWN, Roz	Tel:	(303) 939-6100
Manager, Media Relations	Fax:	(303) 939-5100
rbrown@ball.com		
DEANY, Thomas M.	Tel:	(303) 533-5380
Vice President, Communications	Fax:	(303) 939-5100
tdeany@ball.com		
SCHIFF, Vikki A.	Tel:	(303) 939-6100
Vice President, Human Resources	Fax:	(303) 939-5100
SCOTT, Ann T.	Tel:	(303) 460-3537
Director, Investor Relations	Fax:	(303) 939-5100
ascott@ball.com		
UNGER, William T.	Tel:	(303) 939-6100
Vice President, Finance	Fax:	(303) 939-5100
wunger@ball.com		
Registered Federal Lobbyist		

At Washington Office

BUCKMAN, Hope	Tel:	(703) 284-5440
Federal Lobbyist	Fax:	(703) 284-5449
Registered Federal Lobbyist		
CAMPBELL, John D.	Tel:	(703) 284-5440
Vice President, Legislative Affairs	Fax:	(703) 284-5449
Registered Federal Lobbyist		
LANE, Carol S.	Tel:	(703) 284-5440
Vice President and Lead Executive, Civil and Commercial	Fax:	(703) 284-5449
Space		
Registered Federal Lobbyist		

At Other Offices

DAMPHOUSSE (FORMERLY BUCKMAN), Hope
P.O. Box 1235
Broomfield, CO 80038
Registered Federal Lobbyist

MEDBERY , Alison A.
Vice President, Finance
P.O. Box 1235
Broomfield, CO 80038

POMEROY, Jill
P.O. Box 1235
Broomfield, CO 80038
Registered Federal Lobbyist

Bally Total Fitness Holding Corporation

A holding company for Bally Total Fitness, an owner and operator of health and fitness club facilities.
www.ballyfitness.com
Annual Revenues: $763.20 million
Employees: 19,000
SIC: 7997
Industry/ies: Personal Care/Hygiene

Main Headquarters

Mailing:	8700 W. Bryn Mawr Ave.	Tel:	(773) 380-3000
	Chicago, IL 60631	Fax:	(773) 693-2982
		TF:	(800) 515-2582

Washington Office

Mailing:	P.O. Box 96241
	Washington, DC 20090-6241

Corporate Foundations and Giving Programs

BFIT Communities Program
8700 W. Bryn Mawr Ave.   Tel: (773) 380-3000
Chicago, IL 60631   Fax: (773) 693-2982

Banco Popular

See listing on page 645 under Popular, Inc.

Bancorp South

A financial holding company. It provides commercial banking and financial services to individuals and small-to-medium size businesses. It also offers various deposit products, including interest bearing and noninterest bearing demand deposits, and saving and time deposits.
www.bancorpsouth.com

Annual Revenues: $702.16 million
Employees: 3,820
Ticker: NYSE: BXS
SIC: 6770
Industry/ies: Banking/Finance/Investments

Chairman of the Board and Chief Executive Officer and Director	Tel:	(662) 680-2000
ROLLINS III, James D.	Fax:	(662) 678-7299

Main Headquarters

Mailing:	One Mississippi Plaza	Tel:	(662) 680-2000
	201 S. Spring St.	Fax:	(662) 678-7299
	Tupelo, MS 38804-4826	TF:	(888) 797-7711

Political Action Committees

Bancorp South Bank PAC FKA Bank of Mississippi Officers Voluntary Political Committee
FEC ID: C00183962
Contact: Marty A. Rowe
One Mississippi Plaza   Tel: (662) 680-2000
201 S. Spring St.   Fax: (680) 678-7299
Tupelo, MS 38804

> **Contributions to Candidates:** $21,000 (2015-2016)
> Democrats: $3,000; Republicans: $18,000
>
> **Principal Recipients**
>
> **HOUSE**
> KELLY, JOHN TRENT (REP-MS)

Public Affairs and Related Activities Personnel

At Headquarters

BAGLEY, Chris	Tel:	(662) 680-2000
President and Chief Operating Officer	Fax:	(662) 678-7299
BURCHFIELD, Randy	Tel:	(662) 620-4136
Senior Vice President, Corporate Communications	Fax:	(662) 678-7299
randy.burchfield@bxs.com		
FISACKERLY, Will	Tel:	(662) 680-2475
Senior Vice President and Director, Corporate Finance	Fax:	(662) 678-7299
will.fisackerly@bxs.com		
FREEMAN, Cathy S.	Tel:	(662) 680-2000
Senior Executive Vice President and Chief Administrative Officer	Fax:	(662) 678-7299
PIGNUOLO, Chuck	Tel:	(662) 680-2000
Senior Executive Vice President and General Counsel	Fax:	(662) 678-7299
PRATER, William Lloyd	Tel:	(662) 680-2000
Senior Executive Vice President and Chief Financial Officer	Fax:	(662) 678-7299
ROWE, Marty A.	Tel:	(662) 680-2000
First Vice President, Human Resources and PAC Treasurer	Fax:	(662) 678-7299
THREADGILL, Jr., William James	Tel:	(662) 680-2000
Senior Executive Vice President and Chief Business Development Officer	Fax:	(662) 678-7299

BancWest Corporation

A wholly owned subsidiary of BNP Paribas, and a holding company for Bank of the West and First Hawaiian Bank. BancWest Corporation is a financial services holding company.
www.bancwestcorp.com
Employees: 12,000
SIC: 6022
Industry/ies: Banking/Finance/Investments

Chairman of the Board	Tel:	(415) 765-4800
SHEPHERD, J. Michael		
Chief Executive Officer	Tel:	(415) 765-4800
BAKHSHI, Nandita		

Main Headquarters

Mailing:	180 Montgomery St.	Tel:	(415) 765-4800
	San Francisco, CA 94104		

Political Action Committees

BancWest Corporation PAC
FEC ID: C00418764
Contact: Daniel Beck
180 Montgomery St.   Tel: (415) 765-4884
14th Floor
San Francisco, CA 94104

> **Contributions to Candidates:** $17,500 (2015-2016)
> Democrats: $2,500; Republicans: $15,000

Public Affairs and Related Activities Personnel

At Headquarters

BECK, Daniel	Tel:	(415) 765-4800
PAC Treasurer		
Mail Stop 14th Floor		
FULCONIS, Thibault	Tel:	(415) 765-4800
Vice Chair, Chief Financial Officer and Treasurer		
WASHINGTON, Vanessa	Tel:	(415) 765-4800

Executive Vice President, General Counsel and Secretary

Bank of America Corporation

Headquartered in Charlotte, NC. Acquired FleetBoston Financial Corporation in 2004. Bank of American Corp. acquired MBNA Corporation in June 2006 and acquired Merrill Lynch in January 2009.
www.bankofamerica.com
Annual Revenues: $80.85 billion
Employees: 220,000
Ticker: NYSE: BAC
SIC: 6189
Industry/ies: Banking/Finance/Investments
Legislative Issues: BAN; FIN; POS; RET; TAX; TRD

Chairman of the Board and Chief Executive Officer — Tel: (704) 386-5681
MOYNIHAN, Brian T. — Fax: (704) 403-0968
Brian.T.Moynihan@bankofamerica.com

Main Headquarters
Mailing: Bank of America Corporate Center — Tel: (704) 386-5681
100 N. Tyron St. — Fax: (704) 403-0968
Charlotte, NC 28255 — TF: (800) 299-2265

Washington Office
Mailing: 1455 Pennsylvania Ave. NW — Tel: (202) 661-7100
Suite 950 — Fax: (202) 383-3475
Washington, DC 20004

Political Action Committees
Bank of America Corporation Federal PAC
FEC ID: C00364778
Contact: James R. Carlisle Jr.
1455 Pennsylvania Ave. NW — Tel: (202) 661-7100
Suite 950 — Fax: (202) 383-3475
Washington, DC 20004

> **Contributions to Candidates:** $279,000 (2015-2016)
> Democrats: $79,000; Republicans: $198,000; Other: $2,000

Bank Of America Shareholders Super PAC
FEC ID: C00456434
Contact: Josue Larose
P. O. Box 9961 — Tel: (704) 386-5681
Ft. Lauderdale, FL 33310

Bank of America State and Federal Corporation PAC
FEC ID: C00043489
Contact: Wendy Y. Jamison
1100 N. King St. — Tel: (302) 432-0956
DE5-001-02-07 — Fax: (302)
Wilmington, DE 19884 — 4332-0304

> **Contributions to Candidates:** $6,000 (2015-2016)
> Democrats: $5,000; Republicans: $1,000

Corporate Foundations and Giving Programs
Bank of America Charitable Foundation
Bank of America Corporate Center
100 N. Tyron St., 23rd Floor
Charlotte, NC 28255

Public Affairs and Related Activities Personnel

At Headquarters
FINUCANE, Anne M. — Tel: (704) 386-5681
?Global Chief Strategy and Marketing Officer — Fax: (704) 403-0968

HAGGERTY, Colleen — Tel: (704) 386-5681
Senior Vice President, Public Relations and Communications — Fax: (704) 403-0968
colleen.haggerty@bankofamerica.com

LYNCH, Gary G. — Tel: (704) 386-5681
Global General Counsel — Fax: (704) 403-0968

SMITH, Andrea B. — Tel: (704) 386-5681
Global Head, Human Resources — Fax: (704) 403-0968

STITT, Kevin — Tel: (704) 386-5667
Director, Investor Relations — Fax: (704) 403-0968
kevin.stitt@bankofamerica.com

THOMPSON, Bruce R. — Tel: (704) 386-5681
Chief Financial Officer — Fax: (704) 403-0968

At Washington Office
CARLISLE, Jr., James R. — Tel: (202) 351-0111
Senior Vice President, Federal Government Relations and PAC Treasurer — Fax: (202) 383-3475
Registered Federal Lobbyist

COLLINGWOOD, John E. — Tel: (202) 351-0111
Director, Federal Government Relations & Public Policy — Fax: (202) 383-3475
Mail Stop DC8-455-09-01
john.collingwood@bankoFamerica.cOm
Registered Federal Lobbyist

HILL, Edward J. — Tel: (202) 624-4185
Senior Vice President, Government Relations — Fax: (202) 383-3475
edward.j.hill@bankofamerica.com

Registered Federal Lobbyist
HOBBS, Kelly — Tel: (202) 351-0111
Vice President, Public Policy — Fax: (202) 383-3475

MINOTT, Darrell — Tel: (202) 351-0111
Senior Vice President, State Government Relations — Fax: (202) 383-3475
darrell.minott@bankofamerica.com
Registered Federal Lobbyist

At Other Offices
JAMISON, Wendy Y. — Tel: (302) 432-0956
Vice President, Public Policy and PAC Treasurer — Fax: (302) 432-0304
1100 N. King St., DE5-001-02-07
Wilmington, DE 19884
wendy.jamison@bankofamerica.com

Bank of Hawaii Corporation

Formerly known as the Pacific Century Financial Corp. A banking and financial services company. Parent company of the Bank of Hawaii.
www.boh.com
Annual Revenues: $575.61 million
Employees: 2,156
Ticker: NYSE: BOH
SIC: 6022
Industry/ies: Banking/Finance/Investments

Chairman, President and Chief Executive Officer — Tel: (808) 694-8580
HO, Peter S. — Fax: (808) 537-8440

Main Headquarters
Mailing: 130 Merchant St. — Fax: (808) 537-8440
20th Floor — TF: (888) 643-3888
Honolulu, HI 96813

Political Action Committees
Pacific Century Financial Corporation Special Political Education Committee
FEC ID: C00025668
Contact: Kevin T. Sakamoto
P.O. Box 2900
Honolulu, HI 96846

> **Contributions to Candidates:** $6,500 (2015-2016)
> Democrats: $6,500

Corporate Foundations and Giving Programs
Bank of Hawaii Charitable Foundation
Contact: Donna Tanoue
130 Merchant St.
Honolulu, HI 96813

Public Affairs and Related Activities Personnel

At Headquarters
KIGUCHI, Stafford — Tel: (808) 694-8580
Senior Vice President and Manager, Corporate Communications — Fax: (808) 537-8440
stafford.kaguchi@boh.com

LUCIEN, Kent T. — Tel: (808) 694-8580
Vice Chairman and Chief Financial Officer — Fax: (808) 537-8440

ROSSI, Mark A. — Tel: (808) 694-8580
Vice Chairman and Chief Administrative Officer — Fax: (808) 537-8440

TANOUE, Donna — Tel: (808) 694-8580
Vice Chair and President, Bank of Hawaii Charitable Foundation — Fax: (808) 537-8440

WYRICK, Cindy — Tel: (808) 694-8430
Director, Investor Relations — Fax: (808) 538-4445
cindy.wyrick@boh.com

At Other Offices
SAKAMOTO, Kevin T.
PAC Treasurer
P.O. Box 2900
Honolulu, HI 96846-6000
kevin.sakamoto@boh.com

Bank of Mississippi

See listing on page 103 under Bancorp South

The Bank of New York Mellon Corporation

Established in 2007 from the merger of Mellon Financial Corporation and The Bank of New York Company, Inc., BNY Mellon is a investment management and investment services company, which can act as a single point of contact for clients looking to create, trade, hold, manage, service, distribute or restructure investments.
www.bnymellon.com
Annual Revenues: $15.03 billion
Employees: 51,400
Ticker: NYSE: BK
SIC: 6022
Industry/ies: Banking/Finance/Investments
Legislative Issues: BAN; TAX

Chairman of the Board and Chief Executive Officer   Tel: (212) 495-1784
HASSELL, Gerald L.   Fax: (212) 809-9528

Main Headquarters
Mailing: One Wall St.   Tel: (212) 495-1784
New York City, NY 10286   Fax: (212) 809-9528

Political Action Committees
Bipartisan Political Action Committee/The Bank of New York Mellon
Corporation Bipac/BNYMC
FEC ID: C00017558
Contact: Kurtis R. Kurimsky
One Wall St.   Tel: (212) 495-1784
New York City, NY 10286   Fax: (212) 809-9528

Political Action Committee/The Bank of New York Mellon - Federal
FEC ID: C00494534
Contact: Kurtis R. Kurimsky
One Wall St.   Tel: (212) 495-1784
New York City, NY 10286   Fax: (212) 809-9528

Contributions to Candidates: $146,250 (2015-2016)
Democrats: $66,500; Republicans: $79,750

Principal Recipients
SENATE
BLUNT, ROY (REP-MO)

Corporate Foundations and Giving Programs
BNY Mellon Foundation
One Mellon Bank Center
Pittsburgh, PA 15258

Public Affairs and Related Activities Personnel

At Headquarters
ABBS, Gary E.   Tel: (212) 495-1784
Contact, Government Relations   Fax: (212) 809-9528
BRUECKNER , Richard   Tel: (212) 495-1784
Chief of Staff   Fax: (212) 809-9528
BUCKLEY, John T.   Tel: (412) 236-1198
Global Head, Corporate Social Responsibility   Fax: (212) 809-9258
john.t.buckley@bnymellon.com
COSTELLO, Ann S.   Tel: (212) 495-1784
Managing Director, Global Government Affairs   Fax: (412) 236-5150
GIBBONS, Thomas P.   Tel: (212) 495-1784
Vice Chairman of the Board and Chief Financial Officer   Fax: (212) 809-9528
HEINE, Kevin   Tel: (212) 635-1569
Contact, Global Corporate Communications   Fax: (212) 635-1799
kevin.heine@bnymellon.com
HERENA, Monique R.   Tel: (212) 495-1784
Senior Executive Vice President and Chief Human Resources   Fax: (212) 809-9528
Officer
KEANEY, Timothy F.   Tel: (212) 495-1784
Vice Chairman of the Board and Chief Executive Officer,   Fax: (212) 809-9528
Investment Services
KUMAR, Suresh   Tel: (212) 495-1784
Senior Executive Vice President and Chief Information Officer   Fax: (212) 809-9528
MCCARTHY, J. Kevin   Tel: (212) 495-1784
General Counsel   Fax: (212) 809-9528
PEETZ , Karen B.   Tel: (212) 495-1784
President   Fax: (212) 809-9528
ROYLE, Ivan   Tel: (212) 495-1784
Managing Director, Chief Marketing Officer   Fax: (212) 809-9528
THOMAS, Ruth   Tel: (212) 495-1784
Managing Director, Global Government Affairs   Fax: (212) 809-9528
Registered Federal Lobbyist

At Other Offices
DAY, III, Walter R.   Tel: (412) 234-1537
Senior Vice President, Government Affairs and Community   Fax: (412) 236-5150
Investment
One BNY Mellon Center, Suite 1840
Pittsburgh, PA 15258
Registered Federal Lobbyist
KURIMSKY, Kurtis R.   Tel: (412) 234-1537
PAC Contact   Fax: (412) 236-5150
One BNY Mellon Center, Suite 1840
Pittsburgh, PA 15258
Mail Stop Bny Mellon Center, Room 3225, 500 Grant St.
VANDIVIER, David   Tel: (412) 234-1537
Federal Lobbyist   Fax: (412) 236-5150
One BNY Mellon Center, Suite 1840
Pittsburgh, PA 15258
Registered Federal Lobbyist

Banta Corporation
See listing on page 666 under R. R. Donnelley & Sons

Baptist Health System, Inc.
A not-for-profit, 501(c) corporation that owns and manages four hospitals in the state of Alabama.
www.bhsala.com
Employees: 4,500
Industry/ies: Medicine/Health Care/Mental Health

President and Chief Executive Officer   Tel: (205) 715-5000
PARROTT, Keith

Main Headquarters
Mailing: Ridge Park Place 1130 22nd Street South   Tel: (205) 715-5000
Suite 1000
Birmingham, AL 35205

Corporate Foundations and Giving Programs
Baptist Health Foundation
3201 Fourth Ave. South   Tel: (877) 474-4243
Birmingham, AL 35222

Public Affairs and Related Activities Personnel

At Headquarters
FRANCIS, Beth   Tel: (205) 715-5000
Vice President and Chief Human Resources Officer

At Other Offices
JOHNSTON, Greg   Tel: (205) 715-5339
Chief Financial Officer and Senior Vice President
3201 Fourth Ave., South
Birmingham, AL 35222
MITCHELL, Ross   Tel: (205) 715-5339
Vice President, External and Governmental Affairs
3201 Fourth Ave., South
Birmingham, AL 35222

The Baptista Group, LLC
Lobbying firm.

President   Tel: (202) 257-4178
BAPTISTA, Samuel J.

Main Headquarters
Mailing: 2015 Lorraine Ave.   Tel: (202) 257-4178
McLean, VA 22101

Public Affairs and Related Activities Personnel

At Headquarters
GRAVATT, Laurie Bendall   Tel: (202) 257-4178
Director

Barclays Bank PLC & US Affliates
U.S. operations of Barclays PLC of London, England. U.S. operations consist of Barclaycard, Barclays Capital and Barclays Wealth. Barclays Capital acquired Lehman Brothers North America in 2008, significantly expanding Barclays presence in the U.S.
www.group.barclays.com
Annual Revenues: $34.56 billion
Employees: 132,300
Ticker: NYSE: BCS
SIC: 6029
Industry/ies: Banking/Finance/Investments

Group Chief Executive   Tel: (202) 452-4700
JENKINS, Antony

Main Headquarters
Mailing: 2001 K St. NW   Tel: (202) 452-4700
11th Floor
Washington, DC 20006

Corporate Foundations and Giving Programs
Barclays Bank PLC & US Affliates Contribution Program
745 Seventh Ave.
New York City, NY 10019

Public Affairs and Related Activities Personnel

At Headquarters
BROWN, Irene McDermott   Tel: (202) 452-4700
Director, Group Human Resources
HOYT , Bob   Tel: (202) 452-4700
Group General Counsel
LE BLANC, Robert   Tel: (202) 452-4700
Chief Risk Officer
MORZARIA , Tushar   Tel: (202) 452-4700
Group Finance Director
MOULDS , Jonathan   Tel: (202) 452-4700
Group Chief Operating Officer

At Other Offices
DURKIN, Patrick   Tel: (212) 526-1492
Managing Director

745 Seventh Ave.
New York City, NY 10019

HESTER, Bret   Tel: (212) 526-7000
745 Seventh Ave.
New York City, NY 10019

REGAN, Joseph   Tel: (212) 526-7000
Chief Financial Officer
745 Seventh Ave.
New York City, NY 10019

ROEMER, Michael   Tel: (212) 526-7000
Group Head of Compliance
745 Seventh Ave.
New York City, NY 10019

Bariod Drilling Fluids Division
See listing on page 382 under Halliburton Company

Barnes and Noble College Bookstores
Operates nearly 717 campus stores nationwide.
www.bncollege.com
Annual Revenues: $5.97 billion
Employees: 33,645
Industry/ies: Education; Retail/Wholesale

Chairman of the Board   Tel: (908) 991-2665
RIGGIO, Leonard   Fax: (908) 991-2846

Chief Executive Officer   Tel: (908) 991-2665
ROBERTS, Max J.   Fax: (908) 991-2846

Main Headquarters
Mailing: 120 Mountain View Blvd.   Tel: (908) 991-2665
     Basking Ridge, NJ 07920   Fax: (908) 991-2846

Corporate Foundations and Giving Programs

Barnes and Noble College Bookstores Contributions Program
120 Mountain View Blvd.   Tel: (908) 991-2665
Basking Ridge, NJ 07920   Fax: (908) 991-2846

Public Affairs and Related Activities Personnel

At Headquarters

BROVER, Barry   Tel: (908) 991-2665
Vice President and Chief Financial Officer   Fax: (908) 991-2846

JUERGENSONN, Janine von   Tel: (855) 262-2460
Vice President, Marketing   Fax: (908) 991-2846
jvj@bncollege.com

MAGILL, JoAnn   Tel: (908) 991-2665
Vice President, Human Resources   Fax: (908) 991-2846

MALAT, Lisa   Tel: (908) 991-2665
Vice President, Operations, and Chief Marketing Officer   Fax: (908) 991-2846

MALONEY, Patrick   Tel: (908) 991-2665
President   Fax: (908) 991-2846

Barnes & Noble, Inc.
Barnes & Noble pioneered the concept of the book superstore, combining vast inventory selection in books, music, DVD and magazines with comfortable ambiance.
www.barnesandnobleinc.com
Annual Revenues: $4.16 billion
Employees: 28,225
Ticker: NYSE: BKS
SIC: 5940
Industry/ies: Retail/Wholesale

Founder and Executive Chairman   Tel: (212) 633-3300
RIGGIO, Leonard   Fax: (212) 675-0413

Chief Executive Officer   Tel: (212) 633-3300
BOIRE, Ronald D.   Fax: (212) 675-0413

Main Headquarters
Mailing: 122 Fifth Ave.   Tel: (212) 633-3300
     Second Floor   Fax: (212) 675-0413
     New York City, NY 10011   TF: (800) 422-7717

Corporate Foundations and Giving Programs

Barnes & Noble Contributions Program
Contact: Mary Ellen Keating
122 Fifth Ave.   Tel: (212) 633-3323
Eighth Floor   Fax: (212) 807-6033
New York City, NY 10011

Public Affairs and Related Activities Personnel

At Headquarters

CAREY, Jaime   Tel: (212) 633-3300
President, Development   Fax: (212) 675-0413

FEUER, Brad   Tel: (212) 633-3300
General Counsel   Fax: (212) 675-0413

HERPICH, Peter   Tel: (212) 633-3300
   Fax: (212) 675-0413

*Vice President, Corporate Controller and Principal
Accounting Officer*

KEATING, Mary Ellen   Tel: (212) 633-3300
Senior Vice President, Corporate Communications and Public   Fax: (212) 675-0413
Affairs
mkeating@bn.com

LINDSTROM, Allen W.   Tel: (212) 633-3300
Chief Financial Officer   Fax: (212) 675-0413

MILEVOJ, Andy   Tel: (212) 633-3300
Vice President, Investor Relations   Fax: (212) 675-0413
amilevoj@bn.com

SMITH, Michelle   Tel: (212) 633-3300
Vice President, Human Resources   Fax: (212) 675-0413
msmith@bn.com

WOOD, William E.   Tel: (212) 633-3300
Chief Information Officer   Fax: (212) 675-0413

Barnes Group Inc.
An aerospace and industrial components manufacturer.
www.barnesgroupinc.com
Annual Revenues: $1.18 billion
Employees: 4,735
Ticker: NYSE:B
SIC: 3490
Industry/ies: Management

Chairman of the Board   Tel: (860) 583-7070
BARNES, Thomas O.   Fax: (860) 589-3507

President and Chief Executive Officer   Tel: (860) 583-7070
DEMPSEY, Patrick J.   Fax: (860) 589-3507

Main Headquarters
Mailing: 123 Main St.   Tel: (860) 583-7070
     Bristol, CT 06010-6376   Fax: (860) 589-3507

Corporate Foundations and Giving Programs

Barnes Group Foundation
123 Main St.   Tel: (860) 584-7070
P.O. Box 489   Fax: (860) 589-3507
Bristol, CT 06011

Public Affairs and Related Activities Personnel

At Headquarters

ACKER , Marian   Tel: (860) 583-7070
Vice President, Controller   Fax: (860) 589-3507

BERKLAS, James P.   Tel: (860) 583-7070
Senior Vice President, General Counsel and Secretary   Fax: (860) 589-3507

EDWARDS, Dawn N.   Tel: (860) 583-7070
Senior Vice President, Human Resources   Fax: (860) 589-3507

HOPSON, Kenneth R   Tel: (860) 583-7070
Vice President, Treasurer   Fax: (860) 589-3507

HOVORKA, Lukas   Tel: (860) 583-7070
Vice President, Corporate Development   Fax: (860) 589-3507

PITTS, William   Tel: (860) 583-7070
Director, Planning and Investor Relations   Fax: (860) 589-3507

STEPHENS, Christopher J.   Tel: (860) 583-7070
Senior Vice President, Finance and Chief Financial Officer   Fax: (860) 589-3507

The Barnett Group L.L.C.
Monitors trade in the Middle East each day for its clients, and provides early warning systems for impending commercial problems.
thebarnettgroup.biz/index.htm

President   Tel: (202) 364-6424
BARNETT, Judith   Fax: (775) 367-9774
jbarnett@thebarnettgroup.biz

Main Headquarters
Mailing: 4373 Embassy Park Dr. NW   Tel: (202) 364-6424
     Washington, DC 20016   Fax: (775) 367-9774

Barrick Gold Corporation North America
U.S. subsidiary of Barrick Gold Corporation, a Canadian gold mining company with operations in Nevada and Utah; U.S headquarters in Elko, NV.
www.barrick.com
Annual Revenues: $2.80 million
Employees: 50
Industry/ies: Metals; Mining Industry; Natural Resources
Legislative Issues: ENG; ENV; FOR; NAT; RES; TAX

Chairman of the Board   Tel: (416) 861-9911
THORNTON, John L.   Fax: (416) 861-2492

Co-President   Tel: (416) 861-9911
DUSHNISKY, Kelvin   Fax: (416) 861-2492

Main Headquarters
Mailing: 460 West 50 North   Tel: (416) 861-9911

Suite 500
Salt Lake City, UT 84101

Fax: (416) 861-2492
TF: (800) 720-7415

Washington Office
Mailing: 101 Constitution Ave. NW
Suite 675 East
Washington, DC 20001

Tel: (202) 682-9499
Fax: (801) 359-0875

Political Action Committees
Barrick Goldstrike Mines Inc Political Action Committee 'Barrick Goldstrike PAC'
FEC ID: C00320580
Contact: Be-Be Adams
136 E. South Temple St.
Suite 1300
Salt Lake City, UT 84111

Tel: (801) 990-3900
Fax: (801) 539-0665

Contributions to Candidates: $73,000 (2015-2016)
Democrats: $27,000; Republicans: $46,000

Principal Recipients

SENATE

MASTO, CATHERINE CORTEZ (DEM-NV)

HOUSE

AMODEI, MARK EUGENE (REP-)
HARDY, CRESENT (REP-NV)
TITUS, DINA (DEM-NV)

Corporate Foundations and Giving Programs

Barrick Gold Corporation North America Contributions Program
Contact: Kelvin Dushnisky
136 E. South Temple
Suite 1800
Salt Lake City, UT 84111-1141

Tel: (801) 990-3900
Fax: (801) 359-0875

Public Affairs and Related Activities Personnel

At Headquarters

RAW, Catherine
Executive Vice President, Business Performance

Tel: (416) 861-9911
Fax: (416) 861-2492

RICH, Darian
Executive Vice President, Talent Management

Tel: (416) 861-9911
Fax: (416) 861-2492

SCHWALM, Amy
Vice President, Investor Relations
aschwalm@barrick.com

Tel: (416) 307-7422
Fax: (416) 861-2492

THOMSON, Kevin
Senior Executive Vice President, Strategic Matters

Tel: (416) 861-9911
Fax: (416) 861-2492

USMAR, Shaun
Senior Executive Vice President and Chief Financial Officer

Tel: (416) 861-9911
Fax: (416) 861-2492

At Washington Office

BROWN, Michael J.
Executive Director

Tel: (202) 682-9499
Fax: (202) 682-0391

ERLING, Christina
Director, Federal Affairs
Registered Federal Lobbyist

Tel: (202) 682-9499
Fax: (801) 359-0875

At Other Offices

ADAMS, Be-Be
Manager, Government Affairs and PAC Treasurer
136 E. South Temple, Suite 1800
Salt Lake City, UT 84111-1141

Tel: (801) 990-3900
Fax: (801) 359-0875

LLOYD, Andy
Vice President, Communications
136 E. South Temple, Suite 1800
Salt Lake City, UT 84111-1141
alloyd@barrick.com

Tel: (416) 307-7414
Fax: (801) 359-0875

BASF Catalysts LLC

A manufacturer of chemical and engineered materials.
www.catalysts.basf.com
Employees: 6,000
Industry/ies: Science; Scientific Research
Legislative Issues: MAN

Chairman of the Board
BOCK, Dr. Kurt W.

Tel: (732) 205-5000
Fax: (732) 205-5687

Main Headquarters
Mailing: 25 Middlesex/Essex Tnpk.
Iselin, NJ 08830-0770

Tel: (732) 205-5000
Fax: (732) 205-5687
TF: (800) 889-9845

Corporate Foundations and Giving Programs

BASF Catalysts Contributions Program
25 Middlesex/Essex Tnpk.
Iselin, NJ 08830-0770

Tel: (732) 205-5000
Fax: (732) 205-5687

Public Affairs and Related Activities Personnel

At Headquarters

JONES, Joseph M.
Vice President, Corporate Communications

Tel: (732) 205-5557
Fax: (732) 205-5687

joseph.jones@basf.com

MARCHESE, Melissa
Manager, Global Business
melissa.marchese@basf.com

Tel: (732) 205-5591
Fax: (732) 205-5687

MARINO, Megan
Director, Strategic Planning and Marketing

Tel: (732) 205-5000
Fax: (732) 205-5687

BASF Corporation

A chemical company which holds chemical and chemical-related business including basic, intermediate and specialty chemicals; polymers and fibers; dispersions; automotive and industrial coatings; agricultural products; plant biotechnology and vitamins.
www.basf.com
Employees: 113,000
Industry/ies: Chemicals & Chemical Industry; Pharmaceutical Industry
Legislative Issues: AGR; BUD; CHM; CSP; ENG; ENV; RRR; TAR; TAX; TRD

Chairman of the Board
BOCK, Kurt

Tel: (973) 245-6000
Fax: (973) 895-8002

Main Headquarters
Mailing: 100 Park Ave.
Florham Park, NJ 07932

Tel: (973) 245-6000
Fax: (973) 895-8002
TF: (800) 526-1072

Political Action Committees
BASF Corporation Employees PAC
FEC ID: C00340075
Contact: Bruce Kraemer
100 Park Ave.
Florham Park, NJ 07932

Tel: (973) 245-6000

Contributions to Candidates: $406,236 (2015-2016)
Democrats: $109,500; Republicans: $296,736

Principal Recipients

HOUSE

CALVERT, KEN (REP-CA)

Corporate Foundations and Giving Programs

BASF Corporation Charitable Giving
100 Campus Dr.
Florham Park, NJ 07932

Tel: (973) 245-6000
Fax: (973) 245-6714

Public Affairs and Related Activities Personnel

At Headquarters

BECKER, Andre
Executive Vice President and Chief Financial Officer

Tel: (973) 245-6000
Fax: (973) 895-8002

BLACKWOOD, Jeff
Registered Federal Lobbyist

Tel: (973) 245-6000
Fax: (973) 895-8002

DENNIS, Kathy A.
Manager, Marketing Communications
Kathy.dennis@basf.com

Tel: (973) 245-6288
Fax: (973) 245-6714

ENGEL, Dr. Hans-Ulrich
Member of the Board and Chief Financial Officer

Tel: (973) 245-6000
Fax: (973) 245-6714

GOLDBERG, Steven J.
Vice President, Associate General Counsel, Regulatory & Government Affairs
Registered Federal Lobbyist

Tel: (973) 245-6057
Fax: (973) 245-6002

KRAEMER, Bruce
PAC Treasurer

Tel: (973) 245-6000
Fax: (973) 245-6714

LEPORE, Matthew
Senior Vice President, General Counsel, Chief Compliance Officer

Tel: (973) 245-6000
Fax: (973) 895-8002

MOLL, Magdalena
Senior Vice President, Investor Relations
magdalena.moll@basf.com

Tel: (973) 245-6000
Fax: (973) 245-6714

ODINA, Elizabeth
Manager, Construction Advocacy
Registered Federal Lobbyist

Tel: (973) 245-6000
Fax: (973) 245-6714

WASHKO, Mark J.
Federal Lobbyist
Registered Federal Lobbyist

Tel: (973) 245-6000
Fax: (973) 245-6714

WETTBERG, Dr. Stefanie
Vice President, Corporate Communications
stefanie.wettberg@basf.com

Tel: (621) 609-9223
Fax: (973) 245-6714

Basic American Foods

Manufactures dehydrated potatoes.
www.baf.com
Annual Revenues: $172.60 million
Employees: 1,500
Industry/ies: Food And Beverage Industry

Chairman of the Board
HUML, George H.

Tel: (925) 472-4000
Fax: (925) 472-4360

Main Headquarters
Mailing: 2185 N. California Blvd.

Tel: (925) 472-4000

Suite 215	Fax:	(925) 472-4360
Walnut Creek, CA 94596	TF:	(800) 227-4050

Corporate Foundations and Giving Programs

Basic American Foods Corporate Contributions
2185 N. California Blvd.
Suite 215
Walnut Creek, CA 94596

Tel: (925) 472-4000
Fax: (925) 472-4360

Public Affairs and Related Activities Personnel

At Headquarters

COLLINS, Jim
Vice President and Chief Financial Officer

Tel: (925) 472-4000
Fax: (925) 472-4360

PARK, Gary
Vice President, Human Resources

Tel: (925) 472-4000
Fax: (925) 472-4360

PERETTI, Todd
Vice President, Operations and Technology

Tel: (925) 472-4000
Fax: (925) 472-4360

Basin Coal Company

See listing on page 108 under Basin Electric Power Cooperative

Basin Electric Power Cooperative

An electric generation and transmission (G&T) cooperative.
www.basinelectric.com
Annual Revenues: $953.74 million
Employees: 1,300
Industry/ies: Cooperatives; Energy/Electricity; Utilities
Legislative Issues: ENG; ENV; UTI

Chief Executive Officer and General Manager
SUKUT, Paul
psukut@bepc.com

Tel: (701) 223-0441
Fax: (701) 557-5336

Main Headquarters
Mailing: 1717 E. Interstate Ave.
Bismarck, ND 58501

Tel: (701) 223-0441
Fax: (701) 557-5336

Political Action Committees
Basin Electric Power Cooperative PAC (Basin Electric PAC)
FEC ID: C00220269
Contact: Jean Schafer
171 E. Interstate Ave.
Bismarck, ND 58503

Tel: (701) 223-0441
Fax: (701) 224-5336

Contributions to Candidates: $2,500 (2015-2016)
Republicans: $2,500

Corporate Foundations and Giving Programs
Basin Electric Power Cooperative Contributions Program
Contact: Jennifer Holen
1717 E. Interstate Ave.
Bismarck, ND 58503

Public Affairs and Related Activities Personnel

At Headquarters

EGGL, Mike
Senior Vice President, Communications and Administration
meggl@bepc.com
Registered Federal Lobbyist

Tel: (701) 223-0441
Fax: (701) 224-5336

HOLEN, Jennifer
Event Planner and Coordinator, Charitable Giving
jholen@bepc.com

Tel: (701) 223-0441
Fax: (701) 557-5336

HOLT, Ellen
Vice president, Human Resources

Tel: (701) 223-0441
Fax: (701) 557-5336

JOHNSON, Steve
Senior Vice President and Chief Financial Officer

Tel: (701) 223-0441
Fax: (701) 557-5336

JOHNSON, Stephen
Chief Financial Officer

Tel: (701) 223-0441
Fax: (701) 557-5336

MASSEY, Sheryl R.
Government Relations Coordinator

Tel: (701) 557-5415
Fax: (701) 224-5336

NIEZWAAG, Dale
Senior Legislative Representative
dniezwaag@bepc.com
Registered Federal Lobbyist

Tel: (701) 223-0441
Fax: (701) 557-5336

OLSON, Claire
Senior Vice President and General Counsel
colson@bepc.com

Tel: (701) 223-0441
Fax: (701) 557-5336

RUTTER, Ken
Vice President, Marketing and Trading

Tel: (701) 223-0441
Fax: (701) 557-5336

SCHAFER , Jean
Coordinator, Government Relations
Registered Federal Lobbyist

Tel: (701) 223-0441
Fax: (701) 557-5336

SORENSEN, Susan
Vice President and Treasurer

Tel: (701) 223-0441
Fax: (701) 557-5336

TOMAC, Steve
Senior Legislative Representative
Registered Federal Lobbyist

Tel: (701) 223-0441
Fax: (701) 224-5336

VANDEVENTER, Christopher
Legislative Representative
cvandeventer@bepc.com
Registered Federal Lobbyist

Tel: (701) 223-0441
Fax: (701) 224-5336

Bassett Furniture Industries, Inc.

Manufacturer of home furnishings.
www.bassettfurniture.com
Annual Revenues: $384.27 million
Employees: 1,568
Ticker: NASDAQ: BSET
SIC: 2511
Industry/ies: Furniture/Home Furnishings

Chairman of the Board
FULTON, Paul
Paul.Fulton@bassettfurniture.com

Tel: (276) 629-6000
Fax: (276) 629-6333

President, Chief Executive Officer and Director
SPILMAN, Robert H.

Tel: (276) 629-6000
Fax: (276) 629-6333

Main Headquarters
Mailing: P.O. Box 626
3525 Fairystone Park Hwy.
Bassett, VA 24055

Tel: (276) 629-6000
Fax: (276) 629-6333
TF: (877) 525-7070

Public Affairs and Related Activities Personnel

At Headquarters

DANIEL, J. Michael
Senior Vice President and Chief Financial Officer

Tel: (276) 629-6614
Fax: (276) 629-6333

HERVERY, Jay R.
Vice President, Secretary and General Counsel

Tel: (276) 629-6000
Fax: (276) 629-6333

MOORE, Jay S.
Director, Advertising and Marketing Analytics
jsmoore@bassettfurniture.com

Tel: (276) 629-6450
Fax: (276) 629-6333

Bath Iron Works Corporation

A subsidiary of General Dynamics (see separate listing). Specializes in shipbuilding and repairing. BIW builds private, commercial and military vessels, most of which have been ordered by the United States Navy.
www.gdbiw.com
Annual Revenues: $497.80 million
Employees: 20
SIC: 3731; 3730
Industry/ies: Defense/Homeland Security; Government-Related; Marine/ Maritime/Shipping; Transportation

President
HARRIS, Frederick

Tel: (207) 443-3311
Fax: (207) 442-1156

Main Headquarters
Mailing: 700 Washington St.
Bath, ME 04530

Tel: (207) 443-3311
Fax: (207) 442-1156

Washington Office
Mailing: Maritime Plaza Bldg.
1201 M St. SE, Suite 100
Washington, DC 20003

Tel: (202) 454-2900
Fax: (202) 454-2970

Public Affairs and Related Activities Personnel

At Headquarters

BROWN, Thomas A.
Vice President and Chief Financial Officer

Tel: (207) 443-3311
Fax: (207) 442-1156

DEMARTINI, James
Manager, Communications

Tel: (207) 442-1695
Fax: (207) 442-1009

FITZGERALD, Jon A.
Vice President, General Counsel

Tel: (207) 443-3311
Fax: (207) 442-1567

MULLIGAN, Michael J.
Vice President & General Manager

Tel: (207) 443-3311
Fax: (207) 442-1156

STERGIO, Gerald
Vice President, Human Resources

Tel: (207) 443-3311
Fax: (207) 442-1567

BATS Global Markets, Inc.

Stock exchange.
Industry/ies: Banking/Finance/Investments
Legislative Issues: FIN

Main Headquarters
Mailing: 8050 Marshall Dr.
Lenexa, KS 66214

Tel: (913) 815-7000

Political Action Committees
Direct Edge Holdings LLC PAC AKA Direct Edge PAC
FEC ID: C00458653
Contact: Meredith Lesher
701 Eighth St. NW
Suite 500
Washington, DC 20001

Contributions to Candidates: $17,700 (2015-2016)

Republicans: $17,700

Battelle Memorial Institute

Provides technology development, management and commercialization. Headquartered in Columbus, OH.
www.battelle.org
Annual Revenues: $5.54 billion
Employees: 22,000
Industry/ies: Management; Science; Scientific Research
Legislative Issues: BUD; DEF; ENG; HCR; HOM; LAW; SCI

| **Chairman of the Board** | Tel: | (614) 424-6424 |
| WELCH, John K. | Fax: | (614) 424-5263 |

| **President and Chief Executive Officer** | Tel: | (614) 424-6424 |
| WADSWORTH, Jeffrey | Fax: | (614) 424-5263 |

Main Headquarters
Mailing:	505 King Ave.	Tel:	(614) 424-6424
	Columbus, OH 43201-2696	Fax:	(614) 424-5263
		TF:	(800) 201-2011

Washington Office
Mailing:	2111 Wilson Blvd.,	Tel:	(571) 227-6305
	Suite 900 and 1000		
	Arlington, VA 22201		

Corporate Foundations and Giving Programs

Battelle Memorial Institute Contributions Program
Contact: Courtney Howard-Hodapp
| 505 King Ave. | Tel: | (614) 424-5853 |
| Columbus, OH 43201-2693 | Fax: | (614) 424-5263 |

Public Affairs and Related Activities Personnel

At Headquarters

AUSTIN, Russell	Tel:	(614) 424-6424
Senior Vice President, General Counsel and Secretary	Fax:	(614) 424-5263
DELANEY, Katy	Tel:	(614) 424-7208
Manager, National Media Relations	Fax:	(614) 424-5263
delaneyk@battelle.org		
EVANS, Dave	Tel:	(614) 424-6424
Executive Vice President and Chief Financial Officer	Fax:	(614) 424-5263
JARVIS, Patrick	Tel:	(614) 424-6424
Senior Vice President, Marketing and Communications	Fax:	(614) 424-5263
KENNEDY, Aimee	Tel:	(614) 424-6424
Vice President for Education, STEM Learning and	Fax:	(614) 424-5263
Philanthropy		
MASSEY, T.R.	Tel:	(614) 424-5544
Senior Specialist, Media Relations	Fax:	(614) 424-5263
masseytr@battelle.org		
MORGAN, Erica	Tel:	(614) 424-6424
Federal Lobbyist	Fax:	(614) 424-5263
Registered Federal Lobbyist		
SALMANS, Kristen	Tel:	(614) 424-6424
	Fax:	(614) 424-5263
TACKETT, Leslie L.	Tel:	(614) 424-6587
Paralegal	Fax:	(614) 424-5263

At Other Offices

DOUCETTE, Paul Timothy	Tel:	(202) 646-5228
Federal Lobbyist		
901 D St. SW, Suite 900		
Washington, DC 20024-2169		
doucettep@battelle.org		
Registered Federal Lobbyist		
TOLER, Mary	Tel:	(202) 479-0500
Director, Congressional Affairs		
901 D St. SW, Suite 900		
Washington, DC 20024-2169		
tolerm@battelle.org		
Registered Federal Lobbyist		

Bausch & Lomb, Inc.

A global eye health company. Bausch and Lomb is dedicated to protecting and enhancing the gift of sight for people around the world, from the moment of birth through every phase of life.
www.bausch.com
Employees: 12,000
SIC: 3851
NAICS: 339115
Industry/ies: Medicine/Health Care/Mental Health

Main Headquarters
Mailing:	1400 N. Goodman St.	Tel:	(585) 338-6000
	Rochester, NY 14609	Fax:	(585) 338-6007
		TF:	(800) 344-8815

Corporate Foundations and Giving Programs

The Bausch & Lomb Contribution Programs

One Bausch & Lomb Pl.
Rochester, NY 14604

Public Affairs and Related Activities Personnel

At Headquarters

HEINICK, Rick A.	Tel:	(585) 338-6000
Executive Vice President and Chief Human Resources Officer	Fax:	(585) 338-6007
SARTORI, PhD, Paul H.	Tel:	(585) 338-6000
Corporate Vice President and Chief Human Resources Officer	Fax:	(585) 338-6007

Bavarian Nordic

A biotechnology company.
www.bavarian-nordic.com
Industry/ies: Pharmaceutical Industry
Legislative Issues: BUD; HCR

| **Chairman of the Board** | Tel: | (202) 568-8090 |
| VAN ODIJK, Gerard | Fax: | (202) 595-9822 |

| **President and Chief Executive Officer** | Tel: | (202) 568-8090 |
| CHAPLIN, Paul | Fax: | (202) 595-9822 |

Main Headquarters
Mailing:	3430 Connecticut Ave. NW		
	Suite 4938		
	Washington, DC 20008		

Public Affairs and Related Activities Personnel

At Other Offices

ALTON, Jennifer B.	Tel:	(202) 403-2138
Vice President, Government Affairs	Fax:	(202) 536-1579
2900 K St. NW, Suite 450, North Tower		
Washington, DC 20007		
jennifer.alton@bavarian-nordic.com		
Registered Federal Lobbyist		
LARSEN, Ole	Tel:	(202) 568-8090
Executive Vice President and Chief Financial Officer	Fax:	(202) 595-9822
2900 K St. NW, Suite 450, North Tower		
Washington, DC 20007		
NOLL, PhD, David M.	Tel:	(202) 403-2139
Director, Government Affairs	Fax:	(202) 536-1579
2900 K St. NW, Suite 450, North Tower		
Washington, DC 20007		
david.noll@bavarian-nordic.com		
SORENSEN, Rolf Sass	Tel:	(453) 326-8383
Vice President, Investor Relations and Communications	Fax:	(202) 595-9822
2900 K St. NW, Suite 450, North Tower		
Washington, DC 20007		
investor@bavarian-nordic.com		

Baxter Healthcare Corporation

Manufacturer and supplier of healthcare products, with expertise in medical devices, pharmaceuticals and biotechnology.
www.baxter.com
Annual Revenues: $16.59 billion
Employees: 66,000
Ticker: NYSE: BAX
SIC: 3841; 3842; 5099; 5047
Industry/ies: Medicine/Health Care/Mental Health
Legislative Issues: BUD; HCR; MMM; TAX; TRD

Chairman of the Board and Chief Executive Officer	Tel:	(224) 948-2000
PARKINSON, Jr., Robert L.	Fax:	(847) 948-3642
bob_parkinson@baxter.com		

Main Headquarters
| Mailing: | One Baxter Pkwy. | Tel: | (224) 948-2000 |
| | Deerfield, IL 60015-4625 | Fax: | (847) 948-2016 |

Washington Office
Mailing:	901 15th St. NW		
	Suite 500		
	Washington, DC 20005		

Political Action Committees

Baxter Healthcare Corporation PAC (BAXPAC)
FEC ID: C00117838
Contact: Sarah Creviston
| 1501 K St. NW, Suite 375 | Tel: | (202) 508-8200 |
| Washington, DC 20005 | Fax: | (202) 508-8201 |

Contributions to Candidates: $39,000 (2015-2016)
Democrats: $16,500; Republicans: $22,500

Principal Recipients

HOUSE
DOLD, ROBERT JAMES JR (REP IL)

Corporate Foundations and Giving Programs

Baxter International Foundation
| One Baxter Pkwy. | Tel: | (847) 948-3297 |

Deerfield, IL 60015   Fax: (847) 948-3642

Public Affairs and Related Activities Personnel

At Headquarters

BATCHELOR, Phillip L.   Tel: (224) 948-2000
Corporate Vice President, Quality and Regulatory Affairs   Fax: (847) 948-2016

BOHABOY , Scott A.   Tel: (224) 948-2000
Corporate Vice President, Treasurer and Head, Investor   Fax: (847) 948-2016
Relations

LADONE, Mary Kay   Tel: (224) 948-2000
Corporate Vice President, Investor Relations   Fax: (847) 948-2016
Mary_Kay_Ladone@baxter.com

LAWRENCE, Timothy P.   Tel: (224) 948-2000
Corporate Vice President, Operations   Fax: (847) 948-2016

MASON, Jeanne K.   Tel: (224) 948-2000
Corporate Vice President, Human Resources   Fax: (847) 948-2016

SACCARO, James K.   Tel: (224) 948-2000
Corporate Vice President and Chief Financial Officer   Fax: (847) 948-2016

SCHARF, David P.   Tel: (224) 948-2000
Corporate Vice President and General Counsel and Corporate   Fax: (847) 948-2016
Secretary

SPAK, Deborah G.   Tel: (224) 948-2349
Director, External Communications   Fax: (847) 948-2016
deborah_spak@baxter.com

At Washington Office

BENNETT, Mariko
Registered Federal Lobbyist

BUCCILLI, Maria
Registered Federal Lobbyist

CREVISTON, Sarah
Vice President, Global Government Affairs & Public Policy
sarah_creviston@baxter.com

LESTER, Kelli

RILEY, Crystal
Registered Federal Lobbyist

SASTRY, Bela
Registered Federal Lobbyist

At Other Offices

COIN, Mark   Tel: (202) 508-8200
Director, Public Policy and Reimbursement   Fax: (202) 508-8201
1501 K St. NW, Suite 375
Washington, DC 20005
Registered Federal Lobbyist

MANIKO, Jack   Tel: (202) 508-8200
Director, Federal Legislative Affairs   Fax: (202) 508-8201
1501 K St. NW, Suite 375
Washington, DC 20005
Registered Federal Lobbyist

MILLS LESTER, Kelli A.   Tel: (202) 508-8200
Director, Government Relations   Fax: (202) 508-8201
1501 K St. NW, Suite 375
Washington, DC 20005
Registered Federal Lobbyist

PERRY, Jed   Tel: (202) 508-8200
Director, Federal Legislative Affairs   Fax: (202) 508-8201
1501 K St. NW, Suite 375
Washington, DC 20005

SCHWAN, Joseph V.   Tel: (202) 508-8200
Federal Lobbyist   Fax: (202) 508-8201
1501 K St. NW, Suite 375
Washington, DC 20005
Registered Federal Lobbyist

BayCare Health System Inc.

A community-owned health care services provider.
www.baycare.org
Annual Revenues: $178.61 million
Employees: 1,100
Industry/ies: Medicine/Health Care/Mental Health
Legislative Issues: BUD; HCR

President and Chief Executive Officer   Tel: (727) 820-8200
MASON, Stephen R.

Main Headquarters
Mailing: 16255 Bay Vista Dr.   Tel: (727) 820-8200
Clearwater, FL 33760-3127   TF: (877) 692-2922

Public Affairs and Related Activities Personnel

At Headquarters

EISENBEIS, Keri   Tel: (727) 519-1884
Director, Government Relations
keri.eisenbeis@baycare.org

GANTNER, John J   Tel: (727) 820-8200
Executive vice president and chief financial officer

INZIA, Tommy   Tel: (727) 820-8200
Chief Financial Officer and Chief Administrative Officer

LOVETT, Amy   Tel: (727) 519-1257
Director, Communications
amy.lovett@baycare.org

QUIOCO, Ed   Tel: (727) 519-1239
Manager, Communications
ed.quioco@baycare.org

Bayer Corporation

The North American subsidiary of Bayer AG. A research-based company with major businesses in health care and life sciences.
www.bayerus.com
Employees: 16,000
SIC: 2821; 3841; 5169
NAICS: 325211; 339112; 42269
Industry/ies: Chemicals & Chemical Industry; Medicine/Health Care/Mental Health; Pharmaceutical Industry
Legislative Issues: AGR; BUD; CHM; CPT; ENG; ENV; GOV; HCR; MMM; TAR; TAX; TRA; TRD

Chairman of the Board   Tel: (412) 777-2000
DEKKERS, Dr. Marijn   Fax: (412) 777-3883

President and Chief Executive Officer   Tel: (412) 777-2000
BLOME, James   Fax: (412) 777-2062

Main Headquarters
Mailing: 100 Bayer Rd.   Tel: (412) 777-2000
Pittsburgh, PA 15205-9741   Fax: (412) 777-2062
   TF: (800) 422-9374

Washington Office
Mailing: 801 Pennsylvania Ave. NW   Tel: (202) 737-8900
Suite 745   Fax: (202) 737-8909
Washington, DC 20004

Political Action Committees
Bayer Corporation PAC
FEC ID: C00281162
Contact: Tracy E. Spagnol
100 Bayer Rd.   Tel: (412) 777-2000
Bldg. Four   Fax: (412) 777-2034
Pittsburgh, PA 15205

   Contributions to Candidates: $365,500 (2015-2016)
   Democrats: $74,000; Republicans: $291,500

   Principal Recipients

     HOUSE
     CONAWAY, MICHAEL HONORABLE (REP-TX)
     TIBERI, PATRICK J. (REP-OH)

Corporate Foundations and Giving Programs
Bayer Foundation
Contact: Rebecca L. Lucore
100 Bayer Rd.   Tel: (412) 777-2000
Bldg. Four   Fax: (412) 777-2034
Pittsburgh, PA 15205

Public Affairs and Related Activities Personnel

At Headquarters

BENECKE, Lars   Tel: (412) 777-2000
Contact, General Counsel, Company Secretary and   Fax: (412) 777-2062
Compliance Officer

BIER, Bernd-Peter   Tel: (412) 777-2000
Chief Financial Officer   Fax: (412) 777-2062

CALDERA, Richard   Tel: (412) 777-2000
Senior Vice President, Human Resources   Fax: (412) 777-2062

KERINS, Ray F.   Tel: (412) 777-2000
Senior Vice President, Communications, Government   Fax: (412) 777-2062
Relations and Policy

LUCORE, Rebecca L.   Tel: (412) 777-5725
Executive Director, Bayer USA Foundation   Fax: (412) 777-4432
rebecca.lucore.b@bayer.com

SPAGNOL, Tracy E.   Tel: (412) 777-2000
Vice President and Treasurer   Fax: (412) 777-2034

WALLACE, Lori A.   Tel: (412) 777-2000
Associate Manager, U.S. Reimbursement Strategy   Fax: (412) 777-3883

At Washington Office

BARRON, Edward J.   Tel: (202) 737-8900
Registered Federal Lobbyist   Fax: (202) 737-8909

CORCORAN, Julie   Tel: (202) 737-8900
Federal Lobbyist   Fax: (202) 737-8909
julie.corcoran.b@bayer.com
Registered Federal Lobbyist

LEAHY, Christopher	Tel:	(202) 737-8900
Registered Federal Lobbyist	Fax:	(202) 737-8909
MCCULLOUGH, Brian	Tel:	(202) 737-8900
Registered Federal Lobbyist	Fax:	(202) 737-8909
MCVANEY, James P.	Tel:	(202) 737-8900
Federal Lobbyist	Fax:	(202) 737-8909
Registered Federal Lobbyist		
NAGLE, Brian	Tel:	(202) 737-8900
Registered Federal Lobbyist	Fax:	(202) 737-8909
PERIN, Matthew	Tel:	(202) 737-8900
Federal Lobbyist	Fax:	(202) 737-8909
Registered Federal Lobbyist		
REIMERS, Jean D.	Tel:	(202) 737-8900
Director, Federal Government Relations	Fax:	(202) 737-8909
STEPHENS, Donna	Tel:	(202) 737-8900
Director, Federal Government Relations	Fax:	(202) 737-8909
UTLEY, Hallie	Tel:	(202) 737-8900
Registered Federal Lobbyist	Fax:	(202) 737-8909
WEEKS, Stacie	Tel:	(202) 737-8900
Head of Public Policy	Fax:	(202) 737-8909
WOJCIECHOWSKI, Ursula	Tel:	(202) 737-8900
Registered Federal Lobbyist	Fax:	(202) 737-8909

Bayer CropScience

Formed by the merger of Aventis CropScience and Bayer Crop Protection. Specializes in crop protection products and technology, animal nutrition, and health products. Based in Rhein, Germany. A subsidiary of Bayer AG.
www.bayercropscience.com
Annual Revenues: $7.25 billion
Employees: 21,000
SIC: 2879
NAICS: 32532
Industry/ies: Agriculture/Agronomy; Science; Scientific Research

Chief Executive Officer	Tel:	(919) 549-2000
CONDON, Liam	Fax:	(919) 786-9154

Main Headquarters
Mailing:	Two T.W. Alexander Dr.	Tel:	(919) 549-2000
	P.O. Box 12014	Fax:	(919) 786-9154
	Research Triangle Park, NC 27709	TF:	(866) 992-2937

Washington Office
Mailing:	701 Pennsylvania Ave. NW, Suite 720
	Washington, DC 20004

Corporate Foundations and Giving Programs
Bayer CropScience Foundation
Two T.W. Alexander Dr.
P.O. Box 12014
Research Triangle Park, NC 27709

Public Affairs and Related Activities Personnel

At Headquarters

BROEK, Lykele van der	Tel:	(919) 549-2000
Head, Market Strategy	Fax:	(919) 786-9154
CHERNY, Margaret	Tel:	(919) 549-2000
Vice President, Regulatory, Government Affairs and Communications	Fax:	(919) 786-9154
HAUG , Dr. Michael	Tel:	(919) 549-2000
Head, Human Resources	Fax:	(919) 786-9154
HOLLINRAKE, David	Tel:	(919) 549-2000
Vice President, Marketing and Portfolio Management	Fax:	(919) 786-9154
KREMER, Mathias	Tel:	(919) 549-2000
Head, Strategy	Fax:	(919) 786-9154
MARCHAND, Gerhart	Tel:	(919) 549-2000
Head, Law, Patents and Compliance Services	Fax:	(919) 786-9154
NAAF , Bernd	Tel:	(919) 549-2000
Head Business Affairs and Communications, Director Labor	Fax:	(919) 786-9154
RODEN, Beth	Tel:	(919) 549-2030
Manager, Communications		
beth.roden@bayercropscience.com		
SCHEITZA, Rüdiger	Tel:	(919) 549-2000
Director, Strategy and Business Management Labor Relations	Fax:	(919) 786-9154
SCHULZ, Michael A.	Tel:	(919) 549-2000
Chief Financial Officer	Fax:	(919) 786-9154

Bayer Healthcare Pharmaceuticals Corporation

The U.S.-based pharmaceuticals operation of Bayer HealthCare LLC, a division of Bayer AG.
pharma.bayer.com
Annual Revenues: $2.43 billion
Employees: 39,000
SIC: 2821; 28411 5169
NAICS: 325211; 339112; 42269

Industry/ies: Pharmaceutical Industry

President and Chief Executive Officer	Tel:	(412) 777-2000
BABE, Greg	Fax:	(412) 778-4486

Main Headquarters
Mailing:	100 Bayer Rd.	Tel:	(412) 777-2000
	Building Four	Fax:	(412) 777-3899
	Pittsburgh, PA 15205-9741		

Washington Office
Mailing:	701 Pennsylvania Ave. NW, Suite 720
	Washington, DC 20004

Political Action Committees
Bayer Corporation PAC
FEC ID: C00281162
Contact: Tracy E. Spagnol
100 Bayer Rd.	Tel:	(412) 777-2000
Bldg. Four	Fax:	(412) 777-2034
Pittsburgh, PA 15205		

Contributions to Candidates: $365,500 (2015-2016)
Democrats: $74,000; Republicans: $291,500

Principal Recipients

HOUSE
CONAWAY, MICHAEL HONORABLE (REP-TX)
TIBERI, PATRICK J. (REP-OH)

Corporate Foundations and Giving Programs
Bayer USA Foundation
Contact: Greg Babe
Six W. Belt
Wayne, NJ 07470-6806

Public Affairs and Related Activities Personnel

At Headquarters

SCHERF, Willy	Tel:	(412) 777-2000
Chief Financial Officer	Fax:	(412) 778-4486
SPAGNOL, Tracy E.	Tel:	(412) 777-2000
Vice President and Treasurer	Fax:	(412) 778-4486
YANCOSEK, Rosemarie	Tel:	(973) 305-5213
Head, U.S. External Communications and Women's Healthcare	Fax:	(412) 777-3883
rosemarie.yancosek@bayer.com		

Baylor Health Care System

A health care delivery system company.
www.baylorhealth.com
Annual Revenues: $4.01 billion
Employees: 20,000
Industry/ies: Medicine/Health Care/Mental Health
Legislative Issues: BUD; HCR; MED; MMM; TOR

Chief Executive Officer	Tel:	(214) 820-0111
ALLISON, FACHE, Joel T.	Fax:	(214) 820-7499

Main Headquarters
Mailing:	3500 Gaston Ave.	Tel:	(214) 820-0111
	Dallas, TX 75246-2017	Fax:	(214) 820-7499
		TF:	(800) 422-9567

Corporate Foundations and Giving Programs
Baylor Health Care System Foundation
Contact: Rowland K. Robinson
2001 Bryan St.	Tel:	(214) 820-3055
Suite 750	Fax:	(214) 820-4697
Dallas, TX 75201		

Public Affairs and Related Activities Personnel

At Headquarters

BOYD, William Stephen	Tel:	(214) 820-0111
Chief Legal Officer	Fax:	(214) 820-7499
BROCK , Gary	Tel:	(214) 820-0111
President and Chief Operating Officer	Fax:	(214) 820-7499
COLEMAN, Jennifer	Tel:	(214) 820-0111
Senior Vice President, Consumer Affairs	Fax:	(214) 820-7499
HOLTZ, CPA, Keith	Tel:	(214) 820-0111
Senior Vice President, Chief Human Resources Officer	Fax:	(214) 820-7499
HOYL, Kristi Sherrill	Tel:	(214) 820-0111
Vice President, Government Affairs	Fax:	(214) 820-7499
MICHALSKI , Robert R.	Tel:	(214) 820-0111
Chief Compliance Officer	Fax:	(214) 820-7499
ROBINSON, Rowland K.	Tel:	(214) 820-0111
Foundation President	Fax:	(214) 820 7199
Robinson@BaylorHealth.edu		
SAVELSBERGH, Frederick	Tel:	(214) 820-0111
Chief Financial Officer	Fax:	(214) 820-7499

At Other Offices

MITCHELL, Nikki
Vice President, Public Relations
2001 Bryan St., Suite 750
Dallas, TX 75201
Nikki.Mitchell@BaylorHealth.edu

Tel: (214) 820-6961
Fax: (214) 820-4697

ROBERTS, William L
Senior Vice President and Chief Strategy Development Officer
2001 Bryan St., Suite 750
Dallas, TX 75201

Tel: (214) 820-3055
Fax: (214) 820-4697

BB&T Corporation

A financial holding company that offers clients a complete range of financial services including banking, lending, insurance, trust, and wealth management solutions.
www.bbt.com
Annual Revenues: $8.09 billion
Employees: 33,400
Ticker: NYSE: BBT
SIC: 6021
Industry/ies: Banking/Finance/Investments
Legislative Issues: BAN; FIN

Chairman of the Board and Chief Executive Officer
KING, Kelly S.

Tel: (336) 733-2000
Fax: (336) 733-2470

Main Headquarters
Mailing: 200 W. Second St.
           Winston-Salem, NC 27101

Tel: (336) 733-2000
Fax: (336) 733-2470
TF: (800) 226-5228

Political Action Committees
Branch Bank and Trust PAC
FEC ID: C00075291
150 S. Stratford Rd.
Suite 401
Winston-Salem, NC 27104

Contributions to Candidates: $189,000 (2015-2016)
Democrats: $11,500; Republicans: $177,500

Principal Recipients
SENATE
HECK, JOE (REP-NV)

Public Affairs and Related Activities Personnel
At Headquarters

BIBLE, Daryl N.
Senior Executive Vice President and Chief Financial Officer

Tel: (336) 733-3031
Fax: (336) 733-2470

GJESDAL, Tamera
Senior Vice President, Investor Relations
tgjesdal@BBandT.com

Tel: (336) 733-3058
Fax: (336) 733-2470

HARDAGE, John
Senior Vice President, Government Affairs Manager
Registered Federal Lobbyist

Tel: (336) 733-2000
Fax: (336) 733-2470

JOHNSON, Jr., Robert J
Senior Executive Vice President, General Counsel, Secretary and Chief Corporate Governance Officer

Tel: (336) 733-2000
Fax: (336) 733-2470

MCGRAW, A.C.
Vice President, Media Relations Manger
acmcgraw@bbandt.com

Tel: (336) 733-1471
Fax: (336) 733-2470

SIMPSON, Ed
Senior Vice President

Tel: (336) 733-2000
Fax: (336) 733-2470

WASAFF, Mary
Assistant Vice President, Government and Regulatory Affairs Specialist

Tel: (336) 733-2000
Fax: (336) 733-2470

WIGGS, Steven B.
Senior Executive Vice President and Chief Marketing Officer

Tel: (336) 733-2000
Fax: (336) 733-2470

WILLIAMS, Cynthia A.
Senior Executive Vice President and Chief Communications Officer
cynthia.williams@BBandT.com

Tel: (336) 733-1470
Fax: (336) 733-1476

BBVA Compass Bancshares, Inc.

A financial holding company. Banking subsidiaries include Compass Bank and Central Bank of the South. Compass Bancshares, Inc. is a wholly owned subsidiary of BBVA (NYSE: BBVA)
www.bbvacompass.com
Annual Revenues: $72.08 million
Employees: 11,000
SIC: 6021
Industry/ies: Banking/Finance/Investments

Chairman of the Board, President and Chief Executive Officer
SÁNCHEZ RODRIGUEZ, Manuel

Tel: (205) 297-3000
Fax: (205) 297-7363

Chairman of the Board and Chief Executive Officer
RODRÍGUEZ, Francisco Gonzalez

Tel: (205) 297-3000
Fax: (205) 297-7363

Main Headquarters
Mailing: P.O.Box 10566
           Birmingham, AL 35296

Tel: (205) 297-3000
Fax: (205) 297-7363

Political Action Committees
Compass Bancshares, Inc. PAC
FEC ID: C00142596
Contact: Sandra H. Burson
P.O. Box 10566
Birmingham, AL 35296

Contributions to Candidates: $223,625 (2015-2016)
Democrats: $36,500; Republicans: $187,125

Principal Recipients
SENATE
BENNET, MICHAEL F (DEM-CO)
CRAPO, MICHAEL D (REP-ID)
SHELBY, RICHARD C (REP-AL)
TOOMEY, PATRICK JOSEPH (REP-PA)
HOUSE
LUETKEMEYER, W BLAINE (REP-MO)

Corporate Foundations and Giving Programs
BBVA Compass Foundation
15 S. 20th St.
Suite 1802
Birmingham, AL 35233

Tel: (205) 297-3000
Fax: (205) 297-7363

Public Affairs and Related Activities Personnel
At Headquarters

APOITA, Juan Ignacio
Head, Human Resources and Services

Tel: (205) 297-3000
Fax: (205) 297-7363

ARBIZU, Eduardo
Legal, Tax, Audit and Compliance Services

Tel: (205) 297-3000
Fax: (205) 297-7363

BREWIS, Sue L.
PAC Treasurer
sue.brewis@compassbnk.com

Tel: (205) 297-3000
Fax: (205) 297-7363

BURSON, Sandra H.
PAC Contact

Tel: (205) 297-3000
Fax: (205) 297-7363

HERRICK, Thaddeus
Director, External Communications
Thaddeus.herrick@bbvacompass.com

Tel: (713) 831-5609
Fax: (205) 297-7363

VILA, Carlos Torres
Director de Banca Digital

Tel: (205) 297-3000
Fax: (205) 297-7363

At Other Offices

BUSTILLO, Rafael
Chief Operating Officer
15 S. 20th St.
Birmingham, AL 35233

Tel: (205) 297-3000
Fax: (205) 297-7363

CLANTON, B Shane
General Counsel and Secretary
15 S. 20th St.
Birmingham, AL 35233

Tel: (205) 297-3000
Fax: (205) 297-7363

HESLOP, James
Chief Human Resources Officer
15 S. 20th St.
Birmingham, AL 35233

Tel: (205) 297-3000
Fax: (205) 297-7363

POWELL, David
Head, Corporate and Investment Banking
15 S. 20th St.
Birmingham, AL 35233

Tel: (205) 297-3000
Fax: (205) 297-7363

PRESSLEY, Kirk
Chief Financial Officer
15 S. 20th St.
Birmingham, AL 35233

Tel: (205) 297-3000
Fax: (205) 297-7363

BCBSGA
See listing on page 130 under Blue Cross Blue Shield of Georgia

BCI Coca-Cola Bottling Company of Los Angeles
See listing on page 205 under Coca-Cola Enterprises

BEA Systems Inc.
See listing on page 605 under Oracle Corporation

Beacon Capital Partners LLC
A real estate investment firm.
beaconcapital.com
Annual Revenues: $2.9 million
Employees: 51
SIC: 6798
Industry/ies: Banking/Finance/Investments; Real Estate
Legislative Issues: GOV; RES; TAX

Chairman of the and Chief Executive Officer
LEVENTHAL, Alan M.

Tel: (617) 457-0400
Fax: (617) 457-0499

Main Headquarters
Mailing: 200 State St.

Tel: (617) 457-0400

Fifth Floor   Fax: (617) 457-0499
Boston, MA 02109

Washington Office
Mailing: 1300 Wilson Blvd.   Tel: (703) 894-6257
              Suite 910   Fax: (703) 248-9345
              Arlington, VA 22209

Public Affairs and Related Activities Personnel

At Headquarters

CORNELIUS , Doug   Tel: (617) 457-0400
Chief Compliance Officer   Fax: (617) 457-0499

GOLDEN, Matthew   Tel: (617) 457-0400
Managing Director and General Counsel   Fax: (617) 457-0499

LAMBERT, Brian   Tel: (617) 457-0400
Vice President, Investor Relations   Fax: (617) 457-0499

LAWRENCE, John   Tel: (617) 457-0400
Senior Vice President, Accounting/Finance   Fax: (617) 457-0499

MORRIS, Ann   Tel: (617) 457-0400
Manager, Administration   Fax: (617) 457-0499

SEIGEL , Fred   Tel: (617) 457-0400
President and Chief Operating Officer   Fax: (617) 457-0499

At Other Offices

BACKER, Dan
PAC Treasurer
P.O. Box 1143
Brookline, MA 02446

Beacon Capital Strategies, Inc.

A software company and registered broker-dealer developed to address the inefficiencies in trading in the less liquid fixed income markets, for both round lots and especially odd lots, by allowing participants to trade electronically, directly and anonymously.
www.beacon-cs.com
Employees: 28
Industry/ies: Computer/Technology

Chief Executive Officer   Tel: (212) 946-3989
EPSTEIN, Norman

Main Headquarters
Mailing: 420 Madison Ave.   Tel: (212) 500-0800
              New York City, NY 10017

Public Affairs and Related Activities Personnel

At Headquarters

AUDLEY, David   Tel: (212) 946-3989
Executive Vice President, Strategic Planning

Beal Bank

A federally chartered bank specializing in savings products.
www.bealbank.com
Employees: 300
Industry/ies: Banking/Finance/Investments

Chairman of the Board and Chief Executive Officer   Tel: (469) 467-5000
BEAL, D. Andrew "Andy"   Fax: (469) 241-9564

Main Headquarters
Mailing: 6000 Legacy Dr.   Tel: (469) 467-5000
              Plano, TX 75024   Fax: (972) 309-3800
                                              TF: (877) 879-2325

Public Affairs and Related Activities Personnel

At Headquarters

CHAMBLESS, Jim   Tel: (469) 467-5533
Media Contact   Fax: (469) 241-9564
jchambless@bealservice.com

SHIPMAN, Kim   Tel: (469) 467-5000
Compliance Officer   Fax: (469) 241-9564

Beall's Inc.

Provides planning, control and service in support of Beall's retail business and customers.
www.beallsinc.com
Employees: 10,000
Industry/ies: Management; Retail/Wholesale

Chairman of the Board   Tel: (941) 747-2355
BEALL, II, Robert M.   Fax: (941) 746-1171

Chief Executive Officer   Tel: (941) 747-2355
KNOPIK, Stephen M.   Fax: (941) 746-1171

Main Headquarters
Mailing: 1806 38th Ave., East   Tel: (941) 747-2355
              Bradenton, FL 34208   Fax: (941) 746-1171

Political Action Committees
Beall's PAC USA Inc.
FEC ID: C00378661

Contact: Michael Maddaloni
P.O. Box 1337
Bradenton, FL 34206
   Contributions to Candidates: $2,500 (2015-2016)
   Republicans: $2,500

Corporate Foundations and Giving Programs

Beall's Inc. Contribution Program
1806 38th Ave. East   Tel: (941) 747-2355
Bradenton, FL 34208   Fax: (941) 746-1171

Public Affairs and Related Activities Personnel

At Other Offices

MADDALONI, Michael   Tel: (941) 744-4369
Vice President and PAC Treasurer   Fax: (941) 708-4331
P.O. Box 25030
Bradenton, FL 34206

Beams Global Spirits and Wine

The company was established on October 4, 2011, from the remainder of the Fortune Brands holding company after it sold and spun off various other product lines to form a business focused exclusively on spirits and directly related products.
www.beamsuntory.com
Annual Revenues: $2.31 billion
Employees: 3,200
Ticker: NYSE: BEAM
SIC: 2080
Industry/ies: Beer/Brewers; Beverage Industry; Food And Beverage Industry; Liquor
Legislative Issues: AGR; BEV; BUD; CPT; ENG; FOO; TAX

Chairman & Chief Executive Officer   Tel: (847) 948-8888
SHATTOCK, Matthew J.   Fax: (847) 948-8610
matt.shattock@beamglobal.com

Main Headquarters
Mailing: 510 Lake Cook Rd.   Tel: (847) 948-8888
              Deerfield, IL 60015   Fax: (847) 948-8610

Washington Office
Mailing: 1050 K St. NW
              Suite 1040
              Washington, DC 20001

Corporate Foundations and Giving Programs

Beams Global Spirits and Wine Contributions Program
Contact: Linda Pleuger
510 Lake Cook Rd.
Deerfield, IL 60015

Public Affairs and Related Activities Personnel

At Headquarters

COHEN, Dan   Tel: (847) 444-7657
Director, Public Relations   Fax: (847) 948-8610
Dan.Cohen@BeamGlobal.com

ERICKSON, Paula   Tel: (847) 948-8888
Senior Vice President, Global Chief Human Resources Officer   Fax: (847) 948-8610
paula.erickson@beamglobal.com

GEORGE , Kevin   Tel: (847) 948-8888
Senior Vice President and Global Chief Marketing Officer   Fax: (847) 948-8610
kevin.george@beamglobal.com

HINE, Clarkson   Tel: (847) 948-8888
Senior Vice President, Corporate Communications and Public   Fax: (847) 948-8610
Affairs

PLEUGER, Linda   Tel: (847) 444-7573
Manager, Corporate Communications   Fax: (847) 948-8610
Linda.Pleuger@BeamGlobal.com

RESTREPO, Mauricio   Tel: (847) 948-8888
Senior Vice President and Chief Financial Officer   Fax: (847) 948-8610

RIVEST, Kris   Tel: (847) 948-7117
Foundation Contact   Fax: (847) 948-8610
Kris.Rivest@BeamGlobal.com

ROSE, Kenton R.   Tel: (847) 948-8888
Senior Vice President, Chief Administrative Officer and   Fax: (847) 948-8610
General Counsel and Secretary
kent.rose@beamglobal.com

At Washington Office

STANTON, Matthew R.
Vice President, Public Affairs and PAC Contact

At Other Offices

MCNAUGHTON, Terry   Tel: (202) 962-0551
Fedreal Lobbyist   Fax: (202) 962-0561
1301 K St. NW, Suite 250, West Tower
Washington, DC 20001
Registered Federal Lobbyist

Bear, Stearns and Company Inc.
See listing on page 448 under J. P. Morgan Chase and Company

Bearings, Inc.
See listing on page 70 under Applied Industrial Technologies

Bechtel Corporation
An international engineering and construction company. The Washington office provides domestic and international marketing, government affairs and project financing.
www.bechtel.com
Employees: 55,000
Industry/ies: Chemicals & Chemical Industry; Construction/Construction Materials; Energy/Electricity; Engineering/Mathematics; Environment And Conservation; Fuels See Coal, Gas, Oil, Petroleum; Natural Resources; Petroleum Industry; Pollution And Waste; Transportation; Utilities
Legislative Issues: DEF; ENG; ENV; TAX; TRA; TRD

Chairman of the Board　　　　　Tel:　(415) 768-1234
BECHTEL, Riley P.　　　　　　　　Fax:　(415) 768-9038
rbechtel@bechtel.com

Chief Executive Officer　　　　　Tel:　(415) 768-1234
DUDLEY, Bill　　　　　　　　　　Fax:　(415) 768-9038

Main Headquarters
Mailing:　50 Beale St.　　　　　　Tel:　(415) 768-1234
　　　　　San Francisco, CA 94105　Fax:　(415) 768-9038

Washington Office
Mailing:　12011 Sunset Hills Rd.　Tel:　(571) 392-6300
　　　　　Reston, VA 20190

Political Action Committees
Bechtel Group Inc. PAC (Bechtel PAC)
FEC ID: C00103697
50 Beale St.　　　　　　　　　　Tel:　(202) 828-5200
San Francisco, CA 94105　　　　Fax:　(202) 785-2645

　　Contributions to Candidates: $303,500 (2015-2016)
　　Democrats: $113,500; Republicans: $190,000

　　　　　Principal Recipients

　　　　　　HOUSE
　　　　　　NEWHOUSE, DAN (REP-WA)
　　　　　　SIMPSON, MICHAEL (REP-ID)

Corporate Foundations and Giving Programs
Bechtel Group Foundation
Contact: Charlene Wheeless
50 Beale St.　　　　　　　　　　Tel:　(415) 768-1234
San Francisco, CA 94105　　　　Fax:　(415) 768-9038

Public Affairs and Related Activities Personnel

At Headquarters

BAILEY, Michael　　　　　　　　Tel:　(415) 768-1234
General Counsel　　　　　　　　Fax:　(415) 768-9038

BECHTEL, Brendan　　　　　　　Tel:　(415) 768-1234
President and Chief Operating Officer　Fax:　(415) 768-9038

DAWSON, Peter Anthony　　　　Tel:　(415) 768-1234
Chief Financial Officer　　　　　Fax:　(415) 768-9038

HIGGINS, Nancy　　　　　　　　Tel:　(415) 768-1234
Vice President and Chief Ethics and Compliance Officer　Fax:　(415) 768-9038

SPARKS, Anette　　　　　　　　Tel:　(415) 768-1234
Controller and Business Services　Fax:　(415) 768-9038

At Washington Office

HAYNES, James　　　　　　　　Tel:　(571) 392-6300
Manager, Human Resources

WHEELESS, Charlene　　　　　　Tel:　(571) 392-6300
Principal Vice President, Corporate Affairs
cwheeles@bechtel.com

At Other Offices

BRANNEN, Laura E.　　　　　　Tel:　(202) 828-5200
Vice President and Manager, Government Affairs (BNI)　Fax:　(202) 785-2645
750 Ninth St. NW, Suite 450
Washington, DC 20001
Registered Federal Lobbyist

DEEGAN, Colleen A.　　　　　　Tel:　(202) 828-5200
Vice President and Manager, Government Programs (BNI)　Fax:　(202) 785-2645
750 Ninth St. NW, Suite 450
Washington, DC 20001
Registered Federal Lobbyist

DEGRASSE, Bob　　　　　　　　Tel:　(202) 828-5200
Vice President, Manager Government Programs　Fax:　(202) 785-2645
750 Ninth St. NW, Suite 450
Washington, DC 20001

FARRAR, Jay C.　　　　　　　　Tel:　(202) 828-5200
Principal Vice President and Manager, Washington Office　Fax:　(202) 785-2645
750 Ninth St. NW, Suite 450

Washington, DC 20001
jcfarrar@bechtel.com
Registered Federal Lobbyist

JAMES, Brian　　　　　　　　　Tel:　(202) 828-5200
PAC Manager and Legislative Analyst　Fax:　(202) 785-2645
750 Ninth St. NW, Suite 450
Washington, DC 20001

LEADER, Kevin　　　　　　　　Tel:　(202) 828-5200
PAC Treasurer　　　　　　　　Fax:　(202) 785-2645
750 Ninth St. NW, Suite 450
Washington, DC 20001

Beckman Coulter, Inc.
A manufacturer of biomedical testing instrument systems, tests and supplies that simplify and automate laboratory processes.
www.beckmancoulter.com
Annual Revenues: $3.66 billion
Employees: 12,000
Ticker: NYSE: BEC
SIC: 3826
NAICS: 339112
Industry/ies: Medicine/Health Care/Mental Health

Main Headquarters
Mailing:　250 S. Kraemer Blvd.　　Tel:　(714) 993-5321
　　　　　Brea, CA 92821-6232　　Fax:　(800) 232-3828
　　　　　　　　　　　　　　　　TF:　(800) 526-3821

Corporate Foundations and Giving Programs
Beckman Coulter Foundation
Contact: Marci Raudez
200 S. Kraemer Blvd.　　　　　　Tel:　(714) 961-3904
W363
Brea, CA 92821

Public Affairs and Related Activities Personnel

At Headquarters

BACA, Steve C de　　　　　　　Tel:　(714) 993-5321
Senior Vice President, Quality and Regulatory Affairs　Fax:　(800) 232-3828

GONZALEZ, Evangeline　　　　Tel:　(714) 993-5321
Senior Vice President, Marketing　Fax:　(800) 232-3828

LEE, Grace　　　　　　　　　　Tel:　(714) 993-5321
Senior Vice President, Human Resources and　Fax:　(800) 232-3828
Communications

MCLAUGHLIN, Chuck　　　　　Tel:　(714) 993-5321
Chief Financial Officer　　　　　Fax:　(800) 232-3828

RAUDEZ, Marci　　　　　　　　Tel:　(714) 961-6672
Supervisor　　　　　　　　　　Fax:　(800) 232-3828
mfraudez@beckman.com

Becton Dickinson and Company
Manufactures and sells medical supplies, devices, laboratory equipment and diagnostic products.
www.bd.com
Annual Revenues: $8.45 billion
Employees: 30,619
Ticker: NYSE: BDX
SIC: 3061; 3841
NAICS: 326291; 339112
Industry/ies: Management; Pharmaceutical Industry
Legislative Issues: BUD; HCR; MMM; TAX

Chairman of the Board, Chief Executive Officer and President　Tel:　(201) 847-6800
FORLENZA, Vincent A.　　　　　Fax:　(201) 847-6475

Main Headquarters
Mailing:　One Becton Dr.　　　　Tel:　(201) 847-6800
　　　　　Franklin Lakes, NJ 07417　Fax:　(201) 847-6475
　　　　　　　　　　　　　　　　TF:　(800) 284-6845

Washington Office
Mailing:　700 Sixth St. NW　　　Tel:　(201) 847-5767
　　　　　Suite 400
　　　　　Washington, DC 20001

Political Action Committees
BECTON, DICKINSON AND COMPANY PAC
FEC ID: C00376582
Contact: John E. Gallagher
One Becton Dr.
Frankline Lakes, NJ 07024-1880

　　Contributions to Candidates: $119,500 (2015-2016)
　　Democrats: $54,000; Republicans: $65,500

Corporate Foundations and Giving Programs
Becton Dickinson and Company Contributions Program
One Becton Dr.　　　　　　　　Tel:　(201) 847-6800
Franklin Lakes, NJ 07417　　　　Fax:　(201) 847-6800

Public Affairs and Related Activities Personnel

At Headquarters

DOLECKI, Monique N.
Contact, Investor Relations
monique_dolecki@bd.com
Tel: (201) 847-5453
Fax: (201) 847-6475

GALLAGHER, John E.
Vice President , Corporate Finance, Treasurer and Controller
Tel: (201) 847-6800
Fax: (201) 847-6475

HURWITZ, Jerome V.
Executive Vice President and Chief Human Resources Officer
Tel: (201) 847-6800
Fax: (201) 847-6475

KOZY, William A.
Executive Vice President and Chief Operating Officer
Tel: (201) 847-6800
Fax: (201) 847-6475

NAPLES, Richard J.
Senior Vice President, Regulatory Affairs
Tel: (201) 847-6800
Fax: (201) 847-6475

REIDY, Christopher R.
Chief Financial Officer and Executive Vice President of Administration
Tel: (201) 847-6800
Fax: (201) 847-6475

RUSSELL, Patti E.
Vice President and Chief Ethics and Compliance Officer
Patti_E_Russell@Bd.Com
Tel: (201) 847-6800
Fax: (201) 847-6475

SHABSHAB, Nabil
Senior Vice President and Chief Marketing Officer
Tel: (201) 847-6800
Fax: (201) 847-6475

SHERMAN, Jeffrey S.
Senior Vice President and General Counsel
Tel: (201) 847-6800
Fax: (201) 847-6475

At Washington Office

JOHNSTON, Jessica
Registered Federal Lobbyist
Tel: (201) 847-5767

LURAY, Jennifer
Senior Director, Government Affairs
Registered Federal Lobbyist
Tel: (201) 847-5767

LY, Danny
Contact, Government Relations
Registered Federal Lobbyist
Tel: (201) 847-5767

SPANGLER, Todd
Registered Federal Lobbyist
Tel: (201) 847-5767

At Other Offices

GOSIER, Ann M.
Vice President, Government Relations and Public Policy
1250 H St. NE, 11th Floor, Suite 1102
Washington, DC 20005
ann_gosier@bd.com
Registered Federal Lobbyist
Tel: (202) 777-1589

LAKAVAGE, Anthony P.
Worldwide Vice President, Public Affairs
1250 H St. NE, 11th Floor, Suite 1102
Washington, DC 20005
anthony_lakavage@bd.com
Registered Federal Lobbyist
Tel: (202) 777-1584

WOODY, Elizabeth K.
Federal Lobbyist
1250 H St. NE, 11th Floor, Suite 1102
Washington, DC 20005
Registered Federal Lobbyist
Tel: (202) 777-1584

Bed Bath & Beyond Inc.

A nationwide chain of stores selling domestic merchandise and home furnishings.
www.bedbathandbeyond.com
Annual Revenues: $11.96 billion
Employees: 60,000
Ticker: NASDAQ: BBBY
SIC: 5700
Industry/ies: Furniture/Home Furnishings; Retail/Wholesale

Co-Chairman
EISENBERG, Warren
Tel: (908) 688-0888
Fax: (908) 688-6483

Co-Chairman
FEINSTEIN, Leonard
Tel: (908) 688-0888
Fax: (908) 688-6483

Chief Executive Officer
TEMARES, Steven H.
steven.temares@bedbath.com
Tel: (908) 688-0888
Fax: (908) 688-6483

Main Headquarters
Mailing: 650 Liberty Ave.
Union, NJ 07083
Tel: (908) 688-0888
Fax: (908) 688-6483
TF: (800) 462-3966

Public Affairs and Related Activities Personnel

At Headquarters

CURWIN, Ron
Senior Vice President, Investor Relations
Tel: (908) 688-0888
Fax: (908) 688-6483

DEPRIMA, Paul
Director, Corporate Human Resources
Tel: (908) 688-0888
Fax: (908) 688-6483

FAGIN, Bari
Tel: (631) 420-7050

Director, Public Relations
bari.fagin@bedbath.com
Fax: (908) 688-6483

FRANKEL, Kenneth C.
Director, Investor Relations
Tel: (908) 688-0888
Fax: (908) 688-6483

HAMES, Scott
Vice President, Marketing and Analytics
Tel: (908) 688-0888
Fax: (908) 688-6483

LATTMANN, Susan E.
Chief Financial Officer and Treasurer
Tel: (908) 688-0888
Fax: (908) 688-6483

RAUCH, Allan N.
Vice President, Legal and General Counsel
Tel: (908) 688-0888
Fax: (908) 688-6483

WALTZINGER, Jr., William G.
Vice President, Corporate Development, President Harmon Stores
Tel: (908) 688-0888
Fax: (908) 688-6483

Behavioral Interventions, Inc.

Provides management and monitoring systems for correctional facilities.
www.behaviorinterventions.org
Annual Revenues: $25.40 million
Employees: 600
Industry/ies: Computer/Technology; Law Enforcement/Security

Executive Director
BIBELHEIME, Jerome
Tel: (484) 681-2170
Fax: (484) 320-8307

Main Headquarters
Mailing: 583 Shoemaker Rd.
Suite 230
King of Prussia, PA 19406
Tel: (484) 681-2170
Fax: (484) 320-8307
TF: (800) 241-2911

Public Affairs and Related Activities Personnel

At Headquarters

ACHEE, Jonathan
Billing Administrative Assistant
Tel: (484) 681-2170
Fax: (484) 320-8307

COOPER, Brad
Executive Vice President, Finance and Chief Financial Officer
Tel: (303) 218-1000
Fax: (303) 218-1250

HOOK, Monica
Director, Marketing Communications
monica.hook@bi.com
Tel: (800) 800-2411
Fax: (303) 218-1250

SKERJANEC, Ruth
Vice President, Financial Planning
Tel: (303) 218-1000
Fax: (303) 218-1250

TOMLINSON, Kim
Manager, Human Resources
Tel: (484) 681-2170
Fax: (484) 320-8307

WALDO, Jock
Vice President, Marketing and Electronic Monitoring Operations
jock.waldo@bi.com
Tel: (303) 218-1000
Fax: (303) 218-1250

Behlen Manufacturing Company

A steel fabricator of metal livestock equipment, metal buildings and grain bins.
www.behlenmfg.com
Annual Revenues: $77.40 million
Employees: 900
Industry/ies: Agriculture/Agronomy; Animals; Metals

Chairman of the Board and Coach
RAIMONDO, T.R.
Tel: (402) 564-3111
Fax: (402) 563-7405

President and Chief Executive Officer
RAIMONDO, Phil
phil.raimondo@behlenmfg.com
Tel: (402) 564-3111
Fax: (402) 563-7405

Main Headquarters
Mailing: 4025 E. 23rd St.
P.O. Box 569
Columbus, NE 68602-0569
Tel: (402) 564-3111
Fax: (402) 563-7405
TF: (800) 553-5520

Political Action Committees
Behlen Manufacturing Company PAC
FEC ID: C00449710
Contact: C. Tom Burton
4025 E. 23rd St.
P.O. Box 569
Columbus, NE 68602
Tel: (402) 564-3111

Public Affairs and Related Activities Personnel

At Headquarters

BURTON, C. Tom
PAC Treasurer
Tel: (402) 564-3111
Fax: (402) 563-7405

CASEY, Dick
Senior Vice President, Finance
dick.casey@behlenmfg.com
Tel: (402) 564-3111
Fax: (402) 563-7405

O'CONNELL, Paula
Manager, Human Resource and Media Contact
paula.oconnell@behlenmfg.com
Tel: (402) 564-3111
Fax: (402) 563-7405

RAIMONDO, Jr., Tony
President, International Ag and Diversified Products
tony.raimondo@behlenmfg.com
Tel: (402) 564-3111
Fax: (402) 563-7405

Belden CDT Inc.

Formed from the merger of Cable Design Technologies Corp. and Belden, Inc. in July, 2004.
Designs, manufactures, and markets cable, connectivity, and networking products.
www.belden.com
Annual Revenues: $2.30 billion
Employees: 8,200
Ticker: NYSE: BDC
SIC: 3357
Industry/ies: Communications; Telecommunications/Internet/Cable

| **Chairman of the Board** | Tel: | (314) 854-8000 |
| CRESSEY, Bryan C. | Fax: | (314) 854-8001 |

| **President, Chief Executive Officer and Director** | Tel: | (314) 854-8000 |
| STROUP, John S. | Fax: | (314) 854-8001 |

Main Headquarters

Mailing:	One N. Brentwood Blvd.	Tel:	(314) 854-8000
	15th Floor	Fax:	(314) 854-8001
	St. Louis, MO 63105	TF:	(800) 235-3361

Public Affairs and Related Activities Personnel

At Headquarters

| ALDRICH , David | Tel: | (314) 854-8000 |
| *Director* | Fax: | (314) 854-8001 |

Belk, Inc.

Owns and operates fashion department stores.
www.belk.com
Employees: 24,700
SIC: 5311
Industry/ies: Apparel/Textiles Industry; Retail/Wholesale

| **Chairman of the Board and Chief Executive Officer** | Tel: | (704) 357-1000 |
| BELK, Jr., Thomas M. | Fax: | (704) 357-1876 |

Main Headquarters

Mailing:	2801 W. Tyvola Rd.	Tel:	(704) 357-1000
	Charlotte, NC 28217	Fax:	(704) 357-1876
		TF:	(866) 235-5443

Corporate Foundations and Giving Programs

The Belk Foundation	
2801 W. Tyvola Rd.	Tel: (704) 357-1000
Charlotte, NC 28217	

Public Affairs and Related Activities Personnel

At Headquarters

| BAILEY, Lilicia | Tel: | (704) 357-1000 |
| *Executive Vice President and Chief People Officer* | Fax: | (704) 357-1876 |

| BELK, John R. | Tel: | (704) 357-1000 |
| *President and Chief Operating Officer* | Fax: | (704) 357-1876 |

| ORVOS, Adam M. | Tel: | (704) 357-1000 |
| *Executive Vice President and Chief Financial Officer* | Fax: | (704) 357-1876 |

PITTS, Ralph A.	Tel:	(704) 426-8402
Executive Vice President, General Counsel and Secretary	Fax:	(704) 357-1876
ralph_pitts@belk.com	

Bell Helicopter

A helicopter manufacturing subsidiary of Textron, Inc.
www.bellhelicopter.com
Annual Revenues: $13.55 billion
Employees: 35,000
Ticker: NYSE: TXT
SIC: 3721
NAICS: 336411
Industry/ies: Aerospace/Aviation; Transportation

| **President and Chief Executive Officer** | Tel: | (817) 280-2011 |
| SNYDER, Mitch | Fax: | (817) 280-2321 |

Main Headquarters

Mailing:	P.O. Box 482	Tel:	(817) 280-2011
	Fort Worth, TX 76101	Fax:	(817) 280-2321
		TF:	(800) 851-1367

Corporate Foundations and Giving Programs

Bell Helicopter Textron Charitable Trust	
P.O. Box 482	Tel: (817) 280-2425
Fort Worth, TX 76101	Fax: (817) 280-2425

Public Affairs and Related Activities Personnel

At Headquarters

HALL, Bridget	Tel:	(817) 280-7963
Senior Manager, Global Employee Communications	Fax:	(817) 280-2321
bhall@bellhelicopter.textron.com	

HASTINGS, Jr., Robert T.	Tel:	(817) 280-2011
Senior Vice President, Communications and Government	Fax:	(817) 280-2321
Affairs	
RHastings@bellhelicopter.textron.com	

| MAY, Martha | Tel: | (817) 280-2011 |
| *Senior Vice President and Chief Human Resources officer* | Fax: | (817) 280-2321 |

| VETERE, Al | Tel: | (817) 280-2011 |
| *Chief Financial Officer* | Fax: | (817) 280-2321 |

Bell Plantation Holdings, Inc.

Develops original, healthy and tasty consumer ready products using traditional farm commodities; thereby, positively contributing to national, state, and local economies, providing healthier food choices for all and creating new, higher paying jobs.
www.bellplantation.com
Industry/ies: Energy/Electricity

| **Chief Executive Officer and Chairman of the Board** | Tel: | (229) 387-7238 |
| BELL, James C. | |

Main Headquarters

| *Mailing:* | P.O. Box 943 | Tel: | (229) 387-7238 |
| | Tifton, GA 31793 | |

Corporate Foundations and Giving Programs

Bell Plantation Contribution Program
P.O. Box 943
Tifton, GA 31793

Public Affairs and Related Activities Personnel

At Headquarters

| GAIBLER, Floyd D. | Tel: | (229) 387-7238 |
| *Federal Lobbyist* | |

| SUMNER, Dana | Tel: | (229) 387-7238 |
| *Contact, Commercial Sales* | |

Bell Research Companies Inc.

Food products and renewable energy.
www.bellresearchcompanies.com
SIC: 2000
Industry/ies: Energy/Electricity; Food And Beverage Industry

Chairman and Chief Executive Officer	Tel:	(229) 387-7238
BELL, James C.	
j.c.bell@bellplantation.com	

Main Headquarters

| *Mailing:* | P.O. Box 943 | Tel: | (229) 387-7238 |
| | Tifton, GA 31793 | |

Public Affairs and Related Activities Personnel

At Headquarters

| COMERFORD, James D. | Tel: | (229) 387-7238 |

BellSouth Corporation

See listing on page 89 under AT&T Corporation

Bemis Company, Inc.

Supplier of flexible packaging used by food, consumer products, medical and pharmaceutical companies and pressure sensitive adhesive coated materials.
www.bemis.com
Annual Revenues: $4.00 billion
Employees: 17,696
SIC: 2670
Industry/ies: Paper And Wood Products Industry

| **President and Chief Executive Officer** | Tel: | (920) 727-4100 |
| AUSTEN, William F. | Fax: | (920) 527-7600 |

Main Headquarters

Mailing:	One Neenah Center, Fourth Floor	Tel:	(920) 727-4100
	P.O. Box 669	Fax:	(920) 527-7600
	Neenah, WI 54957-0669	

Corporate Foundations and Giving Programs

Bemis Company Foundation	
Contact: Kim Wetzel	
2800 Schaefer Cir.	Tel: (920) 734-2707
Appleton, WI 54915	

Public Affairs and Related Activities Personnel

At Headquarters

| CLAUER, Michael B. | Tel: | (920) 727-4100 |
| *Vice President and Chief Financial Officer* | Fax: | (920) 527-7600 |

| EDISON, Sheri H. | Tel: | (920) 727-4100 |
| *Vice President, General Counsel and Secretary* | Fax: | (920) 527-7600 |

| FLISS, Timothy S. | Tel: | (920) 727-4100 |
| *Vice President, Human Resources* | Fax: | (920) 527-7600 |

| KREMPA, Jerry S. | Tel: | (920) 727-4100 |
| *Vice President and Controller* | Fax: | (920) 527-7600 |

MILLER, Melanie E.R.	Tel:	(920) 527-5045
Vice President and Treasurer	Fax:	(920) 527-7600
mermiller@bemis.com	

At Other Offices

WETZEL, Kim
Foundation Consultant
2800 Schaefer Cir.
Appleton, WI 54915
kwetzel@bemis.com

Tel: (920) 734-2707
Fax: (920) 527-7600

Ben & Jerry's Homemade Inc.

Manufacturer and distributor of frozen dairy products. Acquired by Unilever United States (see separate listing) in 2000, although the company continues to operate separately from Unilever's current U.S. ice cream business.
www.benjerry.com
Employees: 800
SIC: 2024
NAICS: 31152
Industry/ies: Food And Beverage Industry

Chief Executive Officer
SOLHEIM, Jostein
jostein.solheim@benjerry.com

Tel: (802) 846-1500
Fax: (802) 846-1610

Main Headquarters
Mailing: 30 Community Dr.
             S. Burlington, VT 05403-6828

Tel: (802) 846-1500
Fax: (802) 846-1610
TF: (866) 258-6877

Corporate Foundations and Giving Programs

Ben & Jerry's Foundation
Contact: Rebecca Golden
30 Community Dr.
S. Burlington, VT 05403

Tel: (802) 846-1500
Fax: (802) 846-1610

Public Affairs and Related Activities Personnel

At Headquarters

GOLDEN, Rebecca
Director, Programs

Tel: (802) 846-1500
Fax: (802) 846-1610

GREENWOOD, Sean
Director, Public Relations

Tel: (802) 846-1500
Fax: (802) 846-1556

STEVER, David
Chief Marketing Officer
daves@benjerry.com

Tel: (802) 846-1500
Fax: (802) 846-1610

Benchmark Electronics Inc.

Provides electronics design and manufacturing services.
www.bench.com
Annual Revenues: $2.47 billion
Employees: 10,500
Ticker: NYSE: BHE
SIC: 3679; 3699
NAICS: 335999; 334419
Industry/ies: Electricity & Electronics; Electronics; Energy/Electricity

Chairman of the Board
SCHEIBLE, David W.

Tel: (979) 849-6550
Fax: (979) 848-5270

President and Chief Executive Officer
DELLY, Gayla J.
gayla.delly@bench.com

Tel: (979) 849-6550
Fax: (979) 848-5270

Main Headquarters
Mailing: 3000 Technology Dr.
             Angleton, TX 77515

Tel: (979) 849-6550
Fax: (979) 848-5270

Public Affairs and Related Activities Personnel

At Headquarters

ADAM, Donald F.
Chief Financial Officer

Tel: (979) 849-6550
Fax: (979) 848-5270

PETERSON, Scott R.
General Counsel and Corporate Secretary

Tel: (979) 849-6550
Fax: (979) 848-5270

WEEKS, Lisa K.
Vice President, Strategy and Investor Relations

Tel: (979) 849-6550
Fax: (979) 848-5270

Bendix Commercial Vehicle Systems LLC

Manufacturers of commercial vehicle safety systems.
www.bendix.com
Industry/ies: Automotive Industry; Transportation
Legislative Issues: TRA

Chairman of the Board
MCALEESE , Joseph J.

Tel: (440) 329-9000
Fax: (440) 329-9203

President and Chief Executive Officer
BRACHT , Berend

Tel: (440) 329-9000
Fax: (440) 329-9203

Main Headquarters
Mailing: 901 Cleveland St.
             Elyria, OH 44035

Tel: (440) 329-9000
Fax: (440) 329-9203

Public Affairs and Related Activities Personnel

At Headquarters

ANDERSKY, Frederick
Director, Government Affairs

Tel: (440) 329-9000
Fax: (440) 329-9203

frederick.andersky@bendix.com;fred.andersky@bendix.com

HUNGRIA, Carlos
Chief Operating Officer

Tel: (440) 329-9000
Fax: (440) 329-9203

Bentley Systems, Inc.

Provides comprehensive software solutions for the infrastructure lifecycle: from buildings to bridges, transit to utilities, clean energy to clean water.
www.bentley.com
Annual Revenues: $476.00 million
Employees: 3,000
SIC: 7372
Industry/ies: Computer/Technology

Chief Executive Officer
BENTLEY, Gregory S.

Tel: (610) 458-5000
Fax: (610) 458-1060

Main Headquarters
Mailing: 685 Stockton Dr.
             Exton, PA 19341

Tel: (610) 458-5000
Fax: (610) 458-1060
TF: (800) 236-8539

Washington Office
Mailing: 1250 24th St. NW
             Suite 300
             Washington, DC 20037

Political Action Committees
Bentley Systems Federal PAC
FEC ID: C00408138
Contact: Darlene Foster
685 Stockton Dr.
Exton, PA 19341

Tel: (610) 458-5000

Contributions to Candidates: $3,500 (2015-2016)
Republicans: $3,500

Corporate Foundations and Giving Programs

Bentley Systems Inc. Contributions Program
685 Stockton Dr.
Exton, PA 19341

Public Affairs and Related Activities Personnel

At Headquarters

BARRON, Chris
Vice President, Corporate Communications

Tel: (610) 458-5000
Fax: (610) 458-1060

BYRNE, Christine
Senior Manager, Media Relations
christine.byrne@bentley.com

Tel: (203) 805-0432
Fax: (610) 458-1060

FOSTER, Darlene
PAC Treasurer

Tel: (610) 458-5000
Fax: (610) 458-1060

HOLLISTER, David
Chief Financial Officer

Tel: (610) 458-5000
Fax: (610) 458-1060

KUHFELD, Ron
Manager, Public Relations
ron.kuhfeld@bentley.com

Tel: (610) 321-6493
Fax: (610) 458-1060

MANN, Carey
Chief Marketing Officer

Tel: (610) 458-5000
Fax: (610) 458-1060

NATION, David G.
Senior Vice President, Corporate Affairs, General Counsel and Secretary

Tel: (610) 458-5000
Fax: (610) 458-1060

Berkshire Hathaway Inc

A conglomerate with subsidiaries in property and casualty insurance, shoe and uniform and candy manufacturing, publishing, and home cleaning systems. Subsidiaries include Flight Safety International Inc. and GEICO Corp. (see separate listings.) Acquired Johns Manville and Shaw Industries (see separate listings) in 2001, Fruit of the Loom, Inc. in April of 2002, and McLane Company, Inc. and Clayton Homes, Inc. in 2003 (see separate listings).
www.berkshirehathaway.com
Annual Revenues: $193.90 billion
Employees: 316,000
Ticker: NYSE: BRK-A
SIC: 6331; 3320
Industry/ies: Apparel/Textiles Industry; Food And Beverage Industry; Furniture/Home Furnishings; Insurance Industry; Metals

Chairman of the Board and Chief Executive Officer
BUFFETT, Warren E.

Tel: (402) 346-1400
Fax: (402) 346-3375

Main Headquarters
Mailing: 3555 Farnam St.
             Omaha, NE 68131

Tel: (402) 346-1400
Fax: (402) 346-3375
TF: (888) 395-6349

Corporate Foundations and Giving Programs

Berkshire Hathaway Inc Contributions Program
3555 Farnam St.
Suite 1440
Omaha, NE 68131

Tel: (402) 346-1400

Precision Castparts Corporation Contributions Program
4650 S.W. Macadam Ave.

Tel: (503) 417-4800

Suite 440
Portland, OR 97239-4262

Fax: (503) 417-4817

Public Affairs and Related Activities Personnel

At Headquarters

HAMBURG, Marc D.
Senior Vice President and Chief Financial Officer

Tel: (402) 346-1400
Fax: (402) 346-3375

Berwind Corporation

A company with subsidiaries active in such varied industries as coal mining, specialty chemicals, automotive parts, real estate investment and property management.
www.berwind.com
Employees: 4,500
SIC: 1221; 1382; 2819; 2865; 5169
Industry/ies: Mining Industry; Natural Resources

Main Headquarters

Mailing: 3000 Centre Sq., West
1500 Market St.
Philadelphia, PA 19102

Tel: (215) 563-2800
Fax: (215) 575-2314

Public Affairs and Related Activities Personnel

At Headquarters

LEHN, Alfred M.
Federal Lobbyist

Tel: (202) 456-2420

LEWIS, Charlie
Senior Vice President, Corporate Development
clewis@berwind.com

Tel: (215) 575-2330
Fax: (215) 575-2314

Best Buy Company, Inc.

A specialty retailer of consumer electronics, personal computers, entertainment software and appliances.
www.bestbuy.com
Annual Revenues: $42.41 billion
Employees: 140,000
Ticker: NYSE: BBY
SIC: 5731
Industry/ies: Electricity & Electronics; Electronics; Energy/Electricity; Retail/Wholesale
Legislative Issues: AVI; BUD; CPI; CSP; FIN; LBR; TAX; TRA; TRD

President and Chief Executive Officer
JOLY, Hubert

Tel: (612) 291-1000
Fax: (612) 292-4001

Main Headquarters

Mailing: P.O. Box 9312
Minneapolis, MN 55440

Tel: (612) 291-1000
Fax: (612) 292-4001
TF: (888) 237-8289

Political Action Committees

Best Buy Company Inc. Employee Political Forum PAC
FEC ID: C00405076
Contact: Laura A. Bishop
7601 Penn Ave. South
Richfield, MN 55423

Tel: (612) 291-1000

Contributions to Candidates: $11,273,015 (2015-2016)
Democrats: $70,500; Republicans: $110,500; Other: $11,092,015

Corporate Foundations and Giving Programs

Best Buy Children's Foundation
7601 Penn Ave. South
Richfield, MN 55423

Tel: (612) 291-1000
Fax: (612) 292-4001

Public Affairs and Related Activities Personnel

At Headquarters

BALLARD, Shari
President, U.S. Retail and Chief Human Resources Officer

Tel: (612) 291-1000
Fax: (612) 292-4001

DURCHSLAG, Scott
President, E-Commerce and Marketing

Tel: (612) 291-1000
Fax: (612) 292-4001

FURMAN, Matt
Chief Communications and Public Affairs Officer

Tel: (612) 291-1000
Fax: (612) 292-4001

MCCOLLAM, Sharon
Chief Administrative Officer and Chief Financial Officer

Tel: (612) 291-1000
Fax: (612) 292-4001

NELSEN, Keith
Executive Vice President, General Counsel

Tel: (612) 291-1000
Fax: (612) 292-4001

SZENTE, Andrew
Senior Manager, Government Affairs
Registered Federal Lobbyist

Tel: (612) 291-1000
Fax: (612) 292-4001

WELDON, Amy
Manager, Government Relations
amy.weldon@bestbuy.com

Tel: (612) 291-1000
Fax: (612) 292-4001

At Other Offices

BISHOP, Laura A.
Vice President, Public Affairs
7601 Penn Ave., South
Richfield, MN 55423
laura.bishop@bestbuy.com

Tel: (612) 291-1000
Fax: (612) 292-4001

BRUGGE, Parker
Federal Lobbyist
7601 Penn Ave., South
Richfield, MN 55423
parker.brugge@bestbuy.com
Registered Federal Lobbyist

Tel: (612) 291-1000
Fax: (612) 292-4001

HANLON, Blake
Federal Lobbyist
7601 Penn Ave., South
Richfield, MN 55423
blake.hanlon@bestbuy.com

Tel: (612) 291-1000
Fax: (612) 292-4001

HILTNER, Mike
Manager, Government Relations
7601 Penn Ave., South
Richfield, MN 55423
mike.hiltner@bestbuy.com

Tel: (612) 291-1000
Fax: (612) 292-4001

MORTENSON, Amy
Manager, Government Relations
7601 Penn Ave., South
Richfield, MN 55423
amy.mortenson@bestbuy.com

Tel: (612) 291-6112
Fax: (612) 292-4001

Best Western International

An international hotel chain. Begun in 1946 by hotelier M. K. Guertin and named for its California origins. Best Western has more than 4,000 independently owned and operated hotels throughout the globe (including nearly 2,200 in North America).
www.bestwestern.com
Annual Revenues: $48.40 million
Employees: 1,000
Industry/ies: Travel/Tourism/Lodging

Chairman of the Board
MONTMANEIX, Julie

Tel: (602) 957-4200
Fax: (602) 957-5641

President and Chief Executive Officer
KONG, David T.
david.kong@bestwestern.com

Tel: (602) 957-4200
Fax: (602) 957-5641

Main Headquarters

Mailing: 6201 N. 24th Pkwy.
Phoenix, AZ 85016

Tel: (602) 957-4200
Fax: (602) 957-5641
TF: (800) 780-7234

Corporate Foundations and Giving Programs

Best Western International Contributions Program
6201 N. 24th Pkwy.
Phoenix, AZ 85016

Tel: (602) 957-4200
Fax: (602) 957-5641

Public Affairs and Related Activities Personnel

At Headquarters

BRAS, Barbara
Vice President, Human Resources
barbara.bras@bestwestern.com

Tel: (602) 957-4200
Fax: (602) 957-5641

CUCULIC, Larry
Senior Vice President and General Counsel

Tel: (602) 957-4200
Fax: (602) 957-5641

DOWLING, Dorothy
Senior Vice President, Marketing and Sales
dorothy.dowling@bestwestern.com

Tel: (602) 957-4200
Fax: (602) 957-5641

STRASZYNSKI, Mark
Chief Financial Officer

Tel: (602) 957-4200
Fax: (602) 957-5641

Better Place, Inc.

Better Place is the pioneering electric car network operator enabling mass market adoption of electric cars through innovative network solutions and services.
www.betterplace.com
Employees: 12
Industry/ies: Automotive Industry; Energy/Electricity; Environment And Conservation; Transportation

Chairman of the Board
OFER, Idan

Tel: (650) 845-2800
Fax: (650) 845-2850

Chief Executive Officer
COHEN, Dan

Tel: (650) 845-2800
Fax: (650) 845-2850

Main Headquarters

Mailing: 1070 Arastradero Rd.
Suite 200
Palo Alto, CA 94304

Tel: (650) 845-2800
Fax: (650) 845-2850

Public Affairs and Related Activities Personnel

At Headquarters

AGASSI, Shai
Founder

Tel: (650) 845-2800
Fax: (650) 845-2850

MULLINS, Julie
Contact, Media Relations
julie.mullins@betterplace.com

Tel: (650) 387-0486
Fax: (650) 845-2850

PALUSKA, Joe
Vice President, Communications and Policy

Tel: (650) 845-2800
Fax: (650) 845-2850

joe.paluska@betterplace.com

SHORT , Alastair	Tel:	(650) 845-2800
General Counsel	Fax:	(650) 845-2850

BG and E

See listing on page 121 under Biomass Gas & Electric, LLC

BIC Corporation

The U.S. subsidiary of Society Bic of Clichy, manufactures writing instruments, shavers, lighters, correction fluids and stationery accessories, including sticky notes, erasers, rulers and compasses.
www.bicworld.com
Employees: 6,000
Industry/ies: Personal Care/Hygiene

Chairman of the Board	Tel:	(203) 783-2000
BICH, Bruno	Fax:	(203) 783-2081
brunobich@bicworld.com		

Chief Executive Officer	Tel:	(203) 783-2000
GUEVARA, Maria	Fax:	(203) 783-2081

Main Headquarters

Mailing:	One BIC Way	Tel:	(203) 783-2000
	Suite One	Fax:	(203) 783-2081
	Shelton, CT 06484-6299		

Corporate Foundations and Giving Programs

BIC Corporation Contributions Program
One BIC Way
Suite One
Shelton, CT 06484-6223

Tel: (203) 783-2000

Public Affairs and Related Activities Personnel

At Headquarters

KLIMACK, Jill	Tel:	(203) 783-2051
Supervisor, Communications	Fax:	(203) 783-2081
jill.kilmack@bicworld.om		

Biersack Government Relations Team LLC

A full service lobbying and political consulting firm interacting with both the state and federal government.
biersackgovernmentrelationsteam.com
Legislative Issues: DEF; HCR; HOM; MAR; TEC

Main Headquarters

Mailing:	8197 Cottage Rose Ct.	Tel:	(202) 725-8116
	Fairfax Station, VA 22039		

Public Affairs and Related Activities Personnel

At Headquarters

BIERSACK, Carl	Tel:	(202) 725-8116
carlbiersack@gmail.com		
Registered Federal Lobbyist		

Big Heart Pet Brands

Big Heart Pet Brands is the largest standalone pet food and snacks company in N. America.
www.bigheartpet.com
Annual Revenues: $3.74 billion
Employees: 5,400
Ticker: NYSE: DLM
SIC: 2040
NAICS: 311421
Industry/ies: Food And Beverage Industry
Legislative Issues: AGR

President, Chief Executive Officer and Director	Tel:	(415) 247-3000
WEST, David J.	Fax:	(415) 247-3565

Main Headquarters

Mailing:	One Maritime Plaza	Tel:	(415) 344-4700
	San Francisco, CA 94111		

Political Action Committees

Big Heart Pet Brands PAC
FEC ID: C00522599
Contact: Ralph Lupian
One Maritime Plaza
300 Clay St.
San Francisco, CA 94111

Tel: (415) 247-3379

Corporate Foundations and Giving Programs

Del Monte Foods Contributions Program
One Market
P.O. Box 193575
San Francisco, CA 94105

Public Affairs and Related Activities Personnel

At Headquarters

ERNST, Timothy S.	Tel:	(415) 344-4700
Senior Vice President, General Counsel and Secretary		

FLEMING, Cindy	Tel:	(415) 247-3379
Fedreal Lobbyist		
HUSAIN , Asad	Tel:	(415) 344-4700
Executive Vice President and Chief Human Resources Officer		
JOHNSON, III, M. Carl	Tel:	(415) 344-4700
Executive Vice President, Marketing and Chief Growth Officer		
MADRIAGA, Michael	Tel:	(415) 247-3379
Senior Associate, Government and Industry Relations Registered Federal Lobbyist		
VILLARREAL, Megan	Tel:	(415) 247-3379
Registered Federal Lobbyist		
WEINER, Jonathan R.	Tel:	(415) 344-4700
Senior Vice President, Marketing Strategy, Insights and Activation		

At Other Offices

BODNER, Larry E.	Tel:	(415) 247-3000
Executive Vice President, Chief Financial Officer and Treasurer	Fax:	(415) 247-3565
P.O. Box 193575		
San Francisco, CA 94119		
LUPIAN, Ralph	Tel:	(415) 247-3000
PAC Treasurer	Fax:	(415) 247-3565
P.O. Box 193575		
San Francisco, CA 94119		

Big Lots Inc.

Formerly known as Consolidated Stores Corp. A broadline closeout retailer.
www.biglots.com
Annual Revenues: $5.22 billion
Employees: 11,400
Ticker: NYSE: BIG
SIC: 5331
Industry/ies: Retail/Wholesale

Chief Executive Officer and President	Tel:	(614) 278-6800
CAMPISI , David J.	Fax:	(614) 278-3701

Main Headquarters

Mailing:	300 Phillipi Rd.	Tel:	(614) 278-6800
	Columbus, OH 43228	Fax:	(614) 278-3701

Corporate Foundations and Giving Programs

Big Lots Contributions Program
300 Phillipi Rd.
Columbus, OH 43228-5311

Tel: (614) 278-6800
Fax: (614) 278-6800

Public Affairs and Related Activities Personnel

At Headquarters

BACHMANN, Lisa	Tel:	(614) 278-6800
Executive Vice President, Chief Merchandising and Operating Officer	Fax:	(614) 278-3701
HAUBIEL, II, Charles W.	Tel:	(614) 278-6800
Executive Vice President, Chief Adminstrative Officer, General Counsel and Corporate Secretary	Fax:	(614) 278-6676
JOHNSON, Timothy A.	Tel:	(614) 278-6622
Executive Vice President, Chief Financial Officer and Chief Administrative Officer	Fax:	(614) 278-6666
ROBINS, Rocky	Tel:	(614) 278-6800
Senior Vice President, General Counsel and Corporate Secretary	Fax:	(614) 278-3701
SCHLONSKY, Mike	Tel:	(614) 278-6800
Executive Vice President, Human Resources and Store Operations	Fax:	(614) 278-3701

Big Y Foods Inc.

Most of its stores are Big Y World Class Markets, offering specialty areas such as bakeries and floral shops, as well as banking. The rest consist of Big Y Supermarkets and a single gourmet food and liquor store called Table & Vine in Springfield, Massachusetts. Some Big Y stores provide child care, dry cleaning, photo processing, and even propane sales, and their delis and food courts offer to-go foods.
www.bigy.com
Annual Revenues: $1.38 billion
Employees: 10,000
Industry/ies: Food And Beverage Industry; Retail/Wholesale

Chairman of the Board and Chief Executive Officer	Tel:	(413) 784-0600
D'AMOUR, Donald H.	Fax:	(413) 732-7350
ddamour@bigy.com		

Main Headquarters

Mailing:	2145 Roosevelt Ave.	Tel:	(413) 784-0600
	P. O. Box 7840	Fax:	(413) 732-7350
	Springfield, MA 01102-7840	TF:	(800) 828-2688

Corporate Foundations and Giving Programs

Big Y Foods Contributions Program

Contact: Jill Connors
2145 Roosevelt Ave.
P. O. Box 7840
Springfield, MA 01102-7840

Public Affairs and Related Activities Personnel

At Headquarters

CONNORS, Jill	Tel:	(413) 504-4080
Contact, Foundation	Fax:	(413) 732-7350
D'AMOUR-DALEY, Claire	Tel:	(413) 504-4004
Vice President, Corporate Communications	Fax:	(413) 732-7350

Bill Barrett Corporation

An oil and gas exploration and development company.
www.billbarrettcorp.com
Annual Revenues: $387.71 million
Employees: 202
Ticker: NYSE: BBG
SIC: 1311
Industry/ies: Fuels See Coal, Gas, Oil, Petroleum; Natural Resources; Petroleum Industry

Chief Executive Officer and President	Tel:	(303) 293-9100
WOODALL, R. Scot	Fax:	(303) 291-0420

Main Headquarters

Mailing:	1099 18th St.	Tel:	(303) 293-9100
	Suite 2300	Fax:	(303) 291-0420
	Denver, CO 80202		

Political Action Committees

Bill Barrett Corporation Political Action Committee
FEC ID: C00490441
Contact: Robert W. Howard
1099 18th St.
Suite 2300
Denver, CO 80202

    Contributions to Candidates: $500 (2015-2016)
    Republicans: $500

Public Affairs and Related Activities Personnel

At Headquarters

CRAWFORD, William M.	Tel:	(303) 293-9100
Vice President, Finance and Marketing	Fax:	(303) 291-0420
HOWARD, Robert W.	Tel:	(303) 293-9100
Chief Financial Officer and Treasurer and PAC Treasurer	Fax:	(303) 291-0420
MARTIN, Jennifer C.	Tel:	(303) 312-8155
Vice President, Investor Relations	Fax:	(303) 291-0420
jmartin@billbarretcorp.com		
PARNELL, Larry A.	Tel:	(303) 293-9100
Senior Vice President Engineering, Planning and Business Development	Fax:	(303) 291-0420
VION, Michele	Tel:	(303) 293-9100
Vice President, Human Resources	Fax:	(303) 291-0420
WONSTOLEN, Kenneth A.	Tel:	(303) 293-9100
Senior Vice President and General Counsel	Fax:	(303) 291-0420
ZAVADIL, Duane J.	Tel:	(303) 293-9100
Senior Vice President, Environment, Health and Safety, Government and Regulatory Affairs	Fax:	(303) 291-0420
dzavadil@billbarrettcorp.com		

Binney and Smith

See listing on page 229 under Crayola LLC.

Bio-Rad Laboratories, Inc.

A scientific services provider.
www.bio-rad.com
Annual Revenues: $2.02 billion
Employees: 7,770
Ticker: NYSE: BIO
SIC: 2835; 2836; 2899; 3826
NAICS: 334516; 334510; 541711; 325199
Industry/ies: Science; Scientific Research

Chairman of the Board, President and Chief Executive Officer	Tel:	(510) 724-7000
SCHWARTZ, Norman	Fax:	(510) 741-5817

Main Headquarters

Mailing:	2000 Alfred Noble Dr.	Tel:	(510) 724-7000
	Hercules, CA 94547	Fax:	(510) 741-5817
		TF:	(800) 424-6723

Corporate Foundations and Giving Programs

Bio-Rad Laboratories Community Outreach Program

1000 Alfred Noble Dr.	Tel:	(510) 724-7000
Hercules, CA 94547	Fax:	(510) 741-5815

Public Affairs and Related Activities Personnel

At Headquarters

CUCCIA, Tina	Tel:	(510) 741-6063
Manager, Corporate Communications	Fax:	(510) 741-5817
ERNST, Timothy S.	Tel:	(510) 724-7000
Executive Vice President, General Counsel and Secretary	Fax:	(510) 741-5817
GOETZ, John	Tel:	(510) 724-7000
Executive Vice President, Chief Operating Officer	Fax:	(510) 741-5817
HUTTON, Ronald	Tel:	(510) 724-7000
Vice President, Treasurer	Fax:	(510) 741-5817
MAGNI, Giovanni	Tel:	(510) 724-7000
Executive Vice President, Chief Strategy Officer	Fax:	(510) 741-5817
STARK, James	Tel:	(510) 724-7000
Vice President, Corporate Controller	Fax:	(510) 741-5817
TSINGOS, Christine	Tel:	(510) 724-7000
Executive Vice President and Chief Financial Officer	Fax:	(510) 741-5817
investor_relations@bio-rad.com		

BioBased Systems

www.biobased.net
Industry/ies: Construction/Construction Materials

Main Headquarters

Mailing:	Ten-A Wolfer Industrial Park	Tel:	(202) 498-5642
	Spring Valley, IL 61362	Fax:	(703) 997-0590

Public Affairs and Related Activities Personnel

At Headquarters

HUTCHINSON, Joshua L.	Tel:	(202) 498-5642
Director, Government Affairs	Fax:	(703) 997-0590

BioCryst Pharmaceuticals Inc.

Creates small molecule compounds that inhibit enzymes associated with viral diseases, autoimmune conditions, and cancer.
www.biocryst.com
Annual Revenues: $16.98 million
Employees: 50
Ticker: NASDAQ: BCRX
SIC: 2836
Industry/ies: Pharmaceutical Industry
Legislative Issues: DIS; MED

Chairman of the Board	Tel:	(919) 859-1302
ABERCROMBIE, George B.	Fax:	(919) 859-1314

President and Chief Executive Officer	Tel:	(919) 859-1302
STONEHOUSE, Jon P.	Fax:	(919) 859-1314

Main Headquarters

Mailing:	4505 Emperor Blvd.	Tel:	(919) 859-1302
	Suite 200	Fax:	(919) 859-1314
	Durham, NC 27703		

Public Affairs and Related Activities Personnel

At Headquarters

BARNES, Alane	Tel:	(919) 859-1302
Vice President, General Counsel and Corporate Secretary	Fax:	(919) 859-1314
BENNETT, Rob	Tel:	(919) 859-7910
Vice President, Investor Relations and Operations	Fax:	(919) 859-1314
investorrelations@biocryst.com		
BERGER, PhD, Elliott T.	Tel:	(919) 859-1302
Senior Vice President, Regulatory Affairs	Fax:	(919) 859-1314
STAAB II, Thomas R.	Tel:	(919) 859-1302
Senior Vice President and Chief Financial Officer	Fax:	(919) 859-1314
STONER, Robert	Tel:	(919) 859-1302
Vice President, Human Resources	Fax:	(919) 859-1314
humanresources@biocryst.com		

BioEnergy International, LLC

A biotechnology company focused on developing biorefineries.
www.bioenergyllc.com
Industry/ies: Agriculture/Agronomy; Chemicals & Chemical Industry; Energy/ Electricity; Environment And Conservation; Fuels See Coal, Gas, Oil, Petroleum; Natural Resources; Petroleum Industry; Science; Scientific Research

Main Headquarters

Mailing:	One Pine Hill Dr.	Tel:	(617) 657-5209
	Batterymarch Park II, Suite 301		
	Quincy, MA 02169		

BioFactura

Biodefense and biopharmaceutical development.
www.biofactura.com
Annual Revenues: $0.29 million
Industry/ies: Defense/Homeland Security; Government-Related; Pharmaceutical Industry; Science; Scientific Research
Legislative Issues: DEF

President and Chief Executive Officer
SAMPEY, Darryl
dsampey@biofactura.com

Tel: (301) 315-8002
Fax: (240) 597-6340

Main Headquarters
Mailing: 4539 Metropolitan Ct., Suite 236
Frederick, MD 21704

Tel: (301) 315-8002

Washington Office
Mailing: 9430 Key West Ave.
Suite 125
Rockville, MD 20850

Tel: (301) 315-8002
Fax: (240) 597-6340

BioFire Diagnostics, Inc.

Formerly Idaho Technology, Inc. changed its name in 2012. Pathogen identification and DNA research.
www.biofiredx.com
Industry/ies: Science; Scientific Research
Legislative Issues: DEF

Chairman of the Board and Co-founder
WITTWER, Carl

Tel: (801) 736-6354
Fax: (801) 588-0507

Chief Executive Officer, Director and Founder
RIRIE, Kirk

Tel: (801) 736-6354
Fax: (801) 588-0507

Main Headquarters
Mailing: 79 W 4500 S, Suite 14
Salt Lake City, UT 84107

Tel: (801) 736-6354
Fax: (801) 588-0507
TF: (800) 735-6544

Public Affairs and Related Activities Personnel

At Headquarters

GORRELL, Eric
General Counsel and Corporate Secretary

Tel: (801) 736-6354
Fax: (801) 588-0507

JONES, Rachel R.
Senior Vice President, Sales and Marketing

Tel: (801) 736-6354
Fax: (801) 588-0507

KENDELL, Andrea
Senior Vice President, Finance

Tel: (801) 736-6354
Fax: (801) 588-0507

LOLLINI, Robert J.
Chief Financial Officer and Treasurer

Tel: (801) 736-6354
Fax: (801) 588-0507

Biogen Idec Inc.

A biopharmaceutical company. Formed by the merger of Biogen, Inc. and IDEC Pharmaceuticals Corporation in 2003.
www.biogenidec.com
Annual Revenues: $10.94 billion
Employees: 7,350
Ticker: NASDAQ: BIIB
SIC: 2836
Industry/ies: Medicine/Health Care/Mental Health; Science; Scientific Research
Legislative Issues: BUD; CPT; HCR; MED; MMM; TAX; TRD

Chairman of the Board
PAPADOPOULOS, Stelios

Tel: (781) 464-2000
Fax: (302) 636-5454

Chief Executive Officer
SCANGOS, PhD, George A.
george.scangos@biogenidec.com

Tel: (617) 679-2000
Fax: (617) 679-2617

Main Headquarters
Mailing: 225 Binney St.
Cambridge, MA 02142

Tel: (781) 464-2000
Fax: (302) 636-5454

Washington Office
Mailing: 601 Pennsylvania Ave. NW
Suite 720
Washington, DC 20004

Tel: (202) 383-1440
Fax: (202) 347-1066

Political Action Committees
Biogen Idec PAC
FEC ID: C00390351
Contact: Kathleen Tregoning
133 Boston Post Rd.
Weston, MA 2493

Tel: (617) 679-2000

Contributions to Candidates: $162,500 (2015-2016)
Democrats: $70,000; Republicans: $92,500

Principal Recipients

HOUSE
SANCHEZ, LINDA (DEM-CA)

Corporate Foundations and Giving Programs

Biogen Idec Foundation
Contact: Kara DiGiacomo
14 Cambridge Center
Cambridge, MA 02142

Public Affairs and Related Activities Personnel

At Headquarters

COOPER, Todd
Senior Director, Public Affairs and Contact, Media Relations

Tel: (781) 464-2000
Fax: (302) 636-5454

GLASHOW, Jason
Senior Director, Corporate Communications
jason.glashow@biogenidec.com

Tel: (781) 464-3260
Fax: (302) 636-5454

TREGONING, Kathleen
Vice President, Public Policy, Government Affairs and PAC Treasurer
kathleen.tregoning@biogenidec.com

Tel: (781) 464-2000
Fax: (302) 636-5454

WILLIAMS, Douglas E.
Executive Vice President, Research and Development

Tel: (781) 464-2000
Fax: (302) 636-5454

At Washington Office

BRAND, Adam
Director, Public Policy and Government Affairs
Registered Federal Lobbyist

Tel: (202) 383-1440
Fax: (202) 347-1066

GLUCK, Adam R.
Registered Federal Lobbyist

Tel: (202) 383-1440
Fax: (202) 347-1066

MENDENHALL, Ally
Federal Lobbyist

Tel: (202) 383-1440
Fax: (202) 347-1066

PHILLIPS, Catherine
Registered Federal Lobbyist

Tel: (202) 383-1440
Fax: (202) 347-1066

At Other Offices

ALEXANDER, Susan H.
Executive Vice President, Chief Legal Officer and Corporate Secretary
133 Boston Post Rd.
Weston, MA 02493
susan.alexander@biogenidec.com

Tel: (617) 679-2000
Fax: (617) 679-2617

CLANCY, Paul J.
Executive Vice President and Chief Financial Officer
133 Boston Post Rd.
Weston, MA 02493

Tel: (617) 679-2000
Fax: (617) 679-2617

DIGIACOMO, Kara
Executive Director, Biogen Idec Foundation, Senior Manager of Community Relations and Philanthropy
133 Boston Post Rd.
Weston, MA 02493
kdigiacomo@BiogenIdec.com

Tel: (781) 464-2000
Fax: (617) 679-2617

DIPIETRO, Kenneth
Executive Vice President, Human Resources
133 Boston Post Rd.
Weston, MA 02493

Tel: (617) 679-2000
Fax: (617) 679-2617

HOLTZMAN, Steven H.
Executive Vice President, Corporate Development
133 Boston Post Rd.
Weston, MA 02493

Tel: (617) 679-2000
Fax: (617) 679-2617

KHALEGHPOUR, Kia
Director, Investor Relations
133 Boston Post Rd.
Weston, MA 02493
Kia.Khaleghpour@biogenidec.com

Tel: (781) 464-2442
Fax: (617) 679-2617

STRAIN, Ben
Associate Director, Investor Relations
133 Boston Post Rd.
Weston, MA 02493

Tel: (781) 464-2000
Fax: (617) 679-2617

VINEIS, Tracy
Associate Director, Public Affairs
133 Boston Post Rd.
Weston, MA 02493

Tel: (781) 464-3260
Fax: (617) 679-2617

Biomass Gas & Electric, LLC

Renewable energy technology development and production Company.
www.biggreenenergy.com
Annual Revenues: $0.74 million
Employees: 10
Industry/ies: Energy/Electricity; Environment And Conservation

President and Chief Executive Officer
FARRIS, Glenn
glenn@biggreenenergy.com

Tel: (770) 662-0256
Fax: (770) 662-0287

Main Headquarters
Mailing: 3500 Pkwy. Ln.
Suite 440
Norcross, GA 30092-2861

Tel: (770) 662-0256
Fax: (770) 662-0287

Public Affairs and Related Activities Personnel

At Headquarters

CHANIN, Peter
Contact, Business Development and Regulatory Issues
cpc@biggreenenergy.com

Tel: (770) 662-0256
Fax: (770) 662-0287

MCDERMOTT, Keith J.
Vice President, Marketing and Business Development and Media Relations Contact
kmcdermott@biggreenenergy.com

Tel: (770) 662-0256
Fax: (770) 662-0287

Biomedical Applications of MS, Inc.
See listing on page 343 under Fresenius Medical Care North America

Biosonics, Inc.
Offers hydro acoustic solutions for monitoring and assessing aquatic biological and physical resources.
www.biosonicsinc.com
SIC: 3800
Industry/ies: Science; Scientific Research

President and Chief Executive Officer	Tel:	(206) 782-2211
ACKER, Timothy	Fax:	(206) 782-2244

Main Headquarters
Mailing:	4027 Leary Way NW	Tel:	(206) 782-2211
	Seattle, WA 98107	Fax:	(206) 782-2244

Public Affairs and Related Activities Personnel

At Headquarters
ACKER, Bev	Tel:	(206) 782-2211
Vice President and Chief Financial Officer	Fax:	(206) 782-2244
MUNDAY, Eric	Tel:	(206) 782-2211
Director, Sales and Marketing	Fax:	(206) 782-2244
WOOD, Erin	Tel:	(206) 782-2211
Assistant, Administrative Services and Marketing	Fax:	(206) 782-2244

Biotechnology Research and Development Corporation
A biotechnology consortium that brings government, academia and the private sector together.
Annual Revenues: $1.0 million
Industry/ies: Science; Scientific Research

President and Chief Executive Officer	Tel:	(309) 688-1188
BREWEN, J. Grant	Fax:	(309) 688-1292

Main Headquarters
Mailing:	1815 N. University St.	Tel:	(309) 688-1188
	Peoria, IL 61604-3902	Fax:	(309) 688-1292

Biothera, the Immume Health Company
Biothera is a biotechnology company dedicated to improving immune health.Biothera was founded in 1997 and is based in Eagan, Minnesota, USA.
www.biothera.com
Employees: 100
Industry/ies: Medicine/Health Care/Mental Health; Science; Scientific Research

Chairman of the Board	Tel:	(651) 675-0300
CONNERS, Daniel	Fax:	(651) 675-0400
dconners@biotherapharma.com		

Chief Executive Officer	Tel:	(651) 675-0300
MUELLER, Richard	Fax:	(651) 675-0400
skarel@biotherapharma.com		

Main Headquarters
Mailing:	3388 Mike Collins Dr.	Tel:	(651) 675-0300
	Eagan, MN 55121	Fax:	(651) 452-1421

Public Affairs and Related Activities Personnel

At Headquarters
GACKI, William L.	Tel:	(651) 675-0300
Chief Financial Officer	Fax:	(651) 675-0400
wgacki@biothera.com		
KAREL, Steven	Tel:	(651) 675-0300
Chief Administrative Officer	Fax:	(651) 452-1421
STEINER, Matt	Tel:	(651) 256-4613
Vice President, Sales and Marketing	Fax:	(651) 675-0400
msteiner@biotherapharma.com		
WALSH, David	Tel:	(651) 256-4606
Vice President, Communications	Fax:	(651) 675-0400
dwalsh@biothera.com		

Biovest International, Inc.
A biotechnology company that produces proprietary cell culture systems, biological products and individualized immunotherapies.
www.biovest.com
Annual Revenues: $3.88 million
SIC: 2834
Industry/ies: Pharmaceutical Industry
Legislative Issues: DEF; HCR

General Counsel	Tel:	(813) 864-2554
DUFFEY, Esq., Samuel S.	Fax:	(813) 258-6912

Chief Executive Officer	Tel:	(813) 864-2554
SANTOS, PhD, Carlos F.	Fax:	(813) 258-6912

Main Headquarters
Mailing:	8500 Evergreen Blvd.	Tel:	(763) 786-0302
	Minneapolis, MN 55433		

Public Affairs and Related Activities Personnel

At Headquarters
ENGSTROM, Christiaan	Tel:	(763) 786-0302
President		
MCNAMARA, Chris	Tel:	(763) 786-0302
Account Manager		
SCHUMANN, David	Tel:	(763) 786-0302
Account Manager		

At Other Offices
MOSER, David D.	Tel:	(813) 864-2554
Director, Legal Affairs and Corporate Secretary	Fax:	(813) 258-6912
300 S. Hyde Park Ave., Suite 210		
Tampa, FL 33606		
dmoser@biovest.com		

BIPAC
See listing on page 151 under Business Industry Political Action Committee (BIPAC)

BJ Services Company
A provider of oil to the petroleum industry worldwide. Acquired by Baker Hughes in April 2010.
www.bjservices.com
Ticker: NYSE: BJS
SIC: 1389
Industry/ies: Energy/Electricity

President, North America	Tel:	(713) 439-8600
WILLIAMS, Richard		

Main Headquarters
Mailing:	2929 Allen Pkwy.	Tel:	(713) 439-8600
	Suite 2100	TF:	(800) 229-7447
	Houston, TX 77019-2118		

Public Affairs and Related Activities Personnel

At Headquarters
CHARRETON, Didier	Tel:	(713) 439-8600
Vice President, Human Resources		
CRAIN, Alan	Tel:	(713) 439-8600
Senior Vice President, Chief Legal and Governance Officer		
RAGAUSS, Peter A.	Tel:	(713) 439-8600
Senior Vice President and Chief Financial Officer		

BJ's Wholesale Club, Inc.
Operates a chain of membership warehouse clubs in the eastern United States.
www.bjs.com
Ticker: NYSE: BJ
Industry/ies: Retail/Wholesale

President and Chief Executive Officer	Tel:	(508) 651-7400
SEN, Laura J.	Fax:	(508) 651-6114

Main Headquarters
Mailing:	25 Research Dr.	Tel:	(774) 512-6186
	P.O. Box 5230	Fax:	(774) 512-6859
	Westborough, MA 01581		

Corporate Foundations and Giving Programs
BJ's Charitable Foundation

Black & Veatch
A global engineering, construction and consulting firm. It specializes in infrastructure development for the energy, water, environmental, federal, and telecommunications markets.
www.bv.com
Annual Revenues: $2.26 billion
Employees: 7,000
SIC: 2080
Industry/ies: Engineering/Mathematics
Legislative Issues: DEF; FIN; FOR; FUE; HOM; TAX; TRD; UTI

Chairman, President and Chief Executive Officer	Tel:	(913) 458-2000
EDWARDS, Steven L.	Fax:	(913) 458-2934

Main Headquarters
Mailing:	11401 Lamar Ave.	Tel:	(913) 458-2000
	Overland Park, KS 66211	Fax:	(913) 458-2934
		TF:	(866) 496-9149

Washington Office
Mailing:	1300 N. 17th St.
	Suite 1010
	Arlington, VA 22209

Political Action Committees
Black & Veatch Good Government Fund PAC
FEC ID: C00012310
Contact: Paul W. Weida PLC
8400 Ward Pkwy.
P.O. Box 8405

Kansas City, MO 64114

Contributions to Candidates: $21,000 (2015-2016)
Democrats: $2,500; Republicans: $18,500
Principal Recipients
SENATE
BLUNT, ROY (REP-MO)

Corporate Foundations and Giving Programs

Black & Veatch Contributions Program
11401 Lamar Ave.   Tel: (913) 458-2000
Overland Park, KS 66211   Fax: (913) 458-2934

Building a World of Difference Foundation
11401 Lamar Ave.   Tel: (913) 458-2000
Overland Park, KS 66211   Fax: (913) 458-2934

Public Affairs and Related Activities Personnel

At Headquarters

DANIEL, Karen L.   Tel: (913) 458-2000
Chief Financial Officer   Fax: (913) 458-2934

KELLEHER, Lori   Tel: (913) 458-2000
Chief Human Resources Officer   Fax: (913) 458-2934

LEA, Linda   Tel: (913) 458-4629
Media, Contact   Fax: (913) 458-2934
LeaLA@BV.com

LEWIS, James R.   Tel: (913) 458-2000
Chief Administrative Officer   Fax: (913) 458-2934

MINTER, George   Tel: (913) 458-8001
Director, Media Relations and Communications Fax: (913) 458-2934
MinterGA@bv.com

PETZ, Carl   Tel: (913) 458-4685
Associate Vice President, Communications   Fax: (913) 458-2934
PetzCF@bv.com

TRIPLETT, Timothy W.   Tel: (913) 458-2000
General Counsel   Fax: (913) 458-2934

VAN DYKE, William R   Tel: (913) 458-2000
President, Federal Services   Fax: (913) 458-2934

At Washington Office

HOGAN, John J.
Technician

At Other Offices

WEIDA, PLC, Paul W.   Tel: (913) 458-3897
Vice President, Government Affairs   Fax: (913) 458-2934
8400 Ward Pkwy., P.O. Box 8405
Kansas City, MO 64114
weidapw@bv.com
Registered Federal Lobbyist

Black Hills Corporation

Subsidiaries are classified with two major business groups – Non-regulated Energy and Utilities. The company's non-regulated businesses generate wholesale electricity, produce natural gas, oil and coal, and market energy. Acquired Aquila's natural gas assets in 2008.
www.blackhillscorp.com
Annual Revenues: $1.38 billion
Employees: 2,021
Ticker: NYSE: BKH
SIC: 4911
Industry/ies: Natural Resources

Chairman of the Board, President and Chief Executive Officer Tel: (605) 721-1700
EMERY, David R.   Fax: (605) 721-2599

Main Headquarters
Mailing: 625 Ninth St.   Tel: (605) 721-1700
                Rapid City, SD 57701   Fax: (605) 721-2599
                                              TF: (888) 890-5554

Political Action Committees
Black Hills Corporation PAC
FEC ID: C00125732
Contact: Mary Anne Wingert
P.O. Box 1400   Tel: (605) 721-1700
P.O. Box 13287   Fax: (605) 721-2599
Rapid City, SD 57709

Contributions to Candidates: $11,000 (2015-2016)
Republicans: $11,000

Corporate Foundations and Giving Programs

Black Hills Corporation Contributions Program
Contact: Hillary Dobbs-Davis
625 Ninth St.   Tel: (605) 721-1700
Rapid City, SD 57701   Fax: (605) 721-2599

Public Affairs and Related Activities Personnel

At Headquarters

CLEBERG, Anthony S.   Tel: (605) 721-1700

Executive Vice President and Chief Financial Officer   Fax: (605) 721-2599

DOBBS-DAVIS , Hillary   Tel: (605) 721-2384
Senior Copywriter, Publications   Fax: (605) 721-2599
hillary.dobbs@blackhillscorp.com

HELMERS, Steven J.   Tel: (605) 721-1700
Senior Vice President, General Counsel and Chief Fax: (605) 721-2599
Compliance Officer

IVERSON, Brian   Tel: (605) 721-1700
Senior Vice President, Regulatory and Governmental Affairs Fax: (605) 721-2599
and Assistant General Counsel

MYERS, Robert A.   Tel: (605) 721-1700
Senior Vice President and Chief Human Resources Officer Fax: (605) 721-2599

NICHOLS, Jerome   Tel: (605) 721-1171
Director, Investor Relations   Fax: (605) 721-2599
jerome.nichols@blackhillscorp.com

WHITE, Kyle D.   Tel: (605) 721-1700
Vice President, Resource Planning and Regulatory Affairs Fax: (605) 721-2599
kyle.white@blackhillscorp.com

At Other Offices

WINGERT, Mary Anne
PAC Treasurer
P.O. Box 1400
Rapid City, SD 57709

Black Hills Energy
See listing on page 123 under Black Hills Corporation

Black Knight Financial Services
A mortgage processing and settlement services provider.
www.lpsvcs.com
Annual Revenues: $1.98 billion
Employees: 8,000
Ticker: NYSE: LPS
SIC: 7389
Industry/ies: Banking/Finance/Investments

Chairman of the Board   Tel: (904) 854-5100
KENNEDY, Lee A.   Fax: (904) 854-4124

Chief Executive Officer   Tel: (904) 854-5100
SANZONE, Tom   Fax: (904) 854-4124

Main Headquarters
Mailing: 601 Riverside Ave.   Tel: (904) 854-5100
                Jacksonville Beach, FL 32204 Fax: (904) 854-4124
                                              TF: (800) 991-1274

Washington Office
Mailing: P. O. Box 77693
                Washington, DC 20013

Political Action Committees
Lender Processing Services, Inc. PAC
FEC ID: C00478149
Contact: Kirk Larsen
P. O. Box 77693
Washington, DC 20013

Corporate Foundations and Giving Programs

Lender Processing Services, Inc. Contribution Program
601 Riverside Ave.   Tel: (904) 854-5100
Jacksonville Beach, FL 32204   Fax: (904) 854-4124

Public Affairs and Related Activities Personnel

At Headquarters

CIRCELLI, Melissa   Tel: (904) 854-5100
Senior Vice President, Human Resources   Fax: (904) 854-4124

GLOUDEMAN, Ross   Tel: (904) 854-5100
Chief Compliance and Regulatory Counsel   Fax: (904) 854-4124

GRAVELLE, Mike   Tel: (904) 854-5100
General Counsel   Fax: (904) 854-4124

GRIFFIN, Bill   Tel: (904) 854-5100
Executive Vice President   Fax: (904) 854-4124

KERSCH, Michelle M.   Tel: (904) 854-5043
Senior Vice President, Marketing and Corporate Fax: (904) 854-4124
Communications
michelle.kersah@lpvcs.com

LARSEN, Kirk   Tel: (904) 854-5100
Chief Financial Officer   Fax: (904) 854-4124

MURPHY, Nancy   Tel: (904) 854-5100
Vice President, Investor Relations   Fax: (904) 854-4124
nancy.murphy@lpsvcs.com

OREFICE, Tony   Tel: (904) 854-5100
Chief Operating Officer   Fax: (904) 854-4124

PETERSON, Tom   Tel: (904) 854-5100
Chief Staff   Fax: (904) 854-4124

BlackBerry

Research In Motion (RIM) is a designer, manufacturer and marketer of wireless solutions for the worldwide mobile communications market.BlackBerry Limited, formerly known as Research In Motion Limited.
in.blackberry.com
Ticker: NASDAQ (GS): BBRY
SIC: 3661
Industry/ies: Communications; Telecommunications/Internet/Cable
Legislative Issues: CPT; CSP; HOM; TEC

Executive Chairman and Chief Executive Officer		Tel:	(972) 650-6126
CHEN, John		Fax:	(972) 650-2006

Main Headquarters

Mailing:	122 W. John Carpenter Fwy.	Tel:	(972) 650-6126
	Suite 430	Fax:	(972) 650-2006
	Irving, TX 75038	TF:	(877) 255-2377

Washington Office

Mailing: 1300 I St. NW
             Washington, DC 20005

Political Action Committees

BlackBerry USA Political Action Committee
FEC ID: C00433011
Contact: Clint L. Robinson

1050 K St. NW	Tel:	(202) 204-4749
Tenth Floor		
Washington, DC 20001		

Corporate Foundations and Giving Programs

RIM Corporate Philanthropy

122 W. John Carpenter Pkwy.	Tel:	(972) 650-4266
Suite 430	Fax:	(972) 650-4266
Irving, TX 75039		

Public Affairs and Related Activities Personnel

At Headquarters

BEARD, Marty	Tel:	(972) 650-6126
Chief Operating Officer	Fax:	(972) 650-2006
CHENNAKESHU, Sandeep	Tel:	(972) 650-6126
President	Fax:	(972) 650-2006
MACKEY, James	Tel:	(972) 650-6126
Executive Vice President, Corporate Development and Strategic Planning	Fax:	(972) 650-2006
WHITE-IVY, Nita	Tel:	(972) 650-6126
Executive Vice President, Human Resources	Fax:	(972) 650-2006
YERSH, James	Tel:	(972) 650-6126
Chief Financial Officer	Fax:	(972) 650-2006
ZIPPERSTEIN, Steven E.	Tel:	(972) 650-6126
Chief Legal Officer	Fax:	(972) 650-2006

At Other Offices

NUCKOLLS, Charles Randall	Tel:	(202) 942-0318
LDA Counsel to Blackberry	Fax:	(202) 942-0309
1050 K St. NW, Tenth Floor		
Washington, DC 20001		

Blackboard Inc.

A provider of enterprise learning software applications and related services.
www.blackboard.com
Annual Revenues: $447.32 million
Employees: 1,800
Ticker: NASDAQ: BBBB
SIC: 7372
Industry/ies: Computer/Technology; Education

Chairman of the Board	Tel:	(202) 463-4860
PITTINSKY, Matthew L.	Fax:	(202) 463-4863
President and Chief Executive Officer	Tel:	(202) 463-4860
BHATT , Jay	Fax:	(202) 463-4863

Main Headquarters

Mailing:	650 Massachusetts Ave. NW	Tel:	(202) 463-4860
	Sixth Floor	Fax:	(202) 463-4863
	Washington, DC 20001-3796	TF:	(800) 424-9299

Political Action Committees

Blackboard Inc. Political Action Committee
FEC ID: C00470690
Contact: Michael J. Stanton
650 Massachusetts Ave. NW
Washington, DC 20001

Public Affairs and Related Activities Personnel

At Headquarters

STANTON, Michael J.	Tel:	(202) 463-4860
Senior Vice President	Fax:	(202) 463-4863
mstanton@blackboard.com		

The Blackstone Group

An alternative asset management and financial services company that specializes in investment strategies, as well as financial. It strives to provide solutions that create lasting value for investors, the companies in which they invest and society at large.
www.blackstone.com
Annual Revenues: $8.32 billion
Employees: 2,190
Ticker: NYSE: BX
Industry/ies: Banking/Finance/Investments
Legislative Issues: ENG; FIN; TAX; TRD

Chairman, Chief Executive Officer and Co Founder	Tel:	(212) 583-5000
SCHWARZMAN, Stephen A.	Fax:	(212) 583-5749

Main Headquarters

Mailing:	345 Park Ave., 31st Floor	Tel:	(212) 583-5000
	New York City, NY 10154	Fax:	(212) 583-5749

Washington Office

Mailing: 1455 Pennsylvania Ave. NW, Suite 320
             Washington, DC 20004

Corporate Foundations and Giving Programs

Blackstone Charitable Foundation
Contact: Amy Stursberg

345 Park Ave.	Tel:	(212) 583-5000
New York City, NY 10154	Fax:	(212) 583-5749

Public Affairs and Related Activities Personnel

At Headquarters

ANDERSON, Christine	Tel:	(212) 583-5182
Managing Director, Global Public Affairs	Fax:	(212) 583-5749
Christine.Anderson@blackstone.com		
BERMAN, Wayne L.	Tel:	(212) 583-5000
Senior Advisor, Global Government Affairs	Fax:	(212) 583-5749
BOMBARA, Cynthia	Tel:	(212) 583-5000
Senior Vice President, Human Resources	Fax:	(212) 583-5749
FINLEY, John G.	Tel:	(212) 583-5000
Senior Managing Director and Chief Legal Officer	Fax:	(212) 583-5749
JAMES , Hamilton E.	Tel:	(212) 583-5000
President and Chief Operating Officer	Fax:	(212) 583-5749
MELWANI, Prakash A.	Tel:	(212) 583-5000
Senior Managing Director and Chief Investment Officer	Fax:	(212) 583-5749
ROSE, Peter	Tel:	(212) 583-5871
Senior Managing Director, Public Affairs	Fax:	(212) 583-5749
Peter.Rose@blackstone.com		
SOLOTAR, Joan	Tel:	(212) 583-5000
Senior Managing Director, Head, External Relations and Strategy	Fax:	(212) 583-5749
STURSBERG, Amy	Tel:	(212) 583-5000
Executive Director, Blackstone Charitable Foundation	Fax:	(212) 583-5749
TOSI, Laurence A.	Tel:	(212) 583-5000
Senior Managing Director and Chief Financial Officer	Fax:	(212) 583-5749

Kenneth Blair III (SUNIusa Corporation)

A public policy consulting firm.
Industry/ies: Public Affairs And Public Relations

President	Tel:	(516) 554-4935
BLAIR, III, Kenneth M.		
ken.blair@suniusa.com		

Main Headquarters

Mailing:	68 S. Service Rd., Suite 100	Tel:	(516) 554-4935
	Melville, NY 11747		

Blaylock Robert Van, LLC

An investment banking and financial services company. Formerly Robert Van Securities and Blaylock and Co.
www.brv-llc.com
Employees: 15
Industry/ies: Banking/Finance/Investments

Main Headquarters

Mailing:	600 Lexington Ave.	Tel:	(212) 715-6600
	Third Floor	Fax:	(212) 715-3300
	New York City, NY 10022-6000	TF:	(877) 591-7072

Public Affairs and Related Activities Personnel

At Headquarters

ASHWORTH, Judith	Tel:	(212) 715-6600
Senior Vice President, Administration	Fax:	(212) 715-3300
CIULLA, Alex	Tel:	(212) 715-6600
Senior Vice President, Finance	Fax:	(212) 715-3300
HANLEY, Richard	Tel:	(212) 715-6600
Senior Vice President, Compliance	Fax:	(212) 715-3300
O'BRIEN, Timothy	Tel:	(212) 715-6600

Executive Vice President, Sales and Trading
tobrien@brv-llc.com

STARKMAN, Eric
Contact, Media Relations
erics@starkmanassociates.com

Fax: (212) 715-3300

Tel: (212) 624-9755
Fax: (212) 715-3300

Blessey Marine Service, Inc.

Operates a multi-faceted inland tank barge and towing vessel fleet in the United States.
www.blessey.com
Annual Revenues: $163.50 million
Employees: 600
Industry/ies: Marine/Maritime/Shipping; Transportation

Chairman and Chief Executive Officer
BLESSEY, Jr., Walter E.

Tel: (504) 734-1156
Fax: (504) 734-1195

Main Headquarters
Mailing: 1515 River Oaks Rd., E.
Harahan, LA 70123

Tel: (504) 734-1156
Fax: (504) 734-1195

Public Affairs and Related Activities Personnel

At Headquarters

BETHUNE, Beau
General Counsel and Vice President, Corporate Affairs

Tel: (504) 734-1156
Fax: (504) 734-1195

CALIVA, Liz
Vice President, Human Resources

Tel: (504) 734-1156
Fax: (504) 734-1195

FRIED, David
Vice President, Finance and Controller

Tel: (504) 734-1156
Fax: (504) 734-1195

TODD, Clark A.
President

Tel: (504) 734-1156
Fax: (504) 734-1195

VOSS, Patrick
Chief Financial Officer

Tel: (504) 734-1156
Fax: (504) 734-1195

Blimptech, LLC

Manufacturing outdoor radio-controlled blimps. BlimpTech's mission is to develop innovative state-of-the-art aerobatic blimps that ultimately act as highly effective advertising/camera platforms for a wide variety of high-profile public events.
www.blimptech.com
Industry/ies: Aerospace/Aviation; Transportation

Founder, President and Media Contact
THOMPSON, Mark

Tel: (217) 417-2447

Main Headquarters
Mailing: 803 W. Anthony Dr.
Champaign, IL 61822

Tel: (773) 865-0692

Public Affairs and Related Activities Personnel

At Headquarters

FOURMAN, Brian
Vice President, Advertising, Marketing and Sales
bfourman@blimptech.com

Tel: (773) 865-0692

Bloom Energy Corporation

A manufacturer of semiconductors and related devices.
www.bloomenergy.com
Employees: 200
Industry/ies: Fuels See Coal, Gas, Oil, Petroleum; Natural Resources; Petroleum Industry
Legislative Issues: DEF; ENG; ENV; TAX

Principal Co-Founder and Chief Executive Officer
SRIDHAR, PhD, K.R.

Tel: (408) 543-1500
Fax: (408) 543-1501

Main Headquarters
Mailing: 1299 Orleans Dr.
Sunnyvale, CA 94089

Tel: (408) 543-1500
Fax: (408) 543-1501

Public Affairs and Related Activities Personnel

At Headquarters

BARBER, David
Vice President, Human Resources

Tel: (408) 543-1500
Fax: (408) 543-1501

BRENNAN, Susan
Chief Operations Officer

Tel: (408) 543-1500
Fax: (408) 543-1501

CONVIS, Gary
Senior Advisor

Tel: (408) 543-1500
Fax: (408) 543-1501

FURR, Randy
Chief Financial Officer

Tel: (408) 543-1500
Fax: (408) 543-1501

KURTZ, William
Chief Commercial Officer

Tel: (408) 543-1500
Fax: (408) 543-1501

ROSS, Matt
Chief Marketing Officer

Tel: (408) 543-1500
Fax: (408) 543-1501

THAYER, Bill
Executive Vice President, Sales and Service

Tel: (408) 543-1500
Fax: (408) 543-1501

Bloomberg L.P.

A multimedia company.
www.bloomberg.com
Annual Revenues: $9.00 billion
Employees: 15,500
Industry/ies: Communications; Media/Mass Communication
Legislative Issues: COM; FIN; MIA

Chairman of the Board
GRAUER, Peter

Tel: (212) 318-2000
Fax: (917) 369-5000

Chief Executive Officer
BLOOMBERG, Michael R.

Tel: (212) 318-2000
Fax: (917) 369-5000

Main Headquarters
Mailing: 731 Lexington Ave.
New York City, NY 10022

Tel: (212) 318-2000
Fax: (917) 369-5000

Washington Office
Mailing: 1399 New York Ave. NW
11th Floor
Washington, DC 20005-4711

Tel: (202) 624-1820
Fax: (202) 624-1300

Corporate Foundations and Giving Programs
Bloomberg L.P. Contributions Program
731 Lexington Ave.
New York City, NY 10022

Public Affairs and Related Activities Personnel

At Headquarters

BIGLEY, Deirdre
Chief Marketing Officer

Tel: (212) 318-2000
Fax: (917) 369-5000

FEINBERG, Sarah
Contact, Global Communications and Bloomberg Government

Tel: (212) 318-2000
Fax: (917) 369-5000

GOODKIND, Jill
Director, Communications
jgoodkind@bloomberg.net

Tel: (212) 617-3669
Fax: (917) 369-5000

MCGUIRE, Maureen
Contact, Special Projects

Tel: (212) 318-2000
Fax: (917) 369-5000

MELLER, Lauren
Corporate Communications Contact
lmeller@bloomberg.net

Tel: (212) 617-8185
Fax: (917) 369-5000

At Washington Office

BABYAK, Gregory R.
gbabyak@bloomberg.net
Registered Federal Lobbyist

Tel: (202) 624-1820
Fax: (202) 624-1300

MORGAN, Madeline
Business Development
morgan.madeline796@gmail.com

Tel: (202) 624-1820
Fax: (202) 624-1300

WEBSTER, Meridith
Director, Communications and Public Affairs
mwebster27@bloomberg.net

Tel: (202) 624-1820
Fax: (202) 624-1300

Bloomingdale's, Inc.

A retail store chain, a subsidiary of Macy's, Inc.
www.bloomingdales.com
Employees: 10,500
Industry/ies: Apparel/Textiles Industry; Retail/Wholesale

Chairman and Chief Executive Officer
GOULD, Michael

Tel: (212) 705-2000
Fax: (212) 705-2805

Main Headquarters
Mailing: 1000 Third Ave.
New York City, NY 10022

Tel: (212) 705-2000
Fax: (212) 705-2805
TF: (800) 777-0000

Corporate Foundations and Giving Programs

Bloomingdale's Contributions Program
Contact: Anne Keating
New York City, NY

Tel: (212) 705-2000

Public Affairs and Related Activities Personnel

At Headquarters

KEATING, Anne
Senior Vice President, Public Relations and Corporate Philanthropy

Tel: (212) 705-2000
Fax: (212) 705-2805

QUARTA, Elizabeth
Vice President, Corporate Media
elizabeth.quarta@bloomingdales.com

Tel: (212) 705-2439
Fax: (212) 705-2805

VITAGLIANO, Marissa
Operating Vice President, National Media Relations
marissa.vitagliano@bloomingdales.com

Tel: (212) 705-2000
Fax: (212) 705-2805

Blue Bell Creameries, Inc.

Ice cream makers.
www.bluebell.com
Annual Revenues: $490.00 million
Employees: 3,200
SIC: 2024

Bloomberg L.P.

A multimedia company.

NAICS: 311520
Industry/ies: Food And Beverage Industry

Chairman of the Board　　　Tel:　(979) 836-7977
KRUSE, Edward F.　　　　　　 Fax:　(979) 830-2198

President and Chief Executive Officer　 Tel:　(979) 836-7977
KRUSE, Paul W.　　　　　　　 Fax:　(979) 830-2198

Main Headquarters
Mailing:　　P.O. Box 1807　　　　Tel:　(979) 836-7977
　　　　　Brenham, TX 77834　　 Fax:　(979) 830-2198
　　　　　　　　　　　　　　 TF:　(800) 327-8135

Political Action Committees
Blue Bell Creameries USA Inc. PAC
FEC ID: C00166892
Contact: Samuel Sommer
P.O. Box 1807　　　　　　　　 Tel:　(979) 836-7977
Brenham, TX 77834

　　Contributions to Candidates: $2,500 (2015-2016)
　　Republicans: $2,500

Corporate Foundations and Giving Programs
Blue Bell Creameries, Inc. Contributions Program
P.O. Box 1807　　　　　　　　 Tel:　(979) 836-7977
Brenham, TX 77834

Public Affairs and Related Activities Personnel

At Headquarters
RANKIN, W.J.　　　　　　　　 Tel:　(979) 836-7977
PAC Treasurer　　　　　　　 Fax:　(979) 830-2198
SOMMER, Samuel　　　　　　　 Tel:　(979) 836-7977
PAC Treaurer　　　　　　　　 Fax:　(979) 830-2198

Blue Cross and Blue Shield of Alabama

A health benefits provider. An independent licensee of the Blue Cross and Blue Shield Association.
www.bcbsal.org
Annual Revenues: $116.60 million
Employees: 2,500
Industry/ies: Insurance Industry

President and Chief Executive Officer　 Tel:　(205) 220-2100
KELLOGG, Terry D.　　　　　　 Fax:　(205) 220-6477

Main Headquarters
Mailing:　　450 Riverchase Pkwy., East　 Tel:　(205) 220-2100
　　　　　Birmingham, AL 35244　　 Fax:　(205) 220-6477

Political Action Committees
Blue Cross Blue Shield of Alabama PAC
FEC ID: C00457242
Contact: Robin Stone
Two N. Jackson St.
Suite 202
Montgomery, AL 36104

　　Contributions to Candidates: $65,000 (2015-2016)
　　Democrats: $5,000; Republicans: $60,000

　　　　　　Principal Recipients

　　　　　　　HOUSE
　　　　　　　BROOKS, MO (REP-AL)
　　　　　　　BYRNE, BRADLEY ROBERTS (REP-AL)
　　　　　　　PALMER, GARY (REP-AL)
　　　　　　　ROBY, MARTHA (REP-AL)
　　　　　　　ROGERS, MICHAEL DENNIS (REP-AL)

Corporate Foundations and Giving Programs
Alabama Child Caring Foundation
Post Office Box 830870　　　　　 Tel:　(205) 220-5929
Birmingham, AL 35283-0870

The Caring Foundation (TCF)
Contact: Koko Mackin
450 Riverchase Pkwy. East
Birmingham, AL 35244

Public Affairs and Related Activities Personnel

At Headquarters
MACKIN, Koko　　　　　　　　 Tel:　(205) 220-2713
Vice President, Corporate Communications and Community　 Fax:　(205) 220-6477
Relations
kmackin@bcbsal.org
MIZELL, Cynthia　　　　　　　 Tel:　(205) 220-2100
Vice President, Audit and Security　 Fax:　(205) 220-6477

At Other Offices
STONE, Robin
PAC Treasurer
Two N. Jackson St., Suite 202
Montgomery, AL 36104

Blue Cross and Blue Shield of Arizona

A health insurance company.
www.azblue.com
Employees: 1,300
Industry/ies: Medicine/Health Care/Mental Health
Legislative Issues: BUD; HCR; INS; MMM; TAX

President and Chief Executive Officer　 Tel:　(602) 864-4400
BOALS, Richard L.　　　　　　 Fax:　(602) 864-3116

Main Headquarters
Mailing:　　P.O. Box 13466　　　　Tel:　(602) 864-4400
　　　　　Phoenix, AZ 85002-3466　 Fax:　(602) 864-3116
　　　　　　　　　　　　　　 TF:　(800) 232-2345

Corporate Foundations and Giving Programs
Blue Cross and Blue Shield of Arizona Contributions Program
Contact: Maribel Barrios
P.O. Box 13466　　　　　　　　 Tel:　(602) 864-5107
Phoenix, AZ 85002-3466　　　　 Fax:　(602) 864-3116

Public Affairs and Related Activities Personnel

At Headquarters
ABRAHAM, Karen　　　　　　　 Tel:　(602) 864-4400
Senior Vice President and Chief Financial Officer　 Fax:　(602) 864-5160
BARRIOS, Maribel　　　　　　　 Tel:　(602) 864-5107
Senior Community and Multicultural Relations Manager　 Fax:　(602) 864-3116
MBarrios@azblue.com
HUNT, Renee　　　　　　　　　 Tel:　(602) 864-5182
Senior Manager, Public Relations and Internal　 Fax:　(602) 864-3116
Communications
rhunt@azblue.com
SALAZAR , Deanna　　　　　　　 Tel:　(602) 864-4400
Senior Vice President and General Counsel　 Fax:　(602) 864-3116
STELNIK , Jeff　　　　　　　　 Tel:　(602) 864-4400
Senior Vice President, Strategy, Sales and Marketing　 Fax:　(602) 864-3116

Blue Cross and Blue Shield of California

A health insurance company.
www.blueshieldca.com
Annual Revenues: $13.4 billion
Employees: 6,800
Industry/ies: Insurance Industry; Medicine/Health Care/Mental Health
Legislative Issues: HCR

Chairman of the Board　　　Tel:　(415) 229-5000
LEE, Robert　　　　　　　　　 Fax:　(415) 229-5070

President and Chief Executive Officer　 Tel:　(415) 229-5000
MARKOVICH, Paul　　　　　　 Fax:　(415) 229-5070

Main Headquarters
Mailing:　　50 Beale St.　　　　 Tel:　(415) 229-5000
　　　　　San Francisco, CA 94105-1808　 Fax:　(415) 229-5070
　　　　　　　　　　　　　　 TF:　(800) 329-2742

Political Action Committees
Blue Shield of California PAC
FEC ID: C00340364
Contact: Emily Glidden
50 Beale St.　　　　　　　　　 Tel:　(415) 229-5000
17-C356　　　　　　　　　　 Fax:　(415) 229-5000
San Francisco, CA 94105

　　Contributions to Candidates: $115,500 (2015-2016)
　　Democrats: $80,500; Republicans: $35,000

Corporate Foundations and Giving Programs
Blue Shield of California Foundation
Contact: Peter Long PhD
50 Beale St.　　　　　　　　　 Tel:　(415) 229-6080
San Francisco, CA 94105　　　　 Fax:　(415) 229-5070

Public Affairs and Related Activities Personnel

At Headquarters
BARRY, Sean　　　　　　　　　 Tel:　(415) 229-5627
Manager, Corporate Communications　 Fax:　(415) 229-5070
sean.barry@blueshieldca.com
EPSTEIN, Tom　　　　　　　　 Tel:　(415) 229-5110
Vice President, Public Affairs　　 Fax:　(415) 229-5070
tom.epstein@blueshieldca.com
GLIDDEN, Emily　　　　　　　 Tel:　(415) 229-5000
PAC Treasurer　　　　　　　 Fax:　(415) 229-5070
Mail Stop 17-C356
JACOBS, Seth A.　　　　　　　 Tel:　(415) 229-5000
Senior Vice President and General Counsel　 Fax:　(415) 229-5070
seth.jacobs@blueshieldca.com
LONG, PhD, Peter　　　　　　　 Tel:　(415) 229-5000
President and Chief Executive Officer, Blue Shield of　 Fax:　(415) 229-5070
California Foundation

peter.long@blueshieldcafoundation.org

MCGUE, Clinton	Tel:	(415) 229-6457
Contact, Corporate Communications	Fax:	(415) 229-5070
clinton.mcgue@blueshieldca.com		

MURRAY, Michael A. "Mick"	Tel:	(415) 229-5000
Senior Vice President and Chief Financial Officer	Fax:	(415) 229-5070

O'HARA, Mary	Tel:	(415) 229-5000
Senior Vice President and Chief Human Resources Officer	Fax:	(415) 229-5070

ROBERTSON , Jeffrey	Tel:	(415) 229-5000
Senior Vice President and Chief Marketing Officer	Fax:	(415) 229-5070

SHIVINSKY, Steve	Tel:	(415) 229-5000
Vice President, Corporate Communications	Fax:	(415) 229-5070
steve.shivinsky@blueshieldca.com		

SWEERIS, Esq., Charles	Tel:	(415) 229-5000
Vice President and Deputy General Counsel	Fax:	(415) 229-5070
charles.sweeris@blueshieldca.com		

TURAN, K. C.	Tel:	(415) 229-5000
Vice President, Chief Risk Officer and Chief Compliance Officer	Fax:	(415) 229-5070
kc.turan@blueshieldca.com		

WIDMANN, Janet	Tel:	(415) 229-5000
Executive Vice President, Markets	Fax:	(415) 229-5070

Blue Cross and Blue Shield of Kansas City

A health insurance company.
www.bcbskc.com
Annual Revenues: $1.84 billion
Employees: 1,000
Industry/ies: Insurance Industry; Medicine/Health Care/Mental Health

Chairman of the Board	Tel:	(816) 395-3558
MORRISSEY, CPA, Michael F.	Fax:	(816) 395-2726

President and Chief Executive Officer	Tel:	(816) 395-2222
WILSON, Danette	Fax:	(816) 395-2726

Main Headquarters

Mailing:	One Pershing Sq.	Tel:	(816) 395-3558
	2301 Main St.	Fax:	(816) 395-2726
	Kansas City, MO 64108	TF:	(888) 989-8842

Corporate Foundations and Giving Programs

The Caring Program for Children
Contact: Matthew Fuller

One Pershing Sq.	Tel:	(816) 395-2222
2301 Main St.		
Kansas City, MO 64108		

Public Affairs and Related Activities Personnel

At Headquarters

CAMERLINCK, Bryan	Tel:	(816) 395-2222
Chief Financial Officer	Fax:	(816) 395-2726

ELLISON, Alice	Tel:	(816) 395-2222
Vice President, Community Relations	Fax:	(816) 395-2726
alice.ellison@bcbskc.com		

FRIES, Coni K.	Tel:	(816) 395-3558
Vice President, Government Relations	Fax:	(816) 395-2726

KASTNER, Rick	Tel:	(816) 395-2222
General Counsel and Chief Administrative Officer	Fax:	(816) 395-2726

SCHNEIDER-STUCKY, CPA, Erin	Tel:	(816) 395-3558
Senior Vice President, Sales and Marketing	Fax:	(816) 395-2726

SPARKS, Kevin	Tel:	(816) 395-2222
Group Executive, Enterprise Strategy, Information Technology and Chief Strategy Officer	Fax:	(816) 395-2726

TROMANS, Marilyn	Tel:	(816) 395-2222
Vice President and Chief Financial Officer	Fax:	(816) 395-2726

At Other Offices

FULLER, Matthew
Community Investment Specialist
1055 Broadway, Suite 130
Kansas City, MO 64105

Blue Cross and Blue Shield of Massachusetts

A health care provider.
www.bluecrossma.com
Employees: 3,000
Industry/ies: Insurance Industry

Chairman of the Board	Tel:	(617) 246-5000
YALE, Phyllis R.	Fax:	(617) 246-3992

President and Chief Executive Officer	Tel:	(617) 246-5000
DREYFUS, Andrew	Fax:	(617) 246-4832

Main Headquarters

Mailing:	101 Huntington Ave.	Tel:	(617) 246-5000
	Suite 1300	Fax:	(617) 246-3992

Boston, MA 02199-7611	TF:	(800) 262-2583

Political Action Committees

FED CAREPAC, The Blue Cross and Blue Shield of Massachusetts PAC
FEC ID: C00199166
Contact: Deirdre W. Savage

The Landmark Center	Tel:	(617) 246-5000
401 Park Dr.		
Boston, MA 02215		

Corporate Foundations and Giving Programs

Blue Cross and Blue Shield of Massachusetts Foundation
Contact: Audrey Shelto

The Landmark Center	Tel:	(617) 246-3744
401 Park Dr.	Fax:	(617) 246-3744
Boston, MA 02215		

Public Affairs and Related Activities Personnel

At Headquarters

DEVAUX, Deborah	Tel:	(617) 246-5000
Chief Operating Officer	Fax:	(617) 246-3992

LOVELL, Stephanie	Tel:	(617) 246-5000
Executive Vice President, Medicare and Chief Legal Officer	Fax:	(617) 246-4832
Stephanie.Lovell@bcbsma.com		

MALTZ, Allen P.	Tel:	(617) 246-5000
Executive Vice President and Chief Financial Officer	Fax:	(617) 246-4832
allen.maltz@bcbsma.com		

MCQUAIDE , Jay	Tel:	(617) 246-5000
Senior Vice President, Corporate Communications	Fax:	(617) 246-4832
jay.mcquaide@bcbsma.com		

SAVAGE, Deirdre W.	Tel:	(617) 246-5000
Senior Director	Fax:	(617) 246-4832
newenglandcouncilDC@msn.com		

SGROI, Susan L.	Tel:	(617) 246-5000
Senior Vice President , Organizational Effectiveness and Chief Human Resources Officer	Fax:	(617) 246-3992

SHELTO, Audrey	Tel:	(617) 246-5000
President, Blue Cross Blue Shield of Massachusetts Foundation	Fax:	(617) 246-3992
audrey.shelto@bcbsma.com		

Blue Cross and Blue Shield of Montana

Offers several coverage options in health plan for individuals and families.
www.bcbsmt.com
Annual Revenues: $28.40 million
Employees: 700
Industry/ies: Insurance Industry

Chairman of the Board	Tel:	(406) 437-5000
LUSK, Jerry E.	Fax:	(406) 447-3454

President and Chief Executive Officer	Tel:	(406) 437-5000
FRANK, Michael	Fax:	(406) 447-3454

Main Headquarters

Mailing:	560 N. Park Ave.	Tel:	(406) 437-5000
	P.O. Box 4309	Fax:	(406) 447-3454
	Helena, MT 59604-4309	TF:	(800) 447-7828

Corporate Foundations and Giving Programs

BCBS Foundation for Healthy Montanans
Contact: Michael McGuire MD

560 N. Park Ave.	Tel:	(406) 437-6153
P.O. Box 4309		
Helena, MT 59604		

Caring Foundation of Montana		
PO Box 872	Tel:	(406) 444-8200
Helena, MT 59624	TF:	(877) 543-7669

Public Affairs and Related Activities Personnel

At Headquarters

BELCHER, Mary	Tel:	(406) 437-5000
General Counsel and Corporate Secretary	Fax:	(406) 447-3454

BURZYNSKI, Mark	Tel:	(406) 437-5000
Vice President, Health Affairs	Fax:	(406) 447-3454
mark_burzynski@bcbsmt.com		

COTE, Frank	Tel:	(406) 437-5000
Chief Sales Officer and Media Contact	Fax:	(406) 447-3454
frank_cote@bcbsmt.com		

DORAN, John	Tel:	(406) 437-5000
Director, Strategic Marketing Services	Fax:	(406) 447-3454

Blue Cross and Blue Shield of Nebraska

Provides health care plans to customers in Nebraska.
www.nebraskablue.com
Annual Revenues: $1.33 billion
Employees: 1,000
Industry/ies: Insurance Industry; Medicine/Health Care/Mental Health

Chairperson of the Board BEATTIE, George G.	Tel: Fax:	(402) 982-7000 (402) 398-3736
Chief Executive Officer MARTIN, Steven S.	Tel: Fax:	(402) 390-1800 (402) 398-3736

Main Headquarters

Mailing: 1919 Aksarben Dr.	Tel:	(402) 982-7000
P.O. Box 3248	Fax:	(402) 398-3736
Omaha, NE 68180	TF:	(800) 422-2763

Corporate Foundations and Giving Programs

Blue Cross and Blue Shield of Nebraska Contributions Program
Contact: Carol Vidlak

P.O. Box 3248	Tel:	(402) 390-1820
Omaha, NE 68180-0001	Fax:	(402) 390-1820

Public Affairs and Related Activities Personnel

At Headquarters

BARBEE, Ovell *Vice President, Human Resources and Organizational Development*	Tel: Fax:	(402) 982-7000 (402) 398-3736
BYERS , Gerald *Senior Vice President and Chief Financial Officer*	Tel: Fax:	(402) 982-7000 (402) 398-3736
COLLINS, Russell *Vice President, General Counsel and Board Secretary*	Tel: Fax:	(402) 982-7000 (402) 398-3736
FLOWERS, Shari *Vice President, Compliance and Ethics*	Tel: Fax:	(402) 982-7000 (402) 398-3736
HALL, Joy *Vice President, Brand Management and External Communications*	Tel: Fax:	(402) 982-7000 (402) 398-3736
RICHARDSON, Jennifer *Senior Vice President, Operations*	Tel: Fax:	(402) 982-7000 (402) 398-3736
TROWBRIDGE, Lewis E. *President and Chief Operating Officer*	Tel: Fax:	(402) 390-1820 (402) 398-3736
VIDLAK, Carol *Executive Assistant and Community Relations Specialist* carol.vidlak@bcbsne.com	Tel: Fax:	(402) 398-3734 (402) 398-3736
WALDMAN , Sarah *Senior Vice President, Administration*	Tel: Fax:	(402) 982-7000 (402) 398-3736

At Other Offices

BOURNE, Patrick J.
Senior Vice President, Sales And Account Services
7261 Mercy Rd., P.O. Box 3248
Omaha, NE 68180
pat.bourne@bcbsne.com

Blue Cross and Blue Shield of New Jersey

See listing on page 410 under Horizon Blue Cross Blue Shield of New Jersey Inc.

Blue Cross and Blue Shield of North Carolina

A health insurance company.
www.bcbsnc.com
Industry/ies: Insurance Industry; Medicine/Health Care/Mental Health

Chairman of the Board NELSON, Lars Steven	Tel: Fax:	(919) 489-7431 (919) 765-7818
President and Chief Executive Officer WILSON , J. Bradley (Brad)	Tel: Fax:	(919) 489-7431 (919) 765-7818

Main Headquarters

Mailing: 5901 Chapel Hill Rd.	Tel:	(919) 489-7431
Durham, NC 27707	Fax:	(919) 765-7818
	TF:	(800) 250-3630

Political Action Committees

Blue Cross and Blue Shield of North Carolina Employee PAC
FEC ID: C00312223
Contact: Kenneth Wright
P.O. Box 2291
Durham, NC 27702

   Contributions to Candidates: $14,000 (2015-2016)
   Democrats: $1,000; Republicans: $13,000

Corporate Foundations and Giving Programs

BCBSNC Foundation
Contact: Kathy Higgins

5901 Chapel Hill Rd.	Tel:	(919) 765-4104
Durham, NC 27707	Fax:	(919) 765-4837

Public Affairs and Related Activities Personnel

At Headquarters

BORMAN, Lew *Contact, Corporate Communications*	Tel: Fax:	(919) 765-3005 (919) 765-7818
HIGGINS, Kathy *President, BCBSNC Foundation and Vice President,* *Corporate Affairs*	Tel: Fax:	(919) 765-7345 (919) 765-7288

kathy.higgins@bcbsnc.com

PALUMBO, Fara M. *Senior Vice President and Chief Human Resources Officer*	Tel: Fax:	(919) 489-7431 (919) 765-7818
PARQUET, Cheryl *Community Relations Program Manager* cheryl.parquet@bcbsnc.com	Tel: Fax:	(919) 489-7431 (919) 765-7818
PETKAU, Gerald *Senior Vice President and Chief Financial Officer*	Tel: Fax:	(919) 489-7431 (919) 765-7818
PRATHER , N. King *Senior Vice President, General Counsel and Corporate Secretary*	Tel: Fax:	(919) 489-7431 (919) 765-7818
ROOS, John T. *Senior Vice President, Sales, Marketing and Communications*	Tel: Fax:	(919) 489-7431 (919) 765-7818
WRIGHT, Kenneth *PAC Treasurer*	Tel: Fax:	(919) 489-7431 (919) 765-7818

Blue Cross and Blue Shield of Oklahoma

A health insurance provider.
www.bcbsok.com
Industry/ies: Insurance Industry; Medicine/Health Care/Mental Health

Main Headquarters

Mailing: P.O. Box 3283	Tel:	(918) 560-3500
Tulsa, OK 74102-3283	Fax:	(918) 560-3060

Corporate Foundations and Giving Programs

The Oklahoma Caring Foundation, Inc.
Contact: Paula Huck

P.O. Box 3283	Tel:	(918) 560-3500
Tulsa, OK 74102	Fax:	(918) 560-3060

Public Affairs and Related Activities Personnel

At Headquarters

BINKOWSKI, Beverly *Manager, Public Affairs* bbinkowski@bcbsok.com	Tel: Fax:	(918) 560-3500 (918) 560-3060
HUCK, Paula *Director, Community Affairs* paula_huck@hcsc.net	Tel: Fax:	(918) 551-2160 (918) 560-3060

Blue Cross & Blue Shield of Rhode Island

A health care provider.
www.bcbsri.com
Annual Revenues: $48.60 million
Employees: 1,100
Industry/ies: Insurance Industry

Chairman of the Board WYROFSKY, CPA, Randy A.	Tel: Fax:	(401) 459-1000 (401) 459-1333
President and Chief Executive Officer ANDRUSZKIEWICZ, Peter	Tel: Fax:	(401) 459-1000 (401) 459-1333

Main Headquarters

Mailing: 500 Exchange St.	Tel:	(401) 459-1000
Providence, RI 02903	Fax:	(401) 459-1333
	TF:	(800) 637-3718

Corporate Foundations and Giving Programs

BlueAngel Community Outreach

444 Westminster St.	Tel:	(401) 459-1000
Providence, RI 02903	Fax:	(401) 459-1333

Public Affairs and Related Activities Personnel

At Headquarters

HUDSON, Michael *Executive Vice President and Chief Financial Officer*	Tel: Fax:	(401) 459-1000 (401) 459-1333
LEDERBERG, Michele B. *Executive Vice President and General Counsel and Chief Administrative Officer*	Tel: Fax:	(401) 459-1000 (401) 459-1333
NERONHA, Monica *Legal Services and Government Affairs*	Tel: Fax:	(401) 459-1000 (401) 459-1333
REINGOLD, Kim *Director, Public Relations and External Affairs* kimberly.reingold@bcbsri.org	Tel: Fax:	(401) 459-5611 (401) 459-1333
WOLFKIEL, Bob *Vice President and Chief Sales Officer*	Tel: Fax:	(401) 459-1000 (401) 459-1333

Blue Cross and Blue Shield of Texas, Inc.

A health care provider.
www.bcbstx.com
Industry/ies: Insurance Industry; Medicine/Health Care/Mental Health

Main Headquarters

Mailing: P.O. Box 660044	Tel:	(972) 766-6900
Richardson, TX 75266-0044	Fax:	(972) 766-6234
	TF:	(800) 735-2989

Corporate Foundations and Giving Programs

Blue Cross and Blue Shield of Texas Contributions Program
Contact: Bobby Romero
P.O. Box 660044
Richardson, TX 75266

Caring for Children Foundation, Inc
P.O. Box 660044
Richardson, TX 75266

Public Affairs and Related Activities Personnel

At Headquarters

BUJAK, Denise	Tel:	(972) 766-6900
Chief Financial Officer	Fax:	(973) 766-6234
HUNT, Sue	Tel:	(972) 766-6900
Vice President, Human Resources	Fax:	(972) 766-5298
JARVIS, Margaret	Tel:	(972) 766-7165
Senior Manager, Media and Public Relations	Fax:	(973) 766-6234
margaret_jarvis@bcbstx.com		
LANE, Mark	Tel:	(972) 766-6900
Director, Public Relations	Fax:	(973) 766-6234
ROBERTSON, Kathryn	Tel:	(972) 766-6900
Financial Coordinator	Fax:	(972) 766-6234
kathryn@caravan.org		
ROMERO, Bobby	Tel:	(972) 766-7960
Contact, Community Relations	Fax:	(972) 766-6234
robert_romero@bcbstx.com		

Blue Cross and Blue Shield of Vermont

Offers quality, financially sound health benefit products, community-based health care system, primarily in Vermont. It is an independent, local, not-for-profit Vermont company, governed and managed locally.
www.bcbsvt.com
Employees: 340
Industry/ies: Insurance Industry

Chiarwoman	Tel:	(802) 223-6131
NYSTROM-MEYER, Karen	Fax:	(802) 223-4229
President and Chief Executive Officer	Tel:	(802) 223-6131
GEORGE, Don C.	Fax:	(802) 223-4229

Main Headquarters

Mailing: P.O. Box 186	Tel:	(802) 223-6131
Montpelier, VT 05601	Fax:	(802) 223-4229

Corporate Foundations and Giving Programs

Vermont Caring Foundation
Contact: Kathy Parry
P.O. Box 186	Tel:	(802) 223-6131
Montpelier, VT 05601	Fax:	(802) 223-6131

Public Affairs and Related Activities Personnel

At Headquarters

GANNON, Christopher R.	Tel:	(802) 223-6131
Vice President, General Counsel and Chief Administrative Officer	Fax:	(802) 223-4229
gannonc@bcbsvt.com		
GARLAND, Andrew	Tel:	(802) 223-6131
Vice President, Client Relations and External Affairs	Fax:	(802) 223-4229
GODDARD, Kevin	Tel:	(802) 223-6131
Vice President, External Affairs and sales	Fax:	(802) 223-4229
goddardk@bcbsvt.com		
GREENE, Ruth K.	Tel:	(802) 223-6131
Vice President, Treasurer and Chief Financial Officer	Fax:	(802) 223-4229
HAMILTON, Catherine	Tel:	(802) 223-6131
Vice President, Consumer Services and Planning	Fax:	(802) 223-4229
PARRY, Kathy	Tel:	(802) 371-3205
Coordinator, External Affairs and Contact, Corporate Giving	Fax:	(802) 223-4229
parryk@bcbsvt.com		
YAKUBIK, Ellen	Tel:	(802) 223-6131
Chief Marketing Executive	Fax:	(802) 223-4229

Blue Cross and Blue Shield of Wyoming

Offers a broad range of health insurance products.
www.bcbswy.com
Annual Revenues: $20.40 million
Employees: 200
Industry/ies: Insurance Industry

Chairman of the Board	Tel:	(307) 634-1393
KIRK, Cliff	Fax:	(307) 634-5742
President and Chief Executive Officer and secretary	Tel:	(307) 634-1393
CRILLY, Tim J.	Fax:	(307) 634-5742

Main Headquarters

Mailing: 4000 House Ave.	Tel:	(307) 634-1393
Cheyenne, WY 82001	Fax:	(307) 634-5742

	TF:	(800) 442-2376

Corporate Foundations and Giving Programs

Caring Foundation of Wyoming Inc.
Contact: Karen Rich
P.O. Box 2266	Tel:	(307) 634-1393
Cheyenne, WY 82003	Fax:	(307) 634-5742

Public Affairs and Related Activities Personnel

At Headquarters

GORE, Diane	Tel:	(307) 634-1393
Chief Financial Officer	Fax:	(307) 634-5742
RICH, Karen	Tel:	(307) 432-1393
Foundation Coordinator	Fax:	(307) 638-6929

Blue Cross Blue Shield of Florida

A health insurance company for the people of Florida with every aspect of their health and wellness, to offer quality health services, products and solutions.
www.bcbsfl.com
Annual Revenues: $6.13 Billion
Employees: 6,000
Industry/ies: Insurance Industry

Chairman of the Board and Chief Executive Officer	Tel:	(904) 791-6111
GERAGHTY, Patrick	Fax:	(904) 905-6638

Main Headquarters

Mailing: P.O. Box 1798	Tel:	(904) 791-6111
Jacksonville Beach, FL 32231-0014	Fax:	(904) 905-6638
	TF:	(800) 477-3736

Political Action Committees

Florida Health PAC (The PAC of Blue Cross and Blue Shield of Florida Inc.)
FEC ID: C00161141
Contact: Gary M. Healy
4800 Deerwood Campus Pkwy.
P.O. Box 6936
Jacksonville Beach, FL 32236

> **Contributions to Candidates:** $84,999 (2015-2016)
> Democrats: $36,499; Republicans: $48,500

Principal Recipients

SENATE
MURPHY, PATRICK E (DEM-FL)

Corporate Foundations and Giving Programs

The Blue Foundation for a Healthy Florida
Contact: Susan B. Towler
4800 Deerwood Campus Pkwy.	Tel:	(904) 791-6111
Jacksonville Beach, FL 32246	Fax:	(904) 905-4486

Public Affairs and Related Activities Personnel

At Headquarters

ALTMIRE, Hon. Jason	Tel:	(904) 791-6111
Federal Lobbyist	Fax:	(904) 905-6638
DIVITA, III, Charles "Chuck"	Tel:	(904) 791-6111
Senior Vice President and Chief Financial Officer	Fax:	(904) 905-6638
FURRY, Joseph	Tel:	(904) 791-6111
Consultant, Public Policy Research & Educational	Fax:	(904) 905-6638
HARRISON, Camille	Tel:	(904) 791-6111
Vice President, Chief Customer Experience Officer and Chief of Staff	Fax:	(904) 905-6638
Camille.harrison@bcbsfl.com		
HIGHTOWER, Michael R.	Tel:	(904) 905-6268
Vice President, Governmental and Legislative Relations	Fax:	(904) 905-6638
JOSEPH, Charlie	Tel:	(904) 791-6111
Senior Vice President, Corporate Affairs and General Counsel	Fax:	(904) 905-6638
KLUDING, Paul C.	Tel:	(904) 905-3404
?Senior Director, Public Relations	Fax:	(904) 905-6638
paul.kluding@bcbsfl.com		
SMITH, Steven D.	Tel:	(904) 905-6742
Director, Government Relations	Fax:	(904) 905-6638
THOMAS, Craig	Tel:	(904) 791-6111
Senior Vice President and Officer, Chief Strategy and Marketing	Fax:	(904) 905-6638
TOWLER, Susan B.	Tel:	(904) 791-6111
Vice President, Foundation	Fax:	(904) 905-6638
thebluefoundation@bcbsfl.com		
WALL, Bob	Tel:	(904) 791-6111
Senior Vice President, Human Services Group and Chief Human Resource Officer	Fax:	(904) 905-6638

At Other Offices

EASTERLING-CHARLES, Deborah
Specialist, Governmental & Legislative Relations
4800 Deerwood Campus Pkwy. (DCC 3-4), P.O. Box 6936
Jacksonville, FL 32246

GILES, Tom
Senior Director
4800 Deerwood Campus Pkwy. (DCC 3-4), P.O. Box 6936
Jacksonville, FL 32246

HEALY, Gary M.
Vice President, Corporate Tax and PAC Treasurer
4800 Deerwood Campus Pkwy. (DCC 3-4), P.O. Box 6936
Jacksonville, FL 32246
Mail Stop DC3-4

VIDRINE, James Eric
4800 Deerwood Campus Pkwy. (DCC 3-4), P.O. Box 6936
Jacksonville, FL 32246

Blue Cross Blue Shield of Georgia

A provider of healthcare benefits. Blue Cross and Blue Shield of Georgia, Inc. is independent licensees of the Blue Cross Blue Shield Association and is an operating subsidiary of Anthem, Inc. (formerly WellPoint Inc.) a publicly traded commercial health benefits company.
www.bcbsga.com
Annual Revenues: $1.13 billion
Employees: 3,000
Industry/ies: Insurance Industry

President and Chief Executive Officer	Tel:	(404) 842-8000
SWEDISH, Joseph R.	Fax:	(404) 842-8100

Main Headquarters

Mailing:	3350 Peachtree Rd., NE	Tel:	(404) 842-8000
	Atlanta, GA 30326	Fax:	(404) 842-8100

Corporate Foundations and Giving Programs

Blue Cross and Blue Shield Foundation
Contact: Lance Chrisman

3350 Peachtree Rd., NE	Tel:	(404) 842-8000
Atlanta, GA 30326	Fax:	(404) 842-8100

Public Affairs and Related Activities Personnel

At Headquarters

ANDREWS, Darlene	Tel:	(404) 842-8000
Director, Human Resources	Fax:	(404) 842-8100
DARLENE.ANDREWS@BCBSGA.COM		

CHRISMAN, Lance	Tel:	(404) 842-8000
Executive Director, Anthem Foundation	Fax:	(404) 842-8100

COMBS, Kelly	Tel:	(404) 842-8000
Strategic Planning Director	Fax:	(404) 842-8100

DIAMOND, Debbie	Tel:	(404) 479-8735
Contact, Media Relations	Fax:	(404) 842-8100
Deborah.diamond@anthem.com		

HARDEN, Sandi	Tel:	(404) 842-8000
Director, Sales Support and Support	Fax:	(404) 842-8100

KENDRICK, Morgan	Tel:	(404) 842-8000
President and General Manager	Fax:	(404) 842-8100

Blue Cross Blue Shield of Kansas

A health and life insurance company.
www.bcbsks.com
Annual Revenues: $1.70 billion
Employees: 1,541
Industry/ies: Insurance Industry
Legislative Issues: BUD; HCR; MMM; PHA; TAX

Chairman of the Board	Tel:	(785) 291-4180
SLOAN, Steve W.	Fax:	(785) 290-0711

President and Chief Executive Officer	Tel:	(785) 291-7000
CORBIN, Andrew C.	Fax:	(785) 291-8216
andy.corbin@bcbsks.com		

Main Headquarters

Mailing:	1133 S.W. Topeka Blvd.	Tel:	(785) 291-4180
	Topeka, KS 66629-0001	Fax:	(785) 290-0711
		TF:	(800) 432-3990

Political Action Committees

Blue Cross and Blue Shield of Kansas Employee PAC
FEC ID: C00197202
Contact: Jason Droge

1133 SW Topeka Blvd.	Tel:	(785) 291-8262
CC:855 - B3	Fax:	(785) 290-0711
Topeka, KS 66629		

Corporate Foundations and Giving Programs

Blue Cross and Blue Shield of Kansas Foundation
Contact: Marlou Wegener

1133 SW Topeka Blvd.	Tel:	(785) 291-7000
Topeka, KS 66629	Fax:	(785) 290-0711

Public Affairs and Related Activities Personnel

At Headquarters

ALL, Matthew D.	Tel:	(785) 291-7000
Senior Vice President and General Counsel	Fax:	(785) 290-0711

matt.all@bcbsks.com

BAILEY, S. Graham	Tel:	(785) 291-8846
Vice President, Corporate Communications and Public Relations	Fax:	(785) 291-7664
graham.bailey@bcbsks.com		

CHAMBERS, Mary Beth	Tel:	(785) 291-8869
Manager, Corporate Communications	Fax:	(785) 291-7664
Media.Inquiries@bcbsks.com		

DOLSKY, Mark G.	Tel:	(785) 291-4180
Vice President, Sales and Account Management	Fax:	(785) 290-0711
mark.dolsky@bcbsks.com		

DROGE, Jason	Tel:	(785) 291-4180
PAC Treasurer	Fax:	(785) 290-0711
Mail Stop CC:855 - B3		

MASON, Treena	Tel:	(785) 291-4180
Vice President, External Sales and Marketing	Fax:	(785) 290-0711

MICKLE, Sunee N.	Tel:	(785) 291-7194
Director, Government Relations	Fax:	(785) 290-0711
sunee.mickle@bcbsks.com		
Registered Federal Lobbyist		

PALENSKE, Fredrick D.	Tel:	(785) 291-4180
Senior Vice President, Provider and Government Affairs	Fax:	(785) 290-0711

SIMMONS, Ron	Tel:	(785) 291-4180
Vice President, Finance	Fax:	(785) 290-0711

SINGERLING, Chris	Tel:	(785) 291-4180
PAC Contact	Fax:	(785) 290-0711

WEGENER , Marlou	Tel:	(785) 291-7246
Chief Operating Officer, Blue Cross Blue Shield of Kansas Foundation	Fax:	(785) 291-8997
marlou.wegener@bcbsks.com		

YOUNG , Bob	Tel:	(785) 291-4180
Vice President, Administrative Services and Human Development	Fax:	(785) 290-0711

Blue Cross Blue Shield of Louisiana

A health insurance provider.
www.bcbsla.com
Annual Revenues: $53.3 Million
Employees: 1,500
Industry/ies: Insurance Industry

Chairman of the Board	Tel:	(225) 295-3307
MCCOY, Charles	Fax:	(225) 295-2054

Chairman, BCBSLA Foundation	Tel:	(225) 295-3307
ATKINS, DDS, C. Richard	Fax:	(225) 298-7772

President and Chief Executive Officer	Tel:	(225) 295-3307
REITZ, Mike	Fax:	(225) 295-2054

Main Headquarters

Mailing:	P.O. Box 98029	Tel:	(225) 295-3307
	Baton Rouge, LA 70898-9029	Fax:	(225) 298-7772
		TF:	(800) 392-4089

Corporate Foundations and Giving Programs

Blue Cross and Blue Shield of Louisiana Foundation
Contact: C. Richard Atkins DDS

5525 Reitz Ave.	Tel:	(225) 298-7051
Baton Rouge, LA 70809		

Public Affairs and Related Activities Personnel

At Headquarters

CALANDRO, Michele	Tel:	(225) 295-3307
Senior Vice President and General Counsel	Fax:	(225) 295-2054
Michele.Calandro@bcbsla.com		

KELLER, Brian	Tel:	(225) 295-3307
Senior Vice President and Chief Marketing Officer	Fax:	(225) 295-2054

LANGLOIS, Darrell	Tel:	(225) 295-3307
Vice President, Compliance, Privacy and Fraud	Fax:	(225) 295-2054
Darrell.Langlois@bcbsla.com		

MAGINNIS, Jr., John J.	Tel:	(225) 295-2405
Vice President, Corporate Communications and Company Spokesman	Fax:	(225) 295-2054
john.maginnis@bcbsla.com		

PAQUIN, Dan	Tel:	(225) 295-3307
Senior Vice President, Government Programs	Fax:	(225) 298-7772

RONE, Rodney	Tel:	(225) 295-3307
Vice President, Planning, Projects and Financial Systems	Fax:	(225) 298-7772

SCHEXNAYDER, Todd G.	Tel:	(225) 295-3307
Senior Vice President, Human Resources	Fax:	(225) 295-2054
todd.schexnayder@bcbsla.com		

Blue Cross Blue Shield of Michigan (BCBSM)

An Insurance and health care company for people of Michigan. It is a member of Blue Cross Blue Shield.
www.bcbsm.com
Annual Revenues: $21.3 billion
Employees: 7,800
Industry/ies: Medicine/Health Care/Mental Health
Legislative Issues: BUD; HCR; INS; MMM; PHA; TAX

Chairman of the Board
SUDDERTH, Gregory A.
Tel: (313) 225-9000
Fax: (313) 225-6764

President and Chief Executive Officer
LOEPP, Daniel J.
dloepp@bcbsm.com
Tel: (313) 225-9000
Fax: (313) 225-6764

Main Headquarters
Mailing: P.O. Box 2888
Detroit, MI 48231
Tel: (313) 225-9000
Fax: (313) 225-6764

Washington Office
Mailing: 1301 Pennsylvania Ave. NW
Suite 500
Washington, DC 20004

Political Action Committees
Blue Cross Blue Shield of Michigan PAC
FEC ID: C00084061
Contact: Mark Cook
232 S. CAPITOL
MC L10A
Lansing, MI 48933
Tel: (517) 371-7908

Contributions to Candidates: $59,500 (2015-2016)
Democrats: $25,500; Republicans: $34,000

Principal Recipients

HOUSE
UPTON, FREDERICK STEPHEN (REP-MI)

Corporate Foundations and Giving Programs
Blue Cross Blue Shield of Michigan Foundation
Contact: Ira Strumwasser PhD
600 E. Lafayette Blvd.
Detroit, MI 48226
Tel: (313) 225-6399
Fax: (313) 225-7730

Public Affairs and Related Activities Personnel

At Headquarters

BARTLETT, Mark R.
Executive Vice President, Chief Financial Officer and President, Emerging Markets
Mark.Bartlett@bcbsm.com
Tel: (313) 225-9000
Fax: (313) 225-6764

DALLAFIOR, Kenneth R.
Senior Vice President, Group Business and Corporate Marketing
Tel: (313) 225-9000
Fax: (313) 225-6764

HETZEL, APR, R. Andrew
Vice President, Corporate Communications
Tel: (313) 225-9000
Fax: (313) 225-6764

KANGAS-KRAFT, Kris
Director, State Relations
kkangas-kraft@bcbsm.com
Tel: (313) 225-9000
Fax: (313) 225-6764

ROSSI, Lynda M.
Executive Vice President, Strategy, Government and Public Affairs
Tel: (313) 225-9000
Fax: (313) 225-6764

RUMLEY, Jeffrey P.
Vice President and General Counsel
Tel: (313) 225-9000
Fax: (313) 225-6764

SAMUELS, Michele A.
Senior Vice President, General Auditor and Corporate Compliance
Tel: (313) 225-9000
Fax: (313) 225-6764

STRUMWASSER, PhD, Ira
Executive Director and Chief Executive Officer, BCBS of Michigan Foundation
istrumwasser@bcbsm.com
Tel: (313) 225-8706
Fax: (313) 225-6764

At Other Offices

COOK, Mark
Vice President, Government Affairs and PAC Treasurer
232 S. Capitol, MC L10A
Lansing, MI 48933
mcook@bcbsm.com
Tel: (313) 225-9000
Fax: (313) 225-6764

KEITH, Tricia A.
Senior Vice President, Corporate Secretary and Services
600 E. Lafayette Blvd.
Detroit, MI 48226
Tel: (313) 225-9000
Fax: (313) 225-6764

MODLIN, Amy E.
Vice President, Federal Affairs
1310 G St. NW, Suite 900
Washington, DC 20005
amodlin@bcbsm.com
Registered Federal Lobbyist
Tel: (202) 289-3904

Blue Cross Blue Shield of Minnesota

A health insurance company dedicated to providing quality, cost-effective health plans and unique health programs in the state of Minnesota.
www.bluecrossmn.com
Annual Revenues: $10.08 million
Employees: 3,500
Industry/ies: Insurance Industry; Medicine/Health Care/Mental Health
Legislative Issues: BUD; HCR; MMM; TAX

Chairman of the Board
HEISE, Rita J.
Tel: (651) 662-8000
Fax: (651) 662-2777

President and Chief Executive Officer
GUYETTE, Michael J.
Tel: (651) 662-8000
Fax: (651) 662-2777

Main Headquarters
Mailing: P.O. Box 64560
St. Paul, MN 55164-0560
Tel: (651) 662-8000
Fax: (651) 662-2777

Corporate Foundations and Giving Programs
Blue Cross and Blue Shield of Minnesota Foundation
Contact: Julie Ann Eastling
3535 Blue Cross Rd.
Eagan, MN 55122
Tel: (651) 662-8000
Fax: (651) 662-2777

Public Affairs and Related Activities Personnel

At Headquarters

CONNORS, Corey
Senior Vice President, Human Resources, Communications, Community Relations and Facilities
Tel: (651) 662-8000
Fax: (651) 662-2777

EASTLING, Julie Ann
Foundation and Community Affairs Communications Consultant
julie.eastling@bluecrossmn.com
Tel: (651) 662-6574
Fax: (651) 662-2777

MCMANUS, Jim
Principal Public Relations Consultant
james.mcmanus@bluecrossmn.com
Tel: (651) 662-2882
Fax: (651) 662-2777

NELSON, Lin M.
Director , Legislative Affairs & Chief Lobbyist
Registered Federal Lobbyist
Tel: (651) 662-8000
Fax: (651) 662-2777

PHILLIPPE, Paula
Senior Vice President, Human Resources, Communications & External Relations
Tel: (651) 662-8000
Fax: (651) 662-2777

RILEY, Patricia
Senior Vice President, Government Programs, Policy and Legislative Affairs and Chief Government Officer
patricia_a_riley@bluecrossmn.com
Tel: (651) 662-8000
Fax: (651) 662-2777

STUMP, MaryAnn
Senior Vice President and Chief Strategy and Innovation Officer
MaryAnn_Stump@bluecrossmn.com
Tel: (651) 662-8000
Fax: (651) 662-2777

At Other Offices

KEEFER, Scott
Federal Lobbyist
1750 Yankee Doddle Rd., N179
Eagan, MN 55121
Scott_Keefer@bluecrossmn.com
Registered Federal Lobbyist
Tel: (651) 662-8000
Fax: (651) 662-2777

MATUSHAK, Jay
Senior Vice President and Chief Financial Officer
1750 Yankee Doddle Rd., N179
Eagan, MN 55121
Tel: (651) 662-8000
Fax: (651) 662-2777

RICE, Jamison
Senior Vice President and Chief Transformational Officer
1750 Yankee Doddle Rd., N179
Eagan, MN 55121
Tel: (651) 662-8000
Fax: (651) 662-2777

WATTMAN, Lois
Senior Policy Counsel
1750 Yankee Doddle Rd., N179
Eagan, MN 55121
Tel: (651) 662-8000
Fax: (651) 662-2777

Blue Cross Blue Shield of Mississippi

A health care provider in all Mississippi counties. It is a member of Blue Cross & Blue Shield.
www.bcbsms.com
Annual Revenues: $84.52 million
Employees: 1,000
Industry/ies: Medicine/Health Care/Mental Health

Chairman of the Board
HALE, Richard J.
Tel: (601) 932-3704
Fax: (601) 939-7035

Chief Executive Officer and President
PIGOTT , Mary Carol
Tel: (601) 932-3704
Fax: (601) 939-7035

Main Headquarters
Mailing: 3545 Lakeland Dr
Flowood, MS 39232
Tel: (601) 932-3704
Fax: (601) 939-7035
TF: (800) 222-8046

Corporate Foundations and Giving Programs

Blue Cross and Blue Shield of Mississippi Foundation
P.O. Box 1043
Jackson, MS 39215

Public Affairs and Related Activities Personnel

At Headquarters

LEBER, Jeff	Tel:	(601) 932-3704
Chief Financial Officer	Fax:	(601) 939-7035

Blue Cross Blue Shield of South Carolina

A health insurance and benefits management company.
www.bcbssc.com
Annual Revenues: $678.3 million
Employees: 11,000
Industry/ies: Medicine/Health Care/Mental Health
Legislative Issues: DEF; HCR; MMM

Chairman of the Board	Tel:	(803) 264-5455
SELLERS, M. Edward	Fax:	(301) 447-1928

President and Chief Executive Officer	Tel:	(803) 264-5455
PANKAU, David S.	Fax:	(301) 447-1928

Main Headquarters

Mailing:	I-20 East@ Alpine Rd.	Tel:	(803) 264-7258
	Mail Code - AX-E01	Fax:	(803) 264-7257
	Columbia, SC 29219-0001	TF:	(800) 288-2227

Washington Office

Mailing:	One Massachusetts Ave. NW	Tel:	(202) 243-7575
	Suite 850		
	Washington, DC 20001		

Political Action Committees
Blue Cross Blue Shield of South Carolina Federal Government Programs
FEC ID: C00406850
Contact: Dave Mason

I-20 @ Alpine Rd.	Tel:	(803) 788-0222
Mail Code - AX-212	Fax:	(301) 447-1928
Columbia, SC 29219-0001		

   Contributions to Candidates: $31,500 (2015-2016)
   Democrats: $2,500; Republicans: $29,000

Corporate Foundations and Giving Programs
Blue Cross Blue Shield of South Carolina Foundation
Contact: Harvey L. Galloway

2501 Faraway Dr.	Tel:	(803) 788-0222
Columbia, SC 29219-0001	Fax:	(803) 264-8077

Public Affairs and Related Activities Personnel

At Headquarters

CLOSE, Carol	Tel:	(803) 264-5455
Manager, Public Affairs	Fax:	(301) 447-1928
carol.close@bcbssc.com		

D'ALESSIO, James	Tel:	(803) 264-5455
Vice President, Government Affairs	Fax:	(301) 447-1928
James.D'Alessio@bcbssc.com		

DAVIS, Judith	Tel:	(803) 264-5455
Executive Vice President and Chief Legal Officer	Fax:	(301) 447-1928

GALLOWAY, Harvey L.	Tel:	(803) 264-5455
Executive Director, Bluecross Blueshield -South Carolina Foundation	Fax:	(301) 447-1928

HAMMOND, Elizabeth	Tel:	(803) 264-4626
Manager, Media Relations	Fax:	(301) 447-1928
elizabeth.hammond@bcbssc.com		

MASON, Dave	Tel:	(803) 264-5455
PAC Treasurer	Fax:	(301) 447-1928

Blue Cross Blue Shield of Tennessee

The company offers PPO and traditional indemnity health insurance plans. BlueCross BlueShield of Tennessee also provides Medicare supplement plans as well as vision and dental plans.
www.bcbst.com
Industry/ies: Medicine/Health Care/Mental Health
Legislative Issues: BUD; HCR; MMM; PHA; TAX

President and Chief Executive Officer	Tel:	(423) 535-5600
HICKEY, JD	Fax:	(423) 535-6255

Main Headquarters

Mailing:	One Cameron Hill Circle	Tel:	(423) 535-5600
	Chattanooga, TN 37402	Fax:	(423) 535-6255

Political Action Committees
BCBSTN PAC
FEC ID: C00503003
Contact: Brad Traverse
One Cameron Hill Circle
Chattanooga, TN 37402

   Contributions to Candidates: $8,700 (2015-2016)

   Democrats: $4,200; Republicans: $4,500

Corporate Foundations and Giving Programs
The Blue Cross Blue Shield of Tennessee Health Foundation, Inc.
Contact: Dawn Abel

801 Pine St.	Tel:	(423) 535-7163
Chattanooga, TN 37402	Fax:	(423) 535-7173

Public Affairs and Related Activities Personnel

At Headquarters

ABEL, Dawn	Tel:	(423) 535-5600
Foundation Manager	Fax:	(423) 535-6255
dawn_abel@bcbst.com		

HICKEY, J.D.	Tel:	(423) 535-5600
	Fax:	(423) 535-6255

At Other Offices

ANDERSON, Calvin	Tel:	(901) 544-2111
Senior Vice President, Corporate Affairs and Chief of Staff		
85 N. Danny Thomas Blvd.		
Memphis, TN 38103		
calvin_anderson@bcbst.com		

HUGHES, Tavarski	Tel:	(901) 544-2111
Federal Lobbyist		
85 N. Danny Thomas Blvd.		
Memphis, TN 38103		
Registered Federal Lobbyist		

TRAVERSE, Brad	Tel:	(901) 544-2111
Director, Federal Government Relations		
85 N. Danny Thomas Blvd.		
Memphis, TN 38103		
brad_traverse@bcbst.com		
Registered Federal Lobbyist		

Blue Cross of Idaho Health Service, Inc.

A health insurance company.
www.bcidaho.com
Annual Revenues: $1.33 billion
Employees: 900
Industry/ies: Insurance Industry; Medicine/Health Care/Mental Health

Chairman of the Board	Tel:	(208) 387-6817
SHIRLEY, Michael J.	Fax:	(208) 331-7321

President and Chief Executive Officer and Chair, Blue Cross of Idaho Foundation for Health, Inc.	Tel:	(208) 345-4550
	Fax:	(208) 331-7311
GEYER-SYLVIA, Zelda		

Main Headquarters

Mailing:	P.O. Box 7408	Tel:	(208) 345-4550
	Boise, ID 83707	Fax:	(208) 331-7311
		TF:	(800) 274-4018

Corporate Foundations and Giving Programs
Blue Crew

P.O. Box 7408	Tel:	(208) 345-4550
Boise, ID 83707	Fax:	(208) 345-4550

Blue Cross of Idaho Foundation for Health
Contact: Zelda Geyer-Sylvia

P.O. Box 7408	Tel:	(208) 387-6817
Boise, ID 83707	Fax:	(208) 331-7321

Public Affairs and Related Activities Personnel

At Headquarters

EARLY, Karen	Tel:	(208) 345-4550
Director, Corporate Communications	Fax:	(208) 331-7311

FELLNER, Brian	Tel:	(208) 345-4550
Chief Financial Officer	Fax:	(208) 331-7311

HENRY, Debra M.	Tel:	(208) 345-4550
Vice President, Human Resources and Organizational Development	Fax:	(208) 331-7311
dhenry@bcidaho.com		

JEPPESEN, David	Tel:	(208) 345-4550
Senior Vice President, Sales and Marketing	Fax:	(208) 331-7311

JORDAN, Josh	Tel:	(208) 345-4550
Manager, Corporate Communications	Fax:	(208) 331-7311

MYERS, Jack A.	Tel:	(208) 345-4550
Executive Vice President and Chief Financial Officer	Fax:	(208) 331-7311
jmyers@bcidaho.com		

TAYLOR, Julie M.	Tel:	(208) 331-7357
Director, Governmental Affairs	Fax:	(208) 331-7320
jtaylor@bcidaho.com		

TOBIASON, Steve	Tel:	(208) 345-4550
General Counsel, Senior Vice President, Legal Services and Government Affairs	Fax:	(208) 331-7311
stobiason@bcidaho.com		

Blue Cross of Northeastern Pennsylvania

See listing on page 412 under Hospital Service Association of Northeastern Pennsylvania

Blue Diamond Growers

Founded in 1910. Blue Diamond Growers is the tree nut processing and marketing company.
www.bluediamond.com
Employees: 1,100
SIC: 0173; 2068
NAICS: 311911; 111335
Industry/ies: Food And Beverage Industry
Legislative Issues: AGR; BUD; FOO; IMM; LBR; TRD

Chairman of the Board
CUMMINGS, Dan

President and Chief Executive Officer
JANSEN, Mark D.

Tel: (916) 442-8500
Fax: (916) 446-8461

Main Headquarters
Mailing: 1701 C St.
             Sacramento, CA 95811

TF: (800) 987-2329

Political Action Committees
Blue Diamond Growers Political Action Committee
FEC ID: C00080135
Contact: Richard J. Eichman
1802 C St.
Sacramento, CA 95814

Tel: (916) 446-8354

Contributions to Candidates: $89,200 (2015-2016)
Democrats: $29,000; Republicans: $60,200

Principal Recipients

HOUSE
BERA, AMERISH (DEM-CA)
COSTA, JIM MR. (DEM-CA)
DENHAM, JEFF (REP-CA)
MCCARTHY, KEVIN (REP-CA)
NUNES, DEVIN G (REP-CA)
VALADAO, DAVID (REP-CA)

Corporate Foundations and Giving Programs
Blue Diamond's Charitable Contribution Program
Contact: Richard J. Eichman
P.O. Box 1768
Sacramento, CA 95812

Public Affairs and Related Activities Personnel

At Headquarters
LAVALLEE, Dean
Chief Financial Officer

At Other Offices
EICHMAN, Richard J.
PAC Treasurer
1127-11th St., Suite 300
Sacramento, CA 95814

Blue Source, LLC

A developer of greenhouse gas reduction projects.
www.bluesource.com
Industry/ies: Energy/Electricity

Chief Executive Officer
TOWNSEND, Eric

Tel: (801) 322-4750
Fax: (801) 363-3248

Main Headquarters
Mailing: 1935 E. Vine St.
             Suite 300
             Murray, UT 84121

Tel: (801) 322-4750
Fax: (801) 363-3248

Corporate Foundations and Giving Programs
Globe Foundation
3165 E. Millrock Dr.
Suite 340
Holladay, UT 84121

Tel: (801) 322-4750

Public Affairs and Related Activities Personnel

At Headquarters
MIHELIC, Tracey
General Counsel

Tel: (801) 322-4750
Fax: (801) 363-3248

BlueFire Renewables, Inc.

An ethanol company. BlueFire was established to deploy the Arkenol Process Technology ("Technology") for the conversion of cellulosic waste materials into renewable fuels and other products. Its bio-refineries would convert organic materials, such as agricultural residues, high-content biomass crops, wood residues, and cellulose from municipal solid wastes into ethanol.
bfreinc.com
Annual Revenues: $1.02 million
Employees: 5

Ticker: NYSE:BFRE --Other OTC
SIC: 2860
Industry/ies: Energy/Electricity

Chairman, President and Chief Executive Officer
KLANN, Arnold R.

Tel: (949) 588-3767
Fax: (949) 588-3972

Main Headquarters
Mailing: 31 Musick
             Irvine, CA 92618

Tel: (949) 588-3767
Fax: (949) 588-3972

Corporate Foundations and Giving Programs
Bluefire Ethanol Contributions Program
31 Musick
Irvine, CA 92618-1638

Public Affairs and Related Activities Personnel

At Headquarters
KLANN, Richard
Director, Business Development and Finance
rgklann@bfreinc.com

Tel: (949) 588-3767
Fax: (949) 588-3972

SHIN, Soo Kwan
Executive Vice President, Operations

Tel: (949) 588-3767
Fax: (949) 588-3972

At Other Offices
FINLAYSON, Laura
Contact, Media Relations
One University Plaza, Suite 508
Hackensack, NJ 07601
lfinlayson@beckermanpr.com

Tel: (201) 465-8007
Fax: (201) 465-8000

KITCHER, Scott
Contact, Investor Relations
2201 Dupont Dr., Suite 100
Irvine, CA 92612
skitcher@ecofinconsulting.com

Tel: (949) 435-2056

BMC Software

Provider of enterprise management software used for a variety of functions, including recovery and storage management, business process scheduling and integration, service management, and application and database performance management.
www.bmc.com
Annual Revenues: $2.20 billion
Employees: 6,700
Ticker: NASDAQ: BMC
SIC: 7372
Industry/ies: Computer/Technology
Legislative Issues: CPI; SCI

Chairman of the Board, President and Chief Executive Officer
BEAUCHAMP, Robert E.
bob_beauchamp@bmc.com

Tel: (713) 918-8800
Fax: (713) 918-8000

Main Headquarters
Mailing: 2101 City West Blvd.
             Houston, TX 77042-2827

Tel: (713) 918-8800
Fax: (713) 918-8000
TF: (800) 841-2031

Washington Office
Mailing: Greensboro Corporate Center, 8401
             Greensboro Dr.
             Suite 100
             McLean, VA 22102

Tel: (703) 744-3500
Fax: (703) 744-3501

Corporate Foundations and Giving Programs
BMC Software Community Relations
Contact: Dan D'Armond
2101 City West Blvd.
Houston, TX 77042

Tel: (713) 918-1371
Fax: (713) 918-8000

Public Affairs and Related Activities Personnel

At Headquarters
BERGDOLL, Brian
Executive Vice President, Sales

Tel: (713) 918-8800
Fax: (713) 918-8000

D'ARMOND, Dan
Director, Community and Government Relations
dan_darmond@bmc.com

Tel: (713) 918-8800
Fax: (713) 918-8000

FAHLBUSCH, Monika
Senior Vice President, Chief People and Administrative Officer

Tel: (713) 918-8800
Fax: (713) 918-8000

HINTON, Clarence
Vice President and Head, Corporate Development

Tel: (713) 918-8800
Fax: (713) 918-8000

SOLCHER, Stephen B.
Senior Vice President, Finance and Chief Financial Officer

Tel: (713) 918-8800
Fax: (713) 918-8000

TAGTOW, Patrick K.
Senior Vice President, General Counsel, Corporate Secretary and Chief Compliance Officer

Tel: (713) 918-8800
Fax: (713) 918-8000

BMO Harris Bank

See listing on page 385 under Harris Bank

BMW (U.S.) Holding Corporation

The American import and sales subsidiary of the German manufacturer of automobiles and motorcycles.
www.bmwusa.com
Annual Revenues: $16.80 billion
Employees: 2,200
SIC: 5012
NAICS: 42111
Industry/ies: Automotive Industry; Transportation
Legislative Issues: AUT; MAN; TRD

Main Headquarters

Mailing:	The Executive Tower	Tel:	(202) 393-2150
	1399 New York Ave. NW, Suite 425	Fax:	(202) 393-2151
	Washington, DC 20005		

Corporate Foundations and Giving Programs

BMW of North America, Inc. Contributions Program
300 Chestnut Ridge Rd. — Tel: (201) 307-4000
Woodcliff, NJ 07677-7731 — Fax: (201) 307-0880

Public Affairs and Related Activities Personnel

At Headquarters

HELSING, Craig R.	Tel:	(202) 393-2150
Vice President, Government Relations	Fax:	(202) 393-2151
Registered Federal Lobbyist		
JACOBS, Bryan	Tel:	(202) 393-2150
Vice President	Fax:	(202) 393-2151
Registered Federal Lobbyist		
SENGEWALD, Stefan	Tel:	(202) 393-2150
Senior Vice President, organizational development and	Fax:	(202) 393-2151
process management		
Stefan.Sengewald@bmwusa.com		

At Other Offices

BRANDING, John
300 Chestnut Ridge Rd.
Woodcliff Lake, NJ 07677-7731
Registered Federal Lobbyist

WALMRATH , Stefan
Executive Vice President, Finance and Chief Financial Officer
300 Chestnut Ridge Rd.
Woodcliff Lake, NJ 07677-7731

BNY Mellon

See listing on page 104 under The Bank of New York Mellon Corporation

Bob Evans Farms, Inc.

A producer of food products and owner and operator of a chain of family restaurants.
www.bobevans.com
Annual Revenues: $1.34 billion
Employees: 7,973
Ticker: NASDAQ; BOBE
SIC: 2077; 2099; 2096; 2013
NAICS: 311712; 311919; 311991; 311612
Industry/ies: Food And Beverage Industry

Non-Executive Chair of the Board	Tel:	(614) 491-2225
HABEN , Mary Kay	Fax:	(614) 492-4949

Chief Executive Officer and Chief Financial Officer	Tel:	(614) 491-2225
HOOD, Mark	Fax:	(614) 492-4949

Main Headquarters

Mailing:	3776 S. High St.	Tel:	(614) 491-2225
	Columbus, OH 43207	Fax:	(614) 492-4949
		TF:	(800) 272-7675

Corporate Foundations and Giving Programs

Bob Evans Corporate Philanthropy
3776 S. High St.
Columbus, OH 43207

Public Affairs and Related Activities Personnel

At Headquarters

TAGGART, Scott C.	Tel:	(614) 491-2225
Vice President, Investor Relations and Corporate	Fax:	(614) 492-4949
Communications		

Boehringer Ingelheim Pharmaceuticals, Inc.

The firm is the pharmaceuticals unit of Boehringer Ingelheim Corporation, which is the US headquarters of Germany's Boehringer Ingelheim.
www.boehringer-ingelheim.com
Annual Revenues: $147.00 million
Employees: 1,800
SIC: 2834
NAICS: 325412
Industry/ies: Medicine/Health Care/Mental Health
Legislative Issues: ANI; BUD; CSP; HCR; MMM

Chairman of the Board	Tel:	(203) 798-9988
BARNER, Dr. Andreas	Fax:	(203) 791-6234

President and Chief Executive Officer	Tel:	(203) 798-9988
FONTEYNE, Paul	Fax:	(203) 791-6234

Main Headquarters

Mailing:	900 Ridgebury Rd.	Tel:	(203) 798-9988
	Ridgefield, CT 06877	Fax:	(203) 791-6234
		TF:	(800) 243-0127

Washington Office

Mailing: 1120 G St. NW
Suite 1050
Washington, DC 20005

Political Action Committees

Boehringer Ingelheim USA Corporation Political Action Committee
FEC ID: C00420398
Contact: Frank Pomer
900 Ridgebury Rd. — Tel: (202) 833-0085
Suite 1102 — Fax: (202) 833-0086
Ridgefield, CT 06877

Contributions to Candidates: $141,000 (2015-2016)
Democrats: $71,500; Republicans: $69,500

Principal Recipients

HOUSE
SWALWELL, ERIC MICHAEL (DEM-CA)

Corporate Foundations and Giving Programs

Boehringer Ingelheim Cares Foundation
Contact: Lilly Ackley
900 Ridgebury Rd. — Tel: (203) 798-9988
P.O. Box 368 — Fax: (203) 791-6234
Ridgefield, CT 06877

Public Affairs and Related Activities Personnel

At Headquarters

ACKLEY, Lilly	Tel:	(203) 798-9988
Director and Foundation President	Fax:	(203) 791-6234
CARROLL, J. Martin	Tel:	(203) 798-9988
Contact, Corporate Strategy and Development	Fax:	(203) 791-6234
CREW, Erin	Tel:	(203) 798-5564
Media Contact	Fax:	(203) 791-6234
erin.crew@boehringer-ingelheim.com		
DORST, Jonathan	Tel:	(203) 798-9988
Registered Federal Lobbyist	Fax:	(203) 791-6234
EFANTIS, Amy	Tel:	(202) 347-8270
Executive Director, Federal Government Affairs	Fax:	(203) 791-6234
amy.efantis@boehringer-ingelheim.com		
Registered Federal Lobbyist		
MCPHERSON, Jonathan	Tel:	(203) 798-9988
Federal Lobbyist	Fax:	(203) 791-6234
jonathan.mcpherson@boehringer-ingelheim.com		
Registered Federal Lobbyist		
POMER, Frank	Tel:	(203) 798-9988
PAC Treasurer	Fax:	(203) 791-6234
Mail Stop Suite 315		
RINN, Stefan	Tel:	(203) 798-9988
Senior Vice President, Finance and Chief financial officer	Fax:	(203) 791-6234
ROMNESS, Paul	Tel:	(203) 798-9988
Vice President, Government Affairs & Public Policy	Fax:	(203) 791-6234
TEMME, Alanna	Tel:	(203) 798-9988
Director, Government Affairs	Fax:	(203) 791-6234
Registered Federal Lobbyist		

The Boeing Company

A global aerospace company that specializes in satellites, commercial jetliners, launch systems and services, human space flight and military aircraft.
www.boeing.com
Annual Revenues: $92.45 billion
Employees: 165,500
Ticker: NYSE: BA
SIC: 3721
Industry/ies: Aerospace/Aviation; Defense/Homeland Security; Government-Related; Transportation
Legislative Issues: AER; AVI; BAN; BUD; CPI; CPT; DEF; EDU; ENV; FIN; FOR; GOV; HCR; HOM; INT; LBR; TAX; TRA; TRD

President and Chief Executive Officer	Tel:	(312) 544-2000
MUILENBURG, Dennis A.	Fax:	(312) 544-2082

Main Headquarters

Mailing:	100 N. Riverside	Tel:	(312) 544-2000
	Chicago, IL 60606	Fax:	(312) 544-2082

Washington Office

Mailing:	929 Long Bridge Dr.	Tel:	(703) 414-6493

Arlington, VA 22202

Political Action Committees

Boeing Company PAC, The (BPAC)
FEC ID: C00142711
Contact: Jennifer M. Lowe
1200 Wilson Blvd.   Tel: (703) 465-3500
Arlington, VA 22209-2305

Contributions to Candidates: $1,534,635 (2015-2016)
Democrats: $649,500; Republicans: $877,135; Other: $8,000

Principal Recipients

SENATE

MCCAIN, JOHN S (REP-VA)
MURPHY, PATRICK E (DEM-FL)
SCOTT, TIMOTHY E (REP-SC)

HOUSE

BOUSTANY, CHARLES W. DR. JR. (REP-LA)
CALVERT, KEN (REP-CA)
CARTER, JOHN R. REP. (REP-DC)
CARTWRIGHT, MATT (DEM-PA)
CROWLEY, JOSEPH (DEM-NY)
CULBERSON, JOHN (REP-TX)
CURBELO, CARLOS (REP-FL)
DELBENE, SUZAN K (DEM-WA)
DIAZ-BALART, MARIO (REP-FL)
DINGELL, DEBBIE (DEM-MI)
FRANKEL, LOIS J. (DEM-FL)
FRELINGHUYSEN, RODNEY P. (REP-NJ)
GRANGER, KAY (REP-TX)
HARTZLER, VICKY (REP-MO)
HECK, DENNIS (DEM-WA)
HECK, JOE (REP-NV)
JOYCE, DAVID P (REP-OH)
LOBIONDO, FRANK A. (REP-NJ)
LONG, BILLY MR. (REP-MO)
MEEHAN, PATRICK L. MR. (REP-PA)
PALAZZO, STEVEN MCCARTY (REP-MS)
PELOSI, NANCY (DEM-CA)
ROBY, MARTHA (REP-AL)
ROGERS, MICHAEL DENNIS (REP-AL)
SEWELL, TERRYCINA ANDREA (DEM-AL)
SLAUGHTER, LOUISE M (DEM-NY)
STEFANIK, ELISE M. (REP-NY)
THORNBERRY, MAC (REP-TX)
VALADAO, DAVID (REP-CA)
VISCLOSKY, PETER J. (DEM-IN)
WALDEN, GREGORY P MR. (REP-OR)
WATERS, MAXINE MS (DEM-CA)

Corporate Foundations and Giving Programs

The Global Corporate Citizenship (GCC)
Contact: Anna Eleanor Roosevelt
100 N. Riverside   Tel: (312) 544-2000
Chicago, IL 60606   Fax: (312) 544-2000

Public Affairs and Related Activities Personnel

At Headquarters

CAMERON, Arthur E.   Tel: (312) 544-2000
Vice President, Advocacy and Strategy   Fax: (312) 544-2082
Registered Federal Lobbyist

CHADWICK, Christopher M.   Tel: (312) 544-2000
Executive Vice President   Fax: (312) 544-2082

DOWNEY, Thomas J.   Tel: (312) 544-2002
Senior Vice President, Communications   Fax: (312) 544-2082

LUTTIG, J. Michael   Tel: (312) 544-2000
Executive Vice President, General Counsel   Fax: (312) 544-2082
michael.luttig@boeing.com

PARASIDA, Tony   Tel: (312) 544-2000
Senior Vice President, Human Resources and Administration   Fax: (312) 544-2082

ROOSEVELT, Anna Eleanor   Tel: (312) 544-2000
Vice President, Global Corporate Citizenship   Fax: (312) 544-2082

SMITH, Greg   Tel: (312) 544-2000
Executive Vice President, Business Development and Strategy   Fax: (312) 544-2082
and Chief Financial Officer

VILHAUER, Robert J.   Tel: (703) 465-3671
Vice President, Public Policy Advocacy   Fax: (703) 465-3040

At Washington Office

CAMERON, Tammy F.
Registered Federal Lobbyist

DOLE, Greg S.   Tel: (703) 414-6493
Federal Lobbyist

FERGUSON, Jr., Edward L. L.   Tel: (703) 414-6493
Federal Lobbyist

LOWE, Jennifer M.

Vice President, State and Local Government Operations

PAGANO, Peter   Tel: (703) 414-6493
Registered Federal Lobbyist

SHOCKEY, Jeff   Tel: (703) 414-6493
Vice President, Legislative Affairs
Registered Federal Lobbyist

SHOCKEY, Jeffrey S.
Vice President of Legislative Affairs

At Other Offices

ABRAMCZYK, Nicholas A.   Tel: (703) 465-3500
Director, Federal Lobbyist   Fax: (703) 465-3002
1200 Wilson Blvd.
Arlington, VA 22209-2305

AUSTELL, Theodore   Tel: (703) 465-3876
Vice President, Executive, Legislative and Regulatory Affairs   Fax: (703) 465-3018
1200 Wilson Blvd.
Arlington, VA 22209-2305
theodore.austell@boeing.com

BACHMMAN, Steve E.   Tel: (703) 465-3500
Federal Lobbyist   Fax: (703) 465-3002
1200 Wilson Blvd.
Arlington, VA 22209-2305
steven.e.bachmann@boeing.com
Registered Federal Lobbyist

BLAZEY, III, John T.   Tel: (703) 465-3686
Federal Lobbyist   Fax: (703) 465-3002
1200 Wilson Blvd.
Arlington, VA 22209-2305
Registered Federal Lobbyist

BROOKS, Darcie D.   Tel: (703) 465-3500
Federal Lobbyist   Fax: (703) 465-3002
1200 Wilson Blvd.
Arlington, VA 22209-2305
Registered Federal Lobbyist

BROSNAHAN MCINTYRE, Jennifer   Tel: (703) 465-3500
Federal Lobbyist   Fax: (703) 465-3003
1200 Wilson Blvd.
Arlington, VA 22209-2305

BUMGARDNER, Heath D.   Tel: (703) 465-3500
Federal Lobbyist   Fax: (703) 465-3002
1200 Wilson Blvd.
Arlington, VA 22209-2305
Registered Federal Lobbyist

COX, Daniel J.   Tel: (703) 465-3500
Federal Lobbyist   Fax: (703) 465-3985
1200 Wilson Blvd.
Arlington, VA 22209-2305
Registered Federal Lobbyist

DION, Stacey A.   Tel: (703) 465-3500
Vice President, Corporate Public Policy   Fax: (703) 465-3040
1200 Wilson Blvd.
Arlington, VA 22209-2305
Registered Federal Lobbyist

FALLON, Willard G.   Tel: (703) 465-3876
Federal Lobbyist   Fax: (703) 465-3002
1200 Wilson Blvd.
Arlington, VA 22209-2305

FERKO, Jacqueline   Tel: (703) 465-3686
Federal Lobbyist   Fax: (703) 465-3002
1200 Wilson Blvd.
Arlington, VA 22209-2305
jacqueline.ferko@boeing.com
Registered Federal Lobbyist

GRIFFIN, Virgil   Tel: (703) 465-3500
Federal Lobbyist   Fax: (703) 465-3001
1200 Wilson Blvd.
Arlington, VA 22209-2305
virgil.g.lew@boeing.com
Registered Federal Lobbyist

HEILIG, Paul T.   Tel: (703) 465-3500
Manager, Legislative Affairs, Homeland Security and   Fax: (703) 465-3004
Phantom Works
1200 Wilson Blvd.
Arlington, VA 22209-2305

HOFGARD, Jefferson S.   Tel: (703) 465-3500
Vice President, International Operations   Fax: (703) 465-3041
1200 Wilson Blvd.
Arlington, VA 22209-2305

KEATING, Timothy J.   Tel: (703) 465-3500
Senior Vice President, Government Operations   Fax: (703) 465-3002
1200 Wilson Blvd.
Arlington, VA 22209-2305

tim.keating@boeing.com
Registered Federal Lobbyist

KRAFT, Kenneth — Tel: (703) 465-3686
Federal Lobbyist — Fax: (703) 465-3002
1200 Wilson Blvd.
Arlington, VA 22209-2305
Registered Federal Lobbyist

MCCARDLE, Matthew — Tel: (703) 465-3686
Director, Aviation and Transportation, Government — Fax: (703) 465-3002
Operations
1200 Wilson Blvd.
Arlington, VA 22209-2305
Registered Federal Lobbyist

MCGLAUN, Joy — Tel: (703) 465-3500
Federal Lobbyist — Fax: (703) 465-3002
1200 Wilson Blvd.
Arlington, VA 22209-2305
Registered Federal Lobbyist

MELLODY, Meredith — Tel: (703) 465-3500
Federal Lobbyist — Fax: (703) 465-3002
1200 Wilson Blvd.
Arlington, VA 22209-2305
Registered Federal Lobbyist

MOLONEY, John M. — Tel: (703) 465-3500
Director, Legislative Affairs — Fax: (703) 465-3362
1200 Wilson Blvd.
Arlington, VA 22209-2305
Registered Federal Lobbyist

MORRISON, David H. — Tel: (703) 465-3500
Test & Integration Engineering — Fax: (703) 465-3002
1200 Wilson Blvd.
Arlington, VA 22209-2305

NASH-SCHWARTZ, D. Elizabeth — Tel: (703) 465-3668
Director, Legislative Affairs — Fax: (703) 465-3003
1200 Wilson Blvd.
Arlington, VA 22209-2305
Registered Federal Lobbyist

RAMSDELL, Christine H. — Tel: (703) 465-3500
Federal Lobbyist — Fax: (703) 465-3002
1200 Wilson Blvd.
Arlington, VA 22209-2305
Registered Federal Lobbyist

ROZELSKY, Kevin — Tel: (703) 465-3686
Director, Legislative Affairs — Fax: (703) 465-3002
1200 Wilson Blvd.
Arlington, VA 22209-2305
Registered Federal Lobbyist

SCHWAB, Richard F. — Tel: (703) 465-3500
Director, Legislative Affairs — Fax: (703) 765-3341
1200 Wilson Blvd.
Arlington, VA 22209-2305

SHAHEEN, Frederick F. — Tel: (703) 465-3500
Chief Counsel, Global Trade — Fax: (703) 465-3985
1200 Wilson Blvd.
Arlington, VA 22209-2305

SHANK, John G. — Tel: (703) 465-3500
Vice President, Federal Legislative Affairs — Fax: (703) 465-3002
1200 Wilson Blvd.
Arlington, VA 22209-2305

SMITH, Amy B. — Tel: (703) 465-3500
Administrative Assistant — Fax: (703) 465-3002
1200 Wilson Blvd.
Arlington, VA 22209-2305
Registered Federal Lobbyist

SUTTON, Howard G. — Tel: (703) 465-3500
Federal Lobbyist — Fax: (703) 465-3002
1200 Wilson Blvd.
Arlington, VA 22209-2305
Registered Federal Lobbyist

TAPPAN, Joan S. — Tel: (703) 465-3500
Chief, Staff, Strategy and Advocacy — Fax: (703) 465-3045
1200 Wilson Blvd.
Arlington, VA 22209-2305

WACLAWSKI, Michael — Tel: (703) 465-3686
Federal Lobbyist — Fax: (703) 465-3002
1200 Wilson Blvd.
Arlington, VA 22209-2305
Registered Federal Lobbyist

WILSON, Karen L. — Tel: (703) 465-3500
Federal Lobbyist — Fax: (703) 465-3985
1200 Wilson Blvd.
Arlington, VA 22209-2305
Registered Federal Lobbyist

YOUNG, Jr., David Anthony A. — Tel: (703) 465-3500
Federal Lobbyist — Fax: (703) 465-3002
1200 Wilson Blvd.
Arlington, VA 22209-2305
Registered Federal Lobbyist

Boiron USA

Homeopathic medicine manufacturer
www.boironusa.com
Industry/ies: Medicine/Health Care/Mental Health

President and Chief Executive Officer — Tel: (610) 325-7464
BOUDAZIN, Janick

Main Headquarters
Mailing: Six Campus Blvd. — Tel: (610) 325-7464
Newton Square, PA 19073 — TF: (800) 264-7661

Boise Cascade, LLC

Manufactures wood products and distributes building materials. In February 2008, Boise Cascade sold its Paper, Packaging & Newsprint, and Transportation businesses; they are now operating as Boise Inc.
www.bc.com
Annual Revenues: $3.70 billion
Employees: 6,180
Ticker: NYSE: BCC
SIC: 2421; 2653; 2499; 5112; 5031
Industry/ies: Paper And Wood Products Industry

Chairman of the Board — Tel: (208) 384-6161
CARLILE , Thomas — Fax: (208) 384-7189

Chief Executive Officer — Tel: (208) 384-6161
CORRICK, Thomas — Fax: (208) 384-7189

Main Headquarters
Mailing: P.O. Box 50 — Tel: (208) 384-6161
Boise, ID 83728 — Fax: (208) 384-7189

Corporate Foundations and Giving Programs

Boise Cascade, LLC Contributions Program
P.O. Box 50
Boise, ID 83728

Public Affairs and Related Activities Personnel

At Headquarters

GADDA, Dave — Tel: (208) 384-6161
Vice President, Legal — Fax: (208) 384-7189

HIBBS, Kelly — Tel: (208) 384-6161
Vice President, Controller — Fax: (208) 384-7189

RANCOURT, Wayne — Tel: (208) 384-6073
Senior Vice President, Chief Financial Officer and Treasurer — Fax: (208) 384-7189
investor@bc.com

SAHLBERG, John — Tel: (208) 384-6451
Vice President, Human Resources, General Counsel and — Fax: (208) 384-7189
Secretary
MediaInquiries@bc.com

BOK Financial Corporation

A multi-bank holding company.
investor.bokf.com
Annual Revenues: $1.31 billion
Employees: 4,741
Ticker: NASDAQ: BOKF
SIC: 6021
Industry/ies: Banking/Finance/Investments

Chairman of the Board — Tel: (918) 588-6000
KAISER, George B. — Fax: (918) 588-6853

President and Chief Executive Officer — Tel: (918) 588-6000
BRADSHAW, Steven G. — Fax: (918) 588-6853

Main Headquarters
Mailing: Bank of Oklahoma Tower, P.O. Box 2300 — Tel: (918) 588-6000
Tulsa, OK 74192 — Fax: (918) 588-6853

Political Action Committees
BOK Financial Corporation PAC
FEC ID: C00351924
Contact: Joseph Crivelli
201 Robert S. Kerr Ave.
Mezzanine
Oklahoma City, OK 73102

   Contributions to Candidates: $15,750 (2015-2016)
   Democrats: $500; Republicans: $15,250

Corporate Foundations and Giving Programs

Bank of Oklahoma Foundation
Contact: Leslie Paris
P.O. Box 2300 — Tel: (918) 588-6000

Tulsa, OK 74192   Fax: (918) 588-6853

Public Affairs and Related Activities Personnel

At Headquarters

CRIVELLI, Joseph   Tel: (918) 588-6000
PAC Treasurer   Fax: (918) 588-6853

GROSSI, Stephen D.   Tel: (918) 588-6000
Executive Vice President, Chief Human Resources Officer Fax: (918) 588-6853

HINKLE, Susie   Tel: (918) 588-6752
Director, Internal Audit   Fax: (918) 588-6853
shinkle@bokf.com

MYERS, Andrea   Tel: (918) 594-7794
Manager, Media Relations   Fax: (918) 588-6853
amyers@bokf.com

NELL, Steven E.   Tel: (918) 588-6000
Executive Vice President and Chief Financial Officer Fax: (918) 588-6853

PARIS, Leslie   Tel: (918) 588-6000
Senior Vice President and Director, Corporate Community Fax: (918) 588-6853
Relations

At Other Offices

HIGGINBOTHAM, John D.   Tel: (918) 588-6000
President
201 Robert S. Kerr Ave., Mezzanine
Oklahoma City, OK 73102

THEDFORD, Joyce M.   Tel: (918) 588-6000
Executive Assistant
201 Robert S. Kerr Ave., Mezzanine
Oklahoma City, OK 73102

Bombardier

An airplane and rail transportation systems manufacturer headquartered in Montreal, Canada.
Purchased Learjet Corp. in 1990.
www.bombardier.com
Annual Revenues: $20.10 billion
Employees: 74,000
Industry/ies: Aerospace/Aviation; Railroads; Transportation
Legislative Issues: AER; DEF; TRA

Chairman of the Board   Tel: (316) 946-2000
BEAUDOIN, Laurent   Fax: (316) 946-2220

President and Chief Executive Officer   Tel: (514) 861-9481
BELLEMARE, Alain   Fax: (514) 861-2420

Main Headquarters
Mailing: 800 Rene-Levesque Blvd., West   Tel: (514) 861-9481
              Montreal, QC H3B 1Y8   Fax: (514) 861-2420

Washington Office
Mailing: 2200 Pennsylvania Ave. NW
              Suite 660 West
              Washington, DC 20037

Political Action Committees
Bombardier Corporation Political Action Committee
FEC ID: C00546473
Contact: Kimba Sjogren
2200 Pennsylvania Ave. NW
Suite 660 W
Washington, DC 20037

   Contributions to Candidates: $31,000 (2015-2016)
   Democrats: $6,000; Republicans: $25,000

Bombardier Transportation (Holdings) USA Inc Employees Political Fund
FEC ID: C00255356
Contact: John M Bigley
1501 Lebanon Church Rd.
Pittsburgh, PA 15236

Corporate Foundations and Giving Programs
Bombardier Corporate Social Responsibility
Contact: Janine Bombardier
P.O.Box 7707
Wichita, KS 67277

Public Affairs and Related Activities Personnel

At Headquarters

DESJARDINS, Mtre Daniel   Tel: (514) 861-9481
Senior Vice President, General Counsel and Secretary Fax: (514) 861-2420

At Washington Office

HUNTER, James
Director, Government Affairs
Registered Federal Lobbyist

SJOGREN, Kimba
PAC Contact

At Other Offices

ALARY, Pierre   Tel: (316) 946-2287

Senior Vice President and Chief Financial Officer   Fax: (316) 946-2220
One Learjet Way
Wichita, KS 67209-2924

BERTLING, Lutz   Tel: (202) 414-8989
President and Chief Operating Officer   Fax: (202) 955-8498
1808 Eye St. NW, Suite 400
Washington, DC 20006

BIGLEY, John M   Tel: (412) 655-5700
Treasurer, Bombardier Transportation PAC   Fax: (412) 655-5860
1501 Lebanon Church Rd.
Pittsburgh, PA 15236

BOMBARDIER, Janine   Tel: (316) 946-2000
President and Governor, J. Armand Bombardier Foundation Fax: (316) 946-2220
One Learjet Way
Wichita, KS 67209-2924

MACDONALD, John Paul   Tel: (514) 855-5000
Senior Vice President, Human Resources and Public Affairs Fax: (316) 946-2220
One Learjet Way
Wichita, KS 67209-2924

SLACK, David H.   Tel: (202) 414-8989
Vice President, Federal Government Affairs   Fax: (202) 955-8498
1808 Eye St. NW, Suite 400
Washington, DC 20006
david.slack@bombardier.com
Registered Federal Lobbyist

Bomgar Corporation

Bomgar Corporation specializes in appliance-based remote desktop access solutions for
support professionals.
www.bomgar.com
Annual Revenues: $20 million
Employees: 100
Industry/ies: Communications; Telecommunications/Internet/Cable

Founder and Chairman   Tel: (601) 519-0123
BOMGAR, Joel   Fax: (601) 510-9080

Chief Executive Officer   Tel: (601) 519-0123
DIRCKS, Matt   Fax: (601) 510-9080

Main Headquarters
Mailing: 578 Highland Colony Pkwy.   Tel: (601) 519-0123
              Paragon Centre, Suite 300   Fax: (601) 510-9080
              Ridgeland, MS 39157   TF: (877) 826-6427

Washington Office
Mailing: 11921 Freedom Dr., Two Fountain Sq.,   Tel: (703) 736-8361
              Suite 588   Fax: (866) 823-0280
              Reston, VA 20190

Public Affairs and Related Activities Personnel

At Headquarters

DUNER, Bruce   Tel: (601) 519-0123
Chief Financial Officer   Fax: (601) 510-9080

NORMAN, Patrick   Tel: (601) 519-0123
Co-Founder and Vice President, Online Marketing   Fax: (601) 510-9080

NORTON, Jim   Tel: (601) 519-0123
Executive Vice President, Sales and Marketing   Fax: (601) 510-9080
jim.norton@bomgar.com

SHULOF, Liz   Tel: (770) 407-1876
Senior Director, Public Relations   Fax: (601) 510-9080
LShulof@bomgar.com

WILLOUGHBY, Martin   Tel: (601) 519-0123
Chief Legal Counsel   Fax: (601) 510-9080

Bon Secours Richmond Health System

Provides health care. It is a body of people who share the healing ministry of the Sisters
of Bon Secours and the Catholic Church. It provides healthcare services to those in need,
especially the poor and dying, for the purpose of alleviating human suffering and affirming
human meaning in the midst of pain and loss.
www.richmond.bonsecours.com
Employees: 12,500
SIC: 5912; 6512; 6513; 6732
Industry/ies: Medicine/Health Care/Mental Health

Chairman of the Board   Tel: (804) 342-1500
SEITZ, Donald G.   Fax: (804) 225-1725

Chief Executive Officer, Bon Secours Richmond   Tel: (804) 285-2011
ARDABELL, Toni R.   Fax: (804) 225-1725

Main Headquarters
Mailing: P.O. Box 28538   Tel: (804) 342-1500
              Richmond, VA 23228   Fax: (804) 225-1725
                                                      TT: (877) 342-1500

Corporate Foundations and Giving Programs

The Bon Secours Richmond Healthcare Foundation
Contact: Cynthia C. Reynolds

5875 Bremo Rd.
Suite 710
Richmond, VA 23226

Tel: (804) 287-7700
Fax: (804) 287-7316

Public Affairs and Related Activities Personnel

At Other Offices

MACK, Sister Anne Marie
Senior Vice President, Sponsorship
5801 Bremo Rd.
Richmond, VA 23226

Tel: (804) 285-2011
Fax: (804) 225-1725

REYNOLDS, Cynthia C.
Chief Executive Officer, Bon Secours Richmond Health Care Foundation
7229 Forest Ave., Suite 200
Richmond, VA 23226

Tel: (804) 287-7700

The Bon Ton Stores, Inc.
A regional department store chain.
www.bonton.com
Annual Revenues: $2.83 billion
Employees: 25,200
Ticker: NASDAQ: BONT
SIC: 5311
Industry/ies: Apparel/Textiles Industry; Retail/Wholesale

Chairman Emeritus of the Board and Strategic Initiatives Officer
GRUMBACHER, Tim

Tel: (717) 757-7660
Fax: (717) 751-3108

President and Chief Executive Officer
BUFANO , Kathryn

Tel: (717) 757-7660
Fax: (717) 751-3108

Main Headquarters
Mailing: 2801 E. Market St.
York, PA 17402

Tel: (717) 757-7660
Fax: (717) 751-3108
TF: (800) 233-7626

Corporate Foundations and Giving Programs

Bon Ton Stores, Inc. Contributions Program
2801 E. Market St.
York, PA 17402

Tel: (717) 757-7660
Fax: (717) 751-3108

Public Affairs and Related Activities Personnel

At Headquarters

CLOUSER, Dennis R.
Executive Vice President, Information Systems & Administration

Tel: (717) 757-7660
Fax: (717) 751-3108

KERR, Mary
Vice President, Investor and Public Relations
mkerr@bonton.com

Tel: (717) 751-3071
Fax: (717) 751-3108

PLOWMAN, Keith E.
Executive Vice President, Chief Financial Officer and Principal Accounting Officer
kplowman@bonton.com

Tel: (717) 757-7660
Fax: (717) 751-3108

Bond & Associates
Consultants on Trade, Higher Education and Overseas Development
bondco.org
Legislative Issues: FOR

Main Headquarters
Mailing: 2111 Wilson Blvd.
Suite 700
Arlington, VA 22201

Tel: (703) 351-5058

Public Affairs and Related Activities Personnel

At Headquarters

BOND, James D.
Registered Federal Lobbyist

Tel: (703) 351-5058

WEARS, T.L. Alexis L. Alexis
alex@collinsandcompany.com

Tel: (703) 351-5058

Booz Allen Hamilton
A global management and technology consulting firm.
www.boozallen.com
Annual Revenues: $5.41 billion
Employees: 22,600
Ticker: NYSE: BAH
SIC: 8742
Industry/ies: Business; Computer/Technology; Consultants
Legislative Issues: HCR

Chairman of the Board
SHRADER, Dr. Ralph W.

Tel: (703) 902-5000
Fax: (703) 902-3333

President and Chief Executive Officer
ROZANSKI, Horacio D.

Tel: (703) 902-5000
Fax: (703) 902-3333

Main Headquarters
Mailing: 8283 Greensboro Dr.

Tel: (703) 902-5000

McLean, VA 22102

Fax: (703) 902-3333

Corporate Foundations and Giving Programs

Booz Allen Hamilton Contributions Program
8283 Greensboro Dr.
McLean, VA 22102-3838

Tel: (703) 902-5000
Fax: (703) 902-3333

Public Affairs and Related Activities Personnel

At Headquarters

BOSTEL, Sylvia Von
Corporate Director, Government Affairs

Tel: (703) 902-5000
Fax: (703) 902-3333

BUTT, JOSEPH
Consultant
josephbutt@gmail.com

Tel: (703) 902-5000
Fax: (703) 902-3333

COOK, Kevin
Executive Vice President, Chief Financial Officer and Treasurer

Tel: (703) 902-5000
Fax: (703) 902-3333

FISHER, James
Senior Manager, Media Relations
fisher_james_w@bah.com

Tel: (703) 377-7595
Fax: (703) 902-3333

GOCHEV, Stefan
Consultant
Go4gochev@gmail.com

Tel: (703) 902-5000
Fax: (703) 902-3333

LABEN, Nancy
Executive Vice President and General Counsel

Tel: (703) 902-5000
Fax: (703) 902-3333

MAHAFFEE, Joseph W.
Executive Vice President and Chief Administrative Officer

Tel: (703) 902-5000
Fax: (703) 902-3333

MCCONNELL, John M. "Mike"
Senior Executive Advisor

Tel: (703) 902-5000
Fax: (703) 902-3333

VEITH, Craig G.
Vice President, External Affairs

Tel: (703) 902-5000
Fax: (703) 902-3333

WEST, Kimberly
Senior Associate, Media Relations
west_kimberly@bah.com

Tel: (703) 377-1403
Fax: (703) 902-3333

Borders Group, Inc.
A retailer of books, music, video, and other products.
www.bordersreorganization.com
Employees: 16,000
Ticker: OTCMKTS: BGPIQ
SIC: 5940
Industry/ies: Retail/Wholesale

Chairman of the Board and Chief Executive Officer
LEBOW, Bennett

Tel: (734) 477-1100
Fax: (734) 477-1955

Main Headquarters
Mailing: 100 Phoenix Dr.
Ann Arbor, MI 48108

Tel: (734) 477-1100
Fax: (734) 477-1955

Corporate Foundations and Giving Programs

Borders Group Foundation
100 Phoenix Dr.
Ann Arbor, MI 48108

Tel: (734) 477-1100
Fax: (734) 477-1285

BorgWarner Inc.
A manufacturer of auto components and systems.
www.borgwarner.com
Annual Revenues: $8.31 billion
Employees: 30,000
Ticker: NYSE: BWA
SIC: 3714
NAICS: 336399
Industry/ies: Automotive Industry; Transportation
Legislative Issues: AUT; TRD

Non-Executive Chairman
MICHAS, Alexis P.

Tel: (248) 754-9200
Fax: (248) 754-9397

President and Chief Executive Officer
VERRIER, James R.

Tel: (248) 754-9200
Fax: (248) 754-9397

Main Headquarters
Mailing: 3800 Automation Ave.
Auburn Hills, MI 48326

Tel: (248) 754-9200
Fax: (248) 754-9397

Corporate Foundations and Giving Programs

BorgWarner Inc. Contributions Program
3850 Hamlin Rd.
Auburn Hills, MI 48326

Tel: (248) 754-9200

Public Affairs and Related Activities Personnel

At Headquarters

GALLETT, Scott D.
Vice President, Marketing, Public Relations, Communications and Government Affairs
sgallett@borgwarner.com

Tel: (248) 754-9200
Fax: (248) 754-9397

GASPAROVIC, John J.

Tel: (248) 754-9200

Vice President, General Counsel and Secretary
jgasparovic@borgwarner.com | Fax: | (248) 754-9397

HORISZNY , Laurene H. | Tel: | (248) 754-9200
Vice President and Chief Compliance Officer | Fax: | (248) 754-9397

HUNDZINSKI, Ronald T. | Tel: | (248) 754-9200
Vice President and Chief Financial Officer | Fax: | (248) 754-9397

JENETT, Kim R. | Tel: | (248) 754-9200
Vice President,Human Resources | Fax: | (248) 754-9397

MCGILL, Thomas J. | Tel: | (248) 754-9200
Vice President and Treasurer | Fax: | (248) 754-9397

NIELSEN, Erika | Tel: | (248) 754-0422
Director, Marketing and Public Relations | Fax: | (248) 754-9397
enielsen@borgwarner.com

VANCE , Chris H. | Tel: | (248) 754-9200
Vice President, Business Development | Fax: | (248) 754-9397

Borrego Solar

Borrego Solar Systems, Inc. is a developer, designer and installer of commercial, government and residential grid-connected solar electric systems.
www.borregosolar.com
Industry/ies: Energy/Electricity; Environment And Conservation; Natural Resources; Utilities

Chief Executive Officer | Tel: | (888) 898-6273
HALL, Mike | Fax: | (888) 843-6778

Main Headquarters
Mailing: 1810 Gillespie Way | Tel: | (619) 792-1198
Suite 108 | Fax: | (888) 843-6778
El Cajon, CA 92020 | TF: | (888) 898-6273

Public Affairs and Related Activities Personnel

At Other Offices

BERWICK, Dan | Tel: | (888) 898-6273
Vice President, Business Development | Fax: | (888) 843-6778
360 22nd St., Suite 600
Oakland, CA 94612

BUSH, Bill | Tel: | (888) 898-6273
Chief Financial Officer | Fax: | (888) 843-6778
360 22nd St., Suite 600
Oakland, CA 94612

HALL, Philip | Tel: | (888) 898-6273
Director, Marketing | Fax: | (888) 843-6778
360 22nd St., Suite 600
Oakland, CA 94612
phall@borregosolar.com

HALL, Andrew | Tel: | (888) 898-6273
General Counsel | Fax: | (888) 843-6778
360 22nd St., Suite 600
Oakland, CA 94612

HALL, Aaron | Tel: | (888) 898-6273
President | Fax: | (888) 843-6778
360 22nd St., Suite 600
Oakland, CA 94612

MEYERS, David | Tel: | (888) 898-6273
Executive Vice President, Marketing and Sales | Fax: | (888) 843-6778
360 22nd St., Suite 600
Oakland, CA 94612

NEAGLE, Brendan | Tel: | (888) 898-6273
Chief Operations Officer | Fax: | (888) 843-6778
360 22nd St., Suite 600
Oakland, CA 94612

Bosch Rexroth Corporation

U.S. subsidiary of Bosch Rexroth AG, headquartered in Lohr, Germany. Manufactures electric drives, hydraulic systems, bushings and shafts and pneumatic valves and actuators.
www.boschrexroth-us.com
SIC: 5085; 3492; 3594; 5099
NAICS: 42183; 332912; 333996; 42199
Industry/ies: Automotive Industry; Engineering/Mathematics; Transportation

President and Chief Executive Officer | Tel: | (847) 645-3600
COOKE, Paul | Fax: | (847) 645-6201

Main Headquarters
Mailing: 14001 S. Lakes Dr. | Tel: | (847) 645-3600
Charlotte, NC 28273 | Fax: | (847) 645-6201
| TF: | (800) 739-7684

Public Affairs and Related Activities Personnel

At Headquarters

ROBERTS, Steve | Tel: | (847) 645-3600
Executive Vice President and Chief Financial Officer | Fax: | (847) 645-6201

The BOSE Corporation

A manufacturer of consumer electronics and audio equipment.

www.bose.com
Employees: 8,000
SIC: 3556; 3651
NAICS: 333294
Industry/ies: Arts, The; Electricity & Electronics; Electronics; Energy/Electricity; Performing Arts/Music
Legislative Issues: HCR; TRD

Main Headquarters
Mailing: 100 The Mountain Rd. | Tel: | (508) 879-7330
Framingham, MA 01701 | Fax: | (508) 766-7543
| TF: | (800) 999-2673

Public Affairs and Related Activities Personnel

At Headquarters

BERTHIAUME, Joanne | Tel: | (508) 879-7330
Manager, Public Relations | Fax: | (508) 766-7543
Mail Stop 2C3
joanne_berthiaume@bose.com

GRADY, Daniel | Tel: | (508) 879-7330
Consultant | Fax: | (508) 766-7543

Boston Beer Company

A brewer of handcrafted, full-flavored beers.
www.bostonbeer.com
Annual Revenues: $918.66 million
Employees: 1,325
Ticker: NYSE: SAM
SIC: 2082
Industry/ies: Food And Beverage Industry
Legislative Issues: BUD; TAX

Chairman of the Board | Tel: | (617) 368-5000
KOCH, C. James | Fax: | (617) 368-5500

President and Chief Executive Officer | Tel: | (617) 368-5000
ROPER, Martin F. | Fax: | (617) 368-5500

Main Headquarters
Mailing: One Design Center Pl. | Tel: | (617) 368-5000
Suite 850 | Fax: | (617) 368-5500
Boston, MA 02210 | TF: | (800) 372-1131

Corporate Foundations and Giving Programs

Samuel Adams Brewing the American Dream
One Design Center
Suite 850 | Tel: | (617) 368-5000
Boston, MA 02210 | Fax: | (617) 368-5500

Public Affairs and Related Activities Personnel

At Headquarters

GEIST, John C. | Tel: | (617) 368-5000
Vice President, Sales | Fax: | (617) 368-5500

GREIN, Jr., Esq., Frederick H. | Tel: | (617) 345-6117
General Counsel | Fax: | (617) 368-5500

LANCE, Thomas W. | Tel: | (617) 368-5000
Vice President, Operations | Fax: | (617) 368-5500

LARSON, Jennifer | Tel: | (617) 368-5152
Contact, Investor Relations | Fax: | (617) 368-5500

LIM, Ai-Li | Tel: | (617) 368-5000
Vice President, Human Resources | Fax: | (617) 368-5500

PAAR, Jessica | Tel: | (617) 368-5060
Director, Public Relations | Fax: | (617) 368-5500

SULLIVAN, Michelle | Tel: | (617) 368-5165
Head, Marketing for Twisted Tea & Twisted Lemonade | Fax: | (617) 368-5500
michelle.sullivan@bostonbeer.com

URICH, William F. | Tel: | (617) 368-5000
Chief Financial Officer and Treasurer | Fax: | (617) 368-5500

WADE, Kathleen H. | Tel: | (617) 368-5000
Vice President, Legal and Corporate Secretary | Fax: | (617) 368-5500

Boston Scientific Corporation

A manufacturer and distributor of less-invasive medical devices. Guidant Corporation merged with Boston Scientific in April 2006 and became the Cardiac Rhythm Management division of Boston Scientific Corporation.
www.bostonscientific.com
Annual Revenues: $7.60 billion
Employees: 25,000
Ticker: NYSE: BSX
SIC: 3841; 2835; 2869; 3599; 3679
NAICS: 325199; 325412; 333999; 334419; 339112
Industry/ies: Medicine/Health Care/Mental Health; Pharmaceutical Industry
Legislative Issues: BUD; CPT; HCR; TAX; TRA; TRD; VET

Chairman of the Board | Tel: | (508) 683-4000
NICHOLAS, Peter M. | Fax: | (508) 650-8910

President and Chief Executive Officer | Tel: | (508) 683-4000

MAHONEY, Michael F.

Main Headquarters
Mailing: 300 Boston Scientific Way   Tel: (508) 683-4000
             Marlborough, MA 01752-1234   TF: (800) 876-9960

Washington Office
Mailing: 1455 Pennsylvania Ave. NW   Tel: (202) 637-8020
             Suite 925   Fax: (202) 637-8028
             Washington, DC 20004

Political Action Committees
Boston Scientific Corporation PAC (BSC PAC)
FEC ID: C00357863
Contact: Robert Castagna
One Boston Scientific Pl.
Natick, MA 01760

   Contributions to Candidates: $285,500 (2015-2016)
   Democrats: $68,500; Republicans: $217,000

         Principal Recipients

              HOUSE
              BOUSTANY, CHARLES W. DR. JR. (REP-LA)
              MCCARTHY, KEVIN (REP-CA)

Corporate Foundations and Giving Programs

Boston Scientific Foundation
One Scientific Pl.   Tel: (508) 650-8554
Mailstop B2   Fax: (508) 650-8932
Natick, MA 01760

Public Affairs and Related Activities Personnel

At Headquarters

BRENNAN, Daniel J.   Tel: (508) 683-4000
Executive Vice President and Chief Financial Officer

CARRUTHERS, Wendy   Tel: (508) 683-4000
Senior Vice President, Human Resources

CASTAGNA, Robert   Tel: (508) 683-4000
Vice President and PAC Treasurer

KAIGLER, Denise   Tel: (508) 683-4000
Vice President, Corporate Affairs and External Relations

PRATT, Timothy A.   Tel: (508) 683-4000
Executive Vice President, Chief Administrative Officer,
General Counsel and Secretary

At Washington Office

BARRY, Paul E.   Tel: (202) 637-8023
Vice President, State and International Government Affairs   Fax: (202) 637-8028
Registered Federal Lobbyist

BECKER, Brenda L.   Tel: (202) 637-8024
Senior Vice President, Global Government Affairs   Fax: (202) 637-8028
Registered Federal Lobbyist

FORDJOUR, Isaac A.   Tel: (202) 637-8020
Federal Lobbyist   Fax: (202) 637-8028
Registered Federal Lobbyist

HEDSTROM, MPH, Kristen E.   Tel: (202) 637-8024
Director, Healthcare Policy   Fax: (202) 637-8028

LAPIERRE, Steven N.   Tel: (202) 637-8024
Vice President, Government Affairs   Fax: (202) 637-8028
lapierrs@bsci.com
Registered Federal Lobbyist

TIMMERMAN, Christopher   Tel: (202) 637-8020
Federal Lobbyist   Fax: (202) 637-8028
Registered Federal Lobbyist

Bourns, Inc.

A manufacturer of electronic components and scientific instruments.
www.bourns.com
Employees: 4,000
Industry/ies: Electricity & Electronics; Electronics; Energy/Electricity; Science;
Scientific Research

Chairman of the Board and Chief Executive Officer   Tel: (951) 781-5690
BOURNS, Gordon L.   Fax: (951) 781-5273

Main Headquarters
Mailing: 1200 Columbia Ave.   Tel: (951) 781-5690
             Riverside, CA 92507-2129   Fax: (951) 781-5273
                                             TF: (877) 426-8767

Corporate Foundations and Giving Programs

Bourns Foundation
1200 Columbia Ave.   Tel: (951) 781-5690
Riverside, CA 92507   Fax: (951) 781-5273

Public Affairs and Related Activities Personnel

At Headquarters

BRIDGES, Mike   Tel: (951) 781-5397
Manager, Marketing Services and Media Contact   Fax: (909) 781-5122

mike.birdges@bourns.com

MCKENNA, William P.   Tel: (951) 781-5690
Chief Financial Officer and Treasurer   Fax: (951) 781-5273

Boyd Gaming Corporation

A casino entertainment company.
www.boydgaming.com
Annual Revenues: $2.20 billion
Employees: 18,243
Ticker: NYSE: BYD
SIC: 7011
Industry/ies: Sports/Leisure/Entertainment
Legislative Issues: GAM; IND; LBR; TAX

Executive Chairman   Tel: (702) 792-7200
BOYD, William S.   Fax: (702) 792-7266

President and Chief Executive Officer   Tel: (702) 792-7200
SMITH, Keith E.   Fax: (702) 792-7313
keithsmith@boydgaming.com

Main Headquarters
Mailing: 3883 Howard Hughes Pkwy.   Tel: (702) 792-7200
             Ninth Floor   Fax: (702) 792-7313
             Las Vegas, NV 89169

Political Action Committees
Boyd Gaming PAC
FEC ID: C00142315
Contact: William J. Noonan
6465 S Rainbow Blvd.
Las Vegas, NV 89118

   Contributions to Candidates: $97,000 (2015-2016)
   Democrats: $25,500; Republicans: $71,500

         Principal Recipients

              HOUSE
              LOBIONDO, FRANK A. (REP-NJ)

Corporate Foundations and Giving Programs

Boyd Gaming Corporation Contributions Program
3883 Howard Hughes Pkwy.
Ninth Floor
Las Vegas, NV 89169

Public Affairs and Related Activities Personnel

At Headquarters

BOUGHNER, Robert L.   Tel: (702) 792-7200
Executive Vice President and Chief Business Development   Fax: (702) 792-7313
Officer

FREEDMAN , Cathy   Tel: (702) 792-7200
Executive Assistant   Fax: (702) 792-7313

HIRSBERG, Josh   Tel: (702) 792-7234
Senior Vice President, Chief Financial Officer and Treasurer   Fax: (702) 792-7313
joshhirsberg@boydgaming.com

JAMES, CNS, MS, RN, Michelle   Tel: (702) 792-7200
Executive Secretary   Fax: (702) 792-7313

LARSON, Brian   Tel: (702) 792-7200
Executive Vice President, General Counsel and Secretary   Fax: (702) 792-7313
brianlarson@boydgaming.com

MCPHERSON, Thomas   Tel: (702) 792-7200
Federal Lobbyist   Fax: (702) 792-7266
tommcpherson@boydgaming.com
Registered Federal Lobbyist

NOONAN, William J.   Tel: (702) 792-7200
PAC Treasurer   Fax: (702) 792-7313

SOULTZ, Ryan   Tel: (702) 792-7200
Director, Governmental Affairs   Fax: (702) 792-7266
Registered Federal Lobbyist

SULLIVAN, Kevin F.   Tel: (702) 792-7200
Senior Vice President, Development   Fax: (702) 792-7313
Registered Federal Lobbyist

BP America, Inc.

A wholly-owned subsidiary of BP P.L.C. Its core businesses are petroleum exploration and
production, refining and marketing, chemicals, and solar.
www.bp.com
Annual Revenues: $316.05 billion
Employees: 79,200
Ticker: NYSE: BP
Industry/ies: Energy/Electricity
Legislative Issues: ENG; ENV; FUE; HOU; MAR; TAX

Chairman of the Board   Tel: (800) 333-3991
SVANBERG, Carl-Henric

Group Chief Executive   Tel: (800) 333-3991
DUDLEY, Robert
robert.dudley@bp.com

Main Headquarters
Mailing: 501 Westlake Park Blvd.　　Tel: (281) 366-2000
　　　　　Houston, TX 77079-2696

Washington Office
Mailing: 1101 New York Ave. NW　　Tel: (202) 785-4888
　　　　　Suite 700　　　　　　　　Fax: (202) 457-6597
　　　　　Washington, DC 20005

Corporate Foundations and Giving Programs

BP Foundation, Inc.
4101 Winfield Rd.　　　　　　　　　Tel: (630) 821-3174
Warrenville, IL 60555

Public Affairs and Related Activities Personnel

At Headquarters

BONDY, Rupert　　　　　　　　　　Tel: (800) 333-3991
Group General Counsel

GILVARY, Dr. Brian　　　　　　　　Tel: (800) 333-3991
Group Chief Financial Officer

HOPWOOD, Andy　　　　　　　　　Tel: (281) 366-2000
Chief Operating Officer, Strategy and Regions

SCHUSTER, Helmut　　　　　　　　Tel: (800) 333-3991
Executive Vice President and Director, Group Human Resources
helmut.schuster@bp.com

At Washington Office

BRIEN, Michael P.　　　　　　　　Tel: (202) 457-6573
Senior Director, Regulatory Affairs　Fax: (202) 457-6597
brienmp@bp.com

CUNNEFF, Suzanne　　　　　　　　Tel: (202) 785-4888
Registered Federal Lobbyist　　　　Fax: (202) 457-6597

DEMPSEY, Ray　　　　　　　　　　Tel: (202) 457-6585
Vice President & Head, External Affairs　Fax: (202) 457-6597

GUIDO, Rob　　　　　　　　　　　Tel: (202) 785-4888
Federal Lobbyist　　　　　　　　　Fax: (202) 457-6597
Registered Federal Lobbyist

HYLAND, Karen　　　　　　　　　　Tel: (202) 457-6585
Director, Public Affairs　　　　　　Fax: (202) 457-6597
karen.hyland@bp.com

LYONS, Troy M.　　　　　　　　　　Tel: (202) 457-6585
Associate Director, US Government Affairs　Fax: (202) 457-6597

MATTHEWS, Jason　　　　　　　　　Tel: (202) 457-6585
Federal Lobbyist　　　　　　　　　Fax: (202) 457-6597
Registered Federal Lobbyist

NAGEL, David　　　　　　　　　　　Tel: (202) 785-4888
Federal Lobbyist　　　　　　　　　Fax: (202) 457-6597

ROGERS, Susan　　　　　　　　　　Tel: (202) 785-4888
Director, Tax Policy　　　　　　　　Fax: (202) 457-6597

SAUNDERS, Greg　　　　　　　　　Tel: (202) 785-4888
Federal Lobbyist　　　　　　　　　Fax: (202) 457-6597
Registered Federal Lobbyist

STREETT, Mary M.　　　　　　　　　Tel: (202) 785-4888
Vice President, U.S. Government Affairs　Fax: (202) 457-6597

SWINK, Suzanne　　　　　　　　　　Tel: (202) 457-6585
Federal Lobbyist　　　　　　　　　Fax: (202) 457-6597
Registered Federal Lobbyist

VAN HOOGSTRATEN, David　　　　　Tel: (202) 457-6585
Federal Lobbyist　　　　　　　　　Fax: (202) 457-6597
Registered Federal Lobbyist

WALKER, Ryan　　　　　　　　　　　Tel: (202) 785-4888
Registered Federal Lobbyist　　　　Fax: (202) 457-6597

BP Exploration - Alaska Inc.

See listing on page 140 under BP America, Inc.

BPL Global, Ltd.

A smart grid technology company.
www.bplglobal.net
Annual Revenues: $1.40 million
Industry/ies: Energy/Electricity

Chairman　　　　　　　　　　　Tel: (724) 933-7700
HARVEY, Francis J.　　　　　　　　Fax: (724) 933-7715

Chief Executive Officer　　　　　Tel: (724) 933-7700
LONDA, Peter　　　　　　　　　　　Fax: (724) 933-7715

Main Headquarters
Mailing: Foster Plaza 5　　　　　　Tel: (724) 933-7700
　　　　　Suite 300 Dr.
　　　　　Pittsburgh, PA 15220

Corporate Foundations and Giving Programs

BPL Global, Ltd. Contributions Program

---

500 Cranberry Woods Dr.　　　　　Tel: (724) 933-7700
Suite 170
Cranberry, PA 16066

Brady Corporation

Formally known as W.H. Brady Co., Manufactures identification products and specialty coated material products.
www.bradycorp.com
Annual Revenues: $1.13 billion
Employees: 6,560
Ticker: NYSE: BRC
SIC: 3953; 3993; 5734
NAICS: 339943; 33995; 44312
Industry/ies: Machinery/Equipment

President, Chief Executive Officer and Director　Tel: (414) 358-6600
NAUMAN , J. Michael　　　　　　　Fax: (800) 292-2289

Main Headquarters
Mailing: P.O. Box 571　　　　　　Tel: (414) 358-6600
　　　　　6555 W. Good Hope Rd.　Fax: (800) 292-2289
　　　　　Milwaukee, WI 53201-0571

Corporate Foundations and Giving Programs

The Brady Corporation Foundation
P.O. Box 571　　　　　　　　　　Tel: (414) 358-6600
Milwaukee, WI 53201

Public Affairs and Related Activities Personnel

At Headquarters

BOLOGINI , Louis　　　　　　　　　Tel: (414) 358-6600
Senior Vice President, General Counsel and Secretary　Fax: (800) 292-2289

CURRAN , Bentley　　　　　　　　　Tel: (414) 358-6600
Chief Information Officer and Vice President, Digital Business　Fax: (800) 292-2289

FELMER, Thomas J.　　　　　　　　Tel: (414) 358-6600
President　　　　　　　　　　　　Fax: (800) 292-2289

JOHNSON, Kathy　　　　　　　　　Tel: (414) 358-6600
Vice President, Finance and Chief Accounting Officer　Fax: (800) 292-2289

NELLIGAN, Helena　　　　　　　　　Tel: (414) 358-6600
Senior Vice President, Human Resources　Fax: (800) 292-2289

PEARCE, Aaron　　　　　　　　　　Tel: (414) 438-6895
Senior Vice President and Chief Financial Officer　Fax: (800) 292-2289
Aaron_Pearce@Bradycorp.com

Brain Matters, Inc.

See listing on page 180 under Cerescan

Brainscope Company Inc.

Privately held neurotechnology company focused initially on Traumatic Brain Injury.
www.brainscope.com
Annual Revenues: $1.5 million
Employees: 100
Industry/ies: Electricity & Electronics; Electronics; Energy/Electricity; Medicine/Health Care/Mental Health

Chairman of the Board　　　　　Tel: (240) 752-7680
MOORE, Daniel J.

President and Chief Executive Officer　Tel: (240) 752-7680
SINGER, Michael

Main Headquarters
Mailing: 4350 East-West Hwy.　　Tel: (240) 752-7680
　　　　　Suite 1050
　　　　　Bethesda, MD 20814

Public Affairs and Related Activities Personnel

At Headquarters

SILVER, Laurie　　　　　　　　　　Tel: (240) 752-7680
Chief Financial Officer

Bravo Health Inc.

A HealthSpring Company, is a subsidiary of HealthSpring and health insurer.
www.bravohealth.com
Industry/ies: Medicine/Health Care/Mental Health

Main Headquarters
Mailing: 3601 O'Donnell St.　　　Tel: (443) 529-1339
　　　　　Baltimore, MD 21224　　TF: (800) 235-9188

Washington Office
Mailing: 1250 I St. NW　　　　　Tel: (202) 262-2411
　　　　　Washington, DC 20005

Public Affairs and Related Activities Personnel

At Washington Office

CIORLETTI, Julia　　　　　　　　　Tel: (202) 262-2411
Senior Vice President, Government Relations

---

julia.cioretti@bravohealth.com

The Brewer Group (formerly Powers Brewer)

A law firm.
www.thebrewergroup.com
Legislative Issues: TRA

Chief Executive Officer
BREWER, Amb Jack

Main Headquarters
Mailing: 80 S. 8th St.
             Suite 900
             Minneapolis, MN 55402

Public Affairs and Related Activities Personnel

At Headquarters

BERMAN, Danielle
Managing Director

COLEMAN, Al
General Counsel

MEEHAN, Jesse
President

POWERS, Donald L.
Don@powersbrewer.com
Registered Federal Lobbyist

At Other Offices

BREWER, James D.
17421 W. Muirfield Dr.
Baton Rouge, LA 70810
Registered Federal Lobbyist

BrickStreet Mutual Insurance Company

Workers compensation insurance.
www.brickstreet.com
Industry/ies: Employees & Employment; Insurance Industry
Legislative Issues: TAX

| **Chair of the Board** | Tel: | (304) 941-1000 |
| FLAHERTY, Thomas V | Fax: | (304) 941-1151 |

| **President and Chief Executive Officer** | Tel: | (304) 941-1000 |
| BURTON, Gregory A. | Fax: | (304) 941-1151 |

Main Headquarters

Mailing: 400 Quarrier St.	Tel:	(304) 941-1000
Charleston, WV 25301	Fax:	(304) 941-1151
	TF:	(866) 452-7425

Corporate Foundations and Giving Programs

BrickStreet Insurance Corporate Giving		
400 Quarrier St.	Tel:	(304) 941-1000
Charleston, WV 25301	Fax:	(304) 941-1151

Public Affairs and Related Activities Personnel

At Headquarters

| BECKER, W Marston (Marty) | Tel: | (304) 941-1000 |
| *Chair, Corporate Governance and Nominating* | Fax: | (304) 941-1151 |

| HOWAT, J. Christopher | Tel: | (304) 941-1000 |
| *Senior Vice President, Treasurer and Chief Financial Officer* | Fax: | (304) 941-1151 |

| OBROKTA, T. J. | Tel: | (304) 941-1000 |
| *President and Corporate Secretary* | Fax: | (304) 941-1151 |

| RADER, David L | Tel: | (304) 941-1000 |
| *Chair, Finance and Investment Committee* | Fax: | (304) 941-1151 |

Bridgeborn, LLC

A systems design, engineering and integration company providing IT services and solutions to domestic and international customers within the federal government and commercial markets. Designed and developed by Bridgeborn, Bridgeworks™ is a software platform for the creation of interactive, rich media and data driven visualization solutions.
www.bridgeborn.com
Annual Revenues: $8 million
Industry/ies: Aerospace/Aviation; Computer/Technology; Defense/Homeland Security; Government-Related; Transportation

| **President and Chief Executive Officer** | Tel: | (757) 437-5000 |
| AMBROSINO, Timothy | Fax: | (757) 531-7460 |

Main Headquarters

| *Mailing:* 596 Lynnhaven Pkwy. | Tel: | (757) 437-5000 |
| Virginia Beach, VA 23452 | Fax: | (757) 531-7460 |

Washington Office

Mailing: 2200 Wilson Blvd.	Tel:	(703) 993-0004
Suite 850		
Arlington, VA 22201		

Public Affairs and Related Activities Personnel

At Headquarters

| BARBER, Raymond | Tel: | (757) 437-5000 |
| *Chief Financial Officer* | Fax: | (757) 531-7460 |

| KNUTH, Bob | Tel: | (757) 437-5000 |
| *Chief Operating Officer* | Fax: | (757) 531-7460 |

| SARRO, Matt | Tel: | (757) 437-5000 |
| *Executive Vice President* | Fax: | (757) 531-7460 |

At Washington Office

MURPHY, Katharine M.	Tel:	(703) 993-0004
Executive Vice President, Federal Sector		
kmurphy@bridgeborn.com		

Bridgestone/Firestone, Inc.

A tire and rubber company, Bridgestone Americas Holdings, Inc., is the U.S. subsidiary of Bridgestone Corporation, which is headquartered in Tokyo, Japan.
www.bridgestone-firestone.com
Employees: 45,000
SIC: 3011
NAICS: 326211
Industry/ies: Automotive Industry; Rubber Industry; Transportation
Legislative Issues: AUT; FOR; TAX; TRA; TRD

| **Executive Chairman of the Board** | Tel: | (615) 937-1000 |
| MORIMOTO, Yoshiyuki | Fax: | (615) 937-3621 |

| **President and Chief Executive Officer** | Tel: | (615) 937-1000 |
| GARFIELD , Gary | Fax: | (615) 937-3621 |

Main Headquarters

Mailing: 535 Marriott Dr.	Tel:	(615) 937-1000
P.O Box 140990	Fax:	(615) 937-3621
Nashville, TN 37214	TF:	(877) 201-2373

Washington Office

Mailing: 607 14th St. NW	Tel:	(202) 354-8220
Suite 500	Fax:	(202) 354-8201
Washington, DC 20005		

Political Action Committees

Bridgestone America's Inc. PAC
FEC ID: C00371948
Contact: Charles Johnson

607 14th St. NW	Tel:	(202) 354-8220
Suite 500	Fax:	(202) 354-8201
Washington, DC 20005		

    Contributions to Candidates: $23,000 (2015-2016)
    Democrats: $7,000; Republicans: $16,000

Corporate Foundations and Giving Programs

Bridgestone Americas Trust Fund
535 Marriott Dr.
P.O. Box 140990
Nashville, TN 37214-0990

Public Affairs and Related Activities Personnel

At Headquarters

| FUKUDA, Tom | Tel: | (615) 937-1000 |
| *Executive Vice President, Business Strategy and Enterprise Support* | Fax: | (615) 937-3621 |

| KARBOWIAK, Christine | Tel: | (615) 937-1000 |
| *Chief Administrative Officer, Chief Risk Officer and Chief Human Resources Officer* | Fax: | (615) 937-3621 |

| KARBOWIAK, Christine | Tel: | (615) 937-1000 |
| *Chief Administrative Officer and Chief Risk Officer* | Fax: | (615) 937-3621 |

| KNAPP, Gordon | Tel: | (615) 937-1000 |
| *Chief Operating Officer* | Fax: | (615) 937-3621 |

| STEINMETZ, Jan | Tel: | (615) 937-1000 |
| *Chief Human Resources Officer* | Fax: | (615) 937-3621 |

| SUZUKI, Mick | Tel: | (615) 937-1000 |
| *Executive Vice President, Business Strategy and Enterprise Support* | Fax: | (615) 937-3621 |

| THOMPSON, Bill | Tel: | (615) 937-1000 |
| *Chief Financial Officer* | Fax: | (615) 937-3621 |

At Washington Office

AKEY, Steven J.	Tel:	(202) 354-8220
Vice President, Government Affairs	Fax:	(202) 354-8201
akeysteven@bfusa.com		
Registered Federal Lobbyist		

GULLOTT, Christian	Tel:	(202) 354-8220
Director, State and Federal Government Affairs	Fax:	(202) 354-8201
Registered Federal Lobbyist		

| JOHNSON, Charles | Tel: | (202) 354-8220 |
| *PAC Treasurer* | Fax: | (202) 354-8201 |

Briggs & Stratton

A manufacturer of gasoline engines and automotive locking devices.
www.briggsandstratton.com

Annual Revenues: $1.85 billion
Employees: 5,695
Ticker: NYSE: BGG
SIC: 3510; 3519
NAICS: 336399
Industry/ies: Machinery/Equipment

Chairman of the Board, President and Chief Executive Officer Tel: (414) 259-5333
TESKE, Todd J.

Main Headquarters
Mailing: P.O. Box 702 Tel: (414) 259-5333
Milwaukee, WI 53201-0702 TF: (800) 444-7774

Corporate Foundations and Giving Programs

Briggs & Stratton Corporation Foundation
Contact: Robert F. Heath
P.O. Box 702 Tel: (414) 259-5333
Milwaukee, WI 53201 Fax: (414) 479-1245

Public Affairs and Related Activities Personnel

At Headquarters

CARPENTER, Randall R. Tel: (414) 259-5333
Vice President, Marketing

COAD, Jeff Tel: (414) 259-5333
Vice President, Engine Products

HEATH, Robert F. Tel: (414) 259-5333
Vice President, General Counsel and Secretary

MAHLOCH, Jeffrey G. Tel: (414) 259-5333
Vice President, Human Resources

REITMAN, William H. Tel: (414) 259-5333
*Senior Vice President - Managing Director Europe and
Global Service*

RODGERS, David J. Tel: (414) 259-5333
Senior Vice President and Chief Financial Officer

TIMM, Laura Tel: (414) 259-5333
Vice President Corporate Communications
timm.laura@basco.com

At Other Offices

BALADY, Shaunna L Tel: (414) 259-5333
Vice President, Corporate Development Fax: (414) 259-5773
12301 W. Wirth St.
Wauwatosa, WI 53222

BUONO, Kathryn M Tel: (414) 259-5333
Vice President, General Counsel and Secretary Fax: (414) 259-5773
12301 W. Wirth St.
Wauwatosa, WI 53222

GOLVACH, Andrea L Tel: (414) 259-5333
Vice President and Treasurer Fax: (414) 259-5773
12301 W. Wirth St.
Wauwatosa, WI 53222

SCHWERTFEGER, Mark A Tel: (414) 259-5333
Vice President and Controller Fax: (414) 259-5773
12301 W. Wirth St.
Wauwatosa, WI 53222

Bright House Networks

Advance communications.
Industry/ies: Communications; Telecommunications/Internet/Cable

Main Headquarters
Mailing: 5823 Widewaters Pkwy Tel: (315) 463-7675
East Syracuse, NY 13067

Political Action Committees
Bright House Networks LLC Political Action Committee (BHN PAC)
FEC ID: C00402875
Contact: Meredith Lesher
701 Eighth St. NW
Suite 500
Washington, DC 20001

Contributions to Candidates: $27,300 (2015-2016)
Democrats: $14,000; Republicans: $13,300

Public Affairs and Related Activities Personnel

At Headquarters

LESHER, Meredith Tel: (315) 463-7675
PAC Contact

Bright Source Energy

Utility scale solar power development.
www.brightsourceenergy.com
Ticker: NASDAQ (GS): BRSE
Industry/ies: Energy/Electricity; Utilities
Legislative Issues: ENG

Chairman of the Board and Chief Executive Officer Tel: (510) 550-8161
DAVID RAMM, H. Fax: (510) 550-8165

Main Headquarters
Mailing: 1999 Harrison St. Tel: (510) 550-8161
Suite 2150 Fax: (510) 550-8165
Oakland, CA 94612

Public Affairs and Related Activities Personnel

At Headquarters

BRETT, Mathew Tel: (510) 550-8161
Senior Vice President, Business Development Fax: (510) 550-8165

DESMOND, Joseph Tel: (510) 550-8161
Senior Vice President, Marketing and Government Affairs Fax: (510) 550-8165

GOERS, Steven Tel: (510) 550-8161
Senior Vice President, Operations Fax: (510) 550-8165

HAGAMAN, Kenzel Tel: (510) 550-8161
Associate General Counsel Fax: (510) 550-8165

JOHNSON, Catherine Tel: (510) 550-8161
Senior Vice President, Human Resources Fax: (510) 550-8165

JUDGE, Daniel T. Tel: (510) 550-8161
General Counsel and Corporate Secretary Fax: (510) 550-8165

LEHRMANN, Doug Tel: (510) 550-8161
Interim Chief Financial Officer Fax: (510) 550-8165

Brijot Imaging Systems

Provider of millimeter wave object detection and people-screening technology.
www.brijot.com
Annual Revenues: $5.10 million
Industry/ies: Defense/Homeland Security; Government-Related

Chairman of the Board, President and Chief Executive Officer Tel: (407) 641-4370
LASKEY, Mitchel J. Fax: (407) 351-9455

Main Headquarters
Mailing: 1064 Greenwood Blvd. Tel: (407) 641-4370
Suite 124 Fax: (407) 351-9455
Lake Mary, FL 32746 TF: (866) 723-3796

The Brink's Company

*Provides secure transportation, cash management, and other security-related services. In late
2008, Brink's spun-off Brink's Home Security Holdings, Inc. (BHS).*
www.brinkscompany.com
Annual Revenues: $3.39 billion
Employees: 63,350
Ticker: NYSE: BCO
SIC: 4731
Industry/ies: Law Enforcement/Security
Legislative Issues: FIN; GOV; HCR; LBR; TAX; TRD

Chairman of the Board, President and Chief Executive Officer Tel: (804) 289-9600
SCHIEVELBEIN, Thomas C. Fax: (804) 289-9746

Main Headquarters
Mailing: 1801 Bayberry Ct. Tel: (804) 289-9600
P.O. Box 18100 Fax: (804) 289-9746
Richmond, VA 23226-8100

Political Action Committees
Brink's Company PAC
FEC ID: C00207472
Contact: Jonathan A. Leon
1801 Bayberry Ct. Tel: (804) 289-9600
Suite 400
Richmond, VA 23226

Contributions to Candidates: $2,350 (2015-2016)
Republicans: $2,350

Corporate Foundations and Giving Programs

The Brink's Company Charitable Foundation
Contact: Frank T. Lennon
1801 Bayberry Ct. Tel: (804) 289-9660
P.O. Box 18100 Fax: (804) 289-9770
Richmond, VA 23226

Public Affairs and Related Activities Personnel

At Headquarters

DZIEDZIC, Joseph W. Tel: (804) 289-9709
Vice President and Chief Financial Officer Fax: (804) 289-9770

LENNON, Frank T. Tel: (804) 289-9660
Vice President and Chief Administrative Officer Fax: (804) 289-9753

LEON, Jonathan A. Tel: (804) 289-9600
PAC Treasurer Fax: (804) 289-9770

MARSHALL, II, McAlister C. Tel: (804) 289-9600
Vice President, Secretary and General Counsel Fax: (804) 289-9770

MCCUE, Darren M. Tel: (804) 289-9600
Vice President and Chief Commercial Strategy Officer Fax: (804) 289-9746

TYSON, Holly R.
Vice President and Chief Human Resources Officer
Tel: (804) 289-9600
Fax: (804) 289-9746

WATSON, Patricia A.
Vice President and Chief Information Officer
Tel: (804) 289-9600
Fax: (804) 289-9746

Brinker International

Owns, develops, operates, and franchises full-service casual dining restaurants.
www.brinker.com
Annual Revenues: $3.14 billion
Employees: 53,000
Ticker: NYSE: EAT
SIC: 5812
Industry/ies: Food And Beverage Industry

Chairman of the Board
DEPINTO, Joseph M.
Tel: (972) 980-9917
Fax: (972) 770-9593

President and Chief Executive Officer
ROBERTS, Wyman
Tel: (972) 980-9917
Fax: (972) 770-9593

Main Headquarters
Mailing: 6820 LBJ Fwy.
Suite 200
Dallas, TX 75240
Tel: (972) 980-9917
Fax: (972) 770-9593

Political Action Committees
Brinker International Inc. PAC
FEC ID: C00241851
Contact: Bryan Mccrory
6820 LBJ Fwy.
Dallas, TX 75240
Tel: (972) 770-7228

Contributions to Candidates: $88,372 (2015-2016)
Democrats: $7,259; Republicans: $81,113

Corporate Foundations and Giving Programs
Brinker International Charitable Committee
6820 LBJ Fwy.
Suite 200
Dallas, TX 75240
Fax: (972) 770-5977

Public Affairs and Related Activities Personnel

At Headquarters

EDWARDS , Jr., Thomas
Executive Vice President and Chief Financial Officer
Tel: (972) 980-9917
Fax: (972) 770-9593

GIBSON, Krista
Senior Vice President and Chief Marketing Officer
Tel: (972) 980-9917
Fax: (972) 770-9593

GOLDEN, Nan
Director, Public Affairs
nan.golden@brinker.com
Tel: (972) 980-9917
Fax: (972) 770-9593

MAY, Scarlett
Senior Vice President, General Counsel and Secretary
Tel: (972) 980-9917
Fax: (972) 770-9593

MCCRORY, Bryan
PAC Contact
Tel: (972) 980-9917
Fax: (972) 770-9593

TAYLOR, Joseph G.
Vice President, Corporate Affairs
Tel: (972) 980-9917
Fax: (972) 770-9400

THOMSON, Roger F.
Executive Vice President and Chief Development Officer
roger.thomson@brinker.com
Tel: (972) 980-9917
Fax: (972) 770-9593

VALADE, Kelli
Executive Vice President and Chief Operating Officer
Tel: (972) 980-9917
Fax: (972) 770-9593

Bristol-Myers Squibb Company

Pharmaceutical company. The company's cardiovascular lineup includes heart disease drug Plavix and Avapro for hypertension. BMS also makes antipsychotic medication Abilify and HIV treatments Reyataz and Sustiva.
www.bms.com
Annual Revenues: $16.11 billion
Employees: 25,000
Ticker: NYSE: BMY
SIC: 2834
NAICS: 325412
Industry/ies: Pharmaceutical Industry
Legislative Issues: BUD; CPT; HCR; HOM; MMM; TAX; TRD

Executive Chairman
ANDREOTTI, Lamberto
lamberto.andreotti@bms.com
Tel: (212) 546-4000
Fax: (212) 546-4020

Chief Executive Officer
CAFORIO, Giovanni
Tel: (212) 546-4000
Fax: (212) 546-4020

Main Headquarters
Mailing: 345 Park Ave.
New York City, NY 10154
Tel: (212) 546-4000
Fax: (212) 546-4020
TF: (800) 332-2056

Washington Office
Mailing: 801 Pennsylvania Ave. NW
Suite 325
Washington, DC 20004

Political Action Committees
Bristol-Myers Squibb Company Employee Political Advocacy Fund for Innovation PAC
FEC ID: C00035675
Contact: David Levi
801 Pennsylvania Ave. NW
Suite 325
Washington, DC 20004

Contributions to Candidates: $270,375 (2015-2016)
Democrats: $116,000; Republicans: $154,375

Corporate Foundations and Giving Programs
Bristol-Myers Squibb Foundation
Contact: John L. DaMonti
345 Park Ave.
New York City, NY 10154
Fax: (212) 546-4020

Bristol-Myers Squibb Patient Assistance Foundation, Inc.
345 Park Ave.
New York City, NY 10154
Fax: (212) 546-4020

Public Affairs and Related Activities Personnel

At Headquarters

BANCROFT, Charles
Executive Vice President and Chief Financial Officer
charles.bancroft@bms.com
Tel: (212) 546-4000
Fax: (212) 546-4020

DAMONTI, John L.
President, Bristol-Myers Squibb Foundation
john.damonti@bms.com
Tel: (212) 546-4000
Fax: (212) 546-4020

HORTAS, Laura
Corporate, Media Contact
laura.hortas@bms.com
Tel: (609) 252-4587
Fax: (212) 546-4020

LEUNG, Sandra
General Counsel and Corporate Secretary
sandra.leung@bms.com
Tel: (212) 546-4000
Fax: (212) 546-4020

REILLY, Joseph
Director, Reporting and Consolidations
Reilly@bms.com
Tel: (212) 546-4000
Fax: (212) 546-4020

At Washington Office

WILLIAMS, Paul
Federal Lobbyist
Registered Federal Lobbyist

WILLIAMS, Dinorah
Executive Associate

At Other Offices

CHRIS, Pernie
Director, Federal Affairs
655 15th St. NW., Suite 300
Washington, DC 20005
Registered Federal Lobbyist
Tel: (202) 783-8617

EGENOLF, Fred
Director, Community Affairs and Philanthropy
Route 206 and Province Line Rd.
Princeton, NJ 08540
frederick.egenolf@bms.com
Tel: (609) 252-3377

ELICKER, John
Senior Vice President, Public Affairs and Investor Relations
Route 206 and Province Line Rd.
Princeton, NJ 08540
john.elicker@bms.com
Tel: (609) 252-4875

LANE, Penry
Manager, Federal Government Affairs
655 15th St. NW., Suite 300
Washington, DC 20005
Registered Federal Lobbyist
Tel: (202) 783-8617

LEVI, David
PAC Treasurer
777 Scudders Mill Rd., Building 3, #5165
Plainsboro, NJ 08536

MAUER, Jennifer Fron
Executive Director, Corporate Communications
Route 206 and Province Line Rd.
Princeton, NJ 08540
Tel: (609) 252-4875

MILLER, Ronald
Vice President, Global Policy and Government Affairs
655 15th St. NW., Suite 300
Washington, DC 20005
Miller@bms.com
Registered Federal Lobbyist
Tel: (202) 783-8617

PENRIE, Lane
Federal Lobbyist
655 15th St. NW., Suite 300
Washington, DC 20005
Penrie@bms.com
Tel: (202) 783-8617

Registered Federal Lobbyist

PERNIE, Christopher   Tel: (202) 783-8617
Director, Federal Affairs
655 15th St. NW., Suite 300
Washington, DC 20005
christopher.pernie@bms.com
Registered Federal Lobbyist

British Airways PLC

A commercial air carrier. U.S. corporate office is in Jackson Heights, NY.
www.britishairways.com
SIC: 4512
Industry/ies: Aerospace/Aviation; Airlines; Transportation; Travel/Tourism/
Lodging

Chairman   Tel: (347) 418-4250
WILLIAMS, Keith

Main Headquarters
Mailing: P.O. Box 690457   Tel: (718) 335-7070
        E. Elmhurst, NY 11369   TF: (800) 452-1201

Public Affairs and Related Activities Personnel

At Headquarters

JASINSKI, Paul C   Tel: (718) 335-7070
General Counsel, Americas

At Other Offices

BLANEY, James B.   Tel: (212) 716-0461
Senior Counsel, Americas
Two Park Ave., Suite 1100
New York City, NY 10016

Broadcast Music Inc. (BMI)

A non-profit organization for the rights of performing artists. BMI issues licenses to various users of music, including television and radio stations and networks, and distributes royalty payments to the performers. BMI is a music rights organization, nurturing new talent and new music.
www.bmi.com
Employees: 600
Industry/ies: Communications; Entertainment; Media/Mass Communication;
Sports/Leisure/Entertainment
Legislative Issues: CPT

President and Chief Executive Officer   Tel: (212) 220-3000
O'NEILL, Michael   Fax: (212) 245-8986

Main Headquarters
Mailing: Seven World Trade Center   Tel: (212) 220-3000
        250 Greenwich St.   Fax: (212) 245-8986
        New York City, NY 10007-0030

Corporate Foundations and Giving Programs

BMI Foundation, Inc.
Contact: Deirdre Chadwick
7 World Trade Center
250 Greenwich St.
New York City, NY 10007-0030

Public Affairs and Related Activities Personnel

At Headquarters

CHADWICK, Deirdre   Tel: (212) 220-3000
President, BMI Foundation and Executive Director, Classical   Fax: (212) 245-8986
Writer/Publisher Relations, New York

ESWORTHY, Bruce A.   Tel: (212) 220-3000
Senior Vice President, Finance and Administration, Chief   Fax: (212) 245-8986
Financial Officer

JACKSON, Ralph N.   Tel: (212) 586-2000
President, Foundation   Fax: (212) 245-8986

PANTLE, Hanna   Tel: (212) 220-3000
Assistant Vice President, Corporate Communications and   Fax: (212) 245-8986
Media Relations
hpantle@bmi.com

ROSEN, Stuart   Tel: (212) 220-3000
Senior Vice President and General Counsel   Fax: (212) 245-8986

SAAL, Jodi H.   Tel: (212) 220-3000
Vice President, Corporate Planning   Fax: (212) 245-8986

SMITH, Alison   Tel: (212) 220-3000
Senior Vice President, Distribution and Administration   Fax: (212) 245-8986
Services

SWEENEY, Ann   Tel: (212) 220-3000
Senior Vice President, Global Policy   Fax: (212) 245-8986

At Other Offices

MERAZ, Marlene   Tel: (310) 289-6325
Director, Public Relations
8730 Sunset Blvd., Third Floor West
W. Hollywood, CA 90069-2211

mmeraz@bmi.com

Broadcom Corporation

Designs and develops semiconductor solutions that enable broadband communications and networking of voice, video and data services.
www.broadcom.com
Annual Revenues: $8.50 billion
Employees: 10,650
Ticker: NASDAQ: BRCM
SIC: 3674
Industry/ies: Business; Computer/Technology; Small Business

Co-Founder, Chairman of the Board and Chief Technical Officer Tel: (949) 926-5000
SAMUELI, PhD, Henry   Fax: (949) 926-5203

President and Chief Executive Officer   Tel: (949) 926-5000
MCGREGOR, Scott A.   Fax: (949) 926-6589

Main Headquarters
Mailing: 5300 California Ave.   Tel: (949) 926-5000
        Irvine, CA 92617   Fax: (949) 926-5203
                     TF: (877) 577-2726

Political Action Committees
Broadcom Corporation PAC
FEC ID: C00477919
Contact: Thomas Peter Andrew
5300 California Ave.
Irvine, CA 92617

   Contributions to Candidates: $7,000 (2015-2016)
     Republicans: $7,000

Corporate Foundations and Giving Programs

Broadcom Foundation
Contact: Paula Golden
5300 California Ave.   Tel: (949) 926-5000
Irvine, CA 92617   Fax: (949) 926-5203

LSI Corporation Contributions Program
1621 Barber Ln.   Tel: (610) 712-7369
Milpitas, CA 95035

Public Affairs and Related Activities Personnel

At Headquarters

ANDREW, Thomas Peter   Tel: (949) 926-5000
PAC Treasurer   Fax: (949) 926-5203

BRANDT, Eric K.   Tel: (949) 926-5000
Executive Vice President and Chief Financial Officer   Fax: (949) 926-6589

CHONG, Arthur   Tel: (949) 926-5000
Executive Vice President, General Counsel and Secretary   Fax: (949) 926-6589

FIORILLO, Cindy   Tel: (949) 926-5000
Senior Vice President, Finance and Corporate Controller   Fax: (949) 926-5203

GOLDEN, Paula   Tel: (949) 926-5000
Executive Director, Foundation   Fax: (949) 926-9244
broadcomfoundation@broadcom.com

HURLSTON, Michael E.   Tel: (949) 926-5000
Executive Vice President, Worldwide Sales   Fax: (949) 926-5203

KAHN, Karen   Tel: (949) 926-5000
Vice President, Corporate Marketing and Communications   Fax: (949) 926-5203

KIM, Neil Y.   Tel: (949) 926-5000
Executive Vice President, Operations and Central Engineering Fax: (949) 926-5203

PHILLIPS, Nancy   Tel: (949) 926-5000
Executive Vice President, Human Resources   Fax: (949) 926-5203

ZEGARELLI, Chris   Tel: (949) 926-5000
Senior Director, Investor Relations   Fax: (949) 926-5203
czegarel@broadcom.com

Broadridge, Inc.

A provider of technology-based solutions to the financial services industry. Includes Broadridge Financial Solutions and Broadridge Securities Processing Solutions. Spun off from ADP in 2007.
www.broadridge.com
Annual Revenues: $2.85 billion
Employees: 7,400
Ticker: NYSE: BR
SIC: 7389
Industry/ies: Computer/Technology

Chairman of the Board   Tel: (516) 472-5400
BRUN, Leslie A.

President and Chief Executive Officer   Tel: (516) 472-5400
DALY, Richard J.

Main Headquarters
Mailing: 5 Dakota Dr.   TF: (800) 353-0103
        Suite 300
        Lake Success, NY 11042

Political Action Committees

Broadridge Financial Solutions PAC
FEC ID: C00478107
Contact: Steven J. Rosenthal
1981 Marcus Ave.
Lake Success, NY 10041

Corporate Foundations and Giving Programs

The Broadridge Foundation
Contact: Patricia Sacristan
1981 Marcus Ave.
Lake Success, NY 11042

Public Affairs and Related Activities Personnel

At Headquarters

GOKEY, Timothy C.
Senior Vice President and Chief Operating Officer

MAYADAS, Vijay
Senior Vice President, Strategy and Mergers and Acquisitions

TAYLOR, Julie R.
Corporate Vice President and Chief Human Resources Officer

YOUNG , James M.
Corporate Vice President and Chief Financial Officer

At Other Offices

AMSTERDAM, Adam D.   Tel: (516) 472-5400
Corporate Vice President, General Counsel and Secretary
1981 Marcus Ave.
Lake Success, NY 11042

DAMPEER , Lyell   Tel: (516) 472-5400
Corporate Vice President and President, the U.S. Investor
Communication Solutions business
1981 Marcus Ave.
Lake Success, NY 11042

DESCHUTTER, Douglas R.   Tel: (516) 472-5400
Corporate Vice President, U.S. Regulatory and Digital
Communications
1981 Marcus Ave.
Lake Success, NY 11042

HOGAN , John   Tel: (516) 472-5400
Senior Managing Director Technology
1981 Marcus Ave.
Lake Success, NY 11042

NAMIAS, Linda   Tel: (631) 254-7711
Senior Director, Corporate Communications
1981 Marcus Ave.
Lake Success, NY 11042
Linda.Namias@broadridge.com

ORGON, Ed   Tel: (212) 681-1700
Contact, Media Relations   Fax: (212) 681-6961
60 E. 42nd St., Suite 2112
New York City, NY 10165-2112
ed@torrenzano.com

PAREKH , Dev   Tel: (516) 472-5400
Head, Financial Planning and Analysis
1981 Marcus Ave.
Lake Success, NY 11042

ROSENTHAL, Steven J.   Tel: (516) 472-5400
PAC Treasurer
1981 Marcus Ave.
Lake Success, NY 11042

SACRISTAN, Patricia   Tel: (516) 472-5400
Immigration Program Manager, Compliance Project Manager
1981 Marcus Ave.
Lake Success, NY 11042
patricia.sacristan@broadridge.com

SCAVELLI, Gerard F.   Tel: (516) 472-5400
Corporate Vice President, Investor Communication Solutions-
Mutual Funds
1981 Marcus Ave.
Lake Success, NY 11042

SCHIFELLITE, Robert   Tel: (516) 472-5400
President, Investor Communication Solutions and Corporate
Officer
1981 Marcus Ave.
Lake Success, NY 11042

SHELLEY, Stefanie   Tel: (516) 472-5400
Chief Marketing Officer
1981 Marcus Ave.
Lake Success, NY 11042

BroadVision, Inc.

Supplies application solutions for large-scale, personalized business on the Internet.
www.broadvision.com
Annual Revenues: $13.09 million

Employees: 163
Ticker: NASDAQ: BVSN
SIC: 7372
Industry/ies: Communications; Computer/Technology; Telecommunications/
Internet/Cable

Chairman of the Board, President and Chief Executive Officer   Tel: (650) 331-1000
CHEN, Dr. Pehong   Fax: (650) 364-3425

Main Headquarters
Mailing: 1700 Seaport Blvd.   Tel: (650) 331-1000
    Suite 210   Fax: (650) 364-3425
    Redwood City, CA 94603

Public Affairs and Related Activities Personnel

At Headquarters

CHU, Peter   Tel: (650) 331-1000
Vice President, Strategy, Product Management and   Fax: (650) 364-3425
Marketing
ir1@broadvision.com

LEVINE, Ty   Tel: (650) 331-1000
Vice President, Marketing and Business Development   Fax: (650) 364-3425

TZOU, Shin-Yuan   Tel: (650) 331-1000
Chief Financial Officer   Fax: (650) 364-3425

Broin Companies LLC

See listing on page 642 under Poet, LLC

Brookfield Atlantic Corporation

A multi disciplinary science and advanced engineering management company that conducts contractual research, development, testing projects for organizations.
www.brookfieldatlantic.us
Industry/ies: Science; Scientific Research
Legislative Issues: DEF; FOR

Main Headquarters
Mailing: 581 Boylston St.   Tel: (617) 867-9000
    Suite 707C   Fax: (617) 867-9001
    Boston, MA 02116

Washington Office
Mailing: 2101 Crystal Plaza Arcade   Tel: (703) 348-7757
    Arlington, VA 22202   Fax: (617) 867-9001

Corporate Foundations and Giving Programs

Brookfield Atlantic Corporation Contributions Program
581 Boylston St.   Tel: (617) 867-9000
Suite 707C
Boston, MA 02116

Public Affairs and Related Activities Personnel

At Washington Office

DANTON, Nolia   Tel: (703) 348-7757
Federal Lobbyist   Fax: (617) 867-9001

HOWARD, Nolia   Tel: (703) 348-7757
Federal Lobbyist   Fax: (617) 867-9001

Brookfield Power U.S. Asset Management

Brookfield Asset Management Inc. is a global asset manager focused on property, renewable power.
www.brookfield.com
Industry/ies: Banking/Finance/Investments; Energy/Electricity
Legislative Issues: ENG

Senior Managing Partner and the Chief Executive Officer   Tel: (212) 417-7000
FLATT , Bruce   Fax: (212) 417-7196

Main Headquarters
Mailing: Brookfield Place   Tel: (212) 417-7000
    250 Vesey Street, 15th Floor   Fax: (212) 417-7196
    New York City, NY 10281-1023

Corporate Foundations and Giving Programs

Brookfield U.S. Foundation
Brookfield Place
250 Vesey Street, 15th Floor
New York City, NY 10281-1023

Public Affairs and Related Activities Personnel

At Headquarters

BLIDNER, Jeff   Tel: (212) 417-7000
Senior Managing Partner, Strategic Planning   Fax: (212) 417-7196

DADYBURJOR, Dinaz   Tel: (212) 417-7000
Managing Partner, Corporate Operations   Fax: (212) 417-7196

FOX , Brett   Tel: (212) 417-7000
Managing Partner, Corporate Operations   Fax: (212) 417-7196

LAWSON, Brian   Tel: (212) 417-7000
Senior Managing Partner and Chief Financial Officer   Fax: (212) 417-7196

WILLIS , Andrew   Tel: (416) 369-8236

Senior Vice President, Communications and Media
andrew.willis@brookfield.com   Fax: (212) 417-7196

At Other Offices

AMES, Shannon
Director, Community and Stakeholder Relations
200 Donald Lynch Blvd., Suite 300
Marlborough, MA 01752

Brooks Bawden LLC

Consulting.
Legislative Issues: HOM; LAW

Main Headquarters

Mailing: 401 Massachusetts Ave. NW   Tel: (202) 930-0897
         Suite 509
         Washington, DC 20001

Public Affairs and Related Activities Personnel

At Headquarters

BAWDEN, Ben   Tel: (202) 930-0897
Principal & Founder
Registered Federal Lobbyist

Brookshire Grocery Company

An online grocery shopping company.
www.brookshires.com
Annual Revenues: $1.3 Billion
Employees: 12,000
SIC: 2051
NAICS: 311812
Industry/ies: Food And Beverage Industry

Vice Chairman of the Board   Tel: (903) 534-3000
BROOKSHIRE, Timothy   Fax: (903) 534-2198

President and Chief Executive Officer   Tel: (903) 534-3000
RAYFORD, Richard   Fax: (903) 534-2206

Main Headquarters

Mailing: P. O. Box 1411   Tel: (903) 534-3000
         Tyler, TX 75710-1411   Fax: (903) 534-2206

Political Action Committees

Brookshire Grocery Company PAC
FEC ID: C00449546
Contact: Daniel Kyle McCoy
1600 W. South West Loop 323   Tel: (903) 534-3000
Tyler, TX 75701   Fax: (903) 534-2206

Corporate Foundations and Giving Programs

Brookshire Grocery Company Contributions Program
Contact: Carolyn Langston
P. O. Box 1411   Tel: (903) 534-3000
Tyler, TX 75710-1411   Fax: (903) 534-2206

Public Affairs and Related Activities Personnel

At Headquarters

HUTSON, Carolyn   Tel: (903) 534-3000
Executive Vice President, Chief Financial Officer and   Fax: (903) 534-2206
Treasurer

LANGSTON, Carolyn   Tel: (903) 534-3076
Marketing Specialist   Fax: (903) 534-2206

At Other Offices

MCCOY, Daniel Kyle
PAC Treasurer
1600 WSW Loop 323
Tyler, TX 75701-8532

Brown and Brown, Inc.

An insurance agency.
www.bbinsurance.com
Annual Revenues: $1.68 billion
Employees: 7,807
Ticker: NYSE: BRO
SIC: 6411
Industry/ies: Insurance Industry

Chairman of the Board   Tel: (386) 252-9601
BROWN, J. Hyatt   Fax: (386) 239-7252

President and Chief Executive Officer   Tel: (386) 252-9601
BROWN, Powell   Fax: (386) 239-5729

Main Headquarters

Mailing: 220 S. Ridgewood Ave.   Tel: (386) 252-9601
         P.O. Box 2412   Fax: (386) 239-5729
         Daytona Beach, FL 32114   TF: (800) 877-2769

Public Affairs and Related Activities Personnel

At Headquarters

FREEBOURN, SR., Richard   Tel: (386) 252-9601
Executive Vice President, Internal Operations and People   Fax: (386) 239-5729
Officer

LLOYD, Robert W.   Tel: (386) 252-9601
Executive Vice President; Secretary and General Counsel   Fax: (386) 239-5729

WATTS, R. Andrew   Tel: (386) 252-9601
Executive Vice President, Chief Financial Officer and   Fax: (386) 239-5729
Treasurer

Brown-Forman Corporation

A producer and marketer of consumer products, including wine and spirits, and consumer
durable goods.
www.brown-forman.com
Annual Revenues: $3.10 billion
Employees: 4,200
Ticker: NYSE: BF-B
SIC: 2085
Industry/ies: Food And Beverage Industry
Legislative Issues: AGR; BEV; BUD; CON; CSP; ENG; FIN; LBR; TAR; TAX; TRD

Chairman of the Board and Chief Executive Officer
VARGA, Paul C.

Main Headquarters

Mailing: P.O. Box 1080   Tel: (502) 774-7690
         Louisville, KY 40210

Political Action Committees

Brown-Forman Corporation Non-partisan Committee for Responsible
Government PAC
FEC ID: C00059733
Contact: Lisa Lisker
850 Dixie Hwy.
Louisville, KY 40210

  Contributions to Candidates: $53,288 (2015-2016)
  Democrats: $18,500; Republicans: $34,788

Corporate Foundations and Giving Programs

Brown-Forman Corporate Contributions Program
Contact: Rusty Cheuvront
P.O. Box 1080
Louisville, KY 40201

Public Affairs and Related Activities Personnel

At Headquarters

CHEUVRONT, Rusty   Tel: (502) 774-7690
Director, Community Relations

DONINGER, Eric   Tel: (502) 774-7690
Vice President, Global Director, Brand Homeplace Operations
eric_doninger@b-f.com

KLEBAN, Carrie   Tel: (502) 774-7690
Vice President Director, New Brand Development and
Director, Global Marketing
carrie_kleban@bf.com

MASICK, Michael   Tel: (502) 774-7690
Director, Strategy and Corporate Development

MCCLELLAN, Jr., Donald W.   Tel: (502) 774-7690
Vice President, Government Relations and Public Policy
Registered Federal Lobbyist

ROSE, Wayne   Tel: (502) 774-7690
Vice President, Brand Director wines
wayne_rose@b-f.com

SMITH, Mark H.   Tel: (502) 774-7334
Vice President, Government Relations and Public Policy
Registered Federal Lobbyist

WILSON, Ken   Tel: (502) 774-7690
Senior Vice President
ken_wilson@b-f.com

YUNT, Jennifer   Tel: (502) 774-7690
Manager, Associate Sales Promotions
JENNIFER_YUNT@B-F.COM

At Other Offices

HAMEL, Matthew E.
Executive Vice President, General Counsel and Secretary
850 Dixie Hwy.
Louisville, KY 40210

HAWLEY, Kirsten
Senior Vice President and Chief Human Resources Officer
850 Dixie Hwy.
Louisville, KY 40210

HAYES, John
Senior Vice President and Chief Marketing Officer
850 Dixie Hwy.
Louisville, KY 40210

KOVAL , Jay

Director, Investor Relations
850 Dixie Hwy.
Louisville, KY 40210
Investor_Relations@b-f.com

LISKER, Lisa
PAC Treasurer
850 Dixie Hwy.
Louisville, KY 40210

LYNCH, Philip J.
Vice President and Director, Corporate Communications
850 Dixie Hwy.
Louisville, KY 40210

MORREAU, Jane
Executive Vice President, Chief Financial Officer
850 Dixie Hwy.
Louisville, KY 40210

STEINER, Lisa
Senior Vice President, Chief of Staff and Director, Global Communications and Services
850 Dixie Hwy.
Louisville, KY 40210

Brunswick Corporation

A manufacturer of marine, recreational and fitness products.
www.brunswick.com
Annual Revenues: $3.93 billion
Employees: 12,165
Ticker: NYSE: BC
SIC: 3510
Industry/ies: Boating; Recreation/Hobby; Sports/Leisure/Entertainment
Legislative Issues: HCR; TAX

| **Chairman of the Board and Chief Executive Officer** | Tel: | (847) 735-4700 |
| MCCOY, Dustan E. | Fax: | (847) 735-4765 |

Main Headquarters		
Mailing: One N. Field Ct.	Tel:	(847) 735-4700
Lake Forest, IL 60045-4811	Fax:	(847) 735-4765

Political Action Committees
Brunswick Corporation Good Government Fund PAC
FEC ID: C00110262
Contact: William L. Metzger
One N. Field Ct.   Tel: (847) 735-4700
Lake Forest, IL 60045

> **Contributions to Candidates:** $68,000 (2015-2016)
> Democrats: $18,000; Republicans: $50,000

> **Principal Recipients**
> **SENATE**
> JOHNSON, RONALD HAROLD (REP-)

Corporate Foundations and Giving Programs

Brunswick Corporation Foundation		
One N. Field Ct.	Tel:	(847) 735-4700
Lake Forest, IL 60045	Fax:	(847) 735-4765

Public Affairs and Related Activities Personnel

At Headquarters

BYOTS, Bruce J.	Tel:	(847) 735-4612
Vice President, Investor and Corporate Relations	Fax:	(847) 735-4765
bruce.byots@brunswick.com		

| DEKKER, Christopher F. | Tel: | (847) 735-4700 |
| *Vice President, General Counsel and Secretary* | Fax: | (847) 735-4765 |

| DUNAWAY, Cambria W. | Tel: | (847) 735-4700 |
| *President & Global Chief Marketing Officer* | Fax: | (847) 735-4765 |

| GRODZKI, Kevin S. | Tel: | (847) 735-4700 |
| *Vice President, Communications and Public Affairs* | Fax: | (847) 735-4765 |

| KUBERA, Daniel | Tel: | (847) 735-4617 |
| *Director, Media Relations and Corporate Communications* | Fax: | (847) 735-4750 |

| LOCKRIDGE, B. Russell | Tel: | (847) 735-4700 |
| *Vice President and Chief Human Resources Officer* | Fax: | (847) 735-4050 |

| METZGER, William L. | Tel: | (847) 735-4700 |
| *Senior Vice President, Chief Financial Officer and PAC Treasurer* | Fax: | (847) 735-4765 |

| RUSSELL LOCKRIDGE, B. | Tel: | (847) 735-4700 |
| *Vice President and Chief Human Resources Officer* | Fax: | (847) 735-4765 |

| SCHWABERO, Mark D. | Tel: | (847) 735-4700 |
| *President and Chief Operating Officer* | Fax: | (847) 735-4765 |

Brush Engineered Materials

See listing on page 516 under Materion Corporation

BSA Lifestructures

Specializes in architecture, engineering, interior design and planning for healthcare, higher education and scientific research.

www.bsalifestructures.com
Annual Revenues: $33.70 million
Employees: 200
Industry/ies: Agriculture/Agronomy; Education; Engineering/Mathematics; Medicine/Health Care/Mental Health; Science; Scientific Research

Main Headquarters

Mailing: 9365 Counselours Row	Tel:	(317) 819-7878
Suite 300	Fax:	(317) 819-7288
Indianapolis, IN 46240-6422		

Public Affairs and Related Activities Personnel

At Headquarters

| COURTNEY, Karen | Tel: | (317) 819-7878 |
| *Director, Marketing* | Fax: | (317) 819-7288 |

HOOVERS, Monte L.	Tel:	(317) 819-7878
Contact, Healthcare Planning	Fax:	(317) 819-7288
mhoover@bsalifestructures.com		

BT Americas Inc.

BT Americas Inc, based in El Segundo City, is the U.S. subsidiary of BT Group plc., headquartered in London, United Kingdom. A global business communications service provider.
www.btglobalservices.com
Industry/ies: Communications; Telecommunications/Internet/Cable
Legislative Issues: TEC

Main Headquarters

Mailing: 2217 S. Culpeper St.
Arlington, VA 22206

Main Headquarters

Mailing: 7301 N State Hwy. 161	Tel:	(972) 830-8100
Suite 400	Fax:	(408) 330-2701
Irving, TX 75039		

Washington Office
Mailing: 1001 G St. NW
Suite 800
Washington, DC 20001

Corporate Foundations and Giving Programs

BT Corporate Responsibility programme
2160 E.Grand Ave.
El Segundo, CA 90245-5024

Public Affairs and Related Activities Personnel

At Headquarters

| KOZAMCHAK, Kris | Tel: | (972) 830-8135 |
| *Head, Public Relations and Corporate Relations (U.S. and Canada)* | Fax: | (408) 330-2701 |

At Washington Office

JONES, Jessica
Manager, Government Relations

WHITEHEAD, Thomas

At Other Offices

MERTSCH, Jill	Tel:	(703) 755-6742
Vice President, U.S. Government Affairs	Fax:	(703) 755-6740
11440 Commerce Park Dr.		
Reston, VA 20191		

TAYLOR, Jennifer	Tel:	(408) 330-2700
Vice President, US Government Affairs	Fax:	(408) 330-2701
11440 Commerce Park Dr.		
Reston, VA 20191		
Registered Federal Lobbyist		

Budd Thyssenkrupp Company

See listing on page 785 under ThyssenKrupp AG

Buffalo Supply Inc.

Medical and surgical equipment supplier.
buffalosupply.com
Annual Revenues: $25.8 Million
Industry/ies: Government-Related; Medicine/Health Care/Mental Health

Chairman of the Board	Tel:	(303) 666-6333
JACKSON, Stonewall	Fax:	(303) 666-8518
stonewall.jackson@buffalosupply.com		

President and Chief Executive Officer	Tel:	(800) 366-1812
JACKSON, T.J.	Fax:	(800) 767-9327
tj.jackson@buffalosupply.com		

Main Headquarters		
Mailing: 1650A Coal Creek Dr.	Tel:	(800) 366-1812
Lafayette, CO 80026	Fax:	(800) 767-9327
	TF:	(800) 366-1812

Public Affairs and Related Activities Personnel

At Headquarters

CARLSEN, Sandy
Vendor Specialist
sandy.carlsen@buffalosupply.com
Tel: (800) 366-1812
Fax: (800) 767-9327

JACKSON, PhD, Betty
Chief Financial Officer
betty.jackson@buffalosupply.com
Tel: (303) 666-6333
Fax: (303) 666-8518

PARKER, Kara
Senior Vice President
Tel: (303) 666-6333
Fax: (303) 666-8518

RUMMER, Caitlyn
Manager, Business Development
caitlyn.rummer@buffalosupply.com
Tel: (800) 366-1812
Fax: (800) 767-9327

Buffalo Wild Wings Inc.

Restaurant Chains.
Legislative Issues: LBR; TAX

Chief Executive Officer and President
SMITH, Sally J
Tel: (952) 593-9943

Main Headquarters
Mailing: 5500 Wayzata Blvd.
Suite 1600
Minneapolis, MN 55416
Tel: (952) 593-9943

Public Affairs and Related Activities Personnel

At Headquarters

BENNING, Kathleen M
Executive Vice President, Chief Strategy Officer and Business Development
Tel: (952) 593-9943

DECKER, Emily
Senior Vice President, General Counsel
Tel: (952) 593-9943

EHLERT, Tim
Director, Government Relations
Registered Federal Lobbyist
Tel: (952) 593-9943

PRIBYL, Heather
Investor Relations, Contact
Tel: (952) 593-9943

SCHMIDT, James M
Chief Operating Officer
Tel: (952) 593-9943

TWINEM , Mary J.
Executive Vice President, Chief Financial Officer and Treasurer
Tel: (952) 593-9943

Bunge North America

The North American operating arm of Bunge Limited. An agribusiness and food processing company.
www.bungenorthamerica.com
Annual Revenues: $535.80 million
Employees: 5,000
NAICS: 311222
Industry/ies: Agriculture/Agronomy; Food And Beverage Industry
Legislative Issues: AGR; ENG; FIN; FOO; FOR; TAX; TRA; TRD

Chief Executive Officer
BASTEAN, Todd A.
Tel: (314) 292-2000
Fax: (314) 292-2110

Chief Executive Officer
SCHRODER, Soren W.
Tel: (314) 292-2000
Fax: (314) 292-2110

Main Headquarters
Mailing: P.O. Box 28500
11720 Borman Dr.
St. Louis, MO 63146-1000
Tel: (314) 292-2000
Fax: (314) 292-2110

Washington Office
Mailing: 25 Massachusetts Ave. NW
Suite 340
Washington, DC 20001
Tel: (202) 216-1780

Political Action Committees
Bunge North America Inc. PAC
FEC ID: C00401687
Contact: Thomas J. Erickson
25 Massachusetts Ave. NW
Suite 340
Washington, DC 20001
Tel: (202) 216-1780

Contributions to Candidates: $61,100 (2015-2016)
Democrats: $6,100; Republicans: $55,000

Principal Recipients

SENATE
BLUNT, ROY (REP-MO)
BLUNT, ROY (REP-NY)

Corporate Foundations and Giving Programs

Bunge North America Foundation
11720 Borman Dr
P.O. Box 2850
St. Louis, MO 63146

Public Affairs and Related Activities Personnel

At Headquarters

FRONTCZAK, Mary L.
Vice President, Corporate and Legal Affairs
Tel: (314) 292-2000
Fax: (314) 292-2110

KANNEGANTI, Premchand
Chief Financial Officer
Tel: (314) 292-2000
Fax: (314) 292-2110

BURNS, Susan
Manager, External Communications
susan.burns@bunge.com
Tel: (914) 684-3246
Fax: (314) 292-2110

HADEN, Mark
Contact, Investor Relations
mark.haden@bunge.com
Tel: (314) 292-2000
Fax: (314) 292-2110

HAYES, Geralyn F.
Vice President, Human Resources
Tel: (314) 292-2000
Fax: (314) 292-2110

KABBES, David G.
General Counsel & Managing Director, Corporate Affairs
Tel: (314) 292-2000
Fax: (314) 292-2110

At Washington Office

FELNER, Diana
Director, Government Affairs
Tel: (202) 216-1780

HILL, Jared
Registered Federal Lobbyist
Tel: (202) 216-1780

JOHNSON BENNETT, Jessica
Director, Government Affairs
Tel: (202) 216-1780

POINDEXTER, Martha Scott
Registered Federal Lobbyist
Tel: (202) 216-1780

THOMPSON, Anne
Registered Federal Lobbyist
Tel: (202) 216-1780

At Other Offices

SABOURIN, John
Treasurer
750 First St., Suite 1070
Washington, DC 20002

Burger King Corporation

A fast-food chain company.
www.bk.com
SIC: 5812
Industry/ies: Food And Beverage Industry
Legislative Issues: FOO; LBR; TAX

Chief Executive Officer
SCHWARTZ, Daniel S.
Tel: (305) 378-3000
Fax: (305) 378-7367

Main Headquarters
Mailing: 5505 Blue Lagoon Dr.
Miami, FL 33126-2029
Tel: (305) 378-3000
Fax: (305) 378-7367
TF: (800) 522-1278

Corporate Foundations and Giving Programs

Have It Your Way Foundation Inc
Contact: Ivette R. Diaz
5505 Blue Lagoon Dr.
Miami, FL 33126
Tel: (305) 378-3186

Public Affairs and Related Activities Personnel

At Headquarters

DIAZ, Ivette R.
Director, Corporate Social Responsibility
idiaz@whopper.com
Tel: (305) 378-3000
Fax: (305) 378-7367

GONCALVES, Heitor
Executive Vice President, Chief Information, Performance and People Officer
Tel: (305) 378-3000
Fax: (305) 378-7367

GRANAT, Jill
Senior Vice President, General Counsel and Secretary
Tel: (305) 378-3000
Fax: (305) 378-7367

SCHWAN, Axel
Executive Vice President, Global Chief Marketing Officer
Tel: (305) 378-3000
Fax: (305) 378-7367

Burlington Coat Factory Warehouse Corporation

A retailer of branded apparel products. It offers fashion-focused merchandise, including women?s ready-to-wear apparel, menswear, youth apparel, baby products, footwear, accessories, home décor and gifts, and coats.
www.burlingtoncoatfactory.com
Annual Revenues: $4.88 billion
Employees: 34,000
Ticker: NYSE:BURL
SIC: 5311; 5099; 5611; 5621
Industry/ies: Apparel/Textiles Industry

President, Chief Executive Officer and Director
KINGSBURY, Thomas A.
Tel: (609) 387-7800
Fax: (609) 387-7071

Main Headquarters
Mailing: 1830 Route 130 North
Burlington, NJ 08016
Tel: (609) 387-7800
Fax: (609) 387-7071
TF: (855) 973-8445

Corporate Foundations and Giving Programs

Burlington Coat Factory Warehouse Corporation Contributions Program
1830 Route 130 North
Burlington, NJ 08016

Tel: (609) 387-7800
Fax: (609) 387-7071

Public Affairs and Related Activities Personnel

At Headquarters

HAIGNEY, Stacy J.
Vice President, Legal
stacy.haigney@coat.com

Tel: (609) 387-7800
Fax: (609) 387-7071

KATZ, Marc
Executive Vice President and Chief Financial Officer

Tel: (609) 387-7800
Fax: (609) 387-7071

LAPENTA, Robert L.
Vice President and Treasurer
bob.lapenta@coat.com

Tel: (855) 973-8445
Fax: (609) 387-7071

MAGRINI, Joyce Manning
Executive Vice President, Human Resources

Tel: (609) 387-7800
Fax: (609) 387-7071

SICHEL, Bart
Executive Vice President and Chief Marketing Officer

Tel: (609) 387-7800
Fax: (609) 387-7071

SISKIND, Wendy
Vice President, Marketing and Contact, Public Relations
Wendy.Siskind@coat.com

Tel: (609) 387-7800
Fax: (609) 387-7071

TANG, Paul
Executive Vice President and General Counsel

Tel: (609) 387-7800
Fax: (609) 387-7071

Burlington Northern and Santa Fe Railway

See listing on page 150 under Burlington Northern Santa Fe Corporation

Burlington Northern Santa Fe Corporation

Formerly Burlington Northern Santa Fe Railway, a subsidiary of Burlington Northern Santa Fe Corporation, the company adopted its current name in 2005.
www.bnsf.com
Annual Revenues: $23.00 billion
Employees: 48,000
Ticker: NYSE: BNI
SIC: 4011
NAICS: 482111
Industry/ies: Railroads; Transportation
Legislative Issues: AGR; BUD; ENG; ENV; HOM; LBR; RRR; TAX; TEC; TRA

Executive Chairman

ROSE, Matthew K.
matthew.rose@bnsf.com

Tel: (817) 867-6100
Fax: (817) 352-7171

Main Headquarters

Mailing: 2650 Lou Menk Dr.
Fort Worth, TX 76131-2830

Tel: (817) 352-1000
Fax: (817) 352-7171
TF: (800) 795-2673

Washington Office

Mailing: 500 New Jersey Ave. NW
Suite 550
Washington, DC 20001

Political Action Committees

Burlington Northern Santa Fe Corporation RAILPAC (BNSF RAILPAC)
FEC ID: C00235739
Contact: Patricia A. Murphy
P.O. Box 961039
Suite 220
Fort Worth, TX 76161

Tel: (817) 352-2326
Fax: (817) 352-2392

Contributions to Candidates: $1,415,510 (2015-2016)
Democrats: $558,700; Republicans: $848,310; Other: $8,500

Principal Recipients

SENATE
BOOKER, CORY A (DEM-NJ)
BOOZMAN, JOHN (REP-AR)
KIRK, MARK STEVEN (REP-IL)
SCHATZ, BRIAN (DEM-HI)

HOUSE
CAPUANO, MICHAEL E (DEM-MA)
CRAMER, KEVIN MR. (REP-ND)
CUMMINGS, ELIJAH E (DEM-DC)
DUNCAN, JOHN J REP. JR. (REP-TN)
FRELINGHUYSEN, RODNEY P. (REP-NJ)
LAHOOD, DARIN MCKAY (REP-IL)
LANKFORD, JAMES PAUL MR. (REP-OK)
LARSEN, RICK (DEM-WA)
LIPINSKI, DANIEL WILLIAM WILLIAM (DEM-IL)
MCGOVERN, JAMES P (DEM-MA)
MICA, JOHN L. MR. (REP-FL)
NEAL, RICHARD E MR. (DEM-MA)

Corporate Foundations and Giving Programs

Burlington Northern Sante Fe Foundation
2500 Lou Menk Dr.

Fort Worth, TX 76131

Public Affairs and Related Activities Personnel

At Headquarters

ACOSTA, Juan M.
Regional Assistant Vice President, State Govt. Affairs
juan.acosta@bnsf.com

Tel: (817) 352-2296
Fax: (817) 352-7171

ANDERSEN, Zak
Vice President, Corporate Relations
Zak.Andersen@bnsf.com

Tel: (817) 867-6250
Fax: (817) 352-7171

BOBB, Stevan B.
Executive Vice President and Chief Marketing Officer

Tel: (817) 352-1000
Fax: (817) 352-7171

BRACKER, Mark
Director, Finance
mark.bracker@bnsf.com

Tel: (817) 352-4813
Fax: (817) 253-7171

CHAND, Riz
Vice President and Chief Human Resources Officer

Tel: (817) 352-1000
Fax: (817) 352-7171

FAUST, Joseph
Director, Public Affairs and Media Contact
joseph.faust@bnsf.com

Tel: (817) 867-6427
Fax: (817) 352-7925

JOHNSEN, Andrew K.
Assistant Vice President, State Government Affairs
andrew.johnsen@bnsf.com

Tel: (817) 352-2325
Fax: (817) 352-2392

JOHNSON, Michelle K.
Legislative Analyst
michelle.johnson@bnsf.com

Tel: (817) 352-2356
Fax: (817) 352-2392

LUND, Roberta
Manager, State Govt. Affairs
Roberta.Lund2@bnsf.com

Tel: (817) 352-2326
Fax: (817) 352-7171

NOBER, Roger
Executive Vice President, Law and Corporate Affairs

Tel: (817) 352-1000
Fax: (817) 352-7171

PIGGOTT, Julie A.
Executive Vice President and Chief Financial Officer

Tel: (817) 352-1000
Fax: (817) 352-7171

SHEWMAKE, Charles W.
Vice President and General Counsel

Tel: (817) 352-1000
Fax: (817) 352-7171

At Washington Office

BIRD, Rachel
Budget and Legislative Affairs Analyst

Tel: (202) 347-8662
Fax: (202) 347-8675

CAVOSSA, Ashley Basquin
Director, Government Affairs

Tel: (202) 347-8662
Fax: (202) 347-8675

HAWKINS, Amy C.
Vice President, Government Affairs
Amy.Hawkins@bnsf.com
Registered Federal Lobbyist

Tel: (202) 347-8662
Fax: (202) 347-8675

ROGERS, Jim
Manager, Public Relations

Tel: (202) 347-8662

SMYTHERS, Jr., Michael
Assistant Vice President, Federal Government Affairs
Michael.Smythers@bnsf.com
Registered Federal Lobbyist

Tel: (202) 347-8662
Fax: (202) 347-8675

SULLIVAN, Gael
General Director, Federal Government Affairs
Registered Federal Lobbyist

Tel: (202) 347-8662
Fax: (202) 347-8675

WORMMEESTER, Justin T.
Director, Government Affairs
Registered Federal Lobbyist

Tel: (202) 347-8662
Fax: (202) 347-8675

At Other Offices

DICAMILLO, LaDonna V.
Executive Director, Government Affairs
One World Trade Center, Suite 1680
Long Beach, CA 90831
ladonna.dicamillo@bnsf.com

Tel: (323) 267-4041
Fax: (909) 946-0490

HOWARD, Roger W.
Director, Government Affairs
3253 E. Chestnut Expwy.
Springfield, MO 75802

Tel: (417) 829-4902
Fax: (417) 829-4903

KEARNS, Dennis A.
Legislative Counsel
1001 Congress Ave., Suite 101
Austin, TX 78701

Tel: (512) 473-2823
Fax: (512) 473-8570

MUNGUIA, Roberto F.
Director, Government Affairs
201 N. Seventh St.
Lincoln, NE 68508-1309

Tel: (402) 458-7738
Fax: (402) 458-7739

MURPHY, Patricia A.
Manager, Legislative Affairs and PAC Treasurer
P.O. Box 96161, Suite 220
Fort Worth, TX 76161
Patricia.Murphy@bnsf.com

Tel: (202) 347-8662

NORRIS, Catherine J.

Tel: (303) 480-7406

Executive Director, Government Affairs   Fax: (303) 480-7407
P.O. Box 630317
Littleton, CO 80163-0317
cathy.norris@bnsf.com

RANF, Barbara A.   Tel: (406) 443-2102
Executive Director, Government Affairs   Fax: (406) 449-8610
825 Great Northern Blvd., Suite 105
Helena, MT 59601-3340
barbara.ranf@bnsf.com

Burns & McDonnell Inc.

A full-service engineering, architecture, construction, environmental and consulting solutions firm. It provides engineering, architecture, construction, environmental and consulting services for the aviation, defense, environmental and utilities markets.
www.burnsmcd.com
Annual Revenues: $200.30 million
Employees: 5,000
Industry/ies: Engineering/Mathematics
Legislative Issues: ECN; ENG; TAX; TRA

Chairman of the Board, President and Chief Executive Officer   Tel: (816) 333-9400
GRAVES, Greg M.   Fax: (816) 822-3412

Main Headquarters
Mailing: 9400 Ward Pkwy.   Tel: (816) 333-9400
Kansas City, MO 64114   Fax: (816) 822-3028

Washington Office
Mailing: 8605 Westwood Center Dr.   Tel: (703) 942-5715
Suite 509   Fax: (703) 942-5603
Vienna, VA 22182

Political Action Committees
Burns and McDonnell Inc. PAC
FEC ID: C00442913
Contact: Dennis W. (Denny) Scott
9400 Ward Pkwy.   Tel: (816) 333-9400
Kansas City, MO 64114   Fax: (816) 822-3412

   Contributions to Candidates: $177,500 (2015-2016)
   Democrats: $45,500; Republicans: $126,500; Other: $5,500

     Principal Recipients

       SENATE
       MURKOWSKI, LISA (REP-AK)
       ROBERTS, PAT (REP-KS)

       HOUSE
       BOEHNER, JOHN A. (REP-OH)
       PAULSEN, ERIK (REP-MN)
       YODER, KEVIN (REP-KS)

Corporate Foundations and Giving Programs
Burns and McDonnell Foundation
Contact: Julee Koncak
9400 Ward Pkwy.   Tel: (816) 333-9400
Kansas City, MO 64114   Fax: (816) 822-3412

Public Affairs and Related Activities Personnel

At Headquarters

GARTELOS, Renee   Tel: (816) 333-9400
Director, Human Resources   Fax: (816) 822-3028

KONCAK, Julee   Tel: (816) 822-4391
Director, Burns & McDonnell Foundation   Fax: (816) 822-3028
jkoncak@burnsmcd.com

LAVIN-HICKEY, Melissa   Tel: (816) 822-3024
Director, Corporate Marketing   Fax: (816) 822-3516
mlavin@burnsmcd.com

SCOTT, Dennis W. (Denny)   Tel: (816) 333-9400
Chief Financial Officer and PAC Treasurer   Fax: (816) 822-3412

WALTER, John   Tel: (816) 822-3226
Director, Corporate Communications   Fax: (816) 822-3028
jwalter@burnsmcd.com

Burns and Roe Enterprises, Inc.

A comprehensive engineering, procurement, construction, operations and maintenance company providing services to private and governmental clients worldwide.
www.roe.com
Annual Revenues: $70.76 million
Employees: 400
Industry/ies: Construction/Construction Materials; Energy/Electricity; Engineering/Mathematics; Environment And Conservation

President and Chief Executive Officer   Tel: (201) 986-4000
ROE, Keith   Fax: (201) 986-4459
kroe@roe.com

Main Headquarters
Mailing: 800 Kinderkamack Rd.   Tel: (201) 265-7000
Oradell, NJ 07649   Fax: (201) 986-4459

Washington Office

Mailing: 1133 20th St. NW   Tel: (202) 898-1500
Suite 400   Fax: (202) 898-1561
Washington, DC 20036-3439

Political Action Committees
Burns and Roe Group Inc. PAC
FEC ID: C00318519
Contact: Michael A. Marcopoto
800 Kinderkamack Rd.   Tel: (202) 898-1500
Oradell, NJ 07649   Fax: (202) 898-1561

Public Affairs and Related Activities Personnel

At Headquarters

MARCOPOTO, Michael A.   Tel: (201) 265-2000
PAC Treasurer   Fax: (201) 986-4459

ROE, Hollace L.   Tel: (201) 265-2000
Senior Vice President, Human Resources & Administration   Fax: (201) 986-4459

SMITH, Jr., Russell F.   Tel: (201) 986-4636
Senior Vice President and Chief Financial Officer   Fax: (201) 986-4459

At Washington Office

ROE, Randall   Tel: (202) 898-1500
Vice Chairman & Government Relations   Fax: (202) 898-1561
rroe@roe.com

Business Industry Political Action Committee (BIPAC)

Founded in 1963. Supported by over 1,000 associations and corporations. Publishes The BIPAC Action Report and Elections In Sight. *BIPAC's goal is to help the business community play a more active role in the public policy process.*
bipac.org
Industry/ies: Business; Politics/Political Science; Small Business

Chairman   Tel: (202) 833-1880
PALLAT, John   Fax: (202) 833-2338

President & Chief Executive Officer   Tel: (202) 833-1880
GERLACH, Jim   Fax: (202) 833-2338

Main Headquarters
Mailing: 888 16th St. NW, Suite 305   Tel: (202) 833-1880
Washington, DC 20006   Fax: (202) 833-2338

Public Affairs and Related Activities Personnel

At Headquarters

BOGERT, Terri   Tel: (202) 833-1880
Secretary   Fax: (202) 833-2338

ACKLER, Jeffrey   Tel: (202) 833-1880
Manager, New Media ,Communications   Fax: (202) 833-2338

ARCHULETA, Mark   Tel: (202) 833-1880
Chief Financial Officer   Fax: (202) 833-2338
archuleta@bipac.org

BLASCOVICH, Andrew   Tel: (202) 833-1880
Director, Political Affairs   Fax: (202) 833-2338

CORS, Allan D.   Tel: (202) 833-1880
PAC Contact   Fax: (202) 833-2338

CRAIG, Melissa   Tel: (202) 833-1880
Vice President, Member Relations   Fax: (202) 833-2338

DAVISON, Matt   Tel: (202) 833-1880
Regional Director - Eastern   Fax: (202) 833-2338

HARMON, Bo   Tel: (202) 833-1880
Senior Vice President, Political Affairs   Fax: (202) 833-2338

Business Psychology Associates

Provides behavioral healthcare solutions.
www.bpahealth.com
Annual Revenues: $23.17 million
Employees: 100
Industry/ies: Management; Medicine/Health Care/Mental Health

Chairman of the Board   Tel: (208) 947-4376
JONES, Dr. Whit   Fax: (208) 344-7430
wjones@bpahealth.com

Chief Executive Officer   Tel: (208) 947-4376
WOODLEY, Sarah   Fax: (208) 344-7430

Main Headquarters
Mailing: 380 E. ParkCenter Blvd.   Tel: (208) 336-4275
Suite 300   Fax: (208) 344-7430
Boise, ID 83706   TF: (800) 211-9477

Corporate Foundations and Giving Programs
Business Psychology Associates, Inc Contributions Proogram
380 E. ParkCenter Blvd.
Suite 300
Boise, ID 83706

Public Affairs and Related Activities Personnel

At Headquarters

ARRIOLA, Carl	Tel:	(208) 336-4275
President	Fax:	(208) 344-7430
BATES, Kevin	Tel:	(208) 336-4275
Chief Financial Officer	Fax:	(208) 344-7430

Butler Manufacturing Company

A manufacturer of pre-engineered buildings and of construction materials for non-residential structures. A wholly-owned subsidiary of BlueScope Steel Co., based in Australia. On 27 April 2004 Butler Manufacturing Company was acquired by BlueScope Steel Limited of Melbourne, Australia.
www.butlermfg.com
Employees: 5,000
SIC: 3448
Industry/ies: Construction/Construction Materials

President   Tel: (816) 968-4775
FINAN, Patrick

Main Headquarters
Mailing: 1540 Genessee St.   Tel: (816) 968-4775
Kansas City, MO 64102

Corporate Foundations and Giving Programs

Butler Manufacturing Company Foundation
1540 Genesee St.   Tel: (816) 968-3000
P.O. Box 419917   Fax: (816) 968-3279
Kansas City, MO 64102

Public Affairs and Related Activities Personnel

At Headquarters

CLARK, Leslie	Tel:	(816) 968-4775
Director, Marketing		
GILLIGAN, Tom	Tel:	(816) 968-4775
President		
VERTOVEC, Katie	Tel:	(262) 901-2775
Contact, Media Relations		
kvertovec@bader-rutter.com		

Buzzi Unicem USA

Formed by the merger of Lone Star Industries and RC Cement in 2004 and a subsidiary of Buzzi Unicem SPA of Italy. produces portland cement, masonry cement and ready-mixed concrete.
www.buzziunicemusa.com
Annual Revenues: $94.90 million
Employees: 1,500
Industry/ies: Construction/Construction Materials

President & Chief Executive Officer   Tel: (610) 866-4400
NEPERENY, David A.   Fax: (610) 866-9430

Main Headquarters
Mailing: 100 Broadhead Rd.   Tel: (610) 882-5000
Bethlehem, PA 18017   Fax: (610) 866-9430

Political Action Committees
Buzzi Unicem USA Inc. PAC
FEC ID: C00281675
Contact: Nancy L Krial
100 Brodhead Rd.   Tel: (610) 886-4400
Suite 230   Fax: (610) 886-9430
Bethlehem, PA 18017

   Contributions to Candidates: $500 (2015-2016)
   Republicans: $500

Public Affairs and Related Activities Personnel

At Headquarters

KRIAL, Nancy L	Tel:	(610) 882-5000
PAC Contact	Fax:	(610) 866-9430

BWX Technologies

See listing on page 521 under McDermott International, Inc

C. R. Bard, Inc.

Designs, manufactures, packages, distributes, and sells medical, surgical, diagnostic, and patient care devices worldwide.
www.crbard.com
Annual Revenues: $3.34 billion
Employees: 13,900
Ticker: NYSE: BCR
SIC: 3841
Industry/ies: Medicine/Health Care/Mental Health
Legislative Issues: HCR

Chairman of the Board and Chief Executive Officer   Tel: (908) 277-8000
RING, Timothy M.   Fax: (908) 277-8412
Tim.Ring@crbard.com

Main Headquarters
Mailing: 730 Central Ave.   Tel: (908) 277-8000
Murray Hill, NJ 07974   Fax: (908) 277-8412

   TF: (800) 367-2273

Political Action Committees
C.R. Bard Inc. Active Citizenship Committee
FEC ID: C00359125
Contact: Scott T. Lowry
730 Central Ave.   Tel: (908) 277-8000
Murray Hill, NJ 07974   Fax: (908) 277-8412

   Contributions to Candidates: $5,000 (2015-2016)
   Democrats: $2,000; Republicans: $3,000

Public Affairs and Related Activities Personnel

At Headquarters

CASPER, Andrea J	Tel:	(908) 277-8000
Vice President, Regulatory Affairs	Fax:	(908) 277-8412
CHRISTIAN, Patricia G.	Tel:	(908) 277-8000
Vice President, Quality, Regulatory and Medical Affairs	Fax:	(908) 277-8412
DAILEY, Teri	Tel:	(908) 277-8000
Senior Manager, Strategic Events	Fax:	(908) 277-8412
teri.dailey@crbard.com		
GARNER, Todd W.	Tel:	(908) 277-8065
Vice President, Investor Relations	Fax:	(908) 277-8412
GOTTLIEB, David	Tel:	(908) 277-8000
Senior Vice President, Strategy and Business Development	Fax:	(908) 277-8412
HOLLAND, Christopher S.	Tel:	(908) 277-8000
Senior Vice President and Chief Financial Officer	Fax:	(908) 277-8412
HREVNACK, Linda A.	Tel:	(908) 277-8000
Manager, Community Affairs and Contributions	Fax:	(908) 277-8412
KHICHI, Samrat	Tel:	(908) 277-8000
Senior Vice President, General Counsel and Secretary	Fax:	(908) 277-8412
LARSON, Betty	Tel:	(908) 277-8000
Vice President, Human Resources	Fax:	(908) 277-8412
LOWRY, Scott T.	Tel:	(908) 277-8365
Vice President and Treasurer	Fax:	(908) 277-8412
LUPISELLA, Frank	Tel:	(908) 277-8000
Vice President and Controller	Fax:	(908) 277-8412
ROCHE, Patrick D.	Tel:	(908) 277-8000
Vice President, Information Technology	Fax:	(908) 277-8412
WEILAND, John H	Tel:	(908) 277-8000
President and Chief Operating Officer	Fax:	(908) 277-8412

C. V. Starr

See listing on page 237 under C.V. Starr & Company, Inc.

C.H. Robinson Worldwide, Inc.

A global provider of transportation services and logistics, outsource solutions, produce sourcing, and information services through a network of offices in North America, South America, Europe, and Asia.
www.chrobinson.com
Annual Revenues: $13.25 billion
Employees: 13,159
Ticker: NASDAQ: CHRW
Industry/ies: Transportation
Legislative Issues: BUD; TAX; TRA

Chairman of the Board and Chief Executive Officer   Tel: (952) 937-8500
WIEHOFF, John P.   Fax: (952) 937-6740

Main Headquarters
Mailing: 14701 Charlson Rd.   Tel: (952) 683-2500
Suite 1100   Fax: (952) 937-6714
Eden Prairie, MN 55347   TF: (855) 229-6128

Political Action Committees
C.H. Robinson Worldwide Inc. PAC
FEC ID: C00512673
Contact: Jason Craig
14701 Charlson Rd.   Tel: (952) 683-2500
Suite 1100
Eden Prairie, MN 55347

   Contributions to Candidates: $20,691 (2015-2016)
   Democrats: $3,500; Republicans: $17,191

Corporate Foundations and Giving Programs

The C.H. Robinson Worldwide Foundation
14701 Charlson Rd.
Eden Prairie, MN 55347

Public Affairs and Related Activities Personnel

At Headquarters

CAMPBELL, Ben G.	Tel:	(952) 937-8500
Chief Legal Officer and Secretary	Fax:	(952) 937-6714
CLARKE, Andrew C.	Tel:	(952) 683-2500
Chief Financial Officer	Fax:	(952) 937-6714
CRAIG, Jason	Tel:	(952) 683-3761

Manager, Government Affairs	Fax:	(952) 937-6714
jason.craig@chrobinson.com		
Registered Federal Lobbyist		
FREEMAN, Angela Kay	Tel:	(952) 837-7847
Chief Human Resources Officer	Fax:	(952) 937-6714
angie.freeman@chrobinson.com		
Registered Federal Lobbyist		
LINDBLOOM, Chad M.	Tel:	(952) 937-7779
Chief Information Officer	Fax:	(952) 937-6740
WILKEN, Mike	Tel:	(952) 937-6761
Manager, Public Relations	Fax:	(952) 937-6714
mike.wilken@chrobinson.com		

CA Technologies

Specializes in mission-critical business computing. Provides software, support, and integration services. Formerly Computer Associates International, Inc.
www.ca.com
Annual Revenues: $4.26 billion
Employees: 11,600
Ticker: NASDAQ: CA
SIC: 7372
Industry/ies: Computer/Technology
Legislative Issues: HOM; TAX; TRD

Independent Board Director	Tel:	(631) 342-2391
ALDER, Jens	Fax:	(631) 342-6800
Chief Executive Officer	Tel:	(631) 342-2391
GREGOIRE, Michael P.	Fax:	(631) 342-6800

Main Headquarters
Mailing: One CA Plaza	Fax:	(631) 342-6800
Islandia, NY 11749	TF:	(800) 225-5224

Washington Office
Mailing: 607 14th St. NW	Tel:	(202) 513-6311
Suite 775	Fax:	(202) 513-6395
Washington, DC 20005		

Public Affairs and Related Activities Personnel

At Headquarters
BECKERT, Richard	Tel:	(631) 342-2391
Executive Vice President Chief Financial Officer	Fax:	(631) 342-6800
FLAHERTY, Lauren	Tel:	(631) 342-2391
Executive Vice President and Chief Marketing Officer	Fax:	(631) 342-6800
HEALY, Michelle	Tel:	(631) 342-4701
Director, Corporate Communications	Fax:	(631) 342-6800
michelle.healy@ca.com		
KAFERLE, Daniel	Tel:	(631) 342-2111
Senior Vice President, Corporate Communications	Fax:	(631) 342-4295
daniel.kaferle@ca.com		

At Washington Office
BISIGNANO, Michael	Tel:	(202) 513-6311
Executive Vice President, General Counsel	Fax:	(202) 513-6395
BOUDRIAS, Claude P.	Tel:	(202) 513-6312
Director, Global Government Relations	Fax:	(202) 513-6395
claude.boudrias@ca.com		
Registered Federal Lobbyist		
HOFSTETTER, Patrick	Tel:	(202) 513-6311
Director, Sales Accounting	Fax:	(202) 513-6395
LAMM, Jacob	Tel:	(202) 513-6311
Executive Vice President Strategy and Corporate Development, and Acting Chief Product Officer	Fax:	(202) 513-6395
MYERS, Karen Magee	Tel:	(202) 513-6311
Vice President, Global Government Relations	Fax:	(202) 513-6395
Registered Federal Lobbyist		
PETER, Brendan M.	Tel:	(202) 513-6321
Director, Global Government Relations	Fax:	(202) 513-6395
brendan.peter@ca.com		
Registered Federal Lobbyist		
PRONSATI, Paul	Tel:	(202) 513-6311
Executive Vice President Global Operations and Information Technology	Fax:	(202) 513-6395

Cablevision Systems Corporation

A cable television programming and broadcasting company. Acquired Newsday from the Tribune Co. in 2008.
www.cablevision.com
Annual Revenues: $6.50 billion
Employees: 13,656
Ticker: NYSE: CVC
SIC: 5731; 7832; 4841
NAICS: 512131; 513210; 513220
Industry/ies: Communications; Media/Mass Communication; Telecommunications/Internet/Cable

Legislative Issues: TAX; TEC

Chairman of the Board	Tel:	(516) 803-2300
DOLAN, Charles F.	Fax:	(516) 803-1179
Chief Executive Officer	Tel:	(516) 803-2300
DOLAN, James L.	Fax:	(516) 803-1179
james.dolan@cablevision.com, jamesdolan@cablevision.com		

Main Headquarters
Mailing: 1111 Stewart Ave.	Tel:	(516) 803-2300
Bethpage, NY 11714-3581	Fax:	(516) 803-1179

Washington Office
Mailing: 1099 New York Ave. NW	Tel:	(516) 803-2300
Suite 675	Fax:	(516) 803-3134
Washington, DC 20001		

Political Action Committees
Cablevision Systems Corporation PAC
FEC ID: C00197863
Contact: Elizabeth Losinski
1111 Stewart Ave.	Tel:	(516) 803-2300
Bethpage, NY 11714-3581	Fax:	(516) 803-1179

Contributions to Candidates: $25,700 (2015-2016)
Democrats: $17,000; Republicans: $8,700

Public Affairs and Related Activities Personnel

At Headquarters
BUCKWALTER, Cindi	Tel:	(516) 803-2300
Senior Vice President, Investor Relations	Fax:	(516) 803-1179
ELLEN, David	Tel:	(516) 803-2300
Executive Vice President and General Counsel	Fax:	(516) 803-1179
KAPELL, Sandra	Tel:	(516) 803-2300
Executive Vice President, Human Resources and Administration	Fax:	(516) 803-1179
MARTIN, Ken	Tel:	(516) 803-2300
Vice President, Investor Relations	Fax:	(516) 803-1179
ROSENBLUM, Lisa	Tel:	(516) 803-2300
Executive Vice President, Government and Public Affairs	Fax:	(516) 803-1179
SCHUELER, Charles	Tel:	(516) 803-1013
Executive Vice President, Media and Community Relations	Fax:	(516) 803-1179
cshuele@cablevision.com		
SULLIVAN, Robert	Tel:	(516) 803-2300
Executive Vice President, Sales and Marketing	Fax:	(516) 803-1179
SWEENEY, Brian	Tel:	(516) 803-2300
President and Chief Financial Officer	Fax:	(516) 803-1179

At Washington Office
BURR, Geoff	Tel:	(516) 803-2300
Vice President, Government Affairs	Fax:	(516) 803-3134
LOSINSKI, Elizabeth	Tel:	(516) 803-2300
PAC Treasurer	Fax:	(516) 803-3134

Cabot Corporation

Manufacturer of carbon black and other specialty chemicals and materials. The primary products are rubber and specialty grade carbon blacks, inkjet colorants, fumed metal oxides, aerogel, tantalum and related products, and cesium formate drilling fluids, among others.
www.cabot-corp.com
Annual Revenues: $3.36 billion
Employees: 4,737
Ticker: NYSE: CBT
SIC: 2890
Industry/ies: Chemicals & Chemical Industry

Non-executive Chairman	Tel:	(678) 297-1300
O'BRIEN, John F.	Fax:	(678) 297-1245
President and Chief Executive Officer	Tel:	(678) 297-1300
PREVOST, Patrick M.	Fax:	(678) 297-1245

Main Headquarters
Mailing: 4400 N. Point Pkwy.	Tel:	(678) 297-1300
Suite 200	Fax:	(678) 297-1245
Alpharetta, GA 30022		

Corporate Foundations and Giving Programs

Cabot Corporation Foundation
Contact: Jane A. Bell
Two Seaport Ln.	Tel:	(617) 345-0100
Suite 1300	Fax:	(617) 342-6103
Boston, MA 02210		

Public Affairs and Related Activities Personnel

At Headquarters
BELL, Jane A.	Tel:	(678) 297-1300
Corporate Secretary and Chief Counsel Securities and Governance	Fax:	(678) 297-1243
jane_bell@cabot-corp.com		
BERUBE, Brian	Tel:	(678) 297-1300

Senior Vice President, General Counsel	Fax: (678) 297-1245
CORDEIRO, Eduardo	Tel: (678) 297-1300
Executive Vice President, Chief Financial Officer	Fax: (678) 297-1245
ROBINSON, Susannah	Tel: (678) 297-1300
Director, Investor Relations	Fax: (678) 297-1245
susannah_robinson@cabot-corp.com	
SISCO, Robby D.	Tel: (678) 297-1300
Senior Vice President, Human Resources	Fax: (678) 297-1245

At Other Offices

DOMURAD, Loretta A.	Tel: (617) 345-0100
PAC Treasurer	Fax: (617) 342-6103
Two Seaport Ln., Suite 1300	
Boston, MA 02210	

CACI

Provides information solutions and services to the U.S. federal government and commercial markets in North America and internationally.
www.caci.com
Annual Revenues: $3.50 billion
Employees: 16,600
Ticker: NYSE: CACI
SIC: 7373
Industry/ies: Banking/Finance/Investments; Computer/Technology
Legislative Issues: BUD; DEF; GOV; HCR; TRA; VET

Executive Chairman and Chairman of the Board	Tel: (703) 841-7800
LONDON, Dr. J.P.	Fax: (703) 841-7882

President and Chief Executive Officer	Tel: (703) 841-7800
ASBURY, Kenneth	Fax: (703) 841-7882

Main Headquarters

Mailing:	1100 N. Glebe Rd.	Tel: (703) 841-7800
	Arlington, VA 22201	Fax: (703) 841-7882

Public Affairs and Related Activities Personnel

At Headquarters

BAILEY, Marjorie R.	Tel: (703) 841-7800
Executive Vice President, Chief Human Resources Officer	Fax: (703) 841-7882
BROWN, Jody A.	Tel: (703) 841-7801
Executive Vice President, Public Relations, Corporate Communications and Congressional Relations	Fax: (703) 841-7882
jbrown@caci.com	
DRAGICS, David	Tel: (703) 841-7800
Senior Vice President, Investor Relations Contact	Fax: (703) 841-7882
ddragics@caci.com	
GAFFNEY, Mike	Tel: (703) 841-7800
Executive Vice President, Business Development	Fax: (703) 841-7882
KASS, Dr. Lani	Tel: (703) 841-7800
Corporate Strategic Advisor	Fax: (703) 841-7882
KOEGEL, Jr., J William	Tel: (703) 841-7800
Executive Vice President, General Counsel and Secretary	Fax: (703) 841-7882
MENGUCCI, John S.	Tel: (703) 841-7800
Chief Operating Officer and President, U.S. Operations	Fax: (703) 841-7882
MUTRYN, Thomas A.	Tel: (703) 841-7800
Executive Vice President, Chief Financial Officer and Corporate Treasurer	Fax: (703) 841-7882
tmutryn@caci.com	
WEISS, Steven H.	Tel: (703) 841-7800
Executive Vice President Government Business Operations	Fax: (703) 841-7882

Cadence Design Systems, Inc.

Develops and markets electronic design automation software products.
www.cadence.com
Annual Revenues: $1.61 billion
Employees: 6,100
Ticker: NASDAQ: CDNS
SIC: 5045; 7371; 5734; 7373; 7372
Industry/ies: Computer/Technology; Electricity & Electronics; Electronics; Energy/Electricity

Chairman of the Board	Tel: (408) 943-1234
SHOVEN, Dr. John B.	Fax: (408) 428-5001

President and Chief Executive Officer	Tel: (408) 943-1234
TAN, Lip-Bu	Fax: (408) 428-5001

Main Headquarters

Mailing:	2655 Seely Ave.	Tel: (408) 943-1234
	San Jose, CA 95134	Fax: (408) 428-5001
		TF: (800) 746-6223

Corporate Foundations and Giving Programs

Cadence Design Systems Community Involvement Program	
2655 Seely Ave.	Tel: (408) 428-5993
San Jose, CA 95134	Fax: (408) 943-0513

Public Affairs and Related Activities Personnel

At Headquarters

COWIE, Jim	Tel: (408) 943-1234
Senior Vice President, General Counsel and Secretary	Fax: (408) 428-5001
HSU, Chi-Ping	Tel: (408) 943-1234
Senior Vice President, Chief Strategy Officer	Fax: (408) 428-5001
JONES, Tina	Tel: (408) 943-1234
Senior Vice President, Global Human Resources	Fax: (408) 428-5001
LINDSTROM, Alan J.	Tel: (408) 944-7100
Director, Investor Relations	Fax: (408) 428-5001
investor_relations@cadence.com	
PLUNGY, Mark	Tel: (408) 943-1234
Director, Public Relations	Fax: (408) 428-5001
RIBAR, Geoff	Tel: (408) 943-1234
Senior Vice President and Chief Financial Officer	Fax: (408) 428-5001
SZYMANSKI, Nancy	Tel: (408) 473-8382
Director, Corporate Campaign Marketing	Fax: (408) 944-0747
nancy@cadence.com	

Cadiz Inc.

A publicly traded land and water resource development company.
cadizinc.com
Annual Revenues: $1.02 million
Employees: 10
Ticker: NASDAQ: CDZI
SIC: 4941
Industry/ies: Agriculture/Agronomy
Legislative Issues: ENV; NAT; RRR

Chairman of the Board	Tel: (213) 271-1600
BRACKPOOL, Keith	Fax: (213) 271-1614

President and Chief Executive Officer	Tel: (213) 271-1600
SLATER, Scott S.	Fax: (213) 271-1614

Main Headquarters

Mailing:	550 S. Hope St.	Tel: (213) 271-1600
	Suite 2850	Fax: (213) 271-1614
	Los Angeles, CA 90071	

Corporate Foundations and Giving Programs

Cadiz Inc. Contributions Program	
550 S. Hope St.	Tel: (213) 271-1600
Suite 2850	
Los Angeles, CA 90071	

Public Affairs and Related Activities Personnel

At Headquarters

DEGENER, Courtney	Tel: (213) 271-1600
Vice President, Investor Relations	Fax: (213) 271-1614
cdegener@cadizinc.com	
SHAHEEN, Timothy J.	Tel: (213) 271-1600
Chief Financial Officer	Fax: (213) 271-1614

Caesars Entertainment Corporation

Formerly known as Harrah's Entertainment Inc.
www.caesars.com
Annual Revenues: $4.56 billion
Employees: 33,000
Ticker: NASDAQ: CZR
Industry/ies: Travel/Tourism/Lodging
Legislative Issues: GAM; LAW; RET

Chairman of the Board, President and Chief Executive Officer	Tel: (702) 407-6000
LOVEMAN, Gary W.	Fax: (702) 407-6037

Chief Executive Officer and President	Tel: (702) 407-6000
FRISSORA, Mark P.	Fax: (702) 407-6037

Main Headquarters

Mailing:	One Caesars Palace Dr.	Tel: (702) 407-6000
	Las Vegas, NV 89109	Fax: (702) 407-6037

Political Action Committees

Ceasars Entertainment Political Action Committee
FEC ID: C00239947
Contact: Kelley Magdaluyo

One Caesar's Palace Dr.	Tel: (702) 407-6000
Las Vegas, NV 89109	Fax: (702) 407-6037

Contributions to Candidates: $123,200 (2015-2016)
Democrats: $59,700; Republicans: $63,500

Principal Recipients

SENATE
GRASSLEY, CHARLES E SENATOR (REP-IA)

HOUSE
HECK, JOE (REP-NV)
ROBERSON, MICHAEL (REP-NV)

Corporate Foundations and Giving Programs

Caesars Foundation
One Caesars Palace Dr.   Tel: (702) 880-4728
Las Vegas, NV 89109   Fax: (702) 407-6037

Public Affairs and Related Activities Personnel

At Headquarters

BROOME, Richard   Tel: (702) 407-6000
Executive Vice President, Public Affairs and Communications   Fax: (702) 407-6037

DONOVAN, Tim   Tel: (702) 407-6000
Executive Vice President and General Counsel and Chief   Fax: (702) 407-6037
Regulatory and Compliance Officer

HESSION, Eric   Tel: (702) 407-6000
Chief Financial Officer   Fax: (702) 407-6037

JONES, Janis   Tel: (702) 407-6387
Executive Vice President, Government Relations and   Fax: (702) 407-6388
Corporate Responsibility
jajones@harrahs.com

LA SANE, II, Karlos   Tel: (702) 407-6204
Federal Lobbyist   Fax: (702) 407-6037
Registered Federal Lobbyist

MADDOX, John   Tel: (702) 407-6204
Regional Vice President   Fax: (702) 407-6037
jmaddox@caesars.com
Registered Federal Lobbyist

MAGDALUYO, Kelley   Tel: (702) 407-6000
Manager, Compliance   Fax: (702) 407-6037
magdaluyok@caesars.com

SATZ, David   Tel: (702) 407-6204
Vice President, Government Relations   Fax: (702) 407-6037
Registered Federal Lobbyist

THOMAS, Mary   Tel: (702) 407-6000
Executive Vice President, Human Resources   Fax: (702) 407-6037

THOMPSON, Gary   Tel: (702) 407-6529
Director, Corporate Communications   Fax: (702) 407-6037
gthompson@caesars.com

Cal-Chip Electronics

Specializes in surface mounted devices.
www.calchipelectronics.com
Annual Revenues: $6.40 million
Employees: 55
Industry/ies: Electricity & Electronics; Electronics; Energy/Electricity

Main Headquarters
Mailing: 59 Steamwhistle Dr.   Tel: (215) 942-8900
     Ivyland, PA 18974-1451   Fax: (215) 942-6400
     TF: (800) 884-0864

Public Affairs and Related Activities Personnel

At Headquarters

GIULIANO, Greg   Tel: (215) 942-8900
General Manager   Fax: (215) 942-6400
ggiuliano@calchip.com

MEAKIM, John   Tel: (215) 942-8900
Manager, International Sales   Fax: (215) 942-6400
jmeakim@calchip.com

Caladrius

Caladrius (formerly NeoStem) Provides adult stem cell collection.
www.caladrius.com
Annual Revenues: $17.06 million
Employees: 182
Ticker: NYSE:CLBS
SIC: 8090
Industry/ies: Medicine/Health Care/Mental Health

Chairman of the Board   Tel: (212) 584-4180
SMITH, MD, MBA, Robin L.   Fax: (646) 514-7787
rsmith@neostem.com

Chief Executive Officer and Director   Tel: (212) 584-4180
MAZZO, PhD, David J.   Fax: (646) 514-7787

Main Headquarters
Mailing: 420 Lexington Ave.   Tel: (212) 584-4180
     Suite 350   Fax: (646) 514-7787
     New York City, NY 10170

Corporate Foundations and Giving Programs

Stem For Life Foundation
Contact: Robin L. Smith MD, MBA
420 Lexington Ave.   Tel: (212) 584-4176
Suite 450
New York City, NY 10170

Public Affairs and Related Activities Personnel

At Headquarters

LOSORDO, MD, FACC, Douglas W.   Tel: (212) 584-4180
Senior Vice President, Clinical, Medical and Regulatory   Fax: (646) 514-7787
Affairs and Chief Medical Officer

SCHLOSS, David   Tel: (212) 584-4180
Vice President, Human Resources   Fax: (646) 514-7787

VATERS, Robert S.   Tel: (212) 584-4180
President, Chief Financial Officer and Director   Fax: (646) 514-7787

CalAtlantic Group, Inc.

A residential construction company.
www.standardpacifichomes.com
Annual Revenues: $2.45 billion
Employees: 1,250
Ticker: NYSE: SPF
SIC: 1531
NAICS: 236115
Industry/ies: Architecture And Design; Banking/Finance/Investments;
Construction/Construction Materials; Housing

Founder and Chairman of the Board   Tel: (949) 789-1600
FOELL, Ronald R.   Fax: (949) 789-1609

Chief Executive Officer and President   Tel: (949) 789-1600
STOWELL, Scott D.   Fax: (949) 789-1609

Main Headquarters
Mailing: 15360 Barranca Pkwy.   Tel: (949) 789-1600
     Irvine, CA 92618-2215   Fax: (818) 223-7667

Corporate Foundations and Giving Programs

Standard Pacific Corporation Contributions Program
26 Technology Dr.   Tel: (949) 789-1600
Irvine, CA 92618   Fax: (949) 789-1609

Public Affairs and Related Activities Personnel

At Headquarters

BABEL, John P.   Tel: (949) 789-1600
Executive Vice President, General Counsel and Secretary   Fax: (949) 789-1609

MARLETT, Wendy   Tel: (949) 789-1600
Executive Vice President and Chief Marketing Officer   Fax: (949) 789-1609

MCCALL, Jeffrey J.   Tel: (949) 789-1600
Executive Vice President and Chief Financial Officer   Fax: (949) 789-1609
jmccall@stanpac.com

TOCCO, Danielle   Tel: (949) 789-1600
Director, Communications   Fax: (949) 789-1609
dtocco@stanpac.com

CalCot

Cooperative cotton marketing organization.
www.calcot.com
Annual Revenues: $399.64 million
Employees: 100
SIC: 5099; 0724; 2211; 5159
Industry/ies: Agriculture/Agronomy; Cooperatives

Chairman of the Board   Tel: (661) 327-5961
RAYNER, F. Ronald   Fax: (661) 861-9870

President and Chief Executive Officer   Tel: (661) 327-5961
NEEPER, Jarral T.   Fax: (661) 861-9870
jneeper@calcot.com

Main Headquarters
Mailing: P.O. Box 259   Tel: (661) 327-5961
     Bakersfield, CA 93302-0259   Fax: (661) 861-9870

Political Action Committees
Calcot Ltd. Federal PAC
FEC ID: C00172775
Contact: Miguel Mory
P.O. Box 259   Tel: (661) 327-5961
Bakerfield, CA 93302   Fax: (661) 861-9870

     Contributions to Candidates: $11,000 (2015-2016)
     Democrats: $500; Republicans: $10,500

Corporate Foundations and Giving Programs

The Calcot-Seitz Foundation
Contact: Marci Cunningham
P.O. Box 259   Tel: (661) 395-6874
Bakersfield, CA 93302   Fax: (661) 861-9870

Public Affairs and Related Activities Personnel

At Headquarters

BAGBY, Mark   Tel: (661) 395-6885
Director, Communications   Fax: (661) 861-9870
mbagby@calcot.com

CUNNINGHAM, Marci   Tel: (661) 395-6874
Scholarship Chair, Calcot-Seitz Foundation   Fax: (661) 861-9870
mcunningham@calcot.com

MORY, Miguel   Tel: (661) 327-5961

PAC Treasurer mmory@calcot.com	Fax:	(661) 861-9870
WANG, Roxanne *Chief Financial Officer* rwang@calcot.com	Tel: Fax:	(661) 327-5961 (661) 861-9870

Calera Corporation

Calera Corporation was founded in 2007. Calera's focus is capturing CO2 from stationary emitters- including power plants and cement plants- and permanently converting it to mineral forms. The ultimate goal is to develop valuable products, such as cementitious materials, out of the captured carbon dioxide.
www.calera.com
Annual Revenues: $12.20 million
Employees: 80
Industry/ies: Construction/Construction Materials; Environment And Conservation

Main Headquarters

Mailing:	485 Alberto Way Suite 210 Los Gatos, CA 95032	Tel: Fax:	(408) 340-4600 (408) 340-4650

Public Affairs and Related Activities Personnel

At Headquarters

ALFRICHT, CPA, Jill *Chief Financial Officer*	Tel: Fax:	(408) 340-4600 (408) 340-4650
DEVENNEY, Martin *Chief Operating Officer and President, CO2 to Products*	Tel: Fax:	(408) 340-4600 (408) 340-4650

Caleres

Formerly known as Brown Shoe Company, Inc. A footwear company with worldwide operations.
www.caleres.com
Annual Revenues: $2.51 billion
Employees: 11,200
Ticker: NYSE: BWS
SIC: 3140
Industry/ies: Apparel/Textiles Industry

President, Chief Executive Officer and Chairman of the Board SULLIVAN , Diane M. rfromm@brownshoe.com	Tel: Fax:	(314) 854-4000 (314) 854-4274

Main Headquarters

Mailing:	8300 Maryland Ave. St. Louis, MO 63105	Tel: Fax:	(314) 854-4000 (314) 854-4274

Corporate Foundations and Giving Programs

Brown Shoe's Charitable Trust
8300 Maryland Ave.
St. Louis, MO 63105

Public Affairs and Related Activities Personnel

At Headquarters

HAMMER, Russ *Senior Vice President and Chief Financial Officer*	Tel: Fax:	(314) 854-4000 (314) 854-4274
KOCH, Douglas *Senior Vice President and Chief Talent and Strategy Officer*	Tel: Fax:	(314) 854-4000 (314) 854-4274
OBERLANDER, Michael *Senior Vice President, General Counsel and Corporate Secretary*	Tel: Fax:	(314) 854-4000 (314) 854-4274
THARP, Peggy Reilly *Vice President, Investor Relations* ptharp@brownshoe.com	Tel: Fax:	(314) 854-4000 (314) 854-4274

Calgon Carbon Corporation

A global manufacturer and supplier of activated carbon and innovative treatment systems, provides value-added technologies and services for optimizing production processes and safely purifying the environment.
www.calgoncarbon.com
Annual Revenues: $559.17 million
Employees: 1,096
Ticker: NYSE: CCC
SIC: 2810; 2819; 2899; 5169; 2834
NAICS: 325998; 325998; 325412
Industry/ies: Energy/Electricity
Legislative Issues: DEF; ENV; HOM; MAR

Chairman of the Board, President and Chief Executive Officer DEARTH, Randall S.	Tel: Fax:	(412) 787-6700 (412) 787-6676

Main Headquarters

Mailing:	3000 GSX Dr. Moon Township, PA 15108	Tel:	(412) 787-6700

Political Action Committees

Calgon Carbon Corporation PAC Inc DBA CCC PAC or Calgon Carbon
FEC ID: C00543876
Contact: Peter K. Lee

400 Calgon Carbon Dr. Pittsburgh, PA 15205	Tel: Fax:	(412) 787-6700 (412) 787-6676

Contributions to Candidates: $25,050 (2015-2016)
Democrats: $4,500; Republicans: $20,550

Public Affairs and Related Activities Personnel

At Headquarters

COCCAGNO, James A. *Vice President, Global Procurement and Strategic Initiatives*	Tel:	(412) 787-6700
GERONO, Gail A. *Vice President, Investor Relations and Corporate Communications*	Tel:	(412) 787-6700
O'BRIEN, Robert P. *Executive Vice President and Chief Operating Officer*	Tel:	(412) 787-6700
ROSE, Richard D. *Senior Vice President, General Counsel and Secretary*	Tel:	(412) 787-6700
SCHOTT , Stevan R. *Senior Vice President, Chief Financial Officer*	Tel:	(412) 787-6700

At Other Offices

ADAMS, John *Director, Government Affairs* 400 Calgon Carbon Dr. Pittsburgh, PA 15230 jadams@calgoncarbon-us.com *Registered Federal Lobbyist*	Tel: Fax:	(412) 787-6700 (412) 787-6676

LEE, Peter K.
PAC Treasurer
400 Calgon Carbon Dr.
Pittsburgh, PA 15205

California Dairies Inc.

A dairy processing cooperative company.
www.californiadairies.com
Annual Revenues: $3.00 billion
Employees: 800
Industry/ies: Food And Beverage Industry
Legislative Issues: AGR; ENV; FOO; IMM; TAX; TRD

Chairman of the Board AZEVEDO, John	Tel: Fax:	(559) 625-2200 (559) 625-5433
President and Chief Executive Office MIKHALEVSKY, Andrei	Tel: Fax:	(559) 625-2200 (559) 625-5433

Main Headquarters

Mailing:	2000 N. Plaza Dr. Visalia, CA 93291	Tel: Fax:	(559) 625-2200 (559) 625-5433

Political Action Committees

California Dairies Federal PAC
FEC ID: C00349746
Contact: Eric Erba

475 S. Tegner Turlock, CA 95380	Tel: Fax:	(209) 668-6150 (209) 668-6162

Contributions to Candidates: $169,000 (2015-2016)
Democrats: $26,000; Republicans: $140,500; Other: $2,500

Corporate Foundations and Giving Programs

California Dairies Inc. Contributions Program 2000 N. Plaza Dr. Visalia, CA 93291	Tel:	(559) 625-2200

Public Affairs and Related Activities Personnel

At Headquarters

CAMP, CPA, David *Senior Vice President and Chief Financial Officer*	Tel: Fax:	(559) 625-2200 (559) 625-5433

At Other Offices

ERBA , Eric *Senior Vice President, Chief Strategy Officer and PAC Treasurer* 475 S. Tegner Turlock, CA 95380	Tel: Fax:	(209) 668-6150 (209) 668-6162

California Portland Cement Company

Cement manufacturing company.
www.calportland.com
Annual Revenues: $67.30 million
Employees: 800
SIC: 5032
Industry/ies: Construction/Construction Materials

President & Chief Executive Officer HAMBLEN, Allen	Tel: Fax:	(626) 852-6200 (626) 963-9630

Main Headquarters

Mailing:	2025 E. Financial Way Suite 200 Glendora, CA 91741-4692	Tel: Fax:	(626) 852-6200 (626) 963-9630

Corporate Foundations and Giving Programs
California Portland Cement Company Contributions Program
2025 E. Financial Way   Tel: (626) 852-6200
Glendora, CA 91741   Fax: (626) 963-9630

Public Affairs and Related Activities Personnel

At Headquarters

CABRERA, Irma   Tel: (626) 852-6200
PAC Treasurer, Senior Financial Analyst Fax: (626) 963-9630
WARE, Annette   Tel: (626) 852-6200
Vice President, Operations and Planning Fax: (626) 963-9630

California Water Service Company
Provides water supply and related services.
www.calwater.com
Annual Revenues: $583.17 million
Employees: 1,100
Ticker: NYSE: CWT
SIC: 4941
Industry/ies: Utilities

Chairman of the Board   Tel: (408) 367-8200
NELSON, Peter C.   Fax: (408) 367-8430

President and Chief Executive Officer Tel: (408) 367-8200
KROPELNICKI, Martin A.   Fax: (408) 367-8430

Main Headquarters
Mailing: 1720 N. First St.   Tel: (408) 367-8200
               San Jose, CA 95112-4508   Fax: (408) 367-8430
                                         TF: (800) 750-8200

Political Action Committees
California Water Service Group PAC
FEC ID: C00357608
Contact: Francis S. Ferraro
1720 N. First St.   Tel: (408) 367-8200
San Jose, CA 95112   Fax: (408) 367-8430

   Contributions to Candidates: $1,000 (2015-2016)
   Democrats: $1,000

Corporate Foundations and Giving Programs
California Water Service Company Contributions Program
1720 N. First St.
San Jose, CA 95112-4508

Public Affairs and Related Activities Personnel

At Headquarters

DEAN, Shannon C.   Tel: (310) 258-1435
Vice President, Corporate Communications and Community Fax: (408) 367-8430
Affairs
sdean@calwater.com
FERRARO, Francis S.   Tel: (408) 367-8200
Vice President, Corporate Development and PAC Treasurer Fax: (408) 367-8430
MCGHEE, Lynne P.   Tel: (408) 367-8200
Vice President and General Counsel   Fax: (408) 367-8430
SMEGAL, III, Thomas F.   Tel: (408) 367-8200
Vice President, Chief Financial Officer and Treasurer Fax: (408) 367-8430
TOWNSLEY, Paul G.   Tel: (408) 367-8200
Vice President, Regulatory Matters and Corporate Relations Fax: (408) 367-8430
WEBB, Ronald D.   Tel: (408) 367-8200
Vice President, Human Resources   Fax: (408) 367-8430

Calista
Regional corporation formed under the Alaska Native Claims Settlement Act.
www.calistacorp.com
Annual Revenues: $$401.90 million
Employees: 12,500
Industry/ies: Natural Resources
Legislative Issues: IND; TRA

Chairman of the Board   Tel: (907) 275-2800
KASAYULIE, Willie   Fax: (907) 275-2919

President and Chief Executive Officer Tel: (907) 275-2800
GUY, Andrew   Fax: (907) 275-2919
aguy@calistacorp.com

Main Headquarters
Mailing: 5015 Business Park Blvd. Tel: (907) 275-2800
               Suite 3000   Fax: (907) 275-2919
               Anchorage, AK 99503   TF: (800) 277-5516

Corporate Foundations and Giving Programs
The Calista Education and Culture, Inc.
Contact: Mark John
5015 Business Park Blvd.   Tel: (907) 275-2800
Suite 3000   Fax: (907) 275-2919
Anchorage, AK 99503

Public Affairs and Related Activities Personnel

At Headquarters

BURNS, Sharon   Tel: (907) 275-2800
Chief Financial Officer   Fax: (907) 275-2919
CHARLES, Bob   Tel: (907) 275-2800
Vice President, Management Services   Fax: (907) 275-2919
Registered Federal Lobbyist
FLANDERS, Su   Tel: (907) 275-2800
Legal Assistant   Fax: (907) 275-2919
GEORGE, Jim   Tel: (907) 275-2800
Registered Federal Lobbyist   Fax: (907) 275-2919
JAMES, Monica   Tel: (907) 275-2800
Chief Operating Officer   Fax: (907) 275-2919
Registered Federal Lobbyist
JOHN, Mark   Tel: (907) 275-2800
Cultural Advisor   Fax: (907) 275-2919
mjohn@calistacorp.com
OWLETUCK, George   Tel: (907) 275-2800
Liason, Government Relations   Fax: (907) 275-2919
Registered Federal Lobbyist
PASKVAN, Bonnie   Tel: (907) 275-2800
General Counsel   Fax: (907) 275-2919
PORTER, Robert   Tel: (907) 275-2800
Registered Federal Lobbyist   Fax: (907) 275-2919

Calix Networks
A telecommunications equipment supplier.
www.calix.com
Annual Revenues: $406.45 million
Employees: 782
Ticker: NYSE: CALX
SIC: 4899
Industry/ies: Communications; Telecommunications/Internet/Cable

Chairman of the Board   Tel: (707) 766-3000
LISTWIN, Donald   Fax: (707) 283-3100

President and Chief Executive Officer Tel: (707) 766-3000
RUSSO, Carl   Fax: (707) 283-3100

Main Headquarters
Mailing: 1035 N. McDowell Blvd.   Tel: (707) 766-3000
               Petaluma, CA 94954   Fax: (707) 283-3100

Public Affairs and Related Activities Personnel

At Headquarters

ATKINS, William   Tel: (707) 766-3000
Executive Vice President and Chief Financial Officer Fax: (707) 283-3100
BASS, Carolyn   Tel: (415) 445-3232
Contact, Investor Relations   Fax: (707) 766-3100
carolyn.bass@calix.com
BRADARAN, Mehdi   Tel: (707) 766-3000
Senior Vice President, Product Operations Fax: (707) 283-3100
KOO, Catherine   Tel: (415) 992-4400
Contact, Media Relations   Fax: (707) 766-3100
calix@lewispr.com
LOCKHART, Andy   Tel: (707) 766-3000
Senior Vice President, International Sales and Marketing Fax: (707) 283-3100
MATHENY, Neila   Tel: (707) 766-3512
Contact, Media   Fax: (707) 283-3100
Neila.matheny@calix.com
ORTBERG, Todd   Tel: (707) 766-3000
Senior Vice President, Strategic Development Fax: (707) 283-3100
QUINLAN, Denis   Tel: (707) 766-3000
Contact, General Counsel   Fax: (707) 283-3100
SEDA, David   Tel: (707) 766-3000
Vice President, Marketing   Fax: (707) 283-3100

Callaway Golf Company
A marketer and designer of golf products.
www.callawaygolf.com
Annual Revenues: $819.25 million
Employees: 1,700
Ticker: NYSE: ELY
SIC: 3949; 5091
NAICS: 33992
Industry/ies: Sports/Leisure/Entertainment

Chairman of the Board   Tel: (760) 931-1771
BEARD, Ronald S.   Fax: (760) 930-5015

President and Chief Executive Officer Tel: (760) 931-1771
BREWER, Oliver G.   Fax: (760) 930-5015

Main Headquarters
Mailing: 2180 Rutherford Rd.   Tel: (760) 931-1771

Carlsbad, CA 92008-7328	Fax:	(760) 930-5015
	TF:	(800) 588-9836

Corporate Foundations and Giving Programs

Callaway Golf Foundation
2180 Rutherford Rd.   Tel: (760) 931-1771
Carlsbad, CA 92008   Fax: (760) 930-5015

Public Affairs and Related Activities Personnel

At Headquarters

THORNLEY, Anthony S.   Tel: (760) 931-1771
Director   Fax: (760) 930-5015

WEST, Barb   Tel: (760) 931-1771
Senior Assistant Executive Chief Fincial Officer   Fax: (760) 930-5015

Calpine Corporation

An independent electric power producer, headquartered in San Jose, Calif.
www.calpine.com
Annual Revenues: $7.20 billion
Employees: 2,052
Ticker: NYSE: CPN
SIC: 4911
NAICS: 221122
Industry/ies: Energy/Electricity
Legislative Issues: CAW; ENG; ENV; HOM; TAX

Executive Chairman   Tel: (713) 830-2000
FUSCO, Jack A.   Fax: (713) 830-2001

President and Chief Executive Officer   Tel: (713) 830-2000
HILL, Thad   Fax: (713) 830-2001

Main Headquarters
Mailing: 717 Texas Ave.   Tel: (713) 830-2000
              Suite 1000   Fax: (713) 830-2001
              Houston, TX 77002

Washington Office
Mailing: 875 15th St. NW   Tel: (202) 589-0909
              Suite 700   Fax: (202) 589-0922
              Washington, DC 20005

Political Action Committees

Calpine Corporation PAC
FEC ID: C00362640
Contact: Joseph E. Ronan Jr.
4160 Dublin Blvd.
Suite 100
Dublin, CA 94568

> **Contributions to Candidates:** $12,252,215 (2015-2016)
> Democrats: $78,700; Republicans: $81,500; Other: $12,092,015

Corporate Foundations and Giving Programs

Calpine Contributions Program
717 Texas Ave.
Suite 1000
Houston, TX 77002

Public Affairs and Related Activities Personnel

At Headquarters

DEIDIKER, Jim   Tel: (713) 830-2000
Senior Vice President, Chief Accounting Officer   Fax: (713) 830-2001

DUNN, Norma F.   Tel: (713) 830-8883
Vice President, Corporate Communications   Fax: (713) 830-2001
norma.dunn@calpine.com

FLUMERFELT, John   Tel: (713) 570-4878
Director, Government Relations and Regulatory Affairs   Fax: (408) 995-0505

MCMAHON, Kevin G.   Tel: (713) 830-2000
Senior Vice President, Internal Audit and Chief Compliance   Fax: (713) 830-2001
Officer

MILLER, W. Thaddeus   Tel: (713) 830-2000
Executive Vice President, Chief Legal Officer and Secretary   Fax: (713) 830-2001

NOVOSEL, Sarah   Tel: (713) 830-2000
Senior Vice President, Government Affairs   Fax: (713) 830-2001

RAUF, Zamir   Tel: (713) 830-2000
Executive Vice President and Chief Financial Officer   Fax: (713) 830-2001

RONAN, Jr., Joseph E.   Tel: (713) 830-2000
Senior Vice President, Government and Regulatory Affairs   Fax: (713) 830-2001
and PAC Treasurer
joer@calpine.com

SCHLEIMER, Steven   Tel: (713) 830-2000
Senior Vice President, Government and Regulatory Affairs   Fax: (713) 830-2001

WALKER, Andrew K.   Tel: (713) 830-8775
Contact, Investor Relations   Fax: (713) 830-2001
andrew@calpine.com

At Washington Office

MCINTYRE, Yvonne A.   Tel: (202) 589-0909

Vice President, Federal Affairs   Fax: (202) 589-0922
ymcintyre@calpine.com
Registered Federal Lobbyist

Calumet Electronics Corporation

Manufacturer of mission-critical printed circuit boards.
www.calumetelectronics.com
SIC: 3679; 3672
Industry/ies: Electricity & Electronics; Electronics; Energy/Electricity

President and Chief Executive Officer   Tel: (906) 337-1305
VAIRO, Stephen   Fax: (906) 337-5359
svairo@calumetelectronics.com

Main Headquarters
Mailing: 25830 Depot St.   Tel: (906) 337-1305
              Calumet, MI 49913   Fax: (906) 337-5359

Public Affairs and Related Activities Personnel

At Headquarters

BRASSARD, Todd   Tel: (906) 337-1305
Vice President, Chief Operating Officer   Fax: (906) 337-5359

KADLEC, Mike   Tel: (906) 337-1305
Vice President, Corporate Development   Fax: (906) 337-5359
mkadlec@calumetelectronics.com

MARSHALL, Stephen J.   Tel: (906) 337-1305
Manager, Business Development   Fax: (906) 337-5359
smarshall@calumetelectronics.com

TAIVALKOSKI, Brian   Tel: (906) 337-1305
Vice President, Cheif Financial Officer   Fax: (906) 337-5359
btaivalkoski@calumetelectronics.com

Calvin Klein (client of Conopco, Inc.)

A clothing and cosmetics manufacturer and distributor.
explore.calvinklein.com/en_US
Annual Revenues: $33.40 million
Employees: 700
SIC: 2337; 2329; 2331; 2335; 2339
NAICS: 315234; 315228; 315232; 315233; 315239
Industry/ies: Apparel/Textiles Industry

President and Chief Executive Officer   Tel: (212) 719-2600
MURRY, III, Paul Thomas   Fax: (212) 221-4541

Main Headquarters
Mailing: 205 W. 39th St.   Tel: (212) 719-2600
              New York City, NY 10018   Fax: (212) 221-4541
                                                      TF: (866) 214-6694

Public Affairs and Related Activities Personnel

At Headquarters

GLAHN, John Van   Tel: (212) 719-2600
Executive Vice President, Finance and Administration   Fax: (212) 221-4541

Calypso Medical Technologies, Inc.

Calypso Medical Technologies, Inc., is a medical device company involved in shaping the future of radiation therapy delivery and management.
www.calypsomedical.com
Annual Revenues: $24.20 million
Employees: 200
Industry/ies: Machinery/Equipment; Medicine/Health Care/Mental Health

President and Chief Executive Officer   Tel: (206) 254-0600
VERTATSCHITSCH, PhD, Edward   Fax: (206) 254-0606

Main Headquarters
Mailing: 2101 Fourth Ave., Fourth and Blanchard Bldg. Tel: (206) 254-0600
              Suite 500   Fax: (206) 254-0606
              Seattle, WA 98121-2348

Corporate Foundations and Giving Programs

Calypso Medical Technologies, Inc. Contributions Program
2101 Fourth Ave.
Suite 500
Seattle, WA 98121-2348

Public Affairs and Related Activities Personnel

At Headquarters

BETZ, David   Tel: (206) 330-2621
Manager, Marketing, Communications and Public Relations   Fax: (206) 254-0606
dbetz@calypsomedical.com

GINSBERG, Meryl   Tel: (650) 424-6444
Contact, Media   Fax: (206) 254-0606

PAGE, Marcia   Tel: (206) 254-0600
Vice President, Quality Assurance and Regulatory Affairs   Fax: (206) 254-0606

WELCH, Greg   Tel: (206) 254-0600
Senior Director, Human Resources   Fax: (206) 254-0606

Camber Corporation

Serves the U.S. military with a wide range of information technology and training services.
www.camber.com
Employees: 2,300
Industry/ies: Defense/Homeland Security; Government-Related

Chairman of the Board Tel: (256) 922-0200
BATSON, Jr., Walter Fax: (256) 922-3599

Chief Executive Officer Tel: (256) 922-0200
NOLAN, Philip O. Fax: (256) 922-3599

Main Headquarters
Mailing: 670 Discovery Dr. Tel: (256) 922-0200
  Huntsville, AL 35806 Fax: (256) 922-3599
  TF: (800) 998-7988

Political Action Committees
Camber Corporation PAC (Camber PAC)
FEC ID: C00364851
Contact: Mike Whyte
635 Discovery Dr. Tel: (256) 922-0200
Huntsville, AL 35806 Fax: (256) 922-3599

Contributions to Candidates: $5,400 (2015-2016)
Republicans: $5,400

Public Affairs and Related Activities Personnel

At Headquarters

BRABSTON, James Tel: (256) 922-0200
President and Chief Operating Officer Fax: (256) 922-3599

BROOKS, Randy Tel: (256) 922-0200
Chief Strategy Officer Fax: (256) 922-3599

CORMIER, Joseph Tel: (256) 922-0200
Executive Vice President and Chief Financial Officer Fax: (256) 922-3599

KAKALEC, Gene Tel: (256) 922-0200
Executive Vice President and Chief Growth Officer Fax: (256) 922-3599

WHYTE, Mike Tel: (256) 922-0200
Senior Vice President, Finance and PAC Treasurer Fax: (256) 922-3599
Whyte@Chamber.com

Cambium Learning

Educational publishing and learning tools company.
www.cambiumlearning.com
Annual Revenues: $142.14 million
Employees: 518
Ticker: NASDAQ: ABCD
SIC: 2741
Industry/ies: Education

Chief Executive Officer Tel: (214) 932-9500
CAMPBELL, John

Main Headquarters
Mailing: 17855 Dallas Pkwy. Tel: (214) 932-9500
  Suite 400 TF: (888) 399-1995
  Dallas, TX 75287

Corporate Foundations and Giving Programs

Cambium Learning Contributions Program
17855 Dallas Pkwy. Tel: (214) 932-9500
Suite 400
Dallas, TX 75287

Public Affairs and Related Activities Personnel

At Headquarters

BENSON, Barbara Tel: (214) 932-9500
Chief Financial Officer

GETRIDGE, Carolyn M. Tel: (214) 932-9500
Senior Vice President, Strategic Partnerships

LOGUE, George A. Tel: (214) 932-9500
President

WRIGHT, Elaine Gantz Tel: (214) 932-9500
Contact, Media Relations
elaine.wright@cambiumlearning.com

Cameron International Corporation

Manufacturer of oil and gas pressure control equipment and provider of flow equipment products, systems and services to worldwide oil, gas and process industries.
www.c-a-m.com
Annual Revenues: $10.32 billion
Employees: 28,000
Ticker: NYSE: CAM
SIC: 3533
NAICS: 333132
Industry/ies: Machinery/Equipment

Chairman, President and Chief Executive Officer Tel: (713) 513-3300
MOORE, Jack B. Fax: (713) 513-3456

Main Headquarters
Mailing: 1333 West Loop., South Tel: (713) 513-3300

  Suite 1700 Fax: (713) 513-3456
  Houston, TX 77027

Public Affairs and Related Activities Personnel

At Headquarters

BALDWIN, Dennis S Tel: (713) 513-3300
Vice President, Controller and Chief Accounting Officer Fax: (713) 513-3456

GEIGER, Steven P Tel: (713) 513-3300
Vice President and Chief Administrative Officer Fax: (713) 513-3456

HOLMES, Grace B. Tel: (713) 513-3300
Corporate Secretary and Chief Governance Officer Fax: (713) 513-3456

JENNINGS, H. Keith Tel: (713) 513-3300
Vice President and Treasurer Fax: (713) 513-3456

LAMB, Scott Tel: (713) 513-3300
Vice President, Investor Relations Fax: (713) 513-3456

LARKEY, Roslyn Tel: (713) 513-3300
Vice President, Human Resources Fax: (713) 513-3456

LEMMER, William C. Tel: (713) 513-3300
Senior Vice President and General Counsel Fax: (713) 513-3456
William.Lemmer@c-a-m.com

ROWE, R Scott Tel: (713) 513-3300
President and Chief Operating Officer Fax: (713) 513-3456

SLEDGE, Charles M. Tel: (713) 513-3300
Senior Vice President and Chief Financial Officer Fax: (713) 513-3456

WILL, Edward E. Tel: (713) 513-3300
Vice President, Marketing and Strategy Fax: (713) 513-3456

Camp Dresser and McKee, Inc.
See listing on page 174 under CDM Smith Inc.

Campbell Soup Company

A manufacturer of processed prepared foods. Subsidiaries include Pepperidge Farm.
www.campbellsoupcompany.com
Annual Revenues: $8.31 billion
Employees: 19,400
Ticker: NYSE: CPB
SIC: 2000; 2034; 2032; 2033
Industry/ies: Food And Beverage Industry
Legislative Issues: FOO; GOV; TRD

President and Chief Executive Officer Tel: (856) 342-4800
MORRISON, Denise Fax: (856) 342-3878

Main Headquarters
Mailing: One Campbell Pl. Tel: (856) 342-4800
  Camden, NJ 08103-1701 Fax: (856) 342-3878
  TF: (800) 257-8443

Political Action Committees
Campbell Soup Company PAC
FEC ID: C00415166
Contact: Kelly D. Johnston
One Campbell Pl. Tel: (856) 342-4800
MS43K Fax: (856) 342-4800
Camden, NJ 08103

Contributions to Candidates: $48,500 (2015-2016)
Democrats: $10,500; Republicans: $38,000

Principal Recipients

SENATE
BOOZMAN, JOHN (REP-AR)

Corporate Foundations and Giving Programs

Campbell Soup Foundation
One Campbell Pl. Tel: (856) 968-4367
Camden, NJ 08103 Fax: (856) 342-3878

Public Affairs and Related Activities Personnel

At Headquarters

DISILVESTRO, Anthony P. Tel: (856) 342-4800
Senior Vice President and Chief Financial Officer Fax: (856) 342-3878

JOHNSTON, Kelly D. Tel: (856) 342-4800
Vice President, Government Affairs Fax: (856) 342-3878
Mail Stop MS43K
kelly_johnston@campbellsoup.com
Registered Federal Lobbyist

MORRISSEY, Robert W. Tel: (856) 342-4800
Senior Vice President, Chief Human Resources Office Fax: (856) 342-3878

REARDON, Nancy Tel: (856) 342-4800
Senior Vice President, Chief Human Resources and Fax: (856) 342-3878
Communications Officer

SANZIO, Anthony Tel: (856) 968-4390
Vice President, Communications Fax: (856) 342-3878

SENACKERIB, Michael P. Tel: (856) 342-4800
Senior Vice President and Chief Marketing Officer Fax: (856) 342-3878

Canadian Snowbird Association

Lobbying for the passge of S. 1746, a bill to amend the Immigration and Nationality Act.
www.snowbirds.org
Annual Revenues: $0.67 million
Legislative Issues: TOU

President Tel: (416) 391-9000
SLACK, Robert Fax: (416) 441-7007

Main Headquarters
Mailing: 180 Lesmill Rd. Tel: (416) 391-9000
  Toronto, ON M3B 2T5 Fax: (416) 441-7007
  TF: (800) 265-3200

Corporate Foundations and Giving Programs
Canadian Snowbird Association Corporate Contributions
180 Lesmill Rd. Tel: (800) 265-3200
Toronto, ON M3B 2T5 Fax: (416) 441-7007

Public Affairs and Related Activities Personnel

At Headquarters

BECKSTEAD, Sharon Tel: (416) 391-9000
Member Services, Manager Fax: (416) 441-7007
csaadmin@snowbirds.org

MACKENZIE, Michael Tel: (416) 391-9000
Executive Director Fax: (416) 441-7007
Michael.MacKenzie@snowbirds.org
Registered Federal Lobbyist

PONIKOWSKI, Gabriel Tel: (416) 391-9000
Manager, Finance Fax: (416) 441-7007
csastaff@snowbirds.org

RACHKOVSKY, Evan Tel: (416) 391-9000
Director, Research and Communications Fax: (416) 441-7007
Evan.rachkovsky@snowbirds.org

WEYLIE, Wallace Tel: (416) 391-9000
Legal Counsel Fax: (416) 441-7007
Registered Federal Lobbyist

Canandaigua Brands, Inc.

See listing on page 217 under Constellation Brands, Inc.

Canon USA, Inc.

Imports, markets and distributes photographic products and equipment. A subsidiary of Canon, Inc. of Tokyo, Japan.
www.usa.canon.com
Annual Revenues: $33.74 billion
Employees: 189,571
Ticker: NYSE:CAJ
SIC: 3579; 3861
NAICS: 333313; 333315
Industry/ies: Electricity & Electronics; Electronics; Energy/Electricity

Chairman of the Board and Chief Executive Officer Tel: (631) 330-5000
ADACHI, Joe
JADACHI@usa.canon.com

Main Headquarters
Mailing: One Canon Park Tel: (631) 330-5000
  Melville, NY 11747

Corporate Foundations and Giving Programs
Canon USA, Inc. Contributions Program
One Canon Plaza Tel: (516) 328-5000
Lake Success, NY 11042 Fax: (516) 328-5000

Public Affairs and Related Activities Personnel

At Headquarters

ISHIZUKA, Yuichi Tel: (631) 330-5000
President and Chief Operating Officer

LIEBMAN, Seymour Tel: (631) 330-5000
Executive Vice President, Chief Administrative Officer, General Counsel and Secretary

SHIMONO, Yoshinori Tel: (631) 330-5000
Senior Vice President, Chief Financial Officer and Treasurer Finance and Accounting

WARREN, Joseph G. Tel: (631) 330-5000
Executive Vice President and General Manager, Corporate Human Resources

Canton Drop Forge

Manufacturer of of closed die forgings for high performance applications.
www.cantondropforge.com
Annual Revenues: $23 million
Employees: 300
SIC: 3462
Industry/ies: Metals

Main Headquarters

Mailing: 4575 Southway St. SW Tel: (330) 477-4511
  Canton, OH 44706 Fax: (330) 477-2046

Public Affairs and Related Activities Personnel

At Headquarters

ELLET, Christen Tel: (330) 477-4511
Manager, Human Resources Fax: (330) 477-2046

GRAY, Todd Tel: (330) 477-4511
Vice President, Finance Fax: (330) 477-2046
tgray@cantondropforge.com

MAYKOWSKI, Bill Tel: (330) 445-2547
Vice President, Sales and Marketing Fax: (330) 477-2046
bmaykowski@cantondropforge.com

Capella Healthcare, Inc.

Healthcare company held privately with significant financial resources.
www.capellahealth.com
Employees: 6,500
SIC: 8062
Industry/ies: Medicine/Health Care/Mental Health

Founder and Executive Chairman of the Board Tel: (615) 764-3000
SLIPKOVICH, Daniel S. Fax: (615) 764-3030

President and Chief Executive Officer Tel: (615) 764-3000
"MIKE" WIECHART, Michael A. Fax: (615) 764-3030

Main Headquarters
Mailing: 501 Corporate Center Dr. Tel: (615) 764-3000
  Suite 200 Fax: (615) 764-3030
  Franklin, TN 37067-2659

Political Action Committees
Capella Healthcare Inc. Government Affairs Committee PAC
FEC ID: C00421420
Contact: James R. Wisman
501 Corporate Center
Suite 200
Franklin, TN 37067

  Contributions to Candidates: $15,000 (2015-2016)
  Democrats: $10,000; Republicans: $5,000

Corporate Foundations and Giving Programs
Capella Healthcare Contributions Program
501 Corporate Center Dr.
Suite 200
Franklin, TN 37067-2659

Public Affairs and Related Activities Personnel

At Headquarters

HANCOCK, Anne Tel: (615) 254-0575
Media Contact Fax: (615) 764-3030

KUNKEL, Neil W. Tel: (615) 764-3000
Executive Vice President, Chief Legal and Administrative Fax: (615) 764-3030
Officer

LYNCH, Morgan Tel: (615) 254-0575
Media Contact Fax: (615) 764-3030

SCHNEIDER, Carolyn Tel: (615) 764-3000
Senior Vice President, Human Resources Fax: (615) 764-3030

WARREN, Denise Wilder Tel: (615) 764-3000
Executive Vice President, Chief Financial Officer Fax: (615) 764-3030
Investor.Relations@CapellaHealth.com

WISMAN, James R. Tel: (615) 764-3000
PAC Treasurer Fax: (615) 764-3030

WRIGHT, Beth B. Tel: (615) 764-3000
Senior Vice President, Corporate Communications and Fax: (615) 764-3030
Strategic Marketing
Beth.Wright@CapellaHealth.com

Capewell Components Company

Designs and delivers cargo handling equipment, parachute safety equipment, and precision aerial delivery systems to the U.S. military and to its customers.
www.capewell.com
Employees: 200
Industry/ies: Defense/Homeland Security; Disaster; Government-Related; Machinery/Equipment; Military/Veterans

Main Headquarters
Mailing: 105 Nutmeg Rd., South Tel: (860) 610-0700
  S. Windsor, CT 06074 Fax: (860) 610-0120

Public Affairs and Related Activities Personnel

At Headquarters

EHLER, William (Bill) Tel: (860) 282-5047
Director, Business Fax: (860) 610-0120
ehlerw@capewell.com

HICKEY, Brig. Gen. Michael P. Tel: (860) 282-5045

Director, Global Business Development and Executive Director
hickeym@capewell.com

Fax: (860) 610-0120

KNIGHT, Catherine
Administrative Coordinator
knightc@capewell.com

Tel: (860) 610-0700
Fax: (860) 610-0120

Capital Automotive, LLC
A finance company for automotive retail and real estate.
www.capitalautomotive.com
Annual Revenues: $201.93 million
Employees: 33
SIC: 6798
Industry/ies: Automotive Industry; Transportation

Chairman of the Board
ECKERT, Thomas D.
teckert@capitalautomotive.com

Tel: (703) 394-1300
Fax: (703) 288-3375

President and Chief Operating Officer
FERRIERO, Jay M.
jferriero@capitalautomotive.com

Tel: (703) 394-1319
Fax: (703) 288-3375

Main Headquarters
Mailing: 8270 Greensboro Dr.
Suite 950
McLean, VA 22102

Tel: (703) 288-3075
Fax: (703) 288-3375
TF: (877) 422-7288

Corporate Foundations and Giving Programs

Capital Automotive, LLC Contributions Program
8270 Greensboro Dr.
Suite 950
McLean, VA 22102

Tel: (703) 288-3075

Public Affairs and Related Activities Personnel

At Headquarters

KAY, David S.
Chief Investment Officer and Chief Financial Officer
dkay@capitalautomotive.com

Tel: (703) 394-1302
Fax: (703) 288-3375

POTTER, Catherine
Senior Vice President, Secretary and General Counsel

Tel: (703) 288-3075
Fax: (703) 288-3375

Capital Blue Cross (Pennsylvania)
Provider of health insurance products to individuals and employer groups.
www.capbluecross.com
Industry/ies: Medicine/Health Care/Mental Health

Chairman of the Board
LEHR, Jr., William

Tel: (717) 541-7000
Fax: (717) 541-6915

President and Chief Executive Officer
HILAIRE, Gary D. St.

Tel: (717) 541-7000
Fax: (717) 541-6915

Main Headquarters
Mailing: 2500 Elmerton Ave.
P.O. Box 779519
Harrisburg, PA 17177-9519

Tel: (717) 541-7000
Fax: (717) 541-6915
TF: (800) 962-2242

Corporate Foundations and Giving Programs

Capital Blue Cross Contributions Program
P.O. Box 779519
Harrisburg, PA 17177-9519

Tel: (717) 541-7000
Fax: (717) 541-7000

Public Affairs and Related Activities Personnel

At Headquarters

ABRAHAM, Aji
Senior Vice President, Business and Network Development
aji.abraham@capbluecross.com

Tel: (717) 541-7000
Fax: (717) 541-6915

BAKER, Jr., Robert E.
Vice President, Government Affairs
bob.baker@capbluecross.com

Tel: (717) 541-6785
Fax: (717) 541-6915

BASKIN, Sherry E.
Corporate Secretary and Chief Compliance Officer

Tel: (717) 541-7000
Fax: (717) 541-6915

BUTERA, Joseph
Manager, Public Relations
joe.butera@capbluecross.com

Tel: (717) 541-6139
Fax: (717) 541-6915

CLEARY, Michael R.
Senior Vice President, Chief Finance Officer and Treasurer

Tel: (717) 541-7000
Fax: (717) 541-6915

HEISEY, Glenn
Vice President, Strategy and Business Operations
glenn.heisey@capbluecross.com

Tel: (717) 541-7000
Fax: (717) 541-6915

KRUPINSKI, Steve J.
Senior Vice President, Human Resources and Facilities
steve.krupinski@capbluecross.com

Tel: (717) 541-7000
Fax: (717) 541-6915

LENCKI, Donna K.
Senior Vice President, Consumer Experience and Chief Marketing Officer

Tel: (717) 541-7000
Fax: (717) 541-6915

MELUSKY, Linda M.
Government Affairs Representative

Tel: (717) 541-6135
Fax: (717) 541-6915

linda.melusky@capbluecross.com

SKERPON, David
Vice President, Retail Strategies and Brand Management
david.skerpon@capbluecross.com

Tel: (717) 541-7000
Fax: (717) 541-6915

SULLIVAN, Esq., Brian L.
Vice President and General Counsel
Brian.Sullivan@CapBlueCross.COM

Tel: (717) 541-7000
Fax: (717) 541-6915

Capital Business Development Associates, LLC
Support client site selection, business development and incentive applications
cb-da.com
Annual Revenues: $1.40 million
Industry/ies: Business

Chief Executive Officer
SMITH, Thomas
thomas.smith@cb-da.com

Tel: (703) 980-0332

Main Headquarters
Mailing: 6411 Casperson Rd.
Alexandria, VA 22315

Tel: (703) 980-0332

Capital One Financial Corporation
A financial services company which provide various financial products and services.
www.capitalone.com
Annual Revenues: $18.86 billion
Employees: 45,800
Ticker: NYSE: COF
SIC: 6021
Industry/ies: Banking/Finance/Investments
Legislative Issues: BAN; CIV; CPT; CSP; DEF; FIN; POS; TAX

Founder, Chairman and Chief Executive Officer
FAIRBANK, Richard D.
richard.fairbank@capitalone.com

Tel: (703) 720-1000
Fax: (703) 720-2306

Main Headquarters
Mailing: 1680 Capital One Dr., 12th Floor
12th Floor
McLean, VA 22102-3491

Tel: (703) 720-2500
Fax: (703) 720-2306
TF: (800) 801-1164

Political Action Committees

Capital One Financial Corporation Associates Political Fund PAC
FEC ID: C00326595
Contact: Vincent R. Tallman
1680 Capitol One Dr.
Attn: 19050-1204
McLean, VA 22102

Contributions to Candidates: $599,500 (2015-2016)
Democrats: $172,500; Republicans: $425,000; Other: $2,000

Principal Recipients

SENATE
MURPHY, PATRICK E (DEM-FL)
SCOTT, TIMOTHY E (REP-SC)
SHELBY, RICHARD C (REP-AL)

HOUSE
BARR, GARLAND ANDY (REP-KY)
COMSTOCK, BARBARA J HONORABLE (REP-VA)
DOLD, ROBERT JAMES JR (REP-IL)
FINCHER, STEVE MR. (REP-TN)
HUIZENGA, WILLIAM P THE HON. (REP-MI)
LUETKEMEYER, W BLAINE (REP-MO)
MCCARTHY, KEVIN (REP-CA)
MCHENRY, PATRICK TIMOTHY (REP-NC)
RYAN, PAUL D. (REP-WI)
SCOTT, DAVID ALBERT (DEM-GA)
SESSIONS, PETE MR. (REP-TX)
TIPTON, SCOTT R. (REP-CO)

Corporate Foundations and Giving Programs

Capital One Financial Contributions Program
1680 Capital One Dr.
12th Floor
McLean, VA 22102-3491

Tel: (703) 720-1000
Fax: (703) 720-1000

Public Affairs and Related Activities Personnel

At Headquarters

BERSON, Jory A.
Chief Human Resources Officer
jory.berson@capitalone.com

Tel: (703) 720-1000
Fax: (703) 720-2306

BOMS, Steven
Federal Lobbyist
Registered Federal Lobbyist

Tel: (703) 720-1000
Fax: (703) 720-2306

BONNER, Katherine
Registered Federal Lobbyist

Tel: (703) 720-2500
Fax: (703) 720-2306

FINNERMAN, Jr., John G.
General Counsel and Corporate Secretary

Tel: (703) 720-1000
Fax: (703) 720-2306

MALLOY, Kathleen	Tel:	(703) 448-3747
Senior Vice President and Manager	Fax:	(703) 720-2306
kathleen.malloy@capitalone.com		
NORRIS, Jeff	Tel:	(703) 720-2455
Managing Vice President, Investor Relations	Fax:	(703) 720-2306
OLSON, Rick	Tel:	(703) 720-2500
	Fax:	(703) 720-2306
RAKES, Julie	Tel:	(804) 284-5800
Director, Media Relations	Fax:	(703) 720-2306
julie.rakes@capitalone.com		
REDMON, Ronald	Tel:	(703) 448-3747
Senior Vice President	Fax:	(703) 720-2306
ronald.redmonjr@capitalone.com		
STEIN, Larry	Tel:	(703) 720-1000
Federal Lobbyist	Fax:	(703) 720-2306
Mail Stop 12th Floor		
TALLMAN, Vincent R.	Tel:	(703) 448-3747
Contact, Government Relations, Lobbyist/Registrant Pac	Fax:	(703) 720-2306
WEEMS, Emily Pfeiffer	Tel:	(703) 720-2295
Federal Lobbyist	Fax:	(703) 720-2306
Mail Stop 12th Floor		
Registered Federal Lobbyist		
ZUPANCIC, Nicholas J.	Tel:	(703) 720-2500
Registered Federal Lobbyist	Fax:	(703) 720-2306

Capitol Pacific Group

Advisory firm for government relations and finance.
cappacificgroup.com

Main Headquarters

Mailing:	120 Broadway	Tel:	(310) 576-2256
	Suite 300	Fax:	(310) 496-1938
	Santa Monica, CA 90401		

Washington Office

Mailing:	418 C St. NE	Tel:	(202) 547-8978
	Washington, DC 20002	Fax:	(202) 547-8532

Public Affairs and Related Activities Personnel

At Headquarters

EMMONS, D.M.A., Rachel A.	Tel:	(310) 576-2256
Government and Public Sector, Appropriations and Public	Fax:	(310) 496-1938
Policy		
SHRAGA, William	Tel:	(310) 576-2252
Managing Director and Chief Financial Officer	Fax:	(310) 496-1938
bshraga@cappacificgroup.com		
WHITE, Eric	Tel:	(310) 576-2252
Senior Managing Partner	Fax:	(310) 496-1938

Capitol Strategies Group, LLC

A private investment banking company.
capitalstrategiesgroup.com
Legislative Issues: PHA

Main Headquarters

Mailing:	39111 W. Six Mile Rd.	Tel:	(734) 929-1115
	Livonia, MI 48152		

Public Affairs and Related Activities Personnel

At Headquarters

BOGLE, David M.	Tel:	(734) 929-1115
Of Counsel		
dmbogle12@sbcglobal.net		
CIMINI, P.J.	Tel:	(734) 929-1115
Principal		
Registered Federal Lobbyist		
PENKALA, Ed	Tel:	(734) 929-1115
Principal		

At Other Offices

MCCABE, Patrick
Principal
36 Trumbull St.
Hartford, CT 06103
Registered Federal Lobbyist

Capstone Group NCH, LLC

Association Management and consulting.
www.capstone-nch.com
Annual Revenues: $0.15 million

Main Headquarters

Mailing:	51 South View Rd.	Tel:	(202) 445-9955
	Rising Sun, MD 21911		

Public Affairs and Related Activities Personnel

At Headquarters

CONNELLY, Steven	Tel:	(202) 445-9955
Partner		

Capstone Turbine Corporation

A microturbine systems producer.
www.capstoneturbine.com
Annual Revenues: $122.03 million
Employees: 225
Ticker: NASDAQ: CPST
SIC: 3510
Industry/ies: Energy/Electricity; Environment And Conservation; Machinery/Equipment

President and Chief Executive Officer

JAMISON, Darren	Tel:	(818) 734-5300
	Fax:	(818) 734-5320

Main Headquarters

Mailing:	21211 Nordhoff St.	Tel:	(818) 734-5300
	Chatsworth, CA 91311	Fax:	(818) 734-5320
		TF:	(866) 422-7786

Public Affairs and Related Activities Personnel

At Headquarters

BROOKS, Jayme	Tel:	(818) 734-5300
Chief Financial Officer and Chief Accounting Officer	Fax:	(818) 734-5320
CROUSE, James	Tel:	(818) 734-5300
Executive Vice President, Sales and Marketing	Fax:	(818) 734-5320
HOVSEPIAN, Clarice	Tel:	(818) 734-5300
Vice President, Human Resources and Corporate Counsel	Fax:	(818) 734-5320
LEWIS, Richard B	Tel:	(818) 734-5300
Vice President, Operations	Fax:	(818) 734-5320
REICH, Edward	Tel:	(818) 407-3628
Executive Vice President and Chief Financial Officer	Fax:	(818) 407-3770

Caradigm

Formerly, Sentillion aquired by Microsoft in 2010. It is committed to helping organizations improve care, reduce costs and manage risk.
www.sentillion.com
Employees: 45
Industry/ies: Medicine/Health Care/Mental Health

Chief Executive Officer and President

SIMPSON, Michael	Tel:	(978) 689-9095
	Fax:	(978) 688-2313

Main Headquarters

Mailing:	500 108th Ave. NE	Tel:	(425) 201-2500
	Suite 300		
	Bellevue, WA 98004		

Washington Office

Mailing:	4330 East-West Hwy.
	Suite 220
	Bethesda, MD 20814

Public Affairs and Related Activities Personnel

At Other Offices

BOYLE, Christine	Tel:	(978) 689-9095
Chief Marketing Officer and Senior Vice President	Fax:	(978) 688-2313
40 Shattuck Rd., Suite 200		
Andover, MA 01810-2455		
CABLE, Caitlin	Tel:	(978) 689-9095
Vice President, Human Resources	Fax:	(978) 688-2313
40 Shattuck Rd., Suite 200		
Andover, MA 01810-2455		
DOMESHEK, David	Tel:	(508) 873-7068
Media Contact	Fax:	(978) 688-2313
40 Shattuck Rd., Suite 200		
Andover, MA 01810-2455		
david.domeshek@sentillion.com		
HAAS, Jennifer	Tel:	(978) 689-9095
Director, Communications	Fax:	(978) 688-2313
40 Shattuck Rd., Suite 200		
Andover, MA 01810-2455		
jennifer.haas@sentillion.com		
LEBLANC, Brian	Tel:	(978) 689-9095
Vice President, Finance and PAC Treasurer	Fax:	(978) 688-2313
40 Shattuck Rd., Suite 200		
Andover, MA 01810-2455		
RATLIFF, Warren	Tel:	(978) 689-9095
Senior Vice President, Corporate Development and General	Fax:	(978) 688-2313
Counsel		
40 Shattuck Rd., Suite 200		
Andover, MA 01810-2455		
WILLINGHAM, Mike	Tel:	(978) 689-9095
Vice President, Quality Assurance and Regulatory Affairs	Fax:	(978) 688-2313

40 Shattuck Rd., Suite 200
Andover, MA 01810-2455

WOOD, Matt	Tel:	(978) 689-9095
Chief Financial Officer and Senior Vice President	Fax:	(978) 688-2313

40 Shattuck Rd., Suite 200
Andover, MA 01810-2455

Caraustar Industries, Inc.
Manufactures recycled paperboard products.
www.caraustar.com
Annual Revenues: $396.00 million
Employees: 3,200
Ticker: NASDAQ: CSAR
SIC: 2631; 2671; 2675
NAICS: 322221; 322299
Industry/ies: Paper And Wood Products Industry

Chairman of the Board	Tel:	(770) 948-3101
MURNANE, William P.	Fax:	(770) 732-3401
President and Chief Executive Officer	Tel:	(770) 948-3101
PATTON, Michael C. (Mike)	Fax:	(770) 732-3401

Main Headquarters

Mailing:	5000 Austell Powder Springs Rd.	Tel:	(770) 948-3101
	Suite 300	Fax:	(770) 732-3401
	Austell, GA 30106	TF:	(800) 223-1373

Public Affairs and Related Activities Personnel

At Headquarters

MAYS, Nan	Tel:	(770) 948-3101
Vice President, Human Resources	Fax:	(770) 732-3401
NIX, William A.	Tel:	(770) 948-3101
Vice President, Finance and Chief Accounting Officer	Fax:	(770) 732-3401
william.nix@caraustar.com		
PEALOR, Angela	Tel:	(770) 745-3788
Contact, Investor Relations, Senior Executive Assistant to	Fax:	(770) 732-3401
Chief Executive Officer and Chief Financial Officer		
apealor@caraustar.com		

Cardinal Health Inc.
A manufacturer of healthcare products. Cardinal Health spun off its medical equipment manufacturing and clinical technologies operations as CareFusion Corporation in 2009. It also franchises Medicine Shoppe retail pharmacies. Its medical division parcels out medical, laboratory, and surgical supplies and provides logistics, consulting, and data management.
www.cardinal.com
Annual Revenues: $117.71 billion
Employees: 34,500
Ticker: NYSE:CAH
SIC: 5122
NAICS: 325412
Industry/ies: Medicine/Health Care/Mental Health
Legislative Issues: ALC; ENG; HCR; MED; MMM; PHA; TAX; TEC; TRD; VET

Chairman of the Board and Chief Executive Officer	Tel:	(614) 757-5000
BARRETT, George S.	Fax:	(614) 757-8871

Main Headquarters

Mailing:	7000 Cardinal Pl.	Tel:	(614) 757-5000
	Dublin, OH 43017	Fax:	(614) 757-8871
		TF:	(800) 234-8701

Political Action Committees
Cardinal Health Inc. PAC
FEC ID: C00332833
Contact: Cassi Baker

7000 Cardinal Pl.	Tel:	(614) 757-5000
Dublin, OH 43017		

Contributions to Candidates: $369,000 (2015-2016)
Democrats: $107,500; Republicans: $261,500

Principal Recipients

SENATE
ALEXANDER, LAMAR (REP-VA)
MCCONNELL, MITCH (REP-KY)
MURRAY, PATTY (DEM-WA)

HOUSE
BEATTY, JOYCE (DEM-OH)
LATTA, ROBERT EDWARD MR (REP-OH)
MARINO, THOMAS ANTHONY (REP-PA)
MCCARTHY, KEVIN (REP-CA)
MCMORRIS RODGERS, CATHY (REP-WA)
PALLONE, FRANK JR (DEM-NJ)
PAULSEN, ERIK (REP-MN)
SCALISE, STEVE MR. (REP-LA)
STIVERS, STEVE MR. (REP-OH)
TIBERI, PATRICK J. (REP-OH)

Corporate Foundations and Giving Programs

Cardinal Health Foundation
Contact: Dianne Radigan

7000 Cardinal Pl.	Tel:	(614) 757-5000
Dublin, OH 43017	Fax:	(614) 757-8871

Public Affairs and Related Activities Personnel

At Headquarters

BAKER, Cassi	Tel:	(614) 757-5000
Vice President, Government Relations and PAC Treasurer	Fax:	(614) 757-8871
BIRD, Shelley	Tel:	(614) 757-5000
Executive Vice President, Public Affairs	Fax:	(614) 757-8871
Shelley.Bird@cardinal.com		
CALLINICOS, Sean	Tel:	(614) 757-5000
Senior Vice President, Government Relations	Fax:	(614) 757-8871
Registered Federal Lobbyist		
CURLEY, Sally	Tel:	(614) 757-7115
Senior Vice President, Investor Relations	Fax:	(614) 757-8871
sally.curley@cardinalhealth.com		
ELLIS, G Brian	Tel:	(614) 757-5000
Executive Vice President, Enterprise Corporate Accounts	Fax:	(614) 757-8871
FALK, Steve	Tel:	(614) 757-5000
Executive Vice President, General Counsel and Corporate	Fax:	(614) 757-8871
Secretary		
steve.falk@cardinal.com		
JACOBSON, Susan	Tel:	(614) 757-5000
Deputy General Counsel	Fax:	(614) 757-8871
KAUFMANN, Mike	Tel:	(614) 757-5000
Chief Financial Officer	Fax:	(614) 757-8871
MCGRATH, Rebecca	Tel:	(614) 757-5000
Vice President, Government Relations	Fax:	(614) 757-8871
Registered Federal Lobbyist		
MORFORD, Craig	Tel:	(614) 757-5000
Chief Legal and Compliance Officer	Fax:	(614) 757-8871
NOVELLI, Thomas C.	Tel:	(614) 757-5000
Vice President, Government Relations	Fax:	(614) 757-8871
OWAD, Bill	Tel:	(614) 757-5000
Senior vice president, Operational Excellence	Fax:	(614) 757-8871
RADIGAN, Dianne	Tel:	(614) 757-5000
Vice President, Community Relations	Fax:	(614) 757-8871
dianne.radigan@cardinalhealth.com		
WATKINS, Carole	Tel:	(614) 757-5000
Chief Human Resources Officer	Fax:	(614) 757-8871
Carole.Watkins@cardinal.com		
WOODBURN, Connie R.	Tel:	(614) 757-7769
Senior Vice President, Government and Community Relations	Fax:	(614) 757-8871

Cardiovascular Systems Inc. (CSI)
Formerly Replidyne, Inc. A biopharmaceutical company. It is a medical device company, which develops, manufactures, and markets devices for the treatment of vascular diseases.
www.csi360.com
Annual Revenues: $172.65 million
Employees: 479
Ticker: NASDAQ: CSII
SIC: 3841
Industry/ies: Medicine/Health Care/Mental Health
Legislative Issues: MMM

Chairman of the Board	Tel:	(651) 259-1600
WARD, Scott	Fax:	(612) 677-3355
President, Chief Executive Officer and Director	Tel:	(651) 259-1600
MARTIN, David L.	Fax:	(612) 677-3355

Main Headquarters

Mailing:	1225 Old Highway Eight NW	Tel:	(651) 259-1600
	St. Paul, MN 55112	Fax:	(612) 677-3355
		TF:	(877) 274-0360

Corporate Foundations and Giving Programs

Cardiovascular Systems Contributions Program

651 Campus Dr.	Tel:	(651) 259-1600
St. Paul, MN 55112	Fax:	(612) 677-3355

Public Affairs and Related Activities Personnel

At Headquarters

BETTERLEY, Laurence L.	Tel:	(651) 259-1600
Chief Financial Officer	Fax:	(612) 677-3355
FLAHERTY , James E.	Tel:	(651) 259-1600
Chief Administrative Officer	Fax:	(612) 677-3355
GILLUND , Laura	Tel:	(651) 259-1600
Vice President, Human Resources and Professional	Fax:	(612) 677-3355
Development		
KENNY, Kevin J.	Tel:	(651) 259-1600
Chief Operating Officer	Fax:	(612) 677-3355
NIELSEN, Jack	Tel:	(651) 202-4919

Senior Director, Corporate Communications and Investor Relations
j.nielsen@csi360.com

Fax: (612) 677-3355

Care Action Now, Inc.

Care is a leading humanitarian organization fighting global poverty.
www.care.org
Industry/ies: Charities And Foundations; Nonprofit
Legislative Issues: BUD; FOR

Main Headquarters

Mailing:	1899 L St. NW, Suite 500	Tel:	(202) 595-2800
	Suite 500		
	Washington, DC 20036		

Public Affairs and Related Activities Personnel

At Headquarters

DELANEY, Porter	Tel:	(202) 595-2800
Registered Federal Lobbyist		
KENNEDY, Erin	Tel:	(202) 595-2800
Technical Advisor, Advocacy		
LANE, Jan	Tel:	(202) 595-2800
Director of Advocacy		
MARCEY, Elizabeth	Tel:	(202) 595-2800
Registered Federal Lobbyist		
MILLER, Michael	Tel:	(202) 595-2800
Registered Federal Lobbyist		
PHILLIPS-BARRASSO, Kate	Tel:	(202) 595-2800
kpillips@dc.care.org		
Registered Federal Lobbyist		
PORTER, Katie	Tel:	(202) 595-2800
RAWE, Tonya M.	Tel:	(202) 595-2800
trawe@care.org		
RAY, David	Tel:	(202) 595-2800
Vice President, Advocacy		
SELZER, Blake	Tel:	(202) 595-2800
SMITH, Chris	Tel:	(202) 595-2800
Registered Federal Lobbyist		
SMITH, Chris	Tel:	(202) 595-2800
Registered Federal Lobbyist		
SULLIVAN, Chris	Tel:	(202) 595-2800
Registered Federal Lobbyist		
WEINGROD, Benjamin	Tel:	(202) 595-2800
Registered Federal Lobbyist		
WINTERHOF, JoDee L.	Tel:	(202) 595-2800
Vice President, Policy & Advocacy		
ZIOLKOWSKI, John	Tel:	(202) 595-2800
Registered Federal Lobbyist		

Career Education Corporation

A postsecondary education provider with campus-based and online curriculum.
www.careered.com
Annual Revenues: $725.51 million
Employees: 4,214
Ticker: NASDAQ: CECO
SIC: 8200
Industry/ies: Education; Employees & Employment

Chairman of the Board, Interim President and Chief Executive Officer	Tel:	(847) 781-3600
	Fax:	(847) 781-3610
MCCRAY, Ron		

Main Headquarters

Mailing:	231 N. Martingale Rd.	Tel:	(847) 781-3600
	Schaumburg, IL 60173	Fax:	(847) 781-3610

Washington Office

Mailing:	P.O. Box 77693	Tel:	(847) 585-3600
	Washington, DC 20013	Fax:	(847) 781-3610

Political Action Committees

Career Education Corporation PAC (CEC PAC)
FEC ID: C00461574
Contact: Mark J. Sobota
P. O. Box 77693
Washington, DC 20013

> **Contributions to Candidates:** $9,000 (2015-2016)
> Democrats: $2,000; Republicans: $7,000

Corporate Foundations and Giving Programs

Career Education Corporation Contributions Program

231 N. Martingale Rd.	Tel:	(847) 781-3600
Schaumburg, IL 60173	Fax:	(847) 781-3610

Public Affairs and Related Activities Personnel

At Headquarters

AYERS, Jeffrey D.	Tel:	(847) 781-3600
Senior Vice President, General Counsel and Corporate Secretary	Fax:	(847) 781-3610
COOPER, Jeffrey R.	Tel:	(847) 781-3600
Senior Vice President and Chief Compliance Officer	Fax:	(847) 781-3610
DEYOUNG, Robert T.	Tel:	(847) 781-3600
Vice President, Regulatory Operations	Fax:	(847) 781-3610
JONES, Diane Auer	Tel:	(847) 781-3600
Senior Vice President, Chief External Affairs Officer, and President of the Career Education Scholarship Fund (CESF)	Fax:	(847) 781-3610
RAWDEN, Dave	Tel:	(847) 781-3600
Interim Chief Financial Officer	Fax:	(847) 781-3610
SPENCER, Mark	Tel:	(847) 585-3802
Senior Director, Corporate Communications	Fax:	(847) 781-3610
mdspencer@careered.com		

At Washington Office

SOBOTA, Mark J.	Tel:	(847) 585-3600
PAC Treasurer	Fax:	(847) 781-3610

CareerBuilder.com

An online recruitment and career advancement source for employers, recruiters and job seekers.
www.careerbuilder.com
Annual Revenues: $41.50 million
Employees: 1,700
Industry/ies: Computer/Technology; Employees & Employment

Chief Executive Officer	Tel:	(773) 527-3600
FERGUSON, Matt	Fax:	(773) 399-6313
matthew.ferguson@careerbuilder.com		

Main Headquarters

Mailing:	200 N. LaSalle St.	Tel:	(773) 527-3600
	Suite 1100	Fax:	(773) 353-2452
	Chicago, IL 60601	TF:	(800) 638-4212

Public Affairs and Related Activities Personnel

At Headquarters

GREEN, Alex	Tel:	(773) 527-3600
General Counsel	Fax:	(773) 399-6313
alex.green@careerbuilder.com		
HAEFNER, Rosemary	Tel:	(773) 527-3600
Chief Human Resources Officer	Fax:	(773) 399-6313
KNAPP, Kevin	Tel:	(773) 527-3600
Chief Financial Officer and Chief Operating Officer	Fax:	(773) 399-6313
kevin.knapp@careerbuilder.com		
SULLIVAN-GRASZ , Jennifer	Tel:	(773) 527-3600
Vice President, Corporate Communications	Fax:	(773) 399-6313
jennifer.grasz@careerbuilder.com		

CareFirst Blue Cross Blue Shield

A health care insurance company.
www.carefirst.com
Employees: 4,000
Industry/ies: Insurance Industry; Medicine/Health Care/Mental Health
Legislative Issues: HCR; INS

Chair	Tel:	(410) 581-3000
WAECHTER, Stephen L.	Fax:	(410) 998-5351
President and Chief Executive Officer	Tel:	(410) 528-7000
BURRELL, Chester "Chet"	Fax:	(410) 998-5351

Main Headquarters

Mailing:	Canton Tower	Tel:	(410) 581-3000
	1501 S. Clinton St.	Fax:	(410) 998-5351
	Baltimore, MD 21224	TF:	(800) 321-3497

Washington Office

Mailing:	840 First St. NE	Tel:	(202) 479-8000
	Washington, DC 20065	Fax:	(202) 479-7601

Political Action Committees

CareFirst BlueCross BlueShield Associates Federal PAC
FEC ID: C00286922
Contact: Jeanne A. Kennedy
10455 Mill Run Cir.
Owings Mills, MD 21117

> **Contributions to Candidates:** $14,500 (2015-2016)
> Democrats: $13,000; Republicans: $1,500

Corporate Foundations and Giving Programs

CareFirst BlueCross BlueShield Contributions Program
10455 Mill Run Cir.
Owings Mills, MD 21117

Public Affairs and Related Activities Personnel

At Headquarters

BURGIN , Meryl *Executive Vice President, General Counsel and Corporate Secretary*	Tel: Fax:	(410) 581-3000 (410) 998-5351
CHANEY, G. Mark *Executive Vice President and Chief Financial Officer* mark.chaney@carefirst.com	Tel: Fax:	(410) 528-7000 (410) 998-5351
DEVOU, Gregory A. *Executive Vice President and Chief Marketing Officer*	Tel: Fax:	(410) 528-7000 (410) 998-5351
JENKINS, Lawanda *Manager, Community Relations*	Tel: Fax:	(410) 998-6010 (410) 998-5351
MCSHANE, Michael A. *Vice President, Human Resources*	Tel: Fax:	(410) 581-3000 (410) 998-5351
TILDON, Maria *Senior Vice President, Public Policy and Community Affairs* maria.tildon@carefirst.com	Tel: Fax:	(410) 528-7000 (410) 998-5351
WOLF, Sarah *Contact, Media Relations* sarah.wolf@carefirst.com	Tel: Fax:	(800) 914-6394 (410) 998-5351

At Washington Office

DEUTERMAN, Pamela *Senior Vice President, Federal Programs*	Tel: Fax:	(202) 479-8000 (202) 479-7601
HATTON, Julie *Director, Government Affairs*	Tel: Fax:	(202) 479-8000 (202) 479-7601
RIVKIN , Deborah R. *Vice President, Government Affairs*	Tel: Fax:	(202) 680-5001 (202) 479-7601

At Other Offices

KENNEDY, Jeanne A.
PAC Treasurer
10455 Mill Run Cir.
Owings Mills, MD 21117

CareFirst of Maryland, Inc

See listing on page 164 under CareFirst Blue Cross Blue Shield

CareSource Management Group Company

A nonprofit Ohio-based health plan and provider of Medicaid managed health care plans. CareSource offers managed health care plans for the uninsured and people who need it most.
www.caresource.com
Industry/ies: Management; Medicine/Health Care/Mental Health
Legislative Issues: MMM

President and Chief Executive Officer MORRIS, Pamela	Tel: Fax:	(937) 224-3300 (937) 224-2272

Main Headquarters

Mailing:	230 N. Main St. Dayton, OH 45402	Tel: Fax: TF:	(937) 224-3300 (937) 224-2272 (800) 605-0137

Corporate Foundations and Giving Programs

CareSource Foundation
Contact: Cathy Ponitz
230 N. Main St.
Dayton, OH 45402

Tel: (937) 224-3300
Fax: (937) 224-2272

Public Affairs and Related Activities Personnel

At Headquarters

CHILSON, Mark *Executive Vice President and General Counsel*	Tel: Fax:	(937) 224-3300 (937) 224-2272
GRANT, Janet *Executive Vice President , External Affairs and Corporate Compliance Officer*	Tel: Fax:	(937) 224-3300 (937) 224-2272
JONES, Bobby *Chief Operating Officer*	Tel: Fax:	(937) 224-3300 (937) 224-2272
MCCABE, Daniel J. *Chief Administrative Officer*	Tel: Fax:	(937) 224-3300 (937) 224-2272
MICHAEL, Jenny *Director, Public Relations* jenny.michael@caresource.com	Tel: Fax:	(937) 531-3103 (937) 224-2272
PONITZ, Cathy *Executive Director, CareSource Foundation* cathy.ponitz@caresource.com	Tel: Fax:	(937) 224-3300 (937) 224-2272
THOMAS, Tarlton *Chief Financial Officer*	Tel: Fax:	(937) 224-3300 (937) 224-2272

CARFAX, Inc.

A provider of vehicle history reports. Subsidiary of R.L. Polk & Co.
www.carfax.com
Employees: 400
Industry/ies: Automotive Industry; Communications; Telecommunications/ Internet/Cable; Transportation
Legislative Issues: AUT, TRA

Main Headquarters

Mailing:	5860 Trinity Pkwy. Suite 600 Centreville, VA 20120-1998	Tel: Fax:	(703) 934-2664 (703) 691-2861

Public Affairs and Related Activities Personnel

At Headquarters

BASSO, Christopher *Manager, Public Relations* chrisbasso@carfax.com	Tel: Fax:	(703) 934-2664 (703) 691-2861
HASAN, Faisal H. *North American Director, Data Acquisition & Government Relations* faisalhasan@carfax.com *Registered Federal Lobbyist*	Tel: Fax:	(703) 934-2664 (703) 691-2861

Cargill, Inc.

Specializes in international commodity merchandising, processing and distribution.
www.cargill.com
SIC: 2033; 2037
NAICS: 311411; 311421
Industry/ies: Agriculture/Agronomy; Commodities
Legislative Issues: AGR; CPT; ENG; ENV; FOO; FOR; IMM; LBR; TRA; TRD

Executive Chairman of the Board PAGE, Gregory B.	Tel: Fax:	(952) 742-5799 (952) 742-7224
President and Chief Executive Officer MACLENNAN , David W.	Tel: Fax:	(952) 742-5799 (952) 742-7224

Main Headquarters

Mailing:	P.O. Box 9300 Minneapolis, MN 55440-9300	Tel: Fax:	(952) 742-5799 (952) 742-7224

Washington Office

Mailing:	1030 15th St. NW Suite 650 West Washington, DC 20005	Tel: Fax: TF:	(202) 530-8160 (202) 530-8180 (800) 227-4455

Political Action Committees

Cargill Inc. PAC
FEC ID: C00067884
Contact: Jane Allen
P.O. Box 9300
Minneapolis, MN 55440

Contributions to Candidates: $112,750 (2015-2016)
Democrats: $21,250; Republicans: $91,500

Corporate Foundations and Giving Programs

Cargill Foundation
Contact: Mark Murphy
P.O. Box 9300
Minneapolis, MN 55440

Tel: (952) 742-2792
Fax: (952) 742-7224

Public Affairs and Related Activities Personnel

At Headquarters

ALLEN, Jane *PAC Treasurer* Mail Stop C/O Cargill, Inc. / Cfr / Department Number Five jane_allen@cargill.com	Tel: Fax:	(952) 742-5799 (952) 742-7224
CLEMENS, Lisa *Senior Research Chemist* lisa_clemens@cargill.com	Tel: Fax:	(952) 742-6405 (952) 742-7224
FERNANDEZ, Michael A. *Vice President, Corporate Affairs*	Tel: Fax:	(952) 742-5799 (952) 742-7224
FLIGGE, Lori *Director, Media Relations* lori_fligge@cargill.com	Tel: Fax:	(952) 742-2275 (952) 742-7224
JOHNSON, Lori *Vice President, Corporate Affairs and Director, Global Communications* Lori_Johnson@cargill.com	Tel: Fax:	(952) 742-6194 (952) 742-7224
KLEIN, Mark *Director, Media Relations* mark_klein@cargill.com	Tel: Fax:	(952) 742-6211 (952) 742-7224
LIN, Sarena *President, Cargill Feed and Nutrition*	Tel: Fax:	(952) 742-5799 (952) 742-7224
MURPHY, Mark *Executive Director, Cargill Foundation and Manager, Stakeholder Relations* mark_murphy@cargill.com *Registered Federal Lobbyist*	Tel: Fax:	(952) 742-2792 (952) 742-7224
VRIJSEN, Peter *Corporate Vice President, Human Resources*	Tel: Fax:	(952) 742-5799 (952) 742-7224
WITTE, Laura *Corporate Vice President, General Counsel and Corporate Secretary*	Tel: Fax:	(952) 742-5799 (952) 742-7224

At Washington Office

BOUGHNER, Devry
Director, International Business Relations
devry_boughner@cargill.com
Registered Federal Lobbyist
Tel: (202) 530-8168
Fax: (202) 530-8180

HARRIS, Dominique
Contact, Government Relations
Registered Federal Lobbyist
Tel: (202) 530-8160
Fax: (202) 530-8180

HIXSON, Jon
Vice President, Corporate Affairs
Jon_Hixson@Cargill.com
Registered Federal Lobbyist
Tel: (202) 530-8166
Fax: (202) 530-8180

HOUSTON, Kate
Federal Lobbyist
Registered Federal Lobbyist
Tel: (202) 530-8168
Fax: (202) 530-8180

KOHNS, Jacob
Registered Federal Lobbyist
Tel: (202) 530-8160
Fax: (202) 530-8180

KUHNS, Jake E.
Director, Federal Government Relations
Registered Federal Lobbyist
Tel: (202) 530-8160
Fax: (202) 530-8180

LAI, dinh
Contact, Government Relations
Tel: (202) 530-8160
Fax: (202) 530-8180

MULLINS, Michael L
Vice President, Corporate Affairs
mike_mullins@cargill.com
Tel: (202) 530-8160
Fax: (202) 530-8180

MURPHY, Anne
Registered Federal Lobbyist
Tel: (202) 530-8160
Fax: (202) 530-8180

YEUTTER, Van
Vice President
v_yeutter@cargill.com
Registered Federal Lobbyist
Tel: (202) 530-8160
Fax: (202) 530-8180

Caribbean Tourism Development Company

The Caribbean Tourism Development Company (CTDC) is a marketing and business development unit, owned equally by the Caribbean Hotel Association (CHA) and the Caribbean Tourism Organization (CTO).
www.caribbeantravel.com

CEO and Director General
COMITO, Frank J.
frank@caribbeanhotelandtourism.com
Tel: (786) 476-8617

Main Headquarters
Mailing: 2655 Le Jeune Rd.
Suite 910
Coral Gables, FL 33134
Tel: (305) 443-3040

Public Affairs and Related Activities Personnel

At Headquarters

COOPER, Matt
Chief marketing officer
matt@caribbeanhotelandtourism.com
Tel: (786) 476-8620

LEDESMA, Vanessa
Chief Operating Officer
Tel: (305) 443-3040

At Other Offices

RILEY, Hugh
Secretary General
80 Broad St., 32nd Floor
New York City, NY 10004
Tel: (212) 635-9530
Fax: (212) 635-9511

Caritas Christi

See listing on page 751 under Steward Health Care System

Carlisle Companies Inc.

A manufacturing company.
www.carlisle.com
Annual Revenues: $3.63 billion
Employees: 12,000
Ticker: NYSE: CSL
SIC: 3060
Industry/ies: Construction/Construction Materials

Chairman of the Board and Chief Executive Officer
ROBERTS, David A.
Tel: (704) 501-1100
Fax: (704) 501-1190

Main Headquarters
Mailing: 11605 N. Community House Rd.
Suite 600
Charlotte, NC 28277
Tel: (704) 501-1100
Fax: (704) 501-1190
TF: (866) 869-0474

Corporate Foundations and Giving Programs

Carlisle Companies Inc. Contributions Program
11605 N. Community House Rd.
Suite 600
Charlotte, NC 28277
Tel: (704) 501-1100
Fax: (704) 501-1190

Public Affairs and Related Activities Personnel

At Headquarters

FORD, Steven J.
Vice President, Chief Financial Officer, Secretary and General Counsel
Tel: (704) 501-1100
Fax: (704) 501-1190

KOCH, Chris
President and Chief Operating Officer
Tel: (704) 501-1100
Fax: (704) 501-1190

SELBACH, Scott C.
Vice President, Corporate Development
Tel: (704) 501-1100
Fax: (704) 501-1190

Carlson Companies

A privately-held company with subsidiaries active in hotels, resorts, restaurants, travel, loyalty programs, promotional and sales marketing and incentives. Its restaurant and hotel division, Carlson Hospitality Worldwide, includes T.G.I.Friday's and Pick Up Stix restaurants, Radisson Hotels & Resorts Worldwide, Regent International Hotels, Country Inns & Suites By Carlson, Park Inn Hotels, Park Plaza Hotels & Resorts, and Radisson Seven Seas Cruises.
www.carlson.com
Employees: 166,718
Industry/ies: Travel/Tourism/Lodging

Chief Executive Officer
BERG , David P.
Tel: (763) 212-5000
Fax: (763) 212-2219

Main Headquarters
Mailing: 701 Carlson Pkwy.
Minnetonka, MN 55305
Tel: (763) 212-5000
Fax: (763) 212-2219

Corporate Foundations and Giving Programs

Curtis L. Carlson Family Foundation
Contact: C. David Nelson
701 Carlson Pkwy.
Minnetonka, MN 55305
Tel: (763) 212-4000
Fax: (763) 212-2219

Public Affairs and Related Activities Personnel

At Headquarters

HALL, Brad
Executive Vice President, Chief Financial Officer and Treasurer
Tel: (763) 212-5000
Fax: (763) 212-2219

RODAHL, Cindy
Executive Vice President, Human Resources and Communications
Tel: (763) 212-5000
Fax: (763) 212-2219

At Other Offices

NELSON, C. David
Executive Director, Carlson Family Foundation
550 Tonkawa Rd.
Long Lake, MN 55356
dnelson@carlsonfamilyfoundation.org
Tel: (952) 404-5636
Fax: (952) 350-2437

The Carlyle Group

American-based global asset management firm, in private equity.
www.carlyle.com
Annual Revenues: $2.35 billion
Employees: 1,700
Ticker: NASDAQ: CG
SIC: 6282
Industry/ies: Banking/Finance/Investments
Legislative Issues: HCR

Chairman of the Board and Co-founder
D'ANIELLO, Daniel A.
Tel: (202) 347-2626
Fax: (202) 347-1818

Co Chief Executive Officer and Chief Investment Officer
CORBETT, Bryan N.
bryan.corbett@carlyle.com
Tel: (202) 729-5626
Fax: (202) 347-1818

Co-Founder, Co-Chief Executive Officer and Managing Director
CONWAY, William E.
Tel: (202) 347-2626
Fax: (202) 347-1818

Main Headquarters
Mailing: 1001 Pennsylvania Ave. NW
Suite 220 South
Washington, DC 20004
Tel: (202) 729-5626
Fax: (202) 347-1818

Public Affairs and Related Activities Personnel

At Headquarters

ANDERSON, Jeremy W.
Managing Director
Tel: (202) 729-5626
Fax: (202) 347-1818

ARPEY, Michael W.
Managing Director
Tel: (202) 347-2626
Fax: (202) 347-1818

FERGUSON, Jeffrey W.
General Counsel
Tel: (202) 347-2626
Fax: (202) 347-1818

HARRIS, Daniel
Managing Director and Head, Public Investor Relations
daniel.harris@carlyle.com
Tel: (212) 813-4527
Fax: (202) 347-1818

MARCHICK, David M.
Managing Director and Global Head, External Affairs
Tel: (202) 729-5903
Fax: (202) 347-1818

PETRICK, Michael J.
Tel: (202) 347-2626

Head, Global Market Strategies	Fax:	(202) 347-1818
SABET, Lori R.	Tel:	(202) 347-2626
Managing Director and Chief Human Resources Officer	Fax:	(202) 347-1818
ULLMAN, Christopher W.	Tel:	(202) 729-5399
Managing Director, Global Communications	Fax:	(202) 347-1818
christopher.ullman@carlyle.com		
WHITESTONE, Randall	Tel:	(212) 813-4717
Director, Communications for the Americas	Fax:	(202) 347-1818
media@carlyle.com		
YOUNGKIN, Glenn A.	Tel:	(202) 347-2626
President and Chief Operating Officer	Fax:	(202) 347-1818

CarMax Inc.

A used-car retailer that buys, reconditions, and sells cars and light trucks.
www.carmax.com
Annual Revenues: $14.53 billion
Employees: 22,064
Ticker: NYSE: KMX
SIC: 5500
Industry/ies: Automotive Industry; Transportation

Chairman of the Board	Tel:	(804) 747-0422
TIEFEL, William R.	Fax:	(804) 217-6819

President and Chief Executive Officer	Tel:	(804) 747-0422
FOLLIARD, Thomas J.	Fax:	(804) 217-6819

Main Headquarters

Mailing:	12800 Tuckahoe Creek Pkwy.	Tel:	(804) 747-0422
	Richmond, VA 23238	Fax:	(804) 217-6819
		TF:	(800) 519-1511

Corporate Foundations and Giving Programs

The CarMax Foundation
Contact: Michelle Ellwood

12800 Tuckahoe Creek Pkwy.	Tel:	(804) 747-0422
Richmond, VA 23238	Fax:	(804) 217-6819

Public Affairs and Related Activities Personnel

At Headquarters

DONAHUE, Laura	Tel:	(804) 747-0422
Vice President, Advertising	Fax:	(804) 217-6819
laura_donahue@carmax.com		
ELLWOOD, Michelle	Tel:	(804) 747-0422
Contact Foundation and Coordinator, Public Affairs	Fax:	(804) 217-6819
michelle_ellwood@carmax.com		
HILL , Ed	Tel:	(804) 747-0422
Senior Vice President, Service Operations	Fax:	(804) 217-6819
KENNY, Katharine	Tel:	(804) 747-0422
Vice President, Investor Relations	Fax:	(804) 217-6819
katharine_kenny@carmax.com		
LEE, Trina H.	Tel:	(804) 747-0422
Director, Public Relations	Fax:	(804) 217-6819
trina_lee@carmax.com		
LYSKI , Jim	Tel:	(804) 747-0422
Senior Vice President, Chief Marketing Officer	Fax:	(804) 217-6819
MARGOLIN, Eric	Tel:	(804) 747-0422
Senior Vice President, General Counsel and Corporate Secretary	Fax:	(804) 217-6819
NASH, Bill	Tel:	(804) 747-0422
Executive Vice President, Human Resources and Administration	Fax:	(804) 217-6819
REEDY, Tom	Tel:	(804) 747-0422
Executive Vice President and Chief Financial Officer	Fax:	(804) 217-6819

Carmeuse Lime & Stone

A supplier of lime and limestone in North America.
www.carmeusena.com
Annual Revenues: $600 million
Employees: 5,000
Industry/ies: Food And Beverage Industry

Chief Executive Officer	Tel:	(412) 995-5500
WILLEMS, Yves	Fax:	(412) 995-5570

Main Headquarters

Mailing:	11 Stanwix St.	Tel:	(412) 995-5500
	21st Floor	Fax:	(412) 995-5570
	Pittsburgh, PA 15222		

Political Action Committees

Carmeuse PAC
FEC ID: C00460097
Contact: Bruce Inglis

11 Stanwix St.	Tel:	(412) 995-5500
21st Floor	Fax:	(412) 995-5570
Pittsburgh, PA 15222		

   Contributions to Candidates: $3,000 (2015-2016)

Republicans: $3,000

Public Affairs and Related Activities Personnel

At Headquarters

BARDINE, Ralph	Tel:	(412) 995-5500
Vice President, Business Development	Fax:	(412) 995-5570
FAHLER, Jack	Tel:	(412) 995-5500
Vice President, Sales, Marketing and Technology	Fax:	(412) 995-5570
INGLIS, Bruce	Tel:	(412) 995-5500
Chief Financial Officer and PAC Treasurer	Fax:	(412) 995-5570
JOHNSON, Philip	Tel:	(412) 995-5500
Chief Executive Officer Europe	Fax:	(412) 995-5570
OLSON, Lance	Tel:	(412) 995-5500
Director of Technology and Sales Support	Fax:	(412) 995-5570
PALLOTTA, Tony P.	Tel:	(412) 995-4963
Manager, Marketing Communications	Fax:	(412) 995-5570
Tony.Pallotta@carmeusena.com		
ROUTHIEAUX, Bruce	Tel:	(412) 995-5500
Vice President, Chief Operating Officer	Fax:	(412) 995-5570
WHYTE, Kevin	Tel:	(412) 995-5500
Vice President, Safety, Environmental and Legal	Fax:	(412) 995-5570
K.Whyte@carmeusena.com		
WILEY, Kathy	Tel:	(412) 995-5500
Vice President, Human Resources	Fax:	(412) 995-5570
K.Wiley@carmeusena.com		

Carmeuse North America

See listing on page 167 under Carmeuse Lime & Stone

Carmike Cinemas Inc.

Constructs and operates movie theaters.
www.carmike.com
Annual Revenues: $715.34 million
Employees: 7,800
Ticker: NASDAQ: CKEC
SIC: 7830
Industry/ies: Communications; Media/Mass Communication

Chairman of the Board	Tel:	(706) 576-3400
SMITH, Roland C.	Fax:	(706) 576-2812

President and Chief Executive Officer	Tel:	(706) 576-3400
PASSMAN, III, S. David	Fax:	(706) 576-2812

Main Headquarters

Mailing:	1301 First Ave.	Tel:	(706) 576-3400
	Columbus, GA 31901	Fax:	(706) 576-2812

Public Affairs and Related Activities Personnel

At Headquarters

HARE, Richard B.	Tel:	(706) 576-3416
Senior Vice President and Chief Financial Officer	Fax:	(706) 576-2812
MAYTON, Terrell	Tel:	(706) 576-3464
Director, Marketing	Fax:	(706) 576-2812
RINDERMAN, Robert	Tel:	(212) 835-8500
Contact, Investor Relations	Fax:	(706) 576-2812
ckec@jcir.com		

Carnegie Hall Corporation

Musical institution.
www.carnegiehall.org
Employees: 350
Industry/ies: Arts, The; Performing Arts/Music
Legislative Issues: ART; BUD; EDU

Main Headquarters

Mailing:	881 Seventh Ave. 57th St.	Tel:	(212) 247-7800
	New York City, NY 10019	Fax:	(212) 581-6539

Corporate Foundations and Giving Programs

Carnegie Hall Foundation
Contact: Callie Herzog

881 Seventh Ave.	Tel:	(212) 903-9681
New York City, NY 10019		

Public Affairs and Related Activities Personnel

At Headquarters

AMOS, Christopher	Tel:	(212) 247-7800
Chief Digital Officer	Fax:	(212) 581-6539
CARLINO, Synneve	Tel:	(212) 903-9600
Director, Public Relations	Fax:	(212) 581-6539
scarlino@carnegiehall.org		
CASELLA, Catherine	Tel:	(212) 903-9600
Director, Human Resources	Fax:	(212) 581-6539
FISHER, Dori	Tel:	(212) 247-7800
Director, Corporate Relations and Sponsorships	Fax:	(212) 581-6539

FREUDENTHAL, David	Tel:	(212) 903-9600
Director, Government Relations	Fax:	(212) 581-6539
dfreudenthal@carnegiehall.org		
GRABEL, Naomi	Tel:	(212) 247-7800
Director, Marketing and Creative Services	Fax:	(212) 581-6539
HERZOG, Callie	Tel:	(212) 903-9600
Director, Foundation Relations	Fax:	(212) 581-6539
LONG, Patricia	Tel:	(212) 247-7800
Chief Financial Officer	Fax:	(212) 581-6539
MALENKA, Richard	Tel:	(212) 247-7800
Director, Administration	Fax:	(212) 581-6539
O'REILLY, Seamus	Tel:	(212) 247-7800
Director, e-Strategy	Fax:	(212) 581-6539

Carnival Corporation

A cruise line company. Operates as a dual-listed company with UK-based Carnival PLC.
www.carnival.com
Annual Revenues: $15.83 billion
Employees: 94,600
Ticker: NYSE: CCL
SIC: 4400
Industry/ies: Marine/Maritime/Shipping; Transportation; Travel/Tourism/Lodging
Legislative Issues: ENV; TAX; TOU

Chairman of the Board	Tel:	(305) 599-2600
ARISON, Micky	Fax:	(305) 406-4700
President and Chief Executive Officer	Tel:	(305) 599-2600
DONALD, Arnold W.	Fax:	(305) 406-8630

Main Headquarters
Mailing: 3655 N.W. 87th Ave.	Tel:	(305) 599-2600
Miami, FL 33178	Fax:	(305) 406-8630
	TF:	(800) 438-6744

Washington Office
Mailing: 1750 P St. NW	Tel:	(202) 347-7150
PH-3		
Washington, DC 20036		

Corporate Foundations and Giving Programs
Carnival Foundation
Contact: Linda Coll
Carnival Pl.	Tel:	(305) 599-2600
3655 NW 87th Ave.	Fax:	(305) 406-8630
Miami, FL 33178		

Public Affairs and Related Activities Personnel
At Headquarters
BERNSTEIN, David	Tel:	(305) 599-2600
Chief Financial Officer and Chief Accounting Officer	Fax:	(305) 406-4700
COLL, Linda	Tel:	(305) 599-2600
Director, Carnival Foundation	Fax:	(305) 406-8630
lcoll@carnival.com		
FRIZZELL , Roger	Tel:	(305) 599-2600
Chief Communications Officer	Fax:	(305) 406-8630
LEIBOWITZ, Josh	Tel:	(305) 599-2600
Chief Strategy Officer	Fax:	(305) 406-8630
MONTGOMERY, Jerry	Tel:	(305) 599-2600
Chief Human Resources Officer	Fax:	(305) 406-8630
PEREZ, Arnaldo	Tel:	(305) 599-2600
General Counsel and Secretary	Fax:	(305) 406-4700
ROBERTS, Beth	Tel:	(305) 406-5539
Vice President, Investor Relations	Fax:	(305) 406-4700
Mail Stop Mail Stop CD925N		

At Washington Office
DOW, Thomas	Tel:	(202) 347-7150
Vice President, Public Affairs		
Registered Federal Lobbyist		

Carnival Cruise Lines

See listing on page 168 under Carnival Corporation

Carpenter Technology Corporation

A manufacturer of specialty metals.
www.cartech.com
Annual Revenues: $1.91 billion
Employees: 4,900
Ticker: NYSE: CRS
SIC: 3312; 3315; 3356; 3471; 5051
NAICS: 331111; 331221; 331491; 332618; 42151
Industry/ies: Construction/Construction Materials

| **Chairman of the Board** | Tel: | (610) 208-2000 |
| PRATT, Gregory A. | Fax: | (610) 208-3716 |

| **President and Chief Executive Officer** | Tel: | (610) 208-2000 |
| THENE, Tony R. | Fax: | (610) 208-3716 |

Main Headquarters
Mailing: P.O. Box 14662	Tel:	(610) 208-2000
Bldg. L05	Fax:	(610) 208-3716
Reading, PA 19612-4662	TF:	(800) 654-6543

Corporate Foundations and Giving Programs
Carpenter Technology Corporation Contributions Program
P.O. Box 14662
Bldg. L05
Reading, PA 19612-4662

Public Affairs and Related Activities Personnel
At Headquarters
DEE, James D.	Tel:	(610) 208-2000
Vice President, General Counsel and Secretary	Fax:	(610) 208-3716
EDWARDS, Brad	Tel:	(212) 986-6667
Investor Relations Contact	Fax:	(610) 208-3716
RICE, John L.	Tel:	(610) 208-2000
Vice President, Human Resources	Fax:	(610) 208-3716
RUDOLPH, William J.	Tel:	(610) 208-3892
Director, Corporate Communications	Fax:	(610) 208-3716
wrudolph@cartech.com		

CarrAmerica Realty Corporation

See listing on page 300 under Equity Office Management LLC

Carrier Corporation

A manufacturer of heating, air conditioning and refrigeration equipment for commercial, residential, and transportation applications.
www.carrier.com
Employees: 32,000
NAICS: 333415
Industry/ies: Heating And Air Conditioning

Main Headquarters
Mailing: One Carrier Pl.	Tel:	(860) 674-3000
Farmington, CT 06034-4015	Fax:	(860) 674-3139
	TF:	(800) 227-7437

Corporate Foundations and Giving Programs
Carrier Corporation Contributions Program
| One Carrier Pl. | Tel: | (860) 674-3000 |
| Farmington, CT 06034-4015 | | |

Public Affairs and Related Activities Personnel
At Headquarters
| CALDWELL, Michelle | Tel: | (860) 674-3000 |
| *Manager, Marketing and Communications* | Fax: | (860) 674-3139 |

Carrix, Inc.

A privately held marine and rail terminal operator.It loads and unloads ships and provides warehousing and distribution services.
www.carrix.com
Employees: 11,000
Industry/ies: Marine/Maritime/Shipping; Transportation

Chief Executive Officer	Tel:	(206) 382-4490
HEMINGWAY, Jon	Fax:	(206) 623-0179
jon.hemingway@ssamarine.com		

Main Headquarters
Mailing: 1131 S.W. Klickitat Way	Tel:	(206) 382-4490
Seattle, WA 98134	Fax:	(206) 623-0179
	TF:	(800) 422-3505

Corporate Foundations and Giving Programs
Carrix Contributions Program
| 1131 SW Klickitat Way | Tel: | (206) 382-4490 |
| Seattle, WA 98134 | Fax: | (206) 382-4490 |

Public Affairs and Related Activities Personnel
At Headquarters
SADOSKI, Charlie	Tel:	(206) 382-4490
Executive Vice President and Chief Financial Officer	Fax:	(206) 623-0179
STUBKJAER, Knud	Tel:	(206) 382-4490
Chief Strategic Officer	Fax:	(206) 623-0179
WATTERS, Bob	Tel:	(206) 382-4490
Senior Vice President and Director, Business Development	Fax:	(206) 623-0179

Carter Aviation Technologies

Carter Aviation Technologies (also known as CarterCopters) is an aerospace research and development company. It is dedicated to the creation of practical, advanced technology innovations in hybrid aircraft and rotorcraft.
www.cartercopters.com
Annual Revenues: $0.77 million
Industry/ies: Aerospace/Aviation; Transportation

President and Chief Executive Officer Tel: (940) 691-0819
CARTER, Jr., Jay

Main Headquarters
Mailing: 2730 Commerce St. Tel: (940) 691-0819
Suite 600
Wichita Falls, TX 76301

Public Affairs and Related Activities Personnel

At Headquarters

CARTER, Matt Tel: (940) 691-0819
Vice President & Special Advisor to the Chief Executive Officer

INFANTE, Anita C. Tel: (309) 853-5238
Vice President, Marketing
carter4ga@earthlink.net

ROBERTSON, Kerri Tel: (940) 691-0819
Controller / Secretary

TATRO, Jon Tel: (940) 691-0819
President, International Affairs and Executive Vice President Joint Ventures & Licensing
jon.tatro@carteraero.com

Casco Manufacturing Solutions, Inc.
Specializes in the custom design and production of sewn, sealed and upholstered products.
www.cascosolutions.com
Annual Revenues: $18.20 million
Employees: 200
Industry/ies: Construction/Construction Materials; Engineering/Mathematics

Chief Executive Officer Tel: (513) 681-0003
MANGOLD, Melissa Fax: (513) 853-3605
mmangold@cascosolutions.com

Main Headquarters
Mailing: 3107 Spring Grove Ave. Tel: (513) 681-0003
Cincinnati, OH 45225-1821 Fax: (513) 853-3605
TF: (800) 843-1339

CNH Industrial
Formed by the 1999 merger of New Holland N.V. and Case Corporation. Designer, manufacturer, and distributor of agricultural and construction equipment. Also offers financial products and services.
www.cnhindustrial.com
Annual Revenues: $719.90 million
Employees: 69,000
Ticker: NYSE: CNH
SIC: 3531
Industry/ies: Agriculture/Agronomy; Construction/Construction Materials; Machinery/Equipment
Legislative Issues: AGR; FIN; FUE; LBR; TAX; TRA; TRD

Director and Chairman of the Board Tel: (630) 887-2345
MARCHIONNE, Sergio

Chief Executive Officer Tel: (630) 887-2345
TOBIN, Richard

Main Headquarters
Mailing: 700 State St. Tel: (630) 887-2345
Racine, WI 53404

Washington Office
Mailing: 1001 G St. NW Tel: (202) 737-7575
Suite 100 East Fax: (202) 737-9090
Washington, DC 20001

Political Action Committees
Case New Holland Excellence in Government Committee PAC
FEC ID: C00303883
Contact: Steven Nadherny
1001 G St. NW Tel: (202) 737-7575
Suite 100, East Fax: (202) 737-9090
Washington, DC 20001

Contributions to Candidates: $32,000 (2015-2016)
Republicans: $32,000

Public Affairs and Related Activities Personnel

At Headquarters

CATASTA, Federico Tel: (630) 887-2345
Head, Risk Management
wwinvestorrelations@cnh.com

CHIARA, Massimiliano Tel: (630) 887-2345
Chief Financial Officer

GOING, Michael P. Tel: (630) 887-2345
Chief Compliance Officer and Corporate Secretary
Michael.Going@cnh.com

KNOLL, Linda Tel: (630) 887-2345
Chief Human Resources Officer

At Washington Office

HART, Matthew Tel: (202) 737-7575
Registered Federal Lobbyist Fax: (202) 737-9090

NADHERNY, Steven Tel: (202) 737-7575
Vice President, Government Affairs & PAC Contact Fax: (202) 737-9090
steven.nadherny@cnh.com
Registered Federal Lobbyist

Cash America International
A diversified specialty finance company.
www.cashamerica.com
Annual Revenues: $1.08 billion
Employees: 6,426
Ticker: NYSE: CSH
SIC: 5900
Industry/ies: Retail/Wholesale
Legislative Issues: FIN

Chairman of the Board Tel: (817) 335-1100
DAUGHERTY, Jack R. Fax: (817) 570-1225
jdaugherty@casham.com

President and Chief Executive Officer Tel: (817) 335-1100
FEEHAN, Daniel R. Fax: (817) 570-1225
dfeehan@casham.com

Main Headquarters
Mailing: 1600 W. Seventh St. Tel: (817) 335-1100
Fort Worth, TX 76102 Fax: (817) 570-1225
TF: (800) 223-8738

Washington Office
Mailing: 1325 G St. NW, Suite 500
Washington, DC 20036

Political Action Committees
Cash America International, Inc. PAC
FEC ID: C00275529
Contact: Hurshell Brown
1600 W. Seventh St.
Fort Worth, TX 76102

Contributions to Candidates: $76,900 (2015-2016)
Democrats: $10,500; Republicans: $66,400

Corporate Foundations and Giving Programs
Cash America International Contributions Program
1600 W. Seventh St.
Fort Worth, TX 76102

Public Affairs and Related Activities Personnel

At Headquarters

BESSANT, Jr., Thomas A. Tel: (817) 335-1100
Executive Vice President and Chief Financial Officer Fax: (817) 570-1225

BROWN, Hurshell Tel: (817) 335-1100
Treasurer Fax: (817) 570-1225

LINSCOTT, J. Curtis Tel: (817) 335-1100
Executive Vice President, General Counsel and Corporate Fax: (817) 570-1225
Secretary

LITTRELL, Dee Tel: (817) 335-1100
Director, Investor Relations Fax: (817) 570-1645
dlittrell@casham.com

Caspian Alliance, Inc.
Industry/ies: Energy/Electricity

Main Headquarters
Mailing: 5847 San Filipe Tel: (713) 783-7783
Suite 3275
Houston, TX 77057

Public Affairs and Related Activities Personnel

At Headquarters

CRESCENZI, Josh Tel: (713) 783-7783

ETTINGER, Brian Tel: (713) 783-7783
Legal Counsel
ettingelaw@yahoo.com

POLLAND, Gary Tel: (713) 783-7783

STORCH, Ari

Catalina Health Resource, Inc.
Helps clients develop customized, measureable, treatment-related messages that can incite healthier patient outcomes.
www.adheris.com
Annual Revenues: $6.50 million
Employees: 100
Industry/ies: Medicine/Health Care/Mental Health

Chief Executive Officer Tel: (727) 579-5000
EGASTI, Jamie Fax: (727) 563-5687

Main Headquarters

Mailing:	200 Carillon Pkwy.	Tel:	(727) 579-5000
	St. Petersburg, FL 33716	Fax:	(727) 563-5687
		TF:	(800) 803-9360

Public Affairs and Related Activities Personnel

At Headquarters

MORRIS, Todd	Tel:	(727) 579-5000
Executive Vice President, Brand Development and Marketing	Fax:	(727) 563-5687
Innovation		

Catalina Marketing Corporation

Catalina Marketing is the global in shopper-driven marketing solutions, providing brand manufacturers, retailers and healthcare providers with shopper-driven marketing solutions to meet growth objectives.
www.catalinamarketing.com
Annual Revenues: $66.40 million
Employees: 1,200
Ticker: NYSE:POS
SIC: 7311
Industry/ies: Advertising And Marketing; Communications; Media/Mass Communication

Chief Executive Officer

EGASTI, Jamie	Tel:	(727) 579-5000
	Fax:	(727) 556-2700

Main Headquarters

Mailing:	200 Carillon Pkwy.	Tel:	(727) 579-5000
	St. Petersburg, FL 33716	Fax:	(727) 556-2700
		TF:	(877) 210-1917

Corporate Foundations and Giving Programs

Catalina Charitable Foundation
Contact: Debbie Booth

200 Carillon Pkwy.	Tel:	(727) 579-5000
St. Petersburg, FL 33716	Fax:	(727) 556-2700

Public Affairs and Related Activities Personnel

At Headquarters

BARNA, Michael	Tel:	(727) 579-5000
Executive Vice President , Chief Financial Officer (Interim)	Fax:	(727) 556-2700
BOOTH, Debbie	Tel:	(727) 579-5000
Executive Vice President, Global Operations and Chair,	Fax:	(727) 556-2700
Catalina's Charitable Foundation Board		
BORTNER , Andrea R.	Tel:	(727) 579-5000
Executive Vice President, Chief Human Resources Officer	Fax:	(727) 556-2700
MEYER, Tamara	Tel:	(727) 579-5000
Executive Vice President, General Counsel	Fax:	(727) 556-2700
MORRIS, Todd	Tel:	(727) 579-5000
President, Catalina U.S.	Fax:	(727) 556-2700
PARKER, Ira	Tel:	(727) 579-5000
Executive Vice President Corporate & Business Development	Fax:	(727) 556-2700
& General Counsel		

Catalist, LLC

Provides subscription-based access to a database of voting-age Americans.
www.catalist.us
Industry/ies: Advertising And Marketing; Market Research; Marketing

Chief Executive Officer

QUINN, Laura	Tel:	(202) 962-7200
	Fax:	(202) 962-7201

Main Headquarters

Mailing:	1090 Vermont Ave. NW	Tel:	(202) 962-7200
	Suite 300	Fax:	(202) 962-7201
	Washington, DC 20005		

Corporate Foundations and Giving Programs

Catalist, LLC Contributions Program

1101 Vermont Ave. NW	Tel:	(202) 962-7200
Suite 900		
Washington, DC 20005-3521		

Public Affairs and Related Activities Personnel

At Headquarters

BLAEMIRE, Robert	Tel:	(202) 962-7200
Director, Business Development	Fax:	(202) 962-7201
GRUVER, Gary	Tel:	(202) 962-7200
Chief Financial Officer	Fax:	(202) 962-7201
LOMAN, Will	Tel:	(202) 962-7200
General Counsel	Fax:	(202) 962-7201

Caterpillar Inc.

Manufactures and sells construction and mining equipment, diesel and natural gas engines, industrial gas turbines, and diesel-electric locomotives worldwide.
www.cat.com
Annual Revenues: $54.64 billion
Employees: 113,322

Ticker: NYSE: CAT
SIC: 5082; 3531
Industry/ies: Machinery/Equipment; Transportation; Trucking Industry
Legislative Issues: BUD; CPI; CPT; EDU; ENG; FIN; HCR; LBR; NAT; RET; TAR; TAX; TRA; TRD

Chairman of the Board and Chief Executive Officer

OBERHELMAN, Doug	Tel:	(309) 675-1000
	Fax:	(309) 675-1182

Main Headquarters

Mailing:	501 SW Jefferson St.	Tel:	(309) 675-2337
	Peoria, IL 61614	TF:	(888) 614-4328

Washington Office

Mailing:	1425 K St. NW	Tel:	(202) 466-0662
	Suite 400	Fax:	(202) 466-0684
	Washington, DC 20005		

Political Action Committees

Caterpillar Employee PAC
FEC ID: C00148031
Contact: Michael C. Morrison
100 NE Adams St.
Peoria, IL 61629

Contributions to Candidates: $615,625 (2015-2016)
Democrats: $110,000; Republicans: $500,625; Other: $5,000

Principal Recipients

SENATE
BLUNT, ROY (REP-MO)
KIRK, MARK STEVEN (REP-IL)
TOOMEY, PATRICK JOSEPH (REP-PA)
YOUNG, TODD CHRISTOPHER (REP-IN)

HOUSE
BOST, MICHAEL (REP-IL)
BRADY, KEVIN (REP-TX)
DAVIS, RODNEY L (REP-IL)
DENHAM, JEFF (REP-CA)
DOLD, ROBERT JAMES JR (REP-IL)
HILL, JAMES FRENCH (REP-AR)
HULTGREN, RANDY (REP-IL)
KELLY, JOHN TRENT (REP-MS)
KINZINGER, ADAM (REP-IL)
LAHOOD, DARIN MCKAY (REP-IL)
ROSKAM, PETER (REP-IL)
SHIMKUS, JOHN M (REP-IL)

Corporate Foundations and Giving Programs

Caterpillar Inc. Foundation

100 N.E. Adams St.	Tel:	(309) 675-1000
Peoria, IL 61629	Fax:	(309) 675-1182

Public Affairs and Related Activities Personnel

At Washington Office

ALLEN, Joseph	Tel:	(202) 466-0662
Registered Federal Lobbyist	Fax:	(202) 466-0684
BOLTON, Dwayne	Tel:	(202) 466-0662
Manager, Government Affairs	Fax:	(202) 466-0684
Registered Federal Lobbyist		
BRENT, Richard	Tel:	(202) 466-0655
Washington Manager, Solar Turbines	Fax:	(202) 466-0684
Registered Federal Lobbyist		
CORDANI, Benjamin	Tel:	(202) 466-0662
Contact, Government Affairs, Lead Global Manager, Human	Fax:	(202) 466-0684
Resource		
cordani_benjamin_s@cat.com		
GIBBONS, Justin	Tel:	(202) 466-0662
Manager, Washington Operations	Fax:	(202) 466-0684
Registered Federal Lobbyist		
HAYS, Katie	Tel:	(202) 466-0662
Federal Lobbyist	Fax:	(202) 466-0684
Registered Federal Lobbyist		
HIRABAYASHI, Kai	Tel:	(202) 466-0662
Registered Federal Lobbyist	Fax:	(202) 466-0684
KAROL, Kathryn Dickey	Tel:	(202) 466-0662
Vice President, Global Government and Corporate Affairs	Fax:	(202) 466-0684
LANE, William	Tel:	(202) 466-0662
Washington Director	Fax:	(202) 466-0684
Registered Federal Lobbyist		
LYNN, Jason M.	Tel:	(202) 466-0662
Manager, Government Affairs	Fax:	(202) 466-0684
Registered Federal Lobbyist		
MYERS, Christopher	Tel:	(202) 466-0662
Director, Federal Government Affairs	Fax:	(202) 466-0684
Registered Federal Lobbyist		
THOMPSON, Clay	Tel:	(202) 466-0662
Federal Lobbyist	Fax:	(202) 466-0684

Thompson_Clay@cat.com
Registered Federal Lobbyist

At Other Offices

BUDA, James B.
Executive Vice President, Law and Public Policy
100 N.E. Adams St.
Peoria, IL 61629

Tel: (309) 675-1000
Fax: (309) 675-1182

DEWALT, Michael
Vice President, Finance Services
100 N.E. Adams St.
Peoria, IL 61629

Tel: (309) 675-1000
Fax: (309) 675-1182

DUGAN, Jim
Chief Corporate Spokesperson
100 N.E. Adams St.
Peoria, IL 61629
dugan_jim@cat.com

Tel: (309) 675-4100
Fax: (309) 675-1182

HALVERSON, Bradley M.
President and Chief Financial Officer
100 N.E. Adams St.
Peoria, IL 61629

Tel: (309) 675-1000
Fax: (309) 675-1182

HAUER, Kimberly
Chief Human Resource Officer and Vice President
100 N.E. Adams St.
Peoria, IL 61629

Tel: (309) 675-1000
Fax: (309) 675-1182

MORRISON, Michael C.
PAC Treasurer
100 N.E. Adams St.
Peoria, IL 61629

Tel: (309) 675-1000
Fax: (309) 675-1182

RAPP, Ed
President
100 N.E. Adams St.
Peoria, IL 61629

Tel: (309) 675-1000
Fax: (309) 675-1182

SPEARS, Christopher C.
General Counsel Commercial and International Operations
100 N.E. Adams St.
Peoria, IL 61629

Tel: (309) 675-1000
Fax: (309) 675-1182

VEST, Gary L.
PAC Treasurer
100 N.E. Adams St.
Peoria, IL 61629

Tel: (309) 675-1000
Fax: (309) 675-6155

Catskill Mountainkeeper Inc.

Non-profit 501c3 grassroots advocact organization working to protect the Catskills Region.
www.catskillmountainkeeper.org

Executive Director
ADAMS, Ramsay
ramsay@catskillmountainkeeper.org

Tel: (845) 482-5400

Main Headquarters
Mailing: P.O. Box 1000
47 Main St.
Livingston Manor, NY 12758

Tel: (845) 482-5400

Public Affairs and Related Activities Personnel

At Headquarters

GILLINGHAM, Wesley
Director, Program
wes@catskillmountainkeeper.org
Registered Federal Lobbyist

Tel: (845) 482-5400

SCULLION, Beth
Office Manager
beth@catskillmountainkeeper.org

Tel: (845) 482-5400

CB&I

Provider of complete piping systems and comprehensive engineering, procurement and construction services.
www.chicagobridge.com
Annual Revenues: $13.17 billion
Employees: 54,400
Ticker: NYSE: CBI
SIC: 3490
Industry/ies: Construction/Construction Materials; Engineering/Mathematics
Legislative Issues: BUD; DEF; ENG; TRD

President and Chief Executive Officer
ASHERMAN, Philip K.

Tel: (832) 513-1000

Main Headquarters
Mailing: One CB&I Plaza
2103 Research Forest Dr.
The Woodlands, TX 77380

Tel: (832) 513-1000

Washington Office
Mailing: 1050 K St. NW
Suite 620
Washington, DC 20001

Public Affairs and Related Activities Personnel

At Headquarters

BAILEY, Beth . A
Executive Vice President and Chief Administration Officer

Tel: (832) 513-1000

CHANDLER, Jr., Richard E.
Executive Vice President, Chief Legal Officer and Secretary

Tel: (832) 513-1000

CRAIN , Stephen
Vice President, Sales and Marketing
scrain@cbi.com

Tel: (832) 513-1000

RAY, E. Chip
Executive Vice President and Group President of Government Solutions

Tel: (832) 513-1000

TAFF, Michael S.
Executive Vice President and Chief Financial Officer

Tel: (832) 513-1000

THOMS, Christi
Senior Vice President, Corporate Planning and Contact, Investor Relations

Tel: (832) 513-1000

At Washington Office

MARLO, Stephen M.
Senior Vice President, Government Affairs
stephen.marlo@shawgrp.com
Registered Federal Lobbyist

Tel: (202) 261-1901

ROZZI, Paola M.
PAC Treasurer
paol.rozzi@shawgrp.com

Tel: (202) 261-1900

At Other Offices

BRANN, Gentry
Vice President, Global Communications and Marketing
4171 Essen Ln.
Baton Rouge, LA 70809
gentry.brann@shawgrp.com

Tel: (225) 987-7372
Fax: (225) 932-2661

DONOFRIO, John
Executive Vice President, General Counsel and Corporate Secretary
4171 Essen Ln.
Baton Rouge, LA 70809

Tel: (225) 932-2500
Fax: (225) 987-3328

CB Richard Ellis

A commercial real estate services company.
www.cbre.com
Annual Revenues: $11.65 billion
Employees: 70,000
Ticker: NYSE: CBG
SIC: 6500
Industry/ies: Real Estate

President and Chief Executive Officer
SULENTIC, Bob

Tel: (214) 863-3195
Fax: (214) 863-3125

Main Headquarters
Mailing: 400 S. Hope St.
25th Floor
Los Angeles, CA 90071

Tel: (310) 405-8900
Fax: (310) 405-8950

Corporate Foundations and Giving Programs

CB Richard Ellis Foundation
Contact: Calvin W. Frese Jr.
11150 Santa Monica Blvd.
Suite 105-S
Los Angeles, CA 90025

Public Affairs and Related Activities Personnel

At Headquarters

BOROK, Gil
Deputy Chief Financial Officer and Chief Accounting Officer
gil.borok@cbre.com

Tel: (310) 405-8909
Fax: (310) 405-8950

FERGUSON, Ritson
Chief Executive Officer, CBRE Global Investors

Tel: (310) 405-8900
Fax: (310) 405-8950

MIDLER, Laurence
Executive Vice President, General Counsel

Tel: (310) 405-8900
Fax: (310) 405-8950

MIDLER, Laurence J.
Executive Vice President, General Counsel
larry.midler@cbre.com

Tel: (213) 613-3735
Fax: (310) 405-8950

O'BRIEN, Laura
Executive Vice President, Global Brokerage and Sales Management
laura.obrien@cbre.com

Tel: (818) 623-8089
Fax: (310) 405-8950

At Other Offices

ASHLEY, Jennifer
Global Director, Human Resources
200 Park Ave., 19-22 Floors
New York City, NY 10166

Tel: (212) 984-6578
Fax: (212) 984-8040

DURBURG, Jack

Tel: (312) 935-1418

Chief Executive Officer, Americas
321 N. Clark St., Suite 3400
Chicago, IL 60654

Fax: (312) 935-1880

FRESE, Jr., Calvin W.
Global Group President, Geographies and President,
Foundation
321 N. Clark St., Suite 3400
Chicago, IL 60654
cal.frese@cbre.com

Tel: (312) 297-7600
Fax: (312) 935-1880

GROCH, James
Chief Financial Officer and Global Director, Corporate
Development
1200 Liberty Ridge Dr., Suite 320
Wayne, PA 19087
jim.groch@cbre.com

Tel: (215) 921-7401
Fax: (610) 889-9168

KHOURIE, Matt
Chief Executive Officer, Trammell Crow Company
155 Flower St., 31st floor
Los Angeles, CA 90071

Tel: (213) 683-4150
Fax: (213) 683-4301

KIRK, Chris
Chief Administrative Officer
2100 McKinney Ave., Suite 700
Dallas, TX 75201
chris.kirk@cbre.com

Tel: (214) 863-4015
Fax: (214) 863-3125

LAFITTE, Mike
Chief Operating Officer
2100 McKinney Ave., Suite 700
Dallas, TX 75201

Tel: (214) 863-3511
Fax: (214) 979-6393

MCGRATH, Robert W.
Senior Director, Corporate Communications
200 Park Ave., 19-22 Floors
New York City, NY 10166
robert.mcgrath@cbre.com

Tel: (212) 984-8267
Fax: (212) 984-8207

CBeyond Communications, LLC

A telecommunication service provider.
www.cbeyond.net
Annual Revenues: $484.07 million
Employees: 1,700
Ticker: NASDAQ: CBEY
SIC: 4813
Industry/ies: Communications; Telecommunications/Internet/Cable

Founder, Chairman, President and Chief Executive Officer
GEIGER, James F.

Tel: (678) 424-2400
Fax: (678) 424-2500

Main Headquarters
Mailing: 320 Interstate N. Pkwy. SE
Atlanta, GA 30339

Tel: (678) 424-2400
Fax: (678) 424-2500
TF: (866) 424-2600

Political Action Committees
Cbeyond, Inc. PAC
FEC ID: C00445874
Contact: William H. Weber
320 Interstate N. Pkwy. SE
Suite 300
Atlanta, GA 30339

Corporate Foundations and Giving Programs
Cbeyond Contributions Program
320 Interstate N. Pkwy. SE
Suite 300
Atlanta, GA 30339

Public Affairs and Related Activities Personnel

At Headquarters

CARMODY, Paul
Senior Vice President and Chief Marketing Officer

Tel: (678) 424-2400
Fax: (678) 424-2500

FUGATE, J. Robert
Executive Vice President and Chief Financial Officer
bob.fugate@cbeyond.net

Tel: (678) 424-2400
Fax: (678) 424-2500

MORRICE, Robert R.
Executive Vice President, Sales

Tel: (678) 424-2400
Fax: (678) 424-2500

OJINMAH, Helga
Contact, Media Relations
helga.ojinmah@cbeyond.com

Tel: (678) 370-2243
Fax: (678) 424-2500

TOLLIVER, Joan L.
Vice President, Human Resources
joan.tolliver@cbeyond.net

Tel: (678) 424-2400
Fax: (678) 424-2500

WEBER, William H.
General Counsel and PAC Treasurer
william.weber@cbeyond.net

Tel: (678) 424-2400
Fax: (678) 424-2500

CBRL Group, Inc.

Chain of restaurants and gift shops with headquarters in Lebanon. Database of locations, and information about foods, gift items, and collectibles. They are known to providing a friendly home away from home atmosphere.
www.crackerbarrel.com
Annual Revenues: $2.82 billion
Employees: 72,000
Ticker: NASDAQ: CBRL
SIC: 5812
Industry/ies: Food And Beverage Industry; Retail/Wholesale
Legislative Issues: BAN; CPT; FOO; FUE; HCR; LBR; ROD; TAX; TRD

Chairman of the Board
BRADFORD, James W.

Tel: (615) 444-5533
Fax: (888) 263-4304

President and Chief Executive Officer
COCHRAN, Sandra B.

Tel: (615) 444-5533
Fax: (615) 443-9476

Main Headquarters
Mailing: P.O. Box 787
Lebanon, TN 37088-0787

Political Action Committees
Cracker Barrel Old Country Store, Inc. PAC
FEC ID: C00252791
Contact: Charlie Austin
307 Hartmann Dr.
P.O. Box 787
Lebanon, TN 37088

Tel: (615) 444-5533
Fax: (615) 444-5533

    Contributions to Candidates: $61,500 (2015-2016)
    Democrats: $4,000; Republicans: $57,500

Corporate Foundations and Giving Programs

Cracker Barrel Foundation
Contact: Penny D. Carroll
305 Hartmann Dr.
Lebanon, TN 37088-0787

Tel: (615) 444-5533
Fax: (615) 443-9874

Public Affairs and Related Activities Personnel

At Headquarters

GREENE, Edward A.
Senior Vice President, Strategic Initiatives

At Other Offices

AUSTIN, Charlie
PAC Treasurer
305 Hartmann Dr.
Lebanon, TN 37087

Fax: (888) 263-4304

AUSTIN, Charlie
PAC Treasurer
P. O. Box 787
Lebanon, TN 37088-0787

Tel: (615) 444-5533
Fax: (615) 443-9476

CARMICHAEL, Beverly K.
Senior Vice President, Chief People Officer
305 Hartmann Dr.
Lebanon, TN 37087

Fax: (888) 263-4304

CARMICHAEL, Beverly K.
Senior Vice President, Chief People Officer
P. O. Box 787
Lebanon, TN 37088-0787

Tel: (615) 444-5533
Fax: (615) 443-9476

CARROLL, Penny D.
Director, Foundation
P. O. Box 787
Lebanon, TN 37088-0787
pcarroll@crackerbarrel.com

Tel: (615) 444-5533
Fax: (615) 443-9874

CARROLL, Penny D.
Director, Foundation
305 Hartmann Dr.
Lebanon, TN 37087
pcarroll@crackerbarrel.com

Fax: (888) 263-4304

CIAVARRA, Christopher A.
Senior Vice President, Marketing
305 Hartmann Dr.
Lebanon, TN 37087

Fax: (888) 263-4304

CIAVARRA, Christopher A.
Senior Vice President, Marketing
P. O. Box 787
Lebanon, TN 37088-0787

Tel: (615) 444-5533
Fax: (615) 443-9476

ESCOBAR, Maria Janella
Head of Corporate Communications
305 Hartmann Dr.
Lebanon, TN 37087

Tel: (615) 235-4618
Fax: (888) 263-4304

FLANAGAN, Nicholas V.
Senior Vice President, Operations
P. O. Box 787
Lebanon, TN 37088-0787

Tel: (615) 444-5533
Fax: (615) 443-9476

FLANAGAN, Nicholas V.
Senior Vice President, Restaurant and Retail Operations

Tel: (615) 235-4618
Fax: (888) 263-4304

305 Hartmann Dr.
Lebanon, TN 37087

FLANAGAN, Nicholas V.	Tel:	(615) 444-5533

Senior Vice President, Restaurant and Retail Operations
P. O. Box 787
Lebanon, TN 37088-0787

GREENE, Edward A.	Tel:	(615) 444-5533
Senior Vice President, Strategic Initiatives	Fax:	(615) 443-9476

P. O. Box 787
Lebanon, TN 37088-0787

HYATT, Lawrence E.	Tel:	(615) 444-5533
Senior Vice President and Chief Financial Officer	Fax:	(615) 443-9476

P. O. Box 787
Lebanon, TN 37088-0787
lhyatt@crackerbarrel.com

HYATT, Lawrence E.	Fax:	(888) 263-4304

Senior Vice President and Chief Financial Officer
305 Hartmann Dr.
Lebanon, TN 37087
lhyatt@crackerbarrel.com

SHEEHY, Patrick	Tel:	(615) 235-4618
Senior Director, Public Affairs	Fax:	(888) 263-4304

305 Hartmann Dr.
Lebanon, TN 37087
psheehy@crackerbarrel.com
Registered Federal Lobbyist

SHEEHY, Patrick	Tel:	(615) 444-5533

Senior Director, Public Affairs
P. O. Box 787
Lebanon, TN 37088-0787
psheehy@crackerbarrel.com
Registered Federal Lobbyist

SHOAF, N.B. Forrest	Tel:	(615) 444-5533
Senior Vice President	Fax:	(615) 443-9476

P. O. Box 787
Lebanon, TN 37088-0787
fshoaf@crackerbarrel.com

ZYLSTRA, Michael J.	Tel:	(615) 235-4618
Vice President, General Counsel & Corporate Secretary	Fax:	(888) 263-4304

305 Hartmann Dr.
Lebanon, TN 37087

ZYLSTRA, Michael J.	Tel:	(615) 444-5533

Vice President, General Counsel & Corporate Secretary
P. O. Box 787
Lebanon, TN 37088-0787

CBS Corporation

A mass media company.
www.cbscorporation.com
Annual Revenues: $13.74 billion
Employees: 17,310
Ticker: NYSE: CBS
SIC: 4833
Industry/ies: Communications; Media/Mass Communication
Legislative Issues: ADV; AVI; BUD; COM; CPT; GOV; INT; TAX

Executive Chairman
	Tel:	(212) 975-4321
REDSTONE, Sumner M.	Fax:	(212) 975-4516

President and Chief Executive Officer
	Tel:	(212) 975-4321
MOONVES, Leslie	Fax:	(212) 975-4516

Main Headquarters
Mailing: 51 W. 52nd St.	Tel:	(212) 975-4321
New York City, NY 10019-6188	Fax:	(212) 975-4516
	TF:	(877) 227-0787

Washington Office
Mailing: 1101 K St. NW, Suite 400
Washington, DC 20005

Political Action Committees
CBS Corporation PAC
FEC ID: C00423442
Contact: John S. Orlando
601 Pennsylvania Ave. NW	Tel:	(202) 457-4619
Suite 540	Fax:	(202) 457-4619
Washington, DC 20004		

> **Contributions to Candidates:** $77,000 (2015-2016)
> Democrats: $24,000; Republicans: $53,000

Corporate Foundations and Giving Programs
CBS Contributions Program
51 W. 52nd St.	Tel:	(212) 975-4321
New York City NY 10019	Fax:	(212) 975-4321

Public Affairs and Related Activities Personnel

At Headquarters

AMBROSIO, Anthony G.	Tel:	(212) 975-4321
Senior Executive Vice President, Chief Administrative Officer and Chief Human Resources Officer	Fax:	(212) 975-4516

IANNIELLO, Joseph	Tel:	(212) 975-4321
Chief Operating Officer	Fax:	(212) 975-4516

LIDING, Larry	Tel:	(212) 975-4321
Executive Vice President, Controller and Chief Accounting Officer	Fax:	(212) 975-4516

SCHWARTZ, Gil	Tel:	(212) 975-4321
Senior Executive Vice President and Chief Communications Officer	Fax:	(212) 975-4516

STRAKA, Angeline	Tel:	(212) 975-4321
Senior Vice President, Deputy General Counsel and Secretary	Fax:	(212) 975-4516

TOWNSEND, Adam	Tel:	(212) 975-4321
Executive Vice President, Investor Relations	Fax:	(212) 975-4516

TU, Lawrence	Tel:	(212) 975-4321
Senior Executive Vice President and Chief Legal Officer	Fax:	(212) 975-4516

At Washington Office

LUNDBERG, Gregory
Senior Vice President, Investor Relations

SHASSIAN, Donald R.
Executive Vice President & Chief Financial Officer

At Other Offices

BROWN, Josh	Tel:	(202) 457-4619
Director, Government Relations	Fax:	(202) 457-4511

601 Pennsylvania Ave. NW, Suite 540
Washington, DC 20004
Registered Federal Lobbyist

HARLOW, II, Bryce	Tel:	(202) 457-1461
Vice President, Government Relations	Fax:	(202) 457-4511

601 Pennsylvania Ave. NW, Suite 540
Washington, DC 20004
bharlow@cbs.com
Registered Federal Lobbyist

LUCEY, Anne C.	Tel:	(202) 457-4618
Senior Vice President, Regulatory Policy	Fax:	(202) 457-4511

601 Pennsylvania Ave. NW, Suite 540
Washington, DC 20004
alucey@cbs.com
Registered Federal Lobbyist

ORLANDO, John S.	Tel:	(202) 457-4508
Executive Vice President, Washington	Fax:	(202) 457-4511

601 Pennsylvania Ave. NW, Suite 540
Washington, DC 20004
jsorlando@cbs.com
Registered Federal Lobbyist

CCS Medical

A medical supply company.
www.ccsmed.com
SIC: 8090
Industry/ies: Medicine/Health Care/Mental Health; Retail/Wholesale

President and Chief Executive Officer
	Tel:	(972) 628-2100
CARSON, Rodney		

Main Headquarters
Mailing: 1505 LBJ Freeway	Tel:	(972) 628-2100
Suite 600		
Farmers Branch, TX 75234		

Public Affairs and Related Activities Personnel

At Headquarters

BROWNE, Sean	Tel:	(972) 628-2100
Chief Revenue Officer		

POFF, Brian	Tel:	(972) 628-2100
Senior Vice President and Chief Accounting Officer		

RAINES, Monica	Tel:	(972) 628-2100
Senior Vice President, General Counsel and Chief Compliance Officer		

CDI Corporation

Provider of engineering and information technology outsourcing solutions and professional staffing.
www.cdicorp.com
Annual Revenues: $961.56 million
Employees: 900
Ticker: NYSE: CDI
SIC: 7363
Industry/ies: Employees & Employment; Engineering/Mathematics

Chairman of the Board
	Tel:	(215) 569-2200
GARRISON, Walter R.	Fax:	(215) 569-1300

Chief Executive Officer and President
FREIDHEIM, Scott J

Tel: (215) 569-2200
Fax: (215) 569-1300

Main Headquarters
Mailing: 1717 Arch St.
35th Floor
Philadelphia, PA 19103

Tel: (215) 569-2200
Fax: (215) 569-1300
TF: (800) 996-7566

Corporate Foundations and Giving Programs

CDI Corporation Contributions Program
1717 Arch St.
35th Floor
Philadelphia, PA 19103

Tel: (215) 569-2200

Public Affairs and Related Activities Personnel

At Headquarters

CASTLEMAN, Michael
Chief Financial Officer

Tel: (215) 569-2200
Fax: (215) 569-1300

SHORT, Brian D.
Senior Vice President, Chief Administrative Officer and General Counsel

Tel: (215) 569-2200
Fax: (215) 569-1300

CDM Smith Inc.
In 2011, CDM and Wilbur Smith Associates joined forces to become CDM Smith, a leading global consulting, engineering, construction, and operations firm delivering integrated solutions in water, environment, transportation, energy and facilities.
cdmsmith.com
Annual Revenues: $1.01 billion
Employees: 5,000
Industry/ies: Engineering/Mathematics

Chairman of the Board and Chief Executive Officer
HICKOX, PE, Stephen J.

Tel: (617) 452-6000
Fax: (617) 452-8000

Main Headquarters
Mailing: 50 Hampshire St.
Cambridge, MA 02139

Tel: (617) 452-6000
Fax: (617) 452-8000

Washington Office
Mailing: 3201 Jermantown Rd.
Suite 400
Fairfax, VA 22030

Tel: (703) 691-6500
Fax: (703) 267-6083

Political Action Committees
CDM Smith Inc. National PAC
FEC ID: C00398222
Contact: David A. Martin
3201 Jermantown Rd.
Suite 400
Fairfax, VA 22030

Contributions to Candidates: $14,280 (2015-2016)
Democrats: $5,780; Republicans: $8,500

Corporate Foundations and Giving Programs

Camp Dresser and McKee, Inc. Contributions Program
One Cambridge Pl.
50 Hampshire St.
Cambridge, MA 02139

Tel: (617) 452-6000
Fax: (617) 452-8000

Public Affairs and Related Activities Personnel

At Headquarters

DESMARIS, Thierry
Executive Vice President, Finance

Tel: (617) 452-6000
Fax: (617) 452-8000

TUNNICLIFFE, PE, Peter W.
Executive Vice President, Global Market

Tel: (617) 452-6000
Fax: (617) 452-8000

WALL, Timothy B.
President and Chief Operating Officer

Tel: (617) 452-6000
Fax: (617) 452-8000

At Washington Office

MARTIN, David A.
PAC Contact

Tel: (703) 691-6500
Fax: (703) 267-6083

CDO Information Technologies
Founded in 1995. A full-service systems integrator providing technical and professional services.
www.cdotech.com
Annual Revenues: $35.36 million
Employees: 300
Industry/ies: Computer/Technology

President and Chief Executive Officer
WOFFORD, Alphonso
al.wofford@cdotech.com

Tel: (937) 258-0022

Main Headquarters
Mailing: 5200 Springfield St.
Suite 320
Dayton, OH 45431

Tel: (937) 258-0022
TF: (866) 307-6616

Public Affairs and Related Activities Personnel

At Headquarters

ERTEL, Don
Senior Vice President, Operations

Tel: (937) 258-0022

FERRA, Teri
Director, Corporate Affairs

Tel: (937) 258-0022

GREENING, Greg
Vice President, Business Development
reg.Greening@cdotech.com

Tel: (937) 258-0022

CDR Maguire
An architectural, engineering, planning, transportation engineering and construction management firm. Maguire Group now operates as a subsidiary of Duart's Miami-based Metric Engineering.
www.cdrmaguire.com
Annual Revenues: $40.20 million
Employees: 400
Industry/ies: Construction/Construction Materials; Engineering/Mathematics
Legislative Issues: ECN

President and Chief Operating Officer
DUART, Carlos A.

Tel: (786) 235-8534
Fax: (786) 235-8501

Main Headquarters
Mailing: 8669 N.W. 36 St.
Suite 340
Doral, FL 33166

Tel: (786) 235-8534
Fax: (786) 235-8501

Public Affairs and Related Activities Personnel

At Headquarters

KERR, Katrina
Contact, Media Relations
Katrina.Kerr@cdrmaguire.com

Tel: (786) 235-8534
Fax: (786) 235-8501

CDW Corporation
Formerly known as CDW Computer Centers, Inc. A provider of technology products and services for business, government and education.
www.cdw.com
Annual Revenues: $12.18 billion
Employees: 7,254
SIC: 5045; 5734; 5734; 9999; 9999
Industry/ies: Computer/Technology

Chairman and Chief Executive Officer
RICHARDS, Thomas E.

Tel: (847) 465-6000
Fax: (847) 564-6800

Main Headquarters
Mailing: 200 N. Milwaukee Ave.
Vernon Hills, IL 60061-1577

Tel: (847) 465-6000
Fax: (847) 564-6800
TF: (800) 800-6800

Washington Office
Mailing: 13461 Sunrise Valley
Suite 350
Herndon, VA 20171

Tel: (703) 262-8000

Public Affairs and Related Activities Personnel

At Headquarters

BUNKER, Vickey
Investor Relations Specialist

Tel: (847) 419-6328
Fax: (847) 564-6800

CAMPBELL, Neal J.
Senior Vice President and Chief Marketing Officer

Tel: (847) 465-6000
Fax: (847) 564-6800

CARAHER, Kelly
Manager, Markets and Technologies Public Relations
kellyc@cdw.com

Tel: (847) 968-0729
Fax: (847) 564-6800

ECKROTE, Douglas E.
Senior Vice President, Strategic Solutions and Services

Tel: (847) 465-6000
Fax: (847) 564-6800

KEBO, Collin B.
Vice President, Financial Planning and Analysis

Tel: (847) 465-6000
Fax: (847) 564-6800

LEAHY, Christine A.
Senior Vice President, General Counsel and Corporate Secretary
christineleahy@cdw.com

Tel: (847) 465-6000
Fax: (847) 564-6800

MACRIE, Sari L.
Vice President, Investor Relations

Tel: (847) 465-6000
Fax: (847) 564-6800

STEVENS, Jonathan J.
Senior Vice President, Operations and Chief Information Officer

Tel: (847) 465-6000
Fax: (847) 564-6800

ZIEGLER, Ann E.
Senior Vice President and Chief Financial Officer

Tel: (847) 465-6000
Fax: (847) 564-6800

Ceannate Corporation
Higher education BPO, default prevention, borrower support, collections.
Industry/ies: Banking/Finance/Investments
Legislative Issues: COM; EDU

Chairman of the Board
MACFARLANE , Bruce

Chief Executive Officer

RAJAN, Balaji

Main Headquarters
Mailing: 1701 Golf Rd.   TF: (888) 853-8148
         Tower Two-150
         Rolling Meadows, IL 60008

Public Affairs and Related Activities Personnel

At Headquarters

JONES , Rekha
Vice President, Human Capital Management

PETERSON , Maureen
President and Chief Operations Officer

PRYOR, Walter
Vice President, Government Relations
Registered Federal Lobbyist

SOWELL JR., Gary
Vice President, Compliance and Risk Management

Ceisler Jubelirer LLC
See listing on page 175 under Ceisler Media

Ceisler Media
Ceisler Jubelirer executes media relations strategies, issue advocacy and grassroots mobilization programs to position the platforms of its corporate, non-profit and political coalition clients.
www.ceislermedia.com
Industry/ies: Advertising And Marketing

Main Headquarters
Mailing: 1525 Locust St.   Tel: (215) 735-6760
         Sixth Floor   Fax: (215) 735-6758
         Philadelphia, PA 19102

Public Affairs and Related Activities Personnel

At Headquarters

CEISLER, Larry   Tel: (215) 735-6760
Principal   Fax: (215) 735-6758
Mail Stop Tenth Floor
larry@ceislermedia.com

DORN, Kirk   Tel: (215) 735-6760
Contact, Media Relations Fax: (215) 735-6758
kirk@ceislermedia.com

FELDMAN, Dennis   Tel: (215) 735-6760
Social Media Associate   Fax: (215) 735-6758

FERKO, Michael   Tel: (215) 735-6760
Director, Business Development Fax: (215) 735-6758

FRANK, Laura   Tel: (215) 735-6760
Public Relations Associate Fax: (215) 735-6758

GIBSON, Keegan   Tel: (215) 735-6760
Public Relations Associate Fax: (215) 735-6758

SHEPHERD, Colleen   Tel: (215) 735-6760
Chief Operating Officer   Fax: (215) 735-6758
colleen@ceislermedia.com

Celanese Corporation
Chemical, advanced engineering material and fiber manufacturers.
www.celanese.com
Annual Revenues: $6.55 billion
Employees: 7,468
Ticker: NYSE: CE
SIC: 2819; 2820
NAICS: 325188
Industry/ies: Apparel/Textiles Industry; Chemicals & Chemical Industry
Legislative Issues: ENV; SCI; TAR; TAX; TRA

Chairman of the Board, President and Chief Executive Officer Tel: (972) 443-4000
ROHR, Mark C.   Fax: (972) 443-8555

Main Headquarters
Mailing: 222 W. Las Colinas Blvd.   Tel: (972) 443-4000
         Suite 900N   Fax: (972) 443-8555
         Irving, TX 75039

Washington Office
Mailing: 1001 Pennsylvania Ave. NW
         Suite 8143
         Washington, DC 20004

Political Action Committees
Celanese Corporation PAC
FEC ID: C00084871
Contact: Chuck Kyrish
1601 W. LBJ Fwy.
Suite 600
Dallas, TX 75234

   Contributions to Candidates: $129,000 (2015-2016)

Democrats: $58,000; Republicans: $71,000
   Principal Recipients
      SENATE
      VITTER, DAVID B (REP-LA)

      HOUSE
      COSTA, JIM MR. (DEM-CA)
      GREEN, RAYMOND E. 'GENE' (DEM-TX)
      GRIFFITH, H MORGAN (REP-VA)

Corporate Foundations and Giving Programs

The Celanese Foundation
Contact: Dana Smith
222 W. Las Colinas Blvd.   Tel: (972) 443-4000
Suite 900N   Fax: (972) 443-8555
Irving, TX 75039

Public Affairs and Related Activities Personnel

At Headquarters

JENSEN, Chris   Tel: (972) 443-4000
Senior Vice President, Finance, Chief Accounting officer Fax: (972) 443-8555

JACOBSEN, W. Travis   Tel: (972) 443-4000
Global Marketing and Communications Leader Fax: (972) 443-8555
william.jacobsen@celanese.com

JOHNSTON, Lori   Tel: (972) 443-4000
Senior Vice President, Human Resources Fax: (972) 443-8555

KYRISH, Chuck   Tel: (972) 443-4000
PAC Treasurer   Fax: (972) 443-8555

NIVICA, Gjon v   Tel: (972) 443-4000
Senior Vice President and General Counsel Fax: (972) 443-8555

OBERLE, Mark   Tel: (972) 443-4000
Senior Vice President, Corporate Affairs Fax: (972) 443-8555
Mark.Oberle@celanese.com

PUCKETT , Jon   Tel: (972) 443-4000
Vice President, Investor Relations Fax: (972) 443-8555
jon.puckett@celanese.com

SMITH, Dana   Tel: (972) 443-4000
Manager, Foundation   Fax: (972) 443-8555

TOWNSEND, Jay C.   Tel: (972) 443-4000
Senior Vice President, Business Strategy Development, Fax: (972) 443-8555
Procurement and Advanced Fuels Technology

At Other Offices

DAIGLE, Stephanie   Tel: (703) 647-9500
815 King St., Suite 303
Alexandria, VA 22314
stephanie.diagle@celanese.com
Registered Federal Lobbyist

Celara Genomics
Celera Genomics was founded by Applera Corporation and Dr. J. Craig Venter, with the primary mission of sequencing and assembling the human genome within three years. On May 17, 2011 Quest Diagnostics Successfully Completes Acquisition of Celera.
www.celera.com
Ticker: NYSE: CRA
Industry/ies: Medicine/Health Care/Mental Health

President and Chief Executive Officer   Tel: (510) 749-4200
RUSCKOWSKI, Stephen H.   Fax: (510) 749-1600

Main Headquarters
Mailing: 1401 Harbor Bay Pkwy.   Tel: (510) 749-4200
         Alameda, CA 94502-7070   Fax: (510) 749-1600

Public Affairs and Related Activities Personnel

At Headquarters

SAMUELS, Gary   Tel: (973) 520-2800
Contact, Media   Fax: (510) 749-1600

SPEECHLY, David P.   Tel: (510) 749-1853
Vice President, Corporate Affairs Fax: (510) 749-1857
david.speechly@celera.com

VALENTINE, MD, Kathleen   Tel: (973) 520-2900
Contact, Investor Relations Fax: (510) 749-1600

Celerant Government Services, Inc.
Founded in 1987. A consulting firm.
www.celerantconsulting.com
Employees: 600
Industry/ies: Government-Related; Law/Law Firms

President   Tel: (781) 577-6710
MARCEAU, James   Fax: (781) 530-3605

Main Headquarters
Mailing: 303 Wyman St.   Tel: (781) 577-6710
            Suite 300   Fax: (781) 530-3605
            Waltham, MA 02451-1208

Washington Office
Mailing: 1001 N. 19th St
Suite 1200
Arlington, VA 22209

Public Affairs and Related Activities Personnel

At Headquarters

CLARKSON, Ian	Tel:	(781) 577-6710
Founder and Celerant Life President	Fax:	(781) 530-3605
COSTA, Rafael	Tel:	(781) 577-6710
Senior Vice President, Sales	Fax:	(781) 530-3605
DUNNABACK, John	Tel:	(781) 577-6710
President and Chief Financial Officer	Fax:	(781) 530-3605
ELMER, Ken	Tel:	(781) 577-6710
Senior Vice President, Human Resources	Fax:	(781) 530-3605
JOYCE, Enda	Tel:	(781) 577-6710
Media Contact	Fax:	(781) 530-3605
SARNA, Monisha	Tel:	(781) 577-6710
Contact, Media Relations	Fax:	(781) 530-3605
monisha.sarna@celerantgov.com		

Celgene Corporation

A biopharmaceutical company focusing on the discovery, development, and commercialization of products for the treatment of cancer.
www.celgene.com
Annual Revenues: $8.02 billion
Employees: 6,012
Ticker: NASDAQ: CELG
SIC: 2834
Industry/ies: Pharmaceutical Industry
Legislative Issues: CPT; HCR; MMM; PHA; TAX

Chairman of the Board and Chief Executive Officer	Tel:	(908) 673-9000
HUGIN, Robert J.	Fax:	(908) 673-9001

Main Headquarters

Mailing:	86 Morris Ave.	Tel:	(908) 673-9000
	Summit, NJ 07901	Fax:	(908) 673-9001

Washington Office
Mailing: 950 F St. NW
Washington, DC 20004

Political Action Committees
Celgene Corporation PAC
FEC ID: C00514331
Contact: Richard T. Girards
86 Morris Ave.
Summit, NJ 07901

Contributions to Candidates: $166,500 (2015-2016)
Democrats: $73,000; Republicans: $93,500

Principal Recipients

HOUSE
FRELINGHUYSEN, RODNEY P. (REP-NJ)
LANCE, LEONARD (REP-NJ)
SHIMKUS, JOHN M (REP-IL)

Public Affairs and Related Activities Personnel

At Headquarters

ALLES, Mark J.	Tel:	(908) 673-9000
President and Chief Operating Officer	Fax:	(908) 673-9001
EISENBERG, Alan F.	Tel:	(908) 673-9000
Vice President, Government Relations	Fax:	(908) 673-9001
Registered Federal Lobbyist		
FLANIGAN, III, Patrick E.	Tel:	(908) 673-9969
Vice President, Investor Relations	Fax:	(908) 673-9001
ir@celgene.com		
GILL, Brian P.	Tel:	(908) 673-9530
Vice President, Corporate Affairs	Fax:	(908) 673-9001
GIRARDS, Richard T.	Tel:	(908) 673-9000
Corporate Affairs and Strategic Market Access	Fax:	(908) 673-9001
GLIHA, Patrick	Tel:	(908) 673-9000
Federal Lobbyist	Fax:	(908) 673-9001
Registered Federal Lobbyist		
KELLOGG, Peter N.	Tel:	(908) 673-9000
Executive Vice President and Chief Financial Officer	Fax:	(908) 673-9001
MASOUDI, Gerald F.	Tel:	(908) 673-9000
Executive Vice President, General Counsel and Corporate	Fax:	(908) 673-9001
Secretary		
SCHUMAKER, Matthew	Tel:	(908) 673-9000
Federal Lobbyist	Fax:	(908) 673-9001
Registered Federal Lobbyist		

Cellerant Therapeutics, Inc.

A biotechnology company with a portfolio of products based on the regulation of the hematopoietic (blood-forming) system.
www.cellerant.com
Annual Revenues: $2.50 million
Employees: 20
Industry/ies: Medicine/Health Care/Mental Health

Chairman of the Board	Tel:	(650) 232-2122
RATHMANN, Richard G.	Fax:	(650) 232-5495
President and Chief Executive Officer	Tel:	(650) 232-2122
MANDALAM, PhD, Ram	Fax:	(650) 232-5495

Main Headquarters

Mailing:	1561 Industrial Rd.	Tel:	(650) 232-2122
	San Carlos, CA 94070	Fax:	(650) 232-5495

Public Affairs and Related Activities Personnel

At Headquarters

DILLON, PhD, Margaret	Tel:	(650) 232-2122
Senior Vice President, Regulatory Affairs and Quality	Fax:	(650) 232-5495
Assurance		
GIVENS, Sean	Tel:	(650) 232-2122
Vice President, Government Operations and Controller	Fax:	(650) 232-5495
YOON, Jun S.	Tel:	(650) 232-2122
Vice President, Corporate Development	Fax:	(650) 232-5495

CellStar Corporation

See listing on page 428 under Ingram Micro Mobility

CEMEX USA

CEMEX is a global building materials company that provides high quality products and reliable service to customers and communities throughout the Americas, Europe, Africa, the Middle East, and Asia. We produce, distribute, and sell cement, ready-mix concrete, aggregates, and related building materials in more than 50 countries, and we maintain trade relationships in close to 100 nations.
www.cemexusa.com
Annual Revenues: $12.32 billion
Employees: 10,000
Ticker: NYSE:CX
SIC: 1442; 3281; 2951
NAICS: 327320; 212321; 327991; 324121
Industry/ies: Construction/Construction Materials
Legislative Issues: AGR; NAT; TAX; TRA; TRD

President	Tel:	(713) 650-6200
MADRIDEJOS, Ignacio	Fax:	(713) 722-5124

Main Headquarters

Mailing:	929 Gessner Rd.	Tel:	(713) 650-6200
	Suite 1900	Fax:	(713) 722-5124
	Houston, TX 77024	TF:	(800) 999-8529

Political Action Committees
Cemex Inc. Employees PAC
FEC ID: C00111880
Contact: Frank R. Craddock
929 Gessner Rd.
Suite 1900
Houston, TX 77024

Contributions to Candidates: $240,000 (2015-2016)
Democrats: $42,500; Republicans: $197,500

Principal Recipients

HOUSE
CARTER, JOHN R. REP. (REP-DC)
COOK, PAUL (REP-CA)
DEFAZIO, PETER A (DEM-OR)
SHUSTER, WILLIAM MR. (REP-PA)
SPURLINO, JIM (REP-OH)

Corporate Foundations and Giving Programs

Cemex Contributions Program		
920 Memorial City Way	Tel:	(713) 650-6200
Suite 100	Fax:	(713) 653-6815
Houston, TX 77024		

Public Affairs and Related Activities Personnel

At Headquarters

BOUFFARD, Sara	Tel:	(713) 650-6200
Director, Communications	Fax:	(713) 722-5124
sara.bouffard@cemex.com		
CRADDOCK, Frank R.	Tel:	(713) 650-6200
PAC Treasurer, Executive Vice President, Commercial and	Fax:	(713) 653-6815
Public Affairs		
EGAN, Mike	Tel:	(713) 479-5748
Executive Vice President and General Counsel	Fax:	(713) 653-6815
HERRERA, Juan Carlos	Tel:	(713) 650-6200
Executive Vice President, Strategic Planning	Fax:	(713) 722-5124

MARTINEZ, Guillermo
Executive Vice President, Human Resources and Communications
Tel: (713) 650-6200
Fax: (713) 653-6815

SULLIVAN, Robert L.
Vice President, Government Affairs
robertl.sullivan@cemex.com
Registered Federal Lobbyist
Tel: (713) 650-6200
Fax: (713) 653-6815

At Other Offices

RENDON, Eduardo
Contact, Investor Relations
590 Madison Ave., 41st floor
New York, NY 10022
ir@cemex.com
Tel: (212) 317-6000
Fax: (212) 317-6047

Cempra Pharmaceuticals, Inc.

A clinical-stage pharmaceutical company.
www.cempra.com
Industry/ies: Pharmaceutical Industry
Legislative Issues: BUD; HCR; MMM

Chairman of the Board
KONG, MBA, MD, PhD, Garheng
Tel: (919) 467-1716

Founder, President and Chief Executive Officer
FERNANDES, PhD, Prabhavathi
Tel: (919) 467-1716

Main Headquarters
Mailing: 6320 Quadrangle Dr.
Suite 100
Chapel Hill, NC 27517
Tel: (919) 313-6601

Public Affairs and Related Activities Personnel

At Headquarters

FLAMM, PhD, Robert
Contact, Investor Relations
robert.flamm@russopartnersllc.com
Tel: (212) 845-4226

FOSTER, Carl T.
Executive Vice President, Business Development
Tel: (919) 467-1716

FOX, Elliot
Contact, Media Relations
elliot.fox@russopartnersllc.com
Tel: (212) 845-4253

HAHN, Mark W.
Executive Vice President and Chief Financial Officer
Tel: (919) 467-1716

HORWITH, Gary
Executive Vice President, Regulatory Affairs
Tel: (919) 313-6601

RUSSO, Tony
Contact, Media
tony.russo@russopartnersllc.com
Tel: (212) 845-4251

SCOTT, PhD, RAC, Drusilla
Senior Vice President, Regulatory Affairs
Tel: (919) 467-1716

Cendant Car Rental Group

See listing on page 97 under Avis Budget Group

The Centech Group, Inc.

The Centech Group offers a wide range of information technology services primarily to agencies of the US federal government. The company's areas of expertise include systems engineering and integration, network services, computer facility operations, data administration, and document management.
www.centechgroup.com
Annual Revenues: $152.65 million
Employees: 400
Industry/ies: Computer/Technology; Defense/Homeland Security; Engineering/Mathematics; Government-Related

Chairman of the Board, President and Chief Executive Officer
GALAVIZ, Fernando V.
galavizf@centechgroup.com
Tel: (703) 525-4444
Fax: (703) 525-2349

Main Headquarters
Mailing: 6402 Arlington Blvd.
Tenth Floor
Falls Church, VA 22042
Tel: (703) 525-4444
Fax: (703) 525-2349

Corporate Foundations and Giving Programs

The Centech Group Contributions Program
6402 Arlington Blvd.
Tenth Floor
Falls Church, VA 22042
Tel: (703) 525-4444
Fax: (703) 525-4444

Public Affairs and Related Activities Personnel

At Headquarters

KIDALOV, Max
Vice President and General Counsel
Tel: (703) 525-4444
Fax: (703) 525-2349

LILTZKE, Margaret L.
Director, Corporate Communications
Tel: (703) 525-4444
Fax: (703) 525-2349

MARTIN, Lawyer
Tel: (703) 525-4444

Senior Vice President, Human Resources
Fax: (703) 525-2349

WILLIAMS, Ken
Senior Vice President and Chief Financial Officer
williamsk@centechgroup.com
Tel: (703) 525-4444
Fax: (703) 525-2349

Centene Corporation

Provides multi-line managed care programs and related services to individuals receiving benefits under Medicaid, including Supplemental Security Income (SSI) and the State Children's Health Insurance Program (SCHIP).
www.centene.com
Annual Revenues: $17.10 billion
Employees: 13,400
Ticker: NYSE: CNC
SIC: 6324
Industry/ies: Medicine/Health Care/Mental Health
Legislative Issues: FOR; HCR; MMM

Chairman of the Board, President and Chief Executive Officer
NEIDORFF, Michael F.
Tel: (314) 725-4477
Fax: (314) 725-2428

Main Headquarters
Mailing: 7700 Forsyth Blvd.
St. Louis, MO 63105
Tel: (314) 725-4477
Fax: (314) 725-2428

Washington Office
Mailing: 1150 Connecticut Ave. NW
Suite 1000
Washington, DC 20036
Tel: (202) 223-8010

Political Action Committees

Centene Corporation PAC (CENTENEPAC)
FEC ID: C00397851
Contact: William Scheffe
7700 Forsyth Blvd.
Suite 800
St. Louis, MO 63105

Contributions to Candidates: $101,500 (2015-2016)
Democrats: $59,000; Republicans: $40,500; Other: $2,000

Principal Recipients

SENATE
BLUNT, ROY (REP-MO)

HOUSE
WAGNER, ANN L. (REP-MO)

Public Affairs and Related Activities Personnel

At Headquarters

KROLL, Edmund E.
Senior Vice President, Finance and Investor Relations
Tel: (314) 725-4477
Fax: (314) 725-2428

LANE, Deanne
Vice President, Media & Community Affairs
Tel: (314) 725-4477
Fax: (314) 725-2428

SCHEFFE, William
Lobbyist and PAC Treasurer
Tel: (314) 725-4477
Fax: (314) 725-2428

WILLIAMSON, Keith H.
Senior Vice President, Corporate Secretary and General Counsel
Tel: (314) 725-4477
Fax: (314) 725-2428

At Washington Office

DINESMAN, Jonathan
Senior Vice President, Government Relations
Tel: (202) 223-8010

KENNEDY, Christina
Manager, Public Policy
Tel: (202) 223-8010

MUSKER, Joseph
Vice President, Federal Affairs
jmusker@centene.com
Registered Federal Lobbyist
Tel: (202) 223-8010

TIMMONS, Brooke
Director, Legislative Affairs
Registered Federal Lobbyist
Tel: (202) 223-8010

CenterPoint Energy

An electric and natural gas energy delivery company, operations including electric transmission and distribution, natural gas distribution and sales, and pipeline and gathering operations. Formerly known as the regulated operations of Reliant Energy. The unregulated operations of Reliant Energy were spun off to form a separate company called Reliant Resources.
www.centerpointenergy.com
Annual Revenues: $6.94 billion
Employees: 7,505
Ticker: NYSE: CNP
SIC: 4923; 4911; 4924
NAICS: 221210; 221122
Industry/ies: Energy/Electricity
Legislative Issues: NAT

Chairman of the Board
CARROLL, Milton
milton.carroll@centerpointenergy.com
Tel: (713) 207-1111
Fax: (713) 207-3169

President and Chief Executive Officer | Tel: (713) 207-1111
PROCHAZKA, Scott M. | Fax: (713) 207-3169

Main Headquarters
Mailing: P.O. Box 4567 | Tel: (713) 207-1111
Houston, TX 77210-4567 | Fax: (713) 207-3169

Washington Office
Mailing: 1627 I St. NW | Tel: (703) 408-9024
Suite 950
Washington, DC 20006

Political Action Committees
CenterPoint Energy, Inc. PAC
FEC ID: C00333534
Contact: Annette M. Edmonds
P.O. 4567
Houston, TX 77210

Contributions to Candidates: $29,000 (2015-2016)
Democrats: $12,500; Republicans: $16,500

Corporate Foundations and Giving Programs
CenterPoint Energy Charitable Contributions
Contact: Diane Hasell Englet
P.O. Box 4567
Houston, TX 77210-4567

CenterPoint Energy Charitable Foundation
Contact: Lucretia Ahrens
1111 Louisiana St. | Tel: (713) 207-1111
11th Floor | Fax: (713) 207-3169
Houston, TX 77002

Public Affairs and Related Activities Personnel

At Headquarters

EDMONDS, Annette M. | Tel: (713) 207-1111
PAC Treasurer | Fax: (713) 207-3169

LEBLANC, Floyd | Tel: (713) 207-7125
Contact, Media Relations | Fax: (713) 207-3169

LOWE, Leticia | Tel: (713) 207-7702
Contact, Corporate and Financial Information | Fax: (713) 207-3169
leticia.lowe@centerpointenergy.com

O'BRIEN, Dana | Tel: (713) 207-1111
Senior Vice President and General Counsel | Fax: (713) 207-3169

ORTENSTONE , Sue | Tel: (713) 207-1111
Senior Vice President and Chief Human Resources Officer | Fax: (713) 207-3169

OWENS, Sharon Micheal | Tel: (713) 207-1111
Vice President, Corporate Community Relations | Fax: (713) 207-3169
sharon.owens@centerpointenergy.com

ROGERS, William D. | Tel: (713) 207-1111
Executive Vice President and Chief Financial Officer | Fax: (713) 207-3169

At Other Offices

ENGLET, Diane Hasell
Senior Director, Corporate Community Relations
P.O. Box 1700
Houston, TX 77251
Diane.Englet@CenterPointEnergy.com

Centerpoint Properties Corporation
Develops, owns and manages industrial real estate and related rail, road and port infrastructure.
www.centerpoint-prop.com
Annual Revenues: $194.90 million
Employees: 100
SIC: 6798
Industry/ies: Real Estate

Chief Executive Officer | Tel: (630) 586-8000
CHAPMAN, Robert M | Fax: (630) 586-8010

Main Headquarters
Mailing: 1808 Swift Dr. | Tel: (630) 586-8000
Oak Brook, IL 60523 | Fax: (630) 586-8010

Central Pacific Bank
Central Pacific Bank is the primary subsidiary of Central Pacific Financial Corp. Central Pacific Bank provides a full range of banking, investment and trust services. Provider of standard retail banking products as checking and savings accounts, money market accounts, and CDs.
www.centralpacificbank.com
Annual Revenues: $86.63 million
Employees: 900
Industry/ies: Banking/Finance/Investments

Chairman of the Board | Tel: (808) 544-0500
ROSE, Crystal K. | Fax: (808) 531-2875

President and Chief Executive Officer | Tel: (808) 544-0500
NGO, A Catherine | Fax: (808) 531-2875

Main Headquarters

Mailing: P.O. Box 3590 | Tel: (808) 544-0500
Honolulu, HI 96811-3590 | Fax: (808) 531-2875

Political Action Committees
Central Pacific Bank Fed PAC (IKA CPB PAC- FED)
FEC ID: C00130385
Contact: Glenn Kc Ching
220 S. King St. | Tel: (808) 544-0500
Honolulu, HI 96813 | Fax: (808) 544-0500

Contributions to Candidates: $8,000 (2015-2016)
Democrats: $8,000

Corporate Foundations and Giving Programs
Central Pacific Bank Contributions Program
Contact: Glenn Kc Ching
220 S. King St. | Tel: (808) 544-0500
P.O. Box 3590 | Fax: (808) 531-2875
Honolulu, HI 96813

Public Affairs and Related Activities Personnel

At Headquarters

MORIMOTO, David S. | Tel: (808) 544-0500
Executive Vice President, Chief Financial Officer and | Fax: (808) 531-2875
Treasurer

DEAN, John C. | Tel: (808) 544-0500
Executive Chair | Fax: (808) 531-2875

ISONO , Denis K. | Tel: (808) 544-0500
Executive Vice President | Fax: (808) 531-2875
denis.isono@centralpacificbank.com

KIRIHARA, Wayne | Tel: (808) 544-0687
Chief Marketing Officer | Fax: (808) 531-2875
wayne.kirihara@centralpacificbank.com

At Other Offices

CHING, Glenn Kc | Tel: (808) 544-0500
PAC Treasurer | Fax: (808) 531-2875
220 S. King St.
Honolulu, HI 96813

Centrica US Holdings, Inc.
A Lobbying Firm.
www.centrica.com
Industry/ies: Electricity & Electronics; Electronics; Energy/Electricity; Utilities

Chairman | Tel: (202) 870-6624
HAYTHORNTHWAITE, Rick

Chief Executive Officer | Tel: (443) 904-4555
CONN, Iain

Main Headquarters
Mailing: 1620 I St.NW | Tel: (202) 870-6624
Suite 501
Washington, DC 20006

Public Affairs and Related Activities Personnel
At Headquarters

DAWSON, Grant | Tel: (202) 870-6624
General Counsel and Company Secretary

SHEDDEN, Jill | Tel: (202) 870-6624
Group Director, Human Resources

At Other Offices

PERRAULT, Christopher | Tel: (443) 904-4555
Vice President, US Government and Regulatory Affairs
1423 R St. NW, Suite 404
Washington, DC 20009

Centrus Energy Corporation
Supplier of enriched uranium fuel
Industry/ies: Fuels See Coal, Gas, Oil, Petroleum; Natural Resources
Legislative Issues: ENG

Main Headquarters
Mailing: 6903 Rockledge Dr. | Tel: (301) 564-3392
Bethesda, MD 20817

Political Action Committees
Centrus Energy Corp Pac
FEC ID: C00355719
Contact: John Barpoulis
Rockline Drive
Bethesda, MD 20817

Contributions to Candidates: $26,000 (2015-2016)
Democrats: $7,000; Republicans: $19,000

Public Affairs and Related Activities Personnel
At Headquarters

BARPOULIS, John | Tel: (301) 564-3392
Treasurer

DERRYBERRY, Jeremy | Tel: (301) 564-3392
Communications Manager
derryj@centrusenergy.com

DUDUIT , Angie | Tel: (740) 897-2457
Public Affairs Manager
duduitaj@centrusenergy.com

HOWE, James | Tel: (301) 564-3392
Vice President, Government Affairs

Century Aluminum

Produces and sells primary aluminum.
www.centuryca.com
Annual Revenues: $2.10 billion
Employees: 2,400
Ticker: NASDAQ: CENX
SIC: 3334
Industry/ies: Metals
Legislative Issues: TRD

Chairman of the Board | Tel: (312) 696-3101
WILKINSON, Terence | Fax: (312) 696-3102

President and Chief Executive Officer | Tel: (312) 696-3101
BLESS , Michael A. | Fax: (312) 696-3102

Main Headquarters
Mailing: One South Wacker Dr | Tel: (312) 696-3101
Suite 1000 | Fax: (312) 696-3102
Chicago, IL 60606

Political Action Committees
Century Aluminum Company PAC
FEC ID: C00555532
Contact: Jesse E. Gary
1627 State Hwy. 3543
Hawesville, KY 42348

Public Affairs and Related Activities Personnel

At Headquarters

DILDINE, Michael | Tel: (312) 696-3101
Director, Corporate Relations | Fax: (312) 696-3102
mdidline@centuryca.com

DILLON, Rick T. | Tel: (312) 696-3101
Executive Vice President and Chief Financial Officer | Fax: (312) 696-3102

HARRISON , Shelly | Tel: (312) 696-3101
Senior Vice President, Finance and Treasurer | Fax: (312) 696-3102
sharrison@centuryca.com

HOERNER, John E. | Tel: (312) 696-3101
Vice President, North American Operations | Fax: (312) 696-3102

At Other Offices

GARY, Jesse E. | Tel: (270) 685-2493
Executive Vice President, General Counsel and Secretary
1627 State Hwy. 3543
Hawesville, KY 42348

PRICE, Kip | Tel: (270) 852-2807
Contact, Marketing | Fax: (831) 642-9399
2511 Garden Rd., Building A, Suite 200
Monterey, CA 93940
kprice@centuryky.com

CenturyLink

Provides broadband, voice and wireless services to consumers and businesses across the country. Acquired Qwest Communications in 2011.
www.centurylink.com
Annual Revenues: $17.94 billion
Employees: 44,800
Ticker: NYSE: CTL
SIC: 4813
Industry/ies: Communications; Telecommunications/Internet/Cable
Legislative Issues: TAX; TEC

Chairman of the Board | Tel: (318) 388-9000
OWENS, William A. | Fax: (318) 388-9064

Chief Executive Officer and President | Tel: (318) 388-9000
POST, III, Glen F. | Fax: (303) 992-1724
glen.post@centurylink.com

Main Headquarters
Mailing: 100 CenturyLink Dr. | Tel: (318) 388-9000
P.O. Box 4065 | Fax: (318) 388-9562
Monroe, LA 71203 | TF: (800) 833-1188

Washington Office
Mailing: 1099 New York Ave. NW
Suite 250
Washington, DC 20001

Political Action Committees
CenturyLink Inc Federal PAC

FEC ID: C00225524
Contact: John Jones
100 CenturyLink Drive | Tel: (318) 362-1583
Monroe, LA 71203 | Fax: (318) 388-9602

Corporate Foundations and Giving Programs
Clarke M. Williams Charitable Foundation
100 Centurylink Dr. | Tel: (318) 388-9000
Monroe, LA 71201

Public Affairs and Related Activities Personnel

At Headquarters

DAVIS, Steven | Tel: (318) 388-9000
Executive Vice President, Public Policy and Government | Fax: (303) 992-1724
Relations
steve.davis@centurylink.com

EWING, Jr., R. Stewart | Tel: (318) 388-9000
Executive Vice President, Chief Financial Officer and | Fax: (303) 992-1724
Assistant Secretary
stewart.ewing@centurylink.com

GOFF, Stacey W. | Tel: (318) 388-9000
Executive Vice President, General Counsel | Fax: (303) 992-1724
stacey.goff@centurytel.com

JONES, John | Tel: (318) 388-9000
PAC Treasurer | Fax: (303) 992-1724

PETERSON, Debra | Tel: (913) 323-4881
Director, External Communications and Community Relations | Fax: (318) 388-9064
Debra.D.Peterson@CenturyLink.com

PUCKETT, Karen A. | Tel: (318) 388-9000
President, Global Markets | Fax: (318) 388-9562

SARTOR, Annmarie | Tel: (318) 388-9671
Manager, External Communication | Fax: (318) 388-9562
Annmarie.Sartor@CenturyLink.com

TREZISE, Scott | Tel: (318) 388-9000
Executive Vice President, Human Resources | Fax: (318) 388-9562

WAUGH, Kristie | Tel: (318) 340-5627
Director, Investor Relations | Fax: (318) 388-9064
kristina.r.waugh@centurylink.com

At Washington Office

ADKINS, Richard Brian | Tel: (202) 429-3110
Senior Director, Federal Legislative Affairs, PAC Treasurer
brian.adkins@centurylink.com

BARTLETT, David | Tel: (202) 429-3110
Vice President, Federal Government Affairs

HEINER, Brandon | Tel: (202) 429-3110
Director, Federal Legislative Affairs

TURNER, Sharron | Tel: (202) 429-3110
Director, Public Policy

At Other Offices

SCHWEER, Brad | Tel: (202) 393-7112
Director, Federal Legislative Affairs
701 Pennsylvania Ave. NW, Suite 820
Washington, DC 20004

SOLTES, Mark | Tel: (202) 393-7112
Assistant Vice President, Public Policy & Government Affairs
701 Pennsylvania Ave. NW, Suite 820
Washington, DC 20004

CenturyTel, Inc.

See listing on page 179 under CenturyLink

Cepheid

Manufacturer and developer of microfluidics and microelectronics technologies for DNA analysis.
www.cepheid.com
Annual Revenues: $495.87 million
Employees: 1,400
Ticker: NASDAQ: CPHD
SIC: 3826
Industry/ies: Medicine/Health Care/Mental Health; Science; Scientific Research
Legislative Issues: HCR; MED; MMM; SCI

Chairman of the Board and Chief Executive Officer | Tel: (408) 541-4191
BISHOP, John L. | Fax: (408) 541-4192

Main Headquarters
Mailing: 904 Caribbean Dr. | Tel: (408) 541-4191
Sunnyvale, CA 94089 | Fax: (408) 541-4192

Washington Office
Mailing: 1001 G St. NW | Tel: (202) 756-1380
Suite 817
Washington, DC 20001

Public Affairs and Related Activities Personnel

At Headquarters

FITZGERALD, Mike
Executive Vice President, Global Human Resources
Tel: (408) 541-4191
Fax: (408) 541-4192

FLOM, Kerry
Executive Vice President and Chief Regulatory Officer
Tel: (408) 541-4191
Fax: (408) 541-4192

KOCMOND, Warren
Executive Vice President, Chief Operating Officer
Tel: (408) 541-4191
Fax: (408) 541-4192

ROSS, Jacquie
Contact, Investor Relations
investor.relations@cepheid.com
Tel: (408) 400-8329
Fax: (408) 541-4192

SCHOONMAKER, PhD, Michele
Reimbursement Representative
michele.schoonmaker@cepheid.com
Registered Federal Lobbyist
Tel: (408) 541-4191
Fax: (408) 541-4192

SMITH, Joseph H.
Executive Vice President, Corporate Development and General Counsel
Tel: (408) 541-4191
Fax: (408) 541-4192

TIPTON, Jared
Contact, Media Relations
jared.tipton@cepheid.com
Tel: (408) 400-8377
Fax: (408) 541-4192

At Washington Office

LEWIS, Hallie
Senior Manager, Government & Professional Relations
hallie.lewis@cepheid.com
Tel: (202) 756-1380

Cerberus Capital Management

Provides both financial resources and operational expertise to help turn companies into industry leaders.
www.cerberuscapital.com
Employees: 150,000
Industry/ies: Banking/Finance/Investments; Management

Chairman of the Board
SNOW, John W.
Tel: (212) 891-2100
Fax: (212) 891-1540

Co-Founder and Chief Executive Officer
FEINBERG, Stephen A.
Tel: (212) 891-2100
Fax: (212) 891-1540

Main Headquarters
Mailing: 875 Third Ave.
New York City, NY 10022
Tel: (212) 891-2100
Fax: (212) 891-1540

Public Affairs and Related Activities Personnel

At Headquarters

BROSSARD, Catherine
Managing Director, Investor Relations
Tel: (212) 891-2100
Fax: (212) 891-1540

COOPER, Billy J.
Contact, Government Relations
bcooper@cerberuscapital.com
Registered Federal Lobbyist
Tel: (212) 891-2100
Fax: (212) 891-1540

DILLARD, John
Media Contact
Tel: (212) 445-8052
Fax: (212) 891-1540

DUDA, Peter
Media Contact
pduda@webershandwick.com
Tel: (212) 445-8213
Fax: (212) 891-1540

KANDEL, Andrew I.
Chief Compliance Officer, Co-General Counsel and Senior Managing Director
Tel: (212) 891-2100
Fax: (212) 891-1540

KASLOW, Andy
Chief Human Resource Officer, COAC
Tel: (212) 891-2100
Fax: (212) 891-1540

LOMASKY, Jeffrey L.
Chief Financial Officer and Senior Managing Director
Tel: (212) 891-2100
Fax: (212) 891-1540

NEPORENT, Mark A.
Chief Operating Officer, General Counsel and Senior Managing Director
Tel: (212) 891-2100
Fax: (212) 891-1540

PEZESHKIAN, Roudabeh
Managing Director, Human Resources
Tel: (212) 891-2100
Fax: (212) 891-1540

PRICE, Timothy
Managing Director, Media Relations
media@cerberuscapital.com
Tel: (212) 891-2100
Fax: (212) 891-1540

RISSI, J.J.
Media Contact
Tel: (212) 445-8224
Fax: (212) 891-1540

Ceres, Inc.

A vision of a world in which business and the capital markets promote the well-being of human society and the protection of the earth's environment.
www.ceres.org
Industry/ies: Agriculture/Agronomy
Legislative Issues: ENV

President
LUBBER, Mindy S.
lubber@ceres.org
Tel: (617) 247-0700

Main Headquarters

Mailing: 99 Chauncy St.
Sixth Floor
Boston, MA 02111
Tel: (617) 247-0700

Public Affairs and Related Activities Personnel

At Headquarters

BIRGER, Nina
Senior Associate, Foundations, Development
birger@ceres.org
Tel: (617) 247-0700

COBURN, Jim
Senior Manager, Investor Programs
coburn@ceres.org
Tel: (617) 247-0700

DALY, Ellen
Manager, Finance and Operations
daly@ceres.org
Tel: (617) 247-0700

DAVIS, Chris
Senior Program Director, Investor Programs
davis@ceres.org
Tel: (617) 247-0700

DOHERTY, Megan
Senior Associate, Communications
doherty@ceres.org
Tel: (617) 247-0700

FLEMING, Peyton
Senior Program Director, Strategic Communications
fleming@ceres.org
Tel: (617) 247-0700

FORBES, Hilary A.
Senior Program Director, Human Resources and Operations
forbes@ceres.org
Tel: (617) 247-0700

GOFF, Gabriela
Senior Manager, Finance
goff@ceres.org
Tel: (617) 247-0700

KELLY, Anne
Senior Program Director, Policy and BICEP Program
kelly@ceres.org
Registered Federal Lobbyist
Tel: (617) 247-0700

KUNZ, Karl
Chief Financial Officer
kunz@ceres.org
Tel: (617) 247-0700

MACFARLAND, Gordon
Tel: (617) 247-0700

Cerescan

Formerly Brain Matters, Inc. Changed name upon acquisition by CereScan in April 2008. Providers of SPECT (Single Photon Emission Computed Tomography) brain imaging for patients and physicians.
www.cerescan.com
Industry/ies: Medicine/Health Care/Mental Health
Legislative Issues: HCR

Chairman and Chief Executive Officer
KELLEY, John
Tel: (720) 242-9081

Main Headquarters
Mailing: 991 Southpark Dr.
Suite 200
Littleton, CO 80120
Tel: (720) 242-9081
TF: (866) 722-4806

Public Affairs and Related Activities Personnel

At Headquarters

AMMAN, Bradford K.
Chief Financial Officer
Tel: (720) 242-9081

DEGENNARO, Nick
Chief Development Officer
Tel: (720) 242-9081

JENSEN, Andrea D.
Vice President, Marketing and Sales
Tel: (720) 242-9081

Ceridian Corporation

A government relations office specializing in human resources policy, workforce development policy, and tax policy.
www.ceridian.com
Employees: 9,000
Ticker: NYSE: CEN
SIC: 8742
NAICS: 522320; 541214
Industry/ies: Computer/Technology

Chairman of the Board
HARVEY, Stuart C.
Stuart.C.Harvey@ceridian.com
Tel: (952) 853-8100
Fax: (952) 853-4430

Chief Executive Officer
OSSIP, David
Tel: (952) 853-8100
Fax: (952) 853-4430

Main Headquarters
Mailing: 3311 E. Old Shakopee Rd.
Minneapolis, MN 55425
Tel: (952) 853-8100
Fax: (952) 853-4430

Washington Office
Mailing: 4524 Cheltenham Dr.

Bethesda, MD 20814

Public Affairs and Related Activities Personnel

At Headquarters

ELLIOTT, Paul	Tel:	(952) 853-8100
Chief Operating Officer	Fax:	(952) 853-4430
GRIFFITH, Cary	Tel:	(952) 853-7171
Senior Specialist, Communications	Fax:	(952) 853-4430
cary.j.griffith@ceridian.com		
HILL, Sara	Tel:	(952) 853-8100
Chief Human Resources Officer	Fax:	(952) 853-4430
KITCHING, Scott	Tel:	(952) 853-8100
Executive Vice President and General Counsel	Fax:	(952) 853-4430
MARTIN , Lois M.	Tel:	(952) 853-8100
Executive Vice President and Chief Financial Officer	Fax:	(952) 853-4430
ROTTENBERG, Alan	Tel:	(952) 853-8100
Chief Marketing Officer	Fax:	(952) 853-4430
TEGGART, Donna	Tel:	(952) 853-8100
Global Director, External Communications and Brand	Fax:	(952) 853-4430

At Washington Office

O'CONNELL, James J.
Executive Consultant
james.j.oconnell@ceridian.com

Cerner Corporation

A supplier of healthcare information technology solutions.
www.cerner.com
Annual Revenues: $4.49 billion
Employees: 22,200
Ticker: NASDAQ; CERN
SIC: 7373
Industry/ies: Computer/Technology; Medicine/Health Care/Mental Health
Legislative Issues: BUD; DEF; HCR

Chairman of the Board and Chief Executive Officer	Tel:	(816) 201-1024
PATTERSON, Neal L.	Fax:	(816) 474-1742
npatterson@cerner.com		

Main Headquarters

Mailing:	2800 Rockcreek Pkwy.	Tel:	(816) 201-1024
	Kansas City, MO 64117	Fax:	(816) 474-1742
		TF:	(877) 402-7804

Political Action Committees

Cerner Corporation PAC
FEC ID: C00410589
Contact: Marc G. Naughton
2800 Rockcreek Pkwy.
Kansas City, MO 64117

> **Contributions to Candidates:** $87,500 (2015-2016)
> Democrats: $11,000; Republicans: $66,500; Other: $10,000

> > **Principal Recipients**

> > > **HOUSE**
> > > SMITH, JASON T (OTHER-MO)
> > > YODER, KEVIN (REP-KS)

Corporate Foundations and Giving Programs

First Hand Foundation
Contact: Bob Robke
2800 Rockcreek Pkwy.   Tel: (816) 201-1024
Kansas City, MO 64117   Fax: (816) 474-1742

Public Affairs and Related Activities Personnel

At Headquarters

BURKE, Zane	Tel:	(816) 201-1024
President	Fax:	(816) 474-1742
BURNS, Joanne M.	Tel:	(816) 201-1024
Senior Vice President and Chief Strategy Officer	Fax:	(816) 474-1742
KELLS, Allan O.	Tel:	(816) 201-1024
Vice President, Investor Relations	Fax:	(816) 474-1742
akells@cerner.com		
NAUGHTON, Marc G.	Tel:	(816) 201-1024
Executive Vice President, Chief Financial Officer and PAC Treasurer	Fax:	(816) 474-1742
mnaughton@cerner.com		
NILL, Mike	Tel:	(816) 201-1024
Executive Vice President and Chief Operating Officer	Fax:	(816) 474-1742
ROBKE , Bob	Tel:	(816) 201-1024
Vice President and Contact, Foundation	Fax:	(816) 474-1742
SIMS, Randy	Tel:	(816) 201-1024
Senior Vice President, Chief Legal Officer	Fax:	(816) 474-1742
rsims@cerner.com		
WILSON, Julia M.	Tel:	(816) 201-1024
Executive Vice President and Chief People Officer	Fax:	(816) 474-1742

Cerus Corporation

A biomedical products company focused on commercializing the INTERCEPT Blood System (designed to reduce the risk of transfusion-transmitted infections by inactivating a broad range of pathogens such as viruses, bacteria and parasites that may be present in donated blood) to enhance blood safety.
www.cerus.com
Annual Revenues: $36.24 million
Employees: 144
Ticker: NASDAQ; CERS
SIC: 3841
Industry/ies: Medicine/Health Care/Mental Health
Legislative Issues: BUD; GOV

Chairman of the Board	Tel:	(925) 288-6000
SWISHER , Dan	Fax:	(925) 288-6001
President and Chief Executive Officer	Tel:	(925) 288-6150
GREENMAN, William "Obi" M.	Fax:	(925) 288-6001
bd@cerus.com		

Main Headquarters

Mailing:	2550 Stanwell Dr.	Tel:	(925) 288-6000
	Concord, CA 94520	Fax:	(925) 288-6001

Public Affairs and Related Activities Personnel

At Headquarters

CORTEN, Lainie	Tel:	(925) 288-6319
Senior Director, Global Communications and Marketing and Investor Relations Contact	Fax:	(925) 288-0194
ir@cerus.com		
GREEN, Kevin D.	Tel:	(925) 288-6138
Vice President, Finance and Chief Financial Officer	Fax:	(925) 288-6001
MENARD, Chrystal	Tel:	(925) 288-6000
Chief Legal Officer	Fax:	(925) 288-6001
MOORE, Carol M.	Tel:	(925) 288-6000
Senior Vice President, Regulatory Affairs, Quality and Clinical	Fax:	(925) 288-6001
ROLL, Lori L.	Tel:	(925) 288-6000
Vice President, Administration and Corporate Secretary	Fax:	(925) 288-6001
STASSINOPOULOS, Adonis	Tel:	(925) 288-6000
Vice President, Global Scientific Affairs & Research	Fax:	(925) 288-6001

Cessna Aircraft Company

A manufacturer of general aviation aircrafts.
www.cessna.com
Annual Revenues: $969 million
Employees: 9,000
SIC: 3721
Industry/ies: Aerospace/Aviation; Transportation

President and Chief Executive Officer	Tel:	(316) 517-6000
ERNEST, Scott A.	Fax:	(316) 517-5669

Main Headquarters

Mailing:	One Cessna Blvd.	Tel:	(316) 517-6000
	Wichita, KS 67215	Fax:	(316) 517-5669

Corporate Foundations and Giving Programs

Cessna Foundation, Inc.
Contact: Rhonda Fullerton
One Cessna Blvd.   Tel: (316) 517-6000
Wichita, KS 67215   Fax: (316) 517-5669

Public Affairs and Related Activities Personnel

At Headquarters

ANDERSON, Bill	Tel:	(316) 517-6000
Vice President, Military and Government Programs	Fax:	(316) 517-5669
CARNEY, Shanda	Tel:	(316) 517-7387
Manager, External Communications	Fax:	(316) 517-5669
corpcomm@cessna.textron.com		
FULLERTON, Rhonda	Tel:	(316) 517-7810
Director, Events and Promotions	Fax:	(316) 517-5669
HARDER , Stephanie	Tel:	(316) 517-8702
Director, Communications	Fax:	(316) 517-5669
corpcomm@cessna.textron.com		
SALANDER, Eric	Tel:	(316) 517-6000
Senior Vice President and Chief Financial Officer	Fax:	(316) 517-5669
WHITE, Tim	Tel:	(316) 517-6000
Vice President, Sales	Fax:	(316) 517-5669

CF Industries, Inc.

Manufacturer and distributor of nitrogen and phosphate fertilizer products. Acquired Terra Industries in March 2010.
www.cfindustries.com
Annual Revenues: $4.56 billion
Employees: 2,200
Ticker: NYSE: CF

SIC: 2870
Industry/ies: Agriculture/Agronomy; Chemicals & Chemical Industry
Legislative Issues: BUD; CAW; ENG; ENV; TAX; TRA; TRD

Main Headquarters

Mailing:	Four Pkwy., North	Tel:	(847) 405-2400
	Suite 400	Fax:	(847) 405-2711
	Deerfield, IL 60015-2590		

Washington Office

Mailing:	1401 I St. NW	Fax:	(202) 371-9169
	Suite 340	TF:	(800) 462-8565
	Washington, DC 20005-2225		

Political Action Committees

C F Industries, Inc. Employees' Good Government Fund PAC
FEC ID: C00076588
Contact: Renee Cardella
Four Pkwy. North
Suite 400
Deerfield, IL 60015

Contributions to Candidates: $13,000 (2015-2016)
Republicans: $13,000

Corporate Foundations and Giving Programs

CF Industries Contributions Program

Four Pkwy., North	Tel:	(847) 405-2400
Suite 400	Fax:	(847) 405-2711
Deerfield, IL 60015-2590		

Public Affairs and Related Activities Personnel

At Headquarters

BARNARD, Douglas C.	Tel:	(847) 405-2400
Senior Vice President, General Counsel and Secretary	Fax:	(847) 405-2711
CARDELLA, Renee	Tel:	(847) 405-2400
Manager, Information Technology Applications Development	Fax:	(847) 405-2711
FROST, Bert	Tel:	(847) 405-2400
Senior Vice President, Sales and Market Development	Fax:	(847) 405-2711
KELLEHER , Dennis	Tel:	(847) 405-2400
Senior Vice President And Chief Financial Officer	Fax:	(847) 405-2711
SPERTUS JABLOW, Wendy	Tel:	(847) 405-2400
Senior Vice President, Human Resources	Fax:	(847) 405-2711
SWENSON, Dan	Tel:	(847) 405-2515
Treasurer	Fax:	(847) 405-2711
dswenson@cfindustries.com		

At Washington Office

MEADS, Alicia	Fax:	(202) 371-9169
Contact, Government Relations		
Registered Federal Lobbyist		
O'BRIEN, Rosemary L.	Fax:	(202) 371-9169
Vice President, Public Affairs		
robrien@cfindustries.com		
Registered Federal Lobbyist		
PEPE, Janelle	Fax:	(202) 371-9169
Federal Lobbyist		
Registered Federal Lobbyist		

CGU Insurance Group

See listing on page 603 under OneBeacon Insurance Group

CH Energy Group, Inc.

A family of energy supply and service businesses.
www.chenergygroup.com
Employees: 1,300
Ticker: NYSE: CHG
SIC: 4931
Industry/ies: Energy/Electricity

President and Chief Executive Officer

| LAURITO, James P. | Tel: | (845) 452-2000 |
| | Fax: | (845) 486-5465 |

Main Headquarters

Mailing:	284 S. Ave.	Tel:	(845) 452-2000
	Poughkeepsie, NY 12601	Fax:	(845) 486-5465
		TF:	(800) 527-2714

Corporate Foundations and Giving Programs

Central Hudson Gas & Electric Corporation Contributions Program

| 284 South Ave. | Tel: | (845) 452-2000 |
| Poughkeepsie, NY 12601 | Fax: | (845) 471-8323 |

Public Affairs and Related Activities Personnel

At Headquarters

BROCKS, Thomas C.	Tel:	(845) 452-2000
Vice President, Human Resources	Fax:	(845) 486-5465
CAMPAGIORNI, Anthony S.	Tel:	(845) 452-2000
Vice President, Business Development and Governmental Affairs	Fax:	(845) 486-5465

CAPONE, Christopher M.	Tel:	(845) 452-2000
Executive Vice President and Chief Financial Officer	Fax:	(845) 486-5465
COLBERT, Paul A.	Tel:	(845) 452-2000
Associate General Counsel, Regulatory Affairs	Fax:	(845) 486-5465
GOULD, John E.	Tel:	(845) 452-2000
Executive Vice President and General Counsel	Fax:	(845) 486-5465
KOCZKO, Joseph B.	Tel:	(845) 452-2000
General Counsel and Corporate Secretary	Fax:	(845) 486-5465
MOSHER, Michael L.	Tel:	(845) 452-2000
Vice President, Regulatory Affairs	Fax:	(845) 486-5465
RENNER, Stacey A.	Tel:	(845) 486-5730
Treasurer and Investor Relations Contact	Fax:	(845) 486-5465
srenner@cenhud.com		
VANBUREN, Denise Doring	Tel:	(845) 452-2000
Vice President, Corporate Communications and Corporate Secretary	Fax:	(845) 471-8323
dvanburen@cenhud.com		

CH2M HILL

An engineering company. The company (named for its founders Cornell, Howland, Hayes, and Merryfield) is organized into three divisions: government, environment, and nuclear facilities and infrastructure and energy.
www.ch2m.com
Annual Revenues: $5.55 billion
Employees: 30,000
SIC: 8711
Industry/ies: Computer/Technology; Construction/Construction Materials; Engineering/Mathematics; Environment And Conservation; Pollution And Waste; Science; Scientific Research; Transportation
Legislative Issues: BUD; CAW; ENG; ROD; TAX; TRA

Chairman and Chief Executive Officer

| HINMAN, Jacqueline | Tel: | (303) 771-0900 |
| | Fax: | (720) 286-9250 |

Main Headquarters

Mailing:	9191 S. Jamaica St.	Tel:	(303) 771-0900
	Englewood, CO 80112	Fax:	(720) 286-9250
		TF:	(888) 242-6445

Washington Office

Mailing:	901 New York Ave. NW	Tel:	(202) 393-2426
	Suite 4000 East	Fax:	(202) 783-8410
	Washington, DC 20001		

Political Action Committees

CH2M Hill Companies, Ltd. PAC
FEC ID: C00143305
Contact: Scott Ingvoldstad

| 9191 S. Jamaica St. | Tel: | (202) 393-2426 |
| Englewood, CO 80112 | Fax: | (202) 783-8410 |

Contributions to Candidates: $139,020 (2015-2016)
Democrats: $55,200; Republicans: $83,820

Principal Recipients

HOUSE
SIMPSON, MICHAEL (REP-ID)

Corporate Foundations and Giving Programs

CH2M Hill Foundation
9191 S. Jamaica St.
Englewood, CO 80112

Halcrow Foundation		
22 Cortland St.	Tel:	(212) 608-3990
New York City, NY 10007-3142		

Public Affairs and Related Activities Personnel

At Headquarters

ANDERSON, Tessa	Tel:	(720) 286-2246
Corporate Affairs (PR, Community Investment, Government Affairs, Corporate Communications)	Fax:	(720) 286-9250
Tessa.Anderson@ch2m.com		
DAVIS, Howlie	Tel:	(303) 771-0900
Senior Vice President, Government Affairs	Fax:	(720) 286-9250
Howlie.Davis@ch2m.com		
INGVOLDSTAD, Scott	Tel:	(303) 771-0900
Director, Government Affairs	Fax:	(720) 286-9250
scott.ingvoldstad@ch2m.com		
MCARTHUR, Gary L	Tel:	(303) 771-0900
Executive Vice President and Chief Financial Office	Fax:	(720) 286-9250
MCCOY, Tom	Tel:	(303) 771-0900
Executive Vice President, General Counsel and Secretary	Fax:	(720) 286-9250
MEININGER, Steve	Tel:	(303) 771-0900
Senior Vice President and Managing Director, Operations Management Services	Fax:	(720) 286-9250
O'KEEFE, Patrick	Tel:	(303) 771-0900
Senior Vice President and Regional Managing Director, United States	Fax:	(720) 286-9250

SHEA , JoAnn | Tel: | (303) 771-0900
Interim Chief Financial Officer and Chief Accounting Officer | Fax: | (720) 286-9250

SPERANZA, Elisa | Tel: | (303) 771-0900
Corporate Director, Senior Vice President and Chief Communications Officer | Fax: | (720) 286-9250

At Washington Office

CHILLER, Matthew | Tel: | (202) 393-2426
Senior Director, Federal Affairs | Fax: | (202) 783-8410
Registered Federal Lobbyist

CORSI, John | Tel: | (202) 393-2426
Vice President, Global Media and Public Relations and | Fax: | (212) 566-5059
Director, Corporate Affairs
john.corsi@ch2m.com

CUNNINGHAM, William J. | Tel: | (202) 393-2426
Project Coordinator 2 & O&M Electrical SME | Fax: | (202) 783-8410

GARRISH, Theodore J. | Tel: | (202) 393-2426
Vice President, Federal Operation and Strategic Planning | Fax: | (202) 783-8410
Registered Federal Lobbyist

HOOD, Robert | Tel: | (202) 393-2426
Vice President, Government Affairs | Fax: | (202) 783-8410

LOAR, Theresa | Tel: | (202) 393-2426
Senior Vice President, International Government Affairs | Fax: | (202) 783-8410
theresa.loar@ch2m.com

MADIA, John A. | Tel: | (212) 608-3990
Senior Vice President and Chief Human Resources Officer | Fax: | (212) 566-5059

ROSENBLUM, Sam | Tel: | (202) 393-2426
Platform Developer | Fax: | (202) 783-8410
samuel.rosenblum@ch2m.com

Changing World Technologies

Provider of innovative renewable energy techniques, thereby providing a platform for sustainable development.
www.changingworldtech.com
Annual Revenues: $3.60 million
Employees: 40
SIC: 2860
Industry/ies: Energy/Electricity

Chief Executive Officer | Tel: | (516) 486-0100
APPEL, Brian S. | Fax: | (516) 486-0460

Main Headquarters
Mailing: 460 Hempstead Ave. | Tel: | (516) 486-0100
Hempstead, NY 11552 | Fax: | (516) 486-0460

The Charles Group, Inc.

A company that specializes in security, counter-narcotics and communications issues.
charlesgrouppdc.com
Legislative Issues: EDU; HCR; LAW; RET; TAX; VET

President and Managing Member | Tel: | (202) 546-2262
CHARLES, Robert | Fax: | (202) 546-2266

Main Headquarters
Mailing: 18630 Reliant Dr. | Tel: | (202) 546-2262
Gaithersburg, MD 20879 | Fax: | (301) 977-5600

Washington Office
Mailing: 322 Massachusetts Ave. NE | Tel: | (202) 546-2262
Suite A | Fax: | (202) 546-2266
Washington, DC 20002

Public Affairs and Related Activities Personnel

At Headquarters

CHARLES, Marina T. | Tel: | (202) 546-2262
Senior Vice President, Operations | Fax: | (301) 977-5600

COOKE, Brian E. | Tel: | (202) 546-2262
Senior Advisor | Fax: | (301) 977-5600

At Washington Office

ANDREWS, Hayley | Tel: | (202) 546-2262
Registered Federal Lobbyist | Fax: | (202) 546-2266

COOPER, Laura | Tel: | (202) 546-2262
Director, Government Affairs | Fax: | (202) 546-2266
Registered Federal Lobbyist

ERICKSON, Parker | Tel: | (202) 546-2262
Registered Federal Lobbyist | Fax: | (202) 546-2266

HOWLE, Caroline | Tel: | (202) 546-2262
Federal Lobbyist | Fax: | (202) 546-2266
Registered Federal Lobbyist

MARTIN, Connor M. | Tel: | (202) 546-2262
Senior Policy Analyst | Fax: | (202) 546-2266
Registered Federal Lobbyist

RAYBURN, Caroline | Tel: | (202) 546-2262
Associate, Government Affairs | Fax: | (202) 546-2266

Registered Federal Lobbyist

THOMPSON, William | Tel: | (202) 546-2262
Registered Federal Lobbyist | Fax: | (202) 546-2266

THOMPSON, Bill | Tel: | (202) 546-2262
Registered Federal Lobbyist | Fax: | (202) 546-2266

WEIN, Rachel | Tel: | (202) 546-2262
Federal Lobbyist | Fax: | (202) 546-2266

At Other Offices

DAVIS-GROSSMAN, Carol | Tel: | (973) 575-1444
Managing Partner | Fax: | (973) 575-1445
373 Route 46 West, Bldg. E., Suite 215
Fairfield, NJ 07004

Charles Schwab & Company, Inc.

A financial and brokerage services company.
www.schwab.com
Annual Revenues: $6.03 billion
Employees: 14,900
Ticker: NYSE: SCHW
Industry/ies: Banking/Finance/Investments
Legislative Issues: CSP; FIN; LBR; RET; TAX

Chairman of the Board | Tel: | (415) 667-8400
SCHWAB, Charles R. | Fax: | (415) 636-9820

President and Chief Executive Officer | Tel: | (415) 636-7000
BETTINGER, II, Walter W. | Fax: | (415) 636-9820

Main Headquarters
Mailing: 211 Main St. | Tel: | (415) 667-8400
San Francisco, CA 94105 | Fax: | (415) 636-9820
| TF: | (800) 648-5300

Washington Office
Mailing: 325 Seventh St. NW | Tel: | (202) 638-3755
Suite 200
Washington, DC 20004

Political Action Committees
Charles Schwab Corporation PAC
FEC ID: C00370114
Contact: Scott Eckel
211 Main St.
San Fransico, CA 94105

Contributions to Candidates: $275,000 (2015-2016)
Democrats: $135,500; Republicans: $139,500

Principal Recipients

HOUSE
HENSARLING, JEB HON. (REP-TX)

Corporate Foundations and Giving Programs

Charles Schwab Foundation
Contact: Carrie Schwab-Pomerantz
211 Main St. | Tel: | (415) 636-7000
San Francisco, CA 94105 | Fax: | (415) 636-9820

Public Affairs and Related Activities Personnel

At Headquarters

ALLEN, Jay L. | Tel: | (415) 636-7000
Executive Vice President and Chief Administrative Officer | Fax: | (415) 636-9820

ASERON, Alma | Tel: | (415) 636-9748
Senior Public Relations Specialist | Fax: | (415) 636-5970
alma.aseron@schwab.com

BREWSTER, Pamela | Tel: | (415) 636-7000
Vice President and Government Affairs | Fax: | (415) 636-9820
Mail Stop Suite 740

BULGATZ, Sarah | Tel: | (415) 667-0328
Director, Corporate Public Relations | Fax: | (415) 636-9820
sarah.bulgatz@schwab.com

CLENDENING, John S. | Tel: | (415) 636-7000
Executive Vice President, Investor Services | Fax: | (415) 636-9820

CRAIG , Jonathan M. | Tel: | (415) 636-7000
Executive Vice President and Chief Marketing Officer | Fax: | (415) 636-9820

FOWLER, Rich | Tel: | (415) 667-1841
Senior Vice President, Investor Relations | Fax: | (415) 636-9820

GABLE, Greg | Tel: | (415) 667-0473
Senior Vice President, Corporate Public Relations | Fax: | (415) 636-5970
greg.gable@schwab.com

GARFIELD, David R. | Tel: | (415) 667-8400
Executive Vice President, General Counsel and Corporate | Fax: | (415) 636-9820
Secretary

MARTINETTO, Joseph R. | Tel: | (415) 636-7000
Executive Vice President and Chief Financial Officer | Fax: | (415) 636-9820

SCHWAB-POMERANTZ, Carrie | Tel: | (415) 636-7000
President | Fax: | (415) 636-9820

TUMA , Martha	Tel:	(415) 667-8400
Executive Vice President, Human Resources	Fax:	(415) 636-9820

At Washington Office

BROWN, Jeffrey	Tel:	(202) 638-3755
Senior Vice President, Legislative & Regulatory Affairs		
Registered Federal Lobbyist		
ECKEL, Scott	Tel:	(202) 638-3755
Vice President, Legislative and Regulatory Affairs and PAC		
Treasurer		
Registered Federal Lobbyist		
QUISH, Kimberly M.	Tel:	(202) 638-3755
Vice President, Legislative and Regulatory Affairs		
Registered Federal Lobbyist		
TOWNSEND, Michael	Tel:	(202) 638-3755
Vice President, Legislative & Regulatory Affairs		
michael.townsend@schwab.com		
Registered Federal Lobbyist		

Charming Shoppes, Inc.

Operates a chain of ladies apparel shops under the names Fashion Bug, Fashion Bug Plus, Catherines, Accessorize and Lane Bryant.
www.charmingshoppes.com
Employees: 23,000
Ticker: NASDAQ: CHRS
SIC: 5621; 5099; 5611; 5632
Industry/ies: Apparel/Textiles Industry; Retail/Wholesale

Co-Founder and Non-Executive Chairman	Tel:	(551) 777-6700
JAFFE, Elliot S.		
President and Chief Executive Officer	Tel:	(551) 777-6700
JAFFE, David R.		

Main Headquarters

Mailing:	933 MacArthur Blvd.	Tel:	(551) 777-6700
	Mahwah, NJ 07430		

Public Affairs and Related Activities Personnel

At Headquarters

GIAMMATTEO, Robb	Tel:	(551) 777-6700
Executive Vice President, Chief Financial Officer		
HOLLOWAY, Duane	Tel:	(551) 777-6700
Senior Vice President and General Counsel		
PERSHING, John	Tel:	(551) 777-6700
Executive Vice President, Chief Human Resources Officer		

CheckFree Corporation

See listing on page 330 under Fiserv Corporation

Checkpoint Systems Inc.

A manufacturer and provider of end-to-end solutions in shrink management, supply chain visibility and apparel labeling to the retail and apparel industry.
www.checkpointsystems.com
Annual Revenues: $643.18 million
Employees: 4,894
Ticker: NYSE: CKP
SIC: 3669; 5063; 5099; 5099
Industry/ies: Apparel/Textiles Industry

Chairman of the Board	Tel:	(856) 848-1800
ANTLE, William Smoot	Fax:	(856) 848-0937
President and Chief Executive Officer	Tel:	(856) 848-1800
BABICH, Jr., George	Fax:	(856) 848-0937

Main Headquarters

Mailing:	101 Wolf Dr.	Tel:	(856) 848-1800
	Thorofare, NJ 08086	Fax:	(856) 848-0937
		TF:	(800) 257-5540

Public Affairs and Related Activities Personnel

At Headquarters

ABADI , Farrokh	Tel: (856) 848-1800
Chief Strategy and Business Development Officer	Fax: (856) 848-0937
ANDRUS, Eric	Tel: (856) 384-3170
Head, Media Relations	Fax: (856) 848-0937
GERAGHTY, Annette	Tel: (856) 251-2174
Specialist, Investor Relations	Fax: (856) 848-0937
LEVIN, Per H	Tel: (856) 848-1800
President and Chief Sales Officer	Fax: (856) 848-0937
LUCANIA, James M	Tel: (856) 848-1800
Acting Chief Financial Officer and treasurer	Fax: (856) 848-0937
POWERS, Bob	Tel: (215) 553-8323
Vice President, Investor Relations	Fax: (215) 988-9643
bob.powers@checkpt.com	
ROWLAND, Bryan T.R	Tel: (856) 848-1800

Vice President General Counsel and Corporate Secretary	Fax:	(856) 848-0937
ROY, Carol P.	Tel:	(856) 848-1800
Senior Vice President, Global Human Resource Operations	Fax:	(856) 848-0937
WRIGLEY, James	Tel:	(856) 848-1800
President and Chief Operating Officer	Fax:	(856) 848-0937

The Cheesecake Factory

Casual dining restaurants.
www.thecheesecakefactory.com
Annual Revenues: $2.01 billion
Employees: 35,700
Ticker: NASDAQ: CAKE
SIC: 5812
Industry/ies: Food And Beverage Industry

Chairman of the Board and Chief Executive Officer	Tel:	(818) 871-3000
OVERTON, David	Fax:	(818) 871-3001

Main Headquarters

Mailing:	26901 Malibu Hills Rd.	Tel:	(818) 871-3000
	Calabasas Hills, CA 91301	Fax:	(818) 871-3001

Corporate Foundations and Giving Programs

Cheesecake Factory Oscar and Evelyn Overton Charitable Foundation

26901 Malibu Hills Rd.	Tel:	(818) 871-3000
Calabasas Hills, CA 91301	Fax:	(818) 871-3100

Public Affairs and Related Activities Personnel

At Headquarters

BARMASSE, Dina R.	Tel: (818) 871-3000
Senior Vice President, Human Resources	Fax: (818) 871-3001
BENN, W. Douglas	Tel: (818) 871-3000
Executive Vice President and Chief Financial Officer	Fax: (818) 871-3001
BYFUGLIN, Max S.	Tel: (818) 871-3000
President	Fax: (818) 871-3001
CLARK, Matthew E.	Tel: (818) 871-3000
Senior Vice President, Finance and Strategy	Fax: (818) 871-3001
PETERS, Jill S.	Tel: (818) 871-3000
Vice President, Investor Relations	Fax: (818) 871-3001
jpeters@thecheesecakefactory.com	
STRIEWSKI, Kelly	Tel: (310) 248-6164
Media Contact	Fax: (818) 871-3001
ZURZOLO, Debby R.	Tel: (818) 871-3000
Executive Vice President, General Counsel and Secretary	Fax: (818) 871-3001

Chemed Corporation

A diversified corporation with operations in plumbing, drain cleaning, appliance and air-conditioning repair and maintenance; and janitorial supply products and services(in Iowa only). Subsidiaries include Roto-Rooter.
www.chemed.com
Annual Revenues: $1.56 billion
Employees: 14,406
Ticker: NYSE:CHE
SIC: 2819; 2836; 2841; 2842; 7699; 8082
Industry/ies: Medicine/Health Care/Mental Health

Chairman of the Board	Tel:	(513) 762-6900
WALSH, III, George J.	Fax:	(513) 762-6919
President and Chief Executive Officer	Tel:	(513) 762-6900
MCNAMARA, Kevin	Fax:	(513) 762-6919

Main Headquarters

Mailing:	255 E. Fifth St.	Tel:	(513) 762-6690
	Suite 2600	Fax:	(513) 762-6919
	Cincinnati, OH 45202-4726	TF:	(800) 224-3633

Corporate Foundations and Giving Programs

The Chemed Foundation

255 E. Fifth St.	Tel:	(513) 762-6900
Cincinnati, OH 45202	Fax:	(513) 762-6919

Public Affairs and Related Activities Personnel

At Headquarters

DALLOB, Naomi C.	Tel: (513) 762-6900
Vice President, Secretary and Chief Legal Officer	Fax: (513) 762-6919
REINHARD, Lisa A.	Tel: (513) 762-6900
Vice President, Chief Administrative Officer and Assistant Secretary	Fax: (513) 762-6919
WARNER, Sherri L.	Tel: (513) 762-6683
Director, Investor Relations	Fax: (513) 762-6919
WILLIAMS, David P.	Tel: (513) 762-6690
Executive Vice President and Chief Financial Officer	Fax: (513) 762-6919

Chemtura Corporation

A chemical and plastic additives manufacturer. Formed from the merger of Crompton Corporation and Great Lakes Chemical Corporation in 2005.
www.chemtura.com

Annual Revenues: $2.07 billion
Employees: 2,700
Ticker: NYSE: CHMT
SIC: 2820
Industry/ies: Chemicals & Chemical Industry

Chairman of the Board, President and Chief Executive Officer
ROGERSON, Craig A.
Tel: (203) 573-2000
Fax: (203) 573-3711

Main Headquarters
Mailing: 1818 Market St.
Suite 3700
Philadelphia, PA 19103
Tel: (215) 446-3911

Political Action Committees
Chemtura Corporation PAC
FEC ID: C00385609
Contact: Nancy Mary Bissonnette
199 Benson Rd.
Middlebury, CT 06749

Contributions to Candidates: $5,500 (2015-2016)
Republicans: $5,500

Corporate Foundations and Giving Programs
Chemtura Corporation Contributions Program
199 Benson Rd.
Middlebury, CT 06749
Tel: (203) 573-2000
Fax: (203) 573-3711

Public Affairs and Related Activities Personnel
At Headquarters
ORTON, Laurence
Vice President, Corporate Controller and Principal Accounting Officer
Tel: (215) 446-3911

At Other Offices
BISSONNETTE, Nancy Mary
PAC Treasurer
199 Benson Rd.
Middlebury, CT 06749
Tel: (203) 573-2000
Fax: (203) 573-3711

FLAHERTY, Billie S.
Senior Vice President, General Counsel and Corporate Secretary
199 Benson Rd.
Middlebury, CT 06749
Tel: (203) 573-2000
Fax: (203) 573-3711

FORSYTH, Stephen C.
Executive Vice President and Chief Financial Officer
199 Benson Rd.
Middlebury, CT 06749
Tel: (203) 573-2000
Fax: (203) 573-3711

GUSTAVSEN, John
Manager, Corporate Communications
199 Benson Rd.
Middlebury, CT 06749
Tel: (203) 573-3224
Fax: (203) 573-3711

MOON, Lloyd N.
Vice President, Public Affairs
199 Benson Rd.
Middlebury, CT 06749
Tel: (203) 573-2900
Fax: (203) 573-3711

PAYSENO, Brian
Director, Communications
199 Benson Rd.
Middlebury, CT 06749
Tel: (203) 573-2000
Fax: (203) 573-3711

SWIECH, Alan M.
Executive Vice President, Support Services and General Manager
199 Benson Rd.
Middlebury, CT 06749
Tel: (203) 573-2000
Fax: (203) 573-3711

Chenega Corporation

Offers professional services in the areas of information technology, telecommunications, intel and military operations, logistics support, environmental management, security services, and light manufacturing to the federal government.
www.chenega.com
Annual Revenues: $1.11 billion
Employees: 4,500
Industry/ies: Minorities
Legislative Issues: IND

President and Chief Executive Officer
TOTEMOFF, Charles W.
Tel: (907) 277-5706
Fax: (907) 277-5700

Main Headquarters
Mailing: 3000 C St.
Suite 301
Anchorage, AK 99503
Tel: (907) 277-5706
Fax: (907) 277-5700
TF: (888) 442-5388

Political Action Committees
Chenega Corporation PAC (Chenega PAC)
FEC ID: C00549865
Contact: Chris Marston
3000 C St.
Suite 301
Anchorage, 99503

Contributions to Candidates: $23,500 (2015-2016)
Democrats: $3,500; Republicans: $20,000

Corporate Foundations and Giving Programs
Chenega Future Inc.
Contact: Patricia J. Andrews
3000 C St.
Suite 301
Anchorage, AK 99503
Tel: (907) 277-5706
Fax: (907) 277-5700

Chenega Heritage Foundation
Contact: Paul T. Selanoff
3000 C St.
Suite 301
Anchorage, AK 99503
Tel: (907) 277-5706
Fax: (907) 277-5700

Public Affairs and Related Activities Personnel
At Headquarters
ANDREWS, Patricia J.
Manager, Shareholder Services
pandrews@chenegacorp.com
Tel: (907) 277-5706
Fax: (907) 277-5700

MARSTON, Chris
PAC Contact
Tel: (907) 277-5706
Fax: (907) 277-5700

O'KEEFE, Peggy
Vice President, Human Resources
Tel: (907) 277-5706
Fax: (907) 277-5700

ROGINA, Karen
Director, Corporate Communications
karen.rogina@chenega.com
Tel: (907) 677-4909
Fax: (907) 277-5700

SELANOFF, Paul T.
Director, Chenega Heritage Foundation
Tel: (907) 277-5706
Fax: (907) 277-5700

WOOLSTON, Kristina
Vice President, Government Relations
kristina.woolston@chenega.com
Tel: (907) 677-4907
Fax: (907) 277-5700

Cheniere Energy Inc.

An energy company specializing in oil and gas exploration.
www.cheniere.com
Annual Revenues: $270.67 million
Employees: 642
Ticker: NYSE: LNG
SIC: 4924
Industry/ies: Fuels See Coal, Gas, Oil, Petroleum; Natural Resources; Petroleum Industry
Legislative Issues: ENG; TRA

Chairman of the Board, Chief Executive Officer and President
SOUKI, Charif
Tel: (713) 375-6000
Fax: (713) 375-6000

Main Headquarters
Mailing: 700 Milam St.
Suite 1900
Houston, TX 77002
Tel: (713) 375-5000
Fax: (713) 375-6000

Washington Office
Mailing: 1445 Pennsylvania Ave. NW
Suite 550
Washington, DC 20004

Political Action Committees
Cheniere Energy Inc. PAC
FEC ID: C00430157
Contact: Amanda J. Hoyt
1445 Pennsylvania Ave. NW
Suite 550
Washington, DC 20004

Contributions to Candidates: $12,272,115 (2015-2016)
Democrats: $63,400; Republicans: $116,700; Other: $12,092,015

Principal Recipients

HOUSE
BOEHNER, JOHN A. (REP-OH)
BOUSTANY, CHARLES W. DR. JR. (REP-LA)
RYAN, PAUL D. (REP-WI)

Corporate Foundations and Giving Programs
Cheniere Energy Contributions Program
700 Milam St.
Suite 800
Houston, TX 77002

Public Affairs and Related Activities Personnel
At Headquarters
BHATIA, Randy
Director, Finance and Investor Relations
Tel: (713) 375-5479
Fax: (713) 375-6000

FEYGIN, Anatol
Senior Vice President, Strategy and Corporate Development
Tel: (713) 375-5000
Fax: (713) 375-6000

FRENCH, Jason
Director, Government and Public Affairs
Tel: (713) 375-5000
Fax: (713) 375-6000

jason.french@cheniere.com

GENTLE, Meg	Tel:	(713) 375-6000
Executive Vice President, Marketing	Fax:	(713) 375-6000
HAGGARD, Diane	Tel:	(713) 375-5259
Media Relations Manager	Fax:	(713) 375-6000
OUTTRIM, Patricia	Tel:	(713) 375-5212
Vice President, Governmental and Regulatory Affairs	Fax:	(713) 375-6000
pat.outtrim@cheniere.com		
PIPKIN, Katie	Tel:	(713) 375-6000
Senior Vice President, Business Development and Communications	Fax:	(713) 375-6000
RADEN, Ann	Tel:	(713) 375-6000
Vice President, Human Resources and Administration	Fax:	(713) 375-6000
RAYFORD, Greg W.	Tel:	(713) 375-6000
Senior Vice President and General Counsel	Fax:	(713) 375-6000
WORTLEY, Michael	Tel:	(713) 375-5000
Senior Vice President, and Chief Financial Officer	Fax:	(713) 375-6000

At Washington Office

HOYT, Amanda J.
PAC Treasurer

MOURAD, Majida
Vice President, Government Affairs

At Other Offices

DESAI, Ankit	Tel:	(713) 375-5000
Vice President, Government Relations	Fax:	(713) 375-6000
600 14th St. NW, Suite 600 South		
Washington, DC 20005		
NAHAS, Albert G.	Tel:	(713) 375-5000
Vice President, International Government Affairs	Fax:	(713) 375-6000
600 14th St. NW, Suite 600 South		
Washington, DC 20005		
albert.nahas@cheniere.com		

Cherry Road Technologies

Provides systems integration and consulting services that maximize enterprise performance for private and public sector and federal clients.
www.cherryroad.com
Employees: 400
Industry/ies: Management
Legislative Issues: DEF; VET

Chairman of the Board	Tel:	(973) 402-7802
GULBAN, Michael	Fax:	(973) 402-7808

President	Tel:	(973) 402-7802
GULBAN, Jeremy	Fax:	(973) 402-7808

Main Headquarters

Mailing:	301 Gibraltar Dr.	Tel:	(973) 402-7802
	Suite 2C	Fax:	(973) 402-7808
	Morris Plains, NJ 07950	TF:	(877) 402-7804

Public Affairs and Related Activities Personnel

At Headquarters

LANGE, Steve	Tel:	(973) 402-7802
Vice President, Operations	Fax:	(973) 402-7808
ROGERSON, Nancy Hirsch	Tel:	(973) 402-7802
Vice President and Chief Financial Officer	Fax:	(973) 402-7808
VERRONE, Elaine	Tel:	(973) 541-4227
Manager, Marketing and Media Contact	Fax:	(973) 402-7808
everrone@cherryroad.com		

Chesapeake Energy Corporation

An oil and natural gas company.
www.chk.com
Annual Revenues: $11.51 billion
Employees: 4,400
Ticker: NYSE: CHK
SIC: 1311
Industry/ies: Energy/Electricity
Legislative Issues: ENG; ENV; NAT; TAX; TRA; TRD

Chairman of the Board	Tel:	(405) 935-8878
MARTIN, R. Brad	Fax:	(405) 843-0573

President, Chief Executive Officer and Director	Tel:	(405) 935-8000
LAWLER, Robert Douglas "Doug"	Fax:	(405) 843-0573

Main Headquarters

Mailing:	P.O. Box 18496	Tel:	(405) 935-8878
	Oklahoma City, OK 73154-0496	Fax:	(405) 843-0573
		TF:	(877) 245-1427

Political Action Committees

Chesapeake Energy Corporation FED-PAC
FEC ID: C00389288
Contact: John Christopher Dill

P.O. Box 18496
Oklahoma City, OK 73154

Contributions to Candidates: $288,384 (2015-2016)
Democrats: $48,500; Republicans: $239,884

Principal Recipients

HOUSE
COLE, TOM (REP-OK)
CUELLAR, HENRY (DEM-TX)
JOHNSON, BILL (REP-OH)
MULLIN, MARKWAYNE MR. (REP-OK)
SHUSTER, WILLIAM MR. (REP-PA)

Corporate Foundations and Giving Programs

Chesapeake Energy Contributions Program
Contact: Gordon Pennoyer
P.O. Box 18496
Oklahoma City, OK 73154-0496

Public Affairs and Related Activities Personnel

At Headquarters

DELL'OSSO, Jr., Domenic J.	Tel:	(405) 935-8000
Executive Vice President and Chief Financial Officer	Fax:	(405) 843-0573
DILL, John Christopher	Tel:	(405) 935-8000
PAC Contact	Fax:	(405) 843-0573
DUNHAM, Archie W.	Tel:	(405) 935-8000
Chairman Emeritus	Fax:	(405) 843-0573
JOHNSON, Michael A.	Tel:	(405) 935-8878
Senior Vice President, Accounting, Controller and Chief Accounting Officer	Fax:	(405) 843-0573
PENNOYER, Gordon	Tel:	(405) 935-8878
Director, Strategic Communications	Fax:	(405) 843-0573
media@chk.com		
TOMPKINS, Cathy L.	Tel:	(405) 935-8878
Senior Vice President, Information Technology and Chief Information Officer	Fax:	(405) 843-0573
WEBB, James R.	Tel:	(405) 935-8000
Executive Vice President, General Counsel and Corporate Secretary	Fax:	(405) 843-0573

At Other Offices

GAINER, Sarah	Tel:	(405) 935-6192
Director, Federal Government Relations		
6100 N. Western Ave.		
Oklahoma City, OK 73118		
Sarah.Gainer@chk.com		
Registered Federal Lobbyist		

Chevron U.S.A., Inc.

Formerly ChevronTexaco Corporation. A petroleum company formed by the merger of Chevron Corporation and Texaco Inc.
www.chevron.com
Annual Revenues: $173.71 billion
Employees: 64,700
SIC: 2911
Industry/ies: Chemicals & Chemical Industry; Energy/Electricity; Fuels See Coal, Gas, Oil, Petroleum; Natural Resources; Petroleum Industry
Legislative Issues: BUD; ENG; ENV; FOR; FUE; LAW; TAX; TRD

Chairman and Chief Executive Officer	Tel:	(925) 842-1000
WATSON, John S.	Fax:	(925) 842-3530

Main Headquarters

Mailing:	6001 Bollinger Canyon Rd.	Tel:	(925) 842-1000
	San Ramon, CA 94583	Fax:	(925) 790-3987

Washington Office

Mailing:	1401 I St. NW, Suite 1200	Tel:	(202) 408-5865
	Washington, DC 20005-2225	Fax:	(202) 408-5842

Political Action Committees

Chevron Employees PAC - Chevron Corporation
FEC ID: C00035006
Contact: Alana Ms. O'Connell Ruegg
6101 Bollinger Canyon Rd.
Room 3400
San Ramon, CA 94583

Contributions to Candidates: $626,750 (2015-2016)
Democrats: $51,500; Republicans: $570,250; Other: $5,000

Principal Recipients

SENATE
AYOTTE, KELLY A (REP-NH)
BURR, RICHARD (REP-NC)
JOHNSON, RONALD HAROLD (REP-)
KIRK, MARK STEVEN (REP-FL)
KIRK, MARK STEVEN (REP-IL)
LEE, MIKE (REP-UT)
MCCAIN, JOHN S (REP-VA)

MURKOWSKI, LISA (REP-AK)
PORTMAN, ROB (REP-OH)
TOOMEY, PATRICK JOSEPH (REP-PA)

HOUSE
BISHOP, ROBERT (REP-UT)
BOUSTANY, CHARLES W. DR. JR. (REP-LA)
HURD, WILLIAM (REP-TX)
MCHENRY, PATRICK TIMOTHY (REP-NC)
NUNES, DEVIN G (REP-CA)
ROYCE, ED MR. (REP-CA)
SCALISE, STEVE MR. (REP-LA)
UPTON, FREDERICK STEPHEN (REP-MI)
VALADAO, DAVID (REP-CA)
WALDEN, GREGORY P MR. (REP-OR)

Corporate Foundations and Giving Programs

Chevron Corporate Responsibility
6001 Bollinger Canyon Rd.   Tel: (925) 842-1000
Suite 3400   Fax: (925) 790-3987
San Ramon, CA 94583

Public Affairs and Related Activities Personnel

At Headquarters

BEYE, Mamadou   Tel: (925) 842-1000
Manager, International Affairs   Fax: (925) 842-2046

FAGER, Dan L.   Tel: (925) 842-1000
Manager, Federal Relations   Fax: (925) 842-2046
dfager@chevron.com

GANTEN (JENNIFER WALTO), Jennifer   Tel: (925) 842-1000
Manager, International Team and International Affairs   Fax: (925) 790-3987
Registered Federal Lobbyist

HAYNES, Bradley S.   Tel: (925) 842-1000
Manager, International Government Affairs   Fax: (925) 842-2046
Registered Federal Lobbyist

HUDSON, Laura C.   Tel: (925) 842-1000
Manager, International Government Relations   Fax: (925) 842-2046

IRWIN, William   Tel: (925) 842-1000
Manager, International Government Relations   Fax: (925) 842-2046
wirwin@chevron.com

LAYMON, Joe W.   Tel: (925) 842-1000
Vice President, Human Resources and Corporate Services   Fax: (925) 842-3530

OURADA, Jeanette S.   Tel: (925) 842-1000
Vice President and Comptroller   Fax: (925) 842-3530

PATE, R. Hewitt   Tel: (925) 842-1000
Vice President and General Counsel   Fax: (925) 842-2046

PICA KARP, Maria   Tel: (925) 842-1000
Vice President and General Manager, Government Affairs   Fax: (925) 790-3987
Registered Federal Lobbyist

PRYOR, Jay R.   Tel: (925) 842-1000
Vice President, Corporate Business Development   Fax: (925) 842-3530

SEDNEY, Diana   Tel: (925) 842-1000
Manager, International Government Relations   Fax: (925) 842-2046
dsedney@chevron.com

WYLIE, Lydia   Tel: (925) 842-1000
PAC Treasurer   Fax: (925) 842-3530

YARRINGTON, Patricia E.   Tel: (925) 842-1000
Vice President and Chief Financial Officer   Fax: (925) 842-3530

At Washington Office

GREEN, Steve W.   Tel: (202) 408-5865
Vice President, Policy, Government and Public Affairs   Fax: (202) 408-5842

KOETZLE, Bill   Tel: (202) 408-5865
Manager, Federal Team and Government Affairs   Fax: (202) 408-5842
Registered Federal Lobbyist

MARSHALL, Debra S.   Tel: (202) 408-5865
Manager, Government Affairs   Fax: (202) 408-5842
marshall@chevron.com
Registered Federal Lobbyist

SANDER, Dave   Tel: (202) 408-5865
Manager, Government Affairs   Fax: (202) 408-5842
davesander@chevron.com
Registered Federal Lobbyist

VERMA, Puneet   Tel: (202) 408-5865
Manager, Government Affairs   Fax: (202) 408-5842
Registered Federal Lobbyist

WALTO, Jennifer R.   Tel: (202) 408-5864
Manager, International Government Relations   Fax: (202) 408-5842
Jennifer.Walto@Chevron.com
Registered Federal Lobbyist

WASHINGTON, Gregory J.   Tel: (202) 408-5865
Manager, Government Affairs   Fax: (202) 408-5842
Registered Federal Lobbyist

At Other Offices

ALMEIDA, Renato
6101 Bollinger Canyon Rd., Room 3432
San Ramon, CA 95452
Registered Federal Lobbyist

BARRY, Lisa B.
Vice President and General Manager
6101 Bollinger Canyon Rd., Room 3432
San Ramon, CA 95452

CALVERT, Nathan
6101 Bollinger Canyon Rd., Room 3432
San Ramon, CA 95452

GOODMAN, Caitlyn
6101 Bollinger Canyon Rd., Room 3432
San Ramon, CA 95452
Registered Federal Lobbyist

HARRIS, Daeman
Manager, International Affairs
6101 Bollinger Canyon Rd., Room 3432
San Ramon, CA 95452
Registered Federal Lobbyist

KAUNE, Jason D.
Attorney & Agent for Filer
6101 Bollinger Canyon Rd., Room 3432
San Ramon, CA 95452

KOETZLE, William
6101 Bollinger Canyon Rd., Room 3432
San Ramon, CA 95452
Registered Federal Lobbyist

NAYLOR, Joseph M.
Vice President, Strategic Planning
6101 Bollinger Canyon Rd., Room 3432
San Ramon, CA 95452

ONG, Joo-Jin
Manager, International Affairs
6101 Bollinger Canyon Rd., Room 3432
San Ramon, CA 95452
Registered Federal Lobbyist

PRIDDY, Benjamin
Federal Lobbyist
6101 Bollinger Canyon Rd., Room 3432
San Ramon, CA 95452
Registered Federal Lobbyist

RUEGG, Alana Ms. O'Connell
PAC Treasurer
6101 Bollinger Canyon Rd., Room 3432
San Ramon, CA 95452

THOMPSON, James
6101 Bollinger Canyon Rd., Room 3432
San Ramon, CA 95452
Registered Federal Lobbyist

VALDERRAMA, Alexandra
Manager, International Affairs
6101 Bollinger Canyon Rd., Room 3432
San Ramon, CA 95452
Registered Federal Lobbyist

WALTON, Jennifer
Federal Lobbyist
6101 Bollinger Canyon Rd., Room 3432
San Ramon, CA 95452
Registered Federal Lobbyist

ChevronTexaco Corporation

See listing on page 186 under Chevron U.S.A., Inc.

CHF International

See listing on page 367 under Global Communities

Chicago Board of Trade

See listing on page 200 under CME Group, Inc.

Chicago Bridge &amp

See listing on page 171 under CB&I

The Children's Place Retail Stores, Inc.

A specialty retailer of value-priced apparel and accessories for children, newborn to age ten.
www.childrensplace.com
Annual Revenues: $1.74 billion
Employees: 3,500
Ticker: NASDAQ: PLCE
Industry/ies: Apparel/Textiles Industry; Children And Youth; Retail/Wholesale

Chairman of the Board
MATTHEWS, Norman S.

Tel: (201) 558-2400
Fax: (201) 558-2630

Director, President and Chief Executive Officer
ELFERS, Jane

Tel: (201) 558-2400
Fax: (201) 558-2630

Main Headquarters
Mailing: 500 Plaza Dr.
Secaucus, NJ 07094

Tel: (201) 558-2400
Fax: (201) 558-2630
TF: (877) 752-2387

Corporate Foundations and Giving Programs
The Children's Place Retail Stores, Inc. Contributions Program
500 Plaza Dr.
Secaucus, NJ 07094

Tel: (201) 558-2400
Fax: (201) 558-2630

Public Affairs and Related Activities Personnel

At Headquarters

COST, Bradley
Senior Vice President, General Counsel

Tel: (201) 558-2400
Fax: (201) 558-2630

MCCLURE, Larry
Senior Vice President, Human Resources

Tel: (201) 558-2400
Fax: (201) 558-2630

PRUTHI, Anurup
Chief Financial Officer

Tel: (201) 558-2400
Fax: (201) 558-2630

SCARPA, Michael
Chief Operating Officer

Tel: (201) 558-2400
Fax: (201) 558-2630

SWAN, Leah
Senior Vice President, Human Resources

Tel: (201) 558-2400
Fax: (201) 558-2630

Chili's, Inc.

See listing on page 144 under Brinker International

Chimerix Inc.

Chimerix discovers, develops and commercializes orally-available, antiviral therapeutics for a broad range of viral diseases.
www.chimerix.com
Annual Revenues: $4.50 million
Employees: 83
Ticker: Nasdaq : CMRX
SIC: 2834
Industry/ies: Medicine/Health Care/Mental Health
Legislative Issues: HCR

President and Chief Executive Officer
BERREY, Michelle

Tel: (919) 806-1074
Fax: (919) 806-1146

Main Headquarters
Mailing: 2505 Meridian Pkwy.
Suite 340
Durham, NC 27713

Tel: (919) 806-1074
Fax: (919) 806-1146

Public Affairs and Related Activities Personnel

At Headquarters

ALRUTZ , Michael A.
Vice President, General Counsel

Tel: (919) 806-1074
Fax: (919) 806-1146

GUZMAN, Roberto
Vice President, Compliance

Tel: (919) 806-1074
Fax: (919) 806-1146

PLOHOROS, Tony
Contact, Media Relations
tplohoros@6degreespr.com

Tel: (908) 940-0135
Fax: (919) 806-1146

ROSE, Michelle L.
Vice President, Regulatory Affairs

Tel: (919) 806-1074
Fax: (919) 806-1146

STERN, Lilian
Investor Contact
lilian@sternir.com

Tel: (212) 362-1200
Fax: (919) 806-1146

TROST, Timothy W.
Senior Vice President, Chief Financial Officer

Tel: (919) 806-1074
Fax: (919) 806-1146

China Daily Distribution Company

China Daily US Edition is a tailor-made version of China Daily, China's national English-language newspaper, for North American readers.It was launched in 2009
usa.chinadaily.com.cn
Industry/ies: Retail/Wholesale

Main Headquarters
Mailing: 1500 Broadway
Suite 2800
New York City, NY 10036

Tel: (212) 537-8888
Fax: (212) 537-8898

Public Affairs and Related Activities Personnel

At Headquarters

LIU, Zuoyi
Director, Finance

Tel: (212) 537-8888
Fax: (212) 537-8898

XIE, Zhihong
Director, Administration

Tel: (212) 537-8888
Fax: (212) 537-8898

Chiquita Brands International, Inc.

An international marketer and distributor of fresh and processed food products.
www.chiquita.com
Employees: 20,000
Ticker: NYSE: CQB
SIC: 0100; 5148; 0179; 5099; 5148
Industry/ies: Agriculture/Agronomy; Food And Beverage Industry
Legislative Issues: FOR; IMM; TOR; TRD

Interim Chief Executive Officer
KOCHER, Brian W

Tel: (980) 636-5000

Main Headquarters
Mailing: 2051 S.E. 35th St.
Ft Lauderdale, FL 33316

Washington Office
Mailing: P.O. Box 77472
Washington, DC 20013

Corporate Foundations and Giving Programs
Chiquita Brands International, Inc. Contributions Program
250 E. Fifth St.
Cincinnati, OH 45202

Tel: (513) 784-8000
Fax: (513) 665-2629

Public Affairs and Related Activities Personnel

At Headquarters

BOULDON, Allyson
Vice President and Chief Compliance Officer

JOHNSON, Joseph B.
Chief Accounting Officer and Treasurer

At Other Offices

HIMES, Steve
Director, Investor Relations
550 S. Caldwell St.
Charlotte, NC 28202
shimes@chiquita.com

Tel: (980) 636-5000

HOLLAND, Kevin R.
Chief People Officer
550 S. Caldwell St.
Charlotte, NC 28202

Tel: (980) 636-5000

RODRIGUEZ, Manuel
Executive Vice President and Government and International Affairs and Corporate Responsibility Officer
550 S. Caldwell St.
Charlotte, NC 28202

Tel: (980) 636-5000

THOMPSON, James E.
Executive Vice President, General Counsel and Secretary
550 S. Caldwell St.
Charlotte, NC 28202
Webmaster@Chiquita.com

Tel: (980) 636-5000

Christie Strategy Group

Contract lobbying firm.
christiestrategygroup.com
Industry/ies: Business

President
CHRISTIE, Martin
mchristie@christiestrategygroup.com

Tel: (334) 264-0508
Fax: (334) 262-0889

Main Headquarters
Mailing: 445 Dexter Ave.
Suite 4025
Montgomery, AL 36104

Tel: (334) 264-0508
Fax: (334) 262-0889

Public Affairs and Related Activities Personnel

At Headquarters

WALKER, Maeci Martin
Manager, Public Affairs
mmartin@ChristieStrategyGroup.com

Tel: (334) 264-0598
Fax: (334) 262-0889

CHRISTUS Spohn Health System Corporation

A Catholic-related Health system providing healthcare including cardiac care, clinical excellence and oncology in South Texas.
www.christusspohn.org
Employees: 30,000
Industry/ies: Medicine/Health Care/Mental Health

Chairman of the Board
DONNELL, Ben

Tel: (361) 881-3000
Fax: (361) 883-6478

President and Chief Executive Officer
ROBERTSON, Pamela S.

Tel: (361) 881-3000
Fax: (361) 883-6478

Main Headquarters
Mailing: 1702 Santa Fe
Corpus Christi, TX 78404

Tel: (361) 881-3000
Fax: (361) 883-6478

Corporate Foundations and Giving Programs
CHRISTUS Spohn Health System Foundation
Contact: Karen Bonner

600 Elizabeth St.
Corpus Christi, TX 78404

Tel: (361) 881-3533

Public Affairs and Related Activities Personnel

At Headquarters

BROWER, FHFMA, CPA, Pamela L.
Chief Financial Officer

Tel: (361) 881-3000
Fax: (361) 883-6478

ELKINS, MPH, Kelly
Chief Administrative Officer

Tel: (361) 881-3000
Fax: (361) 883-6478

LAFRANCOIS, SPHR, Mary
Vice President, Human Resources

Tel: (361) 881-3000
Fax: (361) 883-6478

MCHUGH, Colleen
Vice President, Compliance, Risk Management and Privacy Officer

Tel: (361) 881-3000
Fax: (361) 883-6478

At Other Offices

BONNER, Karen
Vice President, Philanthropy for CHRISTUS Spohn Health System Foundation
600 Elizabeth St.
Corpus Christi, TX 78404
Karen.Bonner@christushealth.org

Tel: (361) 881-3533
Fax: (361) 884-7276

Chromalloy Gas Turbine Corporation

Global technology company provides coatings, repairs and parts for gas turbine engines.
www.chromalloy.com
Industry/ies: Aerospace/Aviation; Machinery/Equipment; Metals; Natural Resources; Transportation

President
LUZZATTO, Carlo

Tel: (845) 359-4700

Main Headquarters
Mailing: 330 Blaisdell Rd.
Organgeburg, NY 10962

Tel: (845) 359-4700

Political Action Committees
Sequa Corporation/Chromalloy Gas Turbine Corporation PAC
FEC ID: C00235911
Contact: Craig Haines
300 Blaisdell Rd
P.O. Box 200150
Orangeburg, NY 10962

Contributions to Candidates: $5,000 (2015-2016)
Democrats: $5,000

Public Affairs and Related Activities Personnel

At Headquarters

ANDERSON, Scott
Vice President, Business and Financial Processes

Tel: (845) 359-4700

BOLLMAN, John
Vice President, Human Resources

Tel: (845) 359-4700

FARRANT, Andrew
Vice President, Marketing, Strategy and Communications
afarrant@chromalloy.com

Tel: (845) 359-4700

HAINES, Craig
PAC Contact

Tel: (845) 359-4700

LOWSON, Steven R.
Vice President, General Counsel and Corporate Secretary

Tel: (845) 359-4700

SHAMBAUGH, Bob
Chief Operations Officer

Tel: (845) 359-4700

CHS, Inc.

Formerly CENEX, Inc. The forerunner of CHS Inc, Cenex Harvest States, was formed in 1998 by a merger between two regional cooperatives, Cenex, Inc. and Harvest States Cooperatives.An energy, grains and foods company that also operates petroleum refineries/ pipelines and manufactures, markets and distributes Cenex® brand refined fuels, lubricants, propane and renewable energy products.
www.chsinc.com
Annual Revenues: $39.81 billion
Employees: 10,453
Ticker: NASDAQ: CHSCP
SIC: 5150
Industry/ies: Agriculture/Agronomy; Fuels See Coal, Gas, Oil, Petroleum; Natural Resources; Petroleum Industry
Legislative Issues: AGR; BUD; CAW; CSP; FOO; INS; TRD; VET

Chairman of the Board
BIELENBERG, David

Tel: (651) 355-6000
Fax: (651) 355-6432

President and Chief Executive Officer
CASALE, Carl

Tel: (651) 355-6000
Fax: (651) 355-6432

Main Headquarters
Mailing: 5500 Cenex Dr.
Inver Grove Heights, MN 55077

Tel: (651) 355-6000
Fax: (651) 355-6432
TF: (800) 232-3639

Washington Office

Mailing: 1235 S. Clark St.
Suite 505
Arlington, VA 22202

Tel: (703) 413-9620
Fax: (703) 413-9626

Political Action Committees
CHS Inc. PAC
FEC ID: C00149104
Contact: John Engelen
5500 Cenex Dr.
Inver Grove Heights, MN 55077

Contributions to Candidates: $131,500 (2015-2016)
Democrats: $25,500; Republicans: $106,000

Corporate Foundations and Giving Programs

CHS Foundation
5500 Cenex Dr.
Inver Grove Heights, MN 55077

Tel: (651) 355-6000
Fax: (651) 355-5073

Public Affairs and Related Activities Personnel

At Headquarters

BAREKSTEN, Jim
Director, Governmental Affairs

Tel: (651) 355-6000
Fax: (651) 355-6432

COBB, David
Specialist, Federal Affairs
David.Cobb@chsinc.com
Registered Federal Lobbyist

Tel: (651) 355-6000
Fax: (651) 355-6432

CUNNINGHAM, Shirley
Executive Vice President and Chief Operating Officer, Enterprise Strategy

Tel: (651) 355-6000
Fax: (651) 355-6432

DEBERTIN, Jay
Executive Vice President and Chief Operating Officer, Energy and Foods

Tel: (651) 355-6000
Fax: (651) 355-6432

ENGELEN, John
Vice President, Government Affairs
John.Engelen@chsinc.com
Registered Federal Lobbyist

Tel: (651) 355-6000
Fax: (651) 355-6432

GALLO, Sarah
Contact, Government Relations
Registered Federal Lobbyist

Tel: (651) 355-6000
Fax: (651) 355-6432

HENGSTLER, Nancy

Tel: (651) 355-6000
Fax: (651) 355-6432

JORDAN, Lani
Director, Corporate Communications
lani.jordan@chsinc.com

Tel: (651) 355-4946
Fax: (651) 355-6432

SKIDMORE, Timothy
Executive Vice President and Chief Financial Officer

Tel: (651) 355-6000
Fax: (651) 355-6432

ZAPPA, Jim
Executive Vice President and General Counsel

Tel: (651) 355-6000
Fax: (651) 355-6432

ZELL , Lisa
Executive Vice President, Business Solutions
lisa.zell@chsinc.com

Tel: (651) 355-6000
Fax: (651) 355-6432

At Washington Office

HAMLIN, Jake
Director, State Government Affairs

Tel: (703) 413-9620
Fax: (703) 413-9626

Chugach Alaska Corporation

The company derives the bulk of its sales from oil and gas production, mining, commercial timber and tourist activities that occur in the region.
www.chugach-ak.com
Annual Revenues: $936.98 million
Employees: 6,000
Industry/ies: Fish And Fishing; Minorities
Legislative Issues: BUD; DEF; IND; TAX; TRA

Chairman of the Board
BURETTA, Sheri D.
sburetta@chugach-ak.com

Tel: (907) 563-8866
Fax: (907) 563-8402

Chief Executive Officer, PAC Treasurer
KOMPKOFF, Gabriel

Tel: (907) 563-8866
Fax: (907) 563-8402

Main Headquarters
Mailing: 3800 Centerpoint Dr.
Suite 700
Anchorage, AK 99503

Tel: (907) 563-8866
Fax: (907) 563-8402
TF: (800) 858-2768

Corporate Foundations and Giving Programs

Chugach Heritage Foundation
Contact: Stephen Grantier
3800 Centerpoint Dr.
Suite 601
Anchorage, AK 99503

Tel: (907) 563-8866
Fax: (907) 563-8402

Public Affairs and Related Activities Personnel

At Headquarters

ASTLE, Angela
Executive Vice President, Finance

Tel: (907) 563-8866
Fax: (907) 563-8402

FORREST, Gail	Tel:	(907) 563-8866
Executive Vice President, Administration	Fax:	(907) 563-8402
GAUSE, Randi Jo	Tel:	(907) 563-8866
Senior Manager, Corporate Communications	Fax:	(907) 563-8402
GRANTIER, Stephen	Tel:	(907) 563-8866
Contact, Chugach Heritage Foundation	Fax:	(907) 550-4147
stephen.grantier@chugach-ak.com		
OSBORNE, Melanie	Tel:	(907) 563-8866
Executive Vice President, General Counsel and Chief Compliance Officer	Fax:	(907) 563-8402
PETERS, Sarah	Tel:	(907) 563-8866
Administrative Supervisor, Human Resources	Fax:	(907) 563-8402

Church and Dwight Company, Inc.

Household consumer products, animal nutrition products, and sodium bicarbonate.
www.churchdwight.com
Annual Revenues: $3.43 billion
Employees: 4,406
Ticker: NYSE: CHD
SIC: 2840
Industry/ies: Chemicals & Chemical Industry

Chairman	Tel:	(609) 683-5900
CRAIGIE, James R.		
President and Chief Executive Officer	Tel:	(609) 683-5900
FARRELL , Matthew T.		

Main Headquarters

Mailing: Princeton South Corporate Center	Tel:	(609) 683-5900
500 Charles Ewing Blvd.	TF:	(800) 833-9532
Princeton, NJ 08628		

Corporate Foundations and Giving Programs

The Church and Dwight Employee Giving Fund		
469 N. Harrison St.	Tel:	(609) 683-5900
Princeton, NJ 08543		

Public Affairs and Related Activities Personnel

At Headquarters

BOMHARD, Britta	Tel:	(609) 683-5900
Executive Vice President, Chief Marketing Officer		
BROVA, Jacquelin J.	Tel:	(609) 683-5900
Executive Vice President, Human Resources		
CONISH, Mark G.	Tel:	(609) 683-5900
Executive Vice President, Global Operations		
DIERKER, Rick	Tel:	(609) 683-5900
Executive Vice President and Chief Financial Officer		
FLEMING, Bruce F.	Tel:	(609) 683-5900
Executive Vice President and Chief Marketing Officer		
LEVINE, Jim	Tel:	(609) 683-5900
Global Human Resources		
MAYNADIER, Patrick de	Tel:	(609) 683-5900
Executive Vice President, General Counsel and Secretary		

Churchill Downs, Inc.

Owner and operator of horse racing venues throughout the United States, including the Kentucky Derby.
www.churchilldownsincorporated.com
Annual Revenues: $1.25 billion
Employees: 4,530
Ticker: NASDAQ: CHDN
SIC: 7948
Industry/ies: Animals; Sports/Leisure/Entertainment
Legislative Issues: BUD; GAM

Chairman of the Board	Tel:	(502) 636-4400
EVANS, Robert L.		
Chief Executive Officer		
CARSTANJEN, William C.		

Main Headquarters

Mailing: 600 N. Hurstbourne Pkwy.	Tel:	(502) 636-4400
Suite 400		
Louisville, KY 40222		

Political Action Committees

Churchill Downs Inc. FPAC
FEC ID: C00331942
Contact: Ekumene M. Lysonge
600 N. Hurstbourne Pkwy.
Suite 400
Louisville, KY 40208

Corporate Foundations and Giving Programs

Churchill Downs Foundation		
Contact: Lauren Depaso		
700 Central Ave.	Tel:	(502) 636-4400

Louisville, KY 40208	Fax:	(502) 636-4430

Public Affairs and Related Activities Personnel

At Headquarters

DEPASO, Lauren	Tel:	(502) 636-4400
Director, Community Relations		
MUDD, William E.	Tel:	(502) 636-4400
President and Chief Operating Officer		
THELAN, Paul J.	Tel:	(502) 636-4400
President		

At Other Offices

LYSONGE, Ekumene M.
PAC Contact
600 N. Hurstbourne Pkwy., Suite 400
Louisville, KY 40208

Ciba Corporation

Formerly CIBA Speciality Chemicals. Subsidiary of BASF.
www.ciba.com
Industry/ies: Chemicals & Chemical Industry

Main Headquarters

Mailing: 540 White Plains Rd.	Tel:	(914) 785-4494
Tarrytown, NY 10591		

Public Affairs and Related Activities Personnel

At Headquarters

LIVOLI, Vincent	Tel:	(914) 785-4494
Director, Government Relations		
vincent.livoti@ciba.com		

Ciber, Inc.

Provides consulting services for internet strategy and development.
www.ciber.com
Annual Revenues: $847.60 million
Employees: 6,500
Ticker: NYSE: CBR
SIC: 7371
Industry/ies: Computer/Technology
Legislative Issues: DOC

Chief Executive Officer	Tel:	(303) 220-0100
BOUSTRIDGE, Michael	Fax:	(303) 220-7100

Main Headquarters

Mailing: 6363 S. Fiddler's Green Cir.	Tel:	(303) 220-0100
Suite 1400	Fax:	(303) 220-7100
Greenwood Village, CO 80111	TF:	(800) 242-3799

Corporate Foundations and Giving Programs

Ciber Contribution Program		
Contact: Robin Caputo		
6363 S. Fiddler's Green Cir.	Tel:	(303) 220-0100
Suite 1400	Fax:	(303) 220-7100
Greenwood Village, CO 80111		

Public Affairs and Related Activities Personnel

At Headquarters

MEZGER, Christian	Tel:	(303) 267-3857
Chief Financial Officer	Fax:	(303) 220-7100
cmezger@ciber.com		
PIERMARINI, Tina	Tel:	(303) 220-0100
Executive Vice President and Chief Administrative Officer	Fax:	(303) 220-7100
PLISKO, David	Tel:	(303) 220-0100
Vice President, Employee Services	Fax:	(303) 220-7100
RADCLIFFE, M. Sean	Tel:	(303) 220-0100
Senior Vice President, General Counsel and Corporate Secretary	Fax:	(303) 220-7100

Ciena Corporation

The company makes transport and switching equipment that increases the capacity of long-distance fiber-optic networks by transmitting multiple light signals simultaneously over the same circuit. It also sells optical transport systems for metro and enterprise wide-area networks, as well as broadband access products that enable communications companies to deliver Internet protocol (IP) services, such as VoIP, IP video, and DSL.
www.ciena.com
Annual Revenues: $2.35 billion
Employees: 5,108
Ticker: NASDAQ: CIEN
SIC: 3661
Industry/ies: Communications; Telecommunications/Internet/Cable
Legislative Issues: DEF; HOM; SCI; TEC; TRD

Executive Chairman of the Board of Directors	Tel:	(410) 694-5700
NETTLES, PhD, Patrick H.	Fax:	(410) 694-5750
President, Chief Executive Officer and Director	Tel:	(410) 694-5700
SMITH, Gary B.	Fax:	(410) 694-5750

Main Headquarters

Mailing: 7035 Ridge Rd. Tel: (410) 694-5700
 Hanover, MD 21076 Fax: (410) 694-5750
  TF: (800) 921-1144

Corporate Foundations and Giving Programs

Ciena's Habitat for Humanity Update
1201 Winterson Rd.
Linthicum, MD 21090

Public Affairs and Related Activities Personnel

At Headquarters

ANDERSON, Nicole Tel: (410) 694-5700
Contact, Media Relations Fax: (410) 694-5750
pr@ciena.com

COOPER, Douglas C. Tel: (202) 256-8550
Vice President, Regulatory and Market Development Fax: (410) 694-5750
dcooper@ciena.com

DODD, Rick Tel: (410) 694-5700
Senior Vice President, Global Marketing Fax: (410) 694-5750

FRODSHAM, James Tel: (410) 694-5700
Senior Vice President and Chief Strategy Officer Fax: (410) 694-5750

HOBBS, Jane Tel: (410) 694-5700
Senior Vice President, Human Resources Fax: (410) 694-5750

LAMPF, Gregg Tel: (410) 694-5700
Vice President, Investor Relations Fax: (410) 694-5750

MOCK, Thomas Tel: (410) 694-5700
Senior Vice President, Corporate Communications Fax: (410) 694-5750

MOODY, Jamie Tel: (410) 694-5700
Contact, Media Relations Fax: (410) 694-5750
pr@ciena.com

MOYLAN, Jr., James E. Tel: (410) 694-5700
Senior Vice President, Finance and Chief Financial Officer Fax: (410) 694-5750

NACHBAR, David Tel: (410) 694-5700
Chief Human Resources Officer Fax: (410) 694-5750

PETRIK, Andrew Tel: (410) 694-5700
Vice President and Controller Fax: (410) 694-5750

ROTHENSTEIN, David M. Tel: (410) 694-5700
Senior Vice President, General Counsel and Secretary Fax: (410) 694-5750

STARKE, Marcus Tel: (410) 694-5700
Senior Vice President and Chief Marketing Officer Fax: (410) 694-5750

Cigar Rights of America

Manufacture, distribution and sale of premium cigars.
www.cigarrights.org
Industry/ies: Tobacco Industry
Legislative Issues: TAX; TOB

Executive Director Tel: (800) 460-0729
LOOPE, J. Glynn Fax: (800) 460-6207

Main Headquarters

Mailing: 500-B N. Congress Ave.
 Evansville, IN 47715

Washington Office

Mailing: 300 New Jersey Ave. NW Tel: (800) 460-0729
 Suite 900 Fax: (800) 460-6207
 Washington, DC 20001 TF: (800) 460-0729

Public Affairs and Related Activities Personnel

At Washington Office

CARDIN, Cody Tel: (800) 460-0729
Registered Federal Lobbyist Fax: (800) 460-6207

COPPERMAN, Michael Tel: (800) 460-0729
Legislative Director Fax: (800) 460-6207
mikecopperman@gmail.com
Registered Federal Lobbyist

At Other Offices

BERMAN, Brian Tel: (800) 460-0729
Contact, Media Relations
5105 E. Los Angeles Ave., Suite 155
Simi Valley, CA 93063

Cigarworld.com

See listing on page 353 under General Cigar Holdings, Inc.

CIGNA Corporation

A major healthcare and related financial services company formed by the merger of Connecticut General Life Insurance Company and INA in 1982.
www.cigna.com
Annual Revenues: $38.29 billion
Employees: 39,000
Ticker: NYSE: CI
SIC: 6324

Industry/ies: Insurance Industry
Legislative Issues: HCR; HOM; INS; LBR; MMM; TAX; TRD

President and Chief Executive Officer Tel: (215) 761-1000
CORDANI, David Fax: (215) 761-3596

Main Headquarters

Mailing: Two Liberty Pl. Tel: (215) 761-1000
 1601 Chestnut St. Fax: (215) 761-3596
 Philadelphia, PA 19192

Washington Office

Mailing: 601 Pennsylvania Ave. NW Tel: (202) 861-1451
 Suite 500, South Bldg. Fax: (202) 861-6363
 Washington, DC 20004

Political Action Committees

CIGNA Corporation PAC
FEC ID: C00085316
Contact: Kristin Julason Damato
601 Pennsylvania Ave. NW
South Bldg., Suite 835
Washington, DC 20004

Contributions to Candidates: $353,075 (2015-2016)
 Democrats: $142,200; Republicans: $209,875; Other: $1,000

Principal Recipients

SENATE
BLUNT, ROY (REP-MO)
YOUNG, TODD CHRISTOPHER (REP-IN)

HOUSE
MEEHAN, PATRICK L. MR. (REP-PA)
NUNES, DEVIN G (REP-CA)
SCALISE, STEVE MR. (REP-LA)

Corporate Foundations and Giving Programs

CIGNA Foundation
Contact: Gianna Jackson
Two Liberty Pl. Tel: (215) 761-1000
1601 Chestnut St. Fax: (215) 761-5515
Philadelphia, PA 19192

Public Affairs and Related Activities Personnel

At Headquarters

BACUS, Lisa R. Tel: (215) 761-1000
Executive Vice President and Global Chief Marketing Officer Fax: (215) 761-3596

BARONE, Gloria Tel: (215) 761-4758
Contact, Media Relations Fax: (215) 761-3596
gloria.barone@cigna.com

MCCARTHY, Thomas A. Tel: (215) 761-1000
Executive Vice President and Chief Financial Officer Fax: (215) 761-3596

MURABITO, John M. Tel: (215) 761-1000
Executive Vice President, Human Resources and Services Fax: (215) 761-3596

PETREN, Carol Ann Tel: (215) 761-1000
Executive Vice President and General Counsel Fax: (215) 761-3596

At Washington Office

DAMATO, Kristin Julason Tel: (202) 861-1451
Federal Lobbyist and PAC Treasurer Fax: (202) 861-6363
cignapac@cigna.com
Registered Federal Lobbyist

SCHWARTZ, David C. Tel: (202) 861-1451
Registered Federal Lobbyist Fax: (202) 861-6363

At Other Offices

CANINO, Jill Fax: (202) 861-6363
Federal Lobbyist
601 Pennsylvania Ave. NW, Suite 835 South Bldg.
Washington, DC 20004
Registered Federal Lobbyist

DEVINE, Brendan Fax: (202) 861-6363
Federal Lobbyist
601 Pennsylvania Ave. NW, Suite 835 South Bldg.
Washington, DC 20004
Registered Federal Lobbyist

JONES, Nicole
Executive Vice President and General Counsel
900 Cottage Grove Rd.
Bloomfield, CT 06002

MERSKI, Rich P. Fax: (202) 861-6363
Federal Lobbyist
601 Pennsylvania Ave. NW, Suite 835 South Bldg.
Washington, DC 20004
Registered Federal Lobbyist

NONNEMAKER, Karen Lynn Fax: (202) 861-6363
601 Pennsylvania Ave. NW, Suite 835 South Bldg.
Washington, DC 20004
Registered Federal Lobbyist

ZETTLE, Amy
Federal Lobbyist
601 Pennsylvania Ave. NW, Suite 835 South Bldg.
Washington, DC 20004
Registered Federal Lobbyist

Fax: (202) 861-6363

Cincinnati Bell Telephone

Formerly part of Broadwing Communications. An integrated provider of advanced local, long distance, directory, wireless, Internet, and broadband communications services and equipment to residents and businesses.
www.cincinnatibell.com
Annual Revenues: $1.29 billion
Employees: 3,100
Ticker: NYSE: CBB
SIC: 4813
Industry/ies: Communications; Telecommunications/Internet/Cable
Legislative Issues: TEC

Chairman of the Board
COX, Phillip R.

Tel: (513) 397-9900
Fax: (513) 397-5092

President and Chief Executive Officer
TORBECK, Theodore H.

Tel: (513) 397-9900
Fax: (513) 397-5092

Main Headquarters
Mailing: 221 E. Fourth St.
             Cincinnati, OH 45202

Tel: (513) 397-9900
Fax: (513) 397-5092

Political Action Committees
Cincinnati Bell Inc. Federal PAC
FEC ID: C00087478
Contact: Christopher C. Elma
221 E. Fourth St.
Cincinnati, OH 45202

> **Contributions to Candidates:** $9,000 (2015-2016)
> Democrats: $500; Republicans: $8,500

Corporate Foundations and Giving Programs
Cincinnati Bell Telephone Contributions Program
221 E. Fourth St.
Cincinnati, OH 45202

Public Affairs and Related Activities Personnel

At Headquarters

DUCKWORTH, Joshua
Vice President, Investor Relations and Controller
joshua.duckworth@cinbell.com

Tel: (513) 397-2292
Fax: (513) 397-5092

ELMA, Christopher C.
Vice President, Treasury and Tax

Tel: (513) 397-9900
Fax: (513) 397-5092

FOX, Leigh R.
Chief Financial Officer

Tel: (513) 397-9900
Fax: (513) 397-5092

HECKMANN, Ted
Contact, Government Relations
ted.heckmann@cinbell.com

Tel: (513) 397-1375
Fax: (513) 397-5092

PICHLER, Josh
Senior Manager, Communications and Media Relations
josh.pichler@cinbell.com

Tel: (513) 565-0310
Fax: (513) 397-5092

RUPICH, Patricia L.
Contact, Federal Regulatory Issues
pat.rupich@cinbell.com

Tel: (513) 397-6671
Fax: (513) 397-5092

WILSON, Christopher J.
Vice President and General Counsel

Tel: (513) 397-9900
Fax: (513) 397-5092

Cincinnati Financial Group

Provider of life and disability income insurance and annuities.
www.cinfin.com
Annual Revenues: $5.22 billion
Employees: 4,493
Ticker: NASDAQ: CINF
SIC: 6331
Industry/ies: Banking/Finance/Investments
Legislative Issues: CPT; INS; MMM; TAX

Chairman of the Board
STECHER, Kenneth W.

Tel: (513) 870-2000
Fax: (513) 870-2911

President and Chief Executive Officer
JOHNSTON, CFA, MAAA, Steven J.

Tel: (513) 870-2000
Fax: (513) 870-2911

Main Headquarters
Mailing: P.O. Box 145496
             Cincinnati, OH 45250-5496

Tel: (513) 870-2000
Fax: (513) 870-2911
TF: (888) 242-8811

Public Affairs and Related Activities Personnel

At Headquarters

ERTEL, Betsy
Vice President, Corporate Communications
media_inquiries@cinfin.com

Tel: (513) 870-2000
Fax: (513) 870-2911

GILLIAM, Scott A.
Vice President and Government Relations Officer
scott_gilliam@cinfin.com
Registered Federal Lobbyist

Tel: (513) 870-2811
Fax: (513) 881-8988

HOLLENBECK, CFA, CPCU, Martin H.
Chief Investment Officer, Senior Vice President, Assistant Secretary and Assistant Treasurer

Tel: (513) 870-2000
Fax: (513) 870-2911

LOVE, Lisa A.
Senior Vice President, General Counsel and Corporate Secretary

Tel: (513) 870-2000
Fax: (513) 870-2911

MCDANIEL, Dennis E.
Vice President, Investor Relations
investor_inquiries@cinfin.com

Tel: (513) 870-2768
Fax: (513) 870-2911

SEWELL, Michael J.
Chief Financial Officer, Senior Vice President and Treasurer
mike_sewell@cinfin.com

Tel: (513) 870-2000
Fax: (513) 870-2911

ZIEGLER, Gregory J.
Vice President and Director, Personnel and Community Relations

Tel: (513) 870-2000
Fax: (513) 870-2911

Cincinnati Milacron Inc.

See listing on page 541 under Milacron, Inc.

Circadence Corporation

Produces WARP (Web Assured Response Protocol) technology in a network centric space.
www.circadence.com
Annual Revenues: $13 million
Employees: 35
Industry/ies: Computer/Technology
Legislative Issues: DEF

Chairman of the Board
ANDREASSEN, Dr. Alf

Tel: (303) 413-8800
Fax: (303) 449-7099

Chief Executive Officer
MONIZ, Michael J.
mike@circadence.com

Tel: (303) 413-8800
Fax: (303) 449-7099

Main Headquarters
Mailing: 1011 Walnut St.
             Suite 400
             Boulder, CO 80302

Tel: (303) 413-8800
Fax: (303) 449-7099

Washington Office
Mailing: 6715 Whittier Ave.
             Third floor
             McLean, VA 22101

Tel: (303) 809-9981

Public Affairs and Related Activities Personnel

At Headquarters

BLISARD, Christopher T.
Chief Operating Officer

Tel: (303) 413-8800
Fax: (303) 449-7099

KANNEGIETER, Todd L.
Vice President, Finance

Tel: (303) 413-8800
Fax: (303) 449-7099

KELLNHOFER, Sarah
Office Manager & Executive Assistant
sarah@circadence.com

Tel: (303) 413-8800
Fax: (303) 449-7099

OLIVO, Peter-Christian
Executive Vice President and General Counsel
polivo@circadence.com

Tel: (303) 413-8800
Fax: (303) 449-7099

PREWITT, Bradley R.
Vice President, Government Relations and Mississippi Operations
brad@circadence.com

Tel: (303) 413-8800
Fax: (303) 449-7099

Circle P Investments of New Mexico, LLC

Formerly known as The Peters Corporation.
www.peterscorporation.com
Industry/ies: Art/Art Museums; Arts, The; Banking/Finance/Investments

Main Headquarters
Mailing: P.O. Box 30528
             Columbus, OH 43230

Tel: (614) 418-0922
Fax: (614) 418-0822

Public Affairs and Related Activities Personnel

At Other Offices

GREENLAW RAMOMAS, Denise
Chief of Staff
P.O. Box 908
Santa Fe, NM 87504

Tel: (202) 255-1406

Circor International, Inc.

Designs, manufactures and supplies valves and and other highly engineered products and sub-systems used in the energy, aerospace and industrial markets.
www.circor.com
Annual Revenues: $641.21 million
Employees: 2,500

Ticker: NYSE: CIR
SIC: 3490
Industry/ies: Machinery/Equipment
Legislative Issues: DEF

President and Chief Executive Officer
BUCKHOUT, Scott A.
Tel: (781) 270-1200
Fax: (781) 270-1299

Main Headquarters
Mailing: 30 Corporate Dr.
Suite 200
Burlington, MA 01803-4232
Tel: (781) 270-1200
Fax: (781) 270-1299

Public Affairs and Related Activities Personnel

At Headquarters

BHALLA, Rajeev
Executive Vice President and Chief Financial Officer
Tel: (781) 270-1210
Fax: (781) 270-1299

FARNSWORTH, Andrew
Chief Human Resources Officer
Tel: (781) 270-1200
Fax: (781) 270-1299

SHARMA, Arjun "AJ"
Vice President, Business Development
Tel: (781) 270-1200
Fax: (781) 270-1299

Cirrus Logic, Inc.

Cirrus Logic is expertise in developing high-precision analog and mixed-signal integrated circuits (ICs) for a broad range of consumer and industrial markets.
www.cirrus.com
Annual Revenues: $916.57 million
Employees: 1,104
Ticker: NASDAQ: CRUS
SIC: 3674; 3663; 3699; 3825
NAICS: 334413; 334515; 335999
Industry/ies: Communications; Telecommunications/Internet/Cable

Chairman of the Board
HACKWORTH, Michael L.
Tel: (512) 851-4000
Fax: (512) 851-4977

President and Chief Executive Officer
RHODE, Jason
Tel: (512) 851-4000
Fax: (512) 851-4977

Main Headquarters
Mailing: 800 W. 6th St.
Austin, TX 78701
Tel: (512) 851-4000
Fax: (800) 888-5016

Public Affairs and Related Activities Personnel

At Other Offices

BENSON, Jo-Dee M.
Vice President, Corporate Communications and Human Resources
2901 Via Fortuna
Austin, TX 78746
jodee.benson@cirrus.com
Tel: (512) 851-4653
Fax: (512) 851-4977

BRANNAN, Andy
Vice President Worldwide Sales
2901 Via Fortuna
Austin, TX 78746
Tel: (512) 851-4000
Fax: (512) 851-4977

CASE, Thurman K.
Chief Financial Officer, Vice President of Finance and Treasurer
2901 Via Fortuna
Austin, TX 78746
Tel: (512) 851-4125
Fax: (512) 851-4977

SCHNELL, Bill
Manager, Public Relations
2901 Via Fortuna
Austin, TX 78746
bill.schnell@cirrus.com
Tel: (512) 851-4084
Fax: (512) 851-4977

THOMAS, Gregory Scott
Vice President, General Counsel and Corporate Secretary
2901 Via Fortuna
Austin, TX 78746
Tel: (512) 851-4000
Fax: (512) 851-4977

Cisco Systems Inc.

Manufactures end-to-end networking equipment to build a unified information infrastructure.
www.cisco.com
Annual Revenues: $48.68 billion
Employees: 70,942
Ticker: NASDAQ: CSCO
SIC: 3669; 3625; 3663; 3679
NAICS: 334419; 335314; 33429; 33422
Industry/ies: Communications; Computer/Technology; Telecommunications/Internet/Cable
Legislative Issues: CPI; CPT; CSP; HOM; IMM; INT; LAW; TAX; TEC; TRD

Chairman and Chief Executive Officer
CHAMBERS, John T.
Tel: (408) 536-4000
Fax: (408) 526-4100

Main Headquarters
Mailing: 170 W. Tasman Dr.
San Jose, CA 95134
Tel: (408) 526-4000
Fax: (408) 526-4100
TF: (800) 553-6387

Washington Office
Mailing: 1300 Pennsylvania Ave. NW
Suite 250
Washington, DC 20004
Tel: (202) 354-2904

Political Action Committees
Cisco Systems Inc. Federal PAC
FEC ID: C00362707
Contact: Rebecca Olson
400 Capital Mall
Suite 1545
Sacramento, CA 95814

Contributions to Candidates: $230,500 (2015-2016)
Democrats: $147,500; Republicans: $83,000

Principal Recipients

HOUSE
ESHOO, ANNA G. (DEM-CA)
LOFGREN, ZOE (DEM-CA)

Corporate Foundations and Giving Programs
Cisco Systems Foundation
Contact: Tae Yoo
170 W. Tasman Dr.
Bldg. Ten
San Jose, CA 95134
Tel: (408) 526-7659
Fax: (408) 526-6310

Public Affairs and Related Activities Personnel

At Headquarters

CALDERONI, Frank
Executive Vice President and Chief Financial Officer
Tel: (408) 526-4000
Fax: (408) 526-4100

CHANDLER, Mark
Senior Vice President, General Counsel, Secretary and Chief Compliance Officer
Tel: (408) 526-4000
Fax: (408) 526-4100

CHRISTIE, Blair
Senior Vice President and Chief Marketing Officer
Tel: (408) 536-4000
Fax: (408) 526-4100

EARNHARDT, John
Director, Corporate Communications
john.earnhardt@cisco.com
Tel: (408) 526-4000
Fax: (408) 526-4100

MOORE, Gary
President and Chief Operating Officer
Tel: (408) 526-4000
Fax: (408) 526-4100

WESLOCK, Kathleen
Senior Vice President and Chief Human Resources Officer
Tel: (408) 526-4000
Fax: (408) 526-4100

YOO, Tae
Senior Vice President, Corporate Affairs
Tel: (408) 526-7659
Fax: (408) 526-6310

At Washington Office

RAYDER, Ian
Senior Manager, Government Affairs
Registered Federal Lobbyist
Tel: (202) 354-2904

TIMMENY, Michael
Vice President, Corporate Government Affairs
mtimmeny@cisco.com
Registered Federal Lobbyist
Tel: (202) 354-2904

At Other Offices

BROWN, Mary
Director, Government Affairs
601 Pennsylvania Ave. NW, Suite 900, North Building
Washington, DC 20004
marybrow@cisco.com
Registered Federal Lobbyist
Tel: (202) 661-4040

CAMPBELL, Jeffrey
Director, Technology Policy
601 Pennsylvania Ave. NW, Suite 900, North Building
Washington, DC 20004
Registered Federal Lobbyist
Tel: (202) 661-4040

ERIC, Wenger
601 Pennsylvania Ave. NW, Suite 900, North Building
Washington, DC 20004
Registered Federal Lobbyist
Tel: (202) 661-4040

KAUNE, Jason D.
Attorney & Agent for Filer
601 Pennsylvania Ave. NW, Suite 900, North Building
Washington, DC 20004
Tel: (202) 661-4040

OLSON, Rebecca
PAC Treasurer, Lobbyist
400 Capitol Mall, Suite 1545
Sacramento, CA 95814

PESSNER, Kirk Alan
PAC Treasurer
400 Capitol Mall, Suite 1545
Sacramento, CA 95814

REDIFER, Paul
Director, Government Affairs
601 Pennsylvania Ave. NW, Suite 900, North Building
Tel: (202) 661-4040

Washington, DC 20004
predifer@cisco.com
Registered Federal Lobbyist

SANFORD, Jennifer   Tel: (202) 661-4040
Senior Manager, Global Policy and Government Affairs
601 Pennsylvania Ave. NW, Suite 900, North Building
Washington, DC 20004
jennsanf@cisco.com
Registered Federal Lobbyist

WENGER, Eric   Tel: (202) 661-4040
*Director, Cybersecurity and Privacy Policy, Global
Government Affairs*
601 Pennsylvania Ave. NW, Suite 900, North Building
Washington, DC 20004
Registered Federal Lobbyist

CIT Group, Inc.

Offers commercial and consumer financing solutions.
www.cit.com
Annual Revenues: $2.58 billion
Employees: 3,360
Ticker: NYSE: CIT
SIC: 6172
Industry/ies: Banking/Finance/Investments
Legislative Issues: BAN; FIN; TAX

Chairman of the Board and Chief Executive Officer   Tel: (212) 461-5200
THAIN, John A.

Co-Head and President, Corporate Finance   Tel: (212) 461-5200
CONNOLLY, Peter

Main Headquarters
Mailing: 11 W. 42nd St.   Tel: (212) 461-5200
         New York City, NY 10036

Washington Office
Mailing: 500 New Jersey Ave. NW   Tel: (202) 756-3010
         Suite 350
         Washington, DC 20001

Political Action Committees
CIT Group Inc. PAC (CIT PAC)
FEC ID: C00379420
Contact: Israel Kaufman
One CIT Dr.
Suite 2223-1
Livingston, NJ 07039

   Contributions to Candidates: $76,000 (2015-2016)
   Democrats: $37,000; Republicans: $39,000

Corporate Foundations and Giving Programs
CIT Group Contribution Program
Contact: Stacy Papas
11 W. 42nd St.   Tel: (212) 461-5200
New York City, NY 10036

Public Affairs and Related Activities Personnel

At Headquarters

ALLEN, Bryan   Tel: (212) 461-5200
Executive Vice President and Chief Human Resources Officer

BRANDMAN, Andrew T.   Tel: (212) 461-5200
Executive Vice President and Chief Administrative Officer

BRAUSE, Kenneth A.   Tel: (212) 461-5200
Director and Executive Vice President, Investor Relations

CALLAHAN, Barbara   Tel: (212) 461-5200
Senior Vice President and Head, Investor Relations

INFANTI, Daniel   Tel: (973) 740-5172
Senior Vice President, Marketing and Advertising
dan.infanti@cit.com

INGATO, Bob   Tel: (212) 461-5200
Executive Vice President, General Counsel and Secretary
robert.ingato@cit.com

KLEIN, Matt   Tel: (973) 597-2020
Vice President, Media Relations

PAPAS, Stacy   Tel: (212) 461-5200
Director, Philanthropy and Community Involvement
Stacy.Papas@cit.com

PARADISI, John P.   Tel: (212) 461-5200
Managing Director, Corporate Development

PARKER, Scott T.   Tel: (212) 461-5200
Executive Vice President and Chief Financial Officer
scott.parker@cit.com

RITTER, C. Curtis   Tel: (973) 740-5390
Director, Corporate Communications
Curt.Ritter@cit.com

SPRINGER , Fred   Tel: (212) 461-5200

*Executive Vice President, Chief Ethics and Compliance
Officer*

TUTWILER, Margaret D.   Tel: (212) 461-5200
*Executive Vice President, Head of Communications and
Government Relations*

ZONINO, Lisa D.   Tel: (212) 461-5200
Executive Vice President and Global Head, Human Resources

At Washington Office

GOLDSTEIN, Lon N.   Tel: (202) 756-3010
Senior Vice President & Director, Government Relations
lon.goldstein@cit.com
Registered Federal Lobbyist

HADDELAND, Karl   Tel: (202) 756-3010
Federal Lobbyist
Karl.Haddeland@CIT.com
Registered Federal Lobbyist

KAUFMAN, Israel   Tel: (202) 756-3010
PAC Contact

CITGO Petroleum Corporation

A petroleum refining and marketing corporation.
www.citgo.com
SIC: 1311
Industry/ies: Fuels See Coal, Gas, Oil, Petroleum; Natural Resources; Petroleum
Industry
Legislative Issues: BUD; ENG; FOR; FUE; TRA

President and Chief Executive Officer   Tel: (832) 486-4000
MARTÍNEZ, Nelson   Fax: (832) 486-1814

Main Headquarters
Mailing: P.O. Box 4689   Tel: (832) 486-4000
         Houston, TX 77210-4689   Fax: (832) 486-1814

Corporate Foundations and Giving Programs
CITGO Petroleum Corporation Contributions Program
P.O. Box 4689
Houston, TX 77210

Public Affairs and Related Activities Personnel

At Headquarters

GARAY, Fernando   Tel: (832) 486-1489
Manager, Public Affairs   Fax: (832) 486-1843
fgaray@citgo.com

HASSEMAN, Dean M.   Tel: (832) 486-4000
General Counsel   Fax: (832) 486-1814

MERCHAN, Darío   Tel: (832) 486-4000
Vice President, Government & Public Affairs   Fax: (832) 486-1814

PARILLI, Orestes   Tel: (832) 486-4000
Vice President, Legal Affairs   Fax: (832) 486-1814

VELÁSQUEZ, Gustavo   Tel: (832) 486-4000
Vice President, Supply & Marketing   Fax: (832) 486-1814
gvelasq@citgo.com

At Other Offices

GOMEZ, Rafael   Tel: (800) 992-4846
*Vice President, Strategic Shareholder Relations, Government
& Public Affairs*
1293 Eldridge Pkwy.
Houston, TX 77077

PEREIRA , Jose   Tel: (800) 992-4846
Vice President, Finance
1293 Eldridge Pkwy.
Houston, TX 77077

Citigroup Inc.

*A financial services company that provides consumers, corporations, governments and
institutions with financial products and services, including consumer banking and credit,
corporate investment banking, insurance, securities brokerage, and asset management. Major
brand names include Citibank, CitiFinancial, Primerica (see separate listing), Citigroup
Global Markets, Inc. (see separate listing), Banamex, and Travelers Life and Annuity. Spun off
Travelers Property Casualty Corp. (see seperate listing) and acquired Golden State Banncorp,
the parent company of California Federal Bank, in 2002. In 2007, Citigroup, Inc. acquired the
Investment Services Division of BISYS.*
www.citigroup.com
Annual Revenues: $$69.06 billion
Employees: 248,000
Ticker: NYSE: C
SIC: 6021
Industry/ies: Banking/Finance/Investments
Legislative Issues: BAN; BUD; FIN; HOU; NAT; TAX; TRD

Main Headquarters
Mailing: 390 Greenwich St.   Tel: (212) 559-1000
         New York, NY 10022

Washington Office

Mailing:	1101 Pennsylvania Ave. NW Suite 1100 Washington, DC 20004	Tel:	(202) 879-6865

Public Affairs and Related Activities Personnel

At Headquarters

DAVIDSON, John P.   Tel: (212) 559-1000
Chief Compliance Officer

GERSPACH, John C.   Tel: (212) 559-1000
Chief Financial Officer
John.C.Gerspach@citi.com

LEAHY, Deirdre   Tel: (212) 559-1000
Vice President, North American Consumer Banking, Public Affairs

MCKINNON, Paul   Tel: (212) 559-1000
Head, Human Resources
Paul.McKinnon@citi.com

SKYLER, Edward   Tel: (212) 559-1000
Executive Vice President, Global Public Affairs
Edward.Skyler@citigroup.com

WEERASINGHE , Rohan   Tel: (212) 559-1000
General Counsel and Corporate Secretary

At Washington Office

CALLAHAN, Don   Tel: (202) 879-6865
Head of Operations and Technology

At Other Offices

OLSEN, Lynnea   Tel: (916) 321-5529
Vice President and Counsel   Fax: (916) 442-7127
1115 11th St., Suite 205
Sacramento, CA 95814
olsenl@citigroup.com

Citigroup Management Corporation

A multinational financial services company.
www.citigroup.com
Employees: 248,000
Ticker: NYSE: C
SIC: 6021
Industry/ies: Banking/Finance/Investments
Legislative Issues: BAN; BUD; FIN; HOU; NAT; TAX; TRD

Chairman of the Board   Tel: (212) 559-1000
O'NEILL, Michael

Chief Executive Officer   Tel: (202) 879-6865
CORBAT, Michael   Fax: (202) 783-4460

Main Headquarters
Mailing: 399 Park Ave.   Tel: (212) 559-1000
New York City, NY 10022   TF: (800) 285-3000

Washington Office
Mailing: 1101 Pennsylvania Ave. NW   Tel: (202) 879-6865
Suite 1100
Washington, DC 20004

Political Action Committees
Citigroup PAC - Federal/State
FEC ID: C00039305
1101 Pennsylvania Ave. NW
Suite 1000
Washington, DC 20004

Citigroup PAC-Federal
FEC ID: C00008474
Contact: Mark Monborne
1101 Pennsylvania Ave. NW   Tel: (202) 879-6869
Suite 1000   Fax: (202) 783-4460
Washington, DC 20004

    Contributions to Candidates: $603,747 (2015-2016)
    Democrats: $184,500; Republicans: $418,247; Other: $1,000

Principal Recipients

SENATE
JOHNSON, RONALD HAROLD (REP-)

HOUSE
BOEHNER, JOHN A. (REP-OH)
BOUSTANY, CHARLES W. DR. JR. (REP-LA)
BRADY, KEVIN (REP-TX)
HENSARLING, JEB HON. (REP-TX)
HUIZENGA, WILLIAM P THE HON. (REP-MI)
LOVE, MIA (REP-UT)
MCCARTHY, KEVIN (REP-CA)
MCHENRY, PATRICK TIMOTHY (REP-NC)
TIBERI, PATRICK J. (REP-OH)

Corporate Foundations and Giving Programs

Citigroup Foundation

Contact: Pamela P. Flaherty
399 Park Ave.   Tel: (212) 559-1000
New York City, NY 10043

Public Affairs and Related Activities Personnel

At Headquarters

CALLAHAN, Don   Tel: (212) 559-5091
Head, Operations and Technology

DAVIDSON, John P.   Tel: (212) 559-1000
Chief Compliance Officer

FLAHERTY, Pamela P.   Tel: (212) 559-1000
President and Chief Executive Officer, Citi Foundation

GERSPACH, John C.   Tel: (212) 559-1000
Chief Financial Officer
John.C.Gerspach@citi.com

HU, Bradford   Tel: (212) 559-5091
Chief Risk Officer

SKYLER, Edward   Tel: (212) 559-1000
Executive Vice President, Global Public Affairs
Edward.Skyler@citigroup.com

WEERASINGHE , Rohan   Tel: (212) 559-1000
General Counsel and Corporate Secretary

At Washington Office

CLAMAN, Kimberley   Tel: (202) 879-6865
Senior Vice President, International Government Affairs

EMLING, John   Tel: (202) 879-6865
Head, Federal Government Affairs   Fax: (202) 783-4460

JOHNSON, James   Tel: (202) 879-6865
Director, Federal Government Affairs   Fax: (202) 783-4460

LEAHY, Deirdre   Tel: (202) 879-6865
Vice President, North American Consumer Banking, Public Affairs

MCKINNON, Paul   Tel: (202) 879-6865
Head, Human Resources   Fax: (202) 783-4460
Paul.McKinnon@citi.com

MONBORNE, Mark   Tel: (202) 879-6865
PAC Treasurer   Fax: (202) 783-4460

RUSSELL, Theresa A.   Tel: (202) 879-6865
Citi PAC Federal and State Treasurer   Fax: (202) 783-4460
theresa.a.russell@citigroup.com

RYS, William   Tel: (202) 879-6865
Federal Lobbyist   Fax: (202) 783-4460

SOLHEIM, Kristin   Tel: (202) 879-6865
Senior Democratic Lobbyist   Fax: (202) 783-4460

SOLOMON, Maura K.   Tel: (202) 879-6865
Managing Director, Federal Government Affairs   Fax: (202) 783-4460

THORNELL, Paul N. D.   Tel: (202) 879-6800
Managing Director, Federal Government Affairs   Fax: (202) 783-4460
thornellp@citi.com

WARD, L. Courtney   Tel: (202) 879-6865

WOLFF, Candida Perotti   Tel: (202) 879-6865
Executive Vice President, Citi Global Government Affairs   Fax: (202) 783-4460

WOOSLEY, Maura   Tel: (202) 879-6865
Federal Lobbyist   Fax: (202) 783-4460

At Other Offices

OLSEN, Lynnea   Tel: (916) 321-5529
Vice President and Counsel   Fax: (916) 442-7127
1115 11th St., Suite 205
Sacramento, CA 95814
olsenl@citigroup.com

POLICHENE, Briget   Tel: (317) 283-6269
Vice President Counsel, State Government Relations   Fax: (317) 283-6281
527 W. 46th St.
Indianapolis, IN 46208
policheneb@citigroup.com

Citizens Communications Company

See listing on page 344 under Frontier Communications Corporation

Citizens Energy Group

See listing on page 196 under Citizens Water

Citizens Financial Group Inc.

Citizens Financial Group is the US banking arm of Royal Bank of Scotland (RBS). Acquired Charter One Financial, Inc. in August, 2004.
www.citizensbank.com
Annual Revenues: $4.45 billion
Employees: 17,800
SIC: 6022
Industry/ies: Banking/Finance/Investments
Legislative Issues: FIN

Chairman and Chief Executive Officer
SAUN, Bruce Van

Tel: (401) 456-7000

Main Headquarters
Mailing: One Citizens Plaza
Providence, RI 02903

Tel: (401) 456-7000

Political Action Committees
RBS Citizens Financial Group, Inc. Political Committee (RBS Citizens PAC)
FEC ID: C00307249
Contact: Kenneth W. Robinson
One Citizens Plaza
Fifth Floor
Providence, RI 02903

Tel: (401) 456-7000
Fax: (401) 456-7000

  Contributions to Candidates: $79,500 (2015-2016)
  Democrats: $41,500; Republicans: $38,000

Corporate Foundations and Giving Programs

Citizens Charitable Foundation
One Citizens Plaza
Providence, RI 02903

Tel: (401) 456-7000
Fax: (401) 456-7819

Public Affairs and Related Activities Personnel

At Headquarters

ABOAF, Eric
Chief Financial Officer

Tel: (401) 456-7000

BRADY, Donna L.
Federal Lobbyist

Tel: (401) 456-7000

ERICKSON, Cindy M.
Head, Human Resources

Tel: (401) 456-7000

GANNON, Stephen T.
General Counsel and Chief Legal Officer

Tel: (401) 456-7000

GRAVES, Rachel
Contact, Human Resources

Tel: (401) 456-7000

HUGHES, Jim
Senior Vice President, Media Relations
Jim.Hughes@citizensbank.com

Tel: (781) 751-5404

KELLY, Jocelyn
Registered Federal Lobbyist

Tel: (401) 456-7000

LAMONICA, Susan
Director, Human Resources

Tel: (401) 456-7000

MCGINN, Elaine
Head,Planning and Business Support, Human Resources

Tel: (401) 456-7000

NELSON, Robert
Chief Compliance Officer of RBS Citizens Financial Group, Inc

Tel: (401) 456-7000

O'DONNELL, Kathy
Senior Vice President and Director, Public Affairs
kathy.odonnell@citizensbank.com

Tel: (401) 456-7000

ROBBINS, Joanna
Senior Vice President

Tel: (401) 456-7000

ROBINSON, Kenneth W.
Director, Public Policy
kenneth.w.robinson@citizensbank.com
Registered Federal Lobbyist

Tel: (401) 456-7000

TAYLOR, Ellen
Executive Vice President and Head of Investor Relations

Tel: (401) 456-7000

Citizens Water

Formerly Consumers Gas Trust. A water utility privately managed by Veolia Water. In May 2002, the city of Indianapolis acquired the assets of the Indianapolis Water Company and contracted with Veolia Water. In 2001, Citizens acquired the Thermal Energy System. It a broad-based utility service company, providing natural gas, thermal energy, water, and wastewater services to people and businesses in the Indianapolis area.
www.citizensenergygroup.com
Annual Revenues: $8.19 million
Employees: 500
Industry/ies: Natural Resources

Chairman of the Board
APPEL, Daniel C.

Tel: (317) 927-4328
Fax: (317) 927-4372

President and Chief Executive Officer
HARRISON , Jeff

Tel: (317) 927-4328
Fax: (317) 927-4372

Main Headquarters
Mailing: P.O. Box 7056
Indianapolis, IN 46207-7056

Tel: (317) 927-4328
Fax: (317) 927-4372
TF: (800) 427-4217

Corporate Foundations and Giving Programs

Citizens Energy Group Trust
Contact: Yvonne Perkins
1220 Waterway Blvd.
Indianapolis, IN 46202

Public Affairs and Related Activities Personnel

At Headquarters

BREHM, John
Senior Vice President and Chief Financial Officer

Tel: (317) 927-4328
Fax: (317) 927-4372

HILL, Jennett
Senior Vice President and General Counsel

Tel: (317) 927-4328
Fax: (317) 927-4372

HOLSAPPLE , Sarah
Contact, Media Relations
sholsapple@citizensenergygroup.com

Tel: (317) 927-4341
Fax: (317) 927-4372

JOHNSON, Aaron
Vice President, Corporate Development

Tel: (317) 927-4328
Fax: (317) 927-4372

PERKINS, Yvonne
Vice President, Corporate Communications and Chief Diversity Officer

Tel: (317) 927-4328
Fax: (317) 927-4372

PRENTICE, LaTona
Vice President, Regulatory Affairs
lprentice@citizensenergygroup.com

Tel: (317) 927-4328
Fax: (317) 927-4372

STROHL, Michael
Senior Vice President, Customer Relationships and Corporate Affairs

Tel: (317) 927-4328
Fax: (317) 927-4372

WHITAKER, John
Senior Vice President, Chief Legal and Compliance Officer

Tel: (317) 927-4328
Fax: (317) 927-4372

WHITNEY, Jodi
Vice President, Human Resources

Tel: (317) 927-4328
Fax: (317) 927-4372

Citrix Systems, Inc.

The company provides access infrastructure products that enable PCs, IP phones, and other devices to remotely and securely access applications across wired and wireless networks, freeing customers from facing the difficult task of installing and updating software on each piece of hardware.
www.citrix.com
Annual Revenues: $3.15 billion
Employees: 10,081
Ticker: NASDAQ (GS): CTXS
SIC: 7372
Industry/ies: Computer/Technology

Chairman of the Board
BOGAN, Thomas F.
thomas.bogan@citrix.com

Tel: (954) 267-3000
Fax: (954) 267-9319

President and Chief Executive Officer
TEMPLETON, Mark B.

Tel: (954) 267-3000
Fax: (954) 267-3100

Main Headquarters
Mailing: 851 W. Cypress Creek Rd.
Ft. Lauderdale, FL 33309

Tel: (954) 267-3000
Fax: (954) 267-9319
TF: (800) 424-8749

Corporate Foundations and Giving Programs

Citrix Contribution Program
851 W. Cypress Creek Rd.
Ft. Lauderdale, FL 33309

Tel: (954) 267-3000
Fax: (954) 267-9319

Public Affairs and Related Activities Personnel

At Headquarters

ARMSTRONG, Eric
Director, Corporate Communications
eric.armstrong@citrix.com

Tel: (954) 267-2977
Fax: (954) 267-2525

CRISTINZIANO, Michael
Corporate Vice President, Strategic Development

Tel: (954) 267-3000
Fax: (954) 267-9319

FLEITES, Eduardo
Vice President, Investor Relations
eduardo.fleites@citrix.com

Tel: (954) 229-5758
Fax: (954) 267-9319

FRIEDMAN, David R.
Chief of Staff
david.friedman@citrix.com

Tel: (954) 267-3000
Fax: (954) 267-9319

GEER, Julie
Senior Director, Corporate & Thought Leadership PR
julie.geer@citrix.com

Tel: (408) 790-8543
Fax: (954) 267-9319

GILLES, Karin
Director, Corporate Communications

Tel: (408) 790-8544
Fax: (954) 267-9319

GRIEVE, Robson
Chief Marketing Officer

Tel: (954) 267-3000
Fax: (954) 267-9319

HENSHALL, David J.
Chief Operating Officer and Chief Financial Officer
david.henshall@citrix.com

Tel: (954) 267-3000
Fax: (954) 267-9319

RAMLETH, Geir
Chief Strategy Officer

Tel: (954) 267-3000
Fax: (954) 267-9319

WYSE, Jason
Senior Manager, Corporate Communications
jason.wyse@citrix.com

Tel: (786) 449-3740
Fax: (954) 267-9319

City National Corporation

A regional bank holding company.

www.cnb.com
Annual Revenues: $1.31 billion
Employees: 3,578
Ticker: NYSE: CYN
SIC: 6021
Industry/ies: Banking/Finance/Investments

| **Chairman** | Tel: | (213) 673-8740 |
| GOLDSMITH, Bram | Fax: | (310) 888-6045 |

Chairman of the Board, President and Chief Executive Officer	Tel:	(213) 673-8740
GOLDSMITH, Russell D.	Fax:	(310) 888-6045
russell.goldsmith@cnb.com		

Main Headquarters
Mailing: City National Plaza	Tel:	(213) 673-8740
555 S. Flower St.	Fax:	(310) 888-6045
Los Angeles, CA 90071	TF:	(800) 773-7100

Corporate Foundations and Giving Programs

City National Corporation Contribution Program
City National Plaza   Tel: (213) 673-8740
555 S. Flower St.
Los Angeles, CA 90071

Public Affairs and Related Activities Personnel

At Headquarters

CAHILL, Michael B.	Tel:	(213) 673-8740
Executive Vice President, General Counsel and Secretary	Fax:	(310) 888-6045
mike.cahill@cnb.com		

CAREY, Christopher J.	Tel:	(213) 673-8740
Executive Vice President and Chief Financial Officer	Fax:	(310) 888-6045
Chris.Carey@cnb.com		

LAMUTT, Marianne	Tel:	(213) 673-8740
Executive Vice President, Human Resources	Fax:	(310) 888-6045
Marianne.Lamutt@cnb.com		

MILLER, Thomas R.	Tel:	(213) 673-8740
Executive Vice President, Marketing and Product Strategies	Fax:	(310) 888-6045
thomas.miller@cnb.com		

MUELLER, Linda	Tel:	(213) 673-7619
Contact, Investor Relations	Fax:	(310) 888-6045
Linda.Mueller@cnb.com		

STOWELL, Paul	Tel:	(702) 952-4415
Senior Vice President, Media Relations	Fax:	(310) 888-6045
paul.stowell@cnb.com		

WALKER, Cary	Tel:	(213) 673-7615
Senior Vice President, Corporate Communications	Fax:	(310) 888-6045
cary.walker@cnb.com		

| WARMUTH, Christopher J. | Tel: | (213) 673-8740 |
| *President* | Fax: | (310) 888-6045 |

CKE Restaurants, Inc.

A company that franchises, licensees, and operates various fast food chain restaurants.
www.ckr.com
Annual Revenues: $12.80 billion
Employees: 20,000
Ticker: NYSE: CKR
SIC: 5812
Industry/ies: Food And Beverage Industry
Legislative Issues: AGR; SMB

| **Chief Executive Officer** | Tel: | (805) 745-7500 |
| PUZDER, Andrew F. | Fax: | (714) 490-3630 |

Main Headquarters
Mailing: 6307 Carpinterie Ave.	Tel:	(805) 745-7500
Suite A	Fax:	(714) 490-3630
Carpinteria, CA 93013	TF:	(800) 422-4141

Political Action Committees

CKE Restaurants, Inc. PAC
FEC ID: C00461673
Contact: Luis Farias
6307 Carpinteria Ave.
Suite A
Carpinteria, CA 93013

Corporate Foundations and Giving Programs

CKE Restaurants Contributions Program
Contact: Andrew F. Puzder
6307 Carpinterie Ave.
Suite A
Carpinteria, CA 93013

Public Affairs and Related Activities Personnel

At Headquarters

ABAJIAN, Theodore	Tel:	(805) 745-7500
Executive Vice President and Chief Financial Officer	Fax:	(714) 490-3630
tabajian@ckr.com		

CHASNEY, Jeffrey P.	Tel:	(805) 745-7500
Executive Vice President, Strategic Planning and Chief Information Officer	Fax:	(714) 490-3630
jchasney@ckr.com		

| FARIAS, Luis | Tel: | (805) 745-7500 |
| *PAC Contact* | Fax: | (714) 490-3630 |

HALEY, Brad R.	Tel:	(805) 745-7500
Chief Marketing Officer	Fax:	(714) 490-3630
bhaley@ckr.com		

MURPHY, E. Michael	Tel:	(805) 745-7500
President and Chief Legal Officer	Fax:	(714) 490-3630
mmurphy@ckr.com		

| WILLIAMS, Eric | Tel: | (805) 745-7500 |
| *Chief Operating Officer* | Fax: | (714) 490-3630 |

Claire's Stores, Inc.

Acquired by Apollo Management, L.P. on May 29, 2007. Claire's Stores, Inc. is a retailer of value-priced jewelry and accessories for girls and young women through its two store concepts.
www.clairestores.com
Employees: 18,000
Industry/ies: Retail/Wholesale

| **Chairman of the Board** | Tel: | (954) 433-3900 |
| COPSES, Peter P. | Fax: | (954) 433-3999 |

| **Chief Executive Officer** | Tel: | (954) 433-3900 |
| MARSHALL, Ron | Fax: | (954) 433-3999 |

Main Headquarters
Mailing: Three S.W. 129th Ave.	Tel:	(954) 433-3900
Pembroke Pines, FL 33027	Fax:	(954) 433-3999
	TF:	(800) 252-4737

Corporate Foundations and Giving Programs

Claire's Stores Contributions Program
Three S.W. 129th Ave.
Pembroke Pines, FL 33027

Public Affairs and Related Activities Personnel

At Headquarters

| BERRY, Melanie | Tel: | (954) 433-3900 |
| *Senior Vice President, Marketing* | Fax: | (954) 433-3999 |

| BRODIN, J. Per | Tel: | (954) 433-3900 |
| *Executive Vice President and Chief Financial Officer* | Fax: | (954) 433-3999 |

ORAND, Rebecca	Tel:	(954) 433-3900
Senior Vice President, General Counsel and Quality Assurance and Secretary	Fax:	(954) 433-3999
rebecca.orand@claires.com		

Clariant Corporation

A specialty chemicals manufacturing company.
www.clariant.com
Employees: 1,200
SIC: 2865; 2851
NAICS: 32551; 325192
Industry/ies: Chemicals & Chemical Industry
Legislative Issues: TAR

| **Chief Executive Officer** | Tel: | (704) 331-7000 |
| KOTTMANN, Hariolf | Fax: | (704) 377-1063 |

Main Headquarters
| *Mailing:* 4000 Monroe Rd. | Tel: | (704) 331-7000 |
| Charlotte, NC 28205 | Fax: | (704) 377-1063 |

Public Affairs and Related Activities Personnel

At Headquarters

| JANY, Patrick | Tel: | (704) 331-7000 |
| *Chief Financial Officer* | Fax: | (704) 377-1063 |

LEAZER, Sherri	Tel:	(704) 905-0231
Manager, Business Communications	Fax:	(704) 331-7112
Sherri.Leazer@clariant.com		

Clean Energy Fuels Corporation

A vehicular natural gas provider company.
www.cleanenergyfuels.com
Annual Revenues: $419.51 million
Employees: 1,128
Ticker: NASDAQ (GM): CLNE
SIC: 4932
Industry/ies: Energy/Electricity; Environment And Conservation; Fuels See Coal, Gas, Oil, Petroleum; Natural Resources; Petroleum Industry
Legislative Issues: BUD; ENG; FUE; TAX; TRA

| **Chairman of the Board** | Tel: | (562) 493-2804 |
| MITCHELL, Warren J. | Fax: | (562) 493-4532 |

President and Chief Executive Officer
LITTLEFAIR, Andrew J. — Tel: (562) 493-2804; Fax: (949) 724-1397

Main Headquarters
Mailing: 3020 Old Ranch Pkwy.
Suite 400
Seal Beach, DC 20001
Tel: (562) 493-2804
Fax: (562) 493-4532

Public Affairs and Related Activities Personnel

At Headquarters

CAMPBELL, Todd — Tel: (562) 493-2804; Fax: (562) 493-4532
Vice President, Public Policy and Regulatory Affairs
tcampbell@cleanenergyfuels.com

RUSSEL, Bruce — Tel: (310) 559-4955; Fax: (562) 493-4532
Director, Communications
brussell@cleanenergyfuels.com

At Other Offices

BURKE, Raymond — Fax: (949) 724-1397
Vice President, Business Development
4675 MacArthur Ct., Suite 800
Newport Beach, CA 92660

CORBUS, Clay — Fax: (949) 724-1397
Senior Vice President, Strategic Development
4675 MacArthur Ct., Suite 800
Newport Beach, CA 92660

FOSTER, Gary — Fax: (949) 724-1397
Senior Vice President, Corporate Communications
4675 MacArthur Ct., Suite 800
Newport Beach, CA 92660

GLICK, Rich A.
PAC Treasurer
1125 N.W. Couch St., Suite 700
Portland, OR 97209

GRACE, Peter — Fax: (949) 724-1397
Senior Vice President, Sales and Finance
4675 MacArthur Ct., Suite 800
Newport Beach, CA 92660
pgrace@cleanenergyfuels.com

HARGER, James N. — Fax: (949) 724-1397
Senior Advisor to Chief Executive Officer
4675 MacArthur Ct., Suite 800
Newport Beach, CA 92660
jharger@cleanenergyfuels.com

HOOLEY, James L. — Fax: (949) 724-1397
Vice President, Federal Governement Relations
4675 MacArthur Ct., Suite 800
Newport Beach, CA 92660
jhooley@cleanenergyfuels.com
Registered Federal Lobbyist

JENSEN, Nate — Fax: (949) 724-1397
Vice President and General Counsel
4675 MacArthur Ct., Suite 800
Newport Beach, CA 92660
njensen@cleanenergyfuels.com

KRITZER, Tony — Fax: (949) 724-1397
Director, Investor Communications
4675 MacArthur Ct., Suite 800
Newport Beach, CA 92660

PRATT, Mitchell — Fax: (949) 724-1397
Chief Operating Officer
4675 MacArthur Ct., Suite 800
Newport Beach, CA 92660

VREELAND, Robert — Fax: (949) 724-1397
Chief Financial Officer
4675 MacArthur Ct., Suite 800
Newport Beach, CA 92660

Clear Channel Communications Inc.

A diversified media company with operations in radio and television broadcasting, outdoor advertising, and live entertainment. In 2008, the company announced the completion of a merger with an indirect wholly owned subsidiary of CC Media Holdings, Inc.
www.clearchannel.com
Annual Revenues: $6.2 billion
Employees: 15,000
Ticker: NYSE: CCU
SIC: 3993; 4832; 7999
NAICS: 339950; 711320; 515111
Industry/ies: Advertising And Marketing; Communications; Media/Mass Communication
Legislative Issues: ADV; BUD; COM; CPT; TAX; TEC; TRD

Chairman and Chief Executive Officer
PITTMAN, Bob — Tel: (210) 822-2828; Fax: (210) 822-2299

Main Headquarters
Mailing: 200 E. Basse Rd.
San Antonio, TX 78209
Tel: (210) 822-2828
Fax: (210) 822-2299

Washington Office
Mailing: 419 Seventh St. NW
Suite 500
Washington, DC 20004

Political Action Committees
Clear Channel Communications Inc. Leadership PAC
FEC ID: C00498584
Contact: Scott B. Hamilton
200 E. Basse Rd.
San Antonio, TX 78209
Tel: (210) 822-2828
Fax: (210) 822-2299

Corporate Foundations and Giving Programs
Clear Channel Foundation
Contact: Cammy Jones
200 E. Basse Rd.
San Antonio, TX 78209
Tel: (210) 822-2828
Fax: (210) 822-2299

Public Affairs and Related Activities Personnel

At Headquarters

BRESSLER, Richard J. — Tel: (210) 822-2828; Fax: (210) 822-2299
President and Chief Financial Officer

CUTLER, Steven — Tel: (210) 822-2828; Fax: (210) 822-2299
Executive Vice President of Business Development and Corporate Strategy

FEEHAN, Bill — Tel: (210) 822-2828; Fax: (210) 822-2299
Senior Vice President, Human Resources
bill.feehan@clearchannel.com

GOLDBERG, Wendy — Tel: (210) 822-2828; Fax: (210) 822-2299
Executive Vice President and Chief Communications Officer

HAMILTON, Scott B. — Tel: (210) 822-2828; Fax: (210) 822-2299
PAC Treasurer

JONES, Cammy — Tel: (210) 822-2828; Fax: (210) 822-2299
Foundation Contact
cammyjones@clearchannel.com

MAYS, Lowry — Tel: (210) 822-2828; Fax: (210) 822-2299
Founder

WALLS, Jr., Robert H. — Tel: (210) 822-2828; Fax: (210) 822-2299
Executive Vice President, General Counsel

At Washington Office

MORRIS, Sara
Registered Federal Lobbyist

At Other Offices

DUKES, Dan
Federal Lobbyist
701 Eighth St. NW, Suite 350
Washington, DC 20001
Registered Federal Lobbyist

MARVENTANO, Jessica
Senior Vice President, Government Affairs
701 Eighth St. NW, Suite 350
Washington, DC 20001
jessicamarventano@clearchannel.com
Registered Federal Lobbyist

Cleco Corporation

A midstream energy company. Formerly known as the Central Louisiana Electric Co.
www.clecocorp.com
Annual Revenues: $1.28 billion
Employees: 1,206
Ticker: NYSE: CNL
SIC: 4911
NAICS: 221122
Industry/ies: Utilities

Chairman of the Board, President and Chief Executive Officer
WILLIAMSON, Bruce A. — Tel: (276) 880-1034; Fax: (276) 880-3119

Main Headquarters
Mailing: 544 Redbud Hwy.
Rosedale, VA 24280
Tel: (276) 880-1034
Fax: (276) 880-3119
TF: (800) 622-6537

Political Action Committees
Cleco Political Action Committee, Cleco Corporation
FEC ID: C00165878
Contact: Melissa H. Lohman
P.O. Box 5000
Pineville, LA 71361

Contributions to Candidates: $7,500 (2015-2016)
Democrats: $5,000; Republicans: $2,500

Corporate Foundations and Giving Programs
Cleco Corporation Contributions Program

544 Redbud Hwy.   Tel: (276) 880-1034
Rosedale, VA 24280   Fax: (276) 880-3119

Public Affairs and Related Activities Personnel

At Headquarters

BROUSSARD, Susan   Tel: (318) 484-7773
General Manager, Human Resources and Manager,   Fax: (318) 484-7488
Corporate Communications

COOPER, Robbyn   Tel: (318) 484-7136
Contact, Media Relations   Fax: (318) 484-7488

HOEFLING, Wade A.   Tel: (318) 484-7400
Senior Vice President, General Counsel and Director,   Fax: (318) 484-7488
Regulatory Compliance

MILLER, Judy P.   Tel: (276) 880-1034
Vice President, Corporate Services and Information   Fax: (276) 880-3119
Technology

MILLER, Thomas   Tel: (276) 880-1034
Senior Vice President & Chief Financial Officer   Fax: (276) 880-3119

OLAGUES, Darren   Tel: (318) 484-7400
Senior Vice President, Midstream Resources   Fax: (318) 484-7488

At Other Offices

LOHMAN, Melissa H.
PAC Treasurer
P. O. Box 5000
Pineville, LA 71361

Cleveland-Cliffs Inc.

See listing on page 199 under Cliffs Natural Resources

Cliffs Natural Resources

An international mining and natural resources company. Producer of low-volatile metallurgical coal, iron ore pellets, supplier of direct-shipping lump and fines iron ore and producer of high and low volatile metallurgical coal. It was formerly known as Cleveland-Cliffs Inc.
www.cliffsnaturalresources.com
Annual Revenues: $4.45 billion
Employees: 5,386
Ticker: NYSE: CLF
SIC: 1000
Industry/ies: Natural Resources
Legislative Issues: MAN; TRD

Chairman, President and Chief Executive Officer   Tel: (216) 694-5700
GONCALVES, Lourenco   Fax: (216) 694-4880

Main Headquarters
Mailing: 200 Public Sq.   Tel: (216) 694-5700
     Suite 3300   Fax: (216) 694-4880
     Cleveland, OH 44114-2544

Political Action Committees
Cliffs Natural Resources Inc. PAC (CLIFFSPAC)
FEC ID: C00039016
Contact: Dana W. Byrne
200 Public Square
Suite 3300
Cleveland, OH 44114

     Contributions to Candidates: $29,000 (2015-2016)
     Democrats: $9,000; Republicans: $20,000

Corporate Foundations and Giving Programs

Cleveland-Cliffs Foundation
1100 Superior Ave. East   Tel: (216) 694-5700
Cleveland, OH 44114   Fax: (216) 694-4880

Public Affairs and Related Activities Personnel

At Headquarters

BLOOM, Patrick   Tel: (216) 694-5537
Director, Government Relations   Fax: (216) 694-4880
Registered Federal Lobbyist

BYRNE, Dana W.   Tel: (216) 694-5700
PAC Treasurer   Fax: (216) 694-4880

CARTELLA, David T.   Tel: (216) 694-5700
Vice President, Global Government, Environment, Energy &   Fax: (216) 694-4880
Public Affairs and Environmental Counsel

FINAN, Paul   Tel: (216) 694-6544
Manager, Investor Relations   Fax: (216) 694-4880
paul.finan@cliffsnr.com

GRAHAM, James   Tel: (216) 694-5700
Executive Vice President, Chief Legal Officer and Secretary   Fax: (216) 694-4880

HARAPIAK, Maurice   Tel: (216) 694-5700
Executive Vice President, Human Resources   Fax: (216) 694-4880

PERSICO, Patricia   Tel: (216) 694-5316
Director, Global Communications   Fax: (216) 694-4880
patricia.persico@cliffsnr.com

SMITH, Clifford   Tel: (216) 694-5700

Executive Vice President, Business Development   Fax: (216) 694-4880

TOMPKINS, P. Kelly   Tel: (216) 694-5700
Executive Vice President and Chief Financial Officer   Fax: (216) 694-4880

At Other Offices

TERRY, Juliet   Tel: (304) 344-3040
Director, Government Relations and Federal Lobbyist
900 Lee St. East, Suite 1227
Charleston, WV 25301
juliet.terry@cliffsnr.com

Clinical Data, Inc.

Provides comprehensive molecular and pharmacogenomics services as well as clinical diagnostics to improve patient care. Clinical Data was acquired by Forest Laboratories on April 14, 2011.
www.clda.com
Employees: 200
Ticker: NASDAQ (GM): CLDA
SIC: 2834
Industry/ies: Science; Scientific Research

Chairman of the Board   Tel: (617) 527-9933
KIRK, J. Randal   Fax: (617) 527-0445

President and Chief Executive Officer   Tel: (617) 527-9933
FROMKIN, Drew   Fax: (617) 527-0445

Main Headquarters
Mailing: 909 Third Ave.   Tel: (212) 421-7850
     New York City, NY 10022-4731   Fax: (631) 858-5200

Public Affairs and Related Activities Personnel

At Headquarters

FERRUCCI, Lynn   Tel: (617) 527-9933
Vice President, Human Resources   Fax: (617) 527-0445

MCNEELY, Theresa   Tel: (617) 467-6673
Vice President, Corporate Communications   Fax: (617) 527-0445
tmcneely@clda.com

The Clorox Company

A manufacturer of household grocery products and products for the food service industry.
www.thecloroxcompany.com
Annual Revenues: $5.67 billion
Employees: 7,700
Ticker: NYSE: CLX
SIC: 2842; 2819; 2899; 3582; 3633
NAICS: 325612; 325188; 325998; 333312; 335224
Industry/ies: Chemicals & Chemical Industry; Personal Care/Hygiene

Chairman of the Board   Tel: (510) 271-7000
KNAUSS, Donald R.   Fax: (510) 832-1463

Chief Executive Officer   Tel: (510) 271-7000
DORER, Benno   Fax: (510) 832-1463

Main Headquarters
Mailing: 1221 Broadway   Tel: (510) 271-7000
     Oakland, CA 94612   Fax: (510) 832-1463

Political Action Committees
Clorox Company PAC; The (CLORPAC)
FEC ID: C00062224
Contact: Victoria Jones
1221 Broadway   Tel: (510) 271-7000
Oakland, CA 94612   Fax: (510) 832-1463

     Contributions to Candidates: $46,500 (2015-2016)
     Democrats: $25,500; Republicans: $21,000

Corporate Foundations and Giving Programs

The Clorox Company Foundation
Contact: Deborah Napierski
DeDomenico Bldg.   Tel: (510) 836-3223
200 Frank Ogawa Plaza
Oakland, CA 94612

Public Affairs and Related Activities Personnel

At Headquarters

AUSTENFELD, Steve   Tel: (510) 271-7000
Vice President, Investor Relations   Fax: (510) 832-1463
steve.austenfeld@clorox.com

CAULFIELD, Kathryn   Tel: (510) 271-7209
Chief Communications and Corporate Responsibility Leader   Fax: (510) 832-1463
kathryn.caulfield@clorox.com

JONES, Victoria   Tel: (510) 271-7000
Vice President, Government Affairs and Community Affairs   Fax: (510) 832-1463
and PAC Treasurer
victoria.jones@clorox.com

KANE, Jacqueline R. "Jackie"   Tel: (510) 271-7000
Executive Vice President, Human Resources and Corporate   Fax: (510) 832-1463
Affairs

NAPIERSKI, Deborah		Tel:	(510) 271-7000
Manager, Community Relations		Fax:	(510) 832-1463
Mail Stop DeDomenico Building, 200 Frank Ogawa Plaza			
deborah.napierski@clorox.com			
ROBB, Stephen M.		Tel:	(510) 271-7000
Executive Vice President and Chief Financial Officer		Fax:	(510) 832-1463
STAUBLIN, Dan		Tel:	(510) 271-1622
Director, Corporate Communications, Internal and Crisis		Fax:	(510) 832-1463
dan.staublin@clorox.com			
STEIN, Laura		Tel:	(510) 271-7000
Executive Vice President and General Counsel		Fax:	(510) 832-1463
ZERRUDO, Aileen		Tel:	(510) 271-3075
Director, Corporate Communications		Fax:	(510) 832-1463
aileen.zerrudo@clorox.com			

Cloud Peak Energy Resources, LLC

A coal mining company. Cloud Peak Energy operates three wholly owned coal mines located in the Powder River Basin of Montana and Wyoming. The company, formerly a subsidiary of Rio Tinto, produces about 100 million tons of coal annually and controls 1 billion tons in proved and probable reserves. It was formed in 1993 as Kennecott Coal, changed its name to Rio Tinto Energy America (RTEA) in 2006.
www.cldpk.com
Annual Revenues: $951.51 million
Employees: 1,500
Ticker: NYSE: CLD
SIC: 1221
Industry/ies: Energy/Electricity; Mining Industry; Natural Resources
Legislative Issues: ENG; ENV; NAT; TAX; TRD

President and Chief Executive Officer	Tel:	(307) 687-6000
MARSHALL, Colin	Fax:	(307) 687-6015

Main Headquarters			
Mailing:	505 S. Gillette Ave.	Tel:	(307) 687-6000
	P.O. Box 3009		
	Gillette, WY 82716		

Political Action Committees
Cloud Peak Energy Resources LLC Employee PAC
FEC ID: C00485003
Contact: Molly Schwend
385 Interlocken Cresent
Suite 400
Broomfield, CO 80021

> **Contributions to Candidates:** $25,100 (2015-2016)
> Democrats: $1,000; Republicans: $24,100

> **Principal Recipients**
>
> **HOUSE**
> ZINKE, RYAN K (REP-MT)

Corporate Foundations and Giving Programs
Cloud Peak Energy Contributions Program
Contact: Megan Degenfelder
505 S. Gillette Ave.
P.O. Box 3009
Gillette, WY 82716

Public Affairs and Related Activities Personnel

At Headquarters

CURTSINGER, Rick	Tel:	(720) 256-7781
Director, Public Affairs		
Rick.Curtsinger@cldpk.com		
DEGENFELDER, Megan	Tel:	(307) 685-6146
Contact, Corporate Contributions		
HILL, Heath	Tel:	(307) 687-6000
Executive Vice President and Chief Financial Officer		
KELLEY, Mike	Tel:	(720) 566-2906
Director, Sales and Marketing	Fax:	(307) 687-6015
KIMREY, Karla	Tel:	(720) 566-2932
Vice President, Investor Relations	Fax:	(307) 687-6015
karla.kimrey@cldpk.com		
MARTIN, Cary W.	Tel:	(307) 687-6000
Senior Vice President, Human Resources	Fax:	(307) 687-6015
MYERS, Todd	Tel:	(307) 687-6000
Senior Vice President, Business Development Todd Myers		
ORCHARD, Jim	Tel:	(307) 687-6000
Senior Vice President, Marketing and Government Affairs	Fax:	(307) 687-6015
PECHERSKY, Bryan	Tel:	(307) 687-6000
Executive Vice President, General Counsel and Corporate Secretary	Fax:	(307) 687-6015
RIVENES, Gary	Tel:	(307) 687-6000
Executive Vice President, Chief Operating Officer		

At Other Offices

SCHWEND, Molly	Tel:	(720) 566-2900

PAC Treasurer
385 Interlocken Crescent, Suite 400
Broomfield, CO 80021

ClubCorp, Inc.

An operator of private clubs, resorts and public golf courses.
www.clubcorp.com
Annual Revenues: $1.07 billion
Employees: 17,800
Ticker: NYSE:MYCC
SIC: 7997
Industry/ies: Travel/Tourism/Lodging

President and Chief Executive Officer	Tel:	(972) 243-6191
AFFELDT, Eric L.	Fax:	(972) 888-7558
eric.affeldt@clubcorp.com		

Main Headquarters			
Mailing:	3030 LBJ Fwy.	Tel:	(972) 243-6191
	Suite 600	Fax:	(972) 888-7558
	Dallas, TX 75234		

Corporate Foundations and Giving Programs

The Employee Partners Care Foundation		
Contact: Daniel T. Tilley		
3030 LBJ Fwy.	Tel:	(972) 243-6191
Suite 600	Fax:	(972) 888-7558
Dallas, TX 75234		

Public Affairs and Related Activities Personnel

At Headquarters

BURNETT, Mark A.	Tel:	(972) 243-6191
President and Chief Operating Officer	Fax:	(972) 888-7558
JERDE, Patty	Tel:	(972) 888-7790
Specialist, Communications	Fax:	(972) 888-7558
patty.jerde@clubcorp.com		
KEISER, Ingrid	Tel:	(972) 243-6191
General Counsel, Secretary and Executive Vice President, People Strategy	Fax:	(972) 888-7558
Ingrid.Keiser@clubcorp.com		
MCCLELLAN, Curt	Tel:	(972) 243-6191
Chief Financial Officer	Fax:	(972) 888-7558
WALTERS, Jamie	Tel:	(972) 243-6191
Executive Vice President, Sales	Fax:	(972) 888-7558

CMA CGM (America) Inc.

Provider of container shipping services in North America and internationally. The U.S. agent of France-based container shipping giant CMA CGM.
www.cma-cgm.com
Industry/ies: Marine/Maritime/Shipping; Transportation
Legislative Issues: FOR; MAR

Group Chairman and Chief Executive Officer	Tel:	(757) 961-2100
SAADE, Jacques R.	Fax:	(757) 961-2151

Main Headquarters			
Mailing:	5701 Lake Wright Dr.	Tel:	(757) 961-2100
	Norfolk, VA 23502-1868	Fax:	(757) 961-2151
		TF:	(877) 556-6308

Public Affairs and Related Activities Personnel

At Headquarters

ARNOLD, James	Tel:	(757) 961-2100
Senior Vice President and Chief Financial Officer	Fax:	(757) 961-2151
MCCARTHY, Ed	Tel:	(757) 961-2100
Chief Operating Officer	Fax:	(757) 961-2151
RIVES, Todd	Tel:	(757) 961-2100
Chief Commercial Officer	Fax:	(757) 961-2151

CME Group, Inc.

In 2007, the Chicago Mercantile Exchange Holdings Inc. and the Chicago Board of Trade merged to form the CME Group.
www.cmegroup.com
Annual Revenues: $3.18 billion
Employees: 2,680
Ticker: NASDAQ: CME
SIC: 6200
Industry/ies: Computer/Technology
Legislative Issues: AGR; ENG; FIN; TAX

Executive Chairman of the Board and President	Tel:	(312) 930-1000
DUFFY, Terrence A.	Fax:	(312) 446-4410

Chief Executive Officer	Tel:	(312) 930-1000
GILL, Phupinder	Fax:	(312) 446-4410

Main Headquarters			
Mailing:	20 S. Wacker Dr.	Tel:	(312) 930-1000
	Chicago, IL 60606	Fax:	(312) 446-4410
		TF:	(866) 716-7274

Washington Office

Mailing: 325 Seventh St. NW Tel: (202) 638-3838
Suite 525, Liberty Place Fax: (202) 638-5799
Washington, DC 20004

Political Action Committees

CME Group, Inc. PAC
FEC ID: C00076299
Contact: Ronald A. Pankau
20 S. Wacker Dr. Tel: (312) 930-1000
Chicago, IL 60606

Contributions to Candidates: $525,250 (2015-2016)
Democrats: $225,500; Republicans: $299,750

Principal Recipients

SENATE
GRASSLEY, CHARLES E SENATOR (REP-IA)
LEAHY, PATRICK J (DEM-VT)

HOUSE
BARR, GARLAND ANDY (REP-KY)
DAVIS, RODNEY L (REP-IL)
PETERSON, COLLIN CLARK (DEM-MN)
RYAN, PAUL D. (REP-WI)
SCALISE, STEVE MR. (REP-LA)
SCOTT, DAVID ALBERT (DEM-GA)
THOMPSON, MIKE MR. (DEM-CA)
VELA, FILEMON MR. (DEM-TX)

Corporate Foundations and Giving Programs

CBOT Foundation
Contact: Ellen Paparelli
141 W. Jackson Suite 1801
Chicago, IL 60606

CME Group Assistance Fund
20 S. Wacker Dr.
Chicago, IL 60606

CME Group Community Foundation
Contact: Terrence A. Duffy
20 S. Wacker Dr.
Chicago, IL 60606

CME Group Foundation
Contact: Kassie Davis
20 S. Wacker Dr. Tel: (312) 930-3292
Chicago, IL 60606

Matching Gift Program
20 S. Wacker Dr.
Chicago, IL 60606

Public Affairs and Related Activities Personnel

At Headquarters

CRONIN, Kathleen M. Tel: (312) 930-1000
Senior Managing Director, General Counsel and Corporate Fax: (312) 446-4410
Secretary
kathleen.cronin@cmegroup.com

DAVIS, Kassie Tel: (312) 930-3292
Executive Director, CME Group Foundation Fax: (312) 446-4410
kassie.davis@cmegroupfoundation.org

DURKIN, Bryan T. Tel: (312) 930-1000
Chief Commercial Officer Fax: (312) 446-4410

HOLZRICHTER, Julie Tel: (312) 930-1000
Chief Operating Officer Fax: (312) 446-4410

LISKEY, Anita Tel: (312) 466-4613
Managing Director, Corporate Marketing and Fax: (312) 446-4410
Communications
anita.liskey@cmegroup.com

PANKAU, Ronald A. Tel: (312) 930-1000
Independent Trader Fax: (312) 446-4410

PAPARELLI, Ellen Tel: (312) 435-3609
Executive Assistant Fax: (312) 446-4410

PARISI, James E. Tel: (312) 930-1000
Chief Financial Officer and Managing Director, Finance and Fax: (312) 446-4410
Corporate Development

PIELL, Hilda Harris Tel: (312) 930-1000
Senior Managing Director and Chief Human Resources Fax: (312) 446-4410
Officer

PIETROWICZ, John W. Tel: (312) 930-1000
Chief Financial Officer Fax: (312) 446-4410

At Washington Office

HAWK, Raquel Tel: (202) 638-3838
Federal Lobbyist Fax: (202) 638-5799
Registered Federal Lobbyist

JACHYM, Jonathan Tel: (202) 638-3838
Executive Director Fax: (202) 638-5799

KLEIN GRAY, Anne M. Tel: (202) 638-3838
Associate Director, Government Relations Fax: (202) 638-5799
Anne.KleinGray@cmegroup.com
Registered Federal Lobbyist

RICH, Linda Dallas Tel: (202) 638-3838
Senior Managing Director, Government Relations & Fax: (202) 638-5799
Legislative Affairs
Registered Federal Lobbyist

SPENCE, Jason Tel: (202) 638-3838
Federal Lobbyist Fax: (202) 638-5799
jason.spence@cmegroup.com
Registered Federal Lobbyist

At Other Offices

DEZUR, Samantha Tel: (202) 638-3838
Manager, Government Relations Fax: (202) 638-5799
701 Pennsylvania Ave. NW, Suite 01
Washington, DC 20004

CMS Consulting Services Inc.

Consultant.
Legislative Issues: ENG

President Tel: (203) 445-1974
SINAGRA, Chris

Main Headquarters
Mailing: 500 Purdy Hill Rd Tel: (203) 445-1974
Suite 6
Monroe, CT 06468

CMS Energy Company

An integrated energy company.
www.cmsenergy.com
Annual Revenues: $6.15 billion
Employees: 7,711
Ticker: NYSE: CMS
SIC: 4931
NAICS: 221210
Industry/ies: Energy/Electricity; Utilities
Legislative Issues: AGR; BAN; BUD; CAW; CDT; COM; EDU; ENG; ENV; FIN; HOM; LBR; TAX; TRA; UTI

Chairman of the Board Tel: (517) 788-0550
JOOS, David W. Fax: (517) 788-1859

President and Chief Executive Officer Tel: (517) 788-0550
RUSSELL, John G. Fax: (517) 788-1859

Main Headquarters
Mailing: One Energy Plaza Tel: (517) 788-0550
Jackson, MS 49201 Fax: (517) 788-1859

Washington Office
Mailing: 1730 Rhode Island Ave. NW Tel: (202) 778-3340
Suite 1007
Washington, DC 20036

Political Action Committees

CMS Energy Corporation Employees for Better Government- Federal
FEC ID: C00075473
Contact: Tim Denton
One Energy Plaza Tel: (517) 788-0550
Jackson, MS 49201 Fax: (517) 788-1859

Contributions to Candidates: $66,500 (2015-2016)
Democrats: $15,500; Republicans: $51,000

Corporate Foundations and Giving Programs

CMS Energy Contributions Program
One Energy Plaza Tel: (517) 788-0550
Jackson, MS 49201 Fax: (517) 788-1859

Public Affairs and Related Activities Personnel

At Headquarters

ANDERSON, Jan Tel: (517) 788-0550
Manager, Regulatory Filings Fax: (517) 788-1859

BARBA , Glenn P. Tel: (517) 788-0550
Vice President, Controller, Chief Accounting Officer and and Fax: (517) 788-1859
New Business Development

BISHOP, Daniel Tel: (517) 788-2395
Director, Public Information Fax: (517) 788-1859
newsroom@consumersenergy.com

BLOODWORTH, Carolyn Tel: (517) 788-0550
Director, Corporate Giving Fax: (517) 788-1859

DENTON, Tim Tel: (517) 788-0550
PAC Treasurer Fax: (517) 788-1859

DHENUVAKONDA (DV) RAO, Venkat Tel: (517) 788-0550
Vice President, Treasurer, Financial Planning and Investor Fax: (517) 788-1859
Relations

GLEESPEN, Melissa M.
Vice President, Corporate Secretary and Chief Compliance Officer
Tel: (517) 788-0550
Fax: (517) 788-1859

HENDRIAN, Catherine A.
Vice President, Human Resources
Tel: (517) 788-0550
Fax: (517) 788-1859

REYNOLDS, Catherine M.
Senior Vice President and General Counsel
cmreynolds@cmsenergy.com
Tel: (517) 788-0550
Fax: (517) 788-1859

WEBB, Thomas J.
Executive Vice President and Chief Financial Officer
Tel: (517) 788-0550
Fax: (517) 788-1859

At Washington Office

CROUT, Kiran L.
Director, Federal Governmental Affairs
klcrout@cmsenergy.com
Registered Federal Lobbyist
Tel: (202) 778-3340

MENGEBIER, David G.
Senior Vice President, Governmental and Public Affairs
dgmengebier@cmsenergy.com
Registered Federal Lobbyist
Tel: (202) 778-3340

PLASTER, Amy S.
Executive Director
asplaster@cmsenergy.com
Registered Federal Lobbyist
Tel: (202) 778-3340

CN - Canadian National Railway

A transportation company that offers integrated transportation services: rail, intermodal, trucking, freight forwarding, warehousing and distribution.
www.cn.ca
Employees: 225
Industry/ies: Railroads; Transportation
Legislative Issues: HOM; LBR; RRR; TAX; TRA; TRD

President and Chief Executive Officer
MONGEAU, Claude

Main Headquarters
Mailing: 935 de la Gauchetiere St., West
Montreal, QC H3B 2M9

Washington Office
Mailing: 601 Pennsylvania Ave. NW
Suite 500, North Bldg.
Washington, DC 20004
Tel: (202) 347-7196
Fax: (202) 347-8237

Public Affairs and Related Activities Personnel

At Headquarters

DEEGAN , Paul
Vice-President Public and Government Affairs

DRYSDALE, Janet
Vice President, Investor Relations

FINN, Sean
Executive Vice President, Corporate Services and Chief Legal Officer

HEBERT, Francois C
Vice-President, Corporate Development

JOBIN, Luc
Executive Vice President and Chief Financial Officer

MADIGAN, Kimberly A
Vice President, Human Resources

MURRAY, Fiona
Vice-President, Corporate Marketing

PANRAY, Sunil
Vice-President and Treasurer

RUEST, Jean Jacques
Executive Vice President and Chief Marketing Officer

VENA, Jim
Executive Vice-President and Chief Operating Officer

At Washington Office

PHILLIPS, Karen B.
Vice President, Public & Government Affairs
karen.phillips@cn.ca
Tel: (202) 347-7196
Fax: (202) 347-8237

SOUCIE, Kevin
Director, United States Government Affairs
kevin.soucie@cn.ca
Registered Federal Lobbyist
Tel: (202) 347-7196
Fax: (202) 347-8237

WOODRUFF, David
Registered Federal Lobbyist
Tel: (202) 347-7196
Fax: (202) 347-8237

CNA Financial Corporation

A multi-line business and personal insurance agency.
www.cna.com
Annual Revenues: $9.58 billion
Employees: 6,900

Ticker: NYSE: CNA
SIC: 6331
Industry/ies: Banking/Finance/Investments; Insurance Industry

Chairman of the Board and Chief Executive Officer
MOTAMED, Thomas F.
Tel: (312) 822-5000
Fax: (312) 822-6419

Main Headquarters
Mailing: 333 S. Wabash
Chicago, IL 60604
Tel: (312) 822-5000
Fax: (312) 822-6419
TF: (800) 262-2000

Washington Office
Mailing: 2020 K St. NW
Suite 505
Washington, DC 20006
Tel: (202) 416-4740
Fax: (312) 260-4568

Political Action Committees
CNA Financial Corporation Citizens for Good Government PAC
FEC ID: C00078287
Contact: Karen E. Melchert
333 S. Wabash Ave.
Chicago, IL 60604
Tel: (312) 822-5000
Fax: (312) 822-5000

   Contributions to Candidates: $52,000 (2015-2016)
   Democrats: $4,500; Republicans: $47,500

Corporate Foundations and Giving Programs
CNA Foundation
Contact: Gina Lockhart
333 S. Wabash Ave.
Chicago, IL 60604
Tel: (312) 822-5000
Fax: (312) 822-6419

Public Affairs and Related Activities Personnel

At Headquarters

HERMAN, Mark
President and Chief Operating Officer
Tel: (312) 822-5000
Fax: (312) 822-6419

HOTZA , Marie
Contact, Investor Relations
Marie.Hotza@cna.com
Tel: (312) 822-4278
Fax: (312) 822-6419

KANTOR, Jonathan D.
Executive Vice President, General Counsel and Secretary
jonathan.kantor@cna.com
Tel: (312) 822-5000
Fax: (312) 822-6419

LOCKHART, Gina
Program Officer, CNA Foundation
Mail Stop 44th Floor
gina.lockhart@cna.com
Tel: (312) 822-2828
Fax: (312) 822-6419

MELCHERT, Karen E.
Director, State Government Relations and PAC Treasurer
Mail Stop 43-S
karen.melchert@cna.com
Tel: (312) 822-5000
Fax: (312) 822-6419

MENSE, D. Craig
Executive Vice President and Chief Financial Officer
Tel: (312) 822-5000
Fax: (312) 822-6419

NUTLEY , Debbie
Chief Human Resources Officer
Tel: (312) 822-5000
Fax: (312) 822-6419

PANG , Sarah
Senior Vice President, Corporate Communications
Tel: (312) 822-5000
Fax: (312) 822-6419

PONTARELLI , Thomas
Executive Vice President and Chief Administration Officer
Tel: (312) 822-5000
Fax: (312) 822-6419

WARNICK, Michael P.
Senior Vice President & Deputy General Counsel
Tel: (312) 822-5000
Fax: (312) 822-6419

CNA Insurance Cos.

See listing on page 202 under CNA Financial Corporation

CNF, Inc.

See listing on page 214 under Con-way, Inc.

CNL Financial Group, Inc.

A real estate management and investment firm.
www.cnl.com
Employees: 600
Industry/ies: Real Estate

Executive Chairman
SENEFF, Jr., James M.
Tel: (407) 650-1000
Fax: (407) 650-1011

Chief Executive Officer
SITTEMA, Thomas K.
Tel: (407) 650-1000
Fax: (407) 650-1011

Main Headquarters
Mailing: P.O. Box 4920
Orlando, FL 32802-4920
Tel: (407) 650-1000
Fax: (407) 650-1011
TF: (866) 650-0650

Political Action Committees
CNL Financial Group, Inc. PAC
FEC ID: C00454314
Contact: Tracy Turner
P.O. Box 4920
Tel: (407) 650-1000

Suite 1400
Orlando, FL 32801 — Fax: (407) 650-1011

Contributions to Candidates: $6,400 (2015-2016)
Republicans: $6,400

Corporate Foundations and Giving Programs

CNL Charitable Foundation
Contact: James M. Seneff Jr.
P.O. Box 4920 — Tel: (407) 650-1000
450 S. Orange Ave., Suite 950 — Fax: (407) 650-1011
Orlando, FL 32802-4920

Public Affairs and Related Activities Personnel

At Headquarters

GREER , Holly J. — Tel: (407) 650-1000
Chief Legal Officer — Fax: (407) 650-1011

MANOR, Timothy J. — Tel: (407) 650-1000
General Counsel — Fax: (407) 650-1011

SCHMIDT, Tracy G. — Tel: (407) 650-1000
Chief Financial Officer and Chief Operating Officer — Fax: (407) 650-1011

SCHULTZ, Lisa A. — Tel: (407) 650-1223
Chief Services Officer — Fax: (407) 650-1011
llisa.schultz@cnl.com

At Other Offices

TIPTON, Tammy Jo — Tel: (407) 650-1000
Chief Financial Officer
450 South Orange Avenue, Suite 1400
Orlando, FL 32801

TURNER , Tracy — Tel: (407) 650-1000
PAC Treasurer
450 South Orange Avenue, Suite 1400
Orlando, FL 32801

CNO Financial Group, Inc.

A financial services company, which was incorporated in 1979, began operations in 1982, became a public company as Conseco, Inc. in 1985 and re-branded to CNO Financial Group, Inc. in 2010.
cnoinc.com
Employees: 4,200
Ticker: NYSE: CNO
SIC: 6321
Industry/ies: Banking/Finance/Investments
Legislative Issues: INS; LBR; MMM

Chairman — Tel: (317) 817-6100
SCHNEIDER, Neal C. — Fax: (317) 817-2847

Chief Executive Officer — Tel: (317) 817-6100
BONACH, Edward J. — Fax: (317) 817-2847

Main Headquarters
Mailing: 11825 N. Pennsylvania St. — Tel: (317) 817-6100
P.O. Box 1911 — Fax: (317) 817-2847
Carmel, IN 46032

Political Action Committees
Conseco Inc. Concerned Citizens PAC
FEC ID: C00303503
Contact: William D. Fritts Jr.
11825 N. Pennsylvania St.
Carmel, IN 46032

Contributions to Candidates: $12,000 (2015-2016)
Democrats: $1,000; Republicans: $11,000

Corporate Foundations and Giving Programs
CNO Financial Group Contribution Program
11825 N. Pennsylvania St. — Tel: (317) 817-6100
Carmel, IN 46032 — Fax: (317) 817-2847

Public Affairs and Related Activities Personnel

At Headquarters

BAUDE, Bruce — Tel: (317) 817-6100
Executive Vice President, Chief Operations and Technology Officer — Fax: (317) 817-2847

CIESEMIER, Barbara — Tel: (312) 396-7461
Senior Director, Corporate Communications — Fax: (317) 817-2847
Barbara.ciesemier@cnoinc.com

CRAWFORD, Frederick J. — Tel: (317) 817-6100
Executive Vice President and Chief Financial Officer — Fax: (317) 817-2847

FRITTS, Jr., William D. — Tel: (317) 817-6100
Senior Vice President, Regulatory Affairs — Fax: (317) 817-2847
Bill.fritts@cnoinc.com

HELDING, Erik — Tel: (317) 817-6100
Vice President, Finance — Fax: (317) 817-2847
erik.helding@cnoinc.com

MENZEL, Susan L. — Tel: (317) 817-6100
Executive Vice President, Human Resources — Fax: (317) 817-2847

PERRY, Scott R. — Tel: (317) 817-6100
Chief Business Officer — Fax: (317) 817-2847

ZEHNDER, Anthony — Tel: (312) 396-7086
Contact, Media Relations — Fax: (317) 817-2847
azehnder@conseco.com

ZIMPFER, Matthew J. — Tel: (317) 817-6100
Executive Vice President and General Counsel — Fax: (317) 817-2847

CNSI Inc.

A full-service IT company.
www.cns-inc.com
Annual Revenues: $457.93 million
Employees: 2,300
Industry/ies: Computer/Technology
Legislative Issues: HCR

Co-founder and Chief Executive Officer — Tel: (301) 634-4600
CHATTERJEE, B. — Fax: (301) 944-2022

Main Headquarters
Mailing: 2277 Research Blvd. — Tel: (301) 634-4600
Rockville, MD 20850 — Fax: (301) 944-2022

Washington Office
Mailing: 15800 Gaither Dr. — Tel: (301) 634-4600
Gaithersburg, MD 20877-1430 — Fax: (301) 944-2022

Corporate Foundations and Giving Programs
CNSI Inc. Contributions Programs
15800 Gaither Dr. — Tel: (301) 634-4600
Gaithersburg, MD 20877-1430 — Fax: (301) 944-2022

Public Affairs and Related Activities Personnel

At Headquarters

AHMED, Adnan — Tel: (301) 634-4600
Co-founder and President — Fax: (301) 944-2022
adnan.ahmed@cns-inc.com

KANWAL, Jaytee — Tel: (301) 634-4600
Co-Founder and Chief Operating Officer — Fax: (301) 944-2022

MISRA, Vijay — Tel: (301) 634-4600
Senior Vice President, Federal Programs — Fax: (301) 944-2022

MORSE, Arnold — Tel: (301) 634-4600
Senior Vice President and General Counsel — Fax: (301) 944-2022

PATEL, Shailesh — Tel: (301) 634-4600
Senior Vice President, Federal Health — Fax: (301) 944-2022
shailesh.patel@cns-inc.com

SINGH, Reet — Tel: (301) 634-4600
Co-founder and Chief Administrative Officer — Fax: (301) 944-2022

SINNOTT, Lawrence — Tel: (301) 634-4600
Chief Financial Officer — Fax: (301) 944-2022

Coachman Industries, Inc.

See listing on page 35 under All American Group

Coalescent Technologies Corporation

Provides engineering products and services to the federal government and commercial sector.
www.ctcorp.com
Annual Revenues: $7 million
Employees: 100
Industry/ies: Engineering/Mathematics

President and Chief Executive Officer — Tel: (407) 691-7610
WHITMORE, Kenneth N. — Fax: (407) 691-7999

Main Headquarters
Mailing: 422 W. Fairbanks Ave. — Tel: (407) 691-7610
Winter Park, FL 32789-5079 — Fax: (407) 691-7998
TF: (800) 254-8954

Coastal Lumber Company

Hardwood and specialty pine lumber manufacturer and marketer.
www.coastallumber.com/articles/History%20of%20Coas
Employees: 900
NAICS: 321212
Industry/ies: Construction/Construction Materials; Forestry; Paper And Wood Products Industry

Chairman of the Board — Tel: (434) 293-6087
BARRINGER, II, Paul B. — Fax: (434) 294-5622

Main Headquarters
Mailing: 99 Pullman Way — Tel: (408) 995-0791
San Jose, CA 95111

Public Affairs and Related Activities Personnel

At Headquarters

HINKLE, Tim — Tel: (408) 995-0791
Director, Human Resources

thinkle@coastallumber.com

CoBank

Provides funds for long-term real estate loans secured by first mortgages on farm and rural real estate. U.S. AgBank and CoBank merged on January 1, 2012.
Annual Revenues: $733.27 million
Employees: 1,500
Industry/ies: Banking/Finance/Investments

Chairman of the Board	Tel:	(316) 266-5100
EISENHUNT, John	Fax:	(316) 266-5121
President and Chief Executive Officer	Tel:	(316) 266-5100
RHODES, Darryl W.	Fax:	(316) 266-5121

Main Headquarters
Mailing: 245 N. Waco   Tel: (316) 266-5100
              Wichita, KS 67201   Fax: (316) 266-5121

Public Affairs and Related Activities Personnel

At Headquarters

HULTQUIST, Jeana   Tel: (316) 266-5100
Vice President - Legislative Affairs   Fax: (316) 266-5121
jeana.hultquist@usagbank.com

JANISH, David D.   Tel: (316) 266-5100
Senior Vice President, Finance   Fax: (316) 266-5121

Cobham Analytic Solutions

SPARTA's core business areas include strategic defense and offense systems, tactical weapons systems, space systems.
www.sparta.com
Annual Revenues: $350.00 million
Employees: 1,200
SIC: 8711
Industry/ies: Aerospace/Aviation; Computer/Technology; Construction/ Construction Materials; Defense/Homeland Security; Government-Related; Transportation
Legislative Issues: DEF

Main Headquarters
Mailing: 25531 Commercentre Dr.   Tel: (949) 768-8161
              Suite 120   Fax: (949) 583-9113
              Lake Forest, CA 92630-8874

Public Affairs and Related Activities Personnel

At Headquarters

HOFFMAN, Dorothy H.   Tel: (949) 768-8161
Vice President, Business Development   Fax: (949) 583-9113

SCHREIMAN, David   Tel: (949) 768-8161
Chief Financial Officer   Fax: (949) 583-9113

Cobham Holdings, Inc.

Developer of aerospace and defense systems.
www.cobham.com
Industry/ies: Aerospace/Aviation; Defense/Homeland Security; Government-Related; Transportation

Main Headquarters
Mailing: Ten Cobham Dr.   Tel: (703) 414-5300
              Orchard Park, NY 14127

Washington Office
Mailing: 2121 Crystal Dr.   Tel: (703) 414-5300
              Suite 625
              Arlington, VA 22202

Political Action Committees
Cobham Holdings Inc Political Action
FEC ID: C00457051
Contact: Julie Sutton
2121 Crystal Dr.
Arlington, VA 22202

   Contributions to Candidates: $147,750 (2015-2016)
   Democrats: $44,750; Republicans: $103,000

          Principal Recipients

                HOUSE
                DENT, CHARLES W. REP. (REP-PA)
                HUNTER, DUNCAN D. (REP-CA)
                JOLLY, DAVID W. (REP-FL)
                PETERS, SCOTT (DEM-CA)

Public Affairs and Related Activities Personnel

At Headquarters

BARBERO, Maj. Gen. Michael   Tel: (703) 414-5300
Vice President, Government Relations

At Washington Office

SUTTON, Julie   Tel: (703) 414-5300
PAC Treasurer

Cobham Management Services, Inc.

Cobham Management Services. is a mechanical power ransmission equipment manufacturing company located in Huntsville, Ala.
www.cobham.com
Industry/ies: Machinery/Equipment
Legislative Issues: AVI; DEF

Chairman   Tel: (703) 414-5300
DEVANEY, John

Chief Executive Officer   Tel: (703) 414-5300
MURPHY, Robert

Main Headquarters
Mailing: 2231 Crystal Dr.   Tel: (703) 414-5300
              Suite 1116
              Arlington, VA 22202

Public Affairs and Related Activities Personnel

At Headquarters

BARBARO, Michael   Tel: (703) 414-5300
Federal Lobbyist
Registered Federal Lobbyist

CAIRES, Gre Alan   Tel: (703) 414-5310
Vice President, Media Relations
greg.caires@cobham.com

JULIE, Sutton   Tel: (703) 414-5300
Federal Lobbyist
Registered Federal Lobbyist

MICHAEL, Barbero   Tel: (703) 414-5300
Federal Lobbyist
Registered Federal Lobbyist

NICHOLLS, Simon   Tel: (703) 414-5300
Chief Financial Officer, Executive Director

SUTTON, Julie   Tel: (703) 414-5300
Manager, Government Relations
julie.sutton@cobham.com
Registered Federal Lobbyist

Coca-Cola Bottling Company Consolidated

Markets, distributes, and produces bottled and canned beverage products for the Coca-Cola Company
www.cokeconsolidated.com
Annual Revenues: $1.65 billion
Employees: 5,000
Ticker: NASDAQ: COKE
SIC: 2086
Industry/ies: Food And Beverage Industry

Chairman of the Board and Chief Executive Officer   Tel: (704) 557-4400
HARRISON, III, J. Frank   Fax: (704) 551-4646

Main Headquarters
Mailing: P.O. Box 31487   Tel: (704) 557-4000
              Charlotte, NC 28231   Fax: (704) 551-4646
                                      TF: (800) 777-2653

Corporate Foundations and Giving Programs
Coca-Cola Bottling Company Consolidated Contributions Program
4100 Coca-Cola Plaza   Tel: (704) 557-4400
Charlotte, NC 28231   Fax: (704) 551-4646

Public Affairs and Related Activities Personnel

At Headquarters

CHAMBLESS, Robert G.   Tel: (704) 557-4400
Senior Vice President, Sales, Field Operations and Marketing   Fax: (704) 551-4646

DEAL, Clifford M   Tel: (704) 557-4000
Vice President and Treasurer   Fax: (704) 551-4646

FLINT, Henry W.   Tel: (704) 557-4000
President and Chief Operating Officer   Fax: (704) 551-4646

HARRIS, James E.   Tel: (704) 557-4400
Senior Vice President, Shared Services and Chief Financial Officer   Fax: (704) 551-4646

KASBEKAR, Umesh M.   Tel: (704) 557-4000
Senior Vice President, Planning and Administration   Fax: (704) 551-4646

STEELE, Lauren C.   Tel: (704) 551-4551
Vice President, Corporate Affairs and Contact, Media Relations   Fax: (704) 551-4646
Lauren.steele@cokeconsolidated.com

STRONG, Michael A.   Tel: (704) 557-4400
Senior Vice President, Employee Integration and Transition   Fax: (704) 551-4646

The Coca-Cola Company

A beverage company.
www.coca-colacompany.com
Annual Revenues: $46.13 billion
Employees: 129,200

Ticker: NYSE: KO
SIC: 2086
Industry/ies: Food And Beverage Industry
Legislative Issues: AGR; BEV; CDT; DEF; ECN; ENG; ENV; FOO; FOR; HCR; IMM; NAT; TAX; TRD

Chairman of the Board and Chief Executive Officer   Tel: (404) 676-2121
KENT, Muhtar

Main Headquarters
Mailing: One coca-cola Plaza   Tel: (404) 676-2121
P.O. Box 1734   Fax: (404) 676-6792
Atlanta, GA 30301   TF: (800) 438-2653

Washington Office
Mailing: 800 Connecticut Ave. NW, Suite 701
Washington, DC 20006

Political Action Committees
The Coca-Cola Company Non-partisan Committee for Good Government PAC
FEC ID: C00012468
Contact: Larry M. Mark
One Coca-Cola Plaza NW   Tel: (404) 676-2121
Atlanta, GA 30313

Contributions to Candidates: $434,250 (2015-2016)
Democrats: $164,750; Republicans: $268,500; Other: $1,000

Principal Recipients

SENATE
BLUNT, ROY (REP-MO)

HOUSE
GRAVES, JOHN THOMAS MR. JR. (REP-GA)
HOYER, STENY HAMILTON (DEM-DC)
MCCARTHY, KEVIN (REP-CA)
RYAN, PAUL D. (REP-WI)
SCALISE, STEVE MR. (REP-LA)

Corporate Foundations and Giving Programs

The Coca-Cola Foundation, Inc.
Contact: Lisa Borders
P.O. Box 1734   Tel: (404) 676-3525
Atlanta, GA 30301

Coca-Cola Scholars Foundation
Contact: Lisa Borders
P.O. Box 1734   Tel: (404) 733-5427
Atlanta, GA 30301

Public Affairs and Related Activities Personnel

At Headquarters

BLACK, Kathleen   Tel: (404) 676-2121
Director, Government Relations
Registered Federal Lobbyist

BORDERS , Lisa   Tel: (404) 676-2121
Vice President, Global Community Connections and Chair,
The Coca-Cola Foundation

CAHILLANE, Steve   Tel: (404) 676-2121
Executive Vice President and President, Coca-Cola Americas

CLARK, Wendy   Tel: (404) 676-2121
Senior Vice President, Sparkling Brand Center   Fax: (404) 676-6792

CUMMINGS, Alexander B.   Tel: (404) 676-2121
Chief Administrative Officer, Executive Vice President

DAVIS, J. Mark   Tel: (404) 733-5420
President, The Coca-Cola Scholars Foundation
jmdavis@na.ko.com

EBERLY, Ceree   Tel: (404) 676-2121
Chief People Officer

ECHOLS, Matt   Tel: (404) 676-2121
Vice President, Corporate Government Affairs & Diplomatic
Relations
mechols@coca-cola.com

ETHERLY, Curtis   Tel: (494) 676-2683
Registered Federal Lobbyist

FARRELL, John M.   Tel: (404) 676-2121
Vice President, Strategic Planning

GOEPELT, Bernhard   Tel: (404) 676-2121
Senior Vice President and General Counsel

GUTHRIE, Ryan C.   Tel: (404) 676-2121
Director, Government Relations
Registered Federal Lobbyist

HASTIE, Brent   Tel: (494) 676-2683
Vice President, Strategy and Planning

HOPKINS, Douglas W.   Tel: (404) 676-7733
Manager, Corporate Affairs, Finance and Administration   Fax: (404) 515-2272
dhopkins@na.ko.com

HOWARD, Janet   Tel: (404) 676-2121
Sales Executive

IRVIN, Kate   Tel: (494) 676-2683
Group Director, Diplomatic Relations
Registered Federal Lobbyist

KELLNER, Janine   Tel: (404) 676-2121
Manager, U.S. Government Relations
jkellner@na.ko.com
Registered Federal Lobbyist

MARK, Larry M.   Tel: (494) 676-2683
PAC Treasurer

RACKLEY, IV, Eugene   Tel: (494) 676-2683
Director, Government Relations
Registered Federal Lobbyist

RUMBAUGH, Kate   Tel: (404) 676-2121
Group Director, Government Affairs
krumbaugh@coca-cola.com
Registered Federal Lobbyist

SCHAFER, Dan A.   Tel: (404) 676-2121
Vice President, North American Public Affairs and   Fax: (404) 515-6428
Communications

SOUTUS, Sonya   Tel: (404) 515-0044
Senior Vice President, Public Affairs and Communications   Fax: (404) 515-0430

TUGGLE, Clyde C.   Tel: (494) 676-2683
Chief Public Affairs and Communications Officer   Fax: (404) 515-6428

WALLER, Kathy   Tel: (404) 676-2121
Chief Financial Officer

At Other Offices

ETHERLY, Curtis   Tel: (404) 676-7563
One Coca-Cola Plaza
Atlanta, GA 30313
Registered Federal Lobbyist

HASTIE, Brent   Tel: (404) 676-7563
Vice President, Strategy and Planning
One Coca-Cola Plaza
Atlanta, GA 30313

IRVIN, Kate   Tel: (404) 676-7563
Group Director, Diplomatic Relations
One Coca-Cola Plaza
Atlanta, GA 30313
Registered Federal Lobbyist

KELLY, Jackson   Tel: (404) 676-7563
Vice President and Investor Relations Officer
One Coca-Cola Plaza
Atlanta, GA 30313

MARK, Larry M.   Tel: (404) 676-7563
PAC Treasurer
One Coca-Cola Plaza
Atlanta, GA 30313

RACKLEY, IV, Eugene   Tel: (404) 676-7563
Director, Government Relations
One Coca-Cola Plaza
Atlanta, GA 30313
Registered Federal Lobbyist

Coca-Cola Enterprises
Bottler of Coca-Cola products, including energy drinks, still and sparkling waters, juices, sports drinks, fruit drinks, coffee-based beverages and teas.
www.cokecce.com
Annual Revenues: $8.02 billion
Employees: 11,650
Ticker: NYSE: CCE
SIC: 2086
Industry/ies: Food And Beverage Industry

Chairman of the Board and Chief Executive Officer   Tel: (678) 260-3000
BROCK, John F.
jbrock@cokecce.com

Main Headquarters
Mailing: 2500 Windy Ridge Pkwy.   Tel: (678) 260-3000
Atlanta, GA 30339

Political Action Committees
The Coca-Cola Company Non-partisan Committee for Good Government PAC
FEC ID: C00012468
Contact: Larry M. Mark
One Coca-Cola Plaza NW   Tel: (404) 676-2121
Atlanta, GA 30313

Contributions to Candidates: $434,250 (2015-2016)
Democrats: $164,750; Republicans: $268,500; Other: $1,000

Principal Recipients

SENATE
BLUNT, ROY (REP-MO)

HOUSE
GRAVES, JOHN THOMAS MR. JR. (REP-GA)

HOYER, STENY HAMILTON (DEM-DC)
MCCARTHY, KEVIN (REP-CA)
RYAN, PAUL D. (REP-WI)
SCALISE, STEVE MR. (REP-LA)

Corporate Foundations and Giving Programs

Coca Cola Enterprise Corporate Responsibility
2500 Windy Ridge Pkwy.
Atlanta, GA 30339

Public Affairs and Related Activities Personnel

At Headquarters

FORLIDAS, Suzanne N.	Tel:	(678) 260-3000
Vice President, Secretary, and Deputy General Counsel		
BRIGHTWELL, Laura	Tel:	(678) 260-3000
Senior Vice President, Public Affairs and Communications		
lbrightwell@cokecce.com		
DOUGLAS, III, William W.	Tel:	(678) 260-3000
Executive Vice President, Supply Chain		
ERICKSON, Thor	Tel:	(678) 260-3246
Vice President, Investor Relations		
terickson@cokecce.com		
JHANGIANI, Nik	Tel:	(678) 260-3000
Senior Vice President and Chief Financial Officer		
KIMMET, Pamela O.	Tel:	(678) 260-3000
Senior Vice President, Human Resources		
KING-LAVINDER, Joyce	Tel:	(678) 260-3000
Vice President and Treasurer		
PARKER, Jr., John R.	Tel:	(678) 260-3000
Senior Vice President, General Counsel and Strategic Initiatives		
PATTERSON, Suzanne D.	Tel:	(678) 260-3000
Vice President, Controller and Chief Accounting Officer		
ROSELLI, Fred	Tel:	(678) 260-3421
Director, Public Affairs & Executive Communications		

At Other Offices

MARK, Larry M.
PAC Treasurer
One Coca-Cola Plaza NW
Atlanta, GA 30313

WALLER, Kathy
Vice President & Controller
One Coca-Cola Plaza NW
Atlanta, GA 30313

CoCo Communications Corporation

A wireless telecommunications company.
www.cococorp.com
Annual Revenues: $2.30 million
Employees: 23
Industry/ies: Communications; Telecommunications/Internet/Cable

President and Chief Executive Officer	Tel:	(206) 264-9387
STACHOWIAK, John	Fax:	(206) 770-6461
jstachowiak@cococorp.com		

Main Headquarters

Mailing:	800 Fifth Ave.	Tel:	(206) 284-9387
	Suite 3700	Fax:	(206) 770-6461
	Seattle, WA 98104		

Public Affairs and Related Activities Personnel

At Headquarters

ELLER, Riley	Tel:	(206) 284-9387
Chief Technology Officer	Fax:	(206) 770-6461
GRANT, Rebecca	Tel:	(206) 264-9387
General Counsel	Fax:	(206) 770-6461
rgrant@cococorp.com		
ROBERTS, Michael	Tel:	(206) 284-9387
Head, Military Sales	Fax:	(206) 770-6461
TUBBS, Carey V.	Tel:	(206) 284-9387
Vice President, Government Business Development	Fax:	(206) 770-6461
ctubbs@cococorp.com		

Coeur d'Alene Mines Corporation

A silver and gold mining company.
www.coeur.com
Annual Revenues: $629.07 million
Employees: 1,868
Ticker: NYSE: CDE
SIC: 1040
Industry/ies: Mining Industry; Natural Resources
Legislative Issues: NAT

Chairman of the Board	Tel:	(208) 667-3511
MELLOR, Robert E.	Fax:	(208) 667-2213
President and Chief Executive Officer	Tel:	(208) 667-3511
KREBS, Mitchell J.	Fax:	(208) 667-2213

Main Headquarters

Mailing:	104 S. Michigan Ave.	Tel:	(312) 489-5800
	Suite 900	Fax:	(208) 667-2213
	Chicago, IL 60603	TF:	(800) 624-2824

Corporate Foundations and Giving Programs

Coeur d'Alene Mines Corporation Contributions Program
400 Coeur d'Alene Mines Bldg.
505 Front Ave.
Coeur d'Alene, ID 83816

Public Affairs and Related Activities Personnel

At Headquarters

FREAS, Bridget	Tel:	(312) 489-5910
Director, Investor Relations	Fax:	(208) 667-2213
bfreas@coeur.com		
KERR, Keagan J.	Tel:	(208) 667-3511
Senior Vice President, Corporate Affairs and Human Resources	Fax:	(208) 667-2213
MIRANDOLA, Donna M.	Tel:	(312) 489-5842
Director, Corporate Communications	Fax:	(208) 667-2213
dmirandola@coeur.com		
MITCHELL, Peter C.	Tel:	(208) 667-3511
Senior Vice President and Chief Financial Officer	Fax:	(208) 667-2213
NAULT, Casey	Tel:	(208) 667-3511
Vice President, General Counsel and Secretary	Fax:	(208) 667-2213

COGON Systems

A company that provides web services to the healthcare industry.
www.cogonsystems.com
Industry/ies: Computer/Technology; Medicine/Health Care/Mental Health

Chief Executive Officer	Tel:	(850) 429-1633
NGUYEN, Dr. Huy	Fax:	(850) 429-1634

Main Headquarters

Mailing:	1194 N. Eglin Pkwy.	Tel:	(954) 328-4791
	Shalimar, FL 32579		

Public Affairs and Related Activities Personnel

At Other Offices

COTTON, Kathy	Tel:	(850) 429-1633
Director, Administration	Fax:	(850) 429-1634
One Pensacola Plaza, 125 W. Romana St., Suite 210		
Pensacola, FL 32502		
Kathy.cotton@cogonsystems.com		

Coherus Biosciences

Biosimilars Manufacturer.
Industry/ies: Drug And Alcohol Abuse; Pharmaceutical Industry
Legislative Issues: BUD; CPT; HCR; MMM; PHA

Main Headquarters

Mailing:	333 Redwood Shores Pkwy., Suite 600
	Redwood City, CA 94065

Public Affairs and Related Activities Personnel

At Headquarters

REED, Juliana
Registered Federal Lobbyist

The Coleman Company

Maker of outdoor recreation gear, they also produces coolers, backpacks, footwear, camp stoves/grills, and other camping accessories, sold under the BackHome, Coleman, Campingaz, Exponent, and Peak 1 brands. A subsidiary of American Household, Inc.
www.coleman.com
Annual Revenues: $345.90 million
Employees: 3,700
SIC: 3634; 3949; 3648
NAICS: 33992; 335129
Industry/ies: Sports/Leisure/Entertainment
Legislative Issues: TRD

President and Chief Executive Officer	Tel:	(316) 832-2700
MARCOVITCH, Robert F.	Fax:	(316) 832-3060

Main Headquarters

Mailing:	3600 N. Hydraulic St.	Tel:	(316) 832-2700
	Wichita, KS 67219	Fax:	(316) 832-3060
		TF:	(800) 835-3278

Public Affairs and Related Activities Personnel

At Headquarters

HOGAN, Daniel	Tel:	(316) 832-2700

Chief Financial Officer/Chief Operating Officer　Fax:　(316) 832-3060
REID, Jim　Tel:　(316) 219-7535
Senior Manager, Public Relations　Fax:　(316) 832-3060

Colfax Corporation

Develops, engineers, manufactures and distributes pumping and fluid-handling systems.
www.colfaxcorp.com
Annual Revenues: $4.48 billion
Employees: 18,351
Ticker: NYSE: CFX
SIC: 3561
Industry/ies: Marine/Maritime/Shipping; Transportation

Chairman of the Board　Tel:　(804) 560-4070
RALES, Mitchell P.　Fax:　(804) 560-4076

President and Chief Executive Officer　Tel:　(804) 560-4070
SIMMS, Steven E.　Fax:　(804) 560-4076

Main Headquarters
Mailing:　8170 Maple Lawn Blvd.　Tel:　(301) 323-9090
　　　　　Suite 180　Fax:　(301) 323-9001
　　　　　Fulton, MD 20759

Public Affairs and Related Activities Personnel

At Headquarters

CLARK, Lynn　Tel:　(301) 323-9090
Senior Vice President, Global Human Resources　Fax:　(301) 323-9001

At Other Offices

BRANNAN, C. Scott　Tel:　(804) 560-4070
Senior Vice President, Finance and Chief Financial Officer　Fax:　(804) 560-4076
8730 Stony Point Pkwy., Suite 150
Richmond, VA 23235

PRYOR, Daniel A.　Tel:　(804) 560-4070
Senior Vice President, Strategy and Business Development　Fax:　(804) 560-4076
8730 Stony Point Pkwy., Suite 150
Richmond, VA 23235

PUCKETT, A. Lynne　Tel:　(804) 560-4070
Senior Vice President, General Counsel and Secretary　Fax:　(804) 560-4076
8730 Stony Point Pkwy., Suite 150
Richmond, VA 23235

Colgate Palmolive Company

Manufacturer and distributor of consumer products for personal and household care.
www.colgate.com
Annual Revenues: $15.73 billion
Employees: 37,900
Ticker: NYSE: CL
SIC: 2841; 2842; 2844
NAICS: 325611; 325612; 325620
Industry/ies: Personal Care/Hygiene
Legislative Issues: CHM; ECN

Chairman of the Board, President and Chief Executive Officer　Tel:　(212) 310-2000
COOK, Ian M.　Fax:　(212) 310-2475

Main Headquarters
Mailing:　300 Park Ave.　Tel:　(212) 310-2000
　　　　　New York City, NY 10022-7499　Fax:　(212) 310-2475
　　　　　　TF:　(800) 468-6502

Corporate Foundations and Giving Programs

Colgate Palmolive Company Contributions Program
300 Park Ave.　Tel:　(212) 310-2000
New York City, NY 10022-7499　Fax:　(212) 310-2475

Colgate Palmolive foundation
300 Park Ave.　Tel:　(212) 310-2000
New York City, NY 10022-7499　Fax:　(212) 310-2475

Public Affairs and Related Activities Personnel

At Headquarters

COLLINS, Martin J.　Tel:　(212) 310-2000
Vice President, Chief of Legal Operations, Global Legal Organization　Fax:　(212) 310-2475

FOGARTY, Stephen J.　Tel:　(212) 310-2000
Chief Ethics and Compliance Officer　Fax:　(212) 310-2475

GUIFARRO, Janet　Tel:　(212) 310-2000
Vice President, Corporate Communications　Fax:　(212) 310-2475

HICKEY, Dennis　Tel:　(212) 310-2000
Chief Financial Officer　Fax:　(212) 310-2475

THOMPSON, Bina H.　Tel:　(212) 310-3072
Senior Vice President, Investor Relations　Fax:　(212) 310-2475

Colombian Coffee Federation

Association of coffee farmers.
www.federaciondecafeteros.org/particulares/en
Employees: 2,655

Industry/ies: Commodities

President and Chief Executive Officer　Tel:　(212) 421-8300
ORDUZ, Juan Esteban

Main Headquarters
Mailing:　140 E. 57th St.　Tel:　(212) 421-8300
　　　　　New York City, NY 10022

Colonial Life

See listing on page 207 under Colonial Life & Accident Insurance Company

Colonial Life & Accident Insurance Company

Provides benefits communication, service, enrollment, and supplemental insurance to employees and their families at the worksite. A subsidiary of Unum Provident Corporation.
www.coloniallife.com
Annual Revenues: $35.8 Million
Employees: 950
Industry/ies: Insurance Industry

President and Chief Executive Officer　Tel:　(803) 798-7000
ARNOLD, Tim　Fax:　(803) 731-2618

Main Headquarters
Mailing:　1200 Colonial Life Blvd.　Tel:　(803) 798-7000
　　　　　Columbia, SC 29210　Fax:　(803) 731-2618
　　　　　　TF:　(800) 438-6423

Public Affairs and Related Activities Personnel

At Headquarters

BOGGS, L. Kennedy　Tel:　(803) 798-7000
Senior Vice President, Legal and Compliance Officer　Fax:　(803) 731-2618

BROWN, Jeff　Tel:　(803) 798-7000
Senior Vice President and Chief Marketing Officer　Fax:　(803) 731-2618

GARRISON, John　Tel:　(803) 798-7000
Vice President, General Counsel　Fax:　(803) 731-2618

HOUSER, Ann　Tel:　(803) 798-7000
Vice President, Human Resources　Fax:　(803) 731-2618

NORTHAM, Donna　Tel:　(803) 798-7000
Assistant Vice President, Corporate and External Communications　Fax:　(803) 731-2618
dcnortham@coloniallife.com

PARKER, David　Tel:　(803) 798-7000
Senior Vice President, Growth Operations　Fax:　(803) 731-2618

REYNOLDS, Jeanne　Tel:　(803) 678-6274
Media Contact　Fax:　(803) 731-2618
jdreynolds@coloniallife.com

WINSTON, Jacqueline B.　Tel:　(803) 678-2422
Assistant Vice President and Senior Counsel　Fax:　(803) 731-2618

Colonial Pipeline Company

A joint venture of the following major oil companies - CITGO Pipeline Holding I, LLC, Conoco Phillips Pipe Line Company, HUTTS, LLC, Koch Capital Investments Company, LLC, Phillips Petroleum International, and Shell Pipeline Company LP.
www.colpipe.com
Annual Revenues: $45.70 million
Employees: 700
Industry/ies: Energy/Electricity; Fuels See Coal, Gas, Oil, Petroleum; Natural Resources; Petroleum Industry; Transportation
Legislative Issues: ENG; TRA

President and Chief Executive Officer　Tel:　(678) 762-2200
FELT, Tim　Fax:　(678) 762-2813

Main Headquarters
Mailing:　P.O. Box 1624　Tel:　(678) 762-2200
　　　　　Alpharetta, GA 30009　Fax:　(678) 762-2813
　　　　　　TF:　(800) 275-3004

Corporate Foundations and Giving Programs

Colonial Pipeline Contributions Program
P.O. Box 1624
Alpharetta, GA 30009-9934

Public Affairs and Related Activities Personnel

At Headquarters

BAKER, Steve　Tel:　(678) 762-2589
Director, Communications, Public Affairs　Fax:　(678) 762-2813
SBaker@colpipe.com

BELDEN, Doug　Tel:　(678) 762-2200
Vice President, General Manager of Operations　Fax:　(678) 762-2813

BROOKS, Eve　Tel:　(678) 762-2200
Vice President, Human Resources　Fax:　(678) 762-2813

DOUDNA, Dave　Tel:　(678) 762-2200
Vice President, Chief Financial Officer　Fax:　(678) 762-2813

LACKEY, Meredith　Tel:　(678) 762-2200
Vice President, General Counsel　Fax:　(678) 762-2813

Colonial Properties Trust

Colonial Properties Trust is a multifamily real estate investment trust.
www.colonialprop.com
Annual Revenues: $435.29 million
Employees: 911
Ticker: NYSE: CLP
SIC: 6798
Industry/ies: Real Estate

Chairman of the Board and Chief Executive Officer	Tel:	(205) 250-8700
LOWDER, Thomas H.	Fax:	(205) 250-8890

Main Headquarters

Mailing:	2101 Sixth Ave., North	Tel:	(205) 250-8700
	Suite 750	Fax:	(205) 250-8890
	Birmingham, AL 35203-2775	TF:	(866) 620-1130

Political Action Committees

Colonial Properties Trust PAC
FEC ID: C00327668
Contact: John P. Rigrish
2101 Sixth Ave., North
Suite 750
Birmingham, AL 35203

Public Affairs and Related Activities Personnel

At Headquarters

BREWER, Jerry A.	Tel:	(205) 250-8700
Executive Vice President, Finance	Fax:	(205) 250-8890
jbrewer@colonialprop.com		
RIGRISH, John P.	Tel:	(205) 250-8700
Chief Administrative Officer, Corporate Secretary and PAC Treasurer	Fax:	(205) 250-8890
SANDIDGE, Bradley P.	Tel:	(205) 250-8700
Interim Chief Financial Officer and Chief Accounting Officer	Fax:	(205) 250-8890
THOMPSON, III, Reynolds C.	Tel:	(205) 250-8700
President and Chief Financial Officer	Fax:	(205) 250-8890

Colorado Engineering, Inc.

A software and hardware design and engineering company.
coloradoengineeringinc.com
Annual Revenues: $1.10 million
Employees: 11
Industry/ies: Engineering/Mathematics

Chief Executive Officer	Tel:	(719) 388-8582
SCALLY, Nancy E.	Fax:	(719) 265-1962
nancy.scally@coloradoengineeringinc.com		

Main Headquarters

Mailing:	1915 Jamboree	Tel:	(719) 388-8582
	Suite 165	Fax:	(713) 555-1212
	Colorado Springs, CO 80920		

Public Affairs and Related Activities Personnel

At Headquarters

BONATO, Michael J.	Tel:	(719) 388-8582
Vice President, Advanced Programs	Fax:	(719) 265-1962
michael.bonato@coloradoengineeringinc.com		
BROWN, Lance	Tel:	(719) 388-8582
Director, Business Development	Fax:	(713) 555-1212
BURGHARDT, Sherry	Tel:	(719) 388-8582
Vice President, Operations	Fax:	(713) 555-1212
SCALLY, Lawrence J.	Tel:	(719) 388-8582
President and Chief Technical Officer	Fax:	(719) 265-1962
Larry.scally@coloradoengineeringinc.com		

Columbia Pipeline Group

Energy.
Industry/ies: Energy/Electricity
Legislative Issues: TRA

Main Headquarters

Mailing:	10 G St. NE
	Suite 400
	Washington, DC 20002

Public Affairs and Related Activities Personnel

At Headquarters

OEHLER, Alex
Registered Federal Lobbyist

Columbia Power Technologies

Columbia Power Technologies, LLC is an independent company founded in 2005 by Greenlight Energy Resources, Inc., in partnership with Oregon State University. The company is engaged in the development and commercialization of wave energy harvesting devices using novel, off-shore, direct-drive permanent-magnet generator topologies.
www.columbiapwr.com

Annual Revenues: $0.71 million
Industry/ies: Energy/Electricity; Utilities
Legislative Issues: DEF; ENG

Chief Executive Officer	Tel:	(541) 368-5033
LESEMANN, Reenst	Fax:	(541) 230-1498

Main Headquarters

Mailing:	4920A SW Third St.	Tel:	(541) 368-5033
	Corvallis, OR 97333	Fax:	(541) 230-1498

Public Affairs and Related Activities Personnel

At Headquarters

LAMB, Bradford	Tel:	(541) 368-5033
President and Chief Operating Officer	Fax:	(541) 230-1498
TROUSDALE, Jim	Tel:	(541) 368-5033
Vice President, Finance	Fax:	(541) 230-1498

Columbus Castings

Manufactures steel castings for the freight rail, mass transit and heavy industry markets.
www.columbuscastings.com
Annual Revenues: $63.00 million
Employees: 800
SIC: 3325
NAICS: 331513
Industry/ies: Metals

Chairman of the Board	Tel:	(614) 444-2121
PIERCE, Ernie	Fax:	(614) 445-2084

Main Headquarters

Mailing:	2211 Parsons Ave.	Tel:	(614) 444-2121
	Columbus, OH 43207-2448	Fax:	(614) 445-2084

Public Affairs and Related Activities Personnel

At Headquarters

LAIRD, Jeff	Tel:	(614) 444-2121
Vice President, Marketing and Sales	Fax:	(614) 445-2084
jlaird@columbuscastings.com		

Columbus Steel Casting

See listing on page 208 under Columbus Castings

Combat Medical Systems, LLC

Tactical medical solutions provider.
www.combatmedicalsystems.com
Annual Revenues: $3 million
Industry/ies: Defense/Homeland Security; Government-Related; Medicine/Health Care/Mental Health; Military/Veterans
Legislative Issues: DEF

Chief Executive Officer	Tel:	(704) 705-1222
TWEARDY, Lisa	Fax:	(704) 879-2384
ltweardy@combatmedicalsystems.com		

Main Headquarters

Mailing:	5555 Harrisburg Industrial Park Dr.	Tel:	(704) 705-1222
	Harrisburg, NC 28075	Fax:	(704) 879-2384
		TF:	(855) 428-6074

Public Affairs and Related Activities Personnel

At Headquarters

CAULEY , Jason	Tel:	(704) 705-1222
Vice President, Business Development	Fax:	(704) 879-2384
jcauley@combatmedicalsystems.com		

CombinatoRx, Inc

See listing on page 860 under Zalicus Inc.

Comcast Corporation

A digital cable, high-speed Internet and telephone services provider. Acquired AT&T Broadband in 2002.
corporate.comcast.com
Annual Revenues: $69.22 billion
Employees: 139,000
Ticker: NASDAQ: CMCSK
SIC: 4841
Industry/ies: Communications; Media/Mass Communication; Telecommunications/Internet/Cable
Legislative Issues: ADV; AVI; COM; CPI; CPT; CSP; GOV; HOM; IMM; LAW; SCI; TAX; TEC; TRD

Chairman of the Board and Chief Executive Officer	Tel:	(215) 665-1700
ROBERTS, Brian L.		
brian_roberts@comcast.com		

Main Headquarters

Mailing:	1701 JFK Blvd.	Tel:	(215) 286-1700
	Philadelphia, PA 19103	TF:	(800) 266-2278

Washington Office

Mailing: 300 New Jersey Ave.
Suite 700
Washington, DC 20001

Political Action Committees

Comcast Corporation and NBC Universal Political Action Committee - Federal
FEC ID: C00248716
Contact: William Dordelman
1701 JFK Blvd., 49th Floor
Philadelphia, PA 19103

Contributions to Candidates: $1,524,500 (2015-2016)
Democrats: $569,900; Republicans: $950,100; Other: $4,500

Principal Recipients

SENATE

AYOTTE, KELLY A (REP-NH)
BENNET, MICHAEL F (DEM-CO)
BLUNT, ROY (REP-MO)
BLUNT, ROY (REP-TX)
BURR, RICHARD (REP-NC)
CRAPO, MICHAEL D (REP-ID)
GRASSLEY, CHARLES E SENATOR (REP-IA)
JOHNSON, RONALD HAROLD (REP-)
KIRK, MARK STEVEN (REP-IL)
LEAHY, PATRICK J (DEM-VT)
MORAN, JERRY (REP-KS)
MURRAY, PATTY (DEM-WA)
PAUL, RAND (REP-KY)
SCOTT, TIMOTHY E (REP-SC)
SHELBY, RICHARD C (REP-AL)
THUNE, JOHN (REP-SD)

HOUSE

BLACKBURN, MARSHA MRS. (REP-TN)
BOYLE, BRENDAN F (DEM-PA)
BRADY, ROBERT A (DEM-DC)
CHAFFETZ, JASON (REP-UT)
CLYBURN, JAMES E. (DEM-SC)
COSTELLO, RYAN A (REP-PA)
DENT, CHARLES W. REP. (REP-PA)
DOYLE, MIKE (DEM-PA)
GOODLATTE, ROBERT W. (REP-VA)
GREEN, RAYMOND E. 'GENE' (DEM-TX)
HOYER, STENY HAMILTON (DEM-DC)
HUDSON, RICHARD L. JR. (REP-NC)
LUJAN, BEN R MR. (DEM-NM)
MALONEY, SEAN PATRICK (DEM-NY)
MARINO, THOMAS ANTHONY (REP-PA)
MCHENRY, PATRICK TIMOTHY (REP-NC)
MCMORRIS RODGERS, CATHY (REP-WA)
MEEHAN, PATRICK L. MR. (REP-PA)
PALLONE, FRANK JR (DEM-NJ)
RICE, KATHLEEN (DEM-NY)
RYAN, PAUL D. (REP-WI)
SANCHEZ, LINDA (DEM-CA)
SCALISE, STEVE MR. (REP-LA)
SCHRADER, KURT (DEM-OR)
SCHULTZ, DEBBIE WASSERMAN (DEM-FL)
SINEMA, KYRSTEN (DEM-AZ)
WALDEN, GREGORY P MR. (REP-OR)

Corporate Foundations and Giving Programs

The Comcast Foundation
Contact: Charisse R. Lillie
One Comcast Center
Philadelphia, PA 19103   Tel: (215) 981-7607

Public Affairs and Related Activities Personnel

At Headquarters

ANGELAKIS, Michael J.   Tel: (202) 379-1700
Vice Chairman and Chief Financial Officer
michael_angelakis@comcast.com

BLOCK, Esquire, Arthur R.   Tel: (215) 665-1700
Executive Vice President, General Counsel and Secretary

DORDELMAN, William   Tel: (215) 286-1700
Senior Vice President and PAC Treasurer

GILES, Johnnie   Tel: (215) 286-1700
Executive Director, External Affairs
johnnie_giles@cable.comcast.com

KHOURY, Jennifer   Tel: (215) 286-7408
*Senior Vice President, Corporate and Digital
Communications*
Jennifer_Khoury@comcast.com

LILLIE, Charisse R.   Tel: (215) 665-1700
*Vice President, Community Investment and Executive Vice
President, Comcast Foundation*

MCGINLEY, Joseph P.   Tel: (215) 286-1700

Vice President, Corporate Development

PICK, Robert S.   Tel: (215) 665-1700
Senior Vice President, Corporate Development
robert_pick@comcast.com

RUDNAY, D'Arcy F.   Tel: (215) 285-8582
Senior Vice President and Chief Communications Officer
darcy_rudnay@comcast.com

SMITH, Justin B.   Tel: (215) 286-1700
Vice President, Chief Transaction Compliance Officer

At Washington Office

BUONO, Francis M.
*Senior Vice President, Legal Regulatory Affairs & Senior
Deputy General Counsel*

CHARYTAN, Lynn
General Counsel

DAVIS, Andy
Director, Regulatory and Government Affairs

EICH, Louise
Senior Manager, Government Communications

GOMEZ, Paul A.
Registered Federal Lobbyist

JAMES, Judy
Director, Government Affairs, North Bay Area

MCGEE, Ashley
Federal Lobbyist
Registered Federal Lobbyist

OTERO, Juan
Federal Lobbyist
Registered Federal Lobbyist

ROSE, Mitch
Registered Federal Lobbyist

At Other Offices

ARBOGAST, Rebecca   Tel: (202) 379-7100
Senior Vice President, Global Public Policy   Fax: (202) 466-7718
2100 Pennsylvania Ave., Suite 500
Washington, DC 20006

BAKER, Meredith Attwell   Tel: (202) 379-7100
Senior Vice President, Government Affairs, NBCUniversal   Fax: (202) 466-7718
2100 Pennsylvania Ave., Suite 500
Washington, DC 20006

BRIOCHE, Ruby   Tel: (202) 379-7100
Director, Senior and Global Public Policy   Fax: (202) 466-7718
2100 Pennsylvania Ave., Suite 500
Washington, DC 20006

COLTHARP, James R.   Tel: (202) 379-7102
Chief Policy Advisor, FCC and Regulatory Policy   Fax: (202) 466-7718
2100 Pennsylvania Ave., Suite 500
Washington, DC 20006
jim_coltharp@comcast.com
Registered Federal Lobbyist

DICKINSON, Lindsey   Tel: (202) 379-7134
Vice President, Legislative Affairs   Fax: (202) 466-7718
2100 Pennsylvania Ave., Suite 500
Washington, DC 20006
lindsey_dickinson@comcast.com
Registered Federal Lobbyist

FILON, Peter   Tel: (202) 379-7134
Federal Lobbyist   Fax: (202) 466-7718
2100 Pennsylvania Ave., Suite 500
Washington, DC 20006
pete_filon@comcast.com
Registered Federal Lobbyist

FITZMAURICE, Sena   Tel: (202) 379-7107
Vice President, Government Communications   Fax: (202) 466-7718
2100 Pennsylvania Ave., Suite 500
Washington, DC 20006

HUZARSKY, Kathleen   Tel: (202) 379-7100
Director, Federal Government Affairs   Fax: (202) 466-7718
2100 Pennsylvania Ave., Suite 500
Washington, DC 20006
kathleen_huzarsky@comcast.com
Registered Federal Lobbyist

JONES, Earle   Tel: (202) 379-7134
Federal Lobbyist   Fax: (202) 466-7718
2100 Pennsylvania Ave., Suite 500
Washington, DC 20006
earle_jones@cable.comcast.com
Registered Federal Lobbyist

LANCASTER, Samuel   Tel: (202) 379-7134
Vice President, Legislative Affairs   Fax: (202) 466-7718
2100 Pennsylvania Ave., Suite 500

Washington, DC 20006
samuel_lancaster@comcast.com
Registered Federal Lobbyist

MCMANUS, Mary P.   Tel: (202) 379-7113
Senior Director, FCC & Regulatory Affairs   Fax: (202) 466-7718
2100 Pennsylvania Ave., Suite 500
Washington, DC 20006
mary_mcmanus@comcast.com

PERKINS, Bret   Tel: (202) 379-7100
Vice President, External and Government Affairs   Fax: (202) 466-7718
2100 Pennsylvania Ave., Suite 500
Washington, DC 20006

TAHTAKRAN, Phil   Tel: (202) 379-7120
Federal Lobbyist   Fax: (202) 466-7718
2100 Pennsylvania Ave., Suite 500
Washington, DC 20006
Registered Federal Lobbyist

TRAHERN, Joseph   Tel: (202) 379-7134
Federal Lobbyist   Fax: (202) 466-7718
2100 Pennsylvania Ave., Suite 500
Washington, DC 20006
Registered Federal Lobbyist

VACCARO, Sue   Tel: (202) 379-7120
Senior Director, Government Relations, California   Fax: (202) 466-7718
2100 Pennsylvania Ave., Suite 500
Washington, DC 20006

ZACHEM, Kathryn A.   Tel: (202) 379-7134
Senior Vice President, Regulatory and State Legislative   Fax: (202) 466-7718
Affairs
2100 Pennsylvania Ave., Suite 500
Washington, DC 20006
kathy_zachem@comcast.com

ComEd

A subsidiary of Exelon Corp. (see separate listing). An energy delivery company.
www.comed.com
Employees: 6,000
Industry/ies: Energy/Electricity

Chairman and President   Tel: (312) 394-4321
MCNEILL, Jr., Corbin A.   Fax: (312) 394-2231

President and Chief Executive Officer   Tel: (312) 394-4321
PRAMAGGIORE, Anne   Fax: (312) 394-2231

Main Headquarters
Mailing: P.O. Box 805379   Tel: (312) 394-4321
    Chicago, IL 60680-5379   Fax: (312) 394-2231
           TF: (800) 334-7661

Corporate Foundations and Giving Programs

ComEd contributions Program
P.O. Box 805379   Tel: (312) 394-4321
Chicago, IL 60680-5379   Fax: (312) 394-2231

Public Affairs and Related Activities Personnel

At Headquarters

BROOKINS, Kevin B.   Tel: (312) 394-4321
Senior Vice President, Strategy and Administration   Fax: (312) 394-2231

DONNELLY, Terence   Tel: (312) 394-4321
Executive Vice President and Chief Operating Officer   Fax: (312) 394-2231

MARQUEZ, Fidel   Tel: (312) 394-4321
Senior Vice President, Legislative and External Affairs and   Fax: (312) 394-2231
Chief Governmental and Community Relations Officer

O'NEILL, Thomas   Tel: (312) 394-4321
Senior Vice President, Regulatory and Energy Policy and   Fax: (312) 394-2231
General Counsel

TRPIK, Jr., Joseph   Tel: (312) 394-4321
Senior Vice President, Chief Financial Officer and Treasurer   Fax: (312) 394-2231

Comerica, Inc.

Formed by a 1992 merger of Comerica Bank and Manufacturers Bank, N.A. A financial services company.
www.comerica.com
Annual Revenues: $2.49 billion
Employees: 8,533
Ticker: NYSE: CMA
SIC: 6021
Industry/ies: Banking/Finance/Investments

Chairman and Chief Executive Officer   Tel: (214) 969-6476
BABB, Jr., Ralph W.   Fax: (313) 965-4648

Main Headquarters
Mailing: Comerica Bank Tower   Tel: (214) 462-6831
    1717 Main St.   Fax: (214) 462-6810
    Dallas, TX 75201   TF: (800) 925-2160

Political Action Committees
Comerica Inc. PAC
FEC ID: C00393173
Contact: Daniel Donohoe
P.O. Box 75000
Detroit, MI 48275

  Contributions to Candidates: $153,500 (2015-2016)
  Democrats: $28,000; Republicans: $125,500

Principal Recipients

HOUSE
  HENSARLING, JEB HON. (REP-TX)
  SESSIONS, PETE MR. (REP-TX)

Corporate Foundations and Giving Programs

Comerica Charitable Foundation
Contact: Caroline Chambers
Comerica Bank Tower
1717 Main St.
Dallas, TX 75201

Public Affairs and Related Activities Personnel

At Headquarters

BILSTROM, Jon W.   Tel: (214) 969-6476
Executive Vice President, Legal Affairs   Fax: (313) 965-4648

BUCHANAN, John D.   Tel: (214) 462-6831
Executive Vice President Governance, Regulatory Relations   Fax: (214) 462-6810
and Legal Affairs

BURKHART, Megan D.   Tel: (214) 969-6476
Executive Vice President and Chief Human Resources Officer   Fax: (313) 965-4648

CHAMBERS, Caroline   Tel: (214) 462-6831
Vice President & National Director, Diversity Initiatives   Fax: (214) 462-6810

DUPREY, David E.   Tel: (214) 462-6831
Executive Vice President and Chief Financial Officer   Fax: (214) 462-6810

FORTE, Linda D.   Tel: (214) 462-6831
Senior Vice President, Business Affairs   Fax: (214) 462-6810

MICHALAK, Michael H.   Tel: (214) 969-6476
Executive Vice President and Chief Risk Officer   Fax: (313) 965-4648

PERSONS, Darlene P.   Tel: (214) 462-6831
Senior Vice President and Director, Investor Relations   Fax: (214) 462-6810
Mail Stop Third Floor, MC 6500
dppersons@comerica.com

WALKER, Wendy   Tel: (214) 462-4463
Senior Vice President and Director, National   Fax: (214) 462-4440
Communications
wdwalker@comerica.com

At Other Offices

DONOHOE, Daniel
Senior Vice President- Director, Government Relations
P.O. Box 75000
Detroit, MI 48275
ddonohoe@comerica.com

Commerce Bank, N.A.

Financial services and banking company.
www.commercebank.com
Annual Revenues: $1.04 billion
Employees: 4,769
Ticker: NASDAQ: CBSH
SIC: 6022
Industry/ies: Banking/Finance/Investments
Legislative Issues: BAN; FIN

Chairman and Chief Executive Officer   Tel: (314) 746-3657
KEMPER, David W.

Main Headquarters
Mailing: 8000 Forsyth Blvd.   Tel: (314) 746-3657
    St. Louis, MO 63105   TF: (800) 453-2265

Political Action Committees
Commerce Bancs PAC
FEC ID: C00072967
Contact: Robert Lay
1000 Walnut St.
Suite 700, P.O. Box 419248
Kansas City, MO 64141

  Contributions to Candidates: $59,628 (2015-2016)
  Democrats: $13,228; Republicans: $46,400

Corporate Foundations and Giving Programs

Commerce Bancshares Foundation
1000 Walnut St.   Tel: (816) 234-2000
P.O. Box 419248   Fax: (816) 234-2019
Kansas City, MO 64141

Public Affairs and Related Activities Personnel

At Headquarters

ATENCIO, Anthony
Representative, Public Relations, Investor Relations,
Government Relations, Social Media Contact
anthony.atencio@commercebank.com
Tel: (314) 746-3048

HYLAND, Molly
Vice President, Government Relations
molly.hyland@commercebank.com
Registered Federal Lobbyist
Tel: (314) 746-3657

KEMPER, John W.
President and Chief Operating Officer
Tel: (314) 746-3657

KIM, Charles G.
Chief Financial Officer
Tel: (314) 746-3657

At Other Offices

ABERDEEN, Jeffery D.
Contact, Investor Relations
P.O. Box 419248
Kansas City, MO 64141-6248
mymoney@commercebank.com
Tel: (816) 234-2081
Fax: (816) 234-2019

FOSTER, Sara E.
Chief Human Resources Officer
P.O. Box 419248
Kansas City, MO 64141-6248
Tel: (816) 234-2000
Fax: (816) 234-2019

HOWARD, Jeanne
Director, Regional Marketing
P.O. Box 419248
Kansas City, MO 64141-6248
jeanne.howard@commercebank.com
Tel: (816) 234-2000
Fax: (816) 234-2019

LAY, Robert
PAC Treasurer
1000 Walnut, Suite 700, P.O. Box 419248
Kansas City, MO 64141-6248

SCHNOEBELEN, Maura
Representative, Public Relations, Investor Relations and
Government Relations
P.O. Box 419248
Kansas City, MO 64141-6248
maura.schnoebelen@commercebank.com
Tel: (314) 746-8567
Fax: (816) 234-2019

Commercial Metals Company

A producer of metals.
www.cmc.com
Annual Revenues: $4.81 billion
Employees: 9,126
Ticker: NYSE: CMC
SIC: 3312
Industry/ies: Metals

Chairman of the Board, President and Chief Executive Officer
ALVARADO, Joseph
Tel: (214) 689-4300
Fax: (214) 689-5886

Main Headquarters
Mailing: 6565 N. MacArthur Blvd.
Suite 800
Irving, TX 75039
Tel: (214) 689-4300
Fax: (214) 689-5886

Political Action Committees
Commercial Metals Company PAC (CMC PAC)
FEC ID: C00525071
Contact: Paul K. Kirkpatrick
6565 N. MacArthur Blvd.
Suite 800
Irving, TX 75039
Tel: (214) 689-4300

Contributions to Candidates: $2,000 (2015-2016)
Republicans: $2,000

Corporate Foundations and Giving Programs
Commercial Metals Company Contributions Program
6565 N. MacArthur Blvd.
Suite 800
Irving, TX 75039
Tel: (214) 689-4300
Fax: (214) 689-5886

Public Affairs and Related Activities Personnel

At Headquarters

BATCHELOR, Adam B.
Vice President, Strategy and Planning
Tel: (214) 689-4300
Fax: (214) 689-5886

DUBOIS, Carey
Vice President and Treasurer
Tel: (214) 689-4300
Fax: (214) 689-5886

HATTEN, Terry
Vice President and Chief Human Resources Officer
Tel: (214) 689-4300
Fax: (214) 689-5886

HICKEY, Adam
Vice President and Controller
Tel: (214) 689-4300
Fax: (214) 689-5886

KIRKPATRICK, Paul K.
Vice President, General Counsel, Corporate Secretary and
PAC Treasurer
Tel: (214) 689-4300
Fax: (214) 689-5886

LEWALLYN, Susan
Contact, Investor Relations
Tel: (972) 308-5349
Fax: (214) 689-5886

LINDSEY, Mary
Vice President and Chief Financial Officer
Tel: (214) 689-4300
Fax: (214) 689-5886

SMITH, Barbara R.
Chief Operating Officer
Tel: (214) 689-4300
Fax: (214) 689-5886

Common Man's Advocacy Group LLC
Industry/ies: Consumers

Main Headquarters
Mailing: P.O Box 18 1526
Fairfield, OH 45014
Tel: (513) 829-0040

Public Affairs and Related Activities Personnel

At Headquarters

DALTON, Sam
Tel: (513) 829-0040

DALTON, Lynn
Tel: (513) 829-0040

DALTON, Marshall
Tel: (513) 829-0040

GRAHAM, Julian
Tel: (513) 829-0040

Commonwealth Advisors, Inc.
A financial investment firm.
www.common.com
Annual Revenues: $1.30 million
Employees: 11
Industry/ies: Banking/Finance/Investments

Vice President
O'BEIRNE, James F.
Tel: (225) 343-9342
Fax: (225) 343-1645

Main Headquarters
Mailing: 315 Third St.
Baton Rouge, LA 70801
Tel: (225) 343-9342
Fax: (225) 343-1645

Public Affairs and Related Activities Personnel

At Headquarters

MORALES, CFA, CFP, Walter A.
President and Chief Investment Officer
Tel: (225) 343-9342
Fax: (225) 343-1645

SCHULTE, Tayler
Contact, Investor Relations and Marketing
Tel: (225) 343-9342
Fax: (225) 343-1645

WARRINGTON, Jerry
Chief Compliance Officer
Tel: (225) 343-9342
Fax: (225) 343-1645

Commonwealth Brands, Inc.
The cigarette manufacturer in the United States, manufacturing five brands of cigarettes.
www.commonwealthbrands.com
Annual Revenues: $92.70 million
Employees: 700
Industry/ies: Tobacco Industry

Chairman of the Board
COATES, Spencer
Tel: (270) 781-9111
Fax: (270) 781-7651

Main Headquarters
Mailing: P.O. Box 51587
Bowling Green, KY 42102
Tel: (270) 781-9100
Fax: (270) 781-7651
TF: (800) 481-5814

Political Action Committees
Commonwealth-Altadis, inc. Employee PAC
FEC ID: C00455600
Contact: Hines Hattie
5900 N. Andrews Ave.
Suite 1100
Ft. Lauderdale, FL 33309
Tel: (954) 772-9000
Fax: (954) 267-1198

Contributions to Candidates: $33,000 (2015-2016)
Democrats: $2,500; Republicans: $30,500

Public Affairs and Related Activities Personnel

At Headquarters

MCINTIRE, Bonita
Vice President, Human Resources
Tel: (270) 781-9100
Fax: (270) 781-6728

MERCER, John
Chief Financial Officer
Tel: (270) 781-9100
Fax: (270) 781-7651

At Other Offices

HATTIE, Hines
PAC Treasurer
5900 N. Andrews Ave., Suite 1100
Ft. Lauderdale, FL 33309

Commonwealth Edison Company
See listing on page 210 under ComEd

CommScope
Formed in 1997 as a spin-off of General Instruments Corp. The company helps companies around the world design, build and manage their wired and wireless networks. It helps

customers increase bandwidth; maximize existing capacity; improve network performance and availability; increase energy efficiency; and simplify technology migration. In 2008, CommScope acquired Andrew Corporation.
www.commscope.com
Annual Revenues: $4.13 billion
Employees: 23,000
Ticker: NASDAQ: COMM
SIC: 3357; 3663; 5063
NAICS: 335929
Industry/ies: Communications; Defense/Homeland Security; Government-Related; Telecommunications/Internet/Cable

| **Chairman of the Board** | Tel: | (828) 324-2200 |
| DRENDEL, Frank M. | Fax: | (828) 328-3400 |

| **President and Chief Executive Officer** | Tel: | (828) 324-2200 |
| EDWARDS, Jr., Marvin S. | Fax: | (828) 328-3400 |

Main Headquarters
Mailing:	1100 CommScope Pl. SE	Tel:	(828) 324-2200
	Hickory, NC 28602	Fax:	(828) 328-3400
		TF:	(800) 982-1708

Public Affairs and Related Activities Personnel

At Headquarters

ARMSTRONG, Philip M.	Tel:	(828) 323-4848
Senior Vice President, Corporate Finance	Fax:	(828) 328-3400
investor.relations@commscope.com		

ASPAN, APR, Richard	Tel:	(708) 236-6568
Vice President, Corporate Communications	Fax:	(828) 328-3400
publicrelations@commscope.com		

| CRENSHAW, Randall W. | Tel: | (828) 324-2200 |
| *Executive Vice President and Chief Operating Officer* | Fax: | (828) 328-3400 |

| NOLAN, Fiona | Tel: | (828) 324-2200 |
| *Senior Vice President, Global Marketing* | Fax: | (828) 328-3400 |

| OLSON, Mark A. | Tel: | (828) 324-2200 |
| *Executive Vice President and Chief Financial Officer* | Fax: | (828) 328-3400 |

| TAYLOR, Wendy | Tel: | (828) 324-2200 |
| *Vice President, Corporate Compliance* | Fax: | (828) 328-3400 |

| TOWNSEND, Joanne | Tel: | (828) 324-2200 |
| *Senior Vice President, Human Resources* | Fax: | (828) 328-3400 |

WYATT, II, Frank B.	Tel:	(828) 324-2200
Senior Vice President, General Counsel and Secretary	Fax:	(828) 328-3400
fbwyatt@commscope.com		

CommScope Holding Company, Inc.
See listing on page 211 under CommScope

Communications & Power Industries

Communications & Power Industries, Inc. provides microwave, radio frequency, power and control solutions for defense, communications, medical, scientific and other applications.
www.cpii.com
Annual Revenues: $332.88 million
Employees: 1,500
Ticker: NASDAQ: CPII
SIC: 3670
Industry/ies: Communications; Defense/Homeland Security; Energy/Electricity; Government-Related; Telecommunications/Internet/Cable

| **Chairman of the Board** | Tel: | (650) 846-2900 |
| TARGOFF, Michael B. | Fax: | (650) 846-3276 |

| **Chief Executive Officer** | Tel: | (650) 846-2900 |
| CALDARELLI, O. Joe | Fax: | (650) 846-3276 |

Main Headquarters
| Mailing: | 607 Hansen Way | Tel: | (650) 846-2900 |
| | Palo Alto, CA 94304-1015 | Fax: | (650) 846-3276 |

Corporate Foundations and Giving Programs
Communications and Power Industries Contributions Program
| 607 Hansen Way | Tel: | (650) 846-2900 |
| Palo Alto, CA 94304-1015 | Fax: | (650) 846-3276 |

Public Affairs and Related Activities Personnel

At Headquarters

BEIGHLEY, John R.	Tel:	(650) 846-2900
Vice President, Sales	Fax:	(650) 846-3276
john.beighley@cpii.com		

| FICKETT, Robert A. | Tel: | (650) 846-2900 |
| *President and Chief Operating Officer* | Fax: | (650) 846-3276 |

| LITTMAN, Joel A. | Tel: | (650) 846-2900 |
| *Chief Financial Officer* | Fax: | (650) 846-3276 |

Community Health Systems, Inc.
Triad Hospitals was merged into Community Health Systems in 2007.
www.chs.net
Annual Revenues: $19.52 billion

Employees: 109,000
Ticker: NYSE: CYH
SIC: 8062
Industry/ies: Medicine/Health Care/Mental Health
Legislative Issues: HCR; MMM

Chairman of the Board and Chief Executive Officer	Tel:	(615) 465-7000
SMITH, Wayne T.		
wayne_smith@chs.net		

Main Headquarters
| Mailing: | 4000 Meridian Blvd. | Tel: | (615) 465-7000 |
| | Franklin, TN 37067 | | |

Political Action Committees
Community Health Systems Professional Services Corp PAC (AKA CHS PAC)
FEC ID: C00485896
Contact: Rachel A. Seifert
4000 Meridian Blvd.
Franklin, TX 37067

Contributions to Candidates: $70,500 (2015-2016)
Democrats: $21,500; Republicans: $49,000
Principal Recipients
SENATE
SCHUMER, CHARLES E (DEM-NY)

Corporate Foundations and Giving Programs
Community Health Systems, Inc. Contributions Program
4000 Meridian Blvd.
Franklin, TN 37067

Public Affairs and Related Activities Personnel

At Headquarters

BOSSHART, Andi	Tel:	(615) 465-7000
Vice President, Corporate Compliance Officer and Privacy Officer		
andi_bosshart@hq.chs.net		

| CASH, W. Larry | Tel: | (615) 465-7000 |
| *President, Financial Services and Chief Financial Officer* | | |

| DOUCETTE, James W. | Tel: | (615) 465-7000 |
| *Senior Vice President, Treasurer* | | |

| GALIN, Tomi | Tel: | (615) 465-7000 |
| *Senior Vice President, Corporate Communications, Marketing and Public Affairs* | | |

| GALLIVAN , Matthew S. | Tel: | (615) 465-7000 |
| *Vice President, Government Relations* | | |

| HAMMONS, Kevin | Tel: | (615) 465-7000 |
| *Senior Vice President and Chief Accounting Officer* | | |

| HORRAR, Robert A. | Tel: | (615) 465-7000 |
| *Vice President, Division II Operations* | | |

| LYND, Michael M. | Tel: | (615) 465-7000 |
| *Senior Vice President, Financial Services* | | |

| MILLER, David L. | Tel: | (615) 465-7000 |
| *President and Chief Operating Officer* | | |

| SCHWEINHART, Martin G. | Tel: | (615) 465-7000 |
| *Executive Vice President, Administration* | | |

SEIFERT, Rachel A.	Tel:	(615) 465-7000
Executive Vice President, Secretary and General Counsel		
rachel.seifert@chs.net,rachel_seifert@chs.net		

| SHAFER, Ronald J. | Tel: | (615) 465-7000 |
| *Senior Vice President, Human Resources* | | |

Company
See listing on page 550 under Morgan Stanley

Competitive Power Ventures, Inc.
An electric power generation development and asset management company.
www.cpv.com
Employees: 35
Industry/ies: Energy/Electricity; Natural Resources
Legislative Issues: ENG

| **Chairman of Board and Chief Executive Officer** | Tel: | (240) 723-2300 |
| EGAN, Doug | Fax: | (240) 723-2339 |

Main Headquarters
Mailing:	8403 Colesville Rd.	Tel:	(240) 723-2300
	Suite 915	Fax:	(240) 723-2339
	Silver Spring, MD 20910-6331		

Corporate Foundations and Giving Programs
CPV Contributions Program
8403 Colesville Rd.
Suite 915
Silver Spring, MD 20910-6331

Public Affairs and Related Activities Personnel

At Headquarters

ATWOOD, Don	Tel:	(240) 723-2300
Vice President and Media Contact	Fax:	(240) 723-2339
datwood@cpv.com		
BUCKOVICH, Paul	Tel:	(240) 723-2300
Chief Financial Officer	Fax:	(240) 723-2339
BURKE, Robert	Tel:	(240) 723-2300
General Counsel	Fax:	(240) 723-2339
KELLY, Esq., Jr., Peter Galbraith	Tel:	(240) 723-2300
Senior Vice President, External Affairs	Fax:	(240) 723-2339
bkelly@cpv.com		
ODELL, Jonathan	Tel:	(240) 723-2300
Senior Vice President, General Counsel	Fax:	(240) 723-2339

Comporium Communications

Formerly known as Rock Hill Telephone Company. Provides support services to all sizes and types of telecommunications carriers and cable television operators.
www.comporium.com
Annual Revenues: $0.87 million
Employees: 11
Industry/ies: Communications; Telecommunications/Internet/Cable

President and Chief Executive Officer	Tel:	(803) 328-2534
BARNES, Bryant G.		
bryant.barnes@comporium.com		

Main Headquarters

Mailing:	P.O. Box 470	Tel:	(803) 328-2534
	Rock Hill, SC 29731		

Political Action Committees

Rock Hill Telephone Company D/B/A Comporium Communications PAC
FEC ID: C00407437
Contact: Matthew L. Dosch
330 E. Black St.
Rock Hill, SC 29730

Corporate Foundations and Giving Programs

Comporium Communications Contributions Program
P.O. Box 470
Rock Hill, SC 29731

Public Affairs and Related Activities Personnel

At Headquarters

BARNES, Jr., John M.	Tel:	(803) 328-2534
Executive Vice President, Marketing and Business Solutions		
john.barnes@comporium.com		
MILLER, Jr., Harry M.	Tel:	(803) 328-2534
Executive Vice President, Planning and Development		
ROBERTSON, Daniel R.	Tel:	(803) 328-2534
Executive Vice President, Chief Financial Officer and Treasurer		

At Other Offices

DOSCH, Matthew L.	Tel:	(803) 328-2534
Senior Vice President, Customer Operations and External	Fax:	(803) 326-5709
Affairs and PAC Treasurer		
330 E. Black St.		
Rock Hill, SC 29730		
matt.dosch@comporium.com		

Composite Technology Corporation

Composite Technology Corporation (CTC), develops, produces, and markets energy efficient products and renewable energy projects for the electrical utility industry.
www.compositetechcorp.com
Annual Revenues: $10.84 million
Employees: 200
SIC: 3600
Industry/ies: Electricity & Electronics; Electronics; Energy/Electricity

Chief Executive Officer and Chairman of the Board	Tel:	(949) 428-8500
WILCOXON, Benton H.	Fax:	(949) 428-8515

Main Headquarters

Mailing:	2026 McGaw Ave.	Tel:	(949) 428-8500
	Irvine, CA 92614-0911	Fax:	(949) 428-8515

Public Affairs and Related Activities Personnel

At Headquarters

CARNEY, D. J.	Tel:	(949) 428-8500
Chief Financial Officer	Fax:	(949) 428-8515
CARSWELL, James	Tel:	(949) 428-8500
Vice President, Investor Relations	Fax:	(949) 428-8515
jcarswell@compositetechcorp.com		

Comprehensive Clinical Development

Develops products for central nervous system disorders
www.comprehensivecd.com

Annual Revenues: $21.20 million
Employees: 300
Industry/ies: Medicine/Health Care/Mental Health

Chief Executive Officer	Tel:	(954) 266-2620
UTTERBACK, James (Jim)		

Main Headquarters

Mailing:	3100 S.W. 145th Ave.	Tel:	(954) 266-2620
	Suite 340		
	Miramar, FL 33027		

Washington Office

Mailing:	4228 Wisconsin Ave. NW	Tel:	(202) 885-5666
	Washington, DC 20016	Fax:	(202) 885-5713

Public Affairs and Related Activities Personnel

At Headquarters

DUBIN, Anne	Tel:	(754) 201-2102
Business Development and Media Contact		
ADubin@ComprehensiveCD.com		
LATEVOLA, Monica	Tel:	(954) 266-2620
Vice President, Client and Legal Affairs		
MILLER, Emily	Tel:	(954) 266-2620
Vice President, Corporate Development and Strategy		
MORALES-PEREZ, CPA, MBA, Margarita	Tel:	(954) 266-2620
Executive Vice President and Chief Financial Officer		
SANTIAGO, MBA, Juan R.	Tel:	(954) 266-2620
Vice President, Finance		

Comprehensive Neuroscience, Inc.

See listing on page 213 under Comprehensive Clinical Development

Compressus, Inc.

Compressus, Inc. is a software technology company offering mission critical, industry-leading solutions that optimize workflow and telemedicine applications for medical image management. Compressus Inc. is also the parent company of Compressus Solutions Inc. and the Vigilent Solutions product line.
compressus.com
Annual Revenues: $3.30 million
Industry/ies: Computer/Technology

Chairman of the Board and Co-Founder	Tel:	(202) 742-4307
CAMPBELL, Thomas D.	Fax:	(202) 742-4286
Chief Executive Officer	Tel:	(202) 742-4307
SCHERDER, Daniel B	Fax:	(202) 742-4286

Main Headquarters

Mailing:	101 Constitution Ave. NW	Tel:	(202) 742-4307
	Suite 800	Fax:	(202) 742-4286
	Washington, DC 20001-2133		

Public Affairs and Related Activities Personnel

At Headquarters

FISCHETTI , Tom	Tel:	(202) 742-4307
Controller	Fax:	(202) 742-4286
GASZTONYI, Laszlo	Tel:	(202) 742-4307
Chief Operating Officer	Fax:	(202) 742-4286
MARTINEZ, Reynaldo	Tel:	(202) 742-4331
Co-Founder	Fax:	(202) 742-4286
SYKES, Laurie	Tel:	(202) 742-4307
Vice President, Corporate Development	Fax:	(202) 742-4286
WAY, Jim	Tel:	(202) 742-4307
Vice President, Operations	Fax:	(202) 742-4286

Computer Sciences Corporation

See listing on page 232 under CSC

Compuware Corporation

Data processing professional services and system software products.
www.compuware.com
Annual Revenues: $720.76 million
Employees: 3,066
Ticker: NASDAQ: CPWR
SIC: 7372
Industry/ies: Computer/Technology
Legislative Issues: SCI

Chief Executive Officer	Tel:	(313) 227-7300
O'MALLEY, Chris	Fax:	(313) 227-7555

Main Headquarters

Mailing:	One Campus Martius	Tel:	(313) 227-7300
	Detroit, MI 48226	Fax:	(313) 227-7555
		TF:	(800) 521-9353

Corporate Foundations and Giving Programs

Compuware Corporation Contributions Program

One Campus Martius
Detroit, MI 48226

Public Affairs and Related Activities Personnel

At Headquarters

AHO, Joe
Chief Financial Officer
Tel: (313) 227-7300
Fax: (313) 227-7555

ELKIN, Lisa
Senior Vice President, Marketing, Communications and Investor Relations
lisa.elkin@compuware.com
Tel: (313) 227-7345
Fax: (313) 227-7555

FOURNIER, Laura
Senior Vice President and Chief Financial Officer and Treasurer
Tel: (313) 227-7300
Fax: (313) 227-7555

HUNTER, Mitzi
Vice President, Marketing
Tel: (313) 227-7300
Fax: (313) 227-7555

OLEJNICZAK, Mike
General Counsel
Tel: (313) 227-7300
Fax: (313) 227-7555

REILLY, Steve
Director, Investor Relations and Corporate Communications
steve.reilly@compuware.com
Tel: (313) 227-1799
Fax: (313) 227-7555

SIEFKER, Kayla
Senior Manager, Public Relations
kayla.siefker@compuware.com
Tel: (313) 227-1402
Fax: (313) 227-7555

STARR, Denise
Chief Administrative Officer
Tel: (313) 227-7300
Fax: (313) 227-7555

Con Edison

See listing on page 217 under Consolidated Edison Company of New York, Inc.

Con-way, Inc.

Con-way Inc. is a freight transportation and logistics services company, which delivers industry-leading services through its primary operating companies and provides high-performance, day-definite less-than-truckload (LTL), full truckload and intermodal freight transportation; logistics, warehousing and supply chain management services; and trailer manufacturing.
www.con-way.com
Annual Revenues: $5.81 billion
Employees: 30,100
Ticker: NYSE: CNW
SIC: 4213
Industry/ies: Transportation
Legislative Issues: TAX

Chairman of the Board
KENNEDY, Jr., Dr. W. Keith
Tel: (650) 378-5200
Fax: (650) 357-9160

President and Chief Executive Officer
STOTLAR, Douglas W.
Tel: (650) 378-5200
Fax: (650) 357-9160

Main Headquarters
Mailing: 2211 Old Earhart Rd.
Suite 100
Ann Arbor, MI 48105
Tel: (734) 757-1444
Fax: (734) 757-1158
TF: (800) 755-2728

Political Action Committees
Con-Way Inc. Political Action Committee
FEC ID: C00110759
Contact: Michael J. Morris
2211 Old Earhart Rd.
Suite 100
Ann Arbor, MI 48105

  Contributions to Candidates: $54,122 (2015-2016)
  Democrats: $7,122; Republicans: $47,000

Corporate Foundations and Giving Programs
Con-way Contributions Program
2211 Old Earhart Rd.
Suite 100
Ann Arbor, MI 48105
Tel: (734) 757-1444
Fax: (734) 757-1153

Public Affairs and Related Activities Personnel

At Headquarters

BASSETT, Robert W.
Vice President, Sales and Marketing
Tel: (734) 994-6600
Fax: (734) 757-1153

MORRIS, Michael J.
Senior Vice President, Finance and Treasurer
Tel: (734) 757-1444
Fax: (734) 757-1153

At Other Offices

BRUFFETT, Stephen L.
Executive Vice President and Chief Financial Officer
2855 Campus Dr., Suite 300
San Mateo, CA 94403
Tel: (650) 378-5200
Fax: (650) 357-9160

FOSSENIER, Patrick J.
Vice President, Investor Relations
2855 Campus Dr., Suite 300
San Mateo, CA 94403
fossenier.patrick@cnf.com
Tel: (650) 378-5200
Fax: (650) 357-9160

FRANTZ, Gary
Director, Communications
2855 Campus Dr., Suite 300
San Mateo, CA 94403
frantz.gary@con-way.com
Tel: (650) 378-5335
Fax: (650) 357-9160

KRULL, Stephen K.
Executive Vice President, General Counsel and Corporate Secretary
2855 Campus Dr., Suite 300
San Mateo, CA 94403
Tel: (650) 378-5200
Fax: (650) 357-9160

LUNDBERG, Leslie P.
Senior Vice President, Human Resources
2855 Campus Dr., Suite 300
San Mateo, CA 94403
Tel: (650) 378-5200
Fax: (650) 357-9160

ConAgra

A packaged food company that serves consumer grocery retailers as well as foodservice establishments.
www.conagrafoods.com
Annual Revenues: $15.84 billion
Employees: 32,900
Ticker: NYSE: CAG
SIC: 2068; 2052; 2096; 5812; 2040
NAICS: 311919; 311919; 722213; 311911
Industry/ies: Agriculture/Agronomy; Chemicals & Chemical Industry; Commodities; Fish And Fishing; Food And Beverage Industry
Legislative Issues: AGR; BUD; FOO; FUE; TAX; TRD

Non Executive Chairman
GOLDSTONE, Steven F.
Tel: (402) 240-4000
Fax: (402) 240-4707

President and Chief Executive Officer
CONNOLLY, Sean M.
Tel: (402) 595-4000
Fax: (402) 595-4707

Main Headquarters
Mailing: One ConAgra Dr.
Omaha, NE 68102-5001
Tel: (402) 240-4000
Fax: (402) 240-4707

Washington Office
Mailing: 1101 Pennsylvania Ave. NW
Suite 600
Washington, DC 20004
Tel: (202) 223-5115
Fax: (202) 223-5118

Political Action Committees
ConAgra Foods Inc. Good Government Association PAC
FEC ID: C00087874
Contact: Scott Messel
One ConAgra Dr.
Omaha, NE 68102
Tel: (202) 223-5115
Fax: (202) 223-5118

  Contributions to Candidates: $83,000 (2015-2016)
  Democrats: $8,500; Republicans: $74,500

Corporate Foundations and Giving Programs
ConAgra Foods Feeding Children Better Foundation
One ConAgra Dr.
Omaha, NE 68102
Tel: (402) 595-4000

ConAgra Foods Foundation
One ConAgra Dr.
Omaha, NE 68102
Tel: (402) 595-4158

Ralcorp Holdings, Inc. Contributions Program
P.O. Box 618
St. Louis, MO 63188-0618
Tel: (314) 877-7000
Fax: (314) 877-7000

Public Affairs and Related Activities Personnel

At Headquarters

BATCHELER, Colleen
Executive Vice President, General Counsel and Corporate Secretary
Tel: (402) 240-4000
Fax: (402) 240-4707

BROCK, Charisse
Executive Vice President, Chief Human Resources Officer
Tel: (402) 240-4000
Fax: (402) 240-4707

DE LA MATER, Derek
Executive Vice President and President of Sales
Tel: (402) 240-4000
Fax: (402) 240-4707

FRIEDMAN, Lanie
Media Contact
lanie.friedman@conagrafoods.com
Tel: (630) 857-1086
Fax: (402) 240-4707

GEHRING, John
Executive Vice President and Chief Financial Officer
Tel: (402) 240-4000
Fax: (402) 240-4707

HARRIS, Jon
Senior Vice President and Chief Communications Officer
Tel: (402) 240-4000
Fax: (402) 240-4707

MESSEL, Scott
PAC Treasurer
Tel: (402) 595-4000
Fax: (402) 595-4707

ROSS, Andrew
Executive Vice President and Chief Strategy Officer
Tel: (402) 240-4000
Fax: (402) 240-4707

SHARPE, Jr., Robert F.
Executive Vice President, Legal and External Affairs
Tel: (402) 595-4000
Fax: (402) 595-4707

At Washington Office

BAGLIEN, Brent A.		Tel:	(202) 223-5115
Vice President, Government Affairs		Fax:	(202) 223-5118
Registered Federal Lobbyist			
GARCIA, Megan		Tel:	(202) 223-5115
Registered Federal Lobbyist		Fax:	(202) 223-5118
SCHMIDT, Megan		Tel:	(202) 223-5115
Federal Lobbyist		Fax:	(202) 223-5118
Registered Federal Lobbyist			

ConAgra

See listing on page 214 under ConAgra

Concurrent Technologies Corporation

An independent, nonprofit, applied research and development professional services organization.
www.ctc.com
Annual Revenues: $242.22 million
Employees: 1,500
Industry/ies: Defense/Homeland Security; Government-Related
Legislative Issues: DEF

Chairman of the Board		Tel:	(814) 269-2592
PICKING, Howard M.		Fax:	(814) 269-6500
President and Chief Executive Officer		Tel:	(814) 269-2592
SHEEHAN, Jr., Edward J.		Fax:	(814) 269-6500
Main Headquarters			
Mailing:	100 CTC Dr.	Tel:	(814) 269-2592
	Johnstown, PA 15904-1935	Fax:	(814) 269-6500
		TF:	(800) 282-4392
Washington Office			
Mailing:	1225 S. Clark St.	Tel:	(703) 310-5688
	Suite 500	Fax:	(703) 310-5655
	Arlington, VA 22202-4376		

Corporate Foundations and Giving Programs

CTC Foundation
Contact: Howard McClintic

1225 S. Clark St.	Tel:	(703) 310-5688
Arlington, VA 22202-4376	Fax:	(703) 310-5688

Public Affairs and Related Activities Personnel

At Headquarters

BEVAN, Mary		Tel:	(814) 269-2490
Director, Corporate Communications		Fax:	(814) 269-6500
bevanm@ctc.com			
DIVIRGILIO, Margaret A.		Tel:	(814) 269-2592
Senior Vice President and Chief Financial Officer		Fax:	(814) 269-6500
HUDSON, Jerry R.		Tel:	(814) 269-2592
Senior Vice President, Strategy and Organizational Development		Fax:	(814) 269-6500
Hudson@ctc.com			

At Washington Office

MCCLINTIC, Howard		Tel:	(202) 689-4586
Executive Director, CTC Foundation	.	Fax:	(703) 310-5655
McclintH@ctc.com			

Conemaugh Health Systems

A healthcare provider.
www.conemaugh.org
Annual Revenues: $519.49 million
Employees: 3,500
Industry/ies: Medicine/Health Care/Mental Health

Chief Executive Officer		Tel:	(814) 534-9000
BECKER, Scott A.		Fax:	(814) 539-0264
Main Headquarters			
Mailing:	1086 Franklin St.	Tel:	(814) 534-9000
	Johnstown, PA 15905	Fax:	(814) 539-0264

Corporate Foundations and Giving Programs

Conemaugh Health Foundation (CHF)
Contact: Susan M. Mann

1086 Franklin St.	Tel:	(814) 534-9000
Johnstown, PA 15905	Fax:	(814) 539-0264

Public Affairs and Related Activities Personnel

At Headquarters

BRADLEY, Amy		Tel:	(814) 534-3121
Director, Marketing Communications		Fax:	(814) 539-0264
abradle@conemaugh.org			
DEPASQUALE, Edward H.		Tel:	(814) 534-9000
Chief Financial Officer		Fax:	(814) 539-0264
MALLEK, Brent J.		Tel:	(814) 534-9000
Chief Human Resources Officer		Fax:	(814) 539-0264
MANN, Susan M.		Tel:	(814) 534-9000

President, Conemaugh Health Foundation		Fax:	(814) 539-0264
smann@conemaugh.com			
MORYKEN, John M.		Tel:	(814) 534-9000
Vice President, Business Development and Governmental Affairs		Fax:	(814) 539-0264

Conexant Systems, Inc.

Provides semiconductor solutions for broadband communications and the digital home. Spun-off Mindspeed Technologies, Inc. in June of 2003.
www.conexant.com
Annual Revenues: $166 million
Employees: 500
Ticker: UTP NASDAQ: CNXT
SIC: 3674
Industry/ies: Communications; Telecommunications/Internet/Cable

Chief Executive Officer		Tel:	(949) 483-4600
REGIMBAL, Denis			
Main Headquarters			
Mailing:	1901 Main St.	Tel:	(949) 483-4600
	Suite 300		
	Irvine, CA 92614		

Public Affairs and Related Activities Personnel

At Headquarters

GALLAGHER, Dennis		Tel:	(949) 483-4600
General Counsel and Vice President, Legal			
JOHANNESSEN, Jan		Tel:	(949) 483-4600
Chief Financial Officer, Cheif Operating officer			
NAM, David		Tel:	(949) 483-4600
Vice President, Sales Operations and Business Development			
NAWAZ, Ahmed		Tel:	(949) 483-4600
Chief Sales Officer			

At Other Offices

JOHUR, Sharon		Tel:	(949) 483-4600
Executive Director, Human Resources		Fax:	(949) 483-4600
4000 MacArthur Blvd.			
Newport Beach, CA 92660			
sharon.johur@conexant.com			
OLSEN, Stephanie		Tel:	(949) 453-8080
Media Contact		Fax:	(949) 483-4600
4000 MacArthur Blvd.			
Newport Beach, CA 92660			
stephanie@lages.com			

Connnected Nation Development Corporation

Promotion of technology advancement efforts of the non-profit Connected Nation, Inc.
www.connectednation.org
Industry/ies: Computer/Technology

President and Chief Operating Officer		Tel:	(877) 846-7710
FERREE, Tom			
Main Headquarters			
Mailing:	P.O. Box 43586	Tel:	(877) 846-7710
	Washington, DC 20010	TF:	(877) 846-7710

Corporate Foundations and Giving Programs

Connnected Nation Contributions Program
P.O. Box 43586
Washington, DC 20010

Public Affairs and Related Activities Personnel

At Headquarters

BAILEY, Samantha		Tel:	(877) 846-7710
Manager, Accounting			
BROWN, Phillip K.		Tel:	(877) 846-7710
Director, Government Affairs and Advocacy			
pbrown@connectednation.org			
DITTO, Jessica		Tel:	(877) 846-7710
Director, Education Program Outreach			
DUNN, James		Tel:	(877) 846-7710
Executive Director			
FREDERICK, Eric		Tel:	(877) 846-7710
Vice President, Community Affairs			
HAMM, John		Tel:	(877) 846-7710
Chief Financial Officer			
HIGHLEY, Adam		Tel:	(877) 846-7710
Director, Strategic Programs			
INGLES, Brad		Tel:	(877) 846-7710
Communications Specialist			
PEDERSEN, Chris		Tel:	(877) 846-7710
Vice President, Development and Planning			
THOMAS, Mandi		Tel:	(877) 846-7710

Manager, Human Resources
At Other Offices

MILLS, R. Eric   Tel: (270) 781-4320
Contact, Counsel
P.O. Box 1318
Bowling Green, KY 42102
emills@connedctednation.com

ConocoPhillips

Formed from the merger between Conoco Inc. and Phillips Petroleum Co. in August of 2002. An international integrated energy company with operations in some 49 countries.
www.conocophillips.com
Annual Revenues: $47.25 billion
Employees: 18,800
Ticker: NYSE: COP
SIC: 2911; 2951
NAICS: 324110
Industry/ies: Fuels See Coal, Gas, Oil, Petroleum; Natural Resources; Petroleum Industry
Legislative Issues: ENG; ENV; FUE; NAT; TAX

Chairman and Chief Executive Officer, ConocoPhillips   Tel: (281) 293-1000
LANCE, Ryan M.   Fax: (281) 293-1000

Main Headquarters
Mailing: 600 N. Dairy Ashford   Tel: (281) 293-1000
     P.O. Box 2197   Fax: (281) 293-1000
     Houston, TX 77079

Washington Office
Mailing: 325 Seventh St. NW
     12th Floor
     Washington, DC 20004

Political Action Committees
ConocoPhillips Spirit PAC
FEC ID: C00112896
Contact: Sherry L. Gamble
720 N. Plaza Office Bldg.
Bartlesville, OK 74004

   Contributions to Candidates: $162,400 (2015-2016)
   Democrats: $7,500; Republicans: $154,900

      Principal Recipients

       SENATE
       HOEVEN, JOHN (REP-ND)

       HOUSE
       LANKFORD, JAMES PAUL MR. (REP-OK)
       MCCARTHY, KEVIN (REP-CA)
       RYAN, PAUL D. (REP-WI)

Public Affairs and Related Activities Personnel
At Headquarters

AHMED, Aftab   Tel: (281) 293-4138
Contact, Media and Senior Coordinator, Financial   Fax: (281) 293-1000
Communications
aftab.ahmed@conocophillips.com

DESANCTIS, Ellen   Tel: (281) 293-1000
Vice President Investor Relations and Communications   Fax: (281) 293-1000

HIRSHBERG, Alan J.   Tel: (281) 293-1000
Executive Vice President, Technology and Projects   Fax: (281) 293-1000

KELLY, Janet Langford   Tel: (281) 293-1000
Senior Vice President, Legal, General Counsel and Corporate   Fax: (281) 293-1000
Secretary

KONG, Davy   Tel: (281) 293-2701
Contact, Media Relations   Fax: (281) 293-1000
davy.kong@conocophillips.com

SHEETS, Jeff W.   Tel: (281) 293-1000
Executive Vice President Finance and Chief Financial Officer   Fax: (281) 293-1000

At Washington Office

AVERY, Kevin
Manager, Federal Government Affairs
Registered Federal Lobbyist

DABBAR, John
Registered Federal Lobbyist

GIBSON, Kari
Director, Government Affairs
Registered Federal Lobbyist

At Other Offices

ATKINS, Caroline   Tel: (202) 833-0900
Director, Federal Government Affairs   Fax: (202) 785-0639
1776 I St. NW, Suite 700
Washington, DC 20006

DRAGER, Kjersten   Tel: (202) 833-0900
Manager, Government Affairs and Advocacy Strategy   Fax: (202) 785-0639

1776 I St. NW, Suite 700
Washington, DC 20006
Registered Federal Lobbyist

FORD, Jim   Tel: (202) 833-0900
Vice President, Federal & State Government Affairs   Fax: (202) 785-0639
1776 I St. NW, Suite 700
Washington, DC 20006

GAMBLE, Sherry L.
CPA, Senior Tax Specialist
720 N. Plaza Office Bldg.
Bartlesville, OK 74004

ICHORD, J. William   Tel: (202) 833-0900
Vice President, International Government Affairs   Fax: (202) 785-0639
1776 I St. NW, Suite 700
Washington, DC 20006

LARCOM, Kay   Tel: (202) 833-0922
Director, Federal Affairs International   Fax: (202) 785-0639
1776 I St. NW, Suite 700
Washington, DC 20006

LUNDQUIST, Andrew   Tel: (202) 833-0900
Senior Vice President, Government Affairs   Fax: (202) 785-0639
1776 I St. NW, Suite 700
Washington, DC 20006

MCNEILL, Don   Tel: (202) 833-0900
Manager, Government Affairs   Fax: (202) 785-0639
1776 I St. NW, Suite 700
Washington, DC 20006

REAMY, Jeff M.   Tel: (202) 833-0900
Manager, Downstream and Environment   Fax: (202) 785-0639
1776 I St. NW, Suite 700
Washington, DC 20006
jmreamy@ppco.com

SHUTE, Melissa   Tel: (202) 833-0900
Manager, Federal Affairs Upstream & Alaska   Fax: (202) 785-0639
1776 I St. NW, Suite 700
Washington, DC 20006

SMITH, Kari L.   Tel: (202) 833-0900
1776 I St. NW, Suite 700   Fax: (202) 785-0639
Washington, DC 20006
Registered Federal Lobbyist

SNYDER, Alan   Tel: (202) 833-0900
Federal Lobbyist   Fax: (202) 785-0639
1776 I St. NW, Suite 700
Washington, DC 20006
Registered Federal Lobbyist

Consol Energy

A publicly-held coal and natural gas producer.
www.consolenergy.com
Annual Revenues: $2.29 billion
Employees: 3,114
Ticker: NYSE: CNX
SIC: 1221
Industry/ies: Energy/Electricity; Natural Resources
Legislative Issues: CAW; ENG; TAX; WAS

Chairman of the Board   Tel: (412) 831-4000
HARVEY, J. Brett   Fax: (412) 831-4103

President and Chief Executive Officer   Tel: (724) 485-4000
DEIULIIS, Nicholas J.   Fax: (412) 831-4103

Main Headquarters
Mailing: 1000 Consol Energy Dr.   Tel: (724) 485-4000
     CNX Center   Fax: (412) 831-4103
     Canonsburg, PA 15317-6506

Political Action Committees
Consol Energy Inc. PAC
FEC ID: C00279331
Contact: Eva Roman
P.O. Box 75000
MC2250
Detroit, MI 48275

   Contributions to Candidates: $47,500 (2015-2016)
   Republicans: $47,500

      Principal Recipients

       SENATE
       TOOMEY, PATRICK JOSEPH (REP-PA)

Corporate Foundations and Giving Programs

Consol Energy Contributions Program
1000 CONSOL Energy Dr.   Tel: (724) 485-4000
Canonsburg, PA 15317

Public Affairs and Related Activities Personnel
At Headquarters

BOLEWITZ, David	Tel:	(724) 485-4000
Director, Internal Control and Business Process	Fax:	(412) 831-4103
BROCK, Jimmy A.	Tel:	(724) 485-4000
Chief Operating Officer	Fax:	(412) 831-4103
JOHNSON, Tommy	Tel:	(724) 485-4390
Vice President, Government Affairs	Fax:	(412) 831-4103
Mail Stop CNX Center		
Registered Federal Lobbyist		
JOHNSON, Stephen W.	Tel:	(724) 485-4000
Executive Vice President, Diversified Business Units	Fax:	(412) 831-4103
JOHNSON, Sam	Tel:	(724) 485-3124
Vice President , Energy Marketing	Fax:	(412) 831-4103
samjohnson@consolenergy.com		
KHANI, David M.	Tel:	(724) 485-4000
Executive Vice President and Chief Financial Officer	Fax:	(412) 831-4103
SALVATORI, Kurt	Tel:	(724) 485-4000
Vice President, Human Resources	Fax:	(412) 831-4103
employment@consolenergy.com		

At Other Offices

ROMAN, Eva
PAC Treasurer and Lobbyist
P.O. Box 75000, MC2250
Detroit, MI 48275-2250

Consolidated Edison Company of New York, Inc.

Provide competitive power supply, renewable energy, cost effective energy solutions.
www.coned.com
Annual Revenues: $12.96 billion
Employees: 14,601
Ticker: NYSE: ED
SIC: 4911; 3511
NAICS: 221119; 333611
Industry/ies: Energy/Electricity; Utilities
Legislative Issues: BUD; CDT; DEF; ENG; HOM; TAX; TRA; UTI

Chairman of the Board and Chief Executive Officer	Tel:	(212) 460-4600
MCAVOY, John J.	Fax:	(212) 477-2536

Main Headquarters
Mailing:	P.O. Box 138	Tel:	(212) 460-4600
	New York City, NY 10276-0138	Fax:	(212) 477-2536

Washington Office
Mailing:	1225 I St. NW	Tel:	(212) 460-2174
	Suite 1150	TF:	(800) 752-6633
	Washington, DC 20005		

Political Action Committees

Consolidated Edison Inc Employees Political Action Committee (CEIPAC
FEC ID: C00407635
Contact: Robert Muccilo
Four Irving Pl.
Room 506
New York City, NY 10003

> **Contributions to Candidates:** $5,000 (2015-2016)
> Democrats: $4,000; Republicans: $1,000

Corporate Foundations and Giving Programs

Consolidated Edison Company of New York, Inc. Contributions Program
Contact: Frances A. Resheske
Four Irving Pl.	Tel:	(212) 460-4600
New York City, NY 10003	Fax:	(212) 477-2536

Public Affairs and Related Activities Personnel

At Headquarters
AYALA, Hilary S.	Tel:	(212) 460-2587
Director, Grassroots Management and Strategic Programs	Fax:	(212) 477-2536
Mail Stop 1650-S		
ayalah@coned.com		
HOGLUND , Robert	Tel:	(212) 460-4600
Senior Vice President and Chief Financial Officer	Fax:	(212) 477-2536
MOORE, Elizabeth D.	Tel:	(212) 460-4600
General Counsel	Fax:	(212) 477-2536
MUCCILO, Robert	Tel:	(212) 460-4600
Vice President, Controller, and Chief Accounting Officer and	Fax:	(212) 477-2536
PAC Treasurer		
SOBIN, Carole	Tel:	(212) 460-4600
Vice President and Corporate Secretary	Fax:	(212) 477-2536

At Washington Office
BANKSON, Jr., John P.	Tel:	(212) 460-2174
Federal Lobbyist		
KIMBALL, Kyle	Tel:	(212) 460-2174
Registered Federal Lobbyist		
LANAHAN, Kevin M.	Tel:	(212) 460-2174
Director, Government Relations		

Lanahank@coned.com
RESHESKE, Frances A.	Tel:	(212) 460-2174
Senior Vice President, Public Affairs		
SPRAYREGEN, Mary	Tel:	(212) 460-2174
Manager, Federal Government Relations		

At Other Offices
CHILDRESS, Jan C.	Tel:	(212) 460-4600
Director, Investor Relations	Fax:	(212) 477-2536
Four Irving Pl.		
New York, NY 10003		
childressj@coned.com		

Consorta, Inc.

Cost management and quality improvement initiatives within health allied services field.
www.consorta.com
Annual Revenues: $1.40 million
Employees: 44
Industry/ies: Medicine/Health Care/Mental Health

Chairman of the Board	Tel:	(847) 592-7800
FIERENS, II, Louis J.	Fax:	(847) 592-7801

Main Headquarters
Mailing:	1475 E. Woodfield Rd.	Tel:	(847) 592-7800
	Suite 400	Fax:	(847) 592-7801
	Schaumburg, IL 60173		

Public Affairs and Related Activities Personnel

At Headquarters
HICKS, Linda	Tel:	(847) 592-7800
Director, Human Resources	Fax:	(847) 592-7801

Constella Group LLC

See listing on page 741 under SRI International

Constellation Brands, Inc.

Constellation Brands is a beer, wine, and spirits maker.Constellation Brands markets premium spirits, including Black Velvet whiskey and SVEDKA vodka.
www.cbrands.com
Annual Revenues: $6.13 billion
Employees: 7,200
Ticker: NYSE: STZ
SIC: 2082; 2085; 2084; 2033
NAICS: 312120; 312140; 312130; 311421
Industry/ies: Food And Beverage Industry

Chairman of the Board	Tel:	(585) 678-7100
SANDS, Richard	Fax:	(585) 218-3601
President and Chief Executive Officer	Tel:	(585) 678-7100
SANDS, Robert	Fax:	(585) 218-3601
rob.sands@cbrands.com		

Main Headquarters
Mailing:	207 High Point Dr.	Tel:	(585) 678-7100
	Building 100	Fax:	(585) 218-3601
	Victor, NY 14564	TF:	(888) 724-2169

Corporate Foundations and Giving Programs

Constellation Brands Contributions Program
207 High Point Dr.	Tel:	(585) 678-7100
Building 100	Fax:	(585) 218-3601
Victor, NY 14564		

Public Affairs and Related Activities Personnel

At Headquarters
CZUDAK, Bob	Tel:	(585) 678-7170
Director, Investor Relations	Fax:	(585) 218-3601
bob.czudak@cbrands.com		
GOSSIN, Cheryl	Tel:	(585) 678-7191
Vice President, Corporate Communications	Fax:	(585) 218-3601
cheryl.gossin@cbrands.com		
HETTERICH, F. Paul	Tel:	(585) 678-7100
Executive Vice President, Business Development and	Fax:	(585) 218-3601
Corporate Strategy		
HINTON , Keri	Tel:	(585) 678-7100
Assoc. Manager, Meeting & Events Planner	Fax:	(585) 218-3601
keri.hinton@crownimportsllc.com		
HUMPHREY, Perry	Tel:	(585) 678-7100
PAC Treasurer	Fax:	(585) 218-3601
KANE, Thomas M.	Tel:	(585) 678-7100
Executive Vice President and Chief Human Resources Officer	Fax:	(585) 218-3601
KLEIN, David E.	Tel:	(585) 678-7100
Executive Vice President and Chief Financial Officer	Fax:	(585) 218-3601
MULLIN, Thomas J	Tel:	(585) 678-7100
Executive Vice President and General Counsel	Fax:	(585) 218-3601
tom.mullin@cbrands.com		

THOMAS, Eric	Tel:	(585) 678-7466
Manager, Corporate Communications	Fax:	(585) 218-3601
eric.thomas@cbrands.com		
YAHN-URLAUB, Patty	Tel:	(585) 678-7483
Vice President, Investor Relations	Fax:	(585) 218-3601
patty.yahn-urlaub@cbrands.com		

Constellation Energy Group, Inc.

A holding company whose subsidiaries include energy related businesses focused on power marketing, generation, portfolio management. Constellation Energy operates independent power plants with 9,030 MW of generating capacity through its Constellation Generation unit. Other operations include HVAC services, appliance sales; nuclear plant development; and energy consulting services.
www.constellation.com
Annual Revenues: $13.8 billion
Employees: 8,000
Ticker: NYSE: CEG-PA
SIC: 4911
Industry/ies: Energy/Electricity; Utilities
Legislative Issues: ENG; FIN

Chief Executive Officer Tel: (410) 470-2800
NIGRO, Joseph Fax: (202) 942-2760

Main Headquarters
Mailing:	100 Constellation Way	Tel:	(410) 470-2800
	Suite 1200C	Fax:	(202) 942-2760
	Baltimore, MD 21202	TF:	(888) 635-0827

Washington Office
Mailing: 400 N. Capitol St. NW
Suite 890
Washington, DC 20001

Corporate Foundations and Giving Programs

Constellation Energy Group Contributions Program
100 Constellation Way Tel: (410) 470-2800
Suite 1200C
Baltimore, MD 21202

Public Affairs and Related Activities Personnel

At Headquarters

BERARDESCO, Charles A.	Tel:	(410) 470-2800
Senior Vice President, General Counsel, Corporate Secretary and Chief Compliance Officer	Fax:	(202) 942-2760
ELLSWORTH, David	Tel:	(410) 470-2800
Chief Operating Officer and Senior Vice President	Fax:	(202) 942-2760
GILBERT, David M.	Tel:	(410) 470-2800
Managing Director, Federal Affairs	Fax:	(202) 942-2760
HUSTON, Mark	Tel:	(410) 470-2800
President	Fax:	(202) 942-2760
MATHEY, Chris	Tel:	(202) 942-2770
Director, Public Sector	Fax:	(202) 942-2760
Chris.Mathey@constellation.com		
STEWART, Bruce	Tel:	(410) 470-2800
Senior Vice President and Chief Marketing Officer	Fax:	(202) 942-2760

Consumers Energy Group

See listing on page 201 under CMS Energy Company

ContiGroup Companies, Inc.

See listing on page 218 under Continental Grain Company

Continental Airlines

See listing on page 813 under United Airlines (UA)

Continental Airlines

See listing on page 814 under United Continental Holdings, Inc.

Continental Grain Company

Formerly ContiGroup Companies, Inc. An international agribusiness company with interests in commodity marketing, feed and flour milling and livestock and poultry production and processing. The company also provides consumer and commercial financial services.
www.contigroup.com
Employees: 14,000
Industry/ies: Agriculture/Agronomy

Chairman of the Board and Chief Executive Officer Tel: (212) 207-5930
FRIBOURG, Paul J. Fax: (212) 207-5499
paul.fribourg@conti.com

Main Headquarters
Mailing:	767 Fifth Ave.	Tel:	(212) 207-5930
	Fifteenth Floor	Fax:	(212) 207-5499
	New York, NY 10153-0028		

Political Action Committees
Continental Grain Company PAC
FEC ID: C00155853

Contact: Michael Mayberry
277 Park Ave.
New York City, NY 10172

Corporate Foundations and Giving Programs

Continental Grain Foundation
Contact: Susan McIntyre
277 Park Ave.
New York City, NY 10172

Public Affairs and Related Activities Personnel

At Headquarters

BAIER , Frank W.	Tel:	(212) 207-5930
Executive Vice President and Chief Financial Officer	Fax:	(212) 207-5499
DERIN, Robin	Tel:	(212) 207-5930
Senior Manager, Human Resources and Communications	Fax:	(212) 207-5499
MCCASLIN, Teresa E.	Tel:	(212) 207-5930
Executive Vice President, Chief Human Resources and Administrative Officer	Fax:	(212) 207-5499

At Other Offices

MAYBERRY, Michael	Tel:	(212) 207-5930
Associate General Counsel and PAC Treasurer	Fax:	(212) 207-5499
277 Park Ave.		
New York City, NY 10172		
michael.mayberry@conti.com		
MCINTYRE, Susan	Tel:	(212) 207-5930
Assistant Secretary and Foundation Administrator	Fax:	(212) 207-5499
277 Park Ave.		
New York City, NY 10172		
susan.mcintyre@conti.com		
TANNER, David A.	Tel:	(212) 207-5930
Executive Vice President, Investments	Fax:	(212) 207-5499
277 Park Ave.		
New York City, NY 10172		
ZIMMERMAN, Michael J.	Tel:	(212) 207-5930
Vice Chairman	Fax:	(212) 207-5499
277 Park Ave.		
New York City, NY 10172		

Continental Tire North America, Inc.

Manufacturer of tires. Continental is the first German company to manufacture pneumatic tires for bicycles.
www.continentaltire.com
Annual Revenues: $2.50 billion
Employees: 3,000
Industry/ies: Automotive Industry; Rubber Industry; Transportation

Main Headquarters
Mailing:	1830 MacMillan Park Dr.	Tel:	(704) 583-4882
	Ft. Mill, SC 29707	Fax:	(704) 583-8546
		TF:	(800) 847-3349

Corporate Foundations and Giving Programs

Continental Tire North America Contributions Program
1830 MacMillan Park Dr.
Ft. Mill, SC 29707

Public Affairs and Related Activities Personnel

At Headquarters

LEDSINGER, Rick	Tel:	(704) 583-4882
Vice President. Human Resources	Fax:	(704) 583-8546
REINHART, Dr. Ariane	Tel:	(704) 583-4882
Executive Board Member, Human Resources and Director, Labor Relations	Fax:	(704) 583-8546
ROGERS, Tim	Tel:	(704) 583-4882
Vice-President, Finance and Treasurer	Fax:	(704) 583-8546

At Other Offices

BLACKWELL, Kathryn	Tel:	(248) 393-6593
Vice President , Communications and Marketing	Fax:	(248) 393-5227
One Continental Dr.		
Auburn Hills, MI 48326		
kathryn.blackwell@us.contiautomotive.com		

ConvaTec

Engaged in developing and marketing innovative wound therapeutics and ostomy care products.
www.convatec.com
Employees: 8,000
SIC: 2834
Industry/ies: Medicine/Health Care/Mental Health
Legislative Issues: MMM

Chairman of the Board Tel: (908) 904-2500
LUNDBERG, Magnus Fax: (908) 904-2780

Chief Executive Officer Tel: (908) 904-2500
MORAVIEC, Paul Fax: (908) 904-2780

Main Headquarters

Mailing:	211 American Ave.	Tel:	(336) 297-3087
	Greensboro, NC 27409	Fax:	(908) 904-2780
		TF:	(800) 422-8811

Corporate Foundations and Giving Programs

ConvaTec Contributions Program
100 Headquarters Park Dr.
Skillman, NJ 08558

Public Affairs and Related Activities Personnel

At Headquarters

BISHOP, Stephen	Tel:	(908) 904-2500
Vice President, Research and Development	Fax:	(908) 904-2780
CLERKIN, Nigel	Tel:	(908) 904-2500
Chief Financial Officer	Fax:	(908) 904-2780
DEUTSCH, Adam	Tel:	(908) 904-2500
Executive Vice President and General Counsel	Fax:	(908) 904-2780
DONOHUE, Punnie	Tel:	(908) 904-2151
Director, Public Relations and Communications	Fax:	(908) 904-2780
punnia.donohue@convatec.com		
LEFORT, Douglas	Tel:	(336) 297-3087
Senior Vice President, Corporate Development	Fax:	(908) 904-2780
REUSS, Marc	Tel:	(336) 297-3087
Executive Vice President, Human Resources	Fax:	(908) 904-2780
RICHARDSON, Alan	Tel:	(908) 904-2500
Vice President, Operational Performance	Fax:	(908) 904-2780
ROLLEY, Joseph	Tel:	(908) 904-2500
Vice President, Government Affairs and Health Policy	Fax:	(908) 904-2780
SGRIGNARI, Michael	Tel:	(336) 297-3087
Executive Vice President, Operations	Fax:	(908) 904-2780
STEELE, Robert	Tel:	(908) 904-2500
Executive Vice President, Quality, Regulatory and Clinical Affairs	Fax:	(908) 904-2780

Convergys Corporation

An integrated outsourced billing and customer service corporation.
www.convergys.com
Annual Revenues: $2.99 billion
Employees: 125,000
Ticker: NYSE: CVG
SIC: 7373
Industry/ies: Accounting; Banking/Finance/Investments

Chairman of the Board	Tel:	(513) 723-7000
FOX, Jeff	Fax:	(513) 421-8624

President and Chief Executive Officer	Tel:	(513) 723-7000
AYERS, Andrea J.	Fax:	(513) 421-8624

Main Headquarters

Mailing:	201 E. Fourth St.	Tel:	(513) 723-7000
	Cincinnati, OH 45202	Fax:	(513) 421-8624
		TF:	(888) 284-9900

Washington Office

Mailing:	22340 Dresden St.
	Suite 100
	Dulles, VA 20166

Political Action Committees

Convergys Corporation PAC
FEC ID: C00350108
Contact: Jarrod Pontius

201 E. Fourth St.	Tel:	(513) 723-7000
P.O. Box 1638	Fax:	(513) 723-7000
Cincinnati, OH 45202		

> **Contributions to Candidates:** $32,000 (2015-2016)
> Democrats: $7,000; Republicans: $25,000

Corporate Foundations and Giving Programs

Convergys Foundation

201 E. Fourth St.	Tel:	(513) 723-7000
P.O. Box 1638	Fax:	(513) 421-8624
Cincinnati, OH 45202		

Public Affairs and Related Activities Personnel

At Headquarters

CLINE, Claudia	Tel:	(513) 723-7000
Executive Vice President and General Counsel	Fax:	(513) 421-8624
CONNELLY, Marjorie	Tel:	(513) 723-7000
Chief Operating Officer	Fax:	(513) 421-8624
O'CONNER, Brian	Tel:	(513) 723-7000
Vice President	Fax:	(513) 421-8624
PONTIUS , Jarrod	Tel:	(513) 723-7000
PAC Treasurer	Fax:	(513) 421-8624
STEIN, David	Tel:	(513) 723-7768

Vice President, Investor Relations	Fax:	(513) 421-8624
investor@convergys.com		
VALENTINE, Andre S.	Tel:	(513) 723-7000
Chief Financial Officer	Fax:	(513) 421-8624

Conwood Company, LLC

See listing on page 56 under American Snuff Company, LLC

Cook Children's Health Care System

Cook Children's Health Care System serves newborns to adolescents in the Ft. Worth area.
www.cookchildrens.org
Annual Revenues: $120 million
Employees: 2,000
Industry/ies: Children And Youth; Medicine/Health Care/Mental Health

Chairman, Cook Children's Health Foundation	Tel:	(682) 885-4000
DUNAWAY, James R.	Fax:	(682) 885-4144

President and Chief Executive Officer	Tel:	(682) 885-4000
MERRILL, Rick W.	Fax:	(682) 885-4144

Main Headquarters

Mailing:	801 Seventh Ave.	Tel:	(682) 885-4000
	Fort Worth, TX 76104	Fax:	(682) 885-4144
		TF:	(800) 934-2665

Corporate Foundations and Giving Programs

Cook Children's Health Foundation
Contact: Rick W. Merrill

801 Seventh Ave.	Tel:	(682) 885-4000
Fort Worth, TX 76104	Fax:	(682) 885-4144

Public Affairs and Related Activities Personnel

At Headquarters

JACK, Deirdre	Tel:	(682) 885-4243
Director, Marketing	Fax:	(682) 885-4144
deirdre.jack@cookchildrens.org		
KING, Winifred	Tel:	(817) 897-7265
Director, Public Relatons	Fax:	(682) 885-4144
winifred.king@cookchildrens.org		
ROSSI, Frank	Tel:	(682) 885-4000
Senior Vice President, Human Resources	Fax:	(682) 885-4144

Cook Group, Inc.

Medical device manufacturer.
www.cookgroup.com
Employees: 1,800
SIC: 3841
NAICS: 339112
Industry/ies: Medicine/Health Care/Mental Health
Legislative Issues: CPT; HCR; MMM; TAX

Chairman of the Board	Tel:	(812) 339-2235
FERGUSON, Steve	Fax:	(800) 554-8335

President & Chief Executive Officer	Tel:	(812) 339-2235
HAWKINS, Kem	Fax:	(800) 554-8335

Main Headquarters

Mailing:	P.O. Box 489	Tel:	(812) 339-2235
	Bloomington, IN 47402-0489	Fax:	(800) 554-8335
		TF:	(800) 457-4500

Washington Office

Mailing:	901 New York Ave. NW	Tel:	(202) 661-3320
	Fifth Floor East		
	Washington, DC 20001		

Political Action Committees

Cook Group Inc. PAC
FEC ID: C00399089
Contact: Thomas A. Connaughton
901 New York Ave. NW
Third Floor
Washington, DC 20001

> **Contributions to Candidates:** $21,000 (2015-2016)
> Democrats: $11,000; Republicans: $10,000

Public Affairs and Related Activities Personnel

At Washington Office

CONNAUGHTON, Thomas A.	Tel:	(202) 509-0887
Vice President, Government Affairs		
tom@cookgroupinc.com		
Registered Federal Lobbyist		
GILES, Allison H.	Tel:	(202) 509-0887
Vice President, Federal Affairs		
Registered Federal Lobbyist		
GUTMAN, Gretchen	Tel:	(202) 661-3320
Vice President, Public Policy		
WILEY, Robin	Tel:	(202) 509-0887

Manager, Legislative and Regulatory Affairs
Registered Federal Lobbyist

Cook Inlet Region Inc. (CIRI)

A regional cooperation firm specialized in investments and business ventures.
www.ciri.com
Annual Revenues: $7 million
Employees: 100
Industry/ies: Minorities; Real Estate
Legislative Issues: BUD; ENG; IND; TAX

Chairman of the Board	Tel:	(907) 274-8638
HUHNDORF, Thomas P.	Fax:	(907) 279-8836
President and Chief Executive Officer	Tel:	(907) 274-8638
MINICH, Sophie	Fax:	(907) 279-8836

Main Headquarters

Mailing:	P.O. Box 93330	Tel:	(907) 274-8638
	Anchorage, AK 99509-9330	Fax:	(907) 279-8836

Corporate Foundations and Giving Programs

CIRI Contributions Program
Contact: Rachel Batres

P.O. Box 9330	Tel:	(907) 274-8638
Anchorage, AK 99509-9330	Fax:	(907) 274-8638

CIRI Foundation
Contact: Susan Anderson

3600 San Jeronimo Dr.	Tel:	(907) 793-3575
Anchorage, AK 99508	Fax:	(907) 793-3585

Public Affairs and Related Activities Personnel

At Headquarters

ANDERSON, Bruce	Tel:	(907) 274-8638
Vice President and General Counsel	Fax:	(907) 279-8836
BATRES, Rachel	Tel:	(907) 274-8638
Corporate Administrator, Community Relations	Fax:	(907) 263-5183
rbatres@ciri.com		
COLBERG, Stig	Tel:	(907) 274-8638
Chief Financial Officer	Fax:	(907) 279-8836
DONATELLI, Barbara A.	Tel:	(907) 274-8638
Senior Vice President and Chief Administrative Officer	Fax:	(907) 279-8836
MOORE, Jason	Tel:	(907) 274-8638
Director, Corporate Communications	Fax:	(907) 279-8836
RAZO, Gregory P.	Tel:	(907) 274-8638
Vice President, Government Contracting	Fax:	(907) 279-8836
grazo@ciri.com		

At Other Offices

ANDERSON, Susan	Tel:	(907) 793-3575
President and Chief Executive Officer, CIRI Foundation	Fax:	(907) 793-3585
2525 C St., Suite 500		
Anchorage, AK 99509		

Cool Clean Technologies, Inc.

Offers liquid-carbon dioxide precision cleaning systems. Develops technologies using CO2 for plastics recycling and oil removal from vitamins.
coolclean.com
Annual Revenues: $3.10 million
Employees: 25
Industry/ies: Environment And Conservation; Science; Scientific Research

Chairman of the Board, President, and Chief Executive Officer	Tel:	(651) 842-8600
WIKSTROM, Jon P.	Fax:	(651) 842-8699

Main Headquarters

Mailing:	915 Blue Gentian Rd.	Tel:	(651) 842-8600
	Suite 400	Fax:	(651) 842-8699
	Eagan, MN 55121-1565	TF:	(866) 262-9274

Public Affairs and Related Activities Personnel

At Headquarters

DUBANOSKI, Mark	Tel:	(651) 842-8600
Director, Supply Chain	Fax:	(651) 842-8699

Cooper Industries, Ltd.

A diversified, worldwide manufacturer of electrical products, tools and hardware.
www.cooperindustries.com
Employees: 25,786
Ticker: NYSE: CBE
SIC: 3640; 3699; 3546; 3429
NAICS: 335999; 333991; 333991
Industry/ies: Electricity & Electronics; Electronics; Energy/Electricity

Chairman and Chief Executive Officer	Tel:	(713) 209-8400
CUTLER, Alexander M.	Fax:	(713) 209-8996

Main Headquarters

Mailing:	P.O. Box 4446	Tel:	(713) 209-8400
	Houston, TX 77210-4446	Fax:	(713) 209-8996

Washington Office

Mailing:	1700 Pennsylvania Ave. NW	
	Washington, DC 20006	

Corporate Foundations and Giving Programs

Cooper Industries Foundation
P.O. 4446
Houston, TX 77210-4446

Public Affairs and Related Activities Personnel

At Headquarters

ARNOLD, Craig	Tel:	(713) 209-8400
Vice Chairman and Chief Operating Officer	Fax:	(713) 209-8996
FEARON, Richard H.	Tel:	(713) 209-8400
Vice Chairman and Chief Financial and Planning Officer	Fax:	(713) 209-8996
HELZ, Terrance V.	Tel:	(713) 209-8400
Associate General Counsel, Secretary and PAC Treasurer	Fax:	(713) 209-8996
TATEN, Bruce M.	Tel:	(713) 209-8400
Senior Vice President, General Counsel and Chief Compliance Officer	Fax:	(713) 209-8995
TAYLOR, Robert L.	Tel:	(713) 209-8400
Chief Marketing Officer	Fax:	(713) 209-8996

At Other Offices

KORKOWSKI, Jeffrey	Tel:	(713) 209-8400
Contact, Media Relations	Fax:	(713) 209-8996
600 Travis St., Suite 5600		
Houston, TX 77002-1001		
Jeffrey.Korkowski@cooperindustries.com		

Cooper Tire & Rubber Company

Makes and sells replacement tires for passenger cars and light trucks, motorcycles, race cars, commercial, and off-road vehicles. Underwent name change in 1946.
www.coopertire.com
Annual Revenues: $2.96 billion
Employees: 9,119
Ticker: NYSE: CTB
SIC: 3011; 3069; 5014; 5099
Industry/ies: Rubber Industry
Legislative Issues: ENV; MAN; TAX; TRA

Chairman of the Board, President and Chief Executive Officer	Tel:	(419) 423-1321
ARMES, Roy V.	Fax:	(419) 424-4108

Main Headquarters

Mailing:	701 Lima Ave.	Tel:	(419) 423-1321
	Findlay, OH 45840	Fax:	(419) 424-4212
		TF:	(800) 854-6288

Political Action Committees

Cooper Tire & Rubber Company PAC
FEC ID: C00370270
Contact: Thomas N. Lause
701 Lima Ave.
Findlay, OH 45840

> **Contributions to Candidates:** $5,000 (2015-2016)
> Republicans: $5,000

Corporate Foundations and Giving Programs

Cooper Tire and Rubber Contribution Program		
701 Lima Ave.	Tel:	(419) 423-1321
P.O. BOX 550	Fax:	(419) 424-4108
Findlay, OH 45840		

Public Affairs and Related Activities Personnel

At Headquarters

HANNEMAN, Christine	Tel:	(419) 423-1321
Investor Relations	Fax:	(419) 424-4212
HARMON, Brenda	Tel:	(419) 423-1321
Senior Vice President and Chief Human Resources Officer	Fax:	(419) 424-4212
HUGHES, Brad	Tel:	(419) 423-1321
Senior Vice President and Chief Operating Officer	Fax:	(419) 424-4212
JONES, Ginger	Tel:	(419) 423-1321
Vice President, Chief Financial Officer	Fax:	(419) 424-4212
LAUSE, Thomas N.	Tel:	(419) 423-1321
PAC Treasurer	Fax:	(419) 424-4212
LONG, Jerry	Tel:	(419) 423-1321
Contact, Investor Relations and Assistant Treasurer	Fax:	(419) 424-4212
MEYERS, Gregory E.	Tel:	(419) 423-1321
Assistant General Counsel	Fax:	(419) 424-4212
REHBEIN, Michelle	Tel:	(419) 423-1321
Manager, Media Relations	Fax:	(419) 424-4212
ROMAN, Anne	Tel:	(419) 423-1321
Vice President, Communications and Public Affairs	Fax:	(419) 424-4212
ZAMANSKY, Steve	Tel:	(419) 423-1321
Vice President, General Counsel and Secretary	Fax:	(419) 424-4212

ZEISLOFT, Michelle	Tel:	(419) 423-1321
Manager, Communications	Fax:	(419) 424-4212

Mr.MichaelCooper

Consult for Defense & Communications Issues.
www.mjwcooper.com.au
Legislative Issues: DEF

Principal	Tel:	(918) 230-7754
COOPER, J. Michael		

Main Headquarters

Mailing:	1913 W. Durham St.	Tel:	(918) 230-7754
	Broken Arrow, OK 74011		

CoorsTek, Inc.

Coorstek, Inc. produces precision-machined metals, technical ceramics, and engineered plastics used in the aerospace, automotive, computer, military contracting, power generation and distribution, and telecommunications industries, among others.
www.coorstek.com
Employees: 2,900
SIC: 3089; 3533; 3674; 3679
NAICS: 333132; 326199; 334413; 334419
Industry/ies: Plastics Industry
Legislative Issues: BUD; DEF; TAX; TRD

Chairman of the Board, President and Chief Executive Officer	Tel:	(303) 271-7000
COORS, Dr. Jonathan K.	Fax:	(303) 271-7009

Main Headquarters

Mailing:	14143 Denver West Pkwy.	Tel:	(303) 271-7000
	Suite 400	Fax:	(303) 271-7009
	Golden, CO 80401	TF:	(800) 821-6110

Public Affairs and Related Activities Personnel

At Headquarters

HAAG, Susan	Tel:	(303) 271-7000
Paralegal	Fax:	(303) 271-7009
HARTMAN, Harrison	Tel:	(303) 277-4559
Director, Marketing	Fax:	(303) 277-4779
hhartman@coorstek.com		
HUNTER, Janis	Tel:	(303) 271-7000
Paralegal	Fax:	(303) 271-7009
LANDRY, Lance	Tel:	(303) 271-7125
Federal Lobbyist	Fax:	(303) 271-7009
llandry@coorstek.com		
Registered Federal Lobbyist		
RASK, Stephan	Tel:	(303) 271-7000
Chief Financial Officer	Fax:	(303) 271-7009

Copperhead Chemical Company Inc.

A chemical company and manufacturer of explosive materials used in propellants, fuel additives, and defense munitions applications.
www.copperheadchemical.com
Annual Revenues: $8.60 million
Employees: 45
Industry/ies: Chemicals & Chemical Industry; Defense/Homeland Security; Government-Related; Pharmaceutical Industry

President and Chief Executive Officer	Tel:	(570) 386-6123
BROOKS, Eric J.	Fax:	(570) 386-6158

Main Headquarters

Mailing:	120 River Rd.	Tel:	(570) 386-6123
	Tamaqua, PA 18252-9446	Fax:	(570) 386-6158

Corinthian Colleges, Inc.

A post-secondary education company in North America.
www.cci.edu
Annual Revenues: $1.48 billion
Employees: 10,100
Ticker: NASDAQ: COCO
SIC: 8200
Industry/ies: Education

Chairman of the Board & Chief Executive Officer	Tel:	(714) 427-3000
MASSIMINO, Jack D.	Fax:	(714) 427-3001

Main Headquarters

Mailing:	Six Hutton Center Dr.	Tel:	(714) 427-3000
	Suite 400	Fax:	(714) 427-5111
	Santa Ana, CA 92707	TF:	(800) 611-2101

Washington Office

Mailing:	401 Ninth St. NW	Tel:	(202) 682-9494
	Suite 620	Fax:	(202) 682-9170
	Washington, DC 20004		

Political Action Committees

Corinthian Colleges, Inc. PAC

FEC ID: C00357640	
Contact: Paul A. De Giusti	
401 Ninth St. NW	
Suite 620	
Washington, DC 20004	

Public Affairs and Related Activities Personnel

At Headquarters

BOSIC, Robert D.	Tel:	(714) 427-3000
Chief Operating Officer	Fax:	(714) 427-5111
BUCHANAN, William B.	Tel:	(714) 427-3000
Executive Vice President, Marketing and Admissions	Fax:	(714) 427-5111
DUNLAP, Anna Marie	Tel:	(714) 424-2678
Senior Vice President, Investor Relations & Corporate Communications	Fax:	(714) 427-3001
FIORETTO, John	Tel:	(714) 427-3000
Assistant Vice President, Tax	Fax:	(714) 427-3001
JENKINS, Kent	Tel:	(714) 427-3000
Vice President, Public Affairs Communications	Fax:	(714) 427-5111
MORTENSEN, Stan A.	Tel:	(714) 427-3000
Executive Vice President and General Counsel and Corporate Secretary	Fax:	(714) 427-3001
ORD, Kenneth S.	Tel:	(714) 427-3000
Chief Administrative Officer	Fax:	(714) 427-5111
OWEN, Robert C.	Tel:	(714) 427-3000
Executive Vice President, Chief Financial Officer	Fax:	(714) 427-5111
TERRIE, Omar	Tel:	(202) 682-9494
Manager	Fax:	(714) 427-3001
VAN DUINEN, Roger	Tel:	(714) 427-3000
Senior Vice President, Marketing	Fax:	(714) 427-5111
WADE, James	Tel:	(714) 427-3000
Senior Vice President and Chief Human Resource Officer	Fax:	(714) 427-3001

At Washington Office

DE GIUSTI, Paul A.	Tel:	(202) 682-9494
Vice President, Government Affairs	Fax:	(202) 682-9170

Corizon, Inc.

A health care company.
www.corizonhealth.com
Employees: 11,000
SIC: 8090
Industry/ies: Charities And Foundations; Medicine/Health Care/Mental Health; Nonprofit

Chairman of the Board	Tel:	(615) 373-3100
CATALANO, Michael	Fax:	(888) 729-0069

Chief Executive Officer	Tel:	(615) 373-3100
MYERS, Jr., MD, Woodrow A.	Fax:	(615) 376-1350

Main Headquarters

Mailing:	105 Westpark Dr.	Fax:	(888) 729-0069
	Suite 200		
	Brentwood, TN 37027		

Political Action Committees

Corizon Health, Inc. PAC
FEC ID: C00345496
Contact: Jeff Sholey

105 Westpark Dr.	Tel:	(615) 373-3100
Suite 200	Fax:	(615) 376-1350
Brentwood, TN 37027		

Public Affairs and Related Activities Personnel

At Headquarters

HOFFMAN, T. Scott	Tel:	(615) 244-1818
Senior Vice President, Chief Administrative Officer and Chief Compliance Officer	Fax:	(888) 729-0069
NOLAN, Pat	Tel:	(615) 244-1818
Contact, Media Relations	Fax:	(888) 729-0069
pat.nolan@dvl.com		
TAYLOR, CPA, Michael W.	Tel:	(615) 244-1818
Executive Vice President and Chief Financial Officer	Fax:	(888) 729-0069
WADE, Dennis	Fax:	(888) 729-0069
Senior Vice President and Chief Human Resources Officer		
WALKER, Jonathan B.	Tel:	(615) 244-1818
Senior Vice President, Business Development and Chief Development Officer	Fax:	(888) 729-0069

At Other Offices

BOWERS, Scott A.	Tel:	(615) 373-3100
President and Chief Operating Officer	Fax:	(615) 376-1350
103 Powell Court		
Brentwood, TN 37027		
CESARIO, MSW, Carla	Tel:	(615) 373-3100

Group Vice President 103 Powell Court Brentwood, TN 37027	Fax:	(615) 376-1350	

HOFFMAN, T. Scott — Tel: (615) 373-3100
Senior Vice President, Chief Administrative Officer and Chief Compliance Officer
103 Powell Court
Brentwood, TN 37027

KING, J. Scott — Tel: (615) 373-3100 / Fax: (615) 376-1350
Executive Vice President and Chief Legal Officer
103 Powell Court
Brentwood, TN 37027

SHOLEY, Jeff — Tel: (615) 373-3100 / Fax: (615) 376-1350
Interim Chief Financial Officer
103 Powell Court
Brentwood, TN 37027

TAYLOR, CPA, Michael W. — Tel: (615) 373-3100
Executive Vice President and Chief Financial Officer
103 Powell Court
Brentwood, TN 37027

WADE, Dennis — Tel: (615) 373-3100 / Fax: (615) 376-1350
Senior Vice President and Chief Human Resources Officer
103 Powell Court
Brentwood, TN 37027

WALKER, Jon — Tel: (615) 373-3100 / Fax: (615) 376-1350
Senior Vice President, Business Development
103 Powell Court
Brentwood, TN 37027
walkerjw@asgr.com

WALKER, Jonathan B. — Tel: (615) 373-3100
Senior Vice President, Business Development and Chief Development Officer
103 Powell Court
Brentwood, TN 37027

Corn Products International
See listing on page 429 under Ingredion

Corning Inc.
A manufacturer of optical fiber, cable and components.
www.corning.com
Annual Revenues: $8.89 billion
Employees: 35,700
Ticker: NYSE: GLW
SIC: 3357
NAICS: 335921
Industry/ies: Glass
Legislative Issues: BUD; CPT; DEF; ENV; HCR; TAR; TAX; TEC; TRD

Chairman and Chief Executive Officer — Tel: (607) 974-9000 / Fax: (607) 974-8551
WEEKS, Wendell P.

Main Headquarters
Mailing: One Riverfront Plaza — Tel: (607) 974-9000
Corning, NY 14831 — Fax: (607) 974-8091
TF: (888) 267-6464

Washington Office
Mailing: 325 Seventh St. NW — Tel: (202) 661-4150
Suite 600 — Fax: (202) 661-4165
Washington, DC 20004

Political Action Committees
Corning Incorporated Employees PAC (CORE PAC)
FEC ID: C00033589
Contact: Timothy J. Regan
325 Seventh St. NW — Tel: (202) 661-4150
Suite 600 — Fax: (202) 661-4165
Washington, DC 20004

   Contributions to Candidates: $12,363,765 (2015-2016)
   Democrats: $102,000; Republicans: $119,750; Other: $12,142,015

     Principal Recipients

       SENATE
       SCHUMER, CHARLES E (DEM-NY)

       HOUSE
       REED, THOMAS W II (REP-NY)

Corporate Foundations and Giving Programs
Corning Inc. Foundation
Contact: Karen C. Martin
One Riverfront Plaza — Tel: (607) 974-9000
Corning, NY 14831 — Fax: (607) 974-5927

Public Affairs and Related Activities Personnel

At Headquarters

COLLINS, Daniel F. — Tel: (607) 974-4197 / Fax: (607) 974-8509

Vice President, Corporate Communication and Media Contacts
collinsdf@corning.com

EVENSON, Dr. Jeffrey — Tel: (607) 974-9000 / Fax: (607) 974-8091
Senior Vice President and Chief Strategy Officer

FERRERO, Lisa — Tel: (607) 974-9000 / Fax: (607) 974-8091
Senior Vice President and Chief Administrative Officer

MARTIN, Karen C. — Tel: (607) 974-8722 / Fax: (607) 974-8091
President, Foundation
Mail Stop MP BH 7

MCRAE, Lawrence D. — Tel: (607) 974-9000 / Fax: (607) 974-5927
Vice Chairman and Corporate Development Officer

PAMBIANCHI, Christine M. — Tel: (607) 974-9000 / Fax: (607) 974-8091
Senior Vice President, Human Resources

STEVERSON, Lewis A. — Tel: (607) 974-9000 / Fax: (607) 974-8091
Senior Vice President and General Counsel

TRIPENY, Tony — Tel: (607) 974-9000 / Fax: (607) 974-8091
Senior Vice President and Chief Financial Officer

At Washington Office

FENDLEY, Stan G. — Tel: (202) 661-4152 / Fax: (202) 661-4165
Director, Legislative and Regulatory Policy
fendleysg@corning.com
Registered Federal Lobbyist

REGAN, Timothy J. — Tel: (202) 661-4155 / Fax: (202) 661-4165
Senior Vice President
regantj@corning.com
Registered Federal Lobbyist

WAGGONER, Debra L. — Tel: (202) 661-4157 / Fax: (202) 661-4165
Director, Global Government Affairs
Registered Federal Lobbyist

Corporate Political Strategies, LLC
Political Consulting.
Industry/ies: Consultants; Politics/Political Science
Legislative Issues: BAN

Main Headquarters
Mailing: 555 13th St. NW
Suite 4 East
Washington, DC 20004

Public Affairs and Related Activities Personnel

At Headquarters

RODRIGUEZ, Leonard

Corporation for Enterprise Development
Non-profit corporation dedicated to helping low-income families build assets and enter the economic mainstream.
www.cfed.org
Industry/ies: Accounting; Banking/Finance/Investments; Economics And Economic Development; Housing; Taxation

President — Tel: (202) 408-9788 / Fax: (202) 408-9793
LEVERE, Andrea
alevere@cfed.org

Main Headquarters
Mailing: 1200 G St. NW — Tel: (202) 408-9788
Suite 400 — Fax: (202) 408-9793
Washington, DC 20005

Corporate Foundations and Giving Programs
The 1:1 Fund
1200 G St. NW — Tel: (202) 408-9788
Suite 400
Washington, DC 20005

Public Affairs and Related Activities Personnel

At Headquarters

BOKHARI, Adnan — Tel: (202) 408-9788 / Fax: (202) 408-9793
Chief Financial Officer
abokhari@cfed.org

BROOKS, Jennifer — Tel: (202) 408-9788 / Fax: (202) 408-9793
Vice President, Field Engagement
jennifer.brooks@cfed.org

COTTON, Keven — Tel: (202) 408-9788 / Fax: (202) 408-9793
Policy Associate
kcotton@cfed.org

CRAIN, Rosalyn — Tel: (202) 408-9788 / Fax: (202) 408-9793
Legislative Manager
rcrain@cfed.org

FRIEDMAN, Robert — Tel: (202) 408-9788 / Fax: (202) 408-9793
General Counsel
rfriedman@cfed.org

GREER, Jeremie — Tel: (202) 408-9788

Vice President, Policy and Research	Fax:	(202) 408-9793

IMOH, Inemesit — Tel: (202) 408-9788
Policy Associate — Fax: (202) 408-9793

JACKSON, Sandra Lee Stevens — Tel: (202) 408-9788
Policy Associate — Fax: (202) 408-9793

LAWTON, Kristin — Tel: (202) 408-9788
Director, Communications — Fax: (202) 408-9793
klawton@cfed.org

LIN, Wes — Tel: (202) 408-9788
Human Resources Generalist — Fax: (202) 408-9793
wlin@cfed.org

PALACIO, Camille — Tel: (202) 408-9788
Policy Associate — Fax: (202) 408-9793
cpalacio@cfed.org

WAYMAN, Carol — Tel: (202) 408-9788
Senior Federal Legislative Director — Fax: (202) 408-9793

WEIS, Veronica — Tel: (202) 408-9788
Marketing and Outreach Specialist — Fax: (202) 408-9793
vweis@cfed.org

Corporation for Public Broadcasting

A private, nonprofit corporation created by Congress in 1967 with a mission to facilitate the development of, and ensure universal access to, non-commercial, high-quality programming and telecommunications services. It is the steward of the federal government's investment in public broadcasting and the largest single source of funding for public radio, television, and related online and mobile services.
www.cpb.org
Annual Revenues: $483.67 million
Employees: 100
Industry/ies: Communications; Media/Mass Communication

Chairman of the Board — Tel: (202) 879-9600
SEMBLER, Elizabeth — Fax: (202) 879-9700

President and Chief Executive Officer — Tel: (202) 879-9600
HARRISON, Patricia de Stacy — Fax: (202) 879-9700
pharrison@cpb.org

Main Headquarters
Mailing: 401 Ninth St. NW — Tel: (202) 879-9600
Washington, DC 20004-2129 — Fax: (202) 879-9700
— TF: (800) 272-2190

Corporate Foundations and Giving Programs

Corporation for Public Broadcasting Contributions Program
401 Ninth St. NW — Tel: (202) 879-9600
Washington, DC 20004-2129 — Fax: (202) 879-9700

Public Affairs and Related Activities Personnel

At Headquarters

BRACHMAN, Anne — Tel: (202) 879-9600
Vice President, Government Affairs — Fax: (202) 879-9700

BROADWAY, Kelly — Tel: (202) 879-9641
Public Affairs and Social Media Professional — Fax: (202) 879-9700
kbroadway@cpb.org

CURREN, Vincent — Tel: (202) 879-9600
Executive Vice President and Chief Operating Officer — Fax: (202) 879-9700

DALRYMPLE, Cara — Tel: (202) 879-9600
Vice President, Human Resources — Fax: (202) 879-9700
cdalrymple@cpb.org

LEVY, Michael — Tel: (202) 879-9600
Executive Vice President and Chief Strategy Officer — Fax: (202) 879-9700
mlevy@cpb.org

LIVESAY, Jackie — Tel: (202) 879-9600
Vice President, Compliance — Fax: (202) 879-9700
jlivesay@cpb.org

SAFON, Teresa — Tel: (202) 879-9600
Senior Vice President, Corporate Secretary and Chief of Staff — Fax: (202) 879-9700

SMITHERS, Jr., Westwood — Tel: (202) 879-9600
Senior Vice President and General Counsel — Fax: (202) 879-9700
wsmithers@cpb.org

TAYMAN, Jr., William P. — Tel: (202) 879-9600
Chief Financial Officer and Treasurer — Fax: (202) 879-9700

Correctional Medical Services, Inc.

A healthcare consulting company for prison inmates.
www.corizonhealth.com
Annual Revenues: $730.00 million
Employees: 6,000
Industry/ies: Medicine/Health Care/Mental Health

Chief Executive Officer — Tel: (314) 919-8501
MYERS, Jr., MD, Woodrow A. — Fax: (314) 919-8864

Main Headquarters
Mailing: 103 Powell Ct. — Tel: (800) 729-0069

Brentwood, TN 37027 — TF: (800) 729-0069

Political Action Committees
Corizon Health, Inc. PAC
FEC ID: C00345496
Contact: Jeff Sholey
105 Westpark Dr. — Tel: (615) 373-3100
Suite 200 — Fax: (615) 376-1350
Brentwood, TN 37027

Correctional Medical Services Inc PAC Aka Cms PAC
FEC ID: C00377861
Contact: Melvin M. Mahoney
12647 Olive Blvd.
St. Louis, MO 63141

Corporate Foundations and Giving Programs
Corizon Contributions Program
105 Westpark Dr. — Tel: (615) 376-1329
Suite 200
Brentwood, TN 37027

Public Affairs and Related Activities Personnel

At Headquarters

BOWERS, Scott A. — Tel: (800) 729-0069
President and Chief Operating Officer

HARRIS, Lynette — Tel: (615) 376-1329
Director, Marketing/Communications

KING, Scott — Tel: (800) 729-0069
Executive Vice President and Chief Legal Officer

SHOLEY, Jeff — Tel: (800) 729-0069
Interim Chief Financial Officer and PAC Contact

WADE, Dennis — Tel: (800) 729-0069
Executive Vice President and Chief Human Resources Officer

WALKER, Jon — Tel: (800) 729-0069
Executive Vice President and Chief Development Officer

At Other Offices

FIELDS, Ken — Tel: (314) 982-0556
Contact, Media Relations — Fax: (314) 640-2529
12647 Olive Blvd.
St. Louis, MO 63141
ken.fields@fleishman.com

MAHONEY, Melvin M. — Tel: (314) 919-8501
Contact, Government Relations and PAC Contact — Fax: (314) 919-8864
12647 Olive Blvd.
St. Louis, MO 63141

MOL, John Van — Tel: (615) 244-1818
Contact, Media Relations — Fax: (314) 919-8864
12647 Olive Blvd.
St. Louis, MO 63141

Corrections Corporation of America

Owns and operates privatized correctional and detention facilities in the United States.
www.cca.com
Annual Revenues: $1.67 billion
Employees: 14,040
Ticker: NYSE: CXW
SIC: 8744
Industry/ies: Construction/Construction Materials
Legislative Issues: BUD; GOV; HOM; LAW; TAX

Chairman of the Board — Tel: (615) 263-3000
FERGUSON, John D. — Fax: (615) 263-3140
john.ferguson@correctionscorp.com

President and Chief Executive Officer — Tel: (615) 263-3000
HININGER, Damon T. — Fax: (615) 263-3140

Main Headquarters
Mailing: Ten Burton Hills Blvd. — Tel: (615) 263-3000
Nashville, TN 37215 — Fax: (615) 263-3140
— TF: (800) 624-2931

Washington Office
Mailing: 601 Pennsylvania Ave. NW
Suite 210, South Building
Washington, DC 20004

Political Action Committees
Corrections Corporation of America PAC
FEC ID: C00366468
Contact: Cole G. Carter
Ten Burton Hills Blvd.
Nashville, TN 37215

Contributions to Candidates: $77,700 (2015-2016)
Democrats: $10,500; Republicans: $67,200

Corporate Foundations and Giving Programs
CCA's Corporate Giving Mission

Contact: Gene Sobczak
Ten Burton Hills Blvd.
Nashville, TN 37215

Tel:	(615) 263-3107	
Fax:	(615) 263-3140	

Public Affairs and Related Activities Personnel

At Headquarters

CARTER , Cole G.
PAC Contact

Tel:	(615) 263-3000
Fax:	(615) 263-3140

CRADDOCK, Scott
Corporate Ethics and Compliance Officer
scott.craddock@cca.com

Tel:	(615) 263-3000
Fax:	(615) 263-3140

DEMLER, Karin
Senior Director, Investor Relations
karin.demler@correctionscorp.com

Tel:	(615) 263-3005
Fax:	(615) 263-3140

GARFINKLE, David
Executive Vice President and Chief Financial Officer

Tel:	(615) 263-3000
Fax:	(615) 263-3140

GROOM, Steve E.
Executive Vice President and General Counsel

Tel:	(615) 263-3000
Fax:	(615) 263-3140

OWEN, MBA, Steve
Senior Director, Public Affairs and Contact, Media Relations
steve.owen@correctionscorp.com

Tel:	(615) 263-3107
Fax:	(615) 263-3140

SOBCZAK, Gene
Executive Director, Foundation Contact
gene.sobczak@ccaurora.edu

Tel:	(303) 360-4833
Fax:	(615) 263-3140

WHITE, Kimberly
Executive Vice President, Human Resources

Tel:	(615) 263-3000
Fax:	(615) 263-3140

At Washington Office

CHEEVER, Kelli
Federal Lobbyist

At Other Offices

QUINLAN, Mike
Senior Vice President
444 N. Capitol St. NW, Suite 601
Washington, DC 20001
mike.quinlan@correctionscorp.com
Registered Federal Lobbyist

Tel:	(202) 347-8717

VERHULST, Bart
Managing Director, Federal Relations
444 N. Capitol St. NW, Suite 601
Washington, DC 20001
Verhulst@correctionscorp.com
Registered Federal Lobbyist

Tel:	(202) 347-8717

WILEY, Jeremy
Managing Director, Federal Partnerships
444 N. Capitol St. NW, Suite 601
Washington, DC 20001
jeremy.wiley@correctionscorp.com
Registered Federal Lobbyist

Tel:	(202) 347-8717

Corridor 67, Inc.

In the U.S. state of Illinois, U.S. Route 67 is a north–south highway through the western portions of the state.
Industry/ies: Transportation

Main Headquarters
Mailing: 155 W. Morton
Jacksonville, IL 62650

Tel:	(217) 245-2174

Political Action Committees
Corridor 67, Inc PAC
FEC ID: C00238691
Contact: Ginni Fanning
155 W. Morton
Jacksonville, IL 62650

   Contributions to Candidates: $350 (2015-2016)
   Republicans: $350

Public Affairs and Related Activities Personnel

At Headquarters

FANNING, Virginia L.
Secretary
chamber@jacksonvilleareachamber.org
Registered Federal Lobbyist

Tel:	(217) 245-2174

FANNING, Ginni
PAC Treasurer

Tel:	(217) 245-2174

MUSCH, Lisa
Secretary

Tel:	(217) 245-2174

Costco Wholesale Corporation

A retail or wholesale chain.
www.costco.com
Annual Revenues: $107.89 billion
Employees: 103,000
Ticker: NASDAQ: COST

SIC: 5331
Industry/ies: Retail/Wholesale

Co-Founder and Chairman of the Board
BROTMAN, Jeffrey H.

Tel:	(425) 313-8100
Fax:	(425) 313-6593

President and Chief Executive Officer
JELINEK, W. Craig
cjelinek@costco.com

Tel:	(425) 313-8100
Fax:	(425) 313-6593

Main Headquarters
Mailing: 999 Lake Dr.
Issaquah, WA 98027

Tel:	(425) 313-8100
Fax:	(425) 313-6593
TF:	(800) 774-2678

Corporate Foundations and Giving Programs
Costco Wholesale Corporation Contributions Program
Contact: Muriel Cooper
999 Lake Dr.
Issaquah, WA 98027

Public Affairs and Related Activities Personnel

At Headquarters

CALLANS, Pat
Senior Vice President, Human Resources and Risk Management

Tel:	(425) 313-8100
Fax:	(425) 313-6593

CAMPBELL, Roger A.
Senior Vice President, Operations

Tel:	(425) 313-8100
Fax:	(425) 313-6593

COOPER, Muriel
Contact, Community Relations and Administration
mcooper@costco.com

Tel:	(425) 313-6182
Fax:	(425) 313-6593

FARIA, PJ
Contact, Membership Services and Marketing

Tel:	(425) 313-8100
Fax:	(425) 313-6593

GALANTI, Richard
Executive Vice President and Chief Financial Officer

Tel:	(425) 313-8203
Fax:	(425) 313-6593

OLIN, Rich
Senior Vice President, and General Counsel

Tel:	(425) 313-8100
Fax:	(425) 313-6593

PETTERSON, David S.
Senior Vice President, Corporate Controller

Tel:	(425) 313-8100
Fax:	(425) 313-6593

COUNTRY Financial

See listing on page 224 under Country Insurance and Financial Services

Country Insurance and Financial Services

Provides Insurance, Investments and financial security.
www.countryfinancial.com
Employees: 5,000
SIC: 6411
Industry/ies: Insurance Industry

Chief Executive Officer
BOCK, Kurt F.

Tel:	(309) 821-3000
Fax:	(309) 821-5160

Main Headquarters
Mailing: 1701 N. Towanda Ave.
P.O. Box 2222
Bloomington, IL 61701-2057

Tel:	(309) 821-3000
Fax:	(309) 821-5160
TF:	(866) 268-6879

Political Action Committees
CC Services Inc COUNTRY PAC
FEC ID: C00390971
Contact: Miles Kilcoin
1701 N. Towanda Ave.
P.O. Box 2020
Bloomington, IL 61702

Tel:	(309) 821-3000
Fax:	(309) 821-5160

Corporate Foundations and Giving Programs
Country Insurance and Financial Services Contributions Program
1701 N. Towanda Ave.
Bloomington, IL 61701-2057

Public Affairs and Related Activities Personnel

At Headquarters

BAURER, Barbara A.
Executive Vice President, Chief Operating Officer

Tel:	(309) 821-3000
Fax:	(309) 821-5160

BISHOP, Paul
Senior Vice President, Sales

Tel:	(309) 821-3000
Fax:	(309) 557-3232

DENAULT, Steve
Executive Vice President, Enterprise Business Services

Tel:	(309) 821-3000
Fax:	(309) 557-3232

KILCOIN, Miles
PAC Treasurer

Tel:	(309) 821-3000
Fax:	(309) 821-5160

SCHILL, Kelvin
Senior Vice President, Financial Services

Tel:	(309) 821-3000
Fax:	(309) 821-5160

WILLIAMS, Doyle J.
Chief Marketing Officer

Tel:	(309) 821-3000
Fax:	(309) 557-3232

CountryMark Cooperative

An oil refining and marketing company.

www.countrymark.com
Annual Revenues: $862.97 million
Employees: 400
Industry/ies: Cooperatives; Fuels See Coal, Gas, Oil, Petroleum; Natural
Resources; Petroleum Industry
Legislative Issues: ENG; FUE

Chief Executive Officer
SMITH, Charlie
Tel: (317) 238-8225
Fax: (317) 692-8510

Main Headquarters
Mailing: 225 S.E. St.
Suite 144
Indianapolis, IN 46202-4059
Tel: (317) 238-8225
Fax: (317) 692-8510
TF: (800) 808-3170

Public Affairs and Related Activities Personnel

At Headquarters

ALESIA, Steve
Vice President, Finance and Administration
Tel: (317) 238-8225
Fax: (317) 692-8510

LANTZ, Jon
Vice President, Marketing
Tel: (317) 238-8225
Fax: (317) 692-8510

PUETZ, Belinda
Brand Manager and Contact, Media Relations
puetz@countrymark.com
Tel: (317) 238-8225
Fax: (317) 692-8510

SMORCH, Matt
Vice President, Supply and Strategy
Tel: (317) 238-8225
Fax: (317) 692-8510

WARD, Pat
Vice President, Operations
Tel: (317) 238-8225
Fax: (317) 692-8510

Countrywide Financial
See listing on page 104 under Bank of America Corporation

The Courier-Journal
A newspaper publishing company.
www.courier-journal.com
Annual Revenues: $53.10 million
Employees: 1,200
SIC: 2711
Industry/ies: Communications; Media/Mass Communication

Chairman of the Board
IVEY, Denise
Tel: (502) 582-4011
Fax: (502) 582-4560

President and Publisher
JACKSON, Wesley
wjackson@courier-journal.com
Tel: (502) 582-4101
Fax: (502) 582-4560

Main Headquarters
Mailing: 525 W. Broadway
P.O. Box 740031
Louisville, KY 40201-7431
Tel: (502) 582-4011
Fax: (502) 582-4560
TF: (800) 866-2211

Public Affairs and Related Activities Personnel

At Headquarters

SIMMONS, Anthony
Director, Market Sales and Distribution
tsimmons@gannett.com
Tel: (502) 582-4745
Fax: (502) 582-4560

Covance Inc.
Covance helps pharmaceutical and biotech companies worldwide develop new drugs by providing preclinical testing services, as well as designing and carrying out human clinical trials to determine if the drugs are safe and effective.
www.covance.com
Employees: 11,863
Ticker: NYSE: CVD
SIC: 8731
Industry/ies: Business; Medicine/Health Care/Mental Health; Small Business
Legislative Issues: FOO; MED

Chief Executive Officer
HERRING, Joseph
Tel: (609) 452-8550
Fax: (609) 452-9375

Main Headquarters
Mailing: 210 Carnegie Center
Princeton, NJ 08540
Tel: (609) 452-8550
Fax: (609) 452-9375
TF: (888) 268-2623

Corporate Foundations and Giving Programs
Covance Contributions Program
210 Carnegie Center
Princeton, NJ 08540
Tel: (609) 452-8550
Fax: (609) 452-9375

Public Affairs and Related Activities Personnel

At Headquarters

BROWN, Nigel
Corporate Vice President, Business Development and Strategy
Tel: (609) 452-8550
Fax: (609) 452-9375

CORNELL, Alison A.
Corporate Vice President and Chief Financial Officer
Tel: (609) 452-9375
Fax: (609) 452-9375

ISIP, Laurene
Executive Director, Corporate Communications and Public Relations
laurene.isip@covance.com
Tel: (609) 452-4440
Fax: (609) 452-9375

KLITGAARD, William
Corporate Senior Vice President and Chief Information Officer
Tel: (609) 452-8550
Fax: (609) 452-9375

LOVETT, James
Corporate Senior Vice President, General Counsel and Secretary
James.Lovett@covance.com
Tel: (609) 452-8550
Fax: (609) 452-9375

WATSON, John
Corporate Senior Vice President, Strategic Partnering
Tel: (609) 452-8550
Fax: (609) 452-9375

Covanta Energy Corporation
Offers power and related infrastructure services.
www.covantaenergy.com
Annual Revenues: $212.70 million
Employees: 3,500
SIC: 4991
Industry/ies: Energy/Electricity
Legislative Issues: BUD; ENG; ENV; TAX; WAS

Chairman of the Board
ZELL, Samuel
Tel: (973) 882-9000
Fax: (973) 882-7234

President and Chief Executive Officer
JONES, Stephen J
Tel: (862) 345-5000
Fax: (973) 882-7234

Main Headquarters
Mailing: 445 South St.
Morristown, NJ 07960
Tel: (862) 345-5000
Fax: (973) 882-7234

Political Action Committees
Covanta Energy Corporation Political Action Committee
FEC ID: C00142158
Contact: Joanne Pagliuca
445 South St.
Morristown, NJ 07960
Tel: (703) 246-0830
Fax: (703) 246-0808

   Contributions to Candidates: $70,500 (2015-2016)
   Democrats: $43,000; Republicans: $27,500

Corporate Foundations and Giving Programs
Covanta Energy Corporation Contribution Program
445 South St.
Morristown, NJ 07960
Tel: (862) 345-5000
Fax: (973) 882-7234

Public Affairs and Related Activities Personnel

At Headquarters

BLAYLOCK, Frazier
Federal Lobbyist
Registered Federal Lobbyist
Tel: (202) 295-1123
Fax: (973) 882-7234

BUCKS, Thomas E
Senior Vice President, Finance
Tel: (862) 345-5000
Fax: (973) 882-7234

HELGESON, Brad
Executive Vice President and Chief Financial Officer
Tel: (862) 345-5000
Fax: (973) 882-7234

KATZ, Alan
Vice President, Investor Relations
akatz@CovantaEnergy.com
Tel: (862) 345-5456
Fax: (973) 882-7234

MULCAHY, Matthew
Senior Vice President and Head of Corporate Development
Tel: (862) 345-5000
Fax: (973) 882-7234

PAGLIUCA, Joanne
PAC Treasurer
Tel: (973) 882-9000
Fax: (973) 882-7234

PARKS, Zachary
Special Counsel
Tel: (862) 345-5000
Fax: (973) 882-7234

REGAN, James
Manager, Media Relations and Corporate Communications
jregan@covantaenergy.com
Tel: (862) 345-5216
Fax: (973) 882-7234

SIMPSON, Timothy J.
Executive Vice President, General Counsel and Secretary
Tel: (973) 882-9000
Fax: (973) 882-7234

SOOS-KOBYLSKI, Paula
Vice President, Government Relations & Federal Lobbyist
Registered Federal Lobbyist
Tel: (202) 295-1123
Fax: (973) 882-7234

WRIGHT, Michael A.
Senior Vice President and Chief Human Resources Officer
Tel: (973) 882-9000
Fax: (973) 882-7234

Covenant HealthCare
A health care facilities north of metro Detroit.
www.covenanthealthcare.com
Annual Revenues: $508.52 million
Employees: 4,400
Industry/ies: Medicine/Health Care/Mental Health
Legislative Issues: MMM

Chairman of the Board
NIEDERSTADT, Terry
Tel: (989) 583-0000
Fax: (989) 583-6457

President and Chief Executive Officer		
BRUFF, Ed	Tel:	(989) 583-0000
	Fax:	(989) 583-6457

Main Headquarters

Mailing: 1447 N. Harrison St.	Tel:	(989) 583-0000
Saginaw, MI 48602	Fax:	(989) 583-6457

Corporate Foundations and Giving Programs

Covenant HealthCare Foundation
Contact: Kathi Spence

1447 N. Harrison St.	Tel:	(989) 583-0000
Saginaw, MI 48602	Fax:	(989) 583-6457

Public Affairs and Related Activities Personnel

At Headquarters

ALBOSTA, Kevin	Tel:	(989) 583-0000
Vice President and Chief Fincial Officer	Fax:	(989) 583-6457
KNOLL, Kristin	Tel:	(989) 583-7655
Specialist, Public Relations	Fax:	(989) 583-6457
kknoll@chs-mi.com		
MCDONALD, Michele	Tel:	(989) 583-4580
Compliance Officer	Fax:	(989) 583-6457
SPENCE , Kathi	Tel:	(989) 583-0000
Chairperson, the Covenant HealthCare Foundation	Fax:	(989) 583-6457

Covenant Retirement Communities

A retirement housing provider.
www.covenantretirement.com
Annual Revenues: $38.70 million
Employees: 800
Industry/ies: Housing

President and Chief Executive Officer		
FISK, Rick K.	Tel:	(773) 878-2294
	Fax:	(773) 878-2289

Main Headquarters

Mailing: 5700 Old Orchard Rd.	Tel:	(773) 878-2294
Suite 100	Fax:	(773) 878-2289
Skokie, IL 60077-1036	TF:	(800) 255-8989

Corporate Foundations and Giving Programs

Covenant Charitable Foundation
Contact: Heidi Behm

5700 Old Orchard Rd.	Tel:	(773) 878-2294
Suite 100	Fax:	(773) 878-2294
Skokie, IL 60077		

Public Affairs and Related Activities Personnel

At Headquarters

BEHM, Heidi	Tel:	(773) 878-4336
Foundation Contact	Fax:	(773) 878-2289
BUIKEMA, Elizabeth B.	Tel:	(773) 878-2294
Senior Vice President and Chief Financial Officer	Fax:	(773) 878-2289
CLAXTON, Colette	Tel:	(954) 752-6872
Contact, Media Relations	Fax:	(773) 878-2289
ClaxtonC@bellsouth.net		
ERICKSON, David G.	Tel:	(773) 878-2294
Senior Vice President and General Counsel	Fax:	(773) 878-2289
WESTERFIELD, Jane	Tel:	(773) 878-2294
National Director, Human Resources	Fax:	(773) 878-2289

Coventry Health Care, Inc.

A health insurance company. Aetna acquired Coventry Health Care, Inc. on May 7, 2013.
www.coventryhealthcare.com
Employees: 14,400
Ticker: NYSE: CVH
SIC: 6324
Industry/ies: Medicine/Health Care/Mental Health

Main Headquarters

Mailing: 6730 - B Rockledge Dr.	Tel:	(301) 581-0600
Suite 700		
Bethesda, MD 20817		

Public Affairs and Related Activities Personnel

At Headquarters

HUTCHINGS, Rohan	Tel:	(773) 687-5419
Contact, Media Relations		
hutchingsr@aetna.com		

Covestro, LLC

Chemical manufacturing company.
Legislative Issues: BUD; CHM; ENG; TAR

Main Headquarters

Mailing: One Covestro Cir.
Pittsburgh, PA 15205

Public Affairs and Related Activities Personnel

At Headquarters

KELLY, Glenn
Registered Federal Lobbyist
NASH, Ian
Registered Federal Lobbyist
SALVAGNO, Stephanie
Registered Federal Lobbyist

Covidien

Develops, manufactures, and sells healthcare products for use in clinical and home settings worldwide. Formerly Tyco Healthcare.
www.covidien.com
Employees: 38,500
Ticker: NYSE: COV
Industry/ies: Medicine/Health Care/Mental Health
Legislative Issues: AVI; HCR; MMM; TAX

Chairman of the Board, President and Chief Executive Officer	Tel:	(508) 261-8000
ALMEIDA, Jose E.	Fax:	(508) 261-8102

Main Headquarters

Mailing: 15 Hampshire St.	Tel:	(508) 261-8000
Mansfield, MA 02048	Fax:	(508) 261-8102

Washington Office

Mailing: 900 Seventh St. NW
Suite 975
Washington, DC 20001

Political Action Committees

Covidien (U.S.) Political Action Committee (Covidien PAC)
FEC ID: C00433490
Contact: Gregory Andrulonis
701 Eighth St. NW
Suite 620
Washington, DC 20001

Contributions to Candidates: $1,000 (2015-2016)
Republicans: $1,000

Corporate Foundations and Giving Programs

Covidien Partnership for Neighborhood Wellness

15 Hampshire St.	Tel:	(508) 261-8000
Mansfield, MA 02048	Fax:	(508) 261-8000

Public Affairs and Related Activities Personnel

At Headquarters

BROWN, Jr., Richard G.	Tel:	(508) 261-8000
Vice President Chief Accounting Officer and Corporate Controller	Fax:	(508) 261-8102
CLEMENCE, Lisa	Tel:	(508) 452-4375
Director, Corporate Communications	Fax:	(508) 261-8102
lisa.clemence@covidien.com		
DOCKENDORFF, Charles J.	Tel:	(508) 261-8000
Executive Vice President and Chief Financial Officer	Fax:	(508) 261-8102
charles.dockendorff@covidien.com		
DUNFORD, Michael P.	Tel:	(508) 261-8000
Senior Vice President, Human Resources	Fax:	(508) 261-8102
FARMER, Bruce	Tel:	(508) 452-4372
Vice President, Public Relations	Fax:	(508) 261-8102
bruce.farmer@covidien.com		
LANNUM, CFA, Coleman	Tel:	(508) 452-4343
Vice President, Investor Relations	Fax:	(508) 261-8102
cole.lannum@covidien.com		
MASTERSON, John H.	Tel:	(508) 261-8000
Senior Vice President, General Counsel	Fax:	(508) 261-8102
john.masterson@covidien.com		
OLSON, David A.	Tel:	(508) 261-8000
Vice President, Regulatory Affairs	Fax:	(508) 261-8102
SGRIGNARI, Michael	Tel:	(508) 261-8000
Senior Vice President, Quality and Operations	Fax:	(508) 261-8102
STRAYER, Jacqueline F.	Tel:	(508) 261-8000
Senior Vice President Corporate Communications	Fax:	(508) 261-8102
WENDELL, Amy A.	Tel:	(508) 261-8000
Senior Vice President, Strategy and Business Development	Fax:	(508) 261-8102
amy.wendell@covidien.com		
YOUNG, David	Tel:	(203) 492-6333
Manager, Media Relations	Fax:	(508) 261-8102
david.young@covidien.com		

At Other Offices

ANDRULONIS, Gregory	Tel:	(202) 310-5110
Vice President, Treasurer and PAC Treasurer	Fax:	(508) 261-8102
701 Eighth St. NW, Suite 620		
Washington, DC 20001		
COLLARD, Jonathan S.	Tel:	(202) 310-5110
Director, Government Affairs, Asia	Fax:	(508) 261-8102

701 Eighth St. NW, Suite 620
Washington, DC 20001
Registered Federal Lobbyist

DASILVA, Kevin	Tel:	(202) 310-5110
Vice President and Group Chief Finanacial Officer	Fax:	(508) 261-8102
701 Eighth St. NW, Suite 620		
Washington, DC 20001		

GARDINER, Whitney   Tel: (202) 310-5110
Director, Government Affairs   Fax: (508) 261-8102
701 Eighth St. NW, Suite 620
Washington, DC 20001
Registered Federal Lobbyist

HALE, Whitney   Tel: (202) 310-5110
Manager, Government Affairs   Fax: (508) 261-8102
701 Eighth St. NW, Suite 620
Washington, DC 20001
Registered Federal Lobbyist

KALAVRITINOS, Jack   Tel: (202) 310-5110
Director, Global Government Affairs   Fax: (508) 261-8102
701 Eighth St. NW, Suite 620
Washington, DC 20001

Cox Communications, Inc.

Provides telecommunications services.
ww2.cox.com
Annual Revenues: $9.1 billion
Employees: 22,000
SIC: 4841
Industry/ies: Communications; Telecommunications/Internet/Cable

Main Headquarters

Mailing:	1400 Lake Hearn Dr.	Tel:	(404) 843-5000
	Atlanta, GA 30319	Fax:	(623) 328-3570
		TF:	(888) 566-7751

Corporate Foundations and Giving Programs

The Cox Kids Foundation
1400 Lake Hearn Dr.   Tel: (404) 843-5000
Atlanta, GA 30319

Public Affairs and Related Activities Personnel

At Headquarters

BOWSER, Mark F.   Tel: (404) 843-5000
Executive Vice President and Chief Financial Officer   Fax: (623) 328-3570
mark.bowser@cox.com

COKER , Susan   Tel: (404) 843-5000
Vice President, Treasurer   Fax: (623) 328-3570
susan.coker@cox.com

DOUGLAS, Mae A.   Tel: (404) 843-5000
Executive Vice President and Chief People Officer   Fax: (623) 328-3570
mae.douglas@cox.com

GARRETT , Jennifer   Tel: (404) 843-5000
Vice President, Sales   Fax: (623) 328-3570

HIGHTOWER, Jennifer W.   Tel: (404) 843-5000
Senior Vice President, Law and Policy Services   Fax: (623) 328-3570
jennifer.hightower@cox.com

HOLLIDAY, Mallard   Tel: (404) 843-5000
Vice President, Corporate Communications and Public Affairs   Fax: (623) 328-3570
Mallard.holliday@cox.com

PLOTT, Todd   Tel: (404) 843-5000
PAC Treasurer   Fax: (623) 328-3570

SAKSENA, Asheesh   Tel: (404) 843-5000
Executive Vice President and Chief Strategy Officer   Fax: (623) 328-3570

TAYLOR, Rhonda   Tel: (404) 843-5000
Executive Vice President and Chief People Officer   Fax: (623) 328-3570

Cox Enterprises, Inc.

A communications company involved in newspaper publishing, radio and TV broadcasting, cable TV and programming. Parent company of Cox Communications.
www.coxenterprises.com
Ticker: NASDAQ TRACE: COX.GB
SIC: 2711
NAICS: 511110
Industry/ies: Communications; Media/Mass Communication; Telecommunications/Internet/Cable
Legislative Issues: AUT; COM; CPI; CPT; FIN; TAX; TEC

Chairman of the Board   Tel: (678) 645-0000
KENNEDY, James C.   Fax: (678) 645-1079

President and Chief Executive Officer   Tel: (678) 645-0000
DYER, John M.   Fax: (678) 645-5002

Main Headquarters

Mailing: 2002 Summit Blvd., Suite 200   Tel: (678) 645-0000
Atlanta, GA 30319   Fax: (678) 645-5002

Washington Office

Mailing:	975 F St. NW	Tel:	(202) 637-1330
	Suite 300	Fax:	(678) 645-1079
	Washington, DC 20004		

Political Action Committees

COX Enterprises PAC (COXPAC) Inc
FEC ID: C00477653
Contact: Joab M. Lesesne III
975 F Str. NW
Suite 300
Washington, DC 20004

Contributions to Candidates: $826,950 (2015-2016)
Democrats: $348,500; Republicans: $478,450

Principal Recipients

SENATE
BLUNT, ROY (REP-MO)
JOHNSON, RONALD HAROLD (REP-)
LANKFORD, JAMES PAUL (REP-OK)
MCCAIN, JOHN S (REP-VA)
SCHATZ, BRIAN (DEM-HI)
SCHUMER, CHARLES E (DEM-NY)

HOUSE
BROOKS, SUSAN MRS. (REP-IN)
CICILLINE, DAVID N (DEM-RI)
CLYBURN, JAMES E. (DEM-SC)
CONYERS, JOHN JR. (DEM-MI)
CRENSHAW, ANDER (REP-FL)
DESANTIS, RONALD D (REP-FL)
GRAVES, JOHN THOMAS MR. JR. (REP-GA)
GREEN, RAYMOND E. 'GENE' (DEM-TX)
GRIFFITH, H MORGAN (REP-VA)
LANKFORD, JAMES PAUL MR. (REP-OK)
MULLIN, MARKWAYNE MR. (REP-OK)
PETERS, SCOTT (DEM-CA)
POMPEO, MICHAEL RICHARD (REP-KS)
PRICE, THOMAS EDMUNDS (REP-GA)
RICHMOND, CEDRIC L. (DEM-LA)
RUSH, BOBBY LEE (DEM-IL)
SCALISE, STEVE MR. (REP-LA)
SINEMA, KYRSTEN (DEM-AZ)
THOMPSON, BENNIE G. (DEM-MS)
WALDEN, GREGORY P MR. (REP-OR)
WALTERS, MIMI (REP-CA)

Corporate Foundations and Giving Programs

James M. Cox Foundation
6205 Peachtree Dunwoody Rd.   Tel: (678) 645-0000
Atlanta, GA 30328   Fax: (678) 645-1079

Public Affairs and Related Activities Personnel

At Headquarters

FRIEDMAN, Maria   Tel: (678) 645-0000
Senior Vice President, Tax and Treasury Services   Fax: (678) 645-5002

JIMENEZ, Roberto I.   Tel: (678) 645-0000
Vice President, Corporate Communications and Public Affairs   Fax: (678) 645-1079

LEAMER, Marybeth N.   Tel: (678) 645-0000
Executive Vice President, Human Resources and   Fax: (678) 645-1079
Administration
marybeth.leamer@cox.com

LEWIS, J. Lacey   Tel: (678) 645-0000
Senior Vice President, Finance   Fax: (678) 645-1079

MUHL, Shauna Sullivan   Tel: (678) 645-0000
Vice President, General Counsel and Corporate Secretary   Fax: (678) 645-1079

OHLSON, Barry   Tel: (678) 645-0000
Vice President, Regulatory Affairs   Fax: (678) 645-1079

OLMSTEAD, Elizabeth   Tel: (678) 645-0000
Manager, Public Relations   Fax: (678) 645-1079
elizabeth.olmstead@coxinc.com

At Washington Office

LESESNE, III, Joab M.   Tel: (202) 637-1330
Vice President, Public Policy and Government Affairs and   Fax: (678) 645-1079
PAC Contact
Joab.lesesne@cox.com
Registered Federal Lobbyist

OBLINGER, Elizabeth   Tel: (202) 637-1330
Registered Federal Lobbyist   Fax: (678) 645-1079

RYCHAK, Laura   Tel: (202) 637-1330
Legislative Counsel   Fax: (678) 645-1079

SCOLESE, Paul G.   Tel: (202) 637-1330
Assistant Vice President, Government Relations   Fax: (678) 645-1079
Registered Federal Lobbyist

WILSON, Alexandra M.   Tel: (202) 637-1330
Senior Vice President, Public Policy and Regulatory Affairs   Fax: (678) 645-1079

Registered Federal Lobbyist

CPU Technology

Develops and supplies Compatible System-on-a-Chip based solutions for complex computing environments.
www.cputech.com
Annual Revenues: $7.60 million
Employees: 100
Industry/ies: Computer/Technology

| **Chairman of the Board** | Tel: | (925) 224-9920 |
| WATTS, Claudius E. | Fax: | (925) 227-0539 |

| **Chief Executive Officer** | Tel: | (925) 224-9920 |
| JOHNSON, Clay | Fax: | (925) 227-0539 |

Main Headquarters
| Mailing: | 5731 W. Las Positas Blvd. | Tel: | (925) 224-9920 |
| | Pleasanton, CA 94588 | Fax: | (925) 227-0539 |

Public Affairs and Related Activities Personnel

At Headquarters

BALL, Jim	Tel:	(925) 224-9920
Senior Vice President, Sales and Media Contact	Fax:	(925) 227-0539
j.ball@cputech.com		

| DOERPINGHAUS, Chris | Tel: | (925) 224-9920 |
| *Vice President, Finance and Administration* | Fax: | (925) 227-0539 |

| GILLIS, Stephen | Tel: | (925) 224-9920 |
| *Vice President, Corporate Services* | Fax: | (925) 227-0539 |

Cracker Barrel Old Country Store Inc.

See listing on page 172 under CBRL Group, Inc.

Crane Aerospace and Electronics

Crane Aerospace & Electronics, a division of Crane Co., includes several aerospace and several electronics businesses. It supplies critical systems and components from engines and landing gear to satellites, missiles and electronic countermeasure devices to the aerospace and defense markets.
www.craneae.com
Employees: 2,800
Ticker: NYSE: CR
Industry/ies: Aerospace/Aviation; Engineering/Mathematics; Transportation

| **Chief Executive Officer** | Tel: | (425) 743-1313 |
| FAST, Eric C. | Fax: | (425) 743-8234 |

Main Headquarters
Mailing:	P.O. Box 97027	Tel:	(425) 743-1313
	16700 13th Ave., West	Fax:	(425) 743-8234
	Lynwood, WA 98046-9727	TF:	(800) 464-0261

Corporate Foundations and Giving Programs
Crane Aerospace and Electronics Contributions Program
P.O. Box 97027
16700 13th Ave., West
Lynwood, WA 98046-9727

Public Affairs and Related Activities Personnel

At Headquarters

| CURRAN, Brendan | Tel: | (425) 743-1313 |
| *President* | Fax: | (425) 743-8234 |

SCHWARTZ, Marilyn	Tel:	(425) 743-8231
Director, Communications	Fax:	(425) 743-8234
marilyn.schwartz@craneaerospace.com		

At Other Offices

MOLINE, MBA, Sarah	Tel:	(425) 895-4037
Manager, Marketing Communications	Fax:	(425) 882-1990
P.O. Box 97005, 10301 Willows Rd.		
Redmond, WA 98073-9705		
Sarah.Moline@Crane-EG.com		

Crane Company

Manufactures and sells vending machines, airplane braking devices, pumps, valves, and other industrial goods.
www.craneco.com
Annual Revenues: $2.72 billion
Employees: 11,200
Ticker: NYSE: CR
SIC: 3490
Industry/ies: Machinery/Equipment

| **Chairman of the Board** | Tel: | (203) 363-7300 |
| EVANS, Robert S. | Fax: | (203) 363-7295 |

| **President and Chief Executive Officer** | Tel: | (203) 363-7300 |
| MITCHELL, Max H. | Fax: | (203) 363-7295 |

Main Headquarters
| Mailing: | 100 First Stamford Pl. | Tel: | (203) 363-7300 |
| | Stamford, CT 06902 | Fax: | (203) 363-7295 |

Corporate Foundations and Giving Programs
Crane Foundation
| 100 First Stamford Pl. | Tel: | (203) 363-7300 |
| Stamford, CT 06902 | Fax: | (203) 363-7295 |

The Crane Fund
| 140 Sylvan Ave. | Tel: | (201) 585-0888 |
| Englewood Cliffs, NJ 07632 | | |

Crane Fund for Widows and Children
| 100 First Stamford Pl. | Tel: | (203) 363-7300 |
| Stamford, CT 06902 | Fax: | (203) 363-7295 |

Public Affairs and Related Activities Personnel

At Headquarters

| BARON, Curtis A. | Tel: | (203) 363-7300 |
| *Vice President, Controller* | Fax: | (203) 363-7295 |

| DUPONT, Augustus I. | Tel: | (203) 363-7300 |
| *Vice President, General Counsel and Secretary* | Fax: | (203) 363-7295 |

FELDMAN, Jason D.	Tel:	(203) 363-7329
Director, Investor Relations	Fax:	(203) 363-7295
investors@craneco.com		

| MAUE, Richard A. | Tel: | (203) 363-7300 |
| *Vice President, Finance and Chief Financial Officer* | Fax: | (203) 363-7295 |

| ROWE, Tazewell S. | Tel: | (203) 363-7300 |
| *Vice President, Treasurer* | Fax: | (203) 363-7295 |

| SALOVAARA, Kris R. | Tel: | (203) 363-7300 |
| *Vice President, Business Development and Strategy* | Fax: | (203) 363-7295 |

Crane Group Company

Private holding and management company based in Columbus, Ohio.
www.cranegroup.com
Industry/ies: Construction/Construction Materials
Legislative Issues: COM; DEF; HCR; HOM; TAX

| **Chairman of the Board Emeritus** | Tel: | (614) 754-3000 |
| CRANE, Jameson | | |

| **President and Chief Executive Officer** | Tel: | (614) 754-3000 |
| CRANE, Tanny | | |

Main Headquarters
| Mailing: | 330 W. Spring St. | Tel: | (614) 754-3000 |
| | Columbus, OH 43215 | | |

Washington Office
| Mailing: | 8005 Lewinsville Rd. | Tel: | (202) 302-1909 |
| | McLean, VA 22102 | | |

Corporate Foundations and Giving Programs
Crane Group Contributions Program
330 W. Spring St.
Columbus, OH 43215

Public Affairs and Related Activities Personnel

At Headquarters

| CRANE, Mike | Tel: | (614) 754-3000 |
| *President* | | |

| MILLER, J.D., Timothy T. | Tel: | (614) 754-3000 |
| *Vice President and General Counsel* | | |

| UTRUP, Chad M. | Tel: | (614) 754-3000 |
| *Chief Financial Officer* | | |

At Washington Office

CRANE, Daniel M.	Tel:	(202) 302-1909
President		
Registered Federal Lobbyist		

GIKOVICH, Lucie	Tel:	(202) 302-1909
Partner		
Registered Federal Lobbyist		

Cray Inc.

A supercomputer company. Formed in 2000 from a merger between Tera Computer Company and Cray Research.
www.cray.com
Annual Revenues: $586.14 million
Employees: 1,138
Ticker: NASDAQ: CRAY
SIC: 3571
Industry/ies: Computer/Technology
Legislative Issues: BUD; GOV; SCI

| **Chairman of the Board** | Tel: | (206) 701-2000 |
| KIELY, Stephen C. | Fax: | (206) 701-2500 |

President and Chief Executive Officer	Tel:	(206) 701-2000
UNGARO, Peter J.	Fax:	(206) 701-2500
ungaro@cray.com		

Main Headquarters
| Mailing: | 901 Fifth Ave. | Tel: | (206) 701-2000 |

Suite 1000
Seattle, WA 98164

Fax: (206) 701-2500

Washington Office
Mailing: 241 18th St.
Suite 610
Arlington, VA 22202

Tel: (703) 248-7100
Fax: (703) 248-7105

Political Action Committees
Cray Inc. Employee PAC AKA (CRAY PAC)
FEC ID: C00458547
Contact: Brian C. Henry
241 18th St.
Suite 610
Arlington, VA 22202

Contributions to Candidates: $65,800 (2015-2016)
Democrats: $31,300; Republicans: $34,500

Corporate Foundations and Giving Programs
Cray Inc. Contributions Program
901 Fifth Ave.
Suite 1000
Seattle, WA 98164

Tel: (206) 701-2000
Fax: (206) 701-2500

Public Affairs and Related Activities Personnel

At Headquarters

BOLDING, Barry C.
Vice President, Storage, Data Management and Corporate Marketing

Tel: (206) 701-2000
Fax: (206) 701-2500

DAVIS, Nick
Manager, Public Relations
pr@cray.com

Tel: (206) 701-2123
Fax: (206) 701-2500

HIEMSTRA, Paul
Contact, Investor Relations
ir@cray.com

Tel: (206) 701-2044
Fax: (206) 701-2500

MORREALE, Charles A.
Vice President, Field Operations

Tel: (206) 701-2000
Fax: (206) 701-2500

PIRAINO, Michael C.
Vice President, Administration, General Counsel and Corporate Secretary

Tel: (206) 701-2000
Fax: (206) 701-2500

At Washington Office

HENRY, Brian C.
Executive Vice President and Chief Financial Officer and PAC Treasurer
brianh@cray.com

Tel: (703) 248-7100
Fax: (703) 248-7105

At Other Offices

GUITON, Mark
Director, Government Programs
2001 Jefferson Davis Hwy., Suite 200
Arlington, VA 22202
mguiton@cray.com
Registered Federal Lobbyist

Tel: (703) 248-7102
Fax: (703) 248-7105

HOPPER, Jill Yacone
Vice President, Government Programs
2001 Jefferson Davis Hwy., Suite 200
Arlington, VA 22202
jhopper@cray.com
Registered Federal Lobbyist

Tel: (703) 248-7102
Fax: (703) 248-7105

Crayola LLC

Formerly Binney and Smith Inc. A manufacturer of children's art products and professional artist materials. A wholly-owned subsidiary of Hallmark Cards, Inc. Major brand names include Silly Putty and Model Magic.
www.crayola.com
Employees: 1,100
Industry/ies: Children And Youth

President and Chief Executive Officer
PERRY, Mike

Tel: (610) 253-6271
Fax: (610) 250-5768

Main Headquarters
Mailing: 1100 Church Ln.
P.O. Box 431
Easton, PA 18044-0431

Tel: (610) 253-6271
Fax: (610) 250-5768
TF: (800) 272-9652

Corporate Foundations and Giving Programs

Crayola LLC Contributions Program
Contact: Margaret Heckman
P.O. Box 431
Easton, PA 18044-0431

Tel: (610) 253-6271
Fax: (610) 250-5768

Public Affairs and Related Activities Personnel

At Headquarters

HECKMAN, Margaret
Foundation Contact

Tel: (610) 253-6271
Fax: (610) 250-5768

HOLLAND, Smith

Tel: (610) 253-6271
Fax: (610) 250-5768

Chief Financial Officer and Executive Vice President, International

LANDO, Julie
Director, Marketing Communications

Tel: (610) 253-6272
Fax: (610) 250-5768

LINDEN, Chuck
Executive Vice President, Global Business Development and Digital Strategy

Tel: (610) 253-6271
Fax: (610) 250-5768

POWERS, Michelle
Executive Vice President, Human Resources and Administration
mpowers@crayola.com

Tel: (610) 253-6271
Fax: (610) 250-5768

Credit Suisse First Boston Corporation
See listing on page 229 under Credit Suisse Securities LLC

Credit Suisse Securities LLC
Provides investment banking, securities brokerage and other financial services.
www.credit-suisse.com/us
Employees: 10,900
SIC: 6200
Industry/ies: Banking/Finance/Investments
Legislative Issues: BAN; FIN; TAX

Chairman, CSFB Foundation
COY, Ginny

Tel: (212) 325-2000
Fax: (212) 325-6665

Chief Executive Officer
THIAM, Tidjane

Tel: (212) 325-2000
Fax: (212) 325-6665

Main Headquarters
Mailing: Eleven Madison Ave.
New York, DC 20004

Tel: (212) 325-2000
Fax: (212) 325-6665

Political Action Committees
Credit Suisse Securities (USA) LLC Political Action Committee
FEC ID: C00111559
Contact: Cecilia Guarin
1201 F St. NW
Suite 450
Washington, DC 20004

Tel: (202) 626-3300
Fax: (202) 626-3310

Contributions to Candidates: $97,950 (2015-2016)
Democrats: $43,200; Republicans: $54,750

Corporate Foundations and Giving Programs

Credit Suisse Americas Foundation (formerly Credit Suisse First Boston Foundation Trust)
Contact: Eric Eckholdt
One Madison Ave.
Third Floor
New York, NY 10010-3663

Tel: (212) 325-2389
Fax: (212) 538-8347

Public Affairs and Related Activities Personnel

At Headquarters

BENSON, Drew
Vice President, Corporate Communications

Tel: (212) 325-0932
Fax: (212) 325-6665

CERUTTI, Romeo
General Counsel

Tel: (212) 325-2000
Fax: (212) 325-6665

MATHERS, David
Chief Financial Officer

Tel: (212) 325-2000
Fax: (212) 325-6665

RADTKE, Eva
Director, Investor Relations

Tel: (212) 538-1177
Fax: (212) 325-6665

THOMAS-GRAHAM, Pamela
Managing Director, Chief Marketing and Talent Officer and Member of Executive Board

Tel: (212) 325-2000
Fax: (212) 325-6665

At Other Offices

ECKHOLDT, Eric
Director, Americas Head of Corporate Citizenship and Executive Director, CS Americas Foundation (Formerly Credit Suisse First Boston Foundation Trust)
One Madison Ave., Third Floor
New York, NY 10010-3663
americas.corporatecitizenship@credit-suisse.com

Tel: (212) 325-2389
Fax: (212) 538-8347

GAGE, Margaret M.
Head, Washington Research and Political Strategies
1201 F St. NW, Suite 450
Washington, DC 20004
Registered Federal Lobbyist

Tel: (202) 626-3301
Fax: (202) 626-3310

GUARIN, Cecilia
1201 F St. NW, Suite 450
Washington, DC 20004

Tel: (202) 626-3300
Fax: (202) 626-3310

MANDEL, Jessica A.
Director, Public Polic
1201 F St. NW, Suite 450
Washington, DC 20004
Registered Federal Lobbyist

Tel: (202) 626-3301
Fax: (202) 626-3310

SEIDEL, Joseph L.

Tel: (202) 626-3301

Managing Director Fax: (202) 626-3310
1201 F St. NW, Suite 450
Washington, DC 20004
Registered Federal Lobbyist

TEEL, Ashlyn Tel: (202) 626-3300
1201 F St. NW, Suite 450 Fax: (202) 626-3310
Washington, DC 20004
Registered Federal Lobbyist

THOMPSON, Terrence Tel: (202) 626-3300
Federal Lobbyist Fax: (202) 626-3310
1201 F St. NW, Suite 450
Washington, DC 20004
Registered Federal Lobbyist

WHALEN, Mary L. Tel: (202) 626-3301
Managing Director and Senior Advisor Fax: (202) 626-3310
1201 F St. NW, Suite 450
Washington, DC 20004

Cree, Inc.

Cree, Inc. develops and manufactures lighting-class light emitting diode (LED) products, lighting products, and semiconductor products for power and radio-frequency (RF) applications. Cree leads the LED lighting revolution and is making energy-wasting traditional lighting technologies obsolete through the use of energy-efficient, environmentally friendly LED lighting. It is also a major manufacturer of semiconductors used in power conversion and wireless communications.
www.cree.com
Annual Revenues: $1.69 billion
Employees: 7,130
Ticker: NASDAQ: CREE
SIC: 3674
Industry/ies: Defense/Homeland Security; Government-Related
Legislative Issues: BUD; DEF; ENG; GOV

President, Chief Executive Officer and Chairman of the Board Tel: (919) 407-5300
SWOBODA, Charles M. Fax: (919) 313-5558

Main Headquarters
Mailing: 4600 Silicon Dr. Tel: (919) 407-5300
Durham, NC 27703 Fax: (919) 313-5558
TF: (800) 533-2583

Political Action Committees
Cree, Inc. PAC (Cree PAC)
FEC ID: C00499665
Contact: Bradley David Kohn
4600 Silicon Dr.
Durham, 27703

Contributions to Candidates: $3,000 (2015-2016)
Republicans: $3,000

Public Affairs and Related Activities Personnel

At Headquarters

GARRABRANT, Raiford Tel: (919) 407-5300
Director, Investor Relations Fax: (919) 313-5558

KOHN, Bradley David Tel: (919) 407-5300
General Counsel and PAC Contact Fax: (919) 313-5558

MERRITT, Greg Tel: (919) 407-5300
Vice President, Marketing Fax: (919) 313-5558

MITCHELL, Kimberley Tel: (919) 287-7702
Federal Lobbyist Fax: (919) 313-5558

Cricket Communications, Inc.

A wireless telephone provider.
www.mycricket.com
Annual Revenues: $27.4 Million
Employees: 800
SIC: 4813
Industry/ies: Communications; Telecommunications/Internet/Cable

President and Chief Executive Officer Tel: (858) 882-6000
HUTCHESON, Stewart Douglas "Doug" Fax: (858) 882-6010

Main Headquarters
Mailing: 5887 Copley Dr. Tel: (858) 882-6000
San Diego, CA 92111 Fax: (858) 882-6010

Washington Office
Mailing: 3213 Duke St.
Suite 246
Alexandria, VA 22314

Political Action Committees
Cricket Communications Inc. PAC (CRICKETPAC)
FEC ID: C00435222
Contact: P. Jonathan Klug
5887 Copley Dr.
Suite 246
San Diego, CA 92111

Corporate Foundations and Giving Programs

Cricket Communications, inc. Contributions program
5887 Copley Dr. Tel: (858) 882-6000
San Diego, CA 92111 Fax: (858) 882-6010

Public Affairs and Related Activities Personnel

At Headquarters

BERGER, Walter Tel: (858) 882-6000
Executive Vice President and Chief Financial Officer Fax: (858) 882-6010

At Other Offices

KLUG, P. Jonathan
PAC Treasurer
208 S. Akard St., Suite 2701
Dallas, TX 75202

MERBETH, Russell C. Tel: (858) 882-6000
PAC Treasurer Fax: (858) 882-6010
565 Pennsylvania Ave. NW, Suite 1204
Washington, DC 20001

SHIPLEY, Patrick Tel: (858) 882-6000
Director, Government Affairs and PAC Treasurer Fax: (858) 882-6010
565 Pennsylvania Ave. NW, Suite 1204
Washington, DC 20001

Critical Homecare Solutions

Provides Medicare, Homecare Certified services and products.
www.criticalhs.com
Annual Revenues: $43.50 million
Employees: 2,000
SIC: 8082
Industry/ies: Medicine/Health Care/Mental Health

President and Chief Executive Officer Tel: (610) 825-2061
CUCUEL, Robert Fax: (610) 834-3231

Main Headquarters
Mailing: Two Tower Bridge, One Fayette St. Tel: (610) 825-2061
Suite 150 Fax: (610) 834-3231
Conshohocken, PA 19428 TF: (866) 666-7390

Public Affairs and Related Activities Personnel

At Headquarters

EVANS, Esq., David J. Tel: (610) 825-2061
Senior Vice President, Strategic Operations Fax: (610) 834-3231

GRAVES, Mary Jane Tel: (610) 825-2061
Chief Financial Officer Fax: (610) 834-3231

LEDERER, Colleen M. Tel: (610) 825-2061
Senior Vice President, Professional Services Fax: (610) 834-3231

RYAN, CPA, MBA, Joey Tel: (610) 825-2061
Senior Vice President, Reimbursement and Compliance Fax: (610) 834-3231
Services

SNEFF, Mark P. Tel: (610) 825-2061
Senior Vice President, Human Resources Fax: (610) 834-3231

The Crosby Group LLC

A government relations consulting firm.
www.thecrosbygroupllc.com
Industry/ies: Government-Related

President Tel: (202) 289-9881
CROSBY, Jr., William D. Fax: (202) 479-4084
bcrosby@livingstongroupdc.com

Main Headquarters
Mailing: 2801 Dawson Rd. Tel: (918) 834-4611
Tulsa, OK 74110

Washington Office
Mailing: 499 S. Capitol St. SW Tel: (202) 289-9881
Suite 600 Fax: (202) 479-4084
Washington, DC 20003

Cross Match Technologies, Inc.

Biometric systems provider.
www.crossmatch.com
Annual Revenues: $23.20 million
Employees: 300
SIC: 7373
Industry/ies: Defense/Homeland Security; Electricity & Electronics; Electronics; Energy/Electricity; Government-Related; Science; Scientific Research

Chief Executive Officer Tel: (561) 622-1650
AGOSTINELLI, Richard Fax: (561) 622-9938

Main Headquarters
Mailing: 3950 RCA Blvd. Tel: (561) 622-1650
Suite 5001 Fax: (561) 622-9938
Palm Beach Gardens, FL 33410 TF: (866) 276-7761

Washington Office
Mailing: 1601 N. Kent St. Tel: (703) 841-6280

Suite 200
Arlington, VA 22209

Public Affairs and Related Activities Personnel

At Headquarters

BLISS, Elaine
Senior Vice President, Marketing and Product Management
Tel: (561) 622-1650
Fax: (561) 622-9938

CAHILL, Jerry
Chief Financial Officer
Tel: (561) 622-1650
Fax: (561) 622-9938

HINMON, John B.
Vice President, Marketing
Tel: (561) 622-1650
Fax: (561) 622-9938

HUTTON, Kathryn
Vice President and General Counsel
kathryn.hutton@crossmatch.com
Tel: (561) 622-1650
Fax: (561) 622-9938

Crowe Horwath

A private equity firm. Formerly Crowe Chizek & Company.
www.crowehorwath.com
Annual Revenues: $498.28 million
Employees: 2,400
Industry/ies: Banking/Finance/Investments

Chief Executive Officer
POWERS, James L
Tel: (630) 574-7878
Fax: (630) 574-1608

Main Headquarters
Mailing: One Mid America Plaza, Suite 700
P. O. Box 3697
Oak Brook, IL 60522-3697
Tel: (630) 574-7878
Fax: (630) 574-1608

Washington Office
Mailing: 1325 G St. NW
Suite 500
Washington, DC 20005-3136
Tel: (202) 624-5555
Fax: (202) 624-8858

Corporate Foundations and Giving Programs

Crowe Foundation
Contact: Suzanne Robinson
330 E. Jefferson Blvd.
South Bend, IN 46624
Tel: (574) 232-3992
Fax: (574) 236-8692

Public Affairs and Related Activities Personnel

At Headquarters

SANTUCCI, Joseph P.
Chief Operating Officer
Tel: (630) 574-7878
Fax: (630) 574-1608

KEELEY, Stephen
General Counsel
Tel: (630) 574-7878
Fax: (630) 574-1608

LATHROP, Ann
Chief Marketing Officer
Tel: (630) 574-7878
Fax: (630) 574-1608

WELU, Todd
Chief Financial Officer
Tel: (630) 574-7878
Fax: (630) 574-1608

WOOD, Julie K
Chief People Officer
Tel: (630) 574-7878
Fax: (630) 574-1608

At Other Offices

LIPPMAN, Jannet
Assistant Director, Media Relations
330 E. Jefferson Blvd.
South Bend, IN 46624-0007
jan.lippman@crowehorwath.com
Tel: (312) 899-8414
Fax: (574) 236-8692

ROBINSON, Suzanne
Director, Communications
330 E. Jefferson Blvd.
South Bend, IN 46624-0007
Tel: (317) 706-2687
Fax: (574) 236-8692

SHAWALUK, Amanda
Media Relations Manager
330 E. Jefferson Blvd.
South Bend, IN 46624-0007
amanda.shawaluk@crowehorwath.com
Tel: (312) 899-8416
Fax: (574) 236-8692

Crowell Strategies, LLC

Consulting Firm.
www.crowellstrategies.com

Main Headquarters
Mailing: 4708 Essex Ave.
Chevy Chase, MD 20815
Tel: (202) 271-1477

Crowley Maritime Corporation

An ocean transportation operating company. It is a U.S.-owned and operated marine solutions, transportation and logistics company providing services in domestic and international markets.
www.crowley.com
Annual Revenues: $2.00 billion
Employees: 5,300
SIC: 4400
Industry/ies: Defense/Homeland Security; Government-Related

Legislative Issues: MAR; TRD

Chairman of the Board and Chief Executive Officer
CROWLEY, Jr., Thomas B.
Tel: (904) 727-2200
Fax: (510) 251-7788

Main Headquarters
Mailing: 9487 Regency Sq. Blvd.
Jacksonville Beach, FL 32225
Tel: (904) 727-2200
Fax: (904) 727-2501
TF: (800) 276-9539

Washington Office
Mailing: 575 Seventh St. NW
Suite E11007
Washington, DC 20004
Tel: (202) 344-4008

Political Action Committees
Crowley Maritime Corporation Federal PAC
FEC ID: C00147231
Contact: Daniel L. Warner
9487 Regency Square Blvd.
Suite 600
Jacksonville Beach, FL 32225
Tel: (202) 344-4000

  Contributions to Candidates: $84,406 (2015-2016)
  Democrats: $35,506; Republicans: $43,500; Other: $5,400

Corporate Foundations and Giving Programs
Crowley Maritime Corporation Contributions Program
9487 Regency Sq. Blvd.
Jacksonville Beach, FL 32225
Tel: (904) 727-2200
Fax: (904) 727-2200

Public Affairs and Related Activities Personnel

At Headquarters

FOX, Carl
Senior Vice President, Corporate Services
Tel: (904) 727-2200
Fax: (904) 727-2501

MILLER, Mark
Director, Corporate and Marketing Communications
mark.miller@crowley.com
Tel: (904) 727-4295
Fax: (904) 727-2501

ROBERTS, Michael
Senior Vice President, General Counsel and Corporate Secretary
Tel: (904) 727-2200
Fax: (904) 727-2501

SMITH, Bryan
Vice President, Tax and Audit
Tel: (904) 727-2200
Fax: (904) 727-2501

SMITH, Amelia
Manager, Corporate Communications
amelia.smith@crowley.com
Tel: (904) 727-2513
Fax: (904) 727-2501

WARNER, Daniel L.
Senior Vice President, Treasurer and Contact, PAC
Tel: (904) 727-2200
Fax: (904) 727-2501

At Washington Office

HEGG, Richard Y.
Senior Legislative Advisor
ryhegg@Venable.com
Tel: (202) 344-4000

JACOBS, Ronald M.
Partner
LDA@venable.com
Tel: (202) 344-8215

Crown Cork and Seal Co.

See listing on page 232 under Crown Holdings, Inc.

Crown Equipment Corporation

A transportation equipment company.
www.crown.com
Employees: 8,000
SIC: 3537
NAICS: 333924
Industry/ies: Machinery/Equipment; Transportation
Legislative Issues: LAW

Chairman of the Board and Chief Executive Officer
DICKE, II, James F.
Tel: (419) 629-2311
Fax: (419) 629-3796

Main Headquarters
Mailing: 44 S. Washington St.
New Bremen, OH 45869
Tel: (419) 629-2311
Fax: (419) 629-2900
TF: (800) 298-4708

Corporate Foundations and Giving Programs
Crown Equipment Corporation Contributions Program
44 S. Washington St.
New Bremen, OH 45869
Tel: (419) 629-2311
Fax: (419) 629-2900

Public Affairs and Related Activities Personnel

At Headquarters

DICKE III, James F.
President
Tel: (419) 629-2311
Fax: (419) 629-2900

HELMSTETTER, Dave
Administrator, Publicity Services
Tel: (419) 629-2220
Fax: (419) 629-2900

KELLER, Thomas J.
Accounts
Tel: (419) 629-2311
Fax: (419) 629-2900

MANUEL, Mark A.	Tel:	(419) 629-2311
Development	Fax:	(419) 629-2900
MAXA, John G.	Tel:	(419) 629-2311
Vice President and General Counsel	Fax:	(419) 629-2900
MORAN, David C.	Tel:	(419) 629-2311
Vice President, Branch Operations	Fax:	(419) 629-2900
NIEKAMP, Randall W.	Tel:	(419) 629-2311
Vice President, Human Resources	Fax:	(419) 629-3796
randy.niekamp@crown.com		
RAHE, Christopher W.	Tel:	(419) 629-2311
Vice President, Sales	Fax:	(419) 629-3796
SPILLE, Kent W.	Tel:	(419) 629-2311
Vice President and Chief Financial Officer	Fax:	(419) 629-2900

Crown Holdings, Inc.

Formerly known as Crown Cork and Seal Co. A manufacturer of packaging products for consumer marketing companies worldwide.
www.crowncork.com
Annual Revenues: $8.66 billion
Employees: 24,000
Ticker: NYSE: CCK
SIC: 3411
Industry/ies: Advertising And Marketing; Manufacturers

President and Chief Executive Officer	Tel:	(215) 698-5100
DONAHUE, Timothy J.	Fax:	(215) 676-7245
ir@crowncork.com		

Main Headquarters		
Mailing: One Crown Way	Tel:	(215) 698-5100
Philadelphia, PA 19154-4599	Fax:	(215) 676-7245

Political Action Committees
Crown Cork and Seal Company Inc. PAC
FEC ID: C00254268
Contact: Thomas Fischer
One Crown Way
Philadelphia, PA 19154

> **Contributions to Candidates:** $5,000 (2015-2016)
> Democrats: $1,000; Republicans: $4,000

Public Affairs and Related Activities Personnel

At Headquarters

ABRAMOWICZ, Daniel A.	Tel:	(215) 698-5100
Executive Vice President, Corporate Technology and Regulatory Affairs	Fax:	(215) 676-7245
FISCHER, Thomas	Tel:	(215) 698-5100
Vice President, Investor Relations, Corporate Affairs and PAC Treasurer	Fax:	(215) 676-7245
GALLAGHER, William T.	Tel:	(215) 698-5100
Senior Vice President, Secretary and General Counsel	Fax:	(215) 676-7245
william.gallagher@crowncork.com		
KELLY, Thomas A.	Tel:	(215) 698-5341
Senior Vice President and Chief Financial Officer	Fax:	(215) 676-7245
ir@crowncork.com		
KREIDER, Torsten J.	Tel:	(215) 698-5100
Vice President, Planning and Development	Fax:	(215) 676-7245

Crump Group, Inc.

An insurance services provider.
www.crump.com
Employees: 3,000
Industry/ies: Insurance Industry

Senior Vice President, Marketing	Tel:	(973) 461-2100
LINDENBERG, Sherri K.		

Main Headquarters		
Mailing: 105 Eisenhower Pkwy.	Tel:	(973) 461-2100
Roseland, NJ 07068	TF:	(888) 305-2191

Cryptek Inc.

Formerly known as Cryptek Secure Communications, LLC. Develops, manufactures and integrates security solutions for both the public and private sectors.
www.apitech.com/Cryptek
Annual Revenues: $9.90 million
Employees: 100
Industry/ies: Communications; Law Enforcement/Security; Telecommunications/Internet/Cable

Chairman of the Board	Tel:	(571) 434-2000
ROBERTS, David N.	Fax:	(571) 434-2001

Chairman of the Board and Chief Executive Officer	Tel:	(571) 434-2000
KAHN, Brian R.	Fax:	(571) 434-2001

Main Headquarters		
Mailing: 1501 Moran Rd.	Tel:	(571) 434-2000

Sterling, VA 20166	Fax:	(571) 434-2001
	TF:	(800) 753-0706

Political Action Committees
Cryptek Political Action Committee
FEC ID: C00386565

1501 Moran Rd.	Tel:	(571) 434-2000
Sterling, VA 20166	Fax:	(571) 434-2001

Public Affairs and Related Activities Personnel

At Headquarters

REHKEMPER, Phil	Tel:	(571) 434-2000
Executive Vice President & Chief Financial Officer	Fax:	(571) 434-2001

Cryptek Secure Communications, LLC

See listing on page 232 under Cryptek Inc.

CSA

See listing on page 160 under Canadian Snowbird Association

CSA Strategies LLC

A law firm.
Industry/ies: Public Affairs And Public Relations
Legislative Issues: CSP; FOO; GAM; HCR; TAX

President	Tel:	(412) 400-0368
URREA, Alejandro		
acurrea@comcast.net		

Main Headquarters		
Mailing: 110 Hidden Valley Rd.	Tel:	(412) 400-0368
Suite B		
Pittsburgh, PA 15317		

CSC

CSC is a global leader of next-generation information technology (IT) services and solutions. Our mission is to enable superior returns on clients' technology investments through best-in-class industry solutions, domain expertise and global scale. Acquired DynCorp in March of 2003.
www.csc.com
Annual Revenues: $12.17 billion
Employees: 70,000
Ticker: NYSE: CSC
SIC: 7373
Industry/ies: Computer/Technology
Legislative Issues: DEF; HOM

President and Chief Executive Officer	Tel:	(703) 876-1000
LAWRIE, Mike	Fax:	(703) 641-2969

Main Headquarters		
Mailing: 3170 Fairview Park Dr.	Tel:	(703) 876-1000
Falls Church, VA 22042	Fax:	(703) 641-2969

Political Action Committees
Computer Sciences Corporation PAC
FEC ID: C00101410
Contact: John Kavanaugh
3170 Fairview Park Dr.
Falls Church, VA 22042

> **Contributions to Candidates:** $53,000 (2015-2016)
> Democrats: $15,000; Republicans: $38,000

Corporate Foundations and Giving Programs
Computer Sciences Corporate Giving Foundation

2100 E. Grand Ave.	Tel:	(310) 615-1722
El Segundo, CA 90245	Fax:	(310) 322-9805

Public Affairs and Related Activities Personnel

At Headquarters

BAYLES, Miriam	Tel:	(703) 876-1000
Contact, Human Resources	Fax:	(703) 641-2969
BERNSTEIN, Harvey N.	Tel:	(703) 876-1000
Vice President, Legal Compliance Services	Fax:	(703) 641-2969
BRADY, Bryan	Tel:	(703) 641-3000
Vice President, Investor Relations	Fax:	(703) 641-2969
Investorrelations@csc.com		
DECKELMAN, Jr., Williams L.	Tel:	(703) 876-1000
Executive Vice President and General Counsel	Fax:	(703) 641-2969
ENG, Nelson	Tel:	(703) 876-1000
Vice President, Strategy and Corporate Business Development	Fax:	(703) 641-2969
GRANDIS, Chris	Tel:	(703) 641-2316
Director, Media Relations	Fax:	(703) 641-2969
cgrandis@csc.com		
HOLZER, Sunita	Tel:	(703) 876-1000
Executive Vice President and Chief Human Resources Officer	Fax:	(703) 641-2969
KASSIR, S. Marie	Tel:	(703) 641-2033

Federal Lobbyist	Fax:	(703) 641-2969
KAVANAUGH, John	Tel:	(703) 876-1000
Vice President, Finance and PAC Contact	Fax:	(703) 641-2969
SALEH, Paul N.	Tel:	(703) 876-1000
Executive Vice President and Chief Financial Officer	Fax:	(703) 641-2969
STOCKMAN, Gary	Tel:	(703) 876-1000
Chief Marketing and Communications Officer	Fax:	(703) 641-2969
WILFONG, Diane	Tel:	(703) 876-1000
Vice President, Controller and Principal Accounting Officer	Fax:	(703) 641-2969

CSC Holdings, Inc.

Operating company of Cablevision Systems Corporation. Through its subsidiaries, owns and operates cable television systems in the United States.
www.cschl.com.sg
Employees: 20,000
SIC: 4841
NAICS: 513220
Industry/ies: Communications; Telecommunications/Internet/Cable
Legislative Issues: DEF; TEC

Chairman of the Board — Tel: (516) 803-2300
DOLAN, Charles F. — Fax: (516) 803-3134

President and Chief Executive Officer — Tel: (516) 803-2300
DOLAN, James L. — Fax: (516) 803-3134

Main Headquarters
Mailing: 1111 Stewart Ave. — Tel: (516) 803-2300
Bethpage, NY 11714 — Fax: (516) 803-3134

Political Action Committees
Cablevision Systems Corporation Political Action Committee
FEC ID: C00197863
Contact: Elizabeth Losinski
1111 Stewart Ave. — Tel: (516) 803-2300
Bethpage, NY 11714 — Fax: (516) 803-3134

Contributions to Candidates: $60,700 (2015-2016)
Democrats: $50,200; Republicans: $10,500

Public Affairs and Related Activities Personnel

At Headquarters

BAECHER, Theodore	Tel:	(516) 803-2300
Vice President	Fax:	(516) 803-3134
ELLEN, David	Tel:	(516) 803-2300
Executive Vice President and General Counsel	Fax:	(516) 803-3134
KAPLAN, Kerri	Tel:	(516) 803-2305
Executive Director, The Lustgarten Foundation	Fax:	(516) 803-2303
kkaplan@cablevision.com		
KERNS, Kim	Tel:	(516) 803-2351
Vice President, Corporate Communications	Fax:	(516) 803-3134
LOSINSKI, Elizabeth	Tel:	(516) 803-2387
Vice President	Fax:	(516) 803-3134
MARTIN, Ken	Tel:	(516) 803-2300
Director, Investor Relations	Fax:	(516) 803-3134
investor@cablevision.com		
O'KEEFE, Emett	Tel:	(516) 803-2300
Registered Federal Lobbyist	Fax:	(516) 803-3134
OO, Diana	Tel:	(516) 803-2300
Federal Lobbyist	Fax:	(516) 803-3134
SCHUELER, Charles	Tel:	(516) 803-1013
Executive Vice President, Media and Community Relations	Fax:	(516) 803-3134
cshuele@cablevision.com		
SEIBERT, Gregg	Tel:	(516) 803-2300
Vice Chairman and Chief Financial Officer	Fax:	(516) 803-3134

CSL Behring LLC

Plasma protein biotherapeutics industry.
www.cslbehring.com
Employees: 10,000
SIC: 2834
NAICS: 325412
Industry/ies: Medicine/Health Care/Mental Health
Legislative Issues: HCR; MMM; TAX; TRD

Chief Executive Officer and Managing Director — Tel: (610) 878-4000
PERREAULT, Paul — Fax: (610) 878-4009

Main Headquarters
Mailing: 1020 First Ave. — Tel: (610) 878-4000
P.O. Box 61501 — Fax: (610) 878-4009
King of Prussia, PA 19406-0901

Political Action Committees
CSL Behring Employees PAC
FEC ID: C00422501
Contact: Patrick Collins
1020 First Ave.

P.O. Box 61501
King of Prussia, PA 19406

Contributions to Candidates: $49,700 (2015-2016)
Democrats: $12,000; Republicans: $37,700

Public Affairs and Related Activities Personnel

At Headquarters

BOSS, Greg	Tel:	(610) 878-4000
Executive Vice President, Legal and Group Counsel	Fax:	(610) 878-4009
BULLARD, Brian	Tel:	(610) 878-4000
Federal Lobbyist	Fax:	(610) 878-4009
Registered Federal Lobbyist		
COLLINS, Patrick	Tel:	(610) 878-4311
Director, Healthcare Policy and External Affairs	Fax:	(610) 878-4009
Patrick.Collins@cslbehring.com		
Registered Federal Lobbyist		
FLORENTZ, Chris	Tel:	(610) 878-4316
Manager, Corporate Communications	Fax:	(610) 290-9316
Christopher.Florentz@cslbehring.com		
HEALY, Greg	Tel:	(610) 878-4841
Senior Manager, Communications and Public Relations	Fax:	(610) 878-4009
greg.healy@cslbehring.com		
JACKMAN, Dennis	Tel:	(610) 878-4000
Senior Vice President, Public Affairs	Fax:	(610) 878-4009
dennis.jackman@cslbehring.com		
Registered Federal Lobbyist		
LAMONT, David	Tel:	(610) 878-4000
Chief Financial Officer	Fax:	(610) 878-4009
NAYLOR, Gordon	Tel:	(610) 878-4000
Chief Financial Officer	Fax:	(610) 878-4009
NEAVE, Karen	Tel:	(610) 878-4000
Senior Vice President, Global Financial Operations	Fax:	(610) 878-4009
REED, Laurie	Tel:	(610) 878-4000
Senior Vice President, Human Resources	Fax:	(610) 878-4009
WILLS, Alan	Tel:	(610) 878-4000
Senior Vice President, Strategy and Business Development	Fax:	(610) 878-4009

CSX Corporation

A multimodal transportation company headquartered in Jacksonville, FL.
www.csx.com
Annual Revenues: $11.40 billion
Employees: 29,410
Ticker: NYSE: CSX
SIC: 4011
NAICS: 482111
Industry/ies: Railroads; Shipping Industry; Transportation
Legislative Issues: AVI; BUD; CAW; CSP; ENG; ENV; GOV; RRR; TAX; TRA

Chairman of the Board, President and Chief Executive Officer — Tel: (904) 359-3200
WARD, Michael J. — Fax: (904) 359-2459

Main Headquarters
Mailing: 500 Water St. — Tel: (904) 359-3200
15th Floor — Fax: (904) 633-3450
Jacksonville Beach, FL 32202 — TF: (800) 769-8437

Washington Office
Mailing: 1331 Pennsylvania Ave. NW — Tel: (202) 783-8124
Suite 560 — Fax: (202) 783-5929
Washington, DC 20004

Political Action Committees
CSX Corporation Good Government Fund PAC
FEC ID: C00163832
Contact: Stephen Flippin
1331 Pennsylvania Ave. NW, Suite 560 — Tel: (202) 783-8124
Washington, DC 20004 — Fax: (202) 783-5929

Contributions to Candidates: $1,231,750 (2015-2016)
Democrats: $475,000; Republicans: $754,750; Other: $2,000

Principal Recipients

SENATE
BLUNT, ROY (REP-MO)
GRASSLEY, CHARLES E SENATOR (REP-IA)
JOHNSON, RONALD HAROLD (REP-)
KIRK, MARK STEVEN (REP-IL)
MCCAIN, JOHN S (REP-VA)
PETERS, GARY (DEM-MI)
SCOTT, TIMOTHY E (REP-SC)

HOUSE
ADAMS, ALMA SHEALEY (DEM-NC)
BUTTERFIELD, G K (DEM-NC)
CLYBURN, JAMES E. (DEM-SC)
COHEN, STEPHEN IRA (DEM-)
CUMMINGS, ELIJAH E (DEM-DC)
DEFAZIO, PETER A (DEM-OR)

DENHAM, JEFF (REP-CA)
DIAZ-BALART, MARIO (REP-FL)
DUNCAN, JOHN J REP. JR. (REP-TN)
FORBES, J. RANDY (REP-VA)
GOODLATTE, ROBERT W. (REP-VA)
GRAVES, SAMUEL B JR 'SAM' (REP-MO)
HOYER, STENY HAMILTON (DEM-DC)
JOHNSON, EDDIE BERNICE (DEM-TX)
JOYCE, DAVID P (REP-OH)
LEWIS, JOHN R. (DEM-GA)
LOWEY, NITA M (DEM-NY)
MCCARTHY, KEVIN (REP-CA)
MCCAUL, MICHAEL (REP-TX)
MCGOVERN, JAMES P (DEM-MA)
MCHENRY, PATRICK TIMOTHY (REP-NC)
MICA, JOHN L. MR. (REP-FL)
NADLER, JERROLD L. MR. (DEM-NY)
NEAL, RICHARD E MR. (DEM-MA)
PASCRELL, WILLIAM J. HON. (DEM-NJ)
PRICE, DAVID E. (DEM-NC)
RICHMOND, CEDRIC L. (DEM-LA)
RUPPERSBERGER, C.A. DUTCH (DEM-MD)
RUSH, BOBBY LEE (DEM-IL)
SCALISE, STEVE MR. (REP-LA)
SHUSTER, WILLIAM MR. (REP-PA)
TIBERI, PATRICK J. (REP-OH)
UPTON, FREDERICK STEPHEN (REP-MI)
WITTMAN, ROBERT J MR. (REP-VA)

Corporate Foundations and Giving Programs

CSX Transportation Contributions Program
500 Water St.
15th Floor
Jacksonville Beach, FL 32202

Public Affairs and Related Activities Personnel

At Headquarters

BAGGS, David
Vice President, Treasurer and Investor Relations
david_baggs@csx.com
Tel: (904) 359-4812
Fax: (904) 359-2459

BOOR, David A.
Vice President-Tax and Treasurer
Tel: (904) 359-3200
Fax: (904) 633-3450

ELIASSON, Fredrik
Executive Vice President, Chief Sales and Marketing Officer
Tel: (904) 359-3200
Fax: (904) 359-2459

FITZSIMMONS, Ellen M.
Executive Vice President, Law and Public Affairs, General Counsel and Corporate Secretary
Tel: (904) 359-3200
Fax: (904) 359-2459

GOODEN, Clarence W.
President
Tel: (904) 359-3200
Fax: (904) 359-2459

LONEGRO, Frank A.
Executive Vice President and Chief Financial Officer
Tel: (904) 359-3200
Fax: (904) 633-3450

MANCINI, Lisa A.
Executive Vice President and Chief Administrative Officer
Tel: (904) 359-3200
Fax: (904) 633-3450

PASSA, Lester M.
Vice President, Strategic Planning
Tel: (904) 359-3200
Fax: (904) 359-2459

SANBORN, Cindy
Executive Vice President and Chief Operating Officer
Tel: (904) 359-3200
Fax: (904) 633-3450

SEASE, Gary
Vice President, Corporate Communications
gary_sease@csx.com
Tel: (904) 359-1719
Fax: (904) 359-1899

SHUDTZ, Peter J.
Vice President, Federal Regulation and General Counsel
Registered Federal Lobbyist
Tel: (202) 783-8124
Fax: (202) 783-5929

SIZEMORE, Carolyn T.
Vice President and Controller
Tel: (904) 359-3200
Fax: (904) 633-3450

At Washington Office

BENN, Rebecca
Federal Lobbyist
Registered Federal Lobbyist
Tel: (202) 783-8124
Fax: (202) 783-5929

DOOLITTLE, Robert E.
Director, Communications and Media Relations
Tel: (202) 783-8124
Fax: (202) 783-5929

FLIPPIN, Stephen
PAC Treasurer
Registered Federal Lobbyist
Tel: (202) 783-8124
Fax: (202) 783-5929

FRANCIS, Garrick
Director, Federal Affairs
Registered Federal Lobbyist
Tel: (202) 783-8124
Fax: (904) 633-3450

HOOVER, Reynold N.
Assistant Vice President Law and Risk Management
Tel: (202) 783-8124
Fax: (202) 783-5929

REINKE, Anne Chettle
Vice President, Federal Legislation
Registered Federal Lobbyist
Tel: (202) 783-8124
Fax: (202) 783-5929

WOLDEHAWARIAT, Alem
PAC Contact
Tel: (202) 783-8124
Fax: (202) 783-5929

CTS Corporation

Designs, manufactures, and sells automotive electronic components, electronic assemblies and provides electronics manufacturing services (EMS) primarily for original equipment manufacturers in the communications and computer industries.
www.ctscorp.com
Annual Revenues: $401.63 million
Employees: 2,948
Ticker: NYSE: CTS
SIC: 4264
Industry/ies: Electricity & Electronics; Electronics; Energy/Electricity

Main Headquarters

Mailing: 905 West Blvd., North
        Elkhart, IN 46514
Tel: (574) 293-7511
Fax: (574) 293-6146

Corporate Foundations and Giving Programs

CTS Corporation Foundation
905 West Blvd. North
Elkhart, IN 46514
Tel: (574) 293-7511
Fax: (574) 293-6146

Public Affairs and Related Activities Personnel

At Headquarters

KROLL, Thomas A.
Vice President and Controller
Tel: (574) 293-7511
Fax: (574) 293-6146

WALORSKI, Mitchell J.
Director, Planning and Investor Relations
Tel: (574) 523-3800
Fax: (574) 293-6146

Cuba Democracy Public Advocacy, Corporation

An advocate for the political, economic and social freedoms in cuba.
Industry/ies: Civil Rights And Liberties
Legislative Issues: FOR

Main Headquarters

Mailing: 2020 Pennsylvania Ave. NW
        Suite 927
        Washington, DC 20006
Tel: (240) 441-8345

Public Affairs and Related Activities Personnel

At Headquarters

CLAVER-CARONE, Mauricio
Executive Director
Registered Federal Lobbyist
Tel: (240) 441-8345

Cubic Corporation

Develops, manufactures, and sells mass transit fare collection systems, air and ground combat training systems, and secure communications products for various federal and regional government agencies.
www.cubic.com
Annual Revenues: $1.39 billion
Employees: 7,900
Ticker: NYSE: CUB
SIC: 5044; 5049; 8299; 8748; 9999
Industry/ies: Computer/Technology; Defense/Homeland Security; Government-Related; Transportation
Legislative Issues: DEF; TRA

Chairman of the Board
ZABLE, Walter J.
Tel: (858) 277-6780
Fax: (858) 277-1878

President and Chief Executive Officer
FELDMANN, Bradley H.
Tel: (858) 277-6780
Fax: (858) 505-1523

Main Headquarters

Mailing: 9333 Balboa Ave.
        San Diego, CA 92123
Tel: (858) 277-6780
Fax: (858) 505-1523
TF: (800) 818-8303

Washington Office

Mailing: Crystal Gateway Two, 1225 S. Clark St.
        Suite 601
        Arlington, VA 22202
Tel: (703) 415-1600

Political Action Committees

Cubic Corporation Employees' Political Action Committee
FEC ID: C00151787
Contact: Bryce Nilsson
9333 Balboa Ave.
M/S 10-2
San Diego, CA 92123

Contributions to Candidates: $58,200 (2015-2016)
Democrats: $11,700; Republicans: $46,500

Corporate Foundations and Giving Programs

Cubic Corporation Contributions Program
P.O. Box 85587
San Diego, CA 92186
Tel: (858) 277-6780
Fax: (858) 277-1878

Cubic Defense Contribution Program
P.O. Box 85587
Tel: (858) 277-6780

San Diego, CA 92186-5587   Fax: (858) 277-1878

Public Affairs and Related Activities Personnel

At Headquarters

ALBERTSON, Darryl S.   Tel: (858) 277-6780
Vice President, Human Resources   Fax: (858) 505-1523

BISHOP, Norman R.   Tel: (858) 277-6780
Vice President, Corporate Development   Fax: (858) 505-1523

DIZON, April D   Tel: (858) 277-6780
PAC Treasurer   Fax: (858) 277-1878
Mail Stop M/S 10-2

EDWARDS, James R.   Tel: (858) 277-6780
Senior Vice President, General Counsel & Secretary   Fax: (858) 277-1878

HOESE, William L.   Tel: (858) 277-6780
Vice President and General Counsel   Fax: (858) 277-1878
Registered Federal Lobbyist

JAZWICK, Andrew V.   Tel: (858) 277-6780
Vice President, Legislative Affairs   Fax: (858) 277-1878

KELLOGG, Jr., Joseph K.   Tel: (858) 277-6780
Vice President, Strategic Initiatives   Fax: (858) 505-1523

LEE, Dale   Tel: (858) 277-6780
Senior Revenue Recognition Analyst   Fax: (858) 505-1523

MARSHALL, Jan L.   Tel: (858) 277-6780
Vice President and Chief Information Officer   Fax: (858) 505-1523

NILSSON, Bryce   Tel: (858) 277-6780
PAC Contact   Fax: (858) 505-1523

ROBERTI, John   Tel: (858) 277-6780
Vice President, Human Resources   Fax: (858) 505-1523
Registered Federal Lobbyist

STEVENS, Jan   Tel: (858) 277-6780
Manager, Corporate Communications   Fax: (858) 277-1878
jan.stevens@cubic.com

THOMAS, John D.   Tel: (858) 277-6780
Executive Vice President and Chief Financial Officer   Fax: (858) 505-1523

Cumberland Farms, Inc.

An operator of convenience stores and gas service stations.
www.cumberlandfarms.com
Employees: 7,000
SIC: 2026; 2023; 2037; 2086
Industry/ies: Automotive Industry; Food And Beverage Industry; Transportation
Legislative Issues: BAN; FOO; FUE; GAM; ROD; TAX; TEC

Chairman of the Board   Tel: (508) 270-1400
BENTAS, Lilly Haseotes   Fax: (781) 828-9624

Chief Executive Officer   Tel: (508) 270-1400
HASEOTES, Ari N.   Fax: (781) 828-9624

Main Headquarters
Mailing: 100 Crossing Blvd.   Tel: (508) 270-1400
Framingham, MA 01702   Fax: (781) 828-9624
   TF: (800) 225-9702

Political Action Committees
Cumberland Farms Inc Gulf Oil Limited Partnership Leadership Fund PAC
FEC ID: C00523225
Contact: Howard Rosenstein
100 Crossing Blvd.   Tel: (508) 270-1400
Framingham, MA 01702   Fax: (781) 828-9624

> **Contributions to Candidates:** $5,000 (2015-2016)
> Democrats: $4,000; Republicans: $1,000

Corporate Foundations and Giving Programs

Cumberland Farms, Inc. Contributions Program
100 Crossing Blvd.   Tel: (508) 270-1400
Framingham, MA 01702

Public Affairs and Related Activities Personnel

At Headquarters

BOISSONNEAULT , Diane   Tel: (508) 270-1400
Associate General Counsel   Fax: (781) 828-9624

FORMAN, Gwen   Tel: (508) 270-1400
Vice President, Marketing   Fax: (781) 828-9624

HOWARD, Esq., Mark G.   Tel: (508) 270-1400
Executive Vice President, Chief Legal and Administrative   Fax: (781) 828-9624
Officer
howard@cumberlandfarms.com

LEATHER, Raymond F.   Tel: (508) 270-1400
Vice President, Environmental and Regulatory Affairs   Fax: (781) 828-9624

LINNANE , Sean   Tel: (508) 270-1400
Vice President, Human Resources   Fax: (781) 828-9624

MCMAHON, John P.   Tel: (508) 270-1400
Senior Vice President and Chief Human Resources Officer   Fax: (781) 828-9624

ROSENSTEIN, Howard   Tel: (508) 270-1400

Senior Vice President and Chief Financial Officer and PAC   Fax: (781) 828-9624
Treasurer

TAITELBAUM, Caroline   Tel: (508) 270-1400
Vice President, Compliance and Financial Reporting   Fax: (781) 828-9624

Cummins Engine Company

See listing on page 235 under Cummins Inc.

Cummins Inc.

A provider of products and services for customers in worldwide markets for engines, power generation and filtration.
www.cummins.com
Annual Revenues: $19.52 billion
Employees: 54,600
Ticker: NYSE: CMI
SIC: 3510
Industry/ies: Automotive Industry; Transportation
Legislative Issues: BUD; CAW; DEF; ENG; ENV; LBR; TAX; TRA; TRD

Chairman of the Board and Chief Executive Officer   Tel: (812) 377-5000
LINEBARGER, Tom   Fax: (812) 377-3334

Main Headquarters
Mailing: 500 Jackson St.   Tel: (812) 377-5000
P.O. Box 3005   Fax: (812) 377-3334
Columbus, IN 47202-3005   TF: (800) 343-7357

Washington Office
Mailing: 601 Pennsylvania Ave. NW   Tel: (202) 393-8585
Suite 1100, North Bldg.   Fax: (202) 393-8111
Washington, DC 20004

Political Action Committees
Cummins Inc. PAC
FEC ID: C00377952
Contact: Catherine Van Way
601 Pennsylvania Ave. NW   Tel: (202) 393-8585
North Bldg., Suite 625   Fax: (202) 393-8111
Washington, DC 20004

> **Contributions to Candidates:** $119,700 (2015-2016)
> Democrats: $44,500; Republicans: $75,200

Corporate Foundations and Giving Programs

Cummins Foundation
500 Jackson St.
M.C. 60633
Columbus, OH 47201

Public Affairs and Related Activities Personnel

At Headquarters

COOK, Jill   Tel: (812) 377-5000
Vice President, Human Resources   Fax: (812) 377-3334
jill.e.cook@cummins.com
Registered Federal Lobbyist

DUGGAL, Vinod   Tel: (812) 377-5000
Federal Lobbyist   Fax: (812) 377-3334
Registered Federal Lobbyist

EWALD, Thad   Tel: (812) 377-5000
Vice President, Corporate Strategy   Fax: (812) 377-3334
Registered Federal Lobbyist

FREELAND, Rich   Tel: (812) 377-5000
President and Chief Operating Officer   Fax: (812) 377-3334

LANGLEY, Gwen   Tel: (812) 377-5000
Director, Global Community Engagement, Corporate   Fax: (812) 377-3334
Responsibility

LEVETT, Mark   Tel: (812) 377-5000
Vice President, Corporate Responsibility   Fax: (812) 377-3334

MORMINO, Brian   Tel: (812) 377-5000
Federal Lobbyist   Fax: (812) 377-3334
brian.c.mormino@cummins.com
Registered Federal Lobbyist

OSOWICK, Mark   Tel: (812) 377-5000
Vice President, Human Resources Operations   Fax: (812) 377-3334

ROSE , Marya   Tel: (812) 377-5000
Chief Administrative Officer   Fax: (812) 377-3334
Registered Federal Lobbyist

SMITH, CAE, PhD, Mark A.   Tel: (812) 377-5000
Executive Director, Investor Relations   Fax: (812) 377-3334
investor_relations@cummins.com

WARD, Patrick J.   Tel: (812) 377-5000
Chief Financial Officer   Fax: (812) 377-3334

At Washington Office

FOSTER, Emily Diedrich   Tel: (202) 393-8585
Director, Government Relations   Fax: (202) 393-8111
emily.d.foster@cummins.com
Registered Federal Lobbyist

FRANZETTI, Chris
PAC Manager
Tel: (202) 654-4280
Fax: (202) 393-8111

KIELY-HEIDER, Shannon
Director, State Government Relations
Registered Federal Lobbyist
Tel: (202) 393-8585
Fax: (202) 393-8111

KRAUS, Traci
Manager, Government Relations
traci.kraus@cummins.com
Registered Federal Lobbyist
Tel: (202) 393-8585
Fax: (202) 393-8111

MAY, Stephen L.
Federal Lobbyist
Registered Federal Lobbyist
Tel: (202) 393-8585
Fax: (202) 393-8111

PRINCE, Erik
Director, Government Relations
Tel: (202) 393-8585
Fax: (202) 393-8111

VAN WAY, Catherine
Executive Director, International Government Relations
catherine.vanway@cummins.com
Registered Federal Lobbyist
Tel: (202) 393-8585
Fax: (202) 393-8111

WILSON, William
Registered Federal Lobbyist
Tel: (202) 393-8585
Fax: (202) 393-8111

At Other Offices

KIELY, Mary
Director, State Government Relations
One American Square, Suite 1800
Indianapolis, IN 46282
Registered Federal Lobbyist
Tel: (317) 610-2542

MCCORMACK, Lawrence
Manger, State Government Relations
One American Square, Suite 1800
Indianapolis, IN 46282
lawrence.mccormack@cummins.com
Registered Federal Lobbyist
Tel: (317) 610-2542

Cummins Allison Corporation

Cummins features advanced technology products that speed currency, ticket and coin processing.
www.cumminsallison.com
SIC: 3579; 2754; 3578; 5044; 9999
Industry/ies: Retail/Wholesale
Legislative Issues: CPT; MAN; SCI; TAX

Main Headquarters
Mailing: 852 Feehanville Dr.
            Mt. Prospect, IL 60056
Tel: (847) 299-9550
TF: (855) 609-4802

Political Action Committees
Cummins-Allison Corp Employees For Good Government PAC
FEC ID: C00408914
Contact: Timothy H. Minor
1919 Algonquin Rd.
Rolling Meadows, 60008

   Contributions to Candidates: $13,500 (2015-2016)
   Democrats: $10,000; Republicans: $3,500

Public Affairs and Related Activities Personnel

At Headquarters

MINOR, Timothy H.
Senior Vice President, Corporate Affairs
minort@cumminsallison.com
Registered Federal Lobbyist
Tel: (847) 299-9550

MINOR, Timothy H.
Senior Vice President Corporate Affairs
Mail Stop timster670@aol.com
timster670@aol.com
Registered Federal Lobbyist
Tel: (847) 299-9550

MOORE, Carol
Vice President, Marketing
moorec@cumminsallison.com
Tel: (847) 299-9550

CUNA Mutual Group

A financial services provider to credit unions and their members worldwide, offering insurance, investment and technological solutions through strategic relationships and multiple service channels. CUNA Mutual Group is the marketing name for CUNA Mutual Holding Company and its affiliates and subsidiaries.
www.cunamutual.com
Employees: 5,300
Industry/ies: Insurance Industry
Legislative Issues: FIN; INS; TAX

President and Chief Executive Officer
TRUNZO, Robert N.

Main Headquarters
Mailing: 5910 Mineral Point Rd.
            P.O. Box 391
            Madison, WI 53705
Tel: (608) 238-5851
Fax: (608) 236-6327
TF: (800) 356-2644

Political Action Committees
Cuna Mutual Holding Company Political Action Committee (Cuna Mutual PAC)
FEC ID: C00402107
Contact: Christopher P. Roe
5910 Mineral Point Rd., P.O. Box 747
MS 5910 4 A2
Madison, WI 53701

   Contributions to Candidates: $67,000 (2015-2016)
   Democrats: $29,000; Republicans: $38,000

Corporate Foundations and Giving Programs
CUNA Mutual Corporate Foundation
Contact: Steve Goldberg
5910 Mineral Point Rd.
Madison, WI 53705
Tel: (608) 238-5851
Fax: (608) 238-0830

Public Affairs and Related Activities Personnel

At Headquarters

ANDERSON, Mike
Chief Legal Officer
Tel: (608) 238-5851
Fax: (608) 236-6327

BELGRADE, Kevin
Senior Vice President, Marketing and Corporate Communications
Tel: (608) 238-5851
Fax: (608) 236-6327

BRIGGS, Michael
Senior Vice President, Large Account Strategy
Tel: (608) 238-5851
Fax: (608) 236-6327

ELLIS, Cedric C.
Chief Human Resources Officer
Tel: (608) 238-5851
Fax: (608) 236-6327

KOVAC, Timothy
Vice President, Corporate and Legislative Affairs
tim.kovac@cunamutual.com
Registered Federal Lobbyist
Tel: (608) 238-5851
Fax: (608) 236-6327

MERFELD, Thomas J.
Chief Financial Officer
Tel: (608) 238-5851
Fax: (608) 236-6327

PATZNER, Faye
Chief Administrative Officer
faye.patzner@cunamutual.com
Tel: (608) 238-5851
Fax: (608) 236-6327

ROE, Christopher P.
Senior Vice President, Corporate, Legislative Affairs and PAC Treasurer
Mail Stop 5910 4 A2
christopher.roe@cunamutual.com
Registered Federal Lobbyist
Tel: (608) 238-5851
Fax: (608) 236-6327

SULESKI, Steve
Chief Governance and Compliance Officer
Tel: (608) 238-5851
Fax: (608) 236-6327

Current Group LLC

Company provides electric utilities a Smart Grid solution that increases the efficiency and reliability of the electric grid while reducing the environmental impact of electric usage.
www.thecurrentgroupllc.com/about.html
Annual Revenues: $23.90 million
Employees: 200
Industry/ies: Communications; Energy/Electricity; Telecommunications/Internet/Cable

Main Headquarters
Mailing: 119 Broadfoot Ave.
            Fayetteville, NC 28305

Washington Office
Mailing: 20420 Century Blvd.
            Suite F
            Germantown, MD 20874-1174
Tel: (301) 944-2700
Fax: (301) 944-2701

Public Affairs and Related Activities Personnel

At Headquarters

KAY, Parker Mary
Independent Beauty Consultant

At Washington Office

HERNANDEZ, Angel
Executive Vice President, World Wide Sales
Tel: (301) 944-2700
Fax: (301) 944-2701

Curtiss-Wright Corporation

Curtiss-Wright Corporation is a provider of engineered technological products and services.
www.curtisswright.com
Annual Revenues: $2.25 billion
Employees: 9,000
Ticker: NYSE: CW
SIC: 3590
Industry/ies: Aerospace/Aviation; Transportation

Chairman of the Board and Chief Executive Officer
ADAMS, David C.
Tel: (704) 869-4600
Fax: (973) 541-3699

Main Headquarters
Mailing: 13925 Ballantyne Corporate Pl.
            Suite 400
            Charlotte, NC 28277
Tel: (704) 869-4600
Fax: (973) 541-3699

Washington Office

Mailing: 2941 Fairview Park Dr.   Tel: (703) 286-2000
          Suite 850   Fax: (703) 286-2035
          Falls Church, VA 22042

Political Action Committees

Curtiss Wright Corporation Employees PAC
FEC ID: C00420596
Contact: David Francis
2941 Fairview Park Dr.
Suite 850
Falls Church, VA 22042

   Contributions to Candidates: $3,000 (2015-2016)
   Republicans: $3,000

Public Affairs and Related Activities Personnel

At Headquarters

FERDENZI, Paul J.   Tel: (704) 869-4600
General Counsel and Corporate Secretary Fax: (973) 541-3699

QUINLY , Thomas P.   Tel: (973) 541-3700
Chief Operating Officer   Fax: (973) 541-3699

RYAN, James M.   Tel: (704) 869-4600
Director, Investor Relations   Fax: (973) 541-3699
Jim.Ryan@curtisswright.com

TYNAN, Glenn E.   Tel: (704) 869-4600
Vice President and Chief Financial Officer Fax: (973) 541-3699
gtynan@cwcorp.curtisswright.com

At Washington Office

FRANCIS, David   Tel: (703) 286-2000
PAC Treasurer   Fax: (703) 286-2035

MILLER , Parker B.   Tel: (703) 286-2000
Senior Vice President, Government Relations Fax: (703) 286-2035

C.V. Starr & Company, Inc.

C.V. Starr & Company, Inc. is a global investment holding company with insurance agencies and a portfolio of global investments.
www.starrcompanies.com
Employees: 400
Industry/ies: Banking/Finance/Investments

Chairman of the Board and Chief Executive Officer   Tel: (212) 230-5050
GREENBERG, Maurice R.   Fax: (212) 230-5092

Main Headquarters

Mailing: 399 Park Ave.   Tel: (646) 227-6300
          Eighth Floor   Fax: (631) 685-6673
          New York City, NY 10022

Political Action Committees

C.V. Starr & Company, Inc. PAC
FEC ID: C00462465
Contact: Howard I. Smith
399 Park Ave.
17th Floor
New York City, NY 10022

Corporate Foundations and Giving Programs

The Starr Foundation
399 Park Ave.
17th Floor
New York City, NY 10022

Public Affairs and Related Activities Personnel

At Headquarters

LUNDQVIST, Bertil   Tel: (212) 230-5050
Executive Vice President and General Counsel Fax: (212) 230-5092

SMITH, Howard I.   Tel: (212) 230-5050
Director and the Vice Chairman, Finance Fax: (212) 230-5092

CVS Caremark, Inc.

Retail chain involved in sale of health/beauty aids and prescription drugs. Formed by the merger of CVS Corporation and Caremark Rx, Inc. In 2008, CVS acquired Longs Drug Stores Company.
www.cvshealth.com/contact
Annual Revenues: $160.17 billion
Employees: 155,000
Ticker: NYSE: CVS
SIC: 5912
Industry/ies: Medicine/Health Care/Mental Health
Legislative Issues: HCR; LBR; MMM; PHA; POS; TAX; TRU

Non-Executive Chairman of the Board   Tel: (401) 765-1500
DORMAN, David W.   Fax: (401) 762-9227

President and Chief Executive Officer   Tel: (401) 765-1500
MERLO, Larry J.   Fax: (401) 762-9227

Main Headquarters

Mailing: One CVS Dr.   Tel: (401) 765-1500

Woonsocket, RI 02895   Fax: (401) 762-9227
                                          TF: (800) 746-7287

Washington Office

Mailing: 1275 Pennsylvania Ave. NW   Tel: (202) 772-3517
          Suite 700
          Washington, DC 20004

Political Action Committees

CVS/Caremark Corporation Employees PAC
FEC ID: C00384818
Contact: Bill Raines
1300 I St. NW
Suite 525W
Washington, DC 20005

   Contributions to Candidates: $144,500 (2015-2016)
   Democrats: $48,500; Republicans: $96,000

Corporate Foundations and Giving Programs

The CVS Caremark Charitable Foundation
Contact: Carolyn Castel
One CVS Dr.   Tel: (401) 765-1500
Woonsocket, RI 02895   Fax: (401) 769-4488

Public Affairs and Related Activities Personnel

At Headquarters

BISACCIA, Lisa   Tel: (401) 765-1500
Senior Vice President and Chief Human Resources Officer Fax: (401) 762-9227

BORATTO, Eva   Tel: (401) 765-1500
Senior Vice President, Controller and Chief Accounting Fax: (401) 762-9227
Officer

BUSH, Lucille   Tel: (401) 765-1500
Director, Community Relations   Fax: (401) 769-4488

CASTEL, Carolyn   Tel: (401) 770-5717
Vice President, Corporate Communications Fax: (401) 762-9227

CRAMER, Christine   Tel: (401) 770-3317
Director, Public Relations   Fax: (401) 762-9227
christine.cramer@cvscaremark.com

DENTON, David M.   Tel: (401) 765-1500
Executive Vice President and Chief Financial Officer Fax: (401) 762-9227

FOULKES, Helena B.   Tel: (401) 765-1500
Executive Vice President   Fax: (401) 762-9227

HOWARD BOONE, Eileen   Tel: (401) 770-4561
Senior Vice President, Corporate Social Responsibility and Fax: (401) 762-9227
Philanthropy

JOYNER, J. David   Tel: (401) 765-1500
Executive Vice President, Sales and Account Services Fax: (401) 762-9227

MCGUIRE, Mike P.   Tel: (401) 770-4050
Vice President, Investor Relations   Fax: (401) 770-4279
mpmcguire@cvs.com

MORIARTY, Thomas M.   Tel: (401) 765-1500
Executive Vice President, Chief Health Strategy Officer and Fax: (401) 762-9227
General Counsel

At Washington Office

AYOTTE, Michael   Tel: (202) 772-3517
Head, Government Relations

BROOKS, Elizabeth   Tel: (202) 772-3517
Registered Federal Lobbyist

BURTON, Larry D.   Tel: (202) 772-3501
Senior Vice President, Government Affairs, CVS Caremark
Inc.
Registered Federal Lobbyist

CUTLER, Heather A.   Tel: (202) 772-3517
Director, Federal, Political Advocacy
heather.cutler@caremark.com
Registered Federal Lobbyist

FILES, Brian   Tel: (202) 772-3517
Federal Lobbyist
Registered Federal Lobbyist

NEWSOM, Mark   Tel: (202) 772-3517
Federal Lobbyist
Registered Federal Lobbyist

RAINES, Bill   Tel: (202) 772-3517
PAC Treasurer
Registered Federal Lobbyist

ROSS, Sol   Tel: (202) 772-3517
Registered Federal Lobbyist

SCHLAIFER, Marissa   Tel: (202) 772-3517
Federal Lobbyist
Registered Federal Lobbyist

SCHULMAN, Melissa   Tel: (202) 772-3517
Registered Federal Lobbyist

WALKER-JENKINS, Ann   Tel: (202) 772-3517

Director, Federal Government Affairs
Registered Federal Lobbyist

At Other Offices

CHRISTAL, Nancy	Tel:	(914) 722-4704
Senior Vice President, Investor Relations	Fax:	(914) 722-0847
670 White Plains Rd., Suite 210		
Scarsdale, NY 10583		
mchristal@cvs.com		

Cybernet Systems

A solutions company that strives to advance human performance through the application of technology. It is a research and development Company in the medical and defense fields developing technology and bringing its research to market.
www.cybernet.com
Annual Revenues: $7.53 million
Employees: 50
Industry/ies: Computer/Technology; Defense/Homeland Security; Government-Related

Chairman of the Board and Chief Executive Officer	Tel:	(734) 668-2567
JACOBUS, Heidi N.	Fax:	(734) 668-8780
President	Tel:	(734) 668-2567
JACOBUS, PhD, Charles J.	Fax:	(734) 668-8780

Main Headquarters

Mailing:	3741 Plaza Dr.	Tel:	(734) 668-2567
	Ann Arbor, MI 48108	Fax:	(734) 668-8780

Public Affairs and Related Activities Personnel

At Other Offices

HELLER, CPA, Norma G.	Tel:	(734) 668-2567
Vice President, Finance and Operations	Fax:	(734) 668-8780
3885 Research Park Dr.		
Ann Arbor, MI 48108		

Cyberonics, Inc.

Medical device company specializing in the treatment of epilepsy.
www.cyberonics.com
Annual Revenues: $292.34 Million
Employees: 639
Ticker: NASDAQ: CYBX
SIC: 3845
NAICS: 334510
Industry/ies: Medicine/Health Care/Mental Health
Legislative Issues: HCR

Chairman of the Board	Tel:	(281) 228-7200
MORRISON, Hugh M.	Fax:	(281) 218-9332
hugh.morrison@cyberonics.com		
President and Chief Executive Officer	Tel:	(281) 228-7200
MOORE, Daniel J.	Fax:	(281) 218-9332
dmoore@cyberonics.com		

Main Headquarters

Mailing:	The Cyberonics Bldg	Tel:	(281) 228-7200
	100 Cyberonics Blvd.	Fax:	(281) 218-9332
	Houston, TX 77058	TF:	(800) 332-1375

Political Action Committees
Cyberonics, Inc Federal PAC
FEC ID: C00481291
Contact: Gregory H. Browne

100 Cyberonics Blvd.	Tel:	(281) 228-7200
Houston, TX 77058	Fax:	(281) 218-9332

> **Contributions to Candidates:** $12,000 (2015-2016)
> Democrats: $3,000; Republicans: $9,000

Corporate Foundations and Giving Programs

Cyberonics Contributions Program

The Cyberonics Building	Tel:	(281) 228-7200
100 Cyberonics Blvd.	Fax:	(281) 228-7200
Houston, TX 77058		

Public Affairs and Related Activities Personnel

At Headquarters

ALCH, Darren	Tel:	(281) 228-7200
Vice President, Corporate Counsel, Compliance Officer and Assistant Secretary	Fax:	(281) 218-9332
BROWNE, Gregory H.	Tel:	(281) 228-7262
Vice President, Finance and Chief Financial Officer	Fax:	(281) 218-9332
ir@cyberonics.com		
HOARE, Rohan J	Tel:	(281) 228-7200
Senior Vice President, Chief Operating Officer	Fax:	(281) 218-9332
PERKINS, Sherrie L.	Tel:	(281) 228-7200
Vice President, Marketing and New Business Development	Fax:	(281) 218-9332
WISE, David S.	Tel:	(281) 228-7200
	Fax:	(281) 218-9332

Senior Vice President, Chief Administrative Officer and Secretary

Cymbet Corporation

A private, venture-backed power solutions company.
www.cymbet.com
Industry/ies: Energy/Electricity

Main Headquarters

Mailing:	18326 Joplin St. NW	Tel:	(763) 633-1780
	Elk River, MN 55330-1773	Fax:	(763) 633-1799

Public Affairs and Related Activities Personnel

At Headquarters

GRADY, Steve C.	Tel:	(763) 633-1792
Vice President, Marketing	Fax:	(763) 633-1799

Cypress Semiconductor Corporation

Designs, manufactures and assembles semiconductor devices.
www.cypress.com
Annual Revenues: $764.35 million
Employees: 3,350
Ticker: NASDAQ: CY
SIC: 5063; 5063
Industry/ies: Computer/Technology; Energy/Electricity

Chairman of the Board	Tel:	(408) 962-2500
BINGHAM, Ray	Fax:	(408) 616-8174
Chairman of the Board	Tel:	(408) 943-2600
BINGHAM, Ray	Fax:	(408) 943-4730
President and Chief Executive Officer and Director	Tel:	(408) 943-2600
RODGERS, T.J.	Fax:	(408) 943-4730

Main Headquarters

Mailing:	198 Champion Ct.	Tel:	(408) 943-2600
	San Jose, CA 95134	Fax:	(408) 943-4730
		TF:	(800) 541-4736

Corporate Foundations and Giving Programs

Cypress Semiconductor Corporation Corporate Giving Program

198 Champion Ct.	Tel:	(408) 943-2600
San Jose, CA 95134	Fax:	(408) 943-4730

Spansion Contributions Program
Contact: John H. Kispert

915 DeGuigne Dr.	Tel:	(408) 962-2500
Sunnyvale, CA 94085	Fax:	(408) 962-2500

Public Affairs and Related Activities Personnel

At Headquarters

KESWICK , Paul	Tel:	(408) 943-2600
Executive Vice President, Marketing and Information Technology, Legal and Human Resources	Fax:	(408) 943-4730
KOTHANDARAMAN , Badri	Tel:	(408) 943-2600
Executive Vice President, Data Communications and Executive Director	Fax:	(408) 943-4730
MCCARTHY, Joseph L.	Tel:	(408) 943-2902
Vice President, Corporate Communications	Fax:	(408) 456-1910
SEAMS, Chris	Tel:	(408) 943-2600
Chief Executive Officer, Deca Technologies	Fax:	(408) 943-4730
TRENT, Thad	Tel:	(408) 943-2600
Executive Vice President, Finance and Administration and Chief Financial Officer	Fax:	(408) 943-4730

At Other Offices

FRANKEN, Mark	Tel:	(408) 616-8410
Contact, Media Relations	Fax:	(408) 616-8174
915 DeGuigne Dr.		
Sunnyvale, CA 94085		
mark.franken@spansion.com		
GRIFFIN , Scot	Tel:	(408) 962-2500
Senior Vice President and General Counsel	Fax:	(408) 616-8174
915 DeGuigne Dr.		
Sunnyvale, CA 94085		
MCCARTHY, Joseph L.	Tel:	(408) 962-2500
Senior Director, Corporate Communications	Fax:	(408) 616-8174
915 DeGuigne Dr.		
Sunnyvale, CA 94085		
POURKERAMATI, Ali	Tel:	(408) 962-2500
Senior Vice President, Strategic Alliances and Business Development	Fax:	(408) 616-8174
915 DeGuigne Dr.		
Sunnyvale, CA 94085		
ali.pourkeramati@spansion.com		

Cyren Call Communications, LLC

Cyren Call assists the PSST in the creation of a nationwide, wireless broadband network that will carry Public Safety communications.
www.cyrencall.com
Industry/ies: Communications; Telecommunications/Internet/Cable

Chairman of the Board		Tel:	(703) 760-4830
O'BRIEN, Morgan			

Main Headquarters
Mailing:	7601 Lewinsville Rd.	Tel:	(703) 760-4830
	Suite 201		
	McLean, VA 22102-2814		

Public Affairs and Related Activities Personnel

At Headquarters

COX, Bruce		Tel:	(703) 760-4830
Senior Vice President, External Affairs			
MELCHER, John		Tel:	(703) 760-4830
Executive Vice President, External Affairs			
O'REGAN, Tim		Tel:	(703) 760-4830
Vice President, Communications			
media@cyrencall.com			
PAULL, IV, James		Tel:	(703) 760-4830
Vice President and Managing Director, Strategic Initiatives			

Cytec Industries

A specialty chemicals and materials company.
www.cytec.com
Annual Revenues: $2.03 billion
Employees: 4,600
Ticker: NYSE: CYT
SIC: 2890
Industry/ies: Business; Small Business
Legislative Issues: DEF

Chairman of the Board, President and Chief Executive Officer		Tel:	(973) 357-3100
FLEMING, Shane D.		Fax:	(973) 357-3065

Main Headquarters
Mailing:	Five Garret Mountain Plaza	Tel:	(973) 357-3100
	Woodland Park, NJ 07424	Fax:	(973) 357-3065
		TF:	(800) 652-6013

Public Affairs and Related Activities Personnel

At Headquarters

ALLEN - DE WAAL, Jodi		Tel:	(973) 357-3283
Global Director, Investor Relations and Strategic Communications		Fax:	(973) 357-3065
Jodi.Allen@cytec.com			
AVRIN, William N.		Tel:	(973) 357-3100
Vice President, Corporate and Business Development		Fax:	(973) 357-3065
william_arvin@gm.cytec.com			
CHARLES, M. Regina		Tel:	(973) 357-3100
Vice President, Human Resources		Fax:	(973) 357-3065
regina.charles@cytec.com			
DARAZSDI, Daniel G.		Tel:	(973) 357-3100
Vice President and Chief Financial Officer		Fax:	(973) 357-3065
SMITH, Roy		Tel:	(973) 357-3100
Vice President, General Counsel and Secretary		Fax:	(973) 357-3065
Roy.Smith@cytec.com			

Cytomedix, Inc.

A biotechnology company.
www.cytomedix.com
Employees: 50
Ticker: NYSE: GTF
SIC: 3841
Industry/ies: Medicine/Health Care/Mental Health; Science; Scientific Research
Legislative Issues: MMM; VET

Chairman of the Board and Contact, Investor Relations		Tel:	(240) 499-2680
JORDEN, David E.		Fax:	(240) 499-2690
Chief Executive Officer		Tel:	(240) 499-2680
ROSENDALE, Martin		Fax:	(240) 499-2690

Main Headquarters
Mailing:	207A Perry Pkwy.	Tel:	(240) 499-2680
	Suite One	Fax:	(240) 499-2690
	Gaithersburg, MD 20877		

Public Affairs and Related Activities Personnel

At Headquarters

RICE, Michael		Tel:	(646) 597-6979
Contact, Investor Relations		Fax:	(240) 499-2690
mrice@lifesciadvisors.com			
SHALLCROSS, Steven A.		Tel:	(240) 499-2680
Chief Financial Officer, Secretary and Treasurer		Fax:	(240) 499-2690

D Squared Tax Strategies LLC

Tax lobbying.
www.dsquaredtax.com
Legislative Issues: ENG; TAX

Chief Executive Officer		Tel:	(703) 623-7317
JADAV, Dhaval		Fax:	(202) 342-1904
dhaval.jadav@alliantgroup.com			

Main Headquarters
Mailing:	3238 P St. NW	Tel:	(703) 623-7317
	Washington, DC 20007	Fax:	(202) 342-1904

Public Affairs and Related Activities Personnel

At Headquarters

LEVY O'DONNELL, Dawn		Tel:	(703) 623-7317
Federal Lobbyist		Fax:	(202) 342-1904
Registered Federal Lobbyist			
MISTR, Christine R.		Tel:	(703) 623-7317
		Fax:	(202) 342-1904

D. E. Shaw and Company

The D. E. Shaw group is a global investment and technology development firm. Its activities range from the deployment of investment strategies based on either mathematical models or human expertise to the acquisition of existing companies and the financing or development of new ones.
www.deshaw.com
Annual Revenues: $49.7 million
Employees: 1,300
Industry/ies: Banking/Finance/Investments
Legislative Issues: FIN

Founder and Chairman of the Board		Tel:	(212) 478-0000
SHAW, David E.		Fax:	(212) 478-0100

Main Headquarters
Mailing:	1166 Avenue of the Americas	Tel:	(212) 478-0000
	Ninth Floor	Fax:	(212) 478-0100
	New York City, NY 10036		

Public Affairs and Related Activities Personnel

At Headquarters

LIFTIN, John M.		Tel:	(212) 478-0000
General Counsel and Managing Director		Fax:	(212) 478-0100
john.liftin@deshaw.com			
ZABACK, Christopher		Tel:	(212) 478-0000
Chief Financial Officer		Fax:	(212) 478-0100

D.E Master Blenders 1753, Inc.

D.E Master Blenders 1753 is an international coffee and tea company, headquartered in the Netherlands.
www.demasterblenders1753.com/en
Annual Revenues: $3.64 Billion
Employees: 7,500
Ticker: AMS:DE
Industry/ies: Beverage Industry; Food And Beverage Industry

Chief Executive Officer		Tel:	(+ 31)
LAUBIES, Pierre			05581753

D.R. Horton, Inc.

Commercial and residential real estate developers. The company engages in the acquisition and development of land; and construction and sale of residential homes.
www.drhorton.com
Annual Revenues: $9.32 billion
Employees: 5,621
Ticker: NYSE: DHI
SIC: 1521
NAICS: 236115
Industry/ies: Real Estate

Chairman of the Board		Tel:	(817) 390-8200
HORTON, Donald R.		Fax:	(817) 390-1715
dhorton@drhorton.com			
President and Chief Executive Officer		Tel:	(817) 390-8200
AULD, David		Fax:	(817) 390-1715

Main Headquarters
Mailing:	301 Commerce St.	Tel:	(817) 390-8200
	Suite 500	Fax:	(817) 390-1715
	Fort Worth, TX 76102		

Public Affairs and Related Activities Personnel

At Headquarters

HANSEN, Jessica		Tel:	(817) 390-8200
Vice President, Communications		Fax:	(817) 390-1715
HARBOUR, Ted I.		Tel:	(817) 390-8200
Chief Legal Officer		Fax:	(817) 390-1715

WHEAT, Bill W.	Tel:	(817) 390-8200	
Executive Vice President and Chief Financial Officer	Fax:	(817) 390-1715	

Daiichi Sankyo

A pharmaceutical company.
www.dsi.com
Annual Revenues: $185.20 million
Employees: 250
Industry/ies: Pharmaceutical Industry
Legislative Issues: HCR; MMM

President and Chief Executive Officer — Tel: (973) 359-2600
GARGIULO, John P. — Fax: (973) 359-2645

Main Headquarters
Mailing: Two Hilton Ct. — Tel: (973) 359-2600
Parsippany, NJ 07054 — Fax: (973) 359-2645

Washington Office
Mailing: 1825 K St. NW — Tel: (202) 223-6572
Suite 425
Washington, DC 20006

Corporate Foundations and Giving Programs
Daiichi Sankyo Contributions Program
Two Hilton Ct. — Tel: (973) 359-2600
Parsippany, NJ 07054 — Fax: (973) 359-2645

Public Affairs and Related Activities Personnel

At Headquarters

DARGENTO, Alyssa — Tel: (973) 944-2913
Director, Product Public Relations — Fax: (973) 359-2645
adargento@dsi.com

MUSKUS, Richard — Tel: (973) 359-2600
Senior Manger, Accounting, Finance, Compliance and Supply — Fax: (973) 359-2645
Chain Operations

At Washington Office

DENG, Qing — Tel: (202) 223-6572
PAC Contact

GILGORE, Lance S. — Tel: (202) 223-6572
Executive Director, Government Affairs & Public Policy
lgilgore@dsi.com
Registered Federal Lobbyist

Daimler AG

A global automotive company and the parent company of Mercedes-Benz. Headquartered in Stuggart, Germany. Demerged with Chrysler in 2007.
www.daimler.com
SIC: 3711
Industry/ies: Automotive Industry; Transportation
Legislative Issues: AUT; BAN; BUD; ENV; TAX; TRD; TRU

President — Tel: (503) 745-8000
DAUM, Martin — Fax: (503) 745-5096

Main Headquarters
Mailing: 4747 Channel Ave. — Tel: (503) 745-8000
Portland, OR 97217 — Fax: (503) 745-5096

Washington Office
Mailing: 1401 H St. NW, Suite 700
Washington, DC 20005

Washington Office
Mailing: 575 Seventh St. NW
W4003
Washington, DC 20004

Public Affairs and Related Activities Personnel

At Headquarters

HOWE, Jörg — Tel: (503) 745-8000
Contact, Global Communications — Fax: (503) 745-8921
joerg.howe@daimler.com

At Other Offices

ALBERT, Cynthia — Tel: (202) 414-6751
State Relations Manager — Fax: (202) 414-6729
1717 Pennsylvania Ave. NW, Suite 825
Washington, DC 20006
cynthia.albert@daimler.com

ALTSCHUL, Jessica — Tel: (202) 414-6704
Manager, Public Policy and CSR Mandates — Fax: (202) 414-6790
1717 Pennsylvania Ave. NW, Suite 825
Washington, DC 20006
jessica.altschul@daimler.com

CRAVEN, William — Tel: (202) 414-6763
Senior Manager, Regulatory Affairs — Fax: (202) 414-6790
1717 Pennsylvania Ave. NW, Suite 825
Washington, DC 20006

FOUST, Joanna — Tel: (202) 414-6752

General Manager, Federal Affairs — Fax: (202) 414-6790
1717 Pennsylvania Ave. NW, Suite 825
Washington, DC 20006
Registered Federal Lobbyist

JONES, Jake — Tel: (202) 414-6746
Executive Director, External Affairs and Public Policy — Fax: (202) 414-6729
1717 Pennsylvania Ave. NW, Suite 825
Washington, DC 20006
jake.jones@daimler.com
Registered Federal Lobbyist

TREBING, David — Tel: (202) 414-6793
General Manager, State and Local Relations — Fax: (202) 414-6790
1717 Pennsylvania Ave. NW, Suite 825
Washington, DC 20006

WERNER, Jeff — Tel: (202) 414-6700
General Manager, International & Public Policy
1717 Pennsylvania Ave. NW, Suite 825
Washington, DC 20006
Registered Federal Lobbyist

Dairy Farmers of America

Manufacturer of cheese and butter, as well as dairy ingredients, and contract manufacturer for consumer products.
www.dfamilk.com
SIC: 2021; 2023; 2026
NAICS: 311512; 311511; 311514
Industry/ies: Agriculture/Agronomy; Dairy Industry; Food And Beverage Industry
Legislative Issues: AGR; BUD; ENV; FOO; IMM; RET; TAX; TRA; TRD

President and Chief Executive Officer — Tel: (816) 801-6455
SMITH, Richard P. — Fax: (816) 801-6456
rsmith@dfamilk.com

Main Headquarters
Mailing: 10220 N. Ambassador Dr. — Tel: (816) 801-6455
Kansas City, MO 64153

Political Action Committees
Dairy Farmers of America, Inc. DEPAC (Dairy Education PAC)
FEC ID: C00001388
Contact: J. Sam Stone
P.O. Box 909700 — Tel: (816) 801-6455
Kansas City, MO 64153 — Fax: (816) 801-6456

Contributions to Candidates: $150,700 (2015-2016)
Democrats: $40,000; Republicans: $109,700; Other: $1,000

Principal Recipients

SENATE
SCHUMER, CHARLES E (DEM-NY)

HOUSE
PETERSON, COLLIN CLARK (DEM-MN)

Corporate Foundations and Giving Programs
DFA Cares Foundation
Contact: Ron Hilmes
10220 N. Ambassador Dr. — Tel: (816) 801-6455
Kansas City, MO 64190 — Fax: (816) 801-6455

Public Affairs and Related Activities Personnel

At Headquarters

GEISLER, David A. — Tel: (816) 801-6455
Senior Vice President, Legal and Administration
dgeisler@dfamilk.com

HILMES, Ron — Tel: (816) 801-6455
Contact, Foundation

HOFF, Stephanie — Tel: (816) 801-6455
Manager, Media Relations
sthoff@dfamilk.com

MASSEY, Monica — Tel: (816) 801-6455
Senior Vice President, Corporate Affairs
mmassey@dfamilk.com

REGAN, Annette — Tel: (816) 801-6455
Senior Vice President, Human Resources
aregan@dfamilk.com

WALDVOGEL, Jay — Tel: (816) 801-6455
Senior Vice President, Strategy and International Development
jwaldvogel@dfamilk.com

WICKHAM, Greg — Tel: (816) 801-6455
Chief Financial Officer

WILSON, John — Tel: (816) 801-6455
Senior Vice President and Chief Fluid Marketing Officer
jwilson@dfamilk.com

At Other Offices

BACHELOR, Alex — Tel: (816) 801-6444

Senior Vice President and General Counsel
P.O. BOX 909700
Kansas City, MO 64190
abachelor@dfamilk.com
Fax: (816) 801-6456

KLIPPENSTEIN, Jackie
Vice President, Industry and Government Affairs
P.O. BOX 909700
Kansas City, MO 64190
jklippenstein@dfamilk.com
Registered Federal Lobbyist
Tel: (816) 801-6455
Fax: (816) 801-6456

MEYER, David
Senior Vice President, Finance
P.O. BOX 909700
Kansas City, MO 64190
dmeyer@dfamilk.com
Tel: (816) 801-6455
Fax: (816) 801-6456

STONE, J. Sam
Vice President, Government Relations
P.O. BOX 909700
Kansas City, MO 64190
sstone@dfamilk.com
Registered Federal Lobbyist
Tel: (816) 801-6474
Fax: (816) 801-6456

Dairylea Cooperative, Inc.

A farmer-owned agricultural marketing and service organization.
www.dairylea.com
Annual Revenues: $1.58 billion
Employees: 100
Industry/ies: Agriculture/Agronomy

Chairman and President
BEEMAN, William
william.beeman@dairylea.com
Tel: (315) 433-0100
Fax: (315) 433-2345

Chief Executive Officer
WICKHAM, Gregory I.
greg.wickham@dairylea.com
Tel: (315) 433-0100
Fax: (315) 433-2345

Main Headquarters
Mailing: P.O. Box 4844
Syracuse, NY 13221
Tel: (315) 433-0100
Fax: (315) 433-2345
TF: (800) 654-8838

Political Action Committees
Dairylea Cooperative PAC AKA (LEAPAC)
FEC ID: C00143818
Contact: Ellen M. O'Connor
P.O. Box 4844
Syracuse, NY 13221
Tel: (315) 433-0100
Fax: (315) 433-2345

Public Affairs and Related Activities Personnel

At Headquarters

CARTIER, Karen
Vice President, Communications and Legislative Affairs
Tel: (315) 433-0100
Fax: (315) 433-2345

GALLAGHER, Ed
Vice President, Economics and Risk Management
ed.gallagher@dairylea.com
Tel: (315) 433-0100
Fax: (315) 433-2345

HUSON, Jennifer
Director, Communications
Jennifer.Huson@dairylea.com
Tel: (800) 654-8838
Fax: (315) 433-2345

O'CONNOR, Ellen M.
PAC Treasurer
Tel: (315) 433-0100
Fax: (315) 433-2345

Dakota Minnesota and Eastern Railroad

Operate services across the midwestern and southeastern United States.
Employees: 1,000
Industry/ies: Railroads; Transportation

Main Headquarters
Mailing: 140 N. Phillips Ave.
Sioux Falls, SD 57104
Tel: (605) 782-1200
Fax: (605) 782-1299

Public Affairs and Related Activities Personnel

At Headquarters

ANDERSON, LA
Senior Vice President, Marketing
Tel: (605) 782-1200
Fax: (605) 782-1299

Dana Holding Corporation

A manufacturer of automotive systems equipment, provides power technologies and service parts.
www.dana.com
Annual Revenues: $6.54 billion
Employees: 23,200
Ticker: NYSE: DAN
SIC: 3714
Industry/ies: Automotive Industry; Machinery/Equipment; Transportation

Chairman of the Board
MUSCARI, Joseph C.
Tel: (419) 887-3000
Fax: (419) 887-5200

President and Chief Executive Officer
WOOD, Roger J.
Tel: (419) 887-3000
Fax: (419) 887-5200

Main Headquarters
Mailing: 3939 Technology Dr.
Maumee, OH 43537
Tel: (419) 887-3000
Fax: (419) 887-5200

Corporate Foundations and Giving Programs
Dana Holding Corporation Foundation
P.O. Box 1000
Toldeo, OH 43697
Tel: (419) 535-4500

Public Affairs and Related Activities Personnel

At Headquarters

BOWEN, Jeff
Chief Administrative Officer
Tel: (419) 887-3000
Fax: (419) 887-5200

COLE, Jeff
Director, Marketing Communications
jeff.cole@dana.com
Tel: (419) 887-3535
Fax: (419) 887-5200

HARTLAGE, Chuck
Manager, Corporate and Executive Communications
chuck.hartlage@dana.com
Tel: (419) 887-5123
Fax: (419) 887-5200

LEVIN, Marc C.
Senior Vice President, General Counsel and Secretary
marc.levin@dana.com
Tel: (419) 535-4500
Fax: (419) 535-4756

QUIGLEY, III, William G.
Executive Vice President and Chief Financial Officer
Tel: (419) 887-3000
Fax: (419) 887-5200

Danaher Corporation

Designs, manufactures, and markets products and services to professional, medical, industrial, and commercial customers.
www.danaher.com
Annual Revenues: $20.12 billion
Employees: 71,000
Ticker: NYSE: DHR
SIC: 3823
NAICS: 332212
Industry/ies: Automotive Industry; Electricity & Electronics; Electronics; Energy/Electricity; Machinery/Equipment; Transportation

Co-Founder
RALES, Steven M.
Tel: (202) 828-0850
Fax: (202) 828-0860

President and Chief Executive Officer
JOYCE JR, Thomas P
Tel: (202) 828-0850
Fax: (202) 828-0860

Main Headquarters
Mailing: 2200 Pennsylvania Ave. NW
Suite 800 West
Washington, DC 20037
Tel: (202) 828-0850
Fax: (202) 828-0860

Corporate Foundations and Giving Programs
Danaher Foundation
2099 Pennsylvania Ave. NW
12th Floor
Washington, DC 20006
Tel: (202) 828-0850
Fax: (202) 828-0850

Public Affairs and Related Activities Personnel

At Headquarters

BECK, Mark A.
Executive Vice President
Tel: (202) 828-0850
Fax: (202) 828-0860

COMAS, Daniel L.
Executive Vice President and Chief Financial Officer
Tel: (202) 828-0850
Fax: (202) 828-0860

ELLIS, Brian W.
Senior Vice President and General Counsel
Tel: (202) 828-0850
Fax: (202) 828-0860

KING, IV, William H.
Senior Vice President, Strategic Development
Tel: (202) 828-0850
Fax: (202) 828-0860

LALOR, Angela S.
Senior Vice President, Human Resources
Tel: (202) 828-0850
Fax: (202) 828-0860

LOWE, Michelle
Executive Assistant
michelle.lowe@danaher.com
Tel: (202) 828-0850
Fax: (202) 828-0860

LUTZ, Robert S.
Senior Vice President and Chief Accounting Officer
Tel: (202) 828-0850
Fax: (202) 828-0860

MCGREW, Matt R.
Group Chief Financial Officer, Life Sciences
matt.mcgrew@danaher.com
Tel: (202) 828-0850
Fax: (202) 828-0860

RASKAS, Daniel A.
Senior Vice President, Corporate Development
daniel.raskas@danaher.com
Tel: (202) 828-0850
Fax: (202) 828-0860

Danfoss, Inc.

Manufacturer of valves and fluid handling components for HVAC equipment.
www.danfoss.com
Industry/ies: Energy/Electricity; Engineering/Mathematics; Heating And Air Conditioning; Machinery/Equipment

| **Chairman, Foundation** | Tel: | (410) 931-8250 |
| CLAUSEN, Peter M. | Fax: | (410) 931-8256 |

| **President and Chief Executive Officer** | Tel: | (410) 931-8250 |
| CHRISTIANSEN, Niels B. | Fax: | (410) 931-8256 |

Main Headquarters

| Mailing: 11655 Crossroads Cir. | Tel: | (410) 931-8250 |
| Baltimore, MD 21220 | Fax: | (410) 931-8256 |

Corporate Foundations and Giving Programs

Danfoss Foundation for Education
Contact: Peter M. Clausen
11655 Crossroads Cir.
Baltimore, MD 21220

Public Affairs and Related Activities Personnel

At Headquarters

| CHRISTENSEN, Jesper V. | Tel: | (410) 931-8250 |
| *Executive Vice Presdient and Chief Financial Officer* | Fax: | (410) 931-8256 |

| FAUSING , Kim | Tel: | (410) 931-8250 |
| *Executive Vice President, Chief Operations Officer* | Fax: | (410) 931-8256 |

HOLLOWAY, Jonathan	Tel:	(410) 513-1158
Manager, Marketing and Contact, Media	Fax:	(410) 931-8256
Jonathan.Holloway@danfoss.com		

Dannenbaum Engineering

A consulting firm that provides civil, structural, environmental and transportation solutions for clients in both the private and public sectors.
www.dannenbaum.com
Annual Revenues: $19.40 million
Employees: 100
Industry/ies: Engineering/Mathematics

| **Chairman of the Board** | Tel: | (713) 520-9570 |
| CHAMBERS, Webb | Fax: | (713) 513-4111 |

| **Chief Executive Officer** | Tel: | (713) 520-9570 |
| DANNEBAUM, James | Fax: | (713) 527-6338 |

Main Headquarters

| Mailing: 3100 W. Alabama St. | Tel: | (713) 520-9570 |
| Houston, TX 77098-2004 | Fax: | (713) 513-4111 |

Public Affairs and Related Activities Personnel

At Headquarters

| AHRENS, Wayne G | Tel: | (713) 520-9570 |
| *Principal and Chief Operating Officer* | Fax: | (713) 513-4111 |

CELAURO, Paul	Tel:	(713) 520-9570
Contact, Corporate Development	Fax:	(713) 527-6338
corporatedevelopment@dannenbaum.com		

MCCORMAC, Christopher	Tel:	(713) 520-9570
Contact, Human Resources	Fax:	(713) 527-6442
c.mccormac@dannenbaum.com		

Darden Restaurants, Inc.

A casual dining company. Restaurant divisions include Red Lobster, Olive Garden, Bahama Breeze and Smokey Bones.
www.darden.com
Annual Revenues: $6.54 billion
Employees: 206,489
Ticker: NYSE: DRI
SIC: 5812
Industry/ies: Food And Beverage Industry
Legislative Issues: TAX

| **Chairman of the Board and Chief Executive Officer** | Tel: | (407) 245-4000 |
| OTIS, Jr., Clarence | Fax: | (407) 245-5389 |

Main Headquarters

| Mailing: P.O. Box 695011 | Tel: | (407) 245-4000 |
| Orlando, FL 32869-5011 | Fax: | (407) 245-5389 |

Political Action Committees

Darden Restaurants, Inc. Employees Good Government Fund PAC
FEC ID: C00108282
Contact: Robert S. McAdam

| 1000 Darden Center Dr. | Tel: | (407) 245-6734 |
| Orlando, FL 32837 | Fax: | (407) 245-4462 |

Contributions to Candidates: $106,000 (2015-2016)
Democrats: $38,500; Republicans: $67,500

Corporate Foundations and Giving Programs

Darden Restaurants Foundation
Contact: Clarence Otis Jr.

| P.O. Box 593330 | Tel: | (407) 245-4000 |
| Orlando, FL 32859 | Fax: | (407) 245-5389 |

Public Affairs and Related Activities Personnel

At Headquarters

| BOJALAD, Ronald | Tel: | (407) 245-4000 |

| | Fax: | (407) 245-5389 |
| *Senior Vice President, Operations Human Resources* | | |

JEFFERS, Rich	Tel:	(407) 245-4189
Director, Media Relations	Fax:	(407) 245-5389
rjeffers@darden.com		

| KIRGAN, Danielle | Tel: | (407) 245-4000 |
| *Senior Vice President, Chief Human Resources Officer* | Fax: | (407) 245-5389 |

| LEE, Eugene | Tel: | (407) 245-4000 |
| *President Chief Operating Officer* | Fax: | (407) 245-5389 |

| LOTHROP, Dave | Tel: | (407) 245-4000 |
| *Senior Vice President Corporate Controller* | Fax: | (407) 245-5389 |

| MCADAM, Robert S. | Tel: | (407) 245-4000 |
| *Senior Vice President, Government & Community Affairs* | Fax: | (407) 245-5389 |

| PARK, Matt | Tel: | (407) 245-4000 |
| *Senior Vice President Chief Marketing Officer* | Fax: | (407) 245-5389 |

| RICHMOND, C. Bradford | Tel: | (407) 245-4000 |
| *Senior Vice President and Chief Financial Officer* | Fax: | (407) 245-5389 |

At Other Offices

CONNELLY, Susan	Tel:	(407) 245-6734
Vice President, State and Local Government Relations	Fax:	(407) 245-4462
1000 Darden Center Dr.		
Orlando, FL 32837		
SConnelly@darden.com		

HULETT, Sherry	Tel:	(407) 245-4000
1000 Darden Center Dr.	Fax:	(407) 245-4462
Orlando, FL 32837		

Darling International Inc.

Rendering, recycling and recovery solutions to the nation's food industry.
www.darlingii.com
Annual Revenues: $3.96 billion
Employees: 10,000
Ticker: NYSE: DAR
SIC: 2048; 2077
NAICS: 311613; 311225
Industry/ies: Animals; Food And Beverage Industry
Legislative Issues: ENV

| **Chairman of the Board and Chief Executive Officer** | Tel: | (972) 717-0300 |
| STUEWE, Randall C. | Fax: | (972) 717-1588 |

Main Headquarters

Mailing: 251 O'Connor Ridge Blvd.	Tel:	(972) 717-0300
Suite 300	Fax:	(972) 717-1588
Irving, TX 75038		

Public Affairs and Related Activities Personnel

At Headquarters

| BULLOCK, John | Tel: | (972) 717-0300 |
| *Executive Vice President and Chief Strategy Officer* | Fax: | (972) 717-1588 |

GAITHER, Melissa A.	Tel:	(972) 281-4478
Director, Investor Relations	Fax:	(972) 717-1588
MGaither@darlingii.com		

| KLOOSTERBOER, Dirk | Tel: | (972) 717-0300 |
| *Chief Operating Officer* | Fax: | (972) 717-1588 |

| MUSE, John O. | Tel: | (972) 717-0300 |
| *Executive Vice President and Chief Financial Officer* | Fax: | (972) 717-1588 |

| STERLING, John F. | Tel: | (972) 717-0300 |
| *Executive Vice President, General Counsel and Secretary* | Fax: | (972) 717-1588 |

Dassault Systèmes

Formerly Intercim. Acquired by Dassault Systemes March 16, 2011. 3D EXPERIENCE Company, provides business and people with virtual universes to imagine sustainable innovations.
www.3ds.com
Annual Revenues: $4.60 million
Employees: 42
SIC: 3089
Industry/ies: Aerospace/Aviation; Automotive Industry; Computer/Technology; Defense/Homeland Security; Government-Related; Pharmaceutical Industry; Transportation

| **Chairman of the Board** | Tel: | (781) 810-3000 |
| EDELSTENNE, Charles | Fax: | (651) 289-3420 |

| **President and Chief Executive Officer** | Tel: | (781) 810-3000 |
| CHARLÈS, Bernard | Fax: | (651) 289-3420 |

Main Headquarters

Mailing: 175 Wyman St.	Tel:	(781) 810-3000
Waltham, MA 02451	Fax:	(651) 289-3420
	TF:	(800) 343-3734

Public Affairs and Related Activities Personnel

At Headquarters

| DALOZ, Pascal | Tel: | (781) 810-3000 |
| | Fax: | (651) 289-3420 |

Executive Vice President, Corporate Strategy and Market Development

FORESTIER, Philippe	Tel:	(781) 810-3000
Executive Vice President, Global Affairs and Communities	Fax:	(651) 289-3420
MENGHINI, Monica	Tel:	(781) 810-3000
Executive Vice President, Industry, Marketing and Corporate Communications	Fax:	(651) 289-3420
TERSANT, Thibault de	Tel:	(781) 810-3000
Senior Executive Vice President and Chief Financial Officer	Fax:	(651) 289-3420
VISCAROLASAGA, Jenny	Tel:	(617) 331-4944
Contact, Media Relations	Fax:	(651) 289-3420
jenny.v@tworoadscommunications.com		

Davenport McKesson Corporation

International Relations & Strategic Communications firm.
davenportmckesson.us
Legislative Issues: TRD

Main Headquarters

Mailing:	100 Oliver St.	Tel:	(617) 571-6689
	Suite 1400	Fax:	(617) 507-6115
	Boston, MA 02110		

Public Affairs and Related Activities Personnel

At Headquarters

DANIELS, Ethan	Tel:	(617) 571-6689
Registered Federal Lobbyist	Fax:	(617) 507-6115
DUNN, Hon. Jennifer	Tel:	(617) 571-6689
	Fax:	(617) 507-6115
MONTGOMERY, Christopher	Tel:	(617) 571-6689
Registered Federal Lobbyist	Fax:	(617) 507-6115

David Thomas

Lobbyist.
www.davidthomas.com

Main Headquarters

Mailing: 2572 Weston St.
           Auburn, AL 36832

Public Affairs and Related Activities Personnel

At Headquarters

BROWNE , Doreen
Administration Director
doreenbrowne@davidthomas.com

FURNISS , Carol
Accounts Manager
carolfurniss@davidthomas.com

MITCHELL , Kevin
Managing Director
kevinmitchell@davidthomas.com

NARRAMORE, Gill
Sales and Marketing Manager
gillnarramore@davidthomas.com

POYSER , Robert
Quality Assurance and Regulatory Manager
robertpoyser@davidthomas.com

ROLFE , Peter
Technical Director
peterrolfe@davidthomas.com

THOMAS, David
Managing Member
Registered Federal Lobbyist

Davis and Floyd Engineering

Provides engineering, architectural, environmental and laboratory services.
www.davisfloyd.com
Employees: 200
Industry/ies: Engineering/Mathematics

Chairman of the Board	Tel:	(864) 229-5211
DAVIS, Jr., Emmett I.	Fax:	(864) 229-7844

President, Chief Executive Officer	Tel:	(864) 229-5211
DAVIS, Stephen L.	Fax:	(864) 229-7844
sldavis@davisfloyd.com		

Main Headquarters

Mailing: 240 Stoneridge Dr.
           Suite 305
           Columbia, SC 29210

Public Affairs and Related Activities Personnel

At Other Offices

EPPLEY, Jason P.	Tel:	(864) 229-5211
Chief Operating Officer	Fax:	(864) 229-7844

1319 Hwy 72/221 East
Greenwood, SC 29649
jeppley@davisfloyd.com

LAWRENCE, Natalie J.	Tel:	(864) 229-5211
Director of Brand and Communications	Fax:	(864) 229-7844

1319 Hwy 72/221 East
Greenwood, SC 29649
nlawrence@davisfloyd.com

REIDENBACH, J. Rhett	Tel:	(864) 229-5211
Chief Strategy Officer	Fax:	(864) 229-7844

1319 Hwy 72/221 East
Greenwood, SC 29649
rreidenb@davisfloyd.com

WARNER, Mark	Tel:	(864) 229-5211
Director of Business Development	Fax:	(864) 229-7844

1319 Hwy 72/221 East
Greenwood, SC 29649
mwarner@davisfloyd.com

DaVita, Inc.

An independent provider of kidney dialysis services.
www.davita.com
Annual Revenues: $13.03 billion
Employees: 57,900
Ticker: NYSE: DVA
SIC: 8090
Industry/ies: Medicine/Health Care/Mental Health
Legislative Issues: HCR; MED; MMM; VET

Co-Chairman of the Board and Chief Executive Officer	Tel:	(303) 405-2100
THIRY, Kent		

Main Headquarters

Mailing:	2000 16th St.	Tel:	(303) 405-2100
	Denver, CO 80202	TF:	(800) 244-0680

Washington Office

Mailing: 500 N. Capitol St. NW
           Suite 300
           Washington, DC 20001

Political Action Committees

Davita Healthcare Partners, Inc. PAC (DAPAC)
FEC ID: C00340943
Contact: Lin Whatcott David
601 Hawaii St.
El Segundo, CA 90245

Contributions to Candidates: $433,250 (2015-2016)
Democrats: $176,000; Republicans: $255,250; Other: $2,000

Principal Recipients

HOUSE
RYAN, PAUL D. (REP-WI)
SHIMKUS, JOHN M (REP-IL)

Corporate Foundations and Giving Programs

DaVita Children's Foundation		
2000 16th St.	Tel:	(303) 405-2100
Denver, CO 80202		

KT Family Foundation		
2000 16th St.	Tel:	(303) 405-2100
Denver, CO 80202		

Public Affairs and Related Activities Personnel

At Headquarters

HILGER, James K.	Tel:	(303) 405-2100
Interim Chief Financial Officer and Chief Accounting Officer		
JIGANTI , Jeanine M.	Tel:	(303) 405-2100
Chief Compliance Officer		
MENZEL, Dr. Garry E.	Tel:	(303) 405-2100
Chief Financial Officer		
RIVERA, Kim M.	Tel:	(303) 405-2100
Chief Legal Officer		
THURMAN, Skip	Tel:	(303) 405-2100
Senior Director, Communications		

At Washington Office

MARTINEZ, Javier D.
Registered Federal Lobbyist

PARKER, Gary
Administration

PARKS, Derron

SANDERS, David
Federal Lobbyist
Registered Federal Lobbyist

WHIDBY, Gary
PAC Manager

At Other Offices

DAVID, Lin Whatcott
PAC Treasurer
32275 32nd Ave., South
Federal Way, WA 98001
lin.whatcott@davita.com

GUSTAFSON, Jim	Tel:	(310) 536-2585
Vice President, Investor Relations	Fax:	(310) 536-2675
601 Hawaii St.		
El Segundo, CA 90245		
ir@davita.com		

MILDENBERGER, Laura — Tel: (310) 536-2400
Chief People Officer — Fax: (310) 536-2675
601 Hawaii St.
El Segundo, CA 90245

PARK, Phil W. — Tel: (202) 789-6910
Federal Lobbyist — Fax: (866) 594-5447
900 Seventh St. NW, Suite 680
Washington, DC 20001
Registered Federal Lobbyist

THORNHILL, Joelle — Tel: (202) 789-6910
Vice President — Fax: (866) 594-5447
900 Seventh St. NW, Suite 680
Washington, DC 20001
joelle.thornhill@davita.com
Registered Federal Lobbyist

ZUMWALT, LeAnne — Tel: (650) 696-8910
Group Vice President — Fax: (310) 536-2675
601 Hawaii St.
El Segundo, CA 90245
ir@davita.com
Registered Federal Lobbyist

Day and Zimmermann, Inc.

Provides engineering and construction, design, plant maintenance, security, staffing, munitions decommissioning, validation, and asset management services worldwide.
www.dayzim.com
Annual Revenues: $8851.40 billion
Employees: 33,200
Industry/ies: Architecture And Design; Engineering/Mathematics; Management; Real Estate
Legislative Issues: BUD; DEF; LBR

Chairman of the Board and Chief Executive Officer — Tel: (215) 299-8000
YOH, III, Harold L. — Fax: (215) 299-8030

Main Headquarters
Mailing: 1500 Spring Garden St. — Tel: (215) 299-8000
Philadelphia, PA 19130 — Fax: (215) 299-8030

Washington Office
Mailing: 1655 N. Fort Myer Dr.
Suite 520
Arlington, VA 22209

Political Action Committees
Day & Zimmerman Inc. Federal PAC (AKA DayPAC -Federal)
FEC ID: C00341271
Contact: Dale Biegelman
1500 Spring Garden St. — Tel: (215) 299-8000
Philadelphia, PA 19130 — Fax: (215) 299-8000

Contributions to Candidates: $61,000 (2015-2016)
Democrats: $15,000; Republicans: $46,000

Principal Recipients

SENATE
BOOZMAN, JOHN (REP-AR)

Public Affairs and Related Activities Personnel

At Headquarters

BIEGELMAN, Dale — Tel: (215) 299-8000
PAC Treasurer — Fax: (215) 299-8030

COADY, Fran — Tel: (215) 299-8000
Senior Vice President, Human Resources — Fax: (215) 299-8030

DIMARCO, John — Tel: (215) 299-8000
President, Government Services — Fax: (215) 299-8030
John.DiMarco@dayzim.com

HAMM, William R. — Tel: (215) 299-8000
Senior Vice President, General Counsel and Secretary — Fax: (215) 299-8030
william.hamm@dayzim.com

MURRAY, Theresa — Tel: (610) 642-8253
Contact, Media Relations — Fax: (215) 299-8030
Theresa@GregoryFCA.com

RITZEL, Joseph — Tel: (215) 299-8000
Senior Vice President, Finance and Chief Financial Officer — Fax: (215) 299-8030

At Other Offices

HICKEY, Jr., James J. J. — Tel: (703) 527-2147
Vice President, Governmental Affairs — Fax: (703) 527-2850
1700 N. Moore St., Suite 1502
Arlington, VA 22209
james.hickey@dayzim.com
Registered Federal Lobbyist

JAMES, Hickey — Tel: (703) 527-2147
Federal Lobbyist
1700 N. Moore St., Suite 1502
Arlington, VA 22209
Registered Federal Lobbyist

Day Kimball Healthcare, Inc.

Day Kimball Healthcare is a non-profit, integrated medical services provider. The mission of Day Kimball Healthcare is to meet the health needs of their community through their core values of clinical quality, customer service, fiscal responsibility and local control.
www.daykimball.org
Employees: 1,000
Industry/ies: Medicine/Health Care/Mental Health

Chairman of the Board — Tel: (860) 928-6541
ADILETTA, Joseph — Fax: (860) 774-3366

President and Chief Executive Officer — Tel: (860) 928-6541
SMANIK, Robert — Fax: (860) 774-3366

Main Headquarters
Mailing: 320 Pomfret St. — Tel: (860) 928-6541
Putnam, CT 06260 — Fax: (860) 774-3366

Public Affairs and Related Activities Personnel

At Headquarters

DUNN, Laura — Tel: (860) 928-6541
Director, Marketing and Communications — Fax: (860) 774-3366

GLAZIER, Douglas — Tel: (860) 928-6541
Interim Chief Financial Officer — Fax: (860) 774-3366

Dayjet Corporation

www.dayjet.com
Industry/ies: Aerospace/Aviation; Transportation

Main Headquarters
Mailing: 3651 FAU Blvd. — Tel: (561) 454-2655
Suite 200
Boca Raton, FL 33431

Public Affairs and Related Activities Personnel

At Headquarters

DURKIN, III, Charles — Tel: (561) 454-2655
Manager, Government and Community Affairs

Dayton Power and Light Company

See listing on page 264 under DPL Inc.

DDB Worldwide Communications Group Inc.

A worldwide marketing communications network.
www.ddb.com

Chairman and Chief Executive Officer — Tel: (212) 415-2000
HEMPEL, Peter — Fax: (212) 415-3414
peter.hempel@ny.ddb.com

Main Headquarters
Mailing: 437 Madison Ave. — Tel: (212) 415-2000
New York City, NY 10022 — Fax: (212) 415-3550

Public Affairs and Related Activities Personnel

At Headquarters

KAM, Marilyn — Tel: (212) 415-2000
Federal Lobbyist — Fax: (212) 415-3414

Dean Foods Company

Fluid milk and other dairy products processing, sales and distribution. A food and beverage company, processes and distributes milk, and other dairy and dairy case products.
www.deanfoods.com
Annual Revenues: $7.95 billion
Employees: 16,960
Ticker: NYSE: DF
SIC: 2021; 2022; 2026
NAICS: 311512; 311511
Industry/ies: Dairy Industry; Food And Beverage Industry
Legislative Issues: AGR; FOO; HCR; RET

Non-Executive Chairman of the Board — Tel: (214) 303-3400
TURNER, Jim L. — Fax: (214) 303-3499

Chief Executive Office — Tel: (214) 303-3400
TANNER , Gregg A. — Fax: (214) 303-3499

Main Headquarters
Mailing: 2711 N. Haskell Ave. — Tel: (214) 303-3400

Suite 3400
Dallas, TX 75204

Fax: (214) 303-3499

Washington Office
Mailing: 2111 Wilson Blvd.
Suite 700
Arlington, VA 22201

Tel: (703) 351-5022
Fax: (703) 351-9772

Political Action Committees
Dean Foods Company PAC
FEC ID: C00340083
Contact: Edgar DeGuia
2711 N. Haskell Ave.
Suite 3400
Dallas, TX 75204

Contributions to Candidates: $74,125 (2015-2016)
Democrats: $23,500; Republicans: $50,625

Corporate Foundations and Giving Programs
Dean Foods Foundation
Contact: Liliana Esposito
2515 McKinney Ave.
Suite 1200
Dallas, TX 75201

Public Affairs and Related Activities Personnel

At Headquarters

BELLAIRS , Chris
Executive Vice President and Chief Financial Officer

Tel: (214) 303-3400
Fax: (214) 303-3499

BRAUN , Shay
Senior Vice President, Operations and Procurement

Tel: (214) 303-3400
Fax: (214) 303-3499

COX, Dustin
Manager, Corporate Communications
media@deanfoods.com

Tel: (214) 721-7766
Fax: (214) 303-3499

DEGUIA, Edgar
Assistant Treasurer and PAC Treasurer

Tel: (214) 303-3400
Fax: (214) 303-3499

SCOZZAFAVA , Ralph
Executive Vice President and Chief Operating Officer

Tel: (214) 303-3400
Fax: (214) 303-3499

SMITH, Timothy
Vice President and Treasurer
Mail Stop Suite 1200

Tel: (214) 303-3400
Fax: (214) 303-3499

WARMBIER , Kim
Executive Vice President, Human Resources

Tel: (214) 303-3400
Fax: (214) 303-3499

At Washington Office

DIVJAK, Anne
Director, Government & Industry Relations
anne_divjak@deanfoods.com
Registered Federal Lobbyist

Tel: (703) 351-5022
Fax: (703) 351-9772

Deere & Company

A manufacturer of agricultural and forestry equipment; a supplier of equipment used in lawn, grounds, and turf care; and a manufacturer of construction equipment. Also manufactures and markets engines used in heavy equipment and provides financial services.
www.deere.com
Annual Revenues: $32.94 billion
Employees: 59,600
Ticker: NYSE: DE
SIC: 3523; 3519; 3524; 3531; 3537
NAICS: 33312; 333112; 333924; 336399; 333111
Industry/ies: Machinery/Equipment
Legislative Issues: AGR; COM; CPT; ENG; ENV; FIN; HCR; TAX; TRD

Chairman and Chief Executive Officer
ALLEN, Samuel R.

Tel: (309) 765-8000
Fax: (309) 765-5671

Main Headquarters
Mailing: One John Deere Pl.
Moline, IL 61265

Tel: (309) 765-8000
Fax: (309) 765-5671
TF: (800) 765-9588

Washington Office
Mailing: 801 17th St. NW
Second Floor
Washington, DC 20006

Tel: (202) 223-4817
Fax: (202) 296-0011

Political Action Committees
Deere and Company PAC
FEC ID: C00204099
Contact: Joanne E. Woodward
One John Deere Pl.
Moline, IL 61265

Contributions to Candidates: $580,250 (2015-2016)
Democrats: $135,000; Republicans: $445,250

Principal Recipients

SENATE
AYOTTE, KELLY A (REP-NH)
BLUNT, ROY (REP-MO)
HOEVEN, JOHN (REP-ND)

ISAKSON, JOHN HARDY (REP-GA)
KIRK, MARK STEVEN (REP-IL)
PORTMAN, ROB (REP-OH)
THUNE, JOHN (REP-SD)

HOUSE
BOST, MICHAEL (REP-IL)
CONAWAY, MICHAEL HONORABLE (REP-TX)
COSTA, JIM MR. (DEM-CA)
CRAMER, KEVIN MR. (REP-ND)
DAVIS, RODNEY L (REP-IL)
DELBENE, SUZAN K (DEM-WA)
DENHAM, JEFF (REP-CA)
DOLD, ROBERT JAMES JR (REP-IL)
FINCHER, STEVE MR. (REP-TN)
FOXX, VIRGINIA ANN (REP-NC)
HULTGREN, RANDY (REP-IL)
JENKINS, LYNN (REP-KS)
KIND, RONALD JAMES (DEM-WI)
KINZINGER, ADAM (REP-IL)
LAHOOD, DARIN MCKAY (REP-IL)
MCCARTHY, KEVIN (REP-CA)
NOEM, KRISTI LYNN (REP-SD)
NUNES, DEVIN G (REP-CA)
PETERS, SCOTT (DEM-CA)
PRICE, THOMAS EDMUNDS (REP-GA)
REICHERT, DAVE (REP-WA)
ROSKAM, PETER (REP-IL)
RYAN, PAUL D. (REP-WI)
SCALISE, STEVE MR. (REP-LA)
SCOTT, JAMES AUSTIN (REP-GA)
SHIMKUS, JOHN M (REP-IL)
SHUSTER, WILLIAM MR. (REP-PA)
VALADAO, DAVID (REP-CA)
WAGNER, ANN L. (REP-MO)
YODER, KEVIN (REP-KS)
YOUNG, DAVID (REP-IA)

Corporate Foundations and Giving Programs
John Deere Foundation
One John Deer Pl.
Moline, IL 61265

Public Affairs and Related Activities Personnel

At Headquarters

DAVIES, Todd E.
Corporate Secretary and Associate General Counsel

Tel: (309) 765-8000
Fax: (309) 765-5671

EMERSON, Frances B.
Vice President, Corporate Communications and Global Brand Management

Tel: (309) 765-8000
Fax: (309) 765-5772

FRANCQUE, Jason
Director, US Government Affairs
francquejasona@johndeere.com
Registered Federal Lobbyist

Tel: (309) 748-5261
Fax: (309) 765-5671

GUINN, Max A.
Senior Vice President, Human Resources, Communications, Public Affairs, and Labor Relations

Tel: (309) 765-8000
Fax: (309) 765-5671

HAIGHT, Timothy V.
Vice President and Deputy General Counsel

Tel: (309) 765-8000
Fax: (309) 765-5671

HOWZE, Marc A.
Vice President, Global Human Resources and Employee Communications

Tel: (309) 765-8000
Fax: (309) 765-5671

HUEGEL, Tony
Director, Investor Relations

Tel: (309) 765-8000
Fax: (309) 765-5671

ILES, Thom
Director, Public Affairs
ilesthomase@johndeere.com

Tel: (309) 765-8000
Fax: (309) 765-5671

JONES, Collis
Manager, Government Sales
jonescollisr@johndeere.com

Tel: (309) 765-8000
Fax: (309) 765-5671

JONES, Mary K W.
Senior Vice President and General Counsel

Tel: (309) 765-8000
Fax: (309) 765-5671

KALATHUR, Rajesh
Senior Vice President and Chief Financial Officer

Tel: (309) 765-8000
Fax: (309) 765-5671

NELSON, Barry
Manager, Media Relations
NelsonBarryE@JohnDeere.com

Tel: (309) 765-8000
Fax: (309) 765-5671

NOE, Gregory R.
Vice President and Deputy General Counsel, International

Tel: (309) 765-8000
Fax: (309) 765-5671

SIMPSON, Laurie S.
Vice President and Chief Compliance Officer

Tel: (309) 765-8000
Fax: (309) 765-5671

SOVEY, Mara
President, John Deere Foundation
soveymaral@johndeere.com

Tel: (309) 765-8000
Fax: (309) 765-5671

SPITZFADEN , Thomas C. Tel: (309) 765-8000
Vice President and Treasurer Fax: (309) 765-5671

WOODWARD, Joanne E. Tel: (309) 765-8000
Administrator and PAC Treasurer Fax: (309) 765-5671
woodwardjoannee@johndeere.com

At Washington Office

CASKIE, Dawn Tel: (202) 423-2280
CaskieDawnT@JohnDeere.com Fax: (202) 296-0011

JOHNSON, Stacey Tel: (202) 223-4817
Director, Public Affairs Fax: (202) 296-0011
johnsonstaceyl@johndeere.com
Registered Federal Lobbyist

RAUBER, John Tel: (202) 223-4817
Director, North American Public Affairs Fax: (202) 296-0011
rauberjohn@johndeere.com
Registered Federal Lobbyist

STAMP, Jr., Charles R. Tel: (202) 223-4817
Vice President, Public Affairs Worldwide Fax: (202) 296-0011
stampcharlie@johndeere.com
Registered Federal Lobbyist

STIFFLER-CLAUS, Vanessa Tel: (202) 223-4817
Director, International Affairs Fax: (202) 296-0011
ClausVanessaG@JohnDeere.com

At Other Offices

LEWELLEN, Mark
Spectrum Manager
One John Deere Plaza
Moline, IL 61265

Defense Consulting Group, LLC

Lobbying/Consulting.
defenseconsultinggroup.com
Legislative Issues: AVI; BUD; DEF; TRU

Main Headquarters
Mailing: 1200 G St. NW Tel: (202) 631-4254
  Suite 800 Fax: (202) 434-8707
  Washington, DC 20005

Public Affairs and Related Activities Personnel

At Headquarters

TAYLOR, Robert Tel: (202) 631-4254
Principal Fax: (202) 434-8707
RT@defenseconsultinggroup.com
Registered Federal Lobbyist

Defense Group, Inc.

Performs work in the national interest, advancing public safety and national security through innovative research, analysis and applied technology.
www.defensegroupinc.com
Annual Revenues: $45.46 million
Employees: 100
Industry/ies: Defense/Homeland Security; Government-Related

Chairman of the Board and Chief Executive Officer Tel: (703) 532-0802
WADE, Jr., Dr. James P. Fax: (703) 532-0806
jwade@defensegroup.org

Main Headquarters
Mailing: 2650 Park Tower Dr. Tel: (571) 421-8300
  Suite 400 Fax: (571) 421-8310
  Vienna, VA 22180-7306

Washington Office
Mailing: 1140 Connecticut Ave. NW Tel: (202) 223-8701
  Suite 1140 Fax: (202) 223-8706
  Washington, DC 20036-4030

Public Affairs and Related Activities Personnel

At Headquarters

CHADSEY, Bill Tel: (571) 421-8300
Senior Vice President, Business Development Fax: (571) 421-8310
william.chadsey@defensegp.com

COHEN, Neil R. Tel: (571) 421-8300
Director, Media Relations Fax: (571) 421-8310
neil.cohen@defensegp.com

ESSA, Mehmood Tel: (571) 421-8300
Contact, Accounts Fax: (571) 421-8310

FREDERICKSON, Tony Tel: (571) 421-8300
Chief Operating Officer Fax: (571) 421-8310

JACKOMIS, William Tel: (571) 421-8300
Contact, Administration and Human Resources Fax: (571) 421-8310
william.jackomis@defensegp.com

At Other Offices

DELANEY, Russell Tel: (703) 532-0802

Chief Financial Officer Fax: (703) 532-0806
307 Annandale Rd., Suite 110
Falls Church, VA 22042-2454

WEBB, Ann C. Tel: (703) 532-0802
Vice President, Administration and Human Resources Fax: (703) 532-0806
307 Annandale Rd., Suite 110
Falls Church, VA 22042-2454
awebb@defensegroup.com

Defense Products Marketing, Inc.

A full-service, specialty marketing firm with a focus on transportation equipment, tactical wheeled vehicles, armoring, civil engineering equipment and component within the federal government and military.
www.defenseproducts.com
Annual Revenues: $2.16 million
Employees: 50
Industry/ies: Trade (Foreign And Domestic)

Chief Executive Officer Tel: (202) 459-0810
KIRBY , Christopher

Main Headquarters
Mailing: 805 15th St. NW Tel: (202) 459-0810
  Suite 1101
  Washington, DC 20005

Public Affairs and Related Activities Personnel

At Headquarters

HAMMAKER, Neil Tel: (202) 459-0810
Vice President and Federal Lobbyist
NHammaker@defenseproducts.com

Delaware Municipal Electric Corporation (DEMEC)

DEMEC is a public corporation constituted as a Joint Action Agency and a wholesale electric utility. representing nine municipal electric distribution utilities located in the state of Delaware.
www.demecinc.net
Industry/ies: Energy/Electricity; Utilities

Chairwoman Tel: (302) 653-2733
SLATCHER, Dolores J. Fax: (302) 653-2734

President and Chief Executive Officer Tel: (302) 653-2733
MCCULLAR, Patrick E. Fax: (302) 653-2734
mccullar@demecinc.com

Main Headquarters
Mailing: 217 Artisan Dr. Tel: (302) 653-2733
  P.O. Box 310 Fax: (302) 653-2734
  Smyrna, DE 19977

Public Affairs and Related Activities Personnel

At Headquarters

DOVE , Stephanie Tel: (302) 653-2733
Accounting Manager Fax: (302) 653-2734

SCHLICHTING, Kimberly Tel: (302) 653-2733
Senior Vice President, Operations & Power Supply Fax: (302) 653-2734

Delaware North Companies

Operates in the foodservice, hospitality, retail and entertainment industries.
www.delawarenorth.com
Employees: 55,000
Industry/ies: Food And Beverage Industry
Legislative Issues: NAT; TAX

Chairman Tel: (716) 858-5000
JACOBS, Sr., Jeremey M. Fax: (716) 858-5479

Chief Executive Officer Tel: (716) 858-5000
JACOBS, Charlie Fax: (716) 858-5479

Main Headquarters
Mailing: 40 Fountain Plaza Tel: (716) 858-5000
  Buffalo, NY 14202 Fax: (716) 858-5479
  TF: (800) 441-5645

Political Action Committees
Delaware North Companies Inc.PAC
FEC ID: C00532887
Contact: Rajat R. Shah
40 Fountain Plaza Tel: (716) 858-5000
Buffalo, NY 14202 Fax: (716) 858-5479

  Contributions to Candidates: $14,700 (2015-2016)
  Democrats: $4,700; Republicans: $10,000

Corporate Foundations and Giving Programs
Delaware North Companies Foundation
40 Fountain Plaza Tel: (716) 858-5000
Buffalo, NY 14202 Fax: (716) 858-5125

Public Affairs and Related Activities Personnel

At Headquarters

ABRAMSON, Rick	Tel:	(716) 858-5000
Executive Vice President and Cheif Operating Officer	Fax:	(716) 858-5479
FEENEY, Christopher J.	Tel:	(716) 858-5000
Executive Vice President and Chief Financial Officer	Fax:	(716) 858-5479
GILL, Kathy	Tel:	(716) 858-5000
Vice President, Marketing and Communications	Fax:	(716) 858-5479
KELLER, Bryan J.	Tel:	(716) 858-5000
Vice President and Senior Counsel	Fax:	(716) 858-5479
MERRY, Todd	Tel:	(716) 858-5000
Chief Marketing Officer	Fax:	(716) 858-5479
MORGAN, Eileen	Tel:	(716) 858-5000
Chief Human Resources Officer	Fax:	(716) 858-5479
SHAH, Rajat R.	Tel:	(716) 858-5000
Vice President, General Counsel and Corporate Secretary	Fax:	(716) 858-5479
VINCENT, Yvette	Tel:	(716) 858-5000
Vice President, Information Technology	Fax:	(716) 858-5479

DELEX Systems, Inc.

www.delex.com
Industry/ies: Computer/Technology

Main Headquarters

Mailing: 1953 Gallows Rd.	Tel:	(703) 893-5338
Suite 700	Fax:	(703) 734-8300
Vienna, VA 22182		

Political Action Committees

DELEX Sytems, Inc. PAC
FEC ID: C00428060

1953 Gallows Rd.	Tel:	(703) 734-8300
Suite 700	Fax:	(703) 893-5338
Vienna, VA 20182		

Contributions to Candidates: $1,503 (2015-2016)
Republicans: $1,503

Delhaize America, Inc.

A supermarket chain. A subsidiary of Delhaize America, the U.S. division of Brussels-based Delhaize Group.
www.delhaizegroup.com
Annual Revenues: $27.56 billion
Employees: 154,000
Ticker: NYSE: DEG
SIC: 5411
Industry/ies: Food And Beverage Industry

Chairman of the Board	Tel:	(704) 633-8250
JANSSON, Mats	Fax:	(704) 636-5024
President and Chief Executive Officer	Tel:	(704) 633-8250
MULLER, Frans	Fax:	(704) 636-5024

Main Headquarters

Mailing: 2110 Executive Dr.	Tel:	(704) 633-8250
P.O. Box 1330	Fax:	(704) 636-5024
Salisbury, NC 28145-1330		

Political Action Committees

Delhaize America, Llc. PAC
FEC ID: C00214304
Contact: W Teross Young

2110 Executive Dr.	Tel:	(704) 633-8250
P.O. Box 1330	Fax:	(704) 636-5024
Salisbury, NC 28145-1330		

Contributions to Candidates: $2,000 (2015-2016)
Republicans: $2,000

Corporate Foundations and Giving Programs

Food Lion Charitable Foundation

2110 Executive Dr.	Tel:	(704) 633-8250
P.O. Box 1330	Fax:	(704) 636-5024
Salisbury, NC 28145-1330		

Public Affairs and Related Activities Personnel

At Headquarters

AMOROSO, Greg	Tel:	(704) 633-8250
Chief Sustainability Officer and Senior Vice President	Fax:	(704) 636-5024
BOUCHUT, Pierre	Tel:	(704) 633-8250
Executive Vice President and Chief Financial Officer	Fax:	(704) 636-5024
CROONEN, Marc	Tel:	(704) 633-8250
Executive Vice President and Chief Human Resources Officer	Fax:	(704) 636-5024
YOUNG, W Teross	Tel:	(704) 633-8250
Vice President, PAC Treasurer	Fax:	(704) 636-5024

Dell Inc.

Designs, manufactures, sells, and services personal computers, laptop computers, and servers. Formerly known as Dell Computer Corporation.
www.dell.com

Annual Revenues: $56.94 billion
Employees: 108,800
Ticker: NASDAQ: DELL
SIC: 3571; 3577
NAICS: 334111; 334119
Industry/ies: Computer/Technology
Legislative Issues: BUD; CPI; CPT; CSP; DEF; EDU; ENV; GOV; HOM; IMM; LBR; SCI; SMB; TAX; TRD; VET

Chairman of the Board and Chief Executive Officer	Tel:	(512) 338-4400
DELL, Michael S.	Fax:	(512) 283-6161

Main Headquarters

Mailing: One Dell Way	Tel:	(512) 338-4400
Round Rock, TX 78682	Fax:	(512) 283-6161
	TF:	(800) 289-3355

Washington Office

Mailing: 440 First St. NW	Tel:	(202) 408-7975
Suite 820	Fax:	(202) 408-7664
Washington, DC 20001		

Political Action Committees

Dell Inc. Employee PAC
FEC ID: C00369751
Contact: Christopher Turner
1225 Eye St. NW
Washington, DC 20005

Contributions to Candidates: $111,500 (2015-2016)
Democrats: $48,500; Republicans: $63,000

Corporate Foundations and Giving Programs

Dell Foundation
Contact: Janet Mountain

One Dell Way	Tel:	(512) 338-4400
Round Rock, TX 78682	Fax:	(512) 728-3653

Public Affairs and Related Activities Personnel

At Headquarters

MOUNTAIN, Janet	Tel:	(512) 338-4400
Foundation Executive Director	Fax:	(512) 728-3653
PRICE, Steve H.	Tel:	(512) 338-4400
Senior Vice President, Human Resources	Fax:	(512) 283-6161
QUINTOS, Karen H.	Tel:	(512) 338-4400
Senior Vice President and Chief Marketing Officer	Fax:	(512) 283-6161
ROTHBERG, Richard J.	Tel:	(512) 338-4400
Senior Vice President and General Counsel	Fax:	(512) 283-6161
SWEET, Thomas W.	Tel:	(512) 338-4400
Senior Vice President, Chief Financial Officer	Fax:	(512) 283-6161
WILLIAMS, Robert	Tel:	(512) 728-7570
Specialist Enterprise Technical Support, Dell Servers	Fax:	(512) 283-6161
robert_williams@dell.com		

At Washington Office

ALSUP, Chris	Tel:	(202) 408-7975
Manager, Government Affairs	Fax:	(202) 408-7664
BEIGHTEL, Hillary	Tel:	(202) 408-7975
Registered Federal Lobbyist	Fax:	(202) 408-7664
CONNORS, Michele	Tel:	(202) 408-7975
Registered Federal Lobbyist	Fax:	(202) 408-7664
HOWARD, John	Tel:	(202) 408-7975
Solutions Executive	Fax:	(202) 408-7664
Registered Federal Lobbyist		
KARNAK, Rebecca	Tel:	(202) 408-7975
Registered Federal Lobbyist	Fax:	(202) 408-7664
KRUPNICK, Matt	Tel:	(202) 408-7975
Director, Global Public Policy	Fax:	(202) 408-7664
Registered Federal Lobbyist		
MATTERN, Kristen	Tel:	(202) 408-7975
Registered Federal Lobbyist	Fax:	(202) 408-7664
MURRAY, Kerry	Tel:	(202) 408-7975
Senior Counsel	Fax:	(202) 408-7664
Registered Federal Lobbyist		
SALAYANDIA, Marisela	Tel:	(202) 408-7975
Registered Federal Lobbyist	Fax:	(202) 408-7664
SRIVASTAVA, Neeraj	Tel:	(202) 408-7975
Federal Lobbyist	Fax:	(202) 408-7664
Registered Federal Lobbyist		
TURNER, Cris	Tel:	(202) 408-7975
Federal Lobbyist	Fax:	(202) 408-7664
Registered Federal Lobbyist		
TURNER, Christopher	Tel:	(202) 408-7975
PAC Treasurer	Fax:	(202) 408-7664
VALLUZZO, Fran	Tel:	(202) 408-7975
Manager, State and Local Government Affairs	Fax:	(202) 408-7664

YOUNG, Michael   Tel: (202) 408-7975
Executive   Fax: (202) 408-7664

Deloitte LLP

A professional services firm. The US member of Deloitte Touche Tohmatsu, a UK private company limited by guarantee.
www.deloitte.com
Employees: 51,000
Industry/ies: Accounting; Banking/Finance/Investments
Legislative Issues: ACC; BUD; FIN; GOV; HCR; HOM; IMM; LBR; MMM; SCI; TAX; TRA; VET

Chairman of the Board   Tel: (212) 489-1600
RENJEN, Punit   Fax: (212) 489-1687
prenjen@deloitte.com

Chief Executive Officer   Tel: (212) 489-1600
ECHEVARRIA, Joe   Fax: (212) 489-1687

Main Headquarters
Mailing: 1633 Broadway   Tel: (212) 489-1600
      New York City, NY 10019-6754   Fax: (212) 489-1687

Washington Office
Mailing: 1919 N. Lynn St.   Tel: (571) 882-5000
      Arlington, VA 22209-1742

Political Action Committees
Deloitte Political Action Committee
FEC ID: C00211318
Contact: Cindy M. Stevens
P.O. Box 365   Tel: (202) 879-5600
Washington, DC 20044

    Contributions to Candidates: $1,441,000 (2015-2016)
    Democrats: $453,500; Republicans: $982,500; Other: $5,000

Principal Recipients

SENATE

AYOTTE, KELLY A (REP-NH)
BLUMENTHAL, RICHARD (DEM-CT)
BLUNT, ROY (REP-MO)
BOOZMAN, JOHN (REP-AR)
BURR, RICHARD (REP-NC)
HOEVEN, JOHN (REP-ND)
ISAKSON, JOHN HARDY (REP-GA)
LEAHY, PATRICK J (DEM-VT)
MCCAIN, JOHN S (REP-VA)
MURKOWSKI, LISA (REP-AK)
MURPHY, PATRICK E (DEM-FL)
SCHATZ, BRIAN (DEM-HI)
SCHUMER, CHARLES E (DEM-NY)
SCOTT, TIMOTHY E (REP-SC)
SHELBY, RICHARD C (REP-AL)

HOUSE

ADERHOLT, ROBERT BROWN (REP-AL)
BEYER, DONALD STERNOFF JR. (DEM-VA)
BOUSTANY, CHARLES W. DR. JR. (REP-LA)
BROOKS, SUSAN MRS. (REP-IN)
CARTER, JOHN R. REP. (REP-DC)
COLE, TOM (REP-OK)
COMSTOCK, BARBARA J HONORABLE (REP-VA)
CONAWAY, MICHAEL HONORABLE (REP-TX)
CONNOLLY, GERALD EDWARD (DEM-VA)
CRENSHAW, ANDER (REP-FL)
DELBENE, SUZAN K (DEM-WA)
DENT, CHARLES W. REP. (REP-PA)
DIAZ-BALART, MARIO (REP-FL)
EMMER, THOMAS EARL JR. (REP-MN)
FLORES, BILL (REP-TX)
FORBES, J. RANDY (REP-VA)
FRELINGHUYSEN, RODNEY P. (REP-NJ)
GOODLATTE, ROBERT W. (REP-VA)
GRANGER, KAY (REP-TX)
GRAVES, JOHN THOMAS MR. JR. (REP-GA)
GRIFFITH, H MORGAN (REP-VA)
GUTHRIE, S. BRETT HON. (REP-KY)
HENSARLING, JEB HON. (REP-TX)
HOLDING, GEORGE E MR. (REP-NC)
HOYER, STENY HAMILTON (DEM-DC)
JENKINS, LYNN (REP-KS)
KING, PETER T. HON. (REP-NY)
LOFGREN, ZOE (DEM-CA)
LOWEY, NITA M (DEM-NY)
MCCARTHY, KEVIN (REP-CA)
MCCAUL, MICHAEL (REP-TX)
MCHENRY, PATRICK TIMOTHY (REP-NC)
MEEHAN, PATRICK L. MR. (REP-PA)
MILLER, JEFFERSON B. (REP-FL)
PAULSEN, ERIK (REP-MN)
PERLMUTTER, EDWIN G (DEM-CO)

PRICE, DAVID E. (DEM-NC)
RICE, TOM (REP-SC)
ROBY, MARTHA (REP-AL)
ROSKAM, PETER (REP-IL)
RYAN, PAUL D. (REP-WI)
SCALISE, STEVE MR. (REP-LA)
SERRANO, JOSE E. (DEM-NY)
SHIMKUS, JOHN M (REP-IL)
SMITH, D ADAM (DEM-WA)
THOMPSON, BENNIE G. (DEM-MS)
THORNBERRY, MAC (REP-TX)
TIBERI, PATRICK J. (REP-OH)
WALDEN, GREGORY P MR. (REP-OR)
WITTMAN, ROBERT J MR. (REP-VA)

Corporate Foundations and Giving Programs

The Deloitte Foundation
1633 Broadway   Tel: (212) 492-1600
New York City, NY 10019   Fax: (212) 489-1687

Public Affairs and Related Activities Personnel

At Headquarters

JARRETT, Madonna   Tel: (212) 492-3738
Associate Director, Programs, Global Regulatory and Public   Fax: (212) 489-1687
Policy Group
mjarrett@deloitte.com

At Washington Office

FEUER, Martin   Tel: (571) 882-5000
Sales Executive

At Other Offices

BIGALKE, John   Tel: (202) 879-5600
Senior Partner, Global Health Care   Fax: (202) 879-5309
701 Pennsylvania Ave. NW, Suite 530
Washington, DC 20004

BRADY, P. James   Tel: (202) 879-5600
Federal Lobbyist   Fax: (202) 879-5309
701 Pennsylvania Ave. NW, Suite 530
Washington, DC 20004
Registered Federal Lobbyist

BROWN, Peter   Tel: (202) 879-5600
Director, Federal Government Relations   Fax: (202) 879-5309
701 Pennsylvania Ave. NW, Suite 530
Washington, DC 20004
pdbrown@deloitte.com
Registered Federal Lobbyist

DAVIS, III, Thomas M.   Tel: (202) 879-5600
Director, Federal Government Relations   Fax: (202) 879-5309
701 Pennsylvania Ave. NW, Suite 530
Washington, DC 20004
Registered Federal Lobbyist

GIVENS, Patrick   Tel: (202) 879-5600
Manager, Government Relations   Fax: (202) 661-1052
701 Pennsylvania Ave. NW, Suite 530
Washington, DC 20004
Registered Federal Lobbyist

IANDOLI, Matthew   Tel: (202) 879-5600
Federal Lobbyist   Fax: (202) 879-5309
701 Pennsylvania Ave. NW, Suite 530
Washington, DC 20004
Registered Federal Lobbyist

NORRIS, Jane   Tel: (571) 882-8829
National Public Relations Lead, Federal Government Services   Fax: (202) 879-5309
701 Pennsylvania Ave. NW, Suite 530
Washington, DC 20004
jannorris@deloitte.com

PROCKNOW, Gene A.   Tel: (202) 879-5600
Principal & Senior Client Service Partner   Fax: (202) 879-5309
701 Pennsylvania Ave. NW, Suite 530
Washington, DC 20004

STEVENS, Cindy M.
Principal, Government Affairs & Public Policy
P.O. Box 365
Washington, DC 20044
cistevens@deloitte.com
Registered Federal Lobbyist

WILLIAMS, David   Tel: (202) 879-5600
701 Pennsylvania Ave. NW, Suite 530   Fax: (202) 879-5309
Washington, DC 20004

WOMACK, Bill   Tel: (202) 879-5600
Senior Manager, Government Relations   Fax: (202) 879-5309
701 Pennsylvania Ave. NW, Suite 530
Washington, DC 20004
wwomack@deloitte.com
Registered Federal Lobbyist

Delphi Corporation

Designs, engineers and manufactures automobile components and vehicle electronics.
www.delphi.com
Employees: 117,000
Ticker: NYSE: DLPH
SIC: 3714; 3678; 3679
NAICS: 334417; 334418; 336322
Industry/ies: Automotive Industry; Transportation

Chairman of the Board   Tel: (248) 813-2000
GUPTA, Rajiv L.   Fax: (248) 813-2673

President and Chief Executive Officer   Tel: (248) 813-2000
CLARK, Kevin P.   Fax: (248) 813-2673

Main Headquarters
Mailing: 5725 Delphi Dr.   Tel: (248) 813-2000
             Troy, MI 48098-2815   Fax: (248) 813-2673

Washington Office
Mailing: 975 F St. NW   Tel: (202) 824-0401
             Suite 540   Fax: (202) 628-5815
             Washington, DC 20004

Corporate Foundations and Giving Programs

Delphi Foundation
Contact: Lindsey Williams
5725 Delphi Dr.   Tel: (248) 813-2000
Troy, MI 48098   Fax: (248) 813-2673

Public Affairs and Related Activities Personnel

At Headquarters

HOLSCOTT, Jessica L.   Tel: (248) 813-2000
Vice President, Investor Relations   Fax: (248) 813-2673

MURPHY, Mark J.   Tel: (248) 813-2000
Executive Vice President and Chief Financial Officer   Fax: (248) 813-2673

PREUSS, J. Christopher   Tel: (248) 813-2000
Senior Vice President, Marketing and Communications   Fax: (248) 813-2673

SHERBIN, David M.   Tel: (248) 813-2000
Senior Vice President, General Counsel, Secretary and Chief   Fax: (248) 813-2670
Compliance Officer

SUVER, Susan M.   Tel: (248) 813-2000
Senior Vice President and Chief Human Resources Officer   Fax: (248) 813-2673

TAPIA, Claudia   Tel: (248) 813-2000
Vice President, Corporate Communications   Fax: (248) 813-2673

WILLIAMS, Lindsey   Tel: (248) 813-2528
Vice President, Government Affairs & Technology   Fax: (248) 813-2673
Communications
lindsey.c.williams@delphi.com

At Washington Office

CUSHMAN, Nancy   Tel: (202) 824-0401
PAC Treasurer   Fax: (202) 628-5815

Delta Airlines

Provides air transportation services.
www.delta.com
Annual Revenues: $40.57 billion
Employees: 83,817
Ticker: NYSE: DAL
SIC: 4512
Industry/ies: Aerospace/Aviation; Airlines; Transportation; Travel/Tourism/
Lodging
Legislative Issues: AVI; BUD; FIN; FUE; HOM; IMM; TAX; TRA; TRD

Executive Director of the Board of Directors   Tel: (404) 715-2600
ANDERSON, Richard H.   Fax: (404) 715-5042

Chief Executive Officer   Tel: (404) 715-2600
BASTIAN, Edward H.   Fax: (404) 715-5042

Main Headquarters
Mailing: P.O. Box 20706   Tel: (404) 715-2600
             Atlanta, GA 30320-6001

Washington Office
Mailing: 1212 New York Ave. NW   Tel: (202) 216-0700
             Suite 200
             Washington, DC 20005

Political Action Committees
Delta Air Lines PAC
FEC ID: C00104802
Contact: Sametta Barnett
1212 New York Ave. NW, Suite 200   Tel: (202) 842-3193
Washington, DC 20005   Fax: (202) 289-6834

Contributions to Candidates: $222,500 (2015-2016)
Democrats: $79,500; Republicans: $143,000

Principal Recipients

HOUSE

Corporate Foundations and Giving Programs

The Delta Air Lines Foundation
Contact: Scarlet Pressley-Brown
1030 Delta Blvd.   Tel: (404) 715-2600
Atlanta, GA 30354   Fax: (404) 715-5042

Delta's Force for Global Good
Contact: Scarlet Pressley-Brown
1030 Delta Blvd.   Tel: (404) 715-2600
P.O. Box 20706   Fax: (404) 715-2600
Atlanta, GA 30320-6001

Public Affairs and Related Activities Personnel

At Headquarters

WEST, Gil   Tel: (404) 715-2600
Senior Executive Vice President and Chief Operating Officer

At Washington Office

BARNETT, Sametta   Tel: (202) 216-0700
Director, Government Affairs and PAC Treasurer
sametta.c.barnett@delta.com
Registered Federal Lobbyist

BECKER, Jonathan H.   Tel: (202) 216-0700
Public Policy Consultant

BRANIFF, Mimi   Tel: (202) 216-0700
Federal Lobbyist
Registered Federal Lobbyist

KINZEL, Will   Tel: (202) 216-0700
Federal Lobbyist
Registered Federal Lobbyist

LETTENEY, Robert   Tel: (202) 216-0700
Federal Lobbyist
Registered Federal Lobbyist

NEWMAN, Andrea Fischer   Tel: (202) 216-0700
Senior Vice President, Government Affairs
andrea.newman@delta.com
Registered Federal Lobbyist

YOHE, D. Scott   Tel: (202) 216-0700
Senior Vice President, Government Affairs
Registered Federal Lobbyist

At Other Offices

CARTER, Peter   Tel: (404) 715-2600
Executive Vice President And Chief Legal Officer And   Fax: (404) 715-5042
Corporate Secretary
1030 Delta Blvd.
Atlanta, GA 30354-1989

HAUENSTEIN, Glen   Tel: (404) 715-2600
President   Fax: (404) 715-5042
1030 Delta Blvd.
Atlanta, GA 30354-1989

HIRST, Richard   Tel: (404) 715-2600
Senior Vice President and Chief Legal Officer   Fax: (404) 715-5042
1030 Delta Blvd.
Atlanta, GA 30354-1989

JACOBSON, Paul   Tel: (404) 715-2600
Executive Vice President and Chief Financial Officer   Fax: (404) 715-5042
1030 Delta Blvd.
Atlanta, GA 30354-1989

KARNES, April   Tel: (404) 715-2600
UX Strategy and Design Manager   Fax: (404) 715-5042
1030 Delta Blvd.
Atlanta, GA 30354-1989
april.karnes@nwa.com

MATHEIS, Diane   Tel: (404) 715-2600
Manager, Meetings, Events and Trade Shows   Fax: (404) 715-5042
1030 Delta Blvd.
Atlanta, GA 30354-1989

SHINKLE, Kevin   Tel: (404) 715-2600
Senior Vice President and Chief Communications Officer   Fax: (404) 715-5042
1030 Delta Blvd.
Atlanta, GA 30354-1989

SMITH , Joanne   Tel: (404) 715-2600
Executive Vice President and Chief Human Resources Officer   Fax: (404) 715-5042
1030 Delta Blvd.
Atlanta, GA 30354-1989

Delta Petroleum Corporation

Delta Petroleum Corporation is an independent energy company.
www.deltapetro.com
Annual Revenues: $146.81 million
Employees: 39
Ticker: NASDAQ: DPTR
SIC: 1311

Industry/ies: Energy/Electricity; Natural Resources

Chairman of the Board
TAYLOR, Daniel J.

Tel: (303) 293-9133
Fax: (303) 298-8251

Chief Executive Officer
LAKEY, Carl E.

Tel: (303) 293-9133
Fax: (303) 298-8251

Main Headquarters
Mailing: 370 17th St.
             Suite 4300
             Denver, CO 80202

Tel: (303) 293-9133
Fax: (303) 298-8251

Public Affairs and Related Activities Personnel

At Headquarters

BROWN, Andrea
Manager, Investor Relations
investorrelations@deltapetro.com

Tel: (303) 293-9133
Fax: (303) 298-8251

FREEDMAN, Stanley F.
Executive Vice President, General Counsel and Secretary

Tel: (303) 293-9133
Fax: (303) 298-8251

NANKE, Kevin K.
Treasurer and Chief Financial Officer

Tel: (303) 293-9133
Fax: (303) 298-8251

DeltaHawk Engines, Inc.

Aviation diesel engine development.
www.deltahawkengines.com
Industry/ies: Aerospace/Aviation; Transportation

Main Headquarters
Mailing: 2300 South St.
             Racine, WI 53404

Tel: (262) 634-9660
Fax: (262) 833-1007
TF: (800) 434-2958

Public Affairs and Related Activities Personnel

At Other Offices

LYSSENKO, Taras
Government Relations
2903 Golf Ave.
Racine, WI 53404

Fax: (262) 634-9625

Deluxe Corporation

Subsidiaries provide personal and business checks; business forms and self-inking stamps; and fraud prevention services and customer retention programs to banks, credit unions, financial services companies, consumers, and small businesses. Services are distributed via direct mail, the Internet, telephone, and the company's national sales force.
www.deluxe.com
Annual Revenues: $1.80 billion
Employees: 5,874
Ticker: NYSE: DLX
SIC: 2780; 2761; 2782
NAICS: 323116
Industry/ies: Banking/Finance/Investments

Non Executive Chairman
REDGRAVE, Martyn R.

Tel: (651) 483-7111
Fax: (651) 481-4371

Chief Executive Officer
SCHRAM, Lee J.

Tel: (651) 483-7111
Fax: (651) 481-4163

Main Headquarters
Mailing: 3680 Victoria St., North
             Shoreview, MN 55126-2966

Tel: (651) 483-7111
Fax: (651) 481-4371

Corporate Foundations and Giving Programs

Deluxe Foundation
Contact: Jennifer A. Anderson
3680 Victoria St., North
Shoreview, NJ 55126

Tel: (651) 483-7842

Public Affairs and Related Activities Personnel

At Headquarters

ANDERSON, Jennifer A.
Director, Foundation and Community Affairs
jenny.anderson@deluxe.com

Tel: (651) 483-7842
Fax: (651) 481-4477

BRINKMAN, Amanda
Chief Brand and Communications Officer

Tel: (651) 787-1314
Fax: (651) 481-4371

FILBY, John D.
Senior Vice President, Financial Services

Tel: (651) 483-7111
Fax: (651) 481-4371

LOOSBROCK, Julie M.
Senior Vice President, Human Resources

Tel: (651) 483-7111
Fax: (651) 481-4163

MCROBERTS, Malcolm J.
Senior Vice President, Small Business Services

Tel: (651) 483-7111
Fax: (651) 481-4371

MERRITT, Edward
Treasurer and Vice President, Investor Relations

Tel: (651) 483-7111
Fax: (651) 481-4371

NACHTSHEIM, Stephen P.
Director

Tel: (651) 483-7111
Fax: (651) 481-4163

PETERSON, Terry D.
Chief Financial Officer and Senior Vice President
terry.peterson@deluxe.com

Tel: (651) 787-1068
Fax: (651) 481-4163

POTTS, Cameron
Vice President, Public Relations

Tel: (651) 787-1353
Fax: (651) 481-4371

SCHROEDER, J. Michael
Senior Vice President, General Counsel and Secretary

Tel: (651) 483-7111
Fax: (651) 481-4371

Denbury Resources, Inc.

An oil and gas company.
www.denbury.com
Annual Revenues: $2.09 billion
Employees: 1,496
Ticker: NYSE: DNR
SIC: 1311; 1382
NAICS: 213112; 211111
Industry/ies: Fuels See Coal, Gas, Oil, Petroleum; Natural Resources; Petroleum Industry
Legislative Issues: ENG; ENV; TAX; TRA

Chairman of the Board
WETTSTEIN, Wieland F.

Tel: (972) 673-2000

President and Chief Executive Officer
RYKHOEK, Phil
phil.rykhoek@denbury.com

Tel: (972) 673-2050

Main Headquarters
Mailing: 5320 Legacy Dr.
             Plano, TX 75024

Tel: (972) 673-2000

Corporate Foundations and Giving Programs

Denbury Resources Contributions Program
5100 Tennyson Pkwy.
Suite 1200
Plano, TX 75024

Tel: (972) 673-2000
Fax: (972) 673-2000

Public Affairs and Related Activities Personnel

At Headquarters

ALLEN, Mark C.
Senior Vice President, Chief Financial Officer, Treasurer and Assistant Secretary
mark.allen@denbury.com

Tel: (972) 673-2007

ARNOLD, Rina
Executive Administrative Assistant

Tel: (972) 673-2000

CAMPBELL, Ross
Manager, Investor Relations
ross.campbell@denbury.com

Tel: (972) 673-2825

COLE, Dan E.
Vice President, Marketing and Business Development and Government Relations
dan.cole@denbury.com

Tel: (972) 673-2000

MATTHEWS, James S.
Vice President, Secretary and General Counsel

Tel: (972) 673-2000

MCPHERSON, Craig
Senior Vice President and Chief Operating Officer

Tel: (972) 673-2000

NELSON, Ben
Financial Analyst, Investor Relations

Tel: (972) 673-2787

SHELLEY, Whitney
Vice President and Chief Human Resources Officer

Tel: (972) 673-2000

At Other Offices

RHOADES, Alan
Vice President and Chief Accounting Officer
5100 Tennyson Pkwy., Suite 1200
Plano, TX 75024

Tel: (972) 673-2000
Fax: (972) 673-2150

SCHNACKE, John
Federal Lobbyist
5100 Tennyson Pkwy., Suite 1200
Plano, TX 75024
Registered Federal Lobbyist

Tel: (972) 673-2000
Fax: (972) 673-2150

SHAW, Rachel
Executive Assistant
5100 Tennyson Pkwy., Suite 1200
Plano, TX 75024
rachel.shaw@denbury.com

Tel: (972) 673-2275
Fax: (972) 673-2150

Denny's Corporation

A full-service family restaurant chain.
www.dennys.com
Annual Revenues: $480.55 million
Employees: 8,300
Ticker: NASDAQ: DENN
SIC: 5812
Industry/ies: Food And Beverage Industry

Chairman of the Board
SMITHART-OGLESBY, Debra

Tel: (864) 597-8000
Fax: (864) 597-8780

Chief Executive Officer and President
MILLER, John C.

Tel: (864) 597-8000
Fax: (864) 597-8780

Main Headquarters

Mailing: 203 E. Main St., P-8-6   Tel: (864) 597-8000
Spartanburg, SC 29319   Fax: (864) 597-8780
    TF: (800) 733-6697

Public Affairs and Related Activities Personnel

At Headquarters

AUTRY, C. Patrick   Tel: (864) 597-8000
Ethics and Compliance Officer   Fax: (864) 597-8780

BODE, Christopher D.   Tel: (864) 597-8000
Senior Vice President, Chief Operating Officer   Fax: (864) 597-8780

BRADY, Liz   Tel: (646) 277-1226
Contact, Media Relations   Fax: (864) 597-8780

DILLON, John W.   Tel: (864) 597-8000
Senior Vice President, Chief Marketing Officer   Fax: (864) 597-8780

FLEMMING, Timothy E.   Tel: (864) 597-8000
Senior Vice President, General Counsel and Chief Legal   Fax: (864) 597-8780
Officer

GILMORE, Jay C.   Tel: (864) 597-8000
Vice President, Chief Accounting Officer and Corporate   Fax: (864) 597-8780
Controller

KINCAID, Whit   Tel: (877) 784-7167
Director, Financial Planning and Contact, Investor relations   Fax: (864) 597-8780
ir@dennys.com

MELTON, Scott   Tel: (864) 597-8000
Assistant General Counsel, Corporate Governance Officer   Fax: (864) 597-8780
and Secretary

NELL, Ross B.   Tel: (864) 597-8000
Vice President, Tax and Treasurer   Fax: (864) 597-8780

VAN PELT, Jill A.   Tel: (864) 597-8000
Senior Vice President, Chief People Officer   Fax: (864) 597-8780

VEROSTEK, Robert P.   Tel: (864) 597-8000
Vice President, Financial Planning and analysis and Investor   Fax: (864) 597-8780
Relations

WOLFINGER, F. Mark   Tel: (864) 597-8000
Executive Vice President, Chief Administrative Officer and   Fax: (864) 597-8780
Chief Financial Officer

DENTSPLY International

A manufacturer of dental equipment and supplies.
www.dentsply.com
Annual Revenues: $2.79 billion
Employees: 11,400
Ticker: NASDAQ: XRAY
SIC: 3843
NAICS: 339114
Industry/ies: Machinery/Equipment; Medicine/Health Care/Mental Health

Chairman of the Board   Tel: (717) 845-7511
WISE, Bret W.   Fax: (717) 849-4760

Chief Executive Officer   Tel: (717) 845-7511
SLOVIN, Jeffrey T.   Fax: (717) 849-4760

Main Headquarters
Mailing: 221 W. Philadelphia St.   Tel: (717) 845-7511
P.O. Box 872   Fax: (717) 849-4760
York, PA 17405-0872   TF: (800) 877-0200

Corporate Foundations and Giving Programs

Dentsply International Foundation
221 W. Philadelphia St.   Tel: (717) 845-7511
P.O. Box 872   Fax: (717) 849-4762
York, PA 17405

Public Affairs and Related Activities Personnel

At Headquarters

CLARK, Christopher T.   Tel: (717) 845-7511
President and Chief Operating Officer   Fax: (717) 849-4760

LECKOW, Derek   Tel: (717) 849-7863
Vice President, Investor Relations   Fax: (717) 849-4760
Derek.Leckow@dentsply.com

MACINNIS, Maureen J.   Tel: (717) 845-7511
Vice President, Chief Human Resources   Fax: (717) 849-4760

MICHEL, Ulrich   Tel: (717) 845-7511
Executive Vice President and Chief Financial Officer   Fax: (717) 849-4760

MOSCH, James G.   Tel: (717) 845-7511
President and Chief Operating Officer   Fax: (717) 849-4760

REARDON, William E   Tel: (717) 845-7511
Vice President and Treasurer   Fax: (717) 849-4760

WAGNER, Richard M.   Tel: (717) 845-7511
Vice President and Corporate Controller   Fax: (717) 849-4760

Depository Trust and Clearing Corporation

Provides clearance, settlement and information services for equities, corporate and municipal bonds, government and mortgage-backed securities, over-the-counter credit derivatives and emerging market debt. Also provides custody and asset servicing for more than two million securities issues from the U.S. and 100 other countries and territories. Also processes mutual funds and insurance transactions.
www.dtcc.com
Annual Revenues: $948.58 million
Employees: 2,700
Industry/ies: Banking/Finance/Investments
Legislative Issues: FIN; HOM

Executive Chairman of the Board   Tel: (212) 855-1000
DRUSKIN, Robert   Fax: (212) 855-8440

President and Chief Executive Officer   Tel: (212) 855-1000
BODSON, Michael C.   Fax: (212) 855-8440

Main Headquarters
Mailing: 55 Water St.   Tel: (212) 855-1000
22nd Floor   Fax: (212) 855-8440
New York City, NY 10041   TF: (888) 382-2721

Washington Office
Mailing: 1455 Pennsylvania Ave. NW
Suite 725
Washington, DC 20005

Political Action Committees

Depository Trust and Clearing Corporation PAC - DTCC PAC
FEC ID: C00497917
Contact: Larry E. Thompson
The Homer Bldg.   Tel: (202) 383-2675
601 13th St. NW, Suite 580 South
Washington, DC 20005

    Contributions to Candidates: $356,800 (2015-2016)
    Democrats: $173,600; Republicans: $183,200

       Principal Recipients

        SENATE
        KIRK, MARK STEVEN (REP-IL)
        MURPHY, PATRICK E (DEM-FL)

        HOUSE
        CONAWAY, MICHAEL HONORABLE (REP-TX)
        HIMES, JIM (DEM-CT)
        HOYER, STENY HAMILTON (DEM-DC)

Corporate Foundations and Giving Programs

Depository Trust and Clearing Corporation Contributions Program
55 Water St.
22nd Floor
New York City, NY 10041

Public Affairs and Related Activities Personnel

At Headquarters

COLBY, Robert L.D.   Tel: (212) 855-1000
Chief Legal Officer   Fax: (212) 855-8440

COMPTON , Paul H.   Tel: (212) 855-1000
Chief Administrative Officer   Fax: (212) 855-8440

COSGROVE , Susan   Tel: (212) 855-1000
Managing Director and Chief Financial Officer   Fax: (212) 855-8440

INOSANTO, Judy   Tel: (212) 855-5424
Vice President and Contact, Communications   Fax: (212) 855-8440
jinsosanto@dtcc.com

PORTANNESE, Anthony   Tel: (212) 855-1000
Managing Director, Human Resources   Fax: (212) 855-8440

At Washington Office

THOMPSON, Larry E.
PAC Treasurer, Vice Chairman, General Counsel and
Chairman of the Board

At Other Offices

WOLPERT, Alison   Tel: (202) 383-2675
Vice President, Government Relations
601 13th St. NW, Suite 580 South
Washington, DC 20005

DeSales Media Group, Inc

Catholic media group.

President and Chairman   Tel: (718) 499-9705
HARRINGTON, Monsignor Kieran

Chief Executive Officer   Tel: (718) 499-9705
DIGNAM, Arthur

Main Headquarters
Mailing: 1712 Tenth Ave.   Tel: (718) 499-9705
Brooklyn, NY 11215

Public Affairs and Related Activities Personnel

At Headquarters

CAWLEY, Christine Mohan   Tel: (718) 499-9705
Sales, Marketing and Digital Operations

GUTIERREZ , Stefanie   Tel: (718) 499-9705
Director, Public Relations

LEVIEN, Vincent   Tel: (718) 499-9705
Director, External Affairs
Registered Federal Lobbyist

MCKEON-SLATTERY, Matthew   Tel: (718) 499-9705
Registered Federal Lobbyist

RAIL, Mary Kay   Tel: (718) 499-9705
Director, Human Resources

Desimone Consulting LLC

A consulting firm.
www.de-simone.com
Employees: 250
Legislative Issues: AGR; BUD; DEF; ECN; EDU; ENG; FUE; GAM; HCR; IND; MAR; MED; MMM; NAT; SCI; TRD

Founder and Chairman of the Board   Tel: (212) 532-2211
DESIMONE, PE, FACI, Vincent J.   Fax: (212) 481-6108

President and Chief Executive Officer   Tel: (212) 532-2211
DESIMONE, PE, LEED AP, Stephen V.   Fax: (212) 481-6108

Main Headquarters
Mailing: 18 West 18th St.   Tel: (212) 532-2211
       Tenth Floor   Fax: (212) 481-6108
       New York, NY 10011

Public Affairs and Related Activities Personnel

At Headquarters

DESIMONE, Rick   Tel: (212) 532-2211
President   Fax: (212) 481-6108
Registered Federal Lobbyist

At Other Offices

KRISTJANSSON, Brian
Federal Lobbyist
78 Orchard Rd., North
Tacoma, WA 98406
Registered Federal Lobbyist

Detroit Edison

An investor-owned electric utility company. A subsidiary of DTE Energy, headquartered in Detroit, MI.
www2.dteenergy.com
Ticker: NYSE: DTE
Industry/ies: Energy/Electricity; Utilities

Chairman of the Board and Chief Executive Officer
ANDERSON, Gerard M.

Main Headquarters
Mailing: One Energy Plaza
       Detroit, MI 48226

Washington Office
Mailing: 601 Pennsylvania Ave. NW   Tel: (202) 347-8420
       North Bldg., Suite 350   Fax: (202) 347-8423
       Washington, DC 20004

Public Affairs and Related Activities Personnel

At Washington Office

BRITTO, Karen   Tel: (202) 347-8420
Manager, Federal Affairs   Fax: (202) 347-8423

Deutsche Bank

A bank holding company. Deutsche Bank Alex.Brown provides a range of advisory, brokerage, and investment services to high-net-worth and ultra-high-net-worth individual investors, as well as institutional and corporate clients in the US.
www.db.com
Employees: 78,000
Industry/ies: Banking/Finance/Investments

Chairman of the Board   Tel: (410) 727-1700
ACKERMANN, Josef   Fax: (410) 895-3450

Chief Executive Officer, Human Resources   Tel: (410) 727-1700
LEITHNER, Stephan   Fax: (410) 895-3450

Co-Chief Executive Officer   Tel: (410) 727-1700
FITSCHEN, Jurgen   Fax: (410) 895-3450

Main Headquarters
Mailing: 100 International Dr,   Tel: (410) 727-1700
       22nd Floor   Fax: (410) 895-3450
       Baltimore, MD 21202   TF: (800) 638-2596

Washington Office
Mailing: 801, 17th St.NW
       Suite 300

Washington, DC 20006

Political Action Committees
Deutsche Bank Americas PAC
FEC ID: C00428896
Contact: Richard W. Ferguson
1399 New York Ave. NW   Tel: (202) 626-7022
Suite 500   Fax: (202) 626-7032
Washington, DC 20005

   Contributions to Candidates: $36,700 (2015-2016)
   Democrats: $5,200; Republicans: $31,500

Corporate Foundations and Giving Programs
Deutsche Bank Contribution Program
One South St.   Tel: (410) 727-1700
28th Floor   Fax: (410) 895-3450
Baltimore, MD 21202

Public Affairs and Related Activities Personnel

At Headquarters

LEWIS, Stuart   Tel: (410) 727-1700
Chief Risk Officer   Fax: (410) 895-3450

SCHENCK, Marcus   Tel: (410) 727-1700
Chief Financial Officer   Fax: (410) 895-3450

SEWING, Christian   Tel: (410) 727-1700
Contact, Private and Business Clients, Legal   Fax: (410) 895-3450

WINKER, Klaus   Tel: (410) 727-1700
Contact, Media Relations   Fax: (410) 895-3450
klaus.winker@db.com

At Washington Office

FERGUSON, Richard W.
PAC Treasurer

Deutsche Bank Securities Inc.

A financial services company.
www.db.com
Industry/ies: Banking/Finance/Investments
Legislative Issues: BAN; FIN; HOM; TAX

Main Headquarters
Mailing: 60 Wall St.   Tel: (212) 250-2500
       New York, NY 10005

Washington Office
Mailing: 801 17th St. NW   Fax: (202) 626-7056
       Suite 300
       Washington, DC 20005

Political Action Committees
Deutsche Bank Americas PAC
FEC ID: C00428896
Contact: Richard W. Ferguson
1399 New York Ave. NW   Tel: (202) 626-7022
Suite 500   Fax: (202) 626-7032
Washington, DC 20005

   Contributions to Candidates: $36,700 (2015-2016)
   Democrats: $5,200; Republicans: $31,500

Public Affairs and Related Activities Personnel

At Washington Office

FERGUSON, Richard W.   Tel: (202) 626-7022
PAC Treasurer   Fax: (202) 626-7056

KELLY, Francis J.   Tel: (202) 626-7022
Managing Director and Head Communications & Public   Fax: (202) 626-7056
Affairs
francis.j.kelly@db.com

Deutsche Post World Net-USA, Inc. (DPWN USA)

Deutsche Post World Net-USA, Inc. (DPWN USA), based in Washington City, is the U.S. subsidiary of Deutsche Post DHL., headquartered in Bonn, Germany. Serves the transportation, logistics and air services industries.
www.deutschepost.de
Industry/ies: Communications; Telecommunications/Internet/Cable
Legislative Issues: TRD

President, Chief Executive Officer and PAC Treasurer
PORDZIK, Wolfgang G.

Main Headquarters
Mailing: 900 17th St. NW   Tel: (202) 293-9380
       Suite 920
       Washington, DC 20006

Washington Office
Mailing: 1667 K St. NW
       Suite 410
       Washington, DC 20006

Political Action Committees
DPWN Holdings (USA) Inc./DHL PAC

FEC ID: C00417915
Contact: Wolfgang G. Pordzik
900 17TH St. NW   Tel: (202) 419-8110
Suite 920
Washington, DC 20006

   Contributions to Candidates: $3,000 (2015-2016)
   Republicans: $3,000

Public Affairs and Related Activities Personnel

At Headquarters

LIBBY, Roger   Tel: (202) 419-1880
Senior Director, Corporate Public Policy
Registered Federal Lobbyist

STANLEY, Kriss   Tel: (202) 419-1880
Federal Lobbyist
kriss.stanley@DPDHL-USA.com
Registered Federal Lobbyist

At Other Offices

GARCIA, Bea   Tel: (954) 701-9265
Director, Media Relations - Americas
1210 South Pine Island Rd., Third Floor
Plantation, FL 33324

Deutsche Telekom, Inc.

Headquartered in Bonn, Germany, with American headquarters in New York, NY. It is one of the four largest wireless carriers in the United States.
www.telekom.com/americas
Industry/ies: Communications; Telecommunications/Internet/Cable
Legislative Issues: TEC

Main Headquarters
Mailing: 1020 19th St.   Tel: (202) 452-9100
         Suite 850   Fax: (202) 452-9555
         Washington, DC 20036

Public Affairs and Related Activities Personnel

At Headquarters

HEDBERG, James I.   Tel: (202) 452-9100
Manager, Regulatory and Government Affairs   Fax: (202) 452-9555

HUSSONG, Annette   Tel: (202) 452-9100
Director, Public & Regulatory Affairs   Fax: (202) 452-9555

SHINGLETON, A. Bradley   Tel: (202) 452-9100
General Counsel   Fax: (202) 452-9555
bradley.shingleton@usa.telekom.de

Devon Energy Production Company, L.P.

Engaged in oil and gas exploration, production and property acquisitions. Devon is an independent oil and gas producer and processor of natural gas and natural gas liquids in North America. The company also has operations in selected international areas. Acquired Santa Fe Snyder Corp. in 2000, Mitchell Energy & Development Corp. in January of 2002, Anderson Exploration in 2001, and Ocean Energy in 2004.
www.dvn.com
Annual Revenues: $16.50 billion
Employees: 6,600
Ticker: NYSE: DVN
SIC: 1311
Industry/ies: Energy/Electricity
Legislative Issues: ENG; FUE

Chairman of the Board   Tel: (405) 235-3611
NICHOLS, Larry J.   Fax: (405) 552-4667
nichols@dvn.com

President and Chief Executive Officer   Tel: (405) 235-3611
RICHELS, John   Fax: (405) 552-4550

Main Headquarters
Mailing: 20 N. Broadway   Tel: (405) 235-3611
         Oklahoma City, OK 73102   Fax: (405) 552-4550
             TF: (800) 732-0330

Washington Office
Mailing: 101 Constitution Ave. NW
         Washington, DC 20001

Corporate Foundations and Giving Programs

Devon's Corporate Giving
Contact: Christina Rehkop
20 N. Broadway   Tel: (405) 235-3611
Suite 1500   Fax: (405) 552-4550
Oklahoma City, OK 73102

Public Affairs and Related Activities Personnel

At Headquarters

ALBERTI, Sue   Tel: (405) 235-3611
Senior Vice President, Marketing   Fax: (405) 552-4550

BROCKMAN , Carla   Tel: (405) 235-3611
Vice President, Corporate Governance and Secretary   Fax: (405) 552-4550

COODY, Scott   Tel: (405) 552-4735
Director, Investor Relations   Fax: (405) 552-4550

HAGER, David A.   Tel: (405) 235-3611
Chief Operating Officer   Fax: (405) 552-4550

HARRIS, David G.   Tel: (405) 235-3611
Senior Vice President, Business Development   Fax: (405) 552-4550

HENSON, Gregg L.   Tel: (405) 235-3611
Vice President and Corporate Controller   Fax: (405) 552-4550

HUMPHERS, Jeremy D.   Tel: (405) 235-3611
Senior Vice President and Chief Accounting Officer   Fax: (405) 552-4550

MARCUM, R. Alan   Tel: (405) 235-3611
Executive Vice President, Administration   Fax: (405) 552-4550

MINTY, Chip   Tel: (405) 228-8647
Manager, Media Relations   Fax: (405) 552-4550
chip.minty@dvn.com

MITCHELL, Thomas L.   Tel: (405) 235-3611
Executive Vice President and Chief Financial Officer   Fax: (405) 552-4550

PENHALL, Bill   Tel: (405) 235-3611
Senior Vice President, Exploration and Strategic Services   Fax: (405) 552-4550

REHKOP, Christina   Tel: (405) 235-3611
Supervisor, Community Affairs   Fax: (405) 552-4550
christins.rehkop@dvn.com

RITENOUR, Jeff   Tel: (405) 235-3611
Senior Vice President, Corporate Finance and Treasurer   Fax: (405) 552-4550

ROSEN, Rebecca   Tel: (405) 235-3611
Vice President, Federal Government Affairs   Fax: (405) 552-4550
Registered Federal Lobbyist

RUDOLPH, Frank   Tel: (405) 235-3611
Executive Vice President, Human Resources   Fax: (405) 552-4550
frank.rudolph@dvn.com

SMETTE, Darryl G.   Tel: (405) 235-3611
Executive Vice President, Marketing, Facilities, Pipeline and   Fax: (405) 552-4550
Supply Chain

SNYDER, Shea   Tel: (405) 552-4782
Director, Investor Relations   Fax: (405) 552-4550
shea.snyder@dvn.com

TAYLOR, Lyndon C.   Tel: (405) 235-3611
Executive Vice President and General Counsel   Fax: (405) 552-4550
lyndon.taylor@dvn.com

THILL, Howard J.   Tel: (405) 235-3611
Senior Vice President, Communications and Investor   Fax: (405) 552-4550
Relations

WHITSITT, William F.   Tel: (405) 235-3611
Executive Vice President, Public Affairs   Fax: (405) 552-4550
wfwhitsitt@aol.com

WILLIAMS, Ben   Tel: (405) 235-3611
Vice President and Chief Information Officer   Fax: (405) 552-4550

WRIGHT, Allen   Tel: (405) 552-5394
Vice President, Public and Government Affairs   Fax: (405) 552-4550

At Other Offices

BARGAS, Jon
Supervisor, Political Affairs
333 W. Sheridan Ave.
Oklahoma City, OK 73102

SANDLIN, Jesse
Federal Lobbyists
333 W. Sheridan Ave.
Oklahoma City, OK 73102
Registered Federal Lobbyist

DeVry, Inc.

An institute of higher learning.
www.devryinc.com
Annual Revenues: $1.85 billion
Employees: 10,136
Ticker: NYSE: DV
SIC: 8200
Industry/ies: Education
Legislative Issues: EDU

President and Chief Executive Officer   Tel: (630) 571-7700
WARDELL, Lisa   Fax: (630) 990-1890

Main Headquarters
Mailing: 3005 Highland Pkwy.   Tel: (630) 571-7700
         Downers Grove, IL 60515-5799   Fax: (630) 990-1890
             TF: (800) 733-3879

Political Action Committees
DeVry Inc. PAC
FEC ID: C00198606
Contact: Patrick Unzicker
3005 Highland Pkwy.

Suite 1000
Downers Grove, IL 60515

Contributions to Candidates: $23,000 (2015-2016)
Democrats: $9,000; Republicans: $14,000

Corporate Foundations and Giving Programs

DeVry Foundation
Contact: Sharon Thomas Parrott
3005 Highland Pkwy.   Tel: (630) 571-7700
Downers Grove, IL 60515-5799   Fax: (630) 990-1890

Public Affairs and Related Activities Personnel

At Headquarters

DAVIS, Gregory S.   Tel: (630) 571-7700
General Counsel and Secretary

DENTZER, Susan   Tel: (630) 574-1982
Senior Administrator, External Relations   Fax: (630) 990-1890
sdentzer@devry.com

GIBBLE, Ernie   Tel: (630) 353-9920
Senior Director, Global Communications   Fax: (630) 990-1890
egibble@devrygroup.com

JENNINGS, Donna N.   Tel: (630) 571-7700
Senior Vice President, Human Resources   Fax: (630) 571-0317

PARROTT, Sharon Thomas   Tel: (630) 571-7700
Senior Vice President, Government, Regulatory Affairs, Chief Fax: (630) 571-1991
Compliance Officer and President

SODEIKA, Lisa M.   Tel: (630) 571-7700
Senior Vice President, External Relations and Regulatory Fax: (630) 990-1890
Affairs

TAYLOR, Ronald L.   Tel: (630) 571-7700
Director and Senior Advisor   Fax: (630) 990-1890

UNZICKER, Patrick   Tel: (630) 571-7700
Senior Vice President, Chief Financial Officer, Treasurer and Fax: (630) 990-1890
PAC Treasurer

WALTER, Joan   Tel: (630) 571-7700
Senior Director, Investor and Media Relations Fax: (630) 990-1890
jwalter@devrygroup.com

DFB Pharmaceuticals, Inc.

Provides branded products, services and technologies to the global healthcare industry.
www.dfb.com
Annual Revenues: $322.45 million
Employees: 700
Industry/ies: Pharmaceutical Industry

Chairman and Chief Executive Officer   Tel: (817) 900-4050
DORMAN, Paul H.

Main Headquarters
Mailing: 3909 Hulen St.   Tel: (817) 900-4050
             Fort Worth, TX 76107

DHB Industries Inc.

See listing on page 642 under Point Blank Solutions, Inc.

DHL Worldwide Express, Inc.

Provides international air express services. A wholly owned subsidiary of Deutsche Post World Net, headquartered in Bonn, Germany. Acquired Airborne, Inc. (ground operations only) in August, 2003.
www.dhl-usa.com
Employees: 6,500
Industry/ies: Aerospace/Aviation; Transportation

Chief Executive Officer   Tel: (954) 888-7000
PARRA, Mike   Fax: (954) 888-7310

Main Headquarters
Mailing: 1210 S. Pine Island Rd.   Tel: (954) 888-7000
             Fourth Floor   Fax: (954) 888-7310
             Plantation, FL 33324   TF: (800) 225-5345

Washington Office
Mailing: 1667 K St. NW
             Suite 410
             Washington, DC 20006

Political Action Committees
DPWN Holdings (USA) Inc./DHL PAC
FEC ID: C00417915
Contact: Wolfgang G. Pordzik
900 17TH St. NW   Tel: (202) 419-8110
Suite 920
Washington, DC 20006

Contributions to Candidates: $3,000 (2015-2016)
Republicans: $3,000

Public Affairs and Related Activities Personnel

At Headquarters

ESTEVEZ, Rafael   Tel: (954) 888-7000
Chief Financial Officer   Fax: (954) 888-7310

GARCIA, Bea   Tel: (954) 626-2419
Director, Media Relations   Fax: (954) 888-7310
bea.garcia@dhl.com

MINTZ, Robert   Tel: (425) 368-2163
Manager, Communications   Fax: (954) 888-7310
robertmintz@earthlink.net

At Other Offices

LANEY, Jr., Eugene   Tel: (202) 661-6118
Head, International Trade Affairs
1200 G St. NW, Suite 800
Washington, DC 20006

PORDZIK, Wolfgang G.
PAC Treasurer
900 17th St. NW, Suite 920
Washington, DC 20006

Diageo North America

Producer and distributor of alcoholic beverages.
www.diageo.com
Employees: 8,000
Ticker: NYSE: DEO
Industry/ies: Food And Beverage Industry
Legislative Issues: AGR; ALC; BEV; FOO; TAX; TRD

Chairman of the Board   Tel: (203) 229-2100
HUMER, Dr. Franz   Fax: (203) 229-8901

Chief Executive Officer   Tel: (203) 229-2100
MENEZES , Ivan   Fax: (203) 229-8901

Main Headquarters
Mailing: 801 Main Ave.   Tel: (203) 229-2100
             Norwalk, CT 06851   Fax: (203) 229-8901

Washington Office
Mailing: 600 Pennsylvania Ave. SE   Tel: (202) 715-1115
             Suite 304
             Washington, DC 20003

Political Action Committees
Diageo North America Employees' Political Participation Committee PAC
FEC ID: C00034470
Contact: Michael F. Mulhall
801 Main St.
Norwalk, CT 06851

Contributions to Candidates: $38,842 (2015-2016)
Democrats: $8,342; Republicans: $30,500

Corporate Foundations and Giving Programs

Diageo Foundation
801 Main St.   Tel: (203) 229-2100
Norwalk, CT 06851   Fax: (203) 229-8901

Public Affairs and Related Activities Personnel

At Headquarters

LAMBKIN, Charlotte   Tel: (203) 229-2100
Director, Corporate Relations   Fax: (203) 229-8901

MAHLAN, Deirdre   Tel: (203) 229-2100
Chief Financial Officer   Fax: (203) 229-8901

FENNELL , Andy   Tel: (203) 229-2100
President   Fax: (203) 229-8901

MANZ, Anna   Tel: (203) 229-2100
Director, Strategy   Fax: (203) 229-8901

MORIARTY, Siobhan   Tel: (203) 229-2100
General Counsel   Fax: (203) 229-8901

MULHALL, Michael F.   Tel: (203) 229-2100
Vice President, Federal Relations   Fax: (203) 229-8901

SALLER , Syl   Tel: (203) 229-2100
Chief Marketing Officer   Fax: (203) 229-8901

SCHILLING, Jessica   Tel: (203) 229-2100
Vice President, Human Resources   Fax: (203) 229-8901

SCHWARTZ, Larry   Tel: (203) 229-2100
President   Fax: (203) 229-8901

SMITH, Guy   Tel: (203) 229-2100
Executive Vice President, Corporate Relations Fax: (203) 229-8901

WOOD, Leanne   Tel: (203) 229-2100
Director, Human Resources   Fax: (203) 229-8901

At Washington Office

BERTMAN, Mike   Tel: (202) 715-1115
Vice President, Federal Relations
michael.bertman@diageo.com
Registered Federal Lobbyist

JOHNSON, Erica   Tel: (202) 715-1115

Contact, Government Relations
Registered Federal Lobbyist
WISE, Elizabeth   Tel: (202) 715-1115
Federal Lobbyist
Registered Federal Lobbyist

At Other Offices

JEFFORDS, Maura   Tel: (202) 715-1115
Federal Lobbyist   Fax: (202) 715-1114
1301 K St. NW, Suite 1000 East
Washington, DC 20005
Registered Federal Lobbyist

The Dial Corporation

A subsidiary of Henkel Corporation (see separate listing). A consumer products manufacturer.
www.dialsoap.com
Employees: 2,900
SIC: 2840
Industry/ies: Personal Care/Hygiene
Legislative Issues: CHM; CSP; ENG; TAX; TRD

President and Chief Executive Officer   Tel: (480) 754-3425
CASPER, Bradley A.   Fax: (480) 754-1098

Main Headquarters
Mailing: 7201 E Henkel Way   Tel: (480) 754-3425
             Scottsdale, AZ 85255   Fax: (480) 754-1098

Political Action Committees
Dial Corporation Employees' PAC
FEC ID: C00321083
Contact: James K. Barnhouse
19001 N. Scottsdale Rd.
Scottsdale, AZ 85255

Public Affairs and Related Activities Personnel

At Headquarters

DEMERS, Cynthia A.   Tel: (480) 754-3425
Vice President, Corporate Communications
demers@dialcorp.com

At Other Offices

BARNHOUSE, James K.
PAC Treasurer
19001 N. Scottsdale Rd.
Scottsdale, AZ 85255

Dialysis Clinic, Inc.

Dialysis provider company.
www.dciinc.org
Industry/ies: Medicine/Health Care/Mental Health

Chairman of the Board   Tel: (615) 327-3061
JOHNSON, H. Keith   Fax: (615) 329-2513

Main Headquarters
Mailing: 1633 Church St.   Tel: (615) 327-3061
             Suite 500   Fax: (615) 329-2513
             Nashville, TN 37203   TF: (866) 424-1990

Diamond Foods Inc.

Diamond Foods is the premier processor and marketer of culinary, inshell snack and ingredient nuts.
www.diamondfoods.com
Employees: 1,266
Ticker: NASDAQ: DMND
SIC: 2090
Industry/ies: Food And Beverage Industry

Chairman   Tel: (415) 912-3180
ZOLLARS, Robert J.

President and Chief Executive Officer   Tel: (415) 912-3180
DRISCOLL, Brian J.

Main Headquarters
Mailing: 600 Montgomery St.   Tel: (415) 912-3180
             13th Floor
             San Francisco, CA 94111

Political Action Committees
Diamond Foods Inc. PAC
FEC ID: C00126466
Contact: Troy Bryce
1050 S. Diamond St.
P.O. Box 9024
Stockton, CA 95205

Public Affairs and Related Activities Personnel

At Headquarters

COLO, David   Tel: (415) 912-3180
Executive Vice President and Chief Operating Officer

JOHNSON, Lloyd J.   Tel: (415) 912-3180
Executive Vice President and Chief Sales Officer

JONES, Isobel   Tel: (415) 912-3180
Executive Vice President and General Counsel

SEGRE, Linda   Tel: (415) 445-7444
Senior Vice President, Corporate Strategy and People Officer
lsegre@diamondfoods.com

SILCOCK, Ray   Tel: (415) 912-3180
Executive Vice President and Chief Financial Officer

At Other Offices

BRYCE , Troy   Tel: (209) 467-6000
PAC Treasurer   Fax: (209) 461-7309
1050 S. Diamond St., P.O. Box 1727
Stockton, CA 95205-7087

Diebold, Inc.

Manufacturer of financial self-service transaction systems and security products.
www.diebold.com
Annual Revenues: $2.35 billion
Employees: 15,000
Ticker: NYSE: DBD
SIC: 3669; 3499; 3578; 5044; 5063
NAICS: 333313; 332999; 45321; 42161; 334119
Industry/ies: Computer/Technology

Chairman of the Board   Tel: (330) 490-4000
WALLACE, Henry D. G.   Fax: (330) 490-3794

President and Chief Executive Officer   Tel: (330) 490-4000
MATTES, Andy W.   Fax: (330) 490-3794

Main Headquarters
Mailing: 5995 Mayfair Rd.   Tel: (330) 490-4000
             P.O. Box 3077   Fax: (330) 490-3794
             N. Canton, OH 44720-8077   TF: (800) 999-3600

Public Affairs and Related Activities Personnel

At Headquarters

BAST , Christopher   Tel: (330) 490-6908
Contact, Investor Relations   Fax: (330) 490-3794
christopher.bast@diebold.com

CHAPMAN, Christopher A.   Tel: (330) 490-4000
Senior Vice President and Chief Financial Officer Fax: (330) 490-3794

FINEFROCK, Jamie   Tel: (330) 490-6319
Contact, Investor Relations   Fax: (330) 490-3794
jamie.finefrock@diebold.com

HESSE, Chad F.   Tel: (330) 490-4000
Vice President, General Counsel and Secretary   Fax: (330) 490-3794

JACOBSEN, Michael   Tel: (330) 490-3786
Senior Director, Corporate Communications and Investments Fax: (330) 490-3794
michael.jacobsen@diebold.com

KRISTOFF, John D.   Tel: (330) 490-4000
Vice President and Chief Communications Officer Fax: (330) 490-3794
john.kristoff@diebold.com

LEIKEN, Jonathan B.   Tel: (330) 490-4000
Senior Vice President, Chief Legal Officer and Secretary Fax: (330) 490-3794

RADIGAN, Elizabeth C.   Tel: (330) 490-4000
Vice President, Chief Ethics and Compliance Officer Fax: (330) 490-3794

RUTT, Sheila M.   Tel: (330) 490-4000
Vice President and Chief Human Resources Officer Fax: (330) 490-3794

Diffusion Pharmaceuticals, LLC

A clinical-stage drug-development company.
www.diffusionpharma.com
Employees: 10
Industry/ies: Pharmaceutical Industry

Co-Founder and Chief Executive Officer   Tel: (434) 220-0718
KALERGIS, David G.   Fax: (434) 220-0722
dkalergis@diffusionpharma.com

Main Headquarters
Mailing: 2020 Avon Ct.   Tel: (434) 220-0718
             Suite Four   Fax: (434) 220-0722
             Charlottesville, VA 22902

Public Affairs and Related Activities Personnel

At Headquarters

HOY, Kelly   Tel: (434) 220-0718
Senior Project Manager   Fax: (434) 220-0722

SHEALY, CFA, MBA, Ben   Tel: (434) 220-0718
Chief Financial Officer   Fax: (434) 220-0722

Digimarc Corporation

A security software company and supplier of secure identity and media management solutions.
www.digimarc.com

Annual Revenues: $24.44 million
Employees: 150
Ticker: NASDAQ: DMRC
SIC: 7373
Industry/ies: Computer/Technology

Chairman of the and Chief Executive Officer
DAVIS, Bruce

Tel: (503) 469-4800
Fax: (503) 469-4777

Main Headquarters
Mailing: 9405 S.W. Gemini Dr.
               Beaverton, OR 97008

Tel: (503) 469-4800
Fax: (503) 469-4777
TF: (800) 344-4627

Public Affairs and Related Activities Personnel

At Headquarters

BECK, Charles
Chief Financial Officer and Treasurer

Tel: (503) 469-4800
Fax: (503) 469-4777

CHAMNESS, Robert
Chief Legal Officer and Secretary

Tel: (503) 469-4800
Fax: (503) 469-4777

GIACHETTI, Gina
Contact, Media Relations
pr@digimarc.com

Tel: (510) 858-8111
Fax: (503) 469-4777

KNUDSON, Ed
Executive Vice President, Sales and Marketing

Tel: (503) 469-4800
Fax: (503) 469-4777

LIOLIOS, Scott
Contact, Investor Relations

Tel: (949) 574-3860
Fax: (503) 469-4777

Digital Angel

Digital Angel (formerly Applied Digital Solutions, Inc.) is a technology company in the field of animal identification and emergency identification solutions. Its products are applications as pet identification, using its patented, FDA-approved implantable microchip; livestock identification and herd management using visual and radio frequency identification (RFID) ear tags; and global positioning systems (GPS) search and rescue beacons for army, navy and air force applications worldwide.
www.digitalangel.com
Annual Revenues: $37.72 million
Employees: 200
Ticker: NASDAQ: DIGA
SIC: 3669
Industry/ies: Computer/Technology
Legislative Issues: DEF; ECN; TRD

Interim Chief Executive Officer, President and Chairman of the board
PENNI, Daniel E.

Tel: (651) 552-6301
Fax: (651) 455-0413

Main Headquarters
Mailing: 300 State St.
               New London, CT 06320

Tel: (651) 900-0776
Fax: (651) 455-0413

Public Affairs and Related Activities Personnel

At Headquarters

BREECE, Lorraine M.
Chief Financial Officer

Tel: (651) 900-0776
Fax: (651) 455-0413

FINK, Rob
Contact, Investor Relations and Media Relations

Tel: (212) 896-1206
Fax: (651) 455-0413

PETERSEN, Patricia
General Counsel

Tel: (651) 900-0776
Fax: (651) 455-0413

DigitalGlobe, Inc.

A satellite imagery company.
www.digitalglobe.com
Annual Revenues: $667.50 million
Employees: 1,339
Ticker: NYSE: DGI
SIC: 4899
Industry/ies: Aerospace/Aviation; Science; Scientific Research; Transportation
Legislative Issues: AER; BUD; DEF; INT; SCI

Chairman of the Board
ESTES, Howell

Tel: (303) 684-4000
Fax: (303) 684-3848

President and Chief Executive Officer
TARR, Jeffrey R.

Tel: (303) 684-4000
Fax: (303) 684-3848

Main Headquarters
Mailing: 1601 Dry Creek Dr.
               Suite 260
               Longmont, CO 80503

Tel: (303) 684-4000
Fax: (303) 684-4221
TF: (800) 655-7929

Washington Office
Mailing: 2325 Dulles Corner Blvd.
               Herndon, VA 20171

Tel: (703) 480-7500

Political Action Committees
DigitalGlobe PAC Inc.
FEC ID: C00370585
Contact: Gary W. Ferrera
1601 Dry Creek Dr.

Suite 260
Longmont, CO 80503
   Contributions to Candidates: $79,800 (2015-2016)
   Democrats: $22,050; Republicans: $57,750

Public Affairs and Related Activities Personnel

At Headquarters

BAER, Julie
Government Affairs Associate

Tel: (303) 684-4000
Fax: (303) 684-4221

BANKS, David
Vice President, Investor Relations
ir@digitalglobe.com

Tel: (303) 684-4210
Fax: (303) 684-3848

COMFORT, Stephanie
Senior Vice President, Corporate Strategy, Communications and Marketing

Tel: (303) 684-4000
Fax: (303) 684-4221

FERRERA, Gary W.
Executive Vice President and Chief Financial Officer

Tel: (303) 684-4000
Fax: (303) 684-4221

FRAZIER, Tony
Senior Vice President, Government Solutions

Tel: (303) 684-4000
Fax: (303) 684-4221

HASCALL, Timothy M.
Executive Vice President and Chief Operations Officer

Tel: (303) 684-4000
Fax: (303) 684-4221

JABLONSKY, Dan
Senior Vice President, General Counsel and Corporate Secretary

Tel: (303) 684-4000
Fax: (303) 684-3848

PAULES, USMC (Ret.), Terry
Federal Lobbyist
Paul@geoeye.com
Registered Federal Lobbyist

Tel: (703) 480-7500
Fax: (703) 450-9570

SHAPERO, Amy
Senior Vice President, Strategy and Corporate Development

Tel: (303) 684-4000
Fax: (303) 684-4221

SIMMONS, Vernon N.
Federal Lobbyist
Registered Federal Lobbyist

Tel: (703) 480-7500
Fax: (703) 450-9570

STEINKE, Marcy
Senior Vice President, Government Relations
Registered Federal Lobbyist

Tel: (303) 684-4000
Fax: (303) 684-3848

TROUP, Nathan M.
Vice President, Chief Accounting Officer

Tel: (303) 684-4000
Fax: (303) 684-4221

TURNER, Bert
Senior Vice President, Diversified Commercial Sales and Marketing

Tel: (303) 684-4000
Fax: (303) 684-4221

VAN UUM, Abigail
Contact, Media Relations
digitalglobe@edelman.com

Tel: (512) 634-3642
Fax: (303) 684-3848

WRAY, Grover N.
Senior Vice President and Chief Human Resource Officer

Tel: (303) 684-4000
Fax: (303) 684-3848

YASUMURA, Karen
Federal Lobbyist
Registered Federal Lobbyist

Tel: (303) 684-4000
Fax: (303) 684-4221

Dilas Diode Laser, Inc.

Dilas Diode Laser, Inc., based in Tucson City, is the U.S. subsidiary of DILAS Diodenlaser GmbH, headquartered in Mainz, Germany. Develops and manufactures laser components.
www.dilas.com
Employees: 200
Industry/ies: Electricity & Electronics; Electronics; Energy/Electricity
Legislative Issues: DEF

Main Headquarters
Mailing: 9070 S. Rita Rd.
               Suite 1500
               Tucson, AZ 85747-6104

Tel: (520) 232-3480
Fax: (520) 300-8230

Public Affairs and Related Activities Personnel

At Headquarters

GARCIA, Sandra
Contact, Global Marketing and Media Relations
s.garcia@DILAS-INC.com

Tel: (520) 232-3480
Fax: (520) 300-8230

Dillard's Inc.

Formerly known as the Dillard Department Stores, Inc. A fashion apparel, cosmetics and home furnishing retailer.
www.dillards.com
Annual Revenues: $6.68 billion
Employees: 21,200
Ticker: NYSE: DDS
SIC: 5311
Industry/ies: Apparel/Textiles Industry; Retail/Wholesale

Chairman and Chief Executive Officer
DILLARD, II, William

Tel: (501) 376-5200
Fax: (501) 376-7831

Main Headquarters
Mailing: P. O. Box 486

Tel: (501) 376-5200

Little Rock, AR 72203 | Fax: (501) 376-5917

Public Affairs and Related Activities Personnel

At Headquarters

BULL, Julie Johnson | Tel: (501) 376-5965
Director, Investor Relations | Fax: (501) 376-5885
julie.bull@dillards.com

ELLIOT, Dean | Tel: (501) 376-5200
Director, Government Affairs | Fax: (501) 376-7831

WORLEY, Dean L. | Tel: (501) 376-5200
VicePresident and General Counsel | Fax: (501) 376-7831

DIRECTV Group Inc.

DIRECTV provides digital television entertainment services. It acquires, promotes, sells, and distributes digital entertainment programming primarily through satellite to residential and commercial subscribers.
www.directv.com
Annual Revenues: $33.55 billion
Employees: 29,700
Ticker: NASDAQ: DTV
SIC: 4899
Industry/ies: Communications; Telecommunications/Internet/Cable
Legislative Issues: COM; TAX; TEC

Chairman of the Board, President and Chief Executive Officer | Tel: (310) 964-5000
WHITE, Michael | Fax: (310) 535-5225

Main Headquarters
Mailing: 2230 E. Imperial Hwy. | Tel: (310) 964-5000
El Segundo, CA 90245 | Fax: (310) 535-5225

Washington Office
Mailing: 444 N. Capitol St. NW | Tel: (202) 383-6330
Suite 600 | TF: (800) 490-4388
Washington, DC 20001

Political Action Committees
DIRECTV Group Inc. Fund - Federal (DirecTV PAC)
FEC ID: C00331991
Contact: Andrew Reinsdorf
901 F St. NW
Suite 600
Washington, DC 20004

Contributions to Candidates: $233,500 (2015-2016)
Democrats: $111,500; Republicans: $122,000

Principal Recipients

HOUSE
SCALISE, STEVE MR. (REP-LA)

Corporate Foundations and Giving Programs
DIRECTV Disasters Relief Fund
2230 E. Imperial Hwy. | Tel: (310) 964-5000
El Segundo, CA 90245 | Fax: (310) 535-5225

DIRECTV Employee Gift Matching
2230 E. Imperial Hwy. | Tel: (310) 964-5000
El Segundo, CA 90245 | Fax: (310) 535-5225

Public Affairs and Related Activities Personnel

At Headquarters

BALCERZAK, Ed | Tel: (310) 964-5000
Senior Vice President, Customer Care | Fax: (310) 535-5225

BOSCH, Joseph A. | Tel: (310) 964-5000
Executive Vice President and Chief Human Resources Officer | Fax: (310) 535-5225

CHEW, Allen | Tel: (310) 964-5000
Director, Government Affairs | Fax: (310) 535-5225

DOYLE, Patrick T. | Tel: (310) 964-5000
Executive Vice President and Chief Financial Officer | Fax: (310) 535-5225

EKSTEDT, Jade | Tel: (310) 964-3429
Senior Manager, Public Relations | Fax: (310) 535-5225
jlekstedt@directv.com

GIESELMAN, Jon | Tel: (310) 964-5000
Senior Vice President, Advertising and Communications | Fax: (310) 535-5225
jtgieselman@directv.com

MERCER, Robert | Tel: (310) 726-4683
Director, Public Relations | Fax: (310) 535-5225
rgmercer@directv.com

At Washington Office

GRINGERI, Darris | Tel: (202) 383-6330
Vice President, Public Relations
dagringeri@directv.com

HUNTER, Larry D. | Tel: (212) 205-0882
Executive Vice President and General Counsel

REINSDORF, Andrew | Tel: (202) 383-6330
Senior Vice President, Government Affairs
areinsdorf@directv.com

Discover Financial Services

Discover Financial Services is a credit card issuer and electronic payment services company.
www.discoverfinancial.com
Annual Revenues: $7.24 billion
Employees: 15,036
Ticker: NYSE: DFS
SIC: 6141
Industry/ies: Banking/Finance/Investments
Legislative Issues: BAN; BNK; EDU; FIN; HOM; INT; POS

Chairman and Chief Executive Officer | Tel: (224) 405-0900
NELMS, David W. | Fax: (224) 405-4993
david.w.nelms@discoverfinancial.com

Main Headquarters
Mailing: 2500 Lake Cook Rd. | Tel: (224) 405-0900
Riverwoods, IL 60015 | Fax: (224) 405-4993
| TF: (800) 347-2683

Washington Office
Mailing: 500 Eighth St. NW | Tel: (202) 863-7278
Suite 210
Washington, DC 20004

Political Action Committees
DISCOVER FINANCIAL SERVICES POLITICAL ACTION COMMITTEE
FEC ID: C00438051
Contact: Tod Gordon
500 Eighth St. NW | Tel: (202) 863-7278
Suite 210
Washington, DC 20004

Corporate Foundations and Giving Programs
Discover Financial Services Contributions Program
2500 Lake Cook Rd. | Tel: (877) 807-0203
Riverwoods, IL 60015

Public Affairs and Related Activities Personnel

At Headquarters

GRAF, R. Mark | Tel: (224) 405-0900
Executive Vice President and Chief Financial Officer | Fax: (224) 405-4993

HOCHSCHILD, Roger C. | Tel: (224) 405-0900
President and Chief Operating Officer | Fax: (224) 405-4993

LOEGER, Julie | Tel: (224) 405-0900
Executive Vice President, Chief Marketing Officer | Fax: (224) 405-4993

MCNAMARA CORLEY, Kathy | Tel: (224) 405-0900
Executive Vice President, General Counsel and Secretary | Fax: (224) 405-4993

ROSE, R. Douglas | Tel: (224) 405-0900
Senior Vice President, Chief Human Resources Officer | Fax: (224) 405-4993

TOWSON, Matthew | Tel: (224) 405-5649
Director, Community Affairs | Fax: (224) 405-4993
matthewtowson@discover.com

At Washington Office

GORDON, Tod | Tel: (202) 863-7278
Senior Vice President and Treasurer

MESSINA, Raymond A. | Tel: (202) 863-7278
Assistant General Counsel and Vice President, Government Relations
raymessina@discover.com

PEMBROKE, Mary Dwyer | Tel: (202) 863-7278
Federal Lobbyist
Registered Federal Lobbyist

SANTORO, Richard | Tel: (202) 863-7278
Vice President
Registered Federal Lobbyist

Discovery Communications, Inc.

A global media and entertainment company.
corporate.discovery.com
Annual Revenues: $6.39 Billion
Employees: 6,800
Ticker: NASDAQ: DISCA
SIC: 4841
Industry/ies: Communications; Education; Media/Mass Communication

President and Chief Executive Officer | Tel: (240) 662-2000
ZASLAV, David

Main Headquarters
Mailing: One Discovery Pl. | Tel: (240) 662-2000
Silver Spring, MD 20910

Public Affairs and Related Activities Personnel

At Headquarters

CAMPBELL, Bruce | Tel: (240) 662-2000
Chief Development Officer and General Counsel

LEAVY, David | Tel: (240) 662-2000

Chief Communications Officer, Senior Executive, Vice President, Corporate Marketing and Affairs

ROMM , Adria Alpert   Tel: (240) 662-2000
Chief Human Resources and Global Diversity Officer
Adria_Alpert-Romm@discovery.com

VERVEER, Alexa   Tel: (240) 662-2000
Senior Vice President, Public Policy and Government Relations

WARREN, Andrew   Tel: (240) 662-2000
Senior Executive Vice President and Chief Financial Officer

Dish Network

Provider of satellite-based pay-tv.
www.dish.com
Annual Revenues: $14.77 billion
Employees: 19,000
Ticker: NASDAQ: DISH
SIC: 4841
Industry/ies: Communications; Media/Mass Communication; Telecommunications/Internet/Cable
Legislative Issues: COM; CPT; TEC

Co-founder and Chairman of the Board   Tel: (303) 723-1000
ERGEN, Charles W.   Fax: (303) 723-1399

Main Headquarters
Mailing: 9601 S. Meridian Blvd.   Tel: (303) 723-1000
         Englewood, CO 80112   Fax: (303) 723-1999

Washington Office
Mailing: 1101 Vermont Ave. NW   Tel: (202) 293-0981
         Washington, DC 20005

Political Action Committees
EchoStar Corporation and Dish Network Corporation PAC (EchoStar Dish Network PAC)
FEC ID: C00330647
Contact: Jeffrey Blum
1110 Vermont Ave. NW   Tel: (202) 293-0981
Suite 750   Fax: (202) 293-0984
Washington, DC 20005

    Contributions to Candidates: $103,340 (2015-2016)
    Democrats: $36,000; Republicans: $67,340

       Principal Recipients

          SENATE
          GARDNER, CORY (REP-CO)
          GRASSLEY, CHARLES E SENATOR (REP-IA)
          LEAHY, PATRICK J (DEM-VT)

          HOUSE
          MCMORRIS RODGERS, CATHY (REP-WA)

Public Affairs and Related Activities Personnel

At Headquarters

AHMED, Amir   Tel: (303) 723-1000
Senior Vice President, Sales   Fax: (303) 723-1999

CULLEN, Thomas   Tel: (303) 723-1000
Executive Vice President, Corporate Development   Fax: (303) 723-1999

DODGE, R. Stanton   Tel: (303) 723-1000
Executive Vice President, General Counsel and Secretary   Fax: (303) 723-1399

HAN, Bernie   Tel: (303) 723-1000
Executive Vice President and Chief Operating Officer   Fax: (303) 723-1999

JOHNSON, Danielle   Tel: (720) 514-5351
Manager, Corporate Communications   Fax: (303) 723-1999
danielle.johnson@dish.com

KUELLING, Chris   Tel: (303) 723-1000
Senior Vice President, International Business and Legal Affairs   Fax: (303) 723-1999

MCCLASKEY, Mike   Tel: (303) 723-1000
Executive Vice President and Chief Human Resources Officer   Fax: (303) 723-1999

MOORHEAD, James   Tel: (303) 723-1000
Senior Vice President and Chief Marketing Officer   Fax: (303) 723-1999

NEYLON, Brian   Tel: (303) 723-1000
Senior Vice President, Sales   Fax: (303) 723-1999

SAYEEDI, Nick   Tel: (303) 723-1000
Senior Vice President, Deputy General Counsel   Fax: (303) 723-1999

SCHLICHTING, Warren   Tel: (303) 723-1000
Senior Vice President, Programming and Media Sales   Fax: (303) 723-1999

SCHNEIDER, Kathy   Tel: (303) 723-1000
Senior Vice President, Operations   Fax: (303) 723-1999

SWAIN, Steve   Tel: (303) 723-1000
Senior Vice President and Chief Financial Officer   Fax: (303) 723-1999

At Other Offices

BLUM, Jeffrey   Tel: (202) 293-0981

Senior Vice President & Deputy General Counsel   Fax: (202) 293-0984
1110 Vermont Ave. NW, Suite 750
Washington, DC 20005
Jeffrey.Blum@dish.com
Registered Federal Lobbyist

LEWIS, Peter C.   Tel: (202) 293-0981
Federal Lobbyist   Fax: (202) 293-0984
1110 Vermont Ave. NW, Suite 750
Washington, DC 20005
Registered Federal Lobbyist

STRAUS, Jessica T.   Tel: (202) 293-0981
Director, Government Affairs   Fax: (202) 293-0984
1110 Vermont Ave. NW, Suite 750
Washington, DC 20005
Jessica.Straus@dish.com
Registered Federal Lobbyist

The Walt Disney Company (Disney Worldwide Services)

A family entertainment company.
thewaltdisneycompany.com
Annual Revenues: $54.83 billion
Employees: 185,000
Ticker: NYSE: DIS
SIC: 4841
Industry/ies: Communications; Media/Mass Communication; Retail/Wholesale; Sports/Leisure/Entertainment; Travel/Tourism/Lodging
Legislative Issues: ADV; CHM; COM; CPT; IMM; TAX; TRA; TRD

Chairman and Chief Executive Officer   Tel: (818) 560-1000
IGER, Robert A.   Fax: (818) 560-1930

Main Headquarters
Mailing: 500 S. Buena Vista St.   Tel: (818) 560-1000
         Burbank, CA 91521-4944   Fax: (818) 560-1930

Washington Office
Mailing: 425 Third St. SW
         Suite 1100
         Washington, DC 20024

Political Action Committees
Walt Disney Productions Employees PAC
FEC ID: C00197749
Contact: Richard M. Bates
425 Third St. SW   Tel: (202) 222-4700
Suite 1100
Washington, DC 20024

    Contributions to Candidates: $179,500 (2015-2016)
    Democrats: $99,000; Republicans: $80,500

       Principal Recipients

          HOUSE
          NADLER, JERROLD L. MR. (DEM-NY)

Corporate Foundations and Giving Programs
The Walt Disney Company Foundation
Contact: Zenia Mucha
500 S. Buena Vista St.   Tel: (818) 560-1000
Burbank, CA 91521-4944   Fax: (818) 560-1930

Public Affairs and Related Activities Personnel

At Headquarters

BRAVERMAN, Alan   Tel: (818) 560-1000
Senior Executive Vice President, General Counsel and Secretary   Fax: (818) 560-1930

MAYER, Kevin   Tel: (818) 560-1000
Senior Executive Vice President and Chief Strategy Officer   Fax: (818) 560-1930

MCCARTHY, Christine M.   Tel: (818) 560-1000
Senior Executive Vice President and Chief Financial Officer   Fax: (818) 560-1930

MUCHA, Zenia   Tel: (818) 560-5300
Executive Vice President, Chief Communications Officer   Fax: (818) 560-1930
zenia.mucha@corp.disney.com

PARKER, Jayne   Tel: (818) 560-1000
Executive Vice President and Chief Human Resources Officer   Fax: (818) 560-1930

RASULO, Jay   Tel: (818) 560-1000
Senior Executive Vice President and Chief Financial Officer   Fax: (818) 560-1930

SINGER, Lowell   Tel: (818) 560-6601
Senior Vice President, Investor Relations   Fax: (818) 560-1930

At Washington Office

BAILEY, Bill
Vice President, Government Relations
bill.bailey@disney.com
Registered Federal Lobbyist

BATES, Richard M.
Senior Vice President, Government Relations
Registered Federal Lobbyist

CASTELLANO, Michael

Vice President, Government Relations
Registered Federal Lobbyist

DOW, Troy
Vice President, Government Relations and Counsel
troy.dow@disney.com
Registered Federal Lobbyist

FOX, Susan
Vice President, Government Relations
susan.fox@disney.com
Registered Federal Lobbyist

MOORE, Jessica
Director, Government Relations
jessica.moore@disney.com
Registered Federal Lobbyist

PADDEN, Preston R.
Executive Vice President, Government Relations
Registered Federal Lobbyist

DIT-MCO

Engaged in automated product testing solutions for wired assemblies and provides reliable services to industrial, commercial, and military customers.
www.ditmco.com
Annual Revenues: $16.10 million
Employees: 100
Industry/ies: Computer/Technology; Defense/Homeland Security; Electricity & Electronics; Electronics; Energy/Electricity; Government-Related; Machinery/Equipment

President and Chief Executive Officer
THOMPSON, Rick

Tel: (816) 444-9700
Fax: (816) 444-9737

Main Headquarters
Mailing: 5612 Brighton Terr.
Kansas City, MO 64130-4530

Tel: (816) 444-9700
Fax: (816) 444-9737
TF: (800) 821-3487

Diversicare Healthcare Services, Inc.

Formerly Advocat Inc. Provider of long-term care services to nursing home patients.
www.advocat-inc.com
Annual Revenues: $361.62 million
Employees: 4,200
Ticker: NASDAQ: DVCR
SIC: 8051
Industry/ies: Medicine/Health Care/Mental Health

Chief Executive Officer, President and Director
GILL, Kelly J.

Tel: (615) 771-7575
Fax: (615) 771-7409

Main Headquarters
Mailing: 1621 Galleria Blvd.
Brentwood, TN 37027

Tel: (615) 771-7575
Fax: (615) 771-7409

Political Action Committees
Advocat Inc. PAC
FEC ID: C00421735
Contact: Kelly J. Gill
1621 Galleria Blvd.
Brentwood, TN 37027

Tel: (615) 771-7575
Fax: (615) 771-7409

Contributions to Candidates: $3,500 (2015-2016)
Democrats: $2,500; Republicans: $1,000

Corporate Foundations and Giving Programs

Advocat, Inc. Contributions Program
1621 Galleria Blvd.
Brentwood, TN 37027

Tel: (615) 771-7575

Public Affairs and Related Activities Personnel

At Headquarters

CAMPBELL, Leslie
Chief Operating Officer and Executive Vice President

Tel: (615) 771-7575
Fax: (615) 771-7409

MCKNIGHT, Jr., James R.
Chief Financial Officer and Executive Vice President

Tel: (615) 771-7575
Fax: (615) 771-7409

The Dixie Group, Inc.

A manufacturer of carpet yarns and floor coverings. Changed its name from Dixie Yarns, Inc. in 1997.
www.thedixiegroup.com
Annual Revenues: $417.36 million
Employees: 1,740
Ticker: NASDAQ: DXYN
Industry/ies: Construction/Construction Materials

Chairman of the Board and Chief Executive Officer
FRIERSON, Daniel K.

Tel: (423) 510-7000
Fax: (706) 876-5896

Main Headquarters
Mailing: 2208 South Hamilton St.
Dalton, GA 30721-1974

Tel: (706) 876-5800

Corporate Foundations and Giving Programs

Dixie Group Foundation
104 Nowlin Ln.
Suite 101
Chattanooga, TN 37421

Tel: (423) 510-7000
Fax: (706) 876-5896

Public Affairs and Related Activities Personnel

At Other Offices

DAVIS, W. Derek
Vice President, Human Resources
104 Nowlin Ln., Suite 401
Chattanooga, TN 37421

Tel: (706) 876-5804
Fax: (706) 876-5898

FAULKNER, Jon A.
Vice President, Chief Financial Officer
104 Nowlin Ln., Suite 401
Chattanooga, TN 37421
jon.faulkner@dixiegroup.com

Tel: (706) 876-5814
Fax: (706) 876-5896

DJO, Inc.

A developer, manufacturer and distributor of medical devices that provide solutions for musculoskeletal health, vascular health and pain management.
www.djoglobal.com
Annual Revenues: $965.97 million
Employees: 4,700
SIC: 3842
Industry/ies: Medicine/Health Care/Mental Health
Legislative Issues: MMM

Chairman of the Board
ZAFIROVSKI, Mike S.

Tel: (760) 727-1280
Fax: (800) 936-6569

President, Chief Executive Officer and Director
MOGUL, Michael P.
MICHAEL.MOGUL@DJOGLOBAL.COM

Tel: (760) 727-1280
Fax: (800) 936-6569

Main Headquarters
Mailing: 1430 Decision St.
Vista, CA 92081

Tel: (760) 727-1280
Fax: (800) 936-6569
TF: (800) 936-6569

Public Affairs and Related Activities Personnel

At Headquarters

CRAWFORD, Susan
Executive Vice President, Chief Financial Officer

Tel: (760) 727-1280
Fax: (800) 936-6569

MCDONNELL, Gerry
Executive Vice President, Global Operations

Tel: (760) 727-1280
Fax: (800) 936-6569

MURPHY, Stephen J.
President, Sales and Marketing, International Commercial Business

Tel: (760) 727-1280
Fax: (800) 936-6569

ROBERTS, Donald M.
Executive Vice President, General Counsel and Secretary
don.roberts@djoglobal.com

Tel: (760) 727-1280
Fax: (760) 734-3566

SIMONS, Matt
Senior Vice President, Business Development and Investor Relations
matt.simons@djoglobal.com

Tel: (760) 727-1280
Fax: (800) 936-6569

DKRW Energy LLC

Coal-to-liquids energy technology.
www.dkrwenergy.com
Employees: 4
Industry/ies: Energy/Electricity

Main Headquarters
Mailing: 5444 Westheimer
Suite 1560
Houston, TX 77056

Tel: (713) 425-6500
TF: (855) 876-4595

Public Affairs and Related Activities Personnel

At Other Offices

JIMENEZ, Maria
Project Specialist
Two Riverway, Suite 1780
Houston, TX 77056
mjimenez@dkrwenergy.com

Tel: (713) 425-6520
Fax: (713) 355-3201

DNV - Det Norske Veritas Classification (Americas), Inc.

An international company based in Oslo, Norway that works in risk management, environmental protection, maritime classification and safety.
www.dnv.us
Industry/ies: Environment And Conservation; Marine/Maritime/Shipping; Transportation
Legislative Issues: DEF; ENG; HOM; TRA

Main Headquarters
Mailing: One International Blvd.
Suite 406
Mahwah, NJ 07495

Tel: (201) 512-8900

Washington Office

Mailing: 1560 Wilson Blvd.
            Suite 800
            Arlington, VA 22209

Public Affairs and Related Activities Personnel

At Headquarters

COLLINS, Blaine   Tel: (201) 512-8900
Director, External Affairs
Registered Federal Lobbyist

The Doctors' Company

Provides protection and risk management for sole practitioners, doctors groups, and physicians working in clinics, hospitals, and managed care organizations.
www.thedoctors.com
Annual Revenues: $8.90 million
Employees: 300
Industry/ies: Insurance Industry
Legislative Issues: HCR; TOR

Chairman of the Board and Chief Executive Officer   Tel: (707) 226-0100
ANDERSON, FACP, MD, Richard E.   Fax: (707) 226-0111

Main Headquarters
Mailing: P.O. Box 2900   Tel: (707) 226-0100
            185 Greenwood Rd.   Fax: (707) 226-0111
            Napa, CA 94558   TF: (800) 421-2368

Political Action Committees
Doctors' Company Federal PAC (Doc PAC)
FEC ID: C00300376
Contact: Harry Dasinger
185 Greenwood Rd.
Napa, CA 94558

  Contributions to Candidates: $114,200 (2015-2016)
  Democrats: $68,700; Republicans: $45,500

Principal Recipients
HOUSE
            RUIZ, RAUL DR. (DEM-CA)

Corporate Foundations and Giving Programs

The Doctors Company Foundation
Contact: Leona Egeland Siadek
185 Greenwood Rd.
Napa, CA 94558

Public Affairs and Related Activities Personnel

At Headquarters

DASINGER, Harry   Tel: (707) 226-0100
PAC Treasurer   Fax: (707) 226-0111

EGELAND SIADEK, Leona   Tel: (707) 226-0373
Senior Vice President, Government Relations and Executive Fax: (707) 226-0153
Director, Foundation
lsiadek@thedoctors.com

LAWTON, Bryan   Tel: (707) 226-0100
Chief Governance Officer and Chief, Corporate Development Fax: (707) 226-0111

MCHALE, David   Tel: (707) 226-0100
Senior Vice President and General Counsel   Fax: (707) 226-0111

PREIMESBERGER, David G.   Tel: (707) 226-0100
Senior Vice President and Chief Financial Officer Fax: (707) 226-0111

The Doe Run Company

A privately held natural resources company that is engaged in the recycling and fabrication of lead and lead products. The company also has an affiliate-Doe Run Peru.
www.doerun.com
Annual Revenues: $8851.40 million
Employees: 33,200
SIC: 1000
Industry/ies: Mining Industry; Natural Resources
Legislative Issues: CAW; ENV; MAN; NAT; RES

Chairman of the Board   Tel: (310) 453-7100
RENNERT, Ira Leon   Fax: (310) 453-7177

President and Chief Executive Officer   Tel: (314) 453-7100
PYATT, Jerry L.   Fax: (314) 453-7177

Main Headquarters
Mailing: 1801 Park, 270 Dr.   Tel: (314) 453-7100
            Suite 300   Fax: (314) 453-7177
            St. Louis, MO 63146   TF: (800) 356-3786

Political Action Committees
Doe Run Political Action Committee
FEC ID: C00552109
Contact: Terry P. Fox
1801 Park, 270 Dr.
Suite 300
St. Louis, MO 63146

  Contributions to Candidates: $11,400 (2015-2016)

Democrats: $2,500; Republicans: $4,900; Other: $4,000

Corporate Foundations and Giving Programs
The Doe Run Company Contribution Program
Contact: Mark Coomes
1801 Park, 270 Dr.   Tel: (314) 453-7100
Suite 300   Fax: (314) 453-7177
St. Louis, MO 63146

Public Affairs and Related Activities Personnel

At Headquarters

COOMES, Mark   Tel: (314) 453-7100
Vice President, Human Resources and Community Relations Fax: (314) 453-7177

FOX, Terry P.   Tel: (314) 453-7100
Vice President, Finance and Chief Financial Officer, PAC Fax: (314) 453-7177
Treasurer

HANSEN, Jose   Tel: (314) 453-7100
Vice President, Sales and Marketing   Fax: (314) 453-7177

WOHL, Matthew D.   Tel: (314) 453-7100
Vice President, Law   Fax: (314) 453-7177

Dole Food Company

Provider of fresh fruit, vegetables and other food products, along with fresh-cut flowers.
www.dole.com
Annual Revenues: $4.21 billion
Employees: 34,800
Ticker: NYSE: DOLE
SIC: 0100
Industry/ies: Food And Beverage Industry

Chairman of the Board and Chief Executive Officer   Tel: (818) 879-6600
MURDOCK, David H.   Fax: (818) 879-6615

President and Chief Executive Officer   Tel: (818) 879-6600
DELORENZO, David A.   Fax: (818) 879-6615

Main Headquarters
Mailing: One Dole Dr.   Tel: (818) 879-6600
            Westlake Village, CA 91362-7300   Fax: (818) 879-6615

Political Action Committees
Dole Food Company, Inc. PAC
FEC ID: C00109363
Contact: Johan Malmqvist
One Dole Dr.
Westlake Village, CA 91362

Corporate Foundations and Giving Programs
Dole Food Company Contributions Program
Contact: Marty Ordman
One Dole Dr.   Tel: (818) 879-6600
Westlake Village, CA 91362   Fax: (818) 879-6890

Public Affairs and Related Activities Personnel

At Headquarters

CARTER, C. Michael   Tel: (818) 879-6600
Executive Vice President and General Counsel   Fax: (818) 879-6615
michael.carter@dole.com

MALMQVIST, Johan   Tel: (818) 879-6600
Chief Financial Officer and PAC Contact   Fax: (818) 879-6615

ORDMAN, Marty   Tel: (818) 874-4834
Vice President, Marketing and Communications   Fax: (818) 879-6890
marty.ordman@dole.com

POTILLO, Beth   Tel: (818) 879-6600
Vice President and Treasurer, Investor Relations Fax: (818) 879-6628

TESORIERO, Joseph S.   Tel: (818) 879-6600
Executive Vice President and Chief Financial Officer Fax: (818) 879-6615

Dollar General Corporation

A company-owned and franchised discount store chain located in eastern and southeastern states.
www.dollargeneral.com
Annual Revenues: $19.31 billion
Employees: 105,500
Ticker: NYSE: DG
SIC: 5331
Industry/ies: Retail/Wholesale

Chairman of the Board   Tel: (615) 855-4000
DREILING, Richard W.   Fax: (615) 855-5252

Chief Executive Officer   Tel: (615) 855-4000
VASOS, Todd   Fax: (615) 386-9936

Main Headquarters
Mailing: 100 Mission Ridge   Tel: (615) 855-4000
            Goodlettsville, TN 37072   Fax: (615) 386-9936
                                                   TF: (800) 678-9258

Corporate Foundations and Giving Programs

Dollar General Literacy Foundation
Contact: Susan S. Lanigan
100 Mission Ridge   Tel: (615) 855-4000
Goodlettsville, TN 37072   Fax: (615) 855-5252

Public Affairs and Related Activities Personnel

At Headquarters

BROPHY, Steve J.   Tel: (615) 855-5150
Vice President, Government Affairs   Fax: (615) 855-5252
sbrophy@dollargeneral.com

D'AREZZO, Dave   Tel: (615) 855-4000
Executive Vice President and Chief Merchandising Officer   Fax: (615) 386-9936

ELLIOTT, Anita   Tel: (615) 855-4000
Senior Vice President and Controller   Fax: (615) 386-9936

GARRATT, John W.   Tel: (615) 855-4000
Interim Chief Financial Officer   Fax: (615) 855-5252

GORDON, Mary Winn   Tel: (615) 855-5536
Vice President, Investor Relations and Public Relations   Fax: (615) 855-5252

LANIGAN, Susan S.   Tel: (615) 855-4000
Executive Vice President and General Counsel   Fax: (615) 855-5252

MACDONALD, Dan   Tel: (615) 855-5209
Senior Director, Corporate Communication   Fax: (615) 386-9936
dmacdona@dollargeneral.com

RAVENER, Bob   Tel: (615) 855-4000
Executive Vice President and Chief People Officer   Fax: (615) 855-5252

TAYLOR, Rhonda   Tel: (615) 855-4000
Executive Vice President and General Counsel   Fax: (615) 386-9936

Dollar Tree Inc.

The company operates more than 4,100 Dollar Tree, Deal$, Dollar Giant, and Dollar Bills discount stores in 48 US states and the District of Columbia, as well as about 85 stores in Canadian provinces. Stores carry a mix of housewares, toys, seasonal items, food, health and beauty aids, gifts, and books.Founded in 1986 as Dollar Tree Stores, the company reorganized in 2008 and changed its name to Dollar Tree, Inc.
www.dollartree.com
Annual Revenues: $18.41 billion
Employees: 55,300
Ticker: NASDAQ: DLTR
SIC: 5331
Industry/ies: Retail/Wholesale

Chairman of the Board   Tel: (757) 321-5000
BROCK, Jr., Macon F.   Fax: (757) 321-5292

Chief Executive Officer   Tel: (757) 321-5000
SASSER, Robert   Fax: (757) 321-5292

Main Headquarters
Mailing: 500 Volvo Pkwy.   Tel: (757) 321-5000
    Chesapeake, VA 23320   Fax: (757) 321-5111
    TF: (877) 530-8733

Corporate Foundations and Giving Programs

Dollar Tree Stores Contributions Program
500 Volvo Pkwy.
Chesapeake, VA 23320

Operation Homefront
500 Volvo Pkwy.
Chesapeake, VA 23320

Public Affairs and Related Activities Personnel

At Headquarters

JACOBS, David A.   Tel: (757) 321-5000
Chief Strategy Officer   Fax: (757) 321-5111

MATACUNAS, Mike   Tel: (757) 321-5000
Chief Administrative Officer   Fax: (757) 321-5111

OLD, Jr., William A.   Tel: (757) 321-5000
Chief Legal Officer and Corporate Secretary   Fax: (757) 321-5111

WAMPLER, Kevin S.   Tel: (757) 321-5000
Chief Financial Officer   Fax: (757) 321-5111

WITYNSKI, Michael A.   Tel: (757) 321-5000
Chief Operating Officer   Fax: (757) 321-5111

Dominion

An energy company. Acquired Consolidated Natural Gas in 1999. Subsidiaries include Dominion Virginia Power, Dominion North Carolina Power, Dominion East Ohio (formerly East Ohio Gas Co.), Dominion Hope, Dominion Peoples (formerly Peoples Natural Gas Co.), Dominion Exploration & Production, and Dominion Transmission (formerly CNG Transmission), among others. In July 2008 it was announced that Dominion Peoples was being sold to Babcock & Brown Infrastructure Fund North America; the transaction is expected to be closed in 2009.
www.dom.com
Annual Revenues: $12.22 Billion
Employees: 14,400
Ticker: NYSE: D
SIC: 4911

Industry/ies: Utilities
Legislative Issues: BAN; CAW; ENG; ENV; HOM; TAX; TRA; UTI

Chairman of the Board, President and Chief Executive Officer   Tel: (804) 819-2000
FARRELL, II, Thomas F.   Fax: (804) 819-2233
thomas.farrellii@dom.com

Main Headquarters
Mailing: P.O. Box 26532   Tel: (804) 819-2000
    Richmond, VA 23261   Fax: (804) 819-2233

Washington Office
Mailing: 400 N. Capitol St. NW   Tel: (202) 585-4200
    Suite 875   Fax: (202) 737-3874
    Washington, DC 20001

Political Action Committees
Dominion Resources, Inc. Political Action Committee - Dominion PAC
FEC ID: C00108209
Contact: Hunter Applewhite
One James River Plaza, 20th Floor
P.O. Box 26666
Richmond, VA 23261

    Contributions to Candidates: $393,450 (2015-2016)
    Democrats: $129,700; Republicans: $263,750
    Principal Recipients

       SENATE
       BOOZMAN, JOHN (REP-AR)

       HOUSE
       HOYER, STENY HAMILTON (DEM-DC)
       SHIMKUS, JOHN M (REP-IL)
       UPTON, FREDERICK STEPHEN (REP-MI)

Corporate Foundations and Giving Programs

Dominion Foundation
One James River Plaza, 20th Floor   Tel: (804) 771-4491
P.O. Box 26666
Richmond, VA 23261

Public Affairs and Related Activities Personnel

At Headquarters

CARDIFF , Michele L   Tel: (804) 819-2000
Vice President, Controller and Chief Accounting Officer   Fax: (804) 819-2233

MCGETTRICK, Mark F.   Tel: (804) 819-2000
Executive Vice President and Chief Financial Officer   Fax: (804) 819-2233

REID, Carter M.   Tel: (804) 819-2000
Senior Vice President-Administrative Services and Corporate   Fax: (804) 819-2233
Secretary
carter.reid@dom.com

WADE, Chet G.   Tel: (804) 775-5697
Vice President, Corporate Communications   Fax: (804) 819-2233
chet.wade@dom.com

WOHLFARTH, Thomas P.   Tel: (804) 819-2000
Senior Vice President, Regulatory Affairs   Fax: (804) 819-2233
Thomas_Wohlfarth@dom.com

At Washington Office

PLAUTZ, Molly   Tel: (202) 585-4200
Registered Federal Lobbyist   Fax: (202) 737-3874

WEEKLEY, Dan A.   Tel: (202) 585-4200
Vice President, Corporate Affairs   Fax: (202) 737-3874
Daniel.A.Weekley@dom.com

At Other Offices

APPLEWHITE, Hunter   Tel: (804) 771-4650
Director, Advertising and Creative Services and PAC   Fax: (804) 819-2233
Treasurer
701 East Cary St., P.O. Box 26666
Richmond, VA 23219
hunter.applewhite@dom.com

VARLEY, Robert W.   Tel: (216) 736-6207
Director, State & Local Affairs
1201 E. 55th St.
Cleveland, OH 44103

Dominion Peoples
See listing on page 625 under Peoples Natural Gas

Domino Foods
A sugar refinery company.
www.dominosugar.com
Industry/ies: Food And Beverage Industry

Main Headquarters
Mailing: 30 Frank Lloyd Wright Dr   Tel: (734) 930-3030
    Ann Arbor, MI 48106

Political Action Committees
Domino PAC

FEC ID: C00352591
One Federal St.
Suite 800
Yonkers, NY 10702

Tel: (202) 347-2980
Fax: (202) 347-2992

Domino's Pizza

Pizza delivery company-operates a network of company-owned & franchise-owned stores and dedicated to making and delivering great pizza with high quality ingredients from the start.
www.dominos.com
Annual Revenues: $2.25 billion
Employees: 11,900
Ticker: NYSE: DPZ
SIC: 5140
Industry/ies: Food And Beverage Industry

Chairman
BRANDON, David A.
brandod@dominos.com

Tel: (734) 930-3030
Fax: (734) 930-4346

President and Chief Executive Officer
DOYLE, J. Patrick

Tel: (734) 930-3030
Fax: (734) 747-6210

Main Headquarters
Mailing: 30 Frank Lloyd Wright Dr.
P.O. Box 997
Ann Arbor, MI 48106-0997

Tel: (734) 930-3030
Fax: (734) 747-6210
TF: (888) 366-4667

Corporate Foundations and Giving Programs

Domino's Pizza Contributions Program
30 Frank Lloyd Wright Dr.
P.O. Box 997
Ann Arbor, MI 48106-0997

Tel: (734) 930-3030
Fax: (734) 668-1946

Public Affairs and Related Activities Personnel

At Headquarters

HINSHAW, Scott
Executive Vice President, Franchise Operations and Development

Tel: (734) 930-3030
Fax: (734) 747-6210

LAWTON, Michael
Executive Vice President and Chief Financial Officer

Tel: (734) 930-3030
Fax: (734) 747-6210

LIDDLE, Lynn M.
Executive Vice President, Communications, Legislative Affairs and Investor Relations
investorrelations@dominos.com

Tel: (734) 930-3008
Fax: (734) 747-6210

MCINTYRE, Tim
Vice President, Communications

Tel: (734) 930-3563
Fax: (734) 668-1946

ROLLIN, Kenneth B.
Executive Vice President and General Counsel
Kennth.rollin@dominos.com

Tel: (734) 930-3030
Fax: (734) 747-6210

Donaldson Company, Inc.

A manufacturer of filtration systems and replacement parts.
www.donaldson.com
Annual Revenues: $2.24 billion
Employees: 12,500
Ticker: NYSE: DCI
SIC: 3564
NAICS: 33341
Industry/ies: Machinery/Equipment

President and Chief Executive Officer
CARPENTER, Tod E.

Tel: (952) 887-3131
Fax: (952) 887-3155

Main Headquarters
Mailing: 1400 W. 94th St.
Minneapolis, MN 55431

Tel: (952) 887-3131
Fax: (952) 887-3155

Corporate Foundations and Giving Programs

The Donaldson Foundation
Contact: Jessica Exley
P.O. Box 1299
Minneapolis, MN 55440

Tel: (952) 703-4999

Public Affairs and Related Activities Personnel

At Headquarters

BECKER, Amy C
Vice President, General Counsel and Secretary

Tel: (952) 887-3131
Fax: (952) 887-3155

EXLEY, Jessica
Product Manager
donaldsonfoundation@donaldson.com

Tel: (952) 887-3131
Fax: (952) 887-3155

GRAFE, Timothy H.
Vice President, New Business Development

Tel: (952) 887-3131
Fax: (952) 887-3155

ROBINSON, Scott J.
Vice President, Chief Financial Officer

Tel: (952) 887-3131
Fax: (952) 887-3155

At Other Offices

CALLAHAN, Mary
Director, Engine Group Marketing
P.O. Box 1299

Tel: (952) 887-3034
Fax: (952) 887-3155

Minneapolis, MN 55440
mary.callahan@donaldson.com

KRAMER, Sheila G.
Vice President, Human Resources
P.O. Box 1299
Minneapolis, MN 55440

Tel: (952) 887-3131
Fax: (952) 887-3155

PERUSHEK, Mary Lynne
Vice President and Chief Information Officer
P.O. Box 1299
Minneapolis, MN 55440

Tel: (952) 887-3131
Fax: (952) 887-3155

Donohoe Companies, Inc.

A real estate firm. Formerly 400 C Street Associates, LP.
www.donohoe.com
Annual Revenues: $23.90 million
Employees: 600
Industry/ies: Real Estate
Legislative Issues: RES

Chairman of the Board and Chief Executive Officer
DONOHOE, Robert B.

Tel: (202) 333-0880
Fax: (202) 342-5394

Main Headquarters
Mailing: 2101 Wisconsin Ave. NW
Washington, DC 20007

Tel: (202) 333-0880
Fax: (202) 342-5394

Corporate Foundations and Giving Programs

Donohoe Companies, Inc. Contributions Program
2101 Wisconsin Ave. NW
Washington, DC 20007

Tel: (202) 333-0880
Fax: (202) 333-5394

Public Affairs and Related Activities Personnel

At Headquarters

DONOHOE, III, James A.
Senior Vice President

Tel: (202) 333-0880
Fax: (202) 342-5394

GOEKE, Gerard M.
Executive Vice President and Chief Financial Officer

Tel: (202) 333-0880
Fax: (202) 342-5394

ROBINSON, Deirdre K.
Vice President, Human Resources

Tel: (202) 333-0880
Fax: (202) 342-5394

TWOHIG, Stephen
Chief Operating Officer and Chief Financial Officer

Tel: (202) 333-0880
Fax: (202) 342-5394

Doosan Fuel Cell America, Inc.

Formerly ClearEdge Power, Inc. It is a provider of on-site energy generation systems for homes and small businesses.
www.doosanfuelcell.com
Employees: 15
Industry/ies: Energy/Electricity

President and Chief Executive Officer
CHUNG, Jeff Hyungrak

Tel: (860) 727-2200

Main Headquarters
Mailing: 195 Governor's Hwy.
South Windsor, CT 06074

Tel: (860) 727-2200

Public Affairs and Related Activities Personnel

At Headquarters

CHE, Howie Hooseok
Chief Financial Officer

Tel: (860) 727-2200

MCCORD, Kent
Director, Marketing Strategy

Tel: (860) 727-2200

MOTUPALLY, Sathya
Chief Operating Officer

Tel: (860) 727-2200

STRAYER, Eric
Vice President, Sales and Business Development

Tel: (860) 727-2200

At Other Offices

SIMMONS, Mari
Vice President, Human Resources
7175 NW Evergreen Pkwy., Building 100
Hillsboro, OR 97124

Tel: (503) 693-9600

DoubleClick Inc.

A global internet advertising company.
www.double-click.org
Annual Revenues: $43.80 million
Employees: 900
SIC: 7372
Industry/ies: Communications; Telecommunications/Internet/Cable

President and Webmaster
MACAK, Jim

Main Headquarters
Mailing: 322 McCall St.
Waukesha, WI 53186-5586

Public Affairs and Related Activities Personnel

At Headquarters

BRAUN, Eugene
Contact, Communications

Dow AgroSciences LLC

Technology provider for crop production, crop nutrition, and crop protection.
www.dowagro.com
Employees: 3,500
Industry/ies: Agriculture/Agronomy; Chemicals & Chemical Industry
Legislative Issues: AGR; ENV; FOO; TAR

| **President and Chief Executive Officer** | Tel: | (317) 337-3000 |
| HASSINGER, Tim | Fax: | (317) 334-7409 |

Main Headquarters

| *Mailing:* | 9330 Zionsville Rd. | Tel: | (317) 337-3000 |
| | Indianapolis, IN 46268 | Fax: | (317) 334-7409 |

Washington Office

Mailing:	1776 Eye St. NW	Tel:	(202) 429-3400
	Suite 1050	Fax:	(202) 429-3467
	Washington, DC 20006		

Political Action Committees

Dow AgroSciences LLC Employee PAC (AGPAC)
FEC ID: C00247981
Contact: Mary B. Ayers

| 9330 Zionsville Rd. | Tel: | (202) 429-3495 |
| Indianapolis, IN 46268 | Fax: | (202) 429-3467 |

> **Contributions to Candidates:** $20,200 (2015-2016)
> Democrats: $4,500; Republicans: $15,700

Corporate Foundations and Giving Programs

Dow AgroSciences Corporate Giving Foundation
Contact: Robyn Heine

| 9330 Zionsville Rd. | Tel: | (317) 337-4359 |
| Indianapolis, IN 46368 | Fax: | (317) 337-4880 |

Public Affairs and Related Activities Personnel

At Headquarters

AYERS, Mary B.	Tel:	(317) 337-3000
Global Finance Leader	Fax:	(317) 334-7409
GRIMM, Audrey	Tel:	(317) 337-3000
Contact, Human Resources	Fax:	(317) 334-7409
HAMLIN, Garry	Tel:	(317) 337-4799
Manager, Media Relations	Fax:	(317) 334-7409
garryhamlin@dow.com		
HEINE, Robyn	Tel:	(317) 337-4807
Global Leader, Public Affairs	Fax:	(317) 334-7409
rheine@dow.com		
ISLEY, Kenneth D.	Tel:	(317) 337-3000
Contact, Legal	Fax:	(317) 334-7409
NICHOLAS, Beth	Tel:	(317) 337-3000
Contact, Finance	Fax:	(317) 334-7409
SHURDUT, Bradley A.	Tel:	(317) 337-3000
Global Director, Corporate Strategy, Government and and Public Policy	Fax:	(317) 334-7409

The Dow Chemical Company

A science and technology company providing innovative chemical, plastic and agricultural products and services to many consumer markets.
www.dow.com
Annual Revenues: $56.08 billion
Employees: 52,217
Ticker: NYSE: DOW
SIC: 3084; 3999; 5169; 3083; 2821
NAICS: 326122; 326199; 32613; 42269
Industry/ies: Chemicals & Chemical Industry; Plastics Industry
Legislative Issues: AGR; BNK; BUD; CHM; CPT; ENG; ENV; FOO; GOV; HCR; HOM; SCI; TAR; TAX; TRA; TRD

| **Chairman, President and Chief Executive Officer** | Tel: | (989) 636-1000 |
| LIVERIS, Andrew N. | Fax: | (989) 832-1556 |

Main Headquarters

Mailing:	2030 Dow Center	Tel:	(989) 636-1000
	Midland, MI 48674	Fax:	(989) 636-1830
		TF:	(800) 422-8193

Washington Office

Mailing:	500 N. Capitol St. NW	Tel:	(202) 429-3400
	Suite 200	Fax:	(202) 429-3467
	Washington, DC 20001		

Political Action Committees

Dow Chemical Company Employees PAC (DOWPAC), The
FEC ID: C00074096
Contact: Denise A. Baker
2030 Dow Center
Midland, MI 48674

> **Contributions to Candidates:** $498,750 (2015-2016)
> Democrats: $93,000; Republicans: $403,750; Other: $2,000

Principal Recipients

SENATE
PETERS, GARY (DEM-MI)

HOUSE
BOUSTANY, CHARLES W. DR. JR. (REP-LA)
COSTELLO, RYAN A (REP-PA)
DOLD, ROBERT JAMES JR (REP-IL)
HOYER, STENY HAMILTON (DEM-DC)
KINZINGER, ADAM (REP-IL)
MCCARTHY, KEVIN (REP-CA)
MCHENRY, PATRICK TIMOTHY (REP-NC)
MEEHAN, PATRICK L. MR. (REP-PA)
PAULSEN, ERIK (REP-MN)
RYAN, PAUL D. (REP-WI)
SCALISE, STEVE MR. (REP-LA)
SHIMKUS, JOHN M (REP-IL)

Corporate Foundations and Giving Programs

The Dow Chemical Company Foundation
Contact: Robert N. (Bo) Miller

| 2030 Dow Center | Tel: | (989) 636-1463 |
| Midland, MI 48674 | Fax: | (989) 832-1556 |

Public Affairs and Related Activities Personnel

At Headquarters

BAKER, Denise A.	Tel:	(989) 636-1000
Lobbyist and PAC Treasurer	Fax:	(989) 636-1830
Dabaker@dow.com		
BENTLEY, Rebecca	Tel:	(989) 638-8568
Global Director, Financial Communications, Media Relations,	Fax:	(989) 636-1830
Mergers and Acquisitions		
rmbentley@dow.com		
FREIWALD, Gregory M.	Tel:	(989) 636-1000
Executive Vice President, Human Resources, Corporate	Fax:	(989) 832-1556
Affairs and Aviation		
KALIL, Charles J.	Tel:	(989) 636-1000
Executive Vice President, General Counsel and Corporate	Fax:	(989) 832-1556
Secretary		
KRAEF, Torsten	Tel:	(989) 636-1000
Corporate Vice President, Strategy Development and New	Fax:	(989) 636-1830
Business Development		
LAMB, Nancy	Tel:	(989) 638-7251
Director, Corporate Media Relations	Fax:	(989) 636-1830
nelamb@dow.com		
MILLER, Robert N. (Bo)	Tel:	(989) 636-1204
Global Director, Corporate Citizenship and President and	Fax:	(989) 636-1830
Executive Director The Dow Chemical Company Foundation		
PLISHKA, Bob	Tel:	(989) 638-2288
Director, Communications	Fax:	(989) 636-1830
bplishka@dow.com		
SÖDERSTRÖM, Johanna	Tel:	(989) 636-1000
Corporate Vice President, Human Resources and Aviation	Fax:	(989) 636-1830
WINDER, David	Tel:	(989) 636-0626
Contact, Public Affairs and Government Affairs	Fax:	(989) 832-1556
dwinder@dow.com		

At Washington Office

BEEBE, Brooke Lundquist	Tel:	(202) 429-3440
Director, State Government Affairs	Fax:	(202) 429-3467
blbeebe@dow.com		
Registered Federal Lobbyist		
BOYD, Janet C.	Tel:	(202) 429-3423
Director, Government Relations-Tax and Benefits	Fax:	(202) 429-3467
Registered Federal Lobbyist		
BULLOCK, Latonia	Tel:	(202) 429-3418
Legislative Assistant	Fax:	(202) 429-3467
CULLMAN, Constance	Tel:	(202) 429-3400
Leader, U.S. Government Affairs	Fax:	(202) 429-3467
Registered Federal Lobbyist		
DAVIS, R. Matt	Tel:	(202) 429-3440
Corporate Vice President, Global Government Affairs and	Fax:	(202) 429-3467
Public Affairs		
DEZIEL, Dennis	Tel:	(202) 429-3400
Director, Environment and Regulatory Affairs	Fax:	(202) 429-3467
Registered Federal Lobbyist		
ENGLISH, Katherine E.	Tel:	(202) 429-3440
Director, Government Affairs	Fax:	(202) 429-3467
Registered Federal Lobbyist		
HOUTMAN, Carrie	Tel:	(202) 429-3400
?Associate Director, Government Affairs	Fax:	(202) 429-3467

KOLEVAR, Kevin	Tel:	(202) 429-3400
Vice President, Government Affairs & Public Policy	Fax:	(202) 429-3467
Registered Federal Lobbyist		
LITKENHAUS, Colleen	Tel:	(202) 429-3400
Director, Trade Relations	Fax:	(202) 429-3467
Registered Federal Lobbyist		
SCHROETER, Lisa	Tel:	(202) 429-3407
Global Director, Trade and Investment Policy	Fax:	(202) 429-3467
lmschroeter@dow.com		
Registered Federal Lobbyist		
VERHEGGEN, Theodore	Tel:	(202) 429-3403
Legislative Counsel	Fax:	(202) 429-3467
TFVerheggen@dow.com		

Dow Corning Corporation

A 50/50 joint venture of Dow Chemical and Corning Inc. A manufacturer of specialty chemicals.
www.dowcorning.com
Annual Revenues: $4 billion
Employees: 9,000
Ticker: NASDAQ: DWCR.GB
SIC: 2821; 2819; 2891; 3674
NAICS: 32552; 325211; 325188; 334413
Industry/ies: Chemicals & Chemical Industry
Legislative Issues: ENG; TRD

Chairman of the Board, Chief Executive Officer and President	Tel:	(989) 496-7875
HANSEN, Robert D.		

Main Headquarters

Mailing:	P.O. Box 994	Tel:	(989) 496-7875
	Midland, MI 48686-0994	TF:	(800) 248-2481

Washington Office

Mailing:	Independence Ave. and First St. SW
	Washington, DC 48686

Political Action Committees

Dow Corning Corporation Employee's PAC
FEC ID: C00040246
Contact: Velasquez A. Christian

P.O. Box 994	Tel:	(989) 496-7875
Midland, MI 48686-0994		

Dow Corning Corporation Legislative Action Team PAC
FEC ID: C00386672
Contact: Brian Tessin
2200 W. Salzburg Rd.
P.O. Box 994
Midland, MI 48686

> **Contributions to Candidates:** $20,000 (2015-2016)
> Democrats: $7,500; Republicans: $12,500

Corporate Foundations and Giving Programs

Dow Corning Foundation
Contact: Kathryn Spence

P.O. Box 994	Tel:	(989) 496-4400
P.O. Box 994	Fax:	(989) 496-6731
Midland, MI 48686		

Public Affairs and Related Activities Personnel

At Headquarters

BENECKE, Mary Lou	Tel:	(989) 496-4400
Vice President, Public Affairs and Corporate Communications		
BOGGS, N. Cornell	Tel:	(989) 496-7875
Senior Vice President and General Counsel and Corporate Secretary		
CHRISTIAN , Velasquez A.	Tel:	(989) 496-7875
PAC Treasurer		
CONWAY, Mike	Tel:	(989) 496-4400
Vice President and Chief Human Resource Officer		
COOK, Thomas H.	Tel:	(989) 496-7875
Senior Vice President, Sales and Customer Experience		
ERPELDING, Jarrod	Tel:	(989) 496-4400
Manager, Global Media Relations and Internal Communications		
jarrod.erpelding@dowcorning.com		
SHEETS, J. Donald	Tel:	(989) 496-4400
Executive Vice President and Chief Financial Officer		
SPENCE, Kathryn	Tel:	(989) 496-4614
Director, Foundation		
TESSIN, Brian	Tel:	(989) 496-4400
PAC Treasurer		
brian.tessin@dowcorning.com		

At Washington Office

COULOURIS, Andrew
Vice President, Public Affairs

andy.coulouris@dowcorning.com

Dow Jones & Company, Inc.

A news corporation company.
new.dowjones.com
Annual Revenues: $642.40 billion
Employees: 8,000
Ticker: NYSE: DJ
SIC: 2711
Industry/ies: Banking/Finance/Investments; Communications; Economics And Economic Development; Media/Mass Communication

Chairman of the Board	Tel:	(212) 416-2000
MURDOCH, K. Rupert	Fax:	(413) 592-4783

Main Headquarters

Mailing:	1211 Avenue of the Americas	Tel:	(212) 416-2000
	New York City, NY 10036	Fax:	(413) 592-4783

Washington Office

Mailing:	1025 Connecticut Ave. NW	Tel:	(202) 862-6632
	Suite 1103		
	Washington, DC 20036		

Corporate Foundations and Giving Programs

Dow Jones Foundation		
One World Foundation	Tel:	(212) 416-2000
200 Liberty St.		
New York City, NY 10281		
Dow Jones Newspaper Fund		
Contact: Richard Holden		
P.O. Box 300	Tel:	(609) 520-5927
Princeton, NJ 08543		

Public Affairs and Related Activities Personnel

At Headquarters

JACKSON, Mark H.	Tel:	(212) 416-2000
Executive Vice President and General Counsel	Fax:	(413) 592-4783
mark.jackson@dowjones.com		

At Other Offices

HOLDEN, Richard	Tel:	(609) 452-2820
Executive Director, Dow Jones Newspaper Fund	Fax:	(609) 520-5804
P.O. Box 300		
Princeton, NJ 08543		
richard.holden@dowjones.com		

DPL Inc.

DPL Inc.- a Subsidiary of The AES Corporation-supplies power to 515,000 customers throughout West Central Ohio. Subsidiaries include Dayton Power & Light Co.
www.dplinc.com
Annual Revenues: $1,763.0 million
Employees: 3,000
Ticker: NYSE: DPL
SIC: 4931
Industry/ies: Utilities

Chairman of the Board	Tel:	(937) 224-6000
MILLER, Brian	Fax:	(937) 259-7147
President and Chief Executive Officer	Tel:	(937) 224-6000
ZAGZEBSKI, Kenneth J.	Fax:	(937) 259-7147
President and Chief Executive Officer and PAC Treasurer	Tel:	(937) 224-5940
RAGA, Tom	Fax:	(937) 259-7147

Main Headquarters

Mailing:	1065 Woodman Dr.	Tel:	(937) 224-6000
	Dayton, OH 45432-1423	Fax:	(937) 259-7147

Political Action Committees

Dayton Power and Light Company Employees' Fund for Responsible Citizenship PAC
FEC ID: C00102947
Contact: Tom Raga
1065 Woodman Dr.
Dayton, OH 45432

> **Contributions to Candidates:** $2,350 (2015-2016)
> Democrats: $1,000; Republicans: $1,350

Corporate Foundations and Giving Programs

Dayton Power and Light Foundation and Community
Contact: Ginny Strausburg

1065 Woodman Dr.	Tel:	(937) 259-7925
Dayton, OH 45432	Fax:	(937) 259-7923

Public Affairs and Related Activities Personnel

At Headquarters

HERRINGTON, Phil	Tel:	(937) 224-6000
President, Competitive Generation, AES U.S. Strategic Business Unit	Fax:	(937) 259-7147
JACKSON, Craig L.	Tel:	(937) 224-6000

Senior Vice President, Chief Financial Officer
craig.jackson@dplinc.com
Fax: (937) 259-7147

MACKAY, Jeff
Treasurer and Contact, Investor Relations
communications@dplinc.com
Tel: (937) 224-5940
Fax: (937) 259-7147

MEYER, Arthur G.
Senior Vice President and General Counsel
Tel: (937) 224-6000
Fax: (937) 259-7147

MIZELL, Michael S.
US Business Unit Vice President and General Counsel at
AES
Tel: (937) 224-6000
Fax: (937) 259-7147

RICE, Timothy G.
Vice President, Assistant General Counsel, Corporate
Secretary
timothy.rice@dplinc.com
Tel: (937) 224-6000
Fax: (937) 259-7147

SOBECKI, Judi L.
General Counsel
Tel: (937) 224-6000
Fax: (937) 259-7147

STRAUSBURG, Ginny
Executive Director, Dayton Power and Light Foundation
Tel: (937) 259-7925
Fax: (937) 259-7923

Dr. Pepper Snapple Group

*Operates as a brand owner, manufacturer, and distributor of non-alcoholic beverages and is
the holding company for Cadbury Schweppes Americas Beverages.*
www.drpeppersnapplegroup.com
Annual Revenues: $6.32 billion
Employees: 19,000
Ticker: NYSE:DPS
SIC: 2080
Industry/ies: Food And Beverage Industry

President and Chief Executive Officer
YOUNG, Larry D.
Tel: (972) 673-7000
Fax: (972) 673-7980

Main Headquarters
Mailing: 5301 Legacy Dr.
Plano, TX 75024
Tel: (972) 673-7000
Fax: (972) 673-7980
TF: (800) 696-5891

Political Action Committees
DR Pepper Snapple Group PAC
FEC ID: C00484451
Contact: Christianne Curran
5301 Legacy Dr.
Plano, TX 75024
Tel: (972) 673-7000
Fax: (972) 673-7980

Contributions to Candidates: $66,500 (2015-2016)
Democrats: $6,500; Republicans: $60,000

Principal Recipients

HOUSE
JOHNSON, SAM MR. (REP-TX)

Corporate Foundations and Giving Programs

ACTION Nation Contributions Program
5301 Legacy Dr.
Plano, TX 75024

Public Affairs and Related Activities Personnel

At Headquarters

BALDWIN, Jr., James L.
Executive Vice President and General Counsel
Tel: (972) 673-7000
Fax: (972) 673-7980

CURRAN, Christianne
PAC Treasurer
Tel: (972) 673-7000
Fax: (972) 673-7980

ELLEN, Martin M.
Chief Financial Officer
Tel: (972) 673-7000
Fax: (972) 673-7980

HANCOCK , Lain
Executive Vice President, Human Resources
Tel: (972) 673-7000
Fax: (972) 673-7980

TREBILCOCK, James R.
Executive Vice President and Chief Commercial Officer
Tel: (972) 673-7000
Fax: (972) 673-7980

The DRC Group

A hurricane debris removal company.
www.drcusa.com
Industry/ies: Construction/Construction Materials; Disaster

President and Chief Executive Officer
BUSBY, Lee
Tel: (251) 343-3581
Fax: (251) 343-5554

Chief Executive Officer
STAFFORD, Mark
Tel: (251) 343-3581
Fax: (251) 343-5554

Main Headquarters
Mailing: 1808 Canonero Dr.
Austin, TX 78746
Tel: (512) 418-4361
Fax: (512) 418-4369

Corporate Foundations and Giving Programs

DRC Contribution Program
740 Museum Dr.
Mobile, AL 36608
Tel: (251) 343-3581
Fax: (251) 343-5554

Public Affairs and Related Activities Personnel

At Headquarters
HAMMOCK, Brian
Vice President
Tel: (512) 418-4361
Fax: (512) 418-4369

At Other Offices
BACOTE, Gearle
Vice President, Governmental Affairs
740 Museum Dr.
Mobile, AL 36608
Tel: (251) 343-3581
Fax: (251) 343-5554

COMBS, Thomas B.
Vice President, Governmental Affairs
740 Museum Dr.
Mobile, AL 36608
tom@tomcombs.net
Tel: (251) 343-3581
Fax: (251) 343-5554

DES ROCHES, Cary
General Counsel
740 Museum Dr.
Mobile, AL 36608
Tel: (251) 343-3581
Fax: (251) 343-5554

HODGE, Shaun
Assistant Director, Government Affairs and Project Manager
740 Museum Dr.
Mobile, AL 36608
Tel: (251) 343-3581
Fax: (251) 343-5554

JOHNSON, Don
Chief Financial Officer
740 Museum Dr.
Mobile, AL 36608
Tel: (251) 343-3581
Fax: (251) 343-5554

JORNS, Byron G.
Chief Operating Officer
740 Museum Dr.
Mobile, AL 36608
Tel: (251) 343-3581
Fax: (251) 343-5554

PRIEUR, Chuck
Senior Vice President
740 Museum Dr.
Mobile, AL 36608
Tel: (251) 343-3581
Fax: (251) 343-5554

SHARPE, Clifford C.
Legal Counsel
740 Museum Dr.
Mobile, AL 36608
Tel: (251) 343-3581
Fax: (251) 343-5554

Dreyer's Grand Ice Cream

*Formed from the merger of Dreyer's Grand Ice Cream, Inc. and Nestle Ice Cream Co., LLC
in June of 2003. A manufacturer and distributor of premium ice cream, super-premium ice
cream, yogurt and sherbet products. Dreyer's Grand Ice Cream of America, based in Oakland
city, is the U.S. subsidiary of Nestle, headquartered in Vevey, Switzerland.*
www.dreyers.com
Annual Revenues: $463.20 million
Employees: 7,500
SIC: 2024
Industry/ies: Dairy Industry; Food And Beverage Industry

President and Chief Executive Officer
MITCHELL, Mike
Tel: (510) 652-8187
Fax: (510) 450-4621

Main Headquarters
Mailing: P.O. Box 2178
C/O Nestle Consumer Services
Wilkes-Barre, PA 18703
Tel: (877) 437-3937
Fax: (570) 301-4538

Public Affairs and Related Activities Personnel

At Other Offices
BARBOUR, Steve
Vice President, Division Controller
5929 College Ave.
Oakland, CA 94618
Tel: (510) 652-8187
Fax: (570) 301-4538

The Dreyfus Corporation

*Provided mutual funds and other financial services. A subsidiary of The Bank of New York
Mellon Corporation (see separate listing).*
www.dreyus.com
Employees: 1,100
SIC: 6282
Industry/ies: Banking/Finance/Investments

President and Chief Executive Officer
CARDONA, J. Charles
Tel: (212) 922-6000
Fax: (212) 922-6585

Main Headquarters
Mailing: 200 Park Ave.
New York City, NY 10166
Tel: (212) 922-6000
Fax: (212) 922-6585
TF: (800) 645-6561

Public Affairs and Related Activities Personnel

At Headquarters
CONNOLLY, Joseph W.
Chief Compliance Officer
Tel: (212) 922-6000
Fax: (212) 922-6585

GILL, Jill
Vice President, Human Resources
Tel: (212) 922-6000
Fax: (212) 922-6585

| KOZLOWSKI, Patrice M. | Tel: | (212) 922-6030 |
| *Senior Vice President, Corporate Communications* | Fax: | (212) 922-6585 |

Driscoll Children's Hospital

Offers medical and surgical care for children.
www.driscollchildrens.org
Annual Revenues: $215.69 million
Employees: 1,800
Industry/ies: Medicine/Health Care/Mental Health
Legislative Issues: HCR

Chairman of the Board
| NEAL, Loyd | Tel: | (361) 694-5000 |
| | Fax: | (361) 694-5665 |

President and Chief Executive Officer and Vice Chairman
| WOERNER, Steve | Tel: | (361) 694-5000 |
| | Fax: | (361) 694-5665 |

Main Headquarters
Mailing: 3533 S. Alameda St.	Tel:	(361) 694-5000
Corpus Christi, TX 78411	Fax:	(361) 694-5665
	TF:	(800) 324-5683

Corporate Foundations and Giving Programs
Driscoll Children's Hospital's Foundation
| 3533 S. Alameda St. | Tel: | (361) 694-5000 |
| Corpus Christi, TX 78411 | Fax: | (361) 694-5665 |

Public Affairs and Related Activities Personnel

At Headquarters
ANTHONY, Jeanene	Tel:	(361) 694-5000
Vice President, Business Development and Planning	Fax:	(361) 694-5665
AVERY, Martha	Tel:	(361) 694-5000
Vice President, Development	Fax:	(361) 694-5665
BRATTEN, Mike	Tel:	(361) 694-5662
Manager, Media Communications	Fax:	(361) 808-2120
HAMON, Eric	Tel:	(361) 694-5000
Executive Vice President and Chief Financial Officer	Fax:	(361) 694-5665
LARSEN, Bill	Tel:	(361) 694-5000
Vice President, Human Resources	Fax:	(361) 694-5665
WARD, Greg	Tel:	(361) 694-5000
Vice President, Finance	Fax:	(361) 694-5665
WILSON, Ivan C.	Tel:	(361) 694-5000
Board Member	Fax:	(361) 694-5665

Dropfire, Inc.

Software development for public safety communications.
www.dropfire.com
Industry/ies: Computer/Technology; Disaster; Law Enforcement/Security

Chief Executive Officer
| COHEN, Scott | Tel: | (617) 448-3333 |
| | Fax: | (925) 380-3651 |

Main Headquarters
Mailing: One Boston Pl.	Tel:	(617) 448-3333
Suite 2600	Fax:	(925) 380-3651
Boston, MA 02108		

Washington Office
Mailing: 1001 Connecticut Ave.
Suite 405
Washington, DC 20036

Public Affairs and Related Activities Personnel

At Other Offices
SCOTT, Dick	Tel:	(617) 871-6767
Consultant, Business Development	Fax:	(617) 871-6554
30 Spinelli Pl.		
Cambridge, MA 02138		
scott@dropfire.com		

DRS Technologies, Inc.

A supplier of defense technology systems.
www.drs.com
Employees: 10,000
Ticker: NYSE: DRS
SIC: 3577; 3599; 3679; 3571; 3812
Industry/ies: Aerospace/Aviation; Defense/Homeland Security; Government-Related; Transportation
Legislative Issues: AVI; BUD; DEF; FOR; TRA

Chief Executive Officer
| LYNN III, William J. | Tel: | (703) 416-8000 |
| | Fax: | (973) 898-4730 |

Main Headquarters
Mailing: 2345 Crystal Dr.	Tel:	(703) 416-8000
Suite 1000	Fax:	(973) 898-4730
Arlington, VA 22202		

Political Action Committees
DRS Technologies, Inc. Good Government Fund PAC
FEC ID: C00275123

Contact: Jason Rinsky		
2345 Crystal Dr.	Tel:	(703) 416-8000
Suite 915	Fax:	(703) 416-8010
Arlington, VA 22202		

Contributions to Candidates: $172,400 (2015-2016)
Democrats: $48,500; Republicans: $119,900; Other: $4,000

Principal Recipients

HOUSE
MILLER, JEFFERSON B. (REP-FL)

Corporate Foundations and Giving Programs
DRS Technologies Charitable Foundation
| Five Sylvan Way | Tel: | (973) 898-1500 |
| Parsippany, NJ 07054 | Fax: | (973) 898-4730 |

Public Affairs and Related Activities Personnel

At Headquarters
BREWER, Larry K.	Tel:	(703) 416-8000
Senior Vice President, Washington Operations		
Registered Federal Lobbyist		
CORTESE, Steve J.	Tel:	(703) 416-8000
Executive Vice President, Washington Operations		
DORFMAN, Mark A.	Tel:	(703) 416-8000
Executive Vice President, General Counsel and Secretary	Fax:	(973) 898-4730
GESISKIE, Tami E.	Tel:	(703) 416-8000
Senior Vice President, Human Resources		
GREEN, Matthew	Tel:	(703) 416-8000
Vice President, Legislative Affairs		
Registered Federal Lobbyist		
MILITANO, Joseph P.	Tel:	(703) 416-8000
Senior Vice President, Public Affairs and Communications	Fax:	(973) 898-4730
MURPHY, Terence J.	Tel:	(703) 416-8000
Executive Vice President, Chief Operating Officer		
RINSKY, Jason	Tel:	(703) 416-8000
Senior Vice President and Chief Tax Officer	Fax:	(973) 898-4730
SILVERBERG, Ryan J.	Tel:	(703) 416-8000
Registered Federal Lobbyist		
SPRINGER, Mary	Tel:	(703) 416-8000
Federal Lobbyist		
STAPLEY, David W.	Tel:	(703) 416-8000
Senior Vice President, International Business Development and Government Relations		

At Other Offices
DUNN, Robert	Tel:	(240) 238-3933
Senior Vice President and Chief Finance Officer		
7600 Wisconsin Ave., Suite 1000		
Bethesda, MD 20814		

drugstore.com

The e-tailer sells name-brand and private-label health and beauty items and prescription and OTC drugs.
www.drugstore.com
Annual Revenues: $456.51 million
Employees: 900
Ticker: NASDAQ (GM): DSCM
SIC: 5912
Industry/ies: Communications; Medicine/Health Care/Mental Health; Pharmaceutical Industry; Telecommunications/Internet/Cable

Main Headquarters
Mailing: 411 108th Ave. NE	Tel:	(425) 372-3200
Suite 1400	Fax:	(425) 372-3800
Bellevue, WA 98004	TF:	(800) 378-4786

Corporate Foundations and Giving Programs
Drugstore.com Foundation
411 108th Ave. NE | Tel: | (425) 372-3200 |
Suite 1400
Bellvue, WA 98004

Public Affairs and Related Activities Personnel

At Headquarters
MARSHALL, Anne	Tel:	(425) 372-3200
Director, Public Relations	Fax:	(425) 372-3800
amarshall@drugstore.com		
WRIGHT, Tracy	Tel:	(425) 372-3200
Vice President & Chief Financial Officer	Fax:	(425) 372-3800

Drummond Company, Inc.

A mining company.
www.drummondco.com
Annual Revenues: $2.85 billion
Employees: 6,000
Industry/ies: Mining Industry; Natural Resources

Legislative Issues: TAX; TRD

Chairman of the Board and Chief Executive Officer
DRUMMOND, Garry N.
Tel: (205) 945-6300
Fax: (205) 945-6521

Main Headquarters
Mailing: P.O. Box 10246
Birmingham, AL 35202
Tel: (205) 945-6300
Fax: (205) 945-6440

Political Action Committees
Drummond Company Inc. PAC (DPAC)
FEC ID: C00160630
Contact: Scott O. Stanfield
P.O. Box 10246
Birmingham, AL 35202

Contributions to Candidates: $45,500 (2015-2016)
Democrats: $8,500; Republicans: $37,000

Corporate Foundations and Giving Programs
Drummond Company, Inc. Contribution program
P.O. Box 10246
Birmingham, AL 35202
Tel: (205) 945-6300
Fax: (205) 945-6440

Public Affairs and Related Activities Personnel

At Headquarters

ROBERSON, David L.
Vice President, Government and Regulatory Affairs
Tel: (205) 945-6300
Fax: (205) 945-6440

STANFIELD, Scott O.
PAC Treasurer
Tel: (205) 945-6300
Fax: (205) 945-6440

STILWELL, Jack
Executive Vice President & Chief Financial Officer
jack.stilwell@drummondco.com
Tel: (205) 945-6300
Fax: (205) 945-6440

WEBSTER, Bruce C.
Executive Vice President, General Counsel and Assistant Secretary
Tel: (205) 945-6300
Fax: (205) 945-6440

DSM Dyneema

Manufacturer of fiber.
www.dyneema.com
Annual Revenues: $15.50 million
Employees: 200
Industry/ies: Machinery/Equipment

Chairman of the Board
SIJBESMA, Feike
feike.sijbesma@dsm.com
Tel: (704) 862-5000
Fax: (704) 862-5001

Main Headquarters
Mailing: 1101 Hwy. 27 South
Stanley, NC 28164
Tel: (704) 862-5000
Fax: (704) 862-5001
TF: (800) 833-7404

DST Systems, Inc.

A computer software services provider.
www.dstsystems.com
Annual Revenues: $2.87 billion
Employees: 13,420
Ticker: NYSE: DST
SIC: 7374
Industry/ies: Computer/Technology

Chairman of the Board, President and Chief Executive Officer
HOOLEY, Stephen C.
Tel: (816) 435-1000
Fax: (816) 435-8618

President and Chief Executive Officer
BOEHM, Jonathan
Tel: (816) 435-1000
Fax: (816) 435-8618

Main Headquarters
Mailing: 333 W. 11th St.
Kansas City, MO 64105
Tel: (816) 435-1000
Fax: (816) 435-8618
TF: (888) 378-4636

Corporate Foundations and Giving Programs
DST Systems, Inc. Contributions Program
333 W. 11th St.
Kansas City, MO 64105
Tel: (816) 435-1000

Public Affairs and Related Activities Personnel

At Headquarters

DONALDSON, Craig
Vice President, Chief Ethics and Compliance Officer
Tel: (816) 435-1000
Fax: (816) 435-8618

GIVENS, Gregg
Chief Financial Officer
Tel: (816) 435-1000
Fax: (816) 435-8618

GOLDMAN, Chris
Senior Coordinator, Healthcare Media Relations
ctgoldman@dstsystems.com
Tel: (816) 843-9087
Fax: (816) 435-8618

RILEY, John
Chief Marketing Officer, Communications and Investor Relations
Tel: (816) 435-1000
Fax: (816) 435-8618

SWEETMAN, Beth
Tel: (816) 435-1000

Senior Vice President and Chief Human Resources Officer
Fax: (816) 435-8618

YOUNG, Randall G.
Senior Vice President, General Counsel, and Secretary
Tel: (816) 435-1000
Fax: (816) 435-8618

DSW, inc.

See listing on page 682 under Retail Ventures, Inc.

DTE Energy

Diversified energy company involved in the development and management of energy-related businesses and services nationwide.
www.dteenergy.com
Annual Revenues: $11.36 billion
Employees: 10,000
Ticker: NYSE:DTE
SIC: 4911
Industry/ies: Energy/Electricity; Utilities
Legislative Issues: BUD; CAW; CDT; ENG; ENV; HOM; LBR; TAX; TRA

Chairman and Chief Executive Officer
ANDERSON, Gerard M
Tel: (313) 235-8000
Fax: (313) 235-6743

Main Headquarters
Mailing: One Energy Plaza
Detroit, MI 48226
Tel: (313) 235-8000
Fax: (313) 235-6743

Washington Office
Mailing: 601 Pennsylvania Ave. NW
Suite 350 N
Washington, DC 20004
Tel: (202) 202-2808
Fax: (202) 347-8423

Political Action Committees
DTE Energy Company PAC - Federal
FEC ID: C00081547
Contact: Douglas J. Ziemnick
One Energy Plaza
Detroit, MI 48226
Tel: (313) 235-4000
Fax: (313) 235-4000

Contributions to Candidates: $296,000 (2015-2016)
Democrats: $111,500; Republicans: $184,500

Principal Recipients

SENATE
BLUNT, ROY (REP-MO)

HOUSE
BISHOP, MIKE (REP-MI)
MCCARTHY, KEVIN (REP-CA)
UPTON, FREDERICK STEPHEN (REP-MI)
WALBERG, TIMOTHY L HON. (REP-MI)

Corporate Foundations and Giving Programs
DTE Energy Foundation
One Energy Plaza
Detroit, MI 48226
Tel: (313) 235-9271
Fax: (313) 235-9271

Public Affairs and Related Activities Personnel

At Headquarters

BOYD, Skiles
Federal Lobbyist
Registered Federal Lobbyist
Tel: (313) 235-4000
Fax: (313) 235-8055

CORRIVEAU, Zane
Tel: (313) 235-8000
Fax: (313) 235-6743

KATZ, Alan
Legislative Assistant
Tel: (313) 235-8000
Fax: (313) 235-6743

MEADOR, David E.
Executive Vice President and Chief Financial Officer
Tel: (313) 235-4000
Fax: (313) 235-8055

PETERSON, Bruce D.
Senior Vice President and General Counsel
Tel: (313) 235-4000
Fax: (313) 235-8055

STEWARD, Larry
Vice President, Human Resources
Tel: (313) 235-4000
Fax: (313) 235-8055

TRACEY, Parker
Registered Federal Lobbyist
Tel: (313) 235-8000
Fax: (313) 235-6743

ZIEMNICK, Douglas J.
PAC Treasurer
Mail Stop ROOM 1583 WCB
Tel: (313) 235-4000
Fax: (313) 235-0327

At Washington Office

BRITTO, Karen
Manager, Federal Affairs
Tel: (202) 202-2808
Fax: (202) 347-8423

MOODY, Nancy
Director, Federal Affairs
moodyn@dteenergy.com
Tel: (202) 292-2810
Fax: (202) 347-8423

Duchossois Group, Inc.

A private equity firm specializing acquisitions and investments.
www.duch.com
Employees: 6,000
SIC: 3699; 3442; 3489; 3639; 3669
Industry/ies: Defense/Homeland Security; Government-Related; Transportation

Founder and Chairman of the Board
DUCHOSSOIS, Richard L.

Tel: (630) 279-3600
Fax: (630) 530-6091

Chief Executive Officer
DUCHOSSOIS, Craig J.
cjd@duch.com

Tel: (630) 279-3600
Fax: (630) 530-6091

Main Headquarters
Mailing: 845 Larch Ave.
            Elmhurst, IL 60126

Tel: (630) 279-3600
Fax: (630) 530-6091

Political Action Committees
Duchossois Group PAC
FEC ID: C00212308
Contact: Michael E. Flannery
845 Larch Ave.
Elmhurst, IL 60126

Tel: (630) 279-3600
Fax: (630) 530-6091

    Contributions to Candidates: $17,000 (2015-2016)
    Democrats: $5,000; Republicans: $12,000

Public Affairs and Related Activities Personnel

At Headquarters

BELL, Gaelen
Contact, Media Relations
gbell@msinet.com

Tel: (312) 946-6089
Fax: (630) 530-6091

FLANNERY, Michael E.
Executive Vice President, Chief Financial Officer
mflannery@duch.com

Tel: (630) 279-3600
Fax: (630) 530-6091

MOSKOWITZ, Jason
Senior Director, Business Development
investments@duch.com

Tel: (630) 516-6705
Fax: (630) 530-6091

PLANTE, Judi
Manager, Corporate Human Resources
employment@duch.com

Tel: (630) 530-6753
Fax: (630) 530-6091

REEVES, Eric A.
Vice President and General Counsel

Tel: (630) 279-3600
Fax: (630) 530-6091

Ducks Unlimited

Non-profits conservation organization.
www.ducks.org
Annual Revenues: $183.73 million
Employees: 500
Industry/ies: Animals; Environment And Conservation; Sports/Leisure/
Entertainment
Legislative Issues: CAW; ENV; NAT

Chairman of the Board
NEWMAN, John W.

Tel: (901) 758-3825
Fax: (901) 758-3850

Chief Executive Officer
HALL, H. Dale

Tel: (901) 758-3825
Fax: (901) 758-3850

Main Headquarters
Mailing: One Waterfowl Way
            Memphis, TN 38120

Tel: (901) 758-3825
Fax: (901) 758-3850
TF: (800) 453-8257

Washington Office
Mailing: 1301 Pennsylvania Ave. NW
            Suite 402
            Washington, DC 20004

Tel: (202) 347-1530
Fax: (202) 347-1533

Public Affairs and Related Activities Personnel

At Headquarters

COOPER, Andi
Communications Specialist
acooper@ducks.org

Tel: (601) 956-1936
Fax: (901) 758-3850

DIERKS, Wayne
Director, Human Resources
wdierks@ducks.org

Tel: (901) 758-3825
Fax: (901) 758-3850

FULGHAM, Tom
Chief Communications Officer
tfulgham@ducks.org

Tel: (901) 758-3825
Fax: (901) 758-3850

GASCHLER, Kevin
Director, Membership Marketing
kgaschler@ducks.org

Tel: (901) 758-3825
Fax: (901) 758-3850

GROCHAU, Earl
?Chief Administration Officer and Chief Financial Officer

Tel: (901) 758-3825
Fax: (901) 758-3850

SIMPSON, Tona Jackson
Senior Director, Foundation Relations

Tel: (901) 758-3825
Fax: (901) 758-3850

At Washington Office

EVERSON, Margaret
Chief Policy Officer

Tel: (202) 347-1530
Fax: (202) 347-1533

GARRETT, Caroline
Conservation Policy Specialist
cgarrett@ducks.org

Tel: (202) 347-1530
Fax: (202) 347-1533

MOSS, Kellis

Tel: (202) 347-1530

Director of Public Policy
kmoss@ducks.org

Fax: (202) 347-1533

MURTHA, Katie
Chief Policy Officer

Tel: (202) 347-1530
Fax: (202) 347-1533

TAWNEY, Whitney
Senior Advisor, Water Policy

Tel: (202) 347-1530
Fax: (202) 347-1533

TAYLOR, Gary J.
Director, Governmental Affairs
gtaylor@ducks.org

Tel: (202) 347-1530
Fax: (202) 347-1533

WRINN, Daniel E.
Director, Public Policy

Tel: (202) 347-1530
Fax: (202) 347-1533

Duke Energy

An energy company focused on electric power and gas distribution operations, and other energy services in the Americas. Merged with Progress Energy in July 2012 to form one of the largest electric utilities in America.
www.duke-energy.com
Annual Revenues: $23.30 billion
Employees: 28,344
Ticker: NYSE: DUK
SIC: 4911; 4931
Industry/ies: Energy/Electricity; Utilities
Legislative Issues: BUD; CAW; COM; ENG; ENV; HOM; LBR; TAX; TRA; UTI; WAS

Chairman of the Board
GRAY, Ann Maynard

Tel: (704) 594-6200
Fax: (704) 382-3814

President and Chief Executive Officer
GOOD, Lynn J.
Lynn.Good@duke-energy.com

Tel: (704) 382-3853
Fax: (704) 382-3814

Main Headquarters
Mailing: 550 S. Tryon St.
            Charlotte, NC 28202

Tel: (704) 382-3853
TF: (800) 559-3853

Washington Office
Mailing: 801 Pennsylvania Ave. NW
            Suite 250
            Washington, DC 20004

Political Action Committees
Duke Energy Corporation PAC
FEC ID: C00083535
Contact: Lawrence Valenti
550 S. Tryon St.
Charlotte, NC 28202

    Contributions to Candidates: $656,500 (2015-2016)
    Democrats: $151,500; Republicans: $504,000; Other: $1,000

        Principal Recipients

           SENATE
           BURR, RICHARD (REP-NC)
           SCOTT, TIMOTHY E (REP-SC)

           HOUSE
           BOUSTANY, CHARLES W. DR. JR. (REP-LA)
           DUNCAN, JEFFREY D MR. (REP-SC)
           MULVANEY, JOHN MICHAEL 'MICK' (REP-SC)
           RICE, TOM (REP-SC)

Corporate Foundations and Giving Programs
The Duke Energy Foundation
526 S. Church St.
Charlotte, NC 28202

Tel: (704) 594-6200
Fax: (704) 382-3814

Public Affairs and Related Activities Personnel

At Headquarters

ANDERSON, Melissa H.
Senior Vice President and Chief Human Resources Officer

Tel: (704) 382-3853

BEACH, Richard G.
Associate General Counsel & Assistant Corporate Secretary

Tel: (704) 382-3853

BINGOL, Selim
Senior Vice President and Chief Communications Officer

Tel: (704) 382-3853

CURRENS, Bill
Vice President, Investor Relations

Tel: (704) 382-3853

DE MAY, Stephen G.
Senior Vice President and Treasurer

Tel: (704) 382-3853

JANSON, Julie S.
Executive Vice President, Chief Legal Officer and Corporate Secretary

Tel: (704) 382-3853

MANLY, Marc E.
Executive Vice President
marc.manly@duke-energy.com

Tel: (704) 382-3853

ROCHE, Cathy S.
Senior Vice President and Chief Communications Officer
csroche@duke-energy.com

Tel: (704) 382-3853

STONE, Jeffrey M.

Tel: (704) 382-3853

Vice President, Internal Audit and Chief Ethics and Compliance Officer

TRAUSCHKE, R. Sean   Tel: (704) 382-3853
Senior Vice President, Investor Relations and Financial Planning

VALENTI, Lawrence   Tel: (704) 594-6200
Consultant, Human Resources and PAC Treasurer

VALENTI, Larry   Tel: (704) 382-3853
PAC Contact

WEBER, Jennifer L.   Tel: (704) 382-3853
Executive Vice President, External Affairs and Strategic Policy
Jennifer.Weber@duke-energy.com

YOUNG, Steven K.   Tel: (704) 382-3853
Executive Vice President and Chief Financial Officer

At Other Offices

CRAIG, Thomas
325 Seventh St. NW, Suite 300
Washington, DC 20004
Registered Federal Lobbyist

HAYSBERT, John   Tel: (704) 594-6200
Federal Lobbyist   Fax: (704) 382-3814
526 S. Church St.
Charlotte, NC 28202
Registered Federal Lobbyist

KAVENEY, Colleen
325 Seventh St. NW, Suite 300
Washington, DC 20004
Registered Federal Lobbyist

LOWELL, Brandi
Federal Lobbyist
325 Seventh St. NW, Suite 300
Washington, DC 20004

MCARTHUR, John R.   Tel: (919) 546-6111
Executive Vice President, Regulated Utilities   Fax: (919) 546-2920
P.O. Box 1551
Raleigh, NC 27602

PENNINGTON NATONSKI, Pepper
325 Seventh St. NW, Suite 300
Washington, DC 20004
Registered Federal Lobbyist

SEWELL, Michael B.   Tel: (919) 546-6111
Federal Lobbyist   Fax: (919) 546-2920
P.O. Box 1551
Raleigh, NC 27602
Registered Federal Lobbyist

SHIEL, Tom   Tel: (704) 382-2355
Contact, Corporate Media Relations   Fax: (704) 382-3814
526 S. Church St.
Charlotte, NC 28202
tom.shiel@duke-energy.com

SHORT, Toby   Tel: (704) 594-6200
Federal Lobbyist   Fax: (704) 382-3814
526 S. Church St.
Charlotte, NC 28202
Registered Federal Lobbyist

SHULER, Hon. Heath
Senior Vice President, Federal Affairs
325 Seventh St. NW, Suite 300
Washington, DC 20004

TYNDALL, William   Tel: (704) 594-6200
Senior Vice President, Federal Government and Regulatory Affairs   Fax: (704) 382-3814
526 S. Church St.
Charlotte, NC 28202

Dun & Bradstreet

A provider of international and US business credit information and credit reports and pursues an unrelenting quest for quality; use speed and simplicity to achieve goals.
www.dnb.com
Annual Revenues: $1.68 billion
Employees: 4,900
Ticker: NYSE: DNB
SIC: 7320
NAICS: 51112
Industry/ies: Banking/Finance/Investments; Communications; Media/Mass Communication
Legislative Issues: BUD; DEF; FIN; FOO; GOV; HOM

President, Chief Executive Officer and Director   Tel: (973) 921-5500
CARRIGAN, Bob   Fax: (973) 921-6056

Main Headquarters
Mailing: 103 JFK Pkwy.   Tel: (973) 921-5500

Short Hills, NJ 07078   Fax: (973) 921-6056
         TF: (800) 234-3867

Corporate Foundations and Giving Programs
The Dun & Bradstreet Corporation Foundation
22761 Pacific Coast Hwy.   Tel: (973) 921-5500
Malibu, CA 90265   Fax: (973) 921-6056

Public Affairs and Related Activities Personnel

At Headquarters

DAVE, Rishi   Tel: (973) 921-5500
Chief Marketing Officer   Fax: (973) 921-6056

GUINNESSEY, Kathy   Tel: (973) 921-5892
Corporate Treasurer and North America Chief Financial Officer   Fax: (973) 921-6056
guinnesseyk@dnb.com

HILL, Christie A.   Tel: (973) 921-5500
Chief Legal Officer   Fax: (973) 921-6056

PEIREZ, Josh   Tel: (973) 921-5500
Chief Operating Officer   Fax: (973) 921-6056

PROWER, Julian   Tel: (973) 921-5500
Senior Vice President and Chief Human Resources Officer   Fax: (973) 921-6056

REID-DODICK, John   Tel: (973) 921-5500
Chief People Officer   Fax: (973) 921-6056

SACHS, CFA, Roger   Tel: (973) 921-5914
Director, Investor Relations   Fax: (973) 921-6056
sachsr@dnb.com

VELDRAN, Richard H.   Tel: (973) 921-5500
Senior Vice President and Chief Financial Officer   Fax: (973) 921-6056
veldranr@dnb.com

YELEN, Harvey   Tel: (973) 921-5500
Chief of Staff - Global Legal Team   Fax: (973) 921-6056
yelenh@dnb.com

Dunavant Enterprises

A cotton merchandiser. The firm's two other divisions focus on real estate development and investments under the Dunavant Investments umbrella.
www.dunavant.com
Employees: 1,700
Industry/ies: Agriculture/Agronomy

Chairman of the Board   Tel: (901) 369-1500
DUNAVANT, Jr., III, William Buchanan   Fax: (901) 369-1608
wbdjr@dunavant.com

President and Chief Executive Officer   Tel: (901) 369-1500
DUNAVANT, William B.   Fax: (901) 369-1608

Main Headquarters
Mailing: 959 Ridgeway Loop Rd.   Tel: (901) 369-1500
      Suite 205   Fax: (901) 369-1608
      Memphis, TN 38120   TF: (888) 955-3547

Public Affairs and Related Activities Personnel

At Headquarters

CHERRY, Russel   Tel: (901) 369-1500
Senior Vice President, General Counsel and Secretary   Fax: (901) 369-1608
russ.cherry@dunavant.com

HJERPE, Karen   Tel: (901) 369-1500
Vice President, Quality and Compliance Services   Fax: (901) 369-1608
karen.hjerpe@dunavant.com

LOMAX, Kelly   Tel: (901) 369-1500
Executive Vice President and Chief Financial Officer   Fax: (901) 369-1608
kelly.lomax@dunavant.com

MCDUFFIE, Richard   Tel: (901) 369-1500
Senior Vice President, Chief Operating Officer   Fax: (901) 369-1608

Duncan Solutions

Parking and enforcement management.
www.duncansolutions.com
Annual Revenues: $1.20 million
Industry/ies: Law Enforcement/Security

Main Headquarters
Mailing: 633 W. Wisconsin Ave.   Tel: (414) 847-3773
      Suite 1600   TF: (888) 993-8622
      Milwaukee, WI 53203

Public Affairs and Related Activities Personnel

At Headquarters

KENNEDY, James   Tel: (414) 847-3773
Senior Vice President, Sales and Marketing; Media Contact
jkennedy@duncansolutions.com

Dunkin Brands

Formerly operated as Allied Domecq Quick Service Restaurants. Includes Dunkin' Donuts, Baskin Robbins, and Togo's. A division of Allied Domecq plc of Bristol, England.
www.dunkinbrands.com
Annual Revenues: $762.67 million
Employees: 1,584
Ticker: NASDAQ: DNKN
SIC: 5810
Industry/ies: Food And Beverage Industry
Legislative Issues: LBR; TAX

Chairman of the Board and Chief Executive Officer	Tel:	(781) 737-3000
TRAVIS, Nigel	Fax:	(781) 737-4000
Nigel.Travis@dunkinbrands.com		

Main Headquarters

| *Mailing:* | 130 Royall St. | Tel: | (781) 737-3000 |
| | Canton, MA 02021 | Fax: | (781) 737-4000 |

Washington Office

Mailing: 888 16th St. NW
       Suite 800
       Washington, DC 20006

Political Action Committees
Dunkin' Brands Inc. PAC
FEC ID: C00431544
Contact: Karen Raskopf
130 Royall St.
Suite 100
Canton, MA 02021

  Contributions to Candidates: $2,000 (2015-2016)
    Democrats: $1,000; Republicans: $1,000

Corporate Foundations and Giving Programs

Dunkin' Donuts & Baskin-Robbins Community Foundation		
130 Royall St.	Tel:	(781) 737-3587
Canton, MA 02021		

Public Affairs and Related Activities Personnel

At Headquarters

CARBONE, Paul	Tel:	(781) 737-3000
Chief Financial Officer	Fax:	(781) 737-4000
CLARE, Jack	Tel:	(781) 737-3000
Chief Information and Strategy Officer	Fax:	(781) 737-4000
COSTELLO, John	Tel:	(781) 737-3000
President, Global Marketing and Innovation	Fax:	(781) 737-4000
DRAKE, Justin	Tel:	(781) 737-3000
Senior Manager, Public Relations	Fax:	(781) 737-4000
EMMETT, Richard	Tel:	(781) 737-3000
Chief Legal and Human Resources Officer	Fax:	(781) 737-4000
KING, Michelle	Tel:	(781) 737-5200
Senior Director, Global Media Relations	Fax:	(781) 737-4000
michelle.king@dunkinbrands.com		
RASKOPF, Karen	Tel:	(781) 737-3000
Senior Vice President, Corporate Communications	Fax:	(781) 737-4000
karen.raskopf@dunkinbrands.com		

E.I. du Pont de Nemours & Company (DuPont)

A science-based products and services company.
www.dupont.com
Annual Revenues: $33.95 billion
Employees: 63,000
Ticker: NYSE: DD
SIC: 2820
NAICS: 325910
Industry/ies: Chemicals & Chemical Industry; Pharmaceutical Industry
Legislative Issues: AGR; AVI; CHM; CPT; DEF; ENG; ENV; FOO; SCI; TAR; TAX; TRD

Chairman of the Board and Chief Executive Officer	Tel:	(302) 774-1000
KULLMAN, Ellen J.	Fax:	(302) 999-4399
ellen.j.kullman@usa.dupont.com		

Main Headquarters

Mailing:	1007 N. Market St.	Tel:	(302) 774-1000
	Wilmington, DE 19898	Fax:	(302) 999-4399
		TF:	(800) 441-7515

Washington Office

Mailing:	601 Pennsylvania Ave. NW	Tel:	(202) 628-6320
	Suite 325, North Bldg.	Fax:	(202) 728-3649
	Washington, DC 20004		

Political Action Committees
E.I. Du Pont De Nemours Company Good Government Fund (Dupont Good Government Fund) PAC
FEC ID: C00171926
Contact: Jessica Galarza
974 Centre Rd.
Wilmington, DE 19805

  Contributions to Candidates: $99,750 (2015-2016)
    Democrats: $30,000; Republicans: $69,750

Corporate Foundations and Giving Programs
DuPont Center for Collaborative Research and Education
P.O. Box 80357
Wilmington, DE 19880-0357

E.I. du Pont de Nemours & Company (DuPont) Contributions Program		
1007 Market St.	Tel:	(302) 774-1000
Wilmington, DE 19898	Fax:	(302) 999-4399

Public Affairs and Related Activities Personnel

At Headquarters

BELETTI, Marie	Tel:	(302) 996-8355
Coordinator, Media Relations	Fax:	(302) 999-4399
marie.l.beletti-2@usa.dupont.com		
BILLS, David G.	Tel:	(302) 774-1000
Senior Vice President, Corporate Strategy	Fax:	(302) 999-4399
G.Bills@usa.dupont.com		
CACHINERO-SANCHEZ, Benito	Tel:	(302) 774-1000
Senior Vice President, Human Resources	Fax:	(302) 999-4399
CAPTAIN, Lorie	Tel:	(302) 773-3551
Manager, Business Communications and Media Relations	Fax:	(302) 999-4399
lori.a.captain@usa.dupont.com		
DESALVA, AnnaMaria	Tel:	(302) 774-1000
Vice President, Corporate Communications	Fax:	(302) 999-4399
FANANDAKIS, Nicholas C.	Tel:	(302) 774-1000
Executive Vice President and Chief Financial Officer	Fax:	(302) 999-4399
FOX, Stacy	Tel:	(302) 774-1000
Senior Vice President and General Counsel	Fax:	(302) 999-4399
GRANGER, Barry M.	Tel:	(202) 728-3633
Vice President, Government Affairs	Fax:	(302) 999-4399
Barry.M.Granger@usa.dupont.com		
HANRETTA, Mike	Tel:	(302) 774-4005
Media Relations Leader	Fax:	(302) 999-4399
michael.j.hanretta@usa.dupont.com		
LUKACH, Carl J.	Tel:	(302) 774-1000
Vice President, Investor Relations	Fax:	(302) 999-4399

At Washington Office

ANGELO, Maria	Tel:	(202) 628-6320
Federal Lobbyist and Manager, DuPont Government Affairs	Fax:	(202) 728-3649
ATWELL, Tiffany M.	Tel:	(202) 628-6320
Director, International Government Affairs	Fax:	(202) 728-3649
BOYKIN, Celeste	Tel:	(202) 728-3600
Senior Manager, Government Affairs	Fax:	(202) 728-3649
CLARK, Nancy	Tel:	(202) 628-6320
Registered Federal Lobbyist	Fax:	(202) 728-3649
DICLEMENTI, James N.	Tel:	(202) 728-3601
Senior Manager, Federal Business Development Initiatives	Fax:	(202) 728-3649
GALARZA, Jessica	Tel:	(202) 628-6320
PAC Treasurer	Fax:	(202) 728-3649
GUTTER, Karis	Tel:	(202) 628-6320
Registered Federal Lobbyist	Fax:	(202) 728-3649
HARDEN, Krysta	Tel:	(202) 628-6320
	Fax:	(202) 728-3649
HOLLAND, Gilbert	Tel:	(202) 628-6320
Federal Lobbyist	Fax:	(202) 728-3649
HOPPER, Sara	Tel:	(202) 628-6320
Federal Lobbyist	Fax:	(202) 728-3649
Registered Federal Lobbyist		
KOUNTZ, Dennis	Tel:	(202) 628-6320
Contact, Government Relations	Fax:	(202) 728-3649
LEFTWICH, Joel T.	Tel:	(202) 628-6320
Senior Director, Public Policy	Fax:	(202) 728-3649
Registered Federal Lobbyist		
MOUNTJOY, Brittany	Tel:	(202) 628-6320
Registered Federal Lobbyist	Fax:	(202) 728-3649
OLSEN, Elaine	Tel:	(202) 728-3600
Federal Lobbyist	Fax:	(202) 728-3649
PARR, Michael	Tel:	(202) 728-3661
Senior Manager, Government Affairs	Fax:	(202) 728-3649
SHERIDAN, Kelly	Tel:	(202) 728-3634
Contact, Government Relations	Fax:	(202) 728-3649
Kelly.Sheridan@dupont.com		
Registered Federal Lobbyist		
STRACHAN, Linda Avery	Tel:	(202) 728-3600
Director, Federal Government Affairs	Fax:	(202) 728-3649
Registered Federal Lobbyist		
WHITESEL, Aaron	Tel:	(202) 628-6320
Senior Manager, Government Affairs	Fax:	(202) 728-3649

Registered Federal Lobbyist

DuPont Danisco Cellulosic Ethanol LLC

Provides development and commercialization of cellulosic ethanol.
www.ddce.com
Employees: 6
Industry/ies: Chemicals & Chemical Industry

Main Headquarters
Mailing: 500 Park Blvd.   Tel: (630) 250-9300
            Suite 545
            Itasca, IL 60143-1267

Duquesne Light Company

See listing on page 271 under Duquesne Light Holdings

Duquesne Light Holdings

Formerly known as DQE, Inc. A utility holding company.
www.duquesnelight.com
Employees: 1,400
Ticker: OTC: DQUEK
SIC: 4911
Industry/ies: Energy/Electricity; Utilities

President and Chief Executive Officer   Tel: (412) 393-6000
RIAZZI, Richard   Fax: (412) 393-5517

Main Headquarters
Mailing: 411 Seventh Ave. (Six - One)   Tel: (412) 393-6000
            Pittsburgh, PA 15219   Fax: (412) 393-5517
                                                    TF: (888) 393-7100

Corporate Foundations and Giving Programs

Power of Light Corporate Giving
411 Seventh Ave. (Six - One)
Pittsburgh, PA 15219

Public Affairs and Related Activities Personnel

At Headquarters

DORAN, Mike   Tel: (412) 393-6000
Vice President, Operations   Fax: (412) 393-5517

FAULK, Todd W.   Tel: (412) 393-6000
Vice President, Human Resources   Fax: (412) 393-5517

FISFIS, David T.   Tel: (412) 393-6000
Vice President , General Counsel and Corporate Secretary   Fax: (412) 393-5517

KAPLAN, Mark   Tel: (412) 393-6000
Senior Vice President and Chief Financial Officer Fax: (412) 393-5517

LABRIOLA , Elisa C.   Tel: (412) 393-6000
Chief Compliance Officer   Fax: (412) 393-5517

MIKO, Mark S.   Tel: (412) 393-6000
Vice President, Information Technology and Chief   Fax: (412) 393-5517
Information Officer

MILLIGAN, James   Tel: (412) 393-1216
Manager, Treasury Operations   Fax: (412) 393-5517
jmilligan@duqlight.com

PEKNY, Anthony   Tel: (412) 393-6000
Vice President   Fax: (412) 393-6448

ROCK, Jessica   Tel: (412) 393-4606
Contact, Corporate Communications   Fax: (412) 393-5517
jrock@duqlight.com

SIEBER, Rich   Tel: (412) 232-6848
Manager, Corporate Communications   Fax: (412) 393-6825
rsieber@dqe.com

Dura Automotive Systems, Inc.

Manufacturer of automotive components. It is an independent designer and manufacturer of driver control systems, seating control systems, safety hardware, structural body systems, exterior trim and integrated glass systems.
www.duraauto.com
Annual Revenues: $1.25 billion
Employees: 12,000
SIC: 3714
Industry/ies: Automotive Industry; Transportation

Executive Chairman of the Board   Tel: (248) 299-7500
LEULIETTE, Timothy D.   Fax: (248) 299-7501

Chief Executive Officer   Tel: (248) 299-7500
TILTON, Lynn   Fax: (248) 475-4378

Main Headquarters
Mailing: 1780 Pond Run   Tel: (248) 299-7500
            Auburn Hills, MI 48326   Fax: (248) 475-4378

Public Affairs and Related Activities Personnel

At Headquarters

BECKER, Martin   Tel: (248) 299-7500
Executive Vice President & Chief Operating Officer Fax: (248) 475-4378

BEYER, Pierre   Tel: (248) 299-7500
Executive Vice President, Global Human Resources   Fax: (248) 475-4378

KOHLER, Bill   Tel: (248) 299-7500
Chief Legal Officer & Corporate Secretary   Fax: (248) 475-4378

STOUVENOT, Francois   Tel: (248) 299-7500
Executive Vice President and Chief Commercial Officer   Fax: (248) 299-7501

URSELMANN , Sabine   Tel: (248) 299-7500
Vice President, Human Resources   Fax: (248) 475-4378

WHITE, Richard   Tel: (212) 825-6836
Media Contact   Fax: (248) 299-7501
Richard.White@patriarchpartners.com

Dynalene

Dynalene supplies industrial heat transfer fluids, glycols, brines, potassium formate, secondary refrigerants, such as Liquidow Calcium Chloride, and high performance coolant.
www.dynalene.com
Employees: 10
Industry/ies: Chemicals & Chemical Industry

Chairman of the Board   Tel: (610) 262-9686
LOIKITS, Daniel   Fax: (610) 262-7437
danl@dynalene.com

President and Chief Executive Officer   Tel: (610) 262-9686
MOHAPATRA, Dr. Satish   Fax: (610) 262-7437

Main Headquarters
Mailing: 5250 W. Coplay Rd.   Tel: (610) 262-9686
            Whitehall, PA 18052-2212   Fax: (610) 262-7437
                                                    TF: (877) 244-5525

Public Affairs and Related Activities Personnel

At Headquarters

ARCURY, David   Tel: (610) 262-9686
Chief Operating Officer   Fax: (610) 262-7437

ARMENTI, Carmen   Tel: (610) 262-9686
Contact, Corporate Affairs   Fax: (610) 262-7437

CHAYA, John   Tel: (610) 262-9686
Contact, Marketing   Fax: (610) 262-7437

LUTZ, Keith   Tel: (610) 262-9686
Contact, Finance   Fax: (610) 262-7437

Dynameos, LLC

A homeland security and military affairs consultant.
www.dynameos.net
Industry/ies: Defense/Homeland Security; Government-Related; Military/Veterans

Main Headquarters
Mailing: 11601 Pleasant Ridge Rd.   Tel: (225) 202-5661
            Suite 301
            Little Rock, AR 72212

Dynamic Industries Inc.

Integrated full service construction.
www.dynamicind.com
Annual Revenues: $76.40 million
Employees: 4,000
Industry/ies: Construction/Construction Materials

Senior Vice President   Tel: (337) 237-1898
SANDLIN, Jimmy   Fax: (337) 291-7401

Main Headquarters
Mailing: 400 Poydras St.   Tel: (504) 708-5434
            Suite 1800   Fax: (504) 608-6702
            New Orleans, LA 70130

Corporate Foundations and Giving Programs

Dynamic Industries Contribution Program
6005 Port Rd.   Tel: (337) 560-8700
New Iberia, LA 70560   Fax: (337) 365-8329

Public Affairs and Related Activities Personnel

At Headquarters

DAVIS, Missy   Tel: (337) 237-1898
Executive Assistant, Marketing Coordinator and Media   Fax: (504) 608-6702
Contact

At Other Offices

CLEMENT, Lynette   Tel: (337) 560-8700
Chief Financial Officer   Fax: (337) 365-8329
6005 Port Rd.
New Iberia, LA 70560

LAFLEUR, Dennis   Tel: (337) 237-1898
Vice President, International Sales   Fax: (337) 291-7401
600 Jefferson St., Suite 1400
Lafayette, LA 70501

NICHOLS, Logan
Vice President, Sales
600 Jefferson St., Suite 1400
Lafayette, LA 70501

Tel: (337) 237-1898
Fax: (337) 291-7401

Dynamics Research Corporation

A provider of mission-critical technology management services and solutions for government programs.
www.drc.com
Employees: 1,250
Ticker: NASDAQ: DRCO
SIC: 7373
Industry/ies: Defense/Homeland Security; Government-Related

Chairman of the Board, President and Chief Executive Officer
REGAN, James P.

Tel: (978) 289-1500
Fax: (978) 289-1887

Main Headquarters
Mailing: Two Tech Dr.
          Andover, MA 01810-2434

Tel: (978) 289-1500
Fax: (978) 289-1887

Washington Office
Mailing: 650 Massachusetts Ave. NW
          Suite 510
          Washington, DC 20001

Tel: (202) 525-6900
Fax: (202) 898-4193

Political Action Committees
Dynamics Research Corporation PAC
FEC ID: C00362582
Contact: Pisey Sar
Two Tech Dr.
Andover, MA 01810

Public Affairs and Related Activities Personnel

At Headquarters

COVEL, Richard A.
Vice President and General Counsel

Tel: (978) 289-1616
Fax: (978) 474-9204

KELEHER, David
Senior Vice President and Chief Financial Officer and Treasurer
dkeleher@drc.com

Tel: (978) 289-1500
Fax: (978) 289-1887

SAR, Pisey
PAC Treasurer

Tel: (978) 289-1500
Fax: (978) 289-1887

STRASSER, Paul
Senior Vice President and General Manager, Federal Group

Tel: (978) 289-1500
Fax: (978) 289-1887

TSINGOS, Helen E.
Chief Legal Officer

Tel: (978) 289-1500
Fax: (978) 289-1887

WITTY, Chris
Vice President, Investor Relations
cwitty@darrowir.com

Tel: (646) 438-9385
Fax: (978) 289-1887

At Washington Office

TRUONG, Duyen
Vice President, Public Relations
duyent@aboutsage.com

Tel: (703) 584-5645
Fax: (202) 898-4193

Dynamis Advisors, Inc.

A consulting and a comprehensive service organization dedicated to helping clients find effective solutions through partnerships and collaborations. They assist healthcare providers and the communities they serve transform from fee-for-service to value-based care, specifically by helping build healthier communities.
www.dynamis-hc.com
Annual Revenues: $1.20 million
Industry/ies: Medicine/Health Care/Mental Health

President and Chief Executive Officer
KELLER, Scott J.

Tel: (440) 247-7876
Fax: (440) 247-4960

Main Headquarters
Mailing: 7209-A Chagrin Rd.
          Chagrin Falls, OH 44023

Tel: (440) 247-7876
Fax: (440) 247-4960

Corporate Foundations and Giving Programs

Dynamis Advisors, Inc. Contributions Program
7209-A Chagrin Rd.
Chagrin Falls, OH 44023-1131

Tel: (440) 247-7876
Fax: (440) 247-4960

Public Affairs and Related Activities Personnel

At Headquarters

DAY, Vincent
Vice President

Tel: (440) 247-7876
Fax: (440) 247-4960

LEECH, John D.
Principal

Tel: (440) 247-7876
Fax: (440) 247-4960

PEEL, Marlena Rennie
Project Administrator

Tel: (440) 247-7876
Fax: (440) 247-4960

Dynavox

Provider of augmentative and alternative communication (AAC) products and services.
www.dynavoxtech.com

Annual Revenues: $75.00 million
Employees: 395
Ticker: Nasdaq:DVOX
SIC: 7373
Industry/ies: Communications; Disabilities; Telecommunications/Internet/Cable

Chairman of the Board
HOLSTEIN, Roger C.

Tel: (412) 381-4883
Fax: (412) 381-5241

Main Headquarters
Mailing: 2100 Wharton St.
          Suite 400
          Pittsburgh, PA 15203

Tel: (412) 381-4883
Fax: (412) 381-5241
TF: (866) 396-2869

Public Affairs and Related Activities Personnel

At Headquarters

BERTNER, Sherry L.
Contact, Investor Relations

Tel: (646) 277-1200
Fax: (412) 381-5241

CUNNINGHAM, Robert E.
Chief Strategy and Clinical Officer

Tel: (412) 381-4883
Fax: (412) 381-5241

MERK, Raymond J.
Chief Financial Officer and Corporate Secretary
Ray.Merk@dynavoxtech.com

Tel: (412) 381-4883
Fax: (412) 381-5241

Dyncorp International

DynCorp International is a global government services provider in support of U.S. national security and foreign policy objectives, delivering support.
www.dyn-intl.com
SIC: 7389
Industry/ies: Computer/Technology
Legislative Issues: BUD; DEF; FOR; GOV

Main Headquarters
Mailing: 1700 Old Meadow Rd.
          McLean, VA 22102

Tel: (571) 722-0210

Political Action Committees
Dyncorp International LLC PAC
FEC ID: C00409979
Contact: John Gastright Jr.
3190 Fairview Park Dr.
Suite 350
Falls Church, VA 22042

  Contributions to Candidates: $158,500 (2015-2016)
  Democrats: $79,500; Republicans: $79,000

Public Affairs and Related Activities Personnel

At Headquarters

GASTRIGHT, Jr., John
Vice President, Government Affairs, Communications and International Operations and PAC Treasurer
john.gastright@dyn-intl.com
Registered Federal Lobbyist

Tel: (571) 722-0210

At Other Offices

CRUMPLER, Jane
Manager, Government Relations
3190 Fairview Park Dr., Suite 700
Falls Church, VA 22042
jane.crumpler@dyn-intl.com

Tel: (703) 462-7276

ROSSBACH, Jason A.
Senior Director, Government Affairs
3190 Fairview Park Dr., Suite 700
Falls Church, VA 22042
Jason.Rossbach@Dyn-Intl.com
Registered Federal Lobbyist

Tel: (571) 722-0210

Dynegy, Inc.

Produces and delivers energy, including natural gas, power, natural gas liquids, and coal through its owned and contractually controlled network of pipelines and other physical assets. Subsidiaries include Illinois Power Co. (see separate listing). Merged with Illinova Corp. in 2000.
www.dynegy.com
Annual Revenues: $4.36 billion
Employees: 2,591
Ticker: NYSE: DYN
SIC: 4911; 2911
NAICS: 324110; 221119
Industry/ies: Energy/Electricity

Chairman of the Board
WOOD, Pat

Tel: (713) 507-6400
Fax: (713) 507-6808

President and Chief Executive Officer
FLEXON, Robert C.

Tel: (713) 507-6400
Fax: (713) 507-6808

Main Headquarters
Mailing: 601 Travis St.
          Suite 1400
          Houston, TX 77002

Tel: (713) 507-6400
Fax: (713) 507-6808
TF: (800) 633-4704

Political Action Committees

Dynegy Inc. Good Government Fund
FEC ID: C00579367
Contact: Dean Ellis
601 Travis St. — Tel: (713) 507-6400
Suite 1400 — Fax: (713) 507-6808
Houston, TX 77002

Contributions to Candidates: $1,000 (2015-2016)
Democrats: $1,000

Public Affairs and Related Activities Personnel

At Headquarters

ALONSO, Mario E — Tel: (713) 507-6400
Executive Vice President, Strategic Development — Fax: (713) 507-6808

BLODGETT, J. Kevin — Tel: (713) 507-6400
Senior Vice President, Human Resources — Fax: (713) 507-6808

BURKE, Carolyn J. — Tel: (713) 507-6400
Executive Vice President, Business Operations and Systems — Fax: (713) 507-6808

BYFORD, David W. — Tel: (713) 767-5800
Director — Fax: (713) 507-6808
david.w.byford@dynegy.com

COX, Julius — Tel: (713) 507-6400
Executive Vice President and Chief Administrative Officer — Fax: (713) 507-6808

ELLIS, Dean — Tel: (713) 507-6400
PAC Treasurer — Fax: (713) 507-6808

FREELAND, Clint C. — Tel: (713) 507-6400
Executive Vice President and Chief Financial Officer — Fax: (713) 507-6808

JAMES, Catherine C. — Tel: (713) 507-6400
Executive Vice President, General Counsel and Chief — Fax: (713) 507-6808
Compliance Officer

JONES, Henry D. — Tel: (713) 507-6400
Executive Vice President and Chief Commercial Officer — Fax: (713) 507-6808

LUNDY, Norelle — Tel: (713) 507-6466
Vice President, Investor and Public Relations — Fax: (713) 507-6808

Dynetics Inc.

Ballistic missile defense and earned radar system analysis.
www.dynetics.com
Employees: 1,300
Industry/ies: Aerospace/Aviation; Automotive Industry; Defense/Homeland Security; Engineering/Mathematics; Government-Related; Science; Scientific Research; Transportation
Legislative Issues: AER; BUD; DEF; HOM

Chief Executive Officer — Tel: (256) 964-4000
BENDICKSON, PhD, Dr. Marc J. — Fax: (256) 922-9260

Main Headquarters
Mailing: 1002 Explorer Blvd. NW — Tel: (256) 964-4000
Huntsville, AL 35806-2806 — Fax: (256) 922-9260
— TF: (800) 964-4291

Political Action Committees
Dynetics PAC
FEC ID: C00380709
Contact: Randy Charles Reynolds
1000 Explorer Blvd. NW
Huntsville, AL 35806

Contributions to Candidates: $52,700 (2015-2016)
Republicans: $52,700

Principal Recipients

SENATE
BOOZMAN, JOHN (REP-AR)

HOUSE
ADERHOLT, ROBERT BROWN (REP-AL)
BROOKS, MO (REP-AL)

Corporate Foundations and Giving Programs

Dynetics Inc. Contributions Program
1002 Explorer Blvd. NW — Tel: (256) 922-9230
Huntsville, AL 35806-2806

Public Affairs and Related Activities Personnel

At Headquarters

COOK, Steve — Tel: (256) 964-4000
Vice President, Corporate Development — Fax: (256) 922-9260

FELTS, Janet — Tel: (256) 713-5439
Specialist, Marketing Communications — Fax: (256) 964-4031
janet.felts@dynetics.com

REYNOLDS, Randy Charles — Tel: (256) 964-4000
Vice President, Finance and PAC Treasurer — Fax: (256) 922-9260

E

See listing on page 121 under Biomass Gas & Electric, LLC

E*TRADE Financial Corporation

An innovative financial services company offering a full suite of easy-to-use online brokerage, investing and related banking solutions, delivered at a competitive price. It empowers individuals to take control of their financial futures by providing the products, tools and services they need to meet their near- and long-term investing goals.
us.etrade.com
Annual Revenues: $1.76 billion
Employees: 3,221
Ticker: NASDAQ: ETFC
Industry/ies: Banking/Finance/Investments; Communications; Telecommunications/Internet/Cable

Chief Executive Officer — Tel: (646) 521-4300
IDZIK, Paul T. — Fax: (212) 826-2803

Main Headquarters
Mailing: 671 N.Glebe Rd. — Tel: (703) 247-3700
Arlington, VA 22203

Political Action Committees
E*Trade Financial Corporation PAC
FEC ID: C00356345
Contact: Doug Hollowell
671 N. Glebe Rd. — Tel: (800) 387-2331
Ballston Tower — Fax: (800) 387-2331
Alexandria, VA 22203

Corporate Foundations and Giving Programs

E*TRADE Financial Corporation Contributions Program
Contact: Vickie Tassan
671 N. Glebe Rd. — TF: (800) 470-0999
Ballston Tower
Arlington, VA 22203

Public Affairs and Related Activities Personnel

At Headquarters

LAVERA, Christina — Tel: (703) 247-3700
Associate General Counsel

TASSAN, Vickie — Tel: (703) 236-8414
Director, Community Investment
vickie.tassan@etrade.com

At Other Offices

AUDETTE, Matthew J. — Tel: (646) 521-4300
Chief Financial Officer — Fax: (212) 826-2803
1271 Avenue of the Americas, 14th Floor
New York City, NY 10020-1302

FOLEY, Michael E. — Tel: (646) 521-4300
Executive Vice President and Chief Administrative Officer — Fax: (212) 826-2803
1271 Avenue of the Americas, 14th Floor
New York City, NY 10020-1302

GOODMAN, Brett — Tel: (646) 521-4406
Senior Vice President, Investor Relations and Corporate — Fax: (212) 826-2803
Communications
1271 Avenue of the Americas, 14th Floor
New York City, NY 10020-1302
brett.goodman@etrade.com

HOLLOWELL, Doug — Tel: (646) 521-4300
PAC Treasurer — Fax: (212) 826-2803
1271 Avenue of the Americas, 14th Floor
New York City, NY 10020-1302

LANDSMAN, Liza K. — Tel: (646) 521-4300
Chief Marketing Officer — Fax: (212) 826-2803
1271 Avenue of the Americas, 14th Floor
New York City, NY 10020-1302

NANDRA, Navtej S. — Tel: (646) 521-4300
President — Fax: (212) 826-2803
1271 Avenue of the Americas, 14th Floor
New York City, NY 10020-1302

ROESSNER, Karl A. — Tel: (646) 521-4300
General Counsel — Fax: (212) 826-2803
1271 Avenue of the Americas, 14th Floor
New York City, NY 10020-1302
karl.roessner@etrade.com

E.F. Johnson Technologies, Inc.

Develops and markets secure communications technology.
www.efjohnsontechnologies.com
Annual Revenues: $92.34 million
Employees: 200
Ticker: NASDAQ: EFJI
SIC: 3663
Industry/ies: Communications; Telecommunications/Internet/Cable
Legislative Issues: BUD; DEF; GOV

President and Chief Executive Officer — Tel: (972) 819-0700
SUZUKI, John — Fax: (972) 819-0639

Main Headquarters

Mailing: 1440 Corporate Dr.	Tel:	(972) 819-0700
Irving, TX 75038-2401	Fax:	(972) 819-0639
	TF:	(800) 328-3911

Public Affairs and Related Activities Personnel

At Headquarters

CAGLE, John R	Tel:	(972) 819-0700
Senior Vice President, Sales	Fax:	(972) 819-0639
COOKE, Ryan	Tel:	(972) 819-0700
Vice President, Operations	Fax:	(972) 819-0639
DILLMAN, Julie	Tel:	(972) 819-0700
Vice President, Human Resources	Fax:	(972) 819-0639
JACKSON, Timi	Tel:	(972) 819-2336
Vice President and General Counsel	Fax:	(972) 819-0639
POLITTE-CORN, Karen	Tel:	(972) 819-0700
Vice President, Marketing Communications	Fax:	(972) 819-0639
kpolittecorn@efji.com		
RANGARAJAN, Karthik	Tel:	(972) 819-0700
Vice President, Marketing	Fax:	(972) 819-0639

E.W. Scripps Company

A communications conglomerate.
www.scripps.com
Annual Revenues: $802.13 million
Employees: 3,800
Ticker: NYSE: SSP
SIC: 2711
Industry/ies: Communications; Media/Mass Communication

Board Chairman, President and Chief Executive Officer	Tel:	(513) 977-3000
BOEHNE, Richard A.	Fax:	(513) 977-3024

Main Headquarters

Mailing: 312 Walnut St.	Tel:	(513) 977-3000
2800 Scripps Center	Fax:	(513) 977-3024
Cincinnati, OH 45202		

Corporate Foundations and Giving Programs

Scripps Howard Foundation
Contact: Mike Philipps

P.O. Box 5380	Tel:	(513) 977-3035
2800 Scripps Center	Fax:	(513) 977-3800
Cincinnati, OH 45201-5380		

Public Affairs and Related Activities Personnel

At Headquarters

APPLETON, William	Tel:	(513) 977-3000
Senior Vice President and General Counsel	Fax:	(513) 977-3024
DAVIS, Robin A.	Tel:	(513) 977-3000
Vice President, Finance and Development	Fax:	(513) 977-3024
GILES, David M.	Tel:	(513) 977-3000
Vice President and Deputy General Counsel	Fax:	(513) 977-3024
KNUTSON, Lisa A.	Tel:	(513) 977-3000
Chief Administrative Officer	Fax:	(513) 977-3024
KOORS, Mark L.	Tel:	(513) 977-3000
Vice President, Audit and Compliance	Fax:	(513) 977-3024
MICHELI, Carolyn	Tel:	(513) 977-3000
Vice President, Corporate Communications and Investor Relations	Fax:	(513) 977-3024
WESOLOWSKI, Timothy M.	Tel:	(513) 977-3000
Senior Vice President, Chief Financial Officer and Treasurer	Fax:	(513) 977-3024

EA

See listing on page 283 under Electronic Arts

EaglePicher Corporation

See listing on page 298 under EP Management Corporation

Earth Networks, Inc.

Provider of global technology solutions for businesses connection and communication.In early 2011, AWS Convergence Technologies, Inc. changed its name to Earth Networks, Inc.
www.earthnetworks.com
Annual Revenues: $44.40 million
Industry/ies: Communications; Media/Mass Communication
Legislative Issues: AGR; BUD; ENV; FOR

President and Chief Executive Officer	Tel:	(301) 258-8390
MARSHALL, Robert S.		
marshall@earthnetworks.com		

Main Headquarters

Mailing: 12410 Milestone Center Dr.	Tel:	(301) 250-4000
Suite 300	TF:	(800) 544-4429
Germantown, MD 20876		

Public Affairs and Related Activities Personnel

At Headquarters

CALLAHAN, Bill	Tel:	(301) 258-8390
Vice President, Federal Programs		
HUNT, Rachel	Tel:	(301) 250-4046
Manager, Corporate Communications and Public Relations		
rhunt@earthnetworks.com		
LOMBARDI, Michael	Tel:	(301) 258-8390
Senior Vice President, Domestic Sales		
O'CONNELL, Dan	Tel:	(301) 258-8390
General Counsel and Chief Privacy Officer		
SPAULDING, Rich	Tel:	(301) 258-8390
President and Chief Operating Officer		

Earth Tech, Inc.

A consulting firm built upon sound scientific and engineering principles, specialized in civil, mining, and geotechnical engineering, surveying, geology, environmental science, construction oversight, and various analytical services.
www.earthtechinc.net
Industry/ies: Construction/Construction Materials; Engineering/Mathematics; Environment And Conservation

President	Tel:	(814) 266-6402
RIBBLETT, Hiram C.	Fax:	(814) 266-6530
etihiram@atlanticbb.net		

Main Headquarters

Mailing: 336 Bloomfield St.	Tel:	(814) 266-6402
Suite 201	Fax:	(814) 266-6530
Johnstown, PA 15904		

Public Affairs and Related Activities Personnel

At Headquarters

HORNER, Jason P.	Tel:	(814) 266-6402
Corporate Secretary, Assistant Operations	Fax:	(814) 266-6530
STAIRS, Ryan D.	Tel:	(814) 266-6402
Vice President, Manager, Operations	Fax:	(814) 266-6530

Earth911.com

An environmental services company that addresses solutions for products' end-of-life for both businesses and consumers.
earth911.com
Annual Revenues: $2.20 million
Industry/ies: Environment And Conservation

Chief Executive Officer	Tel:	(480) 889-2650
MONHEIT, Barry		

Main Headquarters

Mailing: 1375 N. Scottsdale Rd.	Tel:	(480) 889-2650
Suite 140		
Scottsdale, AZ 85257		

Public Affairs and Related Activities Personnel

At Headquarters

ZEIDLER, Karl	Tel:	(480) 889-2650
Director, Finances and Controller		

EarthLink, Inc.

IT services and communications providers.
www.earthlink.net
Annual Revenues: $1.16 billion
Employees: 2,402
Ticker: NASDAQ: ELNK
SIC: 7370
Industry/ies: Communications; Telecommunications/Internet/Cable
Legislative Issues: TEC

Chief Executive Officer and President	Tel:	(404) 815-0770
EAZOR, Joseph F.	Fax:	(404) 892-7616

Main Headquarters

Mailing: 1170 Peachtree St.	Tel:	(404) 815-0770
Atlanta, GA 30309		

Washington Office

Mailing: 4711 Fort Sumner Dr.	
Bethesda, MD 20816	

Public Affairs and Related Activities Personnel

At Headquarters

ORTH, Elizabeth	Tel:	(404) 815-0770
Senior Vice President, Chief Customer Officer		
TOPLISEK, Michael D.	Tel:	(404) 815-0770
Executive Vice President, Sales and Marketing,		

At Other Offices

ALTERMAN, Louis	Tel:	(404) 748-7650
Executive Vice President, Chief Financial Officer	Fax:	(678) 472-3252
1375 Peachtree St.		

Atlanta, GA 30309
altermanlo@corp.earthlink.net

BENJAMIN, Valerie C.　Tel:　(404) 815-0770
Senior Vice President, Human Resources　Fax:　(404) 892-7616
1375 Peachtree St.
Atlanta, GA 30309

DESIMONE, Jr., Samuel R.　Tel:　(404) 815-0770
Executive Vice President, General Counsel and Secretary　Fax:　(404) 892-7616
1375 Peachtree St.
Atlanta, GA 30309

FERGUSON, Bradley A.　Tel:　(404) 815-0770
Executive Vice President and Managing Director, Consumer　Fax:　(404) 892-7616
and Small Business
1375 Peachtree St.
Atlanta, GA 30309

GOBBI, Alexandra　Tel:　(404) 815-0770
Senior Vice President, Corporate Marketing and　Fax:　(404) 892-7616
Communications
1375 Peachtree St.
Atlanta, GA 30309

HAGAN, Stacie　Tel:　(404) 815-0770
Executive Vice President, Customer Operations　Fax:　(404) 892-7616
1375 Peachtree St.
Atlanta, GA 30309

MURRAY, Chris　Tel:　(404) 815-0770
Senior Vice President, Public Policy　Fax:　(404) 892-7616
1375 Peachtree St.
Atlanta, GA 30309

OSTROSKI, Raymond B.　Tel:　(781) 362-5700
PAC Treasurer　Fax:　(781) 522-8711
Five Wall St.
Burlington, MA 01803

EarthRenew

A private clean tech company, has developed, patented and commercialized technologies that apply the exhaust from an industrial turbine directly in heat processing while the turbine generates electricity.
www.earthrenew.com
Industry/ies: Energy/Electricity; Environment And Conservation; Pollution And Waste

Chief Executive Officer　Tel:　(416) 861-1685
MEADOW, Douglas　Fax:　(650) 712-8287
dmeadow@earthrenew.com

Main Headquarters
Mailing:　504 Ave. Alhambra, Suite 203　Tel:　(650) 712-8285
　P.O. Box 3148　Fax:　(650) 712-8287
　Half Moon Bay, CA 94019-3148

EarthRenew Organics Ltd.

See listing on page 275 under EarthRenew

East Energy Corporation

See listing on page 420 under Iberdrola USA

Easter Seals, Inc.

A nonprofit health organization headquartered in Chicago, Illinois.
www.easterseals.com
Industry/ies: Disabilities; Medicine/Health Care/Mental Health; Social Service/ Urban Affairs
Legislative Issues: BUD; CIV; EDU; FOR; HCR; INS; LBR; MED; TAX; TRA; VET

Chairman of the Board　Tel:　(800) 221-6827
DAVIDSON, Rick

Chief Executive Officer and President　Tel:　(202) 347-3066
RUTTA, Randall L.　Fax:　(202) 737-7914
rrutta@easterseals.com

Main Headquarters
Mailing:　233 S. Wacker Dr.　Tel:　(800) 221-6827
　Suite 2400　Fax:　(312) 726-1494
　Chicago, IL 60606　TF:　(800) 221-6827

Washington Office
Mailing:　1425 K St. NW　Tel:　(202) 347-3066
　Suite 200　Fax:　(202) 737-7914
　Washington, DC 20005

Corporate Foundations and Giving Programs

Easter Seals Contributions Program
233 S. Wacker Dr.
Suite 2400
Chicago, IL 60606

Public Affairs and Related Activities Personnel

At Headquarters

BARNFIELD, Kristen　Tel:　(312) 551-7147
Contact, Media Relations　Fax:　(312) 726-1494
kbarnfield@easterseals.com

At Washington Office

ANDRUS, Mary　Tel:　(202) 347-3066
Assistant Vice President, Government Relations　Fax:　(202) 737-7914
mandrus@easterseals.com
Registered Federal Lobbyist

DEXTER, Jennifer　Tel:　(202) 347-3066
Assistant Vice President, Government Relations　Fax:　(202) 737-7914
Registered Federal Lobbyist

DOMBROWSKI, Eileen　Tel:　(202) 347-3066
Federal Lobbyist　Fax:　(202) 737-7914
Registered Federal Lobbyist

FREISZ, Maynard　Tel:　(202) 347-3066
Contact, Government Relations　Fax:　(202) 737-7914
mfriesz@easterseals.com
Registered Federal Lobbyist

KAMNIK, Lauren　Tel:　(202) 347-3066
Contact, Government Relations　Fax:　(202) 737-7914

NEAS, Katy Beh　Tel:　(202) 347-3066
Vice President, Government Relations　Fax:　(202) 737-7914
kneas@easterseals.com
Registered Federal Lobbyist

ROZELL, Denise M.　Tel:　(202) 347-3066
Assistant Vice President, State Government Relations　Fax:　(202) 737-7914
drozell@easterseals.com

Eastern Kentucky Power Cooperative

EKPC provides affordable, reliable electricity to its owner-member cooperatives. EKPC and each of its 16 owner-member cooperatives is owned and democratically governed by the people who use their energy and services. All are not-for-profit organizations.
www.ekpc.coop
Annual Revenues: $952.8 million
Employees: 666
Industry/ies: Energy/Electricity
Legislative Issues: BUD; CAW; ENV

Chairman of the Board　Tel:　(859) 744-4812
HAWKINS, Paul　Fax:　(859) 744-6008

President and Chief Executive Officer　Tel:　(859) 744-4864
CAMPBELL, Anthony "Tony"　Fax:　(859) 744-6008

Main Headquarters
Mailing:　4775 Lexington Rd.　Tel:　(859) 744-4812
　P.O. Box 707　Fax:　(859) 744-6008
　Winchester, KY 40392-0707

Public Affairs and Related Activities Personnel

At Headquarters

COMER, Nick　Tel:　(859) 745-9450
Manager, External Affairs　Fax:　(859) 744-6008
nick.comer@ekpc.coop

HOHMAN, Jeff　Tel:　(859) 744-4864
Member, Marketing & Natural Resources　Fax:　(859) 744-6008
jeff.hohman@ekpc.coop

MAYFIELD, Barry　Tel:　(859) 744-4864
Vice President, Stategic Planning and External Affairs　Fax:　(859) 744-6008

MCCLURE , Steve　Tel:　(859) 744-4812
Director, Human Resurses and Support Services　Fax:　(859) 744-6008

MCNALLEY, Mike　Tel:　(859) 744-4864
Chief Financial Officer and Executive Vice President　Fax:　(859) 744-6008

MOSIER, Don　Tel:　(859) 744-4812
Chief Operating Officer and Executive Vice President　Fax:　(859) 744-6008

SMART, David　Tel:　(859) 744-4864
General Counsel　Fax:　(859) 744-6008
david.smart@ekpc.coop

STRATTON, Wayne　Tel:　(859) 744-4864
Chair　Fax:　(859) 744-6008

Eastman Chemical Company

Eastman Chemical Company was once part of film giant Eastman Kodak. The company has developed into a major producer of chemicals, fibers, and plastics. Among Eastman's operating segments are its CASPI (coatings, adhesives, specialty polymers, and inks), Specialty Plastics (engineering polymers), and Fibers (acetate tow and textile fibers) units. The largest segment manufactures Performance Chemicals and Intermediates (PCI).
www.eastman.com
Annual Revenues: $9.66 billion
Employees: 15,000
Ticker: NYSE: EMN
SIC: 2800; 2821
NAICS: 325220
Industry/ies: Chemicals & Chemical Industry

Legislative Issues: CHM; DEF; ENG; GOV; TAR; TAX; TRD

Chairman and Chief Executive Officer
COSTA, Mark J.
Tel: (423) 229-2000
Fax: (423) 224-0502

Main Headquarters
Mailing: P.O. Box 431
Kingsport, TN 37662
Tel: (423) 229-2000
Fax: (423) 224-0502
TF: (800) 325-4330

Washington Office
Mailing: 300 New Jersey Ave.
Suite 1050
Washington, DC 20001
Tel: (202) 347-9547
Fax: (202) 347-9512

Political Action Committees
Eastman PAC-PAC of Eastman Chemical Company
FEC ID: C00113159
Contact: Christine Hampton
P.O. Box 431
Kingsport, TN 37662
Tel: (703) 524-7700
Fax: (703) 524-7707

    Contributions to Candidates: $132,000 (2015-2016)
    Democrats: $9,000; Republicans: $123,000

          Principal Recipients
          HOUSE
          BLACK, DIANE L MRS. (REP-TN)

Corporate Foundations and Giving Programs
Eastman Chemical Company Foundation
P.O. Box 1973
Building 284
Kingsport, TN 37662-5284

Solutia Inc. Contributions Program
P.O. Box 66760
St. Louis, MO 63166

Public Affairs and Related Activities Personnel

At Headquarters

BROADWATER, Tracy
Contact, Media Relations
tkbroadwater@eastman.com
Tel: (423) 224-0498
Fax: (423) 224-0502

CLARK, Etta
Vice President, Global Affairs & Policy
eclark@eastman.com
Registered Federal Lobbyist
Tel: (423) 229-2000
Fax: (423) 224-0502

ESPELAND, Curt E.
Executive Vice President and Chief Financial Officer
Tel: (423) 229-2000
Fax: (423) 224-0502

GOLDEN, David A.
Senior Vice President, Chief Legal Officer, and Corporate Secretary
Tel: (423) 229-2000
Fax: (423) 224-0502

HALL, Mary
Vice President and Treasurer
Tel: (423) 229-2000
Fax: (423) 224-0502

HAMPTON, Christine
PAC Contact
Tel: (423) 229-2000
Fax: (423) 224-0502

LINDSAY, Ronald C.
Chief Operating Officer
Tel: (423) 229-2000
Fax: (423) 224-0502

MCCORD, CeeGee
Manager, State Government Affairs
ceegeemccord@eastman.com
Tel: (423) 229-2000
Fax: (423) 224-0502

PAYNE, Betty
Director, Corporate Communications
bpayne@eastman.com
Tel: (423) 229-4965
Fax: (423) 229-1008

STUCKEY, Perry
Senior Vice President and Chief Human Resources Officer
Tel: (423) 229-2000
Fax: (423) 224-0502

At Washington Office

PERRY, Brent
Manager, Federal Government Relation
bperry@eastman.com
Registered Federal Lobbyist
Tel: (202) 347-9568
Fax: (202) 347-9512

POE, Charles T.
Registered Federal Lobbyist
Tel: (202) 347-9547
Fax: (202) 347-9512

RATHEAL, Ray
Tel: (202) 347-9547
Fax: (202) 347-9512

SAGO, Brett
Senior Counsel
bsago@eastman.com
Tel: (202) 347-9568
Fax: (202) 347-9512

SCHURGER, Marc
Director, Sustainability Strategic Initiatives
Registered Federal Lobbyist
Tel: (202) 347-9568
Fax: (202) 347-9512

WILSON WHITE, Brandi
Federal Lobbyist
Registered Federal Lobbyist
Tel: (202) 347-9568
Fax: (202) 347-9512

At Other Offices

RIDDLE, Gregory A.
Tel: (212) 835-1620

Director, Investor Relations
Five Penn Plaza, 19th Floor
New York City, NY 10001
griddle@eastman.com
Registered Federal Lobbyist

Eastman Kodak Company

A manufacturer of photographic equipment and materials. Also manufactures health care products and office equipment.
www.kodak.com
Annual Revenues: $2.04 billion
Employees: 7,300
Ticker: NYSE: KODK
SIC: 3861; 3825; 3577; 3229; 3081
NAICS: 333315; 335921; 334514; 334119; 326113
Industry/ies: Electricity & Electronics; Electronics; Energy/Electricity
Legislative Issues: MAN

Chief Executive Officer
CLARKE, Jeffrey J.
Tel: (585) 724-4000
Fax: (585) 724-1089

Main Headquarters
Mailing: 343 State St.
Rochester, NY 14650
Tel: (585) 724-4000
Fax: (585) 724-1089
TF: (800) 698-3324

Washington Office
Mailing: 1200 G St. NW
Suite 800
Washington, DC 20005
Tel: (202) 857-3463
Fax: (202) 857-3401

Political Action Committees
Eastman Kodak Company Employee PAC
FEC ID: C00297085
343 State St.
Rochester, NY 14650

    Contributions to Candidates: $17,000 (2015-2016)
    Democrats: $9,000; Republicans: $8,000

Corporate Foundations and Giving Programs
Eastman Kodak Charitable Trust
Contact: Augustin Melendez
343 State St.
Rochester, NY 14650
Tel: (585) 724-1980
Fax: (585) 724-1376

Public Affairs and Related Activities Personnel

At Headquarters

GREEN, Mark
Chief Human Resources Officer and Senior Vice President
Tel: (585) 724-4000
Fax: (585) 724-1089

KEHOE, Louise
Vice President, Media Relations
Tel: (585) 724-4000
Fax: (585) 724-1089

KORIZNO, Michael A.
Vice President, Worldwide Strategic Account Management and New Business Development
Tel: (585) 724-4000
Fax: (585) 724-1089

LOVE, William G.
Treasurer
Tel: (585) 724-4000
Fax: (585) 724-1089

MAHE, Eric-Yves
President, Software and Solutions Division and Senior Vice President
Tel: (585) 724-4000
Fax: (585) 724-1089

MELENDEZ, Augustin
Chief Diversity and Community Affairs Officer, Director, Human Resources, Commercial Segment
Augustin.Melendez@kodak.com
Tel: (585) 724-4000
Fax: (585) 724-1089

SAMUELS, Eric H.
Chief Accounting Officer and Corporate Controller
Tel: (585) 724-4000
Fax: (585) 724-1089

VERONDA, Chris
Director, Global Corporate Communications
christopher.veronda@kodak.com
Tel: (585) 724-4000
Fax: (585) 724-1089

At Washington Office

ALBERT, Stacey Stern
Vice President, Public Affairs
Tel: (202) 857-3464
Fax: (202) 857-3401

BULLWINKLE, David
PAC Contact
Tel: (202) 857-3463
Fax: (202) 857-3401

WILLIAMS, Kristin
Federal Lobbyist
Registered Federal Lobbyist
Tel: (202) 857-3400
Fax: (202) 857-3401

Eat'N Park Hospitality Group, Inc.

Family-style restaurants group.
www.eatnpark.com
Employees: 11,000
Industry/ies: Food And Beverage Industry

Chairman of the Board and Chief Executive Officer
BROADHURST, James S.
Tel: (412) 461-2000
Fax: (412) 461-6000

Chief Executive Officer
BROADHURST, Jeff
Tel: (412) 461-2000
Fax: (412) 461-6000

Main Headquarters

Mailing:	285 E. Waterfront Dr.	Tel:	(412) 461-2000
	Homestead, PA 15120	Fax:	(412) 461-6000

Political Action Committees

Eat'N Park Restaurants Inc. PAC
FEC ID: C00251132
Contact: Joseph A. Sawinski

285 E. Waterfront Dr.	Tel:	(412) 461-2000
Homestead, PA 15120	Fax:	(412) 461-6000

Contributions to Candidates: $4,500 (2015-2016)
Democrats: $1,000; Republicans: $3,500

Public Affairs and Related Activities Personnel

At Headquarters

MCARDLE, Rebecca	Tel:	(412) 461-2000
Coordinator, Public Relations and Comunications	Fax:	(412) 461-6000
O'CONNELL, Kevin	Tel:	(412) 461-2000
Senior Vice President, Marketing	Fax:	(412) 461-6000
SAWINSKI, Joseph A.	Tel:	(412) 461-2000
PAC Treasurer	Fax:	(412) 461-6000

Eaton Corporation

An industrial manufacturing corporation.
www.eaton.com
Annual Revenues: $22.28 billion
Employees: 102,000
Ticker: NYSE: ETN
SIC: 3590; 3491; 3593; 3594
NAICS: 333996; 332911; 333995
Industry/ies: Machinery/Equipment
Legislative Issues: AUT; BUD; DEF; ENG; ENV; TAX; TRA

Chairman and Chief Executive Officer	Tel:	(216) 523-5000
CUTLER, Alexander M.	Fax:	(216) 523-4787

Main Headquarters

Mailing:	1000 Eaton Blvd.	Tel:	(440) 523-5000
	Cleveland, OH 44122	Fax:	(216) 523-4787
		TF:	(800) 386-1911

Political Action Committees

Eaton Corporation Public Policy Association PAC
FEC ID: C00034827
Contact: Robert A. Elliott

1000 Eaton Blvd.	Tel:	(216) 523-5000
Cleveland, OH 44114	Fax:	(216) 523-5000

Contributions to Candidates: $46,450 (2015-2016)
Democrats: $7,500; Republicans: $38,950

Corporate Foundations and Giving Programs

Eaton Charitable Trust
Contact: William B. Doggett

1211 Superior Ave.	Tel:	(216) 523-5000
Cleveland, OH 44114		

Public Affairs and Related Activities Personnel

At Headquarters

BOCCADORO, Steven M.	Tel:	(216) 523-4205
Vice President, General Manager	Fax:	(216) 523-4787
BRABANDER, Cynthia K.	Tel:	(216) 523-4205
Executive Vice President and Chief Human Resources Officer	Fax:	(216) 523-4787
BULLOCK, Jr., Donald H.	Tel:	(216) 523-5000
Senior vice President, Investor Relations	Fax:	(216) 523-4787
DonBullock@Eaton.com		
DOGGETT, William B.	Tel:	(216) 523-4664
Senior Vice President, Public & Community Affairs	Fax:	(216) 523-4787
ELLIOTT, Robert A.	Tel:	(216) 523-5000
PAC Treasurer	Fax:	(216) 523-4787
FEARON, Richard H.	Tel:	(216) 523-4205
Vice Chairman and Chief Financial and Planning officer	Fax:	(216) 523-4787
richardfearon@eaton.com		
HESS, Christopher D.	Tel:	(216) 523-4664
Director, Public Affairs	Fax:	(216) 523-4787
christopherdhess@eaton.com		
Registered Federal Lobbyist		
KLASEN, Gary	Tel:	(216) 523-4736
Vice President, External Communications	Fax:	(216) 523-4787
garyklasen@eaton.com		
MCGRATH, Jr., Donald J.	Tel:	(216) 523-5000
Senior Vice President, Communications	Fax:	(216) 523-4787
MCGUIRE, Mark M.	Tel:	(216) 523-5000
Executive Vice President and General Counsel	Fax:	(216) 523-4787
MURPHY, Molly A.	Tel:	(440) 523-5000
Senior Vice President, Sales and Marketing	Fax:	(216) 523-4787
SALUJA, Harpreet	Tel:	(440) 523-5000

Senior Vice President , Corporate Development and Planning	Fax:	(216) 523-4787
SCHROEDER, Scott	Tel:	(216) 523-5150
Contact, Media Relations	Fax:	(216) 523-4787
ScottRSchroeder@Eaton.com		
SEVERS, Deborah R.	Tel:	(440) 523-5000
Senior Vice President, Global Ethics and Compliance	Fax:	(216) 523-4787
SZMAGALA, Taras G	Tel:	(440) 523-5000
	Fax:	(216) 523-4787

At Other Offices

ARNOLD, Craig	Tel:	(269) 342-3462
Vice Chairman and Chief Operating Officer	Fax:	(269) 342-3597
13100 E. Michigan Ave.		
Galesburg, MI 49053		

Eaton Vance

See listing on page 277 under Eaton Vance Investment Managers

Eaton Vance Investment Managers

Investment management firm providing professional investment advice to individuals, trusts, charitable organizations and institutions.
www.eatonvance.com
Annual Revenues: $1.44 billion
Employees: 1,403
Ticker: NYSE: EV
Industry/ies: Banking/Finance/Investments

Chairman of Board, Chief Executive Officer and President	Tel:	(617) 482-8260
FAUST, Jr., Thomas E.	Fax:	(617) 482-8260

Main Headquarters

Mailing:	Two International Pl.	Tel:	(617) 482-8260
	Boston, MA 02110	Fax:	(617) 482-8260
		TF:	(800) 225-6265

Public Affairs and Related Activities Personnel

At Headquarters

BRENGLE, Susan	Tel:	(617) 672-8540
Director, Relationship Management	Fax:	(617) 482-8260
CATALDO , Daniel	Tel:	(617) 482-8260
Treasurer	Fax:	(617) 482-8260
FUREY, Joe	Tel:	(617) 482-8260
Vice President, Business Development	Fax:	(617) 482-8260
HYLTON, Laurie Greenwald	Tel:	(617) 482-8260
Chief Financial Officer	Fax:	(617) 482-8260
MARIUS, Frederick S.	Tel:	(617) 482-8260
Vice President, Secretary and Chief Legal Officer	Fax:	(617) 482-8260
TICE, Robyn S.	Tel:	(617) 482-8260
Director, Media Relations	Fax:	(617) 482-8260

eBay Inc.

An online trading community with an auction-style format. Enables individuals and businesses to trade items at the local, national, and international levels. Acquired PayPal in 2002 (see separate listing).
www.ebayinc.com
Annual Revenues: $18.09 billion
Employees: 32,700
Ticker: NASDAQ: EBAY
SIC: 7389
Industry/ies: Communications; Telecommunications/Internet/Cable
Legislative Issues: CPI; CPT; CSP; ENV; POS; SCI; TAX; TEC; TRD

Chairman of the Board	Tel:	(408) 376-7400
OMIDYAR, Pierre M.	Fax:	(408) 376-7401
pomidyar@ebay.com		

President and Chief Executive Officer	Tel:	(408) 376-7400
DONAHOE, John A.	Fax:	(408) 516-8811

Main Headquarters

Mailing:	2065 Hamilton Ave.	Tel:	(408) 376-7400
	San Jose, CA 95125	Fax:	(408) 516-8811
		TF:	(800) 322-9266

Washington Office

Mailing:	228 S. Washington Ave.
	Suite 115
	Alexandria, VA 22314

Political Action Committees

eBay Inc. Committee for Responsible Internet Commerce PAC
FEC ID: C00342394
Contact: Sharon McBride

228 S. Washington St.	Tel:	(202) 637-5981
Suite 115	Fax:	(202) 637-5940
Alexandria, VA 22314		

Contributions to Candidates: $150,691 (2015-2016)
Democrats: $67,334; Republicans: $83,357

Corporate Foundations and Giving Programs

The eBay Foundation
Contact: Pierre M. Omidyar
2145 Hamilton Ave.   Tel: (408) 376-7400
San Jose, CA 95125

Public Affairs and Related Activities Personnel

At Headquarters

AXELROD, Beth   Tel: (408) 376-7400
Senior Vice President, Human Resources Fax: (408) 376-7401

FORD, Tracey   Tel: (408) 376-7205
Manager, Investor Relations   Fax: (408) 516-8811
tford@ebay.com

JACOBSON, Michael R.   Tel: (408) 376-7400
Senior Vice President, General Counsel, Legal Affairs and   Fax: (408) 516-8811
Secretary
mjacobson@ebay.com

MARKS, Alan   Tel: (408) 376-7400
Senior Vice President, Corporate Communications   Fax: (408) 516-8811

SWAN, Bob   Tel: (408) 376-7400
Senior Vice President, Finance and Chief Financial Officer   Fax: (408) 516-8811

At Washington Office

DOOLEY, Laura
Senior Manager, North American Government Relations

LONDON, David
Registered Federal Lobbyist

MAWAKANA, Tekedra
Vice President of Government Relations

MCBRIDE, Sharon
PAC Treasurer
smcbride@ebay.com

At Other Offices

AHMED, Usman   Tel: (202) 551-0077
Policy Counsel
1250 I St. NW, Suite 1200
Washington, DC 20005
usahmed@ebay.com

BIERON, Brian F.   Tel: (202) 551-0077
Director
1250 I St. NW, Suite 1200
Washington, DC 20005
bbieron@ebay.com

BRIGHTON, Dusty   Tel: (202) 551-0077
Senior Manager, Government Relations
1250 I St. NW, Suite 1200
Washington, DC 20005
Registered Federal Lobbyist

BROSSEAU, Caitlin   Tel: (202) 551-0077
Senior Manager, Government Relations
1250 I St. NW, Suite 1200
Washington, DC 20005
Registered Federal Lobbyist

GABEL, Nancy   Tel: (202) 551-0077
1250 I St. NW, Suite 1200
Washington, DC 20005

HANNIGAN, Megan   Tel: (202) 551-0077
Federal Lobbyist
1250 I St. NW, Suite 1200
Washington, DC 20005

LAWRENCE, John   Tel: (202) 551-0077
Federal Lobbyist
1250 I St. NW, Suite 1200
Washington, DC 20005
Registered Federal Lobbyist

LONDON, David   Tel: (202) 551-0077
1250 I St. NW, Suite 1200
Washington, DC 20005
Registered Federal Lobbyist

NASH, Richard   Tel: (202) 551-0077
Head, GR Americas
1250 I St. NW, Suite 1200
Washington, DC 20005

SHOLLEY WHITE, Lauren   Tel: (202) 551-0077
Senior Manager, External Affairs
1250 I St. NW, Suite 1200
Washington, DC 20005

WHITE, Lauren   Tel: (202) 551-0077
Federal Lobbyist
1250 I St. NW, Suite 1200
Washington, DC 20005
Registered Federal Lobbyist

WOEBER, Amie J.   Tel: (202) 551-0077
1250 I St. NW, Suite 1200
Washington, DC 20005

EBITDA Capital, LLC

A provider of broadband services to rural communities.
ebitdacapital.com
Industry/ies: Banking/Finance/Investments; Communications;
Telecommunications/Internet/Cable

Main Headquarters

Mailing: 2366 N. Glassel Rd.
              Suite D
              Orange, CA 92865

EBSCO Industries, Inc.

*A global sales, service, and manufacturing corporation, which aims to provide a good work
environment, to deliver useful products and services to our customers with excellent service,
and to improve and grow in all our endeavors.*
www.ebscoind.com
Annual Revenues: $2.40 billion
Employees: 6,000
Industry/ies: Machinery/Equipment

Chairman of the Board   Tel: (205) 991-6600
STEPHENS, James T.   Fax: (205) 995-1636

President and Chief Executive Officer Tel: (205) 991-6600
COLLINS, Tim   Fax: (205) 995-1636

Main Headquarters
Mailing: P.O. Box 1943   Tel: (205) 991-6600
              Birmingham, AL 35201-1943   Fax: (205) 995-1636

Public Affairs and Related Activities Personnel

At Headquarters

MCEVOY, Kathleen   Tel: (800) 653-2726
Vice President of Communications   Fax: (205) 995-1636
kmcevoy@ebscohost.com

WILES, Karla   Tel: (205) 991-6600
Vice President Corporate Communications Fax: (205) 995-1636

At Other Offices

THOMPSON, John C.   Tel: (205) 408-4878
Vice President, Human Resources and General Manager   Fax: (205) 408-4785
5724 Hwy. 280 East
Birmingham, AL 35242

WALKER, David   Tel: (205) 408-4878
Vice President, Chief Financial Officer and Chief Operating   Fax: (205) 408-4785
Office
5724 Hwy. 280 East
Birmingham, AL 35242

EchoStar Communications Corporation

See listing on page 258 under Dish Network

Ecolab Inc.

*A developer and marketer of cleaning and sanitizing products, systems and services for the
hospitality, foodservice, and healthcare industries.*
www.ecolab.com
Annual Revenues: $14.24 billion
Employees: 45,400
Ticker: NYSE: ECL
SIC: 2840
Industry/ies: Chemicals & Chemical Industry
Legislative Issues: BUD; CAW; ENG; ENV; FOO; FOR; HCR; LBR; TAX; TRD; VET

Chairman of the Board and Chief Executive Officer   Tel: (651) 293-2233
BAKER, Jr., Douglas M.   Fax: (651) 225-2092
doug.baker@ecolab.com

Main Headquarters
Mailing: 370 N. Wabasha St.   Tel: (651) 293-2233
              St. Paul, MN 55102-2233   Fax: (651) 225-3305
                                          TF: (800) 232-6522

Washington Office
Mailing: 300 New Jersey Ave. NW, Suite 601
              Washington, DC 20001

Political Action Committees
Ecolab Inc. PAC
FEC ID: C00101485
Contact: Andrew Bosl
370 Wabash St., North
St. Paul, MN 55102

Contributions to Candidates: $255,250 (2015-2016)
Democrats: $78,000; Republicans: $177,250

Principal Recipients
SENATE

BLUNT, ROY (REP-MO)
SCHUMER, CHARLES E (DEM-NY)
TOOMEY, PATRICK JOSEPH (REP-PA)

HOUSE
BRADY, KEVIN (REP-TX)
HOYER, STENY HAMILTON (DEM-DC)
RYAN, PAUL D. (REP-WI)
SCALISE, STEVE MR. (REP-LA)
UPTON, FREDERICK STEPHEN (REP-MI)

Corporate Foundations and Giving Programs

Ecolab Foundation
Contact: Kris J. Taylor
370 N. Wabasha St.   Tel: (651) 293-2923
St. Paul, MN 55102   Fax: (651) 225-3191

Public Affairs and Related Activities Personnel

At Headquarters

BLAHOSKI, Roman	Tel:	(651) 293-4385
Director, Global Communications	Fax:	(651) 225-2092
MediaRelations@Ecolab.com		
BOSL, Andrew	Tel:	(651) 293-2233
PAC Treasurer	Fax:	(651) 225-3305
BUSCH, Angela M.	Tel:	(651) 293-2233
Senior Vice President, Corporate Development	Fax:	(651) 225-2092
GREV, Jason	Tel:	(651) 293-2233
Manager, Government Relations	Fax:	(651) 225-2092
jason.grev@ecolab.com		
Registered Federal Lobbyist		
HANDLEY, Thomas W.	Tel:	(651) 293-2233
President and Chief Operating Officer	Fax:	(651) 225-3305
MARSH, Laurie	Tel:	(651) 293-2233
Executive Vice President, Human Resources	Fax:	(651) 225-3305
MONAHAN, Michael J.	Tel:	(651) 293-2809
Senior Vice President, External Relations	Fax:	(651) 225-2092
michael.monahan@ecolab.com		
MOORE, Julie L.	Tel:	(651) 293-2233
Executive Vice President, Global Marketing	Fax:	(651) 225-2092
julie.moore@ecolab.com		
MUSANTE, Ramola	Tel:	(651) 293-2233
Division Vice President, Government Relations	Fax:	(651) 225-2092
Registered Federal Lobbyist		
PETERSON, Jeffrey K.	Tel:	(651) 293-2557
Director, Government Relations	Fax:	(651) 225-2092
SCHMECHEL, Daniel J.	Tel:	(651) 293-2233
Chief Financial Officer	Fax:	(651) 225-3305
SIEFERT , James J.	Tel:	(651) 293-2233
Executive Vice President, General Counsel and Secretary	Fax:	(651) 225-2092
SIMERMEYER, Elizabeth A.	Tel:	(651) 293-2233
Senior Vice President, Global Marketing and	Fax:	(651) 225-3305
Communications		
TAYLOR, Kris J.	Tel:	(651) 293-2259
Vice President, Community Relations	Fax:	(651) 225-2092
WESTERHAUS, Jim	Tel:	(651) 293-2233
Vice President, Government Relations	Fax:	(651) 225-2092
Registered Federal Lobbyist		
WOOD, John	Tel:	(651) 293-2233
Senior Director, Agency Relations	Fax:	(651) 225-2092
Registered Federal Lobbyist		

ECR International

Heating and cooling systems manufacturer.
www.ecrinternational.com
Annual Revenues: $32.20 million
Employees: 500
Industry/ies: Heating And Air Conditioning

President and Chief Executive Officer	Tel:	(315) 797-1310
PASSAFARO, Ronald	Fax:	(315) 797-3762

Main Headquarters
Mailing:	2201 Dwyer Ave.	Tel:	(315) 797-1310
	Utica, NY 13501	Fax:	(315) 797-3762

Public Affairs and Related Activities Personnel

At Headquarters

CAMPOLA, David	Tel:	(315) 797-1310
Director, Human Resources	Fax:	(315) 797-3762
davcam@ecrinternational.com		
REED LUTZ, Maggie	Tel:	(315) 797-1310
Senior Marketing Representative	Fax:	(315) 797-3762
magree@ecrinternational.com		
TOTARO, Paul	Tel:	(315) 797-1310
Vice President and Chief Financial Officer	Fax:	(315) 797-3762

WALSH, David	Tel:	(315) 797-1310
Director, Sales	Fax:	(315) 797-3762

EDF Renewable Energy

Formerly, EnXco, Inc. of America, based in North Palm Springs city, is the U.S. subsidiary of EDF Energies Nouvelles Company, headquartered in Paris, France. The company develops, constructs, operates and manages renewable energy projects throughout the United States. It provides of third-party operations and maintenance services under contract.
www.edf-re.com
Annual Revenues: $32.70 million
Employees: 400
Industry/ies: Energy/Electricity
Legislative Issues: TAX

President and Chief Executive Officer	Tel:	(858) 521-3300
GRIMBERT, Tristan	Fax:	(760) 740-7030

Main Headquarters
Mailing:	15445 Innovation Dr.	Tel:	(858) 521-3300
	San Diego, CA 92128	Fax:	(760) 740-7030
		TF:	(888) 903-6926

Political Action Committees
EDF Renewable Energy PAC
FEC ID: C00523233
Contact: Virinder Singh
517 S.W. Fourth St.
Portland, OR 97204

> **Contributions to Candidates:** $19,250 (2015-2016)
> Democrats: $8,250; Republicans: $11,000

Public Affairs and Related Activities Personnel

At Headquarters

BARR, Larry	Tel:	(858) 521-3300
Executive Vice President, Operations and Maintenance	Fax:	(760) 740-7030
BRINER, Sandi	Tel:	(858) 521-3525
Director, Marketing and Communications	Fax:	(760) 740-7030
sandi.briner@edf-re.com		
CARP, SPHR, Lisa A.	Tel:	(858) 521-3300
Vice President, Human Resources	Fax:	(760) 740-7030
MARCHAND, John	Tel:	(858) 521-3300
Vice President, Market Development, Valuation and	Fax:	(760) 740-7030
Transaction Services		
MILLER, Robert F.	Tel:	(858) 521-3300
Executive Vice President, Legal, General Counsel and	Fax:	(760) 740-7030
Corporate Secretary		
SILVA, Luis	Tel:	(858) 521-3300
Chief Financial Officer	Fax:	(760) 740-7030

At Other Offices

SINGH, Virinder	Tel:	(503) 219-3166
PAC Treasurer and Clean Energy Market Developer		
1000 S.W. Broadway., Suite 1880		
Portland, OR 97205		

Edison International

An electric utility.
www.edison.com
Annual Revenues: $11.45 billion
Employees: 12,768
Ticker: NYSE: EIX
SIC: 4911
Industry/ies: Energy/Electricity; Utilities
Legislative Issues: BUD; CSP; ENG; ENV; NAT; UTI; WAS

Chairman of the Board and Chief Executive Officer	Tel:	(626) 302-2222
CRAVER, Jr., Theodore F.	Fax:	(626) 302-2517

Main Headquarters
Mailing:	2244 Walnut Grove Ave.	Tel:	(626) 302-2222
	P.O. Box 976	Fax:	(626) 302-2517
	Rosemead, CA 91770	TF:	(877) 379-9515

Washington Office
Mailing:	555 12th St. NW	Tel:	(202) 783-2343
	Suite 640	Fax:	(202) 393-1497
	Washington, DC 20004-2505		

Political Action Committees
Edison International PAC
FEC ID: C00019653
Contact: Cary Davidson
3699 Wiltshire Blvd.
Suite 1290
Los Angeles, CA 90010

> **Contributions to Candidates:** $202,200 (2015-2016)
> Democrats: $112,700; Republicans: $89,500

Principal Recipients

HOUSE

CALVERT, KEN (REP-CA)
MCCARTHY, KEVIN (REP-CA)
RYAN, PAUL D. (REP-WI)

Corporate Foundations and Giving Programs

Edison International Corporate Contributions Program
2244 Walnut Grove Ave.   Tel: (626) 302-2222
Rosemead, CA 91770   Fax: (626) 302-2222

Public Affairs and Related Activities Personnel

At Headquarters

BARNETT, Jeff   Tel: (626) 302-2222
Vice President, Tax   Fax: (626) 302-2517

BOADA, Robert C.   Tel: (626) 302-2222
Vice President and Treasurer Fax: (626) 302-2517

CLARKE, Mark   Tel: (626) 302-2222
Vice President and Controller Fax: (626) 302-2517

CLAYTON, Janet   Tel: (626) 302-2222
Senior Vice President, Corporate Communications Fax: (626) 302-2517

CUNNINGHAM, Scott   Tel: (626) 302-2222
Vice President, Investor Relations Fax: (626) 302-2517
scott.cunningham@edisonintl.com

HELLER, David   Tel: (626) 302-2222
Vice President, Enterprise Risk Management and General Fax: (626) 302-2517
Auditor

LITZINGER, Ronald L.   Tel: (626) 302-2222
Executive Vice President   Fax: (626) 302-2517

MATTHEWS, Barbara E.   Tel: (626) 302-2222
Vice President, Associate General Counsel, Chief Governance Fax: (626) 302-2517
Officer and Corporate Secretary

MONTOYA, Michael D.   Tel: (626) 302-2222
Vice President, Chief Ethics and Compliance Officer Fax: (626) 302-2517

RHONE, Oded J.   Tel: (626) 302-2222
Senior Vice President, Strategic Planning Fax: (626) 302-2517

SCILACCI, Jim   Tel: (626) 302-2222
Executive Vice President and Chief Financial Officer Fax: (626) 302-2517

UMANOFF, Adam S.   Tel: (626) 302-2222
Executive Vice President and General Counsel Fax: (626) 302-2517

At Washington Office

BOLTON, Dwayne   Tel: (202) 783-2343
Registered Federal Lobbyist   Fax: (202) 393-1497

DO, Eun Young Alisa   Tel: (202) 393-3075
                                Fax: (202) 393-1497

LIVOY, Laura   Tel: (202) 393-3075
Executive Administrator   Fax: (202) 393-1497
Laura.Livoy@edisonintl.com

MILLER, Matthew   Tel: (202) 393-3075
Director, Regulatory Affairs Fax: (202) 393-1497
matthew.miller@edisonintl.com
Registered Federal Lobbyist

PRESSLER, Amy   Tel: (202) 393-3075
Director, Public Affairs   Fax: (202) 393-1497
amy.pressler@edisonintl.com
Registered Federal Lobbyist

VASQUEZ, Gaddi   Tel: (202) 783-2343
Senior Vice President, Government Affairs Fax: (202) 393-1497

At Other Offices

DAVIDSON, Cary
PAC Treasurer
515 S. Figueroa St., Suite 1110
Los Angeles, CA 90071

EdisonLearning Inc.

A school management company.
www.edisonlearning.com
Employees: 2,300
SIC: 8200
Industry/ies: Education; Management

Chairman of the Board & Founder   Tel: (865) 329-3600
WHITTLE, H. Christopher   Fax: (212) 419-1604

President and Chief Executive Officer Tel: (865) 329-3600
JACKSON, Thomas   Fax: (212) 419-1604

Main Headquarters
Mailing: 900 S. Gay St.   Tel: (865) 329-3600
           Suite 1000   TF: (888) 737-2968
           Knoxville, TN 37902

Political Action Committees
EdisonLearning Inc. Political Action Committee
FEC ID: C00413583
Contact: Frank Ippolito
2910 Plaza Five

11th Floor
Jersey City, NJ 7311

Public Affairs and Related Activities Personnel

At Headquarters

IPPOLITO, Frank   Tel: (865) 329-3600
PAC Treasurer

LINCOLN, Paul   Tel: (865) 329-3600
Chief Operating & Education Officer

RYAN, Maureen   Tel: (865) 329-3600
Chief Financial Officer

SERPE, Michael   Tel: (865) 329-3600
Director, Media Relations
michael.serpe@edisonlearning.com

STANCIL, Curtiss   Tel: (865) 329-3600
Senior Vice President, Sales

At Other Offices

MALLON, Leah M.
Director, Government Affairs
Harborside Financial Center, 2910 Plaza Five
Jersey City, NJ 07311

EDP Renewables North America, LLC

Develops, constructs, owns and operates wind farms throughout North America and generates electricity using renewable energy sources.
www.edpr.com
Annual Revenues: $28.00 million
Employees: 200
Industry/ies: Energy/Electricity
Legislative Issues: TAX

Chairman   Tel: (713) 265-0350
MEXIA, António   Fax: (713) 265-0365

Chief Operating Officer, Cheif Executive Officer Tel: (713) 265-0350
ALONSO, Gabriel   Fax: (713) 265-0365

Main Headquarters
Mailing: 808 Travis St.   Tel: (713) 265-0350
           Suite 700   Fax: (713) 265-0365
           Houston, TX 77002

Public Affairs and Related Activities Personnel

At Headquarters

ANTUNES, Rui   Tel: (713) 265-0350
Director, Investor Relations Fax: (713) 265-0365
rui.antunes@edpr.com

BOERNER, Gary   Tel: (713) 265-0350
PAC Treasurer   Fax: (713) 265-0365

FREIMAN, Leslie   Tel: (713) 265-0350
Contact, General Counsel, Secretary and Regulatory Fax: (713) 265-0365
Compliance Officer

MENDES, Raquel   Tel: (713) 265-0350
Communications Director   Fax: (713) 265-0365

ROBERTS, Roby   Tel: (713) 265-0350
Vice President, Government Affairs and Contact, Media Fax: (713) 265-0365
Relations
media@horizonwind.com

TEIXEIRA, Rui   Tel: (713) 265-0350
Director   Fax: (713) 265-0365

Educational Credit Management Corporation

Nonprofit insures student loans, and services student loans in the event of bankruptcy.
www.ecmc.org
Industry/ies: Banking/Finance/Investments; Education

President and Chief Executive Officer Tel: (651) 325-3010
HAWN, Dave

Main Headquarters
Mailing: One Imation Pl.   Tel: (651) 325-3010
           Bldg. Two
           Oakdale, MN 55128

Corporate Foundations and Giving Programs

ECMC Foundation
Contact: March Kessler
One Imation Pl.   Tel: (651) 325-3010
Bldg. Two
Oakdale, MN 55128

Public Affairs and Related Activities Personnel

At Headquarters

FISHER, Dan   Tel: (651) 325-3010
Executive Vice President and General Counsel

GUILDER, Greg Van   Tel: (651) 325-3010
Chief Financial Officer

KESSLER, March
Executive Director, ECMC Foundation
Tel: (651) 325-3010

MIKULSKI, Matthew T.
Internal Audit
Tel: (651) 325-3010

RENNER, Heather
Federal Lobbyist
Tel: (651) 325-3010

TAYLOR, Peter
President, ECMC Foundation
Tel: (651) 325-3010

Educational Services of America Inc

Educational services company is a provider of behavior therapy and alternative and special education programs for children and young adults. ESA offers children and young people the opportunity to create successful, independent futures by providing behavioral and educational supports to help them reach their full potential.
www.esa-education.com
Annual Revenues: $101.8 million
Employees: 1,500
Industry/ies: Education

President and Chief Executive Officer
CLAYPOOL, Mark
Tel: (615) 361-4000
Fax: (615) 577-5695

Main Headquarters
Mailing: 1321 Murfreesboro Pike
Suite 702
Nashville, TN 37217
Tel: (615) 361-4000
Fax: (615) 577-5695
TF: (888) 979-0004

Public Affairs and Related Activities Personnel

At Headquarters

HANBACK, Shirley W.
Executive Vice President, Human Resources
Tel: (615) 361-4000
Fax: (615) 577-5695

LEFEVER, EdD, Karen
Executive Vice President and Chief Development Officer
klefever@esa-education.com
Tel: (615) 361-4000
Fax: (615) 577-5695

LEWANDOWSKI, Cate
Executive Vice President and Chief Marketing Officer
clewandowski@esa-education.com
Tel: (615) 361-4000
Fax: (615) 577-5695

MCLAUGHLIN, PhD, John M.
Executive Vice President and Director, Research and Analytics
Tel: (615) 361-4000
Fax: (615) 577-5695

MITCHELL, Kevin
Senior Vice President, Finance
Tel: (615) 361-4000
Fax: (615) 577-5695

O'NEILL, Allison
Chief Operating Officer
aoneill@esa-education.com
Tel: (615) 361-4000
Fax: (615) 577-5695

WHITFIELD, Donald B.
Executive Vice President and Chief Financial Officer
Tel: (615) 361-4000
Fax: (615) 577-5695

Edwards Lifesciences

Provides products and technologies to treat structural heart disease and critically ill patients.
www.edwards.com
Annual Revenues: $2.39 billion
Employees: 9,100
Ticker: NYSE: EW
SIC: 3842
Industry/ies: Science; Scientific Research
Legislative Issues: HCR; MMM; TAX

Chairman and Chief Executive Officer
MUSSALLEM, Michael A.
Tel: (949) 250-2500
Fax: (949) 250-2525

Main Headquarters
Mailing: One Edwards Way
Irvine, CA 92614
Tel: (949) 250-2500
Fax: (949) 250-2525
TF: (800) 424-3278

Washington Office
Mailing: 655 15th St. NW
Suite 350 South
Washington, DC 20005
Tel: (202) 783-0466

Political Action Committees
Edwards Lifesciences PAC (EWPAC)
FEC ID: C00411900
Contact: Barry Liden
One Edwards Way
Irvine, CA 92614
Tel: (949) 250-2500
Fax: (949) 250-2500

   Contributions to Candidates: $178,000 (2015-2016)
   Democrats: $72,000; Republicans: $106,000

   Principal Recipients

   HOUSE
   HOYER, STENY HAMILTON (DEM-DC)
   WALTERS, MIMI (REP-CA)

Corporate Foundations and Giving Programs

Edwards Lifesciences Fund
Contact: Amanda Fowler

One Edwards Way
Irvine, CA 92614
Tel: (949) 250-2500
Fax: (949) 250-2733

Public Affairs and Related Activities Personnel

At Headquarters

BOBO, JR., Donald E.
Corporate Vice President, Strategy and Corporate Development
Tel: (949) 250-2500
Fax: (949) 250-2525

ERICKSON, David K.
Vice President, Investor Relations
david_erickson@edwards.com
Tel: (949) 250-6826
Fax: (949) 250-2248

FOWLER, Amanda
Executive Director, Global Corporate Giving
amanda_fowler@edwards.com
Tel: (949) 250-5070
Fax: (949) 250-2733

HUOH, Sarah
Senior Director, Global Communications
sarah_huoh@edwards.com
Tel: (949) 250-2500
Fax: (949) 250-2525

LEHMAN, Dirksen J.
Corporate Vice President, Public Affairs
dirksen_lehman@edwards.com
Tel: (949) 250-6812
Fax: (949) 250-2525

LIDEN, Barry
Vice President, Government Affairs
barry_liden@edwards.com
Registered Federal Lobbyist
Tel: (949) 250-6812
Fax: (949) 250-2525

MCCAULEY, Christine Z.
Corporate Vice President, Human Resources
Tel: (949) 250-2500
Fax: (949) 250-2525

ULLEM, Scott B.
Corporate Vice President and Chief Financial Officer
Tel: (949) 250-2500
Fax: (949) 250-2525

WEISNER, Aimee S.
Corporate Vice President, General Counsel
Tel: (949) 250-2500
Fax: (949) 250-2525

At Washington Office

KEGLER, Leah
Director, Government Relations
Registered Federal Lobbyist
Tel: (202) 783-3900

Effective Communication Strategies LLC

Government and public relations consultant.
ecommunicationstrategies.com
Legislative Issues: AVI; BUD; DEF; HOM; LAW; TRA; VET

BRICKER, Paul
Tel: (202) 558-7284

Main Headquarters
Mailing: 499 South Capitol St
Suite 600
Washington, DC 20003
Tel: (202) 558-7284
Fax: (571) 384-6587

Washington Office
Mailing: P.O. Box 90762
Alexandria, VA 22309

eHealth Insurance Services, Inc.

A licensed health insurance agency and the online source for individuals, self employed, and small businesses to find, compare and buy Individual Health Insurance, Family Health Insurance, Small Business Health Insurance, Self Employed Health Insurance, and Health Savings Accounts (HSA).
www.ehealth.com
Annual Revenues: $190.02 million
Employees: 1,058
Ticker: NASDAQ: EHTH
SIC: 6411
Industry/ies: Insurance Industry; Medicine/Health Care/Mental Health
Legislative Issues: HCR

Chairman and Chief Executive Officer
LAUER, Gary L.
Tel: (650) 584-2700
Fax: (650) 961-2153

Main Headquarters
Mailing: 440 E. Middlefield Rd.
Mountain View, CA 94043-4006
Tel: (650) 584-2700
Fax: (650) 961-2110
TF: (800) 977-8860

Washington Office
Mailing: 1615 L St. NW
Suite 650
Washington, DC 20036
Tel: (202) 506-1096

Political Action Committees
EHealth PAC
FEC ID: C00459289
Contact: John Desser
1615 L St. NW
Suite 540
Washington, DC 20036

   Contributions to Candidates: $23,500 (2015-2016)
   Democrats: $13,500; Republicans: $10,000

   Principal Recipients

SENATE
CARPER, THOMAS R (DEM-DE)

Public Affairs and Related Activities Personnel

At Headquarters

BARRIOS, Karl S.	Tel:	(650) 584-2700
Associate General Counsel	Fax:	(650) 961-2153
karl.barrios@ehealth.com		
BERNSTEIN, Jeff	Tel:	(650) 584-2700
Senior Vice President, Marketing	Fax:	(650) 961-2110
DREW, Sande	Tel:	(916) 207-7674
Senior Media Consultant	Fax:	(650) 961-2110
sande.drew@ehealthinsurance.com		
HUIZINGA, Stuart M.	Tel:	(650) 584-2700
Senior Vice President and Chief Financial Officer	Fax:	(650) 961-2153
stuart.huizinga@ehealthinsurance.com		
HURLEY, Robert S.	Tel:	(650) 584-2700
Senior Vice President, Sales and Operations	Fax:	(650) 961-2110
LEONARD , Scott A.	Tel:	(650) 210-3158
Associate General Counsel	Fax:	(650) 961-2110
MAST, Brian	Tel:	(650) 210-3149
Vice President, Communications	Fax:	(650) 961-2110
brian.mast@ehealth.com		
PURPURA, Nate	Tel:	(650) 210-3115
Director, Public Relations	Fax:	(650) 961-2153
nate.purpura@ehealth.com		
SHAUGHNESSY, Bill	Tel:	(650) 584-2700
President, Chief Operating Officer and Board Member	Fax:	(650) 961-2153
SIDOROVICH, Kate	Tel:	(650) 210-3111
Vice President, Finance and Investor Relations	Fax:	(650) 961-2110
kate.sidorovich@ehealth.com		
SULLIVAN, David	Tel:	(650) 584-2700
Senior Vice President, Business Development and Strategy	Fax:	(650) 961-2110

At Washington Office

DESSER, John	Tel:	(202) 506-1096
Vice President, Public Policy, Government Affairs and PAC Treasurer		
John.desser@ehealth.com		
Registered Federal Lobbyist		

EISAI, Inc.

A research-based human health care (hhc) company. The U.S. pharmaceutical operation of Eisai Co., Ltd, a Japanese pharmaceutical company headquartered in Tokyo, Japan.
www.eisai.com
Annual Revenues: $62.30 million
Employees: 553
SIC: 5122
Industry/ies: Pharmaceutical Industry; Science; Scientific Research
Legislative Issues: BUD; CPT; EDU; FIN; HCR; MMM; PHA; TAX

Main Headquarters

Mailing:	100 Tice Blvd.		Tel:	(201) 692-1100
	Woodcliff Lake, NJ 07677		Fax:	(201) 692-1804

Washington Office

Mailing:	1501 K St. NW		Tel:	(202) 347-7358
	Suite 580			
	Washington, DC 20005			

Political Action Committees

EISAI Inc. PAC
FEC ID: C00429886
Contact: Stephen D. Mcmillan
100 Tice Blvd.
Woodcliff Lake, NJ 07677

Contributions to Candidates: $51,000 (2015-2016)
Democrats: $30,000; Republicans: $21,000

Corporate Foundations and Giving Programs

Eisai Contributions Program
100 Tice Blvd.
Woodcliff Lake, NJ 07677

Public Affairs and Related Activities Personnel

At Headquarters

KENNEY, Lynn	Tel:	(201) 746-2294
Senior Director, U.S. Corporate Communications	Fax:	(201) 692-1804
Lynn_kenney@eisai.com		
MCMILLAN, Stephen D.	Tel:	(201) 692-1100
PAC Treasurer	Fax:	(201) 692-1804
SCOTT, Alex	Tel:	(201) 746-2177
President, Eisai Global Business Development Unit	Fax:	(201) 692-1804
Alex_Scott@eisai.com		

El Paso Electric Company

Previously known as the El Paso Electric Railway Company, a regional electric utility providing generation, transmission and distribution service.
www.epelectric.com
Annual Revenues: $843.93 million
Employees: 1,100
Ticker: NYSE: EE
SIC: 4911; 4939
NAICS: 221122; 221119
Industry/ies: Energy/Electricity; Utilities
Legislative Issues: BUD; CAW; ENG; HOM

Chairman of the Board	Tel:	(915) 543-5711
YAMARONE, Charles A.	Fax:	(915) 521-4787

Chief Executive Officer	Tel:	(915) 543-5711
KIPP, Mary E.	Fax:	(915) 521-4787
mary.kipp@epelectric.com		

Main Headquarters

Mailing:	P.O. Box 982	Tel:	(915) 543-5711
	El Paso, TX 79960	Fax:	(915) 521-4787
		TF:	(800) 592-1634

Corporate Foundations and Giving Programs

El Paso Electric Company Contributions Program
P.O. Box 982
El Paso, TX 79960 Tel: (915) 543-4122

Public Affairs and Related Activities Personnel

At Headquarters

BOOMER, John	Tel:	(915) 543-4347
Senior Vice President, General Counsel	Fax:	(915) 521-4787
John.boomer@epelectric.com		
GUTIÉRREZ, Eduardo	Tel:	(915) 543-5711
Vice President, Public, Government and Customer Affairs	Fax:	(915) 521-4787
HIRSCHI, Nathan T.	Tel:	(915) 543-5711
Senior Vice President and Chief Financial Officer	Fax:	(915) 521-4787
MIRACLE, Rocky	Tel:	(915) 543-5711
Senior Vice President, Corporate Services and Chief Compliance Officer	Fax:	(915) 521-4787
SCHICHTL, James A.	Tel:	(915) 543-5711
Vice President, Regulatory Affairs	Fax:	(915) 521-4787
SILVA, Jr., Guillermo	Tel:	(915) 543-5711
Vice President, Community Outreach	Fax:	(915) 521-4787
SOZA, H. Wayne	Tel:	(915) 543-5711
Vice President, Compliance, and Chief Risk Officer	Fax:	(915) 521-4787
STILLER, William A.	Tel:	(915) 543-5711
Senior Vice President, Public and Customer Affairs and Chief Human Resources Officer	Fax:	(915) 521-4787
WILLIAMS, Rachelle	Tel:	(915) 543-2257
Supervisor, Investor Relations	Fax:	(915) 521-4787
rwilli5@epelectric.com		

At Other Offices

MACIAS, David	Tel:	(915) 543-5803
Analyst, Investor Relations and Investment Oversight		
100 N. Stanton		
El Paso, TX 79901-1341		
david.macias@epelectric.com		

Elbit Systems of America, LLC

Formerly EFW corporation.
www.elbitsystems-us.com
Industry/ies: Aerospace/Aviation; Transportation
Legislative Issues: BUD; DEF; HOM

President and Chief Executive Officer	Tel:	(817) 234-6600
HOROWITZ, Raanan		

Main Headquarters

Mailing:	4700 Marine Creek Pkwy.	Tel:	(817) 234-6600
	Fort Worth, TX 76179		

Corporate Foundations and Giving Programs

Elbit Systems of America Contributions Program
10823 N.E. Entrance Rd.
San Antonio, TX 78216

Public Affairs and Related Activities Personnel

At Headquarters

CARTER, Tom L.	Tel:	(202) 662-5533
COHEN, Brett	Tel:	(817) 234-6600
Vice President, Human Resources and Employee Development		
FORDYCE, Ted	Tel:	(817) 234-6600
Registered Federal Lobbyist		
GLASENER, Cletus C.	Tel:	(817) 234-6600
Vice President and Chief Financial Officer		

MORAN, James — Tel: (202) 662-5533
Contact, Government Relations

PUFFER , R. Chris — Tel: (817) 234-6600
General Counsel and Secretary

QUINLAN, Kenneth — Tel: (817) 234-6600
Vice President, Marketing

ROGERS, David — Tel: (817) 234-6600
Chief Operating Officer

ROSER, Steven A. — Tel: (817) 234-6600
Vice President, Marketing

SIMPSON, George — Tel: (202) 662-5533
Contact, Government Relations

WEISS, Efrat — Tel: (202) 662-5533
Director, Washington Operations

At Other Offices

EVALDS, Andris — Tel: (210) 381-1986
Chief Operating Officer
10823 N.E. Entrance Rd.
San Antonio, TX 78216

Elcousia

Lobbying Firm
Industry/ies: Aerospace/Aviation; Transportation

Main Headquarters
Mailing: 351 Bloom Dr. — Tel: (323) 724-9975
Monterey Park, CA 91755

Public Affairs and Related Activities Personnel

At Headquarters

TAM, Frederick — Tel: (323) 724-9975
Executive Director

Elder Federal Affairs LLC

Government affairs consulting

Main Headquarters
Mailing: PO Box 378
Waterford, VA 20197

Electrochemical Oxygen Concepts, Inc.

A health care technology company.
www.eo2.com
Industry/ies: Medicine/Health Care/Mental Health

President — Tel: (800) 825-2979
MOFFETT, Joe — Fax: (855) 223-6712

Main Headquarters
Mailing: 12500 Network Blvd. — Tel: (800) 825-2979
Suite 310 — Fax: (855) 223-6712
San Antonio, TX 78249 — TF: (800) 825-2979

Washington Office
Mailing: 565 Pennsylvania Ave. NW
Suite 808
Washington, DC 20001

Electrolux North America

Electrolux, a Sweden Company is a global leader in home appliances and appliances for professional use, selling more than 50 million products to customers in 150 markets every year.
www.electroluxusa.com
Industry/ies: Electricity & Electronics; Electronics; Energy/Electricity

President and Chief Executive Officer — Tel: (706) 651-1751
MCLOUGHLIN, Keith R. — Fax: (706) 651-7769
Keith.McLoughlin@electrolux.com

Main Headquarters
Mailing: P.O. Box 212237 — Tel: (706) 651-1751
250 Bobby Jones Expway — Fax: (706) 651-7769
Augusta, GA 30907

Corporate Foundations and Giving Programs

Electrolux Contributions Program
P.O. Box 212237
Augusta, GA 30907

Public Affairs and Related Activities Personnel

At Headquarters

ELIASSON, Tomas — Tel: (706) 651-1751
Chief Financial Officer, Senior Vice President — Fax: (706) 651-7769

HALE, Eloise — Tel: (706) 651-1751
Vice President, Communications & Public Relations, North America — Fax: (706) 651-7769
eloise.hale@electrolux.com

KOPF, MaryKay — Tel: (706) 651-1751
Chief Marketing Officer and Senior Vice President — Fax: (706) 651-7769

PETERSEN, Lars Worsøe — Tel: (706) 651-1751
Head, Human Resources and Organizational Development, — Fax: (706) 651-7769
Senior Vice President

VIEWEG, Cecilia — Tel: (706) 651-1751
Senior Vice President and General Counsel — Fax: (706) 651-7769

Electronic Arts

An international developer, marketer, publisher and distributor of video games.
www.ea.com
Annual Revenues: $4.40 billion
Employees: 8,400
Ticker: NASDAQ: EA
SIC: 7372
Industry/ies: Computer/Technology; Sports/Leisure/Entertainment

Chairman of the Board — Tel: (650) 628-1500
PROBST, III, Lawrence F. — Fax: (650) 628-1415

Chief Executive Officer — Tel: (650) 628-1500
WILSON , Andrew — Fax: (650) 628-1422

Main Headquarters
Mailing: 209 Redwood Shores Pkwy. — Tel: (650) 628-1500
Redwood City, CA 94065 — Fax: (650) 628-1422

Public Affairs and Related Activities Personnel

At Headquarters

BRUZZO, Chris — Tel: (650) 628-1500
Chief Marketing Officer — Fax: (650) 628-1422

JORGENSEN , Blake — Tel: (650) 628-1500
Chief Financial Officer — Fax: (650) 628-1422

LINZNER, Joel — Tel: (650) 628-1500
Executive Vice President, Business and Legal Affairs — Fax: (650) 628-1422
jlinzner@ea.com

MACRAE, Colin — Tel: (604) 456-3685
Senior Director, Communications — Fax: (650) 628-1422
cmacrae@ea.com

SCHATZ, Jacob — Tel: (650) 628-1500
Senior Vice President, General Counsel and Corporate — Fax: (650) 628-1422
Secretary

TOLEDANO, Gabrielle — Tel: (650) 628-1500
Executive Vice President and Chief Talent Officer — Fax: (650) 628-1422

Electronic Recyclers International

Electronic waste recycler company.
electronicrecyclers.com
Annual Revenues: $15.90 million
Industry/ies: Computer/Technology; Environment And Conservation; Pollution And Waste; Waste

Chairman of the Board and Chief Executive Officer — Tel: (800) 884-8466
SHEGERIAN, John S.
jshegerian@electronicrecyclers.com

Main Headquarters
Mailing: 7815 N. Palm Ave. — Tel: (800) 884-8466
Suite 140 — TF: (800) 884-8466
Fresno, CA 93711

Washington Office
Mailing: 1101 Pennsylvania Ave. — Tel: (800) 884-8466
Suite 600
Washington, DC 20004

Corporate Foundations and Giving Programs

Electronic Recyclers International Contributions Program
7815 N. Palm Ave.
Suite 140
Fresno, CA 93711

Public Affairs and Related Activities Personnel

At Headquarters

BLUM, Aaron — Tel: (800) 884-8466
Co-Founder and Chief Compliance Officer

BROWNING, Tyler — Tel: (800) 884-8466
Contact, Corporate Counsel
tyler.browning@electronicrecyclers.com

DEBELLIS, Carol — Tel: (800) 884-8466
Director, Human Resources
kreilly@electronicrecyclers.com

DILLON, Kevin J. — Tel: (800) 884-8466
Co-Founder and Chief Marketing Officer
kdillon@electronicrecyclers.com

At Washington Office

RAMOS, Linda — Tel: (800) 884-8466
Director, Administration

Elekta Inc.

Medical device manufacturer.
Industry/ies: Machinery/Equipment; Medicine/Health Care/Mental Health
Legislative Issues: BUD; HCR; MMM

President and Chief Executive Officer
PUUSEPP, Tomas

Tel: (770) 300-9725
Fax: (770) 448-6338

Main Headquarters
Mailing: 400 Perimeter Center Ter., Suite 50
            Atlanta, GA 30346

Tel: (770) 300-9725
Fax: (770) 448-6338

Political Action Committees
Elekta Holdings Us Inc Political Action Committee Elektapac
FEC ID: C00570895
Contact: Liberty Berman
400 Perimeter Center Ter., Suite 50
Atlanta, GA 30346

   Contributions to Candidates: $33,500 (2015-2016)
   Democrats: $7,000; Republicans: $26,500

Public Affairs and Related Activities Personnel

At Headquarters

ALEXANDER, Ian
Chief Compliance Officer

Tel: (770) 300-9725
Fax: (770) 448-6338

BERGSTROM, Hakan
Cheif Finanacial Officer

Tel: (770) 300-9725
Fax: (770) 448-6338

BERMAN, Liberty
Treasurer

Tel: (770) 300-9725
Fax: (770) 448-6338

BOLANDER, Jonas
Executive Vice President, Legal and Compliance

Tel: (770) 300-9725
Fax: (770) 448-6338

THOMAS, Robert D.
Vice President, Health Policy & Government Relations

Tel: (770) 300-9725
Fax: (770) 448-6338

WOLLESWINKEL, Maurits
Executive Vice President, Marketing and Strategy

Tel: (770) 300-9725
Fax: (770) 448-6338

Eli Lilly and Company

A global research-based pharmaceutical corporation that works with customers to ensure disease prevention and management.
www.lilly.com
Annual Revenues: $19.58 billion
Employees: 39,135
Ticker: NYSE: LLY
SIC: 2834
Industry/ies: Pharmaceutical Industry
Legislative Issues: AGR; BUD; CPT; CSP; FOR; HCR; MAN; MMM; NAT; PHA; TAX; TOR; TRD

Chairman, President, and Chief Executive Officer
LECHLEITER, PhD, John C.

Tel: (317) 276-2000
Fax: (317) 276-4878

Main Headquarters
Mailing: 893 S. Delaware St.
            Indianapolis, IN 46285

Tel: (317) 276-2000
Fax: (317) 276-4878

Washington Office
Mailing: 555 12th St. NW
            Suite 650 South
            Washington, DC 20004

Tel: (202) 393-7950
Fax: (202) 393-7960

Political Action Committees
Eli Lilly and Company PAC
FEC ID: C00082792
Lilly Corporate Center
Indianapolis, IN 46285

   Contributions to Candidates: $465,625 (2015-2016)
   Democrats: $119,500; Republicans: $341,625; Other: $4,500

   Principal Recipients

   HOUSE
   BROOKS, SUSAN MRS. (REP-IN)
   CARSON, ANDRE (DEM-IN)
   MCCARTHY, KEVIN (REP-CA)
   NOEM, KRISTI LYNN (REP-SD)
   PAULSEN, ERIK (REP-MN)
   RYAN, PAUL D. (REP-WI)
   WALDEN, GREGORY P MR. (REP-OR)
   WALORSKI SWIHART, JACKIE (REP-IN)

Corporate Foundations and Giving Programs
Eli Lilly and Company Foundation
Contact: David J. Marbaugh
893 S. Delaware
Indianapolis, IN 46285

Tel: (317) 428-1130

Public Affairs and Related Activities Personnel

At Headquarters

BARNES, Melissa Stapleton

Tel: (317) 276-2000
Fax: (317) 276-4878

Senior Vice President, Enterprise Risk Management, and Chief Ethics and Compliance Officer

FRY, Stephen F.
Senior Vice President, Human Resources and Diversity

Tel: (317) 276-2000
Fax: (317) 276-4878

HARRINGTON, Michael J.
Senior Vice President and General Counsel

Tel: (317) 276-2000
Fax: (317) 276-4878

MARBAUGH, David J.
Director, Corporate Responsibility Communications
marbaugh_david_j@lilly.com

Tel: (317) 276-2000
Fax: (317) 276-4878

PETERSON, Barton R.
Senior Vice President, Corporate Affairs and Communications

Tel: (317) 276-2000
Fax: (317) 276-4878

RICE, Derica W.
Executive Vice President , Global Services and Chief Financial Officer

Tel: (317) 276-2000
Fax: (317) 276-4878

RYKER, Tarra
Vice President, Global Communications
ryker_tarra@lilly.com

Tel: (317) 276-3787
Fax: (317) 276-4878

At Washington Office

ANDERSON, Anjulen
Contact, Government Relations
Registered Federal Lobbyist

Tel: (202) 393-7950
Fax: (202) 393-7960

ARTIM, Bruce
Director, Federal Affairs
Registered Federal Lobbyist

Tel: (202) 393-7950
Fax: (202) 393-7960

BONITT, John E.
Contact, Government Relations
Registered Federal Lobbyist

Tel: (202) 393-7950
Fax: (202) 393-7960

BRIGGS, Kern
Senior Director, Global Corporate Affairs Launch Strategy

Tel: (202) 393-7950
Fax: (202) 393-7960

BROOKS, Dana
Contact, Government Relations

Tel: (202) 393-7950
Fax: (202) 393-7960

COOK, Harrison
Director, International and Public Government Relations
Registered Federal Lobbyist

Tel: (202) 393-7950
Fax: (202) 393-7960

DONOHUE, Sean
Director, Federal Health Affairs
Registered Federal Lobbyist

Tel: (202) 393-7950
Fax: (202) 393-7960

HINKLEY, Catherine
Contact, Government Relations
Registered Federal Lobbyist

Tel: (202) 393-7950
Fax: (202) 393-7960

KELLEY, Joseph P.
Registered Federal Lobbyist

Tel: (202) 393-7950
Fax: (202) 393-7960

KONKA, Kathleen
Contact, Government Relations

Tel: (202) 393-7950
Fax: (202) 393-7960

MILLER, Kathleen
Contact, Government Relations
Registered Federal Lobbyist

Tel: (202) 393-7950
Fax: (202) 393-7960

PRICE, Jesse
PAC Contact
Registered Federal Lobbyist

Tel: (202) 393-7950
Fax: (202) 393-7960

ROGERS, Jennifer
Registered Federal Lobbyist

Tel: (202) 393-7950
Fax: (202) 393-7960

SALO, Jeannie
Director, Global Anti-Counterfeiting and International Government Affairs
Registered Federal Lobbyist

Tel: (202) 393-7950
Fax: (202) 393-7960

SEVCIK, Jesse
Registered Federal Lobbyist

Tel: (202) 393-7950
Fax: (202) 393-7960

SOTAK, Sonya D.
Director, Government Affairs
Registered Federal Lobbyist

Tel: (202) 393-7950
Fax: (202) 393-7960

STEELE, John
Registered Federal Lobbyist

Tel: (202) 393-7950
Fax: (202) 393-7960

STEINER, Eric
Registered Federal Lobbyist

Tel: (202) 393-7950
Fax: (202) 393-7960

TALBOT, Dave
Federal Lobbyist
Registered Federal Lobbyist

Tel: (202) 393-7950
Fax: (202) 393-7960

Elliott Management Corporation

Hedge fund firm.
www.elliottmgmt.com
Employees: 3
Industry/ies: Banking/Finance/Investments
Legislative Issues: FIN; TAX; TRD

Main Headquarters
Mailing: 40 W. 57th St.
            New York City, NY 10019

Tel: (212) 974-6000
Fax: (212) 586-9431

Public Affairs and Related Activities Personnel

At Headquarters

NADELL, Josh
Chief Financial Officer

Tel: (212) 974-6000
Fax: (212) 586-9431

eMagin Corporation

eMagin is a leader in OLED microdisplays and virtual imaging technologies.
www.emagin.com
Annual Revenues: $25.43 million
Employees: 80
Ticker: NYSE: EMAN
SIC: 3674
Industry/ies: Computer/Technology; Sports/Leisure/Entertainment

Chief Executive Officer and President
SCULLEY, Andrew G.
agsculley@emagin.com

Tel: (425) 284-5200
Fax: (425) 749-3601

Main Headquarters
Mailing: 3006 Northup Way
            Suite 103
            Bellevue, WA 98004

Tel: (425) 284-5200
Fax: (425) 284-5201
TF: (877) 362-4461

Washington Office
Mailing: P.O. Box 121
            Vienna, VA 22183

Tel: (202) 664-2222

Public Affairs and Related Activities Personnel

At Headquarters

CAMPBELL, Paul
Chief Financial Officer
pcampbell@emagin.com

Tel: (425) 284-5200
Fax: (425) 749-3601

KOHIN, Margaret
Senior Vice President, Business Development

Tel: (425) 284-5200
Fax: (425) 284-5201

Embarq

See listing on page 179 under CenturyLink

EmblemHealth

See listing on page 285 under EmblemHealth

EmblemHealth

EmblemHealth is committed to providing affordable, quality health coverage in New York state. Group Health Incorporated (GHI) and the Health Insurance Plan of Greater New York (HIP) merged to create EmblemHealth - a health maintenance organization (HMO).
www.emblemhealth.com
Industry/ies: Insurance Industry; Medicine/Health Care/Mental Health

Chairman and Chief Executive Officer
BRANCHINI , Frank

Tel: (646) 447-5000
Fax: (866) 426-1509

Main Headquarters
Mailing: 55 Water St.
            New York City, NY 10041

Tel: (646) 447-5000
Fax: (866) 426-1509

Washington Office
Mailing: 455 Massachusetts Ave. NW
            Suite 440
            Washington, DC 20001

Political Action Committees
Emblemhealth Services Company LLC Federal PAC
FEC ID: C00412247
Contact: Arthur J. Byrd
55 Water St.
New York City, NY 10041

Tel: (646) 447-5000

Contributions to Candidates: $2,500 (2015-2016)
Democrats: $2,500

Public Affairs and Related Activities Personnel

At Headquarters

BRANDT, Harris
Lead Public Relations and Corporate Communications Specialist
hbrandt@emblemhealth.com

Tel: (646) 447-5000
Fax: (866) 426-1509

BYRD , Arthur J.
Chief Financial Officer and PAC Treasurer

Tel: (646) 447-5000
Fax: (866) 426-1509

CHANSLER, Jeffrey D.
Senior Vice President and General Counsel

Tel: (646) 447-5000
Fax: (866) 426-1509

DROHAN, Marianne E.
Vice President, Human Resources

Tel: (646) 447-5000
Fax: (866) 426-1509

DROHAN, Mariann E.
Vice President, Human Resources

Tel: (646) 447-5000
Fax: (866) 426-1509

FITZGIBBON, Shawn M.
Senior Vice President, Government Programs

Tel: (646) 447-5000
Fax: (866) 426-1509

LAMOREAUX, William C.
Executive Vice President, Corporate Operations

Tel: (646) 447-5000
Fax: (866) 426-1509

MAHER , Charlene
Senior Vice President, Commercial Business & Chief Marketing Officer
dmahder@emblemhealth.com

Tel: (646) 447-6520
Fax: (866) 426-1509

MASTRO, William
Senior Vice President, Deputy General Counsel and Corporate Secretary

Tel: (646) 447-5000
Fax: (866) 426-1509

REARDON, Valerie A.
Chief Compliance Officer

Tel: (646) 447-5000
Fax: (866) 426-1509

At Washington Office

IGNAGNI, CAE, Karen M.
Head

Embraer Aircraft Holdings

Embraer Aircraft Holdings, based in Ft. Lauderdale City, is the U.S. subsidiary of Embraer-Empresa Brasileira de Aeronáutica S.A., headquartered in Sao Paulo, Brazil. Manufactures aircrafts.
www.embraer.com
Annual Revenues: $5.02 billion
Employees: 19,167
Ticker: NYSE: ERJ
SIC: 3728
Industry/ies: Aerospace/Aviation; Transportation
Legislative Issues: AVI; DEF

Main Headquarters
Mailing: 276 S.W. 34th St.
            Ft. Lauderdale, FL 33315

Tel: (954) 359-3700
Fax: (954) 359-3701

Washington Office
Mailing: 1700 Pennsylvania Ave. NW
            Suite 200
            Washington, DC 20008

Tel: (202) 626-9110
Fax: (202) 626-3737

Political Action Committees
Embraer Aircraft Holding Inc PAC (Embraer PAC)
FEC ID: C00472225
Contact: Christopher J. Appleton
276 S.W. 34th St.
Ft. Lauderdale, FL 33312

Tel: (954) 359-3700

Contributions to Candidates: $17,700 (2015-2016)
Democrats: $3,000; Republicans: $14,700

Public Affairs and Related Activities Personnel

At Headquarters

APPLETON, Christopher J.
Chief Financial Officer and PAC Treasurer

Tel: (954) 359-3700
Fax: (954) 359-3701

BUCKEY, William
Vice President, Business Development & Sales Defence & Government Market

Tel: (954) 359-3700
Fax: (954) 359-3701

DONEL, Elisa
Manager, Corporate Communication and Media Relations

Tel: (954) 359-3700
Fax: (954) 359-3701

LAUREANO, Maggie
Vice President, Human Resource

Tel: (954) 359-3700
Fax: (954) 359-3701

At Washington Office

BALLOFF, David H.
Vice President, External Relations, North America
dballoff@embraer.com
Registered Federal Lobbyist

Tel: (202) 626-9110
Fax: (202) 626-3737

EMC Corporation

Information technology storage and management company. Develops, delivers, and supports information infrastructure and virtual infrastructure technologies, solutions, and services.
www.emc.com
Annual Revenues: $24.57 billion
Employees: 70,000
Ticker: NYSE: EMC
SIC: 3577; 3572
NAICS: 334119; 334112
Industry/ies: Computer/Technology
Legislative Issues: BUD; CPI; CPT; DEF; ENG; GOV; HOM; IMM; TAX

Chairman of the Board and Chief Executive Officer
TUCCI, Joseph M.

Tel: (508) 435-1000
Fax: (508) 435-7954

Main Headquarters
Mailing: 176 South St.
            Hopkinton, MA 01748

Tel: (508) 435-1000
Fax: (508) 555-1212

Washington Office
Mailing: 1101 K St. NW
            Suite 410
            Washington, DC 20005

Political Action Committees
EMC Corporation Political Action Committee
FEC ID: C00305948
Contact: Christopher Goode

171 South St.
Hopkinton, MA 01748

Tel: (703) 769-6203
Fax: (703) 892-0091

Contributions to Candidates: $62,000 (2015-2016)
Democrats: $38,500; Republicans: $23,500

Corporate Foundations and Giving Programs

EMC Corporation Contributions Program
176 South St.
Hopkinton, MA 01748

Tel: (508) 435-1000
Fax: (508) 555-1212

Public Affairs and Related Activities Personnel

At Headquarters

BURTON, Jeremy
President, Products and Marketing

Tel: (508) 435-1000
Fax: (508) 555-1212

DACIER, Paul T.
Executive Vice President and General Counsel
paul.t.dacier@emc.com

Tel: (508) 435-1000
Fax: (508) 497-6912

ELIAS, Howard D.
President and Chief Operating Officer

Tel: (508) 435-1000
Fax: (508) 555-1212

GALLANT, Michael
Senior Director, Public Relations
gallant_michael@emc.com

Tel: (508) 293-6357
Fax: (508) 435-7954

GOODE, Christopher
PAC Contact

Tel: (508) 435-1000
Fax: (508) 555-1212

GOULDEN, David
Chief Executive Officer, EMC Information Infrastructure

Tel: (508) 435-1000
Fax: (508) 555-1212

KRAKAUER, M L (Mary Louise)
Executive Vice President, Human Resources

Tel: (508) 435-1000
Fax: (508) 555-1212

ROWE, Zane C.
Executive Vice President and Chief Financial Officer

Tel: (508) 435-1000
Fax: (508) 555-1212

At Washington Office

LONG, Jill Lynette
Federal Lobbyist
Registered Federal Lobbyist

SHAPIRO, Jill
Federal Lobbyist
Registered Federal Lobbyist

At Other Offices

COLBERG, David
Federal Lobbyist
2011 Crystal Dr., Suite 907
Arlington, VA 22202
Registered Federal Lobbyist

Tel: (703) 769-6203
Fax: (703) 892-0091

DICK, Darren
Senior Manager, Government Affairs and Public Policy
2011 Crystal Dr., Suite 907
Arlington, VA 22202
Registered Federal Lobbyist

Tel: (703) 769-6202
Fax: (703) 892-0091

HAYES, James
Vice President, Government Affairs and Public Policy
2011 Crystal Dr., Suite 907
Arlington, VA 22202
Registered Federal Lobbyist

Tel: (703) 769-6203
Fax: (703) 892-0091

SALISBURY, Keith
Director, Government Affairs
2011 Crystal Dr., Suite 907
Arlington, VA 22202
salisbury_keith@emc.com
Registered Federal Lobbyist

Tel: (703) 769-6203
Fax: (703) 892-0091

EmCare, Inc.

EmCare provides outsourced physician services to hospital emergency departments, inpatient physician services, inpatient radiology management programs and anesthesiology services.
www.emcare.com
Annual Revenues: $174.6 million
Employees: 8,000
SIC: 8093
Industry/ies: Medicine/Health Care/Mental Health
Legislative Issues: BUD; HCR; LBR; MMM; TAX

Chief Executive Officer

ZIMMERMAN, Todd G.
todd.zimmerman@emcare.com

Tel: (214) 712-2000
Fax: (214) 712-2444

Main Headquarters

Mailing: 13737 Noel Rd.
Suite 1600
Dallas, TX 75240

Tel: (214) 712-2000
Fax: (214) 712-2444
TF: (800) 362-2731

Political Action Committees

Emergency Medical Care Political Action Committee
FEC ID: C00398271
Contact: John Ranieri
6200 S. Syracuse Way
Suite 200

Greenwood Village, CO 80111

Contributions to Candidates: $6,500 (2015-2016)
Democrats: $1,000; Republicans: $5,500

Corporate Foundations and Giving Programs

EmCare, Inc. Contributions Program
1717 Main St.
Suite 5200
Dallas, TX 75201

Tel: (214) 712-2000
Fax: (214) 712-2444

Public Affairs and Related Activities Personnel

At Headquarters

FELDMAN, Lori
Vice President, Human Resources and Management Services

Tel: (214) 712-2000
Fax: (214) 712-2444

HAMM, Mark
Executive Vice President, Corporate Development

Tel: (214) 712-2000
Fax: (214) 712-2444

IANNACCONE, Raymond
President

Tel: (214) 712-2000
Fax: (214) 712-2444

MARKS, David
Chief Operating Officer

Tel: (214) 712-2000
Fax: (214) 712-2444

RUSSO , Kathy
Project Manager
kathy_russo@emcare.com

Tel: (214) 712-2000
Fax: (214) 712-2444

STANDIFIRD, R Jason
Chief Financial Officer

Tel: (214) 712-2000
Fax: (214) 712-2444

TAYLOR, Jay
Chief Executive Officer, Sales, Marketing and Business

Tel: (214) 712-2000
Fax: (214) 712-2444

At Other Offices

RANIERI, John
PAC Treasurer
6200 S. Syracuse Way, Suite 200
Greenwood Village, CO 80111

EMCOR Group Inc.

An electrical and mechanical construction and facilities services company.
www.emcorgroup.com
Annual Revenues: $6.71 billion
Employees: 29,000
Ticker: NYSE: EME
SIC: 1731
Industry/ies: Government-Related

President and Chief Executive Officer

GUZZI, Anthony J.

Tel: (203) 849-7800
Fax: (203) 849-7950

Main Headquarters

Mailing: 301 Merritt Seven
Sixth Floor
Norwalk, CT 06851

Tel: (203) 849-7800
Fax: (203) 849-7950
TF: (866) 890-7794

Public Affairs and Related Activities Personnel

At Headquarters

CAMMAKER, Sheldon I.
Vice Chairman
scammaker@emcorgroup.com

Tel: (203) 849-7800
Fax: (203) 849-7950

HAIGHT, Lisa
Vice President, Human Resources

Tel: (203) 849-7800
Fax: (203) 849-7950

HEFFLER, Mava K.
Vice President, Marketing and Communications
mava_heffler@emcorgroup.com

Tel: (203) 849-7814
Fax: (203) 849-7950

MATZ, Kevin
Executive Vice President, Shared Services
kevin_matz@emcorgroup.com

Tel: (203) 849-7938
Fax: (203) 849-7950

MAURICIO, Maxine Lum
Senior Vice President and Deputy General Counsel
mmauricio@emcorgroup.com

Tel: (203) 849-7834
Fax: (203) 849-7950

POMPA, Mark A.
Executive Vice President and Chief Financial Officer
mark_pompa@emcorgroup.com

Tel: (203) 849-7800
Fax: (203) 849-7950

SERINO, Joseph A
Vice President and Treasurer

Tel: (203) 849-7800
Fax: (203) 849-7950

EMD Serono, Inc.

Pharmaceutical manufacturing, research, and development.
www.emdserono.com
Annual Revenues: $67.10 million
Employees: 1,100
Industry/ies: Pharmaceutical Industry; Science; Scientific Research
Legislative Issues: FAM; HCR; MMM; PHA; TAX; TRD; VET

President and Managing Director

PANAYIOTOPOULOS, Paris

Tel: (781) 982-9000
Fax: (781) 871-6754

Main Headquarters

Mailing: One Technology Pl.
Rockland, MA 02370

Tel: (781) 982-9000
Fax: (781) 871-6754

		TF:	(800) 283-8088

Washington Office

Mailing:	975 F St. NW	Tel:	(202) 626-2595
	Suite 330	Fax:	(202) 626-2593
	Washington, DC 20004	TF:	(800) 283-8088

Political Action Committees

EMD Serono, Inc. PAC
FEC ID: C00258236
Contact: John Pacino

One Technology Pl.	Tel:	(781) 982-9000
Rockland, MA 02370		

Contributions to Candidates: $59,000 (2015-2016)
Democrats: $36,500; Republicans: $22,500

Corporate Foundations and Giving Programs

EMD Serono, Inc. contributions Program

One Technology Pl.	Tel:	(781) 681-9000
Rockland, MA 02370		

Public Affairs and Related Activities Personnel

At Headquarters

BEALS, Erin	Tel:	(781) 681-2850
Associate Director, Communications	Fax:	(781) 871-6754
BUFFINGTON, Lisa	Tel:	(781) 982-9000
Vice President, US Communications	Fax:	(781) 871-6754
COSTANTINO, Lisa	Tel:	(781) 982-9000
Chief Financial Officer	Fax:	(781) 871-6754
HUYCKE, John	Tel:	(781) 982-9000
Vice President, Strategy and Management	Fax:	(781) 871-6754
MOYNIHAN, Daniel	Tel:	(781) 982-9000
Chief Compliance Officer	Fax:	(781) 871-6754
PACINO, John	Tel:	(781) 982-9000
PAC Contact	Fax:	(781) 871-6754
SMITH, Devin	Tel:	(781) 982-9000
Vice president and General Counsel	Fax:	(781) 871-6754

At Washington Office

JANCARIK, Kent	Tel:	(202) 637-7965
Senior Director, Global Public Policy	Fax:	(202) 626-2593
kent.jancarik@emdserono.com		
KAUNE, Jason D.	Tel:	(202) 626-2595
Attorney & Agent for Filer	Fax:	(202) 626-2593
NICHOLS, DAVID	Tel:	(202) 626-2595
Senior Director, Federal Government Affairs	Fax:	(202) 626-2593
david.nichols@emdserono.com		
RUGGIERO, Michael	Tel:	(202) 626-2595
Federal Lobbyist	Fax:	(202) 626-2593
Registered Federal Lobbyist		
TAYLOR , Lynn A.	Tel:	(202) 626-2595
Vice President, Government Affairs	Fax:	(202) 626-2593
lynn.taylor@emdserono.com		
TEMME, Alanna	Tel:	(202) 626-2595
Registered Federal Lobbyist	Fax:	(202) 626-2593

eRx Network, LLC

eRx Network, LLC is acquired by Emdeon.Emdeon is a provider of revenue and payment cycle management and clinical information exchange solutions, connecting payers, providers and patients in the U.S.
www.emdeon.com
SIC: 7389
Industry/ies: Computer/Technology; Pharmaceutical Industry

Chief Executive Officer	Tel:	(615) 932-3000
LAZENBY, IV, George I.		

Main Headquarters

Mailing:	3055 Lebanon Pike	Tel:	(615) 932-3000
	Nashville, TN 37214		

Public Affairs and Related Activities Personnel

At Headquarters

BYRD, Susan	Tel:	(615) 932-3000
Senior Vice President, Human Resource		
GILES, Randy	Tel:	(615) 932-3000
Executive Vice President, Chief Financial Officer		
LEWIS, Tommy	Tel:	(615) 932-3000
Chief Marketing Officer		
MANZELLA, Frank	Tel:	(615) 932-3000
Senior Vice President Corporate Development		
MCENERY, W Thomas	Tel:	(615) 932-3000
Chief Strategic Marketing Officer		
OLSON, John	Tel:	(615) 932-3000
Executive Vice President Operations		

PARAMORE, Miriam	Tel:	(615) 932-3000
Executive Vice President ,Strategy and Product Management		
STEVENS, Gregory T.	Tel:	(615) 932-3000
Executive Vice President, General Counsel and Secretary		
WHITLEY-TAYLOR, Linda	Tel:	(615) 932-3000
Executive Vice President, Chief Human Resources Officer		

At Other Offices

LUDVIGSON, Nathan	Tel:	(817) 887-0305
Manager, Government Affairs		
301 Commerce St., Suite 3150		
Fort Worth, TX 76102		
nathan.ludvigson@erxnetwork.com		

Emergency Recovery Assistance, LLC

Disaster assistance consulting.
Industry/ies: Disaster

Main Headquarters

Mailing:	1506 N 1025 W	Tel:	(502) 227-9066
	Deputy, IN 47250		

Public Affairs and Related Activities Personnel

At Headquarters

FLINT, Michael	Tel:	(502) 227-9066
mflint@flintgroup.net		

Emergent BioSolutions Corporation

Parent company of BioPort (see separate listing). Emergent BioSolutions is a multinational biopharmaceutical company.
www.emergentbiosolutions.com
Annual Revenues: $459.89 million
Employees: 1,280
Ticker: NYSE: EBS
SIC: 2834
Industry/ies: Medicine/Health Care/Mental Health; Pharmaceutical Industry; Science; Scientific Research
Legislative Issues: BUD; DEF; DIS; HCR; HOM; MED

Executive Chairman of the Board	Tel:	(301) 795-1800
EL-HIBRI, Fuad	Fax:	(301) 795-1899
President and Chief Executive Officer	Tel:	(301) 795-1800
ABDUN-NABI, Daniel J.	Fax:	(301) 795-1899
President, Chief Executive Officer and Director	Tel:	(204) 275-4200
SEDOR , John	Fax:	(204) 269-7003

Main Headquarters

Mailing:	400 Professional Dr.	Tel:	(240) 631-3200
	Gaithersburg, MD 20879		

Washington Office

Mailing:	1455 Pennsylvania Ave. NW	Tel:	(301) 795-6788
	Suite 1225	Fax:	(301) 737-0558
	Washington, DC 20004		

Political Action Committees

Emergent BioSolutions Inc. Employees PAC
FEC ID: C00380303
Contact: Thomas Moran

2273 Research Blvd.	Tel:	(301) 795-1800
Suite 400		
Rockville, MD 20850		

Contributions to Candidates: $201,500 (2015-2016)
Democrats: $55,500; Republicans: $146,000

Principal Recipients

SENATE
AYOTTE, KELLY A (REP-NH)
BLUNT, ROY (REP-MO)
BURR, RICHARD (REP-NC)

HOUSE
HARRIS, ANDREW P (REP-MD)

Corporate Foundations and Giving Programs

Canada-Wide Science Fair		
155 Innovation Dr.	Tel:	(204) 275-4200
Winnipeg, MB R3T 5Y3		
Canadian Liver Foundation		
155 Innovation Dr.	Tel:	(204) 275-4200
Winnipeg, MB R3T 5Y3		
Ronald McDonald House Winnipeg		
155 Innovation Dr.	Tel:	(204) 275-4200
Winnipeg, MB R3T 5Y3		
The Children's Cancer and Blood Foundation		
155 Innovation Dr.	Tel:	(204) 275-4200
Winnipeg, MB R3T 5Y3		
United Way		
155 Innovation Dr.		

Winnipeg, MB R3T 5Y3

Public Affairs and Related Activities Personnel

At Headquarters

CRUZ III, AB   Tel: (240) 631-3200
Executive Vice President and General Counsel

At Washington Office

BRATICH, Ashley K.   Tel: (301) 795-6790
Senior Director, Government Affairs   Fax: (301) 795-1899
Registered Federal Lobbyist

FRECH, Christopher   Tel: (301) 795-6790
Vice President, Government Affairs   Fax: (301) 737-0558
Registered Federal Lobbyist

HAMAKER, Jill   Tel: (301) 795-6788
Senior Manager, Government Affairs   Fax: (301) 737-0558
Registered Federal Lobbyist

At Other Offices

BURLINGTON, Bruce D.   Tel: (204) 275-4200
Director & Human Resource & Compensation Committee   Fax: (204) 269-7003
Chair
155 Innovation Dr.
Winnipeg, MB R3T 5Y3

BURROWS, Robert G.   Tel: (301) 795-1877
Vice President, Investor Relations
2273 Research Blvd., Suite 400
Rockville, MD 20850
BurrowsR@ebsi.com

DEEZAR, Les   Tel: (204) 275-4200
Vice President, Human Resources   Fax: (204) 269-7003
155 Innovation Dr.
Winnipeg, MB R3T 5Y3

HILAIRE, Francis St.   Tel: (204) 275-4200
Vice President, General Counsel and Secretary   Fax: (204) 269-7003
155 Innovation Dr.
Winnipeg, MB R3T 5Y3

KRAMER, Robert G.   Tel: (301) 795-1800
Executive Vice President, Corporate Services, Chief Financial   Fax: (301) 795-1899
Officer and Treasurer
2273 Research Blvd., Suite 400
Rockville, MD 20850

LAMOTHE, Jeff   Tel: (204) 275-4200
Chief Financial Officer   Fax: (204) 269-7003
155 Innovation Dr.
Winnipeg, MB R3T 5Y3

LAZARICH, Paula M.   Tel: (301) 795-1800
Senior Vice President, Human Capital   Fax: (301) 795-1899
2273 Research Blvd., Suite 400
Rockville, MD 20850

MORAN, Thomas   Tel: (301) 795-1800
PAC Treasurer   Fax: (301) 795-1899
2273 Research Blvd., Suite 400
Rockville, MD 20850

OCHOA, Jose   Tel: (301) 795-6772
Vice President, Business Development   Fax: (301) 795-1899
2273 Research Blvd., Suite 400
Rockville, MD 20850
BD@ebsi.com

SCHMITT, Tracey
Vice President, Corporate Communications
2273 Research Blvd., Suite 400
Rockville, MD 20850
SchmittT@ebsi.com

SHOFE, Allen M.   Tel: (301) 795-6790
Executive Vice President, Corporate Affairs   Fax: (301) 795-1899
2273 Research Blvd., Suite 400
Rockville, MD 20850
shofea@ebsi.com
Registered Federal Lobbyist

SINCLAIR , Chris   Tel: (204) 275-4200
Vice President, Business Development and Corporate   Fax: (204) 269-7003
Strategic Planning
155 Innovation Dr.
Winnipeg, MB R3T 5Y3

Emerging Markets Development Corporation

www.emergingmarketsgroup.com

Main Headquarters

Mailing: 1024 N. Orange Dr.   Tel: (323) 465-0406
       Suite 120   Fax: (323) 465-0225
       Los Angeles, CA 90038

Washington Office

Mailing: 1111 11th St. NW   Tel: (202) 744-8082

Suite 710
Washington, DC 20001-4353

Public Affairs and Related Activities Personnel

At Headquarters

HOPKINS, Elwood   Tel: (323) 465-0406
Director, Management   Fax: (323) 465-0225

Emerson

The company makes a slew of electrical, electromechanical, and electronic products, many of which are used to control gases, liquids, and electricity. Among its businesses, its InSinkErator is the maker of food waste disposers and hot water dispensers.
www.emerson.com
Annual Revenues: $24.11 billion
Employees: 115,100
Ticker: NYSE: EMR
SIC: 3600
Industry/ies: Machinery/Equipment
Legislative Issues: ENG; HOM; IMM; MAN; RET; TAX; TRA; TRD

Chairman of the Board and Chief Executive Officer   Tel: (314) 335-2000
FARR, David N.   Fax: (314) 553-3527

Main Headquarters

Mailing: 8000 W. Florissant Ave.   Tel: (314) 553-2000
       P.O. Box 4100   Fax: (314) 553-3527
       St. Louis, MO 63136

Washington Office

Mailing: 529 14th St. NW   Tel: (202) 662-8790
       Suite 412   Fax: (202) 662-8793
       Washington, DC 20045

Political Action Committees

Emerson Electric Company Responsible Government Fund PAC
FEC ID: C00080515
Contact: Mark Pfeiffer
8000 W. Florissant Ave.   Tel: (314) 553-2000
Station 2310   Fax: (314) 553-3527
St. Louis, MO 63136

    Contributions to Candidates: $233,000 (2015-2016)
    Democrats: $57,000; Republicans: $171,000; Other: $5,000

       Principal Recipients

         SENATE
         VAN HOLLEN, CHRIS (DEM-MD)

         HOUSE
         BACON, DONALD (REP-NE)
         GRIFFIN, WILLIAM TAYLOR (REP-CA)
         GRIFFIN, WILLIAM TAYLOR (REP-NC)
         HARTZLER, VICKY (REP-MO)
         JOYCE, DAVID P (REP-OH)
         MCSALLY, MARTHA E. MS. (REP-AZ)

Corporate Foundations and Giving Programs

Emerson Charitable Trust
Contact: Patrick J. (Pat) Sly
8000 W. Florissant Ave.   Tel: (314) 553-2000
P.O. Box 4100   Fax: (314) 553-3527
St. Louis, MO 63136

Public Affairs and Related Activities Personnel

At Headquarters

BELL, Kathy Button   Tel: (314) 553-2000
Vice President and Chief Marketing Officer   Fax: (314) 553-3527

DELLAQUILA, Frank J.   Tel: (314) 553-2000
Executive Vice President and Chief Financial Officer   Fax: (314) 553-3527

FLAVIN, Lisa A.   Tel: (314) 553-2000
Vice President, Audit and Chief Compliance Officer   Fax: (314) 553-3527

KLEGSTAD, Anne   Tel: (314) 553-2000
Program Manager, Information Technology   Fax: (314) 553-3527
ANNE.KLEGSTAD@EMERSONCT.COM

MAXEINER, Lynne M.   Tel: (314) 553-2197
Vice President, Planning and Business Development   Fax: (314) 553-3527

MONSER, Edward L.   Tel: (314) 553-2000
President   Fax: (314) 553-3527

PELCH, Steven J.   Tel: (314) 553-2000
Vice President, Organization Planning and Development   Fax: (314) 553-3527

PFEIFFER, Mark   Tel: (314) 553-2000
Director, Cost Accounting and PAC Treasurer   Fax: (314) 553-3527

POLZIN, Mark   Tel: (314) 982-1758
Contact, Media Relations   Fax: (314) 982-9100
EmersonPR@fleishman.com

PURVIS , Edgar M.   Tel: (314) 553-2000
Chief Operating Officer   Fax: (314) 553-3527

ROHRET, Mike G.   Tel: (314) 553-2000
Senior Vice President, Human Resources   Fax: (314) 553-3527

SLY, Patrick J. (Pat)
Executive Vice President
Tel: (314) 553-2000
Fax: (314) 553-3527

STEEVES, Frank L.
Executive Vice President, Secretary and General Counsel
Tel: (314) 553-2000
Fax: (314) 553-3527

At Washington Office

CARTER, Hon. James
Vice President, Government Affairs
Registered Federal Lobbyist
Tel: (202) 662-8790
Fax: (202) 662-8793

JACKSON, Lisa
Director, Federal Goverment Relations
Registered Federal Lobbyist
Tel: (202) 662-8790
Fax: (202) 662-8793

MCDONALD, Robert D.
Vice President Government Affiars
Rob.McDonald@Emerson.com
Tel: (202) 662-8790
Fax: (202) 662-8793

Emmanuel Merck Darmstadt

See listing on page 286 under EMD Serono, Inc.

Emmis Communications

Emmis Communications Corporation (formerly Emmis Broadcasting) was incorporated in Indiana in 1979. A communication company, owns and operates radio and magazine entities.
www.emmis.com
Annual Revenues: $237.94 million
Employees: 785
Ticker: NASDAQ (GS): EMMS
SIC: 4832
Industry/ies: Communications; Media/Mass Communication

Chairman of the Board, President and Chief Executive Officer
SMULYAN, Jeffery H.
Tel: (317) 266-0100
Fax: (317) 631-3750

Main Headquarters
Mailing: One Emmis Plaza
40 Monument Cir., Suite 700
Indianapolis, IN 46204
Tel: (317) 266-0100
Fax: (317) 631-3750

Corporate Foundations and Giving Programs

Emmis Communications Contributions Program
One Emmis Plaza
40 Monument Cir., Suite 700
Indianapolis, IN 46204

Public Affairs and Related Activities Personnel

At Headquarters

DYNES, Karen
Contact, Media and Investor Relations
kdynes@emmis.com
Tel: (317) 266-0100
Fax: (317) 631-3750

ENRIGHT, Scott
Executive Vice President and General Counsel
Tel: (317) 266-0100
Fax: (317) 631-3750

HORNADAY, Ryan A.
Senior Vice President, Finance and Treasurer
Tel: (317) 266-0100
Fax: (317) 631-3750

LOEWEN, Greg
President, Publishing and Chief Strategy Officer
Tel: (317) 266-0100
Fax: (317) 631-3750

SNEDEKER, Kate
Contact, Media and Investor Relations
kate@emmis.com
Tel: (317) 266-0100
Fax: (317) 631-3750

THOMSON, Traci L.
Vice President, Human Resources
Tel: (317) 266-0100
Fax: (317) 631-3750

WALSH, Patrick
Executive Vice President, Chief Financial Officer and Chief Operating Officer
Tel: (317) 266-0100
Fax: (317) 631-3750

Emmis Communications Corporation

See listing on page 289 under Emmis Communications

Empire Blue Cross and Blue Shield

A healthcare provider.
www.empireblue.com
Industry/ies: Medicine/Health Care/Mental Health

President and Chief Executive Officer
WAGAR, Mark
Tel: (212) 476-1000
Fax: (518) 367-4565

Main Headquarters
Mailing: One Liberty Plaza
165 Broadway, 13th and 14th Floors
New York City, NY 10006
Tel: (212) 476-1000
Fax: (518) 367-4565
TF: (800) 809-7328

Corporate Foundations and Giving Programs

Empire BlueCross BlueShield Foundation
Contact: Sally Kweskin
One Liberty Plaza
165 Broadway
New York City, NY 10006
Tel: (212) 476-1000
Fax: (518) 367-4565

Public Affairs and Related Activities Personnel

At Headquarters

KWESKIN, Sally
Director, Public Relations
sally.kweskin@empireblue.com
Tel: (303) 831-5899
Fax: (518) 367-4565

Empire District Electric Company

An electric, water and natural gas service utility serving S.W. Missouri, N.W. Arkansas, N.E. Oklahoma and S.E. Kansas.
www.empiredistrict.com
Annual Revenues: $637.20 million
Employees: 751
Ticker: NYSE: EDE
SIC: 4911
Industry/ies: Energy/Electricity; Utilities
Legislative Issues: ADV; CAW; DIS; ENV; ROD; TAX; TRA; UTI

Chairman of the Board
LANEY, D. Randy
Tel: (417) 652-5100
Fax: (417) 635-5146

President and Chief Executive Officer
BEECHER, Bradley P.
bbeecher@empiredistrict.com
Tel: (417) 652-5100
Fax: (417) 635-5146

Main Headquarters
Mailing: 602 S. Joplin Ave.
P.O. Box 127
Joplin, MO 64802
Tel: (417) 652-5100
Fax: (417) 635-5146
TF: (800) 206-2300

Political Action Committees
Empire District Electric Company PAC
FEC ID: C00208249
Contact: Larry Jay Williams
602 S. Joplin Ave.
P.O. Box 127
Joplin, MO 64802

   Contributions to Candidates: $7,500 (2015-2016)
   Democrats: $1,000; Republicans: $6,500

Public Affairs and Related Activities Personnel

At Headquarters

DELANO, Laurie A.
Vice President, Finance and Chief Financial Officer
ldelano@empiredistrict.com
Tel: (417) 652-5100
Fax: (417) 625-5173

HARRINGTON, Dale W
Corporate Secretary and Director of Investor Relations
Tel: (417) 652-5100
Fax: (417) 635-5146

MAUS, Julie
Manager, Media Relations
jmaus@empiredistrict.com
Tel: (417) 625-5101
Fax: (417) 625-5155

SAGER, Robert W
Controller, Assistant Secretary and Assistant Treasurer
Tel: (417) 652-5100
Fax: (417) 635-5146

TIMPE, Mark T
Treasurer
Tel: (417) 652-5100
Fax: (417) 635-5146

WALTERS, Kelly S
Vice President and Chief Operating Officer
Tel: (417) 652-5100
Fax: (417) 635-5146

WILLIAMS, Vicki
Director, Human Resources
vwilliams@empiredistrict.com
Tel: (417) 625-5109
Fax: (417) 635-5146

WILLIAMS, Larry Jay
PAC Treasurer
Tel: (417) 652-5100
Fax: (417) 625-5155

EnCana Oil & Gas (USA), Inc.

An oil and gas explorer, producer and marketer in North America.
www.encana.com
Employees: 1,400
SIC: 1311
Industry/ies: Energy/Electricity; Fuels See Coal, Gas, Oil, Petroleum; Natural Resources; Petroleum Industry
Legislative Issues: CAW; ENG; FUE; NAT

Chairman of the Board
WOITAS, Clayton H.
Tel: (303) 623-2300
Fax: (303) 623-2400

President and Chief Executive Officer
SUTTLES, Doug
Tel: (303) 623-2300
Fax: (303) 623-2400

Main Headquarters
Mailing: 370 17th St.
Suite 1700
Denver, CO 80202
Tel: (303) 623-2300
Fax: (303) 623-2400

Political Action Committees
EnCana Oil and Gas (USA) Inc. PAC
FEC ID: C00431932
Contact: Tamara Miller-Davison
370 17th St.
Suite 1700
Denver, CO 80202

Corporate Foundations and Giving Programs

EnCana Oil & Gas (USA), Inc. Contributions Program
Contact: Bill Oliver

370 17th St.   Tel: (303) 623-2300
Suite 1700   Fax: (303) 623-2400
Denver, CO 80202

Public Affairs and Related Activities Personnel

At Headquarters

ALEXANDER, Joanne   Tel: (303) 623-2300
Executive Vice-President and General Counsel Fax: (303) 623-2400

BRILLON, Sherri   Tel: (303) 623-2300
Executive Vice President and Chief Financial Officer Fax: (303) 623-2400

HOCK, Doug   Tel: (720) 876-5096
Manager, Media Relations   Fax: (303) 623-2400
douglas.hock@encana.com

MCALLISTER, Michael   Tel: (303) 623-2300
Executive Vice-President and Chief Operating Officer Fax: (303) 623-2400

MCRITCHIE, Ryder   Tel: (303) 623-2300
Vice President, Investor Relations and Communications Fax: (303) 623-2400

MILLER-DAVISON, Tamara   Tel: (303) 623-2300
PAC Treasurer   Fax: (303) 623-2400
Tammy.Miller-Davison@encana.com

OLIVER, Bill   Tel: (303) 623-2300
Executive Vice President and Chief Corporate Officer Fax: (303) 623-2400

WILLIAMS, Mike   Tel: (303) 623-2300
Executive Vice-President, Corporate Services Fax: (303) 623-2400

ZEMLJAK, Renee   Tel: (303) 623-2300
Executive Vice-President, Midstream, Marketing and Fax: (303) 623-2400
Fundamentals

Encyclopaedia Britannica, Inc.

Provider of learning and knowledge products.
www.corporate.britannica.com
Annual Revenues: $29.60 million
Employees: 400
SIC: 5963; 2731; 5099; 5942
Industry/ies: Communications; Media/Mass Communication

Chairman of the Board   Tel: (312) 347-7159
SAFRA, Jacob E.   Fax: (312) 294-2158

President   Tel: (312) 347-7159
CAUZ, Jorge   Fax: (312) 294-2104

Main Headquarters
Mailing: 331 N. LaSalle St.   Tel: (312) 347-7159
               Chicago, IL 60654-2682   Fax: (312) 294-2104
                                                TF: (800) 323-1229

Public Affairs and Related Activities Personnel

At Headquarters

BARLOW, Gregory   Tel: (312) 347-7159
Senior Vice President and Chief Marketing Officer Fax: (312) 294-2104

BOWE, William J.   Tel: (312) 347-7159
Executive Vice President and General Counsel Fax: (312) 294-2158

PANELAS, Tom   Tel: (312) 347-7309
Director, Communications   Fax: (312) 347-7225
tpanelas@us.britannica.com

PINTER, Jason   Tel: (312) 347-7309
Chief Financial Officer   Fax: (312) 347-7225

ROSS, Michael   Tel: (312) 347-7159
Senior Vice President and General Manager, Education Fax: (312) 294-2104

TOBACK, Andrea   Tel: (312) 347-7159
Executive Director, Human Resources and Benefits Fax: (312) 294-2158

Endeavor International Corporation

An independent oil and gas company focused on exploring for and developing oil and gas reserves in the North Sea and United States.
www.endeavourcorp.com
Annual Revenues: $60.09 million
Employees: 100
Ticker: NYSE: END
Industry/ies: Energy/Electricity; Fuels See Coal, Gas, Oil, Petroleum; Natural Resources; Petroleum Industry

Chairman, President and Chief Executive Officer   Tel: (713) 307-8700
TRANSIER, William L.

Main Headquarters
Mailing: 811 Main St.   Tel: (713) 307-8700
               Suite 2100
               Houston, TX 77002

Public Affairs and Related Activities Personnel

At Headquarters

KIRKSEY, J. Michael   Tel: (713) 307-8788
Executive Vice President and Chief Financial Officer
Mike.Kirksey@endeavourcorp.com

MATTHEWS, Darcey   Tel: (713) 307-8711
Director, Investor Relations and Corporate Communications
Darcey.Matthews@endeavourcorp.com

MIDKIFF, Ralph A.   Tel: (713) 307-8700
Senior Vice President and General Counsel

STUBBS, Catherine   Tel: (713) 307-8700
Chief Financial Officer and Senior Vice President

Endicott Biofuels LLC

An LLC formed with the purpose of building/operating second-generation biodiesel facilities.
www.endicottbiofuels.com
Ticker: NYSE: EBF
Industry/ies: Energy/Electricity; Natural Resources

Chief Executive Officer   Tel: (281) 598-2180
ROBINSON, David M.   Fax: (281) 598-2181

Main Headquarters
Mailing: Two Northpoint Dr.   Tel: (281) 598-2180
               Suite 950   Fax: (281) 598-2181
               Houston, TX 77060-3236   TF: (866) 503-1505

Public Affairs and Related Activities Personnel

At Headquarters

ALLEN, Richard G.   Tel: (281) 598-2180
Vice President, Global Supply Chain   Fax: (281) 598-2181

BAILEY, Brandi   Tel: (281) 598-2180
Office Manager   Fax: (281) 598-2181
brandi@endicottbiofuels.com

FRANTZ , Christopher J.   Tel: (281) 598-2180
Principal   Fax: (281) 598-2181

HAYSLETT, Roderick   Tel: (281) 598-2180
Chief Financial Officer   Fax: (281) 598-2181

KOTHARI, Shanoop   Tel: (281) 598-2180
Chief Financial Officer   Fax: (281) 598-2181

Endicott Interconnect Technologies, Inc.

Endicott Interconnect Technologies, Inc. (EI) is a electronic manufacturer of electronic interconnect solutions and electro/mechanical equipment.They are in the fabrication and assembly of complex printed circuit boards, advanced flip chip and wire bond semiconductor packaging and precision equipment manufacturing and integration.
www.endicottinterconnect.com
Annual Revenues: $116.3 million
Employees: 1,500
Industry/ies: Aerospace/Aviation; Computer/Technology; Defense/Homeland Security; Electricity & Electronics; Electronics; Energy/Electricity; Government-Related; Transportation

Main Headquarters
Mailing: 1093 Clark St.   Tel: (607) 755-0123
               Building 258   Fax: (607) 755-7000
               Endicott, NY 13760   TF: (866) 820-4820

Public Affairs and Related Activities Personnel

At Headquarters

SLAVETSKY, Edward   Tel: (607) 755-2829
Market Analyst   Fax: (607) 755-7000

Endo Pharmaceuticals

Pharmaceutical company engaged in the research, development, sale and marketing of prescription pharmaceuticals used primarily to treat and manage pain.
www.endo.com
Annual Revenues: $3.12 billion
Employees: 5,062
Ticker: NASDAQ: ENDP
SIC: 2834; 2833
NAICS: 325411; 325412
Industry/ies: Pharmaceutical Industry
Legislative Issues: CPT; HCR; PHA; TAX

Chairman of the Board   Tel: (202) 479-4449
KIMMEL, Roger H.   Fax: (610) 558-8979

President, Chief Executive Officer and Director   Tel: (202) 479-4449
SILVA, Rajiv De   Fax: (610) 558-8979

Main Headquarters
Mailing: 1400 Atwater Dr.   Tel: (484) 216-0000
               Malvern, PA 19355   Fax: (610) 558-8979
                                                TF: (800) 462-3636

Washington Office
Mailing: 499 S. Capitol St. SW   Tel: (202) 479-4449
               Suite 608A
               Washington, DC 20003

Political Action Committees
Endo Pharmaceuticals Inc. PAC (ENDO PAC)
FEC ID: C00452052
Contact: Joseph P. Rosenthal

1400 Atwater Dr. Tel: (610) 558-9800
Malvern, PA 19355 Fax: (610) 558-8979

Contributions to Candidates: $63,000 (2015-2016)
Democrats: $14,500; Republicans: $48,500

Public Affairs and Related Activities Personnel

At Headquarters

DAVIS, Blaine T. Tel: (610) 558-9800
President, Endo Ventures and Senior Vice President, Fax: (610) 558-8979
Corporate Affairs
Davis.Blaine@Endo.com

HALL, Susan Tel: (484) 216-0000
Executive Vice President, Chief Scientific Officer and Global Fax: (610) 558-8979
Head, Research and Development and Quality

ROSENTHAL, Joseph P. Tel: (484) 216-0000
Manager, Investor Relations Fax: (610) 558-8979

At Washington Office

VARGHESE, Hemanth J. Tel: (202) 479-4449
Executive Vice President Corporate Development and
Strategy

CUNNINGHAM, Larry Tel: (202) 479-4449
Executive Vice President, Human Resources

MALETTA, Matthew J. Tel: (202) 479-4449
Executive Vice President, Chief Legal Officer

MATTOX, Keri P. Tel: (202) 479-4449
Senior Vice President, Investor Relations and Corporate
Affairs

MUNROE, James B. Tel: (202) 479-4449
Senior Vice President, Government Affairs
munroe.brian@endo.com
Registered Federal Lobbyist

PHIPPS, Candice Tel: (202) 479-4449
Federal Lobbyist

RUDIO, Daniel A. Tel: (202) 479-4449
Vice President, Controller and Chief Accounting Officer

SCOTT, Andrew Tel: (202) 479-4449
Registered Federal Lobbyist

SMOLLEN, Jon Tel: (202) 479-4449
Vice President and Chief Compliance Officer

UPADHYAY, Suketu Tel: (202) 479-4449
Chief Financial Officer and Executive Vice President

Enel Green Power North America, Inc.

Formerly, Enel North America, Inc. Renewable energy generation company.
www.enelgreenpower.com
Industry/ies: Energy/Electricity
Legislative Issues: ENG

President and Chief Executive Officer Tel: (978) 681-1900
VENTURINI, Francesco Fax: (978) 681-7727

Main Headquarters
Mailing: One Tech Dr. Tel: (978) 681-1900
Suite 220 Fax: (978) 681-7727
Andover, MA 01810

Washington Office
Mailing: 816 Connecticut Ave. NW Tel: (202) 349-0883
Suite 600
Washington, DC 20006

Public Affairs and Related Activities Personnel

At Washington Office

BOBBO, Vanessa Tel: (202) 349-0883
Federal Lobbyist
Registered Federal Lobbyist

OLIVIERI, Francesco Tel: (202) 349-0883
Head, DC Office of Enel Green Power NA

THIROLF, Jack Tel: (202) 349-0883
Associate, Regulatory Affairs
Registered Federal Lobbyist

Enerdel, Inc.

EnerDel designs, builds and manufactures lithium-ion energy storage solutions and battery
systems with a focus on heavy duty transportation, on- and off-grid electrical, mass transit
and task-oriented applications.
www.enerdel.com
Annual Revenues: $23.50 million
Employees: 200
Industry/ies: Energy/Electricity

Chairman of the Board Tel: (317) 585-3400
SNYDER, Thomas J. Fax: (317) 585-3111

Chief Executive Officer Tel: (317) 703-1800
CANADA, Michael Fax: (317) 585-3444

Main Headquarters
Mailing: 3023 Distribution Way Tel: (317) 703-1800
Suite 100 Fax: (317) 585-3444
Greenfield, IN 46140-6837

Public Affairs and Related Activities Personnel

At Headquarters

BOWMAN, James Tel: (317) 703-1800
Corporate Controller & Operations Director Fax: (317) 585-3444

At Other Offices

DAWSON, Kammy Tel: (317) 585-3400
Director, Human Resources Fax: (317) 585-3444
8740 Hague Rd., Building Seven
Indianapolis, IN 46256-1246

EnerG2, Inc.

Developer of energy storage materials.
www.energ2.com
Annual Revenues: $3.80 million
Employees: 19
Industry/ies: Energy/Electricity; Machinery/Equipment

Chief Executive Officer Tel: (206) 547-0445
LUEBBE, Eric Fax: (425) 650-7012

Main Headquarters
Mailing: 100 N.E. Northlake Way Tel: (206) 547-0445
Seattle, WA 98105 Fax: (425) 650-7012

Public Affairs and Related Activities Personnel

At Headquarters

GOTTLIEB, Steven Tel: (206) 427-9591
Contact, Media Relations Fax: (425) 650-7012
s.gottlieb@greenc3.com

WHEATON, Chris Tel: (206) 547-0445
Chief Operating and Financial Officer Fax: (425) 650-7012

Energen Corporation

An energy company, focusing on natural gas distribution, and oil and gas exploration and
production.
www.energen.com
Annual Revenues: $1.18 billion
Employees: 550
Ticker: NYSE: EGN
SIC: 1311
Industry/ies: Energy/Electricity
Legislative Issues: FUE

Chairman, President and Chief Executive Officer Tel: (205) 326-2700
MCMANUS, II, James T. Fax: (205) 326-2704

Main Headquarters
Mailing: 605 Richard Arrington, Jr. Blvd., North Tel: (205) 326-2700
Birmingham, AL 35203-2707 Fax: (205) 326-2704
TF: (888) 764-5603

Political Action Committees
Energen Corporation PAC
FEC ID: C00135855
Contact: Marvell Bivins Jr.
605 Richard Arrington Jr. Blvd. North
Birmingham, AL 35203

Contributions to Candidates: $10,000 (2015-2016)
Democrats: $2,500; Republicans: $7,500

Corporate Foundations and Giving Programs

Energen Foundation
Contact: Lindsay Reddick
605 Richard Arrington, Jr. Blvd., North
Birmingham, AL 35203-2707

Public Affairs and Related Activities Personnel

At Headquarters

BIBB, William K. Tel: (205) 326-2700
Vice President, Human Resources Fax: (205) 326-2704

BIVINS, Jr., Marvell Tel: (205) 326-2700
Vice President, Audit and Compliance and PAC Treasurer Fax: (205) 326-2704

COOK, Joe E. Tel: (205) 326-8129
Senior Vice President, Legal and Assistant Secretary Fax: (205) 326-2704

MINOR, David J. Tel: (205) 326-2700
Senior Vice President, Operations Fax: (205) 326-2704

PORTER, Jr., Charles W. Tel: (205) 326-2700
Vice President, Chief Financial Officer and Treasurer Fax: (205) 326-2704
CPORTER@ENERGEN.COM

REDDICK, Lindsay Tel: (205) 326-2700

Coordinator, Community Affairs	Fax:	(205) 326-2704
RICHARDSON, John S.	Tel:	(205) 326-2725
President and Chief Operating Officer	Fax:	(205) 326-2704
RYLAND, Julie S.	Tel:	(205) 326-8421
Vice President, Investor Relations	Fax:	(205) 326-2704
SEWELL, Linda M.	Tel:	(205) 326-2700
Vice President, External Affairs	Fax:	(205) 326-2704
WOODRUFF, J. David	Tel:	(205) 326-2700
Vice President, General Counsel and Secretary	Fax:	(205) 326-2704
j.david.woodruff@energen.com		

Energizer Holdings

A consumer goods company of various household and personal care products. It manufactures and markets primary batteries, portable lighting, and personal care products.
www.energizer.com
Annual Revenues: $1.61 billion
Employees: 5,100
Ticker: NYSE: ENR
SIC: 3690
Industry/ies: Cosmetics & Cosmetology; Energy/Electricity; Personal Care/Hygiene

Chairman of the Board	Fax:	(314) 985-2205
MULCAHY, Patrick J.		
Chief Executive Officer	Tel:	(314) 985-2000
HOSKINS, Alan R.	Fax:	(314) 985-2205
Main Headquarters		
Mailing: 533 Maryville University Dr.	Tel:	(314) 985-2000
St. Louis, MO 63141	Fax:	(314) 985-2205
	TF:	(800) 383-7323

Corporate Foundations and Giving Programs

Energizer Battery Manufacturing Contributions Program
533 Maryville University Dr.
St. Louis, MO 63141

Energizer Holdings Contributions Program		
533 Maryville University Dr.	Tel:	(314) 985-2000
St. Louis, MO 63141	Fax:	(314) 985-2205

Public Affairs and Related Activities Personnel

At Headquarters

BURWITZ, Jacqueline E.	Tel:	(314) 985-2000
Vice President, Investor Relations	Fax:	(314) 985-2224
jacquelineE.burwitz@energizer.com		
CEOTTO, Teresa	Tel:	(314) 985-2000
Vice President, Human Resources	Fax:	(314) 985-2205
DRATH, Sue	Tel:	(314) 985-2000
Chief Human Resource Officer	Fax:	(314) 985-2205
GREENMAN, Erin	Tel:	(314) 704-1983
Contact, Media Relations	Fax:	(314) 982-2205
HAMM, Brian K.	Tel:	(314) 985-2000
Executive Vice President and Chief Financial Officer	Fax:	(314) 985-2205
LAVIGNE, Mark S.	Tel:	(314) 985-2000
Executive Vice President and Chief Operating Officer	Fax:	(314) 985-2205
mark.lavigne@energizer.com		

EnergX, LLC

Provides engineering services and management consulting services.
www.energxllc.com
Annual Revenues: $22.80 million
Employees: 100
Industry/ies: Energy/Electricity

President and Chief Executive Officer	Tel:	(865) 483-9288
BUHL, Anthony R.	Fax:	(865) 483-9811
anthonybuhl@energxllc.com		
Main Headquarters		
Mailing: 1000B Clearview Ct.	Tel:	(865) 483-9288
Oak Ridge, TN 37830	Fax:	(865) 483-9811
	TF:	(866) 932-1333

Public Affairs and Related Activities Personnel

At Headquarters

II, Anthony Buhl	Tel:	(865) 298-1376
Director, Operations	Fax:	(865) 483-9811
abuhl2@energxllc.com		

Energy Conversion Devices, Inc.

Manufactures and sells thin-film solar laminates that convert sunlight to energy using proprietary technology.
www.energyconversiondevices.com
Annual Revenues: $232.55 million
Employees: 1,300
Ticker: NASDAQ: ENER

SIC: 3674
Industry/ies: Energy/Electricity; Environment And Conservation

Chairman of the Board	Tel:	(248) 293-0440
RABINOWITZ, Stephen	Fax:	(248) 364-5678
Main Headquarters		
Mailing: 3800 Lapeer Rd.	Tel:	(248) 475-0100
Auburn Hills, MI 48326	Fax:	(248) 364-5678

Corporate Foundations and Giving Programs

Energy Conversion Devices, Inc. Contributions Program		
3800 Lapeer Rd.	Tel:	(248) 293-0440
Auburn Hills, MI 48326	Fax:	(248) 364-5678

Public Affairs and Related Activities Personnel

At Headquarters

"KRISS" ANDREWS, William C.	Tel:	(248) 475-0100
Executive Vice President and Chief Financial Officer	Fax:	(248) 364-5678
AMYUNI, Ted F.	Tel:	(248) 293-0440
Executive Vice President, Global Sales	Fax:	(248) 364-5678

Energy Future Holdings Corporation

A provider of integrated energy solutions. Formerly named TXU Corporation (Texas Utilities). Headquartered in Dallas, TX.
www.energyfutureholdings.com
Annual Revenues: $8.24 billion
Employees: 9,300
SIC: 4911
Industry/ies: Energy/Electricity; Utilities
Legislative Issues: CAW; ENG; ENV; GOV; HOM; INT; TAX; UTI; WAS

Executive Chairman	Tel:	(214) 812-4600
EVANS, Donald L.		
President and Chief Executive Officer	Tel:	(214) 812-4600
YOUNG, John F.		
Main Headquarters		
Mailing: Energy Plaza	Tel:	(214) 812-4600
1601 Bryan St.	TF:	(877) 277-9913
Dallas, TX 75201		
Washington Office		
Mailing: 601 Pennsylvania Ave. NW	Tel:	(202) 628-1020
Suite 850, South Bldg.	Fax:	(202) 628-1007
Washington, DC 20004		

Political Action Committees

Energy PAC of Energy Future Holdings Corporation
FEC ID: C00226548
Contact: Jeff Westerheide
1601 Bryan St.
Dallas, TX 75201

Contributions to Candidates: $81,500 (2015-2016)
Democrats: $16,000; Republicans: $65,500

Corporate Foundations and Giving Programs

Energy Future Holdings Corporation Contributions Program
Energy Plaza
1601 Bryan St.
Dallas, TX 75201

Public Affairs and Related Activities Personnel

At Headquarters

DORÉ, Stacey	Tel:	(214) 812-4600
Executive Vice President and General Counsel		
KEGLEVIC, Paul	Tel:	(214) 812-4600
Executive Vice President and Chief Financial Officer		
paul.keglevic@energyfutureholdings.com		
KIRBY, Carrie	Tel:	(214) 812-4600
Executive Vice President, Human Resources		
KOENIG, Allan	Tel:	(214) 812-4600
Vice President, Corporate Communications		
Media.Relations@energyfutureholdings.com		
LANDY, Richard	Tel:	(214) 812-4600
Chief Human Resource Officer		
WESTERHEIDE, Jeff	Tel:	(214) 812-4600
Director, Information Technology Security and Compliance Services		

At Washington Office

LYNCH, David	Tel:	(202) 628-1020
Vice President, Federal Advocacy	Fax:	(202) 628-1007
Registered Federal Lobbyist		
MCNEILL, Laura	Tel:	(202) 628-1020
Lobbyist	Fax:	(202) 628-1007
Registered Federal Lobbyist		
O'BRIEN, John	Tel:	(202) 628-1020
Executive Vice President, Public Policy and External Affairs	Fax:	(202) 628-1007

Registered Federal Lobbyist

EnergySolutions, Inc.

A U.S. subsidiary of British Nuclear Fuels PLC (see separate listing). A full service nuclear waste management, decommissioning, engineering, spent fuel storage, and nuclear materials handling company. It provides integrated services and solutions to the nuclear industry. Acquired Envirocare of Utah in 2006.
www.energysolutions.com
Annual Revenues: $2.69 billion
Employees: 5,000
Ticker: NYSE:ES
SIC: 4955
Industry/ies: Energy/Electricity; Environment And Conservation; Pollution And Waste
Legislative Issues: ENG

Chief Executive Officer and President   Tel: (801) 649-2000
LOCKWOOD, David   Fax: (801) 321-0453

Main Headquarters
Mailing: 423 W. 300 South   Tel: (801) 649-2000
   Suite 2   Fax: (801) 321-0453
   Salt Lake City, UT 84101

Political Action Committees
EnergySolutions, inc. Fund for Effective Government (EnergySolutions PAC)
FEC ID: C00387878
Contact: J. Casey Hill
423 West 300 South
Suite 300
Saltlake City, UT 84101

   Contributions to Candidates: $25,200 (2015-2016)
   Democrats: $5,000; Republicans: $20,200

Corporate Foundations and Giving Programs

Energy Solutions Foundation
Contact: Golda Addo
P.O. Box 510583   Tel: (801) 649-2286
Salt Lake City, UT 84151   Fax: (801) 413-5697

Public Affairs and Related Activities Personnel

At Headquarters

HILL, J. Casey   Tel: (801) 649-2000
Senior Vice President, Government and Community Relations   Fax: (801) 321-0453
and PAC Treasurer

JONES, Pauline   Tel: (202) 355-9330
Manager, Government Relations   Fax: (202) 293-1829

NAPIER, Victoria   Tel: (801) 649-2000
Senior Vice President, Federal Government Relations   Fax: (801) 321-0453

WALKER, Mark   Tel: (801) 649-2194
Vice President, Marketing and Media Relations   Fax: (801) 321-0453
mwalker@energysolutions.com

WOOD, Greg   Tel: (801) 649-2000
Executive Vice President, Chief Financial Officer   Fax: (801) 321-0453

At Other Offices

ADDO, Golda   Tel: (801) 649-2286
Founder and Managing Director, Foundation   Fax: (801) 413-5697
P.O. Box 510583
Salt Lake City, UT 84151

EnerNOC, Inc.

EnerNOC, Inc. is a developer and provider of energy solutions to utilities and electric power grid operators, as well as commercial, institutional, and industrial customers.
www.enernoc.com
Annual Revenues: $469.99 million
Employees: 1,074
Ticker: NASDAQ: ENOC
SIC: 7370
Industry/ies: Computer/Technology

Chairman of the Board and Chief Executive Officer   Tel: (617) 224-9900
HEALY, Timothy G.   Fax: (617) 224-9910

Main Headquarters
Mailing: One Marina Park Dr.   Tel: (617) 224-9900
   Suite 400   Fax: (617) 224-9910
   Boston, MA 02210

Corporate Foundations and Giving Programs

EnerNOC, Inc. Contributtions Program
101 Federal St.   Tel: (617) 224-9900
Suite 300   Fax: (617) 224-9910
Boston, MA 02110

Public Affairs and Related Activities Personnel

At Headquarters

HISS, Fielder   Tel: (617) 224-9900
Vice President, Marketing and Product Management   Fax: (617) 224-9910

JENKINS, Don   Tel: (617) 224-9900

Vice President, Operations   Fax: (617) 224-9910

LYNCH, Holly   Tel: (617) 224-9900
Senior Vice President, Human Resources   Fax: (617) 224-9910

MCAULEY, Sarah   Tel: (617) 224-9900
Media and Investor Relations Contact   Fax: (617) 224-9910
smcauley@enernoc.com

MOSES, Neil   Tel: (617) 224-9900
Chief Financial Officer   Fax: (617) 224-9910

SAMUELS, David   Tel: (617) 224-9900
Entrepreneur, Advisor   Fax: (617) 224-9910

SCHISLER, Ken   Tel: (617) 224-9900
Vice President, Regulatory Affairs   Fax: (617) 224-9910

At Other Offices

O'NEILL, Patricia   Tel: (617) 224-9900
Vice President, Human Resources   Fax: (617) 224-9910
101 Federal St., Suite 300
Boston, MA 02110

Enersys Energy Products Inc.

A manufacturer, marketer and distributor of industrial batteries, battery chargers, power equipment, battery accessories and outdoor equipment enclosure solutions to customers worldwide.
www.enersys.com
Annual Revenues: $2.51 billion
Employees: 9,500
Ticker: NYSE: ENS
SIC: 3629; 3691; 5063
NAICS: 42161; 335999; 335911; 335912
Industry/ies: Energy/Electricity
Legislative Issues: DEF

Chairman of the Board, President and Chief Executive Officer   Tel: (610) 208-1991
CRAIG, John D.   Fax: (610) 372-8457

Main Headquarters
Mailing: 2366 Bernville Rd.   Tel: (610) 208-1991
   Reading, PA 19605   Fax: (610) 372-8457
   TF: (800) 538-3627

Public Affairs and Related Activities Personnel

At Headquarters

O'NEILL, Thomas L.   Tel: (610) 236-4040
Vice President & Treasurer   Fax: (610) 372-8457
investorrelations@enersys.com

SCHMIDTLEIN, Michael J.   Tel: (610) 208-1991
Senior Vice President, Finance and Chief Financial Officer   Fax: (610) 372-8457

SECHRIST, Todd M.   Tel: (610) 208-1991
President - Americas   Fax: (610) 372-8457

SHAFFER, David M.   Tel: (610) 208-1991
President and Chief Operating Officer   Fax: (610) 372-8457

ZUIDEMA, Richard W.   Tel: (610) 208-1991
Executive Vice President, Media Contact   Fax: (610) 372-8457
mediacontact@enersys.com

Enesco Group Inc.

See listing on page 293 under Enesco, LLC

Enesco, LLC

The company is a global marketer of porcelain and cold-cast collectibles (figurines, cottages), giftware (ornaments, music boxes, plush animals), garden accessories, and home décor (tableware, sculpture). It distributes products to a wide variety of specialty card and gift retailers, home décor boutiques, as well as mass-market chains and direct mail retailers.
www.enesco.com
Annual Revenues: $49.10 million
Employees: 1,100
SIC: 5199; 3469; 5099; 9999; 9999; 5190
Industry/ies: Retail/Wholesale

Chairman of the Board   Tel: (630) 875-5300
BOUSQUETTE, Matthew C.   Fax: (630) 875-5350

Chief Executive Officer   Tel: (630) 875-5300
BOWLES, Thomas G.   Fax: (630) 875-5350

Main Headquarters
Mailing: 225 Windsor Dr.   Tel: (630) 875-5300
   Itasca, IL 60143   Fax: (630) 875-5350
   TF: (800) 436-3726

Public Affairs and Related Activities Personnel

At Headquarters

BERNAR, Doris   Tel: (630) 875-5524
Sr. Executive Assistant to Chief Executive Officer & Chief   Fax: (630) 875-5350
Operating Officer / Chief Financial Offic
dbernar@enesco.com

EISCHEID, Theodore J.   Tel: (630) 875-5300

Chief Operating Officer & Chief Financial Officer	Fax:	(630) 875-5350
FRIGHETTO, Jennifer	Tel:	(847) 702-5304
Senior Public Relations, Communications Consultant	Fax:	(630) 875-5350
jennifer@frighettocommunications.com		
LENTZSCH, Kathi P.	Tel:	(630) 875-5300
Chief Merchandising Officer	Fax:	(630) 875-5350

Engaging Company

Public affairs.

Main Headquarters

Mailing:	4340 E. Indian School Rd.	Tel:	(602) 574-8878
	Suite 21-551	Fax:	(602) 391-2435
	Phoenix, AZ 85018		

Public Affairs and Related Activities Personnel

At Headquarters

RAGAN, John	Tel:	(602) 574-8878
Partner	Fax:	(602) 391-2435
STRONGIN, Camilla	Tel:	(602) 574-8878
Partner	Fax:	(602) 391-2435

Enlink Geoenergy Services, Inc.

EnLink Geoenergy Services is the industry in providing geothermal earth-heat exchange solutions to governments, businesses, institutions and consumers throughout the United States.
www.enlinkgeoenergy.com
Annual Revenues: $7 million
Employees: 46
Industry/ies: Energy/Electricity; Heating And Air Conditioning

Chairman of the Board	Tel:	(310) 217-4150
MACDONALD, Robert	Fax:	(310) 217-4047

President and Chief Executive Officer	Tel:	(310) 217-4150
MIZRAHI , Mark	Fax:	(310) 217-4047

Main Headquarters

Mailing:	879 W. 190th St.	Tel:	(310) 217-4150
	Suite 400	Fax:	(310) 217-4047
	Gardena, CA 90248		

Public Affairs and Related Activities Personnel

At Headquarters

FERNADEZ, Javier	Tel:	(310) 217-4150
Senior Vice President, Finance	Fax:	(310) 217-4047
RUIZ, Rick	Tel:	(310) 393-1561
Contact, Media Relations	Fax:	(310) 217-4047

EnPro Industries

Providers of engineered industrial products for processing, general manufacturing and other industries worldwide.
www.enproindustries.com
Annual Revenues: $1.21 billion
Employees: 4,900
Ticker: NYSE: NPO
SIC: 3050
Industry/ies: Machinery/Equipment

Non-Executive Chairman	Tel:	(704) 731-1500
HARNETT, Gordon D.	Fax:	(704) 731-1511

President and Chief Executive Officer	Tel:	(704) 731-1500
MACADAM, Stephen E.	Fax:	(704) 731-1511

Main Headquarters

Mailing:	5605 Carnegie Blvd.	Tel:	(704) 731-1500
	Suite 500	Fax:	(704) 731-1511
	Charlotte, NC 28209-4674	TF:	(800) 231-5469

Political Action Committees

Enpro Industries Inc. PAC
FEC ID: C00379784
Contact: David S. Burnett
5605 Carnegie Blvd.
Suite 500
Charlotte, NC 28209

> **Contributions to Candidates:** $19,500 (2015-2016)
> Democrats: $10,000; Republicans: $9,500

Public Affairs and Related Activities Personnel

At Headquarters

BURNETT, David S.	Tel:	(704) 731-1500
PAC Treasurer, Vice President, Treasury and Tax	Fax:	(704) 731-1511
CHILDRESS, J. Milton	Tel:	(704) 731-1500
Senior Vice President and Chief Financial Officer	Fax:	(704) 731-1511
MCKINNEY, Robert P.	Tel:	(704) 731-1500
Vice President, General Counsel and Secretary	Fax:	(704) 731-1511
bob.mckinney@enproindustries.com		

MCLEAN, Robert S.	Tel:	(704) 731-1500
Vice President, General Counsel and Secretary	Fax:	(704) 731-1511
robert.mclean@enproindustries.com		
WASHINGTON, Don	Tel:	(704) 731-1527
Director, Investor Relations and Communications	Fax:	(704) 731-1511
don.washington@enproindustries.com		

ENSCO Inc.

Provides engineering, science and advanced technology solutions for the defense, security, transportation and aerospace industries.
www.ensco.com
Annual Revenues: $88.51 million
Employees: 700
Ticker: NYSE: ESV
NAICS: 213111
Industry/ies: Engineering/Mathematics
Legislative Issues: TRA

Executive Chairman of the Board	Tel:	(703) 321-9000
BROOME, Paul W.	Fax:	(703) 321-4529
pbroome3@ensco.com		

President	Tel:	(703) 321-9000
NEJIKOVSKY, Boris	Fax:	(703) 321-4529

Main Headquarters

Mailing:	3110 Fairview Park Dr.	Tel:	(703) 321-9000
	Suite 300	Fax:	(703) 321-4529
	Falls Church, VA 22042	TF:	(800) 367-2682

Public Affairs and Related Activities Personnel

At Headquarters

BOGDANOVIC, Milan J.	Tel:	(214) 397-3000
Treasurer and Chief Financial Officer	Fax:	(703) 321-4529
MCDONALD, Joanne	Tel:	(703) 321-9000
Vice President, Chief Ethics Officer, Corporate Secretary	Fax:	(703) 321-4529
mcdonald@ensco.com		
SIVEK, Karen	Tel:	(703) 321-9000
Division Manager, Human Resources	Fax:	(703) 321-4529

Ensign-Bickford Industries, Inc

Manufacturer of blast-initiation systems and blasting products. Formerly the Ensign-Bickford Company.
www.ensign-bickfordind.com
Annual Revenues: $185.20 million
Employees: 1,600
SIC: 2892; 3531
Industry/ies: Construction/Construction Materials

Chairman of the Board	Tel:	(860) 843-2000
LOVEJOY, Jr., Joseph E.	Fax:	(860) 843-2600

Main Headquarters

Mailing:	125 Powder Forest Dr., Third Floor	Tel:	(860) 843-2000
	P.O. Box SEVEN	Fax:	(860) 843-2600
	Simsbury, CT 06070-0007		

Public Affairs and Related Activities Personnel

At Headquarters

DEAKIN, Scott M.	Tel:	(860) 843-2000
Executive Vice President, Chief Financial Officer	Fax:	(860) 843-2600

Entegris

Entegris has been a provider of critical products and materials used in advanced high-technology manufacturing. These products and materials are often used to make the building blocks of many of the world's most complex microelectronic products, such as computers, mobile devices and phones, data storage components, televisions and monitors, and automobiles.
www.entegris.com
Annual Revenues: $1.08 billion
Employees: 3,419
Ticker: NASDAQ:ENTG
SIC: 3089
Industry/ies: Commodities; Energy/Electricity; Natural Resources; Science; Scientific Research

Chairman of the Board	Tel:	(978) 436-6500
OLSON, Paul L. H.	Fax:	(978) 436-6735

President and Chief Executive Officer	Tel:	(978) 436-6500
LOY, Bertrand	Fax:	(978) 436-6735

Main Headquarters

Mailing:	129 Concord Rd.	Tel:	(978) 436-6500
	Billerica, MA 01821	Fax:	(978) 436-6735

Corporate Foundations and Giving Programs

Entegris Contribution Programs
129 Concord Rd.
Billerica, MA 01821

Public Affairs and Related Activities Personnel

At Headquarters

CANTOR, Steve
Vice President, Corporate Relations
steven_cantor@entegris.com
Tel: (978) 436-6750
Fax: (978) 436-6735

EDLUND , Todd
Senior Vice President and Chief Operating Officer
Tel: (978) 436-6500
Fax: (978) 436-6735

GRAVES, Gregory B.
Senior Vice President and Chief Financial Officer
Tel: (978) 436-6500
Fax: (978) 436-6735

MURPHY, John
Senior Vice President, Human Resources
Tel: (978) 436-6500
Fax: (978) 436-6735

RUCCI, Corey
Vice President, Business Development
Tel: (978) 436-6500
Fax: (978) 436-6735

WALCOTT, Peter
Senior Vice President, General Counsel and Corporate Secretary
Tel: (978) 436-6500
Fax: (978) 436-6735

Enterasys Networks

Computer software and hardware producer.
www.enterasys.com
Annual Revenues: $65.90 million
Employees: 800
Ticker: NYSE: ETS
SIC: 3576
Industry/ies: Computer/Technology

President and Chief Executive Officer
CROWELL, Chris
Tel: (603) 952-5000
Fax: (603) 952-6909

Main Headquarters
Mailing: Nine Northeastern Blvd.
Salem, NH 03079
Tel: (603) 952-5000
Fax: (603) 952-6909
TF: (800) 653-6956

Public Affairs and Related Activities Personnel

At Headquarters

AFSHAR, Vala
Chief Marketing Officer and Chief Customer Officer
vafshar@enterasys.com
Tel: (603) 952-5000
Fax: (603) 952-6909

HAYES, Padraig
Chief Financial Officer
pahayes@enterasys.com
Tel: (603) 952-5000
Fax: (603) 952-6909

KING, Jason
Manager, Corporate Communications
jaking@enterasys.com
Tel: (603) 952-5000
Fax: (603) 952-6909

Entergy Arkansas, Inc.

A subsidiary of Entergy Corporation.
www.entergy-arkansas.com
Annual Revenues: $2.17 billion
Employees: 1,160
Ticker: NYSE: EHA
SIC: 4911
Industry/ies: Energy/Electricity

Chairman of the Board and Chief Executive Officer
DENAULT, Leo P.
Tel: (501) 377-4000
Fax: (501) 377-4448

President and Chief Executive Officer
MCDONALD, Hugh
Tel: (501) 377-4000
Fax: (501) 377-4448

Main Headquarters
Mailing: P.O. Box 551
Little Rock, AR 72203
Tel: (501) 377-4434
Fax: (501) 377-4448
TF: (800) 368-3749

Corporate Foundations and Giving Programs

Entergy Charitable Foundation
Contact: Marsha Udouj
1600 Perdido St.
Bldg. 529
New Orleans, LA 70112

Public Affairs and Related Activities Personnel

At Headquarters

BROWN, Marcus V.
Senior Vice President and General Counsel
Tel: (501) 377-4434
Fax: (501) 377-4448

DAUGHERTY, Dan H.
Manager, Communications
DDAUGHE@entergy.com
Tel: (501) 377-4000
Fax: (501) 377-4448

DESPEAUX, Kimberly H.
Senior Vice President, (Federal Policy, Regulatory & Governmental Affairs)
Tel: (501) 377-4434
Fax: (501) 377-4448

KULAKOWSKI, Anne
Director, Investor Relations
akulako@entergy.com
Tel: (504) 576-6674
Fax: (501) 377-4448

MARSH, Andrew "Drew"
Tel: (501) 377-4434

Executive Vice President and Chief Financial Officer
Fax: (501) 377-4448

PETTY, Claire
Manager, Investor Relations
cpetty@entergy.com
Tel: (504) 576-5621
Fax: (501) 377-4448

SAVOFF, Mark T.
Executive Vice President and Chief Operating Officer
Tel: (501) 377-4434
Fax: (501) 377-4448

THOMPSON, James
Senior Communications Specialist
jthomp5@entergy.com
Tel: (501) 377-4000
Fax: (501) 377-4448

UDOUJ, Marsha
Contributions Coordinator
Tel: (501) 377-3522
Fax: (501) 377-4448

VINCI, Don
Senior Vice President, Human Resources and Chief Diversity Officer
Tel: (501) 377-4434
Fax: (501) 377-4448

WATERS, Paula
Vice President, Investor Relations
pwater1@entergy.com
Tel: (504) 576-4380
Fax: (501) 377-4448

WEST, Rod
Executive Vice President and Chief Administrative Officer
Tel: (501) 377-4434
Fax: (501) 377-4448

Entergy Corporation

An electric utilities holding company and power producer. The integrated utility holding company's subsidiaries distribute electricity to more than 2.7 million customers in four southern states (Arkansas, Louisiana, Mississippi, and Texas) and provide natural gas to 191,000 customers in Louisiana.
www.entergy.com
Annual Revenues: $11.20 billion
Employees: 13,579
Ticker: NYSE: ETR
SIC: 4911
Industry/ies: Energy/Electricity; Utilities
Legislative Issues: AGR; BUD; CAW; COM; ENG; ENV; HOM; TAX; TRA; UTI

Chairman of the Board and Chief Executive Officer
DENAULT, Leo P.
Tel: (504) 576-4000
Fax: (504) 576-4428

Main Headquarters
Mailing: 639 Loyola Ave.
New Orleans, LA 70113
Tel: (504) 576-4000
Fax: (504) 576-4428
TF: (800) 368-3749

Washington Office
Mailing: 101 Constitution Ave. NW
Suite 200 E
Washington, DC 20001
Tel: (202) 530-7300
Fax: (202) 530-7350

Political Action Committees
Entergy Corporation PAC (EnPAC)
FEC ID: C00363879
Contact: Andrea Weinstein
425 W. Capitol Ave.
Suite 24B
Little Rock, AR 72201
Tel: (202) 530-7300
Fax: (202) 530-7350

Contributions to Candidates: $267,000 (2015-2016)
Democrats: $64,500; Republicans: $202,500

Principal Recipients

HOUSE
BOEHNER, JOHN A. (REP-OH)
HOYER, STENY HAMILTON (DEM-DC)
SCALISE, STEVE MR. (REP-LA)
UPTON, FREDERICK STEPHEN (REP-MI)

Corporate Foundations and Giving Programs

Entergy Charitable Foundation
Contact: Patty Riddle-Barger
1600 Perdido St.
Bldg. 529
New Orleans, LA 70112

Public Affairs and Related Activities Personnel

At Headquarters

BROWN, Marcus V.
Executive Vice President and General Counsel
Tel: (504) 576-4000
Fax: (504) 576-4428

HINNENKAMP, Paul D.
Senior Vice President and Chief Operating Officer
Tel: (504) 576-4000
Fax: (504) 576-4428

LAGARDE, Chanel
Contact, Media Relations
clagar1@entergy.com
Tel: (504) 576-4000
Fax: (504) 576-4428

MARSH, Andrew "Drew"
Executive Vice President and Chief Financial Officer
Tel: (504) 576-4000
Fax: (504) 576-4428

RIDDLE-BARGER, Patty
Director, Corporate Contributions
driddl1@entergy.com
Tel: (504) 576-6116
Fax: (504) 576-4428

SAVOFF, Mark T.
Executive Vice President and Chief Operating Officer
Tel: (501) 576-4000
Fax: (504) 576-4428

VINCI, Don
Tel: (504) 576-4000

Executive Vice President, Shared Services and Human Resources and Chief Diversity Officer	Fax:	(504) 576-4428
WEST, Rod	Tel:	(504) 576-4000
Executive Vice President	Fax:	(504) 576-4428

At Washington Office

DESPEAUX, Kimberly H.	Tel:	(202) 530-7300
Senior Vice President, Federal Policy, Regulatory and Governmental Affairs	Fax:	(202) 530-7350
GRAVES, Allison L.	Tel:	(504) 576-4214
Federal Lobbyist	Fax:	(202) 530-7350
agrave1@entergy.com		
Registered Federal Lobbyist		
HALL, Robert	Tel:	(202) 530-7300
Registered Federal Lobbyist	Fax:	(202) 530-7350
PETERS, Darren	Tel:	(202) 530-7300
Government Affairs Manager	Fax:	(202) 530-7350
Registered Federal Lobbyist		
PRIDE, Ann L.	Tel:	(202) 530-7300
Director, Public Affairs Policy and Strategy	Fax:	(202) 530-7350
apride@entergy.com		
SCHATTE, Conrad	Tel:	(202) 530-7300
Director, Federal Government Affairs	Fax:	(202) 530-7350
Registered Federal Lobbyist		
WILLIAMS, Jeffrey L.	Tel:	(202) 530-7300
Federal Lobbyist	Fax:	(202) 530-7350
jwill35@entergy.com		
Registered Federal Lobbyist		

At Other Offices

ARNOLD, Kay Kelly	Tel:	(501) 377-3553
Vice President		
425 W. Capitol Ave., Suite 24B		
Little Rock, AR 72201		
karnold@entergy.com		
DREHER, Murphy A.	Tel:	(225) 381-5849
Vice President, Government Affairs		
446 North Blvd.		
Baton Rouge, LA 70802		
mdreher@entergy.com		
GRAHAM, Sally	Tel:	(501) 377-4382
Contact, Media		
P.O. Box 61000, L-ENT-8B		
New Orleans, LA 70161		
sgraha3@entergy.com		
SLOAN, Robert D.	Tel:	(501) 377-4382
Executive Vice President, General Counsel and Secretary		
P.O. Box 61000, L-ENT-8B		
New Orleans, LA 70161		
rsloan@entergy.com		
TRAHAN, Beverly	Tel:	(225) 381-5764
Manager, External Affairs		
446 North Blvd.		
Baton Rouge, LA 70802		
btraha1@entergy.com		
UDOUJ, Marsha	Tel:	(501) 377-3522
Contributions Coordinator		
P.O. Box 61000, L-ENT-8B		
New Orleans, LA 70161		
WEINSTEIN, Andrea	Tel:	(501) 377-3553
PAC Treasurer		
425 W. Capitol Ave., Suite 24B		
Little Rock, AR 72201		

Entergy Gulf States, Inc.

See listing on page 295 under Entergy Corporation

Entergy Mississippi

Formerly known as Mississippi Power and Light Co. An electric utility subsidiary of Entergy Corp. (see separate listing).
www.entergy-mississippi.com
Annual Revenues: $1.27 billion
Employees: 800
Ticker: NYSE: EFM
SIC: 4911
Industry/ies: Energy/Electricity

President and Chief Executive Officer	Tel:	(601) 368-5000
FISACKERLY, Haley	Fax:	(601) 969-2583

Main Headquarters

Mailing:	308 E. Pearl St.	Tel:	(601) 368-5000
	Jackson, MS 39201	Fax:	(601) 969-2583
		TF:	(800) 368-3749

Corporate Foundations and Giving Programs

Entergy Charitable Foundation
Contact: Valarie Mabry
1600 Perdido St.
Bldg. 529
New Orleans, LA 70112

Public Affairs and Related Activities Personnel

At Headquarters

ARLEDGE, John	Tel:	(601) 368-5000
Vice President, Public Affairs	Fax:	(601) 969-2583
CASE, Darron	Tel:	(601) 368-5000
Director, Resource Planning and Market Operations	Fax:	(601) 969-2583
DESPEAUX, Kimberly H.	Tel:	(601) 368-5000
Senior Vice President, Federal Policy, Regulatory and Governmental Affairs	Fax:	(601) 969-2583
GRENFELL, Robert	Tel:	(601) 368-5000
Vice President, Regulatory Affairs	Fax:	(601) 969-2583
JETER, James "Robbin"	Tel:	(601) 368-5000
Vice President, Customer Service	Fax:	(601) 969-2583
MABRY, Valarie	Tel:	(601) 969-4825
Coordinator, Contributions	Fax:	(601) 969-2583
vmabry@entergy.com		

Entergy New Orleans, Inc.

An electric and gas utility serving Orleans Parish.
www.entergy-neworleans.com
Annual Revenues: $650.42 million
Employees: 298
Ticker: NYSE: ENJ
SIC: 4931
Industry/ies: Utilities

President and Chief Executive Officer	Tel:	(504) 576-4000
RICE, Charles	Fax:	(504) 576-4269

Main Headquarters

Mailing:	1600 Perdido St.	Tel:	(504) 576-4000
	Building 529	Fax:	(504) 576-4269
	New Orleans, LA 70112	TF:	(800) 368-3749

Corporate Foundations and Giving Programs

Entergy Charitable Foundation
1600 Perdido St.
Bldg. 529
New Orleans, LA 70112

Public Affairs and Related Activities Personnel

At Headquarters

CORCORAN, Theresa	Tel:	(504) 670-3632
Coordinator, Contributions	Fax:	(504) 576-4269
tcorcor@entergy.com		
GARIBALDI, Alvin	Tel:	(504) 576-4000
Governmental Affairs Executive	Fax:	(504) 576-4001
MOLNAR, Steve	Tel:	(504) 670-3635
Project Manager	Fax:	(504) 576-4269
imolnar@entergy.com		

At Other Offices

ARNOLD, Kay Kelly	Fax:	(501) 337-4448
PAC Contact		
425 W. Capitol Ave., Suite 24B		
Little Rock, AR 72201		

Entergy Texas

An electric utility formerly known as Gulf States Utilities Co. A subsidiary of Entergy Corp. (see separate listing).
www.entergy-texas.com
Annual Revenues: $98 million
Employees: 1,000
Ticker: NYSE : EDT
SIC: 4911
Industry/ies: Energy/Electricity

President and Chief Executive Officer	Tel:	(409) 838-6631
RAINER, Sallie	Fax:	(409) 839-3074

Main Headquarters

Mailing:	P.O. Box 2951	Tel:	(409) 838-6631
	Beaumont, TX 77704	Fax:	(409) 839-3074
		TF:	(800) 729-7483

Corporate Foundations and Giving Programs

Entergy Texas Charitable Foundation
Contact: Mary Young
350 Pine St.
Beaumont, TX 77701

Public Affairs and Related Activities Personnel

At Headquarters

BLAKLEY, Jack
Vice President, Regulatory Affairs
Tel: (409) 838-6631
Fax: (409) 839-3074

DERRICK, Debi
Senior Communications Specialist
dderric@entergy.com
Tel: (409) 838-6631
Fax: (409) 839-3074

YOUNG, Mary
Coordinator, Contributions
myoung2@entergy.com
Tel: (409) 981-2656
Fax: (409) 839-3074

Enterprise Holdings Inc. (Enterprise Rent-A-Car)

An automobile rental company.
www.enterpriseholdings.com
Annual Revenues: $17.80 billion
Employees: 83,000
Industry/ies: Automotive Industry; Transportation
Legislative Issues: AUT; LBR; TAX; TOR; TRA; TRD

Chairman of the Board
TAYLOR, Andrew C.
Tel: (314) 512-1000
Fax: (314) 512-4706

President and Chief Executive Officer
NICHOLSON, Pamela
Tel: (314) 512-1000
Fax: (314) 512-4706

Main Headquarters
Mailing: 600 Corporate Park Dr.
St. Louis, MO 63105
Tel: (314) 512-1000
Fax: (314) 512-4706
TF: (800) 264-6350

Political Action Committees
Enterprise Holdings, Inc. PAC
FEC ID: C00219642
Contact: William W. Snyder
600 Corporate Park Dr.
St. Louis, MO 63105
Tel: (314) 512-1000
Fax: (314) 512-1000

Contributions to Candidates: $412,250 (2015-2016)
Democrats: $126,750; Republicans: $285,500

Principal Recipients

SENATE
KIRK, MARK STEVEN (REP-IL)

HOUSE
RYAN, PAUL D. (REP-WI)

Corporate Foundations and Giving Programs

Enterprise Holdings Foundation
Contact: Jo Ann Taylor Kindle
600 Corporate Park Dr.
St. Louis, MO 63105
Tel: (314) 512-1000
Fax: (314) 512-4706

Public Affairs and Related Activities Personnel

At Headquarters

ADAMS, Edward
Senior Vice President, Human Resources
eadams@ehi.com
Tel: (314) 512-1000
Fax: (314) 512-4706

BRYANT, Laura
Assistant Vice President, Corporate Communications
laura.t.bryant@ehi.com
Tel: (314) 512-4178
Fax: (314) 512-4706

FARRELL, Patrick T.
Chief Marketing and Communications Officer
Tel: (314) 512-1000
Fax: (314) 512-4706

GERBER, Tomi
Assistant Vice President, Government Public Affairs
Registered Federal Lobbyist
Tel: (314) 512-1000
Fax: (314) 512-4706

KAPLAN, Lee
Senior Vice President and Chief Administrative Officer
Tel: (314) 512-1000
Fax: (314) 512-4706

KINDLE, Jo Ann Taylor
Foundation President
Tel: (314) 512-1000
Fax: (314) 512-4706

LANGHORST, Rose
Senior Vice President and Treasurer
Tel: (314) 512-1000
Fax: (314) 512-4706

MARTINI, Lisa
Contact, Public Relations
lisa.martini@ehi.com
Tel: (314) 512-2352
Fax: (314) 512-4706

REEL, Gordon
Assistant Vice President, Government & Public Affairs
greel@ehi.com
Registered Federal Lobbyist
Tel: (314) 512-2979
Fax: (314) 512-4706

ROTHERY, Brian
Assistant Vice President, Government and Public Affairs
Tel: (314) 512-5000
Fax: (314) 512-4706

SNYDER, William W.
Executive Vice President and Chief Financial Officer and PAC Treasurer
Tel: (314) 512-1000
Fax: (314) 512-4706

STUBBLEFIELD, Greg
Chief Strategy Officer and Executive Vice President, Global Sales and Marketing
Tel: (314) 512-1000
Fax: (314) 512-4706

WAGNER, Jr., Raymond T.
Vice President, Government and Public Affairs
rwagner@ehi.com
Tel: (314) 512-2897
Fax: (314) 512-4706

Registered Federal Lobbyist

Enterprise Products Company

Also known as Epco, Inc. Natural gas and liquid pipelines.
www.enterpriseproducts.com
Annual Revenues: $42.51 billion
Employees: 7,000
Ticker: NYSE: EPD
SIC: 4922
Industry/ies: Energy/Electricity; Fuels See Coal, Gas, Oil, Petroleum; Natural Resources; Petroleum Industry
Legislative Issues: TAX

Chairman of the Board
WILLIAMS, Randa Duncan
Tel: (713) 381-6500
Fax: (713) 381-8200

Director and Chief Executive Officer
CREEL, Michael A.
Tel: (713) 381-6500
Fax: (713) 381-8200

Main Headquarters
Mailing: P.O. Box 4735
Houston, TX 77210
Tel: (713) 381-6500
Fax: (713) 381-8200
TF: (888) 806-8152

Political Action Committees
Enterprise Products Partners L.P. Political Action Committee
FEC ID: C00496752
Contact: S. Wade Williams
1100 Louisiana St.
Houston, TX 77002
Tel: (713) 381-6500
Fax: (713) 381-8200

Contributions to Candidates: $90,800 (2015-2016)
Democrats: $1,500; Republicans: $89,300

Principal Recipients

HOUSE
BOUSTANY, CHARLES W. DR. JR. (REP-LA)

Public Affairs and Related Activities Personnel

At Headquarters

FOWLER, Randall Randy
Director and Chief Administrative Officer
Tel: (713) 381-6500
Fax: (713) 381-8200

FORE, Delbert W.
Vice President, Government Affairs
dfore@eprod.com
Registered Federal Lobbyist
Tel: (713) 381-6500
Fax: (713) 381-8200

GLAZE, Steve
Registered Federal Lobbyist
Tel: (713) 381-6500
Fax: (713) 381-8200

RAINEY, Rick
Vice President, Public Relations
Tel: (713) 381-3635
Fax: (713) 381-8200

SMITH, Gary P.
Senior Vice President, Human Resources
Tel: (713) 381-6500
Fax: (713) 381-8200

TEAGUE, Jim
Director and Chief Operating Officer
Tel: (713) 381-6500
Fax: (713) 381-8200

At Other Offices

BURKHALTER, Randy
Vice President, Investor Relations
1100 Louisiana St.
Houston, TX 77002
Tel: (713) 381-6500
Fax: (713) 381-8200

DENNIS, James
Federal Lobbyist
1100 Louisiana St.
Houston, TX 77002
djames@enterpriseproduts.com
Registered Federal Lobbyist
Tel: (713) 381-6500
Fax: (713) 381-8200

STINSON, John M.
Federal Lobbyist
1100 Louisiana St.
Houston, TX 77002
jstinson@forstin.com
Registered Federal Lobbyist
Tel: (713) 381-2531
Fax: (713) 381-8200

WILLIAMS , S. Wade
PAC Treasurer
1100 Louisiana St.
Houston, TX 77002
Tel: (713) 381-6500
Fax: (713) 381-8200

Enterra Solutions, LLC

A management consulting and technology firm.
www.enterrasolutions.com
Annual Revenues: $2.60 million
Industry/ies: Computer/Technology; Management

President and Chief Executive Officer
DEANGELIS, Stephen F.
sdeangelis@enterrasolutions.com
Tel: (215) 497-3100
Fax: (215) 497-3114

Main Headquarters
Mailing: 17 Blacksmith Rd.
Suite 200
Tel: (215) 497-3100
Fax: (215) 497-3114

Newtown, PA 18940

Washington Office

Mailing:	1133 20th St. NW	Tel:	(202) 466-7391
	Suite 400	Fax:	(202) 429-0365
	Washington, DC 20036		

Public Affairs and Related Activities Personnel

At Headquarters

ELIAS, Glenn	Tel:	(215) 497-3100
Vice President, Client Operations Group	Fax:	(215) 497-3114
HAYES, Bradd C.	Tel:	(215) 497-3100
Senior Director, Communications and Research	Fax:	(215) 497-3114
bhayes@enterrasolutions.com		
HENRY, Keith S.	Tel:	(215) 497-3100
Senior Vice President, Strategic Consulting and Business	Fax:	(215) 497-3114
Development		
LOWERY, Darrel	Tel:	(215) 497-3100
Vice President, Program Management	Fax:	(215) 497-3114
MCAULIFFE, Denise	Tel:	(215) 497-3100
Vice President, Human Resources	Fax:	(215) 497-3114
SKLUTE, USAF (Retired), MAJ Nolan	Tel:	(215) 497-3100
Chief Administrative Officer and General Counsel	Fax:	(215) 497-3114
nsklute@enterrasolutions.com		

Entrust, Inc.

Secures digital identities and information for consumers, enterprises and governments.
www.entrust.com
Annual Revenues: $98.90 million
Employees: 400
Ticker: NASDAQ: ENTU
SIC: 7371
Industry/ies: Defense/Homeland Security; Government-Related
Legislative Issues: BUD; CPI; CSP

Main Headquarters

Mailing:	Three Lincoln Centre	Tel:	(972) 728-0447
	5430 LBJ Fwy., Suite 1250	Fax:	(972) 728-0440
	Dallas, TX 75240	TF:	(888) 690-2424

Political Action Committees

Entrust Inc. PAC
FEC ID: C00373787
Contact: David Wagner
One Hanover Park
16633 Dallas Pkwy., Suite 800
Addison, TX 75001

Contributions to Candidates: $21,552 (2015-2016)
Democrats: $1,552; Republicans: $20,000

Public Affairs and Related Activities Personnel

At Headquarters

ATKINSON, Rusty	Tel:	(972) 728-0447
Vice President, Customer Operations	Fax:	(972) 728-0440
ROCKVAM, David	Tel:	(972) 728-0447
Vice President Product Management and Marketing	Fax:	(972) 728-0440
Communications		
david.rockvam@entrust.com		
VANKIRK, Robert (Bob)	Tel:	(972) 728-0447
Vice President, Americas Sales and Field Services	Fax:	(972) 728-0440

At Other Offices

WAGNER, David
President, PAC Contact
One Hanover Park, 16633 Dallas Pkwy., Suite 800
Addison, TX 75001

Environmental Tectonics Corporation

Environmental Tectonics Corporation makes flight simulators, disaster simulators, and motion-based simulation rides for the amusement industry. Its NASTAR center provides space training and research services. ETC's control systems group makes steam and gas sterilizers, hyperbaric chambers (used for high-altitude training, decompression, and wound care), and environmental control devices. ETC has operations in Egypt, Malaysia, Poland, Singapore, Turkey, the UK, the United Arab Emirates, and the US.
www.etcusa.com
Annual Revenues: $39.63 million
Employees: 316
Ticker: OTC: ETCC
SIC: 3728; 3690; 3699; 3564; 3569; 3812
Industry/ies: Environment And Conservation

Chairman of the Board	Tel:	(215) 355-9100
LENFEST, H. F. "Gerry"	Fax:	(215) 357-4000
Chief Executive Officer and President	Tel:	(215) 355-9100
LAURENT, Jr., Robert L.	Fax:	(215) 357-4000
rlaurent@etcusa.com		

Main Headquarters

| Mailing: | 125 James Way | Tel: | (215) 355-9100 |
| | Southampton, PA 18966 | Fax: | (215) 357-4000 |

Corporate Foundations and Giving Programs

NASTAR Foundation
Contact: Gregory P. Kennedy

| 125 James Way | Tel: | (215) 355-9100 |
| Southampton, PA 18966 | Fax: | (215) 357-4000 |

Public Affairs and Related Activities Personnel

At Headquarters

KENNEDY, Gregory P.	Tel:	(215) 355-9100
Director, Educational Services	Fax:	(215) 357-4000
gkennedy@etcusa.com		
PRUDENTI, Mark	Tel:	(215) 355-9100
Chief Financial Officer	Fax:	(215) 357-4000
mprudenti@etcusa.com		

EnviroServ, Inc.

A patent holding company that focuses on research, development and eventual commercialization of new technologies.
www.ttinternationalcorp.com
Employees: 3
Ticker: OTCMKTS:EVSV
SIC: 5940
Industry/ies: Computer/Technology; Copyrights, Patents And Trademarks

Chairman of the Board, Chief Executive Officer and Chief	Tel:	(813) 708-9910
Financial Officer	Fax:	(813) 428-5990
TRINA, Chris		

Main Headquarters

Mailing:	3404 W Bay Vista Ave.	Tel:	(813) 708-9910
	First Floor		
	Tampa, FL 33611		

Public Affairs and Related Activities Personnel

At Other Offices

HENRIE, Gary R.	Tel:	(813) 388-6891
Legal Counsel	Fax:	(813) 428-5990
2240 12 Oaks Way, Suite 101-1		
Wesley Chapel, FL 33544-6970		
MERRELL, George	Tel:	(813) 388-6891
Chief Operating Officer and President, Organic Products	Fax:	(813) 428-5990
International		
2240 12 Oaks Way, Suite 101-1		
Wesley Chapel, FL 33544-6970		
gmerrell@opitampa.com		
TELLONE, Angelina	Tel:	(727) 244-7401
Director, Corporate Communications	Fax:	(813) 428-5990
2240 12 Oaks Way, Suite 101-1		
Wesley Chapel, FL 33544-6970		

Enwave Seattle

Formerly Seattle Steam Company. A privately-owned utility.
www.enwaveseattle.com
Industry/ies: Utilities

| **President and Chief Executive Officer** | Tel: | (206) 658-2024 |
| GENT, A. Stanley | Fax: | (206) 467-6394 |

Main Headquarters

Mailing:	1325 Fourth Ave.	Tel:	(206) 623-6366
	Suite 1440	Fax:	(206) 467-6394
	Seattle, WA 98101		

Public Affairs and Related Activities Personnel

At Headquarters

HERSEY, Barbara	Tel:	(206) 658-2020
Office Manager,Executive Assistant	Fax:	(206) 467-6394
WEDEKING, Ann	Tel:	(206) 658-2021
Accountant	Fax:	(206) 467-6394

EP Management Corporation

Formerly EaglePicher Corporation. A manufacturer of chemicals, electronic and precision products, machinery, plastic coatings and rubber products for automotive, industrial and machinery use.
www.epcorp.com
Annual Revenues: $119 million
Employees: 1,400
SIC: 3295
Industry/ies: Chemicals & Chemical Industry; Construction/Construction Materials; Electricity & Electronics; Electronics; Energy/Electricity; Metals; Plastics Industry; Rubber Industry
Legislative Issues: DEF

| **Chairman of the Board, President and Chief Executive Officer** | Tel: | (313) 749-5500 |
| TREADWELL, David L. | Fax: | (313) 749-5502 |

Main Headquarters

Mailing:	5850 Mercury Dr.	Tel:	(313) 749-5500
	Suite 250	Fax:	(313) 749-5502
	Dearborn, MI 48126		

Public Affairs and Related Activities Personnel

At Headquarters

AUBRY, Patrick S.
Vice President, Chief Financial Officer, Secretary and Treasurer
Tel: (313) 749-5500
Fax: (313) 749-5502

KOZAK, Tina
Contact, Media Relations
kozak@franco.com
Tel: (313) 550-1901
Fax: (313) 749-5502

EPCO, Inc.

See listing on page 297 under Enterprise Products Company

Epsilon Systems Solutions, Inc.

A diversified professional and technical services company. Company serves clients in the applied technology, energy, environmental, industrial, and marine sectors.
www.epsilonsystems.com
Annual Revenues: $93.77 million
Employees: 800
Industry/ies: Business; Computer/Technology; Defense/Homeland Security; Engineering/Mathematics; Government-Related; Management; Small Business

Founder and Chief Executive Officer
MIN, Bryan B.
Tel: (619) 702-1700
Fax: (619) 702-1711

Main Headquarters

Mailing:	9242 Lightwave Ave.	Tel:	(619) 702-1700
	Suite 100	Fax:	(619) 702-1711
	San Diego, CA 92123		

Corporate Foundations and Giving Programs

ESSential Foundation
1565 Hotel Cir. South
Suite 200
San Diego, CA 92108

Public Affairs and Related Activities Personnel

At Headquarters

DUFRESNE, Dan
Director, Government Relations
ddufresne@epsilonsystems.com
Tel: (619) 702-1700
Fax: (619) 705-1711

JESTER, Debby
Marketing and Proposal Coordinator
djester@epsilonsystems.com
Tel: (619) 702-1700
Fax: (619) 702-1711

NORTON, Steve
Senior Vice President, Human Resources
Tel: (619) 702-1700
Fax: (619) 702-1711

STAPLES, Ralph
Senior Vice President, Corporate Business Development
rstaples@epsilonsystems.com
Tel: (619) 702-1700
Fax: (619) 702-1711

TESHIMA, Stuart
Executive Vice President and Chief Financial Officer
Tel: (619) 702-1700
Fax: (619) 702-1711

EQT Corporation

An integrated energy company.
www.eqt.com
Annual Revenues: $2.11 billion
Employees: 1,750
Ticker: NYSE: EQT
SIC: 4923
Industry/ies: Energy/Electricity; Fuels See Coal, Gas, Oil, Petroleum; Natural Resources; Petroleum Industry
Legislative Issues: CAW; ENG; FUE; LBR

Chairman of the Board, President and Chief Executive Officer
PORGES, David L.
Tel: (412) 553-5700
Fax: (412) 553-7781

Main Headquarters

Mailing:	625 Liberty Ave.	Tel:	(412) 553-5700
	Suite 1700	Fax:	(412) 553-7781
	Pittsburgh, PA 15222	TF:	(800) 242-1776

Political Action Committees

EQT Corporation PAC
FEC ID: C00151175
Contact: Tobhiyah Engel
EQT Plaza, 625 Liberty Ave.
Suite 1700
Pittsburgh, PA 15222
Tel: (412) 553-5700
Fax: (412) 553-7781

Contributions to Candidates: $33,000 (2015-2016)
Democrats: $3,000; Republicans: $30,000

Principal Recipients

HOUSE
SHUSTER, WILLIAM MR. (REP-PA)

Corporate Foundations and Giving Programs

EQT Foundation
Contact: Bruce Bickel
Two PNC Plaza, 620 Liberty Ave.
30th Floor
Pittsburgh, PA 15222-2719
Tel: (412) 553-5700
Fax: (412) 553-7781

Public Affairs and Related Activities Personnel

At Headquarters

CONTI, Philip P.
Senior Vice President and Chief Financial Officer
Tel: (412) 553-5700
Fax: (412) 553-7781

COX, Natalie
Corporate Director, Communications
ncox@eqt.com
Tel: (412) 395-3941
Fax: (412) 553-7781

DODDS, Audric
Operations Manager, External Affairs
adodds@eqt.com
Tel: (412) 553-5700
Fax: (412) 553-7781

ENGEL, Tobhiyah
PAC Treasurer
Tel: (412) 553-5700
Fax: (412) 553-7781

GARDNER, Lewis B.
Vice President and General Counsel
Tel: (412) 553-5700
Fax: (412) 553-7781

KANE, CFA, Patrick J.
Chief Investor Relations Officer
pkane@eqt.com
Tel: (412) 553-5700
Fax: (412) 553-7781

KILLION, Michael
Manager, Government Affairs
Tel: (412) 553-5700
Fax: (412) 553-7781

PETRELLI, SPHR, Charlene G.
Vice President and Chief Human Resources Officer
Tel: (412) 553-5700
Fax: (412) 553-7781

WEST, Kevin
Managing Director, External Affairs
Tel: (412) 553-5700
Fax: (412) 553-7781

At Other Offices

BICKEL, Bruce
Executive Director, EQT Foundation
One PNC Plaza, 249 Fifth Ave., Third Floor
Pittsburgh, PA 15222
bruce.bickel@pncadvisors.com
Tel: (412) 553-5700
Fax: (412) 553-7781

Equifax Inc.

A provider of credit scores, history information, and risk analysis.
www.equifax.com
Annual Revenues: $2.50 billion
Employees: 7,500
Ticker: NYSE: EFX
SIC: 7320
Industry/ies: Communications; Telecommunications/Internet/Cable
Legislative Issues: GOV; HCR; IMM; TAX

Chairman of the Board and Chief Executive Officer
SMITH, Richard F.
Fax: (404) 885-8988

Main Headquarters

Mailing:	P.O. Box 740241	TF:	(888) 567-8688
	Atlanta, GA 30374		

Washington Office

Mailing:	1900 K St. NW
	Washington, DC 20006

Political Action Committees

Equifax Inc. PAC
FEC ID: C00143867
Contact: Paul Zurawski
1550 Peachtree St. NW
Atlanta, GA 30309

Contributions to Candidates: $87,000 (2015-2016)
Democrats: $10,000; Republicans: $77,000

Corporate Foundations and Giving Programs

Equifax Inc. Contributions Program
1550 Peachtree St. NW
Atlanta, GA 30309
Tel: (404) 885-8000
Fax: (404) 885-8988

Public Affairs and Related Activities Personnel

At Headquarters

DODGE, Jeff
Senior Vice President, Investor Relations
jeff.dodge@equifax.com

HARTMAN, John
Senior Vice President, Corporate Development

KELLEY, III, John J.
Corporate Vice President, Chief Legal Officer

POWELL, Steven
Legislative & Compliance Professional
steven.powell@equifax.com

RUSHING, Coretha M.
Chief Human Resource Officer

SPRINGMAN, Paul
Chief Marketing Officer
paul.springman@equifax.com
WEBB, David
Chief Information Officer
At Other Offices

ZURAWSKI, Paul
Contact, Government Relations and PAC Contact
1550 Peachtree St. NE
Atlanta, GA 30309
Registered Federal Lobbyist

Tel: (404) 885-8000
Fax: (404) 885-8988

Equitable Life Assurance Society of the United States

See listing on page 99 under AXA Equitable Life Insurance Company

Equitable Resources Energy Company

See listing on page 299 under EQT Corporation

Equity Office Management LLC

An owner and manager of office properties. Acquired by Blackstone Group in 2007.
www.equityoffice.com
Annual Revenues: $3 billion
SIC: 6798
Industry/ies: Real Estate
Legislative Issues: TAX

President and Chief Executive Officer
AUGUST, Tom

Tel: (312) 466-3300
Fax: (312) 454-0332

Main Headquarters
Mailing: 222 S. Riverside Dr., Suite 2000
Chicago, IL 60606

Tel: (312) 466-3300

Public Affairs and Related Activities Personnel

At Headquarters

ANDERSON, Keith
Chief Investment Officer

Tel: (312) 466-3300

HEISTER, Kurt
Chief Financial Officer

Tel: (312) 466-3300

HENDRICKS, Chris
Director, Market Management

Tel: (312) 466-3300

KLIMENKO, Laura
Vice President, Human Resources
laura_klimenko@equityoffice.com

Tel: (312) 466-3300

KORITZ , Matt
Vice President, General Counsel

Tel: (312) 466-3300

Equity Residential

An owner of apartment complexes.
www.equityapartments.com
Annual Revenues: $2.65 billion
Employees: 3,500
Ticker: NYSE: EQR
SIC: 6798
NAICS: 52593
Industry/ies: Housing

Chairman of the Board
ZELL, Samuel

Tel: (312) 474-1300
Fax: (312) 454-8703

President and Chief Executive Officer
NEITHERCUT, David J.

Tel: (312) 474-1300
Fax: (312) 454-8703

Main Headquarters
Mailing: Two N. Riverside Plaza
Chicago, IL 60606

Tel: (312) 474-1300
Fax: (312) 454-8703

Corporate Foundations and Giving Programs

Equity Residential Foundation
Two N. Riverside Plaza
Suite 450
Chicago, IL 60606

Tel: (312) 474-1300

Public Affairs and Related Activities Personnel

At Headquarters

MCKENNA, Marty
Vice President, Investor and Public Relations
mmckenna@eqrworld.com

Tel: (312) 928-1901
Fax: (312) 454-8703

PARRELL, Mark J.
Executive Vice President and Chief Financial Officer

Tel: (312) 474-1300
Fax: (312) 454-8703

POWERS, John
Executive Vice President, Human Resources

Tel: (312) 474-1300
Fax: (312) 454-8703

SANTEE, David S.
Executive Vice President and Chief Operating Officer

Tel: (312) 474-1300
Fax: (312) 454-8703

STROHM, Bruce C.
Executive Vice President, General Counsel and Corporate Secretary

Tel: (312) 474-1300
Fax: (312) 454-8703

Ergon, Inc.

Ergon, Inc., a privately held company, operates under six primary business segments including refining and marketing, asphalt and emulsions, transportation and terminating, oil and gas, embedded computing and real estate.
www.ergon.com
Annual Revenues: $203.80 million
Employees: 2,200
SIC: 2911; 2992; 5169
NAICS: 324191
Industry/ies: Construction/Construction Materials
Legislative Issues: FUE; SCI; TRA

Chairman of the Board and Chief Executive Officer
LAMPTON, Sr., Leslie B.

Tel: (601) 933-3000
Fax: (601) 933-3350

Main Headquarters
Mailing: P.O. Box 1639
Jackson, MS 39215-1639

Tel: (601) 933-3000
Fax: (601) 933-3350
TF: (800) 824-2626

Public Affairs and Related Activities Personnel

At Headquarters

ALLEN, Ricky
Human Resources

Tel: (601) 933-3000
Fax: (601) 933-3350

BUSBY, Patrick A.
Executive Vice President and Chief Financial Officer

Tel: (601) 933-3000
Fax: (601) 933-3350

TEMPLE, James
Director, Communications
jim.temple@ergon.com

Tel: (601) 933-3000
Fax: (601) 933-3350

Erickson Air-Crane Incorporated

See listing on page 300 under Erickson Inc.

Erickson Inc.

Owns, operates, and maintains a fleet of heavy-duty S-64 Aircrane helicopters.
www.ericksonaircrane.com
Annual Revenues: $338.59 million
Employees: 1,000
Ticker: NASDAQ: EAC
SIC: 3720
Industry/ies: Transportation

Chairman of the Board
SCOTT, Gary R.

Tel: (503) 505-5800
Fax: (541) 664-7613

President and Chief Executive Officer
RIEDER, Udo

Tel: (503) 505-5800
Fax: (541) 664-7613

Main Headquarters
Mailing: 5550 S.W. Macadam Ave.
Suite 200
Portland, OR 97239

Tel: (503) 505-5800
Fax: (541) 664-7613
TF: (800) 424-2413

Public Affairs and Related Activities Personnel

At Headquarters

ELLIOTT, Susie
Communications Specialist
selliott@ericksonaviation.com

Tel: (503) 505-5885
Fax: (541) 664-7613

HAYNES, Yolanda
Director, Human Resources

Tel: (503) 505-5800
Fax: (541) 664-7613

PALCZYNSKI, James
Contact, Investor Relations
jp@icrinc.com

Tel: (203) 682-8229
Fax: (541) 664-7613

RIZZUTI, Edward
Vice President, General Counsel and Corporate Secretary

Tel: (503) 505-5800
Fax: (541) 664-7613

RYAN, Charles
Vice President and Chief Financial Officer

Tel: (503) 505-5800
Fax: (541) 664-7613

SPLIETH, Glenn
Vice President, Global Human Resources

Tel: (503) 505-5800
Fax: (541) 664-7613

STRUIK, Eric
Chief Financial Officer

Tel: (503) 505-5800
Fax: (541) 664-7613

Erickson Living

A developer and operator of retirement communities.
www.ericksonliving.com
Annual Revenues: $19.50 million
Employees: 600
Industry/ies: Aging; Medicine/Health Care/Mental Health
Legislative Issues: HCR

Chairman of the Board
DAVIS, Jim

Tel: (410) 242-2880
Fax: (410) 737-8854

Chief Executive Officer
BUTLER, R. Alan

Tel: (410) 242-2880
Fax: (410) 737-8854

Main Headquarters
Mailing: 701 Maiden Choice Ln.
Baltimore, MD 21228

Tel: (410) 242-2880
Fax: (410) 737-8854

TF:	(800) 920-0856

Political Action Committees

Erickson Living Federal PAC
FEC ID: C00436238
Contact: Scott Sawicki
5525 Research Park Dr.
Catonsville, MD 21228

Corporate Foundations and Giving Programs

The Erickson Mission Partner Initiative
701 Maiden Choice Ln.   Tel: (410) 242-2880
Baltimore, MD 21228   Fax: (410) 242-2880

Public Affairs and Related Activities Personnel

At Headquarters

DOYLE, Debra B   Tel: (410) 242-2880
Chief Operating Officer   Fax: (410) 737-8854

KANE, Esq., Adam   Tel: (410) 242-2880
Senior Vice President, Corporate Affairs Fax: (410) 737-8854

MACHICOTE, Joseph   Tel: (410) 242-2880
Senior Vice President, Human Resources Fax: (410) 737-8854

MATTHIESEN, Todd A.   Tel: (410) 242-2880
Chief Financial Officer   Fax: (410) 737-8854

NEUBAUER, Tom   Tel: (410) 242-2880
Executive Vice President, Sales and Marketing Fax: (410) 737-8854

TANSILL, Mel   Tel: (410) 241-7614
Regional Public Affairs Manager Fax: (410) 737-8854
Mel.Tansill@Erickson.com

At Other Offices

SAWICKI, Scott
PAC Treasurer
5525 Research Park Dr.
Catonsville, MD 21228
scott.sawicki@erickson.com

Erickson Retirement Communities

See listing on page 300 under Erickson Living

Ericsson Inc.

A manufacturer of business communicators and telecommunications systems.
www.ericsson.com
Annual Revenues: $28.36 billion
Employees: 118,706
Ticker: NASDAQ: ERIC
SIC: 3663; 3669
NAICS: 334220; 334290
Industry/ies: Communications; Media/Mass Communication;
Telecommunications/Internet/Cable
Legislative Issues: CPT; TEC; TRD

President and Chief Executive Officer   Tel: (972) 583-0000
VESTBERG, Hans

Main Headquarters

Mailing: 6300 Legacy Dr.   Tel: (972) 583-0000
Plano, TX 75024

Washington Office

Mailing: 1776 Eye St. NW   Tel: (972) 583-5694
Suite 600
Washington, DC 20006

Corporate Foundations and Giving Programs

Ericsson's Research Foundation
6300 Legacy Dr.   Tel: (972) 583-0000
Plano, TX 75024

Public Affairs and Related Activities Personnel

At Headquarters

CHAURASIA, Bina   Tel: (972) 583-0000
Senior Vice President, Chief Human Resources Officer

EGAN, Kathy   Tel: (972) 583-0000
Vice President, Communications
kathy.egan@ericsson.com

FRYKHAMMAR, Jan   Tel: (972) 583-0000
Executive Vice President and Chief Financial Officer

MACPHERSON, Nina   Tel: (972) 583-0000
Senior Vice President, Chief Legal Officer

MOZDINIEWICZ, Nathalie   Tel: (972) 583-0000
Program Manager, Investor Relations
nathalie.mozdiniewicz@ericsson.com

NORRMAN, Helena   Tel: (972) 583-0000
*Senior Vice President, Chief Marketing and Communications
Officer*

QURESHI, Rima   Tel: (972) 583-0000
Senior Vice President, Chief Strategy Officer

WÄREBY, Jan   Tel: (972) 583-0000
Senior Vice President and Head, Sales and Marketing

At Washington Office

ACKERMAN, Graham   Tel: (972) 583-5694
*Vice President, Strategic Development & Director, Investment
Management*

At Other Offices

BAFFER, Barbara   Tel: (202) 783-2200
Vice President, Corporate Affairs & Communications Fax: (202) 783-2206
1634 Eye St. NW, Suite 600
Washington, DC 20006-4083
Barbara.Baffer@ericsson.com

JONES, Brian   Tel: (202) 783-2200
Director, Government Relations & Public Policy Fax: (202) 783-2206
1634 Eye St. NW, Suite 600
Washington, DC 20006-4083
Registered Federal Lobbyist

Erie Indeminity Company

*A multi-line insurance company. The company provides sales, underwriting, and policy
issuance services for the policyholders on behalf of the Erie Insurance Exchange.*
www.erieinsurance.com
Annual Revenues: $6.22 billion
Employees: 4,700
Ticker: NASDAQ: ERIE
SIC: 6411
Industry/ies: Insurance Industry

Chairman of the Board   Tel: (814) 451-5000
HAGEN, Thomas B.   Fax: (814) 451-5209

President and Chief Executive Officer   Tel: (814) 451-5000
CAVANAUGH, Terrence W.   Fax: (814) 451-5209

Main Headquarters

Mailing: 100 Erie Insurance Pl.   Tel: (814) 451-5000
Erie, PA 16530-1104   Fax: (814) 451-5209
TF: (877) 771-3743

Political Action Committees

Erie Indeminity Company PAC - Federal
FEC ID: C00153577
Contact: Gary D. Veshecco
100 Erie Insurance Pl.
Erie, PA 16530

Contributions to Candidates: $41,800 (2015-2016)
Democrats: $12,000; Republicans: $29,800

Corporate Foundations and Giving Programs

Erie Insurance Giving Network
Contact: Kathy Olsen
100 Erie Insurance Pl.   Tel: (814) 870-7403
Erie, PA 16530-1104   Fax: (814) 870-3126

Public Affairs and Related Activities Personnel

At Headquarters

BEILHARZ, Scott   Tel: (814) 870-7312
Vice President, Capital Management and Investor Relations Fax: (814) 451-5209

DALL, Marcia A.   Tel: (814) 451-5000
Executive Vice President and Chief Financial Officer Fax: (814) 451-5209

DOMBROWSKI, Mark   Tel: (814) 870-2285
Vice President, Government Relations Fax: (814) 870-3126
mark.dombrowski@erieinsurance.com

EUSTON, Megan   Tel: (814) 451-5000
Leader, Local & Digital Marketing Fax: (814) 451-5209
megan.euston@erieinsurance.com

KEARNS, John F.   Tel: (814) 451-5000
Executive Vice President, Sales and Marketing Fax: (814) 451-5209

KNAPP , Leah   Tel: (814) 449-6792
Contact, Media   Fax: (814) 451-5209
leah.knapp@erieinsurance.com

MARSH, CPA, Christina M.   Tel: (814) 870-2000
Senior Vice President, Services Fax: (814) 870-3126

MCLAUGHLIN , Sean   Tel: (814) 451-5000
Executive Vice President, Secretary and General Counsel Fax: (814) 451-5209

OLSEN, Kathy   Tel: (814) 870-2000
Administrator, Contributions & Diversity Fax: (814) 870-3126

PHILLIPS, Karen Kraus   Tel: (814) 870-4665
Vice President, Corporate Marketing Services Fax: (814) 870-2717
karenkraus.phillips@erieinsurance.com

VESHECCO, Gary D.   Tel: (814) 451-5000
Senior Vice President and Deputy General Counsel, Law and Fax: (814) 451-5209
Government Affairs and PAC Treasurer
gary.veshecco@erieinsurance.com

Ernest & Julio Gallo Winery

A family-owned Californian wine producer and distributing company.
www.gallo.com
Employees: 5,000
Industry/ies: Food And Beverage Industry

Co-Chairman	Tel:	(209) 341-3111
GALLO, Robert	Fax:	(209) 341-3569

Main Headquarters
Mailing:	600 Yosemite Blvd.	Tel:	(209) 341-3111
	Modesto, CA 95354	Fax:	(209) 341-3569
		TF:	(877) 687-9463

Corporate Foundations and Giving Programs
Ernest and Julio Gallo Winery Contributions Program
600 Yosemite Blvd. Tel: (209) 341-3111
Modesto, CA 95354

Public Affairs and Related Activities Personnel

At Headquarters
GALLO, Stephanie	Tel:	(209) 341-3111
Vice President, Marketing	Fax:	(209) 341-3569
KENNEDY, Kerrie	Tel:	(209) 341-3111
Senior Human Resources Representative	Fax:	(209) 341-3569
LANNING, Judith	Tel:	(209) 341-3111
Shareholder and Community Relations Manager	Fax:	(209) 341-3569
VILAS, Doug	Tel:	(209) 341-3111
Chief Financial Officer	Fax:	(209) 341-3569

Ernst & Young LLP

Ernst & Young provides assurance, tax, transactions, and advisory services to public and private companies in a wide variety of industries from about 80 offices throughout the US, including Puerto Rico.
www.ey.com
Annual Revenues: $2.46 billion
Employees: 27,000
Industry/ies: Accounting; Banking/Finance/Investments; Taxation
Legislative Issues: ACC; BAN; BUD; ECN; ENG; ENV; FIN; GOV; HCR; HOU; LBR; MMM; RET; SCI; TAX; TEC; TOR; TRD

Chairman and Chief Executive Officer	Tel:	(212) 773-3000
TURLEY, James S.	Fax:	(212) 773-6350
james.turley@ey.com		

Chairman & Chief Executive Officer-elect	Tel:	(202) 327-6032
WEINBERGER, Mark		

Main Headquarters
Mailing:	1001 Pennsylvania Ave. NW
	Suite 601 N. Concourse
	Washington, DC 20004

Political Action Committees
Ernst & Young PAC
FEC ID: C00227744
Contact: Kathryn Sabatini
1101 New York Ave. NW Tel: (202) 327-6000
Washington, DC 20005

Contributions to Candidates: $1,126,125 (2015-2016)
Democrats: $407,000; Republicans: $710,125; Other: $9,000

Principal Recipients

SENATE
JOHNSON, RONALD HAROLD (REP-)
MURPHY, PATRICK E (DEM-FL)
SCOTT, TIMOTHY E (REP-SC)
SHELBY, RICHARD C (REP-AL)

HOUSE
DELANEY, JOHN K (DEM-MD)
ELLMERS, RENEE JACISIN (REP-NC)
HOLDING, GEORGE E MR. (REP-NC)
HOYER, STENY HAMILTON (DEM-DC)
KELLY, GEORGE J JR (REP-PA)
LANKFORD, JAMES PAUL MR. (REP-OK)
LUCAS, FRANK D. (REP-OK)
MALONEY, CAROLYN B. (DEM-NY)
MCCARTHY, KEVIN (REP-CA)
MULVANEY, JOHN MICHAEL 'MICK' (REP-SC)
PERLMUTTER, EDWIN G (DEM-CO)
POLIQUIN, BRUCE L (REP-ME)
RENACCI, JAMES B. (REP-OH)
ROSS, DENNIS ALAN (REP-FL)
RUPPERSBERGER, C.A. DUTCH (DEM-MD)
SCALISE, STEVE MR. (REP-LA)
SHERMAN, BRAD (DEM-CA)
STIVERS, STEVE MR. (REP-OH)
THOMPSON, MIKE MR. (DEM-CA)
TIBERI, PATRICK J. (REP-OH)

Corporate Foundations and Giving Programs
Ernst & Young Foundation
Contact: Deborah K. Holmes
200 Plaza Dr.	Tel:	(201) 872-1724
Secaucus, NJ 07094	Fax:	(201) 872-1724

Public Affairs and Related Activities Personnel

At Headquarters
ALEXANDER, James	Tel:	(202) 327-6846
Principal, Risk Management		
ANGUS, Barbara M.	Tel:	(202) 327-6846
Principal		
barbara.angus@ey.co		
Registered Federal Lobbyist		
BENDALL, Jennifer L.		
BRORSEN, Leslie J.	Tel:	(202) 327-6846
les.brorsen@ey.com		
CARROLL, Robert J.	Tel:	(202) 327-6846
CARROLL, Robert J	Tel:	(202) 327-6846
COBLENCE, Alain	Tel:	(202) 327-6846
CREECH, Cathy L.	Tel:	(202) 327-6846
Principal		
Registered Federal Lobbyist		
CUNNIFFE, Amy Jensen	Tel:	(202) 327-6846
Registered Federal Lobbyist		
EGGE, Sarah	Tel:	(202) 327-6846
Senior Manager		
sarah.egge@wc.ey.com		
Registered Federal Lobbyist		
FLYNN, Donna Steele S.	Tel:	(202) 327-6846
Principal		
donna.flynn@ey.com		
Registered Federal Lobbyist		
FRANCIS, Stephen Adam		
Senior Manager		
Registered Federal Lobbyist		
HALLMARK, John		
Registered Federal Lobbyist		
JACOBS, Terry	Tel:	(202) 327-6846
KUEHL, Sarah		
Member		
sarah.egge@wc.ey.com		
Registered Federal Lobbyist		
LEVERY, Jeff	Tel:	(202) 327-6846
Executive Director, WCEY		
MOE, Lee	Tel:	(202) 327-6846
Manager		
Registered Federal Lobbyist		
OMAN, Eric	Tel:	(202) 327-6846
PEARSON, Mary Frances	Tel:	(202) 327-6846
Partner Global Public Policy		
Registered Federal Lobbyist		
VANDERWOLK, Jefferson	Tel:	(202) 327-6846
Executive Director		
Registered Federal Lobbyist		
WICHINSKI, Randall	Tel:	(202) 327-6846
Executive Director		
randall.wichinski@ey.com		

At Other Offices
ALEXANDER, James	Tel:	(202) 327-6000
Principal, Risk Management		
1101 New York Ave. NW, Suite 601		
Washington, DC 20005		
ALEXANDER, James	Tel:	(212) 773-3000
Principal, Risk Management		
Five Times Sq., 14th Floor		
New York City, NY 10036		
ALEXANDER, James	Tel:	(202) 293-7474
Principal, Risk Management		
1001 Pennsylvania Ave. NW, Suite 601 North		
Washington, DC 20004		
ALEXANDER, James	Tel:	(202) 327-6032
Principal, Risk Management		
1101 New York Ave. NW, Suite 500		
Washington, DC 20005		
ALEXANDER, James	Tel:	(201) 872-2200
Principal, Risk Management		
200 Plaza Dr.		
Secaucus, NJ 07094		
ANGUS, Barbara M.	Tel:	(202) 327-6000

Principal
1101 New York Ave. NW, Suite 601
Washington, DC 20005
barbara.angus@ey.co
Registered Federal Lobbyist

ANGUS, Barbara M. Tel: (212) 773-3000
Principal
Five Times Sq., 14th Floor
New York City, NY 10036
barbara.angus@ey.co
Registered Federal Lobbyist

ANGUS, Barbara M. Tel: (202) 293-7474
Principal
1001 Pennsylvania Ave. NW, Suite 601 North
Washington, DC 20004
barbara.angus@ey.co
Registered Federal Lobbyist

ANGUS, Barbara M. Tel: (202) 327-6032
Principal
1101 New York Ave. NW, Suite 500
Washington, DC 20005
barbara.angus@ey.co
Registered Federal Lobbyist

ANGUS, Barbara M. Tel: (201) 872-2200
Principal
200 Plaza Dr.
Secaucus, NJ 07094
barbara.angus@ey.co
Registered Federal Lobbyist

BEEMAN, E. Ray
1001 Pennsylvania Ave. NW, Suite 601 North
Washington, DC 20004
Registered Federal Lobbyist

BRADSHAW, Tara Fax: (202) 293-8811
Senior Manager
1225 Connecticut Ave. NW, Suite 601 North
Washington, DC 20036
Registered Federal Lobbyist

BRAY, Hillary Tel: (202) 293-7474
1001 Pennsylvania Ave. NW, Suite 601 North Fax: (202) 293-8811
Washington, DC 20004
Registered Federal Lobbyist

BRORSEN, Leslie J. Tel: (202) 327-6000
1101 New York Ave. NW, Suite 601
Washington, DC 20005
les.brorsen@ey.com

BRORSEN, Leslie J. Tel: (212) 773-3000
Five Times Sq., 14th Floor
New York City, NY 10036
les.brorsen@ey.com

BRORSEN, Leslie J. Tel: (202) 293-7474
1001 Pennsylvania Ave. NW, Suite 601 North
Washington, DC 20004
les.brorsen@ey.com

BRORSEN, Leslie J. Tel: (202) 327-6032
1101 New York Ave. NW, Suite 500
Washington, DC 20005
les.brorsen@ey.com

BRORSEN, Leslie J. Tel: (201) 872-2200
200 Plaza Dr.
Secaucus, NJ 07094
les.brorsen@ey.com

CARROLL, Robert J. Tel: (202) 327-6032
1101 New York Ave. NW, Suite 500
Washington, DC 20005

CARROLL, Robert J Tel: (202) 327-6032
1101 New York Ave. NW, Suite 500
Washington, DC 20005

CARROLL, Robert T.
1001 Pennsylvania Ave. NW, Suite 601 North
Washington, DC 20004

CARROLL, Robert J. Tel: (202) 327-6000
1101 New York Ave. NW, Suite 601
Washington, DC 20005

CARROLL, Robert J. Tel: (212) 773-3000
Five Times Sq., 14th Floor
New York City, NY 10036

CARROLL, Robert J. Tel: (202) 293-7474
1001 Pennsylvania Ave. NW, Suite 601 North
Washington, DC 20004

CARROLL, Robert J. Tel: (201) 872-2200
200 Plaza Dr.

Secaucus, NJ 07094

CARROLL, Robert J Tel: (202) 327-6000
1101 New York Ave. NW, Suite 601
Washington, DC 20005

CARROLL, Robert J Tel: (212) 773-3000
Five Times Sq., 14th Floor
New York City, NY 10036

CARROLL, Robert J Tel: (202) 293-7474
1001 Pennsylvania Ave. NW, Suite 601 North
Washington, DC 20004

CARROLL, Robert J Tel: (201) 872-2200
200 Plaza Dr.
Secaucus, NJ 07094

COBLENCE, Alain Tel: (202) 327-6000
1101 New York Ave. NW, Suite 601
Washington, DC 20005

COBLENCE, Alain Tel: (212) 773-3000
Five Times Sq., 14th Floor
New York City, NY 10036

COBLENCE, Alain Tel: (202) 293-7474
1001 Pennsylvania Ave. NW, Suite 601 North
Washington, DC 20004

COBLENCE, Alain Tel: (202) 327-6032
1101 New York Ave. NW, Suite 500
Washington, DC 20005

COBLENCE, Alain Tel: (201) 872-2200
200 Plaza Dr.
Secaucus, NJ 07094

COULAM, Weston J. Fax: (202) 293-8811
Executive Director
1225 Connecticut Ave. NW, Suite 601 North
Washington, DC 20036
Registered Federal Lobbyist

COYLE, Emily Elaine Tel: (202) 327-6000
Director, Public Policy Fax: (202) 327-6200
1101 New York Ave. NW, Suite 601
Washington, DC 20005
Registered Federal Lobbyist

CREECH, Cathy L. Tel: (202) 327-6000
Principal
1101 New York Ave. NW, Suite 601
Washington, DC 20005
Registered Federal Lobbyist

CREECH, Cathy L. Tel: (212) 773-3000
Principal
Five Times Sq., 14th Floor
New York City, NY 10036
Registered Federal Lobbyist

CREECH, Cathy L. Tel: (202) 293-7474
Principal
1001 Pennsylvania Ave. NW, Suite 601 North
Washington, DC 20004
Registered Federal Lobbyist

CREECH, Cathy L. Tel: (202) 327-6032
Principal
1101 New York Ave. NW, Suite 500
Washington, DC 20005
Registered Federal Lobbyist

CREECH, Cathy L. Tel: (201) 872-2200
Principal
200 Plaza Dr.
Secaucus, NJ 07094
Registered Federal Lobbyist

CUNNIFFE, Amy Jensen Tel: (202) 327-6000
1101 New York Ave. NW, Suite 601
Washington, DC 20005
Registered Federal Lobbyist

CUNNIFFE, Amy Jensen Tel: (212) 773-3000
Five Times Sq., 14th Floor
New York City, NY 10036
Registered Federal Lobbyist

CUNNIFFE, Amy Jensen Tel: (202) 293-7474
1001 Pennsylvania Ave. NW, Suite 601 North
Washington, DC 20004
Registered Federal Lobbyist

CUNNIFFE, Amy Jensen Tel: (202) 327-6032
1101 New York Ave. NW, Suite 500
Washington, DC 20005
Registered Federal Lobbyist

CUNNIFFE, Amy Jensen Tel: (201) 872-2200
200 Plaza Dr.
Secaucus, NJ 07094

Registered Federal Lobbyist

DONEY, John L.   Fax: (202) 293-8811
Senior Manager
1225 Connecticut Ave. NW, Suite 601 North
Washington, DC 20036
john.doney@wc.ey.com
Registered Federal Lobbyist

EGGE, Sarah   Tel: (202) 327-6000
Senior Manager
1101 New York Ave. NW, Suite 601
Washington, DC 20005
sarah.egge@wc.ey.com
Registered Federal Lobbyist

EGGE, Sarah   Tel: (212) 773-3000
Senior Manager
Five Times Sq., 14th Floor
New York City, NY 10036
sarah.egge@wc.ey.com
Registered Federal Lobbyist

EGGE, Sarah   Tel: (202) 293-7474
Senior Manager
1001 Pennsylvania Ave. NW, Suite 601 North
Washington, DC 20004
sarah.egge@wc.ey.com
Registered Federal Lobbyist

EGGE, Sarah   Tel: (202) 327-6032
Senior Manager
1101 New York Ave. NW, Suite 500
Washington, DC 20005
sarah.egge@wc.ey.com
Registered Federal Lobbyist

EGGE, Sarah   Tel: (201) 872-2200
Senior Manager
200 Plaza Dr.
Secaucus, NJ 07094
sarah.egge@wc.ey.com
Registered Federal Lobbyist

ETHRIDGE, George T.
Partner, Risk Management
1001 Pennsylvania Ave. NW, Suite 601 North
Washington, DC 20004

FLYNN, Donna Steele S.   Tel: (202) 327-6000
Principal
1101 New York Ave. NW, Suite 601
Washington, DC 20005
donna.flynn@ey.com
Registered Federal Lobbyist

FLYNN, Donna Steele S.   Tel: (212) 773-3000
Principal
Five Times Sq., 14th Floor
New York City, NY 10036
donna.flynn@ey.com
Registered Federal Lobbyist

FLYNN, Donna Steele S.   Tel: (202) 293-7474
Principal
1001 Pennsylvania Ave. NW, Suite 601 North
Washington, DC 20004
donna.flynn@ey.com
Registered Federal Lobbyist

FLYNN, Donna Steele S.   Tel: (202) 327-6032
Principal
1101 New York Ave. NW, Suite 500
Washington, DC 20005
donna.flynn@ey.com
Registered Federal Lobbyist

FLYNN, Donna Steele S.   Tel: (201) 872-2200
Principal
200 Plaza Dr.
Secaucus, NJ 07094
donna.flynn@ey.com
Registered Federal Lobbyist

GASPER, Gary J.   Fax: (202) 293-8811
Partner
1225 Connecticut Ave. NW, Suite 601 North
Washington, DC 20036
gary.gasper@wc.ey.com
Registered Federal Lobbyist

GIORDANO, Nick   Fax: (202) 293-8811
Principal
1225 Connecticut Ave. NW, Suite 601 North
Washington, DC 20036
Registered Federal Lobbyist

GRAB, Francis   Fax: (202) 293-8811

Principal
1225 Connecticut Ave. NW, Suite 601 North
Washington, DC 20036
Registered Federal Lobbyist

HAILEY, Sean
1001 Pennsylvania Ave. NW, Suite 601 North
Washington, DC 20004
Registered Federal Lobbyist

HEYNIGER, Will   Fax: (202) 293-8811
Senior Manager
1225 Connecticut Ave. NW, Suite 601 North
Washington, DC 20036
will.heyniger@wc.ey.com
Registered Federal Lobbyist

HOLMES, Deborah K.   Tel: (212) 773-3000
Director, Corporate Responsibility   Fax: (212) 773-6350
Five Times Sq., 14th Floor
New York City, NY 10036

HOWE JR, Stephen
Managing Partner – Americas
Five Times Sq.
New York City, NY 10036-6530

JACOBS, Terry   Tel: (202) 327-6000
1101 New York Ave. NW, Suite 601
Washington, DC 20005

JACOBS, Terry   Tel: (212) 773-3000
Five Times Sq., 14th Floor
New York City, NY 10036

JACOBS, Terry   Tel: (202) 293-7474
1001 Pennsylvania Ave. NW, Suite 601 North
Washington, DC 20004

JACOBS, Terry   Tel: (202) 327-6032
1101 New York Ave. NW, Suite 500
Washington, DC 20005

JACOBS, Terry   Tel: (201) 872-2200
200 Plaza Dr.
Secaucus, NJ 07094

KOCH, Cathleen M.   Tel: (202) 327-6032
Principal
1101 New York Ave. NW, Suite 500
Washington, DC 20005
Registered Federal Lobbyist

KOSHGARIAN, Dave   Fax: (202) 293-8811
Federal Lobbyist
1225 Connecticut Ave. NW, Suite 601 North
Washington, DC 20036
Registered Federal Lobbyist

LEE, Yuelin   Tel: (202) 327-6032
Senior Manager, International Tax
1101 New York Ave. NW, Suite 500
Washington, DC 20005

LEVERY, Jeff   Tel: (202) 327-6000
Executive Director, WCEY
1101 New York Ave. NW, Suite 601
Washington, DC 20005

LEVERY, Jeff   Tel: (212) 773-3000
Executive Director, WCEY
Five Times Sq., 14th Floor
New York City, NY 10036

LEVERY, Jeff   Tel: (202) 293-7474
Executive Director, WCEY
1001 Pennsylvania Ave. NW, Suite 601 North
Washington, DC 20004

LEVERY, Jeff   Tel: (202) 327-6032
Executive Director, WCEY
1101 New York Ave. NW, Suite 500
Washington, DC 20005

LEVERY, Jeff   Tel: (201) 872-2200
Executive Director, WCEY
200 Plaza Dr.
Secaucus, NJ 07094

LEVEY, Jeff   Fax: (202) 293-8811
Executive Director
1225 Connecticut Ave. NW, Suite 601 North
Washington, DC 20036
jeff.levey@wc.ey.com
Registered Federal Lobbyist

MACPHERSON, John
1001 Pennsylvania Ave. NW, Suite 601 North
Washington, DC 20004

MEADE, Heather   Fax: (202) 293-8811
Senior Manager

1225 Connecticut Ave. NW, Suite 601 North
Washington, DC 20036
Registered Federal Lobbyist

MOE, Lee	Tel:	(202) 327-6000

Manager
1101 New York Ave. NW, Suite 601
Washington, DC 20005
Registered Federal Lobbyist

MOE, Lee	Tel:	(212) 773-3000

Manager
Five Times Sq., 14th Floor
New York City, NY 10036
Registered Federal Lobbyist

MOE, Lee	Tel:	(202) 293-7474

Manager
1001 Pennsylvania Ave. NW, Suite 601 North
Washington, DC 20004
Registered Federal Lobbyist

MOE, Lee	Tel:	(202) 327-6032

Manager
1101 New York Ave. NW, Suite 500
Washington, DC 20005
Registered Federal Lobbyist

MOE, Lee	Tel:	(201) 872-2200

Manager
200 Plaza Dr.
Secaucus, NJ 07094
Registered Federal Lobbyist

OCASAL, Chris
Principal
1001 Pennsylvania Ave. NW, Suite 601 North
Washington, DC 20004
Registered Federal Lobbyist

OMAN, Eric	Tel:	(202) 327-6000

1101 New York Ave. NW, Suite 601
Washington, DC 20005

OMAN, Eric	Tel:	(212) 773-3000

Five Times Sq., 14th Floor
New York City, NY 10036

OMAN, Eric	Tel:	(202) 293-7474

1001 Pennsylvania Ave. NW, Suite 601 North
Washington, DC 20004

OMAN, Eric	Tel:	(202) 327-6032

1101 New York Ave. NW, Suite 500
Washington, DC 20005

OMAN, Eric	Tel:	(201) 872-2200

200 Plaza Dr.
Secaucus, NJ 07094

PEARSON, Mary Frances	Tel:	(202) 327-6000

Partner Global Public Policy
1101 New York Ave. NW, Suite 601
Washington, DC 20005
Registered Federal Lobbyist

PEARSON, Mary Frances	Tel:	(212) 773-3000

Partner Global Public Policy
Five Times Sq., 14th Floor
New York City, NY 10036
Registered Federal Lobbyist

PEARSON, Mary Frances	Tel:	(202) 293-7474

Partner Global Public Policy
1001 Pennsylvania Ave. NW, Suite 601 North
Washington, DC 20004
Registered Federal Lobbyist

PEARSON, Mary Frances	Tel:	(202) 327-6032

Partner Global Public Policy
1101 New York Ave. NW, Suite 500
Washington, DC 20005
Registered Federal Lobbyist

PEARSON, Mary Frances	Tel:	(201) 872-2200

Partner Global Public Policy
200 Plaza Dr.
Secaucus, NJ 07094
Registered Federal Lobbyist

PETRICH, Jeff	Fax:	(202) 293-8811

Executive Director
1225 Connecticut Ave. NW, Suite 601 North
Washington, DC 20036
jeffrey.petrich@wc.ey.com
Registered Federal Lobbyist

PORTER, John D.	Fax:	(202) 293-8811

Consultant
1225 Connecticut Ave. NW, Suite 601 North

Washington, DC 20036
john.porter@wc.ey.com
Registered Federal Lobbyist

RITTERSPUSCH, Kurt	Fax:	(202) 293-8811

Senior Manager
1225 Connecticut Ave. NW, Suite 601 North
Washington, DC 20036
kurt.ritterpusch@wc.ey.com
Registered Federal Lobbyist

ROZEN, Robert M.	Fax:	(202) 293-8811

Federal Lobbyist
1225 Connecticut Ave. NW, Suite 601 North
Washington, DC 20036
Registered Federal Lobbyist

SABATINI, Kathryn	Tel:	(202) 327-6000
	Fax:	(202) 327-6200

PAC Treasurer
1101 New York Ave. NW, Suite 601
Washington, DC 20005

SCHELLHAS, Robert	Fax:	(202) 293-8811

Principal
1225 Connecticut Ave. NW, Suite 601 North
Washington, DC 20036
bob.schellhas@wc.ey.com
Registered Federal Lobbyist

SPRINGER, Linda	Tel:	(703) 747-0388
	Fax:	(202) 327-6200

Executive Director, Americas Government and Public Sector
1101 New York Ave. NW, Suite 601
Washington, DC 20005
linda.springer@ey.com.

URBAN, Timothy J.	Fax:	(202) 293-8811

Federal Lobbyist
1225 Connecticut Ave. NW, Suite 601 North
Washington, DC 20036
Registered Federal Lobbyist

VANDERWOLK, Jefferson	Tel:	(202) 327-6000

Executive Director
1101 New York Ave. NW, Suite 601
Washington, DC 20005
Registered Federal Lobbyist

VANDERWOLK, Jefferson	Tel:	(212) 773-3000

Executive Director
Five Times Sq., 14th Floor
New York City, NY 10036
Registered Federal Lobbyist

VANDERWOLK, Jefferson	Tel:	(202) 293-7474

Executive Director
1001 Pennsylvania Ave. NW, Suite 601 North
Washington, DC 20004
Registered Federal Lobbyist

VANDERWOLK, Jefferson	Tel:	(202) 327-6032

Executive Director
1101 New York Ave. NW, Suite 500
Washington, DC 20005
Registered Federal Lobbyist

VANDERWOLK, Jefferson	Tel:	(201) 872-2200

Executive Director
200 Plaza Dr.
Secaucus, NJ 07094
Registered Federal Lobbyist

WABEKE, Stacy	Tel:	(202) 327-6032

Senior Manager, International Tax
1101 New York Ave. NW, Suite 500
Washington, DC 20005

WICHINSKI, Randall	Tel:	(202) 327-6000

Executive Director
1101 New York Ave. NW, Suite 601
Washington, DC 20005
randall.wichinski@ey.com

WICHINSKI, Randall	Tel:	(212) 773-3000

Executive Director
Five Times Sq., 14th Floor
New York City, NY 10036
randall.wichinski@ey.com

WICHINSKI, Randall	Tel:	(202) 293-7474

Executive Director
1001 Pennsylvania Ave. NW, Suite 601 North
Washington, DC 20004
randall.wichinski@ey.com

WICHINSKI, Randall	Tel:	(202) 327-6032

Executive Director
1101 New York Ave. NW, Suite 500
Washington, DC 20005
randall.wichinski@ey.com

WICHINSKI, Randall   Tel: (201) 872-2200
Executive Director
200 Plaza Dr.
Secaucus, NJ 07094
randall.wichinski@ey.com

ESA

See listing on page 281 under Educational Services of America Inc

ESCO Technologies Inc.

Manufactures highly engineered products. Formerly ESCO Electronics Corporation.
www.escotechnologies.com
Annual Revenues: $531.40 million
Employees: 2,103
Ticker: NYSE: ESE
SIC: 3669
Industry/ies: Engineering/Mathematics; Machinery/Equipment

Chairman of the Board, President and Chief Executive Officer   Tel: (314) 213-7200
RICHEY, Jr., Victor L.   Fax: (314) 213-7250

Main Headquarters
Mailing: 9900A Clayton Rd.   Tel: (314) 213-7200
        St. Louis, MO 63124-1186   Fax: (314) 213-7250
                        TF: (888) 622-3726

Corporate Foundations and Giving Programs

ESCO Technologies Foundation
Contact: Kathleen Lowrey
9900A Clayton Rd.   Tel: (314) 213-7200
Suite 200   Fax: (314) 213-7200
St. Louis, MO 63124

Public Affairs and Related Activities Personnel

At Headquarters

BARCLAY, Alyson Schlinger   Tel: (314) 213-7200
Senior Vice President, Secretary & General Counsel   Fax: (314) 213-7250

HANLON, Deborah J.   Tel: (314) 213-7200
Vice President, Human Resources   Fax: (314) 213-7250
dhanlon@escotechnologies.com

LOWREY, Kathleen   Tel: (314) 213-7277
Director, Investor Relations & Foundation Chairman   Fax: (314) 213-7250
klowrey@escotechnologies.com

MUENSTER, Gary E.   Tel: (314) 213-7200
Executive Vice President & Chief Financial Officer   Fax: (314) 213-7250

Essendant

Formerly called United Stationers. A business products distributor.
www.unitedstationers.com
Employees: 6,100
Ticker: NASDAQ: USTR
SIC: 5110
Industry/ies: Furniture/Home Furnishings; Machinery/Equipment

Chairman of the Board   Tel: (847) 627-7000
CROVITZ, Charles K.   Fax: (847) 627-7001

President and Chief Executive Officer   Tel: (847) 627-7000
AIKEN JR., Robert B.   Fax: (847) 627-7001

Main Headquarters
Mailing: One Pkwy. N. Blvd.   Tel: (847) 627-7000
        Suite 100   Fax: (847) 627-7001
        Deerfield, IL 60015

Corporate Foundations and Giving Programs

United Stationers Charitable Foundation
Contact: Tracey Horwich
One Pkwy. North Blvd.   Tel: (847) 627-7000
Suite 100   Fax: (847) 627-7000
Deerfield, IL 60015-2559

Public Affairs and Related Activities Personnel

At Headquarters

BLANCHARD, Eric A.   Tel: (847) 627-7000
Senior Vice President, General Counsel and Secretary   Fax: (847) 627-7001

CONNOLLY, Tim   Tel: (847) 627-7000
Chief Operating Officer   Fax: (847) 627-7001

HORWICH, Tracey   Tel: (847) 627-7000
Executive Director, United Stationers Charitable Foundation   Fax: (847) 627-7001
thorwich@ussco.com

SHANKS, Earl   Tel: (847) 627-7000
Senior Vice President and Chief Financial Officer   Fax: (847) 627-7001

TOMKO, Carole   Tel: (847) 627-7000
Senior Vice President, Human Resources   Fax: (847) 627-7001

Essent Guaranty, Inc.

Provider of mortgage guaranty insurance and related services.
www.essent.us

Industry/ies: Banking/Finance/Investments; Insurance Industry
Legislative Issues: FIN; HOU; INS

President and Chief Executive Officer   Tel: (610) 230-0555
CASALE, Mark A.   Fax: (610) 386-2396

Main Headquarters
Mailing: Two Radnor Corporate Center
        100 Matsonford Rd.
        Radnor, PA 19087

Public Affairs and Related Activities Personnel

At Headquarters

SHORE, Anthony D.
Vice President/ Deputy General Counsel & Chief Compliance Officer

TULLY, Matthew D.
Vice President, Government & Industry Relations
Registered Federal Lobbyist

At Other Offices

CASHMER, Jeff   Tel: (610) 230-0555
Senior Vice President and Chief Business Officer   Fax: (610) 386-2396
100 Matsonford Rd.
Radnor, PA 19087

CURRAN, Christopher G.   Tel: (610) 230-0555
Vice President, Corporate Development   Fax: (610) 386-2396
100 Matsonford Rd.
Radnor, PA 19087

GIBBONS, Mary Lourdes   Tel: (610) 230-0555
Senior Vice President, Chief Legal Officer and Secretary   Fax: (610) 386-2396
100 Matsonford Rd.
Radnor, PA 19087

HIGGINS, Bill   Tel: (610) 230-0555
Senior Vice President Strategic Initiatives   Fax: (610) 386-2396
100 Matsonford Rd.
Radnor, PA 19087

KAISER, William D.   Tel: (610) 230-0555
Senior Vice President and Chief Operations Officer   Fax: (610) 386-2396
100 Matsonford Rd.
Radnor, PA 19087

MCALEE, Lawrence E.   Tel: (610) 230-0555
Senior Vice President and Chief Financial Officer   Fax: (610) 386-2396
100 Matsonford Rd.
Radnor, PA 19087

MCALEE, Lawrence E.   Tel: (610) 230-0555
Senior Vice President and Chief Financial Officer   Fax: (610) 386-2396
100 Matsonford Rd.
Radnor, PA 19087

TULLY, Matthew D.   Tel: (610) 230-0555
Vice President, Government & Industry Relations   Fax: (610) 386-2396
100 Matsonford Rd.
Radnor, PA 19087
Registered Federal Lobbyist

WALKER, Janice   Tel: (610) 230-0556
Contact, Media Relations   Fax: (610) 386-2396
100 Matsonford Rd.
Radnor, PA 19087
media@essent.us

Essex Corporation

A full-service corporate provider to the senior's living industry.
www.essexseniorliving.com
Employees: 1,144
Ticker: NYSE:ESS
SIC: 8711
Industry/ies: Defense/Homeland Security; Government-Related

President & Chief Executive Officer
SCHALL, Michael

Main Headquarters
Mailing: 11606 Nicholas St.   Tel: (402) 431-0500
        Suite 100   Fax: (402) 431-0345
        Omaha, NE 68154

Public Affairs and Related Activities Personnel

At Headquarters

WARREN, Phil   Tel: (800) 279-0253
Chief Financial Officer   Fax: (402) 431-0345

Essroc Cement Corporation

A cement producer.
www.essroc.com
Annual Revenues: $4.50 billion
Employees: 2,000
SIC: 3241

NAICS: 3273l
Industry/ies: Construction/Construction Materials

Chairman of the Board
VITALETTI, Federico

Tel: (610) 837-6725
Fax: (610) 837-9614

President and Chief Executive Officer
CARANTANI, Francesco

Tel: (610) 837-6725
Fax: (610) 837-9614

Main Headquarters
Mailing: 3251 Bath Pike
Nazareth, PA 18064

Tel: (610) 837-6725
Fax: (610) 837-9614
TF: (800) 437-7762

Corporate Foundations and Giving Programs
Essroc Cement Corporation Contributions Program
3251 Bath Pike
Nazareth, PA 18064

Tel: (610) 837-6725
Fax: (610) 837-6725

Public Affairs and Related Activities Personnel

At Headquarters

ANDREWS, Gordon C.
General Council and Secretary

Tel: (610) 837-6725
Fax: (610) 837-9614

BECKER, Craig C.
Senior Vice President, Human Resources
craig.becker@essroc.com

Tel: (610) 837-6725
Fax: (610) 837-9614

CAR, Alex
Senior Vice President, Cement Sales and Marketing and General Manager, Construction Materials
alex.car@essroc.com

Tel: (610) 837-6725
Fax: (610) 837-9614

DALRYMPLE, Glenn R.
Senior Vice President, Chief Financial Officer and PAC Treasurer

Tel: (610) 837-6725
Fax: (610) 837-9614

HOLLAND, Sherry L.
Vice President, General Counsel and Secretary

Tel: (610) 837-6725
Fax: (610) 837-9614

JONES, Kevin A.
Treasurer

Tel: (610) 837-6725
Fax: (610) 837-9614

PERRIN, Francois M.
Senior Vice President, Strategic Planning and Business Development

Tel: (610) 837-6725
Fax: (610) 837-9614

Estee Lauder, Inc.

Estée Lauder founded this company in 1946 armed with four products and an unshakeable belief: that every woman can be beautiful.
www.esteelauder.com
Annual Revenues: $11.14 billion
Employees: 44,000
Ticker: NYSE: EL
SIC: 2844
NAICS: 325620
Industry/ies: Personal Care/Hygiene
Legislative Issues: CHM; CSP; MAN; TRD

Executive Chairman
LAUDER, William P.

Tel: (212) 572-4200
Fax: (212) 572-3941

President and Chief Executive Officer
FREDA, Fabrizio

Tel: (212) 572-4200
Fax: (212) 572-3941

Main Headquarters
Mailing: 767 Fifth Ave.
New York City, NY 10153

Tel: (212) 572-4200
Fax: (212) 572-3941

Corporate Foundations and Giving Programs
Estée Lauder Contribution Programme
767 Fifth Ave.
New York City, NY 10153

Tel: (212) 572-4200

Public Affairs and Related Activities Personnel

At Headquarters

D'ANDREA, Dennis
Vice President, Investor Relations
ddandrea@estee.com

Tel: (212) 572-4384
Fax: (212) 572-3941

MOSS, Sara E.
Executive Vice President and General Counsel

Tel: (212) 572-4200
Fax: (212) 572-3941

O'HARE, Michael
Executive Vice President, Global Human Resources

Tel: (212) 572-4200
Fax: (212) 572-3941

POWELL, Eleanor F.
Executive Director, Investor Relations
epowell@estee.com

Tel: (212) 572-4088
Fax: (212) 572-3941

TRAVIS, Tracey T.
Executive Vice President and Chief Financial Officer

Tel: (212) 572-4200
Fax: (212) 572-3941

TROWER, Alexandra C.
Executive Vice President, Global Communications
mediarequests@estee.com

Tel: (212) 572-4430
Fax: (212) 572-3941

Ethan Allen Interiors

Furniture and interior design company.
www.ethanallen.com

Annual Revenues: $730.08 million
Employees: 4,900
Ticker: NYSE: ETH
SIC: 2511
Industry/ies: Furniture/Home Furnishings

Chairman of the Board, President and Chief Executive Officer
KATHWARI, M. Farooq
fkathwari@ethanalleninc.com

Tel: (203) 743-8000
Fax: (203) 743-8298

Main Headquarters
Mailing: P.O. Box 1966
Danbury, CT 06813-1966

Tel: (203) 743-8000
Fax: (203) 743-8298

Corporate Foundations and Giving Programs
Ethan Allen Interiors Contributions Program
P.O. Box 1966
Danbury, CT 06813-1966

Tel: (203) 743-8000
Fax: (203) 743-8298

Public Affairs and Related Activities Personnel

At Headquarters

COMO-PUSWICZ, Sandra
Style Communications Specialist
scomopuswicz@ethanalleninc.com

Tel: (203) 743-8503
Fax: (203) 743-8298

DEPASQUALE, Bridget
Vice President, Marketing services

Tel: (203) 743-8000
Fax: (203) 743-8298

GROW, Daniel M.
Senior Vice President, Business Development
dgrow@ethanalleninc.com

Tel: (203) 743-8000
Fax: (203) 743-8298

KOSTER, Eric D.
Vice President, General Counsel and Secretary

Tel: (203) 743-8000
Fax: (203) 743-8298

RAWLINGS, November
Manager, Media Relations and Public Relations
nrawlings@ethanalleninc.com

Tel: (203) 743-8293
Fax: (203) 743-8298

WHITELY, Corey
Executive Vice President, Administration, Chief Financial Officer and Treasurer

Tel: (203) 743-8000
Fax: (203) 743-8298

Etihad Airways PJSC

Commercial airline providing passenger and cargo service to/from the United States.
Legislative Issues: AVI

Main Headquarters
Mailing: 500 Eighth St. NW
Suite 210
Washington, DC 20004

Public Affairs and Related Activities Personnel

At Headquarters

JENNINGS, Matthew
Senior Manager, Public Affairs
Registered Federal Lobbyist

Evas Worldwide

Emergency Vision Assurance System (EVAS) provides a clear space of air through which a pilot can see flight instruments and out the front windshield for landing.
evasworldwide.com
Industry/ies: Aerospace/Aviation; Transportation

Main Headquarters
Mailing: 300 Corporate Dr.
Suite Two
Mahwah, NJ 07430

Tel: (201) 995-9571
Fax: (201) 995-9504

Public Affairs and Related Activities Personnel

At Headquarters

SASSE, Lisa
Vice President, Marketing and Sales
l.sasse@evasworldwide.com

Tel: (201) 995-9571
Fax: (201) 995-9504

Evergreen Energy

Formerly known as KFx, Inc. Provides combined energy, environmental and economic solutions, producing clean, efficient and affordable energy.
www.evgenergy.com
Employees: 23
Ticker: NYSE: EEE
SIC: 1221
Industry/ies: Natural Resources

President and Chief Executive Officer
SMITH, Ken

Tel: (651) 290-2812
Fax: (651) 292-9709

Main Headquarters
Mailing: 345 St Peter St.
Suite 1350
St. Paul, MN 55102

Tel: (651) 290-2812
Fax: (651) 292-9709

Public Affairs and Related Activities Personnel

At Headquarters

AUGER, Michael	Tel:	(651) 290-2812
General Counsel	Fax:	(651) 292-9709
AXELSON, Nina	Tel:	(651) 290-2812
Vice President, Public Relations	Fax:	(651) 292-9709
BURNS, Michael	Tel:	(651) 290-2812
Senior Vice President, Operations	Fax:	(651) 292-9709
HART, Cathy	Tel:	(651) 290-2812
Senior Vice President, Human Resources and Administration	Fax:	(651) 292-9709
KASID, Andrew	Tel:	(651) 290-2812
Executive Vice President, Chief Financial Officer	Fax:	(651) 292-9709
LAUGHLIN, William G.	Tel:	(651) 290-2812
Vice President, General Counsel and Secretary	Fax:	(651) 292-9709
SARNE, Pam	Tel:	(651) 290-2812
Vice President, Accounting Services	Fax:	(651) 292-9709

Evergreen International Aviation

Privately held global aviation services company.
www.evergreenaviation.com
Employees: 3,900
SIC: 4522
Industry/ies: Aerospace/Aviation; Airlines; Transportation
Legislative Issues: AVI; DIS

Chairman of the Board	Tel:	(503) 472-9361
VINSON, Murray E.	Fax:	(503) 472-1048
President and Chief Executive Officer	Tel:	(503) 472-9361
WHEELER, Jim	Fax:	(503) 472-1048

Main Headquarters

Mailing:	3850 Three Mile Ln.	Tel:	(503) 472-9361
	McMinnville, OR 97128-9496	Fax:	(503) 472-1048

Washington Office

Mailing:	805 15th St. NW	Tel:	(202) 638-5500
	Suite 530	Fax:	(202) 638-4593
	Washington, DC 20005-2147		

Corporate Foundations and Giving Programs

Evergreen Humanitarian and Relief Services, Inc.
3850 Three Mile Ln.
McMinnville, OR 97128

Public Affairs and Related Activities Personnel

At Headquarters

CLARK, Michael D.	Tel:	(503) 472-9361
Vice President and Chief Financial Officer	Fax:	(503) 472-1048
HINES, Mike	Tel:	(503) 472-9361
Contact, Media	Fax:	(503) 472-1048
KLUMP, Dan	Tel:	(503) 472-9361
Vice President, Human Resources	Fax:	(503) 472-1048

Eversource Energy

Eversource Energy formerly known as Northeast Utilities. To act as liaison with NH Congressional Delegation on transmission issues to NE utilities.
www.eversource.com
Annual Revenues: $7.30 billion
Employees: 8,697
Ticker: NYSE: NU
SIC: 4911
Industry/ies: Energy/Electricity; Utilities
Legislative Issues: BUD; CAW; COM; ENG; TAX; TRA; UTI

Chairman, President and Chief Executive Officer	Tel:	(860) 665-5000
MAY, Thomas J.	Fax:	(860) 665-5418

Main Headquarters

Mailing:	P.O. Box 270	Tel:	(860) 665-5000
	Hartford, CT 06141	Fax:	(860) 665-5418
		TF:	(800) 286-5000

Washington Office

Mailing:	901 F St. NW	Tel:	(202) 508-0900
	Suite 602	Fax:	(202) 347-7064
	Washington, DC 20004		

Political Action Committees

Northeast Utilities Employees' PAC -Federal
FEC ID: C00102160
Contact: Sheri L. Lauten

901 F St. NW	Tel:	(202) 508-0900
Suite 602	Fax:	(202) 347-7064
Washington, DC 20004		

Contributions to Candidates: $75,000 (2015-2016)
Democrats: $44,500; Republicans: $30,500

Principal Recipients

HOUSE

GUINTA, FRANK (REP-NH)
KUSTER, ANN MCLANE (DEM-NH)

Corporate Foundations and Giving Programs

Northeast Utilities Foundation
Contact: Shirley M. Payne
P.O. Box 870
Hartford, CT 06141

NSTAR Foundation
800 Boyslan St.
Boston, MA 02199

Public Affairs and Related Activities Personnel

At Headquarters

BUTH, Jay S.	Tel:	(860) 665-5000
Vice President, Controller and Chief Accounting Officer	Fax:	(860) 665-5418
BUTLER, Gregory B.	Tel:	(860) 665-5000
Senior Vice President, General Counsel & Corporate Secretary	Fax:	(860) 665-5418
JUDGE, James J.	Tel:	(860) 665-5000
Executive Vice President and Chief Financial Officer	Fax:	(860) 665-5418
KOTKIN, Jeffrey R.	Tel:	(860) 665-5154
Vice President, Investor Relations and Media Contact	Fax:	(860) 665-5418
jeffrey.kotkin@nu.com		
LARA, Al	Tel:	(860) 728-4616
Media Relations Specialist	Fax:	(860) 665-5418
albert.lara@nu.com		
LAVIN, Todd	Tel:	(860) 665-5000
Executive Director, Federal Government Affairs	Fax:	(860) 665-5418
lavintw@nu.com		
Registered Federal Lobbyist		
MORTON, Margaret L.	Tel:	(860) 665-5000
Vice President, Government Affairs	Fax:	(860) 665-5418
mortonml@nu.com		
NIEMAN, Barbara	Tel:	(860) 665-3249
Investor Relations and Media Contact	Fax:	(860) 665-5418
NOLAN, Jr., Joseph R.	Tel:	(860) 665-5000
Senior Vice President, Customer and Corporate Relations		
joseph_nolan@nstaronline.com		
OLIVIER , Leon J.	Tel:	(860) 665-5000
Executive Vice President, Enterprise Energy Strategy and Business Development	Fax:	(860) 665-5418
SCHWEIGER, Werner J.	Tel:	(860) 665-5000
Executive Vice President and Chief Operating Officer	Fax:	(860) 665-5418
THIBDAUE, Lisa	Tel:	(860) 665-5000
Vice President, Regulatory and Government Affairs	Fax:	(860) 665-4853

At Washington Office

LAUTEN, Sheri L.	Tel:	(202) 508-0900
Federal Governmental Affairs Associate	Fax:	(202) 347-7064
Registered Federal Lobbyist		
NOLAN, Jr., Joseph R.	Tel:	(202) 508-0900
Senior Vice President, Customer and Corporate Relations		
joseph_nolan@nstaronline.com		

At Other Offices

HORAN, Douglas S.	Tel:	(617) 424-2635
Seniro Vice President and General Counsel	Fax:	(617) 424-2421
800 Boylston St.		
Boston, MA 02199		
Mail Stop P1700		
JUDGE, James	Tel:	(617) 424-2410
Senior Vice President and Chief Financial Officer		
800 Boylston St.		
Boston, MA 02199		
MOREIRA, John M.	Tel:	(781) 441-8338
Director, Investor Relations and Financial Reporting		
800 Boylston St.		
Boston, MA 02199		
ir@nstar.com		
NOLAN, Jr., Joseph R.	Tel:	(617) 424-2635
Senior Vice President, Customer and Corporate Relations		
800 Boylston St.		
Boston, MA 02199		
joseph_nolan@nstaronline.com		
NOLAN, Jr., Joseph R.	Tel:	(617) 424-2000
Senior Vice President, Customer and Corporate Relations		
One NSTAR Way		
Westwood, MA 02090		
joseph_nolan@nstaronline.com		
PRETYMAN, Caroline	Tel:	(617) 424-2000
Media Contact	Fax:	(781) 441-8886
One NSTAR Way		
Westwood, MA 02090		
caroline.pretyman@nu.com		
REED, Mark	Tel:	(617) 424-2000

PAC Treasurer
One NSTAR Way
Westwood, MA 02090
mark_reed@nstaronline.com

Fax: (781) 441-8886

Evertz Group LLC

Provides business activities for medium-scaled companies which include supply services, development and design of vendor parts and machines for the metallurgical industry.
www.evertz-group.com
Employees: 600
Legislative Issues: HCR

Main Headquarters
Mailing: 2440 Virginia Ave. NW   Tel: (202) 230-1770
      Suite D1207
      Washington, DC 20037

Public Affairs and Related Activities Personnel

At Other Offices

EVERTZ, Scott   Tel: (202) 478-3020
Consultant, International Affairs & Governmental Relations
2029 K St. NW, Seventh Floor
Washington, DC 20006
Registered Federal Lobbyist

Evonik Corporation

The North America arm of German chemical giant.
north-america.evonik.com/region/north_ameri
Annual Revenues: $532.90 million
Employees: 3,700
SIC: 2819
NAICS: 325998
Industry/ies: Chemicals & Chemical Industry
Legislative Issues: CHM; TAR; TAX; TRD

Chairman of the Board   Tel: (973) 929-8000
ENGEL, Dr. Klaus   Fax: (973) 929-8100

Corporate Foundations and Giving Programs

Evonik Degussa Corporation Contributions Program
379 Interpace Pkwy.   Tel: (973) 541-8000
Parsippany, NJ 07054   Fax: (973) 541-8013

Public Affairs and Related Activities Personnel

At Headquarters

NEUHART, Jeremy   Tel: (973) 929-8000
Director & Regional Head Communications, North America   Fax: (973) 574-8013

SHERIDAN, Mike   Tel: (973) 541-8812
Contact, Media Relations   Fax: (973) 574-8013
mike.sheridan@evonik.com.

WESSEL, Thomas   Tel: (973) 929-8000
Chief Human Resources Officer   Fax: (973) 929-8100

Evonik Degussa Corporation

See listing on page 309 under Evonik Corporation

Evraz Inc. NA

Produces steel products. Formerly known as Oregon Steel, Rocky Mountain Steel, Claymont Steel and IPSCO.
www.evrazincna.com
Employees: 2,000
Industry/ies: Metals
Legislative Issues: TRD

President and Chief Executive Officer   Tel: (312) 533-3555
WINKLER, Conrad   Fax: (312) 533-3611

Main Headquarters
Mailing: 200 E. Randolph St.   Tel: (312) 533-3555
      Suite 7800   Fax: (312) 533-3611
      Chicago, IL 60601

Corporate Foundations and Giving Programs

Gilmore Foundation
1000 S.W. Broadway   Tel: (503) 240-5226
Suite 2200   Fax: (503) 240-5226
Portland, OR 97205

Public Affairs and Related Activities Personnel

At Headquarters

CRUZ, Dario   Tel: (312) 533-3555
Senior Vice President, Human Capital   Fax: (312) 533-3611

KING, Caryn   Tel: (312) 533-3555
Senior Director, Marketing and Communications   Fax: (312) 533-3611

MESSMACHER, Christian   Tel: (312) 533-3555
Vice President, Investor Relations   Fax: (312) 533-3611

TIERNEY , Eileen   Tel: (312) 533-3555
General Counsel and Corporate Secretary   Fax: (312) 533-3611

At Other Offices

MINOR, Glenda   Tel: (503) 240-5226
Senior Vice President and Chief Financial Officer   Fax: (503) 240-5232
1000 S.W. Broadway, Suite 2200
Portland, OR 97205

EVT LLC

Engineering services.
Industry/ies: Engineering/Mathematics

Main Headquarters
Mailing: 3501 Mayflower Blvd.   Tel: (815) 692-8176
      Springfield, IL 62707   Fax: (815) 692-6069

Public Affairs and Related Activities Personnel

At Headquarters

DAVSKO, Lawrence   Tel: (815) 692-8176
Chief Financial Officer   Fax: (815) 692-6069

Excellus Inc.

See listing on page 491 under The Lifetime Healthcare Companies

Excelsior Energy, Inc.

An independent energy development company.
www.excelsiorenergy.com
Annual Revenues: $1.10 million
Industry/ies: Energy/Electricity

Co-President & Chief Executive Officer   Tel: (952) 847-2360
JORGENSEN, Julie   Fax: (612) 333-3042

Main Headquarters
Mailing: 225S. Sixth St.   Tel: (952) 847-2360
      Suite 2560   Fax: (612) 333-3042
      Minneapolis, MN 55402

Public Affairs and Related Activities Personnel

At Headquarters

STANLEY, Leanne   Tel: (952) 847-2360
Representative, Public Affairs and Community Affairs   Fax: (612) 333-3042

Exegy, Inc.

Information technology company.
www.exegy.com
Annual Revenues: $8.70 million
Employees: 60
Industry/ies: Computer/Technology

Chairman of the Board and Chief Executive Officer   Tel: (314) 218-3600
O'DONNELL, Jim

Main Headquarters
Mailing: 349 Marshall Ave.   Tel: (314) 218-3600
      Suite 100   TF: (877) 247-5534
      St. Louis, MO 63119-1862

Washington Office
Mailing: 6701 Democracy Plaza
      Suite 555
      Bethesda, MD 20817

Public Affairs and Related Activities Personnel

At Headquarters

ARBAUGH , Rod   Tel: (314) 218-3600
Chief Operating Officer

STUPP, J.J.   Tel: (314) 218-3600
Chief Financial Officer and Founder

WELLS, Jeff   Tel: (314) 503-1912
Vice President, Product Management and Contact, Media Relations
jwells@exegy.com

Exelon Corporation

A diversified energy company created in 2000 by the merger of PECO Energy Company of Philadelphia and Unicom Corporation. Headquartered in Chicago, IL. Subsidiaries include Exelon Transmission Company, Exelon Generation, PECO, and ComEd.
www.exeloncorp.com
Annual Revenues: $29.02 billion
Employees: 28,993
Ticker: NYSE: EXC
SIC: 4931
Industry/ies: Energy/Electricity; Natural Resources; Utilities
Legislative Issues: AGR; BUD; CAW; COM; ENG; ENV; HOM; TAX; TRA; WAS

Chairman   Tel: (202) 347-7500
SHATTUCK, III, Mayo A.   Fax: (202) 347-7501

President and Chief Executive Officer   Tel: (312) 394-7398
CRANE, Christopher M.   Fax: (312) 394-8941
christopher.crane@exeloncorp.com

Main Headquarters

Mailing:	Ten S. Dearborn St., 48th Floor	Tel:	(312) 394-7398
	P.O. Box 805398	Fax:	(312) 394-8941
	Chicago, IL 60680-5398	TF:	(800) 483-3220

Washington Office

Mailing:	101 Constitution Ave. NW	Tel:	(202) 347-7500
	Suite 400 East	Fax:	(202) 347-7501
	Washington, DC 20001		

Corporate Foundations and Giving Programs

Exelon Foundation
Contact: Steve Solomon

Public Affairs and Related Activities Personnel

At Headquarters

BEST, Amy E.	Tel:	(312) 394-7398
Senior Vice President and Chief Human Resources Officer	Fax:	(312) 394-8941
BRADFORD, Darryl	Tel:	(312) 394-7398
Senior Vice President and General Counsel	Fax:	(312) 394-8941
DOMINGUEZ, Joseph	Tel:	(312) 394-7398
Senior Vice President, Governmental and Regulatory Affairs	Fax:	(312) 394-8941
and Public Policy		
joseph.dominguez@exeloncorp.com		
ELSBERG, Paul	Tel:	(312) 394-7417
Senior Manager, Corporate Communications	Fax:	(312) 394-7945
paul.elsberg@exeloncorp.com		
FIRTH, James D	Tel:	(312) 394-7398
Communications, public policy advocacy, and corporate	Fax:	(312) 394-8941
philanthropy.		
FRANK, Stacie	Fax:	(312) 394-8941
Vice President and Treasurer		
stacie.frank@exeloncorp.com		
GANTI, Ravi	Tel:	(312) 394-7398
Senior Vice President and Chief Commercial Risk Officer	Fax:	(312) 394-8941
Ravi.Ganti@exeloncorp.com		
MCALLISTER, Sally Downs	Tel:	(312) 394-7398
Registered Federal Lobbyist	Fax:	(312) 394-8941
OTT, Katie	Tel:	(312) 394-7398
Registered Federal Lobbyist	Fax:	(312) 394-8941
SOLOMON, Steve	Tel:	(312) 394-2200
President, Exelon Foundation	Fax:	(312) 394-8941
steve.solomon@exeloncorp.com		
TILLMAN, David	Tel:	(610) 765-5530
Senior Manager, Communications	Fax:	(312) 394-8941
david.tillman@exeloncorp.com		
VON HOENE, Jr., William A.	Tel:	(312) 394-7398
Senior Executive Vice President and Chief Strategy Officer	Fax:	(312) 394-8941
william.vonhoene@exeloncorp.com		

At Washington Office

BROWN, R. Scott	Tel:	(202) 347-7500
Vice President, Policy Development	Fax:	(202) 347-7501
scott.brown@exeloncorp.com		
BROWN, Jr., David A.	Tel:	(202) 347-7500
Senior Vice President, Federal Government Affairs & Public	Fax:	(202) 347-7501
Policy		
davidc.brown@exeloncorp.com		
Registered Federal Lobbyist		
CARNEY, Jacqueline	Tel:	(202) 347-7500
Director, Federal Government Affairs	Fax:	(202) 347-7501
jackie.carney@exeloncorp.com		
Registered Federal Lobbyist		
FITZPATRICK, Maggie	Tel:	(202) 347-7500
Senior Vice President	Fax:	(202) 347-7501
GILBERT, David M.	Tel:	(202) 347-7500
Managing Director	Fax:	(202) 347-7501
Registered Federal Lobbyist		
MATHEY, Chris	Tel:	(202) 347-7500
Manager	Fax:	(202) 347-7501
Registered Federal Lobbyist		
THAYER, Jonathan W.	Tel:	(202) 347-7500
Executive Vice President and Chief Financial Officer	Fax:	(202) 347-7501
WATSON, Joseph	Tel:	(202) 347-7500
Director, Federal Government Affairs	Fax:	(202) 347-7501
joseph.watson@exeloncorp.com		

Expedia, Inc.

Provider of online travel services.
www.expedia.com
Annual Revenues: $5.94 billion
Employees: 18,210
Ticker: NASDAQ: EXPE
SIC: 4700

Industry/ies: Travel/Tourism/Lodging
Legislative Issues: AVI; BUD; HOM; TAX; TOU; TRA

Chairman of the Board and Senior Executive

	Tel:	(425) 679-7200
DILLER, Barry	Fax:	(425) 679-7240

President and Chief Executive Officer

	Tel:	(425) 679-7200
KHOSROWSHAHI, Dara	Fax:	(425) 679-7240
darakh@expedia.com		

Main Headquarters

Mailing:	3150 139th Ave. SE	Tel:	(425) 679-7200
	Bellevue, WA 98005	Fax:	(425) 679-7240
		TF:	(800) 397-3342

Washington Office

Mailing:	1120 G St. NW
	Suite 410
	Washington, DC 20005

Political Action Committees

Expedia Inc PAC
FEC ID: C00462879
Contact: Brett Thompson
333 108th Ave. NE
Bellevue, WA 98004

Contributions to Candidates: $40,000 (2015-2016)
Democrats: $13,600; Republicans: $26,400

Public Affairs and Related Activities Personnel

At Headquarters

DZIELAK, Robert	Tel:	(425) 679-7200
Executive Vice President, General Counsel and Secretary	Fax:	(425) 679-7240
bdzielak@expedia.com		
OKERSTROM , Mark	Tel:	(425) 679-7200
Executive Vice President, Operations and Chief Financial	Fax:	(425) 679-7240
Officer		

At Washington Office

MINARDI, Philip J.
Director, Policy Communications

PARK, Jason
Director, Government and Corporate Affairs
Registered Federal Lobbyist

THOMPSON, Brent

Experian Information Solutions

See listing on page 310 under Experian North America

Experian North America

Global supplier of information services relating to consumer and business credit.
www.experian.com
Annual Revenues: $2.06 billion
Employees: 6,000
Industry/ies: Banking/Finance/Investments; Consumers
Legislative Issues: CSP; FIN

Chairman of the Board

	Tel:	(714) 830-7000
ROBERT, Donald	Fax:	(714) 830-2449
donald.robert@experian.com		

Chief Executive Officer

	Tel:	(714) 830-7000
CASSIN, Brian	Fax:	(714) 830-2449

Main Headquarters

Mailing:	475 Anton Blvd.	Tel:	(714) 830-7000
	Costa Mesa, CA 92626	Fax:	(714) 830-2449

Washington Office

Mailing:	1401 K St. NW	Tel:	(202) 682-4612
	Suite 501		
	Washington, DC 20005		

Political Action Committees

Experian North America Inc. PAC (Experian PAC)
FEC ID: C00379768
Contact: Anthony Reeves

475 Anton Blvd.	Tel:	(714) 830-7000
Costa Mesa, CA 92626	Fax:	(714) 830-7000

Contributions to Candidates: $349,000 (2015-2016)
Democrats: $129,500; Republicans: $219,500

Principal Recipients

HOUSE
FOSTER, G. WILLIAM (BILL) (DEM-IL)
HENSARLING, JEB HON. (REP-TX)

Corporate Foundations and Giving Programs

The Heart of Experian

475 Anton Blvd.	Tel:	(714) 830-7000
Costa Mesa, CA 92626		

Public Affairs and Related Activities Personnel

At Headquarters

ANDERSON, Scott
Director, Public Relations and Marketing Services
scott.n.anderson@experian.com
Tel: (714) 830-7000
Fax: (714) 830-2449

DEPASQUALE , Donna
Senior Vice President, Global Marketing
donna.depasquale@experian.com
Tel: (714) 830-7000
Fax: (714) 830-2449

DESOTO, Laura
Senior Vice President Marketing and Product Management
laura.desoto@experian.com
Tel: (714) 830-7000
Fax: (714) 830-2449

DINICOLA, Mark
Business Development Director
mark.dinicola@experian.com
Tel: (714) 830-7000
Fax: (714) 830-2449

DRESSLER, Eric
Senior Vice President, Vertical Markets
eric.dressler@experian.com
Tel: (714) 830-7000
Fax: (714) 830-2449

GALLAGHER, Rick
Director, Group Corporate Strategy and Development
Tel: (714) 830-7000
Fax: (714) 830-2449

GIBSON, Darryl
Group General Counsel
Tel: (714) 830-7000
Fax: (714) 830-2449

HAYWOOD, Melanie
Manager, Corporate Events
melanie.haywood@experian.com
Tel: (714) 830-7000
Fax: (714) 830-2449

HENSON, Susan
Senior Director, Public Relations
susan.henson@experian.com
Tel: (714) 830-5129
Fax: (714) 830-2449

KING , Brenda
Specialist, Sales and Marketing
brenda.king@experian.com
Tel: (714) 830-7000
Fax: (714) 830-2449

MAGUIRE, James G.
Senior Director, Marketing
james.maguire@experian.com
Tel: (714) 830-7000
Fax: (714) 830-2449

NILSON, Luci
Manager, Trade Shows and Events
luci.nelson@experian.com
Tel: (714) 830-7000
Fax: (714) 830-2449

PITCHFORD, Lloyd
Chief Financial Officer
Tel: (714) 830-7000
Fax: (714) 830-2449

RAMIREZ, Nelson Ramirez
Senior Relationship Manager
nelson.ramirez@experian.com
Tel: (714) 830-7000
Fax: (714) 830-2449

REEVES, Anthony
PAC Treasurer
Tel: (714) 830-7000
Fax: (714) 830-2449

RIDOUT-JAMIESON, Nadia
Director, Investor Relations and Communications
Tel: (714) 830-7000
Fax: (714) 830-2449

SHEEHAN, Andrew
Senior Vice President
andrew.sheehan@experian.com
Tel: (714) 830-7000
Fax: (714) 830-2449

SMITH, Peg
Executive Vice President, Investor Relations
peg.smith@experian.com
Tel: (714) 830-7000
Fax: (714) 830-2449

STEPHENSON, Kelli
Vice President, Global Sales Operations
kelli.stephenson@experian.com
Tel: (714) 830-7000
Fax: (714) 830-2449

STEPHENSON , Kelli
Vice President, Global Sales Operations
kelli.stephenson@experian.com
Tel: (714) 830-7000
Fax: (714) 830-2449

TOUCHBERRY, Laurie
Director, Corporate Events
laurie.tourhberry@experian.com
Tel: (714) 830-7000
Fax: (714) 830-2449

TRONCALE, Michael
Senior Public Relations Manager, Corporate
michael.troncale@experian.com
Tel: (714) 830-5462
Fax: (714) 830-2449

TSCHOPP, Gerry
Senior Vice President, Public Affairs
gerry.tschopp@experian.com
Tel: (714) 830-7756
Fax: (714) 830-2449

WELLS, Mark
Director, Group Human Resources
Tel: (714) 830-7000
Fax: (714) 830-2449

WHITEHURST, Roslyn
Senior Manager, Public Relations
Tel: (714) 830-5578
Fax: (714) 830-2449

WILLIAMS, Kerry
Deputy Chief Operating Officer
Tel: (714) 830-7000
Fax: (714) 830-2449

At Washington Office

HANCOCK, Jeremy
Federal Lobbyist
jeremy.hancock@experian.com
Registered Federal Lobbyist
Tel: (202) 682-4612

At Other Offices

HADLEY, Anthony L.
Senior Vice President, Government Affairs and Public Policy
Tel: (202) 682-4613

900 17th St. NW, Suite 1050
Washington, DC 20006
tony.hadley@experian.com
Registered Federal Lobbyist

JOHNSTON, Murray L.
Director, State Government Affairs
900 17th St. NW, Suite 1050
Washington, DC 20006
murray.johnston@experian.com
Registered Federal Lobbyist
Tel: (202) 682-4614

OESTERLE, Elizabeth
Federal Lobbyists
900 17th St. NW, Suite 1050
Washington, DC 20006
Registered Federal Lobbyist
Tel: (202) 682-4613

Expert Global Solutions, Inc.

EGS Customer Care, Inc., formerly APAC Customer Services, Inc. (APAC), and EGS Financial Care, Inc., formerly NCO Financial Systems, Inc. (NCO). NCO delivers real world results around the real world. It is group of collection agencies, BPO companies, or call center outsourcing providing clients with successful business solutions.
www.egscorp.com
Employees: 33,000
SIC: 7320
Industry/ies: Banking/Finance/Investments
Legislative Issues: BAN; FIN; TAX

Main Headquarters

Mailing: 507 Prudential Rd.
Horsham, PA 19044
Tel: (215) 441-3000
Fax: (866) 269-8669
TF: (800) 220-2274

Public Affairs and Related Activities Personnel

At Headquarters

ERHARDT, Thomas
Executive Vice President & Chief Financial Officer
Tel: (215) 441-3000
Fax: (866) 269-8669

GRANDELLI, Pete
Senior Vice President, Strategic Business Units
Tel: (215) 441-3000
Fax: (866) 269-8669

L'ABBATE, Tony
Senior Vice President, Accounts Receivable Management Operations Control
Tel: (215) 441-3000
Fax: (866) 269-8669

MORSE, Margie
Vice President, Marketing and Communications
Margie.Morse@egscorp.com
Tel: (623) 580-6226
Fax: (866) 269-8669

Express Scripts, Inc.

A specialty managed care and full-service pharmacy benefit management company. Acquired NextRx, a subsidiary of WellPoint, in 2009. Express Scripts was founded in 1986.
www.medcohealth.com
Annual Revenues: $102.10 billion
Employees: 29,500
Ticker: NASDAQ: ESRX
SIC: 5912
Industry/ies: Management; Medicine/Health Care/Mental Health; Pharmaceutical Industry
Legislative Issues: DEF; HCR; MMM; PHA; POS; TAX

Chairman of the Board, President and Chief Executive Officer
PAZ, George
Tel: (314) 996-0900
Fax: (314) 702-7037

Chairman
SNOW, Jr., David B.
Tel: (201) 269-3400
Fax: (201) 269-1109

Main Headquarters
Mailing: One Expwy.
HQ21-03
St. Louis, MO 63121
Tel: (314) 996-0900
Fax: (314) 702-7037

Washington Office
Mailing: 300 New Jersey Ave. NW
Suite 600
Washington, DC 20001
Tel: (202) 383-7980

Corporate Foundations and Giving Programs

Express Scripts Foundation
Contact: James E. McLeod PhD
One Expwy.
St. Louis, MO 63121
Tel: (314) 996-0900

Public Affairs and Related Activities Personnel

At Headquarters

EBLING, Keith
Executive Vice President and General Counsel
keblillg@express-scripts.com
Tel: (314) 996-0900
Fax: (314) 702-7037

HARPER, Matthew
Vice President, Financial Planning and Analysis
Tel: (314) 996-0900
Fax: (314) 702-7037

HAVEL, Jim
Executive Vice President and Interim Chief Financial Officer
Tel: (314) 996-0900
Fax: (314) 702-7037

HENRY, Brian		Tel:	(314) 684-6438
Vice President, Corporate Communications		Fax:	(314) 702-7037
bhenry@express-scripts.com			
IGNACZAK, Ed		Tel:	(314) 996-0900
Executive Vice President, Sales and Marketing		Fax:	(314) 702-7037
MCLEOD, PhD, James E.		Tel:	(314) 996-0900
Chairman, Foundation		Fax:	(314) 702-7037
MYERS, David		Tel:	(314) 810-3115
Vice President, Investor Relations		Fax:	(314) 702-7037
WADE, Sara		Tel:	(314) 996-0900
Senior Vice President and Chief Human Resources Officer		Fax:	(314) 702-7037

At Washington Office

DAVIS, Chris		Tel:	(202) 383-7980
Director, Government Affairs			
Registered Federal Lobbyist			
DONNELLY, Michael		Tel:	(202) 383-7984
Registered Federal Lobbyist			
GILBRIDE, Nancy		Tel:	(202) 383-7984
Vice President and General Manager, TRICARE Pharmacy Division			
HOUTS, Jonah		Tel:	(202) 383-7984
Vice President, Government Affairs			
Registered Federal Lobbyist			
KATZ, Emily		Tel:	(202) 383-7980
Registered Federal Lobbyist			
KLINE, Gary		Tel:	(202) 383-7984
Contact, Government Relations			
Registered Federal Lobbyist			
SANTIVIAGO, Sergio		Tel:	(202) 383-7984
Federal Lobbyist			
Registered Federal Lobbyist			
SMITH, Timothy		Tel:	(202) 383-7980
PAC Contact			

At Other Offices

BISHOP, Sandy		Tel:	(201) 269-6701
Executive Assistant		Fax:	(201) 268-1109
100 Parsons Pond Dr.			
Franklin Lakes, NJ 07417			
sandy_bishop@medco.com			
KAUNE, Jason D.			
PAC Treasurer			
2350 Kerner Blvd., Suite 250			
San Rafael, CA 94901			
PRINCIVALLE, Karen		Tel:	(201) 269-3400
Senior Vice President, Human Resources		Fax:	(201) 268-1109
100 Parsons Pond Dr.			
Franklin Lakes, NJ 07417			
SMITH, Ann		Tel:	(201) 269-5984
Contact, Media Relations		Fax:	(201) 268-1109
100 Parsons Pond Dr.			
Franklin Lakes, NJ 07417			
ann_smith@medco.com			

Exxon Mobil Corporation

A multinational oil and gas company created through the merger of Exxon and Mobil. Headquartered in Irving, Texas.
www.exxonmobil.com
Annual Revenues: $394.10 billion
Employees: 75,300
Ticker: NYSE: XOM
SIC: 2992; 2673; 2821; 3081; 3089; 2911
NAICS: 324191; 325211; 325211; 326113; 326199
Industry/ies: Fuels See Coal, Gas, Oil, Petroleum; Natural Resources; Petroleum Industry
Legislative Issues: ANI; AVI; BUD; CAW; CHM; CPI; CPT; DEF; EDU; ENG; ENV; FOR; FUE; GOV; NAT; ROD; SCI; TAX; TRA; TRD

Chairman and Chief Executive Officer

TILLERSON, Rex W.	Tel:	(972) 444-1000
	Fax:	(972) 444-1350

Main Headquarters

Mailing:	5959 Las Colinas Blvd.	Tel:	(972) 444-1000
	Irving, TX 75039	Fax:	(972) 444-1348

Washington Office

Mailing:	3225 Gallows Rd.	Tel:	(703) 846-3000
	Fairfax, VA 22037		

Political Action Committees

Exxon Mobil Corporation PAC
FEC ID: C00121368
Contact: Allan R. Sutherlin
P.O. Box 20503
Suite 1300
Indianapolis, IN 46220

Contributions to Candidates: $1,139,750 (2015-2016)
Democrats: $92,500; Republicans: $1,042,250; Other: $5,000

Principal Recipients

SENATE
AYOTTE, KELLY A (REP-NH)
BENNET, MICHAEL F (DEM-CO)
BLUNT, ROY (REP-MO)
BOOZMAN, JOHN (REP-AR)
BURR, RICHARD (REP-NC)
CORNYN, JOHN (REP-TX)
GRASSLEY, CHARLES E SENATOR (REP-IA)
HOEVEN, JOHN (REP-ND)
ISAKSON, JOHN HARDY (REP-GA)
JOHNSON, RONALD HAROLD (REP-)
LEE, MIKE (REP-UT)
MCCAIN, JOHN S (REP-VA)
MCCONNELL, MITCH (REP-KY)
MORAN, JERRY (REP-KS)
PAUL, RAND (REP-KY)
SCOTT, TIMOTHY E (REP-SC)
SHELBY, RICHARD C (REP-AL)
YOUNG, TODD CHRISTOPHER (REP-IN)

HOUSE
BARTON, JOE LINUS (REP-TX)
BISHOP, ROBERT (REP-UT)
BRADY, KEVIN (REP-TX)
COSTA, JIM MR. (DEM-CA)
GOODLATTE, ROBERT W. (REP-VA)
LANKFORD, JAMES PAUL MR. (REP-OK)
MCCARTHY, KEVIN (REP-CA)
MCHENRY, PATRICK TIMOTHY (REP-NC)
MCSALLY, MARTHA E. MS. (REP-AZ)
RYAN, PAUL D. (REP-WI)
SCALISE, STEVE MR. (REP-LA)
SHIMKUS, JOHN M (REP-IL)
UPTON, FREDERICK STEPHEN (REP-MI)

Corporate Foundations and Giving Programs

Exxon Mobil Foundation		
Contact: Suzanne McCarron		
P.O. Box 7288	TF:	(877) 807-0204
Princeton, NJ 08543		

Public Affairs and Related Activities Personnel

At Headquarters

COHEN, Kenneth P.	Tel:	(972) 444-1000
Vice President, Public and Government Affairs	Fax:	(927) 444-1130
COLTON, W.M.	Tel:	(972) 444-1000
Vice President, Corporate and Strategic Planning	Fax:	(972) 444-1350
EASLEY, Daniel	Tel:	(972) 444-1000
Registered Federal Lobbyist	Fax:	(972) 444-1348
FARIELLO, Theresa	Tel:	(972) 444-1000
Vice President	Fax:	(972) 444-1348
Registered Federal Lobbyist		
MATUSIC, Karen	Tel:	(972) 444-1000
Director, Senior Federal Relations	Fax:	(972) 444-1348
MCCARRON, Suzanne	Tel:	(972) 444-1125
President, ExxonMobil Foundation and General Manager, Public and Government Affairs,	Fax:	(972) 444-1139
MCCOY, Keith	Tel:	(972) 444-1000
Senior Director, Federal Relations	Fax:	(972) 444-1348
Registered Federal Lobbyist		
NOLAN, Robert	Tel:	(972) 444-1000
Senior Government Relations Advisor	Fax:	(972) 444-1350
Registered Federal Lobbyist		
RAYMOND, Tim	Tel:	(972) 444-1000
Federal Lobbyist	Fax:	(972) 444-1350
Registered Federal Lobbyist		
ROMAN, Michael	Tel:	(972) 444-1000
Federal Lobbyist	Fax:	(972) 444-1350
Registered Federal Lobbyist		
ROSENTHAL, David	Tel:	(972) 444-1000
Vice President, Investor Relations and Secretary	Fax:	(972) 444-1350
SPELLINGS, Jr., J. M.	Tel:	(972) 444-1000
Vice President and General Tax Counsel	Fax:	(972) 444-1350
SWIGER, Andrew P.	Tel:	(972) 444-1000
Senior Vice President and Principal Financial Officer	Fax:	(972) 444-1348
WALKER, Courtney S.	Tel:	(972) 444-1181
Corporate Issues Advisor	Fax:	(972) 444-1350
courtney.s.walker@exxonmobil.com		

At Other Offices

BAILEY, David

Manager, Climate Policy
4500 Dacoma St., BH3-739
Houston, TX 77092

BOUDREAUX, Mark
Senior Director, Federal Relations
4500 Dacoma St., BH3-739
Houston, TX 77092

CARTER, S. E.
Washington Representative, Government Agencies
4500 Dacoma St., BH3-739
Houston, TX 77092
Registered Federal Lobbyist

JOHNSON, Lonnie
Senior Director, Federal Relations, Exxon Mobil Corporation
4500 Dacoma St., BH3-739
Houston, TX 77092

KELLER, Laura
Advisor, Regulatory Affairs
4500 Dacoma St., BH3-739
Houston, TX 77092
laura.h.keller@exxonmobil.com
Registered Federal Lobbyist

MITCHELL, Jeanne
Senior Director, Federal Relations
4500 Dacoma St., BH3-739
Houston, TX 77092
Registered Federal Lobbyist

SUTHERLIN, Allan R.
PAC Treasurer
P.O. Box 20503, Suite 1300
Indianapolis, IN 46220

ExxonMobil

See listing on page 312 under Exxon Mobil Corporation

Ezcorp Inc.

Owners of pawnshops. Provides consumer financial services.
www.ezcorp.com
Annual Revenues: $770.82 million
Employees: 7,000
Ticker: NASDAQ: EZPW
SIC: 5900
Industry/ies: Retail/Wholesale

Chief Executive Officer Tel: (512) 314-3400
GRIMSHAW, Stuart I. Fax: (512) 314-3404

Main Headquarters
Mailing: 2500 Bee Cave Rd., Suite 200 Tel: (512) 314-3400
Bldg. One Fax: (512) 314-3404
Rollingwood, TX 78746

Political Action Committees
EZCORP INC. POLITICAL ACTION COMMITTEE
FEC ID: C00414185
Contact: Kelly Kauffman
2500 Bee Cave Rd., Suite 200 Tel: (512) 314-3400
Bldg. One Fax: (512) 314-3404
Rollingwood, TX 78746

Corporate Foundations and Giving Programs
EZCORP Foundation
1901 Capital Pkwy. Tel: (512) 314-3400
Austin, TX 78746 Fax: (512) 314-3404

Public Affairs and Related Activities Personnel

At Headquarters

ALOMES, Scott Tel: (512) 314-3400
Chief Human Resources Officer Fax: (512) 314-3404

ASHBY, Mark Tel: (512) 314-3400
Chief Financial Officer Fax: (512) 314-3404

KAUFFMAN, Kelly Tel: (512) 314-3400
PAC Treasurer Fax: (512) 314-3404

WEDIN, Jacob Tel: (512) 314-3400
Chief Business Development Officer Fax: (512) 314-3404

WELCH, Tom Tel: (512) 314-3400
Senior Vice President, Secretary and General Counsel Fax: (512) 314-3404
tom_welch@ezcorp.com

Ezenia Inc.

Provider of real-time collaboration solutions for corporate networks and the Internet.
www.ezenia.com
Annual Revenues: $2.42 million
Employees: 25
Ticker: OTC: EZLNQ
SIC: 3576

Industry/ies: Computer/Technology

Chairman of the Board Tel: (253) 509-7850
KIDSTON, Samuel

President Tel: (253) 509-7850
SNYDER, Larry

Main Headquarters
Mailing: 115 Hall Brothers Loop Tel: (253) 509-7850
Suite 102 TF: (866) 269-0532
Bainbridge Island, WA 98110

Public Affairs and Related Activities Personnel

At Headquarters

MCCANN, Thomas Tel: (253) 509-7850
Chief Financial Officer

Facebook, Inc.

Online social network.
www.facebook.com
Annual Revenues: $13.51 billion
Employees: 10,082
Ticker: NASDAQ: FB
SIC: 7370
Industry/ies: Communications; Media/Mass Communication;
Telecommunications/Internet/Cable
Legislative Issues: CPI; CPT; CSP; EDU; GOV; HOM; IMM; INT; LAW; MIA; TAX;
TEC; TRD

Founder, Chairman and Chief Executive Officer Tel: (650) 308-7300
ZUCKERBERG, Mark

Main Headquarters
Mailing: 1601 S. California Ave. Tel: (650) 308-7300
Palo Alto, CA 94304

Washington Office
Mailing: 1611 Connecticut Ave. NW
Suite 300
Washington, DC 20009

Political Action Committees
Facebook Inc. PAC
FEC ID: C00502906
Contact: Joel Kaplan
1299 Pennsylvania Ave. NW
Suite 800
Washington, DC 20004

> **Contributions to Candidates:** $292,000 (2015-2016)
> Democrats: $128,500; Republicans: $163,500
>
> **Principal Recipients**
>
> **SENATE**
> LEE, MIKE (REP-UT)

Public Affairs and Related Activities Personnel

At Headquarters

FISCHER, David B. Tel: (650) 308-7300
Vice President, Business and Marketing Partnerships

SANDBERG, Sheryl Tel: (650) 308-7300
Chief Operating Officer

SCHROEPFER, Mike Tel: (650) 308-7300
Chief Technology Officer and Vice President, Engineering

STRETCH, Colin S. Tel: (650) 308-7300
Vice President, General Counsel, and Secretary

WEHNER , Dave Tel: (650) 308-7300
Chief Financial Officer

At Washington Office

STONE, Andy
Policy Communications Manager

At Other Offices

EGAN, Erin M.
Senior Policy Advisor and Director, Privacy
1155 F St. NW, Suite 475
Washington, DC 20004
Registered Federal Lobbyist

GONZALES, Susan
Contact, External Affairs
1155 F St. NW, Suite 475
Washington, DC 20004

HERNDON, Christopher
Manager, Public Policy
1155 F St. NW, Suite 475
Washington, DC 20004
Registered Federal Lobbyist

JORDAN, Myriah L.
Policy Manager

1155 F St. NW, Suite 475
Washington, DC 20004
Registered Federal Lobbyist

MAURER, Greg
Director, Public Policy
1155 F St. NW, Suite 475
Washington, DC 20004
Registered Federal Lobbyist

O'NEILL, Catlin W.
Federal Lobbyist
1155 F St. NW, Suite 475
Washington, DC 20004
Registered Federal Lobbyist

RICE, Brian
Federal Lobbyist
1299 Pennsylvania Ave. NW, Suite 800
Washington, DC 20004
Registered Federal Lobbyist

TERRELL, Louisa
Director, Public Policy
1155 F St. NW, Suite 475
Washington, DC 20004

Fair Isaac Corporation

Predictive analytics solutions.
www.fairisaac.com
Annual Revenues: $815.84 million
Employees: 2,748
Ticker: NYSE: FICO
Industry/ies: Management
Legislative Issues: BAN; FIN

| **Chairman of the Board** | Tel: | (408) 535-1500 |
| BATTLE, George | Fax: | (408) 535-1776 |

| **Chief Executive Officer** | Tel: | (408) 535-1500 |
| LANSING , William | Fax: | (408) 535-1776 |

Main Headquarters

Mailing:	181 Metro Dr.	Tel:	(408) 535-1500
	Suite 700	Fax:	(408) 535-1776
	San Jose, CA 95110		

Corporate Foundations and Giving Programs

FICO Contributions Program
901 Marquette Ave.
Suite 3200
Minneapolis, MN 55402

Public Affairs and Related Activities Personnel

At Headquarters

DEAL , Richard S.	Tel:	(408) 535-1500
Senior Vice President and Chief Human Resources Officer	Fax:	(408) 535-1776
HUYARD, Wayne	Tel:	(408) 535-1500
Executive Vice President, Sales, Services and Marketing	Fax:	(408) 535-1776
PUNG , Michael J.	Tel:	(408) 535-1500
Executive Vice President, Chief Financial Officer and Investor Relations	Fax:	(408) 535-1776
SCADINA, Mark R.	Tel:	(408) 535-1500
Executive Vice President, General Counsel and Corporate Secretary	Fax:	(408) 535-1776

At Other Offices

GUDMUNDSEN, Vance
Vice President, Government Affairs & Data Privacy
901 Marquette Ave., Suite 3200
Minneapolis, MN 55402

NESTEL, Daniel
Contact, Government Relations
901 Marquette Ave., Suite 3200
Minneapolis, MN 55402
Registered Federal Lobbyist

Fairchild Semiconductor International Inc.

Fairchild Semiconductor International is one of the world's oldest chip companies, Fairchild makes semiconductors for tens of thousands of customers in the automotive, computer, consumer electronics, industrial, mobile, and communications markets.Its diversified product line includes logic chips, discrete power and signal components, optoelectronics, and many types of analog and mixed-signal chips.
www.fairchildsemi.com
Annual Revenues: $1.44 billion
Employees: 8,272
Ticker: NYSE: FCS
SIC: 3674
Industry/ies: Energy/Electricity

| **Chairman of the Board, President and Chief Executive Officer** | Tel: | (207) 775-8100 |
| THOMPSON, Mark S. | Fax: | (207) 761-6139 |

Main Headquarters

| *Mailing:* | 3030 Orchard Pkwy. | Tel: | (408) 822-2000 |
| | San Jose, CA 95134 | Fax: | (207) 761-3415 |

Corporate Foundations and Giving Programs

Fairchild Semiconductor Contributions Program
3030 Orchard Pkwy.
San Jose, CA 95134

Public Affairs and Related Activities Personnel

At Other Offices

ALLEXANDRE, Chris	Tel:	(207) 775-8100
Senior Vice President, Worldwide Sales and Marketing	Fax:	(207) 761-6139
82 Running Hill Rd.		
S. Portland, ME 04106		

DELVA, Paul D.	Tel:	(207) 775-8100
Senior Vice President, General Counsel and Corporate Secretary	Fax:	(207) 761-6139
82 Running Hill Rd.		
S. Portland, ME 04106		
paul.delva@fairchildsemi.com		

FREY, Mark S.	Tel:	(207) 775-8100
Executive Vice President, Chief Financial Officer and Treasurer	Fax:	(207) 761-6139
82 Running Hill Rd.		
S. Portland, ME 04106		

JANSON, Dan	Tel:	(207) 775-8100
Vice President, Investor Relations	Fax:	(207) 761-6139
82 Running Hill Rd.		
S. Portland, ME 04106		
investor@fairchildsemi.com		

LONDON, Kevin B.	Tel:	(207) 775-8100
Senior Vice President, Human Resources and Administration	Fax:	(207) 761-6139
82 Running Hill Rd.		
S. Portland, ME 04106		

LONES, Paul	Tel:	(207) 775-8100
Senior Vice President, Human Resources	Fax:	(207) 761-6139
82 Running Hill Rd.		
S. Portland, ME 04106		

FairPoint Communications, Inc.

A telecommunications provider. Provides communications services primarily in rural communities and small urban markets. It offers Internet access, high-speed data, and local and long distance voice services, as well as Ethernet, high capacity data transport, and other IP-based services to residential, business, and wholesale customers.
www.fairpoint.com
Annual Revenues: $884.81 million
Employees: 3,052
Ticker: NASDAQ: FRP
SIC: 4813
Industry/ies: Communications; Telecommunications/Internet/Cable

| **Chairman of the Board** | Tel: | (704) 344-8150 |
| HOROWITZ, Edward D. | Fax: | (704) 344-8121 |

Chief Executive Officer	Tel:	(704) 344-8150
SUNU, Paul	Fax:	(704) 344-8121
psunu@fairpoint.com		

Main Headquarters

Mailing:	521 E. Morehead St.	Tel:	(704) 344-8150
	Suite 250, Box F	Fax:	(704) 344-8121
	Charlotte, NC 28202	TF:	(866) 377-3747

Corporate Foundations and Giving Programs

FairPoint Communications, Inc. Contributions Program		
521 E. Morehead St.	Tel:	(704) 344-8150
Suite 240, Box F		
Charlotte, NC 28202		

Public Affairs and Related Activities Personnel

At Headquarters

LINN, Shirley	Tel:	(704) 344-8150
Executive Vice President, General Counsel	Fax:	(704) 344-8121
AMBURN, Kenneth W.	Tel:	(704) 344-8150
Executive Vice President, Operations and Engineering	Fax:	(704) 344-8121
CASTLE, Gregory W.	Tel:	(704) 344-8150
Executive Vice President, Human Resources	Fax:	(704) 344-8121
LINN, Shirley J.	Tel:	(704) 344-8150
Executive Vice President and General Counsel	Fax:	(704) 344-8121
slinn@fairpoint.com		
NIXON, Peter G.	Tel:	(704) 344-8150
Executive Vice President, External Affairs and Operational Support	Fax:	(704) 344-8121
nixonfam@fairpoint.net		
SABHERWAL, Ajay	Tel:	(704) 344-8150
Executive Vice President and Chief Financial Officer	Fax:	(704) 344-8121

VAN OSDELL, James Garrett   Tel: (704) 344-8150
PAC Treasurer   Fax: (704) 344-8121

Falcon Waterfree Technologies

Provider of a widely installed brand of water-free urinal.
www.falconwaterfree.com
Annual Revenues: $12 million
Employees: 30
Industry/ies: Computer/Technology; Utilities

Chairman of the Board   Tel: (310) 209-7250
NATHANSON, Marc B.   Fax: (310) 209-7260
mnathanson@falconwaterfree.com

Chief Executive Officer and Board Member   Tel: (310) 209-7250
DAVIS, Simon A.   Fax: (310) 209-7260

Main Headquarters
Mailing: 2255 Barry Ave.   Tel: (310) 209-7250
         Los Angeles, CA 90064   Fax: (310) 209-7260

Public Affairs and Related Activities Personnel

At Headquarters

BENNETT, Will   Tel: (310) 209-7250
Vice President, Corporate Development   Fax: (310) 209-7260
wbennett@falconwaterfree.com

CHASE, Andrea   Tel: (310) 209-7250
Manager, Marketing   Fax: (310) 209-7260

KORCINSKY, Matthew   Tel: (310) 209-7250
Managing Director and Chief Financial Officer   Fax: (310) 209-7260
mkorcinsky@falconwaterfree.com

NUSKIEWICZ, Steve   Tel: (310) 209-7250
Senior Vice President, National Sales and Media Contact   Fax: (310) 209-7260
snuskiewicz@falconwaterfree.com

Fallbrook Technologies

A research and development company manufacturing advanced transmission systems.
www.fallbrooktech.com
Annual Revenues: $43 million
Employees: 100
SIC: 3714
Industry/ies: Automotive Industry; Transportation

Chairman of the Board and Chief Executive Officer   Tel: (858) 623-9557
KLEHM, III, William G.   Fax: (858) 623-9563

Main Headquarters
Mailing: 2620 Brushy Creek Loop   Tel: (512) 519-5300
         Cedar Park, TX 78613   Fax: (512) 519-5287
                       TF: (888) 688-4624

Public Affairs and Related Activities Personnel

At Headquarters

BERKOV, Barry F.   Tel: (858) 623-9557
Director, Business Support   Fax: (858) 623-9563
bberkov@fallbrooktech.com

GREY, Robin   Tel: (512) 519-5300
Chief Financial Officer   Fax: (512) 519-5287

MERRILL, Kim   Tel: (619) 857-2782
Media Contact   Fax: (858) 623-9563
kmerrill@fallbrooktech.com

O'LEARY, Sharon A.   Tel: (858) 623-9557
Chief Legal Officer, Secretary and Vice President, Human   Fax: (858) 623-9563
Resources

OATES, David   Tel: (858) 750-5560
Media Contact   Fax: (858) 623-9563
doates@fallbrooktech.com

SMITHSON, Robert A.   Tel: (858) 623-9557
Vice President, Business Development and Chief Technical   Fax: (858) 623-9563
Officer

Family Dollar Stores, Inc.

A discount store chain. Family Dollar operates about 6,600 stores in 45 states and the District of Columbia.
www.familydollar.com
Employees: 34,000
Ticker: NYSE: FDO
SIC: 5331
Industry/ies: Retail/Wholesale

Chairman of the Board & Chief Executive Officer   Tel: (704) 847-6961
LEVINE, Howard R.   Fax: (704) 847-0189
hlevine@familydollar.com

Main Headquarters
Mailing: P.O. Box 1017   Tel: (704) 847-6961
         Charlotte, NC 28201-1017   Fax: (704) 847-0189
                       TF: (877) 377-6420

Corporate Foundations and Giving Programs
Family Dollar Stores Contributions Programs
P.O. Box 1017
Charlotte, NC 28201-1017

Public Affairs and Related Activities Personnel

At Headquarters

RAWLINS, CFA, Kiley F.   Tel: (704) 849-7496
Vice President, Investor Relations   Fax: (704) 847-0189
krawlins@familydollar.com

SNYDER, James C.   Tel: (704) 847-6961
Senior Vice President, General Counsel and Secretary   Fax: (704) 847-0189

VENBERG, Bryan   Tel: (704) 847-6961
Senior Vice President, Human Resources   Fax: (704) 847-0189

WINBURN, Bryn   Tel: (704) 708-1653
Manager, Public & Media Relations   Fax: (704) 847-0189
bwinburn@familydollar.com

WINSTON, Mary A.   Tel: (704) 847-6961
Executive Vice President and Chief Financial Officer   Fax: (704) 847-0189

WONG, Jocelyn   Tel: (704) 847-6961
Senior Vice President and Chief Marketing Officer   Fax: (704) 847-0189

Fareway Stores, Inc.

Regional supermarket chain.
www.fareway.com
Employees: 7,000
Industry/ies: Food And Beverage Industry; Retail/Wholesale

Chairman of the Board   Tel: (515) 432-2623
BECKWITH, Rick   Fax: (515) 433-4416

Chief Executive Officer   Tel: (515) 432-2623
CRAMER, Reynolds   Fax: (515) 433-4416

Main Headquarters
Mailing: 715 Eighth St.   Tel: (515) 432-2623
         P.O. Box 70   Fax: (515) 433-4416
         Boone, IA 50036

Corporate Foundations and Giving Programs
Fareway Stores Contribution Programs
2300 E. Eighth St.
Boone, IA 50036

Public Affairs and Related Activities Personnel

At Headquarters

SHEPLEY, Craig A.   Tel: (515) 432-2623
Chief Financial Officer   Fax: (515) 433-4416

Farm Bureau Mutual Insurance Company of Arkansas

An insurance company.
www.afbic.com
Annual Revenues: $10.60 million
Employees: 400
Industry/ies: Agriculture/Agronomy; Insurance Industry

Main Headquarters
Mailing: 10720 Kanis Rd.   Tel: (501) 228-1404
         P.O. Box 31   Fax: (501) 228-1506
         Little Rock, AR 72203-0031

Corporate Foundations and Giving Programs
Farm Bureau Foundation
10720 Kanis Rd.
P.O. Box 31
Little Rock, AR 72203-0031

Public Affairs and Related Activities Personnel

At Headquarters

EDDINGTON, Steve   Tel: (501) 228-1383
Director, Public relations   Fax: (501) 228-1506

MOORE, David   Tel: (501) 224-4400
Vice President, general manager   Fax: (501) 228-1506

SIMS, Richard   Tel: (501) 228-1404
Manager, Actuarial and Regulatory Affairs   Fax: (501) 228-1506
richard.sims@afbic.com

Farmers Alliance Mutual Insurance Company

Farmers Alliance Companies include three regional insurance companies providing property and casualty insurance for homes, autos, businesses and farms. The companies include Farmers Alliance Mutual Insurance Company (the parent company), Alliance Insurance Company, Inc. and Alliance Indemnity Company.
www.fami.com
Annual Revenues: $25.3 million
Employees: 600
Industry/ies: Insurance Industry

Chairman of the Board, President and Chief Executive Officer   Tel: (620) 241-2200
BIRKHEAD, CPCU, Keith L.   Fax: (620) 241-5482

keith-birkhead@fami.com

Main Headquarters

Mailing:	1122 N. Main	Tel:	(620) 241-2200
	P.O. Box 1401	Fax:	(620) 241-5482
	McPherson, KS 67460-1401		

Public Affairs and Related Activities Personnel

At Headquarters

BROSSARD, Joe	Tel:	(620) 241-2200
President and Chief Operating Officer	Fax:	(620) 241-5482
MCCULLOUGH, Greg	Tel:	(620) 241-2200
Vice President, Human Resources	Fax:	(620) 241-5482
RADER, Jack	Tel:	(620) 241-2200
Chief Marketing Officer and Vice President, Marketing and	Fax:	(620) 241-5482
Reinsurance		
jack-rader@fami.com		
TALIAFERRO, CPA, CPCU, W. Paul	Tel:	(620) 241-2200
Chief Financial Officer and Treasurer	Fax:	(620) 241-5482
paul-taliaferro@fami.com		

Farmers Group Inc.

A major personal lines insurance carrier.
www.farmers.com
Annual Revenues: $5.52 billion
Employees: 24,000
SIC: 6331
Industry/ies: Insurance Industry
Legislative Issues: INS; TAX

Chief Executive Officer   Tel: (323) 932-3200
DAILEY, Jeff

Main Headquarters

Mailing:	4680 Wilshire Blvd.	Tel:	(323) 932-3200
	Los Angeles, CA 90010	TF:	(800) 327-6377

Washington Office

Mailing:	1201 F St. NW	Tel:	(202) 737-1445
	Suite 250	Fax:	(202) 737-1446
	Washington, DC 20004		

Political Action Committees
Farmers Group Inc. PAC
FEC ID: C00135681
Contact: Vigo G. Nielsen Jr.
2350 Kerner Blvd.
Suite 250
San Rafael, CA 94901

   Contributions to Candidates: $286,822 (2015-2016)
   Democrats: $66,122; Republicans: $220,700

Principal Recipients

    HOUSE
     CURBELO, CARLOS (REP-FL)
     HENSARLING, JEB HON. (REP-TX)
     STIVERS, STEVE MR. (REP-OH)
     VALADAO, DAVID (REP-CA)

Corporate Foundations and Giving Programs

Farmers Group Inc. Corporate Contributions Program
4680 Wilshire Blvd.   Tel: (323) 932-3200
Los Angeles, CA 90010

Public Affairs and Related Activities Personnel

At Headquarters

DAVIES, Jerry	Tel:	(323) 932-3662
Director, Media Relations	Fax:	(323) 932-3101
jerry.davies@farmersinsurance.com		
GARAVAGLIA, Burt	Tel:	(323) 932-3200
Assistant Vice President, Regulatory Affairs	Fax:	(323) 932-3101
LINDQUIST, Scott	Tel:	(323) 932-3200
Chief Financial Officer		
LINTON, Michael	Tel:	(323) 932-3200
Chief Marketing Officer		
STRANSKY, Paul	Tel:	(323) 932-3200
Assitant Vice President, State Legislative Affairs		
paul.stransky@farmers.com		
TOOHEY, Mark	Tel:	(805) 907-2216
Head, Political Action and Industry Affairs	Fax:	(323) 964-8095
mark.toohey@farmers.com		
TRAVERS, David	Tel:	(323) 932-3200
Chief Operations Officer		

At Washington Office

GANNON, Matthew	Tel:	(202) 737-1445
Head, Federal Affairs	Fax:	(202) 737-1446
Registered Federal Lobbyist		

LUCIANO, Blaire A.	Tel:	(202) 737-1445
Federal Lobbyist	Fax:	(202) 737-1446
Registered Federal Lobbyist		

At Other Offices

BENSCHNEIDER, Mike	Tel:	(303) 283-6126
Director, Regulatory Affairs	Fax:	(303) 283-6117
7535 E. Hampden Ave., Suite 310		
Denver, CO 80321		
mike.benschneider@farmers.com		
DECKER, Kim	Tel:	(405) 603-4134
Director, Government and Industry Affairs		
5314 S. Yale Dr.		
Tulsa, OK 84135		
NIELSEN, Jr., Vigo G.	Tel:	(415) 389-6800
Attorney & Agent for Filer		
2350 Kerner Blvd., Suite 250		
San Rafael, CA 94901		
CNIELSEN@NMGOVLAW.COM		

Farmers Insurance of Columbus Inc., Farmers Insurance Group of Companies, Farmers Mutual Insurance Company of Nebraska

See listing on page 316 under Farmers Group Inc.

Farmers Investment Company

Farming and agriculture.
Industry/ies: Agriculture/Agronomy

Main Headquarters

Mailing:	1525 E. Sahuarita Rd.	Tel:	(520) 791-2852
	Sahuarita, AZ 85629		

Public Affairs and Related Activities Personnel

At Headquarters

WALDEN, Nan S.	Tel:	(520) 791-2852
Vice President & Counsel		
farmersinvco@greenvalleypecan.com		
Registered Federal Lobbyist		

Farmers Mutual Hail Insurance Company of Iowa

The Farmers Mutual Hail Insurance was established on March 4, 1893 and provides crop insurance in 15 Midwestern states.
www.fmh.com
Annual Revenues: $27.40 million
Employees: 200
Industry/ies: Agriculture/Agronomy; Insurance Industry

Chairman of the Board, President and Chief Executive Officer	Tel:	(515) 282-9104
RUTLEDGE, Ronald P.	Fax:	(515) 282-1220

Main Headquarters

Mailing:	6785 Westown Pkwy.	Tel:	(515) 282-9104
	W. Des Moines, IA 50266	Fax:	(515) 282-1220
		TF:	(800) 247-5248

Political Action Committees
Farmers Mutual Hail Insurance Company Of Iowa PAC (FMH PAC)
FEC ID: C00117614
Contact: Scott Mcentee
6785 Westown Pkwy.
Des Moines, IA 50266

   Contributions to Candidates: $8,600 (2015-2016)
   Republicans: $8,600

Public Affairs and Related Activities Personnel

At Headquarters

FISCHER, Steven G.	Tel:	(515) 282-9104
Vice President, Human Resources	Fax:	(515) 282-1220
LADEHOFF, Debbie	Tel:	(515) 282-9104
Assistant Vice President, Training and Development	Fax:	(515) 282-1220
Coordinator		
MCENTEE, Scott	Tel:	(515) 282-9104
PAC Treasurer	Fax:	(515) 282-1220
SCOTTM@FMH.COM		
ROGGENBURG, Darin L.	Tel:	(515) 282-9104
Chief Financial Officer and Treasurer	Fax:	(515) 282-1220

Fastenal Company

Manufactures and distributes fasteners, industrial products and construction products.
www.fastenal.com
Annual Revenues: $3.92 billion
Employees: 20,324
Ticker: NASDAQ: FAST
SIC: 5200
Industry/ies: Construction/Construction Materials

Chairman	Tel:	(507) 454-5374
OBERTON, Williard D.	Fax:	(507) 453-8049

President and Chief Executive Officer
FLORNESS, Daniel L.
daniel.florness@fastenal.com
Tel: (507) 454-5374
Fax: (507) 453-8049

Main Headquarters
Mailing: 2001 Theurer Blvd.
Winona, MN 55987
Tel: (507) 454-5374
Fax: (507) 453-8049
TF: (877) 507-7555

Public Affairs and Related Activities Personnel

At Headquarters

HEIN, Leland J.
Senior Executive Vice President, Sales
Tel: (507) 454-5374
Fax: (507) 453-8049

JANSEN, James C
Executive Vice President, Manufacturing
Tel: (507) 454-5374
Fax: (507) 453-8049

LISOWSKI, Sheryl A
Interim Chief Financial Officer, Controller, and Chief Accounting Officer
Tel: (507) 454-5374
Fax: (507) 453-8049

LUNDQUIST, Nicholas J.
Executive Vice President, Operations
Tel: (507) 454-5374
Fax: (507) 453-8049

POLIPNICK, Gary A.
Executive Vice President, FAST Solutions
Tel: (507) 454-5374
Fax: (507) 453-8049

WISECUP, Reyne K.
Executive Vice President, Human Resources
Tel: (507) 454-5374
Fax: (507) 453-8049

Fate Therapeutics, Inc.
Founded in 2007 on the leading stem cell and developmental biology research.
www.fatetherapeutics.com
Annual Revenues: $1.80 million
Employees: 50
Ticker: NASDAQ:FATE
Industry/ies: Pharmaceutical Industry; Science; Scientific Research

Chairman of the Board
RASTETTER, William H.
Tel: (858) 875-1800

President and Chief Executive Officer
WEYER, Christian
Tel: (858) 875-1800

Main Headquarters
Mailing: 3535 General Atomics Ct.
Suite 200
San Diego, CA 92121
Tel: (858) 875-1800
TF: (866) 875-1833

Public Affairs and Related Activities Personnel

At Headquarters

DANIELS, Moya M
Vice President of Regulatory Affairs
Tel: (858) 875-1800

GRUBB, Walter
Vice President, Business Development
Tel: (858) 875-1800

MASUDA, Seizo
Corporate Communications
masuda_seizo@takeda.co.jp
Tel: (858) 875-1800

TAHL, Cindy
Senior Director, Intellectual Property and Corporate Counsel
Tel: (858) 875-1800

WOLCHKO, Scott
Chief Financial Officer
Tel: (858) 875-1800

FBL Financial Group, Inc.
Provides markets and distributes life insurance, annuities and mutual funds to individuals and small businesses. Subsidiaries include Farm Bureau Life Insurance Company and EquiTrust Life Insurance Company
www.fblfinancial.com
Annual Revenues: $691.72 million
Employees: 1,589
Ticker: NYSE: FFG
SIC: 6311
Industry/ies: Banking/Finance/Investments; Insurance Industry

Chairman
HILL, Craig D.
Tel: (515) 225-5400
Fax: (515) 226-6053

Chief Executive Officer
BRANNEN, James P.
Jim.Brannen@FBLFinancial.com
Tel: (515) 225-5400
Fax: (515) 226-6053

Main Headquarters
Mailing: 5400 University Ave.
West Des Moines, IA 50266-5997
Tel: (515) 225-5400
Fax: (515) 226-6053

Political Action Committees
FBL Financial Group, Inc. PAC
FEC ID: C00317297
Contact: David A. McNeill
5400 University Ave.
Des Moines, IA 50266

Contributions to Candidates: $3,000 (2015-2016)
Republicans: $3,000

Corporate Foundations and Giving Programs
FBL Financial Group Contributions Program
5400 University Ave.
Des Moines, IA 50266

Public Affairs and Related Activities Personnel

At Headquarters

CHICOINE, Jerry L.
Vice Chairman and Corporate Secretary
Tel: (515) 225-5400
Fax: (515) 226-6053

HAPPEL, Charles T.
Executive Vice President, Chief Investment Officer
Tel: (515) 225-5400
Fax: (515) 226-6053

MCNEILL, David A.
Vice President, General Counsel, Secretary and PAC Treasurer
dave.mcneill@fblfinancial.com
Tel: (515) 225-5400
Fax: (515) 226-6053

SEIBEL, Donald J.
Chief Financial Officer and Treasurer
Tel: (515) 225-5400
Fax: (515) 226-6053

STANGE, Kathleen Till
Vice President, Investor Relations and Corporate Affairs
Kathleen.TillStange@FBLFinancial.com
Tel: (515) 226-6780
Fax: (515) 226-6053

STICE, Scott
Chief Marketing Officer
Tel: (515) 225-5400
Fax: (515) 226-6053

WASILEWSKI, Raymond W.
Chief Operating Officer
Tel: (515) 225-5400
Fax: (515) 226-6053

FCX
See listing on page 342 under Freeport-McMoRan Copper & Gold Inc.

Featherlite Inc.
A provider of aluminum specialty trailers, specialized transporters and custom mobile marketing trailers.
www.fthr.com
Employees: 1,300
SIC: 3715
NAICS: 336212
Industry/ies: Automotive Industry; Metals; Transportation

Main Headquarters
Mailing: Hwy. 63 and Nine
P.O. Box 320
Cresco, IA 52136
Tel: (563) 547-6000
Fax: (563) 547-6100
TF: (800) 800-1230

Public Affairs and Related Activities Personnel

At Headquarters

HALL, John K.
Director, Marketing and Corporate Communications
jhall@fthr.com
Tel: (563) 547-6000
Fax: (563) 547-6100

RUDEN, Rick
Director, Human Resources
Tel: (563) 547-6000
Fax: (563) 547-6100

Federal Agricultural Mortgage Corporation (Farmer Mac)
Farmer Mac is a federally chartered corporation created by Congress to establish a secondary market for agricultural real estate and rural housing mortgage loans, and facilitate capital market funding for USDA-guaranteed farm program and rural development loans.
www.farmermac.com
Annual Revenues: $104.71 million
Employees: 71
Ticker: NYSE: AGM
Industry/ies: Agriculture/Agronomy; Banking/Finance/Investments; Real Estate
Legislative Issues: AGR; FIN

Chairman of the Board
JUNKINS, Lowell L.
Tel: (202) 872-7700
Fax: (202) 872-7713

President and Chief Executive Officer
BUZBY, Timothy L.
Tel: (202) 872-7700
Fax: (202) 872-7713

Main Headquarters
Mailing: 1999 K St. NW
Fourth Floor
Washington, DC 20006
Tel: (202) 872-7700
Fax: (202) 872-7713
TF: (800) 879-3276

Washington Office
Mailing: 1133 21st St. NW
Suite 600
Washington, DC 20036

Political Action Committees
Federal Agricultural Mortgage Corporation Political Action Committee
FEC ID: C00253468
Contact: Christopher A. Bohanon
1133 21st St. NW, Suite 600
Washington, DC 20036
Tel: (202) 872-7700
Fax: (202) 872-7713

Contributions to Candidates: $33,500 (2015-2016)
Democrats: $12,000; Republicans: $21,500

Principal Recipients

HOUSE

LUCAS, FRANK D. (REP-OK)

Public Affairs and Related Activities Personnel

At Headquarters

ACKERMAN, Kenneth D.
Contact, Government Relations
Registered Federal Lobbyist
Tel: (202) 872-7700
Fax: (202) 872-7713

BOHANON, Christopher A.
Vice President, Corporate Affairs
Registered Federal Lobbyist
Tel: (202) 872-7700
Fax: (202) 872-7713

LYNCH, R. Dale
Senior Vice President, Chief Financial Officer and Treasurer
Tel: (202) 872-7700
Fax: (202) 872-7713

MULLERY, Stephen P.
Senior Vice President, General Counsel and Corporate
Secretary
Tel: (202) 872-7700
Fax: (202) 872-7713

STENHOLM, Hon. Charles W.
Contact, Government Relations
Registered Federal Lobbyist
Tel: (202) 872-7700
Fax: (202) 872-7713

STENSON , Tom D.
Executive Vice President, Chief Operating Officer
Tel: (202) 872-7700
Fax: (202) 872-7713

Federal Engineers and Constructors

Construction and environmental remediation company.
www.feandc.com
Annual Revenues: $19 million
Employees: 100
Industry/ies: Construction/Construction Materials; Engineering/Mathematics

Chairman of the Board, President, Chief Executive Officer and PAC Contact
FRENCH, Richard T.
rfrenchjr@feandc.com
Tel: (509) 375-1608
Fax: (509) 375-3427

Main Headquarters
Mailing: 3240 Richardson Rd.
Richland, WA 99354-5501
Tel: (509) 375-1608
Fax: (509) 375-3427

Public Affairs and Related Activities Personnel

At Headquarters

BLANKENSHIP, Jessica
Contact, General Counsel
jblankenship@feandc.com
Tel: (509) 375-1608
Fax: (509) 375-3427

FRENCH, Jr., Richard
Executive Vice President, Business Development
Tel: (509) 375-1608
Fax: (509) 375-3427

YOUNES, Bassel
Chief Financial Officer
Tel: (509) 375-1608
Fax: (509) 375-3427

Federal Home Loan Bank of Cincinnati

FHLB Cincinnati is part of the Federal Home Loan Bank System. Federal Home Loan Bank of Cincinnati provides funds for residential mortgages and community development loans to member commercial banks, thrifts, credit unions, and insurance companies.
www.fhlbcin.com
Employees: 200
SIC: 6111
Industry/ies: Banking/Finance/Investments
Legislative Issues: BAN; FIN

Chairman of the Board
WICK, Carl F.
Tel: (513) 852-7500
Fax: (513) 852-7655

President and Chief Executive Officer
HOWELL, Andrew S.
Tel: (513) 852-7500
Fax: (513) 852-7655

Main Headquarters
Mailing: P.O. Box 598
Cincinnati, OH 45201-0598
Tel: (513) 852-7500
Fax: (513) 852-7655
TF: (888) 852-6500

Corporate Foundations and Giving Programs

Federal Home Loan Bank of Cincinnati Contributions Program
P.O. Box 598
Cincinnati, OH 45201-0598

Public Affairs and Related Activities Personnel

At Headquarters

ABLE, Donald R.
Executive Vice President, Chief Operating Officer and Chief Financial Officer
Tel: (513) 852-7500
Fax: (513) 852-7655

BAUER, Jerome C.
Assistant Vice President, Investment Services
bauerjc@fhlbcin.com
Tel: (513) 852-7018
Fax: (513) 852-7655

COSSE, Carole L.
Senior Vice President and Chief Financial Officer
Tel: (513) 852-7500
Fax: (513) 852-7655

DALLAS, Melissa A.
Vice President, Counsel and Corporate Secretary
Tel: (513) 852-7084
Fax: (513) 852-7655

LAWLER, R. Kyle
Executive Vice President and Chief Business Officer
Tel: (513) 852-7500
Fax: (513) 852-7655

RUSSO, Karla
Vice President, Human Resources
Tel: (513) 852-7500
Fax: (513) 852-7655

SPONAUGLE, Stephen J.
Senior Vice President, Chief Risk and Compliance Officer
Tel: (513) 852-7500
Fax: (513) 852-7655

Federal Home Loan Bank of San Francisco

Provides loans and other products and services to member financial institutions. It is a cooperative, wholesale bank that helps meet community credit needs by providing readily available, competitively priced credit products and services to member financial institutions through all phases of the economic cycle.
www.fhlbsf.com
Employees: 300
SIC: 6111
Industry/ies: Banking/Finance/Investments; Housing
Legislative Issues: BAN; BUD; FIN; HOU

Chairman
(TAD) LOWREY, Douglas H.
Tel: (415) 616-1000
Fax: (415) 616-2626

President and Chief Executive Officer
SEIBLY, Greg
Tel: (415) 616-1000
Fax: (415) 616-2626

Main Headquarters
Mailing: P.O. Box 7948
San Francisco, CA 94120-7948
Tel: (415) 616-1000
Fax: (415) 616-2626
TF: (800) 283-0700

Corporate Foundations and Giving Programs

Federal Home Loan Bank of San Francisco Contributions Program
Contact: Stephen P. Traynor
P.O. Box 7948
San Francisco, CA 94120
Tel: (415) 616-1000

Public Affairs and Related Activities Personnel

At Headquarters

FONTENOT, Gregory P.
Senior Vice President, Human Resources
Tel: (415) 616-1000
Fax: (415) 616-2626

MACMILLEN, Lisa B.
Executive Vice President and Chief Operating Officer
Tel: (415) 616-1000
Fax: (415) 616-2626

MILLER, Kenneth C.
Senior Vice President and Chief Financial Officer
millerk@fhlbsf.com
Tel: (415) 616-1000
Fax: (415) 616-2626

PARKS, Lawrence H.
Senior Vice President, External and Legislative Affairs
Tel: (415) 616-1000
Fax: (415) 616-2626

REMCH, Patricia M.
Senior Vice President, Sales and Marketing
Tel: (415) 616-1000
Fax: (415) 616-2626

STEWART, Amy
Vice President, Corporate Communications
stewarta@fhlbsf.com
Tel: (415) 616-2605
Fax: (415) 616-2626

TITUS-JOHNSON, Suzanne
Senior Vice President, General Counsel and Corporate Secretary
titus-johnsons@fhlbsf.com,titusjos@fhlbsf.com
Tel: (415) 616-1000
Fax: (415) 616-2626

TRAYNOR, Stephen P.
Senior Vice President, Financial Services and Community Investment
traynors@fhlbsf.com
Tel: (415) 616-1000
Fax: (415) 616-2626

At Other Offices

MARTENS, David H.
Senior Vice President and Chief Risk Officer
600 California St.
San Francisco, CA 94108
Tel: (415) 616-1000
Fax: (415) 616-2626

Federal Home Loan Bank of Topeka

U.S. government-sponsored banks that provide stable, on-demand, low-cost funding to American financial institutions (not individuals) for home mortgage loans, small business, rural, agricultural, and economic development lending.
www.fhlbtopeka.com
Annual Revenues: $475.51 million
Employees: 100
SIC: 6111
Industry/ies: Banking/Finance/Investments
Legislative Issues: FIN; HOU

Chairman of the Board
COX, G. Bridger
Tel: (785) 233-0507
Fax: (785) 234-1716

President and Chief Executive Officer
JETTER, Andrew J.
Tel: (785) 233-0507
Fax: (785) 234-1716

Main Headquarters
Mailing: P.O. Box 176
Topeka, KS 66601-0176
Tel: (785) 233-0507
Fax: (785) 234-1716

Corporate Foundations and Giving Programs

Federal Home Loan Bank of Topeka Contribution Program
P.O. Box 176
Topeka, KS 66601-0176
Tel: (785) 233-0507
Fax: (785) 234-1716

Public Affairs and Related Activities Personnel

At Headquarters

DEVADER, Julie
*Vice President and Director, Public Relations and
Communications*
julie.devader@fhlbtopeka.com
Tel: (785) 438-6044
Fax: (785) 438-6190

DORAN, Patrick C.
Senior Vice President and General Counsel
pat.doran@fhlbtopeka.com
Tel: (785) 438-6045
Fax: (785) 234-1716

At Other Offices

FISHER, David S.
Senior Executive Vice President and Chief Operating Officer
One Security Benefit Pl.
Topeka, KS 66606-2444
Tel: (785) 233-0507
Fax: (785) 234-1716

HAAR, Eric T.
Vice President, Government Relations and PAC Treasurer
One Security Benefit Pl.
Topeka, KS 66606-2444
Tel: (785) 438-6010
Fax: (785) 234-1716

HESS , Dan
Senior Vice President, Chief Business Officer
One Security Benefit Pl.
Topeka, KS 66606-2444
dan.hess@fhlbtopeka.com
Tel: (785) 438-6039
Fax: (785) 234-1716

SILER, Stephen
Head of Human Resources
One Security Benefit Pl.
Topeka, KS 66606-2444
steve.siler@fhlbtopeka.com
Tel: (785) 233-0507
Fax: (785) 234-1716

YARDLEY, Mark E.
Executive Vice President and Chief Risk Officer
One Security Benefit Pl.
Topeka, KS 66606-2444
Tel: (785) 233-0507
Fax: (785) 234-1794

Federal Home Loan Mortgage Corporation

*Freddie Mac (officially Federal Home Loan Mortgage Corporation) and Fannie Mae were
established to buy residential mortgages. Mission is to stabilize the nation's residential
mortgage markets and expand opportunities for homeownership and affordable rental housing.*
www.freddiemac.com
Annual Revenues: $69.17 billion
Employees: 5,000
Ticker: OTCQB: FMCC
SIC: 6111
Industry/ies: Banking/Finance/Investments; Real Estate

Non-Executive Chairman
LYNCH, Christopher
Tel: (703) 903-3993

Chief Executive Officer
LAYTON, Donald H.
Tel: (703) 903-3993
Fax: (202) 434-8641

Main Headquarters
Mailing: 8200 Jones Branch Dr.
McLean, VA 22102-3110
Tel: (703) 903-2000
TF: (800) 424-5401

Corporate Foundations and Giving Programs

Freddie Mac Foundation
Contact: Wendell J. Chambliss
8200 Jones Branch Dr.
McLean, VA 22102
Tel: (703) 903-2000
Fax: (703) 903-2447

Public Affairs and Related Activities Personnel

At Headquarters

CHAMBLISS, Wendell J.
Executive Director, Freddie Mac Foundation
Tel: (703) 903-3552

COSGROVE, Michael
Contact, Media Relations
Tel: (703) 903-3993

GERMAN, Brad
Senior Director, Public Relations
brad_german@freddiemac.com
Tel: (703) 903-3993

HUTCHINS, Michael
Senior Vice President, Investments and Capital Markets
Tel: (703) 903-2000

MACKEY, James G.
Executive Vice President and Chief Financial Officer
Tel: (703) 903-2000

MCDAVID, William
*General Counsel, Executive Vice President and Corporate
Secretary*
Tel: (703) 903-3993

MCHALE, Sharon
Vice President, Public Relations and Corporate Marketing
sharon_mchale@freddiemac.com
Tel: (703) 903-3993

MCLOUGHLIN, Hollis
Senior Vice President, External Relations
Tel: (703) 903-3993

ROBINSON, Dwight
*Senior Vice President, Human Resources, Diversity and
Outreach and Chief Diversity Officer*
Tel: (703) 903-2000

WAMBEKE, Carol
Senior Vice President and Chief Compliance Officer
Tel: (703) 903-3993

WANDLER, Chad
Contact, Media
Chad_Wandler@FreddieMac.com
Tel: (703) 903-2446

WEISS, Jerry
Executive Vice President and Chief Administrative Officer
Tel: (703) 903-2000

WILLIAMS, Wade S.
PAC Contact
Tel: (703) 903-2000

At Other Offices

FOX, Barbara Matheson
Vice President, Government Affairs
325 Seventh St. NW, Suite 500
Washington, DC 20004
Mail Stop 600
Tel: (202) 434-8618
Fax: (202) 434-8641

Federal Mogul Corporation

*A global manufacturer of a broad range of precision parts primarily for automobiles, trucks,
and farm and construction vehicles.*
www.federalmogul.com
Employees: 44,300
Ticker: NASDAQ: FDML
SIC: 3714; 2891; 3069; 3751
NAICS: 336991; 315999; 339932; 326299
Industry/ies: Automotive Industry; Transportation

Non-executive Chairman of the Board
ICAHN, Carl C.
Tel: (248) 354-7700
Fax: (248) 354-8950

Co-Chief Executive Officer
JUECKSTOCK, Rainer
Tel: (248) 354-7700
Fax: (248) 354-8950

Main Headquarters
Mailing: 27300 West 11 Mile Rd.
Southfield, MI 48034
Tel: (248) 354-7700
Fax: (248) 354-8950
TF: (800) 325-8886

Political Action Committees

Federal Mogul Corporation Employees' PAC
FEC ID: C00084582
Contact: Irv Morse
26555 Northwest Hwy.
Southfield, MI 48033

Public Affairs and Related Activities Personnel

At Headquarters

CALDWELL, Michelle
Contact Communication
michelle.caldwell@federalmogul.com
Tel: (248) 354-7060
Fax: (248) 354-8950

FAULS, Kathy
Investor Relations Representative
kathy.fauls@federalmogul.com
Tel: (248) 354-9942
Fax: (248) 354-8950

FISCHER, Horst
Senior Vice President, Sales and Marketing
Tel: (248) 354-7700
Fax: (248) 354-8950

GOACHET, Pascal
*Senior Vice President, Global Human Resources and
Organization*
Tel: (248) 354-7700
Fax: (248) 354-8950

MORSE, Irv
PAC Treasurer
Tel: (248) 354-7700
Fax: (248) 354-8950

PEPIN, Scott
Senior Vice President, Global Human Resources
Tel: (248) 354-7700
Fax: (248) 354-8950

PYNNONEN, Brett
*Senior Vice President, General Counsel and Chief
Compliance Officer*
brett.pynnonen@federalmogul.com
Tel: (248) 354-7700
Fax: (248) 354-8950

SHAH, Rajesh
Senior Vice President and Chief Financial Officer
Tel: (248) 354-7700
Fax: (248) 354-8950

Federal National Mortgage Association

See listing on page 319 under Fannie Mae

Fannie Mae

*Fannie Mae was established as a federal agency in 1938, and was chartered by Congress
in 1968 as a private shareholder-owned company. Formerly the Federal National Mortgage
Association, the company legally changed its name in 1997. Fannie Mae has three lines
of business - Single-Family, Multifamily and Capital Markets - that provide services and
products to lenders and a broad range of housing partners.*
www.fanniemae.com
Annual Revenues: $39.45 billion
Employees: 7,400
Ticker: OTC: FNMA
SIC: 6111
Industry/ies: Banking/Finance/Investments; Housing; Real Estate

Director and Chairman of the Board
LASKAWY, Philip A.
Tel: (202) 752-7000
Fax: (202) 752-0137

President and Chief Executive Officer
MAYOPOULOS, Timothy J.
timothy_mayopoulos@fanniemae.com

Tel: (202) 752-7000
Fax: (202) 752-0137

Main Headquarters
Mailing: 3900 Wisconsin Ave. NW
Washington, DC 20016-2892

Tel: (202) 752-7000
Fax: (202) 752-0137
TF: (800) 732-6643

Political Action Committees
Fannie Mae Affiliated Mortgage Lenders Super PAC
FEC ID: C00456368
Contact: Josue Larose
P.O. Box 9961
Fort Lauderdale, FL 33310

Tel: (202) 752-7000
Fax: (202) 752-0137

Corporate Foundations and Giving Programs
Fannie Mae Foundation
3900 Wisconsin Ave. NW
Washington, DC 20016

Tel: (202) 752-6112
Fax: (202) 752-6099

Public Affairs and Related Activities Personnel

At Headquarters

BENSON, David
Executive Vice President and Chief Financial Officer

Tel: (202) 752-7000
Fax: (202) 752-0137

BOILLAT, Pascal
Senior Vice President Operations and Technology

Tel: (202) 752-7000
Fax: (202) 752-0137

BROOKS, Brian P.
Executive Vice President, General Counsel and Corporate Secretary

Tel: (202) 752-7000
Fax: (202) 752-0137

DAVENPORT, Maureen
Senior Vice President Chief and Communications Officer

Tel: (202) 752-7000
Fax: (202) 752-0137

DUNN, Judith C.
Senior Vice President, Principal Deputy General Counsel

Tel: (202) 752-7000
Fax: (202) 752-0137

EDWARDS, Terry
Executive Vice President and Chief Operating Officer

Tel: (202) 752-7000
Fax: (202) 752-0137

FORLINES, John
Senior Vice President and Chief Audit Executive

Tel: (202) 752-7000
Fax: (202) 752-0137

JARDINI, Nancy
Senior Vice President and Chief Compliance Officer

Tel: (202) 752-7000
Fax: (202) 752-0137

MCQUAID, Brian
Senior Vice President and Chief Human Resources Officer

Tel: (202) 752-7000
Fax: (202) 752-0137

POPE, Justine
Vice President, Regulatory Affairs

Tel: (202) 752-7000
Fax: (202) 752-0137

Federal Signal Corporation

Designer and manufacturer of various emergency and disaster use products for municipal, governmental, industrial and institutional customers.
www.federalsignal.com
Annual Revenues: $744.30 million
Employees: 2,200
Ticker: NYSE: FSS
SIC: 3599; 3711
NAICS: 333999
Industry/ies: Machinery/Equipment

Executive Chairman of the Board
MARTIN, Dennis J.

Tel: (630) 954-2000
Fax: (630) 954-2030

Chief Executive Officer
SHERMAN, Jennifer L.
jsherman@federalsignal.com

Tel: (630) 954-2000
Fax: (630) 954-2030

Main Headquarters
Mailing: 1415 W. 22nd St.
Suite 1100
Oak Brook, IL 60523

Tel: (630) 954-2000
Fax: (630) 954-2030

Public Affairs and Related Activities Personnel

At Headquarters

COOK, Julie A.
Vice President, Human Resources

Tel: (630) 954-2000
Fax: (630) 954-2030

COOPER, Brian S.
Senior Vice President and Chief Financial Officer

Tel: (630) 954-2000
Fax: (630) 954-2030

DUPRÉ, Daniel A.
Vice President, General Counsel and Secretary

Tel: (630) 954-2000
Fax: (630) 954-2030

GOODWIN, James E.
Director

Tel: (630) 954-2000
Fax: (630) 954-2030

NOEL, Lana J.
Paralegal
lnoel@federalsignal.com

Tel: (630) 954-2008
Fax: (630) 954-2030

VINOKUR, Svetlana
Vice President, Treasurer and Corporate Development

Tel: (630) 954-2000
Fax: (630) 954-2030

Federated Department Stores

See listing on page 504 under Macy's Inc.

Federated Investors, Inc.

Provides investment advisory and administrative services.
www.federatedinvestors.com
Annual Revenues: $868.28 million
Employees: 1,435
Ticker: NYSE: FII
SIC: 6282
Industry/ies: Banking/Finance/Investments
Legislative Issues: FIN

Chairman of the Board and Co-founder
DONAHUE, John F.

Tel: (412) 288-1900
Fax: (412) 288-1171

President and Chief Executive Officer
DONAHUE, J. Christopher

Tel: (412) 288-1900
Fax: (412) 288-1171

Main Headquarters
Mailing: 1001 Liberty Ave.
1001 Liberty Ave.
Pittsburgh, PA 15222

Tel: (412) 288-1900
Fax: (412) 288-1171
TF: (800) 341-7400

Public Affairs and Related Activities Personnel

At Headquarters

BONNEWELL, G. Andrew
Senior Vice President & Chief Government Affairs Officer
Registered Federal Lobbyist

Tel: (412) 288-1900
Fax: (412) 288-1171

BOUDA, Brian P.
Vice President and Chief Compliance Officer

Tel: (412) 288-1900
Fax: (412) 288-1171

COSTELLO, Edward
Manager, Corporate Communications
ecostello@federatedinv.com

Tel: (412) 288-1900
Fax: (412) 288-1171

DONAHUE, Thomas R.
President, Chief Financial Officer and Treasurer

Tel: (412) 288-1900
Fax: (412) 288-1171

FRANK, Frederick
Esq.

Tel: (412) 288-1900
Fax: (412) 288-1171

MCANDREW, Meghan
Contact, Media Relations
mmcandrew@federatedinv.com

Tel: (412) 288-8103
Fax: (412) 288-1171

MCGONIGLE, John W.
Vice Chairman, Executive Vice President, Chief Legal Officer and Secretary

Tel: (412) 288-1900
Fax: (412) 288-1171

RYAN, Melissa
Manager, Corporate Communications
mryan@federatedinv.com

Tel: (412) 288-8079
Fax: (412) 288-1171

FedEx Corporation

Provides transportation, e-commerce, and business services in the United States and internationally.
www.fedex.com/us
Annual Revenues: $49.50 billion
Employees: 246,000
Ticker: NYSE: FDX
SIC: 4513
Industry/ies: Aerospace/Aviation; Airlines; Postal And Mail Services; Transportation
Legislative Issues: AVI; BUD; ENV; HOM; INT; LBR; POS; TAX; TRA; TRD; TRU

President, Chairman of the Board and Chief Executive Officer
SMITH, Frederick W.

Tel: (901) 369-3600
Fax: (901) 395-2000

Main Headquarters
Mailing: 942 S. Shady Grove Rd.
Memphis, TN 38120

Tel: (901) 369-3600

Washington Office
Mailing: 101 Constitution Ave. NW
Suite 801 East
Washington, DC 20005

Tel: (202) 218-3800
Fax: (202) 218-3803

Political Action Committees
FedEx PAC Federal Express PAC
FEC ID: C00068692
Contact: Clement E. Klank
942 S. Shady Grove Rd.
Memphis, TN 38120

Tel: (901) 369-3600

Contributions to Candidates: $362,625 (2015-2016)
Democrats: $128,000; Republicans: $231,625; Other: $3,000

Corporate Foundations and Giving Programs
FedEx Global Community Relations
Contact: Rose Flenorl
1669 Kirby Pkwy.
Suite 202
Memphis, TN 38125

Tel: (901) 818-7500
Fax: (901) 395-2000

Public Affairs and Related Activities Personnel

At Headquarters

FLENORL, Rose
Manager, Social Responsibility

Tel: (901) 369-3600

FOSTER, Mickey   Tel: (901) 369-3600
Vice President, Investor Relations

GLENN, T. Michael   Tel: (901) 369-3600
Executive Vice President, Market Development and Corporate Communications
t.michael.glenn@fedex.com

GRAF, Jr., Alan B.   Tel: (901) 369-3600
Executive Vice President and Chief Financial Officer
ABGRAF@fedex.com

KLANK, Clement E.   Tel: (901) 369-3600
PAC Treasurer

RICHARDS, Christine P.   Tel: (901) 369-3600
Executive Vice President, General Counsel and Secretary

At Washington Office

ADAMS, Gina F.   Tel: (202) 218-3800
Corporate Vice President, Government Affairs   Fax: (202) 218-3803
Registered Federal Lobbyist

DICKEY, Ann S.   Tel: (202) 218-3800
Federal Lobbyist   Fax: (202) 218-3803
Registered Federal Lobbyist

HUGHES, Gerald F.   Tel: (202) 218-3800
Federal Lobbyist   Fax: (202) 218-3803
gerald.hughes@fedex.com
Registered Federal Lobbyist

KAMARA, Mayealie   Tel: (202) 218-3800
Manager, Government Affairs   Fax: (202) 218-3803

KORKOIAN, David   Tel: (202) 218-3800
Registered Federal Lobbyist   Fax: (202) 218-3803

MANGUM, Lance   Tel: (202) 218-3800
Senior Federal Affairs Representative   Fax: (202) 218-3803
Registered Federal Lobbyist

RAND, Kathryn   Tel: (202) 218-3800
Federal Lobbyist   Fax: (202) 218-3803
kathryn.rand@fedex.com
Registered Federal Lobbyist

RODGERS, Richard F.   Tel: (202) 218-3800
Staff Vice President, Government Affairs   Fax: (202) 218-3803
Registered Federal Lobbyist

FedEx Freight Corporation

A less-than-truckload subsidiary of FedEx Corp. (see separate listing) that consists of FedEx Freight East (formerly known as American Freightways) and FedEx Freight West (formerly known as Viking Freight).
www.fedex.com/us/freight/index.html
Annual Revenues: $4.9 billion
Employees: 33,000
Ticker: NYSE: FDX
Industry/ies: Transportation

Executive Vice President and Chief Operating Officer   Tel: (901) 346-4400
LOGUE, William J.   Fax: (901) 434-3118

Main Headquarters
Mailing: Renaissance Center   Tel: (901) 346-4400
     1715 Aaron Brenner Dr., Suite 600   Fax: (901) 434-3118
     Memphis, TN 38120

Public Affairs and Related Activities Personnel

At Headquarters

BROWN, Donald C.   Tel: (901) 346-4400
Executive Vice President, Finance, Administration and Chief   Fax: (901) 434-3118
Financial Officer

PHILLIPS, Debra   Tel: (901) 434-3122
Managing Director, Communications   Fax: (901) 434-3155
debra.phillips@fedex.com

Feld Entertainment Inc.

The owner of Ringling Brothers/Barnum & Bailey Circus, Disney on Ice, Ringling Brothers and Barnum & Bailey Center for Elephant Conservation, Disney Live!, and Doodlebops. Produces and presents live touring family entertainment shows in the United States and internationally.
www.feldentertainment.com
Annual Revenues: $81.20 million
Employees: 1,700
Industry/ies: Sports/Leisure/Entertainment
Legislative Issues: ANI; CSP; HCR; TAX

Chairman of the Board and Chief Executive Officer   Tel: (703) 448-4000
FELD, Kenneth   Fax: (703) 448-4091

Main Headquarters
Mailing: 2001 US Hwy. 301   Tel: (941) 721-1200
     Palmetto, FL 34221

Washington Office
Mailing: 8607 Westwood Center Dr.   Tel: (703) 448-4000
     Vienna, VA 22182   Fax: (703) 448-4100

    TF: (800) 844-3545

Corporate Foundations and Giving Programs
Feld Entertainment Contributions Program
8607 Westwood Center Dr.   Tel: (703) 448-4000
Vienna, VA 22182   Fax: (703) 448-4100

Feld Family Foundation
8607 Westwood Center Dr.   Tel: (703) 448-4000
Vienna, VA 22182   Fax: (703) 448-4100

Public Affairs and Related Activities Personnel

At Washington Office

ALBERT, Thomas L.   Tel: (703) 448-4000
Vice President, Government Relations   Fax: (703) 448-4100
Registered Federal Lobbyist

BITSOFF, Jason   Tel: (703) 448-4000
Vice President, Sponsorship and Strategic Alliances and   Fax: (703) 448-4100
General Manager

DENNY, Hartwig   Tel: (630) 566-6305
Director, Communications   Fax: (703) 448-4100
dhartwig@feldinc.com

GROSSMAN, Michelle   Tel: (703) 448-4000
    Fax: (703) 448-4100

MOYERS, Leigh   Tel: (703) 448-4000
Federal Lobbyist   Fax: (703) 448-4100
Registered Federal Lobbyist

PAYNE, Stephen   Tel: (703) 749-5505
Vice President, Corporate Communications   Fax: (703) 448-4100
spayne@feldinc.com

SENGLAUB, Keith   Tel: (703) 448-4000
Senior Vice President, Finance, Chief Financial Officer and   Fax: (703) 448-4100
Treasurer

Fellowes, Inc.

Manufacturer and marketer of business machines, records storage and office accessories. It sells its products both offline in retail outlets and online via e-commerce stores worldwide.
www.fellowes.com
Annual Revenues: $700.00 million
Employees: 1,500
SIC: 2652
NAICS: 322213
Industry/ies: Machinery/Equipment

Chairman of the Board (Non-Executive)   Tel: (630) 893-1600
FELLOWS, James E.   Fax: (630) 893-1683

Chief Executive Officer   Tel: (630) 893-1600
FELLOWES, II, John E.   Fax: (630) 893-1683

Main Headquarters
Mailing: 1789 Norwood Ave.   Tel: (630) 893-1600
     Itasca, IL 60143   Fax: (630) 893-1683
     TF: (800) 955-3344

Corporate Foundations and Giving Programs
Fellowes Charitable Giving Program
1789 Norwood Ave.
Itasca, IL 60143-1095

Public Affairs and Related Activities Personnel

At Headquarters

BULMAN, Lyn   Fax: (630) 893-1683
Executive Vice President, Global Human Resources

MOORE, Maureen   Tel: (630) 671-8434
Vice President, Corporate Marketing and Contact, Public   Fax: (630) 893-1683
Relations
mmoore@fellowes.com

PARKER, Mike   Tel: (630) 893-1600
President, Global Sales   Fax: (630) 893-1683

Ferrell Companies, Inc.

A construction software and services company. They have been serving the construction industry by providing cutting-edge technology and business solutions designed to save time and money for contractors.
www.ferrell.net
Employees: 1,500
SIC: 5900
Industry/ies: Computer/Technology

President and Chief Executive Officer   Tel: (303) 233-2400
FERRELL, Jerry T.   Fax: (303) 234-5645

Main Headquarters
Mailing: 7456 W. Fifth Ave.   Tel: (303) 233-2400
     Lakewood, CO 80226   Fax: (303) 234-5645

Ferro Corporation

A manufacturer of specialty materials and chemicals.

www.ferro.com
Annual Revenues: $1.09 billion
Employees: 4,846
Ticker: NYSE: FOE
SIC: 2821; 2869; 2899; 3087; 2851
NAICS: 325211; 325131; 32551; 325998
Industry/ies: Chemicals & Chemical Industry

Chairman, President and Chief Executive Officer　Tel:　(216) 875-5600
THOMAS, Peter T.　Fax:　(216) 875-5627

Main Headquarters
Mailing:　6060 Parkland Blvd.　Tel:　(216) 875-5600
　　　Mayfield Heights, OH 44124　Fax:　(216) 875-5627

Corporate Foundations and Giving Programs

Ferro Foundation
Contact: Don Katchman
1000 Lakeside Ave.　Tel:　(216) 641-8580
Cleveland, OH 44114

Public Affairs and Related Activities Personnel

At Headquarters

RUTHERFORD, Jeffrey L.　Tel:　(216) 875-5600
Vice President and Chief Financial Officer　Fax:　(216) 875-5627

TORTAJADA, Jose　Tel:　(216) 875-5600
Vice President, Human Resources　Fax:　(216) 875-5627

At Other Offices

ABOOD, Mary E.　Tel:　(216) 875-5401
Director, Corporate Communications　Fax:　(216) 875-7205
1000 Lakeside Ave.
Cleveland, OH 44114-1147
aboodm@ferro.com

DUESENBERG, Mark H.　Tel:　(216) 641-8580
Vice President, General Counsel and Secretary　Fax:　(216) 875-7205
1000 Lakeside Ave.
Cleveland, OH 44114-1147

Fev Engines
Designer and developer of internal combustion engines, and a supplier of advanced testing and instrumentation products and services to some of the world's largest power train OEMs.
www.fev.com
Employees: 400
Industry/ies: Machinery/Equipment

President and Chief Executive Officer　Tel:　(284) 373-6000
PISCHINGER, Dr. Stefan　Fax:　(284) 373-8084

Main Headquarters
Mailing:　4554 Glenmeade Ln.　Tel:　(284) 373-6000
　　　Auburn Hills, MI 48326-1766　Fax:　(284) 373-8084

Public Affairs and Related Activities Personnel

At Headquarters

ALBERS, Andreas　Tel:　(284) 373-6000
Contact, Corporate Communication　Fax:　(284) 373-8084
presse@fev.com

PAULSEN, Rainer　Tel:　(284) 373-6000
Executive Vice President, Operations　Fax:　(284) 373-8084

ROHATYNSKI, Joe　Tel:　(284) 378-6570
Public Relations Contact　Fax:　(284) 373-8084
joe@joepr.com

SAGUR, Betriebsw Sami　Tel:　(284) 373-6000
Executive Vice President, Finance　Fax:　(284) 373-8084

FFF Enterprises
A healthcare company providing solutions in biopharmaceutical management and distribution, health information management and consumer healthcare services. Distributor of plasma products, vaccines and other biopharmaceuticals in the U.S.
www.fffenterprises.com
Annual Revenues: $36.60 million
Employees: 200
Industry/ies: Pharmaceutical Industry

Chief Executive Officer　Tel:　(961) 296-2500
SCHMIDT, Patrick M.　Fax:　(800) 418-4333

Main Headquarters
Mailing:　41093 County Center Dr.　Tel:　(951) 296-2500
　　　Temecula, CA 92591　Fax:　(800) 418-4333
　　　　　TF:　(800) 843-7477

Corporate Foundations and Giving Programs

FFF Enterprises Contributions Program
Contact: Patrick M. Schmidt
41093 County Center Dr.　Tel:　(951) 296-2500
Temecula, CA 92591　Fax:　(800) 418-4333

Public Affairs and Related Activities Personnel

At Headquarters

COOPER, Brad　Tel:　(951) 296-2500
Chief Financial Officer　Fax:　(800) 418-4333

GROUND, Chris　Tel:　(951) 296-2500
Chief Operating Officer　Fax:　(800) 418-4333

HUBACH, Michele　Tel:　(951) 296-2500
Vice President Finance and Operations　Fax:　(800) 418-4333

NEIER, Greg　Tel:　(951) 296-2500
Vice President, Business Development　Fax:　(800) 418-4333

PEREZ, Sheryl　Tel:　(961) 296-2500
Vice President, Marketing and Communications　Fax:　(800) 418-4333

PRIMOVIC, Jeff　Tel:　(951) 296-2500
Senior Vice President, Strategic Relationships　Fax:　(800) 418-4333

RICHTER, Sue　Tel:　(951) 296-2500
Vice President, Marketing and Communications　Fax:　(800) 418-4333

FHLB Cincinnati
See listing on page 318 under Federal Home Loan Bank of Cincinnati

FHLBank Topeka
See listing on page 318 under Federal Home Loan Bank of Topeka

Fibertower Corporation
A backhaul and access transport provider focused primarily on the wireless carrier market.
www.fibertower.com
Annual Revenues: $86.84 million
Employees: 138
Ticker: NASDAQ: FTWRQ
SIC: 4812
Industry/ies: Communications; Telecommunications/Internet/Cable
Legislative Issues: TEC

Main Headquarters
Mailing:　185 Berry St.　Tel:　(415) 659-3500
　　　Suite 4800　Fax:　(415) 659-0007
　　　San Francisco, CA 94107

Washington Office
Mailing:　1730 Rhode Island Ave. NW
　　　Suite 304
　　　Washington, DC 20036

Public Affairs and Related Activities Personnel

At Headquarters

MATTISON, Cathy　Tel:　(415) 433-3777
Contact, Investor Relations　Fax:　(415) 659-0007
cmattison@lhai.com

SANDRI, Jr., Joseph M.　Tel:　(415) 659-3500
Senior Vice President, Regulatory and Government Affairs　Fax:　(415) 659-0007
jsandri@fibertower.com

Fidelity Engineering
Specializes in emergency power systems and building mechanical systems.
fidelityengineering.com
Annual Revenues: $29.20 million
Employees: 300
Industry/ies: Energy/Electricity; Engineering/Mathematics

Chairman of the Board, Treasurer　Tel:　(410) 771-9400
GOULD, Thorne

Chief Executive Officer　Tel:　(410) 771-9400
LANPHAR, Dave

Main Headquarters
Mailing:　25th Loveton Cir.　Tel:　(410) 771-9400
　　　P.O. Box 2500　TF:　(800) 787-6000
　　　Sparks, MD 21152

Corporate Foundations and Giving Programs

Fidelity Engineering Contributions Program
25th Loveton Cir.
P.O. Box 2500
Sparks, MD 21152

Public Affairs and Related Activities Personnel

At Headquarters

ALDRIDGE, Wayne　Tel:　(410) 771-9400
Vice President, Administration, Controller

Fidelity Investment Advisors
Government relations.
advisor.fidelity.com
Legislative Issues: BUD; DEF; ENG; HOU; PHA

Main Headquarters
Mailing:　3800 Pentagon Blvd.　Tel:　(937) 269-4245
　　　Suite 120

Beavercreek, OH 45431

Political Action Committees
Fidelity Investments Investors Super PAC
FEC ID: C00457531
Contact: Josue Larose
P.O. Box 9961
Fort Lauderdale, 33310

Public Affairs and Related Activities Personnel

At Headquarters

COLVIN, Laurea

HOBSON, Hon. David L.	Tel:	(937) 269-4245
Registered Federal Lobbyist		

Fidelity Investments
See listing on page 336 under FMR LLC (Fidelity Investments)

Fidelity National Financial
Provider of title insurance, mortgage services and diversified services.
www.fnf.com
Annual Revenues: $8.61 billion
Employees: 63,861
Ticker: NYSE: FNF
SIC: 6361
Industry/ies: Banking/Finance/Investments

Chairman of the Board	Tel:	(904) 854-8100
FOLEY, II, William P.	Fax:	(904) 357-1007

Chief Executive Officer	Tel:	(904) 854-8100
QUIRK, Raymond R.	Fax:	(904) 357-1007

Main Headquarters

Mailing:	601 Riverside Ave.	Tel:	(904) 854-8100
	Jacksonville Beach, FL 32204	Fax:	(904) 357-1007
		TF:	(888) 934-3354

Political Action Committees
Fidelity National Financial Inc PAC 2001
FEC ID: C00364455
Contact: John M. Benton
601 Riverside Ave.
Jacksonville Beach, FL 32204

Contributions to Candidates: $51,770 (2015-2016)
Democrats: $16,200; Republicans: $35,570

Principal Recipients

SENATE
HECK, JOE (REP-NV)

Public Affairs and Related Activities Personnel

At Headquarters

BENTON, John M.	Tel:	(904) 854-8100
PAC Treasurer	Fax:	(904) 357-1007

BICKETT, Brent B.	Tel:	(904) 854-8100
President	Fax:	(904) 357-1007

GIRION, Sherwood	Tel:	(904) 854-8100
Senior Vice President, Government Relations	Fax:	(904) 357-1007

GRAVELLE, Michael L.	Tel:	(904) 854-8100
Executive Vice President, General Counsel and Corporate Secretary	Fax:	(904) 357-1007

PARK, Anthony J.	Tel:	(904) 854-8100
Chief Financial Officer	Fax:	(904) 357-1007

SADOWSKI, Peter T.	Tel:	(904) 854-8100
Executive Vice President, Chief Legal Officer and PAC Treasurer	Fax:	(904) 357-1007

Fiesta Mart, Inc.
Retail supermarkets. Products include Bakery, beer, dairy, delicatessen, frozen foods, gasoline, general merchandise, meat, pharmacy, seafood and wine.
www.fiestamart.com
Annual Revenues: $1.48 billion
Employees: 8,000
SIC: 4215
NAICS: 492210
Industry/ies: Food And Beverage Industry; Retail/Wholesale

Main Headquarters

Mailing:	5235 Katy Fwy.	Tel:	(713) 869-5060
	Houston, TX 77007	Fax:	(713) 869-6197
		TF:	(800) 123-4567

Corporate Foundations and Giving Programs

Fiesta Club Party
5235 Katy Fwy.
Houston, TX 77007

	Tel:	(713) 869-5060

Fiesta Super Sports Club

5235 Katy Fwy.
Houston, TX 77007

	Tel:	(713) 869-5060

Public Affairs and Related Activities Personnel

At Headquarters

PARISH, Wanda	Tel:	(713) 869-5060
Director, Human Resources	Fax:	(713) 869-6197

WALKER, Stacey Spurlin	Tel:	(713) 869-5060
Director, Area Operations	Fax:	(713) 869-6197

Fifth &amp
See listing on page 463 under Kate Spade & Company

Fifth Third Bank
Provides personal, business, and commercial banking products and services in the United States. Its personal banking products and services include checking and savings accounts, credit and debit cards, gift cards, Internet and mobile banking services, mortgages, equity lines and loans, vehicle financing, student loans, and investment and wealth management services.
www.53.com
Annual Revenues: $5.78 billion
Employees: 18,471
Ticker: NASDAQ: FITB
SIC: 5099; 6021; 6022
Industry/ies: Banking/Finance/Investments
Legislative Issues: BAN; LBR; TAX

Vice Chairman and Chief Executive Officer	Tel:	(513) 579-5300
KABAT, Kevin T.	Fax:	(513) 534-0629
kevin.kabat@53.com		

Main Headquarters

Mailing:	38 Fountain Sq. Plaza	Tel:	(513) 579-5300
	Cincinnati, OH 45263	Fax:	(513) 534-0629
		TF:	(800) 972-3030

Washington Office

Mailing:	25 Massachusetts Ave. NW	Tel:	(202) 347-8405
	Suite 830		
	Washington, DC 20001		

Corporate Foundations and Giving Programs

Fifth Third Foundation
Contact: Heidi B. Jark
38 Fountain Sq. Plaza
Cincinnati, OH 45236

	Tel:	(513) 579-5300

Public Affairs and Related Activities Personnel

At Headquarters

HONAN, Stephanie	Tel:	(513) 534-6957
Assistant Vice President and Manager, Public Relations	Fax:	(513) 534-0629
stephanie.honan@53.com		

JARK, Heidi B.	Tel:	(513) 579-5300
Manager, Foundation	Fax:	(513) 534-0629
heidi.jark@53.com		

POSTON, Daniel T.	Tel:	(513) 579-5300
Executive Vice President and Chief Strategy and Administrative Officer	Fax:	(513) 534-0629
daniel.poston@53.com		

RICHARDSON, Jeff	Tel:	(513) 579-5300
Senior Vice President and Director, Corporate Development and Capital Planning	Fax:	(513) 534-0629
Jeff.Richardson@53.com		

TANNER, Teresa J.	Tel:	(513) 579-5300
Executive Vice President and Chief Human Resources Officer	Fax:	(513) 534-0629

TUUK, Mary E.	Tel:	(513) 579-5300
Executive Vice President, Corporate Services and Board Secretary	Fax:	(513) 534-0629

TUZUN, Tayfun	Tel:	(513) 579-5300
Executive Vice President and Chief Financial Officer	Fax:	(513) 534-0629

At Washington Office

CARMICHAEL, Greg D.	Tel:	(202) 347-8405
President and Chief Operating Officer		

ENGLISH, Damielle	Tel:	(202) 347-8405
Federal Lobbyist		
Registered Federal Lobbyist		

ENGLISH, Dan	Tel:	(202) 347-8405
Federal Lobbyist		
Registered Federal Lobbyist		

RIZZO, Eric	Tel:	(202) 347-8405
Vice President, Government Affairs Officer		
Registered Federal Lobbyist		

At Other Offices

RUEBEL, Thomas J.
Director, Government Affairs and PAC Treasurer
550 E. Walnut St.

Columbus, OH 43215
thomas.ruebel@53.com
Registered Federal Lobbyist

Fincantieri Marine Systems North America, Inc.

Government contractor. Formerly FDGM, Inc. It operates in the design and construction of complex ships with high technological content such as merchant and naval vessels, offshore and mega yachts.
www.fincantierimarinesystems.com
Annual Revenues: $33.65 million
Employees: 100
Industry/ies: Automotive Industry; Transportation

Main Headquarters
Mailing: 800-C Principal Ct.   Tel: (757) 548-6000
          Chesapeake, VA 23320-3681   Fax: (757) 548-6012

Public Affairs and Related Activities Personnel

At Headquarters

COOPER, Joelle   Tel: (757) 548-6000
Contact, Media Relations   Fax: (757) 548-6012
jcooper@fmsna.com

Finch Paper Holdings, LLC

Manufactures and supplies uncoated printing and writing papers.
finchpaper.com
Industry/ies: Paper And Wood Products Industry
Legislative Issues: TAX

Main Headquarters
Mailing: One Glen St.   Tel: (518) 793-2541
          Glen Falls, NY 12801   TF: (800) 833-9983

Corporate Foundations and Giving Programs
Finch Paper Community Giving
One Glen St.   Tel: (518) 793-2541
Glen Falls, NY 12801

Public Affairs and Related Activities Personnel

At Headquarters

POVIE, Beth A.   Tel: (518) 793-2541
Director, Marketing

Findlay & Western Strategies, LLC

Business and public policy consulting.
Legislative Issues: ENG; GOV

President   Tel: (703) 967-0736
GRONE, Philip
pgrone@me.com

Main Headquarters
Mailing: 7700 Hilltopper Ct.   Tel: (703) 967-0736
          Springfield, VA 22153

Finisar Corporation

Finisar provides optical components and modules for network equipment vendors, instruments and software for communications designers, and products and services for large enterprise storage networks.
www.finisar.com
Annual Revenues: $1.26 billion
Employees: 13,400
Ticker: NASDAQ: FNSR
SIC: 3674
Industry/ies: Communications; Telecommunications/Internet/Cable

Executive Chairman and Chief Executive Officer   Tel: (408) 548-1000
RAWLS, Jerry S.   Fax: (408) 541-6138

Main Headquarters
Mailing: 1389 Moffett Park Dr.   Tel: (408) 548-1000
          Sunnyvale, CA 94089   Fax: (408) 541-6138
                                              TF: (888) 746-6484

Political Action Committees
Finisar Corporation PAC
FEC ID: C00463034
Contact: Kurt Adzema
1389 Moffett Park Dr.   Tel: (408) 548-1000
Sunnyvale, CA 94089   Fax: (408) 548-1000

Public Affairs and Related Activities Personnel

At Headquarters

ADZEMA, Kurt   Tel: (408) 548-1000
PAC Treasurer , Executive Vice President and Chief Financial Fax: (408) 541-6138
Officer

BROWN , Chris   Tel: (408) 548-1000
Executive Vice President and Chief Counsel Fax: (408) 541-6138

MCDONALD, Victoria   Tel: (408) 542-4261
Director, Corporate Communications   Fax: (408) 541-6138

victoria.mcdonald@finisar.com
SWANSON, Todd   Tel: (408) 548-1000
Executive Vice President, Global Sales and Marketing Fax: (408) 541-6138
todd.swanson@finisar.com

WATT , Katherine   Tel: (408) 548-1000
Vice President, Global Employee Services   Fax: (408) 541-6138

YOUNG, Joseph   Tel: (408) 548-1000
Executive Vice President, Global Operations Fax: (408) 541-6138

First Advantage

A provider of risk mitigation and business solutions.
www.fadv.com
Annual Revenues: $780 million
Employees: 4,000
Ticker: NASDAQ: FADV
SIC: 7389
Industry/ies: Insurance Industry

Chief Executive Officer
PARISE, Mark

Main Headquarters
Mailing: One Concourse Pkwy. NE   TF: (866) 400-3238
          Suite 200
          Atlanta, GA 30328

Public Affairs and Related Activities Personnel

At Headquarters

DUFFEY, Mike
Chief Financial Officer

GRECCO, Nick
Senior Vice President, Technology Operations

JARDINE, Bret
Executive Vice President, General Counsel
bret.jardine@fadv.com

LORCH, Kerri
Senior Vice President, Marketing and Communications

PILNICK, Michael
Executive Vice President and Head, Human Resources

First American Financial Corporation

A provider of services through its Title Insurance and Services segment and its Specialty Insurance segment.
www.firstam.com
Annual Revenues: $5.27 billion
Employees: 17,955
Ticker: NYSE: FAF
SIC: 6361
Industry/ies: Banking/Finance/Investments; Real Estate
Legislative Issues: HOU

Chairman of the board   Tel: (714) 250-3000
KENNEDY, Parker S.   Fax: (714) 800-4790

Chief Executive Officer   Tel: (714) 250-3000
GILMORE, Dennis J.   Fax: (714) 800-4790

Main Headquarters
Mailing: One First American Way   Tel: (714) 250-3000
          Santa Ana, CA 92707   Fax: (714) 800-4790
                                              TF: (800) 854-3643

Political Action Committees
The First American Corporation PAC
FEC ID: C00346726
Contact: Kenneth DeGiorgio
One First American Way
Santa Ana, CA 92707

   Contributions to Candidates: $42,000 (2015-2016)
   Democrats: $9,000; Republicans: $33,000
                Principal Recipients
                    HOUSE
                ROYCE, ED MR. (REP-CA)

Corporate Foundations and Giving Programs
The First American Homeownership Foundation
One First American Way   Tel: (714) 250-3000
Santa Ana, CA 92707

Public Affairs and Related Activities Personnel

At Headquarters

ANDERSON, Anthony K.   Tel: (714) 250-3000
Director   Fax: (714) 800-4790

BARBERIO, Craig   Tel: (714) 250-5214
Contact, Investor Relations   Fax: (714) 800-4790
investor.relations@firstam.com

BELL, Sandra   Tel: (714) 250-3000

Contact, Corporate Communications	Fax:	(714) 800-4790
DEGIORGIO, Kenneth	Tel:	(714) 250-3000
Executive Vice President and PAC Treasurer	Fax:	(714) 800-4790
kdegiorgio@firstam.com		
GASKA, Carrie	Tel:	(714) 250-3298
Contact, Media and Public Relations	Fax:	(714) 800-4790
cgaska@firstam.com		
RUTHERFORD, Mark E.	Tel:	(714) 250-3000
Senior Vice President, Human Resources	Fax:	(714) 800-4790
SEATON, Mark E.	Tel:	(714) 250-3000
Chief Financial Officer	Fax:	(714) 800-4790

First Choice Armor

Manufactures surgical appliances and clothing.
www.firstchoicearmor.com
Annual Revenues: $12.60 million
Employees: 100
Industry/ies: Law Enforcement/Security

President and Chief Executive Officer	Tel:	(508) 559-0777
WALSH, Daniel	Fax:	(508) 941-6841

Main Headquarters
Mailing: 178 Forbes Rd.	Tel:	(508) 559-0777
Braintree, MA 02184	Fax:	(508) 941-6841
	TF:	(800) 822-7667

Public Affairs and Related Activities Personnel

At Headquarters

BEVERLEY, William	Tel:	(804) 833-6161
Director, Government Services	Fax:	(828) 288-6740
bbeverley@firstchoicearmor.com		
DWYER, Sue	Tel:	(828) 288-6680
Contact, Marketing and Sales Operations	Fax:	(828) 288-6740
dwyer@firstchoicearmor.com		
PIPER, Christine	Tel:	(828) 288-6680
Director, Marketing	Fax:	(828) 288-6748

First Citizens BancShares

A bank holding company.
www.firstcitizens.com
Annual Revenues: $1.34 B
Employees: 5,734
Ticker: NASDAQ: FCNCA
SIC: 6022
Industry/ies: Banking/Finance/Investments

Chairman of the Board and Chief Executive Officer	Tel:	(919) 716-7000
HOLDING, Jr., Frank B.	Fax:	(919) 716-7074

Main Headquarters
Mailing: P.O. Box 27131	Tel:	(919) 716-7000
Raleigh, NC 27611-7131	Fax:	(919) 716-7074
	TF:	(888) 323-4732

Political Action Committees
First Citizens BancShares Inc. PAC
FEC ID: C00334193
Contact: Elizabeth Bunn
4300 Six Forks Rd.
FCC81
Raleigh, NC 27609

> **Contributions to Candidates:** $2,500 (2015-2016)
> Republicans: $2,500

Corporate Foundations and Giving Programs
First Citizens BancShares Contributions Program
4300 Six Forks Rd.	Tel:	(919) 716-7000
FCC07	Fax:	(919) 716-7000
Raleigh, NC 27609		

Public Affairs and Related Activities Personnel

At Headquarters
BRISTOW, Peter M	Tel:	(919) 716-7000
President	Fax:	(919) 716-7074
HAGGERTY, Terry	Tel:	(919) 716-7459
Senior Vice President, Communications	Fax:	(919) 716-7074
THOMPSON, Barbara W.	Tel:	(919) 716-2716
Senior Vice President and Manager, Corporate Communications and Brand Marketing	Fax:	(919) 716-7074

At Other Offices
BUNN, Elizabeth	Tel:	(919) 716-7000
PAC Treasurer	Fax:	(919) 716-7074
4300 Six Forks Rd., FCC81		
Raleigh, NC 27609		
GEASLEN, Don P.	Tel:	(919) 716-7000
PAC Contact	Fax:	(919) 716-7074

4300 Six Forks Rd., FCC81
Raleigh, NC 27609

First Coast Service Options, Inc.

A medicare program administrator.
www.fcso.com
Annual Revenues: $60.6 million
Employees: 1,500
Industry/ies: Medicine/Health Care/Mental Health

President and Chief Executive Officer	Tel:	(904) 791-0130
COSTON, Sandy		
sandy.coston@fcso.com		

Main Headquarters
Mailing: 532 Riverside Ave.	Tel:	(904) 791-8000
Jacksonville Beach, FL 32202-4914	TF:	(800) 633-4227

Public Affairs and Related Activities Personnel

At Headquarters
BARNETT, Harold	Tel:	(904) 791-0130
Contact, Media Relations		
harold.barnett@fcso.com		

First Command Financial Services, Inc.

Financial services for military personnel. First Command Financial Services, Inc. is the parent company of First Command Financial Planning, Inc. and First Command Bank (Member FDIC). First Command is recognized by the Financial Planning Association (FPA) for commitment to professionalism in financial planning.
www.firstcommand.com
Annual Revenues: $72.2 million
Employees: 1,300
Industry/ies: Banking/Finance/Investments; Defense/Homeland Security; Government-Related; Military/Veterans
Legislative Issues: FIN

Chairman of the Board	Tel:	(817) 731-8621
LANIER, James N.	Fax:	(817) 738-1023
Chief Executive Officer	Tel:	(817) 731-8621
SPIKER, J. Scott	Fax:	(817) 738-1023

Main Headquarters
Mailing: One FirstComm Plaza	Tel:	(817) 731-8621
Fort Worth, TX 76109-4999	Fax:	(817) 738-1023
	TF:	(800) 443-2104

Political Action Committees
First Command Financial Planning, Inc. PAC
FEC ID: C00325647
Contact: Hugh A. Simpson
One First Comm Plaza	Tel:	(817) 731-8621
Fort Worth, TX 76109	Fax:	(817) 738-1023

> **Contributions to Candidates:** $94,700 (2015-2016)
> Democrats: $8,000; Republicans: $86,700

Corporate Foundations and Giving Programs
First Command Package Brigade
Contact: Mark Leach
P.O. Box 2387	Tel:	(817) 569-2419
Fort Worth, TX 76113	Fax:	(817) 569-2419

Public Affairs and Related Activities Personnel

At Headquarters
LEACH, Mark	Tel:	(817) 569-2419
Vice President, Media Relations	Fax:	(817) 738-1023
msleach@firstcommand.com		
LYTTLE, Jill	Tel:	(817) 731-8621
Executive Vice President, Human Resources & Leadership Development	Fax:	(817) 738-1023
MORRISON, Michael F.	Tel:	(817) 731-8621
Executive Vice President and Chief Financial Officer	Fax:	(817) 738-1023
SIMPSON, Hugh A.	Tel:	(817) 731-8621
Executive Vice President, General Counsel and Secretary	Fax:	(817) 738-1023

First Commonwealth Financial Corporation

A holding company for First Commonwealth Bank.
www.fcbanking.com
Annual Revenues: $234.85 million
Employees: 1,259
Ticker: NYSE: FCF
SIC: 6021
Industry/ies: Banking/Finance/Investments

Chairman of the Board	Tel:	(724) 349-7220
DAHLMANN, David S.	Fax:	(888) 711-2329
ddahlmann@fcbanking.com		
Chief Executive Officer	Tel:	(724) 349-7220
PRICE, Thomas Michael	Fax:	(888) 711-2329

Main Headquarters

Mailing: 601 Philadelphia St.
              Indiana, PA 15701

Tel: (724) 349-7220
Fax: (888) 711-2329
TF: (800) 711-2265

Political Action Committees

First Commonwealth Financial Corporation PAC
FEC ID: C00348185
Contact: Teresa Ciambotti
22 N. Sixth St.
P.O. Box 400
Indiana, PA 15701

   Contributions to Candidates: $2,250 (2015-2016)
      Republicans: $2,250

Corporate Foundations and Giving Programs

First Commonwealth Financial Corporation Contributions Program
22 N. Sixth St.
P.O. Box 400
Indiana, PA 15701-0400

Public Affairs and Related Activities Personnel

At Headquarters

LAWRY, Donald A.
Contact, Investor Relations
dlawry@fcbanking.com

Tel: (724) 349-7220
Fax: (888) 711-2329

TOMB, Matthew C.
Executive Vice President, Chief Risk Officer, General Counsel and Secretary

Tel: (724) 349-7220
Fax: (888) 711-2329

At Other Offices

CIAMBOTTI, Teresa
PAC Treasurer
22 N. Sixth St., P.O. Box 400
Indiana, PA 15701

First Data Corporation

First Data is a global technology and payments processing Company. First Data also provides payment processing solutions such as fraud protection and authentication solutions, check guarantee and verification services and point-of-sale (POS) devices and service.
www.firstdata.com
Employees: 24,000
SIC: 7374
Industry/ies: Banking/Finance/Investments; Business; Small Business
Legislative Issues: BAN; CSP; FIN

Chairman and Chief Executive Officer
BISIGNANO, Frank

Tel: (404) 890-2000
Fax: (303) 967-7000

Main Headquarters

Mailing: 5565 Glenridge Connector NE
              Suite 2000
              Atlanta, GA 30342

Tel: (404) 890-2000
Fax: (303) 967-7000
TF: (800) 735-3362

Washington Office

Mailing: 1015 15th St. NW
              Suite 975
              Washington, DC 20005

Tel: (202) 478-1110
Fax: (202) 478-0018

Corporate Foundations and Giving Programs

First Data Foundation
5565 Glenridge Connector NE
Atlanta, GA 30342

Tel: (303) 967-8000
Fax: (303) 967-7000

Public Affairs and Related Activities Personnel

At Headquarters

ELKINS, John
President, International Regions

Tel: (303) 967-8000
Fax: (303) 967-7000

GELB, Andrew
Executive Vice President and Head, Financial Services

Tel: (404) 890-2000
Fax: (303) 967-7000

HIGGINS, Tom
Chief Administrative Officer

Tel: (404) 890-2000
Fax: (303) 967-7000

LARSEN, Christine
Executive Vice President, Chief Operations Officer

Tel: (404) 890-2000
Fax: (303) 967-7000

MARINO, Anthony S.
Executive Vice President and Head, Human Resources

Tel: (404) 890-2000
Fax: (303) 967-7000

MCCARTHY, Barry
President, Financial Services

Tel: (404) 890-2000
Fax: (303) 967-7000

MONEY, David R.
Vice Chairman

Tel: (303) 488-8000
Fax: (303) 967-6705

MOURAD, Gregory W.
PAC Contact

Tel: (303) 967-8000
Fax: (303) 967-7000

NEBORAK, Michael
Executive Vice President and Director, Finance

Tel: (404) 890-2000
Fax: (303) 967-7000

PATEL, Himanshu
Executive Vice President, Strategy and Business Development, Public Affairs

Tel: (404) 890-2000
Fax: (303) 967-7000

ROSMAN, Adam

Tel: (404) 890-2000

Executive Vice President and General Counsel

Fax: (303) 967-7000

SWEARNGAN, Chip
Senior Vice President, Communications and Investor Relations
chip.swearngan@firstdata.com

Tel: (404) 890-3000
Fax: (303) 967-7000

TRENT, Grace Chen
Executive Vice President, Communications

Tel: (303) 488-8000
Fax: (303) 967-7000

At Washington Office

FORD, Kim
Federal Lobbyist
Registered Federal Lobbyist

Tel: (202) 478-1110
Fax: (202) 478-0018

JACKSON, Hon. Alphonso

Tel: (202) 478-1110
Fax: (202) 478-0018

At Other Offices

HALL, Kim
PAC Treasurer
6200 S. Quebec St., Suite 420
Greenwood Village, CO 80111
kimberly.hall@firstdata.com
Registered Federal Lobbyist

Tel: (303) 967-7195
Fax: (303) 967-6705

HUSSEY, Mike
Federal Lobbyist
6200 S. Quebec St., Suite 420
Greenwood Village, CO 80111
Registered Federal Lobbyist

Tel: (303) 967-7195
Fax: (303) 967-6705

KAYES, Kevin
Federal Lobbyist
6200 S. Quebec St., Suite 420
Greenwood Village, CO 80111
Registered Federal Lobbyist

Tel: (303) 967-7195
Fax: (303) 967-6705

KLEIN, Israel
Federal Lobbyist
6200 S. Quebec St., Suite 420
Greenwood Village, CO 80111

Tel: (303) 967-7195
Fax: (303) 967-6705

LAMPKIN, Marc
Federal Lobbyist
6200 S. Quebec St., Suite 420
Greenwood Village, CO 80111
Registered Federal Lobbyist

Tel: (303) 967-7195
Fax: (303) 967-6705

LUGAR, David
Federal Lobbyist
6200 S. Quebec St., Suite 420
Greenwood Village, CO 80111
Registered Federal Lobbyist

Tel: (303) 967-7195
Fax: (303) 967-6705

SAMUEL, Joe
Federal Lobbyist
6200 S. Quebec St., Suite 420
Greenwood Village, CO 80111

Tel: (303) 967-7195
Fax: (303) 967-6705

First Energy Corporation

A registered public utility holding company. First Energy subsidiaries and affiliates are involved in the generation, transmission and distribution of electricity, energy management, and other energy-related services.
www.firstenergycorp.com
Annual Revenues: $14.35 billion
Employees: 15,557
Ticker: NYSE: FE
SIC: 4911
Industry/ies: Energy/Electricity; Utilities
Legislative Issues: ACC; BUD; CAW; CDT; COM; ENG; ENV; FIN; HOM; TAX; TRA; UTI

Non-executive Chairman of the Board
SMART, George M.

Tel: (330) 384-5596

President and Chief Executive Officer
JONES, Charles E.

Tel: (330) 384-5596

Main Headquarters

Mailing: 76 S. Main St.
              18th Floor
              Akron, OH 44308

Tel: (330) 384-5596
TF: (888) 544-4877

Washington Office

Mailing: 801 Pennsylvania Ave.
              Suite 310
              Washington, DC 20004

Tel: (202) 434-8140
Fax: (202) 434-8156

Political Action Committees

FirstEnergy Corporation PAC
FEC ID: C00140855
Contact: Steven Stubb
76 S. Main St.
Akron, OH 44308

   Contributions to Candidates: $327,000 (2015-2016)
      Democrats: $77,000; Republicans: $250,000

Principal Recipients

HOUSE
BEATTY, JOYCE (DEM-OH)
DOYLE, MIKE (DEM-PA)
FUDGE, MARCIA L (DEM-OH)
GRIFFITH, H MORGAN (REP-VA)
JENKINS, EVAN H (REP-WV)
JOYCE, DAVID P (REP-OH)
KAPTUR, MARCY C HON. (DEM-OH)
LATTA, ROBERT EDWARD MR (REP-OH)
MCKINLEY, DAVID B. MR. (REP-WV)
MOONEY, ALEXANDER XAVIER (REP-WV)
MURPHY, TIMOTHY (REP-PA)
RENACCI, JAMES B. (REP-OH)
ROTHFUS, KEITH MR. (REP-PA)
SHIMKUS, JOHN M (REP-IL)
TIBERI, PATRICK J. (REP-OH)

Corporate Foundations and Giving Programs

FirstEnergy Foundation
Contact: Dee Lowery
76 S. Main St.   Tel: (330) 761-4112
Akron, OH 44308   Fax: (330) 834-8788

Public Affairs and Related Activities Personnel

At Headquarters

ALEXANDER, Anthony J.   Tel: (330) 384-5596
President
Registered Federal Lobbyist

BAILEY, Joel D.   Tel: (330) 384-5596
Vice President, Local Affairs and Business Development
cordead@firstenergycorp.com

BENZ, Gary   Tel: (330) 384-5596
Senior Vice President, Strategy

CAVALIER, Lynn M.   Tel: (330) 384-5596
Senior Vice President, Human Resources

CHACK, Dennis   Tel: (330) 384-5596
Senior Vice President, Marketing and Branding

CLARK, Mark T.   Tel: (330) 384-5596
Executive Vice President, Finance and Strategy

DOWLING, Michael J.   Tel: (330) 384-5596
Senior Vice President, External Affairs

ECKARD, Mike   Tel: (330) 384-5596
Registered Federal Lobbyist

GAINES, Bennett L.   Tel: (330) 384-5596
Senior Vice President, Corporate Services and Chief Information Officer

GREALY, Anne   Tel: (330) 384-5596
Director, Federal Regulatory Affairs
Registered Federal Lobbyist

HALL, Marty   Tel: (330) 384-5596
Registered Federal Lobbyist

HALL, Karen   Tel: (330) 384-5596
Federal Lobbyist
Registered Federal Lobbyist

LOWERY, Dee   Tel: (330) 384-5022
President, FirstEnergy Foundation

MILLER, Ebony L.   Tel: (330) 384-5596
Executive Director, State and Legal Affairs

MOUNT, S. Colin   Tel: (330) 384-5596
Director, Federal Regulatory Affairs
Registered Federal Lobbyist

PEARSON, James F.   Tel: (330) 384-5596
Senior Vice President and Chief Financial Officer
pearsonj@firstenergycorp.com

PREZELJ, Irene M.   Tel: (330) 384-5596
Manager, Investor Relations
prezelji@firstenergycorp.com

SCHNEIDER, Todd   Tel: (330) 384-5596
President, FirstEnergy Solutions
tmschneider@firstenergycorp.com

SEKULICH, Gretchen   Tel: (330) 384-5596
Vice President, Communications

STUBB, Steven   Tel: (330) 384-5596
Lobbyist and PAC Treasurer

VESPOLI, Leila L.   Tel: (330) 384-5596
Executive Vice President, Markets, and Chief Legal Officer

WISHAM, Lorna   Tel: (330) 384-5596
Senior Advisor, Federal Affairs
Registered Federal Lobbyist

First Global Consulting & Management Corporation

1st Global is the independently owned wealth management partner for accounting and legal firms.
www.1stglobal.com
Industry/ies: Defense/Homeland Security; Government-Related

Chief Executive Officer   Tel: (214) 294-5000
BATMAN, Stephen A.

Main Headquarters
Mailing: 12750 Merit Dr.   Tel: (214) 294-5000
            Suite 1200   TF: (877) 959-8400
            Dallas, TX 75251

Public Affairs and Related Activities Personnel

At Headquarters

FINNIGAN, Brian M.   Tel: (214) 294-5000
Vice President and Chief Marketing Officer

GEORGE, Ryan   Tel: (214) 294-5430
Director, Marketing Communications
rgeorge@1stGlobal.com

KNOCH, David C   Tel: (214) 294-5000
President

PAGANO, Michael   Tel: (214) 294-5000
Executive Vice President and Chief Compliance Officer

PRENTICE, Al   Tel: (214) 294-5000
Vice President, Strategic Relationships

STEWART, Paul   Tel: (214) 294-5000
Executive Vice President and Chief Operating Officer

At Other Offices

FEKETE, Gabor
Contact, Government Relations
2800 S.W. Fourth Ave., Suite Four
Ft. Lauderdale, FL 33315

First Hawaiian Bank
See listing on page 103 under BancWest Corporation

First Health Group Corporation

A wholly-owned subsidiary of Coventry Health Care that provides health benefits services to self-funded national employers across the country.
www.firsthealth.com
Employees: 6,000
SIC: 6324
Industry/ies: Medicine/Health Care/Mental Health

Chief Executive Officer   Tel: (630) 737-7900
FAULKNER, Blaine   Fax: (630) 737-7856

Main Headquarters
Mailing: 10260 Meanley Dr.   Tel: (630) 737-7900
            San Diego, IL 92131   Fax: (630) 737-7856
                                          TF: (800) 247-2898

Washington Office
Mailing: 6720-b Rockledge Dr.
            Suite 800
            Bethesda, MD 20817

Public Affairs and Related Activities Personnel

At Headquarters

DORNIG, Kara   Tel: (630) 737-7900
Vice President, Business Development   Fax: (630) 737-7856

LENT , Tamra   Tel: (630) 737-7900
Vice President, Marketing   Fax: (630) 737-7856

WRIGHT, Kelly   Tel: (630) 737-7900
Vice President, Operations and Integration Fax: (630) 737-7856

First Horizon National Corporation

A financial services company.
www.fhnc.com
Annual Revenues: $1.17 billion
Employees: 4,269
Ticker: NYSE: FHN
SIC: 6021
Industry/ies: Banking/Finance/Investments
Legislative Issues: BAN

Chairman of the Board, President and Chief Executive Officer Tel: (901) 523-4444
JORDAN, D. Bryan   Fax: (901) 523-4266

Main Headquarters
Mailing: 165 Madison Ave.   Tel: (901) 523-4444
            Memphis, TN 38103   Fax: (901) 523-4266
                                          TF: (800) 489-4040

Political Action Committees
First Horizon National Corporation Federal PAC
FEC ID: C00008151
Contact: Kimberley C. Cherry

165 Madison Ave.
Eighth Floor
Memphis, TN 38103

Contributions to Candidates: $3,500 (2015-2016)
Republicans: $3,500

Corporate Foundations and Giving Programs

First Tennessee Foundation
Contact: Kimberley C. Cherry
165 Madison Ave.   Tel: (901) 523-4307
Memphis, TN 38103   Fax: (901) 523-4307

Public Affairs and Related Activities Personnel

At Headquarters

BOWMAN, Aarti   Tel: (901) 523-4017
Head, Investor Relations   Fax: (901) 523-4266

CHERRY, Kimberley C.   Tel: (901) 523-4444
Executive Vice President, Corporate Communications and   Fax: (901) 523-4266
PAC Treasurer and Contact, Community Relations
Mail Stop Legal Division

DANIEL, John M.   Tel: (901) 523-4444
Executive Vice President and Chief Human Resources Officer   Fax: (901) 523-4266

LOSCH, III, William C.   Tel: (901) 523-4444
Executive Vice President and Chief Financial Officer   Fax: (901) 523-4266

TUGGLE, Jr., Charlie T.   Tel: (901) 523-4444
Executive Vice President and General Counsel   Fax: (901) 523-4266

First Interstate Bancsystem, Inc.

Financial holding company.
www.firstinterstatebank.com
Annual Revenues: $370.25 million
Employees: 1,705
Ticker: NASDAQ: FIBK
SIC: 6022
Industry/ies: Banking/Finance/Investments

Chairman of the Board   Tel: (406) 255-5390
SCOTT, Thomas W.   Fax: (406) 255-5160

President and Chief Executive Officer   Tel: (406) 255-5390
GARDING, Edward   Fax: (406) 255-5160

Main Headquarters
Mailing: 401 N. 31st St.   Tel: (406) 255-5390
        Billings, MN 59116   Fax: (406) 255-5160

Corporate Foundations and Giving Programs

First Interstate Bancsystem Foundation
Contact: Kelly Bruggeman
401 N. 31st St.   Tel: (406) 255-5393
Billings, MT 59116

Public Affairs and Related Activities Personnel

At Headquarters

BRUGGEMAN, Kelly   Tel: (406) 255-5393
Executive Director, Bancsystem Foundation and Media   Fax: (406) 255-5311
Relations

KNIGHT, Lyle R.   Tel: (406) 255-5390
President   Fax: (406) 255-5160
lyle.knight@fib.com

LYLE, Cindy   Tel: (406) 255-5337
Senior Vice President and Marketing Director   Fax: (406) 255-5351

MUTCH, Marcy   Tel: (406) 255-5322
Contact, Investor Relations   Fax: (406) 255-5160
investor.relations@fib.com

RILEY, Kevin P   Tel: (406) 255-5390
Executive Vice President and Chief Financial Officer   Fax: (406) 255-5160

First Marblehead Corporation

A private, non-governmental education lending company. It works with lenders and schools to help meet the growing demand for private student loans.
www.firstmarblehead.com
Annual Revenues: $46.08 million
Employees: 280
Ticker: NYSE: FMD
SIC: 6141
Industry/ies: Education
Legislative Issues: EDU

Chairman of the Board and Chief Executive Officer   Tel: (617) 638-2000
MEYERS, Daniel Maxwell   Fax: (617) 638-2100

Main Headquarters
Mailing: 800 Boylston St.   Tel: (617) 638-2000
        34th Floor   Fax: (617) 638-2100
        Boston, MA 02199   TF: (800) 895-4283

Public Affairs and Related Activities Personnel

At Other Offices

BERTRAND, Deirdre   Tel: (617) 638-2000
Managing Director, Product Strategy   Fax: (617) 638-2100
One Cabot Rd., Suite 200
Medford, MA 02155

BREITMAN, Alan   Tel: (617) 638-2065
Managing Director and Chief Financial Officer   Fax: (617) 638-2100
One Cabot Rd., Suite 200
Medford, MA 02155

BURNHAM, Jo-Ann   Tel: (617) 638-2000
Managing Director, Human Resources   Fax: (617) 638-2100
One Cabot Rd., Suite 200
Medford, MA 02155

GELBER, Seth   Tel: (617) 638-2000
President and Chief Operating Officer   Fax: (617) 638-2100
One Cabot Rd., Suite 200
Medford, MA 02155

HENEGHAN, Barry   Tel: (617) 638-2000
Managing Director, Business Development and Product   Fax: (617) 638-2100
Strategy
One Cabot Rd., Suite 200
Medford, MA 02155

MURRAY, Suzanne   Tel: (617) 638-2000
Managing Director, General Counsel and Secretary   Fax: (617) 638-2100
One Cabot Rd., Suite 200
Medford, MA 02155

First Midwest Bancorp, Inc.

A bank holding company. Operates as the holding company for First Midwest Bank, which provides various commercial and retail banking services to individual, business, institutional, and governmental customers.
www.firstmidwest.com
Annual Revenues: $398.19 million
Employees: 1,788
Ticker: NASDAQ: FMBI
SIC: 6021
Industry/ies: Banking/Finance/Investments

Chairman of the Board   Tel: (630) 875-7450
O'MEARA, Robert P.   Fax: (630) 875-7369

President and Chief Executive Officer   Tel: (630) 875-7450
SCUDDER, Michael L.   Fax: (630) 875-7369

Main Headquarters
Mailing: One Pierce Pl., Suite 1500   Tel: (630) 875-7450
        P.O. Box 459   Fax: (630) 875-7369
        Itasca, IL 60143   TF: (800) 322-3623

Political Action Committees
First Midwest Bancorp, Inc. Government Affairs Fund PAC
FEC ID: C00192906
Contact: Paul F. Clemens
One Pierce Pl.
Suite 1500
Itasca, IL 60143

Contributions to Candidates: $15,700 (2015-2016)
Democrats: $1,000; Republicans: $14,700

Public Affairs and Related Activities Personnel

At Headquarters

CHULOS, Nicholas J.   Tel: (630) 875-7450
Executive Vice President, Corporate Secretary and General   Fax: (630) 875-7369
Counsel

CLEMENS, Paul F.   Tel: (630) 875-7347
Executive Vice President, Chief Financial Officer and PAC   Fax: (630) 875-7369
Treasurer
paul.clemens@firstmidwest.com

GUINTA, Caryn J.   Tel: (630) 875-7450
Executive Vice President and Director, Employee Resources   Fax: (630) 875-7369

HOTCHKISS, James P   Tel: (630) 875-7450
Executive Vice President and Treasurer   Fax: (630) 875-7369

ROOLF, James M.   Tel: (630) 875-7450
Senior Vice President, Corporate Relations Officer and   Fax: (630) 875-7369
Contact, Investor Relations
Jim.Roolf@firstmidwest.com

SANDER, Mark G   Tel: (630) 875-7450
Senior Executive Vice President and Chief Operating Officer   Fax: (630) 875-7369

First National Bank of Jackson

See listing on page 802 under Trustmark National Bank

First National Bank of Nebraska

First National of Nebraska, Inc., through its subsidiary, First National Bank, provides commercial banking services. It operates as a subsidiary of Lauritzen Corporation.
www.fnni.com

Annual Revenues: $1.17 billion
Employees: 6,209
Ticker: NYSE:FINN
SIC: 6021
Industry/ies: Banking/Finance/Investments

Chairman of the Board	Tel:	(402) 341-0500
LAURITZEN, Bruce R.	Fax:	(402) 342-4332

Main Headquarters

Mailing:	1620 Dodge St.	Tel:	(402) 602-3777
	Mail Stop 8143	Fax:	(402) 342-4332
	Omaha, NE 68197-8143	TF:	(800) 642-0014

Political Action Committees
First National of Nebraska PAC
FEC ID: C00300863
Contact: Anna Castner Wightman
1620 Dodge St.
Omaha, NE 68197

> **Contributions to Candidates:** $2,800 (2015-2016)
> Democrats: $2,500; Republicans: $300

Public Affairs and Related Activities Personnel

At Headquarters

BAXTER, Nicholas W.	Tel:	(402) 602-3777
Chief Risk Officer and Secretary	Fax:	(402) 342-4332
HART, Timothy D.	Tel:	(402) 341-0500
Senior Vice President, Treasurer and Investor Relations	Fax:	(402) 342-4332
SIMS, Jeffrey A.	Tel:	(402) 341-0500
Senior Vice President, Marketing	Fax:	(402) 342-4332
SUMMERS, Michael A.	Tel:	(402) 341-0500
Chief Financial Officer	Fax:	(402) 342-4332
WIGHTMAN, Anna Castner	Tel:	(402) 341-0500
Vice President, Government Relations and PAC Treasurer	Fax:	(402) 342-4332

Mail Stop Stop 3395
ACastner@fnni.com

First Principles LLC

Consulting
www.firstprinciplesllc.com

President	Tel:	(281) 980-6331
DELAY, Thomas Dale		

Main Headquarters

Mailing:	2806 St. Annes Dr.	Tel:	(202) 543-3816
	Sugar Land, TX 77479		

Political Action Committees
First Principles Fund PAC
FEC ID: C00531822
Contact: Eric Robinson
133 South Harbour Dr.
Venice, FL 34285

> **Contributions to Candidates:** $73,900 (2015-2016)
> Republicans: $73,900

> **Principal Recipients**
>
> **SENATE**
> HECK, JOE (REP-NV)
> STUTZMAN, MARLIN A (REP-IN)
>
> **HOUSE**
> ZINKE, RYAN K (REP-MT)

Public Affairs and Related Activities Personnel

At Headquarters

BEVAN, Carol	Tel:	(281) 980-6331
Federal Lobbyist		
FLAHERTY, Shannon	Tel:	(202) 543-3816
Contact, Media Relations		

askdelay@tomdelay.com

At Other Offices

ROBINSON, Eric
PAC Treasurer
133 South Harbour Dr.
Venice, FL 34285

First Quality Enterprises, Inc.

Manufacturers of feminine hygiene products, baby diapers and adult incontinence disposables for retail and institutional distribution.
www.firstquality.com
Employees: 3,400
Industry/ies: Manufacturers; Personal Care/Hygiene

Main Headquarters

Mailing:	80 Cuttermill Rd.	Tel:	(519) 829-3030
	Suite 500	Fax:	(519) 829-4949
	Great Neck, NY 11021	TF:	(800) 227-3551

Public Affairs and Related Activities Personnel

At Headquarters

GAROFALO, Chris	Tel:	(519) 829-3030
Senior Executive Counsel	Fax:	(519) 829-4949
KEEN, Kenneth A.	Tel:	(519) 829-3030
Contact, Corporate Communications	Fax:	(519) 829-4949
LUCARELLI, Tom	Tel:	(516) 498-2420
Contact, Investor Relations	Fax:	(519) 829-4949

First Solar Inc.

Designs and manufactures solar modules.
www.firstsolar.com
Annual Revenues: $2.91 billion
Employees: 6,060
Ticker: NASDAQ: FSLR
SIC: 3674
Industry/ies: Science; Scientific Research
Legislative Issues: ENG; NAT; TAX

Chairman of the Board	Tel:	(419) 662-6899
AHEARN, Michael J.	Fax:	(602) 414-9400

Chief Executive Officer	Tel:	(419) 662-6899
HUGHES, James A.	Fax:	(602) 414-9400

Main Headquarters

Mailing:	350 W. Washington St.	Tel:	(419) 662-6899
	Suite 600	Fax:	(602) 414-9400
	Tempe, AZ 85281	TF:	(877) 850-3757

Washington Office

Mailing:	6420 Wood Haven Rd.
	Alexandria, VA 22307

Political Action Committees
First Solar Inc Political Action Committee
FEC ID: C00489534
Contact: Kathleen Weiss
575 Seventh St. NW
Suite 400
Washington, DC 20004

Public Affairs and Related Activities Personnel

At Headquarters

ANTOUN, Georges	Tel:	(419) 662-6899
Chief Operating Officer	Fax:	(602) 414-9400
KALETA, Paul	Tel:	(419) 662-6899
Executive Vice President and General Counsel	Fax:	(602) 414-9400
WIDMAR, Mark	Tel:	(419) 662-6899
Chief Financial Officer and Chief Accounting Officer	Fax:	(602) 414-9400

At Other Offices

WEISS, Kathleen
Vice President, Federal Goverment Affairs
575 Seventh St. NW, Suite 400
Washington, DC 20004
mwessels@firstsolar.com
Registered Federal Lobbyist

First Tennessee Nat'l Corp

See listing on page 327 under First Horizon National Corporation

First Wind Energy, LLC

A wind energy company focused on the development, ownership and operation of wind farms.
www.firstwind.com
SIC: 4911
Industry/ies: Energy/Electricity; Environment And Conservation
Legislative Issues: ENG; NAT; TAX

Chairman of the Board	Tel:	(617) 960-2888
MOGG, James	Fax:	(617) 960-2889

Chief Executive Officer	Tel:	(617) 960-2888
GAYNOR, Paul J.	Fax:	(617) 960-2889

Main Headquarters

Mailing:	179 Lincoln St.	Tel:	(617) 960-2888
	Suite 500	Fax:	(617) 960-2889
	Boston, MA 02111		

Washington Office

Mailing:	601 Pennsylvania Ave. NW	Tel:	(202) 220-3174
	Suite 900, South	Fax:	(202) 639-8238
	Washington, DC 20004		

Corporate Foundations and Giving Programs

First Wind Contributions Program
179 Lincoln St.
Suite 500

Boston, MA 02111

Public Affairs and Related Activities Personnel

At Headquarters

ALVAREZ, Michael   Tel: (617) 960-2888
President and Chief Financial Officer   Fax: (617) 960-2889

BEASLEY, Michele   Tel: (617) 960-2888
Senior Vice President and General Counsel   Fax: (617) 960-2889

ERICKSON, Lori   Tel: (617) 960-2888
Senior Vice President, Human Resources   Fax: (617) 960-2889

GRANT, Carol J.   Tel: (617) 960-2888
Senior Vice President, External Affairs   Fax: (617) 960-2889

KEEL, Pete   Tel: (617) 960-2888
Senior Vice President, Finance   Fax: (617) 960-2889

LAMONTAGNE, Johnson   Tel: (617) 960-9521
Director, Communications   Fax: (617) 964-3342
jlamontagne@firstwind.com

FirstGroup America

A surface transportation provider.
www.firstgroup.com/north_america
Employees: 86,000
Industry/ies: Transportation
Legislative Issues: RRR; TRA

Chairman   Tel: (513) 241-2200
HAUSER, Wolfhart   Fax: (513) 419-3242

Chief Executive Officer   Tel: (513) 241-2200
O'TOOLE, JD, Tim   Fax: (513) 419-3242

Main Headquarters
Mailing: 600 Vine St.   Tel: (513) 241-2200
Suite 1400   Fax: (513) 419-3242
Cincinnati, OH 45202

Corporate Foundations and Giving Programs

FirstGroup America Contributions Program
600 Vine St.   Tel: (513) 241-2200
Suite 1400   Fax: (513) 419-3242
Cincinnati, OH 45202

Public Affairs and Related Activities Personnel

At Headquarters

GREGORY, Matthew   Tel: (513) 241-2200
Chief Financial Officer   Fax: (513) 419-3242

Firstline Transportation

See listing on page 727 under SMS Holdings Corporation

FirstMerit Corporation

A financial services holding company.
www.firstmerit.com
Annual Revenues: $966.71 million
Employees: 3,949
Ticker: NASDAQ: FMER
SIC: 6021
Industry/ies: Banking/Finance/Investments

Chairman of the Board, President and Chief Executive Officer   Tel: (330) 996-6300
GREIG, Paul G.   Fax: (330) 384-7133
paul.greig@firstmerit.com

Main Headquarters
Mailing: Three Cascade Plaza   Tel: (330) 996-6300
Seventh Floor   Fax: (330) 384-7133
Akron, OH 44308-1103   TF: (888) 554-4362

Corporate Foundations and Giving Programs

FirstMerit Foundation
Three Cascade Plaza   Tel: (330) 996-6300
Seventh Floor   Fax: (330) 384-7133
Akron, OH 44308

Public Affairs and Related Activities Personnel

At Headquarters

BICHSEL, Terrence E.   Tel: (330) 996-6300
Executive Vice President and Chief Financial Officer   Fax: (330) 384-7133
Terry.Bichsel@firstmerit.com

LANGER, Carlton E.   Tel: (330) 996-6300
Executive Vice President, Chief Legal Officer and Corporate   Fax: (330) 384-7133
Secretary

MAURER, Christopher J.   Tel: (330) 996-6300
Executive Vice President, Human Resources   Fax: (330) 384-7133

O'MALLEY, Thomas P.   Tel: (330) 384-7109
Director, Corporate Communications and Investor Relations   Fax: (330) 384-7133

TOWNSEND, Robert   Tel: (330) 996-6300
Vice President, Media Relations Officer   Fax: (330) 384-7133

robert.townsend@firstmerit.com

TUTKOVICS, Julie C.   Tel: (330) 996-6300
Executive Vice President, Chief Marketing Officer   Fax: (330) 384-7133

Fiserv Corporation

A financial data processing company operating in three segments: financial services, insurance services and payments; and industry products. In 2008, Fiserv acquired CheckFree Corporation.
www.fiserv.com
Annual Revenues: $5.31 billion
Employees: 22,000
Ticker: NASDAQ: FISV
SIC: 5044
Industry/ies: Banking/Finance/Investments

President and Chief Executive Officer   Tel: (262) 879-5000
YABUKI, Jeffrey W.   Fax: (262) 879-5660

Main Headquarters
Mailing: P.O. Box 979   Tel: (262) 879-5000
Brookfield, WI 53008-0979   Fax: (262) 879-5013
   TF: (800) 872-7882

Public Affairs and Related Activities Personnel

At Headquarters

CAVE, Ann S.   Tel: (678) 375-4039
Director, Public Relations   Fax: (262) 879-5013
ann.cave@fiserv.com

COLEMAN, Wade   Tel: (706) 225-9233
Director, Thought Leadership and Social Media   Fax: (262) 879-5013
wade.coleman@fiserv.com

COX, James W.   Tel: (262) 879-5000
Executive Vice President, Corporate Development   Fax: (262) 879-5660

DONOVAN, Shawn   Tel: (262) 879-5000
Chief Sales Officer   Fax: (262) 879-5013

ERNST, Mark A.   Tel: (262) 879-5000
Chief Operating Officer   Fax: (262) 879-5013

HAU, Robert W.   Tel: (262) 879-5000
Chief Financial Officer and Treasurer   Fax: (262) 879-5013

MCCREARY, Lynn S.   Tel: (262) 879-5000
Chief Legal Officer and Secretary   Fax: (262) 879-5013

NELSON, Eric   Tel: (262) 879-5350
Vice President, Investor Relations   Fax: (262) 879-5013
eric.nelson@fiserv.com

PENNINGTON, Kevin   Tel: (262) 879-5000
Chief Human Resources Officer   Fax: (262) 879-5013

ZARLING, Britt   Tel: (262) 879-5000
Vice President, Corporate Communications   Fax: (262) 879-5013
britt.zarling@fiserv.com

Fisher Scientific International, Inc

See listing on page 783 under Thermo Fisher Scientific Inc.

Fisker Automotive, Inc.

Fisker Automotive is an American premium plug-in hybrid electric vehicle manufacturer with a mission to redefine the luxury automobile with an unwavering dedication to sustainability.
www.fiskerautomotive.com
Annual Revenues: $30.80 million
Employees: 300
Industry/ies: Automotive Industry; Transportation

Chief Executive Officer   Tel: (714) 888-4255
POSAWATZ, Tony   Fax: (714) 888-4256

Main Headquarters
Mailing: 5515 E. La Palma   Tel: (714) 888-4255
Anaheim, CA 92807   Fax: (714) 888-4256

Public Affairs and Related Activities Personnel

At Headquarters

FISKER, Henrik   Tel: (714) 888-4255
Founder   Fax: (714) 888-4256

PAROLY, Matthew   Tel: (714) 888-4255
Vice President, Chief Legal   Fax: (714) 888-4256

YOST, Jim   Tel: (714) 888-4255
   Fax: (714) 888-4256

Fitch Ratings

Formerly Fitch Publishing Company. Provides credit markets with credit opinions, research and data.
www.fitchratings.com
Annual Revenues: $112.70 million
Employees: 2,000
Industry/ies: Banking/Finance/Investments; Economics And Economic Development

Legislative Issues: BAN

President & Chief Executive Officer, Fitch Atlantic Ratings — Tel: (212) 908-0500
JOYNT, Stephen W. — Fax: (212) 480-4435

President and Chief Executive Officer — Tel: (212) 908-0500
TAYLOR, Paul — Fax: (212) 480-4435

Main Headquarters
Mailing: One State St. Plaza — Tel: (212) 908-0500
New York City, NY 10004 — Fax: (212) 480-4435
TF: (800) 893-4824

Public Affairs and Related Activities Personnel

At Headquarters

BROWN, Charles D. — Tel: (212) 908-0500
General Counsel and Secretary — Fax: (212) 480-4435

DUIGNAN, Kevin — Tel: (212) 908-0630
Group Managing Director and Head, Structured Finance — Fax: (212) 480-4435
kevin.duignan@fitchratings.com

JACKSON, Andy — Tel: (212) 908-0500
Head of Human Resources — Fax: (212) 480-4435

JORDAN, Peter — Tel: (212) 908-0500
Vice President, Global Business Management — Fax: (212) 480-4435

NIEDERMAYER, Theodore E. — Tel: (212) 908-0500
Chief Financial Officer — Fax: (212) 480-4435

NOONAN, Daniel — Tel: (212) 908-0706
Global Head, Corporate Communications — Fax: (212) 480-4435

OLERT, John — Tel: (212) 908-0500
Chief Risk Officer and Interim Chief Compliance Officer — Fax: (212) 480-4435

Fix the Debt Coalition Inc.
To educate on the need for a comprehensive plan to fix the US long term debt and deficits.
www.fixthedebt.org

Main Headquarters
Mailing: 1900 M St. NW — Tel: (202) 596-3597
Suite 850 — Fax: (202) 478-0681
Washington, DC 20036

Public Affairs and Related Activities Personnel

At Other Offices

FRANK, Simone — Tel: (202) 596-3420
Senior Advisor — Fax: (202) 986-3696
1900 M St. NW, Suite 850
Washington, DC 20036
frank@fixthedebt.org

SPENCER, Campbell — Tel: (202) 596-3597
Lobbyist — Fax: (202) 986-3696
1900 M St. NW, Suite 850
Washington, DC 20036

WROE, Elizabeth M. — Tel: (202) 596-3597
Vice President, Legislative Strategy — Fax: (202) 986-3696
1900 M St. NW, Suite 850
Washington, DC 20036

Flat Rock Metal, Inc.
A flat polisher of carbon steel engaged in coil processing, automotive blanking and specialty sheet processing.
www.frm.com
Employees: 700
Industry/ies: Metals

Chairman of the Board — Tel: (734) 782-4454
SHIELDS, Peter — Fax: (734) 782-5640

President — Tel: (734) 782-4454
KING, Keith — Fax: (734) 782-5640

Main Headquarters
Mailing: 26601 W. Huron River Rd. — Tel: (734) 782-4454
P.O. Box 1090 — Fax: (734) 782-5640
Flat Rock, MI 48134-1090

Public Affairs and Related Activities Personnel

At Headquarters

ATTERBERRY, Diane — Tel: (734) 782-4454
Manager, Human Resources — Fax: (734) 782-5640

Fleetwood Enterprises, Inc.
A manufacturer of mobile homes and recreational vehicles.
www.fleetwood.com
Annual Revenues: $1.66 billion
Employees: 6,400
SIC: 3716
Industry/ies: Automotive Industry; Housing; Transportation

President and Chief Executive Officer — Tel: (951) 351-3623
SMITH, Elden L. — Fax: (909) 351-3931

Main Headquarters
Mailing: P.O. Box 31 — TF: (800) 322-8216
1031 US 224 East
Decatur, IN 46733

Public Affairs and Related Activities Personnel

At Headquarters

PEROLIO-BULLINGER, Laurie
Contact, Media Relations

Fleming and Company Pharmaceuticals
See listing on page 331 under Fleming Pharmaceuticals

Fleming Pharmaceuticals
Specializes in the discovery, development, and manufacture of prescription and over-the-counter (OTC) therapies.
www.flemingpharma.com
Annual Revenues: $10.80 million
Employees: 100
Industry/ies: Pharmaceutical Industry

President — Tel: (636) 343-5306
DRITSAS, Phillip — Fax: (636) 343-5322

Main Headquarters
Mailing: 1733 Gilsinn Ln. — Tel: (636) 343-5306
Fenton, MO 63026 — Fax: (636) 343-5322
TF: (800) 343-0164

Public Affairs and Related Activities Personnel

At Headquarters

LOVE, George — Tel: (636) 343-5306
General Counsel and Vice President, Legal and Regulatory Affairs — Fax: (636) 343-5322

MENGWASSER, Thomas — Tel: (636) 343-5306
Chief Financial Officer — Fax: (636) 343-5322

Flextronics International Ltd.
Flextronics International Ltd., based in San Jose City, is the U.S. subsidiary of Flextronics International Ltd., headquartered in Singapore. An electronics manufacturer.
www.flextronics.com
Annual Revenues: $24.41 billion
Employees: 200,000
Ticker: NASDAQ: FLEX
SIC: 3672
NAICS: 334412
Industry/ies: Electricity & Electronics; Electronics; Energy/Electricity
Legislative Issues: AER; AUT; CPI; DEF; ENG; MAN; SCI; TEC; TRD

Chairman of the Board — Tel: (408) 576-7000
BINGHAM, H. Raymond

Chief Executive Officer — Tel: (408) 576-7000
MCNAMARA, Michael

Main Headquarters
Mailing: 6201 America Center Dr., 6th Floor - Legal — Tel: (408) 576-7000
Dept.
6th Fl - Legal Dept.
San Jose, CA 95002

Washington Office
Mailing: 1855 Saintt Francis St., Suite 1109
Reston, VA 20190

Corporate Foundations and Giving Programs

Flextronics Foundation
Contact: Lori Kenepp
2090 Fortune Dr. — Tel: (408) 576-7000
San Jose, CA 95131

Public Affairs and Related Activities Personnel

At Headquarters

BALDASSARI, Paul — Tel: (408) 576-7000
Chief Human Resources Officer

BENNETT, David — Tel: (408) 576-7000
Chief Accounting Officer

BROTHERTON, Renee — Tel: (408) 576-7000
Vice President, Corporate Communications
renee.brotherton@flextronics.com

COLLIER, Christopher — Tel: (408) 576-7000
Chief Financial Officer and Chief Accounting Officer

HOAK, Jonathan S. — Tel: (408) 576-7000
Executive Vice President and General Counsel
jon.hoak@flextronics.com

KENEPP, Lori — Tel: (408) 576-7000
Marketing Communications Manager and Community Relations Manager
lori.kenepp@flextronics.com

KESSEL, Kevin
Vice President, Investor Relations
kevin.kessel@flextronics.com
Tel: (408) 576-7000

MENDENHALL , Michael
Chief Marketing and Communications Officer
Tel: (408) 576-7000

SHAIBEL, Ruvi Shaibel
President, Strategic Partnerships
Tel: (408) 576-7000

FlightSafety International

Provides classroom, simulator, and flight training for aircraft pilots and maintenance technicians.
www.flightsafety.com
Annual Revenues: $960.70 million
Employees: 4,100
SIC: 3699; 8200
NAICS: 333319
Industry/ies: Aerospace/Aviation; Electricity & Electronics; Electronics; Energy/Electricity; Transportation
Legislative Issues: TRA

Chairman of the Board, President and Chief Executive Officer
WHITMAN, Bruce N.
Tel: (718) 565-4100
Fax: (718) 565-4134

Main Headquarters
Mailing: Marine Air Terminal
           La Guardia Airport
           Flushing, NY 11371
Tel: (718) 565-4100
Fax: (718) 565-4134
TF: (800) 877-5343

Washington Office
Mailing: 1101 King St.
           Suite 325
           Alexandria, VA 22314
Tel: (703) 518-8931
Fax: (703) 518-8932

Public Affairs and Related Activities Personnel

At Headquarters

D'ANGELO, Mario
Treasurer
Tel: (718) 565-4100
Fax: (718) 565-4134

FERA, Scott
Vice President, Marketing
Tel: (718) 565-4100
Fax: (718) 565-4134

GROSS, Steve
Vice President, Sales
Tel: (718) 565-4100
Fax: (718) 565-4134

MACLELLAN , Daniel
Vice President, Operations
Tel: (718) 565-4100
Fax: (718) 565-4134

MOSTSCHWILLER , Ken
Senior Vice President and Chief Financial Officer
Tel: (718) 565-4100
Fax: (718) 565-4134

NUGENT, Bill
Vice President Government Contracts and Training
Tel: (718) 565-4100
Fax: (718) 565-4134

PHILLIPS, Steve
Vice President, Communications
steve.phillips@flightsafety.com
Tel: (718) 801-9027
Fax: (718) 565-4134

At Washington Office

EFF, Thomas
Senior Vice President, General Counsel and Secretary, PAC Treasurer
Tel: (703) 518-8931
Fax: (703) 518-8932

MARINO, John J.
Vice President, Government Operations
Tel: (703) 518-8931
Fax: (703) 518-8932

Flint Group, Inc.

A manufacturer of printing inks, pigments and dispersions.
www.flintgrp.com
Annual Revenues: $3 billion
Employees: 7,000

Chairman of the Board
KNOTT, Charles
Tel: (734) 781-4600
Fax: (734) 781-4699

Chief Executive Officer
FADY, Antoine
Tel: (734) 781-4600
Fax: (734) 781-4699

Main Headquarters
Mailing: 14909 N. Beck Rd.
           Plymouth, MI 48170
Tel: (734) 781-4600
Fax: (734) 781-4699

Public Affairs and Related Activities Personnel

At Headquarters

STONE, Kim
Director, Corporate Communications
kim.stone@flintgrp.com
Tel: (734) 781-4690
Fax: (734) 781-4699

TAYLOR, Russell
Senior Vice President, Global Human Resources and Communications
russell.taylor@flintgrp.com
Tel: (734) 781-4600
Fax: (734) 781-4699

At Other Offices

DRYDEN, Steve
Chief Financial Officer
130 Waverly Ct.
Tel: (502) 583-6645
Fax: (502) 583-6458

Louisville, KY 40206

FLINT, Michael G.
President
130 Waverly Ct.
Louisville, KY 40206
mflint@flintgroup.net
Tel: (502) 583-6645
Fax: (502) 583-6458

Flint Hills Resources, LP

A refinery and petrochemicals company that is wholly owned by Koch Industries, Inc.
www.fhr.com
Employees: 1,000
Industry/ies: Energy/Electricity

President and Chief Executive Officer
RAZOOK, Bradley J.
Tel: (316) 828-5500

Main Headquarters
Mailing: P.O. Box 2917
           Wichita, KS 67201
Tel: (316) 828-3477

Corporate Foundations and Giving Programs

Flint Hills Resources Contributions Program
P.O. Box 64596
St. Paul, MN 55164-0596
Tel: (316) 828-5500

Public Affairs and Related Activities Personnel

At Headquarters

SCYOC, DeeAnn Van
Manager, Commercial Compliance
deeann.vanscyoc@fhr.com
Tel: (316) 828-3477

STAVINOHA, Katie
Media Contact
Katie.Stavinoha@fhr.com
Tel: (281) 363-7260

FLIR Systems, Inc.

Designs, manufactures and markets thermal imaging and stabilized camera systems.
www.flir.com
Annual Revenues: $1.59 billion
Employees: 3,003
Ticker: NASDAQ: FLIR
SIC: 3812
Industry/ies: Computer/Technology; Defense/Homeland Security; Electricity & Electronics; Electronics; Energy/Electricity; Government-Related; Military/Veterans
Legislative Issues: BUD; DEF; HOM

President and Chief Executive Officer
TEICH, Andrew C.
Tel: (703) 416-6666
Fax: (703) 416-1517

Main Headquarters
Mailing: 27700 S.W. Pkwy. Ave.
           Wilsonville, OR 97070
Tel: (503) 498-3547
Fax: (503) 498-3904
TF: (800) 727-3547

Washington Office
Mailing: 2800 Crystal Dr.
           Suite 330
           Arlington, VA 22202
Tel: (703) 416-6666
Fax: (703) 416-1517

Political Action Committees
FLIR Systems, Inc. Employees PAC (FLIRPAC)
FEC ID: C00411454
Contact: Heather Christiansen
2700A S.W. Parkway Ave.
Suite 300
Wilsonville, OR 97070
Tel: (703) 416-6666
Fax: (703) 416-1517

   Contributions to Candidates: $34,500 (2015-2016)
   Democrats: $15,000; Republicans: $19,500

Public Affairs and Related Activities Personnel

At Headquarters

CHRISTIANSEN, Heather
PAC Treasurer
Tel: (503) 498-3547
Fax: (503) 498-3904

DUCHENE , Todd M
Senior Vice President, General Counsel, Secretary, and Chief Ethics and Compliance Officer
Madangeology@gmail.com
Tel: (503) 498-3547
Fax: (503) 498-3904

MERRILL , Travis D.
Senior Vice President and Chief Marketing Officer
Tel: (503) 498-3547
Fax: (503) 498-3904

MUESSLE , David A
Vice President, Corporate Controller
Tel: (503) 498-3547
Fax: (503) 498-3904

SURRAN , Thomas A.
Senior Vice President and Chief Operating Officer
Tel: (503) 498-3547
Fax: (503) 498-3904

At Washington Office

FRANK , Jeffrey D.
Senior Vice President, Global Product Strategy
Tel: (703) 416-6666
Fax: (703) 416-1517

HARRISON, Shane
Senior Vice President, Corporate Development and Strategy
Tel: (703) 416-6666
Fax: (703) 416-1517

LAVACH, Beth | Tel: (703) 416-6666
Registered Federal Lobbyist | Fax: (703) 416-1517

SEIGLE, Robert N. | Tel: (703) 416-6666
Lobbyist | Fax: (703) 416-1517
Registered Federal Lobbyist

SINGHI, Amit | Tel: (703) 416-6666
Senior Vice President, Finance, and Chief Financial Officer | Fax: (703) 416-1517

VAN DEUSEN, Karl J | Tel: (703) 416-6666
Lobbyist | Fax: (703) 416-1517
Registered Federal Lobbyist

Florida Blue

See listing on page 129 under Blue Cross Blue Shield of Florida

Florida Crystals Corporation

A sugar producer.
www.floridacrystals.com
Employees: 2,000
Industry/ies: Agriculture/Agronomy; Commodities
Legislative Issues: AGR; BUD; ENG; ENV; FOO; TAX; TRD

Chairman of the Board and Chief Executive Officer | Tel: (561) 366-5100
FANJUL, Jr., Alfonso | Fax: (561) 366-5158

Main Headquarters
Mailing: One N. Clematis St. | Tel: (561) 366-5100
Suite 200 | Fax: (561) 366-5158
Palm Beach, FL 33401 | TF: (877) 835-2828

Washington Office
Mailing: 401 Ninth St. NW | Tel: (202) 661-6340
Suite 640 | Fax: (202) 661-6357
Washington, DC 20004

Political Action Committees
Florida Crystals Corporation PAC
FEC ID: C00296624
Contact: Parks D. Shackelford
401 Ninth St. NW | Tel: (202) 661-6340
Suite 640
Washington, DC 20004

    Contributions to Candidates: $1,500 (2015-2016)
    Democrats: $500; Republicans: $1,000

Corporate Foundations and Giving Programs

Florida Crystals Corporation Community Giving
Contact: Alfonso Fanjul Jr.
One N. Clematis St. | Tel: (561) 366-5100
Suite 200 | Fax: (561) 366-5158
Palm Beach, FL 33401

Public Affairs and Related Activities Personnel

At Headquarters
FERNANDEZ, Luis J. | Tel: (561) 366-5100
Executive Vice President and Chief Financial Officer | Fax: (561) 366-5158

At Washington Office
CANTENS, Gaston | Tel: (202) 661-6340
Vice President | Fax: (202) 661-6357

SHACKELFORD, Parks D. | Tel: (202) 661-6340
Vice President | Fax: (202) 661-6357
Mail Stop Suite 800
Registered Federal Lobbyist

Florida Power and Light Company

*Investor-owned utility company providing electric power throughout Florida, a national
provider of electricity services.*
www.fpl.com
SIC: 4911
Industry/ies: Energy/Electricity; Utilities
Legislative Issues: AGR; ENG; TAX; UTI

Chief Executive Officer | Tel: (305) 552-3888
HAY, III, Lewis
lew_hay@fpl.com

President and Chief Executive Officer | Tel: (305) 552-3888
SILAGY, Eric E.
eric.e.silagy@fpl.com

Main Headquarters
Mailing: P.O. Box 025576 | Tel: (305) 552-3888
Miami, FL 33102

Corporate Foundations and Giving Programs

FPL Contributions Program
700 Universe Blvd. | Tel: (561) 694-4000
Juno Beach, FL 33408

Public Affairs and Related Activities Personnel

At Headquarters

BARRETT, Jr., Robert E. | Tel: (305) 552-3888
Vice President, Finance

LITCHFIELD, R. Wade | Tel: (305) 552-3888
Vice President and General Counsel
Wade-Litchfield@fpl.com

OUSDAHL, Kimberly | Tel: (305) 552-3888
Vice President, Controller and Chief Accounting Officer

RAUCH, Pamela M. | Tel: (305) 552-3888
Vice President, Development and External Affairs
Pamela_m_rauch@fpl.com

TOBIN, Brian | Tel: (305) 442-0388
PAC Treasurer
Brian.Tobin@nexteraenergy.com

At Other Offices
CLARK, Jr., Delmar J. | Tel: (305) 552-3888
PAC Treasurer
P.O. Box 33042
St. Petersburg, FL 33733

Florida Turbine Technologies Inc.

Designs, develops, and manufactures gas turbines.
www.fttinc.com
Annual Revenues: $19.50 million
Employees: 200
Industry/ies: Machinery/Equipment

Chief Executive Officer | Tel: (561) 427-6400
BROSTMEYER, Shirley | Fax: (561) 427-6191

Main Headquarters
Mailing: 1701 Military Trail | Tel: (561) 427-6400
Suite 110 | Fax: (561) 427-6191
Jupiter, FL 33458-6331

Political Action Committees
Florida Turbine Technologies, Inc. PAC
FEC ID: C00371526
Contact: Jack W. Wilson
1701 Military Trail
Suite 110
Jupiter, FL 33458

Public Affairs and Related Activities Personnel

At Headquarters

CUNNINGHAM, PhD, Dr. Susan E. | Tel: (561) 427-6525
Director, Marketing and Contact, Public Relations | Fax: (561) 427-6191
scunningham@fttinc.com

WILSON, Jack W. | Tel: (561) 427-6400
PAC Treasurer | Fax: (561) 427-6191
jwilson@fttinc.com

Flowers Foods

*Producer and marketer of packaged bakery foods for retail and foodservice customers. Among
the company's brands are Nature's Own, Cobblestone Mill, Bluebird, Mrs. Freshley's, and
European Bakers.*
www.flowersfoods.com
Annual Revenues: $3.78 billion
Employees: 10,500
Ticker: NYSE: FLO
SIC: 2000
NAICS: 311812
Industry/ies: Food And Beverage Industry

Executive Chairman of the Board | Tel: (229) 226-9110
DEESE, George E. | Fax: (229) 225-3806

President and Chief Executive Officer | Tel: (229) 226-9110
SHIVER, Allen L. | Fax: (229) 225-3806

Main Headquarters
Mailing: 1919 Flowers Cir. | Tel: (229) 226-9110
Thomasville, GA 31757 | Fax: (229) 225-3806

Political Action Committees
Flowers Industries Inc. PAC
FEC ID: C00033555
Contact: Vandy T. Davis
1919 Flowers Cir. | Tel: (229) 226-9110
Thomasville, GA 31757 | Fax: (229) 225-3806

    Contributions to Candidates: $25,000 (2015-2016)
    Republicans: $25,000

Corporate Foundations and Giving Programs

Flowers Foods Corporate Giving
Contact: Marta Jones Turner
1919 Flowers Cir. | Tel: (229) 227-2348
Thomasville, GA 31757

Public Affairs and Related Activities Personnel

At Headquarters

TAYLOR, Tonja W.
Senior Vice President, Human Resources
Tel: (229) 226-9110
Fax: (229) 225-3806

ALEXANDER , Bradley K.
Executive Vice President and Chief Operating Officer
Tel: (229) 226-9110
Fax: (229) 225-3806

AVERA, Stephen R.
Executive Vice President, Secretary and General Counsel
Tel: (229) 226-9110
Fax: (229) 225-3806

BALTZER, Paul
Managing Director, Media Relations and Human Resources Communications
Tel: (229) 226-9110
Fax: (229) 225-3806

COURTNEY, H. Mark
Senior Vice President, Sales
Tel: (229) 226-9110
Fax: (229) 225-3806

DAVIS, Vandy T.
PAC Treasurer
Tel: (229) 226-9110
Fax: (229) 225-3806

HUBBARD, David A.
Senior Vice President and Chief Information Officer
Tel: (229) 226-9110
Fax: (229) 225-3806

KINSEY, R. Steve
Executive Vice President and Chief Financial Officer
Tel: (229) 226-9110
Fax: (229) 225-3806

KRIER, Mary
Vice President, Communications
Tel: (229) 227-2333
Fax: (229) 225-3806

TURNER, Marta Jones
Executive Vice President, Corporate Relations
Tel: (229) 227-2348
Fax: (229) 225-3816

Flowserve Corporation

A manufacturer and aftermarket service provider of flow control products and services.
www.flowserve.com
Annual Revenues: $4.49 billion
Employees: 19,000
Ticker: NYSE: FLS
SIC: 3561; 5084; 7699
NAICS: 42183; 23511; 333911
Industry/ies: Machinery/Equipment

Chairman of the Board
RUSNACK, William C.
Tel: (972) 443-6500
Fax: (972) 443-6800

President and Chief Executive Officer
BLINN, Mark A.
Tel: (972) 443-6500
Fax: (972) 443-6800

Main Headquarters
Mailing: 5215 N. O'Connor Blvd.
Suite 2300
Irving, TX 75039
Tel: (972) 443-6500
Fax: (972) 443-6800
TF: (800) 728-7867

Corporate Foundations and Giving Programs

Flowserve Corporation Contribution Program
5215 N. O'Connor Blvd.
Suite 2300
Irving, TX 75039
Tel: (972) 443-6500
Fax: (972) 443-6800

Public Affairs and Related Activities Personnel

At Headquarters

GILLESPIE, Keith E.
Senior Vice President, Chief Strategy Officer
Tel: (972) 443-6500
Fax: (972) 443-6800

MULLIN, Mike
Director, Investor Relations
MMullin@flowserve.com
Tel: (972) 443-6636
Fax: (972) 443-6800

O'CONNOR, Carey A.
Senior Vice President, General Counsel and Secretary
Tel: (972) 443-6500
Fax: (972) 443-6800

OVELMEN, Karyn F.
Executive Vice President and Chief Financial Officer
Tel: (972) 443-6500
Fax: (972) 443-6800

PAJONAS, Thomas L.
Executive Vice President and Chief Operating Officer
Tel: (972) 443-6500
Fax: (972) 443-6800

ROSENE, Lars E.
Vice President, Global Communications and Public Affairs
lrosene@flowserve.com
Tel: (972) 443-6500
Fax: (972) 443-6800

ROUECHE, III, John E. (Jay)
Vice President, Investor Relations and Treasurer
Tel: (972) 443-6560
Fax: (972) 443-6800

ROUECHE, John (Jay)
Vice President, Investor Relations and Treasurer
Tel: (972) 443-6500
Fax: (972) 443-6800

STEPHENS, Dave M.
Senior Vice President and Chief Human Resources Officer
Tel: (972) 443-6500
Fax: (972) 443-6800

SULLIVAN, Scott E.
Vice President, Chief Ethics and Compliance Officer
Tel: (972) 443-6500
Fax: (972) 443-6800

FluGen, Inc.

Develops, produces and delivers influenza vaccines and related infectious disease products.
flugen.com
Employees: 9
Industry/ies: Medicine/Health Care/Mental Health; Science; Scientific Research

President and Chief Executive Officer
RADSPINNER, Paul V.
pradspinner@flugen.com
Tel: (608) 442-6561

Main Headquarters
Mailing: 597 Science Dr.
Madison, WI 53711
Tel: (608) 441-2729

Fluke Corporation

A manufacturer of precision test and measurement tools. A wholly owned subsidiary of Danaher Corp.
www.fluke.com
Employees: 2,400
SIC: 3825
Industry/ies: Machinery/Equipment; Science; Scientific Research

President
PRINGLE, Wes
Tel: (425) 347-6100
Fax: (425) 446-5116

Main Headquarters
Mailing: P.O. Box 9090
Everett, WA 98206
Tel: (425) 347-6100
Fax: (425) 446-5116
TF: (800) 443-5853

Public Affairs and Related Activities Personnel

At Headquarters

ACKERMAN, Monti
Vice President and Chief Financial Officer
Tel: (425) 347-6100
Fax: (425) 446-5116

FRIBERG, Leah
Contact, Industry Relations And Content Strategy
leah.friberg@fluke.com
Tel: (425) 446-5905
Fax: (425) 446-5116

LAUBER, Ernie
Vice President, Sales
Tel: (425) 347-6100
Fax: (425) 446-5116

Fluor Corporation

A global engineering and construction company with investments in low-sulphur coal headquartered in Aliso Viejo, California.
www.fluor.com
Annual Revenues: $20.70 billion
Employees: 37,508
Ticker: NYSE: FLR
SIC: 1600
Industry/ies: Construction/Construction Materials; Engineering/Mathematics
Legislative Issues: BAN; BUD; DEF; EDU; ENG; FIN; GOV; HCR; LBR; TAX; TRA

Chairman of the board and Chief Executive Officer
SEATON, David T.
Tel: (469) 398-7000
Fax: (469) 398-7255

Main Headquarters
Mailing: 6700 Las Colinas Blvd.
Irving, TX 75039
Tel: (469) 398-7000
Fax: (469) 398-7255

Washington Office
Mailing: 403 E. Capitol St. SE
Washington, DC 20003
Tel: (202) 548-5800
Fax: (202) 548-5810

Political Action Committees
Fluor Corporation PAC (FLUOR PAC)
FEC ID: C00034132
Contact: Edward Kowalchuk
6700 Las Colinas Blvd.
Irving, TX 75039

Contributions to Candidates: $272,500 (2015-2016)
Democrats: $86,500; Republicans: $186,000

Principal Recipients

SENATE
BLUNT, ROY (REP-MO)

HOUSE
CLYBURN, JAMES E. (DEM-SC)
SCALISE, STEVE MR. (REP-LA)
SHUSTER, WILLIAM MR. (REP-PA)

Corporate Foundations and Giving Programs

Fluour Foundation
Contact: Lee C. Tashjian
6700 Las Colinas Blvd.
Irving, TX 75039
Tel: (469) 398-7000
Fax: (469) 398-7000

Public Affairs and Related Activities Personnel

At Headquarters

BUSTAMANTE, Jose
Executive Vice President Business Development and Strategy
Tel: (469) 398-7000
Fax: (469) 398-7255

FLUOR, II, J. Robert
Vice President, Global Public Affairs
j.robert.fluor.ii@fluor.com
Tel: (469) 398-7000
Fax: (469) 398-7255

GILKEY, Glenn
Senior Vice President, Human Resources and Administration
Tel: (469) 398-7000
Fax: (469) 398-7255

HALLGREN, Wendy
Vice President, Corporate Compliance
Tel: (469) 398-7000
Fax: (469) 398-7255

HERNANDEZ, Carlos M.
Senior Vice President,Chief Legal Officer and Secretary
Tel: (469) 398-7000
Fax: (469) 398-7255

KOWALCHUK, Edward — Tel: (469) 398-7000 / Fax: (469) 398-7255
Vice President, Financial Operations

LUCAS, James M — Tel: (469) 398-7000 / Fax: (469) 398-7255
Senior Vice President, Tax, Treasury and Treasurer

OOSTERVEER, Peter — Tel: (469) 398-7000 / Fax: (469) 398-7255
Chief Operating Officer

PORTER, Biggs C. — Tel: (469) 398-7000 / Fax: (469) 398-7255
Senior Vice President and Chief Financial Officer

SMALLEY, Gary — Tel: (469) 398-7000 / Fax: (469) 398-7255
Senior Vice President and Controller

STEPHENS, Keith — Tel: (469) 398-7624 / Fax: (469) 398-7255
Senior Director, Global Media Relations
media.relations@fluor.com

TASHJIAN, Lee C. — Tel: (469) 398-7000 / Fax: (469) 398-7255
Consultant

TELFER, Geoff — Tel: (469) 398-7000 / Fax: (469) 398-7255
Vice President, Corporate Finance and Investor Relations

WEBB, R. Clifton — Tel: (469) 398-7000 / Fax: (469) 398-7255
Senior Vice President, Corporate Affairs

At Washington Office

BONNIN, Nydia — Tel: (202) 548-5800 / Fax: (202) 548-5810
Director, Government Relations
nydia.bonnin@fluor.com
Registered Federal Lobbyist

CATES, Dwight — Tel: (202) 548-5800 / Fax: (202) 548-5810
Director, Government Relations
Dwight.Cates@fluor.com
Registered Federal Lobbyist

GALLAGHER, John — Tel: (202) 548-5800 / Fax: (202) 548-5810
Federal Lobbyist
Registered Federal Lobbyist

MARVENTANO, David — Tel: (202) 548-5800 / Fax: (202) 548-5810
Senior Vice President, Government Relations
david.marventano@fluor.com
Registered Federal Lobbyist

RUTTEN, Timothy M. — Tel: (202) 548-5800 / Fax: (202) 548-5810
Senior Director, Government Relations
tim.rutten@fluor.com
Registered Federal Lobbyist

VAUGHN, Philip — Tel: (202) 548-5800 / Fax: (202) 548-5810
Registered Federal Lobbyist

Flytecomm, Inc

An information services company.
www.flytecomm.com
Industry/ies: Aerospace/Aviation; Transportation

Main Headquarters
Mailing: 6829 K Ave., Suite 101, Plano, TX 75074 — Tel: (650) 404-8100 / Fax: (650) 404-8108

Public Affairs and Related Activities Personnel
At Headquarters
CERRILLOS, Eben — Tel: (650) 404-8100 / Fax: (650) 404-8108
Vice President, Engineering and Chief Architect

FMC Corporation

Manufacturer of insecticides, termiticides, and related products.
www.fmc.com
Annual Revenues: $3.42 billion
Employees: 6,000
Ticker: NYSE: FMC
SIC: 2800
Industry/ies: Chemicals & Chemical Industry; Machinery/Equipment
Legislative Issues: AGR; AVI; BUD; CHM; ENG; ENV; FOO; TAX; TRD

President, Chairman of the Board and Chief Executive Officer — Tel: (215) 299-6000 / Fax: (215) 299-5998
BRONDEAU, Pierre
pierre.brondeau@fmc.com

Main Headquarters
Mailing: 1735 Market St., Philadelphia, PA 19103 — Tel: (215) 299-6000 / Fax: (215) 299-5999 / TF: (800) 845-0187

Washington Office
Mailing: 1050 K St. NW, Suite 600, Washington, DC 20001

Political Action Committees
FMC Corporation Good Government Program PAC
FEC ID: C00033704
Contact: Joseph E Pattison
1101 Pennsylvania Ave. NW — Tel: (202) 956-5200
Suite 325
Washington, DC 20004

Contributions to Candidates: $46,500 (2015-2016)
Democrats: $11,000; Republicans: $35,500
Principal Recipients
HOUSE
CONAWAY, MICHAEL HONORABLE (REP-TX)

Corporate Foundations and Giving Programs
FMC Corporation Contributions Program
Contact: Barbara Del Duke
1735 Market St. — Tel: (215) 299-6000 / Fax: (215) 299-5998
Philadelphia, PA 19103

Public Affairs and Related Activities Personnel
At Headquarters
CRAWFORD, Barry — Tel: (215) 299-6000 / Fax: (215) 299-5999
Vice President, Operations

FITZWATER, Jim — Tel: (215) 299-6633 / Fax: (215) 299-5998
Director, Corporate Communications

GEDAKA, Kenneth A. — Tel: (215) 299-6000 / Fax: (215) 299-5999
Vice President, Communications and Public Affairs

GRAVES, Paul — Tel: (215) 299-6000 / Fax: (215) 299-5999
Executive Vice President and Chief Financial Officer

MATTHEWS, Kyle — Tel: (215) 299-6000 / Fax: (215) 299-5999
Vice President, Human Resources

SANDIFER, Andrew D. — Tel: (215) 299-6000 / Fax: (215) 299-5998
Vice President, Corporate Transformation

UTECHT, Andrea E. — Tel: (215) 299-6000 / Fax: (215) 299-5998
Executive Vice President, General Counsel and Secretary
andrea.utecht@fmc.com

At Washington Office
PATTISON, Joseph E
PAC Treasurer

At Other Offices
DAVIS, Lizanne H. — Tel: (202) 956-5211 / Fax: (202) 956-5235
Director, Government Affairs
1001 Pennsylvania Ave. NW, Suite 7125
Washington, DC 20004
lizanne_davis@fmc.com
Registered Federal Lobbyist

RIPPERGER, Patricia — Tel: (202) 956-5209 / Fax: (202) 956-5235
Office Manager
1001 Pennsylvania Ave. NW, Suite 7125
Washington, DC 20004
patricia_ripperger@fmc.com
Registered Federal Lobbyist

SEYFERT, Mike J. — Tel: (202) 956-5200 / Fax: (202) 956-5235
Director, Government Relations, FMC Agricultural Solutions
1001 Pennsylvania Ave. NW, Suite 7125
Washington, DC 20004
Registered Federal Lobbyist

WHITMAN, Shawn — Tel: (202) 956-5200 / Fax: (202) 956-5235
Vice President, Government Affairs
1001 Pennsylvania Ave. NW, Suite 7125
Washington, DC 20004
Registered Federal Lobbyist

FMC Technologies, Inc.

Involved in the energy, food processing and air transportation industries. Spun off from FMC Corp.
www.fmctechnologies.com
Annual Revenues: $5.88 billion
Employees: 17,400
Ticker: NYSE: FTI
SIC: 3533
Industry/ies: Defense/Homeland Security; Government-Related; Military/Veterans

Chairman and Chief Executive Officer — Tel: (281) 591-4000 / Fax: (281) 591-4102
GREMP, John T.

Main Headquarters
Mailing: 5875 N. Sam Houston Pkwy., W. Houston, TX 77086 — Tel: (281) 591-4000 / Fax: (281) 591-4102

Political Action Committees
FMC Technologies Employee PAC
FEC ID: C00366211
Contact: Matthew Acosta
1803 Gears Rd. — Tel: (281) 591-4000 / Fax: (281) 591-4000
Houston, TX 77067

Contributions to Candidates: $25,400 (2015-2016)
Republicans: $25,400

Principal Recipients
HOUSE
POE, TED (REP-TX)

Public Affairs and Related Activities Personnel

At Headquarters

ALEXANDER, Bradley	Tel:	(281) 405-6345
Director, Investor Relations	Fax:	(281) 591-4102
InvestorRelations@fmcti.com		
BHATIA, Sanjay	Tel:	(281) 591-4000
Vice President, Corporate Development	Fax:	(281) 591-4102
CARR, Jeffrey W.	Tel:	(281) 591-4000
Vice President, General Counsel and Secretary	Fax:	(281) 591-4102
KIMBALL, Patrick	Tel:	(281) 405-6178
Manager, Public Relations	Fax:	(281) 591-4102
media.request@fmcti.com		
MANNEN, Maryann	Tel:	(281) 591-4000
Executive Vice President and Chief Financial Officer	Fax:	(281) 591-4102
PFERDEHIRT, Douglas J.	Tel:	(281) 591-4000
President and Chief Operating Officer	Fax:	(281) 591-4102
RALSTON, Dianne B.	Tel:	(281) 591-4000
Senior Vice President, General Counsel and Secretary	Fax:	(281) 591-4102
SCOTT , Mark	Tel:	(281) 591-4000
Vice President, Administration	Fax:	(281) 591-4102

At Other Offices

ACOSTA, Matthew	Tel:	(281) 591-4000
PAC Treasurer	Fax:	(281) 591-4291
1803 Gears Rd.		
Houston, TX 77067		

FMR LLC (Fidelity Investments)
Manages a large family of mutual funds, provides fund distribution and investment advice services, as well as providing discount brokerage services, retirement services, wealth management, securities execution and clearance, life insurance and a number of other services.
www.fidelity.com
Employees: 41,000
Ticker: NASDAQ: IXIC
Industry/ies: Banking/Finance/Investments
Legislative Issues: BAN; FIN; RET; TAX

Chairman of the Board and Chief Executive Officer	Tel:	(617) 563-7000
JOHNSON, III, Edwards C.	Fax:	(617) 476-6150

Main Headquarters

Mailing:	245 Summer St.	Tel:	(617) 563-7000
	V5A	Fax:	(617) 476-6150
	Boston, MA 02210		

Washington Office

Mailing:	325 Seventh St. NW	Tel:	(202) 737-9084
	Suite 650		
	Washington, DC 20004		

Political Action Committees
FMR LLC PAC (Fidelity PAC)
FEC ID: C00215046
Contact: Kathryn Dunn
82 Devonshire St.
Boston, MA 2109

FMR LLC PAC- Federal (Fidelity PAC)
FEC ID: C00380550
Contact: Kathryn Dunn
82 Devonshire St.
Boston, MA 02109

Contributions to Candidates: $417,700 (2015-2016)
Democrats: $151,500; Republicans: $265,200; Other: $1,000

Principal Recipients
HOUSE
NEAL, RICHARD E MR. (DEM-MA)
RYAN, PAUL D. (REP-WI)

Corporate Foundations and Giving Programs
Fidelity Charitable
Contact: Amy N. Danforth

82 Devonshire St.	Tel:	(617) 563-7000
N5A	Fax:	(617) 476-6150
Boston, MA 02109		

Fidelity Foundation
Contact: Anne-Marie Soulliere

82 Devonshire St.	Tel:	(617) 563-7000
Boston, MA 02109		

Public Affairs and Related Activities Personnel

At Headquarters

DANFORTH, Amy N.	Tel:	(617) 563-7000

President, Fidelity Charitable	Fax:	(617) 476-6150
DUNN, Kathryn	Tel:	(617) 563-7000
PAC Treasurer	Fax:	(617) 476-6150
EVERHART, Pam	Tel:	(202) 408-0999
Senior Vice President	Fax:	(617) 476-6150
Registered Federal Lobbyist		
FEBEO, Jr., James F.	Tel:	(202) 408-0999
Senior Vice President, Government Relations	Fax:	(617) 476-6150
Registered Federal Lobbyist		
JOHNSON, Abigail P.	Tel:	(617) 563-7000
President of Fidelity Financial Services	Fax:	(617) 476-6150
KNIGHT, Shahira	Tel:	(202) 408-0999
Vice President	Fax:	(617) 476-6150
Registered Federal Lobbyist		
MAHLER, Samuel	Tel:	(617) 563-7000
	Fax:	(617) 476-6150
MARKIEWICZ, Stephanie	Tel:	(202) 378-5601
Senior Vice President	Fax:	(617) 476-6150
Stephanie.Markiewicz@fmr.com		
Registered Federal Lobbyist		
ORR, Scott	Tel:	(617) 563-7000
Registered Federal Lobbyist	Fax:	(617) 476-6150
SOULLIERE, Anne-Marie	Tel:	(617) 563-7000
President, Foundation	Fax:	(617) 476-6150
VERMILYE, Andrew	Tel:	(202) 408-0999
Vice President, Public Policy	Fax:	(617) 476-6150
andrew.vermilye@fmr.com		
Registered Federal Lobbyist		
WEST, Yolanda	Tel:	(617) 563-7000
Senior Executive Secretary	Fax:	(617) 476-6150

FMW Composite Systems
Manufacturer of fabricated rubber products and aircraft space vehicle equipment.
www.fmwcomposite.com
Annual Revenues: $4.70 million
Employees: 40
Industry/ies: Defense/Homeland Security; Government-Related

Chairman, President and Chief Executive Officer	Tel:	(304) 628-8028
MCBRIDGE, Dale	Fax:	(304) 842-1972

Main Headquarters

Mailing:	1200 W. Benedum Industrial Dr.	Tel:	(304) 624-8028
	Bridgeport, WV 26330	Fax:	(304) 842-1972

Public Affairs and Related Activities Personnel

At Headquarters

HENSON, Lisa	Tel:	(304) 628-8028
Chief Financial Officer and Treasurer	Fax:	(304) 842-1972

Food Directions, LLC
Operates at the intersection of where public affairs meets food policy.
fooddirectionsllc.com
Industry/ies: Consultants

JOHNSON, MS, RD, Elizabeth	Tel:	(410) 353-6032
BethJohnson@FoodDirectionsDC.com		

Main Headquarters

Mailing:	1101 K St NW	Tel:	(410) 353-6032
	Suite 650		
	Washington, DC 20005		

Washington Office

Mailing:	50 F. St. NW	Tel:	(410) 353-6032
	Suite 900		
	Washington, DC 20001		

Public Affairs and Related Activities Personnel

At Headquarters

SOMMERS, Margaret	Tel:	(410) 353-6032
Senior Director, Food and Nutrition Policy		
MaggieSommers@FoodDirectionsDC.com		
Registered Federal Lobbyist		
SWARY, Ellen	Tel:	(410) 353-6032
Policy and Regulatory Specialist		
YARABEK, Lindsay	Tel:	(410) 353-6032
Director, Food Policy and Communications		

Foot Locker Inc.
A retail holding company.
www.footlocker-inc.com
Annual Revenues: $7.20 billion
Employees: 14,567
Ticker: NYSE: FL
SIC: 3144; 3149; 3143; 2389; 2369

NAICS: 316214; 315991; 315999; 316213; 316219
Industry/ies: Apparel/Textiles Industry; Retail/Wholesale

| **Chairman of the Board, President and Chief Executive Officer** | Tel: | (212) 720-3700 |
| HICKS, Ken C. | Fax: | (212) 720-4397 |

Main Headquarters
| Mailing: | 112 W. 34th St. | Tel: | (212) 720-3700 |
| | New York City, NY 10120 | Fax: | (212) 720-4397 |

Corporate Foundations and Giving Programs
Foot Locker Foundation
| 112 W. 34th St. | | |
| New York City, NY 10120 | Tel: | (212) 720-3700 |

Public Affairs and Related Activities Personnel

At Headquarters
ALVITI, Paulette	Tel:	(212) 720-3700
Senior Vice President and Chief Human Resources Officer	Fax:	(212) 720-4397
CLARKE, Sheilagh M.	Tel:	(212) 720-3700
Vice President, Associate General Counsel	Fax:	(212) 720-4397
KOBER, Lori Ann	Tel:	(212) 720-4169
Vice President, Public Affairs	Fax:	(212) 720-4397
lkober@footlocker-inc.com		
MAURER, John A.	Tel:	(212) 720-4092
Vice President, Treasurer and Investor Relations	Fax:	(212) 720-4397
PETERS, Lauren B.	Tel:	(212) 720-3700
Executive Vice President and Chief Financial Officer	Fax:	(212) 720-4397
PETRUCCI, Laurie J.	Tel:	(212) 720-4403
Senior Vice President, Human Resources	Fax:	(212) 720-4397
lpetrucci@footlocker.com		

Forbes, Inc.
Publishes a business and financial magazine.
www.forbes.com
Annual Revenues: $24.80 million
Employees: 400
SIC: 2721
NAICS: 511120
Industry/ies: Communications; Media/Mass Communication

| **Editor in Chief** | Tel: | (212) 366-8900 |
| FORBES, Malcolm | Fax: | (212) 620-2245 |

Main Headquarters
| Mailing: | 499 Washington Blvd. | Tel: | (800) 295-0893 |
| | Jersey, NJ 07310 | | |

Corporate Foundations and Giving Programs
Forbes Foundation
| 90 Fifth Ave. | | |
| New York City, NY 10011 | Tel: | (212) 366-8900 |

Public Affairs and Related Activities Personnel

At Headquarters
| KRUSE, CAE, Kevin | Tel: | (800) 295-0893 |
| Leadership Columnist | | |

At Other Offices
ADLER, Edward J.	Tel:	(212) 366-8900
Executive Vice President, Corporate Communications	Fax:	(212) 620-2245
90 Fifth Ave.		
New York City, NY 10011		
CARBONELL, Mia	Tel:	(212) 366-8900
Senior Vice President, Corporate Communications	Fax:	(212) 620-2245
90 Fifth Ave.		
New York City, NY 10011		
WEATHERS, Debbie	Tel:	(212) 366-8848
Director, Communications	Fax:	(212) 620-2245
90 Fifth Ave.		
New York City, NY 10011		
dweathers@forbes.net		

Force Protection, Inc.
Designer, developer and manufacturer of survivability solutions.
www.gdls.com
Annual Revenues: $655.97 million
Employees: 1,300
Ticker: NASDAQ: FRPT
SIC: 3790
Industry/ies: Automotive Industry; Defense/Homeland Security; Government-Related; Military/Veterans; Transportation

| **Chairman of the Board and Chief Executive Officer** | Tel: | (586) 825-4000 |
| MOODY, Michael | Fax: | (586) 825-4013 |

Main Headquarters
| Mailing: | 38500 Mound Rd. | Tel: | (586) 825-4000 |
| | Sterling Heights, MI 48310 | Fax: | (586) 825-4013 |

Washington Office

Mailing:	2450 Crystal Dr.	Tel:	(571) 214-7942
	Suite 1060		
	Arlington, VA 22202		

Public Affairs and Related Activities Personnel

At Washington Office
GARRELL, Mark Lennon	Tel:	(571) 214-7942
Senior Vice President, Government Affairs		
mark.garrell@forceprotection.net		
GHAZAL, Jay C.	Tel:	(571) 214-7942
Federal Lobbyist		

Ford & Huff, LC
Ford & Huff LC enjoys a reputation as one of the most innovative law firms in America. We specialize in matters that require special attention and a high level of sophistication.
fordhuff.com

Main Headquarters
Mailing:	4161 North	
	Suite 300	
	Lehi, UT 84043	

Washington Office
Mailing:	1101 17th St. NW	Tel:	(202) 775-0571
	Suite 1220	Fax:	(202) 775-0581
	Washington, DC 20036		

Ford Motor Company
Automotive industry.
www.ford.com
Annual Revenues: $142.10 billion
Employees: 187,000
Ticker: NYSE: F
SIC: 3711; 3519
Industry/ies: Automotive Industry; Transportation
Legislative Issues: AUT; BAN; BUD; CAW; COM; CPT; CSP; ENG; ENV; FUE; HCR; LBR; MAN; RET; RRR; SCI; TAX; TRA; TRD

| **Executive Chairman** | Tel: | (313) 322-3000 |
| FORD, Jr., William Clay | Fax: | (313) 845-6073 |

| **President and Chief Executive Officer** | Tel: | (313) 322-3000 |
| FIELDS, Mark | Fax: | (313) 845-6073 |

Main Headquarters
| Mailing: | P.O. Box 6248 | Tel: | (313) 322-3000 |
| | Dearborn, MI 48126 | Fax: | (313) 845-6073 |

Washington Office
| Mailing: | 6510 Little River Turnpike | |
| | Alexandria, VA 22312 | |

Political Action Committees
Ford Motor Company Civic Action Fund PAC
FEC ID: C00046474
Contact: James M. Carroll
P.O. Box 75000, PAC Svcs.	Tel:	(202) 962-5400
MC 2250	Fax:	(202) 336-7223
Detroit, MI 48275		

Contributions to Candidates: $595,000 (2015-2016)
Democrats: $225,000; Republicans: $366,000; Other: $4,000

Principal Recipients

SENATE
BURR, RICHARD (REP-NC)
MORAN, JERRY (REP-KS)

HOUSE
DINGELL, DEBBIE (DEM-MI)
KAPTUR, MARCY C HON. (DEM-OH)
KELLY, ROBIN L. (DEM-IL)
SHIMKUS, JOHN M (REP-IL)
UPTON, FREDERICK STEPHEN (REP-MI)

Corporate Foundations and Giving Programs
Ford Motor Company Fund
Contact: Jim Vella
One American Rd.	Tel:	(313) 845-8711
Suite 1026		
Dearborn, MI 48126		

Public Affairs and Related Activities Personnel

At Headquarters
DAY, Raymond F.	Tel:	(313) 322-3000
Group Vice President, Communications	Fax:	(313) 845-6073
FARLEY, James D.	Tel:	(313) 322-3000
Executive Vice President, Global Marketing Sales and Service and Lincoln	Fax:	(313) 845-6073
FIELDS, Felicia J.	Tel:	(313) 322-3000
Group Vice President, Human Resources and Corporate Services	Fax:	(313) 845-6073

LEITCH, David G.	Tel:	(313) 322-3000
Group Vice President and General Counsel	Fax:	(313) 845-6073
MORAN, Mike	Tel:	(313) 322-3000
Global News Manager	Fax:	(313) 845-6073
mmoran@ford.com		
RICHMOND, Raphael	Tel:	(313) 322-3000
Global Director, Compliance	Fax:	(313) 845-6073
SHANKS, Robert L.	Tel:	(313) 322-3000
Executive Vice President and Chief Financial Officer	Fax:	(313) 845-6073
VELLA, Jim	Tel:	(313) 322-3000
President, Ford Motor Company Fund and Community Services	Fax:	(313) 845-6073

At Washington Office

SCALES, Samuel A.		
Manager, Government Affairs		
Registered Federal Lobbyist		

At Other Offices

ARAPIS, Peter	Tel:	(202) 962-5391
Legislative Manager	Fax:	(202) 962-5402
1350 I St. NW, Suite 450		
Washington, DC 20005		
Registered Federal Lobbyist		
BAKER, Christin Tinsworth	Tel:	(202) 962-5368
Political Communications Manager	Fax:	(202) 962-5417
1350 I St. NW, Suite 450		
Washington, DC 20005		
cbake117@ford.com		
BIEGUN, Stephen E.	Tel:	(202) 962-5371
Vice President, International Government Affairs	Fax:	(202) 962-5372
1350 I St. NW, Suite 450		
Washington, DC 20005		
sbiegun@ford.com		
CARROLL, James M.	Tel:	(202) 962-5367
Legal Counsel and PAC Treasurer	Fax:	(202) 962-5401
1350 I St. NW, Suite 450		
Washington, DC 20005		
Registered Federal Lobbyist		
DEESE, Benna	Tel:	(202) 962-5457
International Coordinator	Fax:	(202) 962-5459
1350 I St. NW, Suite 450		
Washington, DC 20005		
bdeese@ford.com		
DENOYER, Casey	Tel:	(202) 962-5400
1350 I St. NW, Suite 450	Fax:	(202) 962-5401
Washington, DC 20005		
DONOFRIO, Jeffrey	Tel:	(202) 962-5400
Federal Lobbyist	Fax:	(202) 962-5401
1350 I St. NW, Suite 450		
Washington, DC 20005		
JONES, Alison	Tel:	(202) 962-5381
Director, Government Affairs	Fax:	(202) 962-5401
1350 I St. NW, Suite 450		
Washington, DC 20005		
Registered Federal Lobbyist		
KING, Emma	Tel:	(202) 962-5400
Legislative Analyst	Fax:	(202) 962-5401
1350 I St. NW, Suite 450		
Washington, DC 20005		
Registered Federal Lobbyist		
MAGLEBY, Curt	Tel:	(202) 962-5400
Vice President, Government Affairs	Fax:	(202) 962-5401
1350 I St. NW, Suite 450		
Washington, DC 20005		
Registered Federal Lobbyist		
OJAKLI, Ziad	Tel:	(202) 962-5457
Group Vice President, Government and Community Relations	Fax:	(202) 962-5458
1350 I St. NW, Suite 450		
Washington, DC 20005		
zojakli@ford.com		
Registered Federal Lobbyist		
ROUSSEL, Jerry	Tel:	(202) 962-5386
Director, Government Affairs	Fax:	(202) 962-5402
1350 I St. NW, Suite 450		
Washington, DC 20005		
groussel@ford.com		
Registered Federal Lobbyist		
VERDI, Simonetta	Tel:	(202) 962-5384
Manager, International Strategy and Trade	Fax:	(202) 962-5401
1350 I St. NW, Suite 450		
Washington, DC 20005		
sverdi@ford.com		

VICK , Jane	Tel:	(202) 962-5400
Legislative Analyst	Fax:	(202) 962-5401
1350 I St. NW, Suite 450		
Washington, DC 20005		
WOELFLING, Andrew	Tel:	(202) 962-5400
1350 I St. NW, Suite 450	Fax:	(202) 962-5401
Washington, DC 20005		
Registered Federal Lobbyist		
YOUNG, J. T.	Tel:	(202) 962-5379
Legislative Manager	Fax:	(202) 962-5401
1350 I St. NW, Suite 450		
Washington, DC 20005		
jyoun134@ford.com		
Registered Federal Lobbyist		
YOUNG, James	Tel:	(202) 962-5400
1350 I St. NW, Suite 450	Fax:	(202) 962-5401
Washington, DC 20005		
Registered Federal Lobbyist		

Ford Motor Credit Company

See listing on page 337 under Ford Motor Company

Foremost Insurance Company

A specialty insurance firm.
www.foremost.com
Annual Revenues: $68.40 million
Employees: 1,600
SIC: 6331
Industry/ies: Insurance Industry

Main Headquarters

Mailing:	5600 Beach Tree Ln.	Tel:	(616) 942-3000
	Caledonia, MI 49316	Fax:	(616) 956-3990

Public Affairs and Related Activities Personnel

At Headquarters

PEPPER, Jeff	Tel:	(616) 942-3000
Assistant Vice President, Finance and Accounting	Fax:	(616) 956-3990

Forest City Enterprises

Engages in the ownership, development, management, and acquisition of commercial and residential real estate and land in 26 states and the District of Columbia.
www.forestcity.net
Annual Revenues: $953.60 million
Employees: 2,626
Ticker: NYSE: FCE-A
SIC: 6512; 6552; 5031; 6159; 6513
Industry/ies: Real Estate
Legislative Issues: BUD; TRA

Chairman of the Board	Tel:	(216) 621-6060
RATNER, Charles A.	Fax:	(216) 263-4808

President and Chief Executive Officer	Tel:	(216) 621-6060
LARUE, David J.	Fax:	(216) 263-4808

Main Headquarters

Mailing:	1100 Terminal Tower	Tel:	(216) 621-6060
	50 Public Sq.	Fax:	(216) 263-4808
	Cleveland, OH 44113-2203		

Corporate Foundations and Giving Programs

Forest City Enterprises Charitable Foundation
Contact: Jeffrey B. Linton

1100 Terminal Tower	Tel:	(216) 621-6060
50 Public Sq.		
Cleveland, OH 44113		

Public Affairs and Related Activities Personnel

At Headquarters

DORSEY, Stephanie W.	Tel:	(216) 621-6060
Senior Vice President, Strategic Initiatives and Corporate Operations	Fax:	(216) 263-4808
FRERICKS, Jeff	Tel:	(216) 416-3546
Director, Financial Operations and Contact, Investor Relations	Fax:	(216) 263-4808
jeffreyfrericks@forestcity.net		
KANE, Linda M.	Tel:	(216) 621-6060
Senior Vice President and Treasurer	Fax:	(216) 263-4808
KRULAK, Allan C.	Tel:	(216) 621-6060
Vice President and Director, Community Affairs	Fax:	(216) 263-4808
LINTON, Jeffrey B.	Tel:	(216) 416-3558
Senior Vice President, Corporate Communications and Community Relations	Fax:	(216) 263-4808
jefflinton@forestcity.net		
MCCANN, Nancy	Tel:	(216) 416-3004
Senior Vice President, Marketing and Public Relations	Fax:	(216) 263-4808

nancymccann@forestcity.net

O'BRIEN, Robert G. Tel: (216) 621-6060
Executive Vice President, Chief Financial Officer and PAC Fax: (216) 263-4808
Contact
bobobrien@forestcity.net

OBERT, Charles D. Tel: (216) 621-6060
Senior Vice President , Chief Accounting Officer and Fax: (216) 263-4808
Controller

PASSEN, Andrew J. Tel: (216) 621-6060
Executive Vice President, Human Resources Fax: (216) 263-4808

PRESTI, Geralyn M. Tel: (216) 621-6060
Executive Vice President, General Counsel and Secretary Fax: (216) 263-4808
geripresti@forestcity.net

Forest Laboratories

Actavis completed the acquisition of Forest Laboratories July 1, 2014. A pharmaceutical
manufacturer and marketer.
www.frx.com
Annual Revenues: $3.65 billion
Employees: 5,800
Ticker: NYSE: FRX
SIC: 2834
Industry/ies: Pharmaceutical Industry
Legislative Issues: HCR

Chairman of the Board, Chief Executive Director and President Tel: (212) 421-7850
SOLOMON, Howard Fax: (212) 750-9152
howard.solomon@frx.com

Main Headquarters
Mailing: 909 Third Ave. Tel: (212) 421-7850
New York City, NY 10022 Fax: (212) 750-9152
TF: (800) 947-5227

Public Affairs and Related Activities Personnel

At Headquarters

BAILEY, Bob Tel: (212) 421-7850
Secretary and Chief Legal Officer Fax: (212) 750-9152

KELLY, Alex Tel: (212) 421-7850
Senior Vice President, Public Affairs and Chief Fax: (212) 750-9152
Communications Officer

LING, Karen Tel: (212) 421-7850
Senior Vice President and Chief Human Resources Officer Fax: (212) 750-9152

PERIER, Frank Tel: (212) 421-7850
Executive Vice President, Chief Financial Officer Fax: (212) 750-9152

WALSH, Kevin Tel: (212) 421-7850
Senior Vice President, Operations Fax: (212) 750-9152

WEINSTEIN, Herschel S. Tel: (212) 421-7850
Senior Vice President, General Counsel Fax: (212) 750-9152

ZIMMERMAN, Joe Tel: (212) 421-7850
Senior Vice President, Chief Compliance Officer Fax: (212) 750-9152

Fortune Brands, Inc.

An international consumer products company.
www.fortunebrands.com
Annual Revenues: $4.08 billion
Employees: 18,000
Ticker: NYSE: FBHS
SIC: 1520
Industry/ies: Food And Beverage Industry

Chief Executive Officer Tel: (847) 484-4400
KLEIN , Christopher Fax: (847) 478-0073

Main Headquarters
Mailing: 520 Lake Cook Rd. Tel: (847) 484-4400
Deerfield, IL 60015 Fax: (847) 478-0073

Washington Office
Mailing: 1301 K St. NW
250 West
Washington, DC 20005

Political Action Committees
Fortune Brands Inc PAC
FEC ID: C00473553
Contact: Jean E. Hope
1050 K St. NW
Suite 1040
Washington, DC 20001

Corporate Foundations and Giving Programs

Fortune Brands, Inc. Contributions Program
520 Lake Cook Rd. Tel: (847) 484-4400
Deerfield, IL 60015

Public Affairs and Related Activities Personnel

At Headquarters

BIGGART, Robert Tel: (847) 484-4400
Senior Vice President, General Counsel and Corporate Fax: (847) 478-0073
Secretary

GRISSOM, Sheri Tel: (847) 484-4400
Senior Vice President, Human Resources Fax: (847) 478-0073

LANTZ, Brian C. Tel: (847) 484-4400
Vice President, Investor Relations and Corporate Fax: (847) 478-0073
Communications
investorquestions@FBHS.com

WYATT , E. Lee Tel: (847) 484-4400
Senior Vice President and Chief Financial Officer Fax: (847) 478-0073

At Washington Office

MCNAUGHTON, Terry
Federal Lobbyist

At Other Offices

HOPE, Jean E. Tel: (202) 962-0551
PAC Contact Fax: (202) 962-0561
1050 K St. NW, Suite 1040
Washington, DC 20001

Fossil Inc.

Manufactures and markets fashion accessories.
www.fossil.com
Annual Revenues: $3.46 billion
Employees: 15,200
Ticker: NASDAQ: FOSL
SIC: 3873; 3199
NAICS: 334518; 334518
Industry/ies: Apparel/Textiles Industry

Chairman of the Board and Chief Executive Officer Tel: (972) 234-2525
KARTSOTIS, Kosta N. Fax: (972) 234-4669
kkartsotis@fossil.com

Main Headquarters
Mailing: 2280 N. Greenville Ave. Tel: (972) 234-2525
Richard, TX 75082 Fax: (972) 234-4669

Public Affairs and Related Activities Personnel

At Headquarters

FONTAMILLAS, Mary Tel: (972) 234-2525
Vice President, Public Relations Fax: (972) 234-4669

HART , Darren Tel: (972) 234-2525
Vice President, Finance Fax: (972) 234-4669

HYNE, Randy S. Tel: (972) 699-2115
Vice President, General Counsel and Secretary Fax: (972) 498-9615

KING, Christopher Tel: (972) 234-2525
Vice President, Chief Compliance and Risk Officer Fax: (972) 234-4669

SECOR , Dennis Tel: (972) 234-2525
Executive Vice President, Chief Financial Officer and Fax: (972) 234-4669
Treasurer

L.B. Foster Company

A manufacturer, fabricator and distributor of quality transportation and construction materials.
It manufactures, fabricates, and distributes products and services for the rail, construction,
energy, and utility markets.
www.lbfoster.com
Annual Revenues: $633.68 million
Employees: 1,113
Ticker: NASDAQ (GS): FSTR
SIC: 3317; 3312; 3321; 3363; 5088
Industry/ies: Construction/Construction Materials; Railroads; Transportation

Chairman of the Board Tel: (412) 928-3400
FOSTER, II, Lee B. Fax: (412) 928-7891
lfoster@lbfosterco.com

President and Chief Executive Officer Tel: (412) 928-3400
BAUER, Robert P. Fax: (412) 928-7891
bbauer@lbfoster.com

Main Headquarters
Mailing: 415 Holiday Dr. Tel: (412) 928-3400
Pittsburgh, PA 15220 Fax: (412) 928-7891
TF: (800) 255-4500

Corporate Foundations and Giving Programs

L.B. Foster Company Charitable Trust
Contact: Lee B. Foster II
415 Holiday Dr. Tel: (412) 928-3459
Pittsburgh, PA 15220

Public Affairs and Related Activities Personnel

At Headquarters

FUELLHART, Jake Tel: (412) 928-5645
Manager, Marketing Communications Fax: (412) 928-7891
jfuellhart@lbfoster.com

GUINEE, Patrick J.
Vice President, General Counsel and Corporate Secretary
pguinee@lbfoster.com
Tel: (412) 928-3400
Fax: (412) 928-7891

KELLY, Brian H.
Vice President, Human Resources and Administration
bkelly@lbfosterco.com
Tel: (412) 928-3400
Fax: (412) 928-7891

RUSSO, David J.
Senior Vice President, Chief Financial Officer and Treasurer
drusso@lbfosterco.com
Tel: (412) 928-3417
Fax: (412) 928-7891

SAUDER, David R.
Vice President, Global Business Development
dsauder@lbfosterco.com
Tel: (412) 928-3400
Fax: (412) 928-7891

WOODS, Heather
Manager, Employee Relations
hwoods@lbfosterco.com
Tel: (412) 928-3459
Fax: (412) 928-7891

Foster Miller Inc.

A technology and product development company.
www.foster-miller.qinetiq-na.com
Employees: 300
Industry/ies: Engineering/Mathematics

President and Chief Executive Officer
RIBICH, Dr. William
Tel: (781) 684-4000

Main Headquarters
Mailing: 350 Second Ave.
            Waltham, MA 02451-1196
Tel: (781) 684-4000

Washington Office
Mailing: 2001 Jefferson Davis Hwy.
            Suite 802
            Arlington, VA 22202

Public Affairs and Related Activities Personnel

At Headquarters

AZARIAN, Stephen
Vice President and General Counsel
Tel: (781) 684-4000

DOYLE, Kathrin
Vice President, Human Resources
Tel: (781) 684-4000

Foster Poultry Farms

Provider of poultry products.
www.fosterfarms.com
Annual Revenues: $1.153 billion
Employees: 10,500
SIC: 5144; 5099
Industry/ies: Food And Beverage Industry

Chief Executive Officer
FOSTER, Ron
Tel: (209) 357-1121
Fax: (209) 394-6342

Main Headquarters
Mailing: P.O. Box 306
            Livingston, CA 95334
Tel: (209) 357-1121
Fax: (209) 394-6342
TF: (800) 255-7227

Political Action Committees
Foster Poultry Farms PAC
FEC ID: C00303628
Contact: Randall C. Boyce
P.O. Box 457
Livingston, CA 95334

> **Contributions to Candidates:** $7,000 (2015-2016)
> Democrats: $7,000

Corporate Foundations and Giving Programs
Foster Poultry Farms Contribution Program
P.O. Box 306
Livingston, CA 95334
Tel: (209) 357-1121
Fax: (209) 394-6342

Public Affairs and Related Activities Personnel

At Other Offices

BOYCE, Randall C.
PAC Contact, Senior Vice President and General Counsel
P.O. Box 457
Livingston, CA 95334

BUSH, Lorna
Contact, Public Relations
330 Townsend St., Suite 119
San Francisco, CA 94107
lornabush@finemanpr.com
Tel: (415) 392-1000
Fax: (415) 392-1099

FINEMAN, Michael
Contact, Public Relations
330 Townsend St., Suite 119
San Francisco, CA 94107
mfineman@finemanpr.com
Tel: (415) 392-1000
Fax: (415) 392-1099

Foster Wheeler Ltd.

Operates in engineering and construction, as well as power generating equipment businesses worldwide.
www.fwc.com
Annual Revenues: $3.25 billion
Employees: 14,000
Ticker: NASDAQ: FWLT
SIC: 1600
Industry/ies: Environment And Conservation

President and Chief Executive Officer
MASTERS, J. Kent
Tel: (908) 730-4000
Fax: (908) 713-3245

Main Headquarters
Mailing: Perryville Corporate Park
            Clinton, NJ 08809-4000
Tel: (908) 730-4000
Fax: (908) 713-3245

Public Affairs and Related Activities Personnel

At Headquarters

BASEOTTO, Franco
Executive Vice President, Chief Financial Officer and Treasurer
Tel: (908) 730-4000
Fax: (908) 713-3245

BINGERT, Maureen
Contact, Corporate Communications
maureen_bingert@fwc.com
Tel: (908) 740-4444
Fax: (908) 713-3245

DAVIES, Michelle K.
Executive Vice President, General Counsel and Secretary
Tel: (908) 730-4000
Fax: (908) 713-3245

LAMB, W. Scott
Vice President, Investor Relations and Corporate Communications
scott_lamb@fwc.com
Tel: (908) 730-4155
Fax: (908) 713-3245

ROSTRON, Stephen
Vice President and Chief Corporate Compliance Officer
Tel: (908) 730-4000
Fax: (908) 713-3245

SEXTON, Beth B.
Executive Vice President, Human Resources
beth_sexton@fwc.com
Tel: (908) 730-4000
Fax: (908) 713-3245

THAU, Ronald R.
Assistant Treasurer
Tel: (908) 730-4000
Fax: (908) 713-3245

Foundation Coal Corporation

See listing on page 39 under Alpha Natural Resources, Inc.

The Fox Group, Inc.

A privately-held US corporation with a portfolio of proprietary intellectual property (IP) relating to growth of compound semiconductor crystals and crystal layers.
www.tradewithfox.com
Legislative Issues: ART

President
FOX, Ryan
rfox@tradewithfox.com
Tel: (312) 756-0945
Fax: (312) 756-0947

Main Headquarters
Mailing: 141 W. Jackson Blvd
            Suite 1521
            Chicago, IL 60604
Tel: (312) 756-0945
Fax: (312) 756-0947

Public Affairs and Related Activities Personnel

At Headquarters

KRAL, Herb
Director, Business Development
hkral@tradewithfox.com
Tel: (312) 756-0936
Fax: (312) 756-0947

Franciscan Alliance, Inc.

A hospital system serving Indiana and parts of Illinois.
www.franciscanalliance.org
Employees: 9,000
Industry/ies: Medicine/Health Care/Mental Health
Legislative Issues: MMM

President and Chief Executive Officer
LEAHY, Kevin D.
Tel: (574) 256-3935
Fax: (574) 256-0267

Main Headquarters
Mailing: 1515 Dragoon Trail
            Mishawaka, IN 46544
Tel: (574) 256-3935
Fax: (574) 256-0267

Public Affairs and Related Activities Personnel

At Headquarters

CREEVEY, Tom
Vice President, Human Resources
Tel: (574) 256-3935
Fax: (574) 256-0267

MARION, Jennifer
Senior Vice President, Finance and Chief Financial Officer
Tel: (574) 256-3935
Fax: (574) 256-0267

Franklin Resources Inc.

See listing on page 341 under Franklin Templeton Investments

Franklin Templeton Investments

A financial services holding company.
www.franklintempleton.com
Annual Revenues: $8.36 billion
Employees: 9,400
Ticker: NYSE: BEN
Industry/ies: Banking/Finance/Investments
Legislative Issues: BNK; FIN; TAX

Chairman of the Board and Chief Executive Officer
JOHNSON, Gregory E.

Tel:	(650) 312-4091
Fax:	(650) 312-5606

Main Headquarters
Mailing: P.O. Box 997152
  Sacramento, CA 95899-7152

Tel:	(650) 312-2245

Corporate Foundations and Giving Programs
Franklin Templeton Investments Contribution Program
One Franklin Pkwy.
Building 970, First Floor
San Mateo, CA 94403

Tel:	(650) 312-2100
Fax:	(650) 312-5606

Public Affairs and Related Activities Personnel

At Headquarters

COLEMAN, Stacey
Head, Corporate Communications
scoleman@frk.com

Tel:	(650) 525-7458

GEARY, Sharon H.
Vice President, Human Resources

Tel:	(650) 312-2245

GIBSON, Holly E.
Vice President, Corporate Communications
hgibson@frk.com

Tel:	(650) 312-2245

LEWIS, Kenneth A.
Executive Vice President and Chief Financial Officer

Tel:	(650) 312-2245

TYLE, Craig S.
Executive Vice President and General Counsel

Tel:	(650) 312-2245

WALSH, Matt
Contact, Corporate Communications
mwalsh1@frk.com

Tel:	(650) 312-2245

At Other Offices

GEARY, Sharon H.
Vice President, Human Resources
One Franklin Pkwy., Building 970, First Floor
San Mateo, CA 94403

Tel:	(650) 312-4091
Fax:	(650) 312-5606

GIBSON, Holly E.
Vice President, Corporate Communications
One Franklin Pkwy., Building 970, First Floor
San Mateo, CA 94403
hgibson@frk.com

Tel:	(650) 312-4091
Fax:	(650) 312-5606

JOHNSON, Jennifer M.
Executive Vice President Chief Operating Officer
One Franklin Pkwy., Building 970, First Floor
San Mateo, CA 94403

Tel:	(650) 312-2100
Fax:	(650) 312-5606

LEWIS, Kenneth A.
Executive Vice President and Chief Financial Officer
One Franklin Pkwy., Building 970, First Floor
San Mateo, CA 94403

Tel:	(650) 312-4091
Fax:	(650) 312-5606

LUSK, John M.
Executive Vice President, Investment Management
One Franklin Pkwy., Building 970, First Floor
San Mateo, CA 94403

Tel:	(650) 312-2100
Fax:	(650) 312-5606

RADOSEVICH, Becky
Corporate Communications
One Franklin Pkwy., Building 970, First Floor
San Mateo, CA 94403
rebecca.radosevich@franklintempleton.com

Tel:	(650) 312-2100
Fax:	(650) 312-5606

SANCLEMENTE, Cheryl
Corporate Communications
One Franklin Pkwy., Building 970, First Floor
San Mateo, CA 94403
cheryl.sanclemente@franklintempleton.com

Tel:	(650) 312-3270
Fax:	(650) 312-5606

SEVILLA, Brian
Director, Investor Relations and Corporate Development
One Franklin Pkwy., Building 970, First Floor
San Mateo, CA 94403

Tel:	(650) 312-4091
Fax:	(650) 312-5606

TYLE, Craig S.
Executive Vice President and General Counsel
One Franklin Pkwy., Building 970, First Floor
San Mateo, CA 94403

Tel:	(650) 312-4091
Fax:	(650) 312-5606

YUN, William Y.
Executive Vice President, Alternative Strategies
One Franklin Pkwy., Building 970, First Floor
San Mateo, CA 94403

Tel:	(650) 312-2100
Fax:	(650) 312-5606

Fred Meyer Stores

In 1999 The Kroger co. acquires Fred Meyer,inc.Fred Meyer offers everything from apparel and home goods to groceries, consumer electronics, fuel, and jewelry.
www.fredmeyer.com
Employees: 30,000
SIC: 2099; 3999; 2329; 2339
Industry/ies: Apparel/Textiles Industry; Food And Beverage Industry; Retail/Wholesale

Main Headquarters
Mailing: 3800 S.E. 22nd Ave.
  Portland, OR 97202

Tel:	(503) 232-8844
Fax:	(503) 797-7878
TF:	(800) 576-4377

Corporate Foundations and Giving Programs
Fred Meyer Fund
Contact: Melinda Merrill
3800 S.E. 22nd Ave.
Portland, OR 97202

Tel:	(503) 232-8844
Fax:	(503) 797-5609

Public Affairs and Related Activities Personnel

At Headquarters

DEATHERAGE, David
Vice President and Chief Financial Officer
david.deatherage@fredmeyer.com

Tel:	(503) 232-8844
Fax:	(503) 797-5609

FIKE, Carin
Director and Assistant Treasurer

Tel:	(513) 762-4969
Fax:	(503) 797-5609

MCINTOSH , Jill
Vice President, Human Resources

Tel:	(503) 232-8844
Fax:	(503) 797-7878

MERRILL, Melinda
Manager, Community Affairs
melinda.merrill@fredmeyer.com

Tel:	(503) 797-3830
Fax:	(503) 797-5609

SWEARINGEN, Kim
Manager, Customer Communications

Tel:	(503) 232-8844
Fax:	(503) 797-7878

WOJCIECHOWSKI, Carl
Group Vice President, Human Resources
carl.wojciechowski@fredmeyer.com

Tel:	(503) 232-8844
Fax:	(503) 797-5609

Fred's Inc.

A dollar and drug store operator.
www.fredsinc.com
Annual Revenues: $2.19 billion
Employees: 4,870
Ticker: NASDAQ: FRED
SIC: 5331
Industry/ies: Retail/Wholesale

Chief Executive Officer
SHORE, Jerry A.

Tel:	(901) 365-3733
Fax:	(901) 328-0354

Main Headquarters
Mailing: 4300 New Getwell Rd.
  Memphis, TN 38118

Tel:	(901) 365-8880
Fax:	(901) 328-0354
TF:	(800) 374-7417

Corporate Foundations and Giving Programs
Fred's Contributions Program
Contact: David Mueller
4300 New Getwell Rd.
Memphis, TN 38118

Tel:	(901) 365-8880

Public Affairs and Related Activities Personnel

At Headquarters

BLOOM, Michael K
President and Chief Operating Officer

Tel:	(901) 365-8880
Fax:	(901) 328-0354

DELY, Mark C.
Senior Vice President, Chief Legal Officer, General Counsel and Corporate Secretary

Tel:	(901) 365-8880
Fax:	(901) 328-0354

HANS, Rick
Executive Vice President, Chief Financial Officer

Tel:	(901) 365-8880
Fax:	(901) 328-0354

HAYES, Michael J.
Chairman Emeritus

Tel:	(901) 365-8880
Fax:	(901) 328-0354

TAGG, Sherri L
Chief Accounting Officer

Tel:	(901) 365-8880
Fax:	(901) 328-0354

Freddie Mac

See listing on page 319 under Federal Home Loan Mortgage Corporation

Free Flow Power Corporation

A clean renewable energy company focusing on hydropower, hydrokinetic and hydro pumped storage as reliable, cost-effective sources of electricity and grid stability.
www.free-flow-power.com
Annual Revenues: $2.00 million
Employees: 10
Industry/ies: Energy/Electricity; Marine/Maritime/Shipping; Natural Resources; Ports And Waterways; Transportation
Legislative Issues: ENG

Chairman of the Board　Tel: (978) 283-2822
IRVIN, Daniel R.　Fax: (617) 367-3372
dirvin@free-flow-power.com

President and Chief Executive Officer　Tel: (978) 283-2822
DORMITZER, Henry　Fax: (617) 367-3372
hdormitzer@free--flow--power.com

Main Headquarters
Mailing:　239 Causeway St.　Tel: (978) 283-2822
　　　Suite 300　Fax: (617) 367-3372
　　　Boston, MA 02114-2130

Public Affairs and Related Activities Personnel

At Headquarters

DEVALLES, Melissa　Tel: (978) 283-2822
Director, Business Development　Fax: (617) 367-3372

FELDMAN, Thomas　Tel: (978) 283-2822
Vice President, Regulatory Affairs　Fax: (617) 367-3372

JACOB, Paul　Tel: (978) 283-2822
Chief Commercial Officer　Fax: (617) 367-3372

LISSNER, Daniel　Tel: (978) 283-2822
General Counsel　Fax: (617) 367-3372

MUJANOVIC, Elvir　Tel: (978) 283-2822
Vice President, Finance　Fax: (617) 367-3372

Free Market Petroleum, Inc.

A firm involved with the marketing and financing of crude oil.
Industry/ies: Fuels See Coal, Gas, Oil, Petroleum; Natural Resources; Petroleum Industry; Trade (Foreign And Domestic)

Main Headquarters
Mailing:　1270 Avenue of Americas　Tel: (212) 332-7959
　　　Suite 2110
　　　New York City, NY 10020

Public Affairs and Related Activities Personnel

At Headquarters

HICKMAN, William　Tel: (212) 332-7959

Freedom Communications Inc.

A newspaper and magazine publisher.
www.freedom.com
Annual Revenues: $531.80 million
Employees: 8,000
SIC: 6719; 2711; 2721; 4833
Industry/ies: Communications; Media/Mass Communication

Main Headquarters
Mailing:　625 N. Grand Ave.　Tel: (714) 796-7000
　　　Santa Ana, CA 92701

Public Affairs and Related Activities Personnel

At Headquarters

MORGAN, Eric　Tel: (714) 796-2460
Contact, Communications
emorgan@freedom.com

Freeport-McMoRan Copper & Gold Inc.

A natural resource company formed by the merger of Freeport Minerals Co. and McMoRan Oil and Gas Co. Active in the mining of gold and copper. Acquired Phelps Dodge Corporation.
www.fcx.com
Annual Revenues: $21.32 billion
Employees: 35,000
Ticker: NYSE: FCX
SIC: 1000
Industry/ies: Metals; Mining Industry; Natural Resources
Legislative Issues: CHM

Chairman of the Board　Tel: (504) 582-4000
MOFFETT, James R.　Fax: (504) 582-1847

Vice Chairman, President and Chief Executive Officer　Tel: (504) 582-4000
ADKERSON, Richard C.　Fax: (504) 582-1847

Main Headquarters
Mailing:　333 N. Central Ave.　Tel: (602) 366-8100
　　　Phoenix, AZ 85004　Fax: (504) 582-1847

Washington Office
Mailing:　499 S. Capitol St. SW
　　　Suite 600
　　　Washington, DC 20003

Political Action Committees
Freeport-McMoRan Copper and Gold Citizenship Committee PAC
FEC ID: C00320101
Contact: Tiffanie Figueroa-Phillips
333 N. Central Ave.
Phoenix, AZ 85004

Contributions to Candidates: $126,000 (2015-2016)
Democrats: $28,000; Republicans: $98,000
Principal Recipients
　SENATE
　　MCCAIN, JOHN S (REP-VA)
　HOUSE
　　GOSAR, PAUL ANTHONY (REP-AZ)

Corporate Foundations and Giving Programs
Freeport-McMoRan Copper & Gold Foundation
One N. Central Ave.　Tel: (602) 366-8100
Phoenix, AZ 85004

Public Affairs and Related Activities Personnel

At Headquarters

ARNOLD, Michael J.　Tel: (603) 366-8100
Executive Vice President and Chief Administrative Officer　Fax: (504) 582-1847

COLLIER, William L.　Tel: (504) 583-1750
Vice President, Communications　Fax: (504) 582-1847

FIGUEROA-PHILLIPS, Tiffanie　Tel: (602) 366-7812
PAC Treasurer　Fax: (504) 582-1847
tiffanie_figueroa@fmi.com

JOINT, David P.　Tel: (504) 582-4203
Director, Investor Relations　Fax: (504) 582-1847
ir@fmi.com

KING, W. Russell　Tel: (603) 366-8100
Senior Vice President, International Relations and Federal　Fax: (504) 582-1847
Government Affairs

KINNEBERG, Eric E.　Tel: (602) 366-7994
Director, External Communications　Fax: (504) 582-1847
mr@fmi.com

QUIRK, Kathleen L.　Tel: (602) 366-8016
Executive Vice President, Chief Financial Officer and　Fax: (504) 582-1847
Treasurer

Freeport-McMoran Energy LLC

Resource Development
Industry/ies: Fuels See Coal, Gas, Oil, Petroleum; Natural Resources; Petroleum Industry

Chairman　Tel: (713) 579-6000
R, Moffett James

Vice Chairman, President and Chief Executive Officer　Tel: (713) 579-6000
ADKERSON , Richard C

Main Headquarters
Mailing:　1615 Poydras St.
　　　New Orleans, LA 70112

Public Affairs and Related Activities Personnel

At Headquarters

KATHLEEN, Quirk L　Tel: (713) 579-6000
Executive Vice President, Chief Financial Officer and
Treasurer

JOINT, David　Tel: (713) 579-6000
Director, Investor Relations

MICHAEL, Arnold J　Tel: (713) 579-6000
Executive Vice President and Chief Administrative Officer

MYERS , III, Hance V.　Tel: (713) 579-6000
Vice President and Corporate Information Director　Fax: (713) 579-6611
investor@pxp.com

RUSCH, Steven P.　Tel: (713) 579-6000
Vice President, Environmental, Health, Safety and
Government Affairs
sn1sch@pxp.com

WINTERS, Scott　Tel: (713) 579-6000
Vice President, Corporate Planning and Research　Fax: (713) 579-6611
winters@pxp.com

WOMBWELL, John F.　Tel: (713) 579-6000
Executive Vice President, General Counsel and Corporate　Fax: (713) 579-6500
Secretary

Freightliner Corporation

A division of Daimler Trucks North America, a manufacturer of heavy-duty vehicles and medium-duty vehicles.
www.freightlinertrucks.com
Employees: 20,000
Industry/ies: Transportation; Trucking Industry

President and Chief Executive Officer　Tel: (503) 745-8000
DAUM, Martin　Fax: (503) 745-8921

Main Headquarters
Mailing:　4435 N. Channel Ave.　Tel: (503) 745-8000
　　　Portland, OR 97217　Fax: (503) 745-8921

Public Affairs and Related Activities Personnel

At Headquarters

KRITSCHGAU, Juergen	Tel:	(503) 745-8000
Chief Financial Officer	Fax:	(503) 745-8921

Fresenius Medical Care North America

A provider of kidney dialysis services and renal care products. It provides dialysis care services related to the dialysis treatment a patient receives with end stage renal disease (ESRD); and other health care services.
www.fmcna.com
Annual Revenues: $14.6 billion
Employees: 90,690
Ticker: NYSE: FMS
Industry/ies: Medicine/Health Care/Mental Health
Legislative Issues: HCR; MMM

Chief Executive Officer

KUERBITZ, Ronald	Tel:	(781) 699-9000
ron.kuerbitz@fmc.na.com	Fax:	(781) 402-9005

Main Headquarters

Mailing:	920 Winter St.	Tel:	(781) 699-9000
	Waltham, MA 02451	Fax:	(781) 402-9005
		TF:	(800) 662-1237

Washington Office

Mailing:	801 Pennsylvania Ave. NW	Tel:	(202) 393-7713
	Suite 255		
	Washington, DC 20004		

Political Action Committees

Fresenius Medical Care North America PAC
FEC ID: C00401299
Contact: Eric Bishop

801 Pennsylvania Ave. NW	Tel:	(202) 393-7713
Suite 255	Fax:	(202) 296-8634
Washington, DC 20004		

Contributions to Candidates: $158,500 (2015-2016)
Democrats: $73,000; Republicans: $83,500; Other: $2,000

Principal Recipients

SENATE
BLUMENTHAL, RICHARD (DEM-CT)
CASSIDY, WILLIAM M (REP-LA)
CRAPO, MICHAEL D (REP-ID)

Public Affairs and Related Activities Personnel

At Headquarters

GAUGER, Brian	Tel:	(781) 699-9000
Chief Development Officer and Senior Vice President	Fax:	(781) 402-9005
HEINOLD, Rosemary	Tel:	(781) 699-4171
Director, Communications	Fax:	(781) 402-9005
rosemary.heinold@fmc-na.com		
KEMBEL, David	Tel:	(781) 699-9000
Chief Compliance Officer and Senior Vice President	Fax:	(781) 402-9005
KOTT, Doug	Tel:	(781) 699-9000
Senior Vice President and General Counsel	Fax:	(781) 402-9005
MOESSLANG, Angelo	Tel:	(781) 699-9000
Chief Financial Officer	Fax:	(781) 402-9005
SILVA, Brian	Tel:	(781) 699-9000
Chief Human Resources Officer and Senior Vice President, Administration	Fax:	(781) 402-9005
SONNEN, Kim	Tel:	(781) 699-9000
Senior Vice President, Payor Relations, Government Affairs and Integrated Care	Fax:	(781) 402-9005
STONE, Jonathan D.	Tel:	(781) 699-9704
Director, Communications	Fax:	(781) 402-9005
Jonathan.d.stone@fmc-na.com		

At Washington Office

ANNA, Yvonne Santa	Tel:	(202) 393-7713
Vice President, Congressional Relations		
BISHOP, Eric	Tel:	(202) 393-7713
Vice President, Finance, Administration and PAC Treasurer		
LYNCH, C.M. Cameron	Tel:	(202) 393-7713
Federal Lobbyist		
Registered Federal Lobbyist		
SEPUCHA, Robert	Tel:	(202) 393-7713
Senior Vice President, Corporate Affairs		
robert.sepucha@fmc-na.com		
Registered Federal Lobbyist		
SMITH, Kathleen T.	Tel:	(202) 393-7713
Vice President, Government Affairs		
kathleen.smith@fmc-na.com		
Registered Federal Lobbyist		
SMITH, KATHLEEN	Tel:	(202) 393-7713

Vice President, Government Affairs
Registered Federal Lobbyist

At Other Offices

MORRIS, Terry	Tel:	(800) 948-2538
Vice President, Investor Relations and Corporate Communications	Fax:	(615) 345-5605
5412 Maryland Way, Suite 208		
Brentwood, TN 37027		

Friendly's Ice Cream Corporation

A restaurant company acquired by Tennessee Restaurant Co.
www.friendlys.com
Annual Revenues: $518.40 million
Employees: 13,000
Ticker: AMEX: FRN
SIC: 2024; 5812
NAICS: 31152
Industry/ies: Food And Beverage Industry

President and Chief Executive Officer

MAGUIRE, John M.	Tel:	(413) 731-4000
	Fax:	(413) 731-4471

Main Headquarters

Mailing:	1855 Boston Rd.	Tel:	(413) 731-4000
	Wilbraham, MA 01095	Fax:	(413) 731-4471
		TF:	(800) 966-9970

Corporate Foundations and Giving Programs

Friendly's Ice Cream Corporation Contributions Program
Contact: Gillian Begin

1855 Boston Rd.	Tel:	(413) 731-4243
Wilbraham, MA 01095	Fax:	(413) 731-4471

Public Affairs and Related Activities Personnel

At Headquarters

BEGIN, Gillian	Tel:	(413) 731-4243
Contact, Media	Fax:	(413) 731-4471
gillian.begin@friendlys.com		
BOLTON, Lynn	Tel:	(413) 731-4000
Contact, Media Relations	Fax:	(413) 731-4471
lynn.bolton@friendlys.com		
DAVIS, Randy	Tel:	(413) 731-4000
Executive Vice President, Chief Marketing Officer	Fax:	(413) 731-4471
LENNICK, Connie	Tel:	(413) 731-4000
Senior Vice President, Human Resources	Fax:	(413) 731-4471
SAWYER, Bob	Tel:	(413) 731-4000
Senior Vice President General Counsel and Secretary	Fax:	(413) 731-4471
SCHWENDENMANN, Todd	Tel:	(413) 731-4000
Executive Vice President, Chief Financial Officer	Fax:	(413) 731-4471
WEIGEL, Steve	Tel:	(413) 731-4000
Executive Vice President, Chief Operating Officer	Fax:	(413) 731-4471

Frito-Lay, Inc.

A snack food producer. A separate operating division of PepsiCo, Inc. (see separate listing).
www.fritolay.com
Employees: 40,000
SIC: 2096; 2099
NAICS: 311919; 111998
Industry/ies: Food And Beverage Industry

President and Chief Executive Officer

GRECO, Thomas	Tel:	(972) 334-7000
	Fax:	(972) 334-5418

Main Headquarters

Mailing:	7701 Legacy Dr.	Tel:	(972) 334-7000
	Plano, TX 75024	Fax:	(972) 334-5418

Corporate Foundations and Giving Programs

Frito-Lay Inc. Contributions Program

P.O. Box 660634	Tel:	(972) 334-7000
Dallas, TX 75266		

Public Affairs and Related Activities Personnel

At Headquarters

AVULA, Hari	Tel:	(972) 334-7000
Chief Financial Officer	Fax:	(972) 334-5418
FLAVELL, David	Tel:	(972) 334-7000
Senior Vice President and General Counsel	Fax:	(972) 334-5418
KUECHENMEISTER, Chris	Tel:	(972) 334-7000
Vice President, Communications	Fax:	(972) 334-5418
MCLAUGHLIN, Patrick	Tel:	(972) 334-7000
Senior Vice President, Human Resources and Chief Human Resources Officer	Fax:	(972) 334-5418
SAENZ, Jennifer	Tel:	(972) 334-7000
Senior Vice President and Chief Marketing Officer	Fax:	(972) 334-5418
SANKARAN, Vivek	Tel:	(972) 334-7000
President and Chief Operating Officer	Fax:	(972) 334-5418

TURNER, Chris	Tel:	(972) 334-7000
Senior Vice President, Strategy	Fax:	(972) 334-5418

Frontier Airlines

Provider of budget airline services.
www.frontierairlines.com/frontier/home.do
Annual Revenues: $479.60 million
Employees: 6,000
SIC: 4512
Industry/ies: Aerospace/Aviation; Airlines; Transportation

Main Headquarters

Mailing:	P.O. Box 492085	Tel:	(720) 374-4200
	Denver, CO 80249	Fax:	(720) 374-4375
		TF:	(800) 265-5505

Corporate Foundations and Giving Programs

Frontier Airlines Contributions Program		
7001 Tower Rd.	Tel:	(720) 374-4200
Denver, CO 80249	Fax:	(720) 374-4375

Public Affairs and Related Activities Personnel

At Headquarters

ASHCROFT, Robert	Tel:	(720) 374-4200
Senior Vice President, Finance	Fax:	(720) 374-4375
PURVES, Lindsey	Tel:	(720) 374-4200
Senior Manager, Public Relations	Fax:	(720) 374-4375
SHAH, Ashok	Tel:	(720) 374-4200
Vice President, Finance	Fax:	(720) 374-4375
SHURZ, Daniel	Tel:	(720) 374-4200
Vice President, Commercial	Fax:	(720) 374-4375

Frontier Communications Corporation

Voice, broadband, satellite video, wireless Internet data access, data security solutions.
www.frontier.com
Annual Revenues: $4.99 billion
Employees: 17,800
Ticker: NYSE: FTR
SIC: 4813
Industry/ies: Communications; Telecommunications/Internet/Cable
Legislative Issues: COM; TEC

Chairman of the Board and Chief Executive Officer	Tel:	(203) 614-5600
WILDEROTTER, Maggie	Fax:	(203) 614-4602
President and Chief Executive Officer	Tel:	(203) 614-5600
MCCARTHY, Daniel	Fax:	(203) 614-4602

Main Headquarters

Mailing:	Three High Ridge Park	Tel:	(203) 614-5600
	Stamford, CT 06905-1390	Fax:	(203) 614-4602

Political Action Committees
Citizens Utilities Company PAC
FEC ID: C00355065
Contact: Kenneth Mason
180 S. Clinton St.
Fifth Floor
Rochester, NY 14646

Public Affairs and Related Activities Personnel

At Headquarters

ABERNATHY, Kathleen Q.	Tel:	(203) 614-5600
Executive Vice President, External Affairs	Fax:	(203) 614-4602
kathleen.abernathy@frontiercorp.com		
CROSBY, Steve	Tel:	(203) 614-5600
Senior Vice President, Government and Regulatory Affairs	Fax:	(203) 614-4602
and Public Relations		
steven.crosby@frontiercorp.com		
DEPASQUALE, Pete	Tel:	(203) 614-5600
Vice President, Communications & Corporate Affairs	Fax:	(203) 614-4602
JURELLER, John M	Tel:	(203) 614-5600
Executive Vice President and Chief Financial Officer	Fax:	(203) 614-4602
LASS, John	Tel:	(203) 614-5600
Executive Vice President, Field Operations	Fax:	(203) 614-4602
MCKENNEY, Cecilia K.	Tel:	(203) 614-5600
Executive Vice President, Human Resources and and	Fax:	(203) 614-4602
Administrative Services		
NIELSEN, Mark D	Tel:	(203) 614-5600
Executive Vice President, General Counsel and Secretary	Fax:	(203) 614-4602
Corporate Secretary		
SCHNEIDER, Jennifer	Tel:	(203) 614-5600
Vice President, Legislative Affairs	Fax:	(203) 614-4602
Registered Federal Lobbyist		
SMITH, Brigid M.	Tel:	(203) 614-5042
Assistant Vice President, Corporate Communications	Fax:	(203) 614-4602
brigid.smith@frontiercorp.com		

At Other Offices
MASON, Kenneth
PAC Treasurer
180 S. Clinton St., Fifth Floor
Rochester, NY 14646

Frost Capital Group

See listing on page 344 under Frost National Bank

Frost National Bank

A bank holding company. Also known as Cullen/Frost Bankers, Inc. It offers commercial and consumer banking services in Texas. It provides commercial banking services to corporations and other business clients.
www.frostbank.com
Annual Revenues: $1.02 billion
Employees: 4,154
Ticker: NYSE :CFR
Industry/ies: Banking/Finance/Investments

Chairman of the Board and Chief Executive Officer	Tel:	(210) 220-4011
EVANS, Jr., Richard W.	Fax:	(210) 220-4325

Main Headquarters

Mailing:	P.O. Box 1600	Tel:	(210) 220-4011
	San Antonio, TX 78296	Fax:	(210) 220-4325
		TF:	(800) 513-7678

Corporate Foundations and Giving Programs

Frost National Bank Contributions Program		
100 W. Houston St.	Tel:	(210) 220-4011
San Antonio, TX 78205-1400		

Public Affairs and Related Activities Personnel

At Headquarters

GREEN, Phillip D.	Tel:	(210) 220-4011
President	Fax:	(210) 220-4325
PARKER, Greg	Tel:	(210) 220-5632
Executive Vice President and Director, Investor Relations	Fax:	(210) 220-4325
gparker@frostbank.com		
SABEL, Renee	Tel:	(210) 220-5416
Senior Vice President, Corporate Communications	Fax:	(210) 220-4325
rsabel@frostbank.com		
SALINAS, Jerry	Tel:	(210) 220-4011
Group Executive Vice President & Chief Financial Officer	Fax:	(210) 220-4325

Fruit of the Loom

Products include active wear, casual wear, and children's underwear sold under names such as Russell, Fun pals, Fun gals, and Underoos (which feature licensed characters).
www.fruitoftheloom.com
Employees: 23,000
SIC: 2250; 2322; 2341
NAICS: 315221; 315231
Industry/ies: Apparel/Textiles Industry
Legislative Issues: TRD

Chief Sales and Business Officer	Tel:	(270) 781-6400
NEWTON, William G.	Fax:	(270) 781-6588

Main Headquarters

Mailing:	One Fruit of the Loom Dr.	Tel:	(270) 781-6400
	P.O. Box 90015	Fax:	(270) 781-6588
	Bowling Green, KY 42102	TF:	(855) 253-4534

Corporate Foundations and Giving Programs

Fruit of the Loom Contributions Program		
One Fruit of the Loom Dr.	Tel:	(270) 781-6400
P.O. Box 90015	Fax:	(270) 781-6588
Bowling Green, KY 42102		

FSCC HealthCare Ministry, Inc.

Health care system office
fsccm.org
Industry/ies: Health Care; Hospitals; Medicine/Health Care/Mental Health

President	Tel:	(920) 648-7071
WOLF, Sister Laura	Fax:	(920) 684-6417

Main Headquarters

Mailing:	1415 S. Rapids Rd.	Tel:	(920) 648-7071
	Manitowoc, WI 54220	Fax:	(920) 684-6417

Public Affairs and Related Activities Personnel

At Headquarters

AASEN, Karen	Tel:	(920) 648-7071
Manager, Business and Human Resource	Fax:	(920) 684-6417
HOLLEN, Terri	Tel:	(920) 648-7071
Manager, Quality, Compliance and Risk	Fax:	(920) 684-6417
MCCONNAHA, Scott	Tel:	(920) 648-7071
Vice President	Fax:	(920) 684-6417

smcconnaha@fhcm.org

SCHAEFER, Julie   Tel: (920) 648-7071
Executive Assistant for Governance and Communication   Fax: (920) 684-6417

VOPAT, James   Tel: (920) 648-7071
Senior Vice President, Finance   Fax: (920) 684-6417

FT Industries, Inc.

See listing on page 197 under Claire's Stores, Inc.

Fuel Cell Energy Corporation

Engaged in the development and production of stationary fuel cells for commercial, industrial, municipal and utility customers.
www.fuelcellenergy.com
Annual Revenues: $177.53 million
Employees: 620
Ticker: NASDAQ: FCEL
SIC: 3690
Industry/ies: Energy/Electricity

President and Chief Executive Officer   Tel: (203) 825-6000
BOTTONE, Chip   Fax: (203) 825-6100

Main Headquarters
Mailing: Three Great Pasture Rd.   Tel: (203) 825-6000
    Danbury, CT 06813   Fax: (203) 825-6100

Political Action Committees
FuelCell Energy PAC
FEC ID: C00204180
Contact: Ross Levine
Three Great Pasture Rd.   Tel: (203) 825-6000
Danbury, CT 06813   Fax: (203) 825-6000

    Contributions to Candidates: $28,500 (2015-2016)
    Democrats: $24,000; Republicans: $4,500

       Principal Recipients
       PRESIDENT
       CLINTON, HILLARY RODHAM (DEM-NY)

Public Affairs and Related Activities Personnel
At Headquarters

BISHOP, Michael   Tel: (203) 825-6000
Senior Vice President, Chief Financial Officer, Treasurer and   Fax: (203) 825-6100
Corporate Secretary

GODDARD, Kurt   Tel: (203) 830-7494
Vice President, Investor Relationss   Fax: (203) 825-6100
ir@fce.com

LEVINE, Ross   Tel: (203) 825-6000
PAC Treasurer   Fax: (203) 825-6100
rlevine@fce.com

RAUSEO, Anthony F.   Tel: (203) 825-6000
Senior Vice President and Chief Operating Officer   Fax: (203) 825-6100

TOBY, Ben   Tel: (203) 825-6114
Contact, Sales   Fax: (203) 825-6100
btoby@fce.com

WOLAK, Frank   Tel: (413) 357-9060
Contact, Policy   Fax: (203) 825-6100
fwolak@fce.com

FUJIFILM Holdings America Corporation

A sales and marketing subsidiary of Tokyo's Fujifilm Holdings.
www.fujifilmusa.com
Annual Revenues: $205.60 million
Employees: 3,500
Industry/ies: Communications; Media/Mass Communication

Main Headquarters
Mailing: 200 Summit Lake Dr.   Tel: (914) 789-8100
    Floor Two   TF: (800) 755-3854
    Valhalla, NY 10595-1356

Public Affairs and Related Activities Personnel
At Other Offices

FIORE, Julie M.   Tel: (781) 271-4400
Manager, Human Resources
45 Crosby Dr.
Bedford, MA 01730-1401
jfiore@fujibedford.com

FUJIFILM SonoSite, Inc.

See listing on page 730 under SonoSite, Inc.

Fulcrum BioEnergy, Inc.

A biofuel manufacturer.
www.fulcrum-bioenergy.com
Employees: 19
SIC: 2860

Industry/ies: Energy/Electricity; Fuels See Coal, Gas, Oil, Petroleum; Natural Resources; Petroleum Industry; Science; Scientific Research
Legislative Issues: ENG

Chairman of the Board   Tel: (925) 730-0150
MCDERMOTT, James A.C.   Fax: (925) 730-0157

President and Chief Executive Officer   Tel: (925) 730-0150
MACIAS, E. James   Fax: (925) 730-0157

Main Headquarters
Mailing: 4900 Hopyard Rd.   Tel: (925) 730-0150
    Suite 220   Fax: (925) 730-0157
    Pleasanton, CA 94588

Public Affairs and Related Activities Personnel
At Headquarters

BARRAZA, Richard   Tel: (925) 224-8244
Vice President, Administration   Fax: (925) 730-0157

BUNTON, Karen   Tel: (925) 224-8252
Manager, Administration   Fax: (925) 730-0157
kbunton@fulcrum-bioenergy.com

KNIESCHE, Theodore M.   Tel: (925) 730-0150
Vice President, Business Development   Fax: (925) 730-0157

PRYOR, Eric N.   Tel: (925) 730-0150
Vice President and Chief Financial Officer   Fax: (925) 730-0157

H.B. Fuller Company

A manufacturer of adhesives, sealants, coatings, paints, and other specialty chemicals with comprehensive adhesive technology portfolio to improve wide-ranging production processes from closing a carton to facilitating high tech solar panel manufacturing.
www.hbfuller.com/north-america
Annual Revenues: $2.09 billion
Employees: 3,650
Ticker: NYSE: FUL
SIC: 2891
Industry/ies: Chemicals & Chemical Industry

President and Chief Executive Officer   Tel: (651) 236-5900
OWENS, Jim   Fax: (651) 236-5426

Main Headquarters
Mailing: 1200 Willow Lake Blvd.   Tel: (651) 236-5900
    P.O. Box 64683   Fax: (651) 236-5426
    St. Paul, MN 55164-0683   TF: (888) 423-8553

Corporate Foundations and Giving Programs

H.B. Fuller Company Foundation
Contact: Joel Hedberg
1200 Williow Lake Rd.   Tel: (651) 236-5217
P.O. Box 64683
St. Paul, MN 55164

Public Affairs and Related Activities Personnel
At Headquarters

GIERTZ, James   Tel: (651) 236-5900
Senior Vice President, Chief Financial Officer   Fax: (651) 236-5426

HEDBERG, Joel   Tel: (651) 236-5835
Interim Director, Public Relations   Fax: (651) 236-5056
Joel.Hedberg@hbfuller.com

KEENAN, Timothy   Tel: (651) 236-5900
Vice President, General Counsel and Corporate Secretary   Fax: (651) 236-5426

MARCY, Maximillian   Tel: (651) 236-5062
Senior Manager, Treasury and Investor Relations   Fax: (651) 355-9310
Mail Stop Max.Marcy@hbfuller.com
mailto:max.marcy@hbfuller.com

PARRIOTT, Ann   Tel: (651) 236-5900
Vice President, Human Resources   Fax: (651) 236-5426

SINCLAIR, Kimberlee   Tel: (651) 236-5823
Director, Corporate Communications   Fax: (651) 236-5426
kimberlee.sinclair@hbfuller.com

TRIPPEL, Pat   Tel: (651) 236-5900
Senior Vice President, Market Development   Fax: (651) 236-5426

Fulton Financial Corporation

A U.S. regional financial services holding company.
www.fult.com
Annual Revenues: $676.19 million
Employees: 3,480
Ticker: NASDAQ: FULT
SIC: 6021
Industry/ies: Banking/Finance/Investments

Chairman of the Board, President and Chief Executive Officer   Tel: (717) 291-2411
WENGER, E. Philip   Fax: (717) 295-4792

Main Headquarters
Mailing: One Penn Sq.   Tel: (717) 291-2411
    P.O. Box 4887   Fax: (717) 295-4792

Lancaster, PA 17604   TF: (800) 752-9580

Political Action Committees

Fulton Financial Corporation PAC
FEC ID: C00400317
Contact: Michael J. Deporter
One Penn Sq.
P.O. Box 4887
Lancaster, PA 17604

   Contributions to Candidates: $6,250 (2015-2016)
   Democrats: $1,250; Republicans: $5,000

Fulton Financial Corporation PAC
FEC ID: C00414243
Contact: Karl J Sichelstiel
83 W. Washington St.   Tel: (717) 291-2411
P.O. Box 189   Fax: (717) 295-4792
Hagerstown, MD 21741

Public Affairs and Related Activities Personnel

At Headquarters

BARRETT, Patrick   Tel: (717) 291-2411
Senior Executive Vice President and Chief Financial Officer   Fax: (717) 295-4792

DEPORTER, Michael J.   Tel: (717) 291-2411
Senior Vice President, Controller and Chief Accounting   Fax: (717) 295-4792
Officer

HILL, Craig H.   Tel: (717) 291-2411
Senior Executive Vice President, Human Resources   Fax: (717) 295-4792
Chill@Fult.com

HOSTETTER, David C.   Tel: (717) 291-2456
Executive Vice President, Marketing, Corporate   Fax: (717) 295-4792
Communications and Strategy
dhostetter@fult.com

SHREINER, James E.   Tel: (717) 291-2411
Senior Executive Vice President, Operations and Credit   Fax: (717) 295-4792

WAKELEY, Laura J.   Tel: (717) 291-2616
Vice President, Corporate Communications   Fax: (717) 295-4792

At Other Offices

SICHELSTIEL, Karl J.
Senior Vice President and Trust Controller, PAC Treasurer
83 W. Washington St., P.O. Box 189
Hagerstown, MD 21741

SICHELSTIEL , Karl J
Treasurer
83 W. Washington St., P.O. Box 189
Hagerstown, MD 21741

Furmanite Corporation

Provides technology-based and technical services worldwide.
www.furmanite.com
Annual Revenues: $526.59 million
Employees: 3,017
Ticker: NYSE: FRM
SIC: 1700
Industry/ies: Communications; Telecommunications/Internet/Cable

Chairman of the Board and Chief Executive Officer   Tel: (713) 634-7777
COX, Charles R.

Chief Executive Officer   Tel: (713) 634-7777
MILLIRON, Joseph E.

Main Headquarters
Mailing: 10370 Richmond Ave.   Tel: (713) 634-7777
         Suite 600
         Houston, TX 77042

Public Affairs and Related Activities Personnel

At Headquarters

MUFF, Robert S.   Tel: (713) 634-7777
Chief Financial Officer

FXI

Formerly Foamex Innovations and Foamex International. A manufacturer of flexible polyurethane foam and foam products for the home, healthcare, electronics, industrial, personal care and transportation markets. Its products include finished goods, sub-assemblies, services and raw materials for OEMs, fabricators and retailers.
www.fxi.com
Annual Revenues: $1.17 billion
Employees: 2,000
SIC: 3086
NAICS: 32615
Industry/ies: Chemicals & Chemical Industry

President and Chief Executive Officer   Tel: (610) 744-2300
COWLES, John   Fax: (610) 859-3035

Main Headquarters

Mailing: Rose Tree Corporate Center II   Tel: (610) 744-2300
        1400 Providence Rd., Suite 2000   Fax: (610) 859-3035
        Media, PA 19063-2076   TF: (800) 355-3626

Public Affairs and Related Activities Personnel

At Headquarters

ADAMS, Diane F.   Tel: (610) 744-2300
Senior Vice President, Chief Marketing Officer   Fax: (610) 859-3035

BONADDIO, Vincenzo A.   Tel: (610) 744-2300
Senior Vice President, Research and Development   Fax: (610) 859-3035

DIMARTINO, Robert   Tel: (610) 744-2300
Senior Vice President, Human Resources   Fax: (610) 859-3035

DUNN, Darryl M.   Tel: (610) 744-2300
Senior Vice President, Controller   Fax: (610) 859-3035

EARLEY, Harold J.   Tel: (610) 744-2300
Executive Vice President and Chief Financial Officer   Fax: (610) 859-3035

PRUSKY, Andrew R.   Tel: (610) 859-3000
Senior Vice President, Legal   Fax: (610) 859-3035

SCRIPTER, Jay   Tel: (610) 744-2300
Senior Vice President, Operations   Fax: (610) 859-3035

G

See listing on page 658 under Public Service Enterprise Group (PSE&G)

G4S Secure Solutions (USA) Inc.

A business services company providing security and investigation solutions, facility management and security staffing services in North America. Owned by the UK-based firm, G4S (was acquired in 2002 by Danish company 4 Falck, which merged with Securicor in 2004 to form G4S). Officially changed its name name to G4S Secure Solutions in 2010.
www.g4s.com
Annual Revenues: $2.50 billion
Employees: 57,000
SIC: 7381
Industry/ies: Disaster; Law Enforcement/Security

Group Chief Executive Officer   Tel: (561) 622-5656
ALMANZA, Ashley   Fax: (561) 622-6423

Main Headquarters
Mailing: 515 King St., Suite 300
        Alexandria, VA 22314

Political Action Committees

G4S Secure Solutions (USA) PAC
FEC ID: C00165365
Contact: Celia Fletcher
1395 University Dr.   Tel: (561) 622-5656
Jupiter, FL 33458

   Contributions to Candidates: $12,700 (2015-2016)
   Democrats: $7,700; Republicans: $5,000

Corporate Foundations and Giving Programs

G4S Secure Solutions Contributions Program
4200 Wackenhut Dr. 100   Tel: (561) 622-5656
Palm Beach Gardens, FL 33410-4242   Fax: (561) 622-6423

Public Affairs and Related Activities Personnel

At Other Offices

BENSCHOTEN, Richard Van   Tel: (561) 691-6669
PAC Contact   Fax: (561) 622-6423
1395 University Blvd.
Jupiter, FL 33458

CAPALLATTI, Jeff   Tel: (561) 622-5656
Corporate Treasurer /Risk Manager and PAC Treasurer   Fax: (561) 622-6423
4200 Wackenhut Dr. 100
Palm Beach Gardens, FL 33410-4242

CONNOLLY, Rick   Tel: (561) 691-6669
Senior Vice President, Sales and Marketing, G4S Secure   Fax: (561) 622-6423
Solutions (USA)
1395 University Blvd.
Jupiter, FL 33458

FLETCHER, Celia   Tel: (561) 691-6669
Pac Treasurer   Fax: (561) 622-6423
1395 University Blvd.
Jupiter, FL 33458

GERKS, Geoff   Tel: (561) 691-6669
Senior Vice President, Corporate Human Resources   Fax: (561) 622-6423
1395 University Blvd.
Jupiter, FL 33458

GRIZZARD, Danny   Tel: (561) 691-6669
Chief Operating Officer, G4S Secure Solutions (USA)   Fax: (561) 622-6423
1395 University Blvd.
Jupiter, FL 33458

KENNING, John   Tel: (561) 691-6669
   Fax: (561) 622-6423

*Regional Chief Executive Officer, North America &
Technology*
1395 University Blvd.
Jupiter, FL 33458

LEVINE, Drew	Tel:	(561) 691-6669
President, G4S Secure Solutions North America	Fax:	(561) 622-6423

1395 University Blvd.
Jupiter, FL 33458

LUNDSBERG-NIELSEN, Soren	Tel:	(561) 622-5656
Group General Counsel	Fax:	(561) 622-6423

4200 Wackenhut Dr. 100
Palm Beach Gardens, FL 33410-4242

PARRIS, Helen	Tel:	(561) 622-5656
Director, Investor Relations	Fax:	(561) 622-6423

4200 Wackenhut Dr. 100
Palm Beach Gardens, FL 33410-4242

RAJA, Himanshu	Tel:	(561) 622-5656
Group Chief Financial Officer	Fax:	(561) 622-6423

4200 Wackenhut Dr. 100
Palm Beach Gardens, FL 33410-4242

SHAPIRO, Marc	Tel:	(561) 691-6443
Senior Vice President, Global Partnerships	Fax:	(561) 691-6738

4200 Wackenhut Dr. 100
Palm Beach Gardens, FL 33410-4242
mshapiro@wackenhut.com

WALKER, Debbie	Tel:	(561) 622-5656
Director, Group Communications	Fax:	(561) 622-6423

4200 Wackenhut Dr. 100
Palm Beach Gardens, FL 33410-4242

Galaxy Global Corporation

Galaxy Global Corporation is a Small Business with offices in West Virginia, Maryland, Michigan and Ohio. For over 21 years, Galaxy Global has been providing Information Technology Services in support of several Federal Government customers and major Federal Prime Contractors.
www.galaxyglobal.com
Annual Revenues: $3.10 million
NAICS: 541511
Industry/ies: Computer/Technology; Defense/Homeland Security; Government-Related

President and Chief Executive Officer	Tel:	(304) 363-0602
LINGER, Wade	Fax:	(304) 363-0604

Main Headquarters

Mailing:	2063 Winners Dr.	Tel:	(304) 363-0602
	Suite 202	Fax:	(304) 363-0604
	Fairmont, WV 26554		

Public Affairs and Related Activities Personnel

At Headquarters

CUNANAN, Zeny	Tel:	(304) 363-0602
Executive Vice President	Fax:	(304) 363-0604
cunanan@galaxyglobal.com		

HEFNER, Randy	Tel:	(304) 363-0602
Vice President	Fax:	(304) 363-0604
randy.hefner@galaxyglobal.com		

Gambro, Inc.

A medical device producer and provider of other health care services.
www.gambro.com
Employees: 1,900
Industry/ies: Medicine/Health Care/Mental Health

Main Headquarters

Mailing:	14143 Denver W. Pkwy.	Tel:	(303) 232-6800
	Lakewood, CO 80401-3266	Fax:	(303) 222-6810
		TF:	(800) 525-2623

Public Affairs and Related Activities Personnel

At Headquarters

BONELLI, Anne	Tel:	(303) 222-6709
Director, Communications	Fax:	(303) 231-4545
anne.bonelli@us.gambro.com		

SEYEDZADEH, Javad	Tel:	(303) 232-6800
Senior Vice President, Quality Assurance and Regulatory Affairs	Fax:	(303) 222-6810

Gannett Company, Inc.

An international news and information company.
www.gannett.com
Annual Revenues: $6.08 billion
Employees: 31,250
Ticker: NYSE: GCI
SIC: 2711, 4833, 4841
NAICS: 515120; 511110

Industry/ies: Communications; Media/Mass Communication
Legislative Issues: RET

Chairman of the Board	Tel:	(703) 854-6000
MAGNER, Marjorie	Fax:	(703) 854-2053

President and Chief Executive Officer	Tel:	(703) 854-6000
MARTORE, Gracia C.	Fax:	(703) 854-2053

Main Headquarters

Mailing:	7950 Jones Branch Dr.	Tel:	(703) 854-6000
	McLean, VA 22107-0150	Fax:	(703) 854-2053
		TF:	(800) 778-3299

Corporate Foundations and Giving Programs

The Belo Foundation
Contact: Amy M. Meadows

P.O. Box 655237	Tel:	(214) 977-6661
Dallas, TX 75265-5237	Fax:	(214) 977-6661

Gannett Foundation
Contact: Meg Kennedy

7950 Jones Branch Dr.	Tel:	(703) 854-6000
McLean, VA 22107		

Public Affairs and Related Activities Personnel

At Headquarters

ALLMAN, Amber	Tel:	(703) 854-5358
Vice President, Corporate Communications	Fax:	(703) 854-2053
aallman@gannett.com		

BEHAN, William A.	Tel:	(703) 854-6000
Senior Vice President, Gannett Labor Relations	Fax:	(703) 854-2053

COX, Tom R.	Tel:	(703) 854-6000
Vice President, Corporate Development	Fax:	(703) 854-2053

DALTON, Laura	Tel:	(703) 854-6089
Director, Corporate Communications	Fax:	(703) 854-2053
ljdalton@gannett.com		

DICKERSON, Michael	Tel:	(703) 854-6185
Vice President, Investor Relations	Fax:	(703) 854-2053
mdickerson@gannett.com		

GAINES, Jeremy	Tel:	(703) 854-6049
Vice President, Corporate Communications	Fax:	(703) 854-2053
jmgaines@gannett.com		

HARKER, Victoria D.	Tel:	(703) 854-6000
Chief Financial Officer	Fax:	(703) 854-2053

HEINZ, Jeffrey	Tel:	(703) 854-6917
Vice President, Investor Relations	Fax:	(703) 854-2053
jheinz@gannett.com		

KENNEDY , Meg	Tel:	(703) 854-6000
Manager, Gannett Foundation	Fax:	(703) 854-2053
gannettfoundation@gannett.com		

LORD, Kevin E.	Tel:	(703) 854-6000
Senior Vice President and Chief Human Resources Officer	Fax:	(703) 854-2053

MAYMAN, Todd A.	Tel:	(703) 854-6000
Senior Vice President, General Counsel and Secretary	Fax:	(703) 854-2053

STAHL, Saira	Tel:	(703) 854-6000
Vice President, Corporate Strategy	Fax:	(703) 854-2053

At Other Offices

COLEMAN, Russell F.	Tel:	(214) 977-6606
Senior Vice President, General Counsel and Assistant Secretary	Fax:	(214) 977-6603

400 S. Record St.
Dallas, TX 75202-4841

FRY, R. Paul	Tel:	(214) 977-4465
Vice President, Investor Relations and Treasury Operations	Fax:	(214) 977-4418

400 S. Record St.
Dallas, TX 75202-4841
invest@belo.com

HAMERSLY, William L.	Tel:	(214) 977-6606
Vice President, Human Resources	Fax:	(214) 977-6603

400 S. Record St.
Dallas, TX 75202-4841

KERR, Guy H.	Tel:	(214) 977-6692
Executive Vice President, Law and Government	Fax:	(214) 977-6603

400 S. Record St.
Dallas, TX 75202-4841

MATTHEWS, Jill	Tel:	(214) 977-4405
Director, Corporate Communications	Fax:	(214) 977-7051

400 S. Record St.
Dallas, TX 75202-4841

MEADOWS, Amy M.	Tel:	(214) 977-8267
Executive Director and Vice President, Belo Foundation	Fax:	(214) 760-1254

The Belo Foundation, 901 Main St., Suite 609
Dallas, TX 75202
ameadows@belo.com

SPITZBERG, Marian
President, The Belo Foundation
The Belo Foundation, 901 Main St., Suite 609
Dallas, TX 75202

Tel: (214) 977-8267
Fax: (214) 760-1254

Gannett Fleming, Inc.

An international engineering consulting firm.
www.gannettfleming.com
Annual Revenues: $287.66 million
Employees: 800
SIC: 8711
Industry/ies: Engineering/Mathematics

Chairman of the Board and Chief Executive Officer
STOUT, William M.

Tel: (717) 763-7211
Fax: (717) 763-8150

Main Headquarters
Mailing: 207 Senate Ave.
P.O. Box 67100
Harrisburg, PA 17011-2316

Tel: (717) 763-7211
Fax: (717) 763-8150
TF: (800) 233-1055

Political Action Committees
Gannett Fleming, Inc.PAC
FEC ID: C00141382
Contact: Jon H. Kessler
P.O. Box 67100
Harrisburg, PA 17106

> **Contributions to Candidates:** $16,500 (2015-2016)
> Democrats: $2,000; Republicans: $14,500

Public Affairs and Related Activities Personnel

At Headquarters

HRICAK, Judy L.
Vice President and Chief Marketing Officer
jhricak@gfnet.com

Tel: (717) 763-7211
Fax: (717) 763-8150

KESSLER, Jon H.
Vice President, Chief Financial Officer and PAC Treasurer
jkessler@gfnet.com

Tel: (717) 763-7211
Fax: (717) 763-8150

NOWICKI, Paul D.
Senior Vice President, Regional Director
pnowicki@gfnet.com

Tel: (717) 763-7211
Fax: (717) 763-8150

Gap, Inc.

A retailer offering clothing, accessories and personal care products for men, women, and children under the Gap, Banana Republic, Old Navy, Athleta, and Intermix brand names.
www.gapinc.com
Annual Revenues: $16.32 billion
Employees: 141,000
Ticker: NYSE: GPS
SIC: 2329; 2339; 5699; 5651
Industry/ies: Retail/Wholesale
Legislative Issues: LBR; TAX; TRD

Chief Executive Officer
PECK, Art

Tel: (650) 952-4400
Fax: (651) 450-4033

Main Headquarters
Mailing: Two Folsom St.
San Francisco, CA 94105

Tel: (650) 952-4400
Fax: (651) 450-4033
TF: (800) 333-7899

Washington Office
Mailing: 117 C St. SE
Washington, DC 20003

Political Action Committees
The Gap Inc. PAC
FEC ID: C00257246
Contact: Debbie Mesloh
Two Folston St.
14th Floor
San Francisco, CA 94105

Tel: (650) 952-4400

> **Contributions to Candidates:** $21,500 (2015-2016)
> Democrats: $16,500; Republicans: $5,000

Corporate Foundations and Giving Programs

The Gap Foundation
Contact: Bobbi Silten
Two Folsom St.
San Francisco, CA 94105

Tel: (650) 952-4400

Public Affairs and Related Activities Personnel

At Headquarters

BANKS, Michelle
Executive Vice President, General Counsel, Corporate Secretary and Chief Compliance Officer

Tel: (650) 952-4400
Fax: (651) 450-4033

CHANDLER, William
Senior Vice President, Global Corporate Affairs

Tel: (650) 952-4400
Fax: (651) 450-4033

FRANK, Robert
Head, Global Strategy

Tel: (650) 952-4400
Fax: (651) 450-4033

MESLOH, Debbie
Senior Director, Government and Public Affairs, Lobbyist and PAC Treasurer
Mail Stop 14th Floor

Tel: (650) 952-4400
Fax: (651) 450-4033

SAGE-GAVIN, Eva
Executive Vice President, Human Resources and Corporate Affairs

Tel: (650) 952-4400
Fax: (651) 450-4033

SILTEN, Bobbi
Executive Vice President, Global Talent & Sustainability

Tel: (650) 952-4400
Fax: (651) 450-4033

At Washington Office

LESTER, Stephanie
Director, Government Affairs
Registered Federal Lobbyist

Garney Holdings Company

A construction company serving the public, private and industrial sectors.
www.garney.com
Employees: 700
Industry/ies: Construction/Construction Materials

President and Chief Executive Officer
HEITMANN, Mike
mheitmann@garney.com

Tel: (816) 746-7250
Fax: (816) 741-4488

Main Headquarters
Mailing: 1333 N.W. Vivion Rd.
Kansas City, MO 64118

Tel: (816) 741-4600
Fax: (816) 741-4488

Political Action Committees
Garney Holding Company PAC
FEC ID: C00442905
Contact: Thomas James Roberts
1333 NW Vivion Rd.
Kansas City, MO 64118

Tel: (816) 746-7275
Fax: (816) 741-4894

> **Contributions to Candidates:** $70,500 (2015-2016)
> Democrats: $26,500; Republicans: $42,000; Other: $2,000

> **Principal Recipients**
>
> **HOUSE**
> BLUMENAUER, EARL (DEM-OR)
> PAULSEN, ERIK (REP-MN)

Public Affairs and Related Activities Personnel

At Headquarters

KELLY, Mark
Director, Business Development

Tel: (816) 741-4600
Fax: (816) 741-4488

KRASE, Meggan
Director, Corporate Controller

Tel: (816) 741-4600
Fax: (816) 741-4488

LACY, Jeff
Chief Financial Officer
jlacy@garney.com

Tel: (816) 746-7277
Fax: (816) 746-7296

MCQUILLEN, Jay
Director, Federal Operations

Tel: (816) 741-4600
Fax: (816) 741-4488

O'BRIEN, Wayne
Chief Operating Officer

Tel: (816) 741-4600
Fax: (816) 741-4488

ROBERTS, Tom
Director, Financial Reporting

Tel: (816) 741-4600
Fax: (816) 741-4488

ROBERTS, Thomas James
PAC Treasurer

Tel: (816) 741-4600
Fax: (816) 741-4488

SEUBERT, Jason
Chief Operating Officer

Tel: (816) 741-4600
Fax: (816) 741-4488

Garrett Mcnatt Hennessey Carpenter 360 LLC

Law and government relations.
gmhc360.com
Legislative Issues: BUD; ENV; FIN; IMM; NAT; SCI; TAX; TRA

Managing Director
HUNTER, Mitch

Tel: (770) 427-1605
Fax: (678) 909-0286

Main Headquarters
Mailing: 3625 Cumberland Blvd.
Suite 950
Atlanta, GA 30339

Tel: (770) 427-1605
Fax: (678) 909-0286

Washington Office
Mailing: 511 C St. NE
Washington, DC 20002

Public Affairs and Related Activities Personnel

At Headquarters

CARPENTER, Chris
Partner
Registered Federal Lobbyist

Tel: (770) 427-1605
Fax: (678) 909-0286

COOPER, Caitlyn
Business and Financial Contact

Tel: (770) 427-1605
Fax: (678) 909-0286

GARRETT, Heath

Tel: (770) 427-1605

Attorney, Political Advisor, Media Strategist and Public Policy
Affairs Consultant
Registered Federal Lobbyist

GARRETT, William *Partner* *Registered Federal Lobbyist*	Tel: Fax:	(770) 427-1605 (678) 909-0286
HENNESSEY, Heather *Partner* *Registered Federal Lobbyist*	Tel: Fax:	(770) 427-1605 (678) 909-0286
KING, Amanda *Manager & Federal Lobbyist*	Tel: Fax:	(770) 427-1605 (678) 909-0286

At Washington Office

GARETT, Heath
Attorney, Political Advisor, Media Strategist and Public Policy
Registered Federal Lobbyist

At Other Offices

SMITH, Glee *Counsel* P.O. Box 688 Marietta, GA 30061	Tel: Fax:	(770) 427-1605 (678) 909-0286

Gartner Inc.

Provides research and advisory services.
www.gartner.com
Annual Revenues: $2.25 billion
Employees: 8,019
Ticker: NYSE: IT
SIC: 8741
Industry/ies: Communications; Media/Mass Communication

Chairman of the Board SMITH, James C.	Tel: Fax:	(203) 964-0096 (203) 316-6488
Chief Executive Officer HALL, Eugene A.	Tel: Fax:	(203) 964-0096 (203) 316-6488

Main Headquarters

Mailing:	56 Top Gallant Rd. Stamford, CT 06902-7700	Tel: (203) 964-0096 Fax: (203) 316-6488

Corporate Foundations and Giving Programs

Gartner Enterprise Architecture Foundation
56 Top Gallant Rd.
Stamford, CT 06904

Public Affairs and Related Activities Personnel

At Headquarters

GODFREY, David *Senior Vice President, Global Sales*	Tel: Fax:	(203) 964-0096 (203) 316-6488
KRANICH, Robin *Senior Vice President, Human Resources*	Tel: Fax:	(203) 964-0096 (203) 316-6488
SAFIAN, Craig *Senior Vice President and Chief Financial Officer*	Tel: Fax:	(203) 964-0096 (203) 316-6488
SCHWARTZ, Lewis *Senior Vice President, General Counsel, Corporate Secretary* *and Chief Compliance Officer* lewis.schwartz@gartner.com	Tel: Fax:	(203) 964-0096 (203) 316-6488
SPENDER, Andrew *Vice President, Branding, Public Relations and Marketing* *Communications* andrew.spender@gartner.com	Tel: Fax:	(203) 316-3286 (203) 316-6488

At Other Offices

MCCALL, Tom *Vice President, Public Relations* 2350 Mission College Blvd., 14th Floor Santa Clara, CA 95054 tom.mccall@gartner.com	Tel:	(408) 709-8096
PETTEY, Christy *Director, Public Relations* 2350 Mission College Blvd., 14th Floor Santa Clara, CA 95054 christy.pettey@gartner.com	Tel:	(408) 709-8124

Gary-Williams Energy Corporation

An independent oil and gas company.
www.gwec.com
Employees: 300
SIC: 2911
Industry/ies: Energy/Electricity

Chairman of the Board and Foundation Contact GARY, Samuel	Tel: Fax:	(303) 628-3800 (303) 628-3834
President and Chief Executive Officer WILLIAMS, Ronald	Tel: Fax:	(303) 628-3800 (303) 628-3834

Main Headquarters

Mailing:	370 17th St. Suite 5300 Denver, CO 80202	Tel: (303) 628-3800 Fax: (303) 628-3834

Corporate Foundations and Giving Programs

The Piton Foundation Contact: Samuel Gary 370 17th St. Suite 5300 Denver, CO 80202	Tel:	(303) 628-3800

Public Affairs and Related Activities Personnel

At Headquarters

YOUNGGREN, Dave *Senior Vice President, Finance*	Tel: Fax:	(303) 628-3800 (303) 628-3834

Gates Corporation

Formerly known as Gates Rubber Company. A manufacturer of automotive and industrial
rubber and fiber products and automotive power transmission accessories. A wholly-owned
subsidiary of Tomkins Plc.
www.gates.com
Annual Revenues: $1.32 billion
Employees: 13,000
SIC: 3052
NAICS: 32622
Industry/ies: Automotive Industry; Machinery/Equipment; Rubber Industry;
Transportation

Chief Executive Officer JUREK , Ivo	Tel: Fax:	(303) 744-1911 (303) 744-4443

Main Headquarters

Mailing:	1551 Wewatta St. Denver, CO 80202	Tel: (303) 744-1911 Fax: (303) 744-4443

Public Affairs and Related Activities Personnel

At Headquarters

BHATTACHARYA , Rasmani *Executive Vice President and General Counsel*	Tel: Fax:	(303) 744-1911 (303) 744-4443
CARROLL , Dave *Executive Vice President and Chief Administrative Officer*	Tel: Fax:	(303) 744-1911 (303) 744-4443
DUMAS , Heather *Senior Vice President, Human Resources*	Tel: Fax:	(303) 744-1911 (303) 744-4443
NAEMURA , David *Chief Financial Officer*	Tel: Fax:	(303) 744-1911 (303) 744-4443

Gates Rubber Co.

See listing on page 349 under Gates Corporation

Gateway, Inc.

A manufacturer and marketer of personal computers.
www.gateway.com
Employees: 1,700
Ticker: NYSE: GTW
SIC: 3571
Industry/ies: Computer/Technology

President and Chief Executive Officer BRITTON, Thomas P	Tel: Fax:	(949) 471-7000 (949) 471-7041

Main Headquarters

Mailing:	7565 Irvine Center Dr. Irvine, CA 92618	Tel: (949) 471-7000 Fax: (949) 471-7041

Corporate Foundations and Giving Programs

Gateway Foundation Contact: Thomas P Britton 7565 Irvine Center Dr. Irvine, CA 92618	Tel: Fax:	(949) 471-7000 (949) 471-7041

GATX Corporation

A finance and leasing company specializing in railcar, locomotive and aircraft operating
leasing.
www.gatx.com
Annual Revenues: $1.48 billion
Employees: 2,213
Ticker: NYSE: GMT
SIC: 4700
Industry/ies: Banking/Finance/Investments; Railroads; Transportation
Legislative Issues: TRA

Chairman of the Board, President and Chief Executive Officer KENNEY, Brian A.	Tel: Fax:	(312) 621-6200 (312) 621-6648

Main Headquarters

Mailing:	222 W. Adams St. Chicago, IL 60606	Tel: (312) 621-6200 Fax: (312) 621-6648 TF: (800) 428 0161

Political Action Committees

GATX Good Government Program
FEC ID: C00118703
Contact: Eric D. Harkness
222 W. Adams St. Tel: (312) 621-6200
Chicago, IL 60606 Fax: (312) 621-6648

Contributions to Candidates: $1,500 (2015-2016)
Republicans: $1,500

Corporate Foundations and Giving Programs

GATX Community Partnerships Program
Contact: Allison Dean
222 W. Adams St. Tel: (312) 621-4274
Chicago, IL 60606

Public Affairs and Related Activities Personnel

At Headquarters

BROOKS, Michael T. Tel: (312) 621-6200
Senior Vice President, Operations and Technology Fax: (312) 621-6648

CONNIFF, James M. Tel: (312) 621-6200
Senior Vice President, Human Resources Fax: (312) 621-6648

DEAN, Allison Tel: (312) 621-6200
Specialist, Market Analysis, Event Planning, and Community Affairs Fax: (312) 621-6648
allison.dean@gatx.com

GOLDEN, Deborah A. Tel: (312) 621-6240
Executive Vice President, General Counsel and Corporate Secretary Fax: (312) 499-7274
deborah.golden@gatx.com

HARKNESS, Eric D. Tel: (312) 621-6200
Vice President, Treasurer and Chief Risk Officer and PAC Contact Fax: (312) 621-6648

HASEK, William J. Tel: (312) 621-6200
Senior Vice President and PAC Treasurer Fax: (312) 621-6648

LYONS, Robert C. Tel: (312) 621-6200
Executive Vice President and Chief Financial Officer Fax: (312) 621-6648

PORZENHEIM, Clifford J. Tel: (312) 621-6200
Senior Vice President, Strategic Growth Fax: (312) 621-6648

VAN AKEN, Jennifer Tel: (312) 621-6689
Director, Investor Relations Fax: (312) 621-6648
jennifer.vanaken@gatx.com

Gay & Robinson, Inc.
Former sugar producer, currently focusing on producing ethanol.
Annual Revenues: $17.5 million
Industry/ies: Food And Beverage Industry

President and CEO
KENNETT, Alan

Main Headquarters
Mailing: P.O.Box 156
Kaumakani, HI 96747-0156

Washington Office
Mailing: 1301 Pennsylvania Ave. NW, Suite 401 Tel: (202) 785-4070
Washington, DC 20004 Fax: (202) 659-8581

Gaylord Entertainment Company
A hospitality and entertainment company which owns and operates Gaylord Hotels branded properties. Entertainment brands include the Grand Ole Opry, Ryman Auditorium and General Jackson Showboat, among others. Other interests include two radio stations and the Nashville Predators.
www.gaylordentertainment.com
Annual Revenues: $952.14 million
Employees: 10,000
Ticker: NYSE: GET
SIC: 7011
Industry/ies: Communications; Media/Mass Communication

Chairman and Chief Executive Officer Tel: (615) 316-6000
REED, Colin V. Fax: (615) 316-6555
creed@gaylordentertainment.com

Main Headquarters
Mailing: One Gaylord Dr. Tel: (615) 316-6000
Nashville, TN 37214 Fax: (615) 316-6555

Political Action Committees
Ryman Hospitality Properties Political Action Committee
FEC ID: C00183707
Contact: Jennifer Hutcheson
One Gaylord Dr.
Nashville, TN 37214

Contributions to Candidates: $500 (2015-2016)
Democrats: $500

Corporate Foundations and Giving Programs
Gaylord Entertainment Foundation

Contact: Jacque Layfield
One Gaylord Dr. Tel: (615) 316-6000
Nashville, TN 37214 Fax: (615) 316-6555

Public Affairs and Related Activities Personnel

At Headquarters

ABRAHAMSON, Brian Tel: (615) 316-6302
Senior Vice President, Corporate Communications Fax: (615) 316-6555
babrahamson@gaylordentertainment.com

CONNOR, Rod Tel: (615) 316-6000
PAC Treasurer Fax: (615) 316-6555

FIORAVANTI, Mark Tel: (615) 316-6588
Senior Vice President and Chief Financial Officer Fax: (615) 316-6555
mfioravanti@gaylordentertainment.com

HUTCHESON, Jennifer Tel: (615) 316-6000
PAC Contact Fax: (615) 316-6555

LAYFIELD, Jacque Tel: (615) 316-6000
Foundation Contact Fax: (615) 316-6555

ROGERS, Dan Tel: (615) 458-8543
Senior Manager, Media Relations Fax: (615) 316-6555
drogers@opry.com

SCHAETZ, Barb Tel: (615) 458-8544
Vice President, Marketing Fax: (615) 316-6555
bshaetz@opry.com

GDF SUEZ Energy North America, Inc.
SUEZ Energy North America becomes GDF SUEZ Energy North America in conjunction with its parent company's merger with Gaz de France. The company is involved in electricity generation and cogeneration, natural gas and liquefied natural gas (LNG) distribution and sales, renewable resources and retail energy sales and related services to commercial and industrial customers.
www.gdfsuezna.com
Annual Revenues: $29.90 million
Employees: 2,300
Industry/ies: Energy/Electricity
Legislative Issues: ENG

President and Chief Executive Officer Tel: (713) 636-0000
SMATI, Zin Fax: (713) 636-1364

Main Headquarters
Mailing: 1990 Post Oak Blvd. Tel: (713) 636-0000
Suite 1900 Fax: (713) 636-1364
Houston, TX 77056-3831 TF: (888) 232-6206

Political Action Committees
GDF Suez Energy North America, Inc. Political Action Commitee (Gsena PAC)
FEC ID: C00375568
1990 Post Oak Blvd.
Suite 1900
Houston, TX 77056

Contributions to Candidates: $47,500 (2015-2016)
Democrats: $20,000; Republicans: $27,500

Corporate Foundations and Giving Programs
GDF SUEZ Energy North America Inc. Contribution Programs
1990 Post Oak Blvd. Tel: (713) 636-0000
Suite 1900 Fax: (713) 636-1364
Houston, TX 77056-3831

Public Affairs and Related Activities Personnel

At Headquarters

ALEWINE, Jennifer Tel: (713) 636-0000
  Fax: (713) 636-1364

BARBIR, Karim Tel: (713) 636-0000
Executive Vice President, Business Development Fax: (713) 636-1364

BAYER, Brenda Tel: (713) 636-0000
Senior Vice President of Human Resources and Shared Services Fax: (713) 636-1364

BRADEN, Guy Tel: (713) 636-0000
  Fax: (713) 636-1364

BRADLEY, Eric Tel: (713) 636-0000
Senior Vice President, Strategy Fax: (713) 636-1364

CAHILL, Kevin Tel: (713) 636-0000
Vice President, Regulatory Compliance Fax: (713) 636-1364

CAVICCHI, Paul Tel: (713) 636-0000
Executive Vice President Strategy, Risk and Portfolio Fax: (713) 636-1364

CLARK, Bart Tel: (713) 636-0000
Senior Vice President and General Counsel Fax: (713) 636-1364

DALTON, Joseph William Tel: (713) 636-0000
Director, Government and Regulatory Affairs Fax: (713) 636-1364
joe.dalton@suezenergyna.com

DEMAILLE, Frank Tel: (713) 636-0000
  Fax: (713) 636-1364

GAUSSENT, Patrick Tel: (713) 636-0000

Chief Financial Officer	Fax:	(713) 636-1364
KATULAK, Frank	Tel:	(713) 636-0000
	Fax:	(713) 636-1364
KILPATRICK, Rachel W.	Tel:	(713) 636-0000
PAC Treasurer and VicePresident Tax	Fax:	(713) 636-1364
Mail Stop Suite 1900		
MINTER, James Robert	Tel:	(713) 636-0000
Senior Vice President, Government & Regulatory Affairs	Fax:	(713) 636-1364
rob.minter@gdfsuezna.com		
SABOTA, Danni	Tel:	(713) 636-1039
Manager, Communications	Fax:	(713) 636-1364
danni.sabota@suezenergyna.com		
SERCU, Stefaan	Tel:	(713) 636-0000
President and Chief Executive Officer, GDF SUEZ Energy	Fax:	(713) 636-1364
Marketing NA		
VITEK, Julie	Tel:	(713) 636-1962
Vice President, Communications	Fax:	(713) 636-1364
julie.vitek@suezenergyna.com		

GEICO Corporation

An insurance and financial services subsidiary of Berkshire Hathaway Inc.
www.geico.com
Employees: 23,000
SIC: 6331
Industry/ies: Insurance Industry

Chairman of the Board and Chief Executive Officer	Tel:	(301) 986-3000
NICELY, Tony		
tnicely@geico.com		

Main Headquarters

Mailing:	5260 Western Ave.		Tel:	(301) 986-3000
	Chevy Chase, MD 20815		TF:	(800) 424-3426

Political Action Committees
GEICO PAC
FEC ID: C00343749
Contact: Michael H. Campbell

One GEICO Plaza	Tel:	(301) 986-3000
Washington, DC 20076-		

> **Contributions to Candidates:** $11,500 (2015-2016)
> Democrats: $2,500; Republicans: $9,000

Corporate Foundations and Giving Programs
GEICO Philanthropic Foundation
Contact: Rynthia Manning Rost

One GEICO Plaza	Tel:	(301) 986-3000
Washington, DC 20076		

Public Affairs and Related Activities Personnel

At Headquarters

ROBERTS, Bill	Tel:	(301) 986-3000
President and Chief Operating Officer		
ROST, Rynthia Manning	Tel:	(301) 986-3000
Vice President, Public Affairs and Contact, Foundation		
rrost@geico.com		
STEWART, Jan	Tel:	(301) 986-3000
Vice President, Human Resources		
janstewart@geico.Com		

At Other Offices

CAMPBELL, Michael H.	Tel:	(301) 986-3000
PAC Treasurer	Fax:	(301) 986-2888
One GEICO Plaza		
Washington, DC 20076		
HINTON, Larry	Tel:	(301) 986-3000
Senior Attorney	Fax:	(301) 986-2888
One GEICO Plaza		
Washington, DC 20076		
rrost@geico.com		

Gel-Del Technology, Inc.

A biomedical device company that makes biomaterial products.
www.gel-del.com
Employees: 5
Industry/ies: Machinery/Equipment; Medicine/Health Care/Mental Health
Legislative Issues: BUD

Chairman of the Board, President and Chief Technology Officer	Tel:	(651) 209-0762
MASTERS, PhD, Dr. David B.	Fax:	(651) 209-0706
dmasters@gel-del.com		

Main Headquarters

Mailing:	1000 Westgate Dr.	Tel:	(651) 209-0762
	St. Paul, MN 55114	Fax:	(651) 209-0706

Public Affairs and Related Activities Personnel

At Headquarters

DOLAN, John F	Tel:	(651) 209-0762
Director	Fax:	(651) 209-0706

Gemalto, Inc.

Manufacturer of Smart Cards and secure identification technologies for electronic documents.
www.gemalto.com
Employees: 500
Industry/ies: Computer/Technology; Law Enforcement/Security
Legislative Issues: CPI; CSP; FIN; HCR; IMM; MMM; VET

Chairman of the Board	Tel:	(512) 257-3900
MANDL, Alex		
Chief Executive Officer	Tel:	(512) 257-3900
PIOU, Olivier		

Main Headquarters

Mailing:	9442 Capitol of Texas Hwy., North	Tel:	(512) 257-3900
	Arboretum Plaza II, Suite 400	TF:	(888) 343-5773
	Austin, TX 78759		

Washington Office

Mailing:	4401 Wilson Blvd.	Tel:	(877) 291-1312
	Suite 210		
	Arlington, VA 22203		

Corporate Foundations and Giving Programs
Gemalto Charitable Giving
9442 Capitol of Texas Hwy., North
Arboretum Plaza II, Suite 400
Austin, TX 78759

Public Affairs and Related Activities Personnel

At Headquarters

BEVERLY, Paul	Tel:	(512) 257-3900
Executive Vice President, Marketing		
BIJZITTER, Eke	Tel:	(512) 257-3900
Compliance, Governance and Central Officer		
CABANETTES, Philippe	Tel:	(512) 257-3900
Executive Vice President, Human Resources		
philippe.cabanettes@gemalto.com		
CHARLET, Jean-Pierre	Tel:	(512) 257-3900
Executive Vice President, General Counsel and Company Secretary		
MARAND, Isabelle	Tel:	(512) 257-3900
Executive Vice President, Corporate Communications		
Isabelle.Marand@gemalto.com		
MCCOURT, Martin	Tel:	(512) 257-3900
Executive Vice President, Strategy and Innovation		
TIERNY , Jacques	Tel:	(512) 257-3900
Executive Vice President and Chief Financial Officer		
VALLEE, Philippe	Tel:	(512) 257-3900
Executive Vice President and Chief Operating Officer		
WILLIAMS, Nicole	Tel:	(512) 758-8921
Contact, Media Relations		
nicole.smith@gemalto.com		
WIZBOWSKI, Ray	Tel:	(512) 257-3950
Vice President, Strategic Marketing		
raymond.WIZBOWSKI@gemalto.com		

At Washington Office

EMERICK, Kelli	Tel:	(877) 291-1312
Federal Lobbyist		
Registered Federal Lobbyist		
PATTINSON, Neville	Tel:	(877) 291-1312
Senior Vice President, Government Affairs		
neville.pattinson@gemalto.com		
Registered Federal Lobbyist		

Gemini Global Group

Procurement, Business and Legislative Consultant
geminiglobalgroup.com
Industry/ies: Business

Co-Founder	Tel:	(512) 628-8800
BARNES, Ben	Fax:	(512) 628-8809

Main Headquarters

Mailing:	901 S. Mopac Expy.	Tel:	(512) 628-8800
	Suite 1-100	Fax:	(512) 628-8809
	Austin, TX 78746		

Washington Office

Mailing:	1215 19th St. NW	Tel:	(202) 467-4141
	Washington, DC 20036	Fax:	(202) 467-1625

Gen-Probe, Inc.

Gen-Probe is in the development, manufacture and marketing of rapid, accurate and cost-effective nucleic acid tests (NATs) used primarily to diagnose human diseases and screen

donated human blood. As on August 1st Gen-Probe Incorporated is a part of Hologic Incorporated.
www.gen-probe.com
Annual Revenues: $2.3 billion
Employees: 1,391
Ticker: NASDAQ: GPRO
SIC: 2835; 8731
Industry/ies: Medicine/Health Care/Mental Health

President and Chief Executive Officer
MACMILLAN, Stephen P.
Tel: (781) 999-7300
Fax: (858) 410-8625

Main Headquarters
Mailing: 35 Crosby Dr.
Bedford, MA 01730
Tel: (781) 999-7300
Fax: (858) 410-8625
TF: (800) 523-5001

Political Action Committees
Hologic Gen-Probe Inc PAC (Hologic Gen-Probe PAC)
FEC ID: C00405100
Contact: April C. Boling
10210 Genetic Center Dr.
San Diego, CA 92121

Contributions to Candidates: $9,750 (2015-2016)
Republicans: $9,750

Corporate Foundations and Giving Programs
Hologic's Grant Program
35 Crosby Dr.
Bedford, MA 01730
Tel: (781) 999-7300
Fax: (781) 280-0669

Public Affairs and Related Activities Personnel

At Headquarters

BRADY, David J.
Senior Vice President, Human Resources
Tel: (781) 999-7300
Fax: (858) 410-8625

COMPTON, Eric B.
Chief Operating Officer
Tel: (781) 999-7300
Fax: (858) 410-8625

GARGAN, PhD, Paul
Senior Vice President, Business Development
Tel: (858) 410-8000
Fax: (858) 410-8625

MCMAHON, Robert W.
Chief Financial Officer
Tel: (781) 999-7300
Fax: (858) 410-8625

MUIR, Glenn P.
Executive Vice President, Finance and Administration and Chief Financial Officer
Tel: (781) 999-7300
Fax: (858) 410-8625

WATTS, Michael
Vice President, Investor Relations and Corporate Communications
michaelw@gen-probe.com
Tel: (858) 410-8673
Fax: (858) 410-8625

At Other Offices

BOLING, April C.
PAC Treasurer
10210 Genetic Center Dr.
San Deigo, CA 92121
Fax: (800) 288-3141

Gencorp, Inc.

See listing on page 18 under Aerojet Rocketdyne Holdings, Inc.

Genentech, Inc.

Biotechnology and pharmaceutical company. Subsidiary of Hoffman-La Roche Ltd.
www.gene.com
SIC: 2834
Industry/ies: Medicine/Health Care/Mental Health; Pharmaceutical Industry
Legislative Issues: BUD; CPT; HCR; HOM; MED; MMM; PHA; TAX; TRD

Chief Executive Officer, Head of North American Commercial Operations
CLARK, Ian T.
Tel: (650) 225-1000
Fax: (650) 225-6000

Main Headquarters
Mailing: One DNA Way
S. San Francisco, CA 94080
Tel: (650) 225-1000
Fax: (650) 225-6000

Washington Office
Mailing: 1399 New York Ave. NW
Suite 300
Washington, DC 20005

Political Action Committees
Genentech Inc. PAC
FEC ID: C00199257
Contact: Robert Andreatta
One DNA Way
San Francisco, CA 94080

Contributions to Candidates: $298,500 (2015-2016)
Democrats: $124,500; Republicans: $172,000; Other: $2,000

Principal Recipients

SENATE
BLUMENTHAL, RICHARD (DEM-CT)

BOOZMAN, JOHN (REP-AR)
MURPHY, PATRICK E (DEM-FL)

HOUSE
HUDSON, RICHARD L. JR. (REP-NC)
SPEIER, JACKIE (DEM-CA)

Corporate Foundations and Giving Programs
Genentech Contributions Program
One DNA Way
S. San Francisco, CA 94080
Tel: (650) 225-1000
Fax: (650) 225-6000

Public Affairs and Related Activities Personnel

At Headquarters

KENTZ, Frederick C.
Senior Vice President, Secretary and Chief Compliance Officer and Head of Legal Affairs, North America
kentz.frederick@gene.com
Tel: (650) 225-1000
Fax: (650) 225-6000

KROGNES, Steve
Senior Vice President, Regional Head, Finance, Information Technology and Chief Financial Officer
Tel: (650) 225-1000
Fax: (650) 225-6000

VITALE, Nancy
Vice President, Human Resources
Tel: (650) 225-1000
Fax: (650) 225-6000

At Washington Office

BURT, David
Federal Lobbyist
Registered Federal Lobbyist

BURT, Eli
Federal Lobbyist
Registered Federal Lobbyist

CLARKE, Karron

GRIFFIN, Anna
Federal Lobbyist
Registered Federal Lobbyist

KOGAN, Eli V.
Federal Lobbyist

MARTIN, Katherine
Federal Lobbyist
Registered Federal Lobbyist

RAAB, Katherine
Registered Federal Lobbyist

SAGELY, Anna
Federal Lobbyist
Registered Federal Lobbyist

WOMACK, Andrew
Registered Federal Lobbyist

General Atomics

Research and development of high-end UAV, nuclear, fusion, sensor, radar, electromagnetic, Maglev, environmental cleanup and laser technology.
www.ga.com
Annual Revenues: $210 million
Employees: 2,000
SIC: 3821; 3826; 8731; 3571
Industry/ies: Defense/Homeland Security; Engineering/Mathematics; Government-Related
Legislative Issues: BUD; DEF; ENG; FOR; GOV; HOM; SCI

Chairman and Chief Executive Officer
BLUE, James N.
Tel: (858) 455-3000
Fax: (858) 455-3621

Main Headquarters
Mailing: P.O. Box 85608
San Diego, CA 92186-5608
Tel: (858) 455-3000
Fax: (858) 455-3621

Washington Office
Mailing: 3000 K St.
Suite 250
Washington, DC 20007
Tel: (202) 496-8200
Fax: (202) 695-1110

Political Action Committees
General Atomics PAC
FEC ID: C00215285
Contact: Karen Nichols
P.O. Box 85608
San Diego, CA 92168

Contributions to Candidates: $325,500 (2015-2016)
Democrats: $76,500; Republicans: $249,000

Principal Recipients

SENATE
AYOTTE, KELLY A (REP-NH)
HOEVEN, JOHN (REP-ND)
LEE, MIKE (REP-UT)

HOUSE
CALVERT, KEN (REP-CA)
CRAMER, KEVIN MR. (REP-ND)

DAVIS, SUSAN (DEM-CA)
ENGEL, ELIOT L. REP. (DEM-DC)
GRANGER, KAY (REP-TX)
GRAVES, SAMUEL B JR 'SAM' (REP-MO)
PETERS, SCOTT (DEM-CA)
ROYCE, ED MR. (REP-CA)
TURNER, MICHAEL R (REP-OH)

Corporate Foundations and Giving Programs

General Atomics Sciences Education Foundation
Contact: Lawrence D. Woolf PhD
P.O. Box 85608 Tel: (858) 455-3000
San Diego, CA 92186 Fax: (858) 455-3621

Public Affairs and Related Activities Personnel

At Headquarters

BALDWIN, Karen A. Tel: (858) 455-3000
Manager, Treasury Fax: (858) 455-3621

KASITZ, Kimberly Tel: (858) 312-2294
Manager, Public Relations Fax: (858) 455-3621
kimberly.kasitz@ga-asi.com

NICHOLS, Karen Tel: (858) 455-3000
PAC Contact Fax: (858) 455-3621

WOOLF, PhD, Lawrence D. Tel: (858) 455-3000
President, Foundation Fax: (858) 455-3621
Mail Stop 78-110
Larry.Woolf@ga.com

At Washington Office

COTTERELL, Cheryl Tel: (202) 496-8200
Federal Lobbyist Fax: (202) 695-1110
Registered Federal Lobbyist

HOPPER, Gary B. Tel: (202) 496-8200
Vice President - Strategic Development & Washington Fax: (202) 659-1110
Operations
Gary.Hopper@ga.com
Registered Federal Lobbyist

RICE, William Tel: (202) 496-8200
Federal Lobbyist Fax: (202) 695-1110
Registered Federal Lobbyist

ROPER, Barton B. Tel: (202) 496-8200
Vice President, Strategic Development Fax: (202) 695-1110
bart.roper@ga.com
Registered Federal Lobbyist

TELSON, Michael Tel: (202) 496-8200
Vice President Fax: (202) 695-1110
mike.telson@ga.com
Registered Federal Lobbyist

WOOD, Cheryl Tel: (202) 496-8200
Contact, Government Relations Fax: (202) 695-1110
Registered Federal Lobbyist

General Atomics Aeronautical Systems Inc.

See listing on page 352 under General Atomics

General Cable Industries, Inc.

Develops, designs, manufactures, markets and distributes copper, aluminum and fiber optic wire and cable products.
www.generalcable.com
Annual Revenues: $6.31 billion
Employees: 13,000
Ticker: NYSE: BGC
SIC: 3357
Industry/ies: Sports/Leisure/Entertainment

Non-Executive Chairman of the Board Tel: (859) 572-8000
WELSH, III, John E. Fax: (859) 572-8458

President and Chief Executive Officer Tel: (859) 572-8000
KENNY, III, Gregory B. Fax: (859) 572-8458

Main Headquarters
Mailing: Four Tessenner Dr. Tel: (859) 572-8000
Highland Heights, KY 41076 Fax: (859) 572-8458

Corporate Foundations and Giving Programs

General Cable Contributions Program
Four Tessenner Dr. Tel: (859) 572-8000
Highland Heights, KY 41076-9136

Public Affairs and Related Activities Personnel

At Headquarters

DRAKE, Kurt L. Tel: (859) 572-8000
Senior Vice President and Chief Compliance Officer Fax: (859) 572-8458

LAWSON, Lisa B. Tel: (859) 572-8052
Vice President, Corporate Communications Fax: (859) 572-8458
llawson@generalcable.com

MOSER, Emerson C. Tel: (859) 572-8000
Senior Vice President, General Counsel and Corporate Fax: (859) 572-8458
Secretary

ROBINSON, Brian J. Tel: (859) 572-8000
Executive Vice President and Chief Financial Officer Fax: (859) 572-8458

SIVERD, Robert J. Tel: (859) 572-8000
Attorney and Counsellor Fax: (859) 572-8458

TEXTER, Len Tel: (859) 572-8373
Vice President, Investor Relations and Contact, Media Fax: (859) 572-8458

General Cigar Holdings, Inc.

Manufacturer and marketer of imported, hand-made or hand-rolled cigars in the United States.
www.cigarworld.com
Employees: 5,000
SIC: 2100
Industry/ies: Tobacco Industry
Legislative Issues: BUD; TAX; TOB; TRD

President and Chief Executive Officer Tel: (804) 302-1700
CULLMAN, Jr., Edgar M. Fax: (804) 302-1760

Main Headquarters
Mailing: 7300 Beaufont Springs Dr. Tel: (804) 302-1700
Suite 400 Fax: (804) 302-1760
Richmond, VA 23225

Political Action Committees
General Cigar PAC
FEC ID: C00488320
Contact: Steve Hicks
10900 Nuckols Rd.
Suite 100
Glen Allen, VA 23060

Contributions to Candidates: $15,000 (2015-2016)
Democrats: $1,000; Republicans: $13,500; Other: $500

Public Affairs and Related Activities Personnel

At Headquarters

CARR, Dan Tel: (804) 302-1700
President Fax: (804) 302-1760

JAWORSKI, Victoria McKee Tel: (804) 302-1700
Director, Public Relations Fax: (804) 302-1760

MARTINEZ, Gus Tel: (804) 302-1700
Director, Marketing Fax: (804) 302-1760

WILLNER, Alan Tel: (804) 302-1700
Vice President, Marketing Fax: (804) 302-1760

At Other Offices

HICKS, Steve Tel: (804) 302-1700
PAC Contact Fax: (804) 302-1760
10900 Nuckols Rd., Suite 100
Glen Allen, VA 23060

General Communication Inc.

An Alaska residential and business telecommunications service provider.
www.gci.com
Annual Revenues: $925.00 million
Employees: 2,255
Ticker: NASDAQ: GNCMA
Industry/ies: Communications; Telecommunications/Internet/Cable
Legislative Issues: COM; TAX; TEC

President and Chief Executive Officer and Co-Founder Tel: (907) 276-6222
DUNCAN, Ronald

Main Headquarters
Mailing: 2350 Denali St. Tel: (907) 276-6222
Suite 1000 TF: (800) 390-2782
Anchorage, AK 99503

Washington Office
Mailing: 1900 L St. NW Tel: (202) 457-8812
Suite 700
Washington, DC 20036

Public Affairs and Related Activities Personnel

At Headquarters

BEHNKE, William C. Tel: (907) 276-6222
Senior Vice President, Strategic Initiatives

BROQUET, Bruce Tel: (907) 868-6660
Vice President, Finance

POUNDS, Peter Tel: (907) 276-6222
Senior Vice President, Chief Financial Officer, and Secretary

At Washington Office

CHAPADOS, Gregory Tel: (202) 457-8812
Executive Vice President and Chief Operating Officer
gchapados@gci.com

Registered Federal Lobbyist

JENSEN, Lindsay	Tel:	(202) 457-8812
LASALA, Barry	Tel:	(202) 457-8812

Registered Federal Lobbyist

MAY, Jim	Tel:	(202) 457-8812

Federal Lobbyist
Registered Federal Lobbyist

PIDGEON, Tina M.	Tel:	(202) 457-8812

General Counsel and Senior Vice President, Governmental Affairs
tpidgeon@gci.com

SOLIE, Lindsay	Tel:	(202) 457-8812

Manager, Federal Affairs

SUTHERLAND, Lisa	Tel:	(202) 457-8812

Federal Lobbyist
Registered Federal Lobbyist

General Communications Corporation

Provides telecommunications solutions and services.
www.gcctel.com
Industry/ies: Communications; Telecommunications/Internet/Cable

President	Tel:	(781) 756-5100
DENARO, Paul F.	Fax:	(781) 932-0540

Main Headquarters

Mailing:	114 Cummings Park	Tel:	(781) 756-5100
	Woburn, MA 01801	Fax:	(781) 932-0540
		TF:	(800) 443-6372

Public Affairs and Related Activities Personnel

At Headquarters

STERLING, Michaela	Tel:	(781) 756-5100
Vice President, Administration	Fax:	(781) 932-0540

General Dynamics Bath Iron Works

See listing on page 108 under Bath Iron Works Corporation

General Dynamics Corporation

General Dynamics' military operations include Information Systems & Technology (information technology and collection, and command control systems).
www.generaldynamics.com
Annual Revenues: $31.41 billion
Employees: 99,900
Ticker: NYSE: GD
SIC: 3730
Industry/ies: Defense/Homeland Security; Government-Related
Legislative Issues: AER; BUD; DEF; EDU; FIN; FOR; GOV; HCR; HOM; INT; MAR; TAX; TRA

Chairman of the Board and Chief Executive Officer	Tel:	(703) 876-3000
NOVAKOVIC, Phebe N.	Fax:	(703) 876-3125

Main Headquarters

Mailing:	2941 Fairview Park Dr.	Tel:	(703) 876-3000
	Suite 100	Fax:	(703) 876-3555
	Falls Church, VA 22042-4513		

Political Action Committees
General Dynamics Corporation Political Action Committee (GDC PAC)
FEC ID: C00078451
Contact: Hong Guo

2941 Fairview Park Dr.	Tel:	(703) 876-3000
Suite 100	Fax:	(703) 876-3125
Falls Church, VA 22042-4523		

Contributions to Candidates: $5,091,766 (2015-2016)
Democrats: $277,000; Republicans: $582,750; Other: $4,232,016

Principal Recipients

SENATE
BLUMENTHAL, RICHARD (DEM-CT)
BURR, RICHARD (REP-NC)
MCCAIN, JOHN S (REP-VA)
PORTMAN, ROB (REP-OH)
SHELBY, RICHARD C (REP-AL)
THUNE, JOHN (REP-SD)

HOUSE
ADERHOLT, ROBERT BROWN (REP-AL)
BISHOP, SANFORD D JR (DEM-GA)
CALVERT, KEN (REP-CA)
CRENSHAW, ANDER (REP-FL)
DIAZ-BALART, MARIO (REP-FL)
FRELINGHUYSEN, RODNEY P. (REP-NJ)
GRANGER, KAY (REP-TX)
JOLLY, DAVID W. (REP-FL)
KENNEDY, JOSEPH P III (DEM-MA)
MCCARTHY, KEVIN (REP-CA)
MCCOLLUM, BETTY (DEM-MN)

ROGERS, MICHAEL DENNIS (REP-AL)

Public Affairs and Related Activities Personnel

At Headquarters

AIKEN, Jason W.	Tel:	(703) 876-3000
Senior Vice President and Chief Financial Officer	Fax:	(703) 876-3125
ANDRE, Lorraine	Tel:	(703) 876-3000
Manager, Legislative Affairs	Fax:	(703) 876-3507
GAINES, Theresa	Tel:	(703) 876-3000
Federal Lobbyist	Fax:	(703) 876-3507
Registered Federal Lobbyist		
GALLOPOULOS, Gregory	Tel:	(703) 876-3000
Senior Vice President, General Counsel and Secretary	Fax:	(703) 876-3125
GILLILAND, Amy	Tel:	(703) 876-3000
Senior Vice President, Human Resources and Administration	Fax:	(703) 876-3555
agilliland@generaldynamics.com		
GUO, Hong	Tel:	(703) 876-3000
PAC Treasurer	Fax:	(703) 876-3125
HELM, Robert W.	Tel:	(703) 876-3000
Senior Vice President, Planning and Development	Fax:	(703) 876-3125
Registered Federal Lobbyist		
LAMB, Gerry F.	Tel:	(703) 876-3000
Director, Government Relations	Fax:	(703) 876-3507
ccolburn@generaldynamics.com		
Registered Federal Lobbyist		
MADSON, Thomas R.	Tel:	(703) 876-3000
Director, Government Relations	Fax:	(703) 876-3507
tmadson@gd.com		
Registered Federal Lobbyist		
MORRISS, David M.	Tel:	(703) 876-3000
Director, Government Relations	Fax:	(703) 876-3507
Registered Federal Lobbyist		
NAVARRO, Jennifer	Tel:	(703) 876-3000
Director, Government Relations	Fax:	(703) 876-3507
Registered Federal Lobbyist		
PAULSON, Adam	Tel:	(703) 876-3000
Director, Government Relations	Fax:	(703) 876-3507
Registered Federal Lobbyist		
RITTER, Douglas	Tel:	(703) 876-3000
Staff Vice President	Fax:	(703) 876-3507
Registered Federal Lobbyist		
SCHMID, Betsy	Tel:	(703) 876-3000
Director, Government Relations	Fax:	(703) 876-3507
Registered Federal Lobbyist		
WACLAWSKI, Mark	Tel:	(703) 876-3000
Federal Lobbyist	Fax:	(703) 876-3507
Registered Federal Lobbyist		

General Electric Company

General Electric Company operates as an infrastructure and financial services company worldwide. Merged its NBC subsidiary with Vivendi Universal's subsidiary, Vivendi Universal Enterainment to form NBC Universal.
www.ge.com
Annual Revenues: $144.27 billion
Employees: 305,000
Ticker: NYSE: GE
SIC: 3600; 3643; 6141
Industry/ies: Defense/Homeland Security; Electricity & Electronics; Electronics; Energy/Electricity; Fuels See Coal, Gas, Oil, Petroleum; Government-Related; Natural Resources; Petroleum Industry
Legislative Issues: AER; AVI; BAN; BUD; CAW; CPT; DEF; ENG; ENV; FIN; HCR; HOM; NAT; RRR; SCI; TAX; TEC; TRA; TRD

Chairman and Chief Executive Officer	Tel:	(203) 373-2211
IMMELT, Jeffrey R.	Fax:	(203) 373-3131
jeffrey.immlet@ge.com		

Main Headquarters

Mailing:	4424 West Sam Houston Pkwy. North	Tel:	(713) 683-2400
	Suite 100	Fax:	(713) 683-2421
	Houston, TX 77041		

Washington Office

Mailing:	1299 Pennsylvania Ave. NW	Tel:	(202) 637-4000
	Suite 900	Fax:	(202) 637-4400
	Washington, DC 20004		

Political Action Committees
General Electric Company Political Action Committee
FEC ID: C00024869
Contact: Marie Talwar

1299 Pennsylvania Ave. NW	Tel:	(202) 637-4000
Suite 900	Fax:	(202) 637-4006
Washington, DC 20004-		

Contributions to Candidates: $3,494,516 (2015-2016)

Democrats: $419,500; Republicans: $896,000; Other: $2,179,016

Principal Recipients

SENATE
BLUNT, ROY (REP-MO)
CRAPO, MICHAEL D (REP-ID)

HOUSE
BOUSTANY, CHARLES W. DR. JR. (REP-LA)
DENT, CHARLES W. REP. (REP-PA)
KINZINGER, ADAM (REP-IL)
SCALISE, STEVE MR. (REP-LA)
SHUSTER, WILLIAM MR. (REP-PA)
STIVERS, STEVE MR. (REP-OH)
WALORSKI SWIHART, JACKIE (REP-IN)

Corporate Foundations and Giving Programs

GE Foundation
Contact: Robert Corcoran
3135 Easton Tnpk.   Tel: (203) 373-2211
Fairfield, CT 06828

Public Affairs and Related Activities Personnel

At Headquarters

KNUTSON, Karen   Tel: (713) 683-2400
Leader, Government Affairs and Policy   Fax: (713) 683-2421
Registered Federal Lobbyist

At Washington Office

BECKER, Darby M. R.   Tel: (202) 637-4000
Federal Lobbyist   Fax: (202) 637-4400
Registered Federal Lobbyist

BEHRENS, William   Tel: (202) 637-4000
Manager, Government Relations   Fax: (202) 637-4400
Registered Federal Lobbyist

BHATIA, Karan K.   Tel: (202) 637-4000
Vice President and Senior Counsel, International Law &   Fax: (202) 637-4400
Policy
karan.bhatia@ge.com

BOGGS, Larry A.   Tel: (202) 637-4000
Senior Counsel and Director, CEP, Environmental Legislative   Fax: (202) 637-4400
Affairs

BORSKEY, Carol   Tel: (202) 637-4000
Director , Government Affairs   Fax: (202) 637-4400
Registered Federal Lobbyist

BORSKEY, Chrissy   Tel: (202) 637-4000
Registered Federal Lobbyist   Fax: (202) 637-4400

BURNS, Thaddeus   Tel: (202) 637-4000
Senior Counsel IP and Trade   Fax: (202) 637-4400
Registered Federal Lobbyist

CAMPBELL, Amanda Mertens   Tel: (202) 637-4000
Federal Lobbyist   Fax: (202) 637-4400
Registered Federal Lobbyist

CASANO, Patricia   Tel: (202) 637-4000
Counsel, Government Affairs   Fax: (202) 637-4400
pat.casano@ge.com

COBB, Chance   Tel: (202) 637-4000
Federal Lobbyist   Fax: (202) 637-4400
Registered Federal Lobbyist

DORN, Nancy P.   Tel: (202) 637-4000
Vice President, Government Relations   Fax: (202) 637-4400
Registered Federal Lobbyist

DOUCETTE, Paul   Tel: (202) 637-4000
Global Leader, Public Policy and External Funding Services   Fax: (202) 637-4400
paul.doucette@ge.com
Registered Federal Lobbyist

FREEDMAN, Jon   Tel: (202) 637-4000
Contact, Government Relations   Fax: (202) 637-4400
Registered Federal Lobbyist

FRENKEL, Orit   Tel: (202) 637-4000
Senior Manager, International Law and Policy   Fax: (202) 637-4400
orit.frenkel@ge.com
Registered Federal Lobbyist

GISSENDANNER, Dean   Tel: (202) 637-4000
Executive, Government Programs   Fax: (202) 637-4400

HALL, III, Robert P.   Tel: (202) 637-4000
Executive Counsel   Fax: (202) 637-4400

HORTON, Carl   Tel: (202) 637-4000
Vice President and Chief Intellectual Property Counsel   Fax: (202) 637-4400
carl.horton@ge.com

HOWLETT, Steve   Tel: (202) 637-4000
Federal Lobbyist   Fax: (202) 637-4400
Registered Federal Lobbyist

ITZKOFF, Donald M.   Tel: (202) 637-4000

Federal Lobbyist   Fax: (202) 637-4400
Donald.itzkoff@ge.com
Registered Federal Lobbyist

JOHNSON, Michele   Tel: (202) 637-4000
                                                     Fax: (202) 637-4400

KLEE, Ann R.   Tel: (202) 637-4000
Vice President, Environment, Health and Safety   Fax: (202) 637-4400
Ann.Klee@ge.com

KNUTSON, Karen   Tel: (202) 637-4000
Leader, Government Affairs and Policy   Fax: (202) 637-4400
Registered Federal Lobbyist

MARCELLA, Orrin   Tel: (202) 637-4000
Manager, Government Relations   Fax: (202) 637-4400
Registered Federal Lobbyist

MARRS, Peter   Tel: (202) 637-4000
Global Tax Director, Treasury and Capital Markets   Fax: (202) 637-4400
Registered Federal Lobbyist

MATTOX, Barbara   Tel: (202) 637-4000
Federal Lobbyist   Fax: (202) 637-4400
Registered Federal Lobbyist

MCGOVERN, Tom   Tel: (202) 637-4000
Federal Lobbyist   Fax: (202) 637-4400
Registered Federal Lobbyist

MCMAHON, Joanne   Tel: (202) 637-4000
Leader, Governmental Compliance   Fax: (202) 637-4400

MEADOR, Daniel   Tel: (202) 637-4000
Government Program Executive, Naval Programs   Fax: (202) 637-4400
daniel.meador@ae.ge.com

MERBER, Selig S.   Tel: (202) 637-4000
Counsel, International Trade Regulation & Sourcing   Fax: (202) 637-4400

MINER, Paul   Tel: (202) 637-4000
                                                     Fax: (202) 637-4400

MOREHEAD, Clifton   Tel: (202) 637-4000
Federal Lobbyist   Fax: (202) 637-4400
clifton.morehead@ge.com
Registered Federal Lobbyist

NEWBOLD, Stephen   Tel: (202) 637-4000
Manager, USAF Programs   Fax: (202) 637-4400

O'CONNOR, Stanley   Tel: (202) 637-4000
Director, Civil Advanced Technology Marketing   Fax: (202) 637-4400

OKUN, Hon. Bob   Tel: (202) 637-4000
Federal Lobbyist   Fax: (202) 637-4400
Registered Federal Lobbyist

PARIS, Thomas   Tel: (202) 637-4000
Federal Lobbyist   Fax: (202) 637-4400
Registered Federal Lobbyist

PELLETIER, Eric   Tel: (202) 637-4000
Senior Manager, Government Relations   Fax: (202) 637-4400

PETERS, Susan P.   Tel: (202) 637-4000
Senior Vice President, Human Resources   Fax: (202) 637-4400

PETERSON, Theresa   Tel: (202) 637-4000
Federal Lobbyist   Fax: (202) 637-4400
theresa.peterson@ge.com
Registered Federal Lobbyist

PICKART, George A.   Tel: (202) 637-4000
Federal Lobbyist   Fax: (202) 637-4400
george.pickart@ge.com
Registered Federal Lobbyist

PROWITT, Peter D.   Tel: (202) 637-4000
Manager, Federal Government Relations   Fax: (202) 637-4400
peter.prowitt@ge.com
Registered Federal Lobbyist

RAYMOND, Joshua H.   Tel: (202) 637-4000
Senior Manager, Government Relations   Fax: (202) 637-4400
Registered Federal Lobbyist

REESE, Gary A.   Tel: (202) 637-4000
Federal Lobbyist   Fax: (202) 637-4400
Registered Federal Lobbyist

REGG, James   Tel: (202) 637-4000
Federal Lobbyist   Fax: (202) 637-4400
Registered Federal Lobbyist

RENIGAR, Del   Tel: (202) 637-4000
Senior Counsel, Global Government Affairs and Policy   Fax: (202) 637-4400

RICHARDS, Timothy   Tel: (202) 637-4000
Federal Lobbyist   Fax: (202) 637-4400
Registered Federal Lobbyist

SANDBERG, James C.   Tel: (202) 637-4000
Contact, Government Relations   Fax: (202) 637-4400
Registered Federal Lobbyist

SCHAEFFLER, John   Tel: (202) 637-4000

Federal Lobbyist *Registered Federal Lobbyist*	Fax:	(202) 637-4400
SMITH, Madeleine *Federal Lobbyist* *Registered Federal Lobbyist*	Tel: Fax:	(202) 637-4000 (202) 637-4400
SPARKS, Russ *Federal Lobbyist* *Registered Federal Lobbyist*	Tel: Fax:	(202) 637-4000 (202) 637-4400
STERN, Ronald A. *Vice President and Senior Counsel, Antitrust*	Tel: Fax:	(202) 637-4000 (202) 637-4400
TALWAR, Marie *PAC Treasurer* Mail Stop Suite 900 W Marie.Talwar@ge.com	Tel: Fax:	(202) 637-4000 (202) 637-4400
THOMSON, Lynn *Manager, Federal Government Relations* lynn.thomson@corporate.ge.com *Registered Federal Lobbyist*	Tel: Fax:	(202) 637-4000 (202) 637-4400
VENZKE, Pamela *Federal Lobbyist* *Registered Federal Lobbyist*	Tel: Fax:	(202) 637-4000 (202) 637-4400
WALLACE, George J. *Federal Lobbyist*	Tel: Fax:	(202) 637-4000 (202) 637-4400
WALSH, Kelcy *Senior Analyst, Tax Policy* *Registered Federal Lobbyist*	Tel: Fax:	(202) 637-4000 (202) 637-4400
WILLIAM, Matthew *Federal Lobbyist* *Registered Federal Lobbyist*	Tel: Fax:	(202) 637-4000 (202) 637-4400
WOLSKI, Lisa M. *Senior Manager, Government Affairs and Policy* *Registered Federal Lobbyist*	Tel: Fax:	(202) 637-4000 (202) 637-4400

At Other Offices

BORNSTEIN, Jeffrey S. *Senior Vice President and Chief Financial Officer* 3135 Easton Tnpk. Fairfield, CT 06828-0001	Tel: Fax:	(203) 373-2211 (203) 373-3131
COMSTOCK, Beth *Senior Vice President and Chief Marketing Officer* 3135 Easton Tnpk. Fairfield, CT 06828-0001	Tel: Fax:	(203) 373-2211 (203) 373-3131
CORCORAN, Robert *Vice President, Corporate Citizenship, Chief Learning Office* *and President, Foundation* 3135 Easton Tnpk. Fairfield, CT 06828-0001 robert.corcoran@ge.com	Tel: Fax:	(203) 373-2211 (203) 373-3131
DENNISTON, III, Brackett B. *Senior Vice President, Secretary and General Counsel* 3135 Easton Tnpk. Fairfield, CT 06828-0001 brackett.denniston@ge.com	Tel: Fax:	(203) 373-2211 (203) 373-3131
DIMITRIEF , Alex *Vice President and Senior Counsel, Litigation and Legal* *Policy* 3135 Easton Tnpk. Fairfield, CT 06828-0001	Tel: Fax:	(203) 373-2211 (203) 373-3131
MORRIS, JoAnna H. *Director, Corporate Investor Communications* 3135 Easton Tnpk. Fairfield, CT 06828-0001	Tel: Fax:	(203) 373-2211 (203) 373-3131
SCHAUENBERG, Trevor A. *Vice President, Corporate Investor Communications* 3135 Easton Tnpk. Fairfield, CT 06828-0001	Tel: Fax:	(203) 373-2211 (203) 373-3131
SHEFFER, Gary *Vice President, Corporate Communications and Public Affairs* 3135 Easton Tnpk. Fairfield, CT 06828-0001 gary.sheffer@ge.com	Tel: Fax:	(203) 373-2211 (203) 373-3131
SHERIN, Keith S. *Vice Chairman and Chief Financial Officer* 3135 Easton Tnpk. Fairfield, CT 06828-0001 keith.sherin@ge.com	Tel: Fax:	(203) 373-2211 (203) 373-3131

General Electric Healthcare

Provides services in medical imaging and information technologies, medical diagnostics,
patient monitoring systems, disease research, drug discovery.
www.gehealthcare.com
Industry/ies: Medicine/Health Care/Mental Health

Main Headquarters

Mailing:	101 Carnegie Center Princeton, NJ 08540	Tel: Fax:	(609) 514-6593 (609) 514-6574

Washington Office

Mailing:	1299 Pennsylvania Ave. NW Suite 1100-W Washington, DC 20004

Public Affairs and Related Activities Personnel

At Headquarters

FOX, Benjamin *Director, External Relations* benjamin.fox@ge.com	Tel: Fax:	(609) 514-6593 (609) 514-6574

At Washington Office

SCHAEFFLER, John
General Manager, General Electric Healthcare
john.schaeffler@ge.com

General Mills Inc.

A consumer foods producer. Acquired the Pillsbury Company in 2002. Brands include the
Cheerios, Chex, and Wheaties, Häagen-Dazs, Progresso, and Pillsbury. It manufactures,
markets branded consumer foods also supplies branded and unbranded food products to the
foodservice and commercial baking industries.
www.generalmills.com
Annual Revenues: $17.62 billion
Employees: 43,000
Ticker: NYSE: GIS
SIC: 2040
Industry/ies: Food And Beverage Industry
Legislative Issues: FOO

Chairman of the Board, Chief Executive Officer		
POWELL, Kendall J.	Tel: Fax:	(763) 764-7600 (763) 764-8330

Main Headquarters

Mailing:	P.O. Box 9452 Minneapolis, MN 55440	Tel: Fax: TF:	(763) 764-7600 (763) 764-8330 (800) 248-7310

Washington Office

Mailing:	601 13th St. NW Suite 510 South Washington, DC 20005	Tel: Fax:	(202) 737-8200 (202) 638-4914

Political Action Committees
General Mills, Inc. PAC (GM PAC)
FEC ID: C00062646
Contact: Gerald Morris
One General Mills Blvd.
Minneapolis, MN 55426

> **Contributions to Candidates:** $188,000 (2015-2016)
> Democrats: $54,500; Republicans: $133,500

> **Principal Recipients**
>
> **SENATE**
> BLUNT, ROY (REP-MO)

Corporate Foundations and Giving Programs

General Mills Foundation
Contact: Kimberly A. Nelson
One General Mills Blvd.   Tel: (763) 764-7600
Minneapolis, MN 55426

Public Affairs and Related Activities Personnel

At Headquarters

ALLENDORF, Richard C. *Senior Vice President, General Counsel and Secretary*	Tel: Fax:	(763) 764-7600 (763) 764-8330
ANDERSON, Lee A. *Director, Issues Management & State Government Relations*	Tel: Fax:	(763) 764-7600 (763) 764-8330
BELTON, Y. Marc *Executive Vice President, Global Strategy, Growth and* *Marketing Innovation*	Tel: Fax:	(763) 764-7600 (763) 764-8330
CHRISTENSON, Bridget *Manager, Corporate Communications* bridget.christenson@genmills.com	Tel: Fax:	(763) 764-6364 (763) 764-8330
FOSTER, Kristie *Director of Corporate and Brand Communications*	Tel: Fax:	(763) 764-7600 (763) 764-8330
MULLIGAN, Donal L. *Executive Vice President and Chief Financial Officer*	Tel: Fax:	(763) 764-7600 (763) 764-8330
SIMONDS, Ann W.H. *Senior Vice President and Chief Marketing Officer*	Tel: Fax:	(763) 764-7600 (763) 764-8330
WENKER, Kristen S. *Senior Vice President, Investor Relations*	Tel: Fax:	(763) 764-2607 (763) 764-8330
WILLIAMS-ROLL, Jacqueline R. *Senior Vice President, Human Resources*	Tel: Fax:	(763) 764-7600 (763) 764-8330

At Washington Office

BAUM, Erika Lee — Tel: (202) 737-8200 / Fax: (202) 638-4914
Washington Representative
Registered Federal Lobbyist

IGNOSH, Carol — Tel: (202) 737-8200 / Fax: (202) 638-4914
Office Manager
carol.ignosh@genmills.com

JONGEN, Corinne — Tel: (202) 737-8200 / Fax: (202) 638-4914

TOKER, Mary Catherine — Tel: (202) 737-8200 / Fax: (202) 638-4914
Vice President, Government and Public Affairs
mary.toker@genmills.com
Registered Federal Lobbyist

WILSON, Kent — Tel: (202) 737-8200 / Fax: (202) 638-4914
Washington Representative, Government and Public Affairs
KENT.WILSON@GENMILLS.COM
Registered Federal Lobbyist

At Other Offices

MORRIS, Gerald — Tel: (763) 764-7600 / Fax: (763) 764-8330
?Vice President & Chief Tax Office and PAC Treasurer
One General Mills Blvd.
Minneapolis, MN 55426

NELSON, Kimberly A. — Tel: (763) 764-7600 / Fax: (763) 764-8330
Senior Vice President, External Relations and President,
General Mills Foundation
One General Mills Blvd.
Minneapolis, MN 55426

O'LEARY, Christopher D. — Tel: (763) 764-7600 / Fax: (763) 764-8330
Executive Vice President and Chief Operating Officer,
International
One General Mills Blvd.
Minneapolis, MN 55426

General Motors Company

An automaker. Headquartered in Detroit, MI.
www.gm.com
Annual Revenues: $154.23 billion
Employees: 216,000
Ticker: NYSE: GM
SIC: 3711
Industry/ies: Automotive Industry; Transportation
Legislative Issues: AUT; BUD; CAW; COM; CPI; CPT; CSP; EDU; ENG; ENV; FIN; FOR; HCR; HOM; RET; TAR; TAX; TEC; TRA; TRD

Chief Executive Officer, General Motors Company — Tel: (313) 556-5000 / Fax: (313) 556-5108
BARRA, Mary T.

Main Headquarters
Mailing: 399 Renaissance Center — Tel: (313) 556-5000 / Fax: (313) 556-5108
P.O. Box 300
Detroit, MI 48265-3000

Washington Office
Mailing: 25 Massachusetts Ave. NW — Tel: (202) 775-5027 / Fax: (202) 775-5097
Suite 400
Washington, DC 20001

Political Action Committees
General Motors Corporation Political Action Committee (GM PAC)
FEC ID: C00076810
Contact: Adam Snider
25 Massachusetts Ave. NW
Suite 400
Washington, DC 20001

Contributions to Candidates: $706,750 (2015-2016)
Democrats: $284,500; Republicans: $418,750; Other: $3,500

Principal Recipients

SENATE
BLUNT, ROY (REP-MO)
KIRK, MARK STEVEN (REP-IL)
MURRAY, PATTY (DEM-WA)
PORTMAN, ROB (REP-OH)
THUNE, JOHN (REP-SD)

HOUSE
MCCARTHY, KEVIN (REP-CA)
SCALISE, STEVE MR. (REP-LA)
SHUSTER, WILLIAM MR. (REP-PA)
SLAUGHTER, LOUISE M (DEM-NY)

Corporate Foundations and Giving Programs
General Motors Cancer Research Foundation
Contact: Heather Rosenker
300 Renaissance Center — Tel: (313) 556-5000 / Fax: (313) 556-5108
Detroit, MI 48265

General Motors Foundation
Contact: Heather Rosenker
300 Renaissance Center — Tel: (313) 556-5000

Detroit, MI 48265 — Fax: (313) 556-5108

Public Affairs and Related Activities Personnel

At Headquarters

BRINKLEY, Cynthia J. — Tel: (313) 556-5000 / Fax: (313) 556-5108
Vice President, Global Human Resources

CERVONE, Tony — Tel: (313) 556-5000 / Fax: (313) 556-5108
Senior Vice President, Global Communications

FERGUSON, Robert E. — Tel: (313) 556-5000 / Fax: (313) 556-5108
Senior Vice President, Global Public Policy

GLIDDEN, Craig — Tel: (313) 556-5000 / Fax: (313) 556-5108
Executive Vice President and General Counsel

PICKARD, Vivian R. — Tel: (313) 556-5000 / Fax: (313) 556-5108
Director, General Motors Foundation

QUATTRONE, John J. — Tel: (313) 556-5000 / Fax: (313) 556-5108
Senior Vice President, Human Resources

RAMDEV, Niharika Taskar — Tel: (313) 556-5000 / Fax: (313) 556-5108
Vice President, Finance and Treasurer

SHROSBREE, Robert C. — Tel: (313) 556-5000 / Fax: (313) 556-5108
Secretary and Executive Director Legal, Corporate and
Securities

STEVENS, Chuck — Tel: (313) 556-5000 / Fax: (313) 556-5108
Executive Vice President and Chief Financial Officer

TIMKO, Thomas S. — Tel: (313) 556-5000 / Fax: (313) 556-5108
Vice President, Controller and Chief Accounting Officer

TREMBLAY, Diana — Tel: (313) 556-5000 / Fax: (313) 556-5108
Vice President, Global Business Services

At Washington Office

BARNES, Victoria E. — Tel: (202) 775-5030 / Fax: (202) 775-5097
Executive Director, Federal Affairs
victoria.barnes@gm.com
Registered Federal Lobbyist

FINNERTY, Sean — Tel: (202) 775-5027 / Fax: (202) 775-5097
Manager, Political Affairs and GM PAC
Registered Federal Lobbyist

GEHRING, Stephen G. — Tel: (202) 775-5071 / Fax: (202) 775-5097
Manager, Washington Liaison, Safety Regulations and
Consumer Information Services
stephen.g.gehring@gm.com
Registered Federal Lobbyist

GODOWN, Lee R. — Tel: (202) 775-5033 / Fax: (202) 775-5023
Vice President, Global Government Relations
lee.godown@gm.com
Registered Federal Lobbyist

GUZZO, Joseph L. — Tel: (202) 775-5033 / Fax: (202) 775-5023
Director, Advanced Technology and Federal Affairs
joseph.guzzo@gm.com
Registered Federal Lobbyist

JUNG, Jasper — Tel: (202) 775-5027 / Fax: (202) 775-5097
Senior Analyst, Sustainability

KEMMER, Mark L. — Tel: (202) 775-5066 / Fax: (202) 775-5023
Director, Federal Affairs
mark.l.kemmer@gm.com
Registered Federal Lobbyist

KILEY, Jim — Tel: (202) 775-5055 / Fax: (202) 775-5023
Director, Federal Affairs
jim.kiley@gm.com
Registered Federal Lobbyist

LERNER, Ashley — Tel: (202) 775-5027 / Fax: (202) 775-5097
Grassroots Coordinator

LIGHTSEY, Harry — Tel: (202) 775-5027 / Fax: (202) 775-5097
Executive Director, Global Connected Consumer
Registered Federal Lobbyist

MAGDALENO, John — Tel: (202) 775-5027 / Fax: (202) 775-5097
Senior Manager, NC 460

MCDONNELL, Richard — Tel: (202) 775-5027 / Fax: (202) 775-5097
Manager, Political Affairs and GMPAC

NEER, Marie — Tel: (202) 775-5027 / Fax: (202) 775-5097
Executive Assistant to Lee Godown
marie.neer@gm.com

REESE, Eleanor — Tel: (202) 775-5027 / Fax: (202) 775-5097
Manager, Government Relations

RICE, Toni — Tel: (202) 775-5027 / Fax: (202) 775-5097
Grassroots Analyst

ROOSA, Bryan R. — Tel: (202) 775-5056 / Fax: (202) 775-5023
Regional Director
bryan.roosa@gm.com

SNIDER, Adam — Tel: (202) 775-5027 / Fax: (202) 775-5097
PAC Treasurer

TOOLE, Laura L. — Tel: (202) 775-5027

Senior Manager, Communications	Fax:	(202) 775-5097
TURTON, Daniel A.	Tel:	(202) 775-5027
Contact, Federal Affairs	Fax:	(202) 775-5097
Registered Federal Lobbyist		
UPCHURCH, Jeff	Tel:	(202) 775-5027
Senior Staff Engineer	Fax:	(202) 775-5097
WELLING, Brad	Tel:	(202) 775-5027
Director, Federal Affairs, International Trade and Finance	Fax:	(202) 775-5097
Registered Federal Lobbyist		
WILSON, Cherie	Tel:	(202) 775-5027
Registered Federal Lobbyist	Fax:	(202) 775-5097
YORK, Andrew	Tel:	(202) 775-5027
Registered Federal Lobbyist	Fax:	(202) 775-5097

General Motors Financial Company

Formerly known as AmeriCredit and acquired by General Motors in 2010. An in-house auto financing arm of General Motors and committed to providing best-in-class customer service, while promoting open, honest communication at all levels.
www.gmfinancial.com
Annual Revenues: $154.23 billion
Employees: 216,000
Ticker: NYSE: GM
SIC: 6199
Industry/ies: Automotive Industry; Banking/Finance/Investments; Transportation

President and Chief Executive Officer	Tel:	(817) 302-7000
BERCE, Daniel E.	Fax:	(817) 302-7101

Main Headquarters

Mailing:	801 Cherry St.	Tel:	(817) 302-7000
	Suite 3900	Fax:	(817) 302-7897
	Fort Worth, TX 76102	TF:	(800) 644-2297

Corporate Foundations and Giving Programs

General Motors Financial Company Contributions Program

801 Cherry St.	Tel:	(817) 302-7000
Suite 3900	Fax:	(817) 302-7101
Fort Worth, TX 76102		

Public Affairs and Related Activities Personnel

At Headquarters

BICKMORE, Dan	Tel:	(817) 302-7000
Senior Vice President and Chief Compliance Officer	Fax:	(817) 302-7897
BIRCH, Kyle	Tel:	(817) 302-7000
Executive Vice President & Chief Operating Officer - North America	Fax:	(817) 302-7897
BURT, Chris	Tel:	(817) 302-7000
Executive Vice President and Chief Human Resources Officer	Fax:	(817) 302-7897
CHOATE, Chris A.	Tel:	(817) 302-7000
Executive Vice President , Chief Financial Officer and Treasurer	Fax:	(817) 302-7101
HOLLANDSWORTH, Jonas	Tel:	(817) 302-7000
Executive Vice President, U.S. Sales and Credit Operations	Fax:	(817) 302-7897
JOHNSON, Doug	Tel:	(817) 302-7000
Executive Vice President, Chief Legal Officer	Fax:	(817) 302-7897
SHEFFIELD, Susan	Tel:	(817) 302-7000
Executive Vice President and Treasurer	Fax:	(817) 302-7897

Generali USA Life Reassurance

Generali USA Life Reassurance located at Lenexa, KS.
www.generaliusalifere.com
Annual Revenues: $45.20 million
Employees: 100
Industry/ies: Insurance Industry

Chairman of the Board and Chief Executive Officer	Tel:	(913) 901-4663
CARNICELLI, Chris	Fax:	(913) 901-4778
ccarnicelli@generaliusalifere.com		

Main Headquarters

Mailing:	Seven World Trade Center	Tel:	(212) 602-7600
	250 Greenwich St. 33rd Floor	Fax:	(212) 587-9537
	New York, NY 10007		

Corporate Foundations and Giving Programs

Generali USA Life Reassurance Contributions Program
P.O. Box 419076
Kansas City, MO 64114

Public Affairs and Related Activities Personnel

At Headquarters

ALONZO, Bernadita	Tel:	(212) 602-7600
Human Resources	Fax:	(212) 587-9537
FURNARI, Salvo	Tel:	(212) 602-7600
Controller	Fax:	(212) 587-9537
MARTINI, John	Tel:	(212) 602-7600

President and Chief Financial officer	Fax:	(212) 587-9537
OUTUMURO, Joe	Tel:	(212) 602-7600
Treasurer	Fax:	(212) 587-9537

At Other Offices

GATES, David	Tel:	(913) 901-4665
Senior Vice President, General Counsel and Secretary	Fax:	(913) 901-4778
P.O. Box 419076		
Kansas City, MO 64114-6076		
SWANSON, CLU, FSA, MAAA, Mark	Tel:	(913) 901-4742
Vice President, Marketing Actuary	Fax:	(913) 901-4778
P.O. Box 419076		
Kansas City, MO 64114-6076		

Genesee & Wyoming Inc.

An operator of short line and regional freight railroads in the U.S., Canada, Mexico, Australia and Bolivia. The company operates in five countries on three continents over 8,100 miles of owned and leased track. It also operates over more than 3,000 miles under track access arrangements.
www.gwrr.com
Annual Revenues: $1.66 billion
Employees: 7,700
Ticker: NYSE: GWR
SIC: 4011
Industry/ies: Railroads; Transportation
Legislative Issues: AVI; TAX; TRA

Chairman of the Board	Tel:	(203) 202-8900
FULLER, III, Mortimer B.	Fax:	(203) 656-1092
President and Chief Executive Officer	Tel:	(203) 202-8900
HELLMANN, John C.	Fax:	(203) 656-1092

Main Headquarters

Mailing:	20 West Ave.	Tel:	(203) 202-8900
	Darien, CT 06820	Fax:	(203) 656-1092

Political Action Committees

Genesee & Wyoming Inc. PAC
FEC ID: C00289058
Contact: Jerry Vest
3601 Concord Rd.
Second Floor
York, PA 17402

Contributions to Candidates: $109,100 (2015-2016)
Democrats: $28,700; Republicans: $80,400

Principal Recipients

SENATE
MORAN, JERRY (REP-KS)
WICKER, ROGER F (REP-MS)

HOUSE
BLUMENAUER, EARL (DEM-OR)

Corporate Foundations and Giving Programs

Genesee & Wyoming Inc. Contributions Program		
66 Field Point Rd.	Tel:	(203) 629-3722
Greenwich, CT 06830	Fax:	(203) 661-4106

Public Affairs and Related Activities Personnel

At Headquarters

BROWN, Jack N.	Tel:	(203) 202-8900
Vice President, Compliance and Security	Fax:	(203) 656-1092
BROWN, David A.	Tel:	(203) 202-8900
Chief Operating Officer	Fax:	(203) 656-1092
FERGUS, Allison M.	Tel:	(203) 202-8900
General Counsel and Secretary	Fax:	(203) 656-1092
afergus@gwrr.com		
GALLAGHER, Timothy J.	Tel:	(203) 202-8900
Chief Financial Officer	Fax:	(203) 656-1092
GATES, Gerald T.	Tel:	(203) 202-8900
Senior Vice President, Operations	Fax:	(203) 656-1092
HANSEN, Niels	Tel:	(203) 202-8900
Vice President, Employee and Labor Relations	Fax:	(203) 656-1092
JAMES, Tyrone C.	Tel:	(203) 202-8900
Senior Vice President, Safety and Compliance	Fax:	(203) 656-1092
LIUCCI, Christopher F.	Tel:	(203) 202-8900
Chief Accounting Officer and Global Controller	Fax:	(203) 656-1092
LONG, Mike	Tel:	(203) 202-8900
Senior Vice President, Compliance	Fax:	(203) 656-1092
LUNDELL, Michael F.	Tel:	(203) 202-8900
Vice President, Compliance and Safety	Fax:	(203) 656-1092
RUSSELL, Mary Ellen	Tel:	(203) 202-8900
Chief Human Resource Officer	Fax:	(203) 656-1092
SAVAGE, Thomas D.	Tel:	(203) 202-8900
Vice President, Corporate Development and Treasurer	Fax:	(203) 656-1092

SMITH, Kimberly B.
Federal Lobbyist
Registered Federal Lobbyist

Tel: (203) 202-8900
Fax: (203) 656-1092

WALSH, Matthew O.
Senior Vice President, Corporate Development
mwalsh@gwrr.com

Tel: (203) 202-8900
Fax: (203) 656-1092

WILLIAMS, Michael E.
Vice President, Corporate Communications
mwilliams@gwrr.com

Tel: (203) 413-2116
Fax: (203) 656-1092

At Other Offices

VEST, Jerry
Senior Vice President, Government & Industry Affairs
3601 Concord Rd., Second Floor
York, PA 17402
jvest@gwrr.com
Registered Federal Lobbyist

Tel: (412) 963-1805
Fax: (717) 771-1775

Genesis HealthCare Corporation

Specializes in geriatric healthcare services.
www.genesishcc.com
Employees: 43,000
SIC: 8051
Industry/ies: Medicine/Health Care/Mental Health
Legislative Issues: MMM

Chief Executive Officer
HAGER, Jr., George V.

Tel: (443) 949-9867
Fax: (610) 925-4000

Main Headquarters
Mailing: 101 E. State St.
Kennett Sq., PA 19348

Tel: (610) 444-6350
Fax: (610) 925-4000
TF: (800) 944-7776

Political Action Committees
GHC Ancillary Corporation Political Action Committee
FEC ID: C00292094
Contact: Laurence F. Lane
101 E. State St.
Kennett Square, PA 19348

Tel: (610) 444-6350
Fax: (610) 925-4000

Contributions to Candidates: $137,034 (2015-2016)
Democrats: $38,500; Republicans: $98,534

Public Affairs and Related Activities Personnel

At Headquarters

BETHEA, Lashuan
Registered Federal Lobbyist

Tel: (610) 444-6350
Fax: (610) 925-4000

DIVITTORIO, Tom
Senior Vice President and Chief Financial Officer

Tel: (610) 444-6350
Fax: (610) 925-4000

FEUERMAN, Jason H.
Senior Vice President, Strategic Development and Managed Care

Tel: (610) 444-6350
Fax: (610) 925-4000

GUPTA, Meghna
Marketing Manager
meghna.gupta@viverae.com

Tel: (972) 677-1614
Fax: (610) 925-4000

LANE, Laurence F.
Vice President, Government Relations
laurence.lane@genesishcc.com
Registered Federal Lobbyist

Tel: (610) 444-8430
Fax: (610) 925-4242

PHILLIPS, Jeanne
Senior Vice President and Chief Human Resources Officer

Tel: (610) 444-6350
Fax: (610) 925-4000

REITZ, Robert A.
Executive Vice President and Chief Operating Officer

Tel: (610) 444-6350
Fax: (610) 925-4000

SHERMAN, Michael
Senior Vice President, General Counsel

Tel: (610) 444-6350
Fax: (610) 925-4000

TABAK, James W.
Senior Vice President, Administration and Government Affairs

Tel: (610) 444-6350
Fax: (610) 925-4000

THIVIERGE, Ray
Chief Strategy Officer

Tel: (610) 444-6350
Fax: (610) 925-4000

Genmobi Technologies, Inc.

A software technology company for identity protection.
www.genmobi.com
Industry/ies: Computer/Technology; Defense/Homeland Security; Government-Related

Chairman of the Board
JONES, Glyn

Tel: (408) 324-1508
Fax: (801) 640-9352

Main Headquarters
Mailing: 5046 Russo Dr.
Suite 111
San Jose, CA 95134

Tel: (408) 324-1508
Fax: (801) 640-9352

Genomic Health, Inc.

A life science company conducting genomic research to develop clinically validated molecular diagnostics.
www.genomichealth.com
Annual Revenues: $276.86 million
Employees: 752
Ticker: NASDAQ: GHDX
SIC: 8071
Industry/ies: Medicine/Health Care/Mental Health
Legislative Issues: HCR; MED

Chairman of the Board, Chief Executive Officer and President
POPOVITS, Kimberly J.

Tel: (650) 556-9300
Fax: (650) 556-1132

Main Headquarters
Mailing: 301 Penobscot Dr.
Redwood City, CA 94063

Tel: (650) 556-9300
Fax: (650) 556-1132
TF: (866) 662-6897

Public Affairs and Related Activities Personnel

At Headquarters

CASSEL, Jon
Senior Vice President, Operations

Tel: (650) 556-9300
Fax: (650) 556-1132

COLE, Bradley
Chief Operating Officer and Chief Financial Officer

Tel: (650) 556-9300
Fax: (650) 556-1132

HIBBS, Esq., Kathy
Senior Vice President and General Counsel

Tel: (650) 556-9300
Fax: (650) 556-1132

LEBER, Laura
Senior Vice President, Corporate Communications

Tel: (650) 556-9300
Fax: (650) 556-1132

MCEACHRON, Kim
Chief People Officer

Tel: (650) 556-9300
Fax: (650) 556-1132

GENTEX Corporation

Develops, manufactures and markets interior and exterior automatic-dimming automotive rearview mirrors that utilize the proprietary electro chromic technology.
www.gentex.com
Annual Revenues: $1.58 billion
Employees: 4,757
Ticker: NASDAQ: GNTX
SIC: 3714
Industry/ies: Chemicals & Chemical Industry; Defense/Homeland Security; Government-Related
Legislative Issues: DEF

Chairman of the Board and Chief Executive Officer
BAUER, Fred D.

Tel: (616) 772-1800
Fax: (616) 772-7348

Main Headquarters
Mailing: 600 N. Centennial St.
Zeeland, MI 49464

Tel: (616) 772-1800
Fax: (616) 772-7348

Political Action Committees
GENTEX Corporation PAC
FEC ID: C00386128
Contact: Heather M. Acker
P.O. Box 315
Carbondale, PA 18407

Tel: (616) 772-1800
Fax: (616) 772-7348

Contributions to Candidates: $13,103 (2015-2016)
Democrats: $12,103; Republicans: $1,000

Public Affairs and Related Activities Personnel

At Headquarters

DOWNING, Steve
Vice President, Finance and Chief Financial Officer

Tel: (616) 772-1800
Fax: (616) 772-7348

FLYNN , Paul
Vice President, Operations

Tel: (616) 772-1800
Fax: (616) 772-7348

HAMBLIN, Connie
Consultant, Investor Relations

Tel: (616) 772-1800
Fax: (616) 772-7348

PIERSMA, Craig
Director, Product Marketing

Tel: (616) 772-1800
Fax: (616) 772-7348

At Other Offices

ACKER, Heather M.
PAC Treasurer
P.O. Box 315
Carbondale, PA 18407
hmacker@gentexcorp.com

Tel: (616) 772-1800

Gentiva Health Services

A home health care services firm.
www.gentiva.com
Annual Revenues: $1.80 billion
Employees: 17,200
Ticker: NASDAQ: GTIV
SIC: 8082
Industry/ies: Medicine/Health Care/Mental Health

Chief Executive Officer, President and Director
STRANGE, Tony

Tel: (770) 951-8450
Fax: (631) 501-7148

Main Headquarters

Mailing:	3350 Riverwood Pkwy.	Tel:	(770) 951-6450
	Suite 1400	Fax:	(631) 501-7148
	Atlanta, GA 30339		

Washington Office

Mailing:	600 Cameron St.	Tel:	(703) 340-1633
	Alexandria, VA 22314		

Corporate Foundations and Giving Programs

Gentiva Hospice Foundation
Contact: Mary Griffin
3350 Riverwood Pkwy.
Suite 1400
Atlanta, GA 30339

Public Affairs and Related Activities Personnel

At Headquarters

CAMPERLENGO, John N.	Tel:	(631) 501-7000
Senior Vice President, General Counsel and Secretary	Fax:	(631) 501-7148
CAUSBY, David	Tel:	(770) 951-6450
President, Chief Operating Officer	Fax:	(631) 501-7148
CIANCIULLI, Scott	Tel:	(212) 986-6667
Contact, Media Relations	Fax:	(631) 501-7148
cianciulli@braincomm.com		
DAHLGARD, Douglas	Tel:	(703) 340-1633
Vice President, Tax and Federal Lobbyist	Fax:	(631) 501-7148
GRIFFIN, Mary	Tel:	(770) 951-6208
Executive Director, Gentiva Hospice Foundation	Fax:	(631) 501-7148
ghf@gentiva.com		
SLUSSER, Eric	Tel:	(770) 951-6101
Executive Vice President, Chief Financial Officer	Fax:	(631) 501-7148
eric.slusser@gentiva.com		

At Washington Office

BENNER, Mara	Tel:	(703) 340-1633
Vice President, Government Affairs		
HILL, Kimberly N.	Tel:	(703) 340-1633
Senior Vice President, Tax		

Genuine Parts Company

A service company that distributes automotive products.
www.genpt.com
Annual Revenues: $15.45 billion
Employees: 39,000
Ticker: NYSE: GPC
SIC: 5013
Industry/ies: Automotive Industry; Transportation

Chairman, President and Chief Executive Officer	Tel:	(770) 953-1700
GALLAGHER, Thomas C.	Fax:	(770) 956-2211
tom_gallagher@genpt.com		

Main Headquarters

Mailing:	2999 Cir. 75 Pkwy.	Tel:	(770) 953-1700
	Atlanta, GA 30339	Fax:	(770) 956-2211

Public Affairs and Related Activities Personnel

At Headquarters

CLAYTON, Bruce R.	Tel:	(770) 953-1700
Senior Vice President, Human Resources	Fax:	(770) 956-2211
JONES, Sidney G.	Tel:	(770) 953-1700
Vice President, Investor Relations	Fax:	(770) 956-2211
SMITH, Scott C.	Tel:	(770) 953-1700
Senior Vice President, Corporate Counsel	Fax:	(770) 956-2211
scott_smith@genpt.com		
SPENCER, Gaylord	Tel:	(770) 953-1700
Vice President, Marketing Strategy	Fax:	(770) 956-2211
gaylord_spencer@genpt.com		

Genworth Financial, Inc.

Financial services.
www.genworth.com
Annual Revenues: $9.58 billion
Employees: 5,300
Ticker: NYSE: GNW
SIC: 6311
Industry/ies: Insurance Industry
Legislative Issues: ACC; BAN; FIN; HCR; HOU; INS; RET; TAX

Chairman of the Board	Tel:	(804) 281-6000
RIEPE, James S.	Fax:	(804) 662-2414

Chief Executive Officer, President and Director	Tel:	(804) 281-6000
MCINERNEY, Thomas J.	Fax:	(804) 662-2414

Main Headquarters

Mailing:	6620 W. Broad St.	Tel:	(804) 281-6000
	Richmond, VA 23230	Fax:	(804) 662-2414

	TF:	(888) 436-9678

Washington Office

Mailing:	700 12th St. NW	Tel:	(202) 662-2560
	Suite 710	Fax:	(202) 662-2575
	Washington, DC 20005		

Political Action Committees

Genworth Financial Inc. PAC (Genworth PAC)
FEC ID: C00404194
Contact: Matt Farney

6620 W. Broad St.	Tel:	(804) 281-6000
Richmond, VA 23230	Fax:	(804) 281-6000

Contributions to Candidates: $175,750 (2015-2016)
Democrats: $43,500; Republicans: $132,250

Principal Recipients

HOUSE
MCHENRY, PATRICK TIMOTHY (REP-NC)
ROYCE, ED MR. (REP-CA)
RYAN, PAUL D. (REP-WI)

Corporate Foundations and Giving Programs

Genworth Foundation		
6620 W. Broad St.	Tel:	(804) 281-6000
Richmond, VA 23230	Fax:	(804) 662-2414

Public Affairs and Related Activities Personnel

At Headquarters

FARNEY, Matt	Tel:	(804) 281-6000
PAC Treasurer	Fax:	(804) 662-2414
KLEIN, Martin P.	Tel:	(804) 281-6000
Executive Vice President and Chief Financial Officer	Fax:	(804) 662-2414
LAMING, Michael S.	Tel:	(804) 281-6000
Senior Vice President, Human Resources	Fax:	(804) 662-2414
ORENDORFF, Al	Tel:	(804) 662-2534
Media Contact, Corporate and Financial	Fax:	(804) 662-2414
al.orendorff@genworth.com		
PEHOTA, Joseph J.	Tel:	(804) 281-6000
Senior Vice President, Corporate Development	Fax:	(804) 662-2414
RODAY, Leon E.	Tel:	(804) 281-6000
Senior Vice President, General Counsel and Secretary	Fax:	(804) 662-2414
leon.roday@genworth.com		
SHEEHAN, IV, Daniel J.	Tel:	(804) 281-6000
Chief Investment Officer	Fax:	(804) 662-2414

At Washington Office

DUNCAN, Duane S.	Tel:	(202) 662-2560
Senior Vice President, Government and Industry Relations	Fax:	(202) 662-2575
Registered Federal Lobbyist		
LAGANZA, Dennis	Tel:	(202) 662-2560
Vice President and Director, State Government Relations	Fax:	(202) 662-2575
LEVY, Roger N.	Tel:	(202) 662-2560
Senior Vice President, Government Relations	Fax:	(202) 662-2575
MORGANTE, Sam	Tel:	(202) 662-2560
Vice President, Government Relations	Fax:	(202) 662-2575
Sam.Morgante@genworthcom		

Genzyme Corporation

A biotechnology company focused on developing therapeutic and diagnostic products and services to treat major unmet medical needs. Headquartered in Cambridge, MA.
www.genzyme.com
Employees: 12,000
Ticker: NASDAQ (GS): GENZ
SIC: 2836; 2835
Industry/ies: Medicine/Health Care/Mental Health; Pharmaceutical Industry
Legislative Issues: BUD; CPT; HCR; MMM; PHA; TAX; TRD

Chief Executive Officer and Chairman	Tel:	(617) 252-7500
VIEHBACHER, Christopher A.	Fax:	(617) 252-7600

President and Chief Executive Officer	Tel:	(617) 252-7500
MEEKER, MD, David	Fax:	(617) 252-7600
david.meeker@genzyme.com		

Main Headquarters

Mailing:	500 Kendall St.	Tel:	(617) 252-7500
	Cambridge, MA 02142	Fax:	(617) 252-7600

Washington Office

Mailing:	1850 K St. NW	Tel:	(202) 296-3280
	Suite 500	Fax:	(202) 296-3411
	Washington, DC 20006		

Political Action Committees

Genzyme Corporation PAC (GENZ-PAC)
FEC ID: C00393736
Contact: Joseph C. Tauras

1850 K St. NW	Tel:	(202) 296-3280
Suite 650	Fax:	(202) 296-3411

Washington, DC 20006

Contributions to Candidates: $43,500 (2015-2016)
Democrats: $36,500; Republicans: $7,000

Corporate Foundations and Giving Programs

Genzyme Grants and Charitable Contributions
500 Kendall St.   Tel: (617) 252-7500
Cambridge, MA 02142   Fax: (617) 252-7600

Public Affairs and Related Activities Personnel

At Headquarters

AITCHISON, William   Tel: (617) 252-7500
Head, Global Industrial Operations   Fax: (617) 252-7600

ARNSTEIN, Caren P.   Tel: (617) 252-7500
Head, Corporate Communications   Fax: (617) 252-7600
caren.arnstein@genzyme.com

BARRETT , Mark   Tel: (617) 252-7500
Vice President, Global Head, Strategy and Business   Fax: (617) 252-7600
Development

ESTEVA, Marc   Tel: (617) 252-7500
Chief Financial Officer   Fax: (617) 252-7600

GANSLER, Jayne M.   Tel: (617) 252-7500
Senior Vice President and Head, Human Resources   Fax: (617) 252-7600

GORSKI, Lori   Tel: (617) 768-9344
Director, Communications   Fax: (617) 252-7600
lori.gorski@genzyme.com

HILLBACK, Elliott D.   Tel: (617) 252-7500
Senior Vice President, Corporate Affairs   Fax: (617) 252-7600
elliott.hillback@genzyme.com

NESTOR, Edward   Tel: (617) 252-7500
PAC Treasurer   Fax: (617) 252-7600

PIELA, Bo   Tel: (617) 252-7500
Vice President, Corporate Communications   Fax: (617) 252-7600
bo.piela@genzyme.com

QUARLES, Tracey L.   Tel: (617) 252-7500
Senior Vice President and General Counsel   Fax: (617) 252-7600

TURENNE, G. Andre   Tel: (617) 252-7500
Head, Strategy and Business Development   Fax: (617) 252-7600

At Washington Office

BARTLETT, Melissa   Tel: (202) 296-3280
Federal Lobbyist   Fax: (202) 296-3411
Registered Federal Lobbyist

FROELICH, Sara   Tel: (202) 296-3280
Vice President & Head, Government Relations   Fax: (202) 296-3411
Registered Federal Lobbyist

MCGRANE, Mary   Tel: (202) 296-3280
Senior Vice President   Fax: (202) 296-3411

TAURAS, Joseph C.   Tel: (202) 296-3280
PAC Treasurer   Fax: (202) 296-3411

GEO Command

Offers mobile GIS mapping solutions. Its suite of technologies addresses with an innovative turnkey solution is designed for everyday use: scaling seamlessly from ordinary incidents to multi-agency mass response.
www.geocommand.com
Industry/ies: Medicine/Health Care/Mental Health; Transportation

President, Chief Executive Officer and Chairman of the Board   Tel: (561) 347-9215
KOENIGSBERG, Albert   Fax: (561) 347-9219
albiek@geocommand.com

Main Headquarters
Mailing: 3700 Airport Rd.   Tel: (561) 347-9215
   Suite 410   Fax: (561) 347-9219
   Boca Raton, FL 33431   TF: (888) 766-1766

Public Affairs and Related Activities Personnel

At Headquarters

AIELLO, Paul J.   Tel: (561) 347-9215
Director, Sales and Marketing   Fax: (561) 347-9219

EVANS, Eric   Tel: (561) 347-9215
Director, Business Development   Fax: (561) 347-9219

The GEO Group, Inc.

The GEO Group is into delivery of private correctional and detention management, community residential re-entry services as well as behavioral and mental health services to federal, state and local government agencies. It offers a diversified array of turnkey services which include design, construction, financing, and operations.
www.geogroup.com
Annual Revenues: $1.93 billion
Employees: 15,806
Ticker: NYSE: GEO
SIC: 0/9b
Industry/ies: Law Enforcement/Security

Legislative Issues: HOM; IMM; LAW

Chairman of the Board, Chief Executive Officer and Founder   Tel: (561) 893-0101
ZOLEY, George C.   Fax: (561) 999-7635

Main Headquarters
Mailing: One Park Pl., 621 N.W. 53rd St   Tel: (561) 893-0101
   Suite 700   Fax: (561) 999-7635
   Boca Raton, FL 33487   TF: (866) 301-4436

Political Action Committees
Geo Group, Inc. PAC
FEC ID: C00382150
Contact: Brian R Evans
One Park Pl. 621 NW 53rd St.   Tel: (561) 893-0101
Suite 700   Fax: (561) 999-7635
Boca Raton, FL 33487

Contributions to Candidates: $116,695 (2015-2016)
Democrats: $15,940; Republicans: $100,755

Principal Recipients

SENATE
LEE, MIKE (REP-UT)
LOPEZ-CANTERA, CARLOS (REP-FL)
SCOTT, TIMOTHY E (REP-SC)

HOUSE
NEGRON, REBECCA (REP-FL)

Corporate Foundations and Giving Programs

GEO Group Foundation
Contact: Ann M. Schlarb PhD
One Park Pl. 621 NW 53rd St.   Tel: (561) 893-0101
Suite 700   Fax: (561) 999-7635
Boca Raton, FL 33487

Public Affairs and Related Activities Personnel

At Headquarters

BULFIN, John J.   Tel: (561) 893-0101
Senior Vice President, General Counsel and Corporate   Fax: (561) 999-7635
Secretary

EVANS, Brian R   Tel: (561) 893-0101
Senior Vice President and Chief Financial Officer   Fax: (561) 999-7635

FULLER, Stephen V.   Tel: (561) 893-0101
Senior Vice President, Human Resources   Fax: (561) 999-7635

SCHLARB, PhD, Ann M.   Tel: (561) 893-0101
Senior Vice President and President, GEO Community   Fax: (561) 999-7635
Services

VENTURELLA, David J.   Tel: (561) 893-0101
Senior Vice President, Business Development   Fax: (561) 999-7635

Geo-Enterprises

Participant in Northwest Explorations Joint Venture owner of mineral property in Alaska.
www.geo-enterprises.com
Industry/ies: Minerals; Natural Resources

Founder   Tel: (918) 379-0193
SCHOEN, Philip   Fax: (918) 379-0471

Main Headquarters
Mailing: 2660 N. Hwy. 167   Tel: (918) 379-0193
   Catoosa, OK 74015   Fax: (918) 379-0471
   TF: (800) 994-0428

GeoEye, Inc.

See listing on page 256 under DigitalGlobe, Inc.

The Georgia Aquarium, Inc.

Aquarium and education/research facility. Georgia Aquarium provides an entertaining, engaging and educational experience inspiring stewardship in conservation, research and the appreciation for the animal world.
www.georgiaaquarium.org
Industry/ies: Animals
Legislative Issues: ANI; MAR

Chairman of the Board and Chief Executive Officer   Tel: (404) 581-4000
MARCUS, Bernard

Chairman and Chief Executive Officer   Tel: (404) 581-4000
LEVEN, Mike

Main Headquarters
Mailing: 225 Baker St. NW   Tel: (404) 581-4000
   Atlanta, GA 30313

Public Affairs and Related Activities Personnel

At Headquarters

GIBBONS, Meghann   Tel: (404) 581-4109
Senior Director, Communications

HANNANS, Camille   Tel: (404) 581-4000
Vice President, Human Resources

HIGLEY, Scott	Tel:	(404) 581-4106
Vice President, Marketing and Communications, External Affairs		
PALINSKI, David	Tel:	(404) 581-4000
Senior Vice President and Chief Financial Officer		
RAMSEY, Will	Tel:	(404) 581-4000
Vice President of Sales		
ROGERS, Bailey	Tel:	(404) 581-4277
Specialist, Public Relations		
ROUNTREE, Carey	Tel:	(404) 581-4000
Senior Vice President, Sales and Marketing		
SCHAFER, Mark	Tel:	(404) 581-4000
Executive Vice President and Chief Operating Officer		

Georgia Gulf Corporation

See listing on page 100 under Axiall Corporation

Georgia Power Company

Georgia Power is the largest subsidiary of Southern Company.
www.georgiapower.com
Employees: 8,000
Ticker: NYSE:GPE-A
SIC: 4911
Industry/ies: Energy/Electricity; Utilities

Chairman, President and Chief Executive Officer	Tel:	(404) 506-6526
BOWERS, W. Paul	Fax:	(404) 506-3771

Main Headquarters

Mailing:	241 Ralph McGill Blvd. NE	Tel:	(404) 506-6526
	Atlanta, GA 30308	Fax:	(404) 506-3771

Political Action Committees

Georgia Power Company Federal PAC
FEC ID: C00119776
Contact: Pedro Cherry
241 Ralph McGill Blvd. NE
Atlanta, GA 30308

Contributions to Candidates: $107,500 (2015-2016)
Democrats: $20,500; Republicans: $87,000

Principal Recipients

SENATE

ISAKSON, JOHN HARDY (REP-GA)

HOUSE

BISHOP, SANFORD D JR (DEM-GA)
CARTER, EARL LEROY (REP-GA)
COLLINS, DOUGLAS ALLEN (REP-GA)
GRAVES, JOHN THOMAS MR. JR. (REP-GA)
PRICE, THOMAS EDMUNDS (REP-GA)
WOODALL, ROB REP. (REP-GA)

Corporate Foundations and Giving Programs

Georgia Power Charitable Giving
Contact: Mike Anderson

241 Ralph McGill Blvd. NE	Tel:	(404) 506-6526
Atlanta, GA 30308	Fax:	(404) 506-3771

Georgia Power Foundation, Inc.
Contact: Mike Anderson

241 Ralph McGill Blvd. NE	Tel:	(404) 506-6784
Atlanta, GA 30308	Fax:	(404) 506-1485

Public Affairs and Related Activities Personnel

At Headquarters

ANDERSON, Mike	Tel:	(404) 506-6526
Senior Vice President, Charitable Giving	Fax:	(404) 506-3771
BARRS, Craig	Tel:	(404) 506-7740
Executive Vice President, Customer Service and Operations	Fax:	(404) 506-3771
BELL, Chris	Tel:	(404) 506-6526
Vice President, Energy Planning and Sales	Fax:	(404) 506-3771
BISHOP, Thomas P.	Tel:	(404) 506-6526
Senior Vice President, Compliance Officer, General Counsel and Corporate Secretary	Fax:	(404) 506-3771
CHERRY, Pedro	Tel:	(404) 506-6526
Contact, PAC	Fax:	(404) 506-3771
COLEMAN, Kenny	Tel:	(404) 506-6526
Senior Vice President, Marketing	Fax:	(404) 506-3771
CUMMISKEY , Chris	Tel:	(404) 506-6526
Executive Vice President, External Affairs	Fax:	(404) 506-3771
HINSON, Ron	Tel:	(404) 506-6526
Executive Vice President, Chief Financial Officer, Treasurer and Comptroller	Fax:	(404) 506-3771
OWENS, Leonard	Tel:	(404) 506-6526
Vice President, Human Resources and Labor Relations	Fax:	(404) 506-3771

Georgia Transmission Corporation

Power generation and transmission company providing services to multiple Georgia EMCs.
www.gatrans.com
Industry/ies: Utilities

Chairman of the Board	Tel:	(770) 270-7400
FENDLEY, Charles		
President and Chief Executive Officer	Tel:	(770) 270-7400
DONOVAN, Jerry		

Main Headquarters

Mailing:	2100 E. Exchange Pl.	Tel:	(770) 270-7400
	Tucker, GA 30084	TF:	(800) 241-5374

Public Affairs and Related Activities Personnel

At Headquarters

CULLEN, Terry	Tel:	(770) 270-7207
Manager, Communications		
terry.cullen@gatrans.com		
HAMPTON, Barbara	Tel:	(770) 270-7400
Senior Vice President and Chief Financial Officer		
PARKER, Tom	Tel:	(770) 270-7050
Vice President, External Affairs and Member Relations		
SHEFFIELD, Angela	Tel:	(770) 270-7400
Vice President, General Auditor and Chief Regulatory Compliance Officer		
TYUS, Shaunna	Tel:	(770) 270-7895
Contact, Human Resources		
shaunna.tyus@gatrans.com		
WINKLE, David Van	Tel:	(770) 270-7400
Vice President, Operations and Maintenance		

Georgia-Pacific LLC

A manufacturer of building products, pulp, paper and related chemicals. A subsidiary of Koch Industries (see separate listing).
www.gp.com
Annual Revenues: $17.94 billion
Employees: 40,000
SIC: 2600
Industry/ies: Chemicals & Chemical Industry; Paper And Wood Products Industry

President and Chief Executive Officer	Tel:	(404) 652-4000
HANNAN, James	Fax:	(404) 230-1674

Main Headquarters

Mailing:	133 Peachtree St. NE	Tel:	(404) 652-4000
	Atlanta, GA 30303	Fax:	(404) 749-2454
		TF:	(800) 284-5347

Washington Office

Mailing:	665 15th St. NW	Tel:	(202) 879-8555
	Washington, DC 20005		

Corporate Foundations and Giving Programs

Georiga-Pacific Foundation
Contact: Curley M. Dossman Jr.

133 Peachtree St. NE	Tel:	(404) 652-4182
Atlanta, GA 30303	Fax:	(404) 654-4789

Public Affairs and Related Activities Personnel

At Headquarters

BREHM, Julie	Tel:	(404) 652-4000
Senior Vice President, Human Resources	Fax:	(404) 230-1674
DARLAND, Tye	Tel:	(404) 652-4000
Senior Vice President, General Counsel	Fax:	(404) 230-1674
DOSSMAN, Jr., Curley M.	Tel:	(404) 652-4182
President, Georgia-Pacific Foundation	Fax:	(404) 654-4789
JONES , W. Wesley	Tel:	(404) 652-4000
Executive Vice President, Operations Excellence and Compliance	Fax:	(404) 749-2454
PARK, David	Tel:	(404) 652-4000
Senior Vice President, Strategy and Business Development	Fax:	(404) 654-4789
WALTERS , Kathleen A.	Tel:	(404) 652-4000
Executive Vice President, Consumer Products Group	Fax:	(404) 749-2454
WEIDMAN, Sheila M.	Tel:	(404) 652-4000
Senior Vice President, Communications, Government and Public Affairs	Fax:	(404) 654-4789
sweidman@gapac.com		
WOOLSON, Tyler	Tel:	(404) 652-4000
Senior Vice President and Chief Financial Officer	Fax:	(404) 230-1674

GeoSyn Fuels

Focused on the development of proprietary low cost processes for the production of "advanced biofuels" using renewable feedstocks.
www.geosynfuels.com

Industry/ies: Energy/Electricity; Natural Resources

| **Chairman** | Tel: | (303) 215-0740 |
| SHAPIRO, Steven J. | Fax: | (303) 215-0745 |

President and Chief Executive Officer	Tel:	(303) 215-0740
HARVEY, BSc, MBA, MSc, PhD, J. Todd	Fax:	(303) 215-0745
tjh@geosynfuels.com		

Main Headquarters

Mailing:	14818 W. Sixth Ave.	Tel:	(303) 215-0740
	Suite A1	Fax:	(303) 215-0745
	Golden, CO 80401		

Public Affairs and Related Activities Personnel

At Headquarters

| FLEMMING, Andrew W. | Tel: | (303) 215-0740 |
| *Vice President, Strategy* | Fax: | (303) 215-0745 |

| LEONARD, Terrie | Tel: | (303) 215-0740 |
| *Contact, Human Resources* | Fax: | (303) 215-0745 |

SPILCHEN, BS, Tim P.	Tel:	(303) 215-0740
Vice President, Business Development	Fax:	(303) 215-0745
tps@geosynfuels.com		

SROGE, BS, Joshua A.	Tel:	(303) 215-0740
Controller and Vice President, Finance	Fax:	(303) 215-0745
jas@geosynfuels.com		

Gerdau Long Steel North America

A steel company and producer of minimill steel. Serves customers in the eastern two-thirds of North America.
www.gerdau.com
Employees: 5,000
Ticker: NYSE: GNA
SIC: 3312; 3441
NAICS: 332312
Industry/ies: Construction/Construction Materials; Metals

Main Headquarters

Mailing:	4221 W. Boy Scout Blvd.	Tel:	(813) 286-8383
	Suite 600	Fax:	(813) 207-2355
	Tampa, FL 33607		

Corporate Foundations and Giving Programs

Gerdau Ameristeel Contributions Program
4221 W. Boy Scout Blvd.
Suite 600
Tampa, FL 33607

Public Affairs and Related Activities Personnel

At Headquarters

| CZARNIK, Carl | Tel: | (813) 286-8383 |
| *Electrician* | Fax: | (813) 207-2355 |

| DANAHY, Terry | Tel: | (813) 286-8383 |
| *Vice President and Chief Human Resources Officer* | Fax: | (813) 207-2355 |

| JOHANNPETER, Guilherme Gerdau | Tel: | (813) 286-8383 |
| *Vice President* | Fax: | (813) 207-2355 |

Gerson Lehrman Group

Gerson Lehrman Group (GLG) maintains a network of industry experts in the fields of health care, telecom, insurance, financial services, energy, and other who offer consulting and advice to investors.
www.glgresearch.com
Annual Revenues: $41.10 million
Employees: 300
SIC: 3241
Industry/ies: Banking/Finance/Investments; Consultants; Investments/Securities Industry
Legislative Issues: ENG; FIN; FOR; TRD

Chairman of the Board	Tel:	(212) 984-8500
GERSON, Mark	Fax:	(212) 984-8538
mgerson@glgroup.com		

President and Chief Executive Officer	Tel:	(212) 984-8500
SAINT-ARMAND, Alex	Fax:	(212) 984-8538
alexander@glgroup.com		

Main Headquarters

Mailing:	60 E. 42nd St.	Tel:	(212) 984-8500
	3rd Floor		
	New York, NY 10165		

Political Action Committees

Gerson Lehrman Group Inc. PAC Inc. (Gerson Lehrman Group PAC Inc.)
FEC ID: C00419556
Contact: Laurence Herman
850 Third Ave.
Ninth Floor
New York City, NY 10022

Public Affairs and Related Activities Personnel

At Headquarters

| CATALANE , Bart | Tel: | (212) 984-8500 |
| *Chief Financial Officer* | | |

DONOGHUE, John	Tel:	(212) 984-8500
Head, New Markets		
jdonoghue@glgroup.com		

HERMAN, Laurence	Tel:	(212) 984-8500
General Counsel, Managing Director and PAC Treasurer		
lherman@glgroup.com		

| KING , Michael | Tel: | (212) 984-8500 |
| *Chief Compliance Counsel* | | |

| LEGG , David | Tel: | (212) 984-8500 |
| *Head, International Markets and Managing Director* | | |

| SOCARIDES , Richard | Tel: | (212) 984-8500 |
| *Head, Public Affairs* | | |

At Other Offices

GOLDMAN, Andrew	Tel:	(212) 984-8500
Senior Vice President	Fax:	(212) 984-8538
850 Third Ave., Ninth Floor		
New York City, NY 10022		

SERVES, Brian	Tel:	(212) 984-8500
Head of Products and Marketing	Fax:	(212) 984-8538
850 Third Ave., Ninth Floor		
New York City, NY 10022		

Gesconti Group, Inc.

Trade (domestic and foreign).
Industry/ies: Trade (Foreign And Domestic)

President	Tel:	(202) 434-8779
MARTINDALE, Walter Reed	Fax:	(202) 434-8707
wrmgesconti@verizon.net		

Main Headquarters

Mailing:	1200 G St. NW	Tel:	(202) 434-8779
	Suite 800	Fax:	(202) 434-8707
	Washington, DC 20005		

GFI Group, Inc.

Provides inter-dealer brokerage services in a multitude of global cash and derivatives markets.
www.gfigroup.com
Annual Revenues: $832.24 million
Employees: 1,984
Ticker: NASDAQ: GFIG
SIC: 6200
Industry/ies: Banking/Finance/Investments

| **Executive Chairman of the Board** | Tel: | (212) 968-4100 |
| GOOCH, Michael | Fax: | (212) 968-2386 |

| **Chief Executive Officer** | Tel: | (212) 968-4100 |
| HEFFRON, Colin | Fax: | (212) 968-2386 |

Main Headquarters

| Mailing: | 55 Water St. | Tel: | (212) 968-4100 |
| | New York City, NY 10041 | Fax: | (212) 968-2386 |

Washington Office

| Mailing: | P.O. Box 77472 | |
| | Washington, DC 20013 | |

Corporate Foundations and Giving Programs

GFI Group, Inc. Contributions Program		
Second and D St. SW	Tel:	(212) 968-4100
Washington, DC 20515	Fax:	(212) 968-2386

Public Affairs and Related Activities Personnel

At Headquarters

CASABURRI, Chris Ann	Tel:	(212) 968-4167
Manager, Investor Relations	Fax:	(212) 968-2386
chris.casaburri@gfigroup.com		

| D'ANTUONO, Christopher | Tel: | (212) 968-4100 |
| *General Counsel* | Fax: | (212) 968-2386 |

| GIANCARLO, Christopher J. | Tel: | (212) 968-2992 |
| *Executive Vice President, Corporate Development* | Fax: | (212) 968-2386 |

GUTIERREZ, Patricia	Tel:	(212) 968-2964
Vice President, Public Relations	Fax:	(212) 968-6600
patricia.gutierrez@gfigroup.com		

| LEVI, Ron | Tel: | (212) 968-4100 |
| *Chief Operating Officer* | Fax: | (212) 968-2386 |

At Washington Office

PEERS, James A.
Chief Financial Officer and PAC Treasurer

GGNSC Holdings LLC

Operating under the name Golden Horizons, this privately-held company owns and leases nursing homes and assisted living facilities under the Golden Living and Beverly brands.
www.goldenliving.com
Annual Revenues: $2.06 billion
Employees: 700
Industry/ies: Aging; Medicine/Health Care/Mental Health
Legislative Issues: BUD; LBR; MMM; VET

President and Chief Executive Officer
KURTZ, Neil

Tel: (479) 201-2000
Fax: (479) 201-1101

Main Headquarters
Mailing: 1000 Fianna Way
              Ft. Smith, AR 72919

Tel: (479) 201-2000
Fax: (479) 201-1101
TF: (877) 823-8375

Washington Office
Mailing: 700 13th St.
              Second Floor
              Washington, DC 20005

Political Action Committees
GGNSC Holdings LLC/Golden Horizons Care PAC
FEC ID: C00346346
Contact: Jack A. MacDonald
700 13th St. NW
Second Floor
Washington, DC 20005

Contributions to Candidates: $49,000 (2015-2016)
Democrats: $12,500; Republicans: $36,500

Principal Recipients
HOUSE
RYAN, PAUL D. (REP-WI)

Public Affairs and Related Activities Personnel
At Washington Office
STACIE, Aman
Contact, Government Relations
Registered Federal Lobbyist

At Other Offices
AMAN, Stacie
Federal Lobbyist
1099 New York Ave. NW, Suite 500
Washington, DC 20001
Registered Federal Lobbyist

Tel: (202) 393-2800
Fax: (202) 393-7180

BARTLETT, R. Candace
Federal Lobbyist
1099 New York Ave. NW, Suite 500
Washington, DC 20001
candace.bartlett@goldenliving.com
Registered Federal Lobbyist

Tel: (202) 393-2800
Fax: (202) 393-7180

LUNEBORG, Kelli
Director, Public Relations
7160 Dallas Pkwy., Suite 400
Plano, TX 75024
media@goldenliving.com

Tel: (972) 372-6300

MACDONALD, Jack A.
Executive Vice President
1099 New York Ave. NW, Suite 500
Washington, DC 20001
jack_macdonald@beverlycorp.org

Tel: (202) 393-2800
Fax: (202) 393-7180

WARE, Barbara
Senior Director, Public Relations
1099 New York Ave. NW, Suite 500
Washington, DC 20001

Tel: (202) 393-2800
Fax: (202) 393-7180

GGP Limited Partnership

Formerly General Growth Properties, Inc. A fully integrated, self-managed and self-administered real estate investment trust focused exclusively on owning, managing, leasing, and redeveloping high-quality regional malls throughout the United States.
www.ggp.com
Annual Revenues: $2.62 billion
Employees: 1,800
Ticker: NYSE: GGP
SIC: 6798
Industry/ies: Economics And Economic Development; Real Estate

Chairman of the Board
FLATT, J. Bruce

Tel: (312) 960-5000
Fax: (312) 960-5475

Chief Executive Officer
MATHRANI, Sandeep

Tel: (312) 960-5000
Fax: (312) 960-5475

Main Headquarters
Mailing: 110 N. Wacker Dr.
              Chicago, IL 60606

Tel: (312) 960-5000
Fax: (312) 960-5475

Political Action Committees
General Growth Properties Inc. PAC

FEC ID: C00345355
Contact: Marvin J. Levine
110 N. Wacker Dr.
Chicago, IL 60606

Contributions to Candidates: $11,000 (2015-2016)
Democrats: $5,000; Republicans: $6,000

Corporate Foundations and Giving Programs
GGP Contributions Program
110 N. Wacker Dr.
Chicago, IL 60606

Public Affairs and Related Activities Personnel
At Headquarters
BERMAN, Michael
Executive Vice President and Chief Financial Officer

Tel: (312) 960-5000
Fax: (312) 960-5475

BERRY, Kevin
Vice President, Investor Relations
kevin.berry@ggp.com

Tel: (312) 960-5000
Fax: (312) 960-5475

CHEERS, Lesley
Senior Director, Corporate Communications
Lesley.Cheers@ggp.com

Tel: (312) 960-2646
Fax: (312) 960-5475

KHAN, Shobi
Executive Vice President, Chief Operating Officer

Tel: (312) 960-5000
Fax: (312) 960-5475

KNUDSON, Julie
Senior Vice President and Chief Human Resources Officer

Tel: (312) 960-5000
Fax: (312) 960-5475

LEVINE, Marvin J.
Executive Vice President and Chief Legal Officer and PAC Treasurer

Tel: (312) 960-5000
Fax: (312) 960-5475

MARSZEWSKI, Tara
Senior Vice President, Chief Accounting Officer

Tel: (312) 960-5000
Fax: (312) 960-5475

Giant Cement Holding, Inc.

A subsidiary of Spain's Cementos Portland Valderrivas, produces cement, concrete and aggregate for residential, commercial, and infrastructure projects.Its subsidiaries include Giant Cement Company, Inc., Keystone Cement Company, Giant Resource Recovery, Inc. (GRR!), and Dragon Products Company, LLC.
www.gchi.com
Employees: 650
SIC: 3241
Industry/ies: Construction/Construction Materials

Chief Executive Officer
LLONTOP, José

Tel: (843) 851-9898
Fax: (843) 851-9881

Main Headquarters
Mailing: 320-D Midland Pkwy.
              Summerville, SC 29485

Tel: (843) 851-9898
Fax: (843) 851-9881
TF: (800) 845-1174

Corporate Foundations and Giving Programs
Giant Cement Holding Contributions Program
320-D Midland Pkwy.
Summerville, SC 29485

Public Affairs and Related Activities Personnel
At Headquarters
CANNON, Erin
Legal Counsel

Tel: (843) 851-9898
Fax: (843) 851-9881

GEIER, Jerry
Vice President, Human Resources

Tel: (843) 851-9898
Fax: (843) 851-9881

ROBLEDO, Fernando
Vice President, Administration and Finance

Tel: (843) 851-9898
Fax: (843) 851-9881

Giant Eagle

A grocery retailer.
www.gianteagle.com
SIC: 5411; 5099; 5149; 5912; 9999
NAICS: 44511; 42199; 42249; 44611; 99999
Industry/ies: Food And Beverage Industry; Retail/Wholesale
Legislative Issues: FOO; TAX

Chief Executive Officer
SHAPIRA KARET, Laura
Laura.karet@gianteagle.com

Tel: (412) 963-6200
Fax: (412) 968-1617

Main Headquarters
Mailing: 101 Kappa Dr.
              Pittsburgh, PA 15238-2833

Tel: (412) 963-6200
Fax: (412) 968-1617
TF: (800) 553-2324

Political Action Committees
Giant Eagle Inc. PAC
FEC ID: C00426072
Contact: Mark J. Minnaugh
101 Kappa Dr.
RIDC Park
Pittsburgh, PA 15238

Tel: (412) 963-6200
Fax: (412) 968-1617

Contributions to Candidates: $10,200 (2015-2016)
Democrats: $1,000; Republicans: $9,200

Corporate Foundations and Giving Programs

Giant Eagle Corporate Contributions Program
101 Kappa Dr.   Tel: (412) 963-6200
RIDC Park   Fax: (412) 963-6200
Pittsburgh, PA 15238-2833

Public Affairs and Related Activities Personnel

At Headquarters

LUCOT, John   Tel: (412) 963-6200
Executive Vice President and Chief Operating Officer   Fax: (412) 968-1617

MINNAUGH, Mark J.   Tel: (412) 963-6200
Executive Vice President, Secretary and PAC Treasurer   Fax: (412) 968-1617

Giant Food LLC

A supermarket chain.
www.giantfood.com
Annual Revenues: $4.78 billion
Employees: 28,000
SIC: 2026; 2097; 5411
Industry/ies: Food And Beverage Industry; Retail/Wholesale

Main Headquarters

Mailing: 8301 Professional Pl.   Tel: (301) 341-4100
Suite 115   Fax: (301) 618-4998
Landover, MD 20785   TF: (888) 469-4426

Public Affairs and Related Activities Personnel

At Headquarters

ASTRACHAN, Andrea   Tel: (301) 341-4365
Vice President, Consumer Affairs   Fax: (301) 618-4968

MILLER, Jamie   Tel: (301) 341-8776
Manager, Public & Community Relations   Fax: (301) 618-4998
jmiller@giantofmaryland.com

Giant Industries

See listing on page 849 under Western Refining, Inc.

Giant Tire and Rubber Company

See listing on page 220 under Cooper Tire & Rubber Company

GigOptix Company

Created in the merger between Lumera and GigOptix in 2008. Designs electro-optic components based on proprietary polymer compounds for the telecommunications and computing industries.
www.gigoptix.com
Annual Revenues: $34.62 million
Employees: 77
Ticker: NYSE MKT : GIG
SIC: 3674
Industry/ies: Computer/Technology

Chairman of the Board, Chief Executive Officer and President   Tel: (408) 522-3100
KATZ, Dr. Avi   Fax: (402) 522-3102
avi@gigoptix.com

Main Headquarters

Mailing: 130 Baytech Dr.   Tel: (408) 522-3100
San Jose, CA 95134   Fax: (402) 522-3102

Public Affairs and Related Activities Personnel

At Headquarters

CHAUDHRY, Anil   Tel: (408) 522-3100
Vice President, Government Affairs and Strategic Accounts   Fax: (402) 522-3102

CHOATE, Steve   Tel: (408) 522-3100
Vice President, Operations   Fax: (402) 522-3102

DINU, Dr. Raluca   Tel: (408) 522-3100
Senior Vice President Sales and Marketing   Fax: (402) 522-3102

FANUCCHI, Jim   Tel: (408) 404-5400
Contact, Investor Relations   Fax: (402) 522-3102
ir@gigoptix.com

MA, Darren   Tel: (408) 522-3100
Vice President and Chief Financial Officer   Fax: (402) 522-3102

Gilbane Building Company

Plans, designs and constructs behavioral health facilities.
www.gilbaneco.com
Employees: 2,100
Industry/ies: Construction/Construction Materials

Chairman of the Board   Tel: (401) 456-5800
GILBANE, Jr., Thomas F.   Fax: (401) 456-5404

President and Chief Executive Officer   Tel: (401) 456-5800
MCKELVY, Michael L.   Fax: (401) 456-5404

Main Headquarters

Mailing: Seven Jackson Walkway   Tel: (401) 456-5800
Providence, RI 02903   Fax: (401) 456-5404
   TF: (800) 445-2263

Corporate Foundations and Giving Programs

Gilbane Contributions Program
1230 W. Morehead St.
Charlotte, NC 28208-5214

Public Affairs and Related Activities Personnel

At Headquarters

CORNICK, Dennis M.   Tel: (401) 456-5800
Executive Vice President and Global Director Sales and Marketing   Fax: (401) 456-5404

COTTER, Wes   Tel: (401) 456-5405
Director, Communications   Fax: (401) 456-5404
wcotter@gilbaneco.com

LAIRD, Thomas M.   Tel: (401) 456-5800
Executive Vice President   Fax: (401) 456-5404

RUGGIERI, John T.   Tel: (401) 456-5800
Senior Vice President and Chief Financial Officer   Fax: (401) 456-5404

Gilbarco Veeder-Root

See listing on page 365 under Gilbarco, Inc.

Gilbarco, Inc.

Gilbarco represents the brands of solutions and technologies that provide convenience, control, and environmental integrity for retail fueling and adjacent markets.
www.gilbarco.com
Annual Revenues: $650 million
Employees: 4,000
SIC: 3586
Industry/ies: Fuels See Coal, Gas, Oil, Petroleum; Natural Resources; Petroleum Industry
Legislative Issues: ENG

Main Headquarters

Mailing: P.O. Box 22087   Tel: (336) 547-5000
7300 W. Friendly Ave.   Fax: (336) 547-5299
Greensboro, NC 27420   TF: (800) 800-7498

Public Affairs and Related Activities Personnel

At Headquarters

SACKETT, Lucy   Tel: (336) 547-5607
Director, Marketing Communications   Fax: (336) 547-5890
lucy.sackett@gilbarco.com

Gilead Sciences

A bio-pharmaceutical company.
www.gilead.com
Annual Revenues: $27.48 billion
Employees: 7,000
Ticker: NASDAQ: GILD
SIC: 2836
Industry/ies: Pharmaceutical Industry
Legislative Issues: BUD; CPT; DEF; FOR; HCR; LAW; MMM; PHA; TRD; VET

Chairman of the Board and Chief Executive Officer   Tel: (650) 574-3000
MARTIN, PhD, John   Fax: (650) 578-9264
JMartin@Gilead.com

Main Headquarters

Mailing: 333 Lakeside Dr.   Tel: (650) 574-3000
Foster City, CA 94404   Fax: (650) 578-9264
   TF: (800) 445-3235

Washington Office

Mailing: 601 13th St. NW
Floor 11
Washington, DC 20005

Political Action Committees

Gilead Sciences Inc. Healthcare Policy PAC
FEC ID: C00396895
Contact: Andrew Rittenberg
333 Lakeside Dr.   Tel: (650) 574-3000
Foster City, CA 94404   Fax: (650) 574-3000

Contributions to Candidates: $69,000 (2015-2016)
Democrats: $43,500; Republicans: $25,500

Principal Recipients

SENATE
BENNET, MICHAEL F (DEM-CO)
MURRAY, PATTY (DEM-WA)

Corporate Foundations and Giving Programs

Gilead Foundation
Contact: Amy Flood

333 Lakeside Dr.
Foster City, CA 94404

Tel: (650) 574-3000
Fax: (650) 578-9264

Public Affairs and Related Activities Personnel

At Headquarters

ALTON, Gregg H.
Executive Vice President, Corporate and Medical Affairs
gregg.alton@gilead.com

Tel: (650) 574-3000
Fax: (650) 578-9264

FLOOD, Amy
Vice President, Public Affairs
aflood@gilead.com

Tel: (650) 574-3000
Fax: (650) 578-9264

GROGAN, Joseph
Director, Federal Government Affairs
joe.grogan@gilead.com
Registered Federal Lobbyist

Tel: (650) 574-3000
Fax: (650) 578-9264

JONES, II, Aranthan

Tel: (650) 574-3000
Fax: (650) 578-9264

KAISER, Nathan
Associate Director, Public Affairs
nathan.kaiser@gilead.com

Tel: (650) 522-1853
Fax: (650) 522-5853

MILLIGAN, PhD, John F.
President and Chief Operating Officer
John.Milligan@Gilead.com

Tel: (650) 574-3000
Fax: (650) 578-9264

O'BRIEN, Patrick
Contact, Investor Relations

Tel: (650) 522-1936
Fax: (650) 578-9264

PULLIAM, David
Federal Lobbyist
Registered Federal Lobbyist

Tel: (650) 574-3000
Fax: (650) 578-9264

RITTENBERG, Andrew
Contact, Corporate Counsel and PAC Treasurer

Tel: (650) 574-3000
Fax: (650) 578-9264

WASHINGTON, Robin L.
Executive Vice President and Chief Financial Officer

Tel: (650) 522-5688
Fax: (650) 522-5853

WATSON, Katie L.
Senior Vice President, Human Resources

Tel: (650) 574-3000
Fax: (650) 578-9264

At Other Offices

LIS, Cristin
Vice President, Government Affairs
199 E. Blaine St.
Seattle, WA 98102

Tel: (206) 728-5090
Fax: (206) 728-5095

RAMESH, Rekha
Associate Director, Government Affairs
199 E. Blaine St.
Seattle, WA 98102

Tel: (206) 728-5090
Fax: (206) 728-5095

GKN Aerospace Services, Inc.

A supplier of structures, components, assemblies and engineering services to aircraft and aero engine manufacturers.
www.gkn.com/aerospace
Annual Revenues: $86.60 million
Employees: 700
SIC: 3728; 3429; 3548; 4581
NAICS: 336413; 332919; 333992; 48819
Industry/ies: Aerospace/Aviation; Transportation

Chief Executive Officer
BRYSON, Marcus

Tel: (619) 448-2320
Fax: (619) 258-5270

Main Headquarters
Mailing: 1150 W. Bradley Ave.
El Cajon, CA 92020

Tel: (619) 448-2320
Fax: (619) 258-5270

Political Action Committees
GKN Aerospace Inc. PAC (GKN Aerospace Chem-Tronics PAC)
FEC ID: C00210559
Contact: Craig A. Purser CAE
1150 W. Bradley Ave.
El Cajon, CA 92020

> **Contributions to Candidates:** $9,500 (2015-2016)
> Democrats: $5,500; Republicans: $4,000

Public Affairs and Related Activities Personnel

At Headquarters

BATTAGLIA, Tom
Senior Vice President, Political Affairs

Tel: (619) 448-2320
Fax: (619) 258-5270

FARRELL, Enid
PAC Treasurer

Tel: (619) 448-2320
Fax: (618) 258-5279

HARVEY, Andrew
Senior Vice President, Human Resources

Tel: (619) 448-2320
Fax: (619) 258-5270

PATERSON, Charles
General Manager

Tel: (619) 448-2320
Fax: (619) 258-5270

PURSER, CAE, Craig A.
PAC Contact

Tel: (619) 448-2320
Fax: (619) 258-5270

WATERS, Nick
Chief Financial Officer

Tel: (619) 448-2320
Fax: (619) 258-5270

GKV Associates of McLean LLC

A special interest's lobbying activity may go up or down over time, depending on how much attention the federal government is giving their issues. Particularly active clients often retain multiple lobbying firms, each with a team of lobbyists, to press their case for them.
Industry/ies: Construction/Construction Materials

President
ARMENIAN, Garabed K.
GKArmenian@gmail.com

Tel: (202) 434-4816

Main Headquarters
Mailing: 6006 Balsam Dr.
McLean, VA 22101

Tel: (202) 434-4816

Glaxo Wellcome Inc.

See listing on page 366 under GlaxoSmithKline

GlaxoSmithKline

Researches, develops, manufactures, and markets pharmaceuticals, vaccines, over-the-counter medicines, and health-related consumer goods. Formed through the merger of Glaxo Wellcome and SmithKline Beecham in 2000.
www.gsk.com
Annual Revenues: $35.42 billion
Employees: 97,921
Ticker: NYSE:GSK
SIC: 5122
NAICS: 424210
Industry/ies: Pharmaceutical Industry
Legislative Issues: BUD; CPT; HCR; MMM; TAX; TRD

Non-Executive Chairman
HAMPTON, Sir Philip

Tel: (215) 751-4000
Fax: (919) 315-3344

Chief Executive Officer
WITTY, Andrew
Andrew.Witty@gsk.com

Tel: (215) 751-4000
Fax: (215) 751-4306

Main Headquarters
Mailing: Five Crescent Dr.
P.O. Box 7929
Philadelphia, PA 19112

Tel: (215) 751-4000
Fax: (919) 315-3344
TF: (888) 825-5249

Washington Office
Mailing: 227 N. Royal St.
Alexandria, VA 22315

Tel: (703) 684-3973

Political Action Committees
GlaxoSmithKline LLC PAC
FEC ID: C00199703
Contact: Mark J. Santry
Five Moore Dr.
P.O. Box 13398
Research Triangle Park, NC 27709

> **Contributions to Candidates:** $292,000 (2015-2016)
> Democrats: $105,000; Republicans: $186,000; Other: $1,000

> **Principal Recipients**
>
> **SENATE**
> BURR, RICHARD (REP-NC)

Corporate Foundations and Giving Programs
GlaxoSmithKline Foundation
Contact: Marilyn Foote-Hudson
Five Moore Dr.
P.O. Box 13398
Research Triangle Park, NC 27709

Tel: (919) 483-2100
Fax: (919) 549-7459

Public Affairs and Related Activities Personnel

At Headquarters

ANDERSON, Roy
Independent Non-Executive Director

Tel: (215) 751-4000
Fax: (919) 315-3344

BURNS, Stephanie
Non-Executive Director

Tel: (215) 751-4000
Fax: (919) 315-3344

CARTWRIGHT, Stacey
Independent Non-Executive Director

Tel: (215) 751-4000
Fax: (919) 315-3344

DINGEMANS, Simon
Chief Financial Officer

Tel: (215) 751-4000
Fax: (919) 315-3344

ELSENHANS, Lynn
Independent Non-Executive Director

Tel: (215) 751-4000
Fax: (919) 315-3344

HIRONS, Nick
Senior Vice President, Global Ethics and Compliance

Tel: (215) 751-4000
Fax: (919) 315-3344

LEWENT, Judy
Independent Non-Executive Director

Tel: (215) 751-4000
Fax: (919) 315-3344

MAUGHAN, Deryck
Senior Independent Non-Executive Director

Tel: (215) 751-4000
Fax: (919) 315-3344

PODOLSKY, Daniel
Independent Non-Executive Director

Tel: (215) 751-4000
Fax: (919) 315-3344

RHYNE, Mary Anne

Tel: (919) 483-0492

Media Contact, Corporate, Financial and Global Public Health
Mary.A.Rhyne@gsk.com | Fax: | (919) 315-3344

ROHNER , Urs | Tel: | (215) 751-4000
Independent Non-Executive Director | Fax: | (919) 315-3344

THOMSON , Philip | Tel: | (215) 751-4000
Senior Vice President, Communications and Government Affairs | Fax: | (919) 315-3344

WIJERS , Hans | Tel: | (215) 751-4000
Independent Non-Executive Director | Fax: | (919) 315-3344

At Washington Office

BURRUS, Jan | Tel: | (703) 684-3973
State Government Affairs

FOOTE-HUDSON, Marilyn | Tel: | (703) 684-3973
Executive Director, GlaxoSmith Kline Foundation
marilyn.e.foote-hudson@gsk.com

MCGOWAN, Joseph | Tel: | (703) 684-3973
Federal Government Relations
Registered Federal Lobbyist

At Other Offices

CAUSEY, Jonathan | Tel: | (202) 715-1031
1050 K St. NW, Suite 800 | Fax: | (202) 715-1001
Washington, DC 20001
Registered Federal Lobbyist

CHRISTENSEN, Julie Veneers
Federal Lobbyist
1500 K St. NW, Suite 800
Washington, DC 20001

GARY, Heimberg | Tel: | (202) 715-1031
1050 K St. NW, Suite 800 | Fax: | (202) 715-1001
Washington, DC 20001

HEIMBERG, Gary A. | Tel: | (202) 715-1000
Director, Federal Government Relations | Fax: | (202) 715-1001
1050 K St. NW, Suite 800
Washington, DC 20001
Registered Federal Lobbyist

KILCOYNE, Shira | Tel: | (202) 715-1000
Director, Government Affairs International | Fax: | (202) 715-1001
1050 K St. NW, Suite 800
Washington, DC 20001
Registered Federal Lobbyist

LORBER, Leah | Tel: | (202) 715-1000
Assistant General Counsel, Policy / Director, Public Policy & | Fax: | (202) 715-1001
Advocacy
1050 K St. NW, Suite 800
Washington, DC 20001
leah.l.lorber@gsk.com

MANTHO, Mary Catherine | Tel: | (202) 715-1000
Director, Policy | Fax: | (202) 715-1001
1050 K St. NW, Suite 800
Washington, DC 20001

REDFERN, David | Tel: | (215) 751-4000
Chief Strategy Officer | Fax: | (215) 751-4306
1600 Vine St.
Philadelphia, PA 19101

SALLY, Walsh | Tel: | (202) 715-1031
1050 K St. NW, Suite 800 | Fax: | (202) 715-1001
Washington, DC 20001

SANTRY, Mark J. | Tel: | (919) 483-2100
Director and PAC Contact | Fax: | (919) 549-7459
Five Moore Dr., P.O. BOX 13358
Research Triangle Park, NC 27709

SCANGO, Stephen | Tel: | (202) 715-1000
Manager, Federal Government Relations | Fax: | (202) 715-1001
1050 K St. NW, Suite 800
Washington, DC 20001
Registered Federal Lobbyist

SCHUYLER, William J. | Tel: | (202) 715-1025
Vice President, Government Relations | Fax: | (202) 715-1001
1050 K St. NW, Suite 800
Washington, DC 20001
william.j.schuyler@gsk.com
Registered Federal Lobbyist

SLAUOI, Dr. Moncef | Tel: | (215) 751-4000
Chairman, Research and Development | Fax: | (215) 751-4306
1600 Vine St.
Philadelphia, PA 19101

THOMAS, Claire | Tel: | (215) 751-4000
Senior Vice President, Human Resources | Fax: | (215) 751-4306
1600 Vine St
Philadelphia, PA 19101

Claire.x.Thomas@gsk.com

TROY, Dan | Tel: | (215) 751-4000
Senior Vice President and General Counsel | Fax: | (215) 751-4306
1600 Vine St.
Philadelphia, PA 19101

WALSH, Sarah J. | Tel: | (202) 715-1015
Federal Lobbyist | Fax: | (202) 715-1001
1050 K St. NW, Suite 800
Washington, DC 20001
sarah.j.walsh@gsk.com
Registered Federal Lobbyist

WILLIAMS, Kimberly A. | Tel: | (202) 715-1031
Contact, Government Relations | Fax: | (202) 715-1001
1050 K St. NW, Suite 800
Washington, DC 20001
Registered Federal Lobbyist

Glidepath LLC

Based in Grand Prairie city, U.S. subsidiary of Glidepath Group., headquartered in Auckland, New Zealand. A supplier of turnkey baggage handling systems.
www.glidepathgroup.com
Annual Revenues: $7.90 million
Industry/ies: Aerospace/Aviation; Airlines; Machinery/Equipment; Transportation

Chairman of the Board and Managing Director | Tel: | (972) 641-4200
STEVENS, Ken | Fax: | (972) 641-4203
ken.stevens@glidepathgroup.com

Main Headquarters
Mailing: 1713 S. Great S.W. Pkwy. | Tel: | (972) 641-4200
Grand Prairie, TX 75051 | Fax: | (972) 641-4203

Public Affairs and Related Activities Personnel

At Headquarters

MEAD, David | Tel: | (972) 641-4200
Vice President, Sales and Marketing | Fax: | (972) 641-4203
david.mead@glidepathgroup.com

Global Brass and Copper Holdings, Inc.

A converter, fabricator, distributor and processor of specialized copper and brass products in North America. Subsidiaries and Joint Venture Companies include Bryan Metals, Somers Thin Strip, Dowa-Olin Brass Metals, Olin Brass Luotong Metals, Olin Brass Fineweld Tube, and Olin Brass Fabricated Products. A. J. Oster and Chase Brass are affiliated companies.
www.gbcmetals.com
Annual Revenues: $1.43 billion
Employees: 1,900
Ticker: NYSE: BRSS
Industry/ies: Metals

Chief Executive Officer | Tel: | (847) 240-4700
WASZ, John J.

Main Headquarters
Mailing: 475 N. Martingale Rd. | Tel: | (847) 240-4700
Suite 1050
Schaumburg, IL 60173

Public Affairs and Related Activities Personnel

At Headquarters

HAMILTON, Scott B. | Tel: | (847) 240-4700
General Counsel and Secretary

MICCHELLI, Robert T. | Tel: | (847) 240-4700
Chief Financial Officer and Contact, Media Relations

Global Communities

Formerly known as CHF International and before that, the Cooperative Housing Foundation. It is an non-profit international development and humanitarian aid organization and works in more than 25 countries serving as a catalyst for long-lasting positive change in low and moderate income communities.
www.globalcommunities.org
Industry/ies: Construction/Construction Materials

Chairman of the Board | Tel: | (301) 587-4700
MOSBACHER, Jr., Robert A. | Fax: | (301) 587-7315

President and Chief Executive Officer | Tel: | (301) 587-4700
WEISS, David A. | Fax: | (301) 587-7315

Main Headquarters
Mailing: 8601 Georgia Ave. | Tel: | (301) 587-4700
Suite 800 | Fax: | (301) 587-7315
Silver Spring, MD 20910

Corporate Foundations and Giving Programs

Caterpillar Inc. Foundation
Contact: Michele Sullivan
100 N.E. Adams St. | Tel: | (309) 675-1000
Peoria, IL 61629 | Fax: | (309) 675-1182

Philippine American Foundation

Contact: Mya Grossman
8601 Georgia Ave.
Suite 800
Silver Spring, MD 20910

	Tel:	(301) 587-4700
	Fax:	(301) 587-7315

Public Affairs and Related Activities Personnel

At Headquarters

BHASIN, Abhishek
Chief Financial Officer

Tel:	(301) 587-4700
Fax:	(301) 587-7315

GROSSMAN, Mya
President, Philippine American Foundation
mylenegrossman@gmail.com

Tel:	(240) 441-6941
Fax:	(301) 587-7315

HUMPHRIES, David
Vice President, Communications and Public Affairs
dhumphries@chfinternational.org

Tel:	(301) 587-4700
Fax:	(301) 587-7315

O'NEILL, Eric
General Counsel and Chief Ethics Officer

Tel:	(301) 587-4700
Fax:	(301) 587-7315

SALE, Chris
Executive Vice President and Chief Operating Officer

Tel:	(301) 587-4700
Fax:	(301) 587-7315

At Other Offices

SULLIVAN, Michele
President, Caterpillar Foundation
100 N.E. Adams St.
Peoria, IL 61629

Tel:	(309) 675-1000

Global Green Holdings, LLC

A group of vertically integrated companies that focus on utilizing materials historically been viewed as "waste" and converting them into useable, eco-friendly products.
Industry/ies: Environment And Conservation; Natural Resources; Pollution And Waste

Main Headquarters

Mailing: 320 Harbor Blvd.
                Suite 205
                Destin, FL 32541

Tel:	(850) 837-1530

Public Affairs and Related Activities Personnel

At Headquarters

SPENCE, David W.
Manager

Tel:	(850) 837-1530

Global Security Systems

A systems integrator, service provider and manufacturer of FM radio-based alert and messaging system.
www.alertfm.com
Industry/ies: Defense/Homeland Security; Disaster; Government-Related
Legislative Issues: COM

President & Chief Executive Officer
ADAMS, Robert L.
rladams@gssnet.us

Tel:	(601) 709-4240
Fax:	(601) 709-4241

Main Headquarters

Mailing: 346 Rheem Blvd., Suite 202
                Moraga, CA 94556

Tel:	(925) 377-8411
Fax:	(925) 377-0144

Globe Specialty Metals, Inc.

Produces and sells silicon metal and silicon-based specialty alloys. Its silicon metal is used as a primary raw material in making silicone compounds, aluminum, and polysilicon. Its silicon-based alloys are used as raw materials in making steel, automotive components, and ductile iron.
www.glbsm.com
Annual Revenues: $804.11 million
Employees: 1,569
Ticker: NASDAQ: GSM
SIC: 3330
NAICS: 331112
Industry/ies: Metals

Executive Chairman of the Board
KESTENBAUM, Alan

Tel:	(986) 509-6900
Fax:	(302) 655-5049

Chief Executive Officer and Chief Operating Officer
BRADLEY, Jeff
jbradley@glbsm.com

Tel:	(786) 509-6908
Fax:	(302) 655-5049

Main Headquarters

Mailing: 600 Brickell Ave.
                Suite 3100
                Miami, FL 33131

Tel:	(986) 509-6900
Fax:	(302) 655-5049

Public Affairs and Related Activities Personnel

At Headquarters

LEBOWITZ, Stephen
Chief Legal Officer

Tel:	(986) 509-6900
Fax:	(302) 655-5049

RAGAN, Joe
Chief Financial Officer
jragan@glbsm.com

Tel:	(786) 509-6925
Fax:	(302) 655-5049

GoDaddy.com

Provides individuals and businesses with domain name registration, website hosting, and related services and software.
www.godaddy.com
Annual Revenues: $264.70 million
Employees: 2,000
Industry/ies: Computer/Technology

Executive Chairman and Founder
PARSONS, Bob

Tel:	(480) 505-8800
Fax:	(480) 505-8844

Chief Executive Officer
IRVING, Blake

Tel:	(480) 505-8800
Fax:	(480) 505-8844

Main Headquarters

Mailing: 14455 N. Hayden Rd.
                Suite 226
                Scottsdale, AZ 85260

Tel:	(480) 505-8800
Fax:	(480) 505-8844

Washington Office

Mailing: 400 N. Capitol St.
                Suite 585
                Washington, DC 20001

Tel:	(202) 624-3547

Political Action Committees
Godaddy.Com Inc. PAC
FEC ID: C00432328
Contact: Meredith Lesher
14455 N. Hayden Rd.
Suite 219
Scottsdale, AZ 85260

Tel:	(480) 505-8800
Fax:	(480) 505-8800

Corporate Foundations and Giving Programs
Go Daddy Contribution Program
14455 N. Hayden Rd.
Suite 226
Scottsdale, AZ 85260

Tel:	(480) 505-8800
Fax:	(480) 505-8844

Public Affairs and Related Activities Personnel

At Headquarters

BIENERT, Phil
Chief Marketing Officer and Executive Vice President

Tel:	(480) 505-8800
Fax:	(480) 505-8844

DRISCOLL, Elizabeth
Vice President, Public Relations
PR@GoDaddy.com

Tel:	(480) 505-8800
Fax:	(480) 505-8878

FULLER, Nick
Director, Public Relations
nfuller@godaddy.com

Tel:	(480) 505-8800
Fax:	(480) 505-8844

JONES, Christine
Executive Vice President, General Counsel and Corporate Secretary

Tel:	(480) 505-8800
Fax:	(480) 505-8844

KELLY, Nima
General Counsel

Tel:	(480) 505-8800
Fax:	(480) 505-8844

LESHER, Meredith
PAC Treasurer

Tel:	(480) 505-8800
Fax:	(480) 505-8844

POPOWITZ, David
Senior Vice President, Corporate Development

Tel:	(480) 505-8800
Fax:	(480) 505-8844

RECHTERMAN, Barb
Senior Executive Vice President and Chief Marketing Officer

Tel:	(480) 505-8800
Fax:	(480) 505-8844

WAGNER, Scott
Chief Operating Officer and Chief Financial Officer

Tel:	(480) 505-8800
Fax:	(480) 505-8844

ZIMMERMAN, Michael
Executive Vice President, Finance

Tel:	(480) 505-8800
Fax:	(480) 505-8844

At Washington Office

JOHNSTON, Martha R.
Vice President, Government Relations

Tel:	(202) 624-3547

Gold Bond Stamp Company

See listing on page 166 under Carlson Companies

Gold Kist Inc.

See listing on page 636 under Pilgrim's Pride Corporation

Golden Grain Energy LLC

An ethanol production company.
www.goldengrainenergy.com
Annual Revenues: $208.46 million
Employees: 50
SIC: 2860
Industry/ies: Energy/Electricity

Chairman of the Board
SOVEREIGN, Dave

Tel:	(563) 547-3687
Fax:	(641) 421-8457

President and Chief Executive Officer
WENDLAND, Walter

Tel:	(641) 423-8525
Fax:	(641) 421-8457

Main Headquarters

Mailing: 1822 43rd St. SW

Tel:	(641) 423-8525

Mason City, IA 50401   Fax: (641) 421-8457
TF: (888) 443-2676

Political Action Committees
Golden Grain Energy LLC PAC
FEC ID: C00414490
Contact: Chris N. Schwarck
1822 43rd St. SW
Mason City, IA 50401

  Contributions to Candidates: $5,750 (2015-2016)
  Republicans: $5,750

Public Affairs and Related Activities Personnel

At Headquarters

CALEASE, Jerry   Tel: (319) 275-4493
Director, Public Relations   Fax: (641) 421-8457

FREIN, Sarah   Tel: (641) 423-8525
Manager, Human Resources   Fax: (641) 421-8457
sfrein@ggecorn.com

KUHLERS , Chad   Tel: (641) 423-8525
Chief Operations Officer   Fax: (641) 421-8457

MARCHAND, Christy   Tel: (641) 423-8525
Chief Financial Officer   Fax: (641) 421-8457

SCHWARCK, Chris N.   Tel: (641) 423-8525
PAC Treasurer   Fax: (641) 421-8457

Golden Living
See listing on page 363 under GGNSC Holdings LLC

Golden Peanut Company
Golden Peanut changed its name to Golden Peanut and Tree Nuts in 2013. It is a subsidiary of Archer Daniels Midland Company which shells, delivers quality nuts from farms to families and processes peanuts for retail and commercial distribution to customers worldwide.
www.goldenpeanut.com
Employees: 1,000
Industry/ies: Food And Beverage Industry

President, Chief Executive Officer and PAC Treasurer   Tel: (770) 752-8205
DORSETT, James W.   Fax: (770) 752-8306

Main Headquarters
Mailing: 100 North Point Center., East   Tel: (770) 752-8205
     Suite 400   Fax: (770) 752-8306
     Alpharetta, GA 30022

Public Affairs and Related Activities Personnel

At Headquarters

MILLS, Greg   Tel: (770) 752-8205
President   Fax: (770) 752-8306

Golden Rule Insurance Company
See listing on page 821 under UnitedHealthOne

The Goldenberg Group, Inc.
A real estate development company.
www.goldenberggroup.com
Employees: 12,000
Industry/ies: Real Estate

Founder, President and Chief Executive Officer   Tel: (610) 260-9600
GOLDENBERG, Kenneth N.   Fax: (610) 260-0269

Main Headquarters
Mailing: 630 Sentry Pkwy.   Tel: (610) 260-9600
     Suite 300   Fax: (610) 260-0269
     Blue Bell, PA 19422

Corporate Foundations and Giving Programs
The Goldenberg Group's People Helping People Foundation
Contact: Ellen Lissy Rosenberg
630 Sentry Pkwy.   Tel: (610) 260-9600
Suite 300   Fax: (610) 260-0269
Blue Bell, PA 19422

Public Affairs and Related Activities Personnel

At Headquarters

FARNUM, Peter R.   Tel: (610) 260-9600
Senior Vice President and Director, Sales and Leasing   Fax: (610) 260-0269
pfarnum@goldenberggroup.com

FOGEL, Jeremy   Tel: (610) 260-9600
Executive Vice President and Director, Development   Fax: (610) 260-0269
jfogel@goldenberggroup.com

FREEDMAN, Robert W.   Tel: (610) 260-9600
Senior Vice President and General Counsel   Fax: (610) 260-0269
rfreedman@goldenberggroup.com

LAFONTANT, Georges D.   Tel: (610) 260-9600
Director, Creative Services   Fax: (610) 260-0269

glafontant@goldenberggroup.com

REDICAN, Jr., CPA, MBA, William P.   Tel: (610) 260-9600
Chief Financial Officer   Fax: (610) 260-0269
bredican@goldenberggroup.com

ROSENBERG, Ellen Lissy   Tel: (610) 260-9600
Director, Civic Engagement   Fax: (610) 260-0269
erosenberg@goldenberggroup.com

SHAPIRO, Seth   Tel: (610) 260-9600
Chief Operating Officer   Fax: (610) 260-0269
sshapiro@goldenberggroup.com

Goldhaber Policy Services LLC
A firm that focuses on government relations and issues management, primarily in the areas of housing, mortgage finance, and financial services.
www.goldhaberps.com
Legislative Issues: FIN; HOU

GOLDHABER, Mark   Tel: (919) 510-6847
mark@goldhaberps.com

Main Headquarters
Mailing: 4112 Garden Lake Dr.   Tel: (919) 510-6847
     Raleigh, NC 27612

Goldman Sachs Group, Inc.
The Goldman Sachs Group, Inc. provides investment banking, securities, and investment management services, as well as financial services to corporations, financial institutions, governments, and high-net-worth individuals worldwide.
www.goldmansachs.com
Annual Revenues: $35.82 billion
Employees: 34,400
Ticker: NYSE: GS
SIC: 6211
NAICS: 326211
Industry/ies: Banking/Finance/Investments
Legislative Issues: BAN; ECN; ENG; FIN; TAX; TRD

Chairman of the Board and Chief Executive Officer   Tel: (212) 902-1000
BLANKFEIN, Lloyd C.   Fax: (212) 902-3000
lloyd.blankfein@gs.com

Main Headquarters
Mailing: 200 West St.   Tel: (212) 902-1000
     New York City, NY 10282   Fax: (212) 902-9316

Washington Office
Mailing: 101 Constitution Ave. NW   Tel: (202) 637-3700
     Suite 1000 East   Fax: (202) 637-3773
     Washington, DC 20001

Political Action Committees
GOLDMAN SACHS GROUP, INC. PAC
FEC ID: C00350744
Contact: Robert O'Connor
101 Constitution Ave. NW
Suite 1000 East
Washington, DC 20001

  Contributions to Candidates: $421,500 (2015-2016)
  Democrats: $135,000; Republicans: $285,500; Other: $1,000

Corporate Foundations and Giving Programs
Goldman Sachs Foundation
Contact: Stephanie Bell-Rose
375 Park Ave.   Tel: (212) 357-5296
Suite 1008
New York City, NY 10152

Public Affairs and Related Activities Personnel

At Headquarters

COHEN, Alan M.   Tel: (212) 902-1000
Executive Vice President and Global Head of Compliance   Fax: (212) 902-9316

COHN , Gary D.   Tel: (212) 902-1000
President, Chief Operating Officer and Director   Fax: (212) 902-9316

PALM, Gregory K.   Tel: (212) 902-1000
Executive Vice President, General Counsel and Secretary   Fax: (212) 902-9316

POWELL, Dina Habib   Tel: (212) 902-5400
Global Head, Global Corporate Engagement   Fax: (212) 902-9316

SCHWARTZ, Harvey M.   Tel: (212) 902-1000
Executive Vice President and Chief Financial Officer   Fax: (212) 902-9316

SIEWERT, Jake   Tel: (212) 902-5400
Head, Corporate communications   Fax: (212) 902-9316

At Washington Office

BRAYBOY, Joyce   Tel: (202) 637-3700
Registered Federal Lobbyist   Fax: (202) 637-3773

CONNOLLY, Kenneth   Tel: (202) 637-3700
Federal Lobbyist   Fax: (202) 637-3773
Registered Federal Lobbyist

MAZZUCHI, Matt Niemeyer	Tel:	(202) 637-3700
Federal Lobbyist	Fax:	(202) 637-3773
Registered Federal Lobbyist		

| NIEMEYER, Matthew | Tel: | (202) 637-3700 |
| *Registered Federal Lobbyist* | Fax: | (202) 637-3773 |

O'CONNOR, Robert	Tel:	(202) 637-3700
Vice President and PAC Treasurer	Fax:	(202) 637-3773
Registered Federal Lobbyist		

OVERTON, Amy E.	Tel:	(202) 637-3700
Vice President, Government Relations	Fax:	(202) 637-3773
Registered Federal Lobbyist		

PAESE, Michael	Tel:	(202) 637-3700
Managing Director	Fax:	(202) 637-3773
michael.paese@gs.com		
Registered Federal Lobbyist		

SHIRZAD, Faryar	Tel:	(202) 637-3700
Managing Director	Fax:	(202) 637-3773
faryar.shirzad@gs.com		
Registered Federal Lobbyist		

| THOMPSON, Michael D | Tel: | (202) 637-3700 |
| *Registered Federal Lobbyist* | Fax: | (202) 637-3773 |

WALL, Joe	Tel:	(202) 637-3700
VicePresident, Government Affairs	Fax:	(202) 637-3773
Registered Federal Lobbyist		

| WESTINE, Lezlee | Tel: | (202) 637-3700 |
| *PAC Contact* | Fax: | (202) 637-3773 |

At Other Offices

BELL-ROSE, Stephanie	Tel:	(212) 357-5296
Managing Director		
375 Park Ave., Suite 1008		
New York City, NY 10152		

Golub Corporation

Golub Corporation offers come-ons such as table-ready meals, gift certificates, automatic discount cards, and a hotline where cooks answer food-related queries
www.pricechopper.com
Employees: 23,000
Industry/ies: Food And Beverage Industry

Chairman of the Board and Chief Executive Officer

| GOLUB, Neil M. | Tel: | (518) 355-5000 |
| | Fax: | (518) 379-3536 |

Main Headquarters

| *Mailing:* | 461 Nott St. | Tel: | (518) 355-5000 |
| | Schenectady, NY 12308 | Fax: | (518) 379-3536 |

Corporate Foundations and Giving Programs

Golub Foundation		
501 Duanesburg Rd.	Tel:	(518) 355-5000
Schenectady, NY 12306		

Public Affairs and Related Activities Personnel

At Headquarters

| ENDRES, John | Tel: | (518) 355-5000 |
| *Chief Financial Officer and Senior Vice President, Finance* | Fax: | (518) 379-3536 |

| GOLUB, Mona | Tel: | (518) 355-5000 |
| *Vice President, Public Relations* | Fax: | (518) 279-3515 |

Goodman Properties, Inc.

A real estate development and management firm that owns more than 125 properties.
www.goodmanproperties.org
Employees: 7
Industry/ies: Real Estate

Main Headquarters

Mailing:	636 Old York Rd.	Tel:	(215) 885-8383
	Second Floor	Fax:	(215) 885-4789
	Jenkintown, PA 19046		

Public Affairs and Related Activities Personnel

At Headquarters

GAFFIN, Andee	Tel:	(215) 885-8383
Manager, Human Resources and Assistant Controller	Fax:	(215) 885-4789
Andee@goodmanproperties.org		

| PHILLIPS, Warren | Tel: | (215) 885-8383 |
| *Director, Operations* | Fax: | (215) 885-4789 |

| STERNBERG, Nina | Tel: | (215) 885-8383 |
| *Controller, Accounting* | Fax: | (215) 885-4789 |

TATE, Karen	Tel:	(215) 885-8383
Manager, Legal Department	Fax:	(215) 885-4789
karen@goodmanproperties.org		

Goodrich Corporation

See listing on page 820 under United Technologies Corporation

Goodyear Tire and Rubber Company

A manufacturer of tires, rubber and chemical products, with a subsidiary operation in oil pipelines.
www.goodyear.com
Annual Revenues: $17.69 billion
Employees: 67,000
Ticker: NYSE: GT
SIC: 3011; 2821; 3061
NAICS: 325211; 326291; 326211
Industry/ies: Automotive Industry; Chemicals & Chemical Industry; Fuels See Coal, Gas, Oil, Petroleum; Natural Resources; Petroleum Industry; Plastics Industry; Rubber Industry; Transportation
Legislative Issues: BUD; DEF; FOR; HCR; RET; TAR; TAX

Chairman of the Board, President and Chief Executive Officer

| KRAMER, Richard J. | Tel: | (330) 796-2121 |
| | Fax: | (330) 796-2222 |

Main Headquarters

Mailing:	200 Innovation Way	Tel:	(330) 796-2121
	Akron, OH 44316-0001	Fax:	(330) 796-2222
		TF:	(800) 321-2136

Washington Office

Mailing:	300 New Jersey Ave. NW	Tel:	(202) 682-9250
	Suite 601	Fax:	(202) 682-1533
	Washington, DC 20001		

Political Action Committees

Goodyear Tire and Rubber Company Good Government Fund (Goodyear Good Government Fund)
FEC ID: C00100131
Contact: Victor Pausin

| 200 Innovation Way | Tel: | (330) 796-2121 |
| Akron, OH 44316-0001 | Fax: | (330) 796-2222 |

   Contributions to Candidates: $70,625 (2015-2016)
   Democrats: $17,000; Republicans: $53,625

Corporate Foundations and Giving Programs

The Goodyear Tire & Rubber Company Contributions Program
Contact: Faith S. Stewart

| 1144 E. Market St. | Tel: | (330) 796-8928 |
| Akron, OH 44316 | Fax: | (330) 796-2806 |

Public Affairs and Related Activities Personnel

At Headquarters

BIALOSKY, David L.	Tel:	(330) 796-2121
Senior Vice President, General Counsel and Secretary	Fax:	(330) 796-2222
dave.bialosky@goodyear.com		

| FITZHENRY, Paul | Tel: | (330) 796-5536 |
| *Senior Vice President, Global Communications* | Fax: | (330) 796-2222 |

| HONNOLD, Scott | Tel: | (330) 796-2121 |
| *Vice President, Business Development* | Fax: | (330) 796-2222 |

| KACZYNSKI, Tom | Tel: | (330) 796-2121 |
| *Vice President, Treasurer and Investor Relations* | Fax: | (330) 796-2222 |

| KELLAM, Richard | Tel: | (330) 796-2121 |
| *Senior Vice President, Global Sales and Marketing* | Fax: | (330) 796-2222 |

| KING, Scott | Tel: | (330) 796-2121 |
| *Senior Vice President, Strategy and Business Development* | Fax: | (330) 796-2222 |

| LUCAS, John | Tel: | (330) 796-2121 |
| *Senior Vice President, Global Human Resources and Chief Human Resources Officer* | Fax: | (330) 796-2222 |

| PAUSIN, Victor | Tel: | (330) 796-2121 |
| *PAC Treasurer* | Fax: | (330) 796-2222 |

PRICE, Keith J.	Tel:	(330) 798-1863
Director, National Media Relations and Business Communications	Fax:	(330) 796-1817
kprice@goodyear.com		

| RUOCCO, Joseph B. | Tel: | (330) 796-2121 |
| *Senior Vice President, Global Human Resources* | Fax: | (330) 796-2222 |

| STEWART, Faith S. | Tel: | (330) 796-8928 |
| *Director, Community Affairs* | Fax: | (330) 796-2806 |

| THOMPSON, Laura | Tel: | (330) 796-2121 |
| *ExecutiveVice President and Chief Financial Officer* | Fax: | (330) 796-2222 |

At Washington Office

FACEY, Nathan A.	Tel:	(202) 682-9250
Director, Federal and State Affairs	Fax:	(202) 682-1533
Registered Federal Lobbyist		

JOHNSON, Phala	Tel:	(202) 682-9250
Manager, Government Relations	Fax:	(202) 682-1533
Phala_johnson@goodyear.com		
Registered Federal Lobbyist		

RILEY, Brian	Tel:	(202) 682-9250
Vice President, Government Relations	Fax:	(202) 682-1533
Registered Federal Lobbyist		

Google Inc.

An internet search engine.
www.google.com/corporate
Annual Revenues: $67.84 billion
Employees: 55,419
Ticker: NASDAQ: GOOG
SIC: 7370
Industry/ies: Computer/Technology
Legislative Issues: ADV; AUT; AVI; BUD; COM; CPI; CPT; CSP; EDU; ENG; FOR; GOV; HCR; HOM; IMM; INT; LAW; LBR; SCI; SMB; TAX; TEC; TRA; TRD

Executive Chairman
SCHMIDT, Dr. Eric E.
Eric.Schmidt@google.com
Tel: (650) 253-0000
Fax: (650) 253-0001

Chief Executive Officer and Co-Founder
PAGE , Larry
Tel: (650) 253-0000
Fax: (650) 253-0001

Main Headquarters
Mailing: 1600 Amphitheater Pkwy.
Mountain View, CA 94043
Tel: (650) 253-0000
Fax: (650) 253-0001

Washington Office
Mailing: 25 Massachusetts Ave. NW, Suite 900
Ninth Floor
Washington, DC 20001
Tel: (202) 346-1100

Political Action Committees
Google Inc. NetPAC
FEC ID: C00428623
Contact: Johanna Shelton
1101 New York Ave. NW
Second Floor
Washington, DC 20005

Contributions to Candidates: $4,944,766 (2015-2016)
Democrats: $397,000; Republicans: $474,750; Other: $4,073,016

Principal Recipients

SENATE
BURR, RICHARD (REP-NC)
HARRIS, KAMALA D (DEM-CA)
ISAKSON, JOHN HARDY (REP-GA)
MURKOWSKI, LISA (REP-AK)

HOUSE
BRADY, KEVIN (REP-TX)
CLYBURN, JAMES E. (DEM-SC)
FARENTHOLD, RANDOLPH BLAKE (REP-TX)
GOODLATTE, ROBERT W. (REP-VA)
JORDAN, JAMES D. (REP-OH)
MCCAUL, MICHAEL (REP-TX)
PAULSEN, ERIK (REP-MN)
PELOSI, NANCY (DEM-CA)
ROSKAM, PETER (REP-IL)
ROYCE, ED MR. (REP-CA)
SENSENBRENNER, F. JAMES JR. (REP-WI)

Corporate Foundations and Giving Programs

Google Foundation
1600 Amphitheater Pkwy.
Mountain View, CA 94043
Tel: (650) 253-0000

Public Affairs and Related Activities Personnel

At Headquarters

BOCK, Laszlo
Senior Vice President, People Operations
Tel: (650) 253-0000
Fax: (650) 253-0001

DRUMMOND, David C.
Senior Vice President, Corporate Development and Chief Legal Officer
david.drummond@google.com
Tel: (650) 253-0000
Fax: (650) 253-0001

KORDESTANI, Omid
Senior Vice President and Chief Business Officer
Tel: (650) 253-0000
Fax: (650) 253-0001

TWOHILL, Lorraine
Senior Vice President, Global Marketing
Tel: (650) 253-0000
Fax: (650) 253-0001

WALKER, Kent
Senior Vice President and General Counsel
Tel: (650) 253-0000
Fax: (650) 253-0001

At Washington Office

ATKINSON, Caroline
Head of Global Public Policy
Tel: (202) 346-1100

BERNAL, Jennifer
Public Policy
Registered Federal Lobbyist
Tel: (202) 346-1100

BURCHETT, John
Director, Policy Counsel
Tel: (202) 346-1100

CANO, Mistique
Director, Policy & Public Affairs
Tel: (202) 346-1100

DEVRIES, Will
Privacy Counsel
Tel: (202) 346-1100

DUNN, Lee
Federal Lobbyist
Tel: (202) 346-1100

FISHER, Sarah
Federal Lobbyist
Tel: (202) 346-1100

JEFFRIES, E. Stewart
Policy Counsel
Registered Federal Lobbyist
Tel: (202) 346-1100

LADNER, Andrew
Federal Policy Analyst
Registered Federal Lobbyist
Tel: (202) 346-1100

LASALA, Frannie
Federal Lobbyist
Registered Federal Lobbyist
Tel: (202) 346-1100

LIEBER, David
Senior Privacy Policy Counsel
Registered Federal Lobbyist
Tel: (202) 346-1100

MOLINARI, Hon. Susan
Registered Federal Lobbyist
Tel: (202) 346-1100

OYAMA, Katie
Senior Policy Counsel
Tel: (202) 346-1100

PEARSON, Nick
Manager, Public Policy & Government Affairs
Registered Federal Lobbyist
Tel: (202) 346-1100

SAAR, Malika
Senior Counsel, Civil & Human Rights
Tel: (202) 346-1100

SHELTON, Johanna
PAC Treasurer and Federal Lobbyist
Tel: (202) 346-1100

SULLIVAN, John
Director
Registered Federal Lobbyist
Tel: (202) 346-1100

TAI, Robert
Policy Manager
Tel: (202) 346-1100

VALENCIA, Stephanie
Managers of Strategic Outreach & Partnerships
Tel: (202) 346-1100

WEBB, Seth
Senior Policy Manager
Registered Federal Lobbyist
Tel: (202) 346-1100

WELLINGS, Frannie
Senior Policy Manager
Registered Federal Lobbyist
Tel: (202) 346-1100

The Gorlin Group

A consulting firm providing strategic advice and analysis on intellectual property and international trade issues.
www.gorlingroup.com

President
GORLIN, Jacques J.
jgorlin@gorlingroup.com
Tel: (202) 973-2870
Fax: (202) 296-8407

Main Headquarters
Mailing: 2300 M St. NW
Suite 800
Washington, DC 20037
Tel: (202) 973-2870
Fax: (202) 296-8407

Goss International Corporation

Manufactures advanced press and post-press equipment for newspapers and commercial web printing companies.
www.gossinternational.com
Annual Revenues: $207.40 million
Employees: 2,000
Industry/ies: Communications; Media/Mass Communication; Printing Industry

President and Chief Executive Officer
NICHOLS, Richard
Tel: (603) 749-6600

Main Headquarters
Mailing: 121 Technology Dr.
Durham, NH 03824
Tel: (603) 749-6600

Government Consulting Solutions, Inc

A government consulting to advance client interests through the political process.
www.govconsulting.net

President, Government Consulting Solutions
STONE, Chris
cstone@govconsulting.net
Tel: (217) 528-9120
Fax: (217) 544-4026

Main Headquarters
Mailing: 420 W.Capitol Ave.
Suite One
Springfield, IL 62704
Tel: (217) 528-9120
Fax: (217) 544-4026

Public Affairs and Related Activities Personnel

At Headquarters

HANNEY, Jill		Tel:	(217) 528-9120
Administrative, Financial and Customer service Operations		Fax:	(217) 544-4026
RIEMER, Jim		Tel:	(217) 528-9120
Political consultant and Governmental Affairs		Fax:	(217) 544-4026
jriemer@govconsulting.net			
ZAHN, Steve		Tel:	(217) 528-9120
Exclusive Lobbyist		Fax:	(217) 544-4026
szahn@govconsulting.net			

Goya Foods, Inc

A wholesale food distributor.
www.goya.com
Annual Revenues: $1.70 billion
Employees: 3,500
SIC: 5141; 2033; 2035; 2037; 2099
Industry/ies: Food And Beverage Industry

Main Headquarters

Mailing:	350 County Rd.	Tel:	(201) 348-4900
	Jersey City, NJ 07307	Fax:	(201) 348-6609

Public Affairs and Related Activities Personnel

At Headquarters

LUGO, Miguel		Tel:	(201) 348-4900
Vice President, Finance		Fax:	(201) 348-6609
ORTIZ, Carlos		Tel:	(201) 348-4900
Vice President and General Counsel		Fax:	(201) 348-6609
carlos.ortiz@goya.com			
TORO, Rafael		Tel:	(201) 348-4900
Director, Public Relations		Fax:	(201) 348-6609
rafael.toro@goya.com			

Graco Children's Products Inc.

A juvenile products company.
www.gracobaby.com
Annual Revenues: $96 million
Employees: 1,400
Ticker: NASDAQ: GGG
SIC: 3944
Industry/ies: Children And Youth; Machinery/Equipment

Main Headquarters

Mailing:	4110 Premier Dr.	Tel:	(770) 418-7268
	High Point, NC 27265	TF:	(800) 345-4109

Public Affairs and Related Activities Personnel

At Headquarters

FIGUEREO, Juan R.	Tel:	(770) 418-7268
Chief Financial Officer		
MOWREY, Ashley Feldhaus	Tel:	(770) 418-7268
Public Relations and Consumer Engagement Manager		
Ashley.mowrey@newellco.com		

Graco Inc.

An international manufacturer and marketer of industrial fluid handling and spray finishing equipment and systems.
www.graco.com
Annual Revenues: $1.24 billion
Employees: 3,100
Ticker: NYSE: GGG
SIC: 3561
Industry/ies: Chemicals & Chemical Industry

President and Chief Executive Officer	Tel:	(612) 623-6000
MCHALE, Patrick J.	Fax:	(612) 378-3505

Main Headquarters

Mailing:	88 11th Ave. NE	Tel:	(612) 623-6000
	Minneapolis, MN 55413	Fax:	(612) 623-6777

Corporate Foundations and Giving Programs

The Graco Foundation		
Contact: Kristi Lee		
88 11th Ave. NE	Tel:	(612) 623-6684
Minneapolis, MN 55413		

Public Affairs and Related Activities Personnel

At Headquarters

AHLERS, David M.		Tel:	(612) 623-6000
Vice President, Human Resources and Corporate Communications		Fax:	(612) 378-3505
GALLIVAN, Karen Park		Tel:	(612) 623-6000
Vice President, General Counsel and Secretary		Fax:	(612) 623-6640
GRANER, James A.		Tel:	(612) 623-6635
Chief Financial Officer		Fax:	(612) 378-3505
jgraner@graco.com			
STEINKRAUS, Pamela		Tel:	(612) 623-6000

Coordinator, Investor Relations	Fax:	(612) 378-3505
psteinkraus@graco.com		

At Other Offices

LEE, Kristi		Tel:	(605) 333-6767
Manager, Community Relations & Human Resources		Fax:	(612) 623-6777
P.O. Box 1441			
Sioux Falls, SD 55440-1441			

Graham Holdings Company

See listing on page 844 under The Washington Post Company

Grainger

A distributor of maintenance, repair, and operating supplies and related information to the commercial, industrial, contractor and institutional markets in North America.
www.grainger.com
Annual Revenues: $10.02 billion
Employees: 22,300
Ticker: NYSE: GWW
SIC: 5000
Industry/ies: Automotive Industry; Machinery/Equipment; Transportation

Chairman of the Board, President and Chief Executive Officer	Tel:	(847) 535-1000
RYAN, James T.	Fax:	(847) 535-0878

Main Headquarters

Mailing:	100 Grainger Pkwy.	Tel:	(847) 535-1000
	Lake Forest, IL 60045-5201	Fax:	(847) 535-0878
		TF:	(888) 361-8649

Corporate Foundations and Giving Programs

Grainger Contribution Programs
100 Grainger Pkwy.
Lake Forest, IL 60045-5201

Public Affairs and Related Activities Personnel

At Headquarters

BROWN, Laura D.		Tel:	(847) 535-0065
Senior Vice President, Communications and Investor Relations		Fax:	(847) 535-0878
CHAPMAN, William D.		Tel:	(847) 535-0881
Senior Director, Investor Relations		Fax:	(847) 535-0878
william.chapman@grainger.com			
GRANACK, Sara		Tel:	(847) 535-8089
Senior Director, Global Communications		Fax:	(847) 535-0878
sara.granack@grainger.com			
HIGH, Joseph C.		Tel:	(847) 535-1000
Senior Vice President and Chief People Officer		Fax:	(847) 535-0878
HOWARD, John L.		Tel:	(847) 535-1000
Senior Vice President and General Counsel		Fax:	(847) 535-0878
JADIN, Ronald L.		Tel:	(847) 535-1000
Senior Vice President and Chief Financial Officer		Fax:	(847) 535-0878
MICUCCI, Joe		Tel:	(847) 535-5678
Director, Media Relations		Fax:	(847) 535-0878
joe.micucci@grainger.com			
MULVIHILL, Maureen J.		Tel:	(847) 535-9011
Manager, Community Affairs		Fax:	(847) 535-0878
maureen.mulvihill@grainger.com			
MURREN, Katelyn		Tel:	(847) 535-1000
Specialist, Media Relations		Fax:	(847) 535-0878
katelyn.murren@grainger.com			

Grange Insurance

See listing on page 372 under Grange Mutual Casualty Company

Grange Mutual Casualty Company

Provides auto, home, life and business insurance protection to grangers and others.
www.grangeinsurance.com
Annual Revenues: $65.20 million
Employees: 1,500
Industry/ies: Insurance Industry

Main Headquarters

Mailing:	650 S. Front St.	Tel:	(614) 445-2900
	Columbus, OH 43206	Fax:	(614) 445-2337
		TF:	(800) 422-0550

Political Action Committees

Grange Mutual Casualty Company PAC
FEC ID: C00302695
Contact: Andrea Ensign
671 S. High St.
Columbus, OH 43216

Contributions to Candidates: $20,200 (2015-2016)
Democrats: $3,000; Republicans: $17,200

Public Affairs and Related Activities Personnel

At Headquarters

DRAKE, Carol L.
Vice President, National Accounts
Tel: (614) 445-2900
Fax: (614) 445-2337

MCCAFFREY, Jr., J. Paul
Vice President, Chief Financial Officer and Treasurer
Tel: (614) 445-2900
Fax: (614) 445-2337

At Other Offices

ENSIGN, Andrea
PAC Contact
P.O. Box 1218, 671 S. High St.
Columbus, OH 43216

VAN VLERAH, Andrea B.
PAC Treasurer
P.O. Box 1218, 671 S. High St.
Columbus, OH 43216

Granite Construction Company

A heavy construction company. Builds roads, dams, bridges and other infrastructure related projects.
www.graniteconstruction.com
Annual Revenues: $2.32 billion
Employees: 1,700
Ticker: NYSE: GVA
SIC: 1600
Industry/ies: Construction/Construction Materials

President and Chief Executive Officer
ROBERTS, James H.
Tel: (831) 724-1011
Fax: (831) 722-9657

Main Headquarters
Mailing: 585 W. Beach St.
Watsonville, CA 95076
Tel: (831) 724-1011
Fax: (831) 722-9657

Political Action Committees
Granite Construction Inc. Employee PAC - GRANITEPAC
FEC ID: C00337394
Contact: Cindy Walker
555 Capitol Mall
Suite 1425
Sacramento, CA 95814

   Contributions to Candidates: $5,000 (2015-2016)
   Democrats: $1,000; Republicans: $4,000

Corporate Foundations and Giving Programs

Granite Construction Inc., Contributions Program
585 W. Beach St.
Watsonville, CA 95076
Tel: (831) 724-1011
Fax: (831) 722-9657

Public Affairs and Related Activities Personnel

At Headquarters

BOTOFF, Ronald E.
Director of Investor Relations
Ronald.Botoff@gcinc.com
Tel: (831) 728-7532
Fax: (831) 722-9657

DECOCCO, Philip
Senior Vice President, Human Resources
Tel: (831) 724-1011
Fax: (831) 722-9657

DESAI, Jigisha
Vice President, Treasurer and Assistant Financial Officer
Tel: (831) 724-1011
Fax: (831) 722-9657

FOURCHY, Jacqueline B.
Vice President, Investor Relations and Corporate Communications
jacque.fourchy@gcinc.com
Tel: (831) 724-1011
Fax: (831) 722-9657

GRAHAM, Bradley G.
Vice President, Controller and Assistant Financial Officer
Tel: (831) 724-1011
Fax: (831) 722-9657

KRZEMINSKI, Laurel J.
Senior Vice President and Chief Financial Officer
Tel: (831) 724-1011
Fax: (831) 722-9657

MARSHALL, Kent H.
Vice President and Director, Business Development
Tel: (831) 724-1011
Fax: (831) 722-9657

MILLER, Christopher S.
Executive Vice President and Chief Operating Officer
Tel: (831) 724-1011
Fax: (831) 722-9657

POWELL, William H.
Director
Tel: (831) 724-1011
Fax: (831) 722-9657

WATTS, Richard A.
Senior Vice President, General Counsel, Corporate Compliance Officer and Secretary
Tel: (831) 724-1011
Fax: (831) 722-9657

At Other Offices

WALKER, Cindy
PAC Treasurer
555 Capitol Mall, Suite 1425
Sacramento, CA 95814

Grant Thornton

An accounting, audit, tax, and business advisory services provider working with a broad range of publicly and privately held companies, government agencies, financial institutions, and civic and religious organizations. It is the American member firm of Grant Thornton International.
www.grantthornton.com
Annual Revenues: $5.6 billion
Employees: 6,456

Industry/ies: Accounting; Banking/Finance/Investments
Legislative Issues: GOV; TAX

Chief Executive Officer
MCGUIRE, J. Michael (Mike)
Tel: (312) 856-0200
Fax: (312) 602-8099

Main Headquarters
Mailing: 175 W. Jackson Blvd.
20th Floor
Chicago, IL 60604-2687
Tel: (312) 856-0200
Fax: (312) 602-8099

Washington Office
Mailing: 1250 Connecticut Ave. NW
Suite 400
Washington, DC 20036
Tel: (202) 296-7800

Political Action Committees
Grant Thornton LLP
FEC ID: C00408260
Contact: Trent Gazzaway
171 N. Clark St.
Suite 200
Chicago, IL 60601
Tel: (312) 856-0200
Fax: (312) 602-8099

   Contributions to Candidates: $388,000 (2015-2016)
   Democrats: $142,500; Republicans: $243,000; Other: $2,500

   Principal Recipients

   HOUSE
   HUDSON, RICHARD L. JR. (REP-NC)
   MEEHAN, PATRICK L. MR. (REP-PA)
   REED, THOMAS W II (REP-NY)
   RENACCI, JAMES B. (REP-OH)

Public Affairs and Related Activities Personnel

At Headquarters

BUGARIS, Kristen
External Communications Leader
kristen.bugaris@us.gt.com
Tel: (312) 602-8277
Fax: (312) 602-8099

CUNNINGHAM , Ken
Chief Legal Officer
ken.cunningham@gt.com
Tel: (312) 856-0200
Fax: (312) 602-8099

GAZZAWAY, Trent
National Managing Partner of Professional Standards
trent.gazzaway@gt.com
Tel: (312) 856-0200
Fax: (312) 602-8099

HARLESS, Pamela
Chief People & Culture Officer
Tel: (312) 856-0200
Fax: (312) 602-8099

WIEMAN, Russ
Chief Financial Officer
Tel: (248) 213-4200
Fax: (312) 602-8099

At Washington Office

BRADY, Patrick
Central Region Managing Partner
Tel: (202) 296-7800

BROFFMAN, Marjorie
Associate
mbroffman@gmail.com
Tel: (202) 296-7800

HAMRICK, Mary Moore
National Managing Principal, Public Policy
MaryMoore.Hamrick@us.gt.com
Tel: (202) 296-7800

MURRAY, Fred
Managing Director, Tax Practice Policy and Quality Group
fred.murray@gt.com
Tel: (202) 296-7800

SCHWARZ, Melvin
Federal Lobbyist
Registered Federal Lobbyist
Tel: (202) 296-7800

At Other Offices

MALINCONICO, Kristen
Director, Public Policy and Governmental Affairs
333 John Carlyle St., Suite 500
Alexandria, VA 22314
kristen.malinconico@us.gt.com
Registered Federal Lobbyist
Tel: (202) 521-1521
Fax: (202) 833-9165

Graphic Packaging International

A provider of paperboard packaging solutions for a wide variety of products to multinational and other consumer products companies.
www.graphicpkg.com
Annual Revenues: $4.18 billion
Employees: 11,500
Ticker: NYSE: GPK
SIC: 2631
Industry/ies: Food And Beverage Industry; Machinery/Equipment; Paper And Wood Products Industry
Legislative Issues: ENG; ENV; TAX

Chairman of the Board, President and Chief Executive Officer
SCHEIBLE, David W
Tel: (770) 644-3000
Fax: (770) 644-2070

Main Headquarters

Mailing:	814 Livingston Ct. Marietta, GA 30067	Tel: (770) 644-3000 Fax: (770) 644-2970 TF: (800) 793-2571

Political Action Committees
Graphic Packaging International Inc. PAC
FEC ID: C00282566
Contact: Andrew Johnson
1500 Riveredge Parkway   Tel: (770) 644-3000
Suite 100   Fax: (770) 644-2962
Atlanta, GA 30328

> **Contributions to Candidates:** $22,000 (2015-2016)
> Democrats: $11,000; Republicans: $11,000

Public Affairs and Related Activities Personnel
At Headquarters

ANKERHOLZ, Brad   Tel: (770) 240-7971
Contact, Investor Relations   Fax: (770) 644-2970

CHANEY, Carla J.   Tel: (770) 644-3000
Senior Vice President, Human Resources   Fax: (770) 644-2970

DOSS, Michael P.   Tel: (770) 644-3000
Chief Operating Officer   Fax: (770) 644-2970

JOHNSON, Andy   Tel: (770) 644-3000
Vice President, Government Affairs & Sustainability   Fax: (770) 644-2970

TASHMA, Lauren S.   Tel: (770) 644-3000
Senior VicePresident, General Counsel and Secretary   Fax: (770) 644-2970

At Other Offices

JOHNSON, Andrew
PAC Treasurer
1500 Riveredge Pkwy., Suite 100
Atlanta, GA 30328

SCHERGER, Stephen R
Senior Vice President and Chief Financial Officer
1500 Riveredge Pkwy., Suite 100
Atlanta, GA 30328

Gray Communications Inc.
A television broadcast company.
www.graycommunicationsinc.com
Industry/ies: Communications; Media/Mass Communication

President   Tel: (312) 212-2000
GRAY, Anthony
gary@graycommunicationsinc.com

Main Headquarters
Mailing: 619 S. LaSalle St.   Tel: (312) 212-2000
Suite 101B
Chicago, IL 60605

Graybar Services, Inc.
A wholesale distribution business.
www.graybar.com
SIC: 5063
Industry/ies: Electricity & Electronics; Electronics; Energy/Electricity

Chairman of the Board, President and Chief Executive Officer   Tel: (314) 573-9200
MAZZARELLA, Kathleen M.   Fax: (314) 573-9455

Main Headquarters
Mailing: 34 N. Meramec Ave.   Tel: (314) 573-9200
St. Louis, MO 63105   Fax: (314) 573-9455

Corporate Foundations and Giving Programs
Graybar Foundation
34 N. Meramac Ave.   Tel: (314) 573-9200
St. Louis, MO 63105

Public Affairs and Related Activities Personnel
At Headquarters

GEEKIE, Matthew W.   Tel: (314) 573-9200
Senior Vice President, Secretary and General Counsel   Fax: (314) 573-9455

HARWOOD, Randall R.   Tel: (314) 573-9200
Senior Vice President and Chief Financial Officer   Fax: (314) 573-9455

MANSFIELD, William P.   Tel: (314) 573-9200
Senior Vice President, Sales and Marketing   Fax: (314) 573-9455

PROPST, Beverly L.   Tel: (314) 573-9200
Senior Vice President, Human Resources   Fax: (314) 573-9455

SOMMER, Tim   Tel: (314) 573-5700
Manager, Corporate Communications   Fax: (314) 573-9455
timothy.sommer@graybar.com

Great American Insurance Company
A subsidiary of American Financial Group (AFG).
www.greatamericaninsurancegroup.com
Annual Revenues: $3.60 billion

Employees: 800
SIC: 6411
Industry/ies: Insurance Industry

Co-Chief Executive Officer and Co-President and Director   Tel: (513) 369-5000
LINDNER, III, Carl H.

Main Headquarters
Mailing: 301 E. Fourth St.   Tel: (513) 369-5000
Cincinnati, OH 45202   TF: (800) 545-4269

Public Affairs and Related Activities Personnel
At Headquarters

CONSOLINO, Joseph E. (Jeff)   Tel: (513) 369-5000
Executive Vice President and Chief Financial Officer

The Great Atlantic and Pacific Tea Company
A supermarket chain retailer.
aptea.com
Annual Revenues: $8.07 billion
Employees: 39,000
SIC: 5411
Industry/ies: Food And Beverage Industry; Retail/Wholesale

Chairman of the Board   Tel: (201) 573-9700
MAYS, Greg   Fax: (201) 505-3054

President and Chief Executive Officer   Tel: (201) 573-9700
HERTZ, Paul   Fax: (201) 505-3054

Main Headquarters
Mailing: Two Paragon Dr.   Tel: (201) 573-9700
Montvale, NJ 07645   Fax: (201) 505-3054
  TF: (866) 443-7374

Corporate Foundations and Giving Programs
A&P Foundation
Two Paragon Dr.   Tel: (201) 573-9700
Montvale, NJ 07645   Fax: (201) 573-9700

Public Affairs and Related Activities Personnel
At Headquarters

KRISHNAMURTHY, Nirup   Tel: (201) 573-9700
Chief Strategy Officer   Fax: (201) 505-3054

LACK, Krystyna   Tel: (201) 571-4320
Vice President, Treasury Services   Fax: (201) 505-3054

Great Plains Energy
An electric utility. Subsidiaries include Kansas City Power and Light Co. and KLT Inc.
www.greatplainsenergy.com
Annual Revenues: $2.53 billion
Employees: 2,935
Ticker: NYSE: GXP
SIC: 4911
Industry/ies: Energy/Electricity; Utilities
Legislative Issues: BUD; ENG; UTI

Chairman of the Board, President and Chief Executive Officer   Tel: (816) 556-2200
BASSHAM, Terry   Fax: (816) 556-2992

Main Headquarters
Mailing: 1200 Main St.   Tel: (816) 556-2200
P.O. Box 418679   Fax: (816) 556-2992
Kansas City, MO 64105   TF: (800) 245-5275

Washington Office
Mailing: 818 Connecticut Ave. NW
Suite 1100
Washington, DC 20006

Political Action Committees
KCPL Power PAC - Federal
FEC ID: C00111310
Contact: Paul Schmiege
P.O. Box 418679
Kansas City, MO 64141

> **Contributions to Candidates:** $25,500 (2015-2016)
> Democrats: $1,000; Republicans: $22,000; Other: $2,500

Corporate Foundations and Giving Programs
Great Plains Energy Contributions Program
P.O. Box 418679
1200 Main St.
Kansas City, MO 64141-9679

Public Affairs and Related Activities Personnel
At Headquarters

BRYANT, Kevin   Tel: (816) 556-2782
Vice President, Strategic Planning   Fax: (816) 556-2418
kevin.bryant@kcpl.com

BUSSER, Steven   Tel: (816) 556-2200
Vice President, Business Planning and Controller   Fax: (816) 556-2992

CAISLEY, Chuck	Tel:	(816) 556-2200
Vice President, Marketing and Public Affairs	Fax:	(816) 556-2992
DEGGENDORF, Michael	Tel:	(816) 556-2200
Senior Vice President, Corporate Services	Fax:	(816) 556-2992
Registered Federal Lobbyist		
FAIRCHILD, Ellen	Tel:	(816) 556-2083
Vice President, Corporate Secretary and Chief Compliance	Fax:	(816) 556-2992
Officer		
ellen.fairchild@kcpl.com		
HEIDTBRINK, Scott	Tel:	(816) 556-2200
Executive Vice President and Chief Operating Officer	Fax:	(816) 556-2992
HOOVER , Cara	Tel:	(816) 556-2200
Registered Federal Lobbyist	Fax:	(816) 556-2992
HUMPHREY, Heather	Tel:	(816) 556-2200
Senior Vice President, Human Resources and General	Fax:	(816) 556-2992
Counsel		
IVES, Darrin	Tel:	(816) 556-2200
Vice President, Regulatory Affairs	Fax:	(816) 556-2992
MCDONALD, Katie	Tel:	(816) 556-2365
Director, Corporate Communications	Fax:	(816) 556-2992
katie.mcdonald@kcpl.com		
POLING, Michael A.	Tel:	(202) 824-4546
Federal Government Affairs	Fax:	(816) 556-2992
mike.poling@kcpl.com		
Registered Federal Lobbyist		
SCHMIEGE, Paul	Tel:	(816) 556-2200
PAC Treasurer	Fax:	(816) 556-2992
SHAY, Jim	Tel:	(816) 556-2200
Senior Vice President, Finance and Strategic Planning and	Fax:	(816) 556-2992
Chief Financial Officer		
WRIGHT, Lori	Tel:	(816) 556-2200
Vice President , Investor Relations and Treasurer	Fax:	(816) 556-2992

At Washington Office

HAUER, James
PAC Contact

Great River Energy

An electric utility cooperative. It is a member-owned cooperative which supplies electricity in Minnesota.
www.greatriverenergy.com
Annual Revenues: $1020.2 million
Employees: 880
Industry/ies: Energy/Electricity

Chairman of the Board	Tel:	(763) 445-5000
HOLL, Donald	Fax:	(763) 445-5050
President and Chief Executive Officer	Tel:	(763) 445-5000
SAGGAU, David	Fax:	(763) 445-5050

Main Headquarters

Mailing:	12300 Elm Creek Blvd.	Tel:	(763) 445-5000
	Maple Grove, MN 55369-4718	Fax:	(763) 445-5050

Political Action Committees

Great River Energy Action Team (GREAT) PAC
FEC ID: C00352674
Contact: Robert P. Ambrose
15803 Holdridge Rd.
Wayzata, MN 55391

   Contributions to Candidates: $2,000 (2015-2016)
   Republicans: $2,000

Corporate Foundations and Giving Programs

Great River Energy Contributions Program		
12300 Elm Creek Blvd.	Tel:	(763) 445-5000
Maple Grove, MN 55369-4718	Fax:	(763) 445-5050

Public Affairs and Related Activities Personnel

At Headquarters

AMBROSE, Robert P.	Tel:	(763) 445-5216
Director, Governmental Affairs and PAC Treasurer	Fax:	(763) 445-5050
ANDERSON, Lyndon	Tel:	(701) 442-7036
Supervisor, North Dakota Communications	Fax:	(763) 445-5050
landerson1@grenergy.com		
BECCHETTI, Daniel	Tel:	(763) 445-5706
Communications Specialist	Fax:	(763) 445-5050
LACANNE, Therese	Tel:	(763) 445-5710
Manager, Corporate Communications	Fax:	(763) 445-5050
tlacanne@grenergy.com		
OLSEN, Eric T.	Tel:	(763) 445-5201
Vice President and General Counsel	Fax:	(763) 445-5050
eolsen@grenergy.com		
OLSEN, Kandance	Tel:	(763) 241-2293
Vice President, Communications and Human Resources	Fax:	(763) 445-5050

kolsen@grenergy.com		
SCHMID, Larry	Tel:	(763) 445-5000
Vice President and Chief Financial Officer	Fax:	(763) 445-5050

Great Southern Savings Bank

Bank offering checking and savings accounts.
www.greatsouthernbank.com
Annual Revenues: $202.31 million
Employees: 951
Ticker: NASDAQ: GSBC
Industry/ies: Banking/Finance/Investments

Chairman of the Board	Tel:	(417) 887-4400
TURNER, William V.		
President and Chief Executive Officer	Tel:	(417) 887-4400
TURNER, Joseph W.		

Main Headquarters

Mailing:	1451 E. Battlefield Rd.	Tel:	(417) 887-4400
	Springfield, MO 65804	TF:	(800) 749-7113

Political Action Committees

Great Southern Bank Employees Good Government Committee PAC
FEC ID: C00224147
Contact: Lindsey Teresa Hutchison
1451 E. Battlefield
Springfield, MO 65804

   Contributions to Candidates: $1,000 (2015-2016)
   Democrats: $1,000

Corporate Foundations and Giving Programs

Great Southern Caring and Sharing		
P. O. Box 9009	Tel:	(417) 887-4400
Springfield, MO 65808		

Public Affairs and Related Activities Personnel

At Headquarters

COPELAND, Rex A.	Tel:	(417) 887-4400
Senior Vice President and Chief Financial Officer		
FARRIS, Stacie Jo	Tel:	(417) 887-4400
Training Manager		
MARRS, Doug	Tel:	(417) 887-4400
Director, Operations		
POLONUS, Kelly	Tel:	(417) 895-5242
VicePresident, Director, Corporate Communications		
kpolonus@greatsouthernbank.com		
SNYDER, Matt	Tel:	(417) 887-4400
Director, Human Resources		
MSnyder@greatsouthernbank.com		
TERESA HUTCHISON , Lindsey	Tel:	(417) 887-4400
PAC Treaurer		

Great Wolf Resorts

Owns and operates a handful of resorts under the Great Wolf Lodge name.
corp.greatwolfresorts.com
Annual Revenues: $296.71 million
Employees: 4,600
Ticker: NASDAQ: WOLF
SIC: 7011
Industry/ies: Sports/Leisure/Entertainment; Travel/Tourism/Lodging

Chief Executive Officer	Tel:	(608) 662-4700
SCHAEFER, Kimberly K.	Fax:	(608) 662-4281
kschaefer@greatwolf.com		

Main Headquarters

Mailing:	525 Junction Rd.	Tel:	(608) 662-4700
	Suite 6000 S. Tower	Fax:	(608) 662-4701
	Madison, WI 53717		

Public Affairs and Related Activities Personnel

At Headquarters

BLACK , Timothy	Tel:	(608) 662-4700
Chief Operating Officer	Fax:	(608) 662-4701
CASTELLINO, Rajiv W.	Tel:	(608) 662-4700
Chief Information Officer	Fax:	(608) 662-4701
COHEN, Brad	Tel:	(203) 682-8211
Contact, Investor Relations	Fax:	(608) 662-4281
Brad.Cohen@icrinc.com		
DONOFRIO, Nikki	Tel:	(608) 662-4700
Senior Vice President, Strategic Brand Marketing	Fax:	(608) 662-4701
GENIN, Alan	Tel:	(608) 662-4700
Vice President, Revenue Management	Fax:	(608) 662-4701
LOMBARDO, Alex	Tel:	(608) 662-4700
Senior Vice President, Development	Fax:	(608) 662-4281
alombardo@greatwolf.com		

SHATTUCK, Steve
Corporate Director, Communications
sshattuck@greatwolf.com
Tel: (608) 662-4700
Fax: (608) 662-4281

STOKES, Julie
Senior Vice President, Sales
jstokes@greatwolf.com
Tel: (608) 662-4700
Fax: (608) 662-4281

Greatpoint Energy

A technology-driven natural resources company and the developer of a proprietary, highly-efficient catalytic process, known as hydromethanation, by which coal, petroleum coke and biomass are converted directly into low-cost, clean, pipeline quality natural gas, while allowing for the capture and sequestration of carbon dioxide ($CO2$).
www.greatpointenergy.com
Annual Revenues: $14 million
Employees: 100
Industry/ies: Energy/Electricity

Co-Founder and Chief Executive Officer
PERLMAN, Andrew
Tel: (617) 500-2676
Fax: (617) 500-2676

Main Headquarters
Mailing: 101 Main St.
14th Floor
Cambridge, MA 02142
Tel: (617) 500-2676
Fax: (617) 500-2676

Public Affairs and Related Activities Personnel

At Headquarters
GOLDMAN, Daniel P.
President and Chief Financial Officer
dgoldman@greatpointenergy.com
Tel: (617) 500-2676
Fax: (617) 500-2676

At Other Offices
RICHARD, David Gerzof
Contact, Media Inquiries
2215 W. Harrison St.
Chicago, IL 60612
dgerzof@greatpointenergy.com
Tel: (312) 564-4684

Green Bay Packaging, Inc.

A paperboard packaging manufacturer.
www.gbp.com
Employees: 2,900
SIC: 2672
Industry/ies: Paper And Wood Products Industry

Director, Emeritus
KRESS, James
Tel: (920) 433-5111
Fax: (920) 433-5471

Senior Vice President
BAEMMERT, Joseph
Tel: (920) 433-5111
Fax: (920) 433-5471

Main Headquarters
Mailing: 1700 N. Webster Ct.
P.O. Box 19017
Green Bay, WI 54307-9017
Tel: (920) 433-5111
Fax: (920) 433-5471
TF: (800) 236-8400

Corporate Foundations and Giving Programs
George Kress Foundation
Contact: John Kress
1700 N. Webster Ct.
Green Bay, WI 54307
Tel: (920) 433-5111

Public Affairs and Related Activities Personnel

At Headquarters
BAHDE, Rachel C.
Environmental Communications Associate
rbahde@gbp.com
Tel: (920) 433-5132
Fax: (920) 433-5471

KRESS, John
Secretary, George Kress Foundation
Tel: (920) 433-5111
Fax: (920) 433-5471

Green Earth Fuels, LLC

Biodiesel refining company.
www.greenearthfuelsllc.com
Employees: 33
Industry/ies: Energy/Electricity; Environment And Conservation; Fuels See Coal, Gas, Oil, Petroleum; Natural Resources; Petroleum Industry

President and Chief Executive Officer
BEIRNE, Martin D.
Tel: (713) 237-2800
Fax: (713) 237-2808

Main Headquarters
Mailing: 550 Clinton Dr.
Galena Park, TX 77547
Tel: (713) 237-2800
Fax: (713) 237-2808

Public Affairs and Related Activities Personnel

At Headquarters
GRANDA, Steve
Chief Financial Officer
Tel: (713) 237-2800
Fax: (713) 237-2808

The Greenbrier Companies

A manufacturer of railroad equipment.
www.gbrx.com
Annual Revenues: $2.34 billion
Employees: 9,244
Ticker: NYSE: GBX
SIC: 3743
Industry/ies: Railroads; Transportation
Legislative Issues: RRR; TAX; TRA; TRD

Chairman
WHITELEY, Benjamin R.
Tel: (503) 684-7000
Fax: (503) 684-7553

Chairman, Board, President and Chief Executive Officer
FURMAN, Bill A.
bill.furman@gbrx.com
Tel: (503) 684-7000
Fax: (503) 684-7553

Main Headquarters
Mailing: One Centerpoint Dr.
Suite 200
Lake Oswego, OR 97035
Tel: (503) 684-7000
Fax: (503) 684-7553
TF: (800) 343-7188

Corporate Foundations and Giving Programs
Greenbrier Companies Contributions Program
One Centerpoint Dr.
Suite 200
Lake Oswego, OR 97035

Public Affairs and Related Activities Personnel

At Headquarters
BAKER, Martin R.
Senior Vice President, Chief Compliance Officer and General Counsel
martin.baker@gbrx.com
Tel: (503) 684-7000
Fax: (503) 684-7553

CORBETT, Sherrill A.
Corporate Secretary
Tel: (503) 684-7000
Fax: (503) 684-7553

DOWNES, Adrian J.
Senior Vice President, Chief Accounting Officer
Tel: (503) 684-7000
Fax: (503) 684-7553

GLENN, William A.
Senior Vice President, Chief Commercial Officer
william.glenn@gbrx.com
Tel: (503) 684-7000
Fax: (503) 684-7553

HANNAN, Walter T.
Senior Vice President, Chief Human Resources Officer
Tel: (503) 684-7000
Fax: (503) 684-7553

MALIK, Maren J.
Vice President, Administration
Tel: (503) 684-7000
Fax: (503) 684-7553

MANNING, Anne T.
Vice President, Corporate Controller
Tel: (503) 684-7000
Fax: (503) 684-7553

RITTENBAUM, Mark J.
Executive Vice President and Chief Financial Officer
investor.relations@gbrx.com
Tel: (503) 684-7000
Fax: (503) 684-7553

TEKORIUS, Lorie L.
Senior Vice President, Corporate Finance and Treasurer
Tel: (503) 684-7000
Fax: (503) 684-7553

TURNER, Rick M.
Senior Vice President, Wheels and Strategic Execution
Tel: (503) 684-7000
Fax: (503) 684-7553

GreenHunter Energy, Inc.

Assembles and manages a portfolio of renewable energy assets and clean fuels assets.
www.greenhunterenergy.com
Annual Revenues: $23.79 million
Employees: 114
Ticker: NYSE: GRH
SIC: 2860
Industry/ies: Energy/Electricity; Fuels See Coal, Gas, Oil, Petroleum; Natural Resources; Petroleum Industry

Founder, Chairman, and Interim Chief Executive Officer
EVANS, Gary C.
Tel: (972) 410-1044
Fax: (972) 410-1066

Main Headquarters
Mailing: 28407 State Route 7
Marietta, TX 45750
Tel: (972) 410-1044
Fax: (972) 410-1066

Public Affairs and Related Activities Personnel

At Headquarters
JOHNSTON, Morgan F.
Senior Vice President, General Counsel and Secretary
Tel: (972) 410-1044
Fax: (972) 410-1066

MCCLUNG, Ronald
Senior Vice President and Chief Financial Officer
Tel: (972) 410-1044
Fax: (972) 410-1066

PAGEN , Melissa
Vice President, Business Development
Tel: (972) 410-1044
Fax: (972) 410-1066

SLOAN, Robert
Senior Vice President, Operations
Tel: (972) 410-1044
Fax: (972) 410-1066

TROSCLAIR, Kirk J.
Executive Vice President and Chief Operating Officer
Tel: (972) 410-1044
Fax: (972) 410-1066

Greif, Inc.

Manufacturer of shipping and corrugated containers.
www.greif.com
Annual Revenues: $3.99 billion

Employees: 13,325
Ticker: NYSE: GEF
SIC: 2650
NAICS: 322224
Industry/ies: Metals; Packaging

Chairman of the Board
GASSER, Michael J.
michael.gasser@grief.com

Tel: (740) 549-6000
Fax: (740) 549-6100

President and Chief Executive Officer
FISCHER, David B.

Tel: (740) 549-6000
Fax: (740) 549-6100

Main Headquarters
Mailing: 425 Winter Rd.
            Delaware, OH 43015

Tel: (740) 549-6000
Fax: (740) 549-6100

Corporate Foundations and Giving Programs

Greif Contributions Program
Contact: Debra Strohmaier
425 Winter Rd.
Delaware, OH 43015

Tel: (740) 549-6000
Fax: (740) 549-6100

Public Affairs and Related Activities Personnel

At Headquarters

HILSHEIMER, Larry A.
Executive Vice President and Chief Financial Officer

Tel: (740) 549-6000
Fax: (740) 549-6100

LANE, Karen P.
Senior Vice President, People Services and Talent Development

Tel: (740) 549-6000
Fax: (740) 549-6100

LENTZ, Robert A.
Contact, Investor Relations

Tel: (614) 876-2000
Fax: (740) 549-6100

MARTZ, Gary R.
Executive Vice President and General Counsel

Tel: (740) 549-6000
Fax: (740) 549-6100

WATSON, Peter G.
Chief Operating Officer

Tel: (740) 549-6000
Fax: (740) 549-6100

Gresham Consulting Group LLC

A Other Management Consulting Services company located in Augusta.
greshamconsulting.com

Main Headquarters
Mailing: 25 Skunk Hollow Rd.
            Chalfont, PA 18914

Tel: (215) 997-0645

Public Affairs and Related Activities Personnel

At Headquarters

GRILES, J. Steven
Partner
Registered Federal Lobbyist

Tel: (215) 997-0645

WOOLDRIDGE, Sue Ellen
Managing Member
Registered Federal Lobbyist

Tel: (215) 997-0645

Grey Global Group Inc.

An advertising company.
www.grey.com
Annual Revenues: $594.4 million
Employees: 10,000
SIC: 7311
Industry/ies: Advertising And Marketing

Chairman of the Board and Chief Executive Officer
HEEKIN, III, James R.

Tel: (212) 546-2021
Fax: (212) 546-2001

Main Headquarters
Mailing: 200 Fifth Ave.
            New York City, NY 10010

Tel: (212) 546-2000
Fax: (212) 546-2001

Public Affairs and Related Activities Personnel

At Headquarters

DOUGHERTY, Owen
Executive Vice President and Chief Communications Officer
odougherty@grey.com

Tel: (212) 546-2551
Fax: (212) 546-2001

ESPOSITO, Chris
Chief Financial Officer

Tel: (212) 546-2000
Fax: (212) 546-2001

NAIR, Suresh
Director, Global Strategic Planning
snair@grey.com

Tel: (212) 546-2020
Fax: (212) 546-2001

REISS, Jane
Chief Marketing Officer

Tel: (212) 546-2000
Fax: (212) 546-2001

Greyhound Lines

A commercial bus line and intercity bus transportation services company.
www.greyhound.com
Employees: 100
SIC: 4141; 4142; 4173; 4100
NAICS: 488490; 485510

Industry/ies: Transportation
Legislative Issues: TRA

President and Chief Executive Officer
LEACH, Dave

Tel: (214) 849-8000
Fax: (972) 789-7234

Main Headquarters
Mailing: P.O. Box 660362
            MS 470
            Dallas, TX 75266-0691

Tel: (214) 849-8000
Fax: (972) 387-1874
TF: (800) 268-9000

Washington Office
Mailing: 1920 L St. NW
            Suite 525
            Washington, DC 20036

Political Action Committees
Greyhound Lines PAC
FEC ID: C00215129
Contact: William J. Gieseker
350 N. St. Paul St.
Dallas, TX 75201

Tel: (214) 849-8000

Contributions to Candidates: $12,000 (2015-2016)
Democrats: $2,500; Republicans: $9,500

Corporate Foundations and Giving Programs
Greyhound Lines Contributions Program
P.O. Box 660362
Dallas, TX 75266

Tel: (214) 849-8000

Public Affairs and Related Activities Personnel

At Headquarters

BLANKENSHIP, Bill
Chief Operating Officer

Tel: (214) 849-8000
Fax: (972) 387-1874

BOULT, Chris
Chief Information Officer

Tel: (214) 849-8000
Fax: (972) 387-1874

BURK, Ted F.
Senior Vice President, Corporate Development

Tel: (214) 849-8000
Fax: (972) 387-1874

KAPLINSKY, Andrew
Chief Financial Officer

Tel: (214) 849-8000
Fax: (972) 387-1874

MACANDREW, Rhonda Piar
Senior Vice President, Human Resources

Tel: (214) 849-8000
Fax: (972) 387-1874

At Other Offices

GIESEKER, William J.
Controller and PAC Treasurer
350 N. St. Paul St.
Dallas, TX 75201

Gridpoint

Builds energy management appliances to improve power reliability. It provides comprehensive, data-driven energy management solutions (EMS) that leverage the power of real-time data collection, big data analytics and cloud computing to maximize energy savings, operational efficiency, capital utilization and sustainability benefits.
www.gridpoint.com
Annual Revenues: $31.70 million
Employees: 400
Industry/ies: Energy/Electricity

Chairman and founder
CORSELL, Peter L.

Tel: (703) 667-7000
Fax: (703) 667-7001

President and Chief Executive Officer
RABA, Todd M.

Tel: (703) 667-7000
Fax: (703) 667-7001

Main Headquarters
Mailing: 2801 Clarendon Blvd.
            Suite 100
            Arlington, VA 22201

Tel: (703) 667-7000
Fax: (703) 667-7001
TF: (888) 998-4743

Public Affairs and Related Activities Personnel

At Headquarters

CHINNICI, Joseph R.
Executive Vice President and Chief Financial Officer

Tel: (703) 667-7000
Fax: (703) 667-7001

CURRAN, Denis A.
Executive Vice President and General Counsel

Tel: (703) 667-7000
Fax: (703) 667-7001

DANZENBAKE, Mark A.
Senior Vice President, Sales, Marketing and Product

Tel: (703) 667-7000
Fax: (703) 667-7001

MITCHELL, Laurene M.
Senior Vice President, Operations

Tel: (703) 667-7000
Fax: (703) 667-7001

TRAINOR, Sarah
Communications Specialist
media@gridpoint.com

Tel: (703) 667-7173
Fax: (703) 667-7001

Griffco Quality Solutions

Griffco Quality Solutions provides services such as third party containment, supplier representation, warehousing, sub-assembly and sequencing.
Annual Revenues: $2 million
Employees: 150

Industry/ies: Automotive Industry; Transportation

Chief Executive Officer	Tel:	(502) 412-7221
THOMPSON, Deborah L.	Fax:	(502) 412-3771

Main Headquarters

Mailing: 12305 Westport Rd.	Tel:	(502) 412-7221
Suite 206	Fax:	(502) 412-3771
Louisville, KY 40245-2714		

Public Affairs and Related Activities Personnel

At Headquarters

MAGRE, John	Tel:	(502) 412-7221
Contact, Public Relations	Fax:	(502) 412-3771
jmagre@griffco.com		

The Griffith Corporation

A company focused on promoting homeland, family and person security issues.
www.griffithscorp.com
Industry/ies: Defense/Homeland Security; Government-Related

Main Headquarters

Mailing: 2533 N. Carson St.	Tel:	(775) 841-1534
Suite 3815		
Carson City, NV 89706		

Public Affairs and Related Activities Personnel

At Headquarters

BURKE, Bryan	Tel:	(775) 841-1534
Chief of Staff		
GRIFFITH, Will	Tel:	(775) 841-1534
Owner		
KEISER, Jessica	Tel:	(775) 841-1534
Missing Persons Liaison		
KLINE, Jason	Tel:	(775) 841-1534
Federal Lobbyist		
SAXE, Mark	Tel:	(775) 841-1534
Internet Division Chief		

Griffon Corporation

Manufacturer of electronic communications systems and equipment. Griffon currently conducts its operations through three segments: Home & Building Products, Clopay Plastic Products Company ("Plastics"), and Telephonics Corporation ("Telephonics").
www.griffoncorp.com
Annual Revenues: $2.01 billion
Employees: 6,000
Ticker: NYSE: GFF
SIC: 3442
NAICS: 334210
Industry/ies: Communications; Electricity & Electronics; Electronics; Energy/Electricity; Telecommunications/Internet/Cable

Chairman of the Board	Tel:	(212) 957-5000
BLAU, Harvey R.		

Chief Executive Officer	Tel:	(212) 957-5000
KRAMER, Ronald J.		

Main Headquarters

Mailing: 712 Fifth Ave.	Tel:	(212) 957-5000
18th Floor	TF:	(800) 937-5449
New York City, NY 10019		

Public Affairs and Related Activities Personnel

At Headquarters

HARRIS, Brian G.	Tel:	(212) 957-5000
Senior Vice President and Chief Financial Officer		
KAPLAN, Seth	Tel:	(212) 957-5000
Senior Vice President, General Counsel and Secretary		
kaplan@griffoncorp.com		
MEHMEL, Robert F.	Tel:	(212) 957-5000
President and Chief Operating Officer		

Gronberg Consulting, LLC

Monitors and provides expert analysis on Congressional and Executive Branch policies and actions.
www.gronbergconsulting.com
Industry/ies: Consultants
Legislative Issues: BUD; DEF; HOM; LAW; TEC; VET

President	Tel:	(703) 634-3669
GRONBERG, Katherine		

Main Headquarters

Mailing: 6920 Braddock Rd.	Tel:	(703) 634-3669
Suite B170		
Annandale, VA 22003		

Group 1 Automotive, Inc.

Operates in the automotive retail industry.
www.group1auto.com
Annual Revenues: $10.11 billion
Employees: 12,200
Ticker: NYSE: GPI
SIC: 5500
Industry/ies: Automotive Industry; Transportation

Chairman of the Board	Tel:	(713) 647-5700
ADAMS, John L.	Fax:	(713) 647-5800

President and Chief Executive Officer	Tel:	(713) 647-5700
HESTERBERG, Earl J.	Fax:	(713) 647-5800

Main Headquarters

Mailing: 800 Gessner	Tel:	(713) 647-5700
Suite 500	Fax:	(713) 647-5888
Houston, TX 77024		

Public Affairs and Related Activities Personnel

At Headquarters

BURMAN, Darryl M.	Tel:	(713) 647-5700
Vice President, General Counsel and Corporate Secretary	Fax:	(713) 647-5800
dburman@group1auto.com		
DELONGCHAMPS, Peter C.	Tel:	(713) 647-5700
Vice President, Financial Services and Manufacturer Relations	Fax:	(713) 647-5800
pdelongchamps@group1auto.com		
IUPPENLATZ, Mark J.	Tel:	(713) 647-5700
Vice President, Corporate Development	Fax:	(713) 647-5888
O'HARA, J. Brooks	Tel:	(713) 647-5700
Vice President, Human Resources	Fax:	(713) 647-5800
bohara@group1auto.com		
PARKER, Lance A.	Tel:	(713) 647-5700
Vice President and Corporate Controller	Fax:	(713) 647-5888
RICKEL, John C.	Tel:	(713) 647-5700
Senior Vice President and Chief Financial Officer	Fax:	(713) 647-5888
jrickel@group1auto.com		
WELCH, Michael D.	Tel:	(713) 647-5700
Vice President and Treasurer	Fax:	(713) 647-5888

Group Health Cooperative

A nonprofit health care system.
www.ghc.org
Annual Revenues: $3.20 billion
Employees: 9,000
Industry/ies: Cooperatives; Medicine/Health Care/Mental Health
Legislative Issues: HCR; MED; MMM; TAX

Chairman of the Board	Tel:	(206) 448-5600
BYINGTON, Susan	Fax:	(206) 448-4010

President and Chief Executive Officer	Tel:	(206) 448-5600
ARMSTRONG, Scott	Fax:	(206) 448-4010
armstrong.s@ghc.org		

Main Headquarters

Mailing: 320 Westlake Ave., North	Tel:	(206) 448-5600
Suite 100	Fax:	(206) 448-4010
Seattle, WA 98109-5233	TF:	(800) 848-4259

Corporate Foundations and Giving Programs

Group Health Foundation
320 Westlake Ave. North	Tel:	(206) 448-7330
Suite 100	Fax:	(206) 448-4010
Seattle, WA 98109		

Public Affairs and Related Activities Personnel

At Headquarters

(OTTO) GRANT, Madeline	Tel:	(206) 448-5600
Director, Federal Government Relations	Fax:	(206) 448-4010
DESMERAIS, Coletta	Tel:	(206) 448-5849
Director, Federal Affairs	Fax:	(206) 448-4010
Registered Federal Lobbyist		
HESSELBROCK, Rose	Tel:	(206) 448-5600
Community Benefit Program Manager	Fax:	(206) 448-4010
KNACKSTEDT, Chris	Tel:	(206) 448-5600
Executive Vice President and Chief Financial Officer	Fax:	(206) 448-4010
LAMP, Tami	Tel:	(206) 448-5600
Executive Vice President, Human Resources	Fax:	(206) 448-4010
LOELIGER, Dawn	Tel:	(206) 448-5600
Executive Vice President, Strategic Planning and Development	Fax:	(206) 448-4010
MALPASS, Liam	Tel:	(206) 448-5600
Administrative Coordinator	Fax:	(206) 448-4010
MCCARTHY, Katie	Tel:	(206) 448-5849
Market and Digital Communications Partner	Fax:	(206) 448-4010

mccarthy.kx@ghc.org

PUTMAN, Melissa Benish	Tel:	(206) 448-5600
Registered Federal Lobbyist	Fax:	(206) 448-4010
RAKOW, Diana Birkett	Tel:	(206) 448-5600
Executive vice president, Marketing and Public Affairs	Fax:	(206) 448-4010
birkett.d@ghc.org		
REED, Victoria	Tel:	(206) 448-5600
External Affairs Coordinator	Fax:	(206) 448-4010
TURCOTTE, Joe	Tel:	(206) 448-7301
Philanthropy Contact	Fax:	(206) 448-4010
turcotte.j@ghc.org		
WATT, Bob	Tel:	(206) 448-5600
Vice Chairman of Board	Fax:	(206) 448-4010
WOODS, Rick	Tel:	(206) 448-5600
Executive Vice President & Chief Legal Officer	Fax:	(206) 448-4010
woods.r@ghc.org		
YATES, Sally	Tel:	(206) 448-5600
Executive Vice President and General Counsel	Fax:	(206) 448-4010

At Other Offices

GOODWIN, Jeffrey L.
PAC Treasurer
441 Ninth Ave.
New York City, NY 10001

GUARD Insurance Group Inc.

An Insurance group.
www.guard.com
Employees: 300
Industry/ies: Insurance Industry

President and Chief Executive Officer	Tel:	(570) 825-9900
FOGUEL, Sy	Fax:	(570) 823-5930

Main Headquarters

Mailing:	16 S. River St.	Tel:	(570) 825-9900
	P.O. Box A-H	Fax:	(570) 823-5930
	Wilkes-Barre, PA 18703-0020	TF:	(800) 673-2465

Public Affairs and Related Activities Personnel

At Headquarters

AICHENBAUM, CPA, Eitan	Tel:	(570) 825-9900
Chief Financial Officer and Treasurer	Fax:	(570) 823-5930
DULIN, Esq., Michael J.	Tel:	(570) 825-9900
General Counsel	Fax:	(570) 823-5930
THOMAS, Robert	Tel:	(570) 825-9900
Director, Communications	Fax:	(570) 823-5930
bthomas@guard.com		

Guardian Industries Corporation

Manufactures float glass, fabricated glass products, fiberglass insulation and other building materials for commercial, residential and automotive markets. Formerly known as Guardian Glass Company.
www.guardian.com
Annual Revenues: $4.48 billion
Employees: 17,000
SIC: 3465
NAICS: 33637
Industry/ies: Glass
Legislative Issues: DEF; TAX; TRD

Main Headquarters

Mailing:	2300 Harmon Rd.	Tel:	(248) 340-1800
	Auburn Hills, MI 48326	Fax:	(248) 340-9988

Political Action Committees

Guardian Industries Corporation Federal PAC
FEC ID: C00239285
Contact: Jonathan Joyce

2300 Harmon Rd.	Tel:	(248) 340-1800
Auburn Hills, MI 48326		

Contributions to Candidates: $9,500 (2015-2016)
Republicans: $9,500

Corporate Foundations and Giving Programs

Guardian Industries Corporation Contribution Program

2300 Harmon Rd.	Tel:	(248) 340-1800
Auburn Hills, MI 48326	Fax:	(248) 340-9988

Public Affairs and Related Activities Personnel

At Headquarters

HENNES, Amy	Tel:	(248) 340-2109
Director, Corporate Communications and Public Affairs	Fax:	(248) 340-9988
ahennes@guardian.com		
JOYCE, Jonathan	Tel:	(248) 340-1800
PAC Treasurer	Fax:	(248) 340-9988
KNIGHT, Jeffrey	Tel:	(248) 340-1800

Vice President, Finance / Chief Financial Officer / Director	Fax:	(248) 340-9988

Guardian Life Insurance Company of America

Insurance and related financial products and services. Guardian continues to be there for the people and businesses who put their trust in us through innovative technology, products, and services. At the same time, we remain true to our founding spirit—putting people first, continually building on our financial strength, and maintaining the highest ethical standards.
www.guardianlife.com
Annual Revenues: $7.80 billion
Employees: 8,000
Industry/ies: Insurance Industry
Legislative Issues: FIN; HCR; INS; RET; TAX; WEL

Executive Chairman & Manager	Tel:	(212) 598-8000
MANNING, Dennis J.	Fax:	(212) 949-2170
President and Chief Executive Officer	Tel:	(212) 598-8000
MULLIGAN, Deanna M.	Fax:	(212) 919-2170
deanna_mulligan@glic.com		

Main Headquarters

Mailing:	Seven Hanover Sq.	Tel:	(212) 598-8000
	New York City, NY 10004	Fax:	(212) 919-2170
		TF:	(866) 425-4542

Washington Office

Mailing:	101 Constitution Ave. NW	Tel:	(202) 594-3700
	Suite 705 East		
	Washington, DC 20001		

Political Action Committees

Guardian Life Insurance Company of America PAC (Guardian Life PAC)
FEC ID: C00173393
Contact: Walter Skinner
Seven Hanover Sq.
New York City, NY 10004

Contributions to Candidates: $127,000 (2015-2016)
Democrats: $60,000; Republicans: $67,000

Principal Recipients

HOUSE
KIND, RONALD JAMES (DEM-WI)

Public Affairs and Related Activities Personnel

At Headquarters

AHN, Dong H.	Tel:	(212) 598-8000
Executive Vice President, Group and Worksite Markets	Fax:	(212) 919-2170
BROATCH, Robert E.	Tel:	(212) 598-8000
Executive Vice President, Chief Financial Officer, Risk and Operational Excellence	Fax:	(212) 919-2170
robert_broatch@glic.com		
COSTANTINI, Marc	Tel:	(212) 598-8000
Executive Vice President and Chief Financial Officer	Fax:	(212) 919-2170
DOLFI, D. Scott	Tel:	(212) 598-8000
Chief Operating Officer	Fax:	(212) 919-2170
JONES, Richard	Tel:	(212) 598-8338
Vice President, State Affairs and Chief Communications Officer	Fax:	(212) 919-2170
Richard_Jones@glic.com		
RICH, Tracy L.	Tel:	(212) 598-8000
Executive Vice President, General Counsel, and Corporate Secretary	Fax:	(212) 919-2170
SKINNER, Walter	Tel:	(212) 598-8000
Vice President & Treasurer and PAC Treasurer	Fax:	(212) 919-2170
SORELL, CFA, Thomas G.	Tel:	(212) 598-8000
Executive Vice President and Chief Investment Officer	Fax:	(212) 919-2170

At Washington Office

PRESUTTI, Robert	Tel:	(202) 594-3700
Federal Affairs Specialist		
RENFREW, Jonathan W.	Tel:	(202) 742-4401
Vice President, Federal Affairs		
jonathan_renfrew@glic.com		
Registered Federal Lobbyist		
ROSENBLUM, Jay	Tel:	(202) 594-3700
Senior Vice President, Government Affairs		
Registered Federal Lobbyist		
STRIKOWSKY, Lisa	Tel:	(202) 594-3700
Manager, Federal Affairs		
Registered Federal Lobbyist		

Guggenheim Investment Management, LLC

A private equity investment firm.
guggenheimpartners.com
Employees: 2,200
Industry/ies: Banking/Finance/Investments

Executive Chairman	Tel:	(312) 827-0100

SCHWARTZ, Alan D.
Chief Executive Officer   Tel: (312) 827-0100
WALTER, Mark R.
mark.walter@guggenheimpartners.com

Main Headquarters
Mailing: 227 W. Monroe St.   Tel: (312) 827-0100
               Chicago, IL 60606

Corporate Foundations and Giving Programs
Guggenheim Investment Management, LLC Contributions Program
227 W. Monroe St.
Chicago, IL 60606

Public Affairs and Related Activities Personnel

At Headquarters

MINERD, Scott   Tel: (312) 827-0100
Global Chief Investment Officer

Guggenheim Partners, LLC
See listing on page 379 under Guggenheim Investment Management, LLC

Guidant Corporation
See listing on page 139 under Boston Scientific Corporation

GuideWell Mutual Holding Corporation
Health insurance.
Legislative Issues: MMM

Main Headquarters
Mailing: 4800 Deerwood Campus Pkwy.
               Jacksonville Beach, FL 32246

Public Affairs and Related Activities Personnel

At Headquarters

EASTERLING (CHARLES), Deborah L.
Governmental & Legislative Relations Specialist
FURRY, Joseph
GILES, Tom
Registered Federal Lobbyist
VIDRINE, James Eric

Guilford Performance Textiles
A manufacturer of textiles.
www.guilfordtextiles.com
Annual Revenues: $468.87 million
Employees: 2,600
SIC: 2250
Industry/ies: Apparel/Textiles Industry

President, Chief Executive Officer and Director   Tel: (910) 794-5800
SIMONCINI, Matthew J.   Fax: (336) 316-4057

Main Headquarters
Mailing: 1001 Military Cutoff Rd.   Tel: (910) 794-5800
               Suite 300   Fax: (336) 316-4057
               Wilmington, NC 28405

Gulf Power Company
An electric utility subsidiary of Southern Company (see separate listing).
www.gulfpower.com
Employees: 1,300
Ticker: NYSE: GUI
SIC: 4911
Industry/ies: Energy/Electricity; Utilities

Chairman, President and Chief Executive Officer   Tel: (850) 444-6111
CONNALLY, Stan

Main Headquarters
Mailing: P.O. Box 830660   Tel: (850) 444-6243
               Birmingham, AL 35283-0660   TF: (800) 225-5797

Political Action Committees
Responsible Federal Government Committee of Gulf Power Company
Employees, Inc.
FEC ID: C00610782
Contact: Christopher B. Stadler
One Energy Pl.   Tel: (850) 444-6111
Pensacola, FL 32520   Fax: (850) 444-6448

Corporate Foundations and Giving Programs
Gulf Power Foundation
One Energy Pl.   Tel: (850) 444-6111
Pensacola, FL 32520

Public Affairs and Related Activities Personnel

At Headquarters

ERICKSON, Lynn   Tel: (850) 444-6243
Specialist, Communications

FLETCHER, Jim   Tel: (850) 444-6243
Vice President, External Affairs and Corporate Services
LIU, Xia   Tel: (850) 444-6243
Vice President and Chief Financial Officer
ROGERS, Jeff   Tel: (850) 444-6243
Manager, Corporate Communications
jerogers@southernco.com
SIMS, Sandy   Tel: (850) 444-6243
District General Manager
sfsims@southernco.com
SMITH, Natalie   Tel: (850) 444-6784
Specialist, Communications
ncsmith@southernco.com
TERRY, Bentina   Tel: (850) 444-6243
Vice President, Customer Service and Sales

At Other Offices

ERICKSON, Lynn   Tel: (850) 444-6111
Specialist, Communications   Fax: (850) 444-6448
One Energy Pl.
Pensacola, FL 32520
FLETCHER, Jim   Tel: (850) 444-6111
Vice President, External Affairs and Corporate Services
One Energy Pl.
Pensacola, FL 32520
LIU, Xia   Tel: (850) 444-6111
Vice President and Chief Financial Officer
One Energy Pl.
Pensacola, FL 32520
SIMS, Sandy   Tel: (850) 444-6111
District General Manager   Fax: (850) 444-6448
One Energy Pl.
Pensacola, FL 32520
sfsims@southernco.com
STADLER, Christopher B.   Tel: (850) 444-6111
PAC Treasurer   Fax: (850) 444-6448
One Energy Pl.
Pensacola, FL 32520
TERRY, Bentina   Tel: (850) 444-6111
Vice President, Customer Service and Sales Fax: (850) 444-6448
One Energy Pl.
Pensacola, FL 32520

Gulf Stream Coach, Inc.
A privately held RV manufacturer.
www.gulfstreamcoach.com
Annual Revenues: $109 million
Employees: 1,200
Industry/ies: Automotive Industry; Transportation

Main Headquarters
Mailing: 503 S. Oakland Ave.   Tel: (574) 773-7761
               P.O. Box 1005   Fax: (571) 773-5761
               Nappanee, IN 46550   TF: (800) 289-8787

Public Affairs and Related Activities Personnel

At Headquarters

OLSEN, Chuck   Tel: (574) 773-5761
Chief Financial Officer   Fax: (574) 773-5717

Gulfstream Aerospace Corporation
Gulfstream Aerospace Corporation, a wholly-owned subsidiary of General Dynamics (NYSE: GD), designs, develops, manufactures, markets, services and supports technologically-advanced business jet aircraft.
www.gulfstream.com
Employees: 8,000
SIC: 3721
Industry/ies: Aerospace/Aviation; Defense/Homeland Security; Government-Related; Transportation

President   Tel: (912) 965-3000
BURNS, Mark   Fax: (912) 965-3084

Main Headquarters
Mailing: P.O. Box 2206   Tel: (912) 965-3000
               Savannah, GA 31402-2206   Fax: (912) 965-3084

Washington Office
Mailing: 1000 Wilson Blvd.   Tel: (703) 276-9500
               Suite 2701
               Arlington, VA 22209

Corporate Foundations and Giving Programs

Gulfstream Aerospace Corporation Charitable Contributions
P. O. Box 2206
Savannah, GA 31402-2206

Public Affairs and Related Activities Personnel

At Headquarters

BERMAN, Ira
Senior Vice President, Administration and General Counsel
ira.berman@gulfstream.com
Tel: (912) 965-3000
Fax: (912) 965-3084

CASS, Steve
Vice President, Communications
steve.cass@gulfstream.com
Tel: (912) 965-4908
Fax: (912) 965-3084

CHONG, Leda
Senior Vice President, Government Programs and Sales
Tel: (912) 965-3000
Fax: (912) 965-3084

CLARE, Dan
Chief Financial Officer
Tel: (912) 965-3000
Fax: (912) 965-3084

FEDAK, Heidi
Senior Manager, Social Media and External Communications
heidi.fedak@gulfstream.com
Tel: (912) 395-8574
Fax: (912) 965-3084

NEAL, Scott
Senior Vice President, Sales and Marketing
Tel: (912) 965-3000
Fax: (912) 965-3084

STULIGROSS, Dennis
Senior Vice President, Operations
Tel: (912) 965-3000
Fax: (912) 965-3084

H & R Block, Inc.

A tax, accounting, and financial services company.
www.hrblock.com
Annual Revenues: $3.04 billion
Employees: 2,400
Ticker: NYSE: HRB
SIC: 7200
Industry/ies: Banking/Finance/Investments; Taxation
Legislative Issues: BUD; TAX

Chairman of the Board
GERARD, Robert A.
Tel: (816) 854-3000
Fax: (816) 854-8500

President and Chief Executive Officer
COBB, William C.
Tel: (816) 854-4513
Fax: (816) 854-8500

Main Headquarters
Mailing: One H & R Block Way
              Kansas City, MO 64105
Tel: (816) 854-3000
Fax: (816) 854-8500
TF: (800) 472-5625

Washington Office
Mailing: 1401 Eye St. NW
              Suite 240
              Washington, DC 20005
Tel: (202) 962-0075
Fax: (202) 962-0119

Political Action Committees
H & R Block Political Action Committee
FEC ID: C00188177
Contact: Jeremy Stohs
700 13th St. NW, Suite 700
Washington, DC 20005-
Tel: (202) 508-6363
Fax: (816) 854-8500

  Contributions to Candidates: $138,700 (2015-2016)
  Democrats: $49,000; Republicans: $86,700; Other: $3,000

  Principal Recipients

   SENATE
   BLUNT, ROY (REP-MO)
   YOUNG, TODD CHRISTOPHER (REP-IN)

Corporate Foundations and Giving Programs
The H & R Block Foundation
Contact: David P. Miles
4400 Main St.
Kansas City, MO 64111
Tel: (816) 854-4361
Fax: (816) 854-4361
TF: (800) 472-5625

Public Affairs and Related Activities Personnel

At Headquarters

BOWEN, Tony
Chief Financial Officer
Tel: (816) 854-3000
Fax: (816) 854-8500

BROWN, Colby
Vice President, Investor Relations
colby.brown@hrblock.com
Tel: (816) 854-4559
Fax: (816) 854-8500

COLLINS, Kathy
Chief Marketing Officer
Tel: (816) 854-3000
Fax: (816) 854-8500

GERKE, Tom
General Counsel and Chief Administrative Officer
Tel: (816) 854-3000
Fax: (816) 854-8500

GILL, Erin L.
Manager, Financial Reporting
Tel: (816) 854-3000
Fax: (816) 854-8500

KING, Gene
Director, Corporate Communications
gene.king@hrblock.com
Tel: (816) 854-4287
Fax: (816) 854-8500

MACFARLANE, Gregory J.
Senior Vice President, U.S. Retail Products and Operations
Tel: (816) 854-3000
Fax: (816) 854-8500

MILES, David P.
President
davmiles@hrblock.com
Tel: (816) 854-4372
Fax: (816) 854-8500

PATTARA, Theresa
Director, Public Policy and Advocacy
Registered Federal Lobbyist
Tel: (816) 854-3000
Fax: (816) 854-8500

STOHS, Jeremy
Deputy Director, Government Relations and PAC Treasurer
jeremy.stohs@hrblock.com
Registered Federal Lobbyist
Tel: (816) 854-3000
Fax: (816) 854-8500

VAN LULING, Marie T.
Chief Government Relations Officer
Registered Federal Lobbyist
Tel: (816) 854-3000
Fax: (816) 854-8500

WILKINS, Aileen
Chief People Officer
Tel: (816) 854-3000
Fax: (816) 854-8500

At Washington Office

JENNISON, Andrew
Deputy Director, Government Relations
Registered Federal Lobbyist
Tel: (202) 962-0075
Fax: (202) 962-0119

TURRENTINE, Daniel
Registered Federal Lobbyist
Tel: (202) 962-0075
Fax: (202) 962-0119

At Other Offices

DRYSDALE, Derek
Vice President, Internal Audit
4400 Main St.
Kansas City, MO 64111
derek.drysdale@hrblock.com
Tel: (816) 854-4513
Fax: (816) 854-8500

H. F. Webster

An engineering services company providing services to the Department of Defense and commercial enterprises.
hfwebster.com
Annual Revenues: $1.57 million
Employees: 9
Industry/ies: Aerospace/Aviation; Defense/Homeland Security; Engineering/Mathematics; Government-Related; Transportation

Chief Executive Officer
HRABE, Robert H.
Tel: (605) 343-3260
Fax: (605) 343-1801

Main Headquarters
Mailing: 2160 Dyess Ave.
              Rapid City, SD 57701
Tel: (605) 343-3260
Fax: (605) 343-1801

H.J. Heinz Holding Corporation

See listing on page 476 under Kraft Heinz Company

HA Advisory Services, LLC

Economic and policy consulting on government procurement.
Industry/ies: Economics And Economic Development; Politics/Political Science

Main Headquarters
Mailing: 1997 Annapolis Exchange
              Suite 520
              Annapolis, MD 21401
Tel: (410) 571-6163

Public Affairs and Related Activities Personnel

At Headquarters

KOENIG, Gerald
gkoenig@haadvisory.com
Tel: (410) 571-6163

John I. Haas, Inc.

John I. Haas, Inc. owns and operates its own hop farms, warehouses, pellet and extraction plants as well as isomerisation facilities in the northwestern United States.
www.barthhaasgroup.com
Annual Revenues: $18.50 million
Employees: 200
Industry/ies: Food And Beverage Industry

Chief Executive Officer
BARTH , Alexander
Tel: (202) 777-4800
Fax: (202) 777-4895

Main Headquarters
Mailing: 5185 MacArthur Blvd. NW
              Suite 300
              Washington, DC 20016
Tel: (202) 777-4800
Fax: (202) 777-4895

Public Affairs and Related Activities Personnel

At Headquarters

CONARD, Stephanie
Controller
Tel: (202) 777-4800
Fax: (202) 777-4895

DAVIS, Thomas (Tom)
Chief Financial Officer
Tel: (202) 777-4800
Fax: (202) 777-4895

GERST, Bob
Director, Human Resources
Tel: (202) 777-4800
Fax: (202) 777-4895

THURSTON, Davis
Vice President, Sales and Marketing
Tel: (202) 777-4800
Fax: (202) 777-4895

Hach Company

Manufactures and distributes analytical instruments and reagents used to test the quality of water and other aqueous solutions.
www.hach.com
Employees: 1,100
SIC: 2819; 3826
NAICS: 325188; 334516
Industry/ies: Machinery/Equipment

Main Headquarters

Mailing:	P.O. Box 389	Tel:	(970) 669-3050
	Loveland, CO 80539-0389	Fax:	(970) 669-2932
		TF:	(800) 227-4224

Public Affairs and Related Activities Personnel

At Headquarters

KÖNIG, Ralf	Tel:	(970) 669-3050
Contact, Regulatory Affairs	Fax:	(970) 669-2932
MYER, Liz	Tel:	(970) 663-1377
Contact, Communications	Fax:	(970) 669-2932
emyers@hach.com		

Halliburton Company

Provides products and services to the energy industry.
www.halliburton.com
Annual Revenues: $32.57 billion
Employees: 75,000
Ticker: NYSE: HAL
SIC: 1389; 3499; 3533
NAICS: 332999; 333132
Industry/ies: Construction/Construction Materials; Engineering/Mathematics; Fuels See Coal, Gas, Oil, Petroleum; Natural Resources; Petroleum Industry
Legislative Issues: ENG; ENV; FOR; IMM; LBR; TAX; TRA; TRD

Chairman of the Board, President and Chief Executive Officer	Tel:	(281) 871-2699
LESAR, David J.	Fax:	(713) 759-2635
Dave.Lesar@Halliburton.com		

Main Headquarters

Mailing:	3000 N. Sam Houston Pkwy E.	Tel:	(281) 871-4000
	Houston, TX 77032		

Washington Office

Mailing:	801 17th St. NW	Tel:	(202) 223-0820
	Tenth Floor	Fax:	(202) 223-2385
	Washington, DC 20006		

Political Action Committees

Halliburton Company PAC (HALPAC)
FEC ID: C00035691
Contact: Dale R. French

801 17th St. NW	Tel:	(202) 223-0820
Tenth Floor	Fax:	(202) 223-2385
Washington, DC 20006		

Contributions to Candidates: $367,750 (2015-2016)
Democrats: $12,000; Republicans: $354,750; Other: $1,000

Principal Recipients

SENATE
AYOTTE, KELLY A (REP-NH)
BLUNT, ROY (REP-MO)
THUNE, JOHN (REP-SD)

HOUSE
JOHNSON, BILL (REP-OH)
MCCARTHY, KEVIN (REP-CA)

Corporate Foundations and Giving Programs

Halliburton Foundation		
10200 Bellaire Blvd.	Tel:	(713) 759-2600
1401 McKinney St., Suite 2400		
Houston, TX 77072-5206		

Public Affairs and Related Activities Personnel

At Headquarters

DICKSON, Stacia	Tel:	(281) 871-4000
Senior Manager, Industry Communications		
Stacia.Dickson@Halliburton.com		
FERGUSON, James W.	Tel:	(281) 871-4000
Senior Vice President and Chief Ethics and Compliance Officer		
GARCIA, Christian	Tel:	(281) 871-4000
Senior Vice President of Finance and Acting Chief Financial Officer		
HAYTER, Robert L.	Tel:	(281) 871-4000
Assistant Secretary and Assistant General Counsel		
MCCOLLUM, Mark A.	Tel:	(281) 871-2699
Executive Vice President and Chief Financial Officer		
mark.mccollum@halliburton.com		
MCKEON, Tim	Tel:	(281) 871-4000

Vice President and Treasurer		
METZINGER, Bruce A.	Tel:	(281) 871-4000
Assistant Secretary and Senior Director		
MILLER, Jeff	Tel:	(281) 871-4000
President		
POPE, Lawrence J.	Tel:	(281) 871-2699
Executive Vice President, Administration and Chief Human Resources Officer		
lawrence.pope@halliburton.com		
VOYLES, Robb L.	Tel:	(281) 871-4000
Executive Vice President and General Counsel		
YOUNGBLOOD, Kelly	Tel:	(281) 871-2688
Vice President, Investor Relations		

At Washington Office

BENSCHER, Chris	Tel:	(202) 223-0820
Manager, Government Affairs	Fax:	(202) 223-2385
FRANKS, Jessica	Tel:	(202) 223-0820
Registered Federal Lobbyist	Fax:	(202) 223-2385
FRENCH, Dale R.	Tel:	(202) 223-0820
Director, Financial Controls and PAC Treasurer	Fax:	(202) 223-2385
KNIGHT, Catherine	Tel:	(202) 223-0820
Representative, Government Affairs	Fax:	(202) 223-2385
Catherine.Knight@halliburton.com		
Registered Federal Lobbyist		
MORAN, Robert J.	Tel:	(202) 223-0820
Vice President, Government Affairs	Fax:	(202) 223-2385
bob.moran@halliburton.com		
Registered Federal Lobbyist		
VEST, Catherine	Tel:	(202) 223-0820
Representative, Government Affairs	Fax:	(202) 223-2385

At Other Offices

MANN, Cathy G.	Tel:	(713) 759-2605
Director, Communications		
Five Houston Center, 1401 McKinney St., Suite 2400		
Houston, TX 77010		
cathy.mann@halliburton.com		
NORCROSS, Melissa	Tel:	(713) 759-2608
Public Relations Supervisor		
Five Houston Center, 1401 McKinney St., Suite 2400		
Houston, TX 77010		
melissa.norcross@halliburton.com		

Hallmark Cards, Inc.

A manufacturer and marketer of greeting cards and related personal expression products. Subsidiaries include Crayola LLC (see separate listing).
www.hallmark.com
Annual Revenues: $3.7 billion
Employees: 9,500
SIC: 2771
Industry/ies: Paper And Wood Products Industry
Legislative Issues: POS; TAX

Chairman and Chief Executive Officer	Tel:	(816) 274-5111
HALL, Jr., Donald J.	Fax:	(816) 274-5061

Main Headquarters

Mailing:	P.O. Box 419034	Tel:	(816) 274-5111
	Mail Drop 216	Fax:	(816) 274-5061
	Kansas City, MO 64141	TF:	(800) 425-5627

Political Action Committees

Hallmark Cards PAC
FEC ID: C00000059
Contact: Erin Brower

2501 McGee Trafficway	Tel:	(816) 274-5111
MD # 288	Fax:	(816) 274-5061
Kansas City, MO 64108		

Contributions to Candidates: $58,000 (2015-2016)
Democrats: $19,500; Republicans: $34,500; Other: $4,000

Corporate Foundations and Giving Programs

Hallmark Corporate Foundation		
P.O. Box 419034	Tel:	(816) 274-5111
Mail Drop 216	Fax:	(816) 274-5061
Kansas City, MO 64141-6580	TF:	(800) 425-5627

Public Affairs and Related Activities Personnel

At Headquarters

HALL, Joyce C.	Tel:	(816) 274-5111
Founder	Fax:	(816) 274-5061
HALL, David E.	Tel:	(816) 274-5111
President, North American Division	Fax:	(816) 274-5061
TWIDWELL, Jaci	Tel:	(816) 274-4873
Manager, Publicity	Fax:	(816) 274-5061

newsroom@hallmark.com

At Other Offices

BROWER, Erin
PAC Treasurer
2501 McGee, MD 288
Kansas City, MO 64108

Tel:	(816) 274-5111
Fax:	(816) 274-5061

RODENBOUGH, Dean
Vice President, Corporate Communications and Government Relations
2501 McGee, MD 288
Kansas City, MO 64108

Tel:	(816) 274-5111
Fax:	(816) 274-5061

Hamilton Beach Brands, Inc.

A manufacturer of household appliances. Brands include Hamilton Beach, Proctor-Silex, Eclectrics, and TrueAir.
www.hamiltonbeach.com
Annual Revenues: $45.90 million
Employees: 300
SIC: 3634
Industry/ies: Machinery/Equipment
Legislative Issues: TRD

Chairman of the Board
RANKIN, Jr., Alfred M.

Tel:	(804) 273-9777
Fax:	(804) 527-7142

President and Chief Executive Officer
TREPP, Gregory H.

Tel:	(804) 273-9777
Fax:	(804) 527-7142

Main Headquarters
Mailing: 261 Yadkin Rd.
        Southern Pines, NC 28387

Tel:	(804) 273-9777
Fax:	(804) 527-7142

Public Affairs and Related Activities Personnel

At Headquarters

PERREAULT, Mary Beth
Senior Public Relations Representative
marybeth.dukes@hamiltonbeach.com

Tel:	(804) 418-8868
Fax:	(804) 527-7142

Hamilton Beach/Proctor-Silex , Inc.

See listing on page 383 under Hamilton Beach Brands, Inc.

Hamilton Sundstrand

Manufactures and markets proprietary-technology components and subsystems for industrial and aerospace markets. It was formed from the merger of Hamilton Standard and Sundstrand Corporation in 1999. A subsidiary of United Technologies Corporation.
www.hamiltonsundstrand.com
Annual Revenues: $5.60 billion
Employees: 17,000
SIC: 3724; 3625; 3694; 3822
NAICS: 334512; 335311; 336322; 336412
Industry/ies: Aerospace/Aviation; Transportation

President
DUMAIS, Michael

Tel:	(860) 654-6000
Fax:	(860) 654-2399

Main Headquarters
Mailing: One Hamilton Rd.
        Windsor Locks, CT 06095

Tel:	(860) 654-6000
Fax:	(860) 654-2399

Public Affairs and Related Activities Personnel

At Headquarters

COULOM, Dan
Contact, Media Relations
daniel.coulom@hs.utc.com

Tel:	(860) 654-6000
Fax:	(860) 654-2399

MANN, Elaine
Contact, Media Relations
elaine.mann@hs.utc.com

Tel:	(860) 654-6000
Fax:	(860) 654-2399

SHIRANE, Tatsuo
Vice President, Human Resources

Tel:	(860) 654-6000
Fax:	(860) 654-2399

Hanesbrands, Inc.

A global consumer goods company.
www.hanes.com/corporate
Annual Revenues: $5.47 billion
Employees: 59,500
Ticker: NYSE: HBI
SIC: 2281; 2254; 2269; 2329
NAICS: 313111; 313312; 315192
Industry/ies: Apparel/Textiles Industry; Retail/Wholesale
Legislative Issues: TAX; TRD

Chairman of the Board and Chief Executive Officer
NOLL, Rich A.

Tel:	(336) 519-8080

Main Headquarters
Mailing: 1000 E. Hanes Mill Rd.
        Winston Salem, NC 27105

Tel:	(336) 519-8080

Corporate Foundations and Giving Programs

Hanesbrands Contributions Program
1000 E. Hanes Mill Rd.
Winston Salem, NC 27105

Public Affairs and Related Activities Personnel

At Headquarters

BURGER, Elizabeth L.
Chief Human Resources Officer

Tel:	(336) 519-8080

COHEN, David
Member

Tel:	(336) 519-8080

COOK, Jerry
Vice President, Government and Trade Relations
jerry.cook@hanesbrands.com
Registered Federal Lobbyist

Tel:	(336) 519-5250

EVANS, Jr., Gerald W.
Chief Operating Officer

Tel:	(336) 519-8080

HALL, Matt
Vice President, External Communications
Matt.Hall@Hanesbrands.com

Tel:	(336) 519-3386

JOHNSON, Joia M.
Chief Legal Officer, General Counsel and Corporate Secretary

Tel:	(336) 519-8080

MOSS, Richard D.
Chief Financial Officer

Tel:	(336) 519-8080

ROBILLARD, T.C.
Vice President, Investor Relations
TC.Robillard@Hanesbrands.com

Tel:	(336) 519-2115

Hanger Orthopedic Group Inc.

See listing on page 383 under Hanger, Inc.

Hanger, Inc.

Provides orthotic and prosthetic (O&P) patient care services, distributes O&P devices and components, manages O&P networks, and offers therapeutic solutions in the United States. Formerly known as Hanger Orthopedic Group, Inc.
www.hanger.com
Annual Revenues: $1.06 billion
Employees: 4,800
Ticker: NYSE: HGR
SIC: 8093
Industry/ies: Medicine/Health Care/Mental Health
Legislative Issues: HCR; INS; VET

Chairman of the Board
COOPER, Thomas P.

Tel:	(512) 777-3800

President and Chief Executive Officer
ASAR , Vinit K.

Tel:	(512) 777-3800

Main Headquarters
Mailing: 10910 Domain Dr.
        Suite 300
        Austin, TX 78758

Tel:	(512) 777-3800
TF:	(877) 442-6437

Washington Office
Mailing: 1375 Piccard Dr.
        Suite 300
        Rockville, MD 20850

Tel:	(301) 354-3606
Fax:	(301) 519-2646

Political Action Committees
Hanger Inc. PAC
FEC ID: C00430397
Contact: Russell Allen
10910 Domain Dr.
Suite 300
Austin, TX 78758

Tel:	(301) 986-0701
Fax:	(301) 986-0702

    Contributions to Candidates: $24,000 (2015-2016)
    Democrats: $7,500; Republicans: $16,500

Corporate Foundations and Giving Programs

Hanger Ivan R. Sabel Foundation
1375 Piccard Drive
Suite 300
Rockville, MD 20850

Tel:	(301) 354-3606

The Hanger Charitable Foundation
10910 Domain Dr.
Suite 300
Austin, TX 78758

Tel:	(512) 777-3800

Public Affairs and Related Activities Personnel

At Headquarters

BURKET, Krisita
Media Relations Program Manager
kburket@hanger.com

Tel:	(904) 249-0314

HARTMAN, Thomas E.
Vice President and General Counsel and Secretary

Tel:	(512) 777-3800

KIRALY, Thomas F
Executive Vice President and Chief Financial Officer

Tel:	(512) 777-3800

MORTON, Drew
Vice President and Chief Human Resources Officer

Tel: (512) 777-3800

At Other Offices

BITTNER, Jennifer
Vice President, Public Relations and Corporate Communications
Two Bethesda Metro Center, Suite 1200
Bethesda, MD 20814
jbittner@hanger.com

Tel: (512) 777-3730
Fax: (301) 986-0702

Hannaford Bros. Company

An operator of supermarkets and retail drug stores. A wholly-owned subsidiary of Delhaize America, Inc.
www.hannaford.com
Employees: 26,000
SIC: 5411
Industry/ies: Food And Beverage Industry; Retail/Wholesale

Main Headquarters
Mailing: 145 Pleasant Hill Rd.
Scarborough, ME 04074

Tel: (207) 883-2911
Fax: (207) 885-2859
TF: (800) 442-6049

Corporate Foundations and Giving Programs

Hannaford Charitable Foundation
Contact: Donna Boyce
P.O. Box 1000
Portland, ME 04104

Tel: (207) 883-2911
Fax: (207) 883-2911

Public Affairs and Related Activities Personnel

At Other Offices

BOYCE, Donna
Charitable Giving Specialist
P.O. Box 1000
Portland, ME 04104
dboyce@hannaford.com

Tel: (207) 883-2911
Fax: (207) 885-2859

WISE, Bradford A.
Senior Vice President, Human Resources
P.O. Box 1000
Portland, ME 04104

Tel: (207) 883-2911
Fax: (207) 885-2859

The Hanover Insurance Group

An insurance and financial services company, which provides various property and casualty insurance products and services.
www.hanover.com
Annual Revenues: $4.96 billion
Employees: 4,800
Ticker: NYSE: THG
SIC: 6331
Industry/ies: Banking/Finance/Investments; Insurance Industry

Chairman of the Board
ANGELINI, Michael P.

Tel: (508) 855-1000
Fax: (508) 853-6332

President and Chief Executive Officer
EPPINGER, Frederick H.

Tel: (508) 855-1000
Fax: (508) 853-6332

Main Headquarters
Mailing: 440 Lincoln St.
Worcester, MA 01653-0002

Tel: (508) 855-1000
Fax: (508) 855-8078
TF: (800) 853-0456

Corporate Foundations and Giving Programs

The Hanover Insurance Group Foundation Inc.
Contact: Paul Belsito
440 Lincoln St.
Worcester, MA 01653

Tel: (508) 855-2608
Fax: (508) 853-6332

Public Affairs and Related Activities Personnel

At Headquarters

BERTHIAUME, Mark
Senior Vice President and Chief Administration Officer

Tel: (508) 855-1000
Fax: (508) 855-8078

BILOTTI-PETERSON, Christine
Senior Vice President and Chief Human Resources Officer

Tel: (508) 855-1000
Fax: (508) 855-8078

BULLIS, Eugene
Chief Financial Officer

Tel: (508) 855-1000
Fax: (508) 855-8078

HUBER, J. Kendall
Executive Vice President and General Counsel

Tel: (508) 855-1000
Fax: (508) 853-6332

LAVEY, Richard W.
Executive Vice President, President of Personal Lines and Chief Marketing Officer

Tel: (508) 855-1000
Fax: (508) 853-6332

LUKASHEVA, Oksana
Vice President, Investor Relations
olukasheva@hanover.com

Tel: (508) 855-1000
Fax: (508) 855-8078

ROBINSON, Andrew S.
President, Specialty and Executive Vice President, Corporate Development

Tel: (508) 855-1000
Fax: (508) 853-6332

The Harbour Group

Provides government affairs, communications and public relations counsel.
www.harbourgrp.com

Main Headquarters
Mailing: 1200 New Hampshire Ave. NW
Suite 850
Washington, DC 20036

Tel: (202) 295-8787

Washington Office
Mailing: 2300 N St. NW
Suite 1200
Washington, DC 20009

Tel: (202) 295-8787
Fax: (202) 295-8799

Public Affairs and Related Activities Personnel

At Headquarters

BUCKLEY, John
Managing Director

Tel: (202) 295-8787

CHANDRA, Tara
Manager

Tel: (202) 295-8787

CHANG, Audrey
Managing Director
audrey.chang@harbourgrp.com

Tel: (202) 295-8787

EPPERLY, Matthew
Vice President

Tel: (202) 295-8787

HORTENSTINE , Paul
Director

Tel: (202) 295-8787

HORWITZ, Seth
Vice President

Tel: (202) 295-8787

KANSAGOR, Gayle
Vice President
gayle.kansagor@harbourgrp.com

Tel: (202) 295-8787

MARCUS, Richard
Managing Director

Tel: (202) 295-8787

MINTZ, Richard
Managing Director

Tel: (202) 295-8787

SFORZA, Scott
Senior Counselor

Tel: (202) 295-8787

TRIACA, Matthew
Managing Director
matthew.triaca@harbourgrp.com

Tel: (202) 295-8787

VARNADORE , Langston
Account Coordinator

Tel: (202) 295-8787

At Washington Office

ALKHATIB, Firas
Senior Associate

Tel: (202) 295-8787
Fax: (202) 295-8799

FOGAN, Byron
Managing Member

Tel: (202) 295-8787
Fax: (202) 295-8799

LITTLE, Amy
Public Relations Consultant

Tel: (202) 295-8787
Fax: (202) 295-8799

Hardee's Food Systems Inc.

A system of company and franchise-owned quick-service restaurants. A wholly-owned subsidiary of CKE Restaurants, Inc.
www.hardees.com
Annual Revenues: $650.50 million
Employees: 17,000
Industry/ies: Food And Beverage Industry

Main Headquarters
Mailing: 100 N. Broadway
Suite 1200
St. Louis, MO 63102

Tel: (314) 259-6200
Fax: (314) 621-1778
TF: (877) 799-7827

Political Action Committees

Hardee's Food Systems Inc. Good Government Fund
FEC ID: C00083840
Contact: Doug Isbell
P.O. Box 1619
Rocky Mount, NC 27802

Public Affairs and Related Activities Personnel

At Headquarters

STRASCHIL, Victoria
Senior Vice President, Human Resources

Tel: (314) 259-6200
Fax: (314) 621-1778

At Other Offices

ISBELL, Doug
PAC Contact
P.O. Box 1619
Rocky Mount, NC 27802

Harley-Davidson Motorcycle Company

A manufacturer of motorcycles, recreational and commercial vehicles, parts and accessories.
www.harley-davidson.com

Annual Revenues: $6.18 billion
Employees: 6,500
Ticker: NYSE: HOG
SIC: 3751
Industry/ies: Automotive Industry; Transportation

President and Chief Executive Officer,
LEVATICH, Matthew S.
Tel: (414) 342-4680
Fax: (414) 343-8230

Main Headquarters
Mailing: 3700 W. Juneau Ave.
Milwaukee, WI 53208
Tel: (414) 342-4680
Fax: (414) 343-8230
TF: (800) 258-2464

Washington Office
Mailing: 101 Constitution Ave. NW
Suite 900 East
Washington, DC, DC 20001
Tel: (202) 742-4344

Political Action Committees
Harley-Davidson Inc Political Action Committee (Harley PAC)
FEC ID: C00224725
Contact: Jason Tolleson
3700 W. Juneau Ave.
Milwaukee, WI 53208

Corporate Foundations and Giving Programs
Harley-Davidson Foundation
Contact: Mary Ann Martiny
3700 W. Juneau Ave.
Milwaukee, WI 53208
Tel: (414) 342-4680

Public Affairs and Related Activities Personnel

At Headquarters

ALLEN, Barry K.
Board Member
Tel: (414) 343-4896
Fax: (414) 343-4515

CALAWAY, Tonit M.
Vice President, Human Resources and President, Harley-Davidson Foundation
Tel: (414) 342-4680
Fax: (414) 343-8230

JONES, Paul J.
Vice President, General Counsel and Secretary
Tel: (414) 342-4680
Fax: (414) 343-8230

KLEIN, Bob
Senior Director, Corporate Reputation
bob.klein@harley-davidson.com
Tel: (414) 343-4433
Fax: (414) 343-8230

KRISHOK, Edward M.
Managing Director, International Legal Affairs
edward.krishok@harley-davidson.com
Tel: (414) 343-4056
Fax: (414) 343-8230

MARTINY, Mary Ann
Manager, Harley-Davidson Foundation
Tel: (414) 342-4680
Fax: (414) 343-8230

OLIN, John A.
Senior Vice President and Chief Financial Officer
Tel: (414) 342-4680
Fax: (414) 343-8230

RICHER, Mark-Hans
Senior Vice President and Chief Marketing Officer
Tel: (414) 342-4680
Fax: (414) 343-8230

TOLLESON, Jason
PAC Treasurer
Tel: (414) 342-4680
Fax: (414) 343-8230

Harleysville Group

A regional provider of insurance products and services.
www.harleysvillegroup.com
Annual Revenues: $995.16 million
Employees: 1,717
Ticker: NASDAQ (GS): HGIC
SIC: 6331
Industry/ies: Insurance Industry

Main Headquarters
Mailing: 355 Maple Ave.
Harleysville, PA 19438-2297
Tel: (215) 256-5000
Fax: (215) 256-5799
TF: (800) 523-6344

Corporate Foundations and Giving Programs
Harleyville's Community Involvement Program
Contact: Mark R. Cummins
355 Maple Ave.
Harleysville, PA 19438
Tel: (215) 256-5000

Public Affairs and Related Activities Personnel

At Headquarters

CUMMINS, Mark R.
Executive Vice President, Chief Investment Officer and Treasurer
mcummins@harleysvillegroup.com
Tel: (215) 256-5025
Fax: (215) 256-5601

FRIEL, Beth A.
Assistant Vice President and Assistant General Counsel
Tel: (215) 256-5000
Fax: (215) 256-5799

KEEFE, John B.
Senior Vice President, Corporate Development
Tel: (215) 256-5000
Fax: (215) 256-5799

KELLY, Maria B.
Tel: (215) 256-5000
Fax: (215) 256-5799

Assistant Vice President, Chief Compliance Officer and Assistant General Counsel
mkelly@harleysvillegroup.com

Harp & Poydasheff LLC

Legal services and government relations.
www.hpps-law.com

Main Headquarters
Mailing: 936 Second Ave.
Columbus, GA 31901
Tel: (706) 323-2761

Public Affairs and Related Activities Personnel

At Headquarters

POYDASHEFF, Robert
Partner
RPoydasheff@HandPlaw.com
Tel: (706) 323-2761

Harris Bank

An indirect subsidiary of Bank of Montreal. An integrated financial service organization. It provides a broad range of personal banking products and solutions, which include solutions for everyday banking, financing, investing, as well as a full suite of integrated commercial and financial advisory services.
www.bmoharris.com
Annual Revenues: $1.05 billion
Employees: 14,500
SIC: 6022; 6021; 5099; 6021; 6141
Industry/ies: Banking/Finance/Investments

Chairman of the Board
PRICHARD, J. Robert S.
Tel: (312) 461-2121
Fax: (312) 461-7869

President and Chief Executive Officer
CASPER, Dave
Tel: (312) 461-2121
Fax: (312) 461-7869

Main Headquarters
Mailing: 111 W. Monroe St.
P.O. BOX 755
Chicago, IL 60603-4096
Tel: (312) 461-2121
Fax: (312) 461-7869
TF: (888) 340-2265

Political Action Committees
BMO Harris Bank Government Affairs Fund PAC
FEC ID: C00086256
Contact: Carl Jenkins
111 W. Monroe St.
P.O. Box 755
Chicago, IL 60603

Contributions to Candidates: $31,200 (2015-2016)
Democrats: $17,700; Republicans: $13,500

Corporate Foundations and Giving Programs
Harris Bank Foundation
Contact: Diane Whatton
111 W. Monroe St.
Chicago, IL 60603
Tel: (312) 461-2121

Public Affairs and Related Activities Personnel

At Headquarters

DOWNE, William
Chief Executive Officer of BMO Financial Corp.
Tel: (312) 461-2121
Fax: (312) 461-7869

ELLIS, Jeff
Executive Vice President, General Counsel, Legal, Corporate and Compliance Group, BMO Financial Group
Tel: (312) 461-2121
Fax: (312) 461-7869

FEDAK, Justine
Senior Vice President and Head of Brand, Advertising and Sponsorships of BMO Financial Group
Tel: (312) 461-2121
Fax: (312) 461-7869

JENKINS, Carl
Managing Director, Community Investments, Corporate Finance
carl.jenkins@bmo.com
Tel: (312) 461-2121
Fax: (312) 461-7869

MOSS, Eric
Senior Vice President and Chief Compliance Officer of BMO Financial Group
Tel: (312) 461-2121
Fax: (312) 461-7869

O'HERLIHY, Patrick
Assistant Vice President, Media Relations
patrick.o'herlihy@harrisbank.com
Tel: (312) 461-6970
Fax: (312) 461-7869

RENARD, Paul
Senior Vice President, Human Resources of BMO Financial Group
Tel: (312) 461-2121
Fax: (312) 461-7869

RICE, Judith
Director, Government Relations
Tel: (312) 461-2121
Fax: (312) 461-7869

TAYLOR, Stephen
Chief Financial Officer of BMO Financial Group
Tel: (312) 461-2121
Fax: (312) 461-7869

WHATTON, Diane
Vice President, Community Affairs
Tel: (312) 461-2121
Fax: (312) 461-7869

Harris Corporation

Harris is an international communications and information technology company serving government and commercial markets in more than 125 countries.
harris.com
Annual Revenues: $4.88 billion
Employees: 14,000
Ticker: NYSE: HRS
SIC: 3570
Industry/ies: Electricity & Electronics; Electronics; Energy/Electricity
Legislative Issues: AER; AVI; BUD; COM; DEF; HOM

Chairman, President and Chief Executive Officer
BROWN, William M.
Tel: (321) 727-9100
Fax: (321) 674-4740

Main Headquarters
Mailing: 221 Jefferson Ridge Pkwy.
Lynchburg, VA 24501
Tel: (321) 727-9100
Fax: (321) 674-4740
TF: (800) 442-7747

Washington Office
Mailing: 600 Maryland Ave. SW
Suite 850 E.
Washington, DC 20024
Tel: (202) 729-3709
Fax: (202) 729-3735

Political Action Committees
Harris Corporation PAC
FEC ID: C00100321
Contact: Miguel Lopez
600 Maryland Ave. SW
Suite 850 E
Washington, DC 20024

Contributions to Candidates: $426,500 (2015-2016)
Democrats: $200,000; Republicans: $226,500

Principal Recipients

SENATE
BLUNT, ROY (REP-MO)

HOUSE
HOYER, STENY HAMILTON (DEM-DC)
POSEY, BILL (REP-FL)
SANCHEZ, LORETTA (DEM-CA)
STEFANIK, ELISE M. (REP-NY)

Corporate Foundations and Giving Programs
Harris Foundation
1025 W. NASA Blvd.
Melbourne, FL 32919
Tel: (321) 727-9100

Public Affairs and Related Activities Personnel

At Headquarters
BURKE, Jim
Director, Global Public Relations
jim.burke@harris.com
Tel: (321) 727-9131
Fax: (321) 727-9222

CAVALLUCCI, Eugene S.
Vice President, General Counsel
Tel: (321) 727-9100
Fax: (321) 674-4740

DUFFY, Robert
Senior Vice President, Human Resources and Administration
Tel: (321) 727-9100
Fax: (321) 674-4740

FOX, Sheldon J.
Group President, Government Communications Systems
Tel: (321) 727-9100
Fax: (321) 674-4740

LOPEZ, Miguel
Senior Vice President and Chief Financial Officer and PAC Treasurer
Tel: (321) 727-9100
Fax: (321) 674-4740

MEHNERT, Dana A.
Group President, Communications
Tel: (321) 727-9100
Fax: (321) 674-4740

MIKUEN, Scott
Senior Vice President, General Counsel and Secretary
Tel: (321) 727-9100
Fax: (321) 674-4740

PADGETT, Pamela
Vice President, Investor Relations
ppadge01@harris.com
Tel: (321) 727-9383
Fax: (321) 674-4740

TAYLOR, Todd
Vice President, Principal Accounting Officer
Tel: (321) 727-9100
Fax: (321) 674-4740

At Washington Office
BROWN, Alicia
Federal Lobbyist
Tel: (202) 729-3709
Fax: (202) 729-3735

CHALLAN, Peter H.
Vice President, Government Relations
Tel: (202) 729-3700
Fax: (202) 729-3735

GRAB, Glenn
Federal Lobbyist
Registered Federal Lobbyist
Tel: (202) 729-3709
Fax: (202) 729-3735

GREENE, Charles J.
Vice President, Tax & Treasurer
Tel: (202) 729-3709
Fax: (202) 729-3735

HANNA, Tania
Vice President, Government Relations
tania.hanna@harris.com
Registered Federal Lobbyist
Tel: (202) 729-3700
Fax: (202) 729-3735

POMEROY, Jill K.
Manager, Government Relations
Tel: (202) 729-3709
Fax: (202) 729-3735

Registered Federal Lobbyist
SULLIVAN, Adam J.
Director, Government Relations
Registered Federal Lobbyist
Tel: (202) 729-3700
Fax: (202) 729-3735

ZEPPIERI, Carla N.
Federal Lobbyist
Registered Federal Lobbyist
Tel: (202) 729-3709
Fax: (202) 729-3735

Harris Teeter Supermarkets, Inc.

A holding company with operating subsidiaries active in supermarkets and industrial sewing thread. Acquired by The Kroger Company in 2013.
www.harristeeter.com
Employees: 10,500
Ticker: NYSE: HTSI
SIC: 5411
NAICS: 5411
Industry/ies: Apparel/Textiles Industry; Food And Beverage Industry

Main Headquarters
Mailing: P. O. Box 10100
Mathews, NC 28106-0100

Public Affairs and Related Activities Personnel

At Other Offices
ROBINSON, Danna
Manager, Communication
701 Crestdale Rd.
Matthews, NC 28105
djones@harristeeter.com
Tel: (704) 844-3904
Fax: (704) 844-3214

WOODLIEF, John B.
Executive Vice President and Chief Financial Officer and Contact, Media Relations
701 Crestdale Rd.
Matthews, NC 28105
jb.woodlief@ruddickcorp.com
Tel: (704) 844-3100
Fax: (704) 372-6409

YACENDA, Douglas J.
Secretary and Contact, Investor Relations
701 Crestdale Rd.
Matthews, NC 28105
dyacenda@harristeeter.com
Tel: (704) 844-7536
Fax: (704) 372-6409

Harry & David

Offers gourmet fruit baskets with entrees, appetizers and home style desserts.
www.harryanddavid.com
Annual Revenues: $379.46 million
Employees: 1,000
SIC: 5990
Industry/ies: Food And Beverage Industry

Chief Executive Officer
JOHNSON, Craig
Tel: (877) 322-1200
Fax: (800) 648-6640

Main Headquarters
Mailing: 2500 S. Pacific Hwy.
P.O. Box 9100
Medford, OR 97501-0700
Tel: (877) 322-1200
Fax: (800) 648-6640
TF: (800) 345-5655

Political Action Committees
Harry and David PAC
FEC ID: C00401729
Contact: Michael Schwindle
2500 S. Pacific Hwy.
P.O. Box 299
Medford, OR 97501

Public Affairs and Related Activities Personnel

At Headquarters
O'CONNELL, Stephen V.
Chief Financial Officer and Chief Administrative Officer
svoconnell@gmail.com
Tel: (877) 322-1200
Fax: (800) 648-6640

SCHWINDLE, Michael
PAC Treasurer
Tel: (877) 322-1200
Fax: (800) 648-6640

HARSCO Corporation

A diversified industrial services and products company serving strategic worldwide industries, including steel, gas and energy and infrastructure development. It designs and manufactures railway track maintenance equipment; and provides track maintenance services, also manufactures air-cooled heat exchangers; industrial grating products; and boilers and water heaters for industrial plants, non-residential, commercial and public construction, and retrofit markets, as well as natural gas, natural gas processing, and petrochemical industries.
www.harsco.com
Annual Revenues: $2.00 billion
Employees: 12,200
Ticker: NYSE: HSC
SIC: 3295; 3312; 3341; 3089; 3441
Industry/ies: Construction/Construction Materials; Metals

| **Non-Executive Chairman** | Tel: | (717) 763-7064 |
| EVERITT, David C. | Fax: | (717) 763-6424 |

| **President and Chief Executive Officer** | Tel: | (717) 763-7064 |
| GRASBERGER , F. Nicholas | Fax: | (717) 763-6424 |

Main Headquarters

| Mailing: | 350 Poplar Church Rd. | Tel: | (717) 763-7064 |
| | Camp Hill, PA 17011 | Fax: | (717) 763-6424 |

Political Action Committees

Harsco Corporation PAC (HARSCOPAC)
FEC ID: C00084145
Contact: Stephen E. Baney
350 Poplar Church Rd.
Camp Hill, PA 17011

Corporate Foundations and Giving Programs

Harsco Corporation Fund
Contact: Robert G. Yocum
P.O. Box 8888
Camp Hill, PA 17001

Public Affairs and Related Activities Personnel

At Headquarters

| BANEY, Stephen E. | Tel: | (717) 763-7064 |
| *Senior Director-Risk Management* | Fax: | (717) 763-6424 |

HOCHMAN, Russell	Tel:	(717) 763-7064
Senior Vice President and General Counsel, Chief	Fax:	(717) 763-6424
Compliance Officer and Corporate Secretary		

JULIAN, Kenneth D.	Tel:	(717) 730-3683
Senior Director, Corporate Communications	Fax:	(717) 763-6424
kjulian@harsco.com		

MARTIN, David	Tel:	(717) 612-5628
Director, Investor Relations	Fax:	(717) 763-6424
damartin@harsco.com		

| MCKENZIE, Tracey | Tel: | (717) 763-7064 |
| *Senior Vice President and Chief Human Resources Officer* | Fax: | (717) 763-6424 |

| MINAN, Peter F. | Tel: | (717) 763-7064 |
| *Senior Vice President and Chief Financial Officer* | Fax: | (717) 763-6424 |

Harte-Hanks Inc.

A nationwide communications company with subsidiaries involved in newspaper publishing, television, advertising publications and direct marketing.
www.harte-hanks.com
Annual Revenues: $542.12 million
Employees: 5,389
Ticker: NYSE: HHS
SIC: 2741
NAICS: 511140
Industry/ies: Communications; Media/Mass Communication

| **Chairman, Chief Executive Officer & President** | Tel: | (210) 829-9120 |
| FRANKLIN, Larry D. | Fax: | (210) 829-9139 |

| **Chairman of the Board** | Tel: | (210) 829-9000 |
| HARTE , Christopher M. | Fax: | (210) 829-9139 |

Main Headquarters

Mailing:	9601 McAllister Fwy.	Tel:	(210) 829-9000
	Suite 610	Fax:	(210) 829-9139
	San Antonio, TX 78216	TF:	(800) 456-9748

Public Affairs and Related Activities Personnel

At Headquarters

| FAY, Sarah | Tel: | (210) 829-9000 |
| *Strategic Advisor* | Fax: | (210) 829-9139 |

| METZGER, Keith | Tel: | (210) 829-9000 |
| *Head, Global Corporate Development* | Fax: | (210) 829-9139 |

| MUNDEN, Robert L. R. | Tel: | (210) 829-9000 |
| *Senior Vice President, General Counsel and Secretary* | Fax: | (210) 829-9139 |

| POMMERNELLE, Gavin | Tel: | (210) 829-9000 |
| *Executive Vice President and Chief Human Resources Officer* | Fax: | (210) 829-9139 |

SHEPARD, Douglas C.	Tel:	(210) 829-9000
Executive Vice President and Chief Financial Officer	Fax:	(210) 829-9139
doug_shepard@hart-hanks.com		

| VOICA, Joseph | Tel: | (210) 829-9000 |
| *Senior Vice President, Sales* | Fax: | (210) 829-9139 |

The Hartford Financial Services Group

The Hartford offers products to meet a broad range of needs, from property-and-casualty insurance for personal and business needs to employee benefits and mutual funds.
www.thehartford.com
Annual Revenues: $18.54 billion
Employees: 17,500
Ticker: NYSE: HIG
SIC: 6331
Industry/ies: Insurance Industry

Legislative Issues: CSP; FIN; HOU; INS; LBR; RET; TAX; TOR

| **Chairman and Chief Executive Officer** | Tel: | (860) 547-5000 |
| SWIFT, Christopher J. | Fax: | (860) 547-2680 |

Main Headquarters

Mailing:	One Hartford Plaza	Tel:	(860) 547-5000
	Hartford Plaza HO-1-11	Fax:	(860) 547-2680
	Hartford, CT 06115		

Washington Office

Mailing:	1445 New York Ave. NW	Tel:	(202) 296-7513
	Suite 801	Fax:	(860) 547-3799
	Washington, DC 20005		

Political Action Committees

The Hartford Financial Services Group, Inc. Federal Pac (Aka Hartford Advocates Federal Fund)
FEC ID: C00511444
Contact: Scott Lewis

One Hartford Plaza	Tel:	(860) 547-5000
Hartford Plaza HO-1-11	Fax:	(860) 547-2680
Hartford, CT 06115		

> **Contributions to Candidates:** $39,600 (2015-2016)
> Democrats: $14,500; Republicans: $25,100

The Hartford Financial Services Group, Inc. PAC (Aka The Hartford Advocates Fund)
FEC ID: C00168864
Contact: Scott Lewis
One Hartford Plaza
HO-1-11
Hartford, CT 6155

> **Contributions to Candidates:** $127,500 (2015-2016)
> Democrats: $56,000; Republicans: $71,500

Corporate Foundations and Giving Programs

The Hartford Foundation
Contact: Lori G. Rabb

One Hartford Plaza	Tel:	(860) 547-5000
Hartford Plaza HO-1-11	Fax:	(860) 547-2680
Hartford, CT 06155		

Public Affairs and Related Activities Personnel

At Headquarters

| BOMBARA, Beth A. | Tel: | (860) 547-5000 |
| *Chief Financial Officer* | Fax: | (860) 547-2680 |

| BRIDGET, Bridget J. | Tel: | (860) 547-5000 |
| *President* | Fax: | (860) 547-2680 |

| DUNN, Bridget J. | Tel: | (860) 547-5000 |
| *President* | Fax: | (860) 547-2680 |

| ELLIOT, Doug | Tel: | (860) 547-5000 |
| *President, Commercial Markets* | Fax: | (860) 547-2680 |

| GERVASI, Martha | Tel: | (860) 547-5000 |
| *Executive Vice President, Human Resources* | Fax: | (860) 547-2680 |

| JOHNSON, Brion | Tel: | (860) 547-5000 |
| *Chief Investment Officer* | Fax: | (860) 547-2680 |

| KIRK, Matthew | Tel: | (860) 547-8480 |
| *Senior Vice President, Sales and Distribution* | Fax: | (860) 547-3799 |

| KRECZKO, Alan | Tel: | (860) 547-5374 |
| *Executive Vice President and General Counsel* | Fax: | (860) 547-2680 |

LAPIERRE, Shannon	Tel:	(860) 547-5624
Senior Vice President, Communications	Fax:	(860) 547-2680
shannon.lapierre@thehartford.com		

LEWIS, Scott	Tel:	(860) 547-5000
Lobbyist and PAC Treasurer	Fax:	(860) 547-2680
Mail Stop HO-1-11		

NAPOLI, Andy	Tel:	(860) 547-5000
President, Consumer Markets and Enterprise Business	Fax:	(860) 547-2680
Services		

PURTILL, CFA, Sabra	Tel:	(860) 547-8691
Senior Vice President, Investor Relations	Fax:	(860) 547-2680
sabra.purtill@thehartford.com		

| QUINN, Jordan | Tel: | (860) 547-5000 |
| *Registered Federal Lobbyist* | Fax: | (860) 547-2680 |

| RUPP, Robert | Tel: | (860) 547-5000 |
| *Executive Vice President and Chief Risk Officer* | Fax: | (860) 547-2680 |

| SPRAGUE, Ray | Tel: | (860) 547-5000 |
| *Executive Vice President, Strategy and Business Development* | Fax: | (860) 547-2680 |

| TRIPP, Karen | Tel: | (860) 547-5000 |
| *Executive Vice President, Marketing and Communications* | Fax: | (860) 547-2680 |

| WILLIAMS, Kelley | Tel: | (860) 547-5000 |
| *Federal Lobbyist* | Fax: | (860) 547-2680 |

At Washington Office

| CLARK , Rachel E. | Tel: | (202) 296-7513 |

Senior Specialist, Government Affairs	Fax:	(860) 547-3799
HAINES, Laura	Tel:	(202) 296-8328
Assistant Vice President, Federal Affairs	Fax:	(860) 547-3799
laura.haines@thehartford.com		
Registered Federal Lobbyist		

At Other Offices

RABB , Lori G.	Tel:	(860) 548-1888
Vice President, Philanthropic Services	Fax:	(860) 524-8346
Ten Columbus Blvd., Eighth Floor		
Hartford, CT 06106		
lrabb@hfpg.org		

Hartford Steam Boiler Inspection and Insurance Company

A property and casualty insurance and engineering company. A wholly-owned subsidiary of American International Group (see separate listing).
www.hsb.com
Annual Revenues: $646.15 million
Employees: 1,400
SIC: 6331
Industry/ies: Engineering/Mathematics; Insurance Industry

Chairman of the Board	Tel:	(860) 722-1866
KUCZINSKI , Anthony J.	Fax:	(860) 722-5106
President and Chief Executive Officer	Tel:	(860) 722-1866
BARATS, Greg M.	Fax:	(860) 722-5106

Main Headquarters

Mailing: One State St.	Tel:	(860) 722-1866
P.O. Box 5024	Fax:	(860) 722-5106
Hartford, CT 06103-3199	TF:	(800) 472-1866

Corporate Foundations and Giving Programs

Hartford Steam Boiler Inspection & Insurance Company Giving Program
Contact: Ann Waller

One State St.	Tel:	(860) 722-1866
P.O. Box 5024		
Hartford, CT 06102		

Public Affairs and Related Activities Personnel

At Headquarters

AHRENS, Susan W.	Tel:	(860) 722-1866
Senior Vice President, Human Resources	Fax:	(860) 722-5106
KMIECIK, Theodore D	Tel:	(860) 722-1866
Senior Vice President and Treasurer	Fax:	(860) 722-5106
MILEWSKI, Dennis	Tel:	(860) 722-5567
Contact, Media Relations	Fax:	(860) 722-5280
dennis_milewski@hsb.com		
O'BRIEN, Roberta A.	Tel:	(860) 722-1866
Senior Vice President, Deputy General Counsel and Compliance Officer	Fax:	(860) 722-5106
O'SHEA, Denis	Tel:	(860) 722-5313
Vice President, Communications	Fax:	(860) 722-5106
denis_o'shea@hsb.com		
ONKEN, Nancy	Tel:	(860) 722-1866
Executive Vice President, General Counsel and Corporate Secretary	Fax:	(860) 722-5106
RICHTER, Peter	Tel:	(860) 722-1866
Chief Financial Officer	Fax:	(860) 722-5106
WALLER, Ann	Tel:	(860) 722-1866
Director, Communications	Fax:	(860) 722-5106
Ann_Waller@HSB.com		

Harvest Natural Resources, Inc.

An independent energy company.
www.harvestnr.com
Annual Revenues: $10.7 million
Employees: 30
Ticker: NYSE: HNR
SIC: 1311
Industry/ies: Energy/Electricity

Chairman of the Board	Tel:	(281) 899-5700
CHESEBRO, Stephen D.	Fax:	(281) 899-5702
President and Chief Executive Officer	Tel:	(281) 899-5700
EDMISTON, James A.	Fax:	(281) 899-5702

Main Headquarters

Mailing: 1177 Enclave Pkwy.	Tel:	(281) 899-5700
Suite 300	Fax:	(281) 899-5702
Houston, TX 77077		

Public Affairs and Related Activities Personnel

At Headquarters

HAYNES, Stephen C.	Tel:	(281) 899-5700
Vice President, Chief Financial Officer and Treasurer	Fax:	(281) 899-5702
HEAD, Keith L.	Tel:	(281) 899-5700
Vice President, General Counsel and Corporate Secretary	Fax:	(281) 899-5702

Hasbro, Inc.

A designer, manufacturer and marketer of games and toys ranging from traditional to high-tech. Brands include Playskool, Kenner, Tonka, Oddzon, Super Soaker, Milton Bradley, Parker Brothers, Tiger, Hasbro Interactive, Microporse, Galloob and Wizards of the Coast.
www.hasbro.com
Annual Revenues: $4.31 billion
Employees: 5,200
Ticker: NYSE: HAS
SIC: 3944
Industry/ies: Children And Youth; Furniture/Home Furnishings
Legislative Issues: CSP

President and Chief Executive Officer	Tel:	(401) 431-8697
GOLDNER, Brian	Fax:	(401) 431-8535

Main Headquarters

Mailing: 1027 Newport Ave.	Tel:	(401) 431-8697
P.O.Box 1059	Fax:	(401) 431-8535
Pawtucket, RI 02861-1059		

Corporate Foundations and Giving Programs

Hasbro Children's Foundation		
1027 Newport Ave.	Tel:	(401) 431-8697
P.O. Box 1059		
Pawtucket, RI 02862		

Public Affairs and Related Activities Personnel

At Headquarters

BILLING, Duncan J.	Tel:	(401) 431-8697
Executive Vice President, Global Operations and Business Development	Fax:	(401) 431-8535
CHARNESS, Wayne S.	Tel:	(401) 727-5983
Senior Vice President, Corporate Communications	Fax:	(401) 431-8535
DUFFY, Julie Collins	Tel:	(401) 727-5931
Vice President, Global Communications	Fax:	(401) 431-8535
julie.duffy@hasbro.com		
FINIGAN, Barbara	Tel:	(401) 431-8697
Senior Vice President, Chief Legal Officer and Secretary	Fax:	(401) 431-8535
FRASCOTTI, John A.	Tel:	(401) 431-8697
President	Fax:	(401) 431-8535
HANCOCK, Debbie	Tel:	(401) 431-8447
Vice President, Investor Relations	Fax:	(401) 431-8535
HARGREAVES, David D.R.	Tel:	(401) 431-8697
Executive Vice President and Chief Strategy Officer	Fax:	(401) 431-8535
THOMAS, Deborah M.	Tel:	(401) 431-8697
Senior Vice President and Chief Financial Officer	Fax:	(401) 431-8535
TRUEB, Martin R.	Tel:	(401) 431-8697
Senior Vice President and Treasurer	Fax:	(401) 431-8535

The Hauser Group

THG or Hauser is a full-service risk management, employee benefits and insurance solutions partner which provides value-added support, resources and expertise to clients and prospects across a multitude of industries.
thehausergroup.com

Chief Executive Officer, Employee Benefits, Hauser Insurance Group	Tel:	(513) 745-9200
	Fax:	(513) 745-9219
STINES, James		

Main Headquarters

Mailing: 8260 Northcreek Dr.	Tel:	(513) 745-9200
Suite 200	Fax:	(513) 745-9219
Cincinnati, OH 45236	TF:	(800) 886-0098

Washington Office

Mailing: 2000 P St. NW	Tel:	(202) 518-8047
Suite 310	Fax:	(202) 904-2826
Washington, DC 20009		

Public Affairs and Related Activities Personnel

At Headquarters

ASTON, Kevin	Tel:	(513) 745-9200
President, Hauser Insurance Group	Fax:	(513) 745-9219
ELMER, Lacy	Tel:	(513) 745-9200
Account Executive, Management & Professional Liability, Hauser Insurance Group	Fax:	(513) 745-9219
WORRALL, Joe	Tel:	(513) 745-9200
President, Corporate Risk at Hauser Insurance Group	Fax:	(513) 745-9219

At Washington Office

APPEL, Julia	Tel:	(202) 518-8047
Communications Assistant	Fax:	(202) 904-2826
julia@publicinterestpr.com		
DRING, Jason	Tel:	(202) 518-8047
Senior Associate	Fax:	(202) 904-2826
jason@publicinterestpr.com		

STREUBER, Crystal   Tel: (202) 518-8047
Communications Assistant   Fax: (202) 904-2826
crystal@publicinterestpr.com

Hawaii Medical Service Association Blue Cross Blue Shield of Hawaii

An independent licensee of the Blue Cross and Blue Shield Association. Provider of health care coverage in the state of Hawaii.
www.hmsa.com
Annual Revenues: $581.70 million
Employees: 1,500
Industry/ies: Insurance Industry; Medicine/Health Care/Mental Health
Legislative Issues: BUD; HCR

Chairman of the Board   Tel: (808) 948-6111
HARRISON, Robert S.   Fax: (808) 948-5567

President and Chief Executive Officer   Tel: (808) 948-6111
GOLD, Michael A.   Fax: (808) 948-5567

Main Headquarters
Mailing: P.O. Box 860   Tel: (808) 948-6111
Honolulu, HI 96808   Fax: (808) 948-5567

Political Action Committees
Hawaii Medical Service Association Employee PAC
FEC ID: C00321992
Contact: Carolyn Gire
818 Keeaumoku St.
Honolulu, HI 96814

> **Contributions to Candidates:** $1,000 (2015-2016)
> Democrats: $1,000

Corporate Foundations and Giving Programs

HMSA Foundation
Contact: Mark L. Forman
818 Keeaumoku St.   Fax: (808) 948-6860
P.O. Box 860
Honolulu, HI 96808-0860

Public Affairs and Related Activities Personnel

At Headquarters

BOLAND, Francie E.   Tel: (808) 948-6111
Vice President, Legal Services   Fax: (808) 948-5567
Francie_Boland@hmsa.com

DIESMAN, Jennifer A.   Tel: (808) 948-6111
Vice President, Government Affairs   Fax: (808) 948-5567
Jennifer_Diesman@hmsa.com

EVENSEN, Stacey K.   Tel: (808) 948-6111
Vice President, Government Affairs   Fax: (808) 948-5567

FORMAN, Mark L.   Tel: (808) 948-6111
Executive Administrator   Fax: (808) 948-6860
mark_forman@hmsa.com

KINOSHITA, Shannon   Tel: (808) 952-7989
Contact, Community and Public Relations   Fax: (808) 948-5567
shannon_kinoshita@hmsa.com

MARTING, Gina L.   Tel: (808) 948-6111
Senior Vice President Accounting and Finance   Fax: (808) 948-5567

MIYASATO, Gwen S.   Tel: (808) 948-6111
Chief Corporate Services Officer and Assistant Secretary   Fax: (808) 948-5567

NAKAGAWA, Janna L.S.   Tel: (808) 948-6111
Senior Vice President, Corporate Services   Fax: (808) 948-5567

RIBBINK, Steven Van   Tel: (808) 948-6111
Executive Vice President, Chief Financial Officer and Treasurer   Fax: (808) 948-5567

TAKAHASHI, Brenda S.K.P.   Tel: (808) 948-6111
Assistant Vice President, Appeals, Compliance and Ethics   Fax: (808) 948-5567
brenda_takahashi@hmsa.com

YADAO, Elisa J.   Tel: (808) 948-6111
Senior Vice President, Consumer Experience   Fax: (808) 948-5567
elisa_yadao@hmsa.co

At Other Offices

GIRE, Carolyn
PAC Treasurer
818 Keeaumoku St.
Honolulu, HI 96814

Hawaiian Commercial and Sugar Company

Works to educate members of Congress and staff regarding sugar farming and U.S. policies and regulations affecting sugar farmers.
www.hcsugar.com
Industry/ies: Agriculture/Agronomy
Legislative Issues: AGR

General Manager   Tel: (202) 785-4070
VOLNER, Rick W.   Fax: (202) 659-8581

Main Headquarters
Mailing: 1301 Pennsylvania Ave. NW   Tel: (202) 785-4070

Suite 401   Fax: (202) 659-8581
Washington, DC 20004

Public Affairs and Related Activities Personnel

At Headquarters

CERVANTES, Jennifer   Tel: (202) 785-4070
Legislative Director

GOTO, Keith A   Tel: (202) 785-4070
Vice President, Human Resources   Fax: (202) 659-8581
kkumar6@jgsi.com

WESTON, Ryan
Washington Representative

At Other Offices

LIGIENZA, Daniel J.
Vice President and Controller
P.O. Box 266
Puunene, Maui, HI 96784

SKROBECKI, Anna M
Senior Vice President, Factory and Power Plant Operations
P.O. Box 266
Puunene, Maui, HI 96784

Hawaiian Electric Company

An electric utility of Hawaiian Electric Industries, Inc.
www.heco.com
Employees: 2,200
SIC: 4911
Industry/ies: Energy/Electricity; Utilities
Legislative Issues: ENG

Chairman   Tel: (808) 548-7311
LAU, Constance H.   Fax: (808) 543-7799

President and Chief Executive Officer   Tel: (808) 548-7311
OSHIMA, Alan M.   Fax: (808) 543-7799

Main Headquarters
Mailing: P.O. Box 3978   Tel: (808) 548-7311
Honolulu, HI 96812-3978   Fax: (808) 543-7799
   TF: (888) 813-2215

Corporate Foundations and Giving Programs

Hawaiian Electric Contributions Program
Contact: Sharon Higa
P.O. Box 3978   Tel: (808) 548-7311
Honolulu, HI 96812-3978

Public Affairs and Related Activities Personnel

At Headquarters

ENDO-OMOTO, Darcy L.   Tel: (808) 548-7311
Vice President, Government and Community Affairs   Fax: (808) 543-7799

HIGA, Sharon   Tel: (808) 548-7311
Senior Communications Consultant and Philanthropy Contact   Fax: (808) 543-7799
sharon.higa@hawaiianelectric.com

HOLLINGER, Suzy P.   Tel: (808) 543-7385
Manager, Treasury and Investor Relations   Fax: (808) 203-1155
shollinger@hei.com

LI, Susan A.   Tel: (808) 548-7311
Senior Vice President, General Counsel, Chief Compliance Officer and Corporate Secretary   Fax: (808) 543-7799

ROSEGG, Peter   Tel: (808) 543-7780
Senior Spokesman   Fax: (808) 543-7799
peter.rosegg@heco.com

SEKIMURA, Tayne S. Y.   Tel: (808) 548-7311
Senior Vice President and Chief Financial Officer   Fax: (808) 543-7799

UNEMORI, Lynne T.   Tel: (808) 226-7853
Vice President, Corporate Relations   Fax: (808) 543-7799
lynne.unemori@heco.com

VIOLA, Joseph P.   Tel: (808) 548-7311
Vice President, Regulatory Affairs   Fax: (808) 543-7799

Hawaiian Holdings, LLC

An airline holding company serving 20 domestic and international destinations in the Pacific region.
www.hawaiianair.com
Annual Revenues: $2.33 billion
Employees: 5,371
Ticker: NASDAQ: HA
SIC: 4512
Industry/ies: Aerospace/Aviation; Airlines; Transportation

Chairman of the Board   Tel: (808) 835-3700
HERSHFIELD, Lawrence S.   Fax: (808) 835-3690

President and Chief Executive Officer   Tel: (808) 835-3700
DUNKERLEY, Mark B.   Fax: (808) 835-3690

Main Headquarters

Mailing:	P.O. Box 30008	Tel:	(808) 835-3700
	Honolulu, HI 96820	Fax:	(808) 835-3690
		TF:	(888) 246-8526

Political Action Committees

Hawaiian Airlines Inc. PAC
FEC ID: C00456939
Contact: Hoyt H. Zia
3375 Koapaka St.
Suite G350
Honolulu, HI 96819

> **Contributions to Candidates:** $29,400 (2015-2016)
> Democrats: $12,400; Republicans: $17,000

Public Affairs and Related Activities Personnel

At Headquarters

ANDERSON-LEHMAN, Ron	Tel:	(808) 835-3700
Executive Vice President and Chief Administrative Officer	Fax:	(808) 835-3690
BOTTICELLI, Ann	Tel:	(808) 835-3700
Senior Vice President, Corporate Communications and Public	Fax:	(808) 835-3690
Affairs		
FALVEY, Barbara D.	Tel:	(808) 835-3700
Senior Vice President, Human Resources	Fax:	(808) 835-3690
FORBES, Christian	Tel:	(808) 835-3700
Vice President Financial Planning & Analysis	Fax:	(808) 835-3690
INGRAM, Peter R.	Tel:	(808) 835-3700
Executive Vice President and Chief Commercial Officer	Fax:	(808) 835-3690
MANNIS, Avi A.	Tel:	(808) 835-3700
Senior Vice President, Marketing	Fax:	(808) 835-3690
TOPPING, Scott E.	Tel:	(808) 835-3700
Executive Vice President Chief Financial Officer and	Fax:	(808) 835-3690
Treasurer		
WAGNER, John R.	Tel:	(808) 835-3700
Vice President, Public Affairs	Fax:	(808) 835-3690

At Other Offices

ZIA, Hoyt H.	Tel:	(808) 835-3700
Senior Vice President, General Counsel, Corporate Secretary	Fax:	(808) 835-3690
and PAC Treasurer		
3375 Koapaka St., G-350		
Honolulu, HI 96819		
Hoyt.Zia@hawaiianair.com		

Hawaiian Telecom Communications Inc.

A provider of communications services, products and solutions in Hawaii.
www.hawaiiantel.com
Annual Revenues: $390.78 million
Employees: 1,336
SIC: 4813
Industry/ies: Communications; Telecommunications/Internet/Cable

Chairman of the Board	Tel:	(808) 546-4511
JALKUT, Richard A.	Fax:	(808) 546-6194

President and Chief Executive Officer	Tel:	(808) 546-4511
BARBER, Scott K.	Fax:	(808) 546-6194

Main Headquarters

Mailing:	1177 Bishop St.	Tel:	(808) 546-4511
	Honolulu, HI 96813	Fax:	(808) 546-6194

Political Action Committees

Hawaiian Telcom Communications Inc. FedPAC
FEC ID: C00413401
Contact: Kenneth T. Hiraki
1177 Bishop St.
Honolulu, HI 96813

Corporate Foundations and Giving Programs

Hawaiian Telcom Ho'olaulima Charitable Giving Program
Contact: Ann Nishida

1177 Bishop St.	Tel:	(808) 546-4511
Honolulu, HI 96813	Fax:	(808) 546-3148

Public Affairs and Related Activities Personnel

At Headquarters

BESSEY, Dan T.	Tel:	(808) 546-4511
Chief Financial Officer	Fax:	(808) 546-6194
HIRAKI, Kenneth T.	Tel:	(808) 546-4511
PAC Treasurer	Fax:	(808) 546-3148
KOMEIJI, John T.	Tel:	(808) 546-4511
Senior Vice President and General Counsel	Fax:	(808) 546-3148
john.komeiji@hawaiiantel.com		
NGUYEN, Ngoc	Tel:	(808) 546-3475
Manager, Investor Relations and Financial Planning	Fax:	(808) 546-6194
NISHIDA, Ann	Tel:	(808) 546-1888

Senior Manager, Corporate Communications	Fax:	(808) 546-3148
ann.nishida@hawaiiantel.com		
PUALANI WALKER TOPPING, Sunshine	Tel:	(808) 546-4511
Vice President, Human Resources	Fax:	(808) 546-6194

Hawker Beechcraft Corporation

See listing on page 781 under Textron Inc.

Haworth Inc.

Designs and manufactures office furniture and organic workspaces, including raised access floors, moveable walls, systems furniture, seating, storage and wood case goods.
www.haworth.com
Employees: 6,000
SIC: 2521
NAICS: 337211
Industry/ies: Furniture/Home Furnishings

Chairman	Tel:	(616) 393-3000
HAWORTH, Dick	Fax:	(616) 393-1570

President & Chief Executive Officer	Tel:	(616) 393-3000
BIANCHI, Franco	Fax:	(616) 393-1570
franco.bianchi@haworth.com		

Main Headquarters

Mailing:	One Haworth Center	Tel:	(616) 393-3000
	Holland, MI 49423-9576	Fax:	(616) 393-1570
		TF:	(800) 344-2600

Corporate Foundations and Giving Programs

Haworth Corporate Contributions Program

One Haworth Center	Tel:	(616) 393-3551
Holland, MI 49423		

Public Affairs and Related Activities Personnel

At Headquarters

BRADLEY, Katrina	Tel:	(616) 210-8613
Director, Development and Community Relations	Fax:	(616) 393-1570
CONKLIN, Virginia	Tel:	(616) 393-3551
Executive Administrative Assistant	Fax:	(616) 393-1570
virginia.conklin@haworth.com		
HARTEN, Ann	Tel:	(616) 393-3000
Vice President, Global Human Resources	Fax:	(616) 393-1570
MOONEY, John	Tel:	(616) 393-3000
Vice Presodent, Global Finance & Chief Financial Officer	Fax:	(616) 393-1570
john.mooney@haworth.com		
SMITH, Julie	Tel:	(616) 393-1453
Manager, Public Relations and Communications	Fax:	(616) 393-1570
julie.smith@haworth.com		

HCA Hospital Corporation of America

Provider of healthcare services comprised of locally managed facilities that includes Hospitals and freestanding surgery centers.
hcahealthcare.com
Annual Revenues: $40.26 billion
Employees: 174,000
Ticker: NYSE: HCA
SIC: 8062
Industry/ies: Medicine/Health Care/Mental Health
Legislative Issues: CSP; HCR; MMM

Chairman and Chief Executive Officer	Tel:	(615) 344-9551
JOHNSON, R. Milton	Fax:	(615) 344-2266

Main Headquarters

Mailing:	One Park Plaza	Tel:	(615) 344-9551
	Nashville, TN 37203	Fax:	(615) 344-2266

Political Action Committees

HCA Inc. Good Government Fund PAC
FEC ID: C00067231
Contact: David Anderson
One Park Plaza
P.O. Box 550
Nashville, TN 37203

> **Contributions to Candidates:** $194,666 (2015-2016)
> Democrats: $80,333; Republicans: $114,333

> **Principal Recipients**
>
> **SENATE**
> BLUNT, ROY (REP-MO)
> MURRAY, PATTY (DEM-WA)

Corporate Foundations and Giving Programs

HCA Foundation
Contact: Lois Abrams

One Park Plaza	Tel:	(615) 344-2390
P.O. Box 550	Fax:	(615) 344-5722
Nashville, TN 37203		

Public Affairs and Related Activities Personnel

At Headquarters

ABRAMS, Lois
Grant Manager, HCA Foundation
lois.abrams@hcahealthcare.com
Tel: (615) 344-2390
Fax: (615) 344-2266

CAMPBELL, Victor L.
Senior Vice President
Tel: (615) 344-9551
Fax: (615) 344-2266

CRITCHLOW, David
Director, Government Relations
david.critchlow@hcahealthcare.com
Tel: (615) 344-9551
Fax: (615) 344-2266

DAVIS, Jana J.
Senior Vice President, Corporate Affairs
Tel: (615) 344-9551
Fax: (615) 344-2266

FISHBOUGH, Ed
Assistant Vice President, Communications
ed.fishbough@hcahealthcare.com
Tel: (615) 344-2810
Fax: (615) 344-2266

HAZEN, Samuel N.
Chief Operating Officer
Tel: (615) 344-9551
Fax: (615) 344-2266

KIMBROUGH, Mark
Vice President, Investor Relations
mark.kimbrough@hcahealthcare.com
Tel: (615) 344-2688
Fax: (615) 344-2266

RUTHERFORD, William B.
Chief Financial Officer and Executive Vice President
Tel: (615) 344-9551
Fax: (615) 344-2266

SOWELL, III, Joseph A.
Senior Vice President and Chief Development Officer
joe.sowell@hcahealthcare.com
Tel: (615) 344-9551
Fax: (615) 344-2266

STEELE, John M.
Senior Vice President, Human Resources
Tel: (615) 344-9551
Fax: (615) 344-2266

WATERMAN, Robert A.
Senior Vice President and General Counsel and General Counsel and Chief Labor Relations Officer
Tel: (615) 344-9551
Fax: (615) 344-2266

YUSPEH, Alan R.
Senior Vice President, Chief Ethics and Compliance Officer
Tel: (615) 344-9551
Fax: (615) 344-2266

At Other Offices

ANDERSON, David
PAC Treasurer, Lobbyist and Senior Vice President, Finance and Treasurer
P.O. Box 550, One Park Plaza
Nashville, TN 37203

HCR-Manor Care, Inc.

An integrated health care provider. Operates nursing centers through its operating company, HCR Manor Care, under the names Heartland, Manor Care and Arden Courts.
www.hcr-manorcare.com
Employees: 60,000
SIC: 5047; 8051
Industry/ies: Medicine/Health Care/Mental Health
Legislative Issues: BUD; HCR; MMM

Chairman, President and Chief Executive Officer
ORMOND, Paul A.
Tel: (419) 252-5500
Fax: (419) 252-6404

Main Headquarters
Mailing: 333 N. Summit St.
P.O. Box 10086
Toledo, OH 43699-0086
Tel: (419) 252-5500
Fax: (419) 252-6404

Political Action Committees
HCR Manor Care PAC
FEC ID: C00260141
Contact: Kevin Jackson
333 N. Summit St.
16th Floor
Toledo, OH 43604
Tel: (419) 252-5500
Fax: (419) 252-5500

> **Contributions to Candidates:** $35,534 (2015-2016)
> Democrats: $13,500; Republicans: $22,034

> **Principal Recipients**
> **HOUSE**
> RYAN, PAUL D. (REP-WI)

Corporate Foundations and Giving Programs
HCR Manor Care Foundation
P.O. Box 10086
Toledo, OH 43699

Public Affairs and Related Activities Personnel

At Headquarters

BURY, Brad
Director, Accounting Services
Tel: (419) 252-5500
Fax: (419) 252-6404

CAVANAUGH, Steven M.
President and Chief Financial Officer
Tel: (419) 252-5500
Fax: (419) 252-6404

FORBES, Jeff
Federal Lobbyist
jforbes@cfwdc.com
Registered Federal Lobbyist
Tel: (419) 252-5500
Fax: (419) 252-6404

JACKSON, Kevin
Tel: (419) 252-5500

PAC Treasurer
Fax: (419) 252-6404

KACZOR, Elizabeth
Vice President, Human Resources and Labor Operations
Tel: (419) 252-5500
Fax: (419) 252-6404

PERRY, Brian
Assistant Vice President, Government Relations
Registered Federal Lobbyist
Tel: (419) 252-5500
Fax: (419) 252-6404

RUMP, Rick
Assistant Vice President, Corporate Communications
rrump@hcr-manorcare.com
Tel: (419) 252-5500
Fax: (419) 252-6404

STRUNK, Jeff
Federal Lobbyist
Registered Federal Lobbyist
Tel: (419) 252-5500
Fax: (419) 252-6404

WILLIAMS, Zachary
Federal Lobbyist
Registered Federal Lobbyist
Tel: (419) 252-5500

WYMA, John
Federal Lobbyist
jwyma@wymastrategies.com
Tel: (419) 252-5500
Fax: (419) 252-6404

HD Supply, Inc.

A distributor of electrical, plumbing and other building supplies.
www.hdsupply.com
Annual Revenues: $8.49 billion
Employees: 15,500
SIC: 5000
Industry/ies: Construction/Construction Materials

Chief Executive Officer
DEANGELO, Joe
Tel: (770) 852-9000

Main Headquarters
Mailing: 3100 Cumberland Blvd.
Suite 1700
Atlanta, GA 30339
Tel: (770) 852-9000

Corporate Foundations and Giving Programs
HD Supply Foundation
3100 Cumberland Blvd.
Suite 1700
Atlanta, GA 30339
Tel: (770) 852-9000

Public Affairs and Related Activities Personnel

At Headquarters

FABERE, Mark
Senior Vice President, Operations
Tel: (770) 852-9000

LEVITT, Evan
Senior Vice President and Chief Financial Office
Tel: (770) 852-9000

MCDEVITT, Dan
General Counsel and Corporate Secretary
Tel: (770) 852-9000

NEWMAN, Meg
Senior Vice President, Human Resources, Community Affairs and Communications
Tel: (770) 852-9000

PINCKNEY, Quiana
Senior Manager, Public Relations and Contact, Media Relations
quiana.pinckney@hdsupply.com
Tel: (770) 852-9057

STENGEL, William P.
Senior Vice President Strategic Business Development and Investor Relations
Tel: (770) 852-9000

STEVENS, Anna
Vice President, Human Resources Strategy, Marketing and Director, Communications
anna.stevens@hdsupply.com
Tel: (770) 852-9000

HDR

HDR is an architecture, engineering, and consulting firm that specializes in projects including bridges, water- and wastewater-treatment plants, and hospitals. HDR also provides mechanical and plumbing services, construction and project management, and utilities planning.
www.hdrinc.com
Annual Revenues: $1.76 billion
Employees: 8,000
Industry/ies: Architecture And Design; Engineering/Mathematics
Legislative Issues: DEF; TAX; TRA

Chairman and Chief Executive Officer
LITTLE, P E, George A.
Tel: (402) 399-1000
Fax: (402) 399-1238

Main Headquarters
Mailing: 8404 Indian Hills Dr.
Omaha, NE 68114-4098
Tel: (402) 399-1000
Fax: (402) 548-5015
TF: (800) 366-4411

Washington Office
Mailing: 8403 Colesville Rd.
Suite 910
Silver Spring, MD 20910-3313
Tel: (240) 485-2600
Fax: (240) 485-2655

Political Action Committees
Chad Hartnett
FEC ID: C00103903
Contact: Chad Hartnett
P.O. Box 75000
MC 2250
Detroit, MI 48275

> **Contributions to Candidates:** $37,500 (2015-2016)
> Democrats: $7,500; Republicans: $30,000

Corporate Foundations and Giving Programs

HDR Contribution Programme
8404 Indian Hills Dr.   Tel: (402) 399-1000
Omaha, NE 68114-4098

HDR Foundation
8404 Indian Hills Dr.   Tel: (402) 399-1000
Omaha, NE 68114-4098   Fax: (402) 399-1238

Public Affairs and Related Activities Personnel

At Headquarters

COX, Terence C.   Tel: (402) 399-1000
Chief Financial Officer   Fax: (402) 399-1238

CUSHMAN, Nancy   Tel: (402) 399-1000
PAC Treasurer   Fax: (402) 399-1238

FOX, Jackie   Tel: (402) 926-7058
Media Contact   Fax: (402) 399-1238
jackie.fox@hdrinc.com

SOSNOWCHIK, Katie   Tel: (402) 926-7080
Director, Communications   Fax: (402) 399-1238
katie.sosnowchik@hdrinc.com

ZGODA , Mary   Tel: (402) 399-1372
Coordinator, Media Relations   Fax: (402) 399-1238
mary.zgoda@hdrinc.com

At Other Offices

COBB, S. David   Tel: (562) 264-1100
Director, Civic Affairs   Fax: (562) 264-1101
100 Oceangate, Suite 1120
Long Beach, CA 90802
david.cobb@hdrinc.com
Registered Federal Lobbyist

COBB, David   Tel: (562) 264-1100
Director, Civic Affairs   Fax: (562) 264-1101
100 Oceangate, Suite 1120
Long Beach, CA 90802
Registered Federal Lobbyist

HARTNETT, Chad
Contact, Government Relations, PAC Contact
P.O. Box 75000, MC 2250
Detroit, MI 48275

MADENBURG, Richard   Tel: (562) 264-1100
100 Oceangate, Suite 1120   Fax: (562) 264-1101
Long Beach, CA 90802

MALONE, Patrick   Tel: (202) 594-3268
Coordinator, Government Relations   Fax: (202) 594-3287
100 M St. SE, Suite 305
Washington, DC 20003-3519
Registered Federal Lobbyist

Headwaters, Inc.

A provider of technologies and service related to fossil fuel utilization.
www.headwaters.com
Annual Revenues: $734.14 million
Employees: 2,355
Ticker: NYSE: HW
SIC: 2990; 3272
Industry/ies: Energy/Electricity; Fuels See Coal, Gas, Oil, Petroleum; Natural Resources; Petroleum Industry

Chairman of the Board and Chief Executive Officer   Tel: (801) 984-9400
BENSON, Kirk A.   Fax: (801) 984-9410

Main Headquarters
Mailing: 10701 S. River Front Pkwy.   Tel: (801) 984-9400
                Suite 300   Fax: (801) 984-9410
                S. Jordan, UT 84095

Corporate Foundations and Giving Programs

Headwaters, Inc. Contributions Program
10653 S. River Front Pkwy.   Tel: (801) 984-9400
Suite 300   Fax: (801) 984-9410
S. Jordan, UT 84095

Public Affairs and Related Activities Personnel

At Headquarters

HATFIELD, Harlan M.   Tel: (801) 984-9400
Vice President, Secretary and General Counsel Fax: (801) 984-9410

hhatfield@headwaters.com

MADDEN, Sharon A.   Tel: (801) 984-9400
Vice President, Investor Relations   Fax: (801) 984-9410
smadden@headwaters.com

NEWMAN, Donald P.   Tel: (801) 984-9400
Chief Financial Officer   Fax: (801) 984-9410

Health Alliance Plan

A Michigan-based nonprofit health plan. By negotiations between Henry Ford Hospital, Metropolitan Hospital and Health Centers, and Metro Health Plan, Inc. a new alliance-- Health Alliance Plan, a newly amalgamated health care delivery system was formed in 1979. It has many commercial and government health plan programs with flexible payment mechanisms and custom benefit designs capable of meeting the needs of a variety of health plan purchasers.
www.hap.org
Employees: 1,034
Industry/ies: Medicine/Health Care/Mental Health
Legislative Issues: HCR; MMM

President and Interim Chief Executive officer   Tel: (313) 872-8100
LASSITER, Wright   Fax: (810) 230-7410

Main Headquarters
Mailing: 2850 W. Grand Blvd.   Tel: (313) 872-8100
              Detroit, MI 48202   Fax: (810) 230-7410
                                               TF: (800) 422-4641

Political Action Committees
Health Alliance Plan PAC
FEC ID: C00410670
Contact: Rory Lafferty
2850 W. Grand Blvd.   Tel: (313) 872-8100
Detroit, MI 48202

> **Contributions to Candidates:** $500 (2015-2016)
> Republicans: $500

Corporate Foundations and Giving Programs

Health Alliance Plan Contributions Program
2850 W. Grand Blvd.   Tel: (313) 872-8100
Detroit, MI 48202

Public Affairs and Related Activities Personnel

At Headquarters

ADAMS, Derick   Tel: (313) 872-8100
Vice President, Human Resources   Fax: (810) 230-7410
dadams@hap.org

BAKER, Tiffany   Tel: (248) 443-1072
Team Leader, Communications   Fax: (810) 230-7410
tbaker3@hap.org

BERRY, Ronald   Tel: (313) 872-8100
Chief Financial Officer, Michigan   Fax: (810) 230-7410

CHAMPNEY, Dan E.   Tel: (313) 872-8100
Deputy General Counsel   Fax: (810) 230-7410

CLARK, Doug   Tel: (313) 872-8100
Interim Chief Compliance Officer   Fax: (810) 230-7410

DUNK, Jeanne   Tel: (313) 872-8100
General Counsel   Fax: (810) 230-7410

HIRT, Donald   Tel: (313) 872-8100
Senior Vice President, Planning and Marketing Strategy   Fax: (810) 230-7410

HUTCHISON, Todd   Tel: (313) 872-8100
Senior Vice President and Chief Financial Officer   Fax: (810) 230-7410

LAFFERTY, Rory   Tel: (313) 872-8100
Director, Government Affairs and PAC Treasurer   Fax: (810) 230-7410

MACDERMOTT, JD, MPA, Alice   Tel: (313) 872-8100
Vice President and Associate General Counsel   Fax: (810) 230-7410

MCMURRAY, Maurice E.   Tel: (313) 872-8100
Corporate Secretary   Fax: (810) 230-7410

SCHWANDT, APR, Susan   Tel: (248) 443-1076
Director, Public Relations   Fax: (810) 230-7410
sschwan1@hap.org

TOURNOUX, Mary Ann   Tel: (313) 872-8100
Senior Vice President, Chief Marketing Officer   Fax: (810) 230-7410
mtournou@hap.org

WALSH, Matthew   Tel: (313) 872-8100
Senior Vice President and Chief Operating Officer   Fax: (810) 230-7410

Health Care Services Corporation

A health insurer.
www.hcsc.com
Employees: 23,000
Industry/ies: Medicine/Health Care/Mental Health
Legislative Issues: BUD; HCR; INS; MMM; TAX

President and Chief Executive Officer   Tel: (312) 653-7581
STEINER, Paula A.   Fax: (312) 819-1220

Main Headquarters

Mailing: 300 E. Randolph St.
Chicago, IL 60601

Tel: (312) 653-7581
Fax: (312) 819-1220
TF: (800) 654-7385

Political Action Committees

Health Care Service Corporation Employees PAC
FEC ID: C00199711
Contact: Gerard T. Mallen
300 E. Randolph St.
Chicago, IL 60601

Contributions to Candidates: $257,000 (2015-2016)
Democrats: $91,000; Republicans: $166,000

Principal Recipients

SENATE
CASEY, ROBERT P JR (DEM-PA)

HOUSE
BRADY, KEVIN (REP-TX)
BURGESS, MICHAEL C. DR. (REP-TX)
DAVIS, DANNY K. MR. (DEM-IL)
DOLD, ROBERT JAMES JR (REP-IL)
JOHNSON, SAM MR. (REP-TX)
KINZINGER, ADAM (REP-IL)
LANKFORD, JAMES PAUL MR. (REP-OK)
LUJAN, BEN R MR. (DEM-NM)
ROSKAM, PETER (REP-IL)
SHIMKUS, JOHN M (REP-IL)

Corporate Foundations and Giving Programs

Health Care Services Corporation Contribution Program
300 E. Randolph St.
Chicago, IL 60601

Tel: (312) 653-6000
Fax: (312) 819-1220

Public Affairs and Related Activities Personnel

At Headquarters

AVNER, Kenneth S.
Senior Vice President and Chief Financial Officer

Tel: (312) 653-6000
Fax: (312) 819-1220

CANNON, John
Executive Vice President and Chief Administrative Officer

Tel: (312) 653-7581
Fax: (312) 819-1220

DOYLE, Theresa
Divisional Senior Vice President
Theresa_Doyle@hcsc.net
Registered Federal Lobbyist

Tel: (312) 653-6000
Fax: (312) 819-1220

FELDSTEIN, Eric
Senior Vice President and Chief Financial Officer

Tel: (312) 653-7581
Fax: (312) 819-1220

GLEASON, John
Federal Lobbyist
gleasonj@HCSC.net
Registered Federal Lobbyist

Tel: (312) 653-7934
Fax: (312) 819-1220

LUBBEN, Thomas C.
Senior Vice President, Compliance, Audit, Security, Special Investigations, Privacy and Regulatory Oversight and Enterprise Risk Management, Chief Ethics and Compliance Officer
lubbent@bcbsil.com

Tel: (312) 653-7934
Fax: (312) 819-1220

MALLEN, Gerard T.
PAC Treasurer
Mail Stop Legal Dept.

Tel: (312) 653-6000
Fax: (312) 819-1220

RAZI, Nazneen
Senior Vice President and Chief Human Resources Officer

Tel: (312) 653-7581
Fax: (312) 819-1220

ROHAN, Sue
Vice President, Health Policy

Tel: (312) 653-6000
Fax: (312) 819-1220

STEFFL, Jerry
Registered Federal Lobbyist

Tel: (312) 653-7581
Fax: (312) 819-1220

THOMPSON, Greg
Executive Director, Media and Public Relations
Greg_Thompson@hcsc.net

Tel: (312) 653-7581
Fax: (312) 819-1220

Health Management Associates

A premier operator of general acute care, non-urban hospitals located throughout the United States but primarily in the Southeast and Southwest.
www.healthmanagement.com
Annual Revenues: $5.86 billion
Employees: 31,600
Ticker: NYSE: HMA
SIC: 8062
Industry/ies: Medicine/Health Care/Mental Health

President and Chief Executive Officer
NEWSOME, Gary D.

Tel: (239) 598-3131
Fax: (239) 598-2705

Chief Executive Officer
EVERT, Marilynn Y.
MEvert@healthmanagement.com

Tel: (517) 482-9236
Fax: (850) 222-0318

Main Headquarters

Mailing: 120 N. Washington Sq.
Suite 705
Lansing, MI 48933

Tel: (517) 482-9236
Fax: (517) 482-0920
TF: (800) 678-2299

Corporate Foundations and Giving Programs

HMA Contributions Program
120 N. Washington Sq.
Suite 705
Lansing, MI 48933

Public Affairs and Related Activities Personnel

At Headquarters

JOHNSON, Kelly
Vice President and Chief Operating Officer

Tel: (517) 482-9236
Fax: (517) 482-0920

LOMBARDO, Patrick E.
Senior Vice President, Human Resources

Tel: (517) 482-9236
Fax: (517) 482-0920

ROSEN, Jay
President
jrosen@healthmanagement.com

Tel: (517) 482-9236
Fax: (517) 482-0920

WALLER, Eric L.
Chief Marketing Officer

Tel: (517) 482-9236
Fax: (517) 482-0920

At Other Offices

FARNHAM, Robert E.
Senior Vice President, Finance
5811 Pelican Bay Blvd., Suite 500
Naples, FL 34108

Tel: (239) 598-3104
Fax: (239) 598-2705

GOULD, Bruce
Vice President and Chief Financial Officer
301 South Bronough St., Suite 500
Tallahassee, FL 32301
bgould@healthmanagement.com

Fax: (850) 222-0318

HURST, Paul
Senior Vice President, Government Relations
5811 Pelican Bay Blvd., Suite 500
Naples, FL 34108
paul.hurst@hma.com

Tel: (239) 598-3131
Fax: (239) 598-2705

Health Management Systems, Inc.

Provides cost containment solutions for government-funded, commercial, and private entities.
www.hms.com
Annual Revenues: $88.40 million
SIC: 7389; 7374
Industry/ies: Medicine/Health Care/Mental Health
Legislative Issues: HCR; MMM

Chairman of the Board
HOLST, Robert M.

Tel: (212) 857-5000
Fax: (212) 857-5973

President and Chief Executive Officer
LUCIA, Bill

Tel: (212) 857-5000
Fax: (212) 857-5973

Main Headquarters

Mailing: 401 Park Ave., S.
New York City, NY 10016

Tel: (212) 857-5000
Fax: (212) 857-5004
TF: (877) 467-0184

Washington Office

Mailing: 1101 14th St. NW
Suite 810
Washington, DC 20005

Tel: (202) 448-2020
Fax: (202) 448-2032

Political Action Committees

HMS Holdings Corporation PAC (HMS PAC)
FEC ID: C00440453
Contact: Walter Hosp
401 Park Ave. South
Ninth Floor
New York City, NY 10016

Contributions to Candidates: $11,000 (2015-2016)
Republicans: $11,000

Corporate Foundations and Giving Programs

Health Management Systems Contribution Program
401 Park Ave., South
New York City, NY 10016

Tel: (212) 857-5000
Fax: (212) 857-5973

HMS Holdings Corporation charitable Program
401 Park Ave., South
New York City, NY 10016

Tel: (212) 857-5000

Public Affairs and Related Activities Personnel

At Headquarters

DAUB GLENN, Kimberly
Senior Vice President, Government Services East
kglenn@hms.com

Tel: (212) 725-7965
Fax: (212) 857-5973

HOLT, CHC, Alexandra
Chief Compliance Officer
aholt@hms.com

Tel: (212) 857-5000
Fax: (212) 857-5973

MARRARO, Francesca

Tel: (212) 857-5442

Vice President, Marketing and Communications		
fmarraro@hms.com		
MARSHALL, Edith	Tel:	(212) 857-5000
Chief Counsel	Fax:	(212) 857-5973
Edith.marshall@hms.com		
PERRIN, Maria	Tel:	(212) 857-5000
Chief Marketing Officer	Fax:	(212) 857-5973
mperrin@hmsy.com		
SOUTH, Tracy	Tel:	(212) 857-5000
Senior Vice President, Human Resource	Fax:	(212) 857-5973

At Washington Office

PIERCE, JD, Arika L.	Tel:	(202) 448-2020
Director, Federal Government Relations	Fax:	(202) 448-2032
VICKERY, Jaimie	Tel:	(202) 448-2020
Registered Federal Lobbyist	Fax:	(202) 448-2032

Health Net Federal Services, LLP

Health Net Federal Services provides health insurance and related services to military personnel and their families via the military's TRICARE program. Health Net Federal Services also provides Veterans Affairs services including preferred pricing, claims validation, and outpatient clinic contracting.
www.healthnetfederalservices.com
Annual Revenues: $68.80 million
Employees: 1,000
Industry/ies: Medicine/Health Care/Mental Health
Legislative Issues: BUD; DEF; VET

Chairman of the Board	Tel:	(916) 935-5000
GREAVES, Roger F.	Fax:	(916) 353-6809
President and Chief Executive Officer	Tel:	(916) 935-5000
GELLERT, Jay M.	Fax:	(916) 353-6809

Main Headquarters

Mailing:	2025 Aerojet Dr.	Tel:	(916) 935-5000
	Rancho Cordova, CA 95742	Fax:	(916) 353-6809
		TF:	(877) 874-2273

Washington Office

Mailing:	2107 Wilson Blvd.	Tel:	(703) 527-0366
	Suite 900	Fax:	(571) 227-6714
	Arlington, VA 22201		

Corporate Foundations and Giving Programs

Health Net Federal Services Contributions Program
Contact: Pat Mitchell

2107 Wilson Blvd.	Fax:	(571) 227-6714
Suite 900		
Arlington, VA 22201		

Public Affairs and Related Activities Personnel

At Headquarters

MONTGOMERY, Marie	Tel:	(916) 935-5000
Senior Vice President and Corporate Controller	Fax:	(916) 353-6809
SULAYMAN, Ramsey	Tel:	(916) 935-5000
Manager, Public Affairs	Fax:	(916) 353-6809
Registered Federal Lobbyist		
TOUGH, Steven D.	Tel:	(916) 935-5000
President, Government Programs	Fax:	(916) 353-6809
TUTTLE, Molly	Tel:	(916) 351-5355
Director, Communications	Fax:	(916) 353-6809
molly.tuttle@healthnet.com		
WATERS, Kathleen A.	Tel:	(916) 935-5000
Senior Vice President, General Counsel and Secretary	Fax:	(916) 353-6809
WOYS, James E.	Tel:	(916) 935-5000
Executive Vice President, Chief Financial and Operating Officer and Interim Treasurer	Fax:	(916) 353-6809

At Washington Office

HOFFMEIER, Donna L.	Tel:	(571) 227-6474
Vice President and Veterans Affairs Program Executive	Fax:	(571) 227-6714
Mail Stop Suite 900		
donna.hoffmeier@healthnet.com		
SCHWARTZ, Susan M.	Tel:	(571) 227-6553
Vice President, Beneficiary Coalition and Congressional Services	Fax:	(571) 227-6714
susan.schwartz@healthnet.com		
Registered Federal Lobbyist		

Health Net, Inc.

Formerly known as FHS. A publicly-traded managed health care company. The company's health plans and government contracts subsidiaries provide health benefits to about 6.7 million people. Its behavioral health subsidiary, MHN, provides mental health benefits.
www.healthnet.com
Annual Revenues: $14.86 billion
Employees: 7,922
Ticker: NYSE: HNT

SIC: 6324
Industry/ies: Medicine/Health Care/Mental Health
Legislative Issues: HCR; MMM; VET

Chairman of the Board	Tel:	(818) 676-6000
GREAVES, Roger F.	Fax:	(818) 676-8591
President and Chief Executive Officer	Tel:	(818) 676-6000
GELLERT, Jay M.	Fax:	(818) 676-6616
jay.m.gellert@healthnet.com		

Main Headquarters

Mailing:	21650 Oxnard St.	Tel:	(818) 676-6000
	Woodland Hills, CA 91367	Fax:	(818) 676-8591
		TF:	(800) 291-6911

Washington Office

Mailing:	2107 Wilson Blvd.
	Suite 900
	Arlington, VA 22201

Political Action Committees

Health Net, Inc. Political Action Committee
FEC ID: C00230789
Contact: Julie Hill

455 Capitol Mall	Tel:	(818) 676-6000
Suite 600	Fax:	(818) 676-6616
Sacramento, CA 95814		

> **Contributions to Candidates:** $97,000 (2015-2016)
> Democrats: $41,500; Republicans: $55,500

> **Principal Recipients**
>
> **HOUSE**
> MCCARTHY, KEVIN (REP-CA)

Corporate Foundations and Giving Programs

Health Net Contribution Program
Contact: Patricia T. Clarey

21650 Oxnard St.	Tel:	(818) 676-6000
Woodland, CA 91367	Fax:	(818) 676-6000

Public Affairs and Related Activities Personnel

At Headquarters

BOUCHARD, Angelee F.	Tel:	(818) 676-6000
Senior Vice President, General Counsel and Secretary	Fax:	(818) 676-8591
CAPEZZA, CPA, Joseph C.	Tel:	(818) 676-6000
Executive Vice President, Chief Financial Officer and Treasurer	Fax:	(818) 676-8591
CLAREY, Patricia T.	Tel:	(818) 676-6000
Senior Vice President, Chief Regulatory and External Relations Officer and Chief Compliance Officer	Fax:	(818) 676-8591
patricia.t.clarey@healthnet.com		
LONG, Lori	Tel:	(818) 676-6000
Director, Public Policy and Government Relations	Fax:	(818) 676-8591
lori.long@healthnet.com		
Registered Federal Lobbyist		
MORRELL, Adrienne	Tel:	(571) 227-6561
Vice President, Government Relations	Fax:	(571) 227-6714
adrienne.b.morrell@healthnet.com		
Registered Federal Lobbyist		
SMITH, Haley	Tel:	(818) 676-6000
Contact, PAC	Fax:	(818) 676-8591
Mail Stop 25th Floor		
WOYS, James E.	Tel:	(818) 676-6000
Executive Vice President, Chief Financial and Operating Officer, and Interim Treasurer	Fax:	(818) 676-8591

At Other Offices

HILL, Julie	Tel:	(818) 676-6000
PAC Treasurer		
455 Capitol Mall, Suite 600		
Sacramento, CA 95814		
KIEFFER, Brad	Tel:	(818) 676-6833
Director, Communications		
21281 Burbank Blvd.		
Woodland, CA 91367		
Brad.Kieffer@healthnet.com		

HealthCare Corporation

See listing on page 359 under Genesis HealthCare Corporation

HealthNow New York Inc.

A healthcare company. Parent company of Blue Cross and Blue Shield of Western New York and Blue Cross and Blue Shield of North Eastern New York.
www.healthnowny.com
Annual Revenues: $2.40 billion
Employees: 2,000
Industry/ies: Medicine/Health Care/Mental Health

| **Chairman of the Board** | Tel: | (716) 887-6900 |
| HOOK , Thomas J. | Fax: | (716) 887-8981 |

Main Headquarters

Mailing:	P.O. Box 80	Tel:	(716) 887-6900
	1901 Main St.	Fax:	(716) 887-8981
	Buffalo, NY 14240-0080	TF:	(800) 856-0480

Corporate Foundations and Giving Programs

HealthNow New York Inc. Contributions Program
1901 Main St.

| | Tel: | (716) 887-6900 |
| Buffalo, NY 14240 | Fax: | (716) 887-8981 |

Public Affairs and Related Activities Personnel

At Headquarters

DICKERSON, Jr., James H.	Tel:	(716) 887-6900
Executive Vice President and Chief Financial Officer	Fax:	(716) 887-8981
MERKEL-LIBERATORE, Karen	Tel:	(716) 887-8811
Senior Director, Public Relations and Communications	Fax:	(716) 887-8981
merkel-liberatore.karen@healthnow.org		

HealthSouth Corporation

A healthcare services provider.
www.healthsouth.com
Annual Revenues: $2.52 billion
Employees: 17,402
Ticker: NYSE: HLS
SIC: 8060
Industry/ies: Medicine/Health Care/Mental Health
Legislative Issues: HCR; MMM

| **Chairman of the Board** | Tel: | (205) 967-7116 |
| HIGDON, Jr., Leo I. | Fax: | (205) 969-3543 |

| **President and Chief Executive Officer** | Tel: | (205) 967-7116 |
| GRINNEY, Jay | Fax: | (205) 969-6889 |

Main Headquarters

Mailing:	3660 Grandview Pkwy.	Tel:	(205) 967-7116
	Suite 200	Fax:	(205) 969-3543
	Birmingham, AL 35243	TF:	(800) 765-4772

Washington Office

Mailing: 950 F St. NW
Washington, DC 20004

Political Action Committees

HealthSouth Corporation PAC
FEC ID: C00414649
Contact: Edmund M. Fay
3660 Grandview Pkwy.
Suite 200
Birmingham, AL 35243

Contributions to Candidates: $68,500 (2015-2016)
Democrats: $15,500; Republicans: $51,000; Other: $2,000

Public Affairs and Related Activities Personnel

At Headquarters

ARICO, Mary Ann	Tel:	(205) 969-6175
Chief Investor Relations Officer	Fax:	(205) 969-3543
maryann.arico@healthsouth.com		
BRIMMER, Andy	Tel:	(205) 410-2777
Contact, Public Relations	Fax:	(205) 969-6889
COLTHARP, Doug	Tel:	(205) 967-7116
Executive Vice President and Chief Financial Officer	Fax:	(205) 969-3543
EWING, Cleaster	Tel:	(205) 967-7116
Chief Compliance Officer	Fax:	(205) 969-3543
FAY, Edmund M.	Tel:	(205) 967-7116
PAC Treasurer	Fax:	(205) 969-3543
LEVY, Cheryl	Tel:	(205) 967-7116
Chief Human Resources Officer	Fax:	(205) 969-3543
WHITTINGTON, John P.	Tel:	(205) 967-7116
Executive Vice President, General Counsel and Secretary	Fax:	(205) 969-6889

At Washington Office

BAIRD, Andrew
Director, Government Relations
Registered Federal Lobbyist

HUNTER, Justin
Senior Vice President, Public Policy, Legislation &
Regulations
Registered Federal Lobbyist

Healthspring Management, Inc.

A health care services company focused on the senior population.
www.healthspring.com
Industry/ies: Medicine/Health Care/Mental Health

Main Headquarters

Mailing:	9009 Carothers Pkwy.	Tel:	(615) 291-7000
	Suite 501		
	Franklin, TN 37067		

Public Affairs and Related Activities Personnel

At Headquarters

BAILEY, Gary	Tel:	(615) 291-7000
Director, Government Affairs		
gary.bailey@healthspring.com		
DETRICK, Ted	Tel:	(215) 761-1414
Vice President, Investor Relations		
edwin.detrick@cigna.com		
HARRISON, Graham	Tel:	(615) 234-6710
Director, Corporate Communications and Public Relations		
Graham.Harrison@healthspring.com		

Healthways, Inc.

A provider of health and care support solutions.
www.healthways.com
Annual Revenues: $755.27 million
Employees: 2,700
Ticker: NASDAQ: HWAY
SIC: 8090
Industry/ies: Medicine/Health Care/Mental Health
Legislative Issues: HCR; MMM

| **Chairman of the Board** | Tel: | (615) 614-4929 |
| BALLANTINE, John W. | Fax: | (615) 665-7697 |

| **President and Chief Executive Officer** | Tel: | (615) 665-1122 |
| LEEDLE, Jr., Ben R. | Fax: | (615) 665-7697 |

Main Headquarters

Mailing:	701 Cool Springs Blvd.	Tel:	(615) 614-4929
	Franklin, TN 37067	Fax:	(615) 665-7697
		TF:	(800) 327-3822

Political Action Committees

Healthways Inc. Federal PAC
FEC ID: C00411918
Contact: Glenn Hargreaves
701 Cool Springs Blvd.
Franklin, TN 37067

Contributions to Candidates: $6,000 (2015-2016)
Democrats: $1,000; Republicans: $5,000

Corporate Foundations and Giving Programs

Healthways Foundation
Contact: Katherine Gilliland

| 701 Cool Springs Blvd. | Tel: | (615) 614-4929 |
| Franklin, TN 37067 | | |

Public Affairs and Related Activities Personnel

At Headquarters

ELROD, James W.	Tel:	(615) 614-4929
Vice President, General Counsel and Secretary	Fax:	(615) 665-7697
FLIPSE, Mary S.	Tel:	(615) 614-4929
Senior Vice President and General Counsel	Fax:	(615) 665-7697
GILLILAND, Katherine	Tel:	(615) 614-4929
Foundation Contact	Fax:	(615) 665-7697
Katherine.Gilliland@healthways.com		
HARGREAVES, Glenn	Tel:	(615) 614-4929
PAC treasurer	Fax:	(615) 665-7697
LUMSDAINE, Alfred	Tel:	(615) 614-4929
Executive Vice President and Chief Financial Officer	Fax:	(615) 665-7697
MICHELA, Matthew A	Tel:	(615) 614-4929
Executive Vice President and Chief Operating Officer	Fax:	(615) 665-7697
MIDDLEBROOKS, Bruce	Tel:	(615) 614-4463
Director, Communications	Fax:	(615) 665-7697
bruce.middlebrooks@healthways.com		

The Hearst Corporation

A publisher of newspapers, magazines and books. Also active in radio and TV broadcasting
and news service.
www.hearst.com
Employees: 20,000
SIC: 2721
NAICS: 511120
Industry/ies: Communications; Media/Mass Communication; Public Affairs And
Public Relations
Legislative Issues: CPT; CSP; HCR; MIA

| **Chairman of the Board** | Tel: | (212) 649-2000 |
| HEARST, III, William R. | Fax: | (212) 649-2108 |

| **President and Chief Executive Officer** | Tel: | (212) 649-2000 |
| SWARTZ, Steven R. | Fax: | (212) 649-2108 |

Main Headquarters

Mailing:	300 W. 57th St.	Tel:	(212) 649-2000
	New York City, NY 10019	Fax:	(212) 649-2108

Corporate Foundations and Giving Programs

Hearst Foundation		
300 W. 57th St.	Tel:	(212) 586-5405
New York City, NY 10019		

Public Affairs and Related Activities Personnel

At Headquarters

ASHER, James M.	Tel:	(212) 649-2000
Senior Vice President and Chief Legal and Development	Fax:	(212) 649-2108
Officer		
jasher@hearst.com		
BRONFIN, Kenneth A.	Tel:	(212) 649-2000
Senior Managing Director	Fax:	(212) 649-2108
kbronfin@hearst.com		
BURTON, Eve	Tel:	(212) 649-2000
Senior Vice President and General Counsel	Fax:	(212) 649-2108
LUTHRINGER, Paul	Tel:	(212) 649-2540
Vice President, Corporate and Marketing Communications	Fax:	(212) 649-2108
pluthringer@hearst.com		
SCHERZER, Mitchell	Tel:	(212) 649-2000
Senior Vice President and Chief Financial Officer	Fax:	(212) 649-2108
mscherzer@hearst.com		

Heartcare Midwest S.C.

Provides on-site cardiology services throughout Central Illinois.
www.heartcaremw.com
Annual Revenues: $13.90 million
Employees: 200
Industry/ies: Medicine/Health Care/Mental Health

Main Headquarters

Mailing:	5405 N. Knoxville Ave.	Tel:	(309) 691-4410
	Peoria, IL 61614-5016	Fax:	(309) 692-4730
		TF:	(800) 352-4410

Public Affairs and Related Activities Personnel

At Headquarters

DANKOFF, Shelli	Tel:	(309) 655-3897
Media Relations Specialist	Fax:	(309) 692-4730
THURMOND, Jane	Tel:	(309) 691-4410
Chief Financial Officer	Fax:	(309) 674-9477

Heartland Payment Systems, Inc.

Heartland Payment Systems performs credit card and debit card processing services for large national clients in the petroleum industry.
www.heartlandpaymentsystems.com
Annual Revenues: $2.39 billion
Employees: 3,734
Ticker: NYSE: HPY
SIC: 7389
Industry/ies: Banking/Finance/Investments

Chairman of the Board and Chief Executive Officer	Tel:	(609) 683-3831
CARR, Robert O.	Fax:	(609) 683-3815

Main Headquarters

Mailing:	90 Nassau St.	Tel:	(609) 683-3831
	Princeton, NJ 08542	Fax:	(609) 683-3815
		TF:	(888) 798-3131

Public Affairs and Related Activities Personnel

At Headquarters

CAPUCILLE, Tony	Tel:	(609) 683-3831
Chief Sales Officer	Fax:	(609) 683-3815
HASSETT, Joseph	Tel:	(610) 228-2110
Contact, Investor Relations	Fax:	(609) 683-3815
JoeH@GregoryFCA.com		
HOLBROOK, Randy	Tel:	(609) 683-3831
Relationship Manager	Fax:	(609) 683-3815
KALLENBACH, Charles	Tel:	(609) 683-3831
General Counsel and Chief Legal Officer	Fax:	(609) 683-3815
charles.kallenbach@e-hps.com		
LANE, Conan A.	Tel:	(609) 683-3831
Chief of Operations	Fax:	(609) 683-3815
ZABANEH, Samir Michael	Tel:	(609) 683-3831
Chief Financial Officer	Fax:	(609) 683-3815

HEB Grocery Company

Supermarket chain in Texas and Mexico. Includes store locator, careers, pharmacy refills, recipes and more.
www.heb.com
Industry/ies: Food And Beverage Industry; Retail/Wholesale
Legislative Issues: AGR; CPT; FOO; HCR; IMM; LBR; TAX; TRU

Chairman and Chief Executive Officer	Tel:	(210) 938-8000
BUTT, Charles C.	Fax:	(210) 938-8169
butt.charles@heb.com		

Main Headquarters

Mailing:	P.O. Box 839999	Tel:	(210) 938-8357
	San Antonio, TX 78283-3999		

Corporate Foundations and Giving Programs

HEB Grocery Company Corporate Contributions Program		
P.O. Box 839999	Tel:	(210) 938-8357
San Antonio, TX 78283		

Public Affairs and Related Activities Personnel

At Headquarters

CAMPOS, Dya	Tel:	(210) 938-8357
Director, Public Affairs		
campos.dya@heb.com		
GARZA-ROBERTS, Cindy	Tel:	(210) 938-8357
Director, Public Affairs		

At Other Offices

HERRON, Winnell	Tel:	(210) 938-8000
Group Vice President, Public Affairs	Fax:	(210) 938-8169
646 S. Main Ave.		
San Antonio, TX 78204		
herron.winnell@heb.com		

Hecla Mining Company

Explores and processes silver and gold in the United States, Venezuela and Mexico.
www.hecla-mining.com
Annual Revenues: $494.09 million
Employees: 1,354
Ticker: NYSE: HL
SIC: 1400
Industry/ies: Mining Industry; Natural Resources
Legislative Issues: NAT

Chairman of the Board	Tel:	(208) 769-4100
CRUMLEY, Ted	Fax:	(208) 769-7612
President and Chief Executive Officer	Tel:	(208) 769-4100
BAKER, Jr., Phillip S.	Fax:	(208) 769-7612

Main Headquarters

Mailing:	6500 N. Mineral Dr.	Tel:	(208) 769-4100
	Suite 200	Fax:	(208) 769-7612
	Coeur d'Alene, ID 83815-9408		

Political Action Committees

Hecla Mining Company/Hecla Ltd. PAC
FEC ID: C00124016
Contact: Carolyn S. Turner
6500 N. Mineral Dr.
Suite 200
Coeur d'Alene, ID 83815

> **Contributions to Candidates:** $7,500 (2015-2016)
> Republicans: $7,500

Corporate Foundations and Giving Programs

Hecla Charitable Foundation		
Contact: Jeanne DuPont		
6500 N. Mineral Dr.	Tel:	(208) 769-4177
Suite 200		
Coeur d'Alene, ID 83815		

Public Affairs and Related Activities Personnel

At Headquarters

DUPONT, Jeanne	Tel:	(208) 769-4177
Coordinator, Corporate Communications, Investor and Public	Fax:	(208) 769-7612
Relations and Contact, Foundation		
POIRIER, Don	Tel:	(208) 769-4100
Vice President, Corporate Development	Fax:	(208) 769-7612
dpoirier@hecla-mining.com		
RUSSELL, Luke	Tel:	(208) 769-4100
Vice President, External Affairs	Fax:	(208) 769-7612
SABALA, James A.	Tel:	(208) 769-4100
Senior Vice President and Chief Financial Officer	Fax:	(208) 769-7612
SIENKO, David C.	Tel:	(604) 694-7729
Vice President and General Counsel	Fax:	(208) 769-7612
TURNER, Carolyn S.	Tel:	(208) 769-4100
Director, Budgeting and Forecasting and PAC Treasurer	Fax:	(208) 769-7612

Heineken USA Inc.

U.S. importer of European beer. A subsidiary of Heineken N.V. of Amsterdam, The Netherlands.
www.heinekenusa.com
Annual Revenues: $24.30 million
Employees: 400

SIC: 5181
NAICS: 422810
Industry/ies: Food And Beverage Industry
Legislative Issues: BEV

Managing Director
VAN DEN BRINK, Dolf

Tel: (914) 681-4100
Fax: (914) 681-1900

Main Headquarters
Mailing: 360 Hamilton Ave.
Suite 1103
White Plains, NY 10601

Tel: (914) 681-4100
Fax: (914) 681-1900
TF: (800) 811-4951

Washington Office
Mailing: 1850 M St. NW
Suite 570
Washington, DC 20036

Tel: (202) 736-1333

Political Action Committees
Heineken USA Inc. Good Government Committee PAC
FEC ID: C00358234
Contact: Rush Tara
360 Hamilton Ave.
Suite 1103
White Plains, NY 10601

Tel: (914) 681-4100

Contributions to Candidates: $34,500 (2015-2016)
Democrats: $19,000; Republicans: $15,500

Corporate Foundations and Giving Programs
Heineken USA Contributions Program
360 Hamilton Ave.
Suite 1103
White Plains, NY 10601

Public Affairs and Related Activities Personnel

At Headquarters

KINCH, Julie
Senior Vice President and Chief Legal Officer

Tel: (914) 681-4100
Fax: (914) 681-1900

MOORE, Tamara
Senior Director, Corporate Communications
tmoore@heinekenusa.com

Tel: (914) 681-4153
Fax: (914) 681-1900

TARA, Rush
Treasurer

Tel: (914) 681-4100
Fax: (914) 681-1900

TEARNO, T. Daniel
Senior Vice President and Chief Corporate Relations Officer

Tel: (914) 681-4100
Fax: (914) 681-1900

At Washington Office

KISSINGER, Justin
Contact, Government Relations

Tel: (202) 736-1333

Hemcon, Inc.

A fully integrated medical device company that exists to advance the standard of care in the civilian and Armed Forces markets. Acquired by TriStar Wellness Solutions.
www.hemcon.com
Annual Revenues: $14.70 million
Employees: 100
Industry/ies: Pharmaceutical Industry

Co-Founder and Chairman of the Board
WIESMANN, MD, William P.

Tel: (503) 245-0459
Fax: (503) 245-1326

President and Chief Executive Officer
WAX, Michael

Tel: (503) 245-0459
Fax: (503) 245-1326

Main Headquarters
Mailing: 720 S.W. Washington St.
Suite 200
Portland, OR 97205-3504

Tel: (503) 245-0459
Fax: (503) 245-1326
TF: (877) 247-0196

Corporate Foundations and Giving Programs
The foundation of HemCon
10575 S.W. Cascade Ave.
Suite 130
Portland, OR 97223-4363

Tel: (503) 245-0459
Fax: (503) 245-1326

Public Affairs and Related Activities Personnel

At Headquarters

BEILLIU, Maire Ni
Vice President, Regulatory Affairs and Quality Systems

Tel: (503) 245-0459
Fax: (503) 245-1326

BUERGI, Simona
Chief Scientist and Contact, Media Relations
simona.buergi@hemcon.com

Tel: (503) 245-0459
Fax: (503) 245-1326

SANDS, Stuart
Chief Financial Officer and Chief Operating Officer

Tel: (503) 245-0459
Fax: (503) 245-1326

At Other Offices

MORGAN, John W.
PAC Treasurer
10575 S.W. Cascade Ave., Suite 130
Tigard, OR 97223

Tel: (503) 245-0459
Fax: (503) 245-1326

Gregory Hendricks

Identity management solutions.
www.eidpassport.com
Industry/ies: Management

Main Headquarters
Mailing: 10450 SW Nimbus Ave.
Portland, OR 97223

Tel: (503) 924-5306

Public Affairs and Related Activities Personnel

At Headquarters

HENDRICKS, Gregory
ghendricks@eidpassport.com

Tel: (503) 924-5306

Henkel of America, Inc. & The Henkel Corporation

U.S. subsidiary of Henkel., headquartered in Dusseldorf, Germany. A producer of industrial chemicals and adhesives.
www.henkelna.com
Annual Revenues: $734.30 million
Employees: 7,000
SIC: 2891; 3479; 3586
NAICS: 32552; 332812; 333913
Industry/ies: Electricity & Electronics; Electronics; Energy/Electricity

President and Chief Financial Officer
PICCOLOMINI, Jeffrey C.

Tel: (860) 571-5100
Fax: (860) 571-5465

President
SCHWAERZLER, Jens-Martin

Tel: (860) 571-5100
Fax: (860) 571-5465

Main Headquarters
Mailing: One Henkel Way
Rocky Hill, CT 06067-3581

Tel: (860) 571-5100
Fax: (860) 571-5465
TF: (800) 562-8483

Public Affairs and Related Activities Personnel

At Headquarters

DEMERS, Cynthia A.
Head of Corporate Communications

Tel: (480) 754-4090
Fax: (480) 754-3789

SYZDEK, Alan
Corporate Senior Vice President

Tel: (860) 571-5100
Fax: (860) 571-5465

Henkels & McCoy Inc.

Engaged in construction and maintenance of communications and energy utility lines.
www.henkels.com
Employees: 5,500
Industry/ies: Communications; Energy/Electricity; Telecommunications/Internet/Cable

President and Chief Executive Officer
HENKELS, T. Roderick "Rod"
rhenkels@henkels.com

Tel: (215) 283-7600
Fax: (215) 283-7659

Main Headquarters
Mailing: 985 Jolly Rd.
Blue Bell, PA 19422-0900

Tel: (215) 283-7600
Fax: (215) 283-7659

Public Affairs and Related Activities Personnel

At Headquarters

DEMARA, Paul G.
Manager, Corporate Marketing Communications and Research

Tel: (215) 283-7578
Fax: (215) 283-7939

Henry Schein, Inc.

A provider of health care products and services to office-based practitioners.
www.henryschein.com
Annual Revenues: $10.40 billion
Employees: 18,000
Ticker: NASDAQ: HSIC
SIC: 5047; 5049
NAICS: 421450; 421490
Industry/ies: Machinery/Equipment; Medicine/Health Care/Mental Health
Legislative Issues: ANI

Chairman of the Board and Chief Executive Officer
BERGMAN, Stanley M.
stanleym.bergman@henryschein.com

Tel: (631) 843-5500
Fax: (631) 843-5676

Main Headquarters
Mailing: 135 Duryea Rd.
Melville, NY 11747

Tel: (631) 843-5500
Fax: (631) 843-5676
TF: (800) 356-5788

Corporate Foundations and Giving Programs

Henry Schein Cares Foundation
Contact: Stanley M. Bergman
135 Duryea Rd.
Melville, NY 11747

Tel: (631) 843-5500

Public Affairs and Related Activities Personnel

At Headquarters

DAVID, Leonard A.	Tel:	(631) 843-5500
Senior Vice President and Chief Compliance Officer	Fax:	(631) 843-5676
len.david@henryschein.com		
ETTINGER, Michael S.	Tel:	(631) 843-5500
Senior Vice President, Corporate and Legal Affairs, Secretary	Fax:	(631) 843-5676
and Chief of Staff		
MCGLYNN, Lorelei	Tel:	(631) 843-5500
Senior Vice President, Global Human Resources and	Fax:	(631) 843-5676
Financial Operations		
MLOTEK, Mark E.	Tel:	(631) 843-5500
Executive Vice President and Chief Strategic Officer	Fax:	(631) 843-5676
PALADINO, Steven	Tel:	(631) 843-5500
Executive Vice President and Chief Financial Officer	Fax:	(631) 843-5676
steven.paladino@henryschein.com		
SIEGEL, Walter	Tel:	(631) 843-5500
Senior Vice President and General Counsel	Fax:	(631) 843-5676
VASSALLO, Susan	Tel:	(631) 843-5562
Vice President, Corporate Communications	Fax:	(631) 843-5676
susan.vassallo@henryschein.com		

Herald Group

Public affairs firm
www.theheraldgroup.com

Main Headquarters

Mailing:	1800 M St.	Tel:	(202) 347-7947
	Suite 450 S	Fax:	(202) 347-2283
	Washington, DC 20036		

Washington Office

Mailing:	950 F St. NW	Tel:	(202) 347-7947
	Suite 525	Fax:	(202) 347-2283
	Washington, DC 20004		

Public Affairs and Related Activities Personnel

At Headquarters

GOODWIN, Jr., John D.	Tel:	(202) 347-7947
Vice President	Fax:	(202) 347-2283
MOSBY, Hallie	Tel:	(202) 347-7947
Manager, Account	Fax:	(202) 347-2283
SCHOFIELD, Teresa	Tel:	(202) 347-7947
Chief Operating Officer	Fax:	(202) 347-2283
WELL, Matthew	Tel:	(202) 347-7947
Federal Lobbyist	Fax:	(202) 347-2283
Registered Federal Lobbyist		

At Washington Office

BATES, John	Tel:	(202) 347-7947
Manager, Outreach	Fax:	(202) 347-2283
BOBBITT, Amanda	Tel:	(202) 347-7947
Senior Associate	Fax:	(202) 347-2283
GUERRA, Juliet	Tel:	(202) 347-7947
Director	Fax:	(202) 347-2283
HAMMOND, R.C.	Tel:	(202) 347-7947
Vice President	Fax:	(202) 347-2283
HIRSCHHORN, Julie	Tel:	(202) 347-7947
Associate	Fax:	(202) 347-2283
MULLIGAN, Kasia	Tel:	(202) 347-7947
Senior Director	Fax:	(202) 347-2283
RUSH, Caitlin	Tel:	(202) 347-7947
Digital Account Manager	Fax:	(202) 347-2283
TREANOR, Julia	Tel:	(202) 347-7947
Senior Director	Fax:	(202) 347-2283

Herbalife International of America, Inc.

A total wellness company offering nutrition, weight-management and personal-care products.
www.herbalife.com
Annual Revenues: $4.80 billion
Employees: 7,800
Ticker: NYSE: HLF
SIC: 5122
Industry/ies: Food And Beverage Industry; Medicine/Health Care/Mental
Health; Nutrition
Legislative Issues: AGR; BUD; FIN; FOO; HCR; TRD

Chairman of the Board and Chief Executive Officer

	Tel:	(310) 410-9600
JOHNSON, Michael O.	Fax:	(213) 765-9812

Main Headquarters

Mailing:	800 W. Olympic Blvd.	Tel:	(310) 410-9600
	Suite 406	Fax:	(213) 765-9812
	Los Angeles, CA 90015		

Washington Office

Mailing:	607 14th St. NW
	Suite 675

Washington, DC 20005

Political Action Committees
Herbalife PAC
FEC ID: C00393298
Contact: John DeSimone
990 W. 190th St.
Suite 650
Torrance, CA 90502

> **Contributions to Candidates:** $24,600 (2015-2016)
> Democrats: $16,500; Republicans: $8,100

Corporate Foundations and Giving Programs

Herbalife Family Foundation
Contact: Robyn M. Browning

P.O. Box 80210	TF:	(866) 617-4273
Los Angeles, CA 90080		

Public Affairs and Related Activities Personnel

At Headquarters

BERKLAS, Jim	Tel:	(310) 410-9600
Vice President, Counsel, Chief Compliance Officer and	Fax:	(213) 765-9812
Assistant Corporate Secretary		
CorporateSecretary@herbalife.com		
BROWNING, Robyn M.	Tel:	(310) 410-9600
Executive Director, Herbalife Family Foundation	Fax:	(213) 765-9812
Robynb@herbalife.com		
CHAPMAN, Brett R.	Tel:	(310) 410-9600
Strategic Advisor	Fax:	(213) 765-9812
FISCHER, George	Tel:	(213) 745-0519
Worldwide Corporate Communications	Fax:	(213) 765-9812
GOUDIS, Richard P.	Tel:	(310) 410-9600
Chief Operating Officer	Fax:	(213) 765-9812
GREENE, Amy	Tel:	(213) 745-0504
Vice President, Investor Relations	Fax:	(213) 765-9812
amygr@herbalife.com		
HENDERSON, Barbara B.	Tel:	(213) 745-0517
Senior Vice President, Worldwide Corporate Communications	Fax:	(213) 765-9812
HOFFMAN, Alan	Tel:	(310) 410-9600
Executive Vice President, Global Corporate Affairs	Fax:	(213) 765-9812
WALSH, Des	Tel:	(310) 410-9600
President	Fax:	(213) 765-9812

At Washington Office

ROSEN, Eric
Vice President, U.S. Government Relations
Registered Federal Lobbyist

VENARDOS, John
Registered Federal Lobbyist

At Other Offices

ARBOLEDA, Angela	Tel:	(202) 661-6111
Vice President, Community Engagement and Health Policy		
1200 G St. NW, Suite 800		
Washington, DC 20005		
Registered Federal Lobbyist		
DESIMONE, John	Tel:	(310) 410-9600
Chief Financial Officer and PAC Treasurer		
990 W. 190th St., Suite 650		
Torrance, CA 90502		
HOBBY, Ric	Tel:	(202) 661-6111
Senior Vice President, Global Government Affairs		
1200 G St. NW, Suite 800		
Washington, DC 20005		
POPELKA, Randall	Tel:	(202) 661-6111
Vice President, Government and Industry Affairs		
1200 G St. NW, Suite 800		
Washington, DC 20005		
Registered Federal Lobbyist		
TURPIN, S. Diane	Tel:	(202) 661-6111
Vice President, Worldwide Regulatory, Government and		
Industry Affairs		
1200 G St. NW, Suite 800		
Washington, DC 20005		

Herman Miller

A manufacturer of office furniture for industry, laboratory, healthcare, and industrial and residential environments.
www.hermanmiller.com
Annual Revenues: $2.08 billion
Employees: 6,630
Ticker: NASDAQ: MLHR
SIC: 2269; 2522; 2599; 5021; 5051
NAICS: 313312; 337127; 337214; 42151; 42121
Industry/ies: Architecture And Design; Furniture/Home Furnishings

Chairman of the Board	Tel:	(616) 654-3000	
VOLKEMA, Michael A.	Fax:	(616) 654-5234	
michael_volkema@hermanmiller.com			

President and Chief Executive Officer Tel: (616) 654-3000
WALKER, Brian C. Fax: (616) 654-3632

Main Headquarters
Mailing: 855 E. Main Ave. Tel: (616) 654-3000
P.O. Box 302 Fax: (616) 654-5234
Zeeland, MI 49464-0302 TF: (888) 443-4357

Corporate Foundations and Giving Programs

Herman Miller Foundation
855 E. Main Ave. Tel: (616) 654-3000
P.O. Box 302
Zeeland, MI 49464

Public Affairs and Related Activities Personnel

At Headquarters

SCHURMAN, Mark W. Tel: (616) 654-5498
Director, Corporate Communications Fax: (616) 654-5234

STUTZ, Jeff Tel: (616) 654-3000
Chief Financial Officer Fax: (616) 654-5234
jeff_stutz@hermanmiller.com

VELTMAN, Kevin Tel: (616) 654-3000
Vice President, Investor Relations and Treasurer Fax: (616) 654-5234
kevin_veltman@hermanmiller.com

Hershey Chocolate Corporation
See listing on page 399 under The Hershey Company

The Hershey Company
A manufacturer of chocolate, confectionery, and snack products. It manufactures, imports, markets, distributes, and sells confectionery products.
www.hersheys.com
Annual Revenues: $7.49 billion
Employees: 20,800
Ticker: NYSE: HSY
SIC: 2060
Industry/ies: Food And Beverage Industry
Legislative Issues: AGR; BUD; FOO; LBR; TRD

Chairman of the Board, President and Chief Executive Officer Tel: (717) 534-4200
BILBREY, John P. Fax: (717) 534-7015

Main Headquarters
Mailing: P.O. Box 810 Tel: (717) 534-4200
100 Crystal A Dr. Fax: (717) 534-7015
Hershey, PA 17033-0810 TF: (800) 468-1714

Washington Office
Mailing: 601 Pennsylvania Ave. NW Tel: (202) 434-8278
Suite 900, S. Bldg. Fax: (202) 434-8258
Washington, DC 20004

Political Action Committees
Hershey Company Political Action Committee
FEC ID: C00200139
100 Crystal A Dr. Tel: (202) 434-8278
Suite 900, South Bldg. Fax: (202) 434-8258
Hershey, PA 17033

  Contributions to Candidates: $45,000 (2015-2016)
  Democrats: $20,500; Republicans: $24,500

Corporate Foundations and Giving Programs

The Hershey Company Contributions Program
Contact: James D. George
100 Crystal A Dr. Tel: (717) 534-4200
P.O. Box 810
Hershey, PA 17033-0810

Public Affairs and Related Activities Personnel

At Headquarters

BECKMAN, Jeff Tel: (800) 468-1714
Director, Corporate Communications Fax: (717) 534-7015
jbeckman@hersheys.com

GEORGE, James D. Tel: (717) 534-4200
Vice President, Community Relations Fax: (717) 534-7015

IDROVO, Javier J. Tel: (717) 534-4200
Senior Vice President, Strategy and Business Development Fax: (717) 534-7015

LITTLE, Patricia A. Tel: (717) 534-4200
Senior Vice President, Chief Financial Officer Fax: (717) 534-7015

MCCORMICK, Andrew B. Tel: (717) 534-4200
Vice President, Public Affairs Fax: (717) 534-7015

PAPA, William C. Tel: (717) 534-4200
Senior Vice President, Chief Research and Development Officer Fax: (717) 534-7015

POGHARIAN, Mark K. Tel: (717) 534-7556

Vice President, Investor Relations Fax: (717) 534-6550
mpogharian@hersheys.com

RUSSELL, Richard G. Tel: (717) 534-4200
PAC Treasurer Fax: (717) 534-7038
rickrussell@hersheys.com

TURNER, Leslie M. Tel: (717) 534-4200
Senior Vice President, General Counsel and Secretary Fax: (717) 534-7015

WALLING, Kevin R. Tel: (717) 534-4200
Senior Vice President and Chief Human Resources Officer Fax: (717) 534-7015

WEGE, D. Michael Tel: (717) 534-4200
Senior Vice President, Chief Marketing Officer Fax: (717) 534-7015

ZAMAN, Waheed Tel: (717) 534-4200
Senior Vice President, Chief Knowledge, Strategy and Technology Officer Fax: (717) 534-7015

At Washington Office

GRAF, Ronald P P. Tel: (202) 434-8278
Vice President, Global Government Relations Fax: (202) 434-8258

HARLEY, Eileen Tel: (202) 434-8278
Senior Manager, Government Relations Fax: (202) 434-8258
Registered Federal Lobbyist

LAUZON, Eileen Tel: (202) 434-8278
Registered Federal Lobbyist Fax: (202) 434-8258

SMITH, Janine Tel: (202) 434-8278
Registered Federal Lobbyist Fax: (202) 434-8258

TURNER, Joanna Tel: (202) 434-8278
Registered Federal Lobbyist Fax: (202) 434-8258

Hershey Trust Company
An independent trust company founded by Milton S. Hershey, which funds the Milton Hershey School, a school for underprivileged children. The company acts as trustee and provides investment management and administration services for the trust.
www.hersheytrust.com
Annual Revenues: $6.30 million
Employees: 33
Industry/ies: Banking/Finance/Investments
Legislative Issues: BUD

Chairman of the Board Tel: (717) 520-1100
CAVANAUGH, Robert F. Fax: (717) 520-1111

Main Headquarters
Mailing: 100 Mansion Rd. East Tel: (717) 520-1100
P.O. Box 445 Fax: (717) 520-1111
Hershey, PA 17033

Corporate Foundations and Giving Programs

The M.S. Hershey Foundation
Contact: Don Papson
63 W. Chocolate Ave. Tel: (717) 298-2200
Hershey, PA 17033 Fax: (717) 534-8940

Public Affairs and Related Activities Personnel

At Headquarters

BRATTON, Janice L. Tel: (717) 520-1116
Vice President and Investment Officer Fax: (717) 520-1111

BROWN, Jim Tel: (717) 520-1100
Board Of Directors Fax: (717) 520-1111

BUSH, Gayla M. Tel: (717) 520-1125
Vice President, Finance Fax: (717) 520-1111

At Other Offices

PAPSON, Don Tel: (717) 298-2207
Executive Director, Hershey Foundation Fax: (717) 534-8940
63 W. Chocolate Ave.
Hershey, PA 17033
dpapson@mshersheyfoundation.org

Hertz Corporation
A car rental company.
www.hertz.com
Annual Revenues: $10.77 billion
Employees: 30,400
Ticker: NYSE: HTZ
SIC: 7510
Industry/ies: Automotive Industry; Transportation
Legislative Issues: TAX

President and Chief Executive Officer Tel: (201) 307-2000
TAGUE, John P. Fax: (201) 307-2644

Main Headquarters
Mailing: 225 Brae Blvd. Tel: (201) 307-2000
Park Ridge, NJ 07656 Fax: (201) 307-2644

Corporate Foundations and Giving Programs

Dollar Thrifty Community Driven Program
5330 E. 31st St. Tel: (918) 660-7700

P.O. Box 35985	Fax:	(918) 660-2934
Tulsa, OK 74135		

Public Affairs and Related Activities Personnel

At Headquarters

BOOTENHOFF, Anna — Tel: (918) 669-2236
Manager, Corporate Communications and Investor Relations — Fax: (918) 669-2934
Anna.Bootenhoff@dtag.com

BROOME, Richard — Tel: (201) 307-2000
Executive Vice President, Corporate Affairs and — Fax: (201) 307-2856
Communications

FLEISCHNER, Fred J. — Tel: (918) 669-3086
Executive Director, Corporate Communications — Fax: (918) 669-2934
fred.fleischner@dtag.com

HUNZIKER, Leslie — Tel: (201) 307-3100
Senior Vice President, Investor Relations — Fax: (201) 307-2644

KENNEDY, Tom — Tel: (201) 307-2000
Senior Executive Vice President and Chief Financial Officer — Fax: (201) 307-2644

KRAMER, Robin C. — Tel: (201) 307-2000
Senior Vice President, Chief Accounting Officer — Fax: (201) 307-2644

MCMAHON, Michael — Tel: (918) 660-7700
Staff Vice President and Assistant Treasurer — Fax: (918) 669-2934

SABATINO, Thomas — Tel: (201) 307-2000
Senior Executive Vice President, Chief Administrative Officer — Fax: (201) 307-2644
and General Counsel

STUART, Robert J. — Tel: (201) 307-2000
Executive Vice President, Global Sales and Marketing — Fax: (201) 307-2644

VANIMAN, Vicki — Tel: (918) 660-7700
Executive Vice President, General Counsel & Secretary — Fax: (918) 669-2934
vicki.vaniman@dtag.com

ZIMMERMAN, Jeffrey — Tel: (201) 307-2000
Senior Vice President, General Counsel & Secretary — Fax: (201) 307-2644

Hess Corporation

A U.S.-based international oil and gas company with refining, marketing, exploration, and production interests. Formerly the Amerada Hess Corporation.
www.hess.com
Annual Revenues: $9.60 billion
Employees: 3,045
Ticker: NYSE: HES
SIC: 2911
NAICS: 324191
Industry/ies: Fuels See Coal, Gas, Oil, Petroleum; Natural Resources; Petroleum Industry
Legislative Issues: CAW; ENG; ENV; FOR; FUE; NAT; TAX

Chairman of the Board — Tel: (212) 997-8500
WILLIAMS, Mark R. — Fax: (212) 536-8593

Chief Executive Officer — Tel: (212) 997-8500
HESS, John B. — Fax: (212) 536-8593

Main Headquarters
Mailing: 1185 Avenue of the Americas — Tel: (212) 997-8500
40th Floor — Fax: (212) 536-8593
New York City, NY 10036

Washington Office
Mailing: 800 Connecticut Ave. NW — Tel: (202) 263-1010
Suite 601
Washington, DC 20006

Political Action Committees
Hess Corporation PAC (Hess PAC)
FEC ID: C00557322
Contact: Eric Fishman
1501 McKinney St.
Houston, 77010

> **Contributions to Candidates:** $34,000 (2015-2016)
> Democrats: $2,000; Republicans: $32,000

> **Principal Recipients**

> **SENATE**
> HOEVEN, JOHN (REP-ND)

Corporate Foundations and Giving Programs

Hess Corporation Contributions Program
1185 Avenue of the Americas — Tel: (212) 997-8500
40th Floor
New York City, NY 10036

Public Affairs and Related Activities Personnel

At Headquarters

PAVER, Howard — Tel: (212) 997-8500
Senior Vice President, Strategy, Commercial and New — Fax: (212) 536-8593
Business Development

FRANCHINI, Indrani M. — Tel: (212) 997-8500
Vice President, Chief Compliance Officer — Fax: (212) 536-8593

GOODELL, Timothy B. — Tel: (212) 997-8500
Senior Vice President and General Counsel — Fax: (212) 536-8593

HECKER, Lorrie — Tel: (212) 997-8500
Director, Global Communications — Fax: (212) 536-8593
lhecker@hess.com

HILL, Gregory P — Tel: (212) 997-8500
Chief Operating Officer and President, Exploration and — Fax: (212) 536-8593
Production

MALONEY, Drew — Tel: (212) 997-8500
Vice President, Global Government Affairs and Public Policy — Fax: (212) 536-8593

MARCHETTI, Albert — Tel: (212) 997-8500
Vice President, International and Federal Relations — Fax: (212) 536-8593
amarchetti@hess.com
Registered Federal Lobbyist

RIELLY, John P. — Tel: (212) 997-8500
Senior Vice President and Chief Financial Officer — Fax: (212) 536-8593
jrielly@hess.com

WILCOX, Kevin B — Tel: (212) 997-8500
Vice President, Exploration and Production Controller — Fax: (212) 536-8593

WILSON, Jay R. — Tel: (212) 635-8940
Vice President, Investor Relations — Fax: (212) 536-8593
investorrelations@hess.com

ZIOLO, Mykel — Tel: (212) 997-8500
Senior Vice President, Human Resources — Fax: (212) 536-8593

At Other Offices

CONSOLVO, Brandon
External Affairs and Public Policy
1501 Mckinney St.
Houston, TX 77010

FISHMAN, Eric
PAC Contact
1501 Mckinney St.
Houston, TX 77010

HAGEN, Lauren
1501 Mckinney St.
Houston, TX 77010

KALANTZAKIS, George
Manager, International Government Affairs
1501 Mckinney St.
Houston, TX 77010
Registered Federal Lobbyist

LYONS, Troy
1501 Mckinney St.
Houston, TX 77010
Registered Federal Lobbyist

SCHAAFF, Lesley
Senior Manager, Federal and Environmental Affairs
1501 Mckinney St.
Houston, TX 77010
Registered Federal Lobbyist

Hewlett-Packard Company

HP focuses on simplifying technology experiences for all its customers - from individual consumers to the largest businesses, with a portfolio that spans printing, personal computing, software, services and IT infrastructure.
www.hp.com
Annual Revenues: $100.35 billion
Employees: 287,000
Ticker: NYSE: HPQ
SIC: 3570
Industry/ies: Computer/Technology; Electricity & Electronics; Electronics; Energy/Electricity
Legislative Issues: BUD; CPI; CPT; CSP; EDU; GOV; HOM; IMM; SCI; TAX; TRD

Chairman — Tel: (281) 518-3006
WHITMAN, Meg — Fax: (650) 857-5518

President and Chief Executive Officer — Tel: (650) 857-1501
WEISLER, Dion — Fax: (650) 857-5518

Main Headquarters
Mailing: 3000 Hanover St. — Tel: (650) 857-1501
Suite 1300 North — Fax: (650) 857-5518
Palo Alto, CA 94304

Washington Office
Mailing: 1299 Pennsylvania Ave. NW
Suite 450
Washington, DC 20004

Political Action Committees
Hewlett-Packard Company PAC
FEC ID: C00196725
Contact: Jonathan R. Sturz
3000 Hanover St.
Palo Alto, CA 94304

Contributions to Candidates: $245,500 (2015-2016)
Democrats: $106,000; Republicans: $139,500

Principal Recipients

HOUSE
ESHOO, ANNA G. (DEM-CA)

Corporate Foundations and Giving Programs

Hewlett-Packard Company Foundation
Contact: Cathie Lesjak
3000 Hanover St.   Tel: (650) 857-1501
Palo Alto, CA 94304

Public Affairs and Related Activities Personnel

At Headquarters

BROWN, Gwen   Tel: (202) 637-6728
Federal Lobbyist   Fax: (202) 637-6759
Registered Federal Lobbyist

CINO, Maria   Tel: (202) 637-6728
Vice President, Government Relations   Fax: (202) 637-6759

DOVE, Randolph V.   Tel: (202) 637-6728
Executive Director, Government Relations   Fax: (202) 637-6759
randy.dove@hp.com
Registered Federal Lobbyist

HINSHAW, John   Tel: (650) 857-1501
Chief Customer Officer, Executive Vice President, Technology   Fax: (650) 857-5518
and Operations

HURST, Nate   Tel: (202) 637-6728
Global Director, Sustainability and Social Innovation   Fax: (202) 637-6759

STERNHELL, Kristy Skupa   Tel: (202) 637-6728
Director, Congressional Affairs and Federal Lobbyist   Fax: (202) 637-6759
Registered Federal Lobbyist

STURZ, Jonathan R.   Tel: (650) 857-1501
PAC Treasurer   Fax: (650) 857-5518

TOMB, Mark C.   Tel: (202) 637-6728
Director, Corporate Affairs   Fax: (202) 637-6759

VASELL, Shawn M.   Tel: (202) 637-6728
Senior Director, Corporate Affairs   Fax: (202) 637-6759
shawn.vasell@hp.com

At Washington Office

CHAN, Alvin
Registered Federal Lobbyist

WITKOWSKI, Kasia
Registered Federal Lobbyist

WITKOWSKII, Kasia
Registered Federal Lobbyist

At Other Offices

BERMAN, Kristine
Director, Global Government Relations
709 G St. NW, Suite 300
Washington, DC 20001

FLAXMAN, Jon   Tel: (650) 857-1501
Chief Operating Officer   Fax: (650) 857-5518
1501 Page Mill Rd.
Palo Alto, CA 94304

GOMEZ, Henry   Tel: (650) 857-1501
Executive Vice President and Chief Marketing and   Fax: (650) 857-5518
Communications Officer
1501 Page Mill Rd.
Palo Alto, CA 94304

KEOGH, Tracy S.   Tel: (650) 857-1501
Chief Human Resources Officer   Fax: (650) 857-5518
1501 Page Mill Rd.
Palo Alto, CA 94304

LESJAK, Cathie   Tel: (650) 857-1501
Chief Financial Officer   Fax: (650) 857-5518
1501 Page Mill Rd.
Palo Alto, CA 94304

LUCIO, Antonio J.   Tel: (650) 857-1501
Chief Marketing and Communications Officer   Fax: (650) 857-5518
1501 Page Mill Rd.
Palo Alto, CA 94304

RIVERA, Kim M.   Tel: (650) 857-1501
Chief Legal Officer and General Counsel   Fax: (650) 857-5518
1501 Page Mill Rd.
Palo Alto, CA 94304

SCHULTZ, John   Tel: (650) 857-1501
Executive Vice President and General Counsel   Fax: (650) 857-5518
1501 Page Mill Rd.
Palo Alto, CA 94304

WINCUP, Bret
Director, Government Relations

---

709 G St. NW, Suite 300
Washington, DC 20001

Hexcel Corporation

Hexcel Corporation produces composite materials such as honeycomb, prepregs, film adhesives and sandwich panels. It also manufactures composite parts and structures.
www.hexcel.com
Annual Revenues: $1.89 billion
Employees: 5,897
Ticker: NYSE: HXL
SIC: 2821
Industry/ies: Construction/Construction Materials
Legislative Issues: DEF; TRD

President and Chief Executive Officer, Chairman of the Board   Tel: (203) 352-6800
STANAGE, Nick   Fax: (203) 358-3977

Main Headquarters
Mailing: 281 Tresser Blvd.   Tel: (203) 352-6800
  16th Floor   Fax: (203) 358-3977
  Stamford, CT 06901-3261   TF: (800) 688-7734

Political Action Committees
Hexcel Corporation PAC
FEC ID: C00345173
Contact: Michael MacIntyre
281 Tresser Blvd.
Two Stamford Plaza, 16th Floor
Stamford, CT 06901

  Contributions to Candidates: $9,000 (2015-2016)
  Democrats: $2,500; Republicans: $6,500

Corporate Foundations and Giving Programs

Hexcel Foundation
Contact: Wayne C. Pensky
281 Tresser Blvd.   Tel: (203) 969-0666
Two Stamford Plaza, 16th Floor
Stamford, CT 06901

Public Affairs and Related Activities Personnel

At Headquarters

BACAL, Michael W.   Tel: (203) 352-6826
Investor Relations   Fax: (203) 358-3977
michael.bacal@hexcel.com

HENDRICKS, Kimberly A   Tel: (203) 352-6800
Vice President, Corporate Controller and Chief Accounting   Fax: (203) 358-3977
Officer

HENNEMUTH, Robert G.   Tel: (203) 969-0666
Executive Vice President, Human Resources and   Fax: (203) 358-3977
Communications
Rob.hennemuth@hexcel.com

KRAKOWER, Ira J.   Tel: (203) 969-0666
Senior Vice President, General Counsel and Secretary   Fax: (203) 358-3977

MACINTYRE, Michael   Tel: (203) 969-0666
PAC Treasurer   Fax: (203) 358-3977

OWEN, Rachel   Tel: (203) 352-6800
Marketing Communications   Fax: (203) 358-3977

PENSKY, Wayne C.   Tel: (203) 352-6839
Senior Vice President and Chief Financial Officer   Fax: (203) 358-3977
wayne.pensky@hexcel.com

VEAZEY, Kaye   Tel: (203) 352-0339
Corporate Communications   Fax: (203) 358-3977
kaye.veazey@hexcel.com

HID Corporation

Provides access and ID management solutions for the delivery of secure identity.
www.hidglobal.com
Employees: 800
Industry/ies: Computer/Technology

Interim Chief Executive Officer   Tel: (949) 732-2000
SODERGREN, Ulf   Fax: (949) 732-2120

Main Headquarters
Mailing: 15370 Barranca Pkwy.   Tel: (949) 732-2000
  Irvine, CA 92618-3106   Fax: (949) 732-2120
  TF: (800) 237-7769

Public Affairs and Related Activities Personnel

At Headquarters

CARROLL, Kathleen   Tel: (949) 732-2000
Vice President, Corporate Affairs   Fax: (949) 732-2120

CRUMLEY, Laura   Tel: (949) 732-2000
Senior Vice President and Chief Financial Officer   Fax: (949) 732-2120

DEWITT, Michelle   Tel: (949) 732-2000
Senior Vice President, Human Resources   Fax: (949) 598-1690

HASLAM, Rob   Tel: (949) 732-2000

Vice President, Government ID Solutions	Fax:	(949) 732-2120
HYATT, Jeremy	Tel:	(949) 732-2177
Director, Global Public Relations	Fax:	(949) 732-2120
media@hidglobal.com		
MOXON, Tim	Tel:	(949) 732-2000
Vice President, Corporate Development	Fax:	(949) 732-2120
PROCYK, Mary	Tel:	(949) 732-2000
Vice President, Global Finance	Fax:	(949) 732-2120

High Performance Technologies, Inc.

HPTi is a performance-based architecture service provider for the information technology marketplace.
www.drc.com
Annual Revenues: $91 million
Employees: 400
Industry/ies: Computer/Technology

Chairman, President and Chief Executive Officer — Tel: (703) 707-2700
REGAN, James P. — Fax: (703) 707-0103

Main Headquarters
Mailing: 11955 Freedom Dr. — Tel: (703) 707-2700
Suite 1100 — Fax: (703) 707-0103
Reston, VA 20190

Public Affairs and Related Activities Personnel

At Headquarters

CONNELL, Thomas	Tel:	(703) 707-2700
Senior Vice President, Strategic Business Development	Fax:	(703) 707-0103
JONES, Robert S.	Tel:	(703) 707-2700
Vice President, Corporate Development	Fax:	(703) 707-0103

High Point Regional Health System

High Point Regional Health, a member of UNC Health Care, is central North Carolina's premier health care provider and is a private, not-for-profit health care system includes the Rehab Center, the Millis Regional Health Education Center, the Regional Wound Center, the Diabetes Self Care Management Center, The Vascular Center and High Point Behavioral Health.
www.highpointregional.com
Industry/ies: Medicine/Health Care/Mental Health

President and Chief Executive Officer — Tel: (336) 878-6000
BOVIO, Ernie

Main Headquarters
Mailing: P.O. Box HP-5 — Tel: (336) 878-6000
High Point, NC 27261

Corporate Foundations and Giving Programs
High Point Regional Health Foundation
Contact: Katherine Burns
P.O. Box HP-5 — Tel: (336) 878-6291
601 N. Elm St. — Fax: (336) 878-6144
High Point, NC 27261

Public Affairs and Related Activities Personnel

At Headquarters

ALLEY, Becky	Tel:	(336) 878-6711
Director, Marketing & Public Relations		
Becky.Alley@HPRHS.COM		
BUNCH, FACHE, MPH, Rita A.	Tel:	(336) 878-6000
Vice President, Operations		
BURNS, Katherine	Tel:	(336) 878-6291
Vice President, People Services		
CREWS, Kimberly	Tel:	(336) 878-6000
Vice President, Chief Financial Officer		
POTTER, Denise	Tel:	(336) 878-6000
Vice President, Foundation, Public Relations and Marketing		

Highmark Blue Cross Blue Shield

Formed by the merger of Pennsylvania Blue Shield and Blue Cross of Western Pennsylvania. An independent licensee of the Blue Cross and Blue Shield Association and an association of independent Blue Cross and Blue Shield plans.
www.highmark.com
Employees: 35,000
Industry/ies: Insurance Industry; Medicine/Health Care/Mental Health
Legislative Issues: BUD; HCR; MMM; PHA; TAX

Chairman of the Board, President and Chief Executive Officer — Tel: (412) 544-7000
HOLMBERG, David L. — Fax: (412) 544-8368

Main Headquarters
Mailing: Fifth Ave. Pl. — Tel: (412) 544-7000
120 Fifth Ave. — Fax: (412) 544-8368
Pittsburgh, PA 15222-3099

Political Action Committees
Highmark Health PAC of Highmark Inc.
FEC ID: C00302844

Contact: Kenneth B. Gebhard
1800 Center St.
Camp Hill, PA 17089
Contributions to Candidates: $49,900 (2015-2016)
Democrats: $13,900; Republicans: $36,000

Corporate Foundations and Giving Programs
Highmark Caring Foundation
Contact: Mary Anne Papale
Fifth Avenue Pl. — Tel: (412) 544-4032
120 Fifth Ave. — Fax: (412) 544-8368
Pittsburgh, PA 15222-3099

The Highmark Foundation
Contact: Yvonne Cook
Fifth Avenue Pl. — Tel: (412) 544-7000
120 Fifth Ave.
Pittsburgh, PA 15222

Public Affairs and Related Activities Personnel

At Headquarters

ANDERSON, Melissa	Tel:	(412) 544-7000
Executive Vice President and Chief Audit and Compliance Officer	Fax:	(412) 544-8368
BILLGER, Aaron	Tel:	(412) 544-7826
Director, Public Relations	Fax:	(412) 544-8368
aaron.billger@highmark.com		
CARSON, Ray H.	Tel:	(412) 544-7000
Executive Vice President, Chief Human Resources Officer	Fax:	(412) 544-8368
CARTER, David W.	Tel:	(412) 544-7000
Senior Vice President and Chief Communications Officer	Fax:	(412) 544-8368
COOK, Yvonne	Tel:	(800) 789-1726
President, Highmark Foundation and Vice President, Community Affairs	Fax:	(412) 544-6120
yvonne.cook@highmark.com		
FARBACHER, Elizabeth A.	Tel:	(412) 544-7000
Executive Vice President, Chief Auditor and Compliance Officer	Fax:	(412) 544-8368
elizabeth.farbacher@highmark.com		
NELSON, Steven C.	Tel:	(412) 544-7000
Senior Vice President, Health Services, Strategy, Product and Marketing	Fax:	(412) 544-8368
ONORATO, Daniel A.	Tel:	(412) 544-7000
Executive Vice President, Public Policy, Chief Government Relations and Community Affairs Officer	Fax:	(412) 544-8368
PAPALE, Mary Anne	Tel:	(412) 544-4032
Director, Community Affairs	Fax:	(412) 544-8368
RUSH, Jean	Tel:	(412) 544-7000
Executive Vice President, Government Markets	Fax:	(412) 544-8368
SEAY, Lynn	Tel:	(412) 544-7000
Director, Corporate Communications	Fax:	(412) 544-8368
SETZER, Brian D.	Tel:	(412) 544-7000
Senior Vice President, Chief Financial Officer	Fax:	(412) 544-8368
STUART, Alyson B.	Tel:	(412) 544-7000
Executive Secretary, Government Affairs	Fax:	(412) 544-8368
alyson.stuart@highmark.com		
VANKIRK, Thomas L.	Tel:	(412) 544-7000
Secretary	Fax:	(412) 544-8368
WALTON, Aaron	Tel:	(412) 544-7000
Senior Vice President, Corporate Affairs	Fax:	(412) 544-8368

At Other Offices

ENGLERT, Gregory P.	Tel:	(717) 302-3977
Senior Government Affairs Representative		
1800 Center St.		
Camp Hill, PA 17089		
Registered Federal Lobbyist		
GEBHARD, Kenneth B.	Tel:	(717) 302-3977
PAC Treasurer		
1800 Center St.		
Camp Hill, PA 17089		
PORTER, Gayeta C.	Tel:	(717) 302-3977
PAC Treasurer		
1800 Center St.		
Camp Hill, PA 17089		
WARFEL, Michael G.	Tel:	(717) 302-3977
Vice President, Government Affairs		
1800 Center St.		
Camp Hill, PA 17089		
Registered Federal Lobbyist		

Highmark Blue Cross Blue Shield Delaware

A health insurance company. Name changed to Highmark Blue Cross Blue Shield Delaware in 2012.

www.bcbsde.com
Annual Revenues: $468.79 million
Employees: 700
Industry/ies: Insurance Industry

President and Chief Executive Officer
HOLMBERG, David L.

Tel: (302) 421-3333

Main Headquarters
Mailing: P.O. Box 1991
Wilmingto, DE 19899-1991

Tel: (302) 421-3333

Corporate Foundations and Giving Programs

Highmark Blue Cross Blue Shield Delaware Contributions Program
Contact: Melissa Lukach
P.O. Box 1991
Wilmingto, DE 19899-1991

Tel: (302) 421-3333

Public Affairs and Related Activities Personnel

At Headquarters

ALRICH, Christine L.
Vice President, Corporate Marketing

Tel: (302) 421-3333

LUKACH, Melissa
Representative, Community Relations

Tel: (302) 421-3333

Highmark Blue Cross Blue Shield West Virginia

A health insurance company.
www.highmarkbcbswv.com
Annual Revenues: $839.20 million
Employees: 1,000
Industry/ies: Insurance Industry; Medicine/Health Care/Mental Health

President and Chief Executive Officer
HOLMBERG, David L.

Tel: (304) 347-7754
Fax: (304) 424-7704

Main Headquarters
Mailing: P.O. Box 1948
Parkersburg, WV 26102

Tel: (304) 347-7754
Fax: (304) 424-7704
TF: (800) 982-2583

Public Affairs and Related Activities Personnel

At Headquarters

RUSH, Jean
Executive Vice President, Government Markets

Tel: (304) 347-7754
Fax: (304) 424-7704

SETZER, Brian D.
Senior Vice President, Chief Financial Officer

Tel: (304) 347-7754
Fax: (304) 424-7704

VANKIRK, Thomas L.
Secretary

Tel: (304) 347-7754
Fax: (304) 424-7704

Hill-Rom Company, Inc.

A public holding company for three businesses serving the health care (patient care systems and specialty therapy beds); death care (protective metal and hardwood burial caskets, and cremation products); and life insurance (pre-need funeral planning). Spun-off of its funeral services business, Batesville Casket Company in April 2008.
www.hill-rom.com
Annual Revenues: $1.67 billion
Employees: 7,000
Ticker: NYSE: HRC
SIC: 2531
NAICS: 33636
Industry/ies: Medicine/Health Care/Mental Health
Legislative Issues: HCR; MMM; TAX; TEC; TRD

Chairman of the Board
CLASSON, Rolf A.

Tel: (812) 934-7777
Fax: (812) 934-8189

President and Chief Executive Officer
GREISCH, John J.
John.Greisch@hill-rom.com

Tel: (812) 934-7777
Fax: (812) 934-8189

Main Headquarters
Mailing: 1069 State Rd.
46 East
Batesville, IN 47006

Tel: (812) 934-7777
Fax: (812) 934-8189
TF: (800) 445-3730

Washington Office
Mailing: 1875 I St. NW
Suite 500
Washington, DC 20006

Political Action Committees
Hill-Rom Holdings, Inc. PAC (HRPAC)
FEC ID: C00448993
Contact: Dennis R. Zwink
1069 State Route 46 East
Batesville, IN 47006

Contributions to Candidates: $65,000 (2015-2016)
Democrats: $21,000; Republicans: $44,000

Corporate Foundations and Giving Programs

Hospital Beds for Humanity™ Program
1069 State Route 46 East

Batesville, IN 47006

Public Affairs and Related Activities Personnel

At Headquarters

FRANK, Andreas G.
Senior Vice President, Corporate Development and Strategy

Tel: (812) 934-7777
Fax: (812) 934-8189

JEFFERS, Thomas J.
Vice President, Government Affairs
tom.jeffers@hill-rom.com
Registered Federal Lobbyist

Tel: (812) 934-7777
Fax: (812) 934-8189

LICHTENSTEIN, Susan R.
Senior Vice President, Corporate Affairs and Chief Legal Officer
susan.lichtenstein@hill-rom.com

Tel: (812) 934-7777
Fax: (812) 934-8189

MURPHY, Michael
Senior Vice President, Quality Assurance and Regulatory Affairs

Tel: (812) 934-7777
Fax: (812) 934-8189

REITH, Jr., Blair A. "Andy"
Vice President, Investor Relations
andy.reith@hill-rom.com

Tel: (812) 931-2199
Fax: (812) 931-3533

SHULMAN, Ilana
Chief Compliance Officer

Tel: (812) 934-7777
Fax: (812) 934-8189

SOLOMON, Carlyn D.
Chief Operating Officer

Tel: (812) 934-7777
Fax: (812) 934-8189

STROBEL, Steven J.
Senior Vice President and Chief Financial Officer

Tel: (812) 934-7777
Fax: (812) 934-8189

ZWAAN, Michiel de
Senior Vice President and Chief Human Resources Officer

Tel: (812) 934-7777
Fax: (812) 934-8189

ZWINK, Dennis R.
PAC Contact

Tel: (812) 934-7777
Fax: (812) 934-8189

Hillenbrand Industries, Inc.

See listing on page 403 under Hill-Rom Company, Inc.

Hilton Worldwide

Owner and operator of hotels.
www.hiltonworldwide.com
Annual Revenues: $7.17 billion
Employees: 164,000
Ticker: NYSE:HLT
SIC: 7011
Industry/ies: Travel/Tourism/Lodging
Legislative Issues: GOV; HOM; TAX; TOU; TRD

President and Chief Executive Officer
NASSETTA, Christopher J.

Tel: (703) 883-1000

Main Headquarters
Mailing: 7930 Jones Branch Dr., Suite 1100
McLean, VA 22102

Tel: (703) 883-1000

Political Action Committees
Hilton Worldwide Political Action Committee
FEC ID: C00213074
Contact: Jonas Neihardt
7930 Jones Branch Dr.
Suite 1100
McLean, VA 22102

Tel: (703) 883-1000

Contributions to Candidates: $209,500 (2015-2016)
Democrats: $91,000; Republicans: $118,500

Principal Recipients

SENATE
GRASSLEY, CHARLES E SENATOR (REP-IA)
KAINE, TIMOTHY MICHAEL (DEM-VA)

HOUSE
BRADY, KEVIN (REP-TX)
COMSTOCK, BARBARA J HONORABLE (REP-VA)

Corporate Foundations and Giving Programs

Hilton Worldwide Contributions Program
7930 Jones Branch Dr.
Suite 1100
McLean, VA 22102

Tel: (703) 883-1000

Public Affairs and Related Activities Personnel

At Headquarters

CAMPBELL, Kristin
Executive Vice President and General Counsel

Tel: (703) 883-1000

GORDON, Erica
Federal Lobbyist
Registered Federal Lobbyist

Tel: (703) 883-1000

JACOBS, Kevin
Executive Vice President and Chief Financial Officer

Tel: (703) 883-1000

LUCAS, Steven S.
Attorney & Agent for Filer

Tel: (703) 883-1000

MARGARITIS, William		Tel:	(703) 883-1000
Executive Vice President, Corporate Affairs			
MIKESELL, Katherine		Tel:	(703) 883-5806
Director, Global Corporate Communications			
Katherine.mikesell@hilton.com			
NEIHARDT, Jonas		Tel:	(703) 883-5723
Senior Vice President , Governmental Affairs and PAC			
Treasurer			
Mail Stop Suite 1100			
jonas.neihardt@hilton.com			
Registered Federal Lobbyist			
RADELET, Aaron		Tel:	(703) 883-5804
Vice President, Global Corporate Communications			
SCHUYLER, Matthew W.		Tel:	(703) 883-1000
Executive Vice President and Chief Human Resources Officer			

Hinkle Contracting Corporation

A construction company.
www.hinklecontracting.com
Annual Revenues: $74.3 million
Employees: 850
SIC: 3281
Industry/ies: Construction/Construction Materials
Legislative Issues: BUD; NAT

President and Chief Executive Officer Tel: (859) 987-3670
WINKLEMAN, Larry Fax: (859) 987-0727

Main Headquarters
Mailing: 395 N. Middletown Rd. Tel: (859) 987-3670
  P.O. Box 200 Fax: (859) 987-0727
  Paris, KY 40361-0200

Public Affairs and Related Activities Personnel

At Headquarters

HULLETT, Steve		Tel:	(859) 987-3670
Chief Financial Officer		Fax:	(859) 987-0727
STRAUEL, Kurtis		Tel:	(859) 987-3670
Director, Human Resources		Fax:	(859) 987-0727
kurtis.strauel@hinklecontracting.com			

Hitachi America, Ltd.

Supplies North America with a broad range of high-tech products.
www.hitachi-america.us
Annual Revenues: $27.09 billion
Employees: 4,500
SIC: 3663; 3823; 3674; 3651; 3577
NAICS: 334220; 334513; 334413; 334310; 334119
Industry/ies: Computer/Technology; Electricity & Electronics; Electronics; Energy/Electricity

Representative Executive Officer, Chairman adn Chief Executive Tel: (650) 244-7673
Officer Fax: (650) 244-7600
NAKANISHI, Hiroaki

Foundation President and Chief Executive Officer Tel: (202) 296-1098
DYER, Barbara Fax: (202) 296-1098

Main Headquarters
Mailing: 50 Prospect Ave. Tel: (914) 524-6612
  Tarrytown, NY 10591 Fax: (914) 631-3672

Washington Office
Mailing: 1215 17th St. NW Fax: (202) 296-1098
  Washington, DC 20036

Corporate Foundations and Giving Programs

Hitachi America Contribution Program
50 Prospect Ave. Tel: (914) 332-5800
Tarrytown, NY 10591 Fax: (914) 332-5555

The Hitachi Foundation
Contact: Barbara Dyer
1215 17th St. NW Tel: (202) 457-0588
Washington, DC 20036 Fax: (202) 296-1098

Public Affairs and Related Activities Personnel

At Headquarters

GARVEY, Lauren		Tel:	(914) 333-2986
Senior Manager, Community Relations and Corporate		Fax:	(914) 332-5555
Communications			
lauren.garvey@hal.hitachi.com			
HIGASHIHARA, Toshiaki		Tel:	(914) 524-6612
Executive Officer, President and Chief OperationsOfficer		Fax:	(914) 631-3672
KOJIMA, Keiji		Tel:	(914) 524-6612
Vice President and Executive Officer, Chief Technology		Fax:	(914) 631-3672
Officer , and General Manager, Research and Development			

At Other Offices

KUZUOKA, Toshiaki		Tel:	(650) 244-7673

Senior Vice President and Executive Officer, Human Capital,		Fax:	(650) 244-7600
Government and External Relations and General Manager,			
Legal, Communications and Compliance			
1000 Marina Blvd., Sixth Floor			
Brisbane, CA 94005-1835			
MITARAI, Naoki		Tel:	(650) 244-7673
Senior Vice President and Executive Officer, Chief Human		Fax:	(650) 244-7600
Resource Officer and Chief Revenue Officer			
1000 Marina Blvd., Sixth Floor			
Brisbane, CA 94005-1835			
TANABE, Yasuo		Tel:	(650) 244-7673
Vice President and Executive Officer, Deputy General		Fax:	(650) 244-7600
Manager, Legal and Communications Group			
1000 Marina Blvd., Sixth Floor			
Brisbane, CA 94005-1835			
WATANABE, Masaya		Tel:	(650) 244-7673
Vice President and Executive Officer, Global Service,		Fax:	(650) 244-7600
Business Information Promotion and Telecommunication			
Systems Business			
1000 Marina Blvd., Sixth Floor			
Brisbane, CA 94005-1835			

Hitachi, Ltd.

Manufacturing
www.hitachi.com
Industry/ies: Electricity & Electronics; Electronics; Energy/Electricity

Main Headquarters
Mailing: 1900 K St. NW, Suite 800 Tel: (202) 828-9272
  Washington, DC 20006 Fax: (202) 828-9277

Public Affairs and Related Activities Personnel

At Headquarters

GREEN, Carl J.		Tel:	(202) 828-9272
Senior Representative		Fax:	(202) 828-9277
OHDE, Takashi		Tel:	(202) 828-9272
Senior Representative and General Manager		Fax:	(202) 828-9277
ohde@gbd.hitachi.co.jp			

Hmong Advance, Inc.

A non-profit research, education and advocacy organization concerned with the issues faced by the Hmong and Laotian communities. An affiliate of Hmong Advancement, Inc.
hmongadvance.aidpage.com
Industry/ies: Civil Rights And Liberties; Education; Foreign Relations

President
SMITH, P.
hmongadvance@gmail.com

Main Headquarters
Mailing: 4600 Wisconsin Ave. Tel: (202) 629-0377
  Suite 106-318
  Washington, DC 20016

Hmong Advancement, Inc.

A non-profit organization focused on the support and advocacy of the Hmong and Lao American communities. An affiliate of Hmong Advance, Inc. Headquartered in Arlington, VA.
site.hmongadvacement.org
Industry/ies: Foreign Relations

Main Headquarters
Mailing: 2020 Pennsylvania Ave. NW, Suite 322 Tel: (202) 629-0377
  Washington, DC 20006

Public Affairs and Related Activities Personnel

At Headquarters

SMITH, P. Tel: (202) 629-0377
hmongadvance@gmail.com

HNI Corporation

Engaged in designing, manufacturing, and marketing office furniture and hearth products. Its Office Furniture segment offers a range of metal and wood commercial and home office furnitures.
www.hnicorp.com
Annual Revenues: $2.28 billion
Employees: 10,000
Ticker: NYSE: HNI
SIC: 2522
Industry/ies: Furniture/Home Furnishings

Chairman of the Board, President, Director and Chief Executive Tel: (563) 264-7400
Officer Fax: (563) 272-7655
ASKREN, Stan A.

Main Headquarters
Mailing: 408 E. Second St. Tel: (563) 272-7400
  P.O. Box 1109 Fax: (563) 272-7655
  Muscatine, IA 52761-0071

Corporate Foundations and Giving Programs

HNI Charitable Foundation
Contact: Gary L. Carlson
408 E. Second St.
P.O. Box 1109
Muscatine, IA 52761

Public Affairs and Related Activities Personnel

At Headquarters

BRADFORD, Steven M.
Senior Vice President, General Counsel and Secretary
Tel: (563) 272-7400
Fax: (563) 272-7655

CARLSON, Gary L.
Vice President, Community Relations
Tel: (563) 272-7400
Fax: (563) 272-7655

MCGOUGH, Matthew
Vice President, Corporate Finance
Tel: (563) 272-7400
Fax: (563) 272-7655

MEADE, Donna D.
Vice President, Member Relations
Tel: (563) 272-7400
Fax: (563) 272-7655

TJADEN, Kurt A.
Senior Vice President and Chief Financial Officer
Tel: (563) 272-7400
Fax: (563) 272-7655

HNTB Holdings

A national transportation infrastructure firm that offers extensive design, engineering and planning services to federal, state and local public and private clients.
www.hntb.com
Annual Revenues: $229.90 million
Employees: 3,000
Industry/ies: Architecture And Design; Engineering/Mathematics; Government-Related; Transportation
Legislative Issues: BUD; TRA

Executive Chairman of the Board
HAMMOND, Jr., PE, Harvey
Tel: (816) 472-1201
Fax: (816) 472-4060

Chief Executive Officer
SLIMP, Rob
Tel: (816) 472-1201
Fax: (816) 472-4060

Main Headquarters
Mailing: 715 Kirk Dr.
Kansas City, MO 64105-1310
Tel: (816) 472-1201
Fax: (816) 472-4060

Political Action Committees

HNTB Holdings Ltd. PAC
FEC ID: C00386029
Contact: Edward McSpedon PE
715 Kirk Dr.
Kansas City, MO 64105

Contributions to Candidates: $74,750 (2015-2016)
Democrats: $33,250; Republicans: $40,500; Other: $1,000

Principal Recipients

HOUSE
BLUMENAUER, EARL (DEM-OR)
SHUSTER, WILLIAM MR. (REP-PA)

Public Affairs and Related Activities Personnel

At Headquarters

COX, Brian
Senior Public Relations Manager
bcox@hntb.com
Tel: (816) 527-2056
Fax: (816) 472-4060

MCSPEDON, PE, Edward
Executive Vice President, Corporate Development and PAC Treasurer. Lobbyist
emcspedon@hntb.com
Tel: (816) 472-1201
Fax: (816) 472-4060

MOSHER, Patricia
Director, Corporate Communications
pmosher@hntb.com
Tel: (816) 527-2283
Fax: (816) 472-4060

PREM, Sara
Senior Manager, Public Relations
sprem@hntb.com
Tel: (816) 527-2258
Fax: (816) 472-4060

YAROSSI, Paul
Executive Vice President
Tel: (816) 472-1201
Fax: (816) 472-4060

The Hobbs Group LLC

A government affairs lobbying firm.
www.thehobbsgroup.com
Industry/ies: Government-Related
Legislative Issues: AUT; BEV; BUD; COM; CPT; DEF; ENG; TAX; TOR; TRD

President
HOBBS, David
dhobbs@davidhobbsgroup.com
Tel: (202) 534-4970

Main Headquarters
Mailing: 300 New Jersey Ave. NW
Suite 601
Washington, DC 20001
Tel: (202) 534-4970

Holcim (US) Inc.

Manufacturers and Suppliers of cement and aggregates (crushed stone, gravel and sand) as well as ready-mix concrete and asphalt.
www.holcim.us
Annual Revenues: $1.00 billion
Employees: 1,800
Industry/ies: Construction/Construction Materials
Legislative Issues: CAW; ENG; ENV; MAN; ROD; TRA; TRU

Chairman of the Board
TERVER, Bernard
Tel: (734) 647-2501
Fax: (781) 647-2516

President and Chief Executive Officer
RUIZ, Filiberto
Tel: (781) 647-2501
Fax: (781) 647-2516

Main Headquarters
Mailing: 24 Crosby Dr.
Bedford, MA 01730
Tel: (781) 647-2501
Fax: (781) 647-2517
TF: (866) 465-2460

Political Action Committees

Holcim (US) Inc. PAC
FEC ID: C00213348
Contact: David Loomes
201 Jones Rd.
Waltham, MA 02451

Contributions to Candidates: $54,250 (2015-2016)
Democrats: $12,000; Republicans: $39,250; Other: $3,000

Principal Recipients

SENATE
BLUNT, ROY (REP-MO)

Corporate Foundations and Giving Programs

Holcim (US) Inc. Corporate Contributions Program
Contact: Ronald Walker
201 Jones Rd.
Waltham, MA 02451
Tel: (734) 529-2411

Public Affairs and Related Activities Personnel

At Headquarters

DECARLO, Robin
Vice President, Corporate Communications
Tel: (781) 647-2364
Fax: (781) 647-2517

GUERRA, Erika
Federal Lobbyist and Manager, Government Affairs and Corporate Social Responsibility
erika.guerra@holcim.com
Registered Federal Lobbyist
Tel: (781) 647-2501
Fax: (781) 647-2516

JAGGER, Norman L.
Senior Vice President, Sales and Marketing
Tel: (781) 647-2501
Fax: (781) 647-2517

LOOMES, David
Vice President, Commercial Services, PAC Contact and Lobbyist
Tel: (781) 647-2501
Fax: (781) 647-2516

MARTINELLI, Alyse
Senior Vice President, Human Resources
Tel: (781) 647-2501
Fax: (781) 647-2517

PRATT, Cameron
Policy Analyst
cameron.pratt@holcim.com
Registered Federal Lobbyist
Tel: (781) 647-2374
Fax: (781) 647-2548

REINHART, Rick
Senior Vice President and Chief Financial Officer
Tel: (781) 647-2501
Fax: (781) 647-2516

TANGNEY, Jay
Senior Vice President, Chief Legal Officer and Corporate Secretary
Tel: (734) 529-2411
Fax: (734) 529-5268

WALKER, Ronald
Corporate Communications Head and Delegate of the Board of the Holcim Foundation
Tel: (781) 647-2501
Fax: (781) 647-2516

Hollister Inc.

Medical device manufacturer.
www.hollister.com/us
Employees: 2,400
SIC: 3841
NAICS: 339112
Industry/ies: Machinery/Equipment; Medicine/Health Care/Mental Health
Legislative Issues: HCR; LBR; MMM; TAX

Trustee
HERBERT, Alan F.
Tel: (847) 680-1000
Fax: (847) 680-2123

President
GEORGE MALIEKEL, V.
Tel: (847) 680-1000
Fax: (847) 680-2123

Main Headquarters
Mailing: 2000 Hollister Dr.
Libertyville, IL 60048
Tel: (847) 680-1000
Fax: (847) 680-2123
TF: (888) 740-8999

Public Affairs and Related Activities Personnel

At Headquarters

BRILLIANT, Samuel P.	Tel:	(847) 680-1000
Vice President and Chief Financial Officer	Fax:	(847) 680-2123
WHITE, Carl	Tel:	(847) 680-1000
Director, Global Marketing	Fax:	(847) 680-2123

HollyFrontier Corporation

An petroleum refining and marketing company. Formed as merger of Holly Corporation(NYSE: HOC) ("Holly") and Frontier Oil Corporation (NYSE: FTO) ("Frontier"). It produces and markets gasoline, diesel, jet fuel, asphalt, heavy products and specialty lubricant products.
www.hollyfrontier.com
Annual Revenues: $17.98 billion
Employees: 2,686
Ticker: NYSE: HFC
SIC: 2911
Industry/ies: Energy/Electricity; Fuels See Coal, Gas, Oil, Petroleum; Natural Resources
Legislative Issues: BUD; FUE; TAX

Chairman of the Board, Chief Executive Officer and President Tel: (214) 871-3555
JENNINGS, Michael C.   Fax: (214) 871-3560

Main Headquarters
Mailing: 2828 N. Harwood   Tel: (214) 871-3555
            Suite 1300   Fax: (214) 871-3560
            Dallas, TX 75201

Political Action Committees
HollyFrontier Corporation PAC
FEC ID: C00342766
Contact: Douglas S. Aron
2828 N. Harwood St.
Suite 1300
Dallas, TX 75201

   Contributions to Candidates: $82,500 (2015-2016)
   Democrats: $2,000; Republicans: $80,500

Public Affairs and Related Activities Personnel

At Headquarters

ARON, Douglas S.	Tel:	(214) 871-3555
Executive Vice President and Chief Financial Officer	Fax:	(214) 871-3560
DAMIRIS, George J.	Tel:	(214) 871-3555
Executive Vice President and Chief Operating Officer	Fax:	(214) 871-3560
FAUDEL, Gerald B.	Tel:	(214) 871-3555
Vice President, Government Relations and Environmental Affairs	Fax:	(214) 871-3560
HEIDENREICH, Julia	Tel:	(214) 871-3555
Vice President, Investor Relations	Fax:	(214) 871-3560
LAMP, David L.	Tel:	(214) 871-3555
Executive Vice President and Chief Operating Officer	Fax:	(214) 871-3560
MCWATTERS, Denise C.	Tel:	(214) 871-3555
Senior Vice President, General Counsel and Secretary	Fax:	(214) 871-3560
SHAW, Bruce R.	Tel:	(214) 871-3555
President, Holly Energy Partners, L.P.	Fax:	(214) 871-3560

Holnam Inc.

See listing on page 405 under Holcim (US) Inc.

Hologic, Inc.

A biotechnology firm and a provider of healthcare systems for women in the world. Formed by the merger of Cytyc Corporation and Hologic Inc.
www.hologic.com
Annual Revenues: $2.76 billion
Employees: 5,290
Ticker: NASDAQ: HOLX
SIC: 3844
Industry/ies: Science; Scientific Research
Legislative Issues: HCR; MED; MMM

Chairman, President and Chief Executive Officer Tel: (508) 263-2900
MACMILLAN, Stephen P.   Fax: (781) 280-0669

Main Headquarters
Mailing: 250 Campus Dr.   Tel: (508) 263-2900
            Marlborough, MA 01752

Corporate Foundations and Giving Programs
Hologic's Grant Program
35 Crosby Dr.   Tel: (781) 999-7300
Bedford, MA 01730   Fax: (781) 280-0669

Public Affairs and Related Activities Personnel

At Headquarters

MAZUR, Jane   Tel: (508) 263-8764
Senior Director, Divisional Communications
michael.watts@hologic.com

WATTS, Michael J.   Tel: (858) 410-8588

Vice President, Investor Relations and Corporate Communications
michael.watts@hologic.com

At Other Offices

BEBO, Allison	Tel:	(781) 999-7300
Senior Vice President, Human Resources	Fax:	(781) 280-0669
35 Crosby Dr.		
Bedford, MA 01730		
COMPTON, Eric B.	Tel:	(781) 999-7300
Chief Operating Officer	Fax:	(781) 280-0669
35 Crosby Dr.		
Bedford, MA 01730		
CULLEY, PhD, Jim	Tel:	(781) 999-7583
Senior Director, Marketing	Fax:	(781) 280-0669
35 Crosby Dr.		
Bedford, MA 01730		
jim.culley@hologic.com		
DORIA, Frances	Tel:	(781) 999-7377
Director, Investor Relations	Fax:	(781) 280-0669
35 Crosby Dr.		
Bedford, MA 01730		
Frances.Doria@hologic.com		
GRIFFIN, John M.	Tel:	(781) 999-7300
General Counsel	Fax:	(781) 280-0669
35 Crosby Dr.		
Bedford, MA 01730		
MCMAHON, Robert W.	Tel:	(781) 999-7300
Chief Financial Officer	Fax:	(781) 280-0669
35 Crosby Dr.		
Bedford, MA 01730		

Home Box Office (HBO)

A home entertainment programming subsidiary of Time Warner Inc. (see separate listing).
www.hbo.com
Annual Revenues: $3.10 billion
Employees: 2,000
SIC: 7812
Industry/ies: Communications; Media/Mass Communication

Chairman and Chief Executive Officer Tel: (212) 512-1000
PLEPLER, Richard L.   Fax: (212) 512-1182

Main Headquarters
Mailing: 1100 Avenue of the Americas   Tel: (212) 512-1000
            New York City, NY 10036-6712   Fax: (212) 512-1182

Corporate Foundations and Giving Programs
Home Box Office (HBO) Corporate Giving
1100 Avenue of the Americas   Tel: (212) 512-5119
New York City, NY 10036

Public Affairs and Related Activities Personnel

At Headquarters

ENNIS, APR, CPRC, Susan	Tel:	(212) 512-1000
Executive Vice President, Program Planning and Strategy	Fax:	(212) 512-1182
KONSTAN, Eve	Tel:	(212) 512-1000
Executive Vice President and General Counsel	Fax:	(212) 512-1182
LEVINE, Pamela	Tel:	(212) 512-1000
Chief Marketing Officer	Fax:	(212) 512-1182
MCELHONE, Scott	Tel:	(212) 512-1000
Executive Vice President, Human Resources and Administration	Fax:	(212) 512-1182
ROTH, Robert	Tel:	(212) 512-1000
Executive Vice President and Chief Financial Officer	Fax:	(212) 512-1182
SCHAFFER, Quentin M.	Tel:	(212) 512-1329
Executive Vice President, Corporate Communications	Fax:	(212) 512-1182
quentin.schaffer@hbo.com		

Home Buyers Warranty

Provides comprehensive home warranty services to builders, real estate professionals and homeowners.
www.2-10.com
Annual Revenues: $178.20 million
Employees: 600
Industry/ies: Housing

President and Chief Executive Officer Tel: (303) 368-4805
FLUHR, Emory   Fax: (303) 750-3970

Main Headquarters
Mailing: 10375 E. Harvard Ave.   Tel: (303) 368-4805
            Suite 100   Fax: (303) 750-3970
            Denver, CO 80231-3966   TF: (800) 775-4736

The Home Depot

A retailer of home improvement products and services.

www.homedepot.com
Annual Revenues: $83.18 billion
Employees: 371,000
Ticker: NYSE:HD
SIC: 5211
Industry/ies: Construction/Construction Materials; Retail/Wholesale
Legislative Issues: BAN; BUD; CPI; CPT; CSP; ENG; HCR; HOU; LBR; TAX; TRA; TRD

President   Tel: (202) 393-4400
MENEAR, Craig   Fax: (202) 393-4414

Main Headquarters
Mailing: 2455 Paces Ferry Rd.   Tel: (770) 433-8211
             Atlanta, GA 30339-4024   Fax: (302) 636-5454
                                                   TF: (800) 430-3376

Washington Office
Mailing: 1155 F St. NW   Tel: (202) 393-4400
             Suite 400   Fax: (202) 393-4414
             Washington, DC 20004

Political Action Committees
Home Depot Inc. PAC
FEC ID: C00284885
Contact: Scott Bohrer
1155 F St. NW   Tel: (770) 384-2775
Suite 400
Washington, DC 20004

Contributions to Candidates: $1,594,750 (2015-2016)
Democrats: $444,000; Republicans: $1,142,250; Other: $8,500

Principal Recipients

SENATE
BLUNT, ROY (REP-MO)
BLUNT, ROY (REP-TX)
BOOZMAN, JOHN (REP-AR)
BURR, RICHARD (REP-NC)
HARRIS, KAMALA D (DEM-CA)
MURKOWSKI, LISA (REP-AK)
SHELBY, RICHARD C (REP-AL)

HOUSE
BEATTY, JOYCE (DEM-OH)
BISHOP, SANFORD D JR (DEM-GA)
BLACK, DIANE L MRS. (REP-TN)
BONAMICI, SUZANNE MS. (DEM-OR)
BRADY, KEVIN (REP-TX)
BURGESS, MICHAEL C. DR. (REP-TX)
BUSTOS, CHERI (DEM-IL)
BYRNE, BRADLEY ROBERTS (REP-AL)
CARTER, EARL LEROY (REP-GA)
CHAFFETZ, JASON (REP-UT)
COLE, TOM (REP-OK)
COLLINS, DOUGLAS ALLEN (REP-GA)
COMSTOCK, BARBARA J HONORABLE (REP-VA)
COSTELLO, RYAN A (REP-PA)
CRAMER, KEVIN MR. (REP-ND)
CURBELO, CARLOS (REP-FL)
DAVIS, RODNEY L (REP-IL)
DELBENE, SUZAN K (DEM-WA)
DENHAM, JEFF (REP-CA)
DOLD, ROBERT JAMES JR (REP-IL)
DUFFY, SEAN (REP-WI)
EMMER, THOMAS EARL JR. (REP-MN)
FLORES, BILL (REP-TX)
FOXX, VIRGINIA ANN (REP-NC)
GRAVES, JOHN THOMAS MR. JR. (REP-GA)
GUTHRIE, S. BRETT HON. (REP-KY)
HENSARLING, JEB HON. (REP-TX)
HIMES, JIM (DEM-CT)
HOLDING, GEORGE E MR. (REP-NC)
HOYER, STENY HAMILTON (DEM-DC)
HUDSON, RICHARD L. JR. (REP-NC)
HURD, WILLIAM (REP-TX)
ISSA, DARRELL (REP-CA)
KILMER, DEREK (DEM-WA)
KIND, RONALD JAMES (DEM-WI)
KINZINGER, ADAM (REP-IL)
KNIGHT, STEVE (REP-CA)
LAHOOD, DARIN MCKAY (REP-IL)
LEWIS, JOHN R. (DEM-GA)
LOUDERMILK, BARRY (REP-GA)
LUCAS, FRANK D. (REP-OK)
LUJAN, BEN R MR. (DEM-NM)
MALONEY, SEAN PATRICK (DEM-NY)
MATSUI, DORIS (DEM-CA)
MCCARTHY, KEVIN (REP-CA)
MCCAUL, MICHAEL (REP-TX)
MCHENRY, PATRICK TIMOTHY (REP-NC)

MCMORRIS RODGERS, CATHY (REP-WA)
MCSALLY, MARTHA E. MS. (REP-AZ)
MEEHAN, PATRICK L. MR. (REP-PA)
MESSER, ALLEN LUCAS (REP-IN)
MOULTON, SETH (DEM-MA)
MULLIN, MARKWAYNE MR. (REP-OK)
NOEM, KRISTI LYNN (REP-SD)
NUNES, DEVIN G (REP-CA)
PAULSEN, ERIK (REP-MN)
PETERS, SCOTT (DEM-CA)
POLIQUIN, BRUCE L (REP-ME)
PRICE, THOMAS EDMUNDS (REP-GA)
RENACCI, JAMES B. (REP-OH)
RICHMOND, CEDRIC L. (DEM-LA)
ROBY, MARTHA (REP-AL)
RYAN, PAUL D. (REP-WI)
SANCHEZ, LINDA (DEM-CA)
SCALISE, STEVE MR. (REP-LA)
SCHRADER, KURT (DEM-OR)
SCOTT, JAMES AUSTIN (REP-GA)
SESSIONS, PETE MR. (REP-TX)
SEWELL, TERRYCINA ANDREA (DEM-AL)
SHIMKUS, JOHN M (REP-IL)
SINEMA, KYRSTEN (DEM-AZ)
SMITH, ADRIAN (REP-NE)
STEFANIK, ELISE M. (REP-NY)
STIVERS, STEVE MR. (REP-OH)
TIBERI, PATRICK J. (REP-OH)
VALADAO, DAVID (REP-CA)
WALBERG, TIMOTHY L HON. (REP-MI)
WALDEN, GREGORY P MR. (REP-OR)
WALTERS, MIMI (REP-CA)
WELCH, PETER (DEM-VT)
WOMACK, STEVE (REP-AR)
WOODALL, ROB REP. (REP-GA)
YODER, KEVIN (REP-KS)
YOUNG, DAVID (REP-IA)
ZELDIN, LEE M (REP-NY)

Corporate Foundations and Giving Programs

The Home Depot Foundation
2455 Paces Ferry Rd.   Tel: (770) 433-8211
Atlanta, GA 30339   Fax: (770) 433-8211

Public Affairs and Related Activities Personnel

At Headquarters

CROW, Tim   Tel: (770) 433-8211
Executive Vice President, Human Resources   Fax: (770) 384-2356

DAYHOFF, Diane   Tel: (770) 384-2666
Vice President, Investor Relations   Fax: (770) 384-2356
diane_dayhoff@homedepot.com

DECKER, Ted   Tel: (770) 433-8211
Executive Vice President, Merchandising   Fax: (302) 636-5454

DRAKE, Paula   Tel: (770) 384-3439
Senior Manager, Corporate Communications   Fax: (770) 384-2356
paula_drake@homedepot.com

MCPHAIL, Richard   Tel: (770) 433-8211
Senior Vice President, Global Financial Planning, Analysis   Fax: (302) 636-5454
and Strategic Business Development

MUELLER, Trish   Tel: (770) 433-8211
Senior Vice President and Chief Marketing Officer Fax: (770) 384-2356
Trish_Mueller@homedepot.com

ROSEBOROUGH, Teresa Wynn   Tel: (770) 433-8211
Executive Vice President, General Counsel and Corporate   Fax: (770) 384-2356
Secretary

TOME, Carol B.   Tel: (770) 433-8211
Executive Vice President, Corporate Services and Chief   Fax: (770) 384-2356
Financial Officer

At Washington Office

BOHRER, Scott   Tel: (202) 393-4400
PAC Contact   Fax: (202) 393-4414

DENDAS, Michael   Tel: (202) 393-4400
Senior Manager, Government Relations   Fax: (202) 393-4414
Registered Federal Lobbyist

KENNEDY, Heather   Tel: (202) 393-4400
Senior Director, Government Relations   Fax: (202) 393-4414
heather_kennedy@homedepot.com
Registered Federal Lobbyist

KNUTSON, Kent   Tel: (202) 393-4400
Vice President, Government Relations   Fax: (202) 393-4414
kent_knutson@homedepot.com
Registered Federal Lobbyist

MCDONALD, Sarah Jane   Tel: (202) 393-4400
Senior Manager, Political Programs   Fax: (202) 393-4414

sarah_mcdonald@homedepot.com
Registered Federal Lobbyist

TCHOUKALEFF, Tayler — Tel: (202) 393-4400
Registered Federal Lobbyist — Fax: (202) 393-4414

URIBE, Francisco — Tel: (202) 393-4400
Director, Government Relations — Fax: (202) 393-4414
Francisco_Uribe@homedepot.com

Home Federal Bank of Tennessee

A local banking company.
www.homefederalbanktn.com
Annual Revenues: $90.38 million
Employees: 500
Industry/ies: Banking/Finance/Investments

Chairman, President and Chief Executive Officer — Tel: (865) 546-0330
KEASLING, Dale A.

Main Headquarters
Mailing: 515 Market St. — Tel: (865) 544-3995
Knoxville, TN 37902

Public Affairs and Related Activities Personnel

At Headquarters

HUDDLESTON, Jana — Tel: (865) 544-3995
PAC Treasurer

LIGHT, Cheryl E. — Tel: (865) 546-0330
Vice President and Corporate Secretary

WATSON, Crystal — Tel: (865) 544-3995
PAC Contact

HomeStreet Bank/Continental Savings Bank

Offers financial services including business banking, business lending, consumer banking, mortgage lending, residential construction financing, income property financing and insurance services.
www.homestreetbank.com
Annual Revenues: $158.16 million
Employees: 500
Industry/ies: Banking/Finance/Investments

Chairman, President and Chief Executive Officer — Tel: (206) 389-4400
MASON, Mark K. — Fax: (206) 389-4401

Main Headquarters
Mailing: 601 Union St. — Tel: (206) 389-4400
2000 Two Union Sq. — Fax: (206) 389-4401
Seattle, WA 98101 — TF: (800) 654-1075

Corporate Foundations and Giving Programs

HomeStreet Bank Contributions Program
601 Union St. — Tel: (206) 389-4400
2000 Two Union Sq. — Fax: (206) 389-4401
Seattle, WA 98101

Public Affairs and Related Activities Personnel

At Headquarters

EVANS, Godfrey — Tel: (206) 389-4440
Executive Vice President, General Counsel, Chief — Fax: (206) 389-4401
Administrative Officer and Corporate Secretary
godfrey.evans@homestreet.com

HOOSTON, David E. — Tel: (206) 389-4400
Executive Vice President and Chief Financial Officer — Fax: (206) 389-4401

ROLAND, Monica — Tel: (206) 587-5006
Marketing Specialist — Fax: (206) 389-4460
monica.roland@homestreet.com

SILVER, Terri — Tel: (206) 389-6303
Vice President and Manager, Investor Relations and — Fax: (206) 389-4460
Corporate Communications
terri.silver@homestreet.com

STEWART, Cory D. — Tel: (206) 389-4400
Executive Vice President and Chief Accounting Officer — Fax: (206) 389-4401

VAN AMEN, Darrell S. — Tel: (206) 389-4400
Executive Vice President, Chief Investment Officer and — Fax: (206) 389-4401
Treasurer

HON Industries

See listing on page 404 under HNI Corporation

Honeywell International, Inc.

A diversified high technology company involved in energy and safety controls, defense and aerospace and specialized instrumentation industries.
honeywell.com
Annual Revenues: $39.84 billion
Employees: 127,000
Ticker: NYSE: HON
SIC: 3577; 3724; 2813; 2819; 2821; 2822; 3714; 3571; 3669; 5045
NAICS: 33429; 42143; 334111; 334119

Industry/ies: Aerospace/Aviation; Automotive Industry; Chemicals & Chemical Industry; Computer/Technology; Defense/Homeland Security; Electricity & Electronics; Electronics; Energy/Electricity; Engineering/Mathematics; Government-Related; Transportation
Legislative Issues: AER; AVI; BNK; BUD; CAW; CHM; CSP; DEF; ENG; ENV; FIN; FOR; FUE; HOM; IND; LBR; SCI; TAX; TOR; TRA; TRD

Chairman of the Board and Chief Executive Officer — Tel: (973) 455-2000
COTE, David M. — Fax: (973) 455-4807

Main Headquarters
Mailing: 101 Columbia Rd. — Tel: (973) 455-2000
Morristown, NJ 07962 — Fax: (973) 455-4807
— TF: (800) 601-3099

Washington Office
Mailing: 101 Constitution Ave. NW — Tel: (202) 662-2650
Suite 500 W. — Fax: (202) 662-2675
Washington, DC 20001

Political Action Committees
Honeywell International, Inc. PAC
FEC ID: C00096156
Contact: Stacey Farnen Bernards
101 Constitution Ave. NW — Tel: (202) 662-2664
Suite 500 West — Fax: (202) 662-2674
Washington, DC 20001

Contributions to Candidates: $2,201,181 (2015-2016)
Democrats: $817,000; Republicans: $1,374,181; Other: $10,000

Principal Recipients

SENATE
BLUNT, ROY (REP-MO)
BURR, RICHARD (REP-NC)
CRAPO, MICHAEL D (REP-ID)
GRASSLEY, CHARLES E SENATOR (REP-IA)
HOEVEN, JOHN (REP-ND)
JOHNSON, RONALD HAROLD (REP-)
KIRK, MARK STEVEN (REP-IL)
LEAHY, PATRICK J (DEM-VT)
MCCAIN, JOHN S (REP-VA)
MORAN, JERRY (REP-KS)
MURKOWSKI, LISA (REP-AK)
SCHATZ, BRIAN (DEM-HI)
SCOTT, TIMOTHY E (REP-SC)
YOUNG, TODD CHRISTOPHER (REP-IN)

HOUSE
AGUILAR, PETE (DEM-CA)
ASHFORD, BRAD (DEM-NE)
BERA, AMERISH (DEM-CA)
BEYER, DONALD STERNOFF JR. (DEM-VA)
BILIRAKIS, GUS M (REP-FL)
BISHOP, ROBERT (REP-UT)
BLUMENAUER, EARL (DEM-OR)
BOUSTANY, CHARLES W. DR. JR. (REP-LA)
BRADY, KEVIN (REP-TX)
BYRNE, BRADLEY ROBERTS (REP-AL)
CALVERT, KEN (REP-CA)
CLEAVER, EMANUEL II (DEM-MO)
CLYBURN, JAMES E. (DEM-SC)
COOK, PAUL (REP-CA)
DENHAM, JEFF (REP-CA)
FLORES, BILL (REP-TX)
FRELINGHUYSEN, RODNEY P. (REP-NJ)
GRANGER, KAY (REP-TX)
GRAVES, JOHN THOMAS MR. JR. (REP-GA)
GRAVES, SAMUEL B JR 'SAM' (REP-MO)
GREEN, RAYMOND E. 'GENE' (DEM-TX)
HARTZLER, VICKY (REP-MO)
HECK, JOE (REP-NV)
HIGGINS, BRIAN (DEM-NY)
HIMES, JIM (DEM-CT)
HOLDING, GEORGE E MR. (REP-NC)
HOYER, STENY HAMILTON (DEM-DC)
HUNTER, DUNCAN D. (REP-CA)
JENKINS, LYNN (REP-KS)
KELLY, GEORGE J JR (REP-PA)
KIND, RONALD JAMES (DEM-WI)
LAMBORN, DOUGLAS (REP-CO)
LANKFORD, JAMES PAUL MR. (REP-OK)
LARSON, JOHN B (DEM-CT)
LOBIONDO, FRANK A. (REP-NJ)
LOEBSACK, DAVID WAYNE (DEM-IA)
LUETKEMEYER, W BLAINE (REP-MO)
MCCARTHY, KEVIN (REP-CA)
MCCAUL, MICHAEL (REP-TX)
MCHENRY, PATRICK TIMOTHY (REP-NC)
MCMORRIS RODGERS, CATHY (REP-WA)
MCNERNEY, JERRY (DEM-CA)

MEEHAN, PATRICK L. MR. (REP-PA)
MESSER, ALLEN LUCAS (REP-IN)
NEAL, RICHARD E MR. (DEM-MA)
NUNES, DEVIN G (REP-CA)
PAYNE, DONALD M., JR. (DEM-)
PERLMUTTER, EDWIN G (DEM-CO)
PETERS, SCOTT (DEM-CA)
PRICE, DAVID E. (DEM-NC)
PRICE, THOMAS EDMUNDS (REP-GA)
REED, THOMAS W II (REP-NY)
REICHERT, DAVE (REP-WA)
RICE, KATHLEEN (DEM-NY)
ROONEY, TOM MR. (REP-FL)
ROSKAM, PETER (REP-IL)
ROYCE, ED MR. (REP-CA)
SANCHEZ, LINDA (DEM-CA)
SCALISE, STEVE MR. (REP-LA)
SCHULTZ, DEBBIE WASSERMAN (DEM-FL)
SESSIONS, PETE MR. (REP-TX)
SEWELL, TERRYCINA ANDREA (DEM-AL)
SHIMKUS, JOHN M (REP-IL)
SMITH, JASON T (OTHER-MO)
SMITH, LAMAR (REP-TX)
STIVERS, STEVE MR. (REP-OH)
THORNBERRY, MAC (REP-TX)
TIBERI, PATRICK J. (REP-OH)
TURNER, MICHAEL R (REP-OH)
VALADAO, DAVID (REP-CA)
WAGNER, ANN L. (REP-MO)
WALBERG, TIMOTHY L HON. (REP-MI)
WALDEN, GREGORY P MR. (REP-OR)
WALORSKI SWIHART, JACKIE (REP-IN)
WILSON, JOE THE HON. (REP-SC)
WITTMAN, ROBERT J MR. (REP-VA)
WOODALL, ROB REP. (REP-GA)
YODER, KEVIN (REP-KS)

Corporate Foundations and Giving Programs

Honeywell Foundation
101 Columbia Rd.   Tel: (973) 455-2010
Morristown, NJ 07692

Public Affairs and Related Activities Personnel

At Headquarters

ADAMS, Katherine L.   Tel: (973) 455-2000
Senior Vice President and General Counsel   Fax: (973) 455-4807

BENNETT, Mike   Tel: (973) 455-2753
Vice President, Corporate Communications   Fax: (973) 455-3881

FERRIS, Robert C.   Tel: (973) 455-3388
Vice President, External Communications   Fax: (973) 455-4807
rob.ferris@honeywell.com

GERMANY, Rhonda   Tel: (973) 455-2000
Corporate Vice President, Chief Strategy and Marketing   Fax: (973) 455-4807
Officer

JAMES, Mark R.   Tel: (973) 455-2000
Senior Vice President, Human Resources, Procurement and   Fax: (973) 455-4807
Communications
mark.james@honeywell.com

MACALUSO, Mark   Tel: (973) 455-2222
Vice President, Investor Relations   Fax: (973) 455-4807
mark.macaluso@honeywell.com

MIKKILINENI, Krishna   Tel: (973) 455-2000
Senior Vice President, Engineering, Operations and   Fax: (973) 455-4807
Information Technology

SZLOSEK, Tom   Tel: (973) 455-2000
Senior Vice President and Chief Financial Officer   Fax: (973) 455-4807

At Washington Office

BERNARDS, Stacey Farnen   Tel: (202) 662-2650
Vice President, Government Affairs and Lobbyist, PAC   Fax: (202) 662-2674
Treasurer
Registered Federal Lobbyist

BRUNO, Lauren La   Tel: (202) 662-2650
Director, Internal Communications   Fax: (202) 662-2675

CHIANG, Amy   Tel: (202) 662-2650
Federal Lobbyist, Director of International Affairs   Fax: (202) 662-2674
amy.chiang@honeywell.com
Registered Federal Lobbyist

CLIFFORD, Jason   Tel: (202) 662-2629
Vice President, Human Resources   Fax: (202) 662-2675
jason.clifford@honeywell.com

FENGLER, Joseph   Tel: (202) 662-2650
Federal Lobbyist, Director Defense Logistics Policy   Fax: (202) 662-2674
Registered Federal Lobbyist

GOMEZ, Fernando "Nando"   Tel: (202) 662-2650

Vice President, Government Relations   Fax: (202) 662-2674
nando.gomez@honeywell.com
Registered Federal Lobbyist

GRABER, Rick   Tel: (202) 662-2650
Senior Vice President, Global Government Relations   Fax: (202) 662-2675

HOLLENBERG, Jamie   Tel: (202) 662-2650
Manager, Government Relations   Fax: (202) 662-2675
Registered Federal Lobbyist

KAST, Lawrence P.   Tel: (202) 662-2650
Federal Lobbyist, Vice President, Government Relations   Fax: (202) 662-2674
Lawrence.Kast@honeywell.com
Registered Federal Lobbyist

KIRKHORN, Nicholas   Tel: (202) 662-2629
Federal Lobbyist, Director, Government Relations   Fax: (202) 662-2674
nicholas.kirkhorn@honeywell.com
Registered Federal Lobbyist

ROSSMAN, Elizabeth   Tel: (202) 662-2650
Federal Lobbyist, Director, Government Relations, Aviation &   Fax: (202) 662-2674
Aerospace
Registered Federal Lobbyist

SIMONETTI, Art   Tel: (202) 662-2671
Vice President Government Relations, Trade Legislation &   Fax: (202) 662-2674
Regulation
art.simonetti@honeywell.com

WAGNER, Eric   Tel: (202) 662-2650
Vice President, Government Relations High Growth Regions   Fax: (202) 662-2674
eric.wagner@honeywell.com
Registered Federal Lobbyist

At Other Offices

ICENHOWER, Alexandria
101 Constitution Ave. NW
Washington, DC 20001
Registered Federal Lobbyist

Honigman Miller Schwartz and Cohn LLP
Law firm.
www.honigman.com
Legislative Issues: TAX

Chairman and Chief Executive Officer   Tel: (313) 465-7380
FOLTYN, David   Fax: (313) 465-8000
dfoltyn@honigman.com

Main Headquarters
Mailing: 660 Woodward Ave.   Tel: (313) 465-7000
Suite 2290   Fax: (313) 465-8000
Detroit, MI 48226

Public Affairs and Related Activities Personnel

At Headquarters

ANKERS, Julie M.   Tel: (313) 465-7064
Director, Human Resources   Fax: (313) 465-8000
jankers@honigman.com

BANAS, Valerie   Tel: (313) 465-7226
Paralegal   Fax: (313) 465-8000
vbanas@honigman.com

BAUER, Jeffrey R.   Tel: (313) 465-7042
Chief People Officer   Fax: (313) 465-8000

COMBS, James   Tel: (313) 465-7588
Partner   Fax: (313) 465-8000
jcombs@honigman.com
Registered Federal Lobbyist

KUBIC , Robert D   Tel: (313) 465-7000
Chief Operating Officer   Fax: (313) 465-8000
rkubic@honigman.com

MELNICK , Joseph J   Tel: (313) 465-7000
Director, Strategic Business Development Initiatives   Fax: (313) 465-8000

MORSCHES, Frederick J.   Tel: (313) 465-7040
Chief Marketing Officer   Fax: (313) 465-8000
fmorsches@honigman.com

WEIGEL, Robert C.   Tel: (313) 465-7109
Director, Financial Services   Fax: (313) 465-8000
rweigel@honigman.com

Hope and Reid LLC
Supporting Governor of Rhode Island with creating and achieving federal priorities.

Main Headquarters
Mailing: 1344 30th St. NW   Tel: (202) 965-5788
Washington, DC 20007

Public Affairs and Related Activities Personnel

At Headquarters

REID, Samuel S.   Tel: (202) 965-5788

Horace Mann Educators Corporation

Through its subsidiaries, operates as a multiline insurance company in the United States.
www.horacemann.com
Annual Revenues: $1.08 billion
Employees: 1,396
Ticker: NYSE: HMN
SIC: 6331
Industry/ies: Education; Insurance Industry

Director, President and Chief Executive Officer Tel: (217) 789-2500
ZURAITIS, Marita Fax: (217) 788-5161

Main Headquarters
Mailing: One Horace Mann Plaza Tel: (217) 789-2500
Springfield, IL 62715 Fax: (217) 788-5161
TF: (800) 999-1030

Corporate Foundations and Giving Programs

Horace Mann Educators Corporation Contributions Program
One Horace Mann Plaza Tel: (217) 789-2500
Springfield, IL 62715 Fax: (217) 788-5161

Public Affairs and Related Activities Personnel

At Headquarters

GREENIER , Ryan E. Tel: (217) 789-2500
Vice President, Investor Relations Fax: (217) 788-5161
ryan.greenier@horacemann.com

HALLMAN, Dwayne D. Tel: (217) 789-2500
Executive Vice President and Chief Financial Officer Fax: (217) 789-5161

WAPPEL, Paul Tel: (217) 788-5373
Assistant Vice President, Public Relations and Community Fax: (217) 789-5161
Relations
Paul.Wappel@horacemann.com

Horatio O Roberson Group

Human services, community development, economic development, civil right, and commerce

Main Headquarters
Mailing: 822 S. Beaver St. Tel: (717) 779-4961
York, PA 17403

Horizon Bank

A national commercial bank which offers financial services and community activism. It provides commercial and retail banking services in Northwestern and Central Indiana, and Southwestern and Central Michigan.
www.horizonbank.com
Annual Revenues: $90.60 million
Employees: 448
Ticker: NASDAQ: HBNC
Industry/ies: Banking/Finance/Investments

Chairman, President and Chief Executive Officer Tel: (219) 873-2725
DWIGHT, Craig M. Fax: (219) 873-2626
cdwight@horizonbank.com

Main Headquarters
Mailing: 515 Franklin Sq. Tel: (219) 879-0211
Michigan City, IN 46360 Fax: (219) 874-9305
TF: (888) 904-2265

Political Action Committees
Horizon Bank PAC
FEC ID: C00135376
Contact: Mark E. Secor
515 Franklin Sq.
Michigan City, IN 46360

Corporate Foundations and Giving Programs

Horizon Bank Contributions Program
515 Franklin Sq. Tel: (219) 879-0211
Michigan City, IN 46360 Fax: (219) 874-9305

Public Affairs and Related Activities Personnel

At Headquarters

LUCKER, Dona Tel: (219) 879-0211
Contact, Investor Relations Fax: (219) 874-9305
dlucker@horizonbank.com

MCCOLL, Mary Tel: (219) 874-9272
Officer, Shareholder Relations Fax: (219) 873-2626

NEFF, James D. Tel: (219) 874-9395
Executive Vice President and Corporate Secretary Fax: (219) 874-9305
jneff@horizonbank.com

PRESSINELL, Cindy L. Tel: (219) 873-2692
Vice President, Director of Marketing Fax: (219) 874-9305
cpressinell@horizonbank.com

SECOR, Mark E. Tel: (219) 873-2611
Chief Financial Officer and PAC Treasurer Fax: (219) 874-9280
msecor@horizonbank.com

Horizon Blue Cross Blue Shield of New Jersey Inc.

Horizon Blue Cross Blue Shield of New Jersey (Horizon BCBSNJ) is the New Jersey's largest health insurance company and is a not-for-profit, tax paying health insurer. It offers a complete range of laboratory services in hundreds of convenient locations through LabCorp.
www.horizonblue.com
Industry/ies: Medicine/Health Care/Mental Health
Legislative Issues: BUD; HCR; MMM; TAX

President and Chief Executive Officer Tel: (973) 466-4000
MARINO, Robert A. Fax: (973) 466-4317
robert.marino@horizon-bcbsnj.com

Main Headquarters
Mailing: Three Penn Plaza., East Tel: (973) 466-4000
PP-16H Fax: (973) 466-4317
Newark, NJ 07105-2200

Corporate Foundations and Giving Programs

Horizon Foundation for New Jersey
Contact: Jonathan R. Pearson
Three Penn Plaza East
PP-15V
Newark, NJ 07105-2200

Public Affairs and Related Activities Personnel

At Headquarters

BARNARD, Mark Tel: (973) 466-4000
Senior Vice President, Service Fax: (973) 466-4317

COONS, Margaret M. Tel: (973) 466-4000
Senior Vice President, Human Resources Fax: (973) 466-4317
margaret_coons@horizon-bcbsnj.com

HUBER, David R. Tel: (973) 466-4000
Senior Vice President, Administration, Chief Financial Officer Fax: (973) 466-4317
and Treasurer

JONES, Sarah Tel: (973) 466-4000
Registered Federal Lobbyist Fax: (973) 466-4317

LEPRE, Christopher M. Tel: (973) 466-4000
Senior Vice President, Market Business Units Fax: (973) 466-4317

PEARSON, Jonathan R. Tel: (973) 466-4000
Director, Corporate Social Responsibility and Executive Fax: (973) 466-4317
Director, Horizon Foundation for New Jersey
Jonathan_Pearson@HorizonBlue.com

PREITAUER, Erhardt H.L. Tel: (973) 466-4000
Senior Vice President, Government Programs Fax: (973) 466-4317

RUBINO, EdD, Esq., Thomas W. Tel: (973) 466-8755
Director, Public Affairs, Corporate Marketing and Fax: (973) 466-4317
Communications
trubino@horizonblue.com

VINCZ, Thomas Tel: (973) 466-6625
Manager, Public Relations Fax: (973) 466-4317
Thomas_Vincz@horizonblue.com

WILLETT, Linda A. Tel: (973) 466-4000
Senior Vice President, General Counsel and Secretary Fax: (973) 466-4317

Horizon Lines, Inc.

Shipping and transportation services company.
www.horizon-lines.com
Annual Revenues: $1.07 billion
Employees: 1,633
Ticker: NYSE: HRZL
SIC: 4400
Industry/ies: Marine/Maritime/Shipping; Railroads; Transportation; Trucking
Industry

Chairman of the Board Tel: (704) 973-7000
BRODSKY, Jeffrey A. Fax: (704) 973-7075

Main Headquarters
Mailing: 2550 West Tyvola Rd. Tel: (704) 973-7000
Suite 530 Coliseum 3 Fax: (704) 973-7075
Charlotte, NC 28217-4551 TF: (877) 678-7447

Political Action Committees
Horizon Lines LLC Associates Good Government Fund PAC
FEC ID: C00385179
Contact: Mark Blankenship
2001 K St. NW
Suite 400
Washington, DC 20006

Contributions to Candidates: $13,500 (2015-2016)
Democrats: $11,000; Republicans: $2,500

Public Affairs and Related Activities Personnel

At Headquarters

AVARA, Michael T. Tel: (704) 973-7000
Executive Vice President and Chief Financial Officer Fax: (704) 973-7075
mavara@horizonlines.com

BLANKENSHIP, Mark	Tel: (704) 973-7000		
PAC Treasurer	Fax: (704) 973-7075		
mblankenship@horizonlines.com			
FORSYTH, Gordon	Tel: (732) 817-0400		
Media Contact	Fax: (704) 973-7075		
gordon@bsya.com			
HAMLIN, William A.	Tel: (704) 973-7000		
Executive Vice President And Chief Operating Officer	Fax: (704) 973-7075		

Horizon Telecom, Inc.

Horizon Telcom provides telephone, pay television, Internet access, and information technology services to home subscribers and businesses.
www.horizontel.com
Annual Revenues: $50.90 million
Employees: 300
SIC: 4813
Industry/ies: Communications; Telecommunications/Internet/Cable

Chairman of the Board   Tel: (740) 772-8331
MCKELL, Robert   Fax: (740) 775-1259

Chief Executive Officer   Tel: (740) 772-8200
MCKELL, Bill   Fax: (740) 775-1259

Main Headquarters
Mailing: 68 E. Main St.   Tel: (740) 772-8331
    P.O. Box 480   Fax: (740) 775-7606
    Chillicothe, OH 45601

Political Action Committees
Horizon Telecom PAC
FEC ID: C00375519
Contact: Steve Burkhardt
68 E. Main St.
P.O. Box 480
Chillicothe, OH 45601

Public Affairs and Related Activities Personnel

At Headquarters

BURKHARDT, Steve   Tel: (740) 772-8331
PAC Treasurer   Fax: (740) 775-1259
steve.burkhardt@horizontel.com

THOMPSON, Jack   Tel: (740) 772-8331
Corporate Secretary   Fax: (740) 775-7606

Hormel Foods Corporation

A food processor. Involved in manufacturing and marketing of food and meat products including hams, bacon, sausages, franks, canned luncheon meats, stews, chilies, hash, meat spreads. It also offers nutritional food products and supplements, sugar and sugar substitutes, dessert and drink mixes, and industrial gelatin products.
www.hormelfoods.com
Annual Revenues: $9.18 billion
Employees: 20,700
Ticker: NYSE: HRL
SIC: 2011
NAICS: 311611
Industry/ies: Food And Beverage Industry
Legislative Issues: AGR; FOO; IMM; LBR

Chairman of the Board, President and Chief Executive Officer Tel: (507) 437-5611
ETTINGER, Jeffrey M.   Fax: (507) 437-5129

Main Headquarters
Mailing: One Hormel Pl.   Tel: (507) 437-5611
    Austin, MN 55912   Fax: (507) 437-5129
        TF: (800) 523-4635

Political Action Committees
Hormel Foods Corporation PAC: Aka Hormel-PAC
FEC ID: C00282863
Contact: Roland G. Gentzler
One Hormel Pl.
Austin, TX 55912

Corporate Foundations and Giving Programs

The Hormel Foundation
Contact: John Gray Jr.
One Hormel Pl.   Tel: (507) 437-5611
Austin, TX 55912

Public Affairs and Related Activities Personnel

At Headquarters

FERAGEN, Jody H.   Tel: (507) 437-5611
Executive Vice President and Chief Financial Officer Fax: (507) 437-5129

GENTZLER, Roland G.   Tel: (507) 437-5611
Vice President, Finance and Treasurer and PAC Treasurer Fax: (507) 437-5129

GREV, Jeffrey A.   Tel: (507) 437-5611
Vice President, Legislative Affairs Fax: (507) 437-5129
Registered Federal Lobbyist

HALVIN, Fred D.   Tel: (507) 437-5611

Vice President, Corporate Development Fax: (507) 437-5129

HAYNES, Jana L.   Tel: (507) 437-5611
Director, Investor Relations Fax: (507) 437-5129
jlhaynes@hormel.com

JONES, Kevin C.   Tel: (507) 437-5248
Director, Investor Relations Fax: (507) 437-5129
kcjones@hormel.com

LYONS, Larry C.   Tel: (507) 437-5611
Senior Vice President, Human Resources Fax: (507) 437-5129

MARCO, Lori J.   Tel: (507) 437-5611
Senior Vice President, External Affairs and General Counsel Fax: (507) 437-5129

MARCONI, Luis G.   Tel: (507) 437-5611
Vice President, Marketing Fax: (507) 437-5129

SNEE, James P.   Tel: (507) 437-5611
President and Chief Operating Officer Fax: (507) 437-5129

WATKINS, Wendy A.   Tel: (507) 437-5611
Vice President, Corporate Communications Fax: (507) 437-5129
media@hormel.com

At Other Offices

GRAY , Jr., John   Tel: (507) 437-9800
Assistant Secretary-Treasurer Fax: (507) 396-2705
The Hormel Foundation, 329 N. Main St., Suite 102L
Austin, MN 55912-3478
jjgray@thehormelfoundation.com

Hornbeck Offshore Services, Inc.

A provider of marine transportation services to exploration and production, oilfield service, offshore construction and United States military customers. They provide innovative, technologically advanced marine solutions to meet the evolving needs of the deepwater and ultra-deepwater energy industry in domestic and, more recently, foreign locations.
www.hornbeckoffshore.com
Annual Revenues: $632.83 million
Employees: 1,641
Ticker: NYSE: HOS
SIC: 4400
Industry/ies: Fuels See Coal, Gas, Oil, Petroleum; Marine/Maritime/Shipping; Natural Resources; Petroleum Industry; Transportation
Legislative Issues: MAR

Chairman of the Board, President and Chief Executive Officer Tel: (985) 727-2000
HORNBECK, Todd M.   Fax: (985) 727-2006
todd.hornbeck@hornbeckoffshore.com

Main Headquarters
Mailing: 103 Northpark Blvd.   Tel: (985) 727-2000
    Suite 300   Fax: (985) 727-2006
    Covington, LA 70433   TF: (800) 506-6374

Political Action Committees
Hornbeck Offshore Services, Inc. PAC
FEC ID: C00424366
Contact: Samuel A. Giberga
103 Northpark Blvd.
Suite 300
Covington, LA 70433

    Contributions to Candidates: $22,000 (2015-2016)
    Republicans: $22,000

Corporate Foundations and Giving Programs

Hornbeck Offshore Services, Inc. Contributions Program
103 Northpark Blvd.   Tel: (985) 727-2000
Suite 300
Covington, LA 70433

Public Affairs and Related Activities Personnel

At Headquarters

ANNESSA, Carl G.   Tel: (985) 727-2000
Executive Vice President and Chief Operating Officer Fax: (985) 727-2006

COOK, John S.   Tel: (985) 727-2000
Executive Vice President, Chief Commercial Officer, and Chief Fax: (985) 727-2006
Information Officer

FORTIER, Peter   Tel: (713) 830-8951
Vice President, Sales Fax: (985) 727-2006
Sales@hornbeckoffshore.com

GIBERGA, Samuel A.   Tel: (985) 727-2000
Executive Vice President, General Counsel and PAC Treasurer Fax: (985) 727-2006
samuel.giberga@hornbeckoffshore.com

HARP, Jr., James O.   Tel: (985) 727-2000
Executive Vice President and Chief Financial Officer Fax: (985) 727-2006

Hornneck-Leevac Marine Services, Inc.

See listing on page 411 under Hornbeck Offshore Services, Inc.

Hospira, Inc.

A global specialty pharmaceutical and medication delivery company.

www.hospira.com
Annual Revenues: $4.59 billion
Employees: 19,000
Ticker: NYSE: HSP
SIC: 2834
Industry/ies: Medicine/Health Care/Mental Health

Chairman of the Board — Tel: (224) 212-2000
STALEY, John C. — Fax: (224) 212-3350

Chief Executive Officer — Tel: (224) 212-2000
BALL, F. Michael — Fax: (224) 212-3350

Main Headquarters
Mailing: 275 N. Field Dr. — Tel: (224) 212-2000
Lake Forest, IL 60045 — Fax: (224) 212-3350
TF: (877) 946-7747

Political Action Committees
Hospira, Inc. PAC LLC
FEC ID: C00433284
Contact: Mike Chialdikas
275 N. Field Dr.
H1-4S Dept GVAF
Lake Forest, IL 60045

Contributions to Candidates: $46,000 (2015-2016)
Democrats: $18,000; Republicans: $28,000

Corporate Foundations and Giving Programs
The Hospira Foundation
275 N. Field Dr. — Tel: (224) 212-2000
Lake Forest, IL 60045

Public Affairs and Related Activities Personnel

At Headquarters

BEDWARD, Royce R. — Tel: (224) 212-2000
Senior Vice President, General Counsel and Secretary — Fax: (224) 212-3350

CHIALDIKAS, Mike — Tel: (224) 212-2000
PAC Treasurer — Fax: (224) 212-3350
Mail Stop H1 - 4S DEPT GVAF

KING, Karen — Tel: (224) 212-2711
Vice President, Investor Relations — Fax: (224) 212-3350

MEYERS, Ken — Tel: (224) 212-2000
Senior Vice President and Chief Human Resources Officer — Fax: (224) 212-3350

REED, Juliana M. — Tel: (224) 212-2333
Vice President, Global Government Affairs — Fax: (224) 212-3350

SMITH, Brian J. — Tel: (224) 212-2000
Senior Vice President, Special Counsel — Fax: (224) 212-3350

STOBER, Matthew R. — Tel: (224) 212-2000
Senior Vice President, Operations — Fax: (224) 212-3350

WERNER, Thomas E. — Tel: (224) 212-2000
Senior Vice President, Finance and Chief Financial Officer — Fax: (224) 212-3350

YOSKOWITZ, Marc — Tel: (224) 212-2000
Corporate Vice President, Strategy and Corporate Development — Fax: (224) 212-3350

Hospital Service Association of Northeastern Pennsylvania

A provider of health insurance services.
www.bcnepa.com
Annual Revenues: $929.85 million
Employees: 1,000
Industry/ies: Insurance Industry; Medicine/Health Care/Mental Health

President and Chief Executive Officer — Tel: (570) 200-4300
CESARE, Denise S. — Fax: (570) 200-6888

Main Headquarters
Mailing: 19 N. Main St. — Tel: (570) 200-4300
Wilkes-Barre, PA 18711-0302 — Fax: (570) 200-6640
TF: (800) 822-8753

Corporate Foundations and Giving Programs
Blue Ribbon Foundation
Contact: Cynthia Yevich
19 N. Main St. — Tel: (570) 200-6305
Wilkes-Barre, PA 18711 — Fax: (570) 200-6640

Public Affairs and Related Activities Personnel

At Headquarters

FARRELL, William J. — Tel: (570) 200-4300
Chief Financial Officer — Fax: (570) 200-6888

FLETCHER, Suzanne — Tel: (570) 200-4300
Vice President, Finance & Administrative Services — Fax: (570) 200-6888

MATRISCIANO, Anthony — Tel: (570) 200-6310
Contact, Media Relations — Fax: (570) 200-6888
anthony.matrisciano@bcnepa.com

YEVICH, Cynthia — Tel: (570) 200-4300
Executive Director, the Blue Ribbon Foundation — Fax: (570) 200-6888

cynthia.yevich@bcnepa.com

Host Hotels & Resorts

A lodging real estate company. Our goal is to generate superior returns with reduced volatility to our stockholders by investing in the top domestic and international markets in the most profitable lodging properties.
www.hosthotels.com
Annual Revenues: $5.45 billion
Employees: 240
Ticker: NYSE: HST
SIC: 6798
Industry/ies: Real Estate; Travel/Tourism/Lodging

Chairman of the Board — Tel: (240) 744-1000
MARRIOTT, Richard E. — Fax: (240) 744-5125
richard.marriott@hostmarriott.com

President and Chief Executive Officer and Director — Tel: (240) 744-1000
WALTER, W. Edward — Fax: (240) 744-5125

Main Headquarters
Mailing: 6903 Rockledge Dr. — Tel: (240) 744-1000
Suite 1500 — Fax: (240) 744-5125
Bethesda, MD 20817

Public Affairs and Related Activities Personnel

At Headquarters

ABDOO, Elizabeth A. — Tel: (240) 744-1000
Executive Vice President, General Counsel and Secretary — Fax: (240) 744-5125
elizabeth.abdoo@hosthotels.com

HAMILTON, Joanne G. — Tel: (240) 744-1000
Executive Vice President, Human Resources — Fax: (240) 744-5125
joanne.hamilton@hosthotels.com

LARSON, Gregory J. — Tel: (240) 744-5120
Executive Vice President and Chief Financial Officer — Fax: (240) 744-5125
greg.larson@hostmarriott.com

MACNAMARA, Brian G. — Tel: (240) 744-1000
Senior Vice President, Corporate Controller — Fax: (240) 744-5125

ROBERTSON, Struan B. — Tel: (240) 744-1000
Executive Vice President and Chief Investment Officer — Fax: (240) 744-5125

Host Marriott Corporation

See listing on page 412 under Host Hotels & Resorts

Houchens Industries, Inc.

An operator of supermarkets.
www.houchensindustries.com
Annual Revenues: $2.67 billion
Employees: 18,000
SIC: 5411
Industry/ies: Food And Beverage Industry
Legislative Issues: FOO; LBR; TAX

Chairman of the Board & Chief Executive Officer — Tel: (270) 843-3252
GIPSON, James — Fax: (270) 780-2877

Main Headquarters
Mailing: P.O. Box 90009 — Tel: (270) 843-3252
Bowling Green, KY 42102 — Fax: (270) 780-2877

Corporate Foundations and Giving Programs
Houchens Industries Contributions Program
700 Church St.
Bowling Green, KY 42102

Public Affairs and Related Activities Personnel

At Headquarters

LARSEN, Alan — Tel: (270) 780-2848
Director, Marketing and Merchandising and Media contact — Fax: (270) 780-2877

MINTER, Gordon — Tel: (270) 843-3252
Chief Financial Officer — Fax: (270) 780-2877

Houghton Mifflin Company

A publishing company. Acquired in December, 2002, by a group of private investment firms, including, Thomas H. Lee Partners, Bain Capital and funds managed by The Blackstone Group.
www.hmco.com
Annual Revenues: $277.9 million
Employees: 3,100
SIC: 2731
Industry/ies: Communications; Media/Mass Communication

President and Chief Executive officer — Tel: (617) 351-5000
ZECHER, Linda K. — Fax: (617) 351-1125

Main Headquarters
Mailing: 222 Berkeley St. — Tel: (617) 351-5000
Boston, MA 02116 — Fax: (617) 351-1125

Washington Office

Mailing: 1747 Pennsylvania Ave. NW
             Washington, DC 20006

Corporate Foundations and Giving Programs

Houghton Mifflin Foundation
Contact: Mary Cullinane
222 Berkeley St.   Tel: (617) 351-5000
Boston, MA 02116   Fax: (617) 351-1125

Public Affairs and Related Activities Personnel

At Headquarters

BAYERS, William   Tel: (617) 351-5000
Executive Vice President and General Counsel   Fax: (617) 351-1125

BLAKE, Richard   Tel: (617) 351-5000
Senior Vice President, Public and Governmental Affairs   Fax: (617) 351-1125
richard.blake@hmhco.com

BLUMENFELD, Josef   Tel: (617) 351-5000
Vice President, Communications   Fax: (617) 351-1125
josef.blumenfeld@hmhpub.com

CANNON, Dr. Tim   Tel: (617) 351-5000
Executive Vice President, International Markets and Global   Fax: (617) 351-1125
Strategic Alliances

CULLINANE, Mary   Tel: (617) 351-5000
Executive Vice President, Corporate Affairs and Social   Fax: (617) 351-1125
Responsibility
cullinane@hmhco.com

DRAGOON, John K.   Tel: (617) 351-5000
Executive Vice president And Chief Marketing Officer   Fax: (617) 351-1125

PARADISE, Bridgett   Tel: (617) 351-5000
Senior Vice President and Chief People Officer   Fax: (617) 351-1125

SHUMAN, Eric   Tel: (617) 351-5000
Chief Financial Officer   Fax: (617) 351-1125

Houlihan Smith and Company Inc.

A national investment banking firm providing financial opinions, valuation services and corporate advisory to public and private businesses.
www.houlihansmith.com
Annual Revenues: $10.20 million
Employees: 100
Industry/ies: Banking/Finance/Investments

Founder and Chairman of the Board   Tel: (312) 499-5900
HOULIHAN, Richard   Fax: (312) 499-5901
rhoulihan@houlihansmith.com

Main Headquarters
Mailing: 105 W. Madison   Tel: (312) 499-5900
             Suite 1200   Fax: (312) 499-5901
             Chicago, IL 60602-4602   TF: (800) 654-4977

Corporate Foundations and Giving Programs

Houlihan Smith and Company Inc. Contributions Program
Contact: Robert Becker
105 W. Madison   Tel: (312) 499-5946
Suite 1200   Fax: (312) 499-5901
Chicago, IL 60602-4602

Public Affairs and Related Activities Personnel

At Headquarters

BECKER, Robert   Tel: (312) 499-5900
Foundation Contact and Analyst   Fax: (312) 499-5901

BERGER, William   Tel: (312) 499-5986
Contact, Media Relations   Fax: (312) 499-5901

Household International, Inc.

See listing on page 413 under HSBC North America Holdings (HSBC GR) Inc.

Hovnanian Enterprises, Inc.

A construction and homebuilding company.
www.khov.com
Annual Revenues: $2.16 billion
Employees: 2,006
Ticker: NYSE: HOV
SIC: 1531
Industry/ies: Construction/Construction Materials; Housing

Chairman of the Board, President and Chief Executive Officer   Tel: (732) 747-7800
HOVNANIAN, Ara K.   Fax: (732) 383-2945

Main Headquarters
Mailing: 110 W. Front St.   Tel: (732) 747-7800
             P.O. Box 500   Fax: (732) 383-2945
             Red Bank, NJ 07701

Corporate Foundations and Giving Programs

Hovnanian Enterprises, Inc. Contributions Program
110 W. Front St.   Tel: (732) 747-7800
P. O. Box 500   Fax: (732) 747-6835

Red Bank, NJ 07701

Public Affairs and Related Activities Personnel

At Headquarters

O'CONNOR, Brad   Tel: (732) 747-7800
Vice President, Chief Accounting Officer and Corporate   Fax: (732) 383-2945
Controller

O'KEEFE, Jeffrey T.   Tel: (732) 383-2702
Vice President, Investor Relations   Fax: (732) 383-2945
jokeefe@khov.com

SORSBY, J. Larry   Tel: (732) 747-7800
Executive Vice President, Chief Financial Officer and Director   Fax: (732) 383-2945

VALIAVEEDAN, David G.   Tel: (732) 747-7800
Vice President, Finance and Treasurer   Fax: (732) 383-2945

HP Hood LLC

A dairy manufacturing company. It distributes fresh, quality dairy products and also maintains its own research and development operation, which supports the superior product quality and innovation that Hood customers have come to expect.
www.hphood.com
Annual Revenues: $2.20 billion
Employees: 4,500
Industry/ies: Dairy Industry; Food And Beverage Industry

Chairman, President and Chief Executive Officer   Tel: (617) 887-3000
KANEB, John A.   Fax: (617) 887-8484

Main Headquarters
Mailing: Six Kimball Ln.   Tel: (617) 887-3000
             Lynnfield, MA 01940   Fax: (617) 887-8484
                                         TF: (800) 343-6592

Corporate Foundations and Giving Programs

HP Hood Contributions Program
Six Kimball Ln.   Tel: (617) 887-3000
Lynnfield, MA 01940   Fax: (617) 887-8484

Public Affairs and Related Activities Personnel

At Headquarters

BLAKE, H. Scott   Tel: (617) 887-3000
Senior Vice President, Operations   Fax: (617) 887-8484

BOHAN, Lynne M.   Tel: (617) 887-3000
Vice President, Communications and Government Affairs   Fax: (617) 887-8484
Lynne.Bohan@hphood.com

KANEB, Gary R.   Tel: (617) 887-3000
Chief Financial Officer   Fax: (617) 887-8484

NIGHTINGALE, Paul C.   Tel: (617) 887-3000
Senior Vice President, General Counsel Fax: (617) 887-8484

ROSS, Christopher S.   Tel: (617) 887-3000
Vice President, Marketing   Fax: (617) 887-8484
chris.ross@hphood.com

SEITZ, Jane   Tel: (617) 887-3000
Vice President, Human Resources   Fax: (617) 887-8484

HSBC North America Holdings (HSBC GR) Inc.

A provider of consumer finance and credit card products. A subsidiary of HSBC Holdings PLC, headquartered in London, UK.
www.us.hsbc.com
Employees: 29,000
Ticker: NYSE: HBC
SIC: 6022
Industry/ies: Banking/Finance/Investments
Legislative Issues: BAN; FIN; TAX; TEC; TRD

President and Chief Executive Officer   Tel: (224) 544-2000
BURKE, Patrick   Fax: (224) 552-4400

Main Headquarters
Mailing: 452 Fifth Ave.   Tel: (224) 544-2000
             New York City, NY 10018   Fax: (224) 552-4400

Washington Office
Mailing: 1401 Eye St. NW   Tel: (202) 466-3561
             Suite 500   Fax: (202) 466-3583
             Washington, DC 20005

Political Action Committees
HSBC North America Political Action Committee (H*PAC)
FEC ID: C00033423
1401 I St. NW   Tel: (224) 544-2000
Suite 520   Fax: (224) 552-4400
Washington, DC 20005

   Contributions to Candidates: $181,000 (2015-2016)
   Democrats: $58,000; Republicans: $123,000

Principal Recipients

SENATE
   KIRK, MARK STEVEN (REP-IL)

Public Affairs and Related Activities Personnel

At Headquarters

ALDEROTY, Stuart
Senior Executive Vice President and General Counsel
Tel: (224) 544-2000
Fax: (224) 552-4400

BILBREY, Mary E.
Executive Vice President, Head, Human Resources
Tel: (224) 544-2000
Fax: (224) 552-4400

GUTIERREZ, Juanita
Contact, Media Relations
juanita.gutierrez@us.hsbc.com
Tel: (224) 544-2000
Fax: (224) 552-4400

KLUG, Loren
Executive Vice President, Head, Strategy and Planning
Tel: (224) 544-2000
Fax: (224) 552-4400

MATTIA, Gerard
Senior Executive Vice President and Chief Financial Officer
Tel: (224) 544-2000
Fax: (224) 552-4400

PISARCZYK, Karen
Executive Vice President and Corporate Secretary
Tel: (224) 544-2000
Fax: (224) 552-4400

SEVERINO, Vittorio
Senior Executive Vice President and Chief Operating Officer
Tel: (224) 544-2000
Fax: (224) 552-4400

SODEIKA, Lisa M.
Executive Vice President, Corporate Affairs
Lisa.M.Sodeika@us.hsbc.com
Tel: (847) 564-5000
Fax: (224) 552-4400

ST. AMAND, Janet G.
Federal Government Relations
janet.g.st.amand@us.hsbc.com
Registered Federal Lobbyist
Tel: (224) 544-2000
Fax: (224) 552-4400

At Washington Office

FRAZIER, Monique
Vice President, Federal Government Relations
monique.p.frazier@us.hsbc.com
Registered Federal Lobbyist
Tel: (202) 466-3561
Fax: (202) 466-3583

ROSENKOETTER, Thomas J.
Vice President
thomas.j.rosenkoetter@us.hsbc.com
Registered Federal Lobbyist
Tel: (202) 466-3561
Fax: (202) 466-3583

HSN Inc.

An operating unit of IAC.
www.hsn.com
Annual Revenues: $3.65 billion
Employees: 6,900
Ticker: NASDAQ: HSNI
SIC: 5940
Industry/ies: Retail/Wholesale

Chairman of the Board
MARTINEZ, Arthur C.
Tel: (727) 872-1000

Chief Executive Officer and Director
GROSSMAN, Mindy F.
Tel: (727) 872-1000

Main Headquarters
Mailing: One HSN Dr.
St. Petersburg, FL 33729
Tel: (727) 872-1000
TF: (800) 284-3100

Public Affairs and Related Activities Personnel

At Headquarters

ATTINELLA, Michael J.
Chief Financial Officer
Tel: (727) 872-1000

BOHNERT, Brad
Director, Public Relations and Events
brad.bohnert@hsn.net
Tel: (727) 872-1000

BRAND, Bill
Chief Marketing and Business Development officer
Tel: (727) 872-1000

HENCHEL, Gregory J.
Chief Legal Officer and Secretary
Tel: (727) 872-1000

SCHMELING, Judy
Chief Operating Officer and Chief Financial Officer
Tel: (727) 872-1000

At Other Offices

MCKEON, Kevin J
Treasurer
P.O. Box 9090
Clearwater, FL 34618

HSP Direct

A direct mail fundraising company.
Industry/ies: Fundraising

Main Headquarters
Mailing: 13755 Sunrise Valley Dr.
Suite 450
Herndon, VA 20171
Tel: (703) 793-3220
Fax: (703) 793-3221

Political Action Committees
HSP Direct LLC PAC
FEC ID: C00432419
Contact: Matthew Schenk

13755 Sunrise Valley Dr., Suite 450
Herndon, VA 20171
Tel: (703) 793-3220
Fax: (703) 793-3221

Contributions to Candidates: $12,300 (2015-2016)
Republicans: $12,300

Public Affairs and Related Activities Personnel

At Headquarters

SCHENK, Matthew
PAC Contact
Tel: (703) 793-3220
Fax: (703) 793-3221

HTC Americas

A smartphone manufacturer.
www.htc.com
Employees: 200
Industry/ies: Communications; Telecommunications/Internet/Cable; Telephones
Legislative Issues: CPT; CSP; HCR; INT; TEC; TRD

Main Headquarters
Mailing: 13920 S.E. Eastgate Way
Suite 400
Bellevue, WA 98005
Tel: (425) 679-5318
Fax: (425) 861-1715

Washington Office
Mailing: 1001 Pennsylvania Ave. NW
Washington, DC 20004

Public Affairs and Related Activities Personnel

At Headquarters

MACKENZIE, Jason
President, Global Sales
Tel: (425) 679-5318
Fax: (425) 861-1715

WOLVERTON, Amy
Vice President, Government Affairs
amy_wolverton@htc.com
Registered Federal Lobbyist
Tel: (202) 270-8725
Fax: (425) 861-1715

Hubbard Broadcasting Corp, Inc.

A television and radio broadcasting company.
hubbardradio.com
Employees: 1,200
Industry/ies: Communications; Media/Mass Communication
Legislative Issues: COM; TAX; TEC

Chair and Chief Executive Officer
MORRIS, Ginny
Tel: (651) 642-4656
Fax: (651) 647-2932

Main Headquarters
Mailing: 3415 University Ave.
St. Paul, MN 55114
Tel: (651) 642-4656
Fax: (651) 647-2932

Corporate Foundations and Giving Programs
The Hubbard Foundation
Contact: Kathryn Hubbard Rominski
3415 University Ave.
St. Paul, MN 55114
Tel: (651) 642-4305

Public Affairs and Related Activities Personnel

At Headquarters

BESTLER, Dave
Executive Vice President and Chief Financial Officer
Tel: (651) 642-4656
Fax: (651) 647-2932

CRUMP, Harold
Vice President, Public Affairs
Tel: (651) 646-5555
Fax: (651) 642-4103

HOROWITZ, Drew M.
President and Chief Operating Officer
Tel: (651) 642-4656
Fax: (651) 647-2932

HUBBARD ROMINSKI, Kathryn
Executive Director, Hubbard Foundation
Tel: (651) 642-4305
Fax: (651) 642-4103

SEEMAN, Dan
Vice President and Market Manager
Tel: (651) 642-4656
Fax: (651) 647-2932

At Other Offices

REESE, Bruce T.
Special Advisor
6985 Union Park Center, Suite 600
Cottonwood Heights, UT 84047
Tel: (801) 575-7555
Fax: (801) 575-7548

Hubbell, Inc.

A manufacturer of electrical and electronic products.
www.hubbell.com
Annual Revenues: $5.54 billion
Employees: 16,200
Ticker: NYSE: HUB.B
SIC: 3613; 3643; 3644; 3646; 3648
NAICS: 335122; 335129; 335313; 335932; 335931
Industry/ies: Communications; Computer/Technology; Electricity & Electronics; Electronics; Energy/Electricity; Machinery/Equipment; Telecommunications/Internet/Cable

President and Chief Executive Officer, Chairman
NORD, David G.
Tel: (475) 882-4000

Main Headquarters

Mailing:	40 Waterview Dr.	Tel:	(475) 882-4000
	Shelton, CT 06484-1000		

Corporate Foundations and Giving Programs

Harvey Hubbell Foundation
Contact: David G. Nord
584 Derby Milford Rd.   Tel: (203) 799-4100
Orange, CT 06477

Public Affairs and Related Activities Personnel

At Headquarters

CAPOZZOLI, Joseph A	Tel:	(475) 882-4000
Vice President and Corporate Controller		
HSIEH, An-Ping	Tel:	(475) 882-4000
Senior Vice President, General Counsel		
LEE, Maria R.	Tel:	(475) 882-4000
Treasurer and Vice President, Corporate Strategy and Investor Relations		
MAIS, Stephen M.	Tel:	(475) 882-4000
Senior Vice President, Human Resources		
MURPHY, W. Robert	Tel:	(475) 882-4000
Executive Vice President, Marketing and Sales		
PIZZOLI, Louis G	Tel:	(475) 882-4000
Vice President, Operations		
SPERRY, William R.	Tel:	(475) 882-4000
Senior Vice President and Chief Financial Officer		

Hudson Clean Energy Partners, L.P.

A private equity firm dedicated solely to investing in renewable power, alternative fuels, energy efficiency and storage.
www.hudsoncep.com
Annual Revenues: $3.30 million
Industry/ies: Banking/Finance/Investments; Energy/Electricity; Environment And Conservation

Chairman and Managing Partner	Tel:	(201) 287-4100
CAVALIER, John		
Founder, Chief Executive Officer and Managing Partner	Tel:	(201) 287-4100
AUERBACH , Neil Z.		

Main Headquarters

Mailing:	400 Frank W. Burr Blvd.	Tel:	(201) 287-4100
	Suite 37		
	Teaneck, NJ 07666		

Public Affairs and Related Activities Personnel

At Headquarters

FARQUHARSON, Natasha	Tel:	(201) 287-4100
Vice President and Director of Investor Relations		
HENRY, Larry L.	Tel:	(201) 287-4100
Head, Investor Relations		
ROBINSON-LEON, Jeremy	Tel:	(201) 287-4100
Contact, Media Relations		
jrl@groupgordon.com		
TUOHY, David	Tel:	(201) 287-4100
Operating Partner		

Hudson Hollister LLC

Lobbying and consulting firm.

Main Headquarters

Mailing:	431 13th St. NE	Tel:	(202) 415-4025
	Washington, DC 20002		

Public Affairs and Related Activities Personnel

At Headquarters

JONES, Glynn	Tel:	(202) 415-4025
Communications Specialist		

Hughes Electronics Corporation

See listing on page 257 under DIRECTV Group Inc.

Hughes Network Systems, LLC

A satellite communications network provider.
www.hughes.com
Employees: 1,900
SIC: 4899
Industry/ies: Electricity & Electronics; Electronics; Energy/Electricity
Legislative Issues: COM; DEF

President, Hughes Network Systems	Tel:	(301) 428-5500
KAUL, Pradman P.	Fax:	(301) 428-1868

Main Headquarters

Mailing:	11717 Exploration Ln	Tel:	(301) 428-5500
	Germantown, MD 20876	Fax:	(301) 428-1868

Public Affairs and Related Activities Personnel

At Headquarters

BARBER, Grant	Tel:	(301) 428-5500
Executive Vice President and Chief Financial Officer	Fax:	(301) 428-1868
DOIRON, Steve	Tel:	(301) 428-5500
Senior Director, Regulatory Affairs	Fax:	(301) 428-1868

Hughes Telematics, Inc.

See listing on page 833 under Verizon Telematics

Hulcher Services, Inc.

Provider of railroad, engineering, environmental and disaster response services.
www.hulcher.com
Employees: 600
SIC: 4789
NAICS: 488210
Industry/ies: Disaster; Engineering/Mathematics; Environment And Conservation; Railroads; Transportation

Main Headquarters

Mailing:	611 Kimberly Dr.	Tel:	(940) 387-0099
	P.O. Box 271	Fax:	(940) 382-4550
	Denton, TX 76202-0271	TF:	(800) 659-8032

Public Affairs and Related Activities Personnel

At Headquarters

HART, Carmelita	Tel:	(940) 387-0099
Specialist, Marketing	Fax:	(940) 382-4550
HILLEN, Robert	Tel:	(940) 387-0099
Director, Sales and Marketing	Fax:	(940) 382-4550
rhillen@hulcher.com		

Humana Inc.

A health insurance company including, HMOs, PPOs, POSs, and dental coverage.
www.humana.com
Annual Revenues: $54.26 billion
Employees: 50,100
Ticker: NYSE: HUM
SIC: 6324
Industry/ies: Insurance Industry; Medicine/Health Care/Mental Health
Legislative Issues: DEF; HCR; LBR; MMM; TAX

Chairman of the Board	Tel:	(502) 580-1000
HILZINGER, Kurt J.	Fax:	(502) 580-3677
President and Chief Executive Officer	Tel:	(502) 580-1000
BROUSSARD, Bruce D.	Fax:	(502) 580-3677

Main Headquarters

Mailing:	500 W. Main St.	Tel:	(502) 580-1000
	Louisville, KY 40202	Fax:	(502) 580-3677
		TF:	(800) 486-2620

Washington Office

Mailing:	975 F St. NW	Tel:	(202) 467-5821
	Suite 550	Fax:	(202) 347-1462
	Washington, DC 20004	TF:	(800) 486-2620

Political Action Committees

Humana PAC
FEC ID: C00271007
Contact: Douglas Stoss
975 F St. NW   Tel: (202) 467-5821
Suite 550   Fax: (202) 467-5825
Washington, DC 20004

Contributions to Candidates: $511,500 (2015-2016)
Democrats: $235,500; Republicans: $273,500; Other: $2,500

Principal Recipients

SENATE
PAUL, RAND (REP-KY)

HOUSE
BARR, GARLAND ANDY (REP-KY)
BUCHANAN, VERNON (REP-FL)
FRANKEL, LOIS J. (DEM-FL)
TIBERI, PATRICK J. (REP-OH)

Corporate Foundations and Giving Programs

Humana Foundation
500 W. Main St.   Tel: (502) 580-1000
Louisville, KY 40202

Public Affairs and Related Activities Personnel

At Headquarters

BENNETT, Carol	Tel:	(502) 580-1000
Consultant, Communications	Fax:	(502) 580-3677
BILNEY, Jody L.	Tel:	(502) 580-1000
Senior Vice President and Chief Consumer Officer	Fax:	(502) 580-3677
BURGER-KUGLE, Susan	Tel:	(502) 580-1000

Director, Regional Policy	Fax:	(502) 580-3677
HOAK, Mike	Tel:	(502) 580-1000
Lead, Health Policy	Fax:	(502) 580-3677
HUNTER, Christopher H.	Tel:	(502) 580-1000
Senior Vice President and Chief Strategy Officer	Fax:	(502) 580-3677
HUVAL, Tim	Tel:	(502) 580-1000
Senior Vice President, Chief Human Resources Officer	Fax:	(502) 580-3677
ICE, Julie	Tel:	(502) 580-1000
Director, Legislative, Public Affairs and Humana Government Business	Fax:	(502) 580-3677
KANE, Brian	Tel:	(502) 580-1000
Senior Vice President and Chief Financial Officer	Fax:	(502) 580-3677
LECLAIRE, Brian	Tel:	(502) 580-1000
Senior Vice President and Chief Information Officer	Fax:	(502) 580-3677
MAGNUSON, Rachel	Tel:	(502) 580-1000
Federal Lobbyist	Fax:	(502) 580-3677
Registered Federal Lobbyist		
MCCULLEY, Steven E.	Tel:	(502) 580-1000
Vice President, Principal Accounting Officer and Controller	Fax:	(502) 580-3677
MURRAY, James E.	Tel:	(502) 580-1000
Executive Vice President and Chief Operating Officer	Fax:	(502) 580-3677
NETHERY, Regina C.	Tel:	(502) 580-3644
Vice President, Investor Relations	Fax:	(502) 508-1210
rnethery@humana.com		
NOLAND, Thomas	Tel:	(502) 580-3674
Senior Vice President, Corporate Communications	Fax:	(502) 580-3677
OBERMAN, Debra	Tel:	(502) 580-1000
Vice President Public Affairs and Executive Leader, Strategic Policy	Fax:	(502) 580-3677
Registered Federal Lobbyist		
PATEK, Allan	Tel:	(502) 580-1000
Federal Lobbyist	Fax:	(502) 580-3677
Registered Federal Lobbyist		
PAUL, Jacqueline	Tel:	(502) 580-1000
Federal Lobbyist	Fax:	(502) 580-3677
Registered Federal Lobbyist		
SNYDER, Timothy C.	Tel:	(502) 580-1000
Vice President and National Practice Leader	Fax:	(502) 580-3677
TODOROFF, Christopher M.	Tel:	(502) 580-1000
Senior Vice President and General Counsel	Fax:	(502) 580-3677
ZIPPERLE, Cynthia H.	Tel:	(502) 580-1000
Vice President, Chief Accounting Officer and Controller	Fax:	(502) 580-3677

At Washington Office

MARGULIS, Heidi S.	Tel:	(202) 467-5821
Senior Vice President, Corporate Affairs	Fax:	(202) 347-1462
Registered Federal Lobbyist		
STOSS, Douglas	Tel:	(202) 467-5821
Registered Federal Lobbyist	Fax:	(202) 347-1462

Humanetics Corporation

A biotechnology research company.
www.humaneticscorp.com
Annual Revenues: $1.00 million
Industry/ies: Science; Scientific Research
Legislative Issues: DEF; SCI

Founder, President and Chief Executive Officer	Tel:	(952) 937-7660
ZENK, Ronald J.	Fax:	(952) 937-7667

Main Headquarters

Mailing:	1550 Utica Ave., South	Tel:	(952) 937-7660
	Suite 770	Fax:	(952) 937-7667
	Minneapolis, MN 55416		

Public Affairs and Related Activities Personnel

At Headquarters

DYKSTRA, John C	Tel:	(952) 937-7660
Chief Operating Officer	Fax:	(952) 937-7667

Hunt Oil Company

A petroleum exploration and production company.
www.huntoil.com
Employees: 2,100
SIC: 2911
NAICS: 324110
Industry/ies: Natural Resources

Chairman of the Board, President and Chief Executive Officer	Tel:	(214) 978-8000
HUNT, Ray L.	Fax:	(214) 978-8888

Main Headquarters

Mailing:	1900 N. Akard St.	Tel:	(214) 978-8000
	Dallas, TX 75201-2300	Fax:	(214) 978-8888

Political Action Committees
Hunt Consolidated, Inc. PAC
FEC ID: C00141945
Contact: Donald F. Robillard Jr.

1900 N. Akard St.	Tel:	(214) 978-8000
Dallas, TX 75201-2300	Fax:	(214) 978-8888

Corporate Foundations and Giving Programs
Hunt Oil Company Contribution Program

1900 N. Akard St.	Tel:	(214) 978-8000
Dallas, TX 75201-2300	Fax:	(214) 978-8888

Public Affairs and Related Activities Personnel

At Headquarters

ARMAYOR, Travis	Tel:	(214) 978-8000
Senior Vice President, Corporate Finance and Business Development	Fax:	(214) 978-8888
GRAHAM, James R.	Tel:	(214) 978-8247
PAC Treasurer	Fax:	(214) 978-8888
GRINDINGER, Dennis	Tel:	(214) 978-8000
Executive Vice President, South America	Fax:	(214) 978-8888
KUYKENDALL , Steve	Tel:	(214) 978-8000
Vice President, Strategic Purchasing Services	Fax:	(214) 978-8888
MONROE, Michael	Tel:	(214) 978-8000
Vice President, Assistant General Counsel and Assistant Secretary	Fax:	(214) 978-8888
RAY, Dan	Tel:	(214) 978-8000
Senior Vice President, Marketing	Fax:	(214) 978-8888
ROBILLARD, Jr., Donald F.	Tel:	(214) 978-8000
Senior Vice President and Chief Financial Officer	Fax:	(214) 978-8888
SUELLENTROP , Steve	Tel:	(214) 978-8000
President	Fax:	(214) 978-8888

Hunter and Company Communications, LLC

Public relations consulting.

President
HUNTER, Jan
jan@HunterCoPR.com

Main Headquarters
Mailing: 44 School St.
            Suite 250
            Boston, MA 02108

Public Affairs and Related Activities Personnel

At Other Offices

HUNTER, Stephen	Tel:	(801) 336-7795

Principal
55 Cold Creek Way
Layton, UT 84041

Hunter Engineering Company

Designs, manufactures and sells a wide range of passenger car and truck service equipment.
www.hunter.com
SIC: 3549
NAICS: 333518
Industry/ies: Engineering/Mathematics

Chairman of the Board	Tel:	(314) 731-3020
BRAUER, Stephen F.	Fax:	(314) 731-1776

sfbrauer@hunter.com

Main Headquarters

Mailing:	11250 Hunter Dr.	Tel:	(314) 731-0000
	Bridgeton, MO 63043	Fax:	(314) 731-1776
		TF:	(800) 448-6848

Political Action Committees
Hunter Engineering Company PAC
FEC ID: C00214379
Contact: Joseph A. Staniszewski

11250 Hunter Dr.	Tel:	(314) 731-3020
Bridgeton, MO 63044	Fax:	(314) 731-1776

Public Affairs and Related Activities Personnel

At Headquarters

BRUCE, Robert	Tel:	(314) 716-0443
Advertising Manager	Fax:	(314) 731-1776
KARR, Matt	Tel:	(314) 731-3020
Director, Human Resources	Fax:	(314) 731-1776
STANISZEWSKI, Joseph A.	Tel:	(314) 731-3020
Vice President, Finance and PAC Treasurer	Fax:	(314) 731-1776
ZENTZ, John	Tel:	(314) 731-3020
Vice President, Sales	Fax:	(314) 731-1776

Hunter Fan Company

Maker of celing fans, air purifiers, humidifiers, thermostats, portable fans, and bath exhaust fans.
www.hunterfan.com
Annual Revenues: $57.90 million
Employees: 700
NAICS: 335211
Industry/ies: Furniture/Home Furnishings; Retail/Wholesale

Main Headquarters

Mailing: 7130 Goodlett Farms Pkwy., Suite 400 Tel: (901) 743-1360
Memphis, TN 38016 TF: (888) 830-1326

Huntington Bancshares Inc.

A bank holding company.
www.huntington.com
Annual Revenues: $2.77 billion
Employees: 11,914
Ticker: NASDAQ: HBAN
SIC: 6021
Industry/ies: Banking/Finance/Investments
Legislative Issues: BAN; FIN; TAX

Chairman, President and Chief Executive Officer Tel: (614) 480-8300
STEINOUR, Stephen D. Fax: (614) 480-5284
steve.steinour@huntington.com

Main Headquarters

Mailing: 41 S. High St. Tel: (614) 480-8300
Columbus, OH 43215 Fax: (614) 480-5284
TF: (800) 480-2265

Political Action Committees

Huntington Bancshares Inc. PAC (HBI-PAC)
FEC ID: C00165589
Contact: Dave S. Anderson
41 S. High St. Tel: (614) 480-8300
Columbus, OH 43287 Fax: (614) 480-8300

Contributions to Candidates: $127,500 (2015-2016)
Democrats: $30,300; Republicans: $97,200

Principal Recipients

HOUSE
STIVERS, STEVE MR. (REP-OH)
TIBERI, PATRICK J. (REP-OH)

Corporate Foundations and Giving Programs

Huntington Bancshares Inc. Contributions Program
Contact: Steven Fields
41 S. High St. Tel: (614) 480-4483
Columbus, OH 43287 Fax: (614) 480-4973

Public Affairs and Related Activities Personnel

At Headquarters

ANDERSON, Dave S. Tel: (614) 480-8300
PAC Treasurer Fax: (614) 480-5284

BEER, Michael Tel: (614) 480-8300
Federal Lobbyist Fax: (614) 480-5284
Registered Federal Lobbyist

BENHAM, Barbara Tel: (614) 480-4718
Executive Vice President, Chief Communications Officer Fax: (614) 480-5284
barbara.benham@huntington.com
Registered Federal Lobbyist

BROWN, Maureen Tel: (614) 480-5512
Public Relations Director, Corporate Communications Fax: (614) 480-5746

CHEAP, Richard A. Tel: (614) 480-8300
Executive Vice President, General Counsel & Secretary Fax: (614) 480-5284

FIELDS, Steven Tel: (614) 480-3278
Vice President and Director, Community Engagement and Fax: (614) 480-4973
President, The Huntington Foundation
steven.fields@huntington.com

HATCHER, Christopher Tel: (614) 480-4718
Federal Lobbyist Fax: (614) 480-5284

KALLNER, Mathew Tel: (614) 480-4718
Federal Lobbyist Fax: (614) 480-5284

MCCULLOUGH III, Howell D. "Mac" Tel: (614) 480-8300
Senior Executive Vice President, Chief Financial Officer Fax: (614) 480-5284

THOMPSON, Denise Love Tel: (614) 480-8300
Senior Executive Vice President and Director, Corporate Fax: (614) 480-5284
Operations and Huntington Insurance

THOMPSON, Mark Tel: (614) 480-8300
Senior Executive Vice President, Director of Corporate Fax: (614) 480-5284
Operations

WILKINS, Craig Tel: (614) 480-8300
Senior Vice President, Interim Chief Human Resources Officer Fax: (614) 480-5284

Huntington Ingalls Industries Inc.

Formerly known as the Newport News and Ship Systems and most recently a Northrop Grumman sector. A builder of the US Navy's nuclear aircraft carriers and designs, builds and maintain ships for the U.S. Navy and U.S. Coast Guard at Ingalls Shipbuilding and Newport News Shipbuilding. AMSEC is a subsidiary of Huntington Ingalls Industries.
www.huntingtoningalls.com
Annual Revenues: $6.93 billion
Employees: 38,000
Ticker: NYSE: HII
SIC: 3730
Industry/ies: Construction/Construction Materials; Marine/Maritime/Shipping; Transportation
Legislative Issues: BUD; DEF; ENG; HOM; MAR; TAX

Chairman of the Board Tel: (757) 380-2000
FARGO, Thomas B. Fax: (757) 380-4713

President and Chief Executive Officer Tel: (757) 380-2000
PETTERS, Mike Fax: (757) 380-4713

Main Headquarters

Mailing: 4101 Washington Ave. Tel: (757) 380-2000
Newport News, VA 23607

Washington Office

Mailing: 300 M St. SE
Suite 250
Washington, DC 20003

Political Action Committees

Huntington Ingalls Industries PAC (SHIPPAC)
FEC ID: C00325092
Contact: Barbara A. Niland
300 M St. SE
Suite 350
Washington, DC 20003

Contributions to Candidates: $576,000 (2015-2016)
Democrats: $186,000; Republicans: $390,000

Principal Recipients

HOUSE
BYRNE, BRADLEY ROBERTS (REP-AL)
CARTER, JOHN R. REP. (REP-DC)
COURTNEY, JOSEPH D (DEM-CT)
CRENSHAW, ANDER (REP-FL)
FORBES, J. RANDY (REP-VA)
FRELINGHUYSEN, RODNEY P. (REP-NJ)
HARPER, GREGG (REP-MS)
PALAZZO, STEVEN MCCARTY (REP-MS)
THORNBERRY, MAC (REP-TX)
WITTMAN, ROBERT J MR. (REP-VA)

Public Affairs and Related Activities Personnel

At Headquarters

APOSTOLOU, Carolyn Tel: (757) 380-2000
Vice President, Legislative Affairs
Registered Federal Lobbyist

BLAKE, Dwayne Tel: (757) 380-2104
Corporate Vice President, Investor Relations
investor.relations@hii-co.com

BRENTON, Beci Tel: (202) 264-7143
Corporate Director, Public Affairs
Beci.Brenton@hii-co.com

CHAWLK, Walter Tel: (757) 380-2000
Corporate Manager, Advertising and Marketing
Walter.Chawlk@hii-co.com

DICKSESKI, Jerri Fuller Tel: (757) 380-2000
Corporate Vice President, Communications Fax: (757) 380-3867
jerri.dickseski@hii-co.com

EBBS, William Tel: (757) 380-2000
Vice President Legislative Affairs

ERMATINGER, Bill Tel: (757) 380-2000
Corporate Vice President and Chief Human Resources Officer

HAWTHORNE, Bruce N. Tel: (757) 380-2000
Corporate Vice President and Chief Legal Officer Fax: (757) 380-4713

HICKS, Charles Andrew Tel: (757) 380-2000
Contact, Government Relations
Registered Federal Lobbyist

KASTNER, Christopher D. Tel: (757) 380-2000
Corporate Vice President and General Manager, Corporate
Development

MILLER, Christie Tel: (757) 380-3581
Manager, Media Relations
Christine.Miller@hii-co.com

SENTELL, Sandra Tel: (757) 380-2000

WALDMAN, Mitchell Tel: (757) 380-2000
Corporate Vice President Government and Customer Fax: (757) 380-4713
Relations

Registered Federal Lobbyist

WALKER, Kellye *Corporate Vice President and General Counsel*	Tel:	(757) 380-2000
WEST, Roger *Manager, Legislative Affairs and Federal Policy* *Registered Federal Lobbyist*	Tel:	(757) 380-2000

At Other Offices

COURTNEY, Peter *Federal Lobbyist* 300 M St. SE, Suite 350 Washington, DC 20003 *Registered Federal Lobbyist*	Tel:	(202) 264-7168
NILAND, Barbara A. *PAC Treasurer, Corporate Vice President, Business* *Management and Chief Financial Officer* 300 M St. SE, Suite 350 Washington, DC 20003	Tel:	(202) 264-7168

Huntsman Corporation

A global manufacturer and marketer of differentiated chemicals.
www.huntsman.com
Annual Revenues: $10.06 billion
Employees: 15,000
Ticker: NYSE: HUN
SIC: 2800
Industry/ies: Chemicals & Chemical Industry
Legislative Issues: CHM; FUE; TAX; TRD

Executive Chairman and Director

HUNTSMAN, Jon M.	Tel: Fax:	(281) 719-6000 (281) 719-6416

President, Chief Executive Officer and Director

HUNTSMAN, Peter R.	Tel: Fax:	(281) 719-6000 (281) 719-6416

Main Headquarters

Mailing:	10003 Woodloch Forest Dr. The Woodlands, TX 77380	Tel: Fax:	(281) 719-6000 (281) 719-6416

Political Action Committees

Huntsman L.L.C. PAC (HUNTSMAN PAC)
FEC ID: C00363838
Contact: Shaun J. Nail
10003 Woodlock Forest Dr.
Woodlands, TX 77380

Contributions to Candidates: $3,000 (2015-2016)
Republicans: $3,000

Corporate Foundations and Giving Programs

Huntsman Cancer Foundation
500 Huntsman Way
Salt Lake City, UT 84108

Public Affairs and Related Activities Personnel

At Headquarters

CHAPMAN, Gary *Vice President, Global Communications*	Tel: Fax:	(281) 719-4324 (281) 719-6416
DOUGLAS, Sean *Vice President, Corporate Development* sean_douglas@huntsman.com	Tel: Fax:	(281) 719-6000 (281) 719-6416
ESPLIN, J. Kimo *Executive Vice President and Chief Financial Officer*	Tel: Fax:	(281) 719-6000 (281) 719-6416
KELLER, Troy M. *Vice President, Government Affairs and Associate General* *Counsel*	Tel: Fax:	(281) 719-6000 (281) 719-6416
NAIL, Shaun J. *PAC Treasurer*	Tel: Fax:	(281) 719-6000 (281) 719-6416
OGDEN, Kurt D. *Vice President, Investor Relations*	Tel: Fax:	(281) 719-6000 (281) 719-6416
ROGERS, Wade R. *Senior Vice President, Global Human Resources*	Tel: Fax:	(281) 719-6000 (281) 719-6416
STOLLE, Russ R. *Senior Vice President, Deputy General Counsel*	Tel: Fax:	(281) 719-6000 (281) 719-6416
STRYKER, David *Executive Vice President, General Counsel, Chief Compliance* *Officer and Secretary*	Tel: Fax:	(281) 719-6000 (281) 719-6416

Hy-Vee, Inc.

A food and drug retailer.
www.hy-vee.com
Employees: 56,000
Industry/ies: Food And Beverage Industry
Legislative Issues: HCR; MMM

Main Headquarters

Mailing:	5820 Westown Pkwy. W. Des Moines, IA 50266-8223	Tel: Fax: TF:	(515) 267-2800 (515) 267-2817 (800) 289-8343

Political Action Committees

Hy-Vee Inc. Employees PAC
FEC ID: C00243659
Contact: John Ortner
5820 Westown Pkwy.
West Des Moines, IA 50266

Contributions to Candidates: $17,500 (2015-2016)
Republicans: $17,500

Corporate Foundations and Giving Programs

Hy-Vee Food Stores Inc. Corporate Giving Program
Contact: Lynn Hoskins

5820 Westown Pkwy. Des Moines, IA 50266	Tel:	(515) 267-2800

Public Affairs and Related Activities Personnel

At Headquarters

BRIGGS, John C. *Vice President*	Tel: Fax:	(515) 267-2800 (515) 267-2817
BRUMMIT, John *Assistant Treasurer* jbrummit@hy-vee.com	Tel: Fax:	(515) 267-2800 (515) 267-2817
HOSKINS , Lynn *Foundation Contact* lhoskins@hy-vee.com	Tel: Fax:	(515) 267-2915 (515) 267-2817
MCINTYRE-GRESKOVIAK, Tara *Manager, Human Resource*	Tel: Fax:	(515) 267-2800 (515) 267-2817
ORTNER, John *Contact, PAC*	Tel: Fax:	(515) 267-2800 (515) 267-2817

Hyatt Corporation

The company is one of the operators of luxury hotels and resorts with more than 450 managed, franchised, and owned properties in some 45 countries. Its core Hyatt Regency brand offers hospitality services targeted primarily to business travelers and upscale vacationers. The firm also operates the upscale, full service Hyatt, Grand Hyatt, and Andaz brands, as well as Park Hyatt (luxury), Hyatt Place (select service), and Hyatt Summerfield Suites (extended stay) brands.
www.hyatt.com
Annual Revenues: $2.55 billion
Employees: 45,000
Ticker: NYSE: H
SIC: 7011
Industry/ies: Travel/Tourism/Lodging

Chairman of the Board

PRITZKER, Thomas J.	Tel: Fax:	(312) 750-1234 (312) 750-8550

President, Chief Executive Officer and Director

HOPLAMAZIAN, Mark S. mark.hoplamazian@hyatt.com	Tel: Fax:	(312) 750-1234 (312) 750-8550

Main Headquarters

Mailing:	71 S. Wacker Dr. 12th Floor Chicago, IL 60606	Tel: Fax: TF:	(312) 750-1234 (312) 750-8550 (800) 323-7249

Corporate Foundations and Giving Programs

Hyatt Thrive
71 S. Wacker Dr.
Chicago, IL 60606

Public Affairs and Related Activities Personnel

At Headquarters

BANIKARIM, Maryam *Global Chief Marketing Officer*	Tel: Fax:	(312) 750-1234 (312) 750-8550
GRISMER, Patrick *Chief Financial Officer*	Tel: Fax:	(312) 750-1234 (312) 750-8550
REISS, Rena Hozore *General Counsel and Secretary*	Tel: Fax:	(312) 750-1234 (312) 750-8550
WALLIS, John *Senior Vice President*	Tel: Fax:	(312) 750-1234 (312) 750-8550
WEBB, Robert W.K. *Chief Human Resources Officer* robb.webb@hyatt.com	Tel: Fax:	(312) 750-1234 (312) 750-8550

Hydro Green Energy, LLC

A renewable energy development company. The company's project pipeline will result in the development of nearly 1,000 MW of clean, renewable energy.
www.hgenergy.com
Industry/ies: Energy/Electricity

Chairman of the Board, Executive Vice President, Technology and Founder

KROUSE, Wayne F. wayne@hgenergy.com	Tel: Fax:	(877) 556-6566 (713) 339-9537

President and Chief Executive Officer

MALEY, Michael P.	Tel: Fax:	(877) 556-6566 (713) 339-9537

mike@hgenergy.com

Main Headquarters
Mailing: 900 Oakmont Ln.   Tel: (877) 556-6566
            Suite 310   Fax: (630) 325-5145
            Westmont, IL 60559   TF: (877) 556-6566

Public Affairs and Related Activities Personnel

At Headquarters

HAMMOND, Michael J.   Tel: (877) 556-6566
Senior Vice President, Finance   Fax: (630) 325-5145

Hydrogen Energy International LLC
Provides electric services.
www.hydrogenenergy.com
Annual Revenues: $6.20 million
Employees: 25
Industry/ies: Chemicals & Chemical Industry; Energy/Electricity

Main Headquarters
Mailing: 30 Monument Sq., Suite 125
            Concord, MA 01742

Hyperdynamics Corporation
Oil and gas business.
www.hyperdynamics.com
Annual Revenues: $3 million
Employees: 17
Ticker: NYSE: HDY
SIC: 1311
Industry/ies: Energy/Electricity; Fuels See Coal, Gas, Oil, Petroleum; Natural Resources; Petroleum Industry

President and Chief Executive Officer   Tel: (713) 353-9400
LEONARD, Ray   Fax: (713) 353-9421

Main Headquarters
Mailing: 12012 Wickchester Ln.   Tel: (713) 353-9400
            Suite 475   Fax: (713) 353-9421
            Houston, TX 77079

Public Affairs and Related Activities Personnel

At Headquarters

AMORUSO, Paolo G.   Tel: (713) 353-9400
Vice President, Commercial and Legal Affairs Fax: (713) 353-9421

WESSON , David W.   Tel: (713) 353-9400
Vice President and Chief Financial Officer   Fax: (713) 353-9421

Hyundai Motor America
An automobile manufacturer. Parent company is Hyundai Motor Co. of Seoul, Korea.
www.hyundaiusa.com
Employees: 550
SIC: 5099; 9999; 9999; 5012
Industry/ies: Automotive Industry; Transportation
Legislative Issues: AUT; LBR; TAX; TRD

Main Headquarters
Mailing: P.O. Box 20850   Tel: (714) 965-3000
            Fountain Valley, CA 92728-0850   Fax: (714) 965-3149
                                       TF: (800) 826-2277

Washington Office
Mailing: 1600 L St. NW   Tel: (202) 296-5550
            Suite 620   Fax: (202) 296-6436
            Washington, DC 20036   TF: (800) 633-5151

Public Affairs and Related Activities Personnel

At Headquarters

FERRARA, Frank   Tel: (714) 965-3000
Executive Vice President, Corporate Planning and Customer   Fax: (714) 965-3149
Satisfaction

HOSFORD, Chris L.   Tel: (714) 965-3470
Executive Director, Corporate Communications   Fax: (714) 965-3149
chosford@hmausa.com

At Washington Office

CHO, Hyun R.   Tel: (202) 296-5550
Representative   Fax: (202) 296-6436
Registered Federal Lobbyist

EUM, Hong Seok   Tel: (202) 296-5550
Contact, Government Relations   Fax: (202) 296-6436

KIM, Kyoung Soo   Tel: (202) 296-5550
Director   Fax: (202) 296-6436

SPEAR, Christopher Thomas   Tel: (202) 296-5550
Vice President, Government Affairs   Fax: (202) 296-6436
Registered Federal Lobbyist

SPEAR, Chris   Tel: (202) 296-5550
Vice President, Government Affairs   Fax: (202) 296-6436

Registered Federal Lobbyist

WHEELER, Erin   Tel: (202) 296-5550
Manager, Government Affairs   Fax: (202) 296-6436
Registered Federal Lobbyist

Hyundai Technical Center, Inc.
The design, technology and engineering arm for all North American models of the Korean-based Hyundai-KIA Automotive Group.
www.hatci.com
Employees: 100
Industry/ies: Automotive Industry; Transportation

Main Headquarters
Mailing: 6800 Geddes Rd.   Tel: (734) 337-2500
            Superior Township, MI 48198   Fax: (734) 337-3168

Washington Office
Mailing: 1660 L St. NW   Tel: (202) 296-5550
            Suite 620
            Washington, DC 20036

Public Affairs and Related Activities Personnel

At Washington Office

MACLEOD, William William   Tel: (202) 296-5550
Senior Manager
bmacleod@hatci.com

TORIGIAN, Mark S.   Tel: (202) 296-5550

IAC
IAC is an interactive conglomerate operating in five sectors. The Internet conglomerate owns more than 50 brands, including search engine Ask.com, local guide Citysearch (part of advertising network CityGrid Media), dating site Match.com, and home service provider network ServiceMagic.
www.iac.com
Annual Revenues: $4.50 billion
Employees: 5,000
Ticker: NASDAQ: IACI
SIC: 5990
Industry/ies: Computer/Technology

Chairman and Senior Executive   Tel: (212) 314-7300
DILLER, Barry   Fax: (212) 314-7379

Chief Executive Officer and Chairman, The Match Group   Tel: (212) 314-7300
BLATT, Greg   Fax: (212) 314-7379

Chief Executive Officer   Tel: (212) 314-7300
LEVIN, Joey

Main Headquarters
Mailing: 555 W. 18th St.   Tel: (212) 314-7300
            New York City, NY 10011

Political Action Committees
InterActiveCorp PAC
FEC ID: C00371088
Contact: Nicholas Stoumpas
555 W. 18th St.
New York City, NY 10011

   Contributions to Candidates: $16,200 (2015-2016)
   Democrats: $16,200

Corporate Foundations and Giving Programs

The IAC Foundation
555 W. 18th St.   Tel: (212) 314-7300
New York City, NY 10011

Public Affairs and Related Activities Personnel

At Headquarters

SCHIFFMAN, Glenn H.   Tel: (212) 314-7300
Executive Vice President and Chief Financial Officer

SCHNEIDER, Mark   Tel: (212) 314-7400
Senior Vice President, Finance and Investor Relations

STEIN, Mark   Tel: (212) 314-7300
Executive Vice President and Chief Strategy Officer

STEWART, Jason   Tel: (212) 314-7300
Senior Vice President and Chief Administrative Officer

STOUMPAS, Nicholas   Tel: (212) 314-7300
Senior Vice President and PAC Treasurer
Nick.stoumpas@iac.com

WINIARSKI, Gregg   Tel: (212) 314-7300
Executive Vice President, General Counsel

IAP Worldwide Services, Inc.
Provider of global-scale logistics, facilities management, and advanced professional and technical services.
www.iapws.com
Annual Revenues: $304.70 million
Employees: 5,300

Industry/ies: Construction/Construction Materials
Legislative Issues: AVI; BUD; DEF

Chief Executive Officer and Director
KITANI, Douglas

Tel: (321) 784-7100
Fax: (321) 784-7336

Main Headquarters
Mailing: 7315 N. Atlantic Ave.
Cape Canaveral, FL 32920

Tel: (321) 784-7100
Fax: (321) 784-7336

Washington Office
Mailing: 2011 Crystal Dr.
Suite 903
Arlington, VA 22202

Tel: (703) 253-2800
Fax: (703) 920-1898

Political Action Committees
IAP Worldwide Services PAC
FEC ID: C00414425
Contact: Charles David Peiffer
7315 N. Atlantic Ave.
Cape Canaveral, FL 32920

Contributions to Candidates: $6,000 (2015-2016)
Democrats: $5,000; Republicans: $1,000

Public Affairs and Related Activities Personnel

At Headquarters

COOPER, Rochelle Shelly
Senior Vice President, General Counsel and Corporate Secretary

Tel: (321) 784-7100
Fax: (321) 784-7336

DEROSA, Terry
Executive Vice President and Chief Financial Officer

Tel: (321) 784-7100
Fax: (321) 784-7336

JERICH, Barbara
Vice President, Human Resources and Communications

Tel: (321) 784-7100
Fax: (321) 784-7336

NOHMER, Rick
Vice President, Operations

Tel: (321) 784-7100
Fax: (321) 784-7336

PEIFFER, Charles David
PAC Treasurer

Tel: (321) 784-7100
Fax: (321) 784-7336

THORNTON, Dale
Vice President, Business Development

Tel: (321) 784-7100
Fax: (321) 784-7336

Iberdrola Renewables

Energy project development, wholesale energy sales and natural gas storage.
www.iberdrolarenewables.us
Annual Revenues: $44.50 million
Employees: 200
Industry/ies: Energy/Electricity
Legislative Issues: BUD; COM; ENG; ENV; HOM; LBR; TAX; TRA

President and Chief Executive Officer
BURKHARTSMEYER, Frank

Tel: (503) 796-7000

Main Headquarters
Mailing: 1125 N.W. Couch St.
Portland, OR 97209

Washington Office
Mailing: 607 14th St. NW.
Suite 225
Washington, DC 20005

Public Affairs and Related Activities Personnel

At Headquarters

BAKSHI, Vikram
Vice President, Strategic Transactions

Tel: (503) 796-7000

CARROLL, Marni
Federal Lobbyist
Registered Federal Lobbyist

Tel: (503) 796-7000
Fax: (503) 796-6901

COPLEMAN, Paul
Communications Manager, US East
pcopleman@IberdrolaRen.com

Tel: (207) 351-3284
Fax: (503) 796-6901

CURREY, Ralph
Director, Board

Tel: (503) 796-7000
Fax: (503) 796-6901

GLICK, Rich A.
Vice President, Government Affairs
richard.glick@ppmenergy.com

Tel: (503) 796-7000
Fax: (503) 796-6901

JACOBSON, Scott
Vice President, Finance

Tel: (503) 796-7000

LACKEY, Ben
General Counsel

Tel: (503) 796-7000

LYNCH, Kevin A
Managing Director, External Affairs

Tel: (503) 796-7000

PERRYMAN, Mark
Vice President, Operations

Tel: (503) 796-7000

RAVIV, Rany
Vice President, Business Development

Tel: (503) 796-7000

SASSE, Art
Director, Communications and Brand

Tel: (503) 796-7740
Fax: (503) 796-6901

diana.scholtes@iberdrolaren.com

SCHWARTZ, Staci
Vice President, Human Resources

Tel: (503) 796-7000
Fax: (503) 796-6901

TAIT, Alex
Managing Director, Investment and Business Performance and Chief Compliance Officer

Tel: (503) 796-7000

At Washington Office

DEBOISSIERE, Alex
Registered Federal Lobbyist

ROBERTSON, Kelsey
Manager, Government Affairs
Registered Federal Lobbyist

At Other Offices

LEVIN, Elissa
Director, Federal Government Affairs
605 14th St. NW, Suite 225
Washington, DC 20005
Registered Federal Lobbyist

Iberdrola USA

Formerly known as East Energy Corporation. A regional energy services and delivery company. Subsidiaries include Central Maine Power Co., Connecticut Natural Gas Corp., New York State Electric & Gas Corp., Rochester Gas and Electric Corp., The Berkshire Gas Co., and The Southern Connecticut Gas Co.
www.iberdrolausa.com
Annual Revenues: $4.36 billion
Employees: 6,000
SIC: 4911
Industry/ies: Energy/Electricity

Chairman of the Board
GALAN, Ignacio Sanchez

Tel: (207) 688-6300
Fax: (207) 688-4354

Chief Executive Officer
KUMP, Robert D.

Tel: (207) 688-6300
Fax: (207) 688-4354

Main Headquarters
Mailing: 70 Farm View Dr.
New Gloucester, ME 04260

Tel: (207) 688-6300
Fax: (207) 688-4354

Political Action Committees
Iberdrola USA PAC
FEC ID: C00406801
Contact: Darlene E. Beach
52 Farm View Dr.
New Gloucester, ME 04260

Contributions to Candidates: $2,335,216 (2015-2016)
Democrats: $46,200; Republicans: $27,000; Other: $2,262,016

Corporate Foundations and Giving Programs
Iberdrola USA Contributions Program
52 Farm View Dr.
New Gloucester, ME 04260

Tel: (207) 688-6300
Fax: (207) 688-4354

Public Affairs and Related Activities Personnel

At Headquarters

ADAMS, Steven R.
Vice President, Regulatory Policy
steven.adams@iberdrolausa.com

Tel: (207) 688-6300
Fax: (207) 688-4354

BEACH, Darlene E.
PAC Treasurer and Lobbyist
darlene.beach@iberdrolausa.com

Tel: (207) 688-6300
Fax: (207) 688-4354

DICKINSON, Thorn
Vice President, Business Development
thorn.dickinson@iberdrolausa.com

Tel: (207) 688-6300
Fax: (207) 688-4354

HUCKO, Dan
Director, Communications
Daniel.Hucko@IberdrolaUSA.com

Tel: (585) 724-8825
Fax: (207) 688-4354

LAMOUREUX, Sheri
Vice President, Human Resources, Environmental, Health and Safety

Tel: (207) 688-6300
Fax: (207) 688-4354

MAHONEY, R. Scott
Vice President, General Counsel and Secretary
scott.mahoney@iberdrolausa.com

Tel: (207) 688-6300
Fax: (207) 688-4354

TORRES, Jose Maria
Vice President and Chief Financial Officer

Tel: (207) 688-6300
Fax: (207) 688-4354

Iberiabank Corporation

A banking company.
www.iberiabank.com
Annual Revenues: $646.05 million
Employees: 2,883
Ticker: NASDAQ: IBKC
SIC: 6022
Industry/ies: Banking/Finance/Investments

Chairman of the Board
FENSTERMAKER, William H.
Tel: (337) 521-4012
Fax: (337) 364-1171

President and Chief Executive Officer
BYRD, Daryl G.
Tel: (337) 521-4012
Fax: (337) 364-1171

Main Headquarters
Mailing: 200 W. Congress St.
12th Floor
Lafayette, LA 70501
Tel: (337) 521-4012
Fax: (337) 364-1171
TF: (800) 968-0801

Political Action Committees
Iberiabank Corporation FED PAC
FEC ID: C00406066
Contact: Patrick R. Vance
200 W. Congress St.
Lafayette, LA 70501
Tel: (337) 521-4012
Fax: (337) 364-1171

Contributions to Candidates: $17,500 (2015-2016)
Republicans: $17,500

Corporate Foundations and Giving Programs
Iberiabank Corporation Contribution Program
Contact: Elizabeth A. Ardoin
200 W. Congress St.
Lafayette, LA 70501
Tel: (337) 521-4012
Fax: (337) 364-1171

Public Affairs and Related Activities Personnel

At Headquarters

ARDOIN, Elizabeth A.
Senior Executive Vice President and Director, Communications, Facilities and Human Resources
Tel: (337) 521-4701
Fax: (337) 364-1171

BROWN, Michael J.
Vice Chairman, Chief Operating Officer
Tel: (337) 521-4012
Fax: (337) 364-1171

DAVIS, John R.
Senior Executive Vice President and Director, Financial Strategy
Tel: (337) 521-4012
Fax: (337) 364-1171

RESTEL, Anthony J.
Senior Executive Vice President and Chief Financial Officer and Treasurer
Tel: (337) 521-4012
Fax: (337) 364-1171

VANCE, Patrick R.
PAC Treasurer
Tel: (337) 521-4012
Fax: (337) 364-1171

WORLEY, Jr., Robert B.
Executive Vice President, Corporate Secretary and General Counsel
Tel: (337) 521-4012
Fax: (337) 364-1171

Icahn Associates LLC

A holding company.
www.ielp.com
Annual Revenues: $13.84 billions
Employees: 73,807
Ticker: NASDAQ: IEP
Industry/ies: Banking/Finance/Investments

Chairman of the Board
ICAHN, Carl C.
Tel: (212) 702-4380

Director; President and Chief Executive Officer
COZZA, Keith
Tel: (212) 702-4380

Main Headquarters
Mailing: 767 Fifth Ave.
Suite 4700
New York City, NY 10153
Tel: (212) 702-4380
TF: (800) 255-2737

Public Affairs and Related Activities Personnel

At Headquarters

CHO, SungHwan
Director and Chief Financial Officer
Tel: (212) 702-4300

RECK, Peter
Chief Accounting Officer
Tel: (212) 702-4380

SCHAITKIN, Keith
Associate General Counsel
Tel: (212) 702-4380

ICAP

Interdealer broker and provider of post trade risk and information services.
www.icap.com
Industry/ies: Banking/Finance/Investments
Legislative Issues: FIN

Managing Director and Chief Executive Officer
PAULHAC, Laurent
Tel: (212) 341-9900

Main Headquarters
Mailing: Harborside Financial Center
1100 Plaza Five
Jersey City, NJ 07311
Tel: (212) 341-9900

Political Action Committees
ICAP North America, Inc. PAC
FEC ID: C00555979

Contact: Glenn Worman
1100 Plaza Five
Harborside Financial Ctr.
Jersey City, 7922

Contributions to Candidates: $18,500 (2015-2016)
Democrats: $3,500; Republicans: $15,000

Public Affairs and Related Activities Personnel

At Headquarters

MCCARTY, Kevin Patrick
Federal Lobbyist
Registered Federal Lobbyist
Tel: (212) 341-9900

MCCARTY, Patrick
Registered Federal Lobbyist
Tel: (212) 341-9900

PIGAGA, Ken
Group Chief Operating Officer
Tel: (212) 341-9900

WALES, Duncan
Group General Counsel
Tel: (212) 341-9900

WEXLER, Stuart
General Counsel, Americas
stuart.wexler@us.icap.com
Tel: (212) 341-9900

WORMAN, Glenn
PAC Contact
Tel: (212) 341-9900

Ice Energy, Inc.

An energy technology company developing energy storage and advanced cooling and refrigeration products and technologies.
www.ice-energy.com
Annual Revenues: $5.50 million
Employees: 100
Industry/ies: Heating And Air Conditioning

Chief Executive Officer
HOPKINS, Mike
mhopkins@ice-energy.com
Tel: (970) 545-3630
Fax: (970) 545-3634

Main Headquarters
Mailing: 823 Milford St.
Glendale, CA 91203
Tel: (877) 542-3232
Fax: (818) 478-2287
TF: (877) 542-3232

Public Affairs and Related Activities Personnel

At Headquarters

MILLER, Greg
Executive Vice President, Market Development
gmiller@ice-energy.com
Tel: (877) 542-3232
Fax: (818) 478-2287

At Other Offices

MCNEIL, Brandon
Executive Vice President, Manufacturing and Operations
3 E. De La Guerra St.
Santa Barbara, CA 93101
bmcneil@ice-energy.com
Tel: (877) 542-3232

WHITE, James
Chief Financial Officer
3 E. De La Guerra St.
Santa Barbara, CA 93101
jwhite@ice-energy.com
Tel: (877) 542-3232

ICF International

A global professional services firm.
www.icfi.com
Annual Revenues: $1.14 Billion
Employees: 5,000
Ticker: NASDAQ: ICFI
SIC: 8742
Industry/ies: Computer/Technology; Economics And Economic Development; Education; Management

Chairman of the Board and Chief Executive Officer
KESAVAN, Sudhakar
Tel: (703) 934-3603
Fax: (703) 934-3740

Main Headquarters
Mailing: 9300 Lee Hwy.
Fairfax, VA 22031-1207
Tel: (703) 934-3603
Fax: (703) 934-3740
TF: (800) 532-4783

Corporate Foundations and Giving Programs
ICF International Contribution Program
9300 Lee Hwy.
Fairfax, VA 22031-1207
Tel: (703) 934-3603
Fax: (703) 934-3740

Public Affairs and Related Activities Personnel

At Headquarters

ANDERSON, Steve
Senior Director, Public Affairs and Government Relations
steve.anderson@icfi.com
Tel: (703) 934-3847
Fax: (703) 934-3740

BECK, Dr. Douglas
Tel: (703) 934-3603

Senior Consultant
dbeck@icfi.com
Fax: (703) 934-3740

DANIEL, James E.
Senior Vice President and General Counsel
Tel: (703) 934-3603
Fax: (703) 934-3740

LAFORCE, Colette
Senior Vice President and Chief Marketing Officer
Tel: (703) 934-3603
Fax: (703) 934-3740

MORGAN, James C.
Executive Vice President and Chief Financial Officer
Tel: (703) 934-3603
Fax: (703) 934-3740

REIFF, Isabel
Senior Consultant
Tel: (703) 934-3603
Fax: (703) 934-3740

SPEISER , Dr. David
Executive Vice President, Strategic Planning and Corporate development
Tel: (703) 934-3603
Fax: (703) 934-3740

WASSON, John
President and Chief Operating Officer
Tel: (703) 934-3603
Fax: (703) 934-3740

ID Analytics Inc.

An identity risk management company.
www.idanalytics.com
Annual Revenues: $10.20 million
Employees: 90
Industry/ies: Computer/Technology; Law Enforcement/Security

Chief Executive Officer
MCINTOSH, Larry
Tel: (858) 312-6200
Fax: (858) 451-9051

Main Headquarters
Mailing: 15253 Ave. of Science
San Diego, CA 92128
Tel: (858) 312-6200
Fax: (858) 451-9051
TF: (866) 248-7344

Public Affairs and Related Activities Personnel

At Headquarters

BARTLETT, Kellyn
Contact, Media and Analyst Inquiries
pr@idanalytics.com
Tel: (858) 312-6261
Fax: (858) 451-9051

CARTER, Scott
Chief Operating Officer
Tel: (858) 312-6200
Fax: (858) 451-9051

LAUGHLIN, Timothy
Chief Financial Officer
Tel: (858) 312-6200
Fax: (858) 451-9051

MCALUNEY, Matt
Senior Vice President, Sales
Tel: (858) 312-6200
Fax: (858) 451-9051

MCGEE, Karen
General Counsel and Privacy Officer
Tel: (858) 312-6200
Fax: (858) 451-9051

IDACORP Inc.

A holding company with operations in independent power production and affordable housing. Its mission is to be regarded as an exceptional company and earn profit by providing reliable, responsible, fair-priced energy services, today and tomorrow.
www.idacorpinc.com
Annual Revenues: $1.27 billion
Employees: 2,002
Ticker: NYSE: IDA
SIC: 4911
Industry/ies: Energy/Electricity
Legislative Issues: ENG

President and Chief Executive Officer
ANDERSON, Darrel T.
Tel: (208) 388-2200
Fax: (208) 388-6955

Main Headquarters
Mailing: 1221 W. Idaho St.
Boise, ID 83702-5627
Tel: (208) 388-2200
Fax: (208) 388-6955

Political Action Committees
IDA-PAC PAC
FEC ID: C00083832
Contact: Frances J. Martin
1220 W. Idaho St.
P.O. Box 70
Boise, ID 83707

   Contributions to Candidates: $14,500 (2015-2016)
   Democrats: $5,000; Republicans: $9,500

Public Affairs and Related Activities Personnel

At Headquarters

BLACKBURN, Rex
Senior Vice President and General Counsel
Tel: (208) 388-2200
Fax: (208) 388-6955

HARRINGTON, Patrick A.
Corporate Secretary
Tel: (208) 388-2200
Fax: (208) 388-6955

KEEN, Steve R.
Senior Vice President, Chief Financial Officer and Treasurer
Tel: (208) 388-2200
Fax: (208) 388-6955

KRAWL , Lonnie G.
Senior Vice President, Administrative Services and Chief Human Resources Officer
Tel: (208) 388-2200
Fax: (208) 388-6955

MALMEN, Jeffrey L.
Tel: (208) 388-2200

Vice President, Public Affairs
Registered Federal Lobbyist
Fax: (208) 388-6955

MARTIN, Frances J.
Senior Executive Assistant
fmartin@idahopower.com
Tel: (208) 388-2200
Fax: (208) 388-6955

MCCURDY, Stephanie
Specialist, Corporate Communication
smccurdy@idahopower.com
Tel: (208) 388-6973
Fax: (208) 388-6955

SPENCER, Lawrence F.
Director, Investor Relations
lspencer@idahopower.com
Tel: (208) 388-2664
Fax: (208) 388-6916

TATUM, Tim
Vice President, Regulatory Affairs
Tel: (208) 388-2200
Fax: (208) 388-6955

At Other Offices

PETERSEN, Ken
Vice President, Controller and Chief Accounting Officer
P.O. Box 70
Boise, ID 83707-0070
Tel: (208) 388-2200
Fax: (208) 388-6955

Idaho Power Company

Idaho Power lights up the potato farms and factories in southern Idaho and eastern Oregon. The utility provides electricity to about 492,000 residential, commercial, and industrial customers over nearly 32,000 miles of transmission and distribution lines. A subsidiary of IDACORP.
www.idahopower.com
Annual Revenues: $1.27 billion
Employees: 2,021
Ticker: NYSE: IDA
SIC: 4911
Industry/ies: Utilities
Legislative Issues: ENG

President and Chief Executive Officer
ANDERSON, Darrel T.
Tel: (208) 388-2200
Fax: (208) 388-6955

Main Headquarters
Mailing: 1221 W. Idaho St.
Boise, ID 83702
Tel: (208) 388-2200
Fax: (208) 388-6955

Corporate Foundations and Giving Programs

Idaho Power Contributions Program
1221 W. Idaho St.
Boise, ID 83702
Tel: (208) 388-2200
Fax: (208) 388-2200

Public Affairs and Related Activities Personnel

At Other Offices

BLACKBURN, Rex
Senior Vice President and General Counsel
P.O. Box 70
Boise, ID 83707
Tel: (208) 388-2200
Fax: (208) 388-6955

FOLEY, Michael
Director, Corporate Communications, Marketing and Creative Services
P.O. Box 70
Boise, ID 83707
mfoley@idahopower.com
Tel: (208) 388-2200
Fax: (208) 388-6955

HARRINGTON, Patrick A.
Corporate Secretary
P.O. Box 70
Boise, ID 83707
pharrington@idahopower.com
Tel: (208) 388-2200
Fax: (208) 388-6955

KEEN, Steve R.
Senior Vice President, Chief Financial Officer and Treasurer
P.O. Box 70
Boise, ID 83707
Tel: (208) 388-2200
Fax: (208) 388-6955

MALMEN, Jeffrey L.
Vice President, Public Affairs
P.O. Box 70
Boise, ID 83707
jmalmen@idahopower.com
Tel: (208) 388-2200
Fax: (208) 388-6955

MCCURDY, Stephanie
Contact, Media Relations
P.O. Box 70
Boise, ID 83707
smccurdy@idahopower.com
Tel: (208) 388-6973
Fax: (208) 388-6955

MCDONALD, Luci K.
Vice President, Human Resources and Corporate Services
P.O. Box 70
Boise, ID 83707
Tel: (208) 388-2200
Fax: (208) 388-6955

SAID, Gregory W.
Vice President, Regulatory Affairs
P.O. Box 70
Boise, ID 83707
Tel: (208) 388-2200
Fax: (208) 388-6955

Idexx Laboratories, Inc.

Provides diagnostic testing systems and drugs for pets and livestock.
www.idexx.com
Annual Revenues: $1.64 billion
Employees: 6,800
Ticker: NASDAQ: IDXX
SIC: 3841; 2835
NAICS: 339112
Industry/ies: Animals; Medicine/Health Care/Mental Health; Science; Scientific Research

Chairman of the Board, President and Chief Executive Officer Tel: (207) 556-0300
AYERS, Jonathan W. Fax: (207) 556-4346

Main Headquarters
Mailing: One IDEXX Dr. Tel: (207) 556-0300
Westbrook, ME 04092 Fax: (207) 556-4346
TF: (800) 548-6733

Public Affairs and Related Activities Personnel

At Headquarters

MCKEON, Brian P. Tel: (207) 556-0300
Executive Vice President and Chief Financial Officer Fax: (207) 556-4346
REID, Bonnie Tel: (207) 556-0300
Specialist, Investor Relations Fax: (207) 556-4346
STUDER , Jacqueline L. Tel: (207) 556-0300
Corporate Vice President, General Counsel and Secretary Fax: (207) 556-4346
TWIGGE , Giovani Tel: (207) 556-0300
Corporate Vice President and Chief Human Resources Officer Fax: (207) 556-4346
giovani-twigge@idexx.com

iDirect Technologies, Inc.

Designs, develops and markets the industries top satellite-based broadband access solutions. Its satellite-based IP communications technology enables constant connectivity for voice, video and data applications in diverse and challenging environments.
www.idirect.net
Annual Revenues: $100 million
Employees: 600
Industry/ies: Communications; Computer/Technology; Telecommunications/Internet/Cable

Chief Executive Officer Tel: (703) 648-8000
COTTON, Mary Fax: (703) 648-8014

Main Headquarters
Mailing: 13865 Sunrise Valley Dr. Tel: (703) 648-8000
Suite 100 Fax: (703) 648-8014
Herndon, VA 20171 TF: (866) 345-0983

Public Affairs and Related Activities Personnel

At Headquarters

BETTINGER, Julie Tel: (703) 648-8155
Vice President, Corporate Marketing Fax: (703) 648-8015
jbettinger@idirect.net
CAHOON, Amy B. Tel: (703) 648-8000
Vice President, Human Resources Fax: (703) 648-8014
GRIFFLER, Dean Tel: (703) 648-8000
Senior Vice President, Global Sales Fax: (703) 648-8014
NOREM, Chris Tel: (703) 648-8000
Chief Financial Officer Fax: (703) 648-8014
RUDNICKI , Toni Lee Tel: (703) 648-8000
Chief Marketing Officer Fax: (703) 648-8014
STEEN, Kevin Tel: (703) 648-8000
Chief Operating Officer Fax: (703) 648-8014

IDT Corporation

A communications and media company. It provides retail domestic and international long-distance access mainly in the US, as well as wholesale voice and data services.
www.idt.net
Annual Revenues: $1.53 billion
Employees: 1,230
Ticker: NYSE: IDT
SIC: 4813
Industry/ies: Communications; Telecommunications/Internet/Cable

Chief Executive Officer, President and Co-Chairman Tel: (973) 438-1000
PEREIRA, Bill Fax: (973) 482-3971

Chief Executive Officer Tel: (973) 438-1000
JONAS, Samuel (Shmuel) Fax: (973) 482-3971

Main Headquarters
Mailing: 520 Broad St. Tel: (973) 438-1000
Newark, NJ 07102 Fax: (973) 482-3971

Washington Office
Mailing: 1150 18th St. NW Tel: (202) 367-7600
Suite 501 Fax: (202) 296-2983
Washington, DC 20036

Political Action Committees

IDT Corporation PAC (IDT PAC)
FEC ID: C00367383
Contact: William B. Ulrey
520 Broad St.
Newark, NJ 07102

Contributions to Candidates: $22,700 (2015-2016)
Republicans: $22,700

Corporate Foundations and Giving Programs

IDT Corporation Contributions Program
520 Broad St. Tel: (973) 438-1000
Newark, NJ 07102

Public Affairs and Related Activities Personnel

At Headquarters

ASH, Menachem Tel: (973) 438-1000
Executive Vice President, Strategy and Legal Affairs Fax: (973) 482-3971
FISCHER , Marcelo Tel: (973) 438-1000
Senior Vice President, Finance Fax: (973) 482-3971
MASON, Joyce J. Tel: (973) 438-1000
Executive Vice President, General Counsel and Corporate Secretary Fax: (973) 482-3971
SILBERMAN, Mitch Tel: (973) 438-1000
Chief Accounting Officer and Controller Fax: (973) 482-3971
ULREY, William B. Tel: (973) 438-3838
Contact, Investor Relations and PAC Treasurer Fax: (973) 482-3971
william.ulrey@idt.net

IGOV, Inc.

iGov offers a full line of IT products; security, storage, wireless, and networking iSolutions consulting practices; and asset information management solutions.
www.igov.com
Employees: 100
Industry/ies: Defense/Homeland Security; Government-Related

Chief Executive Officer and Chairman of the Board Tel: (703) 356-1160
NEVEN, Patrick Fax: (703) 356-2023

Main Headquarters
Mailing: 12030 Sunrise Valley Dr. Tel: (703) 356-1160
Suite 300 Fax: (703) 356-2023
Reston, VA 20191

Corporate Foundations and Giving Programs

IGOV, Inc. Contribution Programs
8200 Greensboro Dr. Tel: (703) 777-9375
Suite 1200 Fax: (703) 356-2023
McLean, VA 22102

Public Affairs and Related Activities Personnel

At Headquarters

HAMRIC , Steve Tel: (703) 356-1160
Chief Financial Officer Fax: (703) 356-2023
HUPALO, Walter Tel: (703) 356-1160
Co-Founder and Senior Vice President, Corporate Development Fax: (703) 356-2023
POOLEY, Jack Tel: (703) 356-1160
Senior Vice President, Sales Fax: (703) 356-2023
jpooley@igov.com
REICHE, Chuck Tel: (703) 356-1160
Corporate Vice-President, Business Development Fax: (703) 356-2023
SCHMITT, Kim Tel: (703) 356-1160
Vice President, Human Resources Fax: (703) 356-2023
kschmitt@igov.com
TYRRELL, Mike Tel: (703) 356-1160
President and Chief Operating Officer Fax: (703) 356-2023

II-VI Incorporated

Develops, refines, manufactures, and markets engineered materials and opto-electronic components and products worldwide. II-VI Incorporated and its divisions and subsidiaries utilize expertise in synthetic crystal materials growth, optics fabrication, electronics component manufacture, and more to create high-tech products for a wide range of applications and industries.
www.ii-vi.com
Annual Revenues: $733.20 million
Employees: 6,796
Ticker: NASDAQ: IIVI
SIC: 3827; 3823; 3841; 3851; 5048
Industry/ies: Defense/Homeland Security; Government-Related
Legislative Issues: DEF

Co-founder and Chairman of the Board Tel: (724) 352-4455
JOHNSON, Dr. Carl J. Fax: (724) 352-5284

President and Chief Executive Officer Tel: (724) 352-4455
KRAMER, Francis J. Fax: (724) 352-5284

Main Headquarters

Mailing: 375 Saxonburg Blvd.   Tel: (724) 352-4455
Saxonburg, PA 16056-9499   Fax: (724) 352-5284

Political Action Committees
II-VI Incorporated PAC
FEC ID: C00377960
Contact: Timothy A. Challingsworth
375 Saxonburg Blvd.
Saxonburg, PA 16056

Contributions to Candidates: $14,200 (2015-2016)
Republicans: $14,200

Public Affairs and Related Activities Personnel

At Headquarters

CHALLINGSWORTH, Timothy A.   Tel: (724) 352-4455
Director, Corporate Research and Development and Business   Fax: (724) 352-5284
Development

MATTERA, Jr., Vincent D. (Chuck)   Tel: (724) 352-4455
President, Chief Operating Officer and Director   Fax: (724) 352-5284

RAYMOND, Mary Jane   Tel: (724) 352-4455
Chief Financial Officer and Treasurer   Fax: (724) 352-5284
mjraymond@ii-vi.com

IIT Engineered For Life

A manufacturer of engineered critical components and customized technology solutions for the energy, transportation and industrial markets. A subsidiary of the ITT Corporation.
www.itt.com
Industry/ies: Automotive Industry; Defense/Homeland Security; Electricity & Electronics; Electronics; Energy/Electricity; Government-Related; Transportation

Chief Executive Officer and President   Tel: (914) 641-2000
RAMOS , Denise   Fax: (914) 696-2950

Main Headquarters
Mailing: 1133 Westchester Ave.   Tel: (914) 641-2000
White Plains, NY 10604   Fax: (914) 696-2950

Washington Office
Mailing: 1650 Tysons Blvd.
Suite 1700
McLean, VA 22102

Political Action Committees
Exelis Inc. Employees PAC
FEC ID: C00141002
Contact: Andrew Renauld
1650 Tysons Blvd., Suite 1700   Tel: (703) 790-6300
McLean, VA 22102-4827   Fax: (703) 790-6365

Contributions to Candidates: $53,500 (2015-2016)
Democrats: $21,000; Republicans: $32,500

Public Affairs and Related Activities Personnel

At Headquarters

CREAMER, Vicky   Tel: (914) 641-2000
Chief Human Resources Officer   Fax: (914) 696-2950

FEALING, Burt   Tel: (914) 641-2000
Executive Vice President, General Counsel and Corporate   Fax: (914) 696-2950
Secretary

GUSTAFSSON, Mary Beth   Tel: (914) 641-2000
General Counsel and Chief Compliance Officer   Fax: (914) 696-2950

SCALERA, Tom   Tel: (914) 641-2000
Senior Vice President and Chief Financial Officer   Fax: (914) 696-2950

At Washington Office

DUGAN, Phaedra

GERNHARDT, Gary
Vice President

PATTERSON , Ian
Vice President, Government Relations

RENAULD, Andrew
PAC Treasurer

RIZZO, Lee

SCHRAMEK, Mark

STERNER, Suzy
Director, Government Relations

SYERS, William A.
Vice-President, Congressional Relations

Illinois Tool Works

ITW manufactures and services equipment used in the automotive, construction, electronics, food and beverage, packaging, power system, and pharmaceutical industries.
www.itw.com
Annual Revenues: $14.26 billion
Employees: 49,000
Ticker: NYSE: ITW
SIC: 3089; 3544; 3545; 3565; 3452

Industry/ies: Machinery/Equipment
Legislative Issues: CPT; ENV; MAN; TAX

Chairman, Chief Executive Officer   Tel: (847) 724-7500
SANTI, E. Scott   Fax: (847) 657-4261

Director   Tel: (847) 724-7500
MORRISON, Robert S.   Fax: (847) 657-4261

Main Headquarters
Mailing: 155 Harlem Ave.   Tel: (847) 724-7500
Glenview, IL 60025   Fax: (847) 657-4261

Washington Office
Mailing: 1725 I St. NW
Suite 300
Washington, DC 20006

Political Action Committees
Illinois Tool Works For Better Government Committee PAC
FEC ID: C00000042
Contact: Michael J. Lynch II
3600 W. Lake Ave.   Tel: (847) 724-7500
Glenview, IL 60026

Corporate Foundations and Giving Programs
Illinois Tool Works Foundation
3600 W. Lake Ave.   Tel: (847) 724-7500
Glenview, IL 60026   Fax: (847) 724-7500

Public Affairs and Related Activities Personnel

At Headquarters

BROOKLIER, John L.   Tel: (847) 657-4104
Vice President, Investor Relations   Fax: (847) 657-4268

DONNELLY, Alison   Tel: (847) 657-4565
Director Communications, Investor relation   Fax: (847) 657-4261
adonnelly@itw.com

GREEN, Maria C.   Tel: (847) 724-7500
Senior Vice President, General Counsel and Secretary   Fax: (847) 657-4261

LARSEN, Michael M.   Tel: (847) 724-7500
Senior Vice President and Chief Financial Officer   Fax: (847) 657-4261

LAWLER, Mary K.   Tel: (847) 724-7500
Senior Vice President, Chief Human Resources Officer   Fax: (847) 657-4261

SMITH, Karen   Tel: (847) 724-7500
President   Fax: (847) 657-4261

WASHINGTON, Kevin   Tel: (847) 724-7500
Federal Lobbyist   Fax: (847) 657-4261
Registered Federal Lobbyist

At Other Offices

LYNCH, II, Michael J.
Vice President, Government Affairs
3600 W. Lake Ave.
Glenview, IL 60026
mlynch@htg.net

Imagetree Corporation

A forest resource management company.
geodigital.com
Industry/ies: Computer/Technology; Forestry

Chairman of the Board   Tel: (805) 740-0077
UNGERER, Scott   Fax: (805) 740-4977

President and Chief Executive Officer   Tel: (805) 740-0077
WARRINGTON, Chris   Fax: (805) 740-4977

Main Headquarters
Mailing: 137 W.Central Ave.   Tel: (805) 740-0077
Lompoc, CA 93436   Fax: (805) 740-4977

Public Affairs and Related Activities Personnel

At Headquarters

BRAATVEDT, James   Tel: (805) 740-0077
Chief Marketing Officer   Fax: (805) 740-4977

SCURR, Liza   Tel: (805) 740-0077
Vice President, Human Resources   Fax: (805) 740-4977

STELZ, Bill   Tel: (805) 740-0077
Executive Vice President, Sales   Fax: (805) 740-4977

Imation Corporation

A manufacturer of data storage and removable media products.
www.imation.com/en-US
Annual Revenues: $729.50 million
Employees: 910
Ticker: NYSE: IMN
SIC: 3695
NAICS: 333293
Industry/ies: Engineering/Mathematics

Non-Executive Chairman of the Board
MATTHEWS, L. White

Tel: (651) 704-4000
Fax: (651) 704-4200

President and Chief Executive Officer
LUCAS, Mark E.

Tel: (651) 704-4000
Fax: (651) 704-4200

Main Headquarters
Mailing: One Imation Way
Oakdale, MN 55128-3421

Tel: (651) 704-4000
Fax: (651) 704-4200
TF: (888) 466-3456

Corporate Foundations and Giving Programs

Imation Corporation Contributions Program
Contact: Tonnja Magee
One Imation Way
Oakdale, MN 55128

Public Affairs and Related Activities Personnel

At Headquarters

BREEDLOVE, John P.
Vice President, General Counsel and Corporate Secretary

Tel: (651) 704-4000
Fax: (651) 704-4200

ELLIS, James C.
Vice President, Global OEM Business

Tel: (651) 704-4000
Fax: (651) 704-4200

HERRLEIN, Timothy P.
Executive Director, Human Resources

Tel: (651) 704-4000
Fax: (651) 704-4200

MAGEE, Tonnja
Specialist, Human Resource Program Services
Tlmagee@imation.com

Tel: (651) 704-3280
Fax: (651) 704-7029

ROBINSON, Scott
Vice President, Chief Financial Officer

Tel: (651) 704-4000
Fax: (651) 704-4200

SPRENGER, Jason
Contact, Communications
media@imation.com

Tel: (651) 704-4000
Fax: (651) 704-4200

IMCORP

IMCORP is a provider of underground power cable reliability enhancement solutions.
www.imcorp.com
Annual Revenues: $1.8 million
Industry/ies: Energy/Electricity

Chief Technical Officer and Chief Executive Officer
MASHIKAN, Matthew

Tel: (860) 427-7620
Fax: (860) 427-7619

Main Headquarters
Mailing: 50 Utopia Rd.
Manchester, CT 06042

Tel: (860) 783-8000

Public Affairs and Related Activities Personnel

At Headquarters

MODOS, Dave
Director
dave.modos@imcorptech.com

Tel: (860) 783-8000

IMI Services USA, Inc.

A manufacturer of defense products.
www.imi-israel.com
Industry/ies: Defense/Homeland Security; Government-Related
Legislative Issues: AER; DEF

President & Chief Executive Officer
FELDER, Avi

Tel: (301) 215-4800
Fax: (301) 657-1446

Main Headquarters
Mailing: 7910 Woodmont Ave.
Suite 1410
Bethesda, MD 20814

Tel: (301) 215-4800
Fax: (301) 657-1446

Public Affairs and Related Activities Personnel

At Headquarters

SHECHTER, Avraham
President

Tel: (301) 215-4800
Fax: (301) 657-1446

Imperial Machine and Tool Company

Manufacturers of electrical measuring instruments and industrial machinery. Precision Engineered Technologies, LLC ("Precision"), precision machining platform company of Joshua Partners acquired Imperial Machine and Tool Company ("Imperial" or the "Company") in July 2013.
www.imperialmachine.com
Annual Revenues: $4.20 million
Industry/ies: Defense/Homeland Security; Government-Related; Machinery/Equipment

President and Chief Executive Officer
JOEST, Chris

Tel: (908) 496-8100
Fax: (908) 496-8102

Main Headquarters
Mailing: Eight W. Crisman Rd.
Columbia, NJ 07832

Tel: (908) 496-8100
Fax: (908) 496-8102

Public Affairs and Related Activities Personnel

At Headquarters

CLIFFORD, Michael
Director, Operations

Tel: (908) 496-8100
Fax: (908) 496-8102

GOLEMBESKI, Tom
Chief Financial Officer

Tel: (908) 496-8100
Fax: (908) 496-8102

JOEST, Christian G.
Contact, Business Development

Tel: (908) 496-8100
Fax: (908) 496-8102

MASKER, Sharon
Office Manager & Administrative Assistant to the CEO

Tel: (908) 496-8100
Fax: (908) 496-8102

Imperial Sugar Company

A domestic refiner and processor of refined sugar.
www.imperialsugarcompany.com
Annual Revenues: $847.98 million
Employees: 500
Ticker: NASDAQ: IPSU
SIC: 2062; 2063
NAICS: 311312; 311313
Industry/ies: Food And Beverage Industry

Main Headquarters
Mailing: Three Sugar Creek Center Blvd.
Suite 500
Sugar Land, TX 77478

Tel: (281) 491-9181
Fax: (281) 490-9530
TF: (800) 727-8427

Corporate Foundations and Giving Programs

Imperial Sugar Company Contributions Program
Three Sugar Creek Center Blvd.
Suite 500
Sugar Land, TX 77478

Tel: (281) 491-9181
Fax: (281) 490-9530

Public Affairs and Related Activities Personnel

At Headquarters

MELCHER, Hal
Senior Vice President and Chief Financial Officer
hal.melcher@imperialsugar.com

Tel: (281) 490-9652
Fax: (281) 490-9530

IMS Health Inc.

Provides sales management and market research services to clients in the pharmaceutical and health care industries.
www.imshealth.com
Annual Revenues: $2.63 billion
Employees: 10,200
Ticker: NYSE: IMS
SIC: 7374
Industry/ies: Medicine/Health Care/Mental Health
Legislative Issues: HCR

Chairman of the Board and Chief Executive Officer
BOUSBIB, Ari

Tel: (203) 448-4600

Main Headquarters
Mailing: 83 Wooster Heights Rd.
Danbury, CT 06810

Tel: (203) 448-4600

Washington Office
Mailing: 228 S. Washington St.
Suite 115
Alexandria, VA 22314

Tel: (203) 319-4700
TF: (877) 530-8879

Political Action Committees
IMS Health PAC
FEC ID: C00445387
Contact: Keith A. Davis
228 S. Washington St.
Suite 115
Alexandria, VA 22314

Corporate Foundations and Giving Programs

IMS Health Contributions Program
83 Wooster Heights Rd.
Danbury, CT 06810

Tel: (203) 448-4600

Public Affairs and Related Activities Personnel

At Headquarters

ASHMAN, Harvey A.
Senior Vice President, General Counsel and External Affairs

Tel: (203) 448-4600

BHANGDIA, Harshan
Vice President, Controller and Principal Accounting Officer

Tel: (203) 448-4600

BRUEHLMAN, Ronald
Senior Vice President and Chief Financial Officer

Tel: (203) 448-4600

GATYAS, Gary J.
Director, Public Relations
ggatyas@us.imshealth.com

Tel: (610) 834-5338

GUENAULT, Karl
Chief Information Officer and Vice President, Operations

Tel: (203) 448-4600

KINSLEY, Thomas

Tel: (203) 448-4600

Vice President, Financial Planning and Analysis and Investor Relations

LINN, Stefan	Tel:	(203) 448-4600

Senior Vice President, Strategy and Global Pharma Solutions

PECK, Darcie	Tel:	(203) 845-5237

Vice President, Finance and Investor Relations
dpeck@imshealth.com

WOLFE, Clint	Tel:	(203) 448-4600

Vice President, Human Resources

Independence Blue Cross Family of Companies

A health insurer.
www.ibx.com
Annual Revenues: $512.80 Million
Employees: 9,500
Industry/ies: Insurance Industry; Medicine/Health Care/Mental Health

Chairman of the Board	Tel:	(215) 241-2920
D'ALESSIO, M. Walter		

President and Chief Executive Officer	Tel:	(215) 241-2920
HILFERTY, Daniel J.		

Main Headquarters

Mailing:	1901 Market St.	Tel:	(215) 241-2920
	36th Floor		
	Philadelphia, PA 19103-1480		

Political Action Committees
Independence Blue Cross PAC (IBC PAC)
FEC ID: C00450056

1901 Market St.	Tel:	(215) 636-9559
38th Floor	Fax:	(215) 241-0403
Philadelphia, PA 19103		

Contributions to Candidates: $47,150 (2015-2016)
Democrats: $18,000; Republicans: $29,150

Corporate Foundations and Giving Programs
Independence Blue Cross (Pennsylvania) Caring Foundation
Contact: Lorina Marshall-Blake

1901 Market St.	Tel:	(215) 636-9559
38th Floor	Fax:	(215) 241-0403
Philadelphia, PA 19103		

Public Affairs and Related Activities Personnel

At Headquarters

BROWN, Royal E.	Tel:	(215) 241-2920

PAC Treasurer
royal.brown@ibx.com

DRENAN, Meghan	Tel:	(215) 241-2920

Associate Director, Federal Government Relations

FERA, Stephen P.	Tel:	(215) 241-2920

Vice President, Government Programs and Social Mission Programs
Stephen.fera@ibx.com

HUTTON, Thomas	Tel:	(215) 241-2920

Senior Vice President, General Counsel and Corporate Secretary

KRIGSTEIN, Alan	Tel:	(215) 241-2920

Executive Vice President, Chief Financial Officer, and Treasurer

LOPEZ , Juan R.	Tel:	(215) 241-2920

PAC Treasurer

MARSHALL-BLAKE, Lorina	Tel:	(215) 241-2920

Vice President, Government Relations and President, Independence Blue Cross Foundation
lorina.marshall@ibx.com

THOMAS, Judimarie	Tel:	(215) 241-2920

Senior Director, External Affairs

TUFANO, Paul A.	Tel:	(215) 241-2920

Executive Vice President and President, Government Markets
paul.tufano@ibx.com

UDVARHELYI, MD, I. Steven	Tel:	(215) 241-2920

Executive Vice President, Health Services and Chief Strategy Officer

Independence Mining Company, Inc.

See listing on page 65 under AngloGold Ashanti North America, Inc.

Independent Health Association, Inc.

A not-for-profit organization that provides a range of health insurance and related products to some 375,000 members primarily in western New York (it's licensed in 35 states).
www.independenthealth.com
Employees: 900
Industry/ies: Medicine/Health Care/Mental Health

President and Chief Executive Officer	Tel:	(716) 631-5392
CROPP, MBA, MD, Michael W.	Fax:	(716) 631-0430

Main Headquarters

Mailing:	511 Farber Lakes Dr.	Tel:	(716) 631-3001
	Buffalo, NY 14221	Fax:	(716) 631-0430
		TF:	(800) 453-1910

Political Action Committees
Independent Health Association Inc. Political Alliance PAC
FEC ID: C00323758
Contact: Sidney N. Weiss
2495 Kensington Ave.
Buffalo, NY 14226

Contributions to Candidates: $7,000 (2015-2016)
Democrats: $5,000; Republicans: $2,000

Corporate Foundations and Giving Programs

Independent Health Foundation		
511 Farber Lakes Dr.	Tel:	(716) 631-5392
Buffalo, NY 14221		

Public Affairs and Related Activities Personnel

At Headquarters

CLABEAUX, Patricia	Tel:	(716) 631-3001
	Fax:	(716) 631-0430

Senior Vice President, Human Resources and Organizational Development

JOHNSON, Mark	Tel:	(716) 631-3001
	Fax:	(716) 631-0430

Executive Vice President and Chief Finance Officer

MINEO, John	Tel:	(716) 631-3001
	Fax:	(716) 631-0430

Executive Vice President, General Counsel

RODGERS, John	Tel:	(716) 631-3001
	Fax:	(716) 631-0430

Executive Vice President, Chief Operating Officer

SAVA, Frank	Tel:	(716) 635-3885
	Fax:	(716) 631-0430

Director, Corporate Communications
fsava@independenthealth.com

At Other Offices

WEISS, Sidney N.
PAC Treasurer
2495 Kensington Ave.
Buffalo, NY 14226

Indiana University Health, Inc.

A nonprofit healthcare center and a unique partnership with Indiana University School of Medicine, one of the leading medical schools, giving patients access to innovative treatments and therapies.
iuhealth.org
Employees: 29,395
Industry/ies: Medicine/Health Care/Mental Health
Legislative Issues: BUD; HCR; MMM; TAX

President and Chief Executive Officer	Tel:	(317) 963-7988
MURPHY, Dennis	Fax:	(317) 963-5394

Main Headquarters

Mailing:	I-65 AT 21ST St.	Tel:	(317) 963-7988
	P.O. Box 1367	Fax:	(317) 963-5394
	Indianapolis, IN 46206		

Corporate Foundations and Giving Programs
IU Health Contributions Program
1701 N. Senate Blvd.
Indianapolis, IN 46202

Public Affairs and Related Activities Personnel

At Headquarters

CASTOR, J. Victoria	Tel:	(317) 963-7988
	Fax:	(317) 963-5394

Vice President, Government Affairs
Registered Federal Lobbyist

GATMAITAN, Al	Tel:	(317) 963-7988
	Fax:	(317) 963-5394

Executive Vice President and Chief Operating Officer

KITCHELL, Ryan C.	Tel:	(317) 963-7988
	Fax:	(317) 963-5394

Executive Vice President and Chief Administrative Officer

LINDER, Jeffrey	Tel:	(312) 962-9779
	Fax:	(317) 963-5394

Vice President, Government Relations
Registered Federal Lobbyist

MILLS, Jon M.	Tel:	(317) 982-3193
	Fax:	(317) 963-5394

Director, Corporate Public Relations
jmills3@clarian.org
Registered Federal Lobbyist

Indianapolis Motor Speedway

Owner and operator of a 2.5 mile race track.
www.indianapolismotorspeedway.com
Annual Revenues: $14.70 million
Employees: 200

Industry/ies: Automotive Industry; Sports/Leisure/Entertainment; Transportation

Chairman of the Board   Tel: (317) 481-8500
HULMAN GEORGE, Mari

Main Headquarters
Mailing: 4790 W. 16th St.   Tel: (317) 492-8500
Indianapolis, IN 46222

Indra Systems Inc.
Indra Systems Inc is in the design and manufacture of training systems, automated test equipment, and ticketing and transportation solutions.
www.indra-systems.com
Annual Revenues: $15.60 million
Employees: 100
Industry/ies: Defense/Homeland Security; Government-Related
Legislative Issues: DEF

Chief Executive Officer   Tel: (407) 673-1500
HUNT, Bill   Fax: (407) 673-1510

Main Headquarters
Mailing: 6969 University Blvd.   Tel: (407) 673-1500
Winter Park, FL 32792-6713   Fax: (407) 673-1510

Public Affairs and Related Activities Personnel

At Headquarters

MOSES, Melanie   Tel: (407) 673-1500
Director, Finance   Fax: (407) 673-1510

Industrial Defender, Inc.
The company offers security software designed to monitor and protect the control systems of industrial operations such as pipelines and power plants.
www.industrialdefender.com
Annual Revenues: $12.80 million
Employees: 100
Industry/ies: Computer/Technology

Main Headquarters
Mailing: 225 Foxborough Blvd.   Tel: (508) 718-6700
Foxborough, MA 02035   Fax: (508) 718-6701

Public Affairs and Related Activities Personnel

At Headquarters

LEGELIS, Kim   Tel: (508) 718-6700
Vice President, Marketing   Fax: (508) 718-6701
klegelis@industrialdefender.com

At Other Offices

RILEY, John   Tel: (508) 718-6700
Contact, Media   Fax: (508) 718-6701
16 Chestnut St., Suite 300
Foxborough, MA 02035
jriley@industrialdefender.com

Industrial Origami, Inc.
Provider of sheet material manufacturing design solutions. Its technology allows thinner sheet material to be folded into complex, innovative, high load-bearing structures with simple, low cost fixtures, at the point of assembly.
www.industrialorigami.com
Annual Revenues: $2.10 million
Industry/ies: Computer/Technology

Chairman of the Board   Tel: (440) 260-0000
FISHKIN, Stan   Fax: (440) 260-0015

President and Chief Executive Officer   Tel: (440) 260-0000
CORRIGAN, V. Gerry   Fax: (440) 260-0015

Main Headquarters
Mailing: 6755 Engle Rd.   Tel: (440) 260-0000
Middleburg Heights, OH 44130   Fax: (440) 260-0015

Public Affairs and Related Activities Personnel

At Headquarters

MABREY, Bernie   Tel: (440) 260-0000
Director, Business Development   Fax: (440) 260-0015

WALZ, Kevin   Tel: (440) 260-0000
Vice President, Sales and Marketing   Fax: (440) 260-0015

Infinite Group
A provider of technology services.
www.igius.com
Annual Revenues: $8.72 million
Employees: 83
Ticker: OTC: IMCI
SIC: 7370
Industry/ies: Computer/Technology

Main Headquarters

Mailing: 80 Office Pkwy.   Tel: (585) 385-0610
Pittsford, NY 14534   Fax: (585) 385-0614
    TF: (855) 385-0610

Corporate Foundations and Giving Programs

Infinite Group, Inc. Contributions Program
60 Office Pkwy.   Tel: (585) 385-0610
Pittsford, NY 14534   Fax: (585) 385-0614

Public Affairs and Related Activities Personnel

At Headquarters

FREED, Jr., William   Tel: (707) 658-2843
Contact, Media and Investor Relations   Fax: (585) 385-0614
william@motv-marketing.com

HOYEN, Andrew   Tel: (585) 385-0610
Chief Administrative Officer   Fax: (585) 385-0614

SLAVNY, David   Tel: (585) 385-0610
Director, Business Development   Fax: (585) 385-0614

WITZEL, James C.   Tel: (585) 385-0610
Chief Financial Officer   Fax: (585) 385-0614

WOHLSCHLEGEL, Deanna   Tel: (585) 385-0610
Director, Human Resources and Controller   Fax: (585) 385-0614
DWohlschlegel@IGIus.com

InfoCision
A telemarketing services provider. InfoCision specializes in political, Christian and nonprofit fundraising, and sales and customer care. InfoCision offers outbound and inbound call center services (sales and customer care) as well as fund raising and e-commerce support services. The company also offers product fulfillment services, such as credit card transactions, product delivery, and the production and mailing of marketing collateral. Chairman Gary Taylor founded the company in 1982.
www.infocision.com
Employees: 4,400
Industry/ies: Communications; Telecommunications/Internet/Cable

Chairman of the Board   Tel: (330) 668-1400
TAYLOR, Karen   Fax: (330) 668-1401

Chief Executive Officer   Tel: (330) 668-1400
TAYLOR, Craig   Fax: (330) 668-1401

Main Headquarters
Mailing: 325 Springside Dr.   Tel: (330) 668-1400
Akron, OH 44333   Fax: (330) 668-1401

Political Action Committees
Infocision Management Corporation PAC
FEC ID: C00407098
Contact: Dave Hamrick
325 SpringsideDr.
Akron, OH 44333

    Contributions to Candidates: $3,250 (2015-2016)
    Republicans: $3,250

Public Affairs and Related Activities Personnel

At Headquarters

BRUBAKER, Steve   Tel: (330) 668-1400
Chief of Staff   Fax: (330) 668-1401
Steve.Brubaker@infocision.com

HAMRICK, Dave   Tel: (330) 668-1400
Chief Financial Officer, PAC Treasurer   Fax: (330) 668-1401

SCYOC, Mike Van   Tel: (330) 668-1400
Chief Strategy Officer   Fax: (330) 668-1401
mikev@infocision.com

WELLS, Samantha   Tel: (330) 670-1729
Senior Manager, Corporate Communications   Fax: (330) 668-1401
samantha.wells@infocision.com

Information Systems Laboratories, Inc.
Engineers advanced sensors, communications, adaptive signal processing, nuclear systems analysis, and space/missile system technology.
www.islinc.com
Annual Revenues: $19.70 million
Employees: 100
Industry/ies: Computer/Technology; Defense/Homeland Security; Energy/Electricity; Government-Related

Executive Vice President, Chairman and Chief Technology Officer   Tel: (858) 535-9680
    Fax: (959) 535-9848
CARLOS, John Don
jdc@islinc.com

President and Chief Executive Officer   Tel: (858) 535-9680
MILLER, Richard G.   Fax: (959) 535-9848
rmiller@islinc.com

Main Headquarters
Mailing: 10070 Barnes Canyon Rd.   Tel: (858) 535-9680
San Diego, CA 92121   Fax: (858) 535-9848

Public Affairs and Related Activities Personnel

At Headquarters

KUEBLER, Peter F.   Tel: (858) 535-9680
Chief Financial Officer   Fax: (959) 535-9848
pkuebler@islinc.com

InfoZen

Information technology consulting.
www.infozen.com
Annual Revenues: $30.94 million
Employees: 200
Industry/ies: Computer/Technology

Chairman of the Board, President and Chief Executive Officer   Tel: (301) 605-8000
ANANTHANPILLAI, Raj   Fax: (301) 605-8007

Main Headquarters
Mailing: 6700A Rockledge Dr.   Tel: (301) 605-8000
              Suite 300   Fax: (301) 605-8007
              Bethesda, MD 20817

Public Affairs and Related Activities Personnel

At Headquarters

KILINSKI, Aaron   Tel: (301) 605-8000
Vice-President, Strategy and Solutions   Fax: (301) 605-8007
lmackay@infozen.com

KNOBLOCK, Ronald   Tel: (301) 605-8000
Vice President, Contracts and Compliance   Fax: (301) 605-8007
rknoblock@infozen.com

PENYAK, Stephen C.   Tel: (301) 605-8000
Senior Vice President, Business Operations   Fax: (301) 605-8007

ING North America Insurance Corporation

See listing on page 840 under Voya Financial, Inc.

Ingersoll-Rand Company

A manufacturer of industrial and commercial equipment and components. Headquartered in Bermuda with U.S. executive headquarters in Piscataway, New Jersey.
company.ingersollrand.com
Annual Revenues: $14.08 billion
Employees: 59,000
SIC: 3563
Industry/ies: Machinery/Equipment
Legislative Issues: ENG; ENV; TAX; TRD; TRU

Chairman of the Board, President and Chief Executive Officer   Tel: (704) 655-4000
LAMACH, Michael W.

Main Headquarters
Mailing: 800-E Beaty St.   Tel: (704) 655-4000
              Davidson, NC 28036

Washington Office
Mailing: 601 13th St. NW   Tel: (202) 742-6982
              Suite 290 North
              Washington, DC 20005

Political Action Committees
Ingersoll Rand Company PAC
FEC ID: C00492314
Contact: David Modi
P.O. Box 75000
Detroit, MI 48275

   Contributions to Candidates: $24,500 (2015-2016)
   Democrats: $3,500; Republicans: $21,000

Public Affairs and Related Activities Personnel

At Headquarters

AVEDON, Marcia J.   Tel: (704) 655-4000
Senior Vice President, Human Resources and
Communications
marcia_avedon@irco.com

CARTER, Susan   Tel: (704) 655-4000
Senior Vice President and Chief Financial Officer

FIMBIANTI, Joseph   Tel: (704) 655-4000
Finance
joseph_fimbianti@irco.com

KUEHN, Chris   Tel: (704) 655-4000
Vice President and Chief Accounting Officer

PFEFFER, Janet   Tel: (704) 655-4000
Vice President, Treasury and Investor Relations

At Washington Office

GREEN, Maria L.   Tel: (202) 742-6982

MODI, David   Tel: (202) 742-6982
Vice President, Government Affairs
dmodi@irco.com
Registered Federal Lobbyist

Ingles Markets Inc.

A supermarket chain.
www.ingles-markets.com
Annual Revenues: $3.82 billion
Employees: 8,740
Ticker: NASDAQ: IMKTA
SIC: 5411
Industry/ies: Food And Beverage Industry

Chairman of the Board and Chief Executive Officer   Tel: (828) 669-2941
INGLE, II, Robert P.   Fax: (828) 669-3667
ringle@ingles-markets.com

Main Headquarters
Mailing: P.O. Box 6676   Tel: (828) 669-2941
              Asheville, NC 28816   Fax: (828) 669-3678

Corporate Foundations and Giving Programs
Ingles Markets Inc. Contributions Program
P.O. Box 6676
Asheville, NC 28816

Public Affairs and Related Activities Personnel

At Headquarters

FREEMAN , Ronald B.   Tel: (828) 669-2941
Chief Financial Officer, Vice President, Finance and Director   Fax: (828) 669-3678

LANNING , James W.   Tel: (828) 669-2941
President, Chief Operating Officer and Director   Fax: (828) 669-3678

Ingram Barge Company

Marine transport towing of dry and liquid bulk commodities on U.S. inland waterways.
www.ingrambarge.com
Employees: 2,300
Industry/ies: Transportation
Legislative Issues: ENV; TRA

Chairman and Cheif Executive Officer   Tel: (615) 298-8200
INGRAM, Orrin H.   Fax: (615) 298-7579
orrin.ingram@ingram.com

Main Headquarters
Mailing: 4400 Harding Rd.   Tel: (615) 298-8200
              Nashville, TN 37205-2290   Fax: (615) 298-8213
                                                    TF: (800) 876-2047

Political Action Committees
Ingram Barge Company PAC
FEC ID: C00364471
Contact: Daniel P. Mecklenborg
4400 Harding Rd.
One Belle Meade Pl.
Nashville, TN 37205

   Contributions to Candidates: $110,665 (2015-2016)
   Democrats: $29,500; Republicans: $81,165

Public Affairs and Related Activities Personnel

At Headquarters

MARTIN, Daniel T.   Tel: (615) 298-8373
Senior Vice President and Chief Commercial Officer   Fax: (615) 695-3373
Dan.Martin@IngramBarge.com

MECKLENBORG, Daniel P.   Tel: (615) 298-8209
Senior Vice President, Chief Legal Officer and Secretary and   Fax: (615) 695-3209
PAC Treasurer
dan.mecklenborg@ingrambarge.com

NOWELL, Kim   Tel: (615) 298-8200
Chief People Officer   Fax: (615) 298-8213
Kim.Nowell@ingrambarge.com

RAFFERTY, Brian   Tel: (615) 298-8364
Vice President, Customer Service and Logistics   Fax: (615) 298-8213
Brian.Rafferty@IngramBarge.com

SEHRT, David G.   Tel: (615) 298-8200
Senior Vice President and Chief Engineering Officer   Fax: (615) 298-8213
David.Sehrt@IngramBarge.com

SHAH, PB   Tel: (615) 298-8338
President and Chief Operating Officer   Fax: (615) 695-3338
PB.Shah@IngramBarge.com

TAYLOR, Crystal   Tel: (615) 298-8200
Chief Financial Officer   Fax: (615) 298-8213

Ingram Micro Mobility

Formerly known as Brightpoint Inc., the company adopted its current name in 2012. A global provider of wireless communications products. Acquired Cellstar's U.S. and Latin American operations in 2007. It ships the equipment to companies that sell mobile phones and accessories, including wireless carriers, dealers, and retailers; customers include Vodafone, Best Buy, and Sprint Nextel. Brightpoint also offers a range of services that includes warehousing, product fulfillment, purchasing, contract manufacturing, call center outsourcing, customized packaging, activation, and Web marketing.

www.ingrammicro.com
Annual Revenues: $5.24 billion
Employees: 6,200
Ticker: NYSE: IM
SIC: 5045; 5045; 5734; 9999; 9999
Industry/ies: Communications; Computer/Technology; Telecommunications/Internet/Cable
Legislative Issues: TEC

Chairman of the Board   Tel: (714) 566-1000
LAURANCE, Dale R.   Fax: (714) 566-7900

Chief Executive Officer   Tel: (714) 566-1000
MONIE, Alain   Fax: (714) 566-7900

Main Headquarters
Mailing: 1600 E. St. Andrew Pl.   Tel: (714) 382-5013
Santa Ana, CA 92705

Corporate Foundations and Giving Programs

Brightpoint Contributions Program
501 Airtech Pkwy.
Plainfield, IN 46168

Ingram Micro's Corporate Giving Program
Contact: Nicole Trombly
P.O. Box 25125
Santa Ana, CA 92799

Public Affairs and Related Activities Personnel

At Headquarters

BOYD, Larry C.   Tel: (714) 566-1000
Executive Vice President, Secretary and General Counsel   Fax: (714) 566-7900
larry.boyd@ingrammicro.com

DAVE, Nimesh   Tel: (714) 566-1000
Executive Vice President, Global Business Process and Cloud   Fax: (714) 566-7900
Computing

HUMES, William D.   Tel: (714) 566-1000
Chief Financial Officer   Fax: (714) 566-7900

KAMEL, G. Sam   Tel: (714) 566-1000
Senior Vice President, Corporate Development and Strategy

PARK, Ernest   Tel: (714) 566-1000
Senior Executive Vice President and Chief Information Officer

READ, Paul   Tel: (714) 566-1000
President and Chief Operating Officer

SHERMAN, Scott D.   Tel: (714) 566-1000
Executive Vice President, Human Resources

TROMBLY, Nicole   Tel: (714) 382-5581
Senior Specialist, Public and Community Relations   Fax: (714) 566-7918
nicole.trombly@ingrammicro.com

TYLER, Andrew   Tel: (714) 566-1000
Manager, Marketing
andrew.tyler@brightpoint.com

WRIGHT, Damon   Tel: (714) 382-5013
Contact, Investor Relations
damon.wright@ingrammicro.com

ZWICK, Lisa   Tel: (949) 230-8794
Contact, Corporate Communications
lisa.zwick@ingrammicro.com

At Other Offices

CARPENTER, Craig M.   Tel: (317) 707-2355
Vice President & Associate General Counsel   Fax: (317) 707-2512
7635 Interactive Way, Suite 200
Indianapolis, IN 46278
craig.carpenter@brightpoint.com

KAMEL, G. Sam   Tel: (317) 707-2355
Senior Vice President, Corporate Development and Strategy
7635 Interactive Way, Suite 200
Indianapolis, IN 46278

PARK, Ernest   Tel: (317) 707-2355
Senior Executive Vice President and Chief Information Officer
7635 Interactive Way, Suite 200
Indianapolis, IN 46278

READ, Paul   Tel: (317) 707-2355
President and Chief Operating Officer
7635 Interactive Way, Suite 200
Indianapolis, IN 46278

SHERMAN, Scott D.   Tel: (317) 707-2355
Executive Vice President, Human Resources
7635 Interactive Way, Suite 200
Indianapolis, IN 46278

TYLER, Andrew   Tel: (317) 707-2355
Manager, Marketing
7635 Interactive Way, Suite 200
Indianapolis, IN 46278
andrew.tyler@brightpoint.com

Ingredion

A supplier of food and industrial ingredients derived from the processing of corn and other starch-based materials.
www.ingredion.com
Employees: 11,900
Ticker: NYSE: CPO
SIC: 2040; 2046; 5149
NAICS: 311221; 42249
Industry/ies: Agriculture/Agronomy; Food And Beverage Industry

Chairman of the Board, President and Chief Executive Officer   Tel: (708) 551-2600
GORDON, Ilene S.   Fax: (708) 551-2700

Main Headquarters
Mailing: Five Westbrook Corporate Center   Tel: (708) 551-2600
Westchester, IL 60154   Fax: (908) 685-5096
   TF: (800) 443-2746

Corporate Foundations and Giving Programs

The Corn Products International Educational Foundation
Five Westbrook Corporate Center   Tel: (708) 551-2600
Westchester, IL 60154   Fax: (708) 551-2700

Public Affairs and Related Activities Personnel

At Headquarters

CASTELLANO, Christine M.   Tel: (708) 551-2600
Senior Vice President, General Council, Corporate Secretary   Fax: (708) 551-2700
and Chief Compliance Officer

FORTNUM, Jack C.   Tel: (708) 551-2600
Executive Vice President and Chief Financial Officer   Fax: (708) 551-2700

FRISCH, Diane J.   Tel: (708) 551-2676
Senior Vice President, Human Resources   Fax: (708) 551-2580
diane.frisch@cornproducts.com

SONNTAG, Martin   Tel: (708) 551-2600
Senior Vice President, Strategy and Global Business   Fax: (708) 551-2700
Development

Injured Workers Pharmacy

A national retail pharmacy for injured workers.
www.iwpharmacy.com
Industry/ies: Pharmaceutical Industry

President and Chief Executive Officer   Fax: (800) 305-0499
MARTINO, CPCU, Kenneth F.

Main Headquarters
Mailing: P.O. Box 338   Fax: (800) 305-0499
Methuen, MA 01844   TF: (888) 321-7945

Public Affairs and Related Activities Personnel

At Headquarters

RIPPENS, Pamela J.   Fax: (800) 305-0499
Vice President of Strategy and Business Development

BODYCOTE, Kari   Fax: (800) 305-0499
Paralegal

CANNAVA, Jayne   Fax: (800) 305-0499
Vice President, Legal & Government Affairs
jcannava@iwpharmacy.com
Registered Federal Lobbyist

CAYER, George A.   Fax: (800) 305-0499
Vice President Operations

CIRILLO, Michael A.   Fax: (800) 305-0499
Vice President, Sales and Marketing

ESQ, Jayne Cannava.   Fax: (800) 305-0499
Vice President of Legal and Government Affairs

PRINCE, Kerrin   Fax: (800) 305-0499
Specialist, Legal Document
kprince@iwpharmacy.com

RIPPENS, ARM, Pamela J.   Fax: (800) 305-0499
Vice President, Strategy and Business Development

STANDISH, CPA, James F.   Fax: (800) 305-0499
Chief Financial Officer

Inman Mills

Producer of textiles.
www.inmanmills.com
Annual Revenues: $62 million
Employees: 700
Industry/ies: Apparel/Textiles Industry; Communications; Telecommunications/Internet/Cable

Chairman and Chief Executive Officer and Treasurer   Tel: (864) 472-2121
CHAPMAN, III, Robert H.   Fax: (864) 472-0261

Main Headquarters
Mailing: 300 Park Rd.   Tel: (864) 472-2121
P.O. Box 207   Fax: (864) 472-0261

Inman, SC 29349

Political Action Committees

Inman Mills Good Government Fund PAC
FEC ID: C00142893
Contact: James C. Pace Jr.
300 Park Rd.
P.O. Box 207
Inman, SC 29349

Contributions to Candidates: $3,000 (2015-2016)
Republicans: $3,000

Public Affairs and Related Activities Personnel

At Headquarters

CHAPMAN, Norman H	Tel:	(864) 472-2121
Chief Operating Officer and President	Fax:	(864) 472-0261
PACE, Jr., James C.	Tel:	(864) 472-2121
PAC Treasurer	Fax:	(864) 472-0261
jpace@inmanmills.com		

Inmarsat

Headquartered in London. Provides mobile satellite services.
www.inmarsat.com
Industry/ies: Aerospace/Aviation; Communications; Telecommunications/
Internet/Cable; Transportation
Legislative Issues: DEF; INT

Non-executive Chairman	Tel:	(785) 431-4800
SUKAWATY, Andrew	Fax:	(785) 431-4749
Chief Executive Officer	Tel:	(785) 431-4800
PEARCE, Rupert	Fax:	(785) 431-4749

Main Headquarters

Mailing:	175 S.W. Seventh St.	Tel:	(785) 431-4800
	Suite 1910	Fax:	(785) 431-4749
	Miami, FL 33130		

Washington Office

Mailing:	1101 Connecticut Ave. NW	Tel:	(202) 248-5150
	Suite 1200	Fax:	(202) 248-5177
	Washington, DC 20036		

Public Affairs and Related Activities Personnel

At Headquarters

SLATER, Laura	Tel:	(785) 431-4800
Contact, Investor Relations	Fax:	(785) 431-4749
laura.slater@inmarsat.com		

At Washington Office

BATES, Tony	Tel:	(202) 248-5150
Chief Financial Officer	Fax:	(202) 248-5177

InnoSys, Inc.

Provider of access solutions for airline and GDS/CRS systems to developers, travel suppliers, and travel resellers
www.innosys.com
Employees: 30
Industry/ies: Aerospace/Aviation; Airlines; Electricity & Electronics; Electronics;
Energy/Electricity; Transportation

Main Headquarters

Mailing:	6400 Hollis St.	Tel:	(510) 222-7717
	Suite 15	Fax:	(510) 722-0311
	Emeryville, CA 94608		

Public Affairs and Related Activities Personnel

At Headquarters

PECTOL, Vic	Tel:	(510) 222-7717
Chief Financial Officer	Fax:	(510) 722-0311
WILSON, Lee	Tel:	(510) 222-7717
Contact, Sales	Fax:	(510) 722-0311
lee.wilson@innosys.com		

Innova Dynamics

Innova Materials is a materials technology company spun out of the University of Pennsylvania.
www.innovadynamics.com
Industry/ies: Computer/Technology

Chairman of the Board	Tel:	(415) 796-6445
DAVIS, Wes	Fax:	(415) 796-6445
President and Chief Executive Officer	Tel:	(415) 796-6445
BUTTON, PhD, Dr. Daniel	Fax:	(415) 796-6445

Main Headquarters

Mailing:	1700 Owens St.	Tel:	(415) 796-6445
	Suite 405	Fax:	(415) 796-6445
	San Francisco, CA 94158		

Public Affairs and Related Activities Personnel

At Headquarters

ARNDT, Richard	Tel:	(415) 796-6445
Vice Presdident, Finance	Fax:	(415) 796-6445
KALHORI, Bijhan	Tel:	(415) 796-6445
Vice President, Operations and Process Engineering	Fax:	(415) 796-6445
KUWADA, Ryosuke	Tel:	(415) 796-6445
Vice President, Business Development and Sales	Fax:	(415) 796-6445
SRINIVAS, Arjun	Tel:	(415) 796-6445
Co-Founder and Chief Strategy Officer	Fax:	(415) 796-6445

Innova Materials LLC

See listing on page 430 under Innova Dynamics

Innovation Works, Inc.

Single investor in seed-stage companies. It provides counseling and expert advice to startup companies. IW is the Ben Franklin Technology Partner of Southwestern PA and is supported by the Department of Community and Economic Development.
www.innovationworks.org
Annual Revenues: $7.78 million
Employees: 68
Industry/ies: Banking/Finance/Investments; Computer/Technology

Chairman of the Board	Tel:	(412) 681-1520
BIANCHINI , Jr., Ronald	Fax:	(412) 681-2625
President and Chief Executive Officer	Tel:	(412) 681-1520
LUNAK, Richard	Fax:	(412) 681-2625

Main Headquarters

Mailing:	Nova Tower Two	Tel:	(412) 681-1520
	Two Allegheny Center, Suite 100	Fax:	(412) 681-2625
	Pittsburgh, PA 15212		

Public Affairs and Related Activities Personnel

At Headquarters

GLAUSSER, Gary	Tel:	(412) 681-1520
Chief Investment Officer	Fax:	(412) 681-2625
GLUECK, Terri	Tel:	(412) 894-9514
Director, Community Development and Communications	Fax:	(412) 681-2625
tglueck@innovationworks.org		
KIJOWSKI, Susan	Tel:	(412) 681-1520
Controller	Fax:	(412) 681-2625
MITCHELL, Kathy	Tel:	(412) 894-9519
Human Resources Strategist	Fax:	(412) 681-2625
STARZYNSKI, Bob	Tel:	(412) 681-1520
Director, Business Development	Fax:	(412) 681-2625
WALKER , Deborah	Tel:	(412) 681-1520
Legal Counsel	Fax:	(412) 681-2625

Innovative Emergency Management

Specializes in risk-based solutions for measuring and managing threats to people, infrastructure, and information
www.iem.com
Annual Revenues: $24.50 million
Employees: 300
Industry/ies: Management

President and Chief Executive Officer	Tel:	(225) 952-8191
BERIWAL, Madhu	Fax:	(919) 237-7468

Main Headquarters

Mailing:	P.O.Box 110265	Tel:	(919) 990-8191
	Research Triangle Park, NC 27709	Fax:	(919) 237-7468
		TF:	(800) 977-8191

Corporate Foundations and Giving Programs

Innovative Emergency Management Contributions Program

Public Affairs and Related Activities Personnel

At Headquarters

BOUDREAUX, Staci	Tel:	(919) 237-7556
Contact, Media Relations	Fax:	(919) 237-7468
LATHAM, Greg	Tel:	(225) 952-8191
General Counsel	Fax:	(225) 952-8282
LEMCKE, Ted	Tel:	(919) 990-8191
Chief Operating Officer	Fax:	(919) 237-7468
MERRYMAN, Terry	Tel:	(919) 990-8191
Coordinator, Marketing	Fax:	(225) 952-8122
terry.merryman@iem.com		
MICHAEL, Daniel	Tel:	(919) 990-8191
Chief Financial Officer	Fax:	(919) 237-7468

Insight Enterprise Consulting, LLC

A government affairs management and international agribusiness development consulting firm.
www.insightenterpriseconsulting.com

Employees: 5,000
SIC: 5961
Legislative Issues: AGR; ENV; FOO; TRD

Main Headquarters
Mailing: 701 S. State St.   Tel: (507) 766-1930
          New Ulm, MN 56073

Public Affairs and Related Activities Personnel

At Headquarters

FOSTER, Brian   Tel: (507) 766-1930
Founder and Principal
brian@InsightEnterpriseConsulting.com
Registered Federal Lobbyist

Insight Enterprises, Inc.

IE provider of hardware, software, cloud solutions and IT services to business, government, education and healthcare clients. It focuses on business-to-business and information technology (IT) capabilities for enterprises.
insight.com
Annual Revenues: $5.32 billion
Employees: 5,406
Ticker: NASDAQ: NSIT
SIC: 5961
Industry/ies: Computer/Technology

Founder and Chairman of the Board   Tel: (480) 902-1001
CROWN, Timothy A.   Fax: (480) 902-1157
tcrown@insight.com

President and Chief Executive Officer   Tel: (480) 902-1001
LAMNECK, Kenneth   Fax: (480) 902-1157

Main Headquarters
Mailing: 6820 S. Harl Ave.   Tel: (480) 902-1001
           Tempe, AZ 85283   Fax: (480) 902-1157
                                                             TF: (800) 467-4448

Corporate Foundations and Giving Programs

Insight Enterprises Contributions Program
6820 S. Harl Ave.
Tempe, AZ 85283

Public Affairs and Related Activities Personnel

At Headquarters

BERKLEY, Rosalind   Tel: (480) 333-3420
Contact, Investor Relations   Fax: (480) 902-1157
rosalind.berkley@insight.com

BRYAN, Glynis   Tel: (480) 902-1001
Chief Financial Officer   Fax: (480) 902-1157
glynis.bryan@insight.com

DODENHOFF, Steven W.   Tel: (480) 902-1001
President   Fax: (480) 902-1157

JOHNSON, Helen K.   Tel: (480) 333-3234
Senior Vice President, Treasurer and Contact, Investor   Fax: (480) 902-1157
Relations
helen.johnson@insight.com

KING, Chuck   Tel: (480) 409-6390
Senior Manager, Communications   Fax: (480) 902-1157
chuck.king@insight.com

Insitu, Inc.

Insitu designs, develops and produces small autonomous aircraft for Unmanned Aircraft Systems (UAS), including advanced integrated command, control, and video tools for Intelligence, Surveillance and Reconnaissance (ISR).
www.insitu.com
Annual Revenues: $1.5 billion
Employees: 100
Industry/ies: Defense/Homeland Security; Government-Related

President and Chief Executive Officer   Tel: (509) 493-8600
HARTMAN, Ryan   Fax: (509) 493-8601

Main Headquarters
Mailing: 118 E. Columbia River Way   Tel: (509) 493-8600
           Bingen, WA 98605   Fax: (509) 493-8601

Corporate Foundations and Giving Programs

Insitu Contributions Program
Contact: Jill Vacek
118 E. Columbia River Way
Bingen, WA 98605

Public Affairs and Related Activities Personnel

At Headquarters

ALIC, Esina   Tel: (509) 493-8600
Vice President, Strategy   Fax: (509) 493-8601

ALLEN, Paul   Tel: (509) 493-8600
Director, International Operations   Fax: (509) 493-8601

CLARK, Bill   Tel: (509) 493-8600

Chief Operating Officer   Fax: (509) 493-8601

JACKSON, Alvin   Tel: (509) 493-8600
Vice President, Sales and Marketing   Fax: (509) 493-8601

LINDSTROM, Chris   Tel: (509) 493-8600
Vice President, Human Resources   Fax: (509) 493-8601

MCDUFFEE, Paul   Tel: (509) 493-8600
Associate Vice President, Government Relations and Strategy Fax: (509) 493-8601

MCNAMARA, Suzanne   Tel: (509) 493-8600
Vice President, Business Development   Fax: (509) 493-8600

SIDDIQUI, Nikki   Tel: (509) 493-8600
Chief Financial Officer   Fax: (509) 493-8601

THOM, Jeff   Tel: (509) 493-8600
Vice President, Corporate Operations and Chief Financial   Fax: (509) 493-8601
Officer

VACEK, Jill   Tel: (509) 493-6439
Manager, Communications   Fax: (509) 493-8601
jill.vacek@insitu.com

Insperity

Company provides human resource and business solutions designed to help improve business performance. Also offers include MidMarket Solutions, Performance Management, Expense Management, Time and Attendance, Organizational Planning, Recruiting Services, Employment Screening, Retirement Services, Business Insurance and Technology Services.
www.insperity.com
Annual Revenues: $2.71 billion
Employees: 2,400
Ticker: NYSE: NSP
SIC: 7363
Industry/ies: Employees & Employment
Legislative Issues: HCR; IMM; TAX

Management Director, Chairman and Chief Executive Officer Tel: (281) 358-8986
SARVADI, Paul J.   Fax: (281) 348-3718

Main Headquarters
Mailing: 19001 Crescent Springs Dr.   Tel: (281) 358-8986
           Kingwood, TX 77339-3802   Fax: (281) 348-3718
                                                             TF: (800) 237-3170

Corporate Foundations and Giving Programs

Adminstaff Inc. Contributions Program
19001 Crescent Springs Dr.   Tel: (281) 358-8986
Kingwood, TX 77339   Fax: (281) 348-3718
                                                             TF: (800) 237-3170

Public Affairs and Related Activities Personnel

At Headquarters

ARIZPE, A. Steve   Tel: (281) 358-8986
Executive Vice President of Client Services and Chief   Fax: (281) 348-3718
Operating Officer

COLLINS, Betty L.   Tel: (281) 358-8986
Senior Vice President, Corporate Human Resources   Fax: (281) 348-3718

HERINK, Daniel D.   Tel: (281) 358-8986
Senior Vice President, Legal, General Counsel and Secretary Fax: (281) 348-3718

MINCKS, Jay E.   Tel: (281) 358-8986
Executive Vice President of Sales and Marketing   Fax: (281) 348-3718

RAWSON, Richard G   Tel: (281) 358-8986
Management Director, President   Fax: (281) 348-3718

SHARP, Douglas S.   Tel: (281) 348-3232
Senior Vice President, Finance, Chief Financial Officer and Fax: (281) 348-3718
Treasurer
douglas_sharp@adminstaff.com

Instructional Systems, Inc.

A computer software program provider.
www.isinj.com
Annual Revenues: $2.70 million
SIC: 5045
Industry/ies: Computer/Technology; Education

Chief Executive Officer   Tel: (201) 343-3003
KAMINER, Martin   Fax: (201) 343-8883

Main Headquarters
Mailing: 401 Hackensack Ave.   Tel: (201) 343-3003
           Seventh Floor   Fax: (201) 343-8883
           Hackensack, NJ 07601   TF: (800) 706-5476

Public Affairs and Related Activities Personnel

At Headquarters

HODGES, Virgil   Tel: (201) 343-3003
Vice President, Government Relations   Fax: (201) 343-8883
Hodges.virgil@isinj.com

SAMPLE, Barry   Tel: (201) 343-3003
President   Fax: (201) 343-8883

Integra

See listing on page 432 under Integra Telecom, Inc.

Integra Telecom, Inc.

A facilities-based telecommunications carrier. Founded in 1996 through the acquisition of OGI Telecomm.
www.integratelecom.com
Annual Revenues: $616 million
Employees: 2,000
Industry/ies: Communications; Telecommunications/Internet/Cable
Legislative Issues: TEC

Chairman of the Board
SUNU, Paul
Tel: (503) 453-8000
Fax: (503) 453-8221

Chief Executive Officer
GUTH, Robert
Tel: (503) 453-8000
Fax: (503) 453-8221

Main Headquarters
Mailing: 1201 N.E. Lloyd Blvd.
Suite 500
Portland, OR 97232
Tel: (503) 953-7000
Fax: (503) 453-8221

Washington Office
Mailing: 1101 Pennsylvania Ave. NW
Sixth Floor
Washington, DC 20004

Political Action Committees
Integra PAC of Integra Telecom Holdings Inc.
FEC ID: C00428094
Contact: Dale Perry
1201 N.E. Lloyd Blvd.
Suite 500
Portland, OR 97232

> **Contributions to Candidates:** $28,250 (2015-2016)
> Democrats: $13,500; Republicans: $14,750

Corporate Foundations and Giving Programs
Community Matters Program
1201 NE Lloyd Blvd.
Suite 500
Portland, OR 97232

Public Affairs and Related Activities Personnel

At Headquarters

CLAUSON , Karen
Senior Vice President, General Counsel, Corporate Secretary
klclauson@integratelecom.com
Tel: (503) 453-8000
Fax: (503) 453-8221

O'HERRON, Felicity
Senior Vice President, Human Resources
Tel: (503) 453-8000
Fax: (503) 453-8221

SELNICK, Jesse
Chief Financial Officer
Tel: (503) 453-8000
Fax: (503) 453-8221

SHARPE, Michael
Senior Vice President, Operations
Tel: (503) 453-8000
Fax: (503) 453-8221

SHIPLEY, Scenna
Contact, Media Relations
scenna.shipley@integratelecom.com
Tel: (503) 453-8808
Fax: (503) 453-8221

At Other Offices

PERRY, Dale
Senior Cost Analyst and PAC Treasurer
18110 SE 34th St., Building One
Vancouver, WA 98683
dale.perry@integratelecom.com
Tel: (360) 558-6900

Integrated Device Technology, Inc.

A manufacturer of semiconductor solutions for communications companies.
www.idt.com
Annual Revenues: $487.24 million
Employees: 1,748
Ticker: NASDAQ (GS): IDTI
SIC: 5065; 3674
NAICS: 334413; 42169
Industry/ies: Machinery/Equipment

Chairman of the Board
SCHOFIELD, John
Tel: (408) 284-8200
Fax: (408) 284-2775

President and Chief Executive Officer
WATERS, Gregory L
Tel: (408) 284-8200
Fax: (408) 284-2775

Main Headquarters
Mailing: 6024 Silver Creek Valley Rd.
San Jose, CA 95138
Tel: (408) 284-8200
Fax: (408) 284-2775
TF: (800) 223-1366

Public Affairs and Related Activities Personnel

At Headquarters

BRANDALISE, Matthew
Vice President, General Counsel and Corporate Secretary
Tel: (408) 284-8200
Fax: (408) 284-2775

CHITTIPEDDI, Sailesh
Vice President, Global Operations and Chief Technology Officer
Tel: (408) 284-8200
Fax: (408) 284-2775

HAMILTON, Anja
Vice President, Global Human Resources
Tel: (408) 284-8200
Fax: (408) 284-2775

MONTANA, Mario
Vice President and Chief Sales Officer
Tel: (408) 284-8200
Fax: (408) 284-2775

ROBERTSON, Graham
Vice President, Corporate Marketing and Contact, Media Relations
graham.robertson@IDT.com
Tel: (408) 284-2644
Fax: (408) 284-2776

WHITE, Brian C
Vice President and Chief Financial Officer
Tel: (408) 284-8200
Fax: (408) 284-2775

Integrated Medical Systems International, Inc.

Surgical procedure-based medical service company for the healthcare industry providing equipment-renewal services for several categories of equipment and accessories.
www.imsready.com
Annual Revenues: $31.30 million
Employees: 650
Industry/ies: Medicine/Health Care/Mental Health

Main Headquarters
Mailing: 3316 Second Ave., North
Birmingham, AL 35222
Tel: (205) 879-3840
Fax: (205) 803-4057
TF: (800) 783-9251

Corporate Foundations and Giving Programs
Integrated Medical Systems International Contributions Program
1823 27th Ave., South
Birmingham, AL 35209

Public Affairs and Related Activities Personnel

At Headquarters

DAVIS, Barry
Vice President, Finance
Tel: (205) 879-3840
Fax: (205) 803-4057

MUNDY, III, James R. "Bo"
Vice President, Global Sales
Tel: (205) 879-3840
Fax: (205) 803-4057

PHILLIPS, William C.
President, Sales Division
Tel: (205) 879-3840
Fax: (205) 803-4057

ROBINSON, Lee
Vice President, Operations
Tel: (205) 879-3840
Fax: (205) 803-4057

ROBINSON, Debra
President, Administrative Division and Managing Partner
Tel: (205) 879-3840
Fax: (205) 803-4057

STREVY, David
Chief Financial Officer
Tel: (205) 879-3840
Fax: (205) 803-4057

UPCHURCH, Kellie
Vice President, Administration
Tel: (205) 879-3840
Fax: (205) 803-4057

Integrity Global Security

Provides certified high IT security solutions for government, military, and commercial enterprises.
www.integrityglobalsecurity.com
Annual Revenues: $8.40 million
Employees: 100
Industry/ies: Computer/Technology; Defense/Homeland Security; Government-Related

Chief Executive Officer
CHANDLER, David W.
Tel: (805) 882-2500
Fax: (805) 965-6343

Main Headquarters
Mailing: 30 W. Sola St.
Santa Barbara, CA 93101
Tel: (805) 882-2500
Fax: (805) 965-6343
TF: (888) 882-0019

Washington Office
Mailing: 1100 New York Ave. NW
Suite 620 West
Washington, DC 20005
Tel: (202) 289-7776

Public Affairs and Related Activities Personnel

At Headquarters

SORRELLS, Jimmy
Senior Vice President
Tel: (805) 882-2500
Fax: (805) 965-6343

Intel Corporation

A manufacturer of semiconductors, computer components, modules and systems for the computer industry.
www.intel.com
Annual Revenues: $56.28 billion
Employees: 107,300
Ticker: NASDAQ: INTC
SIC: 3674; 8711
NAICS: 334413; 54133
Industry/ies: Computer/Technology; Electricity & Electronics; Electronics; Energy/Electricity

Legislative Issues: AVI; BUD; CIV; CPI; CPT; DEF; EDU; ENG; ENV; HCR; HOM;
IMM; INT; LBR; SCI; TAX; TEC; TRA; TRD

| **Chairman of the Board** | Tel: | (408) 765-8080 |
| BRYANT, Andy D. | Fax: | (408) 765-3804 |

| **Chief Executive Officer** | Tel: | (202) 626-4381 |
| KRZANICH, Brian | Fax: | (202) 628-2525 |

Main Headquarters

Mailing:	2200 Mission College Blvd.	Tel:	(408) 765-8080
	Santa Clara, CA 95054	Fax:	(408) 765-3804
		TF:	(800) 628-8686

Washington Office

Mailing:	1155 F St. NW	Tel:	(202) 626-4381
	Suite 1025	Fax:	(202) 628-2525
	Washington, DC 20004		

Political Action Committees

Intel Corporation PAC
FEC ID: C00125641
Contact: Peter M. Cleveland

1155 F St. NW	Tel:	(202) 628-3838
Suite 1025	Fax:	(202) 628-2525
Washington, DC 20004		

Contributions to Candidates: $2,812,498 (2015-2016)
Democrats: $275,783; Republicans: $294,699; Other: $2,242,016

Principal Recipients

SENATE
AYOTTE, KELLY A (REP-NH)
MCCAIN, JOHN S (REP-VA)
SCHUMER, CHARLES E (DEM-NY)
TOOMEY, PATRICK JOSEPH (REP-PA)

HOUSE
BERA, AMERISH (DEM-CA)
BLUMENAUER, EARL (DEM-OR)
BONAMICI, SUZANNE MS. (DEM-OR)
BUCK, KENNETH R (REP-CO)
GOODLATTE, ROBERT W. (REP-VA)
HONDA, MIKE (DEM-CA)
ISSA, DARRELL (REP-CA)
PALLONE, FRANK JR (DEM-NJ)
SALMON, MATT (REP-AZ)
SMITH, LAMAR (REP-TX)

Corporate Foundations and Giving Programs

Intel Foundation
Contact: Wendy Hawkins

| 5300 Northeast Elam Young Pkwy. | Tel: | (503) 456-1539 |
| Hillsboro, OR 97124 | | |

Public Affairs and Related Activities Personnel

At Headquarters

BROWN, Rebecca A. (Becky)	Tel:	(408) 765-8080
Vice President, Global Marketing and Communications	Fax:	(408) 765-3804
Director, Digital Marketing and Media Group		

| FUND, Steven | Tel: | (408) 765-8080 |
| *Corporate Vice President and Chief Marketing Officer* | Fax: | (408) 765-3804 |

| JAMES, Renée J. | Tel: | (408) 765-8080 |
| *President* | Fax: | (408) 765-3804 |

| KILROY, Thomas M. | Tel: | (408) 765-8080 |
| *Executive Vice President, Corporate Strategy* | Fax: | (408) 765-3804 |

MANGANO, Claudine	Tel:	(408) 887-2706
Corporate PR and Executive Communications Group Director	Fax:	(408) 765-3804
claudine.a.mangano@intel.com		

MULLOY, Chuck	Tel:	(408) 765-3484
Contact, Media Relations	Fax:	(408) 765-3804
chuck.mulloy@intel.com		

| MURRAY, Patricia | Tel: | (408) 765-8080 |
| *Senior Vice President, Human Resources* | Fax: | (408) 765-3804 |

RODGERS, Steven R.	Tel:	(408) 765-8080
Senior Vice President and General Counsel, Legal and	Fax:	(408) 765-3804
Corporate Affairs		

| SMITH, Stacy J. | Tel: | (408) 765-8080 |
| *Executive Vice President and Chief Financial Officer* | Fax: | (408) 765-3804 |

| TAYLOR, Richard G. A. | Tel: | (408) 765-8080 |
| *Senior Vice President and Director, Human Resources* | Fax: | (408) 765-3804 |

WALDROP, Tom	Tel:	(408) 765-8478
Director, Issues and Policy Communications	Fax:	(408) 765-6008
tom.waldrop@intel.com		

At Washington Office

| BARBER , Lindel | Tel: | (202) 626-4381 |
| | Fax: | (202) 628-2525 |

| BORRELLI, Alice Baker | Tel: | (202) 626-4380 |
| *Director, Global Health and Workforce Policy* | Fax: | (202) 628-2528 |

Registered Federal Lobbyist

CLEVELAND, Peter M.	Tel:	(202) 628-3838
Vice President, Legal and Corporate Affairs and Director,	Fax:	(202) 628-2525
Global Public Policy, PAC Treasurer		
Registered Federal Lobbyist		

COMER, Douglas B.	Tel:	(202) 626-4385
Director, Legal Affairs and Technology Policy	Fax:	(202) 628-2525
Registered Federal Lobbyist		

DICKMAN, Marjorie	Tel:	(202) 628-3838
Global Director and Managing Counsel, Internet of Things	Fax:	(202) 628-2525
Policy and Federal Lobbyist		
marjorie.dickman@intel.com		
Registered Federal Lobbyist		

| FAVA, Andrea | Tel: | (202) 626-4384 |
| *Director , Global Policy* | Fax: | (202) 628-2525 |

| GANN, Tom | Tel: | (202) 626-4381 |
| *Registered Federal Lobbyist* | Fax: | (202) 628-2525 |

HARPER, Stephen F.	Tel:	(202) 626-4399
Global Director, Environmental and Energy Policy	Fax:	(202) 628-2525
stephen.harper@intel.com		

JAHANIAN, Noushin	Tel:	(202) 626-4381
Senior Director and Head of Federal Government Relations	Fax:	(202) 628-2525
Registered Federal Lobbyist		

KOKINDA, Terri	Tel:	(202) 626-4381
Federal Lobbyist	Fax:	(202) 628-2525
terri.kokinda@intel.com		
Registered Federal Lobbyist		

| LOUIS, Jaclyn Suzanne | Tel: | (202) 626-4381 |
| *Government Relations* | Fax: | (202) 628-2525 |

MACDONALD, Donald J.	Tel:	(202) 626-4381
Vice President, Sales and Marketing Group and General	Fax:	(202) 628-2525
Manager, Global Marketing		

| MALLOY, Lisa | Tel: | (202) 626-4381 |
| *Registered Federal Lobbyist* | Fax: | (202) 628-2525 |

MILLER, John S.	Tel:	(202) 626-4381
Director and Managing Counsel, Cybersecurity and Privacy	Fax:	(202) 628-2525
Policy, Government Relations		

| MINTHORN, Cisco | Tel: | (202) 626-4381 |
| *Government Relations* | Fax: | (202) 628-2525 |

| MULVENY, Jennifer | Tel: | (202) 626-4381 |
| *Director, Government Affairs and Federal Lobbyist* | Fax: | (202) 628-2525 |

PALACIOS, Mario	Tel:	(202) 626-4381
Contact, Government Relations	Fax:	(202) 628-2525
Registered Federal Lobbyist		

| PITSCH, Peter K. | Tel: | (202) 626-4382 |
| *Associate General Counsel* | Fax: | (202) 628-2525 |

ROSE, David	Tel:	(202) 626-4390
Federal Lobbyist	Fax:	(202) 628-2525
Registered Federal Lobbyist		

SALINAS, Norberto P.	Tel:	(202) 626-4381
Government Relations	Fax:	(202) 628-2525
Registered Federal Lobbyist		

| SESSOMS, Julia-Feliz | Tel: | (202) 626-4381 |
| *Registered Federal Lobbyist* | Fax: | (202) 628-2525 |

| SESSOMS, Julia | Tel: | (202) 626-4381 |
| *Registered Federal Lobbyist* | Fax: | (202) 628-2525 |

SLATER, Greg	Tel:	(202) 628-3838
Senior Counsel, Director, Global Trade and Competition	Fax:	(202) 628-2525
Policy		
Registered Federal Lobbyist		

Intellectual Ventures

Intellectual Ventures invests in both expertise and capital in the development of inventions.
www.intellectualventures.com
Industry/ies: Copyrights, Patents And Trademarks
Legislative Issues: CPT; TAX; TRD

| **Founder and Chief Executive Officer** | Tel: | (425) 467-2300 |
| MYHRVOLD, Nathan | | |

Main Headquarters

Mailing:	3150 139th Ave. SE	Tel:	(425) 467-2300
	Building Four		
	Bellevue, WA 98005		

Washington Office

Mailing:	1100 H St. NW
	Suite 900
	Washington, DC 20005

Political Action Committees

Intellectual Ventures NPM, Inc. PAC (Intellectual Ventures PAC)
FEC ID: C00557165
Contact: Russel C. Merbeth

1100 H St. NW
Suite 900
Washington, 20005

Contributions to Candidates: $115,500 (2015-2016)
Democrats: $82,000; Republicans: $33,500

Public Affairs and Related Activities Personnel

At Headquarters

GROGAN, Nicole	Tel:	(425) 467-2300
Senior Vice President, Human Resources		
KRIS, David	Tel:	(425) 467-2300
Executive Vice President and General Counsel		
LOCKE, Mona	Tel:	(425) 467-2300
Senior Vice President, Corporate Communications and Marketing		
MERBETH, Robert	Tel:	(425) 467-2300
Chief Policy Counsel		
STEIN, Russell	Tel:	(425) 467-2300
Executive Vice President and Chief Financial Officer		

At Washington Office

MERBETH, Russel C.
PAC Contact

Intellicheck Mobilisa, Inc.

Intellicheck Mobilisa, Inc. develops and markets wireless technology and identity systems for various applications.
www.icmobil.com
Annual Revenues: $7.73 million
Employees: 37
Ticker: AMEX: IDN
SIC: 7372
Industry/ies: Computer/Technology
Legislative Issues: HOM

Chairman	Tel:	(360) 344-3233
MALONE, Michael D.	Fax:	(360) 344-3323

Chief Executive Officer	Tel:	(360) 344-3233
ROOF, PHD, William	Fax:	(360) 344-3323

Main Headquarters

Mailing:	191 Otto St.	Tel:	(360) 344-3233
	Port Townsend, WA 98368	Fax:	(360) 344-3323
		TF:	(888) 942-6624

Washington Office

Mailing:	1800 Diagonal Rd.	Tel:	(703) 683-4313
	Suite 440		
	Alexandria, VA 22314		

Public Affairs and Related Activities Personnel

At Headquarters

COLONTRELLE, Laura	Tel:	(212) 825-3210
Contact, Media Relations	Fax:	(360) 344-3323
SANFELIPPO, Bob	Tel:	(360) 344-3233
Vice President, Sales	Fax:	(360) 344-3323
WHITE, Bill	Tel:	(360) 344-3233
Chief Financial Officer	Fax:	(360) 344-3323
WILLIAMSEN, Robert N.	Tel:	(360) 344-3233
Chief Revenue Officer	Fax:	(360) 344-3323

Intelligent Micro Patterning

Offers thin film solutions through smart filter technology.
www.intelligentmp.com
Employees: 10
Industry/ies: Computer/Technology; Science; Scientific Research

Chief Executive Officer	Tel:	(727) 522-0334
SASSERATH, PhD, Jay N.		
jays@intelligentmp.com		

Main Headquarters

Mailing:	9790 16th St., North	Tel:	(727) 522-0334
	St. Petersburg, FL 33716		

Public Affairs and Related Activities Personnel

At Headquarters

LOWRY, Frank	Tel:	(727) 522-0334
Contact, Sales		
frankl@intelligentmp.com		

Intelligent Optical Systems, Inc.

Develops cutting edge-technologies in optical sensing and instrumentation.
www.intopsys.com
Annual Revenues: $3.40 million
Employees: 45
Industry/ies: Computer/Technology

Cheif Business Officer	Tel:	(424) 263-6300
FARINA, John	Fax:	(310) 530-7417

Chief Executive Officer	Tel:	(424) 263-6300
SANDLER, PhD, Dr. Reuben	Fax:	(310) 530-7417
RSandler@intopsys.com		

Main Headquarters

Mailing:	2520 W. 237th St.	Tel:	(424) 263-6300
	Torrance, CA 90505-5217	Fax:	(310) 530-7417

Public Affairs and Related Activities Personnel

At Headquarters

BESHAY, Manal	Tel:	(424) 263-6300
Cheif Operating Officer	Fax:	(310) 530-7417
HAMILL, Michael	Tel:	(424) 263-6300
Chief Financial Officer	Fax:	(310) 530-7417
OLINS, JD, Jay	Tel:	(424) 263-6300
Vice President, Legal and Administration	Fax:	(310) 530-7417

INTELSAT

Offers Internet, broadcast, telephony, and corporate networks solutions via a geosynchronous satellite fleet, by using a combination of satellite and terrestrial connectivity technology to help enterprises, governments and service providers deliver content around the world quickly, securely and reliably — to people at home, in the office or on the move.
www.intelsat.com
Annual Revenues: $2.45 billion
Employees: 1,082
Ticker: NYSE: I
SIC: 4899
Industry/ies: Communications; Telecommunications/Internet/Cable
Legislative Issues: TEC

Chairman and Chief Executive Officer	Tel:	(404) 381-2000
MCGLADE, David	Fax:	(404) 381-2088
david.mcglade@intelsat.com		

Main Headquarters

Mailing:	7900 Tysons One Pl.	Tel:	(703) 559-6800
	McLean, VA 22102	Fax:	(703) 559-7898

Political Action Committees

Intelsat Corporation Political Action Committee
FEC ID: C00412403
Contact: Stephen Chernow

3400 International Dr. NW	Tel:	(202) 944-6800
Washington, DC 20008-3090	Fax:	(202) 944-8125

Contributions to Candidates: $62,000 (2015-2016)
Democrats: $20,500; Republicans: $41,500

Principal Recipients

HOUSE
BRIDENSTINE, JAMES FREDERICK (REP-OK)
ROGERS, MICHAEL DENNIS (REP-AL)

Corporate Foundations and Giving Programs

INTELSAT Contributions Program
2875 Fork Creek Church Rd.
Ellenwood, GA 30294

Public Affairs and Related Activities Personnel

At Headquarters

RIEGELMAN, Kurt	Tel:	(703) 559-6800
Senior Vice President, Sales and Marketing	Fax:	(703) 559-7898

At Other Offices

BRYAN, Michelle	Tel:	(404) 381-2000
Executive Vice President, General Counsel and Chief Administrative Officer	Fax:	(404) 381-2088
2875 Fork Creek Church Rd.		
Ellenwood, GA 30294		
michelle.bryan@intelsat.com		
CASEY, Patricia A.	Tel:	(202) 944-6800
PAC Treasurer	Fax:	(202) 944-8125
3400 International Dr. NW		
Washington, DC 20008-3006		
CHERNOW, Stephen	Tel:	(202) 944-6800
Vice President & Deputy General Counsel	Fax:	(202) 944-8125
3400 International Dr. NW		
Washington, DC 20008-3006		
COOPER, Patricia	Tel:	(202) 944-6800
Vice President, Government Affairs & Policy	Fax:	(202) 944-8125
3400 International Dr. NW		
Washington, DC 20008-3006		
CRANDALL, Susan	Tel:	(202) 944-6800
Assistant General Counsel	Fax:	(202) 944-7890
3400 International Dr. NW		
Washington, DC 20008-3006		
susan.crandall@intelsat.com		

Registered Federal Lobbyist

MCDONNELL, Michael
Executive Vice President and Chief Financial Officer
2875 Fork Creek Church Rd.
Ellenwood, GA 30294
Tel: (404) 381-2000
Fax: (404) 381-2088

VANBEBER, Dianne
Vice President, Investor Relations and Communications
3400 International Dr. NW
Washington, DC 20008-3006
dianne.vanbeber@intelsat.com
Tel: (202) 944-7406
Fax: (202) 944-7898

Intelsat General Corporation

A wholesaler of commercial satellite services. It IGC provides a wide range of customized, secure, end-to-end communications solutions for commercial, government and military customers.
www.intelsatgeneral.com
Annual Revenues: $9.80 million
Employees: 90
Industry/ies: Aerospace/Aviation; Defense/Homeland Security; Government-Related; Transportation
Legislative Issues: BUD; COM; DEF; SCI

President
SEARS, Kay
Tel: (703) 270-4200

Main Headquarters
Mailing: 6550 Rock Spring Dr.
Suite 450
Bethesda, MD 20817
Tel: (301) 571-1210

Washington Office
Mailing: 7900 Tysons One Pl.
Suite 12
McLean, VA 22102
Tel: (703) 270-4200
TF: (800) 814-7717

Public Affairs and Related Activities Personnel

At Headquarters

DALBELLO, Richard
Vice President, Government Affairs
Tel: (301) 571-1210

NOLTING, Nancy
Marketing Program Manager
nancy.nolting@intelsatgeneral.com
Tel: (301) 571-1210

PRIDE, Myland
Director, Legislative & Government Affairs
Registered Federal Lobbyist
Tel: (301) 571-1210

At Washington Office

AGATSTON, David
Vice President, Finance & Accounting
Tel: (703) 270-4200

BEARZOTTI, Matthew
Manager, Government Affairs
Tel: (703) 270-4200

LEWIS , Britt
Vice President, Marketing and Business Strategy
Tel: (703) 270-4200

UGLIALORO, Joseph
General Counsel and Corporate Secretary
Tel: (703) 270-4200

InterActive Corporation, InterActiveCorp

See listing on page 419 under IAC

Intercell USA, Inc.

See listing on page 829 under Valneva

Intercontinental Exchange

Operates a network of regulated exchanges and clearing houses for financial commodities, indexes and FX, as well as equities and equity options.
www.theice.com
Annual Revenues: $3.14 billion
Employees: 2,887
Ticker: NYSE: ICE
Industry/ies: Energy/Electricity
Legislative Issues: CDT; FIN; HOU

Chairman of the Board and Chief Executive Officer
SPRECHER, Jeffrey C.
Tel: (770) 857-4700
Fax: (770) 937-0020

Main Headquarters
Mailing: 5660 New Northside Dr.
3rd Floor
Atlanta, GA 30328
Tel: (770) 857-4700
Fax: (770) 937-0020

Washington Office
Mailing: 801 Pennsylvania Ave. NW
Suite 630
Washington, DC 20004
Tel: (202) 347-4300

Political Action Committees
Intercontinental Exchange Inc. PAC
FEC ID: C00443168
Contact: Dean S. Mathison

2100 Riveredge Pkwy.
Suite 500
Atlanta, GA 30328
Contributions to Candidates: $195,000 (2015-2016)
Democrats: $74,000; Republicans: $121,000
Principal Recipients
SENATE
PERDUE, DAVID (REP-GA)
STABENOW, DEBBIE (DEM-MI)
HOUSE
CONAWAY, MICHAEL HONORABLE (REP-TX)
SCOTT, DAVID ALBERT (DEM-GA)
SCOTT, JAMES AUSTIN (REP-GA)

Corporate Foundations and Giving Programs
Intercontinental Exchange Corporate Contribution
2100 Riveredge Pkwy.
Suite 500
Atlanta, GA 30328
Tel: (770) 857-4700
Fax: (770) 857-4755

Public Affairs and Related Activities Personnel

At Headquarters

FOLEY , Douglas
Senior Vice President, Human Resources & Administration
Tel: (770) 857-4700
Fax: (770) 937-0020

GOONE, David C.
Senior Vice President and Chief Strategic Officer
Tel: (770) 857-4700
Fax: (770) 937-0020

HILL, Scott A.
Senior Vice President and Chief Financial Officer
Tel: (770) 857-4700
Fax: (770) 937-0020

LOEFFLER, Kelly L.
Senior Vice President of Corporate Communications, Marketing and Investor Relations
kelly.loeffler@theice.com
Tel: (770) 857-4700
Fax: (770) 937-0020

MATHISON, Dean S.
Chief Accounting Officer, Controller and PAC Treasurer
Tel: (770) 857-4700
Fax: (770) 937-0020

NUCKOLLS, Charles Randall
Washington Counsel
Tel: (770) 857-4700
Fax: (770) 937-0020

SHORT, Jonathan H.
Senior Vice President, General Counsel and Corporate Secretary
Tel: (770) 857-4700
Fax: (770) 937-0020

VICE, Charles
Washington Counsel
Tel: (770) 857-4700
Fax: (770) 937-0020

At Washington Office

ALBERT, Alexander
Vice President, Government Affairs
Registered Federal Lobbyist
Tel: (202) 347-4300

ROBERSON, Peter S.
Vice President, Government Relations
robertson@theice.com
Registered Federal Lobbyist
Tel: (202) 347-4300

WEISS, Brendan
Co-Head, Government Affairs
Registered Federal Lobbyist
Tel: (202) 347-4300

Intercontinental Hotels Group

A lodging franchising and management company.
www.ihgplc.com
Annual Revenues: $1.86 billion
Employees: 7,797
Ticker: NYSE: IHG
SIC: 7011
Industry/ies: Travel/Tourism/Lodging
Legislative Issues: CPT; DEF; ENG; TOU

Non-Executive Chairman
CESCAU, Patrick
Tel: (770) 604-2000
Fax: (770) 604-5275

Chief Executive Officer
MAALOUF , Elie
Tel: (770) 604-2000
Fax: (770) 604-5275

Main Headquarters
Mailing: Three Ravinia Dr.
Suite 100
Atlanta, GA 30346
Tel: (770) 604-2000
Fax: (770) 604-5275

Corporate Foundations and Giving Programs
Intercontinental Hotels Group Contributions Program
Three Ravinia Dr.
Suite 100
Atlanta, GA 30346-2149
Tel: (770) 604-2000

Public Affairs and Related Activities Personnel

At Headquarters

ANHUT, James F.
Senior Vice President
Tel: (770) 604-2000
Fax: (770) 604-5275

BALSLEY, Heather
Tel: (770) 604-2000

Senior Vice President	Fax:	(770) 604-5275
BULLEY, Jolyon	Tel:	(770) 604-2000
Chief Operating Officer	Fax:	(770) 604-5275
COUNIHAN, Caroline	Tel:	(770) 604-2090
Senior Manager, Public Relations and Media Contact	Fax:	(770) 604-5275
caroline.counihan@ihg.com		
ECKARD , Jeff	Tel:	(770) 604-2000
Vice President	Fax:	(770) 604-5275
EDGECLIFFE-JOHNSON, Paul	Tel:	(770) 604-2000
Chief Financial Officer	Fax:	(770) 604-5275
GAYTAN, Lori	Tel:	(770) 604-8347
Senior Vice President, Americas Human Resource and Global Reward	Fax:	(770) 604-5275
lori.gaytan@ichotelsgroup.com		
GULLETT, Natasha	Tel:	(770) 604-5597
Director, Brand Communications	Fax:	(770) 604-2059
natasha.gullett@ihg.com		
GUNKEL, Bob	Tel:	(770) 604-2000
Senior Vice President and Chief Financial Officer	Fax:	(770) 604-5275
ROBBINS, Tracy	Tel:	(770) 604-2000
Executive Vice President, Global Human Resources and and Group Operations Support	Fax:	(770) 604-5275
SCHULWOLF, Francie	Tel:	(770) 604-2000
Vice President, Corporate Communications	Fax:	(770) 604-5275
francie.schulwolf@ichotelsgroup.com		
SMITH, Steven W.	Tel:	(770) 604-2000
Senior Vice President and General Counsel	Fax:	(770) 604-5275
SPECK, Gina	Tel:	(770) 604-2000
Senior Vice President and Chief Financial Officer	Fax:	(770) 604-5275
TURNER, George	Tel:	(770) 604-2000
Executive Vice President, General Counsel and Company Secretary	Fax:	(770) 604-5275

InterDigital Communications Corporation

A wholly-owned subsidiary of InterDigital, Inc. It designs and develops technologies that enable and enhance mobile communications and capabilities.
www.interdigital.com
Annual Revenues: $468.36 million
Employees: 320
Ticker: NASDAQ: IDCC
SIC: 3663; 5065; 3661; 5999
Industry/ies: Communications; Computer/Technology; Electricity & Electronics; Electronics; Energy/Electricity; Telecommunications/Internet/Cable
Legislative Issues: CPT

Chairman of the Board	Tel:	(302) 281-3600
HUTCHESON, S. Douglas (Doug)	Fax:	(302) 281-3763
President and Chief Executive Officer	Tel:	(302) 281-3600
MERRITT, William J.	Fax:	(302) 281-3763

Main Headquarters

Mailing:	200 Bellevue Pkwy.	Tel:	(302) 281-3600
	Suite 300	Fax:	(302) 281-3763
	Wilmington, DE 19809		

Washington Office

Mailing:	515 C St. NE	Tel:	(302) 281-3685
	Washington, DC 20002		

Political Action Committees
Interdigital Inc. PAC
FEC ID: C00400333
Contact: Jannie K. Lau
200 Bellevue Parkway
Suite 300
Wilmington, DE 19809

>   **Contributions to Candidates:** $75,450 (2015-2016)
>   Democrats: $39,200; Republicans: $36,250

Public Affairs and Related Activities Personnel

At Headquarters

BREZSKI, Richard J.	Tel:	(302) 281-3600
Chief Financial Officer	Fax:	(302) 281-3763
LAU, Jannie K.	Tel:	(302) 281-3600
Executive Vice President, General Counsel and Secretary, PAC Contact	Fax:	(302) 281-3763
WILLE, Patrick Van de	Tel:	(858) 210-4814
Chief Communications Officer	Fax:	(302) 281-3763
patrick.vandewille@interdigital.com		

At Washington Office

STIEN, Robert Sean	Tel:	(302) 281-3685
Vice President, Government Relations and Regulatory Affairs		
WATTERS, Blair	Tel:	(302) 281-3685
Senior Director, Government Affairs		

Interface Inc.

Provides sales and marketing support to clients represented in their dealings with federal government agencies.
www.interfacinc.com
Annual Revenues: $987.51 million
Employees: 3,346
Ticker: NASDAQ: TILE
SIC: 2273

Chief Executive Officer	Tel:	(703) 225-0025
NESSEL, Rudy R.	Fax:	(703) 225-0020

Main Headquarters

Mailing:	9720 Capital Ct.	Tel:	(703) 225-0025
	Suite 306	Fax:	(703) 225-0020
	Fairfax, VA 22030		

Public Affairs and Related Activities Personnel

At Headquarters

KNAPP, David C.	Tel:	(703) 225-0025
Contact, Business Development	Fax:	(703) 225-0020
WILLIAMS, Robert G.	Tel:	(703) 225-0025
Contact, Federal Government Sales, Marketing and Legislative Affairs	Fax:	(703) 225-0020
ZENTNER, Michele	Tel:	(703) 225-0025
Director, Government Accounts	Fax:	(703) 225-0020
mzentner@internfacinc.com		

Intergraph Corporation

A manufacturer of interactive computer graphics systems.
www.intergraph.com
Employees: 4,000
SIC: 7373
Industry/ies: Computer/Technology

Chief Executive Officer	Tel:	(256) 730-2000
ROLLEN , Ola	Fax:	(256) 730-2048

Main Headquarters

Mailing:	P.O. Box 240000	Tel:	(256) 730-2000
	Huntsville, AL 35813	Fax:	(256) 730-2048

Political Action Committees
Intergraph Corporation PAC
FEC ID: C00201491
Contact: Kerry M. Fehrenbach
170 Graphics Dr.
ISG Mailstop W 1501
Madison, AL 35758

Public Affairs and Related Activities Personnel

At Headquarters

COST, Steven	Tel:	(256) 730-2000
President	Fax:	(256) 730-2048
steven.cost@intergraph.com		
DEEMER, Stephanie	Tel:	(256) 730-1075
Executive Manager, SG and I Public Relations and Government Relations	Fax:	(256) 730-2048
stephanie.deemer@intergraph.com		
FELTS, Jerry	Tel:	(256) 730-3074
Manager, Marketing and Communications	Fax:	(256) 730-2048
jerry.felts@intergraph.com		
FRECHETTE, Angela	Tel:	(256) 730-2000
Manager, Corporate Communications	Fax:	(256) 730-2048
JACKS , Blair	Tel:	(256) 730-2000
Chief Financial Officer	Fax:	(256) 730-2048
LESKO, Myriah	Tel:	(256) 730-2000
Specialist, Senior Communications	Fax:	(256) 730-2048
myriah.lesko@intergraph.com		
MOORE, Scott	Tel:	(256) 730-2000
Chief Financial Officer and Chief Operating Officer	Fax:	(256) 730-2048
PORTER, Ed	Tel:	(256) 730-2000
Executive Vice President, Human Resources	Fax:	(256) 730-2048
ed.porter@intergraph.com		
SALLINGER, Gerhard	Tel:	(256) 730-2000
President	Fax:	(256) 730-2048
WAGNER, Renee	Tel:	(404) 751-2554
Manager, Corporate Communications	Fax:	(256) 730-2048

At Other Offices

DEAVER, John	Tel:	(256) 730-2000
Executive Director, Corporate Communications	Fax:	(256) 730-2048
170 Graphics Dr.		
Madison, AL 35758		
john.deaver@intergraph.com		
FEHRENBACH, Kerry M.	Tel:	(256) 730-2000

PAC Treasurer
170 Graphics Dr.
Madison, AL 35758
kerry.fehrenbach@intergraph.com

Fax: (256) 730-2048

JOFFRION, David
Manager, Corporate Communications
170 Graphics Dr.
Madison, AL 35758
david.joffrion@intergraph.com

Tel: (256) 730-2000
Fax: (256) 730-2048

Interinvest

Global asset management.
www.interinvest.com/english/home/home.html
Industry/ies: Banking/Finance/Investments

Chairman of the Board and Chief Investment Officer
BLACK, Dr. Hans P.
hblack@interinvest.com

Tel: (617) 723-7870

Contact, Investor Relations and President
SCHMIDT, CFA, Stanley T.

Tel: (617) 723-7870

Main Headquarters
Mailing: 192 South St.
Suite 600
Boston, MA 02111

Tel: (617) 723-7870

Interleukin Genetics

Develops genetic tests to identify individual's chances of developing certain diseases.
www.ilgenetics.com
Annual Revenues: $2.05 million
Employees: 30
Ticker: OTC: ILIU
SIC: 2835
Industry/ies: Medicine/Health Care/Mental Health; Science; Scientific Research

Chairman of the Board
WEAVER, James M.

Tel: (781) 398-0700
Fax: (781) 398-0720

Chief Executive Officer
CARBEAU, Mark B.

Tel: (781) 398-0700
Fax: (781) 398-0720

Main Headquarters
Mailing: 135 Beaver St.
Waltham, MA 02452

Tel: (781) 398-0700
Fax: (781) 398-0720
TF: (800) 529-8772

Public Affairs and Related Activities Personnel

At Headquarters

DIPALMA, Steve
Chief Financial Officer

Tel: (781) 398-0700
Fax: (781) 398-0720

KORNMAN, Kenneth S.
President and Chief Scientific Officer

Tel: (781) 398-0700
Fax: (781) 398-0720

SNYDER, Scott A.
Chief Marketing Officer

Tel: (781) 398-0700
Fax: (781) 398-0720

VIOLETTE, Jennifer
Contact, Media
jviolette@ilgenetics.com

Tel: (781) 398-0700
Fax: (781) 398-0720

WALKER, Todd Anthony
Vice President, Marketing

Tel: (781) 398-0700
Fax: (781) 398-0720

Intermet Corporation

An automotive manufacturing supplier.
www.intermet.com
Employees: 2,300
Industry/ies: Automotive Industry; Transportation

President and Chief Executive Officer
TAMBURRINO, Bob

Tel: (817) 348-9190
Fax: (866) 833-3583

Main Headquarters
Mailing: 301 Commerce St.
Suite 2901
Fort Worth, TX 76102

Tel: (817) 348-9190
Fax: (866) 833-3583

Intermountain Gas Company

Intermountain Gas Company ("Intermountain") is a subsidiary of MDU Resources Group, Inc., a multidimensional natural resources enterprise.
www.intgas.com
Annual Revenues: $52.40 million
Employees: 200
Industry/ies: Natural Resources

Chairman of the Board
HOKIN, Richard

Tel: (208) 377-6840
Fax: (208) 377-6081

Main Headquarters
Mailing: P.O. Box 7608
Boise, ID 83707

Tel: (208) 377-6839
Fax: (208) 377-6097
TF: (800) 548-3679

Corporate Foundations and Giving Programs
Eco Fund
P.O. Box 7608
Boise, ID 83707

Public Affairs and Related Activities Personnel

At Headquarters

HANSON, Mark
Contact, Media Relations
mark.hanson@mduresources.com

Tel: (710) 530-1093
Fax: (208) 377-6097

WILDE, Brent
Manager, Marketing and Industrial Services
brent.wilde@intgas.com

Tel: (208) 377-6053
Fax: (208) 377-6097

International Alternative Energy Resources

Sustainable alternative fuel production firm.
Industry/ies: Energy/Electricity

Main Headquarters
Mailing: 4858 S. Cottage Grove
Suite 1
Chicago, IL 60652

Tel: (313) 446-3930

Public Affairs and Related Activities Personnel

At Headquarters

TAYLOR, John

Tel: (313) 446-3930

International Aviation Consulting Services, LLC

Commercial aviation related consulting and services.
Industry/ies: Aerospace/Aviation; Aviation; Transportation

Main Headquarters
Mailing: 209 Glenburn Ave.
Cambridge, MD 21613-1529

Tel: (678) 230-9429

Washington Office
Mailing: PO Box 23710
Washington, DC 20026

Tel: (678) 478-6322

Public Affairs and Related Activities Personnel

At Washington Office

VEATCH , Raymond
Founder and legal counsel

Tel: (678) 478-6322

International Bank of Commerce

A bank holding company.
www.ibc.com
Annual Revenues: $677.55 million
Employees: 3,700
Ticker: NASDAQ (GS): IBOC
Industry/ies: Banking/Finance/Investments
Legislative Issues: BAN; TAX

Chairman, President and Chief Executive Officer
NIXON, Dennis E.

Tel: (956) 722-7611
Fax: (956) 726-6637

Main Headquarters
Mailing: 1200 San Bernardo Ave.
Laredo, TX 78042

Tel: (956) 722-7611
Fax: (956) 726-6637

Political Action Committees
IBC Committee for Improvement and Betterment of the Country
FEC ID: C00276592
Contact: Chris Edward Aldrete
1200 San Bernardo Ave.
Laredo, TX 78042

Tel: (956) 722-7611
Fax: (956) 726-6637

Contributions to Candidates: $14,500 (2015-2016)
Republicans: $14,500

Public Affairs and Related Activities Personnel

At Headquarters

ALDRETE, Chris Edward
PAC Treasurer

Tel: (956) 722-7611
Fax: (956) 726-6637

CARRIEDO, Gabriela
Assistant Vice President, Marketing

Tel: (956) 726-6636
Fax: (956) 726-6637

GARCIA, Noe
Outside Federal Lobbyist

Tel: (956) 722-7611
Fax: (956) 726-6637

GONZALEZ, Rosalinda Eliza
Investment Relations Officer

Tel: (956) 726-6651
Fax: (956) 726-6618

NAVARRO, Imelda
Senior Executive Vice President, Chief Financial Officer, Treasurer

Tel: (956) 722-7611
Fax: (956) 726-6637

International Business Machines Corporation (IBM)

A provider of computer products and services.
www.ibm.com
Annual Revenues: $90.15 billion
Employees: 379,592

Ticker: NYSE: IBM
SIC: 3679; 7379; 7372
NAICS: 334419; 511210; 541519
Industry/ies: Computer/Technology; Electricity & Electronics; Electronics; Energy/Electricity
Legislative Issues: BUD; CPI; CPT; DEF; EDU; LBR; TAX; TRD

Chairman, President and Chief Executive Officer
ROMETTY, Virginia M. (Ginni)   Tel: (914) 499-1900
  Fax: (914) 499-7382

Main Headquarters
Mailing: One New Orchard Rd.   Tel: (914) 499-1900
  Armonk, NY 10504-1722   Fax: (914) 765-6021
  TF: (800) 426-4968

Washington Office
Mailing: 1301 K St. NW, Suite 1200
  Washington, DC 20005

Corporate Foundations and Giving Programs
International Business Machines Corporation Contributions Program
One New Orchard Rd.   Tel: (914) 499-1900
Armonk, NY 10504

Public Affairs and Related Activities Personnel

At Headquarters

BROWDY, Michelle H.   Tel: (914) 499-1900
Senior Vice President, Legal, Regulatory Affairs, and General   Fax: (914) 765-6021
Counsel

GHERSON, Diane   Tel: (914) 499-1900
Senior Vice President, Human Resources   Fax: (914) 765-6021

HORN, Tammy   Tel: (914) 499-1900
Senior Counsel   Fax: (914) 765-6021

IWATA, Jon C.   Tel: (914) 499-1900
Senior Vice President, Marketing and Communications   Fax: (914) 499-7382

KEVERIAN, Ken   Tel: (914) 499-1900
Senior Vice President, Corporate Strategy   Fax: (914) 765-6021

ROSWELL, Clint   Tel: (914) 766-2422
Director, External Communications   Fax: (914) 499-7382

SCHROETER, Martin   Tel: (914) 499-1900
Senior Vice President and Chief Financial Officer, Finance   Fax: (914) 765-6021
and Enterprise Transformation

SHELTON , Doug   Tel: (914) 499-6533
Contact, Media Relations   Fax: (914) 499-7382
doshelton@us.ibm.com

UNDERWEISER, Marian   Tel: (914) 499-1900
  Fax: (914) 765-6021

At Other Offices

BARNES, David N.   Tel: (202) 515-4036
Vice President, Global Workforce Policy   Fax: (202) 515-5194
600 14th St. NW, Suite 300, Third Floor
Washington, DC 20005
dnbarnes@us.ibm.com

BRUNER, Cheryl   Tel: (202) 515-4031
Executive, Governmental Programs   Fax: (202) 515-4943
600 14th St. NW, Suite 300, Third Floor
Washington, DC 20005
cheryl_bruner@us.ibm.com
Registered Federal Lobbyist

BURY, Craig E.   Tel: (202) 551-9502
Federal Lobbyist   Fax: (202) 551-9693
600 14th St. NW, Suite 300, Third Floor
Washington, DC 20005
cbury@us.ibm.com
Registered Federal Lobbyist

DIPAULA-COYLE, Michael   Tel: (202) 515-5000
Senior Executive, Governmental Programs   Fax: (202) 551-9693
600 14th St. NW, Suite 300, Third Floor
Washington, DC 20005
mdipaula-coyle@us.ibm.com
Registered Federal Lobbyist

DOCKTOR, Roslyn   Tel: (202) 551-9499
600 14th St. NW, Suite 300, Third Floor   Fax: (202) 551-9693
Washington, DC 20005
Registered Federal Lobbyist

EDINGTON, P.J.   Tel: (202) 515-5000
Executive, Governmental Program   Fax: (202) 515-5088
600 14th St. NW, Suite 300, Third Floor
Washington, DC 20005
pjeding@us.ibm.com

EVANS, Linda C.   Tel: (202) 515-5526
Executive, Worldwide Tax Policy   Fax: (202) 515-4943
600 14th St. NW, Suite 300, Third Floor
Washington, DC 20005
levans@us.ibm.com

Registered Federal Lobbyist

GILLESPIE, Edward A.   Tel: (202) 515-5187
Federal Lobbyist   Fax: (202) 515-5551
600 14th St. NW, Suite 300, Third Floor
Washington, DC 20005
eag@us.ibm.com

GRAY, Dana   Tel: (202) 515-5000
Federal Lobbyist   Fax: (202) 515-5088
600 14th St. NW, Suite 300, Third Floor
Washington, DC 20005
dgray@us.ibm.com

IGNASZEWSKI, Katie   Tel: (202) 515-5000
Federal Lobbyist   Fax: (202) 515-5088
600 14th St. NW, Suite 300, Third Floor
Washington, DC 20005
Registered Federal Lobbyist

MARKS, Debra   Tel: (202) 515-5184
Federal Lobbyist   Fax: (202) 515-5906
600 14th St. NW, Suite 300, Third Floor
Washington, DC 20005
debmarks@us.ibm.com
Registered Federal Lobbyist

MCCULLOCH, Edgar   Tel: (202) 515-4019
Executive, Governmental Programs   Fax: (202) 515-5194
600 14th St. NW, Suite 300, Third Floor
Washington, DC 20005
Registered Federal Lobbyist

O'RILEY, Mark C.   Tel: (202) 515-5102
Federal Lobbyist   Fax: (202) 515-5906
600 14th St. NW, Suite 300, Third Floor
Washington, DC 20005
mcoriley@us.ibm.com

PADILLA, Christopher A.   Tel: (202) 515-5000
Vice President, Government & Regulatory Affairs   Fax: (202) 551-9693
600 14th St. NW, Suite 300, Third Floor
Washington, DC 20005
padillac@us.ibm.com

PERRY, Edmund   Tel: (202) 551-9499
Director, Governmental Programs   Fax: (202) 551-9693
600 14th St. NW, Suite 300, Third Floor
Washington, DC 20005

PERRY, Edward F.   Tel: (202) 515-5039
Director, Political Programs   Fax: (202) 515-5906
600 14th St. NW, Suite 300, Third Floor
Washington, DC 20005
efp@us.ibm.com
Registered Federal Lobbyist

PHELPS, Lauren   Tel: (202) 515-5109
Federal Lobbyist   Fax: (202) 515-5078
600 14th St. NW, Suite 300, Third Floor
Washington, DC 20005
lphelps@us.ibm.com

RHONE, Adrienne G.   Tel: (202) 515-5103
Director, Governmental Programs   Fax: (202) 515-5906
600 14th St. NW, Suite 300, Third Floor
Washington, DC 20005
aag@us.ibm.com
Registered Federal Lobbyist

SHEEHY, Timothy J.   Tel: (202) 515-5077
Director, Governmental Programs   Fax: (202) 515-4943
600 14th St. NW, Suite 300, Third Floor
Washington, DC 20005
sheehy@us.ibm.com
Registered Federal Lobbyist

SINGER, Meredith   Tel: (202) 515-5000
Federal Lobbyist   Fax: (202) 515-5088
600 14th St. NW, Suite 300, Third Floor
Washington, DC 20005
singerme@us.ibm.com
Registered Federal Lobbyist

SOUTHWORTH, George   Tel: (202) 515-5000
Federal Lobbyist   Fax: (202) 515-5088
600 14th St. NW, Suite 300, Third Floor
Washington, DC 20005
Registered Federal Lobbyist

STEWART, Steve W.   Tel: (202) 515-5054
Director, Governmental Programs   Fax: (202) 515-4943
600 14th St. NW, Suite 300, Third Floor
Washington, DC 20005
Registered Federal Lobbyist

TUTTLE, Susan C.   Tel: (202) 515-5503
Executive, Governmental Programs   Fax: (202) 515-5078
600 14th St. NW, Suite 300, Third Floor

Washington, DC 20005
Registered Federal Lobbyist

VAYNBERG, Yelena
600 14th St. NW, Suite 300, Third Floor
Washington, DC 20005
Registered Federal Lobbyist
Tel: (202) 551-9499
Fax: (202) 551-9693

WILLIAMS, Marcus P.
Executive, Governmental Programs
600 14th St. NW, Suite 300, Third Floor
Washington, DC 20005
marcwill@us.ibm.com
Registered Federal Lobbyist
Tel: (202) 515-5522
Fax: (202) 515-5551

International Data Corporation

IDC is a global provider of market intelligence, advisory services, and events for the information technology, telecommunications, and consumer technology markets.
www.idc.com
Annual Revenues: $3.02 billion
Employees: 1,500
Industry/ies: Advertising And Marketing

Founder and Chairman of the Board
MCGOVERN, Patrick J.
patrick_mcgovern@idg.com
Tel: (617) 534-1200
Fax: (617) 859-8642

President and Chief Executive Officer
CAMPBELL, Kirk
Tel: (508) 872-8200
Fax: (508) 935-4168

Main Headquarters
Mailing: Five Speen St.
Framingham, MA 01701
Tel: (508) 872-8200
Fax: (508) 935-4168
TF: (800) 343-4952

Public Affairs and Related Activities Personnel

At Headquarters

BERNARDI, Debra
Vice President, Human Resources and Education
Tel: (508) 872-8200
Fax: (508) 935-4168

DEL PRETE, Crawford
Executive Vice President, Worldwide Research Products and Chief Research Officer
Tel: (508) 872-8200
Fax: (508) 935-4168

SULLIVAN, Mark
Chief Financial Officer
msullivan@idc.com
Tel: (508) 872-8200
Fax: (508) 935-4168

THORPE, Brad
Chief Sales Officer
Tel: (508) 872-8200
Fax: (508) 935-4168

WHALEN, Meredith
Senior Vice President, Information Technology Executive, Industry and Financial Research
Tel: (508) 872-8200
Fax: (508) 935-4168

International Derivatives Exchange Group, LLC

Focuses on the trading and clearing of derivatives.
www.idcg.com
Industry/ies: Banking/Finance/Investments; Trade (Foreign And Domestic)

Main Headquarters
Mailing: 105 E. 52nd St.
New York City, NY 10022
Tel: (202) 256-3001

International Flavors and Fragrances, Inc.

A creator and manufacturer of flavors, fragrances and aroma chemicals.
www.iff.com
Annual Revenues: $3.03 billion
Employees: 6,732
Ticker: NYSE: IFF
SIC: 2087; 2844
NAICS: 311942; 325620
Industry/ies: Chemicals & Chemical Industry

Chairman and Chief Executive Officer
FIBIG, Andreas
Tel: (212) 765-5500
Fax: (212) 708-7132

Main Headquarters
Mailing: 521 W. 57th St.
New York City, NY 10019
Tel: (212) 765-5500
Fax: (212) 708-7132

Corporate Foundations and Giving Programs

IFF Foundation
521 W. 57th St.
New York City, NY 10019

Public Affairs and Related Activities Personnel

At Headquarters

CANTLON, Angelica T.
Executive Vice President, Chief Human Resources Officer
Angelica.cantlon@iff.com
Tel: (212) 708-7164
Fax: (212) 708-7147

CHWAT, Anne
Senior Vice President, General Counsel and Corporate Secretary
Tel: (212) 765-5500
Fax: (212) 708-7132

anne.chwat@iff.com

CORNELL, Alison A.
Executive Vice President and Chief Financial Officer
Tel: (212) 765-5500
Fax: (212) 708-7132

DEVEAU, Michael
Vice President, Global Corporate Communications and Investor Relations
michael.deveau@iff.com
Tel: (212) 765-5500
Fax: (212) 708-7132

FORTANET, Francisco
Executive Vice President, Operations
Tel: (212) 765-5500
Fax: (212) 708-7132

MORDKOWSKI, Micaela
Coordinator, Communications
Tel: (212) 708-7211
Fax: (212) 708-7147

YOUNG, Shelley
Head, Investor Relations
shelley.young@iff.com
Tel: (212) 708-7271
Fax: (212) 708-7132

International Game Technology (IGT)

Designs, manufactures and markets gaming machines and systems equipment, software, and network systems worldwide.
www.igt.com
Annual Revenues: $3.44 billion
Employees: 8,627
Ticker: NYSE: IGT
SIC: 3990
Industry/ies: Sports/Leisure/Entertainment
Legislative Issues: CPT; GAM; IND; TAX

Chairman of the Board
SATRE, Philip G.
Tel: (775) 448-7777
Fax: (775) 448-0719

Chief Executive Officer
SALA, Marco
Tel: (775) 448-7777
Fax: (775) 448-0719

Main Headquarters
Mailing: 6355 S. Buffalo Dr.
Las Vegas, NV 89113
Tel: (775) 448-7777
Fax: (775) 448-0719
TF: (866) 296-4232

Political Action Committees
International Game Technology (IGT) PAC
FEC ID: C00316331
Contact: Romina Macias
6355 S. Buffalo Dr.
Las Vegas, NV 89113

Contributions to Candidates: $20,000 (2015-2016)
Democrats: $13,000; Republicans: $7,000

Principal Recipients

SENATE
REID, HARRY (DEM-NV)

Corporate Foundations and Giving Programs

International Game Technology Contributions Program
9295 Prototype Dr.
Reno, NV 89521
Tel: (775) 448-7777

Public Affairs and Related Activities Personnel

At Headquarters

BERG, Eric A.
Chief Operations Officer
Tel: (775) 448-7777
Fax: (775) 448-0719

BROOKE, Charles
Senior Vice President, Government Affairs
Tel: (775) 448-1528
Fax: (775) 448-0719

DAMONTE, Audrey
PAC Treasurer
Tel: (775) 448-7777
Fax: (775) 448-0719

FORNARO, Alberto
Executive Vice President and Chief Financial Officer
Tel: (775) 448-7777
Fax: (775) 448-0719

HART, Patti S.
Vice Chairman
Tel: (775) 448-7777
Fax: (775) 448-0719

KNUDSON, Knute
Vice President, Native American Development
knute.knudson@IGT.com
Tel: (775) 448-7777
Fax: (775) 448-0719

MACIAS, Romina
PAC Contact
Tel: (775) 448-7777
Fax: (775) 448-0719

TOM, Eric P.
Executive Vice President, Global Sales
Tel: (775) 448-7777
Fax: (775) 448-0719

VANDEMORE, John
Chief Financial Officer and Treasurer
Tel: (775) 448-7777
Fax: (775) 448-0719

VINCENT, Robert
Senior Vice President, Human Resources and Public Affairs
Tel: (775) 448-7777
Fax: (775) 448-0719

International Harvester

See listing on page 566 under Navistar International Corporation

International Harvester Company

See listing on page 566 under Navistar International Corporation

International Paper

A manufacturer of paper, paperboard and packaging products, wood products, specialty products. Merged with Federal Paper Board Co. in 1996, Union Camp Corp in 1999, and Champion International Corp. in 2000.
www.internationalpaper.com
Annual Revenues: $23.41 billion
Employees: 58,000
Ticker: NYSE: IP
SIC: 2621
Industry/ies: Energy/Electricity; Paper And Wood Products Industry
Legislative Issues: BUD; ENG; ENV; GOV; POS; TAX; TRD

Chairman of the Board and Chief Executive Officer   Tel: (901) 419-9000
SUTTON, Mark S.   Fax: (904) 214-9682

Main Headquarters
Mailing: 6400 Poplar Ave.   Tel: (901) 419-9000
Memphis, TN 38197   Fax: (904) 214-9682
  TF: (800) 223-1268

Washington Office
Mailing: 1101 Pennsylvania Ave. NW   Tel: (202) 628-1223
Suite 200   Fax: (202) 628-1368
Washington, DC 20004

Political Action Committees
International Paper PAC (IP PAC)
FEC ID: C00034405
Contact: Meaghan Killion Joyce
1101 Pennsylvania Ave. NW   Tel: (202) 628-1223
Suite 200   Fax: (202) 628-1368
Washington, DC 20004

Contributions to Candidates: $672,250 (2015-2016)
Democrats: $189,500; Republicans: $481,750; Other: $1,000

Principal Recipients

SENATE
AYOTTE, KELLY A (REP-NH)
BLUNT, ROY (REP-MO)
BURR, RICHARD (REP-NC)
MURKOWSKI, LISA (REP-AK)
MURRAY, PATTY (DEM-WA)
SCHUMER, CHARLES E (DEM-NY)
THUNE, JOHN (REP-SD)

HOUSE
BRADY, KEVIN (REP-TX)
FINCHER, STEVE MR. (REP-TN)
LANKFORD, JAMES PAUL MR. (REP-OK)
RYAN, PAUL D. (REP-WI)
SEWELL, TERRYCINA ANDREA (DEM-AL)
STEFANIK, ELISE M. (REP-NY)

Corporate Foundations and Giving Programs

International Paper Foundation
Contact: Deano Orr
6400 Poplar Ave.   Tel: (800) 236-1996
Memphis, TN 38197

Public Affairs and Related Activities Personnel

At Headquarters

ROYALTY, Jay   Tel: (901) 419-1731
Vice President, Investor Relations   Fax: (904) 214-9682

ALSUP, Julie   Tel: (901) 419-9000
Manager, Government Relations   Fax: (904) 214-9682
julie.alsup@ipaper.com
Registered Federal Lobbyist

CLEVES, Tom   Tel: (901) 419-7566
Vice President and General Manager, Containerboard and   Fax: (904) 214-9682
Recycling

EALY, C. Cato   Tel: (901) 419-9000
Senior Vice President, Corporate Development   Fax: (904) 214-9682

KADIEN, Thomas G.   Tel: (901) 419-9000
Senior Vice President, Human Resources, Communications   Fax: (904) 214-9682
and Government Relations

KARRE, Paul J.   Tel: (901) 419-9000
Senior Vice President, Human Resources and   Fax: (904) 214-9682
Communications

NICHOLLS, Tim S.   Tel: (800) 207-4003
Senior Vice President, Industrial Packaging   Fax: (904) 214-9682

ORR, Deano   Tel: (800) 236-1996
Executive Director and Grant Reviewer, IP Foundation   Fax: (904) 214-9682
deano.orr@ipaper.com

ROBERTS, Carol L.   Tel: (901) 419-9000
Senior Vice President and Chief Financial Officer   Fax: (904) 214-9682

RYAN , Tom   Tel: (901) 419-4333
Global Director, Media Relations   Fax: (904) 214-9682
Thomas.ryan2@ipaper.com

RYAN, Sharon   Tel: (901) 419-9000

Senior Vice President, General Counsel & Corporate   Fax: (904) 214-9682
Secretary
sharon.ryan@ipaper.com

At Washington Office

GEHLHAART, Donna   Tel: (202) 628-1309
Director, State Government Relations   Fax: (202) 628-1368
donna.gehlhaart@ipaper.com
Registered Federal Lobbyist

JOYCE, Meaghan Killion   Tel: (202) 628-1223
Political Affairs Manager Political Action Committee,   Fax: (202) 628-1368
Grassroots
meaghan.killion@ipaper.com

KEULEMAN, Christopher   Tel: (202) 628-7251
Director, Government Relations   Fax: (202) 628-1368
chris.keuleman@ipaper.com
Registered Federal Lobbyist

MANN, Mary M.   Tel: (202) 638-1319
Senior Manager, Government Relations   Fax: (202) 628-1368
mary.mann@ipaper.com
Registered Federal Lobbyist

WROBLESKI, Ann B.   Tel: (202) 628-1315
Vice President, Global Government Relations   Fax: (202) 628-1368
ann.wrobleski@ipaper.com

International Shipholding Corporation

Operates a diversified fleet of U.S. and foreign flag vessels through its subsidiaries, that provide international and domestic maritime transportation services to commercial and governmental customers primarily under medium to long-term charters and contracts.
www.intship.com
Annual Revenues: $259.42 million
Employees: 593
Ticker: NYSE: ISH
SIC: 4412
Industry/ies: Marine/Maritime/Shipping; Transportation
Legislative Issues: MAR; TAX

Chairman of the Board and Chief Executive Officer   Tel: (251) 243-9100
JOHNSEN, Niels M.

Main Headquarters
Mailing: 11 N. Water St.   Tel: (251) 243-9100
Suite 18290   TF: (800) 826-3513
Mobile, AL 36602

Political Action Committees
International Shipholding Corporation PAC
FEC ID: C00327122
Contact: Donna L. Johnson
11 N. Water St.
Suite 18290
Mobile, AL 36602

Contributions to Candidates: $10,750 (2015-2016)
Democrats: $3,500; Republicans: $7,250

Public Affairs and Related Activities Personnel

At Headquarters

ESTRADA, Manuel G.   Tel: (251) 243-9100
Vice President and Chief Financial Officer
estradmg@intship.com

JANASHVILI, Lev   Tel: (212) 227-7098
Contact, Media Relations
ljanashvili@igbir.com

JOHNSON, Donna L.   Tel: (251) 243-9100
Assistant Treasurer and PAC Contact

WILSON, Kevin M.   Tel: (251) 243-9100
Corporate Controller
wilsonkm@intship.com

International Speedway Corporation

International Speedway Corporation (ISC) is a corporation whose primary business is the ownership and management of NASCAR race tracks.
www.internationalspeedwaycorporation.com
Annual Revenues: $656.70 million
Employees: 845
Ticker: NASDAQ: ISCA
SIC: 7948
Industry/ies: Sports/Leisure/Entertainment; Transportation
Legislative Issues: BUD; TAX

Chairman of the Board   Tel: (386) 254-2700
FRANCE, James C.

Chief Executive Officer   Tel: (386) 254-2700
KENNEDY, Lesa France

Main Headquarters
Mailing: One Daytona Blvd.   Tel: (386) 254-2700
International Motorsports Center

Daytona Beach, FL 32114

Corporate Foundations and Giving Programs

International Speedway Corporation Contributions Program
Contact: Christi C. McGee
P.O. Box 2801
Daytona Beach, FL 32120

Public Affairs and Related Activities Personnel

At Headquarters

CROTTY, W. Garrett   Tel: (386) 254-2700
Executive Vice President, Chief Administration Officer and
Chief Legal Counsel

HOUSER, Daniel W.   Tel: (386) 254-2700
Executive Vice President, Chief Financial Officer and
Treasurer

JACKSON, Laura   Tel: (386) 254-2700
Senior Vice President, Corporate Services and Chief Human
Resources Officer

MILTHORPE, Kathy   Tel: (386) 254-2700
Contact, Government Relations
Registered Federal Lobbyist

MOTTO, Greg S.   Tel: (386) 254-2700
Vice President, Finance and Accounting and ISC Controller

SAUNDERS, John R   Tel: (386) 254-2700
President

SCHARBACK, Brett   Tel: (386) 254-2700
Senior Vice President, Legal and Chief Compliance Officer

WOLFE, Daryl Q.   Tel: (386) 254-2700
Executive Vice President and Chief Marketing Officer

At Other Offices

MCGEE, Christi C.
Director, Community and Governmental Affairs
P.O. Box 2801
Daytona Beach, FL 32120
cmcgee@iscmotorsports.com
Registered Federal Lobbyist

International Textile Group

Formed from the merger of Burlington Industries LLC and Cone Mills Corp. in the spring of
2004.
www.itg-global.com
Annual Revenues: $625.47 million
Employees: 4,800
Ticker: OTC: ITXN
SIC: 2200
Industry/ies: Apparel/Textiles Industry
Legislative Issues: DEF

Chairman of the Board   Tel: (336) 379-6220
ROSS, Jr., Wilbur L.   Fax: (336) 379-6287

President and Chief Executive Officer   Tel: (336) 379-6220
KUNBERGER, Kenneth T.   Fax: (336) 379-6287

Main Headquarters
Mailing: 804 Green Valley Rd.   Tel: (336) 379-6220
                Suite 300   Fax: (336) 379-6287
                Greensboro, NC 27408

Political Action Committees

ITG Good Government Committee PAC
FEC ID: C00040238
Contact: Faye Morton
804 Green Valley Rd.   Tel: (336) 379-6220
Suite 300   Fax: (336) 379-6287
Greensboro, NC 27408

   Contributions to Candidates: $1,000 (2015-2016)
   Republicans: $1,000

Public Affairs and Related Activities Personnel

At Headquarters

GARREN, Robert E.   Tel: (336) 379-6220
Vice President, Human Resources and Corporate   Fax: (336) 379-6287
Communications

KOONCE, Neil W.   Tel: (336) 379-6220
Vice President and General Counsel   Fax: (336) 379-6287

KUCZKOWSKI, CPA, Gail   Tel: (336) 379-6220
Executive Vice President and Chief Financial Officer Fax: (336) 379-6287

MORTON, Faye   Tel: (336) 379-6220
PAC Treasurer   Fax: (336) 379-6287
faye.morton@itg-iglobal.com

Internet Corporation for Assigned Names and Numbers (ICANN)

A not-for-profit public-benefit organization responsible for the management of the Internet's
domain name system (DNS), allocation of Internet protocol (IP) addresses, and assignment
of protocol parameters. It keeps the Internet secure, stable and interoperable and promotes
competition and develops policy on the Internet's unique identifiers.
www.icann.org
Annual Revenues: $68.32 million
Employees: 60
Industry/ies: Communications; Telecommunications/Internet/Cable
Legislative Issues: CPI; CPT; TEC

Chairman of the Board   Tel: (310) 823-9358
CROCKER, Stephen   Fax: (310) 823-8649

President and Chief Executive Officer   Tel: (310) 823-9358
CHEHADE, Fadi   Fax: (310) 823-8649

Main Headquarters
Mailing: 12025 Waterfront Dr.   Tel: (650) 684-0200
                Suite 300   Fax: (650) 328-2659
                Los Angeles, CA 90094-2536

Washington Office
Mailing: 801 17th St NW   Tel: (202) 570-7240
                Suite 400   Fax: (202) 789-0104
                Washington, DC 20006

Public Affairs and Related Activities Personnel

At Headquarters

BENNETT, Susan   Tel: (650) 684-0200
Chief Operating Officer   Fax: (650) 328-2659

BURNS, Duncan   Tel: (650) 684-0200
Senior Vice President, Global Communications   Fax: (650) 328-2659

CALVEZ, Xavier   Tel: (650) 684-0200
Chief Financial Officer   Fax: (650) 328-2659

CARPENTER, Tony   Tel: (650) 684-0200
Assitant, Administration   Fax: (650) 328-2659

CARVER, Kathryn A.   Tel: (650) 684-0200
Vice President, Governmental Engagement   Fax: (650) 328-2659

At Other Offices

ANTONOFF, Steve   Tel: (310) 823-9358
Senior Director, Human Resources   Fax: (310) 823-8649
4676 Admiralty Way, Suite 330
Marina Del Ray, CA 90292-6601
steve.antonoff@icann.org

BURNETTE, Stacy   Tel: (310) 823-9358
Director, Contractual Compliance   Fax: (310) 823-8649
4676 Admiralty Way, Suite 330
Marina Del Ray, CA 90292-6601
stacy.burnette@icann.org

BURNS, Duncan   Tel: (202) 570-7240
Senior Vice President, Global Communications   Fax: (202) 789-0104
1101 New York Ave. NW, Suite 930
Washington, DC 20005

HEDLUND, Jamie   Tel: (202) 570-7118
Vice President, Strategic Programs   Fax: (202) 789-0104
1101 New York Ave. NW, Suite 930
Washington, DC 20005
jamie.hedlund@icann.org
Registered Federal Lobbyist

HOGGARTH, Robert L.   Tel: (310) 823-9358
Senior Director, Policy   Fax: (310) 823-8649
4676 Admiralty Way, Suite 330
Marina Del Ray, CA 90292-6601
robert.hoggarth@icann.org

JEFFREY, John   Tel: (310) 823-9358
General Counsel and Secretary   Fax: (310) 823-8649
4676 Admiralty Way, Suite 330
Marina Del Ray, CA 90292-6601
jeffrey@icann.org

KING, Tanzanica S.   Tel: (310) 823-9358
Senior Manager, Meeting Strategy and Design   Fax: (310) 823-8649
4676 Admiralty Way, Suite 330
Marina Del Ray, CA 90292-6601
tanzanica.king@icann.org

MICHEL, Denise   Tel: (310) 823-9358
Vice President, Strategic Initiatives & Advisor to President Fax: (310) 823-8649
4676 Admiralty Way, Suite 330
Marina Del Ray, CA 90292-6601

Internet Poker Solutions, LLC

Consulting regarding the legalization of internet gaming in the USA.

Main Headquarters
Mailing: 10349 Watson Rd.
                Suite 100
                St. Louis, MO 63127

Public Affairs and Related Activities Personnel

At Headquarters

FEARS, Gary
Manager

Tel: (314) 795-7444

Interpublic Group of Companies

A global marketing communications company. It provides consumer advertising, digital marketing, communications planning and media buying, public relations and specialty marketing.
www.interpublic.com
Annual Revenues: $7.58 billion
Employees: 48,000
Ticker: NYSE: IPG
SIC: 7311
Industry/ies: Communications; Telecommunications/Internet/Cable

Chairman and Chief Executive Officer
ROTH, Michael I.
mroth@interpublic.com

Tel: (212) 704-1200
Fax: (212) 704-1201

Main Headquarters
Mailing: 1114 Avenue of the Americas
New York City, NY 10036

Tel: (212) 704-1200
Fax: (212) 704-1201

Corporate Foundations and Giving Programs

IPG Gives Back
Contact: Jemma Gould
1114 Ave.of the Americas
New York City, NY 10036

Tel: (212) 704-1200
Fax: (212) 704-1201

Public Affairs and Related Activities Personnel

At Headquarters

BONZANI, Andrew
Senior Vice President, General Counsel and Secretary
andrew.bonzani@interpublic..com

Tel: (212) 704-1200
Fax: (212) 704-1201

CUNNINGHAM, Thomas
Vice President, Corporate Communications
tom.cunningham@interpublic.com

Tel: (212) 704-1326
Fax: (212) 704-1201

GOULD, Jemma
Director, Content Creation
Jemma.Gould@Interpublic.com.

Tel: (212) 704-1327
Fax: (212) 704-1201

HARAY, Richard J.
Senior Vice President, Corporate Services

Tel: (212) 704-1200
Fax: (212) 704-1201

KRAKOWSKY, Philippe
Executive Vice President, Chief Strategy and Talent Officer
pkrakowsky@interpublic.com

Tel: (212) 704-1328
Fax: (212) 704-1201

LEINROTH, Peter
Senior Vice President and Managing Director
peter.leinroth@interpublic.com

Tel: (212) 704-1418
Fax: (212) 704-1201

LESHNE, Jerome J.
Senior Vice President, Investor Relations
jleshne@interpublic.com

Tel: (212) 704-1439
Fax: (212) 704-1201

MERGENTHALER, Frank
Executive Vice President and Chief Financial Officer
fmergenthaler@interpublic.com

Tel: (212) 704-1200
Fax: (212) 704-1201

POPIELARZ, Beverly
Senior Vice President, Global Director of Talent

Tel: (212) 704-1200
Fax: (212) 704-1201

Intevac, Inc.

A spin-off from Varian Associates; manufactures electro-optic laser illuminated viewing and ranging (LIVAR) systems used by the Air Force and Army. Produces equipment using magnetic media deposition technology.
www.intevac.com
Annual Revenues: $68.42 million
Employees: 265
Ticker: NASDAQ: IVAC
SIC: 3559
Industry/ies: Electricity & Electronics; Electronics; Energy/Electricity; Machinery/Equipment

Founder and Chairman of the Board
POND, Norman H.

Tel: (408) 986-9888
Fax: (408) 988-8145

President and Chief Executive Officer
BLONIGAN, Wendell T.

Tel: (408) 986-9888
Fax: (408) 988-8145

Main Headquarters
Mailing: 3560 Bassett St.
Santa Clara, CA 95054

Tel: (408) 986-9888
Fax: (408) 988-8145

Public Affairs and Related Activities Personnel

At Headquarters

ANDERSON, Jeff
Executive Vice President, Finance, Administration and Chief Financial Officer, Treasurer

Tel: (408) 986-9888
Fax: (408) 988-8145

BURK, Kimberly
Vice President, Human Resources

Tel: (408) 986-9888
Fax: (408) 988-8145

MCADAMS, Claire

Tel: (408) 986-9888

Investor Relations Counsel

Fax: (408) 988-8145

MONIZ, James
Chief Financial Officer, Treasurer and Secretary

Tel: (408) 986-9888
Fax: (408) 988-8145

RUSSAK, Michael A.
Executive Advisor

Tel: (408) 986-9888
Fax: (408) 988-8145

SMITH, Christopher
Vice President, Business Development

Tel: (408) 986-9888
Fax: (408) 988-8145

Intrepid Potash

A producer of potash (potassium chloride).
www.intrepidpotash.com
Annual Revenues: $370.33 million
Employees: 928
Ticker: NYSE: IPI
SIC: 1400
Industry/ies: Mining Industry; Natural Resources
Legislative Issues: NAT

Executive Chairman of the Board, President and Chief Executive Officer
JORNAYVAZ, III, Robert P.
robert.jornayvaz@intrepidpotash.com

Tel: (303) 296-3006
Fax: (303) 298-7502

Main Headquarters
Mailing: 707 17th St.
Suite 4200
Denver, CO 80202

Tel: (303) 296-3006
Fax: (303) 298-7502
TF: (800) 418-6423

Public Affairs and Related Activities Personnel

At Headquarters

FEIST, Kelvin G.
Senior Vice President, Marketing and Sales

Tel: (303) 296-3006
Fax: (303) 298-7502

FRANTZ, Brian D.
Interim Chief Financial Officer

Tel: (303) 296-3006
Fax: (303) 298-7502

HARVEY, JR, Hugh E.
Executive Vice Chairman of the Board

Tel: (303) 296-3006
Fax: (303) 298-7502

KOHN, Gary A.
Vice President, Investor Relations and Treasurer

Tel: (303) 296-3006
Fax: (303) 298-7502

MANSANTI, John G.
Senior Vice President, Strategic Initiatives and Technical Services

Tel: (303) 296-3006
Fax: (303) 298-7502

MCCANDLESS, Margaret E.
Vice President, General Counsel and Secretary

Tel: (303) 296-3006
Fax: (303) 298-7502

TAYLOR, Kenneth G.
Vice President, Corporate Development

Tel: (303) 296-3006
Fax: (303) 298-7502

WHYTE, James N.
Executive Vice President, Human Resources and Risk Management
jamie.whyte@intrepidpotash.com

Tel: (303) 296-3006
Fax: (303) 298-7502

Intuit, Inc.

Software company that develops financial and tax preparation software and related services.
www.intuit.com
Annual Revenues: $4.58 billion
Employees: 8,000
Ticker: NASDAQ: INTU
SIC: 7372
Industry/ies: Banking/Finance/Investments; Communications; Computer/Technology; Telecommunications/Internet/Cable
Legislative Issues: BUD; CPI; CPT; CSP; FIN; HCR; IMM; LBR; SCI; SMB; TAX; TRD

Chairman of the Board
CAMPBELL, Bill

Tel: (650) 944-6000
Fax: (650) 944-3699

President and Chief Executive Officer
SMITH, Brad D.

Tel: (650) 944-6000
Fax: (650) 944-3699

Main Headquarters
Mailing: 601 Pennsylvania Ave. NW
North Building, Suite 200
Washington, DC 20004

Tel: (202) 484-1491

Political Action Committees
Intuit 21st Century Leadership Fund PAC
FEC ID: C00361741
Contact: Lauren Hotz
2700 Coast Ave.
Mountain View, CA 94043

Tel: (650) 944-6000
Fax: (650) 944-6000

Contributions to Candidates: $99,000 (2015-2016)
Democrats: $52,000; Republicans: $47,000

Corporate Foundations and Giving Programs

Intuit Financial Freedom Foundation
601 Pennsylvania Ave. NW
North Bldg., Suite 200
Washington, DC 20004

Tel: (202) 484-1491

The Intuit Foundation
2632 Marine Way
Mountain View, CA 94043

Tel: (650) 944-6000
Fax: (650) 944-3699

Public Affairs and Related Activities Personnel

At Headquarters

MARTINEZ, Jr., Miguel A.
Registered Federal Lobbyist

Tel: (202) 484-1491

MCKAY, Bernard F.
Chief Public Policy Officer, Vice President, Global Corporate Affairs
bernie_mckay@intuit.com
Registered Federal Lobbyist

Tel: (202) 484-1491

NETRAM, Melissa
Senior Public Policy Manager and Counsel
Registered Federal Lobbyist

Tel: (202) 484-1491

PEDIGO, Amanda
Federal Lobbyist
Registered Federal Lobbyist

Tel: (202) 484-1491

RAINS, Laurie D.
Federal Lobbyist
Registered Federal Lobbyist

Tel: (202) 484-1491

At Other Offices

DONAHUE, Caroline
Senior Vice President, Chief Marketing and Sales Officer
2632 Marine Way
Mountain View, CA 94043

Tel: (650) 944-6000
Fax: (650) 944-3699

FENNELL, Laura
Senior Vice President, General Counsel and Secretary
2632 Marine Way
Mountain View, CA 94043
laura.fennell@intuit.com

Tel: (650) 944-6000
Fax: (650) 944-3699

FLOURNOY, Mark
Vice President, Corporate Controller & Chief Accounting Officer
2700 Coast Ave.
Mt. View, CA 94043

HOTZ, Lauren
PAC Treasurer
2700 Coast Ave.
Mt. View, CA 94043

LANESEY, Rob
Chief Communications Officer
2632 Marine Way
Mountain View, CA 94043
rob_lanesey@intuit.com

Tel: (650) 450-0028
Fax: (650) 944-3699

WHITELEY, Sherry
Senior Vice President and Chief Human Resources Officer
2632 Marine Way
Mountain View, CA 94043

Tel: (650) 944-6000
Fax: (650) 944-3699

WILLIAMS, R. Neil
Senior Vice President and Chief Financial Officer
2632 Marine Way
Mountain View, CA 94043

Tel: (650) 944-6000
Fax: (650) 944-3699

Intuitive Surgical, Inc.

Intuitive Surgical designs and builds the da Vinci Surgical System, the breakthrough platform for robotically assisted minimally invasive surgery.
www.intuitivesurgical.com
Annual Revenues: $2.18 billion
Employees: 2,978
Ticker: NASDAQ: ISRG
SIC: 3842
Industry/ies: Medicine/Health Care/Mental Health
Legislative Issues: HCR; MED; MMM; SCI

Chairman of the Board
SMITH, Lonnie M.

Tel: (408) 523-2100
Fax: (408) 523-1390

President and Chief Executive Officer
GUTHART, Gary S.

Tel: (408) 523-2100
Fax: (408) 523-1390

Main Headquarters
Mailing: 1020 Kifer Rd.
Bldg. 108
Sunnyvale, CA 94086

Tel: (408) 523-2100
Fax: (408) 523-1390

Public Affairs and Related Activities Personnel

At Headquarters

BISCHOFF, Paige A.
Vice President, Corporate Communications

Tel: (408) 523-2100
Fax: (408) 523-1390

CHILD, Craig
Vice President, Human Resources

Tel: (408) 523-2100
Fax: (408) 523-1390

CURIC, Aleks
Vice President, Strategy

Tel: (408) 523-2100
Fax: (408) 523-1390

JENNINGS, Steve
Federal Lobbyist
Registered Federal Lobbyist

Tel: (408) 523-2100
Fax: (408) 523-1390

JOHNSON, Mark
Senior Vice President, Senior Vice President Regulatory and Quality

Tel: (408) 523-2100
Fax: (408) 523-1390

JONES, Dan
Director, External Affairs
dan.jones@intusurg.com
Registered Federal Lobbyist

Tel: (408) 523-2100
Fax: (408) 523-1390

MCNAMARA, Jerry J.
Executive Vice President, Worldwide Sales and Marketing

Tel: (408) 523-2100
Fax: (408) 523-1390

MELTZER, Mark J.
Senior Vice President, General Counsel and Chief Compliance Officer

Tel: (408) 523-2100
Fax: (408) 523-1390

MOHR, Marshall L.
Senior Vice President and Chief Financial Officer

Tel: (408) 523-2100
Fax: (408) 523-1390

ROZYNSKI, Edward
Vice President, Government Affairs

Tel: (408) 523-2100
Fax: (408) 523-1390

STOFFEL, David
Vice President, Marketing and New Business Development

Tel: (408) 523-2100
Fax: (408) 523-1390

VAVOSO, Glenn
Senior Vice President, Global Sales Operations and Strategy

Tel: (408) 523-2100
Fax: (408) 523-1390

WONSON, Angela
Vice President, Communications

Tel: (408) 523-2100
Fax: (408) 523-1390

Invacare Corporation

Manufactures home healthcare equipment.
www.invacare.com
Annual Revenues: $1.11 billion
Employees: 4,700
Ticker: NYSE: IVC
SIC: 3842
NAICS: 339113
Industry/ies: Medicine/Health Care/Mental Health
Legislative Issues: BUD; HCR; MMM

Chairman, President and Chief Executive Officer
MONAGHAN, Matthew E.

Tel: (440) 329-6000
Fax: (877) 619-7996

Main Headquarters
Mailing: One Invacare Way
Elyria, OH 44035-4190

Tel: (440) 329-6000
Fax: (877) 619-7996
TF: (800) 333-6900

Washington Office
Mailing: 9323 Old Mansion Rd.
Suite 402
Alexandria, VA 22314

Tel: (440) 329-6226
TF: (800) 333-6900

Political Action Committees
Invacare Corporation PAC (Inva PAC)
FEC ID: C00249896
Contact: Jerome E. Fox Jr.
One Invacare Way
P.O. Box 4028
Elyria, OH 44035

Contributions to Candidates: $24,250 (2015-2016)
Democrats: $2,750; Republicans: $21,500

Corporate Foundations and Giving Programs

The Invacare Foundation
One Invacare Way
P.O. Box 4028
Elyria, OH 44035

Tel: (440) 329-6000

Public Affairs and Related Activities Personnel

At Headquarters

FOX, Jr., Jerome E.
PAC Treasurer

Tel: (440) 329-6000
Fax: (877) 619-7996

GUDBRANSON, Robert K.
Senior Vice President and Chief Financial Officer
rgudbranson@invacare.com

Tel: (440) 329-6111
Fax: (877) 619-7996

LAPLACA, Anthony C.
Senior Vice President and General Counsel

Tel: (440) 329-6000
Fax: (877) 619-7996

MAHONEY, Lara
Director, Investor Relations and Corporate Communications
lmahoney@invacare.com

Tel: (440) 329-6393
Fax: (877) 619-7996

SLANGEN, Louis F.J.
Senior Vice President

Tel: (440) 329-6000
Fax: (877) 619-7996

STUMPP, Patricia
Senior Vice President, Human Resources

Tel: (440) 329-6000
Fax: (877) 619-7996

At Washington Office

BACHENHEIMER, Cara C.
Senior Vice President, Government Relations

Tel: (440) 329-6226

cbachenheimer@invacare.com
Registered Federal Lobbyist

Invenergy Services
See listing on page 444 under Invenergy, LLC

Invenergy, LLC
Develops, owns, and operates power generation facilities in North America and Europe and is North America's largest independent wind power generation company.
www.invenergyllc.com
Annual Revenues: $10.60 million
Employees: 100
Industry/ies: Energy/Electricity
Legislative Issues: TAX

President and Chief Executive Officer	Tel:	(312) 244-1400
POLSKY, Michael	Fax:	(312) 244-1444

Main Headquarters

Mailing:	One S. Wacker Dr.	Tel:	(312) 244-1400
	Suite 1900	Fax:	(312) 244-1444
	Chicago, IL 60606		

Political Action Committees
Invenergy PAC
FEC ID: C00437244
Contact: Joseph Condo

Contributions to Candidates: $15,200 (2015-2016)
Democrats: $6,200; Republicans: $9,000

Public Affairs and Related Activities Personnel

At Headquarters

CONDO, Joseph	Tel:	(312) 506-1465
PAC Treasurer, Senior Vice President and General Counsel	Fax:	(312) 244-1444
jcondo@invenergyllc.com		
KRINSKY, Alissa	Tel:	(312) 582-1554
Director, Communications	Fax:	(312) 244-1444
akrinsky@invenergyllc.com		
MURPHY, Jim	Tel:	(312) 244-1400
Executive Vice President, Chief Financial Officer and Chief Operating Officer	Fax:	(312) 244-1444
jmurphy2@invenergyllc.com		
SHIELD, Jim	Tel:	(312) 244-1400
Executive Vice President and Chief Development Officer	Fax:	(312) 244-1444
ZADLO, Kris	Tel:	(312) 244-1400
Vice President, Regulatory Affairs and Transmission	Fax:	(312) 244-1444
kzadlo@invenergyllc.com		

Invensys Control Systems
A provider of components, systems, and services used in appliances, heating, air conditioning/ cooling, refrigeration, and aftermarket products.
www.invensyscontrols.com
Employees: 7,000
Industry/ies: Computer/Technology; Machinery/Equipment

Chairman of the Board	Tel:	(630) 260-3400
RUDD, Nigel	Fax:	(630) 260-7325

Main Headquarters

Mailing:	191 E. North Ave.	Tel:	(630) 260-3400
	Carol Stream, IL 60188	Fax:	(630) 260-7325

Inverness Medical Innovations, Inc.
See listing on page 32 under Alere Inc.

Invesco Ltd.
Invesco Ltd. provides an array of enduring solutions for retail, institutional and high-net-worth clients around the world.
www.invesco.com
Annual Revenues: $5.17 billion
Employees: 6,360
Ticker: NYSE: IVZ
Industry/ies: Banking/Finance/Investments
Legislative Issues: TAX

Chairman and Non-Executive Director	Tel:	(404) 479-1095
JOHNSON, Ben F.	Fax:	(404) 439-4911
President and Chief Executive Officer	Tel:	(404) 479-1095
FLANAGAN, CFA, CPA, Martin L.	Fax:	(404) 439-4911

Main Headquarters

Mailing:	Two Peachtree Pointe	Tel:	(404) 479-1095
	1555 Peachtree St. NE, Suite 1800	Fax:	(404) 439-4911
	Atlanta, GA 30309	TF:	(800) 241-5477

Political Action Committees
Invesco PLC PAC
FEC ID: C00253369
Contact: Doug Kidd

1360 Peachtree St. NE
Atlanta, GA 30309

Contributions to Candidates: $38,300 (2015-2016)
Democrats: $12,600; Republicans: $25,700

Principal Recipients

SENATE
ISAKSON, JOHN HARDY (REP-GA)

Corporate Foundations and Giving Programs
Invesco Cares
Two Peachtree Pointe
1555 Peachtree St. NE, Suite 1800
Atlanta, GA 30309

Public Affairs and Related Activities Personnel

At Headquarters

HENSEL, Bill	Tel:	(404) 479-2886
Director, Media Relations	Fax:	(404) 439-4911
bill.hensel@invesco.com		
KRUGMAN, Jordan	Tel:	(404) 439-4605
Contact, Investor Relations and Treasurer	Fax:	(404) 439-4911
jordan.krugman@invesco.com		

At Other Offices

KIDD, Doug	Tel:	(404) 479-2922
Contact, Media Relations and PAC Treasurer	Fax:	(404) 439-4911
1360 Peachtree St. NE		
Atlanta, GA 30309		
doug.kidd@invesco.com		

Investment Professionals Inc.
A private, full-service investment brokerage and asset management firm.
www.invpro.com
Annual Revenues: $37.80 million
Employees: 200
Industry/ies: Banking/Finance/Investments

Chairman and Founder	Tel:	(210) 308-8800
BARNES, Scott	Fax:	(210) 308-8707
President and Chief Executive Officer	Tel:	(210) 308-8800
MCANELLY, Jay	Fax:	(210) 308-8707
jay.mcanelly@invpro.com		

Main Headquarters

Mailing:	16414 San Pedro Ave.	Tel:	(210) 308-8800
	Suite 150	Fax:	(210) 308-8707
	San Antonio, TX 78232	TF:	(800) 593-8800

Public Affairs and Related Activities Personnel

At Headquarters

DULLNIG, Richard	Tel:	(210) 308-8800
Chief Compliance Officer	Fax:	(210) 308-8707
FANCHER, Suzanne	Tel:	(210) 308-8800
Senior Vice President, Operations	Fax:	(210) 308-8707
GARZA, Veronica P.	Tel:	(210) 308-8800
Vice President, Human Resources	Fax:	(210) 308-8707
SACCHETTI, John	Tel:	(210) 308-8800
Seniur Vice President, Capital Markets	Fax:	(210) 308-8707
WATSON, Amy	Tel:	(210) 582-2845
Vice President, Director of Marketing	Fax:	(210) 308-8707
amy.watson@invpro.com		

INVISTA
An integrated fiber, resin and intermediates company. A subsidiary of privately held industrial conglomerate Koch Industries. It produces of chemical intermediates, polymers and fibers. The company's advantaged technologies for nylon, spandex and polyester are used to produce clothing, carpet, car parts and countless other everyday products.
www.invista.com
Employees: 15,000
Industry/ies: Apparel/Textiles Industry

Chairman of the Board and Chief Executive Officer	Tel:	(316) 828-1000
GENTRY, Jeff	Fax:	(316) 828-1801

Main Headquarters

Mailing:	4123 E. 37th St., North	Tel:	(316) 828-1000
	Wichita, KS 67220	Fax:	(316) 828-1160
		TF:	(877) 446-8478

Public Affairs and Related Activities Personnel

At Headquarters

RAMSEYER, Roger	Tel:	(316) 828-1525
Director, Public Affairs	Fax:	(316) 828-1801
STANDIFER, Greg	Tel:	(316) 828-1000
Manager, Marketing Communications	Fax:	(316) 828-1160
STUTZMAN, Jodie	Tel:	(316) 828-1786
Director, Public Affairs and Corporate Communications	Fax:	(316) 828-1801

Jodie.Stutzman@INVISTA.com

Invitrogen Corporation

See listing on page 490 under Life Technologies Corporation

IOGEN Corporation

A biotechnology firm.
www.iogen.ca
Industry/ies: Chemicals & Chemical Industry

| **Chairman of the Board** | Tel: | (613) 733-9830 |
| MATHER, H. Clive | Fax: | (613) 733-0781 |

| **President and Chief Executive Officer** | Tel: | (613) 733-9830 |
| FOODY, Brian | Fax: | (613) 733-0781 |

Main Headquarters		
Mailing: 310 Hunt Club Rd., East	Tel:	(613) 733-9830
Ottawa, ON K1V 1C1	Fax:	(613) 733-0781

Public Affairs and Related Activities Personnel

At Headquarters

| DUMVILLE, Claire | Tel: | (613) 733-9830 |
| *Vice President, Finance* | Fax: | (613) 733-0781 |

| HLADIK, Maurice | Tel: | (613) 733-9830 |
| *Federal Lobbyist* | Fax: | (613) 733-0781 |

| KING, Hannah | Tel: | (613) 733-9830 |
| *General Counsel and Corporate Secretary* | Fax: | (613) 733-0781 |

| MCLENNAN, Gordon | Tel: | (613) 733-9830 |
| *Vice President of Business Development* | Fax: | (613) 733-0781 |

| PIKOR, Heather | Tel: | (613) 733-9830 |
| *Vice President Corporate Affairs* | Fax: | (613) 733-0781 |

Iomega Corporation

A wholly-owned subsidiary of EMC Corporation (see separate listing). Manufactures high performance, removable media disk drives and sub-systems and computer peripherals.
www.iomega.com
Annual Revenues: $400 million
Employees: 300
Ticker: NYSE: IOM
SIC: 3572; 5045
Industry/ies: Computer/Technology

Main Headquarters		
Mailing: 3721 Valley Centre Dr.	Tel:	(858) 314-7000
Suite 200	Fax:	(858) 314-7001
San Diego, CA 92130		

Public Affairs and Related Activities Personnel

At Headquarters

| ROMM, Preston | Tel: | (858) 314-7188 |
| *Chief Financial Officer* | Fax: | (858) 314-7001 |

ROMOSER, Chris	Tel:	(858) 314-7148
Director, Corporate Communications and Public Relations	Fax:	(858) 314-7001
romoser@iomega.com		

WHARTON, Peter	Tel:	(858) 314-7000
Vice President, Marketing	Fax:	(858) 314-7001
p.wharton@iomega.com		

ZOLLMAN, Ron S.	Tel:	(858) 314-7000
General Counsel and Secretary	Fax:	(858) 314-7001
zollman@iomega.com		

ION Media Network, Inc.

ION Media Networks, Inc. owns and operates the U.S. broadcast television station group and ION Television, the independent broadcast television network.
www.ionmedianetworks.com
Annual Revenues: $19.60 million
Employees: 500
SIC: 4832
Industry/ies: Communications; Media/Mass Communication

| **Chairman of the Board and Chief Executive officer** | Tel: | (561) 659-4122 |
| BURGESS, Brandon | Fax: | (561) 655-7343 |

Main Headquarters		
Mailing: 601 Clearwater Park Rd.	Tel:	(561) 659-4122
W. Palm Beach, FL 33401	Fax:	(561) 659-4252

Political Action Committees
ION Media Network, Inc. PAC
FEC ID: C00513606
Contact: Sheila Reinken
601 Clearwater Park Rd.   Tel: (561) 659-4122
W. Palm Beach, FL 33401   Fax: (561) 659-4252

  Contributions to Candidates: $7,900 (2015-2016)
  Democrats: $2,700; Republicans: $5,200

Public Affairs and Related Activities Personnel

At Headquarters

| ADDEO, Chris | Tel: | (561) 659-4122 |
| *Senior Vice President, Marketing* | Fax: | (561) 659-4252 |

| APPEL, Stephen | Tel: | (561) 659-4122 |
| *Advertising Sales* | Fax: | (561) 659-4252 |

| HUBNER, Michael | Tel: | (561) 659-4122 |
| *Senior Vice President, General Counsel and Corporate Secretary* | Fax: | (561) 659-4252 |

| LAVALETTE, Gordon | Tel: | (561) 659-4122 |
| *Finance* | Fax: | (561) 659-4252 |

| QUINN, Jeff | Tel: | (561) 659-4122 |
| *Commercial Operations* | Fax: | (561) 659-4252 |

| REINKEN, Sheila | Tel: | (561) 659-4122 |
| *Treasurer* | Fax: | (561) 659-4252 |

| SANTISI, Terri | Tel: | (561) 659-4122 |
| *Administration* | Fax: | (561) 659-4252 |

Ionatron, Inc.

See listing on page 70 under Applied Energetics, Inc.

Iowa Student Loan Liquidity Corporation

Iowa Student Loan is a nonprofit organization that helps students and parents.
www.iowastudentloan.org
Annual Revenues: $3.1 billion
Employees: 375
Industry/ies: Economics And Economic Development; Education
Legislative Issues: EDU

| **Chairman of the Board** | Tel: | (515) 243-5626 |
| HENSLEY, Christine | Fax: | (515) 223-9535 |

| **President and Chief Executive Officer** | Tel: | (515) 243-5626 |
| MCCULLOUGH, Steven W. | Fax: | (515) 223-9535 |

Main Headquarters		
Mailing: 6775 Vista Dr.	Tel:	(515) 243-5626
West Des Moines, IA 50266-9305	Fax:	(515) 223-9535
	TF:	(800) 243-7552

Public Affairs and Related Activities Personnel

At Headquarters

| BIRD, Joe | Tel: | (515) 243-5626 |
| *Senior Vice President, Business Development and Client Relations* | Fax: | (515) 223-9535 |

| DEBOLT, Mary Kay | Tel: | (515) 243-5626 |
| *Senior Vice President, Operations and Corporate Secretary* | Fax: | (515) 223-9535 |

| LACEY, Erin | Tel: | (515) 243-5626 |
| *Executive Vice President and Corporate Treasurer* | Fax: | (515) 223-9535 |

| NICHOLS, Greg | Tel: | (515) 243-5626 |
| *Senior Vice President, Public Affairs and Community Relations* | Fax: | (515) 223-9535 |

| WITTHOFF, Walter | Tel: | (515) 243-5626 |
| *Senior Vice President and Chief Compliance Officer* | Fax: | (515) 223-9535 |

Iowa Telecom

Iowa Telecom is a telecommunications service provider that offers local telephone, long distance, Internet, broadband and network access services to business and residential customers.
www.iowatelecom.com
Annual Revenues: $254.14 million
Employees: 800
Ticker: NYSE: IWA
SIC: 4813
Industry/ies: Communications; Telecommunications/Internet/Cable

| **Chairman, President and Chief Executive Officer** | Tel: | (641) 787-2000 |
| WELLS, Alan | Fax: | (641) 787-2001 |

Main Headquarters		
Mailing: 403 W. Fourth St., North	Tel:	(641) 787-2000
Newton, IA 50208	Fax:	(641) 787-2001
	TF:	(877) 901-4692

Public Affairs and Related Activities Personnel

At Headquarters

| ANDERSON, David M. | Tel: | (641) 787-2000 |
| *Vice President, External Affairs* | Fax: | (641) 787-2001 |

| HENRY, Donald G. | | |
| *Vice President, General Counsel and Secretary* | | |

INDA, Kevin	Tel:	(407) 566-1180
Contact, Corporate Communications	Fax:	(407) 566-1181
kevin.inda@cci-ir.com		

| KNOCK, Craig | Tel: | (641) 787-2089 |
| *Vice President, Chief Financial Officer and Treasurer* | Fax: | (641) 787-2468 |

IPKeys Technologies, LLC

Operates as an internet protocol, information technology and communications systems. IPKeys expertise includes Network and Telecommunications Engineering; Systems Engineering and Integration; Cyber Security; Systems Acquisition, Production and Fielding; Modeling and Simulation; and Energy/Smart Grid Engineering Services.
www.ipkeys.com
Annual Revenues: $13.90 million
Employees: 40
NAICS: 541511; 541512; 541519; 519190; 541330
Industry/ies: Computer/Technology; Defense/Homeland Security; Government-Related

| **Chief Executive Officer** | Tel: | (732) 389-8112 |
| NAWY, Lanfen C. | Fax: | (732) 389-8149 |

Main Headquarters

Mailing:	One Industrial Way West	Tel:	(732) 389-8112
	Building E, Suites G&H	Fax:	(732) 389-8149
	Eatontown, NJ 07724	TF:	(855) 475-3970

Public Affairs and Related Activities Personnel

At Headquarters

NAWY, Robert M.	Tel:	(732) 389-8112
Managing Director and Chief Financial Officer	Fax:	(732) 389-8149
rnawy@ipkeys.com		

| PAPPAS, Mark A. | Tel: | (732) 389-8112 |
| President | Fax: | (732) 389-8149 |

IPSA International, Inc.

A provider of investigative consulting services.
www.ipsaintl.com
Employees: 4
Industry/ies: Banking/Finance/Investments; Defense/Homeland Security; Government-Related

President and Chief Executive Officer	Tel:	(602) 889-1626
WACHTLER, Dan	Fax:	(602) 296-0008
dwachtler@ipsaintl.com		

Main Headquarters

Mailing:	1185 Avenue of the Americas	Tel:	(602) 889-1626
	Suite 1750	TF:	(800) 997-4772
	New York City, NY 10036		

Washington Office

| Mailing: | 13800 Coppermine Rd. | |
| | Herndon, VA 20171 | |

Public Affairs and Related Activities Personnel

At Headquarters

COLLINS, Trevor	Tel:	(602) 889-1626
Managing Director		
tcollins@ipsaintl.com		

LEMIEUX, Carie	Tel:	(602) 889-1626
Controller		
clemieux@ipsaintl.com		

PAP, Jillian	Tel:	(602) 889-1626
Chief Administrative Officer		
Jillian.Pap@ipsaintl.com		

At Other Offices

BERNAICHE, Jillian	Tel:	(480) 235-2066
Director, Corporate Services	Fax:	(212) 946-4991
206 E. Virginia Ave.		
Phoenix, AZ 85004-1110		
jbernaiche@ipsaintl.com		

Iron Company

See listing on page 171 under CB&I.

Iroquois Gas Transmission System

Iroquois Gas Transmission System, L.P. is the owner of an interstate pipeline extending 411 miles from the US-Canadian border at Waddington, NY, through the state of Connecticut to South Commack, Long Island, NY and Hunts Point, Bronx, NY.
www.iroquois.com
Annual Revenues: $205.04 million
Employees: 100
SIC: 4922
Industry/ies: Natural Resources
Legislative Issues: UTI

| **President** | Tel: | (203) 925-7209 |
| BRUNER, Jeffrey A. | Fax: | (203) 929-9501 |

Main Headquarters

Mailing:	One Corporate Dr.	Tel:	(203) 925-7200
	Suite 600	Fax:	(203) 929-9501
	Shelton, CT 06484	TF:	(800) 253-5152

Corporate Foundations and Giving Programs

Iroquios Community Grant Program

Contact: Ruth Parkins

One Corporate Dr.	Tel:	(203) 925-7209
Suite 600		
Shelton, CT 06484		

Public Affairs and Related Activities Personnel

At Headquarters

| BAILEY, Paul | Tel: | (203) 925-7209 |
| Vice President & Chief Financial Officer | Fax: | (203) 929-9501 |

PARKINS, Ruth	Tel:	(203) 925-7209
Manager, Public Affairs and Foundation Contact	Fax:	(203) 929-9501
ruth_parkins@iroquois.com		

| RUPFF, Scott E. | Tel: | (203) 925-7209 |
| Vice President, Marketing, Development and Commercial Operations | Fax: | (203) 929-9501 |

| WHITE, Todd | Tel: | (203) 925-7284 |
| Director, Business Development and Transportation Services | Fax: | (203) 929-9501 |

| WIELER, Michelle | Tel: | (203) 925-7200 |
| Treasurer and Director, Financial Services | Fax: | (203) 929-9501 |

The Irvine Company

A real estate investment and land development company.
www.irvinecompany.com
Annual Revenues: $93.2 million
Employees: 2,000
Industry/ies: Construction/Construction Materials; Defense/Homeland Security; Government-Related
Legislative Issues: TAX

| **Chairman of the Board** | Tel: | (949) 720-2000 |
| BREN, Donald | Fax: | (949) 720-2218 |

| **President, Community Development** | Tel: | (949) 720-2526 |
| YOUNG, Daniel | Fax: | (949) 720-2575 |

Main Headquarters

| Mailing: | 550 Newport Center Dr. | Tel: | (949) 720-2000 |
| | Newport Beach, CA 92660 | Fax: | (949) 720-2218 |

Political Action Committees

Irvine Company Employees PAC
FEC ID: C00131615
Contact: Daniel T. Miller
550 Newport Center Dr.
Newport Beach, CA 92660

> **Contributions to Candidates:** $19,400 (2015-2016)
> Republicans: $19,400

Corporate Foundations and Giving Programs

The Irvine Company Contributions Program
Contact: Daniel Young

| 550 Newport Center Dr. | Tel: | (949) 720-2000 |
| Newport Beach, CA 92660 | Fax: | (949) 720-2218 |

Public Affairs and Related Activities Personnel

At Headquarters

| FEDALEN, Jr., Chip | Tel: | (949) 720-2000 |
| Group Executive Vice President and Chief Financial Officer | Fax: | (949) 720-2218 |

| HEDIGAN, Dan | Tel: | (949) 720-2000 |
| President, Land Sales and Home Building | Fax: | (949) 720-2218 |

| LEY, Mary | Tel: | (949) 720-2000 |
| Executive Vice President and Chief Information Officer | Fax: | (949) 720-2218 |

LOBDELL, Bill	Tel:	(949) 720-2000
Vice President, Communications	Fax:	(949) 720-2218
blobdell@irvinecompany.com		

| MILLER, Daniel T. | Tel: | (949) 720-2000 |
| PAC Contact | Fax: | (949) 720-2218 |

| RUSSO, Tony | Tel: | (949) 720-2471 |
| Group Senior Vice President, Corporate Affairs | Fax: | (949) 720-2218 |

ISE Corporation

Provides hybrid system evaluations to vehicle OEMs and fleet.
www.isecorp.com
Employees: 100
Industry/ies: Automotive Industry; Transportation

| **Chairman of the Board** | Tel: | (858) 413-1720 |
| GOODMAN, David R. | Fax: | (858) 212-9209 |

Main Headquarters

| Mailing: | 12302 Kerran St. | Tel: | (858) 413-1720 |
| | Poway, CA 92064-6884 | Fax: | (858) 413-1732 |

Public Affairs and Related Activities Personnel

At Headquarters

BERNASCONI, Alex G.	Tel:	(858) 413-1720
Senior Vice President, Sales and Marketing	Fax:	(858) 212-9209
abernasconi@isecorp.com		

PAYNTON, Carolyn
Manager, Marketing and Communication
cpaynton@isecorp.com
Tel: (858) 413-1720
Fax: (858) 212-9209

SPRAGG, Justin M.
Vice President, General Counsel & Corporate Secretary
Tel: (858) 413-1720
Fax: (858) 212-9209

Isle of Capri Casinos

A gaming entertainment company.
www.islecorp.com
Annual Revenues: $982.41 million
Employees: 7,000
Ticker: NASDAQ (GS): ISLE
SIC: 7011
Industry/ies: Sports/Leisure/Entertainment
Legislative Issues: GAM

Executive Chairman of the Board
PERRY, James B.
Tel: (314) 813-9200
Fax: (314) 813-9480

President And Chief Executive Officer
MCDOWELL, Virginia
Tel: (314) 813-9200
Fax: (314) 813-9480

Main Headquarters
Mailing: 600 Emerson Rd.
Suite 300
St. Louis, MO 63141
Tel: (314) 813-9200
Fax: (314) 813-9480
TF: (800) 843-4753

Political Action Committees
Isle of Capri Casinos Inc. PAC
FEC ID: C00323311
Contact: Donn Mitchell II
600 Emerson Rd.
Suite 300
St. Louis, MO 63141

Contributions to Candidates: $10,500 (2015-2016)
Democrats: $7,500; Republicans: $3,000

Corporate Foundations and Giving Programs
Isle of Capri Casinos Contributions Program
600 Emerson Rd.
Suite 300
St. Louis, MO 63141
Tel: (800) 843-4753

Public Affairs and Related Activities Personnel

At Headquarters

ALEXANDER, Jill
Senior Director, Corporate Communications and Contact, Investor Relations
jill.alexander@islecorp.com
Tel: (314) 813-9368
Fax: (314) 813-9480

BLOCK, Arnold
Chief Operating Officer
Tel: (314) 813-9200
Fax: (314) 813-9480

DEWALT, Stacy
Senior Vice President, Marketing
Tel: (314) 813-9200
Fax: (314) 813-9480

GUIDO, Greg D.
Senior Vice President, Development, Legal Affairs and Secretary
Tel: (228) 396-7000
Fax: (314) 813-9480

HAUSLER, Eric
Chief Financial Officer
Tel: (314) 813-9200
Fax: (314) 813-9480

JACKSON, Sarah
Senior Vice President, Human Resources
Tel: (314) 813-9200
Fax: (314) 813-9480

MITCHELL, II, Donn
Chief Administrative Officer
Mail Stop Suite 300
donn.mitchell@islecorp.com
Tel: (314) 813-9200
Fax: (314) 813-9480

QUATMANN, Jr., Edmund L.
Chief Legal Officer
Tel: (314) 813-9200
Fax: (314) 813-9480

Isovac Products LLC

Leak detection and isolation systems.
www.isovacproducts.com
Industry/ies: Defense/Homeland Security; Government-Related; Science; Scientific Research

Main Headquarters
Mailing: 1306 Enterprise Dr., Unit C
Romeoville, IL 60446
Tel: (630) 679-1740
Fax: (630) 679-1750

Public Affairs and Related Activities Personnel

At Headquarters

LYSSENKO, Taras
Federal Lobbyist
Tel: (305) 794-4457
Fax: (630) 679-1750

ITC Holdings Corporation (International Transmission Company)

Independent electric transmission company.
Annual Revenues: $1.04 million
Employees: 587
Ticker: NYSE: ITC
SIC: 4911

Industry/ies: Energy/Electricity
Legislative Issues: ENG; HOM; TAX; UTI

Chairman of the Board, President and Chief Executive Officer
WELCH, Joseph L.
Tel: (248) 374-7100
Fax: (248) 374-7140

Main Headquarters
Mailing: 27175 Energy Way
Novi, MI 48377
Tel: (248) 946-3000
Fax: (248) 374-7140
TF: (800) 482-4829

Washington Office
Mailing: 601 13th St. NW
Washington, DC 20005
Tel: (517) 374-9134

Political Action Committees
ITC Holdings Corporation PAC
FEC ID: C00388462
Contact: Sandra Pennell
201 Townsend St.
Suite 900
Lansing, MI 48933

Contributions to Candidates: $140,500 (2015-2016)
Democrats: $19,000; Republicans: $119,000; Other: $2,500

Principal Recipients

HOUSE
JENKINS, LYNN (REP-KS)
NOEM, KRISTI LYNN (REP-SD)
UPTON, FREDERICK STEPHEN (REP-MI)

Public Affairs and Related Activities Personnel

At Headquarters

BELLER, Louise
Manager, Public Relations
lbeller@itctransco.com
Tel: (248) 946-3479
Fax: (248) 374-7140

BRAIRTON, Michael
Manager, Federal Affairs
Registered Federal Lobbyist
Tel: (248) 946-3000
Fax: (248) 374-7140

BREADY, Cameron M.
Executive Vice President and Chief Financial Officer
Tel: (248) 946-3000
Fax: (248) 374-7140

BURKE, Kevin
Vice President, Human Resources
Tel: (248) 946-3000
Fax: (248) 374-7140

HOLLOWAY, Gretchen L.
Vice President, Finance
Tel: (248) 946-3000
Fax: (248) 374-7140

IOANIDIS, Gregory
Vice President, Business Strategy
Tel: (248) 946-3000
Fax: (248) 374-7140

JIPPING, Jon E.
Executive Vice President and Chief Operating Officer
Tel: (248) 946-3000
Fax: (248) 374-7140

OGINSKY, Daniel J.
Senior Vice President and General Counsel
Tel: (248) 374-7100
Fax: (248) 374-7140

PLAUSHIN, Nina
Vice President, Federal Affairs
nplaushin@itctransco.com
Registered Federal Lobbyist
Tel: (202) 216-9067
Fax: (248) 374-7140

SLOCUM, Brian
Vice President, Operations
Tel: (248) 946-3000
Fax: (248) 374-7140

STIBOR, Fred G.
Vice President and Controller
Tel: (248) 946-3000
Fax: (248) 374-7140

VITEZ, Thomas W.
Vice President, Planning
Tel: (248) 946-3000
Fax: (248) 374-7140

WENZEL, Patricia A.
Director, Treasury and Investor Relations
pwenzel@itctransco.com
Tel: (248) 946-3570
Fax: (248) 374-7140

WHITELOCKE, Simon
Vice President, Chief Compliance Officer
Tel: (248) 946-3000
Fax: (248) 374-7140

At Other Offices

JINKS, Anne
Manager, Federal Affairs
201 Townsend Rd., Suite 900
Lansing, MI 48933
Registered Federal Lobbyist
Tel: (517) 374-9134

PENNELL, Sandra
Manager, External Reporting and Research
201 Townsend Rd., Suite 900
Lansing, MI 48933
Tel: (517) 374-9134

Itel Corporation

See listing on page 66 under Anixter International, Inc.

ITM Marketing Inc.

Provides outbound, inbound, IVR, voice cast and web-chat services to a variety of industries.
www.itmmarketing.com
Annual Revenues: $9 million
Employees: 100

Industry/ies: Advertising And Marketing

President and Chief Executive Officer
FARRELL, Larry W.
lfarrell@itmmarketing.com
Tel: (740) 295-3575
Fax: (740) 295-3581

Main Headquarters
Mailing: 470 Downtowner Plaza
Coshocton, OH 43812
Tel: (740) 295-3575
Fax: (740) 295-3581
TF: (800) 686-4486

Public Affairs and Related Activities Personnel
At Headquarters

AFTERKIRK, Suzanne
Manager, Human Resources
safterkirk@itmmarketing.com
Tel: (740) 295-3575
Fax: (740) 295-3581

BIRKHIMER, Theresa
Director, Human Resources
tbirkhimer@itmmarketing.com
Tel: (740) 295-3575
Fax: (740) 295-3581

COLLEN, Bruce
Chief Financial Officer
bcollen@itmmarketing.com
Tel: (740) 295-3575
Fax: (740) 295-3581

GARDNER, Lianna
Director, Sales
Tel: (740) 295-3575
Fax: (740) 295-3581

JACKSON, Bob
Vice President, Sales
bjackson@itmmarketing.com
Tel: (740) 295-3575
Fax: (740) 295-3581

SCHICK, Walter
Director, Operations
Tel: (740) 295-3575
Fax: (740) 295-3581

ITOCHU Aviation, Inc.

A wholly-owned subsidiary of ITOCHU Corporation, based in Tokyo, Japan. An aerospace-based technologies manufacturer.
www.itochuaviation.com
Annual Revenues: $8.50 million
Employees: 40
SIC: 5099; 5088
Industry/ies: Aerospace/Aviation; Transportation

President and Chief Executive Officer
KASAGAWA, Nobuyuki
Tel: (310) 640-2770
Fax: (310) 647-5662

Main Headquarters
Mailing: 222 N. Sepulveda Blvd.
Suite 2200
El Segundo, CA 90245-5629
Tel: (310) 640-2770
Fax: (310) 647-5662

Public Affairs and Related Activities Personnel
At Headquarters

IKUMA, Gary K.
Senior Vice President, Defense Programs
Tel: (310) 640-2770
Fax: (310) 647-5662

WINNERS, Richard
Director, Human Resources Benefits
Tel: (310) 640-2777
Fax: (310) 647-5662

ITT Corporation

A manufacturer of defense, communications, and space products. It manufactures and sells highly engineered critical components and customized technology solutions for the energy, transportation, and industrial markets. It acquired Hartzell Aerospace on June,16, 2015.
www.itt.com
Annual Revenues: $2.57 billion
Employees: 9,400
Ticker: NYSE: ITT
SIC: 3561
NAICS: 334220; 334417; 333911
Industry/ies: Defense/Homeland Security; Government-Related
Legislative Issues: BUD; CAW; HOM; NAT; TRD

Chief Executive Officer and President
RAMOS, Denise L.
Tel: (914) 641-2000
Fax: (914) 696-2950

Main Headquarters
Mailing: 1133 Westchester Ave.
White Plains, NY 10604
Tel: (914) 641-2000
Fax: (914) 696-2950

Washington Office
Mailing: 1650 Tysons Blvd.
Suite 1700
McLean, VA 22102
Tel: (703) 790-6300
Fax: (703) 790-6360

Corporate Foundations and Giving Programs
ITT Industries Corporate Contributions Program
1133 Westchester Ave.
White Plains, NY 10604
Tel: (914) 641-2000

Public Affairs and Related Activities Personnel
At Headquarters

BARK, Kathleen
Executive Director, Reputation and Media
kathleen.bark@itt.com
Tel: (914) 641-2103
Fax: (914) 696-2950

CHICLES, Aris C.
Executive Vice President and President, Industrial Process
Tel: (914) 641-2000
Fax: (914) 696-2950

CREAMER, Vicky
Chief Human Resources Officer
Tel: (914) 641-2000
Fax: (914) 696-2950

GUSTAFSSON, Mary Beth
General Counsel
Tel: (914) 641-2000
Fax: (914) 696-2950

TROMBETTA, Melissa
Vice President, Investor Relations
melissa.trombetta@itt.com
Tel: (914) 641-2030
Fax: (914) 696-2950

At Washington Office

DUGAN, Phaedra
Federal Lobbyist & Director, Defense Programs and Policy
Tel: (703) 790-6300
Fax: (703) 790-6360

SCALERA, Thomas
Chief Financial Officer
thomas.scalera@itt.com
Tel: (703) 790-6300
Fax: (703) 790-6360

J. P. Morgan Chase and Company

Acquired Bank One Corp. in July, 2004, and Bear Stearns Companies Inc in May, 2008.
www.jpmorganchase.com
Annual Revenues: $91.81 billion
Employees: 241,145
Ticker: NYSE: JPM
SIC: 6021
Industry/ies: Banking/Finance/Investments
Legislative Issues: AGR; BAN; FIN; HOM; HOU; TAX; TRD

Chairman and Chief Executive Officer
DIMON, James
Tel: (212) 270-6000
Fax: (212) 270-1648

Main Headquarters
Mailing: 270 Park Ave.
38th Floor
New York City, NY 10017-2014
Tel: (212) 270-6000
Fax: (212) 270-1648

Washington Office
Mailing: 601 Pennsylvania Ave. NW
North Building, Suite 250
Washington, DC 20004
Tel: (202) 585-3750
Fax: (202) 585-3755

Political Action Committees
J.P. Morgan Chase & Company PAC
FEC ID: C00128512
Contact: Shannon Frack Aimone
10 S. Dearborn St.
IL1-0520
Chicago, IL 60603

> **Contributions to Candidates:** $5,000 (2015-2016)
> Republicans: $5,000

JPMorgan Chase & Company Federal PAC
FEC ID: C00104299
Contact: Shannon Frack Aimone
IL1-0520
Chicago, IL 60603

> **Contributions to Candidates:** $606,000 (2015-2016)
> Democrats: $183,000; Republicans: $420,000; Other: $3,000

Principal Recipients

SENATE
KIRK, MARK STEVEN (REP-IL)
MURRAY, PATTY (DEM-WA)
SHELBY, RICHARD C (REP-AL)

HOUSE
BARR, GARLAND ANDY (REP-KY)
GRIFFIN, WILLIAM TAYLOR (REP-NC)
MCHENRY, PATRICK TIMOTHY (REP-NC)
STIVERS, STEVE MR. (REP-OH)
TIBERI, PATRICK J. (REP-OH)
YODER, KEVIN (REP-KS)

Corporate Foundations and Giving Programs
JPMorgan Chase Foundation
270 Park Ave.
29th Floor
New York City, NY 10017-2070
Tel: (212) 270-6000
Fax: (212) 270-6000

Public Affairs and Related Activities Personnel
At Headquarters

BARTLING, Jack
Federal Lobbyist
Tel: (212) 270-6000
Fax: (212) 270-1648

BEIZER, Emily
Managing Director and Head, International Government Relations
Tel: (202) 585-3757
Fax: (212) 270-1648

BRAUNSTEIN, Douglas L.
Chief Financial Officer
Tel: (212) 270-6000
Fax: (212) 270-1648

CAMPER, Naomi Gendler
Head, Nonprofit Engagement
Tel: (202) 585-3757
Fax: (212) 270-1648

CHILDRESS, Katherine Anne
Senior Vice President, Federal Government Relations
Tel: (202) 585-3757
Fax: (212) 270-1648

CUTLER, Stephen M.
General Counsel
Tel: (212) 270-7325
Fax: (212) 270-1648

DONNELLY, John L.
Analyst
Tel: (212) 270-7325
Fax: (212) 270-1648

DREW, Ina R.
Chief Investment Officer
Tel: (212) 270-6000
Fax: (212) 270-1648

EVANGELISTI, Joseph M.
Managing Director, Corporate Communications
joseph.evangelisti@jpmchase.com
Tel: (212) 270-7438
Fax: (212) 270-1648

GATTEN, Nathan
Managing Director and Head, Federal Government Relations
Tel: (202) 585-3757
Fax: (212) 270-1648

KOONCE, Thomas
Executive Director, Federal Government Affairs
Tel: (212) 270-6000
Fax: (212) 270-1648

LAKE, Marianne
Chief Financial Officer
Tel: (212) 270-6000
Fax: (212) 270-1648

MARTIN, Granville
Managing Director, Sustainable Finance
granville.j.martin@jpmchase.com
Tel: (202) 585-3757
Fax: (212) 270-1648

REILLY, Brendan T.
Federal Lobbyist
Tel: (212) 270-6000
Fax: (212) 270-1648

ROSENBERG, Jason
Federal Lobbyist
Tel: (212) 270-6000
Fax: (212) 270-1648

RYAN, Jr., Timothy
Global Head, Regulatory Strategy and Policy Services and
Vice Chairman
Tel: (212) 270-6000
Fax: (212) 270-1648

SCHER, Amb. Peter L.
Executive Vice President and Head, Corporate Responsibility
Tel: (202) 585-3757
Fax: (212) 270-1648

SCRANTON, Pierce
Executive Director, Global Government Relations and Public
Policy Affairs
Tel: (202) 585-3757
Fax: (212) 270-1648

TOMASIC, Steven S.
Assistant General Cousel
Tel: (212) 270-6000
Fax: (212) 270-1648

WILLIAMSON, Todd
Contact, International Government Relations
Tel: (212) 270-6000
Fax: (212) 270-1648

ZAMES, Matthew E.
Chief Operating Officer
Tel: (212) 270-6000
Fax: (212) 270-1648

ZUCCARELLI, Jennifer
Executive Director
jennifer.zuccarelli@ipmchase.com
Tel: (212) 270-6000
Fax: (212) 270-1648

At Washington Office

AIMONE, Shannon Frack
Vice President and PAC Director
Tel: (202) 585-3750
Fax: (202) 585-3755

BOYD, Valerie
Corporate Responsibility Team
Tel: (202) 585-3750
Fax: (202) 585-3755

WEST, Hilary
Vice President, Federal Government Relations
Tel: (202) 585-3750
Fax: (202) 585-3755

J. Crew Group

A apparel retailer. J.Crew continues its retail expansion with a series of new specialty boutiques.
www.jcrew.com
Annual Revenues: $1.72 billion
Employees: 13,000
Ticker: NYSE: JCG
SIC: 5600
Industry/ies: Apparel/Textiles Industry; Retail/Wholesale

Chairman of the Board and Chief Executive Officer
DREXLER, Millard S.
Tel: (212) 209-2500
Fax: (212) 209-2666

Main Headquarters
Mailing: One Ivy Crescent
           Lynchburg, VA 24513-1001
Tel: (434) 385-5775
Fax: (434) 385-5750

Corporate Foundations and Giving Programs

Council of Fashion Designers of America
65 Bleecker
Floor 11
New York City, NY 10012
Tel: (434) 385-5775
Fax: (434) 385-5750

The Leukemia and Lymphoma Society
One Ivy Crescent
Lynchburg, VA 24513-1001
Tel: (434) 385-5775
Fax: (434) 385-5750

Public Affairs and Related Activities Personnel

At Headquarters

DURKIN, Joan
Senior Vice President, Chief Accounting Officer and Interim
Chief Financial Officer
Tel: (434) 385-5775
Fax: (434) 385-5750

MARKOE, Lynda
Executive Vice President, Human Resources
Tel: (434) 385-5775
Fax: (434) 385-5750

At Other Offices

MALKIN, Allison
Contact, Corporate Relations
770 Broadway
New York City, NY 10003
investorrelations@jcrew.com
Tel: (212) 209-8200
Fax: (212) 209-2666

J.B. Hunt Transport, Inc.

Provides transportation and delivery services.
www.jbhunt.com
Annual Revenues: $6.20 billion
Employees: 20,158
Ticker: NASDAQ : JBHT
SIC: 4213
Industry/ies: Transportation
Legislative Issues: TRA

Chairman of the Board
THOMPSON, Kirk
Tel: (479) 820-0000
Fax: (479) 820-3418

President and Chief Executive Officer
ROBERTS, III, John N.
Tel: (479) 820-0000
Fax: (479) 820-3418

Main Headquarters
Mailing: 615 J.B. Hunt Corporate Dr.
           P.O. Box 130
           Lowell, AR 72745
Tel: (479) 820-0000
Fax: (479) 820-3418
TF: (800) 643-3622

Washington Office
Mailing: 8300 Pennsylvania Ave.
           Upper Marlboro, MD 20772

Corporate Foundations and Giving Programs

J. B. Hunt Transport Services Corporate Contributions Program
Contact: Amy Bain
615 J.B. Hunt Corporate Dr.
P.O. Box 130
Lowell, AR 72745
Tel: (479) 820-8111

Public Affairs and Related Activities Personnel

At Headquarters

BAIN, Amy
Executive Assistant and Manager, Corporate Giving
Tel: (479) 820-0000
Fax: (479) 820-3418

HARPER, Craig
Executive Vice President, Operations
Tel: (479) 820-0000
Fax: (479) 820-3418

MEE, David G.
Executive Vice President, Finance and Administration, Chief
Financial Officer and Corporate Secretary
Tel: (479) 820-8363
Fax: (479) 820-3418

SIMPSON , Shelley
President, Integrated Capacity Solutions and Chief Marketing
Officer
Tel: (479) 820-0000
Fax: (479) 820-3418

J.C. Penney Company, Inc.

A retail department store chain.
www.jcpenney.com
Annual Revenues: $12.31 billion
Employees: 114,000
Ticker: NYSE: JCP
SIC: 5311; 5099; 7221; 7221
Industry/ies: Retail/Wholesale

Chairman of the Board
ENGIBOUS, Thomas
Tel: (972) 431-1000
Fax: (972) 431-9140

Chief Executive Officer
ULLMAN, Mike
Tel: (972) 431-1000
Fax: (972) 431-9140

Main Headquarters
Mailing: 6501 Legacy Dr.
           Plano, TX 75024
Tel: (972) 431-1000
Fax: (972) 431-9140
TF: (800) 322-1189

Political Action Committees
PenneyPAC - J. C. Penney Corporation, Inc. PAC
FEC ID: C00042895
6501 Legacy Dr.
Plano, TX 75024

   Contributions to Candidates: $24,500 (2015-2016)
   Democrats: $7,500; Republicans: $17,000

Corporate Foundations and Giving Programs

J.C. Penney Company Contributions Program
Contact: Janice Howell
6501 Legacy Dr.
Plano, TX 75024
Tel: (972) 431-1000
Fax: (972) 431-9140

Public Affairs and Related Activities Personnel

At Headquarters

EVANSON, Brynn
Executive Vice President, Human Resources
Tel: (972) 431-1000
Fax: (972) 431-9140

GROTHUES, Arnold
Tel: (972) 431-1000

	Fax:	(972) 431-9140
HAYS, Kristin	Tel:	(972) 431-5500
Senior Vice President, Investor Relations and	Fax:	(972) 431-9140
Communications		
klhays@jcpenney.com		
HOWELL, Janice	Tel:	(972) 431-1000
Manager, Community Relations	Fax:	(972) 431-9140
KLUN, Natalie	Tel:	(972) 431-1000
PAC Treasurer	Fax:	(972) 431-9140
LINK, Janet	Tel:	(972) 431-1000
Executive Vice President, General Counsel	Fax:	(972) 431-9140
MUSKET, Leanne	Tel:	(972) 431-1000
Senior Manager, Government Relations	Fax:	(972) 431-9140
PHILLIPS, Paula	Tel:	(972) 431-1250
State Government Relations Supervisor	Fax:	(972) 431-9140
RECORD, Edward	Tel:	(972) 431-1000
Executive Vice President, Chief Financial Officer	Fax:	(972) 431-9140
WEST, Mary Beth	Tel:	(972) 431-1000
Executive Vice President, Chief Customer and Marketing	Fax:	(972) 431-9140
Officer		

J.E. Roberts Companies

JER Partners is a fully integrated private equity, real estate investment management company.
JER Investors Trust Inc. (JERIT) is a specialty finance company.
www.jer.com
Employees: 100
Industry/ies: Real Estate

Main Headquarters

Mailing: 1250 Connecticut Ave. NW	Tel:	(202) 419-1533
Washington, DC 20036		

Corporate Foundations and Giving Programs

Fight For Children
Contact: James H. Tardy

1726 M St. NW	Tel:	(202) 772-0400
Suite 202	Fax:	(202) 772-0400
Washington, DC 20036		

Public Affairs and Related Activities Personnel

At Other Offices

MCGILLIS, J. Michael	Tel:	(703) 714-8000
Managing Director and Chief Financial Officer	Fax:	(703) 714-8100
7950 Jones Branch Dr., Suite 320		
McLean, VA 22107		
Mike.McGillis@jer.com		
ROBINSON, Clyde	Tel:	(703) 714-8016
Managing Director, Capital Markets and Client Relations	Fax:	(703) 714-8100
7950 Jones Branch Dr., Suite 320		
McLean, VA 22107		
clyde.robinson@jer.com		
TARDY, James H.	Tel:	(703) 714-8000
Manager, Special Projects	Fax:	(703) 714-8100
7950 Jones Branch Dr., Suite 320		
McLean, VA 22107		
jim.tardy@jer.com		
WARD, Daniel T.	Tel:	(703) 714-8000
General Counsel	Fax:	(703) 714-8100
7950 Jones Branch Dr., Suite 320		
McLean, VA 22107		

J.M. Smucker Company

A producer of jams and jellies, ice cream toppings, peanut butters, shortening, oils, health and
natural foods and beverages. Acquired Internat'l Multifoods Corp. in June, 2004.
www.smuckers.com
Annual Revenues: $5.69 billion
Employees: 4,900
Ticker: NYSE: SJM
SIC: 2033
Industry/ies: Food And Beverage Industry
Legislative Issues: FOO

Chairman of the Board

SMUCKER, Timothy P.	Tel:	(330) 582-3000
	Fax:	(330) 682-3370

Chief Executive Officer

SMUCKER, Richard K.	Tel:	(330) 582-3000
	Fax:	(330) 682-3370

Main Headquarters

Mailing: One Strawberry Ln.	Tel:	(330) 682-3000
Orrville, OH 44667-0280	Fax:	(330) 684-6410
	TF:	(888) 550-9555

Corporate Foundations and Giving Programs

J.M. Smucker Company Contributions Program

One Strawberry Ln.	Tel:	(330) 682-3000
Orrville, OH 44667-0280	Fax:	(330) 684-6410

Public Affairs and Related Activities Personnel

At Headquarters

BELGYA, Mark R.	Tel:	(330) 582-3000
Senior Vice President and Chief Financial Officer	Fax:	(330) 684-6410
BROHOLM, Aaron	Tel:	(330) 684-7682
Director, Investor Relations	Fax:	(330) 684-6410
aaron.broholm@jmsmucker.com		
DEMPSEY, Brenda	Tel:	(330) 682-3084
Director, Corporate Internal Communications	Fax:	(330) 684-6410
FYNAN, Tamara J.	Tel:	(330) 682-3000
Vice President, Marketing Services	Fax:	(330) 684-6410
KNUDSEN, Jeannette L.	Tel:	(330) 682-3000
Vice President, General Counsel and Corporate Secretary	Fax:	(330) 684-6410
PENROSE , Jill R.	Tel:	(330) 682-3000
Vice President, Human Resources	Fax:	(330) 684-6410
RESWEBER, Christopher P.	Tel:	(330) 582-3000
Senior Vice President, Corporate Communications and Public	Fax:	(330) 684-6410
Affairs		
ROBINSON, Sonal P.	Tel:	(330) 684-3440
Vice President, Investor Relations	Fax:	(330) 684-6410
SABIN, Julia L.	Tel:	(330) 682-3000
Vice President, Industry and Government Affairs	Fax:	(330) 684-6410

J.R. Simplot Company

A privately held food and agribusiness company.
www.simplot.com
Annual Revenues: $4.60 billion
Employees: 10,000
SIC: 2037; 2038; 5142
NAICS: 311411; 42242; 311412
Industry/ies: Agriculture/Agronomy

Chairman of the Board and Executive Committee member

SIMPLOT, Scott R.	Tel:	(208) 336-2110
	Fax:	(208) 389-7515

President and Chief Executive Officer

WHITACRE, William J.	Tel:	(208) 336-2110
	Fax:	(208) 389-7515

Main Headquarters

Mailing: P.O. Box 27	Tel:	(208) 336-2110
Boise, ID 83707	Fax:	(208) 389-7515

Washington Office

Mailing: 4618 Sixth St...South	Tel:	(703) 920-0022
Arlington, VA 22204		

Political Action Committees

J. R. Simplot Company PAC (SIM-PAC)
FEC ID: C00120873
Contact: Mark Dunn
999 Main St.
Boise, ID 83702

> **Contributions to Candidates:** $17,500 (2015-2016)
> Republicans: $17,500

Corporate Foundations and Giving Programs

J.R. Simplot Foundation
P.O. Box 27
Boise, ID 83707

Public Affairs and Related Activities Personnel

At Headquarters

COLE, Doug	Tel:	(208) 761-8354
Director, Company Marketing and Public Relations	Fax:	(208) 389-7515
doug.cole@simplot.com		
ELG, Annette	Tel:	(208) 336-2110
Senior Vice President and Chief Financial Officer	Fax:	(208) 389-7515
PHILLIPS, Rick	Tel:	(208) 389-7377
Manager, Public Affairs	Fax:	(208) 389-7515
rick.phillips@simplot.com		

At Washington Office

DUNN, Mark	Tel:	(703) 920-0022
Vice President, Government Affairs & PAC Treasurer		
mark.dunn@simplot.com		

j2 Global Communications, Inc.

A global messaging and communications network, including faxing, voicemail, document
management and conference calling.
www.j2.com
Annual Revenues: $626.16 million
Employees: 1,410
Ticker: NASDAQ (GS): JCOM
SIC: 4822
Industry/ies: Communications; Telecommunications/Internet/Cable

Chairman of the Board

RESSLER, Richard S.	Tel:	(323) 860-9200
	Fax:	(323) 860-9201

Chief Executive Officer
ZUCKER, Nehemia "Hemi"
Tel: (323) 860-9200
Fax: (323) 860-9201

Main Headquarters
Mailing: 6922 Hollywood Blvd.
Hollywood, CA 90028
Tel: (323) 817-3217
Fax: (323) 860-9201
TF: (888) 817-2000

Public Affairs and Related Activities Personnel

At Headquarters

ADELMAN, Jeff
Vice President, General Counsel and Secretary
Tel: (323) 860-9200
Fax: (323) 860-9201

BRUNTON, Patty
Vice President, Human Resources
pbrunton@j2.com
Tel: (323) 860-9200
Fax: (323) 860-9201

HINSON, Laura
Contact, Investor Relations
laura.hinson@j2.com
Tel: (800) 577-1790
Fax: (323) 860-9201

LOSHITZER, Zohar
Executive Vice President, Corporate Strategy
Tel: (323) 860-9200
Fax: (323) 860-9201

PUGH, Mike
Vice President, Marketing
Tel: (323) 817-3217
Fax: (323) 860-9201

TURICCHI , Scott
President and Chief Financial Officer
Tel: (323) 817-3217
Fax: (323) 860-9201

Jabil Circuit Inc.

Designs and manufactures electronic circuit boards.
www.jabil.com
Annual Revenues: $18.60 billion
Employees: 161,000
Ticker: NYSE: JBL
SIC: 3672
Industry/ies: Communications; Telecommunications/Internet/Cable

Chairman of the Board
MAIN, Timothy L.
tim_maine@jabil.com
Tel: (727) 577-9749
Fax: (727) 579-8529

Chief Executive Officer
MONDELLO, Mark T.
Tel: (727) 577-9749
Fax: (727) 579-8529

Main Headquarters
Mailing: 10560 Martin Luther King Jr. St., North
St. Petersburg, FL 33716
Tel: (727) 577-9749
Fax: (727) 579-8529

Corporate Foundations and Giving Programs
Jabil Circuit Inc. Contributions Program
10560 Martin Luther King Jr. St., North
St. Petersburg, FL 33716
Tel: (727) 577-9749
Fax: (727) 579-8529

Public Affairs and Related Activities Personnel

At Headquarters

ALEXANDER, Forbes I. J.
Chief Financial Officer
Tel: (727) 577-9749
Fax: (727) 579-8529

MCGEE, Joseph A.
Executive Vice President, Strategic Planning and Development
Tel: (727) 577-9749
Fax: (727) 579-8529

MUIR, William D.
Chief Operating Officer
Tel: (727) 577-9749
Fax: (727) 579-8529

MYERS, Donald J.
Senior Vice President, Corporate Development
Tel: (727) 577-9749
Fax: (727) 579-8529

PAVER, Robert L.
Chief Legal Officer and Corporate Secretary
bob_paver@jabil.com
Tel: (727) 577-9749
Fax: (727) 579-8529

PETERS, William E.
President
Tel: (727) 577-9749
Fax: (727) 579-8529

WALTERS, Beth A.
Senior Vice President, Communications and Investor Relations
beth_walters@jabil.com
Tel: (727) 803-3349
Fax: (727) 579-8529

Jack in the Box Inc.

A restaurant company.
www.jackinthebox.com
Annual Revenues: $1.55 billion
Employees: 20,700
Ticker: NASDAQ: JACK
SIC: 5812
Industry/ies: Food And Beverage Industry; Retail/Wholesale

Chairman of the Board and Chief Executive Officer
COMMA, Leonard A.
Tel: (858) 571-2121
Fax: (858) 571-2101

Main Headquarters
Mailing: 9330 Balboa Ave.
San Diego, CA 92123-1516
Tel: (858) 571-2121
Fax: (858) 571-2101

Corporate Foundations and Giving Programs

Jack in the Box Foundation
Contact: Kathleen Kovachevich
9330 Balboa Ave.
San Diego, CA 92123
Tel: (858) 571-2121

Public Affairs and Related Activities Personnel

At Headquarters

ALLEN, Frances L.
President
Tel: (858) 571-2121
Fax: (858) 571-2101

BLANKENSHIP, PhD, Mark H.
Executive Vice President, Chief People, Culture and Corporate Strategy Officer
mark.blankenship@jackinthebox.com
Tel: (858) 571-2121
Fax: (858) 571-2101

DIRAIMO, Carol A.
Vice President, Investor Relations and Corporate Communications
Tel: (858) 571-2121
Fax: (858) 571-2101

GUILBAULT, Keith M.
Incoming President, Qdoba Mexican Eats
Tel: (858) 571-2121
Fax: (858) 571-2101

KOVACHEVICH, Kathleen
Director, The Jack in the Box Foundation
kathy.kovacevich@jackinthebox.com
Tel: (858) 571-2544
Fax: (858) 571-4064

LUSCOMB, Brian
Divisional Vice President, Corporate Communications
brian.luscomb@jackinthebox.com
Tel: (858) 571-2291
Fax: (858) 571-2225

MELANCON, Paul D.
Senior Vice President, Finance, Controller and Treasurer
Tel: (858) 571-2121
Fax: (858) 571-2101

PEPPER, Raymond
Vice President and General Counsel
Tel: (858) 571-2121
Fax: (858) 571-2101

REBEL, Jerry P.
Executive Vice President and Chief Financial Officer
Jerry.rebel@jackinthebox.com
Tel: (858) 571-2121
Fax: (858) 571-2225

RUDOLPH, Phillip H.
Executive Vice President, General Counsel and Corporate Secretary
Tel: (858) 571-2121
Fax: (858) 571-2101

Jackson National Life Insurance

A life insurance company.
www.jackson.com
Employees: 3,000
Industry/ies: Insurance Industry
Legislative Issues: BUD; INS; RET; TAX

Chairman
STOWE , Barry L.
Tel: (517) 381-5500
Fax: (517) 706-5521

Main Headquarters
Mailing: One Corporate Way
Lansing, MI 48951
Tel: (517) 381-5500
Fax: (517) 706-5521
TF: (800) 873-5654

Political Action Committees
Brooke Holdings Inc. and Jackson National Life Insurance Company Separate Segregated Fund PAC
FEC ID: C00254953
Contact: Michael Costello
One Corporate Way
Lansing, MI 48951
Tel: (517) 381-5500
Fax: (517) 706-5521

Contributions to Candidates: $149,500 (2015-2016)
Democrats: $34,500; Republicans: $114,000; Other: $1,000

Corporate Foundations and Giving Programs

Jackson National Community Fund
One Corporate Way
Lansing, MI 48951
Tel: (517) 381-5500
Fax: (517) 381-5500

Public Affairs and Related Activities Personnel

At Headquarters

BOWDEN, Andrew J.
Senior Vice President and General Counsel
Tel: (517) 381-5500
Fax: (517) 706-5521

BROOKS, Bob
Federal Lobbyist
Registered Federal Lobbyist
Tel: (517) 702-2447
Fax: (517) 706-5521

BROWN, John Howard
Vice President, Government Relations
john.brown@jackson.com
Registered Federal Lobbyist
Tel: (517) 702-2447
Fax: (517) 706-5521

COSTELLO, Michael
PAC Treasurer
Tel: (517) 381-5500
Fax: (517) 706-5521

DOLAN, Cynthia
Specialist, Government Relations
Tel: (517) 381-5500
Fax: (517) 706-5522

GOATLEY, Julia A.
Senior Vice President, Chief Compliance and Governance Officer
Tel: (517) 381-5500
Fax: (517) 706-5521

HARKINS, Christopher
Registered Federal Lobbyist
Tel: (517) 381-5500
Fax: (517) 706-5521

HARRIS, Brad O.	Tel:	(517) 381-5500
Senior Vice President and Chief Risk Officer	Fax:	(517) 706-5521
MCADORY, Machelle A.	Tel:	(517) 381-5500
Senior Vice President and Chief Human Resources Officer	Fax:	(517) 706-5521
MYERS, P. Chad	Tel:	(517) 381-5500
Executive Vice President and Chief Financial Officer	Fax:	(517) 706-5521
chad.myers@jackson.com		
PARDO , Emilio	Tel:	(517) 381-5500
Senior Vice President, Chief Marketing and Communications	Fax:	(517) 706-5521
Officer		
PRIESKORN, Laura L.	Tel:	(517) 381-5500
Senior Vice President and Chief Administrative Officer	Fax:	(517) 706-5521
SOPHA, James R.	Tel:	(517) 381-5500
President	Fax:	(517) 706-5521
ZYBLE, David A.	Tel:	(517) 381-5500
Fedral Lobbyist	Fax:	(517) 706-5521
Registered Federal Lobbyist		

At Other Offices

HERNANDEZ, Melissa	Tel:	(303) 224-7572
Senior Specialist, Media Relations	Fax:	(303) 224-7549
7601 Technology Way		
Denver, CO 80237		
melissa.hernandez@jackson.com		

Jacobs & Company Public Affairs

Is a nationally recognized government relations firm specializing in grassroots politics and media relations.
www.jacobandco.com
Industry/ies: Public Affairs And Public Relations

President	Tel:	(323) 463-8992
JACOBS, Stephen A.		
saj@sajacobs.com		

Main Headquarters

Mailing:	48 E. 57th St.	Tel:	(212) 719-5887
	New York City, NY 10022		

Public Affairs and Related Activities Personnel

At Headquarters

ABAS, Shamin	Tel:	(212) 719-5887
Contact, Media Relations		
sabas@jacobandco.com		
FINKELSTEIN, Susan	Tel:	(212) 719-5887
Director, Public Relations and Contact, Marketing and		
Product Placement Services		

Jacobs Engineering Group, Inc.

A professional services firm.
www.jacobs.com
Annual Revenues: $12.54 billion
Employees: 53,500
Ticker: NYSE: JEC
SIC: 1600
Industry/ies: Aerospace/Aviation; Construction/Construction Materials; Defense/Homeland Security; Engineering/Mathematics; Environment And Conservation; Government-Related; Transportation
Legislative Issues: AER; DEF

Chairman of the Board	Tel:	(626) 578-3500
WATSON, Noel G.	Fax:	(626) 578-6875

Main Headquarters

Mailing:	155 N. Lake Ave.	Tel:	(626) 578-3500
	Pasadena, CA 91101	Fax:	(626) 578-6988

Washington Office

Mailing:	1100 N. Glebe Rd.	Tel:	(571) 218-1000
	Suite 500	Fax:	(571) 218-1600
	Arlington, VA 22201		

Political Action Committees

Jacobs Good Government Fund of Jacobs Engineering Group Inc. PAC
FEC ID: C00142299
Contact: Michael Udovic
155 N. Lake Ave.
P.O. Box 7084
Pasadena, CA 91101

> **Contributions to Candidates:** $19,000 (2015-2016)
> Republicans: $19,000

Corporate Foundations and Giving Programs

Jacobs Engineering Foundation		
1111 S. Arroyo Pkwy.	Tel:	(626) 578-6803
P.O. Box 7084		
Pasadena, CA 91109		

Public Affairs and Related Activities Personnel

At Headquarters

HOAG, Kim	Tel:	(626) 578-3500
Vice President, Business Development	Fax:	(626) 578-6875
kim.hoag@jacobs.com		
UDOVIC, Michael	Tel:	(626) 578-3500
PAC Contact	Fax:	(626) 578-6988

At Washington Office

HUDGINS, Kimberly	Tel:	(202) 548-5840
Director, Governmental Affairs	Fax:	(202) 548-5841
SHEPARD, Stacey	Tel:	(202) 548-5840
Vice President	Fax:	(202) 548-5841
stacey.shepard@jacobs.com		

At Other Offices

JONES, Michelle	Tel:	(626) 568-7144
Vice President, Marketing and Corporate Communications		
1111 S. Arroyo Pkwy. 91105, P.O. Box 7084		
Pasadena, CA 91109-7084		
michelle.jones@jacobs.com		

Jacuzzi Brands

Bath and Jacuzzi manufacturer.
www.jacuzzibrands.com
Employees: 5,000
SIC: 3430
Industry/ies: Furniture/Home Furnishings

Main Headquarters

Mailing:	13925 City Center Dr.	Tel:	(909) 247-2920
	Suite 200	Fax:	(909) 606-0195
	Chino Hills, CA 91709	TF:	(866) 234-7727

Public Affairs and Related Activities Personnel

At Headquarters

HELLMAN, David	Tel:	(909) 247-2920
Vice President, Corporate Controller	Fax:	(909) 606-0195
LOVALLO, Anthony	Tel:	(909) 247-2920
Vice President and General Counsel	Fax:	(909) 606-0195
anthony.lovallo@jacuzzibrands.com		

Jadoo Power Systems

A supplier of portable fuel cells.
www.jadoopower.com
Annual Revenues: $2.10 million
Industry/ies: Electricity & Electronics; Electronics; Energy/Electricity

Executive Chairman of the Board	Tel:	(916) 618-9044
CRAWFORD, Jack	Fax:	(916) 608-9017
President and Chief Executive Officer	Tel:	(916) 618-9044
DEVANNA, Leonard	Fax:	(916) 608-9017

Main Headquarters

Mailing:	181 Blue Ravine Rd.	Tel:	(916) 618-9044
	Folsom, CA 95630	Fax:	(916) 608-9017
		TF:	(888) 523-6648

Public Affairs and Related Activities Personnel

At Headquarters

ALLGROVE, David	Tel:	(916) 618-9044
Vice President, Government Programs	Fax:	(916) 608-9017
callgrove@jadoopower.com		
RICH, Al	Tel:	(916) 618-9044
Vice President, Solar Business Development	Fax:	(916) 608-9017
marketing@jadoopower.com		

Jaguar Land Rover North America LLC

Automotive manufacturers.
www.jaguar.com
Industry/ies: Automotive Industry; Transportation
Legislative Issues: AUT; TRA

Main Headquarters

Mailing:	555 MacArthur Blvd.	Tel:	(202) 818-8500
	Mahwah, NJ 07430		

Public Affairs and Related Activities Personnel

At Headquarters

AZRIA, Jacob	Tel:	(201) 456-9448
Regulations Engineer		
Registered Federal Lobbyist		
BLAIR, Clinton	Tel:	(201) 456-9448
Federal Lobbyist		
cblair18@jaguarlandrover.com		
Registered Federal Lobbyist		
KOBYLARZ, John	Tel:	(201) 456-9448
Manager, Safety Compliance		

jkobyla1@jaguarlandrover.com
Registered Federal Lobbyist

SCOTT, Christopher D. Tel: (201) 456-9448
Senior Manager, Automotive Safety
Registered Federal Lobbyist

Janssen Pharmaceutical Corporation

A producer of pharmaceutical products. Subsidiary of Johnson & Johnson Services, Inc.
www.janssenpharmaceuticalsinc.com
Employees: 100
SIC: 2834; 5912; 5099; 9999
Industry/ies: Pharmaceutical Industry

Main Headquarters
Mailing: 1125 Trenton-Harbourton Rd. Tel: (609) 730-2000
          P.O. Box 200 Fax: (908) 218-1416
          Titusville, NJ 08560-0200 TF: (800) 775-5514

Public Affairs and Related Activities Personnel

At Headquarters

NORTON, Jennifer Tel: (609) 730-3771
Senior Director, North America Communications Fax: (908) 218-1416

Japan Bank for International Cooperation

A governmental financial institution that conducts Japan's external economic policy.
www.jbic.go.jp
Industry/ies: Banking/Finance/Investments; Trade (Foreign And Domestic)

Chief Representative Tel: (202) 785-5242
NEGISHI, Yasushi Fax: (202) 785-1787
y-negishi@jbic.go.jp

Main Headquarters
Mailing: 1627 Eye St. NW Tel: (202) 785-1785
          Suite 500 Fax: (202) 785-1787
          Washington, DC 20006

Public Affairs and Related Activities Personnel

At Headquarters

ARASE, Rui Tel: (202) 785-5242
Federal Lobbyist Fax: (202) 785-1787

HORIUCHI, Tadashi Tel: (202) 785-5242
Resident Director Fax: (202) 785-1787
Registered Federal Lobbyist

ITO, Yuki Tel: (202) 785-1785
Federal Lobbyist Fax: (202) 785-1787
Registered Federal Lobbyist

KONDO, Shinya Tel: (202) 785-5242
Senior Representative Fax: (202) 785-1787
s-kondo@jbic.go.jp

KONO, Michiko Tel: (202) 785-1785
                Fax: (202) 785-1787

KOTAKA, Teruaki Tel: (202) 785-5242
Senior Representative Fax: (202) 785-1787

KOYANAGI, Hideo Tel: (202) 785-5242
Federal Lobbyist Fax: (202) 785-1787

MIKITA, Satoshi Tel: (202) 785-1785
Registered Federal Lobbyist Fax: (202) 785-1787

MORITA, Minoru Tel: (202) 785-5242
Senior Representative Fax: (202) 785-1787

NAKATA, Ryosuke Tel: (202) 785-5242
Senior Representative Fax: (202) 785-1787
r-nakata@jbic.go.jp

OKU, Ai Tel: (202) 785-5242
Resident Economist Fax: (202) 785-1787
Registered Federal Lobbyist

ONISHI, Kanjiro Tel: (202) 785-5242
Federal Lobbyist Fax: (202) 785-1787

SAKATA, Wataru Tel: (202) 785-5242
Resident Director Fax: (202) 785-1787

SATO, Takayuki Tel: (202) 785-5242
Senior Representative Fax: (202) 785-1787
ta-sato@jbic.go.jp

SUGIMOTO, Takashi Tel: (202) 785-5242
Representative Fax: (202) 785-1787
ts-sato@jbic.go.jp

SUNOUCHI, Yasushi Tel: (202) 785-1785
Cheif Representative Fax: (202) 785-1787

TERADA, Hiroki Tel: (202) 785-1785
Registered Federal Lobbyist Fax: (202) 785-1787

USHIJIMA, Yoshiaki Tel: (202) 785-5242
Cheif Representative Fax: (202) 785-1787
y-ushijima@jbic.go.jp

YASUI, Maki Tel: (202) 785-1785
Registered Federal Lobbyist Fax: (202) 785-1787

JBS USA

A subsidiary of JBS S.A., headquartered in São Paulo, Brazil. A meat processing and distribution company. Formerly Swift and Company. It processes, prepares, packages and delivers fresh, further-processed and value-added beef, pork, lamb and poultry products.
www.jbssa.com
Employees: 20,200
Ticker: NYSE: JBS
SIC: 2013; 2011
Industry/ies: Food And Beverage Industry
Legislative Issues: AGR; IMM

President and Chief Executive Officer Tel: (970) 506-8000
NOGUEIRA, Andre Fax: (970) 506-8307

Main Headquarters
Mailing: 1770 Promontory Cir. Tel: (970) 506-8000
          Greeley, CO 80634 Fax: (970) 506-8307

Political Action Committees
JBS USA LLC PAC
FEC ID: C00394650
Contact: Gustavo Biscardi
1770 Promontory Cir.
Greeley, CO 80634

    Contributions to Candidates: $27,000 (2015-2016)
    Democrats: $3,500; Republicans: $23,500

Principal Recipients

HOUSE
SMITH, ADRIAN (REP-NE)

Corporate Foundations and Giving Programs

JBS USA Contributions Program
1770 Promontory Cir. Tel: (970) 506-8000
Greeley, CO 80634

Public Affairs and Related Activities Personnel

At Headquarters

BISCARDI, Gustavo Tel: (970) 506-8000
PAC Treasurer Fax: (970) 506-8307

BATISTA, Wesley Tel: (970) 506-8000
President Fax: (970) 506-8307

BRUETT, Cameron Tel: (970) 506-7801
Corporate Affairs and Sustainability Fax: (970) 506-8307
Cameron.Bruett@jbssa.com

DOOLEY, Martin Tel: (970) 506-8000
President and Chief Operating Officer Fax: (970) 506-8307

GADDIS, Chris Tel: (970) 506-8000
Head of Human Resources Fax: (970) 506-8307

MOLINA, Denilson Tel: (970) 506-8000
Chief Financial Officer Fax: (970) 506-8307

JBT Corporation
See listing on page 456 under John Bean Technologies Corporation

JELD-WEN, Inc.
Window and door supplier and manufacturer.
www.jeld-wen.com
Employees: 20,000
Industry/ies: Construction/Construction Materials

President and Chief Executive Officer Tel: (541) 882-3451
HACHIGIAN, Kirk S. Fax: (541) 855-7454

Main Headquarters
Mailing: P.O. Box 1329 Tel: (541) 882-3451
          Klamath Falls, OR 97601 Fax: (541) 855-7454
          TF: (800) 535-3936

Political Action Committees
Jeld-Wen Inc Employee PAC
FEC ID: C00469825
Contact: Dan Crenshaw
1500 S.W. First Ave. Tel: (503) 478-4464
Suite 1100
Portland, OR 97201

    Contributions to Candidates: $2,600 (2015-2016)
    Republicans: $2,600

Corporate Foundations and Giving Programs

JELD-WEN Foundation
Contact: Robert Kingzett
401 Harbor Isles Blvd. Tel: (541) 882-3451
Klamath Falls, OR 97601

Public Affairs and Related Activities Personnel

At Headquarters

COTTRILL, Scott	Tel:	(541) 882-3451
Executive Vice President and Chief Financial Officer	Fax:	(541) 855-7454
KINGZETT, Robert	Tel:	(541) 882-3451
Foundation Executive Director	Fax:	(541) 855-7454
MEIHOFF, Darcie	Tel:	(541) 882-3451
Manager, Public Relations	Fax:	(541) 855-7454
dmeihoff@cmdagency.com		
TATE, Dan	Tel:	(541) 882-3451
Federal Lobbyist	Fax:	(541) 855-7454
Registered Federal Lobbyist		

At Other Offices

CRENSHAW, Dan
PAC Treasurer
1631 N.W. Thurman St., Suite 400
Portland, OR 97209

OLSON, Andrea Wendt
PAC Treasurer
1631 N.W. Thurman St., Suite 400
Portland, OR 97209
Mail Stop Suite 1100
Registered Federal Lobbyist

STORK, David
Senior Vice President & General Counsel
401 Harbor Isles Blvd.
Klamath Falls, OR 97601

Jenny Craig, Inc.

A provider of weight management products and services.
www.jennycraig.com
Annual Revenues: $220.10 million
Employees: 3,500
SIC: 7200
Industry/ies: Medicine/Health Care/Mental Health

Chief Executive Officer

LARCHET, Patricia A.	Tel:	(760) 696-4000
	Fax:	(760) 696-4009

Main Headquarters

Mailing: 5770 Fleet St.	Tel:	(760) 696-4000
Carlsbad, CA 92008	Fax:	(760) 696-4009
	TF:	(800) 597-5366

Corporate Foundations and Giving Programs

Jenny Craig, Inc. Contribution Program
5770 Fleet St.

Carlsbad, CA 92008	Tel:	(760) 696-4000
	Fax:	(760) 696-4009

Public Affairs and Related Activities Personnel

At Headquarters

BATTISTA, Doug	Tel:	(760) 696-4000
Vice President, Human Resources	Fax:	(760) 696-4009
SANDERS, Jae	Tel:	(760) 696-4000
Chief Marketing Officer, North America	Fax:	(760) 696-4009

Jeppesen - A Boeing Company

Specializes in aeronautical and nautical information services. A wholly-owned subsidiary of The Boeing Company.
ww1.jeppesen.com
Annual Revenues: $218.30 million
Employees: 3,200
SIC: 2741; 8299; 8999
Industry/ies: Printing Industry

Chief Executive Officer

TINE, Mark Van	Tel:	(303) 799-9090
	Fax:	(303) 328-4153

Main Headquarters

Mailing: 55 Inverness Dr., East	Tel:	(303) 799-9090
Englewood, CO 80112	Fax:	(303) 328-4153
	TF:	(800) 353-2107

Washington Office

Mailing: 515 Prince St.	Tel:	(703) 519-5295
Alexandria, VA 22314-3115	Fax:	(703) 519-5296

Public Affairs and Related Activities Personnel

At Headquarters

ANDERSON, Eric	Tel:	(303) 328-4767
Contact, Corporate Marketing & Communications	Fax:	(303) 328-4130
eric.anderson@jeppesen.com		
ARAGON, Marilyn	Tel:	(303) 799-9090
Vice President, Quality and Business Operation Services	Fax:	(303) 328-4153
CATRON, John	Tel:	(303) 799-9090
Chief Counsel	Fax:	(303) 328-4153
KURTZ, Bob	Tel:	(303) 799-9090
Senior Vice President and Chief Financial Officer	Fax:	(303) 328-4153
LEWIS, Mike	Tel:	(303) 799-9090

Vice President, Government and Industry Affairs	Fax:	(303) 328-4153
POMORSKI, Christine	Tel:	(303) 328-6166
Specialist, Marine Communications and Contact, Media Relations	Fax:	(303) 328-4153
christine.pomorski@jeppesen.com		
RANTALA , Brian	Tel:	(303) 328-4370
Specialist, Corporate Communications Aviation	Fax:	(303) 328-4153
brian.rantala@jeppesen.com		
VILLANUEVA, Mitchell	Tel:	(303) 328-4300
Vice President, Human Resources	Fax:	(303) 328-4153
mitchell.villanueva@jeppesen.com		
WEDE, Thomas	Tel:	(303) 799-9090
President	Fax:	(303) 328-4153

At Washington Office

GOEHLER, David J.	Tel:	(703) 519-5295
Director	Fax:	(703) 519-5296

Jeppesen Sanderson

See listing on page 454 under Jeppesen - A Boeing Company

JER Partners

See listing on page 450 under J.E. Roberts Companies

JetBlue Airways Corporation

A passenger airline company that provides air transportation services.
www.jetblue.com
Annual Revenues: $5.99 billion
Employees: 14,048
Ticker: NASDAQ; JBLU
SIC: 4512
NAICS: 481111
Industry/ies: Aerospace/Aviation; Transportation
Legislative Issues: AVI; HOM; TOU

Chairman of the Board

PETERSON, Joel	Tel:	(718) 286-7900
	Fax:	(718) 709-3621

President and Chief Executive Officer

HAYES, Robin	Tel:	(718) 286-7900
	Fax:	(718) 709-3621

Main Headquarters

Mailing: 27-01 Queens Plaza North	Tel:	(718) 286-7900
Forest Hills, NY 11101	Fax:	(718) 709-3621
	TF:	(800) 538-2583

Washington Office

Mailing: P.O. Box 34275	Tel:	(202) 898-0945
Washington, DC 20043-4275	Fax:	(202) 898-0946

Political Action Committees

JETBLUE Airways Corporation Crewmember Good Government Fund (JETBLUE PAC)
FEC ID: C00484584
Contact: Gavin Robert Sweitzer

1212 New York Ave. NW	Tel:	(718) 286-7900
Suite 1212	Fax:	(718) 709-3621
Washington, DC 20005		

Contributions to Candidates: $93,000 (2015-2016)
Democrats: $33,500; Republicans: $59,500

Principal Recipients

SENATE
SCHUMER, CHARLES E (DEM-NY)

HOUSE
SHUSTER, WILLIAM MR. (REP-PA)

Corporate Foundations and Giving Programs

The JetBlue Swing for Good Golf Classic

27-01 Queens Plaza N.	Tel:	(718) 709-2202
Long Island City, NY 11101		

Public Affairs and Related Activities Personnel

At Headquarters

ELLIOTT, Mike	Tel:	(718) 286-7900
Executive Vice President People	Fax:	(718) 709-3621
HNAT, James	Tel:	(718) 286-7900
Executive Vice President, Corporate Affairs, General Counsel and Corporate Secretary	Fax:	(718) 709-3621
james.hnat@jetblue.com		
MARTIN, Jeff	Tel:	(718) 286-7900
Executive Vice President Operations	Fax:	(718) 709-3621
POWERS, Mark D.	Tel:	(718) 286-7900
Chief Financial Officer and Executive Vice President	Fax:	(718) 709-3621
SWEITZER, Gavin Robert	Tel:	(718) 286-7900
PAC Treasurer	Fax:	(718) 709-3621

At Other Offices

DOVER, Josh J.

1212 New York Ave. NW, Suite 1212
Washington, DC 20005
Registered Federal Lobbyist

DOVER, Joshua
1212 New York Ave. NW, Suite 1212
Washington, DC 20005
Registered Federal Lobbyist

LAND, Robert Tel: (202) 280-6068
Senior Vice President, Government Affairs Fax: (202) 280-6067
1101 Pennsylvania Ave. NW, Fifth Floor
Washington, DC 20004
robert.land@jetblue.com
Registered Federal Lobbyist

Jewelry Television America's Collectibles Network, Inc.

Formerly America's Collectibles Network. A home shopping network with companion web store. Products sold are fine jewelry, watches, loose gemstones, castings, jewelry-making tools and related books.
www.jtv.com
Annual Revenues: $119.90 million
Employees: 2,000
Industry/ies: Communications; Retail/Wholesale; Telecommunications/Internet/Cable

Chairman of the Board Tel: (865) 692-6000
HALL, F. Robert Fax: (865) 692-1346

President and Chief Executive Officer Tel: (865) 692-6000
MATTHEWS, Tim Fax: (856) 692-1346

Main Headquarters
Mailing: 9600 Parkside Dr. Tel: (865) 692-6000
Knoxville, TN 37922 Fax: (865) 692-1346

Public Affairs and Related Activities Personnel

At Headquarters

ROTH, Stephen E. Tel: (865) 692-6000
General Counsel Fax: (865) 692-1346

At Other Offices

ENGLE, Tim Tel: (865) 692-6000
Chief Strategy Officer Fax: (865) 693-3688
10001 Kingston Pike, Suite 57
Knoxville, TN 37922

KOUNS, William C. Tel: (865) 692-6000
Chief Merchandising Officer Fax: (865) 693-3688
10001 Kingston Pike, Suite 57
Knoxville, TN 37922
bill.kouns@jtv.com

WAGNER, III, Charles A. Tel: (865) 692-6000
Vice Chairman Fax: (856) 692-1346
10001 Kingston Pike, Suite 57
Knoxville, TN 37922
charlie.wagner@jtv.com

WAGNER, Crawford Tel: (865) 692-6000
Chief Financial Officer Fax: (856) 692-1346
10001 Kingston Pike, Suite 57
Knoxville, TN 37922

Jiffy Lube International Inc.

Franchised oil change and lubrication centers. A subsidiary of Shell Oil Co. (see separate listing).
www.jiffylube.com
Annual Revenues: $178.80 million
Employees: 3,000
SIC: 7500
Industry/ies: Automotive Industry; Transportation

Main Headquarters
Mailing: P.O. Box 4427 Tel: (713) 546-4100
Houston, TX 77210-4458 Fax: (713) 546-4041
 TF: (800) 344-6933

Public Affairs and Related Activities Personnel

At Headquarters

CONNOLLY, Nicholle Tel: (617) 939-8378
Media Contact Fax: (713) 546-4041
nconnolly@coneinc.com

FRIEDMANN, Jennifer Tel: (713) 546-4100
Manager, Marketing Communications Fax: (713) 546-4041
jennifer.friedmann@shell.com

JILEK, Karn Tel: (701) 239-4400
Media Contact Fax: (713) 546-4041
karn@jklube.com

LACK, Jeffrey Tel: (713) 546-4100
Chief Marketing Officer Fax: (713) 546-4041

SANCHEZ, Virginia Tel: (713) 546-6272

Manager, Communications Fax: (713) 546-4041
virginia.q.sanchez@shell.com

JLG Industries Inc.

A designer, manufacturer and marketer of access equipment.
www.jlg.com
Annual Revenues: $473.20 million
Employees: 4,100
Ticker: NYSE: OSK
SIC: 3531; 3534; 3536; 3537; 3552
NAICS: 332999; 33312; 333292; 333921; 333923
Industry/ies: Machinery/Equipment

President Tel: (717) 485-5161
NERENHAUSEN , Frank Fax: (717) 485-6417

Main Headquarters
Mailing: One JLG Dr. Tel: (717) 485-5161
McConnellsburg, PA 17233-9533 Fax: (717) 485-6417

Public Affairs and Related Activities Personnel

At Headquarters

CHOLEWICKI, Frank Tel: (717) 485-5161
Vice President, Finance Fax: (717) 485-6417

At Other Offices

WILLETTS, Kent E.
Media Contact
13712 Crayton Blvd.
Hagerstown, MD 21742-2386
kewilletts@jlg.com

JLL Partners

A private equity investment firm.
www.jllpartners.com
Employees: 4,600
Industry/ies: Banking/Finance/Investments

Main Headquarters
Mailing: 450 Lexington Ave. Tel: (212) 286-8600
31st Floor Fax: (212) 286-8626
New York City, NY 10017

Public Affairs and Related Activities Personnel

At Headquarters

MILES, William (Bill) Tel: (212) 286-8600
Managing Director, Head, Investor Relations Fax: (212) 286-8626

PROCTOR, Katherine P. Tel: (212) 286-8600
Vice President, Investor Relations Fax: (212) 286-8626

SCHWARTZ, Michael J. Tel: (212) 286-8600
Chief Financial Officer Fax: (212) 286-8626

JM

See listing on page 457 under Johns Manville

JM Family Enterprises, Inc.

A diversified automotive corporation whose principal businesses focus on vehicle distribution and processing, finance and warranty services and insurance activities.
www.jmfamily.com
Industry/ies: Automotive Industry; Banking/Finance/Investments; Transportation
Legislative Issues: AUT; FIN; TRD

President and Chief Executive Officer Tel: (954) 429-2000
BROWN, Colin Fax: (954) 429-2300

Main Headquarters
Mailing: 100 Jim Moran Blvd. Tel: (954) 429-2000
Deerfield Beach, FL 33443 Fax: (954) 429-2300

Political Action Committees
JM Family Enterprises, Inc. PAC
FEC ID: C00240911
Contact: Sonya R. Deen
100 Jim Moran Blvd.
Deerfield Beach, FL 33442

Contributions to Candidates: $60,500 (2015-2016)
Democrats: $12,000; Republicans: $48,500

Corporate Foundations and Giving Programs

The Jim Moran Foundation
Contact: Dr. Melvin T. Stith
100 Jim Moran Blvd. Tel: (954) 429-2122
Deerfield Beach, FL 33442

Public Affairs and Related Activities Personnel

At Headquarters

BENTLEY, Kim Tel: (954) 418-5037
Assistant Vice President, Corporate Philanthropy Fax: (954) 363-0010
kim.bentley@jmfamily.com

BURNS, Brent	Tel:	(954) 429-2000
Executive Vice President and Chief Financial Officer	Fax:	(954) 429-2300
CALIENDO, Christie	Tel:	(954) 363-6285
Lead, Public Relations	Fax:	(954) 429-2300
christie.caliendo@jmfamily.com		
COOMBS, Ron	Tel:	(954) 429-2000
Chief Operating Officer	Fax:	(954) 429-2300
DEEN, Sonya R.	Tel:	(954) 429-2404
Vice President, Government Relations, PAC Treasurer and Federal Lobbyist	Fax:	(954) 429-2300
sonya.deen@jmfamily.com		
Registered Federal Lobbyist		
FINKELMAN, Ilisa	Tel:	(954) 363-5550
Senior Manager, Communications & Grants	Fax:	(954) 363-6810
ilisa.finkelman@jimmoranfoundation.org		
JOHNSON, Carmen	Tel:	(954) 429-2000
Executive Vice President and General Counsel	Fax:	(954) 429-2300
LINDNER, Donna	Tel:	(954) 363-2404
Senior Government Relations Representative	Fax:	(954) 429-2300
SONYA, Deen	Tel:	(954) 429-2000
Registered Federal Lobbyist	Fax:	(954) 429-2300
STITH, Dr. Melvin T.	Tel:	(954) 429-2122
Founding Director	Fax:	(954) 429-2699

JMB Health Solutions, LLC
Industry/ies: Medicine/Health Care/Mental Health

Main Headquarters
Mailing: 1455 Pennsylvania Ave. NW, Suite 400 Tel: (202) 652-2290
Washington, DC 20004

Public Affairs and Related Activities Personnel

At Headquarters

BURKE, William Tel: (202) 652-2290
kathy@mcgintyandco.com

JMJ Development, Inc.
A real estate firm.
www.jmjdevelopment.net
Annual Revenues: $1.40 million
Employees: 15
Industry/ies: Real Estate

Founder, President and Chief Executive Officer Tel: (972) 385-9934
BARTON, Timothy L. Fax: (972) 241-4484

Main Headquarters
Mailing: 1755 Wittington Pl. Tel: (972) 385-9934
Suite 340 Fax: (972) 241-4484
Dallas, TX 75234

Jo-Ann Stores, Inc.
A chain of specialty craft and fabric stores.
www.joann.com
Employees: 21,000
Ticker: NYSE: JAS
SIC: 5940; 5099; 5714; 5719; 5722
NAICS: 45113; 42199; 314121; 442299; 443111
Industry/ies: Apparel/Textiles Industry; Retail/Wholesale

Chief Executive Officer and President Tel: (330) 656-2600
SOLTAU, Jill Fax: (330) 463-6675

Main Headquarters
Mailing: 5555 Darrow Rd. Tel: (330) 656-2600
Hudson, OH 44236 Fax: (330) 463-6760
TF: (888) 739-4120

Corporate Foundations and Giving Programs
Jo-Ann Stores, Inc. Contributions Program
5555 Darrow Rd.
Hudson, OH 44236

Public Affairs and Related Activities Personnel

At Headquarters

COHEN, Brad	Tel:	(330) 463-6865
Senior Managing Director	Fax:	(330) 463-6675
GOLDSTON, David	Tel:	(330) 656-2600
Senior Vice President, General Counsel and Secretary	Fax:	(330) 463-6675
david.goldston@joann.com		
SKINNER, Margaret	Tel:	(330) 463-6705
Director, Corporate Communications	Fax:	(330) 463-6675
margaret.skinner@joann.com		

John Bean Technologies Corporation
JBT Corporation manufactures industrial equipment for the food processing and air transportation industries. Its JBT FoodTech segment makes commercial-grade refrigeration

systems, freezers, ovens, canning equipment, and food processing systems for fruit, poultry, meat patties, breads, pizzas, seafood, and ready-to-eat meals.
www.jbtcorporation.com
Annual Revenues: $1.15 billion
Employees: 4,200
Ticker: NYSE: JBT
SIC: 3550
Industry/ies: Computer/Technology

Chairman of the Board, President and Chief Executive Officer Tel: (312) 861-5900
GIACOMINI , Thomas W. Fax: (312) 861-5897

Main Headquarters
Mailing: 70 W. Madison Tel: (312) 861-5900
Suite 4400 Fax: (312) 861-5897
Chicago, IL 60602

Political Action Committees
John Bean Technologies Corporation PAC
FEC ID: C00452169
Contact: Gregory Packard
70 W. Madison Ave. Tel: (312) 861-6000
Suite 4400 Fax: (312) 861-6176
Chicago, IL 60602

Public Affairs and Related Activities Personnel

At Headquarters

DECK , Brian A.	Tel:	(312) 861-5900
Executive Vice President, Chief Financial Officer and Treasurer	Fax:	(312) 861-5897
JONES, Ken	Tel:	(312) 861-6791
Contact, Media Relations	Fax:	(312) 861-5897
kenneth.jones@jbtc.com		
MARVIN , James L.	Tel:	(312) 861-5900
Executive Vice President, General Counsel and Secretary	Fax:	(312) 861-5897
MONTAGUE, Mark	Tel:	(312) 861-5900
Executive Vice President, Human Resources	Fax:	(312) 861-5897
PODESTÁ, Juan C.	Tel:	(312) 861-5900
Vice President, Corporate Planning and Development	Fax:	(312) 861-5897
SENGUPTA, Debarshi	Tel:	(312) 861-5900
Contact, Investor Relations	Fax:	(312) 861-5897
debarshi.sengupta@jbtc.com		

At Other Offices
PACKARD, Gregory
PAC Treasurer
200 E. Raldoph St.
Chicago, IL 60601

John Bode LLC
Government relations.

Main Headquarters
Mailing: 100 Forth St. NE
Washington, DC 20002

Public Affairs and Related Activities Personnel

At Headquarters
BODE, John R.
Owner
johnbode@johnbodellc.com
HOVERMALE, Molly

John Hancock Financial Services, Inc.
A provider of insurance, investment and other financial services. A subsidiary of Manulife Financial Corporation based in Canada.
www.johnhancock.com
Annual Revenues: $18.59 billion
Employees: 8,000
Industry/ies: Banking/Finance/Investments
Legislative Issues: FIN; RET; TAX

President and Chief Executive Officer Tel: (617) 663-3000
ARNOTT, Andrew G. Fax: (617) 572-6015

Main Headquarters
Mailing: 601 Congress St. Tel: (617) 663-3000
Z-13-49 Fax: (617) 572-6015
Boston, MA 02210 TF: (800) 225-5291

Political Action Committees
John Hancock Life Insurance Company (USA) Federal Political Action Committee
FEC ID: C00137265
Contact: Thoms Samoluk
601 Congress St.
13th Floor
Boston, MA 2210

Contributions to Candidates: $81,000 (2015-2016)
Democrats: $44,000; Republicans: $37,000

Corporate Foundations and Giving Programs

John Hancock Funds
601 Congress St.
Boston, MA 02217

John Hancock Natural Resources Fund
601 Congress St.
Boston, MA 02217

Public Affairs and Related Activities Personnel

At Headquarters

ALVES, Emanuel	Tel:	(617) 663-3000
Counsel and Corporate Secretary	Fax:	(617) 572-6015
FINCH, Steve	Tel:	(617) 663-3000
Executive Vice President and Chief Financial Officer	Fax:	(617) 572-6015
GALLAGHER, James	Tel:	(617) 663-3000
Executive Vice President, General Counsel and Chief Administrative Officer	Fax:	(617) 572-6015
GORGI, Amir	Tel:	(416) 852-8311
Contact, Investor Relations	Fax:	(617) 572-6015
amir_gorgi@manulife.com		
MCGOLDRICK, Beth	Tel:	(617) 663-3000
Assistant Vice President	Fax:	(617) 572-6015
bmcgoldrick@jhancock.com		
PARIATH, Sebastian	Tel:	(617) 663-3000
Head of Operations, Chief Information Officer	Fax:	(617) 572-6015
PATERSON, David	Tel:	(416) 852-8899
Contact, Media Relations	Fax:	(617) 572-6015
david_paterson@manulife.com		
SAMOLUK, Thoms	Tel:	(617) 663-3000
Lobbyist & PAC Treasurer	Fax:	(617) 572-6015
Registered Federal Lobbyist		

John Wiley & Sons, Inc.

Publishers of print and electronic media.
www.wiley.com
Annual Revenues: $1.82 billion
Employees: 4,900
Ticker: NYSE: JW-A
SIC: 2731
Industry/ies: Printing Industry
Legislative Issues: CPT; GOV

Chairman of the Board	Tel:	(201) 748-6000
WILEY, Peter B.	Fax:	(201) 748-6008

President and Chief Executive Officer	Tel:	(201) 748-6000
SMITH, Stephen	Fax:	(201) 748-6008
stsmith@wiley.com		

Main Headquarters

Mailing:	111 River St.	Tel:	(201) 748-6000
	Hoboken, NJ 07030-5774	Fax:	(201) 748-6008

Public Affairs and Related Activities Personnel

At Headquarters

CAMPBELL, Brian	Tel:	(201) 748-6874
Director, Investor Relations	Fax:	(201) 748-6008
brian.campbell@wiley.com		
GORDON, Brent	Tel:	(201) 748-6000
Senior Vice President & Managing Director	Fax:	(201) 748-6008
HEIDER, Joseph S.	Tel:	(201) 748-6000
Senior Vice President, Global Education	Fax:	(201) 748-6008
KRITZMACHER, John	Tel:	(201) 748-6000
Executive Vice President, Chief Financial Officer	Fax:	(201) 748-6008
O'LEARY, MJ	Tel:	(201) 748-6000
Senior Vice President, Human Resources	Fax:	(201) 748-6008
RINCK, Gary M.	Tel:	(201) 748-6000
Senior Vice President, General Counsel	Fax:	(201) 748-6008
SEMEL, John	Tel:	(201) 748-6000
Executive Vice President and Chief Strategy Officer, Planning and Development	Fax:	(201) 748-6008
STOBAUGH, Clay	Tel:	(201) 748-6000
Executive Vice President, Chief Marketing Officer	Fax:	(201) 748-6008
WILEY, Deborah E.	Tel:	(201) 748-6000
Chairman, Wiley Foundation	Fax:	(201) 748-6008

Johns Manville

A manufacturer and marketer of building insulation, commercial roofing, roof insulation, and specialty products for commercial, industrial and residential applications.
www.jm.com
Employees: 8,000
Ticker: NYSE:JM
SIC: 3296; 3564; 5211; 1742; 3290
NAICS: 333412; 44419; 23542; 327993

Industry/ies: Construction/Construction Materials

Chairman, President and Chief Executive Officer	Tel:	(303) 978-2000
RHINEHART, Mary K.	Fax:	(303) 978-2318

Main Headquarters

Mailing:	P. O. Box 5108	Tel:	(303) 978-4900
	Denver, CO 80217-5108	Fax:	(303) 978-2318
		TF:	(800) 654-3103

Public Affairs and Related Activities Personnel

At Headquarters

HERVIG, Robin	Tel:	(303) 978-3404
Manager, Corporate Affairs and Communications	Fax:	(303) 978-2318
Robin.Hervig@jm.com		
RYAN, Cynthia	Tel:	(303) 978-2000
Senior Vice President and General Counsel	Fax:	(303) 978-2318
SKELLY, David	Tel:	(303) 978-2000
Director, Sales	Fax:	(303) 978-2318

At Other Offices

BROWN, Eric	Tel:	(303) 978-2350
Director, Corporate Communications		
717 17th St.		
Denver, CO 80202		
Eric.Brown@jm.com		
LEIKER, Holly	Tel:	(303) 978-2042
Lead, Media Relations and Internal Communications, Corporate Affairs and Communications		
717 17th St.		
Denver, CO 80202		
Holly.Leiker@jm.com		

Johnson & Johnson Services, Inc.

A manufacturer of personal hygiene and healthcare products. Announced a definitive merger agreement with Guidant Corporation (see separate listing) in December 2004, whereby Guidant would become part of Johnson & Johnson's cardiovascular device unit.
www.jnj.com
Annual Revenues: $73.59 billion
Employees: 126,500
Ticker: NYSE:JNJ
SIC: 2834
Industry/ies: Medicine/Health Care/Mental Health; Personal Care/Hygiene; Pharmaceutical Industry
Legislative Issues: ANI; BUD; CPT; CSP; ENV; HCR; MMM; TAX; TOR; TRD; VET

Chairman, Board of Directors and Chief Executive Officer	Tel:	(732) 524-2455
GORSKY, Alex	Fax:	(732) 214-0332

Main Headquarters

Mailing:	One Johnson and Johnson Plaza	Tel:	(732) 524-2455
	New Brunswick, NJ 08933	Fax:	(732) 214-0332

Washington Office

Mailing:	1350 Eye St. NW, Suite 1210
	Washington, DC 20005

Political Action Committees

Johnson & Johnson Political Action Committee
FEC ID: C00010983
Contact: Don W. Bohn

One Johnson & Johnson Plaza	Tel:	(732) 524-0400
New Brunswick, NJ 08933-7204	Fax:	(732) 214-0332

Contributions to Candidates: $315,800 (2015-2016)
Democrats: $121,600; Republicans: $194,200

Principal Recipients

HOUSE
BRADY, KEVIN (REP-TX)
MCCARTHY, KEVIN (REP-CA)

Corporate Foundations and Giving Programs

Johnson & Johnson Services Community Giving

One Johnson & Johnson plaza	Tel:	(732) 524-2455
New Brunswick, NJ 08933	Fax:	(732) 214-0332

Public Affairs and Related Activities Personnel

At Headquarters

BOHN, Don W.	Tel:	(732) 524-2455
Vice President, Global Government Affairs	Fax:	(732) 214-0332
dbohn@corus.jnj.com		
CANNON, James F.	Tel:	(732) 524-2455
Director, State Government Affairs	Fax:	(732) 214-0332
jcannon@corus.jnj.com		
CARUSO, Dominic J.	Tel:	(732) 524-2455
Vice President, Finance and Chief Financial Officer	Fax:	(732) 214-0332
KELLY, Brian	Tel:	(732) 524-2455
Registered Federal Lobbyist	Fax:	(732) 214-0332
KNEWITZ, Ernie	Tel:	(732) 524-6623

Vice President, Global Media Relations
eknewitz@its.jnj.com

Fax: (732) 214-0332

LEEBAW, Jeffrey
Vice President, Corporate Media Relations
jleebaw@its.jnj.com

Tel: (732) 524-2455
Fax: (732) 214-0332

LICITRA, Karen
Corporate Vice President, Government Affairs & Policy

Tel: (732) 524-2455
Fax: (732) 214-0332

LLOYD, Richard
Executive Director, State Government Affairs
rlloyd@corus.jnj.com

Tel: (732) 524-2455
Fax: (732) 214-0332

MEHROTRA, Louise
Vice President, Investor Relations

Tel: (732) 524-6491
Fax: (732) 214-0332

NAU, Charles
Director, Federal Affairs
Registered Federal Lobbyist

Tel: (732) 524-2455
Fax: (732) 214-0332

NOE, Nancy
Manager, State Government Affairs

Tel: (732) 524-2455
Fax: (732) 214-0332

ODENTHAL, Susan
Vice President, Corporate Communications
sodente@corus.jnj.com

Tel: (732) 524-2455
Fax: (732) 214-0332

OSWALT, Anne
Registered Federal Lobbyist

Tel: (732) 524-2455
Fax: (732) 214-0332

RUMACHIK, Jeff
Corporate Vice President, Government Affairs & Policy

Tel: (732) 524-2455
Fax: (732) 214-0332

ULLMANN, Michael
Vice President, General Counsel

Tel: (732) 524-2455
Fax: (732) 214-0332

At Other Offices

ADAMS, Jane
Vice President, U.S. federal affairs
1350 I St. NW, Suite 1210
Washington, DC 20005-3305
Registered Federal Lobbyist

Tel: (202) 589-1000
Fax: (202) 589-1001

ADAMS, Jane A.
Director, Federal Affairs
1350 I St. NW, Suite 1210
Washington, DC 20005-3305
Registered Federal Lobbyist

Tel: (202) 589-1000
Fax: (202) 589-1001

BOHN, Don W.
Vice President, Global Government Affairs
1350 I St. NW, Suite 1210
Washington, DC 20005-3305
dbohn@corus.jnj.com

Tel: (202) 589-1000
Fax: (202) 589-1001

BURNS, Brian
Executive Director, Federal Affairs
1350 I St. NW, Suite 1210
Washington, DC 20005-3305
bburns7@corus.jnj.com
Registered Federal Lobbyist

Tel: (202) 589-1000
Fax: (202) 589-1001

COHEN, Julie
Federal Lobbyist
1350 I St. NW, Suite 1210
Washington, DC 20005-3305

Tel: (202) 589-1000
Fax: (202) 589-1001

DAVIS, Kimberly
Director, Federal Affairs
1350 I St. NW, Suite 1210
Washington, DC 20005-3305

Tel: (202) 589-1000
Fax: (202) 589-1001

DOOLEY, Cathleen M.
Executive Director, Federal Affairs
1350 I St. NW, Suite 1210
Washington, DC 20005-3305
cdooley@obius.jnj.com
Registered Federal Lobbyist

Tel: (202) 589-1000
Fax: (202) 589-1001

FOWLER, Liz
Vice President, Global Health Policy
1350 I St. NW, Suite 1210
Washington, DC 20005-3305

Tel: (202) 589-1000
Fax: (202) 589-1001

JACKSON, Lauryl
Federal Lobbyist
1350 I St. NW, Suite 1210
Washington, DC 20005-3305
Registered Federal Lobbyist

Tel: (202) 589-1000
Fax: (202) 589-1001

JODREY, Darrel
Executive Director, Federal Affairs
1350 I St. NW, Suite 1210
Washington, DC 20005-3305
Mail Stop M/S 1006
Registered Federal Lobbyist

Tel: (202) 589-1000
Fax: (202) 589-1001

KAVANAUGH, David
Director, Federal Affairs
1350 I St. NW, Suite 1210
Washington, DC 20005-3305

Tel: (202) 589-1000
Fax: (202) 589-1001

Registered Federal Lobbyist

LEPORE, Chris
Vice President, U.S. state affairs
1350 I St. NW, Suite 1210
Washington, DC 20005-3305

Tel: (202) 589-1000
Fax: (202) 589-1001

REARDON, Susan
Director, International Policy
1350 I St. NW, Suite 1210
Washington, DC 20005-3305
Registered Federal Lobbyist

Tel: (202) 589-1000
Fax: (202) 589-1001

REESE, Mark
Executive Director, Federal Affairs
1350 I St. NW, Suite 1210
Washington, DC 20005-3305
Registered Federal Lobbyist

Tel: (202) 589-1000
Fax: (202) 589-1001

Johnson Controls, Inc.

The company makes car batteries and interior parts for combustion engine and hybrid electric vehicles, as well as energy-efficient HVAC systems for commercial buildings. Products include seating, instrument panels, and a slew of electronics.
www.johnsoncontrols.com
Annual Revenues: $42.69 billion
Employees: 168,000
Ticker: NYSE: JCI
SIC: 2531
Industry/ies: Energy/Electricity; Machinery/Equipment
Legislative Issues: BUD; DEF; ENG; MAN; TAX

Main Headquarters
Mailing: P.O. Box 591
        5757 N. Green Bay Ave.
        Milwaukee, WI 53201

Tel: (414) 524-1200
Fax: (414) 524-2077

Washington Office
Mailing: 500 N. Capitol St. NW
        Suite 729
        Washington, DC 20001

Tel: (202) 406-4076
Fax: (202) 406-4067

Political Action Committees
Johnson Controls Inc. Federal PAC
FEC ID: C00343095
Contact: Charles A. Harvey
5757 N. Green Bay Ave.
Milwaukee, WI 53209

Tel: (414) 524-1200

    Contributions to Candidates: $17,500 (2015-2016)
    Democrats: $8,500; Republicans: $9,000

Corporate Foundations and Giving Programs
Johnson Controls Foundation
Contact: Mary Dowell
5757 N. Green Bay Ave.
Milwaukee, WI 53209

Tel: (414) 524-1200

Public Affairs and Related Activities Personnel

At Headquarters

ANDREW, Mike
Director, Government Affairs and External Communications
michael.g.andrew@jci.com

Tel: (414) 524-1200
Fax: (414) 524-2077

DAVIS, Susan F.
Executive Vice President, Human Resources

Tel: (414) 524-1200
Fax: (414) 524-2077

DOWELL, Mary
Director, Global Community Relations
mary.j.dowell@jci.com

Tel: (414) 524-1200
Fax: (414) 524-2077

MCDONALD, R. Bruce
Executive Vice President and Chief Financial Officer

Tel: (414) 524-1200
Fax: (414) 524-2077

METCALF-KUPRES, Kim
Vice President and Chief Marketing Officer

Tel: (414) 524-1200
Fax: (414) 524-2077

OKARMA, Jerome D.
Vice President, Secretary and General Counsel
Jerome.D.Okarma@jci.com
Registered Federal Lobbyist

Tel: (414) 524-1200
Fax: (414) 524-2077

PONCZAK, Glen
Vice President, Investor Relations
glen.l.ponczak@jci.com

Tel: (414) 524-2375
Fax: (414) 524-2077

VOLTOLINA, Frank A.
Vice President and Corporate Treasurer

Tel: (414) 524-1200
Fax: (414) 524-2077

At Washington Office

PROSCH, Geoffrey
Director, Federal Government Relations
Registered Federal Lobbyist

Tel: (202) 406-4063
Fax: (202) 406-4067

WAGNER, Mark
Vice President, Government Relations
Registered Federal Lobbyist

Tel: (202) 406-4061
Fax: (202) 406-4067

At Other Offices

BARBOUR, Erin

Tel: (414) 524-1200

Office Manager
5757 N. Green Bay Ave.
Milwaukee, WI 53209

HARVEY, Charles A.   Tel: (414) 524-1200
Chief Diversity Officer and Vice President Community Affairs
and PAC Treasurer
5757 N. Green Bay Ave.
Milwaukee, WI 53209

TATE, Elizabeth   Tel: (414) 524-1200
5757 N. Green Bay Ave.
Milwaukee, WI 53209
Registered Federal Lobbyist

Jones Apparel Group

See listing on page 459 under The Jones Group, Inc.

The Jones Group, Inc.

Manufacturer of men's and women's apparel. Brand names include Jones New York, Evan-Piccone, Nine West, Easy Spirit, Lauren by Ralph Lauren, Ralph by Ralph Lauren, and Enzo Angiolini, among others.
www.jonesgroupinc.com
Annual Revenues: $3.76 billion
Employees: 5,970
Ticker: NYSE: JNY
SIC: 2330; 5137
NAICS: 422330
Industry/ies: Apparel/Textiles Industry

Chairman of the Board   Tel: (212) 642-3860
KIMMEL, Sydney   Fax: (215) 785-1795

Chief Executive Officer   Tel: (212) 642-3860
CARD, Wesley R.   Fax: (215) 785-1795

Main Headquarters
Mailing: 1411 Broadway   Tel: (212) 642-3860
              New York City, NY 10018   Fax: (215) 785-1795

Corporate Foundations and Giving Programs

The Jones Group Inc. Contribution Program
1411 Broadway   Tel: (215) 642-3860
New York City, NY 10018   Fax: (215) 785-1795

Public Affairs and Related Activities Personnel

At Headquarters

DANSKY, Ira M.   Tel: (212) 642-3860
Executive Vice President, General Counsel and Secretary   Fax: (215) 785-1795

MCCLAIN, John T.   Tel: (212) 703-9189
Chief Financial Officer   Fax: (215) 785-1795
JMcClain@jny.com

STERN, Sharon   Tel: (212) 355-4449
Contact, Media Relations   Fax: (215) 785-1795

Jones Lang LaSalle Americas, Inc.

Real estate investment and management company. It offers a range of real estate services, including agency leasing, project and development management/construction, capital markets, property management, corporate finance, real estate investment banking/merchant banking etc.
www.jll.com
Annual Revenues: $6.10 billion
Employees: 61,500
Ticker: NYSE: JLL
SIC: 6531
Industry/ies: Banking/Finance/Investments; Real Estate

Chairman of the Board   Tel: (312) 782-5800
PENROSE, Sheila A.   Fax: (312) 782-4339

President and Chief Executive Officer   Tel: (312) 782-5800
DYER, Colin   Fax: (312) 782-4339

Main Headquarters
Mailing: 200 E. Randolph Dr.   Tel: (312) 782-5800
              Chicago, IL 60601   Fax: (312) 782-4339

Washington Office
Mailing: 1801 K St. NW   Tel: (202) 719-5000
              Suite 1000   Fax: (202) 719-5001
              Washington, DC 20006

Political Action Committees

Jones Lang LaSalle Americas Inc. PAC
FEC ID: C00396549
Contact: Ernest Fiorante
200 E. Randolph Dr.
Chicago, IL 60601

Corporate Foundations and Giving Programs

Greenprint Foundation
200 E. Randolph Dr.   Tel: (312) 782-5800
Chicago, IL 60601

Public Affairs and Related Activities Personnel

At Headquarters

DOYLE, Charles   Tel: (312) 782-5800
Chief Marketing Officer   Fax: (312) 782-4339

FIORANTE, Ernest   Tel: (312) 782-5800
Chief Financial Officer, Americas Region and PAC Treasurer   Fax: (312) 782-4339

JOHNSON, David   Tel: (312) 782-5800
Chief Information Officer   Fax: (312) 782-4339

KANTRO, Gayle   Tel: (312) 228-2795
Director, Corporate Communications   Fax: (312) 782-4339
gayle.kantro@am.jll.com

KELLY, Christie   Tel: (312) 782-5800
Chief Financial Officer, Global   Fax: (312) 782-4339

MAXSON, Trish   Tel: (312) 782-5800
Chief Human Resources Officer   Fax: (312) 782-4339

OHRINGER, Mark   Tel: (312) 782-5800
General Counsel   Fax: (312) 782-4339
mark.ohringer@jll.com

Jostens, Inc.

A subsidiary of Visant Holding Corp. A producer of class rings, yearbooks and other specialized products.
www.jostens.com
Employees: 6,000
SIC: 3911
Industry/ies: Retail/Wholesale

Chief Executive Officer   Tel: (952) 830-3300
MOOTY, Chuck   Fax: (952) 830-3293

Main Headquarters
Mailing: 3601 Minnesota Dr.   Tel: (952) 830-3300
              Minneapolis, MN 55435   Fax: (952) 830-3293

Corporate Foundations and Giving Programs

Jostens Foundation
3601 Minnesota Dr.   Tel: (952) 830-3235
Minneapolis, MN 55435

Public Affairs and Related Activities Personnel

At Headquarters

CARR, Ann   Tel: (952) 830-3300
Chief Marketing Officer   Fax: (952) 830-3293

KELLY, Mike   Tel: (952) 830-3300
Chief of Strategy and Business Development   Fax: (952) 830-3293

LAMBERT, Patrick   Tel: (952) 830-3300
Vice President, Project Management   Fax: (952) 830-3293

LANDMAN, Cathy   Tel: (952) 830-3300
General Counsel   Fax: (952) 830-3293

PETERSON, Jeff   Tel: (952) 830-3348
jeff.peterson@jostens.com%u200B   Fax: (952) 830-3293

SIMPSON, Jim   Tel: (952) 830-3300
Chief Financial Officer   Fax: (952) 830-3293

VELANI, Murad   Tel: (952) 830-3300
Chief Operating Officer and Vice President   Fax: (952) 830-3293

Journal Media Group

Journal Media Group was formerly Journal Communications Inc. Communications company involved in newspaper publishing, printing, radio and television broadcasting.
www.journalcommunications.com
Annual Revenues: $412.47 million
Employees: 2,600
Ticker: NYSE: JRN
SIC: 2711
Industry/ies: Communications; Media/Mass Communication; Printing Industry

President and Chief Executive Officer   Tel: (414) 224-2000
STAUTBERG, Tim   Fax: (414) 224-2469

Main Headquarters
Mailing: 333 W. State St.   Tel: (414) 224-2000
              P.O. Box 661   Fax: (414) 224-2469
              Milwaukee, WI 53201-0661

Public Affairs and Related Activities Personnel

At Headquarters

BRENNER, Betsy   Tel: (414) 224-2954
Executive Vice President   Fax: (414) 224-2469

EBACH , Hillary   Tel: (414) 224-2000
Vice President, General Counsel   Fax: (414) 224-2469

GRAHAM, Jason   Tel: (414) 224-2884
Senior Vice President and Chief Financial Officer   Fax: (414) 224-2469

IASHINSKY, Trina   Tel: (414) 224-2000
Vice President, Human Resources   Fax: (414) 224-2469

O'REILLY, Dennis   Tel: (414) 224-2935

Director, Treasury Operations and Investor Relations Contact	Fax:	(414) 224-2469
dennis.oreilly@jmg.com		
OZOLINS, Marty	Tel:	(414) 224-2000
Vice President and Corporate Controller	Fax:	(414) 224-2469

Joy Global

A holding company for two subsidiaries involved in the manufacture and marketing original equipment and aftermarket parts and services for the mining industries. Joy Global's products and related services are used extensively for the mining of coal, copper, iron ore, oil sands, gold and other mineral resources.
www.joyglobal.com
Annual Revenues: $2.79 billion
Employees: 13,400
Ticker: NYSE:JOY
SIC: 3532
Industry/ies: Machinery/Equipment

President and Chief Executive Officer	Tel:	(414) 319-8500
DOHENY , II, Edward L.	Fax:	(414) 319-8520

Main Headquarters
Mailing:	100 E. Wisconsin Ave., Suite 2780	Tel:	(414) 319-8500
	P.O. Box 554	Fax:	(414) 319-8520
	Milwaukee, WI 53202		

Political Action Committees
Joy Global Inc. PAC (Joy Global PAC)
FEC ID: C00334581
Contact: Patti J. Effertz
100 E. Wisconsin Ave.
Suite 2780
Milwaukee, WI 53202

> **Contributions to Candidates:** $23,650 (2015-2016)
> Republicans: $23,650

Public Affairs and Related Activities Personnel

At Headquarters

BAKER, Randal W.	Tel:	(414) 319-8500
Executive Vice President and Chief Operating Officer	Fax:	(414) 319-8520
EFFERTZ, Patti J.	Tel:	(414) 319-8500
PAC Treasurer	Fax:	(414) 319-8520
MAJOR, Sean D.	Tel:	(414) 319-8500
Executive Vice President, General Counsel and Secretary	Fax:	(414) 319-8520
MARITZ, Johannes S.	Tel:	(414) 319-8500
Executive Vice President, Human Resources	Fax:	(414) 319-8520
MARITZ, Johan S.	Tel:	(414) 319-8500
Executive Vice President, Human Resources	Fax:	(414) 319-8520
MCKENZIE, Sandra L.	Tel:	(414) 319-8506
Executive Assistant	Fax:	(414) 319-8520
Sandy.McKenzie@joyglobal.com		
STARK, Kenneth J.	Tel:	(414) 319-8500
Assistant Treasurer	Fax:	(414) 319-8520
Mail Stop Suite 2780		
ksta@joyglobal.com		
SULLIVAN, Jame M.	Tel:	(414) 319-8509
Executive Vice President and Chief Financial Officer	Fax:	(414) 319-8520

Joy Global, Inc.

See listing on page 460 under Joy Global

JSJ Corporation

A privately held corporation that designs, develops, markets, and brands a group of durable goods and services throughout the world.
www.jsjcorp.com
Annual Revenues: $198 million
Employees: 2,600
Industry/ies: Machinery/Equipment

Chairman, President and Chief Executive Officer	Tel:	(616) 842-6350
JACOBSON, Nelson	Fax:	(616) 847-3112
jacobsonn@jsjcorp.com		

Main Headquarters
Mailing:	700 Robbins Rd.	Tel:	(616) 842-6350
	Grand Haven, MI 49417	Fax:	(616) 847-3112

Corporate Foundations and Giving Programs
JSJ Foundation
Contact: Dana Plowman
1250 S. Beechtree	Tel:	(616) 842-6350
Grand Haven, MI 49417	Fax:	(616) 847-3112

Public Affairs and Related Activities Personnel

At Headquarters

BUURSMA, Bruce	Tel:	(616) 842-6350
Contact, Media Relations	Fax:	(616) 847-3112
JENNINGS, Martin	Tel:	(616) 842-6350

Executive Vice President, Chief Financial Officer	Fax:	(616) 847-3112
PLOWMAN, Dana	Tel:	(616) 847-7057
Specialist , Strategic Services	Fax:	(616) 847-3112
plowmand@jsjcorp.com		
SHERWOOD, Lynne	Tel:	(616) 842-6350
Vice Chairman and Secretary	Fax:	(616) 847-3112
sherwoodl@jsjcorp.com		
WADE, Clare	Tel:	(616) 458-7421
Director, Branding and Communications	Fax:	(616) 847-3112
clare@clarewade.com		

Juniper Networks

Provides IP infrastructure systems to internet service providers.
www.juniper.net/us/en
Annual Revenues: $4.52 billion
Employees: 8,806
Ticker: NASDAQ: JNPR
SIC: 3576
Industry/ies: Computer/Technology; Management
Legislative Issues: SCI

Chairman of the Board	Tel:	(408) 745-2000
KRIENS, Scott G.	Fax:	(408) 745-2100
skriens@juniper.com		

Chief Executive Officer	Tel:	(408) 745-2000
RAHIM, Rami	Fax:	(408) 745-2100

Main Headquarters
Mailing:	1133 Innovation Way	Tel:	(408) 745-2000
	Sunnyvale, CA 94089-1206	Fax:	(408) 745-2100
		TF:	(888) 586-4737

Washington Office
Mailing:	2251 Corporate Park Dr.,	Tel:	(571) 203-1700
	Suite 100	Fax:	(571) 203-1790
	Herndon, VA 20171-2808		

Corporate Foundations and Giving Programs
Juniper Network Foundation Fund
1194 N. Mathilda Ave. | Tel: | (541) 203-1700 |
Sunnyvale, CA 94089

Public Affairs and Related Activities Personnel

At Headquarters

DENHOLM, Robyn	Tel:	(408) 745-2000
Executive Vice President and Chief Financial and Operations Officer	Fax:	(408) 745-2100
GAYNOR, Mitchell	Tel:	(408) 745-2384
Executive Vice President, General Counsel and Secretary	Fax:	(408) 745-2100
mgaynor@juniper.net		
HAYES, Brendan	Tel:	(978) 589-0230
Product Marketing Manager	Fax:	(978) 589-0087
bhayes@juniper.net		
LOVEGREN, Susan	Tel:	(408) 745-2000
Senior Vice President, Human Resources	Fax:	(408) 745-2100
MARCELLIN, Michael	Tel:	(408) 745-2000
Chief Marketing Officer	Fax:	(408) 745-2100
MILLER, Ken	Tel:	(408) 745-2000
Senior Vice President, Finance	Fax:	(408) 745-2100
RICE, Steven	Tel:	(408) 745-2000
Executive Vice President, Human Resources	Fax:	(408) 745-2100

At Washington Office

BEAN, James B.	Tel:	(571) 203-1700
Director, Government Affairs	Fax:	(571) 203-1790
DIX, Robert	Tel:	(571) 203-1700
Vice President, Government Affairs and Critical Infrastructure Protection	Fax:	(571) 203-1790
GARG, Sampak	Tel:	(571) 203-1700
Director, Legislative Affairs	Fax:	(571) 203-1790

Jupiter Aluminum Corporation

An aluminum mill.
www.jupiteraluminum.com
Industry/ies: Metals

Main Headquarters
Mailing:	4825 Scott St.	Tel:	(847) 928-5930
	Schiller Park, IL 60176	Fax:	(847) 928-0795
		TF:	(800) 392-7265

Jupiter Oxygen Corporation

An oxy fuel technology company.
jupiteroxygen.com
Annual Revenues: $4 million
Industry/ies: Energy/Electricity

Chairman of the Board and Chief Executive Officer Tel: (847) 928-5930
GROSS, Dietrich M. Fax: (847) 928-0795

President Tel: (847) 928-5930
WEBER, Thomas G. Fax: (847) 928-0795

Main Headquarters
Mailing: 4825 N. Scott St. Tel: (847) 928-5930
Suite 200 Fax: (847) 928-0795
Schiller Park, IL 60176

Public Affairs and Related Activities Personnel

At Headquarters

SCHOENFIELD, Mark K. Tel: (847) 928-5930
Senior Vice President, Operations and General Counsel Fax: (847) 928-0795

K2 Pure Solutions

Manufactures water purification and disinfection products using safe, environmentally sustainable technology.
www.k2pure.com
Annual Revenues: $1.0 billion
Employees: 7
Industry/ies: Chemicals & Chemical Industry

Executive Chairman Tel: (330) 899-8574
CYNAMON, David Fax: (330) 899-8610
dcynamon@k2pure.com

Chief Executive Officer and Contact, Media Relations Tel: (330) 899-8574
BRODIE, Howard Fax: (330) 899-8610

Main Headquarters
Mailing: 3515 Massillon Rd. Tel: (330) 899-8574
Suite 290 Fax: (330) 899-8610
Uniontown, OH 44685

Corporate Foundations and Giving Programs

Gerry and Nancy Pencer Brain Trust
Contact: David Cynamon
3515 Massillon Rd. Tel: (330) 899-8574
Suite 290 Fax: (330) 899-8610
Uniontown, OH 44685

Mount Sinai Hospital Foundation
Contact: David Cynamon
3515 Massillon Rd. Tel: (330) 899-8574
Suite 290 Fax: (330) 899-8610
Uniontown, OH 44685

Public Affairs and Related Activities Personnel

At Headquarters

ANTHONY, Rick Tel: (330) 899-8574
Director, Engineering Fax: (330) 899-8610
Ranthony@k2pure.com

Kaba Mas Corporation

A manufacturer and supplier of high-security electronic locking solutions.
www.kaba-mas.com
Employees: 2
Industry/ies: Defense/Homeland Security; Government-Related

Chairman of the Board Tel: (888) 950-4715
GRAF, Ulrich Fax: (859) 255-2655

Main Headquarters
Mailing: 749 W. Short St. Tel: (859) 253-4744
Lexington, KY 40508 Fax: (859) 255-2655
TF: (888) 950-4715

Public Affairs and Related Activities Personnel

At Headquarters

POLLACK, Stephen Tel: (888) 950-4715
Director, Media Contact, Chief Marketing Officer Fax: (859) 255-2655
spollack@kml.kaba.com

At Other Offices

BIRDWELL, Tasha Tel: (859) 977-3512
Contact, Media
2941 Indiana Av.
Winston-Salem, NC 27105
tasha.birdwell@kaba.com

Kadrmas Lee & Jackson, Inc.

An engineering firm.
www.kljeng.com
Annual Revenues: $35.95 million
Employees: 300
Industry/ies: Engineering/Mathematics

Chief Executive Officer Tel: (800) 213-3860
HUSHKA, Niles Fax: (701) 333-0701
niles.hushka@kljeng.com

Main Headquarters
Mailing: 4585 Coleman St. Tel: (800) 213-3860
Bismarck, ND 58503

Corporate Foundations and Giving Programs

Kadrmas Lee and Jackson Contributions Program
128 Soo Line Dr.
Bismarck, ND 58502-1157

Public Affairs and Related Activities Personnel

At Headquarters

PE, Lanny Harris Tel: (800) 213-3860
Senior Executive, Director, Telecommunications Services

ANAGNOST, Dean Tel: (800) 213-3860
Chief Financial Officer
dean.anagnost@kljeng.com

ENNEN, Rick Tel: (800) 213-3860
Governance Officer

SCHUCHARD, Barry Tel: (800) 213-3860
Vice President

At Other Offices

SHAFER, Kayla Tel: (701) 355-8400
Manager, Government Affairs Fax: (701) 255-0943
128 Soo Line Dr.,
Bismarck, ND 58502-1157
Kayla.Shafer@kljeng.com

Kaiser Aluminum & Chemical Corporation

A producer of bauxite, alumina, aluminum and fabricated aluminum products. It offers rolled, extruded, and drawn aluminum products used principally for aerospace and defense, automotive, consumer durables, electronics, electrical, and machinery and equipment applications.
www.kaiseraluminum.com
Annual Revenues: $1.39 billion
Employees: 2,650
Ticker: NASDAQ: KALU
SIC: 3350
Industry/ies: Chemicals & Chemical Industry; Metals

Chairman of the Board, President and Chief Executive Officer Tel: (949) 614-1740
HOCKEMA, Jack A. Fax: (949) 614-1930

Main Headquarters
Mailing: 27422 Portola Pkwy. Tel: (949) 614-1740
Suite 200 Fax: (949) 614-1930
Foothill Ranch, CA 92610-2831

Political Action Committees
Kaiser Aluminum PAC
FEC ID: C00047415
Contact: John M. Donnan Esq.
27422 Portola Pkwy. Tel: (949) 614-1740
Suite 350 Fax: (949) 614-1930
Foothill Ranch, CA 92610

Public Affairs and Related Activities Personnel

At Headquarters

BARNESON, John Tel: (949) 614-1740
Senior Vice President, Corporate Development Fax: (949) 614-1930

DONNAN, Esq., John M. Tel: (949) 614-1740
Executive Vice President, Legal, Compliance and Human Fax: (949) 614-1930
Resources and PAC Treasurer
john.donnan@kaiseraluminum.com

ELLSWORTH, Melinda C. Tel: (949) 614-1757
Contact, Invester Relations, Vice President and Treasurer Fax: (949) 614-1930
ellsworthm@honi.com

HARVEY, Keith Tel: (949) 614-1740
Executive Vice President, Fabricated Products Fax: (949) 614-1930

KROUSE, Mark R. Tel: (949) 614-1740
Vice President, Human Resources Fax: (949) 614-1930

QUAST, Dave Tel: (213) 452-6348
Media Contact Fax: (949) 614-1930

RINKENBERGER, Daniel J. Tel: (949) 614-1740
Executive Vice President and Chief Financial Officer Fax: (949) 614-1930

Kaiser Foundation Health Plan, Inc.

See listing on page 461 under Kaiser Permanente

Kaiser Permanente

A non-profit health maintenance organization.
healthy.kaiserpermanente.org
Annual Revenues: $42.10 billion
Employees: 164,000
Industry/ies: Medicine/Health Care/Mental Health
Legislative Issues: BUD; CPI; CPT; DEF; HCR; MMM; TAX

Main Headquarters

Mailing:	One Kaiser Plaza	Tel:	(510) 271-5800
	27th Floor	Fax:	(510) 267-7524
	Oakland, CA 94612	TF:	(800) 556-7677

Washington Office

Mailing:	700 Second St. NE	Tel:	(202) 296-1314
	Washington, DC 20002		

Corporate Foundations and Giving Programs

Kaiser Permanente Contributions Porgram
One Kaiser Plaza   Tel: (510) 271-5800
Ordway Bldg. 27th Floor
Oakland, CA 94612

Public Affairs and Related Activities Personnel

At Headquarters

BARRUETA, Anthony	Tel:	(510) 271-2626
Senior Vice President, Government Relations	Fax:	(510) 267-7524
anthony.barrueta@kp.org		
Registered Federal Lobbyist		
BROWN, Fish	Tel:	(202) 296-1314
Director, Federal Relations	Fax:	(510) 267-7524
fish.brown@kp.org		
Registered Federal Lobbyist		
CASS, Danielle	Tel:	(510) 267-5354
Contact, National Media Relations	Fax:	(510) 267-7524
danielle.x.cass@kp.org		
GREGG, Sandra R.	Tel:	(510) 271-5800
Vice President, Communications and External Relations	Fax:	(510) 267-7524
greg.a.hughes@kp.org		
LANCASTER, Kathy	Tel:	(510) 271-5800
Executive Vice President and Chief Financial Officer	Fax:	(510) 267-7524
WILLIAMS, Joseph	Tel:	(510) 271-5800
Registered Federal Lobbyist	Fax:	(510) 267-7524
WILLIAMSON, Joe	Tel:	(510) 271-5800
Federal Lobbyist	Fax:	(510) 267-7524
Registered Federal Lobbyist		

At Washington Office

BURNETT, Laird	Tel:	(202) 296-1314
Vice President, Federal Government Relations		
laird.burnett@kp.org		
Registered Federal Lobbyist		

At Other Offices

LOVELAND, Darcy	Tel:	(949) 497-2907
Governmental Relations Counsel	Fax:	(949) 497-2927
Three Rockledge Rd.		
Laguna Beach, CA 92651		
MONTGOMERY, Jacque	Tel:	(303) 344-7410
Director, Media and Public Relations		
10350 E. Dakota Ave.		
Denver, CO 80211		
jacque.montgomery@kp.org		
THOMAS, Beverly	Tel:	(404) 264-4713
Vice President, Public Affairs	Fax:	(404) 364-4794
3495 Piedmont Rd. NE		
Atlanta, GA 30305		

Kalsec, Inc.

A manufacturer of spice and herb flavorings and colorings in forms which are adaptable to modern food processing techniques.
www.kalsec.com
Annual Revenues: $43.30 million
Employees: 300
Industry/ies: Food And Beverage Industry

Chairman and Chief Executive Officer   Tel: (269) 349-9711
TODD, George   Fax: (269) 382-3060

Executive Director, Market Development   Tel: (269) 349-9711
AUGUSTINE, Gary   Fax: (269) 382-3060
gaugustine@kalsec.com

Main Headquarters

Mailing:	P.O. Box 50511	Tel:	(269) 349-9711
	Kalamazoo, MI 49005-0511	Fax:	(269) 382-3060
		TF:	(800) 323-9320

Corporate Foundations and Giving Programs

Kalsec contributions Program
P.O. Box 50511   Tel: (269) 349-9711
Kalamazoo, MI 49005-0511   Fax: (269) 382-3060

Public Affairs and Related Activities Personnel

At Headquarters

BAIRD, Donn	Tel:	(269) 349-9711
Treasurer	Fax:	(269) 382-3060

Kaman Corporation

A manufacturing and distribution company.
www.kaman.com
Annual Revenues: $1.83 billion
Employees: 4,797
Ticker: NASDAQ: KAMN
SIC: 5080
Industry/ies: Aerospace/Aviation; Transportation
Legislative Issues: BUD; DEF

Chairman of the Board, President and Chief Executive Officer   Tel: (860) 243-7100
KEATING, Neal J.   Fax: (860) 243-6365

Main Headquarters

Mailing:	1332 Blue Hills Ave.	Tel:	(860) 243-7100
	P.O. Box 1	Fax:	(860) 243-6365
	Bloomfield, CT 06002-0001		

Political Action Committees

aman Corporation Good Government Fund
FEC ID: C00126847
Contact: Eric B. Remington
1332 Blue Hills Ave.   Tel: (860) 243-7100
P.O. Box 1   Fax: (860) 243-6365
Bloomfield, CT 06002-0001

    Contributions to Candidates: $3,000 (2015-2016)
    Democrats: $1,000; Republicans: $2,000

Public Affairs and Related Activities Personnel

At Headquarters

CHETNANI, Jairaj JC	Tel:	(860) 243-7100
Vice President and Treasurer	Fax:	(860) 243-6365
CLARK, Candance A.	Tel:	(860) 243-7100
Senior Vice President, Chief Legal Officer and Secretary	Fax:	(860) 243-6365
FORSBERG, Richard C.	Tel:	(860) 243-7100
Vice President, Contracts and Compliance	Fax:	(860) 243-6365
GOODRICH, Philip A.	Tel:	(860) 243-7100
Senior Vice President, Corporate Development	Fax:	(860) 243-6365
GRIFFIN, Molly	Tel:	(860) 243-7100
Managing Member	Fax:	(860) 243-6365
Registered Federal Lobbyist		
LISLE, Shawn G.	Tel:	(860) 243-7100
Senior Vice President and General Counsel	Fax:	(860) 243-6365
MORNEAU, Michael J	Tel:	(860) 243-7100
Vice President and Controller	Fax:	(860) 243-6365
O'CALLAGHAN , Theresa	Tel:	(860) 243-7100
Senior Director, Benefit Programs and Corporate Human Resources	Fax:	(860) 243-6365
REMINGTON, Eric B.	Tel:	(860) 243-7100
Vice President, Investor Relations and PAC Treasurer	Fax:	(860) 243-6365
eric.remington@kaman.com		
SHEPARD, Ronald P.	Tel:	(860) 243-7100
Manager Contracts & Purchasing	Fax:	(860) 243-6365
SMITH, Richard S	Tel:	(860) 243-7100
Vice President, Deputy General Counsel and Secretary	Fax:	(860) 243-6365
STARR, Robert D.	Tel:	(860) 243-7100
Senior Vice President and Chief Financial Officer	Fax:	(860) 243-6365
TEDONE, John J	Tel:	(860) 243-7100
Vice President, Finance	Fax:	(860) 243-6365
TROY, Gregory T.	Tel:	(860) 243-7100
Senior Vice President, Human Resources and Chief Human Resources Officer	Fax:	(860) 243-6365

Kamo Electric Cooperative, Inc.

An electric utility cooperative.
www.kamopower.com
Annual Revenues: $332.03 million
Employees: 136
Industry/ies: Electricity & Electronics; Electronics; Energy/Electricity

Chief Executive Officer   Tel: (918) 256-5551
CARIKER, Chris J.   Fax: (918) 256-8023

Main Headquarters

Mailing:	500 S. Kamo Dr.	Tel:	(918) 256-5551
	P.O. Box 577	Fax:	(918) 256-8023
	Vinita, OK 74301		

Public Affairs and Related Activities Personnel

At Headquarters

HARTNESS, Ann	Tel:	(918) 256-5551
Chief Financial Officer	Fax:	(918) 256-8023

KAMO Power

See listing on page 462 under Kamo Electric Cooperative, Inc.

Kaneb Services, Inc and Xanser Corporation.

See listing on page 346 under Furmanite Corporation

Kansas City Life Insurance Company

Kansas City Life Insurance Company was established in 1895. Company markets individual life, annuity and group products. Variable life, variable annuities, mutual funds and other investment options are offered through Sunset Financial Services, Kansas City Life's wholly-owned broker/dealer subsidiary.
www.kclife.com
Annual Revenues: $460.71 million
Employees: 436
Ticker: NASDAQ: KCLI
SIC: 6311
Industry/ies: Insurance Industry

Chairman of the Board, President and Chief Executive Officer Tel: (816) 753-7000
BIXBY, R. Philip   Fax: (816) 753-0138

Main Headquarters
Mailing: P.O. Box 219139   Tel: (816) 753-7000
Kansas City, MO 64121-9139   Fax: (816) 753-0138
   TF: (800) 821-6164

Public Affairs and Related Activities Personnel

At Headquarters

KNAPP, Tracy W.   Tel: (816) 753-7299
Senior Vice President, Finance   Fax: (816) 753-0138

KREBS, Donald E.   Tel: (816) 753-7000
Senior Vice President, Sales and Marketing   Fax: (816) 753-0138

MASON JR., A. Craig   Tel: (816) 753-7000
Senior Vice President, General Counsel and Secretary   Fax: (816) 753-0138
cmason@kclife.com

ROPP , Stephen E.   Tel: (816) 753-7000
Senior Vice President, Operations   Fax: (816) 753-0138

At Other Offices

ROPP, Richard   Tel: (816) 753-7000
PAC Treasurer
3520 Broadway
Kansas City, MO 64111

Kansas City Southern Industries

KCSR is a transportation holding company.
www.kcsouthern.com
Annual Revenues: $2.57 billion
Employees: 6,490
Ticker: NYSE: KSU
SIC: 4011
Industry/ies: Banking/Finance/Investments; Railroads; Transportation; Utilities
Legislative Issues: RRR; TAX

Chairman, President and Chief Executive Officer   Tel: (816) 983-1303
STARLING, David L.   Fax: (816) 983-1108

Main Headquarters
Mailing: P.O. Box 219335   Tel: (816) 983-1303
Kansas City, MO 64121-9335   Fax: (816) 983-1108
   TF: (800) 243-8624

Political Action Committees
Kansas City Southern Employee PAC
FEC ID: C00139451
Contact: Barbara L. Blevins
427 W 12th Street   Tel: (816) 983-1303
Kansas City, MO 64105

   Contributions to Candidates: $30,751 (2015-2016)
   Democrats: $5,500; Republicans: $25,251

Corporate Foundations and Giving Programs
KCS Charitable Fund
Contact: C. Doniele Carlson
P.O. Box 219335   Tel: (816) 983-1303
Kansas City, MO 64121-9335

Public Affairs and Related Activities Personnel

At Headquarters

BANKS, Brian P.   Tel: (816) 983-1303
Associate General Counsel & Corporate Secretary   Fax: (816) 983-1108

BLEVINS, Barbara L.   Tel: (816) 983-1303
PAC Treasurer   Fax: (816) 983-1108
bblevins@kcsouthern.com

CARLSON, C. Doniele   Tel: (816) 983-1303
Associate Vice President, Corporate Communications and   Fax: (816) 983-1108
Community Affairs
dcarlson@kcsouthern.com

CHEATUM, Lisa S.   Tel: (816) 983-1303
Senior Vice President, Human Resources   Fax: (816) 983-1108

ERDMAN, Warren K.   Tel: (816) 983-1303

Executive Vice President, Administration and Corporate   Fax: (816) 983-1108
Affairs
werdman@kcsouthern.com

GALLIGAN, William H.   Tel: (816) 983-1551
Vice President, Investor Relations   Fax: (816) 983-1640
william.h.galligan@kcsr.com

GODDERZ, Adam J.   Tel: (816) 983-1303
Associate General Counsel and Corporate Secretary   Fax: (816) 983-1108

HAVERTY, Michael R.   Tel: (816) 983-1303
Executive Chairman

OTTENSMEYER, Patrick J.   Tel: (816) 983-1303
President   Fax: (816) 983-1108

UPCHURCH, Michael W.   Tel: (816) 983-1303
Executive Vice President and Chief Financial Officer   Fax: (816) 983-1108

WOCHNER, William J.   Tel: (816) 983-1303
Senior Vice President and Chief Legal Officer   Fax: (816) 983-1108
jwochner@kcsouthern.com

At Other Offices

ADAMIAK, Ginger   Tel: (281) 465-7180
Assistant Vice President, Marketing
1610 Woodstead Ct.
The Woodlands, TX 77380
gadamiak@kcsouthern.com

HAVERTY, Michael R.   Tel: (281) 465-7180
Executive Chairman
1610 Woodstead Ct.
The Woodlands, TX 77380

HAVERTY, Michael R.   Tel: (816) 983-1372
Executive Chairman   Fax: (816) 983-1446
P.O. Box 219335, 427 W. 12th St.
Kansas City, MO 64121-9335

KANE, Doniele   Tel: (816) 983-1372
Contact, Media Relations   Fax: (816) 983-1446
P.O. Box 219335, 427 W. 12th St.
Kansas City, MO 64121-9335
dkane@kcsouthern.com

Kaplan, Inc.

Helps individuals achieve their educational and career goals.
www.kaplan.com
Employees: 12,000
Industry/ies: Education
Legislative Issues: CSP; DEF; EDU; VET

Chairman and Chief Executive Officer   Tel: (212) 492-5800
ROSEN, Andrew S.

Main Headquarters
Mailing: 6301 Kaplan Univ. Ave.   Tel: (954) 515-3993
Ft. Lauderdale, FL 33309

Corporate Foundations and Giving Programs

Kaplan Educational Foundation
Contact: Melissa Mack
888 Seventh Ave.   Tel: (212) 492-5800
New York City, NY 10106

Public Affairs and Related Activities Personnel

At Headquarters

BLOCK, Janice L.   Tel: (212) 492-5800
Chief Administrative and Legal Officer

HIRSCHHORN, Beth   Tel: (954) 515-3993
Chief Marketing Officer

HORTON, Tom   Tel: (954) 515-3993
Senior Vice President, Strategy and Integration

MACK, Melissa   Tel: (212) 492-5800
Senior Vice President, Marketing and Communications and
Chairman, Kaplan Educational Foundation

SEELYE, Matthew   Tel: (212) 492-5800
Chief Financial Officer

At Other Offices

CAMPOVERDE, Rebecca   Tel: (212) 492-5800
Senior Vice President, Government Relations   Fax: (212) 492-5933
888 Seventh Ave., Suite 21
New York City, NY 10106
rebecca.campoverde@kaplan.com
Registered Federal Lobbyist

Kate Spade & Company

A designer and marketer of fashion apparel and accessories.
www.katespadeandcompany.com
Annual Revenues: $1.56 billion
Employees: 5,800
Ticker: NYSE: KATE

SIC: 2330
NAICS: 315221
Industry/ies: Apparel/Textiles Industry

Chief Executive Officer
LEAVITT, Craig A.

Main Headquarters
Mailing: Two Park Ave.
            New York, NY 10016

Corporate Foundations and Giving Programs
Fifth & Pacific Foundation
1441 Broadway   Tel: (212) 354-4900
New York City, NY 10018   Fax: (212) 626-3416

Public Affairs and Related Activities Personnel

At Headquarters

BEECH, Mary
Senior Vice President and Chief Marketing Officer

CARRARA, George M.
President and Chief Operating Officer

GARBACCIO, Emily
Vice President, Communications

HIGLEY, William
Senior Vice President, Human Resources

LINKO, Thomas
Chief Financial Officer

MACHACEK, Lisa Piovano
Senior Vice President & Chief Human Resources Officer

NARDO, Christopher Di
Senior Vice President, General Counsel and Corporate Secretary

RINALDO, Michael
Vice President, Corporate Controller and Chief Accounting Officer

VILL, Robert J.
Senior Vice President, Finance, Treasurer and Media Contact
robert_vill@liz.com

Kaufman and Broad Home Corporation.

See listing on page 464 under KB Home

KB Home

A home builder with communities in the Western United States.
www.kbhome.com
Annual Revenues: $2.59 billion
Employees: 1,590
Ticker: NYSE: KBH
SIC: 1531
Industry/ies: Construction/Construction Materials; Housing

Chairman of the Board   Tel: (310) 231-4000
BOLLENBACH, Stephen F.   Fax: (310) 231-4222

President, Chief Executive Officer and Director   Tel: (310) 231-4000
MEZGER, Jeffrey T.   Fax: (310) 231-4222

Main Headquarters
Mailing: 10990 Wilshire Blvd.   Tel: (310) 231-4000
            Los Angeles, CA 90024   Fax: (310) 231-4222
                                         TF: (888) 524-6637

Political Action Committees
KB Home American Dream PAC
FEC ID: C00417139
Contact: Cary Davidson
3699 Wilshire Blvd.
Suite 1290
Los Angeles, CA 90010
   Contributions to Candidates: $5,500 (2015-2016)
   Republicans: $5,500

Public Affairs and Related Activities Personnel

At Headquarters

BRIDLEMAN, Dan   Tel: (310) 231-4000
Senior Vice President, Sustainability, Technology and   Fax: (310) 231-4222
Strategic Sourcing

COHEN, Cory F.   Tel: (310) 231-4000
Senior Vice President, Tax   Fax: (310) 231-4222

HOLLINGER, William R.   Tel: (310) 231-4000
Senior Vice President and Chief Accounting Officer   Fax: (310) 231-4222

KAMINSKI , Jeff   Tel: (310) 231-4000
Executive Vice President and Chief Financial Officer   Fax: (310) 231-4222

MARSHALL, Katoiya   Tel: (310) 893-7446
Manager, Investor Relations   Fax: (310) 231-4140
kmarshall@kbhome.com

NORTON, Thomas   Tel: (310) 231-4000
Senior Vice President, Human Resources   Fax: (310) 231-4222

REEVES, Heather   Tel: (310) 231-4142
Contact, Media Relations   Fax: (310) 231-4222
hreeves-x@kbhome.com

SILK , Tom   Tel: (310) 231-4000
Senior Vice President, Marketing and Communications   Fax: (310) 231-4222

WORAM, Brian   Tel: (310) 231-4000
Executive Vice President, General Counsel and Secretary   Fax: (310) 231-4222

At Other Offices

DAVIDSON, Cary
PAC Treasurer
515 S. Figueroa St., Suite 1110
Los Angeles, CA 90071

KBR (Kellogg-Brown-Root)

A subsidiary of Halliburton Co. (see separate listing). A technology-based engineering, procurement, construction, and maintenance contractor.
www.kbr.com
Annual Revenues: $4.66 billion
Employees: 22,000
Ticker: NYSE: KBR
SIC: 1600
NAICS: 213112; 321920; 332312; 331111
Industry/ies: Construction/Construction Materials; Energy/Electricity; Engineering/Mathematics
Legislative Issues: FOR

President and Chief Executive Officer, Group President,   Tel: (713) 753-2000
Engineering and Construction   Fax: (713) 753-5353
BRADIE, Stuart

Main Headquarters
Mailing: 601 Jefferson St.   Tel: (713) 753-2000
            Houston, TX 77002   Fax: (713) 753-5353

Washington Office
Mailing: 2451 Crystal Dr.   Tel: (703) 526-7500
            Suite 164
            Arlington, VA 22202-4804

Political Action Committees
KBR, INC. PAC
FEC ID: C00431114
Contact: Marit Babin
601 Jefferson St.   Tel: (703) 526-7500
Suite 3746C
Houston, TX 77002
   Contributions to Candidates: $30,500 (2015-2016)
   Democrats: $7,000; Republicans: $23,500

Corporate Foundations and Giving Programs
KBR (Kellogg-Brown-Root) Contributions Program
601 Jefferson St.   Tel: (713) 753-2000
Houston, TX 77002   Fax: (713) 753-5353

Public Affairs and Related Activities Personnel

At Headquarters

AKERSON, Eileen Gallagher   Tel: (713) 753-2000
Executive Vice President and General Counsel   Fax: (713) 753-5353

BABIN, Marit   Tel: (713) 753-2000
PAC Treasurer   Fax: (713) 753-5353
Mail Stop Suite 3746C

BRAENDELAND, Jan Egil   Tel: (713) 753-2000
Executive Vice President, Global Sales   Fax: (713) 753-5353

FERRAIOLI, Brian   Tel: (713) 753-2000
Executive Vice President and Chief Financial Officer   Fax: (713) 753-5353

HILL, Graham   Tel: (713) 753-2000
Executive Vice President, Global Business Development and   Fax: (713) 753-5353
Strategy

KUKLA, Jr., Rob   Tel: (713) 753-5082
Director, Investor Relations   Fax: (713) 753-5353
investors@kbr.com

MACKEY, Ian   Tel: (713) 753-2000
Executive Vice President, Human Resources   Fax: (713) 753-5353

NAGLE, Zac   Tel: (713) 753-2000
Vice President, Investor Relations and Communications   Fax: (713) 753-5353
investors@kbr.com

PRINGLE, Andrew   Tel: (713) 753-2000
President, Government Services   Fax: (713) 753-5353

KCI USA, Inc.

Medical device technology innovation and development.
www.kci1.com/KCI1/home
Legislative Issues: HCR

Main Headquarters

Mailing: 12930 IH-10 West	Tel:	(210) 544-5751
San Antonio, TX 78249		

Public Affairs and Related Activities Personnel

At Headquarters

KRAEMER, Brett	Tel:	(210) 544-5751
Senior Litigation Counsel		

Keane, Inc.

See listing on page 592 under NTT Data Corporation

Kela Energy

Converts coal waste to cost-effective and marketable products.
www.kelaenergy.com
Annual Revenues: $1.50 million
Employees: 15
Industry/ies: Energy/Electricity

Chief Executive Officer and President	Tel:	(407) 363-5774
UMSTADTER, Larry	Fax:	(407) 345-0541

Main Headquarters

Mailing: 7575 Dr. Phillips Blvd.	Tel:	(407) 363-5774
Suite 325	Fax:	(407) 345-0541
Orlando, FL 32819		

Public Affairs and Related Activities Personnel

At Headquarters

NEAL, Charlie	Tel:	(407) 363-5774
Vice President and General Counsel	Fax:	(407) 345-0541

Kellogg Company

A producer of cereal and convenience foods, including cookies, crackers, toaster pastries, cereal bars, fruit-flavored snacks, frozen waffles and veggie foods.
www.kelloggs.com
Annual Revenues: $14.39 billion
Employees: 29,790
Ticker: NYSE: K
SIC: 2053
NAICS: 311813
Industry/ies: Food And Beverage Industry
Legislative Issues: ADV; AGR; ENV; FOO; HCR; RET; TAX

President, Chairman of the Board and Chief Executive Officer	Tel:	(269) 961-2000
BRYANT, John A.	Fax:	(269) 961-2871
john.bryant@kellogg.com		

Main Headquarters

Mailing: One Kellogg Sq.	Tel:	(269) 961-2000
P.O. Box 3599	Fax:	(269) 961-2871
Battle Creek, MI 49016	TF:	(800) 962-1413

Washington Office

Mailing: 801 Pennsylvania Ave. NW, Suite 305	Tel:	(202) 624-3909
Washington, DC 20004		

Political Action Committees

Kellogg Better Government Committee PAC
FEC ID: C00039552
One Kellogg Sq.
P.O. Box 3599
Battle Creek, MI 49017

Contributions to Candidates: $63,000 (2015-2016)
Democrats: $21,000; Republicans: $42,000

Principal Recipients

HOUSE
WALBERG, TIMOTHY L HON. (REP-MI)

Corporate Foundations and Giving Programs

Kellogg Company Contributions Program

One Kellogg Sq.	Tel:	(269) 961-2000
P.O. Box 3599	Fax:	(269) 961-2871
Battle Creek, MI 49016-3599		

Public Affairs and Related Activities Personnel

At Headquarters

BECK, Lauren E.	Tel:	(269) 961-2000
Federal Lobbyist	Fax:	(269) 961-2871
Registered Federal Lobbyist		
BRUCK, Larry	Tel:	(269) 961-2000
Vice President, Global Marketing	Fax:	(269) 961-2871
BURTON, CFA, Simon	Tel:	(269) 961-6636
Vice President, Investor Relations	Fax:	(269) 961-2871
CHARLES, Kris	Tel:	(269) 961-2000
Vice President Global Communications and Philanthropy	Fax:	(269) 961-2871
DIGGINGER, Ronald L.	Tel:	(269) 961-2000
Chief Financial Officer	Fax:	(269) 961-2871
GARZA, Christopher	Tel:	(269) 961-2000

Senior Director, Government Relations	Fax:	(269) 961-2871
GWYN, Brigitte Schmidt	Tel:	(269) 961-2000
Vice President, Global Government Relations	Fax:	(269) 961-2871
brigitte.s.gwyn@kellogg.com		
Registered Federal Lobbyist		
LONG, Sammie	Tel:	(269) 961-2000
Senior Vice President, Global Human Resources	Fax:	(269) 961-2871
LOVETT, Tanisha	Tel:	(269) 961-3770
Federal Lobbyist	Fax:	(269) 961-2871
Registered Federal Lobbyist		
PILNICK, Sr., Gary H.	Tel:	(269) 961-2000
Senior Vice President, General Counsel, Corporate Development and Secretary	Fax:	(269) 961-2871
SANDERS, Tanisha	Tel:	(269) 961-2000
Federal Lobbyist	Fax:	(269) 961-2871
Registered Federal Lobbyist		
SHOLL, James	Tel:	(269) 961-2000
Vice President, Internal Audit and PAC Treasurer	Fax:	(269) 961-2871

At Washington Office

CORCORAN, Christine		
Senior Director, Government Relations		
Registered Federal Lobbyist		
WARD, Erin	Tel:	(202) 624-3909
Associate, Government Relations		
erin.ward@kellogg.com		

Kelly Services, Inc.

A company which provides staffing services and human resources solutions to a broad spectrum of business customers.
www.kellyservices.com
Annual Revenues: $5.55 billion
Employees: 8,300
Ticker: NASDAQ: KELYA
SIC: 7363
Industry/ies: Employees & Employment
Legislative Issues: HCR; TAX

Executive Chairman and Chairman of the Board	Tel:	(248) 362-4444
ADDERLEY, Terence E.	Fax:	(248) 244-7572
President and Chief Executive Officer	Tel:	(248) 362-4444
CAMDEN, Carl T.	Fax:	(248) 244-7572

Main Headquarters

Mailing: 999 W. Big Beaver Rd.	Tel:	(248) 362-4444
Troy, MI 48084-4782	Fax:	(248) 244-4360

Political Action Committees

Kelly Services Inc. PAC (KellyPAC)
FEC ID: C00212522
Contact: Matt Harvill

999 W. Big Beaver Rd.	Tel:	(248) 362-4444
Troy, MI 48084		

Contributions to Candidates: $6,000 (2015-2016)
Democrats: $6,000

Corporate Foundations and Giving Programs

Kelly Services Contributions Program
999 W. Big Beaver Rd.
Troy, MI 48084-4782

Public Affairs and Related Activities Personnel

At Headquarters

CORONA, George S.	Tel:	(248) 362-4444
Executive Vice President and Chief Operating Officer	Fax:	(248) 244-4360
HARVILL , Matt	Tel:	(248) 362-4444
PAC Tresurer	Fax:	(248) 244-4360
PALMER, Carolyn	Tel:	(248) 362-4444
Contact, Global Marketing	Fax:	(248) 244-4360
PARFET, Donald R.	Tel:	(248) 362-4444
Director	Fax:	(248) 244-4360
POLEHNA, James	Tel:	(248) 244-4586
Vice President and Corporate Secretary	Fax:	(248) 255-5515
james_polehna@kellyservices.com		
QUIGLEY, Peter	Tel:	(248) 362-4444
General Counsel	Fax:	(248) 244-4360
RAMSEY, Nina M.	Tel:	(248) 362-4444
Chief Human Resources Officer	Fax:	(248) 244-4360
SAMSON, Kate	Tel:	(248) 362-4444
Manager, Marketing and Communications	Fax:	(248) 244-4360
kate.samson@kellyservices.com		
STEHNEY, Jane	Tel:	(248) 244-5630
Director, Public Relations	Fax:	(248) 244-4360
jane_stehney@kellyservices.com		
THIROT, Olivier	Tel:	(248) 362-4444

Chief Financial Officer	Fax:	(248) 244-4360
THORPE, Debra	Tel:	(248) 362-4444
Contact, Strategic Account Operations	Fax:	(248) 244-4360

Kemet Electronics Company

The name "KEMET" is a blend of the words "chemical" and "metallurgy." A manufacturer of solid tantalum and multilayer ceramic capacitors used in electronic equipment.
www.kemet.com
Annual Revenues: $734.82 million
Employees: 8,800
Ticker: NYSE: KEM
SIC: 3675; 3670
Industry/ies: Electricity & Electronics; Electronics; Energy/Electricity

Chairman of the Board	Tel:	(864) 963-6300
BRANDENBERG, Frank G.	Fax:	(864) 963-6322
Chief Executive Officer and Director	Tel:	(864) 963-6300
LOOF, Per-Olof	Fax:	(864) 963-6322
Main Headquarters		
Mailing: 2835 KEMET Way	Tel:	(864) 963-6300
Simpsonville, SC 29681	Fax:	(864) 963-6322
	TF:	(877) 695-3638

Public Affairs and Related Activities Personnel

At Headquarters

ASSAF, R. James	Tel:	(864) 963-6300
Senior Vice President, General Counsel and Secretary	Fax:	(864) 963-6322
BARKAL, Susan B.	Tel:	(864) 963-6300
Senior Vice President, Quality, Chief Compliance Officer and Chief of Staff	Fax:	(864) 963-6322
BOAN, Dr. John C.	Tel:	(954) 766-2813
Vice President, Marketing	Fax:	(864) 963-6322
johnnyboan@kemet.com		
LOWE, Jr., William M.	Tel:	(864) 963-6484
Executive Vice President and Chief Financial Officer	Fax:	(864) 963-6322
williamlowe@kemet.com		
PERSICO, Dr. Daniel F.	Tel:	(864) 963-6300
Vice President, Strategic Marketing and Business Development	Fax:	(864) 963-6322
VATINELLE, Richard J.	Tel:	(954) 766-2800
Vice President and Treasurer	Fax:	(864) 963-6322
richardvatinelle@kemet.com		
VETRALLA, Stefano	Tel:	(864) 963-6300
Vice President and Chief Human Resources Officer	Fax:	(864) 963-6322

The Kemp Group d.b.a Kemp Partners

Strategic consulting firm. Has a strategic alliance with Whitmer & Worrall (see separate listng).
www.kemppartners.com

Main Headquarters		
Mailing: 1111 19th St. NW	Tel:	(202) 572-4022
Suite 700	Fax:	(202) 833-0708
Washington, DC 20006		

Public Affairs and Related Activities Personnel

At Headquarters

KEMP, James P.	Tel:	(202) 572-4022
Managing Partner	Fax:	(202) 833-0708
jpk@kemppartners.com		
STEINBERG, Moshe	Tel:	(202) 572-4022
	Fax:	(202) 833-0708

Kennametal Inc.

The company offers a host of metal-cutting tools and tooling supplies for machining steel, equipment for mining and highway construction, and engineering services for production processes. It operates via two segments: Metalworking Solutions and Services, and Advanced Materials Solutions. Kennametal and its subsidiaries sell products and services worldwide.
www.kennametal.com
Annual Revenues: $2.21 billion
Employees: 12,718
Ticker: NYSE: KMT
SIC: 3531; 3545; 3549; 3423; 3541
NAICS: 33312; 333515; 333518; 332212; 333512
Industry/ies: Electricity & Electronics; Electronics; Energy/Electricity; Engineering/Mathematics; Machinery/Equipment

President and Chief Executive Officer	Tel:	(724) 539-5000
FEO, Ronald M. De		
Main Headquarters		
Mailing: 1600 Technology Way	Tel:	(724) 539-5000
P.O. Box 231		
Latrobe, PA 15650		

Political Action Committees

Kennametal Inc. Employees for Effective Government PAC
FEC ID: C00409938
Contact: Lorrie Paul Crum

1600 Technology Way	Tel:	(724) 539-5000
P.O. Box 231		
Latrobe, PA 15650		

Corporate Foundations and Giving Programs

Kennametal Foundation
Contact: Erica Clayton Wright

1600 Technology Way	Tel:	(724) 539-5000
P.O. Box 231		
Latrobe, PA 15650		

Public Affairs and Related Activities Personnel

At Headquarters

CRUM, Lorrie Paul	Tel:	(724) 539-5000
Vice President, Corporate Relations and PAC Treasurer		
FUSCO, Martha	Tel:	(724) 539-5000
Vice President, Finance and Corporate Controller		

At Other Offices

BACCHUS, Judith L.	Tel:	(800) 835-3668
Vice President, Chief Human Resources and Corporate Relations Officer	Fax:	(724) 539-6657
1662 MacMillan Park Dr.		
Ft. Mill, SC 29707		
Mail Stop PO Box 231		
judith.bacchus@kennametal.com		
GAALEN, Jan Kees van	Tel:	(800) 835-3668
Vice President and Chief Financial Officer	Fax:	(724) 539-6657
1662 MacMillan Park Dr.		
Ft. Mill, SC 29707		
JACKO, Jr., John H.	Tel:	(800) 835-3668
Vice President and Chief Marketing Officer	Fax:	(724) 539-6657
1662 MacMillan Park Dr.		
Ft. Mill, SC 29707		
MCGUIRE, Quynh	Tel:	(724) 539-6559
Director, Investor Relations	Fax:	(724) 539-6657
1662 MacMillan Park Dr.		
Ft. Mill, SC 29707		
NOWE, Kevin G.	Tel:	(800) 835-3668
Vice President, Secretary and General Counsel	Fax:	(724) 539-6657
1662 MacMillan Park Dr.		
Ft. Mill, SC 29707		
kevin.nowe@kennametal.com		
SUTTER, Christina	Tel:	(724) 539-5708
Manager, Corporate Communications	Fax:	(724) 539-6657
1662 MacMillan Park Dr.		
Ft. Mill, SC 29707		
WRIGHT, Erica Clayton	Tel:	(724) 261-6217
Manager, Public Affairs	Fax:	(724) 539-6657
1662 MacMillan Park Dr.		
Ft. Mill, SC 29707		

Kennecott Land

A land development company.
www.kennecott.com
Annual Revenues: $20 million
Employees: 100
Industry/ies: Natural Resources; Transportation

President and Chief Executive Officer	Tel:	(801) 204-2000
SANDERS, Kelly	Fax:	(801) 204-2887
Managing Director	Tel:	(801) 204-2000
STEWARD, Nigel Ian	Fax:	(801) 204-2887
Main Headquarters		
Mailing: 4700 Daybreak Pkwy.	Tel:	(801) 204-2000
S. Jordan, UT 84095	Fax:	(801) 204-2887

Corporate Foundations and Giving Programs

Kennecott Land Contributions Program
Contact: Deborah Thacker

4700 Daybreak Pkwy.	Tel:	(801) 204-2000
S. Jordan, UT 84095		

Public Affairs and Related Activities Personnel

At Headquarters

KEENAN, Patrick	Tel:	(801) 204-2000
Chief Financial Officer	Fax:	(801) 204-2887
MCCUTCHEON, Ty	Tel:	(901) 204-2000
Vice President, Community Development	Fax:	(801) 204-2887
MCGOWAN-JACKSON, Rohan	Tel:	(801) 204-2000
Vice President, Resource Development and Communities	Fax:	(801) 204-2887
THACKER, Deborah	Tel:	(801) 913-8335

Coordinator,Community Outreach, Government and
Community Relations
debbie.thacker@riotinto.com

Fax: (801) 204-2887

Kennecott Minerals Company

A mining company.
www.kennecottminerals.com
Employees: 1,400
SIC: 1021
Industry/ies: Mining Industry; Natural Resources

Main Headquarters
Mailing: 224 2200 W
Salt Lake City, UT 84116

Tel: (801) 595-7028

Kerr Drug, Inc.

*Provides pharmacy and healthcare services for people in the Carolinas. Kerr Drug operates
about 90 stores in North Carolina in several formats, ranging from large health care centers to
smaller clinical hubs and traditional drugstores.*
www.kerrdrug.com
Annual Revenues: $170 million
Employees: 2,400
Industry/ies: Pharmaceutical Industry

Chairman and Executive Director, Foundation
PATTERSON, Phyllis
ppatterson@kerrdrug.com

Tel: (919) 544-3896
Fax: (919) 544-3796

Main Headquarters
Mailing: 3220 Spring Forest Rd.
Raleigh, NC 27616

Tel: (919) 544-3896
Fax: (919) 544-3796

Political Action Committees
Kerr Drug, Inc. PAC
FEC ID: C00368381
Contact: Kathryn R. Carroll
3220 Spring Forest Rd.
Raleigh, NC 27616

Corporate Foundations and Giving Programs
The Kerr Cares for Kids Foundation
Contact: Phyllis Patterson
3220 Spring Forest Rd.
Raleigh, NC 27616

Tel: (919) 544-3896

Public Affairs and Related Activities Personnel

At Headquarters

CARROLL, Kathryn R.
PAC Treasurer

Tel: (919) 544-3896
Fax: (919) 544-3796

GREGORY, Mark
Senior Vice President, Operations

Tel: (919) 544-3896
Fax: (919) 544-3796

JONES, Kenneth F.
PAC Treasurer

Tel: (919) 544-3896
Fax: (919) 544-3796

Kestrel Enterprises, Inc.

Software assurance company.
www.kestrelei.com
Ticker: NYSE: KEG
Industry/ies: Computer/Technology; Defense/Homeland Security; Government-
Related

Co-Founder
FLANAGAN, William J.

Tel: (410) 579-1487
Fax: (202) 434-8915

Main Headquarters
Mailing: 131 National Business Pkwy.
Suite 120
Annapolis Junction, MD 20701

Tel: (301) 497-2842
Fax: (301) 497-2801

Public Affairs and Related Activities Personnel

At Headquarters

DEROSE, Terrence L.
Executive Vice President and Chief Financial Officer

Tel: (410) 579-1487
Fax: (202) 434-8915

KETA Group

*A provider of information technology services, disaster recovery services, space and defense
engineering services, construction and facility management services.*
www.ketagroup.com
Annual Revenues: $3.10 million
Employees: 40
Industry/ies: Aerospace/Aviation; Construction/Construction Materials;
Defense/Homeland Security; Disaster; Engineering/Mathematics; Environment
And Conservation; Government-Related; Transportation

President and Chief Executive Officer
BORNE, Manville
manville.borne@ketagroup.com

Tel: (225) 761-3673
Fax: (225) 766-5217

Main Headquarters
Mailing: 112 Founders Dr.
Baton Rouge, LA 70810

Tel: (225) 761-3673
Fax: (225) 766-5217

Public Affairs and Related Activities Personnel

At Headquarters

HU, Ben
Chief Operating Officer

Tel: (225) 761-3673
Fax: (225) 766-5217

HUYBRECHTS, Ralph
Chief Financial Officer

Tel: (225) 761-3673
Fax: (225) 766-5217

Key Energy Services, Inc.

*Offers workover services, fluid and logistics services, fishing and rental services, pressure
pumping, wireline, and drilling.*
www.keyenergy.com
Annual Revenues: $1.34 billion
Employees: 8,100
Ticker: NYSE: KEG
SIC: 4212; 1389
NAICS: 484220; 213111
Industry/ies: Energy/Electricity

Chairman of the Board, President and Chief Executive Officer
ALARIO, Richard J.

Tel: (713) 651-4300
Fax: (713) 652-4005

Main Headquarters
Mailing: 1301 McKinney St.
Suite 1800
Houston, TX 77010

Tel: (713) 651-4300
Fax: (713) 652-4005
TF: (866) 902-3438

Washington Office
Mailing: 1031 31st St. NW
Washington, DC 20007-4401

Tel: (202) 944-3339
Fax: (202) 944-9830

Political Action Committees
Key Energy Services Inc. PAC
FEC ID: C00403105
Contact: J. Marshall Dodson
1301 McKinney St.
Suite 1800
Houston, TX 77010

Tel: (713) 651-4300

Contributions to Candidates: $2,000 (2015-2016)
Republicans: $2,000

Corporate Foundations and Giving Programs
Key Energy Services Contributions Program
1301 McKinney St.
Suite 1800
Houston, TX 77010

Tel: (713) 651-4300

Public Affairs and Related Activities Personnel

At Headquarters

CLARKE, Kim B.
*Senior Vice President, Administration and Chief People
Officer*

Tel: (713) 651-4300
Fax: (713) 652-4005

DODSON, J. Marshall
*Senior Vice President and Chief Financial Officer and PAC
Treasurer*

Tel: (713) 651-4300
Fax: (713) 652-4005

FRYE, Kimberly R.
Senior Vice President and General Counsel

Tel: (713) 651-4300
Fax: (713) 652-4005

GRAHAM , Rafael
Managing Director, International Business Development

Tel: (713) 651-4300
Fax: (713) 652-4005

Key Impact Strategies LLC

Government relations consulting.

Main Headquarters
Mailing: 1822 Stinson Creek Rd.
Columbus, MS 39705

Public Affairs and Related Activities Personnel

At Headquarters

HEARD, Brian Keith Keith
Partner

Tel: (202) 251-0435

KeyBank National Association

*Provides consumer banking products and services to individual, corporate, and institutional
clients.*
www.key.com
Annual Revenues: $4.02 billion
Employees: 13,590
Ticker: NYSE: KEY
SIC: 6021
Industry/ies: Banking/Finance/Investments

Chairman and Chief Executive Officer
GORMAN, Christopher M.

Tel: (216) 689-3000
Fax: (216) 689-5115

Chairman & Chief Executive Officer
PUGLIESE, Christopher J.

Tel: (216) 689-3000
Fax: (216) 689-5115

Main Headquarters
Mailing: 127 Public Sq.
OH-01-27-0200

Tel: (216) 689-3000
Fax: (216) 689-5115

Cleveland, OH 44114 TF: (800) 539-2968

Political Action Committees
KeyCorp Advocates Fund PAC
FEC ID: C00073155
Contact: Christopher J. Pugliese
127 Public Sq. Tel: (216) 689-6300
OH-01-27-1816 Fax: (216) 689-0519
Cleveland, OH 44114-1306

   Contributions to Candidates: $2,250 (2015-2016)
   Democrats: $1,000; Republicans: $1,250

Keycorp Advocates Fund-Federal Only PAC
FEC ID: C00399063
Contact: Christopher J. Pugliese
127 Public Sq. Tel: (216) 689-6300
OH-01-27-1816 Fax: (216) 689-0519
Cleveland, OH 44114

   Contributions to Candidates: $21,000 (2015-2016)
   Democrats: $7,000; Republicans: $14,000

Corporate Foundations and Giving Programs
KeyBank Foundation
Contact: Karen White
800 Superior Ave., First Floor Tel: (216) 689-3000
OH-01-02-0126 Fax: (216) 689-5115
Cleveland, OH 44114

Public Affairs and Related Activities Personnel
At Headquarters
BELL, David A. Tel: (800) 539-2968
Director, Federal Government Relations Fax: (216) 689-5115

BUFFIE, Craig A. Tel: (216) 689-3000
Chief Human Resources Officer Fax: (216) 689-5115

CADE, Erskine E. Tel: (216) 689-4486
Senior Vice President and Director, Government Relations Fax: (216) 689-5115
erskine_cade@keybank.com

HARRIS, Paul N. Tel: (216) 689-3000
Executive Vice President, Secretary and General Counsel Fax: (216) 689-5115

HARTMANN, William L. Tel: (216) 689-3000
Chief Risk Officer Fax: (216) 689-5115

KIMBLE, Donald R. Tel: (216) 689-3000
Chief Financial Officer Fax: (216) 689-5115

MIMURA, Laura Tel: (216) 471-2883
Vice President, Corporate Communications at KeyCorp Fax: (216) 689-5115

WHITE, Karen Tel: (216) 828-8539
Senior Vice President, Community Relations Fax: (216) 689-5115
Karen_A_White@KeyBank.com

KeyCorp, Inc.

KeyCorp operates as the holding company for KeyBank National Association that provides various banking services in the United States.
www.key.com
Annual Revenues: $4.04 billion
Employees: 13,403
Ticker: NYSE: KEY
SIC: 6021
Industry/ies: Banking/Finance/Investments

Chairman of the Board and Chief Executive Officer Tel: (216) 689-6300
MOONEY, Beth E. Fax: (216) 689-0519

Main Headquarters
Mailing: 127 Public Sq. Tel: (216) 689-6300
   Cleveland, OH 44114 Fax: (216) 689-0519

Political Action Committees
KeyCorp Advocates Fund PAC
FEC ID: C00073155
Contact: Christopher J. Pugliese
127 Public Sq. Tel: (216) 689-6300
OH-01-27-1816 Fax: (216) 689-0519
Cleveland, OH 44114-1306

   Contributions to Candidates: $2,250 (2015-2016)
   Democrats: $1,000; Republicans: $1,250

Keycorp Advocates Fund-Federal Only PAC
FEC ID: C00399063
Contact: Christopher J. Pugliese
127 Public Sq. Tel: (216) 689-6300
OH-01-27-1816 Fax: (216) 689-0519
Cleveland, OH 44114

   Contributions to Candidates: $21,000 (2015-2016)
   Democrats: $7,000; Republicans: $14,000

Corporate Foundations and Giving Programs
KeyCorp Foundation
Contact: Margot James-Copeland
127 Public Sq. Tel: (216) 689-4724

Cleveland, OH 44114

Public Affairs and Related Activities Personnel
At Headquarters
GREENAN, Shane Tel: (216) 689-6300
Chief Financial Officer and Company Secretary Fax: (216) 689-0519

HARRIS, Paul N. Tel: (216) 689-3000
Executive Vice President, Secretary and General Counsel Fax: (216) 689-0519

JAMES-COPELAND, Margot Tel: (216) 689-4724
Executive Vice President and Director, Corporate Diversity Fax: (216) 689-3865
and Philanthropy
margot_copeland@keybank.com

KIMBLE, Don Tel: (216) 689-6300
Chief Financial Officer Fax: (216) 689-0519

PUGLIESE, Christopher J. Tel: (216) 689-6300
PAC Contact Fax: (216) 689-0519
Mail Stop OH-01-27-0200

TERRELL, Kathleen Tel: (216) 689-6300
Chief Human Resources Officer Fax: (216) 689-0519

Keys Group LLC

Lobbying and consulting services.
Legislative Issues: AGR; IMM

Main Headquarters
Mailing: 1312 W. River Rd.
   Shady Side, MD 20764

Public Affairs and Related Activities Personnel
At Headquarters
BENNETT, Scott Tel: (202) 907-4253
Registered Federal Lobbyist

DUNLAP, Mike
Registered Federal Lobbyist

KEYS, III, G. Chandler Tel: (202) 907-4253
Principal
Registered Federal Lobbyist

STAWICK, David Tel: (202) 907-4253
Registered Federal Lobbyist

Keys Lobbying and Consulting Firm, LLC

Industry/ies: Law/Law Firms

Chief Executive Officer Tel: (877) 345-4078
KEYS, Tawana
keyslobbying@gmail.com

Main Headquarters
Mailing: 11405 Hillsborough Ln. Tel: (877) 345-4078
   Frederickburg, VA 22407

KeySpan Corporation

See listing on page 562 under National Grid USA

KFx, Inc.

See listing on page 307 under Evergreen Energy

Kia Motors Corporation

An automobile manufacturer. Kia Motors Corporation, based in Washington city is the U.S. subsidiary of Kia Motors Corporation, headquartered in Seoul, South Korea.
www.kia.com
Annual Revenues: $4.1 billion
Industry/ies: Automotive Industry; Transportation
Legislative Issues: AUT; MAN; TRD

Main Headquarters
Mailing: 1660 L St. NW Tel: (202) 503-1515
   Suite 201
   Washington, DC 20036

Public Affairs and Related Activities Personnel
At Headquarters
ALVIS, James H. Tel: (202) 503-1515
Manager, Government Affairs
Registered Federal Lobbyist

ANDERSON, John T. Tel: (202) 503-1515
Vice President, Government Affairs
jta@kia-dc.com
Registered Federal Lobbyist

CHOI, Seung-Hoon Tel: (202) 503-1515
Federal Lobbyist
Registered Federal Lobbyist

KIM, Minsoo Tel: (202) 503-1515
Federal Lobbyist
Registered Federal Lobbyist

KIM, Thomas   Tel: (202) 503-1515
Federal Lobbyist
thomas.kim@kia.co.k
Registered Federal Lobbyist

MALECH, David   Tel: (202) 503-1515
Registered Federal Lobbyist

MALECH, David   Tel: (202) 503-1515
General Manager, Trade & Economic Issues
Registered Federal Lobbyist

Kiewit Corporation

A commercial development and construction company.
www.kiewit.com
Annual Revenues: $9.94 billion
Employees: 15,000
Industry/ies: Construction/Construction Materials; Engineering/Mathematics
Legislative Issues: GOV; VET

President and Chief Executive Officer   Tel: (402) 342-2052
GREWCOCK, Bruce E.   Fax: (402) 271-2839

Main Headquarters
Mailing: Kiewit Plaza   Tel: (402) 342-2052
           Omaha, NE 68131   Fax: (402) 271-2829

Corporate Foundations and Giving Programs
Peter Kiewit Foundation
Contact: Tobin Schropp
3555 Farnam St.   Tel: (402) 344-7890
Omaha, NE 68131

Public Affairs and Related Activities Personnel

At Headquarters

SCHROPP, Tobin   Tel: (402) 342-2052
General Counsel   Fax: (402) 271-2839

Kimball International, Inc.

Manufacturer of office, lodging and home furniture, and a contract manufacturer of electronic assemblies and components.
www.kimball.com
Annual Revenues: $1.27 billion
Employees: 6,426
Ticker: NASDAQ: KBALB
SIC: 3672
Industry/ies: Furniture/Home Furnishings

Chairman of the Board   Tel: (812) 482-1600
HABIG, Douglas A.   Fax: (812) 482-8300

Main Headquarters
Mailing: 1600 Royal St.   Tel: (812) 482-1600
           Jasper, IN 47549-1001   Fax: (812) 482-8300
                             TF: (800) 482-1616

Corporate Foundations and Giving Programs
Kimball-Habig Foundation
Contact: Douglas A. Habig
1600 Royal St.
Jasper, IN 47549

Public Affairs and Related Activities Personnel

At Headquarters

KAHLE, John H.   Tel: (812) 482-1600
Executive Vice President, General Counsel and Secretary   Fax: (812) 482-8300

KINCER, R. Gregory   Tel: (812) 482-1600
Vice President, Corporate Development   Fax: (812) 482-8300
greg.kincer@kimball.com

SCHNEIDER, Robert F.   Tel: (812) 482-1600
Executive Vice President, Chief Financial Officer   Fax: (812) 482-8300

VAUGHT, Martin W.   Tel: (812) 482-1600
Director, Public and Investor Relations   Fax: (812) 482-8300

Kimberly-Clark Corporation

A manufacturer of fiber-based products for personal care, health care and other diverse markets.
www.kimberly-clark.com
Annual Revenues: $18.38 billion
Employees: 43,000
Ticker: NYSE: KMB
SIC: 2621; 2676; 2679; 3842
NAICS: 322121; 322121; 322291; 322299
Industry/ies: Paper And Wood Products Industry; Personal Care/Hygiene
Legislative Issues: ENV; HCR; TAX; TRD

Chairman of the Board and Chief Executive Officer   Tel: (972) 281-1200
FALK, Thomas J.   Fax: (972) 281-1490

Main Headquarters
Mailing: P.O. Box 619100   Tel: (972) 281-1440
           Dallas, TX 75261-9100   Fax: (972) 281-1490

                             TF: (800) 639-1352

Washington Office
Mailing: 101 Constitution Ave.   Tel: (202) 682-3000
           Suite 921 East
           Washington, DC 20001

Corporate Foundations and Giving Programs
Kimberly-Clark Foundation
351 Phelps Dr.
Irving, TX 75038

Public Affairs and Related Activities Personnel

At Headquarters

ALEXANDER, Paul J.   Tel: (972) 281-1440
Vice President, Investor Relations   Fax: (972) 281-1490
palexand@kcc.com

BRICKMAN, Christian A.   Tel: (972) 281-1200
Group President   Fax: (972) 281-1490

GOTTUNG, Lizanne C.   Tel: (972) 281-1200
Senior Vice President and Chief Human Resources Officer   Fax: (972) 281-1490

HENRY , Maria   Tel: (972) 281-1440
Senior Vice President and Chief Financial Officer   Fax: (972) 281-1490

LOEWE, Nancy   Tel: (972) 281-1440
Senior Vice President and Chief Strategy Officer   Fax: (972) 281-1490

MIELKE, Thomas J.   Tel: (972) 281-1200
Senior Vice President and General Counsel   Fax: (972) 281-1490

PALMER, Anthony J.   Tel: (972) 281-1200
President, Global Brands and Innovation   Fax: (972) 281-1490

At Washington Office

HEINDL, Brian   Tel: (202) 682-3000
Manager, Government Relations
Registered Federal Lobbyist

PHILLIPS, Susan A.   Tel: (202) 682-3000
Vice President, Government Relations
Registered Federal Lobbyist

SHAFFER, PhD, Fred W.   Tel: (202) 682-3000
Federal Lobbyist

Kimmins Contracting Corporation

Provides contract construction services to public- and private-sector clients.
kimmins.com
Annual Revenues: $27.40 million
Employees: 300
SIC: 1623
Industry/ies: Construction/Construction Materials

President and Chief Executive Officer   Tel: (813) 248-3878
WILLIAMS, Joseph M.   Fax: (813) 367-4263

Main Headquarters
Mailing: 1501 E. Second Ave.   Tel: (813) 247-0147
           Tampa, FL 33605   Fax: (813) 579-1081

Corporate Foundations and Giving Programs
Kimmins Foundation
1501 E. Second Ave.
Tampa, FL 33605

Public Affairs and Related Activities Personnel

At Headquarters

WILLIAMS, Debra L.   Tel: (813) 248-3878
Vice President   Fax: (813) 367-4263
dwilliams@kimmins.com

ZEMINA, John   Tel: (813) 247-0147
Vice President Operations   Fax: (813) 579-1081

Kinder Morgan, Inc.

A transporter and marketer of energy products like natural gas, refined petroleum products, crude oil, ethanol, coal and carbon dioxide in the United States.
www.kindermorgan.com
Annual Revenues: $15.78 billion
Employees: 11,535
Ticker: NYSE: KMI
SIC: 4619; 1311; 1321; 4911; 4923; 4922
NAICS: 486210; 486990; 211111; 221112; 221210; 211112
Industry/ies: Fuels See Coal, Gas, Oil, Petroleum; Natural Resources; Petroleum Industry; Utilities
Legislative Issues: ENG; FUE

Chairman of the Board and Chief Executive Officer   Tel: (713) 369-9000
KINDER, Richard D.   Fax: (713) 369-9100

Main Headquarters
Mailing: 1001 Louisiana St.   Tel: (713) 369-9000
           Suite 1000   Fax: (713) 369-9100
           Houston, TX 77002   TF: (800) 324-2900

Washington Office

Mailing: 2101 L St. NW   Tel: (202) 223-4336
           Tenth Floor
           Washington, DC 20037

Corporate Foundations and Giving Programs

El Paso Corporation Contributions Program
P.O. Box 2511   Tel: (713) 420-2878
Houston, TX 77252-2511

Kinder Morgan Foundation
Contact: Larry S. Pierce
370 Van Gordon St.   Tel: (303) 763-3471
Lakewood, CO 80228

Public Affairs and Related Activities Personnel

At Headquarters

CONOVER, David	Tel:	(713) 369-9000
Vice President	Fax:	(713) 369-9100
DANG, Kimberly Allen	Tel:	(713) 369-9000
Vice President and Chief Financial Officer	Fax:	(713) 369-9100
DEVEAU, David R.	Tel:	(713) 369-9000
Vice President and General Counsel	Fax:	(713) 369-9100
KEAN, Steven J.	Tel:	(713) 369-9000
President and Chief Operating Officer	Fax:	(713) 369-9100
MICHELS, David P.	Tel:	(713) 369-9000
Vice President, Finance and Investor Relations	Fax:	(713) 369-9100
MIR, Emily	Tel:	(713) 369-8060
Corporate Communications Manager	Fax:	(713) 369-9100
Emily_mir@kindermorgan.com		
PIERCE, Larry S.	Tel:	(713) 369-9407
Vice President, Corporate Communications and Public Affairs	Fax:	(713) 369-9100
larry_pierce@kindermorgan.com		
SHORB, Lisa	Tel:	(713) 369-9000
Vice President, Human Resources, Administration and Information Technology	Fax:	(713) 369-9100

At Washington Office

GEORGE, Fiji	Tel:	(202) 223-4336
Federal Lobbyist		
fiji.george@elpaso.com		

At Other Offices

BULKLEY, Maureen	Tel:	(303) 763-3471
Manager, Public Affairs and Corporate Communications		
370 Van Gordon St.		
Lakewood, CO 80228		
SULT, John R.	Tel:	(713) 420-2600
Senior Vice President, Chief Financial Officer & Controller	Fax:	(713) 420-4417
P.O. Box 2511		
Houston, TX 77252-2511		
WHITEHEAD, Dane E.	Tel:	(713) 420-2600
Senior Vice President, Strategy and Enterprise Business Development	Fax:	(713) 420-4417
P.O. Box 2511		
Houston, TX 77252-2511		

Kindred Healthcare, Inc.

A healthcare services company.
www.kindredhealthcare.com
Annual Revenues: $5.43 billion
Employees: 38,700
Ticker: NYSE: KND
SIC: 8050
Industry/ies: Medicine/Health Care/Mental Health
Legislative Issues: HCR; MMM; TOR

President and Chief Executive Officer	Tel:	(502) 596-7300
BREIER, Benjamin A	Fax:	(502) 596-4170

Main Headquarters

Mailing: 680 S. Fourth St.	Tel:	(502) 596-7300
Louisville, KY 40202	Fax:	(502) 596-4170
	TF:	(800) 545-0749

Political Action Committees

Kindred Healthcare Inc. PAC
FEC ID: C00242271
Contact: Raymond Sierpina
680 S. Fourth St.
Louisville, TX 40202

    Contributions to Candidates: $144,513 (2015-2016)
    Democrats: $42,600; Republicans: $101,913

        Principal Recipients

           SENATE
           AYOTTE, KELLY A (REP-NH)
           MCCONNELL, MITCH (REP-KY)
           PORTMAN, ROB (REP-OH)

WYDEN, RONALD L (DEM-OR)
YOUNG, TODD CHRISTOPHER (REP-IN)

HOUSE
BRADY, KEVIN (REP-TX)
RYAN, PAUL D. (REP-WI)

Corporate Foundations and Giving Programs

Kindred Foundation Inc.
Contact: Leigh White
680 S. Fourth St.   Tel: (502) 596-7296
Louisville, KY 40202

Public Affairs and Related Activities Personnel

At Headquarters

ALTMAN, William M.	Tel:	(502) 596-7161
Senior Vice President, Strategy and Public Policy	Fax:	(502) 596-4170
william.altman@kindredhealthcare.com		
Registered Federal Lobbyist		
CUNANAN, Stephen R.	Tel:	(502) 596-7300
Chief People Officer	Fax:	(502) 596-4170
FARBER, Stephen D.	Tel:	(502) 596-7300
Executive Vice President, Chief Financial Officer	Fax:	(502) 596-4170
LANDENWICH, Joseph L.	Tel:	(502) 596-7300
Co-General Counsel and Corporate Secretary	Fax:	(502) 596-4170
Joseph.Landenwich@kindredhealthcare.com		
MOSS, Susan E.	Tel:	(502) 596-7296
Vice President, Communications and Marketing	Fax:	(502) 596-4099
Susan.Moss@kindredhealthcare.com		
RIEDMAN, M. Suzanne	Tel:	(502) 596-7300
General Counsel and Chief Diversity Officer	Fax:	(502) 596-4170
ROBINSON, Hank	Tel:	(502) 596-7300
Senior Vice President, Tax and Contact, Investor Relations	Fax:	(502) 596-4099
SAUBER, Alan	Tel:	(502) 596-7300
Federal Lobbyist	Fax:	(502) 596-4170
Registered Federal Lobbyist		
SIERPINA, Raymond	Tel:	(502) 596-7956
Senior Vice President, Public Policy & Government Affairs	Fax:	(502) 596-4170
raymond.sierpina@kindredhealthcare.com		
Registered Federal Lobbyist		
WALLACE, Kent H	Tel:	(502) 596-7300
Executive Vice President and Chief Operating Officer	Fax:	(502) 596-4170
WHITE, Leigh	Tel:	(502) 596-7300
Senior Director, Communications	Fax:	(502) 596-4170
leigh.white@kindredhealthcare.com		

Kinetic Concepts, Inc.

A medical device manufacturer.
www.kci1.com
Annual Revenues: $2.01 billion
Employees: 7,000
Ticker: NYSE: KCI
SIC: 2515; 2599; 2590
NAICS: 337127; 337910
Industry/ies: Medicine/Health Care/Mental Health

Interim Chairman of the Board	Tel:	(210) 524-9000
GUMINA, William J.	Fax:	(210) 255-6998

President and Chief Executive Officer	Tel:	(210) 524-9000
WOODY, Joe	Fax:	(210) 255-6998

Main Headquarters

Mailing: P.O. Box 659508	Tel:	(210) 524-9000
San Antonio, TX 78265	Fax:	(210) 255-6998
	TF:	(800) 275-4524

Corporate Foundations and Giving Programs

KCI Servant's Heart Foundation
P.O. Box 659508
San Antonio, TX 78265

Public Affairs and Related Activities Personnel

At Headquarters

BIBB, John T.	Tel:	(210) 524-9000
Senior Vice President, General Counsel	Fax:	(210) 255-6998
John.Bibb@kci1.com		
HULSE, Butch	Tel:	(210) 524-9000
Chief Compliance Officer	Fax:	(210) 255-6998
KASHYAP, Rohit	Tel:	(210) 524-9000
Senior Vice President, Strategy and Business Development	Fax:	(210) 255-6998
LILLBACK, David	Tel:	(210) 524-9000
Senior Vice President, Global Human Resources	Fax:	(210) 255-6998
SPEICHER, Nathan	Tel:	(210) 524-9000
Vice President, Treasury and Investor Relations	Fax:	(210) 255-6998
nathan.speicher@kci1.com		

TURBYFILL, Cheston
Contact, Corporate Communications
cheston.turbyfill@acelity.com
Tel: (210) 515-7757
Fax: (210) 255-6998

King Kullen Grocery Company
A food store chain.
www.kingkullen.com
Annual Revenues: $460.2 Million
Employees: 4,500
Industry/ies: Food And Beverage Industry; Retail/Wholesale

Co-chairmen
KENNEDY, Bernard D.
bkennedy@kingkullen.com
Tel: (516) 733-7100
Fax: (516) 827-6325

Main Headquarters
Mailing: 185 Central Ave.
Bethpage, NY 11714
Tel: (516) 733-7100
Fax: (516) 827-6325

King Pharmaceutical, Inc.
See listing on page 630 under Pfizer Inc.

King Ranch
The largest ranch in the US and a national historic landmark that also serves as a museum.
www.king-ranch.com
Annual Revenues: $35.10 million
Employees: 700
Industry/ies: Agriculture/Agronomy; History/Historic Preservation; Museums

Chairman of the Board
CLEMENT, Jr., James H.
Tel: (832) 681-5700
Fax: (832) 681-5759

Adviser
HUNT, Jack
Tel: (832) 681-5700
Fax: (832) 681-5759

Main Headquarters
Mailing: Three Riverway
Suite 1600
Houston, TX 77056
Tel: (832) 681-5700
Fax: (832) 681-5759

Public Affairs and Related Activities Personnel

At Headquarters

FEILD, Justin
Media Contact
jfeild@king-ranch.com
Tel: (361) 221-0311
Fax: (832) 681-5759

GARDINER, William J.
PAC Treasurer
Tel: (832) 681-5700
Fax: (832) 681-5759

Kirby Corporation
Operates inland tank barges and towing vessels transporting petrochemicals, black oil products, refined petroleum products and agricultural chemicals throughout the United States' inland waterway system.
www.kirbycorp.com
Annual Revenues: $2.02 billion
Employees: 4,075
Ticker: NYSE: KEX
SIC: 4789
NAICS: 488999
Industry/ies: Marine/Maritime/Shipping; Ports And Waterways; Transportation
Legislative Issues: BUD; DEF; MAR; TRA

Chairman of the Board
PYNE, Joseph H.
Tel: (713) 435-1000
Fax: (713) 435-1464

President and Chief Executive Officer
GRZEBINSKI, David W.
Tel: (713) 435-1000
Fax: (713) 435-1464

Main Headquarters
Mailing: 55 Waugh Dr.
Suite 1000
Houston, TX 77007
Tel: (713) 435-1000
Fax: (713) 435-1010

Political Action Committees
Kirby Corporation PAC
FEC ID: C00250027
Contact: Mary Tucker
55 Waugh Dr.
Suite 1000
Houston, TX 77007

Contributions to Candidates: $137,000 (2015-2016)
Democrats: $11,000; Republicans: $126,000

Public Affairs and Related Activities Personnel

At Headquarters

FORBES, Mark K.
Vice President, Human Resources
Tel: (713) 435-1000
Fax: (713) 435-1464

HOLCOMB, G. Stephen
Vice President, Investor Relations
Tel: (713) 435-1135
Fax: (713) 435-1464

HUSTED, Amy D.
Vice President, Legal
Tel: (713) 435-1000
Fax: (713) 435-1464

Amy.Husted@kirbycorp.com
O'NEIL, Chrisitian G.
Executive Vice President, Commercial Operations
christian.oneil@kirbycorp.com
Tel: (713) 435-1000
Fax: (713) 435-1464

SMITH, Andrew
Executive Vice President and Chief Financial Officer
Tel: (713) 435-1000
Fax: (713) 435-1464

TUCKER, Mary
PAC Treasurer
Mail Stop Suite 1000
Tel: (713) 435-1000
Fax: (713) 435-1464

Kitchell Corporation
A commercial construction and project management company.
www.kitchell.com
Employees: 1,000
Industry/ies: Construction/Construction Materials

Chairman of the Board
SCHUBERT, Bill
Tel: (602) 264-4411
Fax: (602) 631-9112

President and Chief Executive Officer
SWANSON, Jim
Tel: (602) 264-4411
Fax: (602) 631-9112

Main Headquarters
Mailing: 1707 E. Highland
Suite 100
Phoenix, AZ 85016
Tel: (602) 264-4411
Fax: (602) 631-9112

Corporate Foundations and Giving Programs
Kitchell Corporation Contributions Program
1707 E. Highland
Sutie 100
Phoenix, AZ 85016

Public Affairs and Related Activities Personnel

At Headquarters

SPENCER, Kati
Contact, Media Relations
kspencer@kitchell.com
Tel: (602) 759-8926
Fax: (602) 631-9112

KITCO Fiber Optics
Provider of fiber optic connectorization products and consulting services to the military and commercial communications industry.
www.kitcofo.com
Annual Revenues: $5.20 million
Employees: 49
Industry/ies: Communications; Electricity & Electronics; Electronics; Energy/Electricity; Telecommunications/Internet/Cable

Chairman of the Board
MILLERIII , W. Sheppard
Tel: (757) 518-8100
Fax: (757) 518-9700

President and Chief Executive Officer
CLARK, Geoff
Tel: (757) 518-8100
Fax: (757) 518-9700

Main Headquarters
Mailing: 5269 Cleveland St.
Suite 109
Virginia Beach, VA 23462
Tel: (757) 518-8100
Fax: (757) 518-9700
TF: (888) 548-2636

Kla-Tencor Corporation
A manufacturer of semiconductor inspection equipment.
www.kla-tencor.com
Annual Revenues: $2.82 billion
Employees: 5,880
Ticker: NASDAQ: KLAC
SIC: 3827; 3823; 3829
Industry/ies: Computer/Technology

President and Chief Executive Officer
WALLACE, Rick
Tel: (408) 875-3000
Fax: (408) 875-4144

Main Headquarters
Mailing: One Technology Dr.
Milpitas, CA 95035
Tel: (408) 875-3000
Fax: (408) 875-4144
TF: (800) 600-2829

Corporate Foundations and Giving Programs
KLA-Tencor Foundation
One Technology Dr.
Milpitas, CA 95035
Tel: (408) 875-3000
Fax: (408) 875-4144

Public Affairs and Related Activities Personnel

At Headquarters

HIGGINS, Bren
Chief Financial Officer
Tel: (408) 875-3000
Fax: (408) 875-4144

LOCKWOOD, Ed
Senior Director, Investor Relations
ed.lockwood@kla-tencor.com
Tel: (408) 875-9529
Fax: (408) 875-4144

POWERS, Meggan
Senior Director, Corporate Communications
meggan.powers@kla-tencor.com
Tel: (408) 875-8733
Fax: (408) 875-4144

TSAI, Ben	Tel:	(408) 875-3000
Chief Technology Officer and Executive Vice President, Corporate Alliances	Fax:	(408) 875-4144
WHEELER, Kathy	Tel:	(408) 875-3000
Senior Manager, Global Talent Communications	Fax:	(408) 875-4144

KLC School Partnerships
See listing on page 472 under Knowledge Universe

KLT Inc.
See listing on page 374 under Great Plains Energy

Knight Capital Group, Inc.
Provides electronic and voice trade execution services to the capital markets across multiple asset classes for buy-side, sell-side and corporate clients and asset management for institutions and private clients.
www.knight.com
Annual Revenues: $1.17 Billion
Employees: 972
Ticker: NYSE: KCG
SIC: 6211
Industry/ies: Banking/Finance/Investments; Electricity & Electronics; Electronics; Energy/Electricity

Chief Executive Officer	Tel:	(201) 222-9400
COLEMAN, Daniel B.	Fax:	(201) 557-6853

Main Headquarters
Mailing:	545 Washington Blvd.	Tel:	(201) 222-9400
	Jersey City, NJ 07310	Fax:	(201) 557-6853
		TF:	(800) 544-7508

Political Action Committees
KCG Holdings, Inc. Political Action Committee Aka KCG PAC
FEC ID: C00351205
Contact: John McCarthy
545 Washington Blvd.
Jersey City, NJ 07310

Contributions to Candidates: $3,500 (2015-2016)
Democrats: $3,500

Corporate Foundations and Giving Programs
Knight Capital Group, Inc. Contributions Program
545 Washington Blvd.	Tel:	(201) 222-9400
Jersey City, NJ 07310		

Public Affairs and Related Activities Personnel

At Headquarters
DARK, Jerry	Tel:	(201) 222-9400
Chief Human Resources Officer	Fax:	(201) 557-6853
MAIRS, Jonathan	Tel:	(201) 356-1529
Head of Investor Relations, Financial Communications	Fax:	(201) 557-6853
jmairs@knight.com		
MCCARTHY, John	Tel:	(201) 222-9400
General Counsel, Corporate Secretary and PAC Treasurer	Fax:	(201) 557-6853
OGURTSOV, Nick	Tel:	(201) 222-9400
Chief Operating Officer and Chief Risk Officer	Fax:	(201) 557-6853
PARRATT, Steffen	Tel:	(201) 222-9400
Chief Financial Officer	Fax:	(201) 557-6853
SOHN, Sophie	Tel:	(201) 222-9400
Chief Communications Officer	Fax:	(201) 557-6853
SOHOS, George	Tel:	(201) 222-9400
Senior Managing Director, Head Market Making	Fax:	(201) 557-6853

Knoa Software
A software company.
www.knoa.com
Annual Revenues: $3.80 million
Employees: 35
Industry/ies: Computer/Technology

Chief Executive Officer	Tel:	(212) 807-9608
BERNS, Brian	Fax:	(212) 675-6121

Main Headquarters
Mailing:	Five Union Sq. West	Tel:	(212) 807-9608
	Fourth Floor	Fax:	(212) 675-6121
	New York City, NY 10003-3312		

Public Affairs and Related Activities Personnel

At Headquarters
ADELL, Simon	Tel:	(212) 807-9608
Chief Financial Officer	Fax:	(212) 675-6121
CALDARELLA, Janine	Tel:	(212) 807-9608
Vice President, Marketing	Fax:	(212) 675-6121
D'ERAMO, Katelyn	Tel:	(617) 502-4300
Contact, Media Relations	Fax:	(212) 675-6121

Knoa@pancomm.com

Knowledge Universe
Formerly Knowledge Learning Corporation. Acquired Kindercare in 2005, national child care and education provider.
www.kueducation.com/us
Annual Revenues: $2.43 billion
Employees: 36,000
Industry/ies: Education

Co-Founder and Chairman of the Board	Tel:	(503) 872-1300
MILKEN , Mike	Fax:	(503) 872-1349
Chief Executive Officer	Tel:	(503) 872-1300
WYATT, Tom	Fax:	(503) 872-1349

Main Headquarters
Mailing:	650 N.E. Holladay St.	Tel:	(503) 872-1300
	Portland, OR 97232	Fax:	(503) 872-1349
		TF:	(888) 525-2780

Corporate Foundations and Giving Programs
Knowledge Learning Corporation Contributions Program
Contact: David Roy
650 N.E. Holladay St.	Tel:	(503) 872-1300
Suite 1400		
Portland, OR 97232		

Public Affairs and Related Activities Personnel

At Headquarters
CHONG, Wei-Li	Tel:	(503) 872-1300
Executive Vice President, People and Family Experience	Fax:	(503) 872-1349
GALUPPO, Gail	Tel:	(503) 872-1300
Executive Vice President and Chief Marketing Officer	Fax:	(503) 872-1349
LARGE, Elizabeth	Tel:	(503) 872-1300
Executive Vice President and General Counsel	Fax:	(503) 872-1349
ROY, David	Tel:	(503) 872-1300
Senior Director, Community and Communications	Fax:	(503) 872-1349
droy@klcorp.com		
SCHMITZ, Mark	Tel:	(503) 872-1300
Senior Vice President, Business Development	Fax:	(503) 872-1349

Koch Companies Public Sector, LLC
A shared-services company that provides legal, government and public affairs.
www.kochind.com
Industry/ies: Agriculture/Agronomy; Banking/Finance/Investments; Chemicals & Chemical Industry; Environment And Conservation; Fuels See Coal, Gas, Oil, Petroleum; Natural Resources; Paper And Wood Products Industry; Petroleum Industry; Pollution And Waste
Legislative Issues: AGR; BNK; BUD; CAW; CDT; CHM; CON; CPT; ENG; ENV; FIN; FUE; GOV; HOM; LAW; TAX; TRA; TRD

Chairman of the Board and Chief Executive Officer
KOCH , Charles G.

Main Headquarters
Mailing:	P.O. Box 2256
	Wichita, KS 67201-2256

Washington Office
Mailing:	600 14th St. NW	Tel:	(202) 879-8569
	Suite 800		
	Washington, DC 20005		

Public Affairs and Related Activities Personnel

At Headquarters
KOCH , David H.
Executive Vice President
ROBERTSON , David L.
President and Chief Operating Officer

At Washington Office
ELLENDER, Philip	Tel:	(202) 879-8569
Federal Lobbyist		
Registered Federal Lobbyist		
GRAY, Jennifer Bonar	Tel:	(202) 879-8569
Director, Federal Affairs		
Registered Federal Lobbyist		
HAGGETT, Catherine	Tel:	(202) 879-8569
Federal Lobbyist		
Registered Federal Lobbyist		
HENNBERRY, Brian	Tel:	(202) 879-8569
Registered Federal Lobbyist		
HENNEBERRY, Brian M.	Tel:	(202) 879-8569
Federal Lobbyist		
Registered Federal Lobbyist		
PAUL, Raymond	Tel:	(202) 879-8569
Federal Lobbyist		
Registered Federal Lobbyist		

ZERZAN, Greg   Tel: (202) 879-8569
Federal Lobbyist
Registered Federal Lobbyist

Koch Industries, Inc.

Owns a diverse group of companies engaged in trading, investment and operations worldwide.
Acquired Georgia-Pacific Corporation in 2005.
www.kochind.com
Annual Revenues: $115 billion
Employees: 60,000
Industry/ies: Energy/Electricity; Fuels See Coal, Gas, Oil, Petroleum; Natural
Resources; Petroleum Industry
Legislative Issues: CAW; ENG; HOM; TRA

Chairman of the Board and Chief Executive Officer   Tel: (316) 828-5500
KOCH, Charles G.   Fax: (316) 828-5739
charles.koch@kochind.com

Main Headquarters
Mailing: P.O. Box 2256   Tel: (316) 828-5500
     Wichita, KS 67201-2256   Fax: (316) 828-5739

Washington Office
Mailing: 600 14th St. NW   Tel: (202) 737-1977
     Suite 800   Fax: (202) 737-8111
     Washington, DC 20005

Political Action Committees
Koch Industries, Inc. PAC
FEC ID: C00236489
Contact: Lacye R. Tennille
655 15th St. NW   Tel: (202) 737-1977
Suite 445   Fax: (202) 737-8111
Washington, DC 20005-2001

    Contributions to Candidates: $1,040,900 (2015-2016)
    Democrats: $8,500; Republicans: $1,027,900; Other: $4,500

      Principal Recipients

       SENATE
       BLUNT, ROY (REP-MO)
       BOOZMAN, JOHN (REP-AR)
       CRAPO, MICHAEL D (REP-ID)
       MORAN, JERRY (REP-KS)
       PAUL, RAND (REP-KY)
       PORTMAN, ROB (REP-OH)

       HOUSE
       BLUM, RODNEY (REP-IA)
       COFFMAN, MIKE REP. (REP-CO)
       COMSTOCK, BARBARA J HONORABLE (REP-VA)
       DENT, CHARLES W. REP. (REP-PA)
       DESANTIS, RONALD D (REP-FL)
       FARENTHOLD, RANDOLPH BLAKE (REP-TX)
       FLORES, BILL (REP-TX)
       GARRETT, SCOTT REP. (REP-NJ)
       GRIFFITH, H MORGAN (REP-VA)
       GROTHMAN, GLENN S. (REP-WI)
       GUINTA, FRANK (REP-NH)
       HARDY, CRESENT (REP-NV)
       HUDSON, RICHARD L. JR. (REP-NC)
       HUELSKAMP, TIMOTHY A REPRESENTA (REP-KS)
       HURD, WILLIAM (REP-TX)
       MCCARTHY, KEVIN (REP-CA)
       MCHENRY, PATRICK TIMOTHY (REP-NC)
       MULLIN, MARKWAYNE MR. (REP-OK)
       NUNES, DEVIN G (REP-CA)
       PAULSEN, ERIK (REP-MN)
       SCALISE, STEVE MR. (REP-LA)
       SCOTT, JAMES AUSTIN (REP-GA)
       SHUSTER, WILLIAM MR. (REP-PA)
       STEFANIK, ELISE M. (REP-NY)
       UPTON, FREDERICK STEPHEN (REP-MI)
       WALBERG, TIMOTHY L HON. (REP-MI)
       WALDEN, GREGORY P MR. (REP-OR)
       YODER, KEVIN (REP-KS)
       ZELDIN, LEE M (REP-NY)

Corporate Foundations and Giving Programs

Koch Industries Contributions Program
Contact: Susan Addington
4111 E. 37th St., North   Tel: (316) 828-5500
Wichita, KS 67220

Public Affairs and Related Activities Personnel

At Headquarters

COHLMIA, Melissa   Tel: (316) 828-3756
Director, Corporate Communications   Fax: (316) 828-6997
melissa.cohlmia@kochps.com

OSWALD, Bill   Tel: (316) 828-5500
Director, Government and Regulatory Affairs   Fax: (316) 828-5739

oswaldb@kochind.com

ROBERTSON, David L.   Tel: (316) 828-5500
President and Chief Operating Officer   Fax: (316) 828-5739

At Washington Office

ELLENDER, Philip   Tel: (202) 879-8569
President, Government and Public Affairs   Fax: (202) 737-8111

FINK, Richard H.   Tel: (202) 737-1977
Executive Vice President   Fax: (202) 737-8111
finkr@kochind.com

HAGGETT, Catherine   Tel: (202) 879-8569
Director, Federal Affairs   Fax: (202) 737-8111
catherine.haggett@kochind.com

HENNEBERRY, Brian M.   Tel: (202) 879-8569
Vice President, Federal Affairs   Fax: (202) 737-8111

PAUL, Raymond   Tel: (202) 879-8569
Director, Federal Government Affairs   Fax: (202) 737-8111

TENNILLE, Lacye R.   Tel: (202) 879-8569
PAC Treasurer   Fax: (202) 737-8111
Lacye.Tennille@kochind.com

At Other Offices

ADDINGTON, Susan
Program Manager, Arts, Culture
4111 E. 37th St. North
Wichita, KS 67220
philanthropy@kochind.com

Kohl's Corporation

A general merchandise retailer.
www.kohlscorporation.com
Annual Revenues: $19.05 billion
Employees: 32,000
Ticker: NYSE: KSS
SIC: 5311
Industry/ies: Retail/Wholesale

Chairman of the Board, President and Chief Executive Officer   Tel: (262) 703-7000
MANSELL, Kevin B.   Fax: (262) 703-6143

Main Headquarters
Mailing: N56 W17000 Ridgewood Dr.   Tel: (262) 703-7000
     Menomonee Falls, WI 53501   Fax: (262) 703-6143
                               TF: (855) 564-5705

Corporate Foundations and Giving Programs

Kohl's Cares for Kids
Contact: Brian Miller
N56 W17000 Ridgewood Dr.   Tel: (262) 703-7000
Menomonee Falls, WI 53051

Public Affairs and Related Activities Personnel

At Headquarters

CHAWLA, Sona   Tel: (262) 703-7000
Chief Operating Officer   Fax: (262) 703-6143

GASS, Michelle   Tel: (262) 703-7000
Chief Merchandising and Customer Officer   Fax: (262) 703-6143

JOHNSON , Jen   Tel: (262) 703-5241
Vice President, Corporate Communications   Fax: (262) 703-6143
jen.johnson@kohls.com

MCDONALD, Wesley S.   Tel: (262) 703-1893
Chief Financial Officer   Fax: (262) 703-6143
wes.mcdonald@kohls.com

MILLER, Brian   Tel: (262) 703-1723
Senior Vice President, Finance   Fax: (262) 703-6143
brian.f.miller@kohls.com

SCHEPP, Richard   Tel: (262) 703-7000
Chief Administrative Officer   Fax: (262) 703-6143

Kohler Corporation

A manufacturer of plumbing supplies.
www.kohler.com
Employees: 27,000
Ticker: OTC: KHCO
Industry/ies: Construction/Construction Materials
Legislative Issues: CAW

Chairman of the Board   Tel: (920) 457-4441
KOHLER, Jr., Herbert V.   Fax: (920) 457-1271
herbert.kohler@kohler.com

President and Chief Executive Officer   Tel: (920) 457-4441
KOHLER, David   Fax: (920) 457-1271

Main Headquarters
Mailing: 444 Highland Dr.   Tel: (920) 457-4441
     Kohler, WI 53011   Fax: (920) 457-1271
                               TF: (800) 456-4537

Public Affairs and Related Activities Personnel

At Headquarters

CHENEY, Jeffrey
Senior Vice President, Finance and Chief Financial Officer
Tel: (920) 457-4441
Fax: (920) 457-1271

KULOW, Lynn
Manager, Charitable Contributions & Communications
Tel: (920) 457-4441
Fax: (920) 457-9064

Koinonia Homes, Inc.

Non profit provider of services to people with intellectual and developmental disabilities.
www.koinoniahomes.org
Employees: 500

Chairman of the Board
WATKINS, Fred
Tel: (216) 588-8777
Fax: (216) 588-5670

President and Chief Executive Officer
BEASTROM, Diane
Tel: (216) 588-8777
Fax: (216) 588-5670

Main Headquarters
Mailing: 6161 Oak Tree Blvd.
Suite 400
Independence, OH 44131
Tel: (216) 588-8777
Fax: (216) 588-5670
TF: (877) 398-4770

Public Affairs and Related Activities Personnel

At Headquarters

BONDY, Mary
Chief Business Development Officer
Tel: (216) 588-8777
Fax: (216) 588-5670

DISBROW, Nancy
Chief People Officer
Tel: (216) 588-8777
Fax: (216) 588-5670

DOBRIN, Andy
Chief Operating Officer
Tel: (216) 588-8777
Fax: (216) 588-5670

LAHETA, Mike
Vice President, Controller
Tel: (216) 588-8777
Fax: (216) 588-5670

LAUBENTHAL, David
Chief Administrative Officer
Tel: (216) 588-8777
Fax: (216) 588-5670

MORTON, Carol
Vice President, Finance
Tel: (216) 588-8777
Fax: (216) 588-5670

RAVETTO, Gary
Vice President, External Affairs
Tel: (216) 588-8777
Fax: (216) 588-5670

Kopin Corporation

An electronics company. Manufactures bipolar transistors, semiconductors and other electronic devices.
www.kopin.com
Annual Revenues: $35.70 million
Employees: 197
Ticker: NASDAQ: KOPN
SIC: 3674
Industry/ies: Electricity & Electronics; Electronics; Energy/Electricity

Chairman of the Board, President and Chief Executive Officer
FAN, Dr. John C.C.
Tel: (508) 824-6696
Fax: (508) 824-6958

Main Headquarters
Mailing: 125 N. Dr.
Westboro, MA 01581
Tel: (508) 870-5959
Fax: (508) 870-0660

Public Affairs and Related Activities Personnel

At Other Offices

HOWE, Lauren
Senior Account Executive and Media Contact
200 John Hancock Rd.
Taunton, MA 02780
lhowe@rdwgroup.com
Tel: (401) 553-5106
Fax: (508) 824-6958

MEANS, Calley
Contact, News Media Relations
200 John Hancock Rd.
Taunton, MA 02780
Tel: (508) 824-6696
Fax: (508) 824-6958

PRESZ, Michael
Vice President, Government Programs and Special Projects
200 John Hancock Rd.
Taunton, MA 02780
Tel: (508) 824-6696
Fax: (508) 824-6958

SNEIDER, Richard
Treasurer and Chief Financial Officer
200 John Hancock Rd.
Taunton, MA 02780
rsneider@kopin.com
Tel: (508) 824-6696
Fax: (508) 824-6958

Koppers Industries, Inc.

A global integrated producer of carbon compounds and treated wood products for use by the utility, construction, railroad, aluminum, chemical and steel industries.
www.koppers.com
Annual Revenues: $1.62 billion
Employees: 2,142
Ticker: NYSE: KOP
SIC: 2491; 2400

NAICS: 321114
Industry/ies: Paper And Wood Products Industry

Chairman of the Board
HILLENBRAND, Daniel M.
Tel: (412) 227-2001
Fax: (412) 227-2333

President and Chief Executive Officer
BALL, Jr., Leroy M.
Tel: (412) 227-2118
Fax: (412) 227-2333

Main Headquarters
Mailing: 436 Seventh Ave.
Pittsburgh, PA 15219-1800
Tel: (412) 227-2001
Fax: (412) 227-2333
TF: (800) 321-9876

Political Action Committees
Koppers Inc. PAC
FEC ID: C00391821
Contact: Michael H. Juba
436 Seventh Ave.
Pittsburgh, PA 15219
Tel: (412) 227-2001
Fax: (412) 227-2001

Contributions to Candidates: $19,656 (2015-2016)
Democrats: $4,828; Republicans: $14,828

Principal Recipients

HOUSE
MURPHY, TIMOTHY (REP-PA)

Public Affairs and Related Activities Personnel

At Headquarters

CRERAR, Ken A.
PAC Contact
Tel: (412) 227-2001
Fax: (412) 227-2333

GROVES, Daniel R.
Vice President, Human Resources
Tel: (412) 227-2001
Fax: (412) 227-2333

JUBA, Michael H.
Manager, Production Safety and Health and PAC Contact
jubamh@koppers.com
Tel: (412) 227-2001
Fax: (412) 227-2333

LACY, Steven R.
Senior Vice President, Administration, General Counsel and Secretary
Tel: (412) 227-2001
Fax: (412) 227-2333

PICKUS, Traci M.
PAC Contact
Tel: (412) 227-2001
Fax: (412) 227-2333

SNYDER, Michael W.
Director, Investor Relations
snydermw@koppers.com
Tel: (412) 227-2131
Fax: (412) 227-2333

SPIESS, Markus
Vice President, Global Sales and Marketing
Tel: (412) 227-2001
Fax: (412) 227-2333

TRONSBERG-DEIHLE, Louann
Treasurer
Tel: (412) 227-2001
Fax: (412) 227-2333

TURNER, Walter W.
Director
Tel: (412) 227-2001
Fax: (412) 227-2333

ZUGAY, Michael J.
Chief Financial Officer
Tel: (412) 227-2001
Fax: (412) 227-2333

KOR Trading LLC

Works with exchanges, brokers and advisors on market structure, regulatory and rulemaking.
www.kortrading.com

Founder and Chief Executive Officer
NAGY, Christopher
Christopher.Nagy@KORtrading.com
Tel: (402) 349-5033

Main Headquarters
Mailing: 22030 Stanford Cir.
Elkhorn, NE 68022
Tel: (402) 349-5033

Public Affairs and Related Activities Personnel

At Headquarters

DAS, Rajarshi
Director
Tel: (402) 349-5033

LAUER, David
Co-Founder and Chief Technology Officer
Tel: (402) 349-5033

Koyo Corporation of U.S.A.

Koyo Corporation of USA is the Sales Division of JTEKT North America Corporation. Koyo is the JTEKT Corporation brand for Bearings.
www.koyousa.com
Annual Revenues: $134.50 million
Employees: 5,400
Industry/ies: Automotive Industry; Machinery/Equipment; Transportation
Legislative Issues: TRD

President and Chief Executive Officer
KAIJIMA, Hiroyuki
Tel: (734) 454-1500
Fax: (734) 454-4076

Main Headquarters
Mailing: 29570 Clemens Rd.
Westlake, OH 44145
Tel: (440) 835-1000
Fax: (440) 835-9347

Public Affairs and Related Activities Personnel

At Headquarters

BEARGIE, Paul
Director
Tel: (440) 835-1000
Fax: (440) 835-9347

LOX, Jaime
Manager, Marketing and Business Development
Jaime.Lox@JTEKT.com
Tel: (440) 835-1000
Fax: (440) 835-9347

KPGL Global Energy Resource Group, Inc.

Alternative energy development.
Legislative Issues: ECN; EDU

President
RUSSELL, Lee
Tel: (419) 290-2025

Main Headquarters
Mailing: 2240 Franklin Ave.
#3
Toledo, OH 43620

KPMG LLP

Accounting, tax and audit firm. It is the U.S. member firm of KPMG International Cooperative ("KPMG International").
www.kpmg.com/us
Annual Revenues: $4.89 billion
Employees: 21,000
SIC: 8721; 5099; 8399; 8742
Industry/ies: Accounting; Banking/Finance/Investments
Legislative Issues: ACC; BAN; FIN; IMM; LBR; TAX

Chairman and Chief Executive Officer
VEIHMEYER , John
Tel: (201) 307-8270
Fax: (201) 930-8617

Main Headquarters
Mailing: Three Chestnut Ridge Rd.
Montvale, NJ 07645-0435
Tel: (201) 307-7000
Fax: (201) 930-8617

Washington Office
Mailing: 1801 K St. NW
Suite 12000
Washington, DC 20006
Tel: (202) 533-3000
Fax: (202) 533-8500

Political Action Committees
KPMG Partners/Principals and Employees PAC
FEC ID: C00280222
Contact: Stephen E. Allis
1801 K St. NW
Washington, DC 20006

Contributions to Candidates: $869,000 (2015-2016)
Democrats: $318,000; Republicans: $546,000; Other: $5,000

Principal Recipients

SENATE
MURPHY, PATRICK E (DEM-FL)
SCHATZ, BRIAN (DEM-HI)

HOUSE
BERA, AMERISH (DEM-CA)
CASTRO, JOAQUIN REP. (DEM-TX)
CHAFFETZ, JASON (REP-UT)
CROWLEY, JOSEPH (DEM-NY)
DOLD, ROBERT JAMES JR (REP-IL)
HENSARLING, JEB HON. (REP-TX)
HIMES, JIM (DEM-CT)
KELLY, GEORGE J JR (REP-PA)
KENNEDY, JOSEPH P III (DEM-MA)
KRISHNAMOORTHI, S. RAJA (DEM-IL)
LUJAN, BEN R MR. (DEM-NM)
MALONEY, CAROLYN B. (DEM-NY)
MCHENRY, PATRICK TIMOTHY (REP-NC)
MEEKS, GREGORY W. (DEM-NY)
PALAZZO, STEVEN MCCARTY (REP-MS)
ROYCE, ED MR. (REP-CA)
SESSIONS, PETE MR. (REP-TX)
VARGAS, JUAN C. (DEM-CA)

Corporate Foundations and Giving Programs

KPMG Foundation
Contact: Bernard J. Milano
Three Chestnut Ridge Rd.
Montvale, NJ 07645
Tel: (201) 307-7000

Public Affairs and Related Activities Personnel

At Headquarters

GINSBURG, Dan
Executive Director, Corporate and Functional Communications
dginsburg@kpmg.com
Tel: (201) 307-8270
Fax: (201) 930-8617

MILANO, Bernard J.
President, KPMG Foundation
Tel: (201) 307-8270
Fax: (201) 930-8617

PFAU, Bruce
Tel: (201) 307-8270

Vice Chair- Human Resources and Communications
Fax: (201) 930-8617

ZATORSKI, Karen O.
Executive Director, Communications
kzatorski@kpmg.com
Tel: (201) 505-6454
Fax: (201) 930-8617

At Washington Office

BLESSING, Peter
Registered Federal Lobbyist
Tel: (202) 533-3000
Fax: (202) 533-8500

GIMIGLIANO, John
Principal, Sustainability Tax Practice
Tel: (202) 533-3000
Fax: (202) 533-8500

MCGREW, Landon
Registered Federal Lobbyist
Tel: (202) 533-3000
Fax: (202) 533-8500

PLOWGIAN, Michael
Principal, Washington National Tax & International Tax Registered Federal Lobbyist
Tel: (202) 533-3000
Fax: (202) 533-8500

SAMS, James
Registered Federal Lobbyist
Tel: (202) 533-3000
Fax: (202) 533-8500

WEAVER, Brett
Partner, International Tax
Tel: (202) 533-3000
Fax: (202) 533-8500

At Other Offices

ALLIS, Stephen E.
PAC Treasurer
2001 M St. NW
Washington, DC 20036-3310
sallis@kpmg.com
Registered Federal Lobbyist
Tel: (202) 533-3040
Fax: (202) 533-8516

BREAKS, Katherine M.
Federal Lobbyist
2001 M St. NW
Washington, DC 20036-3310
kbreaks@kpmg.com
Tel: (202) 533-4578
Fax: (202) 533-8546

CHARBONNET, Stephen G.
Federal Lobbyist
2001 M St. NW
Washington, DC 20036-3310
scharbonnet@kpmg.com
Tel: (202) 533-6298
Fax: (202) 533-8546

CONJURA, Carol
Partner, Income Tax and Accounting Group
2001 M St. NW
Washington, DC 20036-3310
cconjura@kpmg.com
Tel: (202) 533-3040
Fax: (202) 533-8546

CULP, David
Federal Lobbyist
2001 M St. NW
Washington, DC 20036-3310
Tel: (202) 533-4104
Fax: (202) 533-8546

DAYANANDA, Priya
Federal Lobbyist
2001 M St. NW
Washington, DC 20036-3310
Registered Federal Lobbyist
Tel: (202) 533-3126
Fax: (202) 533-8516

FEDERING, Eric K.
Executive Director, Business and Public Policy, Office of Government Affairs
2001 M St. NW
Washington, DC 20036-3310
Tel: (202) 533-3126
Fax: (202) 533-8516

GREEN, Seth
Principal, Washington National Tax - ICS
2001 M St. NW
Washington, DC 20036-3310
Tel: (202) 533-3236
Fax: (202) 533-8516

GUTMAN, Harry L.
Principal-in-charge, Federal Tax Legislative & Regulatory Services
2001 M St. NW
Washington, DC 20036-3310
Tel: (202) 315-3088
Fax: (202) 533-8546

MCLUCAS, Scott
Managing Director, Federal Government Affairs
2001 M St. NW
Washington, DC 20036-3310
Registered Federal Lobbyist
Tel: (202) 533-3994
Fax: (202) 533-8516

MINTON, Bennett
Federal Lobbyist
2001 M St. NW
Washington, DC 20036-3310
Tel: (202) 533-3236
Fax: (202) 533-8546

STOUT, Thomas A.
Director of Federal Tax Legislative and Regulatory Services
2001 M St. NW
Washington, DC 20036-3310
tstoutjr@kpmg.com
Registered Federal Lobbyist
Tel: (202) 533-4148
Fax: (202) 533-8546

WESSEL, Thomas F.
Senior Manager, Federal Tax
2001 M St. NW
Tel: (202) 533-5700
Fax: (202) 533-8540

Washington, DC 20036-3310
twessel@kpmg.com

Kraft Heinz Company

A food company and provides delicious, nutritious and convenient foods for families.
www.kraftheinzcompany.com
Annual Revenues: $29.118 billion
Employees: 30,200
Ticker: NYSE: KHC
SIC: 2030
Industry/ies: Food And Beverage Industry

| **Chairman of the Board** | Tel: | (412) 456-5700 |
| BEHRING, Alexandre | Fax: | (412) 456-6128 |

| **Chief Executive Officer** | Tel: | (847) 646-2000 |
| VERNON, Tony | | |

Main Headquarters

Mailing:	P.O. Box 57	Tel:	(412) 456-5700
	Pittsburgh, PA 15230-0057	Fax:	(412) 456-6128
		TF:	(800) 255-5750

Political Action Committees
H.J. Heinz Company PAC
FEC ID: C00336040
Contact: James Liu
One PPG Pl.
Suite 3100
Pittsburgh, PA 15222

  Contributions to Candidates: $21,500 (2015-2016)
  Democrats: $14,000; Republicans: $7,500

Corporate Foundations and Giving Programs
H.J. Heinz Company Foundation
Contact: Jenece Upton

| P.O. Box 57 | Tel: | (412) 456-5700 |
| Pittsburgh, PA 15230 | | |

Public Affairs and Related Activities Personnel

At Headquarters

ABEL, Gregory E.	Tel:	(412) 456-5700
Board Member	Fax:	(412) 456-6128
BASILIO, Paul	Tel:	(412) 456-5700
Chief Financial Officer	Fax:	(412) 456-6128
BUFFETT, Warren E.	Tel:	(412) 456-5700
	Fax:	(412) 456-6128
COOL, Tracy Britt	Tel:	(412) 456-5700
Director	Fax:	(412) 456-6128
COX, Kevin	Tel:	(412) 456-5700
Director	Fax:	(412) 456-6128
HILL, Matt	Tel:	(412) 456-5700
Zone President of Europe	Fax:	(412) 456-6128
JACKSON, Jeanne P.	Tel:	(412) 456-5700
Director	Fax:	(412) 456-6128
KELLY, Beth	Tel:	(412) 456-5700
Associate Director, Corporate Affairs	Fax:	(412) 456-6128
LEMANN, Jorge Paulo	Tel:	(412) 456-5700
Director	Fax:	(412) 456-6128
LIU, James	Tel:	(412) 456-5700
PAC Treasurer	Fax:	(412) 456-6128
MAMMADOV, Emin	Tel:	(412) 456-5700
Zone President of Russia, India, and Middle East, Turkey & Africa	Fax:	(412) 456-6128
MCDONALD, Mackey J.	Tel:	(412) 456-5700
	Fax:	(412) 456-6128
MULLEN, Michael	Tel:	(412) 456-5700
Senior Vice President, Corporate and Government Affairs	Fax:	(412) 456-6128
michael.mullen@us.hjheinz.com		
NOLLEN, Margaret	Tel:	(412) 456-5700
Senior Vice President, Strategy Investor Relations	Fax:	(412) 456-6128
PELLEISSONE, Eduardo	Tel:	(412) 456-5700
Executive Vice President of Global Operations	Fax:	(412) 456-6128
POPE, John C.	Tel:	(412) 456-5700
Director	Fax:	(412) 456-6128
ROMANEIRO, Marcos	Tel:	(412) 456-5700
ZOne President of Asia Pacific	Fax:	(412) 456-6128
SA, Francisco	Tel:	(412) 456-5700
Zone President of Latin America	Fax:	(412) 456-6128
SAVINA, Jim	Tel:	(412) 456-5700
Senior Vice President, General Counsel, Corporate Secretary	Fax:	(412) 456-6128
TELLES, Marcel Herrmann	Tel:	(412) 456-5700
Director	Fax:	(412) 456-6128
TURNER, Michelle	Tel:	(412) 456-5700

Head, Human Resources	Fax:	(412) 456-6128
UPTON, Jenece	Tel:	(412) 456-5700
Manager, Heinz Company Foundation and Community Relations	Fax:	(412) 456-6128
WERNECK, Melissa	Tel:	(412) 456-5700
Senior Vice President Global Human Resources, Performance, and IT	Fax:	(412) 456-6128
WINKLEBLACK, Art	Tel:	(412) 456-5700
Executive Vice President and Chief Financial Officer	Fax:	(412) 456-6128
ZOGHBI, George	Tel:	(412) 456-5700
Chief Operating Officer of U.S. Commercial Business	Fax:	(412) 456-6128

At Other Offices

CAHILL, John T.	Tel:	(847) 646-2000
Vice Chairman		
Three Lakes Dr.		
Northfield, IL 60093		
ELSNER, Deanie	Tel:	(847) 646-2000
EVP and Chief Marketing Officer		
Three Lakes Dr.		
Northfield, IL 60093		
LIST-STOLL, Teri	Tel:	(847) 646-2000
EVP and Chief Financial Officer		
Three Lakes Dr.		
Northfield, IL 60093		
RUCKER, Kim	Tel:	(847) 646-2000
Executive Vice President, Corporate & Legal Affairs,		
Three Lakes Dr.		
Northfield, IL 60093		

Kratos Defense & Security Solutions

Missile defense targets, unmanned aircraft programs, & infrastructure protection products.
SIC: 7373
Industry/ies: Computer/Technology; Defense/Homeland Security; Government-Related
Legislative Issues: AER; BUD; DEF; SCI

Main Headquarters

| *Mailing:* | 4820 Eastgate Mall, Suite 200 | | |
| | San Diego, CA 92121 | | |

Washington Office

| *Mailing:* | 5200 Philadelphia Way | Tel: | (443) 539-5330 |
| | Lanham, MD 20706 | Fax: | (301) 577-1982 |

Public Affairs and Related Activities Personnel

At Washington Office

| WHITE, Yolanda | Tel: | (858) 812-7302 |
| *Contact, Media* | Fax: | (301) 577-1982 |

At Other Offices

FRELK, James	Tel:	(301) 731-4233
Senior Vice President, Corporate Business Development	Fax:	(301) 731-9606
6721 Columbia Gateway Dr.		
Columbia, MD 21046		
HERR, Kathryn	Tel:	(301) 731-4233
Vice President, Marketing and Communications	Fax:	(301) 731-9606
6721 Columbia Gateway Dr.		
Columbia, MD 21046		
kherr@integ.com		

The Kroger Company

A supermarket chain and convenience store operator.
www.kroger.com
Annual Revenues: $109.83 billion
Employees: 431,000
Ticker: NYSE: KR
SIC: 5411; 2026; 2051; 5099
Industry/ies: Food And Beverage Industry
Legislative Issues: AGR; TAX

| **Chairman and Chief Executive Officer** | Tel: | (513) 762-4000 |
| MCMULLEN, W. Rodney | Fax: | (513) 762-1160 |

Main Headquarters

Mailing:	1014 Vine St.	Tel:	(513) 762-4000
	Cincinnati, OH 45202	Fax:	(513) 762-1160
		TF:	(800) 576-4377

Political Action Committees
Kroger PAC
FEC ID: C00059238
Contact: Janet Ausdenmoore
1014 Vine St.
Cincinnati, OH 45202

  Contributions to Candidates: $32,750 (2015-2016)
  Democrats: $4,750; Republicans: $28,000

Corporate Foundations and Giving Programs

The Kroger Company Foundation
1014 Vine St.
Cincinnati, OH 45202

Public Affairs and Related Activities Personnel

At Headquarters

WHEATLEY, Christine S.	Tel:	(513) 762-4000
Group Vice President, Secretary and General Counsel	Fax:	(513) 762-1160
ADELMAN, Jessica C.	Tel:	(513) 762-4000
Group Vice President, Corporate Affairs	Fax:	(513) 762-1160
AUSDENMOORE, Janet	Tel:	(513) 762-4999
PAC Treasurer	Fax:	(513) 762-1295
janet.ausdenmoore@kroger.com		
CULL, Brendon	Tel:	(513) 762-4441
Senior Director, Government Relations	Fax:	(513) 762-1160
brendon.cull@kroger.com		
Registered Federal Lobbyist		
DAILEY, Keith	Tel:	(513) 762-1304
Director, Media Relations and Corporate Communications	Fax:	(513) 762-1160
FIKE, Carin	Tel:	(513) 762-4969
Director and Assistant Treasurer	Fax:	(513) 762-1295
HOLMES, Cindy	Tel:	(513) 762-4000
Senior Director, Pension Investments	Fax:	(513) 762-1160
HUDDLESTON, Gary	Tel:	(972) 785-6004
Director, Consumer Affairs	Fax:	(513) 762-1160
gary.huddleston@kroger.com		
MARMER, Lynn	Tel:	(513) 762-4441
Group Vice President, Corporate Affairs	Fax:	(513) 762-1160
lynn.marmer@kroger.com		
Registered Federal Lobbyist		
MASSA, Timothy A.	Tel:	(513) 762-4000
Group Vice President of Human Resources and Labor Relations	Fax:	(513) 762-1160
SCHLOTMAN, J. Michael	Tel:	(513) 762-4000
Senior Vice President and Chief Financial Officer	Fax:	(513) 762-1160

Ktech Corporation

An employee-owned company that provides technical support services, scientific and engineering work, and management expertise to government and industry clients.
www.ktech.com
Annual Revenues: $30 million
Employees: 400
Industry/ies: Defense/Homeland Security; Energy/Electricity; Government-Related; Military/Veterans
Legislative Issues: BUD; DEF

President, Chairman and Chief Executive Officer	Tel:	(505) 998-5830
DOWNIE, Steven E.	Fax:	(505) 998-6059
downie@ktech.com		

Main Headquarters

Mailing:	1300 Eubank Blvd. SE	Tel:	(505) 998-5830
	Albuquerque, NM 87123	Fax:	(505) 998-6059

Public Affairs and Related Activities Personnel

At Headquarters

CANDELARIA, Arturo	Tel:	(505) 998-5830
Manager, Human Resources	Fax:	(505) 998-6059
acandelaria@ktech.com		
WOMACK, Ronald W.	Tel:	(505) 998-5830
Vice President and Chief Financial Officer	Fax:	(505) 998-6059
rwomack@ktech.com		

L Brands

Formerly knows as Limited Brands, Inc. An international specialty fashion retailer. Stores include Express, Victoria's Secret, and Bath and Body Works, among others.
www.lb.com
Annual Revenues: $11.45 billion
Employees: 20,200
Ticker: NYSE: LB
SIC: 5621
Industry/ies: Apparel/Textiles Industry; Retail/Wholesale
Legislative Issues: TAX

Chairman of the Board and Chief Executive Officer	Tel:	(614) 415-7000
WEXNER, Leslie H.	Fax:	(614) 415-7440

Main Headquarters

Mailing:	Three Limited Pkwy.	Tel:	(614) 415-7000
	Columbus, OH 43230	Fax:	(614) 415-7440

Political Action Committees

Limited Brands Inc. PAC
FEC ID: C00214338
Contact: Theodore Adams
Three Limited Pkwy.
Columbus, OH 43230

Contributions to Candidates: $62,000 (2015-2016)
Democrats: $9,500; Republicans: $50,500; Other: $2,000

Corporate Foundations and Giving Programs

Limited Brands Foundation
Contact: Janelle Simmons
Three Limited Pkwy.
Columbus, OH 43230

Public Affairs and Related Activities Personnel

At Headquarters

ADAMS, Theodore	Tel:	(614) 415-7972
Vice President, Government Affairs and PAC Contact	Fax:	(614) 415-7440
BURGDOERFER, Stuart	Tel:	(614) 415-7000
Executive Vice President and Chief Financial Officer	Fax:	(614) 415-7440
FIELDS, Rhoe	Tel:	(614) 415-7000
Senior Specialist, Government Affairs	Fax:	(614) 415-7440
rpfields@limitedbrands.com		
FRIED, Samuel	Tel:	(614) 415-7000
Executive Vice President, Law, Policy and Governance	Fax:	(614) 415-7440
MYERS, Tammy Roberts	Tel:	(800) 945-5088
Vice President, External Communications	Fax:	(614) 415-7786
communications@lb.com		
PRESTON, Amie	Tel:	(614) 415-6704
Contact, Investor Relations	Fax:	(614) 415-7786
RAMSEY, Jane L.	Tel:	(614) 415-7000
Executive Vice President, Human Resources	Fax:	(614) 415-7440
SIMMONS, Janelle	Tel:	(614) 415-7000
Contact, Philanthropy	Fax:	(614) 415-7440

L-3 Chesapeake Sciences Corporation

Engaged in designing and manufacturing of electronic data acquisition systems. Acquired by L-3 Corporation.
www.csciences.com
Annual Revenues: $7.80 million
Employees: 100
Industry/ies: Defense/Homeland Security; Government-Related; Science; Scientific Research
Legislative Issues: BUD; DEF

President	Tel:	(410) 923-1300
MCDARIS, John	Fax:	(410) 923-2669

Main Headquarters

Mailing:	1121H Benfield Blvd.	Tel:	(410) 923-1300
	Millersville, MD 21108	Fax:	(410) 923-2669

L-3 Communications Corporation

Provides technolgy solutions to clients specializing in communications, information technology, and other high technology products.
www.L-3com.com
Annual Revenues: $11.88 billion
Employees: 45,000
Ticker: NYSE: LLL
SIC: 3812; 3827; 3825; 3769; 3823
NAICS: 334511; 336419; 334413; 334515; 334513
Industry/ies: Aerospace/Aviation; Transportation
Legislative Issues: AER; AVI; BUD; DEF; HOM; TRA; TRD

Chairman of the Board, President and Chief Executive Officer	Tel:	(212) 697-1111
STRIANESE, Michael T.	Fax:	(212) 867-5249

Main Headquarters

Mailing:	600 Third Ave.	Tel:	(212) 697-1111
	New York City, NY 10016	Fax:	(212) 490-0731

Washington Office

Mailing:	201 12th St., South	Tel:	(703) 412-7190
	Suite 800		
	Arlington, VA 22202		

Political Action Committees

L-3 Communications Corporation PAC
FEC ID: C00338087
Contact: Stephen M. Souza
600 Third Ave.   Tel: (703) 412-7190
New York City, NY 10016

Contributions to Candidates: $354,500 (2015-2016)
Democrats: $103,000; Republicans: $251,500

Principal Recipients

HOUSE
CARTER, JOHN R. REP. (REP-DC)
ROGERS, HAROLD DALLAS (REP-KY)

Public Affairs and Related Activities Personnel

At Headquarters

BARCHIE, Paul F.	Tel:	(212) 697-1111

Vice President & Assistant General Counsel

BRUNSON, Curtis	Tel:	(212) 697-1111
Executive Vice President, Corporate Strategy and Development	Fax:	(212) 805-5477
COTTRELL, John	Tel:	(212) 697-1111
Federal Lobbyist	Fax:	(212) 805-5477
john.cottrell@L-3com.com		
D'AMBROSIO, Ralph G.	Tel:	(212) 697-1111
Senior Vice President and Chief Financial Officer	Fax:	(212) 805-5477
MALATESTA, Gino	Tel:	(212) 697-1111
Corporate Vice President, Planning	Fax:	(212) 805-5477
POST, Steven M.	Tel:	(212) 697-1111
Senior Vice President, General Counsel and Corporate Secretary	Fax:	(212) 805-5477
SOUZA, Stephen M.	Tel:	(212) 697-1111
PAC Treasurer	Fax:	(212) 867-5249
SWAIN, Cynthia	Tel:	(212) 697-1111
Vice President, Corporate Communications	Fax:	(212) 867-5249

At Washington Office

BARCHIE, Paul F.	Tel:	(703) 412-7190
Vice President & Assistant General Counsel		
BRAUNSTEIN, Matthew	Tel:	(703) 412-7190
Vice President, Government Affairs		
CODY, Richard A.	Tel:	(703) 412-7190
Senior Vice President, Washington Operations		
DRESSENDORFER, John H.	Tel:	(703) 412-7190
Vice President, Government Relations		
NICHOLSON, Ben		
Federal Lobbyist		
Registered Federal Lobbyist		
TINDAL, D'Anna	Tel:	(703) 412-7190
Vice President, Government Relations		
Registered Federal Lobbyist		
WAHL, Frederick	Tel:	(703) 412-7190
Vice President, Government Relations		
Registered Federal Lobbyist		

L.L. Bean, Inc.

A manufacturer and retailer of outdoor apparel and gear.
www.llbean.com
Employees: 4,600
SIC: 3199; 2394; 3161
NAICS: 316999; 314912; 316991
Industry/ies: Apparel/Textiles Industry

President and Chief Executive Officer	Tel:	(207) 552-3028
MCCORMICK, Christopher J.	Fax:	(207) 552-6821
cmccormick@llbean.com		

Main Headquarters

Mailing:	15 Casco St.	Tel:	(207) 552-3028
	Freeport, ME 04033-0001	Fax:	(207) 552-3080
		TF:	(800) 441-5713

Corporate Foundations and Giving Programs

L.L.Bean Charitable Giving Program
Three Campus Dr.
Freeport, ME 04033

Public Affairs and Related Activities Personnel

At Headquarters

BEEM, Carolyn	Tel:	(207) 552-6022
Manager, Public Affairs	Fax:	(207) 552-6821
cbeem@llbean.com		
OLIVER, John	Tel:	(207) 552-6072
Vice President, Public Affairs	Fax:	(207) 552-6821
joliver@llbean.com		

La Quinta Inns, Inc.

A hotel chain.
www.laquinta.com
Employees: 9,000
SIC: 7011
Industry/ies: Travel/Tourism/Lodging

Chairman of the Board	Tel:	(214) 492-6600
PERLSTEIN, William J.	Fax:	(214) 492-6616

President and Chief Executive Officer	Tel:	(214) 492-6600
GOLDBERG, Wayne B.	Fax:	(214) 492-6616

Main Headquarters

Mailing:	909 Hidden Ridge	Tel:	(214) 492-6600
	Suite 600	Fax:	(214) 492-6616
	Irving, TX 75038	TF:	(800) 753-3757

Public Affairs and Related Activities Personnel

At Headquarters

CARY, Julie M.	Tel:	(214) 492-6600
Executive Vice President and Chief Marketing Officer	Fax:	(214) 492-6616
CHLOUPEK, Mark M.	Tel:	(214) 492-6600
Executive Vice President and General Counsel	Fax:	(214) 492-6616
CLINE, Keith A.	Tel:	(214) 492-6600
Executive Vice President and Chief Financial Officer	Fax:	(214) 492-6616
COOPER, Donna R.	Tel:	(214) 492-6600
Executive Vice President, Sales	Fax:	(214) 492-6616
FERGUSON, Teresa	Tel:	(214) 492-6937
Director, Communications and Public Relations	Fax:	(214) 492-6616
teresa.ferguson@laquinta.com		
FRENKEL, Michael	Tel:	(212) 808-6559
Contact, Media Relations	Fax:	(214) 492-6616
michael@mfcpr.com		
SALAZAR, Susan	Tel:	(214) 492-6600
Executive Vice President and Chief People Officer	Fax:	(214) 492-6616

La-Z-Boy Inc.

A manufacturer of furniture.
www.la-z-boy.com
Annual Revenues: $1.43 billion
Employees: 8,270
Ticker: NYSE: LZB
SIC: 2510; 2511; 2512; 2515; 2521
NAICS: 337121; 337122; 337211
Industry/ies: Furniture/Home Furnishings

Chairman of the Board, President and Chief Executive Officer	Tel:	(734) 242-1444
DARROW, Kurt L.	Fax:	(734) 457-2005

Main Headquarters

Mailing:	One La-Z-Boy Dr.	Tel:	(734) 242-1444
	Monroe, MI 48162	Fax:	(734) 457-2005

Corporate Foundations and Giving Programs

La-Z-Boy Foundation
Contact: Donald Blohm
1284 N. Telegraph Rd.   Tel: (734) 241-3680
Monroe, MI 48162

Public Affairs and Related Activities Personnel

At Headquarters

BLOHM, Donald	Tel:	(734) 242-1444
Administrator, La-Z-Boy Foundation	Fax:	(734) 457-2005
HELLEBUYCK, Amy	Tel:	(734) 384-6221
Manager, Brand Marketing and Public Relations	Fax:	(734) 457-2005
Amy.Hellebuyck@la-z-boy.com		
LIEBMANN, Kathy	Tel:	(734) 242-1444
Director, Investor Relations and Corporate Communications	Fax:	(734) 457-2005
kathy.liebmann@la-z-boy.com		
MEYER, Billy	Tel:	(734) 242-1444
Director, Employee Relations	Fax:	(734) 457-2005
QUINN, Shannon	Tel:	(312) 565-3900
Media Contact	Fax:	(734) 457-2005
RICCIO, Jr., Louis Mike	Tel:	(734) 242-1444
Senior Vice President and Chief Financial Officer	Fax:	(734) 457-2005

Labor and Employment Strategies, LLC

Industry/ies: Employees & Employment

Main Headquarters

Mailing:	819 Massachusetts Ave. NE	Tel:	(202) 546-6832
	Washington, DC 20002		

Public Affairs and Related Activities Personnel

At Headquarters

BOLLES, Kenneth A.	Tel:	(202) 546-6832
kenneth.bolles@vertzon.net		

Labor Ready, Inc.

See listing on page 801 under TrueBlue Inc.

Laboratory Corporation of America

Operates nationwide laboratories that perform diagnostic tests for physicians, health care organizations, industrial companies, and other clinical laboratories.
www.labcorp.com/wps/portal
Annual Revenues: $6.35 billion
Employees: 36,000
Ticker: NYSE: LH
SIC: 8071
Industry/ies: Medicine/Health Care/Mental Health; Science; Scientific Research
Legislative Issues: HCR

Chairman of the Board, President and Chief Executive Officer   Tel: (336) 584-5171
KING, David P.   Fax: (336) 436-1205

Main Headquarters
Mailing: 531 S. Spring St.   Tel: (336) 436-5274
Burlington, NC 27215   Fax: (336) 436-1569

Corporate Foundations and Giving Programs
Laboratory Corporation of America Contributions Program
531 S. Spring St.
Burlington, NC 27215

Public Affairs and Related Activities Personnel

At Headquarters

AYOTTE, Tiana G.   Tel: (336) 436-5010
Senior Vice President, Associate General Counsel   Fax: (336) 436-1569
tayotte@labcorp.com

MACY, Anne D.   Tel: (336) 436-5274
Investor Relations and Media Contact   Fax: (336) 436-1569

SURDEZ, Paul   Tel: (336) 436-5076
Vice President, Investor Relations   Fax: (336) 436-1569

At Other Offices

EBERTS, III, F. Samuel   Tel: (336) 229-1127
Senior Vice President and Chief Legal Officer   Fax: (336) 436-1205
358 S. Main St.
Burlington, NC 27215

STARR, Lisa Hoffman   Tel: (336) 229-1127
Senior Vice President, Human Resources   Fax: (336) 436-1205
231 Maple Ave.
Burlington, NC 27215

Laclede Gas Company
See listing on page 479 under The Laclede Group

The Laclede Group
Formerly known as Laclede Gas Co. A gas distribution company.
www.thelacledegroup.com
Employees: 3,078
Ticker: NYSE: LG
SIC: 4924
Industry/ies: Energy/Electricity; Natural Resources

Chairman of the Board   Tel: (314) 342-0873
GLOTZBACH, Edward L.   Fax: (314) 421-1979

President and Chief Executive Officer   Tel: (314) 342-0500
SITHERWOOD, Suzanne   Fax: (314) 421-1979

Main Headquarters
Mailing: 700 Market St.   Tel: (314) 342-0873
St. Louis, MO 63101   Fax: (314) 421-1979

Corporate Foundations and Giving Programs
The Laclede Group Foundation
720 Olive St.   Tel: (314) 342-0873
Room 1517   Fax: (314) 421-1979
St. Louis, MO 63101

Public Affairs and Related Activities Personnel

At Headquarters

DARRELL, Mark C.   Tel: (314) 342-0873
Senior Vice President, General Counsel and Chief   Fax: (314) 421-1979
Compliance Officer

DOWDY, L. Craig   Tel: (314) 342-0873
Senior Vice President, External Affairs, Corporate   Fax: (314) 421-1979
Communications and Marketing

DUDLEY, Scott W.   Tel: (314) 342-0878
Director, Investor Relations   Fax: (314) 421-1979
Scott.Dudley@thelacledegroup.com

GEISELHART, Michael C.   Tel: (314) 342-0500
Vice President, Strategic Development and Planning   Fax: (314) 421-1979

KULLMAN, Mary Caola   Tel: (314) 342-0873
Senior Vice President, Chief Administrative Officer and   Fax: (314) 421-1979
Corporate Secretary
mkullman@lacledegas.com

LINDSEY, Steven L.   Tel: (314) 342-0873
Executive Vice President, Chief Operating Officer,   Fax: (314) 421-1979
Distribution Operations

RASCHE, Steven P.   Tel: (314) 342-0577
Executive Vice President, Chief Financial Officer and   Fax: (314) 421-1979
Contact, Investor Relations
srasche@lacledegas.com

Lafarge North America Inc.
A producer of construction materials. Lafarge North America is part of global building conglomerate Lafarge Group, based in France.
www.lafarge-na.com

Annual Revenues: $1.46 billion
Employees: 17,000
SIC: 3275; 1422; 3241; 3272; 3273
NAICS: 32742; 32739; 32732; 32731; 212312
Industry/ies: Construction/Construction Materials
Legislative Issues: BUD; CDT; ENV; LBR; MAN; TAX; TRA; TRD

Main Headquarters
Mailing: 8700 W. Bryn Mawr Ave.   Tel: (773) 372-1000
Suite 300
Chicago, IL 60631

Washington Office
Mailing: 13450 Sunrise Valley Dr.   Tel: (703) 480-3600
Suite 220
Herndon, VA 20171

Political Action Committees
Lafarge North America Inc Political Action Committee
FEC ID: C00431007
Contact: Michael LeMonds
12018 Sunrise Valley Dr.   Tel: (703) 480-3600
Suite 500   Fax: (703) 796-2219
Reston, VA 20191

   Contributions to Candidates: $12,500 (2015-2016)
   Democrats: $2,500; Republicans: $10,000

Corporate Foundations and Giving Programs
Lafarge Foundation
12018 Sunrise Valley Dr.   Tel: (703) 480-3600
Suite 500
Reston, VA 20191

Public Affairs and Related Activities Personnel

At Headquarters

JWEIED, Serene   Tel: (703) 480-6647
Director, Communications

LIPSKI-ROCKWOOD, Joëlle   Tel: (303) 895-0455
Director of Communications, United States
joelle.lipski-rockwood@lafarge.com

WINTERS, Hicks   Tel: (773) 372-1000
Registered Federal Lobbyist

At Washington Office

LEMONDS, Michael   Tel: (703) 480-3600
Director, Government & Public Affairs
Michael.LeMonds@Lafarge-na.com
Registered Federal Lobbyist

At Other Offices

CAMPBELL, Craig   Tel: (703) 480-3600
VicePresident, Environment and Public Affairs   Fax: (703) 796-9516
12018 Sunrise Valley Dr., Suite 500
Reston, VA 20191
Registered Federal Lobbyist

Lam Research Corporation
A supplier of wafer fabrication equipment and services to the world's semiconductor industry.
www.lamrc.com
Annual Revenues: $5.03 billion
Employees: 7,000
Ticker: NASDAQ: LRCX
SIC: 3559
Industry/ies: Energy/Electricity; Machinery/Equipment

Chairman of the Board   Tel: (510) 572-0200
NEWBERRY, Stephen G.   Fax: (510) 572-2935

President and Chief Executive Officer   Tel: (510) 572-0200
ANSTICE, Martin   Fax: (510) 572-2935

Main Headquarters
Mailing: 4650 Cushing Pkwy.   Tel: (510) 572-0200
Fremont, CA 94538   Fax: (510) 572-2935
   TF: (800) 526-7678

Corporate Foundations and Giving Programs
Lam Research Corporation Contribution Program
P.O. Box 5010   Tel: (510) 572-0200
Fremont, CA 94536   Fax: (510) 572-2935

Public Affairs and Related Activities Personnel

At Headquarters

ARCHER, Tim   Tel: (510) 572-0200
Chief Operating Officer   Fax: (510) 572-2935

BETTINGER, Doug   Tel: (510) 572-0200
Executive Vice President and Chief Financial Officer   Fax: (510) 572-2935

BULTMAN, Gary   Tel: (510) 572-0200
Senior Vice President Strategic Development, Corporate   Fax: (510) 572-2935
Marketing and Communications

GARBER, Lisa   Tel: (510) 572-0200

Managing Director, Corporate Communications
lisa.garber@lamresearch.com

	Fax:	(510) 572-2935
GOTTSCHO, Richard A.	Tel:	(510) 572-0200
Executive Vice President, Global Products Group	Fax:	(510) 572-2935
richard.gottscho@lamrc.com		
HUDSON, Shanye	Tel:	(510) 572-4589
Senior Director, Investor Relations	Fax:	(510) 572-2935
shanye.hudson@lamresearch.com		
KEMBLE , Terese	Tel:	(510) 572-0200
Senior Vice President, Human Resources	Fax:	(510) 572-2935
O'DOWD , Sarah	Tel:	(510) 572-0200
Senior Vice President and Chief Legal Officer	Fax:	(510) 572-2935

Lamar Advertising Company

Founded in 1902. Owns and operates outdoor advertising and logo structures. It also sells advertising space on almost 30,000 signs placed on buses and at bus stops in more than 15 states, and it maintains more than 100,000 logo signs (highway exit signs with logos of nearby hotels and restaurants).
www.lamar.com
Annual Revenues: $1.39 billion
Employees: 3,200
Ticker: NASDAQ: LAMR
SIC: 7311
NAICS: 339950
Industry/ies: Advertising And Marketing

President and Chairman of the Board	Tel:	(225) 926-1000
REILLY, Jr., Kevin P.	Fax:	(225) 926-1005
Chief Executive Officer	Tel:	(225) 926-1000
REILLY, Sean	Fax:	(225) 926-0492

Main Headquarters

Mailing:	P.O. Box 66338	Tel:	(225) 926-1000
	Baton Rouge, LA 70896	Fax:	(225) 926-1005
		TF:	(800) 235-2627

Political Action Committees
Lamar Corporation PAC (LAMARPAC)
FEC ID: C00174599
Contact: Keith A. Istre

P.O. Box 66338	Tel:	(225) 926-1000
Baton Rouge, LA 70896	Fax:	(225) 926-1005

Contributions to Candidates: $59,500 (2015-2016)
Democrats: $14,000; Republicans: $45,500

Principal Recipients

SENATE
BOUSTANY, CHARLES W JR DR (REP-LA)

HOUSE
BOUSTANY, CHARLES W. DR. JR. (REP-LA)

Public Affairs and Related Activities Personnel

At Headquarters

DUNCAN, Tammy	Tel:	(225) 926-1000
Vice President, Human Resources	Fax:	(225) 926-1192
tduncan@lamar.com		
ISTRE, Keith A.	Tel:	(225) 926-1000
Treasurer and Chief Financial Officer	Fax:	(225) 923-0658
KI@lamar.com		
KILSHAW, Hal	Tel:	(225) 926-1000
Vice President, Governmental Relations	Fax:	(225) 923-0658
hkilshaw@lamar.com		
MCILWAIN, James R.	Tel:	(225) 926-1000
Secretary and General Counsel	Fax:	(225) 924-3400
jmcilwain@lamar.com		
MCILWAIN, Jim	Tel:	(225) 926-1000
Secretary and General Counsel	Fax:	(225) 926-1005
SWITZER, Robert	Tel:	(225) 926-1000
Vice President, Operations	Fax:	(225) 926-1005
TEEPELL, Thomas F.	Tel:	(225) 926-1000
Chief Marketing Officer	Fax:	(225) 216-9816
tteepell@lamar.com		

At Other Offices

MILLER, John	Tel:	(225) 926-1000
Vice President, Director of National Sales		
5321 Corporate Blvd.		
Baton Rouge, LA 70808		

Lance Inc.

See listing on page 728 under Snyder's-Lance

Land O'Lakes

See listing on page 480 under Land O'Lakes Inc.

Land O'Lakes Inc.

Land O'Lakes, Inc. is member-owned cooperative. It offers local cooperatives and agricultural producers across the nation an extensive line of agricultural supplies, as well as state-of-the-art production and business services. It is also a leading marketer of dairy-based food products for consumers, foodservice professionals and food manufacturers.
www.landolakesinc.com
Annual Revenues: $15 Billion
Employees: 9,000
SIC: 2023
NAICS: 326199
Industry/ies: Food And Beverage Industry
Legislative Issues: AGR; BUD; CAW; FOO; FOR; IMM; NAT; RET; TRD

Chairman of the Board	Tel:	(651) 481-2222
KAPPELMAN, Peter	Fax:	(651) 481-2000
President and Chief Executive Officer	Tel:	(651) 481-2222
POLICINSKI, Christopher	Fax:	(651) 481-2000

Main Headquarters

Mailing:	P.O. Box 64101	Tel:	(651) 481-2222
	St. Paul, MN 55164-0101	Fax:	(651) 481-2000
		TF:	(800) 328-9680

Political Action Committees
Land O'Lakes, Inc., PAC
FEC ID: C00009423
Contact: Karen Grabow

P.O. Box 64101	Tel:	(651) 481-2222
St. Paul, MN 55164-0101	Fax:	(651) 481-2000

Contributions to Candidates: $233,700 (2015-2016)
Democrats: $68,500; Republicans: $165,200

Principal Recipients

HOUSE
PETERSON, COLLIN CLARK (DEM-MN)
VALADAO, DAVID (REP-CA)

Corporate Foundations and Giving Programs
Lake O'Lakes Foundation
Contact: Lydia Botham

P.O. Box 64101	Tel:	(651) 481-2470
St. Paul, MN 55164	Fax:	(651) 481-2470

Public Affairs and Related Activities Personnel

At Headquarters

BOTHAM, Lydia	Tel:	(651) 481-2222
Executive Director, Land O'Lakes Foundation	Fax:	(651) 481-2000
lrbotham@landolakes.com		
BROOKS, Dana	Tel:	(651) 481-2222
Senior Director, Government Relations & Industry Affairs	Fax:	(651) 481-2000
Registered Federal Lobbyist		
FIFE, Jim	Tel:	(651) 481-2222
Executive Vice President, Ag Businesses	Fax:	(651) 481-2000
FORD, Beth	Tel:	(651) 481-2222
Executive Vice President, Chief Supply Chain and Operations	Fax:	(651) 481-2000
Officer		
GRABOW, Karen	Tel:	(651) 481-2222
Senior Vice President, Business Development Services and	Fax:	(651) 481-2000
PAC Treasurer		
HEERINGA, Loren	Tel:	(651) 481-2222
Senior Vice President and Chief Human Resources Officer	Fax:	(651) 481-2000
LMHeeringa@landolakes.com		
JANZEN, Peter	Tel:	(651) 481-2222
Senior Vice President, General Counsel and Chief	Fax:	(651) 481-2000
Administrative Officer		
KAMINSKI, Jerry	Tel:	(651) 481-2222
Executive Vice President and Chief Operations Officer,	Fax:	(651) 481-2000
International		
KNUTSON, Dan	Tel:	(651) 481-2222
Executive Vice President and Chief Financial Officer	Fax:	(651) 481-2000
MCBETH, Daryn	Tel:	(651) 481-2222
Director, State Government Affairs and Industry Relations	Fax:	(651) 481-2000
RAUCHBAUER, DeeDee	Tel:	(651) 481-2222
Community Relations Supervisor	Fax:	(651) 481-2000
DJRauchbauer@landolakes.com		
SCOTT, Tim	Tel:	(651) 481-2222
Senior Vice President and Chief Marketing Officer	Fax:	(651) 481-2000
VEAZEY, Autumn	Tel:	(651) 481-2222
Director, Government Relations	Fax:	(651) 481-2000
Registered Federal Lobbyist		
WOLFISH, Barry	Tel:	(651) 481-2222
Senior Vice President, Mergers & Acquisitions and Ventures	Fax:	(651) 481-2000
ZENK, Katie	Tel:	(651) 481-2222
Government Relations Specialist and Government Relations	Fax:	(651) 481-2000
Liaison		

Registered Federal Lobbyist

LandAir Project Resources, Inc.

Landair Project Resources Inc. helps organizations to achieve their real estate business plan goals and maximize their institutional strengths.
www.landairprojectresources.com
Annual Revenues: $1.63 million
Employees: 10
Industry/ies: Banking/Finance/Investments; Economics And Economic Development; Government-Related; Real Estate

Chairman of the Board　Tel:　(212) 685-9680
WEBBER, Sr., William P.　Fax:　(212) 685-9685

President and Chief Executive Officer　Tel:　(212) 685-9680
MEULEN, Leith ter　Fax:　(212) 685-9685
leith@projectresourcesgroup.com

Main Headquarters
Mailing:　39 W. 32nd St.　Tel:　(212) 685-9680
　　　　Suite 1402　Fax:　(212) 685-9685
　　　　New York City, NY 10001

Public Affairs and Related Activities Personnel
At Headquarters
HENRIQUES, Beth　Tel:　(212) 685-9680
Vice President, Professional Services　Fax:　(212) 685-9685
bhenriques@projectresourcesgroup.com

At Other Offices
FLORES, Leonardis　Tel:　(212) 685-9680
Comptroller　Fax:　(212) 685-9685
Ten E. 33rd St.
New York City, NY 10016

ROSENBAUM, Elisabeth　Tel:　(212) 685-9680
President　Fax:　(212) 685-9685
Ten E. 33rd St.
New York City, NY 10016

Landmark Communications, Inc.

A company engaged in newspaper publishing, broadcasting and cable programming.
landmarkcommunications.net
Annual Revenues: $1.75 billion
Employees: 12,000
Industry/ies: Communications; Media/Mass Communication

President　Tel:　(770) 813-1000
ROUNTREE, Mark

Main Headquarters
Mailing:　11300 Atlantis Pl.　Tel:　(770) 813-1000
　　　　Suite F
　　　　Alpharetta, GA 30022

Public Affairs and Related Activities Personnel
At Headquarters
SEIGLE, Mike　Tel:　(770) 813-1000
Director, Research and Database Management

At Other Offices
DOWNEY, Richard　Tel:　(403) 225-7357
Senior Director, Investor Relations　Fax:　(757) 446-2489
P.O. Box 449
Norfolk, VA 23510

FRIDDELL, III, Guy　Tel:　(757) 446-2010
Executive Vice President, Corporate Secretary and General　Fax:　(757) 446-2489
Counsel
P.O. Box 449
Norfolk, VA 23510

Landstar System Inc.

A non-asset based transportation and logistics services company.
www.landstar.com
Annual Revenues: $3.26 billion
Employees: 1,211
Ticker: NASDAQ: LSTR
SIC: 4213
Industry/ies: Transportation

President and Chief Executive Officer　Tel:　(904) 398-9400
GATTONI, Jim B.　Fax:　(904) 390-1437
jgattoni@landstar.com

Main Headquarters
Mailing:　13410 Sutton Park Dr., South　Tel:　(904) 398-9400
　　　　Jacksonville Beach, FL 32224　Fax:　(904) 390-1437
　　　　　　　　　　　　　　　　　TF:　(800) 872-9400

Corporate Foundations and Giving Programs
Landstar Scholarship Fund
Contact: Roberta S. Lee

13410 Sutton Park Dr., South　Tel:　(904) 398-9400
Jacksonville Beach, FL 32224

Public Affairs and Related Activities Personnel
At Headquarters
BEACOM, Joe　Tel:　(904) 398-9400
Vice President, Chief Safety and Operations Officer　Fax:　(904) 390-1437
KNELLER, Michael　Tel:　(904) 398-9400
Vice President, General Counsel and Secretary　Fax:　(904) 390-1437
LEE, Roberta S.　Tel:　(904) 398-9400
Foundation Contact　Fax:　(904) 390-1437
MCMENAMIN, Patricia　Tel:　(904) 390-1230
Vice President, Corporate Communications　Fax:　(904) 390-1437
O'MALLEY, Patrick　Tel:　(904) 398-9400
Vice President and Chief Commercial and Marketing Officer　Fax:　(904) 390-1437
STOUT, Kevin　Tel:　(904) 398-9400
Vice President and Chief Financial Officer　Fax:　(904) 390-1437
TAYLOR, Stacey　Tel:　(904) 390-1530
Manager, Investor Relations　Fax:　(904) 390-1437
staylor@landstar.com
WHITCHER, Ginger　Tel:　(904) 390-1457
Director, Corporate Communications　Fax:　(904) 390-1437
gwhitcher@landstar.com

Lanxess Corporation

Chemical manufacturer of plastics, pigments, and rubber compounds.
www.us.lanxess.com
Employees: 1,600
Industry/ies: Chemicals & Chemical Industry
Legislative Issues: ENG; TRA

President and Chief Executive Officer　Tel:　(412) 809-1000
BJOERNSLEV, Flemming B.　Fax:　(412) 809-3599

Main Headquarters
Mailing:　111 RIDC Park W. Dr.　Tel:　(412) 809-1000
　　　　Pittsburgh, PA 15275-1112　Fax:　(412) 809-3599
　　　　　　　　　　　　　　　　　TF:　(800) 526-9377

Public Affairs and Related Activities Personnel
At Headquarters
FITZPATRICK, Terri　Tel:　(412) 809-1516
Vice President, Communications　Fax:　(412) 809-3603
terri.fitzpatrick@lanxess.com

Las Vegas Sands Corporation

A hotel and casino company.
sands.com
Annual Revenues: $11.39 billion
Employees: 46,500
Ticker: NYSE: LVS
SIC: 7011
Industry/ies: Sports/Leisure/Entertainment; Travel/Tourism/Lodging
Legislative Issues: BUD; GAM

Chairman of the Board and Chief Executive Officer　Tel:　(702) 414-1000
ADELSON, Sheldon G.　Fax:　(702) 414-4884

Main Headquarters
Mailing:　3355 Las Vegas Blvd., South　Tel:　(702) 414-1000
　　　　Las Vegas, NV 89109-8941　Fax:　(702) 414-4884

Corporate Foundations and Giving Programs
Sands Foundation
3355 Las Vegas Blvd., South　Tel:　(702) 414-1000
Las Vegas, NV 89109　Fax:　(702) 414-4884

Public Affairs and Related Activities Personnel
At Headquarters
BRIGGS, Daniel J.　Tel:　(702) 414-1221
Senior Vice President, Investor Relations　Fax:　(702) 414-4884
DUMONT, Patrick　Tel:　(702) 414-1000
Executive Vice President and Chief Financial Officer　Fax:　(702) 414-4884
GOLDSTEIN, Robert G.　Tel:　(702) 414-1000
President and Chief Operating Officer　Fax:　(702) 414-4884
RAPHAELSON, Ira H.　Tel:　(702) 414-1000
Executive Vice President and Global General Counsel　Fax:　(702) 414-4884
REESE, Ron　Tel:　(702) 414-3607
Vice President, Communications　Fax:　(702) 414-4884

Latona Associates, Inc.

A financial services firm.
www.latonaassociates.com
Annual Revenues: $4.80 million
Employees: 20
Industry/ies: Banking/Finance/Investments

Chairman of the Board
MONTRONE, Paul

Tel: (603) 929-2607
Fax: (603) 929-2531

Main Headquarters
Mailing: One Liberty Ln.
           Hampton, NH 03842

Tel: (603) 926-5911
Fax: (603) 929-2531

Public Affairs and Related Activities Personnel

At Headquarters

ANNINO, Anthony
PAC Contact

Tel: (603) 929-2204
Fax: (603) 929-2531

Laureate Education

An education services company.
www.laureate.net
Annual Revenues: $2 billion
Employees: 23,000
SIC: 8200
Industry/ies: Education
Legislative Issues: TRD

Founder, Chairman of the Board and Chief Executive Officer
BECKER, Douglas L.

Tel: (410) 843-6100

Main Headquarters
Mailing: 650 S. Exeter St.
           Baltimore, MD 21202-4382

Tel: (410) 843-6100
TF: (866) 452-8732

Corporate Foundations and Giving Programs

Sylvan/Laureate Foundation
Contact: Carol Maivelett
650 S. Exeter St.
Baltimore, MD 21202

Tel: (410) 843-6100

Public Affairs and Related Activities Personnel

At Headquarters

EPSTEIN, Debra
Vice President, Corporate Communications
debra.epstein@laureate.net

Tel: (443) 627-7763

MAIVELETT, Carol
Foundation Administrator
carol.maivelett@laureate.net

Tel: (410) 843-6100

MARTINEZ, Alfonso
Chief Human Resource Officer

Tel: (410) 843-6100

NICKEL, Daniel M.
Executive Vice President, Corporate Operations

Tel: (410) 843-6100

SERCK-HANSSEN, Eilif
Executive Vice President and Chief Financial Officer

Tel: (410) 843-6100

YALE, Matthew
Senior Vice President, Global Communications and Public Affairs
Matthew.Yale@laureate.net

Tel: (305) 808-2922

ZENTZ, Robert W.
Senior Vice President and General Counsel
robert.zentz@laureate-inc.com

Tel: (410) 843-6100

Lazard Group LLC

A financial advisory and asset management firm. It offers various financial advisory services on mergers and acquisitions, and other strategic matters, as well as on restructurings, capital structure, capital raising, other financial matters and provides investment solutions and investment management services in equity and fixed income strategies.
www.lazard.com
Annual Revenues: $2.27 billion
Employees: 2,629
Ticker: NYSE: LAZ
SIC: 6282
Industry/ies: Banking/Finance/Investments
Legislative Issues: FIN

Chairman and Chief Executive Officer
JACOBS, Kenneth M.

Tel: (212) 632-6000
Fax: (302) 655-5049

Main Headquarters
Mailing: 30 Rockefeller Plaza
           New York City, NY 10112

Tel: (212) 632-6000
Fax: (302) 655-5049

Public Affairs and Related Activities Personnel

At Headquarters

BUCAILLE, Matthieu
Chief Financial Officer

Tel: (212) 632-6000
Fax: (302) 655-5049

HOFFMAN, Scott D.
General Counsel

Tel: (212) 632-6000
Fax: (302) 655-5049

MACKEY, Judi Frost
Director, Global Communications
judi.mackey@lazard.com

Tel: (212) 632-1428
Fax: (302) 655-5049

SADOUGHI, Armand
Managing Director, Investor Relations

Tel: (212) 632-6000
Fax: (302) 655-5049

armand.sadoughi@lazard.com

STERN, Alexander F.
Chief Operating Officer

Tel: (212) 632-6000
Fax: (302) 655-5049

Lear Corporation

A manufacturer of automotive interiors.
Annual Revenues: $17.89 billion
Employees: 125,200
Ticker: NYSE:LEA
SIC: 3714
Industry/ies: Automotive Industry; Transportation

President, Chief Executive Officer and Director
SIMONCINI, Matthew J.

Tel: (248) 447-1500
Fax: (248) 447-1722

Main Headquarters
Mailing: 21557 Telegraph Rd.
           Southfield, MI 48033

Tel: (248) 447-1500
Fax: (248) 447-1722

Public Affairs and Related Activities Personnel

At Headquarters

LARKIN, Terrence B.
Executive Vice President, Business Development and General Counsel

Tel: (248) 447-1500
Fax: (248) 447-1722

MORRIS, Valencia Y.
Director, Corporate Relations
vmorris@lear.com

Tel: (248) 447-5938
Fax: (248) 447-1722

STEPHENS, Melvin
Senior Vice President, Communications, PAC Treasurer and Corporate Relations
mstephens@lear.com

Tel: (248) 447-1624
Fax: (248) 447-1722

VANNESTE, Jeffrey H.
Senior Vice President and Chief Financial Officer

Tel: (248) 447-1500
Fax: (248) 447-1722

Learning.com

A provider of Web-delivered curriculum and assessment.
www.learning.com
Employees: 82
Industry/ies: Education

Chief Executive Officer
OELRICH, Keith

Tel: (503) 284-0100
Fax: (503) 210-0351

Main Headquarters
Mailing: 1620 S.W. Taylor St.
           Suite 100
           Portland, OR 97205

Tel: (800) 580-4640
Fax: (503) 210-0351

Public Affairs and Related Activities Personnel

At Headquarters

GREEN, Clifford
Vice President, Education and Customer Experience

Tel: (503) 284-0100
Fax: (503) 210-0351

Lee Enterprises

A newspaper publishing company. Acquired Pulitzer Inc. in June 2005.
www.lee.net
Annual Revenues: $656.90 million
Employees: 3,500
Ticker: NYSE: LEE
SIC: 2711
Industry/ies: Communications; Media/Mass Communication

Chairman, President and Chief Executive Officer
JUNCK, Mary E.

Tel: (563) 383-2100
Fax: (563) 323-9609

Main Headquarters
Mailing: 201 N. Harrison St.
           Suite 600
           Davenport, IA 52801-1939

Tel: (563) 383-2100
Fax: (563) 323-9609

Public Affairs and Related Activities Personnel

At Headquarters

ARMS, Charles E.
Director, Corporate Communications

Tel: (563) 383-2100
Fax: (563) 323-9609

GARCIA, Astrid J.
Vice President, Human Resources and Legal

Tel: (563) 383-2100
Fax: (563) 323-9609

GULLEDGE, Michael R.
Vice President, Sales and Marketing

Tel: (563) 383-2100
Fax: (563) 323-9609

HAYES, Daniel K.
Vice President, Corporate Communications
dan.hayes@lee.net

Tel: (563) 383-2100
Fax: (563) 323-9609

MAYO, Ronald A.
Vice President, Chief Financial Officer and Treasurer

Tel: (563) 383-2100
Fax: (563) 323-9609

MOWBRAY, Kevin D.
Executive Vice President and Chief Operating Officer

Tel: (563) 383-2100
Fax: (563) 323-9609

SCHERMER, Gregory P.
Vice President, Strategy

Tel: (563) 383-2100
Fax: (563) 323-9609

SCHMIDT, Carl G.
Vice President, Chief Financial Officer and Treasurer
Tel: (563) 383-2100
Fax: (563) 323-9609

J. Leek Associates, Inc.
Technical services organization that provides strategic quality assurance systems in the food and beverage industry.
www.jlaglobal.com
Industry/ies: Agriculture/Agronomy; Food And Beverage Industry; Science; Scientific Research

Chairman of the Board
LEEK, James M.
Tel: (229) 889-8293
Fax: (229) 888-1166

Main Headquarters
Mailing: 3016 Kensington Ct
Albany, GA 31721
Tel: (229) 889-8293
Fax: (229) 888-1166

Public Affairs and Related Activities Personnel

At Headquarters

LEEK, Judy J.
Chief Financial Officer
Tel: (229) 889-8293
Fax: (229) 888-1166

LeFrak Organization
A real estate developer, merchant banking and energy solutions provider.
www.lefrak.com
Employees: 200
Industry/ies: Banking/Finance/Investments; Energy/Electricity; Real Estate
Legislative Issues: DIS; GOV; RES; TRA

Chairman, President and Chief Executive Officer
LEFRAK, Richard S.
Tel: (212) 708-6600
Fax: (212) 708-6641

Main Headquarters
Mailing: 40 W. 57th St.
New York City, NY 10019
Tel: (212) 708-6600
Fax: (212) 708-6641

Public Affairs and Related Activities Personnel

At Headquarters

CORTESE, Edward
Senior Vice President, Marketing and Public Relations
Tel: (212) 708-6600
Fax: (212) 708-6641

PAPERT, Richard N.
Executive Vice President, Chief Investment and Financial Officer
Tel: (212) 708-6600
Fax: (212) 708-6641

Legal Services Corporation
A non-profit organization funded by the Congress to provide grants to legal service programs that provide attorneys for those who cannot afford private attorneys in civil cases.
www.lsc.gov
Industry/ies: Law/Law Firms; Social Service/Urban Affairs

Chairman of the Board
LEVI, John G.
Tel: (202) 295-1500
Fax: (202) 337-6797

President
SANDMAN, James J.
jsandman@lsc.gov
Tel: (202) 295-1500
Fax: (202) 337-6797

Main Headquarters
Mailing: 3333 K St. NW
Third Floor
Washington, DC 20007-3522
Tel: (202) 295-1500
Fax: (202) 337-6797

Public Affairs and Related Activities Personnel

At Headquarters

AZIZ, Treefa
Manager, Government Relations
Tel: (202) 295-1500
Fax: (202) 337-6797

BERGMAN, Carol A.
Director, Government Relations and Public Affairs
bergmanc@lsc.gov
Tel: (202) 295-1500
Fax: (202) 337-6797

FLAGG, Ronald
General Counsel, Corporate Secretary and Vice President, Legal Affairs
Tel: (202) 295-1500
Fax: (202) 337-6797

HIGGINS, Traci
Director, Human Resources
Tel: (202) 295-1500
Fax: (202) 337-6797

RATH, Lora
Director, Compliance and Enforcement Services
Tel: (202) 295-1500
Fax: (202) 337-6797

RAUSCHER, Carl
Director, Media Relations, Government Relations and Public Affairs
Tel: (202) 295-1500
Fax: (202) 337-6797

RICHARDSON, David
Treasurer and Comptroller, Financial and Administrative Services
Tel: (202) 295-1500
Fax: (202) 337-6797

SLOANE, Richard
Chief, Staff and sSpecial Assistant President
Tel: (202) 295-1500
Fax: (202) 337-6797

Leggett & Platt
A manufacturer of components for the home furnishings industry. It designs and produces a range of engineered components and products.

www.leggett.com
Annual Revenues: $3.89 billion
Employees: 20,000
Ticker: NYSE: LEG
SIC: 2299; 2392; 3315; 2399; 2510
NAICS: 314129; 314999; 332618; 31323
Industry/ies: Furniture/Home Furnishings; Retail/Wholesale
Legislative Issues: TAX; TRD

Chairman of the Board
HAFFNER, David S.
Tel: (417) 358-8131
Fax: (417) 358-5840

President and Chief Executive Officer
GLASSMAN, Karl G.
Tel: (417) 358-8131
Fax: (417) 358-5840

Main Headquarters
Mailing: P.O. Box 757
One Leggett Rd.
Carthage, MO 64836
Tel: (417) 358-8131
Fax: (417) 358-5840

Political Action Committees
Leggett & Platt Inc. PAC
FEC ID: C00229435
Contact: Wendy March Watson
One Leggett Rd.
P.O. Box 757
Carthage, MO 64836

Contributions to Candidates: $27,500 (2015-2016)
Republicans: $17,500; Other: $10,000

Principal Recipients

HOUSE
LONG, BILLY MR. (REP-MO)
SMITH, JASON T (OTHER-MO)

Corporate Foundations and Giving Programs
Leggett & Platt Contributions Program
One Leggett Rd.
P.O. Box 757
Carthage, MO 64836

Public Affairs and Related Activities Personnel

At Headquarters

BALDWIN, Dan C.
Vice President, Operations Services
Tel: (417) 358-8131
Fax: (417) 358-5840

BESHORE, Lance G.
Vice President, Public Affairs and Government Relations
lance.beshore@leggett.com
Tel: (417) 358-8131
Fax: (417) 358-8449

DESONIER, David M.
Senior Vice President, Strategy and Investor Relations
david.desonier@leggett.com
Tel: (417) 358-8131
Fax: (417) 358-5840

DOUGLAS, Scott S.
Senior Vice President and General Counsel
Tel: (417) 358-8131
Fax: (417) 358-5840

FLANIGAN, Matthew C.
Executive Vice President and Chief Financial Officer
Tel: (417) 358-8131
Fax: (417) 358-8449

IORIO, Russell J.
Senior Vice President, Corporate Development
Tel: (417) 358-8131
Fax: (417) 358-5840

MCCOY, Susan R.
Staff Vice President, Investor Relations
Tel: (417) 358-8131
Fax: (417) 359-5114

MOORE, John G.
Senior Vice President, Chief Legal and Human Resources Officer and Secretary
Tel: (417) 358-8131
Fax: (417) 358-8449

MOSSBECK, Niels
Vice President, Corporate Business Development
Tel: (417) 358-8131
Fax: (417) 358-5840

WATSON, Wendy March
PAC Treasurer
wendy.watson@leggett.com
Tel: (417) 358-8131
Fax: (417) 358-8449

Lehigh Cement Company
A manufacturer of cement and concrete products. A wholly-owned subsidiary of HeidelbergCement AG of Heidelberg, Germany.
www.lehighcement.com
Annual Revenues: $184.10 million
Employees: 2,200
SIC: 3241
Industry/ies: Construction/Construction Materials

President and Chief Executive Officer
HARRINGTON, Daniel M
Tel: (972) 653-5500

Main Headquarters
Mailing: 300 E John Carpenter Fwy.
Irving, TX 75062
Tel: (972) 653-5500

Public Affairs and Related Activities Personnel

At Headquarters

BÖTTCHER, Henner
Senior Vice President and Cheif Financial Officier
Tel: (972) 653-5500

CHIZMADIA, Tom	Tel:	(972) 653-5500
Senior Vice President, Government Affairs, PR and Sustainability		
VENEMA, Bill	Tel:	(972) 653-5500
Vice President and General Counsel		
WALDROP, R Van	Tel:	(972) 653-5500
Senior Vice President, Human Resources		

Lehigh Hanson, Inc.

Manufacturer and supplier of heavy building materials to the construction industry.
www.lehighhanson.com
Legislative Issues: ENV; TRA

President and Chief Executive Officer   Tel: (972) 653-5500
HARRINGTON, Daniel M.

Main Headquarters
Mailing: 300 E. John Carpenter Fwy.   Tel: (972) 653-5500
          Irving, TX 75062

Political Action Committees
Lehigh Hanson, Inc. PAC
FEC ID: C00493270
Contact: Mark Conte
300 E. John Carpenter Freeway   Tel: (972) 653-5500
Irving, TX 75062

    Contributions to Candidates: $98,500 (2015-2016)
    Democrats: $8,500; Republicans: $90,000

Public Affairs and Related Activities Personnel

At Headquarters

BENNETT, Kelly	Tel:	(972) 653-5500
Vice President, Strategy and Development		
BOTTCHER, Henner	Tel:	(972) 653-5500
Senior Vice President and Chief Financial Officer		
CHIZMADIA, Thomas	Tel:	(972) 653-5631
Senior Vice President, Government Affairs, PR & Sustainability		
Thomas.Chizmadia@LehighHanson.com		
Registered Federal Lobbyist		
CONTE, Mark	Tel:	(972) 653-5500
PAC Treasurer, Corporate Controller and Chief Accounting Officer		
SIEG, Jeff	Tel:	(972) 653-6011
Director, Corporate Communications		
jeff.sieg@hanson.com		
VAN WALDROP, R.	Tel:	(972) 653-5500
Vice President, Human Resources		
VENEMA, Bill	Tel:	(972) 653-5500
Vice President and General Counsel		

Lehigh Valley Health Network

Provides general hospital management services.
www.lvhn.org
Annual Revenues: $1.52 billion
Employees: 7,000
Industry/ies: Medicine/Health Care/Mental Health
Legislative Issues: HCR

Chairman of the Board   Tel: (610) 402-8000
HECHT , William F.   Fax: (610) 402-7523

President and Chief Executive Officer   Tel: (610) 402-8000
NESTER, Brian   Fax: (610) 402-7523

Main Headquarters
Mailing: Cedar Crest Blvd. and I-78   Tel: (610) 402-8000
         P.O. Box 689   Fax: (610) 402-7523
         Allentown, PA 18105-1556   TF: (888) 584-2273

Corporate Foundations and Giving Programs
Lehigh Valley Community Foundation
968 Postal Rd.   Tel: (610) 266-4284
Suite 100
Allentown, PA 18109

Public Affairs and Related Activities Personnel

At Headquarters

BURNS, Matthew	Tel:	(484) 884-0879
Media Relations Coordinator	Fax:	(610) 402-7523
matthew.burns@lvhn.org		
CAPUANO, Terry	Tel:	(610) 402-8000
Chief Operating Officer	Fax:	(610) 402-7523
DOWNS, Brian	Tel:	(484) 884-0825
Director, Media Relations	Fax:	(610) 402-7523
brian.downs@lvhn.org		
ENSSLIN, Mary T.	Tel:	(610) 402-8000
Vice President Government and Legislative Affairs	Fax:	(610) 402-7523

mary.ensslin@lvhn.org
Registered Federal Lobbyist

O'DEA, CPA, MBA, Edward	Tel:	(610) 402-8000
Chief Financial Officer	Fax:	(610) 402-7523
SECHLER, Tracey	Tel:	(484) 884-0819
Coordinator, Public Affairs	Fax:	(610) 402-7523
tracey.sechler@lvhn.org		

At Other Offices

TIRRELL, Mary	Tel:	(484) 884-2724
Vice President, Government & Legislative Affairs	Fax:	(610) 861-7783
2545 Schoenersville Rd., Fourth Floor		
Bethlehem, PA 18017		
Registered Federal Lobbyist		

Lehigh Valley Technologies

A pharmaceutical development and manufacturing company.
www.lvtechinc.com
Annual Revenues: $4.70 million
Employees: 40
Industry/ies: Pharmaceutical Industry

Chief Executive Officer   Tel: (610) 782-9780
MOSHAL, Jeffrey   Fax: (610) 782-9781
JMoshal@LVTechinc.com

Main Headquarters
Mailing: 514 N. 12th St.   Tel: (610) 782-9780
         Allentown, PA 18102-2756   Fax: (610) 782-9781

Public Affairs and Related Activities Personnel

At Headquarters

DALESANDRO, Larry	Tel:	(610) 782-9780
Chief Financial Officer	Fax:	(610) 782-9781
LDalesandro@LVTechinc.com		

Lemko

A communications software company.
www.lemko.com
Annual Revenues: $3.00 million
Employees: 35
Industry/ies: Communications; Telecommunications/Internet/Cable

Chairman of the Board and Chief Executive Officer   Tel: (630) 948-3025
LABUN, Nicholas   Fax: (630) 948-3030

Main Headquarters
Mailing: One Pierce Pl.   Tel: (630) 948-3025
         Suite 700   Fax: (630) 948-3030
         Itasca, IL 60143

Public Affairs and Related Activities Personnel

At Headquarters

BARR, Joe	Tel:	(630) 948-3025
Chief Financial Officer	Fax:	(630) 948-3030
FEKRAT, Norman	Tel:	(630) 948-3025
Chief Strategy and Revenue Officer	Fax:	(630) 948-3030
PYSKIR, Bohdan	Tel:	(630) 948-3025
Chief Operating Officer	Fax:	(630) 948-3030
SISTO, Michael	Tel:	(630) 948-3025
Vice President, Sales	Fax:	(630) 948-3030
VORICK, Faye	Tel:	(847) 240-1990
Vice President, Marketing	Fax:	(847) 240-1700
fvorick@lemko.com		
WHITE, Chris	Tel:	(630) 948-3025
Vice President, Government and Public Safety	Fax:	(630) 948-3030

Lend Lease Project Management & Construction

A project management and construction company.
www.lendlease.com
Annual Revenues: $6.68 billion
Employees: 600
Industry/ies: Construction/Construction Materials; Real Estate

Chairman of the Board   Tel: (212) 592-6700
CRAWFORD, David   Fax: (212) 592-6988

Group Chief Executive Officer and Managing Director   Tel: (212) 592-6700
MCCANN, Steve   Fax: (212) 592-6988

Main Headquarters
Mailing: 200 Park Ave.   Tel: (212) 592-6700
         Floor Nine   Fax: (212) 592-6988
         New York City, NY 10166-0999

Corporate Foundations and Giving Programs
Lend Lease Community Fund
200 Park Ave.   Tel: (212) 592-6700
Floor Nine   Fax: (212) 592-6988

New York City, NY 10166-0999

Public Affairs and Related Activities Personnel

At Headquarters

BOWER, Vivienne	Tel:	(212) 592-6700
Group Head, Corporate Affairs and Investor Relations	Fax:	(212) 592-6988
CHRISTENSEN-SJOGREN, Linda	Tel:	(212) 592-6700
Executive Vice President and General Counsel	Fax:	(212) 592-6988
COSTELLO, Mary	Tel:	(212) 592-6946
Senior Vice President, Corporate Affairs Head and Media	Fax:	(212) 592-6988
Contact		
mary.Costello@bovislendlease.com		
LOMBARDO, Tony	Tel:	(212) 592-6700
Chief Financial Officer	Fax:	(212) 592-6988
MCNAMARA, Robert	Tel:	(212) 592-6700
Group Chief Risk Officer	Fax:	(212) 592-6988
PEDERSEN, Karen	Tel:	(212) 592-6700
Group General Counsel	Fax:	(212) 592-6988
VAVAKIS, Michael	Tel:	(212) 592-6700
Group Head, Human Resources	Fax:	(212) 592-6988

Lennar Corporation

A home builder with operations in Florida, California, Texas, Arizona, and Nevada.
www.lennar.com
Annual Revenues: $8.63 billion
Employees: 6,825
Ticker: NYSE: LEN
SIC: 1531
Industry/ies: Construction/Construction Materials; Housing
Legislative Issues: CAW; IMM

Chief Executive Officer	Tel:	(305) 559-4000
MILLER, Stuart A.	Fax:	(305) 228-8383
Stuart.Miller@lennar.com		

Main Headquarters

Mailing:	700 N.W. 107th Ave.	Tel:	(305) 559-4000
	Miami, FL 33172	Fax:	(305) 228-8383
		TF:	(800) 741-4663

Corporate Foundations and Giving Programs

Lennar Charitable Housing Foundation
700 NW 107th Ave.
Miami, FL 33172   Tel: (305) 559-4000   Fax: (305) 228-8383

Lennar Foundation
700 NW. 107th Ave.
Miami, FL 33172   Tel: (305) 559-4000   Fax: (305) 228-8383

Public Affairs and Related Activities Personnel

At Headquarters

AMES, Marshall	Tel:	(305) 559-4000
Contact, Media Relations	Fax:	(305) 228-8383
marshall.ames@lennar.com		
BATY, Brenda	Tel:	(305) 559-4000
Contact, Strategic Initiatives	Fax:	(305) 228-8383
BECKWITT, Rick	Tel:	(305) 559-4000
President	Fax:	(305) 228-8383
Rick.Beckwitt@Lennar.com		
BOBER, Allison	Tel:	(305) 559-4000
Contact, Investor Relations	Fax:	(305) 229-6452
Allison.Bober@lennar.com		
GARRAFFO, Carl	Tel:	(305) 559-4000
Chief Human Resource Officer	Fax:	(305) 228-8383
GROSS, Bruce E.	Tel:	(305) 559-4000
Vice President and Chief Financial Officer	Fax:	(305) 228-8383
HOWARD, Kay L.	Tel:	(305) 559-4000
Director, Communications	Fax:	(305) 228-8383
kay.howard@lennar.com		
JAFFE, Jonathan M.	Tel:	(305) 559-4000
Vice President and Chief Operating Officer	Fax:	(305) 228-8383
SUSTANA, Mark	Tel:	(305) 559-4000
General Counsel and Secretary	Fax:	(305) 228-8383
mark.sustana@lennar.com		

Lennox International, Inc.

Designs, manufactures, and markets climate control products for the heating, ventilation, air conditioning, and refrigeration markets.
www.lennoxinternational.com
Annual Revenues: $3.36 billion
Employees: 9,800
Ticker: NYSE: LII
SIC: 3585
NAICS: 333414, 333415
Industry/ies: Heating And Air Conditioning
Legislative Issues: ENG; TAX

Chairman of the Board and Chief Executive Officer	Tel:	(972) 497-5000
BLUEDORN, Todd M.	Fax:	(972) 497-5292

Main Headquarters

Mailing:	2140 Lake Park Blvd.	Tel:	(972) 497-5000
	Richardson, TX 75080	Fax:	(972) 497-5292
		TF:	(800) 953-6669

Political Action Committees

Lennox Employee Advocacy Program Lennox International Inc
FEC ID: C00116996
Contact: David Dorsett
P.O. Box 799900   Tel: (972) 497-6670
Dallas, TX 75379-9900   Fax: (972) 497-5292

  Contributions to Candidates: $7,000 (2015-2016)
  Democrats: $1,000; Republicans: $6,000

Corporate Foundations and Giving Programs

Lennox Foundation
P.O. Box 799900
Dallas, TX 75379

Public Affairs and Related Activities Personnel

At Headquarters

BUCKLER, Ozzie	Tel:	(972) 497-7456
Manager, Marketing Programs	Fax:	(972) 497-5292
ozzie.buckler@lennoxintl.com		
GEE, Philip	Tel:	(972) 497-5000
Director, Communications and Public Affairs	Fax:	(972) 497-5292
HURST, John	Tel:	(972) 497-5000
Vice President, Government Affairs & Communications	Fax:	(972) 497-5292
john.hurst@lennoxintl.com		
Registered Federal Lobbyist		
REITMEIER, Joseph W.	Tel:	(972) 497-5000
Executive Vice President and Chief Financial Officer	Fax:	(972) 497-5292
SESSA, Daniel M.	Tel:	(972) 497-5000
Executive Vice President and Chief Human Resources Officer	Fax:	(972) 497-5292
TORRES, John D.	Tel:	(972) 497-5000
Executive Vice President, Chief Legal Officer and Secretary	Fax:	(972) 498-5299
John.torres@lennoxintl.com		

At Other Offices

DORSETT, David	Tel:	(972) 497-6670
Federal Lobbyist and PAC Treasurer	Fax:	(972) 497-5292
P.O. Box 799900		
Dallas, TX 75379-9900		
HARRISON, Steve L.	Tel:	(972) 497-6670
Vice President, Investor Relations	Fax:	(972) 497-5292
P.O. Box 799900		
Dallas, TX 75379-9900		

Lenovo Group Ltd.

Lenovo, a PC vendor and smartphone company.
www.lenovo.com/us/en
SIC: 9721
Industry/ies: Computer/Technology
Legislative Issues: BUD; CPT; TEC

Chairman of the Board and Chief Executive Officer	Tel:	(919) 257-6329
YUANQING, Yang		

Main Headquarters

Mailing:	1009 Think Pl.	Tel:	(919) 294-2500
	Morrisville, NC 27560	TF:	(866) 968-4465

Washington Office

Mailing:	1333 New Hampshire Ave. NW	Tel:	(202) 624-3577
	Washington, DC 20036		

Political Action Committees

Lenovo (United States) Inc. Non-Partisan Committee for Good Government PAC
FEC ID: C00435602
Contact: Rachel A. Adams
1333 New Hampshire Ave. NW   Tel: (202) 624-3577
Washington, DC 20036

Corporate Foundations and Giving Programs

Next Generation Hope Fund
1009 Think Pl.   Tel: (919) 294-2500
Morrisville, NC 27560

Public Affairs and Related Activities Personnel

At Headquarters

CLEMENS, Jay	Tel:	(919) 294-2500
Senior Vice President, General Council		
FAIR, Kristy	Tel:	(919) 257-6329
Contact, Media Relations		
krisfair@lenovo.com		
JIAN, Qiao	Tel:	(919) 294-2500
Senior Vice President, Human Resources		

LANCI, Gianfranco
Tel: (919) 294-2500
Executive Vice President and Chief Operating Officer

MING, Wong Wai
Tel: (919) 294-2500
Executive Vice President and Chief Financial Officer

NG, Gary
Tel: (919) 294-2500
Vice President, Investor relations
ir@lenovo.com

ROMAN, David
Tel: (919) 294-2500
Senior Vice President and Chief Marketing Officer

At Washington Office

ADAMS, Rachel A.
Tel: (202) 419-3580
Vice President, Assistant General Counsel
radams@lenovo.com

LenovoEMC

See listing on page 445 under Iomega Corporation

Leo A. Daly Company

Offers planning, architecture, engineering, and interior design services.
www.leoadaly.com
Annual Revenues: $114.91 million
Employees: 1,100
Industry/ies: Social Service/Urban Affairs

Chairman and Chief Executive Officer
Tel: (402) 391-8111
DALY, III, FAIA, Leo A.
Fax: (402) 391-8546

Main Headquarters
Mailing: 8600 Indian Hills Dr.
Tel: (402) 391-8111
Omaha, NE 68114-4039
Fax: (402) 391-8564

Political Action Committees
Leo A. Daly Company PAC
FEC ID: C00402727
Contact: James B. Brader
8600 Indian Hills Dr.
Omaha, NE 68114

Contributions to Candidates: $7,200 (2015-2016)
Democrats: $2,700; Republicans: $4,500

Public Affairs and Related Activities Personnel

At Headquarters

BENES, JD, PE, Edward G.
Tel: (402) 391-8111
Senior Vice President and General Counsel
Fax: (402) 391-8564

BRADER, James B.
Tel: (402) 391-8111
Chief Financial Officer and PAC Treasurer
Fax: (402) 391-8564

IMBER, Sian
Tel: (402) 955-9124
Vice President, Public Relations
Fax: (402) 391-8546

KRASKIEWICZ, John J.
Tel: (214) 526-1144
Senior Vice President, Chief Operations Officer
Fax: (402) 391-8564
JJKraskiewicz@leoadaly.com

REYES, Ignacio J.
Tel: (561) 688-2111
Vice President and Director, Business Development
Fax: (402) 391-8564
IJReyes@leoadaly.com

Leo Burnett Worldwide

A marketing communications agency.
www.leoburnett.com
Employees: 2,000
Industry/ies: Advertising And Marketing

Chairman and Chief Executive Officer
Tel: (312) 220-5959
BERNARDIN, Tom
Fax: (312) 220-3299

Main Headquarters
Mailing: 35 W. Wacker Dr.
Tel: (312) 220-5959
Chicago, IL 60601
Fax: (312) 220-3299

Corporate Foundations and Giving Programs
Leo Burnett Company Charitable Foundation
Contact: Carla Michelotti
35 W. Wacker Dr.
Tel: (312) 220-5959
Chicago, IL 60601
Fax: (312) 220-3299

Public Affairs and Related Activities Personnel

At Headquarters

CHERONIS, Amy
Tel: (312) 220-5996
Executive Vice President, Reputation and Communications
Fax: (312) 220-3299
amy.cheronis@leoburnett.com

DUMOUCHEL, Patrick
Tel: (312) 220-5959
Executive Vice President and Chief Financial Officer
Fax: (312) 220-3299

HEDGER, Giles
Tel: (312) 220-5959
Chief Strategy Officer
Fax: (312) 220-3299

KRISTULA-GREEN, Michelle
Tel: (312) 220-5959
Executive Vice President, Global Head of People and Culture
Fax: (312) 220-3299

MICHELOTTI, Carla
Tel: (312) 220-5959

Executive Vice President, Chief Legal, Government and Corporate Affairs Officer
Fax: (312) 220-3299

PETERS, Michael
Tel: (312) 220-5959
Global Director, Corporate Strategy Affairs
Fax: (312) 220-3299

Leprino Foods Company

A small, family-owned market selling grocery items and handmade cheese in Denver, Colorado, USA.
www.leprinofoods.com
Industry/ies: Dairy Industry; Food And Beverage Industry

Main Headquarters
Mailing: 1830 W. 38th Ave.
Tel: (303) 480-2600
Denver, CO 80211
Fax: (303) 480-2605

Corporate Foundations and Giving Programs
Leprino Foods Company Contributions Program
1830 W. 38th Ave.
Denver, CO 80211

Public Affairs and Related Activities Personnel

At Headquarters

DEVIGIL, Kim
Tel: (303) 480-2600
Media Contact
Fax: (303) 480-2605
kdevigil@leprinofoods.com

TAYLOR, Sue M.
Tel: (303) 480-2600
Vice President, Dairy Policy & Procurement
Fax: (303) 480-2605
staylor@leprinofoods.com

Lettelleir Consulting Group LLC

Business Development Consultation, Federal, State and Local Lobbying

President
LETTELLEIR, Matthew

Main Headquarters
Mailing: 452 Date Palm Ct. NE
Suite 100
Saint Petersburg, FL 33703

Leucadia National Corporation

An insurance, financial services, real estate, manufacturing, banking and lending company.
www.leucadia.com
Annual Revenues: $10.51 billion
Employees: 13,300
Ticker: NYSE: LUK
SIC: 2011
Industry/ies: Banking/Finance/Investments; Insurance Industry

Chief Executive Officer
Tel: (212) 460-1900
HANDLE, Richard B.

Main Headquarters
Mailing: 520 Madison Ave.
Tel: (212) 460-1900
New York City, NY 10022

Public Affairs and Related Activities Personnel

At Headquarters

FRIEDMAN, Brian P
Tel: (212) 460-1900
President

JACOBS, Stephen E.
Tel: (212) 460-1900
General Counsel

Level 3 Communications Inc.

A worldwide communications and information services company. Acquired Genuity in February, 2003.
www.level3.com
Annual Revenues: $7.22 billion
Employees: 13,500
Ticker: NASDAQ: LVLT
SIC: 4813
Industry/ies: Communications; Telecommunications/Internet/Cable
Legislative Issues: BUD; DEF; GOV; TEC

President and Chief Executive Officer
Tel: (720) 888-1000
STOREY, Jeff
Fax: (720) 888-5085

Main Headquarters
Mailing: 1025 Eldorado Blvd.
Tel: (720) 888-1000
Broomfield, CO 80021
Fax: (720) 888-5085

Political Action Committees
Level 3 Communications, Inc. PAC
FEC ID: C00347385
Contact: Michael Mooney
1025 El Dorado Blvd.
Broomfield, CO 80021

Contributions to Candidates: $10,299,195 (2015-2016)
Democrats: $36,930; Republicans: $50,250; Other: $10,212,015

Corporate Foundations and Giving Programs

Level 3 Communications Contributions Program
Independence and New Jersey Ave. SE   Tel: (973) 937-0146
Washington, DC 20515-1902

Public Affairs and Related Activities Personnel

At Headquarters

CHRISTIE, Anthony	Tel:	(720) 888-1000
Chief Marketing Officer	Fax:	(720) 888-5085
DADD, Cyril	Tel:	(720) 888-1000
Registered Federal Lobbyist	Fax:	(720) 888-5085
DUDREY, Francie	Tel:	(720) 888-5434
Media Relations Manager	Fax:	(720) 888-5085
Francie.Dudrey@Level3.com		
KAVANAUGH, Heather	Tel:	(720) 888-1000
Legal Admin	Fax:	(720) 888-5085
MCANDREWS, Colleen C.	Tel:	(310) 459-1405
PAC Treasurer	Fax:	(720) 888-5085
MOONEY, Michael	Tel:	(720) 888-1000
PAC Treasurer	Fax:	(720) 888-5085
PANG, Laurinda	Tel:	(720) 888-1000
Vice president and chief administrative officer	Fax:	(720) 888-5085
PATEL, Sunit	Tel:	(720) 888-1000
Executive Vice President and Chief Financial Officer	Fax:	(720) 888-5085
sunit.patel@level3.com		
REEVES, Kelsi	Tel:	(720) 888-1000
Federal Public Policy	Fax:	(720) 888-5085
RYAN, John	Tel:	(720) 888-1000
Executive Vice President and Chief Legal Officer	Fax:	(720) 888-5085
John.Ryan@Level3.com		
STOUTENBERG, Mark	Tel:	(720) 888-2518
Director, Investor Relations	Fax:	(720) 888-5085
mark.stoutenberg@level3.com		

Levi Strauss and Company

An apparel manufacturer. Market apparel products are sold under the Levi's, Dockers and Levi Strauss Signature brands.
www.levistrauss.com
Employees: 11,400
SIC: 5136; 2300; 2325; 5099
Industry/ies: Apparel/Textiles Industry
Legislative Issues: TRD

Chairman of the Board	Tel:	(415) 501-6000
NEAL, Stephen C.	Fax:	(415) 501-7112
President and Chief Executive Officer	Tel:	(415) 501-6000
BERGH, Chip	Fax:	(415) 501-7112

Main Headquarters

Mailing:	1155 Battery St.	Tel:	(415) 501-6000
	San Francisco, CA 94111	Fax:	(415) 501-7112
		TF:	(800) 872-5384

Corporate Foundations and Giving Programs

Levi Strauss Foundation
Contact: Merle Lawrence
1155 Battery St.
San Francisco, CA 94111

Public Affairs and Related Activities Personnel

At Headquarters

JAFFE, Seth	Tel:	(415) 501-6000
Senior Vice President and General Counsel	Fax:	(415) 501-7112
LAWRENCE, Merle	Tel:	(415) 501-6000
Senior Manager, Levi Strauss Foundation	Fax:	(415) 501-7112
MCCASLAND, Amber	Tel:	(415) 501-7777
Senior Director, Corporate Affairs	Fax:	(415) 501-7112
amccasland@levi.com		
MCGINNIS, Kelly	Tel:	(415) 501-6000
Senior Vice President and Chief Communications Officer	Fax:	(415) 501-7112
OGLE, Chris	Tel:	(800) 438-0349
Contact, Investor Relations	Fax:	(415) 501-7112
Investor-relations@levi.com		
SINGH, Harmit	Tel:	(415) 501-6000
Executive Vice President and Chief Financial Officer	Fax:	(415) 501-7112
WALKER, Anna	Tel:	(415) 501-6000
Senior Director, Government Affairs and Public Policy	Fax:	(415) 501-7112
WOOD, Elizabeth	Tel:	(415) 501-6000
Chief Human Resources Officer	Fax:	(415) 501-7112

Levine Leichtman Capital Partners, Inc.

Levine Leichtman Capital Partners is an independent investment firm that invests in middle market companies located in the United States.
www.llcp.com
Annual Revenues: $27.60 million

Employees: 500
Industry/ies: Banking/Finance/Investments

Chief Executive Officer and Founding Principal	Tel:	(310) 275-5335
LEICHTMAN, Lauren B.	Fax:	(310) 275-1441

Main Headquarters

Mailing:	335 N. Maple Dr.	Tel:	(310) 275-5335
	Suite 130	Fax:	(310) 275-1441
	Beverly Hills, CA 90210		

Public Affairs and Related Activities Personnel

At Headquarters

CRENSHAW, Janet L.	Tel:	(310) 275-5335
Contact, Investor Relations	Fax:	(310) 275-1441
HOGAN, Stephen J.	Tel:	(310) 275-5335
Chief Financial and Chief Administrative Officer	Fax:	(310) 275-1441
HOLEC, Monica J.	Tel:	(310) 275-5335
Managing Director, Investor Relations	Fax:	(310) 275-1441

LexisNexis

Global provider of content-enabled workflow solutions designed specifically for professionals in the legal, risk management, corporate, government, law enforcement, accounting, and academic markets.
www.lexisnexis.com/en-us/home.page
Industry/ies: Electricity & Electronics; Electronics; Energy/Electricity

Chief Executive Officer	Tel:	(212) 448-2172
WALSH, Mike	Fax:	(212) 309-5451

Main Headquarters

Mailing:	125 Park Ave.	Tel:	(212) 448-2172
	Suite 2200	Fax:	(212) 309-5451
	New York City, NY 10017		

Public Affairs and Related Activities Personnel

At Headquarters

LIVINGSTON, Phil	Tel:	(212) 448-2172
Chief Executive Officer, Marketing and Business Solutions	Fax:	(212) 309-5451
MATUCH, Andrew	Tel:	(212) 448-2172
Executive Vice President, Strategy and Business Development	Fax:	(212) 309-5451
MCDOUGALL, Ian	Tel:	(212) 448-2172
Executive Vice President and General Counsel	Fax:	(212) 309-5451
ian.mcdougall@lexisnexis.com		
SCHMITT, Rebecca	Tel:	(212) 448-2172
Senior Vice President and Chief Financial Officer	Fax:	(212) 309-5451
TYBURSKI, Doreen	Tel:	(212) 448-2172
Global Executive Vice President, Human Resources	Fax:	(212) 309-5451

Lexmark International

Manufactures laser printers and provides enterprise services.
www1.lexmark.com
Annual Revenues: $3.68 billion
Employees: 12,700
Ticker: NYSE: LXK
SIC: 3570; 3579
Industry/ies: Printing Industry
Legislative Issues: ACC; ENG; ENV; TAX; TRA; TRD

Chairman of the Board and Chief Executive Officer	Tel:	(859) 232-2000
ROOKE, Paul	Fax:	(859) 232-2403
rooke@lexmark.com		

Main Headquarters

Mailing:	740 W. New Cir. Rd.	Tel:	(859) 232-2000
	Lexington, KY 40550	Fax:	(859) 232-2403
		TF:	(800) 539-6275

Corporate Foundations and Giving Programs

Lexmark International Contributions Program
740 W. New Circle Rd.   Tel: (859) 232-2000
Lexington, KY 40550

Public Affairs and Related Activities Personnel

At Headquarters

GAWORSKI, Juli	Tel:	(859) 232-2000
OEM Business Development Manager	Fax:	(859) 232-2403
jgaworsk@lexmark.com		
GRASSO, Jerry	Tel:	(859) 232-3546
Corporate Communications and Media Contact	Fax:	(859) 232-2403
ggrasso@lexmark.com		
GRIGSBY, Julie	Tel:	(859) 232-1114
Assistant, Investor Relations	Fax:	(859) 232-2403
ISBELL, Jeri L.	Tel:	(859) 232-2000
Vice President, Human Resources	Fax:	(859) 232-2403
MORGAN, John	Tel:	(859) 232-5568
Director, Investor Relations	Fax:	(859) 232-2403
jmorgan@lexmark.com		

PATTON, Robert J.
Vice President, General Counsel and Secretary
Tel: (859) 232-2000
Fax: (859) 232-2403

REEDER, David
Vice President and Chief Financial Officer
Tel: (859) 232-2000
Fax: (859) 232-2403

STROMQUIST, Gary
Vice President and Interim Chief Financial Officer
Tel: (859) 232-2000
Fax: (859) 232-2403

LG&E and KU

LG&E and KU an energy services company-Louisville Gas and Electric Company, an electric and natural gas utility and Kentucky Utilities Company, an electric utility Formerly known as E.ON US; purchased by PPL Corporation in 2010.
www.lge-ku.com
Employees: 3,500
Industry/ies: Energy/Electricity; Natural Resources
Legislative Issues: CAW; UTI

Chairman, President and Chief Executive Officer
STAFFIERI, Victor
Tel: (502) 627-2000
Fax: (502) 627-3609

Main Headquarters
Mailing: 220 W. Main St.
Louisville, KY 40202
Tel: (502) 627-3313
Fax: (502) 627-3609

Corporate Foundations and Giving Programs

LG&E and KU Corporate Responsibility
220 W. Main St
Louisville, KY 40202

Public Affairs and Related Activities Personnel

At Headquarters

BATES, G. Hunter
Federal Lobbyist
Registered Federal Lobbyist
Tel: (502) 627-3313
Fax: (502) 627-3609

BLAKE, Kent
Chief Financial Officer
Tel: (502) 627-3313
Fax: (502) 627-3609

DOUGLAS, Laura
Vice President Corporate Responsibility and Community Affairs
Tel: (502) 627-2000
Fax: (502) 627-3609

KEISLING, Jennifer
Registered Federal Lobbyist
Tel: (502) 627-3313
Fax: (502) 627-3609

MEIMAN, Greg
Vice President, Human Resources
Tel: (502) 627-3313
Fax: (502) 627-3609

O'BRIEN, Dorothy Dot
Vice President and Deputy General Counsel, Legal and Environmental Affairs
Tel: (502) 627-3313
Fax: (502) 627-3609

POTTINGER, Paula
Senior Vice President, Human Resources
paula.pottinger@lge-ku.com
Tel: (502) 627-2000
Fax: (502) 627-3609

REYNOLDS, Gerald
General Counsel, Chief Compliance Officer and Corporate Secretary
Tel: (502) 627-3313
Fax: (502) 627-3609

SIEMENS, George
Vice President, External Affairs
Registered Federal Lobbyist
Tel: (502) 627-2000
Fax: (502) 627-3609

THOMPSON, Paul W.
Chief Operating Officer
Tel: (502) 627-3313
Fax: (502) 627-3609

WHELAN, Chris
Vice President, Communications
Tel: (502) 627-2000
Fax: (502) 627-3609

LG Electronics USA, Inc.

A manufacturer of electronics products. Subsidiary of LG Electronics, headquartered in Seoul, South Korea.
www.lge.com
Annual Revenues: $844.20 million
Employees: 3,000
Industry/ies: Communications; Electricity & Electronics; Electronics; Energy/Electricity; Telecommunications/Internet/Cable

President and Chief Executive Officer
AHN, Michael
Tel: (800) 243-0000

Main Headquarters
Mailing: 1000 Sylvan Ave.
Englewood Cliffs, NJ 07632
Tel: (201) 816-2000
TF: (800) 243-0000

Washington Office
Mailing: 1776 K St. NW
Washington, DC 20006

Public Affairs and Related Activities Personnel

At Headquarters

REGILLO, Kim
Manager, Public Affairs & Communications
Tel: (847) 941-8184

Libbey, Inc.

Libbey is the producer of glass tableware products in the Western Hemisphere, in addition to supplying to markets throughout the world.

www.libbey.com
Annual Revenues: $861.47 million
Employees: 6,553
Ticker: NYSE: LBY
SIC: 3229; 3220
NAICS: 327212
Industry/ies: Glass
Legislative Issues: TRD

Chairman of the Board
FOLEY, William A.
Tel: (419) 325-2100
Fax: (419) 325-2119

Chief Executive Officer
STREETER, Stephanie A.
Tel: (419) 325-2100
Fax: (419) 325-2119

Main Headquarters
Mailing: 300 Madison Ave.
P.O. Box 10060
Toledo, OH 43699-0060
Tel: (419) 325-2100
Fax: (419) 325-2119

Public Affairs and Related Activities Personnel

At Headquarters

BOERGER, Kenneth A.
Vice President & Treasurer
Tel: (419) 325-2279
Fax: (419) 325-2117

BUCK, Sherry
Vice President and Chief Financial Officer
Tel: (419) 325-2100
Fax: (419) 325-2119

IBELE, Daniel P.
Vice President & General Manager
Tel: (419) 325-2100
Fax: (419) 325-2119

KOVACH, Susan A.
Vice President and General Counsel
susan.kovach@libbey.com
Tel: (419) 325-2100
Fax: (419) 325-2119

PAIGE, Timothy T.
Vice President, Human Resources
Tel: (419) 325-2100
Fax: (419) 325-2119

Liberian International Ship & Corporation Registry

LISCR is commited to safe and secure shipping and provides the convenient, efficient, and tax effective offshore corporate registries in the world.
www.liscr.com
Industry/ies: Foreign Relations; Marine/Maritime/Shipping; Trade (Foreign And Domestic); Transportation

Chairman of the Board
COHEN, Yoram Menchem
ycohen@liscr.com
Tel: (703) 790-3434
Fax: (703) 790-5655

Chief Executive Officer
BERGERON, Scott
sbergeron@liscr.com
Tel: (703) 564-0673
Fax: (703) 790-5655

Main Headquarters
Mailing: 8619 Westwood Center Dr.
Vienna, VA 22182
Tel: (703) 790-3434
Fax: (703) 790-5655

Public Affairs and Related Activities Personnel

At Headquarters

HEWER, Chris
Contact, Media Relations
chris@merlinco.com
Tel: (703) 790-3434
Fax: (703) 790-5655

LEBARTON, John
Chief Financial Officer
jleb@liscr.com
Tel: (703) 251-2401
Fax: (703) 790-5655

Liberty Maritime Corporation

A ship management company, operating dry bulk vessels owned by Liberty Shipping Group LLC, as well as one PCTC-Roll On/Roll Off vessel owned by Alliance New York LLC.
www.libertymar.com
Annual Revenues: $22.20 million
Employees: 300
Industry/ies: Marine/Maritime/Shipping; Transportation
Legislative Issues: AGR; MAR

President and Chief Executive Officer
SHAPIRO, Philip J.
Tel: (516) 488-8800
Fax: (516) 488-8806

Main Headquarters
Mailing: 1979 Marcus Ave.
Suite 200
Lake Success, NY 11042
Tel: (516) 488-8800
Fax: (516) 488-8806

Political Action Committees
Liberty Maritime Corporation PAC
FEC ID: C00485466
Contact: John Sheen
1979 Marcus Ave.
Suite 200
Lake Success, NY 11042

Contributions to Candidates: $9,500 (2015-2016)
Democrats: $2,500; Republicans: $7,000

Public Affairs and Related Activities Personnel

At Headquarters

MOSES, Dale B.
Executive Vice President, Secretary and Chief Financial Officer
Tel: (516) 488-8800
Fax: (516) 488-8806

SHEEN, John
Vice President, Finance and PAC Treasurer
jsheen@libertymar.com
Tel: (516) 488-8800
Fax: (516) 488-8806

Liberty Media Corporation

A cable television programming producer and distributor.
www.libertymedia.com
Annual Revenues: $4.52 billion
Employees: 3,690
Ticker: NASDAQ: LMCA
SIC: 4841
Industry/ies: Communications; Media/Mass Communication
Legislative Issues: COM; TAX

Chairman of the Board
MALONE, John C.
john.malone@libertymedia.com
Tel: (720) 875-5400
Fax: (720) 875-5401

President and Chief Executive Officer
MAFFEI, Gregory B.
Tel: (720) 875-5400
Fax: (720) 875-5401

Main Headquarters
Mailing: 12300 Liberty Blvd.
Englewood, CO 80112
Tel: (720) 875-5400
Fax: (720) 875-5401

Political Action Committees
Liberty Interactive Corporation PAC Aka Liberty Interactive PAC
FEC ID: C00442434
Contact: Laura M. Baldi
12300 Liberty Blvd.
Englewood, CO 80112

Contributions to Candidates: $11,450 (2015-2016)
Democrats: $5,700; Republicans: $5,750

Corporate Foundations and Giving Programs
LibertyGives Foundation
12300 Liberty Blvd.
Englewood, CO 80112

Public Affairs and Related Activities Personnel

At Headquarters

BAER, Richard N.
Senior Vice President and General Counsel
Tel: (720) 875-5400
Fax: (720) 875-5401

BALDI, Laura M.
PAC Treasurer
Tel: (720) 875-5400
Fax: (720) 875-5401

SHEAN , Christopher W.
Senior Vice President and Chief Financial Officer
Tel: (720) 875-5400
Fax: (720) 875-5401

ULRICH, Courtnee
Contact, Investor Relations
Tel: (720) 875-5420
Fax: (720) 875-5401

Liberty Mutual Insurance Group

Offers auto insurance, home insurance, and life insurance. It provides broad, useful and competitively-priced insurance products and services to meet their customers' ever-changing needs.
www.libertymutual.com
Annual Revenues: $39.6 billion
Employees: 50,000
Industry/ies: Insurance Industry; Medicine/Health Care/Mental Health
Legislative Issues: BAN; BUD; CPI; FIN; HCR; HOM; INS; TAX; TOR; TRA; TRD

Main Headquarters
Mailing: 175 Berkeley St.
Boston, MA 02117
Tel: (617) 357-9500
Fax: (617) 350-7648
TF: (800) 837-5254

Washington Office
Mailing: 444 N. Capitol St. NW
Suite 740
Washington, DC 20001
Tel: (202) 289-7472
Fax: (202) 408-1282
TF: (888) 442-0329

Political Action Committees
Liberty Mutual Insurance Company PAC
FEC ID: C00171843
Contact: Laurence H.S. Yahia
175 Berkeley St.
Boston, MA 02117

Contributions to Candidates: $742,350 (2015-2016)
Democrats: $272,600; Republicans: $466,250; Other: $3,500

Principal Recipients

SENATE
BLUNT, ROY (REP-MO)
BOOZMAN, JOHN (REP-AR)
JOHNSON, RONALD HAROLD (REP-)

HOUSE
BECERRA, XAVIER (DEM-CA)

BRADY, KEVIN (REP-TX)
CRENSHAW, ANDER (REP-FL)
CROWLEY, JOSEPH (DEM-NY)
DUFFY, SEAN (REP-WI)
GARRETT, SCOTT REP. (REP-NJ)
HECK, DENNIS (DEM-WA)
HENSARLING, JEB HON. (REP-TX)
HUIZENGA, WILLIAM P THE HON. (REP-MI)
JOHNSON, SAM MR. (REP-TX)
LUETKEMEYER, W BLAINE (REP-MO)
MCCARTHY, KEVIN (REP-CA)
MCHENRY, PATRICK TIMOTHY (REP-NC)
ROSKAM, PETER (REP-IL)
ROYCE, ED MR. (REP-CA)
RYAN, PAUL D. (REP-WI)
SHUSTER, WILLIAM MR. (REP-PA)
VARGAS, JUAN C. (DEM-CA)

Corporate Foundations and Giving Programs
Liberty Mutual Foundation
175 Berkeley St.
Boston, MA 02116
Tel: (617) 357-9500

Public Affairs and Related Activities Personnel

At Headquarters

ARMSTRONG, Jack
Assistant Vice President and Senior Regulatory Counsel
Registered Federal Lobbyist
Tel: (617) 357-9500
Fax: (617) 350-7648

BROSIUS, J. Eric
Senior Vice President, Corporate Actuary
Tel: (617) 357-9500
Fax: (617) 350-7648

CUSOLITO, John
Vice President, Manager, External Relations and Contact, Media Relations
john.cusolito@libertymutual.com
Tel: (617) 574-5512
Fax: (617) 350-7648

ERBIG, Alison
Vice President and Director, Investor Relations
Tel: (617) 357-9500
Fax: (617) 350-7648

FOLEY, Melanie M.
Executive Vice President and Chief Human Resources and Administration Officer
Tel: (617) 357-9500
Fax: (617) 350-7648

FONTANES, A. Alexander
Executive Vice President and Chief Investment Officer
Tel: (617) 357-9500
Fax: (617) 350-7648

GRAYSON, Jonathon Jay
Vice President, Customer Advocacy
jonathon.grayson@libertymutual.com
Tel: (617) 574-6655
Fax: (617) 350-7648

KELLEHER, James F.
Senior Vice President and Chief Legal Officer
Tel: (617) 357-9500
Fax: (617) 350-7648

LANGWELL, Dennis J.
Senior Vice President and Chief Financial Officer
dennis.langwell@libertymutual.com
Tel: (617) 357-9500
Fax: (617) 350-7648

MATTERA, Paul
Senior Vice President & Chief Public Affairs Officer
paul.mattera@libertymutual.com
Registered Federal Lobbyist
Tel: (617) 357-9500
Fax: (617) 350-7648

PETRUZZIELLO , Armando
Director, Investor Relations
Tel: (617) 357-9500
Fax: (617) 350-7648

YAHIA, Laurence H.S.
Senior Vice President and PAC Treasurer
Tel: (617) 357-9500
Fax: (617) 350-7648

At Washington Office

DOWLING, S. Colin
Head, Public Affairs
Colin.Dowling@LibertyMutual.com
Registered Federal Lobbyist
Tel: (202) 289-7472
Fax: (202) 408-1282

RANGASWAMI, Viji L.
Vice President, Federal Affairs
Registered Federal Lobbyist
Tel: (202) 289-7472
Fax: (202) 408-1282

RUSSELL, Christopher
Senior Policy Advisor
Registered Federal Lobbyist
Tel: (202) 289-7472
Fax: (202) 408-1282

Liberty Mutual Middle Market

Formerly Wausau Insurance Company. A financial and multiline carrier in the marketplace. Liberty Mutual Middle Market sells property and casualty insurance products to mid-sized businesses throughout the United States.
www.libertymutualgroupmiddlemarket.com
Annual Revenues: $842.40 million
Employees: 3,500
Industry/ies: Insurance Industry; Medicine/Health Care/Mental Health

Main Headquarters
Mailing: 175 Berkeley St.
Boston, MA 02116
Tel: (617) 357-9500

Corporate Foundations and Giving Programs
Liberty Mutual Foundation

175 Berkeley St.   Tel: (617) 357-9500
Boston, MA 02116

Public Affairs and Related Activities Personnel

At Headquarters

CUSOLITO, John   Tel: (617) 574-5512
Vice President and Manager, Public Relations
john.cusolito@libertymutual.com

ERBIG, Alison B.   Tel: (617) 357-9500
Senior Vice President, Comptroller and Director, Investor
Relations

FOLEY, Melanie M.   Tel: (617) 357-9500
Executive Vice President and Chief Human Resources and
Administration Officer

KELLEHER, James F.   Tel: (617) 357-9500
Executive Vice President and Chief Legal Officer

LANGWELL, Dennis J.   Tel: (617) 357-9500
Executive Vice President and Chief Financial Officer

PETRUZZIELLO, Armando   Tel: (617) 574-6655
Contact, Investor Relations

Life Technologies Corporation

A biotechnology tools company formed from the merger of Applied Biosystems Inc. and
Invitrogen Corporation in November 2008.
www.lifetechnologies.com
Employees: 10,000
Ticker: NASDAQ: LIFE
SIC: 2836
Industry/ies: Science; Scientific Research
Legislative Issues: BUD; HCR; LAW; MED

Main Headquarters
Mailing: 5791 Van Allen Way   Tel: (760) 603-7200
            Carlsbad, CA 92008   Fax: (760) 602-6500

Washington Office
Mailing: 1050 K St. NW   Tel: (202) 347-1708
            Suite 310
            Washington, DC 20001

Corporate Foundations and Giving Programs

Life Technologies Foundation
Contact: Heather Virdo
5791 Van Allen Way   Tel: (760) 746-7204
Carlsbad, CA 92008

Public Affairs and Related Activities Personnel

At Headquarters

CLANCY, Suzanne   Tel: (760) 603-7200
Senior Manager, Public Relations and Contact, Media   Fax: (760) 602-6500
Relations

COTTINGHAM, John   Tel: (760) 603-7200
Chief Legal Officer   Fax: (760) 602-6500

HOFFMEISTER, David F.   Tel: (760) 603-7200
Senior Vice President and Chief Financial Officer   Fax: (760) 602-6500

VIRDO, Heather   Tel: (760) 746-7204
Contact, Community Relations and Corporate   Fax: (760) 602-6500
Communications
heather.virdo@lifetech.com

LifeCare Hospitals

Health care delivery.
www.lifecare-hospitals.com
Annual Revenues: $9.50 million
Employees: 700
Industry/ies: Health Care; Hospitals; Medicine/Health Care/Mental Health
Legislative Issues: HCR

Chairman of the Board and Chief Executive Officer   Tel: (469) 241-2100
DOUGLAS, Phillip B.   Fax: (469) 241-2199
phil.douglas@lifecare-hospitals.com

Main Headquarters
Mailing: 5340 Legacy Dr.   Tel: (469) 241-2100
            Suite 150 -Building Four   Fax: (469) 241-2199
            Plano, TX 75024

Public Affairs and Related Activities Personnel

At Headquarters

BATTAFARANO, Frank   Tel: (469) 241-2100
Chief Operating Officer   Fax: (469) 241-2199

BOWMAN, Maegan   Tel: (469) 241-2100
Vice President, Strategic Projects, Sourcing and Audit Fax: (469) 241-2199

BURTON, Becky   Tel: (469) 241-2100
Vice President, Business Development   Fax: (469) 241-2199

CARPENTER, Stephanie   Tel: (469) 241-2100
Vice President, Finance and Planning   Fax: (469) 241-2199

CONNER, Catherine   Tel: (469) 241-2100
Senior Vice President, Human Resources   Fax: (469) 241-2199
Cconner@lifecare-hospitals.com

PAHL, Erik C.   Tel: (469) 241-2100
General Counsel, Chief Compliance Officer and Secretary Fax: (469) 241-2199

PLORIN, Rosemary   Tel: (615) 297-7766
Media Contact   Fax: (469) 241-2199
rosemary@lovell.com

WALKER, Chris A.   Tel: (469) 241-2100
Chief Financial Officer   Fax: (469) 241-2199
chris.walker@lifecare-hospitals.com

Lifecell Corporation

Develops and markets tissue repair products for use in reconstructive, urogynecologic and
orthopedic surgical procedures.
www.lifecell.com
Employees: 600
Ticker: NASDAQ: LIFC
SIC: 3841
Industry/ies: Medicine/Health Care/Mental Health

Main Headquarters
Mailing: One Millennium Way   Tel: (908) 947-1100
            Branchburg, NJ 08876-3876   Fax: (908) 947-1200
                                                        TF: (800) 367-5737

Public Affairs and Related Activities Personnel

At Headquarters

SOBIESKI, Steven T.   Tel: (908) 947-1100
Vice President, Finance, Administration and Chief Financial Fax: (908) 947-1089
Officer

LifeLock

Specializes in identity theft protection and consumer safety issues.
www.lifelock.com
Annual Revenues: $502.84 million
Employees: 669
Ticker: NYSE: LOCK
SIC: 7374
Industry/ies: Consumers
Legislative Issues: CSP

Chairman of the Board and Chief Executive Officer   Tel: (480) 682-5100
DAVIS, Todd   Fax: (888) 244-9823

Main Headquarters
Mailing: 60 E. Rio Salado Pkwy.   Tel: (480) 457-4500
            Suite 400   Fax: (888) 244-9823
            Tempe, AZ 85281   TF: (800) 543-3562

Corporate Foundations and Giving Programs

LifeLock Contributions Program
Contact: Paige Hanson
60 E. Rio Salado Pkwy.
Suite 400
Tempe, AZ 85281

Public Affairs and Related Activities Personnel

At Headquarters

CERDA, Clarissa   Tel: (480) 457-4500
Chief Legal Strategist   Fax: (888) 244-9823

EISENSTAT, Michelle   Tel: (480) 457-4500
Vice President, Human Resources   Fax: (888) 244-9823

HANSON, Paige   Tel: (480) 457-4500
Manager, Educational Programs   Fax: (888) 244-9823
paige@lifelock.com

HARGIS, Michael   Tel: (480) 457-4500
Senior Vice President, Member Services and Business   Fax: (888) 244-9823
Operations

NASH, Jill   Tel: (480) 457-4500
Chief Communications Officer   Fax: (888) 244-9823

POWER, Chris   Tel: (480) 457-4500
Chief Financial Officer   Fax: (888) 244-9823

PRUSINSKI, Mike   Tel: (480) 457-2101
Vice President, Corporate Communications   Fax: (888) 244-9823
mike@lifelock.com

ROBBINS, Nicholas W.   Tel: (480) 457-4500
Interim Chief Legal Officer and Secretary   Fax: (888) 244-9823

SHAY, Ty   Tel: (480) 457-4500
Chief Marketing Officer   Fax: (888) 244-9823

LifePoint Hospitals, Inc.

Provides healthcare services to non-urban communities.
www.lifepointhospitals.com
Annual Revenues: $5.53 billion
Employees: 40,000

Ticker: NASDAQ: LPNT
SIC: 8062
Industry/ies: Medicine/Health Care/Mental Health
Legislative Issues: HCR; MMM

Chairman of the Board and Chief Executive Officer
CARPENTER, III, William F.

Tel: (615) 372-8500
Fax: (615) 372-8575

Main Headquarters
Mailing: 330 Seven Springs Way
Brentwood, TN 37027

Tel: (615) 372-8500
Fax: (615) 372-8575

Political Action Committees
Lifepoint Hospitals Inc. Good Government Fund PAC
FEC ID: C00347955
Contact: Penny L. Brake
103 Powell Ct.
Suite 200
Brentwood, TN 37027

   Contributions to Candidates: $91,800 (2015-2016)
   Democrats: $25,000; Republicans: $66,800

   Principal Recipients

   SENATE
   BLUNT, ROY (REP-MO)
   SCHUMER, CHARLES E (DEM-NY)

Corporate Foundations and Giving Programs

LifePoint Hospitals Contributions Program
103 Powell Ct.
Brentwood, TN 37027

Public Affairs and Related Activities Personnel

At Headquarters

BRAKE, Penny L.
Vice President, Finance and PAC Treasurer
penny.brake@lpnt.net

Tel: (615) 372-8532
Fax: (615) 372-8575

BUMPUS, John P.
Executive Vice President and Chief Administrative Officer

Tel: (615) 372-8500
Fax: (615) 372-8575

DILL, David M
President and Chief Operating Officer

Tel: (615) 372-8500
Fax: (615) 372-8575

GILBERT, Paul D.
Executive Vice President, Chief Legal Officer

Tel: (615) 372-8500
Fax: (615) 372-8575

HUGGINS, Diane
Vice President, Corporate Communications
diane.huggins@lpnt.net

Tel: (615) 565-1817
Fax: (615) 372-8575

MURPHY, Leif
Executive Vice President and Chief Financial Officer

Tel: (615) 372-8500
Fax: (615) 372-8575

LifeScan, Inc.

A manufacturer of blood glucose monitoring systems.
www.lifescan.com
Employees: 2,500
Industry/ies: Medicine/Health Care/Mental Health

Main Headquarters
Mailing: 1000 Gibraltar Dr.
Milpitas, CA 95035

Tel: (408) 263-9789
Fax: (408) 956-4122
TF: (800) 227-8862

Corporate Foundations and Giving Programs

LifeScan, Inc. Contribution Program
1000 Gibraltar Dr.
Milpitas, CA 95035

Tel: (408) 263-9789
Fax: (408) 946-6070

The Lifetime Healthcare Companies

Formerly known as Blue Cross Blue Shield of Central New York and previously Excellus, Inc. A health insurance company.
www.lifethc.com
Annual Revenues: $5.00 billion
Employees: 6,000
Industry/ies: Medicine/Health Care/Mental Health

Chairman of the Board
CARK, Randall L.

Tel: (585) 454-1700
Fax: (585) 238-4233

President and Chief Executive Officer
BOOTH, Esq., Christopher C.

Tel: (585) 454-1700
Fax: (585) 238-4233

Main Headquarters
Mailing: 165 Court St.
Rochester, NY 14647

Tel: (585) 454-1700
Fax: (585) 238-4233
TF: (800) 847-1200

Public Affairs and Related Activities Personnel

At Headquarters

BURKE, Michael S.
Senior Vice President, Government Programs

Tel: (585) 454-1700
Fax: (585) 238-4233

COLEMAN, Dorothy A.
Executive Vice President and Chief Financial Officer

Tel: (585) 454-1700
Fax: (585) 238-4233

PUCHALSKI, Philip J.
Corporate Vice President, Strategic Communications and Creative Services

Tel: (585) 454-1700
Fax: (585) 238-4400

REDMOND, James
Vice President, Communications
james.redmond@lifethc.com

Tel: (585) 238-4579
Fax: (585) 238-4400

REED, James R.
Senior Vice President, Marketing and Sales

Tel: (585) 454-1700
Fax: (585) 238-4233

SANDERSON, David G.
Senior Vice President, Corporate Human Resources

Tel: (585) 454-1700
Fax: (585) 238-4233

SLOAN, Stephen R.
Executive Vice President and Chief Administrative Officer and General Counsel

Tel: (585) 454-1700
Fax: (585) 238-4233

TAYLOR, Geoffrey E.
Senior Vice President, Corporate Communications and Public Policy

Tel: (585) 454-1700
Fax: (585) 238-4233

Lifetouch Inc.

Provides professional portraits for preschools and schools, houses of worship and the retail market.
www.lifetouch.com
Employees: 22,000
SIC: 2732; 2791
NAICS: 323117; 323122
Industry/ies: Education
Legislative Issues: CPT; CSP; TAX

Chairman of the Board and Chief Executive Officer
HARMEL, Paul
pharmel@lifetouch.com

Tel: (952) 826-4000
Fax: (952) 826-4557

Main Headquarters
Mailing: 11000 Viking Dr., Suite 400
P.O. Box 46993
Eden Prairie, MN 55344

Tel: (952) 826-4000
Fax: (952) 826-4557
TF: (800) 588-9151

Political Action Committees
Lifetouch Inc. PAC
FEC ID: C00405241
Contact: Dale Garton
11000 Viking Dr.
Suite 400
Eden Prairie, MN 55344

   Contributions to Candidates: $29,500 (2015-2016)
   Democrats: $7,000; Republicans: $22,500

Corporate Foundations and Giving Programs

Lifetouch Contributions Program
11000 Viking Dr.
Suite 400
Eden Prairie, MN 55344

Tel: (952) 826-4000

Public Affairs and Related Activities Personnel

At Headquarters

ELO, Glenn M.
Director, Taxes

Tel: (952) 826-4000
Fax: (952) 826-4557

GARTON, Dale
PAC Contact

Tel: (952) 826-4000
Fax: (952) 826-4557

PLADSON, Randolph
Board Member

Tel: (952) 826-4000
Fax: (952) 826-4557

Light-Pod, Inc.

An engineering and design firm focused on solid state lighting applications.
www.light-pod.com
Industry/ies: Electricity & Electronics; Electronics; Energy/Electricity

President
BUDIKE, Jr., Lothar E.S.

Tel: (610) 613-5115
Fax: (215) 689-2181

Main Headquarters
Mailing: 4800 S. 13th St.
Building 100 Innovation Center, Suite 130
Philadelphia, PA 19112

Tel: (610) 613-5115
Fax: (215) 689-2181

Lightbridge Corporation

Developer of nuclear energy and proliferation-resistant nuclear fuels.
www.ltbridge.com
Annual Revenues: $1.18 million
Employees: 10
Ticker: NASDAQ: LTBR
SIC: 8742
Industry/ies: Energy/Electricity

Executive Chairman of the Board
GRAHAM, Jr., Thomas
tgraham@ltbridge.com

Tel: (571) 730-1200
Fax: (571) 730-1259

President and Chief Executive Officer
GRAE, Seth

Tel: (571) 730-1200
Fax: (571) 730-1259

Main Headquarters

Mailing:	1600 Tysons Blvd.	Tel:	(571) 730-1200
	Sutie 550	Fax:	(571) 730-1259
	McLean, VA 22102		

Public Affairs and Related Activities Personnel

At Headquarters

HAYS, Amb. Dennis K.	Tel:	(571) 730-1200
Vice President and Director, Government Relations	Fax:	(571) 730-1259
SHARPE, Gary	Tel:	(571) 730-1213
Contact, Investor Relations and Corporate Communications	Fax:	(571) 730-1259
gsharpe@ltbridge.com		
ZWOBOTA, Linda	Tel:	(571) 730-1200
Chief Financial Officer	Fax:	(571) 730-1259

Lighting Science Group Corporation

LSGC designs, manufactures, and markets Eco-friendly, light-emitting diode (LED) technologies that conserve energy and eliminate the use of hazardous materials.
www.lsgc.com
Annual Revenues: $108.15 million
Employees: 372
SIC: 3640
Industry/ies: Energy/Electricity

Main Headquarters

Mailing: 1830 Penn St.
Melbourne, FL 32901

Public Affairs and Related Activities Personnel

At Other Offices

DI GESU, Jon	Tel:	(603) 770-5731
Contact, Media Relations	Fax:	(321) 779-5521
1227 S. Patrick Dr., Bldg. 2A		
Satellite Beach, FL 32937-3969		
jon.digesu@lsgc.com		

Lightwire, Inc.

Photonics technology development.
lightwireinc.com
Annual Revenues: $4 million
Employees: 38
Industry/ies: Energy/Electricity

Main Headquarters

Mailing:	211 E. Six Forks Rd.	Tel:	(919) 836-1255
	Suite 120 Building A	Fax:	(919) 836-5225
	Raleigh, NC 27609		

Public Affairs and Related Activities Personnel

At Headquarters

PANDYA, C.D.	Tel:	(919) 836-1255
Contact, Media Relations	Fax:	(919) 836-5225
cdpandya@lightwire.com		

Limited Brands, Inc.

See listing on page 477 under L Brands

Lincare Holdings Inc.

A provider of oxygen, respiratory and home infusion produces and services.
www.lincare.com
Annual Revenues: $1.84 billion
Employees: 11,000
Ticker: NASDAQ: LNCR
SIC: 8090
Industry/ies: Medicine/Health Care/Mental Health

Chief Executive Officer	Tel:	(727) 530-7700
HOEFER, Kristen	Fax:	(727) 532-9692

Main Headquarters

Mailing:	19387 U.S. 19 North	Tel:	(727) 530-7700
	Clearwater, FL 33764	Fax:	(727) 532-9692

Public Affairs and Related Activities Personnel

At Headquarters

MCKENZIE, Mickey	Tel:	(727) 530-7700
National Director, Marketing and Business Development	Fax:	(727) 532-9692
SCHABEL, Shawn	Tel:	(727) 530-7700
President & Chief Operating Officer	Fax:	(727) 532-9692
TEUFEL, Crispin	Tel:	(727) 530-7700
Chief Financial Officer	Fax:	(727) 532-9692

Lincoln Electric Company

A manufacturer of arc welding and cutting products.
www.lincolnelectric.com
Annual Revenues: $2.43 billion
Employees: 10,000

Ticker: NASDAQ: LECO
SIC: 3548; 5084
NAICS: 333992
Industry/ies: Energy/Electricity; Machinery/Equipment

Chairman of the Board, President and Chief Executive Officer	Tel:	(216) 481-8100
MAPES, Christopher L.	Fax:	(216) 486-1751

Main Headquarters

Mailing:	22801 St. Clair Ave.	Tel:	(216) 481-8100
	Cleveland, OH 44117	Fax:	(216) 486-1751

Corporate Foundations and Giving Programs

James F. Lincoln Arc Welding Foundation
22801 St. Clair Ave.
Cleveland, OH 44117

Public Affairs and Related Activities Personnel

At Headquarters

BATTLE, Anthony	Tel:	(216) 481-8100
Senior Vice President, Internal Audit and Chief Compliance Officer	Fax:	(216) 486-1751
BRUNO, Gabriel	Tel:	(216) 481-8100
Executive Vice President, Chief Human Resources Officer and Interim Chief Information Officer	Fax:	(216) 486-1751
BUTLER, Amanda H.	Tel:	(216) 383-2534
Director, Investor Relations	Fax:	(216) 486-1751
Amanda_Butler@lincolnelectric.com		
COLEMAN, Greg	Tel:	(216) 383-2462
Group Leader, Marketing Communications	Fax:	(216) 486-1751
greg_coleman@lincolnelectric.com		
HEDLUND, Steven B.	Tel:	(216) 481-8100
Vice President, Strategy and Business Development	Fax:	(216) 486-1751
MINTUN, Michael S.	Tel:	(216) 481-8100
Senior Vice President, Sales and Marketing	Fax:	(216) 486-1751
PETRELLA, Vincent K.	Tel:	(216) 481-8100
Executive Vice President, Chief Financial Officer and Treasurer	Fax:	(216) 486-1751
STUEBER, Frederick G.	Tel:	(216) 481-8100
Executive Vice President, General Counsel and Secretary	Fax:	(216) 486-1751
SUTTELL, Robin	Tel:	(216) 696-0229
Contact, Media	Fax:	(216) 486-1751
rsuttell@fallscommunications.com		
WARD, Earl L.	Tel:	(216) 481-8100
Vice President, Mergers, Acquisitions and Investor Relations	Fax:	(216) 486-1751
Earl_Ward@lincolnelectric.com		

Lincoln Financial Group

An insurance and financial services holding company. Lincoln Financial Group provides advice and solutions that empower Americans to take charge of their financial lives with confidence.
www.lfg.com
Employees: 9,627
Ticker: NYSE: LNC
Industry/ies: Banking/Finance/Investments; Insurance Industry
Legislative Issues: FIN; INS; RET; TAX

President and Chief Executive Officer	Tel:	(260) 455-2000
GLASS, Dennis R.	Fax:	(260) 455-5970
dennis.glass@lfg.com		

Main Headquarters

Mailing:	P.O. Box 2348	Tel:	(260) 455-2000
	Ft. Wayne, IN 46801-2348	Fax:	(260) 455-5970

Washington Office

Mailing:	1455 Pennsylvania Ave. NW	Tel:	(202) 783-0350
	Suite 1110	Fax:	(202) 783-3332
	Washington, DC 20004		

Political Action Committees

Lincoln National Corporation PAC
FEC ID: C00110577
Contact: Jeffrey D. Coutts
1300 S. Clinton St.
Ft. Wayne, IN 46802

Contributions to Candidates: $126,500 (2015-2016)
Democrats: $44,000; Republicans: $82,500

Corporate Foundations and Giving Programs

Lincoln Financial Foundation
Contact: Byron Champlin

1300 S. Clinton St.		
Ft. Wayne, IN 46801	Tel:	(260) 455-2000
	Fax:	(260) 455-5970

Public Affairs and Related Activities Personnel

At Headquarters

ARCARO, Michael	Tel:	(260) 455-2000
Contact, Media Inquiries	Fax:	(260) 455-5970
Michael.Arcaro@LFG.com		

BUCKINGHAM, Lisa M.
Chief Human Resources Officer
Lisa.buckingham@lfg.com
Tel: (260) 455-2000
Fax: (260) 455-5970

CHAMPLIN, Byron
Program Officer
Byron.Champlin@LFG.com
Tel: (260) 455-2000
Fax: (260) 455-5970

COOPER, Ellen
Chief Investment Officer
Tel: (260) 455-2000
Fax: (260) 455-5970

FREITAG, Randal J.
Chief Financial Officer
randy.freitag@lfg.com
Tel: (260) 455-2000
Fax: (260) 455-5970

HICKS , Kirkland
Executive Vice President and General Counsel
Tel: (260) 455-2000
Fax: (260) 455-5970

SOLON, Kenneth S.
Executive Vice President, Chief Information Officer, Head,
Administrative Services
Tel: (260) 455-2000
Fax: (260) 455-5970

At Washington Office

HICKS , Kirkland
Executive Vice President and General Counsel
Tel: (202) 783-0350
Fax: (202) 783-3332

SOLON , Kenneth S.
Executive Vice President, Chief Information Officer and Head,
Administrative Services
Tel: (202) 783-0350
Fax: (202) 783-3332

TRANFA, Janna
Specialist, Federal Relations
janna.tranfa@lfg.com
Tel: (202) 783-0350
Fax: (202) 783-3332

At Other Offices

COUTTS, Jeffrey D.
PAC Treasurer
1300 S. Clinton St.
Ft. Wayne, IN 46801
Tel: (260) 455-2000
Fax: (260) 455-5970

LASORDA , Andrea
Director, Conference and Event Planning
1300 S. Clinton St.
Ft. Wayne, IN 46801
alasorda@us.imshealth.com
Tel: (260) 455-2000
Fax: (260) 455-5970

RAYDER, Helene N.
Vice President & Director of Federal Relations
1300 S. Clinton St.
Ft. Wayne, IN 46801
Registered Federal Lobbyist
Tel: (260) 455-2000
Fax: (260) 455-5970

Lincoln National Corporation

See listing on page 492 under Lincoln Financial Group

Linde North America, Inc.

Supplier of industrial, specialty and medical gases and engineering products.
www.lindeus.com
SIC: 2813; 5172; 2869; 3545; 3812
NAICS: 32512; 42272; 32512; 333515; 334511
Industry/ies: Engineering; Engineering/Mathematics
Legislative Issues: ENV; HCR; NAT; TAX

Main Headquarters
Mailing: 575 Mountain Ave.
Murray Hill, NJ 07974
Tel: (908) 771-1086
TF: (800) 232-4726

Political Action Committees
Linde North America, Inc. Alliance For Good Government (Linde PAC)
FEC ID: C00471193
Contact: Gustave Gallinot
575 Mountain Ave.
Murray Hill, 07974

   Contributions to Candidates: $33,000 (2015-2016)
   Democrats: $12,000; Republicans: $21,000

Public Affairs and Related Activities Personnel

At Headquarters

GALLINOT, Gustave
PAC Contact
Tel: (908) 771-1086

MCGOWAN, Michael
Head, Government Affairs
Tel: (908) 771-1086

Lineage Power

Provides power conversion solutions.
www.lineagepower.com
Annual Revenues: $450 Million
Employees: 1,600
Industry/ies: Energy/Electricity

Main Headquarters
Mailing: 601 Shiloh Rd.
Plano, TX 75074
Tel: (972) 244-9288
Fax: (972) 284-2589
TF: (888) 546-3243

Public Affairs and Related Activities Personnel

At Headquarters

GILHOOLY, Stephen J.
General Counsel and Secretary
Tel: (972) 244-9288
Fax: (972) 284-2589

MORAN, Randi
Vice President, Human Resources
Tel: (972) 244-9288
Fax: (972) 284-2589

SORESON, Skip
Chief Financial Officer
Tel: (972) 244-9288
Fax: (972) 284-2589

LinkedIn Corporation

Professional networking on the internet.
Industry/ies: Computer/Technology; Computers & Databases
Legislative Issues: GOV; LBR; VET

Chief Executive Officer
WEINER, Jeff
Tel: (650) 687-3600

Main Headquarters
Mailing: 2029 Stierlin Ct.
Mountain View, CA 94043
Tel: (650) 687-3600

Public Affairs and Related Activities Personnel

At Headquarters

CALLAHAN, Michael
Vice President, General Counsel and Secretary
Tel: (650) 687-3600

CHAVEZ, Pablo
Vice President, Global Public Policy and Government Affairs
Tel: (650) 687-3600

HOROWITZ, Daniel
Director, Advocacy & Campaigns
Tel: (650) 687-3600

SCOTT, Kevin
Senior Vice President, Engineering and Operations
Tel: (650) 687-3600

SORDELLO, Steve
Senior Vice President and Chief Financial Officer
Tel: (650) 687-3600

STUBO, Shannon
Senior Vice President, Marketing and Communications
Tel: (650) 687-3600

Lion Apparel

Manufacturer of personal protective equipment.
www.lionprotects.com
Annual Revenues: $32.00 million
Employees: 700
SIC: 2326; 5699; 9999
NAICS: 44819; 99999; 315225
Industry/ies: Apparel/Textiles Industry; Defense/Homeland Security;
Government-Related
Legislative Issues: BUD

Chief Executive Officer
SCHWARTZ, Stephen
STEVEDY@lionapparel.com
Tel: (937) 898-1949

Main Headquarters
Mailing: 7200 Poe Ave.
Suite 400
Dayton, OH 45414
Tel: (937) 898-1949
TF: (800) 548-6614

Corporate Foundations and Giving Programs
Lion Foundation Charitable Grants
6450 Poe Ave.
Dayton, OH 45413
Tel: (937) 898-1949

Public Affairs and Related Activities Personnel

At Headquarters

FUDGE, Hayley
Vice President, National Accounts
hfudge@lionapparel.com
Tel: (937) 415-2808

SCHWARTZ, Andrew
Corporate Counsel
Tel: (937) 898-1949

Liquidity Services, Inc.

Provider of full-service solutions to market and sell assets.
liquidityservicesinc.com
Annual Revenues: $473.47 million
Employees: 1,345
Ticker: NASDAQ: LQDT
SIC: 7389
Industry/ies: Advertising And Marketing; Banking/Finance/Investments

Chairman of the Board and Chief Executive Officer
ANGRICK, III, William P.
Tel: (202) 467-6868
Fax: (202) 467-5475

Main Headquarters
Mailing: 1920 L St. NW
Sixth Floor
Washington, DC 20036
Tel: (202) 467-6868
Fax: (202) 467-5475
TF: (800) 310-4604

Public Affairs and Related Activities Personnel

At Headquarters

ALI, APR, Sultana F.
Tel: (202) 467-5723

Senior Public Relations Manager	Fax:	(202) 467-5475
sultana.ali@liquidityservicesinc.com		
DAVIS, Julie	Tel:	(202) 558-6234
Director, Investor Relations	Fax:	(202) 467-5475
julie.davis@liquidityservicesinc.com		
DOMINO, Kathy	Tel:	(202) 467-6868
Chief Accounting Officer	Fax:	(202) 467-5475
LUTZ, Mike	Tel:	(202) 467-6868
Vice President, Human Resources	Fax:	(202) 467-5475
RALLO, James M.	Tel:	(202) 467-6868
Chief Financial Officer and Treasurer	Fax:	(202) 467-5475
jim.rallo@liquidityservicesinc.com		
RUSSELL, Rachel	Tel:	(202) 467-6868
Vice President, Marketing and Business Development	Fax:	(202) 467-5475
WILLIAMS, James E.	Tel:	(202) 467-6868
Vice President, General Counsel and Corporate Secretary	Fax:	(202) 467-5475
james.williams@liquidityservicesinc.com		

Little Caesar Enterprises

Operates and franchises more than 2,500 Little Caesars carryout pizza restaurants throughout the US and in about ten other countries. A subsidiary of Ilitch Holdings, Inc.
www.littlecaesars.com
Annual Revenues: $204.7 million
Employees: 6,000
Industry/ies: Food And Beverage Industry
Legislative Issues: LBR

Chairman of the Board and Chief Executive Officer	Tel:	(313) 983-6000
ILTCH, Michael	Fax:	(313) 983-6197

Main Headquarters		
Mailing:	2211 Woodward Ave.	Tel:	(313) 983-6000
	Detroit, MI 48201	Fax:	(313) 983-6390

Corporate Foundations and Giving Programs

Little Caesar Enterprises Contributions Program		
2211 Woodward Ave.	Tel:	(313) 983-6000
Detroit, MI 48201		

Public Affairs and Related Activities Personnel

At Headquarters

OLDHAM, Kathryn	Tel:	(313) 983-6398
Director, Communications	Fax:	(313) 983-6390
SNYGG, Darrel	Tel:	(313) 983-6000
Senior Vice President, Finance, Accounting and Administration	Fax:	(313) 983-6193

Live Nation Entertainment

An entertainment promoter. Formed with the merger of Live Nation and Ticketmaster in 2010.
www.livenation.com
Annual Revenues: $6.86 billion
Employees: 7,900
Ticker: NYSE: LYV
SIC: 7900
Industry/ies: Arts, The; Performing Arts/Music; Sports/Leisure/Entertainment
Legislative Issues: ART; CPT; CSP

Chairman of the Board	Tel:	(310) 867-7000
MAFFEI, Gregory B.	Fax:	(310) 867-7001

Director, President and Chief Executive Officer	Tel:	(310) 867-7000
RAPINO, Michael	Fax:	(310) 867-7001

Main Headquarters		
Mailing:	9348 Civic Center Dr.	Tel:	(310) 867-7000
	Beverly Hills, CA 90210	Fax:	(310) 867-7001
		TF:	(888) 497-2555

Public Affairs and Related Activities Personnel

At Headquarters

BERCHTOLD, Joe	Tel:	(310) 867-7000
Chief Operating Officer	Fax:	(310) 867-7001
BERGMAN, Maili	Tel:	(310) 867-7000
Senior Vice President, Investor Relations	Fax:	(310) 867-7001
IR@livenation.com		
HOPMANS, John	Tel:	(310) 867-7000
Executive Vice President, Mergers and Acquisitions and Strategic Finance	Fax:	(310) 867-7001
ROWLES, Michael	Tel:	(310) 867-7000
General Counsel and Secretary	Fax:	(310) 867-7001
WILLARD, Kathy	Tel:	(310) 867-7000
Chief Financial Officer	Fax:	(310) 867-7001

At Other Offices

RELIC, Becky	Tel:	(310) 209-3183
Senior Vice President, Government Affairs		
1100 Glendon Ave., Suite 2000		
Los Angeles, CA 90024		

Registered Federal Lobbyist

Live365 Inc.

Serves as a global internet broadcasting community for individuals, businesses, artists and organizations to create, broadcast and listen to Internet radio stations.
www.live365.com
Annual Revenues: $4.20 million
Employees: 35
Industry/ies: Communications; Telecommunications/Internet/Cable

Main Headquarters		
Mailing:	950 Tower Ln.	Tel:	(650) 345-7400
	Suite 1550	Fax:	(650) 345-7497
	Foster City, CA 94404	TF:	(800) 294-4777

Public Affairs and Related Activities Personnel

At Headquarters

ELGAARD, Heidi	Tel:	(650) 345-7400
Director, Marketing	Fax:	(650) 345-7497
FLOATER, Johnie	Tel:	(650) 345-7400
General Manager, Media Relations	Fax:	(650) 345-7497

Livermore Fitzgerald Kunin Doyle & Associates Inc.

A healthcare management services provider.
www.lfkd.net
Industry/ies: Law/Law Firms; Management; Medicine/Health Care/Mental Health

Main Headquarters		
Mailing:	P.O. Box 48417	Tel:	(404) 704-0713
	Washington, DC 20002	TF:	(866) 290-7911

Public Affairs and Related Activities Personnel

At Headquarters

DOYLE, Brian L.	Tel:	(404) 704-0713
Partner		
bdoyle@lfkd.net		
JOHNSON, Travis	Tel:	(404) 704-0713
Associate		
KUNIN, J. Livingston	Tel:	(404) 704-0713
Partner		
LIVERMORE, Diane	Tel:	(404) 704-0713
Senior Partner		
NEADOWS, Darryl	Tel:	(404) 704-0713
Associate		

LKQ Corporation

Provides replacement parts, components, and systems needed to repair cars and trucks. In 2007, LKQ acquired Keystone Automotive Industries.
www.lkqcorp.com
Annual Revenues: $5.49 billion
Employees: 29,500
Ticker: NASDAQ: LKQ
SIC: 5010
Industry/ies: Automotive Industry; Machinery/Equipment; Transportation
Legislative Issues: AUT; CSP

Chairman of the Board	Tel:	(312) 621-1950
HOLSTEN, Joseph M.	Fax:	(312) 621-1969

President and Chief Executive Officer	Tel:	(312) 621-1950
WAGMAN, Robert L.	Fax:	(312) 621-1969

Main Headquarters		
Mailing:	500 W. Madison St.	Tel:	(312) 621-1950
	Suite 2800	Fax:	(312) 621-1969
	Chicago, IL 60661	TF:	(877) 557-2677

Political Action Committees

LKQ Corporation Employee Good Government Fund
FEC ID: C00458158
Contact: Ray Colas

5975 N. Federal Hwy.	Tel:	(954) 492-9092
Suite130		
Ft. Lauderdale, FL 33308		

> **Contributions to Candidates:** $27,000 (2015-2016)
> Democrats: $8,500; Republicans: $18,500

Public Affairs and Related Activities Personnel

At Headquarters

ALBERICO, Robert A.	Tel:	(312) 621-1950
Senior Vice President, Human Resources	Fax:	(312) 621-1969
BOUTROSS , Joseph P.	Tel:	(312) 621-2793
Director, Investor Relations and Contact, Media Relations	Fax:	(312) 621-1969
jpboutross@lkqcorp.com		
CASINI, Victor M.	Tel:	(312) 621-1950
Senior Vice President, General Counsel and Corporate Secretary	Fax:	(312) 621-1969

QUINN, John S.
Chief Executive Officer and Managing Director, European Operations
Tel: (312) 621-1950
Fax: (312) 621-1969

ZARCONE, Dominick
Executive Vice President and Chief Financial Officer
Tel: (312) 621-1950
Fax: (312) 621-1969

At Other Offices

COLAS, Ray
Federal Lobbyist
5975 N. Federal Hwy., Suite130
Ft. Lauderdale, FL 33308
Tel: (954) 492-9092

Local Initiatives Support Corporation

A national non-profit organization based in New York City. Concerns include housing and community development policies and programs.
www.liscnet.org
Industry/ies: Economics And Economic Development; Housing
Legislative Issues: ACC; BUD; TAX

Chairman of the Board
RUBIN, Robert E.
Tel: (212) 455-9800
Fax: (212) 687-1396

President and Chief Executive Officer
RUBINGER, Michael
Tel: (212) 455-9800
Fax: (212) 687-1396

Main Headquarters
Mailing: 1825 K St. NW
Suite 1100
Washington, DC 20006
Tel: (212) 455-9800
Fax: (212) 687-1396

Corporate Foundations and Giving Programs

Local Initiatives Support Corporation Contributions Program
Contact: Beth Marcus
501 Seventh Ave.
New York City, NY 10018

Public Affairs and Related Activities Personnel

At Headquarters

BURNHAM, Barbara Wells
Vice President, Federal Policy
Tel: (202) 785-2908
Fax: (202) 835-8931

ROBERTS, Benson F.
Vice President, Policy
Tel: (202) 785-2908
Fax: (202) 835-8931

At Other Offices

ABRAHAM, Reena
Vice President Education Programs
501 Seventh Ave., Seventh Floor
New York City, NY 10018
Tel: (212) 455-9800
Fax: (212) 682-5929

ALLEN, Mary Jo
Senior Vice President, Human Resources
501 Seventh Ave., Seventh Floor
New York City, NY 10018
mjallen@lisc.org
Tel: (212) 455-9856
Fax: (212) 687-1396

BAUM, Geraldine
Senior Vice President, Marketing and Communications
501 Seventh Ave., Seventh Floor
New York City, NY 10018
Tel: (212) 455-9800
Fax: (212) 687-1396

JOSEPHS, Matthew
Senior Vice President, Policy
501 Seventh Ave., Seventh Floor
New York City, NY 10018
Tel: (212) 455-9861
Fax: (212) 682-5929

LEVINE, Michael
Executive Vice President and General Counsel
501 Seventh Ave., Seventh Floor
New York City, NY 10018
Tel: (212) 455-9800
Fax: (212) 687-1396

LEVY, Tobin
Executive Vice President & Chief Financial Officer
501 Seventh Ave., Seventh Floor
New York City, NY 10018
Tel: (212) 455-9800
Fax: (212) 687-1396

MARCUS, Beth
Senior Vice President, Foundation and Corporate Relations
501 Seventh Ave., Seventh Floor
New York City, NY 10018
Tel: (212) 455-9800
Fax: (212) 687-1396

PONSOR, Andrea R.
501 Seventh Ave., Seventh Floor
New York City, NY 10018
Tel: (212) 455-9800
Fax: (212) 682-5929

Lockheed Martin Aculight Corporation

Defense and commercial laser and electro-optic technology producer.
www.aculight.com
Annual Revenues: $8.90 million
Employees: 100
Industry/ies: Computer/Technology; Defense/Homeland Security; Government-Related

President
RICH, Don
Tel: (425) 482-1100
Fax: (425) 482-1101

Main Headquarters

Mailing: 22121 20th Ave. SE
Bothell, WA 98021
Tel: (425) 482-1100
Fax: (425) 482-1101
TF: (888) 451-9558

Public Affairs and Related Activities Personnel

At Headquarters

BENNETT, Dale P.
Executive Vice President, Mission Systems & Training
Tel: (425) 482-1100
Fax: (425) 482-1101

Lockheed Martin Corporation

Lockheed Martin is a highly diversified global enterprise principally engaged in the research, design, development, manufacture and integration of advanced technology systems, products and services. The Corporation's core businesses span space and telecommunications, electronics, information and services, aeronautics, energy and systems integration. Also represented by Adam Emanuel, of Adam Emanuel and Associates, on behalf of the Office of Zel E. Lipsen.
www.lockheedmartin.com
Annual Revenues: $45.06 billion
Employees: 112,000
Ticker: NYSE: LMT
SIC: 3760
Industry/ies: Defense/Homeland Security; Government-Related
Legislative Issues: AER; AVI; BUD; DEF; ENG; ENV; HOM; INT; NAT; TAX; TEC; TRD; VET

Chairman of the Board, President and Chief Executive Officer
HEWSON, Marillyn
Tel: (301) 897-6000
Fax: (301) 897-6704

Main Headquarters
Mailing: 6801 Rockledge Dr.
Bethesda, MD 20817
Tel: (301) 897-6000
Fax: (301) 897-6704

Political Action Committees
Lockheed Martin Corporation Employees PAC
FEC ID: C00303024
Contact: Lawrence Duncan III
2121 Crystal Dr.
Suite 100
Arlington, VA 22202

Contributions to Candidates: $12,414,265 (2015-2016)
Democrats: $790,500; Republicans: $1,358,750; Other: $10,265,015

Principal Recipients

SENATE
BLUNT, ROY (REP-MO)
CRUZ, RAFAEL EDWARD TED (REP-TX)
JOHNSON, RONALD HAROLD (REP-)
SCOTT, TIMOTHY E (REP-SC)

HOUSE
ADERHOLT, ROBERT BROWN (REP-AL)
BEYER, DONALD STERNOFF JR. (DEM-VA)
BYRNE, BRADLEY ROBERTS (REP-AL)
CALVERT, KEN (REP-CA)
CARTER, JOHN R. REP. (REP-DC)
CLYBURN, JAMES E. (DEM-SC)
COFFMAN, MIKE REP. (REP-CO)
COLE, TOM (REP-OK)
COMSTOCK, BARBARA J HONORABLE (REP-VA)
CONNOLLY, GERALD EDWARD (DEM-VA)
COURTNEY, JOSEPH D (DEM-CT)
DENT, CHARLES W. REP. (REP-PA)
ENGEL, ELIOT L. REP. (DEM-DC)
FLORES, BILL (REP-TX)
FORBES, J. RANDY (REP-VA)
FRELINGHUYSEN, RODNEY P. (REP-NJ)
GABBARD, TULSI (DEM-HI)
GRANGER, KAY (REP-TX)
HECK, JOE (REP-NV)
JOHNSON, HENRY C 'HANK' (DEM-GA)
KAPTUR, MARCY C HON. (DEM-OH)
KATKO, JOHN M (REP-NY)
KEATING, WILLIAM RICHARD (DEM-MA)
KILMER, DEREK (DEM-WA)
KINZINGER, ADAM (REP-IL)
KNIGHT, STEVE (REP-CA)
LAMBORN, DOUGLAS (REP-CO)
LARSON, JOHN B (DEM-CT)
LOBIONDO, FRANK A. (REP-NJ)
LOUDERMILK, BARRY (REP-GA)
MARINO, THOMAS ANTHONY (REP-PA)
MCCARTHY, KEVIN (REP-CA)
MCMORRIS RODGERS, CATHY (REP-WA)
NORCROSS, DONALD W (DEM-NJ)
NUNES, DEVIN G (REP-CA)
PALAZZO, STEVEN MCCARTY (REP-MS)
PELOSI, NANCY (DEM-CA)
POMPEO, MICHAEL RICHARD (REP-KS)
PRICE, THOMAS EDMUNDS (REP-GA)

REED, THOMAS W II (REP-NY)
ROBY, MARTHA (REP-AL)
ROGERS, MICHAEL DENNIS (REP-AL)
ROONEY, TOM MR. (REP-FL)
ROYCE, ED MR. (REP-CA)
RUPPERSBERGER, C.A. DUTCH (DEM-MD)
SCOTT, JAMES AUSTIN (REP-GA)
SEWELL, TERRYCINA ANDREA (DEM-AL)
SIMPSON, MICHAEL (REP-ID)
SLAUGHTER, LOUISE M (DEM-NY)
SMITH, LAMAR (REP-TX)
STEFANIK, ELISE M. (REP-NY)
STEWART, CHRIS (REP-UT)
THORNBERRY, MAC (REP-TX)
TURNER, MICHAEL R (REP-OH)
VEASEY, MARC ALLISON MR. (DEM-TX)
WENSTRUP, BRAD DR. (REP-OH)
WITTMAN, ROBERT J MR. (REP-VA)
WOMACK, STEVE (REP-AR)

Corporate Foundations and Giving Programs

Lockheed Martin Contributions Program
6801 Rockledge Dr.
Bethesda, MD 20817

Public Affairs and Related Activities Personnel

At Headquarters

BROWN, Gwendolyn — Tel: (301) 897-6000 — Fax: (301) 897-6704
Registered Federal Lobbyist

BURTON, Dawn — Tel: (301) 897-6000 — Fax: (301) 897-6704
Federal Lobbyist
Registered Federal Lobbyist

COZAD, Stephanie — Tel: (301) 897-6000 — Fax: (301) 897-6704
Federal Lobbyist

DAVID, Elaine — Tel: (301) 897-6000 — Fax: (301) 897-6704
Senior Director, Government and Regulatory Affairs
Registered Federal Lobbyist

DESMOND, Carrie — Tel: (301) 897-6000 — Fax: (301) 897-6704
Director, Legislative Affairs
Registered Federal Lobbyist

FRASER, Mary Ellen — Tel: (301) 897-6000 — Fax: (301) 897-6704
Director, Government Relations
Registered Federal Lobbyist

GARAVANTA, Lisa — Tel: (301) 897-6000 — Fax: (301) 897-6704
Director, Legislative Affairs
Registered Federal Lobbyist

GASPAR, Mark — Tel: (301) 897-6000 — Fax: (301) 897-6704

GASPARD, Marc — Tel: (301) 897-6000 — Fax: (301) 897-6704
Federal Lobbyist
Registered Federal Lobbyist

JUOLA, Paul W. — Tel: (301) 897-6000 — Fax: (301) 897-6704
Registered Federal Lobbyist

KIRCHER, III, Jerry F. — Tel: (301) 897-6584 — Fax: (301) 897-6704
Vice President, Investor Relations
jerry.f.kircher@lmco.com

LUCAS, John T. — Tel: (301) 897-6000 — Fax: (301) 897-6704
Senior Vice President, Human Resources and Communications
john.t.lucas@lmco.com

MCCOLLUM, Lauren M. — Tel: (301) 897-6000 — Fax: (301) 897-6704
Director, Legislative Affairs
Registered Federal Lobbyist

NELSON, Dan — Tel: (301) 897-6000 — Fax: (301) 897-6704
Vice President, Worldwide Media Relations
dan.nelson@lmco.com

O'DONNELL, John — Tel: (301) 897-6308 — Fax: (202) 413-5908
Contact, Government Relations
Registered Federal Lobbyist

ROSEMARINO, Anthony — Tel: (301) 897-6000 — Fax: (301) 897-6704
Federal Lobbyist
Registered Federal Lobbyist

SCHILPP, Donald — Tel: (301) 897-6000 — Fax: (301) 897-6704
Contact, Government Relations
don.schilpp@lmco.com
Registered Federal Lobbyist

SCHNABEL, Andrew — Tel: (301) 897-6000 — Fax: (301) 897-6704
Federal Lobbyist
Registered Federal Lobbyist

SHERIDAN, Cedric N. — Tel: (301) 897-6000 — Fax: (301) 897-6704
Federal Lobbyist
Registered Federal Lobbyist

SPRINGER SFORZA, Mary — Tel: (301) 897-6000 — Fax: (301) 897-6704
Registered Federal Lobbyist

STEVENS , Robert J. — Tel: (301) 897-6000 — Fax: (301) 897-6704
Executive Chairman of the Board

TANNER, Bruce L. — Tel: (301) 897-6000 — Fax: (301) 897-6704
Executive Vice President and Chief Financial Officer
bruce.tanner@lmco.com

VASAN, Regina M. — Tel: (301) 897-6290 — Fax: (301) 897-6252
Vice President, Corporate Identity

WARREN, Jennifer — Tel: (301) 897-6000 — Fax: (301) 897-6704
Vice President, Technology Policy and Regulation
jennifer.warren@lmco.com
Registered Federal Lobbyist

At Other Offices

BANTON, Linda W. — Tel: (703) 413-5600 — Fax: (703) 413-5958
Vice President, Congressional Relations, Government and Regulatory Affairs
1550 Crystal Dr., Crystal Sq. Two, Suite 300
Arlington, VA 22202
linda.banton@lmco.com
Registered Federal Lobbyist

BROZOST, Jay — Tel: (703) 413-5600
Vice President, General Counsel, Washington Operations
1550 Crystal Dr., Crystal Sq. Two, Suite 300
Arlington, VA 22202
jay.a.brozost@lmco.com

BURNISON, Scott — Tel: (703) 413-5660 — Fax: (703) 413-5958
Federal Lobbyist
1550 Crystal Dr., Crystal Sq. Two, Suite 300
Arlington, VA 22202
Registered Federal Lobbyist

CARUTH, Gabrielle — Tel: (703) 413-5600
Federal Lobbyist
1550 Crystal Dr., Crystal Sq. Two, Suite 300
Arlington, VA 22202
gabrielle.k.carruth@lmco.com
Registered Federal Lobbyist

DUBEE, Melvin — Tel: (703) 413-5600
Vice President, Legislative Affairs, Intelligence, Joint, Science and Technology Programs
1550 Crystal Dr., Crystal Sq. Two, Suite 300
Arlington, VA 22202

DUNCAN, III, Lawrence
PAC Treasurer
2121 Crystal Dr., #100, Suite 100
Arlington, VA 22202
Registered Federal Lobbyist

FAUSER, Kristine — Tel: (703) 413-5600 — Fax: (703) 413-5617
Director, Legislative Affairs
1550 Crystal Dr., Crystal Sq. Two, Suite 300
Arlington, VA 22202
kristine.fauser@lmco.com
Registered Federal Lobbyist

GUDES, Scott — Tel: (703) 413-5600 — Fax: (703) 413-5617
Vice President Legislative Affairs Space Systems and Missile Defense
1550 Crystal Dr., Crystal Sq. Two, Suite 300
Arlington, VA 22202

HARVEY, Gerald — Tel: (703) 413-5859 — Fax: (703) 413-5749
Vice President, Legislative Affairs
1550 Crystal Dr., Crystal Sq. Two, Suite 300
Arlington, VA 22202
gerald.g.harvey@lmco.com
Registered Federal Lobbyist

HEAD, Robert — Tel: (703) 413-5600
Federal Lobbyist
1550 Crystal Dr., Crystal Sq. Two, Suite 300
Arlington, VA 22202
Registered Federal Lobbyist

HERMANDORFER, Wayne — Tel: (703) 413-5777 — Fax: (703) 413-5617
Vice President, Navy Programs Legislative Affairs
1550 Crystal Dr., Crystal Sq. Two, Suite 300
Arlington, VA 22202
Registered Federal Lobbyist

LAVAN, Maryanne — Tel: (301) 897-6000 — Fax: (301) 897-6704
Vice President, Internal Audit
1550 Crystal Dr., Crystal Sq. Two, Suite 300
Arlington, VA 22202
maryanne.lavan@lmco.com

MAYNARD, Ray — Tel: (703) 413-5607 — Fax: (703) 413-5617
Director, Legislative Affairs, Space Systems
1550 Crystal Dr., Crystal Sq. Two, Suite 300

Arlington, VA 22202
Registered Federal Lobbyist

MUSARRA, Gerald   Tel: (703) 413-5791
Vice President, Corporate Government and Regulatory Affairs   Fax: (703) 413-5908
1550 Crystal Dr., Crystal Sq. Two, Suite 300
Arlington, VA 22202
Gerald.Musarra@lmco.com

OVERSTREET, Jack C.   Tel: (703) 413-5634
Vice President, Aeronautical Legislative Affairs   Fax: (703) 413-5737
1550 Crystal Dr., Crystal Sq. Two, Suite 300
Arlington, VA 22202

ROBBINS, Michelle E.   Tel: (703) 413-5612
Director, Space Legislative Affairs, NASA Programs   Fax: (703) 413-5819
1550 Crystal Dr., Crystal Sq. Two, Suite 300
Arlington, VA 22202
Registered Federal Lobbyist

SCHLEGEL, Nancy   Tel: (703) 413-5600
Director, Congressional Relations Government and   Fax: (703) 413-5617
Regulatory Affairs
1550 Crystal Dr., Crystal Sq. Two, Suite 300
Arlington, VA 22202

WALTERS, Gregory   Tel: (703) 413-5933
Vice President, Legislative Affairs   Fax: (703) 413-5958
1550 Crystal Dr., Crystal Sq. Two, Suite 300
Arlington, VA 22202
Registered Federal Lobbyist

Lockheed Martin Electronics and Missiles
See listing on page 495 under Lockheed Martin Corporation

Lockheed Martin Sippican, Inc.
A designer and manufacturer of electronic and mechanical systems and subsystems and associated services.
www.sippican.com
Employees: 400
Industry/ies: Business; Marine/Maritime/Shipping; Small Business; Transportation

Main Headquarters
Mailing: Seven Barnabas Rd.   Tel: (508) 748-1160
   Marion, MA 02738   Fax: (508) 748-3626

Corporate Foundations and Giving Programs
Lockheed Martin Sippican, Inc. Contributions Program
Seven Barnabas Rd.   Tel: (508) 748-1160
Marion, MA 02738   Fax: (508) 748-3626

Public Affairs and Related Activities Personnel

At Headquarters
HICKEY, James J.   Tel: (508) 748-1160
Chief Financial Officer & Vice President   Fax: (508) 748-3626

Loews Corporation
A diversified financial holding company involved in hotels, tobacco, insurance, watches and clocks, oil drilling fleets and gas pipelines.
www.loews.com
Annual Revenues: $13.11 billion
Employees: 16,700
Ticker: NYSE: L
SIC: 3873
Industry/ies: Banking/Finance/Investments
Legislative Issues: ENG; FIN; FUE; INS; INT; NAT; TAX; TOU

Co-Chairman of the Board   Tel: (212) 521-2000
TISCH, Andrew H.   Fax: (212) 521-2525

Co-Chairman of the Board   Tel: (212) 521-2000
TISCH, Jonathan   Fax: (212) 521-2525

President and Chief Executive Officer   Tel: (212) 521-2000
TISCH, James S.   Fax: (212) 521-2525

Main Headquarters
Mailing: 667 Madison Ave.   Tel: (212) 521-2000
   New York City, NY 10065-8087   Fax: (212) 521-2525

Political Action Committees
Loews Corporation Energy Public Affairs Committee
FEC ID: C00473082
Contact: Edmund Unneland
667 Madison Ave.   Tel: (212) 521-2000
New York City, NY 10065-8087   Fax: (212) 521-2525

   Contributions to Candidates: $67,500 (2015-2016)
   Democrats: $13,500; Republicans: $54,000

Loews Corporation Public Affairs Committee PAC
FEC ID: C00416495
Contact: Edmund Unneland
667 Madison Ave.   Tel: (212) 521-2000
New York City, NY 10021   Fax: (212) 521-2525

   Contributions to Candidates: $56,000 (2015-2016)
   Democrats: $21,500; Republicans: $34,500

Public Affairs and Related Activities Personnel

At Headquarters
CUSHING, Laura K.   Tel: (212) 521-2000
Chief Human Resources Officer   Fax: (212) 521-2525

EDELSON, David B.   Tel: (212) 521-2000
Senior Vice President and Chief Financial Officer   Fax: (212) 521-2525

GARSON, Gary W.   Tel: (212) 521-2000
Senior Vice President, Secretary and General Counsel   Fax: (212) 521-2525
ggarson@loews.com

KOPLOVITZ, Jonathan   Tel: (212) 521-2000
Vice President, Corporate Development   Fax: (212) 521-2525

RAMPINELLI, Audrey A.   Tel: (212) 521-2000
Vice President, Risk Management   Fax: (212) 521-2525

SCOTT, Richard W.   Tel: (212) 521-2000
Senior Vice President and Chief Investment Officer   Fax: (212) 521-2525

SKAFIDAS, Mary   Tel: (212) 521-2788
Vice President, Investor and Public Relations   Fax: (212) 521-2525

UNNELAND, Edmund   Tel: (212) 521-2000
PAC Contact   Fax: (212) 521-2525

At Other Offices
MOMEYER, Alan   Tel: (212) 521-2000
Vice President, Human Resources
655 Madison Ave.
New York City, NY 10065-8068

Loews Hotels
See listing on page 497 under Loews Corporation

LogistiCare Solutions
LogistiCare provides Medicaid transportation management solution.
www.logisticare.com
Annual Revenues: $17.60 million
Employees: 600
SIC: 4700
Industry/ies: Medicine/Health Care/Mental Health; Transportation
Legislative Issues: MMM

Chief Executive Officer   Tel: (770) 907-7596
SCHWARZ, Herman M.   Fax: (770) 907-7598

Main Headquarters
Mailing: 1275 Peachtree St. NE   Tel: (404) 888-5800
   6th Floor   Fax: (404) 888-5999
   Atlanta, GA 30309   TF: (800) 486-7647

Corporate Foundations and Giving Programs
The LogistiCare Foundation
Contact: Chinta Gaston
1800 Phoenix Blvd.
Suite 120
Atlanta, GA 30349

Public Affairs and Related Activities Personnel

At Headquarters
BRYARS, Gregg   Tel: (404) 888-5800
Senior Vice President, Operations   Fax: (404) 888-5999

BUCKLEY, David   Tel: (404) 888-5800
Director, Business Development   Fax: (404) 888-5999
david.buckley@logisticare.com

CORTINA, Albert   Tel: (770) 907-7596
Chief Administrative Officer   Fax: (770) 907-7598
lbertc@logisticare.com

GASTON, Chinta   Tel: (770) 907-7596
Chief Legal Officer, General Counsel and Foundation Board   Fax: (770) 907-7598
Secretary
chintag@logisticare.com

LINOWES, Steven D.   Tel: (404) 888-5800
Executive Vice President   Fax: (404) 888-5999

SOUTHERN, Jenny   Tel: (770) 907-7596
Director, Human Resources and Recruitment   Fax: (770) 907-7598

WALTER, Bill   Tel: (404) 888-5800
Vice President, Business Developement   Fax: (404) 888-5999

Logistics Health Incorporated
Provides healthcare solutions to government and commercial organizations.
www.logisticshealth.com
Annual Revenues: $161.85 million
Industry/ies: Defense/Homeland Security; Government-Related

Founder and Chief Executive Officer   Tel: (866) 284-8788
WEBER, Donald J.   Fax: (608) 783-7532

Main Headquarters

Mailing:	328 Front St., South	Tel:	(608) 782-0404
	La Crosse, WI 54601	Fax:	(608) 783-7532

Public Affairs and Related Activities Personnel

At Headquarters

ARMSTRONG, Tracey	Tel:	(608) 782-0404
Director, Marketing and Communications	Fax:	(608) 783-7532
tarmstrong@logisticshealth.com		
HELKE, CPA, Karla	Tel:	(608) 782-0404
Director, Finance and Controller	Fax:	(608) 783-7532
HENRY, Diana	Tel:	(866) 284-8788
Manager, Corporate Communications and Marketing	Fax:	(608) 783-7532
KELEMAN, Robert A.	Tel:	(866) 284-8788
Vice President, Human Resources	Fax:	(608) 783-7532
WITT-BOTCHER, JD, Suzanne	Tel:	(866) 284-8788
Corporate Counsel	Fax:	(608) 783-7532

Lojack Corporation

The company rents tracking computers to law enforcement agencies, then markets transponders to dealers and operators in 27 states and the District of Columbia, and more than 30 countries internationally. It also markets products for tracking people, as well as cargo/equipment tracking and recovery.
www.lojack.com
Annual Revenues: $133.57 million
Employees: 670
Ticker: NASDAQ; LOJN
SIC: 3669
Industry/ies: Automotive Industry; Transportation

Chairman of the Board	Tel:	(781) 251-4700
COWAN, Rory	Fax:	(781) 251-4649
President and Chief Executive Officer	Tel:	(781) 251-4700
ORTIZ, Randy	Fax:	(781) 251-4649

Main Headquarters

Mailing:	200 Lowder Brook Dr.	Tel:	(781) 251-4700
	Suite 1000	Fax:	(781) 251-4649
	Westwood, MA 02090		

Public Affairs and Related Activities Personnel

At Headquarters

CALUSDIAN, David	Tel:	(617) 542-5300
Contact, Investor Relations	Fax:	(781) 251-4649
LOJN@investorrelations.com		
DEWSNAP, Hal	Tel:	(781) 251-4700
Senior Vice President and General Manager, Sales	Fax:	(781) 251-4649
DUMAS, Ken	Tel:	(781) 251-4700
Senior Vice President, Chief Financial Officer and Treasurer	Fax:	(781) 251-4649
LANDRY, Matt	Tel:	(978) 499-9250
Contact, Public Relations	Fax:	(781) 251-4649
lojack@matternow.com		
OXHOLM, Jose M.	Tel:	(781) 251-4700
Senior Vice President, General Counsel and Secretary	Fax:	(781) 251-4649

At Other Offices

BOCK, Jeanne	Tel:	(781) 861-5249
Contact, Public Relations	Fax:	(781) 251-4649
29 Turning Mill Rd.		
Lexington, MA 02420		

The Longaberger Company

Manufactures and markets baskets, pottery and other crafts.
www.longaberger.com
Employees: 7,000
SIC: 5199; 5945
NAICS: 45112; 54189
Industry/ies: Furniture/Home Furnishings; Housewares

Chairman, President and Chief Executive Officer	Tel:	(740) 322-7800
ROCHON, John	Fax:	(740) 322-5240

Main Headquarters

Mailing:	One Market Sq.	Tel:	(740) 322-7800
	1500 E. Main St.	Fax:	(740) 322-5240
	Newark, OH 43055-8847		

Corporate Foundations and Giving Programs

Longaberger Foundation
Contact: Matt Elli
One Market Sq.
1500 E. Main St.
Newark, OH 43055

Public Affairs and Related Activities Personnel

At Headquarters

ELLI, Matt	Tel:	(740) 322-5000
Director, The Longaberger Foundation	Fax:	(740) 322-5240
matt.elli@longaberger.com		
MACK, Russell	Tel:	(740) 322-5119
Contact, Media Relations	Fax:	(740) 322-5240
russ.mack@longaberger.com		

Longs Drug Stores Corporation

See listing on page 237 under CVS Caremark, Inc.

Longview Fibre Paper and Packaging Inc.

A forest and paper products company. Longview Fibre became a wholly-owned subsidiary of Brookfield Asset Management in 2007.
www.kapstonepaper.com
Annual Revenues: $186.70 million
Employees: 1,700
SIC: 2650; 2653; 5113
NAICS: 322211
Industry/ies: Paper And Wood Products Industry

Chairman of the Board	Tel:	(360) 425-1550
WOLLENBERG, Richard H.	Fax:	(360) 230-5135

Main Headquarters

Mailing:	P.O. Box 639	Tel:	(360) 425-1550
	300 Fibre Way	Fax:	(360) 230-5135
	Longview, WA 98632		

Corporate Foundations and Giving Programs

Longview Fibre Paper and Packaging Conrporate Contributions
300 Fibre Way
P.O. Box 639
Longview, WA 98632

Public Affairs and Related Activities Personnel

At Headquarters

ARKELL, Robert B.	Tel:	(360) 425-1550
Senior Vice President, Industrial Relations and General Counsel	Fax:	(360) 575-5934
COPENHAGEN, Curt	Tel:	(360) 425-1550
Director, Public Affairs	Fax:	(360) 575-5934
FITZPATRICK, Michael R.	Tel:	(360) 425-1550
Director, Industrial Relations	Fax:	(360) 575-5934
LOOSBROCK, Lou	Tel:	(360) 425-1550
Vice President, Sales, Marketing and Container	Fax:	(360) 230-5135
PURCELL, Rosemary	Tel:	(360) 575-5126
Contact, Investor Relations	Fax:	(360) 230-5135
InvestorRelations@longfibre.com		
TAYDAS, Sarah	Tel:	(360) 575-5286
Director, Communications and Public Affairs	Fax:	(360) 575-5268
setaydas@longfibre.com		

Loop Capital Markets, LLC

An investment banking and financial services company.
www.loopcap.com
Annual Revenues: $50.13 million
Employees: 200
Industry/ies: Banking/Finance/Investments

Co-founder, Chairman and Chief Executive Officer	Tel:	(312) 913-4900
REYNOLDS, Jr., CFA, James	Fax:	(312) 913-4928
Co-Founder and President	Tel:	(312) 913-4900
GRACE, Albert R.	Fax:	(312) 913-4928

Main Headquarters

Mailing:	111 W. Jackson Blvd.	Tel:	(312) 913-4900
	Suite 1901	Fax:	(312) 913-4928
	Chicago, IL 60604	TF:	(888) 294-8898

Washington Office

Mailing:	1875 I St.NW	Tel:	(202) 429-2077
	Suite 558	Fax:	(202) 429-9574
	Washington, DC 20006		

Corporate Foundations and Giving Programs

Loop Capital Contribtuions Program
111 W. Jackson Blvd.
Suite 1901
Chicago, IL 60604

Public Affairs and Related Activities Personnel

At Headquarters

HENDERSON, CPA, Tasha	Tel:	(312) 913-4900
Chief Financial Officer	Fax:	(312) 913-4928
JOHNSON, James Clarence	Tel:	(312) 913-4900
General Counsel	Fax:	(312) 913-4928

Loral Space and Communications

A satellite communications company with activities in satellite manufacturing and satellite services.
www.loral.com
Annual Revenues: $1.11 billion
Employees: 22
Ticker: NASDAQ: LORL
SIC: 3663
NAICS: 334220
Industry/ies: Aerospace/Aviation; Transportation

Non-Executive Chairman of the Board
RACHESKY, MD, Dr. Mark H.

President, General Counsel and Secretary	Tel:	(212) 697-1105
KATZ, Dr. Avi	Fax:	(212) 338-5662

Main Headquarters
Mailing:	888 Seventh Ave.	Tel:	(212) 697-1105
	40th Fl.	Fax:	(212) 338-5662
	New York City, NY 10016		

Washington Office
Mailing:	2400 Research Blvd.
	Suite 200
	Rockville, MD 20850

Political Action Committees
Loral Space And Communications PAC
FEC ID: C00431676
Contact: Laurence D. Atlas
2400 Research Blvd.
Suite 200
Rockville, MD 20850

Public Affairs and Related Activities Personnel

At Headquarters
CAPOGROSSI, John	Tel:	(212) 697-1105
Vice President, Chief Financial Officer, Treasurer, and Controller	Fax:	(212) 338-5662
LEWIS, Wendy	Tel:	(650) 704-7502
Director, Communications	Fax:	(212) 338-5662
TARGOFF, Michael B.	Tel:	(212) 697-1105
Vice Chairman of the Board	Fax:	(212) 338-5662

At Washington Office
ATLAS, Laurence D.
PAC Contact

Lord Corporation
Designs, manufactures and markets devices and systems to manage mechanical motion and control noise and vibration. Formulates, produces and sells general purpose and specialty adhesives and coatings.
www.lord.com
Employees: 3,000
SIC: 3061
NAICS: 326291
Industry/ies: Defense/Homeland Security; Government-Related
Legislative Issues: BUD

Chairman of the Board	Tel:	(919) 468-5979
AMOS, GEN James F.	Fax:	(919) 469-5777
President and Chief Executive Officer	Tel:	(919) 468-5979
AUSLANDER, Edward L.	Fax:	(919) 469-5777

Main Headquarters
Mailing:	111 Lord Dr.	Tel:	(919) 468-5979
	Cary, NC 27511-7923	Fax:	(919) 469-5777
		TF:	(877) 275-5673

Public Affairs and Related Activities Personnel

At Headquarters
AUMAN, Allison	Tel:	(919) 413-2081
Executive Assistant and Contact, External Affairs	Fax:	(919) 469-5777
allison.auman@lord.com		
BORIS, Mark	Tel:	(919) 468-5979
Vice President, Global Human Resources	Fax:	(919) 469-5777
KAYLER, Kimberly	Tel:	(614) 873-6706
Contact, Communications	Fax:	(919) 469-5777
kkayler@constructivecommunication.com		
MCNEEL, Richard L.	Tel:	(919) 468-5979
Director	Fax:	(919) 469-5777
riok.mcneel@lord.com		
OECHSLE, Jonathan D.	Tel:	(919) 468-5979
Chief Legal Officer and Secretary	Fax:	(919) 469-5777
OECHSLE, Tesa L.	Tel:	(919) 468-5979
Chief Financial Officer and Treasurer	Fax:	(919) 469-5777

Lorillard Tobacco Company
A manufacturer and marketer of cigarettes.

www.lorillard.com
Employees: 2,900
Ticker: NYSE: LO
SIC: 2111
Industry/ies: Tobacco Industry

Chairman of the Board, President and Chief Executive Officer	Tel:	(336) 335-7000
KESSLER, Murray S.	Fax:	(336) 335-7550

Main Headquarters
Mailing:	P.O. Box 10529	Tel:	(336) 335-7000
	Greensboro, NC 27404-0529	Fax:	(336) 335-7550

Political Action Committees
Lorillard Tobacco Company Public Affairs Committee PAC
FEC ID: C00112888
Contact: Randall R. Smith
714 Green Valley Rd.
Greensboro, NC 27408

> **Contributions to Candidates:** $23,762 (2015-2016)
> Republicans: $23,762

> **Principal Recipients**

> **SENATE**
> TILLIS, THOM R (REP-NC)

Public Affairs and Related Activities Personnel

At Headquarters
BANNON, Robert	Tel:	(336) 335-7000
Director, Investor Relations	Fax:	(336) 225-7550
investorrelations@lortobco.com		
MORROW, Michael	Tel:	(336) 335-7000
Director, Government Relations	Fax:	(336) 335-7550
SPELL, Randy B.	Tel:	(336) 335-7000
Executive Vice President, Marketing and Sales	Fax:	(336) 225-7550
TAYLOR, David H.	Tel:	(336) 335-7000
Executive Vice President, Finance, Planning and Chief Financial Officer	Fax:	(336) 335-7550

At Other Offices
MILSTEIN, Ronald S.	Tel:	(336) 335-7000
Executive Vice President, Legal and External Affairs, General Counsel and Secretary	Fax:	(336) 335-7550
714 Green Valley Rd.		
Greensboro, NC 27408		
SMITH, Randall R.	Tel:	(336) 335-7000
PAC Treasurer	Fax:	(336) 335-7550
714 Green Valley Rd.		
Greensboro, NC 27408		

Louis Dreyfus Corporation
A worldwide merchant of agricultural commodities.
www.louisdreyfus.com
Annual Revenues: $7.93 billion
Employees: 1,300
Industry/ies: Agriculture/Agronomy; Commodities

Chairman of the Board	Tel:	(203) 761-2000
LOUIS-DREYFUS, Margarita		
Chief Executive Officer	Tel:	(203) 761-8100
SCHOEN, Serge	Fax:	(203) 761-8119

Main Headquarters
Mailing:	40 Danbury Rd.	Tel:	(203) 761-2000
	Wilton, CT 06897		

Washington Office
Mailing:	1200 G St. NW	Tel:	(202) 842-5114
	Suite 800	Fax:	(202) 842-5099
	Washington, DC 20005		

Public Affairs and Related Activities Personnel

At Headquarters
PITARO, Veronica	Tel:	(203) 761-8100
Director, Human Resources	Fax:	(203) 761-2375
pitarov@louisdreyfus.com		
SUSSMAN, Jeffrey I.	Tel:	(202) 842-5114
President		

Louisiana Health Care Group
A health care provider.
lhcgroup.com
Annual Revenues: $745.35 million
Employees: 6,489
Ticker: NASDAQ: LHCG
SIC: 8082
Industry/ies: Medicine/Health Care/Mental Health
Legislative Issues: HCR; MMM

Chairman of the Board and Chief Executive Officer
MYERS, Keith G.
keith.myers@lhcgroup.com

Tel: (337) 233-1307
Fax: (337) 235-8037

Main Headquarters
Mailing: 901 Hugh Wallis Rd., South
Lafayette, LA 70508

Tel: (985) 859-4541
TF: (800) 489-1307

Political Action Committees
Louisiana Health Care Group Employee Federal PAC, Inc.
FEC ID: C00382796
Contact: Albert Simien
420 W. Pinhook Rd.
Suite A
Lafayette, LA 70503

Tel: (337) 233-1307

Contributions to Candidates: $46,500 (2015-2016)
Democrats: $17,000; Republicans: $29,500

Principal Recipients

HOUSE
BOUSTANY, CHARLES W. DR. JR. (REP-LA)

Public Affairs and Related Activities Personnel

At Headquarters
STELLY, Donald D.
President and Chief Operating Officer

Tel: (985) 859-4541

BROWN, PHR, Lolanda J.
Director, Human Resources
Lolanda.Brown@lhcgroup.com

Tel: (337) 233-1307
Fax: (337) 235-8037

CLEMENT, Trudy
Federal Lobbyist

Tel: (985) 859-4541

ELLIOTT, Eric
Senior Vice President, Finance
eric.elliott@lhcgroup.com

Tel: (337) 233-1307
Fax: (337) 235-8037

LITTLE, JoAnne
Senior Vice President and Chief Compliance Officer

Tel: (985) 859-4541

MACIP, Marcus D.
Executive Vice President and Chief Administrative Officer

Tel: (985) 859-4541

MACMILLAN, Richard A.
Senior Vice President, Legislative and Regulatory Affairs and Senior Counsel
richard.macmillan@lhcgroup.com

Tel: (337) 233-1307
Fax: (337) 235-8037

MYERS, Sarah
Registered Federal Lobbyist

Tel: (985) 859-4541

PROFFITT, Joshua L.
Executive Vice President, General Counsel and Corporate Secretary
Josh.Proffitt@LHCGroup.com

Tel: (337) 233-1307
Fax: (337) 235-8037

SIMIEN, Albert
PAC Treasurer

Tel: (985) 859-4541

TAYLOR, Harold L.
Vice President, Government Affairs
harold.taylor@lhcgroup.com
Registered Federal Lobbyist

Tel: (337) 233-1307
Fax: (337) 235-8037

VIATOR, Dionne E.
Executive Vice President, Chief Financial Officer and Treasurer

Tel: (985) 859-4541

Louisiana Pacific Corporation

A building products manufacturer with 30 mills across North America and one in Chile.
www.LPCorp.com
Annual Revenues: $1.96 billion
Employees: 4,500
Ticker: NYSE: LPX
SIC: 2400
Industry/ies: Construction/Construction Materials; Paper And Wood Products Industry
Legislative Issues: ENV

Chairman of the Board
COOK, E. Gary

Tel: (615) 986-5600
Fax: (615) 986-5666

Chief Executive Officer
STEVENS, Curtis M.

Tel: (615) 986-5600
Fax: (615) 986-5666

Main Headquarters
Mailing: 414 Union St.
Suite 2000
Nashville, TN 37219

Tel: (615) 986-5600
Fax: (615) 986-5610
TF: (800) 648-6893

Political Action Committees
Louisiana Pacific Corporation Federal PAC
FEC ID: C00109165
Contact: Mark Tobin
414 Union St.
Suite 2000
Nashville, TN 37219

Contributions to Candidates: $1,000 (2015-2016)
Republicans: $1,000

Corporate Foundations and Giving Programs
Louisiana Pacific Foundation
414 Union St.
Suite 2000
Nashville, TN 37219

Public Affairs and Related Activities Personnel

At Headquarters
BAILEY, Sallie B.
Executive Vice President, Chief Financial Officer

Tel: (615) 986-5600
Fax: (615) 986-5666

BARCKLEY, Becky
Controller and Contact, Investor Relations

Tel: (615) 986-5600
Fax: (615) 986-5666

COHN, Mary
Manager, Corporate Affairs
mary.cohn@lpcorp.com

Tel: (615) 986-5886
Fax: (615) 986-5666

FUCHS, Mark
Vice President, General Counsel and Corporate Secretary

Tel: (615) 986-5600
Fax: (615) 986-5666

HARTNETT, Tim
Vice President, Human Resources

Tel: (615) 986-5600
Fax: (615) 986-5666

KINNEY, Mike
Contact, Investor Relations

Tel: (615) 986-5600
Fax: (615) 986-5666

SIMS, Mike
Senior Vice President, Sales and Marketing

Tel: (615) 986-5600
Fax: (615) 986-5666

TOBIN, Mark
PAC Treasurer
mark.tobin@lpcorp.com

Tel: (615) 986-5600
Fax: (615) 986-5666

Lowe's Companies, Inc.

A hardware and building materials specialty retailer.
www.lowes.com
Annual Revenues: $60.18 billion
Employees: 180,000
Ticker: NYSE: LOW
Industry/ies: Construction/Construction Materials; Retail/Wholesale
Legislative Issues: BUD; FIN; HCR; LAW; LBR; TAX; TRA

Chairman of the Board, President and Chief Executive Officer
NIBLOCK, Robert A.
Robert.A.Niblock@lowes.com

Tel: (704) 758-1000
Fax: (336) 658-4766

Main Headquarters
Mailing: 1000 Lowe's Blvd.
Mooresville, NC 28117

Tel: (704) 758-1000
Fax: (336) 658-4766
TF: (800) 445-6937

Political Action Committees
Lowe's Companies, Inc. PAC
FEC ID: C00251751
Contact: Cynthia Reins
1000 Lowe's Blvd.
Mooresville, NC 28117

Tel: (704) 758-1000

Contributions to Candidates: $264,250 (2015-2016)
Democrats: $40,500; Republicans: $223,750

Principal Recipients

SENATE
BURR, RICHARD (REP-NC)

Corporate Foundations and Giving Programs
Lowe's Charitable and Educational Foundation
1000 Lowe's Blvd.
Mooresville, NC 28117

Tel: (704) 758-1000

Public Affairs and Related Activities Personnel

At Headquarters
AHEARN, Chris
Vice President, Corporate Communications
chris.b.ahearn@lowes.com
Registered Federal Lobbyist

Tel: (704) 758-2304
Fax: (336) 658-4766

AUSURA, Maureen K.
Executive Vice President, Human Resources

Tel: (704) 758-1000
Fax: (336) 658-4766

DAMRON, Rick D.
Chief Operating Officer

Tel: (704) 758-1000
Fax: (336) 658-4766

HOLLIFIELD, Matthew V.
Senior Vice President and Chief Accounting Officer

Tel: (704) 758-1000
Fax: (336) 658-4766

HULL, JR., Robert F.
Executive Vice President and Chief Financial Officer

Tel: (704) 758-1000
Fax: (336) 658-4766

LAMB, Thomas J.
Senior Vice President, Marketing and Advertising
Thomas.J.Lamb@lowes.com

Tel: (704) 758-1000
Fax: (336) 658-4766

MALTSBARGER, Richard D.
Chief Development Officer and President, International
richard.d.maltsbarger@lowes.com

Tel: (704) 758-1000
Fax: (336) 658-4766

MCCANLESS, Ross W. (Bill) Tel: (704) 758-1000
Chief Legal Officer, Secretary and Chief Compliance Officer Fax: (336) 658-4766

PEACE, Brian N. Tel: (704) 758-1000
Senior Vice President, Corporate Affairs Fax: (336) 658-4766

REINS, Cynthia Tel: (704) 758-1000
Assistant Treasurer, Cash Management and PAC Treasurer Fax: (336) 658-4766

WEBER, Jennifer L. Tel: (704) 758-1000
Chief Human Resources Officer Fax: (336) 658-4766

LPL Financial Corporation
A financial services company and an independent broker/dealer.
lplfinancial.lpl.com
Annual Revenues: $4.25 billion
Employees: 3,267
Ticker: Nasdaq: LPLA
Industry/ies: Banking/Finance/Investments
Legislative Issues: FIN; RET; TAX

Chairman of the Board and Chief Executive Officer Tel: (617) 423-3644
CASADY, Mark S. Fax: (617) 556-2811

Main Headquarters
Mailing: 75 State St. Tel: (617) 423-3644
24th Floor
Boston, MA 02109

Political Action Committees
LPL FINANCIAL LLC POLITICAL ACTION COMMITTEE (LPL PAC)
FEC ID: C00486217
Contact: Keith Shores
75 State St.
24th Floor
Boston, MA 02109

> **Contributions to Candidates:** $288,447 (2015-2016)
> Democrats: $91,449; Republicans: $196,998

> **Principal Recipients**
> **SENATE**
> PETERS, GARY (DEM-MI)

Corporate Foundations and Giving Programs
The Invest in Others Charitable Foundation
Contact: Megan McAuley
One Beacon St.
22nd Floor
Boston, MA 02108

Public Affairs and Related Activities Personnel

At Headquarters

BERGERS , David Tel: (617) 423-3644
Managing Director, General Counsel

CRONIN, John R. Tel: (617) 423-3644
Vice President and Head, State Government Affairs

KOEGEL, Chris Tel: (617) 897-4574
Senior Vice President and Investor Relations

LARSEN , Sallie R. Tel: (617) 423-3644
Managing Director, Chief Human Capital Officer

LUX, Thomas Tel: (617) 423-3644
Acting Chief Financial Officer

MCAULEY, Megan Tel: (617) 423-3644
Executive Director, Foundation

PETROSINO, Nicole Tel: (617) 423-3644
Vice President and Head, Government Relations

SHORES, Keith Tel: (617) 423-3644
PAC Treasurer

WEINBERG, Brett Tel: (617) 423-3644
Contact, Media

At Other Offices

ARNOLD, Dan Tel: (617) 423-3644
Chief Financial Officer
One Beacon St., 22nd Floor
Boston, MA 02108

RANDOLPH CARTER, Heather Tel: (617) 423-3644
Executive Vice President, Corporate Communication Fax: (858) 546-8324
One Beacon St., 22nd Floor
Boston, MA 02108
heather.carter@lpl.com

Lubrizol Advanced Materials, Inc.
A specialty chemical company. Acquired by Berkshire Hathaway in 2011.
www.lubrizol.com
Ticker: NYSE: LZ
SIC: 2899; 2821; 2833; 2851; 3087
NAICS: 325991; 325998; 325211; 325411; 325510
Industry/ies: Chemicals & Chemical Industry

Chairman of the Board, President and Chief Executive Officer Tel: (440) 943-4200
HAMBRICK, James L. Fax: (440) 943-5337

Main Headquarters
Mailing: 29400 Lakeland Blvd. Tel: (440) 943-4200
Wickliffe, OH 44092 Fax: (440) 943-5337

Corporate Foundations and Giving Programs
The Lubrizol Foundation
Contact: Karen Lerchbacher
29400 Lakeland Blvd.
Wickliffe, OH 44092

Public Affairs and Related Activities Personnel

At Headquarters

LERCHBACHER, Karen Tel: (440) 347-1797
Manager, Grants Fax: (440) 943-5337
karen.lerchbacher@lubrizol.com

SUTHERLAND, Mark Sutherland Tel: (440) 943-4200
Corporate Vice President, Global Communications and Public Fax: (440) 943-5337
Affairs

At Other Offices

DAY, Suzanne F. Tel: (440) 943-4200
Corporate Vice President and General Counsel and Chief Fax: (440) 943-5337
Ethics Officer
9911 Brecksville Rd.
Cleveland, OH 44141-3247

MAKOWSKI, Judy Tel: (216) 447-7392
Project Manager, Strategy and Business Development Fax: (440) 943-5337
9911 Brecksville Rd.
Cleveland, OH 44141-3247
judy.makowski@lubrizol.com

PANEGA, Andrew B. Tel: (216) 447-5000
Corporate Vice President, Human Resources Fax: (440) 943-5337
9911 Brecksville Rd.
Cleveland, OH 44141-3247

TAYLOR, Gregory D. Tel: (440) 943-4200
Corporate Vice President, Corporate Strategy and Fax: (440) 943-5337
Development
9911 Brecksville Rd.
Cleveland, OH 44141-3247

VALENTINE, Brian A. Tel: (216) 447-5000
Corporate Vice President, Chief Financial Officer Fax: (440) 943-5337
9911 Brecksville Rd.
Cleveland, OH 44141-3247

YOUNG, Julie S. Tel: (440) 347-4432
Senior Manager, Corporate Communications Fax: (440) 943-5337
9911 Brecksville Rd.
Cleveland, OH 44141-3247
corporate.media@lubrizol.com

Lugar Hellmann Group LLC
Lobbying / Public affairs.
lugargroup.com
Legislative Issues: BAN; BUD; CAW; COM; CPI; FIN; FUE; HOM; HOU; IMM; INS; TAX; TOU; TRA; TRD

President
LUGAR, David
dave@lugargroup.com

Main Headquarters
Mailing: 1950 Rhode Island Ave. Tel: (202) 329-9561
McLean, VA 22101

Washington Office
Mailing: 555 12th St. NW Tel: (202) 329-9561
Suite 770
Washington, DC 20004

Public Affairs and Related Activities Personnel

At Headquarters

HELLMANN, Ralph Tel: (202) 329-9561
Principal
Registered Federal Lobbyist

Lumera Corporation
See listing on page 365 under GigOptix Company

Philips Lumileds Lighting Company
Manufacturer of high-power Light Emitting Diodes (LEDs).
www.lumileds.com
Annual Revenues: $40 million
Employees: 500
Industry/ies: Energy/Electricity

Chief Executive Officer Tel: (408) 964-2900
LESAICHERRE, Pierre Yves Fax: (408) 435-6855

Main Headquarters

Mailing:	370 W. Trimble Rd.	Tel:	(408) 964-2900
	San Jose, CA 95131	Fax:	(408) 435-6855

Public Affairs and Related Activities Personnel

At Headquarters

CARRUTHERS, Nathalie		Tel:	(408) 964-2900
Chief Human Resources Officer		Fax:	(408) 435-6855
DIEPPEDALLE, Emmanuel		Tel:	(408) 964-2900
Senior Vice President, Sales and Marketing		Fax:	(408) 435-6855
LUCIDO, Kevin		Tel:	(408) 964-2900
Director, Global Marketing Communications		Fax:	(408) 435-6855
kevin.lucido@philips.com			
MARATHE, Ajay		Tel:	(408) 964-2900
Chief Operating Officer		Fax:	(408) 435-6855
MEISSNER, Falk		Tel:	(408) 964-2900
Chief Strategy Officer		Fax:	(408) 435-6855

Luminex Corporation

Luminex develops, manufactures and markets biological testing technologies with applications throughout the life science and diagnostic industries.
www.luminexcorp.com
Annual Revenues: $228.16 million
Employees: 745
Ticker: NASDAQ (GM): LMNX
SIC: 3841; 3823; 3829
NAICS: 334519
Industry/ies: Computer/Technology; Science; Scientific Research
Legislative Issues: BUD

Chairman of the Board		Tel:	(512) 219-8020
LOEWENBAUM, G. Walter		Fax:	(512) 219-5195

President and Chief Executive Officer		Tel:	(512) 219-8020
SHAMIR, Nachum Homi		Fax:	(512) 219-5195

Main Headquarters

Mailing:	12212 Technology Blvd.	Tel:	(512) 219-8020
	Suite 130	Fax:	(512) 219-5195
	Austin, TX 78727	TF:	(888) 219-8020

Public Affairs and Related Activities Personnel

At Headquarters

BOURNE, David		Tel:	(512) 219-8020
Vice President, Business Development and Strategic Planning		Fax:	(512) 219-5195
BRADLEY, Russell W.		Tel:	(512) 219-8020
Senior Vice President, Corporate Development, Chief Marketing and Sales Officer		Fax:	(512) 219-5195
CURRIE, Harriss T.		Tel:	(512) 219-8020
Chief Financial Officer, Senior Vice President, Finance and Treasurer		Fax:	(512) 219-5195
hcurrie@luminexcorp.com			
FAIRCHILD, Nancy M.		Tel:	(512) 219-8020
Vice President, Human Resources		Fax:	(512) 219-5195
MARTIN, Kendel B.		Tel:	(512) 219-8020
Vice President, Accounting		Fax:	(512) 219-5195
MEEK, Oliver H.		Tel:	(512) 219-8020
Vice President, Quality Assurance and Regulatory Affairs		Fax:	(512) 219-5195

Lundbeck Research USA, Inc.

A Pharmaceutical company.
www.lundbeck.com/us
Industry/ies: Pharmaceutical Industry
Legislative Issues: HCR

President and Chief Executive Officer		Tel:	(866) 337-6996
SCHULTZ, Kare		Fax:	(847) 282-1001

Main Headquarters

Mailing:	Four Pkwy., North	Tel:	(866) 337-6996
	Deerfield, IL 60015	Fax:	(847) 282-1001

Washington Office

Mailing:	1720 Eye St. NW
	Suite 400
	Washington, DC 20006

Political Action Committees

Lundbeck, Inc. Employee PAC
FEC ID: C00491118
Contact: Gregory Katz
Four Pkwy., North
Suite 200
Deerfield, 60015

> **Contributions to Candidates:** $50,500 (2015-2016)
> Democrats: $16,000; Republicans: $34,500

Public Affairs and Related Activities Personnel

At Headquarters

FLESCH, Matt		Tel:	(847) 282-1154
Director, Public Relations		Fax:	(847) 282-1001
MFLE@lundbeck.com			
GÖTZSCHE, Anders		Tel:	(866) 337-6996
Executive Vice President, Chief Financial Officer		Fax:	(847) 282-1001
KATZ, Gregory		Tel:	(866) 337-6996
PAC Treasurer		Fax:	(847) 282-1001
YOUNG, Sally Benjamin		Tel:	(866) 337-6996
Vice President, Public Affairs		Fax:	(847) 282-1001
syou@lundbeck.com			

At Washington Office

HAKIM, Julie		Tel:	(847) 282-1000
Vice President, Administration and Finance			
LAWSON, Patroski		Tel:	(847) 282-1000
Vice President, Government Affairs			
Registered Federal Lobbyist			

LVP Solutions, LLC

Work with companies on issues related to intellectual property and free trade.
www.lvpsolutions.com/index.html
Legislative Issues: CPT

President	Tel:	(706) 870-6874
PEREZ, Lauren		

Main Headquarters

Mailing:	1647 Palermo Dr.
	Weston, FL 33327

Lynden, Inc.

Delivers completely integrated freight transportation package.
www.lynden.com
Employees: 2,000
Industry/ies: Aerospace/Aviation; Marine/Maritime/Shipping; Transportation; Trucking Industry

Chairman of the Board		Tel:	(206) 241-8778
JANSEN, James A.		Fax:	(206) 243-8415

President and Chief Executive Officer		Tel:	(206) 241-8778
BURDICK, Jon		Fax:	(206) 243-8415

Main Headquarters

Mailing:	18000 International Blvd.	Tel:	(206) 241-8778
	Suite 800	Fax:	(206) 243-8415
	Seattle, WA 98188	TF:	(888) 596-3361

Public Affairs and Related Activities Personnel

At Headquarters

KORPELA, Richard A.		Tel:	(206) 241-8778
Executive Vice President, Secretary and Treasurer		Fax:	(206) 243-8415
ROSENZWEIG, David		Tel:	(206) 439-5527
Vice President, Marketing and Media		Fax:	(206) 243-8415
drosen@lynden.com			

Lyondell Basell Industries

The U.S. subsidiary of LyondellBasell Industries headquarters in Rotterdam, The Netherlands. A refiner of crude oil and a producer of gasoline blending components.
www.lyondellbasell.com
Annual Revenues: $44.53 billion
Employees: 13,300
Ticker: NYSE:LYB
SIC: 2819
NAICS: 325188
Industry/ies: Chemicals & Chemical Industry
Legislative Issues: AVI; BUD; CHM; ENV; FUE; LBR; MAN; TAX; TRD

Senior Vice President		Tel:	(713) 309-7200
GALLOGLY, James		Fax:	(302) 478-2796

Main Headquarters

Mailing:	P.O. Box 3646	Tel:	(713) 309-7200
	Houston, TX 77252-3646	Fax:	(302) 478-2796

Washington Office

Mailing:	1101 Pennsylvania Ave. NW	Tel:	(202) 639-0750
	Suite 515	Fax:	(202) 639-0506
	Washington, DC 20004		

Political Action Committees

Lyondell Chemical Company Political Action Committee
FEC ID: C00306175
Contact: Stephen Wessels

1221 McKinney St.		Tel:	(202) 639-0750
Suite 700		Fax:	(202) 639-0506
Houston, TX 77010			

> **Contributions to Candidates:** $107,000 (2015-2016)
> Democrats: $24,500; Republicans: $82,500

Corporate Foundations and Giving Programs

Lyondell Basell Industries Contributions Program
Two Righter Pkwy.
Suite 300
Wilmington, DE 19803

Public Affairs and Related Activities Personnel

At Headquarters

COVEZZI, Massimo	Tel:	(713) 309-7200
Senior Vice President, Research and Development	Fax:	(302) 478-2796
massimo.covezzi@lyondellbasell.com		
HEILMAN, Joel	Tel:	(202) 469-3438
Manager, Federal Government Affairs	Fax:	(302) 478-2796
joel.heilman@lyondellbasell.com		
Registered Federal Lobbyist		
KAPLAN, Jeff	Tel:	(713) 309-7200
Executive Vice President and Chief Legal Officer	Fax:	(302) 478-2796
PIKE, Douglas J.	Tel:	(713) 309-7141
Contact, Investor Relations	Fax:	(302) 478-2796
doug.pike@lyondellbasell.com		
SEHESTED, Stan	Tel:	(713) 309-7200
Contact, Media	Fax:	(302) 478-2796
Stanley.Sehested@lyondellbasell.com		
TRAVIS, Ann	Tel:	(713) 309-7200
Director, Global Government Affairs	Fax:	(302) 478-2796
Registered Federal Lobbyist		
WOLF, Jacquelyn H.	Tel:	(713) 309-7200
Senior Vice President and Chief Human Resources Officer	Fax:	(302) 478-2796

At Other Offices

WESSELS, Stephen
PAC Treasurer
1221 McKinney St., LyondellBasell Tower, Suite 700
Houston, TX 77010

M & T Bank Corporation

M&T Bank traces its origins to the founding of Manufacturers and Traders Bank in Buffalo, New York. As a result of mergers, acquisitions and name changes, M&T Bank Corporation's principal bank is now known as Manufacturers and Traders Trust Company, or M&T Bank. M&T Bank reorganized under a bank holding company in 1969 called First Empire State Corporation. The name was changed in 1998 to M&T Bank Corporation. M&T Bank has over 725 branches & 1,800 ATM's across Delaware, Maryland, New York, Pennsylvania, Virginia, West Virginia, New Jersey, Washington, D.C., and Ontario, Canada.
www.mtb.com
Annual Revenues: $4.35 billion
Employees: 15,263
Ticker: NYSE: MTB
SIC: 6022
Industry/ies: Banking/Finance/Investments
Legislative Issues: BAN

Chairman of the Board and Chief Executive Officer	Tel:	(716) 842-5445
WILMERS, Robert G.	Fax:	(716) 842-5839

Main Headquarters

Mailing:	One M & T Plaza	Tel:	(716) 842-5138
	13th Floor	Fax:	(716) 842-4306
	Buffalo, NY 14203-2399	TF:	(800) 724-2440

Corporate Foundations and Giving Programs

The M&T Charitable Foundation
One Fountain Plaza   Tel: (716) 848-3804
12th Floor
Buffalo, NY 14203

Public Affairs and Related Activities Personnel

At Headquarters

BRAUNSCHEIDEL, Stephen J.	Tel:	(716) 842-5138
Executive Vice President, Human Resources	Fax:	(716) 842-4306
BRIDGER, Chet	Tel:	(716) 842-5182
Vice President, Corporate Communications	Fax:	(716) 842-4306
cbridger@mandtbank.com		
CZARNECKI, Mark J	Tel:	(716) 842-5138
President	Fax:	(716) 842-4306
JONES, Rene F.	Tel:	(716) 842-5138
Executive Vice President and Chief Financial Officer	Fax:	(716) 842-4306
KIENER, Kurt	Tel:	(716) 842-5138
PAC Treasurer	Fax:	(716) 842-4306
N. WARMAN, D. Scott	Tel:	(716) 842-5138
Executive Vice President and Treasurer	Fax:	(716) 842-4306
PFIRRMAN, Drew J.	Tel:	(716) 842-5138
Senior Vice President and General Counsel	Fax:	(716) 842-4306
SPYCHALA, Michael R	Tel:	(716) 842-5138
Senior Vice President and Controller	Fax:	(716) 842-4306
ZABEL, C. Michael	Tel:	(716) 842-5385

Manager, Corporate Communications	Fax:	(716) 842-5839
mzabel@mtb.com		

At Other Offices

MCCLURE, Donna	Tel:	(716) 848-3804
Senior Vice President and Chief Compliance Officer		
One Fountain Plaza, 12th Floor		
Buffalo, NY 14203		
PRINGLE, Debbie	Tel:	(716) 848-3804
Foundation Contact		
One Fountain Plaza, 12th Floor		
Buffalo, NY 14203		

M Cubed Technologies, Inc.

Provides material solutions and products using combinations of ceramics, carbon fibers, nano-materials and various metals.
www.mmmt.com
Annual Revenues: $21.20 million
Employees: 200
Industry/ies: Defense/Homeland Security; Electricity & Electronics; Electronics; Energy/Electricity; Government-Related; Machinery/Equipment; Metals

President and Chief Executive Officer	Tel:	(203) 452-2513
PRICE, Sr., Randall D.	Fax:	(203) 452-2335

Main Headquarters

Mailing:	921 Main St.	Tel:	(203) 452-2515
	Monroe, CT 06468	Fax:	(203) 452-2335

M/I Homes, Inc.

A builders of single family homes.
www.mihomes.com
Annual Revenues: $1.24 billion
Employees: 905
Ticker: NYSE:MHO
Industry/ies: Construction/Construction Materials; Housing

Chairman of the Board, President and Chief Executive Officer	Tel:	(614) 418-8000
SCHOTTENSTEIN, Robert H.	Fax:	(614) 418-8080
rschottenstein@mihomes.com		

Main Headquarters

Mailing:	Three Easton Oval	Tel:	(614) 418-8000
	Suite 500	Fax:	(614) 418-8080
	Columbus, OH 43219-6011	TF:	(888) 644-4111

Public Affairs and Related Activities Personnel

At Headquarters

CREEK, Philip G.	Tel:	(614) 418-8011
Executive Vice President and Chief Financial Officer	Fax:	(614) 418-8080
pcreek@mihomes.com		
HUNKER, Ann Marie	Tel:	(614) 418-8225
Vice President, Corporate Controller and Chief	Fax:	(614) 418-8080
Administration Officer		
amhunker@mihomes.com		
JOANNE, Vaca	Tel:	(614) 418-8000
PAC Treasurer	Fax:	(614) 418-8080
MASON, J. Thomas	Tel:	(614) 418-8000
Executive Vice President, Chief Legal Officer	Fax:	(614) 418-8080
tmason@mihomes.com		
ROBERTS, Bill	Tel:	(614) 418-8000
PAC Treasurer	Fax:	(614) 418-8030

M2 Technologies Inc.

Provider of design automation solutions for manufacturing companies. It provides consulting services, software, and support to automate mechanical and electrical design, undertake collaborative engineering programs, speed prototype development, add features and new functionality to existing designs.
www.m2t.com
Annual Revenues: $1.8 Million
Industry/ies: Defense/Homeland Security; Government-Related
Legislative Issues: DEF

Main Headquarters

Mailing:	Ten Tara Blvd.	Tel:	(603) 657-3800
	Suite 420	Fax:	(603) 888-3407
	Nashua, NH 03062	TF:	(877) 311-6284

Public Affairs and Related Activities Personnel

At Headquarters

BRODERICK, Shannon	Tel:	(603) 657-3800
Associate, Finance	Fax:	(603) 888-3407
sbroderick@m2t.com		
BURKE, Matthew	Tel:	(603) 657-3800
Principal	Fax:	(603) 888-3407
mburke@m2t.com		
END, Darren	Tel:	(603) 657-3800

Chief Financial Officer	Fax:	(603) 888-3407
dend@m2t.com		
HANSON, Peter	Tel:	(603) 657-3800
Director, Human Resources	Fax:	(603) 888-3407
phanson@m2t.com		
HARRIS, Kristen	Tel:	(603) 657-3800
Director, Marketing	Fax:	(603) 888-3407
kharris@m2t.com		
MARALDO, Carol	Tel:	(603) 657-3800
Senior Human Resource Generalist	Fax:	(603) 888-3407
cmaraldo@m2t.com		
PROKOP, Kristin	Tel:	(603) 657-3800
Director, Marketing	Fax:	(603) 888-3407
kharris@m2t.com		

M2Z Networks, Inc

M2Z Networks provides wireless broadband access.
Industry/ies: Communications; Telecommunications/Internet/Cable

Main Headquarters

Mailing:	2800 Sand Hill Rd.	Tel:	(650) 687-5609
	Suite 150	Fax:	(650) 687-5699
	Menlo Park, CA 94025-7057		

Public Affairs and Related Activities Personnel

At Headquarters

CHIUCO, John	Tel:	(650) 687-5609
Media Contact	Fax:	(650) 687-5699
DUFFUS, Chris	Tel:	(650) 687-5609
Vice President and Chief Financial Officer	Fax:	(650) 687-5699

MacAndrews & Forbes Holdings, Inc.

MacAndrews & Forbes is a holding company that acquires and manages a diversified portfolio of public and private companies.
www.macandrewsandforbes.com
Annual Revenues: $4.90 billion
Employees: 61,000
SIC: 6719; 2844
NAICS: 551112
Industry/ies: Banking/Finance/Investments
Legislative Issues: ANI; BUD; CSP; DEF; EDU; FIN; FOO; GAM; HCR; POS; TAR; TAX; TRA

Chairman of the Board and Chief Executive Officer	Tel:	(212) 572-8600
PERELMAN, Ronald O.	Fax:	(212) 572-8400

Main Headquarters

Mailing:	35 E. 62nd St.	Tel:	(212) 572-8600
	New York City, NY 10065	Fax:	(212) 572-8400

Washington Office

Mailing:	900 Seventh St. NW		
	Suite 970		
	Washington, DC 20001		

Political Action Committees

MacAndrews and Forbes Holdings Inc. PAC (MAFPAC)
FEC ID: C00432856
Contact: Evan Knisely

35 E. 62nd St.	Tel:	(212) 572-8600
New York City, NY 10065		

> **Contributions to Candidates:** $153,678 (2015-2016)
> Democrats: $64,400; Republicans: $89,278

Principal Recipients

HOUSE
JOLLY, DAVID W. (REP-FL)

Corporate Foundations and Giving Programs

MacAndrews and Forbes Holdings Contributions Program
35 E. 62nd St.
New York City, NY 10065

Public Affairs and Related Activities Personnel

At Headquarters

ARONSON, Elise Kenderian	Tel:	(212) 572-8600
Vice President, Government Affairs	Fax:	(212) 572-8400
Registered Federal Lobbyist		
COHEN, Steven M.	Tel:	(212) 572-8600
Executive Vice President, Chief Administrative Officer and	Fax:	(212) 572-8400
General Counsel		
KNISELY, Evan	Tel:	(212) 572-8600
Senior Vice President, Government Affairs	Fax:	(212) 572-8400
Registered Federal Lobbyist		
PERELMAN, Debra G.	Tel:	(212) 572-8600
Executive Vice President, Strategy and New Business	Fax:	(212) 572-8400
Development		
SAVAS, Paul G.	Tel:	(212) 572-8600

Executive Vice President and Chief Financial Officer	Fax:	(212) 572-8400
SCHWARTZ, Barry F.	Tel:	(212) 572-8600
Executive Vice Chairman	Fax:	(212) 572-8400
TAYLOR, Christine M.	Tel:	(212) 572-5988
Executive Vice President, Corporate Communications and	Fax:	(212) 572-8400
External Affairs		
ctaylor@mafgrp.com		
TOWNSEND, Frances F.	Tel:	(212) 572-8600
Executive Vice President, Worldwide Government, Legal and	Fax:	(212) 572-8400
Business Affairs		

At Washington Office

IRWIN, Tyler
Director of Political and Community Affairs, Washington Office

Mack Trucks, Inc.

A truck manufacturer. A subsidiary of Volvo Group North America, Inc. (see separate listing).
www.macktrucks.com
Annual Revenues: $739.50 million
Employees: 4,500
SIC: 3711
Industry/ies: Automotive Industry; Transportation; Trucking Industry

President	Tel:	(336) 291-9001
ROY, Stephen	Fax:	(336) 291-9202

Main Headquarters

Mailing:	P.O. Box 26259	Tel:	(336) 291-9001
	Greensboro, NC 27402	Fax:	(336) 291-9202

Corporate Foundations and Giving Programs

Mack Trucks, Inc. Contributions Program

P.O. Box 26259	Tel:	(336) 291-9001
Greensboro, NC 27402	Fax:	(336) 291-9202

Public Affairs and Related Activities Personnel

At Headquarters

CREECH, Cam	Tel:	(336) 291-9001
Marketing Communications Manager	Fax:	(336) 291-9202
JANIS, Stan	Tel:	(336) 291-9001
Senior Vice President, Finance	Fax:	(336) 291-9202
PUPILLO , APR, Kim	Tel:	(336) 291-9001
Director, Media Relations	Fax:	(336) 291-9202

MACTEC Engineering & Consulting Inc.

Engineering consulting and design firm.
www.mactec.com
Industry/ies: Engineering/Mathematics
Legislative Issues: DEF

Main Headquarters

Mailing:	7251 W. Lake Mead Blvd.	Tel:	(702) 251-5449
	Suite 300		
	Las Vegas, NV 89149		

Public Affairs and Related Activities Personnel

At Headquarters

MINTO, Paul	Tel:	(702) 251-5449
Director, Federal Programs		
Registered Federal Lobbyist		

Macy's Inc.

Operates department stores nationally under the names of Macy's as well as Bloomingdale's. The company acquired The May Department Stores Co. in August of 2005.
www.macysinc.com
Annual Revenues: $26.62 billion
Employees: 157,900
Ticker: NYSE: M
SIC: 5311
Industry/ies: Retail/Wholesale

Chairman of the Board and Chief Executive Officer	Tel:	(513) 579-7000
LUNDGREN, Terry J.	Fax:	(513) 579-7555

Main Headquarters

Mailing:	Seven W. Seventh St.	Tel:	(513) 579-7000
	Cincinnati, OH 45202	Fax:	(513) 579-7555
		TF:	(800) 261-5385

Political Action Committees

Macy's Inc. Retail Issues Fund PAC
FEC ID: C00144311
Contact: Frank G. Julian
611 Olive St.
Suite 1750
St. Louis, MO 63101

> **Contributions to Candidates:** $1,000 (2015-2016)
> Republicans: $1,000

Corporate Foundations and Giving Programs

Macy's Foundation
Seven W. Seventh St.
Cincinnati, OH 45202

Tel: (513) 579-7000
Fax: (513) 579-7000

Public Affairs and Related Activities Personnel

At Headquarters

ALLEN, William S.
Chief Human Resources Officer

Tel: (513) 579-7000
Fax: (513) 579-7555

ALLUMBAUGH, Byron
Professional

Tel: (513) 579-7000
Fax: (513) 579-7555

HAWTHORNE, William
Vice President, Diversity Strategies and Legal Affairs
william.hawthorne@macys.com

Tel: (513) 579-7000
Fax: (770) 913-4674

HOGUET, Karen M.
Chief Financial Officer

Tel: (513) 579-7000
Fax: (513) 579-7555

JULIAN, Frank G.
PAC Treasurer

Tel: (513) 579-7000
Fax: (513) 579-7555

MACFARLANE, Justin
Chief Strategy, Analytics and Innovation Officer

Tel: (513) 579-7000
Fax: (513) 579-7555

REARDON, Martine
Chief Marketing Officer

Tel: (513) 579-7000
Fax: (513) 579-7555

SACHSE, Peter
Chief Growth Officer

Tel: (513) 579-7000
Fax: (513) 579-7555

SLUZEWSKI, James A.
Senior Vice President, Corporate Communications and External Affairs
jim.sluzewski@macys.com

Tel: (513) 579-7764
Fax: (513) 579-7555

STEINES, Ann Munson
Senior Vice President
ann.steines@macys.com

Tel: (513) 579-7000
Fax: (513) 579-7555

Madison Gas & Electric Company

Gas & Electric Company.
www.mge.com
Annual Revenues: $546.38 million
Employees: 700
SIC: 4931
Industry/ies: Utilities
Legislative Issues: ENG

Chairman of the Board, President and Chief Executive Officer
WOLTER, Gary J.

Tel: (608) 252-7000
Fax: (608) 252-7098

Main Headquarters

Mailing: P.O. Box 1231
Madison, WI 53701-1231

Tel: (608) 252-7000
Fax: (608) 252-7098
TF: (800) 245-1123

Corporate Foundations and Giving Programs

Madison Gas and Electric Foundation
P.O. Box 1231
Madison, WI 53701

Tel: (608) 252-7000
Fax: (608) 252-7098

Public Affairs and Related Activities Personnel

At Headquarters

EUCLIDE, Kristine A.
Vice President and General Counsel
keuclide@mge.com

Tel: (608) 252-7000
Fax: (608) 252-7098

KRAUS, Steve
Manager, Media Relations
skraus@mge.com

Tel: (608) 252-7907
Fax: (608) 252-7098

NEWMAN, Jeffrey C.
Vice President, Chief Financial Officer, Secretary and Treasurer

Tel: (608) 252-7000
Fax: (608) 252-7098

PELLITTERI, Joseph P.
Assistant Vice President, Human Resources

Tel: (608) 252-7000
Fax: (608) 252-7098

WALDRON, Peter J.
Vice President and Chief Information Officer

Tel: (608) 252-7000
Fax: (608) 252-7098

Madison Kipp

Producer of precision machined components and system sub assemblies for transportation and industrial end markets.
www.madison-kipp.com
Annual Revenues: $41.10 million
Employees: 500
SIC: 3363; 3364; 3369; 3599
NAICS: 331521; 331522; 331528; 333319
Industry/ies: Automotive Industry; Transportation

Chairman of the Board and Chief Executive Officer
COLEMAN, Reed J.

Tel: (608) 244-3511
Fax: (608) 242-5284

President and Chief Executive Officer
KOBLINSKI, Tony

Tel: (608) 244-3511
Fax: (608) 242-5284

Main Headquarters

Mailing: P.O. Box 8043
Madison, WI 53708-8043

Tel: (608) 244-3511
Fax: (608) 242-5284
TF: (800) 356-6148

Public Affairs and Related Activities Personnel

At Headquarters

COULTHARD, Terese
Director, Information Technology

Tel: (608) 244-3511
Fax: (608) 242-5284

At Other Offices

DANIEL, Mark
Chief Financial Officer
1655 Corporate Center Dr.
Sun Prairie, WI 53590

Tel: (608) 834-1201
Fax: (608) 242-5284

Maersk Inc.

A shipping company involved in a wide range of activities within the energy, shipbuilding, retail and manufacturing industries.
www.maerskline.com/en-us
Annual Revenues: $479.80 million
Employees: 3,000
Industry/ies: Marine/Maritime/Shipping; Transportation
Legislative Issues: MAR; TRA

Group Chief Executive Officer
ANDERSEN, Nils Smedegaard

Tel: (973) 514-5000
Fax: (973) 514-5410

Main Headquarters

Mailing: Two Giralda Farms
P.O. Box 880
Madison, NJ 07940-0880

Tel: (973) 514-5000
Fax: (973) 514-5410
TF: (800) 321-8807

Washington Office

Mailing: 1530 Wilson Blvd.
Suite 650
Arlington, VA 22209

Tel: (703) 351-9200
Fax: (703) 351-0130

Political Action Committees

Maersk Inc. Good Government Fund PAC
FEC ID: C00217471
Contact: Clint Eisenhauer
1530 Wilson Blvd.
Suite 650
Arlington, VA 22209

Contributions to Candidates: $44,000 (2015-2016)
Democrats: $14,500; Republicans: $29,500

Public Affairs and Related Activities Personnel

At Headquarters

CHIVERS, Michael
Senior Vice President, Human Resources

Tel: (973) 514-5000
Fax: (973) 514-5410

CLERC, Vincent
Chief Officer, Trade and Marketing

Tel: (973) 514-5000
Fax: (973) 514-5410

GILBERT, Steve
Director, Human Resources Latin America Region

Tel: (973) 514-5000
Fax: (973) 514-5410

STAUSHOLM, Jakob
Chief Operating Officer

Tel: (973) 514-5000
Fax: (973) 514-5410

WESTLIE, Trond
Chief Financial Officer

Tel: (973) 514-5000
Fax: (973) 514-5410

At Washington Office

BONITT, Jay
Registered Federal Lobbyist

Tel: (703) 351-9200
Fax: (703) 351-0130

EISENHAUER, Clint
Vice President, Government Relations
ceisenhauer@maerskgov.com

Tel: (703) 351-9200
Fax: (703) 351-0130

SCOTT, Brett
Registered Federal Lobbyist

Tel: (703) 351-9200
Fax: (703) 351-0130

Magellan Health Services

A health care management company.
www.magellanhealth.com
Annual Revenues: $4.73 billion
Employees: 6,900
Ticker: NASDAQ: MGLN
SIC: 8060
Industry/ies: Medicine/Health Care/Mental Health
Legislative Issues: HCR; MMM

Chairman and Chief Executive Officer
SMITH, Barry M.

Tel: (860) 507-1900
Fax: (860) 507-1990

Main Headquarters

Mailing: 55 Nod Rd.
Avon, CT 06001

Tel: (860) 507-1900
Fax: (860) 507-1990
TF: (800) 410-8312

Political Action Committees

Magellan Health Services Inc. Employee Committee for Good Government PAC
FEC ID: C00247262

Contact: M. Robin Copeland-Carmon
55 Nod Rd. Tel: (860) 507-1900
Avon, CT 06001 Fax: (860) 507-1990

Corporate Foundations and Giving Programs

Magellan Health Services Contributions Program
55 Nod Rd. Tel: (860) 507-1900
Avon, CT 06001 Fax: (860) 507-1990

Public Affairs and Related Activities Personnel

At Headquarters

COPELAND-CARMON, M. Robin Tel: (860) 507-1900
PAC Treasurer Fax: (860) 507-1990

DELK, Meredith Tel: (860) 507-1900
Senior Vice President, Government Affairs Fax: (860) 507-1990

GREGOIRE, Daniel Tel: (860) 507-1900
General Counsel Fax: (860) 507-1990

LAVELLE, Stewart Tel: (860) 507-1900
Chief Sales and Marketing Officer Fax: (860) 507-1990

LEWIS-CLAPPER, Caskie Tel: (860) 507-1900
Chief Human Resources Officer Fax: (860) 507-1990

ROMBERG, Dawn Tel: (860) 507-1900
Vice President, Communications Fax: (860) 507-1990

RUBIN, Jonathan N. Tel: (860) 507-1900
Chief Financial Officer Fax: (860) 507-1990

SHAPIRO, Renie Tel: (877) 645-6464
Senior Vice President, Corporate Finance Fax: (860) 507-1990

At Other Offices

BOYLE, Jeanine Tel: (410) 953-4701
Federal Lobbyist Fax: (888) 656-2379
6950 Columbia Gateway Dr.
Columbia, MD 21046
jboyle@magellanhealth.com
Registered Federal Lobbyist

DOUTY, Laurel D. Tel: (410) 953-2414
Chief Operating Officer Fax: (888) 656-2379
6950 Columbia Gateway Dr.
Columbia, MD 21046

MCQUILLEN, Michael P. Tel: (410) 953-2414
Senior Vice President and Associate General Counsel Fax: (888) 656-2379
6950 Columbia Gateway Dr.
Columbia, MD 21046
MagellanHealthLDA@venable.com

Magellan Midstream Partners, LP

Magellan Midstream Partners, L.P. is a publicly traded partnership formed to own, operate and acquire a diversified portfolio of energy assets.
www.magellanlp.com
Annual Revenues: $2.18 billion
Employees: 1,640
Ticker: NYSE: MMP
SIC: 4610
Industry/ies: Energy/Electricity; Utilities
Legislative Issues: TAX; TRA

Chairman of the Board, President, and Chief Executive Officer Tel: (918) 574-7000
MEARS, Michael M. Fax: (918) 573-6714
mike.mears@magellanlp.com

Main Headquarters
Mailing: One Williams Center Tel: (918) 574-7000
MD 28-8 Fax: (918) 573-6714
Tulsa, OK 74172 TF: (800) 574-6671

Political Action Committees
Magellan Midstream Holdings GP LLC PAC
FEC ID: C00397711
Contact: Holman Jeff
One Williams Center
Tulsa, OK 74172

Contributions to Candidates: $22,500 (2015-2016)
Republicans: $22,500

Public Affairs and Related Activities Personnel

At Headquarters

AARONSON, Michael Tel: (918) 574-7000
Senior Vice President, Business Development Fax: (918) 573-6714

DAVIED, Larry J. Tel: (918) 574-7000
Senior Vice President, Operations and Technical Services Fax: (918) 573-6714

FARRELL, Paula Tel: (918) 574-7650
Contact, Investor, Analyst and Financial Media Relations Fax: (918) 573-6714
paula.farrell@magellanlp.com

HEINE, Bruce W. Tel: (918) 574-7010
Director, Government & Media Affairs Fax: (918) 573-6714
bruce.heine@magellanlp.com

Registered Federal Lobbyist

JEFF, Holman Tel: (918) 574-7000
Treasurer and PAC Treasurer Fax: (918) 573-6714

KORNER, Lisa J. Tel: (918) 574-7000
Senior Vice President, Human Resources and Administration Fax: (918) 573-6714

MASSIE, James Tel: (918) 574-7000
Federal Lobbyist Fax: (918) 573-6714
Registered Federal Lobbyist

MAY , Douglas J. Tel: (918) 574-7000
Senior Vice President, General Counsel, Compliance and Fax: (918) 573-6714
Ethics Officer and Assistant Secretary

MILFORD, Aaron L. Tel: (918) 574-7000
Senior Vice President, Chief Financial Officer Fax: (918) 573-6714

Magna Services of America, Inc.

Automotive systems and components supplier.
www.magna.com
Industry/ies: Automotive Industry; Engineering/Mathematics; Transportation
Legislative Issues: AUT; BAN; TRD

Chief Executive Officer Tel: (248) 729-2400
WALKER, Donald J.

Main Headquarters
Mailing: 750 Tower Dr. Tel: (248) 729-2400
Troy, MI 48098

Public Affairs and Related Activities Personnel

At Headquarters

ERVIN, III, Frank W. Tel: (248) 729-4097
Director, Government Affairs
frank.ervin@magna.com
Registered Federal Lobbyist

GALIFI, Vincent J. Tel: (248) 729-2400
Executive Vice President and Chief Financial Officer

NEEB, Marc Tel: (248) 729-2400
Executive Vice President and Chief Human Resources Officer

PALMER, Jeffrey O. Tel: (248) 729-2400
Executive Vice President and Chief Legal Officer

MagneMotion

MagneMotion provides assembly automation, material handling, and transportation solutions based on its advanced electro-magnetic technology and controls.
www.magnemotion.com
Annual Revenues: $3.2 million
Employees: 30
Industry/ies: Computer/Technology

Chairman of the Board and Chief Technology Officer Tel: (978) 757-9100
THORNTON, Dr. Richard Fax: (978) 757-9200

President and Chief Executive Officer Tel: (978) 757-9100
WEBBER, Todd Fax: (978) 757-9200
twebber@magnemotion.com

Main Headquarters
Mailing: 139 Barnum Rd. Tel: (978) 757-9100
Devens, MA 01434 Fax: (978) 757-9201

Public Affairs and Related Activities Personnel

At Headquarters

ASHE, Peter Tel: (978) 757-9100
Vice President, Operations Fax: (978) 757-9201

CHIN, Larry Tel: (978) 757-9100
Vice President, Sales Fax: (978) 757-9201

HANNON, Michael Tel: (978) 757-9100
Chief Financial Officer Fax: (978) 757-9200

MATTILA, Peter Tel: (978) 757-9100
Vice President, Business Development Fax: (978) 757-9201

Magnetek, Inc.

A manufacturer of electrical equipment.
www.magnetek.com
Annual Revenues: $112.21 million
Employees: 318
Ticker: NYSE: MAG
SIC: 3679
Industry/ies: Electricity & Electronics; Electronics; Energy/Electricity

Chairman of the Board Tel: (262) 783-3500
QUAIN, Mitchell I. Fax: (800) 298-3503

President and Chief Executive Officer Tel: (800) 288-8178
MCCORMICK, Peter M. Fax: (800) 298-3503

Main Headquarters
Mailing: N49 W13650 Campbell Dr. Tel: (262) 783-3500
Menomonee Falls, WI 53051 Fax: (800) 298-3503

		TF:	(800) 288-8178

Public Affairs and Related Activities Personnel

At Headquarters

BOSTROM, Lynn *Director, Marketing Communications* lbostrom@magnetek.com	Tel: Fax:	(262) 252-2903 (262) 781-1775
CRAMER, Scott S. *Vice President, General Counsel and Corporate Secretary*	Tel: Fax:	(262) 783-3500 (800) 298-3503
HUI, Hungsun *Vice President, Operations*	Tel: Fax:	(262) 783-3500 (800) 298-3503
PINTOR, Linda *Vice President, Human Resources*	Tel: Fax:	(262) 252-6950 (800) 298-3503
SCHWENNER, Marty J. *Vice President and Chief Financial Officer* mschwenner@magnetek.com	Tel: Fax:	(262) 783-3500 (800) 298-3503

Maher Terminals, LLC

An independent marine multi-user container terminal operators.
www.maherterminals.com
Annual Revenues: $16.10 million
Employees: 220
SIC: 7361; 5099
Industry/ies: Marine/Maritime/Shipping; Transportation

President and Chief Executive Officer

CROSS, Gary	Tel: Fax:	(908) 527-8200 (908) 790-5678

Main Headquarters

Mailing: 1210 Corbin St. Elizabeth, NJ 07201	Tel: Fax:	(908) 527-8200 (908) 790-5678

Political Action Committees

Maher Terminals LLC PAC
FEC ID: C00335109
Contact: Jay R. Ruble
1210 Corbin St.
P.O. Box 618
Elizabeth, NJ 07201

Public Affairs and Related Activities Personnel

At Headquarters

FARLEY, Joseph *Vice President, Corporate Compliance & External Affairs*	Tel: Fax:	(908) 527-8200 (908) 790-5678
HRDINA, Frank *Senior Vice President, Human Resources*	Tel: Fax:	(908) 527-8200 (908) 436-4812
RAY, Anthony *Executive Vice President, Operations and Labor relations*	Tel: Fax:	(908) 527-8200 (908) 790-5678
RUBLE, Jay R. *Senior Vice President and General Counsel* jruble@maherterminals.com	Tel: Fax:	(908) 527-8200 (908) 436-4812
TONUZI, Ron *Executive Vice President and Chief Financial Officer*	Tel: Fax:	(908) 527-8200 (908) 790-5678
VAN RIEMSDYK, Frans *Executive Vice President, Corporate Development & Strategy* fvanriemsdyk@maherterminals.com	Tel: Fax:	(908) 527-8200 (908) 790-5678

Mainstream Engineering Corporation, Inc.

Mainstream Engineering Corporation is a solutions-oriented research, development and manufacturing small business.
www.mainstream-engr.com
Employees: 20
Industry/ies: Engineering/Mathematics

Main Headquarters

Mailing: 200 Yellow Pl. Rockledge, FL 32955	Tel: Fax:	(321) 631-3550 (321) 631-3552

Public Affairs and Related Activities Personnel

At Headquarters

BOYLE, Mike *Director, Human Resources*	Tel: Fax:	(321) 631-3550 (321) 631-3552
LEGGETT, Molly *Executive Assistant and Contact, Media Relations* mleggett@mainstream-engr.com	Tel: Fax:	(321) 631-3550 (321) 631-3552

Major League Baseball

Organizes and runs professional baseball in the United States and Canada.
mlb.mlb.com
Annual Revenues: $6.50 billion
Employees: 7
Industry/ies: Baseball; Sports See Also Specific Sport; Sports/Leisure/
Entertainment
Legislative Issues: HOM; SPO; TAX

Main Headquarters

Mailing:	245 Park Ave. 31st Floor New York City, NY 10167	Tel: Fax:	(212) 931-7800 (212) 949-5654

Political Action Committees

Office of The Commissioner of Major League Baseball Political Action
Committee
FEC ID: C00368142
Contact: E. Mark Braden

1050 Connecticut Ave. NW, Suite 1100 Washington, DC 20036	Tel: Fax:	(202) 861-1739 (202) 861-1783

Contributions to Candidates: $237,125 (2015-2016)
Democrats: $82,500; Republicans: $154,625

Principal Recipients

SENATE
BLUNT, ROY (REP-MO)
LEE, MIKE (REP-UT)

Corporate Foundations and Giving Programs

Major League Baseball Contributions Program
Contact: Thomas C. Brasuell
245 Park Ave.
31st Floor
New York City, NY 10167

Public Affairs and Related Activities Personnel

At Headquarters

ALKIN, Josh *Vice President, Government Relations*	Tel: Fax:	(212) 931-7800 (212) 949-5654
BRASUELL, Thomas C. *Vice President, Community Affairs*	Tel: Fax:	(212) 931-7800 (212) 949-8636
BROSNAN , Tim *Business Development Corporation*	Tel: Fax:	(212) 931-7800 (212) 949-5654
CONRAD, Lucy Calautti *Lobbyist*	Tel: Fax:	(212) 931-7800 (212) 949-5654
COURTNEY, Patrick *VP Marketing and Digital Strategy*	Tel: Fax:	(212) 931-7800 (212) 949-8636
HALEM, Dan *Chief Legal Officer*	Tel: Fax:	(212) 931-7800 (212) 949-8636
MANFRED, Rob *Commissioner*	Tel: Fax:	(212) 931-7800 (212) 949-5654
MARINER, Jonathan *Chief Investment Officer*	Tel: Fax:	(212) 931-7800 (212) 949-5654
MCHALE, Jr., John *Executive Vice President, Administration and Chief Information Officer*	Tel: Fax:	(212) 931-7800 (212) 949-8636
PETITTI, Tony *Chief Operating Officer*	Tel: Fax:	(212) 931-7500 (212) 949-8636

At Other Offices

BRADEN, E. Mark *Counsel* 245 Park Ave., Suite 1100 New York, NY 10011	Tel: Fax:	(202) 861-1739 (202) 861-1783
CALAUTTI, Lucy J. *Senior Advisor* 245 Park Ave., Suite 1100 New York, NY 10011	Tel: Fax:	(202) 861-1739 (202) 861-1783

Malcolm Pirnie, Inc.

An environmental engineering and consulting firm.
www.pirnie.com
Employees: 1,800
Industry/ies: Environment And Conservation
Legislative Issues: CAW; ENV; NAT

Chairman and Chief Executive Officer

WESTERHOFF, DEE, P E, Garret P.	Tel: Fax:	(914) 694-2100 (914) 694-9286

Main Headquarters

Mailing: 630 Plaza Dr. Suite 200 Highlands Ranch, CO 80129	Tel: Fax:	(720) 344-3500 (720) 344-3535

Public Affairs and Related Activities Personnel

At Headquarters

CAVALUZZI, Jerry *General Counsel*	Tel: Fax:	(914) 694-2100 (914) 694-9286
PASQUINI, Patricia *Vice President, Diversity, Equal Employment Opportunity and Affirmative Action*	Tel: Fax:	(914) 694-2100 (914) 694-9286

Malden Mills Industries

See listing on page 613 under Polartec, LLC

Management and Training Corporation

An international organization dedicated to helping people realize their learning potential.
www.mtctrains.com
Annual Revenues: $667.37 million
Employees: 8,000
Industry/ies: Education
Legislative Issues: BUD; HOM; LAW; LBR

Chairman of the Board, President and Chief Executive Officer   Tel: (801) 693-2600
MARQUARDT, J.D., MBA, Scott   Fax: (801) 693-2900

Main Headquarters
Mailing: 500 N. Marketplace Dr.   Tel: (801) 693-2600
              Centerville, UT 84014   Fax: (801) 693-2900
                                                         TF: (800) 574-4682

Washington Office
Mailing: 1325 G St. NW   Tel: (202) 552-7399
              Suite 500   Fax: (202) 552-5397
              Washington, DC 20005

Political Action Committees
Management and Training Corporation PAC
FEC ID: C00208322
Contact: Lyle J. Parry
500 N. Marketplace Dr.   Tel: (801) 693-2600
P.O. Box Ten   Fax: (801) 693-2600
Centerville, UT 84403

> **Contributions to Candidates:** $44,900 (2015-2016)
> Democrats: $13,500; Republicans: $31,400

Corporate Foundations and Giving Programs
Management and Training Corporation Contributions Program
500 N. Marketplace Dr.
Centerville, UT 84014

Public Affairs and Related Activities Personnel
At Headquarters

ARAMAKI, SPHR, Teresa N.   Tel: (801) 693-2600
Vice President, Human Resources   Fax: (801) 693-2900
taramaki@mtctrains.com

CALL, CPA, J.D., MBA, Dawn M.   Tel: (801) 693-2600
Vice President, General Counsel   Fax: (801) 693-2900
dawn.call@mtctrains.com

MCDONALD, Celeste   Tel: (801) 693-2600
Vice President, Corporate Communications   Fax: (801) 693-2900
celeste.mcdonald@mtctrains.com

MOLINA, Sergio   Tel: (801) 693-2600
Senior Vice President, Business Development and   Fax: (801) 693-2900
Administration

MURPHY, Mike   Tel: (801) 693-2863
Vice President, Corrections Marketing   Fax: (801) 693-2900
mike.murphy@mtctrains.com

PEDERSEN, John   Tel: (801) 693-2600
Senior Vice President, Education and Training   Fax: (801) 693-2900

At Other Offices

PARRY, Lyle J.
Chief Financial Officer, Senior Vice President, Secretary and
Treasurer
500 N. Marketplace Dr.
Centerville, UT 84403
lyle.parry@mtctrains.com

The Manitowoc Company, Inc.

Founded in the lakeshore community of Manitowoc, Wisconsin, in 1902 as a shipbuilding and ship-repair organization. It serves two very different business-to-business markets: cranes and foodservice equipment, and is a global leader in both, building and supporting some of the most recognizable, trusted brands in their respective industries.
www.manitowoc.com
Annual Revenues: $3.79 billion
Employees: 12,300
Ticker: NYSE: MTW
SIC: 3531
Industry/ies: Machinery/Equipment

Chairman of the Board, President and Chief Executive Officer   Tel: (920) 652-2222
TELLOCK, Glenn E.

Main Headquarters
Mailing: 2400 S. 44th St.   Tel: (920) 652-2222
              P.O. Box 66
              Manitowoc, WI 54221-0066

Washington Office
Mailing: 80 M St.   Tel: (202) 867-3607
              Suite 410
              Washington, DC 20003

Political Action Committees
Manitowoc Company PAC

FEC ID: C00287847
Contact: Carl J. Laurino
2400 S. 44th St.
P.O. Box 66
Manitowoc, MN 54221

> **Contributions to Candidates:** $10,000 (2015-2016)
> Democrats: $2,500; Republicans: $7,500

Public Affairs and Related Activities Personnel
At Headquarters

ETCHART, Eric P.   Tel: (920) 652-2222
Senior Vice President of Business Development

HOULAHAN, Therese   Tel: (920) 652-2222
Corporate Treasurer

JONES, Maurice D.   Tel: (920) 652-2222
Senior Vice President, General Counsel and Secretary
maurice.jones@manitowoc.com

LAURINO, Carl J.   Tel: (920) 652-1720
Senior Vice President and Chief Financial Officer
carl.laurino@manitowoc.com

MUSIAL, Thomas G.   Tel: (920) 652-2222
Senior Vice President, Human Resources and Administration

At Washington Office

BERNARD, Al J.   Tel: (202) 863-3607
Senior Vice President, Washington Operations
Registered Federal Lobbyist

Manitowoc Dry Dock Company

See listing on page 508 under The Manitowoc Company, Inc.

Manning Selvage and Lee

A public relations firm. MSLGROUP North America is part of MSLGROUP, Publicis Groupe's strategic communications and engagement group.
northamerica.mslgroup.com
Annual Revenues: $100.0 million
Employees: 1,000
Industry/ies: Public Affairs And Public Relations

Main Headquarters
Mailing: 375 Hudson St.   Tel: (646) 500-7600
              14th Floor   Fax: (646) 468-4007
              New York City, NY 10014

Washington Office
Mailing: Two Lafeyette Centre, 1133 21st St. NW   Tel: (202) 467-6600
              Suite 300   Fax: (202) 467-5187
              Washington, DC 20036-3326

Public Affairs and Related Activities Personnel
At Headquarters

ECHTER, Michael   Tel: (646) 500-7600
Director, Corporate Communications & Marketing   Fax: (646) 468-4007
Mail Stop 14th Floor
michael.echter@mslgroup.com

LILIEN , Tara   Tel: (646) 500-7600
Senior Vice President, Human Resources   Fax: (646) 468-4007
tara.lilien@mslgroup.com

MILLER, Peter   Tel: (646) 500-7600
Chief Financial Officer   Fax: (646) 468-4007
peter.miller@mslgroup.com

PRENDERGAST, Maree   Tel: (646) 500-7600
Chief Talent Officer, North America   Fax: (646) 468-4007
maree.prendergast@mslgroup.com

SHAPIRO , Maury   Tel: (646) 500-7600
Chief Financial Officer, North America   Fax: (646) 468-4007
maury.shapiro@mslgroup.com

SMITH, Stephanie   Tel: (646) 500-7600
Senior Vice President, Chief Editorial Director, North Fax: (646) 468-4007
America
stephanie.smith@mslgroup.com

WILSON, Renee   Tel: (646) 500-7600
Chief Client Officer   Fax: (646) 468-4007
renee.wilson@mslgroup.com

At Other Offices

NEWMAN, Paul   Tel: (312) 861-5200
President, North America
222 Merchandise Mart, Suite 4-150
Chicago, IL 60654

Manpower Inc.

A provider of staffing and workforce management solutions.
www.manpower.com
Annual Revenues: $19.38 billion

Employees: 27,000
Ticker: NYSE: MAN
SIC: 7363
Industry/ies: Employees & Employment

Chairman and Chief Executive Officer
PRISING, Jonas

Tel: (414) 961-1000
Fax: (414) 906-7822

Main Headquarters
Mailing: 100 Manpower Pl.
Milwaukee, WI 53212

Tel: (414) 961-1000
Fax: (414) 906-7822

Corporate Foundations and Giving Programs
The Manpower Foundation
100 Manpower Pl.
Milwaukee, WI 53212

Tel: (414) 961-1000

Public Affairs and Related Activities Personnel

At Headquarters

BUCHBAND, Richard
Senior Vice President, General Counsel and Secretary

Tel: (414) 961-1000
Fax: (414) 906-7822

COLE , Julie
Vice President, Marketing

Tel: (414) 961-1000
Fax: (414) 906-7822

GREEN, Darryl
President and Chief Operating Officer

Tel: (414) 961-1000
Fax: (414) 906-7822

HANDEL, Michael Van
Senior Executive Vice President
Michael.vanhandel@manpower.com

Tel: (414) 906-6807
Fax: (414) 961-7081

MCGINNIS, Jack
Executive Vice President and Chief Financial Officer

Tel: (414) 961-1000
Fax: (414) 906-7822

SWAN, Mara
Executive Vice President, Global Strategy and Talent

Tel: (414) 961-1000
Fax: (414) 961-7081

TOTH , Mark
Chief Legal Officer

Tel: (414) 961-1000
Fax: (414) 906-7822

ZARLING, Britt
Director, Global Strategic Communications
britt.zarling@manpowergroup.com

Tel: (414) 906-7272
Fax: (414) 526-3107

ManTech International Corporation

Leading the Convergence of National Security and Information Technology. Provider of technology solutions in information systems, environment, telecommunications, defense, and aeronautics.
www.mantech.com
Annual Revenues: $1.57 billion
Employees: 7,200
Ticker: NASDAQ: MANT
Industry/ies: Defense/Homeland Security; Government-Related
Legislative Issues: DEF

Founder, Chairman of the Board and Chief Executive Officer
PEDERSEN, George J.

Tel: (703) 218-6000
Fax: (703) 218-6301

Main Headquarters
Mailing: 12015 Lee Jackson Hwy.
Fairfax, VA 22033

Tel: (703) 218-6000
Fax: (703) 218-6301

Political Action Committees
ManTech International Corporation Political Action Committee
FEC ID: C00208983
Contact: Robert D. Knight
12015 Lee Jackson Hwy.
Suite 841
Fairfax, VA 22033

Tel: (703) 218-6000
Fax: (703) 218-8296

Contributions to Candidates: $43,700 (2015-2016)
Democrats: $25,700; Republicans: $18,000

Principal Recipients

HOUSE
RUPPERSBERGER, C.A. DUTCH (DEM-MD)

Corporate Foundations and Giving Programs
ManTech International Contributions Program
12015 Lee Jackson Hwy.
Fairfax, VA 22033

Public Affairs and Related Activities Personnel

At Headquarters

BROWN, Jeffrey S.
Executive Vice President and General Counsel

Tel: (703) 218-6000
Fax: (703) 218-6301

DAVIS, M. Stuart
Executive Vice President, Strategy and Investor Relations Contact

Tel: (703) 218-8269
Fax: (703) 218-6301

KEEFE, Daniel J.
President and Chief Operating Officer

Tel: (703) 218-6000
Fax: (703) 218-6301

KNIGHT, Robert D.
Vice President and PAC Contact
bob.knight@mantech.com

Tel: (703) 218-8275
Fax: (703) 218-6301

MENTUS, Margo

Tel: (703) 218-6000

Senior Vice President, Human Resources
margo.mentus@mantech.com

Fax: (703) 218-6301

PHILLIPS, Kevin M.
Executive Vice President and Chief Financial Officer

Tel: (703) 218-6000
Fax: (703) 218-6301

Mantria Corporation

Provides real estate, financing, biorefinery industry, global philanthropy, investments and education services
www.mantria.com
Industry/ies: Environment And Conservation; Real Estate

Chairman of the Board and Chief Executive Officer
KNORR, Amanda
aknorr@mantria.com

Tel: (610) 617-4455
Fax: (610) 557-3832

Main Headquarters
Mailing: 555 E. City Ave.
Suite 430
Bala Cynwyd, PA 19004-1112

Corporate Foundations and Giving Programs
Mantria Foundation
Contact: Amanda Knorr
555 E. City Ave.
Suite 430
Bala Cynwyd, PA 19004

Public Affairs and Related Activities Personnel

At Headquarters

PAGE, Sharone
Chief Human Resources Officer

Tel: (610) 617-4455
Fax: (610) 557-3832

Manufacturers and Traders Trust Company
See listing on page 503 under M & T Bank Corporation

Marathon Oil Corporation

A United States-based oil and natural gas exploration and production company.
www.marathonoil.com
Annual Revenues: $9.71 billion
Employees: 3,330
Ticker: NYSE: MRO
SIC: 2911; 2899; 2951
NAICS: 324110
Industry/ies: Fuels See Coal, Gas, Oil, Petroleum; Natural Resources; Petroleum Industry
Legislative Issues: BUD; CAW; ENG; ENV; NAT; TAX

Non-Executive Chairman of the Board
REILLEY , Dennis H.

Tel: (713) 629-6600
Fax: (713) 296-2952

President and Chief Executive Office
TILLMAN, Lee M.

Tel: (713) 629-6600
Fax: (713) 296-2952

Main Headquarters
Mailing: 5555 San Felipe St.
Houston, TX 77056-2723

Tel: (713) 629-6600
Fax: (713) 296-2952
TF: (866) 462-7284

Washington Office
Mailing: 975 F St. NW
Suite 530
Washington, DC 20004

Tel: (202) 654-4499
Fax: (202) 654-4492

Political Action Committees
Marathon Oil Company Employees PAC (MEPAC)
FEC ID: C00040568
Contact: Nancy Cushman
P.O. Box 75040, MC 2250
Detroit, MI 48275

Tel: (713) 629-6600
Fax: (713) 296-2952

Contributions to Candidates: $109,000 (2015-2016)
Democrats: $7,500; Republicans: $101,500

Corporate Foundations and Giving Programs
Marathon Oil Company Foundation
Contact: Donna Boyer
c/o Charitable Contributions
P.O. Box 3128
Houston, TX 77253

Public Affairs and Related Activities Personnel

At Headquarters

CAMPBELL, Eileen M.
Vice President, Human Resources

Tel: (713) 629-6600
Fax: (713) 296-2952

CLARK, Morris R.
Vice President and Treasurer

Tel: (713) 629-6600
Fax: (713) 296-2952

CUSHMAN, Nancy
PAC Treasurer

Tel: (713) 629-6600
Fax: (713) 296-2952

JONES, Deanna L.
Vice President, Human Resources and Administrative Services

Tel: (713) 629-6600
Fax: (713) 296-2952

KERRIGAN, Sylvia J.   Tel: (713) 629-6600
Executive Vice President, General Counsel and Secretary   Fax: (713) 296-2952

STOVER, Michael J.   Tel: (713) 629-6600
Vice President, Operations Services   Fax: (713) 296-2952

SULLENBARGER, Daniel J.   Tel: (713) 629-6600
Vice President, Corporate Compliance and Ethics   Fax: (713) 296-2952

SULT, John R. (J.R.)   Tel: (713) 629-6600
Executive Vice President and Chief Financial Office   Fax: (713) 296-2952

WAGNER, Patrick J.   Tel: (713) 629-6600
Vice President, Corporate Development   Fax: (713) 296-2952

WARREN, Lee   Tel: (713) 629-4103
Contact, Media Relations   Fax: (713) 296-2952
mediarelations@marathonoil.com

WEEDITZ, Paul   Tel: (713) 296-3910
General Manager, Public Affairs   Fax: (713) 296-2952
pweeditz@marathonoil.com

WILSON, Gary E.   Tel: (713) 629-6600
Vice President, Controller and Chief Accounting Officer   Fax: (713) 296-2952

At Washington Office

KIRKHAM, Brendon   Tel: (202) 654-4480
Director, Federal & International Government Affairs   Fax: (202) 654-4490
Registered Federal Lobbyist

LEISTER, Michael E.   Tel: (202) 654-4480
Senior Fuels Advisor   Fax: (202) 654-4490

RICHARDS, Patricia M.   Tel: (202) 654-4499
Vice President, Federal Government Affairs   Fax: (202) 654-4490

At Other Offices

BOYER, Donna   Tel: (713) 296-4149
Foundation Contact   Fax: (202) 654-4490
C/O Charitable Contributions, P.O. Box 3128
Houston, TX 77253
philanthropy@marathonoil.com

SIEMIONTKOWSKI, Ronald S.
Contact, Government Relations
P.O. Box 75000, MC 2250
Detroit, MI 48275

Marcus & Millichap

Provides real estate investment sales, financing, research and advisory services.
www.marcusmillichap.com
Employees: 1,200
SIC: 6531
Industry/ies: Banking/Finance/Investments; Real Estate

Chairman of the Board   Tel: (818) 212-2700
MARCUS, George M.   Fax: (818) 212-2710
gmarcus@mmcrealestate.com

President and Chief Executive Officer   Tel: (818) 212-2700
KERIN, John J.   Fax: (818) 212-2710

Main Headquarters
Mailing: 16830 Ventura Blvd.   Tel: (818) 212-2700
        Suite 100   Fax: (818) 212-2710
        Encino, CA 91436

Public Affairs and Related Activities Personnel

At Headquarters

ANDERSON, Rick   Tel: (818) 212-2700
Director, Human Resources   Fax: (818) 212-2710
Rick.Anderson@marcusmillichap.com

KAISER, Stuart E.   Tel: (818) 212-2700
Senior Vice President, Managing Director and Chief   Fax: (818) 212-2710
Financial Officer

LOUIE, Martin E   Tel: (818) 212-2700
Senior Vice President, Chief Financial Officer   Fax: (818) 212-2710

MUDRICH, Paul S.   Tel: (818) 212-2700
Senior Vice President, Managing Director and Chief Legal   Fax: (818) 212-2710
Officer
paul.mudrich@marcusmillichap.com

Maricopa Integrated Health Systems

A training center for the nation's physicians.
www.mihs.org
Annual Revenues: $18.20 million
Employees: 100
Industry/ies: Medicine/Health Care/Mental Health

President and Chief Executive Officer   Tel: (602) 344-5011
PURVES, Steve   Fax: (602) 344-5190

Main Headquarters
Mailing: 2601 E. Roosevelt St.   Tel: (602) 344-5011
        Phoenix, AZ 85008   Fax: (602) 344-5190
                  TF: (866) 333-6447

Corporate Foundations and Giving Programs

Maricopa Health Foundation
Contact: Thomas G. McKinley
2601 E. Roosevelt St.
Phoenix, AZ 85008

Public Affairs and Related Activities Personnel

At Headquarters

BAYLESS, Betsey   Tel: (602) 344-5011
President Emeritus   Fax: (602) 344-5894

GENDREAU, Luis   Tel: (602) 344-5011
Director, Community Relations   Fax: (602) 344-5190
luis.gendreau@mihs .org

GRAHAM, Joyce   Tel: (602) 344-5011
Director, Strategic Planning   Fax: (602) 344-5894

MCKINLEY, Thomas G.   Tel: (602) 344-1818
President, Foundation   Fax: (602) 344-5894
tom.mckinley@mihs.org

Marine Spill Response Corporation

A national, private, non-profit corporation that offers oil spill response services.
www.msrc.org
Industry/ies: Conservation; Environment And Conservation; Pollution And Waste

President and Chief Executive Officer   Tel: (703) 326-5600
BENZ, Steven T.   Fax: (703) 326-5660
norell@msrc.org

Main Headquarters
Mailing: 220 Spring St.   Tel: (703) 326-5600
        Suite 500   Fax: (703) 326-5660
        Herndon, VA 20170

Public Affairs and Related Activities Personnel

At Headquarters

ROOS, Judith   Tel: (703) 326-5617
Vice President Marketing, Customer Services and Corporate   Fax: (703) 326-5660
Relations
roos@msrc.org

Mariner Post Acute Network

See listing on page 702 under SavaSeniorCare, LLC

Mariner Seafood, LLC

A worldwide network of supply, processing and distribution capabilities to streamline the cost and availability of quality seafood products for its customers in the United States and abroad.
www.marinerseafood.com
Annual Revenues: $2.20 million
Industry/ies: Fish And Fishing; Food And Beverage Industry

President and Chief Executive Officer   Tel: (508) 996-9710
FLYNN, Jack   Fax: (774) 202-6605
jackflynn@marinerseafood.com

Main Headquarters
Mailing: 14 S. St.   Tel: (774) 202-4121
        New Bedford, MA 02740   Fax: (774) 202-6605

Public Affairs and Related Activities Personnel

At Headquarters

FREDERICK, Dale   Tel: (774) 202-4121
Director, Sales and Marketing   Fax: (774) 202-6605
dalef@marinerseafood.com

TASSO, Janice   Tel: (774) 202-4121
Vice President, Finance and Operations   Fax: (774) 202-6605
jtasso@marinerseafood.com

WILKINSON, Ryan   Tel: (774) 202-4121
Sales and Marketing   Fax: (774) 202-6605
Ryanw@marinerseafood.com

Marion Energy Inc.

Is a publicly traded independent oil and gas production company.
www.marionenergy.com.au
Industry/ies: Energy/Electricity

Chief Executive Officer   Tel: (972) 540-2967
CLARKE, Jeffrey   Fax: (972) 547-0442
jclarke@marionenergy.com

Main Headquarters
Mailing: 119 S. Tennesee St.   Tel: (972) 540-2967
        Suite 200   Fax: (972) 547-0442
        McKinney, TX 75069-4321

Public Affairs and Related Activities Personnel

At Headquarters

LOUMAN, Karel   Tel: (972) 540-2967

Executive Director and Chief Financial Officer | Fax: (972) 547-0442

Maritz, Inc.

A provider of integrated performance improvement, incentive travel and consumer market research services.
www.maritz.com
Employees: 3,000
Industry/ies: Advertising And Marketing; Banking/Finance/Investments; Business; Consultants; Conventions/Trade Shows/Exhibits; Retail/Wholesale

Board Chairman and Chief Executive Officer | Tel: (636) 827-4000
MARITZ, Steve | Fax: (636) 827-3312

Main Headquarters
Mailing: 1375 N. Highway Dr. | Tel: (636) 827-4000
Fenton, MO 63099 | Fax: (636) 827-3312
| TF: (877) 462-7489

Corporate Foundations and Giving Programs

Maritz, Inc. Corporate Giving Program
Contact: Debbie Schirmer
1375 N. Highway Dr. | Tel: (636) 827-4000
Fenton, MO 63099 | Fax: (636) 827-4000

Public Affairs and Related Activities Personnel

At Headquarters

GALLANT, Steve | Tel: (636) 827-4000
General Counsel | Fax: (636) 827-3312

HUMMEL, Dennis | Tel: (636) 827-4000
President | Fax: (636) 827-3312

LARSEN, Jennifer | Tel: (636) 837-1523
Senior Director, Public Relations | Fax: (636) 827-8605
jennifer.larsen@maritz.com

RAMOS, Rick | Tel: (636) 827-4000
Executive Vice President and Chief Financial Officer | Fax: (636) 827-3312

SCHIRMER, Debbie | Tel: (636) 827-4000
Senior Community Manager | Fax: (636) 827-3312
debbie.schirmer@maritz.com

Mark IV

Manufacturer of engineered systems and components utilizing mechanical and fluid power transmission, fluid transfer, and power systems and components.
www.mark-iv.com
Annual Revenues: $1.18 billion
Employees: 4,000
SIC: 3050
Industry/ies: Machinery/Equipment; Science; Scientific Research

Chief Executive Officer | Tel: (716) 689-4972
ORCHARD, Jim | Fax: (716) 568-6089

Main Headquarters
Mailing: P.O. Box 810 | Tel: (716) 689-4972
Amherst, NY 14226 | Fax: (716) 568-6089

Corporate Foundations and Giving Programs

Mark IV Foundation
P.O. Box 180
Amherst, NY 14226

Public Affairs and Related Activities Personnel

At Headquarters

BARBERIO, Mark | Tel: (716) 689-4972
Chief Financial Officer | Fax: (716) 568-6089

MURPHREE, Sandra | Tel: (716) 689-4972
VP Global HR | Fax: (716) 568-6089

STEELE, Edward R. | Tel: (716) 689-4972
Vice President, Finance, Secretary and Treasurer | Fax: (716) 568-6089

Marriott International, Inc.

A worldwide hospitality company.
www.marriott.com
Annual Revenues: $2.87 billion
Employees: 127,500
Ticker: NYSE: MAR
SIC: 7011
Industry/ies: Food And Beverage Industry; Travel/Tourism/Lodging
Legislative Issues: CSP; FOR; GOV; IMM; TOU

Executive Chairman and Chairman of the Board | Tel: (301) 380-3000
MARRIOTT, Jr., J.W. | Fax: (301) 380-3969

President and Chief Executive Officer | Tel: (301) 380-3000
SORENSON, Arne M. | Fax: (301) 380-3969

Main Headquarters
Mailing: 10400 Fernwood Rd. | Tel: (301) 380-3000
Bethesda, MD 20817 | Fax: (301) 380-3969

Political Action Committees
Marriott International, Inc. PAC

FEC ID: C00284810
Contact: Phyllis Soo-Hoo
10400 Fernwood Rd. | Tel: (301) 380-3000
Bethesda, MD 20817 | Fax: (301) 380-3969

Contributions to Candidates: $259,500 (2015-2016)
Democrats: $124,500; Republicans: $135,000

Principal Recipients

SENATE
MCCAIN, JOHN S (REP-VA)
SCHATZ, BRIAN (DEM-HI)
SCHUMER, CHARLES E (DEM-NY)
VAN HOLLEN, CHRIS (DEM-MD)

HOUSE
DIAZ-BALART, MARIO (REP-FL)
FLAKE, JEFF MR. (REP-AZ)
RYAN, PAUL D. (REP-WI)

Corporate Foundations and Giving Programs

Marriott Foundation for People with Disabilities
Contact: Thomas Asbury
10400 Fernwood Rd. | Tel: (301) 380-7771
Bethesda, MD 20817

Public Affairs and Related Activities Personnel

At Headquarters

ASBURY, Thomas | Tel: (301) 380-3000
Vice President and Executive Director, Marriott Foundation | Fax: (301) 380-3969
for People with Disabilities

FARRELL, June | Tel: (301) 380-7796
Vice President, International Communications | Fax: (301) 380-4684
june.farrell@marriott.com

FROEHLICH-FLOOD, Melissa | Tel: (301) 380-4839
Vice President, Government Affairs | Fax: (301) 380-8957
melissa.froehlich@marriott.com
Registered Federal Lobbyist

HAMPTON, Stephanie L. | Tel: (301) 380-1217
Senior Director, Global Corporate Relations | Fax: (301) 380-3969
stephanie.hampton@marriott.com

HANDLON, Carolyn B. | Tel: (301) 380-3000
Executive Vice President, Finance and Global Treasurer | Fax: (301) 380-3969

HARRISON, Deborah Marriott | Tel: (301) 380-4839
Global Officer, Culture and Business Councils | Fax: (301) 380-3969
debbie.harrison@marriott.com

LINNARTZ, Stephanie C. | Tel: (301) 380-3000
Executive Vice President and Global Chief Marketing and | Fax: (301) 380-3969
Commerical Officer

MALONEY, Thomas J. | Tel: (301) 380-3000
Federal Lobbyist, Director, Government Affairs | Fax: (301) 380-3969
thomas.maloney@marriott.com
Registered Federal Lobbyist

MCLEMORE, APR, Felicia Farrar | Tel: (301) 380-3000
Director, Global Corporate Relations | Fax: (301) 380-3969
Felicia.McLemore@marriott.com

NEILL, Erin | Tel: (301) 380-3000
Registered Federal Lobbyist | Fax: (301) 380-3969

OBERG, Kathleen K. | Tel: (301) 380-3000
Executive Vice President and Chief Financial Officer | Fax: (301) 380-3969

PAUGH, Laura E. | Tel: (301) 380-7418
Senior Vice President, Investor Relations | Fax: (301) 380-5067
laura.paugh@marriott.com

PRIMROSE, Tricia A. | Tel: (301) 380-3000
Executive Vice President and Global Chief Communications | Fax: (301) 380-3969
and Public Affairs Officer

RODRIGUEZ, David A. | Tel: (301) 380-3000
Executive Vice President and Global Chief Human Resources | Fax: (301) 380-3969
Officer
david.rodriguez@marriott.com

RYAN, Esq., Edward A. | Tel: (301) 380-3000
Executive Vice President and General Counsel | Fax: (301) 380-3969
edward.ryan@marriott.com

SOO-HOO, Phyllis | Tel: (301) 380-3000
PAC Treasurer | Fax: (301) 380-3969

Mars, Inc.

A snack food, main meal and pet food manufacturer. In 2008, Mars, Inc. acquired Wrigley as a wholly owned subsidiary.
www.mars.com
Industry/ies: Food And Beverage Industry
Legislative Issues: AGR; ENG; FOO; TAX

Global President | Tel: (703) 821-4900
REID, Grant F. | Fax: (703) 448-9678

Main Headquarters

Mailing:	6885 Elm St.	Tel:	(703) 821-4900
	McLean, VA 22101	Fax:	(703) 448-9678

Public Affairs and Related Activities Personnel

At Headquarters

CAMPAGNA, Shannon — Tel: (703) 821-4900, Fax: (703) 448-9678
Director, Federal Government Affairs
Registered Federal Lobbyist

DONOFRIO, John — Tel: (703) 821-4900, Fax: (703) 448-9678
Vice President, Secretary and General Counsel

FIGEL, Brad — Tel: (703) 821-4900, Fax: (703) 448-9678
Director, Public Affairs
Registered Federal Lobbyist

GAMORAN, Reuben — Tel: (703) 821-4900, Fax: (703) 448-9678
Chief Financial Officer

KAMENETZKY, David — Tel: (703) 821-4900, Fax: (703) 448-9678
Vice President, Corporate Affairs and Strategic Initiatives

MCCOLL, Bruce — Tel: (703) 821-4900, Fax: (703) 448-9678
Chief Marketing Officer

MINVIELLE, Eric — Tel: (703) 821-4900, Fax: (703) 448-9678
Executive Vice President, People and Organization

OLSEN, Eric — Tel: (202) 857-4471, Fax: (703) 448-9678
Federal Lobbyist
Registered Federal Lobbyist

Marsh & McLennan Companies, Inc.

A global professional services firm with risk and insurance services, investment management, and consulting businesses.
www.mmc.com
Annual Revenues: $12.90 billion
Employees: 57,000
Ticker: NYSE: MMC
SIC: 6411
Industry/ies: Insurance Industry
Legislative Issues: BUD; FIN; HCR; HOM; INS; INT; RET; TAX

Chairman of the Board — Tel: (212) 345-5000, Fax: (212) 345-4808
MOCZARSKI, Alexander S.

President and Chief Executive Officer — Tel: (212) 345-5000, Fax: (212) 345-4808
GLASER, Daniel S.

Main Headquarters

Mailing:	1166 Avenue of the Americas	Tel:	(212) 345-5000
	New York City, NY 10036-2774	Fax:	(212) 345-4808

Washington Office

Mailing:	1050 Connecticut Ave. NW	Tel:	(202) 263-7747
	Washington Sq., Suite 700		
	Washington, DC 20036		

Political Action Committees

Marsh & McLennan Companies, Inc. PAC (MMCPAC)
FEC ID: C00457234
Contact: Karen A. Farrell
1166 Avenue of the Americas — Tel: (212) 345-5000
New York City, NY 10036 — Fax: (212) 345-4808

Contributions to Candidates: $286,650 (2015-2016)
Democrats: $119,500; Republicans: $167,150

Principal Recipients

HOUSE
LUETKEMEYER, W BLAINE (REP-MO)

Public Affairs and Related Activities Personnel

At Headquarters

BESHAR, Peter J. — Tel: (212) 345-5000, Fax: (212) 345-4838
Executive Vice President and General Counsel

BIELER, Alan W. — Tel: (212) 345-5000, Fax: (212) 345-4808
Vice President, Treasurer

BISCHOFF, J. Michael — Tel: (212) 345-5470, Fax: (212) 345-4808
Chief Financial Officer
jmichael.bischoff@mmc.com

CORA, Laura — Tel: (212) 345-2731, Fax: (212) 345-4808
Director, Internal Communications
laura.cora@mmc.com

DANDRIDGE, Edward L. — Tel: (212) 345-9751, Fax: (212) 345-4808
Chief Communications Officer
Ed.Dandridge@mmc.com

FANJUL, Oscar — Tel: (212) 345-5000, Fax: (212) 345-4808
Director

FARRELL, Karen A. — Tel: (212) 345-5000, Fax: (212) 345-4808
Assistant Treasurer, Lobbyist and PAC Treasurer

GILBERT, E. Scott — Tel: (212) 345-5000, Fax: (212) 345-4838
Senior Vice President, Chief Risk and Compliance Officer

LEDFORD, Laurie — Tel: (212) 345-5000, Fax: (212) 345-4808
Senior Vice President and Chief Human Resources Officer

MONKTON, Lord Lang of — Tel: (212) 345-5000, Fax: (212) 345-4808
Contact, Directors and Governance Committee

ROBERTS, Carey — Tel: (212) 345-5000, Fax: (212) 345-4808
Deputy General Counsel and Corporate Secretary

WALSH, Keith — Tel: (212) 345-0057, Fax: (212) 345-4808
Investors Contact
keith.walsh@mmc.com

At Washington Office

BENSON, Tara Anne — Tel: (202) 263-7747
Federal Lobbyist, Assistant Manager, Government Relations
tara.a.benson@mmc.com
Registered Federal Lobbyist

FALL, Kenneth G. — Tel: (202) 263-7747
Senior Litigation & Counsel, Government Relations

GUSTAFSON, Erick — Tel: (202) 263-7788
Vice President, Director, Government Relations
Erick.Gustafson@mmc.com
Registered Federal Lobbyist

HILLIAR, III, Paul L. — Tel: (202) 263-7842
Manager, Government Relations
Paul.Hilliar@mmc.com
Registered Federal Lobbyist

LEHAN, Lawrence M. — Tel: (202) 263-7747

MANVILLE, Geoff — Tel: (202) 263-7747
Federal Lobbyist
Registered Federal Lobbyist

Marsh Supermarkets, Inc.

Operator of supermarkets and convenience stores.
www.marsh.net
Annual Revenues: $1.2 billion
Employees: 9,000
SIC: 5411
Industry/ies: Food And Beverage Industry; Retail/Wholesale

Main Headquarters

Mailing:	9800 Crosspoint Blvd.	Tel:	(317) 594-2100
	Indianapolis, IN 46256	Fax:	(317) 594-2704
		TF:	(800) 382-8798

Corporate Foundations and Giving Programs

The PeyBack Foundation
333 S. Franklin Rd.
Indianapolis, IN 46219

Public Affairs and Related Activities Personnel

At Headquarters

GARDNER, Connie — Tel: (317) 594-2100, Fax: (317) 594-2704
Senior Director, Community Relations

At Other Offices

REDDEN, David M. — Tel: (317) 594-2101, Fax: (317) 594-2104
Senior Vice President, Human Resources
333 S. Franklin Rd.
Indianapolis, IN 46219

THIELEN, Mike — Tel: (317) 594-2121, Fax: (317) 594-2704
Vice President, Educational Development
333 S. Franklin Rd.
Indianapolis, IN 46219
mthielen@marsh.net

Marsh, Inc.

Global risk management and insurance brokerage consulting firm. Formerly known as Johnson & Higgins. A subsidiary of Marsh & McLennan Companies, Inc. (see separate listing).
www.marsh.com
Employees: 57,000
SIC: 6411
Industry/ies: Insurance Industry

Chairman and Chief Executive Officer — Tel: (212) 345-6000, Fax: (212) 345-4808
ESLICK, David L.

Main Headquarters

Mailing:	1166 Avenue of the Americas	Tel:	(212) 345-6000
	New York City, NY 10036-2774	Fax:	(212) 345-4808

Corporate Foundations and Giving Programs

Marsh, Inc. Contribution Program
Contact: Nick Jones
1166 Avenue of the Americas — Tel: (212) 345-6000
New York City, NY 10036-2774 — Fax: (212) 345-4808

Public Affairs and Related Activities Personnel

At Headquarters

BUTCHER, Jack — Tel: (212) 345-6000

Head, Business Development	Fax:	(212) 345-4808
DUNDAS, Doug	Tel:	(212) 345-6000
Chief Marketing Officer	Fax:	(212) 345-4808
ELLIOTT, Mary Anne	Tel:	(212) 345-6000
Chief Human Resources Officer	Fax:	(212) 345-4808
FERSTEL, Alexandra von	Tel:	(212) 345-6000
Chief Counsel	Fax:	(212) 345-4808
JONES, Nick	Tel:	(212) 345-6000
Contact, Philanthropy	Fax:	(212) 345-4808
MCNASBY, James J.	Tel:	(212) 345-6000
General Counsel	Fax:	(212) 345-4808
NEWMAN, Ben	Tel:	(212) 345-6000
Chief Financial Officer	Fax:	(212) 345-4808
PIERONI, Bill	Tel:	(212) 345-6000
Chief Operating Officer	Fax:	(212) 345-4808
ROBERTS, Sally	Tel:	(303) 952-9453
Director, Media Relations	Fax:	(212) 345-4808
Sally.Roberts@marsh.com		
ROSEN, Diane	Tel:	(212) 345-6000
Chief Risk and Compliance Officer	Fax:	(212) 345-4808
WERNER, Sharon	Tel:	(212) 345-6000
Senior Vice President, Human Resources	Fax:	(212) 345-4808
WOERNER, Larry	Tel:	(212) 345-6000
Chief Human Resources Officer and Global Head, Regions	Fax:	(212) 345-4808

Marshall & Ilsley Corporation

A diversified financial services company.
www4.harrisbank.com/us
Annual Revenues: $3.38 billion
Employees: 9,000
Ticker: NYSE: MI
SIC: 6022; 6021
Industry/ies: Banking/Finance/Investments

Chairman of the Board	Tel:	(414) 765-7700
KUESTER, Dennis	Fax:	(414) 298-2921
President and Chief Executive Officer	Tel:	(414) 765-7700
FURLONG, Mark F	Fax:	(414) 298-2921
Main Headquarters		
Mailing: 770 N. Water St.	Tel:	(414) 765-7700
Milwaukee, WI 53202	Fax:	(414) 298-2921

Corporate Foundations and Giving Programs

Marshall & Ilsley Foundation
770 N. Water St.
Milwaukee, WI 53202

Tel:	(414) 765-7700
Fax:	(414) 765-7700

Public Affairs and Related Activities Personnel

At Headquarters

CADORIN, Patricia M.	Tel:	(414) 765-7700
Vice President and Director, Corporate Communications	Fax:	(414) 298-2921
JENKINS, Carl	Tel:	(414) 765-7700
PAC Contact	Fax:	(414) 298-2921
RENARD, Paul J.	Tel:	(414) 765-7700
Senior Vice President and Director, Human Resource	Fax:	(414) 298-2921

The Marshfield Clinic

When six Marshfield physicians pooled their medical expertise in 1916 to form Marshfield Clinic, they built the foundation for what has grown to become one of the largest private, multispecialty group practices in the United States.
www.marshfieldclinic.org
Industry/ies: Medicine/Health Care/Mental Health
Legislative Issues: BUD; HCR; MED; MMM

Chairman of the Board	Tel:	(715) 387-5511
BUGHER, Mark D.	Fax:	(715) 456-6282
Nephrologist	Tel:	(715) 387-5511
EWERT, Brian H.	Fax:	(715) 456-6282
Main Headquarters		
Mailing: 1000 N. Oak Ave.	Tel:	(715) 387-5511
Marshfield, WI 54449	Fax:	(715) 456-6282
	TF:	(800) 782-8581

Corporate Foundations and Giving Programs

Marshfield Clinic Research Foundation
1000 N. Oak Ave.
Marshfield, WI 54449

Tel:	(715) 387-5511
Fax:	(715) 387-5240

Public Affairs and Related Activities Personnel

At Headquarters

COLEMAN, James S.	Tel:	(715) 387-5511
Chief Operating Officer	Fax:	(715) 456-6282
JANKOWSKI, Gary	Tel:	(715) 387-5511
Chief Financial Officer	Fax:	(715) 456-6282

MILLER, Brent V.	Tel:	(715) 387-5511
Director, Federal Government Relations	Fax:	(715) 456-6282
miller.brent@marshfieldclinic.org		
Registered Federal Lobbyist		
NYCZ, Greg R.	Tel:	(715) 387-5511
Federal Lobbyist	Fax:	(715) 456-6282
nycz.greg@marshfieldclinic.org		
Registered Federal Lobbyist		

Martek Biosciences Corporation

Martek Biosciences Corporation is a leading innovator in the development of nutritional products that promote health and wellness through every stage of life. Martek has become a leader in fermentation technology and is an innovator in the research and development of products derived from microalgae.
www.martek.com
Annual Revenues: $450.02 million
Employees: 600
Ticker: NASDAQ: MATK
SIC: 2836
Industry/ies: Machinery/Equipment; Pharmaceutical Industry; Science; Scientific Research

Chief Executive Officer	Tel:	(410) 740-0081
DUBIN, Steve	Fax:	(410) 740-2985
Main Headquarters		
Mailing: 6480 Dobbin Rd.	Tel:	(410) 740-0081
Columbia, MD 21045	Fax:	(410) 740-2985
	TF:	(800) 662-6339

Public Affairs and Related Activities Personnel

At Headquarters

FRANCE-KELLY, Cassie	Tel:	(443) 542-2116
Contact, Public Relations	Fax:	(410) 740-2985
cfrancekelly@martek.com		
OH, Kenneth	Tel:	(410) 740-0081
Vice President, Chief Financial Officer	Fax:	(410) 740-2985
STULTS, Kyle	Tel:	(410) 740-0081
Contact, Investor Relations	Fax:	(410) 740-2985
kstults@martek.com		

Martin Marietta Materials

A producer of construction aggregates.
www.martinmarietta.com
Annual Revenues: $3.37 billion
Employees: 7,300
Ticker: NYSE: MLM
SIC: 3281; 2821; 2951; 3272; 3531
NAICS: 327991; 324121; 325211; 32739; 33312
Industry/ies: Construction/Construction Materials

President, Chief Executive Officer and Chairman of the Board	Tel:	(919) 781-4550
NYE, C. Howard	Fax:	(919) 783-4695
Main Headquarters		
Mailing: 2710 Wycliff Rd.	Tel:	(919) 781-4550
Raleigh, NC 27607-3033	Fax:	(919) 783-4695

Corporate Foundations and Giving Programs

Martin Marietta Materials Contributions Program
2710 Wycliff Rd.
Raleigh, NC 27607-3033

Tel:	(919) 781-4550
Fax:	(919) 783-4695

Public Affairs and Related Activities Personnel

At Headquarters

BAR, Roselyn R.	Tel:	(919) 781-4550
Senior Vice President, General Counsel and Corporate Secretary	Fax:	(919) 781-4695
roselyn.bar@martinmarietta.com		
GRANT, Daniel L.	Tel:	(919) 781-4550
Senior Vice President, Strategy and Development	Fax:	(919) 783-4695
GUZZO, Dana F.	Tel:	(919) 783-4540
Senior Vice President, Chief Accounting Officer and Corporate Controller	Fax:	(919) 783-4695
LLOYD, Anne H.	Tel:	(919) 783-4660
Executive Vice President and Chief Financial Officer	Fax:	(919) 781-4695
MCCUNNIFF, Donald A.	Tel:	(919) 781-4550
Senior Vice President, Human Resources	Fax:	(919) 783-4695

Marubeni America Corporation

International trading, financial, investment and organizing projects. Headquartered in New York, NY.
www.marubeni-usa.com
SIC: 5051; 5162; 5131
NAICS: 421510; 422610; 422310
Industry/ies: Banking/Finance/Investments

Main Headquarters

| Mailing: | 375 Lexington Ave. | Tel: | (212) 450-0100 |
| | New York City, NY 10017-5644 | Fax: | (212) 450-0700 |

Washington Office

Mailing:	1776 I St. NW	Tel:	(202) 331-1167
	Suite 725	Fax:	(202) 331-1319
	Washington, DC 20006		

Corporate Foundations and Giving Programs

Marubeni America Corporation Contributions Program
375 Lexington Ave.
New York City, NY 10017

Public Affairs and Related Activities Personnel

At Washington Office

MIKAMO, Tetsuhide	Tel:	(202) 331-1167
Vice President and General Manager	Fax:	(202) 331-1319
UEHARA, So	Tel:	(202) 331-1167
Assistant Manager	Fax:	(202) 331-1319

Mary Kay Inc.

The holding company for Mary Kay Cosmetics, Inc.
www.marykay.com
Employees: 4,500
SIC: 2844
NAICS: 325620
Industry/ies: Personal Care/Hygiene
Legislative Issues: CSP; HCR; SMB; TRD

Executive Chairman	Tel:	(972) 687-6300
ROGERS, Richard R.	Fax:	(972) 387-1611
rogersr@marykay.com		

| **President and Chief Executive Officer** | Tel: | (972) 687-6300 |
| HOLL, David B. | Fax: | (972) 687-1642 |

Main Headquarters

Mailing:	P.O. Box 799045	Tel:	(972) 687-6300
	Dallas, TX 75379-9045	Fax:	(972) 687-1642
		TF:	(800) 627-9529

Corporate Foundations and Giving Programs

The Mary Kay Foundation
Contact: Ryan Rogers
P.O. Box 799044
Dallas, TX 75379-9044

Mary Kay Museum
Contact: Ryan Rogers

| 16251 Dallas Pkwy. | Tel: | (972) 687-6300 |
| Addison, TX 75001-6801 | Fax: | (972) 687-1642 |

Public Affairs and Related Activities Personnel

At Headquarters

ADKINS-GREEN, Sheryl	Tel:	(972) 687-6300
Chief Marketing Officer	Fax:	(972) 687-1642
CREWS, Anne C.	Tel:	(972) 687-6300
Vice President, Government Relations	Fax:	(972) 687-1642
Registered Federal Lobbyist		
FLORES, Theresa	Tel:	(800) 627-9529
Manager, Government Relations	Fax:	(972) 687-1642
Registered Federal Lobbyist		
GIBBINS, Deborah	Tel:	(972) 687-6300
Chief Financial Officer	Fax:	(972) 687-1642
JODIE, Kregg	Tel:	(972) 687-6300
Chief Information Officer	Fax:	(972) 687-1642
LUNCEFORD, Michael L.	Tel:	(972) 687-6300
Senior Vice President, Government Relations	Fax:	(972) 687-1642
michael.lunceford@mkcorp.com		
Registered Federal Lobbyist		
MOORE, Nathan	Tel:	(972) 687-6300
Chief Legal Officer and Secretary	Fax:	(972) 687-1642
ROGERS, Ryan	Tel:	(972) 687-6300
Board of Director, Chief Investment Officer and Philanthropy	Fax:	(972) 687-1642
Contact		
SELLERS, Melinda Foster	Tel:	(972) 687-6300
Chief People Officer	Fax:	(972) 687-1642
TASSOPOULOS, Kerry	Tel:	(972) 687-6300
Federal Lobbyist	Fax:	(972) 687-1642
Registered Federal Lobbyist		

Masco Corporation

A manufacturer of consumer and specialty products for the home and family.
masco.com
Annual Revenues: $8.57 billion
Employees: 32,000
Ticker: NYSE: MAS
SIC: 5023; 3471

Industry/ies: Construction/Construction Materials; Furniture/Home Furnishings
Legislative Issues: ENG; MAN; TAX

| **Chairman of the Board** | Tel: | (313) 274-7400 |
| MANOOGIAN, Richard A. | Fax: | (313) 792-4177 |

| **President and Chief Executive Officer** | Tel: | (313) 274-7400 |
| ALLMAN, Keith J. | Fax: | (313) 792-4177 |

Main Headquarters

| Mailing: | 21001 Van Born Rd. | Tel: | (313) 274-7400 |
| | Taylor, MI 48180 | Fax: | (313) 792-4177 |

Political Action Committees

Masco PAC
FEC ID: C00341289
Contact: Gregory P. Jenkins
21001 Van Born Rd.
Taylor, MI 48180

Contributions to Candidates: $3,600 (2015-2016)
Republicans: $3,600

Corporate Foundations and Giving Programs

Masco Corporation Foundation
Contact: Lillian Bauder

| 21001 Van Born Rd. | Tel: | (313) 274-7400 |
| Taylor, MI 48180 | Fax: | (313) 274-7400 |

Public Affairs and Related Activities Personnel

At Headquarters

BAUDER, Lillian	Tel:	(313) 274-7400
Chairman and President, Masco Corporation Foundation	Fax:	(313) 792-6262
BHARGAVA, Amit	Tel:	(313) 274-7400
Vice President, Strategy and Corporate Development	Fax:	(313) 792-4177
COLE, Kenneth G.	Tel:	(313) 274-7400
Vice President, General Counsel and Secretary	Fax:	(313) 792-4177
DUEY, Maria C.	Tel:	(313) 792-5500
Vice President, Investor Relations	Fax:	(313) 792-4177
maria_duey@mascohq.com		
JENKINS, Gregory P.	Tel:	(313) 274-7400
PAC Treaurer	Fax:	(313) 792-4177
Registered Federal Lobbyist		
MOORE, Renae	Tel:	(517) 374-9121
Authorized Agent	Fax:	(313) 792-4177
rmoore@dykema.com		
O'REGAN, Richard	Tel:	(313) 274-7400
President	Fax:	(313) 792-4177
ROTHWELL, Sharon J.	Tel:	(313) 792-6028
Vice President, Corporate Affairs	Fax:	(313) 792-6135
SHAH, Jai	Tel:	(313) 274-7400
Vice President, Strategic Planning	Fax:	(313) 792-4177
STRABER, Renee	Tel:	(313) 274-7400
Chief Human Resource Officer	Fax:	(313) 792-4177
SZNEWAJS, John G.	Tel:	(313) 274-7400
Vice President, Treasurer and Chief Financial Officer	Fax:	(313) 792-4177

Mascoma Corporation

A cellulosic ethanol research and development corporation.
www.mascoma.com
Employees: 100
Ticker: NYSE: MCM
SIC: 2860
Industry/ies: Environment And Conservation; Natural Resources

| **President and Chief Executive Officer** | Tel: | (603) 676-3320 |
| BRADY, William J. | Fax: | (603) 676-3321 |

Main Headquarters

Mailing:	610 Lincoln St.	Tel:	(603) 676-3320
	Suite 100	Fax:	(603) 676-3321
	Waltham, MA 02451		

Public Affairs and Related Activities Personnel

At Headquarters

DORAN, Kara	Tel:	(617) 391-9646
Contact, Media Relations	Fax:	(603) 676-3321
kdoran@rasky.com		
LINKKILA, Timothy P.	Tel:	(603) 676-3320
General Counsel	Fax:	(603) 676-3321
ROOYEN, Justin van	Tel:	(603) 676-3320
Vice President, Corporate Development	Fax:	(603) 676-3321

MASN: Mid-Atlantic Sports Network

A team-owned regional sports network.
www.masnsports.com
Industry/ies: Communications; Sports/Leisure/Entertainment;
Telecommunications/Internet/Cable

Main Headquarters

Mailing:	333 W. Camden St.	Tel:	(410) 625-7100
	Baltimore, MD 21201-2435	Fax:	(410) 547-6280

Public Affairs and Related Activities Personnel

At Headquarters

CUDDIHY, Jim   Tel: (410) 625-7100
Executive Vice President, Marketing, Programming, Affiliate   Fax: (410) 547-6280
Relations

DUNN, Charlie   Tel: (410) 547-3063
Vice President and Manager, Local Sales   Fax: (410) 547-6280
cdunn@masnsports.com

GLASS, Chris   Tel: (410) 625-7100
Vice President, Executive Producer, Director of Operations   Fax: (410) 547-6280

HALEY, Michael   Tel: (410) 547-3080
Executive Vice President and Chief Financial Officer   Fax: (410) 547-6280
mhaley@masnsports.com

MCGUINNESS, John J.   Tel: (410) 547-3089
Senior Vice President and General Sales Manager   Fax: (410) 547-6280
jmcguinness@masnsports.com

WEBSTER, Todd   Tel: (410) 685-3776
Media Contact   Fax: (410) 547-6280

Masonite International Corporation

A manufacturer and merchandiser of doors.
www.masonite.com
Annual Revenues: $1.85 billion
Employees: 10,300
Ticker: NYSE: DOOR
SIC: 2430
Industry/ies: Housing

Chairman of the Board   Tel: (813) 877-2726
BYRNE, Robert J.   Fax: (813) 739-0204

President and Chief Executive Officer   Tel: (813) 877-2726
LYNCH, Frederick J.   Fax: (813) 739-0204

Main Headquarters

Mailing:	One Tampa City Center	Tel:	(813) 877-2726
	201 N. Franklin St., Suite 300	Fax:	(813) 739-0106
	Tampa, FL 33602		

Public Affairs and Related Activities Personnel

At Headquarters

AUERBACH, Gail N.   Tel: (813) 877-2726
Senior Vice President, Human Resources   Fax: (813) 739-0106

LEWIS, Robert E.   Tel: (813) 877-2726
Senior Vice President, General Counsel and Secretary   Fax: (813) 739-0106

PRENOVEAU, Brian M.   Tel: (813) 877-2726
Director, Investor Relations and Treasury   Fax: (813) 739-0204
investorrelations@masonite.com

REPAR, Lawrence P.   Tel: (813) 877-2726
Executive Vice President, Global Sales and Marketing, and   Fax: (813) 739-0106
Chief Operating Officer

VIROSTEK , Christopher A.   Tel: (813) 877-2726
Senior Vice President, Strategy Implementation and   Fax: (813) 739-0106
Corporate Development

Massachusetts Higher Education Assistance Corporation

Industry/ies: Education

Main Headquarters

Mailing:	111 St.	Tel:	(617) 728-4676
	Boston, MA 54879		

Public Affairs and Related Activities Personnel

At Headquarters

ROG, Jone   Tel: (617) 728-4676
Administration/Finance

MassMutual Financial Group

A global, diversified financial services organization. The company also goes by the name
Massachusetts Mutual Life Insurance Company.
www.massmutual.com
Annual Revenues: $17.00 billion
Employees: 5,200
Industry/ies: Insurance Industry
Legislative Issues: BNK; FIN; HCR; INS; RET; TAX

Chairman and Chief Executive Officer, Babson Capital   Tel: (413) 744-1000
Management LLC   Fax: (413) 744-6005
FINKE, Thomas M.
tfinke@massmutual.com

Chairman, President and Chief Executive Officer   Tel: (413) 744-1000
CRANDALL, Roger W.   Fax: (413) 744-6005

Main Headquarters

Mailing:	601 Pennsylvania Ave. NW	Tel:	(202) 737-0440
	Suite 420 S. Bldg.	Fax:	(202) 628-2313
	Washington, DC 20004		

Political Action Committees

Massachusetts Mutual Life Insurance Company PAC
FEC ID: C00118943
Contact: Bruce C. Frisbie   Tel: (413) 744-1000
1295 State St.
Springfield, MA 01111

Contributions to Candidates: $649,000 (2015-2016)
Democrats: $262,000; Republicans: $382,000; Other: $5,000

Principal Recipients

SENATE
BLUNT, ROY (REP-MO)
YOUNG, TODD CHRISTOPHER (REP-IN)

HOUSE
LOVE, MIA (REP-UT)
MESSER, ALLEN LUCAS (REP-IN)
REED, THOMAS W II (REP-NY)
ROSKAM, PETER (REP-IL)
RYAN, PAUL D. (REP-WI)
THOMPSON, MIKE MR. (DEM-CA)

Corporate Foundations and Giving Programs

The MassMutual Financial Group Contributions Program
1295 State St.   Tel: (413) 744-1000
Springfield, MA 0111   Fax: (413) 744-6005

Public Affairs and Related Activities Personnel

At Headquarters

PFRANG, Steven   Tel: (202) 737-0440
Federal Lobbyist   Fax: (202) 628-2313
Registered Federal Lobbyist

WEISS, Alison B.   Tel: (202) 737-0440
Vice President   Fax: (202) 628-2313
Registered Federal Lobbyist

At Other Offices

CAMMACK, Ann B.   Tel: (413) 744-8411
Vice President and Senior Counsel   Fax: (413) 767-1000
1295 State St.
Springfield, MA 01111

CICCO, Susan M.   Tel: (413) 744-8411
Senior Vice President and Chief of Staff   Fax: (413) 767-1000
1295 State St.
Springfield, MA 01111

COHEN, Kenneth S.   Tel: (413) 744-8411
Senior Vice President, Federal Government Relations and   Fax: (413) 767-1000
Deputy General Counsel
1295 State St.
Springfield, MA 01111
kcohen@massmutual.com
Registered Federal Lobbyist

CORBETT, M. Timothy   Tel: (413) 744-8411
Executive Vice President and Chief Investment Officer   Fax: (413) 767-1000
1295 State St.
Springfield, MA 01111

CYBULSKI, Mark   Tel: (413) 744-5427
Assistant Vice President, Strategic Communications   Fax: (413) 744-8889
1295 State St.
Springfield, MA 01111
mcybulski@massmutual.com

DAVERN, Nathan   Tel: (413) 744-8411
Federal Lobbyist   Fax: (413) 767-1000
1295 State St.
Springfield, MA 01111
Registered Federal Lobbyist

DONALD, Camille   Tel: (413) 744-1000
Assistant Vice President and Counsel   Fax: (413) 744-6005
1295 State St.
Springfield, MA 01111
Registered Federal Lobbyist

FISHER, William P.   Tel: (413) 744-8411
Vice President, State and Local Government Relations   Fax: (413) 767-1000
1295 State St.
Springfield, MA 01111
Registered Federal Lobbyist

FRISBIE, Bruce C.   Tel: (413) 744-1000
PAC Treasurer   Fax: (413) 744-6005
1295 State St.
Springfield, MA 01111
BFrisbie@MassMutual.com

KERTZ, Mary F.   Tel: (413) 744-8411

Assistant Vice President	Fax:	(413) 767-1000

1295 State St.
Springfield, MA 01111
Registered Federal Lobbyist

LACEY, James — Tel: (413) 744-2365
Vice President, Media and Public Relations — Fax: (413) 744-8889
1295 State St.
Springfield, MA 01111
jlacey@massmutual.com

LUCIDO, Bradley J. — Tel: (413) 744-1000
Senior Vice President, Deputy General Counsel and Chief — Fax: (413) 744-6005
Compliance Officer
1295 State St.
Springfield, MA 01111

PALERMINO, Debra A. — Tel: (413) 744-8411
Executive Vice President, Human Resources — Fax: (413) 744-6005
1295 State St.
Springfield, MA 01111

ROELLIG, Mark D. — Tel: (413) 744-8411
Executive Vice President and General Counsel — Fax: (413) 744-6005
1295 State St.
Springfield, MA 01111
mroellig@massmutual.com

ROLLINGS, Michael T. — Tel: (413) 744-1000
Executive Vice President and Chief Financial Officer — Fax: (413) 744-6005
1295 State St.
Springfield, MA 01111

RUSSELL, Douglas G. — Tel: (413) 744-8411
Senior Vice President, Strategy and Corporate Development — Fax: (413) 767-1000
1295 State St.
Springfield, MA 01111

SIMPSON, Camille — Tel: (413) 744-8411
1295 State St. — Fax: (413) 767-1000
Springfield, MA 01111
Registered Federal Lobbyist

MasterCard Worldwide

A global payments company.
www.mastercard.com
Annual Revenues: $9.53 billion
Employees: 10,300
Ticker: NYSE: MA
SIC: 7389
Industry/ies: Banking/Finance/Investments
Legislative Issues: BAN; CPI; CSP; FIN; FOR; GAM; HOM; TAX; TRD

Chairman of the Board — Tel: (914) 249-2000
HAYTHORNTHWAITE, Richard — Fax: (914) 249-4206

President and Chief Executive Officer — Tel: (914) 249-2000
BANGA, Ajay — Fax: (914) 249-4206
ajay_banga@mastercard.com

Main Headquarters
Mailing: 2000 Purchase St. — Tel: (914) 249-6524
Purchase, NY 10577 — Fax: (914) 249-4206
— TF: (800) 627-8372

Washington Office
Mailing: 1401 I St. NW — Tel: (202) 414-8000
Suite 210 — Fax: (202) 414-8010
Washington, DC 20005

Political Action Committees
Mastercard International Employees PAC
FEC ID: C00410274
Contact: Althea Hutchinson
2000 Purchase St.
Purchase, NY 10577

> **Contributions to Candidates:** $244,900 (2015-2016)
> Democrats: $109,700; Republicans: $135,200

> > **Principal Recipients**

> > > **SENATE**
> > > PORTMAN, ROB (REP-OH)

> > > **HOUSE**
> > > CHAFFETZ, JASON (REP-UT)
> > > HOYER, STENY HAMILTON (DEM-DC)

Corporate Foundations and Giving Programs
The MasterCard Foundation
2000 Purchase St.
Purchase, NY 10577

Public Affairs and Related Activities Personnel

At Headquarters

GANNON, Thomas — Tel: (914) 249-6524
Vice President, Public Policy — Fax: (914) 249-4206

thomas_gannon@mastercard.com
Registered Federal Lobbyist

GARROW, Ronald E. — Tel: (914) 249-6524
Chief Human Resources Officer — Fax: (914) 249-4206

HUND-MEJEAN, Martina — Tel: (914) 249-6524
Chief Financial Officer — Fax: (914) 249-4206

HUTCHINSON, Althea — Tel: (914) 249-6524
PAC Treasurer — Fax: (914) 249-4206

MCWILTON, Chris A. — Tel: (914) 249-6524
President — Fax: (914) 249-4206

MONTEIRO, Chris — Tel: (914) 249-5826
Chief Communications Officer, Worldwide Communications — Fax: (914) 249-4206
chris_monteiro@mastercard.com

MURPHY, Timothy — Tel: (914) 249-6524
General Counsel and Chief Franchise Officer — Fax: (914) 249-4206

At Washington Office

BIRKEL, TJ — Tel: (202) 414-8000
Director. Federal Government Affairs — Fax: (202) 414-8010
Registered Federal Lobbyist

FOOTE, Tucker — Tel: (202) 414-8020
Senior Vice President & Head, U.S. Government Affairs — Fax: (202) 414-8010
tucker_foote@mastercard.com
Registered Federal Lobbyist

FRANCIS-REYNOLDS, Nichole A. — Tel: (202) 414-8000
Director, U.S. Federal Affairs — Fax: (202) 414-8010
Registered Federal Lobbyist

Materion Corporation

A producer of engineered materials, including beryllium, beryllium alloys, beryllia ceramic,
precious metal products and specialty metal systems.
materion.com
Annual Revenues: $970.76 million
Employees: 2,450
Ticker: NYSE: MTRN
SIC: 3460
Industry/ies: Construction/Construction Materials

Chairman of the Board, President and Chief Executive Officer — Tel: (216) 486-4200
HIPPLE, Richard J. — Fax: (216) 383-4091

Main Headquarters
Mailing: 6070 Parkland Blvd. — Tel: (216) 486-4200
Mayfield Heights, OH 44124 — Fax: (216) 383-4091

Political Action Committees
Materion Corporation Political Action Committee
FEC ID: C00216770
Contact: Jianghong Ying
6070 Parkland Blvd. — Tel: (216) 486-4200
Mayfield Heights, OH 44124

> **Contributions to Candidates:** $18,400 (2015-2016)
> Democrats: $6,400; Republicans: $12,000

Corporate Foundations and Giving Programs
Materion Corporation Contributions Program
6070 Parkland Blvd. — Tel: (216) 486-4200
Mayfield Heights, OH 44124 — Fax: (216) 383-4091

Public Affairs and Related Activities Personnel

At Headquarters

CARPENTER, Patrick S. — Tel: (216) 383-6835
Vice President, Global Corporate Communications — Fax: (216) 383-4091
patrick_carpenter@beminc.com

CHEMNITZ, Gregory R. — Tel: (216) 486-4200
Vice President and General Counsel — Fax: (216) 383-4091

HASYCHAK, Michael C. — Tel: (216) 383-6823
Vice President, Treasurer and Secretary — Fax: (216) 383-4091
mike.hasychak@materion.com

KELLEY, Joseph P — Tel: (216) 486-4200
Vice President, Finance and Chief Financial Officer — Fax: (216) 383-4091

MCMULLEN, James P. — Tel: (216) 486-4200
Product Manager — Fax: (216) 383-4091

YING, Jianghong — Tel: (216) 486-4200
Tax Analyst and PAC Treasurer — Fax: (216) 383-4091

Matrix Business Strategies, LLC

Business strategy consultantcy.
www.projectmatrix.net/Matrix

Main Headquarters
Mailing: P.O.Box 611 — Tel: (706) 389-0654
Braselton, GA 30517

Public Affairs and Related Activities Personnel

At Headquarters

TROTTER, Chad   Tel: (706) 389-0654
Federal Lobbyist

Matson Navigation Company

An ocean freight shipping company. Formerly a subsidiary of Alexander & Baldwin.
www.matson.com
Annual Revenues: $1.72 billion
Employees: 1,056
Ticker: NYSE: MATX
SIC: 4400
Industry/ies: Marine/Maritime/Shipping; Transportation
Legislative Issues: MAR; TAX

| **Chairman of the Board** | Tel: | (808) 848-1211 |
| DODS, Jr., Walter A. | Fax: | (510) 628-7380 |

| **President and Chief Executive Officer** | Tel: | (808) 848-1211 |
| COX, Matthew J. | Fax: | (510) 628-7380 |

Main Headquarters
| *Mailing:* 1411 Sand Island Pkwy. | Tel: | (808) 848-1211 |
| Honolulu, HI 96819 | Fax: | (510) 628-7380 |

Washington Office
Mailing: 1735 New York Ave. NW
Suite 500
Washington, DC 20006

Political Action Committees
Matson, Inc. Federal Election Committee PAC
FEC ID: C00024752
Contact: Benedict J. Bowler
555 12th St.	Tel:	(510) 628-4000
Eighth Floor	Fax:	(510) 628-7380
Oakland, CA 94607		

> **Contributions to Candidates:** $47,200 (2015-2016)
> Democrats: $39,000; Republicans: $7,700; Other: $500

> **Principal Recipients**
>> **HOUSE**
>> GABBARD, TULSI (DEM-HI)
>> TAKAI, KYLE MARK (DEM-HI)

Public Affairs and Related Activities Personnel

At Headquarters
FOREST, Ronald J.	Tel:	(808) 848-1211
Senior Vice President, Operations	Fax:	(510) 628-7380
HEILMANN, Peter	Tel:	(808) 848-1211
Senior Vice President and Chief Legal Officer	Fax:	(510) 628-7380
HOLLAND, Jerome	Tel:	(510) 628-4021
Contact, Investor Relations	Fax:	(510) 628-7380
investor-relations@matson.com		
HULL, Jeffrey S.	Tel:	(510) 628-4534
Director, Public Relations	Fax:	(510) 628-7380
jhull@matson.com		
O'ROURKE, Kevin	Tel:	(808) 848-1211
Senior Vice President and General Counsel	Fax:	(510) 628-7380
WINE, Joel M.	Tel:	(808) 848-1211
Senior Vice President and Chief Financial Officer	Fax:	(510) 628-7380

At Washington Office
GRILL, Philip M.
Vice President, Government Relations

At Other Offices
BOWLER, Benedict J.	Tel:	(510) 628-4000
PAC Treasurer	Fax:	(510) 628-7380
555 12th St., Eighth Floor		
Oakland, CA 94607		
DENNEGEN, John Edward	Tel:	(510) 628-4000
PAC Treasurer	Fax:	(510) 628-7380
555 12th St., Eighth Floor		
Oakland, CA 94607		

Mattel, Inc.

A toy manufacturer.
corporate.mattel.com
Annual Revenues: $5.65 billion
Employees: 31,000
Ticker: NASDAQ: MAT
SIC: 3942
Industry/ies: Sports/Leisure/Entertainment

| **Chief Executive Officer** | Tel: | (310) 252-2000 |
| SINCLAIR, Christopher A | Fax: | (310) 252-2179 |

Main Headquarters
| *Mailing:* 333 Continental Blvd. | Tel: | (310) 252-2000 |
| El Segundo, CA 90245-5012 | Fax: | (310) 252-2179 |

Political Action Committees

Mattel Inc. PAC
FEC ID: C00340224
Contact: Mandana Sadigh
| 333 Continental Blvd. | Tel: | (310) 252-2000 |
| El Segundo, CA 90245 | Fax: | (310) 252-2000 |

> **Contributions to Candidates:** $1,500 (2015-2016)
> Democrats: $1,500

Corporate Foundations and Giving Programs

Mattel Children's Foundation
| 333 Continental Blvd. | Tel: | (310) 252-3630 |
| El Segundo, CA 90245 | Fax: | (310) 252-3630 |

Public Affairs and Related Activities Personnel

At Headquarters
DICKSON, Richard	Tel:	(310) 252-2000
President and Chief Operating Officer	Fax:	(310) 252-2179
FARR, Kevin	Tel:	(310) 252-2000
Chief Financial Officer	Fax:	(310) 252-2179
FARR, Kevin M.	Tel:	(310) 252-2000
Chief Financial Officer and PAC Treasurer	Fax:	(310) 252-2179
Kevin.Farr@mattel.com		
MURAT, Corinne	Tel:	(310) 252-6628
Director, Government Affairs	Fax:	(310) 252-4443
corinne.murat@mattel.com		
NORMILE, Bob	Tel:	(310) 252-2000
Executive Vice President, Chief Legal Officer and Secretary	Fax:	(310) 252-2179
Robert.Normile@mattel.com		
SADIGH, Mandana	Tel:	(310) 252-2000
PAC Contact	Fax:	(310) 252-2179

Maui Land and Pineapple Company, Inc.

Grows and processes pineapples on the Hawaiian island of Maui.
mauiland.com
Annual Revenues: $33.33 million
Employees: 17
Ticker: NYSE: MLP
SIC: 2033
Industry/ies: Agriculture/Agronomy; Food And Beverage Industry

| **Chairman of the Board and Chief Executive Officer** | Tel: | (808) 877-1608 |
| HARUKI, Warren H. | Fax: | (808) 665-0641 |

Main Headquarters
| *Mailing:* 200 Village Rd. | Tel: | (808) 877-1608 |
| Lahaina, HI 96761 | Fax: | (808) 665-0641 |

Political Action Committees
Maui Land and Pineapple Company, Inc. Federal PAC
FEC ID: C00401380
Contact: Tim T. Esaki
200 Village Rd.
Lahaina, HI 96761

Public Affairs and Related Activities Personnel

At Headquarters
CARLUCCI, Karee	Tel:	(808) 877-1608
Manager, Communications	Fax:	(808) 665-0641
ESAKI, Tim T.	Tel:	(808) 877-1608
Chief Financial Officer and PAC Contact	Fax:	(808) 665-0641
SUMIDA, Adele	Tel:	(808) 877-1608
Controller and Secretary	Fax:	(808) 665-0641
SUZUKI, Warren A.	Tel:	(808) 877-1608
Senior Vice President, Community Relations and Corporate	Fax:	(808) 665-0641
Communications		

Maven, Inc.

A business development and relationship management firm.
www.maven-inc.com
Industry/ies: Management

President & Chief Executive Officer	Tel:	(215) 965-1587
SHAW, Melonease	Fax:	(866) 861-7808
mel@maven-inc.com		

Main Headquarters
Mailing: 8201 Greensboro Dr.
Suite 300
McLean, VA 22102

Public Affairs and Related Activities Personnel

At Other Offices
JONES, Donald	Tel:	(215) 965-1587
Contact, Media Relations	Fax:	(866) 861-7808
Seven N. Columbus Blvd., Suite 119		
Philadelphia, PA 19106		
Don@maven-inc.com		

Maxim Integrated Products

Design, development, manufacturing and marketing of linear and mixed signal circuits.
www.maximintegrated.com
Annual Revenues: $2.37 billion
Employees: 8,812
Ticker: NASDAQ: MXIM
SIC: 3674; 3679; 3651
Industry/ies: Machinery/Equipment

Chairman of the Board — Tel: (408) 601-1000
HAGOPIAN, B. Kipling

President and Chief Executive Officer — Tel: (408) 601-1000
DOLUCA, Tunc
tunc@maxim-ic.com

Main Headquarters
Mailing: 160 Rio Robles — Tel: (408) 601-1000
San Jose, CA 95134 — TF: (888) 629-4642

Corporate Foundations and Giving Programs
Maxim Integrated Products Corporate Contributions
120 San Gabriel Dr. — Tel: (408) 737-7600
Sunnyvale, CA 94086 — Fax: (408) 774-9139

Public Affairs and Related Activities Personnel
At Headquarters

KIDDOO, Bruce E. — Tel: (408) 601-1000
Senior Vice President and Chief Financial Officer
bruce.kiddoo@maxim-ic.com

MANIAR, Paresh — Tel: (408) 601-1000
Executive Director, Investor Relations
paresh.maniar@maxim-ic.com

MEDLIN, Edwin B. — Tel: (408) 601-1000
Vice President and General Counsel
Ed.Medlin@maxim-ic.com

MILLAN, Ferda — Tel: (408) 601-5429
Manager, Public Relations
Ferda.Millan@maximintegrated.com

MURPHY, Matthew J. — Tel: (408) 601-1000
*Senior Vice President, Communications and Automotive
Solutions Group*

SANGALLI, Walter L. — Tel: (408) 601-1000
Vice President, Worldwide Sales and Marketing

TA, Kathy — Tel: (408) 601-5697
Managing Director, Investor Relations
Kathy.Ta@maximintegrated.com

WALDEN, LuAnn Jenkins — Tel: (408) 601-5430
Director, Corporate Communications
LuAnn.Walden@maximintegrated.com

YAMASAKI, Steve — Tel: (408) 601-1000
Vice President, Human Resources

MAXIMUS

A provider of program management, information technology, and consulting services to state and local government health and human service agencies. Our health and human services solutions are designed to make a meaningful impact on people's lives and strengthen communities through state, federal and local government partnerships.
www.maximus.com
Annual Revenues: $1.80 billion
Employees: 16,000
Ticker: NYSE: MMS
SIC: 7389
Industry/ies: Computer/Technology
Legislative Issues: AVI; BUD; CPI; EDU; ENG; GOV; HCR; LBR; MMM; VET

Chairman of the Board — Tel: (703) 251-8500
POND, Peter B. — Fax: (703) 251-8240

President, Director and Chief Executive Officer — Tel: (703) 251-8500
MONTONI, Richard A. — Fax: (703) 251-8240

Main Headquarters
Mailing: 1891 Metro Center Dr. — Tel: (703) 251-8500
Reston, VA 20199 — Fax: (703) 251-8240
— TF: (800) 629-4687

Washington Office
Mailing: 7950 Jones Branch Dr. — Tel: (703) 251-8500
McLean, VA 22107

Political Action Committees
MAXIMUS Inc. PAC (MAXPAC)
FEC ID: C00343707
Contact: Dominic Corley
1891 Metro Center Dr. — Tel: (703) 926-1310
Reston, VA 20190 — Fax: (703) 251-8240

> **Contributions to Candidates:** $18,800 (2015-2016)
> Democrats: $11,200; Republicans: $7,600

Corporate Foundations and Giving Programs
Maximus Charitable Foundation
Contact: John Boyer
11419 Sunset Hills Rd. — Tel: (703) 251-8500
Reston, VA 20190

Public Affairs and Related Activities Personnel
At Headquarters

ANDREKOVICH, Mark S. — Tel: (703) 251-8500
Chief, Human Capital — Fax: (703) 251-8240

BOYER, John — Tel: (703) 251-8500
Chairman, MAXIMUS Foundation — Fax: (703) 251-8240

CASEY, David — Tel: (703) 251-8500
Senior Vice President, Government Relations & Business — Fax: (703) 251-8240
Development

FRANCIS, David — Tel: (703) 251-8500
General Counsel and Secretary — Fax: (703) 251-8240

MACK, Paul — Tel: (703) 251-8500
Chief Administraive Officer & Special Assistant to the CEO — Fax: (703) 251-8240

MILES, Lisa — Tel: (703) 251-8637
Vice President, Investor Relations & Corporate — Fax: (703) 251-8240
Communications
lisamiles@maximus.com

NADEAU, Richard J. "Rick" — Tel: (703) 251-8500
Chief Financial Officer & Treasurer — Fax: (703) 251-8240

RICHARDSON, David — Tel: (703) 926-1310
Senior Vice President — Fax: (703) 251-8240

TIMMONS, David — Tel: (703) 251-8500
Vice President and Controller (PAC Treasurer for 2014) — Fax: (703) 251-8240
davidtimmons@maximus.com

TRAVIS, Blake — Tel: (703) 251-8398
Director, Public Relations & Health Marketing — Fax: (703) 251-8240
blaketravis@maximus.com

VAUGHN GRAHAM, Christine L. — Tel: (703) 251-8498
Senior Manager, Corporate Communications & Investor — Fax: (703) 251-8240
Relations
christinevaughngraham@maximus.com

At Washington Office

CORLEY, Dominic — Tel: (703) 251-8500
*Director, Finance & Accounting and PAC Treasurer (for
2015)*

ROMEO, Thomas — Tel: (703) 251-8500
President, MAXIMUS Federal

MAXXAM

A holding company that operates in the aluminum, forest products, real estate, and racing industries.
maxxam.ca
Annual Revenues: $17.50 million
Employees: 2,200
Ticker: AMEX: MXM
SIC: 0800
Industry/ies: Environment And Conservation; Science; Scientific Research

Chairman of the Board — Tel: (713) 975-7600
HURWITZ, Charles E. — Fax: (713) 267-3701

President and Chief Executive Officer — Tel: (713) 975-7600
HANTHO, Jon — Fax: (713) 267-3701

Main Headquarters
Mailing: 735 Industrial Rd. — Tel: (650) 576-7765
Suite 212
San Carlos, CA 94070

Political Action Committees
MAXXAM Inc. Federal PAC
FEC ID: C00363093
Contact: M. Emily Madison
1330 Post Oak Blvd.
Suite 2000
Houston, TX 77056

Public Affairs and Related Activities Personnel
At Headquarters

BAILEY, Margaret — Tel: (650) 576-7765
Vice President, Human Resources

JEPPESEN, Chris — Tel: (650) 576-7765
Chief Financial Officer

QUON, Steve — Tel: (650) 576-7765
Vice President, Corporate Development

At Other Offices

MADISON, M. Emily — Tel: (713) 975-7600
Vice President, Finance — Fax: (713) 267-3701

1330 Post Oak Blvd., Suite 2000
Houston, TX 77056

Mayer Electric Supply Company, Inc.

Distributors of electrical supplies.
www.mayerelectric.com
Annual Revenues: $609 million
Employees: 950
Industry/ies: Machinery/Equipment

Chairman of the Board and Chief Executive Officer Tel: (205) 583-3500
GOEDECKE, Nancy Collat   Fax: (205) 252-0315

Main Headquarters
Mailing: 3405 Fourth Ave., South   Tel: (205) 583-3500
         Birmingham, AL 35222-2300   Fax: (205) 252-0315

Political Action Committees
Mayer Electric Supply Company Inc. PAC (Mayer Electric PAC)
FEC ID: C00305599
Contact: Larry E. Parrish
P.O. Box 1328   Tel: (205) 583-3500
Birmingham, AL 35201

  Contributions to Candidates: $250 (2015-2016)
  Republicans: $250

Corporate Foundations and Giving Programs
Mayer Electric Supply Company Contributions Program
P.O. Box 1328
Birmingham, AL 35201-1328

Public Affairs and Related Activities Personnel

At Headquarters

GOEDECKE, Glenn   Tel: (205) 583-3500
Executive Vice President, Sales and Marketing Fax: (205) 252-0315
ggoedecke@mayerelectric.com

At Other Offices

PARRISH, Larry E.
PAC Contact, Director, Planning and Finance
P.O. Box 1328
Birmingham, AL 35201-1328

Mayfield Clinic, Inc.

A physician organization for clinical care, education, and research of the spine and brain.
www.mayfieldclinic.com
Annual Revenues: $10.40 million
Employees: 100
Industry/ies: Medicine/Health Care/Mental Health

Chairman of the Board   Tel: (513) 221-1100
WARNICK, Ronald   Fax: (513) 891-1734

Chief Executive Officer   Tel: (513) 221-1100
FARRINGTON , MBA, Mark D.   Fax: (513) 891-1734

Main Headquarters
Mailing: 506 Oak St.   Tel: (513) 221-1100
         Cincinnati, OH 45219-2507   Fax: (513) 891-1734
                                      TF: (800) 325-7787

Corporate Foundations and Giving Programs

Mayfield Education and Research Foundation
Contact: Kelly Bollinger
506 Oak St.   Tel: (513) 569-5277
Cincinnati, OH 45219-2507   Fax: (513) 569-5365

The Neurosciences Foundation
506 Oak St.   Tel: (513) 221-1100
Cincinnati, OH 45219

Public Affairs and Related Activities Personnel

At Headquarters

BOLLINGER, Kelly   Tel: (513) 569-5277
Development Director, Mayfield Education and Research Fax: (513) 891-1734
Foundation

BROUGHTON, SPHR, Debbie M.   Tel: (513) 569-5231
Director, Organizational Development and Human Resources Fax: (513) 891-1734
dbroughton@mayfieldclinic.com

RADOMSKI, Michael J.   Tel: (513) 569-5210
Vice President, Finance and Chief Financial Officer Fax: (513) 891-1734
mradomski@mayfieldclinic.com

ROSENBERGER, APR, Thomas V.   Tel: (513) 221-1100
Vice President, Communications   Fax: (513) 891-1734

SKELLY, Jene   Tel: (513) 221-1100
Director, Patient Business Services   Fax: (513) 891-1734

STARR, Cindy   Tel: (513) 558-3505
Specialist, Media Relations   Fax: (513) 891-1734
cstarr@mayfieldclinic.com

Mazda North America Operations

Responsible for research and development, sales and marketing, and customer parts and service support of Mazda vehicles in the U.S. Headquartered in Irvine, CA.
www.mazdausa.com
Annual Revenues: $5.00 billion
SIC: 6719
Industry/ies: Automotive Industry; Transportation
Legislative Issues: AUT

President   Tel: (949) 727-1990
O'SULLIVAN, James   Fax: (949) 727-6101
JOSullivan@mazdausa.com

Main Headquarters
Mailing: P.O. Box 19734   Tel: (949) 727-1990
         Irvine, CA 92623-9734   Fax: (949) 727-6101
                                      TF: (800) 222-5500

Washington Office
Mailing: 1025 Connecticut Ave. NW   Tel: (202) 467-5096
         Suite 910
         Washington, DC 20036

Corporate Foundations and Giving Programs

Mazda Foundation (USA) Inc.
1025 Connecticut Ave. NW
Suite 910
Washington, DC 20036

Public Affairs and Related Activities Personnel

At Headquarters

LEWIS, Renee   Tel: (949) 727-1990
Vice President, Human Resources   Fax: (949) 727-6101

At Washington Office

MCMORROW, Sean   Tel: (202) 467-5096
Manager, Government Affairs

RYAN, Dan   Tel: (202) 467-5096
Director, Government & Public Affairs
Registered Federal Lobbyist

Mazzetta, Inc.

Brand for prepackaged seafood products.
www.mazzetta.com
Employees: 20
Industry/ies: Fish And Fishing; Food And Beverage Industry
Legislative Issues: MAR; TRD

Chief Executive Officer   Tel: (847) 433-1150
MAZZETTA, Thomas   Fax: (847) 433-8973

Main Headquarters
Mailing: 1990 St. Johns Ave.   Tel: (847) 433-1150
         Highland Park, IL 60035   Fax: (847) 433-8973

Corporate Foundations and Giving Programs

Mazzetta, Inc. Contributions program
P.O. Box 1126   Tel: (847) 433-1150
Highland Park, IL 60035   Fax: (847) 433-8973

MB Financial Inc.

Provides financial solutions to privately-held, middle-market businesses as well as to small businesses and individuals.
www.mbfinancial.com
Annual Revenues: $645.08 million
Employees: 2,839
Ticker: NASDAQ (GS): MBFI
SIC: 6035
Industry/ies: Banking/Finance/Investments

Chairman of the Board   Tel: (847) 653-1996
HARVEY, Thomas H.   Fax: (847) 653-0080
tharvey@mbfinancial.com

President and Chief Executive Officer Tel: (847) 653-1996
FEIGER, Mitchell   Fax: (847) 653-0080
mfeiger@mbfinancial.com

Main Headquarters
Mailing: 800 W. Madison St.   TF: (888) 422-6562
         Chicago, IL 60607

Corporate Foundations and Giving Programs

MB Financial Charitable Foundation
6111 N. River Rd.
Rosemont, IL 60018

Public Affairs and Related Activities Personnel

At Headquarters

BOUMAN, Rosemarie   Tel: (847) 653-1996
Vice President and Executive Vice President, Administration

YORK, Jill E.   Tel: (847) 653-1991
Vice President and Chief Financial Officer Fax: (847) 653-0080
jyork@mbfinancial.com

At Other Offices

CHARLES, Lewis D
PAC Treasurer
P.O. Box 419226
Kanas, MO 64141

MBDA, Inc.

Designer and manufacturer of missile and weapons systems. MBDA designs and provides missiles and missile systems that correspond to the full range of current and future operational needs via land, sea and air.
www.mbdainc.com
Employees: 10,000
Industry/ies: Defense/Homeland Security; Government-Related
Legislative Issues: BUD; DEF

| **President and Chief Executive Officer** | Tel: | (703) 387-7120 |
| PRANZATELLI, John | Fax: | (703) 875-9104 |

Main Headquarters		
Mailing: 1300 Wilson Blvd.	Tel:	(703) 387-7120
Suite 550	Fax:	(703) 875-9104
Arlington, VA 22209		

Political Action Committees

MBDA, Inc. PAC
FEC ID: C00490037
Contact: Justin Rerko
1300 Wilson Blvd.
Suite 550
Arlington, 22209

Contributions to Candidates: $9,500 (2015-2016)
Republicans: $9,500

Public Affairs and Related Activities Personnel

At Headquarters

GEROKOSTOPOULOS, Jan	Tel:	(818) 735-2516
Director, Communications and Media Relations	Fax:	(703) 875-9104
Jan.Gerokostopoulos@mbda-us.com		

| LAMANTIA, Jim | Tel: | (703) 387-7120 |
| *Vice President, Corporate Finance and Administration* | Fax: | (703) 875-9104 |

RERKO, Justin	Tel:	(703) 387-7120
Director, Business Development & Government Relations	Fax:	(703) 875-9104
Registered Federal Lobbyist		

MBIA, Inc.

A holding company whose subsidiaries provide investment management products and services. It helps clients achieve their financial goals by providing credit protection and markets access.
www.mbia.com
Annual Revenues: $656.00 million
Employees: 170
Ticker: NYSE: MBI
SIC: 6351
Industry/ies: Banking/Finance/Investments

| **Chairman** | Tel: | (914) 273-4545 |
| RINEHART, Charles R. | | |

Chief Executive Officer	Tel:	(914) 273-4545
BROWN, Joseph (Jay) W.	Fax:	(914) 765-3163
joseph.brown@mbia.com		

Main Headquarters		
Mailing: One Manhattanville Rd.	Tel:	(914) 273-4545
Suite 301		
Purchase, NY 10577		

Corporate Foundations and Giving Programs

MBIA Foundation
Contact: Jean McGovern
113 King St.
Armonk, NY 10504

Public Affairs and Related Activities Personnel

At Headquarters

BROWN, Kevin	Tel:	(914) 273-4545
Managing Director		
kevin.brown@mbia.com		

| CHAPLIN, C. Edward | Tel: | (914) 273-4545 |
| *Director* | | |

DIAMOND, Greg	Tel:	(914) 765-3190
Managing Director		
greg.diamond@mbia.com		

| FALLON, William C. | Tel: | (914) 273-4545 |
| *President and Chief Operating Officer* | | |

| MCKIERNAN, Anthony | Tel: | (914) 273-4545 |
| *Executive Vice President and Chief Financial Officer* | | |

| WERTHEIM, Ram D. | Tel: | (914) 273-4545 |
| *Chief Legal Officer* | | |

At Other Offices

MCGOVERN, Jean	Tel:	(914) 765-3834
Manager, Corporate Giving	Fax:	(914) 765-3163
113 King St.		
Armonk, NY 10504		
Jean.mcgovern@mbia.com		

McAfee, Inc

Formerly Network Associates, Inc. Supplies network and systems security products and services.
www.mcafee.com
Annual Revenues: $2.06 billion
Employees: 6,000
Ticker: NYSE: MFE
SIC: 7372
Industry/ies: Computer/Technology
Legislative Issues: BUD; CPI; DEF; GOV; HOM; INT; SCI

Main Headquarters		
Mailing: 2821 Mission College Blvd.	Tel:	(972) 963-8000
Santha Clara, CA 95054		

Corporate Foundations and Giving Programs

McAfee Community Involvement
3965 Freedom Cir.
Santa Clara, CA 95054

Public Affairs and Related Activities Personnel

At Headquarters

| BALDWIN, Penny | Tel: | (972) 963-8000 |
| *Executive Vice President and Chief Marketing Officer* | | |

| FOUNTAIN, Tom | Tel: | (972) 963-8000 |
| *Senior Vice President and General Manager, Strategy and Corporate Development* | | |

GANN, Thomas Michael	Tel:	(301) 613-3966
Vice President, Public Policy		
Thomas_Gann@McAfee.com		
Registered Federal Lobbyist		

| KEMP, Judith | Tel: | (972) 963-8000 |
| *Senior Director, Integrated Marketing Communications* | | |

PALM, Chris	Tel:	(408) 346-3089
Contact, Media Relations		
Chris_Palm@mcafee.com		

| RILEY, Louis | Tel: | (972) 963-8000 |
| *Senior Vice President and General Counsel* | | |

At Other Offices

BERMAN, Janis Schwartz	Tel:	(408) 988-3832
Vice President, Government Relations	Fax:	(408) 970-9727
3965 Freedom Cir.		
Santa Clara, CA 95054		
Registered Federal Lobbyist		

GANN, Peggy	Tel:	(408) 988-3832
Vice President, Government Relations	Fax:	(408) 970-9727
3965 Freedom Cir.		
Santa Clara, CA 95054		
Registered Federal Lobbyist		

HAYDEN, Edward	Tel:	(408) 988-3832
Senior Vice President, Finance & Accounting	Fax:	(408) 970-9727
3965 Freedom Cir.		
Santa Clara, CA 95054		

ROSS, Tracy	Tel:	(408) 346-5965
Director, Public Relations	Fax:	(408) 970-9727
3965 Freedom Cir.		
Santa Clara, CA 95054		
tracy_ross@mcafee.com		

THOMPKINS, Stephen	Tel:	(972) 987-2602
Director	Fax:	(408) 970-9727
3965 Freedom Cir.		
Santa Clara, CA 95054		
stephen_thompkins@mcafee.com		

McAlister's Corporation

Operates deli restaurants.
www.mcalistersdeli.com
Employees: 300
Industry/ies: Food And Beverage Industry

Main Headquarters		
Mailing: 4501 N. Point Pkwy.	Tel:	(770) 360-8300
Suite 100	TF:	(888) 855-3354
Alpharetta, GA 30022		

Public Affairs and Related Activities Personnel

At Other Offices

FRIEDMAN, Philip P.

PAC Contact
731 S. Pear Orchard Rd., Suite 51
Ridgeland, MS 39157

Timothy S. McAnarney

A government relations consultant.

Main Headquarters

Mailing:	417 W. Edwards	Tel:	(217) 522-6121
	Sprindfield, IL 62704		

Public Affairs and Related Activities Personnel

At Headquarters

MCANARNEY, Timothy S.	Tel:	(217) 522-6121
Consultant		

The McClatchy Company

Publisher of a nationwide group of newspapers. Purchased Knight Ridder in 2006.
www.mcclatchy.com
Annual Revenues: $1.13 billion
Employees: 5,780
Ticker: NYSE: MNI
SIC: 2711
Industry/ies: Communications; Media/Mass Communication

Chairman of the Board	Tel:	(916) 321-1855
MCCLATCHY, Kevin S.	Fax:	(916) 321-1964
President and Chief Executive Officer	Tel:	(916) 321-1855
TALAMANTES , Patrick J.	Fax:	(916) 321-1964

Main Headquarters

Mailing:	2100 Q St.	Tel:	(916) 321-1855
	Sacramento, CA 95816-6899	Fax:	(916) 321-1964

Public Affairs and Related Activities Personnel

At Headquarters

ALVAREZ, Lourdes	Tel:	(916) 321-1855
Manager, Media and Programs	Fax:	(916) 321-1964
lalvarez@miamiherald.com		
BERNARD, Stephen	Tel:	(916) 321-1855
Vice President, Advertising	Fax:	(916) 321-1964
KIMBALL, Ryan	Tel:	(916) 321-1849
Assistant Treasurer and Contact, Investor Relations	Fax:	(916) 321-1964
rkimball@mcclatchy.com		
LINTECUM, R. Elaine	Tel:	(916) 321-1846
Vice President, Finance and Chief Financial Officer	Fax:	(916) 321-1964
elintecum@mcclatchy.com		
MCCONKEY, Billie S.	Tel:	(916) 321-1855
Vice President, Human Resources	Fax:	(916) 321-1964
ZIEMAN, Mark	Tel:	(916) 321-1855
Vice President, Operations	Fax:	(916) 321-1964

McCormick & Company, Inc.

A producer of spices, seasonings, flavorings and other specialty foods.
www.mccormick.com
Annual Revenues: $4.36 billion
Employees: 10,000
Ticker: NYSE: MKC
SIC: 2090
Industry/ies: Food And Beverage Industry

Executive Chairman of the Board	Tel:	(410) 771-7301
WILSON, Alan D.	Fax:	(410) 771-7462

Main Headquarters

Mailing:	18 Loveton Cir.	Tel:	(410) 771-7301
	Sparks, MD 21152	Fax:	(410) 771-7462
		TF:	(800) 632-5847

Corporate Foundations and Giving Programs

McCormick & Company Contributions Program		
18 Loveton Cir.	Tel:	(410) 771-7301
Sparks, MD 21152		

Public Affairs and Related Activities Personnel

At Headquarters

BROOKS, Joyce	Tel:	(410) 771-7244
Vice President, Investor Relations	Fax:	(410) 527-8214
joyce_brooks@mccormick.com		
GRIM, Diane E.	Tel:	(410) 771-7301
Manager	Fax:	(410) 771-7462
Mail Stop P.O. Box 6000		
HARRSEN, Laurie	Tel:	(410) 527-8753
Director, Public Relations and Consumer Communications	Fax:	(410) 771-7462
laurie_harrsen@mccormick.com		
KURZIUS, Lawrence E.	Tel:	(410) 771-7301
President and Chief Operating Officer	Fax:	(410) 771-7462

LYNN, Jim	Tel:	(410) 771-7803
Director, Corporate Communications	Fax:	(410) 771-7462
Jim_Lynn@mccormick.com		
MANZONE, Lisa	Tel:	(410) 771-7301
Senior Vice President, Human Relations	Fax:	(410) 771-7462
RIMMER, Nneka	Tel:	(410) 771-7301
Senior Vice President, Corporate Strategy and Development	Fax:	(410) 771-7462
SCHWARTZ , Jeffery	Tel:	(410) 771-7301
Vice President, General Counsel and Corporate Secretary	Fax:	(410) 771-7462
SMITH, Michael R.	Tel:	(410) 771-7301
Senior Vice President, Corporate Finance	Fax:	(410) 771-7462
STETZ, Gordon M.	Tel:	(410) 771-7301
Executive Vice President and Chief Financial Officer	Fax:	(410) 771-7462

McDermott International, Inc

A worldwide energy services company. Its subsidiaries provide engineering, fabrication, installation, procurement, and project management for customers involved in the production of energy and in other industries.
www.mcdermott.com
Annual Revenues: $2.25billion
Employees: 13,800
Ticker: NYSE: MDR
SIC: 3443
Industry/ies: Construction/Construction Materials; Energy/Electricity; Engineering/Mathematics; Marine/Maritime/Shipping; Transportation
Legislative Issues: BUD; DEF

Chairman	Tel:	(281) 870-5000
HANKS, Stephen G.	Fax:	(281) 870-5788
President and Chief Executive Officer	Tel:	(281) 870-5000
DICKSON, David	Fax:	(281) 870-5788

Main Headquarters

Mailing:	757 N. Eldridge Pkwy.	Tel:	(281) 870-5000
	Houston, TX 77079	Fax:	(281) 870-5788

Corporate Foundations and Giving Programs

McDermott International Contributions Progarm
757 N. Eldridge Pkwy.
Houston, TX 77079

Public Affairs and Related Activities Personnel

At Headquarters

ALLEN, Steve	Tel:	(281) 870-5000
Senior Vice President, Human Resources	Fax:	(281) 870-5788
HIGHTOWER, Jeff	Tel:	(281) 870-5901
Vice President, Internal Audit	Fax:	(281) 870-5788
HINRICHS, Liane K.	Tel:	(281) 870-5901
Senior Vice President, General Counsel and Corporate Secretary	Fax:	(281) 870-5788
OLDHAM, Steve	Tel:	(281) 870-5000
Vice President, Treasurer and Investor Relations	Fax:	(281) 870-5788
SCHOOLFIELD , Bruce W.	Tel:	(281) 870-5000
Vice President, Assistant General Counsel	Fax:	(281) 870-5788
SPENCE, Stuart	Tel:	(281) 870-5000
Executive Vice President and Chief Financial Officer	Fax:	(281) 870-5788

At Other Offices

BLACK, David S.	Tel:	(434) 522-6800
Vice President and Controller		
2016 Mt. Athos Rd.		
Lynchburh, VA 24504		

McDonald & Harden, LLC

McDonald & Harden, LLC is a full service federal government affairs firm that assists clients in developing and maintaining funding partnerships and creating public policy.
www.mcdonaldharden.com

President	Tel:	(202) 349-3965
LITTON, Chris		
clitton@mcdonaldharden.com		

Main Headquarters

Mailing:	1629 K St. NW	Tel:	(202) 349-3965
	Suite 300		
	Washington, DC 20006		

Corporate Foundations and Giving Programs

McDonald & Harden Federal Funding
1629 K St. NW
Suite 300
Washington, DC 20006

McDonald's Corporation

A global foodservice retailer.
www.mcdonalds.com
Annual Revenues: $26.70 billion

Employees: 420,000
Ticker: NYSE: MCD
Industry/ies: Food And Beverage Industry
Legislative Issues: AGR; FOO; HCR; IMM; LBR; TAX; VET

President and Chief Executive Officer
EASTERBROOK, Steve

Tel: (630) 620-0457
Fax: (630) 623-5004

Main Headquarters
Mailing: 2915 Jorie Blvd.
Oak Brook, IL 60523

Tel: (630) 620-0457
Fax: (630) 623-5004
TF: (800) 244-6227

Washington Office
Mailing: 1099 New York Ave. NW
Suite 510
Washington, DC 20001

Political Action Committees
McDonald's Corporation Political Action Committee
FEC ID: C00063164
Contact: Mike Soenke
2111 McDonalds Dr.
Dept 213
Oak Brook, IL 60523

Tel: (202) 887-8900
Fax: (202) 887-8907

  Contributions to Candidates: $6,552,391 (2015-2016)
  Democrats: $111,500; Republicans: $168,875; Other: $6,272,016

Principal Recipients

HOUSE
DAVIS, RODNEY L (REP-IL)

Corporate Foundations and Giving Programs
Ronald McDonald Children's Charities
2111 McDonald's Dr.
Oak Brook, IL 60523

Ronald McDonald House Charities
One Kroc Dr.
Oak Brook, IL 60523

Tel: (630) 623-7048
Fax: (630) 623-7488

Public Affairs and Related Activities Personnel

At Headquarters

COFFING, Bridget
Senior Vice President and Chief Communications Officer

Tel: (630) 620-0457
Fax: (630) 623-5004

KRIGER, Adam
Senior Vice President, Corporate Strategy

Tel: (630) 620-0457
Fax: (630) 623-5004

BARKER, Heidi
Vice President, Global External Communications
heidi.barker@us.mcd.com

Tel: (630) 623-3678
Fax: (630) 623-8843

BENSEN, Peter J.
Chief Administrative Officer

Tel: (630) 623-3000
Fax: (630) 623-5004

FLOERSCH, Richard
Executive Vice President and Chief Human Resources Officer

Tel: (630) 623-3000
Fax: (630) 623-8843

GONZALEZ-MENDEZ , J. C.
Senior Vice President, Global Corporate Social Responsibility, Sustainability and Philanthropy

Tel: (630) 620-0457
Fax: (630) 623-5004

GONZALEZ-MENDEZ, J.C.
Senior Vice President Global Inclusion, Community Engagement and Philanthropy

Tel: (630) 620-0457
Fax: (630) 623-5004

HANDY, Tara
Senior Communications Manager
tara.handy@us.mcd.com

Tel: (630) 623-3000
Fax: (630) 623-8843

HOWARD, Lisa
Senior Director, Media Relations
lisa.howard@us.mcd.com

Tel: (630) 623-3678
Fax: (630) 623-5004

MCCOMB, Lisa
Director, Media Relations
lisa.mccomb@us.mcd.com

Tel: (630) 623-3678
Fax: (202) 887-8907

OZAN, Kevin
Executive Vice President and Chief Financial Officer

Tel: (630) 620-0457
Fax: (630) 623-5004

SANTONA, Gloria
Executive Vice President, General Counsel and Secretary

Tel: (630) 623-3000
Fax: (630) 623-5004

TATEVOSYAN, Sam
Registered Federal Lobbyist

Tel: (630) 623-3000

At Washington Office

AGUILERA, Sylvia
Director, Federal Government Relations
Registered Federal Lobbyist

Tel: (202) 469-8020

BRYANT, Chester C.
Senior Director, McDonald's Corporation
bo.bryant@us.mcd.com
Registered Federal Lobbyist

Tel: (202) 887-8900
Fax: (202) 887-8907

CABRERA, Jano
Senior Vice President, U.S. Communications / Global Media / Public Relations

HILTON, Steven M.
Vice President, Government Relations
steve.hilton@mcd.com

Tel: (202) 469-8020

MOCHAL, Jeff
Senior Director, External Communication

Tel: (202) 469-8020

TATEVOSYAN, Sam
Registered Federal Lobbyist

Tel: (202) 469-8020

WILLIAMS, Jimmie
Director, Government Relations

Tel: (202) 469-8020
Fax: (202) 469-8027

At Other Offices

SOENKE, Mike
PAC Treasurer
2111 Mcdonalds 213
Oak Brook, IL 60523

TATEVOSYAN, Sam
26345 Network Pl.
Chicago, IL 60673-1263
Registered Federal Lobbyist

Tel: (630) 623-7048

McGladrey &amp

See listing on page 690 under RSM McGladrey, Inc.

McGraw Hill Financial

Credit rating agency.
Annual Revenues: $5.13 billion
Employees: 17,000
Ticker: NYSE:MHFI
Industry/ies: Banking/Finance/Investments
Legislative Issues: BAN; FIN; HCR; TAX

Main Headquarters
Mailing: 55 Water St.
New York City, NY 10020

Washington Office
Mailing: 1200 G St. NW, Suite 1000
Washington, DC 20005

Political Action Committees
Mcgraw Hill Financial Inc. Political Action Committee
FEC ID: C00494682
Contact: Jack Callahan
1221 Avenue of the Americas
New York City, NY 10020

  Contributions to Candidates: $43,500 (2015-2016)
  Democrats: $8,500; Republicans: $35,000

Public Affairs and Related Activities Personnel

At Headquarters

CALLAHAN, Jack
Treasurer

At Washington Office

HERNDON, Scott
Director, Global Government and Public Policy

The McGraw-Hill Companies

A financial intelligence company. Brands include Standard & Poor's, BusinessWeek, and McGraw-Hill Education.
www.mcgraw-hill.com
Annual Revenues: $4.60 billion
Employees: 16,687
Ticker: NYSE: MHP
SIC: 2731; 2721; 2741; 7375
NAICS: 511140; 511199; 514191; 511130
Industry/ies: Communications; Education; Media/Mass Communication
Legislative Issues: FIN; FUE; HCR; HOM; ROD; TAX

Chairman of the Board
MCGRAW, Harold

Tel: (212) 512-2000
Fax: (212) 512-3840

President and Chief Executive Officer
PETERSON, Douglas L.

Tel: (212) 512-2000
Fax: (212) 512-3840

Main Headquarters
Mailing: 1221 Avenue of the Americas
New York City, NY 10020

Tel: (212) 512-2000
Fax: (212) 512-3840

Washington Office
Mailing: 1200 G St. NW
Suite 200, Tenth Floor
Washington, DC 20005-3802

Tel: (202) 383-3700
Fax: (202) 383-3718

Political Action Committees
McGraw-Hill Financial Inc. Political Action Committee
FEC ID: C00494682
Contact: Jack F. Callahan Jr.
1221 Avenue of the Americas
New York City, NY 10020

  Contributions to Candidates: $160,000 (2015-2016)

Democrats: $43,500; Republicans: $116,500

Corporate Foundations and Giving Programs

The McGraw-Hill Companies Corporate Contributions and Community
Relations
Contact: Louise Raymond
1221 Avenue of the Americas   Tel: (212) 512-2001
New York City, NY 10020   Fax: (212) 512-3611

Public Affairs and Related Activities Personnel

At Headquarters

BERISFORD, John L.	Tel:	(212) 512-2000
Executive Vice President, Human Resources	Fax:	(212) 512-3840
CALLAHAN, Jr., Jack F.	Tel:	(212) 512-2000
Executive Vice President and Chief Financial Officer, PAC Treasurer	Fax:	(212) 512-3840
FATO, Lucy	Tel:	(212) 512-2564
Executive Vice President and General Counsel	Fax:	(212) 512-3116
FEUCHTWANGER, Jason	Tel:	(212) 512-3151
Director, Corporate Media Relations	Fax:	(212) 512-3840
GEDULDIG, Courtney	Tel:	(212) 512-2000
Executive Vice President, Public Affairs	Fax:	(212) 512-3840
GOLD, Jason	Tel:	(212) 512-2000
Federal Lobbyists	Fax:	(212) 512-3840
HERNDON, Scott	Tel:	(212) 512-2000
Federal Lobbyists	Fax:	(212) 512-3840
HOWARD, Donald	Tel:	(212) 512-2000
Head, Enterprise Risk Management; Vice Chairman, Risk Policy Committee	Fax:	(212) 512-3840
HUGHES, Celeste M.	Tel:	(212) 512-2192
Senior Manager, Communications and Shareholder Relations	Fax:	(212) 512-3840
MERRITT, Chip	Tel:	(212) 512-4321
Vice President, Investor Relations	Fax:	(212) 512-3840
chip.merritt@mhfi.com		
MORGAN, Sarah	Tel:	(212) 512-2000
Registered Federal Lobbyist	Fax:	(212) 512-3840
PERRY, Leah	Tel:	(212) 512-2000
Federal Lobbyists	Fax:	(212) 512-3840
RAYMOND, Louise	Tel:	(212) 512-2001
Vice President, Corporate Responsibility and Sustainability	Fax:	(212) 512-3611
louise_raymond@mcgraw-hill.com		
ROSENKOETTER, Darlene	Tel:	(212) 512-2000
Federal Lobbyists	Fax:	(212) 512-3840
Registered Federal Lobbyist		
TRILLI, Shannon	Tel:	(212) 512-4319
Director, Corporate Responsibility Strategy	Fax:	(212) 512-3840
WALLMAN, Susan A.	Tel:	(212) 512-6480
Manager, Corporate Contributions	Fax:	(212) 512-3611
susan_wallman@mcgraw-hill.com		

At Washington Office

BRADDON, Cynthia H.	Tel:	(202) 383-3700
Vice President, International Affairs	Fax:	(202) 383-3718
cindy.braddon@mcgraw-hill.com		
Registered Federal Lobbyist		
DUNCAN, Dan	Tel:	(202) 383-3700
Senior Director, Government Affairs	Fax:	(202) 383-3718
daniel_duncan@mcgraw-hill.com		
GOLDBERG, Christopher	Tel:	(202) 383-3700
Manager, Government Affairs	Fax:	(202) 383-3718

At Other Offices

FITZPATRICK, Jillian
55 Water St.
New York City, NY 10041
Registered Federal Lobbyist

LIPSEY, John
55 Water St.
New York City, NY 10041
Registered Federal Lobbyist

McGraw-Hill Education

Provides proven, research-based content with the best emerging digital technologies to guide assessment, teaching and learning to achieve the best possible outcome for students, instructors and institutions.
www.mheducation.com
Employees: 6,000
SIC: 2731
Industry/ies: Education
Legislative Issues: EDU; TAX

President and Chief Executive Officer	Tel:	(212) 904-2574
LEVIN, David	Fax:	(212) 904-6285

Main Headquarters

Mailing:	Two Penn Plaza	Tel:	(212) 904-2574
	Tenth Floor	Fax:	(212) 904-6285
	New York City, NY 10121-2298		

Washington Office

Mailing:	1200 G St. NW	Tel:	(202) 383-2301
	Washington, DC 20005	Fax:	(202) 383-3718

Corporate Foundations and Giving Programs

McGraw-Hill Research Foundation
Two Penn Plaza
Tenth Floor
New York City, NY 10121-2298

Public Affairs and Related Activities Personnel

At Headquarters

BELARDI, Brian	Tel:	(212) 904-2574
Director, Media Relations	Fax:	(212) 904-6285
Brian.Belardi@mheducation.com		
COHEN, Peter	Tel:	(212) 904-2574
President	Fax:	(212) 904-6285
DEGENARO, Angelo T.	Tel:	(212) 904-2574
Chief Information Officer	Fax:	(212) 904-6285
GUTIERREZ, Jesse M.	Tel:	(212) 904-4021
Executive, Education Policy and Government Affairs	Fax:	(212) 904-6285
jesse_gutierrez@mcgraw-hill.com		
MARTIN-RETORTILLO, Teresa	Tel:	(212) 904-2574
Senior Vice President, Strategy and Business Development	Fax:	(212) 904-6285
MILANO, Patrick	Tel:	(212) 904-2574
Chief Financial Officer and Chief Administrative Officer	Fax:	(212) 904-6285
MORRISON, Heath	Tel:	(212) 904-2574
Senior Vice President, Government Affairs and Education Policy	Fax:	(212) 904-6285
SIEGER, Daniel	Tel:	(212) 904-2574
Vice President, Communications	Fax:	(212) 904-6285
Dan.Sieger@mheducation.com		
STAFFORD , David	Tel:	(212) 904-2574
Senior Vice President and General Counsel	Fax:	(212) 904-6285
VALAITIS , Maryellen	Tel:	(212) 904-2574
Senior Vice President, Human Resources	Fax:	(212) 904-6285

At Washington Office

SNOWHITE, Larry S.	Tel:	(202) 383-2301
Vice President, Public and Government Affairs	Fax:	(202) 383-3718
larry.snowhite@mheducation.com		

McKee Foods Corporation

A manufacturer of baked goods. Brands include Little Debbie and Sunbelt.
www.mckeefoods.com
Employees: 6,000
Industry/ies: Food And Beverage Industry
Legislative Issues: AGR; CDT; FOO; TRU

Chairman of the Board	Tel:	(423) 238-7111
MCKEE, Ellsworth R.	Fax:	(423) 238-7101

President	Tel:	(423) 238-7111
MCKEE, Michael	Fax:	(423) 238-7101

Main Headquarters

Mailing:	10260 McKee Rd.	Tel:	(423) 238-7111
	Collegedale, TN 37315	Fax:	(423) 238-7127
		TF:	(800) 522-4499

Public Affairs and Related Activities Personnel

At Headquarters

GLOEKLER, Michael	Tel:	(423) 238-7111
Manager, Corporate Communications and Public Relations	Fax:	(423) 238-7127
mike_gloekler@mckee.com		
PATTERSON, Barry	Tel:	(423) 238-7111
Chief Financial Officer	Fax:	(423) 238-7101

At Other Offices

SMITH, Melissa	Tel:	(479) 736-2601
Manager, Human Resources		
555 McKee Dr.		
Gentry, AZ 72734		

McKenna Metals Company

See listing on page 466 under Kennametal Inc.

McKesson Corporation

A health care supply and information management company.
www.mckesson.com
Annual Revenues: $190.88 billion
Employees: 68,000
Ticker: NYSE: MCK
SIC: 5122

NAICS: 422210
Industry/ies: Food And Beverage Industry; Pharmaceutical Industry
Legislative Issues: HCR; MMM; PHA; TAX; VET

| **Chairman of the Board, President and Chief Executive Officer** | Tel: | (415) 983-8300 |
| HAMMERGREN, John H. | Fax: | (415) 983-7160 |

Main Headquarters

Mailing:	One Post St.	Tel:	(415) 983-8300
	Suite 3400	Fax:	(415) 983-7160
	San Francisco, CA 94104		

Washington Office

Mailing:	601 Pennsylvania Ave. NW		
	Suite 950 North		
	Washington, DC 20004		

Political Action Committees

McKesson Corporation Employees Political Fund PAC
FEC ID: C00108035
Contact: Frank Starn

One Post St.	Tel:	(415) 983-8300
34th Floor	Fax:	(415) 983-8300
San Francisco, CA 94104		

Contributions to Candidates: $437,500 (2015-2016)
Democrats: $159,500; Republicans: $278,000

Principal Recipients

HOUSE
BERA, AMERISH (DEM-CA)
BLACKBURN, MARSHA MRS. (REP-TN)
CARTER, EARL LEROY (REP-GA)
LATTA, ROBERT EDWARD MR (REP-OH)
SWALWELL, ERIC MICHAEL (DEM-CA)

Corporate Foundations and Giving Programs

McKesson Foundation

| One Post St. | Tel: | (415) 983-8300 |
| San Francisco, CA 94104 | Fax: | (415) 983-8300 |

Public Affairs and Related Activities Personnel

At Headquarters

BEER, James	Tel:	(415) 983-8300
Executive Vice President and Chief Financial Officer	Fax:	(415) 983-7160
FIGUEREDO, Jorge L.	Tel:	(415) 983-8300
Executive Vice President, Human Resources	Fax:	(415) 983-7160
GANLEY, Joseph	Tel:	(415) 983-8300
Vice President, Federal Government Affairs	Fax:	(415) 983-7160
Registered Federal Lobbyist		
JONES, Ben	Tel:	(415) 983-8300
Registered Federal Lobbyist	Fax:	(415) 983-7160
LENIHAN, Keagan	Tel:	(415) 983-8300
Federal Lobbyist	Fax:	(415) 983-7160
Registered Federal Lobbyist		
MCELLIGOTT, Kathy	Tel:	(415) 983-8300
Executive Vice President, Chief Information Officer and Chief	Fax:	(415) 983-7160
Technology Officer		
NAGJI, Bansi	Tel:	(415) 983-8300
Executive Vice President, Corporate Strategy and Business	Fax:	(415) 983-7160
Development		
SCHECHTER, Lori A.	Tel:	(415) 983-8300
Executive Vice President, General Counsel and Chief	Fax:	(415) 983-7160
Compliance Officer		
STARN, Frank	Tel:	(415) 983-8300
President, Global Sourcing and PAC Treasurer	Fax:	(415) 983-7160
Mail Stop 32nd Floor		

At Washington Office

BROW, Matthew E.
Registered Federal Lobbyist

SLONE, Peter
Registered Federal Lobbyist

McLane Company, Inc.

It provides distribution services to customers throughout the U.S. The company delivers food and non-food products to the convenience stores, mass merchandise, quick service restaurants, drug store chains, and movie theater industries.
www.mclaneco.com
Employees: 20,000
SIC: 5141
NAICS: 424410
Industry/ies: Food And Beverage Industry
Legislative Issues: TRA

| **Chief Executive Officer** | Tel: | (254) 771-7500 |
| ROSIER, W. Grady | Fax: | (254) 771-7244 |

Main Headquarters

| *Mailing:* | 4747 McLane Pkwy. | Tel: | (254) 771-7500 |

| | Temple, TX 76504 | Fax: | (254) 771-7244 |
| | | TF: | (800) 299-1401 |

Political Action Committees

McLane Company, Inc. Federal PAC
FEC ID: C00215558
Contact: Kevin Koch
4747 McLane Pkwy.
Temple, TX 76503

Contributions to Candidates: $24,000 (2015-2016)
Democrats: $8,000; Republicans: $16,000

Corporate Foundations and Giving Programs

McLane Company, Inc. Contributions Program

| 4747 McLane Pkwy. | Tel: | (254) 771-7500 |
| Temple, TX 76504 | Fax: | (254) 771-7244 |

Public Affairs and Related Activities Personnel

At Headquarters

GARCIA, Neftali	Tel:	(254) 771-7500
Senior Director, Government Affairs	Fax:	(254) 771-7244
neftali.garcia@mclaneco.com		
KOCH, Kevin	Tel:	(254) 771-7500
Vice President Accounting, Tax, Finance, and PAC Treasurer	Fax:	(254) 771-7244
kkoch@mclaneco.com		

The McManus Group

A healthcare and tax consulting firm.
www.mcmanusgrp.com
Legislative Issues: BUD; HCR; MMM; TAX; VET

President	Tel:	(202) 546-6040
MCMANUS, John	Fax:	(202) 546-0021
jmcmanus@mcmanusgrp.com		

Main Headquarters

Mailing:	610 Tenth St. NW	Tel:	(202) 546-6040
	Suite 300	Fax:	(202) 546-0021
	Washington, DC 20001		

Public Affairs and Related Activities Personnel

At Headquarters

BEALOR, Lindsay	Tel:	(202) 546-6040
Director	Fax:	(202) 546-0021
lbealor@mcmanusgrp.com		
Registered Federal Lobbyist		
GERVASI, Christina	Tel:	(202) 546-6040
Registered Federal Lobbyist	Fax:	(202) 546-0021
SHIPLEY, Nick	Tel:	(202) 546-6040
Vice President	Fax:	(202) 546-0021
nshipley@mcmanusgrp.com		
Registered Federal Lobbyist		
THOMAS, Chase	Tel:	(202) 546-6040
Registered Federal Lobbyist	Fax:	(202) 546-0021
THORNHILL, Barrett P.	Tel:	(202) 546-6040
Principal	Fax:	(202) 546-0021
Registered Federal Lobbyist		

The McPherson Group

A government relations firm.
www.mcphersongroup.us

| **Federal Lobbyist** | Tel: | (202) 289-1011 |
| HOUSTON, Katherine | Fax: | (202) 293-2768 |

Main Headquarters

Mailing:	925 15th St. NW	Tel:	(202) 289-1011
	Fifth Floor	Fax:	(202) 293-2768
	Washington, DC 20005		

Public Affairs and Related Activities Personnel

At Headquarters

BROOKS, Thomas A	Tel:	(202) 289-1011
Federal Lobbyist	Fax:	(202) 293-2768
tbrooks@mcphersongroup.us		
CARROLL, Ward	Tel:	(202) 289-1011
Member, Advisory Board	Fax:	(202) 293-2768
KELLY, John A.	Fax:	(202) 293-2768
Partner		
jkelly@kellylobbyshop.com		
ROYER, Robert Stewart	Fax:	(202) 293-2768
Partner		
rsroyer@mcphersongroup.us		

MDU Resources Group

A natural resources products and related services provider.
www.mdu.com

Annual Revenues: $4.23 billion
Employees: 8,689
Ticker: NYSE: MDU
SIC: 1400
Industry/ies: Law Enforcement/Security
Legislative Issues: CAW; ENG; ENV; HOM; TAX; TRA

Chairman of the Board
PEARCE, Harry J.

Tel: (701) 530-1000
Fax: (701) 530-1698

President and Chief Executive Officer
GOODIN, David L.

Tel: (701) 530-1000
Fax: (701) 530-1698

Main Headquarters
Mailing: 1200 W. Century Ave.
P.O. Box 5650
Bismarck, ND 58506-5650

Tel: (701) 530-1000
Fax: (701) 530-1698
TF: (866) 760-4852

Political Action Committees
MDU Resources Group Good Government Fund PAC
FEC ID: C00163253
Contact: Rita O'Neill
1200 W. Century Ave.
P.O. Box 5650
Bismarck, ND 56506

> **Contributions to Candidates:** $6,000 (2015-2016)
> Republicans: $6,000

Corporate Foundations and Giving Programs

MDU Resources Foundation
Contact: Rita O'Neill
1200 W. Century Ave.
P.O. Box 5650
Bismarck, ND 58506

Tel: (701) 530-1087
Fax: (701) 530-1087

Public Affairs and Related Activities Personnel

At Headquarters

HAIDER, Dennis L.
Executive Vice President, Business Development

Tel: (701) 530-1000
Fax: (701) 530-1698

HOURIGAN, Kirsti
Senior Attorney
kirsti.hourigan@mduresources.com

Tel: (701) 530-1795
Fax: (701) 530-1698

KUNTZ , Daniel S.
General Counsel and Secretary

Tel: (701) 530-1000
Fax: (701) 530-1698

MATTESON, Richard
Director, Communications and Public Affairs

Tel: (701) 530-1000
Fax: (701) 530-1698

O'NEILL, Rita
Manager, Foundation and PAC Treasurer
rita.o'neill@mduresources.com

Tel: (701) 530-1000
Fax: (701) 530-1737

RITTENBACH, Phyllis A.
Director, Investor Relations
phyllis.rittenbach@mduresources.com

Tel: (701) 530-1057
Fax: (701) 530-1698

SCHWARTZ, Doran N.
Vice President and Chief Financial Officer

Tel: (701) 530-1000
Fax: (701) 530-1698

SIMON, Geoff
Director, Government Affairs
Registered Federal Lobbyist

Tel: (701) 530-1086
Fax: (701) 530-1698

STUMPF, John P.
Vice President, Strategic Planning

Tel: (701) 530-1000
Fax: (701) 530-1698

VECCHIO, Mark Del
Vice President, Human Resources

Tel: (701) 530-1000
Fax: (701) 530-1698

Mead Johnson Nutritional Group

A company dealing with infant and children's nutrition with focus on scientific research on nutrition. and has introduced a wide range of innovative infant products, pharmaceuticals, entreal and parenteral nutrition products.
www.meadjohnson.com
Annual Revenues: $3.94 billion
Employees: 7,660
Ticker: NYSE: MJN
SIC: 2000
Industry/ies: Food And Beverage Industry
Legislative Issues: AGR

Chairman of the Board
CORNELIUS, James M.

President and Chief Executive Officer
JAKOBSEN, P. Kasper

Tel: (847) 832-2420
Fax: (800) 828-9119

Main Headquarters
Mailing: 2701 Patriot Blvd.
Fourth Floor
Glenview, IL 60026

Tel: (847) 832-2420
Fax: (800) 828-9119
TF: (800) 457-3550

Corporate Foundations and Giving Programs

Mead Johnson's Charitable
2701 Patriot Blvd.
Fourth Floor

Glenview, IL 60026

Public Affairs and Related Activities Personnel

At Headquarters

CUP, Michel
Senior Vice President, Global Human Resources

Tel: (847) 832-2420
Fax: (800) 828-9119

MACDONALD, Kathy
Vice President, Investor Relations
kathy.macdonald@mjn.com

Tel: (847) 832-2182
Fax: (800) 828-9119

MONTEAGUDO, Graciela I.
Senior Vice President and President, Americas

Tel: (847) 832-2420
Fax: (800) 828-9119

ORMESHER, Ian
Senior Vice President, Global Human Resources

Tel: (847) 832-2420
Fax: (800) 828-9119

PERILLE, Christopher
Vice President Corporate Communications and Public Affairs
chris.perille@mjn.com

Tel: (847) 832-2178
Fax: (800) 828-9119

SHELLER, Patrick M.
Senior Vice President, General Counsel and Secretary

Tel: (847) 832-2420
Fax: (800) 828-9119

URBAIN, Charles M.
Executive Vice President and Chief Operating Officer

Tel: (847) 832-2420
Fax: (800) 828-9119

MeadWestvaco

Formed by the merger between The Mead Corp. and Westvaco Corp. in January of 2002. A producer of packaging, coated and specialty papers, consumer and office products and specialty chemicals.
www.meadwestvaco.com
Annual Revenues: $5.59 billion
Employees: 15,000
Ticker: NYSE: MWV
SIC: 2657; 2621; 2679; 2625; 2653; 2671; 3497; 7389; 2650
NAICS: 322211; 322212; 322299; 322213; 322221; 326112; 322225; 325998
Industry/ies: Paper And Wood Products Industry
Legislative Issues: AGR; ENG; ENV; RET; ROD; RRR; TAX; TRA; TRD; TRU

Chairman and Chief Executive Officer
LUKE, Jr., John A.
jaluke@meadwestvaco.com

Tel: (804) 327-5200

Main Headquarters
Mailing: 501 S. Fifth St.
Richmond, VA 23219-0501

Tel: (804) 444-1000

Washington Office
Mailing: 1101 17th St. NW
Suite 1005
Washington, DC 20036

Tel: (202) 289-0802
Fax: (202) 289-8815

Political Action Committees
MeadWestvaco PAC
FEC ID: C00065987
Contact: Alexander H. Stoddard
501 S. Fifth St.
Suite 1005
Richmond, VA 23219

> **Contributions to Candidates:** $24,200 (2015-2016)
> Democrats: $2,000; Republicans: $22,200

RockTenn Political Action Committee
FEC ID: C00117424
Contact: John D. Stakel
504 Thrasher St.
Norcross, GA 30071

> **Contributions to Candidates:** $150,100 (2015-2016)
> Democrats: $19,000; Republicans: $130,100; Other: $1,000

Corporate Foundations and Giving Programs

MeadWestvaco Foundation
Contact: Kathryn A. Strawn
501 S. Fifth St.
Richmond, VA 23219

Tel: (804) 444-6402
Fax: (804) 444-6402

Rock-Tenn Company Contributions Program
Contact: Roxanne Morgan
P.O. Box 4098
Norcross, GA 30091

Public Affairs and Related Activities Personnel

At Headquarters

COX, Donna Owens
Vice President, Global Communications

Tel: (804) 327-5200

MASSEE, Ned W.
Vice President, Corporate Affairs
nwm1@meadwestvaco.com

Tel: (804) 327-7210
Fax: (804) 327-6575

RAJKOWSKI, E. Mark
Senior Vice President and Chief Financial Officer

Tel: (804) 327-5200

SCHREINER, Linda V.
Senior Vice President, Human Resources and Communications

Tel: (804) 327-5200

STRAWN, Kathryn A.
Vice President and Executive Director, MeadWestvaco Foundation
jason.thompson@mwv.com
Tel: (804) 327-6402
Fax: (804) 444-1971

THOMPSON, Jason
Director, Investor Relations
jft6@meadwestvaco.com
Tel: (804) 201-2556

WILLKIE, II, Wendall L.
Senior Vice President, General Counsel and Secretary
Tel: (804) 327-5200

Meat and Livestock Australia

Meat & livestock Australia (MLA) is a producer-owned company providing marketing and, research and development services to over 47000 cattle, sheep and goat.
www.mla.com.au
Industry/ies: Animals; Food And Beverage Industry
Legislative Issues: ANI; TRD

Main Headquarters
Mailing: 1401 K St. NW
Suite 602
Washington, DC 20005
Tel: (202) 521-2551

Public Affairs and Related Activities Personnel

At Headquarters

DEBECK, Rachel
General Manager, Legal and Human Resources
Tel: (202) 521-2551

EDMONDS, Michael
General Manager, Global Marketing
Tel: (202) 521-2551

EDWARDS, Stephen K
Regional Manager
Tel: (202) 521-2551

FINUCAN, Michael
General Manager, International Markets
Tel: (202) 521-2551

HANSEN, Scott
Managing Director
Tel: (202) 521-2551

HELLWIG, Karen
General Manager, Industry Communication and Engagement
Tel: (202) 521-2551

PIETSCH, Paul
Tel: (202) 521-2551

PIETSCH, David
General Manager, Industry Communication and Engagement
Tel: (202) 521-2551

POTTS, Steve
Chief Operating Officer
Tel: (202) 521-2551

Mechanical Equipment Company, Inc.

Provides engineering solutions to industrial, utility, water/wastewater and commercial growth in the Carolinas.
www.mechequip.com
Annual Revenues: $18.00 million
Employees: 30
Industry/ies: Machinery/Equipment

President, Chief Executive Officer
FLETCHER, PE, Scott
sfletcher@mechequip.com
Tel: (864) 967-3420
Fax: (864) 963-4784

Main Headquarters
Mailing: P.O. Box 689
Matthews, NC 28106
Tel: (704) 847-2100
Fax: (704) 847-2349
TF: (877) 747-7136

Political Action Committees
Mechanical Equipment Company Inc. PAC
FEC ID: C00393884
Contact: Reano Siragusa
13189 Hwy. 190 West
Covington, LA 70433

Public Affairs and Related Activities Personnel

At Headquarters

GODSEY, Mike
Chief Financial Officer
Tel: (704) 847-2100
Fax: (704) 847-2349

At Other Offices

JOHNSON, Chadwick
Manager, Corporate Sales
P O Box 758, 510 Palmetto Dr.
Simpsonville, SC 29681
cjohnson@mechequip.com
Tel: (864) 967-3420
Fax: (864) 963-4784

SIRAGUSA, Reano
PAC Treasurer
1301 Industrial Dr.
Matthews, NC 28105
Tel: (704) 847-2100
Fax: (704) 847-2349

Mechanical Technology, Inc.

Brings new technologies to the markets of dimensional gauging, semiconductors and aviation. Involved in micro fuel cells and high-performance test and measurement instruments development through its subsidiaries.

www.mechtech.com
Annual Revenues: $6.90 million
Employees: 30
SIC: 3826; 3827; 3829
NAICS: 334516; 333314; 334519
Industry/ies: Machinery/Equipment

Chairman and Chief Executive Officer
LYNCH, Kevin G.
plim@mechtech.com
Tel: (518) 533-2200
Fax: (518) 533-2201

Main Headquarters
Mailing: 325 Washington Ave. Extension
Albany, NY 12205
Tel: (518) 218-2500
Fax: (518) 533-2201
TF: (800) 828-8210

Public Affairs and Related Activities Personnel

At Headquarters

JONES, Frederick W.
Vice-President and Chief Financial Officer
Tel: (518) 533-2200
Fax: (518) 533-2201

Meda Pharmaceuticals

Specializes in respiratory, allergy, central nervous system, and cough-cold products. Formerly known as MedPointe Inc. and previously Carter-Wallace, Inc. A subsidiary of Meda AB.
www.medapharma.us
Annual Revenues: $83.40 million
Employees: 700
Industry/ies: Pharmaceutical Industry
Legislative Issues: HCR; PHA

Main Headquarters
Mailing: 265 Davidson Ave.
Somerset, NJ 08873-4120
Tel: (732) 564-2200
Fax: (732) 564-2235

Corporate Foundations and Giving Programs
Meda Pharmaceuticals Contributions Program
265 Davidson Ave.
Suite 300
Somerset, NJ 08873-4120
Tel: (732) 564-2200
Fax: (732) 564-2235

Public Affairs and Related Activities Personnel

At Headquarters

HOSTLER, Jeffrey N.
Chief Financial Officer
Jhostler@medapharma.us
Tel: (732) 564-2331
Fax: (732) 564-2306

MedAssets

Performance improvement company, providing technology-enabled products and services for hospitals, health systems, non-acute healthcare providers, payers, and other service providers and product manufacturers.
www.medassets.com
Annual Revenues: $734.94 million
Employees: 3,350
Ticker: NASDAQ: MDAS
SIC: 7372
Industry/ies: Banking/Finance/Investments; Medicine/Health Care/Mental Health
Legislative Issues: HCR

Chairman and Chief Executive Officer
WISE, R. Halsey
Tel: (678) 323-2500
Fax: (678) 323-2501

Main Headquarters
Mailing: 100 N. Point Center., East
Suite 200
Alpharetta, GA 30022
Tel: (678) 323-2500
Fax: (678) 323-2501

Political Action Committees
MedAssets Inc. PAC
FEC ID: C00458380
Contact: Christopher K. Logsdon
200 North Point Center E
Suite 600
Alpharetta, GA 30022

> **Contributions to Candidates:** $3,700 (2015-2016)
> Democrats: $3,700

Corporate Foundations and Giving Programs
MedAssets Contributions Program
100 N. Point Center East
Suite 200
Alpharetta, GA 30022

Public Affairs and Related Activities Personnel

At Headquarters

BORCHERT, Robert
Senior Vice President, Investor Relations and Corporate Communications
rborchert@medassets.com
Tel: (678) 248-8194
Fax: (678) 323-2501

DONOHUE, Michael
Tel: (678) 323-2500

Senior Vice President, Chief Marketing Officer	Fax:	(678) 323-2501

GARNER, Charles O.
Executive Vice President, Chief Strategy & Transformation Officer
Tel: (678) 323-2500
Fax: (678) 323-2501

GLENN, Jonathan H.
Executive Vice President, Chief Legal Officer and Secretary
jglenn@medassets.com
Tel: (678) 323-2500
Fax: (678) 323-2501

NOLTE, Michael P.
Executive Vice President and Chief Operating Officer
Tel: (678) 323-2500
Fax: (678) 323-2501

SPINUZZI, Nicole
Senior Manager, Corporate Communications
nspinuzzi@medassets.com
Tel: (678) 966-2665
Fax: (678) 323-2501

At Other Offices

COLALUCA , Jr., Anthony
Executive Vice President and Chief Financial Officer
200 N. Point Center., East, Suite 400
Alpharetta, GA 30022
Tel: (678) 248-8200

HICKS, Keith
Senior Vice President and Chief People Officer
200 N. Point Center., East, Suite 400
Alpharetta, GA 30022
Tel: (678) 248-8200

LOGSDON, Christopher K.
Senior Vice President, Governance, Risk and Compliance
200 N. Point Center., East, Suite 400
Alpharetta, GA 30022
Tel: (678) 248-8200

Medcath Corporation

The company started the first stand-alone heart hospital in the US; owns and manages medical facilities specializing in cardiology and cardiovascular services.
phx.corporate-ir.net/phoenix.zhtml?c=129804
Employees: 415
Ticker: NASDAQ: MDTH
SIC: 8062
Industry/ies: Medicine/Health Care/Mental Health

President and Chief Executive Officer
CASEY, John T.
Tel: (704) 708-6600
Fax: (704) 708-5035

Main Headquarters
Mailing: 10800 Sikes Pl.
Suite 200
Charlotte, NC 28277
Tel: (704) 815-7700
Fax: (704) 708-5035

Public Affairs and Related Activities Personnel

At Headquarters

MCCANLESS, Joan
Senior Vice President, Chief Clinical & Compliance Officer
JOAN.MCCANLESS@MEDCATH.COM
Tel: (704) 708-6600
Fax: (704) 708-5035

PARKER, J. Arthur
Senior Vice President and Treasurer
Tel: (704) 708-6600
Fax: (704) 708-5035

RAMSEY, Lora
Chief Financial Officer
Tel: (704) 815-7700
Fax: (704) 708-5035

Media General, Inc.

Owns and Operates television stations. It offers consumers and advertisers premium quality entertainment and information, content and distribution on every screen.
www.mediageneral.com
Annual Revenues: $827.78 million
Employees: 5,300
Ticker: NYSE: MEG
SIC: 2711
Industry/ies: Communications; Media/Mass Communication

Chairman of the Board
BRYAN, III, J. Stewart
sbryan@mediageneral.com
Tel: (804) 649-6000
Fax: (804) 649-6865

President and Chief Executive Officer
SADUSKY, Vincent L.
Tel: (804) 649-6000
Fax: (804) 649-6066

Main Headquarters
Mailing: 333 E. Franklin St.
Richmond, VA 23219
Tel: (804) 649-6000
Fax: (804) 649-6066

Public Affairs and Related Activities Personnel

At Headquarters

CARINGTON, Andrew C.
Vice President, General Counsel and Secretary
Tel: (804) 649-6000
Fax: (804) 649-6066

DAVIS, Kimberly S.
Vice President, Human Resources
Tel: (804) 649-6000
Fax: (804) 649-6066

GUERTIN, Courtney
Director, Marketing & Communications
cguertin@mediageneral.com
Tel: (804) 649-6000
Fax: (804) 649-6066

MACPHERSON, Robert F.
Vice President, Corporate Human Resources
Tel: (804) 649-6000
Fax: (804) 649-6066

MCDERMOTT, Deborah A.
Tel: (804) 649-6000

Senior Vice President and Chief Operating Officer
Fax: (804) 649-6066

NABHAN, Lou Anne J.
Vice President and Director, Corporate Communications
Tel: (804) 649-6103
Fax: (804) 649-6066

WOODWARD, James F.
Vice President, Finance and Chief Financial Officer
Tel: (804) 649-6000
Fax: (804) 649-6066

Mediacom Communications Corporation

A local cable company with a nationwide fiber optic infrastructure to deliver a wide array of advanced products and services including digital cable TV, high-speed Internet and phone service.
mediacomcable.com
Annual Revenues: $1.46 billion
Employees: 4,500
Ticker: NASDAQ: MCCC
SIC: 4841
NAICS: 513220
Industry/ies: Communications; Telecommunications/Internet/Cable
Legislative Issues: TEC

Chairman of the Board and Chief Executive Officer
COMMISSO, Rocco B.
Tel: (845) 695-2600
Fax: (845) 695-2699

Main Headquarters
Mailing: One Mediacom Way
Mediacom Park
New York, NY 10918
Tel: (877) 847-6221

Political Action Committees
Mediacom Communications Corporation PAC
FEC ID: C00477737
Contact: Brian M. Walsh
One Mediacom Way
Mediacom Park, NY 10918
Tel: (845) 695-2600
Fax: (845) 695-2699

> **Contributions to Candidates:** $19,500 (2015-2016)
> Democrats: $2,000; Republicans: $17,500

Corporate Foundations and Giving Programs
Mediacom Communications Corporation contributions Program
100 Crystal Run Rd.
Middletown, NY 10941
Tel: (845) 695-2600
Fax: (845) 695-2600

Public Affairs and Related Activities Personnel

At Other Offices

GRIFFIN, Jack
Director, Corporate Finance
100 Crystal Run Rd.
Middletown, NY 10941
Tel: (845) 695-2654
Fax: (845) 695-2639

MCNAUGHTON, David M.
Senior Vice President, Marketing and Consumer Services
100 Crystal Run Rd.
Middletown, NY 10941
Tel: (845) 695-2600
Fax: (845) 695-2699

PASCARELLI, John G.
Executive Vice President, Operations
100 Crystal Run Rd.
Middletown, NY 10941
Tel: (845) 695-2600
Fax: (845) 695-2699

RAPPAPORT, Marvin S.
Contact, Government Relations
100 Crystal Run Rd.
Middletown, NY 10941
mrappaport@mediacomcc.com
Tel: (845) 695-2600
Fax: (845) 695-2669

STEPHAN, Mark E.
Executive Vice President and Chief Financial Officer
100 Crystal Run Rd.
Middletown, NY 10941
mstephan@mediacomcc.com
Tel: (845) 695-2640
Fax: (845) 695-2639

WALSH, Brian M.
Senior Vice President, Corporate Controller and PAC Treasurer
100 Crystal Run Rd.
Middletown, NY 10941
Tel: (845) 695-2600
Fax: (845) 695-2699

WEINAND, Italia Commisso
Senior Vice President, Programming and Human Resources
100 Crystal Run Rd.
Middletown, NY 10941
Tel: (845) 695-2600
Fax: (845) 695-2699

YOUNG, Joseph E.
Senior Vice President, General Counsel and Secretary
100 Crystal Run Rd.
Middletown, NY 10941
Tel: (845) 695-2600
Fax: (845) 695-2699

Medical Management International, Inc. dba Banfield the Pet Hospital

A veterinary medical services provider.
www.banfield.net
Employees: 7,000
Industry/ies: Animals
Legislative Issues: ANI

President and Chief Executive Officer
BRADLEY, Vincent

Tel: (503) 256-7299
Fax: (503) 922-6000

Main Headquarters
Mailing: 8000 N.E. Tillamook
P.O. Box 13998
Portland, OR 97213-0998

Tel: (503) 256-7299
Fax: (503) 922-6000
TF: (866) 894-7927

Corporate Foundations and Giving Programs
Banfield Charitable Trust
Contact: Paul Lipscomb
8000 NE Tillamook
P.O. Box 13998
Portland, OR 97213

Tel: (503) 922-5801
Fax: (503) 922-6801

Public Affairs and Related Activities Personnel

At Headquarters

FREEMAN, Phil
Senior Vice President and Chief Financial Officer

Tel: (503) 256-7299
Fax: (503) 922-6000

LIPSCOMB, Paul
Interim Executive Director

Tel: (503) 256-7299
Fax: (503) 922-6000

MONETTI, Marta
Senior Vice President, Corporate Affairs

Tel: (503) 256-7299
Fax: (503) 922-6000

TAAFFE, Jeannine
Senior Vice President, Marketing, Sales and Product Management

Tel: (503) 256-7299
Fax: (503) 922-6000

Medical Mutual of Ohio

A health insurance company which operates for the benefit of our members without needing to meet the demands of stockholders or Wall Street analysts and develops products and services that allows to better serve customers and the communities around us and help our members achieve their best possible health and quality of life.
www.medmutual.com
Annual Revenues: $2.08 billion
Employees: 2,500
Industry/ies: Medicine/Health Care/Mental Health

President and Chief Executive Officer
CHIRICOSTA, Rick

Tel: (216) 687-7000
Fax: (216) 687-2623

Main Headquarters
Mailing: 2060 E. Ninth St.
Cleveland, OH 44115

Tel: (216) 687-7000
Fax: (216) 687-2623
TF: (800) 700-2583

Corporate Foundations and Giving Programs
Medical Mutual of Ohio Charitable Foundation
Contact: Douglas Bennett
2060 E. Ninth St.
Cleveland, OH 44115

Public Affairs and Related Activities Personnel

At Headquarters

BENNETT, Douglas
Director, Community Relations and Outreach

Tel: (216) 687-7000
Fax: (216) 687-2623

BYERS, Ed
Manager, Media Relations
Ed.Byers@MedMutual.com

Tel: (216) 687-7000
Fax: (216) 687-2623

CHANEY, Jared
Chief Marketing and Communications Officer
jared.chaney@mmoh.com

Tel: (216) 687-7000
Fax: (216) 687-2623

DUGAN, Patrick
Chief Legal Officer and Executive Vice President

Tel: (216) 687-7000
Fax: (216) 687-2623

GIBBONS, Jr., Joseph F.
Vice President, Government Relations

Tel: (216) 687-7000
Fax: (216) 687-2623

GREENE, Thomas E.
Vice President, Human Resources

Tel: (216) 687-7000
Fax: (216) 687-2623

LARKINS, Steffany
Executive Vice President, Chief of Staff and Chief Diversity Officer

Tel: (216) 687-7000
Fax: (216) 687-2623

MUELLER , Ray
Executive Vice President and Chief Financial Officer

Tel: (216) 687-7000
Fax: (216) 687-2623

OLSON, Don
Director, Corporate Communications

Tel: (216) 687-7000
Fax: (216) 687-2623

PARENT, Joe
Vice President, Strategic Planning and Expansion

Tel: (216) 687-7000
Fax: (216) 687-2623

TAYLOR, Sue M.
Executive Vice President and Chief Experience Officer

Tel: (216) 687-7000
Fax: (216) 687-2623

Medical Planning Resources, Inc. (MPR)

www.mpr-inc.com
Industry/ies: Medicine/Health Care/Mental Health

Main Headquarters
Mailing: 24 E. Wood Dr.
Highland, NJ 08520

Fax: (800) 641-0179

Public Affairs and Related Activities Personnel

At Headquarters

COWAN, Edward
Senior Associate

Tel: (609) 944-9458
Fax: (800) 641-0179

Medical Savings Insurance Company

Industry/ies: Insurance Industry

Main Headquarters
Mailing: 5835 W. 47th St.
Indianapolis, IN 42678

Tel: (202) 531-2553

Public Affairs and Related Activities Personnel

At Headquarters

MCMANUS, Brian
Vice President, Government Relations
brianfmcmanus@yahoo.com

Tel: (202) 531-2553

ROONEY, J. Patrick

Tel: (202) 531-2553

The Medicines Company

A pharmaceutical manufacturer.
www.themedicinescompany.com
Annual Revenues: $673.69 million
Employees: 727
Ticker: NASDAQ: MDCO
SIC: 2834
Industry/ies: Pharmaceutical Industry
Legislative Issues: HCR

Chairman of the Board and Chief Executive Officer
MEANWELL, MD, PhD, Clive A.

Tel: (973) 656-1616
Fax: (972) 656-9898

Main Headquarters
Mailing: Eight Sylvan Way
Parsippany, NJ 07054

Tel: (972) 290-6000
Fax: (973) 656-9898
TF: (800) 388-1183

Political Action Committees
Medicines Company PAC
FEC ID: C00456251
Contact: Paul M. Antinori
Eight Sylvan Way
Parsippany, NJ 07054

Contributions to Candidates: $3,000 (2015-2016)
Republicans: $3,000

Public Affairs and Related Activities Personnel

At Headquarters

ANTINORI, Paul M.
General Counsel

Tel: (973) 656-1616
Fax: (972) 656-9898

LAVERTY, Bob
Contact, Corporate Communications
Robert.Laverty@themedco.com

Tel: (973) 290-6162
Fax: (973) 656-9898

MITCHELL, Michael
Head, Global Communications

Tel: (973) 290-6097
Fax: (973) 656-9898

RODIN, Stephen
Senior Vice President and General Counsel

Tel: (972) 290-6000
Fax: (973) 656-9898

SBLENDORIO, MBA, Glenn
President and Chief Financial Officer

Tel: (972) 290-6000
Fax: (973) 656-9898

VISIOLI, Christopher
Vice President, Business Development

Tel: (972) 290-6000
Fax: (973) 656-9898

Medicis Pharmaceutical Corporation

Medicis Pharmaceutical Corporation.
www.medicis.com
Annual Revenues: $7.21 billion
Employees: 600
Ticker: NYSE: MRX
SIC: 2834
Industry/ies: Pharmaceutical Industry

Chairman and Chief Executive Officer
SHACKNAI, Jonah

Tel: (602) 808-8800
Fax: (602) 808-0822

Main Headquarters
Mailing: 7720 N. Dobson Rd.
Scottsdale, AZ 85256

Tel: (602) 808-8800
Fax: (602) 808-0822

Public Affairs and Related Activities Personnel

At Headquarters

IPPOLITO, Vincent
Executive Vice President, Sales and Marketing

Tel: (602) 808-8800
Fax: (602) 808-0822

PETERSON, Richard D.
Executive Vice President, Chief Financial Officer and Treasurer

Tel: (602) 808-8800
Fax: (602) 808-0822

RODNER, Seth L.

Tel: (602) 808-8800
Fax: (602) 808-0822

Executive Vice President, Chief Legal Officer and Corporate Secretary

MedImmune, Inc.
A biotechnology company.
www.medimmune.com
Employees: 6,000
Ticker: Nasdaq: MEDI
SIC: 2836
Industry/ies: Medicine/Health Care/Mental Health; Science; Scientific Research

Main Headquarters
Mailing: One MedImmune Way   Tel: (301) 398-0000
Gaithersburg, MD 20878   Fax: (301) 398-9000

Washington Office
Mailing: 1350 I St. NW
Suite 440
Washington, DC 20005

Political Action Committees
Medimmune Inc Employee Political Awareness Committee (Medimmune PAC)
FEC ID: C00399725
Contact: Linda Murakami
One MedImmune Way   Tel: (301) 398-4715
Gaithersburg, MD 20878   Fax: (301) 398-9715

Corporate Foundations and Giving Programs
Medimmune Contributions Program
One MedImmune Way
Gaithersburg, MD 20878

Public Affairs and Related Activities Personnel

At Headquarters

BELL, Matt   Tel: (301) 398-0000
Chief Operating Officer   Fax: (301) 398-9000

BRADY, MBA, CPA, CFE, Jim   Tel: (301) 398-0000
Vice President, Finance   Fax: (301) 398-9000

ELLIOT, Kinn   Tel: (301) 398-0000
National Sales Director, Public Health   Fax: (301) 398-9000

JALLAL, PhD, Bahija   Tel: (301) 398-0000
Vice President   Fax: (301) 398-9000

MURAKAMI, Linda   Tel: (301) 398-0000
PAC Treasurer   Fax: (301) 398-9000

O'BRIEN, Mike   Tel: (301) 398-0000
Global Head, Corporate Communications   Fax: (301) 398-9000
ObrienM@medimmune.com

ROSSIN, Tracy   Tel: (301) 398-1468
Head, Corporate Affairs   Fax: (301) 398-9000
rossint@medimmune.com

Medline Industries Inc.
A manufacturer and distributor of medical and surgical supplies.
www.medline.com
Employees: 7,500
SIC: 3841; 2834; 3081; 3089; 3842
Industry/ies: Machinery/Equipment; Medicine/Health Care/Mental Health

Chief Executive Officer   Tel: (847) 949-5500
MILLS, Charles N.   Fax: (800) 351-1512

Main Headquarters
Mailing: One Medline Pl.   Tel: (847) 949-5500
Mundelein, IL 60060   Fax: (800) 351-1512
   TF: (800) 633-5463

Corporate Foundations and Giving Programs
Medline Industries Inc. Contribution Program
One Medline Pl.   Tel: (847) 949-5500
Mundelein, IL 60060   Fax: (800) 351-1512

Public Affairs and Related Activities Personnel

At Headquarters

ABRAMS, Jim   Tel: (847) 949-5500
Chief Operating Officer   Fax: (800) 351-1512

PANAGIOTAKAKOS, Vivika   Tel: (847) 643-3311
Manager, Media Relations   Fax: (800) 351-1512

MedPointe Inc.
See listing on page 526 under Meda Pharmaceuticals

Medrad, Inc.
Worldwide market leader of medical devices and services that enable or enhance diagnostic and therapeutic imaging procedures.
www.medrad.com
Annual Revenues: $141.00 million
Employees: 1,200
NAICS: 339113
Industry/ies: Medicine/Health Care/Mental Health

President and Chief Executive Officer   Tel: (724) 940-6800
LIANG, Samuel M.   Fax: (412) 767-4120

Main Headquarters
Mailing: 100 Global View Dr.   Tel: (724) 940-6800
Warrendale, PA 15086   Fax: (412) 767-4120
   TF: (800) 633-7231

Corporate Foundations and Giving Programs
Medrad Contributions Program
100 Global View Dr.   Tel: (724) 940-6800
Warrendale, PA 15086   Fax: (412) 767-4120

Public Affairs and Related Activities Personnel

At Headquarters

COLETTI, Julie   Tel: (724) 940-6800
Chief Legal Counsel and Corporate Secretary   Fax: (412) 767-4120

HAVRILLA, Joseph   Tel: (724) 940-6800
Chief Technology and Strategy Officer and Senior Vice President, Corporate Development   Fax: (412) 767-4120

RADERMACHER, Luanne   Tel: (724) 940-6800
Director, Corporate Affairs   Fax: (412) 767-4120
lradermacher@medrad.com

MedStar Health, Inc.
MedStar Health is a non-profit healthcare organization.
www.medstarhealth.org
Employees: 24,000
Industry/ies: Medicine/Health Care/Mental Health
Legislative Issues: BUD

President and Chief Executive Officer   Tel: (410) 772-6500
SAMET, Kenneth A.   Fax: (410) 715-3905
kenneth.a.samet@medstar.net

Main Headquarters
Mailing: 5565 Sterrett Pl.   Tel: (410) 772-6500
Fifth Floor   Fax: (410) 715-3905
Columbia, MD 21044   TF: (877) 772-6505

Corporate Foundations and Giving Programs
MedStar Health Contributions Program
Contact: Bruce A. Bartoo
5565 Sterrett Pl.   Tel: (410) 772-6500
Fifth Floor   Fax: (410) 715-3905
Columbia, MD 21044

Public Affairs and Related Activities Personnel

At Headquarters

BARTOO, Bruce A.   Tel: (410) 772-6500
Senior Vice President and Chief Philanthropy Officer   Fax: (410) 715-3905
bruce.bartoo@medstar.net

BRYAN, Joel N.   Tel: (410) 772-6500
Vice President, Treasurer   Fax: (410) 715-3905

CASLOW, Diane   Tel: (410) 772-6500
Vice President, Strategic and Business Planning   Fax: (410) 715-3905

CURRAN, Michael J.   Tel: (410) 772-6500
Executive Vice President, Chief Administrative and Financial Officer   Fax: (410) 715-3905

HITCHCOCK, Jean M.   Tel: (410) 772-6557
Vice President, Public Affairs and Marketing   Fax: (410) 715-3905
jean.hitchcock@medstar.net

JOHNSON, II, Oliver M.   Tel: (410) 772-6500
Executive Vice President and General Counsel   Fax: (410) 715-3905

JOY DRASS, M.   Tel: (410) 772-6500
Executive Vice President and Chief Operating Officer   Fax: (410) 715-3905

MCCONAGHA, Jennie P.   Tel: (410) 772-6500
Chief of Staff and Vice President, Operational Communications   Fax: (410) 715-3905

NELSON, Susan K.   Tel: (410) 772-6500
Senior Vice President, Finance   Fax: (410) 715-3905

NOE, David P.   Tel: (410) 772-6500
Vice President, Human Resources   Fax: (410) 715-3905

NOE, David P.   Tel: (410) 772-6500
Vice President, Corporate Human Resources   Fax: (410) 715-3905

SMITH, Larry L.   Tel: (410) 772-6500
Vice President, Risk Management   Fax: (410) 715-3905

SWEARINGEN, Christine   Tel: (410) 772-6500
Executive Vice President, Planning, Marketing and Community Relations   Fax: (410) 715-3905

TOWNSEND, Pegeen   Tel: (410) 772-6500
Vice President, Government Affairs   Fax: (410) 715-3905

TOWNSEND, Pegeen   Tel: (410) 772-6500
Corporate Vice President, Government Affairs   Fax: (410) 715-3905
Pegeen.a.townsend@medstar.net

WAGNER, Eric R.	Tel:	(410) 772-6500
Executive Vice President, External Affairs and Diversified Operations	Fax:	(410) 715-3905
ZYLICH, Margery E.	Tel:	(410) 772-6500
Vice President, Operational Communications and Chief of Staff	Fax:	(410) 715-3905
E.Zylich@medstar.net		

Medtronic, Inc.

Medtronic develops and manufactures innovative medical device technology.
www.medtronic.com
Annual Revenues: $20.13 billion
Employees: 92,500
Ticker: NYSE: MDT
SIC: 3845
Industry/ies: Medicine/Health Care/Mental Health; Pharmaceutical Industry
Legislative Issues: AVI; COM; CPT; DEF; HCR; HOM; MMM; TAX; TRD

Executive Vice President and Chief Financial Officer, Chairman of the Board, Medtronic Foundation
ELLIS, Gary L.
gary.l.ellis@medtronic.com

Chairman of the Board and Chief Executive Officer	Tel:	(763) 514-4000
ISHRAK, Omar	Fax:	(763) 514-4879

Main Headquarters

Mailing:	710 Medtronic Pkwy.	Tel:	(763) 514-4000
	Mail Stop: L100	Fax:	(763) 514-4879
	Minneapolis, MN 55432-5604	TF:	(800) 633-8766

Washington Office
Mailing: 950 F St. NW
Suite 500
Washington, DC 20004

Political Action Committees
Medtronic Inc. PAC
FEC ID: C00311878
Contact: Gary L. Ellis

950 F St. NW	Tel:	(202) 393-0444
Suite 500		
Washington, DC 20004		

Contributions to Candidates: $214,500 (2015-2016)
Democrats: $90,500; Republicans: $124,000

Corporate Foundations and Giving Programs

The Medtronic Foundation
Contact: Dr. Jacob A. Gayle
710 Medtronic Pkwy.
Mail Stop L100
Minneapolis, MN 55432

Public Affairs and Related Activities Personnel

At Headquarters

GAYLE, Dr. Jacob A.	Tel:	(763) 514-4000
Vice President, Medtronic Philanthropy	Fax:	(763) 514-4879
LERMAN, Brad	Tel:	(763) 514-4000
Senior Vice President, General Counsel and Corporate Secretary	Fax:	(763) 514-4879
MARTHA, Geoffrey S.	Tel:	(763) 514-4000
Senior Vice President, Strategy and Business Development	Fax:	(763) 514-4879
PAGE, Heather Hudnut	Tel:	(763) 514-4000
Vice President, Global Marketing	Fax:	(763) 514-4879
RESMAN, Cindy	Tel:	(763) 505-0291
Director, Communications	Fax:	(763) 514-4879
cindy.resman@medtronic.com		
SCHUMACHER, Tom	Tel:	(763) 514-4000
Vice President, Global Chief Ethics and Compliance Officer	Fax:	(763) 514-4879
SHORT, Amee	Tel:	(202) 393-0444
Government Affairs Assistant	Fax:	(763) 514-4879
SURFACE, Carol A.	Tel:	(763) 514-4000
Senior Vice President and Chief Human Resources Officer	Fax:	(763) 514-4879
WARREN, Jeffrey	Tel:	(763) 505-2696
Vice President, Investor Relations	Fax:	(763) 514-4879
jeff.warren@medtronic.com		

At Washington Office

BATTAGLIA, Jessica
Director, Government Affairs
Registered Federal Lobbyist

GARZA, Rosemary
Associate Director, Federal Government Affairs
Registered Federal Lobbyist

PISANELLI, Kristina M.
Registered Federal Lobbyist

SCHOOLEY, Melissa Dodson

Senior Director, Government Affairs
melissa.d.schooley@medtronic.com
Registered Federal Lobbyist

SLONE, Peter B.
Vice President, Global Government Affairs

MegaPath Corporation

Provides integrated voice and data communications.
www.megapath.com
Employees: 1,000
SIC: 4813
Industry/ies: Communications; Computer/Technology; Telecommunications/Internet/Cable

Chairman of the Board and Chief Executive Officer	Tel:	(408) 952-6400
YOUNG, D. Craig	Fax:	(408) 952-7687

Main Headquarters

Mailing:	2510 Zanker Rd.	Tel:	(408) 952-6400
	San Jose, CA 95131	Fax:	(408) 952-7687
		TF:	(877) 611-6342

Washington Office
Mailing: 1750 K St. NW
Suite 200
Washington, DC 20006

Political Action Committees
MegaPath Corporation Political Action Committee
FEC ID: C00348276
Contact: Katherine Mudge

1835-B Kramer Ln.	Tel:	(202) 220-0400
Suite 100	Fax:	(202) 220-0401
Austin, TX 78758		

Public Affairs and Related Activities Personnel

At Headquarters

CHISHOLM, Steve	Tel:	(408) 952-6400
Senior Vice President, Business Development, Legal and Regulatory	Fax:	(408) 952-7687
FOSTER, Dan	Tel:	(408) 952-6400
Executive, Technology Services and Chief Revenue Officer	Fax:	(408) 952-7687
MILLEY, Paul	Tel:	(408) 952-6400
Chief Financial Officer	Fax:	(408) 952-7687
WELZ, Tony	Tel:	(703) 218-3555
Contact, Media Relations	Fax:	(408) 952-7687
Tony@w2comm.com		

At Other Offices

MUDGE, Katherine	Tel:	(512) 794-6000
PAC Contact		
1835-B Kramer Ln., Suite 100		
Austin, TX 78758		

Meijer Stores Limited Partnership

A privately owned retail store chain.
www.meijer.com
Employees: 72,200
Industry/ies: Retail/Wholesale

Co-Chairman and Chief Executive Officer	Tel:	(616) 453-6711
MEIJER, Hendrink G.	Fax:	(616) 791-2572
Co-Chairman	Tel:	(616) 453-6711
MEIJER, Doug	Fax:	(616) 791-2572

Main Headquarters

Mailing:	2929 Walker Ave. NW	Tel:	(616) 453-6711
	Grand Rapids, MI 49544	Fax:	(616) 791-2572
		TF:	(877) 363-4537

Public Affairs and Related Activities Personnel

At Headquarters

GUGLIELMI, Frank	Tel:	(734) 844-2781
Senior Director, Communications	Fax:	(616) 791-2572
frank.guglielmi@meijer.com		

Melvin Jones

See listing on page 818 under U.S. Jails & Prisons Forum, Inc.

Memphis Light, Gas and Water Division

A public utility company which meets the utility needs of Memphis and Shelby County residents by delivering reliable and affordable electricity, natural gas and water service.
www.mlgw.com
Employees: 3,000
Industry/ies: Energy/Electricity; Natural Resources; Utilities

Chairman of the Board	Tel:	(901) 544-6549
SISNETT , Derwin	Fax:	(901) 528-4758

President and Chief Executive Officer
COLLINS, Jerry
jcollins@mlgw.org
Tel: (901) 528-4011
Fax: (901) 528-4758

Main Headquarters
Mailing: 245 S. main st.
Memphis, TN 38101-0430
Tel: (901) 544-6549
Fax: (901) 528-4758

Corporate Foundations and Giving Programs
Memphis Light, Gas and Water Division Community and Public Education
Program
P.O. Box 430
Memphis, TN 38101-0430
Tel: (901) 528-4820
Fax: (901) 528-4758

Public Affairs and Related Activities Personnel

At Headquarters

CARSON, Gale Jones
Director, Corporate Communications
Tel: (901) 528-4011
Fax: (901) 528-4758

DEBERRY, Cliff
Director of Analysis, Strategy and Performance
Tel: (901) 544-6549
Fax: (901) 528-4758

GOODLOE, Von
Vice President, Human Resources
Tel: (901) 528-4011
Fax: (901) 528-4758

JEANES, Dana
Vice President, Chief Financial Officer, Secretary and Treasurer
Tel: (901) 544-6549
Fax: (901) 528-4758

MCELRATH, Roland
Controller
Tel: (901) 544-6549
Fax: (901) 528-4758

PATTERSON, Cheryl W.
Vice President and General Counsel
cpatterson@mlgw.org
Tel: (901) 528-4011
Fax: (901) 528-4758

WEAVER, Alonzo
Vice President of Engineering and Operations
Tel: (901) 544-6549
Fax: (901) 528-4758

The Men's Warehouse

A retailer of man's apparel.
www.menswearhouse.com
Employees: 18,600
Ticker: NYSE: MW
Industry/ies: Apparel/Textiles Industry; Retail/Wholesale

Vice Chairman of the Board
EDWAB, David
Tel: (281) 776-7000
Fax: (281) 776-7038

President and Chief Executive Officer
EWERT, Douglas S.
Tel: (281) 776-7200
Fax: (281) 776-7038

Main Headquarters
Mailing: 6380 Rogerdale Rd.
Houston, TX 77072
Tel: (281) 776-7000
Fax: (281) 776-7038
TF: (800) 851-6744

Corporate Foundations and Giving Programs
The Men's Warehouse Contribution Program
6380 Rogerdale Rd.
Houston, TX 77072
Tel: (281) 776-7200
Fax: (281) 776-7038

Public Affairs and Related Activities Personnel

At Headquarters

KIMMINS, Jon W.
Executive Vice President, Chief Financial Officer and Treasurer
Tel: (281) 776-7000
Fax: (281) 776-7038

Menasha Corporation

A private company offering packaging, logistics, and marketing services.
www.menasha.com
Employees: 4,000
NAICS: 322211
Industry/ies: Advertising And Marketing

Chairman of the Board
SHEPHARD, III, Donald C.
Tel: (920) 751-1000
Fax: (920) 751-1236

President and Chief Executive Officer
KOTEK, James M.
Tel: (920) 751-1000
Fax: (920) 751-1236

Main Headquarters
Mailing: 1645 Bergstrom Rd.
Neenah, WI 54956
Tel: (920) 751-1000
Fax: (920) 751-1236
TF: (800) 558-5073

Corporate Foundations and Giving Programs
Menasha Corporation Foundation
1645 Bergstrom Rd.
Neenah, WI 54956
Tel: (920) 751-1000
Fax: (920) 751-1000

Public Affairs and Related Activities Personnel

At Headquarters

FANTINI, Rick J.
Vice President, Human Resources
Tel: (920) 751-1000
Fax: (920) 751-1236

FOGARTY, Mark P.
Vice President, General Counsel and Corporate Secretary
Tel: (920) 751-1000
Fax: (920) 751-1236

HAMMEN, Lea Ann
Vice President, Treasurer
Tel: (920) 751-1000
Fax: (920) 751-1236

PRITZ, Evan
Vice President, Corporate Development
Tel: (920) 751-1000
Fax: (920) 751-1236

RETTLER, Thomas M.
Senior Vice President and Chief Financial Officer
Tel: (920) 751-1015
Fax: (920) 751-1236

WHITTON, Nancy
Director, Corporate Communications
nancy.whitton@menasha.com
Tel: (920) 751-1015
Fax: (920) 751-1236

Menssana Research, Inc.

A developer of advanced new breath tests for detection of disease.
www.menssanaresearch.com
Employees: 7
Industry/ies: Medicine/Health Care/Mental Health

Founder and Chief Executive Officer
PHILLIPS, FACP, MD, Michael
mphillips@menssanaresearch.com
Tel: (201) 886-7004
Fax: (201) 886-7004

Main Headquarters
Mailing: One Horizon Rd.
Suite 1415
Ft. Lee, NJ 07024-6510
Tel: (201) 886-7004
Fax: (201) 886-7004

Public Affairs and Related Activities Personnel

At Headquarters

PHILLIPS, Linda
Contact, Human Resources
Tel: (201) 886-7004
Fax: (201) 886-7004

PHILLIPS, Jonah
Contact, Sales and Regulatory and Product Development Coordinator
Tel: (201) 886-7004
Fax: (201) 886-7004

Mentor Graphics Corporation

Markets and designs electronic software.
www.mentor.com
Annual Revenues: $1.14 billion
Employees: 5,700
Ticker: NASDAQ: MENT
SIC: 7373
Industry/ies: Electricity & Electronics; Electronics; Energy/Electricity; Science; Scientific Research

Chairman of the Board and Chief Executive Officer
RHINES, Walden C.
Tel: (503) 685-7000
Fax: (503) 685-7704

Main Headquarters
Mailing: 8005 S.W. Boeckman Rd.
Wilsonville, OR 97070
Tel: (503) 685-7000
Fax: (503) 685-1204
TF: (800) 592-2210

Corporate Foundations and Giving Programs
Mentor Graphics Foundation
8005 S.W. Boeckman Rd.
Wilsonville, OR 97070
Tel: (503) 685-7000

Public Affairs and Related Activities Personnel

At Headquarters

DERRICK, Brian
Vice President, Corporate Marketing
Tel: (503) 685-7000
Fax: (503) 685-7704

FREED, Dean
Vice President and General Counsel
Tel: (503) 685-7000
Fax: (503) 685-7704

GRAHAM, Suzanne
Senior Manager, Public Relations
suzanne_graham@mentor.com
Tel: (503) 685-7789
Fax: (503) 685-7704

REINHART, Joe
Vice President, Corporate Development and Investor Relations
joe_reinhart@mentor.com
Tel: (503) 685-1250
Fax: (503) 685-7704

SALE, Paul
Chief Human Resources Officer
Tel: (503) 685-7000
Fax: (503) 685-1204

TREBING, Richard
Vice President, Finance and Chief Accounting Officer
Tel: (503) 685-7000
Fax: (503) 685-1204

Mercedes-Benz USA LLC

Company imports and distributes Mercedes-Benz cars, and provides other services through dealerships. A subsidiary of Daimler AG.
www.mbusa.com
Annual Revenues: $67.70 million
Employees: 1,600
SIC: 7389
Industry/ies: Automotive Industry; Transportation

Main Headquarters
Mailing: One Mercedes Dr.
P.O. Box 350
Montvale, NJ 07645
Tel: (201) 573-0600
Fax: (201) 573-0117
TF: (800) 367-6372

Washington Office

Mailing:	1717 Pennsylvania Ave. NW	Tel:	(202) 649-4511
	Suite 825		
	Washington, DC 20006		

Corporate Foundations and Giving Programs

Mercedes-Benz USA Contributions Program
Three Mercedes Dr. Tel: (201) 573-0600
Montvale, NJ 07645

Public Affairs and Related Activities Personnel

At Headquarters

BOLAND, Donna Tel: (201) 573-6893
Manager, Corporate Communications Fax: (201) 476-2875
bolandd@mbusa.com

WERNER, Herbert Tel: (201) 573-0600
Vice President, Finance / Chief Financial Officer / Fax: (201) 573-0117
Controlling

At Washington Office

ALBERT, Cynthia Tel: (202) 649-4511
Coordinator, Political Programs
cynthia.albert@daimler.com

FOUST, Joanna Tel: (202) 649-4511
General Manager, Federal Affairs

JONES, Jake Tel: (202) 649-4511
Executive Director, External Affairs & Public Policy

Merck & Company

A pharmaceutical company. In March 2009, Merck announced the acquisition of Schering-Plough. Merck spun off Medco Health Solutions, Inc. (see separate listing) as a separate independent company in August, 2003.
www.merck.com
Annual Revenues: $41.40 billion
Employees: 70,000
Ticker: NYSE: MRK
SIC: 2834
NAICS: 325412
Industry/ies: Pharmaceutical Industry
Legislative Issues: ANI; BUD; CPT; HCR; HOM; MMM; PHA; TAX; TRD; VET

Chairman of the Board, President and Chief Executive Officer Tel: (908) 423-1000
FRAZIER, Kenneth C. Fax: (908) 735-1253

Main Headquarters

Mailing: 2000 Galloping Hill Rd. Tel: (908) 740-4000
Kenilworth, NJ 07003

Washington Office

Mailing: 1700 Rockville Pike, Suite 525
Rockville, MD 20852

Political Action Committees

Merck & Company Inc.
FEC ID: C00097485
Contact: Graeme Bell MBA
601 Pennsylvania Ave. NW, Suite 1200 Tel: (202) 638-4170
North Bldg. Fax: (202) 638-3670
Washington, DC 20004

Contributions to Candidates: $507,250 (2015-2016)
Democrats: $172,500; Republicans: $333,750; Other: $1,000

Principal Recipients

SENATE
BARRASSO, JOHN A (REP-WY)
BENNET, MICHAEL F (DEM-CO)
BLUNT, ROY (REP-MO)
CARPER, THOMAS R (DEM-DE)
CRAPO, MICHAEL D (REP-ID)
MURRAY, PATTY (DEM-WA)
PORTMAN, ROB (REP-OH)
SCOTT, TIMOTHY E (REP-SC)
THUNE, JOHN (REP-SD)

HOUSE
BOEHNER, JOHN A. (REP-OH)
LANCE, LEONARD (REP-NJ)
MCCARTHY, KEVIN (REP-CA)
MEEHAN, PATRICK L. MR. (REP-PA)
RYAN, PAUL D. (REP-WI)
SCALISE, STEVE MR. (REP-LA)

Corporate Foundations and Giving Programs

The Merck Company Foundation
Contact: Brenda Colatrella
One Merck Dr.
P.O. Box 100
Whitehouse Station, NJ 08889

Public Affairs and Related Activities Personnel

At Headquarters

CAREY, USN (Ret.), Rr. Adm. James Tel: (908) 740-4000
Registered Federal Lobbyist

KRISHNAMOORTHY, Jenelle S. Tel: (908) 740-4000
Registered Federal Lobbyist

At Other Offices

ADAMS, Victoria Tel: (202) 638-4170
Director, Political Programs Fax: (202) 638-3670
601 Pennsylvania Ave. NW, North Bldg., Suite 1200
Washington, DC 20004

BELL, MBA, Graeme Tel: (202) 638-4170
Contact, U.S. Markets, Vice President, PAC Contact and Fax: (202) 638-3670
Head, Finance
601 Pennsylvania Ave. NW, North Bldg., Suite 1200
Washington, DC 20004

BLAND, Jennifer Hawks Tel: (908) 423-1000
Executive Director, Federal Government Relations and Fax: (908) 735-1253
Counsel
One Merck Dr., P.O. Box 100
Whitehouse Station, NJ 08889-0100

BROWN, Tammie Tel: (908) 423-1000
One Merck Dr., P.O. Box 100 Fax: (908) 735-1253
Whitehouse Station, NJ 08889-0100
Registered Federal Lobbyist

COLATRELLA, Brenda Tel: (908) 423-2042
Executive Director, Corporate Responsibility Fax: (908) 735-1253
One Merck Dr., P.O. Box 100
Whitehouse Station, NJ 08889-0100

DARLING, Erin L. Tel: (202) 638-4170
Contact, Government Relations Fax: (202) 638-3670
601 Pennsylvania Ave. NW, North Bldg., Suite 1200
Washington, DC 20004
Registered Federal Lobbyist

DAVIS, Robert M. Tel: (908) 423-1000
Executive Vice President and Chief Financial Officer Fax: (908) 735-1253
One Merck Dr., P.O. Box 100
Whitehouse Station, NJ 08889-0100

FERGUSON, Carol Tel: (908) 423-4465
Contact, Invester Relations Fax: (908) 735-1253
One Merck Dr., P.O. Box 100
Whitehouse Station, NJ 08889-0100

FILIPPONE, Robert Tel: (202) 638-4170
Vice President, U.S. Policy and Government Relations Fax: (202) 638-3670
601 Pennsylvania Ave. NW, North Bldg., Suite 1200
Washington, DC 20004
Registered Federal Lobbyist

GRADDICK-WEIR, Mirian M. Tel: (908) 423-1000
Executive Vice President, Human Resources Fax: (908) 735-1253
One Merck Dr., P.O. Box 100
Whitehouse Station, NJ 08889-0100

GREZLAK, PhD, Charles Tel: (202) 638-4170
Vice President, Government Affairs and Policy Fax: (202) 638-3670
601 Pennsylvania Ave. NW, North Bldg., Suite 1200
Washington, DC 20004

HOLSTON, Michael J. Tel: (908) 423-1000
Executive Vice President, Legal Fax: (908) 735-1253
One Merck Dr., P.O. Box 100
Whitehouse Station, NJ 08889-0100

JOSEPH, Eli Tel: (908) 423-1000
Senior Director, Federal Policy and Government Relations Fax: (908) 735-1253
One Merck Dr., P.O. Box 100
Whitehouse Station, NJ 08889-0100

KUHLIK, Bruce N. Tel: (908) 423-1000
Executive Vice President and General Counsel Fax: (908) 735-1253
One Merck Dr., P.O. Box 100
Whitehouse Station, NJ 08889-0100

LAPPETITO, Caroline Tel: (267) 305-7639
Director, Global Media Relations Fax: (908) 735-1253
One Merck Dr., P.O. Box 100
Whitehouse Station, NJ 08889-0100

MCMAHON, Robert Tel: (908) 423-1000
President, US Market Fax: (908) 735-1253
One Merck Dr., P.O. Box 100
Whitehouse Station, NJ 08889-0100

MICHEL, Laurie L. Tel: (202) 638-4170
Senior Director, Counsel, Federal Policy and Government Fax: (202) 638-3670
Relations
601 Pennsylvania Ave. NW, North Bldg., Suite 1200
Washington, DC 20004
Registered Federal Lobbyist

OPPENHEIM, Katie Tel: (202) 638-4170
Executive Director, U.S. Policy & Government Relations Fax: (202) 638-3670
601 Pennsylvania Ave. NW, North Bldg., Suite 1200

Washington, DC 20004
Registered Federal Lobbyist

POLAK, Erin	Tel:	(908) 423-1000
Manager, Political Programs	Fax:	(908) 735-1253

One Merck Dr., P.O. Box 100
Whitehouse Station, NJ 08889-0100
Registered Federal Lobbyist

ROGERS, Ronald	Tel:	(908) 423-6449
Lead, Corporate Communications, Financial Media Relations,	Fax:	(908) 735-1253

Social Media, Litigation Communications
One Merck Dr., P.O. Box 100
Whitehouse Station, NJ 08889-0100
ronald.rogers@merck.com

SPATZ, Ian D.	Tel:	(202) 638-4170
Vice President, Public Policy	Fax:	(202) 638-3670

601 Pennsylvania Ave. NW, North Bldg., Suite 1200
Washington, DC 20004
Registered Federal Lobbyist

STEPHEN , Propper	Tel:	(202) 638-4170
Assistant Treasurer	Fax:	(202) 638-3670

601 Pennsylvania Ave. NW, North Bldg., Suite 1200
Washington, DC 20004

Merck Vaccine Division

See listing on page 532 under Merck & Company

Mercury Computer Systems, Inc.

The company makes real-time digital signal processing (DSP) systems for the homeland security, military/aerospace, and telecommunications markets.Provides specialized, high-performance computing systems and software designed for complex HPC and embedded applications.
www.mrcy.com
Annual Revenues: $224.41 million
Employees: 641
Ticker: NASDAQ: MRCY
SIC: 3670; 3571
Industry/ies: Computer/Technology
Legislative Issues: DEF

Chairman of the Board	Tel:	(978) 256-1300
VITTO, Vincent	Fax:	(978) 256-3599

President and Chief Executive Officer	Tel:	(978) 256-1300
ASLETT, Mark	Fax:	(978) 256-3599

maslett@mc.com

Main Headquarters

Mailing:	201 Riverneck Rd.	Tel:	(978) 256-1300
	Chelmsford, MA 01824	Fax:	(978) 256-3599
		TF:	(866) 627-6951

Political Action Committees
Mercury Computer Systems Inc. PAC
FEC ID: C00518894
Contact: Kevin M. Bisson
201 Riverneck Rd.
Chelmsford, MA 01824

Corporate Foundations and Giving Programs
Mercury Computer Systems Contributions Program

199 Riverneck Rd.	Tel:	(978) 256-1300
Chelmsford, MA 01824	Fax:	(978) 256-3599

Public Affairs and Related Activities Personnel

At Headquarters

BISSON, Kevin M.	Tel:	(978) 256-1300
PAC Contact, Senior Vice President, Chief Financial Officer and Treasurer	Fax:	(978) 256-3599

HAINES II, Gerald M.	Tel:	(978) 256-1300
Executive Vice President, Chief Financial Officer and Treasurer	Fax:	(978) 256-3599

ghaines@mc.com

MCGRAIL, Bob	Tel:	(978) 967-1366
Director, Corporate Communications	Fax:	(978) 256-0852

rmcgrail@mc.com

RUPPERT, Michael	Tel:	(978) 256-1300
Senior Vice President, Strategy and Corporate Development	Fax:	(978) 256-3599

SPEICHER, Charles A.	Tel:	(978) 256-1300
Vice President, Controller and Chief Accounting Officer	Fax:	(978) 256-3599

Meredith Corporation

A publicly held media and marketing services company founded upon serving our customers and committed to building value for our shareholders.
www.meredith.com
Annual Revenues: $1.64 billion
Employees: 3,700
Ticker: NYSE: MDP

SIC: 2721; 2791; 2796
NAICS: 511120
Industry/ies: Advertising And Marketing; Communications; Media/Mass Communication

Chairman of the Board and Chief Executive Officer	Tel:	(515) 284-3000
LACY, Stephen M.	Fax:	(515) 284-2700

Main Headquarters

Mailing:	1716 Locust St.	Tel:	(515) 284-3000
	Des Moines, IA 50309-3023	Fax:	(515) 284-2700
		TF:	(800) 284-4236

Political Action Committees
Meredith Corporation Employees Fund for Better Government PAC
FEC ID: C00010520
Contact: Arthur J. Slusark

1716 Locust St.	Tel:	(515) 284-2780
Des Moines, IA 50309		

Contributions to Candidates: $31,000 (2015-2016)
Democrats: $10,500; Republicans: $20,500

Corporate Foundations and Giving Programs
Meredith Foundation
Contact: Cheri Cipperley
1716 Locust St.
Des Moines, IA 50309

Public Affairs and Related Activities Personnel

At Headquarters

CERYANEC, Joseph H.	Tel:	(515) 284-3000
Vice President and Chief Financial Officer	Fax:	(515) 284-2700

CIPPERLEY, Cheri	Tel:	(515) 284-3000
Executive Assistant, Mell Meredith and Coordinator, Charitable Contributions	Fax:	(515) 284-2700

Cheri.Cipperley@meredith.com

FRAZIER, D. Mell Meredith	Tel:	(515) 284-2656
Chairman, Meredith Corporation Foundation	Fax:	(515) 284-3153

HADENFELDT, Jerry L.	Tel:	(515) 284-2780
Director, Government Relations	Fax:	(515) 284-2700

LOVELL, Mike	Tel:	(515) 284-3622
Director, Investor Relations	Fax:	(515) 284-2700

mike.lovell@meredith.com

SLUSARK, Arthur J.	Tel:	(515) 284-3404
Vice President, Chief Communications Officer and PAC Treasurer	Fax:	(515) 284-2700

art.slusark@meredith.com

ZIESER, John S.	Tel:	(515) 284-3000
Chief Development Officer and General Counsel	Fax:	(515) 284-2700

john.zeiser@meredith.com

Meridian Health

A not-for-profit health care organization.
www.meridianhealth.com
Employees: 14,100
Industry/ies: Medicine/Health Care/Mental Health

Chairperson	Tel:	(732) 751-7500
LITWIN, Gordon N.	Fax:	(732) 751-7541

President and Chief Executive Officer	Tel:	(732) 751-7500
LLOYD, FACHE, John K.	Fax:	(732) 751-7541

Main Headquarters

Mailing:	1350 Campus Pkwy.	Tel:	(732) 751-7500
	Neptune, NJ 07753	Fax:	(732) 751-7541
		TF:	(800) 560-9990

Corporate Foundations and Giving Programs
Meridian Health Affiliated Foundation
Contact: Deborah Allen

1350 Campus Pkwy.	Tel:	(732) 751-7500
Neptune, NJ 07753	Fax:	(732) 751-7541

Public Affairs and Related Activities Personnel

At Headquarters

ALLEN, Deborah	Tel:	(609) 978-3081
Foundation Executive Director	Fax:	(732) 751-7541

dallen@meridianhealth.com

BOARDWICK, Carrie L.	Tel:	(732) 751-5127
Director, Philanthropy Operations	Fax:	(732) 751-5130

cboardwick@meridianhealth.com

GAVZY, Ann B.	Tel:	(732) 751-7500
Senior Vice President, Legal Affairs and General Counsel	Fax:	(732) 751-7541

HAND, Richard	Tel:	(732) 751-7500
Vice President, Finance	Fax:	(732) 751-7541

MOLLOY, Russ	Tel:	(732) 751-7500
Vice President, Government Relations	Fax:	(732) 751-7541

rmolloy@meridianhealth.com

SCOTT, Chrisie A.
Vice President, Marketing and Corporate Communications
Tel: (732) 751-7500
Fax: (732) 751-7541

STRING, Sherrie
Senior Vice President, Human Resources
Tel: (732) 751-7500
Fax: (732) 751-7541

SWINNEY, Alvis R.
Senior Vice President Communications and Marketing
aswinney@meridianhealth.com
Tel: (732) 751-7500
Fax: (732) 751-7541

Meridian Investments Inc.

Meridian Investments, Inc. is a Broker/Dealer and a member of FINRA/SIPC, licensed to sell direct participation programs and other forms of securities.It is a national leader in placing corporate investors in the tax-advantaged investments codified by the IRS:.
www.meridianinvestments.com
Annual Revenues: $2.7 million
Industry/ies: Banking/Finance/Investments

Co-Founder, Chairman of the board and Chief Executive Officer
BOC, John F.
jboc@meridiancompaniesllc.com
Tel: (617) 328-6200
Fax: (617) 471-4624

Main Headquarters
Mailing: 1266 Furnace Brook Pkwy.
Fourth Floor
Quincy, MA 02169
Tel: (617) 328-6200
Fax: (617) 471-4624

Washington Office
Mailing: 10411 Motor City Dr.
Suite 302
Bethesda, MD 20817
Tel: (301) 983-5000
Fax: (301) 983-9012

Public Affairs and Related Activities Personnel

At Headquarters

BRILMAN, Roman
Vice President, Product Development
rbrilman@MeridianInvestments.com
Tel: (617) 328-6200
Fax: (617) 471-4624

MCDONOUGH, John
Executive Vice President, Chief Financial Officer and Chief Compliance Officer
jmcdonough@meridianinvestments.com
Tel: (617) 328-6200
Fax: (617) 471-4624

At Washington Office

CASEY, John P. "Jack"
Co-Founder, Vice-Chairman, Chief Operating Officer
jcasey@meridiancompaniesllc.com
Tel: (301) 983-5000
Fax: (301) 983-9012

Merit Medical Systems Inc.

Manufacturer of medical devices used in diagnostic & interventional cardiology & radiology.
www.merit.com
Annual Revenues: $509.69 million
Employees: 3,100
Ticker: NASDAQ: MMSI
SIC: 3841
NAICS: 339112
Industry/ies: Medicine/Health Care/Mental Health

Chairman and Chief Executive Officer
LAMPROPOULOS, Fred
Tel: (801) 253-1600
Fax: (801) 253-1652

Main Headquarters
Mailing: 1600 W. Merit Pkwy.
S. Jordan, UT 84095
Tel: (801) 253-1600
Fax: (801) 253-1652
TF: (800) 356-3748

Political Action Committees
Merit Medical Systems Inc Employee Good Governance PAC
FEC ID: C00475343
Contact: Greg Fredde
1600 Merit Pkwy.
S. Jordan, UT 84095

Contributions to Candidates: $51,500 (2015-2016)
Democrats: $8,000; Republicans: $43,500

Principal Recipients

HOUSE
LOVE, MIA (REP-UT)

Public Affairs and Related Activities Personnel

At Headquarters

FREDDE, Greg
Vice President, Government Affairs
Registered Federal Lobbyist
Tel: (801) 230-3365
Fax: (801) 253-1652

PERRY, Rashelle
Chief Legal Officer
Tel: (801) 253-1600
Fax: (801) 253-1652

STANGER, Kent
Chief Financial Officer, Secretary and Treasurer
Tel: (801) 253-1600
Fax: (801) 253-1652

STEPHENS, Martin
Executive Vice President, Sales and Marketing
Tel: (801) 253-1600
Fax: (801) 253-1652

WRIGHT, Anne-Marie
Tel: (801) 208-4167
Fax: (801) 253-1652

Vice President, Corporate Communications and Investor Relations Contact
awright@merit.com

Meritage Homes

A homebuilding company.
www.meritagehomes.com
Annual Revenues: $2.66 billion
Employees: 1,409
Ticker: NYSE: MTH
SIC: 1531
Industry/ies: Architecture And Design; Construction/Construction Materials

Chairman of the Board and Chief Executive Officer
HILTON, Steven J.
Tel: (480) 515-8100
Fax: (480) 998-9162

Main Headquarters
Mailing: 8800 E. Raintree Dr.
Suite 300
Scottsdale, AZ 85260
Tel: (480) 515-8100
Fax: (480) 998-9162
TF: (877) 275-6374

Political Action Committees
Meritage Homes Corporation PAC
FEC ID: C00494211
Contact: Hilla Sferruzza
8800 E. Raintree Dr.
Suite 300
Scottsdale, AZ 85260

Contributions to Candidates: $12,000 (2015-2016)
Democrats: $2,000; Republicans: $10,000

Public Affairs and Related Activities Personnel

At Headquarters

ANDERSON, Brent
Vice President, Investor and Media Relations
Brent.Anderson@meritagehomes.com
Tel: (972) 580-6360
Fax: (480) 998-9162

FELICIANO, Javier
Executive Vice President and Chief Human Resources Officer
Tel: (480) 515-8100
Fax: (480) 998-9162

LORD, Phillippe
Executive Vice President and Chief Operating Officer
Tel: (480) 515-8100
Fax: (480) 998-9162

SFERRUZZA, Hilla
Executive Vice President, Chief Financial Officer and PAC Treasurer
Tel: (480) 515-8100
Fax: (480) 998-9162

WHITE, Timothy C.
Executive Vice President, General Counsel and Secretary
tim.white@meritagehomes.com
Tel: (817) 237-7678
Fax: (480) 998-9162

Meritor, Inc.

Supplies components for light, medium and heavy-duty vehicles. Headquartered in Troy, MI., it is a leading global supplier of drive train, mobility, braking and aftermarket solutions for commercial vehicle and industrial markets.
www.meritor.com
Annual Revenues: $3.66 billion
Employees: 9,050
Ticker: NYSE: MTOR
SIC: 3714
NAICS: 336399; 333912; 334416
Industry/ies: Automotive Industry; Transportation

Executive Chairman
EVANS, Ivor J. "Ike"
Tel: (248) 435-1000
Fax: (248) 435-1393

Chief Executive Officer and President
CRAIG, Jeffrey A.
Tel: (248) 435-1000
Fax: (248) 435-1393

Main Headquarters
Mailing: 2135 W. Maple Rd.
Troy, MI 48084-7816
Tel: (248) 435-1000
Fax: (248) 435-1393
TF: (866) 463-6276

Political Action Committees
Meritor Inc PAC - Federal
FEC ID: C00506097
Contact: Carl Anderson
201 Townsend St.
Suite 900
Lansing, MI 48933

Corporate Foundations and Giving Programs
Meritor, Inc. Contribution Program
2135 W. Maple Rd.
Troy, MI 48084-7816
Tel: (248) 435-1000
Fax: (248) 435-1393

Public Affairs and Related Activities Personnel

At Headquarters

ANDERSON, Carl
Vice-President, Treasurer and PAC Treasurer
Tel: (248) 435-1000
Fax: (248) 435-1393

KILBORN, Cheryl
Director, Corporate Communications & Public Relations
cheryl.kilborn@meritor.com
Tel: (248) 435-1000
Fax: (248) 435-1393

NOWLAN, Kevin
Senior Vice President and Chief Financial Officer
Tel: (248) 435-1000
Fax: (248) 435-1393

OTT, Larry E.
Senior Vice President, Human Resources and and Communications
Tel: (248) 435-1000
Fax: (248) 435-1393

QUICK, Sandra
Senior Vice President, General Counsel and Corporate Secretary
Tel: (248) 435-1000
Fax: (248) 435-1393

SOHM (MCCLURE), Krista
Vice President, Communications
krista.sohm@arvinmeritor.com
Tel: (248) 435-1000
Fax: (248) 435-9946

Mesa Air Group Inc.

A regional airline.
www.mesa-air.com
Annual Revenues: $1.33 billion
Employees: 1,800
Ticker: NASDAQ: MESA
SIC: 4512
Industry/ies: Aerospace/Aviation; Transportation

Chairman of the Board and Chief Executive Officer
ORNSTEIN, Jonathan G.
Jonathan.Ornstein@Mesa-Air.com
Tel: (602) 685-4000
Fax: (602) 685-4350

Main Headquarters
Mailing: 410 N. 44th St.
Suite 700
Phoenix, AZ 85008
Tel: (602) 685-4000
Fax: (602) 685-4350

Political Action Committees
Mesa Air Group PAC
FEC ID: C00366534
Contact: Christopher Pappaioanou
410 N. 44th St.
Suite 700
Phoenix, AZ 84008
Tel: (602) 685-4000
Fax: (602) 685-4350

Corporate Foundations and Giving Programs
Mesa Angels Foundation
410 N. 44th St.
Suite 100
Phoenix, AZ 85008

Public Affairs and Related Activities Personnel

At Headquarters

BUTLER, David K.
Senior Vice President
david.butler@mesa-air.com
Tel: (602) 685-4000
Fax: (602) 685-4350

COX, Michelle R.
Director, Audit and Compliance
Tel: (602) 685-4000
Fax: (602) 685-4350

DURST, Jill R.
Controller
Tel: (602) 685-4000
Fax: (602) 685-4350

FERVERDA, Michael L.
Senior Vice President, Regulatory Compliance
Tel: (602) 685-4000
Fax: (602) 685-4350

FOLEY, Paul F.
Executive Vice President and Chief Operating Officer
Tel: (602) 685-4000
Fax: (602) 685-4350

GILLMAN, Brian S.
Executive Vice President, General Counsel and Secretary
Tel: (602) 685-4000
Fax: (602) 685-4350

LOTZ, Michael J.
President and Chief Financial Officer
michael.lotz@mesa-air.com
Tel: (602) 685-4000
Fax: (602) 685-4350

PAPPAIOANOU, Christopher
Senior Vice President, East Coast Operations
christopher.pappaioanou@mesa-air.com
Tel: (602) 685-4010
Fax: (602) 685-4350

SWIGART, James E.
Vice President Treasurer
Tel: (602) 685-4000
Fax: (602) 685-4350

WELLS, John E.
Director, Human Resource Operations
Tel: (602) 685-4000
Fax: (602) 685-4350

ZAPFE, Darren
Vice President, Finance
Tel: (602) 685-4000
Fax: (602) 685-4350

Messer Construction Corporation

Messer Construction Co. was founded seventy-nine years ago in Cincinnati, OH. The region offices include Cincinnati, Columbus, Dayton, Indianapolis, Lexington, Louisville, Knoxville, and Nashville.
www.messer.com
Employees: 900
Industry/ies: Construction/Construction Materials

Assistant to the Chairman
SPANGLER, Kim
kspangler@messer.com
Tel: (513) 242-1541
Fax: (513) 242-6467

President and Chief Executive Officer
KECKEIS, Thomas M.
Tel: (513) 242-1541
Fax: (513) 242-6467

Main Headquarters

Mailing: 5158 Fishwick Dr.
Cincinnati, OH 45216
Tel: (513) 242-1541
Fax: (513) 242-6467

Political Action Committees
Messer Construction Company PAC
FEC ID: C00435990
Contact: Bernard P. Suer
5158 Fishwick Dr.
Cincinnati, OH 45216
Tel: (513) 242-1541

Contributions to Candidates: $55,000 (2015-2016)
Democrats: $18,000; Republicans: $37,000

Corporate Foundations and Giving Programs
Messer Construction Foundation
Contact: Kim Spangler
5158 Fishwick Dr.
Cincinnati, OH 45216
Tel: (513) 242-1541
Fax: (513) 242-6467

Public Affairs and Related Activities Personnel

At Headquarters

HENSLEY, Richard A.
Vice President and Chief Information Officer
Tel: (513) 242-1541
Fax: (513) 242-6467

HITTER, Jr., E. Paul
Senior Vice President and Chief Financial Officer
Tel: (513) 242-1541
Fax: (513) 242-6467

WILLIAMSON, Tiffany D.
Director, Marketing and Corporate Communications
Tel: (513) 242-1541
Fax: (513) 242-6467

WITHAM, Tiffany D.
Director, Marketing and Communications
twitham@messer.com
Tel: (513) 242-1541
Fax: (513) 242-6467

Metaldyne Corporation

A provider of metal components. Formed from the merger of Mascotech, Simpson Industries and GMTI.
www.metaldyne.com
Employees: 4,000
SIC: 3469; 3714; 5051
NAICS: 332116; 336312; 336399
Industry/ies: Automotive Industry; Transportation

Main Headquarters
Mailing: 47659 Halyard Dr.
Plymouth, MI 48170
Tel: (734) 207-6200
Fax: (734) 207-6500

Corporate Foundations and Giving Programs
Metaldyne Corporation Contributions Program
47659 Halyard Dr.
Plymouth, MI 48170
Tel: (734) 207-6200
Fax: (734) 207-6500

Public Affairs and Related Activities Personnel

At Headquarters

BLAUFUSS, Mark
Chief Financial Officer and Treasurer
Tel: (734) 207-6200
Fax: (734) 207-6500

DEPP, Juergen
Vice President, Engineering and Business Development
Tel: (734) 207-6200
Fax: (734) 207-6500

LAWSON, David
Senior Specialist, Communications
DavidLawson@metaldyne.com
Tel: (734) 207-6578
Fax: (734) 207-6500

Metglas, Inc.

Metglas is the producer of amorphous metal ribbon and components used in the production of electrical distribution transformers, high frequency magnetic components for power electronics, material for anti-theft tags, brazing alloys, and solder.
www.metglas.com
Annual Revenues: $24.30 million
Employees: 200
Industry/ies: Metals

Main Headquarters
Mailing: 440 Allied Dr.
Conway, SC 29526
Tel: (843) 349-7319
Fax: (843) 349-6815
TF: (800) 581-7654

Public Affairs and Related Activities Personnel

At Headquarters

JORDAN, Jimmy W.
Manager, Accounts
Tel: (843) 349-7319
Fax: (843) 349-6815

MILLURE, Dave
Senior Vice President Sales and Marketing
Tel: (843) 349-7380
Fax: (843) 349-6815

Methanex Inc.

Engaged in production and marketing of methanol.
www.methanex.com
Annual Revenues: $2.83 billion
Employees: 1,231
Ticker: NASDAQ: MEOH
SIC: 2860
NAICS: 424690

Industry/ies: Chemicals & Chemical Industry; Fuels See Coal, Gas, Oil, Petroleum; Natural Resources; Petroleum Industry; Science; Scientific Research

Chairman of the Board   Tel: (972) 702-0909
HAMILTON, Thomas   Fax: (972) 233-1266

President and Chief Executive Officer   Tel: (972) 702-0909
FLOREN, John   Fax: (972) 233-1266

Main Headquarters
Mailing: 15301 Dalla Pkwy.   Tel: (972) 702-0909
       Suite 900   Fax: (972) 233-1266
       Addison, TX 75001

Corporate Foundations and Giving Programs

Methanex Inc. Corporate Contributions
15301 Dalla Pkwy.   Tel: (972) 702-0909
Suite 900   Fax: (972) 233-1266
Addison, TX 75001

Public Affairs and Related Activities Personnel

At Headquarters

BACH, Wendy   Tel: (972) 702-0909
Senior Vice President, Corporate Resources and General   Fax: (972) 233-1266
Counsel
wbach@methanex.com

CAMERON, Ian   Tel: (972) 702-0909
Senior Vice President, Finance and Chief Financial Officer   Fax: (972) 233-1266

CHESKO, Jason   Tel: (972) 702-0909
Senior Manager, Fuels   Fax: (972) 233-1266

DAYCOCK, Sandra   Tel: (972) 702-0909
Director, Investor Relations   Fax: (972) 233-1266

HERZ, Mike   Tel: (972) 702-0909
Senior Vice President, Corporate Development   Fax: (972) 233-1266

JAMES, Vanessa   Tel: (972) 702-0909
Senior Vice President, Global Marketing and Logistics   Fax: (972) 233-1266

MILNER, Randy   Tel: (972) 702-0909
Senior Vice President, General Counsel and Corporate   Fax: (972) 233-1266
Secretary

Metro-Goldwyn-Mayer Studios, Inc. (MGM)

An entertainment company that provides production and distribution of film and television content.
www.mgm.com
Annual Revenues: $67.20 million
Employees: 1,400
Ticker: NYSE: MGM
SIC: 7812
Industry/ies: Sports/Leisure/Entertainment

Chairman of the Board and Chief Executive Officer   Tel: (310) 449-3000
BARBER, Gary   Fax: (310) 449-8857

Main Headquarters
Mailing: 245 N. Beverly Dr.   Tel: (310) 449-3000
       Beverly Hills, CA 90210

Public Affairs and Related Activities Personnel

At Headquarters

PACKMAN, Scott   Tel: (310) 449-3000
Senior Executive Vice President, Secretary and General
Counsel
spackman@mgm.com

At Other Offices

STRATTON, Dene B.   Tel: (310) 499-3000
Chief Financial Officer   Fax: (310) 449-8857
10250 Constellation Blvd.
Los Angeles, CA 90067-6241

The MetroHealth System

MetroHealth is a leading health care system in Northeast Ohio nationally known for quality care in several areas, including heart and vascular.
www.metrohealth.org
Industry/ies: Medicine/Health Care/Mental Health
Legislative Issues: BUD; HCR; MMM

President and Chief Executive Officer   Tel: (216) 778-5638
BOUTROS, Akram

Main Headquarters
Mailing: 2500 MetroHealth Dr.   Tel: (216) 778-5638
       Cleveland, OH 44109

Corporate Foundations and Giving Programs

MetroHealth Foundation
Contact: Kate Brown
2500 MetroHealth Dr.   Tel: (216) 778-5638
Cleveland, OH 44109

Public Affairs and Related Activities Personnel

At Headquarters

AINSLIE, Virginia   Tel: (216) 778-5638
Federal Lobbyist
Registered Federal Lobbyist

ALLEN, Elizabeth Heller   Tel: (216) 778-5638
Vice President, Marketing and Communications

ANDOLSEN, Rita   Tel: (216) 778-5430
Director, Communications
randolsen@metrohealth.org

BROWN, Kate   Tel: (216) 778-5638
Vice President, Foundation and System Philanthropy

CARTER, Tracy   Tel: (216) 778-5638
Registered Federal Lobbyist

LEWIS, Daniel K.   Tel: (216) 778-5638
Chief Operating Officer

PHILLIPS, Michael   Tel: (216) 778-5638
Chief Legal Officer

RICHMOND, Craig   Tel: (216) 778-5638
Chief Financial Officer

ROSE, Tamiyka   Tel: (216) 778-5638
Registered Federal Lobbyist

SHAERBAN-ARUNDEL, Tina   Tel: (216) 778-5638
Media Relations Manager

MetroPCS Corporation

A wireless communications provider. T-Mobile US combines the leading value brands T-Mobile and MetroPCS.
www.metropcs.com
Employees: 3,600
Ticker: NYSE: TMUS
SIC: 4812
NAICS: 517212
Industry/ies: Communications; Telecommunications/Internet/Cable

Chairman of the Board, President and Chief Executive Officer   Tel: (214) 265-2550
LINQUIST, Roger D.   Fax: (214) 265-2570

Main Headquarters
Mailing: P.O. Box 601119   Tel: (214) 265-2550
       Dallas, TX 75360   Fax: (214) 265-2570

Corporate Foundations and Giving Programs

MetroPCS Community Scholars Program
P.O. Box 601119
Dallas, TX 75360

Metropolitan Life Insurance Company (MetLife)

Provides group benefits products (life and disability insurance, retirement products, prepaid legal plans); its Individual segment offers consumers many of the same types of products.
www.metlife.com
Annual Revenues: $74.60 billion
Employees: 68,000
Ticker: NYSE: MET
SIC: 6411
Industry/ies: Insurance Industry
Legislative Issues: BAN; CDT; CSP; FIN; HCR; INS; LBR; RET; TAX; TRD; VET

Chairman, President and Chief Executive Officer   Tel: (212) 578-2211
KANDARIAN, Steven A.   Fax: (212) 578-3320

Main Headquarters
Mailing: 600 13th St. NW   Tel: (202) 659-3575
       Suite 700   Fax: (202) 659-1026
       Washington, DC 20005

Washington Office
Mailing: 1620 L St. NW
       Suite 800
       Washington, DC 20036

Political Action Committees
Metlife Employees' Political Participation Fund A PAC
FEC ID: C00040923
Contact: Nancy S. Davenport
1095 Avenue of the Americas   Tel: (212) 578-2211
Area 4-D   Fax: (212) 578-3320
New York City, NY 10036

    Contributions to Candidates: $383,000 (2015-2016)
    Democrats: $122,000; Republicans: $260,000; Other: $1,000

       Principal Recipients

          SENATE
          BURR, RICHARD (REP-NC)
          KIRK, MARK STEVEN (REP-IL)

          HOUSE
          BOUSTANY, CHARLES W. DR. JR. (REP-LA)
          NUNES, DEVIN G (REP-CA)
          SANCHEZ, LINDA (DEM-CA)

Metlife Inc. Employees' Pol. Participation Fund A - Federal Only PAC
FEC ID: C00493551
Contact: Nancy S. Davenport
1095 Avenue of the Americas
Area 4-D
New York City, NY 10036

Contributions to Candidates: $315,500 (2015-2016)
Democrats: $137,500; Republicans: $177,000; Other: $1,000

Principal Recipients

HOUSE
BRADY, KEVIN (REP-TX)
DUFFY, SEAN (REP-WI)
HENSARLING, JEB HON. (REP-TX)
HIMES, JIM (DEM-CT)
HOYER, STENY HAMILTON (DEM-DC)
KIND, RONALD JAMES (DEM-WI)
LARSON, JOHN B (DEM-CT)
MCCARTHY, KEVIN (REP-CA)
MCHENRY, PATRICK TIMOTHY (REP-NC)
NEAL, RICHARD E MR. (DEM-MA)
RYAN, PAUL D. (REP-WI)
SCALISE, STEVE MR. (REP-LA)

Corporate Foundations and Giving Programs

MetLife Foundation
Contact: Dennis White
27-01 Queens Plaza North
Long Island City, NY 11101

Public Affairs and Related Activities Personnel

At Headquarters

COLE, Jason — Tel: (202) 659-3575 — Fax: (202) 659-1026
Vice President, Federal Government Relations
Registered Federal Lobbyist

DONNELLAN, James — Tel: (212) 578-3968 — Fax: (202) 659-1026
Government Relations Counsel
jfDonnellan@metlife.com
Registered Federal Lobbyist

GREENWELL, Susan — Tel: (212) 578-2389 — Fax: (212) 578-8869
Vice President, International Government Relations
sgreenwell@metlife.com

HOWARD, Janet — Tel: (212) 578-6433 — Fax: (212) 578-3320
Senior Washington Associate

LEE, Esther — Tel: (202) 659-3575 — Fax: (202) 659-1026
Executive Vice President, Global Chief Marketing Officer

PASTRE, Peter — Tel: (202) 872-8819 — Fax: (202) 659-1026
Vice President
ppastre@metlife.com
Registered Federal Lobbyist

ROGET, Gisele — Tel: (202) 659-3575 — Fax: (202) 659-1026
Registered Federal Lobbyist

SMITH, Kristin — Tel: (212) 578-6433 — Fax: (212) 578-3320
Vice President, Government and Industry Relations
ksmith@metlife.com
Registered Federal Lobbyist

SOLOMON, Irica — Tel: (202) 659-3575 — Fax: (202) 659-1026
Registered Federal Lobbyist

WINGATE, Heather — Tel: (202) 659-3575 — Fax: (202) 659-1026
Head, Federal Government Relations
Registered Federal Lobbyist

ZARCONE, Mike A. — Tel: (202) 659-3575 — Fax: (202) 659-1026
Head of Corporate Affairs and Chief of Staff
mzarcone@metlife.com

At Other Offices

ANZALDUA, Ricardo A. — Tel: (212) 578-2211 — Fax: (212) 578-3320
Executive Vice President and General Counsel
200 Park Ave.
New York City, NY 10166

CALAGNA, John — Tel: (212) 578-6252 — Fax: (212) 578-3320
Vice President, Corporate Communications
1095 Avenue of the Americas, Area 4-D
New York City, NY 10036

CORTES, Clara — Tel: (212) 578-2211 — Fax: (212) 578-3320
Director
200 Park Ave.
New York City, NY 10166
ccortes@metlife.com

DAVENPORT, Nancy S. — Tel: (212) 578-2211 — Fax: (212) 578-3320
1095 Avenue of the Americas, Area 4-D
New York City, NY 10036

HELE, John C. R. — Tel: (212) 578-2211 — Fax: (212) 578-3320
Executive Vice President and Chief Financial Officer

200 Park Ave.
New York City, NY 10166

HIJKOOP, Frans — Tel: (212) 578-2211 — Fax: (212) 578-3320
Executive Vice President and Chief Human Resources Officer
200 Park Ave.
New York City, NY 10166

LIPPERT, Martin J. — Tel: (212) 578-2211 — Fax: (212) 578-3320
Executive Vice President, Global Technology and Operations
200 Park Ave.
New York City, NY 10166

MCFADDEN, Jeanmarie — Tel: (212) 578-2211 — Fax: (212) 578-3320
Senior Vice President and Chief Communications Officer
200 Park Ave.
New York City, NY 10166

WHEELER, William J. — Tel: (212) 578-2211 — Fax: (212) 578-3320
President
1095 Avenue of the Americas, Area 4-D
New York City, NY 10036

WHITE, Dennis — Tel: (212) 578-2211 — Fax: (212) 578-3320
President and Chief Executive Officer, MetLife Foundation
200 Park Ave.
New York City, NY 10166

Metropolitan National Bank

Metropolitan National Bank is a customer-oriented bank offering full-service commercial and retail banking to Southwest Missouri, providing outstanding service, convenient Arkansas banking locations and innovative banking solutions. Bear State Financial, Inc. has announced a Definitive Agreement to Purchase Metropolitan National Bank on 22/06/2015.
www.metronationalbank.com
Annual Revenues: $445.0 million
Employees: 500
Industry/ies: Banking/Finance/Investments

Chairman of the Board — Tel: (417) 862-2022 — Fax: (417) 862-6318
MAGERS, Randall

President and Chief Executive Officer — Tel: (417) 862-2022 — Fax: (417) 862-6318
MCFATRIDGE, Mark
mmcfatridge@metronationalbank.com

Main Headquarters
Mailing: 600 S. Glenstone — Tel: (417) 862-2022 — Fax: (417) 862-6318
Springfield, MO 65802

Political Action Committees
Metropolitan National Bank Political Action Commitee (MPAC)
FEC ID: C00408492
Contact: Jeffrey E. Stevenson
425, W Capitol — Tel: (501) 374-9247 — Fax: (501) 374-9425
Little Rock, AR 72201

Corporate Foundations and Giving Programs

Metropolitan National Bank Contributions Program
Contact: Virgil Miller
425 W. Capitol — Tel: (501) 377-7600 — Fax: (501) 377-7608
Little Rock, AR 72201

Public Affairs and Related Activities Personnel

At Headquarters

DAY, Sharon — Tel: (417) 862-2022 — Fax: (417) 862-6318
Executive Vice President, Chief Financial and Administrative Officer
sterry@metronationalbank.com

EARLY, Michal Moss — Tel: (417) 862-2022 — Fax: (417) 862-6318
Senior Vice President, Business Development and Marketing Officer
mmossearly@metronationalbank.com

LANCASTER, Whitley — Tel: (417) 862-2022 — Fax: (417) 862-6318
Vice President, Human Resources Manager
wlancaster@metronationalbank.com

At Other Offices

BARKACS, Jillian — Tel: (417) 886-9990 — Fax: (417) 882-5231
Vice President, Compliance Officer
3550 S National Ave., Bradford Center
Springfield, MO 65807
jbarkacs@metronationalbank.com

MILLER, Virgil — Tel: (501) 374-9247 — Fax: (501) 374-9425
Senior Vice President, Community Development
200 S. Commerce
Little Rock, AR 72201
vmiller@metbank.com

STEVENSON, Jeffrey E. — Tel: (501) 374-9247 — Fax: (501) 374-9425
Senior Vice President and Controller
200 S. Commerce
Little Rock, AR 72201

MGM Entertainment, Inc.

See listing on page 536 under Metro-Goldwyn-Mayer Studios, Inc. (MGM)

MGM Mirage

A gaming industry company. Acquired Mandalay Resort Group in 2005.
www.mgmresorts.com
Annual Revenues: $9.39 billion
Employees: 52,100
Ticker: NYSE: MGM
SIC: 7011
Industry/ies: Sports/Leisure/Entertainment
Legislative Issues: AVI; GAM; IMM; TAX; TOU

Chairman of the Board and Chief Executive Officer
MURREN, James L.

Tel: (702) 693-7111
Fax: (702) 693-8626

Main Headquarters
Mailing: 3600 Las Vegas Blvd., South
             Las Vegas, NV 89109

Tel: (702) 693-7111
Fax: (702) 693-8585

Political Action Committees
MGM Resorts International PAC
FEC ID: C00299321
Contact: Steven S. Lucas
2350 Kerner Blvd.
Suite 250
San Rafael, CA 94901

   Contributions to Candidates: $76,700 (2015-2016)
   Democrats: $52,200; Republicans: $24,500

           Principal Recipients

                HOUSE
                KIHUEN, RUBEN (DEM-NV)
                ROBERSON, MICHAEL (REP-NV)
                TITUS, DINA (DEM-NV)

Corporate Foundations and Giving Programs
MGM MIRAGE Voice Employee Volunteer program
3260 Industrial Rd.
Las Vegas, NV 89109

MGM Mirage Voice Foundation
Contact: Jocelyn Bluitt-Fisher
3260 Industrial Rd.
Las Vegas, NV 89109

MGM Resorts Foundation
3260 Industrial Rd.
Las Vegas, NV 89109

Public Affairs and Related Activities Personnel

At Headquarters

BLUITT-FISHER, Jocelyn
Director, Corporate Philanthropy
jbluitt@mgmmirage.com

Tel: (702) 650-7429
Fax: (702) 693-8626

D'ARRIGO, Dan
Executive Vice President and Chief Financial Officer

Tel: (702) 693-8895
Fax: (702) 693-8626

FELDMAN, Alan M.
Senior Vice President, Public Affairs

Tel: (702) 650-6974
Fax: (702) 693-8626

At Other Offices

GONZALEZ, David
Manager, Public Relations
3260 Industrial Rd.
Las Vegas, NV 89109

Tel: (702) 650-7565

LUCAS, Steven S.
PAC Treasurer
2350 Kerner Blvd., Suite 250
San Rafael, CA 94901

MHA Management Services Corporation

Provides services concerned to health issues.
web.mhanet.com
Industry/ies: Management

Main Headquarters
Mailing: 4712 Country Club Dr.
             P.O. Box 6766
             Jefferson City, MO 65102

Tel: (573) 893-3700

Public Affairs and Related Activities Personnel

At Headquarters

LANDON, Daniel
Senior Vice President, Governmental Relations
dlandon@mail.mhanet.com

RENEE, Steve
srenne@mail.mhanet.com
Registered Federal Lobbyist

Tel: (573) 893-3700

Michael Baker Corporation

Provides professional engineering and consulting expertise for public and private sector clients worldwide.
www.mbakercorp.com
Employees: 2,646
Ticker: NYSE: BKR
SIC: 8741
Industry/ies: Engineering/Mathematics

Chairman of the Board
CAMPBELL , Thomas J.

Tel: (412) 269-6300
Fax: (412) 375-3980

Chief Executive Officer
BERGMAN, Kurt

Tel: (412) 269-6300
Fax: (412) 375-3980

Main Headquarters
Mailing: Airside Business Park
             100 Airside Dr.
             Moon Township, PA 15108

Tel: (412) 269-6300
Fax: (412) 375-3980
TF: (800) 553-1153

Corporate Foundations and Giving Programs
Michael Baker Corporation Foundation
Airside Business Park
100 Airside Dr.
Moon Township, PA 15108

Tel: (412) 269-6300

Public Affairs and Related Activities Personnel

At Headquarters

BONGIOVI, Joseph
Chief Human Resources Officer

Tel: (412) 269-6300
Fax: (412) 375-3980

CHUNG, Ying-Tzu
Environmental Specialist
ytcevent@aol.com

Tel: (412) 269-6300
Fax: (412) 375-3980

FOLEY, Beth M.
Chief Communications Officer

Tel: (412) 269-6300
Fax: (412) 375-3980

HILL, Jeffrey S.
Chief Operating Officer

Tel: (412) 269-6300
Fax: (412) 375-3980

LUTES, Brian
Chief Financial Officer

Tel: (412) 269-6300
Fax: (412) 375-3980

MCKNIGHT, H. James
Chief Legal Officer
jmcknight@mbakercorp.com

Tel: (412) 269-6300
Fax: (412) 375-3980

Michaels Stores

A retailer of arts, crafts, frames, and home decorations. Michaels sells products including art and hobby supplies, décor, frames, needlecraft kits, party supplies, seasonal products, and silk and dried flowers.
www.michaels.com
Annual Revenues: $4.4 billion
Employees: 41,000
Ticker: NYSE: MIK
SIC: 5945
Industry/ies: Sports/Leisure/Entertainment

Chief Executive Officer
RUBIN, Carl S.

Tel: (972) 409-1300
Fax: (972) 409-1556

Main Headquarters
Mailing: 8000 Bent Branch Dr.
             Irving, TX 75063

Tel: (972) 409-1300
Fax: (972) 409-1556
TF: (800) 642-4235

Public Affairs and Related Activities Personnel

At Headquarters

KAUFFMAN, Kristen
Contact, Media Relations
Michaels@spmcommunications.com

Tel: (817) 329-3257
Fax: (972) 409-1556

SONSTEBY, Charles M.
Chief Administrative Officer and Chief Financial Officer

Tel: (972) 409-1300
Fax: (972) 409-1556

VEITENHEIMER, Michael J.
Senior Vice President and General Counsel and Secretary

Tel: (972) 409-1300
Fax: (972) 409-1556

Michelin North America

Makes and sells tires throughout Canada, Mexico, and the US to consumers, trucking fleets; and auto, aviation, and vehicle manufacturers.
www.michelin.com
Annual Revenues: $3.47 billion
Employees: 24,000
SIC: 3011
Industry/ies: Automotive Industry; Rubber Industry; Transportation
Legislative Issues: BUD; DEF; ECN; ENV; TRA; TRD

Main Headquarters
Mailing: One Pkwy., South
             Greenville, SC 29615

Tel: (864) 458-5000
Fax: (864) 458-6359
TF: (800) 847-3435

Public Affairs and Related Activities Personnel

At Headquarters

EVERED, Stephen A.

Tel: (864) 458-5080

Vice President, Government Affairs
stephen.evered@michelin.com
Fax: (864) 458-6359

HENRY, Marc
Chief Financial Officer
Tel: (864) 458-5000
Fax: (864) 458-6359

HOCK, Lyn
Contact, Media Relations
Lyn.Hock@us.michelin.com
Tel: (864) 458-6321
Fax: (864) 458-6359

MAGLOIRE, Valerie
Investor Relations
valerie.magloire@fr.michelin.com
Tel: (864) 458-5000
Fax: (864) 458-6359

At Other Offices

WILKERSON, Sheryl
P.O. Box 19001
Greenville, SC 29615
Registered Federal Lobbyist
Tel: (864) 270-0375
Fax: (864) 458-6359

Microchip Technology Inc.

Microchip Technology Inc. is a provider of microcontroller and analog semiconductors.
www.microchip.com
Annual Revenues: $2.15 billion
Employees: 9,449
Ticker: NASDAQ: MCHP
SIC: 3674
Industry/ies: Computer/Technology

Chairman of the Board, President and Chief Executive Officer
SANGHI, Steve
Tel: (480) 792-7200
Fax: (480) 899-9210

Main Headquarters
Mailing: 2355 W. Chandler Blvd.
Chandler, AZ 85224-6199
Tel: (480) 792-7200
Fax: (480) 899-9210
TF: (888) 628-6247

Corporate Foundations and Giving Programs
Microchip Technology Charitable Foundation
2355 W. Chandler Blvd.
Chandler, AZ 85224-6199
Tel: (480) 792-7200
Fax: (480) 899-9210

Public Affairs and Related Activities Personnel

At Headquarters

BJORNHOLT, J. Eric
Vice President and Chief Financial Officer
Tel: (480) 792-7200
Fax: (480) 899-9210

CARR, Lauren A.
Vice President, Human Resources
lauren.carr@microchip.com
Tel: (480) 792-7200
Fax: (480) 899-9210

HERK, Kimberly Van
Vice President, General Counsel and Corporate Secretary
kim.vanherk@microchip.com
Tel: (480) 792-7200
Fax: (480) 899-9210

LAWSON, Eric
Manager, Public Relations
eric.lawson@microchip.com
Tel: (480) 792-7182
Fax: (480) 792-4150

LITTLE, Mitchell R.
Vice President, Worldwide Sales and Applications
Tel: (480) 792-7200
Fax: (480) 899-9210

MOORTHY, Ganesh
Chief Operating Officer
Tel: (480) 792-7200
Fax: (480) 899-9210

Micron Technology, Inc.

A manufacturer of semiconductor memory products.
www.micron.com
Annual Revenues: $16.95 billion
Employees: 30,400
Ticker: NASDAQ: MU
SIC: 3571; 3577; 3674
Industry/ies: Electricity & Electronics; Electronics; Energy/Electricity
Legislative Issues: ACC; AUT; CPI; CPT; ENG; ENV; HOM; TAX; TEC; TRD

Chairman of the Board
SWITZ, Robert E.
Tel: (208) 368-4000
Fax: (208) 368-4435

Chief Executive Officer
DURCAN, D. Mark
Tel: (208) 368-4000
Fax: (208) 368-4435

President
ADAMS, Mark W.
Tel: (208) 368-4000
Fax: (208) 368-4435

Main Headquarters
Mailing: 8000 S. Federal Way
Boise, ID 83716
Tel: (208) 368-4000
Fax: (208) 368-4435

Washington Office
Mailing: 300 NJ Ave. NW
Washington, DC 20001

Political Action Committees
Micron Technology Inc. PAC
FEC ID: C00443671
Contact: Jennafer Rae Hopkins
8000 S. Federal Way
P.O. Box Six
Boise, ID 83707

Contributions to Candidates: $2,401,016 (2015-2016)
Democrats: $50,500; Republicans: $88,500; Other: $2,262,016
Principal Recipients
SENATE
CRAPO, MICHAEL D (REP-ID)
HOUSE
CHAFFETZ, JASON (REP-UT)
MCCARTHY, KEVIN (REP-CA)

Corporate Foundations and Giving Programs
Micron Foundation
Contact: Kami Faylor
8000 S. Federal Way
P.O. Box Six
Boise, ID 83707

Public Affairs and Related Activities Personnel

At Headquarters

ARNZEN, April
Vice President, Human Resources
Tel: (208) 368-4000
Fax: (208) 368-4435

BEDARD, Kipp A.
Vice President, Investor Relations
kbedard@micron.com
Tel: (208) 368-4465
Fax: (208) 368-2536

FAYLOR, Kami
Manager, Community Relations
Tel: (208) 363-3675
Fax: (208) 368-2536

FOSTER, Ronald C.
Chief Financial Officer and Vice President, Finance
Tel: (208) 368-4000
Fax: (208) 368-4435

HOGANSON, Jonathan
Federal Lobbyist
Registered Federal Lobbyist
Tel: (208) 368-4000
Fax: (208) 368-4435

HOPKINS, Jennafer Rae
Specialist, Political Law Compliance
Mail Stop 1-407
jhopkins@micron.com
Tel: (208) 363-2394
Fax: (208) 368-4435

POPPEN, Joel L.
Vice President, Legal Affairs, General Counsel, and Corporate Secretary
Tel: (208) 368-4000
Fax: (208) 368-4435

SADLER, Michael W.
Vice President, Corporate Development
Tel: (208) 368-4000
Fax: (208) 368-4435

At Washington Office

THURMOND, Holly
Director, Federal Government Affairs
Registered Federal Lobbyist

Microsoft Corporation

A worldwide computer technology corporation providing a variety of software products and services for computing devices.
www.microsoft.com
Annual Revenues: $83.35 billion
Employees: 99,000
Ticker: NASDAQ: MSFT
SIC: 7372; 2731; 3577; 7371
Industry/ies: Computer/Technology
Legislative Issues: ACC; BUD; COM; CPI; CPT; CSP; DEF; EDU; ENV; GOV; HOM; IMM; INT; LAW; LBR; SCI; TAX; TEC; TRD

Chairman
THOMPSON, John W.
Tel: (425) 882-8080
Fax: (425) 936-7329

Chief Executive Officer
NADELLA, Satya
Tel: (425) 882-8080
Fax: (425) 936-7329

Main Headquarters
Mailing: One Microsoft Way
Redmond, WA 98052-6399
Tel: (425) 882-8080
Fax: (425) 936-7329
TF: (800) 642-7676

Washington Office
Mailing: 901 K St. NW
11th Floor
Washington, DC 20001

Political Action Committees
Microsoft Corporation PAC
FEC ID: C00227546
Contact: Edward Ingle
16011 NE 36th Way
P.O. Box 97017
Redmond, WA 98073
Tel: (425) 882-8080
Fax: (425) 936-7329

Contributions to Candidates: $566,818 (2015-2016)
Democrats: $217,500; Republicans: $347,318; Other: $2,000
Principal Recipients
SENATE
AYOTTE, KELLY A (REP-NH)
LEAHY, PATRICK J (DEM-VT)
PAUL, RAND (REP-KY)

SCHUMER, CHARLES E (DEM-NY)

HOUSE

DELBENE, SUZAN K (DEM-WA)
GOODLATTE, ROBERT W. (REP-VA)
HOYER, STENY HAMILTON (DEM-DC)
ISSA, DARRELL (REP-CA)
MCMORRIS RODGERS, CATHY (REP-WA)
RYAN, PAUL D. (REP-WI)

Corporate Foundations and Giving Programs

Bill and Melinda Gates Foundation
Contact: Susan Desmond-Hellmann
500 Fifth Ave., North   Tel: (206) 709-3100
Seattle, WA 98102

Public Affairs and Related Activities Personnel

At Headquarters

ANDERSON, Curt   Tel: (425) 706-3703
Partner Director   Fax: (425) 936-7329

GATES, Bill   Tel: (425) 882-8080
Founder and Technology Advisor   Fax: (425) 936-7329
bill.gates@microsoft.com

HOOD, Amy   Tel: (425) 882-8080
Executive Vice President & Chief Financial Officer   Fax: (425) 936-7329

SMITH, Brad   Tel: (425) 882-8080
President & Chief Legal Officer   Fax: (425) 936-7329

At Washington Office

BOYD, Paula
Director, Government and Regulatory Affairs
Registered Federal Lobbyist

CAVALIERE, Frank
Contact, Federal Government Affairs
Registered Federal Lobbyist

CURTIN, Caroline
Policy Counsel, Entertainment & Devices
Registered Federal Lobbyist

DWOSKIN, Dorothy
Senior Director, Trade Policy, Strategy and Federal Lobbyist
Registered Federal Lobbyist

GELMAN, Matthew
Senior Director, Congressional Affairs
Registered Federal Lobbyist

HUMPHRIES, Fred
Vice President, Government Affairs
Registered Federal Lobbyist

JACKSON, Adrienne
Project Coordinator

KAHN, Suhail
Director, External Affairs

KAMELA, Bill
Policy Counsel

KNOX, Allyson
Federal Lobbyist
Registered Federal Lobbyist

MAGEE, Conor
Project Coordinator

MANN, Susan O.
Senior Director, Intellectual Property Policy
Registered Federal Lobbyist

PATRON, Michelle
Director, Sustainability Policy

PAYNE, Todd

PEARSON, Christina
Senior Director, Public Relations
Christina.Pearson@microsoft.com

PETERS, Stephanie J.
Director, Federal Government Affairs, Visual Communication Designer
Registered Federal Lobbyist

PRYOR, Jr., David
Director, Government Affairs
Registered Federal Lobbyist

ROESSER, Tom
Senior Director, Tax Affairs
Registered Federal Lobbyist

SALEM, Charles
Managing Director, Public Policy

SAMPSON, John
Director, Federal Government Affairs
jsampson@microsoft.com
Registered Federal Lobbyist

SEITZ, Stephen
Senior Strategist

SMITH, Brad
President & Chief Legal Officer

TORRES, Frank
Director, Consumer Affairs
Registered Federal Lobbyist

At Other Offices

DESMOND-HELLMANN, Susan   Tel: (206) 709-3100
Chief Executive Officer, Foundation
500 Fifth Ave., North
Seattle, WA 98102

INGLE, Edward   Tel: (202) 263-5900
Managing Director of Government Affairs   Fax: (202) 263-5901
16011 N.E. 36th Way, P.O. Box 97017
Redmond, WA 98073
Registered Federal Lobbyist

REISMAN, Matthew
1401 I St. NW, Suite 500, 11th Floor
Washington, DC 20005
Registered Federal Lobbyist

MicroSun Technologies, LLC

Designs and assembles battery packs.
www.palladiumenergy.com
Annual Revenues: $15.10 million
Employees: 125
Industry/ies: Computer/Technology; Electricity & Electronics; Electronics; Energy/Electricity

President and Chief Executive Officer   Tel: (630) 410-7900
GATTI, John J.

Main Headquarters
Mailing: 1200 Internationale Pkwy.   Tel: (630) 410-7900
              Woodridge, IL 60517-4975

Political Action Committees
MicroSun Technologies PAC
FEC ID: C00445247
Contact: Nancie ElShafei
1200 Internationale Pkwy.   Tel: (630) 968-5000
Woodridge, IL 60517

Corporate Foundations and Giving Programs
MicroSun Technologies Corporate Social Responsibility program
1200 Internationale Pkwy.   Tel: (630) 968-5000
Woodridge, IL 60517-4975

Public Affairs and Related Activities Personnel

At Headquarters

ELSHAFEI, Alan   Tel: (630) 968-5000
Founder

ELSHAFEI, Nancie   Tel: (630) 968-5000
PAC Treasurer

LILE, Eileen   Tel: (630) 410-7900
Senior Director, Human Resources

MARTIN, Anson   Tel: (630) 410-7900
Vice President of Global Sales and Business Development

POKONOSKY, Chuck   Tel: (630) 968-5000
Vice President, Sales and Marketing
cpokonosky@microsuntech.com

POMEROY, Michael   Tel: (630) 410-7900
Chief Financial Officer

MidAmerican Energy Holdings Company

CalEnergy acquired Northern Electric and MidAmerican Energy to Form MidAmerican Energy Holdings Company. Produces Electricity and Gas. Subsidiaries are MidAmerican Energy Company, PacifiCorp, CE Electric UK, CalEnergy Generation, Kern River Gas Transmission Company and Northern Natural Gas. Effective April 30, 2014, MidAmerican Energy Holdings Company was renamed Berkshire Hathaway Energy Company.
www.midamerican.com
Annual Revenues: $11.50 billion
Employees: 16,000
Ticker: NYSE: BRK-A
SIC: 4900
Industry/ies: Energy/Electricity
Legislative Issues: AGR; BUD; CAW; CDT; COM; ENG; ENV; FIN; HOM; LBR; TAX; TRA; UTI

Chairman, President and Chief Executive Officer   Tel: (515) 242-4300
ABEL, Gregory E.   Fax: (515) 281-2389

Main Headquarters
Mailing: P.O. Box 657   Tel: (515) 242-4300
              666 Grand Ave.   Fax: (515) 281-2389
              Des Moines, IA 50306-0657   TF: (888) 427-5632

Washington Office
Mailing: 1800 M. St. NW   Tel: (202) 828-1378
Suite 330 North
Washington, DC 20036

Political Action Committees
MidAmerican Energy Company Executive PAC
FEC ID: C00324483
666 Grand Ave.
P.O. Box 657
Des Moines, IA 50306

   Contributions to Candidates: $51,700 (2015-2016)
   Democrats: $23,700; Republicans: $28,000

Corporate Foundations and Giving Programs
MidAmerican Energy Foundation
P.O. Box 657
Des Moines, IA 50306
MidAmerican Energy Holdings Company Contributions Program
P.O. Box 657
Des Moines, IA 50306-0657

Public Affairs and Related Activities Personnel

At Headquarters
ANDERSON, Douglas L.   Tel: (515) 242-4300
Executive Vice President, General Counsel and Corporate   Fax: (515) 281-2389
Secretary
EVANS, Steven R.   Tel: (515) 281-2288
PAC Treasurer   Fax: (515) 242-4080
srevans@midamerican.com
GOODMAN, Patrick J.   Tel: (515) 242-4300
Senior Vice President and Chief Financial officer   Fax: (515) 281-2389
KUNERT, Kathryn   Tel: (515) 281-2287
Vice President, , Business and Community Development   Fax: (515) 242-4395
kmkunert@midamerican.com
SAMMON, Maureen E.   Tel: (515) 242-4300
Senior Vice President and Chief Administrative Officer   Fax: (515) 281-2389

At Washington Office
CARRIERE, Jay Gerand   Tel: (202) 828-1378
Director, Federal Government Affairs
Registered Federal Lobbyist
DAVIS, Kyle L.   Tel: (202) 828-1378
Director, Congressional Relations
MENEZES, Mark W.   Tel: (202) 828-1378
Registered Federal Lobbyist
WEISGALL, Jonathan   Tel: (202) 828-1378
Vice President, Legislative & Regulatory Affairs
jmweisgall@midamerican.com
Registered Federal Lobbyist
WHITE, Julie   Tel: (202) 828-1378
Director, Communications

The Midcontinent Independent System Operator, Inc.
MISO is an independent, not-for-profit regional transmission organizaiton responsible for maintaining reliable transmission of power in 15 U.S. states and the Canadian province of Manitoba.
www.misoenergy.org
Employees: 600
Industry/ies: Energy/Electricity

President and Chief Executive Officer   Tel: (317) 249-5400
BEAR, John R.   Fax: (317) 249-5910

Main Headquarters
Mailing: 720 City Center Dr.   Tel: (317) 249-5400
Carmel, IN 46032-7574   Fax: (317) 249-5910

Public Affairs and Related Activities Personnel

At Headquarters
BIGGERS, Jo   Tel: (317) 249-5400
Vice President, Finance   Fax: (317) 249-5910
BOYD, David   Tel: (317) 249-5400
Vice President, Government and Regulatory Affairs   Fax: (317) 249-5910
DOYING, Richard   Tel: (317) 249-5400
Executive Vice President, Operations & Corporate Services   Fax: (317) 249-5910
KOZEY, Stephen G.   Tel: (317) 249-5400
Senior Vice President, Legal and Compliance Services   Fax: (317) 249-5910
POWELL, Greg   Tel: (317) 249-5400
Vice President, Human Resources   Fax: (317) 249-5910
SCHUG, Wayne   Tel: (317) 249-5400
Vice President, Strategy and Business Development   Fax: (317) 249-5910

MidFirst Bank
MidFirst Bank is a financial company.

www.midfirst.com
Employees: 800
Industry/ies: Banking/Finance/Investments
Legislative Issues: BNK

Chairman & Chief Executive Officer   Tel: (405) 840-7600
RECORD, Jeff   Fax: (405) 767-5400

Main Headquarters
Mailing: 501 NW Grand Blvd.   Tel: (405) 840-7600
Suite 100   Fax: (405) 767-5400
Oklahoma City, OK 73118-6054

Public Affairs and Related Activities Personnel

At Headquarters
ADAMS, Daniel   Tel: (405) 840-7600
Vice President   Fax: (405) 767-5400
LORENSON, Dana M.   Tel: (405) 840-7600
Senior Vice President, Human Resources   Fax: (405) 767-5426
dana.lorenson@midfirst.com

Midland Financial Company
A banking institution.
www.midfirst.com
Annual Revenues: $813.38 million
Employees: 1,400
Industry/ies: Banking/Finance/Investments

Chairman and Chief Executive Officer   Tel: (405) 840-7600
RECORDS, George   Fax: (405) 767-5426

Main Headquarters
Mailing: 501 NW Grand Blvd.   Tel: (405) 840-7600
Oklahoma City, OK 45206   Fax: (405) 767-5426

Public Affairs and Related Activities Personnel

At Headquarters
DOBSON, Todd A.
Executive Vice President and Chief Financial Officer
LORENSON, Dana M.
Senior Vice President, Human Resources
dana.lorenson@midfirst.com

Midwest Independent Transmission System Operator, Inc.
See listing on page 541 under The Midcontinent Independent System Operator, Inc.

Milacron, Inc.
A manufacturer of plastic machinery and industrial fluids.
www.milacron.com
Annual Revenues: $243.50 million
Employees: 4,100
Ticker: NYSE: MZIAP
SIC: 3559; 3089; 3841; 5084; 5084
Industry/ies: Plastics Industry

Chairman of the Board   Tel: (513) 487-5000
BOOTS, Ira   Fax: (513) 487-5086
Chief Executive Officer   Tel: (513) 487-5000
GOEKE, Tom   Fax: (513) 487-5086

Main Headquarters
Mailing: 3010 Disney St.   Tel: (513) 487-5000
Cincinnati, OH 45209   Fax: (513) 487-5086

Corporate Foundations and Giving Programs

Milacron Foundation
Contact: Bruce Chalmers
2090 Florence Ave.
Cincinnati, OH 45206

Public Affairs and Related Activities Personnel

At Headquarters
CHALMERS, Bruce   Tel: (513) 487-5000
Vice President, Finance, Chief Financial Officer, Chief   Fax: (513) 487-5086
Administrative Officer and Treasurer
ELLIS, Mike   Tel: (905) 877-0185
Director, Global Marketing and Communications   Fax: (513) 487-5086
O'DONNELL, Hugh   Tel: (513) 487-5000
Senior Vice President, General Counsel and Secretary   Fax: (513) 487-5086
O'LEARY, EdD, Richard A.   Tel: (513) 487-5000
Corporate Vice President, Chief Human Resources Officer   Fax: (513) 487-5086
STARR, Bob   Tel: (513) 487-5000
Director, Marketing   Fax: (513) 487-5086
bob_starr@milacron.com
WRIGHT, Mark   Tel: (513) 487-5080
Treasury Director   Fax: (513) 487-5086
Mark_Wright@milacron.com

Millennia Corporation
See listing on page 790 under TMG Electronics, Inc.

Millennium Pharmaceuticals, Inc.
See listing on page 542 under Millennium: The Takeda Oncology Company

Millennium: The Takeda Oncology Company
A pharmaceutical company. A subsidiary of Takeda Pharmaceutical. Produces cancer treatments. They are focused exclusively in oncology to improve the treatment of cancer around the world.
www.millennium.com
Annual Revenues: $101.10 million
Employees: 900
Ticker: NASDAQ: MLNM
SIC: 2834
Industry/ies: Pharmaceutical Industry

President   Tel: (617) 679-7000
PROTOPAPAS, Anna   Fax: (617) 374-7788

Main Headquarters
Mailing: 40 Landsdowne St.   Tel: (617) 679-7000
    Cambridge, MA 02139   Fax: (617) 374-7788
    TF: (800) 390-5663

Washington Office
Mailing: 750 Ninth St. NW   Tel: (202) 289-6492
    Suite 575   Fax: (202) 289-7257
    Washington, DC 20001

Political Action Committees
Millennium Pharmaceuticals Inc. PAC
FEC ID: C00407460
Contact: Liz Lewis
750 Ninth St. NW
Suite 575
Washington, DC 20001

Corporate Foundations and Giving Programs
Millennium Makes a Difference
40 Landsdowne St.   Tel: (617) 679-7000
Cambridge, MA 02139   Fax: (617) 679-7000

Public Affairs and Related Activities Personnel

At Headquarters

GOODMAN, Shawn   Tel: (617) 679-7000
Site Head, Corporate Communications   Fax: (617) 374-7788

KASSUM, Tariq   Tel: (617) 679-7000
Vice President, Corporate Development   Fax: (617) 374-7788

KEATING, Laurie Bartlett   Tel: (617) 679-7000
Senior Vice President, General Counsel   Fax: (617) 374-7788

PAI, Manisha   Tel: (617) 551-7877
Associate Director, Corporate Communications   Fax: (617) 374-7788
Manisha.Pai@mpi.com

PINGPANK, Elizabeth   Tel: (617) 444-1495
Manager, Public Relations   Fax: (617) 374-7788
elizabeth.pingpank@takeda.com

At Washington Office

LEWIS, Liz   Tel: (202) 289-6492
Chief Counsel, Chief Compliance Officer and PAC Treasurer   Fax: (202) 289-7257

SHAH, Aarti   Tel: (202) 289-6492
Associate Director, Government Relations & Public Policy   Fax: (202) 289-7257

Miller & Long Concrete Construction
A concrete construction company.
www.millerandlong.com
Industry/ies: Construction/Construction Materials

Chairman of the Board   Tel: (301) 657-8000
MCMAHON, John M.   Fax: (301) 657-8610

Main Headquarters
Mailing: 4824 Rugby Ave.   Tel: (301) 657-8000
    Bethesda, MD 20814   Fax: (301) 657-8610

Corporate Foundations and Giving Programs
Miller & Long Concrete Construction Contributions Program
4824 Rugby Ave.   Tel: (301) 657-8000
Bethesda, MD 20814   Fax: (301) 657-8610

Public Affairs and Related Activities Personnel

At Headquarters

BURLAS, Mike   Tel: (301) 657-8000
Vice President   Fax: (301) 657-8610
mikeburlas@millerandlong.com

GLADSTONE, Myles   Tel: (301) 657-8000
Vice President, Human Resources   Fax: (301) 657-8610

RANDOLPH, Carol   Tel: (301) 657-8000

Vice President, Strategic Communications   Fax: (301) 657-8610

MillerCoors LLC
A joint venture between SABMiller and Molson Coors. Primary brands are Coors and Miller.
www.millercoors.com
Annual Revenues: $662.90 million
Employees: 4,500
SIC: 2082
Industry/ies: Food And Beverage Industry
Legislative Issues: ADV; AGR; ALC; BEV; BUD; CAW; CDT; FOO; HCR; LBR; MAR; TAX; TRA; TRU

Chairman of the Board   Tel: (312) 496-2700
COORS, Peter H.   Fax: (303) 277-6246
peter.coors@millercoors.com

Interim Chief Executive Officer   Tel: (312) 496-2700
HATTERSLEY, Gavin   Fax: (303) 277-6246

Main Headquarters
Mailing: 250 S. Wacker Dr.   Tel: (312) 496-2700
    Suite 800   Fax: (303) 277-6246
    Chicago, IL 60606-5888   TF: (800) 645-5376

Washington Office
Mailing: 1501 M St. NW   Tel: (202) 737-4444
    Suite 330   Fax: (202) 737-0951
    Washington, DC 20005

Political Action Committees
MillerCoors LLC PAC
FEC ID: C00457697
Contact: Timothy H. Scully Jr.
1501 M St. NW, Suite 330   Tel: (202) 737-4444
Washington, DC 20005   Fax: (202) 737-0951

    Contributions to Candidates: $104,500 (2015-2016)
    Democrats: $30,500; Republicans: $74,000

    Principal Recipients

    SENATE
    JOHNSON, RONALD HAROLD (REP-)

Corporate Foundations and Giving Programs
MillerCoors Contributions Program
250 S. Wacker Dr.
Suite 800
Chicago, IL 60606-5888

Public Affairs and Related Activities Personnel

At Headquarters

GREBE, Kelly   Tel: (312) 496-2700
Chief Legal and Corporate Services Officer   Fax: (303) 277-6246

JOUBERT, Tracey   Tel: (312) 496-2700
Executive Vice President and Chief Financial Officer   Fax: (303) 277-6246

KROLL, David   Tel: (312) 496-2700
Chief Marketing Officer   Fax: (303) 277-6246

MARINO, Pete   Tel: (312) 496-2700
Chief Public Affairs and Communications Officer   Fax: (303) 277-6246

NETTLES, Michelle   Tel: (312) 496-2700
Chief Human Resources Officer   Fax: (303) 277-6246

At Washington Office

BLOOM, Seth   Tel: (202) 737-4444
Registered Federal Lobbyist   Fax: (202) 737-0951

CRAWFORD, Richard C.   Tel: (202) 737-4444
Federal Lobbyist   Fax: (202) 737-0951
Richard.Crawford@millercoors.com
Registered Federal Lobbyist

HASTINGS, Lance   Tel: (202) 737-4444
Registered Federal Lobbyist   Fax: (202) 737-0951

SCULLY, Jr., Timothy H.   Tel: (202) 737-4444
Vice President, Government Affairs & PAC Treasurer   Fax: (202) 737-0951
scully.timothy@millercoors.com
Registered Federal Lobbyist

YOUNG, Bill   Tel: (202) 737-4444
Federal Lobbyist   Fax: (202) 737-0951
Registered Federal Lobbyist

Milliken and Company
A privately-held textile and chemical manufacturer.
www.milliken.com
Annual Revenues: $2.54 billion
Employees: 91,000
Industry/ies: Apparel/Textiles Industry
Legislative Issues: APP; CHM; DEF; TAR; TRD

Chairman and Co-Founder, Milken Family Foundation
MILKEN, Lowell

Chief Executive Officer

SALLEY, Joe

Main Headquarters
Mailing: P.O. Box 1926
             Spartanburg, SC 29304

Washington Office
Mailing: 910 16th St.
             Suite 700
             Washington, DC 20006

Political Action Committees
Milliken & Company Good Government Committee PAC
FEC ID: C00466672
Contact: Katherine M. Dutilh
910 16th St.
Suite 700
Washington, DC 20006

Corporate Foundations and Giving Programs

Milken Family Foundation
Contact: Lowell Milken
1250 Fourth Street   Tel: (310) 570-4800
Santa Monica, CA 90401-1353   Fax: (310) 570-4801
Milliken Foundation
Long Island City, NY

Public Affairs and Related Activities Personnel

At Headquarters

DILLARD, Richard J.
Director, Corporate Public Affairs

WALKER , Stacy
Global Director, Customer Experience

At Washington Office

DUTILH, Katherine M.
Manager, Government Relations and PAC Contact
Mail Stop Suite 700
kdutilh@millikendc.com
Registered Federal Lobbyist

Milliman Care Guidelines LLC

Formerly known as Milliman Care Guidelines became a part of Hearst Corporation. Develops and produces evidence-based clinical guidelines and software.
www.careguidelines.com
Annual Revenues: $1.50 million
Employees: 30
Industry/ies: Medicine/Health Care/Mental Health

President and Chief Executive Officer   Tel: (206) 381-8100
SHREVE, Jon   Fax: (206) 464-7813
jon.shreve@milliman.com

Main Headquarters
Mailing: 901 Fifth Ave.   Tel: (206) 389-5300
             Suite 2000   Fax: (206) 464-7813
             Seattle, WA 98164   TF: (888) 464-4746

Public Affairs and Related Activities Personnel

At Headquarters

DALY, Kevin   Tel: (206) 389-5300
Vice President, Sales and Market Development   Fax: (206) 464-7813

FREEMAN, Jennifer   Tel: (206) 389-5300
Vice President, Finance   Fax: (206) 464-7813

HERMOSILLO, Jeff   Tel: (206) 389-5300
Senior Vice President, Sales and Marketing   Fax: (206) 464-7813

KERN, Peter   Tel: (206) 389-5300
Chief Financial Officer   Fax: (206) 464-7813

SCHWARTZ, Jay   Tel: (206) 389-5300
Senior Vice President, Sales and Operations   Fax: (206) 464-7813

Millipore Corporation

International bioscience company that provides technologies, tools and services for the discovery, development and production of therapeutic drugs.
www.millipore.com
Annual Revenues: $1.65 billion
Employees: 6,100
SIC: 3826
Industry/ies: Pharmaceutical Industry

Cheif Exceuive Officer and President   Tel: (978) 715-4321
BATRA, Udit   Fax: (800) 645-5439

Main Headquarters
Mailing: 290 Concord Rd.   Tel: (978) 715-4321
             Billerica, MA 01821   Fax: (800) 645-5439
                                        TF: (800) 645-5439

Corporate Foundations and Giving Programs

Millipore Corporate Giving Program

Contact: Tara Duplaga
290 Concord Rd.   Tel: (978) 715-4321
Billerica, MA 01821

Public Affairs and Related Activities Personnel

At Headquarters

BONNEVIER, Bruce   Tel: (978) 715-4321
Corporate Vice President, Global Human Resources   Fax: (800) 645-5439

CONNOLLY, Renee   Tel: (978) 715-4321
Head, Communications   Fax: (800) 645-5439

DAS, Chandreyee   Tel: (978) 762-5147
Specialist, Senior Content Development, Marketing   Fax: (800) 645-5439
Communications
chandreyee_das@millipore.com

DUPLAGA, Tara   Tel: (978) 715-1268
Representative, Corporate Giving   Fax: (800) 645-5439
tara_duplaga@millipore.com

HUTCHINSON, David   Tel: (978) 715-4321
Head, Legal   Fax: (800) 645-5439

JOHNSON, Charleen   Tel: (978) 715-1268
Executive Director, Millipore Foundation   Fax: (978) 715-1385
charleen_johnson@millipore.com

MENNER, Megan Wherry   Tel: (978) 715-4321
Head, Human Resources   Fax: (800) 645-5439

ROSS, Chris   Tel: (978) 715-4321
Head, Operations   Fax: (800) 645-5439

WIRTH, Jean Charles   Tel: (978) 715-4321
Head, Finance and Controlling   Fax: (800) 645-5439

YATES, Robert   Tel: (978) 715-4321
President   Fax: (800) 645-5439

Mindspeed Technologies Inc.

A provider of semiconductor products and systems solutions for internet infrastructure.
www.mindspeed.com
Employees: 554
Ticker: NASDAQ: MSPD
SIC: 3674
Industry/ies: Energy/Electricity

Chairman of the Board   Tel: (949) 579-3000
DECKER, Dwight W.   Fax: (949) 579-3200

Chief Executive Officer and Director   Tel: (949) 579-3000
HALIM, Raouf Y.   Fax: (949) 579-3200

Main Headquarters
Mailing: 4000 MacArthur Blvd.   Tel: (949) 579-3000
             E. Tower   Fax: (949) 579-3020
             Newport Beach, CA 92660

Public Affairs and Related Activities Personnel

At Headquarters

ANANIAS, Stephen N.   Tel: (949) 579-3000
Senior Vice President and Chief Financial Officer Fax: (949) 579-3020

GARCIA, Allison K.   Tel: (949) 579-3000
Senior Vice President, Human Resources   Fax: (949) 579-3020

HAMILTON, Gerald J. (Jerry)   Tel: (949) 579-3000
Senior Vice President, Worldwide Sales   Fax: (949) 579-3020

STEEGE, Brandi   Tel: (949) 579-3000
Vice President and General Counsel   Fax: (949) 579-3020

TROSIAN, Kevin   Tel: (949) 579-3000
Vice President, Corporate Development and Investor Fax: (949) 579-3020
Relations
kevin.trosian@mindspeed.com

Mine Safety Appliances Company (MSA)

Established in 1914, MSA is the manufacturer of safety products designed to protect people throughout the world. MSA's mission is to see to it that men and women may work in safety and that they, their families and their communities may live in health throughout the world.
us.msasafety.com
Annual Revenues: $1.13 billion
Employees: 5,000
Ticker: NYSE: MSA
SIC: 3842; 1799; 2819; 3532; 3577; 5802
NAICS: 339113
Industry/ies: Apparel/Textiles Industry; Mining Industry; Natural Resources

Chairman of the Board   Tel: (724) 776-8600
RYAN, III, John T.   Fax: (724) 776-3280
john.ryan@msanet.com

President and Chief Executive Officer   Tel: (724) 776-8600
LAMBERT, William M.   Fax: (724) 776-3280

Main Headquarters
Mailing: 1000 Cranberry Woods Dr.   Tel: (724) 776-8600
             Cranberry Township, PA 16066 Fax: (724) 776-3280

Political Action Committees
Mine Safety Appliances Company PAC (MSA PAC)
FEC ID: C00173344
Contact: Dennis L. Zeitler
1000 Cranberry Woods Dr.
Cranberry Township, PA 16066

Corporate Foundations and Giving Programs
Mine Safety Appliances Company Charitable Foundation
Contact: Dennis L. Zeitler
P.O. Box 426
Pittsburgh, PA 15230

Public Affairs and Related Activities Personnel

At Headquarters

KRAUSE, Ken	Tel:	(724) 776-8600
Executive Director, Global Finance and Assistant Treasurer	Fax:	(724) 776-3280
MCMAHAN, Stacy	Tel:	(724) 776-8600
Senior Vice President, Chief Financial Officer and Treasurer	Fax:	(724) 776-3280
UHLER, Paul R.	Tel:	(724) 776-8600
Vice President, Global Human Resources	Fax:	(724) 776-3280
paul.uhler@msanet.com		
ZEITLER, Dennis L.	Tel:	(724) 776-8600
Senior Vice President, Chief Financial Officer and PAC Treasurer	Fax:	(724) 776-3280

At Other Offices

DEASY, Mark C.	Tel:	(724) 741-8570
Director, Public Relations and Strategic Communications	Fax:	(412) 967-3451
121 Gamma Dr.		
Pittsburgh, PA 15238-2919		
mark.deasy@msanet.com		
MCCLAINE, Douglas K.	Tel:	(412) 967-3000
Vice President, Secretary and General Counsel	Fax:	(412) 967-3451
121 Gamma Dr.		
Pittsburgh, PA 15238-2919		
douglas.mcclaine@msanet.com		

Mineral Technologies, Inc.

Develops, produces and markets worldwide a broad range of specialty mineral, minerals-based and synthetic minerals products and related systems and services.
www.mineralstech.com
Annual Revenues: $1.75 billion
Employees: 3,868
Ticker: NYSE: MTX
SIC: 2810
NAICS: 327124
Industry/ies: Environment And Conservation; Management; Mining Industry; Natural Resources

Chairman and Chief Executive Officer	Tel:	(212) 878-1800
MUSCARI, Joseph C.	Fax:	(212) 878-1801

Main Headquarters

Mailing:	405 Lexington Ave.	Tel:	(212) 878-1800
	New York City, NY 10174	Fax:	(212) 878-1801

Political Action Committees
Minerals Technologies Inc. Political Action Committee (MTI PAC)
FEC ID: C00378067
Contact: Douglas Todd Dietrich
622 Third Ave.
38th Floor
New York City, NY 10017

> **Contributions to Candidates:** $8,400 (2015-2016)
> Republicans: $8,400

Public Affairs and Related Activities Personnel

At Headquarters

HONEY, Rick B.	Tel:	(212) 878-1831
Vice President, Investor Relations and Corporate Communications	Fax:	(212) 878-1801
rick.honey@mineralstech.com		
III, D.J. Monagle	Tel:	(212) 878-1800
Chief Operating Officer	Fax:	(212) 878-1801
MEEK, Thomas J.	Tel:	(212) 878-1800
Senior Vice President, General Counsel, Secretary, Chief Compliance Officer and Vice President Human Resources	Fax:	(212) 878-1801

At Other Offices

DIETRICH, Douglas Todd	Tel:	(212) 878-1800
Senior Vice President and Chief Financial Officer	Fax:	(212) 878-1801
622 Third Ave., 38th Floor		
New York City, NY 10017		
douglas.dietrich@mineralstech.com		
HASTINGS, Jonathan J.	Tel:	(212) 878-1800
Senior Vice President, Corporate Development	Fax:	(212) 878-1801
622 Third Ave., 38th Floor		

New York City, NY 10017

Minnesota Wire

Minnesota Wire, founded in 1968, is a vertically integrated, custom manufacturing and development house for wire, cable and interconnect assemblies to the Medical, Defense and Industrial markets.
www.mnwire.com
Annual Revenues: $20.87 million
Employees: 400
SIC: 3643
NAICS: 335931
Industry/ies: Electricity & Electronics; Electronics; Energy/Electricity; Metals

Chairman of the Board and Chief Executive Officer	Tel:	(651) 642-1800
WAGNER, Paul J.	Fax:	(651) 642-9201
pwagner@mnwire.com		

Main Headquarters

Mailing:	1835 Energy Park Dr.	Tel:	(651) 642-1800
	St. Paul, MN 55108-2721	Fax:	(651) 642-9201
		TF:	(800) 258-6922

Public Affairs and Related Activities Personnel

At Headquarters

LAINGEN, Chip	Tel:	(651) 642-1800
Director, Communications	Fax:	(651) 642-9201
THOMPSON, Joan	Tel:	(651) 642-1800
Chief Financial Officer	Fax:	(651) 642-9201
jthompson@mnwire.com		

Mission Capital

An investment company.
www.missioncap.com
Annual Revenues: $3.40 million
Employees: 26
Industry/ies: Banking/Finance/Investments

Main Headquarters

Mailing:	32 Avenue of the Americas	Tel:	(212) 925-6692
	Floor 21, Suite 2100	Fax:	(646) 607-8132
	New York City, NY 10013		

Corporate Foundations and Giving Programs

Mission Capital Contributions Program
32 Avenue of the Americas
Floor 21, Suite 2100
New York City, NY 10013

Public Affairs and Related Activities Personnel

At Headquarters

SICILIAN, Chris	Tel:	(212) 925-6692
Chief Financial Officer	Fax:	(646) 607-8132
csicilian@missioncap.com		
VERGARA, Luis	Tel:	(212) 925-6692
Managing Director, Sales and Trading	Fax:	(646) 607-8132
lvergara@missioncap.com		

Mississippi Power Company

An investor-owned electric utility Company - wholly owned subsidiary of Southern Company and serves commercial and residential customers within the 23 counties of southeast Mississippi.
www.mississippipower.com
Employees: 1,253
Ticker: NYSE: MP-PD
SIC: 4911
Industry/ies: Energy/Electricity; Utilities

Chairman of the Board	Tel:	(228) 864-1211
HOLLAND, Jr., G. Edison (Ed)	Fax:	(228) 865-5876

President and Chief Executive Officer	Tel:	(228) 864-1211
WILSON, Anthony	Fax:	(228) 865-5876

Main Headquarters

Mailing:	P.O. Box 4079	Tel:	(228) 864-1211
	Gulfport, MS 39502	Fax:	(228) 865-5876
		TF:	(800) 353-9777

Political Action Committees
Mississippi Power Company Federal PAC A/K/A/ MS PWR CO EMP COMM FOR RESP FED GOV
FEC ID: C00144147
Contact: Rachel V. Newton
2992 W. Beach Blvd.
Gulfport, MS 39501

> **Contributions to Candidates:** $30,000 (2015-2016)
> Democrats: $5,000; Republicans: $25,000
>
> **Principal Recipients**
>
> **HOUSE**
>
> PALAZZO, STEVEN MCCARTY (REP-MS)

Corporate Foundations and Giving Programs

Mississippi Power Education Foundation
P.O. Box 4079
Gulfport, MS 39502

Public Affairs and Related Activities Personnel

At Headquarters

ATHERTON, Johnny W.	Tel:	(228) 864-1211
Vice President, Corporate Services and Community Relations	Fax:	(228) 865-5876
DUVALL, Cindy	Tel:	(228) 865-5543
Manager, Governmental and Community Relations	Fax:	(228) 865-5876
FAULK, Nicole	Tel:	(228) 864-1211
Vice President, Customer Services Organization	Fax:	(228) 865-5876
FEAGIN, Moses	Tel:	(228) 864-1211
Vice President, Treasurer and Chief Financial Officer	Fax:	(228) 865-5876
GETER, Amoi	Tel:	(228) 864-1211
Director, Corporate Communication	Fax:	(228) 865-5876
SHAW, Cindy	Tel:	(228) 864-1211
Comptroller	Fax:	(228) 865-5876
SHEPARD, Jeff	Tel:	(228) 864-1211
Communications Specialist and Media Contact	Fax:	(228) 865-5876
jshepard@southernco.com		
THORNTON, Billy	Tel:	(228) 864-1211
Vice President, External Affairs	Fax:	(228) 865-5876
WEBB, Cindy	Tel:	(228) 864-1211
Director, Human Resources	Fax:	(228) 865-5876

At Other Offices

NEWTON, Rachel V.
PAC Treasurer
2992 W. Beach Blvd.
Gulfport, MS 39502

Missouri Gas Energy

See listing on page 735 under Southern Union Company

Mitsubishi Electric & Electronics, USA

Engaged in the research, marketing, sales, engineering, and manufacturing of electrical and electronic equipment. A subsidiary of Mitsubishi Electric headquartered in Tokyo, Japan.
www.mitsubishielectric-usa.com
Employees: 2,500
Industry/ies: Electricity & Electronics; Electronics; Energy/Electricity

President and Chief Executive Officer	Tel:	(714) 220-2500
TAKAMIYA, Katsuya	Fax:	(714) 229-3854

Main Headquarters

Mailing:	5900-A Katella Ave.	Tel:	(714) 220-2500
	Cypress, CA 90630-5019	Fax:	(714) 229-3854

Washington Office

Mailing:	1300 Wilson Blvd.	Tel:	(703) 276-8240
	Suite 210	Fax:	(703) 276-8260
	Arlington, VA 22209		

Corporate Foundations and Giving Programs

Mitsubishi Electric America Foundation		
Contact: Kevin R. Webb		
1560 Wilson Blvd.	Tel:	(703) 276-8240
Suite 1175		
Arlington, VA 22209		

Public Affairs and Related Activities Personnel

At Headquarters

BLANCHARD, Cayce	Tel:	(714) 229-3837
Senior Vice President, Corporate Communications	Fax:	(714) 229-3854
cayce.blanchard@meus.mea.com		
BRENIZER, Bruce	Tel:	(714) 220-2500
Senior Vice President, Human Resources and Administration	Fax:	(714) 229-3854
PAPPOUS, Perry	Tel:	(714) 220-2500
Executive Vice President and General Counsel	Fax:	(714) 229-3854
perry.pappous@meus.mea.com		
SCOTT, Mark S.	Tel:	(714) 220-6896
Senior Manager, Corporate Communications	Fax:	(714) 229-3954
mark.scott@meus.mea.com		

At Washington Office

SALAVANTIS, Peter J.	Tel:	(703) 276-3519
Senior Vice President	Fax:	(703) 276-8168
peter.salavantis@meus.mea.com		
Registered Federal Lobbyist		
WEBB, Kevin R.	Tel:	(703) 276-8240
Director, Mitsubishi Electric America Foundation	Fax:	(703) 276-8260
kevin.webb@meus.mea.com		

Mitsubishi International Corporation

A wholly owned subsidiary of Mitsubishi Corporation. This multi-industry trading and investment company with 12 locations across the United States deals with businesses that include chemicals, information technology, energy, metals machinery and living essentials.
www.mitsubishicorp.com/us/en
Annual Revenues: $2.048 B
Employees: 800
Industry/ies: Aerospace/Aviation; Transportation

Chairman of the Board	Tel:	(212) 605-2000
KOJIMA, Yorihiko	Fax:	(212) 605-2597
President, Chief Executive Officer and Director	Tel:	(212) 605-2000
MIZUHARA, Hidemoto	Fax:	(212) 605-2597

Main Headquarters

Mailing:	655 Third Ave.	Tel:	(212) 605-2000
	Floor Four	Fax:	(212) 605-2597
	New York City, NY 10017		

Washington Office

Mailing:	2001 Pennsylvania Ave. NW	Tel:	(202) 331-7301
	Suite 700	Fax:	(202) 331-7277
	Washington, DC 20006-1807		

Corporate Foundations and Giving Programs

Mitsubishi International Corporation Foundation
Contact: Tracy L. Austin
655 Third Ave.
New York City, NY 10017

Public Affairs and Related Activities Personnel

At Headquarters

AUSTIN, Tracy L.	Tel:	(212) 605-2121
General Manager, Corporate Communications	Fax:	(212) 605-1908
tracy.austin@mitsubishicorp.com		
GALLOWAY, Jil	Tel:	(212) 605-2000
Senior Vice President, Director, Human Resources and Chief	Fax:	(212) 605-2597
Administration Officer		
KEEGAN, Mark	Tel:	(212) 605-2314
Manager, Investor Relations	Fax:	(212) 605-1908
mark.keegan@mitsubishicorp.com		
KUROSAWA, Akihiro	Tel:	(212) 605-2000
Chief Compliance Officer	Fax:	(212) 605-2597
ROGERS, Julie	Tel:	(212) 605-2000
Contact, Media Relations	Fax:	(212) 605-2597
julie.rogers@mitsubishicorp.com		
STEVENS, Jason	Tel:	(212) 605-2000
Senior Vice President, Chief Legal Officer, Chief Compliance	Fax:	(212) 605-2597
Officer, (Group Head, Legal & Compliance) Secretary and		
Director		
TSURUTA, Naoki	Tel:	(212) 605-2000
Senior Vice President, Chief Financial Officer, Chief	Fax:	(212) 605-2597
Information Officer, (Group Head, Finance & Accounting)		
and Director		

At Washington Office

YANAGIHARA, Tsunehiko	Tel:	(202) 331-7301
Senior Vice President and General Manager, Washington DC	Fax:	(202) 331-7277
Office		
tsunehiko.yanagihara@mitsubishicorp.com		

Mitsubishi Motors North America, Inc.

Headquartered in Cypress, CA. Mitsubishi Motors North America (MMNA) oversees the North American operations of Japan's Mitsubishi Motors. It develops, manufactures, markets, sells, distributes, and finances (through Mitsubishi Motors Credit of America) Mitsubishi brand cars and SUVs through a network of about 400 US dealers.
www.mitsubishicars.com
Annual Revenues: $1.19 billion
Employees: 3,600
SIC: 3711
Industry/ies: Automotive Industry; Transportation

President and Chief Executive Officer	Tel:	(714) 372-6000
FUTAKI, Shiro	Fax:	(714) 373-1020

Main Headquarters

Mailing:	6400 Katella Ave.	Tel:	(714) 372-6000
	P.O. Box 6400	Fax:	(714) 373-1020
	Cypress, CA 90630-9998	TF:	(888) 648-7820

Washington Office

Mailing:	1560 Wilson Blvd., Suite 1200	Fax:	(703) 525-6772
	Arlington, VA 22209		

Mitsubishi Power Systems Americas Inc

Products and services for the electric power generation industry.
Legislative Issues: ENG; ENV; TRD

Main Headquarters

Mailing:	400 Colonial Center Pkwy.	Fax:	(407) 688-6480

Suite 400
Lake Mary, FL 32746

Washington Office

Mailing: 1025 Connecticut Ave.
Suite 1204
Washington, DC 20036

Public Affairs and Related Activities Personnel

At Headquarters

GALLINGER, Jon	Tel:	(407) 688-6480
Director, Government Affairs	Fax:	(407) 688-6480
Registered Federal Lobbyist		
NEWSOM, Bill	Tel:	(407) 688-6480
Executive Vice President of Sales and Marketing	Fax:	(407) 688-6480

Mitsui and Company (U.S.A.), Inc.

Has operations in iron and steel products and materials, infrastructure projects, machinery, information technology, chemicals, plastics and consumer products, among others. A wholly owned subsidiary of Mitsui & Co., Ltd., a global investment and service enterprise based in Tokyo, Japan.
www.mitsui.com
Annual Revenues: $350 million
Employees: 4,500
SIC: 2399; 3441; 3444; 3731
NAICS: 314999; 332312; 336611; 332322
Industry/ies: Trade (Foreign And Domestic)

President and Chief Executive Officer	Tel:	(212) 878-4000
TAKAHASHI, Yasushi	Fax:	(212) 878-4800

Main Headquarters

Mailing: 200 Park Ave.	Tel:	(212) 878-4000
New York City, NY 10166	Fax:	(212) 878-4800

Washington Office

Mailing: 750 17th St. NW	Tel:	(202) 861-0660
Suite 400	Fax:	(202) 861-0437
Washington, DC 20006		

Corporate Foundations and Giving Programs

Mitsui USA Foundation
Contact: Shinichi Hirabayashi
200 Park Ave.
New York City, NY 10166

Public Affairs and Related Activities Personnel

At Headquarters

CAMPBELL, Eric	Tel:	(218) 878-4039
Media Contact	Fax:	(212) 878-4800
GUSHIKEN, Yoshimitsu	Tel:	(212) 878-4000
Senior Vice President and Chief Financial Officer	Fax:	(212) 878-4800
KAWAMURA, Kazuhisa	Tel:	(212) 878-4000
Corporate Communications	Fax:	(212) 878-4800
MENZER, Steven	Tel:	(212) 878-4000
Vice President, Human Resources Division	Fax:	(212) 878-4800
s.menzer@mitsui.com		
SACHIGAI, Mikako	Tel:	(212) 878-4000
Corporate Communications	Fax:	(212) 878-4800
M.Sachigai@mitsui.com		
SERA, Yuichiro	Tel:	(212) 878-4000
Corporate Communications	Fax:	(212) 878-4800
TAKAHASHI, Motomu	Tel:	(212) 878-4000
Representative Director, Executive Vice President	Fax:	(212) 878-4800

At Washington Office

YONEYAMA, Nobuo	Tel:	(202) 861-0666
General Manager	Fax:	(202) 861-0437

MMGL Corporation

Formerly known as Schnitzer Investment Corporation. Investment firm with interests in commercial, industrial and multi-family properties, real estate development projects, ocean shipping, and other industries.
www.mmglcorp.com
Employees: 100
Industry/ies: Banking/Finance/Investments

PAC Treasurer	Tel:	(503) 595-8100
THOMA, John Robert	Fax:	(503) 595-8315

Main Headquarters

Mailing: 818 Stewart St.
Suite 700
Seattle, WA 98101

Mobile Medical International Corporation, Inc.

Provides mobile medical facilities for commercial, military and emergency response applications.
www.mobile-medical.com

Annual Revenues: $11.69 million
Employees: 30
Industry/ies: Medicine/Health Care/Mental Health
Legislative Issues: VET

President and Chief Executive Officer	Tel:	(802) 748-2322
COCHRAN, Rick	Fax:	(802) 748-2323

Main Headquarters

Mailing: 2176 Portland St.	Tel:	(802) 748-2322
P.O. Box 672	Fax:	(802) 748-2323
St. Johnsbury, VT 05819	TF:	(800) 748-2322

Corporate Foundations and Giving Programs

MMIC Cotributions Program		
2176 Portland St.	Tel:	(802) 748-2322
P.O. Box 672	Fax:	(802) 748-2323
St. Johnsbury, VT 05819		

Public Affairs and Related Activities Personnel

At Headquarters

BALDWIN JR., Richard	Tel:	(802) 748-2322
Vice President, International Business Development	Fax:	(802) 748-2323
LUMBRA, Janet	Tel:	(802) 748-2322
Commercial Product Specialist and Media Contact	Fax:	(802) 748-2323
JLumbra@mmicglobal.com		
WELSH, Tim	Tel:	(802) 748-2322
PAC Contact	Fax:	(802) 748-2323

Modine Manufacturing Company

A thermal management company which design, engineer, test, and manufacture heat transfer products for a wide range of applications and markets. We're at work in practically every corner of the world, inside the things you see every day..
www.modine.com
Annual Revenues: $1.35 billion
Employees: 7,100
Ticker: NYSE: MOD
SIC: 3714
NAICS: 336399
Industry/ies: Heating And Air Conditioning

President and Chief Executive Officer	Tel:	(262) 636-1200
BURKE, Thomas A.	Fax:	(262) 636-1424

Main Headquarters

Mailing: 1500 DeKoven Ave.	Tel:	(262) 636-1200
Racine, WI 53403-2552	Fax:	(262) 636-1424
	TF:	(800) 828-4328

Corporate Foundations and Giving Programs

The Modine Manufacturing Company Charity Foundation
Contact: Valerie Madala
1500 DeKoven Ave.
Racine, WI 53403

Public Affairs and Related Activities Personnel

At Headquarters

AGEN, Brian J.	Tel:	(262) 636-1200
Vice President, Human Resources	Fax:	(262) 636-1424
KELSEY, Margaret C.	Tel:	(262) 636-8442
Vice President, Legal and Corporate Communications,	Fax:	(262) 636-1424
General Counsel and Secretary		
m.c.kelsey@na.modine.com		
LUCARELI, Michael B.	Tel:	(262) 636-1200
Vice President, Finance, Chief Financial Officer and Treasurer	Fax:	(262) 636-1424
MADALA, Valerie	Tel:	(262) 636-1200
Coordinator, Foundation	Fax:	(262) 636-1424
MARRY , Thomas F.	Tel:	(262) 636-1200
Executive Vice President, Chief Operating Officer	Fax:	(262) 636-1424
POWERS, Kathleen T.	Tel:	(262) 636-1687
Vice President, Treasurer and Investor Relations	Fax:	(262) 636-1424
k.t.powers@na.modine.com		
WILLIAMS, Marsha C.	Tel:	(262) 636-1200
Board Member	Fax:	(262) 636-1424

Mohawk Industries

A manufacturer and marketer of carpets, washable accents and bath rugs.
www.mohawkind.com
Annual Revenues: $7.87 billion
Employees: 32,300
Ticker: NYSE: MHK
SIC: 2273
Industry/ies: Construction/Construction Materials

Chairman and Chief Executive Officer	Tel:	(706) 629-7721
LORBERBAUM, Jeffrey S.	Fax:	(706) 624-3825
jeff_lorberbaum@mohawkind.com		

Main Headquarters

Mailing: 160 S. Industrial Blvd.	Tel:	(706) 629-7721
Calhoun, GA 30701	Fax:	(706) 624-3825
	TF:	(800) 241-4494

Corporate Foundations and Giving Programs

Mohawk Carpet Foundation
P.O. Box 12069   Tel: (706) 629-7721
Calhoun, GA 30703   Fax: (706) 624-3825

Public Affairs and Related Activities Personnel

At Headquarters

BOYKIN, Frank H.   Tel: (706) 624-2695
Chief Financial Officer   Fax: (706) 624-3825

PATTON, R. David   Tel: (706) 629-7721
Vice President, Business Strategy and General Counsel   Fax: (706) 624-3825

WELLBORN, W. Christopher   Tel: (706) 629-7721
President and Chief Operating Officer   Fax: (706) 624-3825

Molded Fiber Glass Companies

An international manufacturer of composites products.
www.moldedfiberglass.com
Annual Revenues: $141.30 million
Employees: 1,900
SIC: 3089
NAICS: 326199
Industry/ies: Computer/Technology; Construction/Construction Materials

Chief Executive Officer   Tel: (440) 997-5851
MORRISON, Richard S.   Fax: (440) 994-5162

Main Headquarters

Mailing: P.O. Box 675   Tel: (440) 997-5851
2925 MFG Pl.   Fax: (440) 994-5162
Ashtabula, OH 44005-0675   TF: (800) 860-0196

Corporate Foundations and Giving Programs

Molded Fiber Glass Companies Contribution Program
2925 MFG Pl.   Tel: (440) 997-5851
P.O. Box 675   Fax: (440) 994-5162
Ashtabula, OH 44005-0675

Public Affairs and Related Activities Personnel

At Headquarters

COX, Camille   Tel: (805) 391-0378
Contact, Media Relations   Fax: (440) 994-5162
Camille@onrampcomm.com

DAVIS, Larry   Tel: (440) 994-5261
Vice President, Corporate Human Resources   Fax: (440) 994-5162
ldavis@moldedfiberglass.com

FINK, Kurt F.   Tel: (440) 994-5222
Director, Marketing and Media Relations   Fax: (440) 994-5162
kfink@molderfiberglass.com

HENRY, Wendy   Tel: (440) 997-5851
Controller   Fax: (440) 994-5162

JUHOLA, Andy   Tel: (440) 994-5261
Manager, Human Resources   Fax: (440) 994-5162
ajuhola@moldedfiberglass.com

WARNER, Glen   Tel: (440) 994-5152
Corporate Vice President, Marketing   Fax: (440) 994-5162
glwarner@moldedfiberglass.com

Molecular Biometrics

Develops highly specific and sensitive analytical methodologies for molecular diagnostic and monitoring applications in medicine, and for drug discovery and development through pharmacodiagnostics.
www.molecularbiometrics.com
Annual Revenues: $1.50 million
Employees: 16
Industry/ies: Medicine/Health Care/Mental Health; Pharmaceutical Industry

President and Chief Executive Officer   Tel: (781) 501-5600
POSILLICO, PhD, James T.   Fax: (781) 501-5602

Main Headquarters

Mailing: One Edgewater Dr.   Tel: (781) 501-5600
Suite 110   Fax: (781) 501-5602
Norwood, MA 02062-4692

Molex, Inc.

A manufacturer of electronic, electrical, and fiber optic components.
www.molex.com
Annual Revenues: $3.60 billion
Employees: 35,983
Ticker: NASDAQ: MOLX
SIC: 3678
Industry/ies: Electricity & Electronics; Electronics; Energy/Electricity

Co-Chairman of the Board   Tel: (630) 969-4550
KREHBIEL, Frederick A.   Fax: (630) 969-1352

Co-Chairman of the Board   Tel: (630) 969-4550
KREHBIEL, John A.   Fax: (630) 969-1352
john.krehbiel@molex.com

Chief Executive Officer   Tel: (630) 969-4550
SLARK, Martin P.   Fax: (630) 969-1352

Main Headquarters

Mailing: 2222 Wellington Ct.   Tel: (630) 969-4550
Lisle, IL 60532   Fax: (630) 968-8356
    TF: (800) 786-6539

Public Affairs and Related Activities Personnel

At Headquarters

ARMITAGE, Susan   Tel: (630) 527-4561
Senior Director, Corporate Communications   Fax: (630) 512-8627
susan.armitage@molex.com

JOHNSON, David D.   Tel: (630) 969-4550
Executive Vice President, Treasurer and Chief Financial Officer   Fax: (630) 968-8356
dave.johnson@molex.com

LEFORT, Neil G.   Tel: (630) 527-4344
Senior Vice President   Fax: (630) 969-1352

MCCARTHY, Liam   Tel: (630) 969-4550
President and Chief Operating Officer   Fax: (630) 968-8356

RUFF, Tim   Tel: (630) 969-4550
Senior Vice President, Business Development and Corporate Strategy   Fax: (630) 968-8356

ZEITLER, Robert J.   Tel: (630) 969-4550
Senior Vice President, General Counsel and Corporate Secretary   Fax: (630) 968-8356

Molina Healthcare, Inc.

Provides medicaid-related solutions.
www.molinahealthcare.com
Annual Revenues: $14.94 billion
Employees: 21,000
Ticker: NYSE: MOH
SIC: 6324
Industry/ies: Medicine/Health Care/Mental Health
Legislative Issues: MMM

President and Chief Executive Officer   Tel: (562) 435-3666
MOLINA, MD, Joseph Mario   Fax: (562) 499-0790

Main Headquarters

Mailing: 200 Oceangate   Tel: (562) 435-3666
Suite 100   Fax: (562) 499-0790
Long Beach, CA 90802   TF: (888) 562-5442

Washington Office

Mailing: 601 13th St NW   Tel: (888) 562-5442
Suite 800
District of Columbia, DC 20005

Political Action Committees

Molina Healthcare, Inc. PAC
FEC ID: C00430256
Contact: Michael L. Mayers
200 Oceangate
Suite 100
Long Beach, CA 90802

> **Contributions to Candidates:** $150,000 (2015-2016)
> Democrats: $72,750; Republicans: $77,250

> #### Principal Recipients
> #### HOUSE
> MATSUI, DORIS (DEM-CA)

Corporate Foundations and Giving Programs

Molina Healthcare, Inc. Contributions Program
200 Oceangate   Tel: (562) 435-3666
Suite 100
Long Beach, CA 90802

Public Affairs and Related Activities Personnel

At Headquarters

BARLOW, JD, MPH, Jeff D.   Tel: (562) 435-3666
Senior Vice President, General Counsel, and Secretary   Fax: (562) 499-0790

BAYER, Terry   Tel: (562) 435-3666
Chief Operating Officer   Fax: (562) 499-0790

BYRD-JOHNSON, Diana   Tel: (562) 435-3666
Manager, Community Affairs   Fax: (562) 499-0790
diane.byrd-johnson@molinahealthcare.com

MAYERS, Michael L.   Tel: (562) 435-3666
Vice President, Policy & Government Advocacy   Fax: (562) 499-0790

michael.mayers@molinahealthcare.com
Registered Federal Lobbyist

MOLINA, JD, John C.	Tel:	(562) 435-3666
Chief Financial Officer	Fax:	(562) 499-0790
O'GUIN, Kathleen	Tel:	(562) 951-8305
Director, Public Relations	Fax:	(562) 499-0790
ORELLANA, MBA, Juan Jose	Tel:	(562) 435-3666
Senior Vice President, Investor Relations and Marketing	Fax:	(562) 499-0790
WHITE, Joseph W.	Tel:	(562) 435-3666
Chief Accounting Officer	Fax:	(562) 499-0790

At Other Offices

PREEDE, Kenneth M.	Tel:	(888) 562-5442

Director, Federal Affairs
300 University Ave., Suite 100
Sacramento, CA 95825
kpreede@ahca.org
Registered Federal Lobbyist

TENHOUSE, Amy	Tel:	(888) 562-5442

Director, Policy
300 University Ave., Suite 100
Sacramento, CA 95825
Registered Federal Lobbyist

Molybdenum Corporation of America (MCA)

See listing on page 548 under Molycorp Minerals, LLC

Molycorp Minerals, LLC

A mining and technology company that produces and markets rare earth products. Molycorp Inc. is a wholly owned Subsidiary of Chevron. In 2007 Molycorp Inc. merged into Chevron Mining, Inc.
www.molycorp.com
Annual Revenues: $463.51 million
Employees: 2,500
Ticker: NYSE: MCP
SIC: 1000
Industry/ies: Mining Industry; Natural Resources
Legislative Issues: DEF; ENV; MAN

Chairman of the Board	Tel:	(303) 843-8040
KARAYANNOPOULOS, Constantine	Fax:	(303) 843-8082

President, Chief Executive Officer and Chief Operating Officer	Tel:	(303) 843-8040
BEDFORD, Geoffrey R.	Fax:	(303) 843-8082

Main Headquarters

Mailing:	5619 DTC Pkwy.	Tel:	(303) 843-8040
	Suite 1000	Fax:	(303) 843-8082
	Greenwood Village, CO 80111		

Public Affairs and Related Activities Personnel

At Headquarters

ALLEN, James S.	Tel:	(303) 843-8040
Senior Vice President and Treasurer	Fax:	(303) 843-8082
BLACKMAN, Brian	Tel:	(303) 843-8040
Vice President, Investor Relations	Fax:	(303) 843-8082

Brian.Blackman@molycorp.com

CALDWELL, Alexander D.	Tel:	(303) 843-8040
Corporate Secretary and Vice President, Administration	Fax:	(303) 843-8082
DOOLAN, Michael F.	Tel:	(303) 843-8040
Executive Vice President and Chief Financial Officer	Fax:	(303) 843-8082
JOHNSON, Kevin W.	Tel:	(303) 843-8040
Executive Vice President and General Counsel	Fax:	(303) 843-8082
SIMS, James T.	Tel:	(303) 843-8067
Vice President, Corporate Communications	Fax:	(303) 843-8082

jim.sims@molycorp.com
Registered Federal Lobbyist

Momenta Pharmaceuticals, Inc.

A biotechnology company working with the science of sugars and complex biomolecules.
www.momentapharma.com
Annual Revenues: $50.03 million
Employees: 256
Ticker: NASDAQ: MNTA
SIC: 2836
Industry/ies: Pharmaceutical Industry
Legislative Issues: PHA

Chairman of the Board	Tel:	(617) 491-9700
SULAT, James	Fax:	(617) 621-0431

President and Chief Executive Officer	Tel:	(617) 491-9700
WHEELER, Craig A.	Fax:	(617) 621-0431

Main Headquarters

Mailing:	675 W. Kendall St.	Tel:	(617) 491-9700
	Cambridge, MA 02142	Fax:	(617) 621-0431

Public Affairs and Related Activities Personnel

At Headquarters

BELTRAMELLO, Jo-Ann	Tel:	(617) 491-9700
Senior Vice President, Human Resources	Fax:	(617) 621-0431
HOLLEY, Beverly	Tel:	(617) 491-5189
Director, Investor Relations	Fax:	(617) 621-0431

bholley@momentapharma.com

KWON, Young	Tel:	(617) 491-9700
Vice President, Corporate Development and Strategy	Fax:	(617) 621-0431
LEICHER, Bruce A.	Tel:	(617) 491-9700
Senior Vice President and General Counsel, Legal	Fax:	(617) 621-0431
SHEA, Richard P.	Tel:	(617) 491-9700
Senior Vice President and Chief Financial Officer	Fax:	(617) 621-0431

Momentive Performance Materials

Formed in October 2010 from the combination of entities that owned Momentive Performance Materials Inc. and Momentive Specialty Chemicals Inc. (formerly known as Hexion Specialty Chemicals Inc.). A provider of silicones and advanced materials.
www.momentive.com
Annual Revenues: $3.81 billion
Employees: 11,000
SIC: 2821
Industry/ies: Chemicals & Chemical Industry; Construction/Construction Materials
Legislative Issues: TRD

Chief Executive Officer and President	Tel:	(614) 225-2223
BOSS, Jack		

Main Headquarters

Mailing:	260 Hudson River Rd.	Tel:	(614) 225-2223
	Waterford, NY 12188		

Public Affairs and Related Activities Personnel

At Headquarters

ASMUSSEN, Erick	Tel:	(614) 225-2223
Senior Vice President and Chief Financial Officer		
PSUTKA, Stephen	Tel:	(614) 225-2223
Interim General Counsel		

At Other Offices

CARTER, William H.	Tel:	(518) 533-4600
Executive Vice President and Chief Financial Officer	Fax:	(518) 533-4609

180 E. Broad St.
Columbus, OH 43215
william.carter@momentive.com,bill.carter@momentive.com

JOHNSON, Douglas A.	Tel:	(518) 533-4600
Executive Vice President and Secretary	Fax:	(518) 533-4609

180 E. Broad St.
Columbus, OH 43215

KNIGHT, George F.	Tel:	(518) 533-4600
Senior Vice President, Finance and PAC Treasurer	Fax:	(518) 533-4609

180 E. Broad St.
Columbus, OH 43215

KOMPA, John	Tel:	(614) 225-2223
Vice President, Investor Relations and Public Affairs	Fax:	(518) 533-4609

180 E. Broad St.
Columbus, OH 43215
john.kompa@momentive.com

SONNETT, Judith A.	Tel:	(518) 533-4600
Executive Vice President, Human Resources	Fax:	(518) 533-4609

180 E. Broad St.
Columbus, OH 43215

Mondelez International

A food producer, name changed to Mondelez International, Inc. A subsidiary of Altria Group, Inc. (see separate listing). Acquired Nabisco in 2001.
www.mondelezinternational.com
Annual Revenues: $33.36billion
Employees: 104,000
Ticker: NASDAQ: MDLZ
SIC: 2000
Industry/ies: Dairy Industry; Food And Beverage Industry; Food Industry
Legislative Issues: AGR; FOO; TAX; TRD

Chairman and Chief Executive Officer	Tel:	(847) 646-2000
ROSENFELD, Irene B.	Fax:	(847) 646-6005

Main Headquarters

Mailing:	Three Pkwy., North	Tel:	(847) 646-2000
	Suite 300	Fax:	(847) 646-6005
	Deerfield, IL 60015		

Washington Office

Mailing:	975 F St. NW
	Suite 1025
	Washington, DC 20004

Corporate Foundations and Giving Programs

Mondelez International Foundation
Three Pkwy., North
Deerfield, IL 60015 — Tel: (847) 943-4000 / Fax: (847) 943-4901

Public Affairs and Related Activities Personnel

At Headquarters

BREARTON, David — Tel: (847) 646-2000 / Fax: (847) 646-6005
Executive Vice President, Strategic Initiatives

CLOUSE, Mark — Tel: (847) 646-2000 / Fax: (847) 646-6005
Chief Growth Officer

CONGBALAY, Dexter — Tel: (847) 943-5454 / Fax: (847) 646-6005
Vice President, Investor Relations

CRAWFORD, Derek — Tel: (847) 646-2000
Registered Federal Lobbyist

GLADDEN, Brian — Tel: (847) 646-2000 / Fax: (847) 646-6005
Executive Vice President and Chief Financial Officer

JAKUBIK, Chris — Tel: (847) 646-5494 / Fax: (847) 646-6005
Vice President, Finance and Investor Relations
r@kraft.com

MAY, Karen J. — Tel: (847) 646-2000 / Fax: (847) 646-6005
Executive Vice President, Human Resources

MITCHELL, Michael — Tel: (847) 646-2000 / Fax: (847) 646-6005
Senior Director, Corporate External Communications

PERNU, Cathy — Tel: (847) 646-3946 / Fax: (847) 646-6005
Senior Manager, Corporate Communications
cpernu@kraft.com

PLEUHS, Gerhard — Tel: (847) 646-2000 / Fax: (847) 646-6005
Executive Vice President and General Counsel

SINDERS, Paul — Tel: (847) 646-2000
Registered Federal Lobbyist

WEST, Mary Beth — Tel: (847) 646-2000 / Fax: (847) 646-6005
Executive Vice President and Chief Category and Marketing Officer

At Washington Office

BELCOURT, Tracey — Tel: (202) 741-1500
Executive Vice President, Strategy

BLUNT, Abigail — Tel: (202) 741-1500
Global Head, Government Affairs
Mail Stop Suite 1025
Registered Federal Lobbyist

BUCKNER, Tami — Tel: (202) 741-1500
Director, Federal Government Affairs
Tami.Buckner@Kraft.com

CRAWFORD, Derek — Tel: (202) 741-1500
Registered Federal Lobbyist

DAIGLER, Nancy — Tel: (202) 741-1500
Senior Vice President, Corporate and Government Affairs
nancy.daigler@kraft.com

FOLKERTS, Brian — Tel: (202) 741-1500 / Fax: (202) 741-1506
Vice President, Government Affairs and PAC Treasurer
brian.folkerts@mdlz.com
Registered Federal Lobbyist

JACOBY LEMOS, Jessica — Tel: (202) 741-1500
Federal Lobbyist
Registered Federal Lobbyist

MIHAS, Tracy — Tel: (202) 741-1500 / Fax: (202) 741-1506
Director, Corporate and Government Affairs

ROBERTS, Ken J. — Tel: (202) 741-1500 / Fax: (202) 741-1506
Federal Lobbyist
Registered Federal Lobbyist

SINDERS, Paul — Tel: (202) 741-1500
Registered Federal Lobbyist

STEINER, Eric J. — Tel: (202) 741-1500
Director, Government Affairs and Policy

WHITE, Deborah A. — Tel: (202) 741-1500
Director, External Relations

Monsanto Company

Produces and markets high-value agricultural products. Spun off from Pharmacia Corp. in August of 2002. Splits into the divisions: Seeds and Genomics and Agricultural Productivity.
www.monsanto.com
Annual Revenues: $14.95 billion
Employees: 22,400
Ticker: NYSE: MON
SIC: 2870
Industry/ies: Agriculture/Agronomy; Chemicals & Chemical Industry
Legislative Issues: AGR; CHM; CPT; ENG; ENV; FOO; FOR; MAN; NAT; SCI; TAX; TRD

Chairman of the Board and Chief Executive Officer
GRANT, Hugh — Tel: (314) 694-1000 / Fax: (314) 694-8394
hugh.grant@monsanto.com

Main Headquarters
Mailing: 800 N. Lindbergh Blvd. — Tel: (314) 694-1000 / Fax: (314) 694-8394
St. Louis, MO 63167

Washington Office
Mailing: 1300 I St. NW — Tel: (202) 783-2460 / Fax: (202) 789-1819
Suite 450 East
Washington, DC 20005-7211

Political Action Committees
Monsanto Company Citizenship Fund Aka Monsanto Citizenship Fund PAC
FEC ID: C00042069
Contact: Katharine Emerson
800 N. Lindbergh Blvd. — Tel: (314) 694-1000
St. Louis, MO 63167

Contributions to Candidates: $359,000 (2015-2016)
Democrats: $78,000; Republicans: $276,000; Other: $5,000

Principal Recipients

SENATE
CRAPO, MICHAEL D (REP-ID)

HOUSE
BOEHNER, JOHN A. (REP-OH)
CONAWAY, MICHAEL HONORABLE (REP-TX)
DAVIS, RODNEY L (REP-IL)
HOYER, STENY HAMILTON (DEM-DC)
LUCAS, FRANK D. (REP-OK)
PETERSON, COLLIN CLARK (DEM-MN)
SHIMKUS, JOHN M (REP-IL)
SMITH, ADRIAN (REP-NE)
THOMPSON, BENNIE G. (DEM-MS)

Corporate Foundations and Giving Programs
Monsanto Fund
Contact: Janet M. Holloway
800 N. Lindbergh Blvd.
St. Louis, MO 63167

Public Affairs and Related Activities Personnel

At Headquarters

BEGEMANN, Brett D. — Tel: (314) 694-1000 / Fax: (314) 694-8394
President and Chief Operating Officer

COURDUROUX, Pierre — Tel: (314) 694-1000 / Fax: (314) 694-8394
Senior Vice President and Chief Financial Officer

EMERSON, Katharine — Tel: (314) 694-1000 / Fax: (314) 694-8394
PAC Treasurer
Registered Federal Lobbyist

HARTLEY, Tom D. — Tel: (314) 694-1000 / Fax: (314) 694-8394
Vice President and Treasurer

HOLLOWAY, Janet M. — Tel: (314) 694-1000 / Fax: (314) 694-8394
Senior Vice President, Chief of Staff and Community Relations

MIZELL, Steven C. — Tel: (314) 694-1000 / Fax: (314) 694-8394
Executive Vice President, Human Resources
steven.c.mizell@monsanto.com

POWERS, Kelli — Tel: (314) 694-4003 / Fax: (314) 694-8394
Chief of Staff

PREETE, Kerry J. — Tel: (314) 694-1000 / Fax: (314) 694-8394
Executive Vice President, Global Strategy

RINGENBERG, Nicole M. — Tel: (314) 694-1000 / Fax: (314) 694-8394
Vice President and Controller

SNIVELY, David F. — Tel: (314) 694-1000 / Fax: (314) 694-8394
Senior Vice President, Secretary and General Counsel
david.snively@monsanto.com

At Washington Office

AGUSTIN, Melissa — Tel: (202) 383-2873 / Fax: (202) 789-1819
Federal Lobbyist

BURCHETT, Andrew — Tel: (202) 783-2460 / Fax: (202) 789-1819
Director, Government Affairs
andrew.burchett@monsanto.com
Registered Federal Lobbyist

CLARK, Trent — Tel: (202) 783-2460 / Fax: (202) 789-1819
Director, Public Relations and Government Affairs
trent.l.clark@monsanto.com
Registered Federal Lobbyist

DYKES, Michael — Tel: (202) 783-2460 / Fax: (202) 789-1819
Vice President, Government Affairs
michael.d.dykes@monsanto.com

GILLETTE, Kasey — Tel: (202) 783-2460 / Fax: (202) 789-1819
Federal Lobbyist
Registered Federal Lobbyist

HOLLAND, Jr., Mike
Director, Government Affairs
Registered Federal Lobbyist
Tel: (202) 383-2873
Fax: (202) 789-1819

KUSCHMIDER, Scott
Federal Lobbyist
Registered Federal Lobbyist
Tel: (202) 383-2873
Fax: (202) 789-1819

MURPHY, Stephanie
Registered Federal Lobbyist
Tel: (202) 783-2460
Fax: (202) 789-1819

PARRISH, Michael
Director, Government Affairs
Tel: (202) 783-2460
Fax: (202) 789-1819

STUMP, Jeremy
Federal Lobbyist
Registered Federal Lobbyist
Tel: (202) 383-2873
Fax: (202) 789-1819

TRAVIS, Jim
Director, Federal Government Affairs
james.k.travis@monsanto.com
Registered Federal Lobbyist
Tel: (202) 783-2460
Fax: (202) 789-1819

Monster Worldwide

Monster Worldwide, Inc., together with its subsidiaries, provides online and mobile employment solutions worldwide. It offers customized solutions and technologies across a range of public and private sectors.
www.about-monster.com
Annual Revenues: $651.81 Million
Employees: 3,700
Ticker: NYSE: MWW
SIC: 7363
Industry/ies: Communications; Employees & Employment; Telecommunications/Internet/Cable
Legislative Issues: CPI; CPT; DEF; ECN; EDU; GOV; IMM; LAW; LBR; TEC; VET

Chairman of the Board
GIAMBASTIANI, JR., Edmund P.
Tel: (978) 461-8000
Fax: (978) 461-8100

Chief Executive Officer and Chief Financial Officer
YATES, Timothy T.
Tel: (978) 461-8000
Fax: (978) 461-8100

Main Headquarters
Mailing: 133 Boston Post Rd.
Weston, MA 02493
Tel: (978) 461-8000
Fax: (978) 461-8100

Corporate Foundations and Giving Programs
Monster Contributions Program
622 Third Ave.
39th Floor
New York City, NY 10017

Public Affairs and Related Activities Personnel

At Headquarters

COOKER, Steven M.
Executive Vice President, Global Government Solutions
Tel: (978) 461-8000
Fax: (978) 461-8100

KNOTT, Joyce
Federal Lobbyist
Joyce.knott@monster.com
Registered Federal Lobbyist
Tel: (978) 461-8000
Fax: (978) 461-8100

MILLER, Michael C.
Executive Vice President, General Counsel and Secretary
Tel: (978) 461-8000
Fax: (978) 461-8100

MULLANEY, Kimberly
Executive Vice President, Chief Human Resources Officer
Tel: (978) 461-8000
Fax: (978) 461-8100

MUND, Matthew
xecutive Vice President, Chief Product and Marketing Officer
Tel: (978) 461-8000
Fax: (978) 461-8100

POULOS, Lise
Executive Vice President, Chief of Staff
Tel: (978) 461-8000
Fax: (978) 461-8100

STOEVER, Mark
President and Chief Operating Officer
Tel: (978) 461-8000
Fax: (978) 461-8100

At Other Offices

WOJCIAK, Melissa
Vice President, Government Relations
622 Third Ave., 39th Floor
New York City, NY 10017
melissa.wojciak@monster.com
Registered Federal Lobbyist
Tel: (212) 351-7000
Fax: (646) 658-0540

Montana Refining Company

Petroleum refiners.
www.montanarefining.com
Industry/ies: Fuels See Coal, Gas, Oil, Petroleum; Natural Resources; Petroleum Industry

Main Headquarters
Mailing: 1900 Tenth St. NE
Great Falls, MT 56404
Tel: (406) 761-4100

Public Affairs and Related Activities Personnel

At Headquarters

BUSBY, Dexter
Tel: (406) 761-4100

Director, Government and Regulatory Affairs
dbusby@montanarefining.com

DOSSEY, Johnny "J.D."
Vice President, Marketing and Supply
Tel: (406) 761-4100

Moody's Corporation

Provides research data and analytic tools for assessing credit risk, and publishes market-leading credit opinions, deal research and commentary.
www.moodys.com
Annual Revenues: $3.44 billion
Employees: 10,752
Ticker: NYSE: MCO
SIC: 2721
Industry/ies: Banking/Finance/Investments
Legislative Issues: FIN

President and Chief Executive Officer
MCDANIEL, Jr., Raymond W.
Tel: (212) 553-0300
Fax: (212) 553-4820

Main Headquarters
Mailing: Seven World Trade Center
250 Greenwich St.
New York City, NY 10007
Tel: (212) 553-0300
Fax: (212) 553-4820

Corporate Foundations and Giving Programs
Moody's Foundation
Contact: Frances G. Laserson
Seven World Trade Center
250 Greenwich St.
New York City, NY 10007

Public Affairs and Related Activities Personnel

At Headquarters

DOWD, Sean
Senior Vice President, Investor Relations
sean.dowd@moodys.com
Tel: (212) 553-7759
Fax: (212) 553-4820

FAUBER, Robert
Senior Vice President, Corporate and Commercial Development
Tel: (212) 553-0300
Fax: (212) 553-4820

GOGGINS, John J.
Executive Vice President and General Counsel
Tel: (212) 553-0300
Fax: (212) 553-4820

HUBER, Linda S.
Executive Vice President and Chief Financial Officer
Tel: (212) 553-0300
Fax: (212) 553-4820

LASERSON, Frances G.
President, Moody's Foundation
fran.laserson@moodys.com
Tel: (212) 553-0300
Fax: (212) 553-4820

MADELAIN, Michel
President and Chief Operating Officer
Tel: (212) 553-0300
Fax: (212) 553-4820

SCHWARTZ, Salli
Global Head, Investor Relations
sallilyn.schwartz@moodys.com
Tel: (212) 553-4862
Fax: (212) 553-4820

WESTLAKE, Lisa S.
Senior Vice President and Chief Human Resources Officer
Lisa.Westlake@moodys.com
Tel: (212) 553-0300
Fax: (212) 553-4820

Moog Inc.

Designer, manufacturer, and integrator of precision motion control products and systems.
www.moog.com
Annual Revenues: $2.44 billion
Employees: 10,691
Ticker: NYSE: MOG-B
SIC: 3590; 3679; 3728; 3769; 3812; 3823
NAICS: 334511; 335312; 335314; 336413; 336419
Industry/ies: Engineering/Mathematics
Legislative Issues: BUD; DEF; GOV

Chairman of the Board and Chief Executive Officer
SCANNELL, John R.
Tel: (716) 652-2000
Fax: (716) 687-4457

Main Headquarters
Mailing: 500 Jamison Rd.
East Aurora, NY 14052
Tel: (716) 652-2000
Fax: (716) 687-4457
TF: (800) 970-2337

Public Affairs and Related Activities Personnel

At Headquarters

AUBRECHT, Richard A.
Vice President, Strategy and Technology Vice Chairman of the Board
Tel: (716) 652-2000
Fax: (716) 687-4457

FISHBACK, Donald R.
Vice President, Chief Financial Officer
Tel: (716) 652-2000
Fax: (716) 687-4457

GARTLAND, Sean
Vice President, Strategic Growth Initiatives
Tel: (716) 652-2000
Fax: (716) 687-4457

SZAKMARY, Gary A.
Vice President, Chief Human Resources Officer
Tel: (716) 652-2000
Fax: (716) 687-4457

Morgan Stanley

Formed from the merger of Morgan Stanley Group, Inc. and Dean Witter, Discover & Co. A financial advisor to companies, governments and investors from around the world.
www.morganstanley.com
Annual Revenues: $35.30 billion
Employees: 56,087
Ticker: NYSE: MS
SIC: 6211
Industry/ies: Banking/Finance/Investments
Legislative Issues: BAN; BUD; FIN; HOM; HOU; RET; TAX; TRD

Chairman of the Board and Chief Executive Officer　Tel:　(212) 761-4000
GORMAN, James P.　Fax:　(212) 761-0086

Main Headquarters
Mailing:　1585 Broadway　Tel:　(212) 761-4000
　　　　New York City, NY 10036　Fax:　(212) 761-0086
　　　　　　　TF:　(888) 454-3965

Washington Office
Mailing:　401 Ninth St. NW　Tel:　(202) 654-2000
　　　　Suite 630　Fax:　(410) 537-5247
　　　　Washington, DC 20004

Political Action Committees
Morgan Stanley PAC
FEC ID: C00337626
Contact: James Runde
1585 Broadway　Tel:　(212) 761-4000
39th Floor　Fax:　(212) 761-0086
New York City, NY 10036

　Contributions to Candidates: $584,500 (2015-2016)
　　Democrats: $213,000; Republicans: $368,500; Other: $3,000

　　　Principal Recipients

　　　SENATE
　　　KIRK, MARK STEVEN (REP-IL)
　　　MURPHY, PATRICK E (DEM-FL)

　　　HOUSE
　　　BARR, GARLAND ANDY (REP-KY)
　　　ROSKAM, PETER (REP-IL)
　　　RYAN, PAUL D. (REP-WI)

Corporate Foundations and Giving Programs
Morgan Stanley Foundation
1585 Broadway　Tel:　(212) 761-4000
New York City, NY 10036　Fax:　(212) 761-0086

Public Affairs and Related Activities Personnel

At Headquarters

BRODSKY, Jeff　Tel:　(212) 761-4000
Chief Human Resources Officer　Fax:　(212) 761-0086

GROSSMAN, Eric　Tel:　(212) 761-4000
Chief Legal Officer　Fax:　(212) 761-0086

HERNANDEZ, Sandra　Tel:　(212) 761-2446
Associate, Communications　Fax:　(212) 761-0086

PRUZAN, Jonathan　Tel:　(212) 761-4000
Chief Financial Officer and Executive Vice President　Fax:　(212) 761-0086

ROSENTHAL, Jim　Tel:　(212) 761-4000
Chief Operating Officer　Fax:　(212) 761-0086

RUNDE, James　Tel:　(212) 761-4000
PAC Treasurer　Fax:　(212) 761-0086

At Washington Office

KEMPS, David　Tel:　(202) 654-2000
Executive Director　Fax:　(410) 537-5247
Registered Federal Lobbyist

ROESSER, Kristin H.　Tel:　(202) 654-2040
Federal Lobbyist　Fax:　(410) 537-5247
kristin.roesser@morganstanley.com
Registered Federal Lobbyist

STEIN, Michael J.　Tel:　(202) 654-2040
Global Head, Government Relations and Managing Director　Fax:　(410) 537-5247
michael.stein@morganstanley.com
Registered Federal Lobbyist

WILSUSEN, Joshua P.　Tel:　(202) 654-2040
Vice President　Fax:　(410) 537-5247
Registered Federal Lobbyist

Morgan Stanley Dean Witter
See listing on page 550 under Morgan Stanley

Morpho Detection, Inc

A supplier of explosives and narcotics detection systems for government agencies, air and ground transportation, public venues, energy and other high-risk organizations and facilities, and the military.
www.morpho.com
Annual Revenues: $1.5 billion
Employees: 9,300

Industry/ies: Electricity & Electronics; Electronics; Energy/Electricity
Legislative Issues: HOM

Chairman and Chief Executive Officer　Tel:　(510) 739-2400
PETITCOLIN, Philippe　Fax:　(510) 739-6400

Main Headquarters
Mailing:　7151 Gateway Blvd.　Tel:　(510) 739-2400
　　　　Newark, CA 94560　Fax:　(510) 739-6400

Washington Office
Mailing:　1101 Pennsylvania Ave.
　　　　Suite 600
　　　　Washington, DC 20004

Political Action Committees
Morpho Detection, LLC PAC
FEC ID: C00553321
Contact: Lilia Ramirez
7151 Gateway Blvd.
Newark, 94560

　Contributions to Candidates: $12,500 (2015-2016)
　　Democrats: $5,500; Republicans: $7,000

Public Affairs and Related Activities Personnel

At Headquarters

CHENEVIER, Thomas　Tel:　(510) 739-2400
Chief Operating Officer　Fax:　(510) 739-6400

DE TAILLY, Marie Gay　Tel:　(510) 739-2400
Senior Vice President, Human Resources　Fax:　(510) 739-6400

LAHBABI, Pierre　Tel:　(510) 739-2400
Senior Vice President, Strategy　Fax:　(510) 739-6400

RAMIREZ, Lilia　Tel:　(510) 739-2400
Vice President, Government Affairs & PAC Treasurer　Fax:　(510) 739-6400
Registered Federal Lobbyist

Morphotek Inc.

Morphotek is a biotechnology company focused on the generation of proprietary organisms for product discovery and development. It develops novel classes of biological-based products to treat cancer, inflammation and infectious diseases.
www.morphotek.com
Annual Revenues: $30.90 million
Employees: 200
Industry/ies: Medicine/Health Care/Mental Health; Science; Scientific Research

President and Chief Executive Officer　Tel:　(610) 423-6100
NICOLAIDES, PhD, Nicholas　Fax:　(610) 423-6120
Nicolaides@morphotek.com

Main Headquarters
Mailing:　210 Welsh Pool Rd.　Tel:　(610) 423-6100
　　　　Exton, PA 19341　Fax:　(610) 423-6120

Public Affairs and Related Activities Personnel

At Headquarters

DAUSCH, Rodney　Tel:　(610) 423-6100
Vice President, Project Management and Chief Financial Officer　Fax:　(610) 423-6120
dausch@morphotek.com

MorphoTrust USA

A security solutions company.
www.morphotrust.com
Annual Revenues: $650.94 million
Employees: 2,300
Ticker: NYSE: ID
SIC: 7373
Industry/ies: Defense/Homeland Security; Government-Related; Law Enforcement/Security; Law/Law Firms
Legislative Issues: BUD; DEF; GOV; HOM; IMM; TAX; TOU

Chairman, President and Chief Executive Officer　Tel:　(203) 504-1100
LAPENTA, Robert V.　Fax:　(203) 504-1150

Main Headquarters
Mailing:　296 Concord Rd.　Tel:　(978) 215-2400
　　　　Suite 300　Fax:　(978) 215-2500
　　　　Billerica, MA 01821

Washington Office
Mailing:　1255 23rd St. NW
　　　　Suite 800
　　　　Washington, DC 20037

Public Affairs and Related Activities Personnel

At Washington Office

CONLEY, Jason
Federal Lobbyist

SILVERSTEIN, Benjamin
Federal Lobbyist

Registered Federal Lobbyist

TAYLOR, Charles E.
Senior Legal Counsel

At Other Offices

DEPALMA, Jim — Tel: (203) 504-1100 / Fax: (203) 504-1150
Executive Vice President, Chief Financial Officer and Treasurer
177 Broad St., 12th Floor
Stamford, CT 06901

FORDYCE, Doni — Tel: (203) 504-1100 / Fax: (203) 504-1150
Executive Vice President, Corporate Communications
177 Broad St., 12th Floor
Stamford, CT 06901
dfordyce@L1ID.com

MOLINA, Mark S. — Tel: (203) 504-1100 / Fax: (203) 504-1150
Executive Vice President, Chief Legal Officer and Secretary
177 Broad St., 12th Floor
Stamford, CT 06901

ZELAZNY, Frances — Tel: (203) 504-1100 / Fax: (203) 504-1150
Vice President, Marketing and Government Affairs
177 Broad St., 12th Floor
Stamford, CT 06901
Registered Federal Lobbyist

M. A. Mortenson Company

A general contractor providing total facility services.
www.mortenson.com
Employees: 2,200
Industry/ies: Construction/Construction Materials

Chairman — Tel: (763) 522-2100 / Fax: (763) 287-5430
MORTENSON, David

Chief Executive Officer — Tel: (763) 522-2100 / Fax: (763) 287-5430
GUNKEL, Thomas F.

Main Headquarters
Mailing: 700 Meadow Ln., North — Tel: (763) 522-2100 / Fax: (763) 287-5430
Minneapolis, MN 55422

Corporate Foundations and Giving Programs

Mortenson Foundation
700 Meadow Ln. North
Minneapolis, MN 55422

Public Affairs and Related Activities Personnel

At Headquarters

CLEVETTE, Rick — Tel: (763) 522-2100 / Fax: (763) 287-5430
Senior Vice President, Human Resources

JOHNSON, Dan — Tel: (763) 522-2100 / Fax: (763) 287-5430
President

MORTENSON, Mark — Tel: (763) 522-2100 / Fax: (763) 287-5430
Corporate Secretary

SNYDER, Cameron — Tel: (763) 287-5493 / Fax: (763) 287-5430
Senior Manager, Public Relations
Cameron.Snyder@mortenson.com

SPONEM, Sandra G. — Tel: (763) 522-2100 / Fax: (763) 287-5430
Senior Vice President and Chief Financial Officer

WACKER, Tom — Tel: (763) 522-2100 / Fax: (763) 287-5430
Cheif Operating Officer

Mortgage Guaranty Insurance Corporation (MGIC)

A mortgage insurance company, protecting mortgage investors from credit losses.
www.mgic.com
Annual Revenues: $39.10 million
Employees: 1,000
Industry/ies: Banking/Finance/Investments
Legislative Issues: BAN; INS

Chief Executive Officer — Tel: (800) 558-9900
SINKS, Patrick

Main Headquarters
Mailing: 10th Floor — Tel: (800) 558-9900
270 E. Kilbourn Ave.
Milwaukee, WI 53202

Corporate Foundations and Giving Programs

MGIC Contributions Program
250 E. Kilbourn Ave. — Tel: (800) 558-9900 / Fax: (888) 601-4440
Milwaukee, WI 53202

Public Affairs and Related Activities Personnel

At Headquarters

LANE, Jeffrey H. — Tel: (800) 558-9900
Executive Vice President, General Counsel and Secretary

MATTKE, Timothy — Tel: (800) 558-9900
Executive Vice President and Chief Financial Officer

MONFRE, Katie — Tel: (800) 558-9900
Director, Corporate Relations
katie_monfre@mgic.com

ZIMMERMAN, Michael — Tel: (800) 558-9900
Senior Vice President, Investor Relations
mike_zimmerman@mgic.com

The Mosaic Company

The Mosaic Company is a producer and marketer of concentrated phosphate and potash. Its business engages in every phase of crop nutrition development, from the mining of resources to the production of crop nutrients, feed and industrial products.
www.mosaicco.com
Annual Revenues: $8.43 billion
Employees: 8,900
Ticker: NYSE: MOS
Industry/ies: Agriculture; Agriculture/Agronomy; Energy/Electricity; Natural Resources
Legislative Issues: AGR; ENG; ENV; NAT; RES; TAX; TRD

President and Chief Executive Officer — Tel: (763) 577-2700 / Fax: (763) 559-2860
O'ROURKE, Joc C

Main Headquarters
Mailing: 3033 Campus Dr. — Tel: (763) 577-2700 / Fax: (763) 559-2860 / TF: (800) 918-8270
Atria Corporate Center
Plymouth, MN 55441

Political Action Committees
THE MOSAIC COMPANY POLITICAL ACTION COMMITTEE
FEC ID: C00455766
Contact: Catherine Nelsund
3033 Campus Dr. — Tel: (763) 577-2700 / Fax: (763) 559-2860
Atria Corporate Center
Plymouth, MN 55441

Corporate Foundations and Giving Programs

The Mosaic Company Foundation
3033 Campus Dr.
Suite E490
Plymouth, MN 55441

Public Affairs and Related Activities Personnel

At Headquarters

CARD, Lorine — Tel: (763) 577-2700 / Fax: (763) 559-2860
Registered Federal Lobbyist

CLARK, Alison — Tel: (763) 577-2700 / Fax: (763) 559-2860
Contact, Government Relations

GAGNON, Laura — Tel: (763) 577-2700 / Fax: (763) 559-2860
Vice President, Investor Relations

ISAACSON, Mark J — Tel: (763) 577-2700 / Fax: (763) 559-2860
Senior Vice President, General Counsel and Corporate Secretary

KAPLAN, Mark E. — Tel: (763) 577-2700 / Fax: (763) 559-2860
Vice President, Public Affairs

KILDAU, Alicia D. — Tel: (763) 577-2700 / Fax: (763) 559-2860

MACK, Richard L. — Tel: (763) 577-2700
Executive Vice President and Chief Financial Officer

NELSUND, Catherine — Tel: (763) 577-2700 / Fax: (763) 559-2860
PAC Treasurer

PRATT, Ben — Tel: (763) 577-6102 / Fax: (763) 559-2860
Contact, Media Relations

RICARD, Corrine D. — Tel: (763) 577-2700 / Fax: (763) 559-2860
Senior Vice President, Human Resources

STUART, Eileen — Tel: (763) 577-2700 / Fax: (763) 559-2860
Manager, Public Policy and Government Affairs
Registered Federal Lobbyist

Most High, Inc.

Industry/ies: Religion

Main Headquarters
Mailing: P.O. Box 50056 — Tel: (843) 290-5261
Washington, DC 20091

Public Affairs and Related Activities Personnel

At Headquarters

POWELL, Michel — Tel: (843) 290-5261
michelpowell@aim.com

Motor Coach Industries, Inc.

Manufactures luxury buses.
www.mcicoach.com
Employees: 4,200
SIC: 3711
Industry/ies: Transportation

| President and Chief Executive officer | | Tel: | (847) 285-2000 |
| SORRELLS, Thomas | | Fax: | (847) 285-2013 |

Main Headquarters

Mailing:	1700 E. Golf Rd.	Tel:	(847) 285-2000
	Suite 300	Fax:	(847) 285-2079
	Schaumburg, IL 60173	TF:	(866) 624-2622

Public Affairs and Related Activities Personnel

At Headquarters

DENNY, Michael	Tel:	(847) 282-2000
Vice President and General Manager, Financial Services	Fax:	(847) 285-2079
PLODZEEN, Patricia	Tel:	(847) 283-0883
Contact, Public Relations	Fax:	(847) 285-2079

Motorola Mobility

Telecommunications and media services. Spinoff organization of Motorola Inc.
www.motorola.com
SIC: 3663
Industry/ies: Communications; Telecommunications/Internet/Cable; Telephones

| President and Chief Operating Officer | Tel: | (847) 523-5000 |
| OSTERLOH, Rick | | |

Main Headquarters

| Mailing: | 600 N. US Hwy. 45 | Tel: | (847) 523-5000 |
| | Libertyville, IL 60048 | | |

Washington Office

Mailing:	1455 Pennsylvania Ave. NW	Tel:	(202) 371-6835
	Suite 400		
	Washington, DC 20004		

Corporate Foundations and Giving Programs

Motorola Mobility Foundation
| 600 N. U.S. Highway 45 | Tel: | (847) 523-5000 |
| Libertyville, IL 60048 | | |

Public Affairs and Related Activities Personnel

At Headquarters

MORGAN, Bill	Tel:	(847) 523-5000
Senior Vice President, Marketing		
OFFER, Scott	Tel:	(847) 523-5000
Senior Vice President, General Counsel		
SCHAFFER, Eric	Tel:	(847) 523-5000
Corporate Vice President, Human Resources		
STONE, Dale	Tel:	(847) 523-5000
Senior Vice President, Government Relations		
WITTMAN, Vanessa	Tel:	(847) 523-5000
Senior Vice President & Chief Financial Officer		

At Washington Office

ELLINGER, Laura	Tel:	(202) 371-6835
Executive Assistant and Office Manager		
PETERS, Katie	Tel:	(202) 371-6835
Senior Director, Government Relations		
SULLIVAN, Scott	Tel:	(202) 371-6835
Senior Vice President, People Operations		

At Other Offices

MULLEN, Robert	Tel:	(800) 668-6765
Controller		
222 W. Merchandise Mart Plaza, Suite 1800		
Chicago, IL 60654		

Motorola Solutions

A diversified manufacturer of electronic systems, communication equipment, information systems and components. Acquired Symbol Technologies, Inc.
www.motorolasolutions.com
Annual Revenues: $5.88 billion
Employees: 14,000
Ticker: NYSE: MSI
SIC: 3663; 3674; 5065; 3679
NAICS: 334413; 334419
Industry/ies: Communications; Computer/Technology; Electricity & Electronics; Electronics; Energy/Electricity; Telecommunications/Internet/Cable
Legislative Issues: BUD; COM; CPT; DEF; HOM; IMM; LAW; TAX; TEC; TRD; VET

| Chairman of the Board and Chief Executive Officer | Tel: | (847) 576-5000 |
| BROWN, Greg | Fax: | (847) 576-5372 |

Main Headquarters

| Mailing: | 1303 E Algonquin Rd. | Tel: | (847) 576-5000 |
| | Schaumburg, IL 60196 | Fax: | (847) 576-5372 |

Washington Office

Mailing:	1455 Pennsylvania Ave. NW	Tel:	(202) 684-4700
	Suite 900		
	Washington, DC 20004		

Political Action Committees

Motorola Solutions Political Action Committee
FEC ID: C00075341
Contact: Dan Reilly
| 1455 Pennsylvania Ave. NW, Suite 900 | Tel: | (202) 371-6900 |
| Washington, DC 20004 | Fax: | (202) 842-3578 |

Contributions to Candidates: $153,500 (2015-2016)
Democrats: $56,500; Republicans: $97,000

Principal Recipients

HOUSE
FRELINGHUYSEN, RODNEY P. (REP-NJ)

Corporate Foundations and Giving Programs

Motorola Foundation
| 1303 E. Algoquin Rd. | Tel: | (847) 576-6200 |
| Schaumburg, IL 60196 | Fax: | (847) 576-6200 |

Public Affairs and Related Activities Personnel

At Headquarters

BONANOTTE, Gino A.	Tel:	(847) 576-5000
Executive Vice President and Chief Financial Officer	Fax:	(847) 576-5372
CONRADO, Eduardo	Tel:	(847) 576-5000
Senior Vice President and Chief Innovation Officer	Fax:	(847) 576-5372
DUNLAP, Shep	Tel:	(847) 576-6899
Vice President, Investor Relations	Fax:	(847) 576-5372
shep.dunlap@motorolasolutions.com		
HACKER, Mark S.	Tel:	(847) 576-5000
Senior Vice President and General Counsel, Chief Administrative Officer	Fax:	(847) 576-5372
MARK, Kelly S.	Tel:	(847) 576-5000
Corporate Vice President, Strategy	Fax:	(847) 576-5372
MOON, Mark	Tel:	(847) 576-5000
Executive Vice President, President, Sales and Marketing	Fax:	(847) 576-5372
SWEERS, Nick	Tel:	(847) 450-4957
Vice President, Global Communications	Fax:	(847) 576-5372

At Washington Office

BRECHER, Richard	Tel:	(202) 371-6900
Senior Director	Fax:	(202) 842-3578
COX, Bruce	Tel:	(202) 684-4700
Federal Lobbyist		
ELLIS, Andrew K.	Tel:	(202) 684-4700
Senior Mechanical Designer		
HASTINGS, Casey	Tel:	(202) 371-6900
Director, Government Affairs	Fax:	(202) 842-3578
HERRAIZ, Domingo	Tel:	(202) 684-4700
Federal Lobbyist		
MURPHY, James	Tel:	(202) 684-4700
Registered Federal Lobbyist		
NEWMAN, Paul	Tel:	(202) 684-4700
O'KEEFE, Shannon	Tel:	(202) 684-4700
Federal Lobbyist		
Registered Federal Lobbyist		
REILLY, Dan	Tel:	(202) 684-4700
Treasurer	Fax:	(202) 842-3578
paul.newman@motorolasolutions.com		
STARR, Lynn	Tel:	(202) 684-4700
Senior Director, Federal Legislative Affairs, North America Government Affairs		
Registered Federal Lobbyist		
WAVERLEY, Braden	Tel:	(202) 684-4700

Motricity

A mobile content infrastructure service provider.
www.motricity.com
Annual Revenues: $121.70 million
Employees: 300
Ticker: NASDAQ (GM): MOTR
SIC: 7389
Industry/ies: Communications; Telecommunications/Internet/Cable

| Interim Chief Executive Officer | Tel: | (425) 957-6200 |
| SMITH, James | Fax: | (425) 957-6201 |

Main Headquarters

Mailing:	3535 Factoria Blvd. SE	Tel:	(425) 957-6200
	Suite 400	Fax:	(425) 957-6201
	Bellevue, WA 98006		

Public Affairs and Related Activities Personnel

At Headquarters

| CORDIAL, Stephen | Tel: | (425) 957-6200 |
| *Interim Chief Financial Officer* | Fax: | (425) 957-6201 |

STULBAUM, Steven		Tel:	(425) 957-6200
Vice President of Human Resources		Fax:	(425) 957-6201
SWEARINGEN, Gary		Tel:	(425) 957-6200
Vice President and General Counsel		Fax:	(425) 957-6201

Mountain Research, LLC

An employee owned environmental, engineering and laboratory services company.
www.mountainresearch.com
Annual Revenues: $3.90 million
Employees: 41
Industry/ies: Energy/Electricity; Environment And Conservation; Science; Scientific Research

Chairman and Chief Executive Officer	Tel:	(814) 949-2034
REA, James P.	Fax:	(814) 949-9591
jrea@mountainresearch.com		

Main Headquarters			
Mailing:	825 25th St.	Tel:	(814) 949-2034
	Altoona, PA 16601-1901	Fax:	(814) 949-9591
		TF:	(800) 837-4674

Mountain State Blue Cross Blue Shield

See listing on page 403 under Highmark Blue Cross Blue Shield West Virginia

Mountain Top Technologies, Inc.

Provides e-learning solutions, aviation services, wireless broadband solutions, emergency management solutions, and consulting services to commercial and government customers in the United States.
www.mntntp.com
Annual Revenues: $10.50 million
Employees: 100
Industry/ies: Defense/Homeland Security; Government-Related

Main Headquarters			
Mailing:	One Pasquerilla Plaza	Tel:	(814) 536-7676
	Suite 140	Fax:	(814) 535-6810
	Johnstown, PA 15901		

Public Affairs and Related Activities Personnel

At Headquarters

FYOCK, David H.	Tel:	(814) 536-7676
Owner	Fax:	(814) 535-6810

The Moyer Group

A provider of government relations, public affairs and technology services.
www.moyergroup.com
Legislative Issues: BUD; GOV; LAW; POS

President and Chief Executive Officer	Tel:	(404) 229-1127
MOYER, Chris	Fax:	(888) 607-5271

Main Headquarters			
Mailing:	3580 Pierce Dr.	Tel:	(404) 229-1127
	Suite 160	Fax:	(888) 607-5271
	Chamblee, GA 30341		

Washington Office			
Mailing:	6907 Westmoreland Ave.	Tel:	(301) 270-8115
	Takoma Park, MD 20912-4408	Fax:	(301) 270-8255

Public Affairs and Related Activities Personnel

At Washington Office

FISHER, John	Tel:	(301) 270-8115
Federal Lobbyist	Fax:	(301) 270-8255
brumoyer@verizon.net		
MOYER, Bruce	Tel:	(301) 270-8115
President	Fax:	(301) 270-8255
brumoyer@verizon.net		
Registered Federal Lobbyist		

MSE Technology Applications, Inc.

Serves both Government and private industries providing engineering services and testing resources.
www.mse-ta.com
Industry/ies: Aerospace/Aviation; Energy/Electricity; Environment And Conservation; Transportation

Chairman of the Board	Tel:	(406) 494-7100
PEOPLES, Donald	Fax:	(406) 494-7230

Main Headquarters			
Mailing:	200 Technology Way	Tel:	(406) 494-7100
	P. O. Box 4078	Fax:	(406) 494-7230
	Butte, MT 59701-9795		

Public Affairs and Related Activities Personnel

At Headquarters

EGAN, Neal	Tel:	(406) 494-7100
Senior Vice President and Contact, Business Development	Fax:	(406) 494-7230

ROBINSON, William F.		Tel:	(406) 494-7100
PAC Contact		Fax:	(406) 494-7230

MSL Group

See listing on page 508 under Manning Selvage and Lee

MSL Group

Public relations, strategy and communications.
www.mslgroup.com
Employees: 3,400
Industry/ies: Management; Public Affairs And Public Relations; Public Works

President	Tel:	(202) 467-6600
PETRUZZELLO, Michael		

Main Headquarters			
Mailing:	1201 Connecticut Ave. NW	Tel:	(202) 467-6600
	Suite 500		
	Washington, DC 20036		

Public Affairs and Related Activities Personnel

At Headquarters

COLLENDER, Stanley E.	Tel:	(202) 467-6600
Lead Financial Communications Practice		
WILLIAMS, Adam	Tel:	(202) 467-6600
Senior Supervisor, Account		

MTS Systems Corporation

Supplies test systems and position sensors in the Americas, Europe, and Asia.
www.mts.com
Annual Revenues: $575.11 million
Employees: 2,180
Ticker: NASDAQ (GS): MTSC
SIC: 3829
Industry/ies: Computer/Technology; Machinery/Equipment

Chairman of the Board	Tel:	(952) 937-4000
ANDERSON, David J.	Fax:	(952) 937-4515

President and Chief Executive Officer	Tel:	(952) 937-4000
GRAVES, PhD, Dr. Jeffrey A.	Fax:	(952) 937-4515

Main Headquarters			
Mailing:	14000 Technology Dr.	Tel:	(952) 937-4000
	Eden Prairie, MN 55344	Fax:	(952) 937-4515
		TF:	(800) 328-2255

Public Affairs and Related Activities Personnel

At Headquarters

(KENNETH) YU, Chun Hung	Tel:	(952) 937-4000
Director	Fax:	(952) 937-4515
JOHNSON, David D.	Tel:	(952) 937-4000
Director	Fax:	(952) 937-4515
LIGGETT, Emily M.	Tel:	(952) 937-4000
Director	Fax:	(952) 937-4515
MAHON, Steven G.	Tel:	(952) 937-4000
Senior Vice President, General Counsel and Chief Compliance Officer	Fax:	(952) 937-4515
MARTINEZ, Randy J.	Tel:	(952) 937-4000
Director	Fax:	(952) 937-4515
OLDENKAMP, Jeffrey P.	Tel:	(952) 937-4000
Senior Vice President Chief Financial Officer	Fax:	(952) 937-4515
SAMARDZICH, Barb J.	Tel:	(952) 937-4000
Director	Fax:	(952) 937-4515
SCHROCK, Michael V.	Tel:	(952) 937-4000
Director	Fax:	(952) 937-4515
STEINEL, Gail P.	Tel:	(952) 937-4000
Director	Fax:	(952) 937-4515
SYDESKI, Raymond J.	Tel:	(952) 937-4000
PAC Treasurer	Fax:	(952) 937-4515
TRECKER, Kristin E.	Tel:	(952) 937-4000
Senior Vice President and Chief Human Resources Officer	Fax:	(952) 937-4515

Multigig, Inc.

Multigig is a fabless semiconductor company that provides clock and timing solutions for the wired and wireless communications markets.
www.multigig.com
Annual Revenues: $10.00 million
Industry/ies: Energy/Electricity

Chief Executive Officer	Tel:	(408) 514-1350
CANNING, Michael	Fax:	(408) 514-1359

Main Headquarters			
Mailing:	2645 Zanker Rd.	Tel:	(408) 514-1350
	Suite 101	Fax:	(408) 514-1359
	San Jose, CA 95134		

Public Affairs and Related Activities Personnel

At Headquarters

BASIT, Haris	Tel:	(831) 440-0600
Co-Founder and Chief Strategy Officer	Fax:	(831) 440-0601
GOFFIN, Ed	Tel:	(408) 514-1350
Contact, Media Relations and Investor Relations	Fax:	(408) 514-1359

Munich Reinsurance America, Inc.

Munich Reinsurance America, Inc., based in Princeton city, is the U.S. subsidiary of Munich Re Group, headquartered in Munich, Germany. Provides property and casualty reinsurance.
www.munichreamerica.com
Employees: 3,900
Industry/ies: Insurance Industry
Legislative Issues: TAX

Chairman of the Board	Tel:	(609) 243-4200
RÖDER, Dr. Peter	Fax:	(609) 243-4257

President and Chief Executive Officer	Tel:	(609) 243-4200
KUCZINSKI, CPA, CPCU, Anthony J.	Fax:	(609) 243-4257

Main Headquarters		
Mailing: 555 College Rd., East	Tel:	(609) 243-4200
P.O. Box 5241	Fax:	(609) 243-4257
Princeton, NJ 08543		

Public Affairs and Related Activities Personnel

At Headquarters

FISHER, Daniel	Tel:	(609) 243-4200
Regional Head, Human Resources	Fax:	(609) 243-4257
LEVY, CFA, Steven M.	Tel:	(609) 243-4200
Senior Vice President and Chief Financial Officer	Fax:	(609) 243-4257
OLSEN, Richard	Tel:	(609) 243-4200
Chief Financial Officer	Fax:	(609) 243-4257
ROSENTHAL, Terese	Tel:	(609) 243-4339
Head of Marketing Communications	Fax:	(609) 951-8201
trosenthal@munichreinsurance.com		
SALTON, MAAA, Melissa	Tel:	(609) 243-4200
Senior Vice President and Chief Risk Officer	Fax:	(609) 243-4257
UGHETTA, Jennifer	Tel:	(609) 243-4200
Senior Vice President Head of Human Resources	Fax:	(609) 243-4257
WILLCOX, Esq., Robin H.	Tel:	(609) 243-4200
Senior Vice President, General Counsel and Corporate Secretary	Fax:	(609) 243-4257

At Other Offices

FREEMAN, Paige S
Treasurer
56 Perimeter centerEast, Suite 500
Atlanta, GA 30346-2290

Murphy Oil U.S.A.

Gas exploration and production company, engaged in crude oil and natural gas production activities, with refining and marketing operations in the United States and the United Kingdom. Murphy USA is a wholly owned subsidiary of Murphy Oil Corporation.
www.murphyusa.com
Annual Revenues: $4.76 billion
Employees: 1,712
Ticker: NYSE: MUR
SIC: 2911
NAICS: 32411
Industry/ies: Fuels See Coal, Gas, Oil, Petroleum; Natural Resources; Petroleum Industry
Legislative Issues: TAX

Chairman of the Board	Tel:	(870) 862-6411
MURPHY, R. Madison	Fax:	(870) 864-6373

President and Chief Executive Officer	Tel:	(870) 862-6411
CLYDE, Andrew	Fax:	(870) 864-6373

Main Headquarters		
Mailing: P.O. Box 7300	Tel:	(870) 875-7600
El Dorado, AR 71731	Fax:	(870) 864-6373
	TF:	(800) 843-4298

Political Action Committees

Murphy Oil Corporation PAC
FEC ID: C00145722
Contact: John Gardner
200 Peach St.
PO Box 602
El Dorado, AR 71731

> **Contributions to Candidates:** $59,500 (2015-2016)
> Democrats: $3,500; Republicans: $56,000

Corporate Foundations and Giving Programs

Murphy Oil Contributions Program
200 Peach St.

P.O. Box 602
El Dorado, AR 71730

Public Affairs and Related Activities Personnel

At Headquarters

FANNON, Frank R.	Tel:	(870) 862-6411
Federal Lobbyist	Fax:	(870) 864-6373
WEST, Mindy	Tel:	(870) 875-7600
Executive Vice President and Chief Financial Officer	Fax:	(870) 864-6373

At Other Offices

GARDNER, John	Tel:	(870) 862-6411
PAC Treasurer and Treasurer for Murphy Oil Corporation	Fax:	(870) 864-6373
200 Peach St.		
El Dorado, AR 71730		
MOORE, John	Tel:	(870) 862-6411
Senior Vice President, General Counsel and Corporate Secretary	Fax:	(870) 864-6373
200 Peach St.		
El Dorado, AR 71730		
ROCHE, Jacob	Tel:	(870) 862-6411
Director, Government Affairs	Fax:	(870) 864-6373
200 Peach St.		
El Dorado, AR 71730		
TAYLOR , Tammy L.	Tel:	(870) 862-6411
Senior Manager, Investor Relations and Corporate Communications	Fax:	(870) 864-6373
200 Peach St.		
El Dorado, AR 71730		
Mail Stop P.O. Box 7000		
taylotl@murphyusa.com		

Mustang Survival

Designs and manufactures lifesaving solutions.
www.mustangsurvival.com
Annual Revenues: $8.30 million
Employees: 25
Industry/ies: Apparel/Textiles Industry; Defense/Homeland Security; Government-Related

Chairman of the Board	Tel:	(360) 676-1782
ASKEW, Bob	Fax:	(360) 676-5014

Main Headquarters		
Mailing: 1215 Old Fairhaven Pkwy.	Tel:	(360) 676-1782
Suite C	Fax:	(360) 676-5014
Bellingham, WA 98225	TF:	(800) 526-0532

Public Affairs and Related Activities Personnel

At Headquarters

NODA, Dwight	Tel:	(360) 676-1782
Director, Human Resources and Corporate Services	Fax:	(360) 676-5014

Mutual of America

A life insurance, pension and employee benefits company.
www.mutualofamerica.com
Annual Revenues: $2.11 billion
Employees: 1,000
Industry/ies: Insurance Industry

Chairman of the Board, President and Chief Executive Officer	Tel:	(212) 224-1600
MORAN, Thomas J.	Fax:	(212) 224-2539

Chairman and Chief Executive Officer, Foundation	Tel:	(212) 224-1147
GILLIAM, Thomas	Fax:	(212) 207-3001
thomas.gilliam@mutualofamerica.com		

Main Headquarters		
Mailing: 320 Park Ave.	Tel:	(212) 224-1600
New York City, NY 10022-6839	Fax:	(212) 224-2539
	TF:	(800) 468-3785

Washington Office		
Mailing: One Research Ct.	Tel:	(301) 977-6717
Suite 350	Fax:	(301) 977-6907
Rockville, MD 20850-6223		

Corporate Foundations and Giving Programs

Mutual of America Foundation
Contact: Thomas Gilliam
320 Park Ave.
New York City, NY 10022

Public Affairs and Related Activities Personnel

At Headquarters

ANGELO, Jeffrey M.	Tel:	(212) 224-1600
Executive Vice President, Corporate Communications and Strategic Planning	Fax:	(212) 224-2539
GREED, CPA, John R.	Tel:	(212) 224-1600
President	Fax:	(212) 224-2539

LESAFFRE, Daniel J.
Executive Vice President, Human Resources and Corporate Services
Tel: (212) 224-1600
Fax: (212) 224-2539

LU, Kathryn
Executive Vice President and Chief Compliance Officer
Tel: (212) 224-1600
Fax: (212) 224-2539

ROTH, James J.
Executive Vice President and General Counsel
roth@mutualofamerica.com
Tel: (212) 224-1600
Fax: (212) 224-2539

At Washington Office

MANNION, Sean A.
Vice President, Marketing and Corporate Communications
Tel: (301) 977-6717
Fax: (301) 977-6907

Mutual of Omaha Insurance Companies

An insurance company that serves individuals, families and small businesses with life and health insurance, financial services and investment options.
www.mutualofomaha.com
Employees: 5,000
Industry/ies: Insurance Industry
Legislative Issues: BAN; CSP; FIN; INS; LBR; TAX

Chairman of the Board
NEARY, Daniel P.
Tel: (402) 342-7600
Fax: (402) 351-2775

Chief Executive Officer
BLACKLEDGE, James T.
Tel: (402) 342-7600
Fax: (402) 997-1900

Main Headquarters
Mailing: 3300 Mutual of Omaha Plaza
Omaha, NE 68175
Tel: (402) 342-7600
Fax: (402) 997-1900
TF: (800) 843-2455

Washington Office
Mailing: 1455 Pennsylvania Ave. NW
Suite 400
Washington, DC 20004
Tel: (202) 652-2286

Corporate Foundations and Giving Programs

Mutual Omaha Foundation
Contact: Christine Johnson
Mutual of Omaha Plaza
Omaha, NE 68175

Public Affairs and Related Activities Personnel

At Headquarters

ANDERL, Richard C.
Executive Vice President and General Counsel Corporate Secretary
Tel: (402) 342-7600
Fax: (402) 351-2775

ARMSTRONG, Kim
Manager, Community Programs
Tel: (402) 342-7600
Fax: (402) 997-1900

DIAMOND, David A.
Executive Vice President, Chief Financial Officer and Treasurer
dave.diamond@mutualofomaha.com
Tel: (402) 342-7600
Fax: (402) 351-2775

GETSCHER, Jim
Director
JIMGETSCHER@MUTUALOFOMAHA.COM
Tel: (402) 342-7600
Fax: (402) 997-1900

GREEN, Lynn
Director, Event and Meeting
LGREEN@CREATIVEGROUPINC.COM
Tel: (402) 342-7600
Fax: (402) 997-1900

LEBENS, Michelle P
Director
mike.lebens@mutualofomaha.com
Tel: (402) 342-7600
Fax: (402) 997-1900

LECHTENBERGER, Michael A.
Executive Vice President and Chief Information Officer
Tel: (402) 342-7600
Fax: (402) 997-1900

PRITCHETT, Stephanie M.
Executive Vice President and Chief Marketing Officer
Tel: (402) 342-7600
Fax: (402) 997-1900

REXIUS, Chad
Registered Representative
chad.rexius@mutualofomaha.com
Tel: (402) 342-7600
Fax: (402) 997-1900

RICHE, Kelly
Manager, Meeting and Event
kelly.riche@mutualofomaha.com
Tel: (402) 342-7600
Fax: (402) 997-1900

SCHOLTZ, Stacy A.
Executive Vice President, Corporate Operations
stacy.scholtz@mutualofomaha.com
Tel: (402) 351-4310
Fax: (402) 351-2651

ULLSTROM, Galen F.
Vice President
galen.ullstrom@mutualofomaha.com
Tel: (402) 351-5235
Fax: (402) 351-5710

At Washington Office

DENT, Melissa Taylor
Federal Lobbyist
Registered Federal Lobbyist
Tel: (202) 652-2286

HARRY, Kellie
Legislative Issues Consultant
Registered Federal Lobbyist
Tel: (202) 652-2286

REWINKEL, Melissa S.
Vice President, Government Affairs
melissa.rewinkel@mutualofomaha.com
Registered Federal Lobbyist
Tel: (202) 652-2286

TAYLOR, Melissa
Registered Federal Lobbyist
Tel: (202) 652-2286

MVP Health Care, Inc.

MVP Health Care is a regional not-for-profit health benefits company.
www.mvphealthcare.com
Employees: 1,500
Industry/ies: Insurance Industry; Management; Medicine/Health Care/Mental Health

President and Chief Executive Officer
GONICK, Esq., Denise
Tel: (518) 370-4793
Fax: (513) 370-0852

Main Headquarters
Mailing: 625 State St.
P.O. Box 2207
Schenectady, NY 12301-2207
Tel: (518) 370-4793
Fax: (513) 370-0852
TF: (800) 777-4793

Political Action Committees
MVP Health Care Inc. Federal PAC
FEC ID: C00431429
Contact: Jordan T. Estey
625 State St.
Schenectady, NY 12305

Contributions to Candidates: $37,500 (2015-2016)
Democrats: $14,000; Republicans: $23,500

Corporate Foundations and Giving Programs
MVP Health Care Community Support Program
625 State St.
Schenectady, NY 12301
Tel: (518) 370-4793
Fax: (518) 370-4793

Public Affairs and Related Activities Personnel

At Headquarters

AUSTEN, Karla A.
Executive Vice President, Chief Financial Officer
Tel: (518) 370-4793
Fax: (513) 370-0852

BIZZARRO, Dominick
Executive Vice President, Business Development and Informatics
Tel: (518) 370-4793
Fax: (513) 370-0852

ESTEY, Jordan T.
PAC Treasurer
Tel: (518) 370-4793
Fax: (513) 370-0852

GLAVEY, Patrick
Executive Vice President, Medicare Programs
Tel: (518) 370-4793
Fax: (513) 370-0852

JABLONSKI, Dawn
Executive Vice President, Legal and Government Affairs and General Counsel
Tel: (518) 370-4793
Fax: (513) 370-0852

MANNING, Lynn
Vice President, Human Resources
Tel: (518) 370-4793
Fax: (513) 370-0852

VECCHIO, Christopher Del
Chief Operating Officer, Senior Advisor to the President and Chief Executive Officer
Tel: (518) 370-4793
Fax: (513) 370-0852

MWH Global

A global provider of consulting, engineering, construction and management services in most technically advanced water, hydropower, mining, transportation projects, natural resources, and infrastructure sectors.
www.mwhglobal.com
Employees: 7,000
Industry/ies: Construction/Construction Materials; Engineering/Mathematics; Environment And Conservation

Chairman and Chief Executive Officer
KRAUSE, Alan J.
Tel: (303) 533-1900
Fax: (303) 533-1901

Main Headquarters
Mailing: 380 Interlocken Crescent
Suite 200
Broomfield, CO 80021
Tel: (303) 533-1900
Fax: (303) 533-1901

Washington Office
Mailing: 1101 14th St. NW
Suite 1200
Washington, DC 20005
Tel: (202) 223-1733
Fax: (202) 223-0778

Political Action Committees
MCapitol Management / MWH Americas PAC
FEC ID: C00242370
Contact: Thomas G. Payne
380 Interlocken Crescent
Suite 200
Broomfield, CO 80021

Contributions to Candidates: $30,000 (2015-2016)
Democrats: $12,500; Republicans: $17,500

Principal Recipients
HOUSE

BOEHNER, JOHN A. (REP-OH)

Corporate Foundations and Giving Programs

MWH Global, Inc. Contributions Program
380 Interlocken Crescent   Tel: (303) 533-1900
Suite 200   Fax: (303) 533-1901
Broomfield, CO 80021

Public Affairs and Related Activities Personnel

At Headquarters

BARNES, David G.	Tel:	(303) 533-1900
Chief Financial Officer	Fax:	(303) 533-1901
D'AGOSTA, Jeff	Tel:	(303) 533-1900
Chief Legal Officer and General Counsel	Fax:	(303) 533-1901
KUIKEN, Jim	Tel:	(303) 533-1900
Chief Corporate Officer	Fax:	(303) 533-1901
LAPAILLE, Gary J.	Tel:	(303) 533-1900
Vice President, Government Affairs	Fax:	(303) 533-1901
PAYNE, Thomas G.	Tel:	(303) 533-1900
Assistant Treasurer and PAC Treasurer	Fax:	(303) 533-1901
thomas.g.payne@us.mwhglobal.com		
SHANDLEY, Jack	Tel:	(303) 533-1900
Senior Vice President and Chief Human Resources Officer	Fax:	(303) 533-1901
SMITH, David A.	Tel:	(303) 533-1900
Chief Strategy Officer	Fax:	(303) 533-1901
VANDERLAAN, Meg	Tel:	(303) 533-1900
Vice President, Corporate Communications	Fax:	(303) 533-1901
meg.vanderlaan@mwhglobal.com		

Myers Industries Inc.

Manufacturer of polymer products; distributor of tire repair tools, equipment and suppliers.
www.myersindustries.com
Annual Revenues: $629.51 million
Employees: 3,241
Ticker: NYSE: MYE
SIC: 2522; 3089
NAICS: 337214; 326121
Industry/ies: Chemicals & Chemical Industry

Chairman of the Board	Tel:	(330) 253-5592
HEISLER, Jr., Robert B.	Fax:	(330) 761-6156
President and Chief Executive Officer	Tel:	(330) 253-5592
ORR, John C.	Fax:	(330) 761-6156
jorr@myersind.com		

Main Headquarters

Mailing:	1293 S. Main St.	Tel:	(330) 253-5592
	Akron, OH 44301	Fax:	(330) 761-6156

Corporate Foundations and Giving Programs

Myers Industries Inc. Contributions Program
1293 S. Main St.   Tel: (330) 253-5592
Akron, OH 44301   Fax: (330) 761-6156

Public Affairs and Related Activities Personnel

At Headquarters

BRANNING, Gregg	Tel:	(330) 761-6303
Senior Vice President, Chief Financial Officer and Corporate Secretary	Fax:	(330) 761-6156
BRITTON, Paul	Tel:	(330) 253-5592
Vice President, Financial Compliance, Integration and Chief Risk Officer	Fax:	(330) 761-6156
CUNNINGHAM, Ray	Tel:	(330) 253-5592
Vice President, Human Resources, Organization Development and Training	Fax:	(330) 761-6156
VINAY, Monica	Tel:	(330) 761-6212
Vice President, Investor Relations and Treasurer	Fax:	(330) 761-6156

Mylan, Inc.

Formerly known as Mylan Laboratories. A fully integrated pharmaceutical manufacturer.
www.mylan.com
Annual Revenues: $7.88 billion
Employees: 25,000
Ticker: NASDAQ: MYL
SIC: 2834
Industry/ies: Pharmaceutical Industry; Science; Scientific Research
Legislative Issues: BUD; CPT; HCR; MMM; TAX; TRD

Executive Chairman of the Board	Tel:	(724) 514-1800
COURY, Robert J.	Fax:	(724) 514-1870
Chief Executive Officer	Tel:	(724) 514-1800
BRESCH, Heather	Fax:	(724) 514-1870

Main Headquarters

Mailing:	Robert J. Coury Global Center	Tel:	(724) 514-1800
	1000 Mylan Blvd.	Fax:	(724) 514-1870
	Canonsburg, PA 15317		

Washington Office

Mailing:	700 Sixth St. NW	
	Suite 525	
	Washington, DC 20001	

Corporate Foundations and Giving Programs

Mylan Charitable Foundation
1500 Corporate Dr.   Tel: (724) 514-1800
Canonsburg, PA 15317   Fax: (724) 514-1870

Public Affairs and Related Activities Personnel

At Headquarters

JENKINS, Ellen	Tel:	(724) 514-1800
Federal Lobbyist	Fax:	(724) 514-1870
KING, Kris	Tel:	(724) 514-1813
Vice President, Global Investor Relations	Fax:	(724) 514-1870
LOTT, Bruce	Tel:	(724) 514-1800
Vice President, State Government Relations	Fax:	(724) 514-1870
bruce.lott@mylan.com		
LUBOWITZ, Daniel	Tel:	(724) 514-1800
Contact, Government Relations	Fax:	(724) 514-1870
MALIK, Rajiv	Tel:	(724) 514-1800
President	Fax:	(724) 514-1870
MCCLINTIC-COATES, Marcie	Tel:	(724) 514-1800
Head, Global Regulatory Affairs	Fax:	(724) 514-1870
RICE, David	Tel:	(724) 514-1841
Federal Lobbyist	Fax:	(724) 514-1870
david.rice@mylan.com		
Registered Federal Lobbyist		
ROJKJAER, Nawel	Tel:	(724) 514-1800
Federal Lobbyist	Fax:	(724) 514-1870
Registered Federal Lobbyist		
SHEEHAN, John D.	Tel:	(724) 514-1800
Chief Financial Officer	Fax:	(724) 514-1870
jsheehan@mylan.com		
SUMMERS, Leah	Tel:	(724) 514-1849
Vice President, Global Talent Management	Fax:	(724) 514-1870
caire.pena@mylan.com		

At Washington Office

RAMSBURG, Lara
Vice President, Government Relations
lara.ramsburg@mylan.com

SHAH, Nimish
Vice President, Federal Government Relations & PAC Contact
Registered Federal Lobbyist

At Other Offices

SCHLOSS, Marc
1000 Mylan Blvd.
Canonsburg, PA 15317
Registered Federal Lobbyist

Myriad Genetics Inc.

A molecular diagnostic company. It is a genomic company, driven by the vision of elucidating the role genes play in human disease and using this critical information to improve patient care by developing novel molecular diagnostic products.
www.myriad.com
Annual Revenues: $721.98 million
Employees: 1,649
Ticker: NASDAQ: MYGN
SIC: 8731; 2835
Industry/ies: Science; Scientific Research
Legislative Issues: CPT; HCR; MED; MMM

Chairman of the Board	Tel:	(801) 584-3600
HENDERSON, MD, John T.	Fax:	(801) 584-3640
President and Chief Executive Officer	Tel:	(801) 584-3600
MELDRUM , Peter D.	Fax:	(801) 584-3640

Main Headquarters

Mailing:	320 Wakara Way	Tel:	(801) 584-3600
	Salt Lake City, UT 84108	Fax:	(801) 584-3640

Washington Office

Mailing:	1325 G St. NW	Tel:	(202) 449-7738
	Suite 500		
	Washington, DC 20005		

Corporate Foundations and Giving Programs

Myriad Genetics Contributions Program
320 Wakara Way
Salt Lake City, UT 84108

Public Affairs and Related Activities Personnel

At Headquarters

GLEASON, Scott	Tel:	(801) 584-1143

Senior Vice President, Investor Relations	Fax:	(801) 584-3640
sgleason@myriad.com		
HART , Jayne B.	Tel:	(801) 584-3600
Executive Vice President, Human Resources	Fax:	(801) 584-3640
KING, Gary A.	Tel:	(801) 584-3600
Executive Vice President, International Operations	Fax:	(801) 584-3640
MARSH , Richard	Tel:	(801) 584-3600
Executive Vice President, General Counsel and Secretary	Fax:	(801) 584-3640
RIGGSBEE, Bryan	Tel:	(801) 584-3600
Chief Financial Officer	Fax:	(801) 584-3640
ROGERS , Ronald	Tel:	(801) 584-3065
Executive Vice President, Corporate Communications and Media Relations	Fax:	(801) 584-3640

At Washington Office

LINTHICUM, Kimberly J.	Tel:	(202) 449-7738
Vice President, Government Affairs		
Registered Federal Lobbyist		

Mzm, Inc.

Industry/ies: Defense/Homeland Security; Government-Related

Main Headquarters

Mailing:	120 Langley Rd N	Tel:	(301) 858-5542
	Annapolis, MD 21401		

Political Action Committees
Mzm Inc. PAC
FEC ID: C00369884
Contact: Jeanne O'Neil
1523 Connecticut Ave. NW
Washington, DC 20016

Public Affairs and Related Activities Personnel

At Headquarters

O'NEIL, Jeanne	Tel:	(301) 858-5542
PAC Contact		

NABCO, Inc.

NABCO designs and manufactures total explosive containment vessels (TCV) used by military forces, security units, and bomb squads.
www.nabcoinc.com
Annual Revenues: $3.70 million
Employees: 25
Industry/ies: Defense/Homeland Security; Disaster; Government-Related

Chairman and Chief Executive Officer

TOBIN, Frank	Tel:	(724) 746-9617
	Fax:	(724) 746-9709

Main Headquarters

Mailing:	1001 Corporate Dr.	Tel:	(724) 746-9617
	Suite 205	Fax:	(724) 746-9709
	Canonsburg, PA 15317		

Public Affairs and Related Activities Personnel

At Headquarters

KEATING, Amanda	Tel:	(202) 898-0995
Contact, Media Relations	Fax:	(724) 746-9709

Nabi Biopharmaceuticals

Nabi Biopharmaceuticals is headquartered in Boca Raton, Florida with principal R&D offices and laboratories in Rockville, Maryland.
www.biotapharma.com
Industry/ies: Medicine/Health Care/Mental Health; Pharmaceutical Industry

Chief Executive Officer and President

PLUMB, Russell H.	Tel:	(678) 221-3343

Main Headquarters

Mailing:	2500 Northwinds Pkwy.	Tel:	(678) 221-3343
	Suite 100		
	Alpharetta, GA 30009		

Washington Office

Mailing:	12270 Wilkins Ave.	Tel:	(301) 770-3099
	Rockville, MD 20852		

Public Affairs and Related Activities Personnel

At Headquarters

GREEN, Vivienne	Tel:	(678) 221-3343
Vice President, Human Resources		
RYAN, Jane	Tel:	(678) 221-3343
Vice President, Product Development and Strategic Marketing		

Nabors Industries Ltd.

Nabors Industries Ltd., based in Houston city, is the U.S. subsidiary of Nabors Industries Ltd., headquartered in Hamilton, Bermuda. An oil, natural gas and geothermal drilling contractor operating on land throughout the Americas, the Middle East, the Far East, and Africa.
www.nabors.com

Annual Revenues: $6.63 billion
Employees: 24,700
Ticker: NYSE: NBR
SIC: 1381
NAICS: 213111
Industry/ies: Fuels See Coal, Gas, Oil, Petroleum; Natural Resources; Petroleum Industry

Chairman of the Board, President and Chief Executive Officer

PETRELLO, Anthony G.	Tel:	(281) 874-0035
anthony.petrello@nabors.com	Fax:	(281) 872-5205

Main Headquarters

Mailing:	515 W. Greens Rd.	Tel:	(281) 874-0035
	Suite 1200	Fax:	(281) 872-5205
	Houston, TX 77067		

Corporate Foundations and Giving Programs
Nabors Charitable Foundation
515 W. Greens Rd.
Suite 1200
Houston, TX 77067-4599

Public Affairs and Related Activities Personnel

At Headquarters

ANDREWS, Mark	Tel:	(281) 874-0035
Corporate Secretary	Fax:	(281) 872-5205
DOERRE, Laura	Tel:	(281) 874-0035
Vice President and General Counsel	Fax:	(281) 872-5205
GILLENWATER, Carina Lovato	Tel:	(281) 874-0035
Vice President, Human Resources	Fax:	(281) 872-5205
ISENBERG, Eugene M.	Tel:	(281) 874-0035
Chairman Emeritus	Fax:	(281) 872-5205
eisenberg@nabors.com		
RESTREPO, William	Tel:	(281) 874-0035
Chief Financial Officer	Fax:	(281) 872-5205
SMITH, Dennis A.	Tel:	(281) 775-8038
Director, Corporate Development and Investor Relations	Fax:	(281) 872-5205
dsmith@nabors.com		
VALLERU, Sri	Tel:	(281) 874-0035
Vice President and Chief Information Officer	Fax:	(281) 872-5205
WOOD, Clark	Tel:	(281) 874-0035
Officer, Principal Accounting and Finance	Fax:	(281) 872-5205

NACCO Industries

A holding company with operating subsidiaries in forklift truck and related service parts, coal mining, and small electrical appliances.
www.nacco.com
Annual Revenues: $913.10 million
Employees: 4,000
Ticker: NYSE: NC
SIC: 3630
Industry/ies: Automotive Industry; Construction/Construction Materials; Machinery/Equipment; Transportation

Chairman of the Board, President and Chief Executive Officer

RANKIN, Jr., Alfred M.	Tel:	(440) 449-9600
	Fax:	(440) 449-9607

Main Headquarters

Mailing:	5875 Landerbrook Dr.	Tel:	(440) 229-5151
	Suite 220	Fax:	(440) 449-9607
	Cleveland, OH 44124	TF:	(877) 756-5118

Public Affairs and Related Activities Personnel

At Headquarters

BITTENBENDER, Charles A.	Tel:	(440) 449-9600
Vice President, General Counsel and Secretary	Fax:	(440) 449-9607
BUTLER, Jr., J.C.	Tel:	(440) 449-9600
Senior Vice President - Finance, Treasurer and Chief Administrative Officer	Fax:	(440) 449-9607
KMETKO, Christina	Tel:	(440) 229-5151
Investor Relations Consultant and Contact, Media Relations	Fax:	(440) 449-9607
ir@naccoind.com		
MALONEY, Mary D.	Tel:	(440) 229-5151
Associate General Counsel, Assistant Secretary and Senior Director, Benefits and Human Resources	Fax:	(440) 449-9607
NEUMANN, John D.	Tel:	(440) 229-5151
Vice President, General Counsel and Secretary	Fax:	(440) 449-9607

NANA Regional Corporation

Principle business operations in engineering and construction, resource development, facilities management and logistics, real estate and hotel development, and information technology and telecommunications business.
www.nana.com
Employees: 11,576
Industry/ies: Economics And Economic Development
Legislative Issues: DEF; ENG; IND; SMB; TRA

Chairman of the Board   Tel: (907) 442-3301
LEE, Linda Piquk   Fax: (907) 442-4161

President and Chief Executive Officer   Tel: (907) 442-3301
WESTLAKE, Wayne   Fax: (907) 442-4161

Main Headquarters
Mailing: P.O. Box 49   Tel: (907) 442-3301
Kotzebue, AK 99752   Fax: (907) 442-4161
   TF: (800) 478-3301

Political Action Committees
Nana Regional Corp PAC (NANAPAC)
FEC ID: C00385914
Contact: Jamie Clark
909 W. Ninth Ave.
Anchorage, AK 99501

Public Affairs and Related Activities Personnel

At Headquarters

BECK, Jens   Tel: (907) 442-3301
Chief Financial Officer   Fax: (907) 442-4161

GREENE, Chuck   Tel: (907) 442-3301
Vice President, Community and Government Relations   Fax: (907) 442-4161
chuck.greene@nana.com

HANNA, Gia   Tel: (907) 442-3301
Vice President, Shareholder Relations   Fax: (907) 442-4161

HENRY, Lori Manuluk   Tel: (907) 442-3301
Vice President and Chief Operating Officer   Fax: (907) 442-4161

RECKMEYER, Peter R.   Tel: (907) 442-3301
General Counsel   Fax: (907) 442-4161

SEEBERGER, Red   Tel: (907) 442-3301
Vice President, Administration   Fax: (907) 442-4161

WOZNIAK, Shelly   Tel: (907) 265-3776
Senior Director, Corporate Communications   Fax: (907) 343-5715
shelly.wozniak@nana.com

At Other Offices

ADAMS, Steven E.   Tel: (907) 265-4100
Analyst   Fax: (907) 265-4123
1001 E. Benson Blvd.
Seattle, WA 98168

BOLTON, Jeffery   Tel: (907) 265-4100
Director, Government Affairs   Fax: (907) 265-4123
1001 E. Benson Blvd.
Seattle, WA 98168
Registered Federal Lobbyist

CLARK, Jamie   Tel: (907) 265-4100
Vice President - Accounting and Contact, PAC   Fax: (907) 265-4123
909 W. Ninth Ave.
Anchorage, AK 99501

FEDULLO, Charles   Tel: (907) 265-4100
Director, Public Relations   Fax: (907) 265-4123
1001 E. Benson Blvd.
Seattle, WA 98168

MOORE, Elizabeth   Tel: (571) 323-5575
Senior Director, Community and Government Affairs   Fax: (907) 265-4123
1001 E. Benson Blvd.
Seattle, WA 98168
Elizabeth.moore@nana.com
Registered Federal Lobbyist

WEST, Sandy   Tel: (907) 265-4100
Senior Vice President, Human Resources   Fax: (907) 265-4123
909 W. Ninth Ave.
Anchorage, AK 99501

Nando Group LLC

Bipartisan government relations and public affairs firm.
nandogroup.com
Industry/ies: Business; Small Business

Main Headquarters
Mailing: 43980 Mahlon Vail Cir.   Tel: (909) 534-6432
Suite 3103
Temecula, CA 92592

Public Affairs and Related Activities Personnel

At Headquarters

MARTINEZ, Fernando   Tel: (909) 534-6432
Owner

Nano Viricides, Inc.

A development stage company that is creating nanomaterials for viral therapy.
www.nanoviricides.com
Ticker: NYSEMKT:NNVC
Industry/ies: Science; Scientific Research

Chairman of the Board and President   Tel: (203) 937-6137
DIWAN, Dr. Anil R.

Chief Executive Officer   Tel: (203) 937-6137
SEYMOUR, Eugene
eugene@nanoviricides.com

Main Headquarters
Mailing: One Controls Dr.   Tel: (203) 937-6137
Shelton, CT 06484

Public Affairs and Related Activities Personnel

At Headquarters

VYAS, Meeta R.   Tel: (203) 937-6137
Interim Chief Financial Officer

At Other Offices

MENON, Krishna   Tel: (203) 937-6137
Chief Regulatory Officer
135 Wood St., Suite 205
W. Haven, CT 06516

Nanocomp Technologies

A spin-out of Synergy Innovations, Inc., Nanocomp Technologies Inc. is a technology development company.
www.nanocomptech.com
Annual Revenues: $0.73 million
Employees: 8
Industry/ies: Science; Scientific Research
Legislative Issues: DEF

Co-founder, President and Chief Executive Officer   Tel: (603) 442-8992
ANTOINETTE, Peter L.   Fax: (603) 513-7119
jlemons@nanocomptech.com

Main Headquarters
Mailing: 57 Daniel Webster Hwy.   Tel: (603) 442-8992
Merrimack, NH 03054   Fax: (603) 689-2703

Corporate Foundations and Giving Programs
Nanocomp Technologies Contribution Programs
57 Daniel Webster Hwy.   Tel: (603) 442-8992
Merrimack, NH 03054   Fax: (603) 513-7119

Public Affairs and Related Activities Personnel

At Headquarters

BANASH, PhD, Mark A.   Tel: (603) 442-8992
Vice President and Chief Scientist   Fax: (603) 513-7119

DORR, John H.   Tel: (603) 442-8992
Vice President, Business Development   Fax: (603) 513-7119
jdorr@nanocomptech.com

Nanoink

A growth technology company specializing in nanometer-scale manufacturing and applications development for the lifescience and semiconductor industries.
www.nanoink.net
Employees: 27
Industry/ies: Computer/Technology

Chairman of the Board   Tel: (847) 679-6266
SLEZAK, Mark   Fax: (847) 679-8767

Chief Executive Officer   Tel: (847) 679-6266
HUSSEY, James M.   Fax: (847) 679-8767

Main Headquarters
Mailing: 8025 Lamon Ave.   Tel: (847) 679-6266
Skokie, IL 60077   Fax: (847) 679-8767

Public Affairs and Related Activities Personnel

At Headquarters

GUTIERREZ, David   Tel: (312) 726-3600
Contact, Public Relations   Fax: (847) 679-8767
dgutierrez@dresnerco.com

POTHAST, Ben   Tel: (847) 679-6266
Chief Financial Officer   Fax: (847) 679-8767

NanoSonix, Inc.

Develops molecular self-assembly processes.
www.nanosonic.com
Industry/ies: Medicine/Health Care/Mental Health; Science; Scientific Research

President   Tel: (540) 626-6266
LALLI, Jennifer   Fax: (540) 626-6762

Main Headquarters
Mailing: 158 Wheatland Dr.   Tel: (540) 626-6266
Pembroke, VA 24136   Fax: (540) 626-6762

Public Affairs and Related Activities Personnel

At Headquarters

CAMPBELL, Melissa   Tel: (540) 626-6266

Chief Financial Officer	Fax:	(540) 626-6762
CLAUS, Dr. Richard O.	Tel:	(540) 626-6266
Director, Advanced Development	Fax:	(540) 626-6762
roclaus@nanosonic.com		

The NASDAQ OMX Group, Inc.

An electronic-based market listing almost 3,300 companies.
www.nasdaqomx.com
Annual Revenues: $3.46 billion
Employees: 3,730
Ticker: NASDAQ (GS): NDAQ
SIC: 6200
Industry/ies: Banking/Finance/Investments
Legislative Issues: FIN; INT; TRD

Chairman of the Board	Tel:	(212) 401-8700
BALDWIN, H. Furlong	Fax:	(212) 401-1024
Chief Executive Officer	Tel:	(212) 401-8700
GREIFELD, Robert	Fax:	(212) 401-1024

Main Headquarters

Mailing: One Liberty Plaza	Tel:	(212) 401-8700
165 Broadway	Fax:	(212) 401-1024
New York City, NY 10006		

Washington Office

Mailing: 1100 New York Ave. NW	Tel:	(202) 912-3062
Suite 310, E. Lobby		
Washington, DC 20005		

Political Action Committees
NASDAQ OMX Group, Inc. PAC (NASDAQ PAC)
FEC ID: C00366013
Contact: Lee Shavel

1100 New York Ave. NW	Tel:	(202) 912-3060
Suite 310	Fax:	(202) 912-3195
Washington, DC 20005		

> **Contributions to Candidates:** $68,000 (2015-2016)
> Democrats: $29,500; Republicans: $38,500

Corporate Foundations and Giving Programs
NASDAQ OMX Educational Foundation, Inc.

One Liberty Plaza	Tel:	(212) 401-8700
165 Broadway	Fax:	(212) 401-1024
New York City, NY 10006		

Public Affairs and Related Activities Personnel

At Headquarters

CHANEY, Lisa	Tel:	(301) 978-8281
Investor Relations Contact	Fax:	(212) 401-1024
lisa.chaney@nasdaqomx.com		
CHRISTINAT, Joseph	Tel:	(212) 401-8700
Vice President, Media Relations	Fax:	(212) 401-1024
Joseph.Christinat@NASDAQOMX.Com		
CONLEY, Joan	Tel:	(212) 401-8700
Senior Vice President and Corporate Secretary	Fax:	(212) 401-1024
DITMIRE, Ed	Tel:	(212) 401-8737
Vice President, Investor Relations	Fax:	(212) 401-1024
Ed.Ditmire@NASDAQOMX.Com		
LOUIS, Jean-Jacques	Tel:	(212) 401-8700
Senior Vice President, Corporate Strategy	Fax:	(212) 401-1024
SKULE, Jeremy	Tel:	(212) 401-8700
Senior Vice President and Chief Marketing Officer	Fax:	(212) 401-1024
SMITH, Bryan	Tel:	(212) 401-8700
Senior Vice President and Head, Global Human Resources	Fax:	(212) 401-1024
WELLS, Ryan	Tel:	(212) 231-5541
Director, Corporate Communications	Fax:	(212) 401-1024

At Washington Office

AALIM-JOHNSON, Jameel	Tel:	(202) 912-3062
Associate Vice President, Government Relations		
Registered Federal Lobbyist		
CAMPBELL, Terry G.	Tel:	(202) 912-3062
Vice President		
terry.campbell@nasdaq.com		
Registered Federal Lobbyist		
NOLAN, Laura A.	Tel:	(202) 912-3062
Registered Federal Lobbyist		
SHAVEL, Lee	Tel:	(202) 912-3062
Chief Financial Officer and Executive Vice President,		
Corporate Strategy, PAC Treasurer		
YETTER, John	Tel:	(202) 912-3062
Federal Lobbyist		
john.yetter@nasdaq.com		

At Other Offices

KNIGHT, Edward S.	Tel:	(301) 978-8400

Executive Vice President, General Counsel and Chief	Fax:	(301) 978-8472
Regulatory Officer		
9600 Blackwell Rd.		
Rockville, MD 20850		

National Asset Direct

Supports the acquisition and management efforts of various investment funds in the residential debt and real estate related asset classes.
www.nationalassetdirect.com
Annual Revenues: $2.70 million
Employees: 15
Industry/ies: Banking/Finance/Investments

Chairman of the Board	Tel:	(858) 486-2121
DELLACAMERA , Ralph		
Chief Executive Officer	Tel:	(858) 486-2121
KURTZ , Andrew		

Main Headquarters

Mailing: 13520 Evening Creek Dr., North	Tel:	(858) 486-2121
Suite 400		
San Diego, CA 92128		

Public Affairs and Related Activities Personnel

At Headquarters

DANT, Melissa	Tel:	(858) 486-2121
General Counsel		
DELLACAMERA , Christina	Tel:	(858) 486-2121
Director , Marketing and Investor Relations		
SPINNATO, Vincent	Tel:	(858) 486-2121
Chief Financial Officer		

National Association for Stock Car Auto Racing

NASCAR is the sanctioning body of one of America's premier sports. NASCAR consists of three major national series (NASCAR NEXTEL Cup Series, NASCAR Busch Series and the NASCAR Craftsman Truck Series) as well as eight regional series and one local grassroots series.
www.nascar.com
Employees: 40
Industry/ies: Automobiles See Also Motor Vehicles; Automotive Industry; Racing; Sports See Also Specific Sport; Sports/Leisure/Entertainment; Transportation
Legislative Issues: AVI; DEF; TAX; TRA

Chairman and Chief Executive Officer	Tel:	(386) 253-0611
FRANCE, Brian		

Main Headquarters

Mailing: 1 Plaza Entrance	Tel:	(386) 253-0611
Daytona Beach, FL 32114		

Public Affairs and Related Activities Personnel

At Headquarters

FRANCE, Bill	Tel:	(386) 253-0611
President		
JILOTY, Jordan	Tel:	(386) 253-0611
Senior Manager, Public Affairs		
jjiloty@nascar.com		
LYNCH, Michael	Tel:	(386) 253-0611
Vice President		
PEMBERTON, Robin	Tel:	(386) 253-0611
Vice President, Competition		

National Bank for Cooperatives (Co-Bank)

Formed in 1989, CoBank merged with US AgBank in early 2012. Delivers financial solutions to its customers, who include U.S. agribusinesses, agricultural cooperatives, Farm Credit associations, and rural energy, communications and water companies.
www.cobank.com
Employees: 500
SIC: 6141
Industry/ies: Agriculture/Agronomy; Banking/Finance/Investments; Cooperatives
Legislative Issues: AGR; BAN; BUD; FIN; TEC; TRD; UTI

Chairman of the Board	Tel:	(303) 740-4000
DOBRINSKI, Everett M.	Fax:	(303) 741-4001
Chief Executive Officer	Tel:	(303) 740-4000
ENGEL, Robert B.	Fax:	(303) 741-4001

Main Headquarters

Mailing: 6340 S. Fiddlers Green Cir.	Tel:	(303) 740-4000
Greenwood Village, CO 80111	Fax:	(303) 741-4001
	TF:	(800) 542-8072

Washington Office

Mailing: 50 F St. NW	Tel:	(202) 650-5860
Suite 900	Fax:	(202) 650-5861
Washington, DC 20001		

Public Affairs and Related Activities Personnel

At Headquarters

BOWCUTT, Susan *Administration*	Tel: Fax:	(303) 740-4000 (303) 741-4001
BURLAGE, David P. *Chief Financial Officer* dburlage@cobank.com	Tel: Fax:	(303) 740-6464 (303) 741-4001
CAVEY, Brian *Senior Vice President, Government Affairs* *Registered Federal Lobbyist*	Tel: Fax:	(303) 740-4000 (303) 741-4001
HODGES, Arthur *Senior Vice President, Corporate Communications* ahodges@cobank.com	Tel: Fax:	(303) 740-4061 (303) 741-4001
JACOB, Andrew D. *Executive Vice President, Regulatory, Legislative and* *Compliance*	Tel: Fax:	(303) 740-4000 (303) 741-4001
LUNDBERG, Mashenka *Senior Vice President and General Counsel*	Tel: Fax:	(303) 740-4000 (303) 741-4001
MCBRIDE, Mary E. *President*	Tel: Fax:	(303) 740-4000 (303) 741-4001
O'TOOLE, Robert *Chief Human Resources Officer*	Tel: Fax:	(303) 740-4000 (303) 741-4001
STURGEON, Lauren E. *Registered Federal Lobbyist*	Tel: Fax:	(303) 740-4000 (303) 741-4001
TRAKIMAS, Ann *Chief Operating Officer*	Tel: Fax:	(303) 740-4000 (303) 741-4001
WEST, Robert F. *Senior Vice President, Communications Banking Division* rwest@cobank.com	Tel: Fax:	(303) 740-4030 (303) 741-4001

At Washington Office

SVISCO, John *Chief Business Services Officer*	Tel: Fax:	(202) 650-5860 (202) 650-5861
TYREE, Sarah *Vice President, Government Affairs* styree@cobank.com *Registered Federal Lobbyist*	Tel: Fax:	(202) 879-0846 (303) 224-2665

National Bank of South Carolina

A regional banking network.
banknbsc.synovus.com
Annual Revenues: $547.67 million
Employees: 600
Industry/ies: Banking/Finance/Investments

President, Chief Executive Officer and PAC Treasurer GARNETT, Charles W.	Tel:	(803) 929-2010

Main Headquarters

Mailing:	P. O. Box 1798 Sumter, SC 29151-1798	Tel: Fax: TF:	(803) 778-8263 (803) 778-8340 (800) 708-5687

Political Action Committees

NBSC PAC
FEC ID: C00194191
Contact: Charles W. Garnett
1221 Main St.
P.O. Box 1457
Columbia, SC 29201

Tel: (803) 929-2010

Contributions to Candidates: $3,500 (2015-2016)
Republicans: $3,500

National Cooperative Services Corporation

Financing and related business services for rural electric coops and affiliated orgs.
www.ncsc.coop
Industry/ies: Energy/Electricity
Legislative Issues: AGR; BUD; FIN; TEC

Main Headquarters

Mailing:	20701 Cooperative Way Dulles, VA 20166	Tel: TF:	(703) 467-1800 (800) 424-2954

Public Affairs and Related Activities Personnel

At Headquarters

CAPTAIN, Brad *Vice President, Corporate Communications* publicandmediarelations@nrucfc.coop	Tel:	(703) 467-1800
LAIRD, Russell *Vice President* *Registered Federal Lobbyist*	Tel:	(703) 467-1800

National Fuel Gas Company

An integrated energy company.
www.natfuel.com

Annual Revenues: $1.93 billion
Employees: 2,010
Ticker: NYSE: NFG
SIC: 4924
Industry/ies: Fuels See Coal, Gas, Oil, Petroleum; Natural Resources; Petroleum Industry
Legislative Issues: UTI

President and Chief Executive Officer TANSKI, Ronald J.	Tel: Fax:	(716) 857-7000 (716) 857-7195

Main Headquarters

Mailing:	6363 Main St. Williamsville, NY 14221	Tel: Fax:	(716) 857-7000 (716) 857-7195

Political Action Committees

National Fuel Gas Federal PAC
FEC ID: C00083758
Contact: Joseph A. Short
6363 Main St.
Williamsville, NY 14221

Contributions to Candidates: $61,300 (2015-2016)
Democrats: $16,100; Republicans: $45,200

Corporate Foundations and Giving Programs

National Fuel Gas Company Foundation
6363 Main St.
Williamsville, NY 14221

Public Affairs and Related Activities Personnel

At Headquarters

BAUER, David P. *Treasurer and Principal Financial Officer*	Tel: Fax:	(716) 857-7000 (716) 857-7195
CIPRICH, Paula M. *General Counsel and Secretary*	Tel: Fax:	(716) 857-7000 (716) 857-7195
COX, Julia Coppola *Assistant General Manager* coxj@natfuel.com	Tel: Fax:	(716) 857-7079 (716) 857-7195
DAMICO, Edward *Registered Federal Lobbyist*	Tel: Fax:	(716) 857-7000 (716) 857-7195
DECAROLIS, Donna L. *Vice President, Business Development*	Tel: Fax:	(716) 857-7000 (716) 857-7195
GOSSEL, Kenneth M. *Deputy General Counsel*	Tel: Fax:	(716) 857-7000 (716) 857-7195
MERKEL, Karen L. *Contact, Media Relations*	Tel: Fax:	(716) 857-7654 (716) 857-7195
ROSE, Michael *Manager*	Tel: Fax:	(716) 857-7438 (716) 857-7195
SHORT, Joseph A. *PAC Treasurer*	Tel: Fax:	(716) 857-7000 (716) 857-7195
SILVERSTEIN, Timothy *Director, Investor Relations* SilversteinT@natfuel.com	Tel: Fax:	(716) 857-6987 (716) 857-7195

National Geographic Society

Facilitates the increase and diffusion of geographic and scientific knowledge.
www.nationalgeographic.com
Annual Revenues: $445.14 million
Employees: 1,700
SIC: 2721; 2791
Industry/ies: Communications; Media/Mass Communication; Science; Scientific Research

Chairman of the Board FAHEY, Jr., John M.	Tel: Fax:	(202) 857-7000 (202) 828-6141
President and Chief Executive Officer KNELL, Gary E.	Tel: Fax:	(202) 857-7000 (202) 775-6141

Main Headquarters

Mailing:	1145 17th St. NW Washington, DC 20036-4688	Tel: Fax: TF:	(202) 857-7000 (202) 775-6141 (800) 647-5463

Corporate Foundations and Giving Programs

National Geographic Education Foundation
Contact: Daniel C. Edelson
1145 17th St. NW
Washington, DC 20036-4688

Public Affairs and Related Activities Personnel

At Headquarters

ADAMSON, Terrence B. *Chief Legal Officer and Board of Trustees Secretary*	Tel: Fax:	(202) 857-7000 (202) 775-6141
CARRASCO, Emma *Chief Marketing Officer & Senior Vice President, Global* *Strategy*	Tel: Fax:	(202) 857-7000 (202) 775-6141
EDELSON, Daniel C.	Tel:	(202) 857-7000

Vice President, Education and Executive Director, National Geographic Education Foundation	Fax:	(202) 828-6141
HUDSON, Betty	Tel:	(202) 857-7000
Chief Communications Officer	Fax:	(202) 775-6141
KOUMANELIS, Mimi	Tel:	(202) 857-5814
Vice President, Communications	Fax:	(202) 775-6141
mkoumane@ngs.org		
MANIATIS, Amy	Tel:	(202) 857-7000
Executive Vice President and Chief Marketing Officer	Fax:	(202) 775-6141
MOFFET, Barbara S.	Tel:	(202) 857-7756
Senior Director, Communications	Fax:	(202) 775-6141
NICHOLS, Laura	Tel:	(202) 857-7000
Chief Communications Officer	Fax:	(202) 775-6141
RUNNETTE, Brooke	Tel:	(202) 857-7000
Chief Program & Impact Officer	Fax:	(202) 775-6141
SABLO, Thomas A.	Tel:	(202) 857-7000
Chief Talent and Diversity Officer, Human Resources	Fax:	(202) 775-6141
SEITZ, Carol	Tel:	(202) 247-0953
Director, Media Relations	Fax:	(202) 828-6679
ULICA, Michael	Tel:	(202) 857-7000
Chief Financial Officer	Fax:	(202) 775-6141

National Grid USA

An electric utility holding company. A wholly-owned subsidiary of Nat'l Grid Transco Group of the United Kingdom. Acquired Eastern Utilities Associates and New England Electric System in 2000 and Niagara Mohawk Holdings Inc. in 2002.
www.nationalgridus.com
Annual Revenues: $2.49 billion
Employees: 18,000
SIC: 4911
Industry/ies: Energy/Electricity; Utilities
Legislative Issues: ENG; ENV; HOM; TAX; TRA; UTI

Chairman of the Board	Tel:	(781) 907-1000
GERSHON, Peter	Fax:	(508) 389-3198
Chief Executive Officer	Tel:	(781) 907-1000
HOLLIDAY, Steve	Fax:	(508) 389-3198

Main Headquarters

Mailing:	40 Sylvan Rd.	Tel:	(781) 907-1000
	Waltham, MA 02451	Fax:	(508) 389-3198

Washington Office

Mailing:	325 Seventh St. NW	Tel:	(202) 783-7959
	Suite 225		
	Washington, DC 20004		

Corporate Foundations and Giving Programs

The National Grid Foundation
40 Sylvan Rd.
Waltham, MA 02451

Public Affairs and Related Activities Personnel

At Headquarters

BONFIELD, Andrew	Tel:	(781) 907-1000
Director, Finance	Fax:	(508) 389-3198
DREW, Deborah	Tel:	(781) 907-1753
Communications Specialist	Fax:	(508) 389-3198
deborah.drew@us.ngrid.com		
MOSTYN, Chris	Tel:	(781) 907-1726
Head, Corporate Media Relations	Fax:	(508) 389-3198
chris.mostyn@us.ngrid.com		

At Washington Office

DEJESUS, Joel	Tel:	(202) 783-7959
Assistant Deputy Counsel, Federal Affairs		
Registered Federal Lobbyist		
DUNCAN, Emily	Tel:	(202) 783-7959
Registered Federal Lobbyist		
HUYLER, Kevin	Tel:	(202) 783-7959
Registered Federal Lobbyist		
KICHLINE, Edwin	Tel:	(202) 783-7959
General Counsel		
Registered Federal Lobbyist		
MOSHER, Robert J	Tel:	(202) 783-7959
PAC Treasurer		
Mail Stop First Floor East		
MOSHER, Robert	Tel:	(202) 783-7959
Federal Lobbyist		
Registered Federal Lobbyist		
PEREZ, Nelson	Tel:	(202) 783-7959
Vice President, Federal Government Relations		
Registered Federal Lobbyist		
ROEHRENBECK, Jean	Tel:	(202) 783-7959
Registered Federal Lobbyist		

National HealthCare Corporation

Provides long-term health care.
nhccare.com
Annual Revenues: $913.8 million
Employees: 13,225
Ticker: NYSE: NHC
SIC: 8051
Industry/ies: Medicine/Health Care/Mental Health

Chairman of the Board and Chief Executive Officer	Tel:	(615) 890-2020
ADAMS, Robert G.	Fax:	(615) 890-0123

Main Headquarters

Mailing:	100 E. Vine St.	Tel:	(615) 890-2020
	Murfreesboro, TN 37130	Fax:	(615) 890-0123

Political Action Committees

National Health Corporation PAC
FEC ID: C00153445
Contact: J.B. Kinney Jr.

P.O. Box 1398	Tel:	(615) 890-2020
Murfreesboro, TN 37130	Fax:	(615) 890-0123

> **Contributions to Candidates:** $77,034 (2015-2016)
> Democrats: $16,000; Republicans: $61,034

Principal Recipients

HOUSE
DUNCAN, JEFFREY D MR. (REP-SC)

Corporate Foundations and Giving Programs

National HealthCare Corporation Contributions Program
100 E. Vine St.
Murfreesboro, TN 37130

Public Affairs and Related Activities Personnel

At Headquarters

USSERY, Michael	Tel:	(615) 890-2020
Chief Operating Officer	Fax:	(615) 890-0123
COGGIN, D. Gerald	Tel:	(615) 890-2020
Senior Vice President, Corporate Relations	Fax:	(615) 890-0123
DANIEL, Donald K.	Tel:	(615) 890-2020
Senior Vice President and Controller, Principal Accounting Officer	Fax:	(615) 890-0123
FLATT, Stephen F.	Tel:	(615) 890-2020
President	Fax:	(615) 890-0123
LASSITER, David L.	Tel:	(615) 890-2020
Senior Vice President, Corporate Affairs	Fax:	(615) 890-0123
LINES, John K.	Tel:	(615) 890-2020
Senior Vice President, Secretary and General Counsel	Fax:	(615) 890-0123
SWAFFORD, Charlotte A.	Tel:	(615) 890-2020
Senior Vice President and Treasurer	Fax:	(615) 890-0123

At Other Offices

KINNEY, Jr., J.B.
Senior Regional Vice President and PAC Treasurer
P.O. BOX 1398
Murfreesboro, TN 37130

National Interest Security Company, LLC

A provider of information technology solutions, information management, and strategic consulting services in support of national interest and security initiatives.
www.nisc-llc.com
Annual Revenues: $70 million
Employees: 30
Industry/ies: Computer/Technology

Chairman of the Board	Tel:	(517) 229-1300
CAMPBELL, Thomas J.	Fax:	(517) 229-1310
Chief Executive Officer	Tel:	(517) 229-1300
MANER, Andrew B.	Fax:	(517) 229-1310

Main Headquarters

Mailing:	3050 Chain Bridge Rd.	Tel:	(571) 229-1300
	Suite 600	Fax:	(571) 229-1310
	Fairfax, VA 22030		

Public Affairs and Related Activities Personnel

At Headquarters

BURY, Craig E.	Tel:	(571) 229-1300
Senior Advisor	Fax:	(571) 229-1310
KING, William	Tel:	(571) 229-1300
General Counsel	Fax:	(571) 229-1310
LOFTEN, Gina	Tel:	(571) 229-1300
President, NISC LLC	Fax:	(571) 229-1310
VAN DUSEN, James D.	Tel:	(517) 229-1300
Chief Financial Officer	Fax:	(517) 229-1310

National Life Insurance Company

A group of financial service companies that offer a comprehensive portfolio of life insurance, annuity and investment products to help individuals, families and businesses pursue their financial goals.
www.nationallifegroup.com
Employees: 900
Industry/ies: Banking/Finance/Investments; Insurance Industry

Chairman of the Board   Tel: (802) 229-3333
MACLEAY, Thomas H.   Fax: (802) 229-9281

President and Chief Executive Officer   Tel: (802) 229-3333
ASSADI, Mehran   Fax: (802) 229-9281

Main Headquarters
Mailing: One National Life Dr.   Tel: (802) 229-3333
             Montpelier, VT 05604   Fax: (802) 229-9281
                                                       TF: (800) 732-8939

Corporate Foundations and Giving Programs

National Life Group Charitable Foundation
Contact: Beth Rusnock
One National Life Dr.   Tel: (802) 229-7214
Montpelier, VT 05604   Fax: (802) 229-9281

Public Affairs and Related Activities Personnel

At Headquarters

BROWNELL, Thomas H.   Tel: (802) 229-3333
Executive Vice President and Chief Investment Officer Fax: (802) 229-9281

COTTON, Bob   Tel: (802) 229-3333
Executive Vice President and Chief Financial Officer Fax: (802) 229-9281

GRAFF, Chris   Tel: (802) 229-3882
Senior Vice President and Chief Information Officer   Fax: (802) 229-9281
cgraff@nationallife.com

MANOSH, Mallorie   Tel: (802) 229-3333
Director, Corporate Marketing   Fax: (802) 229-9281
MManosh@nationallifegroup.com

WOODROFFE, Sean N.   Tel: (802) 229-3333
Senior Vice President and Chief People Officer   Fax: (802) 229-9281

WOODWORTH, Gregory D.   Tel: (802) 229-3333
Senior Vice President and General Counsel   Fax: (802) 229-9281

National Oilwell Varco Inc.

An oil component manufacturer.
www.nov.com
Annual Revenues: $21.37 billion
Employees: 54,540
Ticker: NYSE: NOV
SIC: 3533; 3462; 3561
NAICS: 332111; 333911; 333132
Industry/ies: Natural Resources

Chairman of the Board   Tel: (713) 346-7500
MILLER, Jr., Merrill A. "Pete"   Fax: (713) 375-3994

President and Chief Executive Officer   Tel: (713) 346-7606
WILLIAMS, Clay C.   Fax: (713) 375-3994
clay.williams@nov.com

Main Headquarters
Mailing: 7909 Parkwood Cir. Dr.   Tel: (713) 375-3700
             Houston, TX 77036   Fax: (713) 375-3994
                                                       TF: (888) 262-8645

Public Affairs and Related Activities Personnel

At Headquarters

BLANCHARD, Robert   Tel: (713) 375-3700
Director, Operations   Fax: (713) 375-3994

PEOPLES, Jack   Tel: (713) 346-7500
Senior Vice President, Human Resources   Fax: (713) 375-3994
jack.peoples@nov.com

RETTIG, Dwight W.   Tel: (713) 375-3700
Executive Vice President and General Counsel   Fax: (713) 375-3994

SINGLETARY, Loren   Tel: (713) 375-3700
Vice President, Global Accounts and Investor Relations Fax: (713) 375-3994
Loren.Singletary@nov.com

THIGPEN, Jeremy   Tel: (713) 375-3700
Senior Vice President and Chief Financial Officer   Fax: (713) 375-3994

National Presto Industries, Inc.

A manufacturer of appliances.
www.gopresto.com
Annual Revenues: $426.81 million
Employees: 1,043
Ticker: NYSE: NPK
SIC: 3480
Industry/ies: Electricity & Electronics; Electronics; Energy/Electricity; Furniture/ Home Furnishings

Chairman of the Board, President and Chief Executive Officer   Tel: (715) 839-2121
COHEN, Maryjo   Fax: (715) 839-2122

Main Headquarters
Mailing: 3925 N. Hastings Way   Tel: (715) 839-2121
             Eau Claire, WI 54703-3703   Fax: (715) 839-2122

Public Affairs and Related Activities Personnel

At Headquarters

AHNEMAN, Spence W.   Tel: (715) 839-2121
Vice President, Sales   Fax: (715) 839-2122

FREDERICK, Douglas J.   Tel: (715) 839-2121
General Counsel and Secretary   Fax: (715) 839-2122

LIEBLE, Randy F.   Tel: (715) 839-2121
Vice President, Chief Financial Officer and Treasurer Fax: (715) 839-2122

National Public Radio

A private, non-profit corporation established in 1970 to provide programming and representation for its member non-commercial radio stations.
www.npr.org
Annual Revenues: $185.60 million
Employees: 900
Industry/ies: Communications; Media/Mass Communication
Legislative Issues: BUD; COM; CPT

Chairman of the Board, Director and General Manager   Tel: (202) 513-3232
EDWARDS, Dave   Fax: (202) 513-3329

President and Chief Executive Officer   Tel: (202) 513-3232
MOHN, Jarl   Fax: (202) 513-3329

Main Headquarters
Mailing: 1111 N. Capitol St. NE   Tel: (202) 513-3232
             Washington, DC 20002   Fax: (202) 513-3329

Corporate Foundations and Giving Programs

NPR Foundation
635 Massachusetts Ave. NW
Washington, DC 20001

Public Affairs and Related Activities Personnel

At Headquarters

COWAN, Deborah A.   Tel: (202) 513-3232
Chief Financial Officer and Vice President, Finance Fax: (202) 513-3329

HANSON, Monique   Tel: (202) 513-3232
Chief Development Officer   Fax: (202) 513-3329

HART, Jonathan   Tel: (202) 513-3232
Chief Legal Officer and General Counsel   Fax: (202) 513-3329

HINGORANEY, Rishi   Tel: (202) 513-2000
Federal Lobbyist   Fax: (202) 513-3329
rhingoraney@npr.org
Registered Federal Lobbyist

MAYOR, Loren   Tel: (202) 513-3232
Chief Operating Officer   Fax: (202) 513-3329

POWELL, Marjorie   Tel: (202) 513-3232
Vice President, Human Resources   Fax: (202) 513-3329

RIKSEN, Michael R.   Tel: (202) 513-3232
Vice President, Policy & Representation   Fax: (202) 513-3329
mriksen@npr.org
Registered Federal Lobbyist

WATSON, Duston   Tel: (202) 513-2000
Director, Government Relations   Fax: (202) 513-3329
dwatson@npr.org
Registered Federal Lobbyist

National Railroad Passenger Corporation

See listing on page 62 under AMTRAK (National Railroad Passenger Corporation)

National Semiconductor

A manufacturer of semiconductor and board-level connectivity products. Founded in 1959. National Semiconductor has now became part of Texas Instruments.
www.ti.com
Annual Revenues: $13.21 billion
Employees: 31,003
Ticker: NYSE: TXN
SIC: 3674
NAICS: 334413
Industry/ies: Computer/Technology

Chairman, President and Chief Executive Officer   Tel: (214) 479-3773
TEMPLETON, Richard K.

Main Headquarters
Mailing: P.O. Box 660199   Tel: (214) 479-3773
             Dallas, TX 75266-0199   TF: (800) 842-2737

Political Action Committees
Texas Instruments, Inc. PAC
FEC ID: C00007070

Contact: Gray Mayes
1341 W. Mockingbird Ln.
Dallas, TX 75247

Contributions to Candidates: $3,116,516 (2015-2016)
Democrats: $37,500; Republicans: $66,000; Other: $3,013,016

Corporate Foundations and Giving Programs

National Semiconductor Foundation
2900 Semiconductor Dr.
P.O. Box 58090
Santa Clara, CA 95052

Public Affairs and Related Activities Personnel

At Headquarters

HUBACH, Joseph F.	Tel:	(214) 479-3773
Senior Vice President, Secretary and General Counsel		
MARCH, Kevin P.	Tel:	(214) 479-3773
Senior Vice President and Chief Financial Officer		
MAYES, Gray	Tel:	(214) 479-3773
Contact, Government Relations, Lobbyist/Registrant Pac		
SZCZSPONIK, John	Tel:	(214) 479-3773
Senior Vice President and Manager of worldwide Sales and Marketing		
WEST, Terri	Tel:	(214) 479-3773
Senior Vice President, Communications, Investor Relations and Public Affairs		
WHITAKER, Darla	Tel:	(214) 479-3773
Senior Vice President, Worldwide Human Resources		

National Technical Systems

Provides a variety of engineering and certification services to customers in such industries as aerospace, defense, transportation, and high technology.
www.nts.com
Annual Revenues: $186.11 million
Employees: 1,200
Ticker: NASDAQ: NTSC
SIC: 8734
Industry/ies: Science; Scientific Research

President and Chief Executive Officer	Tel:	(818) 591-0776
MCGINNIS, William C.	Fax:	(818) 591-0899
bill.mcginnis@nts.com		

Main Headquarters

Mailing:	24007 Ventura Blvd.	Tel:	(818) 591-0776
	Suite 200	Fax:	(818) 591-0899
	Calabasas, CA 91302	TF:	(800) 879-9225

Public Affairs and Related Activities Personnel

At Headquarters

BRISKIE, Douglas	Tel:	(818) 591-0776
Senior Vice President and Chief Strategy Officer	Fax:	(818) 591-0899
CANNON, Dan	Tel:	(818) 591-0776
Corporate Director, Quality and Regulatory Affairs	Fax:	(818) 591-0899
dan.cannon@ntscorp.com		
COPPINGER, Derek	Tel:	(818) 591-0776
Senior Vice President, Chief Marketing and Sales Officer	Fax:	(818) 591-0899
derek.copppinger@nts.com		
EL-HILLOW, Michael	Tel:	(818) 591-0776
Chief Financial Officer and Senior Vice President	Fax:	(818) 591-0899
GLEGHORN, Bruce	Tel:	(818) 591-0776
Senior Vice President and Chief Operating Officer	Fax:	(818) 591-0899
PAWLOWSKI, Nancy	Tel:	(818) 591-0776
Senior Vice President and Chief Information Officer	Fax:	(818) 591-0899
ROBERTSON, Dave	Tel:	(818) 591-0776
Senior Vice President and Chief Human Resources Officer	Fax:	(818) 591-0899

Nationwide Mutual Insurance Company

An insurance company. Acquired Provident Mutual Life Insurance Co. in October of 2002.
www.nationwide.com
Annual Revenues: $12.08 billion
Employees: 33,000
SIC: 6311
Industry/ies: Insurance Industry
Legislative Issues: CPT; HCR; HOU; INS; LBR; RET; TAX; TRA

Chief Executive Officer	Tel:	(614) 249-7111
RASMUSSEN, Stephen S.	Fax:	(614) 249-7705

Main Headquarters

Mailing:	One Nationwide Plaza	Tel:	(614) 249-7111
	Columbus, OH 43215-2220	Fax:	(614) 854-3676
		TF:	(800) 882-2822

Washington Office

Mailing:	1120 G St. NW	Tel:	(202) 434-8771
	Suite 850		

Washington, DC 20005

Political Action Committees

Nationwide Mutual Insurance Company Financial and Investments PAC
FEC ID: C00406215
Contact: Bridget Hagan
One Nationwide Plaza
Columbus, OH 43215-2220

Contributions to Candidates: $450,050 (2015-2016)
Democrats: $158,000; Republicans: $290,050; Other: $2,000

Principal Recipients

HOUSE
BEATTY, JOYCE (DEM-OH)
BOEHNER, JOHN A. (REP-OH)
CROWLEY, JOSEPH (DEM-NY)
LUETKEMEYER, W BLAINE (REP-MO)
MEEHAN, PATRICK L. MR. (REP-PA)
ROYCE, ED MR. (REP-CA)
STIVERS, STEVE MR. (REP-OH)

Nationwide Mutual Insurance Company PAC
FEC ID: C00076174
Contact: Steven M. English
One Nationwide Plaza
Columbus, OH 43215

Contributions to Candidates: $5,000 (2015-2016)
Republicans: $5,000

Corporate Foundations and Giving Programs

Nationwide Insurance Foundation

One Nationwide Plaza	TF:	(877) 764-0418
Columbus, OH 43215-2220		

Public Affairs and Related Activities Personnel

At Headquarters

BREWSTER, Ben	Tel:	(614) 249-7111
Federal Lobbyist	Fax:	(614) 854-3676
Registered Federal Lobbyist		
CASE, Joe	Tel:	(614) 249-7111
Associate Vice President, Corporate Marketing (Public Relations)	Fax:	(614) 249-7705
casej6@nationwide.com		
DOVE, Carol	Tel:	(614) 249-7111
PAC Treasurer	Fax:	(614) 249-7705
dovec@nationwide.com		
GOLDEN, Gerard M.	Tel:	(614) 249-7111
Contact, Government Relations	Fax:	(614) 854-3676
HATLER, Patricia R.	Tel:	(614) 249-7111
Executive Vice President, Chief Legal and Governance Officer	Fax:	(614) 249-7705
JESTER, Chad	Tel:	(614) 249-7111
President, The Nationwide Insurance Foundation	Fax:	(614) 249-7705
KELLER , Michael	Tel:	(614) 249-7111
Executive Vice President and Chief Information Officer	Fax:	(614) 854-3676
KING, Gale V.	Tel:	(614) 249-7111
Executive Vice President, Chief Administrative Officer	Fax:	(614) 249-7705
ROUCH, Jeffrey D.	Tel:	(614) 677-5603
Senior Vice President, Government Relations	Fax:	(614) 854-3676
rouchj@nationwide.com		
THRESHER, Mark	Tel:	(614) 249-7111
Executive Vice President and Chief Financial Officer	Fax:	(614) 854-3676
WILLIAMS, Terrance	Tel:	(614) 249-7111
Executive Vice President and Chief Marketing Officer	Fax:	(614) 854-3676
WYMER, Nathan P.	Tel:	(614) 249-7111
Director, Government Relations	Fax:	(614) 854-3676
Registered Federal Lobbyist		

At Washington Office

DWYER, Timothy	Tel:	(202) 434-8771
Vice President, Assistant Treasurer and PAC Contact		
ENGLISH, Steven M.	Tel:	(202) 434-8771
Senior Vice President, Government Relations		
Registered Federal Lobbyist		
PAPPAS, Dean	Tel:	(202) 434-8771
Vice President, Government Relations		
Registered Federal Lobbyist		
PARMAR, Naveen	Tel:	(202) 434-8771
Director, Government Relations		
Registered Federal Lobbyist		

Nature's Bounty

See listing on page 567 under NBTY Inc.

NAU Country

Insurance Company. QBE NAU was founded to improve the financial security of farming community and is part of QBE Insurance Group Limited.
www.naucountry.com
Annual Revenues: $1.3 million
Employees: 600
Industry/ies: Insurance Industry

Chief Executive Officer
DEAL, Gregory J.
Tel: (763) 427-3770
Fax: (763) 427-6473

Main Headquarters
Mailing: 7333 Sunwood Dr.
Ramsey, MN 55303
Tel: (763) 427-3770
Fax: (763) 427-6473
TF: (800) 942-6557

Public Affairs and Related Activities Personnel

At Headquarters

DEAL, James
Federal Lobbyist
Tel: (763) 427-6473
Fax: (763) 427-6473

DEAL, Michael (Mick)
Chief Marketing Technology Officer
Tel: (763) 427-3770
Fax: (763) 427-6473

JAKWAY, Doug
General Counsel
Tel: (763) 427-6473
Fax: (763) 427-6473

KORIN , CPA, James R.
President
Tel: (763) 427-3770
Fax: (763) 427-6473

Naverus, Inc.

A part of GE Aviation Systems, developer of performance-based navigation for air carriers and fleet operators.
www.naverus.com
Employees: 38
Industry/ies: Defense/Homeland Security; Engineering; Engineering/Mathematics; Government-Related

Main Headquarters
Mailing: 20415 72nd Ave., South
Suite 300
Kent, WA 98032-2357
Tel: (253) 867-3900
Fax: (253) 867-3851
TF: (888) 796-9644

Public Affairs and Related Activities Personnel

At Headquarters

JOHNSON, Amy
Contact, Media Relations
ajohnson@naverus.com
Tel: (206) 779-0416
Fax: (253) 867-3851

SHAPERO, Ken
Director, U.S. Programs
kshapero@naverus.com
Tel: (206) 779-9064
Fax: (253) 867-3851

Navient Solutions, Inc.

Also known as Sallie Mae, Inc. Formerly USA Education, Inc. It originates, acquires, finances, and services private education loans in the United States.
www.navient.com
Annual Revenues: $2.72 Billion
Employees: 6,200
Ticker: NASDAQ:NAVI
SIC: 6141
Industry/ies: Banking/Finance/Investments; Education
Legislative Issues: BAN; BNK; BUD; EDU; TAX

Chairman of the Board
TERRACCIANO, Anthony P.
Tel: (302) 283-8000
Fax: (800) 848-1949

President and Chief Executive Officer
REMONDI , John F.
Tel: (317) 570-7397
Fax: (800) 848-1949

Main Headquarters
Mailing: P.O. Box 9500
Wilkes-Barre, PA 18773-9500
Tel: (317) 570-7397
Fax: (800) 848-1949

Washington Office
Mailing: 701 Pennsylvania Ave. NW
Suite 560
Washington, DC 20004
Tel: (202) 969-8000
Fax: (202) 969-8030

Political Action Committees
Navient Corporation PAC (Navient PAC)
FEC ID: C00331835
Contact: Steve O' Connell
2001 Edmund Halley Dr.
Reston, VA 20191
Tel: (703) 810-3000
Fax: (703) 984-5042

Contributions to Candidates: $10,172,765 (2015-2016)
Democrats: $32,750; Republicans: $48,000; Other: $10,092,015

Corporate Foundations and Giving Programs
The Sallie Mae Fund
Contact: Patricia Nash Christel
12061 Bluemont Way
Reston, VA 20190
Tel: (703) 810-3000
Fax: (703) 810-3000

Public Affairs and Related Activities Personnel

At Headquarters

BEAMON, Andy
Chief Business Development Officer
Tel: (317) 570-7397
Fax: (800) 848-1949

CHIVAVIBUL, Somsak
Chief Financial Officer, Principal Financial and Accounting Officer
Tel: (317) 570-7397
Fax: (800) 848-1949

DISABATO, Michael
Government Relations Professional
Tel: (317) 570-7397

DUCICH, Sarah E.
Registered Federal Lobbyist
Tel: (317) 570-7397

HAUBER, Steve
Senior Vice President and Chief Audit Officer
Tel: (317) 570-7397
Fax: (800) 848-1949

HYNES, Tim
Chief Risk and Compliance Officer
Tel: (317) 570-7397
Fax: (800) 848-1949

KANE, John
Chief Operating Officer
Tel: (317) 570-7397
Fax: (800) 848-1949

LEBENS, Lucia
Tel: (317) 570-7397

RYAN-MACIE, Sheila
Chief of Staff
Tel: (317) 570-7397
Fax: (800) 848-1949

At Washington Office

BUCHANAN, C. Tapscott
Vice President, Government Affairs and Services
Registered Federal Lobbyist
Tel: (202) 969-8000
Fax: (202) 969-8031

DISABATO, Michael
Government Relations Professional
Tel: (202) 969-8000

DUCICH, Sarah E.
Registered Federal Lobbyist
Tel: (202) 969-8000

LEBENS, Lucia
Tel: (202) 969-8000

MAYER , Paul
Senior Vice President, Corporate Development
Tel: (202) 969-8000
Fax: (202) 969-8031

MORRISON, Tim
Senior Vice President, Government Relations
Tel: (202) 969-8000
Fax: (202) 969-8030

At Other Offices

CHRISTEL, Patricia Nash
Vice President, Corporate Communications
300 Continental Dr.
Newark, DE 19713
Patricia.Christel@Navient.com
Tel: (302) 283-8000
Fax: (800) 848-1949

DISABATO, Michael
Government Relations Professional
999 N. Capitol St. NE, Suite 301
Washington, DC 20002
Tel: (202) 460-5646

DISABATO, Michael
Government Relations Professional
12061 Bluemont Way
Reston, VA 20190
Tel: (703) 810-3000

DISABATO, Michael
Government Relations Professional
300 Continental Dr.
Newark, DE 19713
Tel: (302) 283-8000

DUCICH, Sarah E.
12061 Bluemont Way
Reston, VA 20190
Registered Federal Lobbyist
Tel: (703) 810-3000

DUCICH, Sarah E.
300 Continental Dr.
Newark, DE 19713
Registered Federal Lobbyist
Tel: (302) 283-8000

DUCICH, Sarah E.
999 N. Capitol St. NE, Suite 301
Washington, DC 20002
Registered Federal Lobbyist
Tel: (202) 460-5646

HERBST, Ian
Government Relations Coordinator
999 N. Capitol St. NE, Suite 301
Washington, DC 20002
ian.herbst@navient.com
Tel: (202) 460-5646
Fax: (202) 969-8030

LEBENS, Lucia
12061 Bluemont Way
Reston, VA 20190
Tel: (703) 810-3000

LEBENS, Lucia
300 Continental Dr.
Newark, DE 19713
Tel: (302) 283-8000

LEBENS, Lucia
999 N. Capitol St. NE, Suite 301
Washington, DC 20002
Tel: (202) 460-5646

LOWREY, F.A.
Federal Lobbyist
900 Second St. NE, Suite 300
WASHINGTON, DC 20002

LOWREY, Carmen Guzman
999 N. Capitol St. NE, Suite 301
Washington, DC 20002
Registered Federal Lobbyist

MCKAY, Mike
Lobbyist
900 Second St. NE, Suite 300
WASHINGTON, DC 20002

O' CONNELL, Steve
Senior Vice President, Finance, Lobbyist and PAC Treasurer
2001 Edmund Halley Dr.
Reston, VA 20191

Navigenics, Inc.

Personalized Genomic Analysis Service Provider
www.navigenics.com
Industry/ies: Science; Scientific Research
Legislative Issues: CSP; HCR; MED

Chief Executive Officer and President   Tel: (650) 585-7700
VANIER, MD, Vance   Fax: (650) 638-0727

Main Headquarters
Mailing: 1001 E. Hillsdale Blvd.   Tel: (650) 585-7700
           Suite 550   Fax: (650) 638-0727
           Foster City, CA 94404

Public Affairs and Related Activities Personnel

At Headquarters

SWEENEY, Brenna   Tel: (650) 585-7523
Media Contact   Fax: (650) 638-0727
press@navigenics.com

NaviMedix

See listing on page 566 under NaviNet, Inc.

NaviNet, Inc.

Formerly NaviMedix. A real-time healthcare communications network.
www.navinet.net
Employees: 200
Industry/ies: Computer/Technology; Medicine/Health Care/Mental Health

President and Chief Executive Officer   Tel: (617) 715-6000
INGARI, Frank   Fax: (617) 715-7800

Main Headquarters
Mailing: 179 Lincoln St.   Tel: (617) 715-6000
           Boston, MA 02111   Fax: (617) 715-7800
                                              TF: (800) 805-7569

Public Affairs and Related Activities Personnel

At Headquarters

BRIDGEO, Sean W.   Tel: (617) 715-6000
Chief Financial Officer   Fax: (617) 715-7800

DIGATE, Chuck   Tel: (617) 715-6000
Senior Vice President, Sales, Marketing and Business Fax: (617) 715-7800
Development

ROTMAN, Steven   Tel: (617) 715-6000
Vice President, Human Resources   Fax: (617) 715-7800

Navistar International Corporation

Formerly International Harvester and then International Truck and Engine Corporation. A subsidiary of Navistar International. Provides integrated and transportation solutions.
www.navistar.com
Annual Revenues: $11.02 billion
Employees: 14,873
Ticker: NYSE: NAV
SIC: 3711
Industry/ies: Automotive Industry; Machinery/Equipment; Transportation; Trucking Industry
Legislative Issues: BUD; CAW; DEF; ENG; ENV; RET; TAX; TRA; TRD

Non-executive Chairman   Tel: (331) 332-5000
KEYES, James H.   Fax: (630) 753-2303

President and Chief Executive Officer   Tel: (331) 332-5000
CLARKE, Troy   Fax: (630) 753-2303

Main Headquarters
Mailing: 2701 Navistar Dr.   Tel: (331) 332-5000
           Lisle, IL 60532   Fax: (630) 753-2303
                                              TF: (800) 448-7825

Political Action Committees
Navistar, Inc. Good Government Committee PAC
FEC ID: C00040840
Contact: Brien Sheahan
2701 Navistar Dr.   Tel: (630) 753-5000
P.O. Box 1488   Fax: (630) 753-5000
Lisle, IL 60532

Contributions to Candidates: $33,500 (2015-2016)
Democrats: $11,500; Republicans: $22,000

Public Affairs and Related Activities Personnel

At Headquarters

BORST, Walter G.   Tel: (331) 332-5000
Executive Vice President and Chief Financial Officer Fax: (630) 753-2303

CHARBONNEAU, Patrick   Tel: (630) 753-3448
Vice President, Government Relations   Fax: (630) 753-2303
Registered Federal Lobbyist

COVEY, Steven   Tel: (630) 753-5000
Senior Vice President, General Counsel and Chief Ethics Fax: (630) 753-2303
Officer

ELLIOTT, Gregg W.   Tel: (630) 753-5000
Senior Vice President, Human Resources and Administration Fax: (630) 753-2303

GELB, Jacqueline   Tel: (331) 332-3448
Director, Government Relations   Fax: (630) 753-2303
Registered Federal Lobbyist

JACQUELINE, GELB   Tel: (331) 332-5000
PAC Treasurer   Fax: (630) 753-2303

KOS, Heather   Tel: (630) 753-2406
Director, Investor Relations   Fax: (630) 753-2303

KRAMER, Curt A.   Tel: (331) 332-5000
Corporate Secretary   Fax: (630) 753-2303

MAURER, Elissa   Tel: (331) 332-5000
Senior Manager, External Communications   Fax: (630) 753-2303
Elissa.Maurer@navistar.com

SCHRIER, Steve   Tel: (630) 753-2264
Senior Manager, Corporate Communications and External Fax: (630) 753-2303
Communications
Steve.Schrier@navistar.com

TECH, Eric   Tel: (331) 332-5000
Senior Vice President, Strategy and Planning and President, Fax: (630) 753-2303
Global and Specialty Businesses

At Other Offices

FITZGERALD, Raymond M.
Director, Federal Legislative Affairs
P.O. Box 1488, 4201 Winfield Rd.
Warrenville, IL 60555
Registered Federal Lobbyist

QUARANTO, Albert Jason
P.O. Box 1488, 4201 Winfield Rd.
Warrenville, IL 60555
Registered Federal Lobbyist

NBCUniversal

A media and entertainment company. Formed in May 2004 by the merger of General Electric's NBC with Vivendi's Vivendi Universal Entertainment and acquired by Comcast in January 2011. It owns and operates a valuable portfolio of news and entertainment television networks, a premier motion picture company, significant television production operations, a leading television stations group, world-renowned theme parks, and a suite of leading Internet-based businesses. NBCUniversal is a subsidiary of Comcast Corporation.
www.nbcuniversal.com
Annual Revenues: $6.5 billion
Employees: 43,000
SIC: 4841
Industry/ies: Communications; Media/Mass Communication
Legislative Issues: LAW; TEC; TRD

Chairman of the Board   Tel: (212) 664-4444
HARBERT, Ted   Fax: (212) 664-4085
Ted.Harbert@nbcuni.com

Chief Executive Officer   Tel: (212) 664-4444
BURKE, Stephen B.   Fax: (212) 664-4085

Main Headquarters
Mailing: 30 Rockefeller Plaza   Tel: (212) 664-4444
           New York City, NY 10112-0002   Fax: (212) 664-4085

Washington Office
Mailing: 300 New Jersey Ave. NW   Tel: (202) 524-6401
           Suite 700   Fax: (202) 524-6411
           Washington, DC 20001

Political Action Committees
Comcast Corporation and NBC Universal Political Action Committee - Federal
FEC ID: C00248716
Contact: William Dordelman
1701 JFK Blvd., 49th Floor
Philadelphia, PA 19103

Contributions to Candidates: $1,524,500 (2015-2016)
Democrats: $569,900; Republicans: $950,100; Other: $4,500

Principal Recipients

SENATE

AYOTTE, KELLY A (REP-NH)
BENNET, MICHAEL F (DEM-CO)
BLUNT, ROY (REP-MO)
BLUNT, ROY (REP-TX)
BURR, RICHARD (REP-NC)
CRAPO, MICHAEL D (REP-ID)
GRASSLEY, CHARLES E SENATOR (REP-IA)
JOHNSON, RONALD HAROLD (REP-)
KIRK, MARK STEVEN (REP-IL)
LEAHY, PATRICK J (DEM-VT)
MORAN, JERRY (REP-KS)
MURRAY, PATTY (DEM-WA)
PAUL, RAND (REP-KY)
SCOTT, TIMOTHY E (REP-SC)
SHELBY, RICHARD C (REP-AL)
THUNE, JOHN (REP-SD)

HOUSE

BLACKBURN, MARSHA MRS. (REP-TN)
BOYLE, BRENDAN F (DEM-PA)
BRADY, ROBERT A (DEM-DC)
CHAFFETZ, JASON (REP-UT)
CLYBURN, JAMES E. (DEM-SC)
COSTELLO, RYAN A (REP-PA)
DENT, CHARLES W. REP. (REP-PA)
DOYLE, MIKE (DEM-PA)
GOODLATTE, ROBERT W. (REP-VA)
GREEN, RAYMOND E. 'GENE' (DEM-TX)
HOYER, STENY HAMILTON (DEM-DC)
HUDSON, RICHARD L. JR. (REP-NC)
LUJAN, BEN R MR. (DEM-NM)
MALONEY, SEAN PATRICK (DEM-NY)
MARINO, THOMAS ANTHONY (REP-PA)
MCHENRY, PATRICK TIMOTHY (REP-NC)
MCMORRIS RODGERS, CATHY (REP-WA)
MEEHAN, PATRICK L. MR. (REP-PA)
PALLONE, FRANK JR (DEM-NJ)
RICE, KATHLEEN (DEM-NY)
RYAN, PAUL D. (REP-WI)
SANCHEZ, LINDA (DEM-CA)
SCALISE, STEVE MR. (REP-LA)
SCHRADER, KURT (DEM-OR)
SCHULTZ, DEBBIE WASSERMAN (DEM-FL)
SINEMA, KYRSTEN (DEM-AZ)
WALDEN, GREGORY P MR. (REP-OR)

Corporate Foundations and Giving Programs

NBC Universal Foundation
100 Universal City Pl.   Tel: (212) 664-4444
Universal City, CA 91608   Fax: (212) 664-4085

Public Affairs and Related Activities Personnel

At Headquarters

BLANCHARD, Cameron   Tel: (212) 664-4444
Senior Vice President, Corporate Communications Fax: (212) 664-4085
cameron.blanchard@nbcuni.com

COTTON, Richard   Tel: (212) 664-4444
Senior Counsellor for IP Protection   Fax: (212) 664-4085
rick.cotton@nbcuni.com

GREEN, David   Tel: (202) 637-4557
Vice President, Public Policy   Fax: (202) 637-4195
david.green@nbcuni.com

HARRIS, Kimberley D.   Tel: (212) 664-4444
Executive Vice President, General Counsel, NBCUniversal Fax: (212) 664-4085

KELLY-BROWN, Kathy   Tel: (212) 664-4444
Senior Vice President, Global Talent Booking Fax: (212) 664-4085
kathy.kelly-brown@nbcuni.com

KINI, Anand   Tel: (212) 664-4444
Chief Financial Officer, NBCUniversal   Fax: (212) 664-4085

MCSLARROW, Kyle   Tel: (212) 664-4444
President, Comcast/NBC Universal   Fax: (212) 664-4085

YACCARINO, Linda   Tel: (212) 664-4444
Chairman, Advertising Sales and Client Partnerships, Fax: (212) 664-4085
NBCUniversal

At Washington Office

MILLER, Adam   Tel: (202) 524-6401
Executive Vice President, NBCUniversal   Fax: (202) 524-6411
adam.miller@nbcuni.com

ROSE, Mitch   Tel: (202) 524-6401
Senior Vice President, Government Affairs   Fax: (202) 524-6411

TOBEY, Margaret L.   Tel: (202) 524-6401
Vice President, Regulatory Affairs   Fax: (202) 524-6411
margaret.tobey@nbcuni.com

At Other Offices

DORDELMAN, William   Tel: (215) 286-1700

*Senior Vice President and Treasurer for Comcast
Corporation, PAC Treasurer*
1701 JFK Blvd., 49th Floor
Philadelphia, PA 19103

NBT Bank

A full-service community bank. It provides commercial banking and financial services to individuals, corporations, and municipalities.
www.nbtbank.com
Annual Revenues: $359.23 million
Employees: 1,840
Ticker: NASDAQ: NBTB
Industry/ies: Banking/Finance/Investments

Chairman of the Board   Tel: (607) 337-2265
FORSYTHE, Daryl R.   Fax: (607) 336-6545

President and Chief Executive Officer   Tel: (607) 337-2265
DIETRICH, Martin A.   Fax: (607) 336-6545
mdietrich@nbtbank.com

Main Headquarters
Mailing: 52 S. Broad St.   Tel: (607) 337-2265
            P.O. Box 351   Fax: (607) 336-6545
            Norwich, NY 13815   TF: (800) 628-2265

Public Affairs and Related Activities Personnel

At Headquarters

BURNS, Annette L.   Tel: (607) 337-2265
Corporate Controller and PAC Contact   Fax: (607) 336-6545

CHEWENS, Michael J.   Tel: (607) 337-6119
Senior Executive Vice President and Chief Financial Officer Fax: (607) 337-6802

HYLE, Shaunastar M.   Tel: (607) 337-2265
Senior Vice President and Chief Risk Officer (PAC Treasurer Fax: (607) 337-6802
for 2012)

PRENTICE, F. Sheldon   Tel: (607) 337-2265
Corporate Senior Vice President, General Counsel and Fax: (607) 336-6545
Corporate Secretary

SCARLETT, Catherine M.   Tel: (607) 337-2265
Executive Vice President and Director, Human Resources Fax: (607) 336-6545

WEBB, Jack H.   Tel: (607) 337-2265
Executive Vice President, Strategic Support Fax: (607) 336-6545

NBTY Inc.

NBTY is a manufacturer, marketer and distributor of a broad line of high-quality, value-priced nutritional supplements in the United States and throughout the world. Brands include Ester-C, Nature's Bounty, Solgar, and Sundown. NBTY has manufacturing facilities in Canada, China, the UK, and the US and is able to produce and package capsules, tablets, powders, and liquids.
www.nbty.com
Employees: 14,000
Ticker: NYSE: NTY
SIC: 2834
NAICS: 325412
Industry/ies: Food And Beverage Industry

Vice Chairman, Investor Relations   Tel: (631) 200-2020
KAMIL, Harvey   Fax: (631) 567-7148

President and Chief Executive Officer   Tel: (631) 200-2000
CAHILLANE, Steve   Fax: (631) 567-7148

Main Headquarters
Mailing: 2100 Smithtown Ave.   Tel: (631) 200-2000
            Ronkonkoma, NY 11779   Fax: (631) 567-7148

Public Affairs and Related Activities Personnel

At Headquarters

CONBOY, Steve   Tel: (631) 200-2000
Senior Vice President and Chief Financial Officer Fax: (631) 567-7148

PACKER, Karla   Tel: (631) 200-2120
Senior Vice President, Chief Human Resources Officer Fax: (631) 567-7148
humanresources@nbty.com

PHILIPPIS, Stratis   Tel: (631) 200-2000
General Counsel and Chief Compliance Officer Fax: (631) 567-7148

SOUTUS, Sonya   Tel: (631) 200-2000
Senior Vice President, Chief Public Affairs and Fax: (631) 567-7148
Communications Officer

NCAS Pennsylvania

See listing on page 161 under Capital Blue Cross (Pennsylvania)

Ncircle Network Security, Inc.

Provides hardware and software systems that assess and monitor enterprise network security, protecting against hackers and other security threats.
www.ncircle.com
Annual Revenues: $10 million
Employees: 100

Industry/ies: Defense/Homeland Security; Government-Related

Chairman of the Board		Tel:	(415) 625-5900
LUDWICK , Andy		Fax:	(415) 625-5982
President and Chief Executive Officer		Tel:	(415) 625-5900
KLEINFELD, Abe		Fax:	(415) 625-5982

Main Headquarters

Mailing:	101 Second St.	Tel:	(415) 625-5900
	Suite 400	Fax:	(415) 625-5982
	San Francisco, CA 94105	TF:	(888) 464-2900

Public Affairs and Related Activities Personnel

At Headquarters

BOOSE, Shelley	Tel:	(408) 398-6987
Contact, Media Relations	Fax:	(415) 625-5982
sboose@ncircle.com		
D'ELENA, Beverly	Tel:	(415) 625-5900
Vice President, Human Resources	Fax:	(415) 625-5982
ELCHINOFF, Mark	Tel:	(415) 625-5900
Chief Financial Officer	Fax:	(415) 625-5982
IRELAND, Elizabeth	Tel:	(415) 625-5900
Vice President, Marketing	Fax:	(415) 625-5982

NCR Corporation

Provides relationship technology solutions to customers worldwide in the retail, financial, communications, manufacturing, travel and transportation, and insurance markets.
www.ncr.com
Annual Revenues: $6.55 billion
Employees: 30,200
Ticker: NYSE: NCR
SIC: 3571; 3579; 5044
NAICS: 334111; 333313; 42142
Industry/ies: Computer/Technology; Management; Retail/Wholesale
Legislative Issues: CPI; FIN; TAX; TRD

Chairman of the Board, President and Chief Executive Officer	Tel:	(937) 445-5000
NUTI, William	Fax:	(937) 445-1847

Main Headquarters

Mailing:	3097 Satellite Blvd.	Tel:	(937) 445-5000
	Bldg. 700	Fax:	(937) 445-5541
	Duluth, GA 30096	TF:	(800) 225-5627

Washington Office

Mailing:	20 F St. NW
	7th Floor
	Washington, DC 20001

Political Action Committees

NCR Corporation PAC (NCRPAC)
FEC ID: C00324103
Contact: Marija Zivanovic-Smith

20 F St. NW		
Seventh Floor	Tel:	(703) 967-0520
Washington, DC 20001		

   Contributions to Candidates: $14,000 (2015-2016)
   Democrats: $3,500; Republicans: $10,500

Corporate Foundations and Giving Programs

NCR Corporation Foundation
1700 S. Patterson Blvd.
Dayton, OH 45479

Public Affairs and Related Activities Personnel

At Headquarters

CLAY, Justin	Tel:	(937) 445-5000
Manager, Government Relations	Fax:	(937) 445-5541
Registered Federal Lobbyist		
FISHMAN, Bob	Tel:	(937) 445-5000
Senior Vice President, Chief Financial Officer and Chief Accounting Officer	Fax:	(937) 445-5541
HEYMAN, Andrew S.	Tel:	(937) 445-5000
Senior Vice President, Financial Services	Fax:	(937) 445-5541
LEDFORD, Andrea	Tel:	(937) 445-5000
Senior Vice President and Chief Human Resources Officer	Fax:	(937) 445-5541
RUANE, Kevin	Tel:	(212) 589-8553
Director, Corporate Communications	Fax:	(937) 445-5541
kevin.ruane@ncr.com		
SMITH, Cameron	Tel:	(770) 623-7998
Marketing Manager	Fax:	(937) 445-5541
cameron.smith@ncr.com		

At Washington Office

ZIVANOVIC-SMITH, Marija
Vice President
marija.zivanovic-smith@ncr.com
Registered Federal Lobbyist

NCS Pearson, Inc.

Global provider of applications, services and technologies for education, testing, assessment, government and complex data management. Acquired by Pearson in 2000.
www.ncspearson.com
Employees: 7,000
Industry/ies: Computer/Technology

Chief Executive Officer	Tel:	(952) 681-3000
FALLON, John	Fax:	(952) 681-3549

Main Headquarters

Mailing:	5601 Green Valley Dr.	Tel:	(952) 681-3000
	Bloomington, MN 55437	Fax:	(952) 681-3549
		TF:	(800) 431-1421

Public Affairs and Related Activities Personnel

At Headquarters

ASPEY, Susan	Tel:	(952) 681-3000
Vice President, Media Relations	Fax:	(952) 681-3549
GABER, Adam	Tel:	(212) 641-6118
Vice President, Communications	Fax:	(952) 681-3549
Adam.Gaber@Pearson.com		

NCSC Group, LLC

General business consultants.

Main Headquarters

Mailing:	300 E. Evans St.	Tel:	(202) 360-1218
	P-178		
	West Chester, PA 19380		

Public Affairs and Related Activities Personnel

At Headquarters

FALENCKI, Michael	Tel:	(202) 360-1218
Owner		
mjfalencki12@gmail.com		

NEC Corporation

A provider of information technology management solutions. A subsidiary of NEC Corp. of Tokyo, Japan.
www.necam.com
Employees: 3,000
Industry/ies: Computer/Technology
Legislative Issues: SCI

Main Headquarters

Mailing:	6555 N. State Hwy. 161	Tel:	(214) 262-2000
	Irving, TX 75039-2402	Fax:	(214) 262-2586
		TF:	(800) 338-9549

Corporate Foundations and Giving Programs

NEC Foundation of America
6535 N. State Hwy. 161
Irving, TX 70539

Public Affairs and Related Activities Personnel

At Headquarters

COGSWELL-WOJTECKI, Lourdes	Tel:	(631) 755-0720
Vice President	Fax:	(631) 753-7041
lourdes.wojtecki@necam.com		
KAWASHIMA, Isamu	Tel:	(214) 262-2000
Executive Vice President and Chief Financial Officer	Fax:	(214) 262-2586
NIINO, Takashi	Tel:	(214) 262-2000
Senior Executive Vice President, Chief Strategy Officer and Chief Information Officer	Fax:	(214) 262-2586
OKADA, Takayuki	Tel:	(214) 262-2000
Senior Executive Vice President	Fax:	(214) 262-2586
SHIMIZU, Takaaki	Tel:	(214) 262-2000
Senior Vice President and Chief Marketing Officer	Fax:	(214) 262-2586

Nehemiah Corporation of America

Nehemiah Corporation of America is a non-profit corporation specializing in home ownership, affordable housing and community development.
www.nehemiahcorp.org
Annual Revenues: $276.35 million
Industry/ies: Housing

Ex-Officio Director and Chair	Tel:	(816) 231-5246
SYPHAX, Scott	Fax:	(916) 326-5429

Main Headquarters

Mailing:	640 Bercut Dr.	Tel:	(916) 231-1999
	Suite A	Fax:	(916) 326-5429
	Sacramento, CA 95811-0131		

Corporate Foundations and Giving Programs

Nehemiah Community Foundation
Contact: Mary Ackman
424 N. Seventh St.

Suite 250
Sacramento, CA 95811

Public Affairs and Related Activities Personnel

At Headquarters

ACKMAN, Mary
Community Development Analyst
mackman@nehemiahcorp.org
Tel: (916) 231-5246
Fax: (916) 326-5429

BANYAI, Mary
Community Development Associate
mbanyai@nehemiahcorp.org
Tel: (816) 231-5246
Fax: (916) 326-5429

The Nelson Law Firm, LLC

Law firm provides legal services concerning matters of corporate and securities law.
www.thenelsonlawfirm.com

Founder
NELSON, Stephen
sjnelson@nelsonlf.com
Tel: (914) 220-1900
Fax: (914) 220-1911

Main Headquarters
Mailing: White Plains Plaza
One N. Broadway, Suite 712
White Plains, NY 10601
Tel: (914) 220-1900
Fax: (914) 220-1911

Neostem Inc.

See listing on page 155 under Caladrius

Nephron Pharmaceutical Corporation

A pharmaceutical company.
www.nephronpharm.com
Employees: 500
Industry/ies: Pharmaceutical Industry

Chief Executive Officer
KENNEDY, Lou
Tel: (407) 999-2225
Fax: (407) 872-1733

Main Headquarters
Mailing: 4121 S.W. 34th St.
Orlando, FL 32811
Tel: (407) 999-2225
Fax: (407) 872-1733
TF: (800) 443-4313

Public Affairs and Related Activities Personnel

At Headquarters

BRADY, Michelle
Human Resource Manager
Tel: (407) 999-2225
Fax: (407) 872-1733

Neptune Regional Transmission System LLC

Neptune RTS is a consortium of companies with experience in the field of electricity infrastructure development.
neptunerts.com
Annual Revenues: $26.36 million
Employees: 51
Industry/ies: Energy/Electricity

President and Chief Executive Officer
STERN, Edward M.
Tel: (203) 416-5590
Fax: (203) 416-5599

Main Headquarters
Mailing: 501 Kings Hwy., East
Suite 300
Fairfield, CT 06825
Tel: (203) 416-5590
Fax: (203) 416-5599
TF: (877) 466-7344

Public Affairs and Related Activities Personnel

At Headquarters

BEAUMONTE, Thomas G.
Chief Financial Officer and Treasurer
tbeaumonte@neptunerts.com
Tel: (203) 416-5590
Fax: (203) 416-5599

HOCKER, J. Christopher
Vice President, Planning
chocker@neptunerts.com
Tel: (203) 416-5590
Fax: (203) 416-5599

SULLIVAN, James T.
Vice President, Operations
Tel: (203) 416-5590
Fax: (203) 416-5599

Neptunic Technologies, Inc.

A producer of protective material and gear.
www.neptunic.com
Industry/ies: Advertising And Marketing; Business; Small Business

President
ANDREA, Neil

Main Headquarters
Mailing: 1810 Old Okeechobee Rd.
Studio A
W. Palm Beach, FL 33409

Nestle Purina PetCare Company

Acquired the American Ralston Purina Company on December 12, 2001, got merged with Nestlé's Friskies PetCare Company and a subsidiary of Swiss food giant Nestlé S.A. A pet food producer.
www.purina.com
Employees: 7,600
Industry/ies: Agriculture/Agronomy; Animals; Food And Beverage Industry
Legislative Issues: AGR; FOO

Chairman
MCGINNIS, W. Patrick

Chief Executive Officer
SIVEWRIGHT, Joseph R.

Main Headquarters
Mailing: P.O. Box 1326
Wilkes-Barre, PA 18703

Washington Office
Mailing: 818 Connecticut Ave. NW, Suite 950
Washington, DC 20006
Tel: (202) 776-0071
Fax: (202) 776-0083

Political Action Committees
Nestle Purina Petcare Company PAC
FEC ID: C00338335
Contact: Thomas Allgeyer
Checkboard Sq.
St. Louis, MO 63164

Corporate Foundations and Giving Programs
Purina Charitable Giving
Checkboard Sq.
St. Louis, MO 63164
Tel: (314) 982-1000

Public Affairs and Related Activities Personnel

At Other Offices

ALLGEYER, Thomas
PAC Treasurer
Checkboard Sq.
St. Louis, MO 63164
Tel: (314) 982-1000
Fax: (314) 982-2134

FOSTER, Rick
Chief Financial Officer
Checkboard Sq.
St. Louis, MO 63164
Tel: (314) 982-1000
Fax: (314) 982-2134

SCHOPP, Keith
Vice President, Corporate Public Relations Nestlé Purina PetCare Company – North America
Checkboard Sq.
St. Louis, MO 63164
kschopp@purina.com
Tel: (314) 982-2577
Fax: (314) 982-2752

Nestle USA, Inc.

A subsidiary of Nestle S.A., Switzerland. A food company.
www.nestleusa.com
SIC: 2066; 2086; 2099; 5149
NAICS: 312111; 311999; 31132; 42249
Industry/ies: Food And Beverage Industry
Legislative Issues: AGR; BUD; ENV; FOO; LBR; MED; TAX; TRA; TRD

Chairman
MAUCHE, Helmut Oswald
Tel: (818) 549-6000
Fax: (818) 549-6952

Chief Executive Officer
BULCKE, Paul
Tel: (818) 549-6000
Fax: (818) 549-6952

Main Headquarters
Mailing: 800 N. Brand Blvd.
Glendale, CA 91203
Tel: (818) 549-6000
Fax: (818) 549-6952
TF: (800) 225-2270

Washington Office
Mailing: 505 Ninth St. NW
Suite 600
Washington, DC 20004
Tel: (202) 292-2921
Fax: (202) 756-7556

Political Action Committees
Nestle USA, Inc.Political Action Committee
FEC ID: C00087882
Contact: Denise O'Neal
30003 Bainbridge Rd.
Solon, OH 44139

Corporate Foundations and Giving Programs
Nestle USA Foundation
800 N. Brand Blvd.
Glendale, CA 91203

Public Affairs and Related Activities Personnel

At Headquarters

BURGE, Edie
Contact, Media
Mediarelations@nestle.com
Tel: (818) 551-3284
Fax: (818) 549-6952

At Washington Office

COLLIER, Nicole	Tel:	(202) 292-2921	
Director, Government Affairs	Fax:	(202) 756-7556	
Registered Federal Lobbyist			
FOGARTY, Molly	Tel:	(202) 292-2921	
Vice President, Government Relations and Public Affairs	Fax:	(202) 756-7556	
molly.fogarty@us.nestle.com			
Registered Federal Lobbyist			
FREEMAN, Kelsey	Tel:	(202) 292-2921	
Registered Federal Lobbyist	Fax:	(202) 756-7556	

At Other Offices

O'NEAL, Denise
PAC Treasurer
30003 Bainbridge Rd.
Solon, OH 44139

Nestle Waters North America, Inc.

Offers a portfolio of regional water brands, including Arrowhead, Calistoga, Deer Park, Great Bear, Ice Mountain, Ozarka, Poland Spring, and Zephyrhills.
www.nestle-watersna.com
Employees: 7,500
Industry/ies: Food And Beverage Industry
Legislative Issues: ENV

Chairman, Chief Executive Officer and President	Tel:	(203) 531-4100
BROWN, Tim	Fax:	(203) 863-0572

Main Headquarters

Mailing:	900 Long Ridge Rd.	Tel:	(203) 531-4100
	Building Two	Fax:	(203) 863-0572
	Stamford, CT 06902-1138	TF:	(888) 747-7437

Public Affairs and Related Activities Personnel

At Headquarters

BROLL, Charlie	Tel:	(203) 531-4100	
Executive Vice President, General Counsel and Secretary	Fax:	(203) 863-0572	
DONAHUE, Raymond	Tel:	(203) 531-4100	
Senior Manager	Fax:	(203) 863-0572	
LAZGIN, Jane	Tel:	(203) 863-0240	
Director, Corporate Communications	Fax:	(203) 863-0572	
jane.lazgin@waters.nestle.com			
PAUL, Heidi	Tel:	(203) 531-4100	
Executive Vice President, Corporate Affairs	Fax:	(203) 863-0572	
PEARSON, Bill	Tel:	(203) 531-4100	
Executive Vice President, Finance and Chief Financial Officer	Fax:	(203) 863-0572	
SCIUTO, Antonio	Tel:	(203) 531-4100	
Executive Vice President and Chief Marketing Officer	Fax:	(203) 863-0572	
SWINTON, Michael T.	Tel:	(203) 531-4100	
Director	Fax:	(203) 863-0572	
TANNER, Rick	Tel:	(203) 531-4100	
Chief Marketing Officer	Fax:	(203) 863-0572	

At Other Offices

GEISSLER , Christine	Tel:	(203) 531-4100
Vice President, Human Resources		
777 W. Putnam Ave.		
Greenwich, CT 06830		

NetApp

See listing on page 570 under Network Appliance, Inc.

Netflix, Inc.

Provides subscription services for renting videos or viewing "streaming" videos.
www.netflix.com
Annual Revenues: $7.16 billion
Employees: 3,100
Ticker: NASDAQ:NFLX
Industry/ies: Communications; Telecommunications/Internet/Cable
Legislative Issues: COM; LBR; TEC

Chief Executive Officer, President, Chairman of the Board	Tel:	(408) 540-3700
HASTINGS, Reed	Fax:	(302) 655-5049

Main Headquarters

Mailing:	100 Winchester Cir.	Tel:	(408) 540-3700
	Los Gatos, CA 95032	Fax:	(302) 655-5049

Washington Office

Mailing:	1455 Pennsylvania Ave NW, Ste 650
	Washington, DC 20004

Political Action Committees

Netflix Inc PAC (FLIXPAC)
FEC ID: C00518233
Contact: Christopher Libertelli
100 Winchester Cir.
Los Gatos, CA 95032

    Contributions to Candidates: $23,300 (2015-2016)

    Democrats: $13,100; Republicans: $10,200

Public Affairs and Related Activities Personnel

At Headquarters

BENNETT, Kelly	Tel:	(408) 540-3700	
Chief Marketing Officer	Fax:	(302) 655-5049	
FRIEDLAND, Jonathan	Tel:	(408) 540-3700	
Chief Communications Officer	Fax:	(302) 655-5049	
HYMAN, David	Tel:	(408) 540-3700	
General Counsel	Fax:	(302) 655-5049	
KORN, Josh	Tel:	(408) 540-3700	
Registered Federal Lobbyist	Fax:	(302) 655-5049	
LIBERTELLI, Christopher	Tel:	(408) 540-3700	
PAC Treasurer and Vice President, Global Public Policy	Fax:	(302) 655-5049	
WELLS, David	Tel:	(408) 540-3700	
Chief Financial Officer	Fax:	(302) 655-5049	

At Other Offices

WRIGHT, Corie
Federal Lobbyist
1120 G St. NW, Suite 770
Washington, DC 20005
Registered Federal Lobbyist

NetJets

A fractional aircraft ownership company.
www.netjets.com
Annual Revenues: $299 million
Employees: 3,600
Industry/ies: Aerospace/Aviation; Transportation
Legislative Issues: AVI; TAX; TRA

Main Headquarters

Mailing:	4111 Bridgeway Ave.	Tel:	(614) 239-5500
	Columbus, OH 43219-1882	Fax:	(614) 205-0214
		TF:	(877) 356-5823

Political Action Committees

NetJets Inc PAC
FEC ID: C00481309
Contact: Bob E. Tanner
4111 Bridgeway Ave.   Tel: (614) 239-5500
Columbus, OH 43219-1882

    Contributions to Candidates: $36,850 (2015-2016)
    Democrats: $7,000; Republicans: $29,850

Corporate Foundations and Giving Programs

NetJets Family Foundation
Contact: Lynn Wombacher
4111 Bridgeway Ave.   Tel: (614) 849-7695
Columbus, OH 43219-1882   Fax: (614) 205-0214

Public Affairs and Related Activities Personnel

At Headquarters

POWELL, David M.	Tel:	(614) 239-2091
Manager, Maintenance Planning		
Registered Federal Lobbyist		
SMITH, Brent	Tel:	(614) 239-5500
Chief Financial Officer		
TANNER, Bob E.	Tel:	(614) 239-5500
rtanner2@netjets.com		
Registered Federal Lobbyist		
WOMBACHER, Lynn	Tel:	(614) 849-7695
Manager, NetJets Family Foundation	Fax:	(614) 205-0214
lwombacher@netjetsfamily.org		

At Other Offices

AARSETH, Maryann	Tel:	(732) 326-3735
Vice President, Corporate Communications	Fax:	(732) 326-3737
581 Main St.		
Woodbridge, NJ 07095		
maarseth@netjets.com		

NetStart Inc.

See listing on page 164 under CareerBuilder.com

Network Appliance, Inc.

NetApp provides an integrated solution that enables storage, delivery, and management of network data and content to achieve your business goals.
www.netapp.com
Annual Revenues: $6.12 billion
Employees: 12,810
Ticker: NASDAQ: NTAP
SIC: 3572; 3571; 5045
Industry/ies: Computer/Technology
Legislative Issues: GOV

Chief Executive Officer
KURIAN, George
Tel: (408) 822-6000
Fax: (408) 822-4501

Main Headquarters
Mailing: 495 E. Java Dr.
Sunnyvale, CA 94089
Tel: (408) 822-6000
Fax: (408) 822-4501
TF: (800) 445-2234

Washington Office
Mailing: 8405 Greensboro Dr.
Suite 1000
McLean, VA 22102
Tel: (703) 918-7200

Corporate Foundations and Giving Programs
Network Appliance Contributions Programme
495 E. Java Dr.
Sunnyvale, CA 94089
Tel: (408) 822-6000
Fax: (408) 822-4501

Public Affairs and Related Activities Personnel

At Headquarters

FAWCETT, Matthew
Senior Vice President, General Counsel and Secretary
Tel: (408) 822-6000
Fax: (408) 822-4501

HITZ , David
Executive Vice President and Founder
Tel: (408) 822-6000
Fax: (408) 822-4501

KISSANE, Jonathan
Senior Vice President and Chief Strategy Officer
Tel: (408) 822-6000
Fax: (408) 822-4501

MCDONALD, Gwen
Executive Vice President, Human Resources
Tel: (408) 822-6000
Fax: (408) 822-4501

NEWTON, Kris
Senior Director, Investor Relations
Kris.Newton@netapp.com
Tel: (408) 822-6000
Fax: (408) 822-4501

NOVIELLO , Nick
Executive Vice President, Finance and Chief Financial Officer
Tel: (408) 822-6000
Fax: (408) 822-4501

PARRISH, Julie
Senior Vice President and Chief Marketing Officer
Tel: (408) 822-6000
Fax: (408) 822-4501

VILLAREAL, Roger
Public Relations and Press Contact
roger.villareal@netapp.com
Tel: (408) 822-1959
Fax: (408) 822-4501

NetWorth Services, Inc.

A financial information services and software-consulting company.
www.networthservices.com
Annual Revenues: $2 million
Employees: 15
Industry/ies: Banking/Finance/Investments

President and Chief Executive Officer
WILLIS, Nico R.
Tel: (602) 222-6380
Fax: (602) 222-6383

Main Headquarters
Mailing: 3333 E. Camelback Rd.
Suite 260
Phoenix, AZ 85018

Corporate Foundations and Giving Programs
NetWorth Services Contributions Program
1661 E. Camelback Rd.
Suite 200
Phoenix, AZ 85016

Public Affairs and Related Activities Personnel

At Other Offices

COHEN, Barry
Contact, Media Relations
1661 E. Camelback Rd., Suite 200
Phoenix, AZ 85016
bcohen@networthservices.com
Tel: (602) 222-6380
Fax: (602) 222-6383

DIAZ, Marisa K.
Chief Compliance Officer and Vice President, Sales and Marketing
1661 E. Camelback Rd., Suite 200
Phoenix, AZ 85016
diaz@networthservices.com
Tel: (602) 222-6380
Fax: (602) 222-6383

FRANK, Lauren
Contact, Media Relations
1661 E. Camelback Rd., Suite 200
Phoenix, AZ 85016
LFrank@networthservices.com
Tel: (602) 222-6380
Fax: (602) 222-6383

Neural Stem, Inc.

Biotherapeutics company utilizing its patented Human Neural Stem Cell technology to create cures for diseases of the CNS (central nervous system).
www.neuralstem.com
Annual Revenues: $17.58K
Employees: 21
Ticker: NYSE: CUR
SIC: 2836
Industry/ies: Medicine/Health Care/Mental Health

Chairman of the Board, Chief Scientific Officer
JOHE, PhD, Karl
kjohe@neuralstem.com
Tel: (301) 366-4960

President, Chief Executive Officer and Legal Counsel
GARR, JD, I. Richard
irgarr@neuralstem.com
Tel: (301) 366-4960

Main Headquarters
Mailing: 20271 Goldenrod Ln.
Second Floor
Germantown, MD 20876
Tel: (301) 366-4960

Washington Office
Mailing: 9700 Great Seneca Hwy.
Rockville, MD 20850
Tel: (301) 366-4960

Public Affairs and Related Activities Personnel

At Washington Office

CONRON, John
Chief Financial Officer
jconron@neuralstem.com
Tel: (301) 366-4960

ROUSH, Susan
Contact, Investor Relations
Tel: (747) 222-7012

At Other Offices

EAGLE, Deanne
Media Contact
172 W. 82nd St., Suite Four
New York City, NY 10024
deanneeagle@gmail.com
Tel: (917) 837-5866

Neuromonics, Inc.

A medical device company offering tinnitus treatment. It manufactures and distributes the only FDA-cleared, patented and clinically proven medical devices designed for long-term, significant relief of tinnitus.
www.neuromonics.com
Annual Revenues: $2.30 million
Employees: 20
Industry/ies: Medicine/Health Care/Mental Health

Chairman of the Board
WEST, Ronald E.
Tel: (720) 242-6893

Chief Executive Officer
ADAMS, Eula
Tel: (720) 242-6893

Main Headquarters
Mailing: 8774 Yates Dr.
Suite 220
Westminster, CO 80031
Tel: (720) 242-6893

Public Affairs and Related Activities Personnel

At Headquarters

AMANN, Curtis
Vice President, Marketing and Sales
Tel: (720) 242-6893

KNIGHT, Duane
Chief Operating and Chief Financial Officer
duane.knight@neuromonics.com
Tel: (720) 480-1749

Nevada Power Company

An electric utility. Nevada Power, Sierra Pacific Power and Sierra Pacific Resources merged in July 1999 to create one of the fastest growing energy companies listed on the New York Stock Exchange.
www.nvenergy.com
Annual Revenues: $2.95 billion
Employees: 2,699
Ticker: NYSE: NVE
SIC: 4911
Industry/ies: Utilities

Chief Executive Officer
YACKIRA, Michael W.
Tel: (702) 367-5000
Fax: (702) 367-5053

Main Headquarters
Mailing: P.O. Box 98910
Las Vegas, NV 89151-0001
Tel: (702) 367-5000
Fax: (702) 367-5053
TF: (800) 331-3103

Corporate Foundations and Giving Programs
Nevada Power Company Contributions Program
P.O. Box 98910
Las Vegas, NV 89193-8910

NV Energy Foundation
P.O. Box 10100
Reno, NV 89520-3150
Tel: (702) 402-5741

Public Affairs and Related Activities Personnel

At Headquarters

COBB, Alice A.
Tel: (702) 367-5000
Fax: (702) 367-5053

Senior Vice President, Human Resources, Information Technology and Telecommunications

GRAHAM-EASLER, Doretha *Manager, Community Relations*	Tel: Fax:	(702) 367-5741 (702) 579-0801
HALKYARD, Jonathan S. *Executive Vice President and Chief Financial Officer*	Tel: Fax:	(702) 367-5000 (702) 367-5053
SANCHEZ, III, Tony F. *Senior Vice President, Government and Community Strategy*	Tel: Fax:	(702) 367-5000 (702) 367-5053
SCHURICHT, Jennifer *Manager, Communications* JSchuricht@NVEnergy.com	Tel: Fax:	(702) 402-5241 (702) 367-5053
SIMMONS, Mary O. *Vice President, External Affairs*	Tel: Fax:	(702) 367-5000 (702) 367-5053
WALQUIST, Karl *Contact, Communications*	Tel: Fax:	(775) 834-3891 (702) 367-5053

New Balance Athletic Shoe, Inc.

A manufacturer of athletic footwear and apparel.
www.newbalance.com
Annual Revenues: $112.10 million
Employees: 1,500
SIC: 3149; 2329
Industry/ies: Apparel/Textiles Industry; Sports/Leisure/Entertainment
Legislative Issues: DEF

Chairman of the Board

DAVIS, James S. Jim.Davis@newbalance.com	Tel: Fax:	(617) 783-4000 (617) 783-5152

President and Chief Executive Officer

DEMARTINI, Robert T.	Tel: Fax:	(617) 783-4000 (617) 787-9355

Main Headquarters

Mailing:	Brighton Landing 20 Guest St. Boston, MA 02135-2088	Tel: Fax: TF:	(617) 783-4000 (617) 787-9355 (800) 622-1218

Corporate Foundations and Giving Programs

New Balance Foundation
Contact: Mary Lawton
Brighton Landing
20 Guest St.
Boston, MA 02135

Public Affairs and Related Activities Personnel

At Headquarters

DOW, Amy *Senior Manager, Global Corporate Communications* Amy.dow@newbalance.com	Tel: Fax:	(617) 746-2214 (617) 787-9355
LAWTON, Mary *Contact, Media Relations and Contact, Foundation* Mary.lawton@newbalance.com	Tel: Fax:	(617) 746-2525 (617) 787-9355
O'DONNELL, Carol *Vice President, Corporate Human Resources* Carol.O'Donnell@newbalance.com	Tel: Fax:	(617) 783-4000 (617) 783-5152
WITHEE, John *Executive Vice President and Chief Financial Officer* john.withee@newbalance.com	Tel: Fax:	(617) 783-4000 (617) 787-9355

New Bedford Panoramex

Specializes in the airport remote monitoring.
www.nbpcorp.com
Annual Revenues: $5.2 million
Employees: 39
Industry/ies: Aerospace/Aviation; Transportation

Chairman Of the Board

OZUNA, Steven	Tel:	(909) 982-9806

Main Headquarters

Mailing:	1480 N. Claremont Blvd. Claremont, CA 91711	Tel:	(909) 982-9806

Political Action Committees

New Bedford Panoramex Corporation PAC
FEC ID: C00279174
Contact: Bryce L. Nielsen
1480 N. Claremont Blvd.
Claremont, CA 91711

> **Contributions to Candidates:** $1,500 (2015-2016)
> Democrats: $1,250; Republicans: $250

Public Affairs and Related Activities Personnel

At Headquarters

NIELSEN, Bryce L. *PAC Treasurer* bnielsen@nbpcorp.com	Tel:	(909) 982-9806

At Other Offices

BROWN, Mayra *Contact, Human Resources* 1037 W. Ninth St. Upland, CA 91786	Tel: Fax:	(909) 982-9806 (909) 985-6217

New Enterprise Associates

A venture capital firm. It focuses on a variety of investment stages, ranging from seed stage through growth stage across a broad array of industry sectors.
www.nea.com
Employees: 60
Industry/ies: Banking/Finance/Investments
Legislative Issues: ENG; TAX

Main Headquarters

Mailing:	2855 Sand Hill Rd. Menlo Park, CA 94205	Tel: Fax:	(650) 854-9499 (650) 854-9397

Washington Office

Mailing:	5425 Wisconsin Ave. Suite 800 Chevy Chase, MD 20815	Tel: Fax:	(301) 272-2300 (301) 272-1700

Public Affairs and Related Activities Personnel

At Headquarters

MITCHELL, Ashley *Manager, Communications and Marketing*	Tel: Fax:	(650) 854-9499 (650) 854-9397

At Washington Office

BARRETT, Kate *Partner, Marketing* kbarrett@nea.com	Tel: Fax:	(301) 272-2318 (301) 272-1700
BRECHER, Stephanie *General Counsel*	Tel: Fax:	(301) 272-2300 (301) 272-1700
CITRON, Louis *Chief Legal Officer*	Tel: Fax:	(301) 272-2300 (301) 272-1700
SCHALLER, Tim *Chief Financial Officer* tschaller@nea.com	Tel: Fax:	(301) 272-2300 (301) 272-1700

New Flyer of America Inc.

New Flyer is an equal opportunity employer.
www.newflyer.com
SIC: 3713
Industry/ies: Machinery/Equipment
Legislative Issues: TRA

President and Chief Executive Officer

SOUBRY, Paul paul_soubry@newflyer.com	Tel: Fax:	(204) 224-6652 (204) 224-6652

Main Headquarters

Mailing:	711 Kernaghan Ave. Winnipeg, MB R2C 3T4	Tel: Fax:	(204) 224-1251 (204) 224-6652

Public Affairs and Related Activities Personnel

At Headquarters

ABRAHAM, Joel *Federal Lobbyist*	Tel: Fax:	(204) 224-6652 (204) 224-6652
ASHAM, Glenn *Chief Financial Officer*	Tel: Fax:	(204) 224-1251 (204) 224-6652
HARPER, Janice *Vice President, Human Resources* Janice_Harper@newflyer.com	Tel: Fax:	(204) 224-1251 (204) 224-6652
JOSEPH, Wayne *Executive Vice President, Operations* Wayne_Joseph@newflyer.com	Tel: Fax:	(204) 224-1251 (204) 224-6652
KIRSHNER, Alex *Director, Finance* Alex_Kirshner@newflyer.com	Tel: Fax:	(204) 224-1251 (204) 224-6652
PEWARCHUK, Colin *Executive Vice President, General Counsel & Corporate Secretary* Colin_Pewarchuk@newflyer.com	Tel: Fax:	(204) 224-6652 (204) 224-6652
SMITH, Paul *Executive Vice President, Sales and Marketing*	Tel: Fax:	(204) 224-6652 (204) 224-6652
WAYNE, Joseph *Federal Lobbyist*	Tel: Fax:	(204) 224-1251 (204) 224-6652
WOOD, Kevin *Vice President, Manufacturing*	Tel: Fax:	(204) 224-6652 (204) 224-6652

New Generation Biofuels

Producer of liquid biofuel. The fuel can be used to replace diesel, heating oil, kerosene, and other fuel oils. They currently have two product formulations. NGBF Classic and NGBF Ultra HF. While both products can be used in similar applications there are significant differences in Flash Point and Heating Value.
www.newgenerationbiofuels.com

Employees: 9
Ticker: PINK: NGBF
SIC: 2860
Industry/ies: Fuels See Coal, Gas, Oil, Petroleum; Natural Resources; Petroleum Industry

Chairman of the Board　　　　　　　　　Tel:　(321) 363-5100
MACK, John E.　　　　　　　　　　　　　　Fax:　(443) 638-0277

Main Headquarters
Mailing:　1000 Primera Blvd.　　　　　　Tel:　(321) 363-5100
　　　　　Suite 3130　　　　　　　　　　Fax:　(443) 638-0277
　　　　　Lake Mary, FL 32746

Washington Office
Mailing:　4308 Brandywine St. NW
　　　　　Washington, DC 20016

Public Affairs and Related Activities Personnel

At Headquarters

HAINES, Matthew　　　　　　　　　　　　Tel:　(212) 710-9686
Contact, Investor Relations　　　　　　　Fax:　(443) 638-0277

New Health Sciences

Founded in March 2000, New Health Sciences has developed the only quantitative, sensitive, reproducible physiological means of measuring and describing changes in vascular function that signal the presence or risk of conditions that rob organs of adequate blood flow and lead to disabling damage or sudden death. NHSi calls its technology Hemodynamic Vascular Analysis (HDVA).
Industry/ies: Medicine/Health Care/Mental Health; Science; Scientific Research

President and Chief Executive Officer　　　Tel:　(240) 743-4343
CANNON, Martin A.　　　　　　　　　　　Fax:　(301) 493-4360

Main Headquarters
Mailing:　6930 Rockledge Dr.　　　　　　Tel:　(240) 743-4343
　　　　　Suite 230　　　　　　　　　　Fax:　(301) 493-4360
　　　　　Bethesda, MD 20817

Public Affairs and Related Activities Personnel

At Headquarters

BAVONESE, Michael　　　　　　　　　　Tel:　(240) 743-4343
Vice President, Finance and Administration　Fax:　(301) 493-4360

New Jersey Natural Gas Company

See listing on page 573 under New Jersey Resources Corporation

New Jersey Resources Corporation

An energy services company. Subsidiaries include New Jersey Natural Gas Co., NJR Natural Energy Co., and commercial Realty & Resources Corp., among others.
www.njresources.com
Annual Revenues: $3.12 billion
Employees: 968
Ticker: NYSE: NJR
SIC: 4924
Industry/ies: Energy/Electricity; Natural Resources; Utilities

Chairman of the Board and Chief Executive Officer　Tel:　(732) 938-1000
DOWNES, Laurence M.　　　　　　　　　　Fax:　(732) 938-2620

Main Headquarters
Mailing:　1415 Wyckoff Rd.　　　　　　　Tel:　(732) 938-1000
　　　　　Wall, NJ 07719　　　　　　　　Fax:　(732) 938-2620

Corporate Foundations and Giving Programs

New Jersey Resources Corporation Contribution Program
1415 Wyckoff Rd.　　　　　　　　　　　Tel:　(732) 938-1000
Wall, NJ 07719　　　　　　　　　　　　Fax:　(732) 938-2620

Public Affairs and Related Activities Personnel

At Headquarters

DUGAN, Mariellen　　　　　　　　　　　Tel:　(732) 938-1000
Senior Vice President and General Counsel　Fax:　(732) 938-2620
mdugan@njresources.com

FIGUEROA, Rhonda M.　　　　　　　　　Tel:　(732) 938-1000
Corporate Secretary　　　　　　　　　　Fax:　(732) 938-2620

KENT, James　　　　　　　　　　　　　Tel:　(732) 938-1000
Treasurer　　　　　　　　　　　　　　Fax:　(732) 938-2620

KINNEY, Michael　　　　　　　　　　　Tel:　(732) 938-1031
Senior Specialist, Communications　　　　Fax:　(732) 938-3154
njrcommunications@njresources.com

LOCKWOOD, Glenn C.　　　　　　　　　Tel:　(732) 938-1000
Executive Vice President and Chief Financial Officer　Fax:　(732) 938-2620
gclockwood@njresources.com

MIGLIACCIO, Patrick　　　　　　　　　　Tel:　(732) 938-1000
Vice President, Finance and Accounting　　Fax:　(732) 938-2620

PUMA, Dennis R.　　　　　　　　　　　Tel:　(732) 938-1229
Director, Investor Relations　　　　　　　Fax:　(732) 938-3154
investcont@njresources.com

SPERDUTO, Mark R.　　　　　　　　　　Tel:　(732) 938-1000
Senior Vice President, Regulatory and External Affairs　Fax:　(732) 938-2620

New NGC Inc. (National Gypsum Company)

A manufacturer and supplier of producing, marketing, and selling gypsum wallboard and interior finishing products used worldwide in building and construction. National Gypsum Company was purchased and became privately-held in 1995.
www.nationalgypsum.com
Annual Revenues: $1.10 billion
Employees: 1,900
SIC: 3275; 3299; 3270
Industry/ies: Construction/Construction Materials

Chairman, President & Chief Executive Officer　Tel:　(704) 365-7300
NELSON, Thomas C.　　　　　　　　　　Fax:　(704) 329-6421

Main Headquarters
Mailing:　2001 Rexford Rd.　　　　　　Tel:　(704) 365-7300
　　　　　Charlotte, NC 28211　　　　　Fax:　(704) 329-6421
　　　　　　　　　　　　　　　　　　TF:　(800) 628-4662

Corporate Foundations and Giving Programs

National Gypsum Contributions Program
2001 Rexford Rd.
Charlotte, NC 28211

Public Affairs and Related Activities Personnel

At Headquarters

BARBER, Warren　　　　　　　　　　　Tel:　(704) 365-7300
Manager, Construction Design　　　　　　Fax:　(704) 329-6421

CIESLIKOWSKI, Renee　　　　　　　　　Tel:　(704) 365-7329
Manager, Marketing Communications　　　Fax:　(704) 329-6421
RACieslikowski@NationalGypsum.com

RODONO, Nicholas J.　　　　　　　　　Tel:　(704) 365-7300
Vice President, Human Resources　　　　　Fax:　(704) 329-6421
njRodono@nationalgypsum.com

SPURLOCK, Nancy J.　　　　　　　　　Tel:　(704) 365-7556
Director, Corporate Communications　　　Fax:　(704) 329-6421
nhspurlock@nationalgypsum.com

New Way Air Bearings

Designer and manufacturer of air bearing products.
www.newwayairbearings.com
Annual Revenues: $9.60 million
Employees: 94
Industry/ies: Aerospace/Aviation; Transportation

Chairman of the Board and Chief Technology Officer　Tel:　(610) 494-6700
DEVITT, Drew　　　　　　　　　　　　Fax:　(610) 494-0911
ddevitt@newwayairbearings.com

President and Chief Executive Officer　　　Tel:　(610) 494-6700
HACKETT, Nick　　　　　　　　　　　　Fax:　(610) 494-0911
nhackett@newwayairbearings.com

Main Headquarters
Mailing:　50 McDonald Blvd.　　　　　　Tel:　(610) 494-6700
　　　　　Aston, PA 19014-3202　　　　　Fax:　(610) 494-0911

Public Affairs and Related Activities Personnel

At Headquarters

WRIGHT, Michael　　　　　　　　　　　Tel:　(610) 354-3453
Director, Marketing　　　　　　　　　　Fax:　(610) 494-0911
mwright@newwayairbearings.com

New York Community Bancorp Inc.

A bank holding company for New York Community Bank, a branch network operating through seven divisions: Queens Co. Savings Bank; Roslyn Savings Bank; Richmond Co. Savings Bank; Roosevelt Savings Bank; CFS Bank; First Savings Bank of New Jersey; and Ironbound Bank.
ir.mynycb.com
Annual Revenues: $652.13 million
Employees: 3,448
Ticker: NYSE: NYCB
SIC: 6036
Industry/ies: Banking/Finance/Investments

Chairman　　　　　　　　　　　　　Tel:　(516) 683-4100
CIAMPA, Dominick　　　　　　　　　　Fax:　(516) 683-4424

President and Chief Executive Officer　　　Tel:　(516) 683-4100
FICALORA, Joseph R.　　　　　　　　　Fax:　(516) 683-4424

Main Headquarters
Mailing:　615 Merrick Ave.　　　　　　Tel:　(516) 683-4100
　　　　　Westbury, NY 11590　　　　　Fax:　(516) 683-4424
　　　　　　　　　　　　　　　　　　TF:　(800) 394-2010

Corporate Foundations and Giving Programs

New York Community Bancorp, Inc. Contributions Program
615 Merrick Ave.　　　　　　　　　　　Tel:　(516) 683-4100

Westbury, NY 11590   Fax: (516) 683-4424

Public Affairs and Related Activities Personnel

At Headquarters

ANGAROLA, Ilene A.   Tel: (516) 683-4420
Executive Vice President and Director, Investor Relations Fax: (516) 683-4424
ir@mynycb.com

CANGEMI, CPA, Thomas R.   Tel: (516) 683-4100
Senior Executive Vice President and Chief Financial Officer Fax: (516) 683-4424

QUINN, R. Patrick   Tel: (516) 683-4408
Executive Vice President, Chief Corporate Governance Officer Fax: (516) 683-4424
and Corporate Secretary
Patrick.Quinn@mynycb.com

WANN, Robert   Tel: (516) 683-4100
Senior Executive Vice President and Chief Operating Officer Fax: (516) 683-4424

New York Life Insurance Company

In 2008 New York Life International LLC merged with New York Life Insurance Company.
A seller of life insurance, annuities, and long term care insurance. Also provides asset
management services.
www.newyorklife.com
Annual Revenues: $27.29 billion
Employees: 12,000
Industry/ies: Insurance Industry
Legislative Issues: CPI; ECN; FIN; HCR; INS; RET; SCI; TAX

Chairman of the Board, President and Chief Executive Officer Tel: (212) 576-7000
MATHAS, Theodore A.   Fax: (212) 576-8145

Main Headquarters
Mailing: 51 Madison Ave.   Tel: (212) 576-7000
              Suite 1109   Fax: (212) 576-8145
              New York City, NY 10010   TF: (800) 692-3086

Washington Office
Mailing: 901 15th St. NW   Tel: (202) 654-2940
              Suite 600   Fax: (202) 654-2945
              Washington, DC 20005   TF: (800) 692-3086

Political Action Committees
New York Life PAC
FEC ID: C00158881
Contact: Helen Stagias
51 Madison Ave.
Room 1109
New York City, NY 10010

Contributions to Candidates: $13,769,965 (2015-2016)
Democrats: $699,000; Republicans: $884,950; Other: $12,186,015

Principal Recipients

SENATE
FISCHER, DEBRA S (REP-NE)
GRASSLEY, CHARLES E SENATOR (REP-IA)
KIRK, MARK STEVEN (REP-IL)
PAUL, RAND (REP-KY)
PETERS, GARY (DEM-MI)
SCOTT, TIMOTHY E (REP-SC)
VAN HOLLEN, CHRIS (DEM-MD)

HOUSE
AGUILAR, PETE (DEM-CA)
ASHFORD, BRAD (DEM-NE)
BARR, GARLAND ANDY (REP-KY)
BECERRA, XAVIER (DEM-CA)
BOST, MICHAEL (REP-IL)
BROWNLEY, JULIA (DEM-CA)
CARDENAS, TONY (DEM-CA)
CLARKE, YVETTE D (DEM-NY)
CLEAVER, EMANUEL II (DEM-MO)
COFFMAN, MIKE REP. (REP-CO)
COSTA, JIM MR. (DEM-CA)
COSTELLO, RYAN A (REP-PA)
CROWLEY, JOSEPH (DEM-NY)
CURBELO, CARLOS (REP-FL)
DAVIS, RODNEY L (REP-IL)
DENHAM, JEFF (REP-CA)
DOLD, ROBERT JAMES JR (REP-IL)
ESTY, ELIZABETH (DEM-CT)
FRELINGHUYSEN, RODNEY P. (REP-NJ)
GRAVES, GARRET (REP-LA)
GUTHRIE, S. BRETT HON. (REP-KY)
HOYER, STENY HAMILTON (DEM-DC)
HUDSON, RICHARD L. JR. (REP-NC)
HURD, WILLIAM (REP-TX)
KELLY, ROBIN L. (DEM-IL)
KUSTER, ANN MCLANE (DEM-NH)
LARSON, JOHN B (DEM-CT)
LUETKEMEYER, W BLAINE (REP-MO)
LUJAN GRISHAM, MICHELLE (DEM-NM)

LUJAN, BEN R MR. (DEM-NM)
MACARTHUR, THOMAS (REP-NJ)
MALONEY, CAROLYN B. (DEM-NY)
MATSUI, DORIS (DEM-CA)
MCCARTHY, KEVIN (REP-CA)
MCHENRY, PATRICK TIMOTHY (REP-NC)
MCMORRIS RODGERS, CATHY (REP-WA)
MCSALLY, MARTHA E. MS. (REP-AZ)
MEEKS, GREGORY W. (DEM-NY)
MENG, GRACE (DEM-NY)
MESSER, ALLEN LUCAS (REP-IN)
MOORE, GWEN S (DEM-WI)
NEAL, RICHARD E MR. (DEM-MA)
NOLAN, RICHARD M. (DEM-MN)
NUNES, DEVIN G (REP-CA)
PERLMUTTER, EDWIN G (DEM-CO)
PETERS, SCOTT (DEM-CA)
POLIQUIN, BRUCE L (REP-ME)
POMPEO, MICHAEL RICHARD (REP-KS)
REED, THOMAS W II (REP-NY)
RICE, KATHLEEN (DEM-NY)
RUIZ, RAUL DR. (DEM-CA)
RYAN, PAUL D. (REP-WI)
SCALISE, STEVE MR. (REP-LA)
SCOTT, DAVID ALBERT (DEM-GA)
SEWELL, TERRYCINA ANDREA (DEM-AL)
SINEMA, KYRSTEN (DEM-AZ)
STEFANIK, ELISE M. (REP-NY)
STIVERS, STEVE MR. (REP-OH)
TAKANO, MARK (DEM-CA)
TIBERI, PATRICK J. (REP-OH)
TIPTON, SCOTT R. (REP-CO)
VALADAO, DAVID (REP-CA)
VARGAS, JUAN C. (DEM-CA)
WALTERS, MIMI (REP-CA)
YOUNG, DAVID (REP-IA)
ZELDIN, LEE M (REP-NY)

Corporate Foundations and Giving Programs

New York Life Foundation
Contact: Chris Park
51 Madison Ave.
Suite 3200
New York City, NY 10010

Public Affairs and Related Activities Personnel

At Headquarters

BOCCIO, Frank M.   Tel: (212) 576-7000
Executive Vice President and Chief Administrative Officer Fax: (212) 576-8145

DAVIDSON, Sheila K.   Tel: (212) 576-7000
Executive Vice President, Chief Legal Officer and General Fax: (212) 576-8145
Counsel

FLEURANT, John T.   Tel: (212) 576-7000
Executive Vice President and Chief Financial Officer   Fax: (212) 576-8145

KIM, John Y.   Tel: (212) 576-7000
President and Chief Investment Officer   Fax: (212) 576-8145

O'BRIEN, Katherine R.   Tel: (212) 576-7000
Senior Vice President and Chief Human Resources Officer   Fax: (212) 576-8145

PARK, Chris   Tel: (212) 576-7000
President, New York Life Foundation   Fax: (212) 576-8145

STAGIAS, Helen   Tel: (212) 576-7000
PAC Treasurer   Fax: (212) 576-8145

THROPE, Susan A.   Tel: (212) 576-7000
Senior Vice President, Deputy General Counsel and Secretary Fax: (212) 576-8145

WOLCOTT, Terri   Tel: (212) 576-5624
Corporate Vice President, Public Relations   Fax: (212) 576-8145
theresa_m_Wolcott@newyorklife.com

At Washington Office

GONCE, Emily   Tel: (202) 654-2950
Corporate Vice President, Office of Governmental Affairs   Fax: (202) 654-2945
egonce@nyl.com
Registered Federal Lobbyist

HERWIG, Julie E.   Tel: (202) 654-2940
Senior Vice President, Head of Federal Governmental Affairs Fax: (202) 654-2945
Registered Federal Lobbyist

KRMPOTICH, Laurie   Tel: (202) 654-2940
Registered Federal Lobbyist   Fax: (202) 654-2945

LATHROP, Doug   Tel: (202) 654-2940
Corporate Vice President, Legislative Affairs   Fax: (202) 654-2945
Registered Federal Lobbyist

NICHOLS, III, George   Tel: (202) 654-2940
Senior Vice President, Office of Governmental Affairs   Fax: (202) 654-2945
george_nichols@newyorklife.com
Registered Federal Lobbyist

O'DONNELL, Alison	Tel:	(202) 654-2940	
Vice President, Government Affairs	Fax:	(202) 654-2945	
Registered Federal Lobbyist			

OLDHAM, Margaret	Tel:	(202) 654-2940
Legislative Analyst	Fax:	(202) 654-2945

PAONE, Jonathan	Tel:	(202) 654-2940
Vice President, Government Affairs	Fax:	(202) 654-2945
Registered Federal Lobbyist		

VAN ETTEN, John D.	Tel:	(202) 654-2940
Registered Federal Lobbyist	Fax:	(202) 654-2945

WHEELER, Douglas	Tel:	(202) 654-2950
Senior Vice President, Governmental Affairs	Fax:	(202) 654-2945

New York State Higher Education Services Corporation

A state guaranty agency.
www.hesc.ny.gov
Industry/ies: Education

Chairman of the Board	Tel:	(518) 474-3219
KLINGER, Alan M.		

Main Headquarters			
Mailing:	One Commerce Plaza	Tel:	(518) 474-3219
	99 Washington Ave.		
	Albany, NY 12255		

Political Action Committees
New York State Higher Education - PAC
FEC ID: C00496638
Contact: Robert Agyemang
3210 Avenue H
Apt 6C
Brooklyn, 11210

Public Affairs and Related Activities Personnel

At Headquarters

AGYEMANG, Robert	Tel:	(518) 474-3219
PAC Treasurer		

BALLMANN, Frank	Tel:	(518) 474-3219
Director, Federal Relations		

CROWDER, Kathy	Tel:	(518) 402-1448
Senior Vice President, Communications		
kcrowder@hesc.ny.gov		

FISHER, Cheryl B.	Tel:	(518) 474-3219
Supervising Attorney		
Cheryl.Fisher@hesc.ny.gov		

SIMMONS, Joan	Tel:	(518) 474-3219
Contact, Government Relations		

New York Stock Exchange

See listing on page 595 under NYSE Euronext, Inc.

The New York Times Company

A newspaper publisher, TV and radio broadcaster, and an electronic media company.
www.nytco.com
Annual Revenues: $1.58 billion
Employees: 3,588
Ticker: NYSE: NYT
SIC: 2711
NAICS: 511110
Industry/ies: Communications; Media/Mass Communication

Chairman of the Board and Publisher	Tel:	(212) 556-1234
SULZBERGER, Jr., Arthur O.	Fax:	(212) 556-7389

Chief Executive Officer, President and Director	Tel:	(212) 556-1234
THOMPSON, Mark	Fax:	(212) 556-7389

Main Headquarters			
Mailing:	620 Eighth Ave.	Tel:	(212) 556-1234
	New York City, NY 10018	Fax:	(212) 556-7389
		TF:	(888) 698-6397

Corporate Foundations and Giving Programs

The Boston Globe Foundation
620 Eighth Ave.
New York City, NY 10018

The New York Times Company Foundation Inc.
230 W. 41st St.
Suite 1300
New York City, NY 10018

Public Affairs and Related Activities Personnel

At Headquarters

CHRISTIE, Robert H.	Tel:	(212) 556-1981
Senior Vice President, Corporate Communications	Fax:	(212) 556-7389
robert.christie@nytimes		

FOLLO, James M.	Tel:	(212) 556-1234

Executive Vice President and Chief Financial Officer	Fax:	(212) 556-7389

LEVIEN, Meredith Kopit	Tel:	(212) 556-1234
Executive Vice President, Advertising	Fax:	(212) 556-7389

MCNULTY, Diane	Tel:	(212) 556-5244
Executive Director, Community Affairs and Media Relations	Fax:	(212) 556-7389
mcnuldc@nytimes.com		

MURPHY, Eileen M.	Tel:	(212) 556-1982
Vice President, Corporate Communications	Fax:	(212) 556-7389
eileen.murphy@nytimes.com		

PASSALACQUA, Andrea	Tel:	(212) 556-7354
Director, Investor Relations	Fax:	(212) 556-7389

RICHIERI, Kenneth A.	Tel:	(212) 556-1995
Executive Vice President and General Counsel	Fax:	(212) 556-7389

SERPHOS, Abbe	Tel:	(212) 556-4425
Executive Director, Corporate Communications	Fax:	(212) 556-7389
serphos@nytimes.com		

New York Water Taxi

Provides transportation in New York City.
www.nywatertaxi.com
Industry/ies: Marine/Maritime/Shipping; Ports And Waterways; Transportation

Chairman of the Board	Tel:	(212) 742-1969
DURST, Douglas		

President	Tel:	(212) 742-1969
DURST, Helena		

Main Headquarters			
Mailing:	655 Third Ave.	Tel:	(212) 742-1969
	Suite 1404		
	New York City, NY 10017		

Public Affairs and Related Activities Personnel

At Headquarters

SHERMAN, Stacey	Tel:	(203) 855-1600
Contact, Media Relations		
stacey@theshermangroup.com		

Newell-Rubbermaid Inc.

A global manufacturer and full-service marketer of branded consumer products and their commercial extensions, serving the needs of volume purchasers, including department stores, discount stores and warehouse clubs, as well as home centers, hardware stores commercial distributors, office superstores and contract stationers. Brands include Sharpie, Paper Mate, Parker, Waterman, Rubbermaid, Roughneck, Little Tikes, Goody, Graco, Irwin, Lenox, and Marathon.
www.newellrubbermaid.com
Annual Revenues: $5.78 billion
Employees: 17,400
Ticker: NYSE: NWL
SIC: 3089; 5190
Industry/ies: Furniture/Home Furnishings; Machinery/Equipment; Rubber Industry

Chairman of the Board	Tel:	(800) 752-9677
COWHIG, Michael T.	Fax:	(770) 407-3970

President and Chief Executive Officer	Tel:	(770) 407-7000
POLK, Michael B.	Fax:	(770) 407-3970

Main Headquarters			
Mailing:	Three Glenlake Pkwy.	Tel:	(914) 967-9400
	Atlanta, GA 30328	Fax:	(914) 967-9405
		TF:	(800) 752-9677

Corporate Foundations and Giving Programs

Jarden Consumer Solutions Community Fund		
555 Theodore Fremd Ave.		
Suite B-302	Tel:	(914) 967-9400
Rye, NY 10580	Fax:	(914) 967-9405

Newell-Rubbermaid Contribution Program		
Three Glenlake Pkwy.	Tel:	(770) 407-7000
Atlanta, GA 30328	Fax:	(770) 407-3970

Public Affairs and Related Activities Personnel

At Headquarters

BURKE III, William A.	Tel:	(770) 407-7000
Executive Vice President, Chief Operating Officer	Fax:	(770) 407-3970

DAVIES, Richard	Tel:	(770) 407-7000
Chief Marketing and Insights Officer	Fax:	(770) 407-3970

DOOLITTLE, David	Tel:	(770) 418-7519
Vice President, Corporate Communications	Fax:	(770) 407-3970
david.doolittle@newellco.com		

LARSON, Paula S.	Tel:	(770) 407-7000
Executive Vice President, Chief Human Resources Officer	Fax:	(770) 407-3970

O'DONNELL, Nancy	Tel:	(770) 407-7000
Vice President, Investor Relations	Fax:	(770) 407-3970

STIPANCICH, John K.	Tel:	(770) 407-7000

Executive Vice President, Chief Financial Officer	Fax:	(770) 407-3970
john.stipancich@newellco.com		
TARCHETTI, Mark S.	Tel:	(770) 407-7000
Executive Vice President, Chief Development Officer	Fax:	(770) 407-3970
TURNER, Bradford	Tel:	(770) 407-7000
Senior Vice President, General Counsel and Corporate Secretary	Fax:	(770) 407-3970

Newfield Exploration Company

An independent crude oil and natural gas exploration and production company.
www.newfield.com
Annual Revenues: $2.07 billion
Employees: 1,331
Ticker: NYSE: NFX
SIC: 1382
NAICS: 213112
Industry/ies: Energy/Electricity

Chairman of the Board, President and Chief Executive Officer	Tel:	(281) 847-6000
BOOTHBY, Lee K.	Fax:	(281) 405-4242

Main Headquarters

Mailing:	Four Waterway Square Pl.	Tel:	(281) 210-5100
	Suite 100	Fax:	(281) 210-5101
	The Woodlands, TX 77380		

Political Action Committees
Newfield Exploration Company PAC (Newfield PAC)
FEC ID: C00443523
Contact: Susan G. Riggs
Four Waterway Square Pl.
Suite 100
The Woodlands, TX 77380

> **Contributions to Candidates:** $115,500 (2015-2016)
> Democrats: $3,500; Republicans: $112,000

Corporate Foundations and Giving Programs
Newfield Foundation
Contact: Dolores V. Vasquez
363 N. Sam Houston Pkwy. East
Suite 100
Houston, TX 77060

Public Affairs and Related Activities Personnel

At Headquarters

JASEK, John H.	Tel:	(281) 210-5100
Senior Vice President, Operations	Fax:	(281) 210-5101
MASSARO, Larry S.	Tel:	(281) 210-5100
Executive Vice President and Chief Financial Officer	Fax:	(281) 210-5101
PACKER, Gary D.	Tel:	(281) 210-5100
Executive Vice President and Chief Operating Officer	Fax:	(281) 210-5101
SMOUSE, Thomas M.	Tel:	(281) 210-5100
Vice Presiden, Administration and Human Resources	Fax:	(281) 210-5101
VASQUEZ, Dolores V.	Tel:	(281) 210-5100
Contact, Foundation	Fax:	(281) 210-5101

At Other Offices

CAMPBELL, Stephen C.	Tel:	(281) 847-6081
Vice President, Investor Relations	Fax:	(281) 405-4242
363 N. Sam Houston Pkwy., East, Suite 100		
Houston, TX 77060		
MARZIOTTI, John	Tel:	(281) 847-6000
General Counsel and Secretary	Fax:	(281) 405-4242
363 N. Sam Houston Pkwy., East, Suite 100		
Houston, TX 77060		
MCKNIGHT, Penny	Tel:	(281) 405-4284
Contact, Media Relations	Fax:	(281) 405-4255
363 N. Sam Houston Pkwy., East, Suite 100		
Houston, TX 77060		
RATHERT, Terry W.	Tel:	(281) 847-6000
Executive Vice President and Senior Advisor	Fax:	(281) 405-4242
363 N. Sam Houston Pkwy., East, Suite 100		
Houston, TX 77060		
RIGGS, Susan G.	Tel:	(281) 847-6000
PAC Treasurer	Fax:	(281) 405-4242
363 N. Sam Houston Pkwy., East, Suite 100		
Houston, TX 77060		
SCHMIDT, Keith	Tel:	(281) 674-2650
Contact, Media Relations	Fax:	(281) 405-4242
363 N. Sam Houston Pkwy., East, Suite 100		
Houston, TX 77060		
kschmidt@newfield.com		

Newhall Land and Farming Company

A real estate developer.
www.valencia.com

Annual Revenues: $10.60 million
Employees: 200
SIC: 6552
Industry/ies: Agriculture/Agronomy; Real Estate

Chariman of the Board	Tel:	(661) 255-4000
COLEMAN, Kelley	Fax:	(661) 255-3960

Main Headquarters

Mailing:	25124 Springfield Ct.	Tel:	(661) 255-4000
	Suite 300	Fax:	(661) 255-3960
	Valencia, CA 53098		

Political Action Committees
Newhall Land and Farming Company PAC
FEC ID: C00111104
Contact: Donald L. Kimball
25124 Springfield Ct.

Suite 300	Tel:	(661) 255-4000
Valencia, CA 91355	Fax:	(661) 255-4000

> **Contributions to Candidates:** $5,400 (2015-2016)
> Republicans: $5,400

Public Affairs and Related Activities Personnel

At Headquarters

KIMBALL, Donald L.	Tel:	(661) 255-4000
Senior Vice President and Chief Financial Officer and PAC Treasurer	Fax:	(661) 255-3960
Mail Stop Suite 300		

NewMarket Corporation

Serves as a holding entity for two operating subsidiaries: Afton Chemical and Ethyl. Afton Chemical manufactures petroleum additives and Ethyl's main product is the antiknock additive tetraethyl lead (TEL).
www.newmarketservices.com
Annual Revenues: $2.09 billion
Employees: 1,979
Ticker: NYSE: NEU
SIC: 2860
Industry/ies: Chemicals & Chemical Industry; Fuels See Coal, Gas, Oil, Petroleum; Natural Resources; Petroleum Industry; Plastics Industry

Chairman of the Board	Tel:	(804) 788-5000
GOTTWALD, Bruce C.	Fax:	(804) 788-5688
President and Chief Executive Officer	Tel:	(804) 788-5000
GOTTWALD, Thomas E.	Fax:	(804) 788-5688

Main Headquarters

Mailing:	902 N. Ashland St.	Tel:	(866) 595-3792
	Chicago, IL 60622	TF:	(866) 595-3792

Washington Office

Mailing:	700 Second St. NE
	Suite 8200
	Washington, DC 20005

Public Affairs and Related Activities Personnel

At Headquarters

MORGAN, Patrick	Tel:	(866) 595-3792
President		
pmorgan@newmarketservices.com		

At Other Offices

EDMONDS, Steven M.	Tel:	(804) 788-5000
Vice President, General Counsel	Fax:	(804) 788-5688
330 S. Fourth St.		
Richmond, VA 23219-4304		
HAZELGROVE, III, Bruce R.	Tel:	(804) 788-5000
Chief Administrative Officer & Vice President	Fax:	(804) 788-5688
330 S. Fourth St.		
Richmond, VA 23219-4304		
LITTLE, Barbara	Tel:	(202) 223-4411
Vice President, Government Relations		
P.O. Box 2189		
Arlington, VA 23218		
barbara.little@newmarket.com		
MUELLER, Bob	Tel:	(866) 595-3791
Director, Employee and Labor Relations		
P.O. Box 30534		
Phoenix, AZ 85046		
bob@newmarketservices.com		

Newmont Mining Corporation

An international gold mining company.
www.newmont.com
Annual Revenues: $7.79 billion
Employees: 15,600
Ticker: NYSE: NEM
SIC: 1040

Industry/ies: Mining Industry; Natural Resources
Legislative Issues: CAW; ENV; NAT; RES; WAS

Chairman of the Board
CALARCO, Vincent A.
Vincent.calarco@newmont.com
Tel: (303) 863-7414
Fax: (303) 837-5837

President and Chief Executive Officer
GOLDBERG, Gary J.
Tel: (303) 863-7414
Fax: (303) 837-5837

Main Headquarters
Mailing: 6363 S. Fiddler's Green Cir.
Suite. 800
Greenwood Village, CO 80111
Tel: (303) 863-7414
Fax: (303) 837-5837
TF: (800) 810-6463

Washington Office
Mailing: 101 Constitution Ave. NW
Washington, DC 20001
Tel: (202) 742-4277

Political Action Committees
Newmont Mining Corporation PAC
FEC ID: C00206672
Contact: Mary Beth Donnelly
101 Constitution Ave. NW
Suite 800
Washington, DC 20001
Tel: (202) 822-6777

> **Contributions to Candidates:** $35,500 (2015-2016)
> Democrats: $10,500; Republicans: $25,000

Corporate Foundations and Giving Programs
Newmont Contributions Program
6363 S. Fiddler's Green Cir.
Suite. 800
Greenwood Village, CO 80111

Public Affairs and Related Activities Personnel

At Headquarters

BRLAS, Laurie
Executive Vice President and Chief Financial Officer
Tel: (303) 863-7414
Fax: (303) 837-5837

CULPEPPER, Glenn
Senior Vice President and Controller
Tel: (303) 863-7414
Fax: (303) 837-5837

DORWARD-KING, Elaine
Executive Vice President, Sustainability and External Relations
Tel: (303) 863-7414
Fax: (303) 837-5837

ENGEL, Randy
Executive Vice President, Strategic Development
randy.engel@newmont.com
Tel: (303) 863-7414
Fax: (303) 837-5837

FALEY, David
Vice President, Corporate Development
david.faley@newmont.com
Tel: (303) 863-7414
Fax: (303) 837-5837

GOTTESFELD, Stephen P.
Executive Vice President, General Counsel and Corporate Secretary
stephen.gottesfeld@newmont.com
Tel: (303) 863-7414
Fax: (303) 837-5837

HEROLD, Richard
Vice President, Global Government Relations
Tel: (303) 863-7414
Fax: (303) 837-5837

HOLLEMAN, Andy
Associate General Counsel and Chief Compliance Officer
Tel: (303) 863-7414
Fax: (303) 837-5837

JABARA, Omar
Group Executive, Corporate Communications
Mail Stop 800-810-6463
omar.jabara@newmont.com
Tel: (303) 837-5114
Fax: (303) 837-5085

MACGOWAN , Bill
Executive Vice President, Human Resources and Communications
Tel: (303) 863-7414
Fax: (303) 837-5837

PALMER, Tom
Executive Vice President and Chief Operating Officer
Tel: (303) 863-7414
Fax: (303) 837-5837

At Washington Office

ANDERSON, Kai
Registered Federal Lobbyist
Tel: (202) 742-4277

DONNELLY, Mary Beth
Vice President, U.S. Government Relations
mbdonnelly@newmont.com
Registered Federal Lobbyist
Tel: (202) 742-4277

GIANNOTTO, Michael S.
Registered Federal Lobbyist
Tel: (202) 742-4277

JOHNSON, Nils
Registered Federal Lobbyist
Tel: (202) 742-4277

PIEPER, Mike
Registered Federal Lobbyist
Tel: (202) 742-4277

SPIELMAN, Andrew L.
Registered Federal Lobbyist
Tel: (202) 742-4277

SPIELMAN, Andrew
Registered Federal Lobbyist
Tel: (202) 742-4277

News America Marketing

A news and entertainment publisher.
www.newsamerica.com
Annual Revenues: $16.30 million
Employees: 200
SIC: 2711; 2721
NAICS: 511110; 511120
Industry/ies: Communications; Media/Mass Communication

Chief Executive Officer
GAROFALO, Martin
Tel: (212) 782-8000
Fax: (212) 575-5845

Main Headquarters
Mailing: 1185 Avenue of the Americas
27th Floor
New York City, NY 10036
Tel: (212) 782-8000
Fax: (212) 575-5845
TF: (800) 462-0852

Washington Office
Mailing: 444 N. Capitol St. NW
Suite 740
Washington, DC 20001
Tel: (202) 824-6503

Political Action Committees
Twenty-First Century Fox, Inc. PAC (Fox PAC)
FEC ID: C00330019
Contact: Kristopher Jones
444 N. Capitol St. NW, Suite 740
Washington, DC 20001
Tel: (202) 824-6500
Fax: (202) 824-6510

> **Contributions to Candidates:** $240,000 (2015-2016)
> Democrats: $82,000; Republicans: $158,000

> **Principal Recipients**
>
> **HOUSE**
> MCCARTHY, KEVIN (REP-CA)
> UPTON, FREDERICK STEPHEN (REP-MI)

Corporate Foundations and Giving Programs
News America Marketing Contributions Program
1185 Avenue of the Americas
27th Floor
New York City, NY 10036
Tel: (212) 782-8000
Fax: (212) 575-5845

Public Affairs and Related Activities Personnel

At Headquarters

RICHARDS, Laura
Vice President, Corporate Communications
lrichards@newsamerica.com
Tel: (212) 782-8145
Fax: (212) 575-5845

At Washington Office

BLAKE, Evony
Federal Lobbyist
Tel: (202) 824-6503

FARES, David
Federal Lobbyist
Tel: (202) 824-6503

FISHER, Pam
Federal Lobbyist
Tel: (202) 824-6503

LANE, Patrick J.
Senior Vice President, Government Affairs
Mail Stop Suite 740
Tel: (202) 824-6503

O'CALLAGHAN, Janet
Federal Lobbyist
Tel: (202) 824-6503

O'CONNELL, Maureen A.
Federal Lobbyist
Tel: (202) 824-6503

RAMSEY, Kathleen Greenan
Federal Lobbyist
Tel: (202) 824-6503

News Corporation Ltd./FOX

A network of leading companies in the worlds of diversified media, news, education, and information services and has operations spanning film, television, and publishing. It produces and distributes movies through Fox Filmed Entertainment, while its FOX Broadcasting network boasts more than 200 affiliate stations in the US.
www.newscorp.com
Annual Revenues: $8.68 billion
Employees: 22,000
Ticker: NASDAQ: NWS
Industry/ies: Communications; Media/Mass Communication
Legislative Issues: LBR; MIA; TAX; TEC; TRD

Executive Chairman
MURDOCH, K. Rupert
Tel: (212) 852-7000
Fax: (212) 852-7147

Main Headquarters
Mailing: 1667 K St. NW, Suite 350
Eighth Floor
Washington, DC 20006
Tel: (212) 852-7000
Fax: (212) 852-7145

Washington Office
Mailing: 300 New Jersey Ave. NW, Suite 900
Washington, DC 20001

Political Action Committees
News Corporation Political Action Committee

FEC ID: C00546101
Contact: Antoinette Bush
1211 Avenue of the Americas
New York City, NY 10036

Contributions to Candidates: $31,500 (2015-2016)
Democrats: $19,000; Republicans: $12,500

Twenty-First Century Fox, Inc. PAC (Fox PAC)
FEC ID: C00330019
Contact: Patrick J. Lane
444 N. Capitol St. NW, Suite 740   Tel: (202) 824-6500
Washington, DC 20001   Fax: (202) 824-6510

Contributions to Candidates: $240,000 (2015-2016)
Democrats: $82,000; Republicans: $158,000

Principal Recipients

HOUSE
MCCARTHY, KEVIN (REP-CA)
UPTON, FREDERICK STEPHEN (REP-MI)

Public Affairs and Related Activities Personnel

At Headquarters

CAREY, Chase   Tel: (212) 852-7017
President & Chief Operating Officer   Fax: (212) 852-7145

FLORIN, Michael   Tel: (212) 416-3248
Senior Vice President, Head of Investor Relations   Fax: (212) 852-7145
investor@newscorp.com

GAVENCHAK, Genie   Tel: (212) 852-7000
Senior Vice President, Deputy General Counsel, Chief   Fax: (212) 852-7147
Compliance and Ethics Officer

NOLTE, Reed   Tel: (212) 852-7092
Senior Vice President, Investor Relations   Fax: (212) 852-7145
rnolte@newscorp.com

SINGH, Bedi A.   Tel: (212) 852-7000
Chief Financial Officer   Fax: (212) 852-7145

SMITH, Keisha   Tel: (212) 852-7000
Chief Human Resources Officer   Fax: (212) 852-7145

ZWEIFACH, Gerson   Tel: (212) 852-7000
Senior Executive Vice President, Group General Counsel and   Fax: (212) 852-7145
Chief Compliance Officer

At Washington Office

KENNEDY, Jim
Chief Communications Officer

OZERNOY, Ilana
Deputy Head, Communications

At Other Offices

BUSH, Antoinette   Tel: (202) 824-6500
Global Head, Government Affairs   Fax: (202) 824-6510
444 N. Capitol St. NW, Suite 740
Washington, DC 20001

FARES, David   Tel: (202) 824-6500
Senior Vice President, Government Affairs   Fax: (202) 824-6510
444 N. Capitol St. NW, Suite 740
Washington, DC 20001

GUIDERA, Bill   Tel: (202) 824-6500
Senior Vice President, Government Affairs   Fax: (202) 824-6510
444 N. Capitol St. NW, Suite 740
Washington, DC 20001

LANE, Patrick J.   Tel: (202) 824-6500
Senior Vice President and PAC Treasurer   Fax: (202) 824-6510
444 N. Capitol St. NW, Suite 740
Washington, DC 20001

Newsweek/Daily Beast Company LLC

A magazine publisher. Formed after the late stereo equipment magnate Sidney Harman purchased the ailing Newsweek from The Washington Post in 2010 and merged it with IAC/InterActive's online current events magazine Daily Beast in 2011. The Daily Beast became the online home of Newsweek magazine.
www.newsweek.com
Annual Revenues: $87.30 million
Employees: 800
SIC: 2721
NAICS: 511120
Industry/ies: Communications; Media/Mass Communication

Main Headquarters
Mailing: Seven Hanover Sq.   Tel: (212) 445-4600
Fifth Floor   Fax: (212) 445-4425
New York City, NY 10004

Public Affairs and Related Activities Personnel

At Headquarters

FUZESI, Jr., Stephen J.   Tel: (212) 445-4000
Vice President, General Counsel and Secretary   Fax: (212) 445-4425

IMPOCO, Jim   Tel: (212) 445-4600
Editor in Chief   Fax: (212) 445-4425

MARIA, Frank De   Tel: (212) 445-4000
Vice President, Communications   Fax: (212) 445-4425

Newton Dillard

Government Relations Firm.
newtondillard.com

Main Headquarters
Mailing: 1819 N. Capitol St. NE
Washington, DC 20002

Public Affairs and Related Activities Personnel

At Other Offices

NEWTON, Sherry
Principal
611 Pennsylvania Ave., SE 108
Washington, DC 20003-4303

Nexen, Inc.

Nexen is a Canadian-based energy company with operations in strategic locations around the world including the North Sea, the Gulf of Mexico, offshore West Africa, Canada, Yemen and Colombia.
www.nexeninc.com
Annual Revenues: $6.79 billion
Employees: 3,228
SIC: 1311
Industry/ies: Energy/Electricity

Chief Executive Officer   Tel: (832) 714-5000
ZHI, Fang

Main Headquarters
Mailing: 945 Bunker Hill Rd.   Tel: (832) 714-5000
Suite 1400
Houston, TX 77024

Public Affairs and Related Activities Personnel

At Headquarters

NUCKOLLS, Charles Randall   Tel: (202) 496-7176
Federal Lobbyist

O'BRIEN, Alan   Tel: (832) 714-5000
Senior Vice President, General Counsel and Secretary

PAINCHAUD, Denis   Tel: (202) 496-7176
Director, International Government Relations
denis_painchaud@nexeninc.com

POWER, Una   Tel: (832) 714-5000
Chief Financial Officer and Senior Vice President

WILSON, Quinn   Tel: (832) 714-5000
Vice President, Human Resources and Corporate Services

Next IT

A software company.
www.nextit.com
Annual Revenues: $11 million
Industry/ies: Computer/Technology

Chairman of the Board   Tel: (509) 242-0767
HUMPHREYS, Johnny   Fax: (509) 467-8066

Founder and Chief Executive Officer   Tel: (509) 242-0767
BROWN, Fred A.   Fax: (509) 467-8066

Main Headquarters
Mailing: 421 W. Riverside Ave.   Tel: (509) 242-0767
16th Floor   Fax: (509) 467-8066
Spokane, WA 99201

Public Affairs and Related Activities Personnel

At Headquarters

BROWN, Jeff   Tel: (509) 242-0767
Executive Vice President, Sales and Marketing   Fax: (509) 467-8066

GRUMBLY, Cleat   Tel: (509) 242-0767
Vice President, Government Solutions   Fax: (509) 467-8066

LAHAISE, Kevin   Tel: (413) 244-8994
Media Contact   Fax: (509) 467-8066
NextIT@Jones-Dilworth.com

LAWRENCE, Mitch   Tel: (509) 242-0767
President   Fax: (509) 467-8066

REMINGTON, David G   Tel: (509) 242-0767
Acting Chief Financial Officer   Fax: (509) 467-8066

SNELL, Jennifer   Tel: (509) 242-0776
Vice President, Marketing   Fax: (509) 467-8066

NextEra Energy Inc.

NextEra Energy Resources stands for clean energy. Expertise is in wholesale and retail electricity and project development and construction, as well as in offering customers the energy products and services they need.
www.nexteraenergyresources.com
Annual Revenues: $17.45 billion
Employees: 13,800
Ticker: NYSE: NEE
SIC: 4911
Industry/ies: Energy; Energy/Electricity
Legislative Issues: AVI; BUD; CAW; CDT; ENG; HOM; NAT; TAX; TRA

Chairman of the Board and Chief Executive Officer
ROBO, James L.
Tel: (561) 694-4000
Fax: (561) 694-4620

Main Headquarters
Mailing: 700 Universe Blvd.
Juno Beach, FL 33408
Tel: (561) 694-4000
Fax: (561) 694-4620
TF: (888) 867-3050

Washington Office
Mailing: 801 Pennsylvania Ave. NW
Suite 220
Washington, DC 20004

Political Action Committees
NextEra Energy Inc. Political Action Committee
FEC ID: C00064774
Contact: Brian Tobin
801 Pennsylvania Ave. NW
Suite 220
Washington, DC 20004

Contributions to Candidates: $227,350 (2015-2016)
Democrats: $50,750; Republicans: $173,600; Other: $3,000

Corporate Foundations and Giving Programs
FPL Group Foundation
700 Universe Blvd.
P.O. Box 14000
Juno Beach, FL 33408
Tel: (561) 694-4000

Public Affairs and Related Activities Personnel

At Headquarters
BUBRISKI, Mark
Director, Public Affairs
mark.bubriski@fpl.com
Tel: (561) 694-4442
Fax: (561) 694-4620

CAPLAN, Deborah H.
Executive Vice President, Human Resources and Corporate Services
Tel: (561) 694-4000
Fax: (561) 694-4620

CHAPEL, Christopher
Vice President, Government Affairs
christopher_chapel@fpl.com
Registered Federal Lobbyist
Tel: (561) 694-4000
Fax: (561) 694-4620

CUTLER, Paul I.
Treasurer
Tel: (561) 694-4000
Fax: (561) 694-4620

DEWHURST, Moray P.
Vice Chairman, Chief Financial Officer, and Executive Vice President, Finance
Tel: (561) 694-4000
Fax: (561) 694-4620

FROGGATT, Chris N.
Vice President, Controller and Chief Accounting Officer
Tel: (561) 694-4000
Fax: (561) 694-4620

HICKSON, Mark E.
Senior Vice President, Corporate Development, Strategy, Quality and Integration
Tel: (561) 694-4000
Fax: (561) 694-4620

KETCHUM, John W.
Senior Vice President, Finance
Tel: (561) 694-4000
Fax: (561) 694-4620

MARQUEZ, Nadia
Federal Lobbyist
Tel: (561) 694-4000
Fax: (561) 694-4620

SEELEY, Scott
Vice President, Compliance and Corporate Secretary
Tel: (561) 694-4000
Fax: (561) 694-4620

SHER, Lauren
Federal Lobbyist
Registered Federal Lobbyist
Tel: (561) 694-4000
Fax: (561) 694-4620

SIEVING, Charles E.
Executive Vice President and General Counsel
Tel: (561) 694-4000
Fax: (561) 694-4620

At Washington Office
DREW, Whitney E.
Manager, Government Affairs
Registered Federal Lobbyist

O'CONNOR, Kathleen
Manager, Government Affairs
Registered Federal Lobbyist

PENA, Laura
Executive Administrative Assistant

TOBIN, Brian
Vice President and PAC Treasurer

NHS Management, L.L.C.

NHS Management, L.L.C. provides nursing and rehabilitative services for residents, families and employees.
nhsmanagement.com
Annual Revenues: $272.60 million
Employees: 5,000
Industry/ies: Aging; Management; Medicine/Health Care/Mental Health

President and Chief Executive Officer
ESTES, J. Norman
Tel: (205) 391-3600
Fax: (205) 391-3606

Main Headquarters
Mailing: 931 Fairfax Park
Tuscaloosa, AL 35406-2805
Tel: (205) 391-3600
Fax: (205) 391-3606
TF: (800) 489-1046

Corporate Foundations and Giving Programs
NHS Management Contribution Program
931 Fairfax Park
Tuscaloosa, AL 35406-2805
Tel: (205) 391-3600
Fax: (205) 391-3606

Public Affairs and Related Activities Personnel

At Headquarters
LEE, Claude
Vice President and Chief Financial Officer
Tel: (205) 391-3600
Fax: (205) 391-3606

Nicor, Inc.

Principal subsidiaries are Nicor Gas, a gas utility, and Tropical Shipping, a containerized shipping business that operates between Florida and the Caribbean. Nicor also owns several energy-related subsidiaries.
www.nicorinc.net
Annual Revenues: $2.70 billion
Employees: 3,800
Ticker: NYSE: GAS
SIC: 6719; 1311; 1381; 1382; 1389
Industry/ies: Energy/Electricity

Chairman, President and Chief Executive Officer
STROBEL, Russ M.
Tel: (630) 305-9500
Fax: (630) 357-7534

Main Headquarters
Mailing: 100 Commons Rd.
Suite 7-355
Dripping Springs, TX 78620
Tel: (707) 484-0835
Fax: (512) 276-2033

Public Affairs and Related Activities Personnel

At Other Offices
O'CONNOR, Gerald P.
Vice President, Finance and Administration
P.O. Box 190
Aurora, IL 60507-0190
Tel: (630) 305-9500
Fax: (630) 983-4229

Nielsen Media Research

A provider of television audience measurement and advertising information services worldwide.
www.nielsen.com
Employees: 4,000
SIC: 7374
Industry/ies: Communications; Media/Mass Communication
Legislative Issues: BUD; COM; CPT; TAX

Chief Executive Officer
BARNS, Mitch
Tel: (646) 654-8300

Main Headquarters
Mailing: 85 Broad St.
New York City, NY 10004
Tel: (646) 654-8300
TF: (800) 864-1224

Public Affairs and Related Activities Personnel

At Headquarters
BORINO, Mark
Vice President
mark.borino@nielsen.com
Tel: (646) 654-8300

BURBANK, John
President, Strategic Initiatives
Tel: (646) 654-8300

BURKE, Katie
Executive Vice President, Marketing and Communications
Tel: (646) 654-8300

CUMINALE, James W.
Chief Legal Officer
Tel: (646) 654-8300

FINN, Mary Liz
Chief Human Resources Officer
Tel: (646) 654-8300

FORTSON, Joseph
Federal Lobbyist
Registered Federal Lobbyist
Tel: (646) 654-8300

LEITER, Mark
Chief Strategy Officer
Tel: (646) 654-8300

LOWERY, Don
Senior Vice President, Government and Public Affairs
don.lowery@nielsen.com
Tel: (646) 654-8321

Registered Federal Lobbyist

WEST, Brian	Tel:	(646) 654-8300
Chief Operating Officer		

Nike, Inc.

A retailer of footwear and apparel.
www.nike.com
Annual Revenues: $30.60 billion
Employees: 48,000
Ticker: NYSE: NKE
SIC: 3021; 2329; 2339; 5139
Industry/ies: Apparel/Textiles Industry; Retail/Wholesale
Legislative Issues: CPT; CSP; DEF; ENV; HCR; SPO; TAX; TEC; TRD

Chairman of the Board	Tel:	(503) 671-6453
KNIGHT, Philip H.	Fax:	(503) 671-6300

President and Chief Executive Officer	Tel:	(503) 671-6453
PARKER, Mark	Fax:	(503) 671-6300

Main Headquarters

Mailing:	One Bowerman Dr.	Tel:	(503) 671-6453
	Beaverton, OR 97005	Fax:	(503) 671-6300
		TF:	(800) 344-6453

Washington Office

Mailing:	507 Second St. NE	Tel:	(202) 543-6453
	Washington, DC 20002	Fax:	(202) 544-6453

Political Action Committees

Nike Inc. Federal PAC (NIKE Federal PAC)
FEC ID: C00142786
Contact: Wayne George Monfries
One Bowerman Dr.
Beaverton, OR 97005

Contributions to Candidates: $115,500 (2015-2016)
Democrats: $67,000; Republicans: $48,500

Principal Recipients

SENATE
MURRAY, PATTY (DEM-WA)

HOUSE
BONAMICI, SUZANNE MS. (DEM-OR)
WALDEN, GREGORY P MR. (REP-OR)

Corporate Foundations and Giving Programs

Nike Foundation
One Bowerman Dr.
Beaverton, OR 97005

Public Affairs and Related Activities Personnel

At Headquarters

AYRE , David	Tel:	(503) 671-6453
Executive Vice President, Global Human Resources	Fax:	(503) 671-6300
BLAIR, Don	Tel:	(503) 671-6453
Executive Vice President and Chief Financial Officer	Fax:	(503) 671-6300
EITEL, Maria S.	Tel:	(503) 671-6453
President and Chief Executive Officer, Nike Foundation	Fax:	(503) 671-6300
maria.eitel@nike.com		
HALL, Kelley	Tel:	(503) 671-6453
Vice President, Treasurer and Investor Relations	Fax:	(503) 671-6300
KRANE, Hilary K.	Tel:	(503) 671-6453
Executive Vice President, Chief Administrative Officer and	Fax:	(503) 671-6300
General Counsel		
hilary.krane@nike.com		
LEONARD, Kellie	Tel:	(503) 671-6171
Vice President, Global Corporate Communications	Fax:	(503) 671-6300
MONFRIES, Wayne George	Tel:	(503) 671-6453
Vice President and Chief Tax Officer	Fax:	(503) 671-6300
SLUSHER, John	Tel:	(503) 671-6453
Executive Vice President, Global Sports Marketing	Fax:	(503) 671-6300
SPRUNK, Eric	Tel:	(503) 671-6453
Chief Operating Officer	Fax:	(503) 671-6300
STREGE, Kathy	Tel:	(503) 671-6453
Director, Investor Relations	Fax:	(503) 671-6300

At Washington Office

BENDALL, Jennifer L.	Tel:	(202) 543-6453
Director, Government & Public Affairs	Fax:	(202) 544-6453
Registered Federal Lobbyist		
BRIM-EDWARDS, Julia	Tel:	(202) 543-6453
Senior Director, Global Strategy Operations and Government	Fax:	(202) 544-6453
and Public Affairs		
MCCOLLUM, Jesse	Tel:	(202) 543-6453
Federal Lobbyist	Fax:	(202) 544-6453
Registered Federal Lobbyist		
O'HOLLAREN, Sean	Tel:	(202) 543-6453

Senior Vice President, Government and Public Affairs	Fax:	(202) 544-6453

NiSource Inc.

An energy holding company with operations in the natural gas and electric industries.
Formerly known as NIPSCO Industries, Inc. and changed its name to NiSource Inc. in April
1999. Merged with Columbia Energy Group in 2000.
www.nisource.com
Annual Revenues: $6.30 billion
Employees: 8,982
Ticker: NYSE: NI
SIC: 4931
Industry/ies: Energy/Electricity; Natural Resources; Utilities
Legislative Issues: BUD; COM; ENG; ENV; HOM; TAX; TRA; UTI

Chairman of the Board	Tel:	(219) 647-5200
ROLLAND, Ian	Fax:	(219) 647-5589

Chief Executive Officer	Tel:	(219) 647-5990
KETTERING, Glen L.	Fax:	(219) 647-5589

President and Chief Executive Officer	Tel:	(219) 647-5990
SKAGGS, Jr., Robert C.	Fax:	(219) 647-5589

Main Headquarters

Mailing:	801 E. 86th Ave.	Tel:	(219) 647-5990
	Merillville, IN 46410	Fax:	(219) 647-5589
		TF:	(877) 647-5990

Washington Office

Mailing:	601 Pennsylvania Ave. NW	Tel:	(202) 216-9770
	Suite 900	Fax:	(202) 216-9785
	Washington, DC 20004		

Political Action Committees

NiSource Inc. PAC
FEC ID: C00051979
Contact: Timothy J. Tokish Jr.
200 Civic Center Dr.
Columbus, OH 43215

Contributions to Candidates: $213,900 (2015-2016)
Democrats: $40,000; Republicans: $173,900

Principal Recipients
PRESIDENT
KASICH, JOHN R (REP-OH)

HOUSE
VISCLOSKY, PETER J. (DEM-IN)

Corporate Foundations and Giving Programs

NiSource Charitable Foundation
Contact: Jennifer Moench
801 E. 86th Ave.
Merrillville, IN 46410

Public Affairs and Related Activities Personnel

At Headquarters

BANAS, Mike	Tel:	(219) 647-5581
Director, External Communications	Fax:	(219) 647-5589
mbanas@nisource.com		
BRACK , Karl	Tel:	(219) 647-5990
Senior Vice President, Corporate Affairs	Fax:	(219) 647-5589
CAMPBELL, Robert D.	Tel:	(219) 647-5990
Senior Vice President, Human Resources	Fax:	(219) 647-5589
HIGHTMAN, Carrie J.	Tel:	(219) 647-5990
Executive Vice President and Chief Legal Officer	Fax:	(219) 647-5589
HULEN, Randy	Tel:	(219) 647-5688
Vice President, Investor Relations	Fax:	(219) 647-5589
rghulen@nisource.com		
MOENCH, Jennifer	Tel:	(219) 647-6209
Manager, Corporate Affairs	Fax:	(219) 647-5589
MULPAS , Joseph	Tel:	(219) 647-5990
Vice President, Controller and Chief Accounting Officer	Fax:	(219) 647-5589
SMITH , Robert E.	Tel:	(219) 647-5990
Corporate Secretary, Vice President and Deputy General	Fax:	(219) 647-5589
Counsel		
SMITH, Stephen	Tel:	(219) 647-5990
Executive Vice President and Chief Financial Officer	Fax:	(219) 647-5589
VAJDA , David J.	Tel:	(219) 647-5990
Vice President, Chief Risk Officer and Treasurer	Fax:	(219) 647-5589

At Washington Office

GOLDING, Elizabeth	Tel:	(202) 216-9770
Contact, Government Relations	Fax:	(202) 216-9785
Registered Federal Lobbyist		
MORTENSON, Elizabeth A.	Tel:	(202) 216-9770
Contact, Government Relations	Fax:	(202) 216-9785
Registered Federal Lobbyist		
MULLER, Jason	Tel:	(202) 216-9770
Registered Federal Lobbyist	Fax:	(202) 216-9785

SCZUDLO, Rebecca T.
Vice President, Government Affairs
Registered Federal Lobbyist

Tel: (202) 216-9770
Fax: (202) 216-9785

At Other Offices

TOKISH, Jr., Timothy J.
PAC Treasurer
290 W Nationwide Blvd.
Columbus, OH 43215

Tel: (614) 460-4207

Nissan North America Inc.
Manufactures automobiles including passenger cars, buses, trucks.
www.nissanusa.com
Annual Revenues: $100 billion
Employees: 200,000
Industry/ies: Automotive Industry; Transportation
Legislative Issues: AUT; CPT; MAN; TAX; TRD

Chairman of the Board and Chief Executive Officer
GHOSN, Carlos
carlos.ghosn@nissan-usa.com

Tel: (615) 725-1000
Fax: (615) 725-3343

Main Headquarters
Mailing: First Nissan Way
Franklin, TN 37067

Washington Office
Mailing: 11951 Freedom Dr.
Suite 1316
Reston, VA 20190

Tel: (703) 456-2553

Corporate Foundations and Giving Programs
Nissan Foundation
Contact: Scott Becker
P.O. Box 191
Franklin, TN 37076

Public Affairs and Related Activities Personnel

At Headquarters

BECKER, Scott
Senior Vice President, Administration and Finance, and Contact, Nissan Foundation
scott.becker@nissan-usa.com

HANADA, Yuko
Manager, Government Affairs
yuko.hanada@nissan-usa.com
Registered Federal Lobbyist

KELLY, Greg
Vice President, Human Resources and Organization Development

STANDISH, Fred
Director, Corporate Communications
fred.standish@nissan-usa.com

WOODARD, Tracy
Director, Government Affairs
tracy.woodard@nissan-usa.com
Registered Federal Lobbyist

At Other Offices

SIMON, Karl J.
Director, Compliance and Innovative Strategies
P.O. Box 685003
Franklin, TN 37068-5003

Tel: (615) 725-1000
Fax: (615) 725-3343

TAKAHASHI, Yusuke
Corporate Vice President, Human Resources(Japan)
P.O. Box 685003
Franklin, TN 37068-5003

Tel: (615) 725-1000
Fax: (615) 725-3343

Noble Corporation
Drilling contractors serving the worldwide petroleum industry.
www.noblecorp.com
Annual Revenues: $3.16 billion
Employees: 3,700
Ticker: NYSE: NE
SIC: 1381
NAICS: 213111
Industry/ies: Machinery/Equipment; Natural Resources
Legislative Issues: TAX

Chairman of the Board, Chief Executive Officer and President
WILLIAMS, David W.
david.williams@noblecorp.com

Tel: (281) 276-6100
Fax: (281) 491-2092

Main Headquarters
Mailing: 13135 S. Dairy Ashford Rd.
Suite 800
Sugar Land TX 77478

Tel: (281) 276-6100
Fax: (281) 491-2092

Corporate Foundations and Giving Programs
Noble Corporation Contributions Program

13135 S. Dairy Ashford
Suite 800
Sugar Land, TX 77478

Tel: (281) 276-6100
Fax: (281) 491-2092

Public Affairs and Related Activities Personnel

At Headquarters

BREED, John S.
Director, Corporate Communications
jbreed@noblecorp.com

Tel: (281) 276-6729
Fax: (281) 491-2092

CHASTAIN, Jeffrey L.
Vice President, Investor Relations
JChastain@noblecorp.com

Tel: (281) 276-6100
Fax: (281) 491-2092

JACOBSEN, D.E.
Senior Vice President, Operations

Tel: (281) 276-6100
Fax: (281) 491-2092

JOHNSON, Simon W.
Senior Vice President, Marketing and Contracts

Tel: (281) 276-6100
Fax: (281) 491-2092

LUBOJACKY, Dennis J.
Vice President and Controller

Tel: (281) 276-6100
Fax: (281) 491-2092

MACLENNAN, James A.
Senior Vice President and Chief Financial Officer

Tel: (281) 276-6100
Fax: (281) 491-2092

ROBERTSON, Julie J.
Executive Vice President and Corporate Secretary
julie.robertson@noblecorp.com

Tel: (281) 276-6100
Fax: (281) 491-2092

TURCOTTE, William E.
Senior Vice President and General Counsel

Tel: (281) 276-6100
Fax: (281) 491-2092

WOLFORD, Bernie G.
Senior Vice President, Operations

Tel: (281) 276-6100
Fax: (281) 491-2092

Noble Drilling Services
See listing on page 581 under Noble Corporation

Noble Energy, Inc.
Independent energy co with operations that include exploration, development and production.
www.nobleenergyinc.com
Annual Revenues: $4.34 billion
Employees: 2,735
Ticker: NYSE: NBL
SIC: 1311; 1382
NAICS: 213112; 211111
Industry/ies: Fuels See Coal, Gas, Oil, Petroleum; Natural Resources; Petroleum Industry
Legislative Issues: ACC; ENG; ENV; FOR; FUE; NAT

Chairman of the Board, President and Chief Executive Officer
STOVER, David L.

Tel: (281) 872-3100
Fax: (281) 872-3111

Main Headquarters
Mailing: 1001 Noble Energy Way
Houston, TX 77070

Tel: (281) 872-3100
Fax: (281) 872-3111

Political Action Committees
Noble Energy Inc PAC
FEC ID: C00479873
Contact: Bernie J. Dillon
100 Glenborough Dr.
Suite 100
Houston, TX 77067

Tel: (281) 872-3100
Fax: (281) 872-3111

    Contributions to Candidates: $5,000 (2015-2016)
    Republicans: $5,000

Corporate Foundations and Giving Programs
Noble Energy Contributions Program
100 Glenborough Dr.
Suite 100
Houston, TX 77067

Tel: (281) 872-3100

Public Affairs and Related Activities Personnel

At Headquarters

BEMIS, Robert
Contact, Government Relations
Registered Federal Lobbyist

Tel: (281) 872-3100
Fax: (281) 872-3111

FISHER, Kenneth M.
Senior Vice President and Chief Financial Officer

Tel: (281) 872-3100
Fax: (281) 872-3111

JOHNSON, Arnold J.
Senior Vice President, General Counsel and Secretary

Tel: (281) 872-3100
Fax: (281) 872-3111

LARSON, David R.
Vice President, Investor Relations
dlarson@nobleenergyinc.com

Tel: (281) 872-3125
Fax: (281) 872-3111

LEWIS, John T.
Senior Vice President, Corporate Development

Tel: (281) 872-3100
Fax: (281) 872-3111

MILLER, Brian
Federal Lobbyist
Registered Federal Lobbyist

Tel: (281) 872-3100
Fax: (281) 872-3111

ROBISON, Andrea Lee
Senior Vice President, Human Resources and Administration

Tel: (281) 872-3100
Fax: (281) 872-3111

WATKINS, Todd	Tel:	(281) 872-3100
Registered Federal Lobbyist	Fax:	(281) 872-3111
WELCH, Nicholas	Tel:	(281) 872-3100
Federal Lobbyist	Fax:	(281) 872-3111
Registered Federal Lobbyist		
WILLINGHAM, Gary W.	Tel:	(281) 872-3100
Executive Vice President, Operations	Fax:	(281) 872-3111

At Other Offices

DILLON, Bernie J.
Vice President, Communications & Government Relations
100 Glenborough Dr., Suite 100
Houston, TX 77067
Registered Federal Lobbyist

FLAHERTY, Stephen   Tel: (303) 228-4321
Director
1625 Broadway, Suite 2200
Denver, CO 80202
Registered Federal Lobbyist

GRENZE, Michael   Tel: (303) 389-3600
Federal Lobbyist
1625 Broadway, Suite 2200
Denver, CO 80202
Registered Federal Lobbyist

SMITH, Richard   Tel: (303) 389-3600
Manager, Regulatory and Compliance
1625 Broadway, Suite 2200
Denver, CO 80202

STEVENSON, Gerry   Tel: (303) 389-3600
Vice President, Treasurer
1625 Broadway, Suite 2200
Denver, CO 80202

NOKIA Inc.

A manufacturer of cellular telephones. Headquartered in Finland.
www.nokia.com
Employees: 68,500
Ticker: NYSE:NOK
SIC: 3661
Industry/ies: Communications; Electricity & Electronics; Electronics; Energy/
Electricity; Telecommunications/Internet/Cable
Legislative Issues: COM; CPT; CSP; FOR; TEC

Main Headquarters

Mailing:	1401 K St. NW, Suite 450	Tel:	(202) 887-5157
	Suite 450	Fax:	(202) 887-0432
	Washington, DC 20005		

Main Headquarters

Mailing: 200 South Mathilda Ave.
            Sunnyvale, CA 94086 .

Corporate Foundations and Giving Programs

Alcatel-Lucent Foundation
600-700 Mountain Ave.
Murray Hill, NJ 07974

Public Affairs and Related Activities Personnel

At Headquarters

SHULL, Thomas	Tel:	(202) 887-5157
Legislative and Regulatory Associate	Fax:	(202) 887-0432

At Other Offices

PLUMMER, William B
PAC Treasurer
1101 Connecticult Ave.NW, Suite 910
Washington, DC 20036

SHIMAO, Matt   Tel: (914) 368-0555
Head, Investor Relations   Fax: (914) 368-0600
102 Corporate Park Dr.
White Plains, NY 10604
matt.shimao@nokia.com

Nomura Holding America Inc.

A banking financial company.
www.nomuraholdings.com/company/group/holdings/inde
Industry/ies: Banking/Finance/Investments
Legislative Issues: CDT; FIN

Main Headquarters

Mailing:	309 W. 49th St.	Tel:	(212) 667-9000
	New York City, NY 10019	Fax:	(212) 667-9100

Washington Office

Mailing:	1101 Pennsylvania Ave. NW	Tel:	(202) 393-4165
	Washington, DC 20004	Fax:	(202) 737-6929

Political Action Committees

Nomura Holding America Inc. PAC (NOMURAPAC)

FEC ID: C00491951
Contact: Lauren Myrick
1101 Pennsylvania Ave. NW
SUITE 515
Washington, DC 20004

Contributions to Candidates: $81,500 (2015-2016)
Democrats: $32,000; Republicans: $49,500

Principal Recipients

SENATE

CRAPO, MICHAEL D (REP-ID)

Public Affairs and Related Activities Personnel

At Headquarters

ROSS, Randall	Tel:	(212) 667-9000
Registered Federal Lobbyist	Fax:	(212) 667-9100

At Washington Office

HERRERA, Julie M.	Tel:	(202) 393-4165
Director, Washington Operations	Fax:	(202) 737-6929
MYRICK, Lauren	Tel:	(202) 393-4165
Analyst, Public Affairs	Fax:	(202) 737-6929
lauren.myrick@nomura.com		
SCHUERMANN, Mark	Tel:	(202) 393-4164
Managing Director and Head, Public Affairs	Fax:	(202) 737-6929
Mark.schuermann@nomura.com		
Registered Federal Lobbyist		

Nomura Securities International Inc.

A brokerage firm. A subsidiary of Nomura Holding America, Inc.The US-based division of Nomura Holdings, a top Japanese brokerage, provides securities research and trading, asset management, and capital markets services to individual, institutional, corporate, and government clients.Nomura Securities International opened its first US office in New York in 1927, and has expanded its reach to entail all of North and South America.
www.nomura.com
Annual Revenues: $85.3 million
Employees: 1,600
Industry/ies: Banking/Finance/Investments

Director and Chairman	Tel:	(212) 667-9000
KOGA, Nobuyuki	Fax:	(212) 667-9100
Chief Executive Officer	Tel:	(212) 667-9000
NAGAI, Koji	Fax:	(212) 667-9100

Main Headquarters

Mailing:	Worldwide Plaza, 309 W. 49th St.	Tel:	(212) 667-9000
	New York, NY 10019-7316	Fax:	(212) 667-9100

Washington Office

Mailing:	1101 Pennsylvania Ave. NW	Tel:	(202) 393-4165
	Suite 515		
	Washington, DC 20004		

Corporate Foundations and Giving Programs

Nomura charity
Two World Financial Center   Tel: (212) 667-9000
Building B
New York City, NY 10281

Public Affairs and Related Activities Personnel

At Headquarters

KASHIWAGI, Shigesuke	Tel:	(212) 667-9000
Chief Financial Officer	Fax:	(212) 667-9100
MATSUBA, Naoki	Tel:	(212) 667-9000
Co-Head, Global Markets	Fax:	(212) 667-9100
NAGAMATSU, Shoichi	Tel:	(212) 667-9000
Chief of Staff	Fax:	(212) 667-9100
WATANABE, Akihito	Tel:	(212) 667-9000
Senior Corporate Managing Director	Fax:	(212) 667-9100
akihito.watanabe@nomura.com		
YAMAJI, Hiromi	Tel:	(212) 667-9000
Executive Vice President	Fax:	(212) 667-9100
YOSHIKAWA, Atsushi	Tel:	(212) 667-9000
President and Chief Operations Officer	Fax:	(212) 667-9100

Noranda Aluminum Holding Corporation

An integrated producer of value-added primary aluminum products and rolled aluminum coils. Its Bauxite segment mines, produces, and sells bauxite used for alumina production. Its Alumina segment refines and converts bauxite into alumina, which is used in the production of primary aluminum; and sells smelter grade alumina and alumina hydrate, or chemical-grade alumina.
www.norandaaluminum.com
Annual Revenues: $1.39 billion
Employees: 1,600
Ticker: NYSE: NOR
SIC: 3334
Industry/ies: Metals

Legislative Issues: ENV; TRD

Chairman of the Board
EVANS, Richard B.
Tel: (615) 771-5700
Fax: (615) 771-5701

President and Chief Executive Officer
SMITH, Layle K. (Kip)
Tel: (573) 643-2361
Fax: (573) 643-6715

Main Headquarters
Mailing: 801 Crescent Centre Dr.
Suite 600
Franklin, TN 37067
Tel: (615) 771-5700
Fax: (615) 771-5701

Political Action Committees
Noranda Intermediate Holding Corporation PAC
FEC ID: C00468876
Contact: Carol Clifton
801 Crescent Centre Dr.
Suite 600
Franklin, TN 37067
Tel: (615) 771-5700
Fax: (615) 771-5701

Contributions to Candidates: $5,400 (2015-2016)
Other: $5,400

Public Affairs and Related Activities Personnel

At Headquarters

BOYLES, Dale
Chief Financial Officer
Tel: (615) 771-5700
Fax: (615) 771-5701

CLIFTON, Carol
PAC Treasurer
Tel: (615) 771-5700
Fax: (615) 771-5701

LAPINE, Richard
Vice President, Commercial Activities
richard.lapine@noralinc.com
Tel: (615) 771-5783
Fax: (615) 771-5701

LEHMAN, Gail E.
Chief Administrative Officer, General Counsel and Corporate Secretary
Tel: (573) 643-2361
Fax: (573) 643-6715

PARKER, John A.
Vice President, Communication and Investor Relations
john.parker@noralinc.com
Tel: (615) 771-5700
Fax: (615) 771-5701

ROEPE, Chris
Vice President, Governmental Affairs
Tel: (615) 771-5700
Fax: (615) 771-5701

Norcal Mutual Insurance Company

Provides medical professional liability insurance, products and services to its policyholders. It specialize in medical professional liability insurance for Individual physicians and medical groups to offer coverages that will best benefit our policyholder.
www.norcalmutual.com
Annual Revenues: $1.5 billion
Employees: 250
Industry/ies: Insurance Industry

Chairman of the Board
SIDOROV, MD, MHSA, FACP, Jaan E.
Tel: (415) 397-9700
Fax: (415) 835-9817

President and Chief Executive Officer
DIENER, Scott
Tel: (415) 397-9700
Fax: (415) 835-9817

Main Headquarters
Mailing: 560 Davis St.
Suite 200
San Francisco, CA 94111-1966
Tel: (415) 397-9700
Fax: (415) 835-9817
TF: (800) 652-1051

Political Action Committees
Micra Federal PAC of Norcal Mutual Insurance Company
FEC ID: C00398248
Contact: Russell H. Miller
20 Park Rd.
Suite E
Burlingame, CA 94010

Public Affairs and Related Activities Personnel

At Headquarters

BURNS, Julie L.
Senior Vice President & Chief Human Resources Officer
Tel: (415) 397-9700
Fax: (415) 835-9817

CORSO, Joy E.
Vice President, Marketing & Communications
Tel: (415) 397-9700
Fax: (415) 835-9817

FRIERS, Timothy J.
Senior Vice President & Chief Operating Officer
Tel: (415) 397-9700
Fax: (415) 835-9817

HINDERBERG, Philip R.
Senior Vice President, Government Affairs Counsel
Tel: (415) 397-9700
Fax: (415) 835-9817

JOHNSON, Mark D.
Senior Vice President and Chief Financial Officer
Tel: (415) 397-9700
Fax: (415) 835-9817

MILLER, Russell H.
PAC Treasurer
Tel: (415) 397-9700
Fax: (415) 835-9817

RICCI, Kara M.
Senior Vice President, Chief Legal Officer & Corporate Secretary
Tel: (415) 397-9700
Fax: (415) 835-9817

RUMIN, Ronald C.
Senior Vice President & Chief Business Development Officer
Tel: (415) 397-9700
Fax: (415) 835-9817

SIMONS, Neil E.
Vice President, Product Development
Tel: (415) 397-9700
Fax: (415) 835-9817

Nordson Corporation

A manufacturer of industrial equipment for applying adhesives, sealants and coatings.
www.nordson.com
Annual Revenues: $1.72 billion
Employees: 6,100
Ticker: NASDAQ: NDSN
SIC: 3599
NAICS: 333319
Industry/ies: Chemicals & Chemical Industry

President and Chief Executive Officer
HILTON, Michael F.
Tel: (440) 892-1580
Fax: (440) 892-9507

Main Headquarters
Mailing: 28601 Clemens Rd.
Westlake, OH 44145
Tel: (440) 892-1580
Fax: (440) 892-9507

Corporate Foundations and Giving Programs
Nordson Corporation Foundation
Contact: Cecilia H. Render
28601 Clemens Rd.
Westlake, OH 44145

Public Affairs and Related Activities Personnel

At Headquarters

JAYE, James R.
Director, Communications and Investor Relations
jjaye@nordson.com
Tel: (440) 414-5639
Fax: (440) 892-9507

PEET, Shelly M.
Vice President, Human Resources
shelly.peet@nordson.com
Tel: (440) 892-1580
Fax: (440) 892-9507

PRICE, Barbara T.
Manager, Shareholder Relations
bprice@nordson.com
Tel: (440) 414-5344
Fax: (440) 892-9507

RENDER, Cecilia H.
Executive Director, Nordson Corporation Foundation
crender@nordson.com
Tel: (440) 892-1580
Fax: (440) 892-9507

THAXTON, Gregory A.
Senior Vice President and Chief Financial Officer
Tel: (440) 892-1580
Fax: (440) 892-9507

VEILLETTE, Robert E.
Vice President, General Counsel and Secretary
Tel: (440) 892-1580
Fax: (440) 892-9507

Nordstrom, Inc.

A fashion specialty retailer with an unerring eye for what's next in fashion. It has worked to deliver the best possible shopping experience, helping customers possess style—not just buy fashion.
shop.nordstrom.com
Annual Revenues: $14.47 billion
Employees: 78,000
Ticker: NYSE: JWN
SIC: 5651
Industry/ies: Apparel/Textiles Industry; Retail/Wholesale

Main Headquarters
Mailing: 1600 Seventh Ave.
Suite 2600
Seattle, WA 98101
Tel: (206) 628-2111
Fax: (206) 628-1795
TF: (800) 282-6060

Public Affairs and Related Activities Personnel

At Headquarters

DENNEHY, Brian K.
Executive Vice President and Chief Marketing Officer
Tel: (206) 628-2111
Fax: (206) 628-1795

DEPUTY, Christine F.
Executive Vice President, Human Resources
Tel: (206) 628-2111
Fax: (206) 628-1795

JOHNSON, Colin
Director, Public Relations
Mail Stop suite 1000
colin.johnson@nordstrom.com
Tel: (206) 373-3036
Fax: (206) 373-3039

KOPPEL, Michael G.
Executive Vice President and Chief Financial Officer
Tel: (206) 628-2111
Fax: (206) 628-1795

SARI, Robert B.
Executive Vice President, General Counsel and Secretary
Robert.Sari@Nordstrom.com
Tel: (206) 628-2111
Fax: (206) 628-1795

WHITE, Brooke
Vice President, Corporate Communications
Tel: (206) 303-3030
Fax: (206) 628-1795

WORZEL, Ken
Executive Vice President, Strategy and Development
Tel: (206) 628-2111
Fax: (206) 628-1795

At Other Offices

CAMPBELL, Robert E.
Vice President, Full-Line Store Finance
P.O. Box 2737
Seattle, WA 98111-2737
Tel: (206) 303-3200
Fax: (206) 233-6319

invrelations@nordstrom.com

FABRE, Sandy
Director, Planning and Business
P.O. Box 2737
Seattle, WA 98111-2737
sandy.fabre@nordstrom.com

Tel: (206) 233-6563
Fax: (206) 233-6319

Norfolk Southern Corporation

A transportation holding company that operates a freight railroad company, Norfolk Southern Railway. Created in 1982 from the merger of the Norfolk and Western Railway and the Southern Railway Company.
www.nscorp.com
Annual Revenues: $11.50 billion
Employees: 29,482
Ticker: NYSE: NSC
SIC: 4011
Industry/ies: Railroads; Transportation
Legislative Issues: BUD; ENG; ENV; HOM; LBR; ROD; RRR; TAX; TEC; TRA

Chairman of the Board
MOORMAN, IV, Charles W.
wick.moorman@nscorp.com

Tel: (757) 629-2600
Fax: (757) 664-2822

President and Chief Executive Officer
SQUIRES, James A.
james.squires@nscorp.com

Tel: (757) 629-2600
Fax: (757) 664-5069

Main Headquarters
Mailing: Three Commercial Pl.
Norfolk, VA 23510

Tel: (757) 629-2600
Fax: (757) 664-5069
TF: (855) 667-3655

Washington Office
Mailing: One Constitution Ave. NE
Suite 300
Washington, DC 20002

Political Action Committees
Norfolk Southern Corporation Good Government Fund PAC
FEC ID: C00009282
Contact: Marque I. Ledoux
One Constitution Ave NE
DC, DC 20002

Contributions to Candidates: $579,000 (2015-2016)
Democrats: $203,500; Republicans: $375,500

Principal Recipients

SENATE
BURR, RICHARD (REP-NC)
GARDNER, CORY (REP-CO)
PETERS, GARY (DEM-MI)
SCHATZ, BRIAN (DEM-HI)
SCOTT, TIMOTHY E (REP-SC)

HOUSE
BEYER, DONALD STERNOFF JR. (DEM-VA)
DENHAM, JEFF (REP-CA)
GOODLATTE, ROBERT W. (REP-VA)
GRAVES, SAMUEL B JR 'SAM' (REP-MO)
GRIFFITH, H MORGAN (REP-VA)
JOHNSON, EDDIE BERNICE (DEM-TX)
MCCARTHY, KEVIN (REP-CA)
MICA, JOHN L. MR. (REP-FL)
RIGELL, EDWARD SCOTT MR. (REP-VA)
SHUSTER, WILLIAM MR. (REP-PA)

Corporate Foundations and Giving Programs

Norfolk Southern Foundation
Contact: Katie Fletcher
P.O. Box 3040
Norfolk, VA 23514

Public Affairs and Related Activities Personnel

At Headquarters

ALLISON, Clyde H.
Vice President, Audit and Compliance

Tel: (757) 629-2600
Fax: (757) 664-5069

BROWN, Frank S.
Assistant Vice President, Corporate Communications
frank.brown@nscorp.com

Tel: (757) 629-2710
Fax: (757) 664-2822

CUNNINGHAM, Juan K.
Vice President, Human Resources

Tel: (757) 629-2600
Fax: (757) 664-5069

EARHART, Cindy C.
Executive Vice President, Administration

Tel: (757) 629-2600
Fax: (757) 664-2822

FLETCHER, Katie
Executive Director, Norfolk Southern Foundation
katie.fletcher@nscorp.com

Tel: (757) 629-2600
Fax: (757) 664-5069

FRIEDMANN, John H.
Vice President, Strategic Planning

Tel: (757) 629-2600
Fax: (757) 664-5069

HARRIS, Richard W.

Tel: (757) 629-2710

Director, Corporate Communications
rick.harris@nscorp.com
Registered Federal Lobbyist

Fax: (757) 664-2822

HIXON, James A.
Executive Vice President, Law and Corporate Relations
james.hixon@nscorp.com

Tel: (757) 629-2600
Fax: (757) 664-2822

HOSTUTLER, Michael J.
Director, Investor Relations
Michael.Hostutler@nscorp.com

Tel: (757) 629-2600
Fax: (757) 664-5069

MARILLEY, Leanne D.
Director, Distribution Services
leanne.marilley@nscorp.com

Tel: (757) 629-2861
Fax: (757) 664-5069

MEADOR, Chip
Director, Strategic Planning
Chip.Meador@nscorp.com

Tel: (757) 629-2600
Fax: (757) 664-5069

SHAW, Alan H.
Executive Vice President and Chief Marketing Officer

Tel: (757) 629-2600
Fax: (757) 664-5069

STEWART, Marta R.
Executive Vice President Finance and Chief Financial Officer

Tel: (757) 629-2600
Fax: (757) 664-5069

TERPAY, Susan M.
Director, Public Relations
susan.terpay@nscorp.com

Tel: (757) 823-5204
Fax: (757) 664-2822

At Washington Office

LEDOUX, Marque I.
Assistant Vice President, Government Relations and PAC Contact
Registered Federal Lobbyist

MAESTRI, Bruno
Vice President, Government Relations
bruno.maestri@nscrop.com
Registered Federal Lobbyist

MUIR, Scott
Assistant Vice President, Mid-Atlantic States
Scott.Muir@nscorp.com

VOYACK, Frank
Director, Government Relations
Frank.voyack@nscorp.com
Registered Federal Lobbyist

WILSON, Darrell L.
Assistant Vice President, Government Relations
darrell.wilson@nscorp.com
Registered Federal Lobbyist

At Other Offices

HARRELL, III, Joel E.
Resident Vice President, Government Relations
P.O.Box 36, 1200 Peachtree St.
Atlanta, GA 30309-0036
joel.harrell@nscorp.com

Tel: (404) 897-3131
Fax: (404) 589-6973

Noridian Mutual Insurance Company

Offers health, dental, and life insurance, under several brands, including Blue Cross Blue Shield of North Dakota.
www.noridian.com
Annual Revenues: $80.80 million
Employees: 2,000
Industry/ies: Insurance Industry

Chairman of the Board
GROSSMAN, Robert

Tel: (701) 282-1100
Fax: (701) 282-1469

Main Headquarters
Mailing: 4510 13th Ave. SW
Fargo, ND 58121

Tel: (701) 282-1864
Fax: (701) 277-2216
TF: (800) 342-4718

Public Affairs and Related Activities Personnel

At Headquarters

BREUER, David
Senior Vice President, Finance and Chief Financial Officer

Tel: (701) 282-1100
Fax: (701) 277-2454

GAUPER, Larry
Vice President, Corporate Communications
larry.gauper@noridian.com

Tel: (701) 282-1100
Fax: (701) 277-2454

GULLESON, Pam
Vice President, Public Affairs

Tel: (701) 282-1864
Fax: (701) 277-2216

HOUN, Megan

Tel: (701) 282-1864
Fax: (701) 277-2216

JOHNSON, Randy
Vice President, Human Resources

Tel: (701) 297-1595
Fax: (701) 277-2454

NARUM, Jeanne
Vice President, Compliance, Audit and Corporate Ethics

Tel: (701) 282-1100
Fax: (701) 277-2454

ULMER, Dan
Vice President, Government Relations

Tel: (701) 255-5572
Fax: (701) 277-2454

Norm Inc

Government relations.

Chief Executive Officer
HAHN R.S.C, Scott

Main Headquarters
Mailing: Six -18 Burnt Bluff St.
Red Deer, AB T4P 0J6

Nortek Inc.

A manufacturer of commercial and residential building products.
www.nortek-inc.com
Annual Revenues: $2.57 billion
Employees: 11,200
Ticker: NASDAQ: NTK
SIC: 3634
Industry/ies: Construction/Construction Materials

| **Chairman of the Board and President** | Tel: | (401) 751-1600 |
| BREADY, Richard L. | Fax: | (401) 751-4610 |

| **President and Chief Executive Officer** | Tel: | (401) 751-1600 |
| CLARKE, Michael J. | Fax: | (401) 751-4610 |

Main Headquarters

| *Mailing:*   500 Exchange St. | Tel: | (401) 751-1600 |
| Providence, RI 02903 | Fax: | (401) 751-4610 |

Public Affairs and Related Activities Personnel

At Headquarters

| BOTELHO, Michael H. | Tel: | (401) 751-1600 |
| *Vice President, Strategy and Investor Relations* | Fax: | (401) 751-4610 |

| BURLING, Timothy J. | Tel: | (401) 751-1600 |
| *Senior Vice President, Finance* | Fax: | (401) 751-4610 |

DONNELLY, Kevin W.	Tel:	(401) 751-1600
Vice President, General Counsel and Secretary	Fax:	(401) 751-4610
donnelly@nortek-inc.com		

| HALL, Almon C. | Tel: | (401) 751-1600 |
| *Senior Vice President and Chief Financial Officer* | Fax: | (401) 751-4610 |

| PRETE, Andrew W. | Tel: | (401) 751-1600 |
| *Vice President, Business Development, Senior Legal Counsel* | Fax: | (401) 751-4610 |

| REILLY, Donald W. | Tel: | (401) 751-1600 |
| *Vice President, Corporate Controller and Chief Accounting Officer* | Fax: | (401) 751-4610 |

| WESTON, Liam | Tel: | (401) 751-1600 |
| *Chief Human Resources Officer* | Fax: | (401) 751-4610 |

North American Coal

Formerly known as The Cleveland and Western Coal Company, the company changed its name to The North American Coal Corporation in 1925. The North American Coal Corporation, a subsidiary of NACCO Industries, Inc.
www.nacoal.com
Annual Revenues: $129.53 million
Employees: 1,500
Ticker: NYSE: NC
SIC: 1222
NAICS: 212112
Industry/ies: Natural Resources
Legislative Issues: ENG

| **Chairman of the Board** | Tel: | (972) 448-5400 |
| RANKIN, Jr., Alfred M. | Fax: | (972) 387-1328 |

| **President and Chief Executive Officer** | Tel: | (972) 448-5400 |
| BUTLER, J C | Fax: | (972) 387-1328 |

Main Headquarters

Mailing: 5340 Legacy Dr.	Tel:	(972) 448-5400
Building I, Suite 300	Fax:	(972) 387-1328
Plano, TX 75024		

Political Action Committees

North American Coal Corporation PAC (NACPAC)
FEC ID: C00303685
Contact: Donald K. Grischow

5340 Legacy Dr.	Tel:	(972) 239-2625
Bldg. One, Suite 300		
Plano, TX 75024		

Contributions to Candidates: $7,700 (2015-2016)
Republicans: $7,700

Corporate Foundations and Giving Programs

North American Coal Contributions Program

14785 Preston Rd.	Tel:	(972) 239-2625
Suite 1100		
Dallas, TX 75254-7891		

Public Affairs and Related Activities Personnel

At Headquarters

CARLTON, Bob D.	Tel:	(972) 448-5400
Vice President and Chief Financial Officer	Fax:	(972) 387-1328
bob.carlton@nacoal.com		

GREGORY, Michael J.	Tel:	(972) 448-5400
Vice President, International Operations and Special Projects	Fax:	(972) 387-1328
mike.gregory@nacoal.com		

GRISCHOW, Donald K.	Tel:	(972) 448-5400
PAC Treasurer	Fax:	(972) 387-1328
donald.grischow@nacoal.com		

| GRISCHOW, K. Donald | Tel: | (972) 448-5400 |
| *Treasurer* | Fax: | (972) 387-1328 |

| MALONEY, Mary D | Tel: | (972) 448-5400 |
| *Associate General Counsel, Assistant Secretary and Senior Director Benefits and Compensation* | Fax: | (972) 387-1328 |

| NEUMANN, John D. | Tel: | (972) 448-5400 |
| *Vice President, General Counsel and Secretary* | Fax: | (972) 387-1328 |

| POKORNY, John R | Tel: | (972) 448-5400 |
| *Controller* | Fax: | (972) 387-1328 |

SULLIVAN, Jr., J Patrick	Tel:	(972) 448-5400
Vice President and Chief Financial Officer	Fax:	(972) 387-1328
jrawat@jgsi.com		

At Other Offices

STRALEY, David	Tel:	(972) 239-2625
Manager, Government and Public Affairs	Fax:	(972) 387-1328
14785 Preston Rd., Suite 1100		
Dallas, TX 75254-7891		

North Carolina Electric Membership Corporation

Generates and transmits electricity to the state's 26 electric cooperatives (more than 2.5 million people) in 93 of 100 North Carolina counties.
ncemcs.com
Industry/ies: Cooperatives; Electricity & Electronics; Energy/Electricity; Utilities

Executive Vice President and Chief Executive Officer	Tel:	(919) 872-0800
BRANNAN, Joseph P.	Fax:	(919) 645-3410
joe.brannan@ncemcs.com		

Main Headquarters

| *Mailing:*   3400 Sumner Blvd. | TF: | (800) 662-8835 |
| Raleigh, NC 27616 | | |

Public Affairs and Related Activities Personnel

At Headquarters

BURNETTE, Mike
Senior Vice President and Chief Operating Officer

PRITCHARD, Jane
Director, Corporate Communications

ROUSE, Jay	Tel:	(919) 875-3107
Director, Government Affairs		
jay.rouse@ncemcs.com		

SCHWENTKER, Robert B.	Tel:	(919) 875-3107
Senior Vice President, Legal Services and Chief Operating Officer		
bob.schwentker@ncemcs.com		

At Other Offices

ALDRIDGE, Kristie	Tel:	(919) 872-0800
Manager, Digital Communications	Fax:	(919) 645-3410
3400 Sumner Blvd.		
Raleigh, NC 27616		
kristie.aldridge@ncemcs.com		

BURNETTE, Mike	Tel:	(919) 872-0800
Senior Vice President and Chief Operating Officer	Fax:	(919) 645-3410
3400 Sumner Blvd.		
Raleigh, NC 27616		

PRITCHARD, Jane	Tel:	(919) 875-3104
Director, Corporate Communications	Fax:	(919) 645-3410
3400 Sumner Blvd.		
Raleigh, NC 27616		

ROUSE, Jay	Tel:	(919) 872-0800
Director, Government Affairs	Fax:	(919) 645-3410
3400 Sumner Blvd.		
Raleigh, NC 27616		
jay.rouse@ncemcs.com		

SCHWENTKER, Robert B.	Tel:	(919) 872-0800
Senior Vice President, Legal Services and Chief Operating Officer		
3400 Sumner Blvd.		
Raleigh, NC 27616		
bob.schwentker@ncemcs.com		

North Eastern Aeronautical (NEANY) Inc.

A research, development, and engineering firm specializing in unmanned aerial vehicles systems.

www.neanyinc.com
Industry/ies: Aerospace/Aviation; Transportation

President and Chief Executive Officer   Tel: (301) 373-8700
STEPTOE, Steven   Fax: (301) 373-6405

Main Headquarters
Mailing: 44010 Commerce Ave.   Tel: (301) 373-8700
              Suite A   Fax: (301) 373-6405
              Hollywood, MD 20636

Washington Office
Mailing: 2001 Jefferson Davis Hwy.   Tel: (703) 414-8223
              Suite 1101   Fax: (703) 414-8226
              Arlington, VA 22202

Public Affairs and Related Activities Personnel

At Headquarters

WILSON, Heather   Tel: (202) 744-2833
Government Relations Manager   Fax: (301) 373-6405

Northeast Solite Corporation

A construction company. Northeast Solite Corporation produces lightweight aggregates for sale as Solite®, Kenlite® and HydroCure® throughout the entire United States.
www.nesolite.com
Annual Revenues: $15.60 million
Employees: 150
SIC: 1442
NAICS: 212321
Industry/ies: Construction/Construction Materials

Chairman of the Board   Tel: (845) 246-2646
ROBERTS, John W.   Fax: (845) 246-1329

Main Headquarters
Mailing: 1133 Kings Hwy.   Tel: (845) 246-2646
              Saugerties, NY 12477-4343   Fax: (845) 246-1329
                                                         TF: (800) 474-4514

Northeast Utilities Service Company

See listing on page 308 under Eversource Energy

The Northern Trust Company

A bank holding company that provides investment management, asset and fund administration, fiduciary and banking solutions for corporations, institutions and affluent individuals worldwide.
www.northerntrust.com
Annual Revenues: $4.43 billion
Employees: 15,600
Ticker: NASDAQ: NTRS
SIC: 6022
Industry/ies: Banking/Finance/Investments
Legislative Issues: BAN; FIN; FOR

Chairman of the Board and Chief Executive Officer   Tel: (312) 630-6000
WADDELL, Frederick H.   Fax: (312) 630-1512

Main Headquarters
Mailing: 50 S. LaSalle St.   Tel: (312) 630-6000
              Suite M-9   Fax: (312) 630-1512
              Chicago, IL 60603   TF: (877) 651-9156

Political Action Committees
Northern Trust Corporation Federal Political Action Committee (Northern Trust Federal PAC)
FEC ID: C00515148
Contact: Wendy A. Mausolf
50 S. Lasalle St.   Tel: (312) 630-6000
M-9   Fax: (312) 630-1512
Chicago, IL 60603

   Contributions to Candidates: $35,000 (2015-2016)
   Democrats: $11,500; Republicans: $23,500

Northern Trust Corporation PAC (Northern Trust PAC)
FEC ID: C00024935
Contact: Wendy A. Mausolf
50 LaSalle St.   Tel: (312) 630-6000
M-9   Fax: (312) 630-1512
Chicago, IL 60603

Corporate Foundations and Giving Programs

Northern Trust Charitable Trust
Contact: Connie L. Lindsey
50 S. LaSalle St.
Chicago, IL 60603

Public Affairs and Related Activities Personnel

At Headquarters

BOWMAN, S. Biff   Tel: (312) 630-6000
Chief Financial Officer   Fax: (312) 630-1512

DIBBLE, Kelly King   Tel: (312) 630-6000

Senior Vice President and Director, Public Affairs   Fax: (312) 630-1512
Registered Federal Lobbyist

FLEMING, Beverly J.   Tel: (312) 444-7811
Senior Vice President and Director, Investor Relations Fax: (312) 630-1512
beverly_fleming@ntrs.com

HOLT, Doulgas A.   Tel: (312) 557-1571
Head, Global Corporate Communications and Senior Vice Fax: (312) 630-1512
President
Doug_Holt@ntrs.com

LEVY, Susan C.   Tel: (312) 630-6000
Executive Vice President, General Counsel   Fax: (312) 630-1512

LINDSEY, Connie L.   Tel: (312) 630-6000
Head, Corporate Social Responsibility and Global Diversity Fax: (312) 630-1512

MAUSOLF, Wendy A.   Tel: (312) 630-6000
Vice President and Manager, Corporate Tax   Fax: (312) 630-1512
Mail Stop M-9

MULDROW, Wayne S.   Tel: (312) 630-6000
Corporate Counsel   Fax: (312) 630-1512
Mail Stop M-9

O'CONNELL, John   Tel: (312) 444-2388
Asset Management Media Relations   Fax: (312) 630-1512
John_O'Connell@ntrs.com

O'GRADY, Michael G.   Tel: (312) 630-6000
President, Corporate and Institutional Services   Fax: (312) 630-1512

PEMBLETON, Gillian   Tel: (312) 630-6000
Head, Human Resources   Fax: (312) 630-1512

SCHREUDER, Jana R.   Tel: (312) 630-6000
Chief Operating Officer   Fax: (312) 630-1512

TYLER, Jason J.   Tel: (312) 630-6000
Global Head, Client Solutions and Asset Management   Fax: (312) 630-1512

Northrop Grumman Corporation

Aerospace and defense company.
www.northropgrumman.com
Annual Revenues: $24.09 billion
Employees: 64,300
Ticker: NYSE: NOC
SIC: 3721
Industry/ies: Aerospace/Aviation; Defense/Homeland Security; Electricity & Electronics; Electronics; Energy/Electricity; Engineering/Mathematics; Government-Related; Transportation
Legislative Issues: AER; AVI; BUD; DEF; ENG; FOR; GOV; HOM; INT; TAX; TRD

Chairman of the Board, President and Chief Executive Officer   Tel: (703) 280-2900
BUSH, Wes

Main Headquarters
Mailing: 2980 Fairview Park Dr.   Tel: (703) 280-2900
              Falls Church, VA 22042

Political Action Committees
Employees of Northrop Grumman Corporation PAC
FEC ID: C00088591
Contact: Margaret Sidney Ashworth
2980 Fairview Park Dr.
Falls Church, VA 22042

   Contributions to Candidates: $4,903,015 (2015-2016)
   Democrats: $686,500; Republicans: $1,044,500; Other: $3,172,015

   Principal Recipients

   SENATE
   BARRASSO, JOHN A (REP-WY)
   JOHNSON, RONALD HAROLD (REP-)
   NELSON, BILL (DEM-FL)

   HOUSE
   AGUILAR, PETE (DEM-CA)
   BABIN, BRIAN (REP-TX)
   BECERRA, XAVIER (DEM-CA)
   BISHOP, ROBERT (REP-UT)
   BISHOP, SANFORD D JR (DEM-GA)
   BOUSTANY, CHARLES W. DR. JR. (REP-LA)
   BRIDENSTINE, JAMES FREDERICK (REP-OK)
   BROOKS, MO (REP-AL)
   BROOKS, SUSAN MRS. (REP-IN)
   BROWNLEY, JULIA (DEM-CA)
   CALVERT, KEN (REP-CA)
   CARTER, JOHN R. REP. (REP-DC)
   CASTRO, JOAQUIN REP. (DEM-TX)
   CHAFFETZ, JASON (REP-UT)
   CLYBURN, JAMES E. (DEM-SC)
   COLE, TOM (REP-OK)
   COMSTOCK, BARBARA J HONORABLE (REP-VA)
   COOK, PAUL (REP-CA)
   CRAMER, KEVIN MR. (REP-ND)
   CRENSHAW, ANDER (REP-FL)
   CULBERSON, JOHN (REP-TX)

DAVIS, SUSAN (DEM-CA)
DIAZ-BALART, MARIO (REP-FL)
ENGEL, ELIOT L. REP. (DEM-DC)
FLEISCHMANN, CHARLES J (REP-TN)
FORTENBERRY, JEFFREY L. HONORABLE (REP-NE)
FRELINGHUYSEN, RODNEY P. (REP-NJ)
GRANGER, KAY (REP-TX)
HARDY, CRESENT (REP-NV)
HARTZLER, VICKY (REP-MO)
HIMES, JIM (DEM-CT)
KEATING, WILLIAM RICHARD (DEM-MA)
KILMER, DEREK (DEM-WA)
KNIGHT, STEVE (REP-CA)
LAMBORN, DOUGLAS (REP-CO)
LANGEVIN, JAMES R. HONORABLE (DEM-RI)
LARSEN, RICK (DEM-WA)
LOEBSACK, DAVID WAYNE (DEM-IA)
LOWEY, NITA M (DEM-NY)
LUJAN, BEN R MR. (DEM-NM)
MATSUI, DORIS (DEM-CA)
MCCARTHY, KEVIN (REP-CA)
MCCAUL, MICHAEL (REP-TX)
MCMORRIS RODGERS, CATHY (REP-WA)
MCSALLY, MARTHA E. MS. (REP-AZ)
NUNES, DEVIN G (REP-CA)
POSEY, BILL (REP-FL)
ROBY, MARTHA (REP-AL)
ROS-LEHTINEN, ILEANA THE HON. (REP-FL)
ROSKAM, PETER (REP-IL)
ROYCE, ED MR. (REP-CA)
RUPPERSBERGER, C.A. DUTCH (DEM-MD)
RYAN, PAUL D. (REP-WI)
RYAN, TIMOTHY J. (DEM-OH)
SCALISE, STEVE MR. (REP-LA)
SCHIFF, ADAM (DEM-CA)
SCHULTZ, DEBBIE WASSERMAN (DEM-FL)
SHERMAN, BRAD (DEM-CA)
SLAUGHTER, LOUISE M (DEM-NY)
STEWART, CHRIS (REP-UT)
TAKAI, KYLE MARK (DEM-HI)
THORNBERRY, MAC (REP-TX)
VISCLOSKY, PETER J. (DEM-IN)
WALDEN, GREGORY P MR. (REP-OR)
WALORSKI SWIHART, JACKIE (REP-IN)
WOMACK, STEVE (REP-AR)
ZINKE, RYAN K (REP-MT)

Corporate Foundations and Giving Programs

Northrop Grumman Foundation
Contact: Sandra Evers-Manly
1840 Century Park, East   Tel: (888) 478-5478
Los Angeles, CA 90067

Public Affairs and Related Activities Personnel

At Headquarters

ASHWORTH, Margaret Sidney   Tel: (703) 280-2900
Corporate Vice President, Government Relations, Northrop Grumman Corporation
Registered Federal Lobbyist

BEDINGFIELD, Kenneth L.   Tel: (703) 280-2900
Corporate Vice President and Chief Financial Officer

CHESTON, Sheila C.   Tel: (703) 280-2900
Corporate Vice President and General Counsel

EVERS-MANLY, Sandra   Tel: (703) 280-2900
Vice President, Corporate Responsibility

FRASER, Darryl M.   Tel: (703) 280-2900
Corporate Vice President, Communications

GREGORY, Paul   Tel: (703) 280-2900
Vice President, Internal Audit
paul.gregory@ngc.com

GRIFFIN, Spencer   Tel: (703) 280-2900
Federal Lobbyist
Registered Federal Lobbyist

HARDESTY, Michael   Tel: (703) 280-2900
Corporate Vice President, Controller and Chief Accounting Officer

HEATH, Jr., John W.   Tel: (703) 280-2900
Federal Lobbyist
Registered Federal Lobbyist

HENSON, Tom   Tel: (703) 280-2900
Manager, Media Relations
thomas.henson@ngc.com

KOEHN, John Patrick   Tel: (703) 280-2900
Director, Legislative Strategy
Registered Federal Lobbyist

LINN, Meagan S.   Tel: (703) 280-2900
Registered Federal Lobbyist

MCLEMORE, Tom   Tel: (703) 280-2900
Vice President, Legislative Affairs
Registered Federal Lobbyist

MCQUEEN, Matthew   Tel: (703) 280-2900
Sector Director, Strategic and External Communications

MCSWEENEY, Denny   Tel: (703) 280-2900
Director, Investor Relations
denny.mcsweeny@ngc.com

MOVIUS, Stephen C.   Tel: (703) 280-2900
Treasurer and Vice President, Investor Relations

PALMER, James F.   Tel: (703) 280-2900
Corporate Vice President

PEPPARD, Denise   Tel: (703) 280-2900
Corporate Vice President and Chief Human Resources Officer

SCATTERGOOD, Virginia Koenig   Tel: (703) 280-2900
Director, Legislative Affairs
Registered Federal Lobbyist

WIERZBANOWSKI, Ginger   Tel: (703) 280-2900
Vice President, Business Development

WILSON, Brian   Tel: (703) 280-2900
Registered Federal Lobbyist

YOUNG, David A.   Tel: (703) 280-2900
Director, Advanced Concepts, Analysis Center

At Other Offices

ABRAMS, Benjamin   Tel: (703) 875-8400
Director, Government Affairs   Fax: (703) 875-8448
1000 Wilson Blvd., Suite 2300
Arlington, VA 22209
Registered Federal Lobbyist

DRABKIN, David Allan   Tel: (703) 875-8400
Corporate Director, Contracts   Fax: (703) 875-8448
1000 Wilson Blvd., Suite 2300
Arlington, VA 22209

ESPERNE, Jeanine   Tel: (703) 875-8400
Director, Washington Operations   Fax: (703) 875-8448
1000 Wilson Blvd., Suite 2300
Arlington, VA 22209

GULMERT, Gustav   Tel: (703) 875-8400
Corporate Director, Communications   Fax: (703) 875-8448
1000 Wilson Blvd., Suite 2300
Arlington, VA 22209
gus.gulmert@ngc.com

KALAN, Lesley   Tel: (703) 875-8400
Vice President, Legislative Affairs   Fax: (703) 875-8448
1000 Wilson Blvd., Suite 2300
Arlington, VA 22209
lesley.kalan@ngc.com
Registered Federal Lobbyist

LANGKNECHT, John M.   Tel: (703) 875-8400
Corporate Director, Navy Surface Combatant Programs   Fax: (703) 875-8448
1000 Wilson Blvd., Suite 2300
Arlington, VA 22209
Registered Federal Lobbyist

MCINGVALE, Jim   Tel: (703) 875-8400
Director, Government Affairs   Fax: (703) 875-8448
1000 Wilson Blvd., Suite 2300
Arlington, VA 22209
Jim.McIngvale@ngc.com

PERKINS, Peter   Tel: (703) 875-8400
Director, Legislative Affairs   Fax: (703) 875-8448
1000 Wilson Blvd., Suite 2300
Arlington, VA 22209
pete.perkins@ngc.com
Registered Federal Lobbyist

PIERCE, Erin   Tel: (703) 875-8400
Director, Government Relations   Fax: (703) 875-8448
1000 Wilson Blvd., Suite 2300
Arlington, VA 22209
Registered Federal Lobbyist

QUEEN, Matthew   Tel: (703) 875-8400
Vice President, Government and Industry Relations   Fax: (703) 875-8448
1000 Wilson Blvd., Suite 2300
Arlington, VA 22209

WILSON, Timothy   Tel: (703) 875-8400
Contact, Government Relations   Fax: (703) 875-8448
1000 Wilson Blvd., Suite 2300
Arlington, VA 22209
Registered Federal Lobbyist

WINCHALL, Steve   Tel: (703) 875-8400

Director, Congressional Affairs	Fax:	(703) 875-8448
1000 Wilson Blvd., Suite 2300		
Arlington, VA 22209		
Registered Federal Lobbyist		
WINCHELL, Stephen	Tel:	(703) 875-8400
Director, Congressional Affairs	Fax:	(703) 875-8448
1000 Wilson Blvd., Suite 2300		
Arlington, VA 22209		

Northrop Grumman Ship Systems

See listing on page 417 under Huntington Ingalls Industries Inc.

Northwest Natural Gas Company

See listing on page 594 under NW Natural

Northwest Physicians Network

An independent physicians association.
www.npnwa.net
Annual Revenues: $3.40 million
Employees: 35
Industry/ies: Medicine/Health Care/Mental Health

Chief Executive Officer	Tel:	(253) 627-4638
MACCORNACK, Rick		

Main Headquarters

Mailing:	1304 S Fawcett Ave.	Tel:	(253) 627-4638
	Suite 200		
	Tacoma, WA 98402		

Corporate Foundations and Giving Programs

The NPN Foundation
708 Broadway
Suite 400
Tacoma, WA 98402

NorthWestern Corporation

See listing on page 588 under NorthWestern Energy

NorthWestern Energy

NorthWestern Energy is a subsidiary of NorthWestern Corporation, distributes electricity and natural gas to more than 660,000 customers in Montana, Nebraska, and South Dakota.
www.northwesternenergy.com
Annual Revenues: $1.18 billion
Employees: 1,604
Ticker: NYSE: NWE
SIC: 4931
Industry/ies: Energy/Electricity; Utilities
Legislative Issues: CAW; ENG; ENV; TAX; UTI

Chairman of the Board	Tel:	(605) 978-2900
DRAPER, Jr., Dr. E. Linn	Fax:	(605) 353-8286

President and Chief Executive Officer	Tel:	(605) 978-2900
ROWE, Robert C.	Fax:	(605) 353-8286

Main Headquarters

Mailing:	3010 W. 69th St.	Tel:	(605) 978-2900
	Sioux Falls, SD 57108	Fax:	(605) 353-8286
		TF:	(800) 245-6977

Political Action Committees

Northwestern Energy Employees PAC
FEC ID: C00187799
Contact: Mike Williams

3010 W. 69th St.	Tel:	(605) 978-2900
Sioux Falls, SD 57108	Fax:	(605) 353-8286

Corporate Foundations and Giving Programs

NorthWestern Energy Charitable Giving Program

3010 W. 69th St.	Tel:	(605) 978-2900
Sioux Falls, SD 57108	Fax:	(605) 353-8286

Public Affairs and Related Activities Personnel

At Headquarters

BIRD, Brian B.	Tel:	(605) 978-2900
Vice President, Chief Financial Officer and Treasurer	Fax:	(605) 353-8286
BONRUD, Pamela A.	Tel:	(605) 978-2900
Director, Government & Regulatory Affairs	Fax:	(605) 353-8286
pam.bonrud@northwestern.com		
CORCORAN, Patrick R.	Tel:	(605) 978-2900
Vice President, Government and Regulatory Affairs	Fax:	(605) 353-8286
DRISCOLL, Jay	Tel:	(605) 978-2900
Federal Lobbyist	Fax:	(605) 353-8286
Registered Federal Lobbyist		
FORBES, Jeff	Tel:	(605) 978-2900
Federal Lobbyist	Fax:	(605) 353-8286
Registered Federal Lobbyist		
GLANZER, Thomas	Tel:	(605) 978-2900

Media Contact	Fax:	(605) 353-8286
tom.glanzer@northwestern.com		
GRAHAME, Heather H.	Tel:	(605) 978-2900
Vice President and General Counsel	Fax:	(605) 353-8286
heather.grahame@northwestern.com		
KLIEWER, Kendall G.	Tel:	(605) 978-2900
Vice President and Controller	Fax:	(605) 353-8286
NIEMAN, Michael L.	Tel:	(605) 978-2900
Chief Audit and Compliance Officer	Fax:	(605) 353-8286
OLSON, Timothy P.	Tel:	(605) 978-2900
Corporate Secretary	Fax:	(605) 353-8286
tim.olson@northwestern.co		
RAPKOCH, APR, Claudia	Tel:	(605) 978-2900
Director, Corporate Communications	Fax:	(605) 353-8286
claudia.rapkoch@northwestern.com		
SCHROEPPEL, Bobbi L.	Tel:	(605) 978-2900
Vice President, Customer Care, Communications and Human Resources	Fax:	(605) 353-8286
bobbi.schroeppel@northwestern.com		
WELCH, Ryan	Tel:	(605) 978-2900
Federal Lobbyist	Fax:	(605) 353-8286
Registered Federal Lobbyist		
WILLIAMS, Zachary	Tel:	(605) 978-2900
Federal Lobbyist	Fax:	(605) 353-8286
zachary.edstrom@nrgenergy.com		
Registered Federal Lobbyist		
WILLIAMS, Mike	Tel:	(605) 226-4174
Area Manager and PAC Treasurer	Fax:	(605) 353-8286
mike.williams@northwestern.com		

Northwestern Mutual Life Insurance Company

A life insurance and financial services company.
www.northwesternmutual.com
Annual Revenues: $17.0 B
Employees: 5,000
Industry/ies: Insurance Industry
Legislative Issues: BAN; CSP; FIN; INS; LBR; RET; TAX

Chairman and Chief Executive Officer	Tel:	(414) 271-1444
SCHLIFSKE, John E.	Fax:	(414) 665-5756

Main Headquarters

Mailing:	720 E. Wisconsin Ave.	Tel:	(414) 271-1444
	Milwaukee, WI 53202	Fax:	(414) 665-5756

Washington Office

Mailing:	101 Constitution Ave. NW
	Suite 800
	Washington, DC 20001

Political Action Committees

Northwestern Mutual Life Insurance Company Federal PAC
FEC ID: C00197095
Contact: Michelle A. Hinze
720 E. Wisconsin Ave.
Milwaukee, WI 53202

Contributions to Candidates: $401,550 (2015-2016)
Democrats: $119,000; Republicans: $279,550; Other: $3,000

Principal Recipients

SENATE
SCOTT, TIMOTHY E (REP-SC)

HOUSE
KIND, RONALD JAMES (DEM-WI)
KINZINGER, ADAM (REP-IL)
MOORE, GWEN S (DEM-WI)
ROSKAM, PETER (REP-IL)
RYAN, PAUL D. (REP-WI)
TIBERI, PATRICK J. (REP-OH)

Corporate Foundations and Giving Programs

Northwestern Mutual Foundation
Contact: Jennifer Ryan
720 E. Wisconsin Ave.
Milwaukee, WI 53202

Public Affairs and Related Activities Personnel

At Headquarters

BATES, Douglas P.	Tel:	(414) 271-1444
Vice President, Federal Relations	Fax:	(414) 665-5756
CARTER, Michael G.	Tel:	(414) 271-1444
Executive Vice President and Chief Financial Officer	Fax:	(414) 665-5756
EISENHART, Joann M.	Tel:	(414) 271-1444
Senior Vice President, Human Resources	Fax:	(414) 665-5756
GOODE, Kimberley	Tel:	(414) 271-1444
Vice President, Communications and Corporate Affairs	Fax:	(414) 665-5756

HINZE, Michelle A.	Tel:	(414) 271-1444
PAC Treasurer	Fax:	(414) 665-5756
JOELSON, Ronald P.	Tel:	(414) 271-1444
Executive Vice President and Chief Investment Officer	Fax:	(414) 665-5756
MANISTA, Raymond J.	Tel:	(414) 271-1444
Senior Vice President, General Counsel and Secretary	Fax:	(414) 665-5756
OBERLAND, Gregory C.	Tel:	(414) 271-1444
President	Fax:	(414) 665-5756
RADKE, Steven M.	Tel:	(414) 665-1891
Vice President, Government Relations	Fax:	(414) 665-5756
steveradke@northwesternmutual.com		
Registered Federal Lobbyist		
RIMAI, Marcia	Tel:	(414) 271-1444
Executive Vice President, Chief Administrative Officer and	Fax:	(414) 665-5756
Chief Compliance Officer		
RODENHAUS, Bethany M.	Tel:	(414) 271-1444
Vice President, Corporate Planning	Fax:	(414) 665-5756
ROSENTHAL, Thomas	Tel:	(414) 271-1444
Program Officer	Fax:	(414) 665-5756
RYAN, Jennifer	Tel:	(414) 665-3143
Director of Strategic Communications–Philanthropy	Fax:	(414) 665-5756
jenniferryan@northwesternmutual.com		
SCHLUTER, Kathleen H.	Tel:	(414) 271-1444
Federal Lobbyist	Fax:	(414) 665-5756
Registered Federal Lobbyist		
TOWELL, Jean	Tel:	(800) 323-7033
Assistant Director, Media Relations	Fax:	(414) 665-5756
Jeantowell@northwesternmutual.com		
WATSON, Alison F.	Tel:	(414) 271-1444
Federal Lobbyist	Fax:	(414) 665-5756
Registered Federal Lobbyist		
YOUNGMAN, Michael L.	Tel:	(414) 665-1891
Vice President, Government Relations	Fax:	(414) 665-5756
Registered Federal Lobbyist		

Nova Chemicals, Inc.

Nova Chemicals, Inc., based in Coraopolis City, is the U.S. subsidiary of NOVA Chemicals Corporation, headquartered in Calgary, Canada. Manufacturer of plastics and chemicals.
www.novachem.com
Annual Revenues: $5.15 billion
Employees: 3,300
SIC: 2821; 2899
NAICS: 325211; 325998
Industry/ies: Chemicals & Chemical Industry; Plastics Industry

Chairman of the Board	Tel:	(412) 490-4000
AL MAZROUEI, Suhail	Fax:	(412) 490-4155
President, Chief Executive Officer and Chief Financial Officer	Tel:	(412) 490-4000
KARRAN, Todd D.	Fax:	(412) 490-4155

Main Headquarters
Mailing:	U.S. Commercial Center	Tel:	(412) 490-4000
	1555 Coraopolis Heights Rd.	Fax:	(412) 490-4155
	Moon Township, PA 15108		

Political Action Committees
Nova Chemicals Inc and Nova Chemicals Srvcs Inc Committee for Political Action and Engagement
FEC ID: C00335000
Contact: Al Alayon
1555 Corapolis Heights Rd.
Moon Township, PA 15108

   Contributions to Candidates: $1,000 (2015-2016)
   Republicans: $1,000

Corporate Foundations and Giving Programs
NOVA Chemicals Contributions Program		
1555 Coraopolis Heights Rd.	Tel:	(412) 490-4000
Moon Township, PA 15108		

Public Affairs and Related Activities Personnel

At Headquarters
ALAYON, Al	Tel:	(412) 490-4000
Vice President and Business Controller, Finance &	Fax:	(412) 490-4155
Administration and PAC Treasurer		
GREENE, Bill	Tel:	(412) 490-4000
Senior Vice President, Operations	Fax:	(412) 490-4155
MARKOWITZ, Pace	Tel:	(412) 490-4000
Director, Communications	Fax:	(412) 490-4155
pace.markowitz@novachem.com		
SIMPSON, Tracey	Tel:	(412) 490-4000
Leader, External Financial Reporting and Contact, Investor	Fax:	(412) 490-4155
relations		
Tracey.Simpson@novachem.com		

Novartis Corporation

CIBA-GEIGY and Sandoz merged to form Novartis, a pharmaceutical company. Parent company of Chiron Corporation. (see separate listing). Novartis Corporation, based in New York City, is the U.S. subsidiary of Novartis AG, headquartered in Basel, Switzerland. Life sciences company with businesses in pharmaceuticals, nutrition and consumer health.
www.us.novartis.com
Employees: 30,000
Ticker: NYSE: NVS
SIC: 2834
Industry/ies: Agriculture/Agronomy; Chemicals & Chemical Industry; Construction/Construction Materials; Environment And Conservation; Nutrition; Pharmaceutical Industry; Science; Scientific Research
Legislative Issues: BUD; CPT; HCR; MED; MMM; PHA; TAX; TRD

Main Headquarters
| Mailing: | P.O. Box 66556 | |
| | St. Louis, MO 63166-6556 | |

Washington Office
Mailing:	701 Pennsylvania Ave. NW	Tel:	(202) 638-7429
	Suite 725	Fax:	(202) 628-4763
	Washington, DC 20004		

Political Action Committees
Novartis Corporation PAC		
FEC ID: C00033969		
Contact: Shawn O'Neail		
701 Pennsylvania Ave. NW	Tel:	(202) 638-7429
Suite 725	Fax:	(202) 628-4763
Washington, DC 20004		

   Contributions to Candidates: $208,750 (2015-2016)
   Democrats: $104,000; Republicans: $104,750

Corporate Foundations and Giving Programs
Novartis US Foundation
608 Fifth Ave.
New York City, NY 10020

Public Affairs and Related Activities Personnel

At Headquarters
CETANI, Cynthia
Vice President and Chief Compliance Officer
KENDRIS, Thomas
Vice President and General Counsel
PARLAVECCHIO, Caryn
Vice President and Head, Human Resources
RIGBY, Kevin T.
Vice President, Public Affairs
TOMBESI, Paolo
Vice President, Chief Financial and Administrative Officer

At Washington Office
CASSERLY, Daniel P.	Tel:	(202) 638-7429
Vice President & Head, Federal Government Affairs	Fax:	(202) 628-9108
dan.casserly@group.novartis.com		
Registered Federal Lobbyist		
COEN, Mary	Tel:	(202) 638-7429
Federal Lobbyist	Fax:	(202) 628-9108
FARBER, Leo	Tel:	(202) 638-7429
Executive Director, Federal Government Affairs	Fax:	(202) 628-4763
Registered Federal Lobbyist		
HALLER, Sarah E.	Tel:	(202) 638-7429
Executive Director, International and Public Affairs	Fax:	(202) 628-9108
tracy.haller@group.novartis.com		
Registered Federal Lobbyist		
LUCKRITZ, Brenda	Tel:	(202) 638-7429
Vice President, Federal Government Affairs	Fax:	(202) 628-9108
O'NEAIL, Shawn	Tel:	(202) 638-7429
PAC Contact	Fax:	(202) 628-4763
Registered Federal Lobbyist		
PHIPPS, Candie	Tel:	(202) 638-7429
Registered Federal Lobbyist	Fax:	(202) 628-4763
SOLON, Katherine	Tel:	(202) 638-7429
Federal Lobbyist	Fax:	(202) 628-9108
SUSSMAN, Wendy P.	Tel:	(202) 638-7429
Registered Federal Lobbyist	Fax:	(202) 628-4763
VAN PELT, Jason	Tel:	(202) 638-7429
Executive Director	Fax:	(202) 628-4763
Registered Federal Lobbyist		

At Other Offices
BLANCHARD, Brenda	Tel:	(212) 307-1122
Vice President, Public Affairs	Fax:	(212) 246-0185
230 Park Ave., 21st Floor		
New York City, NY 10169		
FRABLE, Anna	Tel:	(862) 778-5388

Vice President, Public Relations	Fax:	(732) 673-5262
230 Park Ave., 21st Floor		
New York City, NY 10169		
JARVIS, Richard	Tel:	(212) 307-1122
Head, Corporate Affairs	Fax:	(212) 246-0185
230 Park Ave., 21st Floor		
New York City, NY 10169		
ZAUSNER, Meryl	Tel:	(212) 307-1122
Executive Vice President and Chief Financial Officer	Fax:	(212) 246-0185
230 Park Ave., 21st Floor		
New York City, NY 10169		

Novelis, Inc.

An aluminum manufacturing and recycling company.
www.novelis.com/en-us
SIC: 3350
Industry/ies: Metals

Chairman of the Board	Tel:	(404) 760-4000
BIRLA, Kumar Mangalam	Fax:	(404) 814-4219
Interim President, Chief Executive Officer, Senior Vice President	Tel:	(404) 760-4000
and Chief Financial Officer	Fax:	(404) 814-4219
FISHER, Steve		
President and Chief Executive officer	Tel:	(404) 760-4000
MARTENS, Philip	Fax:	(404) 814-4219

Main Headquarters

Mailing:	3560 Lenox Rd.	Tel:	(404) 760-4000
	Suite 2000	Fax:	(404) 814-4219
	Atlanta, GA 30326		

Corporate Foundations and Giving Programs

Novelis, Inc. Contributions Program
3560 Lenox Rd.   Tel: (404) 760-4000
Suite 2000
Atlanta, GA 30326

Public Affairs and Related Activities Personnel

At Headquarters

BELBIN, Charles	Tel:	(404) 760-4120
Director, Corporate Communications	Fax:	(404) 814-4219
charles.belbin@novelis.com		
BELL, Fiona	Tel:	(404) 760-6585
Senior Manager, Communications & Government Affairs,	Fax:	(404) 814-4219
Novelis North America		
HIRSCH, Neil	Tel:	(404) 760-4000
Manager, External Communications	Fax:	(404) 814-4219
JOYCE, Leslie	Tel:	(404) 760-4000
Senior Vice President and Chief People Officer	Fax:	(404) 814-4219
PARRETTE, Les	Tel:	(404) 760-4000
Senior Vice President, General Counsel and Compliance	Fax:	(404) 814-4219
Officer		

Novell, Inc.

A manufacturer of computer software and hardware. Novell, Inc., is now part of Micro Focus.
www.novell.com
Annual Revenues: $811.87 million
Employees: 3,600
Ticker: NASDAQ: NOVL
SIC: 7372
Industry/ies: Computer/Technology

President and General Manager	Tel:	(801) 861-4272
OWENS, Kathleen	Fax:	(781) 464-8100

Main Headquarters

Mailing:	1800 S. Novell Pl.	Tel:	(801) 861-4272
	Provo, UT 84606	Fax:	(781) 464-8100

Washington Office

Mailing:	8609 Westwood Center Dr.	Tel:	(703) 663-5500
	Vienna, VA 22182	Fax:	(703) 876-5059

Public Affairs and Related Activities Personnel

At Headquarters

FITZGERALD, Bret	Tel:	(801) 861-5635
Media Contact	Fax:	(781) 464-8100
bfitzgerald@novell.com		
RUSSELL, Dana	Tel:	(801) 861-4272
Senior Vice President and Chief Financial Officer	Fax:	(781) 464-8100
TATE, Katherine	Tel:	(801) 861-4272
Vice President, Global Sales Operations	Fax:	(781) 464-8100
VARNESS, Eric	Tel:	(801) 861-4272
Vice President, Product Management and Marketing	Fax:	(781) 464-8100

Novo Nordisk, Inc.

A diabetes and healthcare manufacturing company.

www.novonordisk-us.com
Annual Revenues: $14.06 billion
Employees: 39,062
Ticker: NYSE: NVO
SIC: 2834
Industry/ies: Pharmaceutical Industry
Legislative Issues: BUD; CPT; DEF; HCR; MMM; PHA; TAX; TRD

President	Tel:	(609) 987-5800
HOILAND, Jesper		

Main Headquarters

Mailing:	800 Scudders Mill Rd.	Tel:	(609) 987-5800
	Plainsboro, NJ 08536	TF:	(800) 727-6500

Washington Office

Mailing:	500 New Jersey Ave. NW	Tel:	(202) 626-4520
	Suite 350	Fax:	(202) 347-9350
	Washington, DC 20001		

Political Action Committees

Novo Nordisk Inc. PAC
FEC ID: C00424838
Contact: Christopher Porter

1155 F St. NW	Tel:	(202) 626-4520
Suite 1150	Fax:	(202) 347-9350
Washington, DC 20004		

Contributions to Candidates: $313,879 (2015-2016)
Democrats: $116,380; Republicans: $196,499; Other: $1,000

Principal Recipients

HOUSE

MCCARTHY, KEVIN (REP-CA)

Corporate Foundations and Giving Programs

Novo Nordisk Foundation
800 Scudders Mill Rd.
Plainsboro, NJ 08536

Public Affairs and Related Activities Personnel

At Headquarters

BIGLEY, Frank	Tel:	(609) 987-5800
Chief Compliance Officer and Vice President, Compliance		
FORNECKER, Phil	Tel:	(609) 987-5800
Corporate Vice President, Strategic Business Operations		
GREEN, Lars	Tel:	(609) 987-5800
Senior Vice President, Finance and Operations		
LAUSTEN, Mads Veggerby	Tel:	(609) 987-5800
Vice President, Strategic Operations		
mlau@novonordisk.com		
LEE, Camille	Tel:	(609) 987-5800
Senior Vice President, Diabetes Marketing		
LINDEGAARD, Jannick	Tel:	(609) 786-4575
Senior Manager, Head of PS Business Plan & Projects - PS		
Business Development		
jlis@novonordisk.com		
OLTMANS, Curt	Tel:	(609) 987-5800
Corporate Vice President and General Counsel		
POWELL, Michelle	Tel:	(609) 786-8598
Manager, Media Relations		
mcpl@novonordisk.com		
SCANLAN, Jacqueline	Tel:	(609) 987-5800
Corporate Vice President, Human Resources		

At Washington Office

BROOKS, Tricia	Tel:	(202) 626-4520
Federal Lobbyist	Fax:	(202) 347-9350
TIIB@novonordisk.com		
Registered Federal Lobbyist		
NUNN, Shaylah	Tel:	(202) 626-4520
Manager, Government Affairs	Fax:	(202) 347-9350
shnu@novonordisk.com		
SEMENIUK, Lauren	Tel:	(202) 626-4520
Manager, Government Affairs	Fax:	(202) 347-9350
Registered Federal Lobbyist		

At Other Offices

BRANTON, Brian E.	Tel:	(202) 626-4520
Federal Lobbyist		
920 Massachusetts Ave. NW, Suite 500		
Washington, DC 20001		
Registered Federal Lobbyist		
MAKKI, Amanda	Tel:	(202) 626-4520
Federal Lobbyist		
920 Massachusetts Ave. NW, Suite 500		
Washington, DC 20001		
Registered Federal Lobbyist		
NORDSTROM, Sarah	Tel:	(202) 626-4520

Federal Lobbyist
920 Massachusetts Ave. NW, Suite 500
Washington, DC 20001
Registered Federal Lobbyist

NOYES, Steve	Tel:	(202) 626-4520
920 Massachusetts Ave. NW, Suite 500		
Washington, DC 20001		
PORTER, Christopher	Tel:	(202) 626-4520
Chief Government Affairs Officer		
920 Massachusetts Ave. NW, Suite 500		
Washington, DC 20001		
cpor@novonordisk.com		
THENIEL, Amy	Tel:	(202) 626-4520
Contact, Government Relations		
920 Massachusetts Ave. NW, Suite 500		
Washington, DC 20001		

Novologix

A health care benefits management company.
www.novologix.net
Employees: 400
Industry/ies: Management; Medicine/Health Care/Mental Health

Chief Executive Officer   Tel: (952) 826-2500
MCLEAN, David J.

Main Headquarters
Mailing: 10400 Viking Dr.   Tel: (952) 826-2500
             Suite 200
             Eden Prairie, MN 55344

Public Affairs and Related Activities Personnel

At Headquarters

MEAD, Sandy	Tel:	(952) 826-2500
Vice President, Finance		
UDINE, Glen	Tel:	(952) 826-2500
Executive Vice President, Sales and Account Management		

Novomer, Inc.

A materials company pioneering a family of high-performance, biodegradable plastics, polymers and other chemicals from renewable substances.
www.novomer.com
Employees: 2
Industry/ies: Plastics Industry

Chairman of the Board   Tel: (781) 419-9860
EISENHUT, Tony   Fax: (781) 672-2525

Chief Executive Officer   Tel: (781) 419-9860
MAHONEY, Jim   Fax: (781) 672-2525

Main Headquarters
Mailing: 200 W. St., Floor Four E Tel: (781) 419-9860
             Waltham, MA 02451   Fax: (781) 672-2525

Public Affairs and Related Activities Personnel

At Headquarters

KOSH, Kevin   Tel: (781) 672-3111
Contact, Media Relations   Fax: (781) 672-2525
kkosh@chenpr.com

Novozymes North America Inc.

A biotech company with a strong focus on enzyme production.
www.novozymes.com
Employees: 1,000
SIC: 2841; 2869
NAICS: 325199; 325611
Industry/ies: Energy/Electricity; Environment And Conservation
Legislative Issues: CHM; ENG; FOO

Chairman of the Board   Tel: (919) 494-3000
GURTLER, Henrik   Fax: (919) 494-3450

President and Chief Executive Officer Tel: (919) 494-3000
NIELSEN, Peder Holk   Fax: (919) 494-3450

Main Headquarters
Mailing: 77 Perry Chapel Church Rd. Tel: (919) 494-3000
             P.O. Box 576   Fax: (919) 494-3450
             Franklinton, NC 27525-9677

Public Affairs and Related Activities Personnel

At Headquarters

BENDER, Chris   Tel: (919) 494-3944
Head, Public Affairs and Communications Fax: (919) 494-3450
csbd@novozymes.com
Registered Federal Lobbyist

DOMHOFF, Thomas Steenbech   Tel: (919) 494-3270
Head, Investor Relations   Fax: (919) 494-3450
tsbm@novozymes.com

DAVIS, Amy	Tel:	(919) 494-3000
Manager, Government Relations	Fax:	(919) 494-3450
Registered Federal Lobbyist		
DONNELLY, Paige	Tel:	(919) 494-3209
Manager, Communications	Fax:	(919) 494-3450
pagd@novoenzymes.com		
EHLERS, Amy	Tel:	(919) 949-3000
Manager, Government Relations	Fax:	(919) 494-3450
Registered Federal Lobbyist		
KELLAR, Robert	Tel:	(919) 494-3000
Federal Lobbyist	Fax:	(919) 494-3450
Registered Federal Lobbyist		
LOFT, Benny Dalgaard	Tel:	(919) 494-3000
Executive Vice President and Chief Financial Officer,	Fax:	(919) 494-3450
Corporate Functions		
MONROE, Adam	Tel:	(919) 494-3000
President	Fax:	(919) 494-3450
Registered Federal Lobbyist		
SCREWS, Jr., Garrett	Tel:	(919) 494-3000
Governmental Relations Manager	Fax:	(919) 494-3450
gasc@novozymes.com		
Registered Federal Lobbyist		
VIDEBÆK, Thomas	Tel:	(919) 494-3000
Executive Vice President, Business Development	Fax:	(919) 494-3450

NRG Energy, Inc.

Power producer and provider. Formerly part of Xcel Energy, Inc. Merged with GenOn in 2012.
www.nrgenergy.com
Annual Revenues: $16.21 billion
Employees: 9,806
Ticker: NYSE: NRG
SIC: 4911
Industry/ies: Energy/Electricity
Legislative Issues: BUD; ENG; ENV; TAX; UTI

Chairman of the Board   Tel: (609) 524-4500
COSGROVE, Howard E.   Fax: (609) 524-4501

President and Chief Executive Officer Tel: (609) 524-4500
CRANE, David W.   Fax: (609) 524-4501

Main Headquarters
Mailing: 211 Carnegie Center   Tel: (609) 524-4500
             Princeton, NJ 08540-6213 Fax: (609) 524-4501

Washington Office
Mailing: 601 13th St. NW
             Washington, DC 20004

Political Action Committees
NRG Energy Inc. PAC
FEC ID: C00366559
Contact: Albert Scerbo
211 Carnegie Center
Princeton, NJ 08540

   Contributions to Candidates: $62,900 (2015-2016)
   Democrats: $27,700; Republicans: $35,200

Corporate Foundations and Giving Programs
NRG Global Giving
211 Carnegie Center
Princeton, NJ 08540

Public Affairs and Related Activities Personnel

At Headquarters

ANDREWS , Kirkland	Tel:	(609) 524-4500
Executive Vice President and Chief Financial Officer	Fax:	(609) 524-4501
BALIFF, Jonathan	Tel:	(609) 524-4500
Executive Vice President, Strategy	Fax:	(609) 524-4501
BLUNTZER, Rick	Tel:	(609) 524-4500
Senior Vice President, Regulatory and Government Affairs	Fax:	(609) 524-4501
CLEEVE, Karen	Tel:	(609) 524-4608
Vice President, Communications	Fax:	(609) 524-4501
karen.cleeve@nrgenergy.com		
CORNELI, Steve	Tel:	(609) 524-4500
Senior Vice President, Sustainabilty, Policy and Strategy	Fax:	(609) 524-4501
steve.corneli@nrgenergy.com		
DICKENSON, Sicily	Tel:	(609) 524-4500
Senior Vice President and Chief Marketing Officer	Fax:	(609) 524-4501
FISHER, Scott	Tel:	(609) 524-4500
Director, Alternative Energy Services	Fax:	(609) 524-4501
scott.fisher@nrgenergy.com		
Registered Federal Lobbyist		
HILL , David	Tel:	(609) 524-4500
Executive Vice President & General Counsel	Fax:	(609) 524-4501
OVITT, Phil	Tel:	(609) 524-4500

Manager, Electric Vehicle (EV) Business Development and Policy
phil.ovitt@nrgenergy.com
Fax: (609) 524-4501

PLOTKIN, Chad | Tel: (609) 524-4526
Vice President, Investor Relations | Fax: (609) 524-4501
Investor.Relations@nrgenergy.com

SCERBO, Albert | Tel: (609) 524-4500
Director, Financial Planning | Fax: (609) 524-4501
Albert.Scerbo@nrgenergy.com

WALLACE, Jennifer | Tel: (609) 524-4500
Senior Vice President, Human Resources | Fax: (609) 524-4501

At Washington Office

BANDERA, Derek | Tel: (202) 585-3800
Registered Federal Lobbyist

At Other Offices

BARBER, Dennis | Tel: (832) 357-3042
Vice President, Investor Relations
1201 Fannin
Houston, TX 77002
dennis.barber@genon.com

HOLDEN, III, J. William | Tel: (832) 357-3000
Executive Vice President and Chief Financial Officer
1201 Fannin
Houston, TX 77002

SOTOS, Christopher | Tel: (832) 357-3000
Senior Vice President, Strategy and Mergers and Acquisitions
1201 Fannin
Houston, TX 77002

WHITTINGTON, Lloyd | Tel: (832) 357-3000
PAC Treasurer
1201 Fannin
Houston, TX 77002

NSK Corporation

NSK Corporation markets, designs and manufactures anti-friction bearings, precision machinery and parts, mechatronics and automotive products.
www.nskamericas.com
SIC: 3562
NAICS: 332991
Industry/ies: Machinery/Equipment

Chairman of the Board, President and Chief Executive Officer | Tel: (734) 913-7500
OTSUKA , Norio | Fax: (734) 913-7426

Main Headquarters
Mailing: 4200 Goss Rd. | Tel: (734) 913-7500
Ann Arbor, MI 48105 | Fax: (734) 913-7426
| TF: (888) 446-5675

Corporate Foundations and Giving Programs

NSK Contributions Program
4200 Goss Rd.
Ann Arbor, MI 48105

Public Affairs and Related Activities Personnel

At Headquarters

LINDSAY, Brian | Tel: (734) 913-7500
President and Chief Operating Officer | Fax: (734) 913-7511

NTT America Inc.

The wholly-owned U.S. subsidiary of NTT Communications, the international and long distance service arm of Nippon Telegraph and Telephone (Tokyo, Japan).
www.us.ntt.com
Annual Revenues: $23.90 million
Employees: 500
Industry/ies: Communications; Telecommunications/Internet/Cable

President and Chief Executive Officer | Tel: (212) 661-0810
GOMI, Kazuhiro | Fax: (212) 661-1078

Main Headquarters
Mailing: 757 Third Ave. | Tel: (212) 661-0810
14th Floor
New York, NY 10017

Public Affairs and Related Activities Personnel

At Other Offices

CARLSON, Christine | Tel: (804) 612-5394
Contact, Communications
1901 E. Franklin St., Suite 111
Richmond, VA 23223
ccarlson@wireside.com

DAVIS, Christopher | Tel: (212) 661-0810
Senior Director, Corporate Marketing Communications | Fax: (212) 661-1078
101 Park Ave., 41st Floor
New York City, NY 10178

c.davis@ntta.com

NTT Data Corporation

IT services and solutions. Acquired Keane Inc. in 2011.
americas.nttdata.com
Annual Revenues: $13 billion
Employees: 75,000
Ticker: NYSE: KEA
SIC: 7371
Industry/ies: Computer/Technology
Legislative Issues: ENG; HOM

Chairman of the Board | Tel: (617) 241-9200
SUBRAMANIAN, Mani | Fax: (617) 241-9507

Chief Executive Officer | Tel: (617) 241-9200
MCCAIN, John | Fax: (617) 241-9507

Main Headquarters
Mailing: 100 City Sq. | Tel: (617) 241-9200
Boston, MA 02129 | Fax: (617) 241-9507
| TF: (877) 885-3263

Corporate Foundations and Giving Programs

Keane, Inc. Contributions Program
Contact: Tara Jantzen
100 City Sq. | Tel: (312) 305-1771
Boston, MA 02129 | Fax: (617) 241-9507

Public Affairs and Related Activities Personnel

At Headquarters

COOKE, Margo | Tel: (617) 241-9200
Senior Director, Industry Analyst Relations | Fax: (617) 241-9507
margo.cooke@keane.com

CROXVILLE, David | Tel: (617) 241-9200
Executive Vice President and Chief Financial Officer | Fax: (617) 241-9507

DICK, John M. | Tel: (617) 241-9200
Executive Vice President, General Counsel and Corporate Development | Fax: (617) 241-9507

MIYAJIMA, Koji | Tel: (617) 241-9200
Executive Vice President, Strategy | Fax: (617) 241-9507

MOUCHAWAR, Marv | Tel: (617) 241-9200
President | Fax: (617) 241-9507

RASMUSSEN , Robb | Tel: (617) 241-9200
Chief Operating Officer | Fax: (617) 241-9507

STEINHEISER, Sylvia | Tel: (617) 241-9200
Executive Vice President, Corporate Development | Fax: (617) 241-9507

THOMAS, Mike | Tel: (617) 241-9200
Executive Vice President, Sales, Marketing, and Client Management | Fax: (617) 241-9507

WILLIAMS, Dean | Tel: (617) 241-9200
Executive Vice President, Human Resources | Fax: (617) 241-9507

Nu Skin International Inc.

A direct selling company that markets premium-quality personal care products under the Nu Skin brand, science-based nutritional supplements under the Pharmanex brand, and technology-based products and services under the Big Planet Brand.
www.nuskin.com
Annual Revenues: $2.18 billion
Employees: 26,800
Ticker: NYSE: NUS
SIC: 5122
Industry/ies: Advertising And Marketing; Personal Care/Hygiene
Legislative Issues: CSP; TRD

Chairman of the Board | Tel: (801) 345-1000
LUND, Steven J. | Fax: (801) 345-2199

President and Chief Executive Officer | Tel: (801) 345-1000
HUNT, Truman | Fax: (800) 487-8000

Main Headquarters
Mailing: 75 W. Center | Tel: (801) 345-1000
Provo, UT 84601 | Fax: (801) 345-2199
| TF: (800) 487-1000

Corporate Foundations and Giving Programs

Nu Skin Force for Good Foundation
Contact: Kara Schneck
One Nu Skin Plaza
75 W. Center St.
Provo, UT 84601

Public Affairs and Related Activities Personnel

At Headquarters

CHARD, Daniel R. | Tel: (801) 345-1000
President, Global Sales and Operations | Fax: (801) 345-2199

DORNY, D. Matthew | Tel: (801) 345-1000
Vice President, General Counsel and Secretary | Fax: (800) 487-8000

FULLER, Kevin
Vice President, Global Product Marketing
Tel: (801) 345-1000
Fax: (801) 345-2199

POND, Scott
Director, Investor Relations
spond@nuskin.com
Tel: (801) 345-2657
Fax: (800) 487-8000

RONEY, Blake M.
Founder
Tel: (801) 345-1000
Fax: (800) 487-8000

SCHNECK, Kara
Senior Director, Corporate Communications
kschneck@nuskin.com
Tel: (801) 345-2116
Fax: (800) 487-8000

WOOD, Ritch N.
Chief Financial Officer
Tel: (801) 345-1000
Fax: (800) 487-8000

Nucor Corporation

A steel product manufacturer. Acquired the assets of Birmingham Steel Corp. in December, 2002.
www.nucor.com
Annual Revenues: $15.76 billion
Employees: 23,700
Ticker: NYSE: NUE
SIC: 3312
Industry/ies: Metals
Legislative Issues: BUD; ENG; ENV; LBR; MAN; TAX; TRA; TRD

Chairman, President and Chief Executive Officer
FERRIOLA, John J.
Tel: (704) 366-7000
Fax: (704) 362-4208

Main Headquarters
Mailing: 1915 Rexford Rd.
Charlotte, NC 28211
Tel: (704) 366-7000
Fax: (704) 362-4208

Washington Office
Mailing: 801 17th St. NW
Suite 201
Washington, DC 20006
Tel: (202) 719-7215

Political Action Committees
Nucor Corporation PAC
FEC ID: C00379628
Contact: Rae A. Eagle
1915 Rexford Rd.
Charlotte, NC 28211

Contributions to Candidates: $229,500 (2015-2016)
Democrats: $59,500; Republicans: $170,000

Principal Recipients

SENATE
BURR, RICHARD (REP-NC)

Corporate Foundations and Giving Programs
Nucor Foundation
1915 Rexford Rd.
Charlotte, NC 28211
Tel: (704) 366-7000
Fax: (704) 362-4208

Public Affairs and Related Activities Personnel

At Headquarters

EAGLE, Rae A.
PAC Treasurer
reagle@Nucor.com
Tel: (704) 366-7000
Fax: (704) 362-4208

FRIAS, James D.
Chief Financial Officer, Treasurer and Executive Vice President
jfrias@nucor.com
Tel: (704) 366-7000
Fax: (704) 362-4208

MCFADDEN, Patrick
Federal Lobbyist
Registered Federal Lobbyist
Tel: (704) 366-7000
Fax: (704) 362-4208

At Washington Office

BRADNER, Eileen
Senior Director & Counsel, Federal Government Affairs
eileen.bradner@nucor.com
Registered Federal Lobbyist
Tel: (202) 719-7215

DIGGINS, Jennifer
Director, Public Affairs
Jennifer.Diggins@nucor.com
Registered Federal Lobbyist
Tel: (202) 719-7215

EHRICH, Anna
Director, Federal Government Affairs
marion@vt.edu
Registered Federal Lobbyist
Tel: (202) 719-7215

NuScale Power, Inc.

NuScale Power develops a modular, scalable nuclear power plant.
www.nuscalepower.com
Employees: 3
Industry/ies: Energy/Electricity

Chairman and Chief Executive Officer
HOPKINS, John L.
Tel: (503) 715-2222
Fax: (503) 746-6041

Main Headquarters
Mailing: 6650 S.W. Redwood Ln.
Suite 210
Portland, OR 97224
Tel: (503) 715-2222
Fax: (503) 746-6041

Public Affairs and Related Activities Personnel

At Headquarters

ATKINSON, Dale
Chief Operating Officer and Chief Nuclear Officer
Tel: (503) 715-2222
Fax: (503) 746-6041

BERGMAN, Tom
Vice President, Regulatory Affairs
Tel: (503) 715-2222
Fax: (503) 746-6041

BRITSCH, Carl
Vice President, Human Resources
Tel: (503) 715-2222
Fax: (503) 746-6041

EUSTERMANN, John
General Counsel
Tel: (503) 715-2222
Fax: (503) 746-6041

MCGOUGH, Michael S.
Chief Commercial Officer
Tel: (503) 715-2222
Fax: (503) 746-6041

MELLOTT, James
Contact, Media Relations
jmellott@nuscalepower.com
Tel: (503) 715-2233
Fax: (503) 746-6041

SURINA, John
Chief Financial Officer
jsurina@nuscalepower.com
Tel: (541) 207-3931
Fax: (503) 746-6041

NuVox Communications

A telecommunications company.
www.nuvox.com
Annual Revenues: $88.30 million
Employees: 1,800
Industry/ies: Communications; Telecommunications/Internet/Cable

Main Headquarters
Mailing: Two N. Main St.
Greenville, SC 29601
Tel: (864) 672-5000
Fax: (864) 672-5105
TF: (800) 672-1450

Public Affairs and Related Activities Personnel

At Headquarters

DELONG, Katie
Media Relations Contact
kdelong@nuvox.com
Tel: (864) 331-8059
Fax: (864) 672-5105

HITE, Susanne
Director, Marketing Communications
hite@nuvox.com
Tel: (864) 672-5097
Fax: (864) 672-5105

NV Energy, Inc.

An electric, gas and water utility serving Nevada's energy needs. Subsidiaries include Nevada Power Co. and Sierra Pacific Power Co. NV Energy was acquired by Berkshire Hathaway Energy in 2013.
www.nvenergy.com
Annual Revenues: $29.61 million
Employees: 2,700
Ticker: NYSE: NVE
SIC: 4931
Industry/ies: Utilities
Legislative Issues: NAT

Chairman of the Board
SATRE, Philip G.
Tel: (702) 402-8400
Fax: (702) 402-0030

President and Chief Executive Officer
CAUDILL, Paul
Tel: (702) 402-8400
Fax: (702) 402-0030

Main Headquarters
Mailing: 6226 W. Sahara Ave.
P.O. Box 98910
Las Vegas, NV 89146
Tel: (702) 402-8400
Fax: (702) 402-0030
TF: (800) 962-0399

Political Action Committees
NV Energy PAC
FEC ID: C00153379
Contact: Steven R. Evans
P.O. Box 81500
Las Vegas, NV 89180

Contributions to Candidates: $57,000 (2015-2016)
Democrats: $25,000; Republicans: $32,000

Principal Recipients

SENATE
MASTO, CATHERINE CORTEZ (DEM-NV)

HOUSE
ROBERSON, MICHAEL (REP-NV)

Corporate Foundations and Giving Programs

NV Energy Foundation
Contact: Stefanie McCaffry
P.O. Box 10100
Reno, NV 89520-3150
Tel: (702) 402-5741

Public Affairs and Related Activities Personnel

At Headquarters

BETHEL, Kevin *Senior Vice President and Chief Financial Officer*	Tel: Fax:	(702) 402-8400 (702) 402-0030
CANNON, Doug *Senior Vice President, General Counsel and Corporate* *Secretary, Chief Compliance Officer*	Tel: Fax:	(702) 402-8400 (702) 402-0030
EVANS, Steven R. *PAC Contact*	Tel: Fax:	(702) 402-8400 (702) 402-0030
OSWALD, Jennifer *Vice President, Human Resources*	Tel: Fax:	(702) 402-8400 (702) 402-0030
SAMIL, Dilek *Executive Vice President, Chief Operating Officer*	Tel: Fax:	(702) 402-8400 (702) 402-0030
SANCHEZ, III, Tony F. *Senior Vice President, Government and Community Strategy*	Tel: Fax:	(702) 402-8400 (702) 402-0030
SIMMONS, Mary O. *Vice President, Business Development and Community* *Strategy*	Tel: Fax:	(702) 402-8400 (702) 402-0030
SMITH, Andrea *Director, Corporate Communications* asmith@nevp.com	Tel: Fax:	(702) 402-8400 (702) 402-0030

At Other Offices

MCCAFFREY, Stefanie *Senior Corporate Communications Specialist and Foundation* *Contact* P.O. Box 10100 Reno, NV 89520 SMccaffrey@nvenergy.com	Tel: Fax:	(775) 834-3615 (775) 834-4204
VINSKI, John *PAC Treasurer* P.O. Box 81500 Las Vegas, NV 89180 JVinski@nvenergy.com	Tel:	(775) 834-4444

NVIDIA Corporation

Manufacturer of advanced computer graphics and software.
www.nvidia.com
Annual Revenues: $5.16 billion
Employees: 9,227
Ticker: NASDAQ: NVDA
SIC: 3674
Industry/ies: Computer/Technology
Legislative Issues: SCI

Co Founder, President and Chief Executive Officer HUANG, Jen-Hsun	Tel: Fax:	(408) 486-2000 (408) 486-2200

Main Headquarters

Mailing: 2701 San Tomas Expwy. Santa Clara, CA 95051	Tel: Fax: TF:	(408) 486-2000 (408) 486-2200 (877) 768-4342

Corporate Foundations and Giving Programs

NVIDIA Foundation
2701 San Tomas Expwy.
Santa Clara, CA 95050

	Tel: Fax:	(408) 486-2000 (408) 486-2200

Public Affairs and Related Activities Personnel

At Headquarters

CABRERA, Brian *Senior Vice President and General Counsel*	Tel: Fax:	(408) 486-2000 (408) 486-2200
CSONGOR, Rob *Vice President and General Manager, Automotive Services* csongor@nvidia.com	Tel: Fax:	(408) 566-6373 (408) 486-2200
HERBST, Jeff *Vice President, Business Development*	Tel: Fax:	(408) 486-2000 (408) 486-2200
KRESS, Colette *Executive Vice President and Chief Financial Officer*	Tel: Fax:	(408) 486-2000 (408) 486-2200
SHANNON, David M. *Executive Vice President, Chief Administrative Officer and* *Secretary*	Tel: Fax:	(408) 486-2000 (408) 486-2200
SHERBIN, Bob *Vice President, Corporate Communications* rsherbin@nvidia.com	Tel: Fax:	(408) 556-5150 (408) 486-2200
SHOQUIST, Debora *Executive Vice President, Operations*	Tel: Fax:	(408) 486-2000 (408) 486-2200

NVR, Inc.

Specializes in homebuilding and financial services.
www.nvrinc.com
Annual Revenues: $5.36 billion
Employees: 4,300
Ticker: NYSE: NVR
SIC: 1531

Industry/ies: Banking/Finance/Investments; Construction/Construction
Materials; Housing

Chairman SCHAR, Dwight C.	Tel: Fax:	(703) 956-4000 (703) 956-4750
President and Chief Executive Officer SAVILLE, Paul C.	Tel: Fax:	(703) 956-4000 (703) 956-4750

Main Headquarters

Mailing: 11700 Plaza America Dr. Plaza America Tower I, Suite 500 Reston, VA 20190	Tel: Fax:	(703) 956-4000 (703) 956-4750

Public Affairs and Related Activities Personnel

At Headquarters

MALZAHN, Daniel David *Senior Vice President, Chief Financial Officer and Treasurer*	Tel: Fax:	(703) 956-4000 (703) 956-4750

NW Natural

A natural gas utility.
www.nwnatural.com
Annual Revenues: $774.04 million
Employees: 1,100
Ticker: NYSE: NWN
Industry/ies: Utilities

Chairman of the Board HAMACHEK, Tod R.	Tel: Fax:	(503) 226-4211 (503) 721-2506
President and Chief Executive Officer KANTOR, Gregg S. gregg.kantor@nwnatural.com	Tel: Fax:	(503) 226-4211 (503) 721-2506

Main Headquarters

Mailing: P.O. Box 6017 Portland, OR 97228-6017	Tel: Fax:	(503) 226-4211 (503) 721-2506

Political Action Committees

Northwest Natural Gas PAC
FEC ID: C00174367
Contact: Gary Bauer
220 NW Second Ave.
Portland, OR 97209

Contributions to Candidates: $9,750 (2015-2016)
Democrats: $9,750

Corporate Foundations and Giving Programs

NW Natural Contributions Program
Contact: Von Summers
P.O. Box 6017
Portland, OR 97228-6017

Public Affairs and Related Activities Personnel

At Headquarters

ANDERSON, David H. *Chief Operating Officer and Executive Vice President* dha@nwnatural.com	Tel: Fax:	(503) 226-4211 (503) 721-2506
DOOLITTLE, Lea Anne *Senior Vice President and Chief Administrative Officer* lad@nwnatural.com	Tel: Fax:	(503) 226-4211 (503) 721-2506
FELTZ, Steve P. *Senior Vice President and Chief Financial Officer*	Tel: Fax:	(503) 226-4211 (503) 721-2506
HEITING, Kimberly A. *Chief Marketing Officer and Vice President, Communications*	Tel: Fax:	(503) 226-4211 (503) 721-2506
KIRKPATRICK, Margaret D. *Senior Vice President, Environmental Policy and Affairs*	Tel: Fax:	(503) 226-4211 (503) 721-2506
MILLER, C. Alex *Vice President, Regulation and Treasurer*	Tel: Fax:	(503) 226-4211 (503) 721-2506
MOORE, Melissa *Manager, Corporate Communications* media@nwnatural.com	Tel: Fax:	(503) 220-2436 (503) 721-2506
SAATHOFF, MardiLyn *Senior Vice President and General Counsel*	Tel: Fax:	(503) 226-4211 (503) 721-2506
SUMMERS, Von *Manager, Community Relations*	Tel: Fax:	(503) 220-2348 (503) 721-2508
WHITE, J. Keith *Vice President Business Development and Energy Supply and* *Chief Strategic Officer*	Tel: Fax:	(503) 226-4211 (503) 721-2506

At Other Offices

BAUER, Gary *PAC Treasurer* 220 N.W. Second Ave. Portland, OR 97209 gary.bauer@nwnatural.com	Tel: Fax:	(503) 226-4211 (503) 273-4824
HESS, Robert S. *Director, Investor Relations* 220 N.W. Second Ave.	Tel: Fax:	(503) 220-2388 (503) 273-4824

Portland, OR 97209
bob.hess@nwnatural.com

NxStage Medical Inc.
A medical device company for those needing dialysis to treat acute kidney failure and end-stage renal disease by new innovations for improving treatment options.
www.nxstage.com
Annual Revenues: $308.76 million
Employees: 3,400
Ticker: NASDAQ: NXTM
SIC: 3845
Industry/ies: Medicine/Health Care/Mental Health

Chairman of the Board
FUNARI, Robert G.
Tel: (978) 687-4700
Fax: (978) 687-4809

Chief Executive Officer
BURBANK, Jeffrey H.
Tel: (978) 687-4700
Fax: (978) 687-4809

Main Headquarters
Mailing: 350 Merrimack St.
Lawrence, MA 01843
Tel: (978) 687-4700
Fax: (978) 687-4809
TF: (866) 697-8243

Political Action Committees
NxStage Medical Inc PAC
FEC ID: C00463745
Contact: Robert S. Brown
350 Merrimack St.
Fifth Floor
Lawrence, MA 01843

Contributions to Candidates: $6,000 (2015-2016)
Democrats: $6,000

Public Affairs and Related Activities Personnel

At Headquarters

BROWN, Robert S.
President, NxStage Kidney Care, Inc and PAC Treasurer
Tel: (978) 687-4700
Fax: (978) 687-4809

RAINS, Jeffrey
Senior Vice President, Sales and Marketing
Tel: (978) 687-4700
Fax: (978) 687-4809

SCANDONE, Darren
Senior Vice President, Human Resources
Tel: (978) 687-4700
Fax: (978) 687-4809

SHEA, Tom
Senior Vice President and Chief Operations Officer
Tel: (978) 687-4700
Fax: (978) 687-4809

SHEPPARD, Esq., Kristen K.
Vice President, Investor & Media Relations
ksheppard@nxstage.com
Tel: (978) 687-4700
Fax: (978) 687-4809

SNELL, Todd M.
Senior Vice President, Quality Assurance, Regulatory and Clinical Affairs
Tel: (978) 687-4700
Fax: (978) 687-4809

SWAN, Esq., Winifred L.
Senior Vice President and General Counsel
Tel: (978) 687-4700
Fax: (978) 687-4809

TOWSE, Matthew W.
Chief Financial Officer
Tel: (978) 687-4700
Fax: (978) 687-4809

TURK, Jr., Joseph E.
President
Tel: (978) 687-4700
Fax: (978) 687-4809

NYSE Euronext, Inc.
Formed from the merger of New York Stock Exchange, Inc. with Euronext. Cross-border exchange with markets in Paris, Brussels, Amsterdam and Lisbon. Acquired the American Stock Exchange in October 2008. A registered national securities exchange. One of the two exchanges of the NYSE Group.
www.nyse.com
Annual Revenues: $3.45 billion
Employees: 3,029
Ticker: NYSE: NYX
SIC: 6200
Industry/ies: Banking/Finance/Investments; Investments/Securities Industry
Legislative Issues: FIN

President and Chief Operating Officer
VICE, Charles
Tel: (212) 656-3000
Fax: (212) 656-2126

Main Headquarters
Mailing: 11 Wall St.
New York City, NY 10005
Tel: (212) 656-3000
Fax: (212) 656-2126

Washington Office
Mailing: 801 Pennsylvania Ave. NW
Suite 630
Washington, DC 20004-5878
Tel: (202) 347-4300
Fax: (202) 347-4370

Public Affairs and Related Activities Personnel

At Headquarters

GOONE, David
Chief Strategy Officer
Tel: (212) 656-3000
Fax: (212) 656-2126

HILL, Scott
Chief Financial Officer
Tel: (212) 656-3000
Fax: (212) 656-2126

SHORT, Johnathan
General Counsel and Corporate Secretary
Tel: (212) 656-3000
Fax: (212) 656-2126

At Washington Office

MATHISON, Dean
PAC Contact
Tel: (202) 347-4300
Fax: (202) 347-4370

RICH, Linda Dallas
Senior Vice President, Government Relations
Tel: (202) 347-4300
Fax: (202) 347-4370

The O Team, LLC
Government affairs consulting firm.
www.theoteam.biz
Legislative Issues: BUD; HCR; MIA; TAX; TEC

OKUN, Hon. Bob
Tel: (202) 403-2150

Main Headquarters
Mailing: 1101 K St. NW
Suite 310
Washington, DC 20005
Tel: (202) 403-2150

Public Affairs and Related Activities Personnel

At Headquarters

COLE, Beth Anne
Tel: (202) 403-2150

O'Donovan Strategies, LLC
Government affairs and corporate strategy.
Industry/ies: Government-Related
Legislative Issues: MAR

Main Headquarters
Mailing: 1455 Pennsylvania Ave. NW
Suite 400
Washington, DC 20004

Public Affairs and Related Activities Personnel

At Headquarters

O'DONOVAN, Kevin
Registered Federal Lobbyist

O'Hara Federal Strategies, LLC
Private consulting firm.
www.ofsdc.com
Legislative Issues: ALC; RRR

Main Headquarters
Mailing: 1875 Eye St. NW
Fifth Floor
Washington, DC 20006
Tel: (202) 429-2019
Fax: (202) 429-9574

Public Affairs and Related Activities Personnel

At Headquarters

GRAVATT, Laurie Bendall
Federal Lobbyist
Tel: (202) 429-2019
Fax: (202) 429-9574

O'HARA, Bartley M.
Principal
Registered Federal Lobbyist
Tel: (202) 429-2019
Fax: (202) 429-9574

O'HARA, Elizabeth
Principal
elizabeth.ohara@ofsdc.com
Registered Federal Lobbyist
Tel: (202) 429-2019
Fax: (202) 429-9574

O'Neill Properties Group
A real estate company engaged in urban development.
www.oneillproperties.com
Annual Revenues: $38.10 million
Employees: 100
Industry/ies: Economics And Economic Development; Real Estate

Founder and Chairman of the Board
O'NEILL, Brian
Tel: (610) 239-6100
Fax: (610) 337-5599

Main Headquarters
Mailing: 2701 Renaissance Blvd.
Fourth Floor
King of Prussia, PA 19406
Tel: (610) 239-6100
Fax: (610) 337-5599

Corporate Foundations and Giving Programs
O'Neill Properties Group Contribution Program
2701 Renaissance Blvd.
Fourth Floor
King of Prussia, PA 19406
Tel: (610) 337-5560
Fax: (610) 337-5599

Public Affairs and Related Activities Personnel

At Headquarters

ANDERSON, Eric
Contact, Corporate Marketing and Communications
Tel: (610) 337-5560
Fax: (610) 337-5599

Oakley Capitol Consulting LLC
Government and community relations consulting.

www.karaoakley.com
Legislative Issues: DEF; HCR; MMM

Main Headquarters

Mailing: 36476 River Oaks Cir.   Tel: (202) 744-9980
             Cumming, IA 50061

Public Affairs and Related Activities Personnel

At Headquarters

OAKLEY, Kara Tollett   Tel: (202) 744-9980
kara@karaoakley.com
Registered Federal Lobbyist

Oakwood Healthcare Inc.

A regional healthcare system providing a comprehensive range of health services.
www.oakwood.org
Annual Revenues: $3.3 billion
Employees: 10,000
Industry/ies: Medicine/Health Care/Mental Health

President and Chief Executive Officer   Tel: (313) 253-6000
CONNOLLY, Brian M.   Fax: (313) 253-6033

Main Headquarters

Mailing: 15500 Lundy Pkwy.   Tel: (313) 586-5234
             Dearborn, MI 48126

Corporate Foundations and Giving Programs

Oakwood Healthcare Foundation
23400 Michigan Ave.   Tel: (313) 586-5234
Suite 301
Dearborn, MI 48124

Public Affairs and Related Activities Personnel

At Headquarters

O'MALLEY, Carla   Tel: (313) 586-5234
*President and Executive Director, Oakwood Healthcare
Foundation*
omalleyc@oakwood.org

At Other Offices

CAMPBELL, David   Tel: (313) 253-6000
Executive Vice President, Operations, System Strategy and Fax: (313) 253-6033
Growth
One Parklane Blvd., Suite 1000
Dearborn, MI 48126

CONWAY, Paul   Tel: (313) 253-6000
Senior Vice President, Human Resources   Fax: (313) 253-6033
One Parklane Blvd., Suite 1000
Dearborn, MI 48126

HANNIS, MD, Mark   Tel: (313) 582-2769
Senior Vice President, Medical Education   Fax: (313) 253-6033
One Parklane Blvd., Suite 1000
Dearborn, MI 48126
jilianj@oakwood.org

KEUTEN, John   Tel: (313) 253-6000
Senior Vice President and Chief Financial Officer   Fax: (313) 253-6033
One Parklane Blvd., Suite 1000
Dearborn, MI 48126

LLOYD, Seth   Tel: (313) 253-6000
Senior Vice President and General Counsel   Fax: (313) 253-6033
One Parklane Blvd., Suite 1000
Dearborn, MI 48126

RIVERA-KERR, Paula   Tel: (313) 791-4817
Contact, Media Relations   Fax: (313) 253-6033
One Parklane Blvd., Suite 1000
Dearborn, MI 48126
riverap@oakwood.org

ZATINA, Mary   Tel: (313) 253-6000
Senior Vice President, Government Relations and Corporate Fax: (313) 253-6033
Communications
One Parklane Blvd., Suite 1000
Dearborn, MI 48126

Occidental Petroleum Corporation

An oil and gas exploration and production company. OxyChem is its subsidiary.
www.oxy.com
Annual Revenues: $17.43 billion
Employees: 11,700
Ticker: NYSE: OXY
SIC: 2911; 1311; 1382; 2899
Industry/ies: Chemicals & Chemical Industry
Legislative Issues: CAW; CHM; ENG; ENV; NAT; TAX; WAS

President and Chief Executive Officer   Tel: (713) 215-7000
CHAZEN, Stephen I.   Fax: (310) 443-6690

Main Headquarters

Mailing: Five Greenway Plaza   Tel: (713) 215-7000

Suite 110
Houston, TX 77046-0506

Washington Office

Mailing: 1717 Pennsylvania Ave. NW   Tel: (202) 857-3000
             Washington, DC 20006-4614

Corporate Foundations and Giving Programs

Occidental Petroleum Corporation Contributions Program
10889 Wilshire Blvd.   Tel: (310) 208-8800
Los Angeles, CA 90024-4201   Fax: (310) 443-6690

Public Affairs and Related Activities Personnel

At Headquarters

COZYN, Martin A.   Tel: (713) 215-7000
Eexecutive Vice President, Human Resources
martin_cozyn@oxy.com

SCHOEB, Melissa E.   Tel: (713) 366-5615
Vice President, Corporate Communications and Public Affairs
melissa_schoeb@oxy.com

At Washington Office

COLLINS, Jr., William A.   Tel: (202) 857-3000
Senior Director, Regulatory Affairs   Fax: (202) 857-3070
al_collins@oxy.com
Registered Federal Lobbyist

DAVIS, Ian   Tel: (202) 857-3000
Vice President, Government Relations   Fax: (202) 857-3030
ian_davis@oxy.com
Registered Federal Lobbyist

FETGATTER, Christopher   Tel: (202) 857-3000
Manager, Government Affairs   Fax: (202) 857-3070
Registered Federal Lobbyist

HASSETT, Jace   Tel: (202) 857-3000
Vice President, Government Affairs and Chemicals   Fax: (202) 857-3030
jace_hassett@oxy.com
Registered Federal Lobbyist

MCPHEE, Gerald T.   Tel: (202) 857-3000
Senior Corporate Director, Government Affairs   Fax: (202) 857-3014
jerry_mcphee@oxy.com
Registered Federal Lobbyist

OSBORNE, Caleb   Tel: (202) 857-3000
Government Affairs Representative

At Other Offices

DEGNER, Christopher M.   Tel: (212) 603-8111
Senior Director, Investor Relations
1230 Avenue of the Americas
New York City, NY 10020-1508
chris_stavros@oxy.com

HASSETT, James
1701 Pennsylvania Ave. NW, Suite 800
Washington, DC 20006
Registered Federal Lobbyist

Ocean Power Technologies, Inc.

Develops and commercializes proprietary systems that generate electricity by harnessing the renewable energy of ocean waves.
www.oceanpowertechnologies.com
Annual Revenues: $3.99 million
Employees: 29
Ticker: NASDAQ: OPTT
SIC: 4911
Industry/ies: Energy/Electricity

Executive Vice Chairman of the Board   Tel: (609) 730-0400
TAYLOR, Dr. George W.   Fax: (609) 730-0404
gtaylor@oceanpowertech.com

Interim Chief Executive Officer   Tel: (609) 730-0400
KELLER, David L   Fax: (609) 730-0404

Main Headquarters

Mailing: 1590 Reed Rd.   Tel: (609) 730-0400
             Pennington, NJ 08534   Fax: (609) 730-0404

Public Affairs and Related Activities Personnel

At Headquarters

FEATHERSTONE, Mark A   Tel: (609) 730-0400
Chief Financial Officer, Secretary & Treasurer   Fax: (609) 730-0404
bposner@oceanpowertech.com

MONTAGNA, Deborah A.   Tel: (609) 730-0400
Vice President, Business and Product Development   Fax: (609) 730-0404
dmontagna@oceanpowertech.com

Ocean Spray Cranberries

A processor of fruit products.
www.oceanspray.com

Employees: 2,000
SIC: 2033; 2037
NAICS: 311421; 311411
Industry/ies: Cooperatives; Food And Beverage Industry
Legislative Issues: AGR; ENV; TAX; TRD

| **President and Chief Executive Officer** | Tel: | (508) 946-1000 |
| PAPADELLIS, Randy C. | Fax: | (508) 946-7704 |

Main Headquarters

Mailing:	One Ocean Spray Dr.	Tel:	(508) 946-1000
	Lakeville-Middleboro, MA 02349	Fax:	(508) 946-7704
		TF:	(800) 662-3263

Political Action Committees

Ocean Spray Cranberries, Inc. PAC
FEC ID: C00114702
Contact: Judith E. Mceachern

   Contributions to Candidates: $82,700 (2015-2016)
   Democrats: $43,500; Republicans: $39,200

Corporate Foundations and Giving Programs

Ocean Spray Cranberries Contributions Program		
One Ocean Spray Dr.	Tel:	(508) 946-1000
Lakeville-Middleboro, MA 02349	Fax:	(508) 946-7704

Public Affairs and Related Activities Personnel

At Headquarters

BIEG, Sonja	Tel:	(508) 946-7688
Manager, Consumer Affairs	Fax:	(508) 946-7704
sbieg@oceanspray.com		

| LEES, Rick | Tel: | (508) 946-1000 |
| *Executive Vice President and Chief Financial Officer* | Fax: | (508) 946-7704 |

| MCEACHERN, Judith E. | Tel: | (508) 946-1000 |
| *PAC Treasurer* | Fax: | (508) 946-7704 |

NEWCOMB, Sharon	Tel:	(508) 946-7185
Senior Public Relations Associate	Fax:	(508) 946-7704
snewcomb@oceanspray.com		

Oceaneering International

Oceaneering International is a provider of engineering services and products for the offshore oil and gas industry, with a focus on deepwater applications.
www.oceaneering.com
Annual Revenues: $3.61 billion
Employees: 12,400
Ticker: NYSE: OII
SIC: 3052; 3429
NAICS: 326220
Industry/ies: Engineering/Mathematics; Fuels See Coal, Gas, Oil, Petroleum; Natural Resources; Petroleum Industry
Legislative Issues: AER; DEF; SCI

| **Chairman of the Board** | Tel: | (713) 329-4500 |
| HUFF, John R. | Fax: | (713) 329-4951 |

| **President and Chief Executive Officer** | Tel: | (713) 329-4500 |
| MCEVOY, M. Kevin | Fax: | (713) 329-4951 |

Main Headquarters

Mailing:	11911 FM 529	Tel:	(713) 329-4500
	Houston, TX 77041	Fax:	(713) 329-4951
		TF:	(800) 829-3483

Corporate Foundations and Giving Programs

Oceaneering International, Inc. Contributions Program		
11911 FM 529	Tel:	(713) 329-4500
Houston, TX 77041	Fax:	(713) 329-4951

Public Affairs and Related Activities Personnel

At Headquarters

CHARLES, Janet G.	Tel:	(713) 329-4500
Vice President Human Resources	Fax:	(713) 329-4951
jcharles@oceaneering.com		

JURKOSHEK, Jack	Tel:	(713) 329-4670
Director, Investor Relations	Fax:	(713) 329-4653
investorrelations@oceaneering.com		

| LARSON, Roderick A. | Tel: | (713) 329-4500 |
| *President and Chief Operating Officer* | Fax: | (713) 329-4951 |

| LAWRENCE, David K. | Tel: | (713) 329-4500 |
| *Vice President, General Counsel and Secretary* | Fax: | (713) 329-4951 |

| MIGURA, Marvin J. | Tel: | (713) 329-4500 |
| *Executive Vice President* | Fax: | (713) 329-4951 |

| PETERSON, Mark | Tel: | (713) 329-4500 |
| *Vice President, Corporate Development* | Fax: | (713) 329-4951 |

OceanFirst Bank

OceanFirst Financial Corp. operates as a holding company for OceanFirst Bank that provides community banking services in retail, government, and business customers. Also known as Ocean Federal Savings Bank.

www.oceanfirstonline.com
Annual Revenues: $88.17 million
Employees: 319
Ticker: NASDAQ:OCFC
Industry/ies: Banking/Finance/Investments

| **Chairman of the Board and Chief Executive Officer** | Tel: | (732) 240-4500 |
| GARBARINO, John R. | Fax: | (732) 349-5070 |

Main Headquarters

Mailing:	975 Hooper Ave.	Tel:	(732) 240-4500
	Toms River, NJ 08753-8320	Fax:	(732) 349-5070
		TF:	(888) 623-2633

Political Action Committees

OceanFirst PAC		
FEC ID: C00304410		
Contact: Nina Anuario		
975 Hooper Ave.	Tel:	(732) 240-4500
Toms River, NJ 08753-8320	Fax:	(732) 349-5070

Corporate Foundations and Giving Programs

OceanFirst Foundation		
Contact: Katherine Durante		
975 Hooper Ave.	Tel:	(732) 240-4500
Toms River, NJ 08753	Fax:	(732) 240-4500

Public Affairs and Related Activities Personnel

At Headquarters

| ANUARIO, Nina | Tel: | (732) 240-4500 |
| *Senior Vice President and PAC Treasurer* | Fax: | (732) 349-5070 |

| FITZPATRICK, Michael J. | Tel: | (732) 240-4500 |
| *Executive Vice President and Chief Financial Officer* | Fax: | (732) 349-5070 |

| HEWITT, Jill Apito | Tel: | (732) 240-4500 |
| *Senior Vice President* | Fax: | (732) 349-5070 |

| MAHER , Christopher D. | Tel: | (732) 240-4500 |
| *President and Chief Operating Officer* | Fax: | (732) 349-5070 |

| TSIMBINOS, Steven J. | Tel: | (732) 240-4500 |
| *First Senior Vice President, General Counsel and Corporate Secretary* | Fax: | (732) 349-5070 |

At Other Offices

DURANTE, Katherine	Tel:	(732) 341-4676
Executive Director, OceanFirst Foundation	Fax:	(732) 473-9641
1415 Hooper Ave., Suite 304		
Toms River, NJ 08753		

Ocera Therapeutics Inc.

A biopharmaceutical company. Merged with Tranzyme Pharma in 2013.
www.ocerainc.com
Employees: 16
Industry/ies: Medicine/Health Care/Mental Health; Pharmaceutical Industry; Science; Scientific Research

| **Chairman of the Board** | Tel: | (858) 436-3900 |
| WEBER, MD, Eckard | Fax: | (858) 436-3999 |

| **President and Chief Executive Officer** | Tel: | (650) 475-0158 |
| GRAIS, Linda S | Fax: | (650) 521-5677 |

Main Headquarters

Mailing:	525 University Ave.	Tel:	(650) 475-0158
	Suite 610	Fax:	(650) 521-5677
	Palo Alto, CA 94301		

Public Affairs and Related Activities Personnel

At Headquarters

| AGGARWAL, Gaurav | Tel: | (650) 475-0158 |
| *Chief Business Officer* | Fax: | (650) 521-5677 |

| BYRNES, Michael | Tel: | (650) 475-0158 |
| *Chief Financial Officer* | Fax: | (650) 521-5677 |

OCP S.A.

A leading exporter of phosphate rock and derivative products.
Industry/ies: Agriculture/Agronomy

| **Chairman and Chief Executive Officer** | Tel: | (706) 771-3415 |
| TERRAB, Mostafa | | |

Main Headquarters

Mailing:	1610 Marvin	Tel:	(706) 771-3415
	Griffin Road		
	Augusta, GA 30906		

Public Affairs and Related Activities Personnel

At Headquarters

| AMEZIANE, Marouane | Tel: | (706) 771-3415 |
| *Executive Director - Strategy and Corporate Development* | | |

| EL KADIRI, Mohamed | Tel: | (706) 771-3415 |
| *Managing Director and General Secretary* | | |

EL OUAFI, Mustapha *Executive Director, Sales, Marketing and Raw Material Procurement*	Tel:	(706) 771-3415
GUEDIRA, Ghislane *Executive Director, Chief Financial Officer*	Tel:	(706) 771-3415
GUENNOUNI, Jamal *Executive Director, Human Capital*	Tel:	(706) 771-3415
LARAKI, Ghita *Investor Relations, Contact* g.laraki@ocpgroup.ma	Tel:	(706) 771-3415
SMIRES, Otmane Bennani- *Executive Director, Legal Division and General Counsel*	Tel:	(706) 771-3415

OEA International, Inc.

A signal integrity software company.
www.oea.com
Annual Revenues: $2 million
Employees: 25
Industry/ies: Computer/Technology; Electricity & Electronics; Electronics; Energy/Electricity

President and Chief Executive Officer
AKCASU, Ersed O.

Tel: (408) 778-6747
Fax: (408) 778-6748

Main Headquarters
Mailing: 155 E. Main Ave.
Suite 110
Morgan Hill, CA 95037-7521

Tel: (408) 778-6747
Fax: (408) 778-6748

Public Affairs and Related Activities Personnel

At Headquarters

TALLINGER, Jerry *Vice President, Marketing and Sales* jerry@oea.com	Tel: Fax:	(512) 382-5575 (408) 778-6748

Office Depot, Inc.

An office supply operator.
www.officedepot.com
Annual Revenues: $12.88 billion
Employees: 64,000
Ticker: NYSE: ODP
SIC: 5940
Industry/ies: Retail/Wholesale

Chairman and Chief Executive Officer
SMITH, Roland C.

Tel: (561) 438-4800
Fax: (561) 438-4001

President
SCHMIDT, Steven M.

Tel: (561) 438-4800
Fax: (561) 438-4001

Main Headquarters
Mailing: 6600 N. Military Trail
Boca Raton, FL 33496

Tel: (561) 438-4800
Fax: (561) 438-4001
TF: (800) 937-3600

Corporate Foundations and Giving Programs

Office Depot Foundation
6600 N. Military Trail Rd.
Boca Raton, FL 33496

Public Affairs and Related Activities Personnel

At Headquarters

ALLISON, Michael *Executive Vice President and Chief People Officer*	Tel: Fax:	(561) 438-4800 (561) 438-4001
GARCIA, Elisa D. *Executive Vice President and Chief Legal Officer* Elisa.Garcia@officedepot.com	Tel: Fax:	(561) 438-4800 (561) 438-4401
HARE, Stephen E. *Executive Vice President and Chief Financial Officer*	Tel: Fax:	(561) 438-4800 (561) 438-4001
JOHANSSON, Juliet *Executive Vice President and Chief Strategy Officer*	Tel: Fax:	(561) 438-4800 (561) 438-4001
REA, Tim *Executive Vice President, Marketing*	Tel: Fax:	(561) 438-4800 (561) 438-4001

OGE Energy Corporation

The holding company for Oklahoma Gas and Electric Co. and Enogex, Inc.
www.oge.com
Annual Revenues: $2.37 billion
Employees: 3,329
Ticker: NYSE: OGE
SIC: 4911
Industry/ies: Energy/Electricity
Legislative Issues: CAW; ENG; ENV; HOM; TAX

Chairman of the Board
DELANEY, Peter B.

Tel: (405) 553-6400
Fax: (405) 553-6498

President and Chief Executive Officer
TRAUSCHKE, Sean

Tel: (405) 553-3000
Fax: (405) 553-3567

Main Headquarters
Mailing: P.O. Box 321
Oklahoma City, OK 73101-0321

Tel: (405) 553-3000
Fax: (405) 553-3567
TF: (888) 988-9747

Political Action Committees

OGE Energy Corp Employee's PAC
FEC ID: C00337808
321 N. Harvey
P.O. Box 321
Oklahoma City, OK 73101

Contributions to Candidates: $30,100 (2015-2016)
Republicans: $30,100

Corporate Foundations and Giving Programs

OGE Energy Corporation Foundation
P.O. Box 321
Oklahoma City, OK 73101-0321

Tel: (405) 553-3000
Fax: (405) 553-3567

Public Affairs and Related Activities Personnel

At Headquarters

BULLARD, William J. *General Counsel*	Tel: Fax:	(405) 553-3000 (405) 553-3567
FORBES, Scott *Controller, Chief Accounting Officer*	Tel: Fax:	(405) 553-3000 (405) 553-3567
HORN, Patricia D *Vice President, Governance and Corporate Secretary*	Tel: Fax:	(405) 553-3000 (405) 553-3567
MCQUISTION, Cristina F. *Vice President, Strategic Planning and PerformanceImprovement and Chief Information Officer*	Tel: Fax:	(405) 553-3000 (405) 553-3567
MERRILL, Stephen E *Chief Financial Officer*	Tel: Fax:	(405) 553-3000 (405) 553-3567
MITCHELL, Keith *Chief Operating Officer*	Tel: Fax:	(405) 553-3000 (405) 553-3567
RENFROW, Paul L. *Vice President, Public Affairs and Corporate Administration*	Tel: Fax:	(405) 553-3287 (405) 553-3760
RHEA, John D. *Assistant Corporate Secretary and Compliance Officer* rheajd@oge.com	Tel: Fax:	(405) 553-3000 (405) 553-6498
ROWLETT, Donald *PAC Treasurer* Mail Stop 321 N. Harvey	Tel: Fax:	(405) 553-3000 (405) 553-3567
WALWORTH, Charles B *Treasurer*	Tel: Fax:	(405) 553-3000 (405) 553-3567

Oglethorpe Power Corporation

A generation cooperative.
www.opc.com
Employees: 200
SIC: 4911
Industry/ies: Energy/Electricity
Legislative Issues: UTI

Chairman of the Board
DENHAM, Benny W.

Tel: (770) 270-7600
Fax: (770) 270-7325

President and Chief Executive Officer
SMITH, Michael L.

Tel: (770) 270-7600
Fax: (770) 270-7325

Main Headquarters
Mailing: 2100 E. Exchange Pl.
Tucker, GA 30084

Tel: (770) 270-7600
Fax: (770) 270-7325
TF: (800) 241-5374

Public Affairs and Related Activities Personnel

At Headquarters

BRENDIAR, Thomas J. *Director, Bank and Investor Relations* tom.brendiar@opc.com	Tel: Fax:	(770) 270-7173 (770) 270-7325
GIVINS, Tara *Vice President, Risk Management and Corporate Compliance*	Tel: Fax:	(770) 270-7600 (770) 270-7325
HIGGINS, Elizabeth B. *Executive Vice President and Chief Financial Officer*	Tel: Fax:	(770) 270-7600 (770) 270-7325
JONES, Greg *Director, Public Relations and Media Contact* greg.jones@opc.com	Tel: Fax:	(770) 270-7890 (770) 270-7560
MITCHELL, Clarence D. *Senior Vice President, Regulatory and Contract Operations*	Tel: Fax:	(770) 270-7600 (770) 270-7325
PRICE, Michael "Mike" W. *Executive Vice President and Chief Operating Officer*	Tel: Fax:	(770) 270-7600 (770) 270-7325
REUSCH, SPHR, Jami G. *Vice President, Human Resources*	Tel: Fax:	(770) 270-7600 (770) 270-7325
ROBBINS, William Clayton *Senior Vice President, Governmental Affairs* clay.robbins@opc.com	Tel: Fax:	(770) 270-7186 (770) 270-7325

Registered Federal Lobbyist

TAYLOR, Jr., George B.	Tel:	(770) 270-7600
Deputy General Counsel	Fax:	(770) 270-7325
george.taylor@opc.com		
USSERY, William F.	Tel:	(770) 270-7600
Executive Vice President, Member and External Relations	Fax:	(770) 270-7325
WHITNEY, Charles W.	Tel:	(770) 270-7600
Senior Vice President and General Counsel	Fax:	(770) 270-7325

Ohio Health

A not-for-profit organization of hospitals and healthcare services.
www.ohiohealth.com
Employees: 15,000
Industry/ies: Medicine/Health Care/Mental Health
Legislative Issues: HCR

President and Chief Executive Officer	Tel:	(614) 544-4412
BLOM, David P.	Fax:	(614) 566-6938

Main Headquarters

Mailing:	180 E. Broad St.	Tel:	(614) 544-4455
	34th Floor	Fax:	(614) 566-6938
	Columbus, OH 43215	TF:	(800) 837-7555

Political Action Committees
OhioHealth Star Corporation PAC DBA OhioHealth PAC
FEC ID: C00210617
Contact: Karen Jefferson Morrison
180 E. Broad St.
34th Floor
Columbus, OH 43215

   Contributions to Candidates: $24,350 (2015-2016)
   Democrats: $6,000; Republicans: $18,350

Corporate Foundations and Giving Programs
OhioHealth Foundation
Contact: Karen Jefferson Morrison
180 E. Broad St.
Columbus, OH 43215

Public Affairs and Related Activities Personnel

At Headquarters

BARNES, Earl	Tel:	(614) 544-4455
Senior Vice President and General Counsel	Fax:	(614) 566-6938
BECKEL, Johnni	Tel:	(614) 544-4403
Senior Vice President and Chief Human Resources Officer	Fax:	(614) 566-6938
HOPKINS, Mark	Tel:	(614) 544-4248
Director, Media Relations	Fax:	(614) 544-4301
mhopkins@ohiohealth.com		
JABLONSKI, Sue	Tel:	(614) 544-4420
Senior Vice President and Chief Communications Officer	Fax:	(614) 566-6938
LOUGE, Michael W	Tel:	(614) 544-4414
Executive Vice President and Chief Operating Officer	Fax:	(614) 566-6938
MORRISON, Karen Jefferson	Tel:	(614) 544-4423
President, OhioHealth Foundation and Senior Vice President,	Fax:	(614) 566-6938
External Affairs		
QUINN, Jessica L	Tel:	(614) 544-4206
Senior Vice President and Chief Compliance Officer	Fax:	(614) 566-6938
YATES, Vinson M.	Tel:	(614) 544-4161
Senior Vice President and Chief Financial Officer	Fax:	(614) 566-6938

Ohio National Financial Services

A group of insurance and financial services companies.
www.ohionational.com
Annual Revenues: $36 Million
Employees: 800
Industry/ies: Banking/Finance/Investments

President and Chief Executive Officer	Tel:	(513) 794-6100
HUFFMAN, Gary	Fax:	(513) 794-4504

Main Headquarters

Mailing:	One Financial Way	Tel:	(513) 794-6100
	Cincinnati, OH 45242	Fax:	(513) 794-4504

Political Action Committees
Ohio National Financial Services Field PAC
FEC ID: C00484089
Contact: Doris Paul
One Financial Way
Cincinnati, OH 45242

Ohio National Financial Services PAC
FEC ID: C00296657
Contact: Doris Paul
One Financial Way
Cincinnati, OH 45242

   Contributions to Candidates: $35,000 (2015-2016)
   Democrats: $4,000; Republicans: $31,000

Principal Recipients
PRESIDENT
   KASICH, JOHN R (REP-OH)

Corporate Foundations and Giving Programs
Ohio National Foundation
One Financial Way
Cincinnati, OH 45242

Public Affairs and Related Activities Personnel

At Headquarters

ESPOSITO, Anthony G.	Tel:	(513) 794-6100
Senior Vice President, Human Resources and Administration	Fax:	(513) 794-4504
GUTBIER, Adrienne	Tel:	(513) 794-6254
Second Vice President, Corporate Marketing	Fax:	(513) 794-4504
HAGENBUCH, Diane S.	Tel:	(513) 794-6313
Senior Vice President, Corporate Relations and	Fax:	(513) 794-4504
Communications		
PAUL, Doris	Tel:	(513) 794-6100
PAC Treasurer	Fax:	(513) 794-4504
SANDER, Joseph R.	Tel:	(513) 794-6100
Vice President and Treasurer	Fax:	(513) 794-4504

Old Dominion Freight Line, Inc.

A lobbying firm.
www.odfl.com
Annual Revenues: $2.42 billion
Employees: 14,073
Ticker: NASDAQ: ODFL
SIC: 4213
Industry/ies: Shipping Industry; Transportation
Legislative Issues: TRU

Executive Chairman of the Board	Tel:	(336) 889-5000
CONGDON, Earl E.	Fax:	(336) 822-5239
Director, President and Chief Executive Officer	Tel:	(336) 889-5000
CONGDON, David S.	Fax:	(336) 822-5239

Main Headquarters

Mailing:	500 Old Dominion Way	Tel:	(336) 889-5000
	Thomasville, NC 27360	Fax:	(336) 822-5239
		TF:	(800) 432-6335

Public Affairs and Related Activities Personnel

At Headquarters

CRANFILL, William	Tel:	(336) 889-5000
Lawyer	Fax:	(336) 822-5239
JACOBS, Ronald M.	Tel:	(336) 889-5000
Counsel	Fax:	(336) 822-5239
MARCHESKI, Maura	Tel:	(336) 889-5000
Counsel	Fax:	(336) 822-5239
OVERBEY, Cecil E.	Tel:	(336) 889-5000
Senior Vice President, Marketing Pricing and Strategic	Fax:	(336) 822-5239
Development		

Old National Bancorp

A financial company.
www.oldnational.com
Annual Revenues: $550.68 million
Employees: 2,938
Ticker: NYSE: ONB
SIC: 6021
Industry/ies: Banking/Finance/Investments

Chairman of the Board	Tel:	(812) 464-1294
DUNIGAN, Larry E.	Fax:	(812) 464-1567
President and Chief Executive Officer	Tel:	(812) 464-1294
JONES, Robert G.	Fax:	(812) 464-1567
bob.jones@oldnational.com		

Main Headquarters

Mailing:	One Main St.	Tel:	(812) 464-1294
	Evansville, IN 47708	Fax:	(812) 464-1567
		TF:	(800) 731-2265

Political Action Committees
Old National Bank PAC
FEC ID: C00165282
Contact: Dean Happe
One Main St.
Evansville, IN 47708

	Tel:	(812) 464-1294
	Fax:	(812) 464-1567

   Contributions to Candidates: $6,300 (2015-2016)
   Democrats: $1,000; Republicans: $5,300

Corporate Foundations and Giving Programs
Old National Bancorp Contributions Program
Contact: Kate Miller

One Main St.
Evansville, IN 47708

Tel: (812) 461-9378
Fax: (812) 461-9378

Public Affairs and Related Activities Personnel

At Headquarters

DAUGHERTY, Julie A. Williams
Executive Vice President, Chief Administrative Officer

Tel: (812) 464-1294
Fax: (812) 464-1567

HAPPE, Dean
PAC Treasurer

Tel: (812) 464-1294
Fax: (812) 464-1567

KNIGHT, Jeffrey L.
Executive Vice President and Chief Legal Counsel

Tel: (812) 464-1294
Fax: (812) 464-1567

MILLER, Kate
Community Relations Officer
kate.miller@oldnational.com

Tel: (812) 461-9378
Fax: (812) 464-1567

RYAN, III, James C.
Executive Vice President, Director, Corporate Strategy

Tel: (812) 464-1294
Fax: (812) 464-1567

SCHOETTLIN, Kathy A.
Executive Vice President, Chief Community Relations and Social Responsibility Officer
kathy.schoettlin@oldnational.com

Tel: (812) 464-7269
Fax: (812) 464-1567

VANZO, Kendra L.
Executive Vice President and Chief Human Resources Officer

Tel: (812) 464-1294
Fax: (812) 464-1567

WALTON, Lynell J.
Senior Vice President, Investor Relations
lynell_walton@oldnational.com

Tel: (812) 464-1366
Fax: (812) 464-1567

WOLKING, Christopher A.
Senior Executive Vice President and Chief Financial Officer

Tel: (812) 464-1294
Fax: (812) 464-1567

Old National Bank

A bank holding company operating 78 banking centers in Indiana, Illinois, Kentucky and Michigan. It provides a comprehensive range of financial services including commercial and retail banking, trust, brokerage, correspondent banking, and insurance.
www.oldnational.com
Annual Revenues: $550.68 million
Employees: 2,938
Ticker: NASDAQ :ONB
Industry/ies: Banking/Finance/Investments

Chairman
DUNIGAN, Larry E.

Tel: (812) 464-9677
Fax: (812) 464-9825

President and Chief Executive Officer
JONES, Robert G.

Tel: (812) 464-9677
Fax: (812) 464-9825

Main Headquarters
Mailing: One Main St.
Evansville, IN 47708

Tel: (812) 464-9677
Fax: (812) 464-9825
TF: (800) 467-1928

Political Action Committees
Old National Bank Political Action Committe
FEC ID: C00165282
Contact: Dean Happe
One Main St.
Evansville, IN 47708

Tel: (812) 464-9677
Fax: (812) 464-9825

Contributions to Candidates: $3,600 (2015-2016)
Democrats: $1,000; Republicans: $2,600

Corporate Foundations and Giving Programs
Old National Bank Foundation
Contact: Kate Miller
One Main St.
Evansville, IN 47708

Tel: (812) 464-9677
Fax: (812) 464-9825

Public Affairs and Related Activities Personnel

At Headquarters

HAPPE, Dean
Senior Vice President, Operations Director

Tel: (812) 464-9677
Fax: (812) 464-9825

KNIGHT, Jeffrey L.
Executive Vice President and Chief Legal Counsel

Tel: (812) 464-9677
Fax: (812) 464-9825

MILLER, Kate
Manager, ?Community Relations
kate.miller@oldnational.com

Tel: (812) 461-9378
Fax: (812) 464-9825

PENCE, George
Vice President and Director, Marketing

Tel: (812) 464-9753
Fax: (812) 464-9825

RICKARD, Candice J.
Executive Vice President and Chief Risk Officer

Tel: (812) 464-9677
Fax: (812) 464-9825

SCHOETTLIN, Kathy A.
Executive Vice President, Chief Community Relations and Social Responsibility Officer
kathy.schoettlin@oldnational.com

Tel: (812) 465-7269
Fax: (812) 464-9825

WALTON, Lynell J.
Senior Vice President, Investors Relations

Tel: (812) 464-1366
Fax: (812) 464-9825

Oldcastle Materials Group

Integrated supplier of aggregates, asphalt, ready mix concrete, and construction and paving services in the United States. A US subsidiary of international building materials group CRH, Celtic Resources Holdings plc.
www.oldcastlematerials.com
Annual Revenues: $172.2 million
Employees: 2,400
Industry/ies: Construction/Construction Materials
Legislative Issues: ROD; TRA

Chief Executive Officer
LAKE, Randy

Tel: (770) 522-5600
Fax: (770) 522-5608

Main Headquarters
Mailing: 900 Ashwood Pkwy.
Suite 700
Atlanta, GA 30338

Tel: (770) 522-5600
Fax: (770) 522-5608
TF: (800) 241-7074

Washington Office
Mailing: 101 Constitution Ave.
Suite 600 West
Washington, DC 20001

Fax: (202) 625-2153

Political Action Committees
Oldcastle Materials Inc. PAC
FEC ID: C00346353
Contact: Steven O. Palmer
101 Constitution Ave.
Suite 600 West
Washington, DC 20001

Contributions to Candidates: $240,930 (2015-2016)
Democrats: $73,280; Republicans: $167,650

Corporate Foundations and Giving Programs
Oldcastle Materials Group Contribution Program
900 Ashwood Pkwy.
Suite 700
Atlanta, GA 30338

Tel: (770) 522-5600
Fax: (770) 522-5602

Public Affairs and Related Activities Personnel

At Headquarters

BROWN, Charles
Chief Financial Officer

Tel: (770) 522-5600
Fax: (770) 522-5602

HAY, John C.
Senior Vice President, Government Relations and Corporate Communications
john.hay@oldcastlematerials.com

Tel: (770) 522-5600
Fax: (770) 522-5602

RANDOLPH, Kirk
Executive Vice President, Strategy and Development

Tel: (770) 522-5600
Fax: (770) 522-5608

At Washington Office

PALMER, Steven O.
Vice President

Fax: (202) 625-2153

Olin Corporation

A manufacturer of chemicals, metals, sporting ammunition, electronic materials and services.
www.olin.com
Annual Revenues: $3.68 billion
Employees: 6,200
Ticker: NYSE: OLN
SIC: 2800
Industry/ies: Chemicals & Chemical Industry; Electricity & Electronics; Electronics; Energy/Electricity; Sports/Leisure/Entertainment
Legislative Issues: CHM; HOM; MAN; TAX; TRA; TRU

Chairman
RUPP, Joseph D.

Tel: (314) 480-1400
Fax: (314) 862-7406

President and Chief Executive Officer
FISCHER, John

Tel: (314) 480-1400
Fax: (314) 862-7406

Main Headquarters
Mailing: 190 Carondelet Plaza
Suite 1530
Clayton, MO 63105-3443

Tel: (314) 480-1400
Fax: (314) 862-7406

Political Action Committees
Olin Corporation Good Government Fund PAC
FEC ID: C00002790
Contact: Todd A. Slater
600 Powder Mill Rd.
P.O. Box 4500
East Alton, IL 62024

Tel: (618) 258-3206

Corporate Foundations and Giving Programs
Olin Charitable Trust
190 Carondelet Plaza
Suite 1530
Clayton, MO 63105-3443

Public Affairs and Related Activities Personnel

At Headquarters

ENNICO, Dolores

Tel: (314) 480-1400

Corporate Vice President, Human Resources	Fax:	(314) 862-7406
KROMIDAS, Larry P.	Tel:	(314) 480-1452
Assistant Treasurer and Director, Investor Relations	Fax:	(314) 862-7406
lpkromidas@olin.com		
LITTLE, Joseph	Tel:	(314) 480-1400
Manager, Government and Public Affairs	Fax:	(314) 862-7406
MULLGARDT, S. Christian	Tel:	(314) 480-1468
Vice President, Regulatory Audit and Senior Counsel	Fax:	(314) 862-7406
corporatemedia.queries@olin.com		
ZIMMERMANN, Theodore A.	Tel:	(618) 258-3451
Vice President, Human Resources	Fax:	(314) 862-7406
tazimmermann@olin.com		

At Other Offices

KRYGIER, Edward J.	Tel:	(618) 258-2000
Federal Lobbyist		
600 Powder Mill Rd.		
E. Alton, IL 62024		
SLATER, Todd A.	Tel:	(618) 258-2000
PAC Treasurer		
600 Powder Mill Rd.		
E. Alton, IL 62024		

Olson Advocacy Group LLC

Consulting and lobbying on housing and financial services issues.
www.olsonadvocacy.com
Legislative Issues: FIN; HOU

President	Tel:	(703) 875-8077
OLSON, Scott		
scott@olsonadvocacy.com		

Main Headquarters

Mailing:	2101 Wilson Blvd.	Tel:	(703) 875-8077
	Suite 610		
	Arlington, VA 22201		

Public Affairs and Related Activities Personnel

At Headquarters

| IGOE, Kevin | Tel: | (703) 875-8077 |
| *Contact, Congressional Relations* | | |

Olympus America, Inc.

A digital imaging company.
www.olympusamerica.com
Annual Revenues: $113.90 million
SIC: 5099
NAICS: 421990
Industry/ies: Electricity & Electronics; Electronics; Energy/Electricity

Main Headquarters

Mailing:	3500 Corporate Pkwy.	Tel:	(484) 896-5000
	P.O. Box 610	Fax:	(484) 896-7130
	Center Valley, PA 18034-0610		

Corporate Foundations and Giving Programs

Olympus America Contributions Program
3500 Corporate Pkwy.   Tel: (484) 894-5000
P.O. Box 610
Center Valley, PA 18034-0610

Public Affairs and Related Activities Personnel

At Headquarters

LEVEY, Michael	Tel:	(484) 896-5000
Contact, Media Relations	Fax:	(484) 896-7130
REED, Jennifer	Tel:	(484) 896-5000
Manager, Marketing Communications	Fax:	(484) 896-7130
STOCKWIN, Virginia	Tel:	(484) 896-5000
Senior Marketing Manager	Fax:	(484) 896-7130
STORMS-TYLER, Laura	Tel:	(484) 896-5000
Vice President, Regulatory Affairs and Quality Assurance	Fax:	(484) 896-7130

OM Group, Inc.

OM Group, Inc. provides specialty chemicals, technologies, and materials worldwide. The company operates through Magnetic Technologies, Specialty Chemicals, and Battery Technologies.
www.omgi.com
Annual Revenues: $1.05 billion
Employees: 6,200
Ticker: NYSE: OMG
SIC: 2899; 3341; 3499; 5169
NAICS: 325998; 331423; 332992; 42269
Industry/ies: Chemicals & Chemical Industry; Metals

| **Chairman and Chief Executive Officer** | Tel: | (800) 519-0083 |
| SCAMINACE, Joseph M. | Fax: | (216) 718-1502 |

Main Headquarters

Mailing:	950 Main Ave.	Tel:	(800) 519-0083
	Suite 1300	Fax:	(216) 718-1502
	Cleveland, OH 44113		

Public Affairs and Related Activities Personnel

At Headquarters

GRIFFITH, Gregory J.	Tel:	(800) 519-0083
Vice President, Strategic Planning and Development	Fax:	(216) 718-1502
greg.griffith@na.omgi.com		
HIX, Christopher M.	Tel:	(800) 519-0083
Vice President and Chief Financial Officer	Fax:	(216) 718-1502
JOHNSON, Michael V.	Tel:	(800) 519-0083
Vice President, Human Resources	Fax:	(216) 718-1502
Mike.Johnson@omgi.com		
KNOWLES, David B.	Tel:	(800) 519-0083
President and Chief Operating Officer	Fax:	(216) 718-1502
SACHS, Valerie Gentile	Tel:	(800) 519-0083
Vice President, General Counsel and Secretary	Fax:	(216) 718-1502
valerie.sachs@omgi.com		

Omaha World-Herald Company

Operates as a daily newspaper publisher in the United States.
www.owh.com
Annual Revenues: $131.50 million
Employees: 2,300
Industry/ies: Communications; Media/Mass Communication

| **President and Publiher** | Tel: | (402) 444-1179 |
| KROEGER, Terry | Fax: | (402) 348-1828 |

Main Headquarters

Mailing:	Omaha World-Herald Bldg.	Tel:	(402) 444-1000
	Omaha, NE 68102-1138	Fax:	(402) 348-1828
		TF:	(800) 284-6397

Corporate Foundations and Giving Programs

Omaha World-Herald Company Contributions Program
1314 Douglas St.
Suite 1500
Omaha, NE 68102

Public Affairs and Related Activities Personnel

At Headquarters

CAMPBELL, Roshelle	Tel:	(402) 444-1150
Director, Human Resources	Fax:	(402) 348-1828
roshelle.campbell@owh.com		
LONG, Joel	Tel:	(402) 444-1493
Director, Public Relations	Fax:	(402) 348-1828
POLODNA, Duane	Tel:	(402) 444-1480
Chief Financial Officer	Fax:	(402) 348-1828
duane.polodna@owh.com		
SEARL, Scott	Tel:	(402) 444-1726
Vice President and General Counsel	Fax:	(402) 348-1828
scott.searl@owh.com		
WARREN, Rich	Tel:	(402) 444-1000
Director, Marketing	Fax:	(402) 348-1828

Omega Protein

An international company primarily involved in marine protein products.
www.omegaprotein.com
Annual Revenues: $316.76 million
Employees: 657
Ticker: NYSE: OME
SIC: 2070; 2077; 2048
NAICS: 311119; 311613
Industry/ies: Fish And Fishing

| **Chairman of the Board** | Tel: | (713) 623-0060 |
| GOODWIN, Gary R. | Fax: | (713) 940-6122 |

| **President and Chief Executive Officer** | Tel: | (713) 623-0060 |
| SCHOLTES, Bret | Fax: | (713) 940-6122 |

Main Headquarters

Mailing:	2105 City West Blvd.	Tel:	(713) 623-0060
	Suite 500	Fax:	(713) 940-6122
	Houston, TX 77042-2838	TF:	(800) 345-8805

Political Action Committees

Omega Protein Inc. PAC
FEC ID: C00085480
Contact: Benjamin M. Landry
2105 City West Blvd.
Suite 500
Houston, TX 77042

   Contributions to Candidates: $1,000 (2015-2016)
   Democrats: $1,000

Corporate Foundations and Giving Programs

Omega Protein Contributions Program
2105 City West Blvd.   Tel: (713) 623-0060
Suite 500   Fax: (713) 940-6122
Houston, TX 77042-2838

Public Affairs and Related Activities Personnel

At Headquarters

HELD, John D.   Tel: (713) 623-0060
Executive Vice President, General Counsel and Secretary   Fax: (713) 940-6122

JOHANNESEN, Andrew C.   Tel: (713) 623-0060
Executive Vice President and Chief Financial Officer   Fax: (713) 940-6122

LANDRY, Benjamin M.   Tel: (225) 383-2326
Director, Public Affairs and PAC Treasurer   Fax: (225) 383-0992
blandry@omegaproteininc.com

LONDON, Sarah   Tel: (713) 623-0060
Marketing Manager   Fax: (713) 940-6122

Omnicare, Inc.

A provider of pharmaceutical care for the elderly.
www.omnicare.com
Annual Revenues: $6.51 billion
Employees: 11,726
Ticker: NYSE: OCR
SIC: 5912
Industry/ies: Medicine/Health Care/Mental Health

Non-Executive Chairman of the Board   Tel: (859) 392-3300
SHELTON, James D.   Fax: (859) 392-3333

President and Chief Executive Officer   Tel: (800) 990-6664
SAHNEY, Nitin

Main Headquarters
Mailing: 900 Omnicare Center   Tel: (800) 990-6664
201 E. Fourth St.
Cincinnati, OH 45202

Washington Office
Mailing: 1301 K St. NW
Suite 1100, East Tower
Washington, DC 20005

Political Action Committees
Omnicare Inc. PAC
FEC ID: C00392886
Contact: Donna Lecky
201 E. Fourth St.
900 Omnicare Center
Cincinnati, OH 45202

Public Affairs and Related Activities Personnel

At Headquarters

KRAFT, Rocky   Tel: (800) 990-6664
Senior Vice President, Chief Financial Officer

LECKY, Donna   Tel: (800) 990-6664
PAC Treasurer

MARRINER, Kirsten   Tel: (800) 990-6664
Senior Vice President, Chief Human Resources Officer

SKWARA, Steve   Tel: (800) 990-6664
Senior Vice President, Chief Compliance Officer

At Washington Office

TERRY, Elizabeth

At Other Offices

KAYNE, Alexander   Tel: (859) 392-3300
Senior Vice President, General Counsel and Secretary   Fax: (859) 392-3333
1600 River Center II, 100 E. River Center Blvd.
Covington, KY 41011

LEE, Patrick C.   Tel: (859) 392-3444
Senior Vice President, Strategy and Investor Relations   Fax: (859) 392-3333
1600 River Center II, 100 E. River Center Blvd.
Covington, KY 41011
patrick.lee@omnicare.com

VORDENBAUMEN, Sr., RPh, Timothy L.   Tel: (859) 392-3300
Vice President, Government Affairs   Fax: (859) 392-3333
1600 River Center II, 100 E. River Center Blvd.
Covington, KY 41011

Omnicom Group Inc.

A marketing communications holding company.
www.omnicomgroup.com
Annual Revenues: $15.16 billion
Employees: 74,900
Ticker: NYSE: OMC
SIC: 7311; 3993
NAICS: 323113
Industry/ies: Advertising And Marketing; Communications; Media/Mass
Communication

Chairman of the Board   Tel: (212) 415-3600
CRAWFORD, Bruce   Fax: (212) 415-3530

President and Chief Executive Officer   Tel: (212) 415-3600
WREN, John D.   Fax: (212) 415-3530

Main Headquarters
Mailing: 437 Madison Ave.   Tel: (212) 415-3600
New York City, NY 10022   Fax: (212) 415-3530

Corporate Foundations and Giving Programs
Omnicom Group Inc. Contributions Program
437 Madison Ave.   Tel: (212) 415-3600
New York City, NY 10022   Fax: (212) 415-3530

Public Affairs and Related Activities Personnel

At Headquarters

ANGELASTRO, Philip J.   Tel: (212) 415-3600
Executive Vice President and Chief Financial Officer   Fax: (212) 415-3530

CASTELLANETA, Andrew L.   Tel: (212) 415-3600
Senior Vice President, Chief Accounting Officer   Fax: (212) 415-3530

HEWITT, Dennis E.   Tel: (212) 415-3600
Treasurer   Fax: (212) 415-3530

O'BRIEN, Michael J.   Tel: (212) 415-3640
Senior Vice President, General Counsel and Secretary   Fax: (212) 415-3574

SWIECICKI, Peter L.   Tel: (212) 415-3600
Senior Vice President, Finance and Controller   Fax: (212) 415-3530

OMNOVA Solutions Inc.

A provider of coatings, specialty chemicals, decorative and functional surfaces.
www.omnova.com
Annual Revenues: $788.20 million
Employees: 1,950
Ticker: NYSE: OMN
SIC: 2295; 2869; 3011
NAICS: 321911; 325188; 31332
Industry/ies: Chemicals & Chemical Industry

Chairman, Chief Executive Officer and President   Tel: (216) 682-7000
MCMULLEN, Kevin M.   Fax: (330) 869-4288
kevin.mcmullen@omnova.com

Main Headquarters
Mailing: 25435 Harvard Rd.   Tel: (216) 682-7000
Beachwood, OH 44122-6201

Political Action Committees
Omnova Solutions Inc. PAC (OPAC)
FEC ID: C00349993
Contact: Vicky Colby
175 Ghent Rd.
Fairlawn, OH 44333

    Contributions to Candidates: $2,000 (2015-2016)
    Republicans: $2,000

Corporate Foundations and Giving Programs

Omnova Solutions Foundation
Contact: Theresa Carter
175 Ghent Rd.
Fairlawn, OH 44333

Public Affairs and Related Activities Personnel

At Headquarters

COLBY, Vicky   Tel: (216) 682-7000
PAC Treasurer

DESANTIS, Paul   Tel: (216) 682-7000
Senior Vice President and Chief Financial Officer

FOX, Chester W.   Tel: (216) 682-7000
*Vice President, Treasurer and Treasurer and Investor
Relations*

LEMAY, James C.   Tel: (216) 682-7000
*Senior Vice President, Corporate Development and General
Counsel*
james.c.lemay@omnova.com

NOAH, Sandi   Tel: (216) 682-7011
Vice President, Communications
sandi.noah@omnova.com

QUINN, Michael A.   Tel: (216) 682-7000
Senior Vice President; Chief Human Resources Officer

At Other Offices

CARTER, Theresa   Tel: (330) 869-4200
President, OMNOVA Solutions Foundation   Fax: (330) 869-4288
175 Ghent Rd.
Fairlawn, OH 44333
theresa.carter@omnova.com

LITZ, Jodie L.   Tel: (330) 869-4200
Executive Assistant   Fax: (330) 869-4288

175 Ghent Rd.
Fairlawn, OH 44333

ON Semiconductor Corporation

Manufactures low-cost, high-volume analog, logic, and discrete semiconductors.
www.onsemi.com
Annual Revenues: $2.83 billion
Employees: 23,000
Ticker: NASDAQ: ONNN
SIC: 3674
Industry/ies: Energy/Electricity

Chairman of the Board	Tel:	(602) 244-6600
MCCRANIE, J. Daneil	Fax:	(602) 244-6609
Director, President and Chief Executive Officer	Tel:	(602) 244-6600
JACKSON, Keith D.	Fax:	(602) 244-6609
Main Headquarters		
Mailing: 5005 E. McDowell Rd.	Tel:	(602) 244-6600
Phoenix, AZ 85008	Fax:	(602) 244-6609
	TF:	(888) 743-7826

Corporate Foundations and Giving Programs

ON Semiconductor Corporation Charitable Giving
5005 E. McDowell Rd.
Phoenix, AZ 85008

Public Affairs and Related Activities Personnel

At Headquarters

AGARWAL, Parag	Tel:	(602) 244-6600
Vice President	Fax:	(602) 244-6609
investor@onsemi.com		
CAVE, George H.	Tel:	(602) 244-6600
Senior Vice President, General Counsel, Chief Compliance	Fax:	(602) 244-6609
and Ethics Officer and Corporate Secretary		
sonny.cave@onsemi.com		
COOKMAN, Tobin	Tel:	(602) 244-6600
Senior Vice President, Human Resources	Fax:	(602) 244-6609
GUTMANN, Bernard	Tel:	(602) 244-6600
Executive Vice President and Chief Financial Officer	Fax:	(602) 244-6609
ROLLS, Paul	Tel:	(602) 244-6600
Executive Vice President, Sales and Marketing	Fax:	(602) 244-6609
SCHROMM, William A.	Tel:	(602) 244-6600
Executive Vice President and Chief Operating Officer	Fax:	(602) 244-6609
SPITZA, Anne	Tel:	(602) 244-6398
Manager, Corporate External Communications	Fax:	(602) 244-4830
anne.spitza@onsemi.com		

Onconova Therapeutics, Inc.

Healthcare firm specializing in cancer research.
www.onconova.com
Annual Revenues: $1.20 million
Employees: 18
Ticker: NASDAQ:ONTX
SIC: 2834
Industry/ies: Medicine/Health Care/Mental Health

Chairman of the Board	Tel:	(267) 759-3680
HOFFMAN, Michael B.	Fax:	(267) 759-3681
President and Chief Executive Officer	Tel:	(267) 759-3680
KUMAR, PhD, Ramesh	Fax:	(267) 759-3681
rkumar@onconova.us		
Main Headquarters		
Mailing: 375 Pheasant Run	Tel:	(267) 759-3680
Newtown, PA 18940-3423	Fax:	(267) 759-3681

Public Affairs and Related Activities Personnel

At Headquarters

ALTLAND, James R.	Tel:	(267) 759-3680
Senior Vice President, Finance and Corporate Development	Fax:	(267) 759-3681
jaltland@onconova.us		
BANSAL, Ajay	Tel:	(267) 759-3680
Chief Financial Officer	Fax:	(267) 759-3681
GUERIN, Mark	Tel:	(267) 759-3680
Chief Accounting Officer	Fax:	(267) 759-3681
HOFFMAN, Benjamin	Tel:	(267) 759-3680
Senior Director, Corporate Affairs and Media contact	Fax:	(267) 759-3681
bhoffman@onconova.us		
KUPREWICZ, Lisa	Tel:	(267) 759-3680
Human Resources and Investor Manager	Fax:	(267) 759-3681
lisa@onconova.com		
MCKEARN, Thomas J.	Tel:	(267) 759-3680
President, Research and Development	Fax:	(267) 759-3681
MORRIS, Kathryn	Tel:	(845) 635-9828
Contact, Media Relations	Fax:	(267) 759-3681

kathryn@proncall.com

Oncor Electric Delivery

Delivers electricity to consumers.
www.oncor.com
Annual Revenues: $3.12 billion
Employees: 3,800
SIC: 4911
Industry/ies: Energy/Electricity
Legislative Issues: ENG; TEC

Chairman and Chief Executive Officer	Tel:	(214) 486-2000
SHAPARD, Bob	Fax:	(214) 486-2175
Main Headquarters		
Mailing: 1601 Bryan St.	Tel:	(214) 486-2039
Suite 2300	Fax:	(214) 486-3367
Dallas, TX 75201		
Washington Office		
Mailing: 601 Pennsylvania Ave.	Tel:	(202) 628-1020
Suite 850, South Bldg.		
Washington, DC 20004		

Political Action Committees

Oncor Political Action Committee of Oncor Electric Delivery Administration
Corporation
FEC ID: C00487447
Contact: Autry Lee Warren
1616 Woodall Rodgers Fwy.
Floor 6C-014
Dallas, TX 75202-1234

Corporate Foundations and Giving Programs

Oncor Community
1601 Bryan St.
Suite 2300
Dallas, TX 75201

Public Affairs and Related Activities Personnel

At Headquarters

CASEY, John	Tel:	(214) 486-4776
Vice President and Treasurer	Fax:	(214) 486-2175
CLEVENGER, Don	Tel:	(214) 486-2000
Senior Vice President, Strategy	Fax:	(214) 486-2175
don.clevenger@oncor.com		
DAVIS, David	Tel:	(214) 486-2000
Senior Vice President and Chief Financial Officer	Fax:	(214) 486-2175
DENNIS, Debbie	Tel:	(214) 486-2000
Senior Vice President, Human Resources and Corporate	Fax:	(214) 486-2175
affairs		
GREER, Jim	Tel:	(214) 486-2039
Senior Vice President and Chief Operating Officer	Fax:	(214) 486-3367
NYE, Allen	Tel:	(214) 486-2000
Senior Vice President, General Counsel and Secretary	Fax:	(214) 486-2175
allen.nye@oncor.com		

At Other Offices

WARREN, Autry Lee
PAC Treasurer
1616 Woodall Rodgers Fwy., Suite 6C-006
Dallas, TX 75202-1234

One Communications Corporation

See listing on page 274 under EarthLink, Inc.

OneBeacon Insurance Group

Formerly One Beacon Corporation, the company changed it when it was acquired by White Mountains Insurance Group of Hamilton, Bermuda in 2001. An insurance company which provides specialty insurance solutions backed by financial strength, expertise and a commitment to excellence in everything we do.
www.onebeacon.com
Employees: 1,200
Ticker: NYSE: OB
SIC: 6331
Industry/ies: Insurance Industry

Chairman of the Board	Tel:	(952) 852-2431
SMITH, Lowndes A.	Fax:	(888) 656-1213
President and Chief Executive Officer	Tel:	(781) 332-7000
MILLER, T. Michael	Fax:	(888) 656-1213
Main Headquarters		
Mailing: 605 Highway 169 N.		
Suite 800		
Plymouth, MN 55441		

Corporate Foundations and Giving Programs

OneBeacon Insurance Group Contributions Program		
One Beacon Ln.	Tel:	(781) 332-7000

Canton, MA 02021 Fax: (888) 656-1213

Public Affairs and Related Activities Personnel

At Other Offices

DUARTE, Carmen Tel: (781) 332-7268
Vice President, Marketing and Communications Fax: (888) 656-1213
601 Carlson Pkwy., Suite 600
Minnetonka, MN 55305
cduarte@onebeacon.com

MCDONOUGH, Paul H. Tel: (877) 248-8765
Senior Vice President and Chief Financial Officer Fax: (888) 656-1213
601 Carlson Pkwy., Suite 600
Minnetonka, MN 55305
ir@onebeacon.com

PHILLIPS, Maureen A. Tel: (952) 852-2431
Senior vice President and General Counsel Fax: (888) 656-1213
601 Carlson Pkwy., Suite 600
Minnetonka, MN 55305

SCHMITT, Thomas N. Tel: (952) 852-2431
Chief Human Resources Officer Fax: (888) 656-1213
601 Carlson Pkwy., Suite 600
Minnetonka, MN 55305

ONEOK, Inc.

Parent company of Oklahoma Natural Gas Co. and Kansas Gas Service Co., natural gas utilities. Engaged also in oil and gas exploration, processing, storage, transmission and gas marketing.
www.oneok.com
Annual Revenues: $10.84 billion
Employees: 2,269
Ticker: NYSE: OKE
SIC: 4923
Industry/ies: Utilities
Legislative Issues: ENG

Chairman of the Board Tel: (918) 588-7000
GIBSON, John W. Fax: (918) 588-7960
john.gibson@oneok.com

President and Chief Executive Officer Tel: (918) 588-7000
SPENCER, Terry K. Fax: (918) 588-7273

Main Headquarters
Mailing: ONEOK Plaza Tel: (918) 588-7000
100 W. Fifth St. Fax: (918) 588-7273
Tulsa, OK 74103 TF: (877) 274-5710

Washington Office
Mailing: 7417 Rebecca Dr. Tel: (202) 257-1779
Alexandria, VA 22307

Political Action Committees
ONEOK Inc. Employee PAC
FEC ID: C00215384
Contact: Ray Poudrier
P.O. Box 871
Tulsa, OK 74102

   Contributions to Candidates: $32,500 (2015-2016)
   Democrats: $1,000; Republicans: $31,500

Corporate Foundations and Giving Programs

ONEOK Foundation Inc.
Contact: Angie Zimmer
P.O. Box 871
Tulsa, OK 74102

Public Affairs and Related Activities Personnel

At Headquarters

BORROR, Brad Tel: (918) 588-7582
Manager, Communications Fax: (918) 588-7960
brad.borror@oneok.com

CHRISTENSEN, Wesley J. Tel: (918) 588-7000
Senior Vice President, Operations Fax: (918) 588-7273

GRIMSHAW, Eric Tel: (918) 588-7000
Vice President, Associate General Counsel and Corporate Fax: (918) 588-7960
Secretary

HARRISON, Dandridge L. Tel: (918) 588-7000
Senior Vice President, Administrative Services and Corporate Fax: (918) 588-7273
Relations
dan.harrison@oneok.com

HULSE III, Walter S. Tel: (918) 588-7000
Executive Vice President Strategic Planning and Corporate Fax: (918) 588-7273
Affairs

LAKE, Stephen W. Tel: (918) 588-7000
Senior Vice President, General Counsel and Assistant Fax: (918) 588-7273
Secretary

MAREBURGER, Robert S. Tel: (918) 588-7000
Senior Vice President, Market Analysis Fax: (918) 588-7273

MARTINOVICH, Robert F. Tel: (918) 588-7000
Executive Vice President, Chief Administrative Officer Fax: (918) 588-7960

MIERS III, Sheppard F. Tel: (918) 588-7000
Vice President, Chief Accounting Officer Fax: (918) 588-7273

REINERS, Derek S. Tel: (918) 588-7000
Senior Vice President, Chief Financial Officer and Treasurer Fax: (918) 588-7273

At Washington Office

WEST, George Tel: (202) 257-1779
Federal Lobbyists
Registered Federal Lobbyist

At Other Offices

POUDRIER, Ray Tel: (877) 208-7318
Contact, PAC
P.O. Box 871
Tulsa, OK 74102

SMITH, Mark W. Tel: (918) 588-7700
Vice President
P.O. Box 871
Tulsa, OK 74102

WILLIAMSON, Christy Tel: (918) 588-7163
Supply Director
P.O. Box 871
Tulsa, OK 74102
christy.williamson@oneok.com

ZIMMER, Angie Tel: (918) 588-7531
Coordinator, Community Investments at ONEOK Foundation
P.O. Box 871
Tulsa, OK 74102
azimmer@oneok.com

Onvia, Inc.

A software solutions provider connecting businesses to government contracts.
www.onvia.com
Annual Revenues: $22.85 million
Employees: 136
Ticker: NASDAQ: ONVI
SIC: 7389
Industry/ies: Construction/Construction Materials; Defense/Homeland Security; Engineering/Mathematics; Government-Related

Chairman of the Board Tel: (206) 282-5170
SKILLING, D. Van Fax: (206) 373-8961

President and Chief Executive Officer Tel: (206) 282-5170
RINER, Henry Fax: (206) 373-8961

Main Headquarters
Mailing: 509 Olive Way Tel: (206) 282-5170
Suite 400 Fax: (206) 373-8961
Seattle, WA 98101

Public Affairs and Related Activities Personnel

At Headquarters

KWON, SoYoung Tel: (206) 373-9404
General Counsel, Corporate Secretary and Vice President, Fax: (206) 373-8961
Human Resources
skwon@onvia.com

PEARL , Travis Tel: (206) 282-5170
Director, Marketing Fax: (206) 373-8961

USHKA, Amber Tel: (206) 282-5170
Director, Human Resources Fax: (206) 373-8961

WAY, Cameron Tel: (206) 373-9034
Senior Vice President and Chief Financial Officer Fax: (206) 373-8961

Open Range Communications, Inc.

A broadband wireless Internet services provider.
www.openrangecomm.com
Industry/ies: Communications; Telecommunications/Internet/Cable

Chief Executive Officer Tel: (303) 376-2111
BEANS, Jr., Bill

Main Headquarters
Mailing: 6430 S. Fiddlers Green Cir. Tel: (303) 376-2111
Suite 500
Greenwood Village, CO 80111

Public Affairs and Related Activities Personnel

At Other Offices

MATTHEWS, Buzz Tel: (303) 376-2103
Senior Vice President, People Services
8100 E. Maplewood Ave., Suite 200
Greenwood Village, CO 80111

Opticomp Corporation

See listing on page 861 under Zephyr Photonics

The Options Clearing Corporation

An equity derivatives clearing organization.
www.optionsclearing.com
Annual Revenues: $158.11 million
Employees: 300
SIC: 6200
Industry/ies: Banking/Finance/Investments
Legislative Issues: BUD; FIN; LBR; TAX

Executive Chairman	Tel:	(312) 322-6200
DONOHUE, Craig S	Fax:	(312) 977-0611

President, Chief Operating Officer and Treasurer	Tel:	(202) 756-1968
CAHILL, Michael E.	Fax:	(202) 756-7518

Main Headquarters
Mailing:	One N. Wacker Dr.	Tel:	(312) 322-6200
	Suite 500	Fax:	(312) 977-0611
	Chicago, IL 60606	TF:	(800) 678-4667

Washington Office
Mailing:	701 Eighth St. NW	Tel:	(202) 507-6201
	Suite 630		
	Washington, DC 20001		

Public Affairs and Related Activities Personnel

At Headquarters

BINDER, Jim	Tel:	(312) 322-9853
Contact, Media Relations	Fax:	(312) 977-0611
jbinder@theocc.com		

BROWN, James E.	Tel:	(312) 322-6200
Executive Vice President and General Counsel	Fax:	(312) 977-0611

CAMLEY, Jean	Tel:	(312) 322-6200
Senior Vice President and Corporate Secretary	Fax:	(312) 977-0611

KAMNIK, Joseph	Tel:	(312) 322-6200
Senior Vice President and General Counsel	Fax:	(312) 977-0611

MACGARRY, Kimberly	Tel:	(312) 322-6200
Senior Vice President and Chief Financial Officer	Fax:	(312) 977-0611

RABEN, Tracy	Tel:	(312) 322-6200
Senior Vice President and Chief Human Resources Officer	Fax:	(312) 977-0611

WALLACE, Richard	Tel:	(312) 322-6200
Senior Vice President and Chief Compliance Officer	Fax:	(312) 977-0611

At Washington Office

CORCORAN, Joseph	Tel:	(202) 507-6201
Vice President		
Registered Federal Lobbyist		

HALL, James	Tel:	(202) 507-6201
Director, Government Relations		
Registered Federal Lobbyist		

At Other Offices

DAHLSTROM, Ted	Tel:	(202) 756-1972
Manager, Government Affairs	Fax:	(202) 756-7518
1101 Pennsylvania Ave. NW, Suite 600		
Washington, DC 20004		

Optosecurity

Develops security products for the transportation and critical infrastructure markets.
www.optosecurity.com
Industry/ies: Defense/Homeland Security; Government-Related

Chairman	Tel:	(418) 653-7665
GRENON, Jean-Francois	Fax:	(418) 657-3851

President and Chief Executive Officer	Tel:	(877) 678-6732
BERGERON, Eric	Fax:	(571) 323-5201

Main Headquarters
Mailing:	1280 Blvd. Lebourgneuf	Tel:	(418) 653-7665
	bureau 420	Fax:	(418) 657-3851
	Quebec, QC G2K 0H1		

Washington Office
Mailing:	13873 Park Center Rd.	Tel:	(418) 653-7665
	Suite 400-N1	Fax:	(571) 323-5201
	Herndon, VA 20171		

Public Affairs and Related Activities Personnel

At Headquarters

BOUCHARD, Gabrielle	Tel:	(418) 653-7665
Contact, Media Relation	Fax:	(418) 657-3851
media@optosecurity.com		

ELLIOTT, Mark	Tel:	(418) 653-7665
Vice president of Sales and Partner Accounts	Fax:	(418) 657-3851

GIASSON, Marjolaine	Tel:	(418) 653-7665
Chief Financial Officer	Fax:	(418) 657-3851

At Washington Office

MATHEWS, Timothy	Tel:	(418) 653-7665

Vice President, Business Development, Sales and Marketing	Fax:	(571) 323-5201

Oracle Corporation

A software provider. In January, 2010, Oracle completes its aquisition of Sun Microsystems. Acquired PeopleSoft in 2005. Acquired BEA Systems, Inc. and Siebel Systems, Inc.
www.oracle.com
Annual Revenues: $38.23 Billion
Employees: 132,000
Ticker: NASDAQ (GS): ORCL
SIC: 7372
Industry/ies: Computer/Technology
Legislative Issues: BUD; CPI; CPT; CSP; DEF; EDU; GOV; HCR; HOM; IMM; INT; LAW; LBR; SCI; TAR; TAX; TEC; TRD; VET

Executive Chairman Board and Chief Technology Officer	Tel:	(650) 506-7000
ELLISON, Lawrence J.	Fax:	(650) 506-7200
larry.ellison@oracle.com		

Chief Executive Officer	Tel:	(650) 506-7000
HURD, Mark V.	Fax:	(650) 506-7200

Chief Executive Officer	Tel:	(650) 506-7000
CATZ, Safra A.	Fax:	(650) 506-7200

Main Headquarters
Mailing:	500 Oracle Pkwy.	Tel:	(650) 506-7000
	Redwood Shores, CA 94065	Fax:	(650) 506-7200
		TF:	(800) 392-2999

Washington Office
Mailing:	1015 15th St. NW	Tel:	(202) 835-7360
	Suite 250	Fax:	(202) 467-4250
	Washington, DC 20005		

Political Action Committees
Oracle America Inc. PAC (ORACLE PAC)
FEC ID: C00323048
Contact: Eric Ball
1015 15th St. NW		
Suite 200	Tel:	(202) 835-7360
Washington, DC 20005	Fax:	(202) 467-4250

> **Contributions to Candidates:** $133,845 (2015-2016)
> Democrats: $66,045; Republicans: $67,800

Corporate Foundations and Giving Programs

Oracle Education Foundation
Contact: Colleen Cassity
500 Oracle Pkwy.
Redwood City, CA 94065

Public Affairs and Related Activities Personnel

At Headquarters

AKBAR, Sara	Tel:	(650) 506-7000
Registered Federal Lobbyist	Fax:	(650) 506-7200

BOND, Ken	Tel:	(650) 607-0349
Vice President, Investor Relations	Fax:	(650) 506-7200
ken.bond@oracle.com		

CASSITY, Colleen	Tel:	(650) 506-7000
Senior Director, Corporate Citizenship	Fax:	(650) 506-7200
Mail Stop 5OP-8		

DALEY, Dorian	Tel:	(650) 506-7000
Senior Vice President, General Counsel and Secretary	Fax:	(650) 506-7200
dorian.daley@oracle.com		

GLUECK, Kenneth	Tel:	(650) 506-7000
Senior Vice President, Office of the Chief Executive Officer	Fax:	(650) 506-7200

GOLEMON-ANDERSON, Meredith	Tel:	(650) 506-7000
Federal Lobbyist	Fax:	(650) 506-7200
Registered Federal Lobbyist		

HENLEY, Jeffrey O.	Tel:	(650) 506-7000
Vice Chairman of the Board	Fax:	(650) 506-7200

HINZMAN, Joel	Tel:	(650) 506-7000
Federal Lobbyist	Fax:	(650) 506-7200
Registered Federal Lobbyist		

JOURNOUD, Franck	Tel:	(650) 506-7000
Federal Lobbyist	Fax:	(650) 506-7200
Registered Federal Lobbyist		

KEHRING, Douglas	Tel:	(650) 506-7000
Executive Vice President, Chief of Staff and Head of	Fax:	(650) 506-7200
Corporate Development		

MAHLER, Jason	Tel:	(650) 506-7000
Federal Lobbyist	Fax:	(650) 506-7200
Registered Federal Lobbyist		

PAVLOVIC, Dejan	Tel:	(650) 506-7000
Senior Director, Government and Corporate Affairs	Fax:	(650) 506-7200
Registered Federal Lobbyist		

SIM, Judith	Tel:	(650) 506-7000
Chief Marketing Officer	Fax:	(650) 506-7200

At Washington Office

BALL, Eric	Tel:	(202) 835-7360
Senior Vice President and Treasurer	Fax:	(202) 467-4250
LORD, Peter	Tel:	(202) 835-7360
Director, Technology Policy	Fax:	(202) 467-4250
Registered Federal Lobbyist		

Orange and Rockland Utilities, Inc.

An electric and gas utility. A wholly owned subsidiary of Consolidated Edison Co. of New York.
www.oru.com
Employees: 1,100
SIC: 4931; 4911; 4924
NAICS: 221210; 221122
Industry/ies: Utilities

President and Chief Executive Officer
CAWLEY, Timothy P.	Tel:	(845) 352-6000
	Fax:	(845) 577-6913

Main Headquarters
Mailing:	One Blue Hill Plaza	Tel:	(845) 352-6000
	Pearl River, NY 10965	Fax:	(845) 577-6913
		TF:	(800) 533-5325

Corporate Foundations and Giving Programs

The Neighbor Fund
Contact: Linda Feger
One Blue Hill Plaza	Tel:	(845) 577-2545
Pearl River, NY 10965		

Public Affairs and Related Activities Personnel

At Headquarters

BRIZZOLARA, Thomas L.	Tel:	(845) 352-6000
Director, Public Affairs	Fax:	(845) 577-6989
DONOVAN, Michael W.	Tel:	(845) 577-2430
Contact, Media Relations	Fax:	(845) 577-6913
mdonovan@oru.com		
FEGER, Linda	Tel:	(845) 577-2545
Foundation Contact	Fax:	(845) 577-6913
FegerL@oru.com		
PEVERLY, Francis W.	Tel:	(845) 352-6000
Vice President, Operations	Fax:	(845) 577-6913
WOLFF, Joanna	Tel:	(845) 352-6000
Director, Human Resources Support Services	Fax:	(845) 577-6913

Orasure Technologies

Develops, manufactures and markets point-of-care, oral fluid specimen collection devices that leverage proprietary oral fluid technologies, diagnostic products, including immunoassays and other in vitro diagnostic tests, and other medical devices.
www.orasure.com
Annual Revenues: $110.01 million
Employees: 320
Ticker: NASDAQ (GM): OSUR
SIC: 2835; 5122; 3841
NAICS: 325413
Industry/ies: Computer/Technology; Medicine/Health Care/Mental Health
Legislative Issues: BUD; HCR

Chairman of the Board
WATSON, Douglas G.	Tel:	(610) 882-1820
	Fax:	(610) 882-1830

President and Chief Executive Officer
MICHELS, Douglas A.	Tel:	(610) 882-1820
	Fax:	(610) 882-1830

Main Headquarters
Mailing:	220 E. First St.	Tel:	(610) 882-1820
	Bethlehem, PA 18015	Fax:	(610) 882-1830
		TF:	(800) 869-3538

Corporate Foundations and Giving Programs

Orasure Technologies Contributions Program
220 E. First St.
Bethlehem, PA 18015

Public Affairs and Related Activities Personnel

At Headquarters

CLARKE, Judy	Tel:	(610) 882-1820
Executive Administrative	Fax:	(610) 882-1830
COHEN, Henry B.	Tel:	(610) 882-1820
Senior Vice President, Human Resources	Fax:	(610) 882-1830
FRASER-HOWZE, Debra Y.	Tel:	(610) 882-1820
Vice President, Government and External Affairs	Fax:	(610) 882-1830
dfraser-howze@orasure.com		
GEORGE-BECK, Rena	Tel:	(610) 882-1820
Contact, Investor Relations	Fax:	(610) 882-1830
investorinfo@orasure.com		
JERRETT, Jack E.	Tel:	(610) 882-1820
Senior Vice President, General Counsel and Secretary	Fax:	(610) 882-1830

MORITZ, Jennifer	Tel:	(917) 748-4006
Contact, Media Relations	Fax:	(610) 882-1830
jmoritz@0to5.com		
SPAIR, Ronald H.	Tel:	(610) 882-1820
Chief Operating Officer and Chief Financial Officer	Fax:	(610) 882-1830
TICHO, Ron	Tel:	(610) 882-1820
Senior Vice President, Corporate Communications	Fax:	(610) 882-1830
ZEZZO, Tony	Tel:	(610) 882-1820
Executive Vice President, Marketing and Sales	Fax:	(610) 882-1830

Orbital Sciences Corporation

A space technology company that designs, manufactures, operates and markets space products and services.
www.orbital.com
Employees: 3,300
Ticker: NYSE: ORB
SIC: 3663
Industry/ies: Aerospace/Aviation; Defense/Homeland Security; Government-Related; Transportation

President and Chief Executive Officer
THOMPSON, David W.	Tel:	(703) 406-5000
thompson.david@orbital.com	Fax:	(703) 406-3502

Main Headquarters
Mailing:	45101 Warp Dr.	Tel:	(703) 406-5000
	Dulles, VA 20166	Fax:	(703) 406-3502

Washington Office
Mailing:	21839 Atlantic Blvd.
	4th Floor
	Dulles, VA 20166

Public Affairs and Related Activities Personnel

At Headquarters

BENESKI, Barron	Tel:	(703) 406-5000
Vice President, Investor Relations and Communications	Fax:	(703) 406-3502
investor.relations@orbitalatk.com		
FORTUNATO, Edward M.	Tel:	(703) 406-5000
Senior Vice President, Government Relations	Fax:	(703) 406-3502
KHOURI, Amer	Tel:	(703) 948-8600
Vice President, Marketing ad Business Development	Fax:	(703) 406-3502
geomarketing@orbital.com		
KRONMILLER, Kathleen B.	Tel:	(703) 406-5000
Senior Vice President, Government Relations	Fax:	(703) 406-3502
LARSON, Blake E.	Tel:	(703) 406-5000
Chief Operating Officer	Fax:	(703) 406-3502
MCCABE, Thomas E.	Tel:	(703) 406-5000
Senior Vice President, General Counsel and Secretary	Fax:	(703) 406-3502
PIERCE, Garrett	Tel:	(703) 406-5000
Chief Financial Officer	Fax:	(703) 406-3502
ROZELSKY, Kevin	Tel:	(703) 406-5000
Senior Director, Government Relations	Fax:	(703) 406-5572
WOLF, Christine A.	Tel:	(703) 406-5000
Senior Vice President, Human Resources	Fax:	(703) 406-3502
YOUNG, Beverly	Tel:	(703) 406-5000
Executive Assistant and PAC Administrator	Fax:	(703) 406-3502

ORC Industries Inc

ORC Industries provides employment opportunities for people with disabilities in manufacturing and assembly operations and related services.
www.orcind.com
Employees: 1,000
Industry/ies: Apparel/Textiles Industry; Defense/Homeland Security; Government-Related

Main Headquarters
Mailing:	2700 Commerce St.	Tel:	(608) 781-7727
	La Crosse, WI 54603	Fax:	(608) 781-1464

Oregon Aero, Inc.

Designer and manufacturer of products for general aviation, military, and specialty industries.
www.oregonaero.com
Annual Revenues: $15.7 million
Industry/ies: Aerospace/Aviation; Defense/Homeland Security; Government-Related; Machinery/Equipment; Military/Veterans; Transportation

Founder, President and Chief Executive Officer
DENNIS, Mike	Tel:	(503) 543-7399
	Fax:	(503) 543-4820

Main Headquarters
Mailing:	34020 Skyway Dr.	Tel:	(503) 543-7399
	Scappoose, OR 97056	Fax:	(503) 543-4820
		TF:	(800) 888-6910

Public Affairs and Related Activities Personnel

At Headquarters

DENNIS, Jude	Tel:	(503) 543-7399
Vice President	Fax:	(503) 543-4820
KRAMER, Marjorie	Tel:	(330) 466-2307
Contact, Media Relations	Fax:	(503) 543-4820
kramcom@sssnet.com		

Orexigen Therapeutics, Inc.

A biopharmaceutical company focused on the treatment of obesity.
www.orexigen.com
Annual Revenues: $59.02 million
Employees: 47
Ticker: NASDAQGS : OREX
SIC: 2834
Industry/ies: Biology; Medicine/Health Care/Mental Health; Science
Legislative Issues: HCR

President and Chief Executive Officer

NARACHI, Michael	Tel:	(858) 875-8600
	Fax:	(858) 875-8650

Main Headquarters

Mailing:	3344 N. Torrey Pines Ct.	Tel:	(858) 875-8600
	Suite 200	Fax:	(858) 875-8650
	La Jolla, CA 92037-1024		

Public Affairs and Related Activities Personnel

At Headquarters

HAGAN, Joseph	Tel:	(858) 875-8600
Executive Vice President, Chief Business and Financial Officer	Fax:	(858) 875-8650
MCDONALD, Suzanne	Tel:	(858) 875-8600
Vice President, Managed Markets & Government Affairs	Fax:	(858) 875-8650
TURNER, Heather	Tel:	(858) 875-8600
Senior Vice President and General Counsel	Fax:	(858) 875-8650
hturner@orexigen.com		
VIVEASH, Dawn	Tel:	(858) 875-8600
Senior Vice President, Head, Global Regulatory Affairs and Quality Assurance	Fax:	(858) 875-8650

Orion Networking

Provides technology customized for individual client needs.
orionnetwork.net
Employees: 5
Industry/ies: Communications; Telecommunications/Internet/Cable

President and Chief Executive Officer

ADAGIO, Floyd	Tel:	(703) 406-4001
	Fax:	(703) 406-4002
floyd.adagio@orionnetwork.net		

Main Headquarters

Mailing:	11211 Birmingham Ct.	Tel:	(703) 406-4001
	Great Falls, VA 22066	Fax:	(703) 406-4002

Public Affairs and Related Activities Personnel

At Headquarters

ADAGIO, Stacy	Tel:	(703) 406-4001
Vice President and Contact, Administration and Human Resources	Fax:	(703) 406-4002
stacy.adagio@orionnetwork.net		

Oshkosh Corporation

Designs, manufactures, and markets specialty vehicles, vehicle bodies and access equipment.
www.oshkoshcorporation.com
Annual Revenues: $6.51 billion
Employees: 12,000
Ticker: NYSE: OSK
SIC: 3711
NAICS: 333924
Industry/ies: Automotive Industry; Transportation; Trucking Industry
Legislative Issues: DEF

Chairman of the Board

DONNELLY, Richard M.	Tel:	(920) 235-9150
	Fax:	(920) 233-9268

Chief Executive Officer

SZEWS, Charles L.	Tel:	(920) 235-9150
	Fax:	(920) 233-9268

Main Headquarters

Mailing:	2307 Oregon St.	Tel:	(920) 235-9150
	Oshkosh, WI 54902	Fax:	(920) 233-9268
		TF:	(866) 222-4059

Washington Office

Mailing:	1300 N. 17th St.	Tel:	(920) 235-9150
	Suite 1040	Fax:	(920) 233-9268
	Arlington, VA 22209		

Political Action Committees

Oshkosh Corporation Employees PAC (OCEPAC)
FEC ID: C00304477

Contact: Corey R. Braun
2307 Oregon St.
P.O. Box 2566
Oshkosh, WI 54903

Contributions to Candidates: $153,000 (2015-2016)
Democrats: $40,000; Republicans: $113,000

Principal Recipients

SENATE
KIRK, MARK STEVEN (REP-IL)
MCCAIN, JOHN S (REP-VA)

HOUSE
CRENSHAW, ANDER (REP-FL)
DUCKWORTH, L. TAMMY (DEM-IL)
GROTHMAN, GLENN S. (REP-WI)
JOLLY, DAVID W. (REP-FL)
TURNER, MICHAEL R (REP-OH)

Corporate Foundations and Giving Programs

Oshkosh Corporation Foundation
Contact: Connie S. Stellmacher
P.O. Box 2566
Oshkosh, WI 54903

Public Affairs and Related Activities Personnel

At Headquarters

BLANKFIELD, Bryan J.	Tel:	(920) 235-9150
Executive Vice President, General Counsel and Secretary	Fax:	(920) 233-9268
BRAUN, Corey R.	Tel:	(920) 235-9150
Assistant Secretary and PAC Contact	Fax:	(920) 233-9268
Mail Stop 2307 Oregon St.		
DAGGETT, John	Tel:	(920) 233-9247
Vice President, Communications	Fax:	(920) 233-9251
jdaggett@oshkoshcorp.com		
DAVIDSON, Patrick N.	Tel:	(920) 966-5939
Vice President, Investor Relations	Fax:	(920) 233-9268
pdavidson@oshkoshcorp.com		
GRENNIER, Scott R.	Tel:	(920) 235-9150
Senior Vice President and Treasurer	Fax:	(920) 233-9268
HILL, Bettye J.	Tel:	(920) 235-9150
Vice President, Chief Ethics & Compliance Officer	Fax:	(920) 233-9268
HOGAN , Janet L.	Tel:	(920) 235-9150
Executive Vice President, Chief Human Resources Officer	Fax:	(920) 233-9268
JONES, Wilson R.	Tel:	(920) 235-9150
President and Chief Operating Officer	Fax:	(920) 233-9268
SAGEHORN, David M.	Tel:	(920) 235-9150
Executive Vice President, Chief Financial Officer	Fax:	(920) 233-9268
STELLMACHER, Connie S.	Tel:	(920) 235-9150
Vice President, Oshkosh Corporation Foundation and Assistant Secretary	Fax:	(920) 233-9268

At Washington Office

KIMMITT, Joseph	Tel:	(920) 235-9150
Executive Vice President, Government Operations and Industry Relations	Fax:	(920) 233-9268
jkimmitt@oshtruck.com		

OSI Restaurant Partners, LLC

A hospitality company that owns several casual dining chains. Subsidiaries include Carrabba's Italian Grill, Bonefish Grill, Roy's Restaurant and Fleming's Prime Steakhouse & Wine Bar.
www.bloominbrands.com
Annual Revenues: $3.8 billion
Employees: 91,000
SIC: 5812
Industry/ies: Food And Beverage Industry
Legislative Issues: FOO; TAX; TRA

Chief Executive Officer & Partner, Fleming Prime Steakhouse - a unit of OSI Restaurant

	Tel:	(813) 282-1225
	Fax:	(813) 282-2114
ALLEN, William A.		

Chief Executive Officer

SMITH, Elizabeth	Tel:	(813) 282-1225
	Fax:	(813) 282-2114

Main Headquarters

Mailing:	2202 N. Westshore Blvd.	Tel:	(813) 282-1225
	Fifth Floor	Fax:	(813) 282-2114
	Tampa, FL 33607		

Political Action Committees

Blooming Brands, Inc. Political Action Committee
FEC ID: C00253153
Contact: Joseph J Kadow
2202 N. Westshore Blvd.
Fifth Floor
Tampa, FL 33607

Contributions to Candidates: $257,725 (2015-2016)

Democrats: $34,100; Republicans: $221,125; Other: $2,500

Principal Recipients

SENATE
MURPHY, PATRICK E (DEM-FL)

HOUSE
COFFMAN, MIKE REP. (REP-CO)
MCCARTHY, KEVIN (REP-CA)

Public Affairs and Related Activities Personnel

At Headquarters

AMBERG, Stephanie L.	Tel:	(813) 282-1225
Vice President, Public Relations	Fax:	(813) 282-2114
stephanieamberg@outback.com		
HALME, Matthew P.	Tel:	(813) 282-1225
Vice President, Government Affairs and Corporate Counsel	Fax:	(813) 282-2114
Registered Federal Lobbyist		
KADOW, Joseph J	Tel:	(813) 282-1225
Treasurer	Fax:	(813) 282-2114
REUSING, Vincent P.	Tel:	(813) 282-1225
Federal Lobbyist	Fax:	(813) 282-2114
Registered Federal Lobbyist		
SALIBA, Khalil G.	Tel:	(813) 282-1225
Registered Federal Lobbyist	Fax:	(813) 282-2114

OSI Systems, Inc.

A technology and electronics company. OSI Systems is committed to both comprehensive research into technology solutions to make the world safer and healthier.
www.osi-systems.com
Industry/ies: Electricity & Electronics; Energy/Electricity

Chairman, President and Chief Executive Officer	Tel:	(310) 978-0516
CHOPRA, Deepak		

Main Headquarters
Mailing:	12525 Chadron Ave.	Tel:	(310) 978-0516
	Hawthorne, CA 90250		

Political Action Committees
OSI Systems Inc. PAC
FEC ID: C00414896
Contact: Peter Kant
2900 Crystal Dr.
Suite 910
Arlington, VA 22202

Contributions to Candidates: $22,000 (2015-2016)
Democrats: $9,000; Republicans: $13,000

Public Affairs and Related Activities Personnel

At Headquarters

DOLCE, Frank	Tel:	(310) 978-0516
Director, Global Corporate Travel, Expense and Meetings		
FDOLCE@OSI-SYSTEMS.COM		
EDRICK, Alan	Tel:	(310) 978-0516
Executive Vice President and Chief Financial Officer		
MANSOURI, Manoocher	Tel:	(310) 978-0516
President, OSI Optoelectronics		
manoocher.mansouri-aliabadi@osi-systems.com		
SZE, Victor	Tel:	(310) 978-0516
Executive Vice President, General Counsel and Corporate Secretary		

Osiris Therapeutics, Inc.

Manufacturer of vaccines and drugs.
www.osiristx.com
Annual Revenues: $70.82 million
Employees: 211
Ticker: NASDAQ: OSIR
SIC: 2836
Industry/ies: Pharmaceutical Industry
Legislative Issues: MMM

Chairman of the Board	Tel:	(443) 545-1800
FRIEDLI, Peter	Fax:	(443) 545-1701
President and Chief Executive Officer	Tel:	(443) 545-1800
DEBRABANDERE, Lode	Fax:	(443) 545-1701

Main Headquarters
Mailing:	7015 Albert Einstein Dr.	Tel:	(443) 545-1800
	Columbia, MD 21046	Fax:	(443) 545-1701

Public Affairs and Related Activities Personnel

At Headquarters

BADILLO, Amanda	Tel:	(443) 545-1834
Contact, Communications	Fax:	(443) 545-1701
OsirisPR@Osiris.com		

JACOBY, Jr., Phillip R.	Tel:	(443) 545-1800
Chief Financial Officer and Corporate Secretary	Fax:	(443) 545-1701
MOLLO, Adrian P.	Tel:	(443) 545-1800
General Counsel	Fax:	(443) 545-1701

Osmotica Pharmaceutical

A global pharmaceutical company of drug delivery technologies and neurology based therapies.
www.osmoticausa.com
Annual Revenues: $25.7 Million
Industry/ies: Pharmaceutical Industry

President and Chief Executive Officer	Tel:	(770) 509-4500
TYLE, Praveen	Fax:	(770) 509-3944

Main Headquarters
Mailing:	895 Sawyer Rd.	Tel:	(770) 509-4500
	Marietta, GA 30062	Fax:	(770) 509-3944

Public Affairs and Related Activities Personnel

At Headquarters

AIKMAN, Mark S.	Tel:	(770) 509-4500
Vice President, Regulatory Affairs and Quality Assurance	Fax:	(770) 509-3944
CAVAGNARO , Albert	Tel:	(770) 509-4500
General Counsel	Fax:	(770) 509-3944
cavagnaro@osmotica.com		
DENTISTE, Angela	Tel:	(770) 509-4500
Vice President, Clinical Operations and Contracts Officer	Fax:	(770) 509-3944
GAYRON, Ken	Tel:	(770) 509-4500
Vice President and Chief Financial Officer	Fax:	(770) 509-3944
NOTARANTONIO, Kathy	Tel:	(770) 509-4500
Director of Human Resources	Fax:	(770) 509-3944
UNDERWOOD, William H.	Tel:	(770) 509-4500
Senior Vice President, Corporate Development and Business Development	Fax:	(770) 509-3944

Otsuka America Inc.

Otsuka American is oversees pharmaceutical research and development, marketing, and distribution of both prescription pharmaceuticals and OTC vitamins.
www.otsuka-america.com
Annual Revenues: $159.80 million
Employees: 2,100
Industry/ies: Pharmaceutical Industry

Chairman of the Board and Chief Executive Officer	Tel:	(415) 986-5300
YOSHIKAWA, Hiromi	Fax:	(415) 986-5361

Main Headquarters
Mailing:	One Embarcadero Center	Tel:	(415) 986-5300
	Suite 2020	Fax:	(415) 986-5361
	San Francisco, CA 94111		

Washington Office
Mailing:	2440 Research Blvd.
	Rockville, MD 20850

Otter Tail Power Company

An electric utility.
www.otpco.com
Annual Revenues: $787.14 million
Employees: 1,893
Ticker: NASDAQ: OTTR
SIC: 4911
Industry/ies: Energy/Electricity; Utilities

Chairman of the Board	Tel:	(218) 739-8200
PARTAIN , Nathan I.	Fax:	(218) 998-3165
President	Tel:	(218) 739-8200
ROGELSTAD, Timothy J.	Fax:	(218) 998-3165

Main Headquarters
Mailing:	215 S. Cascade St.	Tel:	(218) 739-8200
	Fergus Falls, MN 56537	Fax:	(218) 998-3165
		TF:	(800) 257-4044

Political Action Committees
Otter Tail Corporation PAC
FEC ID: C00292136
Contact: Rebecca J. Luhning
215 S. Cascade St.	Tel:	(218) 739-8200
Fergus Falls, MN 56537	Fax:	(218) 998-3165

Corporate Foundations and Giving Programs
Community Connections program
Contact: Rebecca J. Luhning
215 S. Cascade St.	Tel:	(202) 608-4758
P.O. Box 496		
Fergus Falls, MN 56537		

Public Affairs and Related Activities Personnel

At Headquarters

BELL, George D. — Tel: (218) 739-8200 / Fax: (218) 998-3165
Chief Financial Officer

BRAUSE, Thomas R. — Tel: (218) 739-8200 / Fax: (218) 998-3165
Vice President, Administration

BRING, Mark B. — Tel: (218) 739-8200 / Fax: (218) 998-3165
Associate General Counsel and Director, Legislative Affairs

HANSON, Loren — Tel: (218) 739-8481 / Fax: (218) 998-3165
Manager, Investor Relations

LUHNING, Rebecca J. — Tel: (218) 739-8206 / Fax: (218) 739-8218
Contact, Community Relations and PAC Treasurer
bluhning@otpco.com

OEHLER, Cris M. — Tel: (218) 531-0099 / Fax: (218) 739-8762
Director, Public Relations
ckling@otpco.com

SMESTAD, Jennifer O. — Tel: (218) 739-8200 / Fax: (218) 998-3165
General Counsel

TOLLERSON, Bradley E. — Tel: (218) 739-8200 / Fax: (218) 998-3165
Vice President, Planning and Strategy

WASBERG, Peter E. — Tel: (218) 739-8200 / Fax: (218) 998-3165
Director, Human Resources and Safety

Out-Front

Develops, manufactures, and markets products to wheelchair users, clinicians, and researchers. Formerly Three Rivers Holdings LLC.
www.out-front.com
Annual Revenues: $30.22 million
Employees: 100
Industry/ies: Medicine/Health Care/Mental Health

President and Chief Executive Officer — Tel: (480) 833-1829 / Fax: (480) 833-1837
BLANK, John P.

Main Headquarters
Mailing: 1826 W. Broadway Rd. — Tel: (480) 833-1829 / Fax: (480) 833-1837
Suite 43
Mesa, AZ 85202

Public Affairs and Related Activities Personnel

At Headquarters

ELLISOR, Gabriel — Tel: (480) 833-1829 / Fax: (480) 833-1837
Chief Financial Officer

Outback Steakhouse, Inc.

Outback Steakhouse is an Australian themed steakhouse restaurant. Although beef and steak items make up a good portion of the menu, the concept offers a variety of chicken, ribs, seafood, and pasta dishes. Outback Steakhouse is owned and operated by Bloomin' Brands, Inc.
www.outback.com
Annual Revenues: $2.30 billion
Employees: 105,000
SIC: 5812
Industry/ies: Agriculture/Agronomy; Food And Beverage Industry
Legislative Issues: FOO

Chief Executive Officer and Chairman of the Board — Tel: (813) 282-1225 / Fax: (813) 282-2114
SMITH, Elizabeth

Main Headquarters
Mailing: 2202 N.W. Shore Blvd. — Tel: (813) 282-1225 / Fax: (813) 282-2114
Suite 500
Tampa, FL 33607

Corporate Foundations and Giving Programs
Outback Steakhouse, Inc. Contributions Program
2202 N. West shore Blvd. — Tel: (813) 282-1225
Suite 500
Tampa, FL 33607-5747

Public Affairs and Related Activities Personnel

At Headquarters

AMBERG, Stephanie L. — Tel: (813) 282-1225 / Fax: (813) 282-2114
Vice President, Public relations
stephanieamberg@outback.com

SMITH, Jeff — Tel: (813) 282-1225 / Fax: (813) 282-2114
President

Outdoor Venture Corporation

Manufacturer, supplier and subcontractor of military tent systems, components and accessories for the United States Department of Defense.
www.outdoorventure.com
Annual Revenues: $11.90 million
Employees: 250
SIC: 2394
Industry/ies: Apparel/Textiles Industry; Defense/Homeland Security; Government-Related

President and Contracts Administrator — Tel: (606) 376-5021 / Fax: (606) 376-3341
EGNEW, James C.
jc.egnew@outdoorventure.com

Main Headquarters
Mailing: 30 Venture Dr. — Tel: (606) 376-5021 / Fax: (606) 376-3341
Stearns, KY 42647

Public Affairs and Related Activities Personnel

At Headquarters

BRADEN, Anita — Tel: (606) 376-5021 / Fax: (606) 376-3341
Business Development Manager
Anita.Braden@outdoorventure.com

FIELDS, Joe W. — Tel: (606) 376-5021 / Fax: (606) 376-3341
Vice President, Business Development
joe.fields@outdoorventure.com

MILLER, Lori — Tel: (606) 376-5021 / Fax: (606) 376-3341
Vice President, Finance

Overseas Shipholding Group

Operates vessels that transport crude oil, refined petroleum products and gas worldwide.
www.osg.com
Annual Revenues: $1.06 billion
Employees: 2,860
Ticker: NYSE: OSGIQ
SIC: 4491; 4412
NAICS: 483111; 488320
Industry/ies: Marine/Maritime/Shipping; Transportation
Legislative Issues: TAX

Chairman of the Board — Tel: (212) 953-4100 / Fax: (212) 578-1832
WHEAT, Douglas

President and Chief Executive Officer — Tel: (212) 953-4100 / Fax: (212) 578-1832
BLACKLEY, CAPT Ian T.

Main Headquarters
Mailing: 1301 Avenue of the Americas — Tel: (212) 953-4100 / Fax: (212) 578-1832
New York City, NY 10019

Political Action Committees
Overseas Shipholding Group Inc. PAC
FEC ID: C00411389
Contact: James I. Edelson
1301 Avenue of the Americas — Tel: (212) 953-4100 / Fax: (212) 953-4100
New York City, NY 10019

Contributions to Candidates: $2,000 (2015-2016)
Democrats: $1,000; Republicans: $1,000

Corporate Foundations and Giving Programs
Overseas Shipholding Group Contributions Program
666 Third Ave.
New York City, NY 10017

Public Affairs and Related Activities Personnel

At Headquarters

CARPENTER, Geoff — Tel: (212) 953-4100 / Fax: (212) 578-1832
Vice President and Treasurer

ORICCHIO, Rick — Tel: (212) 953-4100 / Fax: (212) 578-1832
Senior Vice President and Chief Financial Officer

OSHODI, Adewale — Tel: (212) 953-4100 / Fax: (212) 578-1832
Vice President and Controller

SMALL, James D. — Tel: (212) 953-4100 / Fax: (212) 578-1832
Senior Vice President, Secretary and General Counsel

At Other Offices

COLLINS, Jr., John F. — Tel: (212) 578-1699 / Fax: (212) 578-1832
Vice President, Investor Relations
666 Third Ave.
New York City, NY 10017

EDELSON, James I. — Tel: (212) 953-4100 / Fax: (212) 578-1832
Senior Vice President, General Counsel, Secretary and PAC Treasurer
666 Third Ave.
New York City, NY 10017

ITKIN, Myles — Tel: (212) 953-4100 / Fax: (212) 578-1832
Executive Vice President, Chief Financial Officer
666 Third Ave.
New York City, NY 10017

OverStock.com, Inc.

An internet retailer.
www.overstock.com
Annual Revenues: $1.55 billion
Employees: 1,700
Ticker: NASDAQ (GM): OSTK
SIC: 5961
Industry/ies: Retail/Wholesale

Legislative Issues: CPT; CSP; FIN; TAX; TEC

Chairman of the Board
JOHNSON III, Jonathan E.
Tel: (801) 947-3100
Fax: (801) 453-7798

Chief Executive Officer and Board Member
BYRNE, Dr. Patrick M.
Tel: (801) 947-3100
Fax: (801) 453-7798

Main Headquarters
Mailing: 6350 S. 3000 East St.
Salt Lake City, UT 84121
Tel: (801) 947-3100
Fax: (801) 453-7798
TF: (800) 989-0135

Public Affairs and Related Activities Personnel

At Headquarters

BURDEN, Kirstie
Contact, Media Relations
kirstie@overstock.com
Tel: (801) 947-3116
Fax: (801) 453-7798

GRIFFIN, Mark J.
Senior Vice President and General Counsel
Tel: (801) 947-3100
Fax: (801) 453-7798

HARDEN, Mark
Corporate Treasurer and Contact, Investor Relations
Tel: (801) 947-3100
Fax: (801) 453-7798

HARDEN, Mark
Contact, Investor Relations
mharden@overstock.com
Tel: (801) 947-5409
Fax: (801) 453-7798

HUGHES, Robert P.
Senior Vice President, Finance and Risk Management
Tel: (801) 947-3100
Fax: (801) 453-7798

MOON, Kevin
Director, Investor Relations
kmoon@overstock.com
Tel: (801) 947-3282
Fax: (801) 947-3149

SIMON, Stormy D.
President and Board Member
Tel: (801) 947-3100
Fax: (801) 453-7798

TRYON, Stephen P.
Senior Vice President, Human Capital Management
Tel: (801) 947-3100
Fax: (801) 453-7798

Overture Technologies

Software for the loan and mortgage industry.
www.overturecorp.com
Annual Revenues: $4.10 million
Employees: 40
Industry/ies: Computer/Technology

Chairman of the Board and Chief Executive Officer
PINGHO, LeRoy
Tel: (301) 492-2140
Fax: (301) 652-8599

Main Headquarters
Mailing: 6900 Wisconsin Ave.
Suite 200
Bethesda, MD 20815
Tel: (301) 492-2140
Fax: (301) 652-8599

Owens and Minor Distributions Inc.

A national wholesale distributor of surgical, medical and related supplies to the acute-care market and a leading provider of healthcare supply chain management solutions.
www.owens-minor.com
Annual Revenues: $9.57 billion
Employees: 7,800
Ticker: NYSE: OMI
SIC: 5047
Industry/ies: Commodities; Medicine/Health Care/Mental Health
Legislative Issues: HCR; MMM; TAX

Chairman of the Board and Chief Executive Officer
SMITH, Craig R.
Tel: (804) 723-7000
Fax: (804) 723-7100

Main Headquarters
Mailing: P.O. Box 27626
Richmond, VA 23261-7626
Tel: (804) 723-7000
Fax: (804) 723-7100

Corporate Foundations and Giving Programs

Owens & Minor, Inc., Contributions Program
9120 Lockwood Blvd.
Mechanicsburg, VA 23166
Tel: (804) 723-7000
Fax: (804) 723-7100

Public Affairs and Related Activities Personnel

At Headquarters

ALLCOTT, Truitt
Director, Investor and Media Relations
truitt.allcott@owens-minor.com
Tel: (804) 723-7555
Fax: (804) 723-7100

BIERMAN, James L.
President and Chief Operating Officer
Tel: (804) 723-7000
Fax: (804) 723-7100

COLPO, Charles C.
Senior Vice President, Strategic Relationships
Tel: (804) 723-7000
Fax: (804) 723-7100

DAVIS, Erika T.
Senior Vice President, Administration and Operations
Tel: (804) 723-7000
Fax: (804) 723-7100

DEN HARTOG, Grace R.
Senior Vice President, General Counsel and Corporate Secretary
Tel: (804) 723-7000
Fax: (804) 723-7100

GRAVES, Chuck
Tel: (804) 723-7556

Director, Finance and Investor Relations
chuck.graves@owens-minor.com
Fax: (804) 723-7100

MEIER, Richard A. (Randy)
Executive Vice President and Chief Financial Officer
Tel: (804) 723-7000
Fax: (804) 723-7100

MINOR, III, G. Gilmore
Chairman Emeritus
Tel: (804) 723-7000
Fax: (804) 723-7100

Owens Corning

A manufacturer of building materials.
www.owenscorning.com
Annual Revenues: $5.20 billion
Employees: 14,000
Ticker: NYSE: OC
SIC: 3290
Industry/ies: Construction/Construction Materials
Legislative Issues: HOU; TAX; TRD

Chairman of the Board, President and Chief Executive Officer
THAMAN, Michael H.
mike.thaman@owenscorning.com
Tel: (419) 248-8000
Fax: (419) 248-6227

Main Headquarters
Mailing: One Owens Corning Pkwy.
Toledo, OH 43659
Tel: (419) 248-8000
Fax: (419) 248-6227
TF: (800) 438-7465

Washington Office
Mailing: 900 19th St. NW, Suite 250
Washington, DC 20006

Corporate Foundations and Giving Programs

The Owens Corning Foundation
Contact: Steve Krull
One Owens Corning Pkwy.
Toledo, OH 43659

Public Affairs and Related Activities Personnel

At Headquarters

DEFILIPPIS, Victor
Administration
Mail Stop 2G
Tel: (419) 248-8000
Fax: (419) 248-6227

DENIS, Thierry J.
Vice President, Investor Relations
Tel: (419) 248-5748
Fax: (419) 248-6227

LIBONATI, John J.
Vice President, Government and Public Affairs
john.libonati@owenscorning.com
Registered Federal Lobbyist
Tel: (419) 248-8000
Fax: (419) 248-6227

MURDOCH, John
Federal Lobbyist
Registered Federal Lobbyist
Tel: (419) 248-8000
Fax: (419) 248-6227

SCHANZE, Christopher
Director, Government and Public Affairs
Registered Federal Lobbyist
Tel: (419) 248-8000
Fax: (419) 248-6227

SCHRODER, Matt
Senior Leader, Corporate Communications and Media Relations
matt.schroder@owenscorning.com
Tel: (419) 248-8987
Fax: (419) 248-6227

WILKE, Jeffery S.
Vice President, Assistant General Counsel and Assistant Secretary
Tel: (419) 248-8000
Fax: (419) 248-6227

Owens-Illinois, Inc. (O-I)

A manufacturer of glass and plastic specialty products.
www.o-i.com
Annual Revenues: $6.57 billion
Employees: 21,100
Ticker: NYSE: OI
SIC: 3085; 3221
NAICS: 32616
Industry/ies: Glass; Plastics Industry
Legislative Issues: CPT; ENG; ENV; GOV; LBR; MAN; NAT; RET; TAX; TRA; TRD

Chairman, President and Chief Executive Officer
STROUCKEN, Albert P.L.
Tel: (567) 336-5000
Fax: (419) 247-7107

Main Headquarters
Mailing: One Michael Owens Way
Perrysburg, OH 43551-2999
Tel: (567) 336-5000
Fax: (419) 247-7107

Washington Office
Mailing: 1401 Wilson Blvd.
Suite 1005
Arlington, VA 22209

Political Action Committees
Owens-Illinois Employee Good Citizenship Fund
FEC ID: C00034330
Contact: Daniel K. Steen
One Michael Owens Way
Tel: (567) 336-5000

Perrysburg, OH 43551-2999

Contributions to Candidates: $13,500 (2015-2016)
Democrats: $5,000; Republicans: $8,500

Fax: (419) 247-7107

Public Affairs and Related Activities Personnel

At Headquarters

BAEHREN, James W.
Senior Vice President, and General Counsel
Tel: (567) 336-5000
Fax: (419) 247-7107

BRAMLAGE, Steve
Senior Vice President and Chief Financial Officer
Tel: (567) 336-5000
Fax: (419) 247-7107

HAUDRICH, John
Acting Chief Financial Officer
Tel: (567) 336-5000
Fax: (419) 247-7107

JARRELL, Paul
Senior Vice President and Chief Administrative Officer
Tel: (567) 336-5000
Fax: (419) 247-7107

JOHNSON, Dave
Vice President, Investor Relations
dave.johnson@o-i.com
Tel: (567) 336-2600
Fax: (419) 247-7107

OWENS, Barbara
Senior Communications Advisor
barbara.owens@o-i.com
Tel: (567) 336-5000
Fax: (419) 247-7107

STEEN, Daniel K.
Vice President, Government Affairs and PAC Treasurer
daniel.steen@o-i.com
Registered Federal Lobbyist
Tel: (567) 336-1381
Fax: (419) 247-7107

At Other Offices

MODLIN, Ryan N.
Vice President, North American Government Relations
2107 Wilson Blvd., Suite 420
Arlington, VA 22201
Registered Federal Lobbyist
Tel: (567) 336-1381
Fax: (703) 717-9746

VANCIL, Jennifer L.
Senior Specialist, Government & Community Affairs
2107 Wilson Blvd., Suite 420
Arlington, VA 22201
jennifer.vancil@o-i.com
Tel: (567) 336-1381
Fax: (703) 717-9746

Oxbow Carbon LLC

A resource recovery company. Oxbow's primary businesses are the mining and marketing of energy and commodities such as coal, natural gas, petroleum, metallurgical and calcined coke.
www.oxbow.com
Annual Revenues: $3.70 billion
Employees: 1,200
Industry/ies: Energy/Electricity; Fuels See Coal, Gas, Oil, Petroleum; Natural Resources; Petroleum Industry

Chief Executive Officer and Chairman of the Board
KOCH, William I
Tel: (561) 907-5400
Fax: (561) 640-8747

Main Headquarters
Mailing: 1601 Forum Pl.
Suite 1400
W. Palm Beach, FL 33401
Tel: (561) 907-5400
Fax: (561) 640-8747

Washington Office
Mailing: 801 Pennsylvania Ave. NW
Suite 247
Washington, DC 20004
Tel: (202) 347-0794

Political Action Committees
Oxbow Carbon & Minerals Holdings Inc PAC
FEC ID: C00436550
Contact: Mcauiffe Michael
1601 Forum Pl.
Suite 1400
Palm Beach, FL 33401

Contributions to Candidates: $1,750 (2015-2016)
Republicans: $1,750

Corporate Foundations and Giving Programs
Oxbow Carbon Contribution Program
1601 Forum Pl.
Suite 1400
W. Palm Beach, FL 33401
Tel: (561) 697-4300
Fax: (561) 697-1876

Public Affairs and Related Activities Personnel

At Headquarters

"BILL" PARMELEE , William D.
Chief Financial Officer
bill.parmelee@oxbow.com
Tel: (561) 907-5400
Fax: (561) 640-8747

CALLAHAN, Richard P.
General Counsel, Director and Executive Vice President
Tel: (561) 697-4300
Fax: (561) 697-1876

CLARK, David
Tel: (561) 907-5400
Fax: (561) 640-8747

FRENEY, James R.
Executive Vice President, Activated Carbon and Special Projects
Tel: (561) 907-5400
Fax: (561) 640-8747

JOHNSON, Eric
President
Tel: (561) 907-5400
Fax: (561) 640-8747

MCAULIFFE, Michael F.
General Counsel Corporate Secretary
Tel: (561) 907-5400
Fax: (561) 640-8747

MICHAEL, Mcauiffe
PAC Treasurer
Tel: (561) 907-5400
Fax: (561) 640-8747

SCHORSCH, Roy J.
Senior Vice President, Operations
Tel: (561) 907-5400
Fax: (561) 640-8747

SZEREMETA, Caroline Martin
Fedaral Lobbyist
Registered Federal Lobbyist
Tel: (561) 697-4300
Fax: (561) 697-1876

Oxbow Corporation

See listing on page 611 under Oxbow Carbon LLC

PACCAR, Inc.

Designs, manufactures, and distributes light, medium, and heavy-duty trucks and related aftermarket parts worldwide.
www.paccar.com
Annual Revenues: $19.45 billion
Employees: 23,300
Ticker: NASDAQ: PCAR
SIC: 3711
Industry/ies: Automotive Industry; Manufacturers; Transportation; Trucking Industry

Chief Executive Officer
ARMSTRONG, Ronald E.
Tel: (425) 468-7400
Fax: (425) 468-8216

Main Headquarters
Mailing: 777 106th Ave. NE
Bellevue, WA 98004
Tel: (425) 468-7400
Fax: (425) 468-8216

Political Action Committees
PACCAR Political Interest Committee
FEC ID: C00034355
Contact: Michael K. Walton
777 106th Ave. NE
Bellevue, WA 98004
Tel: (425) 468-7400
Fax: (425) 468-8216

Contributions to Candidates: $8,000 (2015-2016)
Democrats: $1,000; Republicans: $7,000

Corporate Foundations and Giving Programs
PACCAR Foundation
Contact: Ken Hastings
P.O. Box 1518
Bellevue, WA 98009

Public Affairs and Related Activities Personnel

At Headquarters

ANDERSON, David C.
Vice President & General Counsel
Tel: (425) 468-7400
Fax: (425) 468-8216

CHRISTENSEN, Robert J.
President & Chief Financial Officer
Tel: (425) 468-7400
Fax: (425) 468-8216

EASTON, Robin
Managing Director
Tel: (425) 468-7676
Fax: (425) 468-8216

FEENSTRA, Paul
Director, Government Relations
Tel: (425) 468-7400
Fax: (425) 468-8216

WALTON, Michael K.
PAC Treasurer
Tel: (425) 468-7400
Fax: (425) 468-8216

At Other Offices

HASTINGS, Ken
Contact, Corporate Development
P.O. Box 1518
Bellevue, WA 98009
ken.hastings@paccar.com

Pace Global Energy Services LLC

A firm that offers services in engineering, fuel, power, resource and risk management, finance and regulatory affairs to energy companies. This energy consulting and management firm was acquired by Siemens Industry, Inc. in 2012.
www.paceglobal.com
Industry/ies: Energy/Electricity; Natural Resources

Founder, Chairman and Chief Executive Officer
SUTHERLAND, Timothy F.
Tel: (703) 818-9100
Fax: (703) 818-9108

Main Headquarters
Mailing: 4401 Fair Lakes Ct.
Suite 400
Fairfax, VA 22033
Tel: (703) 818-9100
Fax: (703) 818-9108

Public Affairs and Related Activities Personnel

At Headquarters

VESSEY, Robert Christopher
Vice President
bob.vessey@paceglobal.com
Tel: (703) 818-9100
Fax: (703) 818-9108

Pacific Capital Bank, N.A.

Banking company. The company operates under the local brand names of Santa Barbara Bank & Trust, First National Bank of Central California, South Valley National Bank, San Benito Bank, and First Bank of San Luis Obispo.Change name to Union Bank.
www.pacificcapitalbank.com
Annual Revenues: $330.31 million
Employees: 1,400
Ticker: NASDAQ (GS): PCBC
Industry/ies: Banking/Finance/Investments

Chairman of the Board Tel: (818) 865-3300
BIRCH, Edward E.

Chief Executive Officer Tel: (818) 865-3300
WEBB, Carl B.

Main Headquarters
Mailing: 29015 Thousand Oaks Blvd Tel: (818) 706-4848
Agoura Hills, CA 91301

Corporate Foundations and Giving Programs
Pacific Capital Bancorp Giving
30343 Canwood St.
Suite 100
Agoura Hills, CA 91301

Public Affairs and Related Activities Personnel

At Headquarters

BRUTON, Noma J. Tel: (818) 865-3300
Chief Human Resources Officer

CLOUGH, Frederick W. Tel: (818) 865-3300
Executive Vice President and General Counsel

LEIS, George S. Tel: (818) 865-3300
President

OLSON, Mark K. Tel: (818) 865-3300
Chief Financial Officer
mark.olson@pcbancorp.com

WHITE, Deborah A. Tel: (805) 884-6680
Executive Vice President, Investor Relations, Public Relations and Marketing

ZEPKE, Carol M. Tel: (805) 564-6298
Corporate Secretary
carol.zepke@pcbancorp.com

Pacific Companies, Inc.

See listing on page 463 under Kate Spade & Company

Pacific Consolidated Industries

PCI manufactures ruggedized onsite liquid and gaseous oxygen and nitrogen generators for a variety of markets; including Military, Medical, Water & Wastewater Treatment, Industrial, and Oil & Gas markets.
pci-intl.com
Annual Revenues: $15.80 million
Employees: 100
Industry/ies: Natural Resources; Utilities

Chairman of the Board Tel: (951) 479-0860
CHERINGTON, Charles Fax: (951) 479-0861

Chief Executive Officer Tel: (951) 479-0860
ENG, Bob Fax: (951) 479-0861

Main Headquarters
Mailing: 12201 Magnolia Ave. Tel: (951) 479-0860
Riverside, CA 92503-4820 Fax: (951) 479-0861
TF: (800) 309-8935

Corporate Foundations and Giving Programs
Pacific Consolidated Industries Contributions Program
12201 Magnolia Ave.
Riverside, CA 92503-4820

Public Affairs and Related Activities Personnel

At Headquarters

STEVENS, Paul T. Tel: (951) 479-0860
Chief Financial Officer, Vice President and General Manager, Fax: (951) 479-0864
Military Solutions

ZELAS, Barbara Tel: (951) 479-0860
Vice President, Human Resources Fax: (951) 479-0864

Pacific Gas and Electric Company

Combined natural gas and electric utility provider for northern and central California.
www.pge.com
Annual Revenues: $16.91 billion
Employees: 23,000
Ticker: NYSE: PCG
Industry/ies: Utilities
Legislative Issues: AVI; BUD; CAW; ENG; ENV; HOM; INT; LBR; TAX; TRA; UTI; VET

Chairman of the Board Tel: (202) 638-3500
EARLEY, Jr., Anthony F. Fax: (202) 638-3522

Manager, Federal Governmental Relations, Chief of Staff, Office Tel: (202) 638-3502
of the Chairman and Chief Executive Officer Fax: (202) 638-3522
FOSTER, Chris
c1f2@pge.com

Main Headquarters
Mailing: P.O. Box 997300 TF: (800) 743-5000
Sacramento, CA 95899-7300

Washington Office
Mailing: 900 Seventh St. NW Tel: (202) 638-3500
Suite 950 Fax: (202) 638-3522
Washington, DC 20001-3886

Corporate Foundations and Giving Programs
PG&E Corporation Foundation
Contact: Helen A. Burt
One Market, Spear Tower
Suite 2400
San Fracisco, CA 94105-1126

Public Affairs and Related Activities Personnel

At Headquarters

ANGALAKUDATI, Mallik
Vice President, Corporate Strategy

CAIRNS, Stephen J.
Vice President, Internal Audit and Compliance

FITZPATRICK, Tim
Vice President, Corporate Relations and Chief Communications Officer

LODUCA, Janet C.
Vice President, Investor Relations

SIMON, John R.
Executive Vice President, Corporate Services and Human Resources

STAVROPOULOS, Nick
President, Gas

THOMASON, David S.
Vice President, Chief Financial Officer, and Controller

At Washington Office

ALDANA, Silvia R. Tel: (202) 638-3500
Manager, Federal Governmental Relations Fax: (202) 638-3522
Registered Federal Lobbyist

BLACK, Patricia Tel: (202) 638-3521
Executive Assistant Fax: (202) 638-3522
pjb5@pge.com

BURT, Helen A. Tel: (202) 638-3521
Senior Vice President, External Affairs and Public Policy and Chairman, Foundation

DYE, Richard Tel: (202) 638-3521

GARRETT, Ezra C. Tel: (202) 638-3500
Executive Director, Foundation Fax: (202) 638-3522

HOGLE , Jessica C. Tel: (202) 638-3503
Director, Federal Affairs and Chief of Staff Fax: (202) 638-3522
j8h1@pge.com
Registered Federal Lobbyist

MALNIGHT, Steve Tel: (202) 638-3500
Senior Vice President, Regulatory Affairs Fax: (202) 638-3522

MILLER, Matt R. Tel: (202) 638-3500
Manager, Federal Governmental Relations Fax: (202) 638-3522
Registered Federal Lobbyist

At Other Offices

BURT, Helen A. Tel: (415) 973-8719
Senior Vice President, External Affairs and Public Policy and Chairman, Foundation
77 Beale St., P.O. Box 770000, Mail Code B 29H
San Francisco, CA 94177

CHENG, Linda Y.H. Tel: (415) 973-8719
Vice President, Corporate Governance and Corporate Secretary
77 Beale St., P.O. Box 770000, Mail Code B 29H
San Francisco, CA 94177

DYE, Richard Tel: (415) 973-8719
77 Beale St., P.O. Box 770000, Mail Code B 29H
San Francisco, CA 94177

LAVINSON, Melissa A.
Federal Lobbyist
77 Beale St., P.O. Box 770000, Mail Code B 29H
San Francisco, CA 94177
Registered Federal Lobbyist

LUCAS, Steven S.

Attorney & Agent for Filer
77 Beale St., P.O. Box 770000, Mail Code B 29H
San Francisco, CA 94177

Pacific Life Insurance Company
Formerly known as Pacific Mutual Life Insurance Co. Became Pacific Life Insurance Co. in 1997.
www.pacificlife.com/PL
Employees: 3,800
Industry/ies: Insurance Industry
Legislative Issues: FIN; LBR; TAX

Chairman, Foundation and Chief Executive Officer
MORRIS, FSA, James T.   Tel: (949) 219-3011   Fax: (949) 219-7614

Main Headquarters
Mailing: P.O. Box 9000
Newport Beach, CA 92658-9030   Tel: (949) 219-3011   Fax: (949) 219-7614   TF: (800) 800-7646

Political Action Committees
Pacific Life Insurance Company PAC
FEC ID: C00068528
Contact: Patricia S. Douglass
700 Newport Center Dr.
Newport Beach, CA 92660

  Contributions to Candidates: $12,598,515 (2015-2016)
  Democrats: $189,000; Republicans: $303,000; Other: $12,106,515

    Principal Recipients

    HOUSE
    BRADY, KEVIN (REP-TX)
    MCCARTHY, KEVIN (REP-CA)
    PAULSEN, ERIK (REP-MN)
    ROYCE, ED MR. (REP-CA)
    WALTERS, MIMI (REP-CA)

Corporate Foundations and Giving Programs
Pacific Life Foundation
Contact: James T. Morris FSA
P.O. Box 9000
Newport Beach, CA 92658

Public Affairs and Related Activities Personnel

At Headquarters

BROWN, FSA, MAAA, Mary Ann   Tel: (949) 219-3011   Fax: (949) 219-7614
Executive Vice President, Corporate Development

CHEEVER, Sharon A.   Tel: (949) 219-3011   Fax: (949) 219-7614
Senior Vice President and General Counsel

GOODMAN, Milda C.   Tel: (949) 219-3011   Fax: (949) 219-7614
Assistant Vice President, Corporate Advertising
mgoodman@pacificlife.com

GRIGGS, Adrian S.   Tel: (949) 219-3011   Fax: (949) 219-7614
Executive Vice President and Chief Financial Officer

OLEKSIW, Andrew   Tel: (949) 219-3011   Fax: (949) 219-7614
Senior Vice President, Corporate Development

OYLER, Tennyson   Tel: (949) 219-3248   Fax: (949) 219-7614
Vice President, Brand Management and Public Affairs
tennyson.oyler@pacificlife.com

SCHINDLER, CLU, FLMI, Richard J.   Tel: (949) 219-3011   Fax: (949) 219-7614
Executive Vice President

SUDBECK, Carol R.   Tel: (949) 219-3011   Fax: (949) 219-7614
Senior Vice President, Corporate

TRAN, Khanh T.   Tel: (949) 219-3011   Fax: (949) 219-7614
President

ZEMBLES, Andrew   Tel: (949) 219-3058   Fax: (949) 219-7614
Assistant Vice President, Corporate Compliance
Andrew.Zembles@Pacificlife.com

At Other Offices

DOUGLASS, Patricia S.   Tel: (949) 219-3011   Fax: (949) 219-7614
Federal Lobbyist and PAC Treasurer
700 Newport Center Dr.
Newport Beach, CA 92660-6397
Registered Federal Lobbyist

Pacific Pulmonary Services
Pacific Pulmonary Services (PPS) was founded in 1978 in Bakersfield, California, as "Med-Mart", a full-service durable medical equipment (DME) company serving the Central Valley of California. It is a medical equipment and services provider for patients with chronic respiratory diseases.
www.ppsc.com
Annual Revenues: $130 million
Employees: 1,000
Industry/ies: Medicine/Health Care/Mental Health

Main Headquarters
Mailing: 773 San Marin Dr.   Tel: (800) 572-7522

Suite 2230
Novato, CA 94945

Public Affairs and Related Activities Personnel
At Other Offices

DOTY, Jim   Tel: (800) 572-7522
Vice President, Marketing and General Manager, Sleep Therapy
88 Rowland Way, Suite 300
Novato, CA 94945

MCELROY, Carolyn   Tel: (800) 572-7522
Vice President and General Counsel
88 Rowland Way, Suite 300
Novato, CA 94945

PacifiCorp
An electric utility headquartered in Portland, OR. Acquired by MidAmerican Energy Holdings Company.
www.pacificorp.com
Annual Revenues: $5.21 billion
Employees: 5,900
SIC: 1221
NAICS: 212111
Industry/ies: Energy/Electricity; Utilities
Legislative Issues: ENG; GOV; MAR; NAT; UTI

Chairman and Chief Executive Officer
ABEL, Gregory E.   Tel: (503) 813-5000   Fax: (503) 813-7247

Main Headquarters
Mailing: 825 N.E. Multnomah St.
Portland, OR 97232   Tel: (503) 813-5000   Fax: (503) 813-7247   TF: (888) 221-7070

Political Action Committees
Pacificorp - Pacific Power/Rocky Mountain Power PAC
FEC ID: C00082800
Contact: Steven R. Evans
825 N.E. Multnomah St.
Portland, OR 97232   Tel: (503) 813-5000   Fax: (503) 813-7247

  Contributions to Candidates: $21,500 (2015-2016)
  Democrats: $11,000; Republicans: $10,500

Corporate Foundations and Giving Programs
Pacificorp Foundation
Contact: Lilisa C. Hall
825 NE Multnomah
Suite 2000
Portland, OR 97232   Tel: (503) 813-5000   Fax: (503) 813-7247

Public Affairs and Related Activities Personnel
At Headquarters

EVANS, Steven R.   Tel: (503) 813-5000   Fax: (503) 813-7247
PAC Treasurer
Mail Stop Suite 2000
srevans@midamerican.com

HALL, Lilisa C.   Tel: (503) 813-5000   Fax: (503) 813-7247
Executive Director, PacifiCorp Foundation and Director, Community Affairs and Strategic Programs

STUVER, Douglas   Tel: (503) 813-5000   Fax: (503) 813-7247
Senior Vice President and Chief Financial Officer

Pactiv Corporation
Packaging company. Manufactures, markets and sells consumer products and food/food service packaging. Brand names include Hefty, Baggies, Hefty One-Zip, Kordite, and E-Z Foil.
www.pactiv.com
Employees: 11,000
Ticker: NYSE: PTV
SIC: 3081
NAICS: 326113
Industry/ies: Food And Beverage Industry; Plastics Industry

Main Headquarters
Mailing: 1900 W. Field Ct.
Lake Forest, IL 60045   Tel: (847) 482-2000   Fax: (770) 232-9864   TF: (888) 828-2850

Corporate Foundations and Giving Programs
Pactiv Corporation Contributions Program
1900 W. Field Ct.   Tel: (847) 482-2000
Lake Forest, IL 60045

Public Affairs and Related Activities Personnel
At Headquarters

BERNDT, Tori   Tel: (847) 482-3148   Fax: (770) 232-9864
Manager, Communications
vberndt@pactiv.com

DOYLE, Joseph E.   Tel: (847) 482-2000

General Counsel
jdoyle@pactiv.com
Fax: (770) 232-9864

WALTERS, Edward T.
Vice President and Controller
Tel: (847) 482-2000
Fax: (770) 232-9864

Padraic Riley Communications LLC
Communications consulting, public affairs, media relations, and government relations.

Main Headquarters
Mailing: 25 Nassau Rd.
Larchmont, NY 10538

Public Affairs and Related Activities Personnel

At Headquarters

RILEY, Padraic
Principal
Tel: (914) 309-7114

Paetec Holding Corporation
Telecommunications provider.
www.paetec.com
Employees: 4,788
Ticker: NASDAQ:PAET
SIC: 4813
NAICS: 513390
Industry/ies: Communications; Telecommunications/Internet/Cable

Chairman and Chief Executive Officer
CHESONICS, Arunas S.
Tel: (585) 340-2500
Fax: (585) 340-2801

Main Headquarters
Mailing: 600 Willow Brook Office Park
Fairport, NY 14450
Tel: (585) 340-2500
Fax: (585) 340-2801
TF: (877) 472-3832

Corporate Foundations and Giving Programs

Paetec Holding Corporation Contributions Program
600 Willow Brook Office Park
Fairport, NY 14450
Tel: (585) 340-2500

Public Affairs and Related Activities Personnel

At Headquarters

CONNOY, Pete
Vice President, Corporate Finance
peter.connoy@paetec.com
Tel: (585) 340-2649
Fax: (585) 340-2801

MULLLER, Chris
Contact, Communications
cchristopher.muller@paetec.com
Tel: (585) 340-8218
Fax: (585) 340-2801

PainTherapeutics, Inc.
A biopharmaceutical company.
www.paintrials.com
Annual Revenues: $20.56 million
Employees: 9
Ticker: NASDAQ: PTIE
SIC: 2834
Industry/ies: Pharmaceutical Industry

Chairman of the Board, President and Chief Executive Officer
BARBIER, Remi
Tel: (512) 501-2444
Fax: (512) 614-0414

Main Headquarters
Mailing: 7801 N Capital of Texas Hwy.
Suite 260
Austin, TX 78731
Tel: (512) 501-2444
Fax: (512) 614-0414

Corporate Foundations and Giving Programs

PainTherapeutics, Inc. Contributions Program
7801 N Capital of Texas Hwy.
Suite 260
Austin, TX 78731
Tel: (512) 501-2444

Public Affairs and Related Activities Personnel

At Headquarters

RODDY, Peter S.
Vice President and Chief Financial Officer
proddy@paintrials.com
Tel: (512) 501-2450
Fax: (512) 614-0414

Palantir Technologies
Designs analytical tools and software for government agencies and financial institutions.
www.palantirtech.com
Annual Revenues: $7.30 million
Employees: 200
Industry/ies: Computer/Technology; Defense/Homeland Security; Government-Related
Legislative Issues: BUD; DEF; SCI; TAX

Chief Executive Officer
KARP, Alexander C.
Tel: (650) 815-0200

Main Headquarters
Mailing: 100 Hamilton Ave.
Tel: (650) 815-0200

Suite 300
Palo Alto, CA 94301

Washington Office
Mailing: 1660 International Dr.
McLean, VA 22102
Tel: (650) 815-0333

Political Action Committees
Palantir Technologies Inc. PAC
FEC ID: C00498691
Contact: Lisa Gordon
100 Hamilton Ave.
Suite 300
Palo Alto, CA 94301

Contributions to Candidates: $1,000 (2015-2016)
Democrats: $1,000

Public Affairs and Related Activities Personnel

At Headquarters

ATKIN, James
Contact, Public Affairs
Tel: (650) 815-0200

GORDON, Lisa
Contact, Media and Government Relations and PAC Treasurer
lgordon@palantirtech.com
Tel: (650) 815-0200

LONG, Matthew
Legal Counsel
Tel: (650) 815-0200

MIKOLAY, Justin
Tel: (650) 815-0200

PHILIPPONE, Douglas
Federal Lobbyist
dougp@palantirtech.com
Tel: (650) 815-0200

Pall Corporation
A manufacturer of filtration, separation and purification products and systems.
www.pall.com
Employees: 10,400
Ticker: NYSE: PLL
SIC: 3569
Industry/ies: Chemicals & Chemical Industry

Chairman and Chief Executive Officer
KINGSLEY, Lawrence D.
Tel: (516) 484-5400
Fax: (516) 801-9754

Main Headquarters
Mailing: 25 Harbor Park Dr.
Port Washington, NY 11050
Tel: (516) 484-5400
Fax: (516) 801-9754
TF: (800) 645-6532

Public Affairs and Related Activities Personnel

At Headquarters

BEHNIA, Roya
Senior Vice President, General Counsel and Corporate Secretary
Tel: (516) 484-5400
Fax: (516) 801-9754

HOFFMAN, Ronald
Lead Director
Tel: (516) 484-5400
Fax: (516) 801-9754

JONES, R. Brent
Interim Chief Financial Officer
Tel: (516) 484-5400
Fax: (516) 801-9754

KIM, H. Alex
Senior Vice President, Corporate Strategy
Tel: (516) 484-5400
Fax: (516) 801-9754

ROUSE, Angelina
Vice President, Corporate Controller and Group Financial Officer, Global Operations
Tel: (516) 484-5400
Fax: (516) 801-9754

TAYLOR, Julie R.
Chief Human Resources Officer
Tel: (516) 484-5400
Fax: (516) 801-9754

Palm, Inc.
Manufactures hand-held computer systems and smartphones. Spun-off PalmSource, Inc. (see separate listing) in October, 2003.
www.palm.com
Annual Revenues: $735.87 million
Employees: 900
Ticker: NASDAQ: PALM
Industry/ies: Computer/Technology; Machinery/Equipment

Chairman and Chief Executive Officer
RUBINSTEIN, Jon
Tel: (408) 617-7000
Fax: (408) 617-0100

Main Headquarters
Mailing: 950 W. Maude Ave.
Sunnyvale, CA 94085
Tel: (408) 617-7000
Fax: (408) 617-0100

Corporate Foundations and Giving Programs

The Pam Foundation
Contact: Gisela Bushey
950 W. Maude Ave.
Sunnyvale, CA 94085
Tel: (408) 617-7000
Fax: (408) 617-7000

Public Affairs and Related Activities Personnel

At Headquarters

BUSHEY, Gisela
Foundation Manager
gisela.bushey@palm.com
Tel: (408) 617-7000
Fax: (408) 224-7563

KLEIN, Teri
Vice President, Investor Relations
teri.klein@palm.com
Tel: (408) 617-8825
Fax: (408) 617-0100

LETTS, Leslie
Director, Product Public Relations
leslie.letts@palm.com
Tel: (408) 617-8671
Fax: (408) 617-0100

PalmSource Inc.

See listing on page 8 under ACCESS Systems Americas, Inc.

Palo Alto Networks Inc

Developing network security and cybersecurity for government and private enterprise.
Legislative Issues: DEF; HOM; VET

Main Headquarters

Mailing: 4401 Great America Pkwy.
c/o Jeff True
Santa Clara, CA 95054
Tel: (408) 753-4000

Public Affairs and Related Activities Personnel

At Headquarters

GILLIS, Ryan
Registered Federal Lobbyist
Tel: (408) 753-4000

Pan American Life Insurance Company

PALIG offers financial planning services, life insurance, brokerage services and international financial services. It provides top-rated life, accident and health insurance, employee benefits and financial services.
www.palig.com
Annual Revenues: $704.00 million
Employees: 1,500
Industry/ies: Insurance Industry

Chairman, President and Chief Executive Officer

SUQUET, Jose S.
Tel: (504) 566-1300
Fax: (504) 566-3950

Main Headquarters

Mailing: 601 Poydras St.
New Orleans, LA 70130
Tel: (504) 566-1300
Fax: (504) 566-3950
TF: (877) 939-4550

Corporate Foundations and Giving Programs

Pan American Life Insurance Company Contributions Program
601 Poydras St.
New Orleans, LA 70130
Tel: (504) 566-1300
Fax: (504) 566-1300

Public Affairs and Related Activities Personnel

At Headquarters

FRAIZER, Patrick
Senior Vice President, Human Resources and General Counsel
Tel: (504) 566-1300
Fax: (504) 566-3950

MICKAN, Carlos F.
Vice Chairman of the Board and Chief Financial Officer
Tel: (504) 566-1300
Fax: (504) 566-3950

REEVES, Marta
Vice President, Corporate Marketing and Communications
MReeves@palig.com
Tel: (504) 566-1300
Fax: (504) 566-3950

REITAN , Scott
Senior Vice President, Administration and Information Technology
Tel: (504) 566-1300
Fax: (504) 566-3950

REVUELTA, CFA, Rodolfo J. "Rudy"
Senior Vice President and Chief Investment Officer
Tel: (504) 566-1300
Fax: (504) 566-3950

TEMPLATE, Jennifer
Compliance Analyst
Tel: (504) 566-3419
Fax: (504) 566-3950

Panasonic Corporation of North America

Panasonic Corporation of North America, based in Secaucus, NJ, is the principal North American subsidiary of Osaka, Japan-based Panasonic Corporation (NYSE: PC) and the hub of its branding, marketing, sales, service, product development and R&D operations in the U.S. and Canada.
www.panasonic.com
Employees: 12,000
SIC: 3559; 3563; 3575; 3621; 3679
Industry/ies: Electricity & Electronics; Electronics; Energy/Electricity
Legislative Issues: AUT; AVI; COM; EDU; ENG; ENV; GOV; HCR; SCI; TAX; TEC; TRA

Chairman and Chief Executive Officer

TAYLOR, Joe
Tel: (201) 348-7000
Fax: (201) 348-7016

Main Headquarters

Mailing: Two Riverfront Plaza
Newark, NJ 07102-5490

Washington Office

Mailing: 1130 Connecticut Ave. NW
Suite 1100
Washington, DC 20036

Corporate Foundations and Giving Programs

Panasonic Corporate Outreach Program
Contact: Marilyn Joseph
One Panasonic Way
Secaucus, NJ 07094

The Panasonic Foundation
Contact: Lawrence Leverett
One Panasonic Way
Seacaucus, NJ 07094

Public Affairs and Related Activities Personnel

At Washington Office

NONISHI, Masakazu

YOSHIKAWA, Shuichi
Senior Representative
Registered Federal Lobbyist

At Other Offices

FANNON, Peter M.
Vice President, Corporate and Government Affairs
3042 Connecticut Ave. NW, Suite 1100
Washington, DC 20036
Registered Federal Lobbyist
Tel: (202) 912-3800

IWATSU, Yuko
Manager, Investor Relations
One Panasonic Way, 3G-7
Secaucus, NJ 07094
Tel: (212) 698-1365
Fax: (201) 392-6007

JASIONOWSKI, Anthony
Senior Group Manager
3042 Connecticut Ave. NW, Suite 1100
Washington, DC 20036
Registered Federal Lobbyist
Tel: (202) 912-3800

JOSEPH, Marilyn
Vice President, Community Relations and Corporate Outreach
One Panasonic Way, 3G-7
Secaucus, NJ 07094
penny.joseph@us.panasonic.com
Tel: (201) 348-7000
Fax: (201) 392-6007

LEVERETT, Lawrence
Executive Director, The Panasonic Foundation
Three Panasonic Way, 2I-1
Secaucus, NJ 07094
Tel: (201) 392-4132
Fax: (201) 392-4126

MARIN, Robert
Special Counsel
One Panasonic Way, 3G-7
Secaucus, NJ 07094
Tel: (201) 348-7000
Fax: (201) 392-6007

MONAHAN, Charles
Federal Lobbyist
3042 Connecticut Ave. NW, Suite 1100
Washington, DC 20036
monahanc@us.panasonic.com
Registered Federal Lobbyist
Tel: (202) 912-3800

REILLY, James
Vice President, Corporate Communications
One Panasonic Way, 3G-7
Secaucus, NJ 07094
jim.reilly@us.panasonic.com
Tel: (201) 392-6067
Fax: (201) 392-6007

RICCIO, Mike J.
Chief Financial Officer and Treasurer
One Panasonic Way, 3G-7
Secaucus, NJ 07094
Tel: (201) 348-7000
Fax: (201) 348-7016

SCHOMBURG, Paul
Senior Manager, Government & Public Affairs
3042 Connecticut Ave. NW, Suite 1100
Washington, DC 20036
paul.schomburg@us.panasonic.com
Registered Federal Lobbyist
Tel: (202) 912-3800

SEENEY, Terri
Manager, Corporate Outreach Programs
One Panasonic Way, 3G-7
Secaucus, NJ 07094
terri.seeney@us.panasonic.com
Tel: (201) 348-7000
Fax: (201) 392-6007

SHARP, Mark
Group Manager, Corporate Environmental Department
3042 Connecticut Ave. NW, Suite 1100
Washington, DC 20036
mark.sharp@us.panasonic.com
Registered Federal Lobbyist
Tel: (202) 912-3800

THAME, Clarece P.
Federal Lobbyist
3042 Connecticut Ave. NW, Suite 1100
Washington, DC 20036
Tel: (202) 912-3800

THOMPSON, David A.　　　　　　　　Tel:　(202) 912-3800
Federal Lobbyist
3042 Connecticut Ave. NW, Suite 1100
Washington, DC 20036
thompsond@us.panasonic.com
Registered Federal Lobbyist

YOSHIKAWA, Shuichi　　　　　　　　Tel:　(201) 348-7000
Senior Representative　　　　　　　　Fax:　(201) 348-7016
One Panasonic Way, 3G-7
Secaucus, NJ 07094
Registered Federal Lobbyist

Panera Bread Company

A quick service restaurant chain and bakery.
www.panerabread.com
Annual Revenues: $2.57 billion
Employees: 19,900
Ticker: NASDAQ: PNRA
SIC: 5812
Industry/ies: Food And Beverage Industry

Chairman of the Board and Chief Executive Officer　Tel:　(314) 984-1000
SHAICH, Ronald M.　　　　　　　　　　Fax:　(314) 909-3350
Ronald.Shaich@panerabread.com

Main Headquarters
Mailing:　　3630 S. Geyer Rd.　　　　Tel:　(314) 984-1000
　　　　　　Suite 100　　　　　　　　Fax:　(314) 909-3350
　　　　　　St. Louis, MO 63127

Corporate Foundations and Giving Programs

Panera Bread Company Contributions Program
6710 Clayton Rd.　　　　　　　　　　Tel:　(314) 633-7100
Richmond Heights, MO 63117　　　　　Fax:　(314) 633-7200

Public Affairs and Related Activities Personnel

At Headquarters

BLAIR, Scott　　　　　　　　　　　　Tel:　(314) 984-1000
Senior Vice President and Chief Legal and Franchise Officer　Fax:　(314) 909-3350
scott.blair@panerabread.com

BUFANO, Mike　　　　　　　　　　　Tel:　(314) 984-1000
Chief Financial Officer　　　　　　　Fax:　(314) 909-3350

CHAPMAN, Charles J　　　　　　　　Tel:　(314) 984-1000
Executive Vice President and Chief Operating Officer　Fax:　(314) 909-3350

DUNLAP, Elizabeth A　　　　　　　　Tel:　(314) 984-1000
Senior Vice President and Chief People Officer　Fax:　(314) 909-3350

DUNLAP, Liz　　　　　　　　　　　　Tel:　(314) 984-1000
Senior Vice President and Chief People Officer　Fax:　(314) 909-3350

MORETON, William W.　　　　　　　Tel:　(314) 984-1000
Executive Vice Chairman　　　　　　Fax:　(314) 909-3350
william.moreton@panerabread.com

SIMON, Michael　　　　　　　　　　Tel:　(314) 984-1000
Executive Vice President & Chief Marketing Officer　Fax:　(314) 909-3350
michael.simon@panerabread.com

The Pantry, Inc.

A convenience store operator in the southeastern US with more than 1,660 shops in about a dozen states.
www.thepantry.com
Annual Revenues: $6.64 billion
Employees: 6,042
Ticker: NASDAQ: PTRY
SIC: 5500
Industry/ies: Retail/Wholesale

President and Chief Executive Officer　　Tel:　(919) 774-6700
HATCHELL, Dennis G.　　　　　　　　Fax:　(919) 774-3329

Main Headquarters
Mailing:　　305 Gregson Dr.　　　　　Tel:　(919) 774-6700
　　　　　　Cary, NC 27511　　　　　Fax:　(919) 774-3329

Public Affairs and Related Activities Personnel

At Headquarters

BRYCE, Brandon　　　　　　　　　　Tel:　(919) 459-6451
Contact, Media Relations　　　　　　Fax:　(919) 774-3329

CARNEY, Thomas D.　　　　　　　　Tel:　(919) 774-6700
Senior Vice President, General Counsel and Secretary　Fax:　(919) 774-3329

EPLEY, Berry　　　　　　　　　　　Tel:　(919) 774-6700
Media Contact　　　　　　　　　　Fax:　(919) 774-3329

ORESON, Keith　　　　　　　　　　Tel:　(919) 774-6700
Senior Vice President, Human Resources　Fax:　(919) 774-3329

PRESLAR, Clyde B.　　　　　　　　Tel:　(919) 774-6700
Senior Vice President and Chief Financial Officer　Fax:　(919) 774-3329

SCHMIDT, Gordon　　　　　　　　　Tel:　(919) 774-6700
Senior Vice President, Operations　　Fax:　(919) 774-3329

Papa John's International, Inc.

A pizza company.
www.papajohns.com
Annual Revenues: $1.63 billion
Employees: 22,350
Ticker: NASDAQ: PZZA
SIC: 5812
Industry/ies: Food And Beverage Industry

Founder, Chairman of the Board and Chief Executive Officer　Tel:　(502) 261-7272
SCHNATTER, John H.　　　　　　　　Fax:　(502) 261-4315

Main Headquarters
Mailing:　　2002 Papa John's Blvd.　　Tel:　(502) 261-7272
　　　　　　Louisville, KY 40299　　　Fax:　(502) 261-4315
　　　　　　　　　　　　　　　　　　TF:　(888) 777-7272

Corporate Foundations and Giving Programs

Papa John's International Contributions Program
2002 Papa John's Blvd.　　　　　　　Tel:　(502) 261-7272
P.O. Box 99900
Louisville, KY 40269

Public Affairs and Related Activities Personnel

At Headquarters

MULDOON, Tish　　　　　　　　　　Tel:　(502) 261-4987
Senior Director, Public Relations　　Fax:　(502) 261-4315
tish_muldoon@papajohns.com

O'HERN, Timothy C.　　　　　　　　Tel:　(502) 261-7272
Senior Vice President and Chief Development Officer　Fax:　(502) 261-4315

RITCHIE, Steve M　　　　　　　　　Tel:　(502) 261-7272
Senior Vice President and Chief Operating Officer　Fax:　(502) 261-4315

TUCKER, Lance F.　　　　　　　　　Tel:　(502) 261-4218
Senior Vice President, Chief Financial Officer, Chief　Fax:　(502) 261-4315
Administrative Officer and Treasurer

Paperwork Services

Private document preparer.
www.paperworkservices.com
SIC: 5940
Industry/ies: Paper And Wood Products Industry

Main Headquarters
Mailing:　　P.O. Box 327　　　　　　Tel:　(646) 895-3914
　　　　　　New York City, NY 10116-4744

Public Affairs and Related Activities Personnel

At Headquarters

BRASSELL, Jr., NP, Robert J.　　　　Tel:　(646) 895-3914
Federal Lobbyist
Darklovin2004@aol.com

At Other Offices

JUSTIN, Karen T.　　　　　　　　　Tel:　(973) 831-0181
Contact, Communications
22 Post Ln., Second Floor
Riverdale, NJ 07457-1108
kjustin@paperworkservices.com

PaperWorks Industries, Inc.

Producer of clay-coated and recycled paperboard.
www.paperwrks.com
Employees: 1,800
Industry/ies: Environment And Conservation; Paper And Wood Products Industry
Legislative Issues: ENG; ENV; TAX

President and Chief Executive Officer　　Tel:　(215) 984-7000
KWILINSKI, Kevin　　　　　　　　　Fax:　(215) 984-7181

Main Headquarters
Mailing:　　5000 Flat Rock Rd.　　　　Tel:　(215) 984-7000
　　　　　　Philadelphia, PA 19127　　Fax:　(215) 984-7181

Public Affairs and Related Activities Personnel

At Headquarters

SASSI, Dan　　　　　　　　　　　　Tel:　(215) 984-7175
Vice President, Human Resources　　Fax:　(215) 984-7181
dan.sassi@paperwrks.com

PAR Technology Corporation

Creates and markets technology solutions that help hospitality operators around the world to manage money, materials, people and the guest experience. It has developed hospitality solutions: restaurant point of sale, hotel management software, spa, retail POS and cruise ship point of sale.
www.partech.com
Annual Revenues: $236.69 million
Employees: 1,221
Ticker: NYSE: PAR

SIC: 3578
Industry/ies: Banking/Finance/Investments; Travel/Tourism/Lodging

Chief Executive Officer and President, PAC Treasurer
CASCIANO, Ronald J.

Tel: (315) 738-0600
Fax: (315) 738-0411

Main Headquarters
Mailing: 8383 Seneca Tnpk.
New Hartford, NY 13413

Tel: (315) 738-0600
Fax: (315) 738-0411
TF: (800) 448-6505

Political Action Committees
PAR Technology Corporation PAC
FEC ID: C00387969
Contact: Ronald J. Casciano
8383 Seneca Tnpk.
New Hartford, NY 13413

Corporate Foundations and Giving Programs
PAR Technology Corporation Contributions Program
8383 Seneca Tnpk.
New Hartford, NY 13413

Tel: (315) 738-0600
Fax: (315) 738-0600

Public Affairs and Related Activities Personnel

At Headquarters

BYRNES, Christopher R.
*Vice President, Business, Financial Relations and Public
Relations Contact*
cbyrnes@partech.com

Tel: (315) 738-0600
Fax: (315) 738-0411

MILDE, Denise C.
Vice President, Human Resources

Tel: (315) 738-0600
Fax: (315) 738-0411

MURDOCK, Viola A.
Vice President, General Counsel and Secretary

Tel: (315) 738-0600
Fax: (315) 738-0411

Parabel Inc.

A biofuel company
www.parabel.com
Employees: 38
Ticker: OTC: PABL
Industry/ies: Agriculture/Agronomy; Energy/Electricity; Environment And
Conservation; Fuels See Coal, Gas, Oil, Petroleum; Natural Resources; Petroleum
Industry; Science; Scientific Research

Chairman of the Board and Chief Executive Officer
TIARKS, Anthony

Tel: (321) 409-7970

Main Headquarters
Mailing: 1901 S. Harbor City Blvd.
Sixth Floor
Melbourne, FL 32901

Tel: (321) 409-7970

Public Affairs and Related Activities Personnel

At Headquarters

BOULDING , Jamie
Contact, Media Relations

Tel: (321) 409-7970

CHAUDHRI, Assad
Chief Financial Officer

Tel: (321) 409-7970

GALE, Michael
Federal Lobbyist
mgale@petroalgae.com

Tel: (321) 409-7484

LEBBOS, Nazih
Chief Operating Officer

Tel: (321) 409-7970

LYONS, George
Federal Lobbyist

Tel: (321) 409-7484

Parametric Technology Corporation

Makers of software for product development.
www.ptc.com
Annual Revenues: $1.18 billion
Employees: 5,705
Ticker: NASDAQ: PTC
SIC: 7372
Industry/ies: Computer/Technology

Chairman
SCHECHTER, Robert P.

Tel: (781) 370-5000
Fax: (781) 370-6000

President and Chief Executive Officer
HEPPELMANN, James E.
jheppelmann@ptc.com

Tel: (781) 370-5000
Fax: (781) 370-6000

Main Headquarters
Mailing: 140 Kendrick St.
Needham, MA 02494

Tel: (781) 370-5000
Fax: (781) 370-6000

Washington Office
Mailing: 11710 Plaza America Dr.
Suite 2000
Reston, VA 20190

Tel: (703) 944-8361

Political Action Committees
Parametric Technology Corporation PAC (PTC PAC)

FEC ID: C00410688
Contact: Charles Cash
11710 Plaza America Dr.
Suite 200
Reston, VA 20190

Tel: (703) 944-8361

Corporate Foundations and Giving Programs
PTC Contributions Program
140 Kendrick St.
Needham, MA 02494

Public Affairs and Related Activities Personnel

At Headquarters

AMBARUCH, Beth
Senior Director, Academic Community

Tel: (781) 370-5000
Fax: (781) 370-6000

COHEN, PhD, Barry F.
Executive Vice President, Strategy
bcohen@ptc.com

Tel: (781) 370-5000
Fax: (781) 370-6000

FOX, Tim
Vice President, Investor Relations
tifox@ptc.com

Tel: (781) 370-5961
Fax: (781) 370-6000

GREMLEY, Rob
Executive Vice President Technology Platforms

Tel: (781) 370-5000
Fax: (781) 370-6000

MILLER, Andrew D.
Executive Vice President and Chief Financial Officer

Tel: (781) 370-5000
Fax: (781) 370-6000

SNOW, Eric
Vice President, Corporate Communications
esnow@ptc.com

Tel: (781) 370-6210
Fax: (781) 370-6000

STUART, John
Manager

Tel: (781) 370-5979
Fax: (781) 370-5536

UNGASHICK, Charlie
Executive Vice President and Chief Marketing Officer

Tel: (781) 370-5000
Fax: (781) 370-6000

VON STAATS, Aaron C.
Corporate Vice President, General Counsel and Secretary
staats@ptc.com

Tel: (781) 370-5000
Fax: (781) 370-6000

At Washington Office

CASH, Charles
PAC Treasurer

Tel: (703) 944-8361

RAY, Ronald E.
Executive Adviser

Tel: (703) 944-8361

Pardee Homes Construction Company

*A company of homebuilders and residential developers in the Southern California and Las
Vegas metro markets.*
www.pardeehomes.com
Annual Revenues: $12.40 million
Employees: 300
Industry/ies: Construction/Construction Materials

President and Chief Executive Officer
MCGEE, Michael V.

Tel: (310) 475-3525
Fax: (310) 446-1290

Main Headquarters
Mailing: 10880 Wilshire Blvd.
Suite 1900
Los Angeles, CA 90024

Tel: (310) 475-3525
Fax: (310) 446-1290

Corporate Foundations and Giving Programs
Pardee Homes Construction Company Contributions Program
10880 Wilshire Blvd.
Suite 1900
Los Angeles, CA 90024

Tel: (310) 475-3525
Fax: (310) 446-1290

Parion Sciences

*A development-stage pharmaceutical company focused on the discovery and development of
new treatments for serious diseases in multiple therapeutic areas. It is dedicated to research,
development, and commercialization of treatments to restore patient's innate mucosal surface
defenses.*
www.parion.com
Annual Revenues: $1.6 million
Employees: 10
Industry/ies: Medicine/Health Care/Mental Health; Pharmaceutical Industry

Co-Founder and Chairman of the Board
BOUCHER, MD, Dr. Richard
pboucher@parion.com

Tel: (919) 313-1180
Fax: (919) 313-1190

Co-Chairman and Founder
JOHNSON, Dr. M. Ross

Tel: (919) 313-1180
Fax: (919) 313-1190

President and Chief Executive Officer
BOUCHER, MBA, Paul
pboucher@parion.com

Tel: (919) 313-1195
Fax: (919) 313-1190

Main Headquarters
Mailing: 2800 Meridian Pkwy.
Suite 195
Durham, NC 27713

Tel: (919) 313-1180
Fax: (919) 313-1190

Public Affairs and Related Activities Personnel

At Headquarters

SCHACHLE, Joe	Tel:	(919) 313-1180
Chief Operating Officer	Fax:	(919) 313-1190

Parker Drilling Company

Provides drilling services on land and offshore including drilling rigs, project management and rental tools to the energy industry.
www.parkerdrilling.com
Annual Revenues: $943.53 million
Employees: 3,443
Ticker: NYSE: PKD
SIC: 1381
NAICS: 213111
Industry/ies: Fuels See Coal, Gas, Oil, Petroleum; Natural Resources; Petroleum Industry

Chairman of the Board, President and Chief Executive Officer	Tel:	(281) 406-2000
RICH, Gary G.	Fax:	(281) 406-2001

Main Headquarters

Mailing:	Five Greenway Plaza	Tel:	(281) 406-2000
	Suite 100	Fax:	(281) 406-2001
	Houston, TX 77046		

Public Affairs and Related Activities Personnel

At Headquarters

BAJENSKI, Richard	Tel:	(281) 406-2030
Director, Investor Relations	Fax:	(281) 406-2001
richard.bajenski@parkerdrilling.com		
DIXON, Stephanie J.	Tel:	(281) 406-2000
Manager, Marketing and Corporate Communications	Fax:	(281) 406-2001
stephanie.dixon@parkerdrilling.com		
DUPLANTIER, Jon-Al	Tel:	(281) 406-2000
Senior Vice President, Chief Administrative Officer and General Counsel	Fax:	(281) 406-2001
jonal.duplantier@parkerdrilling.com		
WEBER, Christopher T.	Tel:	(281) 406-2000
Senior Vice President and Chief Financial Officer	Fax:	(281) 406-2001

At Other Offices

WHITE, Jean Ann
PAC Contact
Eight E. Third St.
Tulsa, OK 74103

Parker Hannifin Corporation

A producer of motion-control components and systems for industrial, automotive, aerospace and commercial markets. Acquired Commercial Intertech Corp. in 2000.
www.parker.com
Annual Revenues: $11.55 billion
Employees: 54,754
Ticker: NYSE: PH
SIC: 3494; 3599; 3728
NAICS: 332912; 336399; 332999
Industry/ies: Machinery/Equipment
Legislative Issues: AER; AGR; AUT; AVI; BUD; CAW; CDT; CHM; CPI; CPT; CSP; DEF; DIS; ECN; EDU; ENG; ENV; FOO; FUE; GOV; HCR; HOM; LBR; MAN; MED; POS; ROD; SCI; TAX; TRA; TRD; TRU; URB; WAS

Chairman and Chief Executive Officer	Tel:	(216) 896-3000
WILLIAMS, Thomas L.	Fax:	(216) 896-4000

Main Headquarters

Mailing:	6035 Parkland Blvd.	Tel:	(216) 896-3000
	Cleveland, OH 44124	Fax:	(216) 896-4000
		TF:	(800) 272-7537

Political Action Committees

Parker Hannifin Corporation PAC (PARKER PAC)
FEC ID: C00135459
Contact: David B. Ostro
6035 Parkland Blvd.
Cleveland, OH 44124

> **Contributions to Candidates:** $22,000 (2015-2016)
> Democrats: $4,500; Republicans: $17,500

Corporate Foundations and Giving Programs

Parker Hannifan Foundation
Contact: Thomas A. Piraino Jr.
6035 Parkland Blvd.
Cleveland, OH 44124

Public Affairs and Related Activities Personnel

At Headquarters

BANKS, Lee C.	Tel:	(216) 896-3000
Executive Vice President and Operating Officer	Fax:	(216) 896-4000
FARAGE, Christopher M.	Tel:	(216) 896-3000
	Fax:	(216) 896-4000

Vice President, International Human Resources and External Affairs
cfarage@parker.com

GORMLEY, Aidan	Tel:	(216) 896-3258
Director, Corporate Communications	Fax:	(216) 896-4000
aidan_gormley@steris.com		
LEONTI , Joseph R.	Tel:	(216) 896-3000
Vice President, General Counsel and Secretary	Fax:	(216) 896-4410
MARTEN, Jon P.	Tel:	(216) 896-3000
Executive Vice President, Finance and Administration and Chief Financial Officer	Fax:	(216) 896-4000
OSTRO, David B.	Tel:	(216) 896-3000
Vice President, Treasurer and PAC Contact	Fax:	(216) 896-4410
SERBIN, Daniel S.	Tel:	(216) 896-3000
Executive Vice President, Corporate Human Resources	Fax:	(216) 896-4000

Parkview Health System, Inc.

Network healthcare provider.
www.parkview.com
Annual Revenues: $309.50 million
Employees: 5,000
Industry/ies: Medicine/Health Care/Mental Health

Chairman of the Board	Tel:	(260) 373-4000
SCHRIMPER, Chuck	Fax:	(260) 373-3620
President and Chief Executive Officer	Tel:	(260) 373-7092
PACKNETT, Michael J.	Fax:	(260) 373-3620

Main Headquarters

Mailing:	10501 Corporate Dr.	Tel:	(260) 373-7092
	Fort Wayne, IN 46845		

Corporate Foundations and Giving Programs

Parkview Foundation		
2200 Randallia Dr.	Tel:	(260) 373-7970
Ft. Wayne, IN 46805		

Public Affairs and Related Activities Personnel

At Headquarters

BROWNING, Mike	Tel:	(260) 373-7092
Chief Financial Officer		
CLABAUGH, Eric	Tel:	(260) 373-7092
Manager, Public Information		
eric.clabaugh@parkview.com		
HENVEY, Rick	Tel:	(260) 373-7092
Chief Operating Officer		

At Other Offices

PERLICH, John	Tel:	(260) 705-4271
Contact, Media	Fax:	(260) 373-3620
3000 Coliseum Blvd., East, Suite 100		
Ft. Wayne, IN 46845		
john.perlich@parkview.com		

Parkway Properties, Inc.

A real estate investment trust specialized in the operation, leasing, acquisition and ownership of office properties.
www.pky.com
Annual Revenues: $471.95 million
Employees: 322
Ticker: NYSE: PKY
SIC: 6798
Industry/ies: Real Estate

Chairman of the Board	Tel:	(407) 650-0593
CANNADA, Charles T.	Fax:	(601) 949-4077
President and Chief Executive Officer	Tel:	(407) 650-0593
HEISTAND, James R.	Fax:	(601) 949-4077

Main Headquarters

Mailing:	390 N. Orange Ave.	Tel:	(407) 650-0593
	Suite 2400	TF:	(800) 748-1667
	Orlando, FL 32801		

Corporate Foundations and Giving Programs

Parkway Properties Contributions Program
Contact: Megan Wylie
One Jackson Pl., 188 E. Capitol St.
Suite 1000
Jackson, MS 39201

Public Affairs and Related Activities Personnel

At Headquarters

BAISDEN, Liz	Tel:	(407) 650-0593
Vice President of Marketing		
BATES, Jason	Tel:	(407) 650-0593
EVP and Chief Investment Officer		

BLALOCK, Thomas E.
Vice President, Investor Relations and Media Contact
tblalock@pky.com

Tel: (407) 650-0593

DORSETT, Jeremy
Executive Vice President, General Counsel

Tel: (407) 650-0593

EGGER, Susan D.
Vice President, Human Resources

Tel: (407) 650-0593

FRANCIS, Scott E
Executive Vice President and Chief Accounting Officer

Tel: (407) 650-0593

GRAY, James W
Vice president, Director of National Accounts

Tel: (407) 650-0593

GREGOIRE, Jack
Vice President and Director of Operations

Tel: (407) 650-0593

LAU, Knicks
Vice President and Corporate Controller

Tel: (407) 650-0593

LIPSEY, Jayson
Executive Vice President, Chief Operating Officer

Tel: (407) 650-0593

O'REILLY, David
Executive Vice President, Chief Investment Officer and Chief Financial Officer

Tel: (407) 650-0593

At Other Offices

WYLIE, Megan
Human Resources Generalist and Customer and Employee Advocate
188 E. Capitol St., Suite 1000
Jackson, MS 39201
recruiter@pky.com

Tel: (601) 948-4091
Fax: (601) 949-4077

Parsons Brinckerhoff Inc.

A civil engineering, planning, and construction management firm headquartered in New York, NY.
www.pbworld.com
Employees: 14,000
Industry/ies: Engineering/Mathematics
Legislative Issues: BUD; TRA

President and Chief Executive Officer
SHOIRY, Pierre

Tel: (212) 465-5000
Fax: (212) 465-5096

Main Headquarters
Mailing: One Penn Plaza
            New York City, NY 10119

Tel: (212) 465-5000
Fax: (212) 465-5096

Washington Office
Mailing: 1015 Half St. SE
            Suite 650
            Washington, DC 20003

Tel: (202) 783-0241
Fax: (202) 783-0229

Political Action Committees
Parsons Brinckerhoff Group Inc. PAC
FEC ID: C00287003
Contact: Andrew Lynn
1401 K St. NW
Suite 701
Washington, DC 20005

Tel: (202) 783-0241
Fax: (202) 783-0229

   Contributions to Candidates: $88,100 (2015-2016)
   Democrats: $51,600; Republicans: $36,500

Corporate Foundations and Giving Programs
PB Foundation
One Penn Plaza
Second Floor
New York City, NY 10119

Public Affairs and Related Activities Personnel

At Headquarters

ADJAHI, Isabelle
Vice President, Investor Relations and Corporate Communications

Tel: (212) 465-5000
Fax: (212) 465-5096

COOPER, Judy DeScenza
Senior Vice President, Corporate Communications
cooperj@pbworld.com

Tel: (212) 465-5000
Fax: (212) 465-5096

DOLLIN, Paul
Chief Operating Officer

Tel: (212) 465-5000
Fax: (212) 465-5096

DONA, Christina
Vice President, Global Brand, Marketing and Internal Communications

Tel: (212) 465-5000
Fax: (212) 465-5096

L'HEUREUX, Alexandre
Chief Financial Officer

Tel: (212) 465-5000
Fax: (212) 465-5096

MCALISTER, Dave
Global Director, Infrastructure

Tel: (212) 465-5000
Fax: (212) 465-5096

ZAMUNER, Valéry
Chief Legal Officer and Corporate Secretary

Tel: (212) 465-5000
Fax: (212) 465-5096

At Washington Office

CONNOR, Catherine

Tel: (202) 783-0241

Senior Vice President and Director, Federal Government Affairs
connor@pbworld.com
Registered Federal Lobbyist

Fax: (202) 783-0229

FISCHETTI, Michelle
Lobbyist and PAC Treasurer

Tel: (202) 783-0241
Fax: (202) 783-0229

LYNN, Andrew
PAC Treasurer

Tel: (202) 783-0241
Fax: (202) 783-0229

Parsons Corporation

A group of companies, operating in both domestic and foreign markets, that provide planning, design, program management and construction management services to private clients as well as federal, state and local governments in the fields of infrastructure, transportation, energy, water, environment, telecommunications, and industrial engineering.
www.parsons.com
Annual Revenues: $3.0 billion
Employees: 11,500
Industry/ies: Construction/Construction Materials; Engineering/Mathematics
Legislative Issues: CAW; ENG; ROD; RRR; TRA

Chairman of the Board and Chief Executive Officer
HARRINGTON, Charles L.

Tel: (626) 440-2000
Fax: (626) 440-2630

Main Headquarters
Mailing: 100 W. Walnut St.
            Pasadena, CA 91124

Tel: (626) 440-2000
Fax: (626) 440-2630

Washington Office
Mailing: 100 M St. SE
            Suite 1200
            Washington, DC 20003-3515

Tel: (202) 775-3300
Fax: (202) 775-3422

Political Action Committees
Parsons Corporation PAC
FEC ID: C00103549
Contact: Richard Henderson
100 W. Walnut St.
T-1110
Pasadena, CA 91124

Tel: (626) 440-2000
Fax: (626) 440-2630

   Contributions to Candidates: $247,000 (2015-2016)
   Democrats: $116,000; Republicans: $131,000

   Principal Recipients

   SENATE
   SHELBY, RICHARD C (REP-AL)

   HOUSE
   BLUMENAUER, EARL (DEM-OR)
   CALVERT, KEN (REP-CA)
   CLYBURN, JAMES E. (DEM-SC)
   FRELINGHUYSEN, RODNEY P. (REP-NJ)
   HOYER, STENY HAMILTON (DEM-DC)
   LARSEN, RICK (DEM-WA)
   LOBIONDO, FRANK A. (REP-NJ)
   MCCARTHY, KEVIN (REP-CA)
   ROYBAL-ALLARD, LUCILLE (DEM-CA)
   RUPPERSBERGER, C.A. DUTCH (DEM-MD)
   SCHIFF, ADAM (DEM-CA)
   SIMPSON, MICHAEL (REP-ID)
   THORNBERRY, MAC (REP-TX)
   WILSON, JOE THE HON. (REP-SC)

Public Affairs and Related Activities Personnel

At Headquarters

BALL, George L.
Executive Vice President and Chief Financial Officer

Tel: (626) 440-2000
Fax: (626) 440-2630

ELLIS, Jr., Clyde E.
Senior Vice President and General Counsel

Tel: (626) 440-2000
Fax: (626) 440-2630

GOODRICH, David R.
Vice President, Human Resources

Tel: (626) 440-2000
Fax: (626) 440-2630

HARPER, Margareth
Vice President, Government Relations
margareth.harper@parsons.com

Tel: (626) 440-2000
Fax: (626) 440-2630

HENDERSON, Richard
PAC Treasurer

Tel: (626) 440-2000
Fax: (626) 440-2630

KUHLMAN, Erin
Vice President, Corporate Relations
erin.kuhlman@parsons.com

Tel: (626) 440-4590
Fax: (626) 440-2630

SHAPPELL, James R.
President

Tel: (626) 440-2000
Fax: (626) 440-2630

Partners Healthcare System, Inc.

A non-profit organization health care system that is committed to patient care, research, teaching, and service to the community locally and globally.
www.partners.org
Employees: 17,000
Industry/ies: Medicine/Health Care/Mental Health
Legislative Issues: BUD; CPT; HCR; MED; MMM; PHA

Chairman of the Board
LAWRENCE, Esq., Edward P.
Tel: (617) 278-1000
Fax: (617) 278-1049

President and Chief Executive Officer
TORCHIANA, Dr. David
Tel: (617) 278-1000
Fax: (617) 278-1049

Main Headquarters
Mailing: 800 Boylston St.
Suite 1150
Boston, MA 02199
Tel: (617) 278-1000
Fax: (617) 278-1049

Corporate Foundations and Giving Programs
Partners Healthcare System Inc. Contributions Program
800 Boylston St.
Suite 1150
Boston, MA 02199-8001
Tel: (617) 278-1000
Fax: (617) 278-1000

Public Affairs and Related Activities Personnel

At Headquarters

ALVIANI, Esq., Joseph D.
Vice President, Government Affairs
Registered Federal Lobbyist
Tel: (617) 278-1000
Fax: (617) 278-1049

COPP, Jr., Richard W.
Director, Communications
rcopp@partners.org
Tel: (617) 278-1031
Fax: (617) 278-1049

DAMIANO, Robert
Vice President, Compliance & Internal Audit
Tel: (617) 278-1000
Fax: (617) 278-1049

EICKHOLT, Lynne J.
Chief Strategy Officer
Tel: (617) 278-1000
Fax: (617) 278-1049

GASPER, Heather
Federal Lobbyist and Government Affairs Associate
Registered Federal Lobbyist
Tel: (617) 278-1000
Fax: (617) 278-1049

GOGGIN, Maureen
Director, Government Relations
megoggin@partners.org
Tel: (617) 278-1041
Fax: (617) 278-1049

GOLBITZ, Aimee
Manager, Federal Affairs
agolbitz@partners.org
Registered Federal Lobbyist
Tel: (617) 278-1000
Fax: (617) 278-1049

HENRY, Brent L.
Vice President and General Counsel
bhenry1@partners.org
Tel: (617) 278-1000
Fax: (617) 278-1049

MARKELL, Peter K.
Executive Vice President, Administration and Finance, Chief Financial Officer and Treasurer
pkmarkell@partners.org
Tel: (617) 278-1000
Fax: (617) 278-1049

Patent Properties, Inc.

A provider of security consulting and investigation services, including risk mitigation, decision support, emergency management, litigation support, anti-fraud solutions, business intelligence, and related security services.
www.globaloptionsgroup.com
Annual Revenues: $1.02 billion
Employees: 800
Ticker: NASDAQ: GLOI
SIC: 8742
Industry/ies: Energy/Electricity; Management

Chairman of the Board
SCHILLER, PhD, Dr. Harvey W.
Tel: (203) 461-7200
Fax: (212) 445-0053

Vice Chairman and Chief Executive Officer
ELLENTHAL, Jonathan
Tel: (203) 461-7200

Main Headquarters
Mailing: Two High Ridge Park
Stamford, CT 06905
Tel: (203) 461-7200

Washington Office
Mailing: 1501 M St. NW
Suite 500
Washington, DC 20005
Tel: (202) 585-0780
Fax: (202) 585-0792

Political Action Committees
Patent Political Action Committee
FEC ID: C00569947
Contact: Scott Wesley Burt
900 19th St.
Eighth floor
Washington, DC 20006

Public Affairs and Related Activities Personnel

At Headquarters

JENNY, Kara
Chief Financial
Tel: (203) 461-7200

SIEGEL, Jonathan
Cheif Administrative officer and General Counsel
Tel: (203) 461-7200

At Washington Office

LIVINGSTON, Bill
Lobbyist
Tel: (202) 293-2490
Fax: (202) 585-0792

At Other Offices

BURFENING, Jody
Contact, Investor Relations
800 Third Ave.
New York City, NY 10022
jburfening@lhai.com
Tel: (212) 838-3777
Fax: (212) 838-4568

BURT, Scott Wesley
Treasurer
900 19th St., Eighth floor
Washington, DC 20006

HANDELSMAN, Adam
Contact, Media Relations
415 Madison Ave., 17th Floor
New York City, NY 10017
ahandelsman@lhai.com
Tel: (212) 445-6262
Fax: (212) 445-0053

HORTON, A. J.
Contact, Communications
235 Peachtree St. NE, Suite 2215
Atlanta, GA 30303
holton@wittassociates.com
Tel: (404) 963-8214
Fax: (404) 880-1769

ONDECK, Thomas
President, International Strategies
415 Madison Ave., 17th Floor
New York City, NY 10017
Tel: (212) 445-6262
Fax: (212) 445-0053

Pathmark Stores Inc.

A supermarket retailer.
pathmark.apsupermarket.com
Annual Revenues: $2.68 billion
Employees: 22,400
SIC: 5411
Industry/ies: Food And Beverage Industry; Retail/Wholesale

Main Headquarters
Mailing: Two Paragon Dr.
Montvale, NJ 07645
Tel: (201) 573-9700
Fax: (201) 505-3054
TF: (866) 443-7374

Corporate Foundations and Giving Programs
Pathmark Stores Inc. Corporate Giving
Two Paragon Dr.
Montvale, NJ 07645

Public Affairs and Related Activities Personnel

At Headquarters

CONNOR, Marcy
Contact, Media Relations
apmedia@aptea.com
Tel: (201) 571-4453
Fax: (201) 505-3054

Patriarch Partners, LLC

A global investment firm designed to manage and monetize the distressed portfolios of financial institutions.
www.patriarchpartners.com
Employees: 18,000
Industry/ies: Banking/Finance/Investments

Founder and Chief Executive Officer
TILTON, Lynn
Tel: (212) 825-0550
Fax: (212) 825-2038

Main Headquarters
Mailing: One Broadway
Fifth Floor
New York City, NY 10004
Tel: (212) 825-0550

Public Affairs and Related Activities Personnel

At Headquarters

POTHIN, John
Managing Director, Human Resources Platform
Tel: (212) 825-0550

WHITE, Richard A.
Director, Communications and Media Relations
Richard.White@PatriarchPartners.com
Tel: (212) 825-0550

Patriot Equities L.P.

A real estate developer and investor.
www.patriotequities.com
Annual Revenues: $1.60 million
Employees: 20
Industry/ies: Banking/Finance/Investments; Real Estate

President and Chief Executive Officer
KOLAR, Erik E.
ekolar@patriotequities.com
Tel: (484) 615-1201
Fax: (610) 993-2624

Main Headquarters
Mailing: 1200 Liberty Ridge Dr.
Suite 115
Tel: (610) 993-2131
Fax: (610) 993-2624

Wayne, PA 19087

Public Affairs and Related Activities Personnel

At Headquarters

GARDNER, Geoffrey
Chief Investment Officer
Tel: (610) 993-2131
Fax: (610) 993-2624

Patton Medical Devices, LP

A provider of medical devices and supplies for individuals living with diabetes.
www.i-port.com
Annual Revenues: $3.10 million
Employees: 34
Industry/ies: Machinery/Equipment; Medicine/Health Care/Mental Health

Executive Chairman of the Board
GREGG, Terrance H.
Tel: (512) 279-4545
Fax: (512) 279-0372

President
BURNS, John S.
Tel: (512) 279-4545
Fax: (512) 279-0372

Main Headquarters
Mailing: 3108 N. Lamar Blvd.
Austin, TX 78705
Tel: (512) 279-4545
Fax: (512) 279-0372
TF: (877) 763-7678

Corporate Foundations and Giving Programs

Patton Medical Devices, LP Contributions Program
3108 N. Lamar Blvd.
Austin, TX 78705-2013
Tel: (512) 279-4545

Public Affairs and Related Activities Personnel

At Headquarters

DONNELLY, Chris C.
Executive Vice President and Chief Financial Officer
Tel: (512) 279-4545
Fax: (512) 279-0372

Payless Shoe Source

A unit of holding company Collective Brands. Provider of family footwear.
www.payless.com
Employees: 750
Ticker: NYSE: PSS
SIC: 5661
Industry/ies: Apparel/Textiles Industry; Retail/Wholesale

Chief Executive Officer
JONES, W. Paul
Tel: (785) 295-6099
Fax: (785) 295-6233

Main Headquarters
Mailing: 3231 S.E. Sixth Ave.
Topeka, KS 66607
Tel: (785) 295-6099
Fax: (785) 295-6233
TF: (877) 474-6379

Political Action Committees
Collective Brands, Inc. PAC
FEC ID: C00319368
Contact: Gary Calvin Madsen
3231 E. Sixth St.
P.O. Box 1189
Topeka, KS 66607

Corporate Foundations and Giving Programs

The Collective Brands Foundation
Contact: Nikki Sloup
3231 S.E. Sixth Ave.
Topeka, KS 66607
Tel: (785) 233-5171
Fax: (785) 368-7510

Payless ShoeSource Foundation
3231 SE Sixth Ave.
Topeka, KS 66607

Public Affairs and Related Activities Personnel

At Headquarters

CLICK, Betty J.
Senior Vice President, Human Resources
Tel: (785) 295-6099
Fax: (785) 295-6233

DESANTIS, Vincent
Senior Vice President and Chief Marketing Officer
Tel: (785) 295-6099
Fax: (785) 295-6233

DONOHOO, Robert
Senior Vice President, General Counsel
Tel: (785) 295-6099
Fax: (785) 295-6233

ELLIS, Tammy
Senior Marketing Executive
tammy.ellis@payless.com
Tel: (785) 295-6099
Fax: (785) 295-6233

VITELLI, Mike
Executive Vice President and Chief Operating Officer
Tel: (785) 295-6099
Fax: (785) 295-6233

ZAPPULLA, Linda
Director Brand Marketing
linda_zappulla@payless.com
Tel: (785) 295-6099
Fax: (785) 295-6233

PC Connection, Inc.

A direct marketer of computer products and solutions. It delivers valuable IT services and advanced technology solutions to business, government, healthcare, and education markets.
www.pcconnection.com

Annual Revenues: $2.57 billion
Employees: 2,155
Ticker: NASDAQ: PCCC
SIC: 5961
Industry/ies: Advertising And Marketing; Computer/Technology

President and Chief Executive Officer
MCGRATH, Timothy
tmcgrath@pcconnection.com
Tel: (603) 683-2000
Fax: (603) 423-5748

Main Headquarters
Mailing: 730 Milford Rd.
Route 101A
Merrimack, NH 03054-4631
Tel: (603) 683-2000
Fax: (603) 423-5748
TF: (800) 800-0009

Public Affairs and Related Activities Personnel

At Headquarters

DRISCOLL, Joseph
Senior Vice President, Treasurer and Chief Financial Officer
Tel: (603) 683-2000
Fax: (603) 423-5748

GALLUP, Patricia
Chief Administrative Officer
Tel: (603) 683-2000
Fax: (603) 683-2041

Peabody Energy (Peabody Holding Company, Inc.)

A coal company with operations in the United States and Australia. Formerly known as the Peabody Group.
www.peabodyenergy.com
Annual Revenues: $6.65 billion
Employees: 8,300
Ticker: NYSE: BTU
SIC: 1221
Industry/ies: Energy/Electricity; Mining Industry; Natural Resources
Legislative Issues: BUD; ENG; ENV; LBR; TAX

Chairman of the Board and Chief Executive Officer
BOYCE, Gregory H.
Tel: (314) 342-3400
Fax: (314) 342-7799

President & Chief Executive Officer
PALMER, Fredrick D.
fpalmer@peabodyenergy.com
Tel: (314) 342-7624
Fax: (314) 342-7799

President and Chief Executive Officer
KELLOW, Glenn
Tel: (314) 342-3400
Fax: (314) 342-7799

Main Headquarters
Mailing: 701 Market St.
St. Louis, MO 63101-1826
Tel: (314) 342-3400
Fax: (314) 342-7799

Washington Office
Mailing: 801 Pennsylvania Ave. NW
Suite 212
Washington, DC 20004-2615
Tel: (202) 942-2586

Political Action Committees
Peabody Energy Corporation PAC (PEABODY PAC)
FEC ID: C00110478
Contact: Walter L. Hawkins Jr.
701 Market St.
St. Louis, MO 63101
Tel: (314) 342-3400
Fax: (314) 342-3400

   Contributions to Candidates: $40,500 (2015-2016)
   Democrats: $4,000; Republicans: $36,500

Corporate Foundations and Giving Programs

Peabody Energy Contributions Program
Contact: Sarah Kramer
701 Market St.
St. Louis, MO 63101-1826
Tel: (314) 342-3400
Fax: (314) 342-7799

Public Affairs and Related Activities Personnel

At Headquarters

GALLI, Bryan A.
Chief Marketing Officer
Tel: (314) 342-3400
Fax: (314) 342-7799

HAGEDORN, Christopher J
Executive, Strategy and Development
Tel: (314) 342-3400
Fax: (314) 342-7799

KRAMER, Sarah
Director, Community Relations
PR@PeabodyEnergy.com
Tel: (314) 342-3400
Fax: (314) 342-7799

MORROW, Christina A.
Director, Operations Planning
Tel: (314) 342-7900
Fax: (314) 342-7799

SCHOCH, Alexander C.
Executive Vice President, Law, Chief Legal Officer and Secretary
Tel: (314) 342-3400
Fax: (314) 342-7799

SCHWETZ, Amy
Chief Financial Officer
Tel: (314) 342-3400
Fax: (314) 342-7799

SLENTZ, Andrew P
Executive Vice President, Human Resources and Administration
Tel: (314) 342-3400
Fax: (314) 342-7799

SUTTON, Beth
Vice President, Global Communications
bsutton@peabodyenergy.com
Tel: (928) 522-7008
Fax: (314) 342-7799

SVEC, Victor P.
Senior Vice President, Investor Relations and Corporate Communications
Tel: (314) 342-7798
Fax: (314) 342-7799

WILLIAMSON, Kemal
President
Tel: (314) 342-3400
Fax: (314) 342-7799

At Washington Office

SHEPHERD, Raymond
Vice President, Federal Government Relations
Tel: (202) 942-2586

Peabody Investment Corporation

A coal mining corporation.
www.peabodyenergy.com
Annual Revenues: $6.65 billion
Employees: 8,300
Ticker: NYSE: BTU
SIC: 1221
Industry/ies: Mining Industry; Natural Resources
Legislative Issues: BUD; ENG; ENV; TAX

Chairman of the Board and Chief Executive Officer
BOYCE, Gregory H.
Tel: (314) 342-3400

Main Headquarters
Mailing: 701 Market St.
St. Louis, MO 63101-1826
Tel: (314) 342-3400

Political Action Committees
Peabody Energy Corporation PAC (PEABODY PAC)
FEC ID: C00110478
Contact: Walter L. Hawkins Jr.
701 Market St.
St. Louis, MO 63101
Tel: (314) 342-3400
Fax: (314) 342-3400

   Contributions to Candidates: $40,500 (2015-2016)
   Democrats: $4,000; Republicans: $36,500

Corporate Foundations and Giving Programs
Peabody Energy Contributions Program
701 Market St.
St. Louis, MO 63101-1826
Tel: (314) 342-3400
Fax: (314) 342-7799

Public Affairs and Related Activities Personnel

At Headquarters

CREWS, Michael C.
Executive Vice President and Chief Financial Officer
Tel: (314) 342-3400

DAVIS, Matt
Vice President, Investor Relations
ir@peabodyenergy.com
Tel: (314) 342-7900

DEMETER, Ruth
Registered Federal Lobbyist
Tel: (314) 342-3400

FLANNIGAN, Michael
Senior Vice President, Global Government Affairs
Tel: (314) 342-3400

HAWKINS, Jr., Walter L.
PAC Treasurer
Tel: (314) 342-3400

PALMER, Fredrick D.
Registered Federal Lobbyist
Tel: (314) 342-3400

SHEPHERD, Raymond
Registered Federal Lobbyist
Tel: (314) 342-3400

SUTTON, Beth
Vice President, Communications and Community Relations
PR@PeabodyEnergy.com
Tel: (314) 342-3400

SVEC, Victor P.
Senior Vice President Investor Relations and Corporate Communications
ir@peabodyenergy.com
Tel: (314) 342-3400

Pearson, Inc.

A media company with market-leading businesses in education, business information and consumer publishing.
www.pearson.com
Annual Revenues: $8.51 billion
Employees: 41,964
Ticker: NYSE: PSO
SIC: 2731
NAICS: 511130
Industry/ies: Communications; Media/Mass Communication
Legislative Issues: CPT; EDU

Chairman of the Board
MORENO, Glen
Tel: (212) 641-2400
Fax: (212) 641-2500

Main Headquarters
Mailing: 330 Hudson St.
New York, NY 10013
Tel: (212) 641-2400

Washington Office
Mailing: 1919 M St. NW
Washington, DC 20036

Washington Office
Mailing: 1919 M. St. NW
Suite 310
Washington, DC 20036
Tel: (800) 745-8489
TF: (800) 745-8489

Corporate Foundations and Giving Programs
The Pearson Foundation
1330 Avenue of the Americas
New York City, NY 10019

Public Affairs and Related Activities Personnel

At Headquarters

KAUNE, Jason D.
Attorney & Agent for Filer
Tel: (212) 641-2400

At Washington Office

ALLISON, Neil
Director, Market Development and Strategy
neil.allison@pearson.com
Tel: (800) 745-8489

BISHOP, Abigail
Director, Corporate Affairs Strategy and Planning
abigail.bishop@pearson.com
Tel: (800) 745-8489

SKELLY, Stacy
Director, Media Relations
stacy.skelly@pearson.com
Tel: (800) 745-8489

At Other Offices

FREESTONE, Robin
Chief Financial Officer
1330 Avenue of the Americas
New York City, NY 10019
robin.freestone@pearson.com
Tel: (212) 641-2400
Fax: (212) 641-2500

MULLANEY, Daniel
Director, Government Affairs
4250 N. Fairfax Dr., Suite 1200
Arlington, VA 22203
Daniel.Mullaney@pearson.com
Registered Federal Lobbyist
Tel: (703) 284-5818

SPIEGEL, Wendy
Media Contact
1330 Avenue of the Americas
New York City, NY 10019
Tel: (212) 641-2400
Fax: (212) 641-2500

TAYLOR, Jeff
Senior Vice President and Contact, Investor Relation
1330 Avenue of the Americas
New York City, NY 10019
Tel: (212) 641-2400
Fax: (212) 641-2500

Pebble East Claims Corporation/Pebble Limited Partnership

Mine exploration, development and operation.
www.pebblepartnership.com
Annual Revenues: $14.90 million
Employees: 200
Industry/ies: Mining Industry; Natural Resources
Legislative Issues: ENG; NAT; SCI

Main Headquarters
Mailing: 3201 C St.
Suite 604
Anchorage, AK 99503
Tel: (907) 339-2600
Fax: (907) 339-2601
TF: (877) 450-2600

Corporate Foundations and Giving Programs
The Pebble Fund
3201 C St.
Suite 604
Anchorage, AK 99503

Public Affairs and Related Activities Personnel

At Headquarters

HEATWOLE, Mike
Vice President, Public Affairs
mikeheatwole@pebblepartnership.com
Tel: (907) 339-2600
Fax: (907) 339-2601

Peckham Industries Inc.

Produces asphalt, crushed stone, ready mix concrete, and liquid calcium chloride.
www.peckham.com
Annual Revenues: $38.40 million
Employees: 400
Ticker: NASDAQ: PKMS
SIC: 1442; 2951
NAICS: 324121; 212321
Industry/ies: Construction/Construction Materials

Chairman of the Board and President
PECKHAM, John R.
Tel: (914) 949-2000
Fax: (914) 949-2075

Main Headquarters
Mailing: 20 Haarlem Ave.
White Plains, NY 10603
Tel: (914) 949-2000
Fax: (914) 949-2075

Political Action Committees

Peckham Industries Inc. Federal PAC
FEC ID: C00343681
Contact: Joanne Leslie Dzibela
20 Haarlem Ave.
White Plains, NY 10603

Contributions to Candidates: $25,500 (2015-2016)
Democrats: $4,000; Republicans: $21,500

Corporate Foundations and Giving Programs

Peckham Family Foundation
Contact: John R. Peckham
20 Haarlem Ave.
White Plains, NY 10603

Public Affairs and Related Activities Personnel

At Headquarters

ANTES, Richard E. *Chief Financial Officer and Controller* rantes@peckham.com	Tel: Fax:	(914) 949-2000 (914) 949-2075
DZIBELA, Joanne Leslie *PAC Treasurer*	Tel: Fax:	(914) 949-2000 (914) 949-2075
REYNOLDS, Jacqui *Manager, Human Resources*	Tel: Fax:	(914) 949-2000 (914) 949-2075

Pegasus Capital Advisors, L.P.

A private equity fund manager that provides creative capital and business solutions to a wide variety of industries.
www.pcalp.com
Annual Revenues: $7.20 million
Employees: 60
Industry/ies: Banking/Finance/Investments

Main Headquarters

Mailing: 99 River Rd. Cos Cob, CT 06807	Tel: Fax:	(203) 869-4400 (203) 869-6940

Public Affairs and Related Activities Personnel

At Headquarters

COGUT, Craig *Founder and Co-Managing Partner*	Tel: Fax:	(203) 869-4400 (203) 869-6940
FRANK-SHAPIRO, Anne *Chief Administrative Officer and Chief Compliance Officer* AFrank-Shapiro@pcalp.com	Tel: Fax:	(203) 869-4400 (203) 869-6940
POLLAK, David *Director, Marketing and Investor Relations* DPollak@pcalp.com	Tel: Fax:	(212) 710-3488 (203) 869-6940
SCHAEFER, Jason *General Counsel* jschaefer@pcalp.com	Tel: Fax:	(212) 710-2500 (203) 869-6940
STENCEL, Daniel *Chief Financial Officer* dstencel@pcalp.com	Tel: Fax:	(203) 869-4400 (203) 869-6940
ZUCKER, Mitchell *Vice President, Marketing and Investor Relations* mzucker@pcalp.com	Tel: Fax:	(203) 869-4400 (203) 869-6940

Pella Corporation

A manufacturer of wood windows and glass doors.
www.pella.com
Employees: 6,000
SIC: 2431; 3442
NAICS: 321911; 332321
Industry/ies: Glass

Chairman of the Board	Tel:	(641) 628-1000
FARVER, Charles	Fax:	(641) 628-6070

President and Chief Executive Officer	Tel:	(641) 628-1000
MEYER, Pat	Fax:	(641) 628-6070

Main Headquarters

Mailing: 102 Main St. P.O. Box 112 Pella, IA 50219	Tel: Fax: TF:	(641) 628-1000 (641) 628-6070 (800) 374-4758

Corporate Foundations and Giving Programs

Pella Rolscreen Foundation Contact: Mary Van Zante 102 Main St. Pella, IA 50219	Tel: Fax:	(641) 621-6224 (641) 621-6224

Public Affairs and Related Activities Personnel

At Headquarters

SAGERS, Elaine *Vice President, Marketing and Customer Support*	Tel: Fax:	(641) 628-1000 (641) 628-6070
VAN ZANTE, Mary	Tel: Fax:	(641) 621-6221 (641) 621-6070

Manager, Corporate Communications and Board Member,
Pella Community Foundation
mavzante@pella.com

The Penn Mutual Life Insurance Company

The company provides life insurance and annuity products.
www.pennmutual.com
Annual Revenues: $169 Million
Employees: 2,000
Industry/ies: Insurance Industry

Chairman, President and Chief Executive Officer	Tel:	(215) 956-8000
MCDONNELL, Eileen C	Fax:	(215) 956-7699

Main Headquarters

Mailing: 600 Dresher Rd. P.O. Box 178 Horsham, PA 19105-0178	Tel: Fax: TF:	(215) 956-8000 (215) 956-7699 (800) 523-0650

Political Action Committees

The Penn Mutual Life Insurance Company PAC
FEC ID: C00142372
Contact: Steven M. Herzberg

600 Dresher Rd.	Tel:	(215) 956-8000
Horsham, PA 19044	Fax:	(215) 956-8000

Contributions to Candidates: $2,700 (2015-2016)
Republicans: $2,700

Public Affairs and Related Activities Personnel

At Headquarters

BEATH, Donna *Executive Secretary and Contributions Coordinator*	Tel: Fax:	(215) 956-8060 (215) 956-7699
BRATZ, Keith *Assistant Vice President, Corporate Communications* bratz.keith@pennmutual.com	Tel: Fax:	(215) 956-7907 (215) 956-7699
DEAKINS, Susan T. *Senior Vice President and Chief Financial Officer*	Tel: Fax:	(215) 956-8000 (215) 956-7699
FLEISCHMAN, Jeffrey *Senior Vice President, Chief Marketing and Digital Officer*	Tel: Fax:	(215) 956-8000 (215) 956-7699
HERZBERG, Steven M. *PAC Treasurer*	Tel: Fax:	(215) 956-8000 (215) 956-7699
MOOSE, Alida *Senior Vice President, Chief Human Resources Officer*	Tel: Fax:	(215) 956-8000 (215) 956-7699
O'MALLEY, David M. *Chief Operating Officer*	Tel: Fax:	(215) 956-8000 (215) 956-7699
REYNOLDS , Kevin T. *Senior Vice President and Chief Legal Officer*	Tel: Fax:	(215) 956-8000 (215) 956-7699
SHERMAN, Peter *Executive Vice President and Chief Investment Officer* peter.sherman@pennmutual.com	Tel: Fax:	(215) 956-8000 (215) 956-7699

Penn National Gaming

A racing and gaming business.
www.pngaming.com
Annual Revenues: $2.93 billion
Employees: 18,204
Ticker: NASDAQ: PENN
SIC: 7011
Industry/ies: Sports/Leisure/Entertainment

Chairman of the Board	Tel:	(610) 373-2400
CARLINO, Peter M.	Fax:	(610) 373-4966

President and Chief Executive Officer	Tel:	(610) 373-2400
WILMOTT , Timothy J.	Fax:	(610) 373-4966

Main Headquarters

Mailing: 825 Berkshire Blvd. Wyomissing, PA 19610	Tel: Fax:	(610) 373-2400 (610) 373-4966

Political Action Committees

Penn National Gaming Inc. PAC
FEC ID: C00423814
Contact: D. Eric Schippers
825 Berkshire Blvd.
Suite 200
Wyomissing, PA 19610

Contributions to Candidates: $23,700 (2015-2016)
Democrats: $10,000; Republicans: $13,700

Principal Recipients

SENATE

CASEY, ROBERT P JR (DEM-PA)

Corporate Foundations and Giving Programs

Penn National Gaming Foundation Inc.

Contact: Amanda Garber		
825 Berkshire Blvd.	Tel:	(610) 373-2400
Suite 200	Fax:	(610) 373-2400

Wyomissing, PA 19610

Public Affairs and Related Activities Personnel

At Headquarters

CLARK, Gene
Senior Vice President, Human Resources
gene.clark@pngaming.com
Tel: (610) 373-2400
Fax: (610) 373-4966

GARBER, Amanda
Manager, Administrative Affairs and Executive Director, Penn National Gaming Foundation
Tel: (610) 378-8325
Fax: (610) 373-4966

REIBSTEIN, Saul V.
Executive Vice President, Finance, Chief Financial Officer and Treasurer
Tel: (610) 373-2400
Fax: (610) 373-4966

SCHIPPERS, D. Eric
Senior Vice President, Public Affairs and PAC Treasurer
eric.schippers@pngaming.com
Tel: (610) 373-2400
Fax: (610) 373-4966

SNOWDEN , Jay
Executive Vice President, Chief Operating Officer
Tel: (610) 373-2400
Fax: (610) 373-4966

SNYDER, Steven T.
Senior Vice President, Corporate Development
Tel: (610) 373-2400
Fax: (610) 373-4966

SOTTOSANTI , Carl
Senior Vice President, General Counsel and Secretary
Tel: (610) 373-2400
Fax: (610) 373-4966

WEISSMAN , Jennifer
Senior Vice President, Chief Marketing Officer
Tel: (610) 373-2400
Fax: (610) 373-4966

Penn National Insurance

A regional, mutual insurance company. It delivers superior property and casualty insurance products and services through independent agents and provides financial security to businesses and individuals that assists them in managing their risk.
www.pennnationalinsurance.com
Annual Revenues: $706.02 million
Employees: 820
Industry/ies: Insurance Industry

Chairman of the Board
ROWE, CPCU, Dennis C.
Tel: (717) 234-4941
Fax: (717) 255-6850

President and Chief Executive Officer
SEARS, CPCU, Christine
Tel: (717) 234-4941
Fax: (717) 255-6317

Main Headquarters
Mailing: P.O. Box 2361
Harrisburg, PA 17105-2361
Tel: (717) 234-4941
Fax: (717) 255-6317
TF: (800) 388-4764

Public Affairs and Related Activities Personnel

At Headquarters

STINE, CTP, FLMI, Gregory R.
Senior Vice Pesident, Chief Financial Officer and Treasurer
Tel: (717) 234-4941
Fax: (717) 255-6317

YARRISH, Esq., Karen C.
Senior Vice President, Secretary and General Counsel
Tel: (717) 234-4941
Fax: (717) 255-6850

At Other Offices

BRANDON, CPCU, Robert B.
Executive Vice President and Chief Operating Officer
Two N. Second St.
Harrisburg, PA 17101
Tel: (717) 234-4941
Fax: (717) 255-6317

BUFFINGTON, William
Vice President Human Resources
Two N. Second St.
Harrisburg, PA 17101
Tel: (717) 234-4941
Fax: (717) 255-6317

MARKLEY, Christopher D.
Vice President, Corporate Communications
Two N. Second St.
Harrisburg, PA 17101
cmarkley@pnat.com
Tel: (717) 255-6895
Fax: (717) 255-6317

Penske Automotive Group

An automobile and truck dealership operator.
www.penskeautomotive.com
Annual Revenues: $19.63 billion
Employees: 22,000
Ticker: NYSE: PAG
SIC: 22000
Industry/ies: Automotive Industry; Transportation

Chairman and Chief Executive Officer
PENSKE, Roger S.
Tel: (248) 648-2500
Fax: (248) 648-2525

Main Headquarters
Mailing: 2555 Telegraph Rd.
Bloomfield Hills, MI 48302-0954
Tel: (248) 648-2500
Fax: (248) 648-2525

Public Affairs and Related Activities Personnel

At Headquarters

BROCHICK, George
Executive Vice President, Strategic Development
Tel: (248) 648-2500
Fax: (248) 648-2525

CARLSON, J. D.
Executive Vice President and Chief Financial Officer
Tel: (248) 648-2500
Fax: (248) 648-2525

DENKER, Claude Bud H
Executive Vice President, Human Resources
Tel: (248) 648-2500
Fax: (248) 648-2525

MULCAHEY, Terri
Executive Vice President, Marketing and Business Development
Tel: (248) 648-2500
Fax: (248) 648-2525

PORDON, Anthony R.
Senior Vice President, Investor Relations and Corporate Development
tpordon@penskeautomotive.com
Tel: (248) 648-2540
Fax: (248) 648-2600

RAMONAT, R. Whitfield
Executive Vice President, Central Operations and Financial Services
Tel: (248) 648-2500
Fax: (248) 648-2525

SPRADLIN, Shane M.
Senior Vice President, General Counsel and Secretary
SSPRADLIN@PENSKEAUTOMOTIVE.com
Tel: (248) 648-2500
Fax: (248) 648-2525

VERMILLION, Nancy
Specialist, Corporate Communications
nvermillion@unitedauto.com
Tel: (248) 648-2500
Fax: (248) 648-2525

Penske Truck Leasing

A global transportation services provider.
www.pensketruckleasing.com
Employees: 17,000
SIC: 7510
Industry/ies: Transportation; Trucking Industry
Legislative Issues: TRU

Chairman of the Board
PENSKE, Roger S.
Tel: (610) 775-6000
Fax: (610) 775-2449

President and Chief Executive Officer
HARD, Brian
Tel: (610) 775-6000
Fax: (610) 775-2449

Main Headquarters
Mailing: Route Ten Green Hills
P.O. Box 563
Reading, PA 19603
Tel: (610) 775-6000
Fax: (610) 775-2449
TF: (888) 234-4201

Political Action Committees
Penske Truck Leasing Co LP PAC
FEC ID: C00373217
Contact: Michael A. Duff
P.O. Box 563
Reading, PA 19603

Contributions to Candidates: $53,500 (2015-2016)
Democrats: $8,500; Republicans: $45,000

Principal Recipients

HOUSE
COSTELLO, RYAN A (REP-PA)

Corporate Foundations and Giving Programs
Penske Truck Leasing Contributions Program
2675 Morgantown Rd.
Reading, PA 19607

Public Affairs and Related Activities Personnel

At Headquarters

ALTHEN, Marc
President
Tel: (610) 775-6000
Fax: (610) 775-2449

BELJIN, Alen
Public Relations Manager
alen.beljin@penske.com
Tel: (610) 775-6364
Fax: (610) 775-2449

DUFF, Michael A.
Treasurer
Mail Stop P.O. Box 563
Registered Federal Lobbyist
Tel: (610) 775-6292
Fax: (610) 775-2449

OTT, Paul
Senior Vice President, Finance
Tel: (610) 775-6000
Fax: (610) 775-2449

RYERSON, Randolph P.
Director, Corporate Communications
randolph.ryerson@penske.com
Tel: (610) 775-6408
Fax: (610) 775-2449

STOICHEFF , Jeff
Senior Vice President, Human resources
Tel: (610) 775-6000
Fax: (610) 775-2449

Pentair, Inc.

A diversified manufacturer of water technologies and enclosures for electronic products.
www.pentair.com
Annual Revenues: $6.87 billion
Employees: 28,400
Ticker: NYSE: PNR
SIC: 3550
Industry/ies: Machinery/Equipment

Chairman of the Board and Chief Executive Officer
HOGAN, Randall J.
Tel: (763) 545-1730
Fax: (763) 656-5402

Main Headquarters

Mailing: 5500 Wayzata Blvd. Tel: (763) 545-1730
Suite 800 Fax: (763) 656-5402
Minneapolis, MN 55416

Corporate Foundations and Giving Programs

The Pentair Foundation
Contact: Susan Carter
5500 Wayzata Blvd. Tel: (763) 656-5237
Suite 800
Minneapolis, MN 55416-1261

Public Affairs and Related Activities Personnel

At Headquarters

BORIN, Mark C. Tel: (763) 545-1730
Chief Accounting Officer and Treasurer Fax: (763) 656-5402

DAY, Betsy Tel: (763) 656-5537
Manager, Corporate Communications Fax: (763) 656-5402
Betsy.day@pentair.com

GLEASON, Todd Tel: (763) 656-5570
Senior Vice President, Growth Fax: (763) 656-5402

KOURY, Frederick S. Tel: (763) 545-1730
Senior Vice President, Human Resources Fax: (651) 639-5251

LAGESON, Angela D. Tel: (763) 545-1730
Senior Vice President, General Counsel, and Secretary Fax: (651) 639-5251

STAUCH, John L. Tel: (763) 545-1730
Executive Vice President and Chief Financial Officer Fax: (651) 639-5251

People's United Bank

A financial services company. It is a subsidiary of People's United Financial, Inc. It is a premier, community-based, regional bank in the Northeast offering commercial and retail banking, as well as wealth management services.
www.peoples.com
Annual Revenues: $1.19 billion
Employees: 5,000
SIC: 6035
Industry/ies: Banking/Finance/Investments

Non Executive Chairman of the Board Tel: (203) 338-7171
CARTER, George P. Fax: (203) 338-2310

President and Chief Executive Officer Tel: (203) 338-7171
BARNES, John P. Fax: (203) 338-2310

Main Headquarters

Mailing: P.O. Box 27 Tel: (203) 338-7171
Bridgeport, CT 06601-0027 Fax: (203) 338-2310

Political Action Committees

People'S Bank Federal Political Action Committee
FEC ID: C00178012
Contact: Alexander G. Egelson
850 Main St.
15th Floor
Bridgeport, CT 06604

> **Contributions to Candidates:** $14,000 (2015-2016)
> Democrats: $6,500; Republicans: $7,500

Corporate Foundations and Giving Programs

People's United Community Foundation
Contact: Carolyn Caffrey
850 Main St. Tel: (800) 839-1754
11th Floor
Bridgeport, CT 06604

Public Affairs and Related Activities Personnel

At Headquarters

CAFFREY, Carolyn Tel: (203) 338-7252
Manager, Customer Contact Programs Fax: (203) 338-2310
Carolyn.Caffrey@peoples.com

POWLUS, Lee Tel: (203) 338-7171
Senior Executive Vice President and Chief Administrative Fax: (203) 338-2310
Officer

At Other Offices

CARLSON, Valerie C. Tel: (203) 338-2351
First Vice President, Corporate Communications Fax: (203) 338-2310
850 Main St.
Bridgeport, CT 06604
vccarls@peoples.com

DI GIORGIO, Brent Tel: (203) 338-3135
Director, External Communications Fax: (203) 338-2310
850 Main St.
Bridgeport, CT 06604
bsdigio@peoples.com

EGELSON, Alexander G. Tel: (203) 338-7171
PAC Treasurer Fax: (203) 338-2310
850 Main St.

Bridgeport, CT 06604

GOULDING, Peter Tel: (203) 338-6799
Senior Vice President, Corporate Development and Strategic Fax: (203) 338-2310
Planning
850 Main St.
Bridgeport, CT 06604

HERSOM, Andrew S. Tel: (203) 338-4581
Senior Vice President, Investor Relations Fax: (203) 338-2310
850 Main St.
Bridgeport, CT 06604
Andrew.Hersom@peoples.com

NORTON, David Tel: (203) 338-7171
Senior Executive Vice President, Human Resources Fax: (203) 338-2310
850 Main St.
Bridgeport, CT 06604

ROSATO, David Tel: (203) 338-7171
Senior Executive Vice President and Chief Financial Officer Fax: (203) 338-2310
850 Main St.
Bridgeport, CT 06604

TRAUTMANN, Robert E. Tel: (203) 338-7171
Senior Executive Vice President and General Counsel Fax: (203) 338-2310
850 Main St.
Bridgeport, CT 06604

WALTERS, Kirk W. Tel: (203) 338-7171
Senior Executive Vice President, Corporate Development and Fax: (203) 338-2310
Strategic Planning
850 Main St.
Bridgeport, CT 06604

Peoples Natural Gas

Took over Dominion Peoples in 2013.
www.peoples-gas.com
Annual Revenues: $12.22 billion
Employees: 14,400
Ticker: NYSE: D
Industry/ies: Energy/Electricity

Chief Executive Officer Tel: (800) 764-0111
O'BRIEN, Morgan K.

Main Headquarters

Mailing: PO Box 535323 Tel: (800) 764-0111
Pittsburgh, PA 15253-5323

The Pep Boys - Manny, Moe & Jack

A provider of automotive parts, accessories and services.
www.pepboys.com
Annual Revenues: $2.09 billion
Employees: 18,000
Ticker: NYSE: PBY
SIC: 5531; 5099; 7538; 7549
Industry/ies: Automotive Industry; Transportation

Chairman of the Board Tel: (215) 430-9000
HOTZ , Robert H. Fax: (215) 227-7513

Main Headquarters

Mailing: 3111 W. Allegheny Ave. Tel: (215) 430-9000
Philadelphia, PA 19132 Fax: (215) 227-7513
TF: (800) 737-2697

Public Affairs and Related Activities Personnel

At Headquarters

CIRELLI , Joseph A. Tel: (215) 430-9000
Senior Vice President, Corporate Development Fax: (215) 227-7513

SPOONER, Alexandra Tel: (215) 430-9588
Manager, Communications Fax: (215) 227-7513
mediarelations@pepboys.com

STERN, David Ross Tel: (215) 430-9000
Chief Financial Officer Fax: (215) 227-7513

ZUCKERMAN, Brian M. Tel: (215) 430-9000
Senior Vice President, General Counsel and Secretary Fax: (215) 227-7513

PEPCO Holdings, Inc.

Pepco Holdings, Inc. is a diversified energy holding company with headquarters in Washington, DC. Subsidiaries include Atlantic City Electric, Delmarva Power, Pepco, Conectiv Energy, and Pepco Energy Services. Delivers power to customers in the District of Columbia, Delaware, Maryland, New Jersey and Virginia through its subsidiaries.
www.pepcoholdings.com
Annual Revenues: $4.92 billion
Employees: 5,125
Ticker: NYSE:POM
SIC: 4931
Industry/ies: Energy/Electricity; Utilities
Legislative Issues: ENG

Chairman of the Board, President and Chief Executive Officer
RIGBY, Joseph M.
Tel: (202) 872-2000
Fax: (292) 331-6750

Main Headquarters
Mailing: 701 Ninth St. NW
Washington, DC 20068
Tel: (202) 872-2000
Fax: (202) 331-6750

Political Action Committees
PEPCO Holdings Inc. PEPCO-Conectiv Political Action Committee (PHI PAC)
FEC ID: C00385849
Contact: Julie Beasley
701 Ninth St. NW
Room EP1202
Washington, DC 20068
Tel: (202) 872-2000

 Contributions to Candidates: $23,300 (2015-2016)
 Democrats: $18,500; Republicans: $4,800

Corporate Foundations and Giving Programs
Pepco's Charitable Giving Program
Contact: Pamela Holman
701 Ninth St. NW
Washington, DC 20068
Tel: (202) 872-3488
Fax: (202) 331-6750

Public Affairs and Related Activities Personnel
At Headquarters
BEASLEY, Julie
PAC Treasurer
Tel: (202) 872-2000
Fax: (202) 331-6750

BOYLE, Frederick J.
Senior Vice President and Chief Financial Officer
Tel: (202) 872-2000
Fax: (202) 331-6750

DOVE, Nathaniel E.
PAC Treasurer
Mail Stop Room 1207
Tel: (202) 872-2000
Fax: (202) 331-6750

FITZGERALD , Kevin C.
Executive Vice President and General Counsel
Tel: (202) 872-2000
Fax: (202) 331-6750

GRAHAM , Thomas H.
Vice President, People Strategy and Human Resources
Tel: (202) 872-2000
Fax: (202) 331-6750

HAINEY, Robert
Manager, Media Relations
rshainey@pepcoholdings.com
Tel: (202) 872-2680
Fax: (202) 331-6750

HOLMAN, Pamela
Contact, Philantropy Senior Staff Assistant
contributions@pepcoholdings.com
Tel: (202) 872-3488
Fax: (202) 331-6750

KINZEL, Donna J.
Vice President and Treasurer
dkinzel@pepco.com
Tel: (302) 429-3004
Fax: (302) 429-3188

MONICA, Laura L.
Vice President, Corporate Communications
Tel: (202) 872-2000
Fax: (202) 331-6750

MORA, Suzanne
Federal Lobbyist
Tel: (202) 872-2000
Fax: (202) 331-6750

PARKER, Kenneth J.
Senior Vice President, Government Affairs & Corporate Citizenship
Tel: (202) 872-2000
Fax: (202) 331-6750

REESE, Hallie M.
Vice President, Customer Care
hallie.reese@pepcoholdings.com
Tel: (202) 872-2000
Fax: (292) 331-6750

Pepperwood International Corporation d/b/a Hannaford Enterprises

Main Headquarters
Mailing: 1101 Pennsylvania Ave. NW, Suite 600
Washington, DC 20004

Public Affairs and Related Activities Personnel
At Headquarters
HANNAFORD, Peter D.

PepsiCo, Inc.
A major manufacturer of beverages, snack foods and juices. The company acquired Quaker Oats Co. in 2001.
www.pepsico.com
Annual Revenues: $66.28 billion
Employees: 271,000
Ticker: NYSE: PEP
SIC: 2033; 2086; 2099; 2080
NAICS: 312111; 311421; 311919
Industry/ies: Food And Beverage Industry
Legislative Issues: AGR; BUD; FOO; TAX; TRD

Chairman of the Board and Chief Executive Officer
NOOYI, Indra K.
Tel: (914) 253-2000
Fax: (914) 253-2070

Main Headquarters
Mailing: 700 Anderson Hill Rd.
Purchase, NY 10577
Tel: (914) 253-2000
Fax: (914) 253-2070

Washington Office
Mailing: 325 Seventh St. NW
Suite 400
Washington, DC 20004

Political Action Committees
Pepsico, Inc. Concerned Citizens Fund PAC
FEC ID: C00039321
Contact: Thompson Kenny
700 Anderson Hill Rd.
Purchase, NY 10577

 Contributions to Candidates: $111,000 (2015-2016)
 Democrats: $52,500; Republicans: $58,500

Corporate Foundations and Giving Programs
PepsiCo Foundation
Contact: Tony West
700 Anderson Hill Rd.
Purchase, NY 10577
Tel: (914) 253-2000
Fax: (914) 253-2000

Public Affairs and Related Activities Personnel
At Headquarters
BANNER, Jon
Executive Vice President, Communications
Tel: (914) 253-2000
Fax: (914) 253-2070

BETZ, Kimberly S.
Lobbyist
Tel: (914) 253-2000
Fax: (914) 253-2070

CHILDS, Stephanie
Vice President, Federal Government Affairs and Head, Washington, DC Office
Registered Federal Lobbyist
Tel: (914) 253-2000
Fax: (914) 253-2070

CHILDS, Stephanie
Registered Federal Lobbyist
Tel: (914) 253-2000
Fax: (914) 253-2070

JOHNSTON, Hugh F.
Executive Vice President and Chief Financial Officer
Tel: (914) 253-2000
Fax: (914) 253-2070

KENNY , Thompson
PAC Treasurer
Tel: (914) 253-2000
Fax: (914) 253-2070

LYNCH, Tricia
Contact, Media Relations
Tel: (914) 253-2000
Fax: (914) 253-2070

MARTINELLI, Richard
Senior Representative, Government Affairs
Registered Federal Lobbyist
Tel: (914) 253-2000
Fax: (914) 253-2070

SWINK, Phil
Senior Vice President, Government Affairs
Tel: (914) 253-2000
Fax: (914) 253-2070

TAMONEY, Jr., Thomas H.
Senior Vice President, Deputy General Counsel
Tel: (914) 253-2000
Fax: (914) 253-2070

TRUDELL, Cynthia M.
Senior Vice President, Human Resources and Chief Human Resources Officer
Tel: (914) 253-2000
Fax: (914) 253-2070

At Washington Office
AVERY, Elizabeth
Senior Vice President, Global Public Policy & Govt Affairs

BOYKAS, Paul
Vice President, Public Policy and Government Affairs

CHRISTENSON, Dan
Director, Federal Government Relations & Regulatory Affairs

RUIZ, Diego
Vice President, Global Public Policy and Government Affairs

THOMPSON, Kenneth D.
Director, External Relations

WEST, Tony
Executive Vice President, Government Affairs, General Counsel and Corporate Secretary

At Other Offices
LEZMAN, Steve
Senior Director, Government Affairs
604 13th Ave. E
Bradenton, FL 34208
steve.lezman@pepsico.com

Perdue Farms Inc.
A poultry producer, processor and an agricultural company.
www.perdue.com
Employees: 20,000
SIC: 2015; 2099; 5142
NAICS: 311615; 311999
Industry/ies: Agriculture/Agronomy; Animals; Food And Beverage Industry
Legislative Issues: AGR; TRD

Chairman of the Board and Chief Executive Officer
PERDUE, James A.
Tel: (410) 543-3579
Fax: (410) 543-3532

Main Headquarters
Mailing: 31149 Old Ocean City Rd.
Salisbury, MD 21804
Tel: (410) 543-3579
Fax: (410) 543-3532
TF: (800) 473-7383

Corporate Foundations and Giving Programs

Arthur W. Perdue Foundation
31149 Old Ocean City Rd.
Salisbury, MD 21804

Public Affairs and Related Activities Personnel

At Headquarters

DEYOUNG, Julie
Contact, Media Relations
julie.deyoung@perdue.com

Tel: (410) 341-2533
Fax: (410) 543-3532

Perf Go Green

Develops and markets eco-friendly, non-toxic and biodegradable plastic products.
www.perfgogreen.com
Employees: 9
SIC: 3089
Industry/ies: Environment And Conservation; Plastics Industry

Chairman of the Board and Chief Executive Officer
CARIDI, Michael

Tel: (212) 935-3550
Fax: (917) 210-3110

Main Headquarters
Mailing: 645 Fifth Ave.
8th Floor
New York City, NY 10022-5910

Tel: (212) 935-3550
Fax: (917) 210-3110

Corporate Foundations and Giving Programs

Go Green 21.0 Foundation
12 E. 52nd St.
Fourth Floor
New York City, NY 10022

Public Affairs and Related Activities Personnel

At Headquarters

FULMER, Kim
Manager, Communication and Operations
kim@perfgogreen.com

Tel: (212) 935-3550
Fax: (917) 210-3110

GIUSTO, Louis
Chief Financial Officer

Tel: (212) 935-3550
Fax: (917) 210-3110

Performance Food Group Inc.

A food service distributor. Merged with VISTAR in 2008.
www.pfgc.com
Annual Revenues: $415.40 million
Employees: 10,000
Ticker: NASDAQ (GS): PFGC
SIC: 5141
Industry/ies: Food And Beverage Industry

Chairman of the Board
STEENLAND, Doug

Tel: (804) 484-7700
Fax: (804) 484-7701

President and Chief Executive Officer
HOLM, George L.

Main Headquarters
Mailing: 12500 W. Creek Pkwy.
Richmond, VA 23238

Tel: (804) 484-7700
Fax: (804) 484-7701

Corporate Foundations and Giving Programs

PFG Foundation
12500 W. Creek Pkwy.
Richmond, VA 23242

Public Affairs and Related Activities Personnel

At Headquarters

BERKE, Kent
Senior Vice President, Business Development

Tel: (804) 484-7700
Fax: (804) 484-7701

EVANS, Bob
Senior Vice President and Chief Financial Officer

Tel: (804) 484-7700
Fax: (804) 484-7701

HOPE, Jim
Executive Vice President, Operations

Tel: (804) 484-7700
Fax: (804) 484-7701

MANION, Jane
Senior Vice President, Human Resources

MILLER, Mike
Senior Vice President, General Counsel

Tel: (804) 484-7700
Fax: (804) 484-7701

PRICE, Carol
Senior Vice President, Chief Human Resources Officer

Tel: (804) 484-7700
Fax: (804) 484-7701

VAGI, Joe
Manager, Corporate Communications
jvagi@pfgc.com

Tel: (804) 484-7700
Fax: (804) 484-7701

WILLIAMSON, Jeff
Senior Vice President, Operations

Tel: (804) 484-7700
Fax: (804) 484-7701

Performance Trust Capital Partners, LLC

Provides strategic financial advisory and investment banking services to mid-sized financial institutions
www.performancetrust.com
Annual Revenues: $11.10 million
Employees: 100

Industry/ies: Banking/Finance/Investments

Chairman of the Board
NUSSBAUM, Philip M.

Tel: (312) 521-1000
Fax: (312) 521-1001

Chief Executive Officer
BERG, Richard S.

Tel: (312) 521-1000
Fax: (312) 521-1001

Main Headquarters
Mailing: 500 W. Madison St.
Suite 450
Chicago, IL 60661

Tel: (312) 521-1000
Fax: (312) 521-1001
TF: (800) 843-6284

Public Affairs and Related Activities Personnel

At Headquarters

ELDER, Jason A.
Managing Director, Corporate Strategy

Tel: (312) 521-1000
Fax: (312) 521-1001

GELDMAN, Megan
Director, Marketing and Contact, Communications
mgeldman@performancetrust.com

Tel: (312) 521-1163
Fax: (312) 521-1001

JOHNSON, Craig S.
Managing Director, Sales and Trading

Tel: (312) 521-1000
Fax: (312) 521-1001

Performant Financial Corporation

Performant Financial Corporation, together with its subsidiaries, provides technology-enabled recovery and related analytics services in the United States. It helps commercial and government organizations prevent, identify and recover waste, improper payments and defaulted debts.
www.performantcorp.com
Annual Revenues: $175.31 million
Employees: 1,484
Ticker: NASDAQ:PFMT
Industry/ies: Banking/Finance/Investments

Chairperson and Chief Executive Officer
IM, Lisa

Tel: (925) 960-4800
Fax: (925) 960-4880

Main Headquarters
Mailing: 333 N. Canyons Pkwy.
Suite 100
Livermore, CA 94551

Tel: (925) 960-4800
Fax: (925) 960-4880
TF: (866) 256-0057

Political Action Committees

Performant Financial Corporation PAC
FEC ID: C00411199
Contact: Christopher E. Skinnell
2350 Kerner Blvd.
Suite 250
San Rafael, CA 94901

Contributions to Candidates: $3,000 (2015-2016)
Republicans: $3,000

Public Affairs and Related Activities Personnel

At Headquarters

CRISSMAN, Chris
Federal Lobbyist

Tel: (925) 960-4800
Fax: (925) 960-4880

LEACH, Hal
Chief Operating Officer

Tel: (925) 960-4800
Fax: (925) 960-4880

ORVELL, Hakan L.
Chief Financial Officer

Tel: (925) 960-4800
Fax: (925) 960-4880

PAIK, John
Senior Vice President and Chief Marketing Officer

Tel: (925) 960-4800
Fax: (925) 960-4880

ZUBEK, Richard
Contact, Investor Relations
investors@performantcorp.com

Tel: (925) 960-4988
Fax: (925) 960-4880

At Other Offices

SKINNELL, Christopher E.
PAC Treasurer
2350 Kerner Blvd., Suite 250
San Rafael, CA 94901

PerkinElmer

A global technology company that supplies products and technical services to manufacturers and end-users in industrial and government markets.
www.perkinelmer.com
Annual Revenues: $2.23 billion
Employees: 7,700
Ticker: NYSE: PKI
SIC: 3826; 8733; 3823; 5084; 7372
NAICS: 334513; 334611; 54171; 42183
Industry/ies: Aerospace/Aviation; Electricity & Electronics; Electronics; Energy/Electricity; Transportation

Chairman of the Board, President and Chief Executive Officer
FRIEL, Robert F.

Tel: (781) 663-6900
Fax: (203) 944-4904

Main Headquarters
Mailing: 940 Winter St.
Waltham, MA 02451

Tel: (781) 663-6900
Fax: (203) 944-4904

Corporate Foundations and Giving Programs

PerkinElmer Foundation
Contact: Suzanne Hurley
940 Winter St.   Tel: (781) 663-6900
Waltham, MA 02451   Fax: (781) 663-6052

Public Affairs and Related Activities Personnel

At Headquarters

FRANCISCO, David C.   Tel: (781) 663-5677
Vice President, Investor Relations   Fax: (203) 944-4904
dave.francisco@perkinelmer.com

GOLDBERG, Joel S.   Tel: (781) 663-6900
Senior Vice President, General Counsel and Secretary   Fax: (203) 944-4904

LETCHER, John   Tel: (781) 663-6900
Senior Vice President, Human Resources   Fax: (203) 944-4904

OKUN, Andrew   Tel: (781) 663-6900
Vice President and Chief Accounting Officer   Fax: (203) 944-4904

WASCO, Stephanie R.   Tel: (781) 663-5701
Vice President, Corporate Communications   Fax: (781) 663-5973
stephanie.wasco@perkinelmer.com

WILSON, Frank A.   Tel: (781) 663-6900
Senior Vice President, Chief Financial Officer   Fax: (203) 944-4904

Perma-fix Environmental Services, Inc.

Perma-Fix is a national environmental services company, providing unique mixed waste and industrial waste management services. Perma-Fix has increased its focus on the nuclear services segment, which provides radioactive and mixed waste treatment services to hospitals, research laboratories and institutions, numerous federal agencies including DOE and the U.S. Department of Defense and nuclear utilities.
www.perma-fix.com
Annual Revenues: $60.12 million
Employees: 522
Ticker: NASDAQ; PESI
Industry/ies: Environment And Conservation
Legislative Issues: ENG; WAS

Chairman, President and Chief Executive Officer   Tel: (770) 587-9898
CENTOFANTI, Lou   Fax: (770) 587-9937
lcentofanti@perma-fix.com

Main Headquarters
Mailing: 8302 Dunwoody Pl.   Tel: (770) 587-9898
Suite 250   Fax: (770) 587-9937
Atlanta, GA 30350

Political Action Committees
Perma-fix Environmental Services, Inc. PAC
FEC ID: C00516518
Contact: Ben Naccarato
8302 Dunwoody Pl.   Tel: (770) 587-9898
Suite 250   Fax: (770) 587-9937
Atlanta, GA 30350

   Contributions to Candidates: $2,500 (2015-2016)
   Democrats: $1,000; Republicans: $1,500

Public Affairs and Related Activities Personnel

At Headquarters

LASH, John   Tel: (770) 587-9898
Chief Operating Officer   Fax: (770) 587-9937

NACCARATO, Ben   Tel: (770) 587-9898
Chief Financial Officer, Vice President, and Secretary   Fax: (770) 587-9937
bnaccarato@perma-fix.com

WALDMAN, David K.   Tel: (212) 671-1020
Contact, Investor Relations   Fax: (770) 587-9937
perma-fix@crescendo-ir.com

The Permanente Federation

An entity of the Permanente Medical Groups which focuses on the standardization of patient care and performance.
Industry/ies: Health Care; Hospitals; Medicine/Health Care/Mental Health
Legislative Issues: MMM

Main Headquarters
Mailing: 1800 Harrison St.   Tel: (510) 625-6920
Floor 22
Oakland, CA 94612-3466

Washington Office
Mailing: 900 Seventh St. NW
Suite 590
Washington, DC 20001

Public Affairs and Related Activities Personnel

At Other Offices

KEMPSKI, Ann   Tel: (202) 296-1314
Director, Policy & Government Relations
One Kaiser Plaza

Oakland, CA 94612
ann.x.kempski@kp.org
Registered Federal Lobbyist

Pernod Ricard USA

A manufacturer and distributor of alcoholic and non-alcoholic beverages headquartered in Paris, France.
www.pernod-ricard-usa.com
Annual Revenues: $211 million
Employees: 2,000
Industry/ies: Food And Beverage Industry
Legislative Issues: BUD; CPT; FOR; HOM; TAX; TRD

President and Chief Executive Officer   Tel: (212) 372-5400
FRY, Bryan

Main Headquarters
Mailing: 250 Park Ave.   Tel: (212) 372-5400
New York City, NY 10177

Washington Office
Mailing: 816 Connecticut Ave. NW   Tel: (202) 833-2150
Suite 900   Fax: (202) 833-1733
Washington, DC 20006

Political Action Committees
Pernod Ricard USA LLC PAC
FEC ID: C00380527
Contact: John Gemma
100 Manhattanville Rd.   Tel: (914) 848-4800
Purchase, NY 10577   Fax: (914) 848-4800

   Contributions to Candidates: $4,500 (2015-2016)
   Democrats: $2,500; Republicans: $2,000

Public Affairs and Related Activities Personnel

At Headquarters

CARGILL, Emmanuel   Tel: (212) 372-5400
Senior Vice President, Human Resources and Corporate Services

CHEVLIN , Brian   Tel: (212) 372-5400
Senior Vice President, General Counsel

CRANE, Marty   Tel: (212) 372-5400
Senior Vice President, Spirits Sales

DENISOFF, Dan   Tel: (212) 372-5400
Senior Vice President, Operations

KELLEY, Shawn   Tel: (212) 372-5400
National Senior Manager, Marketing
Shawn.kelley@pernod-ricard-usa.com

O'NEILL, Stephen   Tel: (212) 372-5400
Senior Vice President, Strategy and Transformation

SHEA, Jack   Tel: (212) 372-5400
Vice President, Corporate Communications
jack.shea@pernod-ricard-usa.com

At Washington Office

MACATUNO, Vanessa   Tel: (202) 833-2150
Issues Analyst   Fax: (202) 833-1733
vanessa.macatuno@pernod-ricard-usa.com

ORR, Mark   Tel: (202) 833-2150
Vice President, Public Affairs   Fax: (202) 833-1733
mark.orr@pernod-ricard-usa.com
Registered Federal Lobbyist

At Other Offices

GEMMA, John   Tel: (914) 848-4800
PAC Treasurer   Fax: (914) 848-4777
100 Manhattanville Rd.
Purchase, NY 10577

THOMAS, Guillaume   Tel: (914) 848-4800
Chief Financial Officer   Fax: (914) 848-4777
100 Manhattanville Rd.
Purchase, NY 10577

Perrigo Company

Produces over-the-counter pharmaceuticals and nutritional supplements for store brands as well as generic drugs, active pharmaceutical ingredients and consumer products. It provides affordable healthcare products to consumers worldwide.
www.perrigo.com
Annual Revenues: $5.87 billion
Employees: 13,300
Ticker: NASDAQ : PRGO
SIC: 2834
Industry/ies: Pharmaceutical Industry
Legislative Issues: HCR; PHA; TAX

Chairman of the Board   Tel: (269) 673-8451
BRLAS, Laurie   Fax: (269) 673-9128

Chief Executive Officer
HENDRICKSON, John T.
Tel: (269) 673-8451
Fax: (269) 673-9128

Main Headquarters
Mailing: 515 Eastern Ave.
Allegan, MI 49010
Tel: (269) 673-8451
Fax: (269) 673-9128
TF: (800) 719-9260

Corporate Foundations and Giving Programs

Perrigo Company Charitable Foundation
515 Eastern Ave.
Allegan, MI 49010
Tel: (269) 673-8451
Fax: (269) 673-9128

Public Affairs and Related Activities Personnel

At Headquarters

BROWN, Judy L.
Executive Vice President and Chief Financial Officer
Tel: (269) 673-8451
Fax: (269) 673-9128

JOSEPH, Bradley
Vice President, Global Investor Relations
bradley.joseph@perrigo.com
Tel: (269) 686-3373
Fax: (269) 673-9128

KINGMA, Todd W.
Executive Vice President, General Counsel and Secretary
Tel: (269) 673-8451
Fax: (269) 673-9128

SHANNON, Arthur J.
Vice President, Global Corporate Affairs and European Investor Relations
Tel: (269) 686-1709
Fax: (269) 673-9128

STEWART, Mike
Senior Vice President, Global Human Resources
Tel: (269) 673-8451
Fax: (269) 673-9128

YU, Louis
Senior Vice President, Global Quality and Compliance
Tel: (269) 673-8451
Fax: (269) 673-9128

PETCO Animal Supplies, Inc.

Operates stores with pet-related products and services.
www.petco.com
Employees: 21,000
Ticker: NASDAQ: PETC
SIC: 5990
Industry/ies: Animals; Retail/Wholesale

Chairman of the Board
DEVINE, Brian K.
Tel: (858) 453-7845
Fax: (858) 784-3489

Chief Executive Officer
MYERS, James M.
Tel: (858) 453-7845
Fax: (858) 784-3489

Main Headquarters
Mailing: 9125 Rehco Rd.
San Diego, CA 92121
Tel: (858) 453-7845
Fax: (858) 909-2618
TF: (877) 738-6742

Corporate Foundations and Giving Programs

PETCO Foundation
Contact: Susanne Kogut
7262 N. Rosemead Blvd.
San Gabriel, CA 91775

Public Affairs and Related Activities Personnel

At Headquarters

FARELLO, Tom
Senior Vice President, Operations
Tel: (858) 453-7845
Fax: (858) 909-2618

PISCITELLO, Charlie
President and Chief People Officer
Tel: (858) 453-7845
Fax: (858) 784-3489

STARK, Lisa
Senior Communications Specialist
lisa.stark@petco.com
Tel: (858) 453-7845
Fax: (858) 784-3489

At Other Offices

KOGUT, Susanne
Executive Director, PETCO Foundation
7262 N. Rosemead Blvd.
San Gabriel, CA 91775
Tel: (858) 909-2618

Peter Kiewit Sons', Inc.

See listing on page 469 under Kiewit Corporation

Peter Pan Seafoods

Producer of frozen, canned and fresh seafood products.
www.ppsf.com
Employees: 400
SIC: 2099; 2091; 2092; 5142; 5146; 5421
NAICS: 311712; 311711
Industry/ies: Food And Beverage Industry

President and Chief Executive Officer and PAC Treasurer
COLLIER, Barry D.
Tel: (206) 728-6000
Fax: (206) 441-9090

Main Headquarters
Mailing: 2200 Sixth Ave.
Tenth Floor
Seattle, WA 98121-1820
Tel: (206) 728-6000
Fax: (206) 441-9090

Political Action Committees

Peter Pan Seafoods PAC (1220 Associates)
FEC ID: C00100305
Contact: Barry D. Collier
2200 Sixth Ave.
Suite 1000
Seattle, WA 98121

Contributions to Candidates: $1,250 (2015-2016)
Democrats: $750; Republicans: $500

Public Affairs and Related Activities Personnel

At Headquarters

CHARTIER, Steven
Vice President Sales and Marketing
Tel: (206) 728-6000
Fax: (206) 441-9090

KOCH, Kirk
Vice President, Finance and Accounting
Tel: (206) 728-6000
Fax: (206) 441-9090

The Peterson Companies, Inc.

A full-service real estate development and management company.
www.petersoncos.com
Annual Revenues: $11.70 million
Employees: 150
Industry/ies: Real Estate

Principal and Chairman
PETERSON, Milton V.
Tel: (703) 227-2000
Fax: (703) 631-6481

President
SMITH, William C.
Bsmith@petersoncos.com
Tel: (703) 227-2000
Fax: (703) 631-6481

Main Headquarters
Mailing: 12500 Fair Lakes Cir.
Suite 400
Fairfax, VA 22033
Tel: (703) 227-2000
Fax: (703) 631-6481

Public Affairs and Related Activities Personnel

At Headquarters

ALGIE, Janice
Director, Human Resources
jalgie@petersoncos.com
Tel: (703) 227-2000
Fax: (703) 631-6481

MCGRATH, Nancy Zabriskie
General Counsel
Tel: (703) 227-2000
Fax: (703) 631-6481

SENSI, Claudia
Chief Financial Officer
Tel: (703) 227-2000
Fax: (703) 631-6481

SWEENEY, Angela
Vice President, Marketing and Communications
asweeney@petersoncos.com
Tel: (703) 227-2000
Fax: (703) 631-6481

VECCHIARELLI, James J.
Chief Operating Officer
Tel: (703) 227-2000
Fax: (703) 631-6481

WITT, Garry
Senior Vice President, General Counsel
Tel: (703) 227-2000
Fax: (703) 631-6481

PetSmart, Inc.

A retailer of pet food, supplies and services.
www.petsmart.com
Employees: 26,000
Ticker: NASDAQ: PETM
SIC: 5990
Industry/ies: Animals; Retail/Wholesale

President and Chief Executive Officer
MASSEY, Michael J.
Tel: (623) 580-6100
Fax: (623) 580-6183

Main Headquarters
Mailing: 19601 N. 27th Ave.
Phoenix, AZ 85027
Tel: (623) 580-6100
Fax: (623) 580-6183
TF: (800) 738-1385

Corporate Foundations and Giving Programs

PetSmart Charities
Contact: Julie White
19601 N. 27th Ave.
Phoenix, AZ 85027
Tel: (800) 423-7387

Public Affairs and Related Activities Personnel

At Headquarters

ALPAUGH, John
Senior Vice President and Chief Marketing Officer
Tel: (623) 580-6100
Fax: (623) 580-6183

COOPERMAN, Ron
Executive Vice President, Strategy
Tel: (623) 580-6100
Fax: (623) 580-6183

DODSON, Paulette
Senior Vice President, General Counsel and Secretary
Tel: (623) 580-6100
Fax: (623) 580-6183

GOLDBERG, Erick
Senior Vice President, Human Resources
Tel: (623) 580-6100
Fax: (623) 580-6183

STACEY, Neil
Senior Vice President, Human Resources
Tel: (623) 580-6100
Fax: (623) 580-6183

WHITE, Julie	Tel:	(623) 580-6100
Director, Grants	Fax:	(623) 580-6183

Pfizer Inc.

A research-based health care company with businesses in pharmaceuticals, hospital products, animal health, consumer products, specialty chemicals and specialty minerals. Acquired Warner-Lambert in 2000 and Pharmacia Corp. in 2002.
www.pfizer.com
Annual Revenues: $49.12 billion
Employees: 78,300
Ticker: NYSE: PFE
SIC: 2834
NAICS: 325412
Industry/ies: Pharmaceutical Industry
Legislative Issues: AGR; BUD; CPT; HCR; MMM; PHA; TAX; TOR; TRD

Chairman of the Board and Chief Executive Officer
READ, Ian
Tel: (212) 573-2323
Fax: (212) 338-1525
ian.read@pfizer.com

Main Headquarters
Mailing: 235 E. 42nd St.   Tel: (212) 733-2323
    New York City, NY 10017   Fax: (423) 274-8677

Washington Office
Mailing: 1275 Pennsylvania Ave. NW   Tel: (202) 783-7070
    Suite 1200   Fax: (202) 347-2044
    Washington, DC 20004

Political Action Committees
Pfizer Inc. PAC
FEC ID: C00016683
Contact: Joseph Gruber
235 E. 42nd St.   Tel: (212) 733-2323
New York City, NY 10017

   Contributions to Candidates: $746,250 (2015-2016)
   Democrats: $291,500; Republicans: $449,750; Other: $5,000

      Principal Recipients

         SENATE
         BURR, RICHARD (REP-NC)
         CRAPO, MICHAEL D (REP-ID)
         PAUL, RAND (REP-KY)
         SCOTT, TIMOTHY E (REP-SC)
         THUNE, JOHN (REP-SD)

         HOUSE
         BRADY, KEVIN (REP-TX)
         FRELINGHUYSEN, RODNEY P. (REP-NJ)
         GREEN, RAYMOND E. 'GENE' (DEM-TX)
         KINZINGER, ADAM (REP-IL)
         ROSKAM, PETER (REP-IL)
         UPTON, FREDERICK STEPHEN (REP-MI)
         WALTERS, MIMI (REP-CA)

Corporate Foundations and Giving Programs
Pfizer Contributions Program
235 E. 42nd St.
New York City, NY 10017

Pfizer Foundation
235 E. 42nd St.   Tel: (212) 733-2323
New York City, NY 10017

Public Affairs and Related Activities Personnel

At Headquarters

D'AMELIO, Frank	Tel:	(212) 573-2323
Executive Vice President, Business Operations and Chief Financial Officer	Fax:	(212) 338-1525
GOUDIE, Doug	Tel:	(212) 733-2323
Director, Government Relations	Fax:	(423) 274-8677
Registered Federal Lobbyist		
GRUBER, Joseph	Tel:	(212) 573-2323
Senior Vice President, Global Tax and PAC Treasurer	Fax:	(212) 338-1525
HILL, Chuck	Tel:	(212) 733-2323
Executive Vice President, Worldwide Human Resources	Fax:	(423) 274-8677
chuck.hill@pfizer.com		
JOHNSON, Rady	Tel:	(212) 733-2323
Executive Vice President, Chief Compliance and Risk Officer	Fax:	(423) 274-8677
LANKLER, Doug	Tel:	(212) 573-2323
Executive Vice President and General Counsel	Fax:	(212) 338-1525
Douglas.Lankler@pfizer.com		
SUSMAN, Sally	Tel:	(212) 573-2323
Executive Vice President, Corporate Affairs	Fax:	(212) 338-1525
TERRY, Myron	Tel:	(212) 733-2323
Senior Director, Team Leader, Political Action Committee (PAC) and Grassroots	Fax:	(423) 274-8677
Registered Federal Lobbyist		

At Washington Office

BURG, Paula	Tel:	(202) 783-7070
Senior Director, Federal Government Relations	Fax:	(202) 347-2044
Registered Federal Lobbyist		
COLE, Ken	Tel:	(202) 783-7070
Senior Vice President & Head, DC Office	Fax:	(202) 347-2044
Registered Federal Lobbyist		
HALLIWELL, John Paul	Tel:	(202) 783-7070
Senior Director, Federal Government Relations	Fax:	(202) 347-2044
Registered Federal Lobbyist		
IDELKOPE, Julie	Tel:	(202) 783-7070
Vice President, Government Relations South	Fax:	(202) 347-2044
MCULSKY, Janet	Tel:	(202) 783-7070
Senior Director, Alliance Development	Fax:	(202) 347-2044
janet.mculsky@pfizer.com		
MEEHAN, Matthew	Tel:	(202) 783-7070
US Government Relations and Alliance Development,	Fax:	(202) 347-2044
POPOVIAN, Robert	Tel:	(202) 783-7070
Senior Director, US Government Relations	Fax:	(202) 347-2044
POTEET, Claudia	Tel:	(202) 783-7070
Director, Government Relations	Fax:	(202) 347-2044
RIEMER, Angela W.	Tel:	(202) 783-7070
Senior Director, Federal Government Relations	Fax:	(202) 347-2044
Registered Federal Lobbyist		
SCHELLHAS, Caroline Moody	Tel:	(202) 783-7070
Senior Director, Federal Government Relations, Tax Legislative and Regulatory Affairs	Fax:	(202) 347-2044
Registered Federal Lobbyist		
SWENSON, Jennifer	Tel:	(202) 783-7070
Senior Director, Federal Government Relations	Fax:	(202) 347-2044
Registered Federal Lobbyist		
WALSH, Mary Bridget	Tel:	(202) 783-7070
Vice President, Federal Government Relations	Fax:	(202) 347-2044
Registered Federal Lobbyist		
WILSON, Anne	Tel:	(202) 783-7070
Senior Director, Public Affairs	Fax:	(202) 347-2044
Anne.E.Wilson@pfizer.com		
Registered Federal Lobbyist		

At Other Offices

ALPERT, Dennis W.
Director, Advocacy & Public Affairs - U.S. Government Relations
1275 Pennsylvania Ave. NW, Suite 600
Washington, DC 20004

BLOOM, Seth
Lobbyist
1275 Pennsylvania Ave. NW, Suite 600
Washington, DC 20004

PG&E Corporation

An electric and gas utility. Subsidiaries include Pacific Gas and Electric Co.
www.pge-corp.com
Annual Revenues: $17.10 billion
Employees: 22,581
Ticker: NYSE: PCG
SIC: 4931
Industry/ies: Energy/Electricity; Natural Resources; Utilities
Legislative Issues: ENG; ENV; FIN; TAX; UTI

Chairman of the Board, Chief Executive Officer, and President   Tel: (415) 267-7070
EARLEY, Jr., Anthony F.   Fax: (415) 267-7268

Main Headquarters
Mailing: 77 Beale St.   Tel: (415) 973-8200
    24th Floor, MC B24W   Fax: (415) 973-8719
    San Francisco, CA 94105

Washington Office
Mailing: 900 Seventh St. NW   Tel: (202) 638-3500
    Suite 950
    Washington, DC 20001-3886

Political Action Committees
PG & E Corporation Employees Energy PAC
FEC ID: C00177469
Contact: George R. Opacic
77 Beale St.
Mail Code B29H
San Francisco, CA 94105

   Contributions to Candidates: $411,749 (2015-2016)
   Democrats: $251,000; Republicans: $160,749

      Principal Recipients

         HOUSE
         CALVERT, KEN (REP-CA)
         CARDENAS, TONY (DEM-CA)
         COSTA, JIM MR. (DEM-CA)

HOYER, STENY HAMILTON (DEM-DC)
MCCARTHY, KEVIN (REP-CA)
PELOSI, NANCY (DEM-CA)
PETERS, SCOTT (DEM-CA)
SWALWELL, ERIC MICHAEL (DEM-CA)
UPTON, FREDERICK STEPHEN (REP-MI)
VALADAO, DAVID (REP-CA)
WALTERS, MIMI (REP-CA)

PG&E Corporation Fund for Electric Generation - Federal PAC
FEC ID: C00404079
Contact: George R. Opacic
77 Beale St.
MC B29H
San Francisco, CA 94105

Corporate Foundations and Giving Programs

PG&E Corporation Foundation
Contact: Ezra C. Garrett
One Market, Spear Tower
Suite 2400
San Fracisco, CA 94105-1126

Public Affairs and Related Activities Personnel

At Headquarters

AFFONSA, Deborah T. | Tel: (415) 973-8200
Vice President, Corporate Strategy | Fax: (415) 973-8719

ARNDT, William D. | Tel: (415) 973-8200
Vice President, Electric Operations Strategic Business | Fax: (415) 973-8719
Management

BIJUR, Nicholas M. | Tel: (415) 973-8200
Vice President and Treasurer | Fax: (415) 973-8719

BRINTON, Elisabeth S. | Tel: (415) 973-8200
Vice President, Corporate Strategy Officer | Fax: (415) 973-8719

BURT, Helen A. | Tel: (415) 973-8200
Senior Vice President, Corporate Affairs | Fax: (415) 973-8719

CHENG, Linda Y.H. | Tel: (415) 973-8200
Vice President, Corporate Governance and Corporate | Fax: (415) 973-8719
Secretary

FITZPATRICK, Tim | Tel: (415) 973-8200
Vice President, Corporate Relations and Chief | Fax: (415) 973-8719
Communications Officer

KANE, Julie M. | Tel: (415) 973-8200
Senior Vice President and Chief Ethics and Compliance | Fax: (415) 973-8719
Officer

KIYOTA, Travis | Tel: (415) 973-8200
Vice President, Corporate Affairs | Fax: (415) 973-8719

LODUCA, Janet C. | Tel: (415) 973-8200
Vice President, Investor Relations | Fax: (415) 973-8719

MISTRY, Dinyar B. | Tel: (415) 973-8200
Vice President, Chief Financial Officer and Controller | Fax: (415) 973-8719

OPACIC, George R. | Tel: (415) 267-7000
PAC Treasurer and Lobbyist | Fax: (415) 972-5105
gro2@pge.com

SURI, Anil K. | Tel: (415) 973-8200
Vice President and Chief Risk and Audit Officer | Fax: (415) 973-8719

WELLS, Jason P. | Tel: (415) 973-8200
Vice President, Finance | Fax: (415) 973-8719

At Washington Office

COOPER, Shawn E. | Tel: (202) 638-3545
Director, Corporate Relations
shawn.cooper@pge-corp.com

LAVINSON, Melissa A. | Tel: (202) 638-1958
Vice President, Federal Affairs | Fax: (202) 638-3522
melissa.lavinson@pge-corp.com

At Other Offices

BEDWELL, Edward T. | Tel: (415) 267-7070
Vice President, Government Relations | Fax: (415) 267-7268
One Market, Spear Tower, Suite 2400
San Francisco, CA 94105-1126

BOTTORFF, Thomas E. | Tel: (415) 267-7000
Senior Vice President, Regulatory Relations | Fax: (415) 267-7268
One Market, Spear Tower, Suite 2400
San Francisco, CA 94105-1126

CAIRNS, Stephen J. | Tel: (415) 267-7070
Vice President, Internal Audit and Compliance | Fax: (415) 267-7268
One Market, Spear Tower, Suite 2400
San Francisco, CA 94105-1126

GARRETT, Ezra C. | Tel: (415) 267-7070
Vice President, Community Relations and Chief Sustainability | Fax: (415) 267-7268
Officer
One Market, Spear Tower, Suite 2400
San Francisco, CA 94105-1126

HAPNER, DeAnn | Tel: (415) 267-7000
Vice President, Federal Regulatory Policy and Rates | Fax: (415) 267-7268
One Market, Spear Tower, Suite 2400
San Francisco, CA 94105-1126

HARVEY, Kent M. | Tel: (415) 267-7070
Senior Vice President and Chief Financial Officer | Fax: (415) 267-7268
One Market, Spear Tower, Suite 2400
San Francisco, CA 94105-1126

PARK, Hyun | Tel: (415) 267-7000
Senior Vice President and General Counsel | Fax: (415) 267-7268
One Market, Spear Tower, Suite 2400
San Francisco, CA 94105-1126

SIMON, John R. | Tel: (415) 267-7000
Senior Vice President, Human Resources | Fax: (415) 267-7268
One Market, Spear Tower, Suite 2400
San Francisco, CA 94105-1126

UCHIN, Maria L. | Tel: (415) 267-7080
Manager, Federal Governmental Relations | Fax: (415) 267-7268
One Market, Spear Tower, Suite 2400
San Francisco, CA 94105-1126

Pharmaceutical Product Development, Inc.

Provides global research and development services to pharmaceutical, biotech, and medical device companies seeking regulatory approval for their products. Acquired in 2011 by private investors The Carlyle Group and Hellman & Friedman.
www.ppdi.com
Employees: 12,500
Ticker: NASDAQ: PPDI
SIC: 8731
Industry/ies: Pharmaceutical Industry

Chairman and Chief Executive Officer | Tel: (910) 558-7585
SIMMONS, David | Fax: (910) 558-7056

Main Headquarters
Mailing: 929 N. Front St. | Tel: (910) 251-0081
Wilmington, NC 28401-3331 | Fax: (910) 762-5820

Corporate Foundations and Giving Programs

Pharmaceutical Product Development Contributions Program
929 N. Front St. | Tel: (910) 251-0081
Wilmington, NC 28401-3331 | Fax: (910) 251-0081

Public Affairs and Related Activities Personnel

At Headquarters

BABISS, Lee E. | Tel: (910) 558-7585
Chief Scientific Officer, Executive Vice President of Discovery | Fax: (910) 558-7056
Innovation and Chief Executive Officer

BUCKWALTER, Randy | Tel: (919) 456-4425
Senior Manager, Public Relations | Fax: (910) 762-5820
Randy.Buckwalter@ppdi.com

CAUDLE, Louise | Tel: (910) 558-7585
Executive Director, Corporate Communications | Fax: (910) 558-7056
louise.caudle@rtp.ppdi.com

HARTMAN, Judd B. | Tel: (910) 558-7585
General Counsel | Fax: (910) 762-5820
judd.hartman@ppdi.com

HUMPHREY, Elizabeth | Tel: (910) 558-6096
Manager, Corporate Communications | Fax: (910) 762-5820
Elizabeth.Humphrey@ppdi.com

HUREAU, Robert | Tel: (910) 251-0081
Executive Vice President and Chief Financial Officer | Fax: (910) 762-5820

MURRAY, Ed | Tel: (910) 558-7585
Executive Vice President and Chief Human Resources Officer | Fax: (910) 558-7056

PENTECOST, Sue Ann | Tel: (910) 558-7585
Senior Director, Marketing and Sales Communications | Fax: (910) 558-7056
sueann.pentecost@ppdi.com

RICHARDSON, William W. | Tel: (910) 558-7585
Executive Vice President, Global Business Development | Fax: (910) 558-7056

SHARBAUGH, William J. | Tel: (910) 558-7585
Chief Operating Officer | Fax: (910) 558-7056

Pharmaco Group
See listing on page 11 under Actavis, Inc.

PharmAthene, Inc.

Develops effective countermeasures against a range of potential biological and chemical weapons.
www.pharmathene.com
Annual Revenues: $13.52 million
Employees: 35
Ticker: NYSE AMEX: PIP
SIC: 2834
Industry/ies: Pharmaceutical Industry
Legislative Issues: BUD; HCR; HOM

Chairman of the Board
SAYARE, Dr. Mitchel
Tel: (410) 269-2600
Fax: (410) 269-2601

President and Chief Executive Officer
GILL, John M.
Tel: (410) 269-2600
Fax: (410) 269-2601

Main Headquarters
Mailing: One Park Pl.
Suite 450
Annapolis, MD 21401
Tel: (410) 269-2600
Fax: (410) 269-2601

Political Action Committees
Pharmathene Inc PAC
FEC ID: C00472019
Contact: Linda L. Chang
One Park Pl.
Suite 450
Annapolis, MD 21401

Public Affairs and Related Activities Personnel

At Headquarters

CHANG, Linda L.
Senior Vice President, Chief Financial Officer and PAC Treasurer
Tel: (410) 269-2600
Fax: (410) 269-2601

COOK, Francesca
Senior Vice President, Policy and Government Affairs
francesca.cook@pharmathene.com
Registered Federal Lobbyist
Tel: (443) 610-4196
Fax: (410) 269-2601

JONES, Jeffrey M.
Chief Operating Officer
Tel: (410) 269-2600
Fax: (410) 269-2601

MACNEILL, Philip
Chief Financial Officer
Tel: (410) 269-2600
Fax: (410) 269-2601

Pharmavite LLC

A dietary supplement manufacturer.
www.pharmavite.com
Employees: 850
SIC: 5122; 2833; 2834; 5099; 9999
Industry/ies: Nutrition; Pharmaceutical Industry
Legislative Issues: BUD; FOO; LAW; TAX

Main Headquarters
Mailing: P.O. Box 9606
Mission Hills, CA 91346-9606
Tel: (818) 221-6200
Fax: (818) 221-6618
TF: (800) 423-2405

Washington Office
Mailing: 1909 K St. NW
Suite 400
Washington, DC 20006
Fax: (202) 973-5858
TF: (877) 866-2539

Political Action Committees
Pharmavite LLC PAC (Pharmavite PAC)
FEC ID: C00410654
Contact: John Wilson_
P.O. Box 9606
Mission Hills, CA 91346

Contributions to Candidates: $58,093 (2015-2016)
Democrats: $27,000; Republicans: $31,093

Public Affairs and Related Activities Personnel

At Headquarters

BUATTI , Brett
Vice President of Operations
Tel: (818) 221-6200
Fax: (818) 221-6618

DESHPANDE, Nitin
Executive Vice President and Chief Financial Officer
Tel: (818) 221-6200
Fax: (818) 221-6618

PATOUT , Etienne
Chief Marketing Officer
Tel: (818) 221-6200
Fax: (818) 221-6618

WILSON, John
Director Finance, Corporate Controller
Tel: (818) 221-6200
Fax: (818) 221-6618

At Washington Office

NOVELLI, Porter
Contact, Media Relations
pnbpr@porternovelli.com
Fax: (202) 973-5858

At Other Offices

SABATINI, Carolyn J.
Director, Government Relations
8510 Balboa Blvd., Suite 100
Northridge, CA 91325
csabatini@pharmavite.net
Registered Federal Lobbyist
Tel: (913) 338-2640
Fax: (818) 221-6618

PharMerica Corporation

An institutional pharmacy services company and pharmacy management services for skilled nursing facilities (SNF), long term care facilities (LTC), assisted living facilities (ALF), hospitals and other institutional care settings.
www.pharmerica.com

Annual Revenues: $2.04 billion
Employees: 4,600
Ticker: NYSE: PMC
SIC: 5912
Industry/ies: Pharmaceutical Industry

Chairman of the Board
MEYERS, Geoffrey G.
Tel: (502) 627-7000
Fax: (800) 395-6972

Chief Executive Officer
WEISHAR, Gregory S.
Tel: (502) 627-7000
Fax: (800) 395-6972

Main Headquarters
Mailing: 1901 Campus Pl.
Louisville, KY 40299
Tel: (502) 627-7000
Fax: (800) 395-6972
TF: (866) 209-2178

Political Action Committees
Pharmerica Corporation PAC (PPAC)
FEC ID: C00397455
Contact: David W. Froesel Jr.
1901 Campus Pl.
Louisville, KY 40299
Tel: (502) 627-7000
Fax: (502) 627-7000

Contributions to Candidates: $5,000 (2015-2016)
Republicans: $5,000

Public Affairs and Related Activities Personnel

At Headquarters

CANERIS, Thomas A.
Senior Vice President, General Counsel
Tel: (502) 627-7000
Fax: (800) 395-6972

FROESEL, Jr., David W.
Executive Vice President, Chief Financial Officer, Treasurer and PAC Treasurer
Tel: (502) 627-7959
Fax: (800) 395-6972

Phibro Animal Health Corporation

Formerly Philipp Brothers Chemicals, Inc. A global manufacturer and marketer of animal health pharmaceuticals, animal nutrition products and industrial and fine chemicals.
www.pahc.com
Annual Revenues: $747.32 million
Employees: 1,100
Ticker: NASDAQ: PAHC
SIC: 2040
Industry/ies: Animals; Chemicals & Chemical Industry

Chairman of the Board, President and Chief Executive Officer
BENDHEIM, Jack C.
jack.Bendheim@pahc.com
Tel: (201) 329-7300
Fax: (201) 329-7399

Main Headquarters
Mailing: Glenpointe Centre East, Third Floor
300 Frank W. Burr Blvd., Suite 21
Teaneck, NJ 07666-6712
Tel: (201) 329-7300
Fax: (201) 329-7399

Public Affairs and Related Activities Personnel

At Headquarters

BENDHEIM, Daniel
Director and Executive Vice President, Corporate Strategy
Tel: (201) 329-7300
Fax: (201) 329-7399

CARLSON, Gerald K.
Director and Chief Operating Officer
gerald.carlson@pahc.com
Tel: (201) 329-7300
Fax: (201) 329-7399

DAGGER, Thomas G.
Senior Vice President, General Counsel and Corporate Secretary
Tel: (201) 329-7300
Fax: (201) 329-7399

JOHNSON, Richard G.
Chief Financial Officer
Tel: (201) 329-7300
Fax: (201) 329-7399

WELCH, Daniel A.
Senior Vice President, Human Resources
Tel: (201) 329-7300
Fax: (201) 329-7399

WOLF, Tom
Media Contact
Tel: (312) 983-7109
Fax: (201) 329-7399

Philadelphia Health and Education Corporation (PHEC)

PHEC d/b/a Drexel University College of Medicine is a non-profit subsidiary of Drexel.
www.drexelmed.edu/Home
Industry/ies: Medicine/Health Care/Mental Health
Legislative Issues: DEF

Main Headquarters
Mailing: 1601 Cherry St.
Suite 10627
Philadelphia, PA 19102
Tel: (215) 255-7700
Fax: (215) 255-7702

Public Affairs and Related Activities Personnel

At Headquarters

DAVIS, Tiffany J.
Director, Clinical Education Assessment Center
Tiffany.Davis@drexelmed.edu
Tel: (215) 991-8533
Fax: (215) 255-7702

KEECH, Brian T.
Senior Vice President
Fax: (215) 255-7702

bk34@drexel.edu
Registered Federal Lobbyist

MONTANARO, Gregory — Tel: (215) 895-2109
Registered Federal Lobbyist — Fax: (215) 255-7702

MUNTEAN, Andrei — Fax: (215) 255-7702
Executive Director, Federal Affairs
Registered Federal Lobbyist

NOVACK, MD, Dennis H. — Tel: (215) 991-8537
Associate Dean, Clinical Education & Assessment — Fax: (215) 255-7702
Dennis.Novack@drexelmed.edu

SANDFORT, Donna H. — Tel: (215) 843-0214
Director, Administrative Services — Fax: (215) 255-7702
Donna.Sandfort@drexelmed.edu

SCHINDLER, MD, Barbara — Tel: (215) 991-8561
Vice Dean, Educational & Academic Affairs — Fax: (215) 255-7702
Barbara.Schindler@drexelmed.edu

WILSON, David — Tel: (215) 895-2109
Registered Federal Lobbyist — Fax: (215) 255-7702

ZEISET, George — Tel: (215) 991-8511
Director, Technology in Medical Education — Fax: (215) 255-7702
gzeiset@drexelmed.edu

Philip Morris Companies Inc.

See listing on page 41 under Altria Client Services, Inc.

Philips Lighting

A global leader in lighting products, systems and services.
www.usa.lighting.philips.com
Employees: 6,000
Industry/ies: Electricity & Electronics; Energy/Electricity
Legislative Issues: BUD; CPT; ENG; HOU; SCI; URB

Chief Executive Officer, Philips Lighting — Tel: (732) 563-3000
RONDOLAT, Eric

Main Headquarters
Mailing: 200 Franklin Square Drive — Tel: (732) 563-3000
  Somerset, NJ 08875

Washington Office
Mailing: 1050 K St. NW, Suite 900 — Tel: (202) 962-8567
  Washington, DC 20001 — Fax: (202) 962-8560

Political Action Committees
Philips Electronics North America Corporation PAC
FEC ID: C00239780
1050 K St. NW — Tel: (202) 962-8550
Suite 900 — Fax: (202) 962-8560
Washington, DC 20001

  Contributions to Candidates: $58,250 (2015-2016)
  Democrats: $16,250; Republicans: $42,000

Public Affairs and Related Activities Personnel

At Headquarters

HUNTINGTON, Amy — Tel: (732) 563-3000
President, Lighting Americas

MARTIN, Scott — Tel: (732) 563-3000
Head of Marketing, North America

ROUGEOT, Stephanie — Tel: (732) 563-3000
Chief Financial Officer, Philips Lighting

At Washington Office

CANTRELL, Jean — Tel: (202) 962-8567
Vice President, State and Local Government Relations — Fax: (202) 962-8560
jean.cantrell@philips.com

POULAND, John — Tel: (202) 725-4397
Vice President, Government Affairs and Solutions — Fax: (202) 962-8560
john.pouland@philips.com

SERRES, Anthony — Tel: (202) 962-8559
Technical Policy Manager — Fax: (202) 962-8560
Anthony.serres@philips.com

Philips Lumileds

See listing on page 501 under Philips Lumileds Lighting Company

Philips North America

A diversified health and well-being company and leader in cardiac care, acute care, home healthcare, male grooming and oral healthcare. Headquartered in Netherlands.
www.usa.philips.com
Employees: 15,000
Ticker: NYSE: PHG
Industry/ies: Electricity & Electronics; Electronics; Energy/Electricity
Legislative Issues: BUD; HCR; MMM; TAX; TRA; VET

Chief Executive Officer and Chairman of the Board of — Tel: (140) 274-4947
Management and Executive Committee — Fax: (140) 274-4947
HOUTEN, Frans van

Chief Executive Officer — Tel: (800) 223-1828
SHAFER, Brent

Main Headquarters
Mailing: 3000 Minuteman Rd. — Tel: (800) 223-1828
  Andover, MA 01810 — TF: (800) 223-1828

Washington Office
Mailing: 1050 K St. NW — Tel: (202) 962-8550
  Suite 900 — Fax: (202) 962-8560
  Washington, DC 20001

Political Action Committees
Philips Electronics North America Corporation PAC
FEC ID: C00239780
Contact: Jacquelyn R. Olson
1050 K St. NW — Tel: (202) 962-8550
Suite 900 — Fax: (202) 962-8560
Washington, DC 20001

  Contributions to Candidates: $58,250 (2015-2016)
  Democrats: $16,250; Republicans: $42,000

Public Affairs and Related Activities Personnel

At Headquarters

REVETTI, Clement — Tel: (800) 223-1828
Chief Legal Officer, Philips Electronics North America
clement.revetti@philips.com

STEPHENSON, Mark A. — Tel: (800) 223-1828
Head, Integrated Brand and Communications
mark.stephenson@philips.com

At Washington Office

ARTHUR, Arti — Tel: (202) 316-3612
Vice President, Business Development — Fax: (202) 962-8560
arti.arthur@philips.com

CENTER, Will — Tel: (202) 962-8551
Director, International Funding Organizations — Fax: (202) 962-8560
will.center@philips.com

CLASON, Kristy — Tel: (301) 385-7921
Vice President, Government Business Development — Fax: (202) 962-8560

FANTACONE, Christine — Tel: (202) 962-8550
Administrative Assistant — Fax: (202) 962-8560
Christine.fantacone@philips.com

FELTON, Dan — Tel: (202) 962-8550
Senior Manager, State Government Relations — Fax: (202) 962-8560
Daniel.felton@philips.com

LEE, Tony S. — Tel: (202) 962-8550
Senior Manager, Federal Government Relations, Home — Fax: (202) 962-8560
Healthcare
Tony.lee@philips.com
Registered Federal Lobbyist

OLSON, Jacquelyn R. — Tel: (202) 962-8550
Senior Manager, Government and Political Affairs, PAC — Fax: (202) 962-8560
Treasurer
jj.olson@philips.com
Registered Federal Lobbyist

OMIDVAR, Andrew O. — Tel: (301) 547-0504
Enterprise and Government R&D — Fax: (202) 962-8560
andrew.omidvar@philips.com

SHOULTZ, David — Tel: (202) 962-8550
Head of Government Affairs — Fax: (202) 962-8560
david.shoultz@philips.com
Registered Federal Lobbyist

Phillips 66

Phillips 66 is a energy manufacturing and logistics company.
www.phillips66.com
Annual Revenues: $129.29 billion
Employees: 14,000
Ticker: NYSE: PSX
SIC: 2911
Industry/ies: Fuels See Coal, Gas, Oil, Petroleum; Natural Resources
Legislative Issues: BUD; CAW; CHM; ENV; FUE; TAX; TRA

Chairman and Chief Executive Officer — Tel: (281) 293-6600
GARLAND, Greg C.

Main Headquarters
Mailing: P.O. Box 4428 — Tel: (281) 293-6600
  Houston, TX 77210

Washington Office
Mailing: 601 Pennsylvania Ave. NW
  Suite 1150 North
  Washington, DC 20004

Political Action Committees
Phillips 66 PAC
FEC ID: C00513549

Contact: Charles Rohrs
411 S. Keeler Ave.
670 Adams Bldg.
Bartsville, OK 74003

Contributions to Candidates: $161,250 (2015-2016)
Democrats: $15,000; Republicans: $146,250

Principal Recipients

HOUSE
RYAN, PAUL D. (REP-WI)
UPTON, FREDERICK STEPHEN (REP-MI)

Public Affairs and Related Activities Personnel

At Headquarters

JOHNSON, Paula   Tel: (281) 293-6600
Executive Vice President, Legal, General Counsel and
Corporate Secretary

MAXWELL, Greg G.   Tel: (281) 293-6600
Executive Vice President, Finance and Chief Financial Officer

REASOR, C. C. (Clayton)   Tel: (281) 293-6600
Executive Vice President, Investor Relations, Strategy,
Corprate and Government Affairs

REED, Sonya   Tel: (281) 293-6600
Senior Vice President, Human Resources

TAYLOR, Tim G.   Tel: (281) 293-6600
President

At Washington Office

THANJAN, Dale
Registered Federal Lobbyist

At Other Offices

ELIASSEN, Caroline   Tel: (202) 833-0903
Director, Federal Government Affairs
1776 Eye St. NW, Suite 700
Washington, DC 20006
Registered Federal Lobbyist

REAMY, Jeff M.   Tel: (202) 833-0903
Federal Lobbyist
1776 Eye St. NW, Suite 700
Washington, DC 20006
Registered Federal Lobbyist

ROHRS, Charles   Tel: (918) 977-6009
Lobbyist and PAC Treasurer
411 S. Keeler Ave., 670 Adams Bldg.
Bartsville, OK 74003

STETTNER, Jennifer   Tel: (202) 833-0903
Vice President, Federal and State Government Affairs
1776 Eye St. NW, Suite 700
Washington, DC 20006
Jen.C.Stettner@p66.com

Phillips-Van Heusen Corporation

Operates as an apparel company in the United States and internationally. A manufacturer and
retailer of footwear and apparel.
www.pvh.com
Annual Revenues: $8.06 billion
Employees: 18,200
Ticker: NYSE: PVH
SIC: 2321; 3143; 3144; 5611; 5661
NAICS: 315223; 316213; 316214; 448110; 448210
Industry/ies: Apparel/Textiles Industry; Retail/Wholesale

Chairman and Chief Executive Officer   Tel: (212) 381-3500
CHIRICO, Emanuel   Fax: (212) 381-3950

Main Headquarters
Mailing: 200 Madison Ave.   Tel: (212) 381-3500
                New York City, NY 10016-3903   Fax: (212) 381-3950

Corporate Foundations and Giving Programs

Phillips-Van Heusen Contributions Program
200 Madison Ave.   Tel: (212) 381-3500
New York City, NY 10016-3903

Public Affairs and Related Activities Personnel

At Headquarters

FISCHER, Mark D.   Tel: (212) 381-3500
Executive Vice President, General Counsel and Secretary Fax: (212) 381-3950
markfischer@pvh.com

GOLDSTEIN, Bruce   Tel: (212) 381-3500
Senior Vice President and Corporate Controller   Fax: (212) 381-3950

KELLY, Michael   Tel: (212) 381-3500
Executive Vice President, Marketing   Fax: (212) 381-3950
mikekelly@pvh.com

KOZEL, David F.   Tel: (212) 381-3500
Executive Vice President, Chief Human Resources Officer Fax: (212) 381-3950

PERLMAN, Dana M.   Tel: (212) 381-3502
Senior Vice President, Treasurer, Business Development and Fax: (212) 381-3950
Investor Relations
danaperlman@pvh.com

SHAFFER, Mike A.   Tel: (212) 381-3523
Executive Vice President and Chief Operating and Financial Fax: (212) 381-3950
Officer
michaelshaffer@pvh.com

STEINER, Melanie   Tel: (212) 381-3500
Senior Vice President, Chief Risk Officer   Fax: (212) 381-3950

The Phoenix Companies

A life insurance and investment management company.
www.phoenixwm.phl.com
Annual Revenues: $1.70 billion
Employees: 630
Ticker: NYSE: PNX
SIC: 6311
Industry/ies: Insurance Industry
Legislative Issues: INS; TAX

Chairman of the Board   Tel: (860) 403-5000
FORSGREN , Jr., John H.   Fax: (860) 403-5855

President and Chief Executive Officer   Tel: (860) 403-5000
WEHR, James D.   Fax: (860) 403-5755

Main Headquarters
Mailing: One American Row   Tel: (860) 403-5000
                P.O. Box 5056   Fax: (860) 403-5855
                Hartford, CT 06102-5056   TF: (800) 628-1936

Political Action Committees
Phoenix Companies, Inc. PAC Federal
FEC ID: C00168203
Contact: John H. Beers
One American R ow
Hartford, CT 06102

Contributions to Candidates: $10,000 (2015-2016)
Democrats: $10,000

Corporate Foundations and Giving Programs

The Phoenix Companies Contributions Program
One American Row   Tel: (860) 403-5000
P.O. Box 5056   Fax: (860) 403-5855
Hartford, CT 06102-5056

Public Affairs and Related Activities Personnel

At Headquarters

BEERS, John H.   Tel: (860) 403-5000
Vice President, Litigation, Governance Counsel and PAC   Fax: (860) 403-5755
Treasurer

BERESIN, Jody A.   Tel: (860) 403-5000
Executive Vice President and Chief Administrative Officer Fax: (860) 403-5855

ERICSON, Alice   Tel: (860) 403-5946
Second Vice President, Communications   Fax: (860) 403-5755
alice.ericson@pheonixwm.com

KLEINMAN, Naomi Baline   Tel: (860) 403-7100
Vice President, Investor Relations and Treasurer   Fax: (860) 403-5855

MALLEY, Bonnie J.   Tel: (860) 403-5000
Executive Vice President and Chief Financial Officer   Fax: (860) 403-5755

MULRAIN, John T.   Tel: (860) 403-5000
Executive Vice President, General Counsel and Secretary Fax: (860) 403-5534

O'CONNELL, Gina Collopy   Tel: (860) 403-5000
Senior Vice President and Chief Risk Officer   Fax: (860) 403-5855

Phoenix Footwear Group, Inc.

Phoenix Footwear Group, Inc. manufactures footwear, belts and accessories.
www.phoenixfootwear.com
Annual Revenues: $22.95 million
Employees: 42
Ticker: OTC : PXFG
SIC: 3140
Industry/ies: Apparel/Textiles Industry

Chairman of the Board and Chief Executive Officer   Tel: (760) 602-9688
RIEDMAN, James R.   Fax: (760) 602-9684

Main Headquarters
Mailing: 5937 Darwin Ct.   Tel: (760) 602-9688
                Suite 109   Fax: (760) 602-9684
                Carlsbad, CA 92008

Public Affairs and Related Activities Personnel

At Headquarters

CARTER, Robby L.   Tel: (760) 602-9688
Executive Vice President, Sales   Fax: (760) 602-9684

SLACK, Greg   Tel: (760) 602-9688

Chief Financial Officer, Treasurer and Secretary
gslack@phxg.com

Fax: (760) 602-9684

Phoenix Strategies Inc.

A public affairs consultant. Phoenix Strategies provides alternative dispute resolution services and training in Colorado.
coloradospringsmediators.com
Industry/ies: Public Affairs And Public Relations

President
CULNAN, Sr., Dennis M.
dculnan@phoenixstrategiesinc.com

Tel: (856) 727-9791

President
LICHTENBERGER, Monica

Tel: (719) 266-8181
Fax: (719) 598-8055

Main Headquarters
Mailing: 3730 Sinton Rd.
Suite 150
Colorado Springs, CO 80907

Tel: (719) 266-8181
Fax: (719) 598-8055

Phylogy, Inc.

Designs, develops, and markets communications equipment for telecommunications companies.
Industry/ies: Communications; Machinery/Equipment; Telecommunications/Internet/Cable

Chairman of the Board
MARKEY, Randy

Tel: (866) 749-5649
Fax: (408) 416-3350

Main Headquarters
Mailing: 817 Huron Rd. E
Suite 845
Cleveland, OH 44115-1141

Tel: (866) 749-5649
Fax: (408) 416-3350
TF: (866) 749-5649

Physical Sciences, Inc.

Focuses on providing contract research and development services in a variety of technical areas to both government and commercial customers.
www.psicorp.com
Annual Revenues: $23.1 million
Employees: 200
Industry/ies: Aerospace/Aviation; Energy/Electricity; Environment And Conservation; Transportation
Legislative Issues: DEF; ENG; SMB

Chairman of the Board
CALEDONIA, George E.
caledonia@psicorp.com

Tel: (978) 689-0003
Fax: (978) 689-3232

President and Chief Executive Officer
GREEN, B. David
dgreen@psicorp.com

Tel: (978) 689-0003
Fax: (978) 689-3232

Main Headquarters
Mailing: 20 New England Business Center
Andover, MA 01810-1077

Tel: (978) 689-0003
Fax: (978) 689-3232

Public Affairs and Related Activities Personnel

At Headquarters

GENESTRETI, Steven
Executive Vice President and Chief Financial Officer
genestreti@psicorp.com

Tel: (978) 689-0003
Fax: (978) 689-3232

NAKAMURA, Dr. Takashi
Contact, Media Relations
nakamura@psicorp.com

Tel: (925) 743-1110
Fax: (925) 743-1117

Physiotherapy Associates

Provides occupational, physical and speech rehabilitation services.
www.physiocorp.com
Annual Revenues: $190.90 million
Employees: 3,000
Industry/ies: Medicine/Health Care/Mental Health

Executive Chairman
CONNORS, Dan

Tel: (610) 644-7824
Fax: (610) 644-9065

Chief Executive Officer
BALAVENDER, Hank

Tel: (610) 644-7824
Fax: (610) 644-9065

Main Headquarters
Mailing: 855 Springdale Dr.
Suite 200
Exton, PA 19341

Tel: (610) 644-7824
Fax: (610) 644-9065
TF: (866) 786-8482

Public Affairs and Related Activities Personnel

At Headquarters

FERDINAND, Joel
Vice President, General Counsel and Secretary

Tel: (610) 644-7824
Fax: (610) 644-9065

ARNOLD, Keller
Chief Financial Officer

Tel: (610) 644-7824
Fax: (610) 644-9065

BERESCH, Jennifer

Tel: (610) 884-4882

Manager, Marketing Project
Jennifer.Beresch@physiocorp.com

Fax: (610) 644-9065

HONE, Michael
Vice President Financial Planning Analysis

Tel: (610) 644-7824
Fax: (610) 644-9065

KING, Janna
Senior Vice President, General Counsel
janna.king@physiocorp.com

Tel: (610) 644-7824
Fax: (610) 644-9065

OLIVER, Steve
Vice President, Marketing

Tel: (610) 644-7824
Fax: (610) 644-9065

WOLF, Michael
Vice President Controller

Tel: (610) 644-7824
Fax: (610) 644-9065

ZAPPACOSTA, Jennifer
Vice President Human Resources

Tel: (610) 644-7824
Fax: (610) 644-9065

Piedmont Healthcare PA

Works to develop services, infrastructure and practices that will provide patients with better healthcare.
www.piedmonthealthcare.com
Employees: 700
Industry/ies: Medicine/Health Care/Mental Health

Chairman of the Board
MORAN, Joseph

Tel: (704) 873-4277

Main Headquarters
Mailing: P.O. Box 1845
Statesville, NC 28687-1845

Tel: (704) 873-4277

Public Affairs and Related Activities Personnel

At Headquarters

PRENDERGAST, Mark L.
PAC Treasurer

Tel: (704) 873-4277

At Other Offices

SATLZMAN, Dr. Robert I.
Orthopaedic Surgeon
650 Signal Hill Dr. Extension
Statesville, NC 28625
bob.saltzman@piedmonthealthcare.com

Tel: (704) 873-4277
Fax: (704) 873-5008

Piedmont Natural Gas Company

A natural gas distributor.
www.piedmontng.com
Annual Revenues: $1.15 billion
Employees: 1,923
Ticker: NYSE: PNY
SIC: 4924
Industry/ies: Natural Resources; Utilities

Chairman of the Board, President and Chief Executive Officer
SKAINS, Thomas E.

Tel: (704) 364-3120
Fax: (704) 365-8515

Main Headquarters
Mailing: P.O. Box 33068
Charlotte, NC 28233

Tel: (704) 364-3120
Fax: (704) 365-8515
TF: (800) 752-7504

Political Action Committees
Piedmont Natural Gas PAC
FEC ID: C00144824
Contact: Arnold Garcia
P.O. Box 33068
Charlotte, NC 28233

> **Contributions to Candidates:** $32,000 (2015-2016)
> Democrats: $2,000; Republicans: $30,000

Corporate Foundations and Giving Programs

Piedmont Natural Gas Foundation
Contact: Jane R. Lewis-Raymond
P.O. Box 33068
Charlotte, NC 28233

Public Affairs and Related Activities Personnel

At Headquarters

BALDWIN, George
Managing Director, Government Relations
george.baldwin@piedmontng.com

Tel: (704) 364-3120
Fax: (704) 365-8515

CARPENTER, David
Vice President, Planning and Regulatory Affairs

Tel: (704) 364-3120
Fax: (704) 365-8515

GIAIMO, Nick
Director, Assistant Treasurer
nick.giaimo@piedmontng.com

Tel: (704) 364-3120
Fax: (704) 365-8515

LEWIS-RAYMOND, Jane R.
Senior Vice President and Chief Legal, Compliance and External Relations Officer
jane.lewis-raymond@piedmontng.com

Tel: (704) 364-3120
Fax: (704) 365-8515

MAYO, Judy

Tel: (704) 364-3120
Fax: (704) 365-8515

Vice President, Corporate Secretary and Deputy General Counsel

NEWLIN, Karl W.   Tel: (704) 364-3120
Senior Vice President and Chief Financial Officer   Fax: (704) 365-8515

O'HARA, Kevin M.   Tel: (704) 364-3120
Senior Vice President and Chief Administrative Officer   Fax: (704) 365-8515
kevin.o'hara@piedmontng.com

PRITCHARD, Robert   Tel: (704) 364-3120
Vice President, Treasurer and Chief Risk Officer   Fax: (704) 365-8515

SUTPHIN, John   Tel: (704) 364-3120
Director, Strategic Planning   Fax: (704) 365-8515

TRUSTY, David L.   Tel: (704) 731-4391
Managing Director, Public Relations   Fax: (704) 365-8515
david.trusty@piedmontng.com

VALENTINE, Ken   Tel: (704) 364-3120
Vice President, Business Development and Technology Services   Fax: (704) 365-8515

At Other Offices

GARCIA, Arnold   Tel: (704) 364-3120
PAC Treasurer   Fax: (704) 365-8515
4720 Piedmont Row Dr.
Charlotte, NC 28210

Pier I Imports

Offers a wide selection of indoor and outdoor furniture, wicker, lamps, vases, baskets, ceramics, dinnerware, candles, and other specialty products.
www.pier1.com
Annual Revenues: $1.87 billion
Employees: 5,000
Ticker: NYSE: PIR
SIC: 5700; 5099; 5712
NAICS: 423990; 442299
Industry/ies: Furniture/Home Furnishings

Non-executive Chairman of the Board   Tel: (817) 252-8000
LONDON, Terry E.   Fax: (817) 252-8174

President and Chief Executive Officer   Tel: (817) 252-8000
SMITH, Alexander W.   Fax: (817) 252-8174

Main Headquarters
Mailing: 100 Pier One Pl.   Tel: (817) 252-8000
Fort Worth, TX 76102   Fax: (817) 252-8174
    TF: (800) 245-4595

Public Affairs and Related Activities Personnel

At Headquarters

CARTER, Michael A.   Tel: (817) 252-8000
Senior Vice President, General Counsel and Secretary   Fax: (817) 252-8174

COFFEY, Laura A.   Tel: (817) 252-8000
Executive Vice Preseident and Interim Chief Financial Officer   Fax: (817) 252-8174

HUMENESKY, Gregory S.   Tel: (817) 252-8000
Executive Vice President, Human Resources   Fax: (817) 252-8174

HUNTER, Eric W.   Tel: (817) 252-8000
Executive Vice President, Marketing   Fax: (817) 252-8174

KINNISON, Donald L.   Tel: (817) 252-8000
Senior Vice President, Marketing & Visual Merchandising   Fax: (817) 252-8174

TURNER, Charles H.   Tel: (817) 252-8000
Senior Executive Vice President & Chief Financial Officer   Fax: (817) 252-8174

Pilgrim's Pride Corporation

A chicken products producer. Acquired Gold Kist Inc. in 2007. Acquired by Brazilian beef company JBS SA in 2009.
www.pilgrimspride.com
Annual Revenues: $8.09 billion
Employees: 37,900
Ticker: NASDAQ: PPC
SIC: 2015; 2048
NAICS: 311615; 311119
Industry/ies: Agriculture/Agronomy

Chairman of the Board   Tel: (970) 506-8000
BATISTA , Wesley Mendonca

President and Chief Executive Officer   Tel: (970) 506-8000
LOVETTE, William W.

Main Headquarters
Mailing: 1770 Promontory Cir.   Tel: (970) 506-8000
Greeley, CO 80634   TF: (800) 727-5366

Corporate Foundations and Giving Programs

Pilgrim's Pride Corporation Contributions Program
1770 Promontory Cir.
Greeley, CO 80634

Public Affairs and Related Activities Personnel

At Headquarters

BRUETT, Cameron   Tel: (970) 506-7801
Chief Sustainability Officer; Head, Corporate Communications at JBS USA
cameron.bruett@jbssa.com

NORONHA, Eduardo   Tel: (970) 506-8000
Head, Human Resources

PENN, Jayson   Tel: (970) 506-8000
Executive Vice President, Sales and Operations

SANDRI, Fabio   Tel: (970) 506-8000
Chief Financial Officer

SCHULT, Doug   Tel: (970) 506-8000
Senior Vice President, Human Resources

SHAFER , Walt   Tel: (970) 506-8000
Executive Vice President, Operations

Pilkington North America

Pilkington North America manufactures and markets glass and glazing products for the architectural and automotive markets.
www.pilkington.com
Annual Revenues: $310 million
Employees: 3,700
Industry/ies: Glass
Legislative Issues: ENG

Director, President and Chief Executive Officer   Tel: (419) 247-3731
KNOWLTON, Warren   Fax: (419) 247-4517

Main Headquarters
Mailing: 811 Madison Ave.   Tel: (419) 247-3731
P.O. Box 799   Fax: (419) 247-4517
Toledo, OH 43697-0799   TF: (800) 221-0444

Public Affairs and Related Activities Personnel

At Headquarters

GRAHAM, Alan   Tel: (419) 247-3731
General Counsel, Chief Compliance Officer and Country Manager   Fax: (419) 247-3821

HEPNER, Rachel   Tel: (419) 247-3895
Manager, Marketing and Communications   Fax: (419) 247-4517
rachel.hepner@us.pilkington.com

KRASULA , Michael   Tel: (419) 247-3993
Regional Sales & Marketing Manager   Fax: (419) 247-4517
Michael.Krasula@nsg.com

URBAN, Sharon   Tel: (419) 247-3895
Specialist, Marketing Communications   Fax: (419) 247-4517
sharon.urban@nsg.com

Pinnacle Entertainment, Inc.

A developer, owner and operator of casino gaming resorts.
www.pnkinc.com
Employees: 14,738
Ticker: NYSE: PNK
SIC: 7011
Industry/ies: Computer/Technology

Chairman of the Board   Tel: (702) 541-7777
MARTINEAU, James L.   Fax: (702) 784-7778

Chief Executive Officer   Tel: (702) 541-7777
SANFILIPPO, Anthony   Fax: (702) 784-7778

Main Headquarters
Mailing: 3800 Howard Hughes Pkwy.   Tel: (702) 541-7777
Las Vegas, NV 89169   Fax: (702) 784-7778

Political Action Committees
Pinnacle Entertainment, Inc. PAC AKA Pinnacle Entertainment PAC
FEC ID: C00394122
Contact: Christopher E. Skinnell
2350 Kerner Blvd.
Suite 250
San Rafael, CA 94901

Corporate Foundations and Giving Programs
Pinnacle Entertainment Contributions Program
8918 Spanish Ridge Ave.
Las Vegas, NV 89148

Public Affairs and Related Activities Personnel

At Headquarters

DONELSON, Christina   Tel: (702) 541-7777
Senior Vice President, Human Resources   Fax: (702) 784-7778

KINKADE, APR, Roxann M.   Tel: (702) 541-7777
Director, Public Relations   Fax: (702) 784-7778
roxann.kinkade@pnkmail.com

NEGROTTO, Donna   Tel: (702) 541-7777
Executive Vice President, General Counsel and Secretary   Fax: (702) 784-7778

RUISANCHEZ, Carlos   Tel: (702) 541-7777

President and Chief Financial Officer — Fax: (702) 784-7778

SHANKS, Ginny
Executive Vice President and Chief Administrative Officer
Tel: (702) 541-7777
Fax: (702) 784-7778

STREMMING, Troy
Executive Vice President, Government Relations and Public Affairs
Tel: (702) 541-7777
Fax: (702) 784-7778

ZAHN, CFA, Vincent
Vice President and Treasurer
Tel: (702) 541-7777
Fax: (702) 784-7778

At Other Offices

ANDERSEN, Kerry
Director, Media Relations and Public Affairs
777 Ave. L'Auberge
Lake Charles, LA 70601
Kerry.Andersen@pnkmail.com
Tel: (337) 395-7631

SKINNELL, Christopher E.
PAC Treasurer
2350 Kerner Blvd., Suite 250
San Rafael, CA 94901

Pinnacle West Capital Corporation

Delivers electricity and energy-related products and services. Also involved in real estate development. It generates, transmits, and distributes electricity using coal, nuclear, gas, oil, and solar resources primarily in the State of Arizona.
www.pinnaclewest.com
Annual Revenues: $3.50 billion
Employees: 93
Ticker: NYSE: PNW
SIC: 4911
Industry/ies: Banking/Finance/Investments; Energy/Electricity; Real Estate; Utilities
Legislative Issues: BUD; CAW; ENG; ENV; HOM; TAX; UTI

Chairman of the Board, President and Chief Executive Officer
BRANDT, Donald E.
Tel: (602) 250-1000
Fax: (602) 250-3803

Main Headquarters
Mailing: 400 N. Fifth St.
Phoenix, AZ 85004
Tel: (602) 250-1000
TF: (800) 824-8101

Washington Office
Mailing: 801 Pennsylvania Ave. NW
Suite 214
Washington, DC 20004
Tel: (202) 293-2655
Fax: (202) 293-2666

Political Action Committees
Pinnacle West Capital Corporation PAC
FEC ID: C00015933
Contact: Robert Ekstrom
801 Pennsylvania Ave. NW, Suite 214
Washington, DC 20004
Tel: (202) 293-2655
Fax: (202) 293-2666

Contributions to Candidates: $349,500 (2015-2016)
Democrats: $91,000; Republicans: $257,500; Other: $1,000

Principal Recipients

SENATE
BLUNT, ROY (REP-MO)

HOUSE
BOEHNER, JOHN A. (REP-OH)
CLYBURN, JAMES E. (DEM-SC)
FRANKS, TRENT (REP-AZ)
GOSAR, PAUL ANTHONY (REP-AZ)
HOYER, STENY HAMILTON (DEM-DC)
MCSALLY, MARTHA E. MS. (REP-AZ)
RYAN, PAUL D. (REP-WI)
SALMON, MATT (REP-AZ)
SINEMA, KYRSTEN (DEM-AZ)
UPTON, FREDERICK STEPHEN (REP-MI)

Corporate Foundations and Giving Programs
Pinnacle West Foundation
P.O. Box 53999
Phoenix, AZ 85072

Public Affairs and Related Activities Personnel

At Washington Office
AIKEN, Robert S.
Vice President, Federal Affairs
Mail Stop M/S A112
robbie.aiken@pinnaclewest.com
Registered Federal Lobbyist
Tel: (202) 293-2655
Fax: (202) 293-2666

EKSTROM, Robert
PAC Treasurer
Tel: (602) 250-1000
Fax: (602) 250-2430

At Other Offices
BUNNELL, Alan
Contact, Corporate Communications and Media Relations
P.O. Box 53999
Phoenix, AZ 85072-3999
Tel: (602) 250-3376
Fax: (602) 250-2430

alan.bunnell@pinnaclewest.com

FALCK, David P.
Executive Vice President, General Counsel and Secretary
P.O. Box 53999
Phoenix, AZ 85072-3999
Tel: (602) 250-1000
Fax: (602) 250-2430

GOMEZ, Barbara M.
Vice President, Human Resources
P.O. Box 53999
Phoenix, AZ 85072-3999
Tel: (602) 250-1000
Fax: (602) 250-2430

HATFIELD, James R.
Executive Vice President and Chief Financial Officer
P.O. Box 53999
Phoenix, AZ 85072-3999
Tel: (602) 250-1000
Fax: (602) 250-2430

MOUNTAIN, Paul J.
Director, Investor Relations
P.O. Box 53999
Phoenix, AZ 85072-3999
paul.mountain@pinnaclewest.com
Tel: (602) 250-4952
Fax: (602) 250-2430

Pioneer Electronics (USA) Inc.

A company involved in manufacturing and marketing electronic products.
www.pioneerelectronics.com/PUSA
Annual Revenues: $166.90 million
Employees: 500
SIC: 5065; 3651; 3679; 5098; 9999
Industry/ies: Electricity & Electronics; Electronics; Energy/Electricity

President and Chief Executive Officer
KOTANI, Susumu
Tel: (310) 952-2000
Fax: (310) 952-2199

Main Headquarters
Mailing: 2265 E. 220th St.
Long Beach, CA 90801-1720
Tel: (310) 952-2000
Fax: (310) 952-2199
TF: (800) 746-6337

Washington Office
Mailing: 701 Eighth St. NW
Suite 500
Washington, DC 20001

Political Action Committees
Pioneer Political Action Committee
FEC ID: C00325357
Contact: Virginia D. Ragan
701 Eighth St. NW
Suite 500
Washington, DC 20001

Contributions to Candidates: $330,042 (2015-2016)
Republicans: $327,149; Other: $2,893

Principal Recipients

SENATE
AYOTTE, KELLY A (REP-NH)
PORTMAN, ROB (REP-OH)
TOOMEY, PATRICK JOSEPH (REP-PA)
YOUNG, TODD CHRISTOPHER (REP-IN)

HOUSE
BOST, MICHAEL (REP-IL)
BOUSTANY, CHARLES W. DR. JR. (REP-LA)
DOLD, ROBERT JAMES JR (REP-IL)
HECK, JOE (REP-NV)

Public Affairs and Related Activities Personnel

At Headquarters
ARZADON, Jaed
Manager, Corporate Communications
Tel: (310) 952-2451
Fax: (310) 952-2199

At Washington Office
RAGAN, Virginia D.
PAC Treasurer

Pioneer Hi-Bred International, Inc.

A producer of farm seeds. Formerly known as Pioneer Hi-Bred International, Inc.
www.pioneer.com
Annual Revenues: $522.20 million
Employees: 12,300
SIC: 100
Industry/ies: Agriculture/Agronomy; Horticulture And Landscaping

Main Headquarters
Mailing: P.O. Box 1000
Johnston, IA 50131-0184
Tel: (515) 535-3200
Fax: (515) 535-4590
TF: (800) 247-6803

Washington Office
Mailing: 601 Pennsylvania Ave. NW
North Bldg., Suite 325
Washington, DC 20004
Tel: (202) 728-3613
Fax: (202) 728-3649

Corporate Foundations and Giving Programs

Pioneer Hi-Bred International Contributions Program
P.O. Box 1000
Johnston, IA 50131

Public Affairs and Related Activities Personnel

At Headquarters

BOBST, Christine	Tel:	(515) 535-3200
Director, Executive Plans	Fax:	(515) 535-4590
CONSLATO, Laurie	Tel:	(515) 535-3200
Vice President, Finance	Fax:	(515) 535-4590
FLINT, Jerry	Tel:	(515) 535-3200
Vice President, Biotech Affairs and Regulatory	Fax:	(515) 535-4590
JOHNSON, Tim	Tel:	(515) 535-3200
Director, Investor Relations	Fax:	(515) 535-4590
PATRICK, Michael	Tel:	(515) 535-3200
Director, Human Resources	Fax:	(515) 535-4590
RAGLAND, Lonnetta	Tel:	(515) 535-0029
Senior Consultant, Communications Public Affairs	Fax:	(515) 334-4515
lonnetta.ragland@pioneer.com		
WILLITS, Tracy	Tel:	(515) 535-3200
Director, DuPont Pioneer Communications	Fax:	(515) 535-4590

Pioneer Natural Resources

Pioneer Natural Resources Company was formed through the 1997 merger of Parker & Parsley Petroleum Company and MESA Inc. In September 2004, Pioneer merged with Evergreen Resources, Inc. An independent oil and gas exploration and production company.
www.pxd.com
Annual Revenues: $3.89 billion
Employees: 4,075
Ticker: NYSE: PXD
SIC: 1311; 1381; 1382
NAICS: 213112; 213111
Industry/ies: Natural Resources
Legislative Issues: ENG; FUE; TAX

Chairman of the Board and Chief Executive Officer	Tel:	(972) 444-9001
SHEFFIELD, Scott D.	Fax:	(972) 969-3516

Main Headquarters

Mailing:	5205 N. O'Connor Blvd.	Tel:	(972) 444-9001
	Suite 200	Fax:	(972) 969-3576
	Irving, TX 75039	TF:	(800) 242-2607

Corporate Foundations and Giving Programs

Pioneer's Scholarship Foundation
5205 N. O'Connor Blvd.
Suite 200
Irving, TX 75039

Tel: (972) 444-9001
Fax: (972) 444-9001

Public Affairs and Related Activities Personnel

At Headquarters

ABBOTT, Todd C.	Tel:	(972) 444-9001
Vice President, Finance and Treasurer	Fax:	(972) 969-3576
BERG, Mark S.	Tel:	(972) 444-9001
Executive Vice President, Corporate	Fax:	(972) 969-3576
DEALY, Richard P.	Tel:	(972) 444-9001
Executive Vice President and Chief Financial Officer	Fax:	(972) 969-3516
DISTASO, John C.	Tel:	(972) 444-9001
Vice President, Marketing	Fax:	(972) 969-3576
DOVE, Timothy L.	Tel:	(972) 444-9001
President, Chief Operating Officer and Board Member	Fax:	(972) 969-3576
HOPKINS, Frank E.	Tel:	(972) 969-4065
Senior Vice President, Investor Relations	Fax:	(972) 969-3576
frank.hopkins@pxd.com		
KLEINMAN, Mark H.	Tel:	(972) 444-9001
Senior Vice President, General Counsel and Corporate Secretary	Fax:	(972) 969-3516
PAULSEN, Larry N.	Tel:	(972) 444-9001
Senior Vice President, Administration and Risk Management	Fax:	(972) 969-3576
SPRATLEN, Susan A.	Tel:	(972) 444-4018
Vice President, Communications	Fax:	(972) 969-3576
susan.spratlen@pxd.com		
WALLACE, Roger W.	Tel:	(972) 444-9001
Vice President, Federal Policy	Fax:	(972) 969-3516

Piper Aircraft Inc.

A manufacturer of single and twin engine aircraft.
www.piper.com
Employees: 100
SIC: 3721
Industry/ies: Aerospace/Aviation; Transportation

President and Chief Executive Officer	Tel:	(772) 559-5907
CALDECOTT, Simon	Fax:	(772) 978-6592

Main Headquarters

Mailing:	2926 Piper Dr.	Tel:	(772) 567-4361
	Vero Beach, FL 32960	Fax:	(772) 978-6592

Corporate Foundations and Giving Programs

Piper Aircraft Inc. Contributions Program
2926 Piper Dr.
Vero Beach, FL 32960

Tel: (772) 567-4361
Fax: (772) 978-6592

Public Affairs and Related Activities Personnel

At Headquarters

CALCAGNO, John	Tel:	(772) 567-4361
Chief Financial Officer	Fax:	(772) 978-6592
CARLON, Jackie	Tel:	(772) 559-5907
Director, Marketing and Communications	Fax:	(772) 978-6592
jackie.carlon@piper.com		
FUNK, Jim	Tel:	(772) 567-4361
Vice President, Operations	Fax:	(772) 978-6592
HARKINS, Francis J.	Tel:	(772) 567-4361
Vice President, General Counsel and Corporate Secretary	Fax:	(772) 978-6592
HARKINS, Francis J.	Tel:	(772) 567-4361
Vice President, General Counsel and Corporate Secretary	Fax:	(772) 978-6592
MCEWEN, Drew	Tel:	(772) 567-4361
Vice President, Sales and Marketing	Fax:	(772) 978-6592

Piper Jaffray & Co

PJC operates as an investment bank and asset management firm. It provides a range of investment banking services, including mergers and acquisitions advice, industry research, equity and debt underwriting, sales, and trading for corporate clients, institutional investors, government entities and not-for-profits.
www.piperjaffray.com
Annual Revenues: $641.88 million
Employees: 1,026
Ticker: NYSE: PJC
SIC: 6211
Industry/ies: Banking/Finance/Investments

Chairman of the Board and Chief Executive Officer	Tel:	(612) 303-6000
DUFF, Andrew S.	Fax:	(612) 303-8199

Main Headquarters

Mailing:	800 Nicollet Mall	Tel:	(612) 303-6000
	Suite 1000	Fax:	(612) 303-8199
	Minneapolis, MN 55402	TF:	(800) 333-6000

Washington Office

Mailing:	1747 Pennsylvania Ave. NW
	Suite 210
	Washington, DC 20006

Corporate Foundations and Giving Programs

Piper Jaffray Community Giving
Contact: Christine Esckilsen
800 Nicollet Mall
Suite 800
Minneapolis, MN 55402

Public Affairs and Related Activities Personnel

At Headquarters

ESCKILSEN, Christine	Tel:	(612) 303-6000
Managing Director, Global Head, Human Capital and Assistant General Counsel	Fax:	(612) 303-8199
GEELAN, John	Tel:	(612) 303-6000
Managing Director, General Counsel and Secretary	Fax:	(612) 303-8199
OLSON-GOUDE, Jennifer A.	Tel:	(612) 303-6277
Director, Investor Relations	Fax:	(612) 303-8199
jennifer.a.olson-goude@pjc.com		
SCHONEMAN, Debbra L.	Tel:	(612) 303-6000
Managing Director and Chief Financial Officer	Fax:	(612) 303-8199
SMITH , Tom	Tel:	(612) 303-6336
Contact, Investor Relations, Managing Director, Corporate Development	Fax:	(612) 303-8199
thomas.g.smith@pjc.com		
STEENSLAND, Pamela	Tel:	(612) 303-6000
Principal, Marketing, Events and Travel	Fax:	(612) 303-8199
pamela.k.steensland@pjc.com		

Pitney Bowes, Inc.

A mail and messaging management provider.
www.pitneybowes.com
Annual Revenues: $3.77 billion
Employees: 15,200
Ticker: NYSE: PBI
SIC: 3579
NAICS: 333313
Industry/ies: Machinery/Equipment; Postal And Mail Services
Legislative Issues: BAN; POS; TRD

President and Chief Executive Officer
LAUTENBACH, Marc B.

Tel: (203) 356-5000
Fax: (203) 351-7336

Main Headquarters
Mailing: 3001 Summer St.
Stamford, CT 06926

Tel: (203) 356-5000

Political Action Committees
Pitney Bowes Inc., PAC
FEC ID: C00339499
Contact: Andrew Gold
One Elmcroft Rd.
MSC 63-20
Stamford, CT 06926

Contributions to Candidates: $76,500 (2015-2016)
Democrats: $33,000; Republicans: $43,500

Principal Recipients

SENATE
BLUMENTHAL, RICHARD (DEM-CT)

Corporate Foundations and Giving Programs

Pitney Bowes Foundation
One Elmcroft Rd.
Stamford, CT 06926

Tel: (203) 356-5000
Fax: (203) 351-7336

Public Affairs and Related Activities Personnel

At Headquarters

BRAND , Patrick
Senior Vice President and General Manager, Global SMB Products and Strategy

Tel: (203) 356-5000

DALEY, Ann
Federal Lobbyist
Registered Federal Lobbyist

Tel: (203) 356-5000

GOLD, Andrew
Vice President, Total Rewards and PAC Treasurer
andrew.gold@pb.com

Tel: (203) 356-5000

GOLDSTEIN, Daniel J.
Executive Vice President and Chief Legal and Compliance Officer
daniel.goldstein@pb.com

Tel: (203) 356-5000

KOHNSTAMM, Abby F.
Executive Vice President and Chief Marketing Officer

Tel: (203) 356-5000

MCBRIDE, Charlie F.
Vice President, Investor Relations
charles.mcbride@pb.com

Tel: (203) 356-5000

MONAHAN, Michael
Executive Vice President and Chief Financial Officer

Tel: (203) 356-5000

O'BRIEN MORROW, Polly
Vice President, Community Investments
polly.obrien@pb.com

Tel: (203) 356-5000

SCHMITT , Joseph
Vice President and Chief Information Officer

Tel: (203) 356-5000

TORSONE, Johnna G.
Executive Vice President and Chief Human Resources Officer

Tel: (203) 356-5000

WALLACE, Carol
Director, External Communications
carol.wallace@pb.com

Tel: (203) 356-5000

At Other Offices

ERCOLANO, Joseph
PAC Contact
300 Summer St., MSC 63-20
Stamford, CT 06926

Tel: (203) 356-5000
Fax: (203) 351-7336

LYONS, Ashley
Vice President, Federal Relations
300 Summer St., MSC 63-20
Stamford, CT 06926

Tel: (203) 351-6327
Fax: (203) 351-7336

Pittsburgh Life Sciences Greenhouse

Provides entrepreneurial life sciences enterprises with the resources and tools they need to make advances in research and patient care.
www.plsg.com
Annual Revenues: $15.36 Million
Employees: 43
Industry/ies: Science; Scientific Research

Chairman of the Board
DECOMO, Peter M.

Tel: (412) 201-7370
Fax: (412) 770-1276

President and Chief Executive Officer
MANZETTI, John W.
jwmanzetti@plsg.com

Tel: (412) 201-7370
Fax: (412) 770-1276

Main Headquarters
Mailing: 2425 Sidney St
Pittsburgh, PA 15203

Tel: (412) 201-7270
Fax: (412) 770-1276

Public Affairs and Related Activities Personnel

At Headquarters

JORDAN, James
Vice President and Chief Investment Officer
jjordan@plsg.com

Tel: (412) 201-7370
Fax: (412) 770-1276

PETRAGLIA, CPA, Philip G.
Vice President and Chief Financial Officer
ppetraglia@plsg.com

Tel: (412) 201-7370
Fax: (412) 770-1276

Pixia Corporation

Pixia provides data access, scalability and integration.
www.pixia.com
Industry/ies: Computer/Technology

Main Headquarters
Mailing: One Freedom Sq.
11951 Freedom Dr., 18th Floor
Reston, VA 20190

Tel: (571) 203-9665
Fax: (571) 203-9348

Public Affairs and Related Activities Personnel

At Headquarters

LUNDY, Gina
Vice President, Government Relations and Corporate Communications

Tel: (571) 203-9665
Fax: (571) 203-9348

Placid Refining Company

An independent, privately held petroleum refining company.
www.placidrefining.com
Annual Revenues: $3.7 billion
Employees: 200
SIC: 2911
Industry/ies: Fuels See Coal, Gas, Oil, Petroleum; Natural Resources; Petroleum Industry

President
ROBINSON, Daniel R.

Tel: (225) 387-0278
Fax: (225) 346-7410

Main Headquarters
Mailing: 1940 La Hwy. One North
Port Allen, LA 70767

Tel: (225) 387-0278
Fax: (225) 346-7410

Corporate Foundations and Giving Programs

Placid Refining Company Contributions Program
1940 La Hwy. One North
Port Allen, LA 70767

Tel: (225) 387-0278
Fax: (225) 346-7410

Public Affairs and Related Activities Personnel

At Headquarters

HANCOCK, Ron
Contact, Community Relations

Tel: (225) 387-0278
Fax: (225) 346-7410

HOPKINS, Joy
Credit Manager
Joy.Hopkins@placidrefining.com

Tel: (225) 387-0278
Fax: (225) 346-7410

HURST, Ron
Vice President and General Counsel

Tel: (225) 880-8479
Fax: (225) 346-7410

PFISTER, Matt
Director, Marketing and Business Development

Tel: (225) 346-7404
Fax: (225) 346-7410

PINION, Rita
Manager, Human Resources

Tel: (225) 387-0278
Fax: (225) 346-7410

WEBER, Candace M.
Contact, Media Relations and Administration

Tel: (225) 387-0278
Fax: (225) 346-7410

PlainsCapital Corporation

PlainsCapital Corporation is a middle market independent financial services.
www.plainscapital.com
Industry/ies: Banking/Finance/Investments

Chairman of the Board
WHITE, Alan B.

Tel: (214) 525-9100

President and Chief Executive Officer
SCHAFFNER, Jerry L.

Tel: (214) 525-9100

Main Headquarters
Mailing: 2323 Victory Ave.
Dallas, TX 75219-7657

Tel: (214) 525-9100

Political Action Committees
Plainscapital Corporation PAC
FEC ID: C00482125
Contact: Corbin Cook
2323 Victory Ave.
Suite 1400
Dallas, TX 75219

Contributions to Candidates: $10,000 (2015-2016)
Republicans: $10,000

Corporate Foundations and Giving Programs

PlainsCapital Corporation Contributions Program

2323 Victory Ave.
Dallas, TX 75219

Public Affairs and Related Activities Personnel

At Headquarters

COOK, Corbin	Tel:	(214) 525-9100
PAC Treasurer		
HEFLIN, Brian L.	Tel:	(214) 525-9100
Chief Operating Officer		
IRBY, Linda	Tel:	(214) 525-9100
Chief Human Resources Officer		
RICKS, Eddie	Tel:	(214) 525-9100
Chief Financial Officer		
TOWNE, Carol A.	Tel:	(214) 525-9100
Chief Marketing Officer		

Planning Systems, Inc. (PSI)

Develops technologies with real-world applications for network centric programs, homeland security and the commercial sector. Acquired by QinetiQ North America in 2011.
plansys.qinetiq-na.com
Industry/ies: Computer/Technology; Defense/Homeland Security; Government-Related

Main Headquarters

Mailing:	11091 Sunset Hills Rd.	Tel:	(571) 521-7700
	Suite 500	Fax:	(703) 480-0495
	Reston, VA 20191		

Public Affairs and Related Activities Personnel

At Headquarters

BLACK, Cindy	Tel:	(781) 684-4093
Contact, Media Relations	Fax:	(703) 480-0495
cblack@foster-miller.com		
TRUONG, Hang	Tel:	(703) 788-7700
Director, Human Resources	Fax:	(703) 480-0495

Plantronics Inc.

Manufactures telecommunications products and accessories.
www.plantronics.com
Annual Revenues: $865.01 million
Employees: 3,397
Ticker: NYSE: PLT
SIC: 3661; 3679
Industry/ies: Communications; Telecommunications/Internet/Cable

Director and Chairman of the Board	Tel:	(831) 426-5858
TSEU, Marvin	Fax:	(831) 426-6098

Director, President and Chief Executive Officer	Tel:	(831) 426-5858
KANNAPPAN, S. Kenneth	Fax:	(831) 426-6098
ken.kannappan@plantronics.com		

Main Headquarters

Mailing:	345 Encinal St.	Tel:	(831) 426-5858
	Santa Cruz, CA 95060	Fax:	(831) 426-6098
		TF:	(800) 544-4660

Public Affairs and Related Activities Personnel

At Headquarters

BUSTAMANTE, Alejandro	Tel:	(831) 426-5858
Senior Vice President, Operations	Fax:	(831) 426-6098
CASTRONOVO , Russell	Tel:	(831) 458-7598
Director, Global Communications	Fax:	(831) 426-6098
russell.castronovo@plantronics.com		
HOUSTON, Donald	Tel:	(831) 426-5858
Senior Vice President, Sales	Fax:	(831) 426-6098
KLABEN, Greg		
Vice President, Investor Relations		
greg.klaben@plantronics.com		
LOVEGREN, Susan	Tel:	(831) 426-5858
Senior Vice President, Human Resources	Fax:	(831) 426-6098
MARGERUM, Barry	Tel:	(831) 426-5858
Chief Strategy Officer	Fax:	(831) 426-0162
MERSEREAU , Marilyn	Tel:	(831) 426-5858
Senior Vice President, Marketing and Chief Marketing Officer	Fax:	(831) 426-6098
PICKARD, Richard	Tel:	(831) 426-5858
Vice President, Legal, General Counsel and Secretary	Fax:	(831) 426-6098
STRAYER , Pamela	Tel:	(831) 426-5858
Senior Vice President and Chief Financial Officer	Fax:	(831) 426-6098

Plastipak Packaging

Manufacturer of plastic containers and bottled water products.
www.plastipak.com
Annual Revenues: $242.82 million
Employees: 2,600

SIC: 3089; 3082; 3083; 3084; 3081
Industry/ies: Plastics Industry

President and Chief Executive Officer	Tel:	(734) 455-3600
YOUNG, William C.	Fax:	(734) 354-7391

Main Headquarters

Mailing:	41605 Ann Arbor Rd.	Tel:	(734) 455-3600
	Plymouth, MI 48170	Fax:	(734) 354-7391

Corporate Foundations and Giving Programs

Plastipak Packaging Contribution Program		
41605 Ann Arbor Rd.	Tel:	(734) 455-3600
Plymouth, MI 48170	Fax:	(734) 354-7391

Platinum Equity, LLC

A global investment firm specializing in merger and acquisition of mission-critical services and solutions in diverse industries.
www.platinumequity.com
Employees: 50,000
Industry/ies: Banking/Finance/Investments

Chairman of the Board and Chief Executive Officer	Tel:	(310) 712-1850
GORES, Tom T.	Fax:	(310) 712-1848
tgores@platinumequity.com		

Main Headquarters

Mailing:	360 N. Crescent Dr.	Tel:	(310) 712-1850
	Beverly Hills, CA 90210	Fax:	(310) 712-1848

Corporate Foundations and Giving Programs

Platinum Equity, LLC Contributions Program		
360 N. Crescent Dr.	Tel:	(310) 712-1850
South Bldg.	Fax:	(310) 712-1848
Beverly Hills, CA 90210		

Public Affairs and Related Activities Personnel

At Headquarters

BARNHILL, Mark	Tel:	(310) 228-9514
Partner	Fax:	(310) 712-1848
BOUTRY, David C.	Tel:	(310) 712-1850
Principal, Global Head of Business Development	Fax:	(310) 712-1848
KALAWSKI, Eva	Tel:	(310) 712-1850
Partner, General Counsel, and Secretary	Fax:	(310) 712-1848
SIGLER, Mary Ann	Tel:	(310) 712-1850
Chief Financial Officer and Chief Compliance Officer	Fax:	(310) 712-1848
WHELAN, Dan	Tel:	(310) 282-9202
Senior Vice President, Investor and Media Relations	Fax:	(310) 712-1848
dwhelan@platinumequity.com		

Playboy Enterprises, Inc.

Playboy Enterprises is a brand-driven, international multimedia entertainment company. It publishes Playboy Magazine and creates content for distribution via television networks, websites, mobile platforms and radio.
www.playboyenterprises.com
Annual Revenues: $215.20 million
Employees: 550
Ticker: NYSE: PLA
SIC: 4841
Industry/ies: Sports/Leisure/Entertainment

Chief Executive Officer	Tel:	(312) 751-8000
FLANDERS, Scott N.	Fax:	(312) 751-2818

Main Headquarters

Mailing:	680 N. Lake Shore Dr.	Tel:	(312) 751-8000
	Chicago, IL 60611	Fax:	(312) 751-2818

Corporate Foundations and Giving Programs

Playboy Foundation		
680 N. Lake Shore Dr.	Tel:	(312) 373-2432
Chicago, IL 60611	Fax:	(312) 266-8506

Public Affairs and Related Activities Personnel

At Headquarters

(HENNESSEY) BARCY, Theresa	Tel:	(312) 373-2444
Vice President, Public Relations	Fax:	(312) 751-2818
theresah@playboy.com		
BRIGGS, Kendice K.	Tel:	(312) 751-8000
Senior Vice President, Human Resources	Fax:	(312) 751-2818
ISRAEL, David	Tel:	(312) 751-8000
Chief Operating Officer, Playboy Enterprises and President, Playboy Media	Fax:	(312) 751-2818
PACHLER, Christoph M.	Tel:	(312) 751-8000
Executive Vice President and Chief Financial Officer	Fax:	(312) 751-2818
SAGAN, Rachel	Tel:	(312) 751-8000
Executive Vice President, Business Affairs and General Counsel	Fax:	(312) 751-2818

Plug Power.

Transforms the energy landscape in ways that will positively impact the economy, society and environment.
www.plugpower.com
Annual Revenues: $68.07 million
Employees: 267
Ticker: NASDAQ: PLUG
SIC: 3620
Industry/ies: Fuels See Coal, Gas, Oil, Petroleum; Natural Resources; Petroleum Industry
Legislative Issues: BUD; TAX

| **President and Chief Executive Officer** | Tel: | (518) 782-7700 |
| MARSH, Andy | Fax: | (518) 782-9060 |

Main Headquarters
| Mailing: | 968 Albany Shaker Rd. | Tel: | (518) 782-7700 |
| | Latham, NY 12110 | Fax: | (518) 782-9060 |

Corporate Foundations and Giving Programs

Plug Power Contributions Program		
968 Albany-Shaker Rd.	Tel:	(518) 782-7700
Latham, NY 12110-1401	Fax:	(518) 782-7700

Public Affairs and Related Activities Personnel

At Headquarters

COCOCCIA, John	Tel:	(518) 782-7700
Vice President, Business Development and Investor Relations	Fax:	(518) 782-9060
CONWAY, Jr., Gerard L.	Tel:	(518) 782-7700
Senior Vice President, Governmental Affairs and Corporate Counsel	Fax:	(518) 782-9060
CRESPO, Jose Luis	Tel:	(518) 782-7700
Vice President, Global Sales	Fax:	(518) 782-9060
MIDDLETON, Paul	Tel:	(518) 782-7700
Chief Financial Officer	Fax:	(518) 782-9060
SCHMID, Keith	Tel:	(518) 782-7700
Chief Operating Officer	Fax:	(518) 782-9060

PMI Global Services Inc.

Headquartered in New York, NY. Provides services to Phillip Morris International, a tobacco manufacturing company.
www.pmi.com
SIC: 2111
Industry/ies: Tobacco Industry
Legislative Issues: CPT; HOM; IMM; TAX; TOB; TRD

| **Chairman of the Board** | Tel: | (917) 663-2233 |
| CAMILLERI, Louis C. | | |

| **Chief Executive Officer** | Tel: | (917) 663-2233 |
| CALANTZOPOULOS, Andre | | |

Main Headquarters
| Mailing: | 120 Park Ave. | Tel: | (917) 663-2233 |
| | New York City, NY 10017-5579 | | |

Washington Office
Mailing:	1399 New York Ave. NW	Tel:	(202) 495-2663
	Suite 400		
	Washington, DC 20005		

Public Affairs and Related Activities Personnel

At Headquarters

FIRESTONE, Marc S.	Tel:	(917) 663-2233
Senior Vice President and General Counsel		
MORTENSEN, James R.	Tel:	(917) 663-2233
Senior Vice President, Human Resources		
OLCZAK, Jacek	Tel:	(917) 663-2233
Chief Financial Officer		
POLLES, Jeanne	Tel:	(917) 663-2233
Senior Vice President, Corporate Affairs		
WILDE, Frederic de	Tel:	(917) 663-2233
Senior Vice President, Marketing and Sales		

At Washington Office

DAVIS, Brandie	Tel:	(202) 495-2665
Director, Corporate Affairs		
Registered Federal Lobbyist		
HUENEMANN, Jon E.	Tel:	(202) 495-2663
Federal Lobbyist		
Registered Federal Lobbyist		
JACOBS, Stephen	Tel:	(202) 495-2663
Federal Lobbyist		
Registered Federal Lobbyist		
REIF, Kristin	Tel:	(202) 495-2663
Registered Federal Lobbyist		

The PMI Group, Inc.

PMI Group is a mortgage insurer company that maintains offices in Asia, Europe and Australia.
www.pmi-us.com
Annual Revenues: $641.1 million
Employees: 700
Ticker: NYSE: PMI
SIC: 6351
Industry/ies: Banking/Finance/Investments; Housing; Insurance Industry

| **Chairman of the Board and President** | Tel: | (925) 658-7878 |
| SMITH, L. Stephen | Fax: | (925) 658-6931 |

| **Chief Executive Officer** | Tel: | (925) 658-7878 |
| PRAGER, David W. | Fax: | (925) 658-6931 |

Main Headquarters
Mailing:	PMI Plaza, 3003 Oak Rd.	Tel:	(925) 658-7878
	Walnut Creek, CA 94597	Fax:	(925) 658-6931
		TF:	(800) 288-1970

Washington Office
Mailing:	816 Connecticut Ave. NW	Tel:	(202) 223-4640
	Tenth Floor	Fax:	(202) 223-4845
	Washington, DC 20006		

Corporate Foundations and Giving Programs

The PMI Foundation		
3003 Oak Rd.	Tel:	(925) 658-7878
Walnut Creek, CA 94597		

Public Affairs and Related Activities Personnel

At Headquarters

CAMERON, Andrew D.	Tel:	(925) 658-7878
Executive Vice President, General Counsel and Secretary	Fax:	(925) 658-6931
CHANG, Ray D.	Tel:	(925) 658-7878
Senior Vice President, Corporate Treasurer	Fax:	(925) 658-6931
LOFE, Jr., Donald P.	Tel:	(925) 658-7878
Executive Vice President, Chief Financial Officer and Chief Administrative Officer	Fax:	(925) 658-6931
MOSES, James W.	Tel:	(925) 658-7878
General Counsel	Fax:	(925) 658-6931

At Washington Office

| SHOWELL, Jill | Tel: | (202) 223-4640 |
| *Vice President, Government Relations* | Fax: | (202) 223-4845 |

PMX Industries

PMX Industries fabricates copper, nickel and zinc based alloys.
www.ipmx.com
Annual Revenues: $35.30 million
Employees: 500
Industry/ies: Metals

| **Chairman and Chief Executive Officer** | Tel: | (319) 368-7700 |
| RYU, Jin Roy | Fax: | (319) 368-7721 |

Main Headquarters
| Mailing: | 5300 Willow Creek Dr. SW | Tel: | (319) 368-7700 |
| | Cedar Rapids, IA 52404 | Fax: | (319) 368-7721 |

Corporate Foundations and Giving Programs

PMX Industries Foundation
5300 Willow Creek Dr. SW
Cedar Rapids, IA 52404

Public Affairs and Related Activities Personnel

At Headquarters

PRATT, Rich	Tel:	(319) 368-7700
Director, Marketing, Research and Development	Fax:	(319) 368-7721
SELLERS, Merna	Tel:	(319) 368-7700
Human Resources Contact	Fax:	(319) 368-7721

PNC Financial Services Group, Inc.

A bank holding company providing deposit, lending, cash management and investment services to consumer and small business customers. In 2009, PNC acquired National City Corporation. Acquired Midlantic Corporation in 1995 and Mercantile Bankshares Corporation in 1996.
www.pnc.com
Annual Revenues: $15.10 billion
Employees: 49,745
Ticker: NYSE: PNC
SIC: 6021
Industry/ies: Banking/Finance/Investments
Legislative Issues: FIN

| **President** | Tel: | (412) 762-2000 |
| BINDYKE, Jacqueline | Fax: | (412) 762-7829 |

Main Headquarters
Mailing:	300 Fifth Ave.	Tel:	(412) 762-2000
	Pittsburgh, PA 15222	Fax:	(412) 762-7829
		TF:	(877) 762-2000

Corporate Foundations and Giving Programs

PAC Foundation
249 Fifth Ave.
One PNC Plaza
Pittsburgh, PA 15222

Tel: (412) 762-2748
Fax: (412) 762-7829

Public Affairs and Related Activities Personnel

At Headquarters

BLUM, Eva T.
Chairwoman and President, PNC Foundation
Mail Stop P1-POPP-20-1
eva.blum@pnc.com

Tel: (412) 762-2748
Fax: (412) 705-3584

CALLIHAN, William H.
Senior Vice President, Investor Relations
investor.relations@pnc.com

Tel: (412) 762-8257
Fax: (412) 762-7829

FOSCATO, Tara Wade
Contact, Government Relations
Registered Federal Lobbyist

Tel: (412) 762-2000
Fax: (412) 762-7829

JORDAN, Gregory B.
General Counsel and Head, Regulatory and Government Affairs

Tel: (412) 762-2000
Fax: (412) 762-7829

KOZICH , Gregory
Controller

Tel: (412) 762-2000
Fax: (412) 762-7829

LAMB, Jr., Thomas F.
Senior Vice President
thomas.lamb@pnc.com
Registered Federal Lobbyist

Tel: (412) 762-7558
Fax: (412) 762-2784

LONG, III, George P.
Chief Counsel, Corporate & Securities Group
george.long@pnc.com

Tel: (412) 762-1901
Fax: (412) 762-7829

MARCH, Amy M.
Vice President, Ethics Manager

Tel: (412) 762-2000
Fax: (412) 762-7829

MCMAHON, Patrick
Director, Public Relations
patrick.mcmahon@pnc.com

Tel: (412) 762-2477
Fax: (412) 762-7829

METZ, Mark R.
Manager, Government Affairs

Tel: (412) 762-2000
Fax: (412) 762-7829

MILLER, Andrew
Vice President
Registered Federal Lobbyist

Tel: (412) 762-2000
Fax: (412) 762-7829

SMITH, Erin
Assistant Vice President

Tel: (412) 762-2000
Fax: (412) 762-7829

SMITH, Shawn D.
Vice President, PAC Manager

Tel: (412) 762-2000
Fax: (412) 762-7829

SOLOMON, Fred
Director, External Communications
frederick.solomon@pnc.com

Tel: (412) 762-4550
Fax: (412) 762-7829

VARMECKY, Ronald E.
PAC Treasurer

Tel: (412) 762-2000
Fax: (412) 762-7829

ZANDRA MOSS, C.
Ethics Coordinator/PAC Administrator
Mail Stop 21st Floor

Tel: (412) 762-2000
Fax: (412) 762-7829

PNM Resources

An energy holding company with utility and energy subsidiaries in New Mexico and Texas.
www.pnmresources.com
Annual Revenues: $1.44 billion
Employees: 1,881
Ticker: NYSE: PNM
SIC: 4911
Industry/ies: Utilities
Legislative Issues: CAW; ENG; ENV; TAX

Chairman of the Board, President and Chief Executive Officer
VINCENT-COLLAWN, Pat
pat.collawn@pnmresources.com

Tel: (505) 241-2700
Fax: (505) 241-2367

Main Headquarters

Mailing: 414 Silver Ave. SW
Alvarado Sq.
Albuquerque, NM 87158-1275

Tel: (505) 241-2700
Fax: (505) 241-4311

Washington Office

Mailing: 1717 North St. NW
Fourth Floor
Washington, DC 20036

Tel: (202) 293-1595

Corporate Foundations and Giving Programs

PNM Resources Foundation
Alvarado Sq.
Albuquerque, NM 87158

Tel: (505) 241-2700
Fax: (505) 241-2367

Public Affairs and Related Activities Personnel

At Headquarters

APODACA, Patrick

Tel: (505) 241-2700

Senior Vice President and General Counsel
Patrick.Apodaca@pnmresources.com

Fax: (505) 241-2367

BLOTTER, Jimmie
Contact, Investor Relations

Tel: (505) 241-2227
Fax: (505) 241-4311

DARNELL , Ron
Senior Vice President, Public Policy

Tel: (505) 241-2700
Fax: (505) 241-2367

EDEN, Lisa
Vice President and Treasurer

Tel: (505) 241-2700
Fax: (505) 241-4311

ELDRED, Charles
Executive Vice President and Chief Financial Officer

Tel: (505) 241-2700
Fax: (505) 241-2367

MONFILETTO , Laurie
Vice President, Human Resources

Tel: (505) 246-5700
Fax: (505) 241-4311

SHIPLEY, Pahl
Contact, Media

Tel: (505) 241-2782
Fax: (505) 241-4311

TALBOT, Ron
Senior Vice President and Chief Operating Officer

Tel: (505) 241-2700
Fax: (505) 241-4311

TARRY, Don
Vice President, Corporate Controller and Chief Information Officer

Tel: (505) 241-2700
Fax: (505) 241-4311

At Washington Office

CAMPBELL, Kathleen F
Senior Corporate Governance Analyst
Kathleen.Campbell@pnmresources.com

Tel: (505) 241-4921

Poet, LLC

Production of ethanol and other biorefined products.
www.poetenergy.com
Employees: 1,500
Industry/ies: Chemicals & Chemical Industry; Construction/Construction Materials; Engineering/Mathematics
Legislative Issues: AGR; BUD; ENG; ENV; FUE; TAX; TRD

Executive Chairman and Founder
BROIN, Jeff

Tel: (605) 965-2200
Fax: (605) 965-2203

Chief Executive Officer
LAUTT, Jeff

Tel: (605) 965-2200
Fax: (605) 965-2203

Main Headquarters
Mailing: 4615 N. Lewis Ave.
Sioux Falls, SD 57104

Tel: (605) 965-2200
Fax: (605) 965-2203

Washington Office
Mailing: 900 Seventh St. NW
Suite 820
Washington, DC 20001

Political Action Committees
Poet PAC
FEC ID: C00450692
Contact: Daniel Loveland
4615 N. Lewis Ave.
Sioux Falls, SD 57104

Tel: (605) 965-2200
Fax: (605) 965-2203

Contributions to Candidates: $207,000 (2015-2016)
Democrats: $82,500; Republicans: $124,500

Principal Recipients

SENATE
BENNET, MICHAEL F (DEM-CO)
BLUNT, ROY (REP-MO)
KIRK, MARK STEVEN (REP-IL)
SCHATZ, BRIAN (DEM-HI)
SCHUMER, CHARLES E (DEM-NY)

HOUSE
CRAMER, KEVIN MR. (REP-ND)
WALORSKI SWIHART, JACKIE (REP-IN)
YODER, KEVIN (REP-KS)

Corporate Foundations and Giving Programs

POET Foundation
Contact: Jeff Broin
4615 N. Lewis Ave.
Sioux Falls, SD 57104

Tel: (605) 965-2200
Fax: (605) 965-2203

Public Affairs and Related Activities Personnel

At Headquarters

BERVEN, Doug
Vice President, Corporate Affairs

Tel: (605) 965-2200
Fax: (605) 965-2203

GILLEY, Kyle E.

Tel: (605) 965-2200
Fax: (605) 965-2203

LOVELAND, Daniel
Chief Financial Officer and Director

Tel: (605) 965-2200
Fax: (605) 965-2203

WALTHER, Robert
Director, Federal Affairs

Tel: (605) 965-2200
Fax: (605) 965-2203

Point Blank Solutions, Inc.

Engages in the manufacture and provision of bullet, fragmentation, and stab resistant apparel and related ballistic accessories for military, law enforcement, security, and corrections personnel, as well as government agencies in the United States.
www.pointblanksolutionsinc.com
Annual Revenues: $203.09 million
Employees: 1,300
SIC: 3842
Industry/ies: Defense/Homeland Security; Government-Related; Law Enforcement/Security; Military/Veterans

Chief Executive Officer — Tel: (954) 630-0900
GASTON, Daniel — Fax: (954) 630-9225

Main Headquarters
Mailing: 2102 S.W. Second St. — Tel: (954) 630-0900
Pompano Beach, FL 33069 — Fax: (954) 630-9225
TF: (800) 413-5155

Public Affairs and Related Activities Personnel

At Headquarters

MANCHESTER, Dionne — Tel: (212) 786-6068
Contact, Media Relations — Fax: (954) 630-9225
dionne@GWCco.com

MIRANDA, Deniese — Tel: (954) 630-0900
Director, Human Resources — Fax: (954) 630-9225

TAYLOR, Lisa — Tel: (954) 630-0900
Vice President, Human Resources — Fax: (954) 414-8130

WHITE, Sam — Tel: (954) 630-0900
Executive Vice President, Sales, Marketing and Senior Vice President, Business Development — Fax: (954) 630-9225

PointCare Technologies Inc.

A fully integrated company that invents, develops, manufactures and markets medical diagnostic products.
www.pointcare.net
Annual Revenues: $2.60 million
Employees: 20
Industry/ies: Medicine/Health Care/Mental Health

Chief Executive Officer and Co-Founder — Tel: (508) 281-6925
KRAULEDAT, PhD, Petra B. — Fax: (508) 281-6930

Main Headquarters
Mailing: 257 Simarano Dr. — Tel: (508) 281-6925
Marlborough, MA 01752 — Fax: (508) 281-6930

Public Affairs and Related Activities Personnel

At Headquarters

COLLINS, Jack — Tel: (508) 281-6925
Chief Financial and Operating Officer — Fax: (508) 281-6930
jcollins@pointcare.net

QUILTER, MPA, David — Tel: (508) 281-6925
Director, Marketing and Sales — Fax: (508) 281-6930

Polaris Industries

Designs, manufactures, and markets snowmobiles, all-terrain vehicles, personal watercrafts, motorcycles, sport boats, and professional series workmobiles for recreational and utility use.
www.polarisindustries.com
Annual Revenues: $4.69 billion
Employees: 8,000
Ticker: NYSE: PII
SIC: 3790
Industry/ies: Automotive Industry; Engineering/Mathematics; Transportation
Legislative Issues: CSP; DEF; TAX

Chairman and Chief Executive Officer — Tel: (763) 542-0500
WINE, Scott W. — Fax: (763) 542-0599

Main Headquarters
Mailing: 2100 Hwy. 55 — Tel: (763) 542-0500
Medina, MN 55340-9770 — Fax: (763) 542-0599
TF: (800) 765-2747

Political Action Committees
Polaris Industries Inc. Political Participation Program
FEC ID: C00279497
Contact: Michael W. Malone
2100 Hwy. 55 — Tel: (763) 542-0500
Medina, MN 55340-9770 — Fax: (763) 542-0599

Corporate Foundations and Giving Programs
The Polaris Foundation
2100 Hwy. 55
Medina, MN 55340

Public Affairs and Related Activities Personnel

At Headquarters

BALAN, Todd Michael — Tel: (763) 542-0500
Vice President, Corporate Development — Fax: (763) 542-0599

BOGART, Stacy L. — Tel: (763) 542-0500
Vice President, General Counsel, Compliance Officer and Secretary — Fax: (763) 542-0599

EDWARDS, Richard — Tel: (763) 513-3477
Director, Investor Relations — Fax: (763) 542-0599
richard.edwards@polarisind.com

KNUTSON, Marlys — Tel: (763) 542-0533
External Relations Manager — Fax: (763) 542-0599
marlys.knutson@polaris.com

MALONE, Michael W. — Tel: (763) 542-0500
Vice President, Finance, Chief Financial Officer and PAC Treasurer — Fax: (763) 542-0599

MORGAN, Bennett J. — Tel: (763) 542-0500
President and Chief Operating Officer — Fax: (763) 542-0599

WILLIAMS, James P. — Tel: (763) 542-0500
Vice President, Human Resources — Fax: (763) 542-0599

Polaroid Corporation

A manufacturer of photographic equipment and supplies. Purchased by Hilco Consumer Capital and Gordon Brothers Brands in 2009 and is operated in joint holding with holding company PLR IP Holdings, LLC.
www.polaroid.com
Employees: 1,500
SIC: 3861
Industry/ies: Electricity & Electronics; Electronics; Energy/Electricity

President and Chief Executive Officer — Tel: (952) 936-5000
HARDY, Scott W. — Fax: (781) 386-6441

Main Headquarters
Mailing: 4350 Baker Rd. — Tel: (952) 934-9918
Suite 180 — Fax: (781) 386-6441
Minnetonka, MN 55343 — TF: (800) 765-2764

Corporate Foundations and Giving Programs
Polaroid Corporation Contributions Program
4350 Baker Rd. — Tel: (952) 934-9918
Minnetonka, MN 55343-8609 — Fax: (781) 386-6441

Public Affairs and Related Activities Personnel

At Headquarters

HOISTION, Melissa — Tel: (952) 934-9918
Contact, Media Relations — Fax: (781) 386-6441
mhoistion@randjpr.com

RAASCH, Taylor — Tel: (952) 934-9918
Contact, Media Relations — Fax: (781) 386-6441
TRaasch@webershandwick.com

Polartec, LLC

Formerly Malden Mills Industries. Makes all-season synthetic fabrics.
www.polartec.com
Employees: 1,000
Industry/ies: Apparel/Textiles Industry
Legislative Issues: DEF; TRD

Chairman of the Board — Tel: (978) 685-6341
SEGALL, Greg

Chief Executive Officer — Tel: (978) 685-6341
SMITH, Gary S.

Main Headquarters
Mailing: 46 Stafford St. — Tel: (978) 685-6341
P.O. Box 809 — TF: (800) 252-6688
Lawrence, MA 01842

Policepay.net, Inc.

Policepay develops new models for Pay Studies and Financial Forensic Services.
www.policepay.net
Industry/ies: Employees & Employment

President — Tel: (405) 701-8616
BARNARD, Matthew — Fax: (405) 701-8631
matt@policepay.net

Main Headquarters
Mailing: 219 W. Boyd St., 1824A Atchison Dr. — Tel: (405) 701-8616
Suite 205 — Fax: (405) 701-8631
Norman, OK 73069

PolicyWorks

Software to survey, market, propose, bind, and issue insurance policies. Provides product information, evaluation version and support.
www.policyworks.com
Legislative Issues: EDU

Chairman — Tel: (866) 518-0209
JURY, Patrick S.

Chief Executive Officer — Tel: (515) 224-8957
HUPFER, Justin

Main Headquarters

Mailing:	1500 N.W. 118th St.	Tel:	(866) 518-0209
	Des Moines, IA 50325	TF:	(800) 260-3676

Public Affairs and Related Activities Personnel

At Headquarters

CACCIATORE, John — Tel: (515) 224-8957
johnc@policyworksllc.com
Registered Federal Lobbyist

EARNHARDT, Mary — Tel: (866) 518-0209
Federal Lobbyists

HANER, Chris — Tel: (866) 518-0209
Senior Compliance Officer
chrish@policyworksllc.com

HAUS, Robert — Tel: (866) 518-0209
Federal Lobbyists

MALDONADO, Jessica — Tel: (515) 224-8963
Public Affairs Manager
jessicam@policyworksllc.com

MURPHY, Jon — Tel: (515) 224-8956
Director, Government Affairs
jonm@policyworksllc.com

O'HERN, Erin — Tel: (515) 221-1852
Director, League Compliance Services
erino@policyworksllc.com

RUSSELL, Lisa — Tel: (515) 221-3000
Public Affairs Consultant
lisar@policyworksllc.com

WILLIAMS, Cindy — Tel: (866) 518-0209
Vice President, Regulatory Compliance
cindyw@policyworksllc.com

PoliteView, Inc.

Media content provider.
www.politeview.com
Annual Revenues: $1.10 million
Industry/ies: Communications; Media/Mass Communication

Main Headquarters

Mailing:	Two Park Pl., 4009 Banister Ln.	Tel:	(512) 394-4570
	Suite 102		
	Austin, TX 78704		

Public Affairs and Related Activities Personnel

At Headquarters

COMBS, Randy — Tel: (512) 394-4570
Executive Vice President, Sales
rcombs@politeview.com

Polo Ralph Lauren

Designer and marketer of apparel and home furnishings.
www.ralphlauren.com
Annual Revenues: $7.62 billion
Employees: 15,000
Ticker: NYSE: RL
SIC: 2320
Industry/ies: Apparel/Textiles Industry

Contact, Foundation, President and Founder — Tel: (212) 318-7000
FREEMAN, Harold P. — Fax: (212) 888-5780

Main Headquarters

Mailing:	625 Madison Ave.	Tel:	(212) 318-7000
	Seventh Floor	Fax:	(212) 888-5780
	New York City, NY 10022	TF:	(888) 475-7674

Corporate Foundations and Giving Programs

The Polo Ralph Lauren Foundation
Contact: Harold P. Freeman
650 Madison Ave. — Tel: (212) 318-7000
12th Floor — Fax: (212) 318-7000
New York City, NY 10022

Public Affairs and Related Activities Personnel

At Headquarters

KOSH, Mitchell A. — Tel: (212) 318-7000
Senior Vice President, Human Resources and Legal — Fax: (212) 888-5780

LAUREN, Ralph — Tel: (212) 318-7000
Senior Director, Database Marketing — Fax: (212) 888-5780

PETERSON, Christopher H. — Tel: (212) 318-7000
Senior Marketing Insights Manager eCommerce — Fax: (212) 888-5780

PolyOne Corporation

Formed by the merger of Geon Co. and M. A. Hanna Company in 2000. Manufactures plastic compounds and distributes plastic resins and shapes.
www.polyone.com

Annual Revenues: $3.71 billion
Employees: 6,900
Ticker: NYSE: POL
SIC: 2821; 3089
NAICS: 326199
Industry/ies: Chemicals & Chemical Industry; Plastics Industry
Legislative Issues: CHM; MAN; TAX

Executive Chairman — Tel: (440) 930-1000
NEWLIN, Stephen D. — Fax: (440) 930-3799

President and Chief Executive Officer — Tel: (440) 930-1000
PATTERSON, Robert M. — Fax: (440) 930-3064

Main Headquarters

Mailing:	33587 Walker Rd.	Tel:	(440) 930-1000
	Avon Lake, OH 44012	Fax:	(440) 930-3064
		TF:	(866) 765-9663

Political Action Committees

PolyOne Corporation PAC
FEC ID: C00288712
Contact: Woodrow H. Ban
33587 Walker Rd.
Avon Lake, OH 44012

Contributions to Candidates: $7,500 (2015-2016)
Republicans: $7,500

Corporate Foundations and Giving Programs

PolyOne Contributions Program
33587 Walker Rd.
Avon Lake, OH 44012

Public Affairs and Related Activities Personnel

At Headquarters

BAN, Woodrow H. — Tel: (440) 930-1000
PAC Treasurer — Fax: (440) 930-3799
woodrow.ban@polyone.com

DELUCA, Isaac — Tel: (440) 930-3162
Vice President, Planning and Investor Relations — Fax: (440) 930-3064
Isaac.DeLuca@polyone.com

DODD, Cathy K. — Tel: (440) 930-1000
Vice President, Marketing — Fax: (440) 930-3064

HONEYCUTT, David — Tel: (440) 930-3154
Director, Marketing Communications — Fax: (440) 930-3799
david.honeycutt@polyone.com

KUNKLE, Lisa K. — Tel: (440) 930-1000
Vice President, General Counsel and Secretary — Fax: (440) 930-3064
lisa.kunkle@polyone.com

RICHARDSON , Bradley C. — Tel: (440) 930-1000
Executive Vice President and Chief Financial Officer — Fax: (440) 930-3064

RODRIGUEZ, Ana — Tel: (440) 930-1000
Senior Vice President, Chief Human Resources Officer — Fax: (440) 930-3064

ROSE, Kyle — Tel: (440) 930-1000
Director, Corporate Communications — Fax: (440) 930-3064
Kyle.Rose@polyone.com

SMITH, Kenneth M. — Tel: (440) 930-1313
Senior Vice President, Chief Information Officer and Human — Fax: (440) 930-3799
Resources Officer
ken.smith@polyone.com

Pool Corporation

Formerly SCP Pool Corporation. A wholesale swimming pool supply distributor.
www.poolcorp.com
Annual Revenues: $2.43 billion
Employees: 3,800
Ticker: NASDAQ: POOL
SIC: 5090
Industry/ies: Sports/Leisure/Entertainment

Chairman of the Board — Tel: (985) 892-5521
SEXTON, Wilson B. — Fax: (985) 801-5716

Director, President and Chief Executive Officer — Tel: (985) 892-5521
PEREZ DE LA MESA, Manuel J. — Fax: (985) 801-5716

Main Headquarters

Mailing:	109 Northpark Blvd.	Tel:	(985) 892-5521
	Covington, LA 70433-5521	Fax:	(985) 801-5716

Corporate Foundations and Giving Programs

Pool Corporation Contributions Program
109 Northpark Blvd.
Covington, LA 70433-5521

Public Affairs and Related Activities Personnel

At Headquarters

HOUSEY HART, Melanie M. — Tel: (985) 892-5521
Corporate Controller and Chief Accounting Officer — Fax: (985) 801-5716

HUBBARD, Craig K. *Investor Relations Officer* craig.hubbard@poolcorp.com	Tel: Fax:	(985) 801-5117 (985) 809-1045
JOSLIN, Mark W. *Senior Vice President and Chief Financial Officer* mark.joslin@poolcorp.com	Tel: Fax:	(985) 892-5521 (985) 801-5716
NEIL, Jennifer M. *General Counsel and Secretary* jennifer.neil@poolcorp.com	Tel: Fax:	(985) 892-5521 (985) 801-5716

Popeyes Louisiana Kitchen, Inc.

Develops, operates, and franchises quick-service restaurants under the trade name Popeyes®.In January 2014, AFC Enterprises, Inc. changed its corporate name to Popeyes Louisiana Kitchen, Inc.
popeyes.com
Annual Revenues: $245 million
Employees: 2,200
Ticker: NASDAQ: PLKI
SIC: 5812
Industry/ies: Food And Beverage Industry

Chairman of the Board CRANOR, III, John M.	Tel:	(404) 459-4450
Chief Executive Officer BACHELDER, Cheryl A.	Tel:	(404) 459-4450

Main Headquarters
Mailing:	400 Perimeter Center Terrace Suite 1000 Atlanta, GA 30346	Tel:	(404) 459-4450

Corporate Foundations and Giving Programs

AFC Foundation
555 Glenridge Connector NE Suite 300 Atlanta, GA 30342	Tel:	(404) 459-4450

Public Affairs and Related Activities Personnel

At Headquarters

COHEN, Harold M. *Senior Vice President, Legal Affairs, General Counsel and Corporate Secretary* hcohen@afce.com	Tel:	(404) 459-4450
LYNCH, Richard H. *Chief Brand Experience Officer* rlynch@afce.com	Tel:	(404) 459-4450
MATT, William P. *Chief Financial Officer*	Tel:	(404) 459-4450
ZAPPONE, Lynne *Chief Talent Officer*	Tel:	(404) 459-4450

Popular, Inc.

A commercial banking firm.
www.popular.com
Annual Revenues: $1.11 billion
Employees: 8,203
Ticker: NASDAQ: BPOP
SIC: 6022
Industry/ies: Banking/Finance/Investments

Chairman of the Board, President and Chief Executive Officer CARRION, Richard L.	Tel:	(787) 765-9800

Main Headquarters
Mailing:	P.O. Box 362708 San Juan, PR 00936-2708	Tel: TF:	(787) 765-9800 (888) 724-3659

Washington Office
Mailing:	700 13th St. NW Suite 600 Washington, DC 20005

Political Action Committees
Popular Inc. PAC
FEC ID: C00441303
Contact: Brian Doran
700 13th St. NW
Suite 600
Washington, DC 20005

> **Contributions to Candidates:** $9,000 (2015-2016)
> Democrats: $7,500; Republicans: $1,500

Corporate Foundations and Giving Programs

Banco Popular Foundation
P.O. Box 362708
San Juan, PR 00936-2708

Public Affairs and Related Activities Personnel

At Headquarters

ALVAREZ, Ignacio *President and Chief Operating Officer*	Tel:	(787) 765-9800
NEGRON, Eduardo J. *Executive Vice President, Administration*	Tel:	(787) 765-9800
POLHAMUS, Beatriz M. *Executive Director, Banco Popular Foundation*	Tel:	(787) 765-9800
RULLAN, Teruca *Senior Vice President, Corporate Communications* trullan@bppr.com	Tel:	(787) 281-5170
SCHEINER, Brett *Investor Relations Officer* BScheiner@BPOP.com	Tel:	(212) 417-6721
VAZQUEZ, Carlos J. *Chief Financial Officer*	Tel:	(787) 765-9800

At Washington Office

DORAN, Brian
PAC Treasurer

Porsche Cars North America, Inc.

Car manufacturing company.
www.porsche.com
Annual Revenues: $69.60 million
Employees: 200
Industry/ies: Automotive Industry; Transportation
Legislative Issues: AUT; BUD

President, Chief Executive Officer VON PLATEN, Detlev	Tel: Fax:	(770) 290-3500 (770) 290-3700

Main Headquarters
Mailing:	980 Hammond Dr. Suite 1000 Atlanta, GA 30328	Tel: Fax: TF:	(770) 290-3500 (770) 290-3700 (800) 767-7243

Corporate Foundations and Giving Programs

Porsche Foundation
980 Hammond Dr.
Suite 1000
Atlanta, GA 30328

Public Affairs and Related Activities Personnel

At Other Offices

KARTOCHIAN, Thierry *Executive Vice President, Chief Financial Officer* One Porsche Dr. Atlanta, GA 30354	Tel: Fax:	(770) 290-3500 (770) 290-3700

Porter Gordon Silver Communications, LLC

Consulting Firm. PGS provides insight, advice and resolutions to legislative and regulatory dilemmas at various levels of government.
www.gordonsilver.com/porter-gordon-silver

Main Headquarters
Mailing:	11 D St. SE Washington, DC 20003	Tel: Fax:	(202) 733-4960 (202) 330-5968

Public Affairs and Related Activities Personnel

At Headquarters

CANNON, Jenifer *Assistant* jcannon@gordonsilver.com	Tel: Fax:	(702) 992-1934 (202) 330-5968
HASTIE, Chrissie *PAC Contact*	Tel: Fax:	(202) 742-4562 (202) 330-5968
MAUER, Daniel	Tel: Fax:	(202) 742-4562 (202) 330-5968
MCMULLEN, Sam *Governmental Law, Strategic Positioning, Lobbying and Political Strategy Contact*	Tel: Fax:	(202) 733-4960 (202) 330-5968
ROSS, George *Business, Financial, Legislative, and Governmental and Public Policy issues Contact*	Tel: Fax:	(202) 733-4960 (202) 330-5968

Portland General Electric Company

An integrated electric utility Company, engaged in the generation, purchase, transmission, distribution, and retail sale of electricity in the state of Oregon.
www.portlandgeneral.com
Annual Revenues: $1.88 billion
Employees: 2,600
Ticker: NYSE: POR
SIC: 4911
Industry/ies: Energy/Electricity; Utilities
Legislative Issues: BUD; CAW; CDT; COM; ENG; ENV; HOM; TAX; TRA; UTI

President and Chief Executive Officer PIRO, James	Tel: Fax:	(503) 464-8000 (503) 464-2676

Main Headquarters

Mailing: P.O. Box 4404
  Portland, OR 97208

Tel: (503) 464-8000
Fax: (503) 464-2676

Political Action Committees

Portland General Electric Company Bi-Partisan Committee for Effective Govt
PAC
FEC ID: C00381020
Contact: Sania Radcliffe
121 SW Salmon
1WTC0301
Portland, OR 97204

Contributions to Candidates: $33,500 (2015-2016)
Democrats: $24,750; Republicans: $8,750

Corporate Foundations and Giving Programs

PG&E Corporation Foundation
Contact: Dave Robertson
One Market, Spear Tower
Suite 2400
San Fracisco, CA 94105-1126

Public Affairs and Related Activities Personnel

At Headquarters

DILLIN, Carol A.
Vice President, Customer Strategies and Business Development

Tel: (503) 464-8000
Fax: (503) 464-2676

DUDLEY, Jay
Vice President, General Counsel and Corporate Compliance Officer
Jay.Dudley@pgn.com

Tel: (503) 464-8900
Fax: (503) 464-2676

LOBDELL, James
Senior Vice President, Finance, Chief Financial Officer and Treasurer

Tel: (503) 464-8000
Fax: (503) 464-2676

POPE, Maria
Senior Vice President, Power Supply, Operations, and Resource Strategy

Tel: (503) 464-8000
Fax: (503) 464-2676

VALACH, William
Director, Investor Relations
william.valach@pgn.com

Tel: (503) 464-7395
Fax: (503) 464-2676

At Other Offices

BARNETT, Arleen
Vice President of Human Resources, Diversity & Inclusion and Administration
121 S.W. Salmon St.
Portland, OR 97204

Tel: (503) 464-8000
Fax: (503) 464-2676

DORNFELD, Jill
Federal Lobbyist
121 S.W. Salmon St.
Portland, OR 97204
jill.dornfeld@pgn.com

Tel: (503) 464-8000
Fax: (503) 464-2676

MIRANDA, Michele
121 S.W. Salmon St.
Portland, OR 97204
Registered Federal Lobbyist

Tel: (503) 464-8000
Fax: (503) 464-2676

MOIR, Melanie
Public Information Officer and Media Contact
121 S.W. Salmon St.
Portland, OR 97204

Tel: (503) 464-8790
Fax: (503) 464-2676

RADCLIFFE, Sania
PAC Treasurer
121 S.W. Salmon St.
Portland, OR 97204
Mail Stop 1WTC0301

Tel: (503) 464-7329
Fax: (503) 464-2354

ROBERTSON, Dave
Vice President, Public Policy and President, PGE Foundation
121 S.W. Salmon St.
Portland, OR 97204

Tel: (503) 464-2929
Fax: (503) 464-2676

SPAK, Brian
Manager, Federal Affairs
121 S.W. Salmon St.
Portland, OR 97204

Tel: (503) 464-8900
Fax: (503) 464-2676

Ports America, Inc.

A port operations and maritime facilities management and development company.
www.portsamerica.com
Employees: 400
Industry/ies: Marine/Maritime/Shipping; Ports And Waterways; Transportation

Chief Executive Officer and President
HASSING, Michael F.

Tel: (732) 635-3803
Fax: (201) 216-9366

Main Headquarters

Mailing: 525 Washington Blvd.
  Suite 1660
  Jersey City, NJ 07310

Tel: (732) 635-3899
Fax: (201) 216-9366

Public Affairs and Related Activities Personnel

At Headquarters

BOND, Kathleen C.
Director, Regional Marketing
kathleen.bond@portsamerica.com

Tel: (732) 635-3899
Fax: (201) 216-9366

BROWN, Kevin
Chief Financial Officer

Tel: (732) 635-3818
Fax: (201) 216-9393

HAINES, Colby
Contact, Communications
Colby.Haines@colbycom.com

Tel: (562) 900-6232
Fax: (201) 216-9366

WALSH, Maureen
Treasurer

Tel: (732) 635-3899
Fax: (201) 216-9366

PotashCorp

A producer of fertilizer, industrial and animal feed products.
www.potashcorp.com
Annual Revenues: $6030 billion
Employees: 5,787
Ticker: NYSE:POT
Industry/ies: Agriculture/Agronomy; Food And Beverage Industry

President and Chief Executive Officer
TILK, Jochen E.

Tel: (847) 849-4200
Fax: (847) 849-4695

Main Headquarters

Mailing: 1101 Skokie Blvd.
  Suite 400
  Northbrook, IL 60062

Tel: (847) 849-4200
Fax: (847) 849-4695
TF: (800) 241-6908

Political Action Committees

Potashcorp PAC
FEC ID: C00385039
Contact: Tom Pasztor
1101 Skokie Blvd.
Suite 400
Northbrook, IL 60062

Contributions to Candidates: $10,500 (2015-2016)
Democrats: $1,500; Republicans: $9,000

Principal Recipients

SENATE
KIRK, MARK STEVEN (REP-IL)

Corporate Foundations and Giving Programs

PotashCorp Foundation
Contact: Rhonda Speiss
1101 Skokie Blvd.
Suite 400
Northbrook, IL 60062

Public Affairs and Related Activities Personnel

At Headquarters

BROWNLEE, Wayne R.
Executive Vice President and Chief Financial Officer
wayne.brownlee@potashcorp.com

Tel: (847) 849-4200
Fax: (847) 849-4695

DELANEY, G. David
Executive Vice President and Chief Operating Officer

Tel: (847) 849-4200
Fax: (847) 849-4695

DOWDLE, Stephen F.
President, Sales

Tel: (847) 849-4200
Fax: (847) 849-4695

HERROD, Tim
Senior Director, Global Sourcing
twherrod@potashcorp.com

Tel: (306) 933-8543
Fax: (847) 849-4695

JOHNSON, Bill
Director, Public Affairs
Bjohnson@potashcorp.com

Tel: (306) 933-8849
Fax: (306) 933-8844

KNAFELC, Lee M.
Vice President, Human Resources and Administration
lee.knafelc@potashcorp.com

Tel: (847) 849-4200
Fax: (847) 849-4695

PASZTOR, Tom
PAC Treasurer
tcpasztor@potashcorp.com

Tel: (847) 849-4297
Fax: (847) 849-4695

PODWIKA, Joseph
Senior Vice President, General Counsel and Secretary

Tel: (847) 849-4290
Fax: (847) 849-4695

REYNOLDS, Chet
Senior Director, Global Government Relations

Tel: (306) 933-8665
Fax: (847) 849-4695

SIROIS, Denis A.
Vice President and Corporate Controller

Tel: (847) 849-4200
Fax: (847) 849-4695

SPEISS, Rhonda
Manager, Community Investment

Tel: (306) 933-8544
Fax: (847) 849-4695

STANN, Denita
Vice President, Investor and Public Relations
denita.stann@potashcorp.com

Tel: (847) 849-4277
Fax: (847) 849-4695

Potlatch Corporation

A manufacturer of wood products.

www.potlatchcorp.com
Annual Revenues: $605.5 million
Employees: 850
Ticker: NYSE: PCH
SIC: 6798
Industry/ies: Paper And Wood Products Industry
Legislative Issues: CAW; ENV; NAT; TAX; TRD

Chairman of the Board, President and Chief Executive Officer Tel: (509) 835-1500
COVEY, Mike J.   Fax: (509) 835-1559

Main Headquarters
Mailing: 601 W. First Ave.   Tel: (509) 835-1500
              Suite 1600   Fax: (509) 835-1559
              Spokane, WA 99201

Political Action Committees
Potlatch Employees Political Fund PAC
FEC ID: C00041608
Contact: Eric J. Cremers
601 W. First Ave.
Suite 1600
Spokane, WA 99201

> **Contributions to Candidates:** $63,000 (2015-2016)
> Democrats: $13,000; Republicans: $50,000

> **Principal Recipients**
> **HOUSE**
> MCMORRIS RODGERS, CATHY (REP-WA)

Corporate Foundations and Giving Programs
Potlatch Contributions Program
601 W. First Ave.
Suite 1600
Spokane, WA 99201

Public Affairs and Related Activities Personnel

At Headquarters

BENSON, Mark J.   Tel: (509) 835-1513
Vice President, Government Affairs   Fax: (509) 835-1559
mark.benson@potlatchcorp.com
Registered Federal Lobbyist

CREMERS, Eric J.   Tel: (509) 835-1500
President and Chief Operating Officer and PAC Treasurer Fax: (509) 835-1559
eric.cremers@potlatchcorp.com

RICHARDS , Jerald W.   Tel: (509) 835-1500
Vice President and Chief Financial Officer   Fax: (509) 835-1559

SCHWARTZ, Robert L.   Tel: (509) 835-1500
Vice President, Human Resources   Fax: (509) 835-1559

SCOTT , Lorrie D.   Tel: (509) 835-1500
Vice President, General Counsel and Corporate Secretary Fax: (509) 835-1559

SHERMAN , Lori   Tel: (509) 835-1500
Administrative Assistant   Fax: (509) 835-1559

Powder River Energy Corporation
PRECorp works to keep the power on for every home and business in their service area.
precorp.coop
Industry/ies: Energy/Electricity

Chief Executive Officer   Tel: (307) 283-3531
EASLEY , Mike

Main Headquarters
Mailing: P.O. Box 930   Tel: (307) 283-3531
              221 Main St.   TF: (800) 442-3630
              Sundance, WY 82729

Public Affairs and Related Activities Personnel

At Headquarters

MILLS , Brian   Tel: (307) 283-3531
Human Resources Officer

MOCK , Curtis   Tel: (307) 283-3531
Chief Financial and Administration Officer

PENNING, Les   Tel: (307) 283-3531
Deputy General Manager and Chief Operating Officer

POMMARANE , Mike   Tel: (307) 283-3531
Senior Vice President, System Operations

WILSON , Doug   Tel: (307) 283-3531
Chief Information Officer

Powerspan Corporation
Develops and commercializes proprietary, multi-pollutant control technology for electric power plants.
www.powerspan.com
Annual Revenues: $3.10 million
Industry/ies: Energy/Electricity; Environment And Conservation, Pollution And Waste

Chairman of the Board   Tel: (603) 570-3000
PARRY, Steven E.   Fax: (603) 570-3100

Chief Executive Officer   Tel: (603) 570-3000
ALIX, Frank R.   Fax: (603) 570-3100

Main Headquarters
Mailing: One New Hampshire Ave.   Tel: (603) 570-3000
              Suite 125   Fax: (603) 570-3100
              Portsmouth, NH 03801

Corporate Foundations and Giving Programs
Powerspan Corporation Contributions Program
100 International Dr.
Suite 200
Portsmouth, NH 03801

Public Affairs and Related Activities Personnel

At Headquarters

FRIEDEL, Lynn K.   Tel: (603) 570-3000
Chief Financial Officer   Fax: (603) 570-3100

PowerThru
Manufactures and markets advanced flywheel energy storage systems that provide ride-through power and voltage stabilization for power quality and power recycling applications.
www.power-thru.com
Annual Revenues: $3.40 million
Employees: 30
Industry/ies: Energy/Electricity

Director   Tel: (877) 920-5004
CRAIG, Paul

Main Headquarters
Mailing: 11825 Mayfield   Tel: (877) 920-5004
              Livonia, MI 48150   TF: (877) 920-5004

Public Affairs and Related Activities Personnel

At Headquarters

O'BRIEN, Amanda   Tel: (877) 920-5004
Specialist, Marketing and Media contact
amanda.obrien@pentadyne.com

PPG Industries, Inc.
Manufacturer of coatings, glass and chemical products.
www.ppg.com
Annual Revenues: $15.34 billion
Employees: 46,600
Ticker: NYSE: PPG
SIC: 2819; 2851; 2891; 3211; 5169
NAICS: 325188; 327211; 32551; 32552; 42269
Industry/ies: Chemicals & Chemical Industry; Construction/Construction Materials; Glass
Legislative Issues: BUD; DEF; FIN; MAN; TAX; TRA; TRD

Executive Chairman   Tel: (412) 434-3131
BUNCH, Charles E.   Fax: (412) 434-2011

President and Chief Executive Officer   Tel: (412) 434-3131
MCGARRY, Michael H.   Fax: (412) 434-2011

Main Headquarters
Mailing: One PPG Pl.   Tel: (412) 434-3131
              Pittsburgh, PA 15272   Fax: (412) 434-2011

Political Action Committees
PPG Better Government Team; PPG Industries Inc. PAC
FEC ID: C00034298
Contact: A John Jankowski
One PPG Pl.   Tel: (412) 434-3131
40th Fl.   Fax: (412) 434-4666
Pittsburgh, PA 15272

> **Contributions to Candidates:** $71,100 (2015-2016)
> Democrats: $4,500; Republicans: $66,600

Corporate Foundations and Giving Programs
PPG Global Charitable Contributions Grants
One PPG Pl.
Pittsburgh, PA 15272

PPG Industries Foundation
Contact: Sue Sloan
One PPG Pl.   Tel: (412) 434-3131
40th Floor   Fax: (412) 434-3131
Pittsburgh, PA 15272

Public Affairs and Related Activities Personnel

At Headquarters

BOST, II, Glenn E.   Tel: (412) 434-3131
Senior Vice President and General Counsel   Fax: (412) 434-4666

DAVIES, Jeffrey L.   Tel: (412) 434-3131
Vice President, Corporate Development   Fax: (412) 434-2011

IAMS, Bryan N.
Vice President, Corporate and Government Affairs
Tel: (412) 434-3131
Fax: (412) 434-2011

JAIN, Anup
Vice President, Specialty Coatings and Materials
Tel: (412) 434-3131
Fax: (412) 434-2011

JANKOWSKI, A John
PAC Contact
Mail Stop Gabe Pellathy
Tel: (412) 434-3131
Fax: (412) 434-2011

KENNY , Patrick J.
Director, Marketing and Construction Market Team
Tel: (412) 434-3131
Fax: (412) 434-2011

MORALES, Vincent J.
Vice President, Investor Relations and Treasurer
vmorales@ppg.com
Tel: (412) 434-3740
Fax: (412) 434-4666

PELLATHY, Gabriel
Registered Federal Lobbyist
Tel: (412) 434-3131
Fax: (412) 434-2011

SCHMIDT, Lynne D.
Vice President, Government and Community Affairs
ldschmidt@ppg.com
Tel: (412) 243-4397
Fax: (412) 434-4666

SKLARSKY, Frank S.
Executive Vice President and Chief Financial Officer
Tel: (412) 434-3131
Fax: (412) 434-2011

SLOAN, Sue
Executive Director, PPG Industries Foundation
Tel: (412) 434-3131
Fax: (412) 434-2011

THIELE, Eric K.
Vice President and Business Controller, Architectural Coatings and Protective and Marine Coatings
Tel: (412) 434-3131
Fax: (412) 434-4666

TIBERGHIEN, Herve
Vice President, Human Resources
Tel: (412) 434-3131
Fax: (412) 434-2011

WISE, K.C. McCrory
Supervisor, Public Relations and Corporate Communications
kmccrory@ppg.com
Tel: (412) 434-2445
Fax: (412) 434-2011

PPL Corporation

An energy holding company, distributes electricity. The company has 19,000 MW of generating capacity. Its subsidiaries are PPL Electric Utilities and Western Power Distribution Holdings.
www.pplweb.com
Annual Revenues: $13.47 billion
Employees: 17,391
Ticker: NYSE: PPL
SIC: 4911
Industry/ies: Energy/Electricity; Utilities
Legislative Issues: BUD; CAW; COM; ENG; ENV; HOM; TAX; TRA

Chairman, President and Chief Executive Officer
SPENCE, William H.
Tel: (610) 774-5151
Fax: (610) 774-4198

Main Headquarters
Mailing: Two N. Ninth St.
Allentown, PA 18101
Tel: (610) 774-5151
Fax: (610) 774-4198

Washington Office
Mailing: 900 Seventh St. NW
Suite 510
Washington, DC 20001-3886
Tel: (202) 326-0180
Fax: (202) 326-0191

Corporate Foundations and Giving Programs
PPL Corporation Contributions Program
Two N. Ninth St.
Allentown, PA 18101

Public Affairs and Related Activities Personnel

At Headquarters

BERGSTEIN, Joseph P.
Vice President, Investor Relations
Tel: (610) 774-5609
Fax: (610) 774-6950

CLELLAND, Russell R.
PAC Treasurer
Mail Stop GENTW2
Tel: (610) 774-5151
Fax: (610) 774-5281

FARR, Paul A.
Executive Vice President and Chief Financial Officer
Tel: (610) 774-5151
Fax: (610) 774-4198

GREY, Robert J.
Executive Vice President and Chief Legal Officer
Tel: (610) 774-5151
Fax: (610) 774-5281

MCCARTHY, Daniel J.
Vice President, Corporate Communications and Community Affairs
djmccarthy@pplweb.com
Tel: (610) 774-5758
Fax: (610) 774-4198

RAPHAEL, Joanne H.
Senior Vice President, General Counsel and Corporate Secretary
jhraphael@pplweb.com
Tel: (610) 774-5372
Fax: (610) 774-4751

RUSSO, Stephen R.
Senior Vice President, Human Resources and Services and Chief Human Resources Officer
Tel: (610) 774-5151
Fax: (610) 774-4198

SORGI, Vincent
Senior Vice President and Chief Financial Officer
Tel: (610) 774-5151
Fax: (610) 774-4198

WILTEN, Mark F.
Tel: (610) 774-5151

Vice President, Treasurer and Chief Risk Officer
Fax: (610) 774-4198

WIRTH, Paul G.
Senior Manager, Corporate Communications
pgwirth@pplweb.com
Tel: (610) 774-5532
Fax: (610) 774-4198

At Washington Office

ARTHUR, David
Vice President, Federal Government Relations
dkarthur@pplweb.com
Registered Federal Lobbyist
Tel: (202) 326-0180
Fax: (202) 326-0191

LYNCH, Kenneth
Registered Federal Lobbyist
Tel: (202) 326-0180
Fax: (202) 326-0191

PPL Electric Utilities

See listing on page 648 under PPL Corporation

PPM Energy Inc.

See listing on page 420 under Iberdrola Renewables

Prasco Laboratories

Generic pharmaceutical distributor.
www.prasco.com
Industry/ies: Pharmaceutical Industry

Founder and Chairman of the Board
ARINGTON, E. Thomas
Tel: (513) 618-3333
Fax: (513) 618-3334

Chief Executive Officer
ARINGTON, Christopher
c.arington@prasco.com
Tel: (513) 618-3333
Fax: (513) 618-3334

Main Headquarters
Mailing: 6125 Commerce Ct.
Mason, OH 45040
Tel: (513) 618-3333
Fax: (513) 618-3334
TF: (866) 469-1414

Washington Office
Mailing: 444 N. Capitol St. NW
Suite 821
Washington, DC 20001
Tel: (202) 737-1960
Fax: (202) 737-5585

Corporate Foundations and Giving Programs
The Arington Foundation (AF)
Contact: E. Thomas Arington
6125 Commerce Ct.
Mason, OH 45040
Tel: (513) 204-1234
Fax: (513) 204-1259

Public Affairs and Related Activities Personnel

At Headquarters

FURNISS, David
Chief Financial Officer
Tel: (513) 618-3333
Fax: (513) 618-3334

TRITSCHLER, Gayle L.
Administration
Tel: (513) 618-3333
Fax: (513) 618-3334

At Washington Office

WISE, Nicholas P.
Senior Vice President
Tel: (202) 737-1960
Fax: (202) 737-5585

WISE, Tricia
Federal Lobbyist
Tel: (202) 737-1960
Fax: (202) 737-5585

Pratt & Whitney

The company, a division of United Technologies (UTC), manufactures and maintains commercial, military, and business jet engines and produces space propulsion systems. On the space side, Pratt & Whitney rocket engines help launch NASA space shuttles, space probes, and satellites.
www.pw.utc.com
Annual Revenues: $14.50 billion
Employees: 31,500
SIC: 3724
Industry/ies: Aerospace/Aviation; Transportation

President
ADAMS, Paul
Tel: (860) 565-4321

Main Headquarters
Mailing: 400 Main St.
E. Hartford, CT 06118
Tel: (860) 565-4321

Corporate Foundations and Giving Programs
Pratt and Whitney Contributions Program
Contact: Heather Summerer
400 Main St.
E. Hartford, CT 06108

Public Affairs and Related Activities Personnel

At Headquarters

BAILEY, Bob
Vice President and Chief Financial Officer
Tel: (860) 565-4321

DEFRANK, Jay
Vice President, Communications and Government Relations
Tel: (860) 565-4321

HERNANDEZ, Ray   Tel: (860) 565-2341
Contact, Media
raymond.hernandez@pw.utc.com

SANTOS, Joseph A.   Tel: (860) 565-4321
Vice President and General Counsel

SUMMERER, Heather   Tel: (860) 565-4321
Manager, Public Affairs
heathe.summerer@pw.utc.com

VILLENEUVE, Nadia   Tel: (860) 565-4321
Vice President, Human Resources

ZIMMERMAN, Bernie   Tel: (860) 565-4321
Vice President, Group Strategy and Development

Praxair, Inc.

A producer of industrial gases and specialty coatings. Industrial gases company in the world as determined by customers, employees, shareholders, suppliers and the communities in which the company operate.
www.praxair.com
Annual Revenues: $12.00 billion
Employees: 27,780
Ticker: NYSE: PX
SIC: 2810
Industry/ies: Chemicals & Chemical Industry; Natural Resources
Legislative Issues: BUD; ENG; NAT; TAX; TRA

Chairman of the Board, President and Chief Executive Officer   Tel: (203) 837-2000
ANGEL, Stephen F.   Fax: (800) 772-9985

Main Headquarters
Mailing: 39 Old Ridgebury Rd.   Tel: (203) 837-2000
         Danbury, CT 06810   Fax: (800) 772-9985
                               TF: (800) 772-9247

Washington Office
Mailing: 100 F St. NE
         Washington, DC 20549

Political Action Committees
Praxair Inc. PAC
FEC ID: C00283440
Contact: Michael S. Bourgeault
39 Old Ridgebury Rd.
P.O. Box 2958
Danbury, CT 06813

    Contributions to Candidates: $101,000 (2015-2016)
    Democrats: $42,000; Republicans: $59,000

                Principal Recipients

                    HOUSE
                     REED, THOMAS W II (REP-NY)

Corporate Foundations and Giving Programs
Praxair Foundation
39 Old Ridgebury Rd.   Tel: (203) 837-2000
Danbury, CT 06810   Fax: (203) 837-2311

Public Affairs and Related Activities Personnel

At Headquarters

BICHARA, Guillermo   Tel: (203) 837-2000
Vice President, General Counsel and Corporate Secretary   Fax: (800) 772-9985

BOURGEAULT, Michael S.   Tel: (203) 837-2000
PAC Treasurer   Fax: (800) 772-9985

DEPASQUALE, Pete   Tel: (203) 837-2000
Manager, Government Relations   Fax: (800) 772-9985

ESNEAULT, Lisa A.   Tel: (203) 837-2000
Vice President, Global Communications and Public Relations   Fax: (800) 772-9985

HIRSCH, Elizabeth T.   Tel: (203) 837-2354
Vice President and Controller   Fax: (203) 837-2505
liz_hirsch@praxair.com

KEEGANS, Karen   Tel: (203) 837-2000
Vice President & Chief Human Resources Officer   Fax: (800) 772-9985

KING, Valerie K.   Tel: (203) 837-2037
Director, Government Relations   Fax: (800) 772-9985
valerie_king@praxair.com

SZITA-GORE, Susan   Tel: (203) 837-2311
Director, Corporate Communications   Fax: (203) 837-2454
susan_szita-gore@praxair.com

VARGAS, Omar   Tel: (203) 837-2000
Executive Director, Government Relations   Fax: (800) 772-9985
omar_vargas@praxair.com
Registered Federal Lobbyist

WHITE, Matthew J.   Tel: (203) 837-2000
Senior Vice President & Chief Financial Officer   Fax: (800) 772-9985

At Washington Office

BEUP, Neil
Director, Government Relations

Premera Blue Cross

A regional health plan. Subsidiaries also serve members in Oregon and Arizona.
www.premera.com
Annual Revenues: $3.02 billion
Employees: 1,600
Industry/ies: Medicine/Health Care/Mental Health

President and Chief Executive Officer   Tel: (425) 918-4000
ROE, Jeff   Fax: (425) 918-4791

Main Headquarters
Mailing: 7001 220th St. SW   Tel: (425) 918-4000
         Mountlake Terrace, WA 98043   Fax: (425) 918-4791
                                 TF: (800) 722-1471

Political Action Committees
Premera Blue Cross PAC
FEC ID: C00409227
Contact: Leonard H. Sorrin
7001 220th St. SW
Mountlake Terrace, WA 98043

    Contributions to Candidates: $46,500 (2015-2016)
    Democrats: $22,500; Republicans: $24,000

Corporate Foundations and Giving Programs
Premera Cares
Contact: Teresita Heiser
7001 220th St.   Tel: (425) 918-5933
Mountlake Terrace, WA 98043

Public Affairs and Related Activities Personnel

At Headquarters

CHASTAIN, Sharon   Tel: (425) 918-4000
Senior Vice President, Operations   Fax: (425) 918-4791

COFFEY, Jodi   Tel: (425) 918-5953
Director, Health Care Delivery Systems Operations   Fax: (425) 918-5575
jodi.coffey@premera.com

COON, Melanie   Tel: (425) 918-6238
Contact, Media Relations and Public Affairs   Fax: (425) 918-4791
melanie.coon@premera.com

CRAMER , Katharine   Tel: (425) 918-4000
Senior Vice President, Government and Public Affairs   Fax: (425) 918-4791

EARLING, Eric   Tel: (425) 918-3297
Vice President, Corporate Communications   Fax: (425) 918-5575
eric.earling@premera.com

HALL , Cecily M.   Tel: (425) 918-4000
Director   Fax: (425) 670-5635

KEMP, Kristen   Tel: (425) 918-4000
Senior Vice President, Operations   Fax: (425) 918-4791

MARQUARDT, Kent   Tel: (425) 918-4000
Executive Vice President, Chief Financial Officer   Fax: (425) 918-4791

MESSINA, Jim   Tel: (425) 918-4000
Executive Vice President and Chief Marketing Executive   Fax: (425) 918-4791

MILO, Yoram   Tel: (425) 670-5900
Executive Vice President and Chief Legal Public Policy Officer   Fax: (425) 670-5635
yori.milo@premera.com

OKIGWE, Jaja   Tel: (425) 918-4000
Senior Vice President, Strategic Development   Fax: (425) 918-4791

PIERCE, John   Tel: (425) 918-4000
Senior Vice President, General Counsel   Fax: (425) 670-5635
john.pierce@premera.com

SORRIN, Leonard H.   Tel: (425) 918-4000
Vice President, Congressional and Legislative Affairs and   Fax: (425) 918-4791
PAC Treasurer
leonard.sorrin@premera.com

Premier Exhibitions, Inc.

A provider of museum quality touring exhibitions.
www.prxi.com
Annual Revenues: $29.39 million
Employees: 46
Ticker: NASDAQ: PRXI
SIC: 7900
Industry/ies: History/Historic Preservation

Chairman of the Board   Tel: (404) 842-2600
SELLERS, Mark A.   Fax: (404) 842-2626

Interim President, Chief Executive Officer, Chief Financial   Tel: (404) 842-2600
Officer and Chief Operating Officer   Fax: (404) 842-2626
LITTLE, Michael J.
michael.little@prxi.com

Main Headquarters
Mailing: 3340 Peachtree Rd. NE   Tel: (404) 842-2600
         Suite 900   Fax: (404) 842-2626
         Atlanta, GA 30326

Public Affairs and Related Activities Personnel

At Headquarters

MORGENSTERN, Katherine	Tel:	(404) 842-2675
Director, Public Relations	Fax:	(404) 842-2626
kmorgenstern@prxi.com		
NORMAN, John	Tel:	(404) 842-2600
President	Fax:	(404) 842-2626
WEISER, Samuel	Tel:	(404) 842-2600
Executive Chairman	Fax:	(404) 842-2626

Premier Micronutrient Corporation

A provider of scientific based micronutrient supplements.
premiermicronutrient.com
Employees: 5
Industry/ies: Chemicals & Chemical Industry; Food And Beverage Industry

President and Chief Executive Officer

LOOPER, Randy L.	Tel:	(615) 234-4020
	Fax:	(615) 321-4782

Main Headquarters

Mailing:	1801 W. End Ave.	Tel:	(615) 234-4020
	16th Floor, Suite 910	Fax:	(615) 321-4782
	Nashville, TN 37203		

Public Affairs and Related Activities Personnel

At Headquarters

HAASE, Gerald M.	Tel:	(615) 234-4020
Chief Medical Officer	Fax:	(615) 321-4782

At Other Offices

MCCALLUM, Jennifer M.	Tel:	(303) 828-0655
Contact, Investor Relations	Fax:	(303) 828-2938
The McCallum Law Firm, LLC, 685 Briggs Str., P.O. Box 929		
Erie, CO 80516		

Premier, Inc.

Health care company.
www.premierinc.com
Employees: 1,200
Industry/ies: Medicine/Health Care/Mental Health
Legislative Issues: HCR; MMM

President and Chief Executive Officer

DEVORE, Susan D.	Tel:	(704) 357-0022
susan_devore@premierinc.com	Fax:	(704) 357-6611

Main Headquarters

Mailing:	13034 Ballantyne Corporate Pl.	Tel:	(704) 357-0022
	Charlotte, NC 28277	Fax:	(704) 357-6611
		TF:	(877) 777-1552

Washington Office

Mailing:	444 N. Capitol St. NW	Tel:	(202) 393-0860
	Suite 625	Fax:	(202) 393-0864
	Washington, DC 20001		

Corporate Foundations and Giving Programs

Premier, Inc. Foundation
12255 El Camino Real
Suite 100
San Diego, CA 92130

Public Affairs and Related Activities Personnel

At Headquarters

ALKIRE, Michael J.	Tel:	(704) 357-0022
Chief Operating Officer	Fax:	(704) 357-6611
LEMKIN, Jeffrey W.	Tel:	(704) 357-0022
General Counsel	Fax:	(704) 357-6611
LINN, Terry	Tel:	(704) 357-0022
Senior Vice President, Corporate Development And Strategy	Fax:	(704) 357-6611
LONG, Gary S.	Tel:	(704) 357-0022
Chief Sales Officer	Fax:	(704) 357-6611
MCKASSON, Craig	Tel:	(704) 357-0022
Chief Financial Officer	Fax:	(704) 357-6611
PETRY, Jeffrey M.	Tel:	(704) 357-0022
Senior Vice President, Marketing	Fax:	(704) 357-6611

At Washington Office

CHILDS, Blair G.	Tel:	(202) 879-8009
Senior Vice President, Public Affairs	Fax:	(202) 393-0864
blair_childs@premierinc.com		
Registered Federal Lobbyist		
CHOI, Lauren	Tel:	(202) 879-8009
Senior Director, Federal and International Affairs	Fax:	(202) 393-0864
EDWARDS, Seth	Tel:	(202) 879-8009
Manager, Federal Affairs	Fax:	(202) 393-0864
seth_edwards@premierinc.com		

Registered Federal Lobbyist

LLOYD, Danielle	Tel:	(202) 393-0860
Federal Lobbyist	Fax:	(202) 393-0864
Registered Federal Lobbyist		
PEARSON, Duanne	Tel:	(202) 393-0860
Federal Lobbyist	Fax:	(202) 393-0864
Registered Federal Lobbyist		
REAGAN, Margaret	Tel:	(202) 879-8009
Corporate Vice President, Premier Healthcare Alliance and PAC Treasurer	Fax:	(202) 393-0864
margaret_reagan@premierinc.com		
Registered Federal Lobbyist		

Premiere Global Services, Inc.

Formerly PTEK Holdings, Inc, provides business communications services and business process solutions. It provides collaboration software and services which enables business users and teams to connect and share ideas and manage projects with everywhere-access of the cloud technologies.
www.pgi.com
Annual Revenues: $567.00 million
Employees: 2,250
Ticker: NYSE: PGI
SIC: 7389
Industry/ies: Communications; Telecommunications/Internet/Cable

Founder, Chairman of the Board and Chief Executive Officer

JONES, Boland T.	Tel:	(404) 262-8400
boland.jones@premiereglobal.com	Fax:	(404) 262-8540

Main Headquarters

Mailing:	3280 Peachtree Rd. NE	Tel:	(404) 262-8400
	Suite 1000	Fax:	(404) 262-8540
	Atlanta, GA 30305	TF:	(866) 548-3203

Public Affairs and Related Activities Personnel

At Headquarters

LEONARD, Scott Askins	Tel:	(494) 262-8502
Executive Vice President, Legal, General Counsel and Secretary	Fax:	(404) 262-8540
scott.leonard@pgi.com		
O'BRIEN, Sean P.	Tel:	(404) 262-8462
Executive Vice President, Strategy and Communications and Contact, Investor Relations	Fax:	(404) 262-8540
sean.obrien@pgi.com		
SHEEHAN, Alison	Tel:	(913) 982-1111
Senior Vice President, Human Resources	Fax:	(404) 262-8540
alison.sheehan@premiereglobal.com		
TAPP, J. Scott	Tel:	(404) 262-8400
Executive Vice President, Sales and Marketing	Fax:	(404) 262-8540
THOMAS-AGUILAR, Blakely	Tel:	(404) 262-8429
Manager, Public Relations & Social Media, Content & Communications Strategy	Fax:	(404) 262-8540
blakely.thomas-aguilar@pgi.com		
TRINE, David	Tel:	(404) 262-8400
Chief Financial Officer	Fax:	(404) 262-8540

PRG-Schultz International, Inc.

See listing on page 650 under PRGX Global, Inc.

PRGX Global, Inc.

PRGX Global, Inc. is a analytics and information services firm as well as the leading provider of recovery audit services. It is also pioneering Profit Discover, a unique combination of audit, analytics and advisory services that improves client financial performance.
www.prgx.com
Annual Revenues: $159.42 million
Employees: 1,500
Ticker: NASDAQ: PRGX
SIC: 8700
Industry/ies: Employees & Employment

Chairman of the Board

DILLS, Patrick	Tel:	(770) 779-3900
patrick.dills@prgx.com	Fax:	(770) 779-3133

President and Chief Executive Officer

STEWART, Ron	Tel:	(770) 779-3900
	Fax:	(770) 779-3133

Main Headquarters

Mailing:	600 Galleria Pkwy.	Tel:	(770) 779-3900
	Suite 100	Fax:	(770) 779-3133
	Atlanta, GA 30339	TF:	(800) 752-5894

Public Affairs and Related Activities Personnel

At Headquarters

ALLUMS, Victor A.	Tel:	(770) 779-3900
General Counsel and Secretary	Fax:	(770) 779-3133
vic.allums@prgx.com		

GOBBI, Alexandra
Vice President, Marketing, Communications & Human Resources
alexandra.gobbi@prgx.com
Tel: (770) 779-3900
Fax: (770) 779-3133

LEE, Robert B.
Chief Financial Officer
Tel: (770) 779-6464
Fax: (770) 779-3133

LEE, Catherine
Senior Vice President, Human Resources
Tel: (770) 779-3900
Fax: (770) 779-3133

LIMERI, Pete
Chief Financial Officer
Tel: (770) 779-3900
Fax: (770) 779-3133

PAMNANI, Puneet
Senior Vice President, Corporate Strategy and Mergers and Acquisitions
puneet.pamnani@prgx.com
Tel: (770) 779-3900
Fax: (770) 779-3133

REENE, Michael
Senior Vice President, Growth and Market Development
Tel: (770) 779-3900
Fax: (770) 779-3133

REID, Chip
Vice President, Client Services & Media Relations
chip.reid@prgx.com
Tel: (770) 779-6543
Fax: (770) 779-3133

Price Systems, LLC

Provides software solutions and services that automate the estimating process.
www.pricesystems.com
Industry/ies: Computer/Technology; Management

President and Managing Member
DEMARCO, Anthony A.
anthony.demarco@pricesystems.com
Tel: (856) 608-7200
Fax: (856) 608-7247

Main Headquarters
Mailing: 17000 Commerce Pkwy.
Suite A
Mount Laurel, NJ 08054
Tel: (856) 608-7200
Fax: (856) 608-7247
TF: (800) 437-7423

Washington Office
Mailing: 1501 Lee Hwy.
Suite 206
Arlington, VA 22209
Fax: (703) 740-0088

Public Affairs and Related Activities Personnel

At Headquarters

BECKER, Robert
Vice President, Business Development
Tel: (856) 608-7200
Fax: (856) 608-7247

CIPRIANO, Dominick
Director, Business Operations
Tel: (856) 608-7200
Fax: (856) 608-7247

DEVLIN, Geri
Director, Human Resources
geri.devlin@pricesystems.com
Tel: (856) 608-7200
Fax: (856) 608-7247

MONTGOMERY, Marybeth
Marketing Communications Manager
marybeth.montgomery@pricesystems.com
Tel: (856) 608-7200
Fax: (856) 608-7247

PriceWaterhouseCoopers

An accounting and consulting firm, formed by the merger of Price Waterhouse LLP and Coopers and Lybrand, in February 2002. It is a multinational professional services network.
www.pwc.com/us/en
Annual Revenues: $34.00 billion
Employees: 180,000
Industry/ies: Accounting; Banking/Finance/Investments
Legislative Issues: ACC; FIN; IMM; LBR; TAX; TRD

Chairman
RYAN, Jr., Timothy
Tel: (202) 414-1000
Fax: (202) 414-1301

US Chairman & Senior Partner
MORITZ, Robert
robert.moritz@us.pwc.com
Tel: (646) 471-4000
Fax: (646) 471-4444

Main Headquarters
Mailing: 300 Madison Ave.
24th Floor
New York City, NY 10017-6204
Tel: (646) 471-4000
Fax: (646) 471-4444

Washington Office
Mailing: 600 13th St. NW
Suite 1000
Washington, DC 20005
Tel: (202) 414-1000
Fax: (202) 414-1301

Political Action Committees
Pricewaterhousecoopers PAC I
FEC ID: C00107235
Contact: Laura Cox Cox Kaplan
1301 K St. NW
Suite 800 West
Washington, DC 20005-3333

Contributions to Candidates: $1,336,888 (2015-2016)
Democrats: $433,849; Republicans: $897,039; Other: $6,000

Principal Recipients

SENATE
BLUNT, ROY (REP-MO)
BURR, RICHARD (REP-NC)
ERNST, JONI K (REP-IA)
JOHNSON, RONALD HAROLD (REP-)
KIRK, MARK STEVEN (REP-IL)
MURPHY, PATRICK E (DEM-FL)
SCHUMER, CHARLES E (DEM-NY)
SHELBY, RICHARD C (REP-AL)
TOOMEY, PATRICK JOSEPH (REP-PA)
YOUNG, TODD CHRISTOPHER (REP-IN)

HOUSE
BARR, GARLAND ANDY (REP-KY)
BLACK, DIANE L MRS. (REP-TN)
BROWNLEY, JULIA (DEM-CA)
BUSTOS, CHERI (DEM-IL)
CLYBURN, JAMES E. (DEM-SC)
COFFMAN, MIKE REP. (REP-CO)
COMSTOCK, BARBARA J HONORABLE (REP-VA)
CONAWAY, MICHAEL HONORABLE (REP-TX)
DELBENE, SUZAN K (DEM-WA)
DOLD, ROBERT JAMES JR (REP-IL)
DUFFY, SEAN (REP-WI)
ESTY, ELIZABETH (DEM-CT)
FLORES, BILL (REP-TX)
GABBARD, TULSI (DEM-HI)
HENSARLING, JEB HON. (REP-TX)
HOYER, STENY HAMILTON (DEM-DC)
HUDSON, RICHARD L. JR. (REP-NC)
KELLY, GEORGE J JR (REP-PA)
KUSTER, ANN MCLANE (DEM-NH)
LARSON, JOHN B (DEM-CT)
LOFGREN, ZOE (DEM-CA)
LOVE, MIA (REP-UT)
MALONEY, CAROLYN B. (DEM-NY)
MCCARTHY, KEVIN (REP-CA)
MCHENRY, PATRICK TIMOTHY (REP-NC)
MCMORRIS RODGERS, CATHY (REP-WA)
MCSALLY, MARTHA E. MS. (REP-AZ)
MEEHAN, PATRICK L. MR. (REP-PA)
MESSER, ALLEN LUCAS (REP-IN)
NOEM, KRISTI LYNN (REP-SD)
NUNES, DEVIN G (REP-CA)
PALAZZO, STEVEN MCCARTY (REP-MS)
PAULSEN, ERIK (REP-MN)
POLIQUIN, BRUCE L (REP-ME)
REED, THOMAS W II (REP-NY)
RENACCI, JAMES B. (REP-OH)
RICE, TOM (REP-SC)
ROBY, MARTHA (REP-AL)
ROSS, DENNIS ALAN (REP-FL)
ROYCE, ED MR. (REP-CA)
RYAN, PAUL D. (REP-WI)
SANCHEZ, LINDA (DEM-CA)
SCALISE, STEVE MR. (REP-LA)
SESSIONS, PETE MR. (REP-TX)
SINEMA, KYRSTEN (DEM-AZ)
STEFANIK, ELISE M. (REP-NY)
STIVERS, STEVE MR. (REP-OH)
WALDEN, GREGORY P MR. (REP-OR)
WALTERS, MIMI (REP-CA)
WATERS, MAXINE MS (DEM-CA)

Corporate Foundations and Giving Programs

PricewaterhouseCoopers Foundation
Contact: Shannon Schuyler
300 Madison Ave.
24th Floor
New York City, NY 10017

Public Affairs and Related Activities Personnel

At Headquarters

BURWELL, Mike
Vice Chairman; Transformation
Tel: (646) 471-4000
Fax: (646) 471-4444

CHACHERE, Clare
Director, U.S. Public Relations
clare.chachere@us.pwc.com
Tel: (646) 471-4000
Fax: (646) 471-4444

GITTINGS, Rob
Vice Chairman, Client Service
Tel: (646) 471-4000
Fax: (646) 471-4444

SAWDYE, Carol
Vice Chairman and Chief Financial Officer
Tel: (646) 471-4000
Fax: (646) 471-4444

SCHUYLER, Shannon
Corporate Responsibility Leader
Tel: (312) 867-1164
Fax: (646) 471-4444

SILBER, Steven G.
Director, Public Relations
steven.g.silber@us.pwc.com
Tel: (646) 471-1059
Fax: (646) 394-5355

WEISS, Diana	Tel:	(646) 471-4000
General Counsel	Fax:	(646) 471-4444
Registered Federal Lobbyist		

At Washington Office

ARCHER, Jr., Hon. Bill Reynolds	Tel:	(202) 414-1000
Senior Policy Advisor	Fax:	(202) 414-1301
Registered Federal Lobbyist		
ASKEY, Elizabeth	Tel:	(202) 414-1000
Principal	Fax:	(202) 414-1301
Registered Federal Lobbyist		
ATTICKS, Ethan	Tel:	(202) 414-1000
Registered Federal Lobbyist	Fax:	(202) 414-1301
BROOKS, Roslyn	Tel:	(202) 414-1000
Managing Director	Fax:	(202) 414-1301
Registered Federal Lobbyist		
CAMPBELL, Larry	Tel:	(202) 414-1000
Tax Managing Director	Fax:	(202) 414-1301
larry.campbell@us.pwc.com		
CARLSON, Donald G.	Tel:	(202) 414-1000
Managing Director ,Specializing in Legislative and	Fax:	(202) 414-1301
Regulatory Representation		
donald.g.carlson@us.pwc.com		
Registered Federal Lobbyist		
CHEN, Matt	Tel:	(202) 414-1000
Partner, International Tax, Washington National Tax Services	Fax:	(202) 414-1301
Matthew.m.chen@us.pwc.com		
COUGHLIN, Amy Best	Tel:	(202) 414-1000
Deputy Director, Public Affairs	Fax:	(202) 414-1301
COURTNEY, Patrick	Tel:	(202) 414-1000
	Fax:	(202) 414-1301
COX KAPLAN, Laura Cox	Tel:	(202) 414-1000
Principal-in-Charge of U.S. Government, Regulatory Affairs	Fax:	(202) 414-1301
& Public Policy		
laura.cox.kaplan@us.pwc.com		
DELL'IMPERIO, Dominick	Tel:	(202) 414-1000
Partner	Fax:	(202) 414-1301
dominick.dellimperio@us.pwc.com		
FISCHL, Alan	Tel:	(202) 414-1030
Partner, Tax	Fax:	(202) 414-1301
alan.l.fischl.@us.pwc.com		
FISHER, Patricia Ann	Tel:	(202) 414-1000
Federal Lobbyist	Fax:	(202) 414-1301
FONTENOT, Gray	Tel:	(202) 414-1000
Global Lead Tax Partner	Fax:	(202) 414-1301
gray.fontenot@us.pwc.com		
HARMAN, John R.	Tel:	(202) 414-1000
Director, Tax Policy	Fax:	(202) 414-1301
john.r.harman@us.pwcglobal.com		
KUMAR, Rohit	Tel:	(202) 414-1000
Tax Policy Services Co-Leader and Principal	Fax:	(202) 414-1301
rohit.kumar@us.pwc.com		
Registered Federal Lobbyist		
LAVINE, Jeff	Tel:	(202) 414-1000
Partner, Financial Services Regulatory Practice	Fax:	(202) 414-1301
jeff.lavine@us.pwc.com		
LONGANO, Don R.	Tel:	(202) 414-1000
Principal	Fax:	(202) 414-1301
don.longano@us.pwcglobal.com		
LYON, Andrew	Tel:	(202) 414-1000
Principal, specializing in economic analysis of tax and other	Fax:	(202) 414-1301
legislative & regulatory proposals		
drew.lyon@us.pwc.com		
Registered Federal Lobbyist		
MANOUSOS, George	Tel:	(202) 414-1000
Tax Partner	Fax:	(202) 414-1301
george.manousos@us.pwc.com		
MARKHAM, Charles	Tel:	(202) 414-1000
Registered Federal Lobbyist	Fax:	(202) 414-1301
MAYS, Janice A.	Tel:	(202) 414-1000
Managing Director	Fax:	(202) 414-1301
MAYSTER, Bryan	Tel:	(202) 414-1000
Tax Managing Director specializing in state and local tax	Fax:	(202) 414-1301
bryan.mayster@us.pwc.com		
MCCANDLESS, Scott	Tel:	(202) 414-1000
Principal, Tax Policy Services	Fax:	(202) 414-1301
scott.mccandless@us.pwc.com		
Registered Federal Lobbyist		
MCCLELLAN, Ed	Tel:	(202) 414-1000
Tax Policy Services Co-Leader and Principal	Fax:	(202) 414-1301
ed.mcclellan@us.pwc.com		

Registered Federal Lobbyist		
MCCLEMENTS, Terri	Tel:	(202) 414-1000
US Human Capital Leader and Vice Chair	Fax:	(202) 414-1301
MERRILL, Peter R.	Tel:	(202) 414-1000
Principal and Director, National Economics and Statistics	Fax:	(202) 414-1301
Peter.merrill@us.pwcglobal.com		
Registered Federal Lobbyist		
METCALF, Todd	Tel:	(202) 414-1000
Principal	Fax:	(202) 414-1301
MITCHELL, Gerald L.	Tel:	(202) 414-1000
Director, Regulatory Services	Fax:	(202) 414-1301
gerald.minehan@us.pwc.com		
MULL, Meredith	Tel:	(202) 414-1000
Director of U.S. Government, Regulatory Affairs and Public	Fax:	(202) 414-1301
Policy		
Registered Federal Lobbyist		
NAUHEIM, Steve	Tel:	(202) 414-1000
Managing Director, International Tax Services	Fax:	(202) 414-1301
stephen.a.nauheim@us.pwc.com		
Registered Federal Lobbyist		
O'BRIEN, Michael	Tel:	(202) 414-1000
Managing Director	Fax:	(202) 414-1301
Registered Federal Lobbyist		
OLSON, Pam	Tel:	(202) 414-1000
US Deputy Tax Leader and Washington National Tax	Fax:	(202) 414-1301
Services (WNTS) Practice Leader		
pam.olson@us.pwc.com		
Registered Federal Lobbyist		
PAULL, Lindy	Tel:	(202) 414-1000
Principal – WNTS Tax Policy Services	Fax:	(202) 414-1301
Registered Federal Lobbyist		
PENN, Oren S.	Tel:	(202) 414-1000
Principal, Washington National Tax Services	Fax:	(202) 414-1301
oren.penn@us.pwc.com		
Registered Federal Lobbyist		
PRIOR, Andrew	Tel:	(202) 414-1000
Managing Director, Legislative & Regulatory Services	Fax:	(202) 414-1301
andrew.prior@us.pwc.com		
Registered Federal Lobbyist		
RICCIO, Julie B.	Tel:	(202) 414-1000
Director Regulatory Affairs & Public Policy	Fax:	(202) 414-1301
Registered Federal Lobbyist		
ROSS, Christopher	Tel:	(202) 414-1000
Tax Director	Fax:	(202) 414-1301
SHAPIRO, Bob	Tel:	(202) 414-1000
Partner	Fax:	(202) 414-1301
SMITH, Mark	Tel:	(202) 414-1000
Registered Federal Lobbyist	Fax:	(202) 414-1301
SMITH, Linden C.	Tel:	(202) 414-1000
Managing Director	Fax:	(202) 414-1301
linden.c.smith@us.pwc.com		
Registered Federal Lobbyist		
SMITH, Annette	Tel:	(202) 414-1000
	Fax:	(202) 414-1301
STELL, John	Tel:	(202) 414-1000
Director	Fax:	(202) 414-1301
John.L.Stell@us.pwc.com		
WILES, Daniel	Tel:	(201) 414-4586
Managing Director	Fax:	(202) 414-1301
dan.wiles@us.pwc.com		

At Other Offices

HAFFIELD, Susan	Tel:	(612) 596-6000
Partner	Fax:	(612) 373-7160
225 S. Sixth St., Suite 1400		
Minneapolis, MN 55402		
susan.haffield@us.pwcglobal.com		

Pride Mobility Products Corporation

Pride Mobility Products Corp. is the leader in the design, development and manufacture of mobility products - power chairs, scooters and lift chairs. Lifts and Ramps. They are dedicated to providing expertly designed, engineered, and tested products incorporating technologically innovative features enabling consumers to achieve the highest quality of life and mobility goals.
www.pridemobility.com
Annual Revenues: $82.10 million
Employees: 1,100
SIC: 3842
NAICS: 339113
Industry/ies: Aging; Disabilities; Medicine/Health Care/Mental Health
Legislative Issues: MMM

Chairman of the Board and Chief Executive Officer
MEUSER, Scott

Tel: (570) 655-5574
Fax: (800) 800-1636

Main Headquarters
Mailing: 182 Susquehanna Ave.
Exeter, PA 18643

Tel: (570) 655-5574
Fax: (800) 800-1636
TF: (800) 800-8586

Political Action Committees
Pride Mobility Products Corp PAC
FEC ID: C00388132
Contact: Thomas J. Wychock
182 Susquehanna Ave.
Exeter, PA 18643

Fax: (800) 800-1636

Contributions to Candidates: $40,000 (2015-2016)
Democrats: $10,000; Republicans: $30,000

Corporate Foundations and Giving Programs

Pride Mobility Products Corporation Contributions Program
182 Susquehanna Ave.
Exeter, PA 18643

Public Affairs and Related Activities Personnel

At Headquarters

JOHNSON, Seth N.
Vice President, Government Affairs
sjohnson@pridemobility.com
Registered Federal Lobbyist

Tel: (570) 655-5574
Fax: (800) 800-1636

PIRIANO, Julie
Director, Rehab Industry Affairs
jpiriano@pridemobility.com
Registered Federal Lobbyist

Tel: (570) 655-5574
Fax: (800) 800-1636

WYCHOCK, Thomas J.
PAC Treasurer

Tel: (570) 655-5574
Fax: (800) 800-1636

Prime Therapeutics LLC

A pharmacy benefit company.
www.primetherapeutics.com
Annual Revenues: $16.80 million
Employees: 200
Industry/ies: Insurance Industry; Medicine/Health Care/Mental Health;
Pharmaceutical Industry
Legislative Issues: HCR; MMM; PHA

President and Chief Executive Officer
DUCHARME, Jim

Tel: (612) 777-4000

Main Headquarters
Mailing: 1305 Corporate Center Dr.
Eagan, MN 55121

Tel: (612) 777-4000
TF: (800) 858-0723

Washington Office
Mailing: 1455 Pennsylvania Ave. NW
Suite 400
Washington, DC 20004

Political Action Committees
Prime Therapeutics Employee PAC (PRIMEPAC)
FEC ID: C00498105
Contact: Aaron Rodriguez
1305 Corporate Center Dr.
Eagan, MI 55121

Contributions to Candidates: $8,000 (2015-2016)
Democrats: $4,000; Republicans: $4,000

Public Affairs and Related Activities Personnel

At Headquarters

BEARDSLEY, John
Vice President, Enterprise Strategy and Chief, Staff

Tel: (612) 777-4000

CHASE, Jacqueline A.
Senior Vice President, Human Resources

Tel: (612) 777-4000

FAHRNER, Stacey
Vice President, Government Affairs

Tel: (202) 280-2013

FEIGAL, Erin
Vice President, Human Resources

Tel: (612) 777-4000

FRIES, Scott
*Chief Operating Officer and Senior Vice President,
Government Programs*

Tel: (612) 777-4000

HOSCH, Ellyn
Chief Information Officer

Tel: (612) 777-4000

MAHMOOD, Alec
Chief Financial Officer

Tel: (612) 777-4000

OLIG, Cameron
Senior Vice President, Commercial Markets and Sales

Tel: (612) 777-4000

RODRIGUEZ, Aaron
Vice President, General Counsel and Secretary

Tel: (612) 777-4000

ROOT, David

Tel: (612) 777-4000

SEIBERT, Angela
Manager, Sponsorship and Events
aseibert@primetherapeutics.com

Tel: (612) 777-4000

TOBIN, Ann
Chief Compliance Officer

Tel: (612) 777-4000

VOJTA, Christopher
Senior Vice President, Pharmacy and Network Services

Tel: (612) 777-4000

At Washington Office

CANTOR-WEINBERG, Julie
Federal Lobbyist
Registered Federal Lobbyist

PrimeraDx

Manufacturer of laboratory diagnostics equipment and devices.
www.primeradx.com
Annual Revenues: $3.80 million
Industry/ies: Machinery/Equipment; Science; Scientific Research

Executive Chairman of the Board
MCCARTHY, PhD, Laurence

Tel: (508) 618-2300
Fax: (508) 339-0452

President Chief Executive Officer and Director
MCMANUS, MBA, MD, PhD, Matthew F.

Tel: (508) 618-2300
Fax: (508) 339-0452

Main Headquarters
Mailing: 171 Forbes Blvd.
Suite 1000
Mansfield, MA 02048-1172

Tel: (508) 618-2300
Fax: (508) 339-0452

Public Affairs and Related Activities Personnel

At Headquarters

BOND, Andrew
Contact, Media Relations
abond@primeradx.com

Tel: (508) 618-2300
Fax: (508) 339-0452

JACKSON, PhD, David
Vice President, Business Development

Tel: (508) 618-2300
Fax: (508) 339-0452

MEMON, Fayyaz
Vice President, Regulatory Affairs and Quality Assurance

Tel: (508) 618-2300
Fax: (508) 339-0452

MYLES, Ted
Chief Financial Officer and Vice President, Operations

Tel: (508) 618-2300
Fax: (508) 339-0452

Primerica Financial Services

A financial services company.
www.primerica.com
Annual Revenues: $1.36 billion
Employees: 1,953
Ticker: NYSE: PRI
SIC: 6311
Industry/ies: Advertising And Marketing; Banking/Finance/Investments;
Insurance Industry
Legislative Issues: FIN; RET; TAX

Chairman of the Board
WILLIAMS, D. Richard

Tel: (770) 381-1000
Fax: (770) 564-6216

Chief Executive Officer
WILLIAMS, Glenn J.

Tel: (770) 381-1000
Fax: (770) 564-6216

Main Headquarters
Mailing: One Primerica Pkwy.
Duluth, GA 30099

Tel: (770) 381-1000
Fax: (770) 564-6216

Washington Office
Mailing: 900 Seventh St. NW
Washington, DC 20001

Political Action Committees
Primerica, Inc. PAC (Primerica PAC)
FEC ID: C00521914
Contact: Claudia Herrera
One Primerica Pkwy.
Duluth, 30099

Contributions to Candidates: $120,500 (2015-2016)
Democrats: $44,500; Republicans: $76,000

Corporate Foundations and Giving Programs

PFS Foundation
Contact: Anne Soutter
Houston, TX

Public Affairs and Related Activities Personnel

At Headquarters

ABOLAFIA, Dylan
Federal Lobbyist

Tel: (770) 381-1000
Fax: (770) 564-6216

ADAMS, Michael
*Executive Vice President and Chief Business Technology
Officer*

Tel: (770) 381-1000
Fax: (770) 564-6216

ADDISON, Jr., John A.
Chairman, Primerica Distribution

Tel: (770) 381-1000
Fax: (770) 564-6216

BRITT, Chess	Tel:	(770) 381-1000
Executive Vice President and Chief Marketing Officer	Fax:	(770) 564-6216
FENDLER, Jeffrey S.	Tel:	(770) 381-1000
Chief Compliance and Risk Officer	Fax:	(770) 564-6216
FINE SALTIEL, Karen	Tel:	(770) 381-1000
Executive Vice President	Fax:	(770) 564-6216
GINN , David	Tel:	(770) 381-1000
Assistant General Counsel	Fax:	(770) 564-6216
LOOMIS, Suzanne	Tel:	(770) 381-1000
Senior Vice President	Fax:	(770) 564-6216
suzanne.loomis@primerica.com		
PITTS, Gregory C.	Tel:	(770) 381-1000
Executive Vice President and Chief Operating Officer	Fax:	(770) 564-6216
RAND, Alison S.	Tel:	(770) 381-1000
Executive Vice President and Chief Financial Officer	Fax:	(770) 564-6216
alison.rand@primerica.com		
SCHNEIDER, Peter W.	Tel:	(770) 381-1000
Executive Vice President, General Counsel, Corporate	Fax:	(770) 564-6216
Secretary and Chief Administrative Officer		
SHUSTER, Allison	Tel:	(770) 381-1000
	Fax:	(770) 564-6216
SOUTTER, Anne	Tel:	(770) 381-1000
Vice President, Community and Foundation Relations	Fax:	(770) 564-6216
SUKIN, Karen	Tel:	(770) 381-1000
Executive Vice President	Fax:	(770) 564-6216
THOMAS, Greg	Tel:	(770) 381-1000
Vice President, Federal Government Relations	Fax:	(770) 564-6216
WILLIAMS, Adam	Tel:	(770) 381-1000
Federal Lobbyist	Fax:	(770) 564-6216

At Washington Office

FARRELL, Jeanette
Senior Assistant, Government Relations
jeanette.farrell@primerica.com

HERRERA, Claudia
PAC Contact

Principal Financial Group

Principal Financial Group, Inc. provides retirement savings, investment, and insurance products and services. It operates through Retirement and Investor Services, Principal Global Investors, Principal International, and U.S. Insurance Solutions segments.
www.principal.com
Annual Revenues: $10.66 billion
Employees: 14,873
Ticker: NYSE: PFG
SIC: 6321
Industry/ies: Banking/Finance/Investments; Insurance Industry
Legislative Issues: BAN; BUD; CPT; FIN; HCR; INS; RET; TAX; TRD

Chairman and Chief Executive Officer	Tel:	(515) 247-5111
ZIMPLEMAN, Larry D.	Fax:	(515) 246-5475

Main Headquarters
Mailing:	711 High St.	Tel:	(515) 247-5111
	Des Moines, IA 50392-0001	Fax:	(515) 246-5475
		TF:	(800) 986-3343

Washington Office
Mailing:	1350 I St. NW	Tel:	(202) 682-1280
	Suite 880	Fax:	(202) 682-1412
	Washington, DC 20005-3305		

Political Action Committees
Principal Life Insurance Company PAC
FEC ID: C00128918
711 High St.	Tel:	(515) 247-5111
Des Moines, IA 50392	Fax:	(515) 247-5111

 Contributions to Candidates: $214,000 (2015-2016)
 Democrats: $97,000; Republicans: $117,000

Corporate Foundations and Giving Programs
Principal Financial Group Foundation, Inc.
Contact: Andrew Allen
711 High St.	Tel:	(515) 247-7227
Des Moines, IA 50392		

Public Affairs and Related Activities Personnel

At Headquarters

BRADY, Beth	Tel:	(515) 247-5111
Senior Vice President and Chief Marketing Officer	Fax:	(515) 246-5475
BURMEISTER, Ned A.	Tel:	(515) 247-5111
Senior Vice President and Chief Operating Officer	Fax:	(515) 246-5475
BURROWS, Gregory J.	Tel:	(515) 247-5111
Senior Vice President, Retirement and Investor Services	Fax:	(515) 246-5475
DUNBAR, Timothy M.	Tel:	(515) 247-5111
Executive Vice President and Chief Investment Officer	Fax:	(515) 246-5475

EGAN, John	Tel:	(515) 247-5111
Vice President, Investor Relations	Fax:	(515) 246-5475
egan.john@principal.com		
HALE, Terri	Tel:	(515) 283-8858
Media Relations Officer	Fax:	(515) 246-5475
hale.terri@principal.com		
HOUSER, Susan	Tel:	(515) 248-2268
Assistant Vice President, Corporate Relations	Fax:	(515) 246-5475
houser.susan@principal.com		
KEMPKES, Jill	Tel:	(515) 247-5111
Associate Director, Government Relations	Fax:	(515) 246-5475
LILLIS, Terrance J.	Tel:	(515) 247-5111
Executive Vice President and Chief Financial Officer	Fax:	(515) 246-5475
RAYMOND, Elizabeth L.	Tel:	(515) 247-5111
Senior Vice President and Chief Human Resources Officer	Fax:	(515) 246-5475
SHAFF, Karen E.	Tel:	(515) 247-5111
Executive Vice President, General Counsel and Secretary	Fax:	(515) 246-5475
WIREMAN, Rich	Tel:	(515) 247-5111
Vice President, Tax and PAC Treasurer	Fax:	(515) 246-5475

At Washington Office

BLANCHARD, Laricke D.	Tel:	(202) 682-1280
Assistant Vice President, Government Relations	Fax:	(202) 682-1412
Registered Federal Lobbyist		
BLUMER, Patti R.	Tel:	(202) 682-1280
Director, Federal Government Relations	Fax:	(202) 682-1412
CAVANAUGH, James N.	Tel:	(202) 682-1280
Assistant Director, Federal Government Relations	Fax:	(202) 682-1412
LAWSON, Richard C.	Tel:	(202) 682-1280
Vice President, Federal Government Relations	Fax:	(202) 682-1412
lawson.rick@principal.com		
LIPKA, Jason	Tel:	(202) 682-1280
Assistant Director - Federal Government Relations	Fax:	(202) 682-1412
Registered Federal Lobbyist		
PAYNE, Christopher	Tel:	(202) 682-1280
Vice President, Federal Government Relations	Fax:	(202) 682-1412
payne.chris@principal.com		
Registered Federal Lobbyist		
STANLEY NGUYEN, Rachel A.	Tel:	(202) 682-1280
Assistant Vice President, Federal Government Relations	Fax:	(202) 682-1412
Registered Federal Lobbyist		

Procter & Gamble

A manufacturer and distributor of cleaning and other household products, soap, health care, beauty care, paper products, snacks, and beverages.
www.pg.com
Annual Revenues: $71.28 billion
Employees: 110,000
Ticker: NYSE: PG
SIC: 0174; 2037; 2045; 2076; 2841; 3711
NAICS: 325611
Industry/ies: Chemicals & Chemical Industry; Food And Beverage Industry; Paper And Wood Products Industry; Personal Care/Hygiene; Pharmaceutical Industry
Legislative Issues: ADV; ANI; BAN; CHM; CPT; CSP; ENV; FOR; GOV; HCR; IMM; LAW; LBR; MAN; PHA; TAR; TAX; TRA; TRD

Executive Chairman of the Board	Tel:	(513) 983-1100
LAFLEY, Alan G.	Fax:	(513) 983-9369
lafley.ag@pg.com		

President and Chief Executive Officer	Tel:	(513) 983-1100
TAYLOR, David S.	Fax:	(513) 983-9369

Main Headquarters
Mailing:	One Procer and Gamble Plaza	Tel:	(513) 983-1100
	Cincinnati, OH 45201	Fax:	(513) 983-9369

Washington Office
Mailing:	701 Pennsylvania Ave. NW	Tel:	(202) 393-3400
	Suite 520		
	Washington, DC 20004		

Political Action Committees
The Procter & Gamble Company Good Government Fund (P&G GGF) PAC
FEC ID: C00257329
Contact: Susan Whaley
One Procter & Gamble Plaza
Cincinnati, OH 45202

 Contributions to Candidates: $262,500 (2015-2016)
 Democrats: $89,500; Republicans: $172,000; Other: $1,000

Principal Recipients

 SENATE
  BLUNT, ROY (REP-MO)

 HOUSE
  PALLONE, FRANK JR (DEM-NJ)

Corporate Foundations and Giving Programs

Procter & Gamble Company Contributions Program
Contact: Brian Sasson
P.O. Box 599
Cincinnati, OH 45201

Public Affairs and Related Activities Personnel

At Headquarters

BIEGGER, Mark F.	Tel:	(513) 983-1100
Chief Human Resources Officer	Fax:	(513) 983-9369
CHEVALIER, John	Tel:	(513) 983-1100
Director, Investor Relations	Fax:	(513) 983-9369
chevalier.jt@pg.com		
FROELICHER, Julie	Tel:	(513) 983-1100
	Fax:	(513) 983-9369
LEROY, Jeff	Tel:	(513) 983-1100
Contact, Corporate Communications	Fax:	(513) 983-9369
leroy.jh@pg.com		
MAJORAS, Deborah P.	Tel:	(513) 983-1100
Chief Legal Officer and Secretary	Fax:	(513) 983-9369
MOELLER, Jon R.	Tel:	(513) 983-1100
Chief Financial Officer	Fax:	(513) 983-9369
SASSON, Brian	Tel:	(513) 983-1100
Contact, P and G Fund	Fax:	(513) 983-9369
SHEPPARD, Valarie L.	Tel:	(513) 983-1100
Senior Vice President, Comptroller and Treasurer	Fax:	(513) 983-9369
WHALEY, Susan	Tel:	(513) 983-1100
PAC Treasurer	Fax:	(513) 983-9369

At Washington Office

BREHM, Carolyn L.	Tel:	(202) 393-3400
Vice President, Global Government Relations and Public Policy		
brehm.cl@pg.com		
Registered Federal Lobbyist		
BRODERICK, Sean	Tel:	(202) 393-3400
Senior Manager, Global Government Relations and Public Policy		
Registered Federal Lobbyist		
HOGAN CHARLES, Tara	Tel:	(202) 393-3400
Senior Manager, Global Government Relations and Public Policy		
hogancharles.t@pg.com		
Registered Federal Lobbyist		
ILUYEMI, Adebimpe Temitope	Tel:	(202) 393-3400
Registered Federal Lobbyist		
PENBERTHY, Shannon	Tel:	(202) 393-3400
Associate Director, Global Health and Beauty		
Registered Federal Lobbyist		
ROBERTI, Amy	Tel:	(202) 393-3400
Director, Global Tax and Fiscal Policy		
odonnell.a.1@pg.com		
Registered Federal Lobbyist		

Producers Rice Mill, Inc.

Producers of rice.
www.producersrice.com
Annual Revenues: $499.99 million
Employees: 700
Industry/ies: Agriculture/Agronomy; Food And Beverage Industry

Chairman of the Board	Tel:	(870) 673-4444
SEBREE, Gary	Fax:	(870) 672-4482

President & Chief Executive Officer	Tel:	(870) 673-4444
GLOVER, Keith	Fax:	(870) 672-4482
kglover@producersrice.com		

Main Headquarters

Mailing:	P.O. Box 1248	Tel:	(870) 673-4444
	Stuttgart, AR 72160	Fax:	(870) 672-4482

Political Action Committees

Producers Rice Mill Inc. PAC
FEC ID: C00378083
Contact: Kent Lockwood
P.O. Box 1248
Stuttgart, AR 72160

> **Contributions to Candidates:** $12,300 (2015-2016)
> Republicans: $11,300; Other: $1,000

Public Affairs and Related Activities Personnel

At Headquarters

BADEN, Marvin	Tel:	(870) 673-4444
Senior Vice President, Rice Sales and Marketing	Fax:	(870) 672-4482
mbaden@producersrice.com		

KEY, Michele	Tel:	(870) 673-4444
Human Resources Contact	Fax:	(870) 672-4482
mkey@producersrice.com		
LINDSEY, Kris	Tel:	(870) 673-4444
Director, Human Resources	Fax:	(870) 672-4482
klindsey@producersrice.com		
LOCKWOOD, Kent	Tel:	(870) 673-4444
Vice President, Finance, Administration and PAC Treasurer	Fax:	(870) 672-4482
klockwood@producersrice.com		
MCGILTON, Jennifer	Tel:	(870) 673-4444
Human Resources Contact	Fax:	(870) 672-4482
jmcgilton@producersrice.com		
RUFF, Patricia	Tel:	(870) 673-4444
Human Resources Contact	Fax:	(870) 672-4482
pruff@producersrice.com		

Professional Warranty Service Corporation

Provider of home warranty products in the U.S., including a 10-year insured warranty.
www.pwsc.com
Annual Revenues: $4.00 million
Employees: 40
Industry/ies: Housing; Insurance Industry

President and Chief Executive Officer	Tel:	(703) 750-2701
SOMMERS, Gale	Fax:	(800) 851-2799
galesommers@pwsc.com		

Main Headquarters

Mailing:	4443 Brookfield Corporate Dr.	Tel:	(800) 850-2799
	Suite 300	Fax:	(800) 851-2799
	Chantilly, VA 20151	TF:	(800) 850-2799

Public Affairs and Related Activities Personnel

At Headquarters

COOKE, Terence	Tel:	(703) 750-2701
Senior Vice President and General Counsel	Fax:	(800) 851-2799
terencecooke@pwsc.com		
HARWELL, Ben	Tel:	(703) 750-2701
Vice President, Sales and Advisor	Fax:	(800) 851-2799
BenHarwell@pwsc.com		
LANGFORD, Roger	Tel:	(800) 850-2799
Vice President, Sales and Marketing	Fax:	(800) 851-2799
ROEDER, Angela	Tel:	(800) 850-2799
Vice President and Chief Accounting Officer	Fax:	(800) 851-2799

Progress Energy

See listing on page 268 under Duke Energy

The Progressive Corporation

A property and casualty insurance company.
www.progressive.com
Annual Revenues: $19.56 billion
Employees: 26,501
Ticker: NYSE: PGR
SIC: 6331
Industry/ies: Insurance Industry

Chairman, President and Chief Executive Officer	Tel:	(440) 461-5000
RENWICK, Glenn M.	Fax:	(800) 456-6590

Main Headquarters

Mailing:	6300 Wilson Mills Rd.	Tel:	(440) 461-5000
	Mayfield Village, OH 44143	Fax:	(800) 456-6590
		TF:	(800) 456-6590

Corporate Foundations and Giving Programs

Progressive Insurance Foundation
6300 Wilson Mills Rd.
Mayfield Village, OH 44143

Tel:	(440) 461-5000
Fax:	(800) 456-6590

Public Affairs and Related Activities Personnel

At Headquarters

CHARNEY, Jeffrey	Tel:	(440) 461-5000
Chief Marketing Officer	Fax:	(800) 456-6590
CODY, Bill	Tel:	(440) 461-5000
Chief Investment Officer	Fax:	(800) 456-6590
DOMECK, Brian	Tel:	(440) 461-5000
Vice President and Chief Financial Officer	Fax:	(800) 456-6590
FORNICK, Theresa	Tel:	(440) 461-5000
Contact, Media Relations	Fax:	(800) 456-6590
Theresa_Fornick@progressive.com		
JARRETT, Charles	Tel:	(440) 461-5000
Chief Legal Officer	Fax:	(800) 456-6590
chuck_jarrett@progressive.com		
KRASOWSKI, Valerie	Tel:	(440) 461-5000
Chief Human Resource Officer	Fax:	(800) 456-6590

Prologic, Inc.
See listing on page 809 under Ultra Electronics, Prologic

Promise Healthcare, Inc.
A hospital that provides acute long term care.
www.promisehealthcare.com
Employees: 2,000
Industry/ies: Medicine/Health Care/Mental Health
Legislative Issues: MMM

Chairman of the Board and Chief Executive Officer	Tel:	(561) 869-3100
BARONOFF, Peter R.	Fax:	(561) 869-3101

Main Headquarters

Mailing:	999 Yamato Rd.	Tel:	(561) 869-3100
	Third Floor	Fax:	(561) 869-3101
	Boca Raton, FL 33431	TF:	(800) 485-0885

Public Affairs and Related Activities Personnel

At Headquarters

ARMSTRONG, David J.	Tel:	(561) 869-3100
Executive Vice President, General Counsel, Chief Compliance Officer and Corporate Secretary	Fax:	(561) 869-3101

COHEN, Richard	Tel:	(561) 869-3100
Senior Vice President, Finance and Chief Administrative Officer	Fax:	(561) 869-3101

GOLD, Richard A.	Tel:	(561) 869-3100
President and Chief Operating Officer	Fax:	(561) 869-3101

HOPWOOD, James	Tel:	(561) 869-3100
Chief Financial Officer	Fax:	(561) 869-3101

PERE, RN, Laurie	Tel:	(561) 869-3100
Vice President, Physician Relations and Education	Fax:	(561) 869-3101
lpere@promisehealthcare.com		

SPIVACK, Nancy	Tel:	(561) 869-3100
Senior Vice President, Human Resources	Fax:	(561) 869-3101

WADE, Kimberly	Tel:	(561) 869-3100
Manager, Marketing	Fax:	(561) 869-3101

Prosper Marketplace Inc.
A web-based person-to-person consumer lending company.
www.prosper.com
Annual Revenues: $6.81 million
Employees: 74
SIC: 6199
Industry/ies: Consumers

Executive Chairman	Tel:	(415) 593-5400
VERMUT, Stephan		

Chief Executive Officer	Tel:	(415) 593-5400
VERMUT, Aaron		

Main Headquarters

Mailing:	221 Main St.
	Suite 300
	San Francisco, CA 94105

Corporate Foundations and Giving Programs

Prosper Marketplace Contributions Program
111 Sutter St.
22nd Floor
San Francisco, CA 94104

Public Affairs and Related Activities Personnel

At Headquarters

ADARKAR, Sachin
General Counsel and Chief Compliance Officer

COHEN, Itzik
Vice President, Business Development

LAW, Cheryl
Chief Marketing Officer

LEE, Macy
Chief Financial Officer

PIPER, Dawn
Vice President, Human Resources

SUBER, Ron
President

At Other Offices

AZZANO, Laurie	Tel:	(415) 593-5400
Contact, Media Relations		
101 Second St., 15th Floor		
San Francisco, CA 94105		
laurie@cosmo-pr.com		

Protective Life Insurance Company
An insurance holding company. It is a subsidiary of Protective Life Corporation.

www.protective.com
Annual Revenues: $4.40 billion
Employees: 2,457
SIC: 6311
Industry/ies: Insurance Industry
Legislative Issues: BUD; HOM; INS; TAX

Chairman of the Board, President and Chief Executive Officer	Tel:	(205) 268-1000
JOHNS, John D.	Fax:	(205) 268-3196
johnny.johns@protective.com		

Main Headquarters

Mailing:	2801 Hwy. 280 South	Tel:	(205) 268-1000
	Birmingham, AL 35223	Fax:	(205) 268-3196
		TF:	(800) 866-9933

Corporate Foundations and Giving Programs

The Protective Life Foundation
Contact: Kate H. Cotton

2801 Hwy. 280 South	Tel:	(205) 268-1000
Birmingham, AL 35223	Fax:	(205) 268-3196

Public Affairs and Related Activities Personnel

At Headquarters

ADAMS, D. Scott	Tel:	(205) 268-1000
Senior Vice President and Chief Human Resources Officer	Fax:	(205) 268-3196

BIELEN, Richard J.	Tel:	(205) 268-1000
Vice Chairman and Chief Financial Officer	Fax:	(205) 268-3196

LONG, J D, Deborah J.	Tel:	(205) 268-1000
Executive Vice President, Secretary and General Counsel	Fax:	(205) 268-3196

MEYER, Jennefer	Tel:	(205) 268-4122
Vice President, Communications and Social Engagement	Fax:	(205) 268-3196
jennefer.meyer@protective.com		

ROBERTSON, Eva	Tel:	(205) 268-3912
Vice President, Investor Relations	Fax:	(205) 268-3196
eva.robertson@protective.com		

SOTTOSANTI, Frank R.	Tel:	(205) 268-1000
Senior Vice President, Chief Marketing Officer	Fax:	(205) 268-3196

THIGPEN, Carl S.	Tel:	(205) 268-1000
Executive Vice President and Chief Investment Officer	Fax:	(205) 268-3196

At Other Offices

COTTON, Kate H.	Tel:	(205) 268-4434
Vice President, Community Relations and. Executive Director, Protective Life Foundation		
P.O. Box 2606		
Birmingham, AL 35202		
kate.cotton@protective.com		

WALKER, Steven G.	Tel:	(205) 268-4434
PAC Treasurer, Senior Vice President, Controller and Chief Accounting Officer		
P.O. Box 2606		
Birmingham, AL 35202		
steve.walker@protective.com		

The Providence Journal Company
A newspaper publishing company.
www.providencejournal.com
Annual Revenues: $64.6 million
Employees: 1,100
SIC: 4833
Industry/ies: Communications; Media/Mass Communication

Main Headquarters

Mailing:	75 Fountain St.	Tel:	(401) 277-7000
	Providence, RI 02902	Fax:	(401) 277-7889

Corporate Foundations and Giving Programs

Providence Journal Charitable Foundation
75 Fountain St.
Providence, RI 02902

Public Affairs and Related Activities Personnel

At Headquarters

CONNOLLY, Scott	Tel:	(401) 277-7000
Senior Vice President, Sales and Marketing	Fax:	(401) 277-7889
sconnoll@projo.com		

MCDONOUGH, Thomas	Tel:	(401) 277-7000
Vice President, Human Resources and Labor Relations	Fax:	(401) 277-7461

RADCLIFFE, Sandra	Tel:	(401) 277-7000
Executive Vice President, Finance and Administration and Chief Financial Officer	Fax:	(401) 277-7889

Prudential Financial, Inc.
A financial services company.
www.prudential.com
Annual Revenues: $57.45 billion
Employees: 49,384

Ticker: NYSE: PRU
SIC: 6311
Industry/ies: Economics And Economic Development; Insurance Industry
Legislative Issues: BAN; BUD; CSP; FIN; HCR; HOM; INS; LAW; RET; TAX; TRD

| **Chairman, President and Chief Executive Officer** | Tel: | (973) 802-6000 |
| STRANGEFELD, Jr., John R. | Fax: | (973) 802-4479 |

Main Headquarters

| *Mailing:* | 751 Broad St. | Tel: | (973) 802-6000 |
| | Newark, NJ 07102 | TF: | (800) 346-3778 |

Washington Office

Mailing: 575 Seventh St.
Suite 250
Washington, DC 20004

Political Action Committees

Prudential Financial Inc. Federal Political Action Committee (Aka - Prudential Federal PAC)
FEC ID: C00127779
Contact: Roman Gabriel
751 Broad St.
14th Floor
Newark, NJ 07102

Contributions to Candidates: $488,250 (2015-2016)
Democrats: $286,000; Republicans: $200,250; Other: $2,000

Principal Recipients

HOUSE
LEVIN, SANDER M MR (DEM-MI)
PAYNE, DONALD M., JR. (DEM-)
PERLMUTTER, EDWIN G (DEM-CO)

Corporate Foundations and Giving Programs

The Prudential Foundation
751 Broad St.
Newark, NJ 07102

Public Affairs and Related Activities Personnel

At Headquarters

BRATTON, William J.	Tel:	(973) 802-6000
Director, Regulatory Supervision		
BRUBAKER, Alan	Tel:	(973) 802-6000
Vice President, Government Affairs		
alan.brubaker@prudential.com		
Registered Federal Lobbyist		
CANCIENNE, Lauren	Tel:	(973) 802-6000
Federal Lobbyist		
Registered Federal Lobbyist		
DOYLE, Robert H.	Tel:	(973) 802-6000
Federal Lobbyist		
Registered Federal Lobbyist		
FALZON, Robert	Tel:	(973) 802-6000
Executive Vice President and Chief Financial Officer		
FEENEY, John	Tel:	(973) 802-6000
Federal Lobbyist		
Registered Federal Lobbyist		
GABRIEL, Roman	Tel:	(973) 802-6000
PAC Treasurer		
Mail Stop 14th Floor		
roman.gabriel@prudential.com		
Registered Federal Lobbyist		
GREEN, Desiree	Tel:	(973) 802-6000
Registered Federal Lobbyist		
GREENWOOD, Sheila M.	Tel:	(973) 802-6000
Vice President, Regulatory Affairs		
HARRIS, Timothy P.	Tel:	(973) 802-6000
Executive Vice President and General Counsel		
KELM, Lauren V.	Tel:	(973) 802-6000
Federal Lobbyist		
Registered Federal Lobbyist		
KINSTLICK, Riva	Tel:	(973) 802-6000
Vice President, Government Affairs		
riva.kinstlick@prudential.com		
Registered Federal Lobbyist		
LOWREY, Charles F.	Tel:	(973) 802-6000
Executive Vice President, Chief Operating Officer		
PICKEL, Bryan	Tel:	(973) 802-6000
Federal Lobbyist		
pickel@prudential.com		
Registered Federal Lobbyist		
SARPER, Lauren	Tel:	(973) 802-6000
Registered Federal Lobbyist		
TAYLOR, Sharon C.	Tel:	(973) 802-6000
Senior Vice President, Human Resources	Fax:	(973) 802-4479

sharon.taylor@prudential.com

WACKERLE, Rex	Tel:	(973) 802-6000
Vice President, Government Affairs		
rex.wackerle@prudential.com		
Registered Federal Lobbyist		

At Washington Office

BURNS, David D.	Tel:	(202) 239-4872
Federal Lobbyist	Fax:	(202) 327-5249
Registered Federal Lobbyist		
TYLER, Ralph	Tel:	(202) 239-4872
Manager, Government Affairs	Fax:	(202) 327-5249
ralph.tyler@prudential.com		
Registered Federal Lobbyist		

Prudential Insurance Company of America

See listing on page 656 under Prudential Financial, Inc.

PSE and G

See listing on page 658 under Public Service Enterprise Group (PSE&G)

PSS World Medical Inc.

McKesson Medical-Surgical and PSS World Medical have officially combined as McKesson Medical-Surgical in 2013. McKesson Medical-Surgical, a subsidiary of McKesson, offers products, including its own private-label line of patient exam, wound care, and laboratory supplies to doctors' offices, surgery centers, long-term care facilities, and home care businesses across the country.
www.mckessonpss.com
Annual Revenues: $225.40 million
Employees: 3,000
SIC: 5047
Industry/ies: Machinery/Equipment; Medicine/Health Care/Mental Health

President & Chief Executive Officer	Tel:	(804) 264-7500
CORLESS, Gary A.		
President	Tel:	(804) 264-7500
MCCOMB, Stanton		

Main Headquarters

| *Mailing:* | 4345 S. Point Blvd. | Tel: | (904) 332-3000 |
| | Jacksonville, FL 32216 | | |

Public Affairs and Related Activities Personnel

At Other Offices

FIGUEREDO, Jorge L.	Tel:	(804) 264-7500
Executive Vice President, Human Resources		
8741 Landmark Rd.		
Richmond, VA 23228		
MARSHALL, Kimberly A.	Tel:	(804) 264-7500
Senior Vice President, Human Resources		
8741 Landmark Rd.		
Richmond, VA 23228		
REES, Nigel A.	Tel:	(804) 264-7500
Interim-Chief Financial Officer and Vice President, Controller		
8741 Landmark Rd.		
Richmond, VA 23228		
SEEGER, Laureen E.	Tel:	(804) 264-7500
Executive Vice President, General Counsel and Chief Compliance Officer		
8741 Landmark Rd.		
Richmond, VA 23228		
TYLER, Brian S.	Tel:	(804) 264-7500
Executive Vice President, Corporate Strategy and Business Development,		
8741 Landmark Rd.		
Richmond, VA 23228		

Psychemedics Corporation

Provides testing services for the detection of abused substances through the analysis of hair samples primarily in the United States.
www.psychemedics.com
Annual Revenues: $28.92 million
Employees: 156
Ticker: NASDAQ: PMD
SIC: 8071
Industry/ies: Drug And Alcohol Abuse; Testing

| **Chairman of the Board, President and Chief Executive Officer** | Tel: | (978) 206-8220 |
| KUBACKI, Jr., Raymond C. | Fax: | (978) 264-9236 |

Main Headquarters

Mailing:	125 Nagog Park	Tel:	(978) 206-8220
	Suite 200	Fax:	(978) 264-9236
	Acton, MA 01720	TF:	(800) 628-8073

Public Affairs and Related Activities Personnel

At Headquarters

DYKE, Jim		Tel:	(978) 206-8220
Corporate Vice President, Sales and Marketing		Fax:	(978) 264-9236
LERNER, Neil		Tel:	(978) 206-8220
Vice President, Finance		Fax:	(978) 264-9236
Neill@psychemedics.com			

PTEK Holdings, Inc.
See listing on page 650 under Premiere Global Services, Inc.

PTPN, Inc.
A network of independent outpatient rehabilitation providers.
www.ptpn.com
Employees: 3,500
Industry/ies: Medicine/Health Care/Mental Health

President
WEINPER, DPT, MPH, PT, Michael
Tel: (800) 766-7876
Fax: (818) 737-0270

Main Headquarters
Mailing: 26635 W. Agoura Rd.
Suite 250
Calabasas, CA 91302
Tel: (800) 766-7876
Fax: (818) 737-0270
TF: (800) 766-7876

Corporate Foundations and Giving Programs
PTPN Contribution Program
26635 W. Agoura Rd.
Suite 250
Calabasas, CA 91302
Tel: (800) 766-7876

Public Affairs and Related Activities Personnel

At Headquarters

CONNOLLY, Jerry
Federal Lobbyist
Tel: (800) 766-7876
Fax: (818) 737-0270

MOORE, Stephen
Director, Sales and Marketing
smoore@ptpn.com
Tel: (818) 737-0246
Fax: (818) 737-0270

ROTHENBERG, Nancy
Vice President
nrothenberg@ptpn.com
Tel: (800) 766-7876
Fax: (818) 737-0270

Public Service Company of New Mexico
A energy holding company.
www.pnm.com
Annual Revenues: $1.11 billion
Employees: 1,100
SIC: 4911
Industry/ies: Energy/Electricity; Utilities
Legislative Issues: CAW; CPI; ENG; ENV

Chairman, President and Chief Executive Officer
VINCENT-COLLAWN, Pat
Tel: (505) 241-2700
Fax: (505) 241-2367

Main Headquarters
Mailing: P.O. Box 17970
Denver, CO 80217-0970

Political Action Committees
Public Service Company of New Mexico Responsible Citizens Group PAC
FEC ID: C00025395
Contact: Thomas Sategna
Alvarado Sq.
Albuquerque, NM 87158-0001
Tel: (505) 241-2700

> **Contributions to Candidates:** $17,500 (2015-2016)
> Democrats: $12,500; Republicans: $5,000

Public Affairs and Related Activities Personnel

At Headquarters
MONFILETTO, Laurie
Vice President, Human Resources

At Other Offices
APODACA, Patrick
Senior Vice President and General Counsel
Alvarado Sq., MS 1110
Albuquerque, NM 87158-0001
Patrick.Apodaca@pnmresources.com
Tel: (505) 241-2700
Fax: (505) 241-2367

C' DE BACA, Ernie
Vice President, Government Affairs
Alvarado Sq., MS 1110
Albuquerque, NM 87158-0001
ecdeba@pnm.com
Tel: (505) 241-2700
Fax: (505) 241-2367

DARNELL, Ron
Senior Vice President, Public Policy
Alvarado Sq., MS 1110
Albuquerque, NM 87158-0001
Tel: (505) 241-2700
Fax: (505) 241-2367

ELDRED, Charles
Executive Vice President and Chief Financial Officer
Alvarado Sq., MS 1110
Albuquerque, NM 87158-0001
Tel: (505) 241-2700
Fax: (505) 241-2367

ORTIZ, Gerard
Vice President, Regulatory Affairs
Alvarado Sq., MS 1110
Albuquerque, NM 87158-0001
Tel: (505) 241-2700
Fax: (505) 241-2367

SATEGNA, Thomas
Vice President, Corporate Controller and PAC Treasurer
Alvarado Sq., MS 1110
Albuquerque, NM 87158-0001
Mail Stop 2701
thomas.sategna@pnmresources.com
Tel: (505) 241-2700
Fax: (505) 241-2367

SPONAR, Susan
Senior Communications Representative
Alvarado Sq., MS 1110
Albuquerque, NM 87158-0001
susan.sponar@pnmresources.com
Tel: (505) 241-2768
Fax: (505) 241-2367

TARRY, Joseph Don
Vice President, Corporate Controller and Chief Information Officer and PAC Treasurer
414 Silver SW
Albuquerque, NM 87158

Public Service Enterprise Group (PSE&G)
The Public Service Corporation was formed in 1903. An electric and gas utility Company, subsidiary of the Public Service Enterprise Group.
www.pseg.com
Annual Revenues: $10.80 billion
Employees: 12,689
Ticker: NYSE: PEG
SIC: 4931
Industry/ies: Energy/Electricity; Natural Resources; Utilities
Legislative Issues: BUD; COM; ENG; ENV; HOM; TAX; TRA; UTI

Chairman of the Board, President and Chief Executive Officer
IZZO, Ralph
Tel: (973) 430-7000
Fax: (973) 824-7056

Main Headquarters
Mailing: 80 Park Plaza, T4B - P.O. Box 570
P.O. Box 570
Newark, NJ 07101
Tel: (973) 430-7000
Fax: (973) 824-7056
TF: (800) 350-7734

Washington Office
Mailing: One Massachusetts Ave. NW
Suite 360
Washington, DC 20001
Tel: (202) 408-0800
Fax: (202) 408-0214

Corporate Foundations and Giving Programs
PSEG Foundation
Contact: Sheila Rostiac
80 Park Plaza
P.O. Box 570
Newark, NJ 07102

Public Affairs and Related Activities Personnel

At Headquarters

BOUKNIGHT, Jr., J.A.
Executive Vice President and General Counsel
Tel: (973) 430-7000
Fax: (973) 824-7056

DORSA, Caroline
Executive Vice President and Chief Financial Officer
Tel: (973) 430-7000
Fax: (973) 824-7056

DOW-BRESLIN, Jo Ann
Manager, Community Affairs
joann.dow@pseg.com
Tel: (973) 430-5861
Fax: (973) 824-7056

GUIDA, Arthur S.
Director, External Affairs
arthur.guida@pseg.com
Tel: (973) 650-7194
Fax: (973) 622-4261

JOHNSON, Karen
Director, Communications
karen.johnson2@pseg.com
Tel: (973) 430-7734
Fax: (973) 824-7056

KAHRER, Mark G.
Vice President, Finance, Lobbyist/Registrant Pac
mark.kahrer@pseg.com
Tel: (973) 430-7000
Fax: (973) 824-7056

LAROSSA, Ralph A.
President and Chief Operating Officer
Tel: (973) 430-7000
Fax: (973) 824-7056

MAHONEY, Hugh J.
Chief Compliance Officer
hugh.mahoney@pseg.com
Tel: (973) 430-6405
Fax: (973) 824-7056

MCKOY, Vaughn L.
General State Regulatory Counsel
Vaughn.McKoy@pseg.com
Tel: (973) 430-7000
Fax: (973) 824-7056

PEGO, Margaret M.
Senior Vice President, Human Resources and Chief Human Resources Officer
margaret.pego@pseg.com
Tel: (973) 430-7243
Fax: (973) 824-7056

QUINN, Kevin J.
Vice President, Holdings and Corporate Planning and Analysis
Tel: (973) 430-7000
Fax: (973) 824-7056

ROSTIAC, Sheila
Tel: (973) 430-6047

President, PSEG Foundation and Director, Corporate Social Responsibility
sheila.rostiac@pseg.com

Fax: (973) 824-7056

At Washington Office

CAMERON, Donise
Manager, Federal Affairs
donise.cameron@pseg.com
Registered Federal Lobbyist

Tel: (202) 408-0800
Fax: (202) 408-0214

LUDECKE, Kristen
Vice President, Federal Affairs
kristen.ludecke@pseg.com
Registered Federal Lobbyist

Tel: (202) 408-0800
Fax: (202) 408-0214

NARAINE, Neil
Director, Federal Affairs
Registered Federal Lobbyist

Tel: (202) 408-0800
Fax: (202) 408-0214

Publix Super Markets Inc.

A grocery store chain.
www.publix.com
Annual Revenues: $29.23 billion
Employees: 175,000
Ticker: OTCMKTS:PUSH
SIC: 5411
Industry/ies: Food And Beverage Industry; Retail/Wholesale
Legislative Issues: AGR; BUD; CPT; CSP; FOO; HCR; TAX; TRA

Chairman of the Board
JENKINS, Jr., Charles H.

Tel: (863) 688-1188
Fax: (863) 284-5532

Chief Executive Officer
CRENSHAW, Edward

Tel: (863) 688-1188
Fax: (863) 284-5532

President
JONES, Randall T.

Tel: (863) 688-1188
Fax: (863) 284-5532

Main Headquarters
Mailing: P.O. Box 407
           Lakeland, FL 33802-0407

Tel: (863) 688-1188
Fax: (863) 284-5532
TF: (800) 242-1227

Political Action Committees
Publix Super Markets, Inc. Associates PAC
FEC ID: C00400705
Contact: Shane Kunze
P.O. Box 407
Lakeland, FL 33811

> **Contributions to Candidates:** $365,000 (2015-2016)
> Democrats: $77,000; Republicans: $288,000

> ### Principal Recipients
>
> #### SENATE
> BURR, RICHARD (REP-NC)
> SCOTT, TIMOTHY E (REP-SC)
>
> #### HOUSE
> BUCHANAN, VERNON (REP-FL)
> CLYBURN, JAMES E. (DEM-SC)
> CRENSHAW, ANDER (REP-FL)
> CURBELO, CARLOS (REP-FL)
> DIAZ-BALART, MARIO (REP-FL)
> MCCARTHY, KEVIN (REP-CA)
> ROONEY, TOM MR. (REP-FL)
> ROSS, DENNIS ALAN (REP-FL)
> RYAN, PAUL D. (REP-WI)

Corporate Foundations and Giving Programs
Publix Super Markets Charity
Contact: Sharon Miller
3300 Airport Rd.
Lakeland, FL 33802

Public Affairs and Related Activities Personnel

At Headquarters

ATTAWAY, Jr., John A.
Senior Vice President, General Counsel and Secretary

Tel: (863) 688-1188
Fax: (863) 284-5532

BROUS, Maria
Director, Media and Community Relations
maria.brous@publix.com

Tel: (863) 688-1188
Fax: (863) 284-5532

KUNZE, Shane
PAC Treasurer

Tel: (863) 688-1188
Fax: (863) 284-5532

MILLER, Sharon
Foundation Executive Director

Tel: (863) 688-1188
Fax: (863) 284-5532

MITCHELL, Michael
Director, Government Relations

Tel: (863) 688-1188
Fax: (863) 284-5532

PHILLIPS, David P.
Chief Financial Officer and Treasurer

Tel: (863) 688-1188
Fax: (863) 284-5532

At Other Offices

NAPIER, Lindsey

3300 Publix Corporate Pkwy.
Lakeland, FL 33811
Registered Federal Lobbyist

Puget Sound Energy

Electric utility.
www.pse.com
Annual Revenues: $3.12 billion
Employees: 2,800
Ticker: NYSE: PSD
SIC: 4911
Industry/ies: Energy/Electricity; Utilities
Legislative Issues: BUD; CAW; ENG; ENV; HOM; TAX; TRA

President and Chief Executive Officer
HARRIS, Kimberly J.

Tel: (425) 454-6363

Main Headquarters
Mailing: P.O. Box 97034
           EST-11E
           Bellevue, WA 98009-9269

Tel: (888) 225-5773
TF: (888) 225-5773

Political Action Committees
Puget Sound Energy, Inc. Good Government PAC
FEC ID: C00101592
Contact: Sharmila K. Swenson
10885 NE Fourth St.
P.O. Box 97034
Bellevue, WA 98009

Tel: (425) 454-6363

> **Contributions to Candidates:** $30,814 (2015-2016)
> Democrats: $26,814; Republicans: $4,000

Corporate Foundations and Giving Programs

Puget Sound Energy Foundation
Contact: Sandra M. Carson
10885 NE Fourth St.
P.O. Box 97034
Bellevue, WA 98009

Tel: (425) 454-6363

Public Affairs and Related Activities Personnel

At Headquarters

ALLEN, James
Senior Federal Government Relations Representative

Tel: (425) 462-3990

AMOR, Dom
Manager, Local Government and Community Relations
Mail Stop EST-11E
dom.amor@pse.com

Tel: (425) 454-6363

BUSSEY, Philip K.
Senior Vice President, Chief Customer Officer

Tel: (888) 225-5773

CARSON, Sandra M.
Executive Director, Puget Sound Energy Foundation

Tel: (425) 454-6363

DONEGAN, Christina
Manager, Strategic Communications
Christina.Donegan@pse.com

Tel: (888) 225-5773

DOYLE, Daniel A.
Senior Vice President and Chief Financial Officer

Tel: (888) 225-5773

HOPKINS, Margaret F.
Vice President and Chief Information Officer

Tel: (888) 225-5773

KELLY, Janet
Federal Lobbyist
Registered Federal Lobbyist

Tel: (425) 454-6363

MELLIES, Marla D.
Senior Vice President, Chief Administrative Officer

Tel: (888) 225-5773

ODELL, Nina
Director, Government Affairs & Public Policy
nina.odell@pse.com
Registered Federal Lobbyist

Tel: (425) 462-3990

SECRIST, Steve R.
Vice President, General Counsel, Chief Ethics and Compliance Officer
steve.secrist@pse.com

Tel: (425) 454-6363

SWENSON , Sharmila K.
PAC Contact

Tel: (888) 225-5773

WAPPLER, Andy
Vice President, Corporate Affairs

Tel: (425) 454-6363

WORTHINGTON, Janet
Federal Lobbyist
Registered Federal Lobbyist

Tel: (425) 462-3990

Pullen.
See listing on page 690 under RSM McGladrey, Inc.

Pulmatrix

A clinical stage pharmaceutical company developing inhaled therapies that treat, prevent and help control infectious and progressive respiratory diseases.

---

www.pulmatrix.com
Annual Revenues: $3.52 million
Employees: 13
Industry/ies: Medicine/Health Care/Mental Health; Science; Scientific Research

Chief Executive Officer Tel: (781) 357-2333
CLARKE, PhD, Robert

Main Headquarters
Mailing: 99 Hayden Ave. Tel: (781) 357-2333
  Suite 390
  Lexington, MA 02421-7966

Public Affairs and Related Activities Personnel

At Headquarters

BAKER, Thomas Tel: (781) 357-2333
Contact, Investor and Media Relations

MORRIS, Kathryn Tel: (845) 635-9828
Contact, Communications
kathryn@theyatesnetwork.com

PulseTech Products Corporation

Manufactures a line of 12- and 24-V battery maintenance charges.
www.pulsetech.net
Annual Revenues: $4.60 million
Employees: 25
SIC: 5063
NAICS: 423610
Industry/ies: Defense/Homeland Security; Government-Related
Legislative Issues: TRD

Main Headquarters
Mailing: 1100 S. Kimball Ave. Tel: (817) 329-6099
  Southlake, TX 76092-9009 Fax: (817) 329-5914
    TF: (800) 580-7554

Corporate Foundations and Giving Programs

PulseTech Products Corporation Contributions Program
1100 S. Kimball Ave. Tel: (817) 329-6099
Southlake, TX 76092

Public Affairs and Related Activities Personnel

At Headquarters

BELL, John Tel: (954) 684-5155
Consultant, Public Relations and Contact, Media Relations Fax: (817) 329-5914
johnebell@bellsouth.net

GREGORY, Rick Tel: (817) 329-6099
Manager, Business Development Fax: (817) 329-5914
RGregory@pulsetech.net

JUSTICE, Briza Tel: (817) 329-6099
Government and Military Quotes and Sales Fax: (817) 329-5914
bjustice@pulsetech.net

WHITE, Robert Tel: (817) 329-6099
Vice President, Sales and Marketing Fax: (817) 329-5914
swhite@pulsetech.net

PulteGroup Inc.

Formerly Pulte Corp. A homebuilder and related financial services company. Acquired Del E. Webb Corp. in 2001 and Centex in 2009.
www.pultegroupinc.com
Annual Revenues: $6.28 billion
Employees: 4,542
Ticker: NYSE: PHM
SIC: 1531
Industry/ies: Construction/Construction Materials; Housing
Legislative Issues: TAX

Chairman and Chief Executive Officer Tel: (248) 647-2750
DUGAS, Jr., Richard J. Fax: (248) 433-4599

Main Headquarters
Mailing: 3350 Peachtree Rd. NE Tel: (404) 978-6400
  Atlanta, GA 30326 TF: (800) 777-8583

Political Action Committees
Pultegroup Inc Political Action Committee (Pulte PAC)
FEC ID: C00560839
Contact: Darrin Lim
2350 Kerner Blvd.
Suite 250
San Rafael, CA 94901

  Contributions to Candidates: $16,400 (2015-2016)
  Democrats: $2,500; Republicans: $13,900

Corporate Foundations and Giving Programs

PulteGroup Inc. Charitable Giving Program
100 Bloomfield Hills Pkwy. Tel: (248) 647-2750
Suite 150 Fax: (248) 433-4598
Bloomfield Hills, MI 48304-2950

Public Affairs and Related Activities Personnel

At Headquarters

MARSHALL, Ryan R. Tel: (404) 978-6400
President

SMITH, Harmon D. Tel: (404) 978-6400
Executive Vice President and Chief Operating Officer

At Other Offices

COOK, Steven M. Tel: (248) 647-2750
Senior Vice President, General Counsel and Secretary Fax: (248) 433-4599
100 Bloomfield Hills Pkwy., Suite 300
Bloomfield Hills, MI 48304

ELLINGHAUSEN, James R. Tel: (248) 647-2750
Executive Vice President, Human Resources Fax: (248) 433-4599
100 Bloomfield Hills Pkwy., Suite 300
Bloomfield Hills, MI 48304

LIM, Darrin
PAC Treasurer
2350 Kerner Blvd., Suite 250
San Rafael, CA 94901

O'SHAUGHNESSY, Robert T. Tel: (248) 647-2750
Executive Vice President and Chief Financial Officer Fax: (248) 433-4599
100 Bloomfield Hills Pkwy., Suite 300
Bloomfield Hills, MI 48304

PETROULAKIS, Jacque Tel: (480) 391-6169
Contact, Media Relations Fax: (248) 433-4599
100 Bloomfield Hills Pkwy., Suite 300
Bloomfield Hills, MI 48304
jacque.petroulakis@pultegroup.com

RACHIDE, Mary Tel: (248) 647-2750
Vice President, Strategy Fax: (248) 433-4599
100 Bloomfield Hills Pkwy., Suite 300
Bloomfield Hills, MI 48304

SHRIVASTAVA, Manish M. Tel: (248) 647-2750
Vice President and Chief Marketing Officer Fax: (248) 433-4599
100 Bloomfield Hills Pkwy., Suite 300
Bloomfield Hills, MI 48304

ZEUMER, James Tel: (248) 433-4502
Vice President, Investor Relations and Corporate Fax: (248) 433-4599
Communications
100 Bloomfield Hills Pkwy., Suite 300
Bloomfield Hills, MI 48304
jim.zeumer@pultegroup.com

Purdue Frederick

See listing on page 660 under Purdue Pharma, LP

Purdue Pharma, LP

A pharmaceutical research, development and manufacturing company.
www.purduepharma.com
Annual Revenues: $99 million
Employees: 800
Industry/ies: Pharmaceutical Industry
Legislative Issues: ALC; BUD; CPT; HCR; MMM; PHA

President and Chief Executive Officer Tel: (203) 588-8000
TIMNEY, Mark Fax: (203) 588-8850

Main Headquarters
Mailing: One Stamford Forum Tel: (203) 588-8000
  201 Tresser Blvd. Fax: (203) 588-8850
  Stamford, CT 06901-3431 TF: (800) 877-5666

Washington Office
Mailing: 1001 Pennsylvania Ave. NW
  13th Floor North
  Washington, DC 20004

Political Action Committees
Purdue Pharma Inc. PAC (Purdue PAC)
FEC ID: C00370643
Contact: Brad Griffin
One Stamford Forum
201 Tresser Blvd.
Stamford, CT 06901

  Contributions to Candidates: $19,000 (2015-2016)
  Democrats: $1,000; Republicans: $18,000

Principal Recipients
SENATE
BURR, RICHARD (REP-NC)

Corporate Foundations and Giving Programs

Purdue Pharma Grants and Giving
One Stamford Forum
201 Tresser Blvd.
Stamford, CT 06901-3431

Public Affairs and Related Activities Personnel

At Headquarters

BANNON, Timothy F.	Tel:	(203) 588-8450
Special Counsel and Head, Public Affairs	Fax:	(203) 508-8850
timothy.bannon@pharma.com		
CHARHON, Jean-Jacques JJ	Tel:	(203) 588-8000
Executive Vice President and Chief Financial Officer	Fax:	(203) 588-8850
DAMAS, Raul	Tel:	(203) 588-8000
Vice President, Corporate Affairs and Communications	Fax:	(203) 588-8850
GRIFFIN, Brad	Tel:	(203) 588-8000
Contact, Financial Planning and Analysis and PAC Treasurer	Fax:	(203) 588-8850
HEINS, James W.	Tel:	(203) 588-8069
Senior Director, Public Affairs and Media Contact	Fax:	(203) 508-8850
james.heins@pharma.com		
LONG, David	Tel:	(203) 588-8000
Senior Vice President, Human Resources	Fax:	(203) 588-8850
MALLIN, William	Tel:	(203) 588-8000
Vice President, Strategic Planning and Program Management	Fax:	(203) 588-8850
ROBINSON, Susie	Tel:	(203) 588-8000
Vice President, Human Resources	Fax:	(203) 588-8850
STRASSBURGER, Philip C.	Tel:	(203) 588-8000
Vice President and General Counsel	Fax:	(203) 588-8850
WEINSTEIN, Bert	Tel:	(203) 588-8000
Vice President, Corporate Compliance	Fax:	(203) 588-8850

At Other Offices

ROSEN, Burt E.	Tel:	(202) 508-0181

Federal Government Affairs
1301 K St. NW, Suite 1050 East
Washington, DC 20005
burt.rosen@pharma.com
Registered Federal Lobbyist

PureChoice

Provides building-performance reporting software that helps business and property owners and managers maximize energy conservation and create better indoor environments.
Annual Revenues: $1.50 million
Employees: 15
Industry/ies: Environment And Conservation; Machinery/Equipment

Main Headquarters

Mailing:	6121 Baker Rd.	Tel:	(952) 985-0500
	Suite 101	Fax:	(952) 985-0505
	Minnetonka, MN 55345-5961	TF:	(800) 845-5544

Public Affairs and Related Activities Personnel

At Headquarters

BISGROVE, Richard	Tel:	(952) 985-0500
Director, Founder	Fax:	(952) 985-0505
ODLAUG, Elizabeth	Tel:	(952) 985-0500
Media Contact	Fax:	(952) 985-0505
pr@purechoice.com		

Purple Advocacy LLC

Government affairs consulting firm.
www.purplestrategies.com
Legislative Issues: BUD; DEF; TAX; TRA

Main Headquarters

Mailing:	815C Slaters Ln.	Tel:	(703) 548-7877
	Alexandria, VA 22314		

Public Affairs and Related Activities Personnel

At Headquarters

DONAHUE, Leah	Tel:	(703) 548-7877
Senior Director, Marketing and Business Development		
HAMLETT, Sarah	Tel:	(703) 548-7877
Federal & State Legislative Advocacy		
Registered Federal Lobbyist		
HAYNES, Deb	Tel:	(703) 548-7877
General Counsel		
JOHNSON, Meghan	Tel:	(703) 548-7877
Consultant		
Registered Federal Lobbyist		
JORDAN, Jim	Tel:	(703) 548-7877
Counsel		
MORGANTE, Kristen	Tel:	(703) 548-7877
Chief Operating Officer		

Purple Communications, Inc.

A provider of onsite interpreting services, video relay and text relay services tailored for people who are deaf or hard of hearing.
www.purple.us

Annual Revenues: $109.17 million
Ticker: NASDAQ (CM): PRPL
SIC: 4812
Industry/ies: Communications; Disabilities; Telecommunications/Internet/Cable

Chairman, Purple Foundation	Tel:	(916) 715-9775
OBRAY, Ronald	Fax:	(302) 636-5454
President and Chief Executive Officer	Tel:	(916) 715-9775
RAE, Robert	Fax:	(302) 636-5454

Main Headquarters

Mailing:	595 Menlo Dr.	Tel:	(201) 996-1717
	Rocklin, CA 95765	Fax:	(302) 636-5454
		TF:	(800) 900-9478

Washington Office

Mailing:	1747 Pennsylvania Ave.
	Suite 1000
	Washington, DC 20006

Political Action Committees
Purple PAC Inc
FEC ID: C00544569
Contact: Joseph Coon
1747 Pennsylvania Ave NW
Suite 1000
Washington, DC 20006

> **Contributions to Candidates:** $671,624 (2015-2016)
> Republicans: $671,624

> **Principal Recipients**
> **PRESIDENT**
> PAUL, RAND (REP-DC)

Corporate Foundations and Giving Programs

Purple Foundation	
Contact: Ronald Obray	
773 San Marin Dr.	Tel: (916) 715-9775
Suite 2210	
Novato, CA 94945	

Public Affairs and Related Activities Personnel

At Headquarters

ARTHUR, Brandon	Tel:	(202) 302-4374
Regional Director	Fax:	(302) 636-5454
barthur@purple.us		
BELLA, Mark	Tel:	(201) 996-1717
Vice President, Sales	Fax:	(302) 636-5454
BRICK, Kelby	Tel:	(916) 715-9775
Vice President, Regulatory and Strategic Policy	Fax:	(302) 636-5454
DANIELS, Bob	Tel:	(415) 408-2300
Vice President, Marketing	Fax:	(302) 636-5454
GOODMAN, John	Tel:	(415) 408-2300
Chief Legal Officer	Fax:	(302) 636-5454
HONG, Theresa	Tel:	(415) 408-2300
Public Relations and Marketing Communications Manager	Fax:	(302) 636-5454
Theresa.Hong@purple.us		
KELLEHER, John	Tel:	(201) 996-1717
Chief Financial Officer and Chief Operating Officer	Fax:	(302) 636-5454
LA ROSA, Tony	Tel:	(201) 996-1717
Chief Technology Officer and Chief Information Officer	Fax:	(302) 636-5454
SMITH, Bradley A.	Tel:	(201) 996-1717
PAC Treasurer	Fax:	(302) 636-5454

At Washington Office

COON, Joseph
PAC Contact

QBase Inc.

Specializes in data enhancement, management and analytics.
www.qbase.us
Annual Revenues: $10 million
Employees: 117
NAICS: 518210
Industry/ies: Communications; Computer/Technology; Media/Mass Communication

President and Chief Executive Officer	Tel:	(937) 521-4200
BALDWIN, Steve	Fax:	(937) 521-2434
sbaldwin@4qbase.com		

Main Headquarters

Mailing:	250 Veronia Dr.	Tel:	(937) 521-4200
	Suite 300	Fax:	(937) 521-2434
	Springfield, OH 45505		

Washington Office

Mailing:	12018 Sunrise Valley Dr.	Tel:	(937) 521-4200
	Suite 300	Fax:	(703) 437-3709
	Reston, VA 20191		

Corporate Foundations and Giving Programs

Qbase Homeless REACH
12018 Sunrise Valley Dr.   Tel: (937) 521-4200
Suite 300   Fax: (703) 437-3709
Reston, VA 20191

Public Affairs and Related Activities Personnel

At Other Offices

GREVER, Louis E.   Tel: (937) 458-0345
Senior Vice President, Product and Services Development Fax: (937) 458-0346
2619 Commons Blvd., Suite 120
Dayton, OH 45431-3818
LGrever@4qbase.com

LASTOWSKI, Tina   Tel: (937) 458-0345
Vice President, Human Resources Fax: (937) 458-0346
2619 Commons Blvd., Suite 120
Dayton, OH 45431-3818

WATTERMANN, Eric   Tel: (937) 458-0345
Vice President, Finance and Accounting Fax: (937) 458-0346
2619 Commons Blvd., Suite 120
Dayton, OH 45431-3818
rwattermann@4qbase.com

QC Holdings, Inc.

A customer-focused provider of convenient financial solutions that meet the immediate needs of mainstream consumers.
www.qcholdings.com
Annual Revenues: $149.08 million
Employees: 1,270
Ticker: NASDAQ (GM): QCCO
SIC: 6099
Industry/ies: Banking/Finance/Investments

Chairman of the Board and Director Tel: (913) 234-5000
EARLY, Don   Fax: (913) 234-5500

President and Chief Executive Officer Tel: (913) 234-5000
ANDERSEN, Darrin J.   Fax: (913) 439-1170

Main Headquarters
Mailing: 9401 Indian Creek Pkwy. Tel: (913) 234-5000
    Suite 1500   Fax: (913) 439-1170
    Overland Park, KS 66210-2020 TF: (866) 660-2243

Political Action Committees
QC Holdings Inc. PAC
FEC ID: C00411769
Contact: Douglas E. Nickerson
9401 Indian Creek Pkwy.
Suite 1500
Overland Park, KS 66210

 Contributions to Candidates: $30,000 (2015-2016)
 Democrats: $1,500; Republicans: $28,500

Principal Recipients

HOUSE
JENKINS, LYNN (REP-KS)
YODER, KEVIN (REP-KS)

Corporate Foundations and Giving Programs

The QC Foundation
9401 Indian Creek Pkwy.
Suite 1500
Overland Park, KS 66210

Public Affairs and Related Activities Personnel

At Headquarters

LINAFELT, Thomas   Tel: (913) 234-5237
Director, Corporate Communications Fax: (913) 234-5500
tom.linafelt@qchi.com

NICKERSON, Douglas E.   Tel: (913) 234-5154
Chief Financial Officer and PAC Treasurer Fax: (913) 234-5500
Mail Stop Suite 1500

SMITH, D. Scott   Tel: (913) 234-5000
Vice President Operations   Fax: (913) 439-1170

WALROD , Darren   Tel: (913) 234-5000
Director, Development   Fax: (913) 439-1170

WILTANGER , Matthew Joseph Tel: (913) 234-5000
Vice President, General Counsel Fax: (913) 234-5500

QD Vision

QD Vision is a nanotechnology product company.
www.qdvision.com
Annual Revenues: $11.90 million
Employees: 40
Industry/ies: Chemicals & Chemical Industry

Chairman of the Board   Tel: (781) 652-7400
SHIH, PhD, Dr. Willy   Fax: (617) 926-1388

Main Headquarters
Mailing: 29 Hartwell Ave.   Tel: (781) 652-7400
    Lexington, MA 02421 Fax: (617) 926-1388

Public Affairs and Related Activities Personnel

At Headquarters

FINNEGAN, Martha   Tel: (617) 607-9700
Counsel   Fax: (617) 926-1388
mfinnegan@qdivision.com

MAZZUCHI, Matt Niemeyer   Tel: (617) 607-9700
Vice President, Market and Business Development Fax: (617) 926-1388
mmazzuchi@qdivision.com

VOLKMANN, John   Tel: (781) 652-7400
Chief Marketing Officer   Fax: (617) 926-1388

WOODBURY, Bob   Tel: (781) 652-7400
Chief Financial Officer   Fax: (617) 926-1388

QinetiQ North America

Provides technology solutions to Government and industry. Their goal is not to be a valued vendor, but a strategic partner working closely with customers and able to develop, field, support their missions by delivering resilient, cost-effective solutions. QinetiQ North America is a public company.
www.qinetiq-na.com
Annual Revenues: $2.73 billion
Industry/ies: Computer/Technology; Engineering/Mathematics
Legislative Issues: BUD; DEF

President   Tel: (781) 684-4000
YORSZ, Jeff

Main Headquarters
Mailing: 11091 Sunset Hills Rd. Tel: (619) 725-3700
    Suite 200   Fax: (619) 725-3717
    Reston, VA 20190

Washington Office
Mailing: 19980 Highland Vista Dr.
    Ashburn, VA 20147

Political Action Committees
Qinetiq North America, Inc. PAC (A.K.A. QINETIQ PAC)
FEC ID: C00383992
Contact: Deborah Fox
11091 Sunset Hills Rd.   Tel: (703) 752-9595
Suite 600
Reston, VA 20190

 Contributions to Candidates: $18,800 (2015-2016)
 Democrats: $3,500; Republicans: $15,300

Public Affairs and Related Activities Personnel

At Other Offices

BAUER, Tom   Tel: (781) 684-4000
Senior Vice President, Human Resources
350 Second Ave., Bldg one.
Waltham, MA 02451

FOX, Deborah   Tel: (703) 752-9595
Senior Vice President, Secretary and General Counse, IPAC Fax: (703) 752-9596
Contact
7918 Jones Branch Dr., Suite 350
Mclean, VA 22102

KLEIN, Scott   Tel: (703) 752-9595
Vice President, Government Affairs Fax: (703) 480-0393
7918 Jones Branch Dr., Suite 350
Mclean, VA 22102
Registered Federal Lobbyist

PASKARIS, Katerina   Tel: (703) 752-9595
Manager, Corporate Communications Fax: (703) 752-9596
7918 Jones Branch Dr., Suite 350
Mclean, VA 22102
Katerina.Paskaris@QinetiQ-NA.com

SATERIALE, Paul   Tel: (781) 684-4000
Vice President, Finance
350 Second Ave., Bldg one.
Waltham, MA 02451

Qorvo

Qorvo is an American semiconductor company. Formed by the merger of TriQuint Semiconductor and RF Micro Devices.
www.rfmd.com
Annual Revenues: $1.15 billion
Employees: 4,000
Ticker: NASDAQ: QRVO
SIC: 3674
Industry/ies: Communications; Telecommunications/Internet/Cable

Chairman of the Board   Tel: (336) 664-1233
WILKINSON, Jr., Walter H.   Fax: (336) 664-0454

President and Chief Executive Officer
BRUGGEWORTH, Robert A.

Tel: (336) 664-1233
Fax: (336) 664-0454

Main Headquarters
Mailing: 7628 Thorndike Rd.
Greensboro, NC 27409-9421

Tel: (336) 664-1233
Fax: (336) 664-0454

Public Affairs and Related Activities Personnel

At Headquarters

DELIETO, Doug
Vice President, Investor Relations and Director, Corporate Relations
ddelieto@rfmd.com

Tel: (336) 678-7968
Fax: (336) 678-7849

KNUPP, Ralph
Vice President, Human Resources

Tel: (336) 664-1233
Fax: (336) 664-0454

PRIDDY, William A.
Chief Financial Officer and Corporate Vice President, Administration and Secretary

Tel: (336) 664-1233
Fax: (336) 664-0454

RUDY, Suzanne B.
Vice President, Corporate Treasurer, Compliance Officer and Assistant Secretary

Tel: (336) 664-1233
Fax: (336) 664-0454

SCHWARZ, Hans
Corporate Vice President, Business Development

Tel: (336) 664-1233
Fax: (336) 664-0454

QTC

QTC delivers occupational health and disability-related examination services for customers in the public and private sectors. Acquired by Lockheed Martin in 2011.
www.qtcm.com
Annual Revenues: $37.20 million
Employees: 500
Industry/ies: Medicine/Health Care/Mental Health

Chief Executive Officer
KIM, Grant

Tel: (909) 859-2101
Fax: (909) 610-2603

Main Headquarters
Mailing: P.O. Box 5679
Diamond Bar, CA 91765

Tel: (909) 859-2100
Fax: (909) 610-2603
TF: (800) 260-1515

Washington Office
Mailing: 225 Reinekers Ln.
Suite G4
Alexandria, VA 22314

Tel: (703) 519-6136

Public Affairs and Related Activities Personnel

At Headquarters

ABRAMCHECK, Carla
Vice President, Business Capture

Tel: (909) 859-2100
Fax: (909) 610-2603

KWONG, Valma
Vice President, Finance and Accounting

Tel: (909) 859-2101
Fax: (909) 610-2603

LOZANO, Andy
Marketing Coordinator
alozano@qtcm.com

Tel: (909) 978-3459
Fax: (909) 610-2603

MAO, Virginia
Vice President, Corporate Administration

Tel: (909) 859-2101
Fax: (909) 610-2603

SCHAEFER, Larry
Chief Operating Officer

Tel: (909) 859-2100
Fax: (909) 610-2603

Quad/Graphics, Inc.

A printing company.
www.qg.com
Annual Revenues: $4.63 billion
Employees: 22,500
Ticker: NYSE: QUAD
SIC: 2759
NAICS: 323113
Industry/ies: Printing Industry

Chairman of the Board, President and Chief Executive Officer
QUADRACCI, J. Joel
joel.quadracci@qg.com

Tel: (414) 566-6000
Fax: (414) 566-4650

Main Headquarters
Mailing: N61 W23044 Harry's Ways
Sussex, WI 53089-3995

Tel: (414) 566-6000
Fax: (414) 566-4650
TF: (888) 782-3226

Corporate Foundations and Giving Programs

The Windhover Foundation
Contact: Emmy LaBode
N63 W23075 State Hwy. 74
Sussex, WI 53089

Public Affairs and Related Activities Personnel

At Headquarters

HO, Claire
Director, Corporate Communications

Tel: (414) 566-2955
Fax: (414) 566-4650

HONAN, Dave
Vice President and Chief Financial Officer

Tel: (414) 566-6000
Fax: (414) 566-4650

JAEGER, Steve
Executive Vice President, President, Direct Marketing and Media Solutions, and Chief Information Officer

Tel: (414) 566-6000
Fax: (414) 566-4650

KENT, Jennifer
Executive Vice President, Administration and General Counsel

Tel: (414) 566-6000
Fax: (414) 566-4650

OTT, Nancy
Vice President, Human Resources

Tel: (414) 566-6000
Fax: (414) 566-4650

PACKHAM, Maura
Vice President, Marketing and Communications
maura.packham@qg.com

Tel: (414) 566-6000
Fax: (414) 566-4650

STANIAK, Tony
Vice President and Chief Accounting Officer

Tel: (414) 566-6000
Fax: (414) 566-4650

VANDERBOOM, Kelly
President, Logistics and Vice President and Treasurer
Kelly.Vanderboom@qg.com

Tel: (414) 566-2464
Fax: (414) 566-4650

Quadriserv

Delivers transformational market structure changes to the securities lending industry.
www.quadriserve.com
Annual Revenues: $2 million
Employees: 20
Industry/ies: Banking/Finance/Investments

Chief Executive Officer
CESTARO III , Pat
pat.cestaro@quadriserv.com

Tel: (212) 905-5225
Fax: (212) 421-6709

Main Headquarters
Mailing: 545 Washington Blvd
Seventh Floor
Jersey, NJ 07310

Tel: (201) 499-1412

Public Affairs and Related Activities Personnel

At Headquarters

CLANCY, Michael
Chief Financial Officer

DEPETRIS, Gregory W.
Co-Founder and Chief Strategic Officer
gregory.depetris@quadriserv.com

DOYLE, Martin
Managing Director and General Counsel
martin.doyle@quadriserv.com

SURGENT, John
Chief Operating Officer
opsgroup@quadriserv.com

Tel: (201) 499-1412

Qualcomm Incorporated

Develops, manufactures, distributes and operates communications systems.
www.qualcomm.com
Annual Revenues: $22.61 billion
Employees: 33,000
Ticker: NASDAQ: QCOM
SIC: 3663
Industry/ies: Communications; Telecommunications/Internet/Cable
Legislative Issues: AUT; AVI; BUD; CHM; COM; CPT; CSP; EDU; ENG; ENV; HCR; HOM; IMM; INT; TAX; TEC; TRA; TRD

Chairman of the Board
JACOBS, Dr. Paul E.

Tel: (858) 587-1121
Fax: (858) 658-2100

Chief Executive Officer
MOLLENKOPF, Steve

Tel: (858) 587-1121
Fax: (858) 658-2100

Main Headquarters
Mailing: 5775 Morehouse Dr.
San Diego, CA 92121

Tel: (858) 587-1121
Fax: (858) 658-2100

Washington Office
Mailing: 1730 Pennsylvania Ave. NW
Suite 850
Washington, DC 20006

Tel: (202) 263-0008

Political Action Committees
Qualcomm PAC
FEC ID: C00339085
Contact: Alice R. Tornquist
1730 Pennsylvania Ave. NW
Suite 850
Washington, DC 20006

Tel: (202) 263-0024

Contributions to Candidates: $140,250 (2015-2016)
Democrats: $65,000; Republicans: $75,250

Corporate Foundations and Giving Programs

Qualcomm Foundation
Contact: Allison Kelly
5775 Morehouse Dr.

Tel: (858) 587-1121

San Diego, CA 92121   Fax: (858) 587-1121

Public Affairs and Related Activities Personnel

At Headquarters

BOLD, William   Tel: (858) 587-1121
Senior Vice President, Government Affairs   Fax: (858) 658-2100
wbold@qualcomm.com

BRENNER, Dean R.   Tel: (858) 587-1121
Vice President, Government Affairs   Fax: (858) 658-2100
dbrenner@qualcomm.com
Registered Federal Lobbyist

DAVIS, George S.   Tel: (858) 587-1121
Executive Vice President and Chief Financial Officer   Fax: (858) 658-2100

KELLY, Allison   Tel: (858) 651-4027
Senior Manager, Global Social Responsibility   Fax: (858) 845-4119
allison@qualcomm.com

KILPATRICK, Emily   Tel: (858) 845-5959
Senior Director, Corporate Communications and Public   Fax: (858) 658-2100
Relations

KNEESHAW, Warren   Tel: (858) 658-4813
Vice President, Investor Relations   Fax: (858) 658-2100

ROSENBERG, Donald J.   Tel: (858) 587-1121
Executive Vice President, General Counsel and Corporate   Fax: (858) 658-2100
Secretary

STERLING, Michelle   Tel: (858) 587-1121
Executive Vice President, Human Resources   Fax: (858) 658-2100

TRIMBLE, Christine   Tel: (858) 845-5959
Vice President, Public Affairs   Fax: (858) 658-2100
ctrimble@qualcomm.com

At Washington Office

CROUT, Steve   Tel: (202) 263-0000
Vice President, Government Affairs
Registered Federal Lobbyist

MURPHY, Sean   Tel: (202) 263-0024
Vice President and Counsel
Registered Federal Lobbyist

SELF, Laurie C.   Tel: (202) 263-0008
Vice President and Counsel
Registered Federal Lobbyist

SONI, Ayush   Tel: (202) 263-0008
Government Affairs Analyst

THOENE, Christie   Tel: (858) 651-5130
Director, Public Affairs
cthoene@qualcomm.com

TIBBITS, Nate   Tel: (202) 263-0008
Senior Vice President, Government Affairs

TORNQUIST, Alice R.   Tel: (202) 263-0024
Vice President & PAC Treasurer
alicet@qualcomm.com
Registered Federal Lobbyist

WADSWORTH, Philip   Tel: (202) 263-0023
Vice President and Legal Counsel

WASILEWSKI, Tom   Tel: (202) 263-0000
Vice President, Government Affairs
twaz@qualcomm.com
Registered Federal Lobbyist

Quanex Building Products

A producer of specialized metal products. Quanex Corporation completed a spin-off of its building products segment and the subsequent merger of the remaining Quanex Corporation with a subsidiary of Gerdau SA.
www.quanex.com
Annual Revenues: $603.66 million
Employees: 2,206
Ticker: NYSE: NX
SIC: 3317; 3334; 3354; 3350
NAICS: 331111; 331312; 331316
Industry/ies: Construction/Construction Materials
Legislative Issues: CHM; ENG; ENV; MAN

Chairman, President and Chief Executive Officer   Tel: (713) 961-4600
GRIFFITHS, Bill   Fax: (713) 439-1016

Main Headquarters
Mailing: 1800 W. Loop South   Tel: (713) 961-4600
              Suite 1500   Fax: (713) 439-1016
              Houston, TX 77027   TF: (800) 231-8176

Corporate Foundations and Giving Programs

Quanex Foundation
1900 W. Loop South
Suite 1500
Houston, TX 77027

Public Affairs and Related Activities Personnel

At Headquarters

CALVERT, Valerie   Tel: (713) 877-5305
Manager, Corporate Communications and Investor Relations   Fax: (713) 877-5333
vcalvert@quanex.com

CORNETT, Paul   Tel: (713) 961-4600
Associate General Counsel   Fax: (713) 439-1016
pcornett@quanex.com

DELANEY, Kevin P.   Tel: (713) 961-4600
Senior Vice President, General Counsel and Secretary   Fax: (713) 439-1016

JACKSON, Eric   Tel: (713) 961-4600
Director, External Affairs   Fax: (713) 439-1016
Registered Federal Lobbyist

KETELAAR, Martin P.   Tel: (713) 961-4600
Vice President, Treasurer and Investor Relations   Fax: (713) 439-1016

KORB, Brent L.   Tel: (713) 961-4600
Senior Vice President, Finance and Chief Financial Officer   Fax: (713) 439-1016

WILLIAMS, Dewayne   Tel: (713) 961-4600
Vice President, Controller   Fax: (713) 439-1016

Quantico North NFP Limited North America

Foreign Relations , Export Management & Development
www.quanticonorth.com
Industry/ies: Defense/Homeland Security; Government-Related
Legislative Issues: FOR

Main Headquarters
Mailing: 581 Boylston Street   Tel: (617) 867-9000
              Suite 707C
              Boston, MA 02116

Public Affairs and Related Activities Personnel

At Headquarters

DENT, Jennifer   Tel: (617) 867-9000

DENTON, Jennifer   Tel: (617) 867-9000

MONTGOMERY, Wayne   Tel: (617) 867-9000
montgomery@quanticonorth.com

Quantum Corporation

A mass storage company.
www.quantum.com
Annual Revenues: $553.09 million
Employees: 1,250
Ticker: NYSE: QTM
SIC: 3572
Industry/ies: Computer/Technology

Chairman of the Board   Tel: (408) 944-4000
AUVIL, Paul   Fax: (408) 944-4040

Chief Executive Officer and President   Tel: (408) 944-4000
GACEK, Jon   Fax: (408) 894-3218
jon.gacek@quantum.com

Main Headquarters
Mailing: 224 Airport Pkwy.   Tel: (408) 944-4000
              Suite 300   Fax: (408) 944-4040
              San Jose, CA 95110   TF: (800) 677-6268

Washington Office
Mailing: 4500 Forbes Blvd.   Tel: (301) 955-3000
              Suite 110   Fax: (301) 955-3103
              Lanham, MD 20706

Public Affairs and Related Activities Personnel

At Headquarters

BREARD, Linda   Tel: (408) 944-4000
Chief Financial Officer   Fax: (408) 944-4040

BRITTS, Bill   Tel: (408) 944-4000
Senior Vice President, Worldwide Sales and Marketing   Fax: (408) 944-4040

HALL, Shawn   Tel: (408) 944-4000
Senior Vice President, General Counsel and Secretary   Fax: (408) 944-4040
shawn.hall@quantum.com

LEE, Christi   Tel: (253) 334-9823
Contact, Investor Relations   Fax: (408) 944-4040

LEE, Janae Stow   Tel: (408) 944-4000
Senior Vice President, Strategy   Fax: (408) 944-4040

Quest Diagnostics Inc.

A national provider of diagnostic laboratory testing, information, and services.
www.questdiagnostics.com
Annual Revenues: $7.53 billion
Employees: 45,000
Ticker: NYSE: DGX
SIC: 8071
Industry/ies: Medicine/Health Care/Mental Health; Science; Scientific Research
Legislative Issues: HCR; MED; MMM

President and Chief Executive Officer
RUSCKOWSKI, Stephen H.

Tel: (800) 222-0446
Fax: (201) 462-4169

Main Headquarters
Mailing: Three Giralda Farms
Madison, NJ 07940

Tel: (973) 520-2700
Fax: (201) 462-4169
TF: (800) 222-0446

Washington Office
Mailing: 815 Connecticut Ave. NW
Suite 330
Washington, DC 20006

Tel: (202) 263-6260
Fax: (202) 728-0338

Political Action Committees
Quest Diagnostics Incorporated Political Action Committee
FEC ID: C00329185
Contact: Garrett H. Hansen
1401 K St. NW
Suite 803
Washington, DC 20005

Contributions to Candidates: $56,500 (2015-2016)
Democrats: $17,500; Republicans: $39,000

Corporate Foundations and Giving Programs
The Quest Diagnostics Foundation
Contact: Barbara Short
Three Giralda Farms
Madison, NJ 07940

Public Affairs and Related Activities Personnel

At Headquarters

BOST, Wendy
Director, Media Relations and Senior Communications Professional
wendy.h.bost@questdiagnostics.com

Tel: (973) 520-2800
Fax: (201) 462-4169

CONTI, Nicholas
Vice President, Business Development
Nicholas.J.Conti@questdiagnostics.com

Tel: (973) 520-2901
Fax: (201) 462-4169

CUNNINGHAM, Everett
Senior Vice President, Commercial

Tel: (973) 520-2700
Fax: (201) 462-4169

DAVIS, James E.
Senior Vice President, Operations

Tel: (973) 520-2700
Fax: (201) 462-4169

GUINAN, Mark J.
Senior Vice President and Chief Financial Officer

Tel: (973) 520-2700
Fax: (201) 462-4169

HAEMMERLE , Dan
Executive Director, Investor Relations

Tel: (973) 520-2700
Fax: (201) 462-4169

PARK, Laure
Vice President, Customer Experience
investor@questdiagnostics.com

Tel: (201) 393-5030
Fax: (201) 393-4755

PREVOZNIK, Michael E.
Senior Vice President and General Counsel

Tel: (800) 222-0446
Fax: (201) 462-4169

SAMUELS, Gary D.
Vice President, Corporate Communications
gary.d.samuels@questdiagnostics.com

Tel: (973) 520-2700
Fax: (201) 462-4169

SHARPE, Timothy
Vice President, Compliance Services
timothy.u.sharpe@questdiagnostics.com

Tel: (800) 222-0446
Fax: (201) 462-4169

SHORT, Barbara
Executive Director, Quest Diagnostics Foundation
Barb.X.Short@QuestDiagnostics.com

Tel: (973) 520-2800
Fax: (201) 729-8920

SHORTEN, Dermot
Vice President, Strategy and Ventures

Tel: (973) 520-2700
Fax: (201) 462-4169

SHUMAN, Jeffrey S.
Senior Vice President, Chief Human Resources Officer

Tel: (973) 520-2700
Fax: (201) 462-4169

SOMERS, Jennifer
Manager, External Communications

Tel: (201) 393-5700
Fax: (201) 393-4755

VALENTINE, MD, Kathleen
Director, Investor Relations

Tel: (972) 520-2900
Fax: (201) 462-4169

At Washington Office

HANSEN, Garrett H.
Senior Manager, Benefit and Risk Management Finance

Tel: (202) 263-6260
Fax: (202) 728-0338

JUDGE, Dolly
Vice President, Government Relations
Registered Federal Lobbyist

Tel: (202) 263-6260
Fax: (202) 728-0338

Questar Corporation

An integrated natural gas company involved in the production, processing, storage and distribution of gas.
www.questar.com
Annual Revenues: $1.16 billion
Employees: 1,745
Ticker: NYSE: STR
SIC: 4923; 6710; 1299; 1311

Industry/ies: Energy/Electricity; Fuels See Coal, Gas, Oil, Petroleum; Natural Resources; Petroleum Industry
Legislative Issues: ENG

Chairman, President and Chief Executive Officer
JIBSON, Ronald W.
Ron.Jibson@Questar.com

Tel: (801) 324-5000
Fax: (801) 324-5483

Main Headquarters
Mailing: 333 S. State St.
P.O. Box 45433
Salt Lake City, UT 84145-0433

Tel: (801) 324-5000
Fax: (801) 324-5483

Political Action Committees
Questar Corporation Employee PAC
FEC ID: C00097758
Contact: David Marlow Curtis
333 S. State St.
P.O. Box 45433
Salt Lake City, UT 84145

Contributions to Candidates: $6,500 (2015-2016)
Republicans: $6,500

Corporate Foundations and Giving Programs
Questar Education Foundation
Contact: Debra Hoyt
333 S. State St.
P.O. Box 45433
Salt Lake City, UT 84111

Tel: (801) 324-5000
Fax: (801) 324-5483

Public Affairs and Related Activities Personnel

At Headquarters

BELL, Colleen Larkin
Vice President, General Counsel

Tel: (801) 324-5000
Fax: (801) 324-5483

BUTCHER, Rey
Vice President, Government Relations

Tel: (801) 324-5000
Fax: (801) 324-5483

CURTIS, David Marlow
Vice President, Controller and PAC Treasurer

Tel: (801) 324-5000
Fax: (801) 324-5483

HADLOCK, Kevin W.
Executive Vice President and Chief Financial Officer

Tel: (801) 324-5000
Fax: (801) 324-5483

HOYT, Debra
Director, Corporate Giving and Foundations
Corporate.Giving@Questar.com

Tel: (801) 324-5000
Fax: (801) 324-5483

IVINS, Anthony R.
Vice President, Investor Relations and Corporate Treasurer

Tel: (801) 324-5000
Fax: (801) 324-5483

JEPPERSON, Thomas C.
Chief Operating Officer

Tel: (801) 324-5000
Fax: (801) 324-5483

JONES, Abigail L.
Vice President

Tel: (801) 324-5000
Fax: (801) 324-5483

JONES, Chad
General Manager, Corporate Communication

Tel: (801) 324-5495
Fax: (801) 324-5483

MAXFIELD, Kelly B.
Vice President, Information Technology and Administration

Tel: (801) 324-5000
Fax: (801) 324-5483

WRAY, Julie
Corporate Secretary and General Manager, Human Resources

Tel: (801) 324-5000
Fax: (801) 324-5483

Quicken Loans, Inc.

A residential mortgage lending company.
www.quickenloans.com
Annual Revenues: $91.10 million
Employees: 1,700
Industry/ies: Banking/Finance/Investments; Housing
Legislative Issues: BAN; CPT; HOM; HOU; TAX

Chairman of the Board and Founder
GILBERT, Daniel B.

Tel: (734) 805-5000
Fax: (734) 805-8400

Chief Executive Officer
EMERSON, William

Tel: (734) 805-5000
Fax: (734) 805-8400

Main Headquarters
Mailing: 1050 Woodward Ave.
Detroit, MI 48226

Tel: (800) 863-4332
Fax: (734) 805-8400
TF: (800) 226-6308

Political Action Committees
Quicken Loans Inc. PAC
FEC ID: C00388827
Contact: David Carroll
101 S. Washington Sq.
Suite 620
Lansing, MI 48933

Contributions to Candidates: $220,750 (2015-2016)
Democrats: $47,500; Republicans: $173,250

Principal Recipients

SENATE
MURPHY, PATRICK E (DEM-FL)

Corporate Foundations and Giving Programs

Quicken Loans, Inc. Contributions Program
1050 Woodward Ave.   Tel: (734) 805-5000
Detroit, MI 48226   Fax: (734) 805-8400

Public Affairs and Related Activities Personnel

At Headquarters

BERARDINI, Chris   Tel: (800) 863-4332
Registered Federal Lobbyist   Fax: (734) 805-8400

BOOTH, Julie   Tel: (734) 805-5000
Chief Financial Officer and Treasurer   Fax: (734) 805-8400
juliebooth@quickenloans.com

CARROLL, Pete   Tel: (800) 863-4332
Registered Federal Lobbyist   Fax: (734) 805-8400

EHRBAR, Nicole   Tel: (800) 863-4332
Associate, Government Affairs   Fax: (734) 805-8400
Registered Federal Lobbyist

EMERSON, Aaron   Tel: (800) 863-4332
Vice President, Communications   Fax: (734) 805-8400

FARNER, Jay   Tel: (800) 863-4332
President and Chief Marketing Officer   Fax: (734) 805-8400

GHAZAL, Jay C.   Tel: (734) 805-5000
Federal Lobbyist   Fax: (734) 805-8400
Registered Federal Lobbyist

KRAUSE, Shawn   Tel: (734) 805-5000
Federal Lobbyist   Fax: (734) 805-8400
shawnkrause@quickenloans.com
Registered Federal Lobbyist

ZIMMER, Robert   Tel: (734) 805-5000
Federal Lobbyist   Fax: (734) 805-8400
Registered Federal Lobbyist

At Other Offices

CARROLL, David   Tel: (734) 805-7450
Vice President and PAC Treasurer   Fax: (734) 805-8400
101 S. Washington Sq., Suite 620
Lansing, MI 48933
davidcarroll@quickenloans.com

Quintiles TransNational Corporation

A provider of information, technology and services to the pharmaceutical and healthcare industries.
www.quintiles.com
Annual Revenues: $3.89 billion
Employees: 29,000
Ticker: NYSE: Q
SIC: 8731
Industry/ies: Pharmaceutical Industry
Legislative Issues: HCR

Executive Chairman of the Board   Tel: (919) 998-2000
GILLINGS, PhD, Dennis B.   Fax: (919) 998-2003

Chief Executive Officer   Tel: (919) 998-2000
PIKE, Tom   Fax: (919) 998-2003

Main Headquarters
Mailing: P.O. Box 13979   Tel: (919) 998-2000
            4820 Emperor Blvd.   Fax: (919) 998-2003
            Durham, NC 27703   TF: (866) 267-4479

Washington Office
Mailing: 1133 19th St. NW
            Suite 400
            Washington, DC 20015

Corporate Foundations and Giving Programs

Quintiles Contributions Program
4820 Emperor Blvd.
Durham, NC 27703

Public Affairs and Related Activities Personnel

At Headquarters

BRIDGES, Phil   Tel: (919) 998-1653
Senior Director, Corporate Communications Fax: (919) 998-2003
phil.bridges@quintiles.com

CONNORS, Greg   Tel: (919) 998-2000
Senior Vice President, Corporate Development and Investor Fax: (919) 998-2003
Relations
greg.connors@quintiles.com

ERLINGER, James   Tel: (919) 998-2000
Executive Vice President and General Counsel Fax: (919) 998-2003

GORDON, Kevin   Tel: (919) 998-2000
Executive Vice President and Chief Financial Officer Fax: (919) 998-2003

MANSFIELD, Mari   Tel: (919) 998-2639
Senior Director, Global Corporate Communications Fax: (919) 518-9075
mari.mansfield@quintiles.com

SPREEN, Paul   Tel: (919) 998-2000
Senior Vice President, Enterprise Sales Fax: (919) 998-2003

VERST, PharmD, Cynthia   Tel: (919) 998-2000
Global Head, Real-World and Late Phase Research Fax: (919) 998-2003

WINSTANLY, Derek   Tel: (919) 998-2000
Senior Executive Vice President   Fax: (919) 998-2003

Qwest Communications

See listing on page 179 under CenturyLink

R. R. Donnelley & Sons

R.R. Donnelley, a commercial printing company, produces magazines, catalogs, and books, as well as advertising material, business forms, financial reports, and telephone directories. It also offers graphics and prepress services in conjunction with printing. Acquired Banta Corporation on January 8, 2007.
www.rrdonnelley.com
Annual Revenues: $11.68 billion
Employees: 68,000
Ticker: NASDAQ: RRD
SIC: 2750
Industry/ies: Printing Industry
Legislative Issues: GOV

Chairman of the Board   Tel: (312) 326-8000
WOLF, Stephen M.   Fax: (312) 326-7156
stephen.wolf@rrdonnelley.com

President and Chief Executive Officer   Tel: (312) 326-8000
QUINLAN, III, Thomas J.   Fax: (312) 326-7156
tom.quinlan@rrd.com

Main Headquarters
Mailing: 35 W. Wacker Dr.   Tel: (312) 326-8000
            Chicago, IL 60606-4301   Fax: (312) 326-8001
                                            TF: (800) 742-4455

Political Action Committees
R.R. Donnelley & Sons Company Good Government Fund PAC
FEC ID: C00033977
Contact: George Zengo
111 S. Wacker Dr.   Tel: (312) 326-8000
Chicago, IL 60606   Fax: (312) 326-7156

  Contributions to Candidates: $10,355,515 (2015-2016)
  Democrats: $12,000; Republicans: $41,500; Other: $10,302,015

Corporate Foundations and Giving Programs
R.R. Donnelly Foundation
Contact: Kamala L. Martinez
111 S. Wacker Dr.
Chicago, IL 60606

Public Affairs and Related Activities Personnel

At Headquarters

FITZGERALD, Doug   Tel: (630) 322-6830
Executive Vice President, Communications Fax: (312) 326-7156
doug.fitzgerald@rrd.com

GARDELLA, Dave   Tel: (312) 326-8155
Senior Vice President, Finance and Executive Vice President, Fax: (312) 326-7156
Communications
david.a.gardella@rrd.com

At Other Offices

MARTINEZ , Kamala L.   Tel: (630) 322-6946
Manager, Community Relations
4101 Winfield Rd.
Warrenville, IL 60555
communityrelations@rrd.com

ZENGO, George   Tel: (312) 326-8000
Chief Sales Officer and PAC Treasurer   Fax: (312) 326-7156
111 S. Wacker Dr.
Chicago, IL 60606
george.zengo@rrd.com

R.J. Corman Railroad Group

R. J. Corman Railroad Group is a privately owned holding company for the following key operations: Shortline Railroads,Switching Operations,Rail Construction,Track Material Distribution Warehousing,Aviation Services,Equipment Rental,Derailment Services,Railroad Emergency Response, My Old Kentucky Dinner Train,RailPower,EcoPower.
www.rjcorman.com
Annual Revenues: $73.50 million
Employees: 1,000
Industry/ies: Railroads; Transportation

Chairman of the Board   Tel: (859) 881-7521
MUDGE, Fred N.   Fax: (859) 885-7804

President   Tel: (859) 881-7521
KING, Craig   Fax: (859) 885-7804

Main Headquarters
Mailing: 101 R.J. Corman Dr.   Tel: (859) 881-7521

Nicholasville, KY 40356 | Fax: | (859) 885-7804
| TF: | (800) 772-9091

Public Affairs and Related Activities Personnel

At Headquarters

HENDERSON, Nathan | Tel: | (859) 881-7521
Vice President, Strategic Sales and Marketing | Fax: | (859) 885-7804

MCKEE , Regina | Tel: | (859) 881-7521
Vice President, People Services | Fax: | (859) 885-7804

RUSH, Noel | Tel: | (859) 881-2473
Vice President, Finance and Administration | Fax: | (859) 885-7804
noel.rush@rjcorman.com

SESSA , Joe | Tel: | (859) 881-7521
Advisor | Fax: | (859) 885-7804

Racal Communications

See listing on page 782 under Thales Communications Inc.

Radian Group, Inc.

Credit enhancement provider. Through subsidiaries Radian Guaranty, Amerin Guaranty, and Radian Insurance, Radian Group provides traditional private mortgage insurance coverage to protect lenders from defaults by borrowers who put down a deposit of less than 20% when buying a home.
www.radian.biz
Annual Revenues: $1.11 billion
Employees: 1,702
Ticker: NYSE: RDN
SIC: 6351
Industry/ies: Banking/Finance/Investments; Insurance Industry
Legislative Issues: FIN; HOU; INS

Chairman of the Board | Tel: | (215) 231-1000
WENDER, Herbert | Fax: | (215) 854-1457

Chief Executive Officer | Tel: | (215) 231-1000
IBRAHIM, S. A. | Fax: | (215) 854-1457

Main Headquarters
Mailing: 1601 Market St. | Tel: | (215) 231-1000
Philadelphia, PA 19103 | Fax: | (215) 854-1457
| TF: | (800) 523-1988

Political Action Committees
Radian Group Employees PAC
FEC ID: C00302166
Contact: Robert Radicioni
1601 Market ST.
Philadelphia, PA 19103

Contributions to Candidates: $21,000 (2015-2016)
Democrats: $10,500; Republicans: $10,500

Public Affairs and Related Activities Personnel

At Headquarters

ALTMAN, Richard I. | Tel: | (215) 231-1000
Executive Vice President and Chief Operating Officer | Fax: | (215) 854-1457

BAZEMORE, Teresa Bryce | Tel: | (215) 231-1000
President | Fax: | (215) 854-1457

FRANKEL, Steve | Tel: | (215) 231-1990
Media Contact | Fax: | (215) 854-1457

HALL, J. Franklin | Tel: | (215) 231-1000
Executive Vice President and Chief Financial Officer | Fax: | (215) 854-1457

HOFFMAN, Edward J. | Tel: | (215) 231-1000
Senior Vice President, General Counsel and Corporate | Fax: | (215) 854-1457
Secretary

JACKSON, Catherine M. | Tel: | (215) 231-1000
Senior Vice President and Corporate Controller | Fax: | (215) 854-1457

RADICIONI , Robert | Tel: | (215) 231-1000
PAC Treasurer | Fax: | (215) 854-1457

RILEY, Emily | Tel: | (215) 231-1035
Contact, Media and Investor Relations | Fax: | (215) 854-1457

TOMLJANOVIC, William | Tel: | (215) 231-1000
Senior Vice President, Corporate Development | Fax: | (215) 854-1457

Radiation Therapy Services Inc.

Operator of radiation therapy centers.
www.rtsx.com
Annual Revenues: $544 million
Employees: 1,000
SIC: 8011
Industry/ies: Medicine/Health Care/Mental Health

President,Vice Chairman and Chief Financial Officer | Tel: | (239) 931-7275
CAREY, Bryan J. | Fax: | (239) 931-7380

Chief Executive Officer, Co-Founder and Radiation Oncologist | Tel: | (239) 931-7389
DOSORETZ, Daniel E. | Fax: | (239) 931-7380

Main Headquarters
Mailing: 2270 Colonial Blvd. | Tel: | (239) 931-7275
Ft. Myers, FL 33907 | Fax: | (239) 931-7380
| TF: | (800) 437-1619

Political Action Committees
Radiation Therapy Services Inc. PAC
FEC ID: C00385120
Contact: Daniel E. Dosoretz
2234 Colonial Blvd.
Ft. Myers, FL 33907

Contributions to Candidates: $59,000 (2015-2016)
Democrats: $41,500; Republicans: $17,500

Principal Recipients

SENATE
KANDER, JASON (DEM-MO)

Public Affairs and Related Activities Personnel

At Headquarters

DORNAUS, Madlyn | Tel: | (239) 931-7275
Senior Vice President and Chief Compliance Officer | Fax: | (239) 931-7380
mdornaus@rtsx.com

LAUDICO, Nicholas S. | Tel: | (646) 536-7030
Contact, Investor Relations | Fax: | (239) 931-7380
nlaudico@theruthgroup.com

TRAVIS, Norton L. | Tel: | (239) 931-7275
Executive Vice President and General Counsel | Fax: | (239) 931-7380
jtravis@rtsx.com

RadioShack Corporation

Engaged in the retail sale of consumer electronics goods and services.
www.radioshackcorporation.com
Annual Revenues: $3.43 billion
Employees: 27,500
Ticker: NYSE: RSH
SIC: 3661; 3577; 3663
NAICS: 334220; 334220; 334210
Industry/ies: Electricity & Electronics; Electronics; Energy/Electricity; Retail/Wholesale

Non-Executive Chairman of the Board | Tel: | (817) 415-3011
FEEHAN, Daniel R. | Fax: | (817) 415-2647

Main Headquarters
Mailing: 300 RadioShack Cir. | Tel: | (817) 415-3700
Fort Worth, TX 76102-1964 | Fax: | (817) 415-2647
| TF: | (800) 843-7422

Corporate Foundations and Giving Programs
RadioShack Corporation Contributions Program
300 RadioShack Cir. | Tel: | (817) 415-3699
Fort Worth, TX 76102

Public Affairs and Related Activities Personnel

At Headquarters

DONOHOO, Robert C. | Tel: | (817) 415-3700
Vice President, General Counsel and Corporate Secretary | Fax: | (817) 415-2647

Radius, The Global Travel Company

A travel management network operator. It designs and delivers programs unique to each multinational company through a worldwide network of best-in-market agencies.
www.radiustravel.com
Industry/ies: Travel/Tourism/Lodging

Chairman of the Board | Tel: | (301) 718-9500
HARE, Michael | Fax: | (301) 718-4290

President and Chief Executive Officer | Tel: | (301) 718-9500
HYLAND, Shannon | Fax: | (301) 718-4290

Main Headquarters
Mailing: 7700 Wisconsin Ave. | Tel: | (301) 718-9500
Suite 400 | Fax: | (301) 718-4290
Bethesda, MD 20814-4408

Public Affairs and Related Activities Personnel

At Headquarters

DOODY, Diana | Tel: | (240) 744-3319
Brand Manager | Fax: | (301) 718-4290
ddoody@radiustravel.com

HARTWELL, Kieran | Tel: | (301) 718-9500
Senior Vice President, Global Sales and Service | Fax: | (301) 718-4290

KOZIOL , Kate | Tel: | (773) 774-7847
Contact, Communications (K Squared Communications) | Fax: | (301) 718-4290
kkoziol@ksqrd.com

KWEDER, Tatiana | Tel: | (301) 718-9500
Vice President, Finance & Administration | Fax: | (301) 718-4290

MCANDREWS, Chris | Tel: | (800) 989-3059

Senior Vice President, Product and Partnerships	Fax:	(301) 718-4290
SLAN, Allan G.	Tel:	(301) 718-9500
Executive Vice President and Legal Liaison	Fax:	(301) 718-4290
aslan@radiustravel.com		

Rafael USA, Inc.

A manufacturer of defense equipment.
www.rafael.co.il
Industry/ies: Defense/Homeland Security; Government-Related

President & Chief Executive Officer	Tel:	(240) 482-0252
RAM, Azarel	Fax:	(240) 482-0249

Main Headquarters		
Mailing: 6903 Rockledge Dr.	Tel:	(240) 482-0240
Suite 850	Fax:	(240) 482-0249
Bethesda, MD 20817		

Public Affairs and Related Activities Personnel

At Headquarters

ADAMS, Rachel	Tel:	(240) 482-0240
Assistant to Vice President,Business Development and Marketing	Fax:	(240) 482-0249
Rachel.A@rafael-usa.com		
POLEG, Oren	Tel:	(240) 482-0240
	Fax:	(240) 482-0249
SHOHAM, Debby	Tel:	(240) 482-0252
Executive Assistant & Office Manager	Fax:	(240) 482-0249
Registered Federal Lobbyist		

RailAmerica, Inc.

A railroad management company.
www.railamerica.com
Annual Revenues: $551 million
Employees: 1,800
SIC: 4011
Industry/ies: Management; Railroads; Transportation

Chairman of the Board	Tel:	(904) 538-6100
EDENS, Wesley R.		
President and Chief Executive Officer	Tel:	(904) 538-6100
GILES, John		

Main Headquarters		
Mailing: 7411 Fullteron St.	Tel:	(904) 538-6100
Suite 300	TF:	(800) 342-1131
Jacksonville Beach, FL 32256		

Public Affairs and Related Activities Personnel

At Headquarters

BERGER, Ira	Tel:	(904) 538-6332
Vice President, Investor Relations and PAC Treasurer		
CRIME, Donia	Tel:	(904) 645-6200
Contact, Media Relations		
KING, Michelle	Tel:	(904) 654-2772
Director, Public Relations		
michelle.king@railamerica.com		
RUSSELL, Mary Ellen	Tel:	(904) 538-6100
Chief Human Resource Officer		
WILLIAMS, Scott G.	Tel:	(904) 538-6100
Senior Vice President and General Counsel		

Rajant Corporation

Developer of wireless network systems.
www.rajant.com
Employees: 30
Industry/ies: Communications; Telecommunications/Internet/Cable
Legislative Issues: BUD; DEF

Chairman of the Board, Chief Executive Officer and Co-Founder	Tel:	(484) 595-0233
SCHENA, Robert J.	Fax:	(484) 595-0244

Main Headquarters		
Mailing: 400 E. King St.	Tel:	(484) 595-0233
Suite One	Fax:	(484) 595-0244
Malvern, PA 19355-3258		

Public Affairs and Related Activities Personnel

At Headquarters

ANDERSON, Gary	Tel:	(484) 595-0233
Senior Vice President, Business Development	Fax:	(484) 595-0244
BYLES, Kirk	Tel:	(484) 595-0233
Senior Vice President, Sales and Marketing	Fax:	(484) 595-0244
ONEILL, Charles	Tel:	(484) 595-0233
Special Counsel	Fax:	(484) 595-0244
SCHENA, Dave	Tel:	(484) 595-0233
Vice President, Finance	Fax:	(484) 595-0244

Raley's

A retail supermarket.
www.raleys.com
Annual Revenues: $3.2 billion
Employees: 13,000
Industry/ies: Food And Beverage Industry; Retail/Wholesale

Co-Chairman of the Board	Tel:	(916) 373-3333
TEEL, James E.	Fax:	(916) 371-1323
Co-Chairman of the Board	Tel:	(916) 373-3333
RALEY TEEL, Joyce	Fax:	(916) 371-1323
President and Chief Executive Officer	Tel:	(916) 373-3333
TEEL, Michael	Fax:	(916) 371-1323

Main Headquarters		
Mailing: 500 W. Capitol Ave.	Tel:	(916) 373-3333
West Sacramento, CA 95605	Fax:	(916) 371-1323
	TF:	(800) 925-9989

Corporate Foundations and Giving Programs

Raley's Contribution Program		
500 W. Capitol Ave.	Tel:	(916) 373-3333
P.O. Box 15618	Fax:	(916) 371-1323
West Sacramento, CA 95605		

Public Affairs and Related Activities Personnel

At Headquarters

LANDERS, Gerald	Tel:	(916) 373-3333
Senior Director, Human Resources	Fax:	(916) 371-1323
TOWNSEND, Nicole	Tel:	(916) 373-6209
Senior Director, Talent Development and Communications	Fax:	(916) 371-1323
ntownsen@raleys.com		

Rambus, Inc.

Rambus is a technology licensing company specializing in the invention and design of high-speed chip interfaces.
www.rambus.com
Annual Revenues: $291.18 million
Employees: 505
Ticker: NASDAQ: RMBS
SIC: 3674
Industry/ies: Copyrights, Patents And Trademarks

Chairman of the Board	Tel:	(408) 462-8000
STANG , Eric	Fax:	(408) 462-8001
President and Chief Executive Officer	Tel:	(408) 462-8000
BLACK, PhD, Ronald	Fax:	(408) 462-8001

Main Headquarters		
Mailing: 1050 Enterprise Way	Tel:	(408) 462-8000
Suite 700	Fax:	(408) 462-8001
Sunnyvale, CA 94089		

Corporate Foundations and Giving Programs

Rambus Foundation
Contact: Julie Hopper
2440 W. El Camino Real
Suite 300
Mountain View, CA 94040

Public Affairs and Related Activities Personnel

At Headquarters

ASHMORE, Linda	Tel:	(408) 462-8411
Director, Corporate Marketing	Fax:	(408) 462-8001
lashmore@rambus.com		
BENTLEY, J. Thomas	Tel:	(408) 462-8000
Director	Fax:	(408) 462-8001
KIM, Jae	Tel:	(408) 462-8000
Senior Vice President and General Counsel	Fax:	(408) 462-8001
NADEL, Jerome	Tel:	(408) 462-8000
Senior Vice President and Chief Marketing Officer	Fax:	(408) 462-8001
RISHI, Satish	Tel:	(408) 462-8000
Senior Vice President and Chief Financial Officer	Fax:	(408) 462-8001
SCHROEDER, Michael	Tel:	(408) 462-8000
Senior Vice President, Human Resources	Fax:	(408) 462-8001
STARK, Laura	Tel:	(408) 462-8000
Senior Vice President, Corporate Strategy, Mergers and Acquisitions	Fax:	(408) 462-8001
TRAN, Hoa	Tel:	(408) 462-8000
Foundation Contact	Fax:	(408) 462-8001
httran@siliconvalleycf.org		

At Other Offices

HOPPER, Julie	Tel:	(650) 450-5400
Contact, Foundation		
C/O Silicon Valley Community Foundation, 2440 W. El Camino Real, Suite 300		

Mountain View, CA 94040-1498
jahopper@siliconvalleycf.org

Ramsell Holding Corporation

Consists of three healthcare companies, and a nonprofit foundation, all focused on serving underserved populations.
www.ramsellcorp.com
Industry/ies: Medicine/Health Care/Mental Health

Founder and Chairman of the Board	Tel:	(510) 587-2600
FLOWERS, RPh, Sylester	Fax:	(510) 587-2799
sflowers@ramsellcorp.com		

| **President and Chief Executive Officer** | Tel: | (510) 587-2600 |
| FLOWERS, MBA, Eric | Fax: | (510) 587-2799 |

Main Headquarters
Mailing:	200 Webster St.	Tel:	(510) 587-2600
	Suite 200	Fax:	(510) 587-2799
	Oakland, CA 94607-4108	TF:	(888) 311-7632

Corporate Foundations and Giving Programs
The Flowers Heritage Foundation
Contact: Gregory W. Edwards
200 Webster St.
Suite 200
Oakland, CA 94607

Public Affairs and Related Activities Personnel

At Headquarters

EDWARDS, Gregory W.	Tel:	(510) 587-2600
Foundation Executive Director	Fax:	(510) 587-2799
HERRERA, Gina	Tel:	(510) 587-2600
Vice President, Human Resources	Fax:	(510) 587-2799
KLATT, Jennifer	Tel:	(510) 587-2600
Chief Financial Officer	Fax:	(510) 587-2799
MURRILL, Timothy	Tel:	(510) 587-2600
Executive Vice President, Sales and Marketing	Fax:	(510) 587-2799
tmurrill@ramsellcorp.com		
WOO, Michael	Tel:	(510) 587-2632
Director, Marketing	Fax:	(510) 587-2799
mwoo@ramsellcorp.com		

Ranbaxy Pharmaceuticals, Inc.

Ranbaxy Pharmaceuticals Inc. (RPI), a wholly owned subsidiary of Ranbaxy Laboratories Limited. (RLL), was established in the U.S. in 1994. It is a Seller and distributor of generic and branded prescription products in the U.S. healthcare system.
www.ranbaxy.com/us
Employees: 1,000
SIC: 2834; 5122
Industry/ies: Pharmaceutical Industry

Vice President, Corporate Communications and Government Affairs	Tel:	(609) 720-5615
	Fax:	(609) 720-1155
CAPRARIELLO, Charles		
chuck.caprariello@ranbaxy.com		

Main Headquarters
Mailing:	600 College Rd., East	Tel:	(609) 720-9200
	Suite 2100	Fax:	(609) 720-1155
	Princeton, NJ 08540	TF:	(888) 726-2299

Public Affairs and Related Activities Personnel

At Headquarters

BROTHMAN, Bernard	Tel:	(609) 720-9200
Vice President, Human Resources	Fax:	(609) 720-1155
MEEHAN, James	Tel:	(609) 720-9200
Vice President, Sales and Distribution	Fax:	(609) 720-1155
MEHROTRA, Gaurav	Tel:	(609) 720-9200
Vice President, Finance	Fax:	(609) 720-1155
SAMTANI, Lavesh	Tel:	(609) 720-9200
Vice President and Head, Legal Americas	Fax:	(609) 720-1155
TOMSKY, Scott	Tel:	(609) 720-9200
Vice President, Regulatory Affairs	Fax:	(609) 720-1155
WINTER, Bill	Tel:	(609) 720-9200
Vice President, Sales and Distribution	Fax:	(609) 720-1155

Rand McNally

A private company with operations in map and reference book publishing; retail map and travel stores; and mileage and routing information for commercial trucking and shipping companies.
www.randmcnally.com
Employees: 600
Industry/ies: Communications; Media/Mass Communication; Transportation

Main Headquarters
| Mailing: | P.O. Box 7600 | Tel: | (847) 329-8100 |
| | Chicago, IL 60680-7600 | Fax: | (800) 934-3479 |

| | TF: | (800) 333-0136 |

Corporate Foundations and Giving Programs
Rand McNally Foundation
9855 Woods Dr.
Skokie, IL 60077

Public Affairs and Related Activities Personnel

At Headquarters

KROUSE, Amy	Tel:	(703) 860-2677
Contact, Media Relations	Fax:	(800) 934-3479
akrouse@randmcnally.com		

Rapiscan Systems

Non-intrusive, contraband inspection technologies.
www.rapiscansystems.com
Annual Revenues: $81.80 million
Employees: 900
Industry/ies: Computer/Technology; Defense/Homeland Security; Government-Related
Legislative Issues: BUD; DEF; HOM

| **President** | Tel: | (310) 978-1457 |
| MEHRA, Ajay | Fax: | (310) 349-2491 |

Main Headquarters
| Mailing: | 2805 Columbia St. | Tel: | (310) 978-1457 |
| | Torrance, CA 90503 | Fax: | (310) 349-2491 |

Washington Office
Mailing:	2900 Crystal Dr.	Tel:	(571) 227-6767
	Suite 910	Fax:	(571) 227-6816
	Arlington, VA 22202		

Public Affairs and Related Activities Personnel

At Headquarters

GOLDSMITH, Andrew	Tel:	(703) 812-0322
Vice President, Marketing	Fax:	(310) 349-2491
agoldsmith@rapiscansystems.com		

At Washington Office

KING, James	Tel:	(571) 227-6767
Registered Federal Lobbyist	Fax:	(571) 227-6816
KING, James	Tel:	(571) 227-6767
Registered Federal Lobbyist	Fax:	(571) 227-6816
MCHUGH, Stephen J.	Tel:	(571) 227-6767
	Fax:	(571) 227-6816
ROMIG, CHRISTOPHER C.	Tel:	(571) 227-6767
Vice President, Government Relations	Fax:	(571) 227-6816
SPIVEY, Beth	Tel:	(703) 812-0322
Vice President Legislative Affairs	Fax:	(310) 978-1457
bspivey@rapiscansystems.com		

At Other Offices

NORTON, Jeremy	Tel:	(310) 349-2237
Vice President, Asia Pacific Sales		
12525 Chadron Ave.		
Hawthorne, CA 90250		
jnorton@osi-systems.com		

Ratner Companies

Ratner Companies is the family-owned and operated chain. Its diverse brands include Hair Cuttery, Bubbles, Salon Cielo and Spa, ColorWorks, and Salon Plaza.
www.ratnerco.com
Industry/ies: Personal Care/Hygiene

| **Chief Executive Officer** | Tel: | (703) 269-5400 |
| RATNER, Dennis | Fax: | (703) 269-5409 |

Main Headquarters
Mailing:	1577 Spring Hill Rd.	Tel:	(703) 269-5400
	Suite 500	Fax:	(703) 269-5409
	Vienna, VA 22182	TF:	(800) 874-6288

Corporate Foundations and Giving Programs
Ratner Family Foundation
Contact: Dennis Ratner
1577 Spring Hill Rd.
Suite 500
Vienna, VA 22182

| | Tel: | (703) 269-5400 |
| | Fax: | (703) 269-5409 |

Public Affairs and Related Activities Personnel

At Headquarters

DALY, Diane	Tel:	(703) 269-5338
Director, Public Relations	Fax:	(703) 876-2897
ddaly@ratnerco.com		
GUSTAFSON, Susan	Tel:	(703) 269-5400
President	Fax:	(703) 269-5409

Raydon Corporation

Simulation training products and solutions.
www.raydon.com
Annual Revenues: $57.97 million
Employees: 250
Industry/ies: Computer/Technology; Defense/Homeland Security; Government-Related
Legislative Issues: BUD; DEF

Chairman
ARIEL, Donald
Tel: (386) 267-2936
Fax: (386) 271-2283

Chief Executive Officer
VOLLMAR, Mike
Tel: (386) 267-2936
Fax: (386) 271-2283

Main Headquarters
Mailing: 1420 Hockney Ct.
Port Orange, FL 32128
Tel: (386) 267-2936
Fax: (386) 271-2283
TF: (888) 776-3865

Public Affairs and Related Activities Personnel

At Headquarters

HENRY, Toni
Director, Strategic Communications
thenry@raydon.com
Tel: (386) 267-2936
Fax: (386) 271-2283

MCANDREW, Cory
Contact, Sales Support
cmcandrew@raydon.com
Tel: (386) 267-2936
Fax: (386) 271-2283

MORELLI, John
Specialist, Business Development Operations
Tel: (386) 267-2936
Fax: (386) 271-2283

Raymond James Financial, Inc.

Raymond James is a diversified financial services holding company with subsidiaries engaged primarily in investment and financial planning.
www.raymondjames.com
Annual Revenues: $5.21 billion
Employees: 11,000
Ticker: NYSE: RJF
SIC: 6211
Industry/ies: Banking/Finance/Investments

Executive Chairman of the Board
JAMES, Thomas A.
Tel: (727) 567-1000
Fax: (727) 567-8915

Chief Executive Officer
REILLY, Paul C.
Tel: (727) 567-1000
Fax: (727) 567-8915

Main Headquarters
Mailing: 880 Carillon Pkwy.
St. Petersburg, TX 33716
Tel: (727) 567-1000
Fax: (727) 567-8915
TF: (800) 248-8863

Corporate Foundations and Giving Programs
Raymond James Financial, Inc. Contributions Program
880 Carillon Pkwy.
St. Petersburg, TX 33716
Tel: (727) 567-1000
Fax: (727) 567-8915

Public Affairs and Related Activities Personnel

At Headquarters

ALLAIRE, Bella Loykhter
Executive Vice President, Technology and Operations
Tel: (727) 567-1000
Fax: (727) 567-8915

HOLLISTER, Steve
Director, Public Communications
media.relations@raymondjames.com
Tel: (727) 567-1000
Fax: (727) 567-8915

JULIEN, Jeffrey P.
Executive Vice President, Finance, Chief Financial Officer and and Treasurer
Tel: (727) 567-1000
Fax: (727) 567-8915

SHOUKRY, Paul
Vice President, Finance and Investor Relations
investorrelations@raymondjames.com
Tel: (727) 567-5133
Fax: (727) 567-8915

ZANK, Dennis
Chief Operating Officer
Tel: (727) 567-1000
Fax: (727) 567-8915

Rayonier

A global supplier of specialty pulps, timber and wood products.
www.rayonier.com
Annual Revenues: $600.64 million
Employees: 300
Ticker: NYSE: RYN
SIC: 6798
Industry/ies: Forestry
Legislative Issues: TAX

Chairman, President and Chief Executive Officer
BOYNTON, Paul G.
Tel: (904) 357-9100
Fax: (904) 357-9101

Main Headquarters
Mailing: 1301 Riverplace Blvd.
Suite 2300
Jacksonville Beach, FL 32207
Tel: (904) 357-9100
Fax: (904) 357-9101
TF: (800) 243-2590

Political Action Committees

Rayonier Inc.Good Government Committee PAC
FEC ID: C00451757
Contact: Scott D. Winer
1301 Riverplace Blvd.
Suite 2300
Jacksonville Beach, FL 32207
 Contributions to Candidates: $68,698 (2015-2016)
 Democrats: $11,700; Republicans: $56,998

Corporate Foundations and Giving Programs
Rayonier Foundation
50 N. Laura St.
Suite 1900
Jacksonville Beach, FL 32202

Public Affairs and Related Activities Personnel

At Headquarters

HERMAN, Michael R.
Senior Vice President and General Counsel
michael.herman@rayonier.com
Tel: (904) 357-9000
Fax: (904) 357-9101

HOOD, Charles H.
Senior Vice President, Public Affairs and Communications
Tel: (904) 357-9100
Fax: (904) 357-9101

KIKER, H. Edwin
Senior Vice President and Chief Financial Officer
Tel: (904) 357-9100
Fax: (904) 357-9101

KRAUS, Carl E.
Senior Vice President, Finance
Tel: (904) 357-9158
Fax: (904) 357-9848

PARROTT, Joe R.
Tel: (904) 357-9000
Fax: (904) 357-9101

POSZE, Jr., James L.
Senior Vice President, Human Resources
Tel: (904) 357-9100
Fax: (904) 357-9101

ROWAN, Helen C.
Vice President, Strategic Planning and Communications
Tel: (904) 357-9806
Fax: (904) 357-9101

WINER, Scott D.
Vice President, Taxes and PAC Treasurer
Tel: (904) 357-9000
Fax: (904) 357-9101

Rayovac
See listing on page 739 under Spectrum Brands Inc.

Raytheon Applied Signal Technology, Inc.
Formerly Applied Signal Technology, Inc. Renamed Raytheon Applied Signal Technology, Inc. after acquisition by Raytheon Company in 2011. Designs, develops, manufactures and markets advanced digital signal processing equipment to process a wide range of telecommunications signals for commercial and government applications.
www.raytheon.com
Annual Revenues: $22.61 billion
Employees: 61,000
Ticker: NYSE: RTN
SIC: 3823; 3674; 3812
Industry/ies: Aerospace/Aviation; Defense/Homeland Security; Electricity & Electronics; Electronics; Energy/Electricity; Engineering/Mathematics; Environment And Conservation; Government-Related; Machinery/Equipment; Transportation
Legislative Issues: AER; AVI; BUD; DEF; FOR; GOV; HOM; RET; SCI; TAX; TRD

Chairman and Chief Executive Officer
KENNEDY, Thomas A.
Tel: (781) 522-3000
Fax: (781) 522-3001

Main Headquarters
Mailing: 870 Winter St.
Waltham, MA 02451-1449
Tel: (781) 522-3000
Fax: (781) 522-3001
TF: (866) 729-6271

Washington Office
Mailing: 1100 Wilson Blvd.
Suite 1500
Arlington, VA 22209

Political Action Committees
Raytheon PAC
FEC ID: C00097568
Contact: Dr. Mark T. Esper
1100 Wilson Blvd.
Suite 1500
Arlington, VA 22209
 Contributions to Candidates: $1,268,750 (2015-2016)
 Democrats: $397,000; Republicans: $865,750; Other: $6,000
 Principal Recipients
  SENATE
  HATCH, ORRIN G (REP-UT)
  YOUNG, TODD CHRISTOPHER (REP-IN)

  HOUSE
  BOUSTANY, CHARLES W. DR. JR. (REP-LA)
  BRADY, KEVIN (REP-TX)
  BROOKS, SUSAN MRS. (REP-IN)
  CHABOT, STEVE (REP-OH)
  COFFMAN, MIKE REP. (REP-CO)

CRENSHAW, ANDER (REP-FL)
FORBES, J. RANDY (REP-VA)
FRELINGHUYSEN, RODNEY P. (REP-NJ)
GRANGER, KAY (REP-TX)
GRAVES, SAMUEL B JR 'SAM' (REP-MO)
HUNTER, DUNCAN D. (REP-CA)
JOHNSON, SAM MR. (REP-TX)
JOLLY, DAVID W. (REP-FL)
LAMBORN, DOUGLAS (REP-CO)
LANGEVIN, JAMES R. HONORABLE (DEM-RI)
LIPINSKI, DANIEL WILLIAM WILLIAM (DEM-IL)
MCCARTHY, KEVIN (REP-CA)
MCSALLY, MARTHA E. MS. (REP-AZ)
MICA, JOHN L. MR. (REP-FL)
NEAL, RICHARD E MR. (DEM-MA)
NUNES, DEVIN G (REP-CA)
PAULSEN, ERIK (REP-MN)
PERLMUTTER, EDWIN G (DEM-CO)
REED, THOMAS W II (REP-NY)
ROYCE, ED MR. (REP-CA)
SANCHEZ, LORETTA (DEM-CA)
SCALISE, STEVE MR. (REP-LA)
STEFANIK, ELISE M. (REP-NY)
TAKAI, KYLE MARK (DEM-HI)
THORNBERRY, MAC (REP-TX)
WALORSKI SWIHART, JACKIE (REP-IN)

Corporate Foundations and Giving Programs

Raytheon Charitable Giving Program
Contact: Tina Martineau
870 Winter St.
Waltham, MA 02451-1449

Raytheon Company Contributions Program		
10 Moulton St.	Tel:	(781) 522-3000
Cambridge, MA 02451-1449	Fax:	(781) 522-3001

Public Affairs and Related Activities Personnel

At Headquarters

AYER, Donna	Tel:	(781) 522-5880
Media Contact	Fax:	(781) 522-3001
BARAGAR, Douglas	Tel:	(781) 522-3000
Senior Manager, Legislative Operations	Fax:	(781) 522-3001
douglas_baragar@raytheon.com		
BHIDE, Roopa	Tel:	(781) 522-3000
Contact, Media Relations	Fax:	(781) 522-3001
idspr@raytheon.com		
CARNEVALE, James T.	Tel:	(781) 522-3000
Strategic Development Contact	Fax:	(781) 522-3001
COOPER, Caroline G.	Tel:	(781) 522-3000
Regional Director, Europe	Fax:	(781) 522-3001
caroline_g_cooper@raytheon.com		
CRUMPLER, Ryan Phillip	Tel:	(781) 522-3000
Registered Federal Lobbyist	Fax:	(781) 522-3001
ERNST, Todd	Tel:	(781) 522-5141
Vice President, Investor Relations	Fax:	(781) 522-3001
GALLAGHER, Jennifer	Tel:	(781) 522-3000
Registered Federal Lobbyist	Fax:	(781) 522-3001
HANNIS, Eric	Tel:	(781) 522-3000
Registered Federal Lobbyist	Fax:	(781) 522-3001
HARRINGTON, Lawrence J.	Tel:	(781) 522-3000
Vice President, Internal Audit	Fax:	(781) 522-3001
HARRIS, II, John D.	Tel:	(781) 522-3000
Vice President, Business Development	Fax:	(781) 522-3001
HUGHES, Douglas R.	Tel:	(781) 522-3000
Senior Director, Legislative Operations	Fax:	(781) 522-3001
Registered Federal Lobbyist		
JIMENEZ, Frank R.	Tel:	(781) 522-3000
Vice President, General Counsel and Corporate Secretary	Fax:	(781) 522-3001
KASLE, Jon	Tel:	(781) 522-5110
Vice President, Communications & External Affairs	Fax:	(781) 522-3001
jonathan_d_kasle@raytheon.com		
KENNETT, Bayard "Chip"	Tel:	(781) 522-3000
Federal Lobbyist	Fax:	(781) 522-3001
LEE, William J.	Tel:	(781) 522-3000
Director, Legislative Operations	Fax:	(781) 522-3001
MARSH, William A.	Tel:	(781) 522-3000
Senior Manager, Government Relations	Fax:	(781) 522-3001
Registered Federal Lobbyist		
MARTINEAU, Tina	Tel:	(781) 522-6490
Contact, Community Relations	Fax:	(781) 522-3001
MCFARLAND, Richard	Tel:	(781) 522-3000
Director, Legislative Operations	Fax:	(781) 522-3001

Registered Federal Lobbyist		
MILHORN, Brandon	Tel:	(781) 522-3000
Director, Integrated Defense Business	Fax:	(781) 522-3001
brandon.milhorn@raytheon.com		
Registered Federal Lobbyist		
NEAL, Robert R.	Tel:	(781) 522-3000
Director, Legislative Operations	Fax:	(781) 522-3001
robneal@raytheon.com		
Registered Federal Lobbyist		
NEWSOME, Randa G.	Tel:	(781) 522-3000
Vice President, Human Resources and Global Security	Fax:	(781) 522-3001
O'BRIEN, Anthony F.	Tel:	(781) 522-3000
Vice President, Chief Financial Officer	Fax:	(781) 522-3001
PARKER, Melissa	Tel:	(972) 952-4028
Senior Manager, Integrated Communications and Public Affairs	Fax:	(781) 522-3001
saspr@raytheon.com		
PAUL, Marisa	Tel:	(781) 522-3000
Federal Lobbyist	Fax:	(781) 522-3001
PRINCE, Timothy	Tel:	(781) 522-3000
Registered Federal Lobbyist	Fax:	(781) 522-3001
SASS, Emily	Tel:	(781) 522-3000
Manager, Government Relations	Fax:	(781) 522-3001
Registered Federal Lobbyist		
SINGER, Jim	Tel:	(781) 522-5136
Director, Investor Relations	Fax:	(781) 522-3001
STANDRIDGE, Lea	Tel:	(781) 522-3000
Federal Lobbyist	Fax:	(781) 522-3001
WAGNER, Jennifer	Tel:	(781) 522-3000
Senior Manager, Government Relations	Fax:	(781) 522-3001
Registered Federal Lobbyist		
WAJSGRAS, David C.	Tel:	(781) 522-3000
Vice President	Fax:	(781) 522-3001
WENTLAND, Jane	Tel:	(781) 522-3000
Manger, Senior Contracts Governance	Fax:	(781) 522-3001
Registered Federal Lobbyist		
WICKHAM, Pamela A.	Tel:	(781) 522-3000
Vice President, Corporate Affairs and Communications	Fax:	(781) 522-3001
WOOD, Mike J.	Tel:	(781) 522-3000
Vice President, Controller and Chief Accounting Officer	Fax:	(781) 522-3001
ZUMMO, Joseph E.	Tel:	(781) 522-3000
Senior Manager, Legislative Operations	Fax:	(781) 522-3001
Joseph_E_Zummo@raytheon.com		
Registered Federal Lobbyist		

At Washington Office

WAGNER, Jennifer
Senior Manager, Government Relations
Registered Federal Lobbyist

At Other Offices

ESPER, Dr. Mark T.	Tel:	(703) 841-5700
1555 Wilson Blvd., Suite 703	Fax:	(703) 841-5792
Arlington, VA 22209		
mark.t.esper@raytheon.com		
Registered Federal Lobbyist		
TREICHLER, John R.	Tel:	(703) 417-5300
Co-Founder / Chief Technology Officer / Senior Scientist	Fax:	(703) 841-8395
1555 Wilson Blvd., Suite 703		
Arlington, VA 22209		
WATSON, Courtney G.	Tel:	(703) 841-5702
Federal Lobbyist	Fax:	(703) 841-5792
1555 Wilson Blvd., Suite 703		
Arlington, VA 22209		
courtney_watson@raytheon.com		
Registered Federal Lobbyist		

RBC Bank (USA)

The bank provides deposit and lending services, as well as credit cards, online securities brokerage, asset management, insurance, and retail leasing.
www.rbcbankusa.com
Annual Revenues: $249.3 million
Employees: 4,500
Industry/ies: Banking/Finance/Investments

Main Headquarters

Mailing:	411 Fayetteville St.	Tel:	(919) 839-4400
	Raleigh, NC 27602	Fax:	(919) 839-4806
		TF:	(800) 236-8872

Corporate Foundations and Giving Programs

RBC Bank(USA) Contributions Program
Contact: Molly Sapienza
RBC Plaza, 301 Fayetteville St.

Raleigh, NC 27601

Public Affairs and Related Activities Personnel

At Headquarters

LANDIS, Dorsey
Specialist, Public Relations

Tel: (919) 788-6272
Fax: (919) 839-4806

UCHIDA, Susan
Vice President, Learning & Development

Tel: (919) 839-4400
Fax: (919) 839-4806

WATSON, Robert
Vice President, Human Resources

Tel: (919) 839-4400
Fax: (919) 839-4806

At Other Offices

FULGHUM, Carol
Chief Financial Officer
RBC Plaza, 301 Fayetteville St.
Raleigh, NC 27601

SAPIENZA, Molly
Director, Regional Marketing
RBC Plaza, 301 Fayetteville St.
Raleigh, NC 27601

STEVENSON, Tracy
Executive Vice President
RBC Plaza, 301 Fayetteville St.
Raleigh, NC 27601

RBC Wealth Management

Provides brokerage and investment banking services. A subsidiary of Royal Bank of Canada.
www.rbcwm-usa.com
Annual Revenues: $3.89 billion
Employees: 10,000
SIC: 6211
Industry/ies: Banking/Finance/Investments

Deputy Chairman
MITCHELL, Gay

Tel: (612) 371-2711
Fax: (612) 313-1353

Chief Executive Officer
TAFT, John

Tel: (612) 371-2711
Fax: (612) 313-1353

Main Headquarters
Mailing: 60 S. Sixth St., 19th Floor
Minneapolis, MN 55402-4422

Tel: (612) 371-2711
Fax: (612) 313-1353
TF: (800) 678-3246

Corporate Foundations and Giving Programs

RBC Foundation
60 S. Sixth St.
P20
Minneapolis, MN 55402

Public Affairs and Related Activities Personnel

At Headquarters

BAUMBACH, Martha
Director, Corporate and Community Relations
martha.baumbach@rbcdain.com

Tel: (612) 371-7753
Fax: (612) 313-1353

COURVILLE, J-F
Chief Operating Officer

Tel: (612) 371-2711
Fax: (612) 313-1353

LUNDQUIST, Jonell Rusinko
Advisor, Senior External Communications
jonell.rusinko@rbcdain.com

Tel: (612) 371-2239
Fax: (612) 313-1353

RBS Securities Inc. (Formerly RBS Greenwich Capital)

A wholly-owned subsidiary of The Royal Bank of Scotland that deals in U.S. government securities, sales and trading of asset-backed securities. Formerly known as Greenwich Capital Markets, Inc and RBS Greenwich Capital.
Industry/ies: Banking/Finance/Investments

Main Headquarters
Mailing: 600 Washington Blvd.
Stamford, CT 06901

Tel: (203) 897-7466

Washington Office
Mailing: 700 12th St. NW
Suite 700
Washington, DC 20005

Tel: (202) 625-4880
Fax: (202) 625-4881

Public Affairs and Related Activities Personnel

At Headquarters

MARRINAN , Edward B.
Managing Director and Head of US Macro Credit Strategy and Co-Head, Markets Strategy, Americas
edward.marrinan@rbs.com

Tel: (203) 897-4675

RE/MAX International

A global network of real estate franchises. RE/MAX also conducts real estate auctions and provides advisory and relocation services.
www.remax.com
Annual Revenues: $33.70 million
Employees: 300

Industry/ies: Real Estate

Chief Executive Officer, Chairman and Co-Founder
LINIGER, Dave

Tel: (303) 770-5531
Fax: (303) 796-3599

Main Headquarters
Mailing: 5075 S. Syracuse St.
Denver, CO 80237

Tel: (303) 770-5531
Fax: (303) 796-3599
TF: (800) 525-7452

Corporate Foundations and Giving Programs

RE/MAX, LLC. Contributions program
5075 S. Syracuse St.
Denver, CO 80237

Tel: (303) 770-5531
Fax: (303) 796-3599

Public Affairs and Related Activities Personnel

At Headquarters

KRAMIG, Tom
Vice President, Multi Media and Education

Tel: (303) 770-5531
Fax: (303) 796-3599

LEWIS, Geoff
President
glewis@remax.com

Tel: (303) 770-5531
Fax: (303) 796-3599

METZGER, David M. K.
Executive Vice President, Chief Operating Officer and Chief Financial Officer

Tel: (303) 770-5531
Fax: (303) 796-3599

REAGAN, Mike
Senior Vice President, Brand Marketing

Tel: (303) 770-5531
Fax: (303) 796-3599

RYAN, Mike
Executive Vice President, Global Communications

Tel: (303) 770-5531
Fax: (303) 796-3599

WHITE, Shaun
Vice President, Public Relations
shaunwhite@remax.net

Tel: (303) 796-3405
Fax: (303) 796-3599

ZIMMERMAN, Susan
Senior Vice President, Human Resources

Tel: (303) 770-5531
Fax: (303) 796-3599

RE/MAX, LLC.

See listing on page 672 under RE/MAX International

Reader's Digest Association, Inc.

A multi-brand and multi-platform media and direct marketing company.
www.rd.com
Annual Revenues: $1.71 billion
Employees: 4,700
SIC: 3695
NAICS: 334613
Industry/ies: Communications; Media/Mass Communication; Printing Industry

President and Chief Executive Officer
KINTZER, Bonnie

Tel: (914) 238-1000
Fax: (914) 244-5644

Main Headquarters
Mailing: 750 Third Ave.
New York City, NY 10017

Tel: (914) 238-1000
Fax: (914) 244-5644
TF: (800) 310-6261

Corporate Foundations and Giving Programs

Reader's Digest Foundation
Contact: Susan Fraysse Russ
Reader's Digest Rd.
Pleasantville, NY 10570

Tel: (914) 238-1000
Fax: (914) 238-1000

Reader's Digest Partners for Sight Foundation
Reader's Digest Rd.
Pleasantville, NY 10570

Tel: (914) 238-1000
Fax: (914) 238-1000

Public Affairs and Related Activities Personnel

At Headquarters

COHEN, Pauli
Manager, Public Relations
Pauli_Cohen@rd.com

Tel: (914) 238-1000
Fax: (914) 244-5644

GEBHARDT, Phyllis
Senior Vice President, Global Human Resources and Communications

Tel: (914) 238-1000
Fax: (914) 244-5644

HALLIGAN, Howard
Chief Operating Officer

Tel: (914) 238-1000
Fax: (914) 244-5644

LOEFFEL, Fred
Executive Vice President, Sales and Marketing

Tel: (914) 238-1000
Fax: (914) 244-5644

SIROTA, Mark
Vice President, General Counsel and Secretary

Tel: (914) 238-1000
Fax: (914) 244-5644

At Other Offices

LIBERATORE, Tracy
Investor Relations
44 S. Broadway
White Plains, NY 10601
Tracy_Liberatore@rd.com

Tel: (914) 244-2293

Reading Blue Mountain and Northern Railroad

A privately owned railroad.

www.readingnorthern.com
Annual Revenues: $8.00 million
Industry/ies: Railroads; Transportation

Chairman of the Board and Chief Executive Officer   Tel: (610) 562-2100
MULLER, Jr., Andy M.   Fax: (610) 562-1922

Main Headquarters
Mailing: One Railroad Blvd.   Tel: (610) 562-2100
P.O. Box 218   Fax: (610) 562-0596
Port Clinton, PA 19549-1507

Public Affairs and Related Activities Personnel

At Headquarters

BARKET, Jonathan   Tel: (610) 562-2100
Assistant Vice President, Signals and Communications   Fax: (610) 562-0596
jbarket@readingnorthern.com

BOLTZ, Heather   Tel: (610) 562-2100
Director, Human Resources   Fax: (610) 562-1922

COLLER, Andrea   Tel: (610) 562-2100
Vice President, Finance   Fax: (610) 562-0596

GILCHRIST, Daniel R.   Tel: (610) 562-2100
Vice President, Marketing and Sales   Fax: (610) 562-0596
dgilchrist@readingnorthern.com

GLASS, Tyler A.   Tel: (610) 562-2100
Executive Vice President, Operations   Fax: (610) 562-0596

HESS, Beverly B.   Tel: (610) 562-2100
Director, Employee Relations   Fax: (610) 562-0596

JOHNSON, LT Matthew   Tel: (610) 562-2100
Assistant Vice President, Community Affairs   Fax: (610) 562-0596

MICHEL, Wayne A.   Tel: (610) 562-2100
President   Fax: (610) 562-0596

MULLER-LEVAN, Christina J.   Tel: (610) 562-2100
Vice President, Administration   Fax: (610) 562-0596

Realogy Corporation

Subsidiary of Realogy Holdings Corporation. Providers of real estate and relocation services.
www.realogy.com
Annual Revenues: $5.78 billion
Employees: 11,400
Ticker: NYSE: RLGY
SIC: 6531
Industry/ies: Real Estate

Chairman of the Board, President and Chief Executive Officer   Tel: (973) 407-2000
SMITH, Richard A.   Fax: (973) 407-7004
richard.smith@realogy.com

Main Headquarters
Mailing: 175 Park Ave.   Tel: (973) 407-2000
Madison, NJ 07940   Fax: (302) 636-5454

Political Action Committees
Realogy Holdings Corporation PAC (Realogy PAC)
FEC ID: C00424218
Contact: Alicia Swift
175 Park Ave.
Madison, NJ 7940

Contributions to Candidates: $15,000 (2015-2016)
Democrats: $6,000; Republicans: $9,000

Corporate Foundations and Giving Programs
Realogy Charitable Foundation
One Campus Dr.
Parsippany, NJ 07054

Public Affairs and Related Activities Personnel

At Headquarters

BORRUSO, Kathy   Tel: (973) 407-5041
Vice President, Corporate Communications   Fax: (973) 407-7004
kathy.borruso@realogy.com

GUSTAVSON, Tim   Tel: (973) 407-2000
Senior Vice President, Chief Accounting Officer and   Fax: (302) 636-5454
Controller

HOLZER, Sunita   Tel: (973) 407-2000
Executive Vice President and Chief Human Resources Officer   Fax: (302) 636-5454

HULL, Anthony E.   Tel: (973) 407-2000
Executive Vice President, Chief Financial Officer and   Fax: (973) 407-7118
Treasurer
anthony.hull@realogy.com

PANUS, Mark   Tel: (973) 407-7215
Senior Vice President, Corporate Communications   Fax: (973) 407-7004
mark.panus@realogy.com

SWIFT, Alicia   Tel: (973) 407-2000
Senior Vice President, Investor Relations and PAC Treasurer   Fax: (302) 636-5454
alicia.swift@realogy.com

WASSER, Marilyn J.   Tel: (973) 407-2000
Executive Vice President and General Counsel   Fax: (973) 407-7004
marilyn.wasser@realogy.com

WEAVING, Dave   Tel: (973) 407-2000
Executive Vice President and Chief Administrative Officer   Fax: (973) 407-7004
dave.weaving@realogy.com

Reckitt Benckiser

A subsidiary of U.K.-based Reckitt Benckiser PLC, they have interests in household, health and personal care, and delivering solutions to consumers.
www.reckittprofessional.com
Annual Revenues: $205.30 million
Employees: 1,600
Industry/ies: Chemicals & Chemical Industry; Personal Care/Hygiene
Legislative Issues: ALC; CSP; ENV; FOO; HCR; PHA

Chief Executive Officer   Tel: (973) 404-2600
KAPOOR, Rakesh   Fax: (973) 404-5700

Main Headquarters
Mailing: 399 Interpace Pkwy.   Tel: (973) 404-2600
P.O. Box 225   Fax: (973) 404-5700
Parsippany, NJ 07054   TF: (800) 333-3899

Corporate Foundations and Giving Programs
Reckitt Benckiser Foundation
399 Interpace Pkwy.
Parsippany, NJ 07054

Public Affairs and Related Activities Personnel

At Headquarters

FUNARI, Roberto   Tel: (973) 404-2600
Executive Vice President, Category Marketing   Fax: (973) 404-5700

HENNAH, Adrian   Tel: (973) 404-2600
Chief Financial Officer   Fax: (973) 404-5700

O'HAYER, Patty   Tel: (973) 404-2600
Global Head, External Relations and Affairs   Fax: (973) 404-5700
mediapr@rb.com

YATES, Deborah   Tel: (973) 404-2600
Senior Vice President, Human Resources   Fax: (973) 404-5700

ReconRobotics Inc.

The company develops, manufactures, sells and supports micro-robot systems.
www.reconrobotics.com
Industry/ies: Electricity & Electronics; Electronics; Energy/Electricity

President and Chief Executive Officer   Tel: (952) 935-5515
WILSON, Mary   Fax: (952) 935-5508

Main Headquarters
Mailing: 7620 W. 78th St.   Tel: (952) 935-5515
Edina, MN 55439   Fax: (952) 935-5508
  TF: (866) 398-1921

Public Affairs and Related Activities Personnel

At Headquarters

AYRE, Bob   Tel: (952) 935-5515
Law Enforcement Sales   Fax: (952) 935-5508
bob.ayre@reconrobotics.com

KLOBUCAR, Jack   Tel: (952) 935-5515
Vice President of Marketing and Media Contact   Fax: (952) 935-5508
Jack.Klobucar@ReconRobotics.com

Recreational Equipment Inc.

National retailer of outdoor apparel and recreational equipment.
www.rei.com
Employees: 6,000
Industry/ies: Sports/Leisure/Entertainment
Legislative Issues: ECN; ENG; ENV; NAT

Chairman of the Board   Tel: (253) 395-3780
HAMLIN, John   Fax: (253) 395-8160

President and Chief Executive Officer   Tel: (253) 395-3780
STRITZKE, Jerry   Fax: (253) 395-8160

Main Headquarters
Mailing: P.O. Box 1938   Tel: (253) 437-1100
Sumner, WA 98390-0800   Fax: (253) 395-8160
  TF: (800) 622-2236

Corporate Foundations and Giving Programs
The REI Foundation
Contact: Megan Behrbaum
P.O. Box 1938   Tel: (253) 395-3780
Sumner, WA 98390-0800   Fax: (253) 891-2523

Public Affairs and Related Activities Personnel

At Headquarters

ARTZ, Eric   Tel: (253) 395-3780

Executive Vice President, Chief Operating Officer and Treasurer	Fax:	(253) 395-8160
MEEKER, Jennifer	Tel:	(253) 437-1100
Senior Vice President, General Counsel and Corporate Secretary	Fax:	(253) 395-8160
ROWLEY, Craig	Tel:	(253) 437-1100
Vice President, Marketing	Fax:	(253) 395-8160
THOMPSON, Alex	Tel:	(253) 437-1100
Vice President, Communications and Public Affairs	Fax:	(253) 395-8160
WALKER, Catherine	Tel:	(253) 395-3780
Senior Vice President, General Counsel and Corporate Secretary	Fax:	(253) 891-2523
cwalker@rei.com		
WINBIGLER, Tracie	Tel:	(253) 437-1100
Senior Vice President, Chief Financial Officer	Fax:	(253) 395-8160

Recycled Energy Development, LLC

Developers of decentralized energy recycling projects.
www.recycled-energy.com
Annual Revenues: $2.70 million
Industry/ies: Environment And Conservation

Chairman of the Board	Tel:	(630) 590-6030
CASTEN, Thomas R.	Fax:	(630) 590-6037
President and Chief Executive Officer	Tel:	(630) 590-6030
CASTEN, Sean	Fax:	(630) 590-6037
Main Headquarters		
Mailing: 640 Quail Ridge Dr.	Tel:	(630) 590-6030
Westmont, IL 60559-6147	Fax:	(630) 590-6037

Public Affairs and Related Activities Personnel

At Headquarters

GOTTUNG, Eric	Tel:	(630) 590-6030
Senior Vice President, Business Development	Fax:	(630) 590-6037
KAREGIANES, Myra	Tel:	(630) 590-6030
General Counsel	Fax:	(630) 590-6037
SHADUR, Heather	Tel:	(312) 226-5100
Contact, Media Relations	Fax:	(630) 590-6037
heather@shadur.com		

Red Gold, Inc.

Grows and processes tomatoes into canned goods, pastes, sauces, and juices.
www.redgold.com
Annual Revenues: $750 million
Employees: 1,300
SIC: 2033; 2035; 3556; 5149
NAICS: 311421; 311941; 333294
Industry/ies: Food And Beverage Industry

President and Chief Executive Officer	Tel:	(765) 754-7527
RIECHART, Brian L.	Fax:	(765) 754-3230
Main Headquarters		
Mailing: 1500 Tomato Country Way	Tel:	(765) 557-5500
P.O. Box 83	Fax:	(765) 557-5501
Elwood, IN 46036	TF:	(866) 729-7187

Political Action Committees
Red Gold, Inc. PAC
FEC ID: C00390112
Contact: Robert Savage

P.O. Box 83	Tel:	(765) 754-7527
Elwood, IN 46036	Fax:	(765) 754-7527

 Contributions to Candidates: $9,500 (2015-2016)
 Democrats: $2,000; Republicans: $7,500

Public Affairs and Related Activities Personnel

At Headquarters

METZGER, Greg	Tel:	(765) 557-5500
Director, Marketing	Fax:	(765) 557-5501
REICHART, Selita	Tel:	(765) 557-5500
Senior Vice President	Fax:	(765) 557-5501
SAVAGE, Robert	Tel:	(765) 754-7527
Director, Risk Management and PAC Treasurer	Fax:	(765) 754-3230
bsavage@redgold.com		

At Other Offices

BONS, Pete	Tel:	(765) 754-7527
Vice President, Finance	Fax:	(765) 754-3230
120 E. Oak St.		
Orestes, IN 46063		
pbons@redgold.com		
INGLE, Tim	Tel:	(765) 754-7527
Vice President, Human Resources and Corporate Strategy	Fax:	(765) 754-3230
120 E. Oak St.		
Orestes, IN 46063		

tingle@redgold.com

Redpath Integrated Pathology, Inc.

A cancer molecular diagnostics company.
www.redpathip.com
Annual Revenues: $3.10 million
Employees: 100
Industry/ies: Medicine/Health Care/Mental Health

Chairman of the Board	Tel:	(412) 244-6100
MURPHY, Brian G.	Fax:	(412) 224-6425
Chief Executive Officer	Tel:	(412) 244-6100
SMITH, Jr., MD, Dennis M.	Fax:	(412) 224-6110
Main Headquarters		
Mailing: 2515 Liberty Ave.	Tel:	(412) 244-6100
Pittsburgh, PA 15222	Fax:	(412) 224-6110
	TF:	(800) 495-9885

Reebok International

Designer, marketer, and distributor of sports, fitness, and casual footwear, apparel, and equipment. In 2005, Reebok was acquired by Adidas AG and is now their subsidiary.
www.reebok.com
Annual Revenues: $794 million
Employees: 9,100
SIC: 3021
Industry/ies: Apparel/Textiles Industry
Legislative Issues: TAR; TRD

President and Chief Executive Officer	Tel:	(781) 401-5000
BECKER, Uli	Fax:	(781) 401-7402
Main Headquarters		
Mailing: 1895 J.W. Foster Blvd.	Tel:	(781) 401-5000
Canton, MA 02021	Fax:	(781) 401-7402
Washington Office		
Mailing: 1120 G St. NW	Tel:	(202) 783-3333
Suites 1020	Fax:	(202) 783-4422
Washington, DC 20005		

Political Action Committees
Reebok International Ltd. PAC
FEC ID: C00256313
Contact: Peter Friedmann
1120 G St. NW
Suite 1020 and 613
Washington, DC 20005

Corporate Foundations and Giving Programs

Reebok 4 Real Human Rights Student Advocate Program		
1895 J.W. Foster Blvd.	Tel:	(781) 401-5000
Canton, MA 02021	Fax:	(781) 401-5000
Reebok Employee Charitable program		
1895 J.W. Foster Blvd.	Tel:	(781) 401-5000
Canton, MA 02021	Fax:	(781) 401-5000
Reebok Foundation		
1895 J.W. Foster Blvd.		
Canton, MA 02021		
Reebok Recognition Program		
1895 J.W. Foster Blvd.	Tel:	(781) 401-5000
Canton, MA 02021	Fax:	(781) 401-5000

Public Affairs and Related Activities Personnel

At Headquarters

HOLMES, Bill	Tel:	(781) 401-5000
Senior Vice President, Human Resources Management	Fax:	(781) 401-7402
MARTIN, Yan	Tel:	(781) 401-5000
Vice President , Global Brand Communications	Fax:	(781) 401-7402
O'MEARA, John-Paul	Tel:	(781) 401-5000
Senior Vice President, Strategy	Fax:	(781) 401-7402
RUSCITO, Jessica	Tel:	(781) 401-5000
Director, United States Media and Digital Branding	Fax:	(781) 401-7402
SARRO, Daniel	Tel:	(781) 401-4443
Manager, Corporate Communications	Fax:	(781) 401-7402
daniel.sarro@reebok.com		
WALTER, Nellie	Tel:	(781) 401-5000
Director, Human Resources	Fax:	(781) 401-7402
WARREN, John	Tel:	(781) 401-5000
General Manager, Sports Licensed Division	Fax:	(781) 401-7402
WHITEHEAD, Mark	Tel:	(781) 401-5000
Senior Director, Global Digital Marketing	Fax:	(781) 401-7402

At Washington Office

FRIEDMANN, Peter	Tel:	(781) 401-5000
Director, International Trade Policy and Government Affairs and PAC Treasurer	Fax:	(202) 783-4422
OurManInDC@federalrelations.com		

Referentia Systems, Inc.

Provider of Command, Control, Communications, Computers, and Intelligence (C4I) Systems, Advanced Technology Solutions, and Information Technology & Services (IT&S).Referentia is an applied R&D company dedicated to providing proven high assurance and flexible solutions that meet the critical IT modernization needs of the federal government.
www.referentia.com
Annual Revenues: $6.10 million
Employees: 50
Industry/ies: Defense/Homeland Security; Government-Related

President and Chief Executive Officer	Tel:	(808) 840-8500
KANEMOTO, Nelson	Fax:	(808) 423-1960

Main Headquarters
Mailing:	155 Kapalulu Pl.	Tel:	(808) 840-8500
	Suite 200	Fax:	(808) 423-1960
	Honolulu, HI 96819	TF:	(800) 569-6255

Political Action Committees
Referentia Systems Incorporated PAC
FEC ID: C00408872
Contact: Jill Harper
550 Paiea St.
Suite 236
Honolulu, HI 96819

Corporate Foundations and Giving Programs
Referentia Systems Incorporated Contributions Program		
155 Kapalulu Pl.	Tel:	(808) 840-8500
Suite 200		
Honolulu, HI 96819		

Public Affairs and Related Activities Personnel

At Headquarters
SMITH, Naerilyn	Tel:	(808) 840-8500
Manager, Human Resources	Fax:	(808) 423-1960

At Other Offices
HARPER, Jill
PAC Treasurer
550 Paiea St., Suite 236
Honolulu, HI 96819

The Regence Group

An affiliation of Blue Cross and Blue Shield Plans in Oregon, Washington, Idaho and Utah.
www.regence.com
Annual Revenues: $261.10 billion
Employees: 7,000
Industry/ies: Medicine/Health Care/Mental Health
Legislative Issues: HCR; MMM

President and Chief Executive Officer	Tel:	(503) 225-5221
GANZ, Mark B.	Fax:	(503) 225-5274
Mark.Ganz@regence.com		

Main Headquarters
Mailing:	P.O. Box 1071	Tel:	(503) 225-5221
	Portland, OR 97207	Fax:	(503) 225-5274
		TF:	(800) 452-7278

Washington Office
Mailing:	330 Ninth St. SE	Tel:	(202) 544-1818
	Washington, DC 20003		

Corporate Foundations and Giving Programs
The Regence Foundation
Contact: Julia Sims
P.O. Box 1071
Portland, OR 97207

Public Affairs and Related Activities Personnel

At Headquarters
SIMS, Julia	Tel:	(503) 225-5336
Program Officer	Fax:	(503) 225-5274
jasims@regence.com		

At Washington Office
BANDOLI, Christopher	Tel:	(202) 544-1818
Regulatory and Legislative Analyst		

At Other Offices
DAUGHN, Jason A.	Tel:	(503) 225-6772
Vice President, Public Policy	Fax:	(503) 225-5274
200 S.W. Market St., MS E12C		
Portland, OR 97201		
Mail Stop E12C		

Regions Financial Corporation

A financial services company. Merged with Union Planters Corp. in 2004.
www.regions.com
Annual Revenues: $1.44 billion
Employees: 23,601

Ticker: NYSE: RF
SIC: 6021
Industry/ies: Banking/Finance/Investments
Legislative Issues: BAN; CSP; FIN; HOU; TAX

Chairman, President and Chief Executive Officer	Tel:	(205) 944-1300
HALL, Jr., O. B. Grayson	Fax:	(205) 326-5300

Main Headquarters
Mailing:	1900 Fifth Ave., North	Tel:	(205) 944-1300
	Birmingham, AL 35203	Fax:	(205) 326-5300
		TF:	(800) 734-4667

Washington Office
Mailing:	1015 15th St. NW	Tel:	(202) 737-4747
	Suite 920		
	Washington, DC 20005		

Political Action Committees
Regions Financial Corporation PAC		
FEC ID: C00432252		
Contact: Chris Scribner		
1015 15th St. NW	Tel:	(202) 737-4747
Suite 920		
Washington, DC 20005		

Contributions to Candidates: $127,000 (2015-2016)
Democrats: $40,000; Republicans: $87,000

Corporate Foundations and Giving Programs
Regions Financial Corporation Contributions Program		
1900 Fifth Ave., North	Tel:	(205) 944-1300
Birmingham, AL 35203		

Public Affairs and Related Activities Personnel

At Headquarters
DEIGHTON, Tim	Tel:	(205) 264-5277
Senior Vice President, Corporate Communications	Fax:	(205) 326-5300
tim.deighton@regions.com		
GALE, III, Fournier J. "Boots"	Tel:	(205) 944-1300
Senior Executive Vice President, General Counsel and Corporate Secretary	Fax:	(205) 326-5300
HERRON, C. Keith	Tel:	(205) 944-1300
Senior Executive Vice President, Strategic Planning and Execution	Fax:	(205) 326-5300
KEENAN, David R.	Tel:	(205) 944-1300
Senior Executive Vice President and Director, Human Resources	Fax:	(205) 326-5300
SMITH, Brian Keith	Tel:	(205) 944-1300
Contact, Government Relations	Fax:	(205) 326-5300
Registered Federal Lobbyist		
TURNER, Jr., David J.	Tel:	(205) 944-1300
Senior Executive Vice President, Chief Financial Officer	Fax:	(205) 326-5300
UNDERWOOD, M. List	Tel:	(205) 801-0265
Executive Vice President, Investor Relations	Fax:	(205) 326-5300
list.underwood@regions.com		

At Washington Office
SCRIBNER, Chris	Tel:	(202) 737-4747
Senior Vice President, Public Policy		
Registered Federal Lobbyist		

Regis Corporation

Owner, operator, and franchiser of hair and retail product salons in the United States, Canada, Puerto Rico, the United Kingdom, France, Italy, Spain, Belgium, Switzerland and Poland.
www.regiscorp.com
Annual Revenues: $1.81 billion
Employees: 46,000
Ticker: NYSE: RGS
SIC: 7200
Industry/ies: Education; Personal Care/Hygiene

Chief Executive Officer	Tel:	(952) 947-7777
HANRAHAN, Daniel J.	Fax:	(952) 947-7600

Main Headquarters
Mailing:	7201 Metro Blvd.	Tel:	(952) 947-7777
	Minneapolis, MN 55439	Fax:	(952) 947-7600

Corporate Foundations and Giving Programs
The Regis Foundation for Breast Cancer Research		
7201 Metro Blvd.	Tel:	(952) 947-7777
Minneapolis, MN 55439	Fax:	(952) 947-7600

Public Affairs and Related Activities Personnel

At Headquarters
BAKKEN, Eric A.	Tel:	(952) 947-7777
Executive Vice President, Chief Administrative Officer and General Counsel	Fax:	(952) 947-7600
EVANS, Susan	Tel:	(612) 338-6999

Contact, Media Relations	Fax:	(952) 947-7600
susan@evanslarson.com		
FOSLAND, Mark	Tel:	(952) 806-1707
Senior Vice President, Finance and Investor Relations	Fax:	(952) 947-7600
LAIN, Jim	Tel:	(952) 947-7777
Executive Vice President, Chief Operating Officer	Fax:	(952) 947-7600
PASSE, Heather	Tel:	(952) 947-7777
Senior Vice President, Chief Marketing Officer	Fax:	(952) 947-7600
SPIEGEL, Steven M.	Tel:	(952) 947-7777
Executive Vice President, Chief Financial Officer	Fax:	(952) 947-7600
THIEDE, Carmen	Tel:	(952) 947-7777
Senior Vice President, Chief Human Resources Officer	Fax:	(952) 947-7600

Regscan Inc.

Deals with electronic regulatory publishing.
www.regscan.com
Employees: 100
Industry/ies: Computer/Technology

President and Chief Executive Officer — Tel: (570) 548-2811
ERTEL, Ned — Fax: (570) 323-8082
nertel@regscan.com

Main Headquarters
Mailing:	800 W. Fourth St.	Tel:	(570) 323-1010
	Suite 202	Fax:	(570) 323-8082
	Williamsport, PA 17701	TF:	(800) 734-7226

Public Affairs and Related Activities Personnel

At Headquarters

LANG, Dr. Robert	Tel:	(570) 323-1010
Vice President, Engineering and Marketing	Fax:	(570) 323-8082
rland@regscan.com		
RUCKNO, Heidi	Tel:	(570) 323-1010
Specialist, Marketing Communications	Fax:	(570) 323-8082
hruckno@regscan.com		
VILLEGAS-SNEVELY, Elsa	Tel:	(703) 435-5457
Senior Corporate Account Executive	Fax:	(570) 323-8082
evillegas@regscan.com		

RehabCare Group

Provides physical rehabilitation services including physical, occupational and speech-language therapies, to hospitals, nursing homes and other long-term care facilities. Merged with Triumph HealthCare in November 2009.
www.rehabcare.com
Annual Revenues: $1.33 billion
Employees: 16,000
Ticker: NYSE: RHB
SIC: 8060
Industry/ies: Medicine/Health Care/Mental Health
Legislative Issues: MMM

Chairman of the Board — Tel: (502) 596-7640
WIDMER, Kurt

Chief Executive Officer — Tel: (502) 596-7640
MICHAELSON, Terry

Main Headquarters
Mailing:	680 S. Fourth St.	Tel:	(502) 596-7640
	Louisville, KY 40202	TF:	(800) 545-0749

Public Affairs and Related Activities Personnel

At Headquarters

KELLER, Phil	Tel:	(502) 596-7640
Senior Vice President, Finance		
MACK, Glenda	Tel:	(502) 596-7640
Divisional Vice President, Clinical Operations		
MANN, Marty	Tel:	(502) 596-7640
Senior Vice President, Business Development		
ROUSSEAU, Jon	Tel:	(502) 596-7640
Executive Vice President and President		

REI

See listing on page 673 under Recreational Equipment Inc.

Reichhold, Inc.

A manufacturer of high-performance coating and composite resins. A subsidiary of Dainippon Ink & Chemicals of Japan. Formerly Reichhold Chemicals, Inc.
www.reichhold.com
Annual Revenues: $70.50 million
Employees: 600
SIC: 2821; 2851; 2891; 3479
NAICS: 325211; 32551; 32552; 332812
Industry/ies: Chemicals & Chemical Industry

Chairman of the Board, President and Chief Executive Officer — Tel: (919) 990-7500
GAITHER, John S. — Fax: (919) 990-7749

Main Headquarters
Mailing:	1035 Swabia Ct.	Tel:	(919) 990-7500
	Durham, NC 27703	Fax:	(919) 990-7749

Public Affairs and Related Activities Personnel

At Headquarters

GRACE, Joan	Tel:	(919) 990-7876
Contact, Media Relations	Fax:	(919) 990-7749
WILLIS, Roger	Tel:	(919) 990-7500
Chief Financial Officer	Fax:	(919) 990-7749

Reilly Industries

www.reillyind.com
Annual Revenues: $152 million
Employees: 750
Industry/ies: Chemicals & Chemical Industry

Main Headquarters
Mailing:	300 N. Meridian St.	Tel:	(317) 536-7228
	Suite 1500		
	Indianapolis, IN 46204		

Public Affairs and Related Activities Personnel

At Headquarters

JONES, Glyn	Tel:	(317) 536-7228
Administration		

Reinsurance Association of America

Incorporated in the District of Columbia as the National Association of Property and Casualty Reinsurers. Became the Reinsurance Association of America in 1970. RAA is a trade association of property and casualty reinsurers and is committed to promote a regulatory environment that ensures the industry remains globally competitive and financially robust, unhindered by conflicting state and federal regulation.
www.reinsurance.org
Employees: 23
Industry/ies: Banking/Finance/Investments; Insurance Industry; Investments/Securities Industry
Legislative Issues: FIN; INS; TAX

Main Headquarters
Mailing:	1445 New York Ave. NW	Tel:	(202) 638-3690
	Seventh Floor	Fax:	(202) 638-0936
	Washington, DC 20005		

Political Action Committees
Reinsurance Association of America Political Action Committee
FEC ID: C00256453
Contact: Mary Z. Seidel
1445 New York Ave. NW		
Seventh Floor	Tel:	(202) 638-3690
Washington, DC 20005	Fax:	(202) 638-0936

   Contributions to Candidates: $12,500 (2015-2016)
   Democrats: $2,000; Republicans: $10,500

Public Affairs and Related Activities Personnel

At Headquarters

BURKE, Dennis C.	Tel:	(202) 783-8325
Vice President, State Relations	Fax:	(202) 638-0936
burke@reinsurance.org		
CARROLL, Barbara	Tel:	(202) 638-3690
Director, Membership and Communications and Contact,	Fax:	(202) 638-0936
Media Relations		
COHEN, Marsha A.	Tel:	(202) 783-8329
Senior Vice President and Director, Education	Fax:	(202) 638-0936
GREEN, Geneva P.	Tel:	(202) 638-3690
Coordinator, Financial Affairs Reporting and Federal Affairs	Fax:	(202) 638-0936
green@reinsurance.org		
LAWS, Tracey W.	Tel:	(202) 783-8315
Senior Vice President and General Counsel	Fax:	(202) 638-0936
laws@reinsurance.org		
MORELL, Karalee C.	Tel:	(202) 638-3690
Vice President and Assistant General Counsel	Fax:	(202) 638-0936
morell@ reinsurance.org		
MORRISS, Robyn L.	Tel:	(202) 783-8321
Senior Vice President, Membership Services and Business	Fax:	(202) 638-0936
Operations		
MWOMBELA, Ann-Marie	Tel:	(202) 638-3690
Projects Manager	Fax:	(202) 638-0936
NUTTER, Franklin W.	Tel:	(202) 638-3690
President	Fax:	(202) 638-0936
SHUE, J. Christopher	Tel:	(202) 783-8317
Vice President and Director, Information Services	Fax:	(202) 638-0936
shue@reinsurance.org		

SIEVERLING, Joseph B.
Senior Vice President and Director, Financial Services
sieverling@reinsurance.org
Tel: (202) 783-8312
Fax: (202) 638-0936

TURNER, Sonya
Office Services Manager & HR Generalist
Tel: (202) 638-3690
Fax: (202) 638-0936

WILLIAMSON, W. Scott
Vice President, Financial Analysis
williamson@reinsurance.org
Tel: (202) 783-8311
Fax: (202) 638-0936

WULF, Matthew T.
Vice President, State Relations and Assistant General Counsel
wulf@reinsurance.org
Tel: (202) 783-8381
Fax: (202) 638-0936

At Other Offices

HUGHES, Patrick J.
Associate General Counsel & Assistant Secretary
P.O. Box 5241, 555 College Rd. East
Princeton, NJ 08543
phughes@amre.com
Tel: (609) 243-4642

Reinsurance Group of America, Inc.

An insurance provider for insurance companies.
www.rgare.com
Annual Revenues: $10.77 billion
Employees: 2,070
Ticker: NYSE: RZA
SIC: 6321
Industry/ies: Insurance Industry
Legislative Issues: FIN; INS; TAX; TRD

Chairman of the Board
EASON, J. Cliff
Tel: (636) 736-5445
Fax: (636) 736-7100

President and Chief Executive Officer
WOODRING, FSA, A. Greig
Tel: (636) 736-5445
Fax: (636) 736-7100

Main Headquarters
Mailing: 16600 Swingley Ridge Rd.
Chesterfield, MO 63017-1706
Tel: (636) 736-5445

Political Action Committees
RGA Reinsurance Company Federal PAC
FEC ID: C00461129
Contact: Kent Zimmerman
1370 Timberlake Manor Pkwy.
Chesterfield, MO 63017

Contributions to Candidates: $163,500 (2015-2016)
Democrats: $57,000; Republicans: $102,000; Other: $4,500

Principal Recipients

SENATE
BLUNT, ROY (REP-MO)

HOUSE
CLEAVER, EMANUEL II (DEM-MO)
LUETKEMEYER, W BLAINE (REP-MO)

Public Affairs and Related Activities Personnel

At Headquarters

BURNS, Gay
Senior Vice President and Chief Human Resources Officer
Tel: (636) 736-5445

HUTTON, William L.
Executive Vice President, General Counsel and Secretary
Tel: (636) 736-5445

MUSEN, Robert M.
Executive Vice President and Chief of Staff
Tel: (636) 736-5445

WELSH, Kimberly
Assistant General Counsel
Tel: (636) 736-5445

ZIMMERMAN, Kent
PAC Treasurer
Tel: (636) 736-5445

At Other Offices

HAYDEN, John
Senior Vice President, Controller and Investor Relations
1370 Timberlake Manor Pkwy.
Chesterfield, MO 63017-6039
Tel: (636) 300-8828
Fax: (636) 736-7100

LAY, Jack B.
Senior Executive Vice President and Chief Financial Officer
1370 Timberlake Manor Pkwy.
Chesterfield, MO 63017-6039
Tel: (636) 736-7000
Fax: (636) 736-7100

SMITH, Sally
Vice President, Corporate Communications
1370 Timberlake Manor Pkwy.
Chesterfield, MO 63017-6039
ssmith@rgare.com
Tel: (636) 736-8167
Fax: (636) 736-7100

Related Company

Developer, manager and financier of premier real estate properties.
www.related.com

Employees: 300
Industry/ies: Economics And Economic Development; Real Estate

Chairman and Founder
ROSS, Stephen M.
sross@related.com
Tel: (212) 421-5333
Fax: (212) 801-1003

Chief Executive Officer
BLAU, Jeff T.
Tel: (212) 421-5333
Fax: (212) 801-1003

President
BEAL, Jr., Bruce A.
Tel: (212) 421-5333
Fax: (212) 801-1003

Main Headquarters
Mailing: 60 Columbus Cir.
19th Floor
New York City, NY 10023
Tel: (212) 421-5333
Fax: (212) 801-1003

Public Affairs and Related Activities Personnel

At Headquarters

BRENNER, Michael J.
Executive Vice President and Chief Financial Officer
Tel: (212) 421-5333
Fax: (212) 801-1003

ROSE, Joanna
Senior Vice President, Corporate Communications and Public Affairs
joanna.rose@related.com
Tel: (212) 801-3902
Fax: (212) 801-1003

WONG, Kenneth P.
Chief Operating Officer and Director, International Development
Tel: (212) 421-5333
Fax: (212) 801-1003

Reliance Steel & Aluminum Company

A metals service center company.
www.rsac.com
Annual Revenues: $8.9 billion
Employees: 14,000
Ticker: NYSE: RS
SIC: 5051
Industry/ies: Metals

Chairman of the Board
HANNAH, David H.
dhannah@rsac.com
Tel: (213) 687-7700
Fax: (213) 687-8792

President and Chief Executive Officer
MOLLINS, Gregg J.
Tel: (213) 687-7700
Fax: (213) 687-8792

Main Headquarters
Mailing: 350 S. Grand Ave.
Suite 5100
Los Angeles, CA 90071
Tel: (213) 687-7700
Fax: (213) 687-8792

Corporate Foundations and Giving Programs

Reliance Steel & Aluminum Company Contributions Program
350 S. Grand Ave.
Suite 5100
Los Angeles, CA 90071
Tel: (213) 687-7700
Fax: (213) 687-8792

Public Affairs and Related Activities Personnel

At Headquarters

FEAZLE, Kim P.
Contact, Investor Relations
kfeazle@rsac.com
Tel: (713) 610-9937
Fax: (213) 576-2428

HOFFMAN, James D
Executive Vice President and Chief Operating Officer
Tel: (213) 687-7700
Fax: (213) 687-8792

KOCH, Stephen P
Senior Vice President, Operations
Tel: (213) 687-7700
Fax: (213) 687-8792

LEWIS, Karla R.
Executive Vice President and Chief Financial Officer
klewis@rsac.com
Tel: (213) 687-7700
Fax: (213) 687-8792

MIYAMOTO, Brenda
Vice President, Corporate Initiatives
investor@rsac.com
Tel: (213) 687-7700
Fax: (213) 687-8792

PREBOLA, Donald
Vice President, Human Resources
Tel: (213) 687-7700
Fax: (213) 687-8792

SMITH, II, William A.
Vice President, General Counsel and Corporate Secretary
Tel: (213) 687-7700
Fax: (213) 687-8792

Relyance Bank

Provides traditional banking products, online banking, telephone banking, insurance services and title company services.
www.relybank.com
Annual Revenues: $19.78 million
Employees: 100
Industry/ies: Banking/Finance/Investments

President and Chief Executive Officer
MORGAN, Chuck
Tel: (870) 535-7222
Fax: (870) 540-1212

Main Headquarters
Mailing: 912 S. Poplar St.
Tel: (870) 535-7222

Pine Bluff, AR 71601

Fax: (870) 540-1212
TF: (800) 420-7262

Political Action Committees
Relyance Bank Political Action Committee - Federal
FEC ID: C00278754
Contact: Anita Shafer-Durman
912 S. Poplar St.
P.O. Box 7878
Pine Bluff, AR 71611

   Contributions to Candidates: $6,250 (2015-2016)
   Republicans: $6,250

Public Affairs and Related Activities Personnel

At Headquarters

GARNER, Greg
Senior Vice President, Marketing and Human Resources

Tel: (870) 535-7222
Fax: (870) 540-1212

SHAFER-DURMAN, Anita
Senior Vice President, Controller and PAC Treasurer

Tel: (870) 535-7222
Fax: (870) 540-1212

The Remi Group

Medical equipment manufacturer and maintenance.
www.theremigroup.com
Annual Revenues: $7.00 million
Employees: 60
Industry/ies: Machinery/Equipment; Medicine/Health Care/Mental Health

Founder and Chief Executive Officer
SCHUSTER, Dan

Tel: (888) 451-8916
Fax: (704) 887-2915

President
HOWISON, Brent

Tel: (704) 602-0818
Fax: (704) 887-2915

Main Headquarters
Mailing: 11325 N. Community House Rd.
      Suite 300
      Charlotte, NC 28277

Tel: (704) 602-0818
Fax: (704) 887-2915
TF: (888) 451-8916

Corporate Foundations and Giving Programs
Remi Cares
11325 N. Community House Rd.
Suite 300
Charlotte, NC 28277

Public Affairs and Related Activities Personnel

At Headquarters

BARCLIFT, Laura
Manager, Strategic Accounts

Tel: (704) 602-0818
Fax: (704) 887-2915

FLEISCHACKER, Robert
Vice President, General Counsel and Chief Compliance Officer

Tel: (888) 451-8916
Fax: (704) 887-2915

LANDON, Brian
Chief Financial Officer

Tel: (888) 451-8916
Fax: (704) 887-2915

MCCONICO, Trina
Manager, Inside Sales

Tel: (888) 451-8916
Fax: (704) 887-2915

STEUBER, Chris
Manager, Sales
csteuber@theremigroup.com

Tel: (704) 602-0818
Fax: (704) 887-2915

Remy International, Inc.

Formerly Delco Remy International. A manufacturing holding company. A subsidiary of Citicorp Venture Capital Ltd., a Citigroup company.
www.remyinc.com
Annual Revenues: $1.14 billion
Employees: 6,600
SIC: 3714
Industry/ies: Automotive Industry; Engineering/Mathematics; Machinery/Equipment; Transportation

President and Chief Executive Officer
PITTAS, Jay

Tel: (765) 778-6499
Fax: (765) 778-6404

Main Headquarters
Mailing: 600 Corporation Dr.
      Pendleton, IN 46064

Tel: (765) 778-6499
Fax: (765) 778-6404
TF: (800) 372-3555

Public Affairs and Related Activities Personnel

At Headquarters

BITZER, Barbara
Vice President, Global Controller

Tel: (765) 778-6499
Fax: (765) 778-6404

KRALL, David
Senior Vice President and General Counsel

Tel: (765) 778-6499
Fax: (765) 778-6404

MCFEELY, Mark
Senior Vice President and Chief Operations Officer

Tel: (765) 778-6499
Fax: (765) 778-6404

PALLAGI, Shawn
Senior Vice President and Chief Human Resources Officer

Tel: (765) 778-6499
Fax: (765) 778-6404

POLEN, Victor

Tel: (765) 778-6499

Senior Vice President and Chief Operations Officer

Fax: (765) 778-6404

VANDENBERGH, Al
Senior Vice President and Chief Financial Officer

Tel: (765) 778-6499
Fax: (765) 778-6404

WEBER, John H.
Board Director

Tel: (765) 778-6499
Fax: (765) 778-6404

WESTERMEYER, Guy
Media Contact

Tel: (317) 685-9761
Fax: (765) 778-6404

WILLIAMS, Quinn
General Counsel

Tel: (765) 778-6499
Fax: (765) 778-6404

Renaissance Learning

Assessment technology for pre-K-12 schools.
www.renlearn.com
Annual Revenues: $130.09 million
Employees: 900
Ticker: NASDAQ: RLRN
SIC: 7372
Industry/ies: Education
Legislative Issues: EDU

Chief Executive Officer
LYNCH, Jr., John J.

Tel: (715) 424-3636
Fax: (715) 424-4242

Main Headquarters
Mailing: P.O. Box 8036
      Wisconsin Rapids, WI 54495-8036

Tel: (715) 424-3636
Fax: (715) 424-4242
TF: (800) 338-4204

Public Affairs and Related Activities Personnel

At Headquarters

BORKON, Laurie
Vice President, Educational Partnerships
laurie.borkon@renlearn.com

Tel: (715) 424-3636
Fax: (715) 424-4242

CORRIGALL, John
Senior Vice President, Human Resources and Administration

Tel: (715) 424-3636
Fax: (715) 424-4242

MINCH, Mary T.
Executive Vice President, Finance and Chief Financial Officer

Tel: (715) 424-3636
Fax: (715) 424-4242

MITCHELL, Kim
Chief People Officer

Tel: (715) 424-3636
Fax: (715) 424-4242

MYERS, D. Andrew
Chief Marketing Officer

Tel: (715) 424-3636
Fax: (715) 424-4242

O'GORMAN, Paula
Senior Vice President, Government Affairs

Tel: (715) 424-3636
Fax: (715) 424-4242

PETERSEN, Mark W.
Senior Vice President, Strategy and Business Development

Tel: (715) 424-3636
Fax: (715) 424-4242

POSNY, Dr. Alexa
Senior Vice President, State and Federal Programs

Tel: (715) 424-3636
Fax: (715) 424-4242

RADEMAN, Carolyn
Contact, Media Relations
pr@renlearn.com

Tel: (877) 988-8048
Fax: (715) 424-4242

WALKER, Jeff
Vice President, Marketing
pr@renlearn.com

Tel: (715) 424-3636
Fax: (715) 424-4242

Renewable Energy Group, Inc.

A biodiesel plant and biodiesel processor.
www.regi.com
Annual Revenues: $1.46 billion
Employees: 597
Ticker: NASDAQ: REGI
SIC: 2860
Industry/ies: Energy/Electricity
Legislative Issues: AGR; CHM; ENG; ENV; FUE; TAX; TRD

Chairman of the Board
STROBURG , Jeffrey

Tel: (515) 239-8000
Fax: (515) 239-8009

President and Chief Executive Officer
OH, Daniel

Tel: (515) 239-8000
Fax: (515) 239-8009

Main Headquarters
Mailing: 416 S. Bell St.
      P.O. Box 888
      Ames, IA 50010

Tel: (515) 239-8000
Fax: (515) 239-8009
TF: (888) 734-8686

Political Action Committees
Renewable Energy Group, Inc. PAC (REG PAC)
FEC ID: C00536466
Contact: Anthony Hulen
416 S. Bell Ave.
P.O. Box 888
Ames, 50010

   Contributions to Candidates: $13,500 (2015-2016)
   Democrats: $3,000; Republicans: $10,500

Public Affairs and Related Activities Personnel

At Headquarters

BOWEN, Eric
Vice President, Corporate Business Development and Legal Affairs
Tel: (515) 239-8000
Fax: (515) 239-8009

HACKETT, Jonathan W.
Director, Procurement and Feedstock Development
Registered Federal Lobbyist
Tel: (515) 386-3158
Fax: (515) 239-8009

HAER, Gary
Vice President, Sales and Marketing
Tel: (515) 239-8000
Fax: (515) 239-8009

HULEN, Anthony
Executive Director, Corporate Affairs & PAC Treasurer
Registered Federal Lobbyist
Tel: (515) 386-3158
Fax: (515) 239-8009

MERRILL , Natalie
Chief of Staff and Vice President and Corporate Secretary
Tel: (515) 239-8000
Fax: (515) 239-8009

STONE, Chad
Chief Financial Officer
Tel: (515) 239-8000
Fax: (515) 239-8009

TAYLOR, Sara
Deputy Assistant
Registered Federal Lobbyist
Tel: (515) 386-3158
Fax: (515) 239-8009

Renewable Energy Systems Americas, Inc.

Develops, constructs and owns wind projects. Subsidiary of Renewable Energy Systems Ltd, based in London, United Kingdom.
www.res-americas.com
Industry/ies: Energy/Electricity

Chief Executive Officer
DAVIS, Glen
Tel: (303) 439-4200
Fax: (303) 439-4299

Main Headquarters
Mailing: 11101 W. 120th Ave.
Suite 400
Broomfield, CO 80021
Tel: (303) 439-4200
Fax: (303) 439-4299

Political Action Committees
Renewable Energy Systems Americas Inc. PAC (AKA RESPAC)
FEC ID: C00434142
Contact: Lori Ann Ebbesen
11101 W. 120th Ave.
Suite 400
Broomfield, CO 80021
Tel: (303) 439-4200
Fax: (303) 439-4200

> **Contributions to Candidates:** $14,400 (2015-2016)
> Democrats: $10,400; Republicans: $4,000

Corporate Foundations and Giving Programs
Renewable Energy Systems Americas, Inc. Contributions Program
11101 W. 120th Ave.
Suite 400
Broomfield, CO 80021

Public Affairs and Related Activities Personnel

At Headquarters

EBBESEN, Lori Ann
PAC Treasurer
Tel: (303) 439-4200
Fax: (303) 439-4299

EMMONS , Marcia
General Counsel
Tel: (303) 439-4200
Fax: (303) 439-4299

FOLKERTS, Raheleh
Manager, Marketing and Communications
raheleh.folkerts@res-americas.com
Tel: (303) 439-4200
Fax: (303) 439-4299

FOWLER, Andrew
Chief Operating Officer
Tel: (303) 439-4200
Fax: (303) 439-4299

MORGAN, Rob
Executive Vice President, Business Development and Chief Strategy Officer
Tel: (303) 439-4200
Fax: (303) 439-4299

NIEB, Doug
Vice President, Human Resources
doug.nieb@res-americas.com
Tel: (303) 439-4200
Fax: (303) 439-4299

WALKER , Paul
Chief Financial Officer
Tel: (303) 439-4200
Fax: (303) 439-4299

Renewable Funding, Inc.

Finances renewable energy and energy efficiency installations for property owners.
www.renewfund.com
Industry/ies: Energy; Energy/Electricity

Chairman of the Board
PORTIS, Stephen Compagni
Tel: (510) 451-7900
Fax: (510) 451-7904

President and Chief Executive Officer
DEVRIES, Cisco
Tel: (510) 451-7900
Fax: (510) 451-7904

Main Headquarters
Mailing: 500 12th St.
Suite 300
Oakland, CA 94607
Tel: (510) 451-7900
Fax: (510) 451-7904

Public Affairs and Related Activities Personnel

At Headquarters

BHARADHWAJ, Gannesh
President
Tel: (510) 451-7900
Fax: (510) 451-7904

FRUSHA, Mimi
Chief Operating Officer
Tel: (510) 451-7900
Fax: (510) 451-7904

KARGER, Joanna
Chief Financial Officer
Tel: (510) 451-7900
Fax: (510) 451-7904

STATON, Cliff
Executive Vice President
cliff@renewfund.com
Tel: (510) 451-7900
Fax: (510) 451-7904

RenRe North America Holdings Inc.

An insurance provider. A subsidiary of RenaissanceRe.
www.renre.com
Industry/ies: Insurance Industry
Legislative Issues: DIS; HOU; INS; RES; TAX

President and Chief Executive Officer
O'DONNELL, Kevin J.
Tel: (301) 351-4400

Main Headquarters
Mailing: 805 15th St. NW
Suite 650
Washington, DC 20005
Tel: (301) 351-4400

Public Affairs and Related Activities Personnel

At Headquarters

COHEN, Michael
Vice President, Governmnent Affairs
Registered Federal Lobbyist
Tel: (301) 351-4400

KELLY, Jeffery D.
Executive Vice President and Chief Financial Officer
Tel: (301) 351-4400

PAI, Rohan
Director, Investor Relations
Tel: (301) 351-4400

WEINSTEIN , Stephen H.
Senior Vice President, Chief Compliance Officer, General Counsel and Secretary
Tel: (301) 351-4400

Rent-a-Center, Inc.

A chain of rent to own stores featuring furniture, appliances, and electronics.
www.rentacenter.com
Annual Revenues: $3.21 billion
Employees: 22,200
Ticker: NASDAQ: RCII
SIC: 7359
Industry/ies: Electricity & Electronics; Electronics; Energy/Electricity; Furniture/ Home Furnishings
Legislative Issues: BAN

Chairman of the Board
SPEESE, Mark E.
Tel: (972) 801-1100
Fax: (866) 260-1424

Chief Executive Officer
DAVIS, Robert D.
Tel: (972) 801-1100
Fax: (866) 260-1424

Main Headquarters
Mailing: 5501 Headquarters Dr.
Plano, TX 70524
Tel: (972) 801-1100
Fax: (866) 260-1424
TF: (800) 422-8186

Political Action Committees
Rent-A-Center, Inc. Good Government PAC
FEC ID: C00410324
Contact: Dwight Dumler
5501 Headquarters Dr.
Plano, TX 75024

> **Contributions to Candidates:** $4,359,215 (2015-2016)
> Democrats: $18,500; Republicans: $38,700; Other: $4,302,015
>
> **Principal Recipients**
> **HOUSE**
> HENSARLING, JEB HON. (REP-TX)

Corporate Foundations and Giving Programs

Rent-a-Center Contributions Program
5501 Headquarters Dr.
Plano, TX 75024
Tel: (972) 801-1100
Fax: (972) 801-1100

Public Affairs and Related Activities Personnel

At Headquarters

CARPENTER, David E.
Vice President, Investor Relations
david.carpenter@rentacenter.com
Tel: (972) 801-1214
Fax: (866) 260-1424

CONSTANT, Guy J.
Executive Vice President, Finance, Chief Financial Officer and Treasurer
Tel: (972) 801-1100
Fax: (866) 260-1424

DIAZ, Jody
Senior Vice President, Human Resources, Chief People Officer
Tel: (972) 801-1214
Fax: (866) 260-1424

DOMINICIS, Xavier
Tel: (972) 801-1100

Vice President, Public and Community Affairs	Fax:	(866) 260-1424
Xavier.Dominicis@Rentacenter.com		
DUMLER, Dwight	Tel:	(972) 801-1100
Senior Vice President , Assistant General	Fax:	(866) 260-1424
Counsel ,Regulatory Affairs and PAC Treasurer		
Mail Stop Floor Three		
FADEL, Mitchell E.	Tel:	(972) 801-1100
President and Chief Operating Officer	Fax:	(866) 260-1424
GOIN, Walter R.	Tel:	(972) 801-1214
Vice President , International Human Resources and FSC	Fax:	(866) 260-1424
GUZIEC, Douglas A.	Tel:	(972) 801-1214
Senior Vice President, Strategy and Business Development	Fax:	(866) 260-1424
and Chief Strategy Officer		
HERMAN, Fred E.	Tel:	(972) 801-1100
Executive Vice President, Accounting and Global Controller	Fax:	(866) 260-1424
KORST, Christopher A.	Tel:	(972) 801-1100
Executive Vice President, Chief Administrative Officer	Fax:	(866) 260-1424
MUSSAT, Joel M.	Tel:	(972) 801-1100
Executive Vice President, Emerging Businesses and Strategic	Fax:	(866) 260-1424
Planning		
WOLVERTON, Dawn M.	Tel:	(972) 801-1100
Vice President, Associate General Counsel and Assistant	Fax:	(866) 260-1424
Secretary		

RentPath Inc.

Formerly Primedia Inc . RentPath is a digital media company, builds upon its success and long-standing heritage in the real estate industry to empower people nationwide to find apartments, houses for rent and new homes for sale.
rentpath.com
Employees: 900
Ticker: NYSE: PRM
SIC: 2721
Industry/ies: Advertising And Marketing

President and Chief Executive Officer   Tel: (678) 421-3000
STUBBS, Charles

Main Headquarters
Mailing: 3585 Engineering Dr.   Tel: (678) 421-3000
            Suite 100   TF: (800) 216-1423
            Norcross, GA 30092

Public Affairs and Related Activities Personnel

At Headquarters

ASHER, Scott	Tel:	(678) 421-3000
Vice President, Sales Operations		
BERGERON, Kelly	Tel:	(678) 421-3000
Chief Human Resources Officer		
PAYNE, Kim	Tel:	(678) 421-3000
Senior Vice President and Chief Financial Officer		
kim.payne@primedia.com		
SILVA, Kate	Tel:	(678) 421-3000
Manager, Marketing and Communications		
STARR, Marlon	Tel:	(678) 421-3000
Senior Vice President, General Counsel and Corporate		
Secretary		
STERNOT, Rob	Tel:	(678) 421-3000
Vice President, Corporate Development and Strategy		

At Other Offices

ANDERSON, Duff   Tel: (678) 421-3800
Contact, Investor Relations
400 S. River Rd., Suite 300
New Hope, PA 18938

Replacements Ltd.

Selection of dinnerware, including china, stoneware, crystal, glassware, silver, stainless, and collectibles.
www.replacements.com
Annual Revenues: $80.74 million
Employees: 600
Industry/ies: Furniture/Home Furnishings

President and Chief Executive Officer   Tel: (336) 697-3000
PAGE, Bob   Fax: (336) 697-3100

Main Headquarters
Mailing: P.O. Box 26029   Tel: (336) 697-3000
            Greensboro, NC 27420-6029   Fax: (336) 697-3100
                                        TF: (800) 737-5223

Political Action Committees
Replacements Ltd. PAC
FEC ID: C00427849
Contact: Gary M. Palmer
1089 Knox Rd.   Tel: (336) 697-3000
P.O. Box 26029   Fax: (336) 697-3100

Greensboro, NC 27420
  Contributions to Candidates: $6 (2015-2016)
    Democrats: $6

Public Affairs and Related Activities Personnel

At Headquarters

CONKLIN, Lisa	Tel:	(336) 697-3000
Manager, Public Relations	Fax:	(336) 697-3100
lisa.conklin@replacements.com		
PALMER, Gary M.	Tel:	(336) 697-3000
PAC Treasurer	Fax:	(336) 697-3100
SMITH, Kelly M.	Tel:	(336) 697-3000
Chief Financial Officer	Fax:	(336) 697-3100

Replidyne

See listing on page 163 under Cardiovascular Systems Inc. (CSI)

REPSOL YPF, S.A.

An Oil and gas company.
www.repsol.com
Industry/ies: Fuels See Coal, Gas, Oil, Petroleum; Gas; Natural Resources
Legislative Issues: ENG; FOR

Main Headquarters
Mailing: 2001 Timberloch Pl.   Tel: (281) 297-1000
            Suite 3000
            The Woodlands, TX 77380

Republic Services, Inc.

Specializes in solid waste management. In 2008, merged with Allied Waste Industries, Inc. It is one of the largest waste and recycling companies in the United States.
www.republicservices.com
Annual Revenues: $9.19 billion
Employees: 33,000
Ticker: NYSE: RSG
SIC: 4953
Industry/ies: Environment And Conservation; Pollution And Waste
Legislative Issues: ENG; LBR; TAX; WAS

Chairman of the Board   Tel: (480) 627-2700
RODRIGUEZ , Ramon A.   Fax: (480) 627-7150

President and Chief Executive Officer   Tel: (480) 627-2700
SLAGER, Donald W.   Fax: (480) 627-7150

Main Headquarters
Mailing: 18500 N. Allied Way   Tel: (480) 627-2700
            Phoenix, AZ 85054   Fax: (480) 627-7150

Political Action Committees
Republic Services Inc. Employees for Better Government PAC
FEC ID: C00428391
Contact: Russ Knocke
18500 N. Allied Way
Phoenix, AZ 85054

  Contributions to Candidates: $8,650 (2015-2016)
    Democrats: $3,650; Republicans: $5,000

Corporate Foundations and Giving Programs
Republic Services Employee Relief Fund
18500 N. Allied Way   Tel: (480) 627-2717
Phoenix, AZ 85054

Public Affairs and Related Activities Personnel

At Headquarters

ARK , Jon Vander	Tel:	(480) 627-2700
Executive Vice President, Operations	Fax:	(480) 627-7150
BALES, Brian A.	Tel:	(480) 627-2700
Executive Vice President and Chief Development Officer	Fax:	(480) 627-7150
BROSSART, Darcie	Tel:	(480) 627-2700
Senior Vice President, Communications	Fax:	(480) 627-7150
media@republicservices.com		
CALL, David M.	Tel:	(480) 627-2700
PAC Treasurer	Fax:	(480) 627-7150
CLARK, Jerry	Tel:	(480) 627-2700
Senior Vice President, Operations Controller	Fax:	(480) 627-7150
DELGHIACCIO, Brian	Tel:	(480) 627-2700
Senior Vice President, Finance	Fax:	(480) 627-7150
ELLINGSEN, Catharine	Tel:	(480) 627-2700
Executive Vice President, Chief Legal Officer and Corporate	Fax:	(480) 627-7150
Secretary		
HALNON, Bill	Tel:	(480) 627-2700
Senior Vice President and Chief Information Officer	Fax:	(480) 627-7150
HERTRICH, Judy	Tel:	(480) 627-2837
Executive Assistant	Fax:	(480) 627-7150
jhertrich@republicservices.com		

HUGHES, Jeffrey A.
Executive Vice President and Chief Administrative Officer
Tel: (480) 627-2700
Fax: (480) 627-7150

KNOCKE, Russ
PAC Treasurer
Tel: (480) 627-2700
Fax: (480) 627-7150

SERIANNI , Chuck
Executive Vice President and Chief Financial Officer
Tel: (480) 627-2700
Fax: (480) 627-7150

VAN WEELDEN, James G.
Senior Vice President, Environmental Development and Compliance
Tel: (480) 627-2700
Fax: (480) 627-7150

ResCare Inc.
A provider of home care to the elderly and those with disabilities.
www.rescare.com
Employees: 45,000
Ticker: NASDAQ: RSCR
Industry/ies: Children And Youth; Disabilities; Education
Legislative Issues: EDU; LBR; MMM

President and Chief Executive Officer
GRONEFELD, Jr., Ralph G.
Tel: (502) 394-2100
Fax: (502) 394-2206

Main Headquarters
Mailing: 9901 Linn Station Rd.
Louisville, KY 40223-3808
Tel: (502) 394-2100
Fax: (502) 394-2206
TF: (800) 866-0860

Political Action Committees
ResCare, Inc. Advocacy Fund PAC
FEC ID: C00344663
Contact: Ken Lovan
9901 Linn Stn. Rd.
Louisville, KY 40223

Contributions to Candidates: $12,450 (2015-2016)
Democrats: $1,000; Republicans: $11,450

Public Affairs and Related Activities Personnel
At Headquarters

LOVAN, Ken
PAC Treasurer
klovan@rescare.com
Tel: (502) 394-2100
Fax: (502) 394-2206

TAYLOR, Nel
Chief Communications Officer
Tel: (502) 394-2100
Fax: (502) 394-2206

Reserve Management Corporation
Provides cash management solutions for institutions, banks, brokerages, advisors and individual investors.
Employees: 200
Industry/ies: Banking/Finance/Investments; Management

Chairman and Chief Executive Officer
BENT, Bruce R.
Tel: (212) 401-5765
Fax: (212) 401-5959

Main Headquarters
Mailing: 1250 Broadway
32nd Floor
New York City, NY 10001-3701
Tel: (212) 401-5765
Fax: (212) 401-5959

Public Affairs and Related Activities Personnel
At Headquarters

BENT, Arthur T.
Senior Vice President and Assistant Secretary
Tel: (212) 401-5759
Fax: (212) 401-5959

Resolute Marine Energy
A marine energy company.
www.resolutemarine.com
Annual Revenues: $0.94 million
Industry/ies: Energy/Electricity

Founder and Chief Executive Officer
STABY, Bill
wstaby@resolute-marine-energy.com
Tel: (617) 600-3050

Main Headquarters
Mailing: Three Post Office Sq.
Third Floor
Boston, MA 02109
Tel: (617) 600-3050

Public Affairs and Related Activities Personnel
At Headquarters

CEBERIO, Olivier
Co-Founder and Chief Operating Officer
Tel: (617) 600-3050

Resolution Copper Company
Developing a copper mine near Superior, Arizona.
resolutioncopper.com
Employees: 5
Industry/ies: Mining Industry; Natural Resources
Legislative Issues: ENV; NAT; RES

Main Headquarters
Mailing: 102 Magma Heights Rd.
P.O. Box 1944
Superior, AZ 85173
Tel: (520) 689-9374
Fax: (520) 689-9304

Corporate Foundations and Giving Programs
Resolution Copper Company Contribution Program
402 W. Main St.
P.O. Box 1944
Superior, AZ 85173
Tel: (520) 689-9374
Fax: (520) 689-9304

Public Affairs and Related Activities Personnel
At Headquarters

CHERRY, Jon
Vice President
Tel: (520) 689-9374
Fax: (520) 689-9304

HUNDLEY, Sterling
Financial Operations Officer
Tel: (520) 689-9374
Fax: (520) 689-9304

RICHINS, Dave
Principal Advisor, Government Affairs
Tel: (520) 689-9374
Fax: (520) 689-9304

TAPLIN, Andrew
Project Director
Tel: (520) 689-9374
Fax: (520) 689-9304

Resorb Networks Inc.
A software development company.
www.resorb.net
Employees: 2
Industry/ies: Computer/Technology; Engineering/Mathematics

President and Chief Executive Officer
IANUALE, Robert John
Tel: (908) 316-0610
Fax: (908) 552-1532

Main Headquarters
Mailing: 52 Broad St.
Suite Three
Keyport, NJ 07735
Tel: (732) 264-3084
Fax: (732) 264-3182

Resource Efficiency Incorporated
Materials Reduction and Re-use.
www.resourceefficiencysolutions.com
Legislative Issues: ENG; ENV

President
SPURR, Mark

Main Headquarters
Mailing: P.O. Box 1140
Thonotosassa, FL 33592
Tel: (800) 929-7987
Fax: (888) 731-7201
TF: (800) 929-7987

Response Analytics
A financial services optimization company.
www.responseanalytics.com
Industry/ies: Banking/Finance/Investments; Management

Chairman of the Board and Chief Executive Officer
LIPPMAN, Brent
Tel: (480) 429-4480
Fax: (480) 429-4551

Main Headquarters
Mailing: 6991 E. Camelback Rd.
Suite D-205
Scottsdale, AZ 85251-3568
Tel: (480) 429-4480
Fax: (480) 429-4551

Public Affairs and Related Activities Personnel
At Headquarters

MANNING, Tim
Senior Vice President, Marketing and Contact, Media Relations
tim.manning@responseanalytics.com
Tel: (480) 429-4480
Fax: (480) 429-4551

Resurgent Health and Medical
Delivers employee hygiene technologies to hospitals and healthcare facilities.
www.resurgenthealth.com
Annual Revenues: $2.10 million
Employees: 20
Industry/ies: Machinery/Equipment; Medicine/Health Care/Mental Health

Chief Executive Officer
GLENN, Jim
Tel: (303) 790-4670
Fax: (303) 790-4859

Main Headquarters
Mailing: 400 Corporate Cir.
Suite H
Golden, CO 80401
Tel: (303) 790-4670
Fax: (303) 790-4859
TF: (800) 932-7707

Public Affairs and Related Activities Personnel
At Headquarters

COLBERT, Michele
Vice President, Sales and Marketing
mcolbert@meritech.com
Tel: (303) 790-4670
Fax: (303) 790-4859

STENBERG, Amy
Coordinator, Marketing and Media
astenberg@meritech.com

Tel: (303) 790-4670
Fax: (303) 790-4859

Retail Ventures, Inc.

Formerly known as Value City Department Stores, Inc., a wholly-owned subsidiary of DSW, Inc.
www.retailventuresinc.com
Employees: 13,000
Ticker: NYSE: RVI
SIC: 5331
Industry/ies: Apparel/Textiles Industry; Retail/Wholesale

Chairman of the Board
SCHOTTENSTEIN, Jay L.

Tel: (614) 238-4105
Fax: (631) 254-7268

Chief Executive Officer, President, Chief Financial Officer and Treasurer
MCGRADY, James

Tel: (614) 471-4722
Fax: (631) 254-7268

Main Headquarters
Mailing: 4314 E. Fifth Ave.
Columbus, OH 43219

Tel: (614) 238-4105
Fax: (631) 254-7268
TF: (866) 379-7463

Public Affairs and Related Activities Personnel

At Headquarters

DAVIS, Julia
Executive Vice President, General Counsel and Secretary

Tel: (614) 238-4105
Fax: (631) 254-7268

Revere Data, LLC

Provides data feed, software, index and ETF services.
www.reveredata.com
Annual Revenues: $2.50 million
Employees: 40
Industry/ies: Computer/Technology

Co-Chairman of the Board
ENGMANN, Douglas J.

Tel: (415) 782-0454
Fax: (415) 782-0474

Co-Chairman
ENGMANN, Michael

Tel: (415) 782-0454
Fax: (415) 782-0474

President and Chief Executive Officer
O'BRIEN, Kevin

Tel: (415) 782-0454
Fax: (415) 782-0474

Main Headquarters
Mailing: One California St.
Suite 1900
San Francisco, CA 94111

Tel: (415) 782-0454
Fax: (415) 782-0474

Public Affairs and Related Activities Personnel

At Headquarters

MENDEL, Bill
Contact, Media Relations
bill@mendelcommunications.com

Tel: (212) 397-1030
Fax: (415) 782-0474

RAMOS, Vivian
Chief Operating Officer

Tel: (415) 782-0454
Fax: (415) 782-0474

Revlon Consumer Products Corporation

A cosmetic manufacturer.
www.revlon.com
Annual Revenues: $1.91 billion
Employees: 5,700
Ticker: NYSE: REV
SIC: 2844; 5122
NAICS: 325620
Industry/ies: Personal Care/Hygiene

Chairman of the Board
PERELMAN, Ronald O.

Tel: (212) 527-4000

President and Chief Executive Officer
DELPANI, Lorenzo

Tel: (212) 527-4000

Main Headquarters
Mailing: One New York Plaza
New York, NY 10004

Tel: (212) 527-4000

Public Affairs and Related Activities Personnel

At Headquarters

FIGUEREO, Juan R.
Executive Vice President and Chief Financial Officer

Tel: (212) 527-4000

HORMOZI, Mitra
Executive Vice President, General Counsel and Chief Compliance Officer

Tel: (212) 527-4000

KRETZMAN, Robert K.
Retired Executive Vice President
robert.kretzman@revlon.com

Tel: (212) 527-4000

PAWLAK, Mark
Senior Vice President, Human Resources

Tel: (212) 527-4000

Reyes Beverage Group

Operates as a food and beverage distributor. Chesbay Distributing Company and Windy City Distribution Company joins Reyes Beverage Group in 2012.
www.reyesbeveragegroup.com
Industry/ies: Food And Beverage Industry

Founder & Co-Chairman of The Board
REYES , J. Christopher

Tel: (847) 227-6500
Fax: (847) 227-6550

Co-Chairman of the Board
REYES, Jude

Tel: (847) 227-6500
Fax: (847) 227-6550

Chief Executive Officer, Martin-Brower
NICKELE, Gregory A.

Tel: (847) 227-6500
Fax: (847) 227-6550

Main Headquarters
Mailing: 6250 N. River Rd.
Suite 9000
Rosemont, IL 60018

Tel: (847) 227-6500
Fax: (847) 227-6550

Public Affairs and Related Activities Personnel

At Headquarters

CARLSEN, Jeff
Senior Vice President & Chief Human Capital Officer

Tel: (847) 227-6500
Fax: (847) 227-6550

DOHENY, Daniel P.
Chief Financial Officer

Tel: (847) 227-6500
Fax: (847) 227-6550

GIAMPIETRO, Nicholas L.
Senior Vice President, General Counsel & Secretary

Tel: (847) 227-6500
Fax: (847) 227-6550

Reyes Holdings LLC

A food and beverage distributor. Parent organization of Reyes Beverage Group.
www.reyesholdings.com
Employees: 14,000
Industry/ies: Food And Beverage Industry

Main Headquarters
Mailing: 6250 N. River Rd.
Suite 9000
Rosemont, IL 60018

Tel: (847) 227-6500

Public Affairs and Related Activities Personnel

At Headquarters

BYRNE, Kate
Senior Counsel

Tel: (847) 227-6596

REYES, William
Director, Government Relations

Tel: (847) 227-6596

Reynolds American Inc.

A consumer product company, formerly known as R. J. Reynolds Tobacco Holdings, Inc. The name change resulted from the acquisition of Brown and Williamson Tobacco Corp.'s U.S. operations by subsidiary R. J. Reynolds Tobacco Co. in July, 2004.
www.reynoldsamerican.com
Annual Revenues: $11.54 billion
Employees: 5,600
Ticker: NYSE: RAI
SIC: 2111
Industry/ies: Tobacco Industry
Legislative Issues: ADV; AGR; AVI; BUD; CSP; GOV; TAX; TOB; TRD

Chairman of the Board
WAJNERT, Thomas C.

Tel: (336) 741-2000

President and Chief Executive Officer
CAMERON , Susan M

Tel: (336) 741-4000

Main Headquarters
Mailing: P.O. Box 718
Winston Salem, NC 27102

Washington Office
Mailing: 1201 F St. NW
Suite 1000
Washington, DC 20004

Tel: (202) 626-7200
Fax: (202) 626-7208

Political Action Committees
R. J. Reynolds PAC; Reynolds American Inc.
FEC ID: C00042002
Contact: Laura Leigh Oyler
P.O. Box 718
Winston Salem, NC 27102

Contributions to Candidates: $286,000 (2015-2016)
Democrats: $12,500; Republicans: $273,500

Principal Recipients

SENATE
BOOZMAN, JOHN (REP-AR)
BURR, RICHARD (REP-NC)

HOUSE
BOUSTANY, CHARLES W. DR. JR. (REP-LA)
HUDSON, RICHARD L. JR. (REP-NC)

Corporate Foundations and Giving Programs

R.J. Reynolds Foundation
401 N. Main St.
Winston Salem, NC 27101

Public Affairs and Related Activities Personnel

At Headquarters

CREW, Debra A.
President and Chief Operating Officer

LAMBETH, Julie E.
Executive Vice President and General Counsel

O'BRIEN, J. Brice
Executive Vice President, Public Affairs and Chief Communications Officer

OYLER, Laura Leigh
PAC Treasurer

At Washington Office

ANDERSON, LaKeitha *Senior Manager, Federal Government Relations* *Registered Federal Lobbyist*	Tel: Fax:	(202) 626-7200 (202) 626-7208
BRENNAN, Patrick *Federal Lobbyist* *Registered Federal Lobbyist*	Tel: Fax:	(202) 626-7200 (202) 626-7208
DAWSON, Brennan *Contact, Government Relations*	Tel: Fax:	(202) 626-7200 (202) 626-7208
FISH, John H. *Vice President, Federal Government Relations* fishj@rjrt.com *Registered Federal Lobbyist*	Tel: Fax:	(202) 626-7210 (202) 626-7208
FOREMAN, Donald D. *Director, Federal Government Relations* *Registered Federal Lobbyist*	Tel: Fax:	(202) 626-7230 (202) 626-7208
HOGG, Jeff *Senior Manager, Federal Government Relations* hoggj@rjrt.com *Registered Federal Lobbyist*	Tel: Fax:	(202) 626-7235 (202) 626-7208

At Other Offices

CALDWELL, Lisa J. *Executive Vice President and Chief Human Resources Officer* 401 N. Main St., P.O. Box 2990 Winston Salem, NC 27101 lisa.caldwell@rjrt.com	Tel:	(336) 741-2000
DUNHAM, Robert H. *Executive Vice President, Public Affairs and Chief Communications Officer* 401 N. Main St., P.O. Box 2990 Winston Salem, NC 27101	Tel:	(336) 741-2000
GENTRY , Jeffery S. *Executive Vice President, Operations and Chief Scientific Officer* 401 N. Main St., P.O. Box 2990 Winston Salem, NC 27101	Tel:	(336) 741-4000
GILCHRIST , Andrew D *Chief Financial Officer and Executive Vice President* 401 N. Main St., P.O. Box 2990 Winston Salem, NC 27101	Tel:	(336) 741-4000
HOLTON, Martin L. *Executive Vice President, General Counsel and Assistant Secretary* 401 N. Main St., P.O. Box 2990 Winston Salem, NC 27101	Tel:	(336) 741-2000
PAYNE, Tommy J. *Director, Niconovum AB; President, Niconovum USA, Inc.* 401 N. Main St., P.O. Box 2990 Winston Salem, NC 27101 *Registered Federal Lobbyist*	Tel:	(336) 741-2000
SINGLETON, John *Consulting, Public Relations* 401 N. Main St., P.O. Box 2990 Winston Salem, NC 27101 single@jrjt.com	Tel:	(336) 741-2000

Reynolds and Reynolds Company

A provider of information management systems and related professional services to the automotive retail industry.
www.reyrey.com
Annual Revenues: $467.40 million
Employees: 6,000
SIC: 7373
Industry/ies: Computer/Technology; Management

Chairman and Chief Executive Officer	Tel:	(937) 485-2000
BROCKMAN, Bob	Fax:	(937) 485-8971

Main Headquarters

Mailing: One Reynolds Way Kettering, OH 45430	Tel: Fax: TF:	(937) 485-2000 (937) 485-8971 (800) 756-5310

Corporate Foundations and Giving Programs

Reynolds and Reynolds Company Foundation
Contact: Alice Davisson

One Reynolds Way	Tel:	(937) 485-2000
Kettering, OH 45430	Fax:	(937) 485-2000

Public Affairs and Related Activities Personnel

At Headquarters

DAVISSON, Alice *Community Relations* alice_davisson@reyrey.com	Tel: Fax:	(937) 485-8138 (937) 485-8971
SCHWARTZ, Thomas *Director, Corporate Communications* thomas_schwartz@reyrey.com	Tel: Fax:	(937) 485-8109 (937) 485-8971

R.F. Global Capital LLC

A global business advisory firm.
Industry/ies: Advertising And Marketing

Main Headquarters

Mailing: 1629 K St. NW Suite 300 Washington, DC 20006	Tel:	(910) 691-2006

Public Affairs and Related Activities Personnel

At Headquarters

FUNDERBURK, Hon. David
Principal
ambromdf@aol.com

RFXCEL Corporation

RFXCEL Corporation provides ePedigree Management solutions that allow manufacturers, distributors, and retailers to track the chain of custody of prescription drugs through the pharmaceutical supply chain.
www.rfxcel.com
Annual Revenues: $5.30 million
Employees: 100
Industry/ies: Computer/Technology

Chairman of the Board and Chief Executive Officer	Tel:	(925) 824-0300
ABOOD, Glenn E.	Fax:	(925) 824-0100

Main Headquarters

Mailing: 12657 Alcosta Blvd. Sutie 485 San Ramon, CA 94583-4438	Tel: Fax:	(925) 824-0300 (925) 824-0100

Public Affairs and Related Activities Personnel

At Headquarters

DEVADAS, Roy *Vice President, Operations*	Tel: Fax:	(925) 824-0300 (925) 824-0100
MCCRORY, James *Vice President, Products and Technology and Media Resources* jmccrory@rfxcel.com	Tel: Fax:	(925) 824-0302 (925) 824-0100
TARKOFF, Jack *Chief Strategy Officer, SVP of Field Operations, Co-Founder* jtarkoff@rfxcel.com	Tel: Fax:	(925) 915-1039 (925) 824-0100

Rheem Manufacturing Company

A wholly owned subsidiary of Paloma Industries of Nagoya, Japan since 1988. Produces electric and gas water heaters, central warm air furnaces, air conditioners, storage tanks, swimming pool heaters and commercial boilers in North America.
www.rheem.com
SIC: 3639
NAICS: 335228
Industry/ies: Construction/Construction Materials; Engineering/Mathematics
Legislative Issues: ENG; ENV

President and Chief Executive Officer	Tel:	(770) 351-3000
JONES, J. R.		

Main Headquarters

Mailing: 1100 Abernathy Rd. NE Suite 1400 Atlanta, GA 30328	Tel: TF:	(770) 351-3000 (800) 995-0982

Public Affairs and Related Activities Personnel

At Headquarters

BRUNETTO, Sal *Corporate Manager, National Accounts*	Tel:	(770) 351-3000
UBIAN, William *Corporate Vice President, Human Resources*	Tel.	(770) 351-3000

PARFITT, Simon   Tel: (770) 351-3000
Corporate Vice President, Finance

At Other Offices

MEYERS, Karen   Tel: (479) 648-4747
Corporate Director, Government Relations   Fax: (479) 648-4155
5600 Old Greenwood Rd., P.O. Box 17010
Ft. Smith, AR 72917-7010
karen.meyers@rheem.com
Registered Federal Lobbyist

Rhodia, Inc.

Formerly a subsidiary of Rhone-Poulenc S.A., the company was spun off in 1999. Rhodia is a specialty chemicals company developing value-added products, services and solutions in the areas of cosmetics, clothing, food, health, the environment, and industry.
www.us.rhodia.com
Employees: 1,800
SIC: 5169; 2899; 5099
Industry/ies: Chemicals & Chemical Industry

Chairman of the Board and Chief Executive Officer   Tel: (609) 860-4000
CLAMADIEU, Jean-Pierre   Fax: (609) 860-2250

Main Headquarters
Mailing: Eight Cedar Brook Dr.   Tel: (609) 860-4000
         CN 7500   Fax: (609) 860-2250
         Cranbury, NJ 08512-7500

Public Affairs and Related Activities Personnel

At Headquarters

DAHLINGER, Mark A.   Tel: (609) 860-4000
Executive Vice President, Finance   Fax: (609) 409-8652

DONAHUE, John   Tel: (609) 860-4000
General Counsel   Fax: (609) 860-2250

KLUCSIK, David   Tel: (609) 860-3616
Director, Communications   Fax: (609) 860-2250
david.klucsik@us.rhodia.com

Ricoh Americas Corporation

Manufacturer of office equipment and cameras. subsidiary of Ricoh Company, Ltd., headquartered in Tokyo, Japan.
www.ricoh-usa.com
Employees: 36,000
Industry/ies: Furniture/Home Furnishings
Legislative Issues: BUD; GOV

Chairman of the Board and Chief Executive Officer   Tel: (973) 882-2000
BRODIGAN, Martin   Fax: (973) 882-2048

Main Headquarters
Mailing: Five Dedrick Pl.   Tel: (973) 882-2000
         W. Caldwell, NJ 07006   Fax: (973) 882-2048

Public Affairs and Related Activities Personnel

At Headquarters

CROWE, Gary   Tel: (973) 882-2000
Senior Vice President and Chief Financial Officer   Fax: (973) 882-2048

GRECO, John   Tel: (973) 882-2000
Specialist, Public Relations   Fax: (973) 882-2048

MONTEFUSCO, Linda   Tel: (973) 882-2172
Manager, Advertising and Video Production   Fax: (973) 882-2048

VELLEK, Tim   Tel: (973) 882-2000
Senior Vice President, Marketing   Fax: (973) 882-2048

VENABLE, Donna   Tel: (973) 882-2000
Executive Vice President, Human Resources   Fax: (973) 882-2048

Rio Grande Valley Sugar Growers, Inc.

Works to educate members of Congress and staff regarding sugar farming and U.S. policies and regulations affecting sugar farmers. Sugar Cane producer Company.
www.rgvsugar.com
Annual Revenues: $62.08 million
Employees: 500
SIC: 2061; 2062
NAICS: 311311; 311312
Industry/ies: Agriculture/Agronomy; Commodities; Food And Beverage Industry; Utilities
Legislative Issues: AGR

Chairman of the Board   Tel: (956) 358-8001
MURDEN, Dale   Fax: (956) 262-1138
dalemurden@hotmail.com

Main Headquarters
Mailing: 2.5 Miles W. Hwy. 107   Tel: (956) 636-1411
         P.O. Box 459   Fax: (956) 636-1449
         Santa Rosa, TX 78593

Political Action Committees
Rio Grande Valley Sugar Growers Inc. PAC

FEC ID: C00185686
Contact: Armando Briones
2.5 Miles West Highway 107   Tel: (956) 636-1411
Santa Rosa, TX 78543   Fax: (956) 636-1411

     Contributions to Candidates: $37,500 (2015-2016)
     Democrats: $14,500; Republicans: $23,000

Corporate Foundations and Giving Programs
Rio Grande Valley Sugar Growers, Inc. Contributions Program
2.5 Miles W. Hwy. 107
P.O. Box 459
Santa Rosa, TX 78593

Public Affairs and Related Activities Personnel

At Headquarters

BRIONES, Armando   Tel: (956) 636-1411
PAC Treasurer   Fax: (956) 636-1449

FLEENOR, Wayne   Tel: (512) 565-7527
Contact, Media Relations   Fax: (956) 636-1449

Rio Tinto Energy America, Inc. (RTEA)

See listing on page 200 under Cloud Peak Energy Resources, LLC

Rite Aid Corporation

A chain of drugstores. Acquired eckerd in 2007.
www.riteaid.com
Annual Revenues: $26.53 billion
Employees: 50,730
Ticker: NYSE: RAD
SIC: 5099; 5912; 5122
Industry/ies: Personal Care/Hygiene; Pharmaceutical Industry; Retail/Wholesale
Legislative Issues: FOO; HCR; MMM

Chairman and Chief Executive Officer   Tel: (717) 761-2633
STANDLEY, John   Fax: (717) 975-5871
contacttheboard@riteaid.com

Main Headquarters
Mailing: P.O. Box 3165   Tel: (717) 761-2633
         Harrisburg, PA 17105   Fax: (717) 975-5871
                         TF: (800) 748-3243

Political Action Committees
Rite Aid Corporation PAC
FEC ID: C00104083
Contact: Byron J. Purcell
30 Hunter Ln.   Tel: (717) 761-2633
Camp Hill, PA 17011

     Contributions to Candidates: $97,000 (2015-2016)
     Democrats: $28,500; Republicans: $68,500

Corporate Foundations and Giving Programs
Rite Aid Foundation
P.O. Box 3165
Harrisburg, PA 17105

Public Affairs and Related Activities Personnel

At Headquarters

BELLEZZA, Tony   Tel: (717) 761-2633
Senior Vice President and Chief Compliance Officer   Fax: (717) 975-5871

CASTLE, Dedra N.   Tel: (717) 761-2633
Executive Vice President and Chief Human Resources Officer   Fax: (717) 975-5871

CHOE, Yong   Tel: (717) 761-2633
Vice President, Federal Affairs and Public Policy   Fax: (717) 975-5871
Registered Federal Lobbyist

HENDERSON, Susan   Tel: (717) 761-2633
Senior Vice President and Chief Communications Officer   Fax: (717) 975-5871

HURLEY, Deborah A.   Tel: (717) 975-5979
Administrator, Government Affairs Programs   Fax: (717) 975-5979
dhurley@riteaid.com
Registered Federal Lobbyist

KARST, Darren   Tel: (717) 761-2633
Executive Vice President and Chief Financial Officer   Fax: (717) 975-5871

LEARISH, John   Tel: (717) 761-2633
Senior Vice President, Marketing   Fax: (717) 975-5871

MARTINDALE, Ken   Tel: (717) 761-2633
President and Chief Operating Officer   Fax: (717) 975-5871

POULIOS, George   Tel: (717) 761-2633
Registered Federal Lobbyist   Fax: (717) 975-5871

STRASSLER, Marc A.   Tel: (717) 761-2633
Executive Vice President, Secretary and General Counsel   Fax: (717) 975-5871

At Other Offices

PURCELL, Byron J.   Tel: (717) 761-2633
PAC Trasurer
30 Hunter Ln.
Camp Hill, PA 17011

SCHROEDER, Matthew
Tel: (717) 214-8867
Group Vice President, Strategy, Investor Relations and Treasurer
30 Hunter Ln.
Camp Hill, PA 17011
mschroeder@riteaid.com

Rivada Networks, LLC

Rivada Networks is a designer, integrator and operator of public safety communications and information technology networks for homeland security forces and first responders.
rivada.com
Employees: 25
Industry/ies: Communications; Telecommunications/Internet/Cable

Chairman of the Board and Chief Executive Officer
GANLEY, J. Declan

Main Headquarters
Mailing: 1755 Telstar Dr.
Suite 300
Colorado Springs, CO 80920

Public Affairs and Related Activities Personnel

At Headquarters

BASHAMBU, R. Montu
Secretary & General Counsel

Riverglass, Inc.

Information technology company. Their products includes eDiscovery, Fusion Centers, Custom Solutions. RiverGlass professional services will ensure all hardware and software is installed and running properly.
www.riverglassinc.com
Annual Revenues: $4.10 million
Employees: 30
Industry/ies: Computer/Technology

Main Headquarters
Mailing: 2001 S. First St.
Tel: (630) 578-4268
Suite 103
Fax: (630) 578-4260
Champaign, IL 61820-7480

Public Affairs and Related Activities Personnel

At Headquarters

CARROLL, Peter
Tel: (630) 578-4268
Media Contact
Fax: (630) 578-4260
pcarroll@riverglassinc.com

HALL, Howard
Tel: (630) 578-4268
Vice President, Business Development
Fax: (630) 578-4260

RKO Pictures

American film production and distribution company.
www.rko.com
Annual Revenues: $10 million
Industry/ies: Sports/Leisure/Entertainment

Chairman and Chief Executive Officer
Tel: (310) 277-0707
HARTLEY, Ted
Fax: (310) 566-8940

Main Headquarters
Mailing: 9200 Sunset Blvd.
Tel: (310) 277-0707
Suite 600
Fax: (310) 566-8940
Los Angeles, CA 90069

Public Affairs and Related Activities Personnel

At Headquarters

MATTHEWS, Andrew
Tel: (310) 277-0707
President
Fax: (310) 566-8940

NIELSEN, Loren
Tel: (310) 277-0707
Contact, Strategy and Business Development
Fax: (310) 566-8940

R. L. Polk & Company

Provider of marketing information and services to the auto industry.
usa.polk.com
Employees: 1,400
Industry/ies: Communications; Media/Mass Communication; Paper And Wood Products Industry; Printing Industry

President
Tel: (248) 728-7000
ROGERS, Tim
Fax: (248) 728-7680

Main Headquarters
Mailing: 26955 Northwestern Hwy.
Tel: (248) 728-7000
Southfield, MI 48033
Fax: (248) 728-7680
TF: (800) 464-7655

Public Affairs and Related Activities Personnel

At Headquarters

CULVER, Michelle
Tel: (313) 309-9500
Senior Manager, Corporate Communications
Fax: (248) 728-7680

mculver@lambert-edwards.com

Robert Bosch LLC

Provider of Automotive Technology, Industrial Technology, Consumer Goods, and Energy and Building Technology.
www.bosch.us
Annual Revenues: $10.60 billion
Employees: 24,600
SIC: 3593; 3714
NAICS: 333995; 336322
Industry/ies: Automotive Industry; Transportation
Legislative Issues: AUT; CSP; ENG; TAX; TRA

Chairman
Tel: (248) 876-1000
STRUTH, Werner
Fax: (248) 876-1116

President
Tel: (248) 876-1000
MANSUETTI, Mike
Fax: (248) 876-1116

Main Headquarters
Mailing: 38000 Hills Tech Dr.
Tel: (248) 876-1000
Farmington Hills, MI 48331
Fax: (248) 876-1116

Washington Office
Mailing: 1001 G St. NW
Suite 800
Washington, DC 20001

Corporate Foundations and Giving Programs

Robert Bosch LLC Contributions Program
38000 Hills Tech Dr.
Tel: (248) 876-1000
Farmington Hills, MI 48331
Fax: (248) 876-1116

Public Affairs and Related Activities Personnel

At Headquarters

CARUSO, Michael
Tel: (248) 876-2930
Federal Lobbyist
Fax: (248) 876-1116
Registered Federal Lobbyist

JOHNSON, Norman
Tel: (248) 876-2930
norman.johnson@us.bosch.com
Fax: (248) 876-1116
Registered Federal Lobbyist

KILBORN, Cheryl
Tel: (248) 876-1167
Director of Corporate Communicatons and Public Relations
Fax: (248) 876-1116
Cheryl.Kilborn@us.bosch.com

KIRSCHNER, Ulrich
Tel: (248) 876-1000
Executive Vice President, Controlling, Finance and
Fax: (248) 876-1116
Administration

LEWIS, Chandra
Tel: (248) 876-6731
Vice President, Communications
Fax: (248) 876-1116
chandra.lewis@us.bosch.com

STRAUB, Maximiliane
Tel: (248) 876-1000
Chief Financial Officer, Executive Vice President, Controlling,
Fax: (248) 876-1116
Finance and Administration

TUNICK, Meredith
Tel: (248) 876-1000
Manager, Federal Government Affairs
Fax: (248) 876-1116
Registered Federal Lobbyist

At Washington Office

BRENEMAN, Jeffrey S.
Registered Federal Lobbyist

BRODERICK, William
Registered Federal Lobbyist

IMLAY, Esq., Chris
Registered Federal Lobbyist

MEUWISSEN, Ana
Director, Government Affairs
Registered Federal Lobbyist

Robert Half International, Inc.

A provider of specialized staffing services.
www.rhi.com
Annual Revenues: $4.82 billion
Employees: 14,000
Ticker: NYSE: RHI
Industry/ies: Employees & Employment

Chairman of the Board and Chief Executive Officer
Tel: (650) 234-6000
MESSMER, Jr., Harold M.
Fax: (650) 234-6999

Main Headquarters
Mailing: 2884 Sand Hill Rd.
Tel: (650) 234-6000
Suite 200
Fax: (650) 234-6999
Menlo Park, CA 94025

Corporate Foundations and Giving Programs

Robert Half International Contributions Program
2884 Sand Hill Rd.
Tel: (650) 234-6000
Suite 200
Menlo Park, CA 94025

Public Affairs and Related Activities Personnel

At Headquarters

BECK, Amanda
Media Contact
amanda.beck@rhi.com
Tel: (650) 234-6000
Fax: (650) 234-6999

BUCKLEY , Michael
Executive Vice President, Chief Administrative Officer and Treasurer
Tel: (650) 234-6000
Fax: (650) 234-6999

GENTZKOW, Paul F.
President and Chief Operating Officer, Staffing Services
Tel: (650) 234-6000
Fax: (650) 234-6999

GLASS, Robert W.
Executive Vice President, Corporate Development
glass@rhi-ag.com
Tel: (650) 234-6000
Fax: (650) 234-6999

KAREL, Steven
Executive Vice President, Secretary and General Counsel
Tel: (650) 234-6000
Fax: (650) 234-6999

STATEN, Reesa McCoy
Senior Vice President, Corporate Communications
reesa.staten@rhi.com
Tel: (650) 234-6000
Fax: (650) 234-6999

WADDELL, M. Keith
Vice Chairman of the Board, President and Chief Financial Officer
keith.waddell@rhi.com
Tel: (650) 234-6000
Fax: (650) 234-6999

Roche Diagnostics Corporation

The Roche Diagnostics Division is engaged in five business fields: professional diagnostics, diabetes care, molecular diagnostics, applied science.
www.roche.com
Industry/ies: Medicine/Health Care/Mental Health; Pharmaceutical Industry
Legislative Issues: HCR; MMM

Chairman
FRANZ, Christoph
Tel: (317) 521-2000
Fax: (317) 521-7116

Chief Executive Officer
DIGGELMANN, Roland
Tel: (317) 521-2000
Fax: (317) 521-7116

Main Headquarters
Mailing: 9115 Hague Rd.
Indianapolis, IN 46250-0457
Tel: (317) 521-2000
Fax: (317) 521-7116

Washington Office
Mailing: 1425 K St. NW
Suite 600, E. Tower
Washington, DC 20005

Corporate Foundations and Giving Programs

Roche Diagnostics Contributions Program
9115 Hague Rd.
Indianapolis, IN 46250-0457

Public Affairs and Related Activities Personnel

At Headquarters

AYYOUBI, Silvia
Head, Human Resources
Tel: (317) 521-2000
Fax: (317) 521-7116

EPLETT , Julie
Executive Director, Marketing
jeplett@meetings-incentives.com
Tel: (317) 521-2000
Fax: (317) 521-7116

FELDHAUS, Stephan
Head, Group Communications
Tel: (317) 521-2000
Fax: (317) 521-7116

HIPPE, Dr. Alan
Chief Financial and Information Technology Officer
Tel: (317) 521-2000
Fax: (317) 521-7116

JACKSON , Jennifer
Manager, Marketing
jen.jackson@roche.com
Tel: (317) 521-2000
Fax: (317) 521-7116

KELLER, Gottlieb A.
General Counsel
Tel: (317) 521-2000
Fax: (317) 521-7116

KLAUSER, Alexander
Senior Manager, Communications
Tel: (317) 521-2000
Fax: (317) 521-7116

At Washington Office

BARNETT, Thomas
Director, Federal Government Affairs
Registered Federal Lobbyist

RING, Rusty
Vice President, Government Relations
Registered Federal Lobbyist

TAYLOR, Bruce
Director, Government Strategy and Relations
Registered Federal Lobbyist

At Other Offices

CLAESSENS, Kathleen
Federal Lobbyist
1399 New York Ave., Suite 300
Washington, DC 20005
Registered Federal Lobbyist

CLARKE, Karron
901 F St. NW, Suite 610
Washington, DC 20004

PHILLIPS, Jack
President and Chief Executive Officer, North America
901 F St. NW, Suite 610
Washington, DC 20004

RING, Russell
Federal Lobbyist
901 F St. NW, Suite 610
Washington, DC 20004
Registered Federal Lobbyist

ROTH, Jessica
Federal Lobbyist
901 F St. NW, Suite 610
Washington, DC 20004

STEWARD, Shannon C.
Department Administrator
1399 New York Ave., Suite 300
Washington, DC 20005

UPADHYAY, Ravi
Director, Government Affairs
901 F St. NW, Suite 610
Washington, DC 20004
Registered Federal Lobbyist

Rockwell Automation, Inc.

Rockwell Automation is the industrial automation and information company, serving automotive, food and beverage (including dairy), personal care, life sciences, oil and gas, mining, and paper and pulp markets.
www.rockwellautomation.com
Annual Revenues: $6.56 billion
Employees: 22,500
Ticker: NYSE: ROK
SIC: 3562; 3566; 3612; 3621; 3625
NAICS: 332991; 333612; 333319; 335312; 335314
Industry/ies: Automotive Industry; Transportation
Legislative Issues: DEF; MAN; TRD

Chairman of the Board and Chief Executive Officer
NOSBUSCH, Keith D.
Tel: (414) 382-2000
Fax: (414) 382-4444

Main Headquarters
Mailing: 1201 S. Second St.
Milwaukee, WI 53204-2496
Tel: (414) 382-2000
Fax: (414) 382-4444

Washington Office
Mailing: 5601 Huntington Pkwy.
Bethesda, MD 20814

Corporate Foundations and Giving Programs

Rockwell Automation Charitable Corporation
1201 S. Second St.
Milwaukee, WI 53204-2496
Tel: (414) 382-2000
Fax: (414) 382-2000

Public Affairs and Related Activities Personnel

At Headquarters

BERNADEN, John
Director, External Communications
jabernaden@ra.rockwell.com
Tel: (414) 382-2555
Fax: (414) 382-4444

CRANDALL, Theodore D.
Senior Vice President and Chief Financial Officer
Tel: (414) 382-2000
Fax: (414) 382-4444

HAGERMAN, Douglas
Senior Vice President, General Counsel and Secretary
Tel: (414) 382-2000
Fax: (414) 382-4444

JACOBSON, Kevin
Director, Marketing Communications and Events Global Sales & Marketing
Tel: (414) 382-5878
Fax: (414) 382-4444

LESTER, Keith
Manager, Public Relations
klester@ra.rockwell.com
Tel: (414) 382-4871
Fax: (414) 382-4444

MCDERMOTT, John
Senior Vice President, Global Sales and Marketing
Tel: (414) 382-2000
Fax: (414) 382-4444

ROHR-DRALLE, Rondi
Vice President, Corporate Development and Investor Relations
Tel: (414) 382-8510
Fax: (414) 382-8520

SCHMITT, Susan
Senior Vice President, Human Resources
Tel: (414) 382-2000
Fax: (414) 382-4444

THOMAS, Marty
Senior Vice President, Operations and Engineering Services
Tel: (414) 382-2000
Fax: (414) 382-4444

At Other Offices

QUINN, MD, PhD, Bruce
Vice President, Government Affairs
2800 Clarendon Blvd., Suite W414
Arlington, VA 22210
Registered Federal Lobbyist

Rogers Group, Inc.

Quarries producing crushed stone and hot mix asphalt for road construction.
www.rogersgroupincint.com
Annual Revenues: $186.80 million
Employees: 1,600
SIC: 2951; 3272; 3281; 3295; 3299
NAICS: 324121; 327991; 327992; 327999
Industry/ies: Construction/Construction Materials; Transportation

| **Chief Executive Officer** | Tel: | (615) 242-0585 |
| GERAGHTY, Jerry | Fax: | (615) 780-5700 |

Main Headquarters
| Mailing: | 421 Great Circle Rd., P.O. Box 25250 | Tel: | (615) 242-0585 |
| | Nashville, TN 37202 | Fax: | (615) 780-5700 |

Political Action Committees
Rogers Group Inc. PAC
FEC ID: C00277152
Contact: James A. Patton Jr.
| 421 Great Circle Rd. | Tel: | (615) 242-0585 |
| Nashville, TN 37228 | Fax: | (615) 780-5700 |

Contributions to Candidates: $1,500 (2015-2016)
Republicans: $1,500

Corporate Foundations and Giving Programs

Rogers Group, Inc. Contributions Program
| P. O. Box 25250 | Tel: | (615) 242-0585 |
| Nashville, TN 37202 | Fax: | (615) 780-5700 |

Public Affairs and Related Activities Personnel

At Headquarters

KENLEY, Tom	Tel:	(615) 780-5764
Manager, Corporate Communications	Fax:	(615) 780-5700
tom.kenley@rogersgroupinc.com		

| PATTON, Jr., James A. | Tel: | (615) 242-0585 |
| PAC Treasurer | Fax: | (615) 780-5700 |

| ROSE, Dan | Tel: | (615) 242-0585 |
| Vice President and General Counsel | Fax: | (615) 780-5700 |

Rohm and Haas Company

A chemical manufacturing company headquartered in Philadelphia, PA.
www.rohmhaas.com
Industry/ies: Chemicals & Chemical Industry; Plastics Industry

Main Headquarters
| Mailing: | 100 Independence Mall West |
| | Philadelphia, PA 19106 |

Washington Office
| Mailing: | 1300 Wilson Blvd., Suite 1220 | Fax: | (703) 741-5884 |
| | Arlington, VA 22209 |

Political Action Committees
Rohm and Haas Company Employees Association for Better Government PAC
FEC ID: C00039057
Contact: Colleen A. Keashen
100 Independence Mall West
Philadelphia, PA 19106

Public Affairs and Related Activities Personnel

At Headquarters

KEASHEN, Colleen A.
PAC Treasurer
ckeashen@rohmhaas.com

ROHO Group

A medical device manufacturer.
www.therohogroup.com
Annual Revenues: $13.90 million
Employees: 200
SIC: 2515; 2522; 2822; 3537; 3751
NAICS: 325212; 326199; 337214; 337910
Industry/ies: Medicine/Health Care/Mental Health
Legislative Issues: HCR; MMM

| **Chief Executive Officer** | Tel: | (618) 277-9173 |
| GRAEBE, Bobby | Fax: | (618) 277-9561 |

Main Headquarters
Mailing:	100 N. Florida Ave.	Tel:	(618) 277-9173
	Belleville, IL 62221-5429	Fax:	(618) 277-9561
		TF:	(800) 851-3449

Political Action Committees
ROHO Group PAC (Roho PAC)
FEC ID: C00448530
Contact: Timothy R. Richter
100 N. Florida Ave.
Belleville, IL 62221

Contributions to Candidates: $4,750 (2015-2016)

Democrats: $2,750; Republicans: $2,000

Public Affairs and Related Activities Personnel

At Headquarters

BORCHERDING, Tom	Tel:	(618) 277-9173
President	Fax:	(618) 277-9561
TomB@roho.com		

BRAUN, Whitney	Tel:	(618) 277-9173
Marketing Manager	Fax:	(618) 277-9561
Whitney.Braun@roho.com		

| CHELF, Pat | Tel: | (618) 277-9173 |
| Senior Vice President, Sales and Business Development | Fax: | (618) 277-9561 |

CREMEENS, Cynthia	Tel:	(618) 277-9173
Sales Specialist, Global Operations	Fax:	(618) 277-9561
cynthiac@roho.com		

HARTMANN, Tom	Tel:	(618) 277-9173
Senior Director, Global Sales	Fax:	(618) 277-9561
TomH@roho.com		

JUEN, Bridget	Tel:	(618) 277-9173
Executive Assistant	Fax:	(618) 277-9561
BridgetJ@roho.com		

KLOTZ, Jackie	Tel:	(618) 277-9173
Marketing Services Manager	Fax:	(618) 277-9561
JackieK@roho.com		

LYNCH, Susan	Tel:	(618) 277-9173
Senior Director, Marketing	Fax:	(618) 277-9561
SusanL@roho.com		

MCCAUSLAND, Dave	Tel:	(618) 277-9173
Senior Vice President, Planning and Government Affairs	Fax:	(618) 277-9561
davem@therohogroup.com		

MEEKER, Pat	Tel:	(618) 277-9173
Senior Director, Global Sales	Fax:	(618) 277-9561
patm@roho.com		

| RICHTER, Timothy R. | Tel: | (618) 277-9173 |
| PAC Contact | Fax: | (618) 277-9561 |

RICHTER, Tim	Tel:	(618) 277-9173
Chief Financial Officer and Senior Vice President, Finance	Fax:	(618) 277-9561
Tim.Richter@roho.com		

RITTER, Chris	Tel:	(618) 277-9173
Senior Director, Global Sales	Fax:	(618) 277-9561
ChrisR@roho.com		

Roll Call Group

An economist group business.
www.rollcall.com
Industry/ies: Communications; Media/Mass Communication; Politics/Political Science

Main Headquarters
| Mailing: | 77 K St. NE, Eighth Floor | Tel: | (202) 650-6500 |
| | Washington, DC 20002-4681 | TF: | (800) 432-2250 |

Public Affairs and Related Activities Personnel

At Headquarters

FREEMYER, Kathleen	Tel:	(202) 650-6500
Sales Representative		
kathleen.freemyer@gmail.com		

LEIBOWITZ, Stuart	Tel:	(202) 650-6500
Senior Director, Business Development		
stuartleibowitz@cqrollcall.com		

| RIEDEL, Bunnie | | |
| Federal Lobbyist | | |

| SHAH, Vinay | Tel: | (202) 650-6500 |
| Chief Financial Officer | | |

Roll Global LLC

A private holding company with a diverse set of interests.
www.wonderful.com
Employees: 4,000
Industry/ies: Banking/Finance/Investments

| **President and Chief Executive Officer** | Tel: | (310) 966-5700 |
| RESNICK, Stewart A. | Fax: | (310) 966-5758 |

Main Headquarters
| Mailing: | 11444 W. Olympic Blvd. | Tel: | (310) 966-5700 |
| | Los Angeles, CA 90064 | Fax: | (310) 966-5758 |

Corporate Foundations and Giving Programs

Roll Global Contributions program
Contact: Stewart A. Resnick
| 11444 W. Olympic Blvd. | Tel: | (310) 966-5700 |
| Los Angeles, CA 90064 | Fax: | (310) 966-5758 |

Public Affairs and Related Activities Personnel

At Headquarters

RESNICK, Lynda	Tel:	(310) 966-5700
Co Owner	Fax:	(310) 966-5758

Roll International Corporation
See listing on page 687 under Roll Global LLC

Rollins, Inc.
A service company engaged in pest control.
www.rollins.com
Annual Revenues: $1.43 billion
Employees: 10,936
Ticker: NYSE: ROL
SIC: 7340
Industry/ies: Animals; Furniture/Home Furnishings

Chairman of the Board	Tel:	(404) 888-2000
ROLLINS, R. Randall	Fax:	(404) 888-2662

Vice Chairman and Chief Executive Officer	Tel:	(404) 888-2000
ROLLINS, Gary W.	Fax:	(404) 888-2662

Main Headquarters
Mailing:	P.O. Box 647	Tel:	(404) 888-2000
	Atlanta, GA 30301	Fax:	(404) 888-2662

Political Action Committees
Rollins Inc PAC
FEC ID: C00131219
Contact: Christopher Gorecki
2170 Piedmont Rd. NE
Atlanta, GA 30324

    Contributions to Candidates: $9,650 (2015-2016)
    Democrats: $1,250; Republicans: $8,400

Public Affairs and Related Activities Personnel
At Headquarters

BECK, Sarah	Tel:	(404) 888-2917
Supervisor , Public Relations	Fax:	(404) 888-2662
GORECKI, Christopher	Tel:	(404) 888-2000
PAC Treasurer	Fax:	(404) 888-2662
LUCZYNSKI, Thomas E.	Tel:	(404) 888-2000
Corporate Secretary	Fax:	(404) 888-2662
tluczyns@rollins.com		
NORTHEN, Paul E.	Tel:	(404) 888-2000
Chief Financial Officer and Treasurer	Fax:	(404) 888-2662
SWANN, Ruby	Tel:	(404) 888-2000
Director, Recruiting and Talent Management	Fax:	(404) 888-2662
corprecruiting@rollins.com		
WILSON, John	Tel:	(404) 888-2000
President and Chief Operating Officer	Fax:	(404) 888-2662

Rolls-Royce North America Inc.
A power systems company operating in aerospace, marine and industrial power markets. Produces a broad range of aero engines powering aircraft and helicopters for both commercial and military applications. Also provides industrial equipment for power generation, transmission and distribution, oil and gas, marine propulsion and materials handling.
www.rolls-royce.com
Annual Revenues: $16.70 million
Employees: 200
Industry/ies: Aerospace/Aviation; Defense/Homeland Security; Energy/ Electricity; Government-Related; Transportation; Utilities
Legislative Issues: AVI; BUD; DEF; ECN; ENG

President and Chief Executive Officer	Tel:	(703) 834-1700
GUYETTE, James M.	Fax:	(703) 709-6086

Main Headquarters
Mailing:	1875 Explorer St.	Tel:	(703) 834-1700
	Suite 200	Fax:	(703) 709-6086
	Reston, VA 20190		

Political Action Committees
Rolls-Royce North America PAC
FEC ID: C00296822
Contact: Michael N. Elliott
1875 Explorer St., Suite 200	Tel:	(703) 834-1700
Reston, VA 20190	Fax:	(703) 621-4989

    Contributions to Candidates: $222,325 (2015-2016)
    Democrats: $57,500; Republicans: $164,825

        Principal Recipients

            SENATE
            MCCAIN, JOHN S (REP-VA)

            HOUSE
            CARSON, ANDRE (DEM-IN)
            CONNOLLY, GERALD EDWARD (DEM-VA)
            FORBES, J. RANDY (REP-VA)

Corporate Foundations and Giving Programs
Rolls-Royce North America Contributions Program
1875 Explorer St.
Suite 202
Reston, VA 20190

Public Affairs and Related Activities Personnel
At Headquarters

DALE, Thomas P.	Tel:	(703) 834-1700
Executive Vice President, General Counsel	Fax:	(703) 709-6086
ELLIOTT, Michael N.	Tel:	(703) 834-1700
PAC Treasurer	Fax:	(703) 709-6086
ELSON, Brian	Tel:	(703) 834-1700
Vice President, Government Relations	Fax:	(703) 709-6086
Registered Federal Lobbyist		
LARSON, Kirk	Tel:	(703) 834-1700
Executive Vice President, Human Resources	Fax:	(703) 709-6086
MCINERNEY, Anne	Tel:	(703) 834-1700
Vice President, Legislative Affairs	Fax:	(703) 709-6086
anne.mcinerney@rolls-royce.com		
Registered Federal Lobbyist		
MCVAY, Craig	Tel:	(703) 834-1700
Registered Federal Lobbyist	Fax:	(703) 709-6086
PEASE, Edward A.	Tel:	(703) 621-2808
Senior Vice President, Government Relations	Fax:	(703) 709-6087
ed.pease@rolls-royce.com		
Registered Federal Lobbyist		
PLUMMER, Stephen B.	Tel:	(703) 834-1700
Executive Vice President, Government Business	Fax:	(703) 709-6087
Registered Federal Lobbyist		
POWERS, III, William T.	Tel:	(703) 834-1700
Executive Vice President and Chief Financial Officer	Fax:	(703) 709-6086
REUTER , Joel	Tel:	(703) 834-1700
Vice President, Communications and Marketing Services	Fax:	(703) 709-6086
WOOD, Steve	Tel:	(703) 621-2808
Senior Vice President, Defense Relations	Fax:	(703) 709-6086
Registered Federal Lobbyist		
WORLEY, Mike	Tel:	(703) 621-2808
Federal Lobbyist	Fax:	(703) 709-6086

Ron Kendall & Associates
Real Estate consulting.

President	Tel:	(301) 495-5925
KENDALL, Ronald		

Main Headquarters
Mailing:	2019 Lanier Dr.
	Silver Spring, MD 20910

Roseburg Forest Products Company
A producer of wood products.
www.roseburg.com
Employees: 3,800
SIC: 2436; 2421; 2493; 2411
NAICS: 321212; 321912; 321219; 11331
Industry/ies: Forestry

Chief Executive Officer	Tel:	(541) 679-3311
FORD, Allyn C.	Fax:	(541) 679-9543
allynf@rfpco.com		

Main Headquarters
Mailing:	P.O. Box 1088	Tel:	(541) 679-3311
	Roseburg, OR 97470	Fax:	(541) 679-2543
		TF:	(800) 245-1115

Public Affairs and Related Activities Personnel
At Headquarters

DALEY, Marty	Tel:	(541) 679-3311
Chief Financial Officer and Senior Vice President, Finance	Fax:	(541) 679-9543
KILLGORE, Steve	Tel:	(541) 679-3311
Senior Vice President, Solid Wood and Marketing	Fax:	(541) 679-9543
WISE, Kellye	Tel:	(541) 679-3311
Senior Vice President, Human Resources and Labor Relations	Fax:	(541) 679-2543

Ross Environmental Services Inc.
A privately-owned hazardous waste management company.
www.rossenvironmental.com
Annual Revenues: $4.90 million
Employees: 100
Industry/ies: Environment And Conservation; Pollution And Waste

Chairman of the Board	Tel:	(440) 366-2000
CROMLING, Maureen M.	Fax:	(440) 336-2186

President and Chief Executive Officer
HARGATE, Arthur W.

Tel: (440) 366-2000
Fax: (440) 336-2186

Main Headquarters
Mailing: 150 Innovation Dr.
Elyria, OH 44035-1672

Tel: (440) 366-2000
Fax: (440) 336-2186
TF: (800) 878-7677

Corporate Foundations and Giving Programs

Ross Foundation
Contact: Maggie Kelch
150 Innovation Dr.
Elyria, OH 44035

Tel: (400) 366-2076

Public Affairs and Related Activities Personnel

At Headquarters

CLEMENS, Stefanie
Chief Financial Officer

Tel: (440) 366-2000
Fax: (440) 336-2186

KELCH, Maggie
*Director, Corporate Communications and Community
Relations*
mkelch@rossenvironmental.com

Tel: (400) 366-2076
Fax: (440) 336-2186

LAWSON, Patricia
Vice President, Corporate Compliance and Risk Management

Tel: (440) 366-2000
Fax: (440) 336-2186

VIDMER, Gary
Executive Vice President, Sales and Marketing

Tel: (440) 366-2000
Fax: (440) 336-2186

Ross Stores, Inc.

A retailer of clothing, shoes, home accents, fragrances, and accessories.
www.rossstores.com
Annual Revenues: $12.09 billion
Employees: 77,800
Ticker: NASDAQ: ROST
SIC: 5651
Industry/ies: Retail/Wholesale

Executive Chairman of the Board
BALMUTH, Michael
michael.balmuth@ros.com

Tel: (925) 965-4400
Fax: (925) 965-4388

Chief Executive Officer
RENTLER, Barbara

Tel: (925) 965-4400
Fax: (925) 965-4388

Main Headquarters
Mailing: 5130 Hacienda Dr.
Dublin, CA 94568

Tel: (925) 965-4400
Fax: (925) 965-4388
TF: (800) 945-7677

Corporate Foundations and Giving Programs

Ross Stores, Inc. Contributions Program
5130 Hacienda Dr.
Dublin, CA 94568

Public Affairs and Related Activities Personnel

At Headquarters

CALL, John G.
*Executive Vice President, Finance and Legal, and Corporate
Secretary*

Tel: (925) 965-4400
Fax: (925) 965-4388

CARUANA, Ken
*Executive Vice President, Strategy, Marketing and Human
Resources*

Tel: (925) 965-4400
Fax: (925) 965-4388

FASSIO, James S.
President and Chief Development Officer

Tel: (925) 965-4400
Fax: (925) 965-4388

HARTSHORN, Michael J.
Senior Vice President and Chief Financial Officer

Tel: (925) 965-4400
Fax: (925) 965-4388

O'SULLIVAN, Michael
President and Chief Operating Officer
michael.osullivan@ros.com

Tel: (925) 965-4400
Fax: (925) 965-4388

WONG, Connie
Director, Investor and Media Relations
connie.wong@ros.com

Tel: (925) 965-4668
Fax: (925) 965-4388

Rothschild, Inc.

*Rothschild, Inc., based in New York city, is the U.S. subsidiary of N.M. Rothschild & Sons
Limited, headquartered in London, United Kingdom. An investment banking firm.*
www.rothschild.com
Employees: 3,000
Industry/ies: Banking/Finance/Investments

Chairman of the Board
DE ROTHSCHILD, Baron David

Tel: (212) 403-3500
Fax: (212) 403-3501

Chief Executive Officer
HIGGINS, Nigel
Nigel.Higgins@rothschild.com

Tel: (212) 403-3500
Fax: (212) 403-3501

Main Headquarters
Mailing: 1251 Avenue of the Americas
44th Floor
New York City, NY 10020

Tel: (212) 403-3500
Fax: (212) 403-3501

Washington Office
Mailing: 1101 Connecticut Ave. NW
Seventh floor
Washington, DC 20036

Tel: (202) 862-1660
Fax: (202) 862-1699

Corporate Foundations and Giving Programs

Rothschild, Inc. Community Partnerships
1251 Ave. of the Americas
51st Floor
New York City, NY 10020

Tel: (212) 403-3500
Fax: (212) 403-3501

Public Affairs and Related Activities Personnel

At Headquarters

MCFARLANE, James
Contact, Media Relations

Tel: (212) 403-3500
Fax: (212) 403-3501

Rowan Companies, Inc.

*A provider of oil well drilling, aviation and manufacturing services primarily to the petroleum
industry.*
www.rowancompanies.com
Annual Revenues: $2.09 billion
Employees: 3,496
Ticker: NYSE:RDC
SIC: 3533; 3531
NAICS: 333132; 333120
Industry/ies: Aerospace/Aviation; Fuels See Coal, Gas, Oil, Petroleum; Natural
Resources; Petroleum Industry; Transportation

President and Chief Executive Officer
BURKE, Thomas P.

Tel: (713) 621-7800
Fax: (713) 960-7660

Main Headquarters
Mailing: 2800 Post Oak Blvd.
Sutie 5450
Houston, TX 77056

Tel: (713) 621-7800
Fax: (713) 960-7660

Public Affairs and Related Activities Personnel

At Headquarters

BUTZ, Stephen
Executive Vice President, Chief Financial Officer

Tel: (713) 621-7800
Fax: (713) 960-7660

FAURE, David E.
Vice President, Legal and Associate General Counsel

Tel: (713) 621-7800
Fax: (713) 960-7660

GOBILLOT, Theodore D.
Associate General Counsel

Tel: (713) 621-7800
Fax: (713) 960-7660

KELLER, Mark A.
Executive Vice President, Business Development

Tel: (713) 621-7800
Fax: (713) 960-7660

PITRE , Chris
*Vice President, Investor Relations and Corporate
Development*
chris.pitre@rowancompanies.com

Tel: (713) 621-7800
Fax: (713) 960-7660

POPE, Joe
Vice President, Sales and Marketing

Tel: (713) 621-7800
Fax: (713) 960-7660

SMITH, Pharr
Senior Vice President, Operations Support

Tel: (713) 621-7800
Fax: (713) 960-7660

TRENT, Melanie M.
*Executive Vice President, General Counsel, Chief
Administrative Officer and Company Secretary*

Tel: (713) 621-7800
Fax: (713) 960-7660

Roy Anderson Corporation

A construction firm.
www.rac.com
Employees: 300
Industry/ies: Construction/Construction Materials

President and Chief Executive Officer
ANDERSON, III, Roy

Tel: (228) 896-4000
Fax: (228) 896-4078

Main Headquarters
Mailing: P.O. Box Two
Gulfport, MS 39502-0002

Tel: (228) 896-4000
Fax: (228) 896-4078
TF: (800) 688-4003

Public Affairs and Related Activities Personnel

At Headquarters

BERMOND, Debbie
Vice President, Human Resources
debbie@rac.com

Tel: (228) 896-4000
Fax: (228) 896-4078

HANCOCK, Doug
Chief Financial Officer

Tel: (228) 896-4000
Fax: (228) 896-4078

VOLLENWEIDER, Robert
Executive Vice President, Finance and Risk
robert.vollenweider@rac.com

Tel: (228) 896-4000
Fax: (228) 896-4078

Royal Bank of Canada

Financial Services
www.rbcroyalbank.com
Industry/ies: Banking/Finance/Investments

Legislative Issues: BAN; TAX

President and Chief Executive Officer
MCKAY, David I

Tel: (212) 428-6200

Main Headquarters
Mailing: Three World Financial Center
             200 Vesey St.
             New York City, NY 10281

Tel: (212) 428-6200

Public Affairs and Related Activities Personnel

At Headquarters

DEAN, Jr., Gregory J.
Registered Federal Lobbyist

Tel: (212) 428-6200

FUKAKUSA, Janice
Chief Administrative Officer and Chief Financial Officer

Tel: (212) 428-6200

HIRJI, Zabeen
Chief Human Resources Officer

Tel: (212) 428-6200

MAHER, Shawn
Managing Director & Head , Regulatory
Registered Federal Lobbyist

Tel: (212) 428-6200

MARTIN, LaBrena
Federal Lobbyist
Registered Federal Lobbyist

Tel: (212) 428-6200

MCGREGOR, A. Douglas
Chair and CEO of RBC Capital Markets and Group Head,
Capital Markets and Investor and Treasury Services

Tel: (212) 428-6200

ROSS, Bruce
Group Head, Technology and Operations

Tel: (212) 428-6200

Royal Caribbean Cruises, Ltd.
A cruise line operator.
www.royalcaribbean.com
Annual Revenues: $8.40 billion
Employees: 65,900
Ticker: NYSE: RCL
SIC: 4400
Industry/ies: Sports/Leisure/Entertainment; Transportation; Travel/Tourism/
Lodging
Legislative Issues: CAW; MAR; TAX; TRA

Chairman of the Board and Chief Executive Officer
FAIN, Richard D.

Tel: (305) 539-6000
Fax: (305) 539-0562

Main Headquarters
Mailing: 1050 Caribbean Way
             Miami, FL 33132

Tel: (305) 539-6000
Fax: (305) 539-0562
TF: (800) 398-9819

Corporate Foundations and Giving Programs

Get Involved Volunteer Everywhere (G.I.V.E.)
1050 Caribbean Way
Miami, FL 33132

Tel: (305) 539-6000
Fax: (305) 539-0562

Public Affairs and Related Activities Personnel

At Headquarters

KALISCH, Eleni P.
Vice President, Government Relations
ekalisch@rccl.com
Registered Federal Lobbyist

Tel: (305) 539-6799
Fax: (305) 539-0562

LIBERTY, Jason
Chief Financial Officer

Tel: (305) 539-6000
Fax: (305) 539-0562

SIERRA-CARO, Lyan
Account Executive, Corporate Communications
lsierracaro@rccl.com

Tel: (305) 539-6000
Fax: (305) 539-0562

STEIN, Bradley
Corporate Counsel

Tel: (305) 539-6000
Fax: (305) 539-0562

RPM International, Inc.
RPM International, Inc. manufactures and markets high-performance coatings, sealants
and specialty chemicals, primarily for maintenance and improvement applications. It offers
waterproofing, coatings, and institutional roofing systems; sealants, air barriers, tapes, and
foams; residential home weatherization systems; roofing and building maintenance and related
services; polymer flooring systems; commercial and decorative flooring, etc.
www.rpminc.com
Annual Revenues: $4.76 billion
Employees: 12,864
Ticker: NYSE: RPM
SIC: 2851; 2679; 2899; 2952; 3069
NAICS: 322299; 324122; 325199; 326299; 32551
Industry/ies: Construction/Construction Materials
Legislative Issues: AVI; CHM; ENG; TOR; TRA

Chairman of the Board and Chief Executive Officer
SULLIVAN, Frank C.

Tel: (330) 273-5090
Fax: (330) 225-8743

Main Headquarters
Mailing: 2628 Pearl Rd.

Tel: (330) 273-5090

P.O. Box 777
Medina, OH 44258

Fax: (330) 225-8743

Political Action Committees
RPM International Inc Manufacturing in America PAC
FEC ID: C00402081
Contact: Ronald A. Rice
2628 Pearl Rd.
P.O. Box 777
Medina, OH 44258

Tel: (330) 273-5090
Fax: (330) 273-5090

   Contributions to Candidates: $30,000 (2015-2016)
   Republicans: $30,000

Public Affairs and Related Activities Personnel

At Headquarters

GORDON, Russell L.
Vice President and Chief Financial Officer

Tel: (330) 273-5090
Fax: (330) 225-8743

KRAMER, John F.
Vice President, Corporate Development

Tel: (330) 273-5090
Fax: (330) 225-8743

MCSHEPHARD, Randall
Vice President, Public Affairs

Tel: (330) 273-8857
Fax: (330) 225-8743

MOORE, Edward W.
Vice President, General Counsel and Chief Compliance
Officer
emoore@rpminc.com

Tel: (330) 273-5090
Fax: (330) 225-8743

RICE, Ronald A.
President, Chief Operating Officer and PAC Treasurer

Tel: (330) 273-5090
Fax: (330) 225-8743

ROGERS, Kathie M.
Manager, Investor Relations

Tel: (800) 776-4488
Fax: (330) 225-8743

SLIFSTEIN, Barry M.
Vice President, Investor Relations, Planning and Media
Contact
bslifstein@rpminc.com

Tel: (330) 273-5090
Fax: (330) 225-8743

RSM McGladrey, Inc.
A professional services firm providing accounting, tax and business consulting which provides
clients with the insights they need to make critical business decisions. We seek to provide
strategic guidance from an independent and unbiased perspective, instilling optimism and
inspiring confidence. In December 2011 RSM McGladrey was reunited with McGladrey &
Pullen.
mcgladrey.com
Employees: 8,000
Industry/ies: Accounting; Banking/Finance/Investments; Business;
Management; Small Business

Managing Partner and Chief Executive Officer
ADAMS, Joe

Tel: (952) 921-7700
Fax: (952) 921-7702

Main Headquarters
Mailing: 3600 American Blvd., West
             Third Floor
             Bloomington, MN 55431

Tel: (952) 921-7700
Fax: (952) 921-7702
TF: (800) 274-3978

Corporate Foundations and Giving Programs

McGladrey Foundation
Contact: Linda Gizzi
3600 American Blvd., West
Third Floor
Bloomington, MN 55431

Public Affairs and Related Activities Personnel

At Headquarters

ANDREWS, Terri
Director, National Public Relations
terri.andrews@mcgladrey.com

Tel: (980) 233-4710
Fax: (952) 921-7702

AUDINO, Mark
Chief Marketing Officer

Tel: (952) 921-7700
Fax: (952) 921-7702

GIZZI, Linda
Consulting Manager

Tel: (617) 241-1285
Fax: (952) 921-7702

KIRLEY , Mike
Chief Operating Officer

Tel: (952) 921-7700
Fax: (952) 921-7702

LAMKIN, Katie
National Human Resources Leader

Tel: (952) 921-7700
Fax: (952) 921-7702

OPHEIM, Doug
Chief Finance Officer

Tel: (952) 921-7700
Fax: (952) 921-7702

ORDOGNE, Renee
Chief of Staff & Chief Financial Officer

Tel: (952) 921-7700
Fax: (952) 921-7702

RTD Embedded Technologies Inc.
A Lobbying Firm.
www.rtd.com
Industry/ies: Defense/Homeland Security; Government-Related

Main Headquarters
Mailing: 103 Innovation Blvd.
             State College, PA 16803

Tel: (814) 234-8087
Fax: (814) 234-5218

Public Affairs and Related Activities Personnel

At Headquarters

HARRIS MCCREY, Julie
Government And Industrial Liaison
jharrismccrey@rtd.com

Tel: (814) 234-8087
Fax: (814) 234-5218

RTI International

RTI International-(formerly Research Triangle Institute)-an independent, nonprofit research and development organization offers innovative research and technical solutions to governments and businesses worldwide in the areas of health and pharmaceuticals.
www.rti.org
Industry/ies: Pharmaceutical Industry; Science; Scientific Research
Legislative Issues: BUD; ENG; FOR

President and Chief Executive Officer
HOLDEN, PhD, E. Wayne

Tel: (919) 541-6000
Fax: (919) 541-5985

Main Headquarters
Mailing: 3040 Cornwallis Rd.
            P.O.Box 12194
            Research Triangle Park, NC 27709-2194

Tel: (919) 541-6000
Fax: (919) 541-5985
TF: (800) 334-8571

Washington Office
Mailing: 701 13th St NW
            Suite 750
            Washington, DC 20005-3967

Tel: (202) 728-2080

Public Affairs and Related Activities Personnel

At Headquarters

BISTREICH-WOLFE, Lisa
Manager, Media Relations

Tel: (919) 541-6000
Fax: (919) 541-5985

CABALLERO, Lindsey
Congressional Liaison

Tel: (919) 541-6000
Fax: (919) 541-5985

GIBSON, James J.
Executive Vice President and Chief Operating Officer

Tel: (919) 541-6000
Fax: (919) 541-5985

KAELIN, Jr., Michael H.
Executive Vice President and Chief Financial Officer

Tel: (919) 541-6000
Fax: (919) 541-5985

MAGRUDER, Katherine
Federal Lobbyist

Tel: (919) 541-6000
Fax: (919) 541-5985

MANESS, Reid
Communications and Government Relations Consultant

Tel: (919) 541-7044
Fax: (919) 541-5985

MAY, Lisa
Executive Vice President, Human Resources.

Tel: (919) 541-6000
Fax: (919) 541-5985

ROBERTS, Martha
Senior Vice President, Human Resources and Facility Services

Tel: (919) 541-6000
Fax: (919) 541-5985

SLADICH, Rachel

Tel: (919) 541-6000
Fax: (919) 541-5985

SPANGENBERG, Kami
Senior Director, Communications
kspangenberg@rti.org

Tel: (919) 485-5606
Fax: (919) 541-5985

STORY, George Edward
Executive Vice President, General Counsel and Corporate Secretary

Tel: (919) 541-6000
Fax: (919) 541-5985

TRAINHAM, PhD, Dr. James
Senior Vice President, Strategic Energy Initiatives

Tel: (919) 541-6000
Fax: (919) 541-5985

At Washington Office

O'BRIEN, Dennis
Senior Manager, Government Relations

Tel: (202) 728-2080

PEGANOFF, Bradley
Vice President, Government and Corporate Relations

Tel: (202) 728-2080

RTI International Metals

A producer of titanium mill products and fabricated metal components for the global market.
rtiintl.com
Annual Revenues: $817.53 million
Employees: 2,575
Ticker: NYSE: RTI
SIC: 3350
Industry/ies: Metals

Chairman of the Board
HERNANDEZ, Robert M.

Tel: (412) 893-0026
Fax: (412) 893-0027

Vice Chair, President and Chief Executive Officer
HICKTON, Dawne S.

Tel: (412) 893-0026
Fax: (412) 893-0027

Main Headquarters
Mailing: Westpointe Corporate Center One
            1550 Coraopolis Heights Rd., Fifth Floor
            Pittsburgh, PA 15108-2973

Tel: (412) 893-0026
Fax: (412) 893-0027

Political Action Committees
RTI International Metals Inc. PAC
FEC ID: C00350280
1550 Coraopolis Heights Rd
1550 Coraopolis Heights Rd., Fifth Floor
Coraopolis, PA 15108

Tel: (112) 090 0026
Fax: (412) 893-0026

Contributions to Candidates: $10,768 (2015-2016)
Democrats: $6,000; Republicans: $4,768

Public Affairs and Related Activities Personnel

At Headquarters

CROOKSHANK, Dan
Director, Investor Relations
dcrookshank@rtiintl.com

Tel: (412) 893-0026
Fax: (412) 893-0027

HULL, William T.
PAC Treasurer

Tel: (412) 893-0026
Fax: (412) 893-0027

MCAULEY, Michael G.
Senior Vice President, Chief Financial Officer and Treasurer
mmcauley@rtiintl.com

Tel: (412) 893-0117
Fax: (412) 893-0027

MCCARLEY, James L.
Executive Vice President, Operations

Tel: (412) 893-0026
Fax: (412) 893-0027

WHALEN, Chad
General Counsel and Senior Vice President, Government Relations

Tel: (412) 893-0026
Fax: (412) 893-0027

Rubin Health Policy Consulting, LLC

Consulting firm.
Legislative Issues: HCR

Main Headquarters
Mailing: 5826 Highland Dr.
            Chevy Chase, MD 20815

Public Affairs and Related Activities Personnel

At Headquarters

EISINGER, Neleen
Registered Federal Lobbyist

Ruddick Corporation

See listing on page 386 under Harris Teeter Supermarkets, Inc.

Timothy J. Rudnicki

Main Headquarters
Mailing: 4224 Lynn Ave.
            Edina, MN 55416

Tel: (952) 915-1505

Public Affairs and Related Activities Personnel

At Headquarters

RUDNICKI, Timothy J.

Tel: (952) 915-1505

Rupari Food Services, Inc.

Produces whole packaged frozen goods.
www.rupari.com
Annual Revenues: $164.50 million
Employees: 150
Industry/ies: Food And Beverage Industry

Chairman and Chief Executive Officer
KELLY, Jack

Tel: (708) 225-9411

Main Headquarters
Mailing: 15600 Wentworth Ave.
            S. Holland, IL 60473

Tel: (708) 225-9411

Public Affairs and Related Activities Personnel

At Headquarters

KROEPFL, Kristin
Vice President, Marketing

Tel: (708) 225-9411

Rural Community Insurance Agency, Inc.

Rural Community Insurance Agency provides risk management protection for more than 100 crops.
www.rcis.com
Industry/ies: Insurance Industry

Main Headquarters
Mailing: 3501 Thurston Ave.
            Anoka, MN 55303-1060

Tel: (763) 427-0290
TF: (800) 328-9143

Washington Office
Mailing: 1706 23rd St., S
            Arlington, VA 22202

Rural Community Insurance Services

Rural Community Insurance Services provides comprehensive insurance services to agricultural communities.
www.rcis.com
Annual Revenues: $10 million
Industry/ies: Insurance Industry

President
DAY, Mike

Tel: (763) 427-0290

Main Headquarters

Mailing:	3501 Thurston Ave.	Tel: (763) 427-0290
	Anoka, MN 55303-1060	TF: (800) 328-9143

Rural Technologies Strategies, Inc.
Funding for rural broadband and IT infrastructure.
ruraltechnologiesstrategies.com
Industry/ies: Agriculture/Agronomy; Energy/Electricity
Legislative Issues: SCI

President & Chairman   Tel: (202) 628-0644
RAMO, Tony

Main Headquarters
Mailing: 1050 Connecticut Ave. NW   Tel: (202) 628-0644
Tenth Floor
Washington, DC 20036

Public Affairs and Related Activities Personnel

At Headquarters

HELWIG, Rex R   Tel: (202) 628-0644
Treasurer

Rural/Metro Corporation
Provides ambulance and emergency services throughout North and South America.
www.ruralmetro.com
Annual Revenues: $530.8 million
Employees: 8,000
Ticker: NASDAQ: RURL
SIC: 4100
Industry/ies: Medicine/Health Care/Mental Health; Transportation

President and Chief Executive Officer   Tel: (480) 994-3886
BARTOS, Scott A.   Fax: (480) 606-3338

Main Headquarters
Mailing: 9221 E. Via de Ventura   Tel: (480) 994-3886
Scottsdale, AZ 85258   Fax: (480) 606-3338
TF: (800) 352-2309

Political Action Committees
Rural/Metro Federal Management PAC
FEC ID: C00288613
Contact: Kevin Moore
9221 E. Via de Ventura
Scottsdale, AZ 85258

Public Affairs and Related Activities Personnel

At Headquarters

BURKETT , Jay L.	Tel:	(480) 994-3886
Chief Financial Officer	Fax:	(480) 606-3338
HERBERT, Anne	Tel:	(480) 606-3633
Director, Labor Relations	Fax:	(480) 606-3338
Anne.Herbert@rmetro.com		
JOHNSON, Sven K.	Tel:	(480) 994-3886
Chief Strategy Officer	Fax:	(480) 606-3338
KAROLZAK, John P.	Tel:	(480) 994-3886
Vice President, Operations	Fax:	(480) 606-3338
KEVANE, Christopher E.	Tel:	(480) 994-3886
Senior Vice President and General Counsel	Fax:	(480) 606-3338
LINDBERG, Dave	Tel:	(480) 994-3886
Senior Vice President, Business Development	Fax:	(480) 606-3338
MILTON, Tom	Tel:	(480) 606-3620
Director, Community Relations	Fax:	(480) 606-3338
Thomas.Milton@rmetro.com		
MOORE, Kevin	Tel:	(480) 994-3886
PAC Treasurer	Fax:	(480) 606-3338
REID, Theresa	Tel:	(480) 606-3345
Corporate Human Resource Manager	Fax:	(480) 606-3338
Theresa.Reid@rmetro.com		
SIEGEL, Andrew	Tel:	(212) 355-4449
Contact, Media Relations	Fax:	(480) 606-3338

At Other Offices

CORBEIL, Minda   Tel: (678) 473-1990
Director, South Zone Human Resources
250 Hembree Park Dr., Suite 112
Roswell, GA 30076
Minda.Corbeil@rmetro.com

ERICKSON, Nancy   Tel: (619) 280-6060
Director, Human Resources
10405 San Diego Mission Rd., #200
San Diego, CA 92108
Nancy.Erickson@rmetro.com

Russell Corporation
A designer, manufacturer and marketer of activewear, casualwear, athletic uniforms, and sports equipment.

shop.russellathletic.com
Industry/ies: Apparel/Textiles Industry
Legislative Issues: TRD

President and Chief Executive Officer
HOLLAND, John

Main Headquarters
Mailing: P.O. Box 90015   TF: (877) 879-8410
Bowling Green, KY 42102-9015

Political Action Committees
Russell Corporation PAC
FEC ID: C00093195
Contact: William G. Newton
P.O. Box 272
Alexander City, AL 35010

Public Affairs and Related Activities Personnel

At Headquarters

HOLLIDAY, K. Roger
Vice President, Investor Relations
hollidayroger@russellcorp.com

At Other Offices

NEWTON, William G.
PAC Treasurer
P.O. Box 272
Alexander City, AL 35010

RWC Inc.
RWC is a global leader in the design and production of innovative manufacturing systems, with primary markets in the appliance and automotive industries.
www.rwcinc.com
Legislative Issues: FIN

Principal   Tel: (202) 255-5903
WEISMAN, Robin Mahler
robinmweisman@gmail.com

Main Headquarters
Mailing: 2105 S. Euclid Ave.   Tel: (989) 684-4030
P.O. Box 920   Fax: (989) 684-3960
Bay City, MI 48707-0920

Washington Office
Mailing: 4722 Chesapeake St. NW   Tel: (202) 255-5903
Washington, DC 20016

Ryder System, Inc.
Provider of logistics and transportation services.
www.ryder.com
Annual Revenues: $6.63 billion
Employees: 33,100
Ticker: NYSE: R
SIC: 7510
Industry/ies: Transportation; Trucking Industry
Legislative Issues: BUD; FUE; LBR; ROD; TAX; TRA; TRU

Chairman of the Board and Chief Executive Officer   Tel: (305) 500-3726
SANCHEZ, Robert E.   Fax: (305) 500-3203

Main Headquarters
Mailing: 11690 N. W. 105th St.   Tel: (305) 500-3726
Miami, FL 33178   Fax: (305) 500-3203

Political Action Committees
Ryder System Inc. Employees PAC
FEC ID: C00088435
Contact: Scott Allen
11690 NW 105th St.
Miami, FL 33178

   Contributions to Candidates: $61,000 (2015-2016)
   Democrats: $6,500; Republicans: $54,500

Corporate Foundations and Giving Programs
Ryder Charitable Foundation
Contact: David Bruce
11690 NW 105th St.
Miami, FL 33178

Public Affairs and Related Activities Personnel

At Headquarters

ALLEN, Scott	Tel:	(305) 500-3726
PAC Treasurer	Fax:	(305) 500-3203
BARR, James R.	Tel:	(305) 500-4466
Vice President	Fax:	(305) 500-3203
jbarr@ryder.com		
Registered Federal Lobbyist		
BRUCE, David	Tel:	(305) 500-4999
Vice President, Corporate Communications and Public Affairs	Fax:	(305) 500-3203
and Foundation Executive Director		

david_bruce@ryder.com

BRUNN, Robert S. *Vice President, Corporate Strategy and Investor Relations*	Tel: Fax:	(305) 500-4053 (305) 500-3130
FATOVIC, Robert D. *Executive Vice President, Chief Legal Officer and Corporate Secretary*	Tel: Fax:	(305) 500-3726 (305) 500-4129
GARCIA, Art A. *Executive Vice President and Chief Financial Officer*	Tel: Fax:	(305) 500-3726 (305) 500-3203
GREENE, Gregory F. *Executive Vice President and Chief Administrative Officer*	Tel: Fax:	(305) 500-3726 (305) 500-4129
GRODIN, Joshua *Director, Government Relations* *Registered Federal Lobbyist*	Tel: Fax:	(305) 500-3726 (305) 500-3203
HAAS, Cindy *Director, Corporate Communications and Community Relations* cindy_haas@ryder.com	Tel: Fax:	(305) 500-4526 (305) 500-3203
JONES, Karen *Executive Vice President and Chief Marketing Officer*	Tel: Fax:	(305) 500-3726 (305) 500-3203

Ryerson Inc.

A distributor and processor of metals and industrial plastics. Formerly Inland Materials Distribution Group, Inc.
www.ryerson.com
Employees: 4,200
Ticker: NYSE: RYI
SIC: 5051
Industry/ies: Metals

President and Chief Executive Officer LEHNER, Edward J.	Tel: Fax:	(312) 292-5000 (773) 762-0437

Main Headquarters
Mailing:	227 W. Monroe St. 27th Floor Chicago, IL 60606	Tel: Fax:	(312) 292-5000 (773) 762-0437

Public Affairs and Related Activities Personnel

At Headquarters

LINDSAY, Roger W. *Chief Human Resources Officer* roger.lindsay@ryerson.com	Tel: Fax:	(312) 292-5040 (773) 762-0437
SCHNAUFER, Erich *Interim Chief Financial Officer*	Tel: Fax:	(312) 292-5000 (773) 762-0437

Rypos

Manufactures active exhaust control systems for the reduction of harmful emissions from diesel engines.
www.rypos.com
Annual Revenues: $8.70 million
Employees: 26
Industry/ies: Engineering/Mathematics

Chairman of the Board WATSON, Stephen L.	Tel: Fax:	(508) 429-4552 (508) 429-4553
Chief Executive Officer BRANSFIELD, Peter	Tel: Fax:	(508) 429-4552 (508) 429-4553

Main Headquarters
Mailing:	40 Kenwood Cir. Franklin, MA 02038	Tel: Fax:	(508) 429-4552 (508) 429-4553

S&B Engineers and Constructors, Ltd.

Provides engineering, procurement, and construction services to the refining, petrochemical and chemical, midstream and power industries.
www.sbec.com
Employees: 2,400
SIC: 1629
NAICS: 236210
Industry/ies: Construction/Construction Materials; Engineering/Mathematics

Co-Founder and Chairman of the Board BROOKSHIRE, Dr. William A.	Tel:	(713) 845-4008
President and Chief Executive Officer REDDISH, Harold J.	Tel:	(713) 645-4141

Main Headquarters
Mailing:	7825 Park Place Blvd. Houston, TX 77087	Tel:	(713) 645-4141

Public Affairs and Related Activities Personnel

At Headquarters

AKIN, Richard L. *Senior Vice President, Business Development* rlakin@sbec.com	Tel:	(713) 645-4141
GREEN, Donna	Tel:	(713) 845-4002

Executive Secretary and Contact, Media Relations
degreen@sbec.com
SLAUGHTER, James G. *President*	Tel:	(713) 645-4141

S&T Bank

S &T Bank offers many loan and deposit products created specifically to meet the needs of low and moderate-income customers.
www.stbank.com
Annual Revenues: $173.31 million
Employees: 1,027
Ticker: NASDAQ (GS): STBA
SIC: 6022
Industry/ies: Banking/Finance/Investments

President and Chief Executive Officer BRICE, Todd D.	Tel: Fax:	(724) 465-1487 (724) 465-1488

Main Headquarters
Mailing:	P. O. Box 190 Indiana, PA 15701	Tel: Fax: TF:	(724) 349-1800 (724) 465-6874 (888) 806-3809

Political Action Committees
S and T Bank PAC
FEC ID: C00263483
Contact: William J MckKametz
800 Philadelphia St. P.O. Box 190 Indiana, PA 15701	Tel: Fax:	(724) 349-1800 (724) 465-6874

  Contributions to Candidates: $2,750 (2015-2016)
  Republicans: $2,750

Corporate Foundations and Giving Programs

S&T Foundation
P. O. Box 190 Indiana, PA 15701	Tel: Fax:	(724) 349-1800 (724) 465-6874

Public Affairs and Related Activities Personnel

At Headquarters

AMBROSE, Thomas F. *Senior Auditor*	Tel: Fax:	(724) 349-1800 (724) 465-6874
JORGENSON, Bob *Manager, Executive Vice President Marketing Division*	Tel: Fax:	(724) 465-5448 (724) 465-6874
KOCHVAR , Mark *Senior Executive Vice President, Chief Financial Officer and Contact, Investor Relations*	Tel: Fax:	(724) 349-1800 (724) 465-6874
MCKKAMETZ, William J *PAC Treasurer*	Tel: Fax:	(724) 349-1800 (724) 465-6874
RUDDOCK, David P. *Senior Executive Vice President and Chief Operating Officer*	Tel: Fax:	(724) 349-1800 (724) 465-6874
STAPLETON, Becky *Executive Vice President, Director, Human Resources and Employee Communications* becky.stapleton@stbank.net	Tel: Fax:	(724) 465-4800 (724) 465-3062

S.C. Johnson and Son, Inc.

A global producer and marketer of consumer insect control, home food storage and cleaning products.
www.scjohnson.com
Industry/ies: Chemicals & Chemical Industry
Legislative Issues: AVI; CHM; HCR; TAX; TRD

Chairman of the Board and Chief Executive Officer JOHNSON, Dr. Fisk H.	Tel: Fax:	(262) 260-2000 (262) 260-6004

Main Headquarters
Mailing:	1525 Howe St. Racine, WI 53403-5011	Tel: Fax: TF:	(262) 260-2000 (262) 260-6004 (800) 494-4855

Washington Office
Mailing:	1667 K St. NW Suite 650 Washington, DC 20006	Tel: Fax:	(202) 331-1186 (202) 659-2338

Political Action Committees
S.C. Johnson and Son, Inc. PAC (SCJPAC)
FEC ID: C00342246
Contact: William H. Van Lopik
1525 Howe St. Racine, WI 53403	Tel: Fax:	(262) 260-2000 (262) 260-6004

  Contributions to Candidates: $102,700 (2015-2016)
  Democrats: $18,500; Republicans: $84,200

Corporate Foundations and Giving Programs

SC Johnson Fund, Inc
1525 Howe St. Racine, WI 53403	Tel: Fax:	(262) 260-2000 (262) 260-2000

Public Affairs and Related Activities Personnel

At Headquarters

ANDEREGG, Gregory L.
Director, Community Leadership
Tel: (262) 260-2000
Fax: (262) 260-6189

BREWER, III, F.H.
Director, Government Relations Worldwide
Tel: (262) 260-2493
Fax: (262) 260-2944

HUTTERLY, Jane M.
Executive Vice President, Worldwide Corporate and Environmental Affairs
Tel: (262) 260-2000
Fax: (262) 260-6004

KOSTERMAN, Gayle P.
Executive Vice President, Worldwide Human Resources
Tel: (262) 260-2000
Fax: (262) 260-6004

MEYRAN , Pascale
Senior Vice President, Global Human Resources
Tel: (262) 260-2000
Fax: (262) 260-6004

SEMRAU, Kelly M.
Senior Vice President – Global Corporate Affairs, Communication & Sustainability
Tel: (262) 260-2000
Fax: (262) 260-6004

VAN LOPIK, William H.
PAC Treasurer and Lobbyist
Tel: (262) 260-2000
Fax: (262) 260-6004

At Washington Office

BURKHEAD, Paul
Registered Federal Lobbyist
Tel: (202) 331-1186
Fax: (202) 659-2338

LEVENSON, Nancy R.
Senior Director, Global Government Relations
Tel: (202) 331-1186
Fax: (202) 659-2338

PEARCE, Christopher P.
Director, Government Relations
Registered Federal Lobbyist
Tel: (202) 331-1186
Fax: (202) 659-2338

Saab Sensis

An aerospace and defence company. Acquired Sensis in 2011.
www.saabsensis.com
Industry/ies: Defense/Homeland Security; Government-Related
Legislative Issues: DEF

Chairman of the Board
WALLENBERG , Marcus
Tel: (315) 445-0550
Fax: (315) 445-9401

Main Headquarters
Mailing: 85 Collamer Crossings Pkwy.
E. Syracuse, NY 13057
Tel: (315) 445-0550
Fax: (315) 445-9401

Washington Office
Mailing: 600 Maryland Ave. SW
Suite 605E
Washington, DC 20024
Tel: (202) 264-8753
Fax: (202) 264-8751

Saab Sensis Corporation

Formerly, Sensis Corporation. Absorbed current name in 2011. Offers a wide range of sensors and information processing systems for air defense, air traffic control, airline and airport management.
www.saabsensis.com
Employees: 100
SIC: 3577; 3812; 7371; 7372
NAICS: 334119; 334511; 511210; 541511
Industry/ies: Defense/Homeland Security; Government-Related; Transportation
Legislative Issues: AVI; BUD

President and Chief Executive Officer
BUSKHE , Hakan
Tel: (315) 445-0550
Fax: (315) 445-9401

Main Headquarters
Mailing: 85 Collamer Crossings
E. Syracuse, NY 13057-8800
Tel: (315) 445-0550
Fax: (315) 445-9401

Washington Office
Mailing: 600 Maryland Ave. SW
Suite 605E
Washington, DC 20024
Tel: (202) 264-8753
Fax: (202) 264-8751

Public Affairs and Related Activities Personnel

At Headquarters

BAREMO , Annika
Senior Vice President and Head of Group, Legal Affairs, General Counsel and Secretary
Tel: (315) 445-0550
Fax: (315) 445-9401

BEARDSLEY, Kelly
Senior Financial Analyst
investor_relations@sensis.com
Tel: (315) 445-5728
Fax: (315) 445-9401

DUDARCHIK, Peggy
Senior Vice President, Human Resources
Tel: (315) 445-0550
Fax: (315) 445-9401

ELIASSON, Lena
Senior Vice President and Head, Group Human Resources
Tel: (315) 445-0550
Fax: (315) 445-9401

MORGAN, John
Senior Vice President and Chief Strategy Officer
Tel: (315) 445-0550
Fax: (315) 445-9401

ORNBERG, Magnus
Executive Vice President and Chief Financial Officer
Tel: (315) 445-0550
Fax: (315) 445-9401

THEGSTROM, Asa
Tel: (315) 445-0550

Senior Vice President and Head of Group, Communication   Fax: (315) 445-9401

SABIC Innovative Plastics US LLC

Manufacturer of plastics.
www.sabic.com
Employees: 11,000
Industry/ies: Plastics Industry
Legislative Issues: AUT; CHM; EDU; TRA

Vice-Chairman and Chief Executive Officer
AL-BENYAN, Yousef Abdullah
Tel: (413) 448-7110
Fax: (413) 448-5573

Main Headquarters
Mailing: One Plastics Ave.
Pittsfield, MA 01201
Tel: (413) 448-7110
Fax: (413) 448-5573

Washington Office
Mailing: 1310 G St. NW
Suite 770
Washington, DC 20005
Tel: (202) 621-2540
Fax: (202) 621-2546

Public Affairs and Related Activities Personnel

At Headquarters

ADAMS , Gregory A .
Vice President, Americas Region
Tel: (413) 448-7110
Fax: (413) 448-5573

AL-OHALI, Mosaed
Executive Vice-President, Corporate Finance
Tel: (413) 448-7110
Fax: (413) 448-5573

AL-OUDAN, Abdulaziz
Executive Vice President, Corporate Human Resources
Tel: (413) 448-7110
Fax: (413) 448-5573

AL-SHAMRANI, Ali
Vice President, Corporate Communications
Tel: (413) 448-7110
Fax: (413) 448-5573

AL-ZAMEL, Yousef
Executive Vice President, Corporate Strategy
Tel: (413) 448-7110
Fax: (413) 448-5573

BAYNE, Steve
Senior Director, Finance
Tel: (413) 448-7110
Fax: (413) 448-5573

HARNETT, Lawrence M.
General Counsel
Tel: (413) 448-7110
Fax: (413) 448-5573

KENNEDY, Jodi
Director, Communications Americas Region
Tel: (413) 448-7383
Fax: (413) 448-5573

LEBOURDAIS, Susan
Business Communications Leader
susan.lebourdais@sabic.com
Tel: (413) 448-7795
Fax: (413) 448-5573

SHASTRI, Naveena
Senior Director, Americas Chief Counsel
Tel: (413) 448-7110
Fax: (413) 448-5573

At Washington Office

BATSON, Russell B.
Senior Counsel, Government Relations
russell.batson@sabic.com
Registered Federal Lobbyist
Tel: (202) 621-2542
Fax: (202) 621-2546

MONAGHAN, Jessine A.
Director & Senior Counsel, Government Relations, Americas
jessine.monaghan@sabic.com
Registered Federal Lobbyist
Tel: (202) 621-2544
Fax: (202) 621-2546

Sabre Holdings

An information technology provider for the travel industry.
www.sabre.com
Employees: 9,000
SIC: 4700
Industry/ies: Communications; Computer/Technology; Telecommunications/Internet/Cable; Travel/Tourism/Lodging
Legislative Issues: AVI; CPT; HOM; IMM; LAW; LBR; TOU; TRD

President and Chief Executive Officer
KLEIN, Tom
Tel: (682) 605-1000
Fax: (682) 264-9000

Main Headquarters
Mailing: 3150 Sabre Dr.
Southlake, TX 76092
Tel: (682) 605-1000
Fax: (682) 264-9000

Washington Office
Mailing: 1250 Connecticut Ave. NW
Suite 825
Washington, DC 20036
Tel: (202) 467-8203
Fax: (202) 467-8204

Political Action Committees
Sabre Holdings PAC
FEC ID: C00325811
Contact: Michael Hanson
1250 Connecticut Ave. NW
Suite 825
Washington, DC 20036
Tel: (202) 467-8208
Fax: (202) 467-8204

Contributions to Candidates: $52,500 (2015-2016)
Democrats: $32,000; Republicans: $20,500

Principal Recipients

SENATE
BLUMENTHAL, RICHARD (DEM-CT)

Corporate Foundations and Giving Programs

Sabre Holdings Contributions Program
3150 Sabre Dr.
Southlake, TX 76092

Public Affairs and Related Activities Personnel

At Headquarters

ANDERSON, Clinton	Tel:	(682) 605-1000
Senior Vice President, Strategy and Traveler Experience	Fax:	(682) 264-9000
CHIAMES, Chris	Tel:	(682) 605-1000
Senior Vice President, Corporate Communications	Fax:	(682) 264-9000
GONZALEZ, Rachel	Tel:	(682) 605-1000
Executive Vice President and General Counsel	Fax:	(682) 264-9000
ROBINSON, Bill	Tel:	(682) 605-1000
Executive Vice President and Chief Human Resources Officer	Fax:	(682) 264-9000
SIMONSON, Rick	Tel:	(682) 605-1000
Executive Vice President and Chief Financial Officer	Fax:	(682) 264-9000
WONG, Pam	Tel:	(682) 605-1000
Director, Global External Communications	Fax:	(682) 264-9000

At Washington Office

CHARENDOFF, Bruce	Tel:	(202) 467-8203
Senior Vice President, Government Affairs	Fax:	(202) 467-8204
Mail Stop Suite 825		
bruce.charendoff@sabre-holdings.com		
HANSON, Michael	Tel:	(202) 467-8203
PAC Treasurer	Fax:	(202) 467-8204
Registered Federal Lobbyist		

Sacred Wind Communications, Inc.

Sacred Wind Communications is a privately owned, New Mexico-based company, dedicated to improve telecommunications services to rural areas within New Mexico.
www.sacredwindcommunications.com
Annual Revenues: $3.80 million
Employees: 17
Industry/ies: Communications; Telecommunications/Internet/Cable

Chief Executive Officer	Tel:	(877) 722-3393
BADAL, John	Fax:	(505) 821-0226
jbadal@sacred-wind.com		

Main Headquarters

Mailing: 875 US Hwy 491 North	Tel:	(877) 722-3393
Yatahey, NM 87375		

Corporate Foundations and Giving Programs

Sacred Wind Communications Community Connect
Contact: Janice Badal

5901-J Wyoming Blvd. NE	Tel:	(505) 821-5080
Sutie 266		
Albuquerque, NM 87109		

Public Affairs and Related Activities Personnel

At Headquarters

ARVISO, Gil	Tel:	(877) 722-3393
Manager, Community Relations		
BADAL, Janice	Tel:	(877) 722-3393
Executive Director, Non-profit at Sacred Wind Communications		
jcbadal@sacred-wind.com		
CROSBY, Herb	Tel:	(877) 722-3393
Human Resources		

SAFECO Insurance

A subsidiary of Liberty Mutual Insurance Company. An insurance, financial services and real estate development company.
www.safeco.com
Employees: 7,000
Ticker: NYSE: SAF
SIC: 6331
Industry/ies: Banking/Finance/Investments

President	Tel:	(206) 545-5000
NICKERSON, Matthew	Fax:	(425) 376-6533

Main Headquarters

Mailing: SAFECO Plaza	Tel:	(206) 545-5000
1001 Fourth Ave.	Fax:	(425) 376-6533
Seattle, WA 98154	TF:	(800) 332-3226

Corporate Foundations and Giving Programs

SAFECO Insurance Foundation
1001 Fourth Ave.
Seattle, WA 98154

Public Affairs and Related Activities Personnel

At Headquarters

DESHAW, Donald J.	Tel:	(206) 545-5000

Vice President and General Counsel	Fax:	(425) 376-6533
Don.DeShaw@safeco.com		
HARRISON, Brenda Mann	Tel:	(206) 545-5000
Media Contact	Fax:	(425) 376-6533
Brenda.Harrison@safeco.com		

Safeguard Scientifics, Inc.

An information technology holding company.
www.safeguard.com
Annual Revenues: $34.84 million
Employees: 30
Ticker: NYSE: SFE
SIC: 6799; 2521; 3471; 3577; 3661; 8742
Industry/ies: Computer/Technology

President and Chief Executive Officer	Tel:	(610) 293-0600
ZARRILLI, Stephen T.	Fax:	(610) 293-0601

Main Headquarters

Mailing: 435 Devon Park Dr.	Tel:	(610) 293-0600
Building 800	Fax:	(610) 293-0601
Wayne, PA 19087		

Public Affairs and Related Activities Personnel

At Headquarters

ACEVEDO, Jason	Tel:	(610) 293-0600
Corporate Counsel	Fax:	(610) 293-0601
HUNTER, Heather R.	Tel:	(610) 293-0600
Vice President, Corporate Communications	Fax:	(610) 293-0601
hhunter@safeguard.com		
MCGROARTY, Jeffrey B.	Tel:	(610) 293-0600
Senior Vice President and Chief Financial Officer	Fax:	(610) 293-0601
SHAVE, III, John E.	Tel:	(610) 975-4952
Senior Vice President, Investor Relations and Corporate Communications	Fax:	(610) 293-0601
jshave@safeguard.com		

Safeway, Inc.

A food and drug retailer.
www.safeway.com
Employees: 138,000
Ticker: NYSE: SWY
SIC: 5411
Industry/ies: Food And Beverage Industry; Retail/Wholesale
Legislative Issues: AGR; BUD; CSP; FOO; HCR; LBR; PHA; TAX

Chairman of the Board	Tel:	(925) 467-3000
ROGERS , T. Gary	Fax:	(925) 467-3323
President and Chief Executive Officer	Tel:	(925) 467-3000
EDWARDS, Robert L.	Fax:	(925) 467-3321

Main Headquarters

Mailing: 5918 Stoneridge Mall Rd.	Tel:	(925) 467-3000
Pleasanton, CA 94588	Fax:	(925) 467-3323

Washington Office

Mailing: 11555 Dublin Canyon Rd.
Suite 530E
Pleasanton, DC 20015

Political Action Committees

Safeway PAC
FEC ID: C00194084
Contact: Rachel Zenner Kane

5918 Stoneridge Mall Rd.		
Pleasanton, CA 94588	Tel:	(202) 464-8806

    Contributions to Candidates: $90,499 (2015-2016)
    Democrats: $31,500; Republicans: $58,999

Corporate Foundations and Giving Programs

The Safeway Foundation
Contact: Christy Duncan Anderson
5918 Stoneridge Mall Rd.
Pleasanton, CA 94588

Public Affairs and Related Activities Personnel

At Headquarters

ANDERSON , Christy Duncan	Tel:	(925) 467-3000
Executive Director, Foundation	Fax:	(925) 467-3323
Christy.Duncan-Anderson@safeway.com		
BOCIAN, Peter J.	Tel:	(925) 467-3000
Executive Vice President and Chief Financial Officer	Fax:	(925) 467-3323
COLER, Kate	Tel:	(925) 467-3000
Vice President, Federal Government Relations	Fax:	(925) 467-3323
Registered Federal Lobbyist		
DIETZ, Diane M.	Tel:	(925) 467-3000
Executive Vice President and Chief Marketing Officer	Fax:	(925) 467-3323
DOWLING, Brian G.	Tel:	(925) 467-3787

Vice President, Public Affairs	Fax: (925) 467-3323
brian.dowling@safeway.com	
JACKSON, Russell M.	Tel: (925) 467-3000
Senior Vice President, Human Resources	Fax: (925) 467-3321
KANE, Rachel Zenner	Tel: (925) 467-3102
Federal Lobbyist and PAC Treasurer	Fax: (925) 467-3321
rachel.zenner@safeway.com	
MASSINGILL, Teena	Tel: (925) 467-3810
Contact, Media Relations	Fax: (925) 467-3323
Teena.Massingill@Safeway.com	
MAYES, Jonathan	Tel: (925) 467-3000
	Fax: (925) 467-3323
PLAISANCE, Melissa C.	Tel: (925) 467-3136
Senior Vice President, Finance and Investor Relations	Fax: (925) 467-3321
RENDA, Larree M.	Tel: (925) 467-3000
Executive Vice President	Fax: (925) 467-3323

Safran USA, Inc.

Formerly SNECMA USA. A holding company for aircraft parts manufacturers in North America.
www.safran-na.com
Annual Revenues: $193.50 million
Employees: 4,300
Industry/ies: Business; Small Business
Legislative Issues: BUD; DEF; HOM; TRA

Chief Executive Officer	Tel: (703) 351-9898
PETITCOLIN, Philippe	Fax: (703) 351-9890

Main Headquarters
Mailing:	2300 Clarendon Blvd.	Tel: (703) 351-9898
	Suite 607	Fax: (703) 351-9890
	Arlington, VA 22201	

Public Affairs and Related Activities Personnel

At Headquarters

ABRIAL, Stephane	Tel: (703) 351-9898
Senior Executive Vice President International and Public Affairs	Fax: (703) 351-9890
BERARD, Jean-Luc	Tel: (703) 351-9898
Executive Vice President, Human Resources	Fax: (703) 351-9890
DALBIES, Eric	Tel: (703) 351-9898
Executive Vice President, Strategy, M and A	Fax: (703) 351-9890
DELPIT, Bernard	Tel: (703) 351-9898
Senior Executive Vice President, Finance	Fax: (703) 351-9890
DUBOIS, Pascale	Tel: (703) 351-9898
Executive Vice President, Communication	Fax: (703) 351-9890
FAIN, Alex	Tel: (703) 351-9898
Corporate Secretary	Fax: (703) 351-9890
JORGE, Kaitlyn	Tel: (703) 351-9898
Registered Federal Lobbyist	Fax: (703) 351-9890
LYLE, Michelle	Tel: (703) 351-9898
Director, Marketing Communications	Fax: (703) 351-9890
mlyle@safranusa.com	
MCKAY, Allison	Tel: (703) 351-9898
Director, Public Affairs	Fax: (703) 351-9890
Registered Federal Lobbyist	
MCLNNES, Ross	Tel: (703) 351-9898
Deputy Chief Executive Officer, Finance	Fax: (703) 351-9890
VAN DE WATER, Read	Tel: (703) 351-9898
Registered Federal Lobbyist	Fax: (703) 351-9890

At Other Offices
MELINK, Mark	Tel: (972) 606-7108
PAC Treasurer	Fax: (972) 606-7114
2850 Safran Dr.	
Grand Prairie, TX 75052	

Saga Communications, Inc.

Saga Communications, Inc. is a performing broadcast company, devoted to acquiring, developing, and operating broadcast properties.
sagacom.com
Annual Revenues: $133.64 million
Employees: 761
Ticker: NYSE: SGA
SIC: 4832
Industry/ies: Communications; Telecommunications/Internet/Cable

President, Chief Executive Officer and Chairman	Tel: (313) 886-7070
CHRISTIAN, Edward	Fax: (313) 886-7150
echristian@sagacom.com	

Main Headquarters
Mailing:	73 Kercheval Ave.	Tel: (313) 886-7070
	Suite 201	Fax: (313) 886-7150

Grosse Pointe Farms, MI 48236

Public Affairs and Related Activities Personnel

At Headquarters

BOBINSKI, Cathy	Tel: (313) 886-7070
Senior Vice President, Chief Accounting Officer, Corporate Controller	Fax: (313) 886-7150
BUSH, Samuel D.	Tel: (313) 886-7070
Senior Vice President, Chief Financial Officer and Treasurer	Fax: (313) 886-7150
sbush@sagacom.com	
LADA, Warren	Tel: (313) 886-7070
Executive Vice President Operations	Fax: (313) 886-7150
LOBAITO, Marcia	Tel: (313) 886-7070
Senior Vice President and Director, Business Affairs	Fax: (313) 886-7150

Saint-Gobain Corporation

U.S. subsidiary of Company Saint-Gobain, headquartered in Courbevoie, France. Provides services involving the following materials: building materials, glass containers, glass, ceramics, abrasives, reinforcements and plastics.
www.saint-gobain-northamerica.com
Employees: 26,000
Industry/ies: Construction/Construction Materials
Legislative Issues: ENV

Chairman and Chief Executive Officer	Tel: (610) 341-7000
CHALENDAR, Pierre-André de	Fax: (610) 341-7777

Main Headquarters
Mailing:	750 E. Swedesford Rd.	Tel: (610) 341-7000
	P.O. Box 860	Fax: (610) 341-7777
	Valley Forge, PA 19482	

Corporate Foundations and Giving Programs

Saint-Gobain Corporation Foundation
750 E. Swedesford Rd.
P.O. Box 860
Valley Forge, PA 19482

Public Affairs and Related Activities Personnel

At Headquarters

DIDIER , Fabrice	Tel: (610) 341-7000
Vice President, Marketing	Fax: (610) 341-7777
GENY-STEPHANN, Delphine	Tel: (610) 341-7000
Vice President, Corporate Planning and Strategy	Fax: (610) 341-7777
GUILLOT, Laurent	Tel: (610) 341-7000
President	Fax: (610) 341-7777
HUFNAGEL, Charles	Tel: (610) 341-7000
Vice-President, Communications	Fax: (610) 341-7777
IMAUVEN, Claude	Tel: (610) 341-7000
Chief Operating Officer	Fax: (610) 341-7777
PEDINI, Claire	Tel: (610) 341-7000
Senior Vice President, Human Resources	Fax: (610) 341-7777
PUCCIO, M. Shawn	Tel: (610) 341-7000
Senior Vice President, Finance	Fax: (610) 341-7777
SEIBERLICH, Bill	Tel: (610) 341-7187
Manager, Communications	Fax: (610) 341-7777
TEXIER, Guillaume	Tel: (610) 341-7000
Chief Financial Officer	Fax: (610) 341-7777

Salem Communications Corporation

Salem is a radio broadcaster, Internet content provider, and magazine and book publisher targeting audiences interested in Christian themed content and conservative values.
salem.cc
Annual Revenues: $266.05 million
Employees: 1,230
Ticker: NASDAQ: SALM
SIC: 4832
Industry/ies: Communications; Media/Mass Communication
Legislative Issues: CPT

Chairman of the Board	Tel: (805) 987-0400
EPPERSON, Stuart W.	Fax: (805) 384-4520

Chief Executive Officer and Director	Tel: (805) 987-0400
ATSINGER, III, Edward G.	Fax: (805) 384-4520

Main Headquarters
Mailing:	4880 Santa Rosa Rd.	Tel: (805) 987-0400
	Camarillo, CA 93012	Fax: (805) 384-4520

Political Action Committees

Salem Communications Corporation PAC
FEC ID: C00321158
Contact: Russell R. Hauth
4860 Santa Rosa Rd.
Camarillo, CA 93012

Contributions to Candidates: $56,960 (2015-2016)
Republicans: $56,960

Principal Recipients
SENATE
BLUNT, ROY (REP-MO)

Public Affairs and Related Activities Personnel
At Headquarters

EVANS, David	Tel:	(805) 987-0400
President, New Media	Fax:	(805) 384-4520
HAUTH, Russell R.	Tel:	(805) 987-0400
Senior Vice President	Fax:	(805) 384-4520
russh@salem.cc		
HENDERSON, Christopher J.	Tel:	(805) 987-0400
Senior Vice President, Legal and Human Resources, General Counsel and Corporate Secretary	Fax:	(805) 384-4520
MASYR, Evan D.	Tel:	(805) 987-0400
Senior Vice President and Chief Financial Officer	Fax:	(805) 384-4520
evan@salem.cc		
SOLIS, Tomasita	Tel:	(805) 987-0400
Media Contact	Fax:	(805) 384-4520
tomasitaa@salem.cc		

Salesforce.com
Provider of customer relationship management (CRM) software and cloud computing and help companies connect with customers, partners, and employees in entirely new ways.
www.salesforce.com
Annual Revenues: $5.66 billion
Employees: 16,000
Ticker: NYSE: CRM
SIC: 7372
Industry/ies: Computer/Technology
Legislative Issues: CPI; CPT; GOV; TEC; TRD

Chairman of the Board and Chief Executive Officer	Tel:	(415) 901-7000
BENIOFF, Marc	Fax:	(415) 901-7040

Main Headquarters

Mailing:	One Market St.	Tel:	(415) 901-7000
	Suite 300	Fax:	(415) 901-7040
	San Francisco, CA 94105	TF:	(800) 667-6389

Political Action Committees
Salesforce.com Inc. PAC
FEC ID: C00511600
Contact: Elizabeth Allen
The Landmark at One Market
Suite 300
San Francisco, CA 94105

> **Contributions to Candidates:** $26,500 (2015-2016)
> Democrats: $16,500; Republicans: $10,000

Principal Recipients
SENATE
SCHUMER, CHARLES E (DEM-NY)

Corporate Foundations and Giving Programs

Salesforce.com Foundation
Contact: Suzanne DiBianca

The Landmark at One Market	Tel:	(415) 901-7000
Suite 300	Fax:	(415) 901-7000
San Francisco, CA 94105		

Public Affairs and Related Activities Personnel
At Headquarters

ALLEN, Elizabeth	Tel:	(415) 901-7000
Director, Global Treasury and PAC Treasurer	Fax:	(415) 901-7040
Mail Stop The Landmark at One Market, Suite 300		
CIARALLO, Joe	Tel:	(201) 835-3225
Senior Director, Public Relations	Fax:	(415) 901-7040
jciarallo@salesforce.com		
DIBIANCA, Suzanne	Tel:	(415) 901-7000
Executive Director, The Salesforce.com Foundation	Fax:	(415) 901-7040
GAMBLE, Hugh	Tel:	(415) 901-7000
Senior Director, Government Affairs	Fax:	(415) 901-7040
Registered Federal Lobbyist		
GREEN, James	Tel:	(415) 901-7000
	Fax:	(415) 901-7040
HAWKINS, Mark	Tel:	(415) 901-7000
Chief Financial Officer and Executive Vice President	Fax:	(415) 901-7040
HU, George	Tel:	(415) 901-7000
Chief Operating Officer	Fax:	(415) 901-7040
NORTON, Burke	Tel:	(415) 901-7000
Chief Legal Officer	Fax:	(415) 901-7040
OLIVER , April	Tel:	(415) 901-7000
Global Compliance Attorney	Fax:	(415) 901-7040
VOJVODICH, Lynn	Tel:	(415) 901-7000

Executive Vice President and Chief Marketing Officer	Fax:	(415) 901-7040
WEAVER, Amy	Tel:	(415) 901-7000
General Counsel	Fax:	(415) 901-7040

Sallie Mae, Inc.
See listing on page 565 under Navient Solutions, Inc.

Salt River Project
Provides water to the owners and occupants of lands within the Salt River reclamation district and produces electricity for use within the region.
www.srpnet.com
Employees: 4,500
Industry/ies: Energy/Electricity; Marine/Maritime/Shipping; Ports And Waterways; Transportation; Utilities
Legislative Issues: BAN; BUD; CAW; ENG; NAT; TAX

General Manager and Chief Executive Officer	Tel:	(602) 236-5900
BONSALL, Mark	Fax:	(602) 236-4423

Main Headquarters

Mailing:	1521 N. Project Dr.	Tel:	(602) 236-5900
	Tempe, AZ 85281-1298	Fax:	(602) 236-4423
		TF:	(800) 258-4777

Washington Office

Mailing:	101 Constitution Ave. NW	Tel:	(202) 898-1580
	Suite 300 E	Fax:	(202) 898-1580
	Washington, DC 20001		

Political Action Committees
Salt River Valley Water Users' Association Political Involvement Committee (SRPPIC) PAC
FEC ID: C00048579
Contact: Heidi Rowe Schaefer
P.O. Box 52025
ISB 336
Phoenix, AZ 85072

> **Contributions to Candidates:** $137,000 (2015-2016)
> Democrats: $47,000; Republicans: $90,000

Corporate Foundations and Giving Programs
Salt River Project Contributions Program
P.O. Box 52025
PAB 337
Phoenix, AZ 85072

Public Affairs and Related Activities Personnel
At Headquarters

HARELSON, Scott	Tel:	(602) 236-2500
Manager, Media Relations	Fax:	(602) 236-4423
scott.harelson@srpnet.com		
MCSHEFFREY, Aidan	Tel:	(602) 236-5900
Associate General Manager, Chief Financial Executive, Financial and Corporate Services	Fax:	(602) 236-4423
O'CONNOR, Michael	Tel:	(602) 236-5900
Associate General Manager, Chief Legal Executive, Law and Human Resource Services	Fax:	(602) 236-4423
REED, Stephanie	Tel:	(602) 236-5900
Corporate Secretary	Fax:	(602) 236-4423
ROUSSEAU, David	Tel:	(602) 236-5900
President	Fax:	(602) 236-4423
SULLIVAN, John	Tel:	(602) 236-5900
Deputy General Manager and Executive, Chief Strategic Initiatives	Fax:	(602) 236-4423
TRIMBLE, Gena	Tel:	(602) 236-5900
Associate General Manager, Chief Communications Executive, Marketing and Communications	Fax:	(602) 236-4423

At Washington Office

DICKSON, Lane	Tel:	(202) 898-8089
Representative, Federal Affairs	Fax:	(202) 898-1580
lane.dickson@srpnet.com		
Registered Federal Lobbyist		
EASTMAN, Renee	Tel:	(202) 898-8089
Senior Director, Federal Affairs	Fax:	(202) 898-1580
renee.eastman@srpnet.com		
Registered Federal Lobbyist		
HAYES, Peter	Tel:	(202) 898-8089
Associate General Manager and Chief Public Affairs Executive, Public Affairs	Fax:	(202) 898-1580

At Other Offices
SCHAEFER, Heidi Rowe
PAC Treasurer
P.O. Box 52025
Phoenix, AZ 85072-2025
hrschaef@srpnet.com

Saltchuk Resources

Operates air cargo, marine transport, petroleum distribution, real estate development, and marine services businesses. Originally a marine transportation company.
www.saltchuk.com
Employees: 4,500
Industry/ies: Marine/Maritime/Shipping; Transportation
Legislative Issues: BNK; TAX; TRU

| **Chairman of the Board** | Tel: | (206) 652-1111 |
| TABBUTT, Mark N. | | |

| **President** | Tel: | (206) 652-1111 |
| ENGLE, Tim | | |

Main Headquarters
Mailing: 1111 Fairview Ave., North   Tel: (206) 652-1111
Seattle, WA 98109

Washington Office
Mailing: 1000 Potomac St. NW
Suite 200
Washington, DC 20007

Political Action Committees
Saltchuk Resources, Inc. PAC
FEC ID: C00411694
Contact: Robert A. Lowe
32001 32nd Ave., South
Suite 200
Federal Way, WA 98001

> **Contributions to Candidates:** $95,500 (2015-2016)
> Democrats: $43,500; Republicans: $49,000; Other: $3,000

Public Affairs and Related Activities Personnel

At Headquarters

| GIESE, Steven | Tel: | (206) 652-1111 |
| *Senior Vice President and Chief Financial Officer* | | |

HOERSTER, John	Tel:	(206) 652-1111
Senior Vice President, General Counsel and Chief Ethics Officer		
johnh@saltchuk.com		

| REITER, Emily | Tel: | (206) 652-1111 |
| *Director, Communications and External Affairs* | | |

| ROSAS, Colleen | Tel: | (206) 652-1111 |
| *Senior Vice President, Human Resources* | | |

At Washington Office

COAKLEY, Christopher A.	Tel:	(202) 650-6910
ccoakley@saltchuk.com		
Registered Federal Lobbyist		

At Other Offices

LOWE, Robert A.
PAC Treasurer
32001 32nd Ave., South, Suite 200
Federal Way, WA 98001

The Same Page, LLC

A Lobbying Firm.

President, The Same Page, LLC	Tel:	(703) 971-2875
HAIGWOOD, Michael B		
burl.haigwood@gmail.com		

Main Headquarters
Mailing: 906 Royal Adelade Dr.   Tel: (202) 441-2400
College Station, TX 77845

Washington Office
Mailing: 5704 Shropshire Ct.   Tel: (703) 971-2875
Alexandria, VA 22315

Sammons Enterprises, Inc.

Life insurance and financial services.
www.sammonsenterprises.com
Annual Revenues: $121.20 million
Employees: 3,000
Industry/ies: Taxation

| **Chairman of the Board** | Tel: | (214) 210-5000 |
| CORCORAN, Thomas | Fax: | (214) 210-5099 |

| **Chief Executive Officer** | Tel: | (214) 210-5000 |
| KREAGER, Heather | Fax: | (214) 210-5099 |

Main Headquarters
Mailing: 5949 Sherry Ln.   Tel: (214) 210-5000
Suite 1900   Fax: (214) 210-5099
Dallas, TX 75225

Political Action Committees
Sammons Enterprises Inc. PAC
FEC ID: C00388777

Contact: Pam Doeppe
5949 Sherry Ln.
Suite 1900
Dallas, TX 75225

Corporate Foundations and Giving Programs
Sammons Dallas Foundation
5949 Sherry Ln.   Tel: (214) 210-5000
Suite 1900   Fax: (214) 210-5099
Dallas, TX 75225

Public Affairs and Related Activities Personnel

At Headquarters

ASH, Darron	Tel:	(214) 210-5000
Senior Vice President, Chief Financial Officer	Fax:	(214) 210-5099
DOEPPE, Pam	Tel:	(214) 210-5000
Vice President and PAC Treasurer	Fax:	(214) 210-5099
NEWMAN, Linda	Tel:	(214) 210-5000
Vice President, General Counsel and Secretary	Fax:	(214) 210-5099

Samsung Informations Systems America, Inc.

Engaged in researching emerging technology to create new businesses, and developing core technology to enhance the competitiveness of Samsung's products.
www.sisa.samsung.com
Industry/ies: Communications; Telecommunications/Internet/Cable

Main Headquarters
Mailing: 75 W. Plumeria Dr.   Tel: (408) 383-9486
San Jose, CA 95134

Washington Office
Mailing: 1200 New Hampshire Ave. NW   Tel: (202) 887-5667
Suite 550
Washington, DC 20036

Public Affairs and Related Activities Personnel

At Washington Office

GODFREY, John B.	Tel:	(202) 887-5667
Vice President, Government and Public Affairs		
john.godfrey@samsung.com		

Samtrans

Samtrans is a public transport agency.
www.samtrans.com
Annual Revenues: $17.20 million
Employees: 800
Industry/ies: Transportation
Legislative Issues: TRA

Chairman of the Board	Tel:	(650) 508-6200
MATSUMOTO, Karyl	Fax:	(650) 508-6281
karyl.matsumoto@ssf.net		

Chief Executive Officer	Tel:	(650) 508-6200
SCANLON, Michael J.	Fax:	(650) 508-7917
scanlonm@samtrans.com		

Main Headquarters
Mailing: 1250 San Carlos Ave.   Tel: (650) 508-6200
P.O. Box 3006   Fax: (650) 508-6281
San Carlos, CA 94070-1306   TF: (800) 660-4287

Public Affairs and Related Activities Personnel

At Headquarters

| DUNN, Christine | Tel: | (650) 508-6238 |
| *Media Contact* | Fax: | (650) 508-7917 |

San Diego Gas and Electric

An electric and gas utility. A subsidiary of Sempra Energy Corp.
www.sdge.com
Annual Revenues: $3.69 billion
Employees: 5,000
Ticker: NYSE Amex: SDO-PA
SIC: 4931
Industry/ies: Energy/Electricity; Utilities

| **Chairman** | Tel: | (619) 696-2000 |
| KNIGHT, Jr., Jessie J. | Fax: | (858) 654-1515 |

| **Chief Executive Officer** | Tel: | (619) 696-2000 |
| MARTIN, Jeff | Fax: | (858) 654-1515 |

Main Headquarters
Mailing: P.O. Box 129831   Tel: (619) 696-2000
San Diego, CA 92112-9831   Fax: (858) 654-1515
                             TF: (800) 336-7343

Corporate Foundations and Giving Programs
San Diego Gas and Electric Corporate Contributions
P.O. Box 129831   Tel: (619) 696-2000
San Diego, CA 92112-9831   Fax: (858) 654-1515

Public Affairs and Related Activities Personnel

At Headquarters

BAKER, J. Chris
Senior Vice President And Chief Information Officer
Tel: (619) 696-2000
Fax: (858) 654-1515

DAVIS, Steven D.
President And Chief Operating Officer
Tel: (619) 696-2000
Fax: (858) 654-1515

DONOVAN, Stephanie
Senior Communications Manager
Tel: (877) 866-2066
Fax: (858) 654-1515

DRURY, Scott
Vice President, Human Resources, Diversity and Inclusion
Tel: (619) 696-2000
Fax: (858) 654-1515

MITCHELL, Mitch
Vice President, Legislative and External Affairs
Tel: (619) 696-2000
Fax: (858) 654-1515

SCHAVRIEN, Lee
Senior Vice President, Finance, Regulatory and Legislative Affairs
Tel: (619) 696-2000
Fax: (858) 654-1515

SCHLAX, Robert M.
Vice President, Controller and Chief Financial Officer
Tel: (619) 696-2000
Fax: (858) 654-1515

SKOPEC, Daniel
Vice President, Regulatory and Legislative Affairs
Tel: (619) 696-2000
Fax: (858) 654-1515

SMITH, Davis W.
Senior Vice President, General Counsel and Assistant Secretary
Tel: (619) 696-2000
Fax: (858) 654-1515

The Sandi Group

A real estate development and trading company. Today, TSG is a global, multi-disciplined private company providing turnkey, design, real estate development, fully managed construction services, security, aviation, logistics and life support.
www.thesandigroup.com
Annual Revenues: $6.60 million
Employees: 100
Industry/ies: Government-Related

Chairman and Chief Executive Officer
SANDI, Dr. Rubar S.
Tel: (202) 331-9320
Fax: (202) 331-9321

Main Headquarters
Mailing: 2215 M St. NW
          Washington, DC 20037
Tel: (202) 331-9320
Fax: (202) 331-9321

Public Affairs and Related Activities Personnel

At Headquarters

BLOUNT, III, Buford C.
Chief Operating Officer
Tel: (202) 331-9320
Fax: (202) 331-9321

CREAGHAN, James P.
Senior Advisor
Tel: (202) 331-9320
Fax: (202) 331-9321

HOOD, Michael A.
Managing Director & General Manager (TSG Global Operations)
Tel: (202) 331-9320
Fax: (202) 331-9321

HUGO, Russell
Chief Financial Officer
Tel: (202) 331-9320
Fax: (202) 331-9321

KARSLIOGLU, Muge
Senior Vice President, Business Development
Tel: (202) 331-9320
Fax: (202) 331-9321

MOLLARD, Karin
Vice President, Business Management
Tel: (202) 331-9320
Fax: (202) 331-9321

RAMAIZEL, Esq., Prof. Frank A.
Senior Consultant – Rule of Law
Tel: (202) 331-9320
Fax: (202) 331-9321

SanDisk Corporation

SanDisk designs, develops, manufactures and markets flash storage card products for a wide variety of electronic systems and digital devices. The company is a producer of data storage products based on flash memory, which retains data even when power is interrupted. SanDisk's products include removable and embedded memory cards used in digital still cameras, medical devices, networking equipment, notebook computers, and other electronics.
www.sandisk.com
Annual Revenues: $15.38 billion
Employees: 8,790
Ticker: NASDAQ: SNDK
SIC: 5045; 5734
Industry/ies: Computer/Technology

Co-Founder, President and Chief Executive Officer
MEHROTRA, Sanjay
Tel: (408) 801-1000
Fax: (408) 801-8657

Main Headquarters
Mailing: 951 SanDisk Dr.
          Milpitas, CA 95035-7933
Tel: (408) 801-1000
Fax: (408) 801-8657

Corporate Foundations and Giving Programs

San Disk Contributions Program
601 McCarthy Blvd.
Milpitas, CA 95035
Tel: (408) 801-1000

Public Affairs and Related Activities Personnel

At Headquarters

BAKER, Tom
Tel: (408) 801-1000

Senior Vice President, Human Resources
tom.baker@sandisk.com
Fax: (408) 801-8657

BRAZEAL, Mark
Senior Vice President and Chief Legal Officer
Tel: (408) 801-1000
Fax: (408) 801-8657

BRUNER, Judy
Executive Vice President, Chief Financial Officer
Tel: (408) 801-1000
Fax: (408) 801-8657

NIR, Shuki
Senior Vice President, Corporate Marketing and General Manager, Retail Services
Tel: (408) 801-1000
Fax: (408) 801-8657

SADANA, Sumit
Executive Vice President and Chief Strategy Officer
Tel: (408) 801-1000
Fax: (408) 801-8657

Sanmina-SCI, Inc.

An electronics contract manufacturer, formed from the merger between Sanmina Corp. and SCI Systems, Inc. in December of 2001.
www.sanmina.com
Annual Revenues: $6.32 billion
Employees: 33,966
Ticker: NASDAQ: SANM
SIC: 3672
NAICS: 334412
Industry/ies: Electricity & Electronics; Electronics; Energy/Electricity

Chairman of the Board and Chief Executive Officer
SOLA, Jure
jure.sola@sanmina-sci.com
Tel: (408) 964-3500
Fax: (408) 964-3636

Main Headquarters
Mailing: 2700 N. First St.
          San Jose, CA 95134
Tel: (408) 964-3500
Fax: (408) 964-3440
TF: (800) 416-8749

Public Affairs and Related Activities Personnel

At Headquarters

BOMBINO, Paige
Vice President, Investor Relations
paige.bombino@sanmina-sci.com
Tel: (408) 964-3610
Fax: (408) 964-3636

EULAU, Bob
Executive Vice President and Chief Financial Officer
Tel: (408) 964-3500
Fax: (408) 964-3636

KOSTALNICK, Charles
Executive Vice President and Chief Business Officer
Tel: (408) 964-3500
Fax: (408) 964-3440

REID, Alan
Executive Vice President, Global Human Resources
Tel: (408) 964-3500
Fax: (408) 964-3440

Sanofi-Aventis U.S.

Pharmaceutical manufacturer.
www.sanofi.us
Annual Revenues: $39.29 billion
Employees: 113,500
Ticker: NYSE: SNY
SIC: 2834
Industry/ies: Pharmaceutical Industry
Legislative Issues: ANI; BUD; CPT; ECN; HCR; MMM; PHA; TAX; TOR; TRD

Main Headquarters
Mailing: 55 Corporate Dr.
          P.O. Box 5925
          Bridgewater, NJ 08807
Tel: (908) 981-5560
Fax: (908) 981-7870
TF: (800) 981-2491

Washington Office
Mailing: 1455 Pennsylvania Ave. NW, #500
          Suite 500
          Washington, DC 20004

Political Action Committees
Sanofi-Aventis U.S. Inc. Employees PAC
FEC ID: C00144345
Contact: Alok Goel
55 Corporate Dr,
P.O. Box 5925,
Bridgewater, NJ 08807
Tel: (908) 981-5560
Fax: (908) 981-7870

Contributions to Candidates: $426,975 (2015-2016)
Democrats: $124,500; Republicans: $300,475; Other: $2,000

Principal Recipients

SENATE
SCOTT, TIMOTHY E (REP-SC)

HOUSE
WALDEN, GREGORY P MR. (REP-OR)

Corporate Foundations and Giving Programs

Sanofi-Aventis U.S. Contributions Program
55 Corporate Dr.
Bridgewater, NJ 08807

Public Affairs and Related Activities Personnel

At Headquarters

BROOKS, Susan
Tel: (908) 981-6566

Senior Director
susan.brooks@sanofi.com

Fax: (908) 981-7870

DUNLAP, Mary Anne
Director, Federal Government Affairs
Registered Federal Lobbyist

Tel: (908) 231-4000
Fax: (908) 981-7870

GOEL, Alok
Lobbyist and PAC Treasurer

Tel: (908) 981-5560
Fax: (908) 981-7870

GRILLET , Philippe
Vice President, Finance and Chief Financial Officer

Tel: (908) 231-4000
Fax: (908) 981-7870

GROFIK , George
Senior Director, Investor Relations
George.grofik @sanofi.com

Tel: (908) 981-5560
Fax: (908) 981-7870

IRACE, Gregory
Senior Vice President, Global Services

Tel: (908) 981-5560
Fax: (908) 231-3614

LAUSCHER, Felix
Director, Investor Relations
felix.lauscher@sanofi-aventis.com

Tel: (908) 981-5560
Fax: (908) 981-7870

O'HAGAN, Judy
Vice President, Human Resources

Tel: (908) 231-4000
Fax: (908) 981-7870

At Washington Office

BONEBRAKE, Alison
Director, Federal Government Affair

DEVANEY, Joseph

HARTSFIELD, Jacob
Registered Federal Lobbyist

REDL, Amy L.
Director, Federal Government Affairs
Registered Federal Lobbyist

At Other Offices

CLARK, Timothy
Director, Federal Government Affairs and Federal lobbyist
and PAC Treasurer
801 Pennsylvania Ave. NW, Suite 725
Washington, DC 20004
Registered Federal Lobbyist

Tel: (202) 585-3000
Fax: (202) 682-0538

EVANS, Eddie D.
Vice President, Federal Government Relations
801 Pennsylvania Ave. NW, Suite 725
Washington, DC 20004

Tel: (202) 585-3000
Fax: (202) 682-0538

GREISSING, Jr., Edward F.
Senior Vice President, U.S. Corporate Affairs
801 Pennsylvania Ave. NW, Suite 725
Washington, DC 20004
edward.greissing@sanofi-aventis.com

Tel: (202) 585-3000
Fax: (202) 682-0538

MCLAIN, Patrick M.
Vice President, Federal Government Affairs and Policy
801 Pennsylvania Ave. NW, Suite 725
Washington, DC 20004

Tel: (202) 585-3000
Fax: (202) 682-0538

TAYLOR, Ann
Senior Director, Policy and Strategic Advocacy
801 Pennsylvania Ave. NW, Suite 725
Washington, DC 20004
ann.taylor@sanofi-aventis.com

Tel: (202) 585-3000
Fax: (202) 682-0538

Sanofi-Pasteur, Inc.

The company is the US unit of Sanofi Pasteur SA, the vaccines division of French drugmaker Sanofi. Formerly Aventis Pasteur.
www.sanofipasteur.us
Employees: 3,000
SIC: 2834; 2835; 2836
NAICS: 325412; 325412; 325414
Industry/ies: Pharmaceutical Industry
Legislative Issues: HCR; MMM

Main Headquarters
Mailing: One Discovery Dr.
            Swiftwater, PA 18370

Tel: (570) 957-7187
Fax: (570) 957-0955
TF: (800) 822-2463

Washington Office
Mailing: 801 Pennsylvania Ave. NW
            Suite 725
            Washington, DC 20004-1107

Tel: (202) 628-0500
Fax: (202) 682-0538

Political Action Committees
Sanofi Pasteur PAC
FEC ID: C00215236
Contact: Todd Rehder
Discovery Dr.
P.O. Box 187
Swiftwater, PA 18370

> **Contributions to Candidates:** $101,500 (2015-2016)
> Democrats: $23,000; Republicans: $78,500

Principal Recipients

HOUSE
DENT, CHARLES W. REP. (REP-PA)

Corporate Foundations and Giving Programs
Sanofi-Pasteur, Inc. Contributions Program
P.O. Box 187
Discovery Dr.
Swiftwater, PA 18370-0187

Tel: (570) 957-7187
Fax: (570) 957-0955

Public Affairs and Related Activities Personnel

At Headquarters

BRAGA , Damian
Senior Vice President, Commercial Operations

Tel: (570) 957-7187
Fax: (570) 957-0955

CARY, Donna
Director, Employee Engagement and Corporate Branding
donna.cary@sanofipasteur.com

Tel: (570) 957-0717
Fax: (570) 957-0955

EPIFANO, Frank
Vice President, North America and Global Finance,
Commercial Operations

Tel: (570) 957-7187
Fax: (570) 957-0955

LAVENDA, Len
Vice President, U.S. Communications
len.lavenda@sanofipasteur.com

Tel: (570) 957-7187
Fax: (570) 957-0955

REHDER, Todd
PAC Treasurer

Tel: (570) 957-7187
Fax: (570) 957-0955

At Washington Office

DUNLAP, Mary Anne
Senior Director, Federal Government Affairs

Tel: (202) 344-8215
Fax: (202) 371-1107

Santander Bank

Santander Bank formerly known as Sovereign Bank. A financial services company. Acquired by Banco Santander in 2010.
www.santanderbank.com
Employees: 7,000
SIC: 6035
Industry/ies: Banking/Finance/Investments

Chief Executive Officer
POWELL, Scott

Tel: (610) 320-8400
Fax: (610) 378-6155

Main Headquarters
Mailing: P.O. Box 12646
            Reading, PA 19612

Tel: (610) 320-8400
Fax: (610) 378-6155
TF: (877) 768-2265

Political Action Committees
Sovereign Bancorp Inc. PAC
FEC ID: C00327072
Contact: Richard Kosak
1130 Berkshire Blvd., 11-900-AC5
Wyomissing, PA 19610

Corporate Foundations and Giving Programs
Sovereign Bank Foundation
Contact: John V. Killen
P.O. Box 12646
Reading, PA 19612

Public Affairs and Related Activities Personnel

At Headquarters

KILLEN, John V.
Senior Vice President and CRA Community Development
Managing Director
jkillen@sovereignbank.com

Tel: (610) 320-8400
Fax: (610) 378-6155

At Other Offices

KOSAK, Richard
Senior Vice President
1130 Berkshire Blvd.
Wyomissing, PA 19610
Mail Stop 11-900-AC5

Tel: (610) 320-8400

SAP America

SAP America, Inc. is the U.S. subsidiary of SAP AG, headquartered in Walldorf, Germany. It is a provider of e-business software solutions.
www.sap.com
Annual Revenues: $3.69 billion
Employees: 5,200
Industry/ies: Computer/Technology
Legislative Issues: BUD; CPI; CPT; DEF; GOV; HOM; INT; LAW; SCI; TAX; TRD

Chief Executive Officer
MCDERMOTT, Bill

Tel: (610) 661-1000
Fax: (610) 661-4024

Main Headquarters
Mailing: 399 W. Chester Pike
            Newtown, PA 19073

Tel: (610) 661-1000
Fax: (610) 661-4024
TF: (800) 872-1727

Washington Office

Mailing: 1300 Pennsylvania Ave. NW
Suite 600, North Tower
Washington, DC 20005

Tel: (202) 312-3500
Fax: (202) 312-3501
TF: (800) 872-1727

Political Action Committees

SAP America, Inc. PAC
FEC ID: C00367375
Contact: Cynthia Ann Hirschfeld
3999 W. Chester Pike
Newtown, PA 19073

Contributions to Candidates: $83,000 (2015-2016)
Democrats: $50,000; Republicans: $33,000

Corporate Foundations and Giving Programs

SAP America Contributions Program
3999 W. Chester Pike
Newtown, PA 19073

Public Affairs and Related Activities Personnel

At Headquarters

CARDENUTO, Rodolpho
President, SAP Americas

Tel: (610) 661-1000
Fax: (610) 661-4024

DAVID, Peter
Chief Financial Officer

Tel: (610) 661-1000
Fax: (610) 661-4024

DEVER, James
Vice President, Corporate Affairs
james.dever@sap.com

Tel: (610) 661-2161
Fax: (610) 661-4024

GRUBER, Stefan
Head, Investor Relations
stefan.gruber@sap.com

Tel: (610) 661-1000
Fax: (610) 661-4024

HANSS, Mary Beth
Senior Vice President and General Counsel

Tel: (610) 661-1000
Fax: (610) 661-4024

HIRSCHFELD, Cynthia Ann
PAC Treasurer

Tel: (610) 661-1000
Fax: (610) 661-4024

HUTCHISON, David J.
Senior Vice President, Marketing SAP Sales and Marketing Leadership |

Tel: (610) 661-1000
Fax: (610) 661-4024

KNOWLES, Richard
Chief Operating Officer

Tel: (610) 661-1000
Fax: (610) 661-4024

LAUDAL, Terry W.
Senior Vice President, Human Resources

Tel: (610) 661-4600
Fax: (610) 661-4024

At Washington Office

BURGESS, W. Gregg
Senior International Trade Counsel
gregg.burgess@sap.com

Tel: (202) 312-3500
Fax: (202) 312-3501

GUSMAN, Larry
Commercial and Public Sector Law (federal, state, local, and International) and Regulatory Affairs Specialist
larry.gusman@sap.com

Tel: (202) 312-3500
Fax: (202) 312-3501

RICHARDS, Kevin
Director, Government Relations
Registered Federal Lobbyist

Tel: (202) 312-3500
Fax: (202) 312-3501

SEALE, C. Stevens
State & Local Government Relations

Tel: (202) 312-3500
Fax: (202) 312-3501

SISTI, Tom
Senior Director and Chief Legislative Counsel
tom.sisti@sap.com
Registered Federal Lobbyist

Tel: (202) 312-3500

STEPHENSON, John
Executive Director, Government Relations
Registered Federal Lobbyist

Tel: (202) 312-3500
Fax: (202) 312-3501

Sara Lee Corporation

A global manufacturer comprised of three business segments: food and beverage; intimates and underwear; and household products. Major brands include Sara Lee, Douwe Egberts, Hillshire Farms, Kiwi, Hanes, Playtex, and Bali. In 2001, The Earthgrains Co. merged with Sara Lee Bakery to become Sara Lee Bakery Group, a division of Sara Lee Corporation.
www.saralee.com
Annual Revenues: $8.68 billion
Employees: 21,000
Ticker: NYSE: SLE
SIC: 2000
Industry/ies: Food And Beverage Industry

Chairman of the Board and Director
BENNINK, Jan

Tel: (630) 598-8100
Fax: (630) 598-8482

Main Headquarters
Mailing: P.O. Box 3901
Peoria, IL 61612

Tel: (800) 261-4754
Fax: (630) 598-8482

Corporate Foundations and Giving Programs

Sara Lee Foundation
Contact: Judy E. Schaefer
3500 Lacey Rd.

Downers Grove, IL 60515

Public Affairs and Related Activities Personnel

At Headquarters

CUMMINS, Michael
Director, Corporate Communications
media@saralee.com

Tel: (630) 598-8412
Fax: (630) 598-8653

MATHEU, Sara
Director, Media Development and Communications
sara.matheu@saralee.com

Tel: (630) 598-8722
Fax: (630) 598-8059

SCHAEFER, Judy E.
Director, Foundation

Tel: (630) 598-8459
Fax: (630) 598-8482

SAS Institute Inc.

A software research and development company. SAS transforms your data into insights that give you a fresh perspective on your business. You can identify what's working. Fix what isn't. And discover new opportunities.
www.sas.com
Annual Revenues: $2.72 billion
Employees: 13,000
Industry/ies: Computer/Technology
Legislative Issues: ALC; BUD; CPI; CPT; CSP; FIN; GOV; HCR; HOM; INT; LAW; SCI; TAX; TRA

Chief Executive Officer
GOODNIGHT, PhD, Dr. James H.
jim.goodnight@sas.com

Tel: (919) 677-8000
Fax: (919) 677-4444

Main Headquarters
Mailing: 100 SAS Campus Dr.
Cary, NC 27513-2414

Tel: (919) 677-8000
Fax: (919) 677-4444
TF: (800) 727-0025

Washington Office
Mailing: 1530 Wilson Blvd.
Suite 800
Arlington, VA 22209

Tel: (571) 227-7000
Fax: (571) 227-7010

Corporate Foundations and Giving Programs

SAS Institute Inc. Contributions Program
100 SAS Campus Dr.
Cary, NC 27513-2414

Public Affairs and Related Activities Personnel

At Headquarters

BOSWELL, John
Senior Vice President, Chief Legal Officer and Corporate Secretary
John.Boswell@sas.com

Tel: (919) 677-8000
Fax: (919) 677-4444

DAVIS, Jim
Senior Vice President and Chief Marketing Officer
Jim.Davis@sas.com

Tel: (919) 677-8000
Fax: (919) 677-4444

LAMANNA, Joanne
Senior Campaign & Events Specialist
joanne.lamanna@sas.com

Tel: (919) 531-6080
Fax: (919) 677-4444

MANN, Jennifer
Vice President, Human Resources

Tel: (919) 677-8000
Fax: (919) 677-4444

MEEK, Pamela
Senior Director, Corporate Communications
pamela.meek@sas.com

Tel: (919) 531-7883
Fax: (919) 677-4444

PARKER, Don
Senior Vice President and Chief Financial Officer
Don.Parker@sas.com

Tel: (919) 677-8000
Fax: (919) 677-4444

At Washington Office

HAHN, Katherine
Director, Federal Government Affairs
katherine.hahn@sas.com
Registered Federal Lobbyist

Tel: (571) 227-7000
Fax: (571) 227-7010

SASOL North America, Inc.

The division produces a number of commodity and specialty chemicals from its manufacturing sites and an R&D center in the US. Among the products made by Sasol North America are alcohols, alumina, paraffins, specialty surfactants, and fatty acid esters. A part of South African chemical giant Sasol Limited's Olefins and Surfactants unit (which itself is based in Germany).
www.sasolnorthamerica.com
Annual Revenues: $65.30 million
Employees: 700
SIC: 2841; 2899
NAICS: 325998; 325611
Industry/ies: Chemicals & Chemical Industry; Natural Resources
Legislative Issues: ENG; TAX

Vice President, Human Resources
BOTHA, Cobus

Tel: (281) 588-3000
Fax: (281) 588-3144

Main Headquarters
Mailing: 900 Threadneedle St.

Tel: (281) 588-3000

Suite 100
Houston, TX 77224

Fax: (281) 588-3144

Savantage Solutions, Inc.

Savantage Solutions provides business and technology consulting and related services primarily to federal, state, and local government agencies in Maryland and Washington DC areas.
www.savantage.net
Annual Revenues: $12.10 million
Employees: 100
Industry/ies: Banking/Finance/Investments
Legislative Issues: BUD; GOV

President, Chief Executive Officer and Acting Chief Operational Officer
KAZOR, Lisa R.
lkazor@savantage.net

Tel: (301) 258-5600
Fax: (301) 258-5630

Main Headquarters
Mailing: 1355 Picard Dr.
Suite 425
Rockville, MD 20850

Tel: (301) 258-5600
Fax: (301) 258-5630

Washington Office
Mailing: 1250 Eye St. NW
Suite 505
Washington, DC 20005

Tel: (301) 258-5600
Fax: (301) 258-5630

Public Affairs and Related Activities Personnel
At Headquarters

BARNES, Kelly Moore
Chief Financial Officer and Treasurer
kmoore@savantage.net

Tel: (301) 258-5600
Fax: (301) 258-5630

RAHMAN, Ayesha
Senior Vice President and Media Contact
arahman@savantage.net

Tel: (301) 258-5600
Fax: (301) 258-5630

SavaSeniorCare, LLC

Formerly Mariner Health Care, provides short-term and long-term health care services in the United States.
www.savaseniorcare.com
Employees: 400
Industry/ies: Medicine/Health Care/Mental Health
Legislative Issues: MMM

Chairman of the Board
GRUNSTEIN, Leonard

Tel: (770) 829-5100
Fax: (770) 393-8054

Division Vice President, Sales and Marketing
LUEBE, Melissa

Tel: (770) 829-5100
Fax: (770) 393-8054

Main Headquarters
Mailing: One Ravinia Dr.
Suite 1400
Atlanta, GA 30346

Tel: (770) 829-5100
Fax: (770) 393-8054
TF: (800) 628-7009

Corporate Foundations and Giving Programs
Storms of Life Foundation
One Ravinia Dr.
Suite 1400
Atlanta, GA 30346

Tel: (770) 829-5100
Fax: (770) 393-8054

Public Affairs and Related Activities Personnel
At Headquarters

LYLE, Robert
Vice President and Controller

Tel: (770) 829-5100
Fax: (770) 393-8054

Save Mart Supermarkets

Save Mart Supermarkets was founded in 1952, the company now operates about 245 grocery stores in Northern and Central California and Nevada. About half of the locations house in-store pharmacies. Its supermarkets and warehouse stores operate under the Save Mart Supermarkets, S-Mart, Lucky, and FoodMaxx names.
www.savemart.com
Annual Revenues: $1.09 billion
Employees: 9,400
Industry/ies: Food And Beverage Industry

Chairman of the Board
PICCININI, Robert "Bob" M.

Tel: (209) 577-1600
Fax: (209) 577-3857

Co-President, Chief Financial Officer and Foundation Contact
HILL, Greg

Tel: (209) 577-1600
Fax: (209) 577-3857

Main Headquarters
Mailing: P.O. Box 4278
Modesto, CA 95352

Tel: (209) 577-1600
Fax: (209) 577-3857
TF: (800) 692-5710

Corporate Foundations and Giving Programs
Save Mart Cares
Contact: Greg Hill
P. O. Box 4278

Tel: (209) 577-1600

Modesto, CA 95352

Fax: (209) 577-3857

Public Affairs and Related Activities Personnel
At Headquarters

CAPPS, Frank
Executive Vice President, Operations / Chief Sales Officer / General Manager, Food Maxx

Tel: (209) 577-1600
Fax: (209) 577-3857

JUNQUEIRO, Steve
Co-President and Chief Operating Officer

Tel: (209) 577-1600
Fax: (209) 577-3857

PESCO, Nicole Piccinini
Co-President, Chief Strategy and Branding Officer

Tel: (209) 577-1600
Fax: (209) 577-3857

SCAN HealthPlan

Provides health care coverage and personal care services that allow seniors to remain independent.
www.scanhealthplan.com
Annual Revenues: $1.61 billion
Employees: 900
Industry/ies: Insurance Industry; Medicine/Health Care/Mental Health
Legislative Issues: HCR; MMM

Chairman of the Board
TRIMBLE, Ryan

Tel: (562) 989-5100
Fax: (562) 989-5200

Chief Executive Officer
WING, Chris

Tel: (562) 989-5100
Fax: (562) 989-5200

Main Headquarters
Mailing: 3800 Kilroy Airport way
Suite 100
Long Beach, CA 90806

Tel: (562) 989-5100
Fax: (562) 989-5200
TF: (800) 559-3500

Washington Office
Mailing: 1455 Pennsylvania Ave. NW, Suite 640
Sixth Floor
Washington, DC 20004

Corporate Foundations and Giving Programs
SCAN's Community Giving Program
3800 Kilroy Airport Way
Suite 100
Long Beach, CA 90806

Tel: (562) 989-5100
Fax: (562) 989-5100

Public Affairs and Related Activities Personnel
At Headquarters

BATTEER, Cathy
Senior Vice President and General Manager

Tel: (562) 989-5100
Fax: (562) 989-5200

BEGANS, Peter
Senior Vice President, Public and Government Affairs
Registered Federal Lobbyist

Tel: (562) 989-5100
Fax: (562) 989-5200

BURLACE , Jeannean
Senior Executive Assistant
jburlace@scanhealthplan.com

Tel: (562) 989-5100
Fax: (562) 989-5200

CAIN, Colleen
Co-founder

Tel: (562) 989-5100
Fax: (562) 989-5200

HOKR, Michelle
Contact, Media Relations
michelle@kevinross.net

Tel: (818) 597-8453
Fax: (562) 989-5200

KORNBLATT, Janet
General Counsel

Tel: (562) 989-5100
Fax: (562) 989-5200

MEEK, Alison
Federal Office Manager

Tel: (562) 989-5100
Fax: (562) 989-5200

MOHAN, Vinod
Chief Financial Officer

Tel: (562) 989-5100
Fax: (562) 989-5200

ROTH, Bill
President

Tel: (562) 989-5100
Fax: (562) 989-5200

STANISLAW, Sherry L.
Senior Vice President, General Manager, Southern California

Tel: (562) 989-5100
Fax: (562) 989-5200

TRANQUILLI, Michelle L.
Federal Lobbyist
Registered Federal Lobbyist

Tel: (562) 989-5100
Fax: (562) 989-5200

SCANA Corporation

The holding company for South Carolina Electric & Gas Co.
www.scana.com
Annual Revenues: $4.75 billion
Employees: 5,886
Ticker: NYSE: SCG
SIC: 4931
Industry/ies: Utilities
Legislative Issues: ENG; ENV; TAX

Chairman and Chief Executive Officer
MARSH, Kevin B.

Tel: (803) 217-9000

Main Headquarters
Mailing: 220 Operation Way
Cayce, SC 29033-3701

Tel: (803) 217-9000
TF: (877) 467-2262

Political Action Committees

SCANA Corporation Federal PAC
FEC ID: C00200907
Contact: Mark R. Cannon
100 SCANA Pkwy.
Cayce, SC 29033

Contributions to Candidates: $60,000 (2015-2016)
Democrats: $6,500; Republicans: $53,500

Principal Recipients

SENATE
SCOTT, TIMOTHY E (REP-SC)

Corporate Foundations and Giving Programs

SCANA Corporation Contributions Program
1426 Main St.
Suite 220
Columbia, SC 29201

Public Affairs and Related Activities Personnel

At Headquarters

ADDISON, Jimmy *Executive Vice President and Chief Financial Officer*	Tel:	(803) 217-9000
BOOMHOWER, Eric *Director, Public Affairs* eboomhower@scana.com	Tel:	(803) 217-9000
CANNON, Mark R. *Risk Management Officer and PAC Treasurer*	Tel:	(803) 217-9000
GRIFFIN, Iris *Corporate Compliance and Privacy Officer*	Tel:	(803) 217-9000
HINSON, Byron *Director, Financial Planning and Investor Relations*	Tel:	(803) 217-9000
JACKSON, Kenneth R. *Senior Vice President, Economic Development, Governmental and Regulatory Affairs*	Tel:	(803) 217-9000
LESSLIE, William H. *Senior Analyst*	Tel:	(803) 217-9000
LINDSAY, Ronald *Senior Vice President and General Counsel* ronald.lindsay@scana.com	Tel:	(803) 217-9000
PHALEN, Marty *Senior Vice President, Administration*	Tel:	(803) 217-9000
PUTNAM, CPA, Christina *Manager, Investor Relations*	Tel:	(803) 217-9000

At Other Offices

BURWELL, James D. *Director, Federal Affairs* 1426 Main St., Suite 220 Columbia, SC 29201 jburwell@scana.com *Registered Federal Lobbyist*	Tel: Fax:	(803) 748-3000 (803) 217-8825
CHAMPION, Gina S. *Corporate Secretary, Associate General Counsel and Director, Corporate Governance* 1426 Main St., Suite 220 Columbia, SC 29201	Tel: Fax:	(803) 217-9000 (803) 217-8119
LOVE, Catherine B. *Vice President, Marketing and Communications* 1426 Main St., Suite 220 Columbia, SC 29201 clove@scana.com	Tel: Fax:	(803) 217-9000 (803) 217-8119
MCFADDEN, Charles B. *Senior Vice President, Governmental Relations and Economic Development* 1426 Main St., Suite 220 Columbia, SC 29201	Tel: Fax:	(803) 217-9000 (803) 217-8119
O'BANION, Rhonda *Public Relations Leader* 1426 Main St., Suite 220 Columbia, SC 29201 rhonda.o'banion@scana.com	Tel: Fax:	(800) 562-9308 (803) 217-8119

Schaeffler Group USA Inc.

Manufacturer of rolling bearings, engine and drivetrain components, linear motion products, precision products and plain bearings. It is responsible for the engineering, production, sales and marketing for the INA, LuK, FAG and Barden brands, which provide high-performance, precision technologies for the Automotive OEM, Industrial OEM and Distribution markets as well as the Aerospace industry.
www.schaeffler.us
Annual Revenues: $302.70 million
Employees: 3,200
Industry/ies: Construction/Construction Materials; Engineering/Mathematics

Chief Executive Officer and Chief Financial Officer ROSENFELD, Klaus	Tel: Fax:	(803) 548-8500 (803) 548-8599

Main Headquarters

Mailing:	308 Springhill Farm Rd. Ft. Mill, SC 29715	Tel: Fax:	(803) 548-8500 (803) 548-8599

Political Action Committees

Schaeffler Group USA Inc. PAC
FEC ID: C00405209
Contact: Steve L. Crow
308 Springhill Farm Rd.
Ft. Mill, SC 29715

Public Affairs and Related Activities Personnel

At Headquarters

CROW, Steve L. *General Counsel and PAC Treasurer*	Tel: Fax:	(803) 548-8500 (803) 548-8599
JUNG, Oliver *Chief Operating Officer*	Tel: Fax:	(803) 548-8500 (803) 548-8599
KIER, Lynn *Vice President, Communications and Marketing* lynn.kier@schaeffler.com	Tel: Fax:	(803) 578-2929 (803) 548-8599
NEWTON, Walter *Manager, Industrial Communications and Marketing* walter.newton@schaeffler.com	Tel: Fax:	(803) 396-3680 (803) 547-7988
TINNELL, Greg *Senior Vice President Human Resources, Americas*	Tel: Fax:	(803) 548-8500 (803) 548-8599

Schenck Company

Schenck Company distributes domestic, specialty, and imported beers, as well as alcoholic energy drinks such as Sparks and Liquid Charge.
www.schenckandcompany.com
Annual Revenues: $101.20 million
Employees: 400
Industry/ies: Food And Beverage Industry

Chairman of the Board FULTON, Richard	Tel: Fax:	(407) 299-4773 (407) 296-6655
Co-Chief Executive Officer SCHENCK, Jeffrey C.	Tel: Fax:	(407) 299-4773 (407) 296-6655

Main Headquarters

Mailing:	P. O. Box 70007 Houston, TX 77270	Tel: Fax:	(713) 266-7608 (713) 863-1547

Corporate Foundations and Giving Programs

Schenck Company Contributions Program P.O. Box 685061 Orlando, FL 32868-5061	Tel: Fax:	(407) 299-4773 (407) 299-4773

Public Affairs and Related Activities Personnel

At Headquarters

SCHENCK, Chris *Manager, Operations*	Tel: Fax:	(713) 266-7608 (713) 863-1547

At Other Offices

TALLENT, Nancy *Vice President, Human Capital* P.O. Box 685061 Orlando, FL 32868-5061	Tel: Fax:	(407) 298-2424 (407) 296-6655

Schlumberger Limited

A global technology services company consisting of two business segments. Schlumberger Oilfield Services is a provider of technology services and solutions to the international petroleum industry.
www.slb.com
Annual Revenues: $47.59 billion
Employees: 120,000
Ticker: NYSE: SLB
SIC: 3533; 1382
NAICS: 333132; 213112
Industry/ies: Computer/Technology; Natural Resources

Chairman of the Board and Chief Executive Officer KIBSGAARD , Paal	Tel:	(713) 375-3494

Main Headquarters

Mailing:	5599 San Felipe 17th Fl. Houston, TX 77056	Tel:	(713) 375-3494

Corporate Foundations and Giving Programs

Schlumberger Foundation Contact: Jean-Marc Perraud 5599 San Felipe 17th Floor Houston, TX 77056	Tel:	(713) 513-2000

Public Affairs and Related Activities Personnel

At Headquarters

FARRANT, Simon
Vice President, Investor Relations
Tel: (713) 375-3494

ANDERSON, Malcolm W.
Senior Vice President, Human Resources
Tel: (281) 443-3370
Fax: (281) 233-5199

AYAT, Simon
Executive Vice President and Chief Financial Officer
Tel: (713) 513-2000

COX, Stephanie
Vice President
Tel: (713) 375-3494

DOMERACKI, Dan
Vice President, Government and Community Relations
Tel: (713) 513-2000

HOUSLEY, Shawn
Consultant, Digital Marketing and Communication
Tel: (281) 443-3370
Fax: (281) 233-5199

JUDEN, Alex
Secretary and General Counsel
Tel: (713) 513-2000

MARTELLOZO, Gerard
Vice President, Human Resources
Tel: (713) 375-3494

PERRAUD, Jean-Marc
Chairman and President, Foundation
Tel: (713) 513-2000

POUPEAU, Jean-Francois
Executive Vice President, Corporate Development and Communications
Tel: (713) 513-2000

WHITTAKER, Stephen
Director, Corporate Communications
swhittaker@slb.com
Tel: (314) 062-1330

Schneider Electric

A subsidiary of Schneider Electric of Paris, France. Manufactures electrical equipment and electronic products and components.
www.schneider-electric.us
Annual Revenues: $2.05 billion
Employees: 300
SIC: 3612; 3613; 3625; 3643; 3699
NAICS: 3699
Industry/ies: Energy/Electricity; Machinery/Equipment

President and Chief Executive Officer
TRICOIRE, Jean-Pascal
Tel: (847) 397-2600
Fax: (847) 925-7500

Main Headquarters
Mailing: 1415 Roselle Rd.
Palatine, IL 60067
Tel: (847) 397-2600
Fax: (847) 925-7500
TF: (877) 342-5173

Corporate Foundations and Giving Programs
Schneider Electric/Square D Foundation
1415 S. Roselle Rd.
Palatine, IL 60067
Tel: (847) 397-2600
Fax: (847) 397-2600

Public Affairs and Related Activities Personnel

At Headquarters

BABEAU, Emmanuel
Executive Vice President Finance
Tel: (847) 397-2600
Fax: (847) 925-7500

BLUM, Olivier
Executive Vice President, Global Human Resources
Tel: (847) 397-2600
Fax: (847) 925-7500

CROCHON, Michel
Executive Vice President, Strategy
Tel: (847) 397-2600
Fax: (847) 925-7500

DELORME, Philippe
Executive Vice President, Partner Business
Tel: (847) 397-2600
Fax: (847) 925-7500

HANNA, Martin
Vice President, Communications
martin.hanna@us.schneider-electric.com
Tel: (847) 925-3482
Fax: (847) 925-7500

LEONG, Chris
Chief Marketing Officer
Tel: (847) 397-2600
Fax: (847) 925-7500

RODRÌGUEZ, Julio
Executive Vice President, Global Operations
Tel: (847) 397-2600
Fax: (847) 925-7500

Schnuck Markets, Inc.

A grocery store chain.
www.schnucks.com
Annual Revenues: $1.84 billion
Employees: 16,000
Industry/ies: Food And Beverage Industry; Retail/Wholesale

Chairman of the Board and Chief Executive Officer
SCHNUCK, Todd
Tel: (314) 994-9900
Fax: (314) 994-4465

Main Headquarters
Mailing: 11420 Lackland Rd.
P.O. Box 46928
St. Louis, MO 63146-6928
Tel: (314) 994-9900
Fax: (314) 994-4465
TF: (800) 264-4400

Corporate Foundations and Giving Programs
Schnuck Markets Contributions Program
11420 Lackland Rd.
P.O. Box 46928

St. Louis, MO 63146-6928

Public Affairs and Related Activities Personnel
At Headquarters

BELL, David
Chief Financial Officer
Tel: (314) 994-4400
Fax: (314) 994-4465

WILLIS, Lori
Director, Communications
lwillis@schnucks.com
Tel: (314) 994-4602
Fax: (314) 994-4465

Scholastic, Inc.

A publisher of magazines, books, instructional materials, computer software and video materials for children. Acquired Grolier Inc. in 2001.
www2.scholastic.com/home
Annual Revenues: $1.65 billion
Employees: 8,900
Ticker: NASDAQ: SCHL
SIC: 2731
NAICS: 511130
Industry/ies: Education; Retail/Wholesale
Legislative Issues: EDU

Chairman of the Board, President and Chief Executive Officer
ROBINSON, Richard
Tel: (212) 343-6100
Fax: (212) 343-6934

Main Headquarters
Mailing: 557 Broadway
New York City, NY 10012
Tel: (212) 343-6100
Fax: (212) 343-6934

Corporate Foundations and Giving Programs
Scholastic, Inc. Contributions Program
557 Broadway
New York City, NY 10012
Tel: (212) 343-6100
Fax: (212) 343-6934

Public Affairs and Related Activities Personnel

At Headquarters

AMITIE, Julie
Director, Retail Marketing and Brand Management
jamitie@scholastic.com
Tel: (212) 343-6100
Fax: (212) 343-6934

DISCEPOLO, Kevin
Federal Lobbyist
Registered Federal Lobbyist
Tel: (212) 343-6100
Fax: (212) 343-6934

GOOD, Kyle
Senior Vice President, Corporate Communications and Media Relations
kgood@scholastic.com
Tel: (212) 343-4563
Fax: (212) 343-6934

HEDDEN, Andrew S.
Executive Vice President and General Counsel
Tel: (212) 343-6100
Fax: (212) 343-6934

HITCHCOCK, Nelson
EVP, Marketing
nhitchcock@scholastic.com
Tel: (212) 343-6100
Fax: (212) 343-6934

HYMOWITZ, Gary
Vice President, Sales and Marketing
ghymowitz@scholastic.com
Tel: (212) 343-6100
Fax: (212) 343-6934

JOHNSON, Karen
Federal Lobbyist
Registered Federal Lobbyist
Tel: (212) 343-6100
Fax: (212) 343-6934

KIRKSEY, Suzette
Director, International Sales
skirksey@scholastic.com
Tel: (212) 343-6100
Fax: (212) 343-6934

LICK, Christopher
Vice President and Senior Counsel
click@scholastic.com
Tel: (212) 343-6560
Fax: (212) 343-6934

LYONS, Jessie
Director, Government Relations
jlyons@scholastic.com
Registered Federal Lobbyist
Tel: (202) 343-4817
Fax: (212) 343-6934

MINDLIN, Casey
Regional Director
Tel: (212) 343-6100
Fax: (212) 343-6934

O'CONNELL, Maureen
Executive Vice President, Chief Financial Officer and Chief Administrative Officer
Tel: (212) 343-6100
Fax: (212) 343-6934

PORIS, Betsy
Vice President, Strategic Marketing
bporis@scholastic.com
Tel: (212) 343-6100
Fax: (212) 343-6934

RIBAUDO, Mark
Group Director, Marketing
mribaudo@scholastic.com
Tel: (212) 343-6100
Fax: (212) 343-6934

SMAGLER, Alan
Vice President, Trade Sales
asmagler@scholastic.com
Tel: (212) 343-6100
Fax: (212) 343-6934

STRAATEN, Tracy Van
Trade Books
ernest.fleishman@scholastic.com
Tel: (212) 343-6100
Fax: (212) 343-6934

THOMAS, Lisa
Vice President, Training and Development
lthomas@scholastic.com
Tel: (212) 343-6100
Fax: (212) 343-6934

URBAN, David
Federal Lobbyist
Registered Federal Lobbyist
Tel: (212) 343-6100
Fax: (212) 343-6934

Schott North America, Inc.

A company engaged in advanced glass and glass ceramic materials research, development and manufacturing.
www.us.schott.com
Annual Revenues: $176.3 million
Employees: 3,000
Industry/ies: Glass

Chairman of the Board
HEINRICHT, Frank
Tel: (914) 831-2200
Fax: (914) 831-2201

Main Headquarters
Mailing: 555 Taxter Rd.
Elmsford, NY 10523
Tel: (914) 831-2200
Fax: (914) 831-2201

Washington Office
Mailing: 2451 Crystal Dr.
Suite 450
Arlington, VA 22202
Tel: (703) 418-1409
Fax: (703) 418-4762

Corporate Foundations and Giving Programs

Schott North America Corporate Social Program
Contact: Linda S. Mayer
555 Taxter Rd.
Elmsford, NY 10523
Tel: (914) 831-2200
Fax: (914) 831-2201

Public Affairs and Related Activities Personnel

At Washington Office

STEIN, James C.
Vice President, Government Affairs
Tel: (703) 418-1409
Fax: (703) 418-4762

The Schwan Food Company

A food processor.
www.theschwanfoodcompany.com
Annual Revenues: $2.03 billion
Employees: 14,000
SIC: 2038
NAICS: 311412
Industry/ies: Food And Beverage Industry; Retail/Wholesale

Chairman of the Board
SCHUMAN, Allan
Tel: (507) 532-3274
Fax: (507) 537-8226

Chief Executive Officer
SMYRNIOS, Dimitrios
Tel: (507) 532-3274
Fax: (507) 537-8226

Main Headquarters
Mailing: 115 W. College Dr.
Marshall, MN 56258
Tel: (507) 532-3274
Fax: (507) 537-8226
TF: (800) 533-5290

Political Action Committees
Schwan Food Company Inc. PAC (SCHWAN PAC)
FEC ID: C00360362
Contact: Alan Poff
115 W. College Dr.
Marshall, MN 56258

Contributions to Candidates: $25,500 (2015-2016)
Democrats: $8,000; Republicans: $17,500

Corporate Foundations and Giving Programs

The Schwan Food Company Cotributions Program
115 W. College Dr.
Marshall, MN 56258
Tel: (507) 532-3274
Fax: (507) 537-8226

Public Affairs and Related Activities Personnel

At Headquarters

GALLOWAY, Robin
Executive Vice President, Finance and Chief Financial Officer
Tel: (507) 532-3274
Fax: (507) 537-8226

LEE, Sue Sorensen
Contact, Communications
sue@leepublicrelations.com
Tel: (952) 926-2140
Fax: (507) 537-8226

PETERSON, Scott
Executive Vice President and Chief Human Resources Officer
Tel: (507) 532-3274
Fax: (507) 537-8226

POFF, Alan
PAC Treasurer
Tel: (507) 532-3274
Fax: (507) 537-8226

SATTLER, Brian
Executive Vice President, Business Services and General Counsel
Tel: (507) 532-3274
Fax: (507) 537-8226

Schwan's Global Supply Chain, Inc.

See listing on page 705 under The Schwan Food Company

Schweitzer Engineering Laboratories

Designs and manufactures products for the protection, monitoring, control, automation, and metering of electric power systems
www.selinc.com
Annual Revenues: $171.90 million
Employees: 2,000
Industry/ies: Energy/Electricity; Engineering/Mathematics

President and Chief Executive Officer
SCHWEITZER, III, Edmund O.
Tel: (509) 332-1890
Fax: (509) 332-7990

Main Headquarters
Mailing: 2350 N.E. Hopkins Ct.
Pullman, WA 99163
Tel: (509) 332-1890
Fax: (509) 332-7990

Washington Office
Mailing: 500 Montgomery St.
Suite 400
Alexandria, VA 22314
Tel: (703) 647-6253
Fax: (703) 647-6259

Public Affairs and Related Activities Personnel

At Headquarters

BIELENBERG, Adina
Manager, Public Affairs
public_affairs@selinc.com
Tel: (509) 336-9456
Fax: (509) 332-7990

WILHITE, Kate
Senior Media Specialist
public_affairs@selinc.com
Tel: (509) 334-8893
Fax: (509) 332-7990

At Washington Office

ARTZ, Sharla B.
Director, Government Affairs
sharla_artz@selgs.com
Tel: (703) 647-6253
Fax: (703) 647-6259

Science and Engineering Services, Inc.

Weapon system manufacturing. It has established a new standard in science, engineering, and weapon system manufacturing that provides a quick-response, total turn-key solution for customers throughout the Department of Defense and Homeland Security.
www.sesi-md.com
Annual Revenues: $437.96 million
Employees: 223
Industry/ies: Defense/Homeland Security; Engineering/Mathematics; Government-Related

Chief Executive Officer
SINCLAIR, E.J.
Tel: (443) 539-0139
Fax: (443) 539-1757

Main Headquarters
Mailing: 6992 Columbia Gateway Dr.
Suite 200
Columbia, MD 21046
Tel: (443) 539-0139
Fax: (443) 539-1757

Public Affairs and Related Activities Personnel

At Headquarters

BOGOSIAN, Paul
Executive Vice President, Strategic Planning
Tel: (443) 539-0139
Fax: (443) 539-1757

CHUNN, Russell
Chief Financial Officer and Executive Vice President
Tel: (443) 539-0139
Fax: (443) 539-1757

SANG LEE, Dr. Hyo
President
Tel: (443) 539-0139
Fax: (443) 539-1757

Science Applications International Corporation (SAIC)

An employee-owned provider of high tech products and services. Also involved in research and development.
www.saic.com
Annual Revenues: $4.32 billion
Employees: 15,000
Ticker: NYSE: SAIC
SIC: 7373
Industry/ies: Computer/Technology; Defense/Homeland Security; Government-Related
Legislative Issues: AVI; BUD; DEF; ENG; GOV; HCR; HOM; INT

Chairman of the Board
SANDERSON, Jr., Edward
Tel: (703) 676-4300
Fax: (703) 676-2269

Chief Executive Officer
MORACO, Anthony J.
Tel: (703) 676-4300
Fax: (703) 676-2269

Main Headquarters
Mailing: 1710 SAIC Dr.
McLean, VA 22102
Tel: (703) 676-4300
Fax: (703) 676-2269
TF: (800) 430-7629

Washington Office
Mailing: 8301 Greensboro Dr.
Ms E-12-5
Mclean, VA 22102

Political Action Committees
Science Applications International Corporation Voluntary PAC
FEC ID: C00300418

Contact: Patrick J. Mcgee
1710 SAIC Dr.   Tel: (703) 676-4300
McLean, VA 22102

Corporate Foundations and Giving Programs

SAIC Contributions Program
1710 SAIC Dr.   Tel: (703) 676-4300
McLean, VA 22102

Public Affairs and Related Activities Personnel

At Headquarters

ADMIRE, Kimberly	Tel:	(703) 676-4300
Executive Vice President And Chief Human Resources Officer	Fax:	(703) 676-2269
FITCH, Lucy Reilly	Tel:	(703) 676-4300
Senior Vice President and Chief Communications Officer	Fax:	(703) 676-2269
HARTLEY, John R.	Tel:	(703) 676-4300
Executive Vice President and Chief Financial Officer	Fax:	(703) 676-2269
KEENAN, Brian F.	Tel:	(703) 676-4300
Executive Vice President, Chief Human Capital Officer	Fax:	(703) 676-2269
brian.f.keenan@saic.com		
KENNEDY, Laura	Tel:	(703) 676-4300
Senior Vice President of Ethics and Compliance	Fax:	(703) 676-2269
LEVI, Paul E.	Tel:	(703) 676-2283
Senior Vice President and Director, Investor Relations	Fax:	(703) 676-2269
Paul.E.Levi@saic.com		
MAHON, Steven	Tel:	(703) 676-4300
Executive Vice President and General Counsel	Fax:	(703) 676-2269
MCGEE, Patrick J.	Tel:	(703) 676-4300
PAC Treasurer	Fax:	(703) 676-2269
PRESTI, Lauren	Tel:	(703) 676-4300
Senior Media Relations Specialist	Fax:	(703) 676-2269
lauren.a.presti@saic.com		

At Washington Office

BURKE , Thomas
Assistant General Counsel

At Other Offices

CHILDERS, Amy	Tel:	(703) 676-5745
Vice President and Director, Policy and Political Programs	Fax:	(703) 243-2161
1911 Fort Myer Dr., 11th Floor, Suite 1110		
Arlington, VA 22209		
childersa@saic.com		
ELDRIDGE, Thomas R.	Tel:	(703) 676-5753
Senior Vice President, Government Affairs Counsel	Fax:	(703) 676-4305
1911 Fort Myer Dr., 11th Floor, Suite 1110		
Arlington, VA 22209		
eldridgetr@saic.com		
HESCHELES, Heather	Tel:	(703) 676-5753
Federal Lobbyist	Fax:	(703) 676-4305
1911 Fort Myer Dr., 11th Floor, Suite 1110		
Arlington, VA 22209		
Registered Federal Lobbyist		
KILLEEN, John J.	Tel:	(703) 676-5745
Senior Vice President, Government Affairs	Fax:	(703) 243-2161
1911 Fort Myer Dr., 11th Floor, Suite 1110		
Arlington, VA 22209		
Registered Federal Lobbyist		
LISS, Brian		
Executive Vice President, Chief Human Capital Officer		
11955 Freedom Dr.		
Reston, VA 20190		
NEELEY, Karen		
Senior Counsel, Corporate Legal		
11955 Freedom Dr.		
Reston, VA 20190		
ROBERTS, Kimberley	Tel:	(703) 676-5753
Vice President, Public Policy	Fax:	(703) 676-4305
1911 Fort Myer Dr., 11th Floor, Suite 1110		
Arlington, VA 22209		
SEGALL, Samantha		
11955 Freedom Dr.		
Reston, VA 20190		
Registered Federal Lobbyist		
SEGALL (FORMERLY ANDERSON), Samantha	Tel:	(703) 676-5753
Assistant Vice President	Fax:	(703) 676-4305
1911 Fort Myer Dr., 11th Floor, Suite 1110		
Arlington, VA 22209		
Registered Federal Lobbyist		
THORPE, Kathryne M.	Tel:	(703) 676-5745
Corporate Vice President, Government Affairs	Fax:	(703) 243-2161
1911 Fort Myer Dr., 11th Floor, Suite 1110		
Arlington, VA 22209		
VAUGHAN, Matthew L.	Tel:	(703) 676-5753

Senior Vice President, Program Development	Fax:	(703) 676-4305
1911 Fort Myer Dr., 11th Floor, Suite 1110		
Arlington, VA 22209		
WOODBRIDGE, Alfred	Tel:	(202) 530-8900
Corporate Vice President, Government Affairs	Fax:	(202) 530-5641
1911 Fort Myer Dr., 11th Floor, Suite 1110		
Arlington, VA 22209		

Scientific Games Corporation

Scientific Games Corporation has completed the merger with Bally Technologies, Inc. A gaming company. Formerly known as Alliance Gaming.
www.ballytech.com
Annual Revenues: $2.06 billion
Employees: 9,000
Ticker: NasdaqGS: SGMS
SIC: 3578; 7999; 3999
NAICS: 333313; 713290; 713210
Industry/ies: Sports/Leisure/Entertainment

Main Headquarters

Mailing:	6601 S. Bermuda Rd.	Tel:	(702) 584-7700
	Las Vegas, NV 89119	Fax:	(702) 584-7710
		TF:	(877) 462-2559

Political Action Committees

Bally Technologies Inc. Federal PAC
FEC ID: C00454017
Contact: Evan Knisely
6601 S. Bermuda Rd.   Tel: (702) 584-7700
Las Vegas, NV 89119

Corporate Foundations and Giving Programs

Bally Technologies, Inc. Contributions Program
Contact: Amanda J. Riddle
6601 S. Bermuda Rd.   Tel: (702) 584-7700
Las Vegas, NV 89119

Public Affairs and Related Activities Personnel

At Headquarters

KNISELY, Evan	Tel:	(702) 584-7700
PAC Treasurer	Fax:	(702) 584-7710
OLSON-REYES, Laura	Tel:	(702) 584-7742
Executive Director, Community and Corporate Relations	Fax:	(702) 584-7710
lolson-reyes@ballytech.com		
PARENTE, Robert	Tel:	(702) 584-7700
Senior Vice President and Chief Revenue Officer	Fax:	(702) 584-7710
RIDDLE, Amanda J.	Tel:	(702) 584-7451
Communications Specialist	Fax:	(702) 584-7710
ariddle@ballytech.com		
TRASK, Mike	Tel:	(702) 584-7451
Senior Manager, Corporate Communications	Fax:	(702) 584-7710
mtrask@ballytech.com		

Scott & White Health Plan

A nonprofit Health Maintenance Organization in the Central Texas region. Baylor Health Care System and Scott & White Healthcare merged to form Baylor Scott & White Health in Sep. 2013.
www.swhp.org
Annual Revenues: $660.09 million
Employees: 400
Industry/ies: Medicine/Health Care/Mental Health

Chairman of the Board	Tel:	(254) 298-3000
PRYOR , MD, Robert	Fax:	(254) 298-3012
Interim President and Chief Executive Officer	Tel:	(254) 298-3000
WILLIAMS, Marinan	Fax:	(254) 298-3012

Main Headquarters

Mailing:	2401 S. 31st St.	Tel:	(254) 298-3000
	Temple, TX 76508	Fax:	(254) 298-3012
		TF:	(800) 321-7947

Public Affairs and Related Activities Personnel

At Headquarters

CARROLL, Jimmy	Tel:	(254) 298-3000
Legal Counsel	Fax:	(254) 298-3012
DICKISON, Scott	Tel:	(254) 298-3000
Chief Financial Officer	Fax:	(254) 298-3012
HOLMES, Kristi	Tel:	(254) 298-3415
Director, Community Connections	Fax:	(254) 298-3012
kholmes@SW.org		
O'BANNON, Pamela	Tel:	(254) 298-3000
Compliance Officer	Fax:	(254) 298-3012

Scotts Company, O.M. Scott and Sons

See listing on page 707 under Scotts Miracle-Gro Company

Scotts Miracle-Gro Company

Industry-leading lawn care & gardening advice. Indoor & outdoor lawn and garden products and services.
www.scotts.com
Annual Revenues: $3.21 billion
Employees: 7,900
Ticker: NYSE: SMG
SIC: 2870
Industry/ies: Agriculture/Agronomy
Legislative Issues: AGR

Chief Executive Officer and Chairman of the Board — Tel: (937) 644-0011
HAGEDORN, Jim — Fax: (937) 644-7184

Main Headquarters
Mailing: 14111 Scottslawn Rd. — Tel: (937) 644-0011
Marysville, OH 43041 — Fax: (937) 644-7614
TF: (888) 270-3714

Political Action Committees
Scotts Miracle-Gro Company Stewardship PAC
FEC ID: C00365254
Contact: Brian Herrington
14111 Scottslawn Rd. — Tel: (937) 644-0011
Marysville, OH 43041 — Fax: (937) 644-7614

Contributions to Candidates: $26,500 (2015-2016)
Democrats: $2,500; Republicans: $24,000
Principal Recipients
SENATE
PORTMAN, ROB (REP-OH)

Corporate Foundations and Giving Programs
Scotts Miracle-Gro Company Contributions Program
14111 Scottslawn Rd. — Tel: (937) 644-0011
Marysville, OH 43041 — Fax: (937) 644-7614

Public Affairs and Related Activities Personnel

At Headquarters

COLEMAN, Randy — Tel: (937) 644-0011
Executive Vice President and Chief Financial Officer — Fax: (937) 644-7614
HENDRICK, Scott — Tel: (937) 644-0011
Senior Vice President, Global Supply Chain — Fax: (937) 644-7614
HERRINGTON, Brian — Tel: (937) 644-0011
Director, Government Affairs, PAC Treasurer — Fax: (937) 644-7614
KING, Jim — Tel: (937) 578-5622
Senior Vice President, Investor Relations and Corporate — Fax: (937) 644-7184
Affairs and Chief Communications Officer
Jim.King@Scotts.com
LUKEMIRE, Mike — Tel: (937) 644-0011
President and Chief Operating Officer — Fax: (937) 644-7614
SHANK, PhD, Dr. Richard — Tel: (937) 644-0011
Chief Environmental Officer — Fax: (937) 644-7614
SMITH, Ivan — Tel: (937) 644-0011
Executive Vice President and General Counsel, Corporate — Fax: (937) 644-7614
Secretary and Chief Compliance Officer
STUMP, Denise S. — Tel: (937) 644-0011
Executive Vice President, Global Human Resources and Chief — Fax: (937) 644-7184
Ethics Officer
SWIHART, Dave — Tel: (937) 644-0011
Senior Vice President, Research and Development — Fax: (937) 644-7614

The Scoular Company

A grain marketing and trading company.
www.scoular.com
Annual Revenues: $203.81 million
Employees: 400
Industry/ies: Agriculture/Agronomy; Commodities

Chairman of the Board and President — Tel: (402) 342-3500
FAITH, David — Fax: (402) 342-5568

Chief Executive Officer — Tel: (913) 338-1474
ELSEA, Charles "Chuck"

Main Headquarters
Mailing: 2027 Dodge St. — Tel: (402) 342-3500
Omaha, NE 68102 — Fax: (402) 342-5568
TF: (800) 487-1474

Political Action Committees
Scoular Company Fund for Effective Government PAC
FEC ID: C00293076
Contact: Roger Lee Barber
2027 Dodge St. — Tel: (402) 342-3500
Omaha, NE 68102 — Fax: (402) 342-3500

Corporate Foundations and Giving Programs

Scoular Foundation
2027 Dodge St.

Omaha, NE 68102

Public Affairs and Related Activities Personnel

At Headquarters

BARBER, Roger Lee — Tel: (402) 342-3500
Vice President, Treasurer and PAC Treasurer — Fax: (402) 342-5568
rbarber@scoular.com
FAITH, Marshall E. — Tel: (402) 342-3500
Vice Chairman of the Board — Fax: (402) 342-5568
HECK, John — Tel: (402) 342-3500
Senior Vice President, Asset Management and Business — Fax: (402) 342-5568
Development
jheck@scoular.com
HEILIGER, Julie — Tel: (402) 342-3500
Director, Corporate Communications — Fax: (402) 342-5568
SAGHEER, Omer — Tel: (402) 342-3500
Vice President, Finance — Fax: (402) 342-5568

At Other Offices

MACLIN, Joan — Tel: (612) 335-8205
Senior Vice President and General Counsel
250 Marquette Ave., Suite 1050
Minneapolis, MN 55401
jmaclin@scoular.com
PETERSON, Kurt — Tel: (612) 335-8205
Vice President, Talent and Human Resources
250 Marquette Ave., Suite 1050
Minneapolis, MN 55401

SCP Pool Corporation

See listing on page 644 under Pool Corporation

Scripps Networks Interactive, Inc.

A lifestyle content and interactive services company with television and interactive brands.
www.scrippsnetworksinteractive.com
Annual Revenues: $2.68 billion
Employees: 2,100
Ticker: NYSE: SNI
SIC: 4841
Industry/ies: Communications; Telecommunications/Internet/Cable
Legislative Issues: COM; MIA; TAX

Chairman of the Board, President and Chief Executive Officer — Tel: (865) 694-2700
LOWE, Kenneth W. — Fax: (865) 985-7778

Main Headquarters
Mailing: 9721 Sherrill Blvd. — Tel: (865) 694-2700
Knoxville, TN 37932 — Fax: (865) 985-7778

Washington Office
Mailing: 5425 Wisconsin Ave.
Fifth Floor
Chevy Chase, MD 20815

Corporate Foundations and Giving Programs

Scripps Networks Interactive, Inc. Contributions Program
Contact: Jim Clayton
9721 Sherrill Blvd. — Tel: (865) 694-2700
Knoxville, TN 37932 — Fax: (865) 985-7778

Public Affairs and Related Activities Personnel

At Headquarters

AHN, Henry — Tel: (865) 694-2700
Executive Vice President, Content Distribution and Marketing — Fax: (865) 985-7778
BLISS, Jerilyn — Tel: (865) 560-4181
Vice President, Corporate Communications — Fax: (865) 985-7778
jbliss@scrippsnetworks.com
CLAYTON, Jim — Tel: (865) 694-2700
Executive Vice President, Corporate Giving and Community — Fax: (865) 985-7778
Relations
DEEN, Sameer — Tel: (865) 694-2700
Senior Vice President, Corporate Development — Fax: (865) 985-7778
GALLENTINE, Mike — Tel: (865) 560-4473
Senior Vice President, Investor Relations — Fax: (865) 985-7778
mgallentine@scrippsnetworks.com
GIBSON, Cynthia L. — Tel: (865) 694-2700
Executive Vice President, Chief Legal Officer and Corporate — Fax: (865) 985-7778
Secretary
GIGLIOTTI, Steven J. — Tel: (865) 694-2700
Chief Revenue Officer — Fax: (865) 985-7778
HALL, Lee — Tel: (865) 560-3853
Director, Corporate Communications — Fax: (865) 985-7778
lhall@scrippsnetworks.com
HICKOK, Lori A. — Tel: (865) 694-2700
Chief Financial Officer — Fax: (865) 985-7778
KROEGER, Mark W. — Tel: (865) 560-5007

Executive Vice President and Chief Communications Officer | Fax: | (865) 985-7778
mark.kroeger@scrippsnetworks.com

MCCONKEY, Cindy | Tel: | (865) 560-3976
Senior Vice President, Communications | Fax: | (865) 985-7778
cmcconkey@scrippsnetworks.com

NECASTRO, Joseph G. | Tel: | (865) 694-2700
Chief Development Officer | Fax: | (865) 985-7778

PESCI , NJ | Tel: | (865) 694-2700
Executive Vice President, Human Resources | Fax: | (865) 985-7778

SAMPLES, Jim | Tel: | (865) 694-2700
President, International | Fax: | (865) 985-7778

SCHUERMANN, Mark F. | Tel: | (865) 694-2700
Senior Vice President and Treasurer | Fax: | (865) 985-7778

SMITHERS, Terry L. | Tel: | (865) 694-2700
Senior Vice President, Audit and Compliance | Fax: | (865) 985-7778

TALBOTT, Mary E. | Tel: | (865) 694-2700
Senior Vice President, Deputy General Counsel and | Fax: | (865) 985-7778
Corporate Secretary

Seaboard Corporation

An international food and shipping company.
www.seaboardcorp.com
Annual Revenues: $5.46 billion
Employees: 10,772
Ticker: NYSE: SEB
SIC: 2011
Industry/ies: Fish And Fishing; Food And Beverage Industry; Marine/Maritime/
Shipping; Transportation
Legislative Issues: AGR; ENG; FOO; FOR; TAX; TRD

Chairman of the Board, President and Chief Executive Officer | Tel: | (913) 676-8800
BRESKY, Steven J. | Fax: | (913) 676-8872

Main Headquarters
Mailing: | 9000 W. 67th St. | Tel: | (913) 676-8800
| Shawnee Mission, KS 66202 | Fax: | (913) 676-8872
| | TF: | (800) 262-7907

Washington Office
Mailing: | 818 Connecticut Ave. NW | Tel: | (202) 955-6111
| Suite 801 | Fax: | (202) 955-6118
| Washington, DC 20008

Political Action Committees
Seaboard Corporation PAC
FEC ID: C00246736
Contact: David M. Dannov
9000 W. 67th St.
Shawnee Mission, KS 66201

Contributions to Candidates: $46,350 (2015-2016)
Democrats: $8,000; Republicans: $38,350

Corporate Foundations and Giving Programs
The Seaboard Foundation
Contact: Steven J. Bresky
9000 W. 67th St.
Shawnee Mission, KS 66202

Public Affairs and Related Activities Personnel

At Headquarters

BECKER, David M. | Tel: | (913) 676-8800
Senior Vice President, General Counsel and Secretary | Fax: | (913) 676-8872

DANNOV, David M. | Tel: | (913) 676-8800
Contact, Commodity Trading and Milling | Fax: | (913) 676-8872

OSWALT, David S. | Tel: | (913) 676-8800
Senior Vice President, Finance and Treasurer | Fax: | (913) 676-8872

RANKIN, David H. | Tel: | (913) 676-8800
Vice President, Taxation and Business Development | Fax: | (913) 676-8872

STEER, Robert L. | Tel: | (913) 676-8800
Executive Vice President and Chief Financial Officer | Fax: | (913) 676-8872

TROLLINGER, Michael D. | Tel: | (913) 676-8800
Vice President, Corporate Controller and Chief Accounting | Fax: | (913) 676-8872
Officer

At Washington Office

BURTON, Andrew | Tel: | (202) 955-6111
Federal Lobbyist | Fax: | (202) 955-6118
Registered Federal Lobbyist

CHOINIERE, Ian | Tel: | (202) 955-6111
Registered Federal Lobbyist | Fax: | (202) 955-6118

HIGGINS, Justin | Tel: | (202) 955-6111
Federal Lobbyist | Fax: | (202) 955-6118
Registered Federal Lobbyist

JEREMIAS, John | Tel: | (202) 955-6111
Government Affairs Assistant | Fax: | (202) 955-6118
john_jeremias@seaboard.com

Registered Federal Lobbyist

MCNARY, Andrew | Tel: | (202) 955-6111
Government Affairs Assistant | Fax: | (202) 955-6118
Registered Federal Lobbyist

MOSS, Ralph L. | Tel: | (202) 955-6111
Senior Vice President, Government Affairs | Fax: | (202) 955-6118
ralph_moss@seaboardcorp.com
Registered Federal Lobbyist

QUARRIE, John | Tel: | (202) 955-6111
Registered Federal Lobbyist | Fax: | (202) 955-6118

RUDE, Julian | Tel: | (202) 955-6111
Government Affairs Assistant | Fax: | (202) 955-6118
Registered Federal Lobbyist

STEINBRINK, David | Tel: | (202) 955-6111
Government Affairs Associate | Fax: | (202) 955-6118
Registered Federal Lobbyist

Seagate Technology, LLC

A manufacturer of data storage products. Acquired Maxtor Corporation.
www.seagate.com
Annual Revenues: $14.11 billion
Employees: 52,100
Ticker: NASDAQ: STX
SIC: 3572
Industry/ies: Computer/Technology

Chairman of the Board, President and Chief Executive Officer | Tel: | (408) 658-1000
LUCZO, Stephen J. | Fax: | (831) 438-3320
steve.luczo@seagate.com

Main Headquarters
Mailing: | 10200 S. De Anza Blvd | Tel: | (408) 658-1000
| Cupertino, CA 95014 | Fax: | (831) 438-3320

Public Affairs and Related Activities Personnel

At Headquarters

GRIECI, John | Tel: | (408) 658-1000
Senior Vice President, Customer Advocacy | Fax: | (831) 438-3320

HOGUE, Joanne | Tel: | (408) 658-1000
Director, Member, Audit Committee and Member, Finance | Fax: | (831) 438-3320
Committee

MASSARONI, Ken | Tel: | (408) 658-1000
Executive Vice President, General Counsel and Chief | Fax: | (831) 438-3320
Administrative Officer
kenneth.m.massaroni@seagate.com

MOSLEY, Dave | Tel: | (408) 658-1000
President, Operations and Technology | Fax: | (831) 438-3320

NYBERG, Joy | Tel: | (408) 658-1000
Senior Vice President, Human Resources, Internal | Fax: | (831) 438-3320
Communications and Community Engagement

PIMENTEL, Albert A. "Rocky" | Tel: | (408) 658-1000
President, Global Markets and Customers | Fax: | (831) 438-3320

RICHARZ, D. Kurt | Tel: | (408) 658-1000
Executive Vice President, Global Sales and Sales Operations | Fax: | (831) 438-3320

VOSSOUGHI, John | Tel: | (408) 658-1000
Senior Vice President, Global Strategic Sales | Fax: | (831) 438-3320

At Other Offices

COOPER, Rod J. | Tel: | (408) 658-1222
Vice President, Corporate Finance | Fax: | (831) 438-0558
920 Disc Dr.
Scotts Valley, CA 95066
rod.j.cooper@seagate.com

O'MALLEY, Patrick | Tel: | (831) 438-6550
Executive Vice President and Chief Financial Officer | Fax: | (831) 429-6356
920 Disc Dr.
Scotts Valley, CA 95066

Sealaska Native Corporation

A holding company. Principal business concerns are timber, minerals, telecommunications, entertainment and portfolio management. It is a Native institution representing the rich heritage of the Tlingit, Haida and Tsimshian people.
www.sealaska.com
Annual Revenues: $21.7 million
Employees: 1,400
Industry/ies: Communications; Telecommunications/Internet/Cable
Legislative Issues: IND; NAT

Chairman of the Board | Tel: | (907) 586-1512
NELSON, Joseph | Fax: | (907) 586-2304

President and Chief Executive Officer | Tel: | (907) 586-1512
MALLOTT, Anthony | Fax: | (907) 586-2304
Anthony.Mallott@sealaska.com

Main Headquarters
Mailing: | One Sealaska Plaza | Tel: | (907) 586-1512

Suite 400	Fax:	(907) 586-2304
Juneau, AK 99801	TF:	(800) 848-5921

Political Action Committees

Sealaska Corporation PAC
FEC ID: C00520643
Contact: Melanie A. Tyska
One Sealaska Plaza   Tel: (907) 586-1512
Suite 400   Fax: (907) 586-2304
Juneau, AK 99801

Corporate Foundations and Giving Programs

Sealaska Heritage Institute
Contact: Dr. Rosita Worl
One Sealaska Plaza   Tel: (907) 463-4844
Suite 301   Fax: (907) 463-4844
Juneau, AK 99801

Public Affairs and Related Activities Personnel

At Headquarters

ARAUJO, Jaeleen   Tel: (907) 586-1512
Vice President and General Counsel   Fax: (907) 586-2304
jaeleen.araujo@sealaska.com

CHENEY, PhD, Gail   Tel: (907) 586-1512
Director, Human Resources   Fax: (907) 586-2304

DOWNES, Terry   Tel: (907) 586-1512
Chief Operating Officer   Fax: (907) 586-2304

HUTCHINSON, Dixie   Tel: (907) 586-9297
Manager, Communications   Fax: (907) 586-2304
dixie.hutchinson@sealaska.com

MORRIS, Doug   Tel: (907) 586-1512
Vice President and Chief Financial Officer   Fax: (907) 586-2304

TYSKA, Melanie A.   Tel: (907) 586-1512
Corporate Compliance & Risk Manager and PAC Contact   Fax: (907) 586-2304

At Other Offices

WORL, Dr. Rosita   Tel: (907) 463-4844
President, Sealaska Heritage Institute   Fax: (907) 586-9293
Sealaska Heritage Institute, 105 S. Seward St., Suite 201
Juneau, AK 99801
Mail Stop Suite 301
rosita.worl@sealaska.com

Sealed Air

Manufacturer of specialized packaging materials.
www.sealedair.com
Annual Revenues: $6.88 billion
Employees: 23,000
Ticker: NYSE: SEE
SIC: 2840; 2820
Industry/ies: Construction/Construction Materials; Personal Care/Hygiene

Chairman of The Board   Tel: (201) 791-7600
CODEY , Lawrence R.   Fax: (201) 703-4205

President and Chief Executive Officer   Tel: (201) 791-7600
PERIBERE, Jerome A.   Fax: (201) 703-4205

Main Headquarters
Mailing: 8215 Forest Point Blvd.   Tel: (980) 221-3235
Charlotte, NC 28273

Public Affairs and Related Activities Personnel

At Headquarters

ROPER, Ruth   Tel: (980) 221-3235
Vice President, Strategy and Business Development

At Other Offices

AURICHIO, Ken   Tel: (201) 791-7600
Executive Director, Corporate Communications   Fax: (201) 703-4205
200 Riverfront Blvd.
Elmwood Park, NJ 07407
ken.aurichio@sealedair.com

CHAITMAN , Lori   Tel: (201) 703-4161
Vice President, Investor Relations   Fax: (201) 703-4205
200 Riverfront Blvd.
Elmwood Park, NJ 07407
lori.chaitman@sealedair.com

FINCH, Norman D.   Tel: (201) 791-7600
Vice President, General Counsel and Secretary and Human   Fax: (201) 703-4205
Resources
200 Riverfront Blvd.
Elmwood Park, NJ 07407

LOWE, Carol P.   Tel: (201) 791-7600
Senior Vice President and Chief Financial Officer   Fax: (201) 703-4205
200 Riverfront Blvd.
Elmwood Park, NJ 07407

WHALEY, Jim   Tel: (201) 791-7600

Vice President, Corporate Communications and	Fax:	(201) 703-4205
Sustainability		

200 Riverfront Blvd.
Elmwood Park, NJ 07407

Searfoss Consulting Group, LLC

Consulting firm.
www.jensearfoss.com

Founder Chief Executive Officer   Tel: (410) 703-2635
SEARFOSS, Jennifer   Fax: (443) 628-9178

Main Headquarters
Mailing: P.O. Box 4186   Tel: (410) 703-2635
Ashburn, VA 20148   Fax: (443) 628-9178

Washington Office
Mailing: 42747 Summerhouse Pl.
Ashburn, VA 20148

Public Affairs and Related Activities Personnel

At Headquarters

SWIFT, Carey   Tel: (410) 703-2635
Chief of Staff   Fax: (443) 628-9178

Sears Holdings Corporation

Formed in 2005 by the merger of Sears, Roebuck and Co. and Kmart Holding Corp. Brands and labels include Kenmore, Craftsman, DieHard, Lands' End, Jaclyn Smith, Joe Boxer, Apostrophe, Covington, and Martha Stewart Everyday. it is a leading integrated retailer where members have the ability to earn points and receive benefits across a wide variety of physical and digital formats through shop your way.com and mobile apps.
www.searsholdings.com
Annual Revenues: $31.20 billion
Employees: 196,000
Ticker: NASDAQ: SHLD
SIC: 5311
Industry/ies: Apparel/Textiles Industry; Furniture/Home Furnishings; Retail/Wholesale
Legislative Issues: TAX

Chairman of the Board and Chief Executive Officer   Tel: (847) 286-2500
LAMPERT, Edward S.   Fax: (847) 286-8351

Main Headquarters
Mailing: 3333 Beverly Rd.   Tel: (847) 286-2500
B6-347B   Fax: (847) 286-8351
Hoffman Estates, IL 60179

Political Action Committees

Sears Holdings Corporation PAC(1)
FEC ID: C00038612
Contact: Misty Redman
3333 Beverly Rd.   Tel: (847) 286-2500
B6-347B   Fax: (847) 286-8351
Hoffman Estates, IL 60179

> **Contributions to Candidates:** $20,000 (2015-2016)
> Democrats: $9,000; Republicans: $11,000

Corporate Foundations and Giving Programs

Sears Holdings Company Contributions Program
3333 Beverly Rd.
Hoffman Estates, IL 60179

Public Affairs and Related Activities Personnel

At Headquarters

BRATHWAITE, Chris   Tel: (847) 286-8371
Vice President, Media Relations and Corporate   Fax: (847) 286-8351
Communications

COLEMAN, Kristin M.   Tel: (847) 286-2500
Senior Vice President, General Counsel and Corporate   Fax: (847) 286-8351
Secretary

COSTELLO, Larry   Tel: (847) 286-9036
Director, Public Relations   Fax: (847) 286-8351
Larry.Costello@searshc.com

JAMES, Alasdair   Tel: (847) 286-2500
President and Chief Member Officer   Fax: (847) 286-8351

MARKS, Dan   Tel: (847) 286-2500
Division Vice President, Marketing   Fax: (847) 286-8351

OPPENKOWSKI, Misty   Tel: (847) 286-2500
Registered Federal Lobbyist   Fax: (847) 286-8351

REDMAN, Misty   Tel: (847) 286-1535
Vice President, Government Affairs and PAC Contact   Fax: (847) 286-8351
Mail Stop B6-347B
Registered Federal Lobbyist

RIECKER, Robert A.   Tel: (847) 286-2500
Vice President, Controller and Chief Accounting Officer   Fax: (847) 286-8351

SCHRIESHEIM, Robert A.   Tel: (847) 286-2300
Executive Vice President and Chief Financial Officer   Fax: (847) 286-8351

SCIABARAS, Dawn | Tel: (847) 286-2500
| Fax: (847) 286-8351

The Seattle Times Company

The Seattle Times Company is a private and independent news and information company.
www.seattletimescompany.com
Annual Revenues: $64.20 million
Employees: 1,000
SIC: 2711
Industry/ies: Communications; Media/Mass Communication
Legislative Issues: LBR

Publisher and Chief Executive Officer | Tel: (206) 464-2111
BLETHEN, Frank A. | Fax: (206) 493-0883

Main Headquarters
Mailing: 1000 Denny Way | Tel: (206) 464-2111
Seattle, WA 98109 | Fax: (206) 493-0883

Corporate Foundations and Giving Programs
The Seattle Times Fund For The Needy
P.O. Box 70 | Tel: (206) 464-2119
Seattle, WA 98111-0070 | Fax: (206) 493-0883

Public Affairs and Related Activities Personnel

At Headquarters

FARDELLA, Alayne | Tel: (206) 464-2111
President and Chief Operating Officer | Fax: (206) 493-0883

MACKIE, Jill R. | Tel: (206) 646-2028
Vice President, Public Affairs | Fax: (206) 515-5565
Registered Federal Lobbyist

TAKEUCHI, Eileen | Tel: (206) 464-2111
Vice President and Chief Financial Officer | Fax: (206) 493-0883

SeaWorld Parks & Entertainment Inc.

Operates adventure parks in the United States.
seaworldentertainment.com
Annual Revenues: $1.38 billion
Employees: 5,000
Ticker: NYSE: SEAS
Industry/ies: Animals; Sports/Leisure/Entertainment
Legislative Issues: ANI; BUD; CSP; IMM; MAR; TOU; TRA

President and Chief Executive Officer
MANBY, Joel

Main Headquarters
Mailing: P.O. Box 690129
Orlando, FL 32869

Washington Office
Mailing: 601 Pennsylvania Ave. | Tel: (202) 220-3055
Suite 900
Washington, DC 20004

Corporate Foundations and Giving Programs
SeaWorld Parks & Entertainment Contributions program
P.O. Box 690129
Orlando, FL 32869

Public Affairs and Related Activities Personnel

At Headquarters

BIDES, Becca
Director, Communications
Becca.Bides@seaworld.com

HAMMER, Dave
Chief Human Resources Officer

HEANEY, James
Chief Financial Officer

JACOBS, Fred
Vice President, Communications
Fred.Jacobs@SeaWorld.com

JEANSONNE-BECKA, Aimee
Director, Marketing Communications

TAYLOR, Tony
General Counsel and Chief Legal Officer and Corporate Secretary

At Washington Office

GALBRAITH, James R. | Tel: (202) 220-3055
Federal Lobbyist
Jay.galbraith@seaworld.com
Registered Federal Lobbyist

HEFFERNAN, Barbara D. | Tel: (202) 220-3055
Vice President, National & International Affairs
barbara.heffernan@seaworld.com

HOMER STEWART, Jill | Tel: (202) 220-3055
Registered Federal Lobbyist

KERMES, Jill | Tel: (202) 220-3055

Registered Federal Lobbyist
STEWART, Jill Homer | Tel: (202) 220-3055
Registered Federal Lobbyist

At Other Offices

SWANSON, Marc | Tel: (407) 226-5011
Chief Accounting Officer and Interim Chief Financial Officer
9205 S. Park Center Loop, Suite 400
Orlando, FL 32819

Second Chance

Second Chance was founded in 1993 . It Provides job readiness training, employment placement, affordable housing and life skills for homeless and unemployed men, women and youth.
www.secondchanceprogram.org
Annual Revenues: $4.46 million
Industry/ies: Charities And Foundations; Employees & Employment; Nonprofit

Executive Director | Tel: (619) 234-8888
COLEMAN, Robert | Fax: (619) 234-7787
rcoleman@secondchanceprogram.org

Main Headquarters
Mailing: 6145 Imperial Ave. | Tel: (619) 234-8888
San Diego, CA 92114-4213 | Fax: (619) 234-7787

Public Affairs and Related Activities Personnel

At Headquarters

EINSELE, Cheryl | Tel: (619) 234-8888
Director, Development and Communications | Fax: (619) 234-7787
ceinsele@secondchanceprogram.org

GOOCH, Trisha | Tel: (619) 839-0950
Vice President, Advancement and External Affairs | Fax: (619) 234-7787
tgooch@secondchanceprogram.org

SMITH, Randy | Tel: (619) 839-0956
Chief Financial Officer | Fax: (619) 234-7787

VALDEZ, Ricky | Tel: (619) 839-0961
Vice President, Programs | Fax: (619) 234-7787

SecureInfo Corporation

SecureInfo Corporation is a provider of Information Assurance (IA) solutions.
www.secureinfo.com
Employees: 120
Industry/ies: Computer/Technology; Law Enforcement/Security

President and Chief Executive Officer | Tel: (703) 488-2500
FOUNTAIN, Christopher | Fax: (703) 488-2555

Main Headquarters
Mailing: 14432 Albemarle Cir. | Tel: (703) 488-2500
Suite E-1 | Fax: (703) 488-2555
Chantilly, VA 20151 | TF: (888) 677-9351

Securian Financial Group Inc.

Providers of financial security for individuals and businesses in the form of insurance, retirement plans and investments.
www.securian.com
Employees: 5,000
Industry/ies: Banking/Finance/Investments

Chairman | Tel: (651) 665-3500
SENKLER, Robert L. | Fax: (651) 665-4488
robert.senkler@securian.com

President and Chief Executive Officer | Tel: (651) 665-3500
HILGER, Christopher M. | Fax: (651) 665-4488

Main Headquarters
Mailing: 400 Robert St., North | Tel: (651) 665-3500
St. Paul, MN 55101 | Fax: (651) 665-4488

Political Action Committees
Securian Inc.PAC
FEC ID: C00120006
Contact: John Regal
400 and 401 Robert St., North
St. Paul, MN 55101

Contributions to Candidates: $8,250 (2015-2016)
Democrats: $250; Republicans: $8,000

Corporate Foundations and Giving Programs
Securian Foundation
400 and 401 Robert St., North
St. Paul, MN 55101

Public Affairs and Related Activities Personnel

At Headquarters

BAILEY, Vicki | Tel: (651) 665-3500
Vice President, Investment Law and Chief Compliance Officer | Fax: (651) 665-4488
CAMPBELL, Keith M. | Tel: (651) 665-3500

Senior Vice President, Human Resources and Corporate Services	Fax:	(651) 665-4128
CHRISTENSEN, Gary	Tel:	(651) 665-3500
Senior Vice President, General Counsel and Secretary	Fax:	(651) 665-4488
gary.christensen@securian.com		
JENSEN, Margaret	Tel:	(651) 665-7558
Media Relations Contact	Fax:	(651) 665-4128
margaret.jensen@securian.com		
KOUTSKY, Lori J.	Tel:	(651) 665-3501
Manager, Community Relations and Foundation	Fax:	(651) 665-4488
lori.koutsky@securian.com		
KUPLIC, David M.	Tel:	(651) 665-3500
Senior Vice President and Chief Investment Officer	Fax:	(651) 665-4488
david.kuplic@securian.com		
PINKETT, Kathy L.	Tel:	(651) 665-3500
Senior Vice President, Human Resources and Corporate Services	Fax:	(651) 665-4488
kathleen.pinkett@securian.com		
RADEL, Dwaye	Tel:	(651) 665-3500
Senior Vice President and General Counsel	Fax:	(651) 665-4488
REGAL, John	Tel:	(651) 665-3500
Director, Risk Management	Fax:	(651) 665-4488
john.regal@securian.com		
WILSON, Loyall E.	Tel:	(651) 665-3500
Senior Vice President, Corporate Compliance Officer	Fax:	(651) 665-4488
ZACCARO, Warren J.	Tel:	(651) 665-3500
Executive Vice President and Chief Financial Officer and and Chief Compliance Officer	Fax:	(651) 665-4488

Security Finance Corporation

A consumer loan company.
www.security-finance.com
Employees: 2,500
Industry/ies: Banking/Finance/Investments
Legislative Issues: BAN; FIN

Chief Executive Officer	Tel:	(501) 907-2000
HARDING, Rush F.	Fax:	(864) 582-2532
rharding@crewsfs.com		

Main Headquarters

Mailing:	P. O. Box 811	Tel:	(864) 582-8193
	Spartanburg, SC 29304	Fax:	(864) 582-2532
		TF:	(800) 395-8195

Political Action Committees

Security Finance Corporation Of Spartanburg and Affiliates PAC
FEC ID: C00387753
Contact: Jonathan W. Norwood

P.O. Box 811	Tel:	(864) 582-8193
Spartanburg, SC 29304	Fax:	(864) 582-8193

> **Contributions to Candidates:** $22,000 (2015-2016)
> Democrats: $1,500; Republicans: $20,500

Corporate Foundations and Giving Programs

Securitys Lending Hand Foundation

P. O. Box 811	Tel:	(864) 582-8193
Spartanburg, SC 29304	Fax:	(864) 582-2532

Public Affairs and Related Activities Personnel

At Headquarters

HOLT, Phillip	Tel:	(469) 385-7845
Senior Vice President	Fax:	(864) 582-2532
phillip.holt@security-finance.com		
NORWOOD, Jonathan W.	Tel:	(864) 582-8193
PAC Treasurer	Fax:	(864) 582-2532

SECURUS Technologies

A supplier of detainee communications and information management solutions.
www.securustech.net
Annual Revenues: $25.30 million
Employees: 700
SIC: 4899
Industry/ies: Computer/Technology; Law Enforcement/Security
Legislative Issues: TEC

Chairman of the Board and Chief Executive Officer	Tel:	(972) 277-0300
SMITH, Richard A.	Fax:	(972) 277-0301

Main Headquarters

Mailing:	14651 Dallas Pkwy.	Tel:	(972) 277-0300
	Sixth Floor	Fax:	(972) 277-0301
	Dallas, TX 75254	TF:	(800) 844-6591

Public Affairs and Related Activities Personnel

At Headquarters

BROLSMA, Patrick W.	Tel:	(972) 277-0300

Director, Corporate Development	Fax:	(972) 277-0301
HOPFINGER, Curtis L.	Tel:	(972) 277-0319
Director, Regulatory & Government Affairs	Fax:	(972) 277-0416
chopfinger@securustech.net		
Registered Federal Lobbyist		
LENGYEL, Kate	Tel:	(972) 277-0300
Vice President, Human Resources	Fax:	(972) 277-0301
REINHOLD, Dennis J.	Tel:	(972) 277-0300
Vice President, General Counsel and Secretary	Fax:	(972) 277-0301
DReinhold@securustech.net		
SIDLER, James S.	Tel:	(972) 277-0340
Director, Marketing, Communications and Sales	Fax:	(972) 277-0301
jsidler@securustech.com		

Select Health of South Carolina, Inc.

A healthcare company. It is a part of the AmeriHealth Caritas Family of Companies and provides healthcare for South Carolinians.
www.selecthealthofsc.com
Annual Revenues: $7.80 million
Employees: 300
Industry/ies: Medicine/Health Care/Mental Health

President and Chief Executive Officer	Tel:	(843) 569-1759
JERNIGAN, J. Michael	Fax:	(843) 569-7228
mjernigan@selecthealthofsc.com		

Main Headquarters

Mailing:	P.O. Box 40849	Tel:	(843) 569-1759
	Charleston, SC 29423	Fax:	(843) 569-7228
		TF:	(800) 741-6605

Corporate Foundations and Giving Programs

Select Health of South Carolina, Inc. Contributions Program
Contact: Lillian Suarez

P.O. Box 40849	Tel:	(843) 569-1759
Charleston, SC 29423	Fax:	(843) 569-1759

Public Affairs and Related Activities Personnel

At Headquarters

CRIMMINGER, Tricia	Tel:	(843) 569-1759
Director, Communications	Fax:	(843) 569-7228
tricia.crimminger@selecthealthofsc.com		
ENGELMAN, Rebecca	Tel:	(843) 569-1759
Market President	Fax:	(843) 569-7228
POPSON, Sean	Tel:	(843) 569-1759
Director, Finance	Fax:	(843) 569-7228
POWELL, Michelle	Tel:	(843) 569-1759
Director, Human Resources	Fax:	(843) 569-7228
michelle.powell@selecthealthofsc.com		
SUAREZ, Lillian	Tel:	(843) 569-1759
Director, Community Education	Fax:	(843) 569-7228
Lillian.suarez@selecthealthofsc.com		

Select Medical Corporation

An operator of specialty acute care hospitals and clinics throughout the United States.
www.selectmedicalcorp.com
Annual Revenues: $3.06 billion
Employees: 21,400
Ticker: NYSE: SEM
SIC: 8093
Industry/ies: Medicine/Health Care/Mental Health
Legislative Issues: MMM

Executive Chairman of the Board	Tel:	(717) 972-1100
ORTENZIO, Robert A.	Fax:	(717) 972-1042
President and Chief Executive Officer	Tel:	(717) 972-1100
CHERNOW, David	Fax:	(717) 972-1042

Main Headquarters

Mailing:	4714 Old Gettysburg Rd.	Tel:	(717) 972-1100
	P.O. Box 2034	Fax:	(717) 972-1042
	Mechanicsburg, PA 17055	TF:	(888) 735-6332

Political Action Committees

Select Medical Corporation PAC
FEC ID: C00546119
Contact: William Walters
4716 Old Gettysburg Rd.
P.O. Box 2034
Mechanicsburg, PA 17055

> **Contributions to Candidates:** $186,431 (2015-2016)
> Democrats: $34,000; Republicans: $152,431

> **Principal Recipients**
>
> **SENATE**
> BENNET, MICHAEL F (DEM-CO)
> BLUNT, ROY (REP-MO)
> BURR, RICHARD (REP-NC)

CORNYN, JOHN (REP-TX)
ISAKSON, JOHN HARDY (REP-GA)
JOHNSON, RONALD HAROLD (REP-)
MCCONNELL, MITCH (REP-KY)
PORTMAN, ROB (REP-OH)

HOUSE
BOUSTANY, CHARLES W. DR. JR. (REP-LA)
BRADY, KEVIN (REP-TX)
BUCHANAN, VERNON (REP-FL)
COSTELLO, RYAN A (REP-PA)
PASCRELL, WILLIAM J. HON. (DEM-NJ)
REED, THOMAS W II (REP-NY)
TIBERI, PATRICK J. (REP-OH)

Corporate Foundations and Giving Programs

Select Medical Community Relations Program
4716 Old Gettysburg Rd.
P.O. Box 2034
Mechanicsburg, PA 17055

Public Affairs and Related Activities Personnel

At Headquarters

BODENSIEK, Edwin — Tel: (717) 972-1100
Vice President, Public Relations and Communications — Fax: (717) 972-1042
ebodensiek@selectmedical.com

BREIGHNER, Jr., Robert G. — Tel: (717) 972-1100
Vice President, Compliance and Audit Services and Corporate — Fax: (717) 972-1042
Compliance Officer
rbreighner@selectmedicalcorp.com

CURNANE, Carolyn — Tel: (717) 730-4221
Vice President, Corporate Communications — Fax: (717) 972-1042
ccurnane@selectmedicalcorp.com

JACKSON, Martin F. — Tel: (717) 972-1100
Executive Vice President and Chief Financial Officer — Fax: (717) 972-1042
mjackson@selectmedicalcorp.com

ORTENZIO, Rocco A. — Tel: (717) 972-1100
Vice Chairman and Co-Founder — Fax: (717) 972-1042

SAICH, John A. — Tel: (717) 972-1100
Executive Vice President, Chief Human Resources Officer — Fax: (717) 972-1042
jsaich@selectmedicalcorp.com

TARVIN, Michael E. — Tel: (717) 972-1100
Executive Vice President, General Counsel and Secretary — Fax: (717) 972-1042

VEIT, Joel — Tel: (717) 972-1100
Senior Vice President and Treasurer — Fax: (717) 972-1042
ir@selectmedicalcorp.com

WALTERS, William — Tel: (717) 972-1100
PAC Treasurer — Fax: (717) 972-1042

Selective Insurance Group, Inc.

Selective Insurance Group offers insurance and alternative risk management services.
www.selective.com
Annual Revenues: $2.16 billion
Employees: 2,200
Ticker: NASDAQ: SIGI
SIC: 6331
Industry/ies: Insurance Industry

Chairman, President and Chief Executive Officer — Tel: (973) 948-3000
MURPHY, Gregory E. — Fax: (973) 948-0292

Main Headquarters
Mailing: 40 Wantage Ave. — Tel: (973) 948-3000
Branchville, NJ 07890-1000 — Fax: (973) 948-0292
— TF: (800) 777-9656

Corporate Foundations and Giving Programs

Selective Group Foundation
40 Wantage Ave.
Branchville, NJ 07890

Public Affairs and Related Activities Personnel

At Headquarters

BECK, Jeffrey — Tel: (973) 948-3000
Senior Vice President, Government and Regulatory Affairs — Fax: (973) 948-0292

BURNETT, Kimberly — Tel: (973) 948-3000
Executive Vice President, Chief Human Resource Officer — Fax: (973) 948-0292

LANZA, Michael H. — Tel: (973) 948-3000
Executive Vice President, General Counsel and Chief — Fax: (973) 948-0292
Compliance Officer
Michael.Lanza@selective.com

MARCHIONI, John J. — Tel: (973) 948-3000
President Chief Operating Officer — Fax: (973) 948-0292

THATCHER, Dale A. — Tel: (973) 948-3000
Executive Vice President and Chief Financial Officer — Fax: (973) 948-0292
dale.thatcher@selective.com

SEMCO Energy, Inc.

A diversified energy and infrastructure company distributing natural gas to customers in Michigan and Alaska.
www.semcoenergy.com
Annual Revenues: $1.64 million
Employees: 500
SIC: 4924
Industry/ies: Energy/Electricity; Utilities

Chairman of the Board, President and Chief Executive Officer — Tel: (810) 987-2200
SCHREIBER, Jr., George A. — Fax: (810) 987-7638

Main Headquarters
Mailing: 1411 Third St., Suite A — Tel: (810) 987-2200
P.O. Box 5004 — Fax: (810) 989-4098
Port Huron, MI 48060 — TF: (800) 624-2019

Public Affairs and Related Activities Personnel

At Headquarters

CLARK, Peter — Tel: (810) 987-2200
Executive Vice President and General Counsel — Fax: (810) 989-4098

CONNELLY, Jr., Thomas — Tel: (810) 887-4208
Director, Investor Relations — Fax: (248) 458-6150
Thomas.Connelly@semcoenergy.com

LUBBERS, Timothy J. — Tel: (810) 887-4208
Director, Marketing and External Affairs — Fax: (810) 989-4098

LUKEHART, Terri — Tel: (810) 987-2200
Manager, Human Resources — Fax: (810) 989-4098

WILSON, Andrew — Tel: (810) 987-2200
Chief Financial Officer and Company Secretary — Fax: (810) 989-4098

Sempra Energy

A diversified international energy corporation formed by the merger of Pacific Enterprise and Enova Corporation in 1998.
www.sempra.com
Annual Revenues: $10.92 billion
Employees: 17,046
Ticker: NYSE: SRE
SIC: 4932
Industry/ies: Energy/Electricity; Utilities
Legislative Issues: AVI; BUD; CAW; CDT; ENG; ENV; FUE; HOM; NAT; TAX; TRA; TRD; UTI

Chairman of the Board and Chief Executive Officer — Tel: (619) 696-2000
REED, Debra L. — Fax: (619) 696-2374

President — Tel: (619) 696-2000
SNELL, Mark A. — Fax: (619) 696-2374

Main Headquarters
Mailing: 101 Ash St., HQ18 — Tel: (619) 696-2000
San Diego, CA 92101 — Fax: (619) 696-2374
— TF: (866) 616-5565

Washington Office
Mailing: 1399 New York Ave. NW — Tel: (202) 662-1700
Suite 350
Washington, DC 20005

Political Action Committees

Sempra Energy Employee PAC - Federal
FEC ID: C00008748
101 Ash St.
HQ08C
San Diego, CA 92101-3017

Contributions to Candidates: $197,500 (2015-2016)
Democrats: $80,500; Republicans: $117,000

Corporate Foundations and Giving Programs

Sempra Foundation
Contact: G. Joyce Rowland
101 Ash St.
San Diego, CA 92101

Public Affairs and Related Activities Personnel

At Headquarters

CLARK, Randall L. — Tel: (619) 696-2000
Vice President, Compliance and Governance and Corporate — Fax: (619) 696-2374
Secretary

DAVIS, Steven D. — Tel: (619) 696-2000
Senior Vice President, External Affairs — Fax: (619) 696-2374

GRANT, Andrea — Tel: (619) 696-2000
PAC Contact — Fax: (619) 696-2374

HOUSEHOLDER, Joseph A. — Tel: (619) 696-2000
Executive Vice President and Chief Financial Officer — Fax: (619) 696-2374

ICHORD, J. William — Tel: (202) 662-1700
Vice President, Corporate Relations — Fax: (202) 293-2887

KNIGHT, Jr., Jessie J. — Tel: (619) 696-2000

Executive Vice President , External Affairs	Fax:	(619) 696-2374
LAMBRIGHT, James H.	Tel:	(619) 696-2000
Senior Vice President ,Corporate Development	Fax:	(619) 696-2374
LARSON, Art	Tel:	(619) 696-4307
Contact, Media Relations	Fax:	(619) 696-4379
alarson@sempra.com		
PRASSER, Kelly	Tel:	(619) 696-4230
Regional Manager, Community Relations and Events	Fax:	(619) 696-2500
kprasser@sempra.com		
ROWLAND, G. Joyce	Tel:	(619) 696-2000
Senior Vice President, Human Resources and Foundation President	Fax:	(619) 696-2374
VACCARI, Richard A.	Tel:	(619) 696-2000
Vice President, Investor Relations and Treasurer	Fax:	(619) 696-2374
WYRSCH, Martha L.	Tel:	(619) 696-2000
Executive Vice President & General Counsel	Fax:	(619) 696-2374
YONG, Paul	Tel:	(619) 696-2000
Vice President and Treasurer	Fax:	(619) 696-2374

At Washington Office

CRIDER, Scott B.	Tel:	(202) 662-1700
Vice President, Federal Government Affairs		
Registered Federal Lobbyist		
HAAS, Monica	Tel:	(619) 696-2000
Vice President, Administration and External Affairs	Fax:	(619) 696-2374
HULL, Allison	Tel:	(202) 662-1700
Registered Federal Lobbyist		
LANSINGER, Jr., William C.	Tel:	(202) 662-1712
Director, FERC and Federal Agency Relations	Fax:	(202) 293-2887
wlansinger@sempra.com		
Registered Federal Lobbyist		
MACKEY, Sean	Tel:	(202) 662-1700
Federal Lobbyist		
Registered Federal Lobbyist		
MOALLEM, Sabra	Tel:	(877) 866-2066
Contact, Media and Sempra Foundation		
PRENDERGAST, Danielle	Tel:	(202) 662-1700
Contact, Government Relations	Fax:	(202) 293-2887
Registered Federal Lobbyist		
RANSDELL, Tim H.	Tel:	(202) 662-1700
Contact, Government Relations		
transdell@sempra.com		
Registered Federal Lobbyist		
WILLIAMS, George P.	Tel:	(202) 662-1701
Director, Government Affairs	Fax:	(202) 293-2887

Semprus Biosciences, Inc.

A venture-backed biotechnology company developing functional surfaces to prevent medical device complications.
www.semprusbio.com
Employees: 13
Industry/ies: Science; Scientific Research
Legislative Issues: DEF; HCR

Chairman of the Board	Tel:	(617) 577-7755
ROCKLAGE, PhD, Dr. Scott	Fax:	(617) 577-7756
Chief Executive Officer and Co-Founder	Tel:	(617) 577-7755
LUCCHINO, David L.	Fax:	(617) 577-7756
David.Lucchino@semprusbio.com		

Main Headquarters

Mailing:	One Kendall Sq.	Tel:	(617) 577-7755
	Building 1400W, First Floor	Fax:	(617) 577-7756
	Cambridge, MA 02139-1673		

Public Affairs and Related Activities Personnel

At Headquarters

GLASS, Holly P.	Tel:	(703) 754-2848
Contact, Media Relations	Fax:	(617) 577-7756
holly.glass@semprusbio.com		
HAAS, Gregory	Tel:	(617) 577-7755
Contact, Product Strategy and Regulatory Affairs	Fax:	(617) 577-7756
MCCLELLAN, David N.	Tel:	(617) 577-7755
Contact, Business Development	Fax:	(617) 577-7756

Sensient Technology Corporation

An ingredient manufacturer. Formerly known as Universal Foods Corp.
www.sensient-tech.com
Annual Revenues: $1.37 billion
Employees: 4,032
Ticker: NYSE: SXT
SIC: 2860
Industry/ies: Food And Beverage Industry

Chairman of the Board, President and Chief Executive Officer	Tel:	(414) 271-6755
MANNING , Paul	Fax:	(414) 347-3785

Main Headquarters

Mailing:	777 E. Wisconsin Ave.	Tel:	(414) 271-6755
	Milwaukee, WI 53202-5304	Fax:	(414) 347-3785
		TF:	(800) 558-9892

Public Affairs and Related Activities Personnel

At Headquarters

COLLOPY, John F	Tel:	(414) 271-6755
Vice President and Treasurer	Fax:	(414) 347-3785
HAMMOND, John L.	Tel:	(414) 271-6755
Senior Vice President, General Counsel and Secretary	Fax:	(414) 347-3785
MAKAL, Jeffrey	Tel:	(414) 271-6755
Vice President, Controller and Chief Accounting Officer	Fax:	(414) 347-3785
MORIN, Kimberly A.	Tel:	(414) 271-6755
Vice President, Human Resources	Fax:	(414) 347-3785
ROLFS , Stephen J.	Tel:	(414) 271-6755
Senior Vice President and Chief Financial Officer	Fax:	(414) 347-3785

Sensus Metering Systems. Inc.

Sensus provides Automatic Meter Reading (AMR) and Advanced Metering Infrastructure (AMI) system solutions for water, gas, electric and heat utilities.
www.sensus.com
Employees: 4,000
SIC: 3824
NAICS: 334514
Industry/ies: Energy/Electricity; Environment And Conservation; Machinery/Equipment; Pollution And Waste; Utilities

Chairman of the Board	Tel:	(919) 845-4000
D'AMBROSIO, Louis		
President	Tel:	(919) 845-4000
BAYS, Randy		

Main Headquarters

Mailing:	8601 Six Forks Rd.	Tel:	(919) 845-4000
	Suite 700	TF:	(800) 638-3748
	Raleigh, NC 27615		

Public Affairs and Related Activities Personnel

At Headquarters

BOYLE, Todd	Tel:	(919) 845-4000
Chief People Officer		
ENGHAUSER, Courtney	Tel:	(919) 845-4000
Chief Financial Officer		
FLANNERY, Colin	Tel:	(919) 845-4000
Executive Vice President, General Counsel and Secretary		
colin.flannery@sensus.com		
HARBER, Dale	Tel:	(919) 845-4000
Executive Vice President, Global Marketing and International Programs		
HILTY, James J.	Tel:	(919) 845-4007
Executive Vice President, Corporate Development		
jim.hilty@sensus.com		
PALMER, Linda	Tel:	(919) 845-4021
Manager, Corporate Communications		
linda.palmer@sensus.com		
RIDGE, Ron	Tel:	(919) 845-4000
Vice President and Chief Information Officer		
URAM, George	Tel:	(919) 845-4000
Vice President, Industry and Regulatory Affairs		
george.uram@sensus.com		

Sentinel Worldwide

Sentinel Worldwide, LLC is a Corporate Security and Risk Mitigation company based in Southern Denver, Colorado. Founded in 2005.
sentinelworldwide.com
Industry/ies: Law Enforcement/Security; Security
Legislative Issues: BUD; CPT; TRD

President & Founder	Tel:	(202) 657-3489
TEPP, Steven		

Main Headquarters

Mailing:	9752 Firth Ct.	Tel:	(202) 657-3489
	Vienna, VA 22181		

Sentry Insurance

A mutual insurance company.
www.sentry.com
Annual Revenues: $2.33 billion
Employees: 4,800
Industry/ies: Insurance Industry

Chairman of the Board, President and Chief Executive Officer　Tel:　(715) 346-6000
MCPARTLAND, Pete G.　　　　　　　　　　　　　　　　　　Fax:　(715) 346-7516

Main Headquarters
Mailing:　　1800 N. Point Dr.　　　　　　　　Tel:　(715) 346-6000
　　　　　Stevens Point, WI 54481　　　　　Fax:　(715) 346-7516
　　　　　　　　　　　　　　　　　　　　TF:　(800) 628-3547

Political Action Committees
Sentry Insurance A Mutual Company Federal Political Action Committee
FEC ID: C00545194
Contact: Dwayne A. Gantz
44 E. Mifflin St.
Suite 801
Madison, WI 53703

　　Contributions to Candidates: $52,050 (2015-2016)
　　Democrats: $17,000; Republicans: $35,050

　　　　Principal Recipients
　　　　　HOUSE
　　　　DUFFY, SEAN (REP-WI)

Corporate Foundations and Giving Programs
Sentry Insurance Foundation
1800 N. Point Dr.
Stevens Point, WI 54481

Public Affairs and Related Activities Personnel

At Other Offices

GANTZ , Dwayne A.
PAC Treasurer
Ten E. Doty St., Suite 701
Madison, WI 53703

Sequa Corporation

Sequa Corporation is owned by the Carlyle Group. Company is into aerospace, automotive and metal coating business segments.
www.sequa.com
SIC: 3769
NAICS: 336419
Industry/ies: Aerospace/Aviation; Transportation

Chairman of the Board　　　　　　　　　　　Tel:　(561) 935-3571
CLARE, Peter J.

Chief Executive Officer　　　　　　　　　　Tel:　(561) 935-3571
MEPHAM, Jr., Thomas

Main Headquarters
Mailing:　　3999 RCA Blvd.　　　　　　　　Tel:　(561) 935-3571
　　　　　Palm Beach Gardens, FL 33410　　TF:　(800) 634-7936

Corporate Foundations and Giving Programs
Sequa Corporation Contributions Program
300 Blaisdell Rd.
P.O. Box 200150
Orangeburg, NY 10962

Public Affairs and Related Activities Personnel

At Headquarters

BOLLMAN, John　　　　　　　　　　　　　Tel:　(561) 935-3571
Vice President, Human Resources

COSTELLO, Donna　　　　　　　　　　　Tel:　(561) 935-3571
Chief Financial Officer
donna_costello@sequa.com

FARRANT, Andrew　　　　　　　　　　　Tel:　(561) 935-3571
Vice President, Marketing and Corporate Communications
Andrew_farrant@sequa.com

GEDVILAS, Cathy　　　　　　　　　　　Tel:　(561) 935-3571
Director, Corporate Communications
cathy_gedvilas@sequa.com

LANGELOTTI , James　　　　　　　　　　Tel:　(561) 935-3571
Vice President and Treasurer

LOWSON, Steven R.　　　　　　　　　　Tel:　(561) 935-3571
Vice President, General Counsel and Secretary
steven_lowson@sequa.com

At Other Offices

HAINES, Craig
Vice President & Controller
300 Blaisdell Rd.
Orangeburg, NY 10962

SERMO

SERMO is an online community for physicians founded in 2006. SERMO is a place for physicians to post observations and questions about clinical issues and hear other doctors opinions.
www.sermo.com
Annual Revenues: $8.50 million
Employees: 100

Industry/ies: Communications; Medicine/Health Care/Mental Health; Science; Scientific Research; Telecommunications/Internet/Cable

Chief Executive Officer　　　　　　　　　　Tel:　(212) 358-0800
KIRK , Peter

Main Headquarters
Mailing:　　200 Park Avenue South　　　　Tel:　(212) 358-0800
　　　　　Suite 1310　　　　　　　　　　TF:　(866) 910-6279
　　　　　New York, NY 10003

Public Affairs and Related Activities Personnel

At Headquarters

BENSHOSHAN, Osnat　　　　　　　　　Tel:　(212) 358-0800
Senior Vice President, Marketing and Strategy

SMITH, Gerard　　　　　　　　　　　　Tel:　(212) 358-0800
Chief Financial Officer

STANLEY, Giles　　　　　　　　　　　Tel:　(212) 358-0800
General Counsel

Service Corporation International

Provider of funeral, cremation and cemetery services.
www.sci-corp.com
Annual Revenues: $2.99 billion
Employees: 15,654
Ticker: NYSE: SCI
SIC: 7200
Industry/ies: Cemeteries/Funerals

Chairman of the Board and Chief Executive Officer　Tel:　(713) 522-5141
RYAN, Thomas L.　　　　　　　　　　　　　　　　Fax:　(713) 525-5586

Main Headquarters
Mailing:　　1929 Allen Pkwy.　　　　　　　Tel:　(713) 522-5141
　　　　　Houston, TX 77019　　　　　　Fax:　(713) 525-5586

Political Action Committees
Service Corporation International PAC (SCI/PAC)
FEC ID: C00173096
Contact: Caressa F. Hughes
1929 Allen Pkwy.
Houston, TX 77019

　　Contributions to Candidates: $18,000 (2015-2016)
　　Democrats: $15,000; Republicans: $3,000

Corporate Foundations and Giving Programs
Stewart Enterprises Contributions Program
1333 S. Clearview Pkwy.
Jefferson, LA 70121

Public Affairs and Related Activities Personnel

At Headquarters

HUGHES, Caressa F.　　　　　　　　　　Tel:　(713) 525-5230
PAC Treasurer　　　　　　　　　　　　Fax:　(713) 525-5586

JACOBS, Philip C.　　　　　　　　　　　Tel:　(713) 522-5141
Senior Vice President and Chief Marketing Officer　Fax:　(713) 525-5586

MARSHALL, Lisa　　　　　　　　　　　Tel:　(713) 525-3066
Managing Director, Corporate Communications　Fax:　(713) 525-5586

MOORE , Tammy R.　　　　　　　　　　Tel:　(713) 522-5141
Vice President and Corporate Controller　　Fax:　(713) 525-5586

SANGALIS, Gregory T.　　　　　　　　　Tel:　(713) 522-5141
Senior Vice President, General Counsel and Secretary　Fax:　(713) 525-5586

TANZBERGER, Eric D.　　　　　　　　　Tel:　(713) 522-5141
Senior Vice President, Chief Financial Officer and Treasurer　Fax:　(713) 525-5586

WALTRIP, Robert L.　　　　　　　　　　Tel:　(713) 522-5141
Founder and Chairman Emeritus　　　　Fax:　(713) 525-5586

WEBB, Michael R.　　　　　　　　　　Tel:　(713) 522-5141
President and Chief Operating Officer　　Fax:　(713) 525-5586

WESTERFIELD, Denise B.　　　　　　　Tel:　(713) 522-5141
Manager, Contract Corporate Communications　Fax:　(713) 525-5586
dwesterfield@stei.com

YOUNG, Debbie　　　　　　　　　　　Tel:　(713) 525-9088
Director, Investor Relations　　　　　　Fax:　(713) 525-5586
debbie.young@sci-us.com

The ServiceMaster Company

Commercial and residential services company.
www.servicemaster.com
Annual Revenues: $3.37 billion
Employees: 27,000
SIC: 8741
Industry/ies: Environment And Conservation
Legislative Issues: RES

Chief Executive Officer　　　　　　　　　　Tel:　(901) 597-1400
GILLETTE, Robert J.　　　　　　　　　　　　　Fax:　(630) 663-2001

Main Headquarters

Mailing: 860 Ridge Lake Blvd.	Tel:	(901) 597-1400
Suite 101	Fax:	(630) 663-2001
Memphis, TN 38120	TF:	(888) 937-3783

Political Action Committees

The Servicemaster Company PAC (SERVEPAC)
FEC ID: C00331363
Contact: Thomas Campbell
860 Ridge Lake Rd.
Memphis, TN 38120

Corporate Foundations and Giving Programs

The ServiceMaster Company Contributions Program

860 Ridge Lake Rd.	Tel:	(901) 597-1400
Memphis, TN 38120	Fax:	(630) 663-2001

Public Affairs and Related Activities Personnel

At Headquarters

BISHOP, Alison	Tel:	(866) 397-7921
Senior Public Relations and Corporate Communications	Fax:	(630) 663-2001
Consultant		
Alison.Boyle@servicemaster.com		
CAMPBELL, Thomas	Tel:	(901) 597-1400
PAC Treasurer	Fax:	(630) 663-2001
HAUGHIE, Alan	Tel:	(901) 597-1400
Senior Vice President, Finance and Chief Financial Officer	Fax:	(630) 663-2001
HUNSBERGER, Susan	Tel:	(901) 597-1400
Senior Vice President, Human Resources	Fax:	(630) 663-2001
LUCKE, James T.	Tel:	(901) 597-1400
Senior Vice President and General Counsel	Fax:	(630) 663-2001
TOSCHES, Peter	Tel:	(901) 597-8449
Senior Vice President, Corporate Communications	Fax:	(630) 663-2001
peter.tosches@servicemaster.com		
TURCOTTE, Brian	Tel:	(901) 597-3282
Vice President, Investor Relations	Fax:	(630) 663-2001
Brian.Turcotte@servicemaster.com		

SES World Skies

SES AMERICOM and SES NEW SKIES have joined together to form SES WORLD SKIES. Broadcasters, Internet Service Providers, network integrators, telecommunications carriers, corporations and provide high quality video, Internet, data and voice communications services.
www.ses.com/4232583/en
Employees: 300
Industry/ies: Communications; Telecommunications/Internet/Cable
Legislative Issues: TEC

President and CEO	Tel:	(609) 987-4000
SABBAGH, Karim Michel	Fax:	(609) 987-4517

Main Headquarters

Mailing: Four Research Way	Tel:	(609) 987-4000
Princeton, NJ 08540	Fax:	(609) 987-4517

Washington Office

Mailing: 1129 20th St.	Tel:	(202) 478-7100
Suite 1000		
Washington, DC 20036		

Public Affairs and Related Activities Personnel

At Headquarters

FELTES, Yves	Tel:	(609) 987-4000
Vice President, Corporate Communications	Fax:	(609) 987-4517
MCCARTHY, Padraig	Tel:	(609) 987-4000
Chief Financial Officer	Fax:	(609) 987-4517
NASR, Hanaa	Tel:	(609) 987-4000
Tax Director	Fax:	(609) 987-4517

SESAC

SESAC's purpose is to develop individual relationships with both songwriters and publishers. SESAC are businesses designed to represent songwriters and publishers and their right to be compensated for having their music performed in public.
www.sesac.com
Annual Revenues: $15.70 million
Employees: 100
Industry/ies: Arts, The; Bands See Also Music; Music See Also Bands; Performing Arts/Music
Legislative Issues: ART; CPT

Chairman of the Board and Chief Executive Officer	Tel:	(615) 320-0055
SWID, Stephen C.	Fax:	(615) 963-3527

Main Headquarters

Mailing: 55 Music Sq., East	Tel:	(615) 320-0055
Nashville, TN 37203	Fax:	(615) 963-3527

Public Affairs and Related Activities Personnel

At Headquarters

COLLINS, Pat	Tel:	(615) 320-0055

President and Chief Operating Operator	Fax:	(615) 963-3527
FARMER, Jonathan	Tel:	(615) 320-0055
Senior Counsel, Licensing Operations	Fax:	(615) 963-3527
jfarmer@sesac.com		
GALE, Trevor	Tel:	(212) 586-3450
Vice President, Writer and Publisher Relations	Fax:	(615) 963-3527
GRIZZELL, Cathy	Tel:	(615) 320-0055
Vice President, Human Resources	Fax:	(615) 329-9267
LORD, Dennis	Tel:	(615) 320-0055
Executive Vice President	Fax:	(615) 963-3527
WILLIAMS, Shawn	Tel:	(615) 320-0055
Manager	Fax:	(615) 329-9267

Sesaco Corporation

Sesaco Corporation provides information to U.S. farmers of the option to grow sesame as an alternative, rotation, catch, failed or hailed out crop alternate.
www.sesaco.com
Industry/ies: Agriculture/Agronomy; Science; Scientific Research

Chairman	Tel:	(815) 416-8490
SMITH, Glenn C.		
gcs31@mac.com		

Main Headquarters

Mailing: 6201 E. Oltorf St.	Tel:	(512) 389-0759
Suite 100	Fax:	(512) 389-0790
Austin, TX 78741		

Public Affairs and Related Activities Personnel

At Other Offices

HERON, Jr., Julian B.	Tel:	(815) 416-8490
Federal Lobbyist		
700 W. Center St.		
Paris, TX 75460		
julianheron@msn.com		
SCHWARZ, Frederick	Tel:	(815) 416-8490
Federal Lobbyist		
700 W. Center St.		
Paris, TX 75460		

Severstal North America

Formerly Wheeling-Pittsburgh Steel Corporation. Acquired by Sverstal North America. A manufacturer of steel and steel products.
www.severstalna.com
Annual Revenues: $13.57 billion
Employees: 84,000
SIC: 3312
Industry/ies: Metals

Chairman of the Board	Tel:	(304) 234-2400
CLARK, Christopher	Fax:	(304) 234-2213

Main Headquarters

Mailing: 1134 Market St.	Tel:	(304) 234-2400
Wheeling, WV 26003	Fax:	(304) 234-2213
	TF:	(800) 441-8190

Corporate Foundations and Giving Programs

Severstal North America Contributions Program
14661 Rotunda Dr.
Dearborn, MI 48120

Public Affairs and Related Activities Personnel

At Headquarters

BAGGETT, Melvin E.	Tel:	(304) 234-2400
Vice President, Human Resources	Fax:	(304) 234-2213
KOVALEVA, Elena	Tel:	(495) 926-7766
Head, External Communications	Fax:	(304) 234-2213
ev.kovaleva@severstal.com		
LANDON, Drew	Tel:	(304) 234-2400
PAC Treasurer	Fax:	(304) 234-2213
Mail Stop 12TH FLOOR		
SCHRADER, Douglas C.	Tel:	(304) 234-2400
Vice President, Government Relations	Fax:	(304) 234-2213
SZYMANSKI, Martin	Tel:	(304) 234-2400
Vice President, General Counsel	Fax:	(304) 234-2213
YOST, Mark J.	Tel:	(304) 234-2400
Chief Financial Officer	Fax:	(304) 234-2213
ZALUZHSKY, Vladimir	Tel:	(495) 926-7766
Head, Investor Relations	Fax:	(304) 234-2213
vladimir.zaluzhsky@severstal.com		

At Other Offices

DEY, Saikat
Chief Strategy and Procurement Officer
14661 Rotunda Dr., P.O. Box 1699
Dearborn, MI 48120-1699

FILATOVA, Olga G.
Vice President, Human Resources
14661 Rotunda Dr., P.O. Box 1699
Dearborn, MI 48120-1699

SGI Federal

SGI Federal, a wholly owned SGI subsidiary, provides world-class visualization, storage and computing solutions including visual workstations, scalable servers, high-end supercomputers, and complete storage infrastructure. SGI Federal focuses on providing leading-edge information technology solutions to U.S. federal government customers.
www.sgi.com
Annual Revenues: $510.44 million
Employees: 1,104
Ticker: NASDAQ: SGI
SIC: 3571
NAICS: 334111
Industry/ies: Computer/Technology

| **Chairman of the Board** | Tel: | (650) 960-1980 |
| VERDOORN, Ron D. | Fax: | (408) 321-0293 |

| **President and Chief Executive Officer** | Tel: | (510) 933-8300 |
| TITINGER, Jorge L. | Fax: | (408) 321-0293 |

Main Headquarters
| Mailing: | 900 N. McCarthy Blvd. | Tel: | (669) 900-8000 |
| | Milpitas, CA 95035 | TF: | (800) 800-7441 |

Washington Office
Mailing:	12200-G Plum Orchard Dr.	Tel:	(301) 572-1980
	SGI Federal Headquarters		
	Silver Spring, MD 20904		

Public Affairs and Related Activities Personnel

At Headquarters
CONCEICAO, Cassio	Tel:	(669) 900-8000
Executive Vice President and Chief Operating Officer		
KING, Liz	Tel:	(669) 900-8000
Senior Vice President, Worldwide Sales		

At Other Offices
BRAHAM, Bob	Tel:	(510) 933-8300
Senior Vice President and Chief Marketing Officer	Fax:	(408) 321-0293
46600 Landing Pkwy., SGI Corporate Headquarters		
Fremont, CA 94538		
FINTLAND, Meghan	Tel:	(415) 677-2704
Media Contact	Fax:	(408) 321-0293
46600 Landing Pkwy., SGI Corporate Headquarters		
Fremont, CA 94538		
sgi-opr@ogilvypr.com		
LIAO, Ben	Tel:	(510) 933-8430
Contact, Investor Relations	Fax:	(408) 321-0293
46600 Landing Pkwy., SGI Corporate Headquarters		
Fremont, CA 94538		
bliao@sgi.com		
NIKL, Robert J.	Tel:	(510) 933-8300
Executive Vice President and Chief Financial Officer	Fax:	(408) 321-0293
46600 Landing Pkwy., SGI Corporate Headquarters		
Fremont, CA 94538		
PILEGGI, Jennifer	Tel:	(510) 933-8300
Senior Vice President, General Counsel and Corporate Secretary	Fax:	(408) 321-0293
46600 Landing Pkwy., SGI Corporate Headquarters		
Fremont, CA 94538		
PRATT, Jennifer	Tel:	(650) 960-1980
Senior Vice President, Human Resources	Fax:	(408) 321-0293
46600 Landing Pkwy., SGI Corporate Headquarters		
Fremont, CA 94538		

SGT Inc.

A government contractor aerospace engineering technical service provider company.
www.sgt-inc.com
Annual Revenues: $93.6 million
Employees: 1,500
Industry/ies: Aerospace/Aviation; Engineering/Mathematics; Transportation
Legislative Issues: AER; BUD; ENV; HOM; MMM; SMB; TRA

| **Chairman of the Board** | Tel: | (301) 614-8600 |
| STINGER, Harold | Fax: | (301) 614-8601 |

| **President and Chief Executive Officer** | Tel: | (301) 614-8600 |
| GHAFFARIAN, Dr. Kam S. | Fax: | (301) 614-8601 |

Main Headquarters
Mailing:	7701 Greenbelt Rd.	Tel:	(301) 614-8600
	Suite 400	Fax:	(301) 614-8601
	Greenbelt, MD 20770		

Corporate Foundations and Giving Programs
SGT Inc. Contributions Program

7701 Greenbelt Rd.	Tel:	(301) 614-8600
Suite 400	Fax:	(301) 614-8601
Greenbelt, MD 20770		

Public Affairs and Related Activities Personnel

At Headquarters
GOOREVICH, Charlie	Tel:	(301) 614-8600
President, Business Development	Fax:	(301) 614-8601
JOHNSON, Shelley	Tel:	(301) 489-1108
Chief Human Resources Officer, Corporate Communications	Fax:	(301) 614-8601
sjohnson@sgt-inc.com		
MORWAY, Joe	Tel:	(301) 614-8600
Chief Financial Officer	Fax:	(301) 614-8601
WALL, Mary	Tel:	(301) 614-8600
Benefits Manager	Fax:	(301) 614-8601
mwall@sgt-inc.com		

Shaklee Corporation

A manufacturer of nutritional, personal care and household products.
www.shaklee.com
Annual Revenues: $30.30 million
Employees: 500
SIC: 2833; 2844; 5122; 5169
Industry/ies: Furniture/Home Furnishings; Nutrition; Personal Care/Hygiene

| **Chairman of the Board and Chief Executive Officer** | Tel: | (925) 924-2000 |
| BARNETT, Roger | Fax: | (925) 924-2862 |

Main Headquarters
Mailing:	4747 Willow Rd.	Tel:	(925) 924-2000
	Pleasanton, CA 94588	Fax:	(925) 924-2862
		TF:	(800) 742-5533

Corporate Foundations and Giving Programs
Shaklee Cares		
4747 Willow Rd.	Tel:	(925) 924-2003
Pleasanton, CA 94588	Fax:	(925) 925-2303

Public Affairs and Related Activities Personnel

At Headquarters
BATESOLE, Mike	Tel:	(925) 924-2000
Chief Financial Officer	Fax:	(925) 924-2862
MANUS, Jamie Mc	Tel:	(925) 924-2000
Chairman, Medical Affairs, Health Sciences and Education	Fax:	(925) 924-2862
NEAL, Amy	Tel:	(925) 924-2000
Contact, Media Relations	Fax:	(925) 924-2862
Shaklee@launchsquad.com		
STEEVES-KISS, Jennifer	Tel:	(925) 924-2000
Global Chief Marketing Officer	Fax:	(925) 924-2862
TUCKER, Todd	Tel:	(925) 924-2000
Senior Vice President, General Counsel and Secretary	Fax:	(925) 924-2862

Sharp Electronics Corporation

A manufacturer of electronics.
www.sharpusa.com
Annual Revenues: $22.54 billion
Industry/ies: Electricity & Electronics; Electronics; Energy/Electricity

Main Headquarters
| Mailing: | One Sharp Plaza, Suite 1 | Tel: | (201) 529-8200 |
| | Mahwah, NJ 07495 | Fax: | (201) 529-8425 |

Washington Office
Mailing:	1300 Wilson Blvd.		
	8th Floor		
	Arlington, VA 22209		

Public Affairs and Related Activities Personnel

At Washington Office
| DAWSON, III, Thomas J. | Tel: | (571) 480-5630 |
| *Federal Account Manager* | | |

Shaw Industries, Inc.

A carpet and floor covering manufacturer. Subsidiary of Berkshire Hathaway.
shawfloors.com
Annual Revenues: $4 billion
Employees: 25,000
SIC: 2273
Industry/ies: Construction/Construction Materials; Furniture/Home Furnishings
Legislative Issues: MAN

| **Chief Executive Officer** | Tel: | (706) 275-4710 |
| BELL, Vance D. | | |

Main Headquarters
Mailing:	616 E. Walnut Ave.	Tel:	(706) 275-4710
	P.O. Drawer 2128	TF:	(800) 441-7429
	Dalton, GA 30772-2128		

Public Affairs and Related Activities Personnel

At Headquarters

ALLEN, Mollie J.
Specialist, Public and Media Relations, Marketing Communications
Tel: (706) 275-4710

MERRITT, Randy
President
Tel: (706) 275-4710

Shaw's Supermarkets, Inc.

Operates a chain of supermarkets. A subsidiary of J. Sainsbury PLC of London, England. Shaw's is now part of The New SUPERVALU.
www.shaws.com
Annual Revenues: $663.30 million
Employees: 30,000
Industry/ies: Food And Beverage Industry

President
RICE, Jim
Tel: (508) 313-4000
Fax: (508) 313-3112

Main Headquarters
Mailing: 750 W. Center St.
W. Bridgewater, MA 02379
Tel: (508) 313-4000

Corporate Foundations and Giving Programs

Shaws Supermarkets Contribution Programs
P. O. Box 600
E. Bridgewater, MA 02333
Tel: (508) 313-4000
Fax: (508) 313-4000

Public Affairs and Related Activities Personnel

At Headquarters

GARNETT, Cindy
Vice President, Human Resources and Labor Relations
Tel: (508) 313-4000

GOSSETT, Paul
Vice President, Marketing and Merchandising
Tel: (508) 313-4000

At Other Offices

RINALDI, Ken
Vice President, Retail Operations
P.O. Box 600
E. Bridgewater, MA 02333
Tel: (508) 313-4000
Fax: (508) 313-3112

Sheetz, Inc.

Operator of convenience store chain.
www.sheetz.com
Employees: 9,000
Industry/ies: Food And Beverage Industry; Retail/Wholesale

Chairman of the Board and PAC Treasurer
SHEETZ, Stanton R.
Tel: (814) 946-3611
Fax: (814) 946-4375

President and Chief Executive Officer
SHEETZ, Joe S.
Tel: (814) 946-3611
Fax: (814) 946-4375

Main Headquarters
Mailing: 5700 Sixth Ave.
Altoona, PA 16602
Tel: (814) 946-3611
Fax: (814) 946-4375
TF: (800) 487-5444

Political Action Committees
Sheetz, Inc. PAC
FEC ID: C00219121
Contact: Stanton R. Sheetz
5700 Sixth Ave.
Altoona, PA 16602
Tel: (814) 946-3611
Fax: (814) 946-3611

Contributions to Candidates: $5,200 (2015-2016)
Republicans: $5,200

Corporate Foundations and Giving Programs

Sheetz Family Charities
Contact: Joe S. Sheetz
5700 Sixth Ave.
Altoona, PA 16602
Tel: (814) 946-3611
Fax: (814) 946-3611

Public Affairs and Related Activities Personnel

At Headquarters

SHEETZ, Louie
Executive Marketing Advisor
Tel: (814) 946-3611
Fax: (814) 946-4375

WOODLEY, Dave
Executive Vice President, Sales and Marketing
Tel: (814) 946-3611
Fax: (814) 946-4375

Shell Chemical Company

See listing on page 717 under Shell Oil Company

Shell Oil Company

A producer, refiner and marketer of petroleum products and chemicals. Affiliated with the Royal Dutch/Shell Group of companies.
www.shell.us
Annual Revenues: $77.66 billion
Employees: 24,008
SIC: 1311; 2899

NAICS: 325998; 211111
Industry/ies: Fuels See Coal, Gas, Oil, Petroleum; Natural Resources; Petroleum Industry
Legislative Issues: BUD; CHM; ENG; ENV; FIN; FOR; FUE; GOV; HOM; MAR; NAT; RRR; SCI; TAX; TRA; TRD; TRU

Chairman
OLLILA, Jorma
Tel: (713) 241-6161
Fax: (713) 241-4044

Chief Executive Officer
BEURDEN, Ben van
Tel: (713) 241-6161
Fax: (713) 241-4044

Main Headquarters
Mailing: P.O. Box 2463
Houston, TX 77252
Tel: (713) 241-6161
Fax: (713) 241-4044
TF: (888) 467-4355

Washington Office
Mailing: 1050 K St. NW
Suite 700
Washington, DC 20002
Tel: (202) 466-1405
Fax: (202) 466-1498

Political Action Committees
Shell Oil Company Employees' Political Awareness Committee PAC
FEC ID: C00039503
Contact: Camden Toohey
1050 K St. NW
Suite 700
Washington, DC 20001

Contributions to Candidates: $51,000 (2015-2016)
Democrats: $5,500; Republicans: $45,500

Corporate Foundations and Giving Programs

Shell Oil Company Foundation
P.O. Box 2463
Houston, TX 77252

Public Affairs and Related Activities Personnel

At Headquarters

CHING, Donny
Director, Legal
Tel: (713) 241-6161
Fax: (713) 241-4044

HENRY, Simon
Chief Financial Officer
Tel: (713) 241-6161
Fax: (713) 241-4044

KIRKLEY, Allen
Vice President, Chemicals Strategy
Tel: (713) 241-6161
Fax: (713) 241-4044

LOWREY, Bill
Senior Vice President, General Counsel and Corporate Secretary
Registered Federal Lobbyist
Tel: (713) 241-6161
Fax: (713) 241-4044

MITCHELL, Hugh
Chief Human Resources and Corporate Officer
Tel: (713) 241-6161
Fax: (713) 241-4044

ODUM, Marvin
Director, Upstream Americas
Tel: (713) 241-6161
Fax: (713) 241-4044

At Washington Office

ADLER, Adina
International Government Relations Advisor
Tel: (202) 466-1405
Fax: (202) 466-1498

BUCHERT, Janet
Senior Tax Counsel, Global Planning and Strategy
Registered Federal Lobbyist
Tel: (202) 466-1405
Fax: (202) 466-1498

FUNK, Marnie
Senior Advisor
marnie.funk@shell.com
Registered Federal Lobbyist
Tel: (202) 466-1422
Fax: (202) 466-1498

GLENN, Sara
Director, Federal Government Relations
sara.glenn@shell.com
Registered Federal Lobbyist
Tel: (202) 466-1400
Fax: (202) 466-1498

GRAYDON, Daniel
PAC Treasurer
Tel: (202) 466-1405
Fax: (202) 466-1498

LYNCH, Kristine
Federal Lobbyist
Registered Federal Lobbyist
Tel: (202) 466-1405
Fax: (202) 466-1498

MALNAK, Brian P.
Vice President, Government Relations
brian.malnak@shell.com
Registered Federal Lobbyist
Tel: (202) 466-1410
Fax: (202) 466-1498

MCMINN, Tracey
Director, International Government Relations
Registered Federal Lobbyist
Tel: (202) 466-1405
Fax: (202) 466-1498

SALMON, Scott
Registered Federal Lobbyist
Tel: (202) 466-1405
Fax: (202) 466-1498

SATTERLEE, Kent
Manager Regulatory Policy - Offshore
kent.satterlee@shell.us
Tel: (202) 466-1405
Fax: (202) 466-1498

SMITH, Philip
Tel: (202) 466-1405
Fax: (202) 466-1498

General Manager, Emergency Management and Deepwater
Regulatory Affairs

TALLMAN, Vincent *Treasurer*	Tel: Fax:	(202) 466-1405 (202) 466-1498
TAMEZ, Patricia *Registered Federal Lobbyist*	Tel: Fax:	(202) 466-1405 (202) 466-1498
THOMPSON, Jennifer *Senior Advisor, Government Relations* *Registered Federal Lobbyist*	Tel: Fax:	(202) 466-1405 (202) 466-1498
WHITMAN, Kristin *Manager, Regulatory Affairs and Third Party Advocacy* kristin.whitman@shell.com *Registered Federal Lobbyist*	Tel: Fax:	(202) 466-1485 (202) 466-1498
WHITTENBURG, Emily *Registered Federal Lobbyist*	Tel: Fax:	(202) 466-1405 (202) 466-1498

At Other Offices

CHILDS, Susan *Federal Lobbyist* Two Houston Center, Plaza Level I, 909 Fannin St. Houston, TX 77010 susan.childs@shell.us	Tel:	(713) 767-5400
TOOHEY, Camden *Federal Lobbyist and PAC Treasurer* 3601 C St., Suite 1314 Anchorage, AK 99503	Tel:	(907) 771-7910

Shenandoah Life Insurance Company

A mutual insurance company.
www.shenlife.com
Annual Revenues: $29.40 million
Employees: 300
Industry/ies: Insurance Industry

Chairman of the Board	Tel:	(540) 985-4400
DALHOUSE, Warner	Fax:	(540) 985-4444

Main Headquarters

Mailing:	2301 Brambleton Ave. SW	Tel:	(540) 985-4400
	Roanoke, VA 24015	Fax:	(540) 985-4444
		TF:	(800) 848-5433

Public Affairs and Related Activities Personnel

At Headquarters

COFFMAN, Michael	Tel:	(540) 985-4400
Senior Vice President and Chief Financial Officer	Fax:	(540) 985-4444

Sherwin Williams Company

Sherwin-Williams is a paint manufacturer in the U.S. It develops, manufactures, distributes, and sells paints, coatings, and related products to professional, industrial, commercial, and retail customers.
www.sherwin-williams.com
Annual Revenues: $11.46 billion
Employees: 40,706
Ticker: NYSE: SHW
SIC: 5200
Industry/ies: Chemicals & Chemical Industry

Chairman of the Board	Tel:	(216) 566-2000
CONNOR, Christopher M.	Fax:	(216) 566-3310
President and Chief Executive Officer	Tel:	(216) 566-2000
MORIKIS, John G.	Fax:	(216) 566-3310

Main Headquarters

Mailing:	101 W. Prospect Ave.	Tel:	(216) 566-2000
	Cleveland, OH 44115-1075	Fax:	(216) 566-3310
		TF:	(800) 474-3794

Washington Office

Mailing:	1120 Third St. NE	Tel:	(202) 543-8177
	Washington, DC 20002		

Corporate Foundations and Giving Programs

Sherwin Williams Foundation
Contact: Barbara Gadosik

101 Prospect Ave. NW	Tel:	(216) 566-2000
Cleveland, OH 44115	Fax:	(216) 566-2000

Public Affairs and Related Activities Personnel

At Headquarters

CONWAY, Mike	Tel:	(216) 515-4393
Director, Corporate Communications and Investor Relations mike.conway@sherwin.com	Fax:	(216) 566-2947
GADOSIK, Barbara	Tel:	(216) 566-2000
Director, Corporate Contributions	Fax:	(216) 566-3310
GILLIGAN, Thomas P.	Tel:	(216) 566-2000
Senior Vice President, Human Resources	Fax:	(216) 566-3310
HENNESSY, Sean P.	Tel:	(216) 566-2000

Senior Vice President, Finance and Chief Financial Officer	Fax:	(216) 566-3310
HOPKINS, Thomas E.	Tel:	(216) 566-2000
Senior Vice President, Human Resources	Fax:	(216) 566-3310
KEOUGH, Susan	Tel:	(216) 566-2000
Vice President, Human Resources sdkeough@sherwin.com	Fax:	(216) 566-2947
KILBANE, Catherine M.	Tel:	(216) 566-2000
Senior Vice President, General Counsel and Secretary	Fax:	(216) 566-3310
KNIGHT, Timothy A.	Tel:	(216) 566-2000
Senior Vice President, Corporate Planning, Development and Administration	Fax:	(216) 566-3310
WELLS, Robert J.	Tel:	(216) 566-2244
Senior Vice President, Corporate Communications and Public Affairs rjwells@sherwin.com	Fax:	(216) 566-3310

Shintech, Inc.

Shintech, based in Houston City, is the U.S. subsidiary of Shin-Etsu Chemical Co., based in Tokyo, Japan. Producer of PVC (polyvinyl chloride).
www.shintechinc.com
Annual Revenues: $55.30 million
Employees: 500
SIC: 2821; 3087
NAICS: 325211; 325991
Industry/ies: Chemicals & Chemical Industry

Director & Chairman	Tel:	(713) 965-0713
KANAGAWA, Chihiro	Fax:	(713) 965-0629

Main Headquarters

Mailing:	Three Greenway Plaza	Tel:	(713) 965-0713
	Suite 1150	Fax:	(713) 965-0629
	Houston, TX 77046		

Shionogi USA, Inc.

The US subsidiary of Shionogi, Inc. of Osaka, Japan.
www.shionogi-inc.com
Annual Revenues: $29.50 million
SIC: 2834
Industry/ies: Pharmaceutical Industry

President and Chief Executive Officer	Tel:	(973) 966-6900
KELLER, PhD, John		

Main Headquarters

Mailing:	300 Campus Dr.	Tel:	(973) 966-6900
	Florham Park, NJ 07932	TF:	(800) 849-9707

Corporate Foundations and Giving Programs

Shionogi Contributions Program
300 Campus Dr.
Florham Park, NJ 07932

Public Affairs and Related Activities Personnel

At Headquarters

DICKINSON, Gary	Tel:	(973) 966-6900
Senior Vice President, Human Resources		
HARA, Tadashi	Tel:	(973) 966-6900
Executive Vice President and Chief Financial Officer		
LIPPMAN, Renee	Tel:	(973) 307-3877
Vice President, Commercial Strategy rlippman@shionogi.com		
SPAGNARDI, Joseph M	Tel:	(973) 966-6900
Executive Vice President, Legal and Compliance		

Shire Pharmaceuticals Inc.

A pharmaceutical company focusing on central nervous system (CNS), gastrointestinal (GI), and renal diseases.
www.shire.com
Annual Revenues: $3 billion
Employees: 3,900
SIC: 2834
Industry/ies: Medicine/Health Care/Mental Health; Pharmaceutical Industry
Legislative Issues: HCR; MMM; PHA; TAX

Chairman of the Board	Tel:	(484) 595-8800
EMMENS, Matthew	Fax:	(484) 595-8200
Chairman		
KILSBY, Susan		
Chief Executive Officer	Tel:	(203) 682-7222
ORNSKOV, MD, Flemming	Fax:	(203) 557-0739

Main Headquarters

Mailing:	725 Chesterbrook Blvd.	Tel:	(484) 595-8800
	Wayne, PA 19087	Fax:	(484) 595-8200

Washington Office

Mailing:	1050 Connecticut Ave. NW

Tenth Fl.
Washington, DC 20036

Political Action Committees

Shire Pharmaceuticals, Inc. PAC
FEC ID: C00421065
Contact: Matthew Handel
725 Chesterbrook Blvd.
Wayne, PA 19087

Corporate Foundations and Giving Programs

Shire Pharmaceuticals Contributions Program
Contact: Tatjana May
725 Chesterbrook Blvd.
Wayne, PA 19087

Public Affairs and Related Activities Personnel

At Headquarters

COTRONE, Jessica — Tel: (781) 482-9538 — Fax: (617) 613-4005
Senior Director, Corporate Communications
jcontrone@shire.com

GREENWOOD, Ricki — Tel: (484) 595-8800 — Fax: (484) 585-8686
Corporate Communications and Government Relations Specialist
rgreenwood@shire.com

HANDEL, Matthew — Tel: (484) 595-8800 — Fax: (484) 595-8200
PAC Contact and Senior Director, Commercial Assessment

HETHERINGTON, Graham — Tel: (484) 595-8800 — Fax: (484) 595-8200
Chief Financial Officer

MANN, Jessica — Tel: (484) 595-8800 — Fax: (484) 595-8200
Senior Vice President, Global Corporate Communications
jmann@shire.com

MAY, Tatjana — Tel: (484) 595-8800 — Fax: (484) 595-8200
General Counsel / Chair, Responsibility Steering & Communications Group

MILLER, John F. — Tel: (484) 595-8800 — Fax: (484) 595-8200
Vice President, Behavioral Health Finance

At Washington Office

BUCKLEY, Ted — Tel: (202) 772-1899
Senior Director, US Government Relations and Public Policy
Tbuckley@shire.com
Registered Federal Lobbyist

LENKER, Mark W. — Tel: (202) 772-3325
Director, US Government Relations & Public Policy
mlenker@shire.com
Registered Federal Lobbyist

At Other Offices

BUCKLEY, Edward
Global Government Relations and Public Affairs
11095 Torreyana Rd.
San Diego, CA 92121
Registered Federal Lobbyist

BURKE, Carrie
Federal Lobbyists
1001 Connecticut Ave. NW, Suite 925
Washington, DC 20036

ENYEDY, Mark
Head, Corporate Development
11095 Torreyana Rd.
San Diego, CA 92121

GREGORY, Ginger
Chief Human Resources Officer
11095 Torreyana Rd.
San Diego, CA 92121

GREISSING, John
Federal Lobbyists
1001 Connecticut Ave. NW, Suite 925
Washington, DC 20036
Registered Federal Lobbyist

POULTON, Jeffrey — Tel: (617) 349-0200
Chief Financial Officer
300 Shire Way
Lexington, MA 02421

VICKERS, Phil
Head, Research and Development
11095 Torreyana Rd.
San Diego, CA 92121

Shopko Stores, Inc.

A chain of discount stores.
www.shopko.com
Employees: 23,000
Ticker: NYSE: SKO
SIC: 5331
Industry/ies: Retail/Wholesale

Main Headquarters

Mailing: 700 Pilgrim Way — Tel: (920) 429-2211
P. O. Box 19060 — Fax: (920) 429-4799
Green Bay, WI 54307-9060 — TF: (800) 791-7333

Corporate Foundations and Giving Programs

Shopko Foundation
Contact: Pam Schwanke
700 Pilgrim Way — Tel: (920) 429-2211
P.O. Box 19060 — Fax: (920) 429-2211
Green Bay, WI 54307

Public Affairs and Related Activities Personnel

At Headquarters

SCHWANKE, Pam — Tel: (920) 429-2211 — Fax: (920) 429-4799
Contact, Shopko Foundation

Short, Elliot, and Hendrickson

Provides professional consulting services to local governments, regional and state agencies, federal agencies, and industrial and private-sector clients.
www.sehinc.com
Employees: 700
Industry/ies: Agriculture/Agronomy; Architecture And Design; Engineering/ Mathematics; Law/Law Firms

Chief Executive Officer - President — Tel: (651) 490-2000
CLAASSEN, Sam — Fax: (651) 490-2150
sclaassen@sehinc.com

Main Headquarters

Mailing: 3535 Vadnais Center Dr. — Tel: (651) 490-2000
St. Paul, MN 55110-5196 — Fax: (651) 490-2150
TF: (800) 325-2055

Political Action Committees

Short Elliott Hendrickson Inc. Employees Federal PAC
FEC ID: C00384206
Contact: James A. Fraser
3535 Vadnais Center Dr.
Vadnais Heights, MN 55110

Public Affairs and Related Activities Personnel

At Headquarters

ARRIOLA, Ben — Tel: (651) 490-2000 — Fax: (651) 490-2150
Chief Marketing Officer
barriola@sehinc.com

CARLSON, Pete — Tel: (651) 490-2000 — Fax: (651) 490-2150
Chief Operating Officer
pcarlson@sehinc.com

FRASER, James A. — Tel: (800) 325-2055 — Fax: (651) 490-2150
Chief Financial Officer and PAC Treasurer
jfraser@sehinc.com

LAMPPA, Gary — Tel: (651) 490-2000 — Fax: (651) 490-2150
Director Sales, Government Relations
glamppa@sehinc.com

WILLIAMS, Dawn — Tel: (612) 758-6789 — Fax: (651) 490-2150
Director, Corporate Communications
dwilliams@sehinc.com

ZAMORANO, Jackie — Tel: (651) 490-2000 — Fax: (651) 490-2150
Chief People Officer
jzamorano@sehinc.com

Shotspotter, Inc.

Engaged in the development, sales and installation of gunshot location systems.
www.shotspotter.com
Annual Revenues: $8.30 million
Employees: 50
Industry/ies: Firearms/Gun Control
Legislative Issues: EDU; FIR; HOM

President and Chief Executive Officer — Tel: (510) 794-3144
CLARK, Ralph A. — Fax: (650) 887-2106

Main Headquarters

Mailing: 7979 Gateway Blvd. — Tel: (510) 794-3144
Suite 210 — TF: (888) 274-6877
Newark, CA 94560

Public Affairs and Related Activities Personnel

At Headquarters

ARIALE, John M. — Tel: (510) 794-3144
Lobbyist

BARRETT, Lydia J. — Tel: (510) 794-3144
Vice President, Marketing and Communications

BELDOCK, James G. — Tel: (510) 794-3144
Senior Vice President, Product and Business Development

EINBINDER, Liz	Tel:	(415) 577-8255

Contact, Media
leinbinder@shotspotter.com

HAWKINS, Joe	Tel:	(510) 794-3144

Senior Vice President, Operations

LOPEZ, Erin	Tel:	(510) 794-3144

Manager, Marketing and Corporate Communications
elopez@shotspotter.com

ROWLAND, Gregg	Tel:	(510) 794-3144

Senior Vice President, Sales and Marketing
gregg@shotspotter.com

STRICKLER, Sonya	Tel:	(510) 794-3144

Vice President, Finance and Controller

At Other Offices

HOLLADAY, Gary	Tel:	(650) 960-9200
	Fax:	(408) 608-0340

Vice President, Government Programs
1060 Terra Bella Ave.
Mountain View, CA 94043-1881

SHPS, Inc.

ADP has acquired SHPS, Inc. SHPS is a provider of integrated health solutions that improve personal health.
www.shps.com
Annual Revenues: $211.00 million
Employees: 2,000
Industry/ies: Medicine/Health Care/Mental Health

President and Chief Executive Officer	Tel:	(502) 426-4888
MEHROTRA, Rishabh	Fax:	(502) 420-5590

Main Headquarters

Mailing:	9200 Shelbyville Rd.	Tel:	(502) 426-4888
	Suite 100	Fax:	(502) 420-5590
	Louisville, KY 40222	TF:	(888) 421-7477

Public Affairs and Related Activities Personnel

At Headquarters

HAICK, David	Tel:	(502) 426-4888
Chief Legal Officer	Fax:	(502) 420-5590
JAY, Chris	Tel:	(502) 426-4888
PAC Treasurer	Fax:	(502) 420-5590
MCCARTY, John	Tel:	(502) 426-4888
Executive Vice President and Chief Financial Officer	Fax:	(502) 339-0452
ROSS, LeAnn	Tel:	(502) 426-4888
Director, Corporate Marketing	Fax:	(502) 420-5590
leann.ross@shps.com		
RYAN, Chris	Tel:	(502) 426-4888
Executive Vice President, Chief Strategy and Marketing Officer	Fax:	(502) 420-5590
WEAR, Brad	Tel:	(502) 426-4888
Executive Vice President, Chief Financial Officer	Fax:	(502) 420-5590

Shure Inc.

Manufacturer of electronic devices.
www.shure.com
Employees: 1,000
SIC: 3651
NAICS: 33431
Industry/ies: Arts, The; Performing Arts/Music
Legislative Issues: TEC

Chairman of the Board	Tel:	(847) 600-2000
SHURE, Rose L.	Fax:	(847) 600-1212

President and Chief Executive Officer	Tel:	(847) 600-2000
LAMANTIA, Santo A.	Fax:	(847) 600-1212

Main Headquarters

Mailing:	5800 W. Touhy Ave.	Tel:	(847) 600-2000
	Niles, IL 60714-4608	Fax:	(847) 600-1212
		TF:	(800) 257-4873

Public Affairs and Related Activities Personnel

At Headquarters

LOHMAN, Mike	Tel:	(847) 600-2000
Associate Director, Content and Digital Marketing	Fax:	(847) 600-1212
RAHILLY, Mark	Tel:	(847) 600-2000
Senior Manager, Sales	Fax:	(847) 600-1212

SICPA Product Security LLC

SICPA is a leading worldwide provider of Security Inks and Systems.
www.sicpa.com
Industry/ies: Law Enforcement/Security
Legislative Issues: FOO; GOV

Main Headquarters
Mailing: 277 Park Ave.

47th Floor
New York City, NY 10172

Washington Office
Mailing: 8000 Research Way
Springfield, VA 22153

Public Affairs and Related Activities Personnel

At Headquarters

ENGEL, Peter
Vice President

FINKEL, Charles

OZALTIN, Mariam
Government Affairs Manager
mariam.ozaltin@sicpa.com

Siemens Corporation

Siemens Corporation, based in New York City, is the U.S. subsidiary of Siemens AG, headquartered in Munich, Germany. The holding company for the shares of Siemens companies in the U.S. Provides coordination, corporate services and support to Siemens operating companies.
www.usa.siemens.com
Employees: 362,000
SIC: 3646; 3661; 3674; 3679; 3714
NAICS: 336399; 334419; 335122; 335312; 335999
Industry/ies: Electricity & Electronics; Electronics; Energy/Electricity; Engineering/Mathematics; Medicine/Health Care/Mental Health
Legislative Issues: EDU; ENG; ENV; HCR; MAN; MMM; TAX; TRD

President and Chief Executive Officer	Tel:	(202) 434-4800
SPIEGEL, Eric A.	Fax:	(202) 347-4015

Main Headquarters

Mailing:	300 New Jersey Ave. NW	Tel:	(202) 434-4800
	Suite 1000	Fax:	(202) 347-4015
	Washington, DC 20001		

Political Action Committees
Siemens Corporation Political Action Committee (SCPAC)
FEC ID: C00353797
Contact: Elizabeth A. Reicherts
300 New Jersey Ave. NW
Suite 1000
Washington, DC 20001

  Contributions to Candidates: $208,180 (2015-2016)
  Democrats: $65,180; Republicans: $143,000

Principal Recipients

SENATE
MURKOWSKI, LISA (REP-AK)

Corporate Foundations and Giving Programs
The Siemens Foundation
170 Wood Ave., South
Iselin, NJ 08830

Public Affairs and Related Activities Personnel

At Headquarters

CAMPBELL, Abigail	Tel:	(202) 434-4800
Director	Fax:	(202) 347-4015
abigail.campbell@siemens.com		
Registered Federal Lobbyist		
ESHERICK, Mark	Tel:	(202) 434-4803
Director, Government Affairs & Policy Healthcare	Fax:	(202) 347-4015
mark.esherick@siemens.com		
Registered Federal Lobbyist		
GLAZER, Rose Marie E.	Tel:	(202) 434-4820
Senior Vice President and General Counsel	Fax:	(202) 347-4015
rosemarie.glazer@siemens.com		
JOHNSTON, Camille	Tel:	(202) 434-4800
Senior VP, Corporate Affairs & Communicationas	Fax:	(202) 347-4015
camille.johnston@siemens.com		

At Other Offices

ALVARADO, Christine	Tel:	(212) 258-4478
Executive Assistant, Mergers and Acquisitions	Fax:	(212) 767-0580
527 Madison Ave., Eight Floor		
New York City, NY 10022		
christine.alvarado@siemens.com		
CORDIA, Kim	Tel:	(202) 434-4802
Admin Assistant	Fax:	(202) 347-4015
300 New Jersey Ave. NW, Suite 1000		
Washington, DC 20001		
kimberly.cordia@siemens.com		
KERR, Eleanor	Tel:	(202) 434-4801
Director, Government Affairs Healthcare	Fax:	(202) 347-4015
300 New Jersey Ave. NW, Suite 1000		
Washington, DC 20001		

eleanor.kerr@siemens.com
Registered Federal Lobbyist

KRUKLINSKI, Michael	Tel:	(212) 258-4000
Head of Region Americas	Fax:	(212) 767-0580
527 Madison Ave., Eight Floor		
New York City, NY 10022		
PANIGEL, Mike	Tel:	(212) 258-4000
Senior Vice President and Chief Human Resources Officer	Fax:	(212) 767-0580
527 Madison Ave., Eight Floor		
New York City, NY 10022		
PROELS, Alexander	Tel:	(212) 258-4000
Lead Regional Compliance Officer	Fax:	(212) 767-0580
527 Madison Ave., Eight Floor		
New York City, NY 10022		
REICHERTS, Elizabeth A.	Tel:	(202) 434-4806
300 New Jersey Ave. NW, Suite 1000	Fax:	(202) 347-4015
Washington, DC 20001		
elizabeth.reicherts@siemens.com		
Registered Federal Lobbyist		
STEGEMANN, Klaus P.	Tel:	(212) 258-4000
Chief Financial Officer	Fax:	(212) 767-0580
527 Madison Ave., Eight Floor		
New York City, NY 10022		

Sierra Nevada Corporation

Manufactures high technology electronics, avionics, and communications systems.
www.sncorp.com
Employees: 2,000
SIC: 3663
Industry/ies: Aerospace/Aviation; Transportation
Legislative Issues: DEF; HOM; LAW

Owner and Chief Executive Officer	Tel:	(775) 331-0222
OZMEN, Faith	Fax:	(775) 331-0370
Main Headquarters		
Mailing: 444 Salomon Cir.	Tel:	(775) 331-0222
Sparks, NV 89434	Fax:	(775) 331-0370
Washington Office		
Mailing: 2231 Crystal Dr.	Tel:	(703) 412-1502
11th Floor, Suite 1113		
Arlington, VA 22202		

Political Action Committees

Sierra Nevada Corporation PAC
FEC ID: C00367995
Contact: Eren Akman

444 Salomon Cir.	Tel:	(775) 331-0222
P.O. Box 50193	Fax:	(775) 331-0370
Sparks, NV 89434		

  Contributions to Candidates: $292,500 (2015-2016)
  Democrats: $37,500; Republicans: $255,000

  Principal Recipients

    HOUSE
    COFFMAN, MIKE REP. (REP-CO)
    HECK, JOE (REP-NV)
    LAMBORN, DOUGLAS (REP-CO)
    NUNES, DEVIN G (REP-CA)
    TURNER, MICHAEL R (REP-OH)

Corporate Foundations and Giving Programs

Sierra Nevada Corporation Contributions Program
444 Salomon Cir.
Sparks, NV 89434

Public Affairs and Related Activities Personnel

At Headquarters

MCDONALD, Betsy	Tel:	(775) 849-6435
Contact, Media Relations	Fax:	(775) 331-0370
SNCDreamChaser@sncorp.com		
OZMEN, Eren	Tel:	(775) 331-0222
Owner and President	Fax:	(775) 331-0370

At Other Offices

AKMAN, Eren
PAC Treasurer
P.O. Box 50193
Sparks, NV 89434

Sierra Pacific Resources

See listing on page 593 under NV Energy, Inc.

Sierra Rutile America

Sierra Rutile is a mineral sands company.
www.sierra-rutile.com
Annual Revenues: $179.1 million
Industry/ies: Mining Industry; Natural Resources

Non Executive Chairman of the Board
CASTRO, Jan

Chief Executive Officer
SISAY, John Bonoh

Main Headquarters
Mailing: 2081 W. Lymington Way
  St. Augustine, FL 32084

Public Affairs and Related Activities Personnel

At Headquarters

FOLMER, Derek
Chief Marketing Officer

ILUNGA, Yves
Chief Financial Officer

MCGARVIE, Maxwell
Federal lobbyist

SIG SAUER

A manufacturer of law enforcement and military firearms.
www.sigsauer.com
Annual Revenues: $17.90 million
Employees: 400
Industry/ies: Firearms/Gun Control
Legislative Issues: FIR

President and Chief Executive Officer	Tel:	(305) 823-1212
COHEN, PA, Ronald J.	Fax:	(305) 823-7778
Main Headquarters		
Mailing: 72 Pease Blvd.	Tel:	(603) 772-2302
Newington, NH 03833-4557	Fax:	(603) 772-9082

Public Affairs and Related Activities Personnel

At Headquarters

FINI, Bud	Tel:	(603) 772-2302
Vice President, Marketing	Fax:	(603) 772-9082
SCULLIN, Tim	Tel:	(603) 772-2302
Chief Financial Officer	Fax:	(603) 772-9082
SHAWVER, Steven	Tel:	(603) 772-2302
Vice President, Chief Legal Officer and Secretary	Fax:	(603) 772-9082

SIGA Technologies, Inc.

A drug development company in the biodefense arena.
www.siga.com
Annual Revenues: $8.83 million
Employees: 71
Ticker: NASDAQ (GM): SIGA
SIC: 2834
Industry/ies: Defense/Homeland Security; Government-Related; Pharmaceutical Industry
Legislative Issues: BUD

Chairman of the Board and Chief Executive Officer	Tel:	(212) 672-9100
ROSE, Dr. Eric A.	Fax:	(212) 697-3130
Main Headquarters		
Mailing: 660 Madison Ave.	Tel:	(212) 672-9100
Suite 1700	Fax:	(212) 697-3130
New York City, NY 10065		

Public Affairs and Related Activities Personnel

At Headquarters

FROMER, Todd	Tel:	(212) 672-9100
Contact, Investor Relations, KCSA Strategic Communications	Fax:	(212) 697-3130
Tfromer@kcsa.com		
HAYNES, II, William J.	Tel:	(212) 672-9100
Executive Vice President and General Counsel	Fax:	(212) 697-3130
KOSARAJU, Akhila	Tel:	(212) 672-9100
Vice President, Global Development	Fax:	(212) 697-3130
LUCKSHIRE, Daniel J.	Tel:	(212) 672-9100
Executive Vice President and Chief Financial Officer	Fax:	(212) 697-3130

Sigma-Aldrich Corporation

Manufactures biochemicals and organic chemical products used in scientific and genomic research, biotechnology, pharmaceutical development, disease diagnosis and high technology manufacturing. It is a life science and high technology company, develops, manufactures, purchases, and distributes various chemicals, biochemicals, biochemicals, and equipment products.
www.sigmaaldrich.com
Annual Revenues: $2.77 billion
Employees: 9,400
Ticker: NASDAQ: SIAL
SIC: 2835; 2869
NAICS: 325413; 325199
Industry/ies: Chemicals & Chemical Industry; Pharmaceutical Industry

President and Chief Executive Officer
SACHDEV, Rakesh
Tel: (314) 771-5765
Fax: (314) 771-5757

Main Headquarters
Mailing: 3050 Spruce St.
St. Louis, MO 63103
Tel: (314) 771-5765
Fax: (314) 771-5757
TF: (800) 521-8956

Corporate Foundations and Giving Programs
Sigma-Aldrich Foundation
3050 Spruce St.
St. Louis, MO 63103

Public Affairs and Related Activities Personnel

At Headquarters

BERTSCH, Jan A.
Executive Vice President and Chief Financial Officer
Tel: (314) 771-5765
Fax: (314) 286-7874

LAI , Quintin
Vice President, Investor Relations and Strategy
Tel: (314) 898-4643
Fax: (314) 286-7874

MILLER, Karen J.
Senior Vice President, Corporate Development and Corporate Communications
Tel: (314) 771-5765
Fax: (314) 771-5757

MILLER, George L.
Senior Vice President, General Counsel and Secretary
Tel: (314) 771-5765
Fax: (314) 771-5757

RAU, Douglas W.
Vice President, Human Resources
Tel: (314) 771-5765
Fax: (314) 771-5757

Silicon Graphics International Corporation
See listing on page 716 under SGI Federal

Silicon Valley Technology Center
See listing on page 760 under SVTC Technologies, LLC

Silvaco Inc.
SILVACO International makes technical computer-aided design (TCAD) software that semiconductor manufacturers use to simulate processes in R&D, test, and fabrication of integrated circuits (ICs).
www.silvaco.com
Employees: 200
Industry/ies: Computer/Technology

Executive Chairman of the Board
PESIC, Iliya
Tel: (408) 567-1000
Fax: (408) 496-6080

Chief Executive Officer
DUTTON, David L.
Tel: (408) 567-1000
Fax: (408) 496-6080

Main Headquarters
Mailing: 4701 Patrick Henry Dr.
Bldg. Two
Santa Clara, CA 95054
Tel: (408) 567-1000
Fax: (408) 496-6080

Public Affairs and Related Activities Personnel

At Headquarters

JONES, Stan J.
Director, Human Resources
Tel: (408) 567-1000
Fax: (408) 496-6080

KARELL, Claudia
Manager, Corporate Human Resources
Tel: (408) 567-1000
Fax: (408) 496-6080

MAURER, Mark
Vice President, Business Development
mark.maurer@silvaco.com
Tel: (408) 567-1000
Fax: (408) 496-6080

NANDA, Amit
Vice President, Global Marketing
Tel: (408) 567-1000
Fax: (408) 496-6080

SHER, Tom
Vice President, Finance
Tel: (408) 567-1000
Fax: (408) 496-6080

Silvaco International
See listing on page 722 under Silvaco Inc.

Simmons First National Corporation
Simmons First offers a variety of financial services in Arkansas, Missouri, and Kansas, including: Personal/Commercial Checking and Savings accounts, Personal/Commercial credit cards, as well as various time deposits. Simmons also offers consumer loans, real estate construction loans and single family residential loans; commercial loans; agricultural loans; and loans to financial institutions.
www.simmonsfirst.com
Annual Revenues: $246.46 million
Employees: 1,338
Ticker: NASDAQ: SFNC
SIC: 6021
Industry/ies: Banking/Finance/Investments

Chairman and Chief Executive Officer
MAKRIS, Jr., George A.
Tel: (870) 541-1000
Fax: (870) 541-1154

Main Headquarters
Mailing: 501 Main St.
P.O. Box 7009
Tel: (870) 541-1000
Fax: (870) 541-1154

Pine Bluff, AR 71601
TF: (800) 272-2213

Political Action Committees
Simmons First National Bank PAC (SIMPAC) Federal Fund
FEC ID: C00123885
Contact: Craig Hunt
501 Main St.
P.O. Box 7009
Pine Bluff, AR 71611
Tel: (870) 541-1000
Fax: (870) 541-1000

> **Contributions to Candidates:** $3,500 (2015-2016)
> Republicans: $3,500

Public Affairs and Related Activities Personnel

At Headquarters

BURDINE, Sharon K.
Senior Vice President & Director-Human Resources
Tel: (870) 541-1000
Fax: (870) 541-1154

FEHLMAN, Robert A.
Senior Executive Vice President, Chief Financial Officer and Treasurer
Tel: (870) 541-1000
Fax: (870) 541-1154

GARNER, David W.
Executive Vice President, Controller and Chief Accounting Officer
bankanywhere@simmonsfirst.com
Tel: (870) 541-1243
Fax: (870) 541-1154

HUNT, Craig
President, Corporate Chief Credit Officer and PAC Treasurer
Tel: (870) 541-1000
Fax: (870) 541-1154

LASSEIGNE, Stephen
Vice President and Advertising Manager
stephen.lasseigne@simmonsfirst.com
Tel: (501) 377-7610
Fax: (870) 541-1045

NELSON, Rex
Director, Corporate Communications
rex.nelson@simmonsfirst.com
Tel: (870) 541-1000
Fax: (870) 541-1154

Simon Property Group
Real estate developer.
www.simon.com
Annual Revenues: $5.34 billion
Employees: 3,150
Ticker: NYSE: SPG
SIC: 6798
Industry/ies: Real Estate
Legislative Issues: TAX

Chairman of the Board and Chief Executive Officer
SIMON, David
Tel: (317) 636-1600
Fax: (317) 263-2318

Main Headquarters
Mailing: 225 W. Washington St.
Indianapolis, IN 46204
Tel: (317) 636-1600
Fax: (317) 263-2318

Corporate Foundations and Giving Programs
Simon Youth Foundation
Contact: Dr. Richard Markoff
225 W. Washington St.
Indianapolis, IN 46204

Public Affairs and Related Activities Personnel

At Headquarters

BARKLEY, James M.
Secretary and General Counsel
Tel: (317) 636-1600
Fax: (317) 263-2318

FIVEL, Steven E.
Assistant General Counsel and Assistant Secretary
Tel: (317) 636-1600
Fax: (317) 263-2318

JUSTER, Andrew
Executive Vice President and Chief Financial Officer
ssterrett@simon.com
Tel: (317) 636-1600
Fax: (317) 263-2318

MCDADE, Brian
Senior Vice President and Treasurer
Tel: (317) 636-1600
Fax: (317) 263-2318

MORRIS, Les
Manager, Corporate Public Relations
lmorris@simon.com
Tel: (317) 263-7711
Fax: (317) 263-2318

SOKOLOV, Richard S.
Director, President and Chief Operating Officer
Tel: (317) 636-1600
Fax: (317) 263-2318

Simpson Investment Company
A holding company for a forest products firm. Through Simpson Lumber Company, it operates two facilities in Washington that convert Douglas fir and hemlock logs into dimension lumber for the home construction market; its facilities in Georgia and South Carolina utilize yellow pine. It also owns Simpson Door Company, which manufactures interior and exterior wood doors.
www.simpson.com
Annual Revenues: $305.4 million
Employees: 2,800
Industry/ies: Forestry; Paper And Wood Products Industry

Chairman & Chief Executive Officer
MOSELEY, Colin
Tel: (253) 779-6400
Fax: (253) 280-9000

President	Tel:	(253) 779-6400
TRINKWALD, Allan F.	Fax:	(253) 280-9000

Main Headquarters

Mailing:	917 E. 11th St.	Tel:	(253) 779-6400
	Tacoma, WA 98421	Fax:	(253) 280-9000

Political Action Committees

Simpson Investment Company PAC
FEC ID: C00034934
Contact: Betsy G. Stauffer

917 E. 11th St.	Tel:	(253) 779-6400
Tacoma, WA 98421	Fax:	(253) 779-6400

> **Contributions to Candidates:** $18,500 (2015-2016)
> Democrats: $12,000; Republicans: $6,500

Corporate Foundations and Giving Programs

Simpson Investment Company Contributions Program

917 E. 11th St.	Tel:	(253) 779-6400
Tacoma, WA 98421	Fax:	(253) 280-9000

Public Affairs and Related Activities Personnel

At Headquarters

SLADE, Clifford	Tel:	(253) 779-6400
Director, Human Resources	Fax:	(253) 280-9000

At Other Offices

STAUFFER, Betsy G.
PAC Treasurer
1301 Fifth Ave., Suite 2700
Seattle, WA 98101

Sinclair Oil Corporation

A privately-held company, supplying customers Sinclair gasoline, diesel fuel, and jet fuel, producing 60,000 barrels of petroleum products per day.
www.sinclairoil.com
Employees: 7,000
SIC: 2911
NAICS: 32411
Industry/ies: Energy/Electricity; Fuels See Coal, Gas, Oil, Petroleum; Natural Resources; Petroleum Industry
Legislative Issues: ENG; FUE; TAX

Chief Executive Officer	Tel:	(801) 524-2700
MATTHEWS, Ross	Fax:	(801) 524-2880

Main Headquarters

Mailing:	P.O. Box 30825	Tel:	(801) 524-2700
	Salt Lake City, UT 84130	Fax:	(801) 524-2880

Public Affairs and Related Activities Personnel

At Other Offices

BARGER, Jack	Tel:	(801) 524-2700
Senior Vice President, Marketing	Fax:	(801) 524-2721
550 E. South Temple		
Salt Lake City, UT 84102		
ENSIGN, Clint W.	Tel:	(801) 524-2700
Senior Vice President, Government Relations	Fax:	(801) 524-2880
550 E. South Temple		
Salt Lake City, UT 84102		
jdarrington@sinclairoil.com		
Registered Federal Lobbyist		
HART, Lynn C.	Tel:	(801) 524-2700
Vice President and General Counsel	Fax:	(801) 524-2721
550 E. South Temple		
Salt Lake City, UT 84102		

Sirius XM Radio, Inc.

Formerly known as Sirius XM Radio Inc. and changed its name to Sirius XM Holdings Inc. in November 2013. Provider of satellite digital audio radio service. In 2008, Sirius Satellite Radio, Inc. acquired XM Satellite Radio, Inc. to become Sirius XM Radio, Inc. It creates and broadcasts commercial-free music; premier sports and live events; news and comedy; exclusive talk and entertainment; and the most comprehensive lineup of Latin commercial-free music, sports, and talk programming in radio.
www.siriusxm.com
Employees: 2,327
Ticker: NASDAQ (GS): SIRI
SIC: 4832
NAICS: 513112
Industry/ies: Communications; Telecommunications/Internet/Cable
Legislative Issues: COM; CPT

Chairman of the Board	Tel:	(212) 584-5100
MAFFEI , Gregory B.	Fax:	(212) 584-5200
Chief Executive Officer	Tel:	(212) 584-5100
MEYER, James E.	Fax:	(212) 584-5200

Main Headquarters

Mailing:	P.O. Box 33174	Tel:	(866) 519-7641
	Detroit, MI 48232		

Washington Office

Mailing:	1500 Eckington Pl. NE	Tel:	(202) 380-4000
	Washington, DC 20002	Fax:	(202) 380-4500

Public Affairs and Related Activities Personnel

At Other Offices

ALTMAN, Dara	Tel:	(212) 584-5100
Executive Vice President and Chief Administrative Officer	Fax:	(212) 584-5200
1221 Avenue of the Americas, 36th Floor		
New York City, NY 10020		
DONNELLY, Patrick L.	Tel:	(212) 584-5100
Executive Vice President and General Counsel	Fax:	(212) 584-5200
1221 Avenue of the Americas, 36th Floor		
New York City, NY 10020		
patrick.donnelly@siriusxm.com		
FITZPATRICK, Andrew	Tel:	(212) 584-5100
Vice President, Communications and Sports Programming	Fax:	(212) 584-5200
1221 Avenue of the Americas, 36th Floor		
New York City, NY 10020		
andrew.fitzpatrick@siriusxm.com		
FREAR, David J.	Tel:	(212) 584-5100
Executive Vice President and Chief Financial Officer	Fax:	(212) 584-5200
1221 Avenue of the Americas, 36th Floor		
New York City, NY 10020		
GREENSTEIN, Scott	Tel:	(212) 584-5100
President and Chief Content Officer	Fax:	(212) 584-5200
1221 Avenue of the Americas, 36th Floor		
New York City, NY 10020		
KUNKLE, Jennifer	Tel:	(212) 584-5100
Manager, Business Affairs	Fax:	(212) 584-5200
1221 Avenue of the Americas, 36th Floor		
New York City, NY 10020		
jennifer.kunkle@siriusxm.com		
RESENDEZ, Sal	Tel:	(646) 313-2405
Contact, Media Relations	Fax:	(212) 584-5200
1221 Avenue of the Americas, 36th Floor		
New York City, NY 10020		
sal.resendez@siriusxm.com		

SIRVA, Inc.

A global relocation and moving services business. Brands include Allied Van Lines, North American Van Lines, Global Van Lines, and SIRVA Relocation.
www.sirva.com
Employees: 3,800
Ticker: NYSE: SIR
SIC: 4213
Industry/ies: Furniture/Home Furnishings; Transportation

President and Chief Executive Officer	Tel:	(630) 570-3047
LUCAS, Wes W.	Fax:	(630) 468-4761
wes.lucas@sirva.com		

Main Headquarters

Mailing:	One Parkview Plaza	Tel:	(630) 570-3050
	Oakbrook Terrace, IL 60181		

Public Affairs and Related Activities Personnel

At Other Offices

BORRINK, Chris	Tel:	(630) 570-3686
Director, Interactive Marketing	Fax:	(630) 468-4761
700 Oakmont Ln.		
Westmont, IL 60559		
chris.borrink@sirva.com		
OBERDORF, Thomas W.	Tel:	(630) 570-3047
Chief Financial Officer	Fax:	(630) 468-4761
700 Oakmont Ln.		
Westmont, IL 60559		
PAIS, Margaret E.	Tel:	(630) 570-3047
Executive Vice President, Human Resources	Fax:	(630) 468-4761
700 Oakmont Ln.		
Westmont, IL 60559		

Sisters of St. Francis Health Services Inc.

See listing on page 340 under Franciscan Alliance, Inc.

Six Flags, Inc.

A theme park company.
www.sixflags.com
Annual Revenues: $1.19 billion
Employees: 1,900
Ticker: NYSE: SIX
SIC: 7990
Industry/ies: Sports/Leisure/Entertainment

Chairman of the Board, President and Chief Executive Officer	Tel:	(972) 595-5000
REID-ANDERSON, Jim		

Main Headquarters

Mailing:	924 Ave. J East	Tel:	(972) 595-5000
	Grand Prairie, TX 75050		

Washington Office

Mailing:	P.O. Box 4210	Tel:	(707) 644-4000
	Largo, MD 20775		

Corporate Foundations and Giving Programs

Six Flags Friends Program
1540 Broadway   Tel: (212) 652-9346
15th Floor
New York City, NY 10036

Public Affairs and Related Activities Personnel

At Headquarters

BALK, Lance C.	Tel:	(972) 595-5000
Executive Vice President, General Counsel		
DUFFEY, John M.	Tel:	(972) 595-5000
Executive Vice President, Chief Financial Officer		
HAWRYLAK, Walt	Tel:	(972) 595-5000
Senior Vice President, Administration		
KREJSA, Nancy	Tel:	(972) 595-5083
Senior Vice President, Investor Relations and Corporate Communications		
nkrejsa@sftp.com		
MCKILLIPS, David	Tel:	(972) 595-5000
Senior Vice President, Corporate Alliances		
dmckillips@sftp.com		
PETIT, Brett	Tel:	(972) 595-5000
Senior Vice President, Marketing		

At Other Offices

ANTINORO, Mike	Tel:	(212) 652-9403
Executive Vice President	Fax:	(212) 354-3089
230 Park Ave., 16th Floor		
New York City, NY 10169		
DANIELS, Sandra	Tel:	(212) 652-9393
Vice President, Communications	Fax:	(212) 354-3089
230 Park Ave., 16th Floor		
New York City, NY 10169		
sdaniels@sftp.com		
SCHLEIMER, Andrew	Tel:	(212) 652-9403
Executive Vice President, Strategic Development	Fax:	(212) 354-3089
230 Park Ave., 16th Floor		
New York City, NY 10169		
SCHMITT, William	Tel:	(203) 683-8200
Contact, Investor Relations	Fax:	(212) 354-3089
230 Park Ave., 16th Floor		
New York City, NY 10169		

Skechers U.S.A. Inc.

Provides footwear for men, women and children.
www.skechers.com
Annual Revenues: $2.61 billion
Employees: 2,944
Ticker: NYSE: SKX
SIC: 3140
Industry/ies: Apparel/Textiles Industry

Chairman of the Board and Chief Executive Officer	Tel:	(310) 318-3100
GREENBERG, Robert	Fax:	(310) 318-5019

Main Headquarters

Mailing:	228 Manhattan Beach Blvd.	Tel:	(310) 318-2982
	Manhattan Beach, CA 90266	Fax:	(516) 826-0336

Corporate Foundations and Giving Programs

Skechers Foundation
228 Manhattan Beach Blvd.
Manhattan Beach, CA 90266

Public Affairs and Related Activities Personnel

At Headquarters

CLAY, Jennifer	Tel:	(310) 318-3100
Vice President, Corporate Communications and Marketing	Fax:	(310) 318-5019
PACCIONE, Philip G.	Tel:	(310) 318-3100
General Counsel, Executive Vice President, Business Affairs and Corporate Secretary	Fax:	(310) 318-5019
WEINBERG, David	Tel:	(310) 318-3100
Chief Operating Officer & Chief Financial Officer	Fax:	(310) 318-5019

Skilled Healthcare Group, Inc.

Operates nursing facilities, assisted living facilities, a rehabilitation therapy business, and a hospice business.
www.skilledhealthcaregroup.com
Annual Revenues: $834.51 million

Employees: 15,000
Ticker: NYSE: SKH
SIC: 8051
Industry/ies: Medicine/Health Care/Mental Health

Chief Executive Officer	Tel:	(949) 282-5800
FISH, Robert H.	Fax:	(949) 282-5889

Main Headquarters

Mailing:	27442 Portola Pkwy.	Tel:	(949) 282-5800
	Suite 200	Fax:	(949) 282-5889
	Foothill Ranch, CA 92610		

Political Action Committees

Skilled Healthcare Group, Inc. PAC (Skilled Healthcare PAC)
FEC ID: C00442426
Contact: Pat Ikerd
27442 Portola Pkwy.   Tel: (949) 282-5800
Suite 200   Fax: (949) 282-5800
Foothill Ranch, CA 92610

Public Affairs and Related Activities Personnel

At Headquarters

FELFE, Christopher N.	Tel:	(949) 282-5800
Chief Financial Officer	Fax:	(949) 282-5889
HINTGEN, Kristina	Tel:	(949) 282-5800
Vice President, Human Resources	Fax:	(949) 282-5889
IKERD, Pat	Tel:	(949) 282-5800
PAC Contact	Fax:	(949) 282-5889
MITCHELL, John T.	Tel:	(949) 282-5800
Senior Vice President and Chief Compliance Officer	Fax:	(949) 282-5889
RAPP, Roland	Tel:	(949) 282-5800
Executive Vice President, General Counsel, Secretary and Chief Administrative Officer	Fax:	(949) 282-5889

Skyline Solar

Manufactures solar-power systems.
www.skyline-solar.com
Annual Revenues: $5 million
Employees: 30
Industry/ies: Energy/Electricity; Environment And Conservation; Utilities

Main Headquarters

Mailing:	139 Glendale Ave.	Tel:	(855) 575-9546
	Edison, NJ 08817		

Public Affairs and Related Activities Personnel

At Other Offices

MORRIS, Jason	Tel:	(415) 512-0770
Contact, Media Relations	Fax:	(650) 964-4263
185 E. Dana St.		
Mountain View, CA 94041		
skylinesolar@schwartzmsl.com		

SkyTerra Communication Inc.

Engaged in the supply of mobile satellite communications services.
www.lightsquared.com
Annual Revenues: $34.50 million
Employees: 200
SIC: 4899
Industry/ies: Communications; Science; Scientific Research; Telecommunications/Internet/Cable
Legislative Issues: TEC

Chairman, Chief Executive Officer and President	Tel:	(877) 678-2920
GOOD, Alexander H.	Fax:	(703) 390-2770

Main Headquarters

Mailing:	10802 Parkridge Blvd.	Tel:	(877) 678-2920
	Reston, VA 20191	Fax:	(703) 390-2770

Political Action Committees

Lightsquared Inc. Political Action Committee (Lightsquared PAC)
FEC ID: C00416396
Contact: Jeffrey Carlisle
10802 Parkridge Blvd.
Reston, VA 20191

   Contributions to Candidates: $1,000 (2015-2016)
   Democrats: $1,000

Public Affairs and Related Activities Personnel

At Headquarters

CARLISLE, Jeffrey	Tel:	(703) 390-1899
Executive Vice President, Regulatory Affairs & Public Policy	Fax:	(703) 390-1893
MACLEOD, Scott	Tel:	(703) 390-1899
Executive Vice President, Chief Financial Officer and Treasurer	Fax:	(703) 390-2770
MONTAGNER, Marc	Tel:	(877) 678-2920
Chief Financial Officer	Fax:	(703) 390-2770

SURFACE, Tom
Media Contact
tom.surface@skyterra.com

Tel: (703) 390-1579
Fax: (703) 390-2770

SkyTide, Inc.

A business analytics software company.
www.skytide.com
Industry/ies: Computer/Technology

Chief Executive Officer
O'DONNELL, Michael

Tel: (510) 250-4313
Fax: (510) 250-4276

Main Headquarters
Mailing: One Kaiser Plaza
Suite 785
Oakland, CA 94612

Tel: (510) 250-4275
Fax: (510) 250-4276

Public Affairs and Related Activities Personnel

At Headquarters

HURLEY, Patrick
Vice President, Marketing
phurley@skytide.com

Tel: (510) 435-9865
Fax: (510) 250-4276

Slade Gorton

Federal advocacy.
www.sladegorton.com

Chairman of the Board
GORTON, III, Mike

Tel: (617) 442-5800
Fax: (617) 442-9090

President and Chief Executive officer
GORTON, Kimberly

Tel: (617) 442-5800
Fax: (617) 442-9090

Main Headquarters
Mailing: 225 Southampton St.
Suite 1640
Boston, MA 02118

Tel: (617) 442-5800
Fax: (617) 442-9090
TF: (800) 442-9090

Public Affairs and Related Activities Personnel

At Headquarters

NEWMAN, Dennis
Vice President Finance

Tel: (617) 442-5800
Fax: (617) 442-9090

SLM Corporation

Financial Services.
Legislative Issues: BUD; EDU

Main Headquarters
Mailing: Two Wisconsin Cir.
Suite 700
Chevy Chase, MD 20815

Public Affairs and Related Activities Personnel

At Headquarters

MORRISON, Timothy
Registered Federal Lobbyist

Sloane Strategies, LLC

Government Relations Consulting.

Main Headquarters
Mailing: 292 New Mark Esplanade
Rockville, MD 20850

Tel: (301) 424-0348
Fax: (301) 424-0363

Public Affairs and Related Activities Personnel

At Headquarters

SLOANE, David P.
Principal
dsloane@firststreetstrategies.com

Tel: (301) 424-0348
Fax: (301) 424-0363

Small Business Corporation - Seoul, Korea

Industry/ies: Business; Small Business

Main Headquarters
Mailing: 1952 Gallows Rd.
Suite 110
Vienna, VA 22182

Public Affairs and Related Activities Personnel

At Headquarters

CHUN, Pyong Chon

LEE, Geun Hyung

PARK, Chang Ki

WOO, Do Hyan

Small Business Corporation - USA Office (dba Korea Business Development Center)

Industry/ies: Business; Small Business

Main Headquarters

Mailing: 105 Challenger Rd.
4th Floor
Ridgefield Park, NJ 07660

Public Affairs and Related Activities Personnel

At Headquarters

CHUN, Byungwoo
Director

At Other Offices

LEE, Kun Bok
General Manager
2360 E. Devon Ave., Suite 2010
Des Plaines, IL 60018

LEE, Kwan Woong
General Manager
20280 S. Vermont Ave., Suite 200
Torrance, CA 90502

PARK, Chang Ki
2360 E. Devon Ave., Suite 2010
Des Plaines, IL 60018

SONG, Jung Hye
2360 E. Devon Ave., Suite 2010
Des Plaines, IL 60018

YEOM, Jung Hyeon
Manager
2400 E. Devon Ave., Suite 220
Des Plaines, IL 60018

YOON, In Kyoo
2360 E. Devon Ave., Suite 2010
Des Plaines, IL 60018

SmartSynch, Inc.

Specializes in the two-way delivery of real-time energy usage data over public wireless networks.
www.itron.com
Employees: 100
Industry/ies: Energy/Electricity
Legislative Issues: BUD; DEF

Chairman of the Board
TARR, Jake

Tel: (601) 362-1780
Fax: (601) 362-1787

Chief Executive Officer
JOHNSTON, Stephen D.

Tel: (601) 362-1780
Fax: (601) 362-1787

Main Headquarters
Mailing: 4400 Old Canton Rd.
Jackson, MS 39211

Tel: (888) 362-1780
Fax: (601) 362-1787
TF: (888) 362-1780

Public Affairs and Related Activities Personnel

At Headquarters

GUL, Nancy
Senior Vice President, Strategic Development

Tel: (888) 362-1780
Fax: (601) 362-1787

HABBU, Ajit
Chief Financial Officer

Tel: (888) 362-1780
Fax: (601) 362-1787

MCCOOL, Campbell
Chief Marketing Officer

Tel: (601) 362-1780
Fax: (601) 362-1787

MYERS, Chris
Marketing Director
cmyers@smartsynch.com

Tel: (601) 209-1315
Fax: (601) 362-1787

THORNTON, Matt
Senior Vice President, Corporate Development and Strategy

Tel: (601) 362-1780
Fax: (601) 362-1787

SMH International

Public affairs consultant.
www.smhintl.com

Principal, President and Founder
WARNER, Michael
mike.warner@smhintl.com

Tel: (856) 642-9595
Fax: (609) 784-7898

Main Headquarters
Mailing: 11 Eves Dr.
Suite 100
Marlton, NJ 08053-3130

Tel: (856) 810-0662
Fax: (856) 810-3944

Smith & Nephew, Inc.

Develops and markets advanced medical devices that help healthcare professionals treat patients more effectively in Orthopaedic Reconstruction, Advanced Wound Management, Sports Medicine and Trauma.
www.smith-nephew.com
Annual Revenues: $4.62 billion
Employees: 14,242
Ticker: NYSE: SNN
SIC: 5047; 3842

NAICS: 339113; 42145
Industry/ies: Medicine/Health Care/Mental Health
Legislative Issues: HCR; MMM; TAX

Chairman of the Board
QUARTA, Roberto

Tel: (901) 396-2121
Fax: (901) 399-6174

Chief Executive Officer
BOHUON, Olivier

Tel: (901) 396-2121
Fax: (901) 399-6174

Main Headquarters
Mailing: 1450 Brooks Rd.
            Memphis, TN 38116

Tel: (901) 396-2121
Fax: (901) 399-6174
TF: (800) 821-5700

Washington Office
Mailing: 1090 Vermont Ave. NW
            Suite 220
            Washington, DC 20005

Tel: (202) 898-4801

Political Action Committees
Smith & Nephew, Inc. PAC
FEC ID: C00374066
Contact: Jean W. Mercer
7135 Goodlett Farms Pkwy.
Cordova, 38016

> **Contributions to Candidates:** $45,000 (2015-2016)
> Democrats: $15,000; Republicans: $30,000

Corporate Foundations and Giving Programs
Smith & Nephew Contributions Program
1450 Brooks Rd.
Memphis, TN 38116

Public Affairs and Related Activities Personnel
At Headquarters

BROWN, Julie
Chief Financial Officer

Tel: (901) 396-2121
Fax: (901) 399-6174

BURNS, Andrew
Director, Global Marketing Communications
andrew.burns@smith-nephew.com

Tel: (901) 399-5739
Fax: (901) 399-6174

CAMPO, Jack
Chief Legal Officer

Tel: (901) 396-2121
Fax: (901) 399-6174

COWDY, Phil
Senior Vice President, Corporate Affairs and Strategic Planning
phil.cowdy@smith-nephew.com

Tel: (901) 396-2121
Fax: (901) 399-6174

MAYE, Helen
Chief Human Resources Officer

Tel: (901) 396-2121
Fax: (901) 399-6174

PETIT , Cyrille
Chief Corporate Development Officer

Tel: (901) 396-2121
Fax: (901) 399-6174

RAJARATNAM, Arjun
Chief Compliance Officer

Tel: (901) 396-2121
Fax: (901) 399-6174

REYNOLDS , Charles
Director, Corporate Communications
charles.reynolds@smith-nephew.com

Tel: (901) 396-2121
Fax: (901) 399-6174

At Washington Office

MARTIN, John
Registered Federal Lobbyist

Tel: (202) 898-4801

At Other Offices

MERCER, Jean W.
PAC Contact
7135 Goodlett Farms Pkwy.
Cordova, TN 38016

SELTMAN, Paul
Senior Vice President, Government Affairs & Reimbursement
1701 Pennsylvania Ave. NW, Suite 300
Washington, DC 20006
paul.seltman@smith-nephew.com
Registered Federal Lobbyist

Tel: (202) 441-2342

Smith and Wesson Holding Company
Deals with businesses in safety, security, protection and sport, globally.
www.smith-wesson.com
Annual Revenues: $541.29 million
Employees: 1,758
Ticker: NASDAQ; SWHC
SIC: 2399; 3429; 3479; 3481
NAICS: 332994; 315999; 332812; 332999
Industry/ies: Firearms/Gun Control
Legislative Issues: DEF; MAN; TRD

Chairman of the Board
MONHEIT, Barry M.

Tel: (413) 781-8300
Fax: (413) 747-3317

President and Chief Executive Officer
DEBNEY, P. James

Tel: (413) 781-8300
Fax: (413) 747-3317

Main Headquarters

Mailing: 2100 Roosevelt Ave.
            Springfield, MA 01104

Tel: (413) 781-8300
Fax: (413) 731-8980
TF: (800) 331-0852

Political Action Committees
Smith & Wesson Holding Corporation PAC
FEC ID: C00419051
Contact: Deana Mcpherson
2100 Roosevelt Ave.
Springfield, MA 01104

> **Contributions to Candidates:** $20,000 (2015-2016)
> Republicans: $20,000

Public Affairs and Related Activities Personnel
At Headquarters

BUCHANAN, Jeffrey D.
Executive Vice President, Chief Financial Officer and Treasurer

Tel: (413) 781-8300
Fax: (413) 747-3317

CICERO, Robert J.
Vice President, Chief Compliance Officer, General Counsel, and Secretary
rcicero@smith-wesson.com

Tel: (413) 747-3443
Fax: (413) 747-3317

MCPHERSON, Deana
PAC Contact

Tel: (413) 781-8300
Fax: (413) 747-3317

PASANTES, Mario
Senior Vice President, Marketing and Global Professional Sales
mpasantes@smith-wesson.com

Tel: (413) 781-8300
Fax: (413) 747-3317

SHARP, Elizabeth
Vice President, Investor Relations
lsharp@smith-wesson.com

Tel: (480) 949-9700
Fax: (413) 747-3317

Smithfield Foods Inc.
A meat packing company.
www.smithfieldfoods.com
Annual Revenues: $13.22 billion
Employees: 46,950
Ticker: NYSE: SFD
SIC: 2011
NAICS: 311611
Industry/ies: Food And Beverage Industry
Legislative Issues: AGR; ENG; FOO; FOR; FUE; IMM; LBR; TAX; TRD

Executive Vice President and Foundation Contact
LUTER, III, IV, Joseph W.
iii@smithfieldfoods.com

Tel: (757) 365-3000
Fax: (757) 365-3017

President and Chief Executive Officer
POPE, C. Larry
larrypope@smithfieldfoods.com

Tel: (757) 365-3000
Fax: (757) 365-3017

Main Headquarters
Mailing: 200 Commerce St.
            Smithfield, VA 23430

Tel: (757) 365-3000
Fax: (757) 365-3017

Washington Office
Mailing: 2001 K St. NW
            Suite 400
            Washington, DC 20006

Tel: (202) 857-2411
Fax: (202) 857-1737

Political Action Committees
Smithfield Foods Inc. PAC (HamPAC)
FEC ID: C00359075
Contact: Dennis H. Treacy
2001 K St. NW
Suite 400
Washington, DC 20006

> **Contributions to Candidates:** $68,650 (2015-2016)
> Democrats: $25,650; Republicans: $43,000

Corporate Foundations and Giving Programs

Smithfield-Luter Foundation
200 Commerce St.
Smithfield, VA 23430

Tel: (757) 365-3000
Fax: (757) 365-3017

Public Affairs and Related Activities Personnel
At Headquarters

COLE, Michael H.
Vice President, Chief Legal Officer and Secretary
michaelcole@smithfieldfoods.com

Tel: (757) 365-3000
Fax: (757) 365-3017

DEEL, Jeffrey A.
Vice President and Corporate Controller

Tel: (757) 365-3000
Fax: (757) 365-3017

DYKSTRA , Timothy
Vice President and Corporate Treasurer

Tel: (757) 365-3000
Fax: (757) 365-3017

ELLIS, Bart
Vice President, Operations Analysis

Tel: (757) 365-3000
Fax: (757) 365-3017

FLEMMING, Michael D.
Vice President and Corporate General Counsel

Tel: (757) 365-3000
Fax: (757) 365-3017

HARLOW , Craig R.	Tel:	(757) 365-3000
Vice President, Internal Audit	Fax:	(757) 365-3017
KIRKHAM, Kathleen	Tel:	(757) 365-3000
Director, Corporate Communications	Fax:	(757) 365-3017
LEETH , Stewart T.	Tel:	(757) 365-3000
Vice President, Regulatory Affairs and Sustainability	Fax:	(757) 365-3017
LOMBARDO, Keira L.	Tel:	(757) 365-3050
Senior Vice President, Corporate Affairs	Fax:	(757) 365-3017
keiralombardo@smithfieldfoods.com		
SULLIVAN, Kenneth M.	Tel:	(757) 365-3000
Senior Vice President, Finance and Chief Financial Officer	Fax:	(757) 365-3017
kennethsullivan@smithfieldfoods.com		
TURNER , Vernon T.	Tel:	(757) 365-3000
Vice President, Corporate Tax	Fax:	(757) 365-3017

At Washington Office

TREACY, Dennis H.	Tel:	(202) 857-2411
Executive Vice President and Chief Sustainability Officer and	Fax:	(202) 857-1737
PAC Treasurer		
dennistreacy@smithfieldfoods.com		

SmithKline Beecham

See listing on page 366 under GlaxoSmithKline

Smiths Detection, Inc.

A provider of technologically advanced security solutions.
www.smithsdetection.com
Annual Revenues: $5.19 million
Employees: 2,300
Industry/ies: Computer/Technology; Defense/Homeland Security; Government-Related; Law Enforcement/Security; Machinery/Equipment
Legislative Issues: BUD; DEF; HOM

President	Tel:	(410) 612-2625
INGRAM, Richard	Fax:	(410) 510-9496

Main Headquarters

Mailing: 2202 Lakeside Blvd.	Tel:	(410) 612-2625
Edgewood, MD 21040	Fax:	(410) 510-9496
	TF:	(800) 297-0955

Washington Office

Mailing: 425 Third St. SW	Tel:	(202) 777-8448
Suite 875		
Washington, DC 20024		

Political Action Committees
Smiths Group Services Corporation Political Action Committee (Smiths PAC)
FEC ID: C00448324
Contact: Sarah Riegner
425 Third St. SW
Suite 875
Washington, DC 20024

Contributions to Candidates: $119,700 (2015-2016)
Democrats: $41,000; Republicans: $78,700

Principal Recipients

SENATE
GARDNER, CORY (REP-CO)

Public Affairs and Related Activities Personnel

At Headquarters

ANNING, David	Tel:	(410) 612-2625
Vice President, Global Operations	Fax:	(410) 510-9496
HOUGHTON, Diana	Tel:	(410) 612-2625
Vice President, Strategy and Marketing	Fax:	(410) 510-9496
KNOX-GOWER, Dana	Tel:	(203) 482-6752
Director, Communications and Marketing	Fax:	(410) 510-9496
dana.gower@smithsdetection.com		
LITTLEBOY, Darren	Tel:	(410) 612-2625
Vice President, Human Resources	Fax:	(410) 510-9496
LIU, Lily	Tel:	(410) 612-2625
Vice President, Finance	Fax:	(410) 510-9496
MCSEVENY, Colin	Tel:	(207) 808-5534
Manager, Media Relations	Fax:	(410) 510-9496
colin.mcseveny@smiths.com		
PICCIOTTI, Timothy	Tel:	(410) 510-9100
Federal Lobbyist	Fax:	(410) 510-9496
RAMSAY, Adam	Tel:	(410) 612-2625
Divisional General Counsel	Fax:	(410) 510-9496
RIPIN, Marilyn Joy	Tel:	(410) 510-9100
Vice President, Business Development	Fax:	(410) 510-9496

At Washington Office

HESSENIUS, Elizabeth	Tel:	(202) 777-8448
Federal Lobbyist		

RIEGNER, Sarah	Tel:	(202) 777-8448
PAC Contact		

Smiths Group PLC

Smiths Group has five divisions - Smiths Detection, Smiths Medical, John Crane, Smiths Interconnect and Flex-Tek. They are focused on the threat and contraband detection, medical devices, energy, communications and engineered components markets worldwide.
www.smiths.com
Annual Revenues: $3.08 billion
Employees: 23,000
Ticker: LON: SMIN
Industry/ies: Energy/Electricity
Legislative Issues: AVI; BUD; DEF; ENG; ENV; HOM; MED; TAX; TOR

Chairman	Tel:	(202) 777-8448
BUCKLEY, George		

Chief Executive Officer	Tel:	(202) 777-8448
BOWMAN, Philip		

Main Headquarters

Mailing: 425 Third St. SW	Tel:	(202) 777-8448
Suite 875		
Washington, DC 20024		

Political Action Committees
Smiths Group Services Corporation Political Action Committee (Smiths PAC)
FEC ID: C00448324
Contact: John Drugan
425 Third St. SW
Suite 875
Washington, DC 20024

Contributions to Candidates: $119,700 (2015-2016)
Democrats: $41,000; Republicans: $78,700

Principal Recipients

SENATE
GARDNER, CORY (REP-CO)

Public Affairs and Related Activities Personnel

At Headquarters

CEGLIA, Lisa	Tel:	(202) 777-8448
Vice President, Government Relations		
Registered Federal Lobbyist		
DRUGAN, John	Tel:	(202) 777-8448
PAC Treasurer		
GIBBONS, Meredith	Tel:	(202) 777-8448
Government Relations PAC & Grassroots Coordinator		
HESSENIUS, Elizabeth	Tel:	(202) 777-8448
Federal Lobbyist		
Registered Federal Lobbyist		
MCSEVENY, Colin	Tel:	(202) 777-8448
Media, Head		
PRESSNELL-HESSENIUS, Elizabeth "Sissy"	Tel:	(202) 777-8448
Chair, Security Manufacturers Coalition (SMC)		
SCHMIDT, Kevin	Tel:	(202) 777-8448
Vice President, Government Relations		
kevin.schmidt@smithsdetection.com		
Registered Federal Lobbyist		
SWONGER, Chris R.	Tel:	(202) 777-8447
Senior Vice President, Government Relations		
chris.swonger@smiths.com		
Registered Federal Lobbyist		
TURNER, Peter	Tel:	(202) 777-8448
Director, Finance		

SMS Holdings Corporation

Maintains 340 public facilities across the U.S. Provider of maintenance and housekeeping services.
smsholdings.com
Annual Revenues: $9.70 million
Employees: 500
Industry/ies: Management

Chairman of the Board and Chief Executive Officer	Tel:	(615) 399-1839
WOLKEN, Keith	Fax:	(615) 399-1438

Main Headquarters

Mailing: 7135 Charlotte Pike	Tel:	(615) 399-1839
Suite 100	Fax:	(615) 399-1438
Nashville, TN 37209		

Political Action Committees
Firstline Transportation Security Inc./SMS Holdings PAC
FEC ID: C00398511
Contact: Hiram Cox
7135 Charlotte Pike
Suite 100
Nashville, TN 37209

Contributions to Candidates: $1,000 (2015-2016)
Republicans: $1,000

Public Affairs and Related Activities Personnel

At Headquarters

BURNETT, Jim
Executive Vice President and Chief Development Officer
Jburnett@smsholdings.com
Tel: (615) 399-1839
Fax: (615) 399-1438

COX, Hiram
PAC Contact, Executive Vice President, Chief Financial Officer and Chief Administrative Officer
hcox@smsholdings.com
Tel: (615) 399-1839
Fax: (615) 399-1438

Snap-on Incorporated

Manufactures and markets tools, equipment, diagnostics, and repair information and systems solutions for professional users worldwide.
www.snapon.com
Annual Revenues: $3.54 billion
Employees: 11,400
Ticker: NYSE: SNA
SIC: 3423; 2542; 3559; 3420
NAICS: 332212; 333319; 337215
Industry/ies: Machinery/Equipment

Chairman of the Board and Chief Executive Officer
PINCHUK, Nicholas T.
nicholas.pinchuk@snapon.com
Tel: (262) 656-5200
Fax: (262) 656-5777

Main Headquarters
Mailing: 2801 80th St.
P.O. Box 1410
Kenosha, WI 53141-1410
Tel: (262) 656-5200
Fax: (262) 656-5577

Public Affairs and Related Activities Personnel

At Headquarters

BOYD, Iain
Vice President, Human Resources
Tel: (262) 656-5200
Fax: (262) 656-5777

JOHNSEN, Constance R
Vice President and Controller
Tel: (262) 656-5200
Fax: (262) 656-5777

KOSTRZEWA, Jeffrey F
Vice President and Treasurer
Tel: (262) 656-5200
Fax: (262) 656-5777

KRATCOSKI, Leslie H.
Vice President, Investor Relations
leslie.h.kratcoski@snapon.com
Tel: (262) 656-6121
Fax: (262) 656-5577

PAGLIARI, Aldo J.
Senior Vice President, Finance and Chief Financial Officer
Tel: (262) 656-5200
Fax: (262) 656-5577

SECOR, Richard
Director, Marketing Communications
Tel: (262) 656-5561
Fax: (262) 656-5777

SHUR, Irwin M.
Vice President, General Counsel and Secretary
irwin.m.shur@snapon.com
Tel: (262) 656-5200
Fax: (262) 656-5777

SMALES, Alicia A.
Vice President, Chief Marketing Officer
alicia.a.smales@snapon.com
Tel: (262) 656-5200
Fax: (262) 656-5777

SUDAC, Irene S
Vice President, Financial Services
Tel: (262) 656-5200
Fax: (262) 656-5577

THATCHER, Kevin L
Vice President, Business Development
Tel: (262) 656-5200
Fax: (262) 656-5577

Snyder's-Lance

Snyder's-Lance manufactures, distributes, markets, and sells snacks and other packaged food products. Its products include pretzels, sandwich crackers, potato chips, cookies, tortilla chips, restaurant-style crackers, popcorn, nuts and other snacks.
www.snyderslance.com
Annual Revenues: $1.65 billion
Employees: 5,700
Ticker: NASDAQ: LNCE
SIC: 2052
Industry/ies: Food And Beverage Industry

Chairman of the Board
PREZZANO , W. J.
Tel: (704) 554-1421
Fax: (704) 554-5562

President and Chief Executive Officer
LEE, Jr., Carl E.
Tel: (704) 554-1421
Fax: (704) 554-5562

Main Headquarters
Mailing: 13024 Ballantyne Corporate Pl.
Suite 900
Charlotte, NC 28277
Tel: (704) 554-1421
Fax: (704) 554-5562
TF: (800) 438-1880

Corporate Foundations and Giving Programs
Snyder's-Lance Contribution Programs
13024 Ballantyne Corporate Pl.
Suite 900
Charlotte, NC 28277
Tel: (704) 554-1421
Fax: (704) 554-5562

Public Affairs and Related Activities Personnel

At Headquarters

JAMISON, Jr., Zean
Foundation Director
Tel: (704) 554-1421
Fax: (704) 554-5562

PUCKETT, Rick D.
Executive Vice President, Chief Financial Officer and Chief Administrative Officer
Tel: (704) 554-1421
Fax: (704) 554-5562

WICKLUND, Margaret E.
Vice President, Corporate Controller, Principal Accounting Officer and Assistant Secretary
Tel: (704) 554-1421
Fax: (704) 554-5562

SolarCity, Inc.

A solar power systems manufacturer.
www.solarcity.com
Annual Revenues: $258.96 million
Employees: 9,012
Ticker: NASDAQ: SCTY
Industry/ies: Energy/Electricity; Machinery/Equipment
Legislative Issues: ENG; TAX

Chairman
MUSK, Elon
Tel: (650) 638-1028
Fax: (650) 638-1029

Founder and Chief Executive Officer
RIVE, Lyndon
Tel: (650) 638-1028
Fax: (650) 638-1029

Main Headquarters
Mailing: 3055 Clearview Way
San Mateo, CA 94402
Tel: (650) 638-1028
Fax: (650) 638-1029

Washington Office
Mailing: 9000 Virginia Manor Rd.
Suite 250
Beltsville, MD 20705

Political Action Committees
Solarcity Corporation PAC
FEC ID: C00520569
Contact: John M. Stanton
575 Seventh St. NW
Suite 400
Washington, DC 20004
Tel: (650) 963-5100

Contributions to Candidates: $10,191,675 (2015-2016)
Democrats: $63,900; Republicans: $65,760; Other: $10,062,015

Principal Recipients

SENATE
GARDNER, CORY (REP-CO)

HOUSE
REED, THOMAS W II (REP-NY)

Public Affairs and Related Activities Personnel

At Headquarters

BASS, Jonathan
Vice President, Communications
jbass@solarcity.com
Tel: (650) 963-5156
Fax: (650) 638-1029

BUSS, Brad
Chief Financial Officer
Tel: (650) 638-1028
Fax: (650) 638-1029

GUSSIS, Chrysanthe
Vice President and Deputy General Counsel
Tel: (650) 638-1028
Fax: (650) 638-1029

KELLY, Robert
Chief Financial Officer
Tel: (650) 638-1028
Fax: (650) 638-1029

SERRA, Tanguy
Chief Operating Officer
Tel: (650) 638-1028
Fax: (650) 638-1029

WEISSMAN, Seth
Vice President and General Counsel
sweissman@solarcity.com
Tel: (650) 638-1028
Fax: (650) 638-1029

At Other Offices

HENNESSEY, Scott
Director, Policy & Electricity Markets
505 Ninth St. NW, Suite 800
Washington, DC 20004

NAZAR, Hasan
601 13th St. NW, Suite 900 North
Washington, DC 20005

STANTON, John M.
Vice President, Government Affairs and PAC Treasurer, Executive Vice President, Policy and Markets
601 13th St. NW, Suite 900 North
Washington, DC 20005
gga@dwgp.com

SolarWorld AG

See listing on page 728 under SolarWorld California

SolarWorld California

A solar cell manufacturing Company.

www.solarworld-usa.com
Employees: 20
Industry/ies: Energy/Electricity; Environment And Conservation

Main Headquarters
Mailing: 4650 Adohr Ln.   Tel: (805) 388-6590
Camarillo, CA 93012-8508   Fax: (805) 388-6395

Public Affairs and Related Activities Personnel

At Headquarters

SANTARRIS, Ben   Tel: (503) 693-5189
Contact, Public Relations and Manager, Public Affairs   Fax: (805) 388-6395
ben.santarris@solarworld-usa.com

Solazyme Inc.

A renewable energy firm.
solazyme.com
Annual Revenues: $60.60 million
Employees: 266
Ticker: NASDAQ:SZYM
SIC: 2860
Industry/ies: Energy/Electricity

Chairman of the Board   Tel: (650) 780-4777
FIDDLER, Jerry   Fax: (650) 989-6700

Chief Executive Officer   Tel: (650) 780-4777
WOLFSON, Jonathan S.   Fax: (650) 989-6700

Main Headquarters
Mailing: 225 Gateway Blvd.   Tel: (650) 780-4777
San Francisco, CA 94080   Fax: (650) 989-6700

Public Affairs and Related Activities Personnel

At Headquarters

DAVIDSON , Nicholas   Tel: (650) 780-4777
   Fax: (650) 989-6700

ELLIS, Graham   Tel: (650) 780-4777
   Fax: (650) 989-6700

GARAMENDI, Genet   Tel: (650) 963-5228
Vice President, Corporate Communications   Fax: (650) 989-6700
press@solazyme.com

ISAACS, David   Tel: (650) 780-4777
Senior Vice President, Government Relations   Fax: (650) 989-6700

NOWAK, Kate   Tel: (650) 780-4777
   Fax: (650) 989-6700

PAINTER, Tyler W.   Tel: (650) 780-4777
Chief Financial Officer and Chief Operating Officer   Fax: (650) 989-6700

PINO, Rhawnie   Tel: (650) 780-4777
   Fax: (650) 989-6700

QUINLAN, Paul T.   Tel: (650) 780-4777
Senior Vice President and General Counsel   Fax: (650) 989-6700

ZWILLINGER, Joseph   Tel: (650) 780-4777
Vice President, Industrial Products   Fax: (650) 989-6700

Solexant Corporation

Develops thin film PV technologies, using printable nano-material technologies exclusively licensed from leading universities, Solexant's flexible solar cells harvest energy from the entire solar spectrum.
www.solexant.com
Industry/ies: Energy/Electricity

Member Board of Directors   Tel: (408) 240-8900
DIXON, Donald   Fax: (408) 240-8901

Chief Executive Officer   Tel: (408) 240-8900
MATTSON, Brad   Fax: (408) 240-8901

Main Headquarters
Mailing: 2329 Zanker Rd.   Tel: (408) 240-8900
San Jose, CA 95131-1109   Fax: (408) 240-8901

Public Affairs and Related Activities Personnel

At Headquarters

FLEMING, Dan   Tel: (408) 240-8900
Vice President, Finance   Fax: (408) 240-8901

SETLIFF, Kimberly   Tel: (415) 977-1942
Media Contact   Fax: (408) 240-8901
kimberly@antennagroup.com

Solomon P. Ortiz Holdings, LLC

Multi-faceted business, of which part of its scope is government relations and consulting.
Legislative Issues: WAS

ORTIZ, Hon. Solomon P.   Tel: (888) 658-8484

Main Headquarters
Mailing: 6262 Weber Rd.
Suite102

Corpus Christi, TX 74813

Public Affairs and Related Activities Personnel

At Headquarters

WARD, Mark

Soluble Systems

Soluble Systems, LLC, manufactures and markets a line of sterile wound care dressings under the brand name TheraGauze.
www.solublesystems.com
Annual Revenues: $1.50 million
Employees: 9
Industry/ies: Medicine/Health Care/Mental Health

Chief Executive Officer   Tel: (757) 877-8899
MCCARTER, Thomas   Fax: (757) 877-8870
tkmccarter@solublesystems.com

President   Tel: (757) 877-8899
STALEY, Allan R.   Fax: (757) 877-8870

Main Headquarters
Mailing: 11830 Canon Blvd.   Tel: (757) 877-8899
Suite A   Fax: (757) 877-8870
Newport News, VA 23606   TF: (877) 222-2681

Public Affairs and Related Activities Personnel

At Headquarters

ZENI, Thomas   Tel: (757) 877-8899
Chief Financial Officer   Fax: (757) 877-8870

Solutia Inc.

See listing on page 275 under Eastman Chemical Company

Sonic Automotive, Inc.

Founded with five dealerships in 1997, operates as an automotive retailer in the United States. These dealerships provide comprehensive services, including sales of both new and used cars and light trucks, sales of replacement parts, performance of vehicle maintenance, warranty, paint and collision repair services, and arrangement of extended warranty contracts, financing and insurance for the company's customers.
www.sonicautomotive.com
Annual Revenues: $9.30 billion
Employees: 9,300
Ticker: NYSE: SAH
Industry/ies: Automotive Industry; Transportation

Chairman of the Board and Chief Executive Officer   Tel: (704) 566-2400
SMITH, O. Bruton

Main Headquarters
Mailing: 4401 Colwick Rd.   Tel: (704) 566-2400
Charlotte, NC 28211

Public Affairs and Related Activities Personnel

At Headquarters

ATENHAN, J. Todd   Tel: (888) 766-4218
Contact, Investor Relations
todd.atenhan@sonicautomotive.com

BYRD, Heath R.   Tel: (704) 566-2400
Executive Vice President, Chief Financial Officer

DYKE, Jeff   Tel: (704) 566-2400
Executive Vice President, Operations

SMITH, B. Scott   Tel: (704) 566-2400
President, Chief Strategic Officer and Director

Sonoco Products Company

A manufacturer of packaging products and provider of packaging services.
www.sonoco.com
Annual Revenues: $5.03 billion
Employees: 20,800
Ticker: NYSE: SON
SIC: 2621; 2655; 2675; 3089
NAICS: 322214; 322121; 322231; 326199
Industry/ies: Construction/Construction Materials

Chairman of the Board   Tel: (843) 383-7000
DELOACH, Jr., Harris E.   Fax: (843) 383-7008

President and Chief Executive Officer   Tel: (843) 383-7000
SANDERS, M. Jack   Fax: (843) 383-7008

Main Headquarters
Mailing: One N. Second St.   Tel: (843) 383-7000
Hartsville, SC 29550   Fax: (843) 383-7008
   TF: (800) 377-2692

Corporate Foundations and Giving Programs

Sonoco Foundation
Contact: David Laird
One N. Second St.   Tel: (843) 383-7000

Hartsville, SC 29550		Fax:	(843) 383-7008

Public Affairs and Related Activities Personnel

At Headquarters

BEASLEY, Joyce S.	Tel:	(843) 383-7851
Manager, Communications and Philanthropy Contact	Fax:	(843) 383-7008
joyce.beasley@sonoco.com		
LAIRD, David	Tel:	(803) 254-5601
Director, Community Impact	Fax:	(843) 383-7008
david@yourfoundation.org.		
MCLELAND, Allan H.	Tel:	(843) 383-7000
Senior Vice President, Human Resources	Fax:	(843) 383-7008
SAUNDERS, Barry L.	Tel:	(843) 383-7000
Vice President and Chief Financial Officer	Fax:	(843) 383-7008
barry.saunders@sonoco.com		
SCHRUM, Roger	Tel:	(843) 339-6018
Vice President, Investor Relations and Corporate Affairs	Fax:	(843) 383-7008
roger.schrum@sonoco.com		

SonoSite, Inc.

Manufacturer and distributor of medical devices and point-of-care ultrasound. Provider of high performance, highly miniaturized, hand-carried, all-digital ultrasound imaging devices for use in a variety of clinical applications and settings.
www.sonosite.com
Employees: 450
Ticker: NASDAQ: SONO
SIC: 3841
Industry/ies: Machinery/Equipment; Medicine/Health Care/Mental Health
Legislative Issues: AVI; MMM; VET

President and Chief Executive Officer	Tel:	(425) 951-1430
FUJITANI, Naohiro	Fax:	(425) 951-1201

Main Headquarters

Mailing:	21919 30th Dr. SE	Tel:	(425) 951-1430
	Bothell, WA 98021-3904	Fax:	(425) 951-1201

Political Action Committees
SonoSite, Inc. PAC
FEC ID: C00404251
Contact: Kevin M. Goodwin

21919 30th Dr. SE		
Bothell, WA 98021	Tel:	(425) 951-1430

Public Affairs and Related Activities Personnel

At Headquarters

AMLANI, Anil	Tel:	(425) 951-1430
Chief Commercial Officer	Fax:	(425) 951-1201
GOODWIN, Kevin M.	Tel:	(425) 951-1430
Lobbyist and PAC Treasurer	Fax:	(425) 951-1201
LECK, Brian	Tel:	(425) 951-1430
Vice President & General Manager	Fax:	(425) 951-1201
NOYES, Brian	Tel:	(425) 951-1430
Vice President, Marketing	Fax:	(425) 951-1201
PAULSON, Scott	Tel:	(425) 951-6926
Manager, Regulatory Affairs	Fax:	(425) 951-1201
scott.paulson@sonosite.com		

Sony Corporation of America

The U.S. Headquarters for the electronics, motion picture, music, retail entertainment, new technology and other software operations of the Sony Corporation, headquartered in Tokyo, Japan. Sony Corporation announced plans in 2003 to merge its music unit with the music unit of Bertelsmann AG.
www.sony.com
Employees: 33,000
SIC: 3651; 3679; 3861; 3931; 3944
NAICS: 334220; 334419; 339932; 339992; 34310
Industry/ies: Electricity & Electronics; Electronics; Energy/Electricity
Legislative Issues: CSP

Chairman and Chief Executive Officer	Tel:	(212) 833-6722
LYNTON, Michael M.	Fax:	(212) 833-6938

Main Headquarters

Mailing:	550 Madison Ave.	Tel:	(212) 833-6800
	New York City, NY 10022-3211	Fax:	(212) 833-6938
		TF:	(800) 556-3411

Washington Office

Mailing:	1667 K St. NW, Suite 200	
	Washington, DC 20006	

Corporate Foundations and Giving Programs

Sony USA Foundation Inc.

550 Madison Ave.	Tel:	(212) 833-6722
New York City, NY 10022	Fax:	(212) 833-6722

Public Affairs and Related Activities Personnel

At Headquarters

DAVIDSON, Cary	Tel:	(310) 244-6660
PAC Treasurer	Fax:	(310) 244-2467
HILL, Justin	Tel:	(212) 833-6722
General Manager	Fax:	(212) 833-6938
KOBER, Steven	Tel:	(212) 833-6722
Executive Vice President and Chief Financial Officer	Fax:	(212) 833-6938
SELIGMAN, Nicole	Tel:	(212) 833-6722
President	Fax:	(212) 833-6938
nicole.seligman@am.sony.com		

Sony Electronics, Inc.

Sony Corporation of America's consumer electronics unit makes and markets products to tap into Sony's music, films, games, and other businesses. The electronics arm sells PCs (the Sony VAIO) and their peripherals, as well as TVs, VCRs, PDAs, DVD and MP3 players, digital cameras, camcorders, CD players, and car audio items.
www.sony.com
Annual Revenues: $2.74 billion
Employees: 26,000
Industry/ies: Electricity & Electronics; Electronics; Energy/Electricity

Chairman of the Board	Tel:	(858) 942-2400
STRINGER, Howard		
howard.stringer@am.sony.com		
President and Chief Operating Officer	Tel:	(714) 585-5217
FASULO, Michael		

Main Headquarters

Mailing:	16530 Via Esprillo	Tel:	(714) 585-5217
	San Diego, CA 92127		

Washington Office

Mailing:	1667 K St. NW	Tel:	(202) 429-3652
	Suite 200		
	Washington, DC 20006		

Corporate Foundations and Giving Programs

Community Arts Partnership

16530 Via Esprillo	Tel:	(858) 942-2400
San Diego, CA 92127		

Public Affairs and Related Activities Personnel

At Headquarters

DOLAK, John	Tel:	(714) 585-5217
Vice President, Corporate Communications		
MIYOSHI, Rintaro	Tel:	(858) 942-2400
Executive Vice President and Chief Financial Officer		

At Washington Office

MORGAN, James	Tel:	(202) 429-3652
Director and Counsel, Government and Industry Affairs		
james.morgan@am.sony.com		
MULVIHILL, Christina	Tel:	(202) 429-3652
Director, Government and Public Affairs		
christina.mulvihill@am.sony.com		

Sony Music Entertainment f/k/a Sony BMG Music Entertainment

A global recorded music company and a subsidiary of consumer electronics giant Sony Corporation of America, the United States subsidiary of Japan's Sony Corporation.
www.sonymusic.com
Employees: 3,000
NAICS: 334310
Industry/ies: Arts, The; Performing Arts/Music
Legislative Issues: CPT

Chief Executive Officer	Tel:	(212) 833-8000
MORRIS, Douglas	Fax:	(212) 833-4445

Main Headquarters

Mailing:	25 Madison Ave.	Tel:	(212) 833-8000
	New York, NY 10010	Fax:	(212) 833-4445

Political Action Committees
Sony Music Entertainment Inc PAC
FEC ID: C00293837
Contact: Kevin M. Kelleher
550 Madison Ave.
32nd Floor
New York City, NY 10022

Public Affairs and Related Activities Personnel

At Headquarters

GUZZI, Perry	Tel:	(212) 833-8000
Executive Assistant, Global Industry & Government Relations	Fax:	(212) 833-4445
perry.guzzi@sonymusic.com		
JACOBSEN, Jennifer	Tel:	(212) 833-4203
Federal Lobbyist	Fax:	(212) 833-4445
Registered Federal Lobbyist		
KELLEHER, Kevin M.	Tel:	(212) 833-7100
Executive Vice President and Chief Financial Officer	Fax:	(212) 833-7416

MCDONALD, Deiadre	Tel:	(212) 833-4203
Senior Vice President, Global Industry and Government Registered Federal Lobbyist	Fax:	(212) 833-4445
SWIDLER, Julie	Tel:	(212) 833-8000
Executive Vice President, Business Affairs and General Counsel	Fax:	(212) 833-4445
YOUNG, Liz	Tel:	(212) 833-8000
Executive Vice President, Corporate Communications	Fax:	(212) 833-4445

Sony Pictures Entertainment, Inc.

Sony Pictures Entertainment (SPE) is a subsidiary of Sony Corporation of America, a subsidiary of Tokyo based Sony Corporation. SPE's global operations encompass motion picture production and distribution; television production and distribution; home entertainment acquisition and distribution; a global channel network; digital content creation and distribution; operation of studio facilities; development of new entertainment products, services and technologies; and distribution of entertainment in more than 140 countries.
www.sonypictures.com
Annual Revenues: $241.60 million
Employees: 4,000
Industry/ies: Entertainment; Sports/Leisure/Entertainment
Legislative Issues: CPT; ECN; TAX; TRD

Chairman and Chief Executive Officer	Tel:	(310) 244-4000
LYNTON, Michael	Fax:	(310) 244-2626

Main Headquarters
Mailing:	10202 W. Washington Blvd.	Tel:	(310) 244-4000
	Culver City, CA 90232	Fax:	(310) 244-2626

Political Action Committees
Sony Pictures Entertainment, Inc. PAC
FEC ID: C00282038
Contact: Cary Davidson
10202 W. Washington Blvd.	Tel:	(310) 244-4000
Culver City, CA 90232	Fax:	(310) 244-2626

Contributions to Candidates: $139,500 (2015-2016)
Democrats: $70,500; Republicans: $67,500; Other: $1,500

Principal Recipients

HOUSE
GOODLATTE, ROBERT W. (REP-VA)

Corporate Foundations and Giving Programs
Sony Pictures Entertainment Contributions Program
10202 W. Washington Blvd.	Tel:	(310) 244-4000
Culver City, CA 90232	Fax:	(310) 244-2626

Public Affairs and Related Activities Personnel

At Headquarters
DAVIDSON, Cary	Tel:	(310) 244-4000
PAC Treasurer	Fax:	(310) 244-2626
HENDLER, David C.	Tel:	(310) 244-4000
Senior Executive Vice President and Chief Financial Officer	Fax:	(310) 244-2626
PARKER , Kerry	Tel:	(207) 292-8346
Contact, Public Relations	Fax:	(310) 244-2626
Kerry.Parker@premierpr.com		
POBER, Janice	Tel:	(310) 244-4000
Senior Vice President, Corporate Social Responsibility	Fax:	(310) 244-2626
ROSE, George	Tel:	(310) 244-4000
Executive Vice President, Worldwide People and Organization	Fax:	(310) 244-2626
SELIGMAN, Nicole	Tel:	(310) 244-4000
President	Fax:	(310) 244-2626
WEAVER, Keith	Tel:	(310) 244-4000
Executive Vice President, Global Policy and External Affairs	Fax:	(310) 244-2626
WEIL, Leah	Tel:	(310) 244-4000
Senior Executive Vice President and General Counsel	Fax:	(310) 244-2626

Sopris West Education Services

An education products and services company.
www.soprislearning.com
Industry/ies: Communications; Education; Media/Mass Communication

Main Headquarters
Mailing:	C/O Cambium Learning Group	Tel:	(800) 547-6747
	17855 Dallas Pkwy., Suite 400	Fax:	(888) 819-7767
	Dallas, TX 75287	TF:	(800) 547-6747

Public Affairs and Related Activities Personnel

At Headquarters
PEREIRA, Jahnell	Tel:	(800) 547-6747
Vice President Director, Marketing	Fax:	(888) 819-7767
jahnell.pereira@soprislearning.com		

At Other Offices
BURKE, Laurie	Tel:	(303) 651-2829
Contact, Media Relations	Fax:	(888) 819-7767
Cambium Learning Group, 4093 Specialty Pl.		

Longmont, CO 80504
LBurke@cambiumlearning.com

Sotheby's Holdings Inc.

Operates as an auctioneer of authenticated fine art, decorative art, and jewelry.
www.sothebys.com
Annual Revenues: $912.35 million
Employees: 1,520
Ticker: NYSE: BID
SIC: 7389
Industry/ies: Arts, The; Auctions
Legislative Issues: ART; CPT

President and Chief Executive Officer	Tel:	(212) 606-7000
SMITH, Thomas S.	Fax:	(212) 606-7107

Main Headquarters
Mailing:	1334 York Ave.	Tel:	(212) 606-7000
	New York City, NY 10021	Fax:	(212) 606-7107

Corporate Foundations and Giving Programs
Sotheby's Contribution Program
1334 York Ave.
New York City, NY 10021

Public Affairs and Related Activities Personnel

At Headquarters
ALEXANDER, Susan	Tel:	(212) 606-7204
Executive Vice President, Worldwide Head of Human Resources	Fax:	(212) 606-7107
susan.alexander@sothebys.com		
DAYBELGE, Leyla	Tel:	(212) 606-7000
Contact, Press Office	Fax:	(212) 606-7107
GIOIA, Lauren	Tel:	(212) 606-7000
Executive Vice President, Worldwide Director, Communications	Fax:	(212) 606-7107
GOODMAN, David	Tel:	(212) 606-7000
Executive Vice President, Digital Development and Marketing	Fax:	(212) 606-7107
GOSS, Michael	Tel:	(212) 606-7000
Executive Vice President, Chief Financial Officer	Fax:	(212) 606-7107
KLEMANN, II, Gilbert L.	Tel:	(212) 606-7000
Executive Vice President, Worldwide General Counsel and Secretary	Fax:	(212) 606-7107
LEVINE, Jane A.	Tel:	(212) 606-7000
Senior Vice President and Worldwide Director, Compliance	Fax:	(212) 606-7107
NADLER, Lisa	Tel:	(212) 606-7000
Executive Vice President, Worldwide Head, Human Resources	Fax:	(212) 606-7107
OLSOFF , Jonathan A.	Tel:	(212) 606-7000
Executive Vice President, Worldwide General Counsel	Fax:	(212) 606-7107
PARK, Jennifer	Tel:	(212) 894-1023
Vice President, Strategic Planning and Investor Relations	Fax:	(212) 606-7107
Jennifer.Park@Sothebys.com		
PHILLIPS, Diana	Tel:	(212) 606-7176
Executive Vice President, Worldwide Director, Press and Corporate Affairs	Fax:	(212) 606-7381
diana.phillips@sothebys.com		
SCHWARTZ , David G.	Tel:	(212) 606-7000
Senior Vice President, Chief Securities Counsel and Corporate Secretary	Fax:	(212) 606-7107

SoundExchange

SoundExchange is an independent, nonprofit performance rights organization.
www.soundexchange.com
Annual Revenues: $19.88 million
Employees: 10
Industry/ies: Communications; Media/Mass Communication
Legislative Issues: CPT; CSP; TRD

President and Chief Executive Officer	Tel:	(202) 640-5858
HUPPE, Michael	Fax:	(202) 640-5859
mhuppe@soundexchange.com		

Main Headquarters
Mailing:	733 Tenth St. NW	Tel:	(202) 640-5858
	Tenth Floor	Fax:	(202) 640-5859
	Washington, DC 20001		

Political Action Committees
Soundexchange Inc Legislative Fund PAC
FEC ID: C00540153
Contact: Anjula Singh
733 Tenth St. NW	Tel:	(202) 524-7839
Tenth Floor		
Washington, DC 20001		

Contributions to Candidates: $3,000 (2015-2016)
Republicans: $3,000

Public Affairs and Related Activities Personnel

At Headquarters

DICK , Rebecca
Contact, Communications
Tel: (202) 524-7839
Fax: (202) 640-5859

MASSIMINO, Julia A.
Federal Lobbyist
Registered Federal Lobbyist
Tel: (202) 524-7839
Fax: (202) 640-5859

RUSHING, Colin
Senior Vice President and General Counsel
Tel: (202) 640-5858
Fax: (202) 640-5859

SINGH, Anjula
Chief Financial Officer
Tel: (202) 640-5858
Fax: (202) 640-5859

At Other Offices

EISENBERG, Mark
Senior Vice President, Strategic Initiatives
1121 14th St. NW, Suite 700
Washington, DC 20006
Tel: (202) 640-5880
Fax: (202) 640-5859

GRAVATT, Laurie Bendall
Federal Lobbyist
1121 14th St. NW, Suite 700
Washington, DC 20006
Tel: (202) 640-5858
Fax: (202) 640-5859

PETERSON, Jacqueline
Senior Vice President, Communications
1121 14th St. NW, Suite 700
Washington, DC 20006
Tel: (202) 640-5880
Fax: (202) 640-5859

SIMSON, John
Executive Director
1121 14th St. NW, Suite 700
Washington, DC 20006
Registered Federal Lobbyist
Tel: (202) 640-5858
Fax: (202) 640-5859

Sourcefire

A network assets protection company.
www.sourcefire.com
Employees: 644
Ticker: NASDAQ (GM): FIRE
SIC: 7374
Industry/ies: Computer/Technology; Defense/Homeland Security; Government-Related; Science; Scientific Research

Chairman of the Board
POLK, Steven R.
Tel: (410) 290-1616
Fax: (410) 290-0024

Chief Executive Officer
BECKER, John
Tel: (410) 290-1616
Fax: (410) 290-0024

Main Headquarters
Mailing: 9770 Patuxent Woods Dr.
Suite 200
Columbia, MD 21046
Tel: (410) 290-1616
Fax: (410) 290-0024
TF: (800) 917-4134

Public Affairs and Related Activities Personnel

At Headquarters

HEADLEY, Todd
Chief Financial Officer
todd.headley@sourcefire.com
Tel: (410) 290-1616
Fax: (410) 290-0024

MCDONOUGH, Tom M.
President and Chief Operating Officer
tom.mcdonough@sourcefire.com
Tel: (410) 290-1616
Fax: (410) 290-0024

MCNITT, Douglas
General Counsel
Tel: (410) 290-1616
Fax: (410) 290-0024

PENDERGRAST, Leslie
Chief People Officer
Tel: (410) 290-1616
Fax: (410) 290-0024

PERRY, Michele M.
Chief Marketing Officer
Tel: (410) 290-1616
Fax: (410) 290-0024

SOLOMON , Marc
Chief Marketing Officer
msolomon@sourcefire.com
Tel: (410) 290-1616
Fax: (410) 290-0024

South Jersey Gas Company

Provides natural gas utility service to residential, commercial and industrial customers. Atlantic City Gas Company and People's Gas Company merged to form South Jersey Gas Company.
www.southjerseygas.com
Annual Revenues: $909.65 million
Employees: 720
Ticker: NYSE: SJI
SIC: 4923
Industry/ies: Utilities

Chairman of the Board, President and Chief Executive Officer
GRAHAM, Edward J.
Tel: (609) 561-9000
Fax: (609) 561-8225

Main Headquarters
Mailing: One S. Jersey Plaza
Folsom, NJ 08037
Tel: (609) 561-9000
Fax: (609) 561-8225
TF: (888) 766-9900

Corporate Foundations and Giving Programs

South Jersey Gas Company Contributions Program
One S. Jersey Plaza
Folsom, NJ 08037
Tel: (609) 561-9000
Fax: (609) 561-8225

Public Affairs and Related Activities Personnel

At Headquarters

CLARK, Stephen H.
Chief Financial Officer
sclark@sjindustries.com
Tel: (609) 561-9000
Fax: (609) 561-8225

MCENDY, Kathleen A.
Senior Executive
Tel: (609) 561-9000
Fax: (609) 561-8225

MERRITT-EPPS, Gina
Associate General Counsel and Assistant Secretary
Tel: (609) 561-9000
Fax: (609) 561-8225

TRAVALINE, Marissa
Director, Stakeholder Relations
Tel: (609) 561-9000
Fax: (609) 561-8225

Southcoast Health System

A not-for-profit charitable organization formed from the merged entity of St. Luke's Health Care System, Charlton Health System, and Tobey Health Systems. It has multiple access points, offering an integrated continuum of health services throughout Southeastern Massachusetts and East Bay, Rhode Island.
www.southcoast.org
Annual Revenues: $884.00 million
Employees: 7,200
Industry/ies: Medicine/Health Care/Mental Health
Legislative Issues: MMM

Chairman of the Board
KUNZ, Elizabeth H.
Tel: (508) 961-5000
Fax: (508) 961-5297

President and Chief Executive Officer
HOVAN, Keith A.
Tel: (508) 961-5000
Fax: (508) 961-5297

Main Headquarters
Mailing: 101 Page St.
New Bedford, MA 02740
Tel: (508) 961-5000
Fax: (508) 961-5297
TF: (800) 497-1727

Corporate Foundations and Giving Programs

Southcoast Philanthropy
Contact: Jack Dresser
101 Page St.
New Bedford, MA 02740

Public Affairs and Related Activities Personnel

At Headquarters

BANACH, Ellen
Senior Vice President, Strategic Services
Tel: (508) 679-7234
Fax: (508) 961-5297

BODENMANN, Linda
Executive Vice President & Chief Operating Officer
Tel: (508) 961-5000
Fax: (508) 961-5297

BOYLE, Esq., Lisa
General Counsel & Corporate Compliance
Tel: (508) 961-5000
Fax: (508) 961-5297

CANESSA, Stephen
Vice President, Marketing & Government Affairs
Tel: (508) 961-5000
Fax: (508) 961-5297

COHENNO, Peter
Public Information Officer & New Media Specialist
cohennop@southcoast.org
Tel: (508) 973-5280
Fax: (508) 961-5297

DEJESUS, Jr., David
Senior Vice President, Human Resources
DeJesusD@southcoast.org
Tel: (508) 961-5174
Fax: (508) 961-5297

DRESSER, Jack
Senior Vice President & Chief Philanthropy Officer
Tel: (508) 961-5000
Fax: (508) 961-5297

Southeast Anesthesiology Consultants

A physician anesthesiology and pain management practice in the Carolinas and Virginia.
www.seanesthesiology.com
Annual Revenues: $6.70 million
Industry/ies: Medicine/Health Care/Mental Health

Executive Director and Chief Financial Officer
RAUH, CPA, Richard
richardrauh@seanesthesiology.com
Tel: (704) 355-7150
Fax: (704) 355-7102

Main Headquarters
Mailing: 1000 Blythe Blvd.
Charlotte, NC 28203
Tel: (704) 355-2000
Fax: (704) 355-7102

Corporate Foundations and Giving Programs

Southeast Anesthesiology Consultants Contributions Program
1000 Blythe Blvd.
Charlotte, NC 28203

Public Affairs and Related Activities Personnel

At Headquarters

BOSTEDO-CONWAY, Kristen
Director, Marketing
kbconway@seanesthesiology.com
Tel: (704) 355-7150
Fax: (704) 355-7102

WALTERS, Jamal
Human Resources Generalist
jamalwalters@seanesthesiology.com

Tel: (704) 355-7150
Fax: (704) 355-7102

WALTMAN, Barbara
Contact, Credentialing

Tel: (704) 355-2000
Fax: (704) 355-7102

Southeast Milk, Inc.

Engaged in the manufacture of whole diary products and prepared feeds.
www.southeastmilk.org
Employees: 300
Industry/ies: Dairy Industry; Food And Beverage Industry
Legislative Issues: AGR; FUE; TAX

Chief Executive Officer
BIKOWITZ, Paul W.

Tel: (352) 245-2437
Fax: (352) 245-9434

Main Headquarters
Mailing: P.O. Box 3790
Belleview, FL 34421

Political Action Committees
Southeast Milk, Inc. PAC
FEC ID: C00359984
Contact: Paul W. Bikowitz
P.O. Box 3790
Belleview, FL 34421

Contributions to Candidates: $5,500 (2015-2016)
Democrats: $1,000; Republicans: $4,500

Public Affairs and Related Activities Personnel

At Other Offices

ANTOINE, Albert
Chief Financial Officer
19039 121st Rd.
McAlpin, FL 32062

Tel: (352) 245-9607
Fax: (352) 245-9434

HODGE, Ray
Federal Lobbyist
19039 121st Rd.
McAlpin, FL 32062
rhodge@southeastmilk.org

Tel: (407) 257-6782
Fax: (352) 245-9434

MOSHER, Michele
Manager, Human Resources and Accounting Director
19039 121st Rd.
McAlpin, FL 32062

Tel: (352) 245-9607
Fax: (352) 245-9434

Southeast QSR, LLC

Operates and manages multi-unit quick service restaurants.
Industry/ies: Food And Beverage Industry; Food Industry
Legislative Issues: CIV; ENG; LBR

Main Headquarters
Mailing: 4107 Columbia Rd
Martinez, GA 30907

Tel: (706) 855-6395

Public Affairs and Related Activities Personnel

At Headquarters

STRACZEWSKI, Jason
Vice President, Government Affairs
Registered Federal Lobbyist

Tel: (706) 855-6395

Southern California Edison Company

An electric utility.
www.sce.com
Annual Revenues: $12.56 billion
Employees: 18,069
Ticker: NYSE Amex: SCE/PB
SIC: 4911
Industry/ies: Utilities

President and Chief Executive Officer
CRAVER, JR., Theodore F.

Tel: (626) 302-1212
Fax: (626) 302-2517

Main Headquarters
Mailing: 2244 Walnut Grove Ave.
P.O. Box 800
Rosemead, CA 91770

Tel: (626) 302-1212
Fax: (626) 302-2517
TF: (800) 655-4555

Washington Office
Mailing: 555 12th St. NW
Suite 640
Washington, DC 20004

Tel: (202) 393-3075

Corporate Foundations and Giving Programs
California State University Foundation's Early Assessment Program (EAP)
Contact: James M. Rosser
2244 Walnut Grove Ave.
Rosemead, CA 91770

Tel: (626) 302-1212
Fax: (626) 302-2517

Public Affairs and Related Activities Personnel

At Headquarters

CLAYTON, Janet
Senior Vice President, Corporate Communications

Tel: (626) 302-1212
Fax: (626) 302-2517

COLEMAN, Charles
Contact, Media Relations
colemance@sce.com

Tel: (626) 302-7982
Fax: (626) 302-2517

CONROY, Steve
Director, Corporate Communications
steven.conroy@sce.com

Tel: (626) 695-7843
Fax: (626) 302-2517

CUNNINGHAM, Scott
Vice President, Investor Relations
scott.cunningham@edisonintl.com

Tel: (626) 302-2540

FOSTER, Bruce C.
Senior Vice President, Regulatory Affairs
fosterbc@sce.com

Tel: (626) 302-1212
Fax: (626) 302-2517

GUTIERREZ, Veronica
Vice President, Local Public Affairs
veronica.gutierrez@sce.com

Tel: (626) 302-1212
Fax: (626) 302-2517

KRACKE, Dana
Vice president, Safety, Security and Compliance

Tel: (626) 302-1212
Fax: (626) 302-2517

MATHEWS, Barbara E.
Vice President, Associate General Counsel, Chief Governance Officer and Corporate Secretary
barbara.mathews@sce.com

Tel: (626) 302-1212
Fax: (626) 302-2517

MCLEOD, Christine
Principal Advisor, Regulatory Policy and Affairs

Tel: (626) 302-3947
Fax: (626) 302-2517

MILLER, Patricia
Vice President, Human Resources
patricia.miller@sce.com

Tel: (626) 302-1212
Fax: (626) 302-2517

MONTOYA, Michael D.
Vice President and Compliance Officer

Tel: (626) 302-1212
Fax: (626) 302-2517

PICKETT, Stephen E.
Executive Vice President, External Relations
stephen.pickett@sce.com

Tel: (626) 302-1212
Fax: (626) 302-2517

RIGATTI, Maria
Senior Vice President and Chief Financial Officer

Tel: (626) 302-1212
Fax: (626) 302-2517

STARCK, Leslie E.
Senior Vice President, Regulatory and Policy Affairs
les.starck@sce.com

Tel: (626) 302-1212
Fax: (626) 302-2517

SWARTZ, Russell C.
Senior Vice President and General Counsel

Tel: (626) 302-1212
Fax: (626) 302-2517

VASQUEZ, Lynda L.
Vice President, Public Affairs

Tel: (626) 302-1212
Fax: (626) 302-2517

At Washington Office

MILLER, Matt
Manager and Federal Lobbyist

Tel: (202) 393-3075

Southern California Gas Company

A gas utility company.
www.socalgas.com
Annual Revenues: $3.82 billion
Employees: 7,000
SIC: 4922
Industry/ies: Utilities

President and Chief Executive Officer
ARRIOLA, Dennis

Tel: (213) 244-1200
Fax: (214) 244-3897

Main Headquarters
Mailing: 1801 S. Atlantic Blvd.
Monterey Park, CA 91754

Corporate Foundations and Giving Programs
Southern California Gas Company Contributions Program
555 W. Fifth St.
Los Angeles, CA 90013-1011

Tel: (213) 244-1200
Fax: (213) 244-3897

Public Affairs and Related Activities Personnel

At Other Offices

KEITH, Erbin
Senior Vice President, External Affairs & General Counsel
555 W. Fifth St.
Los Angeles, CA 90013-1011

Tel: (213) 244-1200
Fax: (214) 244-3897

KING, Denise
Contact, Media Relations
555 W. Fifth St.
Los Angeles, CA 90013-1011

Tel: (877) 643-2331
Fax: (214) 244-3897

MENDOZA, Javier
Strategic Communications Professional
555 W. Fifth St.
Los Angeles, CA 90013-1011

Tel: (877) 643-2331
Fax: (214) 244-3897

SCHAVRIEN, Lee
Chief Administrative Officer
555 W. Fifth St.

Tel: (213) 244-1200
Fax: (214) 244-3897

Los Angeles, CA 90013-1011
SCHLAX, Robert M.
Vice President, Controller and Chief Financial Officer
555 W. Fifth St.
Los Angeles, CA 90013-1011 — Tel: (213) 244-1200 Fax: (214) 244-3897

SKOPEC, Daniel
Vice President, Regulatory and Legislative Affairs
555 W. Fifth St.
Los Angeles, CA 90013-1011 — Tel: (213) 244-1200 Fax: (214) 244-3897

SNYDER, Hal D.
Vice President, Human Resources, Diversity and Inclusion
555 W. Fifth St.
Los Angeles, CA 90013-1011 — Tel: (213) 244-1200 Fax: (214) 244-3897

Southern Company

An electric utility holding company. Parent company of Alabama Power, Georgia Power, Gulf Power, Mississippi Power, and Southern Nuclear. Headquartered in Atlanta, GA.
www.southerncompany.com
Annual Revenues: $18.01 billion
Employees: 26,369
Ticker: NYSE: SO
Industry/ies: Energy/Electricity; Utilities
Legislative Issues: BUD; CAW; CDT; ENG; ENV; HOM; INT; NAT; SCI; TAX; TEC; TRA; UTI

Chairman of the Board, President and Chief Executive Officer
FANNING, Thomas A. — Tel: (404) 506-5000 Fax: (404) 506-0455

Main Headquarters
Mailing: 30 Ivan Allen Jr. Blvd. NW
Atlanta, GA 30308 — Tel: (404) 506-5000 Fax: (404) 506-0455 TF: (866) 506-5333

Washington Office
Mailing: 601 Pennsylvania Ave. NW
Suite 800
Washington, DC 20004 — Tel: (202) 261-5000 Fax: (202) 296-7937

Political Action Committees
Southern Company Employees PAC
FEC ID: C00144774
Contact: James A. Mason Jr.
241 Ralph McGill Blvd. NE
BIN 10111
Atlanta, GA 30308

Contributions to Candidates: $300,625 (2015-2016)
Democrats: $71,500; Republicans: $229,125

Principal Recipients

SENATE
BLUNT, ROY (REP-MO)
PAUL, RAND (REP-KY)

HOUSE
CROWLEY, JOSEPH (DEM-NY)
HURD, WILLIAM (REP-TX)
RYAN, PAUL D. (REP-WI)

Corporate Foundations and Giving Programs
Southern Company Contributions Program
30 Ivan Allen Jr. Blvd. NW
Atlanta, GA 30308 — Tel: (404) 506-5000 Fax: (404) 506-0455

Public Affairs and Related Activities Personnel
At Headquarters

BEATTIE, Art P.
Executive Vice President and Chief Financial Officer — Tel: (404) 506-5000 Fax: (404) 506-0455

COHILAS, Terri
Project Manager — Tel: (404) 506-5333 Fax: (404) 506-0455

GREENE, Kimberly S.
Executive Vice President and Chief Operating Officer — Tel: (404) 506-5000 Fax: (404) 506-0455

KERR II, James Y.
Executive Vice President, General Counsel and Chief Compliance Officer — Tel: (404) 506-5000 Fax: (404) 506-0455

KUNDERT, Glen
Vice President, Investor Relations
gakunder2@southernco.com — Tel: (404) 506-5135 Fax: (404) 506-0455

PHILLIPS, Carrie H.
Manager, Public Affairs
chphilli@southernco.com — Tel: (205) 992-5168 Fax: (404) 506-0455

WOMACK, Christopher C.
President, External Affairs — Tel: (404) 506-5000 Fax: (404) 506-0455

At Washington Office

ANDERSON, Bryan
Vice President, Governmental Affairs
Registered Federal Lobbyist — Tel: (202) 261-5000 Fax: (202) 296-7937

BLACK, Noelle — Tel: (202) 261-5000
Vice President, Federal Regulatory Affairs
Registered Federal Lobbyist — Fax: (202) 296-7937

BURKE, Stoney G.
Director, Federal Legislative Affairs
Registered Federal Lobbyist — Tel: (202) 261-5000 Fax: (202) 296-7937

COX, S. Lofton S.
Federal Lobbyist
slcox@southernco.com — Tel: (202) 261-5000 Fax: (202) 296-7937

HARRY, Raymond L.
Director, Environmental Issues
lrharry@southernco.com
Registered Federal Lobbyist — Tel: (202) 261-5000 Fax: (202) 296-7937

LAWRENCE, H. Adam
Director, Federal Legislative Affairs
halawren@southernco.com
Registered Federal Lobbyist — Tel: (202) 261-5000 Fax: (202) 296-7937

MCCOOL, Jr., James M.
Director, Federal Legislative Affairs
Registered Federal Lobbyist — Tel: (202) 261-5000 Fax: (202) 296-7937

MOOR, Karl R.
Senior Vice President and Chief General Counsel
Registered Federal Lobbyist — Tel: (202) 261-5000 Fax: (202) 296-7937

NIX, Leroy
Federal Lobbyist
ldnix@southernco.com
Registered Federal Lobbyist — Tel: (202) 261-5000 Fax: (202) 296-7937

ORMES, Gifford
Federal Lobbyist
Registered Federal Lobbyist — Tel: (202) 261-5000 Fax: (202) 296-7937

ORR, Scott F.
Federal Lobbyist
Registered Federal Lobbyist — Tel: (202) 261-5000 Fax: (202) 296-7937

PEMBERTON, John L.
Vice President, Governmental Affairs
Registered Federal Lobbyist — Tel: (202) 261-5000 Fax: (202) 296-7937

PUNYKO, Carl A.
Federal Lobbyist
capunyko@southernco.com — Tel: (202) 261-5000 Fax: (202) 296-7937

RIITH, Michael
Director, Federal Legislative Affairs
Registered Federal Lobbyist — Tel: (202) 261-5000 Fax: (202) 296-7937

SMITH, Gregory L.
Contact, Government Relations
Registered Federal Lobbyist — Tel: (202) 261-5000 Fax: (202) 296-7937

THORNTON, Billy F.
Federal Lobbyist — Tel: (202) 261-5000 Fax: (202) 296-7937

WOLAK, Jeanne H.
Vice President, Federal Legislative Affairs
Registered Federal Lobbyist — Tel: (202) 261-5000 Fax: (202) 296-7937

WOODS, Robert F.
Federal Lobbyist
RFWoods@southernco.com — Tel: (202) 261-5000 Fax: (202) 296-7937

At Other Offices

MASON, Jr., James A.
PAC Treasurer
241 Ralph McGill Blvd. NE, BIN 10111
Atlanta, GA 30308
Mail Stop BIN 10111 — Tel: (404) 506-7750

Southern Nuclear Operating Company

A subsidiary of Southern Company. Southern Nuclear operates three plants, Farley, Hatch and Vogtle. These plants provide about 20 percent of the electricity used in Alabama and Georgia.
www.southerncompany.com/about-us/our-business/sout
Employees: 3,000
Industry/ies: Energy/Electricity

Chairman, President and Chief Executive Officer
KUCZYNSKI, Stephen — Tel: (205) 992-5000 Fax: (205) 992-5000

Main Headquarters
Mailing: 40 Inverness Center Pkwy.
Birmingham, AL 35242 — Tel: (205) 992-5000 Fax: (205) 992-5000

Political Action Committees
Southern Company - Southern Nuclear Operating Company Inc. PAC
FEC ID: C00250407
Contact: Robert M. Cannon
40 Inverness Center Pkwy.
Birmingham, AL 35242 — Tel: (205) 992-5000

Contributions to Candidates: $58,125 (2015-2016)
Democrats: $4,500; Republicans: $53,625

Public Affairs and Related Activities Personnel
At Headquarters

CANNON, Robert M.
PAC Treasurer

Tel: (205) 992-5000
Fax: (205) 992-5000

At Other Offices

PHILLIPS, Carrie H.
Manager, Public Affairs
30 Ivan Allen Jr. Blvd. NW
Atlanta, GA 30308
chphilli@southernco.com

Tel: (205) 992-5168
Fax: (404) 506-0455

Southern States Cooperative

A farmer-owned cooperative.
www.southernstates.com
Annual Revenues: $1.83 billion
Employees: 4,000
SIC: 5190
Industry/ies: Agriculture/Agronomy

Chairman of the Board
EAST, John

Tel: (804) 281-1000
Fax: (804) 281-1413

President and Chief Executive Officer
SCRIBNER, Thomas R.

Tel: (804) 281-1000
Fax: (804) 281-1413

Main Headquarters
Mailing: P.O. Box 26234
    Richmond, VA 23260-6234

Tel: (804) 281-1000
Fax: (804) 281-1413

Public Affairs and Related Activities Personnel

At Headquarters

NEWTON, Leslie
Chief Financial Officer

Tel: (804) 281-1000
Fax: (804) 281-1413

Southern Union Company

A natural gas distribution, pipeline transmission and storage company. Southern Union Company is a subsidiary of ETP Holdco.
www.southernunionco.com
Annual Revenues: $2.67 billion
Employees: 2,256
Ticker: NYSE: SUG
SIC: 4922
Industry/ies: Fuels See Coal, Gas, Oil, Petroleum; Natural Resources; Petroleum Industry

Chairman of the Board and Chief Executive Officer
LINDEMANN, George L.

Tel: (713) 989-2000
Fax: (713) 989-1121

Main Headquarters
Mailing: 5051 Westheimer Rd.
    Houston, TX 77056

Tel: (713) 989-2000
Fax: (713) 989-1121

Corporate Foundations and Giving Programs

Southern Union Company Charitable Foundation
5444 Westheimer Rd.
Houston, TX 77056

Tel: (713) 989-2000
Fax: (713) 989-1121

Public Affairs and Related Activities Personnel

At Headquarters

GAUDOSI, Monica M.
Senior Vice President and General Counsel

Tel: (713) 989-2000
Fax: (713) 989-1121

MARSHALL, Richard N.
Senior Vice President and Chief Financial Officer

Tel: (713) 989-2000
Fax: (713) 989-1121

At Other Offices

BOUCHARD, Andre C.
PAC Contact
417 Lackawanna Ave.
Scranton, PA 18503

GAVIN, Mara
Federal Lobbyist
767 Fifth Ave., 50th Floor
New York City, NY 10153

Tel: (212) 659-3208
Fax: (212) 754-5789

GRAF, Jon
PAC Contact
1301 S. Mopac, Suite 400
Austin, TX 78746

WALSH, Jack
Vice President, Investor Relations
767 Fifth Ave., 50th Floor
New York City, NY 10153
jack.walsh@sug.com

Tel: (212) 659-3208
Fax: (212) 754-5789

Southern Wine and Spirits of America

A wholesale distributor of wine and distilled beverages.
www.southernwine.com
Industry/ies: Food And Beverage Industry

Chairman
CHAPLIN, Harvey R.
harveychaplin@southernwine.com

Tel: (305) 625-4171
Fax: (305) 625-1720

President and Chief Executive Officer
CHAPLIN, Wayne E.

Tel: (305) 625-4171
Fax: (305) 625-4720

Main Headquarters
Mailing: 1600 N. W. 163rd St.
    Miami, FL 33169

Tel: (305) 625-4171
Fax: (305) 625-4720

Political Action Committees
Southern Wine and Spirits PAC
FEC ID: C00217877
Contact: Steven R. Becker
1600 NW 163rd St.
Miami, FL 33169

Tel: (305) 625-4171
Fax: (305) 625-4720

Contributions to Candidates: $99,800 (2015-2016)
Democrats: $74,800; Republicans: $25,000

Principal Recipients

SENATE
SCHUMER, CHARLES E (DEM-NY)

HOUSE
DEUTCH, THEODORE ELIOT (DEM-FL)
FRANKEL, LOIS J. (DEM-FL)
NEGRON, REBECCA (REP-FL)
ROS-LEHTINEN, ILEANA THE HON. (REP-FL)
SCHULTZ, DEBBIE WASSERMAN (DEM-FL)
SHERMAN, BRAD (DEM-CA)

Corporate Foundations and Giving Programs

The Southern Wine & Spirits Foundation
1600 NW 163rd St.
Miami, FL 33169

Tel: (305) 625-4171
Fax: (305) 625-4720

Public Affairs and Related Activities Personnel

At Headquarters

BECKER, Steven R.
Executive Vice President and PAC Treasurer

Tel: (305) 625-4171
Fax: (305) 625-4720

HAGER, Lee F.
Executive Vice President, Secretary and Chief Administrative Officer

Tel: (305) 625-4171
Fax: (305) 625-4720

KRAUSS, Mark
Vice President, Human Resources

Tel: (305) 625-4171
Fax: (305) 625-4720

PRESTON, John R.
Vice President, Finance and Administration

Tel: (305) 625-4171
Fax: (305) 625-4720

VASSAR, Brad
Executive Vice President and Chief Operating Officer

Tel: (305) 625-4171
Fax: (305) 625-4720

Southstream Seafood

Produces and markets frozen seafood products to food service and retail customers.
www.southstream.com
Industry/ies: Food And Beverage Industry

Main Headquarters
Mailing: 100 Metro Center Blvd.
    Warwick, RI 02886

Tel: (401) 737-2300
Fax: (401) 737-2350
TF: (800) 600-2300

Public Affairs and Related Activities Personnel

At Headquarters

POKORSKI, Christopher
Owner

Tel: (401) 737-2300
Fax: (401) 737-2350

Southwest Airlines

A short haul, low-fare passenger air carrier. The mission of Southwest Airlines is dedication to the highest quality of Customer Service delivered with a sense of warmth, friendliness, individual pride, and Company Spirit.
www.southwest.com
Annual Revenues: $20.06 billion
Employees: 50,911
Ticker: NYSE: LUV
SIC: 4512
NAICS: 481111
Industry/ies: Aerospace/Aviation; Airlines; Transportation; Travel/Tourism/Lodging
Legislative Issues: AVI; BUD; FIN; HOM; TAX

Chairman of the Board, President and Chief Executive Officer
KELLY, Gary C.

Tel: (214) 792-4000
Fax: (214) 792-5015

Main Headquarters
Mailing: 2702 Love Field Dr.
    Dallas, TX 75235

Tel: (214) 792-4000
Fax: (214) 792-5015
TF: (800) 435-9792

Washington Office
Mailing: 1901 L St. NW
    Suite 640
    Washington, DC 20036

Tel: (202) 263-6280
Fax: (202) 263-6291

Political Action Committees
Southwest Airlines Company Freedom Fund PAC

FEC ID: C00341602
Contact: Jose Luis Sanchez
2702 Love Field Dr.
P.O. Box 36611
Dallas, TX 75235

Contributions to Candidates: $99,198 (2015-2016)
Democrats: $27,000; Republicans: $72,198

Corporate Foundations and Giving Programs

Southwest Airlines Contributions Program
2702 Love Field Dr.   Tel: (214) 792-4000
P.O. Box 36611   Fax: (214) 792-4000
Dallas, TX 75235-1647

Public Affairs and Related Activities Personnel

At Headquarters

GREEN, Ryan C.   Tel: (214) 792-4000
Vice President, Marketing   Fax: (214) 792-5015

JORDAN, Robert E.   Tel: (214) 792-4000
Executive Vice President and Chief Commercial Officer   Fax: (214) 792-5015

LAMB, Jeff   Tel: (214) 792-4000
Executive Vice President, Corporate Services   Fax: (214) 792-5015

NEALON , Tom   Tel: (214) 792-4000
Executive Vice President, Strategy and Innovation   Fax: (214) 792-5015

NIETO, Laura   Tel: (214) 792-4000
Senior Manager, Community Affairs and Grassroots   Fax: (214) 792-5015

RICHARDSON, David M.   Tel: (202) 263-6287
Director, Governmental Affairs   Fax: (214) 792-5015
david.richardson@wnco.com
Registered Federal Lobbyist

RICKS, Ron   Tel: (214) 792-4000
Vice Chairman, Board of Directors   Fax: (214) 792-5015

ROMO, Tammy   Tel: (214) 792-4000
Executive Vice President and Chief Financial Officer   Fax: (214) 792-5015

RUTHERFORD, Linda B.   Tel: (214) 792-4625
Vice President, Chief Communications Officer   Fax: (214) 792-5015

SHAW , Mark R.   Tel: (214) 792-4000
Vice President General Counsel and Corporate Secretary   Fax: (214) 792-5015

VAN DE VEN, Michael G.   Tel: (214) 792-4000
Executive Vice President and Chief Operating Officer   Fax: (214) 792-5015

VAN EATON, Jason   Tel: (214) 792-4000
Vice President, Governmental Affairs   Fax: (214) 792-5015

WEBER, Julie   Tel: (214) 792-4000
Vice President, People   Fax: (214) 792-5015

At Other Offices

SANCHEZ, Jose Luis   Tel: (214) 792-4415
PAC Treasurer
P.O. Box 36611
Dallas, TX 75235
Mail Stop HDQ 4GA

SAUVINET, Dorothy   Tel: (214) 792-4415
Federal Lobbyist
P.O. Box 36611
Dallas, TX 75235

Southwest Bank of Texas

See listing on page 46 under Amegy Bank NA

Southwest Gas Corporation

A natural gas company-Southwest Gas Corporation is principally engaged in the business of purchasing, distributing and transporting natural gas to residential, commercial and industrial customers in the southwestern United States.
www.swgas.com
Annual Revenues: $2.46 billion
Employees: 5,876
Ticker: NYSE: SWX
SIC: 4923
Industry/ies: Fuels See Coal, Gas, Oil, Petroleum; Natural Resources; Petroleum Industry

Chairman of the Board   Tel: (702) 876-7011
MELARKEY, Michael J.   Fax: (702) 364-3180

President and Chief Executive Officer   Tel: (702) 876-7011
HESTER, John P.   Fax: (702) 364-3180

Main Headquarters
Mailing: P.O. Box 98512   Tel: (702) 876-7011
             Las Vegas, NV 89193-8512   Fax: (702) 364-3180
                                             TF: (877) 860-6020

Political Action Committees
Southwest Gas Corporation PAC
FEC ID: C00076737
Contact: Roy R. Centrella

5241 Spring Mountain Rd.
Las Vegas, NV 89150

Contributions to Candidates: $45,750 (2015-2016)
Democrats: $9,500; Republicans: $36,250

Corporate Foundations and Giving Programs

Southwest Gas Corporation Foundation
P.O. Box 95812
Las Vegas, NV 98193

Public Affairs and Related Activities Personnel

At Headquarters

BRADDY-MCKOY, Sharon W.   Tel: (702) 876-7011
Vice President, Human Resources   Fax: (702) 364-3180

BROWN, Justin L.   Tel: (702) 876-7011
Vice President, Regulatory Affairs and Public Affairs   Fax: (702) 364-3180

DEBONIS, Eric   Tel: (702) 876-7011
Senior Vice President,Operations   Fax: (702) 364-3180

HALLER, Karen S.   Tel: (702) 876-7011
Vice President, General Counsel and Corporate Secretary   Fax: (702) 364-3180
karen.haller@swgas.com

HEADEN, Sonya   Tel: (702) 364-3411
Contact, Communications and Media   Fax: (702) 364-3180

JANOV , Edward A.   Tel: (702) 876-7011
Senior Vice President, Corporate Development   Fax: (702) 364-3180

KENNY, Kenneth J.   Tel: (702) 876-7237
Vice President, Finance and Treasurer   Fax: (702) 364-3180

MESSINA, Cynthia   Tel: (702) 365-2044
Administrator and Contact, Communications   Fax: (702) 364-3180
cynthia.messina@swgas.com

STANBROUGH, Frank J.   Tel: (702) 876-7011
Vice President,Risk Management and Compliance Officer   Fax: (702) 364-3180

At Other Offices

CENTRELLA, Roy R.   Tel: (702) 364-3128
Senior Vice President, Chief Financial Officer and PAC Treasurer
5241 Spring Mountain Rd.
Las Vegas, NV 89150

Southwestern Energy Company

Natural gas exploration, production, transmission, marketing and distribution.
www.swn.com
Annual Revenues: $3.86 billion
Employees: 2,781
Ticker: NYSE: SWN
SIC: 1382; 4923; 4924; 4932
NAICS: 213112; 221210
Industry/ies: Natural Resources

Executive Chairman of the Board   Tel: (832) 796-1000
KORELL, Harold M.   Fax: (832) 796-4818

Chairman of the Board and Chief Executive Officer   Tel: (832) 796-1000
MUELLER, Steven L.   Fax: (832) 796-4818

Main Headquarters
Mailing: 10000 Energy Dr.   Tel: (832) 796-1000
             Houston, TX 77389   Fax: (832) 796-4818

Political Action Committees
Southwestern Energy Company PAC
FEC ID: C00190652
Contact: Melissa D. McCarty
4100 Corporate Center Dr.   Tel: (479) 521-1141
Suite 330   Fax: (479) 521-1141
Springdale, AR 72762

Contributions to Candidates: $14,600 (2015-2016)
Democrats: $1,000; Republicans: $13,600

Corporate Foundations and Giving Programs

Southwestern Energy Company Contributions Program
2350 N. Sam Houston Pkwy., East   Tel: (281) 618-4700
Suite 125   Fax: (281) 618-4818
Houston, TX 77032

Public Affairs and Related Activities Personnel

At Headquarters

ALE, John C.   Tel: (832) 796-1000
Senior Vice President, General Counsel and Secretary   Fax: (832) 796-4818

BOLING, Mark K.   Tel: (832) 796-1000
President, General Counsel and Secretary   Fax: (832) 796-4818
mark_boling@swn.com

FERGUSON, Danny W.   Tel: (832) 796-1000
Vice President, Government and Community Relations   Fax: (832) 796-4818
danny_ferguson@swn.com

HRESKO, Joanne C.   Tel: (832) 796-1000

Senior Vice President, Corporate Development	Fax:	(832) 796-4818
MCCAULEY, Jennifer N.	Tel:	(832) 796-1000
Senior Vice President, Human Resources	Fax:	(832) 796-4818
OWEN, Craig	Tel:	(832) 796-1000
Senior Vice President and Chief Financial Officer	Fax:	(832) 796-4818
RICHARDSON, Susan	Tel:	(832) 796-1000
Director, Corporate Affairs	Fax:	(832) 796-4818
susan_richardson@swn.com		
SHERRICK, Jeffrey B.	Tel:	(832) 796-1000
Senior Vice President, Corporate Development	Fax:	(832) 796-4818
STUBBLEFIELD, J. Alan	Tel:	(832) 796-1000
Senior Vice President, Operations	Fax:	(832) 796-4818
TRAMUTO, James A.	Tel:	(832) 796-1000
Vice President, Governmental and Regulatory Strategies	Fax:	(832) 796-4818
WAY, William J.	Tel:	(832) 796-1000
President and Chief Operating Officer	Fax:	(832) 796-4818

At Other Offices

MCCARTY, Melissa D.
PAC Treasurer
4100 Corporate Center Dr., Suite 330
Springdale, AZ 72762

SYLVESTER, Bradley D.	Tel:	(281) 618-4847
Vice President, Investor Relations	Fax:	(281) 618-4820

2350 N. Sam Houston Pkwy., East, Suite 125
Houston, TX 77032

Southwestern Great American, Inc.

The oldest direct-selling corporation in the United States.
www.southwestern.com
Annual Revenues: $71.90 million
Employees: 1,000
Industry/ies: Advertising And Marketing

Executive Chairman of the Board	Tel:	(615) 391-2500
HAYS, Spencer	Fax:	(615) 391-2848

Chief Executive Officer	Tel:	(615) 391-2500
BEDFORD, Henry	Fax:	(615) 391-2848

Main Headquarters

Mailing:	2451 Atrium Way	Tel:	(615) 391-2500
	Nashville, TN 37214	Fax:	(615) 316-5459
		TF:	(888) 602-7867

Public Affairs and Related Activities Personnel

At Headquarters

CAMPBELL, Trey	Tel:	(615) 391-2500
Director, Communications	Fax:	(615) 391-2848
trey.campbell@southwestern.com		

OHNSTAD, Kevin	Tel:	(615) 391-2500
Principal	Fax:	(615) 316-5459

Southwire, Inc.

A producer of electrical wire and cable.
www.southwire.com
Employees: 3,900
SIC: 3334; 3341; 3357; 5051
NAICS: 331491; 331312; 331492
Industry/ies: Metals
Legislative Issues: ENG; TAX; TRD

President and Chief Executive Officer	Tel:	(770) 832-4242
THORN, Stuart	Fax:	(770) 838-6981
stu_thorn@southwire.com		

Main Headquarters

Mailing:	One Southwire Dr.	Tel:	(770) 832-4242
	Carrollton, GA 30119	Fax:	(770) 838-6981
		TF:	(800) 444-1700

Corporate Foundations and Giving Programs

Southwire, Inc. Contributions Program		
One Southwire Dr.	Tel:	(770) 832-4242
Carrollton, GA 30119		

Public Affairs and Related Activities Personnel

At Headquarters

COCHRAN, Guyton J.	Tel:	(770) 832-4242
Executive Vice President and Chief Financial Officer	Fax:	(770) 838-6981
HERRIN, Jeff	Tel:	(770) 832-4242
Executive Vice President, Operations	Fax:	(770) 838-6981
LEFTWICH, Gary	Tel:	(770) 832-4884
Manager, Communications	Fax:	(770) 838-6981
gary_leftwich@southwire.com		
SMITH, Floyd	Tel:	(770) 832-4242
Senior Vice President, General Counsel and Secretary	Fax:	(770) 838-6981

WIGGINS, Mike	Tel:	(770) 832-4242
Executive Vice President, Human Resources	Fax:	(770) 838-6981

Space Exploration Technologies Corporation

Commercial space exploration.
www.spacex.com
Annual Revenues: $135 million
Employees: 1,200
Industry/ies: Aerospace/Aviation; Science; Scientific Research; Transportation
Legislative Issues: AER; BUD; DEF; SCI

Founder and Chief Executive Officer	Tel:	(310) 363-6000
MUSK, Elon		

Main Headquarters

Mailing:	One Rocket Rd.	Tel:	(310) 363-6000
	Hawthorne, CA 90250		

Washington Office

Mailing:	1030 15th St. NW		
	Suite 220 East		
	Washington, DC 20005		

Political Action Committees

Space Exploration Technologies Corporation PAC
FEC ID: C00411116
Contact: Ray Kato
1030 15th St. NW
Suite 220 East
Washington, DC 20005

Contributions to Candidates: $171,000 (2015-2016)
Democrats: $71,000; Republicans: $100,000

Principal Recipients

SENATE
MCCAIN, JOHN S (REP-VA)

Public Affairs and Related Activities Personnel

At Headquarters

BEDNAREK, Stephanie	Tel:	(202) 649-2707
Manager, Government Affairs		
stephanie.bednarek@spacex.com		
Registered Federal Lobbyist		
BITTERMAN, Mark E.	Tel:	(310) 363-6000
Federal Lobbyist		
CARDACI, Christopher	Tel:	(310) 363-6000
Senior Counsel		
DUNN, Mathew	Tel:	(310) 363-6000
Federal Lobbyist		
mathew.dunn@spacex.com		
Registered Federal Lobbyist		
FIELDER, Jerry	Tel:	(310) 363-6000
Vice President, Human Resources		
jerry.fielder@spacex.com		
HUGHES, Timothy R.	Tel:	(310) 363-6000
Senior Vice President and General Counsel		
tim.hughes@spacex.com		
SCHENEWERK, Caryn	Tel:	(310) 363-6000
Counsel		
caryn@spacex.com		
Registered Federal Lobbyist		
SHANKLIN, Emily	Tel:	(310) 363-6000
Director, Marketing and Communications		
emily.shanklin@spacex.com		

At Washington Office

HARRIS, David
Deputy General Counsel

KATO, Ray
Finance Director

LAPIDUS, Michael
Federal Lobbyist
Registered Federal Lobbyist

Spangler Strategic Advisors, LLC

Government relations, business development and Congressional strategy.
Industry/ies: Abrasives
Legislative Issues: DEF

Main Headquarters

Mailing:	304 Eatons Landing Dr.		
	Annapolis, MD 21401		

Public Affairs and Related Activities Personnel

At Headquarters

SPANGLER, Jr., JD, Thomas J.
Principal
Registered Federal Lobbyist

SPARTA, Inc.

See listing on page 204 under Cobham Analytic Solutions

SpartaMatrix, Inc.

A security engineering company for government, military and commercial entities.
www.spartamatrix.com
Employees: 4
Industry/ies: Defense/Homeland Security; Engineering/Mathematics;
Government-Related; Law Enforcement/Security; Military/Veterans

Founder and Chief Executive Officer	Tel:	(310) 443-4151
WAINWRIGHT, Dr. Philip H.	Fax:	(310) 443-4220
philip.wainwright@spartamatrix.com		

Main Headquarters

Mailing:	10940 Wilshire Blvd.	Tel:	(310) 443-4151
	Suite 1600	Fax:	(310) 443-4220
	Los Angeles, CA 90024		

Public Affairs and Related Activities Personnel

At Headquarters

MCLENNAN, Andrew	Tel:	(919) 682-9484
Investor Relations Officer	Fax:	(919) 682-9570
SCHULTIS, Jr., Regis W.	Tel:	(919) 251-6295
Chief Financial Officer	Fax:	(919) 238-7019

SpartanNash

A food wholesaler and retailer. Also provides service for conventional super market.
www.spartannash.com
Annual Revenues: $7.90 billion
Employees: 8,500
Ticker: NASDAQ: SPTN
SIC: 5141
Industry/ies: Food And Beverage Industry; Retail/Wholesale

Chairman of the Board	Tel:	(616) 878-2000
STURKEN, Craig C.	Fax:	(616) 878-8561

President and Chief Executive Officer	Tel:	(616) 878-2000
EIDSON, Dennis	Fax:	(616) 878-8561

Main Headquarters

Mailing:	850 76th St. NW	Tel:	(616) 878-2000
	P.O. Box 8700	Fax:	(616) 878-8561
	Grand Rapids, MI 49518-8700	TF:	(800) 343-4422

Corporate Foundations and Giving Programs

NFC Foundation
Contact: Alec C. Covington

7600 Frances Ave. SOuth	Tel:	(952) 832-0534
P.O. Box 355	Fax:	(952) 844-1237
Minneapolis, MN 55440		

Spartan Stores Foundation		
850 76th St. NW	Tel:	(616) 878-2830
P.O. Box 8700		
Grand Rapids, MI 49518-8700		

Public Affairs and Related Activities Personnel

At Headquarters

DEYONKER, Alex	Tel:	(616) 878-2000
Executive Vice President Chief Legal Officer	Fax:	(616) 878-8561
alex_deyonker@spartanstores.com		
DIMOND, Roebrt B.	Tel:	(952) 844-1060
Executive Vice President, Chief Financial Officer and Treasurer	Fax:	(952) 844-1237
MAHONEY, Kathleen M.	Tel:	(952) 832-0534
Executive Vice President, General Counsel and Secretary	Fax:	(952) 844-1237
kathleen.mahoney@nashfinch.com		
NORCROSS, Jeanne	Tel:	(616) 878-2830
Director, Corporate Communications	Fax:	(616) 878-8561
jeanne_norcross@spartanstores.com		
PIERCE, Larry	Tel:	(616) 878-2000
Executive Vice President, Merchandising and Marketing	Fax:	(616) 878-8561
STAPLES, Dave	Tel:	(616) 878-8319
Executive Vice President and Chief Operating Officer	Fax:	(616) 878-8561
david.staples@spartanstores.com		
VANHALL, Tom	Tel:	(616) 878-2000
Vice President, Interim Chief Accounting Officer	Fax:	(616) 878-8561
WARCHOLAK, Steve	Tel:	(724) 543-1275
Investor Relations	Fax:	(616) 878-8561

Sparton Corporation

Designer and manufacturer of technical products for commercial, governmental, industrial and telecommunications customers worldwide.
www.sparton.com
Annual Revenues: $348.87 million
Employees: 1,385

Ticker: NYSE: SPA
SIC: 3672
Industry/ies: Electricity & Electronics; Electronics; Energy/Electricity
Legislative Issues: DEF

Independent Chairman of the Board	Tel:	(847) 762-5800
SWARTWOUT, James R.	Fax:	(847) 762-5820

President, Chief Executive Officer, Board Member and Interim Principle Financial Officer	Tel:	(847) 762-5800
WOOD, Cary B.	Fax:	(847) 762-5820

Main Headquarters

Mailing:	425 N. Martingale Rd.	Tel:	(847) 762-5800
	Suite 2050	Fax:	(847) 762-5820
	Schaumburg, IL 60173-2213	TF:	(800) 772-7866

Public Affairs and Related Activities Personnel

At Headquarters

BRAND, Larry	Tel:	(847) 762-5800
Vice President, Corporate Human Resources	Fax:	(847) 762-5820
MADLOCK, Gordon	Tel:	(847) 762-5800
Senior Vice-President, Operations	Fax:	(847) 762-5820
MCCORMACK, Joseph	Tel:	(847) 762-5800
Senior Financial Consultant	Fax:	(847) 762-5820
MOLFENTER, David P.	Tel:	(847) 762-5800
Director	Fax:	(847) 762-5820
OSBORNE, Mike	Tel:	(847) 762-5814
Senior Vice President, Corporate Development and Contact, Media Relations	Fax:	(847) 762-5820
mosborne@sparton.com		
PACINI, Dick	Tel:	(248) 276-1970
Contact, Media Relations	Fax:	(847) 762-5820
dpacini@millerschingroup.com		
SCHNEIDER, Joseph	Tel:	(847) 762-5800
Senior Vice-President, Sales and Marketing	Fax:	(847) 762-5820

Spatial Corporation

Provider of 3D components for technical applications across a broad range of industries.
www.spatial.com
Employees: 125
Industry/ies: Computer/Technology; Electricity & Electronics; Electronics;
Energy/Electricity

Chief Executive Officer	Tel:	(303) 544-2900
GUILLARD, Jean-Marc	Fax:	(303) 544-3000

Main Headquarters

Mailing:	310 Interlocken Pkwy.	Tel:	(303) 544-2900
	Suite 200	Fax:	(303) 544-3000
	Broomfield, CO 80021-3468		

Public Affairs and Related Activities Personnel

At Headquarters

CARDOSI, Paul	Tel:	(303) 544-2900
Vice President, Chief Financial Officer	Fax:	(303) 544-3000
KING, Connie	Tel:	(303) 544-2900
Director, Human Resources	Fax:	(303) 544-3000
LOKAY, Linda	Tel:	(303) 544-2900
Vice President Marketing and Business Development	Fax:	(303) 544-3000

Spectra Energy

A natural gas infrastructure company.
www.spectraenergy.com
Annual Revenues: $5.68 billion
Employees: 5,900
Ticker: NYSE: SE
SIC: 4923; 4922
Industry/ies: Natural Resources; Utilities
Legislative Issues: BUD; ENG; ENV; FUE; HOM; NAT; TAX; TRA

Chairman, President and Chief Executive Officer	Tel:	(713) 627-5400
EBEL, Gregory L.	Fax:	(713) 627-4691

Main Headquarters

Mailing:	5400 Westheimer Ct.	Tel:	(713) 627-5400
	Houston, TX 77056-5310	Fax:	(713) 627-4691

Washington Office

Mailing:	401 Ninth St. NW	
	Washington, DC 20004	

Political Action Committees

Spectra Energy Corp PAC (Spectra-Dcp Pac)
FEC ID: C00429662
Contact: Ritu K. Talwar
5400 Westheimer Ct.
Houston, TX 77056

> **Contributions to Candidates:** $157,500 (2015-2016)
> Democrats: $29,000; Republicans: $128,500

Corporate Foundations and Giving Programs

Spectra Energy Foundation
Contact: Dorothy M. Ables
5400 Westheimer Ct.
Houston, TX 77056

Public Affairs and Related Activities Personnel

At Headquarters

ABLES, Dorothy M. *Chief Administrative Officer*	Tel: (713) 627-5400 Fax: (713) 627-4691
AVILA, Armando	Tel: (713) 627-5400 Fax: (713) 627-4691
CAPPADONNA, Roni *General Manager, Investor Relations*	Tel: (713) 627-5400 Fax: (713) 627-4691
DILL, Julie *Chief Communications Officer*	Tel: (713) 627-5400 Fax: (713) 627-4691
FITZPATRICK, Patti *General Manager, East Tennessee Natural Gas & Vice President, Audit Services*	Tel: (713) 989-0315 Fax: (713) 627-4691
HEDGEBETH, Reginald D. *General Counsel*	Tel: (713) 627-5400 Fax: (713) 627-4691
KRUSE, Richard *Vice President, Rate Regulatory Affairs and Chief Compliance Officer*	Tel: (713) 627-5368 Fax: (713) 627-4691
OLSON, Wendy *Director, External Affairs*	Tel: (713) 627-4072 Fax: (713) 627-4691
REDDY, John Patrick *Chief Financial Officer*	Tel: (713) 627-5400 Fax: (713) 627-4691
SHEFFIELD, Peter V. *Vice President, Federal & State Government Affairs* pvsheffield@spectraenergy.com *Registered Federal Lobbyist*	Tel: (202) 347-2053 Fax: (713) 627-4691
TALWAR, Ritu K. *PAC Treasurer*	Tel: (713) 627-5400 Fax: (713) 627-4691
TILLMAN, Steven E. *Director, Federal Government Affairs* setillman@spectraenergy.com *Registered Federal Lobbyist*	Tel: (202) 347-2053 Fax: (713) 627-4691

Spectrum Brands Inc.

A consumer products company.
www.spectrumbrands.com
Annual Revenues: $4.44 billion
Employees: 13,400
Ticker: NYSE: SPB
SIC: 3690
Industry/ies: Retail/Wholesale

Chief Executive Officer ROUVE, Andreas	Tel: (608) 275-3340 Fax: (608) 278-6643

Main Headquarters

Mailing: 3001 Deming Way Middleton, WI 53562-1431	Tel: (608) 275-3340 Fax: (608) 278-6643

Public Affairs and Related Activities Personnel

At Headquarters

MARTIN, Douglas L *Executive Vice President and Chief Financial Officer*	Tel: (608) 275-3340 Fax: (608) 278-6643

At Other Offices

FAGRE, Nathan E. *Senior Vice President, General Counsel and Secretary* 601 Rayovac Dr. Madison, WI 53711-2497	Tel: (608) 275-3340 Fax: (608) 278-6643
PRICHARD, Dave *Vice President, Investor Relations and Corporate Communications* 601 Rayovac Dr. Madison, WI 53711-2497 investorrelations@spectrumbrands.com	Tel: (608) 278-6141 Fax: (608) 278-6643
RANEW, Frank *Contact, Media Relations* 601 Rayovac Dr. Madison, WI 53711-2497	Tel: (404) 870-6832 Fax: (608) 278-6643

Spencer & Syed LLC

Provider of advisory, consulting and lobbying services.
www.sandsllp.co.uk
Industry/ies: Law/Law Firms

Spherion Staffing LLC

Formerly Spherion. A human capital management organization.
www.spherion.com

Annual Revenues: $2.19 billion
Employees: 171,000
Ticker: NYSE: SFN
SIC: 7363
Industry/ies: Management

President, Chief Executive Officer and Director KRAUSE, Roy G.	Tel: (954) 308-7600 Fax: (954) 308-7666
President MAZUR, Sandy	Tel: (954) 308-7600 Fax: (954) 308-7666

Main Headquarters

Mailing: 1212 N Washington St. 118
Spokane, WA 99201

Spin Systems, Inc

Computer related consulting services.
www.spinsys.com
SIC: 7373; 7379
NAICS: 541512; 511210; 518210; 541330; 541511; 541513; 541519; 541611; 541990; 611420
Industry/ies: Computer/Technology

President and Chief Executive Officer AL-ALI, Wael walali@spinsys.com	Tel: (703) 318-0803

Main Headquarters

Mailing: 100 Carpenter Dr. Suite 100 Sterling, VA 20164	Tel: (703) 318-0803

Public Affairs and Related Activities Personnel

At Headquarters

BERKOW, Bob *Vice President, Strategy and Programs*	Tel: (703) 318-0803
DUDEK, Chris *Vice President, Government Programs*	Tel: (703) 318-0803
RAY, Shourya *Vice President and Chief Administrative Officer and Contact, Media Relations* sray@spinsys.com	Tel: (703) 318-0803
WEED, Ruth *Director, Marketing and Business Development*	Tel: (703) 318-0803

Spire Corporation

A diversified technology company providing innovative solar energy manufacturing equipment and solar systems, biomedical devices, and optoelectronic components.
www.spirecorp.com
Annual Revenues: $15.29 million
Employees: 82
Ticker: NASDAQ: SPIR
SIC: 3674; 3559; 3827
Industry/ies: Energy/Electricity

Chairman of the Board of Directors LITTLE, Roger G. gttle@spirecorp.com	Tel: (781) 275-6000 Fax: (781) 275-7470
President and Chief Executive Officer LAFAVRE, Rodger W.	Tel: (781) 275-6000 Fax: (781) 275-7470

Main Headquarters

Mailing: One Patriots Park Bedford, MA 01730-2396	Tel: (781) 275-6000 Fax: (781) 275-7470 TF: (800) 510-4815

Public Affairs and Related Activities Personnel

At Headquarters

LIPINSKI, David R. *Director and Chairman of Audit Committee*	Tel: (781) 275-6000 Fax: (781) 275-7470
LITTLE, Mark C. *Director*	Tel: (781) 275-6000 Fax: (781) 275-7470

Spirit Aerosystems, Inc.

Supplier of commercial airplane assemblies and components. Offer products and services in Fuselages, Under-wing components, Composites, Wings and Spares/repairs.
www.spiritaero.com
Annual Revenues: $6.81 billion
Employees: 15,096
Ticker: NYSE: SPR
SIC: 3728
NAICS: 336413
Industry/ies: Aerospace/Aviation; Transportation

President and Chief Executive Officer LAWSON, Larry A	Tel: (316) 526-9000 Fax: (316) 523-8814

Main Headquarters

Mailing: P.O. Box 780008	Tel: (316) 526-9000

Wichita, KS 67278-0008   Fax: (316) 523-8814
    TF: (800) 501-7597

Political Action Committees

Spirit Aerosystems, Inc. PAC
FEC ID: C00428110
Contact: Damon Ward
P.O. Box 780008   Tel: (316) 526-9000
MC K16-21
Wichita, KS 67278

    Contributions to Candidates: $40,000 (2015-2016)
    Democrats: $5,000; Republicans: $35,000

Corporate Foundations and Giving Programs

Spirit Aerosystems, Inc Contributions Program
Contact: Brian Black
P.O. Box 780008
Wichita, KS 67278-0008

Public Affairs and Related Activities Personnel

At Headquarters

BLACK, Brian	Tel:	(316) 523-5691
Senior Manager, Corporate Public Affairs and Global	Fax:	(316) 523-8814
Diversity		
brian.black@spiritaero.com		
FLENTJE, Gloria	Tel:	(316) 526-9000
Senior Vice President, Corporate Administration and Human	Fax:	(316) 523-8814
Resources		
GANN, Deborah	Tel:	(316) 526-3910
Vice President, Communications and Public Affairs	Fax:	(316) 523-8814
KAPOOR, Sanjay	Tel:	(316) 526-9000
Senior Vice President and Chief Financial Officer	Fax:	(316) 523-8814
KONDROTIS, Krisstie	Tel:	(316) 526-9000
Senior Vice President, Business Development	Fax:	(316) 523-8814
LAMMERS, Jon	Tel:	(316) 526-9000
Senior Vice President, General Counsel and Secretary	Fax:	(316) 523-8814
MARNICK , Sam	Tel:	(316) 526-9000
Senior Vice President and Chief Administration Officer	Fax:	(316) 523-8814
RABE, Ron	Tel:	(316) 526-9000
Senior Vice President, Operations	Fax:	(316) 523-8814
WARD, Damon	Tel:	(316) 526-9000
PAC Treasurer	Fax:	(316) 523-8814
WOOD, Heidi	Tel:	(316) 526-9000
Senior Vice President, Strategy and Investor Relations	Fax:	(316) 523-8814

Sports Authority

A sporting goods store operator.
www.sportsauthority.com
Annual Revenues: $1.40 billion
Employees: 15,000
SIC: 5940
Industry/ies: Retail/Wholesale; Sports/Leisure/Entertainment

Chief Executive Officer   Tel: (303) 200-5050
FOSS, Michael E   Fax: (303) 863-2240

Main Headquarters
Mailing: 1050 W. Hampden Ave.   Tel: (303) 200-5050
         Englewood, CO 80110   Fax: (303) 863-2240
             TF: (800) 360-8721

Corporate Foundations and Giving Programs

Sports Authority Contributions Program
705 W. Hampden Ave.   Tel: (303) 789-5266
Englewood, CO 80110

Public Affairs and Related Activities Personnel

At Headquarters

AGUILAR, Jeremy	Tel:	(303) 200-5050
Executive Vice President, Chief Financial Officer	Fax:	(303) 863-2240
FOSTER, Michael	Tel:	(303) 200-5050
Vice President, Business Development and Strategy	Fax:	(303) 863-2240
GARRETT, Douglas	Tel:	(303) 200-5050
Senior Vice President, Chief Counsel and Corporate Secretary	Fax:	(303) 863-2240
GAUDET, Paul	Tel:	(303) 200-5050
Executive Vice President, Store Operations	Fax:	(303) 863-2240
GORDON, Robert	Tel:	(303) 200-5050
Senior Vice President, Human Resources	Fax:	(303) 863-2240
STOUPA, Ron	Tel:	(303) 200-5050
Executive Vice President and Chief Marketing Officer	Fax:	(303) 863-2240

Springs Global, Inc.

Formerly known as Springs Industries, Inc. A manufacturer of finished fabrics and home furnishings. Springs Global US and Brazil's Coteminas are subsidiaries of parent Springs Global Participacoes, a home textiles manufacturer.
www.springs.com

Employees: 6,000
SIC: 2211
NAICS: 31321
Industry/ies: Apparel/Textiles Industry; Furniture/Home Furnishings

Chairman of the Board   Tel: (803) 547-1500
REBELLO DE PAULA, João Gustavo   Fax: (803) 547-1636

Chief Executive Officer   Tel: (803) 547-1500
GOMES DA SILVA, Josue Christiano   Fax: (803) 547-1636

Main Headquarters
Mailing: P.O. Box 70   Tel: (803) 547-1500
         Ft. Mill, SC 29716   Fax: (803) 547-1636
             TF: (888) 926-7888

Corporate Foundations and Giving Programs

Springs Global Contributions Program
P.O. Box 70   Tel: (803) 547-1500
Ft. Mill, SC 29716   Fax: (803) 547-1636

Public Affairs and Related Activities Personnel

At Headquarters

BASTOS NETO, Pedro Garcia	Tel:	(803) 547-1500
Director, Corporate Affairs and Chief Financial Officer	Fax:	(803) 547-1636
KAWASSAKI, Gustavo Shimoda	Tel:	(803) 547-1500
Director, Investor Relations	Fax:	(803) 547-1636

Sprint Corporation

A telecommunications company.
www.sprint.com
Annual Revenues: $34.53 billion
Employees: 31,000
Ticker: NYSE: S
SIC: 4813; 4899
Industry/ies: Communications; Telecommunications/Internet/Cable
Legislative Issues: COM; CPT; LBR; TAX; TEC; TRA

Chairman of the Board   Tel: (913) 624-6000
SON, Masayoshi

Chief Executive Officer   Tel: (913) 624-6000
CLAURE, Marcelo

Main Headquarters
Mailing: 6200 Sprint Pkwy.   Tel: (913) 624-6000
         Overland Park, KS 66251   TF: (800) 829-0965

Washington Office
Mailing: 401 Ninth St.
         Suite 400
         Washington, DC 20004

Political Action Committees

Sprint Corporation PAC
FEC ID: C00089342
Contact: Neil J. Robertson
6450 Sprint Pkwy.
Overland Park, KS 66251

    Contributions to Candidates: $105,500 (2015-2016)
    Democrats: $40,500; Republicans: $64,000; Other: $1,000

Corporate Foundations and Giving Programs

Sprint Foundation
Contact: Douglas Michelman
6450 Sprint Pkwy.
Overland Park, KS 66251

Public Affairs and Related Activities Personnel

At Headquarters

CRULL, Kevin	Tel:	(913) 624-6000
Chief Marketing Officer		
MICHELMAN, Douglas	Tel:	(913) 624-6000
Senior Vice President, Corporate Communications and		
Corporate Social Responsibility		

At Washington Office

ROBERTSON, Neil J.
PAC Contact

At Other Offices

BARLOON, William J.	Tel:	(202) 585-1928
Vice President, State & Federal Legislative Affairs	Fax:	(202) 585-1895
900 Seventh St. NW, Suite 700		
Washington, DC 20001		
bill.barloon@sprint.com		
Registered Federal Lobbyist		
BLALOCK, Paul	Tel:	(425) 636-5828
Investor Relation Contact		
1250 Eye St. NW, Suite 901		
Washington, DC 20005		
paul.blalock@clearwire.com		

CARROLL, Hugh P.
Federal Lobbyist
900 Seventh St. NW, Suite 700
Washington, DC 20001
Registered Federal Lobbyist

Tel: (202) 585-1928
Fax: (202) 585-1895

EUTENEUER, Joseph J.
Chief Financial Officer
6391 Sprint Pkwy.
Overland Park, KS 66251-4300

Tel: (913) 624-6000

HODDER, Broady R.
Senior Vice President, General Counsel
1475 120th Ave. NE
Bellevue, WA 98005

Tel: (425) 216-7600

HOPPER, Scott
Senior Vice President, Strategic Business Development
1475 120th Ave. NE
Bellevue, WA 98005

Tel: (425) 216-7600

MATHIOT, Lawrence K.
PAC Treasurer
150 Fayetteville St. Mall, Suite 2810
Raleigh, NC 27601

MCPHERSON, Laura
Director, Government Affairs
900 Seventh St. NW, Suite 700
Washington, DC 20001
Registered Federal Lobbyist

Tel: (202) 585-1928
Fax: (202) 585-1895

PRICE, Sandra J.
Senior Vice President, Human Resources
6391 Sprint Pkwy.
Overland Park, KS 66251-4300

Tel: (913) 624-6000

RYDER, Alice
Contact, Investor Relations
1475 120th Ave. NE
Bellevue, WA 98005

Tel: (425) 505-6494

SCHWARTZ, Michael
Senior Vice President, Corporate and Business Development
6391 Sprint Pkwy.
Overland Park, KS 66251-4300

Tel: (913) 624-6000

WUNSCH, Charles
General Counsel, Corporate Secretary and Chief Ethics Officer
6391 Sprint Pkwy.
Overland Park, KS 66251-4300
charles.wunsch@mail.sprint.com

Tel: (913) 624-6000

SPX Corporation

A manufacturer and marketer of specialty service tools and original equipment components for the global motor vehicle industry. Acquired General Signal Corp. in 1998 and United Dominion Industries Ltd. in 2001.
www.spx.com
Annual Revenues: $4.59 billion
Employees: 14,000
Ticker: NYSE: SPW
SIC: 3540
Industry/ies: Machinery/Equipment

Chairman, President and Chief Executive Officer
KEARNEY, Christopher J.
chris.kearney@spx.com

Tel: (704) 752-4400
Fax: (704) 752-4505

Main Headquarters
Mailing: 13320 Ballantyne Corporate Pl.
Charlotte, NC 28277

Tel: (704) 752-4400
Fax: (704) 752-4505

Corporate Foundations and Giving Programs

SPX Foundation
13515 Ballantyne Corporate Pl.
Charlotte, NC 28277

Public Affairs and Related Activities Personnel

At Headquarters

EPSTEIN, Jennifer
Chief Communications Officer
jennifer.epstein@spx.com

Tel: (704) 752-7403
Fax: (704) 752-4505

SMELTSER, Jeremy W.
Vice President and Chief Financial Officer

Tel: (704) 752-4400
Fax: (704) 752-4505

TAYLOR, Ryan
Director, Investor Relations
investor@spx.com

Tel: (704) 752-4486
Fax: (704) 752-4505

TSORIS, Stephen A.
Vice President, Secretary and General Counsel

Tel: (704) 752-4400
Fax: (704) 752-4505

WHITTED, Michael
Vice President, Corporate Development

Tel: (704) 752-4400
Fax: (704) 752-4505

Spyrus Inc.

Developer of hardware-based data protection and client authentication products, and integrated identity management solutions.
www.spyrus.com
Annual Revenues: $5.4 million
Employees: 40
Industry/ies: Computer/Technology; Defense/Homeland Security; Government-Related

Chief Executive Officer and President
PONTIUS, Sue

Tel: (408) 392-9131
Fax: (408) 392-0319

Main Headquarters
Mailing: 1860 Hartog Dr.
San Jose, CA 95131-2203

Tel: (408) 392-9131
Fax: (408) 392-0319

Public Affairs and Related Activities Personnel

At Headquarters

CHMIELEWSKI, Dan
Contact, Media Relations
dchm@madisonalexanderpr.com

Tel: (949) 231-2965
Fax: (408) 392-0319

DICKENS, Tom
Chief Operation Officer and Media Contact
tdickens@spyrus.com

Tel: (408) 953-0700
Fax: (408) 392-0319

Square D

See listing on page 704 under Schneider Electric

SRA International, Inc.

Provides IT solutions, mission-specific domain expertise in areas such as energy and environmental consulting; intelligence analysis; advanced research; and bioinformatics. Acquired Adroit Systems in 2003.
www.sra.com
Employees: 6,000
Industry/ies: Computer/Technology

Founder and Chairman
VOLGENAU, Dr. Ernst

Tel: (703) 803-1500
Fax: (703) 803-1509

President and Chief Executive Officer
BALLHAUS, William "Bill" L.

Tel: (703) 803-1500
Fax: (703) 803-1509

Main Headquarters
Mailing: 4300 Fair Lakes Ct.
Fairfax, VA 22033

Tel: (703) 803-1500
Fax: (703) 803-1509

Washington Office
Mailing: 1801 K St. NW
Washington, DC 20006

Tel: (202) 338-6106

Political Action Committees
SRA International Inc. Fund for Better IT in Government PAC
FEC ID: C00393256
Contact: Nathan Brown
4300 Fair Lakes Ct.
Suite 500
Fairfax, VA 22033

Contributions to Candidates: $3,350 (2015-2016)
Democrats: $1,500; Republicans: $1,850

Public Affairs and Related Activities Personnel

At Headquarters

ATKIN, Timothy J.
Executive Vice President, Chief Administrative Officer and Chief of Staff

Tel: (703) 803-1500
Fax: (703) 803-1509

BROWN, Nathan
Lobbyist and PAC Treasurer

Tel: (703) 803-1500
Fax: (703) 803-1509

DONOHUE, Esq., Anne M.
Senior Vice President and General Counsel

Tel: (703) 803-1500
Fax: (703) 803-1509

KEFFER, David
Executive Vice President and Chief Financial Officer

Tel: (703) 803-1500
Fax: (703) 803-1509

PEDUZZI, Lauren
Director, Communications

Tel: (703) 803-1500
Fax: (703) 803-1509

REING, John
Senior Vice President, Human Resources

Tel: (703) 803-1500
Fax: (703) 803-1509

SRI International

A multi-disciplinary research and consulting company. Acquired Constella Group, LLC in 2007.
www.sri.com
Annual Revenues: $495 million
Employees: 2,100
Industry/ies: Law Enforcement/Security
Legislative Issues: BUD; DEF; ENG; HOM; MED; SCI

Chairman
CLARK, Vernon E.

Tel: (650) 859-2000
Fax: (650) 326-5512

President and Chief Executive Officer
JEFFREY, William

Tel: (650) 859-2000
Fax: (650) 326-5512

Main Headquarters

| Mailing: | 333 Ravenswood Ave. | Tel: | (650) 859-2000 |
| | Menlo Park, CA 94025-3493 | Fax: | (650) 326-5512 |

Washington Office

| Mailing: | 1100 Wilson Blvd. | Tel: | (703) 524-2053 |
| | Arlington, VA 22209 | Fax: | (703) 247-8569 |

Corporate Foundations and Giving Programs

SRI International Contributions Program

| 333 Ravenswood Ave. | Tel: | (650) 859-2000 |
| Menlo Park, CA 94025-3493 | Fax: | (650) 326-5512 |

Public Affairs and Related Activities Personnel

At Headquarters

ABRAMSON, Richard	Tel:	(650) 859-2000
Senior Staff Advisor	Fax:	(650) 326-5512
richard.abramson@sri.com		

| CIESINSKI, Stephen | Tel: | (650) 859-2000 |
| *President, Global Partnerships and Vice President* | Fax: | (650) 326-5512 |

| LAU, Luther | Tel: | (650) 859-2000 |
| *Vice President, Treasurer, and Chief Financial Officer* | Fax: | (650) 326-5512 |

| MCINTIRE, John | Tel: | (650) 859-2000 |
| *General Counsel* | Fax: | (650) 326-5512 |

RESNICK, Alice R.	Tel:	(650) 859-2000
Vice President, Corporate and Marketing Communications	Fax:	(650) 326-5512
inquiry.line@sri.com		

| TOOKER, Jean E. | Tel: | (650) 859-2000 |
| *Vice President, Human Resources* | Fax: | (650) 326-5512 |

| ZAROOGIAN, Mark | Tel: | (650) 859-2000 |
| *Vice President, Strategic Initiatives* | Fax: | (650) 326-5512 |

At Washington Office

HARMAN, Phillip	Tel:	(703) 247-8413
Director, Congressional Relations	Fax:	(703) 247-8569
Registered Federal Lobbyist		

SSA Marine

A container terminal operator and cargo handling company.
www.ssamarine.com
Annual Revenues: $779 million
Employees: 10,000
Industry/ies: Marine/Maritime/Shipping; Transportation
Legislative Issues: ENV; LBR; MAR; TAX; TRA; TRD; TRU

Chairman of the Board	Tel:	(206) 623-0304
HEMINGWAY, Jon	Fax:	(206) 623-0179
jon.hemingway@ssamarine.com		

| **Chief Executive Officer** | Tel: | (206) 623-0304 |
| STUBKJAER, Knud | Fax: | (206) 623-0179 |

Main Headquarters

Mailing:	1131 S.W. Klickitat Way	Tel:	(206) 623-0304
	Seattle, WA 98134	Fax:	(206) 623-0179
		TF:	(800) 422-3505

Washington Office

Mailing:	1850 M St. NW
	Suite 910
	Washington, DC 20036

Political Action Committees

SSA Marine Inc. Good Government Fund PAC
FEC ID: C00397893
1131 S.W. Klickitat Way
Seattle, WA 98134

    Contributions to Candidates: $45,000 (2015-2016)
    Democrats: $22,500; Republicans: $22,500

        Principal Recipients

            HOUSE
            SMITH, D ADAM (DEM-WA)

Public Affairs and Related Activities Personnel

At Headquarters

JOHNSON, Mark	Tel:	(206) 623-0304
Vice President, Government Relations & Business	Fax:	(206) 623-0179
Development		
mark.johnson@ssamarine.com		
Registered Federal Lobbyist		

| NEAL, Jaime | Tel: | (206) 623-0304 |
| *Senior Vice President and Treasurer* | Fax: | (206) 623-0179 |

| WATTERS, Bob | Tel: | (206) 654-3575 |
| *Senior Vice President* | Fax: | (206) 623-0179 |

At Washington Office

MELIS, Adam
PAC Contact

SSAB Enterprises, LLC (formerly IPSCO Enterprises Inc.)

Firm.
www.ssab.com
Industry/ies: Metals
Legislative Issues: ENG; ENV; TAX; TRA; TRD

Main Headquarters

| Mailing: | 615 S. Oakland St. | Tel: | (202) 255-1604 |
| | Arlington, VA 22204 | | |

Washington Office

| Mailing: | 101 Constitution Ave. NW |
| | Washington, DC 20001 |

Public Affairs and Related Activities Personnel

At Headquarters

| GIBBONS, Martha | Tel: | (202) 255-1604 |
| *Director, Government Relations* | | |

At Washington Office

LARSON, Katie R.
Registered Federal Lobbyist

St. Elizabeth Healthcare

Established in 1861, providing comprehensive healthcare services to Covington, Edgewood and Grant Counties.
www.stelizabeth.co
Industry/ies: Family & Home Issues/Abortion/Adoption; Medicine/Health Care/ Mental Health

| **President** | Tel: | (859) 655-8800 |
| DUBIS, John S. | | |

Main Headquarters

| Mailing: | 1500 James Simpson Jr. Way | Tel: | (859) 655-8800 |
| | Covington, KY 41011 | | |

The St. Joe Company

A real estate company engaged in town, resort, commercial and industrial development, land sales and commercial real estate services.
www.joe.com
Annual Revenues: $124.88 million
Employees: 100
Ticker: NYSE:JOE
Industry/ies: Real Estate

| **Chairman of the Board** | Tel: | (850) 231-6400 |
| BERKOWITZ, Bruce R. | Fax: | (850) 231-6595 |

| **President and Interim Chief Executive Officer** | Tel: | (850) 231-6400 |
| KEIL, Jeffrey C. | Fax: | (850) 231-6595 |

Main Headquarters

Mailing:	133 S. Watersound Pkwy.	Tel:	(850) 231-6400
	Watersound, FL 32413	Fax:	(850) 231-6595
		TF:	(866) 417-7133

Corporate Foundations and Giving Programs

The St. Joe Community Foundation
Contact: Sue Joffe

| 133 S. Watersound Pkwy. | Tel: | (850) 231-7430 |
| Watersound, FL 32413 | Fax: | (850) 231-7431 |

Public Affairs and Related Activities Personnel

At Headquarters

BAKUN, Marek	Tel:	(866) 417-7132
Chief Financial Officer	Fax:	(850) 231-6595
Marek.Bakun@Joe.com		

BORICK, Kenneth M.	Tel:	(850) 231-6400
Senior Vice President, General Counsel and Corporate	Fax:	(850) 231-6595
Secretary		

GOFF, Rhea	Tel:	(850) 231-6400
Chief Administrative Officer	Fax:	(850) 231-6595
rhea.goff@joe.com		

| GONZALEZ, Jorge | Tel: | (850) 231-6400 |
| *Senior Vice President, Development* | Fax: | (850) 231-6595 |

JOFFE, Sue	Tel:	(850) 588-1957
Manager, Foundation	Fax:	(850) 588-2302
SJoffe@stjcf.com		

| MAYER, Amber | Tel: | (850) 231-6400 |
| *Chief Marketing Officer* | Fax: | (850) 231-6595 |

MCCUSKER, James	Tel:	(203) 682-8245
Contact, Media Relations	Fax:	(850) 231-6595
jmccusker@icrinc.com		

PARK, Bo	Tel:	(646) 277-1222
Contact, Media Relations	Fax:	(850) 231-6595
bo.park@icrinc.com		

St. Jude Medical, Inc.

A medical device developer and manufacturer.

www.sjm.com
Annual Revenues: $5.60 billion
Employees: 16,000
Ticker: NYSE: STJ
SIC: 3845
NAICS: 334517
Industry/ies: Medicine/Health Care/Mental Health
Legislative Issues: HCR; MMM; TRA

Chairman of the Board, President and Chief Executive Officer	Tel:	(651) 756-2000
STARKS, Daniel J.	Fax:	(651) 766-3045

Main Headquarters

Mailing:	One St. Jude Medical Dr.	Tel:	(651) 756-2000
	St. Paul, MN 55117-9983	Fax:	(651) 756-3301
		TF:	(800) 328-9634

Washington Office

Mailing:	One Massachusetts Ave. NW	Tel:	(202) 384-1360
	Suite 330		
	Washington, DC 20001		

Political Action Committees
St. Jude Medical Inc. PAC
FEC ID: C00305029
Contact: Robert Frenz
One Lillehei Plaza
St. Paul, MN 55117

Contributions to Candidates: $173,000 (2015-2016)
Democrats: $63,500; Republicans: $109,500

Principal Recipients

HOUSE
CARDENAS, TONY (DEM-CA)
CRAIG, ANGELA DAWN (DEM-MN)

Corporate Foundations and Giving Programs

St. Jude Medical Foundation		
One Lillehei Plaza	Tel:	(651) 756-2000
St. Paul, MN 55117		

Public Affairs and Related Activities Personnel

At Headquarters

ANDRADE, Lisa M.	Tel:	(651) 756-2000
Vice President, Chief Marketing Officer	Fax:	(651) 756-3301
BAE, Paul	Tel:	(651) 756-2000
Vice President, Global Human Resources and Chief Compliance Officer	Fax:	(651) 756-3301
CRAIG, Angela D.	Tel:	(651) 756-2191
Senior Advisor	Fax:	(651) 756-3301
acraig@sjm.com		
ELLINGSON , Rachel H.	Tel:	(651) 756-2295
Vice President, Global Communications	Fax:	(651) 756-3301
rellingson02@sjm.com		
ROUSSEAU , Michael T.	Tel:	(651) 756-2000
Chief Operating Officer	Fax:	(651) 756-3301
THOME, Scott P.	Tel:	(651) 756-2000
Vice President, Global Operations and Supply Chain	Fax:	(651) 756-3301
WEIGELT, J. C.	Tel:	(651) 756-4347
Director, Investor Relations	Fax:	(651) 756-3301
jweigelt@sjm.com		
ZELLERS, Jason A.	Tel:	(651) 756-2000
Vice President, General Counsel and Corporate Secretary	Fax:	(651) 756-3301
ZURBAY, Donald J.	Tel:	(651) 756-2000
Vice President, Finance and Chief Financial Officer	Fax:	(651) 756-3301

At Washington Office

DOUGLAS, Ashli J.	Tel:	(202) 384-1360
Senior Director, Government Affairs		
adouglas@sjm.com		
Registered Federal Lobbyist		
FARHADIEH, Piran	Tel:	(202) 384-1360
Senior Counsel		
pfarhadieh@sjm.com		

At Other Offices

FRENZ, Robert	Tel:	(651) 756-5833
PAC Treasurer	Fax:	(800) 374-2505
One Lillehei Plaza		
St. Paul, MN 55117		
rfrenz@sjm.com		

St. Lucia National Development Corporation

Invest Saint Lucia is committed to expertly and efficiently promote and facilitate potential investors' access to business development and investment opportunities on the simply beautiful island of Saint Lucia.
www.stluciandc.com
Industry/ies: Banking/Finance/Investments

Main Headquarters

Mailing:	800 Second Ave.	Tel:	(212) 697-9360
	Ninth Floor		
	New York City, NY 10017		

Public Affairs and Related Activities Personnel

At Headquarters

DEVAUX, Odile	Tel:	(212) 697-9360
PILGRIM, Carl	Tel:	(212) 697-9360

St. Luke's Episcopal Health System

A Texas non-profit corporation providing quality, patient-focused care and made headlines with such milestones as the first successful heart transplantation, the first artificial heart implantation, and the first laser angioplasty procedure.
www.stlukestexas.com
Annual Revenues: $1.08 billion
Employees: 600
Industry/ies: Medicine/Health Care/Mental Health

President and Chief Executive Officer	Tel:	(832) 355-1000
COVERT, Michael H.	Fax:	(832) 355-7341

Main Headquarters

Mailing:	6624 Fannin	Tel:	(832) 355-1000
	Suite 1100	Fax:	(832) 355-7341
	Houston, TX 77030		

Corporate Foundations and Giving Programs

St. Luke's Episcopal Health System Contributions Program		
P.O. Box 20269	Tel:	(832) 355-6822
MC 3-206	Fax:	(832) 355-7223
Houston, TX 77225		

Public Affairs and Related Activities Personnel

At Headquarters

BAILEY-NEWELL, JD, Susan	Tel:	(832) 355-1000
Vice President, Chief Human Resources Officer	Fax:	(832) 355-7341
BISHOP, CPA, CIA, Cecelia	Tel:	(832) 355-1000
Vice President, Internal Audit and Chief Compliance Officer	Fax:	(832) 355-7341
BROSIUS, William "Bill"	Tel:	(832) 355-1000
Vice President and Chief Financial Officer	Fax:	(832) 355-7341
LEE-EDDIE, Deborah	Tel:	(832) 355-1000
Interim Chief Operation Officer	Fax:	(832) 355-7341
SPRINGHETTI, JD, David	Tel:	(832) 355-1000
Vice President and General Counsel	Fax:	(832) 355-7341
STANO, Jennifer	Tel:	(832) 355-1000
Assistant Vice President, Strategic Planning	Fax:	(832) 355-7341

Stage Stores, Inc.

Stage Stores, Inc. sells brand name apparel, accessories, cosmetics and footwear to small and mid-size towns and communities.
www.stagestoresinc.com
Annual Revenues: $1.57 billion
Employees: 13,500
Ticker: NYSE: SSI
SIC: 5651
Industry/ies: Retail/Wholesale

President and Chief Executive Officer	Tel:	(713) 667-5601
GLAZER, Michael	Fax:	(713) 663-9780

Main Headquarters

Mailing:	2425 West Loop S.	TF:	(800) 324-3244
	Houston, TX 77027		

Corporate Foundations and Giving Programs

Stage Stores Contributions Program
10201 Main St.
Houston, TX 77025

Public Affairs and Related Activities Personnel

At Other Offices

GENTNER, Bill	Tel:	(713) 667-5601
Executive Vice President and Chief Marketing Officer	Fax:	(713) 663-9780
10201 Main St.		
Houston, TX 77025		
PARSONS, Steve	Tel:	(713) 667-5601
Executive Vice President and Chief Human Resources Officer	Fax:	(713) 663-9780
10201 Main St.		
Houston, TX 77025		
SHEIN, Oded	Tel:	(713) 667-5601
Chief Financial Officer	Fax:	(713) 663-9780
10201 Main St.		
Houston, TX 77025		
SONENSHEIN, Randi	Tel:	(713) 667-5601
Senior Vice President, Finance and Strategy	Fax:	(713) 663-9780
10201 Main St.		
Houston, TX 77025		

rsonenshein@stagestores.com

Stamps.com

Stamps.com provides Internet-based services for mailing or shipping letters, packages or parcels.
www.stamps.com
Annual Revenues: $158.02 million
Employees: 343
Ticker: NASDAQ :STMP
SIC: 7389
Industry/ies: Postal And Mail Services
Legislative Issues: POS; SMB

Chairman of the Board and Chief Executive Officer
MCBRIDE, Ken

Tel: (310) 482-5800
Fax: (310) 483-5900

Co-President and Chief Financial Officer
HUEBNER, Kyle

Tel: (310) 482-5800
Fax: (310) 483-5900

Main Headquarters
Mailing: 1990 E. Grand Ave.
El Segundo, CA 90245-5013

Tel: (310) 482-5800
Fax: (310) 482-5900

Political Action Committees
Stamps.Com Inc. PAC
FEC ID: C00416636
Contact: Cary Davidson
3699 Wilshire Blvd.
Suite 1290
Los Angeles, CA 90010

  Contributions to Candidates: $41,400 (2015-2016)
  Democrats: $16,400; Republicans: $25,000

Public Affairs and Related Activities Personnel

At Headquarters

BORTNAK, James M.
Co-President, Corporate and Business Development Officer

Tel: (310) 482-5800
Fax: (310) 483-5900

BUERBA, Sebastian
Chief Marketing Officer

Tel: (310) 482-5800
Fax: (310) 482-5900

CLEM, John
Chief Product and Strategy Officer

Tel: (310) 482-5800
Fax: (310) 482-5900

WEISBERG, Seth
Chief Legal Officer and Secretary

Tel: (310) 482-5800

At Other Offices

DAVIDSON, Cary
PAC Treasurer
515 S. Figueroa St., Suite 1110
Los Angeles, CA 90071

WEISBERG, Seth
Chief Legal Officer and Secretary
3699 Wilshire Blvd., Suite 1290
Los Angeles, CA 90010

Tel: (310) 482-5800
Fax: (310) 482-5900

Standard Insurance Company

A subsidiary of StanCorp. Financial Group, Inc.
www3.standard.com
Employees: 3,000
Industry/ies: Insurance Industry

Chairman of the Board, President and Chief Executive Officer
NESS, J. Greg

Tel: (503) 321-7000
Fax: (971) 321-6776

Main Headquarters
Mailing: 1100 S.W. Sixth Ave.
Portland, OR 97204

Tel: (800) 262-7111
Fax: (503) 321-7000
TF: (800) 378-5742

Political Action Committees
Standard Insurance Company PAC (Stan PAC)
FEC ID: C00193169
Contact: Justin R. Delaney
1100 S.W. Sixth Ave.
Portland, OR 97204

  Contributions to Candidates: $5,500 (2015-2016)
  Democrats: $3,000; Republicans: $2,500

Corporate Foundations and Giving Programs
Standard Charitable Foundation
1100 S.W. Sixth Ave.
Portland, OR 97204

Tel: (971) 321-8662
Fax: (971) 321-8662

Public Affairs and Related Activities Personnel

At Headquarters

CHADEE, Floyd F.
Senior Vice President and Chief Financial Officer
fchadee@standard.com

Tel: (800) 262-7111
Fax: (503) 321-7000

DELANEY, Justin R.
PAC Treasurer
jdelaney@standard.com

Tel: (800) 262-7111
Fax: (503) 321-7000

DURHAM, Katherine
Vice President, Marketing and Communications

Tel: (800) 262-7111
Fax: (503) 321-7000

FRANKLIN, Holley Y.
Vice President, Corporate Secretary and Associate Counsel
holley.franklin@standard.com

Tel: (503) 321-7000
Fax: (971) 321-6776

HALLIN, Jeff
Assistant Vice President, Investor Relations and Capital Markets
jeff.hallin@standard.com

Tel: (971) 321-6127
Fax: (971) 321-5037

HOOPER, John
Vice President, Human Resources

Tel: (800) 262-7111
Fax: (503) 321-7000

SPELTZ, Bob
Director, Public Affairs
bob.speltz@standard.com

Tel: (971) 321-3162
Fax: (971) 321-6776

Standard Register Corporation

A document management services.
www.standardregister.com
Annual Revenues: $806.65 million
Employees: 3,700
Ticker: NYSE: SR
SIC: 2761; 2752; 2759; 3555; 7389
NAICS: 323116; 323110; 323119; 333293; 56191
Industry/ies: Machinery/Equipment

Chairman of the Board
CLARKE, III, F. David

Tel: (937) 221-1000
Fax: (937) 221-1855

Main Headquarters
Mailing: P.O. Box 1167
Dayton, OH 45401-1167

Tel: (937) 221-1000
Fax: (937) 221-1855
TF: (800) 755-6405

Corporate Foundations and Giving Programs
The Sherman-Standard Foundation
P.O. Box 1167
Dayton, OH 45401

Tel: (937) 221-1000
Fax: (937) 221-1000

Public Affairs and Related Activities Personnel

At Headquarters

CUTTING , Jr., Ben
Chief Financial Officer

Tel: (937) 221-1000
Fax: (937) 221-1855

MODER, Jeff
President, Promotional Marketing

Tel: (937) 221-1000
Fax: (937) 221-1855

SOWAR, Gerard D.
Vice President, General Counsel and Secretary

Tel: (937) 221-1506
Fax: (937) 221-3431

Stanley Black & Decker

A worldwide manufacturer and marketer of tools, hardware and door systems for home improvement, consumer, industrial and professional use. Formed by the merger of The Stanley Works and Black & Decker in 2010.
www.stanleyblackanddecker.com
Annual Revenues: $11.21 billion
Employees: 51,250
Ticker: NYSE: SWK
SIC: 3420
Industry/ies: Construction/Construction Materials
Legislative Issues: BUD; CSP; EDU; ENG; GOV; HOM; MAN; NAT; TAX

Chairman of the Board and Chief Executive Officer
LUNDGREN, John F.

Tel: (860) 225-5111
Fax: (860) 827-3895

Main Headquarters
Mailing: 1000 Stanley Dr.
New Britain, CT 06053

Tel: (860) 225-5111
Fax: (860) 827-3895

Corporate Foundations and Giving Programs
Stanley Black and Decker Citizenship Program
1000 Stanley Dr.
New Britain, CT 06053

Tel: (860) 225-5111
Fax: (860) 827-3895

Public Affairs and Related Activities Personnel

At Headquarters

ALLAN, Jr., Donald
Senior Vice President and Chief Financial Officer

Tel: (860) 225-5111
Fax: (860) 827-3937

BEATT, Bruce H.
Senior Vice President, General Counsel and Secretary

Tel: (860) 225-5111
Fax: (860) 827-3895

GASS, Rhonda
Vice President and Chief Information Officer

Tel: (860) 225-5111
Fax: (860) 827-3895

LOREE, James M.
President and Chief Operating Officer

Tel: (860) 225-5111
Fax: (860) 827-3895

PERRA, Tim
Director, Global Communications
Tim.Perra@swkbdk.com

Tel: (860) 826-3260
Fax: (860) 827-3895

VOELKER, Joe
Senior Vice President, Human Resources

Tel: (860) 225-5111
Fax: (860) 827-3895

WAYBRIGHT, Greg

Tel: (860) 225-5111

Vice President, Investor and Government Relations
investorrelations@sbdinc.com
Fax: (860) 827-3895

WYATT, John
President, Sales and Marketing
Tel: (860) 225-5111
Fax: (860) 827-3895

Stanley Consultants, Inc.

A provider of engineering, environmental, and construction services. Services include consulting, planning, studies, design, environmental, and construction management.
www.stanleyconsultants.com
Annual Revenues: $59 million
Employees: 1,700
Industry/ies: Engineering/Mathematics

Chairman of the Board
THOMOPULOS, PE, Gregs G.
Tel: (563) 264-6600
Fax: (563) 264-6658

President and Chief Executive Officer
ROBERTS, PE, Gayle A.
Tel: (563) 264-6600
Fax: (563) 264-6658

Main Headquarters
Mailing: 225 Iowa Ave.
Muscatine, IA 52761-3764
Tel: (563) 264-6600
Fax: (563) 264-6658

Political Action Committees
Stanley Consultants Inc. PAC
FEC ID: C00415224
Contact: Richard C. Smith
225 Iowa Ave.
Muscatine, IA 52761

Contributions to Candidates: $500 (2015-2016)
Democrats: $500

Corporate Foundations and Giving Programs

The Stanley Foundation
Contact: Richard H. Stanley
225 Iowa Ave.
Muscatine, IA 52761

Public Affairs and Related Activities Personnel

At Headquarters

FINCHUM, Mary Jo
Communications Section Manager and Public Relations Administrator
PublicRelations@StanleyGroup.com
Tel: (563) 264-6485
Fax: (563) 264-6658

SMITH, Richard C.
PAC Treasurer
Tel: (563) 264-6600
Fax: (563) 264-6658

STANLEY, Richard H.
Chairman, Stanley Foundation
Tel: (563) 264-6600
Fax: (563) 264-6658

Stanley Engineering Company

See listing on page 745 under Stanley Consultants, Inc.

Staples, Inc.

Operates as an office products company. Offers various office supplies and services, office machines and related products, computers and related products, and office furniture under Staples, Quill, and other proprietary brands.
www.staples.com
Annual Revenues: $22.10 billion
Employees: 44,400
Ticker: NASDAQ: SPLS
SIC: 5940
Industry/ies: Retail/Wholesale

Chairman of the Board and Chief Executive Officer
SARGENT, Ronald L.
Ron.sargent@Staples.com
Tel: (508) 253-5000
Fax: (508) 253-8989

Main Headquarters
Mailing: 500 Staples Dr.
Framingham, MA 01702
Tel: (508) 253-5000
Fax: (508) 253-8989
TF: (800) 378-2753

Political Action Committees
Staples Political Action Committee (Staples PAC)
FEC ID: C00391409
Contact: Christine T. Komola
500 Staples Dr.
Framingham, MA 01702
Tel: (508) 253-5000
Fax: (508) 253-8989

Corporate Foundations and Giving Programs

Staples Foundation for Learning
Contact: Brian Curran
500 Staples Dr.
Framingham, MA 01702
Tel: (508) 253-0203
Fax: (508) 253-8989

Public Affairs and Related Activities Personnel

At Headquarters

CURRAN, Brian
Manager, Community Relations
Briana.Curran@Staples.com
Tel: (508) 253-0203
Fax: (700) 333-0703

GOODMAN, Shira
President, North American Commercial
Tel: (508) 253-5000
Fax: (508) 253-8989

KOMOLA, Christine T.
Executive Vice President and Chief Financial Officer and PAC Treasurer
Tel: (508) 253-5000
Fax: (508) 253-8989

MCELWEE, Carrie
Director, Public Relations
Carrie.McElwee@Staples.com
Tel: (508) 253-1405
Fax: (508) 253-8989

MULOT, Regis
Executive Vice President, Human Resources
Tel: (508) 253-5000
Fax: (508) 253-8989

POWERS, Christopher
Vice President, Investor Relations
Tel: (508) 253-4632
Fax: (508) 253-8989

WILLIAMS, Michael T.
Senior Vice President, General Counsel and Secretary
Tel: (508) 253-5000
Fax: (508) 253-8989

Star Financial Bank

Provides financial services including banking, equipment leasing, mortgage banking, wealth management, insurance, and trust through three subsidiary organizations.
www.starfinancial.com
Annual Revenues: $107.45 million
Employees: 600
Industry/ies: Banking/Finance/Investments

Chairman of the Board, President and Director
MARCUCCILLI, Thomas M.
Tel: (260) 428-7000
Fax: (260) 428-7050

Chief Executive Officer
MARCUCCILLI, James C.
Tel: (260) 428-7000
Fax: (260) 428-7050

Senior Vice President
HART, Trois K.
Tel: (260) 415-2401
Fax: (260) 479-2549

Main Headquarters
Mailing: P.O. Box 11409
Ft. Wayne, IN 46858-1409
Tel: (260) 428-7000
Fax: (260) 428-7050

Political Action Committees
Star Financial Bank PAC
FEC ID: C00366633
Contact: Karen F. Gregerson
127 W. Berry St.
Suite Two
Ft. Wayne, IN 46802

Contributions to Candidates: $250 (2015-2016)
Democrats: $250

Public Affairs and Related Activities Personnel

At Headquarters

CORNWELL, David D.
General Counsel
Tel: (260) 428-7000
Fax: (260) 428-7050

GOTSCH, Stephen L.
Senior Vice President and Human Resources Director
Tel: (260) 428-7000
Fax: (260) 428-7050

GREGERSON, Karen F.
Chief Financial Officer and PAC Treasurer
karen.gregerson@starfinancial.com
Tel: (260) 428-7000
Fax: (260) 428-7050

The Star Tribune

Newspaper company serving the Minneapolis-St. Paul area and readers around the state of Minnesota, also provides direct marketing services and produces niche publications.
www.startribune.com
Annual Revenues: $147.70 million
Employees: 2,700
Industry/ies: Communications; Media/Mass Communication

Publisher and Chief Executive Officer
KLINGENSMITH, Michael J.
michael.klingensmith@startribune.com
Tel: (612) 673-4256
Fax: (612) 673-4359

Main Headquarters
Mailing: 650 Third Ave., South
Suite 1300
Minneapolis, MN 55488
Tel: (612) 673-4000

Corporate Foundations and Giving Programs

Star Tribune Foundation
425 Portland Ave.
First Floor
Minneapolis, MN 55488

Public Affairs and Related Activities Personnel

At Headquarters

BROWN, Chuck
Senior Vice President, Chief Financial Officer
chuck.brown@startribune.com
Tel: (612) 673-4760

DESMOND, Kevin
Senior Vice President, Operations
kevin.desmond@startribune.com
Tel: (612) 627-8710

KASBOHM, Paul
Chief Revenue Officer
Tel: (612) 673-7207

paul.kasbohm@startribune.com

LEBEDOFF, Randy   Tel: (612) 673-7133
Senior Vice President and General Counsel
randy.lebedoff@startribune.com

SIRANY, Adrienne   Tel: (612) 673-4076
Vice President, Human Resources
adrienne.sirany@startribune.com

At Other Offices

TAYLOR, Ben   Tel: (612) 673-7457
Senior Vice President, Marketing and Communications   Fax: (612) 673-4835
425 Portland Ave., South
Minneapolis, MN 55488
btaylor@startribune.com

Starbucks Corporation

Owner and operator of specialty coffee shops and distributor of coffee and novelty items.
www.starbucks.com
Annual Revenues: $20.16 billion
Employees: 157,000
Ticker: NASDAQ: SBUX
SIC: 5812; 2095; 2090
Industry/ies: Food And Beverage Industry; Retail/Wholesale
Legislative Issues: AGR; CIV; EDU; ENV; FOR; LAW; LBR; TAX; TRD; VET

Chairman of the Board and Chief Executive Officer   Tel: (206) 447-1575
SCHULTZ, Howard   Fax: (206) 447-0828
Howard.Schultz@starbucks.com

Main Headquarters
Mailing: P.O. Box 3717   Tel: (206) 447-1575
        Seattle, WA 98124-3717   Fax: (206) 447-0828

Corporate Foundations and Giving Programs

Starbucks Foundation
P.O. Box 3717
Seattle, WA 98124

Public Affairs and Related Activities Personnel

At Headquarters

DEGRANDE, JoAnn   Tel: (206) 318-7118
Vice President   Fax: (206) 447-0828

JOHNSON, Kevin   Tel: (206) 447-1575
President and Chief Operating Officer   Fax: (206) 447-0828

PITASKY, Scott   Tel: (206) 447-1575
Executive Vice President and Chief Partner Resources Officer   Fax: (206) 447-0828

ROTHSTEIN, Sharon   Tel: (206) 447-1575
Executive Vice President and Global Chief Marketing Officer   Fax: (206) 447-0828

SWAYA, Matthew   Tel: (206) 447-1575
Senior Vice President, Chief Ethics and Compliance Officer,   Fax: (206) 447-0828
Law and Corporate Affairs

VARMA, Vivek   Tel: (206) 447-1575
Executive Vice President, Public Affairs   Fax: (206) 447-0828
Vivek.Varma@starbucks.com

YOUNG-SCRIVNER, Annie   Tel: (206) 447-1575
Executive Vice President and Global Digital and Loyalty   Fax: (206) 447-0828
Development

At Other Offices

ENGSKOV, Kris   Tel: (206) 318-5780
President, Starbucks Europe, Middle East and Africa   Fax: (206) 447-0828
2401 Utah Ave., South, Suite 800
Seattle, WA 98134
Registered Federal Lobbyist

HELM, Lucy Lee   Tel: (206) 447-1575
Executive Vice President, General Counsel, Secretary and   Fax: (206) 447-0828
Law and Corporate Affairs
2401 Utah Ave., South, Suite 800
Seattle, WA 98134

MAW, Scott   Tel: (206) 447-1575
Executive Vice President and Chief Financial Officer   Fax: (206) 447-0828
2401 Utah Ave., South, Suite 800
Seattle, WA 98134

PROSSER , Stephen   Tel: (206) 447-1575
Managing Director, Business Ethics and Compliance   Fax: (206) 447-0828
2401 Utah Ave., South, Suite 800
Seattle, WA 98134

ROTH, Jayme   Tel: (206) 447-1575
2401 Utah Ave., South, Suite 800   Fax: (206) 447-0828
Seattle, WA 98134
Registered Federal Lobbyist

RYAN, Matthew   Tel: (206) 447-1575
Executive Vice President and Global Chief Strategy Officer   Fax: (206) 447-0828
2401 Utah Ave., South, Suite 800
Seattle, WA 98134

Stark Investments

An investment firm.
www.starkinvestments.com
Industry/ies: Banking/Finance/Investments
Legislative Issues: FIN

Chief Executive Officer and Chief Investment Officer   Tel: (414) 294-7000
STARK, Brian

Main Headquarters
Mailing: 3600 S. Lake Dr.   Tel: (414) 294-7000
        St. Francis, WI 53235

Public Affairs and Related Activities Personnel

At Headquarters

MCNALLY , Dan   Tel: (414) 294-7000
Chief Operating Officer and General Counsel

MOREADITH, Kathryn   Tel: (414) 294-7000
Investor Relations

ROTH , Mike   Tel: (414) 294-7000
Head, Business Development

Starr Commonwealth

Operates programs for troubled youth and their families in Michigan and Ohio.
www.starr.org
Annual Revenues: $30.17 million
Employees: 500
Industry/ies: Children And Youth
Legislative Issues: EDU; HCR; LAW

President and Chief Executive Officer   Tel: (517) 629-5591
CAREY, MSW, Elizabeth A.   Fax: (517) 630-2400
careye@starr.org

Main Headquarters
Mailing: 13725 Starr Commonwealth Rd.   Tel: (517) 629-5591
        Albion, MI 49224-9580   Fax: (517) 630-2400
                         TF: (800) 837-5591

Corporate Foundations and Giving Programs

Starr Commonwealth/Montcalm Schools Scholarship Endowment Fund
13725 Starr Commonwealth Rd.
Albion, MI 49224

Public Affairs and Related Activities Personnel

At Headquarters

SMITH, CPA, BBA, Christopher L.   Tel: (517) 629-5591
Executive Vice President and Chief Financial Officer   Fax: (517) 629-2317
smithc@starr.org

Starwood Energy Group

A private equity investment firm that specializes in energy infrastructure investments.
www.starwoodenergygroup.com
Employees: 5
Industry/ies: Energy/Electricity

Chairman of the Board   Tel: (203) 422-7700
STERNLICHT, Barry S.   Fax: (203) 422-7827
sternlicht@starwood.com

Chief Executive Officer and Managing Director   Tel: (203) 422-7700
NORDHOLM, Bradford   Fax: (203) 422-7827
bnordholm@starwood.com

Main Headquarters
Mailing: 591 W. Putnam Ave.   Tel: (203) 422-7700
        Greenwich, CT 06830   Fax: (203) 422-7827

Public Affairs and Related Activities Personnel

At Headquarters

ARBIA, David   Tel: (203) 422-7700
Chief Financial Officer   Fax: (203) 422-7827

BRUCE, Olga   Tel: (203) 422-7727
Investor Relations Coordinator   Fax: (203) 422-7827
obruce@starwood.com

JOHNSON, Tom   Tel: (212) 371-5999
Contact, Media Relations   Fax: (203) 422-7784
tbj@abmac.com

Starwood Hotels and Resorts Worldwide, Inc.

Hotel and leisure companies. Acquired ITT Corp. in 1998. Starwood acquired the Sheraton. It operates about 100 luxury resorts and hotels through its St. Regis and Luxury Collection, while its chain of about 40 W Hotels offers ultra-modern style. Starwood is a fully integrated owner, operator and franchisor of hotels, resorts and residences with internationally renowned brands.
www.starwoodhotels.com
Employees: 180,000
Ticker: NYSE: HOT
SIC: 6798
Industry/ies: Travel/Tourism/Lodging

Legislative Issues: CPT; FOR; IMM; LBR; TAX

Chief Executive Officer
MANGAS, Thomas B.

Tel: (203) 964-6000
Fax: (914) 640-8310

Main Headquarters
Mailing: One StarPoint
Fifth Floor
Stamford, CT 06902

Tel: (203) 964-6000
Fax: (914) 640-8310
TF: (800) 328-6242

Political Action Committees
Starwood Hotels and Resorts Worldwide Inc. PAC (Starwood PAC)
FEC ID: C00219717
Contact: Alisa Rosenberg
15147 N. Scottsdale Rd.
Suite 210
Scottsdale, AZ 85254

Contributions to Candidates: $48,515 (2015-2016)
Democrats: $19,515; Republicans: $28,000; Other: $1,000

Corporate Foundations and Giving Programs
Starwood Hotels and Resorts Worldwide Contributions Program
1111 Westchester Ave.
Third Floor
White Plains, NY 10604

Tel: (914) 640-8100

Public Affairs and Related Activities Personnel

At Headquarters

CAVA, Jeff
Executive Vice President and Chief Human Resources Officer

Tel: (203) 964-6000
Fax: (914) 640-8310

DUNCAN, Bruce W.
Director

Tel: (203) 964-6000
Fax: (914) 640-8310

HORSHAM-BERTELS, Helen
Senior Director, Consumer Affairs
helen.horsham-bertels@starwoodhotels.com

Tel: (203) 964-6000
Fax: (914) 640-8310

KAVANAGH, K.C.
Senior Vice President, Global Communications

Tel: (203) 964-6000
Fax: (914) 640-8310

PETTIBONE, Stephen
Vice President, Investor Relations

Tel: (203) 351-3500
Fax: (914) 640-8310

ROBERTS, Katie
Contact, Public Relations
Katie.Roberts@starwoodhotels.com

Tel: (203) 964-6000
Fax: (914) 640-8310

SCHNAID, Alan M.
Senior Vice President and Chief Financial Officer

Tel: (203) 964-6000
Fax: (914) 640-8310

SIEGEL, Kenneth S.
Chief Administrative Officer and General Counsel
kenneth.siegel@starwoodhotels.com

Tel: (203) 964-6000
Fax: (914) 640-8310

TURNER, Simon
President, Global Development

Tel: (203) 964-6000
Fax: (914) 640-8310

At Other Offices

DADDARIO, Nick
Vice President, Assistant Corporate Controller
15147 N. Scottsdale Rd., Suite H-210
Scottsdale, AZ 85254

Tel: (480) 905-4500

MITCHELL, Mark
Vice President, Corporate Controller
15147 N. Scottsdale Rd., Suite H-210
Scottsdale, AZ 85254

Tel: (480) 905-4500

ROSENBERG, Alisa
PAC Treasurer
15147 N. Scottsdale Rd., Suite H-210
Scottsdale, AZ 85254

Tel: (480) 905-4500

State Farm Insurance Companies

An insurance company.
www.statefarm.com
Employees: 69,000
Industry/ies: Insurance Industry
Legislative Issues: AVI; BAN; CPT; DIS; FIN; HCR; HOM; INS; POS; RET; TAX; TOR; TRA

Chairman of the Board and Chief Executive Officer
RUST, Jr., Edward B.

Tel: (309) 766-2871
Fax: (309) 766-3621

Main Headquarters
Mailing: One State Farm Plaza
Bloomington, IL 61710-0001

Tel: (309) 766-2311
Fax: (309) 766-3621

Washington Office
Mailing: 1900 M St. NW
Suite 730
Washington, DC 20036

Tel: (202) 263-4400
Fax: (202) 263-4435

Political Action Committees
State Farm Mutual Automobile Insurance Company Federal PAC
FEC ID: C00111017
Contact: Mark Schwamberger
One State Farm Plaza

Bloomington, 61710

Contributions to Candidates: $613,125 (2015-2016)
Democrats: $276,250; Republicans: $336,875

Principal Recipients

SENATE
BLUNT, ROY (REP-MO)

HOUSE
KILMER, DEREK (DEM-WA)
MCCARTHY, KEVIN (REP-CA)
ROSS, DENNIS ALAN (REP-FL)
ROYCE, ED MR. (REP-CA)
SINEMA, KYRSTEN (DEM-AZ)

Corporate Foundations and Giving Programs
State Farm Companies Foundation
One State Farm Plaza
Bloomington, IL 61710

Public Affairs and Related Activities Personnel

At Headquarters

CAREY-ODEKIRK, Carol
Business Analyst
carol.carey-odekirk.btdj@statefarm.com

Tel: (309) 766-6781
Fax: (309) 766-3621

DUNDOV, Missy
Media Contact
Missy.Dundov.sg5r@statefarm.com

Tel: (630) 541-4355
Fax: (309) 766-3621

FONES, Dawn
Public Affairs Specialist
dawn.fones.cv9s@statefarm.com

Tel: (309) 766-2259
Fax: (309) 766-3621

SUPPLE, Phil
Senior Director, External Relations

Tel: (309) 766-9921
Fax: (309) 766-3621

At Washington Office

BLUMENTHAL, Bill
Director, Government Affairs
bill.blumenthal.mhdx@statefarm.com
Registered Federal Lobbyist

Tel: (202) 263-4400
Fax: (202) 263-4435

CIMONS, Wayne A.
Counsel
Registered Federal Lobbyist

Tel: (202) 263-4400
Fax: (202) 263-4435

COYLE, Rebecca
Public Policy Analyst

Tel: (202) 263-4400
Fax: (202) 263-4435

DILLARD, Regina K.
Federal Affairs Counsel
Registered Federal Lobbyist

Tel: (202) 263-4400
Fax: (202) 263-4435

JACKSON, Neil
Registered Federal Lobbyist

Tel: (202) 263-4400
Fax: (202) 263-4435

MANESS, Alan
Associate General Counsel
alan.maness.grnd@statefarm.com
Registered Federal Lobbyist

Tel: (202) 263-4400
Fax: (202) 263-4435

ROGERS, Joel
Public Policy Analyst
Registered Federal Lobbyist

Tel: (202) 263-4400
Fax: (202) 263-4435

SCHWAMBERGER, Mark
Vice President and Controller and PAC Treasurer

Tel: (202) 263-4400
Fax: (202) 263-4435

State Street Bank and Trust Company

Provides mutual fund and pension processing and custody services; its target clients include large-scale institutional investors and corporations who can choose from a service menu that includes accounting, foreign exchange, cash management, securities lending, and more.
www.statestreet.com
SIC: 6022
Industry/ies: Banking/Finance/Investments
Legislative Issues: BAN; FIN; RET; TAX

Chairman of the Board and Chief Executive Officer
HOOLEY, Joseph L.

Tel: (617) 786-3000
Fax: (617) 664-4299

Main Headquarters
Mailing: One Lincoln St.
21st Floor
Boston, MA 02111

Tel: (617) 786-3000
Fax: (617) 664-4299

Political Action Committees
State Street Bank and Trust Company Voluntary PAC
FEC ID: C00072751
Contact: J. Barry McDonald Jr.
P.O. Box 5351
Boston, MA 02206

Tel: (617) 786-3000
Fax: (617) 786-3000

Contributions to Candidates: $107,000 (2015-2016)
Democrats: $49,000; Republicans: $57,000; Other: $1,000

Corporate Foundations and Giving Programs
State Street Foundation
Contact: George A. Russell Jr.

P.O. Box 5501   Tel: (617) 786-3000
Boston, MA 02206   Fax: (617) 786-3000

Public Affairs and Related Activities Personnel

At Headquarters

BARRY, Joseph   Tel: (617) 664-1254
Senior Vice President, Regulatory & Government Affairs   Fax: (617) 664-4299
jjbarry@statestreet.com
Registered Federal Lobbyist

CARP, Jeffrey N.   Tel: (617) 664-3000
Executive Vice President and Chief Legal Officer   Fax: (617) 664-4999

CICHON, Carolyn   Tel: (617) 664-8672
Senior Vice President and Global Head, Corporate   Fax: (617) 664-4299
Communications
ccichon@statestreet.com

COULTER, Cuan   Tel: (617) 786-3000
Executive Vice President and Chief Compliance Officer   Fax: (617) 664-4299

GAVELL, Stefan M.   Tel: (617) 786-3000
Executive Vice President, Head, Regulatory, Industry and   Fax: (617) 664-4299
Government Affairs

GROVE, Hannah   Tel: (617) 786-3000
Executive Vice President and Chief Marketing Officer   Fax: (617) 664-4299

KAHN, Melissa   Tel: (617) 786-3000
Registered Federal Lobbyist   Fax: (617) 664-4299

KEATING, Mark R.   Tel: (617) 786-3000
Executive Vice President and International Chief Finance   Fax: (617) 664-4299
Officer, Corporate Finance

KLINCK, John   Tel: (617) 786-3000
Executive Vice President, Head, Global Strategy and New   Fax: (617) 664-4299
Ventures

MCDONALD, Jr., J. Barry   Tel: (617) 786-3000
PAC Treasurer   Fax: (617) 664-4299

NAZZARO, Stephen   Tel: (617) 786-3000
Executive Vice President and Head, Institutional Investor   Fax: (617) 664-4299
Services

PATTERSON, Steven   Tel: (617) 786-3000
Registered Federal Lobbyist   Fax: (617) 664-4299

QUIRK, Alison   Tel: (617) 786-3000
Executive Vice President and Head, Global Human Resources   Fax: (617) 654-4062
and and Citizenship Officer

ROGERS, Michael F.   Tel: (617) 786-3000
President and Chief Operating Officer   Fax: (617) 664-4299

RUSSELL, Jr., George A.   Tel: (617) 786-3000
Executive Vice President and Director, Corporate Citizenship   Fax: (617) 451-6315

State Street Partners L.L.C.

A full-service Government Affairs and Lobbying firm representing clients throughout the United States on federal environmental issues.
www.statestreetpartners.com
Legislative Issues: ENV

Founder & Managing Partner   Tel: (609) 695-8684
IOSSA, Esq., Rocco F.
riossa@statestreetpartners.com

Main Headquarters
Mailing: 156 W. State St.   Tel: (609) 695-6664
       Suite 201
       Trenton, NJ 08608

Public Affairs and Related Activities Personnel

At Headquarters

MCDONOUGH, Peter   Tel: (609) 695-8684
Federal Lobbyist

STEINBERG, Alan J.   Tel: (609) 695-8684
Regional Administrator
asteinberg@statestreetpartners.com
Registered Federal Lobbyist

Station Casinos, Inc.

Provides gaming and entertainment to the residents of Las Vegas, Nevada.
www.sclv.com
Annual Revenues: $944.96 million
Employees: 12,000
SIC: 7011
Industry/ies: Sports/Leisure/Entertainment
Legislative Issues: GAM; IND

Chairman of the Board and Chief Executive Officer   Tel: (702) 495-3000
FERTITTA, III, Frank J.   Fax: (702) 495-3530

Main Headquarters
Mailing: 1505 S. Pavilion Center Dr.   Tel: (702) 495-3000
       Las Vegas, NV 89135   Fax: (702) 495-3530
       TF: (800) 634-3101

Corporate Foundations and Giving Programs
Station Casinos Contributions Program
1505 S. Pavilion Center Dr.   Fax: (702) 495-3310
Las Vegas, NV 89135

Public Affairs and Related Activities Personnel

At Headquarters

CAVALLARO, Stephen L.   Tel: (702) 495-3000
President and Chief Operating Officer   Fax: (702) 495-3530

FALCONE, Marc J.   Tel: (702) 495-3600
Executive Vice President, Chief Financial Officer and   Fax: (702) 495-3530
Treasurer

HASKINS, Richard J.   Tel: (702) 495-3000
Executive Vice President, General Counsel and Secretary   Fax: (702) 495-3530

NELSON, Lori   Tel: (702) 495-3000
Vice President, Corporate Communications   Fax: (702) 495-3530
lori.nelson@stationcasinos.com

STEPHENS, Aimee   Tel: (702) 495-3000
Manager, Public Relations   Fax: (702) 495-3530

Statoil Gulf of Mexico, LLC

A private company categorized under Oil and Gas Exploration and Development.
www.statoil.com/en/about/worldwide/northamerica/us
Industry/ies: Fuels See Coal, Gas, Oil, Petroleum; Natural Resources; Petroleum
Industry

Chairman   Tel: (713) 918-8200
REINERTSEN, Oivind

President and Chief Executive Officer   Tel: (713) 918-8200
SÆTRE, Eldar

Main Headquarters
Mailing: 2103 City West Blvd.   Tel: (713) 918-8200
       Houston, TX 77042

Washington Office
Mailing: 1050 K St. NW   Tel: (202) 370-5210
       Suite 950
       Washington, DC 20001-4417

Public Affairs and Related Activities Personnel

At Headquarters

GJEDREM, Njal   Tel: (713) 918-8200
Federal Lobbyist

KNIGHT, John   Tel: (713) 918-8200
Executive Vice President, Global Strategy and Business
Development

O'BRIEN, Charles   Tel: (713) 918-8200
General Counsel

OPEDAL, Anders   Tel: (713) 918-8200
Chief Operating Officer

REITAN, Torgrim   Tel: (713) 918-8200
Executive Vice President and Chief Financial Officer

Statoil Marketing & Trading (U.S.) Inc.

Statoil Marketing & Trading is a wholesaler of oil and petroleum products.
www.statoil.com
Industry/ies: Advertising And Marketing; Fuels See Coal, Gas, Oil, Petroleum;
Natural Resources; Petroleum Industry; Trade (Foreign And Domestic)

President and Chief Executive Officer   Tel: (203) 976-6988
SMITH, Luann   Fax: (203) 978-6952

Main Headquarters
Mailing: 120 Long Ridge Rd.   Tel: (203) 978-6900
       Suite 3EO1   Fax: (203) 978-6952
       Stamford, CT 06902

Washington Office
Mailing: 1050 K St. NW   Tel: (202) 370-5210
       Suite 950
       Washington, DC 20001-4417

Public Affairs and Related Activities Personnel

At Headquarters

BJORNSTAD, Geir   Tel: (203) 978-6900
Vice President, Investor Relations   Fax: (203) 978-6952
gebjo@statoil.com

JOHANNESSEN, Morten Sven   Tel: (203) 570-2524
Vice President, Investor Relations   Fax: (203) 978-6952
mosvejo@statoil.com

O'BRIEN, Charles   Tel: (203) 978-6900
General Counsel   Fax: (203) 978-6952

TURIANO, Gary   Tel: (203) 978-6900
Chief Financial Officer   Fax: (203) 978-6952

Statoil Natural Gas LLC

Energy company primarily focused on upstream oil and gas operations.
www.statoil.com
Employees: 40
Industry/ies: Natural Resources
Legislative Issues: ENG

Main Headquarters

Mailing:	120 Long Ridge Rd. Suite 3EO1 Stamford, CT 06902	Tel: Fax:	(203) 978-6900 (203) 978-6952

Washington Office

Mailing:	1050 K St. NW Suite 950 Washington, DC 20001-4417	Tel:	(202) 370-5210

Corporate Foundations and Giving Programs

Backing Green Foundation

120 Long Ridge Rd. Suite 3EO1 Stamford, CT 06902	Tel: Fax:	(203) 978-6900 (203) 978-6952

Public Affairs and Related Activities Personnel

At Headquarters

EITRHEIM, Pl *Federal Lobbyist*	Tel: Fax:	(203) 978-6900 (203) 978-6952
JOHANNESSEN, Morten Sven *Vice President, Investor Relations* mosvejo@statoil.com	Tel: Fax:	(203) 570-2524 (203) 978-6952
O'BRIEN, Charles *General Counsel*	Tel:	(203) 978-6988

At Washington Office

TETI, Nate J. *Head, Sustainability*	Tel:	(202) 370-5210

At Other Offices

AANESTAD , Ola Morten *Head, Communications* 2103 City W. Blvd., Suite 800 Houston, TX 77042 oaan@statoil.com	Tel:	(713) 918-8200

StatoilHydro ASA

Formerly Statoil ASA. Norwegian national oil company. Headquartered in Stavanger, Norway. The address shown below is used for its U.S. affiliates, Statoil Marketing & Trading (U.S.) Inc. and Statoil Natural Gas LLC (see separate listings).
www.statoil.com
Industry/ies: Natural Resources
Legislative Issues: ENV; FOR; FUE

Public Affairs and Related Activities Personnel

At Headquarters

FUERY, Evan
Registered Federal Lobbyist

KARLSEN, Jan Karl
Vice President

MASSY, Kevin
Director
Registered Federal Lobbyist

OLSEN, Mike
Senior Director
Registered Federal Lobbyist

At Other Offices

EITRHEIM, Pl 225 High Ridge Rd. Stamford, CT 06905	Tel: Fax:	(203) 978-6988 (203) 978-6952
GJEDREM, Njal *Lobbyist* 225 High Ridge Rd. Stamford, CT 06905	Tel: Fax:	(203) 978-6988 (203) 978-6952
O'BRIEN, Charles *General Counsel* 225 High Ridge Rd. Stamford, CT 06905	Tel: Fax:	(203) 978-6988 (203) 978-6952
TETI, Nate J. *Manager, U.S. Onshore Public and Regulatory Affairs* 225 High Ridge Rd. Stamford, CT 06905	Tel: Fax:	(203) 978-6988 (203) 978-6952

Steelcase Inc.

A designer and manufacturer of architecture, furniture and technology for the office.
www.steelcase.com
Annual Revenues: $3.06 billion
Employees: 10,700
Ticker: NYSE: SCS

SIC: 2522; 2521
NAICS: 337211
Industry/ies: Furniture/Home Furnishings
Legislative Issues: TAX; TRD

President and Chief Executive Officer, Director	Tel:	(616) 247-2710
KEANE, James P.	Fax:	(616) 475-2270

Main Headquarters

Mailing:	901 44th St. SE Grand Rapids, MI 49508	Tel: Fax: TF:	(616) 247-2710 (616) 475-2270 (800) 333-9939

Corporate Foundations and Giving Programs

The Steelcase Foundation
Contact: Phyllis Gebben
P.O. Box 1967
Grand Rapids, MI 49501

Public Affairs and Related Activities Personnel

At Headquarters

ARMBRUSTER, Sara E. *Vice President, Strategy, Research and New Business* *Innovation*	Tel: Fax:	(616) 247-2710 (616) 475-2270
GEBBEN, Phyllis *Coordinator, Donations* pgebben@steelcase.com	Tel: Fax:	(616) 247-2710 (616) 475-2270
MOSSING, Mark T. *Corporate Controller and Chief Accounting Officer*	Tel: Fax:	(616) 247-2710 (616) 475-2270
MOUTREY, Gale *Vice President, Communications*	Tel: Fax:	(616) 247-2710 (616) 475-2270
O'SHAUGHNESSY, Lizbeth S. *Senior Vice President, Chief Administrative Officer, General* *Counsel and Secretary*	Tel: Fax:	(616) 247-2710 (616) 475-2270
SMITH, Allan W. *Vice President, Global Marketing*	Tel: Fax:	(616) 247-2710 (616) 475-2270
SYLVESTER, David C. *Senior Vice President and Chief Financial Officer*	Tel: Fax:	(616) 247-2710 (616) 475-2270
WHITMAN, Sara *Contact, Media Relations* swhitman@peppercom.com	Tel: Fax:	(212) 931-6121 (616) 475-2270

Steele & Utz

Main Headquarters

Mailing:	1700 Pennsylvania Ave. NW Suite 400 Washington, DC 20006	Tel:	(202) 785-2130

Public Affairs and Related Activities Personnel

At Headquarters

UTZ, William Nelson	Tel:	(202) 785-2130

Stego Industries, LLC

Concrete Vapor Barrier Marketing Firm
www.stegoindustries.com

Chief Operations Officer	Tel:	(617) 676-7877
BLASDEL, CSI, Matthew matthewblasdel@stegoindustries.com		

Main Headquarters

Mailing:	216 Avenida Fabricante Suite 101 San Clemente, CA 92672	Tel:	(617) 676-7877

Public Affairs and Related Activities Personnel

At Headquarters

HOUCK, CSI, Bret *Director, Business Development* brethouck@stegoindustries.com	Tel:	(617) 676-7877
KARTUNEN, Dave *Government Relations Executive & Contact, Corporate* *Communications* davekartunen@stegoindustries.com	Tel:	(617) 676-7877
MARKS , Joe *Director of Operations*	Tel:	(617) 676-7877

Stephens Inc.

An investment banking firm.
www.stephens.com
Employees: 500
Industry/ies: Banking/Finance/Investments

Chairman of the Board, President and Chief Executive Officer	Tel:	(501) 377-2148
STEPHENS, Warren A wstephens@stephens.com	Fax:	(501) 377-2666

Main Headquarters

Mailing: 111 Center St.
Suite 225
Little Rock, AR 72201

Tel: (501) 377-2000
Fax: (501) 377-2470
TF: (800) 643-9691

Washington Office

Mailing: 1425 K St.
Suite 350
Washington, DC 20005

Tel: (202) 628-6668
Fax: (202) 628-6669

Political Action Committees

Stephens Inc. Federal PAC
FEC ID: C00166553
Contact: Frank Thomas
111 Center St.
P.O. BOX 3507
Little Rock, AR 72201

Contributions to Candidates: $57,000 (2015-2016)
Republicans: $57,000

Principal Recipients

SENATE
BOOZMAN, JOHN (REP-AR)

Corporate Foundations and Giving Programs

Stephens Inc. Contribution Program
111 Center St.
Little Rock, AR 72201

Tel: (501) 377-2000
Fax: (501) 377-2470

Public Affairs and Related Activities Personnel

At Headquarters

BRADBURY, Curt
Chief Operating Officer

Tel: (501) 377-2000
Fax: (501) 377-2470

DORAMUS, Mark
Chief Financial Officer

Tel: (501) 377-2003
Fax: (501) 377-2470

FITZSIMMONS, Kelly
Media Contact

Tel: (303) 684-6401
Fax: (501) 377-2470

GRAY, Ellen
Executive Vice President, Human Resources and Administrative Services
egray@stephens.com

Tel: (501) 377-2003
Fax: (501) 377-2470

KNIGHT, David
Executive Vice President, General Counsel
dknight@stephens.com

Tel: (501) 377-2000
Fax: (501) 377-2470

THOMAS, Frank
PAC Treasurer
Mail Stop P.O. Box 3507
frank.thomas@stephens.com

Tel: (501) 377-2000
Fax: (501) 377-3453

Stephens Investments Holdings LLC

Specializes in equity investment management focused on small and mid-capitalization growth companies.
www.stephensfunds.com
Industry/ies: Banking/Finance/Investments
Legislative Issues: FIN

Chairman, President, Chief Executive Officer
STEPHENS, Warren A.
wstephens@stephens.com

Tel: (507) 377-2148
Fax: (501) 377-2470

Main Headquarters

Mailing: 111 Center St.
Suite 2500
Little Rock, AR 72201

Tel: (501) 377-2000
Fax: (501) 377-2470
TF: (800) 643-9691

Public Affairs and Related Activities Personnel

At Headquarters

BRYANT, Kathy Riley
Chief Financial Officer
kbryant@stephens.com

Tel: (501) 377-2346
Fax: (501) 377-2470

FARROW, JR., Jackson
General Counsel and Managing Director
jfarrow@stephens.com

Tel: (501) 377-2261
Fax: (501) 377-2470

LANDFAIR, Cherry
Paralegal

Tel: (501) 377-2000
Fax: (501) 377-2470

THOMAS, Frank
Federal Lobbyist
Registered Federal Lobbyist

Tel: (501) 377-2680
Fax: (501) 377-2470

WEAVER, Vernon
Federal Lobbyist
Registered Federal Lobbyist

Tel: (501) 377-2000
Fax: (501) 377-2470

Stericycle, Inc.

Stericycle is a medical and pharmaceutical waste management company.
www.stericycle.com
Annual Revenues: $3.20 billion
Employees: 25,472
Ticker: NASDAQ: SRCL

SIC: 4955
Industry/ies: Environment And Conservation; Medicine/Health Care/Mental Health; Pollution And Waste; Transportation
Legislative Issues: HCR

Chairman of the Board
MILLER, Mark C.
mmiller@stericycle.com

Tel: (847) 367-5910
Fax: (847) 367-9493

President and Chief Executive Officer
ALUTTO, Charles A.
calutto@stericycle.com

Tel: (847) 367-5910
Fax: (847) 367-9493

Main Headquarters

Mailing: 28161 N. Keith Dr.
Lake Forest, IL 60045

Tel: (847) 367-5910
Fax: (847) 367-9493
TF: (800) 643-0240

Political Action Committees

Stericycle, Inc. PAC
FEC ID: C00458018
Contact: Pin Lin
28161 N. Keith Dr.
Suite 300
Lake Forest, IL 60045

Contributions to Candidates: $9,500 (2015-2016)
Democrats: $2,500; Republicans: $7,000

Public Affairs and Related Activities Personnel

At Headquarters

ARNOLD, Brent
Executive Vice President and Chief Operating Officer

Tel: (847) 367-5910
Fax: (847) 367-9493

COLLINS, Mike
Executive Vice President and President, Expert, Environmental Solutions and Communication Solutions

Tel: (847) 367-5910
Fax: (847) 367-9493

FRANK, Brenda R.
Executive Vice President and Chief People Officer

Tel: (847) 367-5910
Fax: (847) 367-9493

GINNETTI, Daniel V.
Executive Vice President and Chief Financial Officer

Tel: (847) 367-5910
Fax: (847) 367-9493

LIN, Pin
PAC Treasurer

Tel: (847) 367-5910
Fax: (847) 367-9493

SCHETZ, John P.
Executive Vice President and General Counsel

Tel: (847) 367-5910
Fax: (847) 367-9493

STERIS Corporation

Provides infection prevention, contamination prevention, and microbial reduction products and services.
www.steris.com
Annual Revenues: $1.84 billion
Employees: 7,600
Ticker: NYSE: STE
SIC: 3842; 3841; 5099
NAICS: 339113
Industry/ies: Medicine/Health Care/Mental Health
Legislative Issues: DEF

Chairman of the Board
WAREHAM, John P.

Tel: (440) 354-2600
Fax: (440) 392-8972

President and Chief Executive Officer
ROSEBROUGH, Jr., Walter M.

Tel: (440) 354-2600
Fax: (440) 392-8972

Main Headquarters

Mailing: 5960 Heisley Rd.
Mentor, OH 44060

Tel: (440) 354-2600
Fax: (440) 392-8972
TF: (800) 548-4873

Political Action Committees

STERIS Corporation Good Government Fund PAC
FEC ID: C00368720
Contact: Michael J. Oleksa
5960 Heisley Rd.
Mentor, OH 44060

Contributions to Candidates: $33,400 (2015-2016)
Democrats: $9,000; Republicans: $24,400

Corporate Foundations and Giving Programs

STERIS Foundation
5960 Heisley Rd.
Mentor, OH 44060

Public Affairs and Related Activities Personnel

At Headquarters

MCGINLEY, Mark D.
Senior Vice President, General Counsel and Secretary

Tel: (440) 354-2600
Fax: (440) 392-8972

NORTON, Stephen
Director, Corporate Communications and Government Affairs
stephen.norton@steris.com

Tel: (440) 392-7482
Fax: (440) 392-8972

OLEKSA, Michael J.

Tel: (440) 354-2600
Fax: (440) 392-8972

Controller and Director Strategic Alliances and PAC
Treasurer

WINTER, Julie — Tel: (440) 392-7245
Director, Investor Relations — Fax: (440) 392-8972
julie_winter@steris.com

Sterling Chemical Company

Manufactures commodity petrochemicals. Subsidiary of Eastman Chemical Company.
www.sterlingchemical.com
Annual Revenues: $114.33 million
Employees: 200
SIC: 2860
Industry/ies: Chemicals & Chemical Industry

President and Chief Executive Officer — Tel: (904) 358-3085
GENOVA, John V. — Fax: (904) 358-3095

Main Headquarters
Mailing: 3414 N. Main St. — Tel: (904) 358-3085
Jacksonville Beach, FL 32206 — Fax: (904) 358-3095

Corporate Foundations and Giving Programs

Sterling Chemical Company Contributions Program
333 Clay St. — Tel: (713) 650-3700
Suite 3600
Houston, TX 77002-4109

Public Affairs and Related Activities Personnel

At Headquarters

JORDAN, Stan — Tel: (904) 358-3085
President — Fax: (904) 358-3095

Stevens Reed Curcio and Potholm

A political/media consulting and placement firm.
www.srcpmedia.com

Media Director — Tel: (703) 683-8326
VONDERHEID, Betsy — Fax: (703) 683-8826

Main Headquarters
Mailing: 201 N. Union St. — Tel: (703) 683-8326
Suite 200 — Fax: (703) 683-8826
Alexandria, VA 22314

Public Affairs and Related Activities Personnel

At Headquarters

BURGER, Ben — Tel: (703) 683-8326
Partner — Fax: (703) 683-8826

CURCIO, Paul — Tel: (703) 683-8326
Partner — Fax: (703) 683-8826
pcurcio@srcmedia.com

DURANT, Lindsey — Tel: (703) 683-8326
Media Assistant — Fax: (703) 683-8826

GILDNER, Lauren — Tel: (703) 683-8326
Director, Production — Fax: (703) 683-8826

LIEBSCHUTZ, Charlie — Tel: (703) 683-8326
Associate Vice President — Fax: (703) 683-8826

PAYNE, Jay — Tel: (703) 683-8326
Vice President, Creative Services — Fax: (703) 683-8826

POTHOLM, Eric — Tel: (703) 683-8326
Partner — Fax: (703) 683-8826
epotholm@srcmedia.com

REED, Rick — Tel: (703) 683-8326
Partner — Fax: (703) 683-8826
rreed@srcmedia.com

STEVENS, Greg — Tel: (703) 683-8326
Founder — Fax: (703) 683-8826

Steward Health Care System

A healthcare provider. Steward Health Care System is a community-based accountable care organization and community hospital network.
www.steward.org
Annual Revenues: $1.33 billion
Employees: 13,000
Industry/ies: Medicine/Health Care/Mental Health
Legislative Issues: ENG; FIN; HCR; HOM; TAX; UTI

Chairman of the Board and Chief Executive Officer — Tel: (617) 789-3000
DE LA TORRE, Ralph
Ralph.delatorre@steward.org

Main Headquarters
Mailing: 500 Boylston St. — Tel: (617) 419-4700
Boston, MA 02116

Public Affairs and Related Activities Personnel

At Headquarters

BERRY, Julie — Tel: (617) 419-4700

Chief Information Officer
CALLUM, Michael G. — Tel: (617) 419-4700
Executive Vice President, Business and Corporate Development

CARTY, Brian — Tel: (617) 789-3350
Chief Marketing Officer
Brian.Carty@caritaschristi.org

GROVE, Denise — Tel: (617) 419-4700
Manager, Marketing and Communications

MAHER, Esq., Jr., Joseph — Tel: (617) 789-3000
General Counsel
joseph.maher@caritaschristi.org

MURRAY, CHC, FACHE, MBA, Karen — Tel: (617) 419-4700
Chief Compliance Officer

RICH, Mark — Tel: (617) 789-3000
Chief Financial Officer

THURSTON, Brooke — Tel: (617) 419-4700
Vice President, Media Relations

TURNER, Esq., Sarah — Tel: (617) 419-4700
Chief Human Resources Officer

Stewart & Stevenson Services, Inc.

A manufacturer and distributor of products and services for the oil and gas, marine, construction, power generation, transportation, material handling, mining and agricultural industries.
www.stewartandstevenson.com
Annual Revenues: $861.23 million
Employees: 2,900
Ticker: NYSE: SNS
SIC: 3533; 3714; 3812; 3625; 3621; 3546
NAICS: 336312; 334511; 335314; 335312; 335312
Industry/ies: Defense/Homeland Security; Energy/Electricity; Government-Related; Machinery/Equipment

Chairman of the Board — Tel: (713) 751-2600
ANSARY, Hushang — Fax: (302) 636-5454

Chief Executive Officer — Tel: (713) 751-2700
SIMMONS, John B. — Fax: (302) 636-5454

Main Headquarters
Mailing: 1000 Louisiana St. — Tel: (713) 751-2700
Suite 5900 — Fax: (302) 636-5454
Houston, TX 77002

Public Affairs and Related Activities Personnel

At Headquarters

HATCHER, Charles — Tel: (713) 751-2700
Vice President, Human Resources — Fax: (302) 636-5454

SULKIS, David — Tel: (713) 751-2700
General Counsel — Fax: (302) 636-5454

Stewart Title Guaranty Company

Provides personnel and underwriting support for Stewart Title Company's land title business.
www.stewart.com
Annual Revenues: $1.93 billion
Employees: 7,400
Ticker: NYSE: STC
Industry/ies: Banking/Finance/Investments

Chairman — Tel: (713) 625-8100
APEL, Thomas G. — Fax: (713) 629-2323

Chief Executive Officer — Tel: (713) 625-8100
MORRIS, Matt — Fax: (713) 629-2323

Main Headquarters
Mailing: 1980 Post Oak Blvd. — Tel: (713) 625-8100
Suite 800 — Fax: (713) 629-2323
Houston, TX 77056 — TF: (800) 729-1900

Political Action Committees
Stewart Title Guaranty Company PAC (STEWPAC)
FEC ID: C00226712
Contact: Malcolm S. Morris
1980 Post Oak Blvd.
Suite 800
Houston, TX 77056

Public Affairs and Related Activities Personnel

At Headquarters

ARCIDIACONO, John — Tel: (713) 625-8100
Chief Marketing Officer — Fax: (713) 629-2323
Mail Stop Suite 230
jarcidia@stewart.com

BERRYMAN, Allen — Tel: (713) 625-8100
Chief Financial Officer — Fax: (713) 629-2323

CLEMENTS, Glenn H — Tel: (713) 625-8100

Contact, Operations	Fax:	(713) 629-2323
HENSHAW, Liz	Tel:	(713) 625-8100
Senior Vice President, Strategy and Program Management	Fax:	(713) 629-2323
Officer		
JONES, PhD, Ted C.	Tel:	(713) 625-8100
Senior Vice President, Chief Economist and Contact, Investor	Fax:	(713) 629-2323
Relations		
KILLEA, John	Tel:	(713) 625-8100
Chief Legal and Compliance Officer	Fax:	(713) 629-2323
MCLAUCHLAN, Susan	Tel:	(713) 625-8100
Chief Human Resources Officer	Fax:	(713) 629-2323
MILLIGAN, Jay	Tel:	(713) 625-8100
Chief Enterprise Sales Officer	Fax:	(713) 629-2323
MORRIS, Malcolm S.	Tel:	(713) 625-8100
Vice Chairman and PAC Treasurer	Fax:	(713) 629-2323
matt@stewart.com		

Stiefel Laboratories, Inc.

A skin care pharmaceutical company.
www.stiefel.com
Annual Revenues: $130.80 million
Employees: 2,000
Ticker: NASDAQ_TRACE: CNCT.GD
SIC: 2834; 2844
NAICS: 325412; 325620
Industry/ies: Personal Care/Hygiene; Pharmaceutical Industry

President	Tel:	(919) 990-6000
JOSE, Simon		

Main Headquarters

Mailing:	20 T.W. Alexander Dr.	Tel:	(919) 990-6000
	P.O. Box 13398		
	Research Triangle Park, NC 27709-4910		

Corporate Foundations and Giving Programs

Stiefel Community Partnership		
20 T.W. Alexander Dr.	Tel:	(919) 990-6000
P.O. Box 13398		
Research Triangle Park, NC 27709-4910		

Public Affairs and Related Activities Personnel

At Headquarters

BIGGS, Michelle	Tel:	(919) 990-6000
Director, Human Resources		
michelle.biggs@stiefel.com		
COLEMAN, Darren M.	Tel:	(919) 990-6000
Vice President, Global Strategy and Operations		
DONOFRIO, John	Tel:	(919) 990-6000
Vice President, Stiefel Global Finance		
ROYAL, Chris	Tel:	(919) 990-6000
Compliance Officer		

Stinson Morrison Hecker LLP

Law Firm.
www.stinson.com

Managing Partner	Tel:	(816) 691-2706
HINDERKS, Mark D.	Fax:	(816) 412-9376
mhinderks@stinson.com		

Main Headquarters

Mailing:	1201 Walnut St.	Tel:	(816) 842-8600
	Suite 2900	Fax:	(816) 691-3495
	Kansas City, MO 64106		

Washington Office

Mailing:	1775 Pennsylvania Ave. NW	Tel:	(202) 785-9100
	Suite 800	Fax:	(202) 785-9163
	Washington, DC 20006		

Corporate Foundations and Giving Programs

Stinson Morrison Hecker Contribution Program		
1201 Walnut St.	Tel:	(816) 691-3398
Suite 2900	Fax:	(816) 412-9376
Kansas City, MO 64106		

Public Affairs and Related Activities Personnel

At Headquarters

BOWLING, Amanda McManigal	Tel:	(816) 691-3478
Director, Marketing Communications	Fax:	(816) 412-9376
abowling@stinson.com		
BRUMMER, Terry E.	Tel:	(816) 842-8600
Chief Operating Officer	Fax:	(816) 691-3495
terry.brummer@stinsonleonard.com		
CRIPE, Ann C.	Tel:	(816) 691-2613
Director, Human Resources	Fax:	(816) 412-9376
ann.cripe@stinsonleonard.com		

DOERFLER, Doug	Tel:	(816) 691-3209
Chief Financial Officer	Fax:	(816) 412-9376
ddoerfler@stinson.com		
MILLER, Ramdy	Tel:	(816) 691-3398
Federal Lobbyist	Fax:	(816) 412-9376
WIBBENZ, Jason	Tel:	(612) 335-7222
Public Relations and Creative Manager	Fax:	(816) 691-3495
jason.wibben@stinsonleonard.com		

At Washington Office

FRAAS, Phillip L.	Tel:	(202) 572-9904
Partner and Attorney	Fax:	(202) 785-9163
pfraas@stinson.com		

At Other Offices

EVERSON, David	Tel:	(816) 691-3108
Partner	Fax:	(314) 863-9388
7700 Forsyth Blvd., Suite 1100		
St. Louis, MO 63105		
deverson@stinson.com		
FRISBY, Jr., H. Russell	Tel:	(202) 572-9904
Partner	Fax:	(202) 572-9958
1150 18th St. NW, Suite 800		
Washington, DC 20036		
RFrisby@stinson.com		
SCHNEIDER, Jonathan	Tel:	(202) 728-3034
Partner	Fax:	(202) 572-9967
1150 18th St. NW, Suite 800		
Washington, DC 20036		
jschneider@stinson.com		

The Stop and Shop Supermarket Company

A chain of supermarkets.
www.stopandshop.com
Annual Revenues: $4.55 billion
Employees: 30,000
SIC: 2026; 2037; 2013
Industry/ies: Food And Beverage Industry; Retail/Wholesale

Main Headquarters

Mailing:	1385 Hancock St.	Tel:	(617) 770-6090
	Quincy, MA 02169	Fax:	(617) 689-4545
		TF:	(800) 453-7467

Corporate Foundations and Giving Programs

The Stop and Shop Family Foundation
P.O. Box 55888
Boston, MA 02205

Public Affairs and Related Activities Personnel

At Headquarters

TRACEY, Phil	Tel:	(617) 770-6090
Contact, Media Relation	Fax:	(617) 689-4545

Strategic Policies LLC

A group of public safety and public policy experts assisting government, public organizations and private institutions.
www.policy-partners.com
Legislative Issues: AGR; FUE

Chairman and Principal	Tel:	(508) 693-8571
WASSERMAN, Robert	Fax:	(508) 693-1404

Main Headquarters

Mailing:	P. O. Box 577	Tel:	(508) 693-8571
	W. Tisbury, MA 02575	Fax:	(508) 693-1404

Washington Office

Mailing:	1201 15th St. NW	
	Suite 450	
	Washington, DC 20005	

Public Affairs and Related Activities Personnel

At Headquarters

GINSBURG, Zachary	Tel:	(508) 693-8571
Staff Associate	Fax:	(508) 693-1404
KELLING, George	Tel:	(508) 693-8571
Counsel Senior Associate	Fax:	(508) 693-1404

At Washington Office

ROSSO, Joseph
Federal Lobbyist
Registered Federal Lobbyist

Strategic Solutions Group

An information technology provider services company.
www.ssg-llc.com
Industry/ies: Communications; Computer/Technology; Defense/Homeland Security; Government-Related; Telecommunications/Internet/Cable

Manager, Human Resources
GONCALVES, Fernando

Tel:	(781) 400-1322
Fax:	(781) 850-4495

Main Headquarters
Mailing: 300 First Ave.
Suite 103
Needham, MA 02494

Tel:	(781) 400-1322
Fax:	(781) 850-4495

Washington Office
Mailing: 3863 Centerview Dr.
Suite 150
Chantilly, VA 20151

Tel:	(703) 956-8200
Fax:	(703) 956-8201

Public Affairs and Related Activities Personnel

At Headquarters

GAERLAN, Beau
Director, Operations

Tel:	(781) 400-1322
Fax:	(781) 850-4495

PODGORNAYA, Inna
Quality Assurance Manager

Tel:	(781) 400-1322
Fax:	(781) 850-4495

SCHAEFFER , John
Co-President

Tel:	(781) 400-1322
Fax:	(781) 850-4495

At Washington Office

BURLESON, Robert
Senior Vice President, Business Operations and Finance

Tel:	(703) 956-8200
Fax:	(703) 956-8201

HEINRICHS, Linda
Vice President, Human Resources

Tel:	(703) 956-8200
Fax:	(703) 956-8201

SCOTT, Damon W.
Senior Director, Marketing and Communications
damon.scott@techteam.com

Tel:	(703) 956-8160
Fax:	(703) 956-8201

Strategies International Ltd.

A business development consultant.
www.strategyinc.com

President
SCHWARZ, Frederick
fritz@fschwarz.com

Tel:	(410) 329-5077
Fax:	(410) 329-5879

Main Headquarters
Mailing: 15820 Carroll Rd.
Monkton, MD 21111

Tel:	(410) 329-5077
Fax:	(410) 329-5879

Stryker Corporation

Manufactures and distributes surgical and medical products.
www.stryker.com
Annual Revenues: $10.06 billion
Employees: 27,000
Ticker: NYSE: SYK
SIC: 3841
Industry/ies: Medicine/Health Care/Mental Health
Legislative Issues: HCR; MMM

Chairman and Chief Executive Officer
LOBO, Kevin A.

Tel:	(269) 385-2600
Fax:	(269) 385-1062

Main Headquarters
Mailing: 2825 Airview Blvd.
Kalamazoo, MI 49002

Tel:	(269) 385-2600
Fax:	(269) 385-1062

Corporate Foundations and Giving Programs

Stryker Contributions Program
2825 Airview Blvd.
Kalamazoo, MI 49002

Tel:	(269) 385-2600
Fax:	(269) 385-2600

Public Affairs and Related Activities Personnel

At Headquarters

BECKER, Yin C.
Vice President, Communications, Public Affairs and Strategic Marketing

Tel:	(269) 385-2600
Fax:	(269) 385-1062

BENSCOTER, Steven P.
Vice President, Business Transformation

Tel:	(269) 385-2600
Fax:	(269) 385-1062

BERGY, Dean H.
Vice President, Corporate Secretary

Tel:	(269) 385-2600
Fax:	(269) 385-1062

BLONDIA, Jeanne M.
Vice President, Finance and Treasurer

Tel:	(269) 385-2600
Fax:	(269) 385-1062

BOEHNLEIN, Glenn S.
Vice President, Chief Financial Officer

Tel:	(269) 385-2600
Fax:	(269) 385-1062

FINK, M. Kathryn (Katy)
Vice President, Chief Human Resources Officer

Tel:	(269) 385-2600
Fax:	(269) 385-1062

HUTCHINSON, Michael D.
General Counsel

Tel:	(269) 385-2600
Fax:	(269) 385-1062

MULLALLY, Anne L.
Vice President, Customer Excellence

Tel:	(269) 385-2600
Fax:	(269) 385-1062

OWEN, Katherine A.
Vice President, Strategy and Investor Relations
katherine.owen@stryker.com

Tel:	(269) 385-2600
Fax:	(269) 385-1062

STAUB, Elizabeth A.
Vice President, Regulatory Affairs and Quality Assurance

Tel:	(269) 385-2600
Fax:	(269) 385-1062

TAYLOR, Bronwen R.
Vice President, Compliance and Risk Management

Tel:	(269) 385-2600
Fax:	(269) 385-1062

TIPTON, Nathaniel
Federal Lobbyist
Registered Federal Lobbyist

Tel:	(269) 385-2600
Fax:	(269) 385-1062

At Other Offices

BENCH, John
Independent
325 Corporate Dr.
Mahwah, NJ 07434-2002
Registered Federal Lobbyist

Tel:	(201) 831-5000
Fax:	(201) 831-4000

KRANBUHL, Page
Director, U.S. Government Affairs
325 Corporate Dr.
Mahwah, NJ 07434-2002
page.kranbuhl@stryker.com
Registered Federal Lobbyist

Tel:	(201) 831-5000
Fax:	(201) 831-4000

LIPEJ, Ned
Senior Vice President
325 Corporate Dr.
Mahwah, NJ 07434-2002
Registered Federal Lobbyist

Tel:	(201) 831-5000
Fax:	(201) 831-4000

RUGO, Eric
Director, Reimbursement
325 Corporate Dr.
Mahwah, NJ 07434-2002
eric.rugo@stryker.com
Registered Federal Lobbyist

Tel:	(201) 831-5000
Fax:	(201) 831-4000

SCHANE, Cindy
Vice President, Hip Team
325 Corporate Dr.
Mahwah, NJ 07434-2002
Registered Federal Lobbyist

Tel:	(201) 831-5000
Fax:	(201) 831-4000

Studley

A real estate brokerage firm.
www.studley.com
Annual Revenues: $17.80 million
Employees: 600
Industry/ies: Banking/Finance/Investments; Real Estate
Legislative Issues: RES

Chairman of the Board and Chief Executive Officer
STEIR, Mitchell S.
msteir@studley.com

Tel:	(212) 326-1096
Fax:	(212) 326-1034

Main Headquarters
Mailing: 399 Park Ave.
11th Floor
New York City, NY 10022

Tel:	(212) 326-1000
Fax:	(212) 326-1034

Washington Office
Mailing: 555 13th St. NW
Suite 420 East
Washington, DC 20004

Tel:	(202) 628-6000
Fax:	(202) 624-8555

Corporate Foundations and Giving Programs

Studley Contributions Program
300 Park Ave.
Third Floor
New York City, NY 10022

Tel:	(212) 326-1000
Fax:	(212) 753-6413

Public Affairs and Related Activities Personnel

At Headquarters

COLACINO , Michael D.
President
mcolacino@studley.com

Tel:	(212) 326-1008
Fax:	(212) 326-1034

PANTAZIS, John
Executive Vice President, Chief Operating Officer
jpantazis@savills-studley.com

Tel:	(212) 326-1071
Fax:	(212) 326-1034

PETRILLO , Al
Executive Vice President, Director and Chief Financial Officer
apetrillo@savills-studley.com

Tel:	(212) 326-1040
Fax:	(212) 326-1034

TOWNE, L. Stanton
Executive Vice President, Director and General Counsel
stowne@savills-studley.com

Tel:	(212) 326-1039
Fax:	(212) 326-1034

At Washington Office

LYNCH, Ann Marie
Senior Vice President, Professional Development
alynch@studley.com

Tel:	(212) 326-8686
Fax:	(212) 753-6413

Studsvik, Inc.

Processor of nuclear waste.
www.studsvik.com

Annual Revenues: $5.30 million
Employees: 100
Industry/ies: Engineering/Mathematics

Chairman of the Board
ULLBERG, Anders

Tel: (404) 497-4900
Fax: (404) 497-4901

Chief Executive Officer
MONONEN, Michael

Tel: (404) 497-4900
Fax: (404) 497-4901

Main Headquarters
Mailing: 5605 Glenridge Dr. NE
Suite 705
Atlanta, GA 30342

Tel: (404) 497-4900
Fax: (404) 497-4901

Public Affairs and Related Activities Personnel

At Headquarters

JARNESS, Pal
Chief Financial Officer

Tel: (404) 497-4900
Fax: (404) 497-4901

USHER, Sam
Senior Vice President, Business Development

Tel: (404) 497-4900
Fax: (404) 497-4901

Sturman Industries, Inc.

Manufactures industrial valves.
www.sturmanindustries.com
Annual Revenues: $3.50 million
Employees: 40
Industry/ies: Automotive Industry; Transportation

Director, Human Resources
DAVEY, Lorie
ldavey@sturmanindustries.com

Tel: (719) 686-6294
Fax: (719) 686-6050

Main Headquarters
Mailing: One Innovation Way
Woodland Park, CO 80863-3308

Tel: (719) 686-6000
Fax: (719) 686-6050

STV Group

A professional firm offering engineering, architectural, planning, environmental and construction management services.
www.stvinc.com
Annual Revenues: $364.55 million
Employees: 1,600
SIC: 8711
Industry/ies: Engineering/Mathematics

Executive Chairman
SERVEDIO, Dominick M.
dominick.servedio@stvinc.com

Tel: (212) 777-4400
Fax: (212) 529-5237

President and Chief Executive Officer
RIVERSO, Milo E.

Tel: (610) 385-8200
Fax: (610) 395-8500

Main Headquarters
Mailing: 205 W. Welsh Dr.
Douglassville, PA 19518-8713

Tel: (610) 385-8200
Fax: (610) 395-8500

Washington Office
Mailing: 1400 I (Eye) St. NW
Suite 400
Washington, DC 20005-2294

Tel: (202) 688-2190
Fax: (202) 380-0219

Political Action Committees
STV Group Inc PAC
FEC ID: C00214866
Contact: Peter W. Knipe
205 W. Welsh Dr.
Douglassville, PA 19518

Tel: (610) 385-8200
Fax: (610) 395-8500

> **Contributions to Candidates:** $32,400 (2015-2016)
> Democrats: $27,900; Republicans: $4,500

Principal Recipients

HOUSE
NADLER, JERROLD L. MR. (DEM-NY)

Public Affairs and Related Activities Personnel

At Headquarters

BUTCHER, CPA, Thomas
Chief Financial Officer

Tel: (610) 385-8200
Fax: (610) 395-8500

AUSTIN, Patrick M.
Director, Human Resources
austinpm@stvinc.com

Tel: (610) 385-8200
Fax: (610) 385-8500

KNIPE, Peter W.
PAC Treasurer
peter.knipe@stvinc.com

Tel: (610) 385-8200
Fax: (610) 385-8500

TRACE, Debra B.
Manager, Corporate Communications
debrat@stvinc.com

Tel: (610) 385-8306
Fax: (610) 395-8500

At Other Offices

BENNETT, Michelle

Tel: (212) 777-4400

Vice President, Chief People Officer
225 Park Ave., South
New York City, NY 10003-1604

Fax: (212) 529-5237

ROSENBERG, Linda
Senior Vice President, Marketing and Communications
225 Park Ave., South
New York City, NY 10003-1604
rosenbl@stvinc.com

Tel: (212) 777-4400
Fax: (212) 529-5237

Subaru of America

A distributor of Subaru's brand vehicles and a subsidiary of Fuji Heavy Industries of Japan.
www.subaru.com
Employees: 700
SIC: 3714; 5013; 5099; 5012
Industry/ies: Automotive Industry; Transportation

Chairman and Chief Executive Officer
NAKAMURA, Tomomi

Tel: (856) 488-8500
Fax: (856) 488-3196

Main Headquarters
Mailing: Subaru Plaza, P.O. Box 6000
Cherry Hill, NJ 08034-6000

Tel: (856) 488-8500
Fax: (856) 488-3196
TF: (800) 782-2783

Corporate Foundations and Giving Programs
Subaru of America Foundation
Contact: Sandra Capell
P.O. Box 6000
Cherry Hill, NJ 08034

Public Affairs and Related Activities Personnel

At Headquarters

DOLL, Thomas J.
President and Chief Operating Officer

Tel: (856) 488-8500
Fax: (856) 488-3196

WALTERS, Jeffrey A.
Senior Vice President, Sales

Tel: (856) 488-8500
Fax: (856) 488-3196

At Other Offices

CAPELL, Sandra
Community Services Manager
2235 Route 70 West
Cherry Hill, NJ 08002
foundation@subaru.com

Tel: (856) 488-8500
Fax: (856) 488-3196

Subsentio, Inc.

A trusted third party vendor to electronic communication service providers.
www.subsentio.com

President
BOCK, Steve

Tel: (303) 794-6936
Fax: (866) 271-3020

Main Headquarters
Mailing: 2001 E. Easter Ave.
Suite 302
Centennial, CO 80122

Tel: (303) 794-6936
Fax: (866) 271-3020
TF: (866) 271-3020

Public Affairs and Related Activities Personnel

At Headquarters

MARGOLIS, Joel
General Counsel and Senior Director, Government Affairs

Tel: (703) 946-9419
Fax: (866) 271-3020

MCDERMOTT, Martin
Chief Operating Officer

Tel: (303) 794-6936
Fax: (866) 271-3020

SuddenLink Communications

A provider of information and communications services.
www.suddenlink.com
Annual Revenues: $2.06 billion
Employees: 6,000
Industry/ies: Communications; Telecommunications/Internet/Cable
Legislative Issues: TEC

Chairman of the Board and Chief Executive Officer
KENT, Jerald L.

Tel: (314) 965-2020
Fax: (314) 965-0500

Main Headquarters
Mailing: 520 Maryville Centre Dr.
Suite 300
St. Louis, MO 63141

Political Action Committees
Suddenlink Communications PAC
FEC ID: C00426601
Contact: Ralph Kelly
12444 Powerscourt Dr.
Suite 420
St. Louis, MO 63131

> **Contributions to Candidates:** $11,250 (2015-2016)
> Democrats: $1,000; Republicans: $10,250

Public Affairs and Related Activities Personnel

At Headquarters

FOX, James B.
Senior Vice President and Chief Accounting Officer

ABEL, Peter M.
Senior Vice President, Corporate Communications
pete.abel@suddenlink.com

BOYLL, Aaron
Vice President, Corporate Development

DOW, Jerry
Chief Marketing and Sales Officer

JOHNSON, Don
Vice President, Human Resources

KELLY, Ralph
Senior Vice President and PAC Treasurer
Mail Stop Suite 300
ralph.kelly@suddenlink.com

MCMILLIN, Thomas P.
Executive Vice President and Chief Operating Officer

MEDUSKI, Mary E.
Executive Vice President and Chief Financial Officer
mary.meduski@suddenlink.com

PFLANTZ, Mike
Vice President, Corporate Finance

PORTER, Mary
Vice President, Human Resources

ROSENTHAL, Craig L.
Senior Vice President and General Counsel
craig.rosenthal@suddenlink.com

WILEY, Douglas G.
Senior Vice President, Human Resources

ZARRILLI, Michael
Vice President, Government Relations and Senior Counsel
mike.zarrilli@suddenlink.com

At Other Offices

FECHTER, Steve
Coordinator, Corporate Communications
12444 Powerscourt Dr., Suite 140
St. Louis, MO 63131
steven.fechter@suddenlink.com
Tel: (314) 315-9335
Fax: (314) 965-0500

SUEZ Energy North America

See listing on page 350 under GDF SUEZ Energy North America, Inc.

Sun Edison

A solar energy services provider. SunEdison finances, installs, and operates solar power plants and systems for customers including corporations, government agencies.
www.sunedison.com
Annual Revenues: $2.11 billion
Employees: 6,300
Ticker: NYSE: SUNE
Industry/ies: Energy/Electricity

Chairman of the Board
HERNANDEZ , CPA, Emmanuel T.
Tel: (636) 474-5000

President and Chief Executive Officer
DOMENECH, Carlos
Tel: (636) 474-5000

President and Chief Executive Officer
CHATILA, Ahmad
Tel: (314) 770-7300

Main Headquarters
Mailing: 13736 Riverport Dr.
Maryland Heights, MO 63043
Tel: (314) 770-7300

Washington Office
Mailing: 12500 Baltimore Ave.
Beltsville, MD 20705
Tel: (443) 909-7200
Fax: (240) 264-8260
TF: (866) 786-3347

Public Affairs and Related Activities Personnel

At Headquarters

ALVAREZ, Michael
Senior Vice President, Global Operations
Tel: (314) 770-7300

BLUNDEN, Julie
Senior Vice President, Chief Strategy Officer
Tel: (314) 770-7300

HARBORNE, Ben
Senior Marketing Manager, Brand and Corporate Communications
bharborne@sunedison.com
Tel: (314) 770-7300

HERZBERG, Matthew
Senior Vice President and and Chief Human Resources Officer
Tel: (314) 770-7300

MORRIS , Phelps
Vice President, Investor Relations and Treasurer
pmorris@sunedison.com
Tel: (314) 770-7345

PEREZ, Pancho
Executive Vice President and Chief Operating Officer
Tel: (314) 770-7300

TRUONG, Martin H.
Senior Vice President, General Counsel and Secretary
Tel: (314) 770-7300

WUEBBELS, Brian
Executive Vice President and Chief Financial Officer
Tel: (314) 770-7300

At Washington Office

TOTH, Attila
Vice President, Marketing
Tel: (443) 909-7200
Fax: (240) 264-8260

WYSE, Robert
Contact, Media Relations
rob@m1pr.com
Tel: (212) 920-1470
Fax: (240) 264-8260

At Other Offices

CHANEY , Chris
Director, Investor Relations
501 Pearl Dr. (City of O'Fallon)
St. Peters, MO 63376
Tel: (636) 474-5226

JACOLICK, Carole
Vice President, Human Resources and Office Management
501 Pearl Dr. (City of O'Fallon)
St. Peters, MO 63376
Tel: (636) 474-5000

MICHALEK , Bill
Director, Corporate Communications
501 Pearl Dr. (City of O'Fallon)
St. Peters, MO 63376
Tel: (636) 474-5443

O'ROURKE, Steve
Chief of Staff, Chief Strategy Officer
501 Pearl Dr. (City of O'Fallon)
St. Peters, MO 63376
Tel: (636) 474-5000

Sun Life Financial

A financial services company. A subsidiary of Sun Life Financial Services of Canada Inc. It provides protection and wealth products and services to individuals and corporate customers.
www.sunlife.com/us
Annual Revenues: $21.77
Employees: 16,275
Ticker: NYSE:SLF
SIC: 6311
Industry/ies: Banking/Finance/Investments

Chairman of the Board
SUTCLIFFE, James H.
Tel: (781) 237-6030
Fax: (888) 863-8311

Senior Vice President and Chief Executive Officer, Sun Life Financial International
DARFOOR, Andrew A.
Tel: (781) 237-6030
Fax: (888) 863-8311

Main Headquarters
Mailing: One Sun Life Executive Park
Wellesley Hills, MA 02481
Tel: (781) 237-6030
Fax: (888) 863-8311
TF: (800) 786-5433

Corporate Foundations and Giving Programs

Sun Life Financial Charity Program
Contact: Kaitlin Jaquez
One Sun Life Executive Park
Wellesley Hills, MA 02481
Tel: (781) 237-6030
Fax: (888) 863-8311

Public Affairs and Related Activities Personnel

At Headquarters

ACCUM, Claude A.
Executive Vice-President and Chief Risk Officer, Corporate Actuarial and Risk Management, Canada
Tel: (781) 237-6030
Fax: (888) 863-8311

BLAIR, Carolyn (Carrie)
Executive Vice-President, Human Resources, Canada
Tel: (781) 237-6030
Fax: (888) 863-8311

CLULOW, Thomas J.
Senior Vice President, Corporate Development and General Counsel, Canada
Tel: (781) 237-6030
Fax: (888) 863-8311

DAVIS, Scott M.
Senior Vice President and General Counsel
Tel: (781) 237-6030
Fax: (888) 863-8311

FISHBEIN, Dan
President, Sun Life Financial U.S.
Tel: (781) 237-6030
Fax: (888) 863-8311

GALLO, Amanda
Contact, Media Relations
amanda.gallo@sunlife.com
Tel: (781) 303-1264
Fax: (888) 863-8311

HAYNES, Neil
Senior Vice President, Chief Financial Officer
Tel: (781) 237-6030
Fax: (888) 863-8311

HEALY, David
Senior Vice President, Client & Technology Services
Tel: (781) 237-6030
Fax: (888) 863-8311

JAQUEZ, Kaitlin
Associate Director, Philanthropy
kaitlin.jaquez@sunlife.com
Tel: (781) 237-6030
Fax: (888) 863-8311

MALEK, Philip G.
Vice President, Investor Relations
Tel: (781) 237-6030
Fax: (888) 863-8311

MILANO, Ed
Vice President, Marketing
Tel: (781) 237-6030
Fax: (888) 863-8311

SCHUR, Emily
Vice President, Human Resources
Tel: (781) 237-6030
Fax: (888) 863-8311

Sun-Maid Growers of California

Sun-Maid Growers of California is an American cooperative of raisin growers. It is the largest dried fruit processor in the world.
www.sunmaid.com
SIC: 2034; 0172
Industry/ies: Food And Beverage Industry
Legislative Issues: AGR; TRD

Main Headquarters
Mailing: 13525 S. Bethel Ave.
Kingsburg, CA 93631-9232
Tel: (555) 896-8000
Fax: (555) 897-6209

Public Affairs and Related Activities Personnel

At Headquarters

MARSHBURN, Gary H.
Federal Lobbyist
Tel: (555) 896-8000
Fax: (555) 897-6209

Sundstrand Corporation Designs.

See listing on page 383 under Hamilton Sundstrand

SunGard Data Systems Inc.

Offers integrated IT services and eProcessing for financial services.
www.sungard.com
Annual Revenues: $4.99 billion
Employees: 20,000
Ticker: NASDAQ: SDS
SIC: 7374
Industry/ies: Computer/Technology

President and Chief Executive Officer
FRADIN, Russ
Tel: (484) 582-2000
Fax: (610) 225-1120

Main Headquarters
Mailing: 680 E. Swedesford Rd.
Wayne, PA 19087-1586
Tel: (484) 582-2000
Fax: (610) 225-1120
TF: (800) 825-2518

Corporate Foundations and Giving Programs
SunGard Data Systems Contributions Program
680 E. Swedesford Rd.
Wayne, PA 19087

Public Affairs and Related Activities Personnel

At Headquarters

BRAB, Regina
Senior Vice President, Professional Services Operations
Tel: (484) 582-2000
Fax: (610) 225-1120

BROWN, Marianne
Chief Operating Officer, Financial Systems
Tel: (484) 582-2000
Fax: (610) 225-1120

MCCURRY, Kevin
Senior Vice President, Corporate Development and Strategy
Tel: (484) 582-2000
Fax: (610) 225-1120

NERAL, Charles
Chief Financial Officer
Tel: (484) 582-2000
Fax: (610) 225-1120

SILBEY, Victoria
Senior Vice President, Legal and Chief Legal Officer
victoria.silbey@sungard.com
Tel: (484) 582-2000
Fax: (610) 225-1120

THOMAS, George
Vice President, Corporate and Internal Communications
george.thomas@sungard.com
Tel: (484) 582-5635
Fax: (610) 225-1120

Sunkist Growers, Inc.

Serves as a marketing cooperative in the fruit and vegetable industry.
www.sunkist.com
Employees: 500
SIC: 0721; 2033; 2037; 5099; 5148
Industry/ies: Agriculture/Agronomy

Chairman of the Board
BOZICK, Nicholas L.
Tel: (818) 986-4800
Fax: (818) 379-7405

President and Chief Executive Officer
HANLIN, Russell L.
Tel: (818) 986-4800
Fax: (818) 379-7405

Main Headquarters
Mailing: P.O. Box 7888
Van Nuys, CA 91409-7405
Tel: (818) 986-4800
Fax: (818) 379-7405

Political Action Committees
Sunkist Growers, Inc. PAC
FEC ID: C00099002
Contact: Jason D. Kaune
14130 Reverside Dr.
P.O. Box 5576
Sherman Oaks, CA 91413

Contributions to Candidates: $32,769 (2015-2016)

Democrats: $13,319; Republicans: $19,450

Public Affairs and Related Activities Personnel

At Headquarters

FRENCH, Richard T.
Vice President and Chief Financial Officer
Tel: (818) 986-4800
Fax: (818) 379-7405

SMITH, Claire J.
Director, Corporate Communications
Tel: (818) 986-4800
Fax: (818) 379-7405

WOLTMANN, Charles L.
Senior Vice President, Law and General Counsel
Tel: (818) 986-4800
Fax: (818) 379-7405

At Other Offices

KAUNE, Jason D.
PAC Contact
27770 N. Entertainment Dr.
Valencia, CA 91355
Tel: (661) 290-8900

WOOTTON, Michael J.
Senior Vice President, Corporate Relations, Administration and PAC Treasurer
14130 Riverside Dr.
Sherman Oaks, CA 91413

Sunoco, Inc.

A refiner and marketer of petroleum, Coal Mining,Shipping, Oil,Gas and chemical products.
www.sunocoinc.com
Annual Revenues: $46.82 billion
Employees: 10,500
Ticker: NYSE: SUN
SIC: 2911; 1221; 1311; 1321; 1382
Industry/ies: Chemicals & Chemical Industry; Fuels See Coal, Gas, Oil, Petroleum; Natural Resources; Petroleum Industry
Legislative Issues: CAW

President and Chief Executive Officer
MACDONALD, Brian P.
Tel: (800) 786-6261
Fax: (215) 977-3409

President and CEO
OWENS, Robert W.
Tel: (215) 977-3000
Fax: (215) 977-3409

Main Headquarters
Mailing: P.O. Box 321
Essington, PA 19029-0321
Tel: (800) 786-6261

Washington Office
Mailing: 901 K St. NW
Suite 1250
Washington, DC 20001
Tel: (202) 628-1010

Corporate Foundations and Giving Programs
The Sunoco Foundation
1735 Market St.
Suite LL
Philadelphia, PA 19103

Public Affairs and Related Activities Personnel

At Washington Office

SCHNEPP, Ryan
Tel: (202) 628-1010

At Other Offices

MCGRORY, Clare
Executive Vice President / Chief Financial Officer / Treasurer
1735 Market St., Suite LL
Philadelphia, PA 19103-7583
Tel: (215) 977-6764
Fax: (215) 977-3409

Sunovion Pharmaceuticals Inc.

Formerly Sepracor. Research-based pharmaceutical company.
www.sunovion.com
Annual Revenues: $302.30 million
Employees: 2,400
Ticker: NASDAQ: SEPR
SIC: 2834
Industry/ies: Medicine/Health Care/Mental Health; Pharmaceutical Industry; Science; Scientific Research
Legislative Issues: HCR; MMM; PHA

Chairman of the Board and Chief Executive Officer
HAMANAKA, Saburo
Tel: (508) 481-6700
Fax: (508) 357-7499

Main Headquarters
Mailing: 84 Waterford Dr.
Marlborough, MA 01752
Tel: (508) 481-6700
Fax: (508) 357-7499

Political Action Committees
Sunovion Pharmaceuticals Inc. Good Governance Fund PAC
FEC ID: C00423236
Contact: Stephen Freeman
84 Waterford Dr.
Marlborough, MA 01752

Contributions to Candidates: $61,500 (2015-2016)
Democrats: $26,500; Republicans: $32,000; Other: $3,000
Principal Recipients

SENATE
CRAPO, MICHAEL D (REP-ID)

Public Affairs and Related Activities Personnel

At Headquarters

BABA, Hiroyuki
Executive Vice President, Corporate Strategy
Tel: (508) 481-6700
Fax: (508) 357-7499

D'AMBROSIO, Matthew
Senior Vice President, Chief Compliance and Ethics Officer
Tel: (508) 481-6700
Fax: (508) 357-7499

FREEMAN, Stephen
Vice President and Chief Financial Officer and PAC Treasurer
Tel: (508) 481-6700
Fax: (508) 357-7499

GREGORIO, Robert
Executive Vice President and Chief Administrative Officer
Tel: (508) 481-6700
Fax: (508) 357-7499

IKEDA, PhD, Yoshiharu
Executive Vice President, Corporate Strategy
Tel: (508) 481-6700
Fax: (508) 357-7499

MAGNETTI, Anthony
Vice President, Government Affairs
tony.magnetti@sepracor.com
Registered Federal Lobbyist
Tel: (508) 481-6700
Fax: (508) 357-7499

MORIARTY, Patricia
Senior Director, Corporate Communications
patricia.moriarty@sunovion.com
Tel: (508) 787-4279
Fax: (508) 357-7499

NOMURA, Hiroshi
Vice Chair, Executive Vice President and Chief Financial Officer
Tel: (508) 481-6700
Fax: (508) 357-7499

RASMUSSEN, MD, FACP, Eric
Senior Director, Federal Government Affairs
Registered Federal Lobbyist
Tel: (508) 481-6700
Fax: (508) 357-7499

TAMURA, Nobuhiko
Vice Chair, President
Tel: (508) 481-6700
Fax: (508) 357-7499

SunPower Corporation
A company that designs, manufactures and delivers solar electric systems worldwide for residential, commercial and utility-scale power plant customers.
www.sunpowercorp.com
Annual Revenues: $1.52 billion
Employees: 8,309
Ticker: NASDAQ: SPWR
SIC: 3674
Industry/ies: Energy/Electricity

President and Chief Executive Officer
WERNER, Thomas H.
Tel: (408) 240-5500
Fax: (408) 240-5400

Main Headquarters
Mailing: 77 Rio Robles
San Jose, CA 95134
Tel: (408) 240-5500
Fax: (408) 240-5400
TF: (800) 786-7693

Political Action Committees
SunPower Corporation PAC
FEC ID: C00451575
Contact: James Walter Parker
77 Rio Robles
San Jose, CA 95134

Corporate Foundations and Giving Programs
SunPower Foundation
1414 Harbor Way South
Richmond, CA 94804

Public Affairs and Related Activities Personnel

At Headquarters

ASCHENBRENNER, Peter
Executive Vice President, Corporate Strategy and Business Development
Tel: (408) 240-5500
Fax: (408) 240-5400

BODENSTEINER, Lisa
Executive Vice President and General Counsel
Tel: (408) 240-5500
Fax: (408) 240-5400

BOYNTON, Charles D.
Executive Vice President and Chief Financial Officer
Tel: (408) 240-5500
Fax: (408) 240-5400

NELSON, Erin Mulligan
Executive Vice President and Chief Marketing Officer
Tel: (408) 240-5500
Fax: (408) 240-5400

PARKER, James Walter
Vice President, Tax and PAC Treasurer
Tel: (408) 240-5500
Fax: (408) 240-5400

RICHARDS, Douglas J.
Executive Vice President, Administration
Tel: (408) 240-5500
Fax: (408) 240-5400

Sunrise Assisted Living, Inc.
See listing on page 757 under Sunrise Senior Living

Sunrise Medical
Manufacturers of homecare and extended care products.
www.sunrisemedical.com
Annual Revenues: $150.30 million
Employees: 1,900

SIC: 3842
Industry/ies: Medicine/Health Care/Mental Health

President and Chief Executive Officer
ROSSNAGEL, Thomas
Tel: (303) 218-4600
Fax: (303) 218-4590

Main Headquarters
Mailing: 2842 Business Park Ave.
Fresno, CA 93727
Tel: (800) 333-4000
Fax: (800) 300-7502
TF: (800) 333-4000

Political Action Committees
Sunrise Medical Inc. PAC
FEC ID: C00436097
Contact: Dustin Henry
6899 Winchester Cir.
Suite 200
Boulder, CO 80301

> **Contributions to Candidates:** $1,000 (2015-2016)
> Democrats: $500; Republicans: $500

Public Affairs and Related Activities Personnel

At Headquarters

BENDSON, Kristyn
Senior Marketing Manager
kristyn.bendson@sunmed.com
Tel: (303) 218-4600
Fax: (303) 218-4590

BINSTOCK, Randi
Vice President, Business Development
Tel: (800) 333-4000
Fax: (800) 300-7502

COBURN, Pete
President Commercial Operations
Tel: (800) 333-4000
Fax: (800) 300-7502

CROMWELL, Roxane
Senior Vice President Operations North America
Tel: (800) 333-4000
Fax: (800) 300-7502

MARSHMAN, Kevin
Controller, North America
Tel: (800) 333-4000
Fax: (800) 300-7502

PROFFITT, Michael
Vice President, Marketing and Product Management
Tel: (303) 218-4600
Fax: (303) 218-4590

RILEY, Peter
Senior Vice President and Chief Financial Officer
Tel: (800) 333-4000
Fax: (800) 300-7502

SMITH, Robert
General Counsel
Tel: (303) 218-4600
Fax: (303) 218-4590

WHITTLE, Pete
Vice President, Human Resources
Tel: (800) 333-4000
Fax: (800) 300-7502

At Other Offices

HENRY, Dustin
Treasury Analyst
6899 Winchester Circle, Suite 200, Attn John Carter
Boulder, CO 80301

Sunrise Research Corporation
A law firm.
www.sunriseresearchcorp.com
Legislative Issues: MMM

President
PACKWOOD, Robert William
bpacky@gmail.com
Tel: (202) 965-9810

Main Headquarters
Mailing: 3227 Sutton Pl. NW
Suite C
Washington, DC 20016
Tel: (202) 965-9810

Public Affairs and Related Activities Personnel

At Headquarters

KORENS, Michael E.
Federal Lobbyist
mkorens@mindspring.com
Tel: (202) 965-9810

Sunrise Senior Living
Formerly Sunrise Assisted Living, Inc. A provider of assisted living for seniors.
www.sunriseseniorliving.com
Annual Revenues: $1.31 billion
Employees: 31,600
Ticker: NYSE: SRZ
SIC: 8050
Industry/ies: Aging

Chairman of the Board
KLAASSEN, Paul J.
paul.klaassen@sunriseseniorliving.com
Tel: (703) 273-7500
Fax: (703) 744-1601

Chief Executive Officer
WINKLE, Chris
Tel: (703) 273-7500
Fax: (703) 744-1601

Main Headquarters
Mailing: 7900 Westpark Dr.
Suite T-900
McLean, VA 22102
Tel: (703) 273-7500
Fax: (703) 744-1601

Public Affairs and Related Activities Personnel

At Headquarters

CLARKE, Heather A.
Specialist, Corporate Marketing and Communications
Tel: (703) 854-0234
Fax: (703) 744-1601

KLAASSEN, Teresa M.
Founder and Chief Cultural Officer
teresa.klaassen@sunriseseniorliving.com
Tel: (703) 273-7500
Fax: (703) 744-1601

LUBLIN, Meghan
Senior Vice President, Corporate Marketing and Communications
Meghan.Lublin@sunriseseniorliving.com
Tel: (703) 854-0299
Fax: (703) 744-1601

RICHARDS , Marc
Chief Financial Officer
marc.richards@sunriseseniorliving.com
Tel: (703) 273-7500
Fax: (703) 744-1601

RODIS, Michael
Senior Vice President, Human Resources
mike.rodis@sunriseseniorliving.com
Tel: (703) 273-7500
Fax: (703) 744-1601

TEHRANI, Farinaz
General Counsel and Chief Compliance Officer
Tel: (703) 273-7500
Fax: (703) 744-1601

SUNRx

Provides technology solutions to federally qualified health centers.
www.sunrx.com
Employees: 25
Industry/ies: Medicine/Health Care/Mental Health; Pharmaceutical Industry

Main Headquarters

Mailing:	3220 Tillman Dr.	Tel:	(267) 525-3430
	Suite 100	Fax:	(267) 525-3427
	Bensalem, PA 19020	TF:	(800) 786-1791

Public Affairs and Related Activities Personnel

At Headquarters

LIEBMANN, Timothy A.
Vice President, Business Developement
tliebmann@sunrx.com
Tel: (856) 675-1406
Fax: (800) 786-7550

SIMOES, Jill
General Manager
Tel: (267) 525-3430
Fax: (267) 525-3427

WARD, Brian
Vice President, Regulatory Affairs and Compliance
Tel: (267) 525-3430
Fax: (267) 525-3427

Sunshine in Government Initiative

A coalition of media groups committed to promoting policies that ensure the government is accessible, accountable and open. It helps support the work of its 9 member organizations promoting open government policies.
www.sunshineingovernment.org
Industry/ies: Communications; Government-Related; Media/Mass Communication

Coordinator
BLUM, Rick
rblum@sunshineingovernment.org
Tel: (202) 795-9305
Fax: (202) 795-9310

Main Headquarters

Mailing:	1156 15th St.	Tel:	(202) 795-9305
	Suite 1250	Fax:	(202) 795-9310
	Washington, DC 20005		

Washington Office

Mailing:	1101 Wilson Blvd.	Tel:	(703) 807-2100
	Suite 1100	Fax:	(703) 807-2109
	Arlington, VA 22209		

SunTrust Banks, Inc.

A commercial banking organization operating through an extensive distribution network in Alabama, Florida, Georgia, Maryland, Tennessee, Virginia and the District of Columbia. It also serves markets nationally.
www.suntrust.com
Annual Revenues: $7.76 billion
Employees: 24,638
Ticker: NYSE: STI
SIC: 6021
Industry/ies: Banking/Finance/Investments
Legislative Issues: BAN

Chairman of the Board and Chief Executive Officer
ROGERS, Jr., William H.
Tel: (404) 335-2682
Fax: (404) 332-3875

Main Headquarters

Mailing:	303 Peachtree St. NE	Tel:	(404) 335-2682
	32nd Floor	Fax:	(404) 332-3875
	Atlanta, GA 30308	TF:	(800) 786-8787

Washington Office

| Mailing: | 1445 New York Ave. | | |
| | Washington, DC 20005 | | |

Political Action Committees

SunTrust Bank Good Government Group - Georgia PAC
FEC ID: C00009639
Contact: Christian D. Beyers
P.O. Box 4418
MC 041
Atlanta, GA 30303

Contributions to Candidates: $75,400 (2015-2016)
Democrats: $12,000; Republicans: $63,400

Principal Recipients

HOUSE
COLLINS, DOUGLAS ALLEN (REP-GA)
GRAVES, JOHN THOMAS MR. JR. (REP-GA)

Suntrust Bank Good Government Group Florida PAC
FEC ID: C00111567
Contact: Linda Brinkley
215 S. Monroe St.
Suite 125
Tallahassee, FL 32301

Contributions to Candidates: $34,000 (2015-2016)
Democrats: $8,500; Republicans: $25,500

Principal Recipients

SENATE
MURPHY, PATRICK E (DEM-FL)

SunTrust Bank Good Government Group-Mid-Atlantic PAC
FEC ID: C00214965
Contact: Brenda L. Skidmore
919 E. Main St.
Richmond, VA 23219

Contributions to Candidates: $48,000 (2015-2016)
Democrats: $3,500; Republicans: $44,500

Principal Recipients

HOUSE
MCHENRY, PATRICK TIMOTHY (REP-NC)

SunTrust Banks of Tennessee, Inc., Good Government Fund PAC
FEC ID: C00043265
Contact: Eugene Hine
9950 Kingston Pike
Knoxville, TN 37922

Contributions to Candidates: $5,500 (2015-2016)
Republicans: $5,500

Corporate Foundations and Giving Programs

Sun Trust Bank Atlanta Foundation
Contact: Kay Miller
303 Peachtree St. NE
Atlanta, GA 30308
Tel: (404) 588-7711
Fax: (404) 588-7711

SunTrust Bank Trusteed Foundation
303 Peachtree St. NE
Atlanta, GA 30308
Tel: (404) 588-7711
Fax: (404) 588-7711

Public Affairs and Related Activities Personnel

At Headquarters

CARRIG, Kenneth J.
Chief Human Resources Officer
Tel: (404) 335-2682
Fax: (404) 332-3875

FORTIN, Raymond D.
General Counsel and Corporate Secretary
raymond.fortin@suntrust.com
Tel: (404) 588-7711
Fax: (404) 332-3875

GILLANI, Aleem
Chief Financial Officer
aleem.gillani@suntrust.com
Tel: (404) 724-3477
Fax: (404) 332-3875

KOLING, Barry R.
Corporate Initiatives Contact and Industry and Strategic Issue
barry.koling@suntrust.com
Tel: (404) 320-5268
Fax: (404) 332-3875

LONG, Autrice Campbell
Manager, Community Development
Tel: (404) 335-2682
Fax: (404) 332-3875

MALLINO, Sue
Senior Vice President and Chief Communications Officer
sue.mallino@suntrust.com
Tel: (404) 813-0463
Fax: (404) 332-3875

MCCOY, Michael
Contact, Corporate Communications Relationship Manager
michael.mccoy@suntrust.com
Tel: (404) 588-7230
Fax: (404) 581-1664

MILLER, Kay
Contact, Foundation
Tel: (404) 588-8250
Fax: (404) 332-3875

At Washington Office

CRITCHFIELD, Amanda N.
Director, Corporate Communications, Legal, and Government Relations

MORROW, Rich
Senior Vice President
rich.morrow@suntrust.com

WRIGHT, Sherry
Analyst

At Other Offices

JOHNSON, Susan S.
Chief Marketing Officer
9950 Kingston Pike
Knoxville, TN 37922

BEYERS, Christian D.
PAC Treasurer
P.O. Box 4418, MC 041
Atlanta, GA 30303
Chris.Beyers@SunTrust.com

BRINKLEY, Linda
PAC Treasurer
215 S. Monroe St., Suite 125
Tallahassee, FL 32301

HINE, Eugene
PAC Treasurer
9950 Kingston Pike
Knoxville, TN 37922

OESTERLE, Mark   Tel: (804) 782-5000
Federal Lobbyist   Fax: (804) 782-7064
919 E. Main St.
Richmond, VA 23219
Registered Federal Lobbyist

SKIDMORE, Brenda L.   Tel: (804) 782-5000
Senior Vice President & Contact, PAC   Fax: (804) 782-7064
919 E. Main St.
Richmond, VA 23219
brenda.skidmore@suntrust.com
Registered Federal Lobbyist

SuperValu, Inc.

Engaged in grocery retail and supply chains.
www.supervalu.com
Annual Revenues: $17.82 billion
Employees: 38,500
Ticker: NYSE: SVU
SIC: 5411
Industry/ies: Food And Beverage Industry

Executive Chairman of the Board   Tel: (952) 828-4000
NODDLE, Jeffrey   Fax: (952) 828-8998

President and Chief Executive Officer   Tel: (952) 828-4000
DUNCAN, Sam   Fax: (952) 828-8998

Main Headquarters
Mailing: 7075 Flying Cloud Dr.   Tel: (952) 828-4000
   Eden Prairie, MN 55344   Fax: (952) 828-8998

Corporate Foundations and Giving Programs

Supervalu Foundation
11840 Valley View Rd.
Eden Prairie, MN 55344

Public Affairs and Related Activities Personnel

At Headquarters

BESANKO, Bruce   Tel: (952) 828-4000
Executive Vice President and Chief Financial Officer   Fax: (952) 828-8998

MURPHY, Michele   Tel: (952) 828-4000
Executive Vice President, Human Resources and Corporate   Fax: (952) 828-8998
Communications

ROBERTSON, Karla   Tel: (952) 828-4000
Executive Vice President, General Counsel and Corporate   Fax: (952) 828-8998
Secretary

SWANSON, Jeff   Tel: (952) 903-1645
Director, Corporate Communications   Fax: (952) 828-8998
jeffrey.s.swanson@supervalu.com

VAN BUSKIRK, Mark   Tel: (952) 828-4000
Executive Vice President, Merchandising and Marketing   Fax: (952) 828-8998

WOSETH, Rob   Tel: (952) 828-4000
Executive Vice President, Chief Strategy Officer   Fax: (952) 828-8998

At Other Offices

BLOOMQUIST, Steve   Tel: (952) 828-4144
Senior Director Investor Relations and Corporate Planning
11840 Valley View Rd.
Eden Prairie, MN 55344
steve.bloomquist@supervalu.com

Surewest Communications

Provides local and long-distance phone service.
www.surewest.com
Annual Revenues: $248.4 million
Employees: 812

Ticker: NASDAQ: SURW
SIC: 4813
Industry/ies: Communications; Telecommunications/Internet/Cable

Chairman of the Board   Tel: (916) 772-2000
DOYLE, Kirk C.   Fax: (916) 786-7170

President and Chief Executive Officer   Tel: (916) 772-2000
OLDHAM, Steven C.   Fax: (916) 786-7170

Main Headquarters
Mailing: P.O. Box 969   Tel: (916) 772-2000
   Roseville, CA 95661   Fax: (916) 786-7170
        TF: (866) 787-3937

Political Action Committees
Surewest Communications PAC (Surewest PAC)
FEC ID: C00372789
Contact: Thomas W. Hiltachk
455 Capitol Mall
Suite 600
Sacramento, CA 95814

Corporate Foundations and Giving Programs

Surewest Foundation
Contact: Robert T. Collins
P.O. Box 969
Roseville, CA 95661

Public Affairs and Related Activities Personnel

At Headquarters

COLLINS, Robert T.   Tel: (916) 772-2000
President, Foundation   Fax: (916) 786-7170

SOMMERS, L. Scott   Tel: (916) 772-2000
Senior Vice President, Finance and Corporate Development   Fax: (916) 786-7170
s.sommers@surewest.com

At Other Offices

HILL, Julie   Tel: (916) 772-2000
PAC Treasurer   Fax: (916) 786-7170
455 Capitol Mall, Suite 600
Sacramento, CA 95814

HILTACHK, Thomas W.   Tel: (916) 772-2000
PAC Contact   Fax: (916) 786-7170
455 Capitol Mall, Suite 600
Sacramento, CA 95814

SVB Financial Group

Provides financial services. Parent company of the Silicon Valley Bank, Santa Clara, CA.
www.svb.com
Employees: 1,737
Ticker: NASDAQ: SIVB
SIC: 6022
Industry/ies: Banking/Finance/Investments
Legislative Issues: BAN; CPI

President and Chief Executive Officer   Tel: (408) 654-7400
BECKER, Greg   Fax: (408) 496-2405

Main Headquarters
Mailing: 3005 Tasman Dr.   Tel: (408) 654-7400
   Santa Clara, CA 95054   Fax: (408) 496-2405

Political Action Committees
SVB Financial Group PAC
FEC ID: C00333658
Contact: Rebecca Olson
3005 Tasman Dr.
Santa Clara, CA 95054

   Contributions to Candidates: $22,600 (2015-2016)
   Democrats: $13,900; Republicans: $8,700

Corporate Foundations and Giving Programs

SVB Foundation
3005 Tasman Dr.
Santa Clara, CA 95054

Public Affairs and Related Activities Personnel

At Headquarters

DESCHENEAUX, Michael   Tel: (408) 654-7400
Chief Financial Officer   Fax: (408) 496-2405

DRAPER, Michelle   Tel: (408) 654-7400
Chief Marketing Officer   Fax: (408) 496-2405

EDMONDS-WATERS, Chris   Tel: (408) 654-7400
Head, Human Resources   Fax: (408) 496-2405

MERRITT, Carrie   Tel: (503) 574-3705
Director, Public Relations   Fax: (408) 496-2405
cmerritt@svb.com

O'LEARY, Meghan   Tel: (650) 255-9934
Director, Investor Relations   Fax: (408) 496-2405
moleary@svb.com

OLSON, Rebecca *PAC Treasurer*	Tel: Fax:	(408) 654-7400 (408) 496-2405
VERISSIMO, Marc J. *Chief Strategy and Risk Officer*	Tel: Fax:	(408) 654-7400 (408) 496-2405
WALLACE, Bruce *Chief Operations Officer and Principal Operating Officer*	Tel: Fax:	(408) 654-7400 (408) 496-2405
ZUCKERT, Michael *General Counsel*	Tel: Fax:	(408) 654-7400 (408) 496-2405

SVTC Technologies, LLC

An association dedicated to supporting public policy initiatives that improve the economic health and development in the Silicon Valley area.
www.svtc.com
Employees: 400
Industry/ies: Computer/Technology

Main Headquarters

Mailing: 3901 N. First St. San Jose, CA 95134	Tel:	(408) 240-7000

Public Affairs and Related Activities Personnel

At Headquarters

CHERIYAN, Anil *Federal Lovbbyist*	Tel:	(408) 240-7000

Swedish Covenant Hospital

Swedish Covenant Hospital is a healthcare facility providing health and wellness services to the communities of Chicago's north and northwest side. Rooted in the Evangelical Covenant Church, the hospital is dedicated to serving the physical, spiritual and psychological needs of our culturally diverse communities.
www.swedishcovenant.org
Annual Revenues: $253.69 million
Employees: 1,800
Industry/ies: Medicine/Health Care/Mental Health

President and Chief Executive Officer
NEWTON, Mark

Tel: (773) 878-8200
Fax: (773) 271-2854

Main Headquarters

Mailing: 5145 N. California Ave. Chicago, IL 60625	Tel: Fax:	(773) 878-8200 (773) 271-2854

Corporate Foundations and Giving Programs

Swedish Covenant Hospital Foundation
Contact: Jennifer Tscherney
5145 N. California Ave.
Chicago, IL 60625

Public Affairs and Related Activities Personnel

At Headquarters

BORENSTEIN, JD, Judith A. *Vice President and General Counsel*	Tel: Fax:	(773) 878-8200 (773) 271-2854
GARVEY, Thomas *Senior Vice President, Operations and Chief Financial Officer*	Tel: Fax:	(773) 878-8200 (773) 271-2854
GUACCIO, Anthony *Senior Vice President, Operations and Chief Operations Officer*	Tel: Fax:	(773) 878-8200 (773) 271-2854
MALSOM, Karen *Senior Director, Marketing and Media Contact* kmalsom@SwedishCovenant.org	Tel: Fax:	(773) 989-1685 (773) 271-2854
MANNS, Carl *Director, Development* cmanns@schosp.org	Tel: Fax:	(773) 878-8200 (773) 271-2854
TSCHERNEY, Jennifer *Executive Director, Swedish Covenant Hospital Foundation* jtscherney@swedishcovenant.org	Tel: Fax:	(773) 293-8877 (773) 271-2854

Swedish Match North America, Inc.

A tobacco company. Formerly the Pinkerton Group, Inc. The company is also called SMNA which makes snuff, as well as cigars, pipe tobacco, and of course, matches and lighters. In the US, its snuff brands include Longhorn, Timber Wolf, and Red Man; pipe tobacco brands are Borkum Riff, Half and Half, Paladin, and Velvet.
www.swedishmatch.com
Annual Revenues: $690.13 million
Employees: 1,001
SIC: 2111
Industry/ies: Tobacco Industry
Legislative Issues: BUD; TAX; TOB; TRD

Chairman of the Board
KARLSSON, Conny

Tel: (804) 787-5100
Fax: (804) 225-7000

President and Chief Executive Officer
DAHLGREN, Lars

Tel: (804) 787-5100
Fax: (804) 225-7000

Main Headquarters

Mailing: Two James Center, 1021 E. Cary St. Suite 1600 Richmond, VA 23219	Tel: Fax:	(804) 787-5100 (804) 225-7000

Political Action Committees

Swedish Match North America, Inc. PAC
FEC ID: C00215053
Contact: Wanda Blake
1021 E. Cary St.
P.O. Box 13297
Richmond, VA 23219

> **Contributions to Candidates:** $34,500 (2015-2016)
> Democrats: $4,500; Republicans: $29,000; Other: $1,000

Corporate Foundations and Giving Programs

The Solstickan Foundation
Contact: Maria Clementsson

Two James Center 1021 E. Cary St., Suite 1600 Richmond, VA 23219	Tel: Fax:	(804) 787-5100 (804) 225-7000

Public Affairs and Related Activities Personnel

At Headquarters

BERGSTROM , Rupini *Director, International Media and Corporate Public Relations* rupini.bergstrom@swedishmatch.com	Tel: Fax:	(468) 658-0106 (804) 225-7000
BLAKE, Wanda *Controller and PAC Treasurer*	Tel: Fax:	(804) 787-5100 (804) 225-7000
BREHMER, Henrik *Senior Vice President, Corporate Comunications* henrik.brehmer@swedishmatch.com	Tel: Fax:	(804) 787-5100 (804) 225-7000
CLEMENTSSON, Maria *Contact, Philanthropy* maria.clementsson@swedishmatch.com	Tel: Fax:	(468) 658-0495 (804) 225-7000
FLAHERTY, Richard *President US Division and Contact, US Investor Relations* rich.flaherty @smna.com	Tel: Fax:	(804) 787-5100 (804) 225-7000
FORSELL, Marlene *Senior Vice President and Chief Financial Officer*	Tel: Fax:	(804) 787-5100 (804) 225-7000
FOWLER-JONES, Sandy *Director Public Relations and Communications, US Division* sandy.fowler-jones @smna.com	Tel: Fax:	(804) 363-0424 (804) 225-7000
HARRISON, Emmett *Senior Vice President, Investor Relations and Corporate Communications* emmett.harrison@swedishmatch.com	Tel: Fax:	(468) 658-0173 (804) 225-7000
HEIMAN, Marie-Louise *Senior Vice President, Legal Affairs and General Counsel*	Tel: Fax:	(804) 787-5100 (804) 225-7000
HILDINGSSON , Patrik *Vice President, Group Public Affairs* patrik.hildingsson@swedishmatch.com	Tel: Fax:	(804) 787-5100 (804) 225-7000
ROERTY, Gerry *Vice President, Legal and General Counsel, US Division* gerry.roerty @smna.com	Tel: Fax:	(804) 400-8553 (804) 225-7000
TILLY, Joakim *President*	Tel: Fax:	(804) 787-5100 (804) 225-7000
WREDBERG, Johan *Director Communications and Media Relations* johan.wredberg@swedishmatch.com	Tel: Fax:	(804) 787-5100 (804) 225-7000

SWF Consulting, L.L.C.

Government Affairs and business consultation.
swfconsultingdc.com

President and Chief Executive Officer
FUJII, Stacie W.

Tel: (202) 294-0658

Main Headquarters

Mailing: 611 Pennsylvania Ave. SE Suite 120 Washington, DC 20003	

Swfit and Company

See listing on page 453 under JBS USA

Swisher International Inc.

A manufacturer of cigars and smokeless tobacco products.
www.swisher.com
Employees: 1,600
SIC: 2121; 2141; 2441; 3634; 3999
NAICS: 31221; 32192; 339999; 312229
Industry/ies: Tobacco Industry
Legislative Issues: HCR; TAX; TOB

Chairman of the Board
ZIEGLER, William

Tel: (904) 353-4311

Chief Executive Officer
GHILONI, Peter

Tel: (904) 353-4311

Main Headquarters

Mailing: 20 Thorndal Cir.
Darien, CT 06820

Tel: (203) 656-8000

Political Action Committees

Swisher International Inc. PAC Fund
FEC ID: C00312785
Contact: Joseph R. Augustus
459 E. 16th St.
Jacksonville Beach, FL 32206

Contributions to Candidates: $98,000 (2015-2016)
Republicans: $98,000

Principal Recipients

SENATE
BURR, RICHARD (REP-NC)
DESANTIS, RONALD D (REP-FL)
ISAKSON, JOHN HARDY (REP-GA)

HOUSE
DESANTIS, RONALD D (REP-FL)
RYAN, PAUL D. (REP-WI)

Public Affairs and Related Activities Personnel

At Headquarters

AUGUSTUS, Joe
Senior Vice President, Global Affairs

Tel: (203) 656-8000

At Other Offices

AUGUSTUS, Joseph R.
Senior Vice President and PAC Treasurer
459 E.16th St.
Jacksonville Beach, FL 32206-3025

Tel: (904) 353-4311

Swiss Re America

A reinsurance company. Swiss Re America, based in Armonk City, is the U.S. subsidiary of Swiss Re, headquartered in Zurich, Switzerland.
www.swissre.com
Annual Revenues: $76.40 million
Employees: 2,000
Industry/ies: Insurance Industry
Legislative Issues: ENG; INS; LAW; TAX; TRD

Chairman
OZENDO, Pierre L.

Tel: (914) 828-8000
Fax: (914) 828-7000

Chairman of the Board
KIELHOLZ, Walter B.

Tel: (914) 828-8000
Fax: (914) 828-7000

Main Headquarters
Mailing: 175 King St.
Armonk, NY 10504

Tel: (914) 828-8000
Fax: (914) 828-7000

Washington Office
Mailing: 101 Constitution Ave. NW
Suite 800
Washington, DC 20001-2133

Tel: (202) 742-4637

Political Action Committees

Swiss Re America Holding Corporation PAC
FEC ID: C00462564
Contact: Elissa Kenny
175 King St.
Armonk, NY 10504

Tel: (914) 828-8000
Fax: (914) 828-7000

Contributions to Candidates: $67,500 (2015-2016)
Democrats: $32,000; Republicans: $35,500

Principal Recipients

SENATE
BLUNT, ROY (REP-MO)

Corporate Foundations and Giving Programs

Swiss Re America Contributions Program
175 King St.
Armonk, NY 10504

Tel: (914) 828-8000
Fax: (914) 828-7000

Public Affairs and Related Activities Personnel

At Headquarters

ALLEN, Nicole
Senior Vice President, State Regulatory Officer and Direct Commercial Insurance
nicole_allen@swissre.com
Registered Federal Lobbyist

Tel: (914) 828-8000
Fax: (914) 828-7000

CODA, Carolyn
Vice President, Regulatory Affairs
Registered Federal Lobbyist

Tel: (914) 828-8000
Fax: (914) 828-7000

GEIGER, Hermann
Group General Counsel

Tel: (914) 828-8000
Fax: (914) 828-7000

KELLER, Anne
Head Corporate Citizenship

Tel: (914) 828-8000
Fax: (914) 828-7000

KENNY, Elissa

Tel: (914) 828-8000

PAC Treasurer

Fax: (914) 828-7000

SOMERS, Jeanette

Tel: (914) 828-8000
Fax: (914) 828-7000

At Washington Office

FRETWELL, Nigel P.
Chief Human Resources Officer

Tel: (202) 742-4637

KAPLAN, Alex
Senior Client Manager
Registered Federal Lobbyist

Tel: (202) 742-4633

PRESTON, Don
Head, Americas Government Affairs
Registered Federal Lobbyist

Tel: (202) 742-4633

SIMON, Cosette R.
Managing Director and Head, Government Affairs
Registered Federal Lobbyist

Tel: (202) 742-4633

Sybase Inc.

A data applications development company.
www.sybase.com
Employees: 3,800
Ticker: NYSE: SY
SIC: 7372
Industry/ies: Computer/Technology

Main Headquarters
Mailing: One Sybase Dr.
Dublin, CA 94568

Tel: (925) 236-5000
Fax: (925) 236-4321
TF: (800) 792-2735

Public Affairs and Related Activities Personnel

At Headquarters

CARL, Dan R.
Former General Counsel

Tel: (925) 236-5000
Fax: (925) 236-4321

GRANT, Stuart
Manager, Business Development

Tel: (925) 236-5000
Fax: (925) 236-4321

Sylvan Learning Systems Inc

See listing on page 482 under Laureate Education

Symantec Corporation

Provides virus protection, intrusion prevention, Internet content and e-mail filtering, and other security services.
www.symantec.com
Annual Revenues: $6.62 billion
Employees: 20,800
Ticker: NASDAQ: SYMC
SIC: 7372
NAICS: 51121
Industry/ies: Computer/Technology
Legislative Issues: CPI; HOM

Interim President and Chief Executive Officer
BROWN, Michael A.

Tel: (650) 527-8000

Main Headquarters
Mailing: 350 Ellis St.
Mountain View, CA 94043

Tel: (650) 527-8000

Washington Office
Mailing: 700 13th St. NW
Suite 1150
Washington, DC 20005

Tel: (408) 517-8324
Fax: (202) 371-6728

Political Action Committees

Symantec Corporation PAC
FEC ID: C00394031
Contact: Cheri F. McGuire
350 Ellis St.
Mountain View, CA 94043

Contributions to Candidates: $58,759 (2015-2016)
Democrats: $31,510; Republicans: $27,249

Corporate Foundations and Giving Programs

Symantec Foundation
Contact: Cecily Joseph
20330 Stevens Creek Blvd.
Cupertino, CA 95014

Public Affairs and Related Activities Personnel

At Headquarters

CAPPELLANTI-WOLF , Amy
Senior Vice President, Chief Human Resources Officer

Tel: (650) 527-8000

CORCOS, Helyn
Vice President, Investor Relations
hcorcos@symantec.com

Tel: (650) 527-5523

JOSEPH, Cecily
Vice President, Corporate Responsibility

Tel: (650) 527-8000

MCGUIRE , Cheri F. Tel: (650) 527-8000
Vice President, Global Government Affairs & Cybersecurity
Policy
Cheri_McGuire@symantec.com

SEIFERT, Thomas Tel: (650) 527-8000
Executive Vice President, Chief Financial Officer

TAYLOR, Scott Tel: (650) 527-8000
Executive Vice President, General Counsel and Secretary
scott.taylor@symantec.com

At Washington Office

GRAZIANO, Dena Tel: (408) 517-8324
Director, Federal Government Affairs Fax: (202) 371-6728
governmentaffairs@symantec.com
Registered Federal Lobbyist

Synagro Technologies, Inc.

Helps government agencies and private industries manage organic residuals.
www.synagro.com
Annual Revenues: $41.80 million
Employees: 900
SIC: 4953
Industry/ies: Agriculture/Agronomy; Management

President and Chief Executive Officer Tel: (713) 369-1700
COLE, Stephen W. Fax: (713) 369-1750

Main Headquarters
Mailing: 1800 Bering Dr. Tel: (713) 369-1700
Suite 1000 Fax: (713) 369-1750
Houston, TX 77057 TF: (800) 370-0035

Public Affairs and Related Activities Personnel

At Headquarters

DUNKERLEY, Chris Tel: (713) 369-1700
Vice President and Chief Financial Officer Fax: (713) 369-1750

RACEY, Pamela K. Tel: (713) 369-1700
Vice President, Sales and Development Fax: (713) 369-1750

Syndetics, Inc.

Specializes in the classified arena, primarily in the federal defense, aerospace, intelligence and homeland security markets.
www.syndetics-inc.com
Employees: 100
Industry/ies: Management

President and Chief Executive Officer Tel: (703) 273-8350
HASSLER, Christopher C. Fax: (703) 273-8353
cchassler@syndetics-inc.com

Main Headquarters
Mailing: 10395 Democracy Ln. Tel: (703) 273-8350
Fairfax, VA 22030 Fax: (703) 273-8353

Public Affairs and Related Activities Personnel

At Headquarters

BRENNAN, Michael J. Tel: (703) 598-2777
Federal Lobbyist Fax: (703) 273-8353

FAULKNER, Joe Tel: (703) 273-8350
Director, Human Resources Fax: (703) 273-8353

RODGERS, Jason A. Tel: (703) 273-8350
Vice President, Business Operations Fax: (703) 273-8353

Synergy Group, Ltd.

Non-residential construction.
www.synergygroupltd.com
Annual Revenues: $7.50 million
Industry/ies: Apparel/Textiles Industry; Commodities

Chief Executive Officer & President Tel: (512) 326-2678
MARSHALL, William
williammarshall@synergygroupltd.com

Main Headquarters
Mailing: 2347 Douglas St. Tel: (512) 326-2678
Suite 1105
Austin, TX 78741

Syngenta Corporation

Agribusiness company. U.S. subsidiary of Syngenta AG, headquartered in Basel, Switzerland.
www.syngenta-us.com
Employees: 5,100
Industry/ies: Agriculture/Agronomy; Chemicals & Chemical Industry
Legislative Issues: AGR; CHM; ENV; FOO; FUE; TAR; TRD

Chairman of the Board, Non-executive Director Tel: (302) 425-2000
DEMARÉ, Michel

Chief Executive Officer Tel: (302) 425-2000
MACK, Michael Fax: (302) 425-2001

Regional Director, North America Tel: (302) 425-2000
HAWKINS, Vern Fax: (302) 425-2001

Main Headquarters
Mailing: 3411 Silverside Rd.
Suite 100
Wilmington, DE 19810

Washington Office
Mailing: 1775 Pennsylvania Ave. NW
Suite 600
Washington, DC 20005

Political Action Committees
Syngenta Corporation Employee PAC
FEC ID: C00363945
Contact: Eddie Bao
1775 Pennsylvania Ave. NW Tel: (202) 347-8348
Suite 600 Fax: (202) 347-8758
Washington, DC 20005

Contributions to Candidates: $204,700 (2015-2016)
Democrats: $61,000; Republicans: $143,700

Principal Recipients

HOUSE
MARINO, THOMAS ANTHONY (REP-PA)

Corporate Foundations and Giving Programs
Syngenta Foundation
Contact: Marco Ferroni
2200 Concord Pike
Wilmington, DE 19803

Public Affairs and Related Activities Personnel

At Headquarters

DELUCIA, Aline
Registered Federal Lobbyist

At Washington Office

BAO, Eddie
PAC Treasurer

At Other Offices

ATKIN , John Tel: (302) 425-2000
Chief Operating Officer
3411 Silverside Rd.
Wilmington, DE 19810

BRYAN, Ann Tel: (336) 632-2486
Contact, Media Relations
3411 Silverside Rd.
Wilmington, DE 19810
ann.bryan@syngenta.com

DETWILER, Mark Tel: (202) 347-8348
Federal Lobbyist Fax: (202) 347-8758
1775 Pennsylvania Ave., Suite 750, Seventh Floor
Washington, DC 20006

DOLCH, Michael Tel: (302) 425-2000
Federal Lobbyist
3411 Silverside Rd.
Wilmington, DE 19810

FERRONI, Marco Tel: (302) 425-2000
Executive Director, Syngenta Foundation Fax: (302) 425-2001
2200 Concord Pike, P. O. Box 8353
Wilmington, DE 19803-8353

KELLY, Angus Tel: (302) 425-2000
Manager, Federal Government Relations Fax: (302) 425-2001
2200 Concord Pike, P. O. Box 8353
Wilmington, DE 19803-8353
angus.kelly@syngenta.com

LENTZ, Christina Q. Tel: (302) 425-2000
Esquire
3411 Silverside Rd.
Wilmington, DE 19810

LUSCOMBE, Caroline Tel: (302) 425-2000
Head, Human Resources
3411 Silverside Rd.
Wilmington, DE 19810

MÄDER, Christoph Tel: (302) 425-2000
Head, Legal and Taxes and Company Secretary
3411 Silverside Rd.
Wilmington, DE 19810

MINEHART, Paul Tel: (202) 347-8348
Head, Corporate Communications Fax: (202) 347-8758
1775 Pennsylvania Ave., Suite 750, Seventh Floor
Washington, DC 20006
paul.minehart@syngenta.com

PETERSON, Laura Wood Tel: (202) 347-8348
Manager, Federal Government Relations Fax: (202) 347-8758

1775 Pennsylvania Ave., Suite 750, Seventh Floor
Washington, DC 20006
Registered Federal Lobbyist

QUAIN, Cheryl	Tel:	(302) 425-2019
Corporate General Counsel & Regional Compliance Officer	Fax:	(302) 425-2001

2200 Concord Pike, P. O. Box 8353
Wilmington, DE 19803-8353
cheryl.quain@syngenta.com

RAMSAY, John	Tel:	(302) 425-2000
Chief Financial Officer	Fax:	(302) 425-2001

2200 Concord Pike, P. O. Box 8353
Wilmington, DE 19803-8353
john.ramsay@syngenta.com

SANDS, Jeff	Tel:	(302) 425-2000

Federal Lobbyist
3411 Silverside Rd.
Wilmington, DE 19810
Registered Federal Lobbyist

SEABROOK , Jonathan	Tel:	(302) 425-2000

Head, Corporate Affairs
3411 Silverside Rd.
Wilmington, DE 19810

THEIS, Greg A.	Tel:	(202) 347-8348
Senior Director, Federal Government Relations	Fax:	(202) 347-8758

1775 Pennsylvania Ave., Suite 750, Seventh Floor
Washington, DC 20006

WOOD, Laura	Tel:	(302) 425-2000

Federal Lobbyist
3411 Silverside Rd.
Wilmington, DE 19810
Registered Federal Lobbyist

Syngenta Crop Protection

Syngenta Crop Protection is the U.S. subsidiary of Syngenta AG , headquartered in Basel, Switzerland and is a supplier manufacturing pesticides, seeds, potting soil and other related agricultural products.
www.syngentacropprotection.com
Annual Revenues: $390.80 million
Employees: 5,000
Industry/ies: Agriculture/Agronomy

Chief Executive Officer		
MACK, Michael	Tel:	(336) 632-6000
	Fax:	(336) 632-7353

Main Headquarters		
Mailing: P.O. Box 18300	Tel:	(336) 632-6000
Greensboro, NC 27419-8300	Fax:	(336) 632-7353
	TF:	(800) 334-9481

Public Affairs and Related Activities Personnel

At Headquarters

ANDERSON , Doug	Tel:	(336) 632-6000
Manager, Marketing	Fax:	(336) 632-7353
FISCHER, Valdemar	Tel:	(336) 632-6000
President	Fax:	(336) 632-7353
LUSCOMBE, Caroline	Tel:	(336) 632-6000
Head Human Resources	Fax:	(336) 632-7353
MÄDER, Christoph	Tel:	(336) 632-6000
Head Legal and Taxes and Company Secretary	Fax:	(336) 632-7353
PARR, Jonathan	Tel:	(336) 632-6000
Chief Operating Officer	Fax:	(336) 632-7353
PEACOCK, Mark	Tel:	(336) 632-6000
Head Global Operations	Fax:	(336) 632-7353
RAMSAY, John	Tel:	(336) 632-6000
Chief Financial Officer	Fax:	(336) 632-7353
SEABROOK, Jonathan	Tel:	(336) 632-6000
Head Corporate Affairs	Fax:	(336) 632-7353

Syniverse Technologies

A telecommunications services company.
www.syniverse.com
Annual Revenues: $482.99 million
Employees: 1,300
Ticker: NYSE: SVR
SIC: 4899
Industry/ies: Communications; Telecommunications/Internet/Cable

Chairman of the Board		
ATTWOOD, James A.	Tel:	(813) 637-5000
	Fax:	(813) 229-1770

President and Chief Executive Officer		
GRAY, Stephen C.	Tel:	(813) 637-5000
	Fax:	(813) 229-1770

Main Headquarters		
Mailing: 8125 Highwoods Palm Way	Tel:	(813) 637-5000
Tampa, FL 33647-1776	Fax:	(813) 229-1770

Political Action Committees

Syniverse Technologies PAC (PAC)
FEC ID: C00395186
Contact: Bobbie Reyes

8125 Highwoods Palm Way	Tel:	(813) 637-5000
Tampa, FL 33647	Fax:	(813) 229-1770

Contributions to Candidates: $2,000 (2015-2016)
Democrats: $1,000; Republicans: $1,000

Corporate Foundations and Giving Programs

Syniverse Technologies Contributions Program

8125 Highwoods Palm Way	Tel:	(813) 637-5000
Suite 600	Fax:	(813) 637-5000
Tampa, FL 33647-1776		

Public Affairs and Related Activities Personnel

At Headquarters

BINION, Laura E.	Tel:	(813) 637-5000
General Counsel and Senior Vice President	Fax:	(813) 229-1770
laura.binion@syniverse.com		
CLARK, Mary	Tel:	(813) 637-5000
Chief Marketing Officer	Fax:	(813) 229-1770
EAGLE, Bobby	Tel:	(813) 637-5050
Senior Manager, Public Relations	Fax:	(813) 229-1770
bobby.eagle@syniverse.com		
HENNEN, Leigh M.	Tel:	(813) 637-5000
Chief Human Resources Officer	Fax:	(813) 229-1770
HITCHCOCK, David W.	Tel:	(813) 637-5000
Executive Vice President, Global Product Management and Development	Fax:	(813) 229-1770
LEWIS, Ed	Tel:	(813) 637-5000
Chief Strategy Officer	Fax:	(813) 229-1770
MCRAE, John	Tel:	(813) 637-5000
Chief Information Officer	Fax:	(813) 229-1770
REICH, Bob	Tel:	(813) 637-5000
Chief Financial Officer	Fax:	(813) 229-1770
REYES, Bobbie	Tel:	(813) 637-5000
PAC Contact	Fax:	(813) 229-1770

Synovus Financial Corporation

A banking and credit card processing company.
www.synovus.com
Annual Revenues: $1.05 billion
Employees: 4,481
Ticker: NYSE: SNV
SIC: 6021
Industry/ies: Banking/Finance/Investments

Chairman of the Board and Chief Executive Officer		
STELLING, Jr., Kessel D.	Tel:	(706) 649-2311
	Fax:	(706) 641-6555

Main Headquarters		
Mailing: P.O. Box 120	Tel:	(706) 649-2311
Columbus, GA 31902	Fax:	(706) 641-6555
	TF:	(888) 796-6887

Political Action Committees

Synovus Financial Corporation Committee for Good Leadership PAC
FEC ID: C00200642
Contact: Alan Kamensky
P.O. Box 120
Columbus, GA 31920

Contributions to Candidates: $1,000 (2015-2016)
Republicans: $1,000

Synovus Financial Corporation Florida Fund for Effective Leadership PAC
FEC ID: C00437418
Contact: Alan Kamensky
P.O. Box 120
Columbus, GA 31902

Synovus Financial Corporation Georgia Fund for Effective Leadership PAC
FEC ID: C00032607
Contact: Alan Kamensky

P.O. Box 120	Tel:	(706) 649-2311
Columbus, GA 31902	Fax:	(706) 641-6555

Contributions to Candidates: $36,700 (2015-2016)
Democrats: $11,000; Republicans: $25,700

Principal Recipients

HOUSE
BISHOP, SANFORD D JR (DEM-GA)

Synovus Financial Corporation Tennessee Fund for Effective Leadership PAC
FEC ID: C00437426
Contact: Alan Kamensky
P.O. Box 120
Columbus, GA 31902

Corporate Foundations and Giving Programs

Synovus Foundation
Contact: Calvin Smyre
P.O. Box 120
Columbus, GA 31902

Public Affairs and Related Activities Personnel

At Headquarters

BANKS, Gloria C.	Tel:	(706) 649-2311
Senior Director, Compliance	Fax:	(706) 641-6555
COPELAND, R. Dallis "D"	Tel:	(706) 649-2311
Executive Vice President and Chief Community Banking Officer	Fax:	(706) 641-6555
DOWE, Alison	Tel:	(706) 641-3781
Senior Director, Corporate Communications	Fax:	(706) 641-6555
alisondowe@synovus.com		
DUKES, Elizabeth K.	Tel:	(706) 649-2311
Chief Strategy Officer	Fax:	(706) 641-6555
HOLLINGSWORTH, Audrey D.	Tel:	(706) 649-2311
Group Executive, Human Resources	Fax:	(706) 641-6555
HUDGISON, Greg	Tel:	(706) 644-0528
Manager, External Communications	Fax:	(706) 641-6555
KAMENSKY, Alan	Tel:	(706) 649-2311
Executive Vice President, General Counsel, Secretary and PAC Treasurer	Fax:	(706) 641-6555
PRESCOTT, Thomas J.	Tel:	(706) 649-2311
Executive Vice President and Chief Financial Officer	Fax:	(706) 641-6555
SMYRE, Calvin	Tel:	(706) 649-2311
Executive Vice President, Corporate Affairs and Chief Executive Officer, Foundation	Fax:	(706) 641-6555
calvinsmyre@synovus.com		

Syntroleum Corporation

The company licenses its patented gas-to-liquids (GTL) process which converts natural gas into synthetic crude oil by using air instead of pure oxygen.
www.syntroleum.com
Employees: 19
Ticker: NASDAQ: SYNM
SIC: 1311
Industry/ies: Defense/Homeland Security; Government-Related

Chairman of the Board	Tel:	(918) 592-7900
ROSENE, Jr., Robert B.	Fax:	(918) 592-7979

President and Chief Executive Officer	Tel:	(918) 592-7900
ROTH, Edward G.	Fax:	(918) 592-7979

Main Headquarters

Mailing:	5416 S. Yale Ave.	Tel:	(918) 592-7900
	Suite 400	Fax:	(918) 592-7979
	Tulsa, OK 74135		

Political Action Committees

Syntroleum Corporation PAC
FEC ID: C00376848
Contact: Carla S. Covey

4322 S. 49th West Ave.	Tel:	(918) 592-7900
Tulsa, OK 74107	Fax:	(918) 592-7979

Public Affairs and Related Activities Personnel

At Headquarters

BIGGER, Jeffery M.	Tel:	(918) 592-7900
Senior Vice President, Business Development	Fax:	(918) 592-7979
GALLAGHER, Karen L.	Tel:	(918) 592-7900
Senior Vice President and Principal Financial Officer	Fax:	(918) 592-7979
STINEBAUGH, Ronald E.	Tel:	(918) 764-3406
Senior Vice President, Finance and Acquisitions	Fax:	(918) 592-7979
rstinebaugh@Syntroleum.com		

At Other Offices

COVEY, Carla S.	Tel:	(918) 592-7900
PAC Contact	Fax:	(918) 592-7979
4322 S. 49th W. Ave.		
Tulsa, OK 74107		

Syracuse Research Corporation

A research and development company working in industries of defense, environment, and intelligence.
www.syrres.com
Annual Revenues: $0.63 million
Employees: 50
Industry/ies: Science; Scientific Research

Chairperson of the Board	Tel:	(315) 452-8000
ROBERTS, Robert U.	Fax:	(315) 452-8090

President	Tel:	(315) 452-8000
TREMONT, Paul G.	Fax:	(315) 452-8090

Main Headquarters

Mailing:	7502 Round Pond Rd.	Tel:	(315) 452-8000
	Syracuse, NY 13212-2510	Fax:	(315) 452-8090
		TF:	(800) 724-0451

Corporate Foundations and Giving Programs

Syracuse Research Corporation Corporate Contributions

7502 Round Pond Rd.	Tel:	(315) 452-8000
Syracuse, NY 13212-2510	Fax:	(315) 452-8090

Public Affairs and Related Activities Personnel

At Headquarters

FAZIO, Philip	Tel:	(315) 452-8000
Executive Vice President, Finance, and Chief Financial Officer	Fax:	(315) 452-8090
HAIR , Kevin	Tel:	(315) 452-8000
Executive Vice President, Strategy and Business Development	Fax:	(315) 452-8090
HOLLAND, James F.	Tel:	(315) 452-8000
Executive Vice President, Administration	Fax:	(315) 452-8090
LANE, Robert P.	Tel:	(315) 452-8000
Executive Vice President, General Counsel	Fax:	(315) 452-8090
blane@srcinc.com		
UPSON, Donald	Tel:	(315) 452-8000
Federal Lobbyist	Fax:	(315) 452-8090

SYSCO Corporation

A wholesale food distributor.
www.sysco.com
Annual Revenues: $49.12 billion
Employees: 51,700
Ticker: NYSE: SYY
SIC: 5085
NAICS: 423830
Industry/ies: Food And Beverage Industry
Legislative Issues: AGR; FOO; LBR; TRA

Non-Executive Chairman of the Board	Tel:	(281) 584-1390
WARD, Jackie L.	Fax:	(281) 584-2721

President and Chief Executive Officer	Tel:	(281) 584-1390
DELANEY, Bill J.	Fax:	(281) 584-2721

Main Headquarters

Mailing:	1390 Enclave Pkwy.	Tel:	(281) 584-1390
	Houston, TX 77077-2099	Fax:	(281) 584-2721

Corporate Foundations and Giving Programs

SYSCO Corporation Contributions Program

1390 Enclave Pkwy.	Tel:	(281) 584-1390
Houston, TX 77077	Fax:	(281) 584-2721

Public Affairs and Related Activities Personnel

At Headquarters

BENE, Tom	Tel:	(281) 584-1390
President and Chief Operating Officer	Fax:	(281) 584-2721
ELMER , Mitch	Tel:	(281) 584-1390
Senior Vice President, Shared Services Finance and Co-Chief Accounting Officer	Fax:	(281) 584-2721
GOETZ , Bill	Tel:	(281) 584-1390
Senior Vice President, Marketing and Chief Marketing Officer	Fax:	(281) 584-2721
GRADE , Joel	Tel:	(281) 584-1390
Senior Vice President, Finance and Chief Accounting Officer	Fax:	(281) 584-2721
HORTON , Nehl	Tel:	(281) 584-1390
Senior Vice President, Chief Communications and Government Relations Officer	Fax:	(281) 584-2721
KARNA , Ajoy	Tel:	(281) 584-1390
Senior Vice President, Finance and Treasury	Fax:	(281) 584-2721
KUNDE, II, Gerald "Chip"	Tel:	(281) 584-1390
Vice President, Government Relations	Fax:	(281) 584-2721
LIBBY, Russel T.	Tel:	(281) 584-1390
Executive Vice President, Administration and Corporate Secretary	Fax:	(281) 584-2721
russell@sysco.com		
MOSKOWITZ , Paul T.	Tel:	(281) 584-1390
Executive Vice President, Human Resources	Fax:	(281) 584-2721
MUNN, Charles A.	Tel:	(281) 584-1390
Vice President, Labor Relations	Fax:	(281) 584-2721
munn.chuck.r059@sysco.com		
RANDT, Thomas P.	Tel:	(281) 584-1390
Vice President, Employee Relations	Fax:	(281) 584-2721
SKORECKI , Adam	Tel:	(281) 584-1390
Senior Vice President and General Counsel	Fax:	(281) 584-2721
SONNEMAKER , Scott	Tel:	(281) 584-1390
Senior Vice President, Sales	Fax:	(281) 584-2721
STONE, Scott B.	Tel:	(281) 584-1390

Vice President, Financial Reporting	Fax: (281) 584-2721
STORY, Wesley	Tel: (281) 584-1390
Vice President, Marketing and Innovative Technology	Fax: (281) 584-2721
WISNOSKI, Mark	Tel: (281) 584-1390
Vice President	Fax: (281) 584-2721

SYSCOM Inc

Information technology services company, which provides enterprise content management, business process management, business intelligence, and enterprise capture solutions and services.
www.syscom.com
Employees: 75
Industry/ies: Computer/Technology

Founder, President and Chief Executive Officer Tel: (410) 539-3737
BAYER, Theodore F. Fax: (410) 837-9535

Main Headquarters
Mailing: 400 E. Pratt St. Tel: (410) 539-3737
Suite 502 Fax: (410) 837-9535
Baltimore, MD 21202 TF: (800) 579-7266

Public Affairs and Related Activities Personnel

At Headquarters

VOYTILLA, Michael Tel: (410) 539-3737
Vice President, Sales and Marketing Fax: (410) 837-9535
mvoytilla@syscom.com

WILLIES, SPHR, Verna Tel: (410) 539-3737
Vice President, Human Resources Fax: (410) 837-9535
vwilles@syscom.com

Systemax Inc.

A direct marketer of brand name and private label products, including industrial, material handling and supplies, personal computers, notebook computers, technology supplies, consumer electronics and computer-related accessories. In May 2009, Systemax acquired defunct retailer Circuit City and now operates internet retail operations under the name of www.circuitcity.com.
www.systemax.com
Annual Revenues: $3.36 billion
Employees: 5,300
Ticker: NYSE: SYX
SIC: 5961; 5044; 5045
NAICS: 421420; 421430
Industry/ies: Computer/Technology

Chairman of the Board and Chief Executive Officer Tel: (516) 608-7000
LEEDS, Richard Fax: (516) 608-7001

Main Headquarters
Mailing: 11 Harbor Park Dr. Tel: (516) 608-7000
Port Washington, NY 11050 Fax: (516) 608-7001

Public Affairs and Related Activities Personnel

At Headquarters

DOOLEY, Bob Tel: (516) 608-7000
President, Global Industrial Fax: (516) 608-7001

LERNER, Eric Tel: (516) 608-7000
Senior Vice President and General Counsel Fax: (516) 608-7001

REINHOLD, Larry Tel: (516) 608-7000
Executive Vice President and Chief Financial Officer Fax: (516) 608-7001

WARD, Natasha Tel: (516) 608-7000
Director, Human Resources Fax: (516) 608-7001

At Other Offices

PASCARELLA, Dianne Tel: (212) 986-6667
Contact, Investor and Media Relations Fax: (212) 986-8302
521 Fifth Ave., Eighth Floor
New York City, NY 10175
pascarella@braincomm.com

SMARGIASSI, Mike Tel: (212) 986-6667
Contact, Investor Relations and Media Fax: (212) 986-8302
521 Fifth Ave., Eighth Floor
New York City, NY 10175
smarg@braincomm.com

SZD Government Advocates, LLC

Main Headquarters
Mailing: P.O. Box 165020 Tel: (614) 462-5052
Columbus, OH 43215

Public Affairs and Related Activities Personnel

At Headquarters
ROBINSON, David J. Tel: (614) 462-5052

T-Mobile USA

Formerly known as Voicestream Wireless Corporation. Provider of wireless voice, messaging, and data services. T-Mobile USA, Inc. is a subsidiary of Deutsche Telekom AG.

www.t-mobile.com
Annual Revenues: $30.47 billion
Employees: 45,000
Ticker: NYSE: TMUS
SIC: 4812
Industry/ies: Communications; Telecommunications/Internet/Cable
Legislative Issues: COM; CPT; DEF; LBR; TAX; TEC

Chairman of the Board Tel: (425) 378-4000
HOTTGES, Timotheus Fax: (425) 378-4040

President and Chief Executive Officer Tel: (425) 378-4000
LEGERE, John J. Fax: (425) 378-4040

Main Headquarters
Mailing: 601 Pennsylvania Ave. NW Tel: (202) 609-8380
Suite 800 North
Washington, DC 20004

Political Action Committees
T-Mobile USA, Inc. PAC (T-PAC)
FEC ID: C00361758
Contact: Anthony M. Russo
601 Pennsylvania Ave. NW Tel: (202) 654-5900
Suite 800
Washington, DC 20004

  Contributions to Candidates: $10,546,015 (2015-2016)
  Democrats: $134,750; Republicans: $129,250; Other: $10,282,015

Corporate Foundations and Giving Programs
T-Mobile USA Contributions Program
12920 S.E. 38th St. Tel: (425) 378-4000
Bellevue, WA 98006 Fax: (425) 378-4000

Public Affairs and Related Activities Personnel

At Headquarters

HAM, Kathleen O'Brien Tel: (202) 654-5900
Vice President, Federal Regulatory Affairs

KURTH, Christine Tel: (202) 609-8380
Registered Federal Lobbyist

LINDERMAN BARKER, Laura Tel: (202) 609-8380
Federal Lobbyist
Registered Federal Lobbyist

MCPHERSON, Laura Tel: (202) 609-8380
Registered Federal Lobbyist

PETERMAN, Adam J. Tel: (202) 609-8380
Federal Lobbyist
Registered Federal Lobbyist

THOMPSON, Derric Tel: (202) 609-8380
Federa Lobbyist

At Other Offices

CALAFF, Robert Tel: (202) 654-5900
Senior Corporate Counsel
401 Ninth St. NW, Suite 550
Washington, DC 20004

CAREY, David R. Tel: (425) 378-4000
Executive Vice President, Corporate Services Fax: (425) 378-4040
12920 S.E. 38th St.
Bellevue, WA 98006

CARTER, J. Braxton Tel: (425) 378-4000
Executive Vice President, Chief Financial Officer Fax: (425) 378-4040
12920 S.E. 38th St.
Bellevue, WA 98006

EWENS, Peter A. Tel: (425) 378-4000
Chief Strategy Officer Fax: (425) 378-4040
12920 S.E. 38th St.
Bellevue, WA 98006
peter.ewens@T-Mobile.com

KELSAY, Brendan Tel: (202) 654-5900
Director
401 Ninth St. NW, Suite 550
Washington, DC 20004

LINDERMAN, Laura Tel: (202) 654-5900
Principal Manager, Federal Government Affairs
401 Ninth St. NW, Suite 550
Washington, DC 20004
Registered Federal Lobbyist

MILLER, David Tel: (425) 378-4000
Executive Vice President, General Counsel and Secretary Fax: (425) 378-4040
12920 S.E. 38th St.
Bellevue, WA 98006
dave.miller@T-Mobile.com

MYERS, Larry Tel: (425) 378-4000
Executive Vice President of Human Resources Fax: (425) 378-4040
12920 S.E. 38th St.
Bellevue, WA 98006

larry.myers@T-Mobile.com

PAELLMANN, Nils
Vice President, Investor Relations
One Park Ave., 14th Floor
New York City, NY 10016
investor.relations@t-mobile.com
Tel: (212) 358-3210
Fax: (212) 358-3224

PERSAUD, Michelle
Senior Corporate Counsel
401 Ninth St. NW, Suite 550
Washington, DC 20004
Registered Federal Lobbyist
Tel: (202) 654-5900

RUSSO, Anthony M.
Vice President, Federal Legislative Affairs & PAC Treasurer
401 Ninth St. NW, Suite 550
Washington, DC 20004
tony.russo@t-mobile.com
Registered Federal Lobbyist
Tel: (202) 654-5900

SHERRARD, J Andrew
Executive Vice President and Chief Marketing Officer
12920 S.E. 38th St.
Bellevue, WA 98006
Tel: (425) 378-4000
Fax: (425) 378-4040

SIEVERT, G. Michael
Executive Vice President and Chief operating Officer
12920 S.E. 38th St.
Bellevue, WA 98006
Tel: (425) 378-4000
Fax: (425) 378-4040

SYLLA-DIXON, Marie
Chief Legislative Counsel, Director Government Affairs
401 Ninth St. NW, Suite 550
Washington, DC 20004
Registered Federal Lobbyist
Tel: (202) 654-5900

T. Rowe Price

Help clients around the world achieve their long-term investment goals. It is a publicly owned asset management holding company, which provides its services to individuals, institutional investors, retirement plans, financial intermediaries, and institutions.
corporate.troweprice.com
Annual Revenues: $4.05 Billion
Employees: 5,905
Ticker: NASDAQ:TROW
Industry/ies: Banking/Credit & Finance/Savings & Loan; Banking/Finance/Investments; Insurance Industry; Investments/Securities Industry

Chairman and Chief Investment Officer
ROGERS, CFA, CIC, Brian C.
Tel: (410) 345-2000
Fax: (410) 345-2394

President and Chief Executive Officer
KENNEDY, CFA, James A. C.
Tel: (410) 345-2000
Fax: (410) 345-2394

Main Headquarters
Mailing: 100 East Pratt St.
Baltimore, MD 21202
Tel: (410) 345-2000
Fax: (410) 345-2394
TF: (800) 638-7890

Corporate Foundations and Giving Programs

T. Rowe Price Foundation
Contact: John Brothers
100 East Pratt St.
Baltimore, MD 21202

Public Affairs and Related Activities Personnel

At Headquarters

BROTHERS, John
President, T. Rowe Price Foundation
Tel: (410) 345-2000
Fax: (410) 345-2394

MORELAND, Kenneth V.
Chief Financial Officer
Tel: (410) 345-2000
Fax: (410) 345-2394

Taco Bell Corporation

A fast food chain. Subsidiary of Yum! Brands.
www.tacobell.com
Industry/ies: Food And Beverage Industry

Chief Executive Officer
NICCOL, Brian
Tel: (949) 863-4000
Fax: (949) 863-2252

Main Headquarters
Mailing: One Glen Bell Way
Irvine, CA 92618
Tel: (949) 863-4000
Fax: (949) 863-2252

Corporate Foundations and Giving Programs

Taco Bell Foundation for Teens
Contact: Michael Ramirez
One Glen Bell Way
Irvine, CA 92618
Tel: (949) 863-4579

Public Affairs and Related Activities Personnel

At Headquarters

BRANDT, Chris
Chief Marketing Officer
Tel: (949) 863-4000
Fax: (949) 863-2252

CORSINITA, Juliet
Tel: (949) 863-4000

Vice President, Media and Brand Partnerships
Fax: (949) 863-2252

RAMIREZ, Michael
Contact, Media Relations
michael.ramirez@edelman.com
Tel: (323) 202-1057
Fax: (949) 863-2252

TUCKER, Frank
Chief People Officer
Tel: (949) 863-4000
Fax: (949) 863-2252

Take-Two Interactive Software, Inc.

Take-Two Interactive Software, Inc. is a publisher and developer of interactive entertainment software.
www.take2games.com
Annual Revenues: $1.41 billion
Employees: 2,933
Ticker: NASDAQ: TTWO
SIC: 7372
Industry/ies: Computer/Technology

Chairman of the Board and Chief Executive Officer
ZELNICK, Strauss
Tel: (646) 536-2842
Fax: (646) 536-2926

Main Headquarters
Mailing: 622 Broadway
New York City, NY 10012
Tel: (646) 536-2842
Fax: (646) 536-2926

Public Affairs and Related Activities Personnel

At Headquarters

EMERSON, Daniel P.
Executive Vice President and General Counsel
Tel: (646) 536-2842
Fax: (646) 536-2926

GOLDSTEIN, Lainie
Chief Financial Officer
Tel: (646) 536-2842
Fax: (646) 536-2926

LEWIS, Alan
Vice President, Corporate Communications and Public Affairs
alan.lewis@take2games.com
Tel: (646) 536-2983
Fax: (646) 536-2926

SLATOFF, Karl
President
Tel: (646) 536-2842
Fax: (646) 536-2926

Takeda Pharmaceuticals America

A pharmaceutical company.
www.takeda.us
Annual Revenues: $196.10 million
Industry/ies: Pharmaceutical Industry
Legislative Issues: BUD; HCR; MED; MMM; TAX; TRD

Director and Chairman of the Board
HASEGAWA, Yasuchika
Tel: (224) 554-6500

Representative Director, President and Chief Executive Officer
WEBER, Christophe
Tel: (224) 554-6500

Main Headquarters
Mailing: One Takeda Pkwy.
Deerfield, IL 60015
Tel: (224) 554-6500
TF: (877) 825-3327

Washington Office
Mailing: 750 Ninth St. NW, Suite 575
Washington, DC 20001-4584

Political Action Committees
Takeda Pharmaceuticals of America Inc. PAC (TAKPAC)
FEC ID: C00441733
Contact: Helen Pring
One Takeda Pkwy.
Deerfield, IL 60015
Tel: (224) 554-6500

Contributions to Candidates: $53,250 (2015-2016)
Democrats: $34,750; Republicans: $18,500

Corporate Foundations and Giving Programs

Takeda Pharmaceuticals Contributions Program
One Takeda Pkwy.
Deerfield, IL 60015
Tel: (224) 554-6500

Public Affairs and Related Activities Personnel

At Headquarters

HIRATE, Haruhiko
Corporate Communications and Public Affairs Officer and Global Head, Public Affairs
Tel: (224) 554-6500

JOHNSEN, Elissa J.
Contact, Media Relations
ejohnsen@tpna.com
Tel: (224) 554-3185

LUGOGO, Mwana
Global Compliance Officer
Tel: (224) 554-6500

NAKAGAWA, Yoshihiro
Global General Counsel
Tel: (224) 554-6500

OSBORNE, David
Global Human Resources Officer
Tel: (224) 554-6500

PRING, Helen
PAC Treasurer
Tel: (224) 554-6500

At Washington Office

BARGATZE, Robert
Federal Lobbyist

CLINE, Laura
Senior Director, Federal Governmental Affairs
laura.cline@tpna.com
Registered Federal Lobbyist

STEWART, Shelly
Director, Federal Government Affairs
Registered Federal Lobbyist

WALTER, Deborah
Director, Federal Health Policy
deborah.walter@tpna.com
Registered Federal Lobbyist

WILKINSON, Andrea L.
Director, Federal Governmental Affairs
Registered Federal Lobbyist

Talbert Manufacturing Inc.
Designs and manufactures heavy haul trailers and specialized transportation equipment.
www.talbertmfg.com
Annual Revenues: $30.10 million
Employees: 200
Industry/ies: Machinery/Equipment; Transportation

| **Vice Chairman of the Board** | Tel: | (219) 866-7141 |
| ODLE, Rick | Fax: | (219) 866-5437 |

rodle@talbertmfg.com

| **President** | Tel: | (219) 866-7141 |
| TANNER, Andy | Fax: | (219) 866-7060 |

atanner@talbertmfg.com

Main Headquarters
Mailing:	1628 W. State Rd. 114	Tel:	(219) 866-7141
	Rensselaer, IN 47978	Fax:	(219) 866-7060
		TF:	(888) 489-1731

Public Affairs and Related Activities Personnel

At Headquarters
| GEISLER, Troy | Tel: | (219) 866-7141 |
| *Vice President, Sales and Marketing* | Fax: | (219) 866-7060 |

tgeisler@talbertmfg.com

Talecris Biotherapeutics, Inc.
Talecris Biotherapeutics produces critical care treatments for life-threatening disorders in therapeutic areas such as immunology, neurology, pulmonology.
www.talecris.com
Industry/ies: Medicine/Health Care/Mental Health; Science; Scientific Research
Legislative Issues: HCR

Main Headquarters
| Mailing: | 79 T.W. Alexander Dr. | Tel: | (919) 316-6383 |
| | Research Triangle Park, NC 27709 | |

Public Affairs and Related Activities Personnel

At Headquarters
BROWN, Eric	Tel:	(919) 316-6383
Corporate Paralegal	
BUNYAN, Bruce	Tel:	(919) 316-6383
Vice President, Public Policy & Government Affairs	

Target Corporation
Specializes in large store general merchandise formats, including discount stores.
www.target.com
Annual Revenues: $72.86 billion
Employees: 341,000
Ticker: NYSE: TGT
SIC: 5331
Industry/ies: Retail/Wholesale
Legislative Issues: CHM; CSP; ENV; FIN; HCR; LBR; TAX; TRA; TRD

| **Chairman of the Board and Chief Executive Officer** | Tel: | (612) 354-5914 |
| CORNELL, Brian | Fax: | (612) 696-5400 |

Main Headquarters
Mailing:	1000 Nicollet Mall	Tel:	(612) 354-5914
	Minneapolis, MN 55403	Fax:	(612) 696-5400
		TF:	(800) 440-0680

Washington Office
Mailing:	1155 F St. NW
	Suite 925
	Washington, DC 20004

Political Action Committees
Target Citizens Political Forum PAC
FEC ID: C00098061
Contact: Isaac A. Reyes
1000 Nicollet Mall
TPN 1101

Minneapolis, MN 55403
Contributions to Candidates: $235,500 (2015-2016)
Democrats: $110,000; Republicans: $125,500
Principal Recipients

SENATE
BLUNT, ROY (REP-MO)

HOUSE
KIND, RONALD JAMES (DEM-WI)
MCCARTHY, KEVIN (REP-CA)
PAULSEN, ERIK (REP-MN)

Corporate Foundations and Giving Programs
Target Foundation
Contact: Laysha L. Ward
1000 Nicollet Mall
Minneapolis, MN 55403

Public Affairs and Related Activities Personnel

At Headquarters
BAER, Timothy R.	Tel:	(612) 304-6073
Executive Vice President, Chief Legal Officer and Corporate Secretary	Fax:	(612) 696-5400
tim.baer@target.com	
CARL, Casey	Tel:	(612) 354-5914
Chief Strategy and Innovation Officer	Fax:	(612) 696-5400
HAGENSON, Anika	Tel:	(612) 696-6866
Federal Lobbyist	Fax:	(612) 696-5400
anika.hagenson@target.com	
Registered Federal Lobbyist	
JONES, Jeffrey J.	Tel:	(612) 354-5914
Executive Vice President and Chief Marketing Officer	Fax:	(612) 696-5400
LUNDQUIST, Stephanie	Tel:	(612) 354-5914
Executive Vice President and Chief Human Resources Officer	Fax:	(612) 696-5400
MULLIGAN, John J.	Tel:	(612) 354-5914
Executive Vice President and Chief Operating Officer	Fax:	(612) 696-5400
OBERHELMAN, Amy	Tel:	(612) 304-6073
Federal Lobbyist	Fax:	(612) 696-5400
Registered Federal Lobbyist	
REYES, Isaac A.	Tel:	(612) 354-5914
Senior Director, Government Affairs and PAC Treasurer	Fax:	(612) 696-5400
Registered Federal Lobbyist	
RICE, Jackie Hourigan	Tel:	(612) 354-5914
Chief Risk and Compliance Officer	Fax:	(612) 696-5400
SMITH, Cathy R.	Tel:	(612) 354-5914
Executive Vice President and Chief Financial Officer	Fax:	(612) 696-5400
WARD, Laysha L.	Tel:	(612) 304-6073
Executive Vice President, Chief Corporate Social Responsibility Officer	Fax:	(612) 696-5400
ZABEL, Matt L.	Tel:	(612) 304-6073
Vice President, Government Affairs	Fax:	(612) 696-5400
Mail Stop TPN 1101	

At Washington Office
CONROY, Erin
Senior Manager, Public Relations
LAZDA, Janis
Registered Federal Lobbyist
OLSON, Breanna
Manager, Government Affairs

Targeted Growth, Inc.
A biotech company that focuses on developing products for agriculture and energy industries.
www.targetedgrowth.com
Annual Revenues: $0.61 million
Industry/ies: Computer/Technology

| **Chairman of the Board and Chief Executive Officer** | Tel: | (206) 336-5570 |
| WOODS, Robert | Fax: | (206) 336-5573 |

Main Headquarters
Mailing:	2815 Eastlake Ave., East	Tel:	(206) 336-5570
	Suite 300	Fax:	(206) 336-5573
	Seattle, WA 98102	

Public Affairs and Related Activities Personnel

At Headquarters
MCCORMICK, Margaret	Tel:	(206) 336-5570
Chief Operations Officer	Fax:	(206) 336-5573
WEITZ, Michael	Tel:	(206) 336-5570
Chief Financial Officer	Fax:	(206) 336-5573
WILLIAMS, John	Tel:	(206) 625-0075
Contact, Media Relations	Fax:	(206) 336-5573
jwilliams@scovillepr.com	

TAS

Clean energy manufacturing company.
www.tas.com
Industry/ies: Energy/Electricity

| **Chairman of the Board** | Tel: (713) 877-8700 |
| HURLBERT, Craig M. | Fax: (713) 440-8892 |

| **President and Chief Executive Officer** | Tel: (713) 877-8700 |
| GRUMSKI, J. T. | Fax: (713) 440-8892 |

Main Headquarters
Mailing: 6110 Cullen Blvd   Tel: (713) 877-8700
Houston, TX 77021   Fax: (713) 440-8892

Public Affairs and Related Activities Personnel
At Headquarters

| ROHR, Steve | Tel: (713) 877-8700 |
| *General Counsel* | Fax: (713) 440-8892 |

WALKER, Kelsey	Tel: (202) 450-3616
Director, Government Relations	Fax: (713) 440-8892
kwalker@tas.com	

Tasty Baking Company

Manufacturer of snack cakes and other bakery items.
www.tastykake.com
Annual Revenues: $171.67 million
Employees: 33
Ticker: NASDAQ: TSTY
SIC: 2050; 2052; 3825; 3861; 5084; 5149
Industry/ies: Food And Beverage Industry

| **President and Chief Executive Officer** | Tel: (215) 221-8500 |
| PIZZI, Charles P. | Fax: (215) 223-3288 |

Main Headquarters
Mailing: 4300 S. 26th St.   Tel: (215) 221-8500
Philadelphia, PA 19112-1608   Fax: (215) 223-3288
  TF: (800) 248-2789

Corporate Foundations and Giving Programs

Tasty Baking Contributions Program
Navy Yard Corporate Center, Three Crescent Dr.   Tel: (215) 221-8500
Suite 200   Fax: (215) 223-3288
Philadelphia, PA 19112

Tasty Baking Foundation
Contact: Marie Mann
2801 Hunting Park Ave.   Tel: (215) 221-8500
Philadelphia, PA 19129   Fax: (215) 221-8500

Public Affairs and Related Activities Personnel
At Headquarters

KRIER, Mary A.	Tel: (229) 227-2333
Contact, Media Relations	Fax: (215) 223-3288
RIDDER, Paul D.	Tel: (215) 221-8500
President	
Paul.Ridder@Tastykake.com	

At Other Offices

MANN, Marie	Tel: (215) 221-8500
Foundation Contact	Fax: (215) 228-3970
2801 Hunting Park Ave.	
Philadelphia, PA 19129	
RIDDER, Paul D.	Tel: (215) 221-8500
President	
2801 Hunting Park Ave.	
Philadelphia, PA 19129	
Paul.Ridder@Tastykake.com	

Tate and Lyle North American Sugars, Inc.

Provider of ingredients and solutions to the food, beverage and other industries. An affiliate of UK ingredient giant Tate & Lyle.
www.tateandlyle.com
Annual Revenues: $267.90 million
Employees: 2,100
Industry/ies: Food And Beverage Industry

Main Headquarters
Mailing: 2200 E. Eldorado St.   Tel: (217) 421-3592
Decatur, IL 62525   Fax: (217) 421-2881
  TF: (800) 348-7414

Political Action Committees
Tate and Lyle PAC of Tate and Lyle Ingredients Americas, Inc.
FEC ID: C00056564
Contact: William C. Olsen
2200 E. Eldorado St.
Decatur, IL 62521

Contributions to Candidates: $12,500 (2015-2016)
Democrats: $500; Republicans: $12,000

Public Affairs and Related Activities Personnel
At Headquarters

BLACK, Pashen	Tel: (217) 358-6512
Marketing Communications Manager, Americas	Fax: (217) 421-2881
pashen.black@tateandlyle.com	
OLSEN, William C.	Tel: (217) 421-2804
PAC Treasurer	Fax: (217) 421-2881

Tax Legislative Solutions, LLC

Lobbying firm.
www.taxlegislativesolutions.com
Legislative Issues: ACC; TAX

| MILLER, James | Tel: (202) 489-3711 |
| jmiller@taxlegislativesolutions.com | Fax: (703) 997-3010 |

Main Headquarters
Mailing: 610 Kings Cloister Cir.   Tel: (202) 489-3711
Alexandria, VA 22302   Fax: (703) 997-3010

TC PipeLines, LP

See listing on page 795 under TransCanada Pipelines, Limited

TCF Financial Corporation

A savings and loan holding company.
www.tcfbank.com
Annual Revenues: $1.23 billion
Employees: 5,522
Ticker: NYSE: TCB
SIC: 6021
Industry/ies: Banking/Finance/Investments
Legislative Issues: BAN; FIN

| **Chairman of the Board** | Tel: (612) 661-6500 |
| COOPER, William A. | Fax: (952) 745-2775 |

| **Chief Executive Officer and Vice Chairman** | Tel: (952) 745-2760 |
| DAHL, Craig R. | Fax: (952) 745-2775 |

Main Headquarters
Mailing: 200 Lake St., East   Tel: (952) 745-2760
Wayzata, MN 55391-1693   Fax: (952) 745-2775

Political Action Committees
TCF Financial Corporation PAC
FEC ID: C00218263
801 Marquette Ave
Minneapolis, MN 55402

Contributions to Candidates: $55,500 (2015-2016)
Democrats: $32,500; Republicans: $23,000

Principal Recipients
SENATE
TOOMEY, PATRICK JOSEPH (REP-PA)

Corporate Foundations and Giving Programs

TCF Foundation
200 Lake St., East   Tel: (602) 716-8985
Wayzata, MN 55391

Public Affairs and Related Activities Personnel
At Headquarters

COSTA, James M.	Tel: (952) 745-2760
Chief Risk Officer	Fax: (952) 745-2775
HAWKINS, Donald	Tel: (952) 745-2760
Senior Vice President, Community Affairs	Fax: (952) 745-2775
JONES, Michael S.	Tel: (952) 745-2760
Executive Vice President, Consumer Banking	Fax: (952) 745-2775
KORSTANGE, Jason	Tel: (952) 745-2755
Senior Vice President and Contact, Investor Relations	Fax: (952) 745-2775
MAASS, Brian W.	Tel: (952) 745-2760
Chief Financial Officer	Fax: (952) 745-2775
RONSHAUGEN, Stacey	Tel: (952) 745-2762
Manager, Investor Relations	Fax: (952) 745-2775
Mail Stop EX0-01-C	
investor@tcfbank.com	
STRATTON, Earl D.	Tel: (952) 745-2760
Chief Information Officer	Fax: (952) 745-2775

At Other Offices

HIATT, Douglass B.	Tel: (612) 661-6500
PAC Treasurer	
801 Marquette Ave.	
Minneapolis, MN 55402	
douglas@douglashiatt.net	
JASPER, Thomas F.	Tel: (612) 661-6500
Chief Operating Officer and Vice Chairman	
801 Marquette Ave.	

Minneapolis, MN 55402

TD Ameritrade Holding Corporation

Provides securities brokerage services and technology-based financial services to retail investors, traders, and independent registered investment advisors (RIAs).
www.amtd.com
Annual Revenues: $3.15 billion
Employees: 5,895
Ticker: NYSE: AMTD
SIC: 6211
Industry/ies: Banking/Finance/Investments
Legislative Issues: FIN; RET; TAX

Chairman of the Board	Tel:	(402) 597-5658
MOGLIA, Joseph H.	Fax:	(402) 597-7789

President and Chief Executive Officer	Tel:	(402) 331-7856
TOMCZYK, Frederic J.	Fax:	(402) 597-7789

Main Headquarters		
Mailing: 200 S. 108th Ave.	Tel:	(402) 331-7856
Omaha, NE 68154	Fax:	(402) 597-7789
	TF:	(800) 237-8692

Political Action Committees
TD Ameritrade Holding Corporation PAC
FEC ID: C00396887
Contact: Ellen Koplow
200 S. 108th Ave.
Omaha, NE 68154

    Contributions to Candidates: $11,000 (2015-2016)
    Democrats: $3,000; Republicans: $8,000

Corporate Foundations and Giving Programs
TD Ameritrade Holding Corporation Contributions Program
Contact: Kristin Petrick
4211 S. 102nd St.   Tel: (402) 331-7856
Omaha, NE 68127

Public Affairs and Related Activities Personnel

At Headquarters

ADAMS , Marv	Tel:	(402) 331-7856
Executive Vice President, Chief Operating Officer	Fax:	(402) 597-7789
BOYLE, Steve	Tel:	(402) 331-7856
Executive Vice President of Finance	Fax:	(402) 597-7789
GANZLIN, Karen	Tel:	(402) 331-7856
Executive Vice President and Chief Human Resources Officer	Fax:	(402) 597-7789
GERBER, Bill	Tel:	(402) 331-7856
Executive Vice President, Chief Financial Officer	Fax:	(402) 597-7789
GOESER, Jeff	Tel:	(402) 597-8464
Director, Finance and Investor Relations	Fax:	(402) 597-7789
jeffrey.goeser@tdameritrade.com		
GOETHE, Christina	Tel:	(201) 369-8541
Manager, Communications and Public Affairs	Fax:	(402) 597-7789
christina.goethe@tdameritrade.com		
HILLYER, Kim	Tel:	(402) 574-6523
Director, Communications and Public Affairs	Fax:	(402) 597-8441
kim.hillyer@tdameritrade.com		
JIGANTI, Paul	Tel:	(402) 331-7856
Managing Director, arket Structure and Client Advocacy	Fax:	(402) 597-7789
Registered Federal Lobbyist		
KOPLOW, Ellen	Tel:	(443) 539-2125
Executive Vice President, General Counsel and Secretary and	Fax:	(402) 597-7789
PAC Treasurer		
ellen.koplow@tdameritrade.com		
Registered Federal Lobbyist		
MARKLE, John S.	Tel:	(402) 331-7856
Deputy General Counsel and Federal Lobbyist	Fax:	(402) 597-7789
Registered Federal Lobbyist		
PETRICK, Kristin	Tel:	(402) 574-6569
Director, Institutional Communications	Fax:	(402) 597-7789
kristin.petrick@tdameritrade.com		

TD Bank, NA

TD Bank, N.A., is a bank holding company in the United States that offers banking, insurance, brokerage, and investment banking services.
www.tdbank.com
Industry/ies: Banking/Finance/Investments
Legislative Issues: FIN; HOU; SMB; TAX

President and Chief Executive Officer	Tel:	(856) 751-2739
PEDERSEN, Mike		

Main Headquarters		
Mailing: 1701 Route 70 E.	Tel:	(856) 751-2739
Cherry Hill, NJ 08034		

Washington Office		
Mailing: 1101 Pennsylvania Ave. NW	Tel:	(202) 347-4668

Suite 600
Washington, DC 20004

Public Affairs and Related Activities Personnel

At Headquarters

PATTERSON, Ellen	Tel:	(856) 751-2739
Executive Vice President and Head, Legal, Compliance, AML and General Counsel		
POLLOCK, Edward B	Tel:	(856) 751-2739
Executive Vice President and Head, Regulatory Relationships and Government Affairs		
SANKOVIC, Rudy	Tel:	(416) 308-9030
Senior Vice President, Investor Relations		
SINGH, Manjit	Tel:	(856) 751-2739
Executive Vice President, Finance and Chief Financial Officer		
VIJAY, Vinoo	Tel:	(856) 751-2739
Executive Vice President and Chief Marketing Officer		

At Other Offices

LEFRANCOIS, Ron J.	Tel:	(207) 756-6863
Senior Vice President		
1611 Wisconsin Ave. NW		
Washington, DC 20007		
Registered Federal Lobbyist		

SILVERMAN, Edward
607 14th St. NW, Suite 650
Washington, DC 20005
Registered Federal Lobbyist

TDG-Phenix Inc.

A lobbying firm.
www.tdgphenix.com
Industry/ies: Banking/Finance/Investments

Main Headquarters		
Mailing: P.O. Box 4065	Tel:	(615) 200-4178
Brentwood, TN 37024		

Public Affairs and Related Activities Personnel

At Other Offices

DE PALMA, Laurence
915B Russell St.
Nashville, TN 37206

TDS Telecommunications

Provides innovative voice, internet, and entertainment services to rural and suburban communities nationwide.
www.tdstelecom.com
Annual Revenues: $795.84 million
Employees: 3,300
Ticker: NYSE: TDS
Industry/ies: Communications; Telecommunications/Internet/Cable
Legislative Issues: TEC

President and Chief Executive Officer	Tel:	(608) 664-4000
WITTWER, Dave	Fax:	(608) 664-4035

Main Headquarters		
Mailing: P.O. Box 5158	Tel:	(608) 664-4000
Madison, WI 53705-0158	Fax:	(608) 830-5569
	TF:	(866) 571-6662

Political Action Committees
TDS Telecomminications Corporation PAC
FEC ID: C00299750
Contact: Andrew S. Petersen
P.O. Box 5158
Madison, WI 53705

    Contributions to Candidates: $13,950 (2015-2016)
    Democrats: $5,000; Republicans: $8,950

Corporate Foundations and Giving Programs
TDS Telecommunications Contributions Program
525 Junction Rd.   Tel: (608) 664-4000
Madison, WI 53717   Fax: (608) 664-4000

Public Affairs and Related Activities Personnel

At Headquarters

CEFALU, Kathy	Tel:	(608) 664-4000
Vice President, Human Resources	Fax:	(608) 830-5569
PETERSEN, Andrew S.	Tel:	(608) 664-4155
Vice President, External Affairs & Communications and PAC Treasurer	Fax:	(608) 830-5569
andrew.petersen@tdstelecom.com		
Registered Federal Lobbyist		

At Other Offices

BOEGLI, DeAnne	Tel:	(608) 664-4428

Manager, Public Relations
525 Junction Rd.
Madison, WI 53717
deanne.boegli@tdstelecom.com

Fax: (608) 830-5519

BUTMAN, Jim
Group President, Marketing, Sales and Customer Operations
525 Junction Rd.
Madison, WI 53717

Tel: (608) 664-4000
Fax: (608) 664-4035

HESS, Kevin
Executive Vice President
525 Junction Rd.
Madison, WI 53717
Kevin.Hess@tdstelecom.com

Tel: (608) 664-4000
Fax: (608) 664-4035

PANDOW, Mike
Senior Vice President , Human Resources and Administration
525 Junction Rd.
Madison, WI 53717

Tel: (608) 664-4000
Fax: (608) 664-4035

TOMLINSON, Cindy
Associate Manager, Public Relations
525 Junction Rd.
Madison, WI 53717
cindy.tomlinson@tdstelecom.com

Tel: (608) 664-4471
Fax: (608) 664-4035

VILLACREZ, Vicki L.
Vice President, Finance and Chief Financial Officer
525 Junction Rd.
Madison, WI 53717

Tel: (608) 664-4000
Fax: (608) 664-4035

TE Connectivity, Inc.

Formerly named Tyco Electronics. A manufacturer of electronic and fiber-optic connectors and interconnection systems components. A subsidiary of Tyco International (U.S.) (see separate listing).
www.te.com
Annual Revenues: $13.28 billion
Employees: 84,000
Ticker: NYSE: TEL
SIC: 3661; 5065
Industry/ies: Communications; Electricity & Electronics; Electronics; Energy/Electricity; Telecommunications/Internet/Cable
Legislative Issues: BUD; DEF; MAR; TAX; TEC

Chairman of the Board and Chief Executive Officer
LYNCH, Tom J.

Tel: (610) 893-9800
Fax: (610) 893-9550

Main Headquarters
Mailing: 1050 Westlake Dr.
              Berwyn, PA 19312

Tel: (610) 893-9800
Fax: (610) 893-9550

Washington Office
Mailing: 607 14th St. NW
              Suite 250
              Washington, DC 20005

Fax: (202) 471-3388

Political Action Committees
TE Connectivity, Inc. Political Action Committee TELPAC
FEC ID: C00433482
Contact: Thomas G. Ernst
607 14th St. NW
Suite 550
Washington, DC 20005

Contributions to Candidates: $99,700 (2015-2016)
Democrats: $32,000; Republicans: $66,700; Other: $1,000

Corporate Foundations and Giving Programs
TE Connectivity Corporate Responsibility
1050 Westlakes Dr.
Berwyn, PA 19312

Tel: (610) 893-9800
Fax: (610) 893-9550

Tyco Electronics Foundation
Contact: Mary Rakoczy
P.O. Box 3608
Harrisburg, PA 17105

Tel: (717) 592-4869

Public Affairs and Related Activities Personnel

At Headquarters

AMBROSE, Kathleen
Head, Global Government Affairs & Corporate Responsibility
Registered Federal Lobbyist

Tel: (610) 893-9800
Fax: (610) 893-9550

CURTIN, Terrence
President, Industrial Solutions

Tel: (610) 893-9800
Fax: (610) 893-9550

DONAHUE, Joe
Executive Vice President and Chief Operating Officer

Tel: (610) 893-9800
Fax: (610) 893-9550

FRIES, Wendy
Executive Assistant to Chief Marketing Officer
wendy.fries@te.com

Tel: (610) 893-9800
Fax: (610) 893-9550

GAMBILL, Brad
Senior Vice President, Strategy and Business Development

Tel: (610) 893-9800
Fax: (610) 893-9550

HAU, Robert
Executive Vice President and Chief Financial Officer

Tel: (610) 893-9800
Fax: (610) 893-9550

JENKINS, Jr., John
Executive Vice President and General Counsel

Tel: (610) 893-9800
Fax: (610) 893-9550

KOLSTROM, Keith
Vice President, Investor Relations
keith.kolstrom@te.com

Tel: (610) 893-9551
Fax: (610) 893-9550

LEIPOLD, Jane
Senior Vice President, Global Human Resources

Tel: (610) 893-9800
Fax: (610) 893-9550

ROSELLI, CFA, John M.
Vice President, Finance and Chief Financial Officer, Data Communications
john.roselli@te.com
Registered Federal Lobbyist

Tel: (610) 893-9559
Fax: (610) 893-9550

SHAH, Amy
Senior Vice President and Chief Marketing Officer
amy.shah@te.com

Tel: (610) 893-9555
Fax: (610) 893-9550

WAINWRIGHT, Joan
President, Channel and Customer Experience
joan.wainwright@te.com

Tel: (610) 893-9800
Fax: (610) 893-9550

At Washington Office

BLAIR, Michele
Director, Political Programs and Legislative Affairs
michele.blair@ te.com

Tel: (202) 471-3354
Fax: (202) 471-3388

ERNST, Thomas G.
PAC Treasurer

Tel: (202) 471-3354
Fax: (202) 471-3388

PICCOLO, Joann
Vice President, Global Government Affairs & Corporate Responsibility

Tel: (202) 471-3355
Fax: (202) 471-3388

POLK, Gregory F.
Director, U.S. Government Affairs
greg.polk@te.com
Registered Federal Lobbyist

Tel: (202) 471-3377
Fax: (202) 471-3388

ROSELLINI, Courtney
Registered Federal Lobbyist

Tel: (202) 471-3354
Fax: (202) 471-3388

At Other Offices

RAKOCZY, Mary
Contact, Foundation
P.O. Box 3608, MS 140-10
Harrisburg, PA 17105
mjrakoczy@te.com

Tel: (717) 592-4869

Teaching Strategies Inc.

An early childhood education publishing company that provides the most innovative and effective curriculum, assessment, professional development, and family connection resources to programs serving children from birth through kindergarten.
www.teachingstrategies.com
Annual Revenues: $17.50 million
Employees: 115
Industry/ies: Education

Founder and President
DODGE, Diane Trister

Tel: (301) 634-0818
Fax: (301) 634-0826

Chief Executive Officer
DAVIES, Ron

Tel: (301) 634-0818
Fax: (301) 634-0826

Main Headquarters
Mailing: 7101 Wisconsin Ave.
              Suite 700
              Bethesda, MD 20814

Tel: (301) 634-0818
Fax: (301) 634-0826
TF: (800) 637-3652

Corporate Foundations and Giving Programs
Teaching Strategies Contributions Program
7101 Wisconsin Ave.
Suite 700
Bethesda, MD 20814

Tel: (301) 634-0818
Fax: (301) 657-0250

Public Affairs and Related Activities Personnel

At Headquarters

BELLES, Mark
President and Chief Operating Officer

Tel: (301) 634-0818
Fax: (301) 634-0826

BLAKE, Ted
Chief Financial Officer

Tel: (301) 634-0818
Fax: (301) 634-0826

HEPPLER, Karen
Senior Vice President, Operations

Tel: (301) 634-0818
Fax: (301) 634-0826

STUART, Jonah
Director, Public Policy and Government Relations
jonahs@teachingstrategies.com

Tel: (301) 634-0818
Fax: (301) 634-0826

Team Eagle

Supplier of snow and ice removal equipment, ARFF vehicles, GPS/GIS situational awareness, Safety Management Systems, and Digital Inspection and Monitoring Systems for airfield management professionals.
www.team-eagle.ca

Main Headquarters

Mailing:	141 Sanborn Rd.	Tel: (603) 729-0046
	Suite 3275	Fax: (603) 729-0276
	Tilton, NH 03276	TF: (855) 835-7171

Public Affairs and Related Activities Personnel

At Headquarters

ETTINGER, Brian — Tel: (603) 729-0046
Federal Lobbyist — Fax: (603) 729-0276
ettingelaw@yahoo.com

Tech Data Corporation

A wholesale distributor of computer-related equipment.
www.techdata.com
Annual Revenues: $26.46 billion
Employees: 9,000
Ticker: NASDAQ: TECD
SIC: 5045
Industry/ies: Computer/Technology

Chairman of the Board — Tel: (727) 539-7429
RAYMUND, Steven A. — Fax: (727) 538-7803
steve.raymund@techdata.com

Chief Executive Officer — Tel: (727) 539-7429
DUTKOWSKY, Robert M. — Fax: (727) 538-7803

Main Headquarters
Mailing: 5350 Tech Data Dr. — Tel: (727) 539-7429
Clearwater, FL 33760 — Fax: (727) 538-7803
— TF: (800) 237-8931

Public Affairs and Related Activities Personnel

At Headquarters

DANNEWITZ, Charles V. — Tel: (727) 539-7429
Executive Vice President and Chief Financial Officer — Fax: (727) 538-7803

HUME, Rich — Tel: (727) 539-7429
Executive Vice President and Chief Operating Officer — Fax: (727) 538-7803

KOSOY, Brian — Tel: (727) 299-8865
Director, Corporate Communications — Fax: (727) 538-7803
brian.kosoy@techdata.com

TONNISON, John — Tel: (727) 539-7429
Executive Vice President and Chief Information Officer — Fax: (727) 538-7803

TREPANI, Joseph B. — Tel: (727) 539-7429
Senior Vice President and Chief Financial Officer — Fax: (727) 538-7803

VETTER, David R. — Tel: (727) 539-7429
Senior Vice President, General Counsel and Secretary — Fax: (727) 538-7803

TechniGraphics, Inc.

Homeland security and GIS.
www.technigraphicsinc.com
Industry/ies: Defense/Homeland Security; Government-Related

Main Headquarters
Mailing: 5750 I-10 Industrial Pkwy. — Tel: (251) 653-7110
Theodore, AL 36582 — Fax: (251) 653-8839

Public Affairs and Related Activities Personnel

At Headquarters

JACQUES, Steven D. — Tel: (251) 653-7110
Federal Lobbyist — Fax: (251) 653-8839

VAN STELTON, Jenna — Tel: (251) 653-7110
Federal Lobbyist — Fax: (251) 653-8839

Technocom Corporation

A wireless location operations and business support systems company.
www.technocom-wireless.com
Employees: 40
Industry/ies: Communications; Telecommunications/Internet/Cable

Founder and Chief Executive Officer — Tel: (760) 438-5115
PROIETTI, Mario — Fax: (760) 438-5815
mproietti@technocom-wireless.com

Main Headquarters
Mailing: 2030 Corte del Nogal — Tel: (760) 438-5115
Suite 200 — Fax: (760) 438-5815
Carlsbad, CA 92011

Public Affairs and Related Activities Personnel

At Headquarters

MOTAMEDI, Masoud — Tel: (760) 438-5115
Founder, President and Chief Operating Officer — Fax: (760) 438-5815

SCHAFER, Brenda — Tel: (760) 438-5115
Contact, Media Relations — Fax: (760) 438-5815
info@technocom-wireless.com

Teck Resources, Ltd.

A mining company. Formerly Teck Cominco American Inc. Teck is Canada's largest diversified resource company, committed to responsible mining and mineral development. We produce materials essential to the quality of life of people around the world – copper, steelmaking coal, zinc and energy
www.teck.com
Annual Revenues: $7.06 billion
Employees: 10,200
Ticker: NYSE:TCK
SIC: 1400
Industry/ies: Mining Industry; Natural Resources

Chairman of the Board — Tel: (509) 747-6111
KEEVIL, Norman B. — Fax: (509) 459-4400

President and Chief Executive Officer — Tel: (509) 747-6111
LINDSAY, Donald R. — Fax: (509) 459-4400

Main Headquarters
Mailing: 501 N. Riverpoint Blvd. — Tel: (509) 747-6111
Suite 300 — Fax: (509) 922-8767
Spokane, WA 99202-1659

Corporate Foundations and Giving Programs

Teck Cominco Community Partnership Initiative
501 N. Riverpoint Blvd.
Suite 300
Spokane, WA 99202

Public Affairs and Related Activities Personnel

At Headquarters

GODLEWSKI, David — Tel: (509) 747-6111
Federal Lobbyist — Fax: (509) 922-8767
dave.godlewski@teck.com

KILGOUR, Ian C. — Tel: (509) 747-6111
Executive Vice President and Chief Operating Officer — Fax: (509) 922-8767

MILLOS, Ronald A. — Tel: (509) 747-6111
Senior Vice President, Finance and Chief Financial Officer — Fax: (509) 459-4400

PESEK, Phillip A. — Tel: (509) 747-6111
Vice President, General Counsel & Secretary — Fax: (509) 922-8767
phil.pesek@teck

ROZEE, Peter C. — Tel: (509) 747-6111
Senior Vice President, Commercial and Legal Affairs — Fax: (509) 922-8767
peter.rozee@teck.com

STONKUS, Andrew A. — Tel: (509) 747-6111
Senior Vice President, Marketing and Sales — Fax: (509) 922-8767

VANCE, Ronald J. — Tel: (509) 747-6111
Senior Vice President, Corporate Development — Fax: (509) 459-4400

WALLER, Gregory A. — Tel: (509) 747-6111
Vice President, Investor Relations and Strategic Analysis — Fax: (509) 459-4400
greg.waller@teck.com

At Other Offices

DUFFY, Alana — Tel: (604) 699-4547
Senior Communications Specialist — Fax: (604) 699-4750
550 Burrard St., Suite 3300, Betall 5
Vancouver, BC V6C 0B3
alana.duffy@teck.com

HORSWILL, Douglas H. — Tel: (604) 699-4000
Senior Vice President — Fax: (604) 699-4750
550 Burrard St., Suite 3300, Betall 5
Vancouver, BC V6C 0B3
Doug.Horswill@teck.com

SMITH, Marcia M. — Tel: (604) 699-4000
Senior Vice President, Sustainability and External Affairs — Fax: (604) 699-4750
550 Burrard St., Suite 3300, Betall 5
Vancouver, BC V6C 0B3
marcia.smith@teck.com

WINSOR, Dean — Tel: (604) 699-4000
Vice President, Human Resources — Fax: (604) 699-4750
550 Burrard St., Suite 3300, Betall 5
Vancouver, BC V6C 0B3

TECO Energy, Inc.

An energy-related holding company with five core businesses, including two regulated utilities.
www.tecoenergy.com
Annual Revenues: $2.57 billion
Employees: 4,400
Ticker: NYSE: TE
SIC: 4911
Industry/ies: Utilities
Legislative Issues: BUD; CAW; COM; ENG; ENV; HOM; TAX; TRA

Chairman of the Board — Tel: (813) 228-4111
HUDSON, Sherrill W. — Fax: (813) 228-4811

President and Chief Executive Officer — Tel: (813) 228-1111
RAMIL, John B. — Fax: (813) 228-4811

Main Headquarters

Mailing:	TECO Plaza	Tel: (813) 228-1111
	702 N. Franklin St.	Fax: (813) 228-4811
	Tampa, FL 33602	

Washington Office

Mailing:	1331 Pennsylvania Ave. NW	Tel: (202) 824-0411
	Suite 510 North	Fax: (202) 824-0419
	Washington, DC 20004	

Political Action Committees

TECO Energy Inc Employees PAC (TEPAC)
FEC ID: C00161422
TECO Plaza
702 N. Franklin St.   Tel: (202) 824-0411
Tampa, FL 33602   Fax: (202) 824-0419

  Contributions to Candidates: $35,500 (2015-2016)
  Democrats: $5,500; Republicans: $30,000

Public Affairs and Related Activities Personnel

At Headquarters

ATTAL, III, Charles A.	Tel: (813) 228-4111
Senior Vice President & General Counsel	Fax: (813) 228-4811
BARRINGER, Phil	Tel: (813) 228-1111
Senior Vice President, Corporate Services and Chief Human Resources Officer	Fax: (813) 228-4811
CALLAHAN , Sandra W.	Tel: (813) 228-1111
Senior Vice President, Finance and Accounting and Chief Financial Officer	Fax: (813) 228-4811
HINSON, III, Charles O.	Tel: (813) 228-4111
Vice President, State and Community Relations	Fax: (813) 228-4811
JACOBS, Cherie	Tel: (813) 228-1111
Manager, Media and Public Relations	Fax: (813) 228-4811
cljacobs@tecoenergy.com	
KILPATRICK, Jr., Burnis	Tel: (813) 228-4418
Corporate Compliance Officer	Fax: (813) 228-4811
bxkilpatrick@tecoenergy.com	
MOSCOVIC, Sandy	Tel: (813) 228-1111
Director of Corporate Ethics and Compliance	Fax: (813) 228-4811
samoscovic@tecoenergy.com	
REMMERS, Chrys A.	Tel: (813) 228-1111
PAC Treasurer	Fax: (813) 228-4811

At Washington Office

BANAGA, Shannon	Tel: (202) 824-0411
Director, Federal Affairs	Fax: (202) 824-0419
Registered Federal Lobbyist	

Tejon Ranch Company

Tejon Ranch is the largest continuous expanse of private land in California. Focuses on residential and commercial real estate development on its land.
www.tejonranch.com
Annual Revenues: $53.35 million
Employees: 157
Ticker: NYSE: TRC
SIC: 6500
Industry/ies: Real Estate
Legislative Issues: RES; TRA

President and Chief Executive Officer	Tel: (661) 248-3000
BIELLI, Gregory S	Fax: (661) 248-3100

Main Headquarters

Mailing:	4436 Lebec Rd.	Tel: (661) 248-3000
	P.O. Box 1000	Fax: (661) 248-3100
	Lebec, CA 93243	

Public Affairs and Related Activities Personnel

At Headquarters

LYDA, Allen	Tel: (661) 248-3000
Executive Vice President, Chief Financial Officer and Corporate Treasurer	Fax: (661) 248-2318
NIXON, Gina	Tel: (661) 248-3000
Vice President, Marketing	Fax: (661) 248-3100
REYNOLDS, Eileen	Tel: (661) 248-3000
Vice President, Government Affairs	Fax: (661) 248-2318
ereynolds@tejonranch.com	
TOBIAS, Greg	Tel: (661) 248-3000
Vice President, General Counsel	Fax: (661) 248-2318
ZOELLER, Barry	Tel: (661) 663-4212
Vice President, Corporate Communications and Marketing	Fax: (661) 248-2318
bzoeller@tejonranch.com	

Tektronix, Inc.

A manufacturer of electronic test and measurement, computer graphics and professional broadcast equipment.
www.tek.com

Employees: 5,000
SIC: 3825; 3575
NAICS: 334113
Industry/ies: Machinery/Equipment

Main Headquarters

Mailing:	14150 S.W. Karl Braun Dr.	Tel: (503) 627-7111
	P.O. Box 500	Fax: (503) 627-6108
	Beaverton, OR 97077-0001	TF: (800) 833-9200

Corporate Foundations and Giving Programs

Tektronix Foundation
14150 S.W. Karl Braun Dr.
P.O. Box 500
Beaverton, OR 97077

Public Affairs and Related Activities Personnel

At Headquarters

AGHDAEI, Amir	Tel: (503) 627-7111
Vice President	Fax: (503) 627-6108
GOFF, Alisha	Tel: (469) 330-4405
Director, Business Communications	Fax: (503) 567-3449
alisha.goff@tektronix.com	
MALAGAMBA, Amy	Tel: (503) 627-7111
Contact, Business and Local Media	Fax: (503) 627-6108

TELACU Industries, Inc.

The group provides affordable housing, constructs private and public facilities, fulfills financial needs of the people through its financial institution, conducts energy related programs.
telacu.com
Annual Revenues: $31.20 million
Employees: 400
Industry/ies: Economics And Economic Development
Legislative Issues: BAN

Founder & Chairman – TELACU Education Foundation	Tel: (323) 721-1655
LIZÁRRAGA, David C.	Fax: (323) 724-3372

President and Chief Executive Officer	Tel: (323) 721-1655
LIZARRAGA, Michael D.	Fax: (323) 724-3372

Main Headquarters

Mailing:	5400 E. Olympic Blvd.	Tel: (323) 721-1655
	Third Floor	Fax: (323) 724-3372
	Los Angeles, CA 90022	

Corporate Foundations and Giving Programs

LINC TELACU Education Foundation (LTEF)
Contact: Velma de la Rosa
5400 E. Olympic Blvd., Third Floor
Suite 300
Los Angeles, CA 90022

Public Affairs and Related Activities Personnel

At Headquarters

DE LA ROSA, Velma	Tel: (323) 721-1655
Senior Vice President, Education Foundation	Fax: (323) 724-3372
GONZALEZ, Ana	Tel: (323) 721-1655
Senior Vice President, Human Resources	Fax: (323) 724-3372
LIZÁRRAGA, Priscilla	Tel: (323) 721-1655
Senior Vice President, TELACU Communications Group	Fax: (323) 724-3372
SAMUEL, Paul	Tel: (323) 721-1655
Senior Vice President and Chief Financial Officer	Fax: (323) 724-3372
VILLALOBOS, José	Tel: (323) 721-1655
Senior Vice President	Fax: (323) 724-3372
jvillalobos@telacu.com	

TelAlaska, Inc.

A statewide, full service telecommunications provider.
www.telalaska.com
Annual Revenues: $27.40 million
Employees: 100
Industry/ies: Communications; Telecommunications/Internet/Cable

Chief Executive Officer and Chief Financial Officer	Tel: (907) 563-2003
SHEPARD, Brenda	Fax: (907) 565-5539

President and General Manager	Tel: (907) 563-2003
GOGGINS, David J.	Fax: (907) 565-5539

Main Headquarters

Mailing:	201 E. 56th Ave.	Tel: (907) 563-2003
	Anchorage, AK 99518	Fax: (907) 565-5539
		TF: (800) 478-3127

Corporate Foundations and Giving Programs

TelAlaska Contributions Program
210 E. 56th Ave.
Anchorage, AK 99518

Public Affairs and Related Activities Personnel

At Headquarters

BRENNAN, Marnie	Tel:	(907) 563-2003
Vice President, Marketing	Fax:	(907) 565-5539
CARTER, Brett	Tel:	(907) 563-2003
Vice President, Finance	Fax:	(907) 565-5539
LOUVIE, Jason	Tel:	(907) 563-2003
Vice President, Operations	Fax:	(907) 565-5539

Telapex Inc.

A telecommunications holding company. Telapex, Inc.'s subsidiaries include Cellular South, Inc., Franklin Telephone Company, Inc., Delta Telephone Company, Inc., Telepak Networks, Inc. and Branch Cable, Inc. The company provides, through its' subsidiaries, wireless, local telephone exchange, broadband, Internet, video and long distance services.
www.telapex.com
Annual Revenues: $20.20 million
Employees: 500
Industry/ies: Communications; Telecommunications/Internet/Cable

Chief Executive Officer	Tel:	(601) 355-1522
HUGHES, Carson	Fax:	(601) 353-0950

Main Headquarters

Mailing:	1018 Highland Colony Pkwy.	Tel:	(601) 355-1522
	Suite 700	Fax:	(601) 353-0950
	Ridgeland, MS 39157		

Political Action Committees

Telapex Inc. PAC
FEC ID: C00408500
Contact: Benjamin C. Pace
1018 Highland Colony Pkwy.
Suite 330
Ridgeland, MS 39157

> **Contributions to Candidates:** $18,100 (2015-2016)
> Republicans: $18,100

Corporate Foundations and Giving Programs

Telapex, Inc. Contributions Program
1018 Highland Colony Pkwy.		
Suite 700	Tel:	(601) 355-1522
Ridgeland, MS 39157		

Public Affairs and Related Activities Personnel

At Headquarters

PACE, Benjamin C.	Tel:	(601) 355-1522
PAC Treasurer	Fax:	(601) 353-0950
STEGALL, Sherry	Tel:	(601) 355-1522
PAC Treasurer	Fax:	(601) 353-0950
Mail Stop Suite 330		

Telcordia Technologies, Inc.

A provider of operations support systems, network software and consulting and engineering services to the telecommunications industry. Formerly known as Bellcore. A subsidiary of Science Applications International Corp. (see separate listing).
www.telcordia.com
Annual Revenues: $238.50 million
Employees: 3,200
Industry/ies: Communications; Telecommunications/Internet/Cable

President and Chief Executive Officer	Tel:	(732) 699-2000
GREENQUIST, Mark	Fax:	(732) 336-2559

Main Headquarters

Mailing:	One Telcordia Dr.	Tel:	(732) 699-2000
	Piscataway, NJ 08854	Fax:	(732) 336-2559
		TF:	(800) 521-2673

Public Affairs and Related Activities Personnel

At Headquarters

COOLEY, Matthew	Tel:	(732) 699-2000
Head, Finance and Business Control	Fax:	(732) 336-2559
DELUKEY, Linda	Tel:	(732) 699-2000
Executive Vice President, Human Resources and Corporate Security	Fax:	(732) 336-2559
GIORDANO, Joseph	Tel:	(732) 699-2000
General Counsel and Secretary	Fax:	(732) 336-2559
MARANO, Rich	Tel:	(732) 699-2000
Executive Vice President, Operations	Fax:	(732) 336-2559
NOONAN, Steve	Tel:	(732) 699-2000
Executive Vice President, Transition Activities and Strategic Special Projects	Fax:	(732) 336-2559
ODDY, Sharon	Tel:	(732) 699-4203
Senior Specialist, Communications	Fax:	(732) 336-2559
oddys@telcordia.com		
WALD, Krista	Tel:	(732) 699-5050
Media Contact	Fax:	(732) 336-2559
kwald@telcordia.com		

Teledyne Technologies Inc.

Operates with four major segments: Digital Imaging, Instrumentation, Engineered Systems, and Aerospace and Defense Electronics.
www.teledyne.com
Annual Revenues: $2.39 billion
Employees: 9,800
Ticker: NYSE: TDY
SIC: 3821
Industry/ies: Computer/Technology

Chairman, President and Chief Executive Officer	Tel:	(805) 373-4545
MEHRABIAN, Robert	Fax:	(805) 373-4775

Main Headquarters

Mailing:	1049 Camino Dos Rios	Tel:	(805) 373-4545
	Thousand Oaks, CA 91360	Fax:	(805) 373-4775

Political Action Committees

Teledyne Technologies, Inc. PAC
FEC ID: C00357285
Contact: Brian Levan
1049 Camino Dos Rios	Tel:	(805) 373-4545
Thousand Oaks, CA 91360	Fax:	(805) 373-4545

Public Affairs and Related Activities Personnel

At Headquarters

BAILEY, Mary	Tel:	(703) 276-4611
Federal Lobbyist	Fax:	(805) 373-4775
BOBB , George C.	Tel:	(805) 373-4545
Chief Compliance Officer, Vice President, Information Technology and Deputy General Counsel, Litigation	Fax:	(805) 373-4775
CIBIK, Melanie S.	Tel:	(805) 373-4545
Senior Vice President, General Counsel and Secretary	Fax:	(805) 373-4775
LEVAN, Brian	Tel:	(805) 373-4545
PAC Treasurer	Fax:	(805) 373-4775
blevan@teledyne.com		
MAIN, Susan (Sue) L.	Tel:	(805) 373-4545
Senior Vice President and Chief Financial Officer	Fax:	(805) 373-4775
MCGOWAN, Robyn E.	Tel:	(805) 373-4540
Vice President, Administration, Human Resources, Assistant Secretary	Fax:	(805) 373-4775
VANWEES, Jason	Tel:	(805) 373-4542
Vice President, Strategy, Mergers and Acquisitions	Fax:	(805) 373-4775

Teleflex Inc.

A global supplier of disposable and single use medical products for critical care and surgical applications.
www.teleflex.com
Annual Revenues: $1.82 billion
Employees: 11,700
Ticker: NYSE: TFX
SIC: 3841
Industry/ies: Machinery/Equipment; Medicine/Health Care/Mental Health

Chairman, President and Chief Executive Officer	Tel:	(610) 948-5100
SMITH, Benson F.	Fax:	(610) 948-5101

Main Headquarters

Mailing:	155 S. Limerick Rd.	Tel:	(610) 948-5100
	Limerick, PA 19468-1699	Fax:	(610) 948-5101
		TF:	(888) 883-1499

Corporate Foundations and Giving Programs

Teleflex Foundation
Contact: Jill Kitchin
155 S. Limerick Ave.		
Limerick, PA 19468	Tel:	(610) 948-2853

Public Affairs and Related Activities Personnel

At Headquarters

BOYLAN, Karen	Tel:	(610) 948-5100
Contact, Global Regulatory Affairs and Quality Assurance	Fax:	(610) 948-5101
ELGUICZE, Jake	Tel:	(610) 948-2836
Treasurer and Vice President, Investor Relations	Fax:	(610) 948-5101
GLENN , Kenney	Tel:	(610) 948-5100
Senior Vice President, Global Marketing	Fax:	(610) 948-5101
HICKS, Cameron	Tel:	(610) 948-5100
Vice President, Global Human Resources	Fax:	(610) 948-5101
KITCHIN, Jill	Tel:	(610) 948-2853
Contact, Teleflex Foundation	Fax:	(610) 948-2858
jmcdowell@teleflex.com		
LEYDEN, James J.	Tel:	(610) 948-5100
Vice President, General Counsel and Secretary	Fax:	(610) 948-5101
MCDOWELL, Julie	Tel:	(610) 948-2836
Vice President, Global Communications	Fax:	(610) 948-5101
POWELL, Thomas E.	Tel:	(610) 948-5100

Executive Vice President and Chief Financial Officer	Fax:	(610) 948-5101
WATANABE, Gwen	Tel:	(610) 948-5100
Vice President, Business Development and Technical Resources	Fax:	(610) 948-5101

Telephone & Data Systems, Inc. (TDS)

TDS is a telecommunications company providing wireless products and services; cable and wireline broadband, TV and voice services; and hosted and managed services.
www.teldta.com
Annual Revenues: $5.17 billion
Employees: 10,400
Ticker: NYSE: TDS
SIC: 4813
Industry/ies: Communications; Telecommunications/Internet/Cable

Non Executive Chairman of the Board	Tel:	(312) 630-1900
CARLSON, Walter C.D.	Fax:	(312) 630-1908
President and Chief Executive Officer	Tel:	(312) 630-1900
CARLSON, Jr., LeRoy T.	Fax:	(312) 630-1908

Main Headquarters
Mailing:	30 N. LaSalle St.	Tel:	(312) 630-1900
	Suite 4000	Fax:	(312) 630-1908
	Chicago, IL 60602		

Public Affairs and Related Activities Personnel

At Headquarters

HANLEY, Joseph R.	Tel:	(312) 630-1900
Senior Vice President, Technology, Services and Strategy	Fax:	(312) 630-1908
HERBERT, C. Theodore	Tel:	(312) 630-1900
Vice President, Human Resources	Fax:	(312) 630-1908
ted.herbert@teldta.com		
KOTYLO, Kenneth M.	Tel:	(312) 630-1900
Vice President, Acquisitions and Corporate Development	Fax:	(312) 630-1908
MATHEWS, Julie D.	Tel:	(312) 592-5341
Manager, Investor Relations	Fax:	(312) 630-1908
julie.mathews@teldta.com		
MCCAHON, Jane W.	Tel:	(312) 592-5379
Senior Vice President, Corporate Relations and Corporate Secretary	Fax:	(312) 630-1908
jane.mccahon@teldta.com		
MEYERS, Kenneth R.	Tel:	(312) 630-1900
President and Chief Executive Officer, U.S. Cellular	Fax:	(312) 630-1908
MURPHY, Heather A.	Tel:	(312) 592-5327
Manager, Corporate Communications	Fax:	(312) 630-1908
heather.murphy@teldta.com		
SEREDA, Peter L.	Tel:	(312) 630-1900
Senior Vice President, Finance and Treasurer	Fax:	(312) 630-1908
SHUMA, Douglas D.	Tel:	(312) 630-1900
Senior Vice President, Finance and Chief Accounting Officer	Fax:	(312) 630-1908
WILLIAMSON, Scott H.	Tel:	(312) 630-1900
Senior Vice President, Acquisitions and Corporate Development	Fax:	(312) 630-1908

Teletech Teleservices, Inc.

Provides a full range of front-to and back-office outsourced solutions.
www.teletech.com
Annual Revenues: $1.27 billion
Employees: 43,000
Ticker: NASDAQ: TTEC
SIC: 7363
Industry/ies: Communications; Telecommunications/Internet/Cable

Chairman of the Board and Chief Executive Officer	Tel:	(303) 397-8100
TUCHMAN, Kenneth	Fax:	(303) 397-8199

Main Headquarters
Mailing:	9197 S. Peoria St.	Tel:	(303) 397-8100
	Englewood, CO 80112-5833	Fax:	(303) 397-8199
		TF:	(800) 835-3832

Corporate Foundations and Giving Programs

TeleTech Community Foundation (TTCF)
9197 S. Peoria St.
Englewood, CO 80112-5833

Tel:	(303) 397-8100
Fax:	(303) 397-8199

Public Affairs and Related Activities Personnel

At Headquarters

GRICE, Elizabeth	Tel:	(303) 397-8100
Director, Corporate Communications	Fax:	(303) 397-8199
HAND, Judi	Tel:	(303) 397-8100
Executive Vice President, Customer Growth Services	Fax:	(303) 397-8199
MCLEAN, Margaret	Tel:	(303) 397-8100
Senior Vice President, General Counsel and Chief Risk Officer	Fax:	(303) 397-8199
MILLER, Paul	Tel:	(303) 397-8641
Senior Vice President, Treasurer and Head, Investor Relations	Fax:	(303) 397-8199

PAOLILLO, Regina	Tel:	(303) 397-8100
Executive Vice President, Chief Administrative and Financial Officer	Fax:	(303) 397-8199
WELLMAN, Michael	Tel:	(303) 397-8100
Chief People Officer, Human Resources	Fax:	(303) 397-8199

Tellabs, Inc.

A communications service provider.
www.tellabs.com
Employees: 2,525
Ticker: NASDAQ: TLAB
SIC: 5065; 2517; 5712; 3357; 3661; 3663; 3674; 4812
NAICS: 33421; 334413; 335929; 513332; 337129; 337122
Industry/ies: Communications; Telecommunications/Internet/Cable

Chairman of the Board	Tel:	(800) 690-2324
TOBKIN, Vincent H.	Fax:	(866) 665-8280
President and Chief Executive Officer	Tel:	(800) 690-2324
DAGENAIS, Mike	Fax:	(866) 665-8280

Main Headquarters
Mailing:	1415 W. Diehl Rd.	Tel:	(800) 690-2324
	Naperville, IL 60563	Fax:	(866) 665-8280
		TF:	(800) 443-5555

Washington Office
Mailing:	9711 Washingtonian Blvd.	Tel:	(301) 978-3007
	Suite 550	Fax:	(866) 665-8280
	Gaithersburg, MD 20878		

Corporate Foundations and Giving Programs

Tellabs Foundation
Contact: Meredith Hilt
1415 W. Diehl Rd.
Naperville, IL 60563

Public Affairs and Related Activities Personnel

At Headquarters

HILT, Meredith	Tel:	(800) 690-2324
Executive Director, Tellabs Foundation	Fax:	(866) 665-8280
meredith.hilt@tellabs.com		
RUVARAC, Thomas	Tel:	(800) 690-2324
Vice President, Global Sales	Fax:	(866) 665-8280

Telos Corporation

Telos company provides networking and security products and services. Its Managed Solutions unit offers networking hardware, software, advanced messaging, and support services. The company also provides identity management software and services through its Telos ID subsidiary
www.telos.com
Annual Revenues: $226.10 million
Employees: 560
Ticker: OTCMKTS:TLSRP
SIC: 7373
Industry/ies: Computer/Technology

Chairman of the Board and Chief Executive Officer	Tel:	(703) 724-3800
WOOD, John B.	Fax:	(703) 724-3868
john.wood@telos.com		

Main Headquarters
Mailing:	19886 Ashburn Rd.	Tel:	(703) 724-3800
	Ashburn, VA 20147	Fax:	(703) 724-3868
		TF:	(800) 444-9628

Political Action Committees

Telos Corporation PAC
FEC ID: C00289041
Contact: Jennifer L. Schneider
19886 Ashburn Rd.
Ashburn, VA 20147

Tel:	(703) 724-3800
Fax:	(703) 724-3868

Contributions to Candidates: $3,600 (2015-2016)
Republicans: $3,600

Public Affairs and Related Activities Personnel

At Headquarters

BUONA, Ralph M.	Tel:	(703) 724-3800
Vice President, Corporate Business Development	Fax:	(703) 724-3868
FLAHERTY, Michael P.	Tel:	(703) 724-3800
Executive Vice President, General Counsel and Chief Administrative Officer	Fax:	(703) 724-3868
NAKAZAWA, Michele	Tel:	(703) 724-3800
Executive Vice President, Chief Financial Officer	Fax:	(703) 724-3868
NEELY, Renate	Tel:	(703) 724-3780
Director, Marketing	Fax:	(703) 724-3868
Renate.Neely@Telos.com		
SCHNEIDER, Jennifer L.	Tel:	(703) 724-3800
PAC Treasurer	Fax:	(703) 724-3868

jen.Schneider@telos.com

WILLIAMS, Edward L.	Tel:	(703) 724-3800
Executive Vice President and Chief Operating Officer	Fax:	(703) 724-3868
WOOD, Emmett	Tel:	(703) 724-3800
Executive Vice President, Marketing and Strategy	Fax:	(703) 724-3868
WRIGHT, Jefferson V.	Tel:	(703) 724-3800
Executive Vice President, General Counsel	Fax:	(703) 724-3868

Temple-Inland, Inc.

A manufacturer of corrugated packaging and building products, with a diversified financial services operation. On February 13, 2012, International Paper has purchased Temple-Inland.
www.templeinland.com
Annual Revenues: $3.79 billion
Employees: 10,500
Ticker: NYSE: TIN
SIC: 2631
Industry/ies: Banking/Finance/Investments; Paper And Wood Products Industry; Real Estate

Chairman of the Board and Chief Executive Officer	Tel:	(512) 434-5800
SIMONS, Doyle R.	Fax:	(512) 434-3750

Main Headquarters		
Mailing: C/O International Paper	Tel:	(901) 419-9000
6400 Poplar Ave.		
Memphis, TN 38197		

Political Action Committees
Committee for Responsible Government of Temple-Inland Inc
FEC ID: C00080721
Contact: Robert G. Samford
401 W. 15th St.
Suite 840
Austin, TX 78701

Corporate Foundations and Giving Programs

Temple-Inland Foundation
Contact: Evonne Nerren
P.O. Box 40
Austin, TX 78767

Public Affairs and Related Activities Personnel

At Headquarters

DAVIS, C. Morris	Tel:	(901) 419-9000
General Counsel		
EALY, C. Cato	Tel:	(901) 419-9000
Senior Vice President, Corporate Development		
KARRE, Paul J.	Tel:	(901) 419-9000
Senior Vice President, Human Resources and Communications		
MATHIS, Chris	Tel:	(901) 419-9000
Contact, Media Relations and Vice President, Investor Relations and Treasury		

At Other Offices

NERREN, Evonne	Tel:	(512) 434-5800
Secretary and Treasurer, Temple-Inland Foundation	Fax:	(512) 434-3750
1300 S. Mopac Expwy., Third Floor		
Austin, TX 78746		
SAMFORD, Robert G.		
PAC Treasurer		
401 W. 15th St., Suite 840		
Austin, TX 78701		

Tenaska, Inc.

An independent power producing company.
www.tenaska.com
Annual Revenues: $10.76 billion
Employees: 700
SIC: 4911
Industry/ies: Electricity & Electronics; Electronics; Energy/Electricity
Legislative Issues: ENG; HOM; TAX

Chairman of the Board	Tel:	(402) 691-9500
HAWKS, Howard L.	Fax:	(402) 691-9526

Vice Chairman and Chief Executive Officer	Tel:	(402) 691-9500
CROUSE, Jerry K.	Fax:	(402) 691-9526

Main Headquarters		
Mailing: 14302 FNB Pkwy.	Tel:	(402) 691-9500
Omaha, NE 68154-5212	Fax:	(402) 691-9526

Political Action Committees
Tenaska Inc. Employees PAC
FEC ID: C00479998
Contact: Ronald N. Quinn

1044 N. 115th St.	Tel:	(402) 691-9500
Suite 400	Fax:	(402) 691-9526
Omaha, NE 68154		

Contributions to Candidates: $91,500 (2015-2016)
Democrats: $17,500; Republicans: $74,000

Corporate Foundations and Giving Programs

Tenaska, Inc. Contributions Program
Contact: Jana Martin

1044 N. 115h St.	Tel:	(402) 691-9500
Suite 400	Fax:	(402) 691-9526
Omaha, NE 68154-4446		

Public Affairs and Related Activities Personnel

At Headquarters

FIORELLI, David G.	Tel:	(402) 691-9500
Consultant & Member of Board of Stakeholders	Fax:	(402) 691-9526
FOSSUM, Drew J.	Tel:	(402) 691-9500
Vice President and General Counsel	Fax:	(402) 691-9526
KIRKWOOD, David W.	Tel:	(402) 691-9500
Vice President and Treasurer	Fax:	(402) 691-9526
KOPIASZ, Corey S.	Tel:	(402) 691-9500
Vice President Finance	Fax:	(402) 691-9526
KUDRON, Timothy G.	Tel:	(402) 691-9500
Senior Vice President, Finance and Administration	Fax:	(402) 691-9526
LAWLER, Michael F.	Tel:	(402) 691-9500
Executive Vice President, Corporate Investments	Fax:	(402) 691-9526
mlawler@tenaska.com		
MARTIN, Jana	Tel:	(402) 691-9500
Director, Government and Public Affairs and Media Contact	Fax:	(402) 691-9526
jmartin@tenaska.com		
OLBERG, Delette J.	Tel:	(402) 691-9500
Vice President, Public and Government Relations	Fax:	(402) 691-9526
QUINN, Ronald N.	Tel:	(402) 691-9500
Executive Vice President and PAC Treasurer	Fax:	(402) 691-9526
Mail Stop Suite 400		
TRUEBLOOD, Sheila R.	Tel:	(402) 691-9500
Vice President and Corporate Controller	Fax:	(402) 691-9526
TRUEBLOOD, Sheila R.	Tel:	(402) 691-9500
Vice President and Corporate Controller	Fax:	(402) 691-9526
VAN DYKE, Gregory A.	Tel:	(402) 691-9500
Chief Financial Officer	Fax:	(402) 691-9526

TenCate Protective Fabrics North America

A manufacturer of protective fabrics.
www.tencate.com/protective-fabrics/default.aspx
Employees: 1,400
Ticker: NYSE Euronext: AMX
Industry/ies: Apparel/Textiles Industry; Defense/Homeland Security; Government-Related
Legislative Issues: BUD; DEF; DIS; LBR; TRA; TRD

President	Tel:	(770) 969-1000
HAUERT, Daniel	Fax:	(770) 969-1010
d.hauert@tencate.com		

Main Headquarters		
Mailing: 6501 Mall Blvd., PO Box 289	Tel:	(770) 969-1000
Union City, GA 30291	Fax:	(770) 969-1010
	TF:	(800) 241-8630

Washington Office		
Mailing: 101 Constitution Ave. NW	Tel:	(770) 639-6244
Ninth Floor, Suite #9C08 E.	Fax:	(678) 658-8032
Washington, DC 20001		

Political Action Committees
Royal TenCate USA PAC aka TenCate PAC
FEC ID: C00523605
Contact: Daniel Trope
101 Constitution Ave. NW
Ninth Floor, Suite #9C08 East
Washington, DC 20001

Contributions to Candidates: $24,500 (2015-2016)
Democrats: $4,000; Republicans: $20,500

Corporate Foundations and Giving Programs

Ten Cate Contribution Program

6501 Mall Blvd., PO Box 289	Tel:	(770) 969-1000
Union City, GA 30291	Fax:	(770) 969-1010

Public Affairs and Related Activities Personnel

At Headquarters

ALLEN, Mike	Tel:	(770) 969-1000
Senior Director, Marketing	Fax:	(770) 969-1010
DUNAWAY, Lavon	Tel:	(770) 969-1000
Vice President, Finance	Fax:	(770) 969-1010
l.dunaway@tencate.com		
HARRIS, Jean	Tel:	(770) 969-1000
Vice President, Human Resources	Fax:	(770) 969-1010

RATCLIFFE, Joyce
Executive Assistant
j.ratcliffe@tencate.com
Tel: (770) 969-1000
Fax: (770) 969-5697

At Washington Office

COLLINS, Laurence Kenyatta
k.collins@tencate.com
Tel: (770) 639-6244
Fax: (678) 658-8032

TROPE, Daniel
President
d.trope@tencate.com
Registered Federal Lobbyist
Tel: (770) 639-6244
Fax: (678) 658-8032

Tenet Healthcare Corporation

Formerly National Medical Enterprises. Owns and operates acute care hospitals and related health care services.
www.tenethealth.com
Annual Revenues: $17.12 billion
Employees: 83,160
Ticker: NYSE: THC
SIC: 8062
Industry/ies: Medicine/Health Care/Mental Health
Legislative Issues: BUD; FIN; HCR; MMM; TEC; VET

Chairman of the Board
KANGAS, Edward A.
Tel: (469) 893-2000
Fax: (469) 893-8600

President and Chief Executive Officer
FETTER, Trevor
trevor.fetter@tenethealth.com
Tel: (469) 893-2000
Fax: (805) 563-7070

Main Headquarters
Mailing: 1445 Ross Ave.
            Suite 1400
            Dallas, TX 75202
Tel: (469) 893-2000

Washington Office
Mailing: 801 Pennsylvania Ave. NW
            Suite 900
            Washington, DC 20004

Political Action Committees
Tenet Healthcare Corporation PAC
FEC ID: C00119354
Contact: Todd Plott
1445 Ross Ave.
Suite 1400
Dallas, TX 75202

> **Contributions to Candidates:** $112,150 (2015-2016)
> Democrats: $59,650; Republicans: $52,500

> **Principal Recipients**
> **SENATE**
> BLUNT, ROY (REP-MO)

Corporate Foundations and Giving Programs
Tenet Healthcare Foundation
P.O. Box 809088
Dallas, TX 75380

Public Affairs and Related Activities Personnel

At Headquarters

ANDREWS, Audrey T.
Senior Vice President and General Counsel
audrey.andrews@tenethealth.com
Tel: (469) 893-2000

CAMPANINI, Steven
Vice President, Corporate Communications
steven.campanini@tenethealth.com
Tel: (469) 893-2000

CANCELMI , Daniel J.
Chief Financial Officer
Tel: (469) 893-2000

FRASER, Cathy Kusaka
Vice-Chair
Tel: (469) 893-2000

PLOTT, Todd
PAC Treasurer
Todd.Plott@Tenethealth.com
Tel: (469) 893-2000

RICE, Thomas
Senior Vice President, Investor Relations
Thomas.Rice@tenethealth.com
Tel: (469) 893-2000

At Washington Office

HUSKEY, Teresa

At Other Offices

GRIFFIN, Aron
Senior Director, Federal Affairs
607 14th St. NW, Suite 500
Washington, DC 20005
Registered Federal Lobbyist
Tel: (202) 359-8289

PHILLIPS, Brock
Federal Lobbyist
607 14th St. NW, Suite 500
Tel: (202) 359-8289

Washington, DC 20005
Registered Federal Lobbyist

WALDMANN, Daniel R.
Senior Vice President, Public Affairs and Government Relations
607 14th St. NW, Suite 500
Washington, DC 20005
daniel.waldmann@tenethealth.com
Tel: (202) 359-8289

Tenneco Automotives, Inc.

Designers, manufacturers and marketers of emission control and risk control products and systems for the automotive original equipment market and aftermarket.
www.tenneco.com
Annual Revenues: $8.35 billion
Employees: 29,000
Ticker: NYSE: TEN
SIC: 3714
Industry/ies: Automotive Industry; Transportation
Legislative Issues: BUD; TRD

Chairman of the Board and Chief Executive Officer
SHERRILL, Gregg M.
Tel: (847) 482-5000
Fax: (847) 482-5049

Main Headquarters
Mailing: 500 N. Field Dr.
            Lake Forest, IL 60045
Tel: (847) 482-5000
Fax: (847) 482-5940

Corporate Foundations and Giving Programs
Tenneco Contributions Program
500 N. Field Dr.
Lake Forest, IL 60045

Public Affairs and Related Activities Personnel

At Headquarters

BOLT, Gregg
Senior Vice President, Global Human Resources and Administration
Tel: (847) 482-5000
Fax: (847) 482-5940

DAWSON, William
Executive Director, Global Communications
bdawson@tenneco.com
Tel: (847) 482-5807
Fax: (847) 482-5940

GIBBONS, Maritza
Vice President, Strategic Planning and Business Development
Tel: (847) 482-5000
Fax: (847) 482-5940

GOLLA, Linae
Executive Director, Investor Relations
lgolla@tenneco.com
Tel: (847) 482-5162
Fax: (847) 482-5320

HARRINGTON, James
Senior Vice President, General Counsel and Corporate Secretary
Tel: (847) 482-5000
Fax: (847) 482-5940

JACKSON, Tim
Executive Vice President, Technology, Strategy and Business Development
Tel: (847) 482-5000
Fax: (847) 482-5940

KLUTH, Barbara A.
Executive Director, Human Resources
Tel: (847) 482-5000
Fax: (847) 482-5940

OSTRANDER, Jane
Vice President, Global Communications
jostrander@tenneco.com
Tel: (847) 482-5607
Fax: (847) 482-5049

TRAMMELL, Kenneth R.
Executive Vice President, Chief Financial Officer
Tel: (847) 482-5000
Fax: (847) 482-5940

Teradata Corporation

Teradata Corporation provides enterprise data warehousing solutions.
www.teradata.com
Annual Revenues: $2.69 billion
Employees: 11,500
Ticker: NYSE: TDC
SIC: 3571
Industry/ies: Computer/Technology
Legislative Issues: BAN; BUD; CPI; FIN; GOV; SCI; TAX

Chairman of the Board
RINGLER, James M.
Tel: (937) 242-4030

President and Chief Executive Officer
KOEHLER, Michael F.
Tel: (937) 242-4030

Main Headquarters
Mailing: 10000 Innovation Dr.
            Dayton, OH 45342
Tel: (937) 242-4030
TF: (866) 548-8348

Washington Office
Mailing: P.O. Box 7026
            Alexandria, VA 22307

Corporate Foundations and Giving Programs
Teradata Cares
Contact: Susan Baxley
2835 Miami Village Dr.
Dayton, OH 45342
Tel: (937) 242-4800

Public Affairs and Related Activities Personnel

At Headquarters

BAXLEY, Susan   Tel: (937) 242-4030
Director, Community Relations
Susan.Baxley@teradata.com

CARVER, Todd   Tel: (937) 242-4030
Vice President, Deputy General Counsel and Chief Ethics and
Compliance Officer
todd.carver@teradata.com

CONWAY, Dan   Tel: (937) 242-4030
Contact, Public Relations
dan.conway@teradata.com

DAVIS, Saundra   Tel: (937) 242-4030
Chief Human Resource Officer

DAY, Timothy   Tel: (937) 242-4030
Vice President, Government Affairs

FAIR , Bob   Tel: (937) 242-4030
Executive Vice President and Chief Marketing and
Information Officer

HOTCHKISS, D'Anne   Tel: (937) 242-4030
Contact, Public Relations
danne.hotchkiss@teradata.com

MCDONALD, Darryl D.   Tel: (937) 242-4030
Chief Strategy Officer
darryl.mcdonald@teradata.com

NYQUIST, Laura   Tel: (937) 242-4030
General Counsel and Secretary

SCHEPPMANN, Stephen   Tel: (937) 242-4030
Executive Vice President and Chief Financial Officer
stephen.scheppmann@teradata.com

SHADOAN, Juliet   Tel: (937) 242-4030
Federal Lobbyist
juliet.shadoan@teradata.com

SWEARINGEN, Gregg   Tel: (937) 242-4030
Vice President, Investor Relations
gregg.swearingen@teradata.com

TREESE, Margaret   Tel: (937) 242-4030

At Washington Office

SIEMIONTKOWSKI, Ronald S.
PAC Treasurer

Teradyne, Inc.

A manufacturer of electronic test systems.
www.teradyne.com
Annual Revenues: $1.73 billion
Employees: 4,100
Ticker: NYSE:TER
SIC: 3825
Industry/ies: Electricity & Electronics; Electronics; Energy/Electricity

Chairman of the Board   Tel: (978) 370-2700
VALLEE, Roy A.   Fax: (978) 370-1440

President and Chief Executive Officer   Tel: (978) 370-2700
JAGIELA , Mark E.   Fax: (978) 370-1440

Main Headquarters
Mailing: 600 Riverpark Dr.   Tel: (978) 370-2700
            N. Reading, MA 01864   Fax: (978) 370-1440

Corporate Foundations and Giving Programs

Teradyne Contributions Program
600 Riverpark Dr.
N. Reading, MA 01864

Public Affairs and Related Activities Personnel

At Headquarters

BEECHER, Gregory R.   Tel: (617) 370-2700
Chief Financial Officer   Fax: (617) 422-2910

BLANCHARD, Andy   Tel: (978) 270-2425
Vice President, Corporate Relations   Fax: (617) 422-2910
andy.blanchard@teradyne.com

FAULKNER, Jessica   Tel: (978) 370-1437
Specialist , Marketing Communications   Fax: (978) 370-1440
jessica.faulkner@teradyne.com

GRAY, Charles   Tel: (617) 370-2700
Vice President, General Counsel and Secretary Fax: (617) 422-2910

GRIFFIS, Bobby   Tel: (978) 370-6354
Manager, Regional Sales   Fax: (978) 370-6305
bobby.griffis@teradyne.com

Terex Corporation

A diversified global manufacturer based in Westport, CT. Terex is involved in a broad range of
construction, infrastructure, recycling and mining-related capital equipment.
www.terex.com

Annual Revenues: $6.47 billion
Employees: 20,400
Ticker: NYSE: TEX
SIC: 3537
Industry/ies: Mining Industry; Natural Resources

Main Headquarters
Mailing: 200 Nyala Farm Rd.   Tel: (203) 222-7170
            Westport, CT 06880   Fax: (203) 222-7976

Political Action Committees

Terex Corporation PAC
FEC ID: C00386284
Contact: Eric I. Cohen
200 Nyala Farm Rd.   Tel: (203) 222-7170
Westport, CT 06880   Fax: (203) 222-7976

Corporate Foundations and Giving Programs

Terex Corporation Contributions Program
200 Nyala Farm Rd.   Tel: (203) 222-7170
Westport, CT 06880   Fax: (203) 222-7976

Public Affairs and Related Activities Personnel

At Headquarters

BABSON-SMITH, Stacey   Tel: (203) 222-7170
Vice President, Chief Ethics and Compliance Officer   Fax: (203) 222-7976

BARR, Kevin A.   Tel: (203) 222-7170
Senior Vice President, Human Resources   Fax: (203) 222-7976

BRADLEY, Kevin   Tel: (203) 222-7170
Senior Vice President and Chief Financial Officer   Fax: (203) 222-7976

COHEN, Eric I.   Tel: (203) 222-7170
Senior Vice President, General Counsel, Secretary and PAC   Fax: (203) 222-7976
Treasurer

FILIPOV, Steve   Tel: (203) 222-7170
President, Material Handling and Port Solutions   Fax: (203) 222-7976

HENRY, Brian J.   Tel: (203) 222-7170
Senior Vice President, Business Development and Investor   Fax: (203) 222-0130
Relations
brian.henry@terex.com

Ternion Bio Industries

A biotechnology company. Ternion Bio Industries generate beneficial raw materials as a by-
product of the carbon recycling process.
www.ternionbio.com
Industry/ies: Agriculture/Agronomy; Energy/Electricity; Environment And
Conservation; Science; Scientific Research

Main Headquarters
Mailing: 1257 Dell Ave.   Tel: (408) 676-8246
            Campbell, CA 95008   Fax: (408) 516-9854

Public Affairs and Related Activities Personnel

At Headquarters

GEISER, Zack   Tel: (408) 676-8246
Director, Marketing   Fax: (408) 516-9854

TerreStar Networks

A mobile network operator.
www.terrestarnetworks.com
Annual Revenues: $17.90 million
Employees: 100
Ticker: NASDAQ: TSTR
SIC: 4899
Industry/ies: Communications; Telecommunications/Internet/Cable

Chairman of the Board   Tel: (703) 483-7800
FREEMAN, William M.   Fax: (703) 476-7143

President and Chief Executive Officer   Tel: (703) 483-7800
EPSTEIN, Jeffrey W.   Fax: (703) 476-7143

Main Headquarters
Mailing: One Discovery Sq.   Tel: (703) 483-7800
            12010 Sunset Hills Rd., Sixth Floor   Fax: (703) 476-7143
            Reston, VA 20190   TF: (877) 878-2701

Political Action Committees

Terrestar Networks Inc PAC
FEC ID: C00432641
Contact: Donald Lefeve
One Discovery Sq.
12010 Sunset Hills Rd., Sixth Floor
Reston, VA 20190

Public Affairs and Related Activities Personnel

At Headquarters

ADAMS, Kelly   Tel: (703) 483-7966
Public Affairs, Marketing and Communications   Fax: (703) 476-7143
kelly.adams@terrestar.com

BRANDON, Douglas
General Counsel and Secretary
doug.brandon@terrestar.com
Tel: (703) 483-7800
Fax: (703) 476-7143

LEFEVE, Donald
PAC Contact
Tel: (703) 483-7800
Fax: (703) 476-7143

LOIACONO, Vincent
Chief Financial Officer
Tel: (703) 483-7800
Fax: (703) 476-7143

Territory & Commonwealth LLC

A lobbying firm.

President
SIMMONS, Brook
Tel: (202) 746-3424

Main Headquarters
Mailing: 20 F St. NW
Seventh Floor
Washington, DC 20001
Tel: (202) 746-3424

Public Affairs and Related Activities Personnel

At Headquarters

BELJIN, Alen
President
Tel: (202) 746-3424

Terumo BCT

Formerly known as Navigant Biotechnologies, CaridianBCT is a wholly-owned subsidiary of Gambro BCT, Inc.
www.terumobct.com
Annual Revenues: $102.20 Million
Industry/ies: Computer/Technology; Medicine/Health Care/Mental Health
Legislative Issues: HCR

President and Chief Executive Officer
PEREZ, David
Tel: (303) 239-2318
Fax: (303) 542-5215

Main Headquarters
Mailing: 10811 W. Collins Ave.
Lakewood, CO 80215
Tel: (303) 231-4357
Fax: (303) 542-5215
TF: (877) 339-4228

Political Action Committees
Terumo BCT Inc. PAC
FEC ID: C00388652
Contact: Mark Ingebritson
10811 W. Collins Ave.
Lakewood, CO 80215

Corporate Foundations and Giving Programs
Terumo BCT Contributions Program
10811 W. Collins Ave.
Lakewood, CO 80215

Public Affairs and Related Activities Personnel

At Headquarters

FUSCO, Laura
Contact, Global Corporate Communications
press@terumobct.com
Tel: (303) 205-2546
Fax: (303) 542-5215

INGEBRITSON, Mark
Vice President, Finance and Accounting and PAC Treasurer
Tel: (303) 231-4357
Fax: (303) 542-5215

JO KIRKLAND, Stacey
Chief Administrative Officer
Tel: (303) 231-4357
Fax: (303) 542-5215

LARSON, Scott
Senior Vice President, Legal, and General Counsel
scott.larson@caridianbct.com
Tel: (303) 231-4357
Fax: (303) 542-5215

RINEHARDT, Craig
Executive Vice President, Global Operations
Tel: (303) 231-4357
Fax: (303) 542-5215

SPINNEY, Rusty
Chief Financial Officer
Rusty.spinney@caridianbct.com
Tel: (303) 231-4357
Fax: (303) 542-5215

Tesla Motors, Inc.

Designer and Manufacturer of Electric Vehicles and Electric Vehicle Powertrain Components.
www.teslamotors.com
Annual Revenues: $3.52 billion
Employees: 10,161
Ticker: NASDAQ: TSLA
SIC: 3711
Industry/ies: Automotive Industry; Transportation
Legislative Issues: AUT; ENG; MAN; ROD; TAX; TRA

Co-Founder, Chairman and Chief Executive Officer
MUSK, Elon
elon.musk@teslamotors.com
Tel: (650) 413-4000
Fax: (650) 413-4099

Main Headquarters
Mailing: 3500 Deer Creek
Palo Alto, CA 94304
Tel: (650) 681-5000
Fax: (650) 681-5101
TF: (888) 518-3752

Washington Office

Mailing: 1050 K St. NW
Suite 101
Washington, DC 20001
Tel: (202) 737-0024

Public Affairs and Related Activities Personnel

At Headquarters

AHUJA, Deepak
Chief Financial Officer
deepak@teslamotors.com
Tel: (650) 413-4000
Fax: (650) 413-4099

EVANSON, Jeff
Vice President, Global Investor Relations
ir@teslamotors.com
Tel: (650) 681-5000
Fax: (650) 681-5101

GESHUR, Arnnon
Vice President, Human Resources
Tel: (650) 681-5000
Fax: (650) 681-5101

GUILLEN, Jerome
Vice President, World Wide Sales and Service
Tel: (650) 681-5000
Fax: (650) 681-5101

O'CONNELL, Diarmuid
Vice President, Business Development
diarmuid@teslamotors.com
Tel: (650) 681-5000
Fax: (650) 413-4099

At Washington Office

BENDALL, MN, Laurie
Federal Lobbyist
Tel: (202) 737-0024

KINTZ, Brooke
Registered Federal Lobbyist
Tel: (202) 737-0024

WITT, Daniel
Manager, Business Development & Policy
dwitt@teslamotors.com
Tel: (408) 482-5570

At Other Offices

PINEDA, Patricia A.
PAC Treasurer
45500 Fremont Blvd.
Fremont, CA 94538
Tel: (510) 498-5500
Fax: (510) 770-4116

POTTS, James Watson
PAC Contact
45500 Fremont Blvd.
Fremont, CA 94538
Tel: (510) 498-5500
Fax: (510) 770-4116

Tesoro Corporation

An independent refiner and marketer of petroleum products.
www.tsocorp.com
Annual Revenues: $36.58 billion
Employees: 5,600
Ticker: NYSE: TSO
SIC: 2911
NAICS: 324110
Industry/ies: Fuels See Coal, Gas, Oil, Petroleum; Natural Resources; Petroleum Industry
Legislative Issues: BUD; CAW; ENG; ENV; FIN; FUE; LBR; NAT; RRR; TAX; TRA

Chairman, President and Chief Executive Officer
GOFF, Gregory J.
Tel: (210) 626-6000
Fax: (210) 579-4574

Main Headquarters
Mailing: 19100 Ridgewood Pkwy.
San Antonio, TX 78259
Tel: (210) 626-6000
Fax: (210) 579-4574
TF: (800) 299-0570

Washington Office
Mailing: 601 Pennsylvania Ave. NW
Suite 900
Washington, DC 20004
Tel: (202) 434-8904

Political Action Committees
Tesoro Petroleum Corporation PAC
FEC ID: C00358366
Contact: Max C. Walters
19100 Ridgewood Pkwy.
San Antonio, TX 78259
Tel: (210) 626-6000
Fax: (210) 626-6000

Contributions to Candidates: $292,500 (2015-2016)
Democrats: $70,500; Republicans: $222,000

Principal Recipients

SENATE
MURKOWSKI, LISA (REP-AK)

HOUSE
HURD, WILLIAM (REP-TX)
MCCARTHY, KEVIN (REP-CA)

Corporate Foundations and Giving Programs
Tesoro Corporation Contributions Program
19100 Ridgewood Pkwy.
San Antonio, TX 78259
Tel: (210) 626-6000
Fax: (210) 626-6000

Public Affairs and Related Activities Personnel

At Headquarters

CASEY, Keith
Tel: (210) 626-6000

Senior Vice President, Strategy and Business Development	Fax:	(210) 579-4574
LATORRE, Craig M.	Tel:	(210) 626-6000
Senior Vice President and Chief Human Resources Officer	Fax:	(210) 579-4574
MOREAU, Claude P.	Tel:	(210) 626-6000
Senior Vice President, Marketing	Fax:	(210) 579-4574
PARRISH, Charles S.	Tel:	(210) 626-6000
Executive Vice President, General Counsel and Secretary	Fax:	(210) 579-4574
charles.s.parrish@tsocorp.com		
PETERSON, Brenda	Tel:	(210) 626-6000
Vice President, Enterprise Business Improvement	Fax:	(210) 579-4574
RAMRAJ, Sam	Tel:	(210) 626-6000
Vice President, Investor Relations	Fax:	(210) 579-4574
RANDECKER, Brian	Tel:	(210) 626-4757
Chief Financial Officer Refining	Fax:	(210) 579-4574
Brian.E.Randecker@tsocorp.com		
STERIN, Steven M.	Tel:	(210) 626-6000
Executive Vice President and Chief Financial Officer	Fax:	(210) 579-4574
SULLIVAN, Brian	Tel:	(210) 626-6000
Vice President, Corporate Affairs	Fax:	(210) 579-4574
WALTERS, Max C.	Tel:	(210) 626-6000
PAC Treasurer	Fax:	(210) 579-4574
WARNER, Cynthia	Tel:	(210) 626-6000
Executive Vice President, Strategy and Business Development	Fax:	(210) 579-4574

At Washington Office

BROWN, Stephen H.	Tel:	(202) 434-8904
Vice President, Federal Government Affairs		
Registered Federal Lobbyist		
MOORE, Jamie	Tel:	(202) 742-6688
Director, Federal Government Affairs		
Registered Federal Lobbyist		

Tesoro Petroleum

See listing on page 778 under Tesoro Corporation

Tessera Technologies, Inc.

Provider of miniaturization technologies for the electronics industry.
www.tessera.com
Annual Revenues: $270.32 million
Employees: 203
Ticker: NASDAQ: TSRA
SIC: 3674
Industry/ies: Copyrights, Patents And Trademarks
Legislative Issues: CPT; TRD

Chief Executive Officer	Tel:	(408) 321-6000
LACEY, Tom	Fax:	(408) 321-8257

Main Headquarters

Mailing:	3025 Orchard Pkwy.	Tel:	(408) 321-6000
	San Jose, CA 95134	Fax:	(408) 321-8257

Political Action Committees
Tessera Technologies, Inc. PAC
FEC ID: C00443739
Contact: John Allen

3025 Orchard Pkwy.	Tel:	(408) 321-6000
San Jose, CA 95134	Fax:	(408) 321-8257

> **Contributions to Candidates:** $38,000 (2015-2016)
> Democrats: $18,000; Republicans: $20,000

Public Affairs and Related Activities Personnel

At Headquarters

ALLEN, John	Tel:	(408) 321-6000
Senior Vice President, Corporate Controller and PAC Contact	Fax:	(408) 321-8257
ANDERSEN, Robert	Tel:	(408) 321-6000
Chief Financial Officer	Fax:	(408) 321-8257
DAVIS, Paul E.	Tel:	(408) 321-6000
General Counsel and Corporate Secretary	Fax:	(408) 321-8257
FARRELL, John	Tel:	(408) 321-6000
Vice President, Sales and Marketing	Fax:	(408) 321-8257
MEHRA, Sumat	Tel:	(408) 321-6000
Senior Vice President, Marketing and Business Development	Fax:	(408) 321-8257
SCHLEZINGER, Eric	Tel:	(408) 321-6000
Senior Vice President, Global Business Strategy and Human Resources	Fax:	(408) 321-8257
WHITE, Chuck	Tel:	(408) 321-6000
Senior Vice President, Corporate Development	Fax:	(408) 321-8257

Tethys Bioscience

Tethys Bioscience is dedicated to the discovery, development and commercialization of biological markers, biomarkers that provide a tool to address the growing global challenge of chronic metabolic diseases such as diabetes.
www.tethysbio.com

Annual Revenues: $19.10 million
Industry/ies: Medicine/Health Care/Mental Health; Science; Scientific Research
Legislative Issues: HCR; MED

Co-Founder, Chairman of the Board and Chief Scientific Officer	Tel:	(888) 483-8497
URDEA, Mickey S.	Fax:	(510) 450-0675

President and Chief Executive Officer	Tel:	(510) 420-6700
STRAHAN, Randall K.	Fax:	(510) 601-0371

Main Headquarters

Mailing:	5858 Horton St.	Tel:	(510) 420-6700
	Suite 280	Fax:	(510) 601-0371
	Emeryville, CA 94608	TF:	(888) 697-7339

Public Affairs and Related Activities Personnel

At Headquarters

FERGUSON, Matthew B.	Tel:	(510) 420-6700
Chief Financial Officer	Fax:	(510) 601-0371
HOLLISTER, John	Tel:	(510) 420-6700
Senior Vice President, Marketing	Fax:	(510) 601-0371

Tetra Tech

Provides consulting, engineering and technical services.
www.tetratech.com
Annual Revenues: $1.79 billion
Employees: 13,000
Ticker: NASDAQ: TTEK
SIC: 8711
Industry/ies: Energy/Electricity

Chairman, Chief Executive Officer and President	Tel:	(626) 351-4664
BATRACK, Dan L.	Fax:	(626) 351-5291

Main Headquarters

Mailing:	3475 E. Foothill Blvd.	Tel:	(626) 351-4664
	Pasadena, CA 91107-6024	Fax:	(626) 351-5291

Corporate Foundations and Giving Programs

Tetra Tech Contribution Program

3475 E. Foothill Blvd.	Tel:	(626) 351-4664
Pasadena, CA 91107-6024	Fax:	(626) 351-5291

Public Affairs and Related Activities Personnel

At Headquarters

BIEBER, Michael A.	Tel:	(626) 351-4664
Vice President, Corporate Development	Fax:	(626) 351-5291
michael.bieber@tetratech.com		
BURDICK, Steven M.	Tel:	(626) 351-4664
Executive Vice President, Chief Financial Officer and Treasurer	Fax:	(626) 351-5291
CARTER, Brian N	Tel:	(626) 351-4664
Senior Vice President, Corporate Controller and Chief Accounting Officer	Fax:	(626) 351-5291
LEMMON , Richard A.	Tel:	(626) 351-4664
Senior Vice President, Corporate Administration	Fax:	(626) 351-5291
MACPHERSON, Charlie	Tel:	(626) 351-4664
Contact, Media and Public Relations	Fax:	(626) 351-5291
charlie.macpherson@tetratech.com		
MCDONALD, Kevin P.	Tel:	(626) 351-4664
Senior Vice President, Corporate Human Resources	Fax:	(626) 351-5291
kevin.mcdonald@tetratech.com		
PAGENKOPF, James R	Tel:	(626) 351-4664
Executive Vice President, Federal Programs	Fax:	(626) 351-5291
SALIN, Janis B.	Tel:	(626) 351-4664
Vice President, General Counsel and Secretary	Fax:	(626) 351-5291
janis.salin@tetratech.com		
SHOEMAKER, Leslie L.	Tel:	(626) 351-4664
Senior Vice President, Corporate Strategy	Fax:	(626) 351-5291
leslie.shoemaker@tetratech.com		
WU, Jim	Tel:	(626) 351-4664
Contact, Investor Relations	Fax:	(626) 351-5291
jim.wu@tetratech.com		

TetraLogic Pharmaceuticals

A privately held biopharmaceutical company.
www.tetralogicpharma.com
Annual Revenues: $1.60 million
Employees: 17
SIC: 2834
Industry/ies: Pharmaceutical Industry

Chairman of the Board	Tel:	(610) 889-9900
PECORA, Andrew	Fax:	(610) 889-9994

President and Chief Executive Officer	Tel:	(610) 889-9900
BUCHI, J. Kevin	Fax:	(610) 889-9994

Main Headquarters

Mailing:	343 Phoenixville Pike	Tel: (610) 889-9900
	Malvern, PA 19355	Fax: (610) 889-9994

Public Affairs and Related Activities Personnel

At Headquarters

MEYERS, Pete A	Tel:	(610) 889-9900
Chief Financial Officer	Fax:	(610) 889-9994
RUSSELL, Lesley	Tel:	(610) 889-9900
Chief Operating Officer	Fax:	(610) 889-9994
SHERMAN, JD, J.D., Richard L.	Tel:	(610) 889-9900
Senior Vice President, Strategic Transactions and General Counsel	Fax:	(610) 889-9994

Teva Pharmaceticals Industries, Ltd

Teva Pharmaceuticals USA develops, manufactures, and supplies generic prescription medications in the United States. Acquired Barr Pharmaceuticals, Inc. in late 2008.
www.tevausa.com
SIC: 2834
Industry/ies: Medicine/Health Care/Mental Health; Pharmaceutical Industry
Legislative Issues: ALC; CPT; HCR; MMM; PHA; TAX; TOR; TRD

President and Chief Executive Officer
VIGODMAN, Erez — Tel: (215) 591-3000 / Fax: (215) 591-8600

Main Headquarters

Mailing:	1090 Horsham Rd.	Tel: (610) 344-0200
	N. Wales, PA 19454	TF: (888) 838-2872

Political Action Committees

Teva Pharmaceuticals USA, Inc. Political Action Committee
FEC ID: C00434811
Contact: Deborah Alice Griffin
25 Masschusetts Ave. NW
Suite 440
Washington, DC 20001

> **Contributions to Candidates:** $129,500 (2015-2016)
> Democrats: $57,500; Republicans: $72,000

Principal Recipients

SENATE
CASEY, ROBERT P JR (DEM-PA)

Corporate Foundations and Giving Programs

CephalonCares Foundation
6900 College Boulevard, Suite 1000 — Tel: (610) 344-0200
Overland Park, KS 66211 — Fax: (877) 438-4404

Teva Pharmaceuticals USA Contiributions Program
1090 Horsham Rd.
N. Wales, PA 19454

Public Affairs and Related Activities Personnel

At Headquarters

BECK-CODNER, Iris	Tel:	(610) 344-0200
Group Execuitve Vice President, Corporate Marketing and Communications		
BRADLEY, Denise	Tel:	(215) 591-8974
Vice President, Corporate Communications		
denise.bradley@tevapharm.com		
DESHEH, Eyal	Tel:	(610) 344-0200
Group Executive Vice President, Chief Financial Officer		
EGOSI, Richard S.	Tel:	(610) 344-0200
Group Executive Vice President, Chief Legal Officer		
HAYDEN, Dr. Michael	Tel:	(610) 344-0200
President, Global Research and Development and Chief Scientific Officer		
MANNIX, Kevin C.	Tel:	(215) 591-8912
Vice President and Head, Investor Relations		
kevin.mannix@tevapharm.com		
SABAG, Mark	Tel:	(610) 344-0200
Group Executive Vice President, Human Resources		
WRIGHT, Timothy R.	Tel:	(610) 344-0200
Executive Vice President, Business Development, Strategy and Commercial Innovation		

At Other Offices

AHN, Susie	Tel:	(215) 591-3000
Federal Lobbyist	Fax:	(215) 591-8600
1090 Horsham Rd., P.O. Box 1090		
N. Wales, PA 19454		
Registered Federal Lobbyist		
BARKSDALE, Denise	Tel:	(877) 237-4881
Senior Manager, Government Affairs and Special Projects	Fax:	(877) 438-4404
25 Massachussets Ave. NW, Suite 440		
Washington, DC 20001		
denise.barksdale@tevausa.com		
BARRETT, Debra S.	Tel:	(215) 591-3000
Senior Vice President, Global Government Affairs & Public Policy	Fax:	(215) 591-8600
1090 Horsham Rd., P.O. Box 1090		
N. Wales, PA 19454		
debra.barrett@tevausa.com		
Registered Federal Lobbyist		
BRADLEY, Denise	Tel:	(215) 591-3000
Vice President, Corporate Communications	Fax:	(215) 591-8600
1090 Horsham Rd., P.O. Box 1090		
N. Wales, PA 19454		
denise.bradley@tevapharm.com		
DZUBIN, Shannon	Tel:	(877) 237-4881
25 Massachussets Ave. NW, Suite 440	Fax:	(877) 438-4404
Washington, DC 20001		
Registered Federal Lobbyist		
ERDEL, Grant	Tel:	(215) 591-3000
Director, Federal Affairs	Fax:	(215) 591-8600
1090 Horsham Rd., P.O. Box 1090		
N. Wales, PA 19454		
Registered Federal Lobbyist		
FALB, Robert J.	Tel:	(215) 591-3000
Federal Lobbyist	Fax:	(215) 591-8600
1090 Horsham Rd., P.O. Box 1090		
N. Wales, PA 19454		
Registered Federal Lobbyist		
GRIFFIN, Deborah Alice	Tel:	(877) 237-4881
PAC Treasurer	Fax:	(877) 438-4404
25 Massachussets Ave. NW, Suite 440		
Washington, DC 20001		
MANSER, Jim	Tel:	(877) 237-4881
Associate Director, State Government Affairs	Fax:	(877) 438-4404
25 Massachussets Ave. NW, Suite 440		
Washington, DC 20001		
SCHUMER, Charles	Tel:	(215) 591-3000
Vice President of Government Affairs	Fax:	(215) 591-8600
1090 Horsham Rd., P.O. Box 1090		
N. Wales, PA 19454		
STEWART, Terri	Tel:	(215) 591-3000
Federal Lobbyist	Fax:	(215) 591-8600
1090 Horsham Rd., P.O. Box 1090		
N. Wales, PA 19454		
Terri.Stewart@tevausa.com		

Texas Industries, Inc.

A producer of steel and construction materials, including cement, aggregates and concrete. Also involved in the real estate industry.
www.txi.com
Employees: 2,040
Ticker: NYSE: TXI
SIC: 3241
Industry/ies: Construction/Construction Materials; Real Estate

Chairman of the Board — Tel: (972) 647-6700
RANSDELL , Thomas R. — Fax: (972) 647-3964

President and Chief Executive Officer — Tel: (972) 647-6700
BREKHUS, Melvin G. — Fax: (972) 647-3878

Main Headquarters

Mailing:	1341 W. Mockingbird Ln.	Tel: (972) 647-6700
	Suite 700 West	Fax: (972) 647-3964
	Dallas, TX 75247	TF: (800) 442-4910

Political Action Committees

Texas Industries, Inc. PAC
FEC ID: C00176388
Contact: Dana L. Link
1341 W. Mockingbird Ln.
Suite 700W
Dallas, TX 75247

> **Contributions to Candidates:** $2,700 (2015-2016)
> Republicans: $2,700

Public Affairs and Related Activities Personnel

At Headquarters

ALLEN, Kenneth R.	Tel:	(972) 647-6730
Vice President, Finance, Chief Financial Officer	Fax:	(972) 647-3964
ANDERSON, Frederick G.	Tel:	(972) 647-6700
Vice President, General Counsel and Secretary	Fax:	(972) 647-3878
fanderson@txi.com		
COLLAR, Michael P.	Tel:	(972) 647-6700
Vice President, Human Resources	Fax:	(972) 647-3878
JONES, D. Randall	Tel:	(972) 647-6701
Vice President, Corporate Communications and Government Affairs	Fax:	(972) 647-3355
LINK , Dana L.	Tel:	(972) 647-6700

| General Manager and PAC Treasurer | Fax: | (972) 647-3964 |

MAYFIELD, Stephen D.
Vice President, Sales and Marketing
Tel: (972) 647-6700
Fax: (972) 647-3964

PERKINS , David S.
Vice President, Environmental, Government and Public Affairs
Tel: (972) 647-6700
Fax: (972) 647-3964

ROGERS , James B.
Vice President and Chief Operating Officer
Tel: (972) 647-6700
Fax: (972) 647-3964

Texas Instruments
See listing on page 563 under National Semiconductor

Texas Instruments
A Texas-based, international digital signal processing and analog technologies company.
www.ti.com
Annual Revenues: $14.39 billion
Employees: 31,003
Ticker: NYSE: TXN
SIC: 3674
NAICS: 334413
Industry/ies: Electricity & Electronics; Electronics; Energy/Electricity
Legislative Issues: AUT; CPI; CPT; CSP; EDU; IMM; SCI; TAX; TRA; TRD

Chairman of the Board, President & Chief Executive Officer
TEMPLETON, Richard K.
Tel: (972) 995-2011
Fax: (972) 927-6377

Main Headquarters
Mailing: P.O. Box 660199
Dallas, TX 75266-0199
Tel: (972) 995-2011
Fax: (972) 927-6377

Washington Office
Mailing: 1455 Pennsylvania Ave. NW, Suite 375
Washington, DC 20004
Tel: (202) 220-9440
Fax: (202) 220-9480

Political Action Committees
Texas Instruments, Inc. PAC
FEC ID: C00007070
1341 W. Mockingbird Ln.
Dallas, TX 75247

Contributions to Candidates: $3,116,516 (2015-2016)
Democrats: $37,500; Republicans: $66,000; Other: $3,013,016

Corporate Foundations and Giving Programs
Texas Instruments Foundation
Contact: Sam Self
12500 TI Blvd.
Dallas, TX 75266

Public Affairs and Related Activities Personnel

At Headquarters

BONNER, Stephen
Registered Federal Lobbyist
Tel: (972) 995-2011
Fax: (972) 927-6377

CUNNINGHAM, Trisha
Director, Worldwide Corporate Citizenship
t-cunningham@ti.com
Tel: (972) 995-2011
Fax: (972) 927-6377

HUBACH, Joseph F.
Senior Vice President, Secretary and General Counsel
j-hubach@ti.com
Tel: (972) 995-2011
Fax: (972) 927-6377

MARCH, Kevin P.
Senior Vice President & Chief Financial Officer
Tel: (972) 995-2011
Fax: (972) 927-6377

MORGAN, Kimberly J.
Director, Corporate Communications
kim-morgan@ti.com
Tel: (972) 995-2011
Fax: (972) 927-6377

SELF, Sam
Chairman, Texas Instruments Foundation
Tel: (972) 995-2011
Fax: (972) 927-6377

SZCZSPONIK, John
Senior Vice President & Manager, Worldwide Sales and Marketing
Tel: (972) 995-2011
Fax: (972) 927-6377

WEST, Teresa Lynne
Senior Vice President & Manager, Communications and Investor Relations
t-west@ti.com
Tel: (972) 995-2011
Fax: (972) 927-6377

WHITAKER, Darla
Senior Vice President, Worldwide Human Resources
Tel: (972) 995-2011
Fax: (972) 927-6377

At Washington Office

BLAYLOCK, William
Vice President and Senior Tax Counsel
Registered Federal Lobbyist
Tel: (202) 220-9440
Fax: (202) 220-9480

COLLINS, Paula J.
Vice President, Government Relations
Mail Stop M/S 4072
pcollins@ti.com
Registered Federal Lobbyist
Tel: (202) 220-9440
Fax: (202) 220-9480

IRISARI, Gene
Director, Government Relations
Tel: (202) 220-9440
Fax: (202) 220-9480

Registered Federal Lobbyist

JOHNSON, Cynthia K.
Director, Government Relations (International Trade and Energy)
Mail Stop M/S 4072
ckjohnson@ti.com
Tel: (202) 220-9440
Fax: (202) 220-9480

At Other Offices

MAYES, Gray
PAC Treasurer
P.O. Box 742496
Dallas, TX 75374
gmayes@ti.com

Textron Inc.
A global, multi-industry company with operations in aircraft, automotive, industrial and finance markets.
www.textron.com
Annual Revenues: $14.10 billion
Employees: 34,000
Ticker: NYSE: TXT
SIC: 3720
Industry/ies: Aerospace/Aviation; Automotive Industry; Banking/Finance/Investments; Transportation
Legislative Issues: AVI; BUD; DEF; HCR; HOM; LAW; SCI; TAX; TRD

Chairman of the Board, President and Chief Executive Officer
DONNELLY, Scott C.
Tel: (401) 421-2800
Fax: (401) 457-2220

Main Headquarters
Mailing: 40 Westminster St.
Providence, RI 02903
Tel: (401) 421-2800
Fax: (401) 457-2220

Washington Office
Mailing: 1101 Pennsylvania Ave. NW
Suite 400
Washington, DC 20004
Tel: (202) 637-3800
Fax: (202) 637-3860

Political Action Committees
Beechcraft Inc. Political Action Committee (Beechcraft PAC)
FEC ID: C00434183
Contact: Douglas R. Scott
9709 E. Central
P.O. Box 85
Wichita, KS 67201-0085

Textron Inc. PAC
FEC ID: C00123612
Contact: Keith Watson
40 Westminster St.
Providence, RI 02903

Contributions to Candidates: $269,000 (2015-2016)
Democrats: $64,000; Republicans: $205,000

Principal Recipients

HOUSE
GRANGER, KAY (REP-TX)
POMPEO, MICHAEL RICHARD (REP-KS)
THORNBERRY, MAC (REP-TX)

Corporate Foundations and Giving Programs
Textron Inc. Contributions Program
40 Westminster St.
Providence, RI 02903
Tel: (401) 421-2800
Fax: (401) 457-2220

Public Affairs and Related Activities Personnel

At Headquarters

ALEXANDER, Nicole
Manager, Communications and Public Affairs
Nicole_Alexander@beechcraft.com
Tel: (316) 676-3212
Fax: (316) 671-3376

BLOUIN, Robert
Vice President
Tel: (316) 676-5031
Fax: (401) 457-2220

CONNOR, Frank T.
Executive Vice President and Chief Financial Officer
Tel: (401) 421-2800
Fax: (401) 457-2220

DUFFY, Julie G.
Vice President and Deputy General Counsel
Tel: (401) 421-2800
Fax: (401) 457-2220

GARTOLL, Paul Mc
Vice President, Strategy and Business Development
Tel: (401) 421-2800
Fax: (401) 457-2220

HESS, Derek
Vice President, Government Affairs
Tel: (316) 676-7111
Fax: (401) 457-2220

JOHNSON, Cheryl H.
Executive Vice President, Human Resources
Tel: (401) 421-2800
Fax: (401) 457-2220

LOVEJOY, Mary F.
Vice President and Treasurer
Tel: (401) 421-2800
Fax: (401) 457-2220

LUPONE, E. Robert
Executive Vice President, General Counsel and Secretary
Tel: (401) 421-2800
Fax: (401) 457-2220

PERKINS, Elizabeth C.
Vice President and Deputy General Counsel
Tel: (401) 421-2800
Fax: (401) 457-2220

QUINTAL, Karen Gordon
Director, Corporate Communications
kgordon@textron.com
Tel: (401) 421-2800
Fax: (401) 457-3598

ROBERTS, Lyndon
Federal Lobbyist
Tel: (316) 676-5031
Fax: (401) 457-2220

ROSENBERG, Dave
Vice President, Strategic Planning and Programs
Tel: (316) 676-7111
Fax: (401) 457-2220

SCOTT, Douglas R.
Vice President, Government Affairs
Tel: (316) 676-5031
Fax: (401) 457-2220

STREKER, Cathy
Vice President, Human Resources
Tel: (401) 421-2800
Fax: (401) 421-2878

VICK, Shawn
Executive Vice President, Sales and Marketing
Tel: (316) 676-7111
Fax: (401) 457-2220

WATSON, Keith
PAC Treasurer
Tel: (401) 421-2800
Fax: (401) 457-2220

WILBURNE, Douglas R.
Vice President, Investor Relations
Tel: (401) 457-2288
Fax: (401) 457-2220

At Washington Office

BRITTAIN, Frank
Director, Government Affairs
Tel: (202) 637-3800
Fax: (202) 637-3860

DAPSON, Matthew
Federal Lobbyist
mdapson@dc.textron.com
Registered Federal Lobbyist
Tel: (202) 637-3800
Fax: (202) 637-3860

EHUDIN, Marc
Federal Lobbyist
Registered Federal Lobbyist
Tel: (202) 637-3800
Fax: (202) 637-3860

FERNANDEZ, Manuel
Director, Government Affairs
Tel: (202) 637-3800
Fax: (202) 637-3860

HARBER, Susan
Registered Federal Lobbyist
Tel: (202) 637-3800
Fax: (202) 637-3860

HOLMES, Stewart
Federal Lobbyist
Registered Federal Lobbyist
Tel: (202) 637-3800
Fax: (202) 637-3860

HOTSENPILLER, Susan
Federal Lobbyist
Registered Federal Lobbyist
Tel: (202) 637-3800
Fax: (202) 637-3860

ROWLAND, Robert
Senior Vice President, Washington Operations
Registered Federal Lobbyist
Tel: (202) 637-3800
Fax: (202) 637-3860

THOMAS, Gordon
Executive Director, Government Affairs
gthomas@dc.textron.com
Registered Federal Lobbyist
Tel: (202) 637-3821
Fax: (202) 637-3860

Textured Coatings of America

A manufacturer of textured coatings.
www.texcote.com
Annual Revenues: $9.0 million
Employees: 100
Industry/ies: Chemicals & Chemical Industry

Chairman of the Board
HAINES, Stuart
Tel: (800) 454-0340
Fax: (850) 913-8619

President and Chief Executive Officer
HAINES, Esq., Jay A.
Tel: (800) 454-0340
Fax: (850) 913-8619

Main Headquarters
Mailing: 2422 E. 15th St.
            Panama City, FL 32405-6348
Tel: (850) 769-0347
Fax: (850) 913-8619
TF: (800) 454-0340

Public Affairs and Related Activities Personnel

At Headquarters

MOWERY, Julie
Chief Financial Officer
Tel: (800) 454-0340
Fax: (850) 913-8619

TG & C Group

A bipartisan boutique government affairs consulting firm.
www.tgandcgroup.com
Legislative Issues: BAN; FIN; HCR; HOM; INS

Main Headquarters
Mailing: 601 13th St. NW
            11th Floor North
            Washington, DC 20005
Tel: (202) 534-1789

Public Affairs and Related Activities Personnel

At Headquarters

CRANE, David F.
Partner
David@TGandCgroup.com
Registered Federal Lobbyist
Tel: (202) 534-1789

DOBEK, Robert F.
Legislative Director, House of Representatives
Registered Federal Lobbyist
Tel: (202) 534-1789

GOULD, J. Eric
Partner & Associate Director, Domestic Policy, EOP
Eric@TGandCgroup.com
Registered Federal Lobbyist
Tel: (202) 534-1789

HOPKINS, Dan
Partner
Dan@TGandCgroup.com
Tel: (202) 534-1789

THURMAN, Hon. Karen L.
Partner
Karen@TGandCgroup.com
Registered Federal Lobbyist
Tel: (202) 534-1789

TH Lee Putnam Ventures

A technology-focused private equity firm whose primary focus is private transactions in later-stage venture companies whose success depends on the deployment and use of information technologies and who have established revenue streams, a clear path to profitability and strong management.
www.thlpv.com
Industry/ies: Banking/Finance/Investments

Main Headquarters
Mailing: 1120 Avenue of the Americas
            Suite 1807
            New York City, NY 10036
Tel: (212) 951-8600

Public Affairs and Related Activities Personnel

At Headquarters

BROWN, Jim
Managing Director
Tel: (212) 951-8600

PHILLIPS, Deirdre B.
Managing Director
Tel: (212) 951-8600

PIPE, Sharon
Managing Director
Tel: (212) 951-8600

RAGHAVENDRAN, Ramanan
Managing Director
Tel: (212) 951-8600

ROSSI, P.J.
Manager, Business Operations
pj.rossi@thlpv.com
Tel: (212) 951-8600

Thales Communications Inc.

Formerly known as Racal Communications. Makes handheld radio equipment.
www.thalescomminc.com
Annual Revenues: $44.00 million
Employees: 600
Industry/ies: Communications; Telecommunications/Internet/Cable
Legislative Issues: AVI; BUD; DEF; GOV

President and Chief Executive Officer
SHEEHAN, Michael
Tel: (240) 864-7000
Fax: (240) 864-7920

Main Headquarters
Mailing: 22605 Gateway Center Dr.
            Clarksburg, MD 20871
Tel: (240) 864-7000
Fax: (240) 864-7920
TF: (800) 258-4420

Corporate Foundations and Giving Programs

Thales Communications Contributions Program
22605 Gateway Center Dr.
Clarksburg, MD 20871
Tel: (240) 864-7000
Fax: (240) 864-7000

Public Affairs and Related Activities Personnel

At Headquarters

BORKEY, Todd
Chief Technology Officer and Vice President, Strategic Initiatives
Tel: (240) 864-7000
Fax: (240) 864-7920

BROSNAN, Aaron
Vice President, Business Development
Tel: (240) 864-7000
Fax: (240) 864-7920

FRANSEN, Dennis
Executive Vice President and Chief Financial Officer
Tel: (240) 864-7000
Fax: (240) 864-7920

Thales North America, Inc.

A subsidiary of Thales Group which is headquartered in France. Serves the U.S. government, defense, aerospace and security markets.
www.thalesgroup.com
Employees: 1,200
Industry/ies: Aerospace/Aviation; Communications; Defense/Homeland Security; Government-Related; Telecommunications/Internet/Cable; Transportation
Legislative Issues: AVI; DEF; HOM

President and Chief Executive Officer
PELLEGRINI, Alan
Tel: (703) 838-9685
Fax: (703) 838-1688

Main Headquarters
Mailing: 2733 S. Crystal Dr.
Tel: (703) 838-9685

Suite 1200
Arlington, VA 22202

Fax: (703) 838-1688

Public Affairs and Related Activities Personnel

At Headquarters

ARBEL, Pierre-Edouard
Chief Financial Officer

Tel: (703) 838-9685
Fax: (703) 838-1688

FOREMAN, Brad
Vice President, Business Development

Tel: (703) 838-9685
Fax: (703) 838-1688

FRASER, Jim
Vice President, Government Relations and Communications

Tel: (703) 838-9685
Fax: (703) 838-1688

FRASER, James H.
Vice President, Government Relations
jim.fraser@us.thalesgroup.com
Registered Federal Lobbyist

Tel: (703) 838-9685
Fax: (703) 838-1688

MARION, Daniel
Vice President, Legal and Contracts

Tel: (703) 838-9685
Fax: (703) 838-1688

MARKS, Adam
Vice President, Strategy, Marketing and Technology

Tel: (703) 838-9685
Fax: (703) 838-1688

RAMASAMY, Raj
Vice President, Information Technology

Tel: (703) 838-9685
Fax: (703) 838-1688

REED, Susanne
Vice President, Communications and Marketing

Tel: (703) 838-9685
Fax: (703) 838-1688

WYMAN-CLARKE, Andria
Vice President, Human Resources

Tel: (703) 838-9685
Fax: (703) 838-1688

The Shaw Group
See listing on page 171 under CB&I

Theragenics Corporation
Manufactures and markets its products, including TheraSeed®, a palladium-103 based device, I-Seed, an iodine-125 based device, and related products and service.
www.theragenics.com
Annual Revenues: $80.66 million
Employees: 534
Ticker: NYSE: TGX
SIC: 3825
Industry/ies: Medicine/Health Care/Mental Health
Legislative Issues: HCR

Chief Executive Officer & President
TARALLO, Francis J.
frankt@theragenics.com

Tel: (770) 271-0233
Fax: (770) 831-5294

Main Headquarters
Mailing: 5203 Bristol Industrial Way
Buford, GA 30518

Tel: (770) 271-0233
Fax: (770) 831-5294
TF: (800) 998-8479

Public Affairs and Related Activities Personnel

At Headquarters

RASSEL, Lisa
Exective Assistant CEO, Competitive Market Intelligence Officer
investor_relations@theragenics.com

Tel: (770) 831-5137
Fax: (770) 831-5294

SMALL, C. Russell
Executive Vice President, Sales and Marketing

Tel: (770) 271-0233
Fax: (770) 831-5294

SMITH, Bruce W.
Executive Vice President, Strategy and Business Development and Corporate Secretary

Tel: (770) 271-0233
Fax: (770) 831-5294

Thermo Electron Corporation
See listing on page 783 under Thermo Fisher Scientific Inc.

Thermo Fisher Scientific Inc.
A scientific technology company. Formed by the merger of Thermo Electron Corp. and Fisher Scientific International Inc.
www.thermofisher.com
Annual Revenues: $16.90 billion
Employees: 51,000
Ticker: NYSE: TMO
SIC: 3829
Industry/ies: Electricity & Electronics; Electronics; Energy/Electricity; Science; Scientific Research
Legislative Issues: BUD; GOV; HCR; HOM; MED; MMM; TAX

Chairman of the Board
MANZI, Jim P.

Tel: (781) 622-1000
Fax: (781) 622-1207

President and Chief Executive Officer
CASPER, Marc N.

Tel: (781) 622-1000
Fax: (781) 622-1207

Main Headquarters
Mailing: 81 Wyman St.
Waltham, MA 02451

Tel: (781) 622-1000
Fax: (781) 622-1207
TF: (800) 678-5599

Washington Office
Mailing: 1050 K St. NW, Suite 310
Washington, DC 20001

Political Action Committees
Thermo Fisher Scientific Inc. PAC
FEC ID: C00292318
Contact: Maura Spellman
81 Wyman St.
P.O. Box 9046
Waltham, MA 02454

Contributions to Candidates: $187,364 (2015-2016)
Democrats: $92,000; Republicans: $95,364

Principal Recipients

HOUSE
DENT, CHARLES W. REP. (REP-PA)

Corporate Foundations and Giving Programs
Thermo Fisher Foundation for Science
81 Wyman St.
Waltham, MA 02454

Thermo Fisher Scientific Contributions Program
81 Wyman St.
Waltham, MA 02454

Tel: (781) 622-1000
Fax: (781) 622-1207

Public Affairs and Related Activities Personnel

At Headquarters

APICERNO, Kenneth J.
Vice President, Investor Relations
ken.apicerno@thermofisher.com

Tel: (781) 622-1111
Fax: (781) 622-1207

BARR, Kerstin
Senior Marketing Manager
kbarr@ahurascientific.com

Tel: (781) 622-1000
Fax: (781) 622-1207

FENTON, Timothy
Federal Lobbyist & Director, Federal Government Relations
tim.fenton@thermofisher.com
Registered Federal Lobbyist

Tel: (781) 622-1000
Fax: (781) 622-1207

HOOGASIAN , Seth H.
Senior Vice President, General Counsel and Secretary

Tel: (781) 622-1000
Fax: (781) 622-1207

JENKINSON, Richard D.
Senior Advisor
rick.jenkinson@thermofisher.com

Tel: (781) 622-1240
Fax: (781) 622-1207

KIRKWOOD, Karen
Vice President, Corporate Communications
karen.kirkwood@thermofisher.com

Tel: (781) 622-1306
Fax: (781) 622-1207

MALUS , Alan J.
Executive Vice President and President, Laboratory Products and Services

Tel: (781) 622-1000
Fax: (781) 622-1207

O'BRIEN, Ron
Director, Public Relations
ron.obrien@thermofisher.com

Tel: (781) 622-1242
Fax: (781) 622-1207

PAK, Chol H.
Registered Federal Lobbyist

Tel: (781) 622-1000
Fax: (781) 622-1207

SPELLMAN, Maura
PAC Treasurer

Tel: (781) 622-1000
Fax: (781) 622-1207

STEVENSON, Mark P.
Executive Vice President and President, Life Sciences Solutions

Tel: (781) 622-1000
Fax: (781) 622-1207

WILVER, Peter M.
Senior Vice President and Chief Financial Officer

Tel: (781) 622-1000
Fax: (781) 622-1207

THIRTEEN WNET
Thirteen, is a non-commercial educational, public television station licensed to Newark, New Jersey, USA which provides educational, informational and cultural products and services, using all media. It is a unique cultural and educational institution that harnesses the power of television and electronic media to inform, enlighten, entertain and inspire.
www.thirteen.org
Annual Revenues: $154.62 million
Employees: 400
Industry/ies: Communications; Education; Media/Mass Communication

Chairman of the Board
TISCH, James S.

Tel: (212) 560-1313
Fax: (212) 560-1314

Main Headquarters
Mailing: 825 Eighth Ave.
New York City, NY 10019

Tel: (212) 560-1313
Fax: (212) 560-1314

Public Affairs and Related Activities Personnel

At Headquarters

DAVIS, Roslyn
Vice President, Media and Broadcast Operations and General Manager, THIRTEEN

Tel: (212) 560-1313
Fax: (212) 560-1314

SPECTER, Kellie
Senior Director, Communications and Marketing

Tel: (212) 560-1313
Fax: (212) 560-1314

specter@wnet.org

Thomas & Betts Corporation

A producer of connectors and components for worldwide electrical, communications, and utility markets.
www.tnb.com
Annual Revenues: $2.29 billion
Employees: 9,400
Ticker: NYSE: TNB
SIC: 3629; 3663; 5063; 5065; 5084
NAICS: 335999
Industry/ies: Electricity & Electronics; Electronics; Energy/Electricity

Main Headquarters

Mailing:	8155 T and B Blvd.	Tel:	(901) 252-5000
	Memphis, TN 38125	Fax:	(901) 252-1354

Public Affairs and Related Activities Personnel

At Headquarters

BERGERON, Patricia A.	Tel:	(901) 252-8000
Vice President, Investor and Corporate Relations	Fax:	(901) 252-1306
GANN, Peggy	Tel:	(901) 252-8000
Senior Vice President, Human Resources and Administration	Fax:	(901) 252-1354
LOCKE, Stanley P.	Tel:	(901) 252-8000
Vice President, Business Development and Strategic Planning	Fax:	(901) 252-1354
RAINES, J. N.	Tel:	(901) 252-8000
Vice President, General Counsel and Secretary	Fax:	(901) 252-1354
SMITH, Jr., W. David	Tel:	(901) 252-8000
Chief Compliance Officer, Assistant Secretary and Assistant General Counsel	Fax:	(901) 252-1354
david.smith@tnb.com		

Thompson Engineering TCO, Inc.

Thompson Engineering is a multi-disciplined engineering design, environmental consulting, construction management, construction inspection and materials testing firm.
thompsonengineering.com
Annual Revenues: $25.4 million
Employees: 325
Industry/ies: Engineering/Mathematics

Chairman of the Board	Tel:	(251) 666-2443
SEAWELL, III, Henry R.	Fax:	(251) 666-6422

Chief Executive Officer	Tel:	(251) 666-2443
SHUMOCK, James H.	Fax:	(251) 666-6422

President	Tel:	(251) 666-2443
BAKER III, John H.	Fax:	(251) 666-6422

Main Headquarters

Mailing:	2970 Cottage Hill Rd.	Tel:	(251) 666-2443
	Suite 190	Fax:	(251) 666-6422
	Mobile, AL 36606-4748		

Corporate Foundations and Giving Programs

Thompson Holding Foundation
Contact: Vester J. Thompson
2970 Cottage Hill Rd.
Suite 190
Mobile, AL 36606

Public Affairs and Related Activities Personnel

At Headquarters

BROWN, Chad R.	Tel:	(251) 666-2443
Chief Legal Officer & General Counsel	Fax:	(251) 666-6422
MANNING, Mike	Tel:	(251) 666-2443
Senior Vice President, Business Development	Fax:	(251) 666-6422
mmanning@thompsonengineering.com		
THOMPSON, Vester J.	Tel:	(251) 666-2443
Founder and Philanthropy Contact	Fax:	(251) 666-6422

Thomson Reuters Corporation

Formed by the merger between The Thomson Corp. and Reuters. A global integrated information solutions provider combining industry expertise with innovative technology to deliver critical information to leading decision makers in the financial and risk, legal, tax and accounting, intellectual property and science and media markets. It sells electronic content and services to professionals primarily on a subscription basis.
thomsonreuters.com
Annual Revenues: $12.52 billion
Employees: 53,000
Ticker: NYSE: TRI
SIC: 2741
Industry/ies: Communications; Computer/Technology; Media/Mass Communication

Chairman of the Board	Tel:	(646) 223-4000
THOMSON, David	Fax:	(646) 223-4547

President and Chief Executive Officer	Tel:	(646) 223-4000
SMITH, James C.	Fax:	(646) 223-4547

Main Headquarters

Mailing:	Three Times Sq.	Tel:	(646) 223-4000
	New York City, NY 10036	Fax:	(646) 223-4547

Washington Office

Mailing:	1333 H St. NW	Tel:	(202) 898-8300
	Washington, DC 20005		

Corporate Foundations and Giving Programs

Thomson Reuters Foundation
Contact: David Binnet
Three Times Sq.
New York City, NY 10036

Public Affairs and Related Activities Personnel

At Headquarters

BELLO, Stephane	Tel:	(646) 223-4000
Executive Vice President and Chief Financial Officer	Fax:	(646) 223-4547
BINNET, David	Tel:	(646) 223-4000
Deputy Chairman	Fax:	(646) 223-4547
CARLSON, Gustav	Tel:	(646) 223-8313
Executive Vice President and Chief Communications Officer	Fax:	(646) 223-4547
gus.carlson@thomsonreuters.com		
CLARK, Abel	Tel:	(646) 223-4000
Managing Director, Marketplaces, Financial and Risk	Fax:	(646) 223-4547
GOLDEN, Frank	Tel:	(646) 223-5288
Senior Vice President, Investor Relations	Fax:	(646) 223-4547
frank.golden@thomsonreuters.com		
KING, Richard H.	Tel:	(646) 223-4000
Executive Vice President and Chief Operating Officer, Technology	Fax:	(646) 223-4547
SHAUGHNESSY, John	Tel:	(651) 687-4749
Vice President, Corporate Communications	Fax:	(646) 223-4547
john.shaughnessy@thomson.com		
STANLEY, Deirdre	Tel:	(646) 223-4000
Executive Vice President, General Counsel and Secretary	Fax:	(646) 223-4547

At Washington Office

COX, Chris	Tel:	(202) 898-8300
Accelus Advisory Board		

Thomson West

A provider of e-information and solutions for the U.S. legal market. A division of The Thomson Corporation (see separate listing).
legalsolutions.thomsonreuters.com
Employees: 16,000
Industry/ies: Communications; Law/Law Firms; Media/Mass Communication

Main Headquarters

Mailing:	610 Opperman Dr.	Tel:	(651) 687-7000
	Eagan, MN 55123	Fax:	(651) 687-7302
		TF:	(800) 344-5008

Public Affairs and Related Activities Personnel

At Headquarters

FRIEDLAND, Edward	Tel:	(651) 687-7000
General Counsel	Fax:	(651) 687-7302
ed.friedland@thomson.com		
MORAN, Tom	Tel:	(651) 687-7000
Senior Vice President, Human Resources	Fax:	(651) 687-7302
thomas.moran@thomson.com		
WARWICK, Peter	Tel:	(651) 687-7000
Chief People Officer	Fax:	(651) 687-7302

Thomson-CSF Inc.

See listing on page 782 under Thales North America, Inc.

Thoratec Corporation

Thoratec provides a mechanical circulatory support portfolio to treat a range of clinical needs.
www.thoratec.com
Annual Revenues: $473.17 million
Employees: 954
Ticker: NASDAQ: THOR
SIC: 3845
Industry/ies: Medicine/Health Care/Mental Health

Chairman of the Board	Tel:	(925) 847-8600
DIMICK, Neil F.	Fax:	(925) 847-8571

President, Chief Executive Officer and Director	Tel:	(925) 847-8600
GROSSMAN, D. Keith	Fax:	(925) 847-8571

Main Headquarters

Mailing:	6035 Stoneridge Dr.	Tel:	(925) 847-8600
	Pleasanton, CA 94588	Fax:	(925) 847-8571
		TF:	(800) 456-1477

Public Affairs and Related Activities Personnel

At Headquarters

HARRIS, Taylor
Vice President and Chief Financial Officer
Tel: (925) 847-8600
Fax: (925) 847-8571

LEHMAN, David A.
Senior Vice President and General Counsel
Tel: (925) 847-8600
Fax: (925) 847-8571

RUSSELL, Susan Benton
Contact, Media Relations
susan@bentoncommunications.com
Tel: (310) 697-3488
Fax: (925) 847-8571

Thorium Power
See listing on page 491 under Lightbridge Corporation

Three Rivers Holdings, LLC
See listing on page 609 under Out-Front

Thrivent Financial for Lutherans
A fraternal benefit society formed from the merger of Aid Association for Lutherans and Lutheran Brotherhood. It is a not-for-profit, membership organization of Christians.
www.thrivent.com
Annual Revenues: $8.94 billion
Employees: 3,000
Industry/ies: Taxation
Legislative Issues: FIN; TAX

Chairman of the Board
MOELLER, Frank H.
Tel: (920) 734-5721
Fax: (800) 205-8348

President and Chief Executive Officer
HEWITT, Brad L.
Tel: (612) 340-7000
Fax: (800) 205-8348

Main Headquarters
Mailing: 4321 N. Ballard Rd.
Appleton, WI 54919-0001
Tel: (920) 734-5721
Fax: (800) 205-8348
TF: (800) 847-4836

Political Action Committees
Thrivent Financial for Lutherans-Employee PAC
FEC ID: C00121319
Contact: Magan A. Devalk
P.O. Box 1892
Appleton, WI 54912

   Contributions to Candidates: $204,500 (2015-2016)
   Democrats: $67,500; Republicans: $134,000; Other: $3,000

   ### Principal Recipients
      #### HOUSE
      DUFFY, SEAN (REP-WI)
      NOEM, KRISTI LYNN (REP-SD)
      PAULSEN, ERIK (REP-MN)
      STIVERS, STEVE MR. (REP-OH)

Corporate Foundations and Giving Programs

Lutheran Community Foundation
625 Fourth Ave., South
Minneapolis, MN 55415
Tel: (800) 365-4172
Fax: (612) 844-4110

Thrivent Financial for Lutherans Foundation
Contact: Marie A. Uhrich
625 Fourth Ave., South
Minneapolis, MN 55415

Public Affairs and Related Activities Personnel

At Headquarters

BOUSHEK, Randy
Senior Vice President, Chief Financial Officer and Treasurer
randy.boushek@thrivent.com
Tel: (612) 340-7000
Fax: (800) 225-2264

GIBSON, Debi
Senior Administrative Assistant
debi.gibson@thrivent.com
Tel: (612) 844-7059
Fax: (800) 205-8348

MORET, Pamela J.
Senior Vice President, Strategic Development
Tel: (612) 340-7000
Fax: (800) 205-8348

SAMPLE, Anne
Senior Vice President, Chief Human Resources Officer
Tel: (920) 734-5721
Fax: (800) 205-8348

SWANSEN, Russell W.
Senior Vice President and Chief Investment Officer
Tel: (612) 340-7000
Fax: (800) 205-8348

UHRICH, Marie A.
Vice President, Membership Marketing
marie.uhrich@thrivent.com
Tel: (612) 340-7000
Fax: (800) 205-8348

WEINBERG, Brett
Director, Public Relations
Tel: (612) 219-3244
Fax: (800) 205-8348

At Other Offices

BRIESE, Callie L.
Senior Media Relations Specialist
625 Fourth Ave., South
Minneapolis, MN 55415-1624
callie.briese@thrivent.com
Tel: (612) 844-7340
Fax: (612) 240-7373

BROSNAN, Sharon
Tel: (612) 844-7216

Director, Government Affairs
625 Fourth Ave., South
Minneapolis, MN 55415-1624
Fax: (612) 240-7373

CASEY, Brian
Federal Lobbyist
625 Fourth Ave., South
Minneapolis, MN 55415-1624
Tel: (612) 844-7216
Fax: (612) 240-7373

DEVALK, Magan A.
PAC Treasurer
P.O. Box 1892
Appleton, WI 54912
Tel: (920) 734-5721
Fax: (800) 205-8348

KLEVEN, Richard
Vice President, Government Affairs
625 Fourth Ave., South
Minneapolis, MN 55415-1624
richard.kleven@thrivent.com
Tel: (612) 844-7216
Fax: (612) 240-7373

RASMUSSEN, Teresa J.
Senior Vice President, General Counsel and Secretary
625 Fourth Ave., South
Minneapolis, MN 55415-1624
teresa.rasmussen@thrivent.com
Tel: (612) 844-7216
Fax: (612) 240-7373

THENELL, Heather
Senior Counsel
625 Fourth Ave., South
Minneapolis, MN 55415-1624
heather.thenell@thrivent.com
Tel: (612) 844-7216
Fax: (612) 240-7373

THOMSEN, James A.
Senior Vice President and Chief Marketing Officer
625 Fourth Ave., South
Minneapolis, MN 55415-1624
Tel: (612) 844-7216
Fax: (612) 240-7373

ThyssenKrupp AG
Formerly known as The Budd Company. A subsidiary of ThyssenKrupp Automotive AG (which is a subsidiary of German company ThyssenKrupp AG). Manufactures automotive body parts.
www.thyssenkrupp.com
Annual Revenues: $5.10 million
Employees: 100
Industry/ies: Automotive Industry; Transportation

Chairman of the Executive Board
HIESINGER, Dr. -Ing. Heinrich
Tel: (248) 530-2900
Fax: (248) 530-2929

Main Headquarters
Mailing: 3331 W. Big Beaver Rd.
Troy, MI 48084-3002
Tel: (248) 530-2900
Fax: (248) 530-2929

TIAA-CREF
A nationwide financial services organization whose full name is Teachers Insurance and Annuity Association-College Retirement Equities Fund, providing lifelong financial security for those in the academic, cultural, governmental, medical and research fields.
www.tiaa-cref.org
Annual Revenues: $33.81 billion
Employees: 12,500
Industry/ies: Education; Insurance Industry
Legislative Issues: BAN; FIN; INS; RET; TAX

Chairman of the Board
THOMPSON, Ronald L.
Tel: (704) 595-1000
Fax: (212) 916-4840

President and Chief Executive Officer
FERGUSON, PhD, Jr., Roger W.
Tel: (704) 595-1000
Fax: (212) 916-4840

Main Headquarters
Mailing: P.O. Box 1259
Charlotte, NC 28201
Tel: (704) 595-1000
Fax: (212) 916-4840
TF: (800) 842-2252

Washington Office
Mailing: 601 13th St. NW
Suite 700, North
Washington, DC 20005
Tel: (202) 637-0090
Fax: (202) 342-0605
TF: (800) 842-2008

Political Action Committees
Teachers Insurance Annuity Assoc of America College Retirement Equit Fund
PAC TIAA-CREF
FEC ID: C00431361
Contact: Larry M. Chadwick
601 13th St. NW
Suite 700, North
Washington, DC 20005
Tel: (202) 637-0090
Fax: (202) 342-0605

   Contributions to Candidates: $210,500 (2015-2016)
   Democrats: $97,000; Republicans: $113,500

Public Affairs and Related Activities Personnel

At Headquarters

BECKER, Brandon
Executive Vice President and Chief Legal Officer
Tel: (704) 595-1000
Fax: (212) 916-4840

PETERSON, Chad
Tel: (212) 916-4808

Senior Director, Corporate Media Relations | Fax: (212) 916-4840
cpeterson@tiaa-cref.org

PRESSMAN, Ron | Tel: (704) 595-1000
Executive Vice President and Chief Operating Officer | Fax: (212) 916-4840

SPRIGGS , III, Otha T. "Skip" | Tel: (704) 595-1000
Executive Vice President and Chief Human Resources Officer | Fax: (212) 916-4840

TETUAN, Mike | Tel: (704) 988-2790
Senior Director, Media Relations | Fax: (212) 916-4840
Michael.Tetuan@tiaa-cref.org

WEAVER, Constance K. | Tel: (704) 595-1000
Executive Vice President and Chief Marketing Officer | Fax: (212) 916-4840

WILSON, Virginia M. (Gina) | Tel: (704) 595-1000
Executive Vice President and Chief Financial Officer | Fax: (212) 916-4840

At Washington Office

CHADWICK, Larry M. | Tel: (202) 637-0090
Vice President, Federal Government Relations Public Policy, | Fax: (202) 342-0605
Lobbyist and PAC Treasurer
Registered Federal Lobbyist

SPENCE, Christopher | Tel: (202) 637-0090
Senior Director, Federal Government Relations & Public | Fax: (202) 342-0605
Policy
Registered Federal Lobbyist

SPRINGER, Edie | Tel: (202) 637-0090
| Fax: (202) 342-0605

At Other Offices

BROWN, Jill | Tel: (202) 637-0090
Federal Lobbyist | Fax: (202) 347-2974
1101 Pennsylvania Ave. NW, Suite 800
Washington, DC 20004
Registered Federal Lobbyist

DILANDRO, Sue | Tel: (202) 637-0090
Vice President, Compliance & Political Programs | Fax: (202) 347-2974
1101 Pennsylvania Ave. NW, Suite 800
Washington, DC 20004
sdilandro@tiaa-cref.org
Registered Federal Lobbyist

ELINSKI, Karen | Tel: (212) 490-9000
Vice President, Associate General Counsel & Acting Head, | Fax: (212) 913-2803
Government Relations
750 Third Ave.
New York City, NY 10017-3206
kelinski@tiaa-cref.org
Registered Federal Lobbyist

HODAS, Samuel | Tel: (202) 637-0090
Lobbyist | Fax: (202) 347-2974
1101 Pennsylvania Ave. NW, Suite 800
Washington, DC 20004
Registered Federal Lobbyist

SNOW, Kimberley | Tel: (202) 637-0090
Director, Compliance and Political Programs | Fax: (202) 347-2974
1101 Pennsylvania Ave. NW, Suite 800
Washington, DC 20004
Registered Federal Lobbyist

Tiber Creek Associates of Capitol Hill, Inc.

A lobbying, public relations and strategic consulting firm.
www.tiberdc.com
Legislative Issues: HOU; IND

Founder and President | Tel: (202) 543-5755
BOESEN, Christopher | Fax: (202) 543-5288
chris@tiberdc.com

Main Headquarters
Mailing: 330 Pennsylvania Ave. SE | Tel: (202) 543-5755
Third Floor | Fax: (202) 543-5288
Washington, DC 20003

Public Affairs and Related Activities Personnel

At Headquarters

BOESEN, Thomas | Tel: (202) 543-5755
Chief Operations Officer | Fax: (202) 543-5288

PARK, Anna | Tel: (202) 543-5755
Legislative Associate | Fax: (202) 543-5288

Tiber Creek Health Strategies, Inc.

Government relations.
www.tchs-dc.com
Legislative Issues: HCR; MED; MMM; PHA; TAX

President | Tel: (202) 496-2122
HALL, Bryant | Fax: (202) 223-0358
bhall@tchs-dc.com

Main Headquarters

Mailing: 1300 Connecticut Ave. NW | Tel: (202) 496-2122
Suite 600 | Fax: (202) 223-0358
Washington, DC 20036

Washington Office
Mailing: 1300 Connecticut Ave. NW
Sixth Floor
Washington, DC 20036

Public Affairs and Related Activities Personnel

At Headquarters

HARRELL, Wanda | Tel: (202) 496-2122
Director, Operations of Peck | Fax: (202) 223-0358

PECK, Jeffrey J. | Tel: (202) 496-2122
Partner | Fax: (202) 223-0358

SMITH, Sarah T. | Tel: (202) 496-2122
Federal Lobbyist | Fax: (202) 223-0358
ssmith@gmail.com

TicketNetwork

A secondary ticketing company.
www.ticketnetwork.com
Industry/ies: Sports/Leisure/Entertainment
Legislative Issues: ART

Director, Government Relations | Tel: (860) 870-3400
PULLIUM, Daniel

Main Headquarters
Mailing: 75 Gerber Rd., East | Tel: (860) 870-3400
South Windsor, CT 06074 | TF: (888) 456-8499

Public Affairs and Related Activities Personnel

At Headquarters

VANDEHOEF, Chris | Tel: (860) 870-3400
Director, Government Relations
Registered Federal Lobbyist

Tidewater Inc.

Provider of marine support services for the offshore energy industry.
www.tdw.com
Annual Revenues: $1.50 billion
Employees: 8,900
Ticker: NYSE: TDW
SIC: 4400
Industry/ies: Marine/Maritime/Shipping; Transportation
Legislative Issues: MAR

Chairman of the Board | Tel: (504) 568-1010
PATTAROZZI, R.A. | Fax: (504) 566-4582

Director, President and Chief Executive Officer | Tel: (504) 568-1010
PLATT , Jeffrey M. | Fax: (504) 566-4582

Main Headquarters
Mailing: 601 Poydras St. | Tel: (504) 568-1010
Suite 1500 | Fax: (504) 566-4582
New Orleans, LA 70130 | TF: (800) 678-8433

Political Action Committees
Tidewater Inc. PAC (TIDEPAC)
FEC ID: C00199471
Contact: Joseph M. Bennett
601 Poydras St.
Suite 1500
New Orleans, LA 70130

Contributions to Candidates: $2,500 (2015-2016)
Republicans: $2,500

Corporate Foundations and Giving Programs
Tidewater Contributions Program
601 Poydras St.
Suite 1900
New Orleans, LA 70130

Public Affairs and Related Activities Personnel

At Headquarters

BENNETT, Joseph M. | Tel: (504) 568-1010
Executive Vice President, Chief Investor Relations Officer and | Fax: (504) 566-4582
PAC Treasurer
Mail Stop Suite 1900

DEMAREST, Craig J. | Tel: (504) 568-1010
Vice President, Principal Accounting Officer and Controller | Fax: (504) 566-4582

FANNING, Quinn P. | Tel: (504) 568-1010
Executive Vice President and Chief Financial Officer | Fax: (504) 566-4582

GORSKI, Jeffrey A. | Tel: (504) 568-1010
Executive Vice President and Chief Operating Officer | Fax: (504) 566-4582

LUNDSTROM, Bruce D. | Tel: (504) 568-1010
Senior Vice President, General Counsel and Secretary | Fax: (504) 566-4582

MANCHESKI, Mathew
Vice President
mmancheski@tdw.com

| Tel: | (504) 568-1010 |
| Fax: | (504) 566-4582 |

WILLINGHAM, Debbie
Chief Human Resources Officer

| Tel: | (504) 568-1010 |
| Fax: | (504) 566-4582 |

At Other Offices

ORTH, Chris
Vice President, Sales
2000 W. Sam Houston Pkwy., South, Suite 1280
Houston, TX 77042

| Tel: | (713) 470-5300 |
| Fax: | (713) 470-0077 |

Tiffany & Company

A retailer of fine jewelry, timepieces, china, crystal, sterling silver, leather goods, fragrances, stationery, and accessories and believes to have a moral imperative to help sustain the natural beauty that inspires designers, customers and employees.
www.tiffany.com
Annual Revenues: $4.03 billion
Employees: 12,200
Ticker: NYSE: TIF
SIC: 3262; 3873; 3911; 3914; 3952
NAICS: 327215; 334518; 339912; 339941; 339911
Industry/ies: Jewelry & Gems
Legislative Issues: NAT; TRD

Chairman of the Board
KOWALSKI, CAE, Michael J.
michaeljkowalski@tiffany.com

| Tel: | (212) 755-8000 |
| Fax: | (212) 605-4465 |

Chief Executive Officer
CUMENAL, Frederic

| Tel: | (212) 755-8000 |
| Fax: | (212) 605-4465 |

Main Headquarters
Mailing: 727 Fifth Ave.
New York City, NY 10022

Tel:	(212) 755-8000
Fax:	(212) 605-4465
TF:	(800) 843-3269

Corporate Foundations and Giving Programs

Tiffany & Company Foundation
Contact: Fernanda M. Kellogg
600 Madison Ave.
New York City, NY 10022

Public Affairs and Related Activities Personnel

At Headquarters

BELLAICHE, Jean-Marc
Senior Vice President, Strategy and Business Development

| Tel: | (212) 755-8000 |
| Fax: | (212) 605-4465 |

BERGER-GROSS, Victoria
Senior Vice President, Global Human Resources

| Tel: | (212) 755-8000 |
| Fax: | (212) 605-4465 |

CLOUD, Pamela H.
Senior Vice President, Global Category Marketing

| Tel: | (212) 755-8000 |
| Fax: | (212) 605-4465 |

GLOVER, Carson
Group Director, Worldwide Media Relations
carson.glover@tiffany.com

| Tel: | (212) 755-8000 |
| Fax: | (212) 605-4465 |

HARLAN, Leigh M.
Senior Vice President, General Counsel and Secretary

| Tel: | (212) 230-5320 |
| Fax: | (212) 605-4465 |

NAGGIAR, Caroline D.
Senior Vice President, Chief Brand Officer

| Tel: | (212) 755-8000 |
| Fax: | (212) 605-4465 |

NICOLETTI, Ralph
Executive Vice President and Chief Financial Officer

| Tel: | (212) 755-8000 |
| Fax: | (212) 605-4465 |

PETTERSON, John S.
Senior Vice President, Global Operations and Customer Services

| Tel: | (212) 755-8000 |
| Fax: | (212) 605-4465 |

At Other Offices

AARON, Mark L.
Vice President, Investor Relations and Media Contact
200 Fifth Ave.
New York City, NY 10010
mark.aaron@tiffany.com

| Tel: | (212) 230-5301 |

Timberland Company

Manufacturer of footwear and apparel.
www.timberland.com
Annual Revenues: $1.5 billion
Employees: 5,600
Ticker: NYSE: TBL
SIC: 2389; 3149
NAICS: 315999; 316219
Industry/ies: Apparel/Textiles Industry
Legislative Issues: TAR; TRD

President
FRISK, Patrik

| Tel: | (603) 772-9500 |
| Fax: | (603) 773-1640 |

Main Headquarters
Mailing: 200 Domain Dr.
Stratham, NH 03885

Tel:	(603) 772-9500
Fax:	(603) 773-1640
TF:	(888) 802-9947

Public Affairs and Related Activities Personnel

At Headquarters

GRUNDY, Leslie
Director, Public Relations and Communications
Leslie_Grundy@vfc.com

| Tel: | (603) 772-9500 |
| Fax: | (603) 773-1640 |

KOMIEGA, Samantha
Manager, Public Relation

| Tel: | (603) 772-9500 |
| Fax: | (603) 773-1640 |

MCGOVERN, Brian
Senior Marketing Manager
bmcgovern@timberland.com

| Tel: | (603) 772-9500 |
| Fax: | (603) 773-1640 |

VANDERBECK, Cara
Corporate Communications Specialist
cvanderbeck@timberland.com

| Tel: | (603) 773-1222 |
| Fax: | (603) 773-1640 |

Time Domain Corporation

Technology product manufacturing company developing and deploying Ultra Wideband (UWB) products. It holds the premier patent portfolio for UWB technology.
www.timedomain.com
Annual Revenues: $11.40 million
Employees: 100
Industry/ies: Science; Scientific Research

Chairman of the Board
YOUNGBLOOD, Kneeland

| Tel: | (256) 922-9229 |
| Fax: | (257) 922-0387 |

President and Chief Executive Officer
REINHARDT, Rachel
rachel.reinhardt@timedomain.com

| Tel: | (256) 922-9229 |
| Fax: | (256) 922-0387 |

Main Headquarters
Mailing: Cummings Research Park
4955 Corporate Dr., Suite 101
Huntsville, AL 35805

Tel:	(256) 922-9229
Fax:	(256) 922-0387
TF:	(888) 826-8378

Public Affairs and Related Activities Personnel

At Headquarters

BUSZKA, Tony
Chief Financial Officer

| Tel: | (256) 922-9229 |
| Fax: | (256) 922-0387 |

GOODMAN, Jennifer
Senior Vice President, Human Resources and Corporate Communications

| Tel: | (256) 922-9229 |
| Fax: | (257) 922-0387 |

HEDGES, Jon
Director, Sales and Marketing
jon.hedges@timedomain.com

| Tel: | (256) 288-6720 |
| Fax: | (256) 922-0387 |

Time Warner Cable

Time Warner Cable offers Digital Cable TV, High-Speed Online and Digital Phone services across the nation.
www.timewarnercable.com
Annual Revenues: $23.01 billion
Employees: 54,430
Ticker: NYSE: TWC
SIC: 4841; 7812
NAICS: 515210
Industry/ies: Communications; Computer/Technology; Media/Mass Communication; Telecommunications/Internet/Cable
Legislative Issues: COM; CPT; LBR; TAX; TEC

Chairman and Chief Executive Officer
MARCUS, Robert D.

| Tel: | (704) 377-9600 |

Main Headquarters
Mailing: 60 Columbus Cir.
17th Floor
New York City, NY 10023

| Tel: | (212) 364-8200 |

Washington Office
Mailing: 901 F St. NW
Suite 800
Washington, DC 20004

| Tel: | (202) 370-4200 |
| TF: | (800) 892-4357 |

Political Action Committees

Charter Communications Inc. PAC
FEC ID: C00426775
Contact: Paul Cancienne
12405 Powerscourt Dr.
St. Louis, MO 63131

| Tel: | (202) 973-3412 |
| Fax: | (202) 973-4499 |

Contributions to Candidates: $329,000 (2015-2016)
Democrats: $148,000; Republicans: $177,000; Other: $4,000

Principal Recipients

SENATE
THUNE, JOHN (REP-SD)

HOUSE
BLACKBURN, MARSHA MRS. (REP-TN)
WAGNER, ANN L. (REP-MO)

Time Warner Cable Inc. Federal Political Action Committee
FEC ID: C00431551

Contact: Rachel Welch
901 F St. NW
Suite 800
Washington, DC 20004

Tel: (202) 530-5454
Fax: (202) 530-7860

Contributions to Candidates: $331,900 (2015-2016)
Democrats: $126,500; Republicans: $205,400

Corporate Foundations and Giving Programs

Charter Communications, Inc. Contributions Program
12405 Powerscourt Dr.
Suite 100
St. Louis, MO 63131

Tel: (314) 965-0555
Fax: (314) 965-9745

Public Affairs and Related Activities Personnel

At Headquarters

EAST, Ellen M.
Executive Vice President and Chief Communications Officer

Tel: (212) 364-8200

GILLMAN, Joan Hogan
Chief Operating Officer

Tel: (212) 364-8200

LAWRENCE-APFELBAUM, Marc
Executive Vice President, General Counsel and Secretary

Tel: (212) 364-8200

OSBOURN, JR., William F.
Senior Vice President, Controller and Chief Accounting Officer and Acting Co-Chief Financial Officer

Tel: (212) 364-8200

ROBEY, Thomas
Senior Vice President, Investor Relations
ir@twcable.com

Tel: (212) 364-8200

STERN, Peter C.
Executive Vice President and Chief Product, People and Strategy Officer

Tel: (212) 364-8200

At Washington Office

AN, Edward
Federal Lobbyist

Tel: (202) 370-4200

BAXTER, Todd
Regional Vice President, Government Relations, Texas Region
todd.baxter@twcable.com

Tel: (202) 370-4200

BOHIGIAN, Catherine
Executive Vice President, Government Affairs
Registered Federal Lobbyist

Tel: (202) 370-4200

CANCIENNE, Paul
PAC Contact
Registered Federal Lobbyist

Tel: (202) 370-4200

DOLLINS, Crystal
Manager, Federal Government Affairs
Registered Federal Lobbyist

Tel: (202) 370-4200

HODGES, C. Howie
Vice President, External Affairs

Tel: (202) 370-4200

MACKINNON, Gail G.
Executive Vice President & Chief Government Relations Officer

Tel: (202) 370-4200

MCMILLAN, Waldo
Registered Federal Lobbyist

Tel: (202) 370-4200

MINSON, Jr., Arthur T.
Executive Vice President and Chief Financial Officer

Tel: (202) 370-4200

ROGERS, Cinnamon
Vice President, Federal Affairs

Tel: (202) 370-4200

TEPLITZ, Steven N.
Federal Lobbyist

Tel: (202) 370-4200

WELCH, Rachel
Lobbyist and PAC Treasurer

Tel: (202) 370-4200

WILLIAMS, Patrick

Tel: (202) 370-4200

At Other Offices

JAIN, Dinesh C.
Chief Operating Officer
7800 Crescent Executive Dr.
Charlotte, NC 28217

Tel: (704) 377-9600

Time Warner Telecom Inc.

See listing on page 804 under TW Telecom Inc.

Time Warner Inc.

A media and entertainment company with businesses in television networks, filmed entertainment and publishing, with multiple distribution outlets.
www.timewarner.com
Annual Revenues: $28.30 billion
Employees: 24,800
Ticker: NYSE: TWX
SIC: 7812
Industry/ies: Communications; Computer/Technology; Media/Mass Communication; Telecommunications/Internet/Cable

Legislative Issues: ADV; AVI; COM; CPI; CPT; CSP; IMM; MIA; TAX; TEC; TRA; TRD

Chairman of the Board and Chief Executive Officer
BEWKES, Jeffrey L.
jeff.bewkes@timewarner.com

Tel: (202) 530-7868
Fax: (202) 530-7860

Main Headquarters
Mailing: One Time Warner Center
New York City, NY 10019-8016

Tel: (212) 484-8000
Fax: (212) 489-6183
TF: (866) 463-6899

Washington Office
Mailing: 800 Connecticut Ave. NW
Suite 1200
Washington, DC 20006

Tel: (202) 530-7878
Fax: (202) 530-7860

Political Action Committees
Time Warner Inc. PAC
FEC ID: C00339291
Contact: Steven F. Vest
800 Connecticut Ave. NW
Suite 1200
Washington, DC 20006

Tel: (202) 530-5454
Fax: (202) 530-7860

Contributions to Candidates: $262,000 (2015-2016)
Democrats: $126,500; Republicans: $133,500; Other: $2,000

Principal Recipients

HOUSE
GOODLATTE, ROBERT W. (REP-VA)

Public Affairs and Related Activities Personnel

At Headquarters

AVERILL, Howard M.
Executive Vice President and Chief Financial Officer

Tel: (212) 484-8000
Fax: (212) 489-6183

CAPPUCCIO, Paul T.
Executive Vice President and General Counsel
Paul.Cappuccio@timewarner.com

Tel: (212) 484-8000
Fax: (212) 489-6183

COCOZZA, Keith
Vice President, Corporate Communications
keith.cocozza@timewarner.com

Tel: (212) 484-8000
Fax: (212) 489-6183

GINSBERG, Gary L.
Executive Vice President, Corporate Marketing and Communications

Tel: (212) 484-8000
Fax: (212) 489-6183

MAGEE , Karen
Executive Vice President and Chief Human Resources Officer

Tel: (212) 484-8000
Fax: (212) 489-6183

OLAFSSON, Olaf J.
Executive Vice President, International and Corporate Strategy
olaf.olafsson@timewarner.com

Tel: (212) 484-8000
Fax: (212) 489-6183

QUIROZ, Lisa
Chief Diversity Officer and Senior Vice President
Lisa.Quiroz@timewarner.com

Tel: (212) 484-8000
Fax: (212) 489-6183

At Washington Office

DIXON, Kyle D.
Vice President, Public Policy
Registered Federal Lobbyist

Tel: (202) 530-7868
Fax: (202) 530-7860

GILREATH, Cameron
Vice President, Public Policy
cameron.gilreath@timewarner.com
Registered Federal Lobbyist

Tel: (202) 530-5454
Fax: (202) 530-7860

HURVITZ, Joshua
Vice President, Public Policy
josh.hurvitz@timewarner.com
Registered Federal Lobbyist

Tel: (202) 530-7868
Fax: (202) 530-7860

MELTON, Carol A.
Executive Vice President, Global Public Policy
Registered Federal Lobbyist

Tel: (202) 530-5454
Fax: (202) 530-7860

VEST, Steven F.
steve.vest@timewarner.com
Registered Federal Lobbyist

Tel: (202) 530-7878
Fax: (202) 530-7860

TIMET

See listing on page 790 under Titanium Metals Corporation

Timex Group USA, Inc.

Watch manufacturer
global.timex.com
Annual Revenues: $180 million
Employees: 2,000
Industry/ies: Jewelry & Gems

Chairman of the Board
OLSEN, Annette

Tel: (203) 346-5000
Fax: (203) 346-5139

President and Chief Executive Officer
COHEN, Gary S.

Tel: (203) 346-5000
Fax: (203) 346-5139

Main Headquarters

Mailing:	555 Christian Rd.	Tel:	(203) 346-5000
	P.O. Box 310	Fax:	(203) 346-5139
	Middlebury, CT 06762	TF:	(800) 448-4639

Public Affairs and Related Activities Personnel

At Headquarters

BURNES, Jeff	Tel:	(203) 346-5000
Contact, Media Relations	Fax:	(203) 346-5139
jeff@burnes.net.au		
MORISSETTE, Arthur	Tel:	(203) 346-5000
Senior Vice President, Finance & Chief Financial Officer	Fax:	(203) 346-5139

The Timken Company

A manufacturer of anti-friction bearings and alloy steel products. Acquired Torrington Co. in February, 2003.
www.timken.com
Annual Revenues: $4.36 billion
Employees: 14,000
Ticker: NYSE: TKR
SIC: 3312; 3316; 3317; 3325; 3562
NAICS: 332991; 331221; 331221; 331513
Industry/ies: Metals
Legislative Issues: BUD; DEF; ENG; ENV; IMM; LBR; TAX; TRD

Chairman of the Board	Tel:	(330) 438-3000
TIMKEN, Jr., Ward J.	Fax:	(330) 471-4041
President and Chief Executive Officer	Tel:	(234) 262-3000
KYLE, Richard G.		

Main Headquarters

Mailing:	4500 Mount Pleasant St. NW	Tel: (234) 262-3000
	N. Canton, OH 44720	

Political Action Committees

The Timken Good Government Fund PAC
FEC ID: C00311308
Contact: Jeffrey R. Dafler
1835 Dueber Ave. SW
Canton, OH 44706-0932

> **Contributions to Candidates:** $56,200 (2015-2016)
> Democrats: $3,500; Republicans: $52,700

> **Principal Recipients**

> > **HOUSE**
> > RENACCI, JAMES B. (REP-OH)

Corporate Foundations and Giving Programs

Timken Charitable Trust
1835 Dueber Ave. SW
Canton, OH 44706

Timken Foundation of Canton
Contact: Ward J. Timken Jr.
1835 Dueber Ave. SW
Canton, OH 44706

Public Affairs and Related Activities Personnel

At Headquarters

BURKHART, William R.	Tel:	(234) 262-3000
Senior Vice President and General Counsel		
william.burkhart@timken.com		
DAFLER, Jeffrey R.	Tel:	(234) 262-3000
Vice President, Government Affairs & PAC Contact		
Registered Federal Lobbyist		
FRACASSA, Philip D.	Tel:	(234) 262-3000
Chief Financial Officer		
GROH, Kari	Tel:	(234) 262-3000
Vice President, Communications and Public Relations		
groh@timken.com		
MENNING, J. Ron	Tel:	(234) 262-3000
Senior Vice President, Strategy and Development		
MYERS, Ronald J.	Tel:	(234) 262-3000
Vice President, Human Resources		
SCHILLING, Michael T.	Tel:	(234) 262-3000
Vice President, Corporate Development		
THARP, Christina	Tel:	(234) 262-3000
Global Manager, Marketing Communications		
christina.tharp@timken.com		
TSCHIEGG, Steven D.	Tel:	(330) 471-7446
Director, Capital Markets and Investor Relations		
Mail Stop WHQ-03		

At Other Offices

CLARK, Jeffrey A.	Tel:	(330) 438-3000
Vice President, Strategic Planning	Fax:	(330) 458-6006
1835 Dueber Ave. SW		

Canton, OH 44706-0932

LAPP, Robert J.	Tel:	(330) 471-4275
Vice President, Government Affairs and Community Relations	Fax:	(330) 471-3810
1835 Dueber Ave. SW		
Canton, OH 44706-0932		
SCHOOLEY, Kathy	Tel:	(330) 471-3071
Senior Vice President, Government Affairs and Community Relations Representative	Fax:	(330) 471-4381
1835 Dueber Ave. SW		
Canton, OH 44706-0932		
WALKER, Donald L.	Tel:	(330) 438-3000
Senior Vice President, Human Resources & Organizational Advancement	Fax:	(330) 471-4041
1835 Dueber Ave. SW		
Canton, OH 44706-0932		

Timken Steel Corporation

Manufacturer of speciality high performance steel for industrial, automotive, energy, etc.
www.timkensteel.com
Legislative Issues: TAX; TRA; TRD

Chief Executive Officer, Chairman and president	Tel:	(330) 471-7000
TIMKEN, JR., Ward J. "Tim"	Fax:	(330) 458-6006

Main Headquarters

Mailing:	1835 Dueber Ave. SW	Tel: (330) 471-7000
	Canton, OH 44706	Fax: (330) 458-6006

Public Affairs and Related Activities Personnel

At Headquarters

"MANDY" STERLING, Amanda J.	Tel:	(330) 471-7000
Vice President and Corporate Controller	Fax:	(330) 458-6006
DREW, Lauren	Tel:	(330) 471-7000
Administration	Fax:	(330) 458-6006
PRICE, Joe	Tel:	(330) 471-7000
Federal Lobbyist	Fax:	(330) 458-6006
Registered Federal Lobbyist		
RUSSELL REOLFI , Elaine M.	Tel:	(330) 471-7000
Vice President, Communications and Community Relations	Fax:	(330) 458-6006
STENGER, Ryan	Tel:	(330) 471-7000
Vice President, Government Affairs	Fax:	(330) 458-6006
Registered Federal Lobbyist		
WALKER, Donald L.	Tel:	(330) 471-7000
Executive Vice President, Human Resources and Organizational Advancement	Fax:	(330) 458-6006

Timothy D. Naegele & Associates

A law firm.
www.naegele.com
Legislative Issues: BAN

Managing Partner	Tel:	(805) 827-0983
NAEGELE, Timothy D.		
tdnaegele.associates@gmail.com		

Main Headquarters

Mailing:	P.O. Box 6408	Tel: (805) 827-0983
	Malibu, CA 90264-6408	

Washington Office

Mailing:	1615 L St. NW
	Washington, DC 26566

Titan America LLC

A producer of concrete products.
www.titanamerica.com
Industry/ies: Construction/Construction Materials

Chief Executive Officer	Tel:	(954) 481-2800
ZARKALIS, Bill		

Main Headquarters

Mailing:	455 Fairway Dr.	Tel: (954) 481-2800
	Suite 200	
	Deerfield Beach, FL 33441	

Public Affairs and Related Activities Personnel

At Headquarters

BROWN, Steve	Tel:	(954) 481-2800
Vice President, Human Resources		
FINK, Russ	Tel:	(954) 481-2800
Vice President, General Counsel and Secretary		
WILT, Lawrence H.	Tel:	(954) 481-2800
Vice President and Chief Financial Officer		

At Other Offices

JOHNSON, Hardy
Chief Government Affairs Officer

7256 N.W. 127th Way
Parkland, FL 33076

Titanium Metals Corporation

A supplier of titanium metal products.
www.timet.com
Annual Revenues: $1.04 billion
Employees: 2,750
Ticker: NYSE: TIE
SIC: 3341
Industry/ies: Metals
Legislative Issues: DEF; TRD

President and Chief Executive Officer   Tel: (972) 934-5300
O'BRIEN, Bobby D.   Fax: (972) 934-5343

Main Headquarters
Mailing: 224 Valley Creek Blvd.   Tel: (610) 968-1300
            Suite 200   Fax: (610) 968-1322
            Exton, PA 19341

Public Affairs and Related Activities Personnel

At Other Offices

ARMSTRONG, Christopher   Tel: (972) 934-5300
Executive Vice President, Strategic Planning and Business   Fax: (972) 934-5343
Initiatives
5430 LBJ Fwy., Suite 1700
Dallas, TX 75240

GRAHAM, Robert D.   Tel: (972) 934-5300
PAC Treasurer   Fax: (972) 934-5343
5430 LBJ Fwy., Suite 1700
Dallas, TX 75240

The TJX Companies, Inc.

An off-price retailer of apparel and home fashions.
www.tjx.com
Annual Revenues: $31.62 billion
Employees: 216,000
Ticker: NYSE: TJX
SIC: 5651
Industry/ies: Retail/Wholesale

Executive Chairman of the Board   Tel: (508) 390-1000
MEYROWITZ, Carol M.   Fax: (508) 390-2828

Chief Executive Officer and President   Tel: (508) 390-1000
HERRMAN, Ernie   Fax: (508) 390-2828

Main Headquarters
Mailing: 770 Cochituate Rd.   Tel: (508) 390-1000
            Framingham, MA 01701   Fax: (508) 390-2828
                                                  TF: (800) 926-6299

Corporate Foundations and Giving Programs

TJX Foundation
Contact: Christine A. Strickland
770 Cochituate Rd.
Framingham, MA 01701

Public Affairs and Related Activities Personnel

At Headquarters

GOLDENBERG , Scott   Tel: (508) 390-1000
Executive Vice President and Chief Financial Officer   Fax: (508) 390-2828

KANGAS, Paul   Tel: (508) 390-1000
Senior Vice President, Human Resources Administration Fax: (508) 390-2828

MCCAULEY, Ann   Tel: (508) 390-1000
General Counsel and Secretary   Fax: (508) 390-2828
AnnMcCauley@tjx.com

MCCONNELL, Debra   Tel: (508) 390-1000
Senior Vice President, Global Communications   Fax: (508) 390-2828

PEIRCE, Dan   Tel: (508) 390-1000
Assistant Vice President, Marketing   Fax: (508) 390-2828

STRICKLAND, Christine A.   Tel: (508) 390-3199
Manager, TJX Foundation   Fax: (508) 390-5722
Christy_Stickland@TJX.com

TKB Global Strategies LLC

Grassroots lobbying and government affairs consulting.
Legislative Issues: HCR

Main Headquarters
Mailing: 555 Massachusetts Ave. NW
            Suite 919
            Washington, DC 20001

Public Affairs and Related Activities Personnel

At Headquarters

BOYD, Tammy   Tel: (202) 207-2854
Registered Federal Lobbyist

TMG Electronics, Inc.

An electronic manufacturing services company.
www.1tmg.com
Annual Revenues: $20.30 million
Employees: 200
Industry/ies: Computer/Technology

Chairman and Chief Executive Officer   Tel: (724) 274-7741
D'AMBROSIO, Jr., Michael   Fax: (724) 274-2234

Main Headquarters
Mailing: 1105 Pittsburgh St.   Tel: (724) 715-2900
            Suite A   Fax: (724) 274-7208
            Cheswick, PA 15024

TMP Worldwide, Inc.

See listing on page 550 under Monster Worldwide

Todd Pacific Shipyards Corporation

Builds and repairs military and commercial vessel.
www.toddpacific.com
Annual Revenues: $180.02 million
Employees: 400
Ticker: NYSE:TOD
Industry/ies: Marine/Maritime/Shipping; Ports And Waterways; Transportation

Chairman, President and Chief Executive Officer   Tel: (206) 623-1635
WELCH, Stephen G.   Fax: (206) 442-8535

Main Headquarters
Mailing: P.O. Box 3806   Tel: (206) 623-1635
            Seattle, WA 98124   Fax: (206) 442-8505

Public Affairs and Related Activities Personnel

At Headquarters

PICKEREL, Hilary   Tel: (206) 623-1635
Executive Assistant   Fax: (206) 442-8505

The Tokyo Electric Power Company, Inc.

A Japanese utility whose Washington office is primarily engaged in research.
www.tepco.co.jp
Industry/ies: Energy/Electricity; Utilities

President   Tel: (202) 457-0790
MASUDA, Tamio   Fax: (202) 457-0810

Main Headquarters
Mailing: 1901 L St. NW, Suite 720   Tel: (202) 457-0790
            Washington, DC 20036   Fax: (202) 457-0810

Toll Brothers, Inc.

A luxury home builder.
www.tollbrothers.com
Annual Revenues: $4.51 billion
Employees: 3,900
Ticker: NYSE: TOL
SIC: 1531
Industry/ies: Architecture And Design; Construction/Construction Materials; Housing; Real Estate

Executive Chairman of the Board   Tel: (215) 938-8000
TOLL, Robert I.   Fax: (215) 938-8010
rtoll@tollbrothersinc.com

Chief Executive Officer and Director   Tel: (215) 938-8000
YEARLEY, Jr., Douglas C.   Fax: (215) 938-8010

Main Headquarters
Mailing: 250 Gibraltar Rd.   Tel: (215) 938-8000
            Horsham, PA 19044   Fax: (215) 938-8010
                                                  TF: (800) 897-8655

Public Affairs and Related Activities Personnel

At Headquarters

CONNOR, Martin P.   Tel: (215) 938-8000
Chief Financial Officer   Fax: (215) 938-8010

COOPER, Frederick N.   Tel: (215) 938-8312
Senior Vice President, Finance, International Development   Fax: (215) 938-8010
and Investor Relations
fcooper@tollbrothersinc.com

HARTMAN, Richard T.   Tel: (215) 938-8000
President and Chief Operating Officer   Fax: (215) 938-8010

SICREE, Joseph R.   Tel: (215) 938-8045
Senior Vice President, Chief Accounting Officer and Director,   Fax: (215) 938-8010
Investor Relations
jsicree@tollbrothersinc.com

STERLING, Kira McCarron   Tel: (215) 938-8220
Senior Vice President and Chief Marketing Officer   Fax: (215) 938-8010
ksterling@tollbrothersinc.com

Tom Dawson & Partners LLC

General Business Consulting and Education on Healthcare Policy

Main Headquarters
Mailing: 1400 Spring St.   Tel: (202) 293-2444
           Suite 330
           Silver Spring, MD 20910

Washington Office
Mailing: 4857 Colorado Ave. NW
           Washington, DC 20011

Public Affairs and Related Activities Personnel

At Headquarters

ATKINS , G. Lawrence   Tel: (202) 293-2444
Senior Advisor

DAWSON , Tom   Tel: (202) 293-2444
Managing Partner

JOHNSON, Charlene   Tel: (202) 293-2444
Assistant, Legal Administrative

Tom Wolfe

Public Affairs Consulting.
www.tomwolfe.com

Registrant
WOLFE, Tom
jtomwolfe@gmail.com

Main Headquarters
Mailing: 6246 Lee Hwy.
           Arlington, VA 22205

Tompkins Strategies, LLC

Government relations consulting.
Industry/ies: Governments (Local/State/Federal/Foreign)
Legislative Issues: HCR

Main Headquarters
Mailing: 3042 Dent Pl. NW
           Washington, DC 20007

Public Affairs and Related Activities Personnel

At Headquarters

TOMPKINS, Elena G.
Principal
Registered Federal Lobbyist

Tops Markets LLC

A food retail chain.
www.topsmarket.com
Annual Revenues: $2.26 billion
Employees: 23,000
SIC: 5411
Industry/ies: Food And Beverage Industry; Retail/Wholesale

President and Chief Executive Officer   Tel: (800) 522-2522
CURCI, Frank   Fax: (716) 515-3021

Main Headquarters
Mailing: P.O. Box 1027   Tel: (800) 522-2522
           Buffalo, NY 14240-1027

Corporate Foundations and Giving Programs

Tops Markets LLC Contributions Program
P.O. Box 1027   Tel: (716) 635-5987
Buffalo, NY 14240-1027

Public Affairs and Related Activities Personnel

At Headquarters

BARRETT, Jack   Tel: (800) 522-2522
Senior Vice President, Human Resources

BROCATO, Andrew   Tel: (800) 522-2522
Director, Community Relations and Special Events

Torch Technologies

Scientific and engineering services provider.
www.torchtechnologies.com
Annual Revenues: $40.21 million
Employees: 100
NAICS: 541330; 541710
Industry/ies: Defense/Homeland Security; Government-Related
Legislative Issues: DEF; SMB

Co-Founder and Chief Executive Officer   Tel: (256) 319-6000
ROARK, Bill   Fax: (256) 319-6016

Main Headquarters
Mailing: 4035 Chris Dr.   Tel: (256) 319-6000
           Suite C   Fax: (256) 319-6016
           Huntsville, AL 35801

Political Action Committees
Torch Technologies Inc. PAC
FEC ID: C00400424
Contact: William Roark
4035 Chris Dr.   Tel: (256) 319-6067
Suite C
Huntsville, AL 35802

   Contributions to Candidates: $32,900 (2015-2016)
   Democrats: $4,500; Republicans: $28,400

Corporate Foundations and Giving Programs

Torch Helps
4035 Chris Dr. SW   Tel: (256) 319-6000
Suite C   Fax: (256) 319-6016
Huntsville, AL 35802-4192

Public Affairs and Related Activities Personnel

At Headquarters

CLARK, Sue   Tel: (256) 319-6067
Chief Financial Officer   Fax: (256) 319-6016

PARKER, Scott   Tel: (256) 319-6000
Chief Operating Officer   Fax: (256) 319-6016

ROARK, William   Tel: (256) 319-6067
PAC Treasurer   Fax: (256) 319-6016
Bill.Roark@torchtechnologies.com

WATSON, John   Tel: (256) 319-6000
President   Fax: (256) 319-6016

Torchmark Corporation

An insurance and financial services holding company.
www.torchmarkcorp.com
Annual Revenues: $3.83 billion
Employees: 2,900
Ticker: NYSE: TMK
SIC: 6311
Industry/ies: Banking/Finance/Investments
Legislative Issues: INS; TAX

Co-Chairman of the Board and Co-Chief Executive Officer   Tel: (972) 569-4000
COLEMAN, Gary L.   Fax: (972) 569-3282

Main Headquarters
Mailing: P.O. Box 8080   Tel: (972) 569-4000
           3700 S. Stonebridge Dr. Fax: (972) 569-3282
           McKinney, TX 75070-8080

Political Action Committees
Torchmark Corporation PAC (Torch-PAC)
FEC ID: C00167460
Contact: Stephen W. Still
2001 Third Ave., South
Birmingham, AL 35233

   Contributions to Candidates: $21,900 (2015-2016)
   Democrats: $2,000; Republicans: $19,900

Corporate Foundations and Giving Programs

Torchmark Benevolent Foundation
Contact: Carol A. McCoy
P.O. Box 8080
McKinney, TX 75070-8080

Public Affairs and Related Activities Personnel

At Headquarters

BOWIE, Arvelia   Tel: (972) 569-4000
Vice President and Director, Human Resources Fax: (972) 569-3282

MAJORS, Mike   Tel: (972) 569-3239
Vice President, Investor Relations and Contact, Media Fax: (972) 569-3282
Relations
tmkir@torchmarkcorp.com

MCCOY, Carol A.   Tel: (972) 569-4000
Vice President, Associate Counsel, Secretary and Contact, Fax: (972) 569-3282
Foundation

MCPARTLAND, James   Tel: (972) 569-4000
Executive Vice President and Chief Information Officer Fax: (972) 569-3282

MITCHELL, R. Brian   Tel: (972) 569-4000
Executive Vice President and General Counsel Fax: (972) 569-3282

SVOBODA, Frank M.   Tel: (972) 569-4000
Executive Vice President and Chief Financial Officer Fax: (972) 569-3282

WILLIAMS, Glenn D.   Tel: (972) 569-4000
Executive Vice President and Chief Marketing Officer Fax: (972) 569-3282

At Other Offices

STILL, Stephen W.
PAC Treasurer
2001 Third Ave., South
Birmingham, AL 35233

sstill@maynardcooper.com

The Toro Company

An independent manufacturer and marketer of outdoor maintenance and irrigation equipment.
www.toro.com
Annual Revenues: $2.41 billion
Employees: 6,874
Ticker: NYSE: TTC
SIC: 3524
Industry/ies: Agriculture/Agronomy; Machinery/Equipment

Chairman, President and Chief Executive Officer	Tel:	(952) 888-8801
HOFFMAN, Michael J.	Fax:	(952) 887-8258

Main Headquarters
Mailing:	8111 Lyndale Ave.,South	Tel:	(952) 888-8801
	Bloomington, MN 55420-1196	Fax:	(952) 887-8258
		TF:	(800) 348-2424

Corporate Foundations and Giving Programs
The Toro Foundation
8111 Lyndale Ave., South
Bloomington, MN 55420

Public Affairs and Related Activities Personnel

At Headquarters

DAHL, Amy E.	Tel:	(952) 888-8801
Vice President, Human Resources	Fax:	(952) 887-8258
DORDELL, Timothy P.	Tel:	(952) 888-8801
Vice President, Secretary and General Counsel	Fax:	(952) 887-8258
HAPPEL, Branden	Tel:	(952) 887-8930
Senior Manager, Public Relations	Fax:	(952) 887-8258
branden.happel@toro.com		
OLSON, Richard M.	Tel:	(952) 888-8801
President and Chief Operating Officer	Fax:	(952) 887-8258
PETERSON, Renee J.	Tel:	(952) 888-8801
Vice President, Chief Financial Officer and Treasurer	Fax:	(952) 887-8258
WRIGHT, John	Tel:	(952) 888-8865
Director, Business Development	Fax:	(952) 887-8258
invest@toro.com		

Toshiba America, Inc.

Toshiba America based in New York City, is the U. S. subsidiary of Toshiba Corp., headquartered in Tokyo, Japan. Toshiba America is the holding company for a group of high technology companies.Toshiba acquires Landis + Gyr AG.
www.toshiba.com/tai
Annual Revenues: $671 million
Employees: 8,000
SIC: 5065
Industry/ies: Electricity & Electronics; Electronics; Energy/Electricity

Director, Chairman	Tel:	(212) 596-0600
MUROMACHI, Masashi	Fax:	(212) 593-3875

Representative Executive Officer President and Cheif Executive Officer	Tel:	(212) 596-0600
	Fax:	(212) 593-3875
TANAKA, Hisao		

Main Headquarters
Mailing:	1251 Avenue of the Americas	Tel:	(212) 596-0600
	Suite 4110	Fax:	(212) 593-3875
	New York City, NY 10020		

Corporate Foundations and Giving Programs
Toshiba Corporate Social Responsibility
1251 Avenue of the Americas
Suite 4110
New York City, NY 10020

Public Affairs and Related Activities Personnel

At Headquarters

MOORE, Marlene	Tel:	(818) 708-1704
Media Contact	Fax:	(212) 593-3875
Marlene@smm-ads.com		
WHITE, Melinda	Tel:	(212) 596-0600
Vice President, Finance	Fax:	(212) 593-3875

Total Petrochemicals USA

Formerly ATOFINA Petrochemicals, Inc. They are a worldwide producer of polypropylene, polyethylene, styrenics (including polystyrene), base chemicals and transportation fuels.
www.totalpetrochemicalsusa.com
Annual Revenues: $164.60 million
Employees: 1,600
Industry/ies: Chemicals & Chemical Industry

Main Headquarters
Mailing:	1201 Louisiana St., Suite 1800	Tel:	(713) 483-5000
	P.O. Box 674411	Fax:	(713) 483-5383
	Houston, TX 77267-4411	TF:	(800) 322-3462

Public Affairs and Related Activities Personnel

At Headquarters

D'OLIVEIRA, Agnes	Tel:	(713) 483-5000
Vice President and Chief Financial Officer	Fax:	(713) 483-5383
FULLER, Tricia	Tel:	(713) 483-5000
Manager, Public Affairs	Fax:	(713) 483-5383
PHELPS, William W.	Tel:	(713) 482-5362
Government Relations	Fax:	(713) 483-5383
SANDERS, Carolyn	Tel:	(800) 322-3462
Vice President, Human Resources and Public Affairs	Fax:	(713) 483-5383
WALSH, Jennifer	Tel:	(713) 483-5461
Communication Advisor	Fax:	(713) 483-5383
jennifer.walsh@total.com		
WATTERMANN, Richard	Tel:	(713) 483-5432
Public Affairs Advisor	Fax:	(713) 483-5466

Total System Services, Inc.

Provides electronic payment services to financial institutions and companies around the globe.
www.tsys.com
Annual Revenues: $2.86 billion
Employees: 10,500
Ticker: NYSE: TSS
SIC: 7389
Industry/ies: Banking/Finance/Investments; Electricity & Electronics; Electronics; Energy/Electricity
Legislative Issues: FIN; HOM

Chairman of the Board, President and Chief Executive Officer	Tel:	(706) 649-2310
WOODS, Troy	Fax:	(706) 649-4266

Main Headquarters
Mailing:	P.O. Box 2567	Tel:	(706) 649-2310
	Columbus, GA 31902-2567	Fax:	(706) 649-4266

Political Action Committees
Total System Services, Inc. PAC (TSYS PAC)
FEC ID: C00441980
Contact: G. Sanders Griffith III
P.O. Box 1755
Columbus, GA 31902

> **Contributions to Candidates:** $92,000 (2015-2016)
> Democrats: $24,500; Republicans: $67,500

Corporate Foundations and Giving Programs
TSYS Future Scholars Foundation
P.O. Box 2567
Columbus, GA 31902

Public Affairs and Related Activities Personnel

At Headquarters

HARRELSON, Ryland L.	Tel:	(706) 649-2310
Executive Vice President and Chief Human Resource Officer	Fax:	(706) 649-4266
MIMS, Cyle	Tel:	(706) 644-3110
Contact, Media Relations and External Communications	Fax:	(706) 649-4266
ROBERTS, Shawn	Tel:	(706) 644-6081
Director, Investor Relations	Fax:	(706) 644-8065
shawnroberts@tsys.com		
TODD, Paul M.	Tel:	(706) 649-2310
Senior Executive Vice President and Chief Financial Officer	Fax:	(706) 649-4266

At Other Offices

GRIFFITH, III, G. Sanders	Tel:	(706) 649-2310
Senior Executive Vice President, General Counsel and Secretary and PAC Treasurer	Fax:	(706) 649-4266
P.O. Box 1755		
Columbus, GA 31902		

Towers Watson

Human resource consulting firm providing services related to employee benefits, risk and financial services, and talent and rewards. Formerly Towers Perrin Forster & Crosby Inc.
www.towerswatson.com
Annual Revenues: $3.64 billion
Employees: 15,400
Ticker: NYSE, NASDAQ: TW
SIC: 8742
Industry/ies: Management
Legislative Issues: RET

Chairman and Chief Executive Officer	Tel:	(212) 725-7550
HALEY, John	Fax:	(914) 745-4180

Main Headquarters
Mailing:	875 Third Ave.	Tel:	(212) 725-7550
	16th Floor	Fax:	(212) 644-7432
	New York City, NY 10022		

Washington Office
Mailing:	901 N. Glebe Rd.	Tel:	(703) 258-8000

Suite 500	Fax:	(703) 258-8585
Arlington, VA 22203	TF:	(800) 666-2871

Public Affairs and Related Activities Personnel

At Headquarters

BAYLIN, Ezra — Tel: (212) 725-7550 / Fax: (212) 644-7432
Managing Director, Strategy and Corporate Development

BODNAR, Anne Donovan — Tel: (212) 725-7550 / Fax: (914) 745-4180
Chief Administrative Officer
bodnara@towers.com

CLARK, Sharon — Tel: (212) 725-7550 / Fax: (914) 745-4180
Chief Marketing Officer

GOULD, Gordon — Tel: (212) 725-7550 / Fax: (914) 745-4180
Managing Director, Strategy and Corporate Development

HICKS, Kirkland — Tel: (212) 725-7550 / Fax: (212) 644-7432
Vice President, General Counsel and Secretary

MCKEE, Gail — Tel: (212) 725-7550 / Fax: (914) 745-4180
Chief Officer, Human Resources

MILLAY, Roger F. — Tel: (212) 725-7550 / Fax: (914) 745-4180
Vice President and Chief Financial Officer
roger.millay@towerswatson.com

At Washington Office

GARDNER, Deseree — Tel: (703) 258-8000 / Fax: (703) 258-8585
Attorney- Delegated Investments

Toyota Motor Engineering and Manufacturing North America, Inc.

Responsible for engineering design, research and development, and manufacturing activities in the US, Canada, and Mexico.
www.toyota.com/about/our_business/engineering_and_
Employees: 3,131
SIC: 8880
Industry/ies: Automotive Industry; Transportation

Chairman of the Board — Tel: (859) 746-4000 / Fax: (859) 746-4190
NIIMI, Atsushi

President and Chief Operating Officer — Tel: (859) 746-4000 / Fax: (859) 746-4190
AGATA, Tetsuo

Main Headquarters
Mailing: 25 Atlantic Ave. — Tel: (859) 746-4000 / Fax: (859) 746-4190
Erlanger, KY 41018

Public Affairs and Related Activities Personnel

At Headquarters

BROWN, Charles (Chuck) — Tel: (859) 746-4000 / Fax: (859) 746-4190
Vice President, Accounting, Finance and Secretary

Toyota Motor North America, Inc.

Car manufacturer.
www.toyota.com
Annual Revenues: $2.95 billion
Employees: 9,000
Industry/ies: Automotive Industry; Retail/Wholesale; Transportation
Legislative Issues: AUT; CAW; CPT; CSP; EDU; ENG; ENV; HOM; LAW; MAN; TAX; TEC; TRA; TRD

President, Chief Executive Officer & Chief Operating Officer — Tel: (212) 715-7483 / Fax: (212) 759-7670
LENTZ III, James E. (Jim)

Main Headquarters
Mailing: 601 Lexington Ave., 49th Floor — Tel: (212) 715-7483
49th Floor — Fax: (212) 759-7670
New York City, NY 10022 — TF: (800) 458-2700

Washington Office
Mailing: 601 13th St. NW — Tel: (202) 775-1700
Suite 910 South — Fax: (202) 463-6859
Washington, DC 20005

Political Action Committees
Toyota Motor North America Inc Political Action Committee (Toyota/Lexus PAC)
FEC ID: C00542365
Contact: Tracey Doi
601 13th St. NW — Tel: (301) 468-4000
Suite 910 S
Washington, DC 20005

Contributions to Candidates: $525,500 (2015-2016)
Democrats: $245,500; Republicans: $280,000

Principal Recipients

SENATE
HARRIS, KAMALA D (DEM-CA)
SCHUMER, CHARLES E (DEM-NY)

HOUSE
JOHNSON, SAM MR. (REP-TX)

Corporate Foundations and Giving Programs
Toyota U.S.A Foundation

Contact: Patricia A. Pineda — Tel: (212) 715-7490
601 Lexington Ave.
49th Floor
New York City, NY 10022

Public Affairs and Related Activities Personnel

At Headquarters

BALLINGER, Chris — Tel: (212) 715-7483 / Fax: (212) 759-7670
Senior Vice President and Chief Financial Officer

PINEDA, Patricia A. — Tel: (212) 715-7483 / Fax: (212) 759-7670
Group Vice President, Philanthropy

ZEIGLER, Zoe — Tel: (212) 715-7492 / Fax: (212) 759-7670
Senior Strategist, Corporate Marketing and Communications

At Washington Office

BRADEN, Amanda — Tel: (202) 463-6817 / Fax: (202) 463-6859
PAC Administrator and Coordinator, Events
amanda_braden@toyota.com

CAIN, Hilary Marie — Tel: (202) 775-1700 / Fax: (202) 463-6859
Director, Technology and Innovation Policy
Registered Federal Lobbyist

CHIAPPETTA, Robert — Tel: (202) 463-6816 / Fax: (202) 463-6859
Manager, Government Affairs
robert_chiappetta@toyota.com
Registered Federal Lobbyist

CICCIONE, Stephen — Tel: (202) 775-1700 / Fax: (202) 463-6859
Group Vice President, Government Affairs
Registered Federal Lobbyist

DOI, Tracey — Tel: (202) 775-1700 / Fax: (202) 463-6859
PAC Treasurer

ING, Charles E. — Tel: (202) 463-6812 / Fax: (202) 463-6859
Director, Government Affairs
Registered Federal Lobbyist

JOHNSON, Mark — Tel: (202) 463-6814 / Fax: (202) 822-0928
National Manager, Government Affairs
mark_johnson@toyota.com
Registered Federal Lobbyist

KIRKHORN, Erik M. — Tel: (202) 463-6845 / Fax: (202) 822-0928
Director, State Government and Industry Affairs
erik_kirkhorn@toyota.com

PHILLIPS, Michelle — Tel: (202) 775-1700 / Fax: (202) 463-6859
Office Manager
MPhillips@tma.toyota.com

RHUDY, Donna — Tel: (202) 463-6832 / Fax: (202) 463-6859
Manager , TMA State Government Affairs
Donna_rhudy@toyota.com

UNNO, Yuri — Tel: (202) 463-6802 / Fax: (202) 463-6859
Senior Manager, International Trade Strategy
yuri_unno@toyota.com
Registered Federal Lobbyist

VAZQUEZ, Tanya — Tel: (202) 775-1700 / Fax: (202) 463-6859
Associate Director, State Government Relations

VOSS, Martha — Tel: (202) 463-6834 / Fax: (202) 822-0928
Manager, National Public Affairs
martha_voss@toyota.com

Toys "R" US

A toy and baby products retailer. In May 2009, it was announced that Toys"R"Us, Inc. was acquiring FAO Schwartz and will continue operate the chain's stores under the FAO Schwartz name.
www.toysrus.com
Ticker: NYSE: TOYS
SIC: 5945
Industry/ies: Children And Youth; Retail/Wholesale

Chairman of the Board and Chief Executive Officer — Tel: (973) 617-3500 / Fax: (973) 617-4006
BRANDON, David A.

Main Headquarters
Mailing: One Geoffrey Way — Tel: (973) 617-3500
Wayne, NJ 07470-2030 — Fax: (973) 617-4006
— TF: (800) 869-7787

Corporate Foundations and Giving Programs
Toys"R"Us Children's Fund
One Geoffrey Way — Tel: (973) 617-3500
Wayne, NJ 07470 — Fax: (973) 617-3500

Public Affairs and Related Activities Personnel

At Headquarters

BARRY, Richard — Tel: (973) 617-3500 / Fax: (973) 617-4006
Executive Vice President, Global Chief Merchandising Officer

SCHWARTZ, David J. — Tel: (973) 617-3500 / Fax: (973) 617-4006
Executive Vice President, General Counsel, Corporate Secretary

SHORT, Michael J.	Tel:	(973) 617-3500
Executive Vice President and Chief Financial Officer	Fax:	(973) 617-4006
WAUGH, Kathleen	Tel:	(973) 617-5888
Vice President, Corporate Communications	Fax:	(973) 617-4006
Kathleen.Waugh@toysrus.com		

TracFone Wireless, Inc.

Wireless phone company.
www.tracfone.com
Annual Revenues: $20.50 million
Employees: 500
Industry/ies: Communications; Telecommunications/Internet/Cable
Legislative Issues: TAX; TEC

Vice-Chairman	Tel:	(305) 640-2000
BLANCO, Gustav	Fax:	(305) 640-2070

President and Chief Executive Officer	Tel:	(305) 640-2000
POLLAK, F.J.	Fax:	(305) 640-2070
fjpollak@tracfone.com		

Main Headquarters

Mailing:	9700 N.W. 112th Ave.	Tel:	(305) 640-2000
	Miami, FL 33178	Fax:	(305) 640-2070
		TF:	(800) 867-7183

Political Action Committees

Tracfone Wireless, Inc. PAC (Tracfone PAC)
FEC ID: C00561522
Contact: Richard Dobrinsky
9700 N.W. 112th Ave.
Miami, FL 33178

> **Contributions to Candidates:** $16,000 (2015-2016)
> Democrats: $7,000; Republicans: $9,000

Public Affairs and Related Activities Personnel

At Headquarters

DOBRINSKY, Richard	Tel:	(305) 640-2000
PAC Contact	Fax:	(305) 640-2070

Traditional Values Coalition

A grass-roots Christian lobby headquartered in Anaheim, CA. Promotes religious liberties and a Christian perspective on sexuality and other social issues. Serves as an information clearinghouse for churchgoers nationwide.
www.traditionalvalues.org
Industry/ies: Coalitions; Family & Home Issues/Abortion/Adoption; Religion
Legislative Issues: BUD; DEF; FAM; FOR; GOV; REL

Chairman	Tel:	(202) 547-8570
SHELDON, Rev. Louis P.	Fax:	(202) 546-6403
tvcwashdc@traditionalvalues.org		

President	Tel:	(202) 547-8570
LAFFERTY, Andrea S.	Fax:	(202) 546-6403

Main Headquarters

Mailing:	139 C St. SE	Tel:	(202) 547-8570
	Washington, DC 20003	Fax:	(202) 546-6403

Public Affairs and Related Activities Personnel

At Headquarters

SHELDON-LAFFERTY, Andrea A.	Tel:	(202) 547-8570
Executive Director	Fax:	(202) 546-6403
tvcwashdc@traditionalvalues.org		
Registered Federal Lobbyist		

Trane

See listing on page 428 under Ingersoll-Rand Company

Trans Union Corporation

TransUnion was created in 1968 by Union Tank Car Company as their holding company.
www.transunion.com
Industry/ies: Banking/Finance/Investments
Legislative Issues: BAN; CSP; GOV; HOM; LAW

Chief Executive Officer	Tel:	(312) 985-2000
PECK, James M.		

Main Headquarters

Mailing:	555 W. Adams St.	Tel:	(312) 985-2000
	Chicago, IL 60661-3614		

Washington Office

Mailing:	300 New Jersey Ave. NW		
	Suite 900		
	Washington, DC 20001		

Political Action Committees

Trans Union Corporation PAC
FEC ID: C00313700
Contact: Jill Griffin
555 W. Adams St.

Chicago, IL 60661-3614

> **Contributions to Candidates:** $79,500 (2015-2016)
> Democrats: $30,500; Republicans: $49,000

Public Affairs and Related Activities Personnel

At Headquarters

AMBACH, Dennis	Tel:	(312) 985-2000
Vice President, Government Relations		
Registered Federal Lobbyist		
BLUMBERG, Dave	Tel:	(312) 972-6646
Director, Public Relations and Corporate Affairs, U.S. and Canada		
dblumbe@transunion.com		
GRIFFIN, Jill	Tel:	(312) 985-2000
PAC Treasurer		
HAMOOD, Samuel A. "Allen"	Tel:	(312) 985-2000
Executive Vice President and Chief Financial Officer		
LEYDEN, Anne	Tel:	(312) 985-2000
Executive Vice President and Head, Human Resources		
O'NEAL, Clifton	Tel:	(312) 985-2540
Vice President, Corporate Communications		
coneal@transunion.com		
ROHRICH, John	Tel:	(312) 985-2000
Senior Director, Marketing		
RYAN, Robert F.	Tel:	(312) 466-7799
Vice President, Government Relations		
rryan@transunion.com		
Registered Federal Lobbyist		

Transamerica

An insurance holding company. A U.S. subsidiary of AEGON N.V. of the Netherlands which is also the parent company of Transamerica Corp.
www.transamerica.com
Annual Revenues: $686.70 million
Employees: 12,000
Industry/ies: Banking/Finance/Investments; Insurance Industry; Taxation
Legislative Issues: BAN; CSP; FIN; HCR; INS; RET; TAX; VET

President and Chief Executive Officer	Tel:	(319) 355-8511
MULLIN, Mark	Fax:	(319) 369-2209

Main Headquarters

Mailing:	4333 Edgewood Rd. NE	Tel:	(319) 355-8511
	Cedar Rapids, IA 52499	Fax:	(319) 369-2209

Washington Office

Mailing:	600 13th St. NW		
	Suite 400B		
	Washington, DC 20005		

Political Action Committees

Aegon USA, LLC/Transamerica Corporation PAC
FEC ID: C00236414
Contact: Jeanne De Cervens

1001 Pennsylvania Ave. NW	Tel:	(410) 576-4529
Suite 500A South	Fax:	(410) 374-8621
Washington, DC 20004		

> **Contributions to Candidates:** $310,000 (2015-2016)
> Democrats: $134,500; Republicans: $175,500
>
> **Principal Recipients**
>
> **SENATE**
> BLUNT, ROY (REP-MO)
>
> **HOUSE**
> BLUM, RODNEY (REP-IA)
> KIND, RONALD JAMES (DEM-WI)

Corporate Foundations and Giving Programs

AEGON Transamerica Foundation		
1111 N. Charles St.	Tel:	(410) 576-4571
Baltimore, MD 21201	Fax:	(410) 374-8621

Public Affairs and Related Activities Personnel

At Washington Office

CERVENS, Jeanne De		
Vice President & Director, Federal Government Affairs		
jdecervens@aegonusa.com		
Registered Federal Lobbyist		
CONSEDINE, Michael		
Registered Federal Lobbyist		

At Other Offices

ANDERSON, Byron E.	Tel:	(410) 576-4571
Vice President, Federal Affairs	Fax:	(410) 347-8621
1111 N. Charles St.		
Baltimore, MD 21201		
Registered Federal Lobbyist		

KAUNE, Jason D.
Attorney & Agent for Filer
1111 N. Charles St.
Baltimore, MD 21201

Tel: (410) 576-4529
Fax: (410) 374-8685

TransCanada Pipelines, Limited

TC PipeLines, LP was formed by TransCanada PipeLines Limited to acquire, own and actively participate in the management of United States based natural gas pipelines and related assets.
www.tcpipelineslp.com
Annual Revenues: $422.00 million
Ticker: TCP
SIC: 4922
Industry/ies: Energy/Electricity; Natural Resources
Legislative Issues: ENG

President and Principle Executive Officer
BECKER, Steven D.

Fax: (508) 871-7047

Main Headquarters
Mailing: 700 Louisiana St.
Suite 700
Houston, TX 77002-2700

Fax: (508) 871-7047
TF: (877) 290-2772

Public Affairs and Related Activities Personnel

At Headquarters

BROWN, Nathan
Controller and Principal Financial Officer

Fax: (508) 871-7047

At Other Offices

ELLIOTT, Paul E.
Director, Government Relations
450 First St. SW
Calgary, AB T2P5H
paul_elliott@transcanada.com
Registered Federal Lobbyist

Tel: (403) 920-2000
Fax: (403) 920-2200

NUCKOLLS, Charles Randall
Washington Counsel
450 First St. SW
Calgary, AB T2P5H

Tel: (403) 920-2000
Fax: (403) 920-2200

Transformation Advisors Group LLC

A small business serving the department of defense.
www.taateam.com
Annual Revenues: $7 million
Employees: 6
Industry/ies: Business; Defense/Homeland Security; Disabilities; Government-Related; Military/Veterans; Small Business

Chairman of the Board
MACENKA, Thomas

Tel: (703) 418-9731

Chief Managing Officer
SHANNON, Campbell P.

Tel: (703) 224-8831
Fax: (703) 418-0155

Main Headquarters
Mailing: 1616 Anderson Rd.
McLean, VA 22102

Tel: (703) 224-8831
Fax: (703) 418-0155

Public Affairs and Related Activities Personnel

At Headquarters

JOHNS, George T.
Director, Business Development and Information Technology

Tel: (703) 224-8831
Fax: (703) 418-0155

KUDLA, Jennifer
Chief Administrative Officer

Tel: (703) 224-8831
Fax: (703) 418-0155

Transgenrx

Manufactures protein therapeutics.
www.tgrxinc.com
Industry/ies: Computer/Technology; Science; Scientific Research

President and Chief Executive Officer
FIORETTI, William C.

Tel: (888) 432-0721

President
COOPER, Richard K.

Tel: (888) 432-0721

Main Headquarters
Mailing: 340 E. Parker Blvd.
Baton Rouge, LA 70803

Tel: (888) 432-0721
TF: (888) 432-0721

Public Affairs and Related Activities Personnel

At Headquarters

GALLAGHER, John
Corporate Counsel

Tel: (888) 432-0721

TransMontaigne Partners L.P.

Trans Montaigne Inc., formerly NYSE:TMG, is a Fortune 500 oil pipeline and terminal company based in Denver, Colorado. Transports, stores and markets refined petroleum products in and crude oil.
www.transmontaigne.com
Annual Revenues: $149.91 million

Employees: 700
Ticker: NYSE: TLP
SIC: 4610
Industry/ies: Fuels See Coal, Gas, Oil, Petroleum; Natural Resources; Petroleum Industry

Chairman of the Board
MUNGER, Stephen R.

Tel: (303) 626-8200
Fax: (303) 626-8228

Chief Executive Officer
DUNLAP, Charles L.

Tel: (303) 626-8200
Fax: (303) 626-8228

Chief Executive Officer
BOUTIN, Frederick W.

Tel: (303) 626-8200
Fax: (303) 626-8228

Main Headquarters
Mailing: P.O. Box 5660
Denver, CO 80217

Tel: (303) 626-8200
Fax: (303) 626-8228

Public Affairs and Related Activities Personnel

At Headquarters

HAMMELL, Michael A.
Executive Vice President, General Counsel and Secretary

Tel: (303) 626-8200
Fax: (303) 626-8228

KINDARD, Judy
Director, Corporate Communications

Tel: (303) 626-8213
Fax: (303) 626-8228

POUND, Gregory J.
President and Chief Operating Officer

Tel: (303) 626-8200
Fax: (303) 626-8228

Transocean Inc.

Formerly known as Transocean Sedco Forex Inc. The offshore drilling contractor, Transocean specializes in deepwater and harsh environment drilling. Acquired GlobalSantaFe Corporation.
www.deepwater.com
Annual Revenues: $8.66 billion
Employees: 13,100
Ticker: NYSE: RIG
SIC: 1381
NAICS: 213111
Industry/ies: Energy/Electricity; Fuels See Coal, Gas, Oil, Petroleum; Natural Resources; Petroleum Industry

Chairman of the Board
STRACHAN, Ian C.

Tel: (713) 232-7500
Fax: (713) 232-7027

President, CEO
THIGPEN, Jeremy D.

Tel: (713) 232-7500
Fax: (713) 232-7027

Main Headquarters
Mailing: P.O. Box 2765
Houston, TX 77252-2765

Tel: (713) 232-7500
Fax: (713) 232-7027

Public Affairs and Related Activities Personnel

At Headquarters

ADAMSON, Keelan I.
Vice President, Human Resources

Tel: (713) 232-7500
Fax: (713) 232-7027

BONNO, Terry B.
Senior Vice President, Marketing

Tel: (713) 232-7500
Fax: (713) 232-7027

CANTWELL, Guy
Director, Corporate Communications

Tel: (712) 232-7647
Fax: (713) 232-7027

EASTON, Pam
Media Contact

Tel: (713) 232-7500
Fax: (713) 232-7027

IKÄHEIMONEN, Esa
Executive Vice President, Chief Financial Officer

Tel: (713) 232-7500
Fax: (713) 232-7027

KATZ, Allen M.
Interim Senior Vice President and General Counsel

Tel: (713) 232-7500
Fax: (713) 232-7027

MUNRO, Michael F.
Vice President, Chief Compliance Officer and Deputy General Counsel

Tel: (713) 232-7500
Fax: (713) 232-7027

SJÖBRING, Lars
Senior Vice President and General Counsel

Tel: (713) 232-7500
Fax: (713) 232-7027

STOBART, John
Executive Vice President and Chief Operating Officer

Tel: (713) 232-7500
Fax: (713) 232-7027

TOMA, Ihab
Executive Vice President, Chief of Staff

Tel: (713) 232-7500
Fax: (713) 232-7027

TONNEL, David A.
Senior Vice President, Finance and Controller

Tel: (713) 232-7500
Fax: (713) 232-7027

VAYDA, R. Thaddeus
Vice President, Investor Relations and Communications
Thad.Vayda@deepwater.com

Tel: (713) 232-7551
Fax: (713) 232-7027

Transportation for America

A broad coalition advocating for transportation policy.
t4america.org
Industry/ies: Coalitions; Transportation
Legislative Issues: ECN; ENG; ENV; HOU; ROD; RRR; TRA; URB

Director, Communications
DAVIS, Stephen Lee
steve.davis@t4america.org

Tel: (202) 971-9302

Main Headquarters

Mailing:	1707 L St. NW	Tel:	(202) 955-5543
	Suite 250		
	Washington, DC 20036		

Public Affairs and Related Activities Personnel

At Headquarters

DONOHUE, Nick — Tel: (202) 251-5501
Policy Director
nick.donohue@t4america.org
Registered Federal Lobbyist

GANN, Georgia — Tel: (202) 251-5501
Federal Lobbyist
Registered Federal Lobbyist

MCANDREW, Joe — Tel: (202) 971-3905
Policy Director
joe.mcandrew@t4america.org

YOUNG, Erika — Tel: (202) 955-5543
Director, Strategic Partnerships
erika.young@t4america.org

The Transportation Institute

Transportation Institute Focuses on research areas such as planning, construction and maintenance to help improve national infrastructure.
transportationinstitute.org
Employees: 25
Industry/ies: Marine/Maritime/Shipping; Ports And Waterways; Shipping Industry; Transportation
Legislative Issues: BAN; MAR; TAX; TRD

Chairman and President — Tel: (301) 423-3335
HENRY, James L. — Fax: (301) 423-0634
jhenry@trans-inst.org

Main Headquarters

Mailing:	5201 Auth Way	Tel:	(301) 423-3335
	Fifth Floor	Fax:	(301) 423-0634
	Camp Springs, MD 20746		

Public Affairs and Related Activities Personnel

At Headquarters

EVANS, Lawrence H. — Tel: (301) 423-3335
Director, Research and Maritime Services — Fax: (301) 423-0634

TravelCenters of America, Inc.

Provides full-service travel center company, which includes full-service restaurants, branded lodging, diesel fuel and gasoline.
www.tatravelcenters.com
Annual Revenues: $5.61 billion
Employees: 13,500
Ticker: AMEX: TA
SIC: 5500
Industry/ies: Retail/Wholesale

Managing Director, President and Chief Executive Officer — Tel: (440) 808-9100
O'BRIEN, Thomas M. — Fax: (440) 808-3306

Main Headquarters

Mailing:	24601 Center Ridge Rd.	Tel:	(440) 808-9100
	Suite 200	Fax:	(440) 808-3306
	Westlake, OH 44145-5639	TF:	(888) 982-5528

Public Affairs and Related Activities Personnel

At Headquarters

BRESNAHAN, Rodney — Tel: (440) 808-9100
Senior Vice President, Retail Marketing and Operations — Fax: (440) 808-3306

LARKIN, Vern D. — Tel: (440) 808-9100
Director, Internal Audit — Fax: (440) 808-3306

LIUTKUS, Tom — Tel: (440) 808-7364
Vice President, Marketing and Public Relations — Fax: (440) 808-4458
liutkus.tom@tatravelcenters.com

LOMBARDI, Michael J. — Tel: (440) 808-9100
Executive Vice President, Sales — Fax: (440) 808-3306

MCGARY, Skip — Tel: (440) 808-9100
Senior Vice President, Truck Service Marketing and — Fax: (440) 808-3306
Operations

MYERS, William E. — Tel: (440) 808-9100
Senior Vice President and Chief Accounting Officer — Fax: (440) 808-3306

REBHOLZ, Andrew J. — Tel: (440) 808-9100
Executive Vice President, Chief Financial Officer and — Fax: (440) 808-9100
Treasurer
rebholz.andrew@tatravelcenters.com

STROHACKER, Katie — Tel: (617) 219-1442
Senior Director, Investor Relations — Fax: (440) 808-3306
kstrohacker@ta-petro.com

YOUNG, Mark R. — Tel: (440) 808-9100

Executive Vice President and General Counsel — Fax: (440) 808-3306

The Travelers Companies, Inc.

A provider of insurance products and services for commercial markets and for auto and homeowners insurance for consumers. Formerly St. Paul Travelers Cos., Inc. assumed its name in February 27, 2007. Formed from the merger of Travelers Property Casualty Corp. and The St. Paul Cos. in April of 2004.
www.travelers.com
Annual Revenues: $26.86 billion
Employees: 30,900
Ticker: NYSE: TRV
SIC: 6331
Industry/ies: Insurance Industry
Legislative Issues: AVI; BAN; BUD; FIN; INS; TAX

Chairman of the Board — Tel: (917) 778-6000
FISHMAN, Jay S. — Fax: (917) 778-7007

Chief Executive Office — Tel: (917) 778-6000
SCHNITZER, Alan D. — Fax: (917) 778-7007

Main Headquarters

Mailing:	485 Lexington Ave.	Tel:	(917) 778-6000
	New York City, NY 10017-2630	Fax:	(917) 778-7007
		TF:	(800) 328-2189

Washington Office

Mailing:	700 13th St. NW	Tel:	(202) 628-2051
	Suite 950		
	Washington, DC 20005		

Political Action Committees

Travelers Companies Inc. PAC
FEC ID: C00376376
Contact: Chipps Katie
One Tower Sq.
Hartford, CT 06183

Contributions to Candidates: $216,000 (2015-2016)
Democrats: $63,500; Republicans: $150,500; Other: $2,000

Principal Recipients

HOUSE
COURTNEY, JOSEPH D (DEM-CT)
HENSARLING, JEB HON. (REP-TX)
HIMES, JIM (DEM-CT)
LUETKEMEYER, W BLAINE (REP-MO)
TIBERI, PATRICK J. (REP-OH)

Corporate Foundations and Giving Programs

Travelers Foundation
Contact: Marlene Ibsen
385 Washington St. — Tel: (860) 277-9039
St. Paul, MN 55102 — Fax: (860) 277-9039

Public Affairs and Related Activities Personnel

At Headquarters

BENET, Jay S. — Tel: (917) 778-6000
Vice Chairman and Chief Financial Officer — Fax: (917) 778-7007

CAPUTO, Lisa — Tel: (917) 778-6000
Executive Vice President, Chief Marketing and — Fax: (917) 778-7007
Communications Officer

CLIFFORD, Jr., John P. — Tel: (917) 778-6000
Executive Vice President, Human Resources — Fax: (917) 778-7007

JONES, Bruce R. — Tel: (917) 778-6000
Executive Vice President and Chief Risk Officer — Fax: (917) 778-7007

MACLEAN, Brian W. — Tel: (917) 778-6000
President and Chief Operating Officer — Fax: (917) 778-7007

NAWI, Gabriella — Tel: (917) 778-6844
Senior Vice President, Investor Relations — Fax: (917) 778-7007
gnawi@travelers.com

SMITH, Kevin C. — Tel: (917) 778-6000
Executive Vice President and President, International — Fax: (917) 778-7007

SPENCE, III, Kenneth F. — Tel: (917) 778-6000
Executive Vice President and General Counsel — Fax: (917) 778-7007

WOODWARD, Joan Kois — Tel: (917) 778-6000
Executive Vice President, Public Policy and & President - — Fax: (917) 778-7007
Travelers Institute

At Washington Office

NOVASCONE, Sarah — Tel: (202) 628-2051
Vice President, Federal Government Affairs
Registered Federal Lobbyist

At Other Offices

IBSEN, Marlene — Tel: (860) 277-9039
Vice President, Community Relations and Chief Executive — Fax: (860) 277-7979
Officer and President, Travelers Foundation
One Tower Sq.
Hartford, CT 06183

---

mibsen@travelers.com

KATIE, Chipps	Tel:	(860) 277-0111
PAC Treasurer	Fax:	(860) 277-7979
One Tower Sq.		
Hartford, CT 06183		

OLIVO, Maria	Tel:	(860) 277-0111
Executive Vice President, Strategic Development and	Fax:	(860) 277-7979
Corporate Treasurer		
One Tower Sq.		
Hartford, CT 06183		

STOWELL, Arlene G.	Tel:	(860) 277-0111
Government Relations Coordinator	Fax:	(860) 277-7979
One Tower Sq.		
Hartford, CT 06183		
astowell@travelers.com		

WESTRICK, Glenn	Tel:	(860) 277-0111
Vice President & Director, Government Relations	Fax:	(860) 277-7979
One Tower Sq.		
Hartford, CT 06183		
Registered Federal Lobbyist		

Travelocity.com

Provider of consumer-direct travel services for the leisure and business traveler.
www.travelocity.com
Annual Revenues: $41.20 million
Employees: 700
Industry/ies: Travel/Tourism/Lodging

Main Headquarters

Mailing: 3150 Sabre Dr.	Tel:	(682) 605-1000
Southlake, TX 76092	TF:	(888) 872-8356

Corporate Foundations and Giving Programs

Travelocity Contributions Program		
3150 Sabre Dr.	Tel:	(682) 605-1000
Southlake, TX 76092		

Public Affairs and Related Activities Personnel

At Headquarters

DUMAINE, Stephen	Tel:	(682) 605-1000
Senior Vice President, Global Strategy and Product		
NOWAK, Keith	Tel:	(214) 443-7590
Director, Marketing and Communications		
keith.nowak@travelocity.com		
QUIGLEY, Scott	Tel:	(682) 605-1000
Vice President, Sales and Customer Care		
TAYLOR, Tran	Tel:	(682) 605-1000
Chief People Officer		

Travelport, Inc.

An online travel service provider.
www.travelport.com
Employees: 6,000
SIC: 4700
Industry/ies: Travel/Tourism/Lodging
Legislative Issues: AVI

Non-Executive Chairman of the Board	Tel:	(770) 563-7400
STEENLAND, Douglas M.	Fax:	(770) 563-7400

President and Chief Executive Officer	Tel:	(770) 563-7400
WILSON, Gordon	Fax:	(770) 563-7400

Main Headquarters

Mailing: 400 Interspace Pkwy.	Tel:	(973) 939-1000
Parsippany, NJ 07054	Fax:	(973) 939-1096

Washington Office

Mailing: 1725 I St. NW	Tel:	(770) 563-7400
Suite 300		
Washington, DC 20006		

Corporate Foundations and Giving Programs

Travelport Contributions Program
300 Galleria Pkwy.
Atlanta, GA 30339

Public Affairs and Related Activities Personnel

At Headquarters

ALDRIDGE, Kate	Tel:	(973) 939-1000
Vice President, Corporate Communications	Fax:	(973) 939-1096
MURPHY, Thomas	Tel:	(973) 939-1000
General Counsel	Fax:	(973) 939-1096
ROBERTS, Christopher	Tel:	(973) 939-1000
Group Vice President, Corporate Strategy and Development	Fax:	(973) 939-1096

At Washington Office

VANDE BEEK, Dirk	Tel:	(770) 563-7400

Senior Vice President, Corporate and Government Affairs and
PAC Treasurer
Registered Federal Lobbyist

At Other Offices

CONWAY, Bryan	Tel:	(770) 563-7400
Chief Marketing Officer	Fax:	(770) 563-7400
300 Galleria Pkwy.		
Atlanta, GA 30339		
EMERY, Philip	Tel:	(770) 563-7400
Executive Vice President and Chief Financial Officer	Fax:	(770) 563-7400
300 Galleria Pkwy.		
Atlanta, GA 30339		
philip.emery@travelport.com		
GROS, Simon	Tel:	(202) 336-5101
Vice President, Government Affairs		
1401 Eye St. NW, Suite 1220		
Washington, DC 20005		
simon.gros@travelport.com		
KOLB, Kelly	Tel:	(202) 336-5101
Vice President, Government Affairs		
1401 Eye St. NW, Suite 1220		
Washington, DC 20005		

Travois, Inc.

An Indian housing consulting company.
travois.com
Industry/ies: Economics And Economic Development; Housing; Minorities

Chairman of the Board and Chief Executive Officer	Tel:	(816) 994-8970
BLAND, David W.	Fax:	(816) 994-8974

Main Headquarters

Mailing: 310 W. 19th Ter.	Tel:	(816) 994-8970
Kansas City, MO 64108	Fax:	(816) 994-8974

Public Affairs and Related Activities Personnel

At Headquarters

GLYNN, Elizabeth Bland	Tel:	(816) 994-8970
Chief Operating Officer	Fax:	(816) 994-8974
HEAP, Beth	Tel:	(816) 994-8970
Director, Communications	Fax:	(816) 994-8974
bheap@travois.com		
SCHWARZ, Brett	Tel:	(816) 994-8970
Chief Financial Officer	Fax:	(816) 994-8974

Tredegar Corporation

Manufactures plastic films and non-ferrous metal extrusions.
www.tredegar.com
Annual Revenues: $869.34 million
Employees: 2,800
Ticker: NYSE: TG
SIC: 3081; 2671; 5162; 3350
NAICS: 322221; 326113
Industry/ies: Metals; Plastics Industry

President and Chief Executive Officer	Tel:	(804) 330-1000
GOTTWALD, John	Fax:	(804) 330-1177

Main Headquarters

Mailing: 1100 Boulders Pkwy.	Tel:	(804) 330-1000
Richmond, VA 23225	Fax:	(804) 330-1177
	TF:	(800) 411-7441

Public Affairs and Related Activities Personnel

At Headquarters

BELLAMY, Neill	Tel:	(804) 330-1211
Contact, Investor Relations and Corporate Communications	Fax:	(804) 330-1177
neill.bellamy@tredegar.com		
EDWARDS, D. Andrew	Tel:	(804) 330-1000
Vice President and Chief Financial Officer	Fax:	(804) 330-1177
GIANCASPRO, Michael W.	Tel:	(804) 330-1000
Vice President, Business Processes and Corporate	Fax:	(804) 330-1177
Development		
SCHEWEL, Michael J.	Tel:	(804) 330-1000
Vice President, General Counsel and Secretary	Fax:	(804) 330-1177

Tremco Incorporated

Manufactures and sells roofing materials and services, as well as industrial coatings and
sealants.
www.tremcoinc.com
Annual Revenues: $512.80 million
Employees: 3,600
SIC: 2952; 2891; 5099; 9999
Industry/ies: Construction/Construction Materials

Main Headquarters

Mailing: 3735 Green Rd.	Tel:	(800) 321-7906

	Fax:	(216) 292-5036
	TF:	(800) 852-9068

Beachwood, OH 44122

Public Affairs and Related Activities Personnel

At Headquarters

DRUMM, Mike — Tel: (216) 292-5000
Vice President and Chief Financial Officer — Fax: (216) 292-5036

POKORNY, Cathy — Tel: (216) 292-5002
Director, Marketing Communications — Fax: (216) 292-5036
cpokorny@tremcoinc.com

Trex Enterprises

Provides solutions and products to improve performance across the electromagnetic spectrum.
www.trexenterprises.com
Annual Revenues: $21.80 million
Employees: 200
Industry/ies: Defense/Homeland Security; Government-Related

Chairman of the Board and Chief Executive Officer — Tel: (858) 646-5300
TANG, PhD, Kenneth Y. — Fax: (858) 646-5301

Main Headquarters
Mailing: 10455 Pacifice Center Ct. — Tel: (858) 646-5300
San Diego, CA 92121 — Fax: (858) 646-5301
— TF: (800) 626-5885

Triangulation Strategies, LLC

Public Affairs Consulting and Commentary.

Main Headquarters
Mailing: 1801 S. Federal Hwy.
Suite 220
Delray Beach, FL 33483

Public Affairs and Related Activities Personnel

At Headquarters

MORRIS, Dick — Tel: (888) 658-8484

Tribune Company

A media company with operations in television and radio broadcasting, publishing, and interactive ventures. The Tribune Company filed for bankruptcy in December 2008.
www.tribunemedia.com
Annual Revenues: $2.90 billion
Employees: 19,600
Ticker: OTC: TRBAA
SIC: 4833
Industry/ies: Communications; Media/Mass Communication
Legislative Issues: COM; TEC

Chairman of the Board — Tel: (312) 222-9100
HARTENSTEIN, Eddy W. — Fax: (312) 222-1573

Chairman of the Board — Tel: (312) 222-9100
KARSH, Bruce A. — Fax: (312) 222-1573

President and Chief Executive Officer — Tel: (312) 222-9100
LIGUORI, Peter — Fax: (312) 222-1573

Main Headquarters
Mailing: 435 N. Michigan Ave. — Tel: (312) 222-9100
Sixth Floor — Fax: (312) 222-1573
Chicago, IL 60611

Washington Office
Mailing: 609 S. Fairfax St. — Tel: (202) 775-7750
Alexandria, VA 22314

Corporate Foundations and Giving Programs

Tribune Company Contributions Program
435 N. Michigan Ave.
Chicago, IL 60611

Public Affairs and Related Activities Personnel

At Headquarters

BERNS, Steven — Tel: (312) 222-9100
Executive Vice President and Chief Financial Officer — Fax: (312) 222-1573

BIGELOW, Chandler — Tel: (312) 222-9100
Executive Vice President and Chief Business Strategies and — Fax: (312) 222-1573
Operations Officer
CBigelow@tribune.com

GRANATO, Donna — Tel: (312) 222-9100
Vice President and Corporate Finance and Investor Relations — Fax: (312) 222-1573

HUGHES, Melanie — Tel: (312) 222-9100
Executive Vice President, Human Resources — Fax: (312) 222-1573

LAZARUS, Edward P. — Tel: (312) 222-9100
Executive Vice President and General Counsel — Fax: (312) 222-1573

WEITMAN, Gary — Tel: (312) 222-3394
Senior Vice President, Corporate Relations — Fax: (312) 222-1573

At Washington Office

SHEEHAN, Shaun M. — Tel: (202) 775-7750
Vice President
ssheehan@tribune.com
Registered Federal Lobbyist

WHITE, Dina — Tel: (202) 775-7750
Office Manager
diwhite@tribune.com

TriHealth, Inc.

TriHealth is a health care organization.
www.trihealth.com
Employees: 800
Industry/ies: Medicine/Health Care/Mental Health

Chairman of the Board — Tel: (513) 569-5000
WALKER , Robert — Fax: (513) 569-6233

President and Chief Executive Officer — Tel: (513) 569-6111
PROUT, John S. — Fax: (513) 569-6233

Main Headquarters
Mailing: 619 Oak St. — Tel: (513) 569-5400
Cincinnati, OH 45206 — Fax: (513) 569-6233

Corporate Foundations and Giving Programs

Bethesda Foundation
Contact: Barbara Boyne
10500 Montgomery Rd. — Tel: (513) 865-1616
Cincinnati, OH 45242

Good Samaritan Hospital Foundation
Contact: Mary L. Rafferty
375 Dixmyth Ave. — Tel: (513) 862-3786
Cincinnati, OH 45220

Public Affairs and Related Activities Personnel

At Headquarters

KELLEY, Joe — Tel: (513) 569-6703
Media Relations Manager — Fax: (513) 569-6233
Joe_Kelley@TriHealth.com

NIENABER, Donna S. — Tel: (513) 569-6111
Assistant Secretary, Chief Legal Counsel and Director, Board — Fax: (513) 569-6233
Operations and Support

At Other Offices

BOYNE, Barbara — Tel: (513) 865-1616
Executive Director, Bethesda North Hospital — Fax: (513) 865-1623
10500 Montgomery Rd.
Cincinnati, OH 45242-4402

RAFFERTY, Mary L. — Tel: (513) 862-3786
President and Chief Executive Officer, Good Samaritan — Fax: (513) 862-3788
Hospital Foundation
375 Dixmyth Ave.
Cincinnati, OH 45220-2475
mary_rafferty@trihealth.com

Trinity Industries, Inc.

A manufacturer of transportation, construction, and industrial products.
www.trin.net
Annual Revenues: $6.34 billion
Employees: 22,070
Ticker: NYSE: TRN
SIC: 3312; 3321; 3441; 3443; 3743
NAICS: 324199; 331511; 332312; 332313
Industry/ies: Construction/Construction Materials
Legislative Issues: ACC; ENG; MAN; MAR; ROD; RRR; TRA

Chairman of the Board, President and Chief Executive Officer — Tel: (214) 631-4420
WALLACE, Timothy R. — Fax: (214) 689-0501

Main Headquarters
Mailing: 2525 Stemmons Fwy. — Tel: (214) 631-4420
Dallas, TX 75207 — Fax: (214) 589-8810
— TF: (800) 631-4420

Political Action Committees
Trinity Industries Employee PAC (SF) Inc.
FEC ID: C00268904
Contact: Mike Mason
2525 Stemmons Fwy.
Dallas, TX 75207

Contributions to Candidates: $210,000 (2015-2016)
Democrats: $18,000; Republicans: $190,000; Other: $2,000

Principal Recipients

SENATE
SCOTT, TIMOTHY E (REP-SC)

HOUSE
HURD, WILLIAM (REP-TX)

Public Affairs and Related Activities Personnel

At Headquarters

GREINER, Jessica L.
Director, Investor Relations and Media Contact
Tel: (214) 631-4420
Fax: (214) 589-8810

JEMENTE, Josh
Registered Federal Lobbyist
Tel: (214) 631-4420
Fax: (214) 589-8810

LAFFMAN-JOHNSON, Elise
Federal Lobbyist
Registered Federal Lobbyist
Tel: (214) 631-4420
Fax: (214) 589-8810

LOVETT, Melendy E.
Senior Vice President and Chief Administrative Officer
Tel: (214) 631-4420
Fax: (214) 589-8810

MASON, Mike
PAC Treasurer
mike.mason@trin.net
Tel: (214) 631-4420
Fax: (214) 689-0501

PEABODY, Paige
Registered Federal Lobbyist
Tel: (214) 631-4420
Fax: (214) 589-8810

PERRY, James E.
Senior Vice President and Chief Financial Officer
Tel: (214) 589-8412
Fax: (214) 589-8810

RICE, S. Theis
Vice President and Chief Legal Officer
Tel: (214) 631-4420
Fax: (214) 589-8810

SEQUENZIA, Madison
Federal Lobbyist
Tel: (214) 631-4420
Fax: (214) 589-8810

TODD, Jack
Vice President, Public Affairs
jack.todd@trin.net
Registered Federal Lobbyist
Tel: (214) 589-8901
Fax: (214) 589-8810

At Other Offices

SICKELS, Linda S.
Vice President, Government Relations
316 W. 12th St., Suite 102
Austin, TX 78701
linda.sickels@trin.net
Registered Federal Lobbyist
Tel: (512) 478-4844

Triple Canopy, Inc.

Private security and mission support contractor.
www.triplecanopy.com
Annual Revenues: $12.1 million
Employees: 600
Industry/ies: Defense/Homeland Security; Government-Related
Legislative Issues: DEF; ENG; FOR; GOV

Co-Chairman
MANN, Matt
Tel: (703) 673-5000
Fax: (703) 673-5001

President
MULLIGAN, Mo
Tel: (703) 673-5000
Fax: (703) 673-5001

Main Headquarters
Mailing: 12018 Sunrise Valley Dr.
Suite 140
Reston, VA 20191
Tel: (703) 673-5000
Fax: (703) 673-5001
TF: (866) 349-1506

Washington Office
Mailing: 300 New Jersey Ave. NW
Suite 900
Washington, DC 20001
Tel: (703) 673-5065

Corporate Foundations and Giving Programs

Triple Canopy Contributions Program
2250 Corporate Park Dr.
Suite 300
Herndon, VA 20171-4835

Public Affairs and Related Activities Personnel

At Headquarters

ANTHONY, Lisa
Director, Human Resources
Tel: (703) 673-5000
Fax: (703) 673-5001

FOX, Dan
Senior Director, Business Management
Tel: (703) 673-5000
Fax: (703) 673-5001

KATIS, Tom
Founder and Board Member
Tel: (703) 673-5000
Fax: (703) 673-5001

LYLE, Timothy
Senior Vice President, Operations
Tel: (703) 673-5000
Fax: (703) 673-5001

MCCUIN, Tom
Registered Federal Lobbyist
Tel: (703) 673-5000
Fax: (703) 673-5001

MOORE, Gearoid E.
General Counsel
Tel: (703) 673-5000
Fax: (703) 673-5001

RANDALL, Ray
Senior Vice President, Strategic Initiatives
ray.randall@triplecanopy.com
Tel: (703) 673-5000
Fax: (703) 673-5001

At Washington Office

GLOVER, Christopher
Compliance Counsel
Tel: (703) 673-5065

Triumph Group Inc.

It designs, engineers, manufactures, repairs and overhauls a broad portfolio of aerostructures, aircraft components, accessories, sub-assemblies and systems.
www.triumphgroup.com
Annual Revenues: $3.89 billion
Employees: 15,153
Ticker: NYSE:TGI
Industry/ies: Aerospace/Aviation; Transportation
Legislative Issues: AER; BUD; DEF

Non-Executive Chairman
EBERHART , GEN Ralph "Ed"
Tel: (610) 251-1000
Fax: (610) 251-1555

President and Chief Executive Officer
C., III, Richard
Tel: (610) 251-1000
Fax: (610) 251-1555

Main Headquarters
Mailing: 8306 Marble Dale Ct.
Alexandria, VA 22308
Tel: (703) 619-1434

Political Action Committees

Triumph Group Inc Pac
FEC ID: C00361949
Contact: Clay Crawford
P. O. Box 655907
Dallas, TX 75265

Contributions to Candidates: $74,000 (2015-2016)
Democrats: $17,000; Republicans: $57,000

Principal Recipients

HOUSE
COOPER, JAMES H S (DEM-TN)
GRANGER, KAY (REP-TX)

Public Affairs and Related Activities Personnel

At Headquarters

MCKEOWN, Frank J.
Vice President, Washington Operations
mmckeown@triumphgroup.com
Registered Federal Lobbyist
Tel: (703) 619-1434

At Other Offices

CRAWFORD, Clay
PAC Treasurer
899 Cassatt Rd., Suite 210
Berwyn, PA 19312
Tel: (610) 251-1000
Fax: (610) 251-1555

DEROGATIS, M. Robin
Vice President, Human Resources
899 Cassatt Rd., Suite 210
Berwyn, PA 19312
Tel: (610) 251-1000
Fax: (610) 251-1555

HARGUS, Wendy
Contact, Financial Services
9314 W. Jefferson Blvd.
Dallas, TX 75211
Tel: (972) 946-2011

KORNBLATT, M. David
Director, Corporate Development.
899 Cassatt Rd., Suite 210
Berwyn, PA 19312
Tel: (610) 251-1000
Fax: (610) 251-1555

MCKEOWN, Frank J.
Vice President, Washington Operations
899 Cassatt Rd., Suite 210
Berwyn, PA 19312
mmckeown@triumphgroup.com
Registered Federal Lobbyist
Tel: (610) 251-1000
Fax: (610) 251-1555

MCRAE, Jeff
President
9314 W. Jefferson Blvd.
Dallas, TX 75211
Tel: (972) 946-2011

MCRAE, Jeffrey L.
Senior Vice President and Chief Financial Officer
899 Cassatt Rd., Suite 210
Berwyn, PA 19312
Tel: (610) 251-1000
Fax: (610) 251-1555

SPAGNOLO , Sheila G.
Vice President, Tax and Investor Relations
899 Cassatt Rd., Suite 210
Berwyn, PA 19312
sspagnolo@triumphgroup.com
Tel: (610) 251-1000
Fax: (610) 251-1555

WRIGHT, II, John B.
Vice President, General Counsel and Secretary
899 Cassatt Rd., Suite 210
Berwyn, PA 19312
Tel: (610) 251-1000
Fax: (610) 251-1555

Triumph HealthCare

A privately owned hospital company. Merged with RehabCare Group in 2009.
www.triumph-healthcare.com
Annual Revenues: $1.40 million
Industry/ies: Medicine/Health Care/Mental Health

Chairman and Chief Executive Officer Tel: (888) 748-6742
ALLEN, Charlie

Main Headquarters
Mailing: 7333 North Fwy. Tel: (888) 748-6742
Suite 500
Houston, TX 77076

Public Affairs and Related Activities Personnel

At Headquarters

HUMPHREY, Larry Tel: (888) 748-6742
Chief Financial Officer

TriWest Healthcare Alliance, Inc.

Provides quality health care and customer service for America's military families.
www.triwest.com
Annual Revenues: $86.50 million
Employees: 2,000
Industry/ies: Medicine/Health Care/Mental Health
Legislative Issues: VET

President and Chief Executive Officer Tel: (602) 564-2000
MCINTYRE, Jr., David J. Fax: (602) 564-2457

Main Headquarters
Mailing: P.O. Box 42049 Tel: (602) 564-2000
Phoenix, AZ 85080-2049 Fax: (602) 564-2457

Washington Office
Mailing: 101 Constitution Ave. NW Tel: (202) 216-9141
Washington, DC 20001

Political Action Committees
TriWest Healthcare Alliance Corporation PAC (TriWest Alliance PAC)
FEC ID: C00459743
Contact: William Cahill
15810 N. 28th Ave.
Phoenix, AZ 85053

Contributions to Candidates: $4,000 (2015-2016)
Democrats: $3,000; Republicans: $1,000

Corporate Foundations and Giving Programs
TriWest Healthcare Alliance Contributions Program
Contact: Lara H. Smith
16010 N. 28th Ave. Tel: (602) 564-2000
Phoenix, AZ 85053

Public Affairs and Related Activities Personnel

At Headquarters

DODD, Elizabeth Tel: (602) 564-2000
Chief Financial Officer Fax: (602) 564-2457
ONG, Jeanne Tel: (602) 564-2000
Vice President, Human Capital Fax: (602) 564-2457

At Washington Office

CAHILL, William Tel: (202) 216-9141
Vice President, Government Relations & General Counsel
wcahill@triwest.com

TSOUCALAS, Charlotte Tel: (202) 216-9141
Senior Advisor, Washington D.C. Office

At Other Offices

GRAY, Glenn Tel: (602) 564-2078
Director, Customer Care & Community Relations Fax: (602) 564-2523
15810 N. 28th Ave.
Phoenix, AZ 85053

TOWNSEND, Julie A. Tel: (602) 564-2000
Vice President, Strategic Planning and Business Development Fax: (602) 564-2457
15451 N. 28th Ave.
Phoenix, AZ 85053-4049

Tronox, Inc.

A producer and marketer of titanium dioxide pigment.
www.tronox.com
Annual Revenues: $1.70 billion
Employees: 3,400
Ticker: NYSE: TROX
SIC: 2810
Industry/ies: Chemicals & Chemical Industry

Chairman of the Board and Chief Executive Officer Tel: (203) 705-3800
CASEY, Tom Fax: (203) 705-3703

Main Headquarters
Mailing: One Stamford Plaza, 263 Tresser Blvd. Tel: (203) 705-3800
263 Tresser Blvd., Suite 1100 Fax: (203) 705-3703
Stamford, CT 06901

Public Affairs and Related Activities Personnel

At Headquarters

ARNDT, Brennen Tel: (203) 705-3800
Vice President, Investor Relations Fax: (203) 705-3703
GREBEY, Bud Tel: (203) 705-3800
Vice President, Corporate Affairs and Communications Fax: (203) 705-3703
HARPER, Katherine Tel: (203) 705-3800
Senior Vice President, Chief Financial Officer Fax: (203) 705-3703
KEEGEL, Machiel Tel: (203) 705-3800
Vice President, Strategy Fax: (203) 705-3703
MERTURI, John Tel: (203) 705-3800
Vice President, Treasurer and Global Head, Financial Fax: (203) 705-3703
Planning and Analysis
MUGLIA, Richard L. Tel: (203) 705-3800
Senior Vice President, General Counsel and Secretary Fax: (203) 705-3703
NARCISSE, Sonja Tel: (203) 705-3800
Senior Vice President, Global Human Resources and Chief Fax: (203) 705-3703
Human Resources Officer
NIEKERK, Willem Van Tel: (203) 705-3800
Senior Vice President, Strategic Planning and Business Fax: (203) 705-3703
Development
SMITH, Michael Tel: (203) 705-3800
Vice President, Buisness Development Fax: (203) 705-3703
Michael.Smith@tronox.com

Trover Solutions Inc.

Provides recovery services to the insurance industry.
www.troversolutions.com
Employees: 700
SIC: 6411
Industry/ies: Insurance Industry

Chief Executive Officer Tel: (502) 214-1340
BADER, Jr., Robert G. Fax: (502) 214-1350

Main Headquarters
Mailing: Trover Plaza Tel: (502) 214-1340
9390 Bunsen Pkwy. Fax: (502) 214-1350
Louisville, KY 40220

Political Action Committees
Trover Solutions, Inc. PAC
FEC ID: C00340828
Contact: Daniel Gibson
9390 Bunsen Pkwy.
Louisville, KY 40220

Public Affairs and Related Activities Personnel

At Headquarters

FRENCH, Glen Tel: (502) 214-1340
Chief Financial Officer Fax: (502) 214-1350
GIBSON, Daniel Tel: (502) 214-1340
Senior Vice President, Human Resources, General Counsel, Fax: (502) 214-1350
Training and Development, PAC Treasurer
GORMAN, Slayton Tel: (502) 214-1340
Executive Vice President, Healthcare Sales, Client Solutions Fax: (502) 214-1350
and Marketing
SHARPS, Douglas R. Tel: (502) 214-1340
Executive Vice President, Business and Organizational Fax: (502) 214-1350
Development and PAC Treasurer

True Value Company

Formerly TruServ Corp. A hardware retailer.
truevaluecompany.com/home/flash.asp
Employees: 3,000
SIC: 5070
Industry/ies: Construction/Construction Materials; Machinery/Equipment;
Retail/Wholesale

Chairman of the Board Tel: (773) 695-5000
BURGER, Brent Fax: (773) 695-6516

President and Chief Executive Officer Tel: (773) 695-5000
HARTMANN, John Fax: (773) 695-6516

Main Headquarters
Mailing: 8600 W. Bryn Mawr Ave. Tel: (773) 695-5000
Chicago, IL 60631-3505 Fax: (773) 695-6516

Corporate Foundations and Giving Programs
True Value Foundation
Contact: Shirley Fugiel
8600 W. Bryn Mawr Ave.
Chicago, IL 60631-3505

Public Affairs and Related Activities Personnel

At Headquarters

ANDERSON, Catherine Tel: (773) 695-5000
Senior Vice President, Human Resources, General Counsel Fax: (773) 695-6516
and Secretary
FOHL, Blake Tel: (773) 695-5000

Senior Vice President, Marketing and Chief Customer Officer	Fax:	(773) 695-6516
FUGIEL, Shirley	Tel:	(773) 695-5000
Contact, Foundation	Fax:	(773) 695-6516
Shirley.fugiel@truevalue.com		
SAELENS, Jean	Tel:	(773) 695-5000
Vice President and Corporate Controller	Fax:	(773) 695-6516
SHUKLA, Abhinav	Tel:	(773) 695-5000
Senior Vice President and Chief Operating Officer	Fax:	(773) 695-6516
WAGNER, Barbara	Tel:	(773) 695-5000
Vice President and Corporate Treasurer	Fax:	(773) 695-6516

TrueBlue Inc.

An employment agency.
www.trueblueinc.com
Annual Revenues: $2.35 billion
Employees: 5,000
Ticker: NYSE: TBI
SIC: 7363
Industry/ies: Employees & Employment
Legislative Issues: EDU; HCR; IMM; LBR; TAX

Chairman of the Board	Tel:	(253) 383-9101
SAMBATARO, Jr., Joseph P.	Fax:	(877) 733-0399
jsambataro@trueblueinc.com		
Director and Chief Executive Officer	Tel:	(253) 383-9101
COOPER, Steven C.	Fax:	(877) 733-0399

Main Headquarters

Mailing:	P.O. Box 2910	Tel:	(253) 383-9101
	Tacoma, WA 98402-2910	Fax:	(877) 733-0399
		TF:	(800) 610-8920

Political Action Committees

True Blue Inc. PAC
FEC ID: C00363853
Contact: John R. Wilson
P.O. Box 2910
Tacoma, WA 98401

Contributions to Candidates: $45,750 (2015-2016)
Democrats: $22,250; Republicans: $23,500

Corporate Foundations and Giving Programs

True Blue Contributions Program		
P.O. Box 2910	Tel:	(253) 383-9101
Tacoma, WA 98401-2910		

Public Affairs and Related Activities Personnel

At Headquarters

BEHARELLE, Patrick	Tel:	(253) 383-9101
President and Chief Operating Officer	Fax:	(877) 733-0399
CANNON, Kimberly A.	Tel:	(253) 383-9101
Executive Vice President, Human Resources	Fax:	(877) 733-0399
DEFEBAUGH, James E.	Tel:	(253) 383-9101
Executive Vice President, General Counsel and Secretary	Fax:	(877) 733-0399
jdefebaugh@trueblueinc.com		
GAFFORD, Derrek L.	Tel:	(253) 383-9101
Executive Vice President and Chief Financial Officer	Fax:	(877) 733-0399
MCNAIR-HUFF, Natalie	Tel:	(253) 680-8473
Director, Government Relations	Fax:	(877) 733-0399
nmcnair-huff@trueblueinc.com		
Registered Federal Lobbyist		
NUBEL, Edward B.	Tel:	(253) 383-9101
Senior Vice President, Sales and Marketing	Fax:	(877) 733-0399
WILSON, John R.	Tel:	(253) 383-9101
PAC Treasurer	Fax:	(877) 733-0399

At Other Offices

BURKE, Stacey	Tel:	(253) 680-8291
Vice President, Corporate Communications		
1015 A St.		
Tacoma, WA 98401		
sburke@trueblueinc.com		

TruePosition Inc.

Provides wireless location technologies and solutions.
www.trueposition.com
Annual Revenues: $20.60 million
Employees: 250
Industry/ies: Communications; Computer/Technology; Telecommunications/Internet/Cable

Chief Executive Officer	Tel:	(610) 680-1000
WAGGY, Craig	Fax:	(610) 680-1199

Main Headquarters

Mailing:	1000 Chesterbrook Blvd.	
	Berwyn, PA 19312	

Public Affairs and Related Activities Personnel

At Headquarters

HOPPMAN, Michael	Tel:	(610) 680-1000
Senior Vice President, Finance and Chief Financial Officer	Fax:	(610) 680-1199
MORRISON, Robert	Tel:	(610) 680-1000
Executive Vice President, Business Operations	Fax:	(610) 680-1199
SALEN, Stuart	Tel:	(610) 680-1000
Senior Vice President, General Counsel	Fax:	(610) 680-1199

At Other Offices

LOGAN, John E.	Tel:	(212) 301-2814
Attorney		
1230 Avenue of the Americas, Suite 810		
New York City, NY 10020		

Truscott Rossman Group, LLC

Truscott Rossman is Michigan's premier strategic communications firm with offices in Lansing, Detroit and Grand Rapids.
www.truscottrossman.com
Industry/ies: Management

Chief Executive Officer and Principal	Tel:	(517) 487-9320
ROSSMAN-MCKINNEY, Kelly		

Main Headquarters

Mailing:	124 W Allegan St.	Tel:	(517) 487-9320
	Suite 800		
	Lansing, MI 48933		

Public Affairs and Related Activities Personnel

At Headquarters

BLUMER, Cathie	Tel:	(517) 487-9320
Executive Assistant to the President		
DAVIS, Graham	Tel:	(517) 487-9320
Director, New Media Relations		
MONTI, Ellen	Tel:	(517) 487-9320
Business Manager		
TIPPETT, Jeff	Tel:	(517) 487-9320
Chief Operating Officer		

TruServ Corp.

See listing on page 800 under True Value Company

Trust Resources Law Firm PC.

Law practice and advocacy.
Legislative Issues: IND

President	Tel:	(703) 887-4675
MCHUGH, Stephen J.		
steve@trlaw.net		

Main Headquarters

Mailing:	1101 30th St. NW
	Suite 500
	Washington, DC 20007

Trusted Computer Solutions

Computer network security.
www.trustedcs.com
Annual Revenues: $13.70 million
Employees: 100
Industry/ies: Computer/Technology

President	Tel:	(703) 318-7134
BROWN, Lisa	Fax:	(703) 318-5041

Main Headquarters

Mailing:	12950 Worldgate Dr.	Tel:	(703) 318-7134
	Suite 600	Fax:	(703) 318-5041
	Herndon, VA 20170	TF:	(866) 230-1307

Public Affairs and Related Activities Personnel

At Headquarters

DORCH, Sherryl	Tel:	(703) 537-4364
Vice President, Marketing	Fax:	(703) 318-5041
sdorch@trustedCS.com		

Trustees of the University of Pennsylvania

The University of Pennsylvania is one of the oldest universities in America.
www.upenn.edu
Industry/ies: Education
Legislative Issues: AGR; BUD; EDU; HCR; MMM; SCI

Vice President, Government & Community Affairs	Tel:	(215) 898-5000
COOPER , Jeffrey		
jeffcoop@upenn.edu		

Main Headquarters

Mailing:	3451 Walnut St.	Tel:	(215) 898-5000

Philadelphia, PA 19104

Corporate Foundations and Giving Programs

University Research Foundation
3451 Walnut St.
Philadelphia, PA 19104

Tel: (215) 898-5000

Public Affairs and Related Activities Personnel

At Headquarters

ANDRESEN, William
Associate Vice President, Federal Affairs
wgajr@upenn.edu
Registered Federal Lobbyist

Tel: (215) 898-1388

BARTOSHESKY, Amanda
Federal Lobbyist
Registered Federal Lobbyist

Tel: (215) 898-1388

BRYAN, Glenn
Assistant Vice President, Community Relations
gbryan@upenn.edu

Tel: (215) 898-5000

DEITCH, Dawn Maglicco
Executive Director
maglicco@upenn.edu

Tel: (215) 898-5000

DIRKS, Courtney
Federal Lobbyist
Registered Federal Lobbyist

Tel: (215) 898-5000

KELLY, Kevin Patrick
Federal Lobbyist
Registered Federal Lobbyist

Tel: (215) 898-5000

MENGEL, Courtney
Federal Lobbyist
Courtney.Mengel@uphs.upenn.edu
Registered Federal Lobbyist

Tel: (215) 898-1388

Trustmark National Bank

Provides banking, wealth management and insurance solutions.
www.trustmark.com
Annual Revenues: $568.99 million
Employees: 3,038
Ticker: NASDAQ: TRMK
Industry/ies: Banking/Finance/Investments

Chairman of the Board
GRAFTON, Daniel A.

Tel: (601) 208-5111
Fax: (604) 208-6684

President and Chief Executive Officer
HOST, Gerard R.

Tel: (601) 208-5111
Fax: (604) 208-6684

Main Headquarters
Mailing: P.O. Box 291
Jackson, MS 39205

Public Affairs and Related Activities Personnel

At Headquarters

REIN, F. Joseph
Assistant Secretary

At Other Offices

COLLIER, III, T. Harris
General Counsel and Secretary
248 E. Capitol St.
Jackson, MS 39201

Tel: (601) 208-5111
Fax: (604) 208-6684

GREER, Louis E.
Treasurer and Principal Financial Officer
248 E. Capitol St.
Jackson, MS 39201
lareer@trustmark.com

Tel: (601) 208-2310
Fax: (604) 208-6684

TRW Automotive

See listing on page 861 under ZF TRW

TSG Solutions

The Tactical Survey System is designed to enhance training, allowing response teams to virtually create and practice response scenarios.
www.tsgsinc.com
Employees: 100
NAICS: 541512; 541513; 541519; 541611; 541620; 541712; 541330; 541511; 541690; 561621; 541990; 561210; 562910
Industry/ies: Defense/Homeland Security; Government-Related

Chief Executive Officer and Chairman of the Board
IFFLAND, John E.

Tel: (909) 475-4080
Fax: (909) 475-4081

Main Headquarters
Mailing: 2701 Loker Ave. West
Suite 110
Carlsbad, CA 92010

Tel: (909) 475-4080
Fax: (909) 475-4081
TF: (877) 475-4080

Public Affairs and Related Activities Personnel

At Headquarters

GRANUM, Dianna
Chief Strategy Officer and Executive Vice President, Business Development

Tel: (909) 475-4080
Fax: (909) 475-4081

LARSON, Adam
Vice President, Finance and Administration

Tel: (909) 475-4080

TTX Company

A rail car pooling and leasing company.
www.ttx.com
Employees: 1,700
SIC: 3743; 3441; 4741
NAICS: 33651; 332312; 532411
Industry/ies: Railroads; Transportation
Legislative Issues: BUD; RRR; TRA

President and Chief Executive Officer
WELLS, Thomas F.

Tel: (312) 853-3223
Fax: (312) 984-3790

Main Headquarters
Mailing: 101 N. Wacker Dr.
Chicago, IL 60606

Tel: (312) 853-3223
Fax: (312) 984-3790
TF: (800) 889-4357

Political Action Committees

TTX PAC
FEC ID: C00138974
Contact: Patrick B. Loftus
101 N. Wacker Dr.
Chicago, IL 60606

Contributions to Candidates: $17,913 (2015-2016)
Democrats: $7,500; Republicans: $10,413

Corporate Foundations and Giving Programs

TTX Company Contributions Program
101 N. Wacker Dr.
Chicago, IL 60606

Public Affairs and Related Activities Personnel

At Headquarters

DUDLEY, Victoria A.
Vice President, Chief Financial Officer and Treasurer

Tel: (312) 853-3223
Fax: (312) 984-3790

LOFTUS, Patrick B.
Senior Vice President, Law and Administration and PAC Treasurer

Tel: (312) 853-3223
Fax: (312) 984-3790

POWERS, Brian R.
Vice President, Human Resources and Labor Relations
Brain.powers@ttx.com

Tel: (312) 984-3701
Fax: (312) 984-3790

TREADWAY, Anne E.
Assistant General Counsel and Assistant Secretary
Anne.Treadway@ttx.com

Tel: (312) 853-3223
Fax: (312) 984-3790

Tufts Health Plan

A Massachusetts-based health plan that provides health care coverage.
www.tuftshealthplan.com
Employees: 2,700
Industry/ies: Medicine/Health Care/Mental Health
Legislative Issues: HCR; INS; MED; MMM

President and Chief Executive Officer
CROSWELL, Thomas A.

Tel: (617) 972-9400
Fax: (617) 973-9048

Main Headquarters
Mailing: 705 Mt. Auburn St.
Watertown, MA 02472

Tel: (617) 972-9400
Fax: (617) 973-9048
TF: (888) 880-8699

Corporate Foundations and Giving Programs

Tufts Health Plan Foundation
Contact: James Roosevelt Jr.
705 Mt. Auburn St.
Watertown, MA 02472

Public Affairs and Related Activities Personnel

At Headquarters

ABRUZESSE, Derek
Senior Vice President and Chief Strategy Officer

Tel: (617) 972-9400
Fax: (617) 973-9048

BACKON, Marc
Senior Vice President and Chief Sales and Marketing Officer, Commercial Products

Tel: (617) 972-9400
Fax: (617) 973-9048

GREENE, Lydia
Senior Vice President and Chief Human Resources Officer

Tel: (617) 972-9400
Fax: (617) 973-9048

HAGOPIAN, Sonya
Vice President, Corporate Communications and Public Relations

Tel: (617) 972-1090
Fax: (617) 973-9048

KELLEY, Tina
Senior Compliance Assistant
Tina_Kelley@tufts-health.com

Tel: (617) 972-9400
Fax: (617) 973-9048

KURPAD, Umesh

Tel: (617) 972-9400

Senior Vice President and Chief Financial Officer	Fax:	(617) 973-9048
MAHONEY, Mary O'Toole	Tel:	(617) 972-9400
Senior Vice President, General Counsel	Fax:	(617) 973-9048
ROOSEVELT, Jr., James	Tel:	(617) 972-9400
President, Tufts Health Plan Foundation	Fax:	(617) 973-9048
TREBINO, Tricia	Tel:	(617) 972-9400
Senior Vice President and Chief Operations Officer	Fax:	(617) 973-9048

Tuggey, Rosenthal, Pauerstein, Sandoloski, Agather, LLP (TRPSA)

Maintains additional offices in Austin, TX and Washington, DC. The law firm collaborates with The Loeffler Group (see separate listing) on selected federal government affairs projects.
www.rpsalaw.com
Legislative Issues: CAW; ENV; ROD; TRA

Main Headquarters

Mailing:	755 E. Mulberry	Tel:	(210) 225-5000
	Suite 200	Fax:	(210) 354-4034
	San Antonio, TX 78212		

Public Affairs and Related Activities Personnel

At Other Offices

BEINKE, Allen	Tel:	(512) 479-8162
Partner	Fax:	(512) 479-8282
1001 Congress Ave., Suite 350		
Austin, TX 78701		
CLEVELAND, Kelli	Tel:	(512) 479-6998
Federal Lobbyist		
1001 Congress Ave., Suite 350		
Austin, TX 78701		
FOWLER, Meredyth D.	Tel:	(512) 479-8282
Federal Lobbyist		
1001 Congress Ave., Suite 350		
Austin, TX 78701		
HESSION, Margaret	Tel:	(512) 479-6403
Principal	Fax:	(512) 479-8282
1001 Congress Ave., Suite 350		
Austin, TX 78701		
HOLTON, Cheryl	Tel:	(512) 479-6403
Federal Lobbyist	Fax:	(512) 479-8282
1001 Congress Ave., Suite 350		
Austin, TX 78701		
LEGGETT, Kimberly	Tel:	(512) 479-6403
Government Affairs Specialist		
611 S. Congress Ave., Suite 340		
Austin, TX 78704		

Tupperware Brands Corporation

In December of 2005, Tupperware Corporation changed its name to Tupperware Brands Corporation. The company makes and sells household products and beauty items.
www.tupperwarebrands.com
Annual Revenues: $2.52 billion
Employees: 13,100
Ticker: NYSE: TUP
SIC: 3089
NAICS: 326199
Industry/ies: Plastics Industry; Rubber Industry

Chairman of the Board and Chief Executive Officer	Tel:	(407) 826-5050
GOINGS, E.V.	Fax:	(407) 826-8268

Main Headquarters

Mailing:	14901 S. Orange Blossom Trail	Tel:	(407) 826-5050
	Orlando, FL 32837	Fax:	(407) 826-8268
		TF:	(800) 366-3800

Political Action Committees
Tupperware Brands Corporation PAC
FEC ID: C00317529
Contact: SLAPPEY BRYAN

14901 S. Orange Blossom Trail	Tel:	(407) 826-5050
Orlando, FL 32837	Fax:	(407) 826-8268

Contributions to Candidates: $6,000 (2015-2016)
Democrats: $1,500; Republicans: $4,500

Corporate Foundations and Giving Programs
Tupperware Brands Foundation
Contact: Yolanda Londono

P.O. Box 2353	Tel:	(407) 826-5050
Orlando, FL 32802	Fax:	(407) 826-8268

Public Affairs and Related Activities Personnel

At Headquarters

BRAUNGARDT, Anna	Tel:	(407) 826-5050
Senior Vice President, Worldwide Human Resources	Fax:	(407) 826-8268
BRYAN, SLAPPEY	Tel:	(407) 826-5050
PAC Treasurer	Fax:	(407) 826-8268
BURCHFIELD, Teresa	Tel:	(407) 826-4475

Vice President, Investor Relations	Fax:	(407) 826-8268
DECKER, Nicole	Tel:	(407) 826-4560
Vice President, Strategy	Fax:	(407) 826-4510
finrel@tupperware.com		
GARCIA, Lillian D.	Tel:	(407) 826-5050
Executive Vice President and Chief Human Resources Officer	Fax:	(407) 826-8268
HAJEK, Josef	Tel:	(407) 826-5050
Senior Vice President, Tax and Government Affairs	Fax:	(407) 826-8268
HEMUS, Simon C.	Tel:	(407) 826-5050
President and Chief Operating Officer	Fax:	(407) 826-8268
LONDONO, Yolanda	Tel:	(407) 826-5050
Vice President, Global Social Responsibility	Fax:	(407) 826-8268
POTESHMAN, Michael	Tel:	(407) 826-5050
Executive Vice President and Chief Financial Officer	Fax:	(407) 826-8268
MikePoteshman@tupperware.com		
ROEHLK, Thomas M.	Tel:	(407) 826-5050
Executive Vice President, Chief Legal Officer and Secretary	Fax:	(407) 826-8268
STEELE-ZEGELBONE, Elinor	Tel:	(407) 826-5050
Vice President, Global Public Relations	Fax:	(407) 826-8268
publicrelations@tupperware.com		
VOLES, Lydia	Tel:	(646) 356-8305
Contact, Media Relations	Fax:	(407) 826-8268
lvoles@maloneyfox.com		

Turi Defense Group Inc.

An international defense and security services firm.
turidefense.com
Industry/ies: Defense/Homeland Security; Government-Related

President and Chief Executive Officer	Tel:	(888) 953-5999
TURI, Marc		

Main Headquarters

Mailing:	7521 W. Lake Mead Blvd.	Tel:	(888) 953-5999
	Suite 300		
	Las Vegas, NV 89128		

Public Affairs and Related Activities Personnel

At Headquarters

BAUER, Dana	Tel:	(888) 953-5999

Turner Broadcasting System

Global media company. It creates and programs branded news, entertainment, animation, young adult and sport media on television and other platforms. It is a Time Warner Company.
www.turner.com
Employees: 7,000
Ticker: NASDAQ TRACE: AOL.HB
SIC: 4833
Industry/ies: Communications; Media/Mass Communication

Chairman and Chief Executive Officer	Tel:	(404) 827-1700
MARTIN, John	Fax:	(404) 827-2437

Main Headquarters

Mailing:	One CNN Center	Tel:	(404) 827-1700
	190 Marietta St NW	Fax:	(404) 827-2437
	Atlanta, GA 30303		

Corporate Foundations and Giving Programs

Turner Broadcasting System Contributions Program		
One CNN Center, 100 International Blvd.	Tel:	(404) 827-1700
Atlanta, GA 30303		

Public Affairs and Related Activities Personnel

At Headquarters

DESROCHES, Pascal	Tel:	(404) 827-1700
Executive Vice President and Chief Financial Officer	Fax:	(404) 827-2437
HURVITZ, Lauren	Tel:	(404) 827-1700
Executive Vice President and Chief Communications and Corporate Marketing Officer	Fax:	(404) 827-2437
LEVY, David	Tel:	(404) 827-1700
President, Turner Broadcasting System, Inc.	Fax:	(404) 827-2437
SAMS, Louise	Tel:	(404) 827-1700
Executive Vice President and General Counsel	Fax:	(404) 827-2024
louise.sams@turner.com		
SANTONE, Angela	Tel:	(404) 827-1700
Executive Vice President and Global Chief Human Resources Officer	Fax:	(404) 827-2437
SHAPIRO, Doug	Tel:	(404) 827-1700
Executive Vice President and Chief Strategy Officer	Fax:	(404) 827-2437
ZEILER, Gerhard	Tel:	(404) 827-1700
President, Turner Broadcasting System International	Fax:	(404) 827-2437

The Turner Corporation

Parent Company of Turner Construction Company. A subsidiary of German construction group HOCHTIEFA. A commercial, industrial, institutional and multi-unit residential construction company.
www.turnerconstruction.com
SIC: 1540
Industry/ies: Construction/Construction Materials

President and Chief Executive Officer
DAVOREN, Peter J.
Tel: (212) 229-6313
Fax: (214) 915-9700

Main Headquarters
Mailing: 433 1st Ave
New York, NY 10010
Tel: (212) 683-7710

Corporate Foundations and Giving Programs
The Turner Corporation Contributions Program
901 Main St.
Suite 4900
Dallas, TX 75202
Tel: (214) 915-9600
Fax: (214) 915-9700

Public Affairs and Related Activities Personnel

At Other Offices

DICIURCIO, John
Chief Operating Officer
901 Main St., Suite 4900
Dallas, TX 75202
Tel: (214) 915-9600
Fax: (214) 915-9700

GOULD, Karen O.
Senior Vice President, Chief Financial Officer
901 Main St., Suite 4900
Dallas, TX 75202
Tel: (214) 915-9600
Fax: (214) 915-9700

LEITNER, Lars
Senior Vice President, Chief Strategy Officer
901 Main St., Suite 4900
Dallas, TX 75202
lleitner@tcco.com
Tel: (212) 229-6052
Fax: (214) 915-9700

MCFADDEN, Chris
Vice President, Communications
901 Main St., Suite 4900
Dallas, TX 75202
Tel: (212) 229-6145
Fax: (212) 229-6390

Tutor.com

Tutoring and homework help services.
www.tutor.com
Annual Revenues: $9.20 million
Employees: 200
Industry/ies: Education

Chief Executive Officer
GINSBERG, Mandy
Tel: (212) 528-3101

Main Headquarters
Mailing: 555 W. 18th St.
Fourth Floor
New York City, NY 10011
Tel: (212) 528-3101
TF: (800) 411-1970

Public Affairs and Related Activities Personnel

At Headquarters

DONALDS, Kevin
Senior Vice President, Operations and Chief Financial Officer
Tel: (212) 528-3101

KOHN, Jennifer
Vice President, Corporate Communications
jkohn@tutor.com
Tel: (212) 528-3101

WHITE, Sandi
Vice President, Institutional Sales and Marketing
swhite@tutor.com
Tel: (212) 528-3101

Tuvin Associates

Lobbying Firm
tuvingovernmentaffairslobbying.com

Main Headquarters
Mailing: 2805 Washington Ave.
Chevy Chase, MD 20815-3009
Tel: (301) 588-8461

Public Affairs and Related Activities Personnel

At Headquarters

TUVIN, Carl R.
Head of Firm
tuvin_associates@juno.com
Tel: (301) 588-8461

TW Telecom Inc.

Provider of managed networking solutions.
www.twtelecom.com
Annual Revenues: $1.59 billion
Employees: 3,397
Ticker: NASDAQ: TWTC
SIC: 4813
Industry/ies: Communications; Telecommunications/Internet/Cable

Legislative Issues: TEC

Chairman of the Board and Chief Executive Officer
HERDA, Larissa L.
larissa.herda@twtelecom
Tel: (303) 566-1000
Fax: (303) 566-1011

Main Headquarters
Mailing: 10475 Park Meadows Dr.
Littleton, CO 80124
Tel: (303) 566-1000
Fax: (303) 566-1011
TF: (800) 829-0420

Political Action Committees
Tw Telecom, Inc. PAC
FEC ID: C00355941
Contact: Reggie Vegliante
10475 Park Meadows Dr.
Littleton, CO 80124
Tel: (303) 566-1000
Fax: (303) 566-1011

Corporate Foundations and Giving Programs
TW Telecom Contributions Program
10475 Park Meadows Dr.
Littleton, CO 80124

Public Affairs and Related Activities Personnel

At Headquarters

BLOUNT, John T.
President and Chief Operating Officer
Tel: (303) 566-1000
Fax: (303) 566-1011

CURTIN, Carole
Vice President, Investor Relations
carole.curtin@twtelecom.com
Tel: (303) 566-1000
Fax: (303) 566-1011

DAVIS, Tina A.
Senior Vice President, General Counsel
Tel: (303) 566-1000
Fax: (303) 566-1011

GASKINS, Robert W.
Senior Vice President, Corporate Development and Strategy
Tel: (303) 566-1000
Fax: (303) 566-1011

HARDARDT, Steve
Senior Vice President, Human Resources and Business Administration
steve.hardardt@twtelecom.com
Tel: (303) 566-1000
Fax: (303) 566-1011

JONES, Paul B.
Executive Vice President, General Counsel and Regulatory Policy
Tel: (303) 566-1000
Fax: (303) 566-1011

MELDRUM, Robert
Vice President, Corporate Communications
bob.meldrum@twtelecom.com
Tel: (303) 324-9588
Fax: (303) 566-1011

PETERS, Mark A.
Executive Vice President and Chief Financial Officer
mark.peters@twtelecom.com
Tel: (303) 566-1545
Fax: (303) 566-1011

ROULEAU, Michael A.
Senior Vice President, Business Development and Public Policy
Tel: (303) 566-1000
Fax: (303) 566-1011

STUART, Jill R.
Senior Vice President, Accounting and Finance and Chief Accounting Officer
Tel: (303) 566-1000
Fax: (303) 566-1011

TAYLOR, Graham
Senior Vice President, Marketing
Tel: (303) 566-1000
Fax: (303) 566-1011

VEGLIANTE, Reggie
Vice President Finance and Treasurer, Lobbyist and PAC Treasurer
Tel: (303) 566-1000
Fax: (303) 566-1011

Twenty-First Century Fox, Inc.

Multinational mass media corporation.
Industry/ies: Communications
Legislative Issues: ADV; COM; CPT; MIA; TAX; TEC; TRD

Chief Executive Officer
MURDOCH , James
Tel: (212) 852-7000

Main Headquarters
Mailing: 444 N. Capitol St. NW
Suite 740
Washington, DC 20001

Political Action Committees
Twenty-First Century Fox, Inc. PAC (Fox PAC)
FEC ID: C00330019
Contact: Kristopher Jones
444 N. Capitol St. NW, Suite 740
Washington, DC 20001
Tel: (202) 824-6500
Fax: (202) 824-6510

Contributions to Candidates: $240,000 (2015-2016)
Democrats: $82,000; Republicans: $158,000

Principal Recipients

HOUSE
MCCARTHY, KEVIN (REP-CA)
UPTON, FREDERICK STEPHEN (REP-MI)

Public Affairs and Related Activities Personnel

At Headquarters

LANE, Rick
Senior Vice President, Government Relations
Registered Federal Lobbyist

O'CALLAHAN, Janet
Federal Lobbyist

RAMSEY, Kathleen
Federal Lobbyist
Registered Federal Lobbyist

REGAN, Jr., Michael
Legal Consultant
Registered Federal Lobbyist

At Other Offices

HENDERSON, Julie   Tel: (212) 852-7000
Executive Vice President, Chief Communications Officer
1211 Avenue of the Americas
New York City, NY 10036

JONES, Kristopher
Federal Lobbyist and PAC Contact
400 N. Capitol St. NW, Suite 890
Washington, DC 20001
Registered Federal Lobbyist

LANE, Patrick J.
Senior Vice President, Government Relations
400 N. Capitol St. NW, Suite 890
Washington, DC 20001

NALLEN, John   Tel: (212) 852-7000
Senior Executive Vice President, Chief Financial Officer
1211 Avenue of the Americas
New York City, NY 10036

NOLTE , Reed   Tel: (212) 852-7000
Senior Vice President, Investor Relations
1211 Avenue of the Americas
New York City, NY 10036

NOVA , Janet   Tel: (212) 852-7000
Executive Vice President, Deputy Group General Counsel
1211 Avenue of the Americas
New York City, NY 10036

SMITH, Chip
Executive Vice President, Global Public Affairs
1101 K St. NW, Suite 400
Washington, DC 20005

ZWEIFACH , Gerson A.   Tel: (212) 852-7000
Senior Executive Vice President and Group General Counsel,
Chief Compliance Officer
1211 Avenue of the Americas
New York City, NY 10036

Twin Star Medical

A medical technology company.
www.twinstarmedical.com
Annual Revenues: $1.00 million
Industry/ies: Medicine/Health Care/Mental Health

President, Chief Executive Officer and Director   Tel: (612) 382-0888
STICE, Jim   Fax: (612) 338-9181
jim.stice@twinstarmedical.com

Main Headquarters
Mailing: 700 S. Tenth Ave.   Tel: (612) 382-0888
          Suite 120   Fax: (612) 338-9181
          Minneapolis, MN 55415

Twitter, Inc.

Online social networking service.
Industry/ies: Communications; Computer/Technology; Telecommunications/
Internet/Cable
Legislative Issues: CPI; CPT; GOV; INT; LAW; TEC

Main Headquarters
Mailing: 1133 15th St. NW, Ninth Floor
          Suite 600
          Washington, DC 20005

Political Action Committees
Twitter, Inc. PAC
FEC ID:
Contact: Vijaya Gadde
1355 Market St.
Suite 900
San Francisco, 94103

Public Affairs and Related Activities Personnel

At Headquarters

CARTY, William
Manager, Public Policy

CROWELL, Colin
Head, Global Public Policy

EVINS, Sean C.
Associate,Government & News

FINN, Mindy
Strategic Partnerships

GADDE, Vijaya
PAC Contact

SHARP, Adam
Government Liaison

TXU Corporation

See listing on page 292 under Energy Future Holdings Corporation

TXU Electric Delivery

See listing on page 603 under Oncor Electric Delivery

Tyco International (US), Inc.

A diversified company that offers products ranging from residential, commercial security,
fire suppression systems to electrical connectors in cars, trucks, and airplanes, as well as
firefighter equipment construction materials. Acquired Broadview Security in 2010.
www.tyco.com
Annual Revenues: $10.28 billion
Employees: 57,000
Ticker: NYSE: TYC
SIC: 7380
Industry/ies: Communications; Electricity & Electronics; Electronics; Energy/
Electricity; Telecommunications/Internet/Cable
Legislative Issues: BUD; CPT; EDU; HOM; TAX; TRA; TRD

Chairman of the Board   Tel: (609) 720-4200
BREEN, Edward D.   Fax: (609) 720-4208

Chief Executive Officer   Tel: (609) 720-4200
OLIVER, George R.   Fax: (609) 720-4208

Main Headquarters
Mailing: Nine Roszel Rd.   Tel: (609) 720-4200
          Princeton, NJ 08540   Fax: (609) 720-4208

Washington Office
Mailing: 607 14th St. NW   Tel: (202) 471-3355
          Suite 550   Fax: (202) 393-5110
          Washington, DC 20005

Political Action Committees
Tyco International Management Company Employees PAC (Tyco Employees
PAC)
FEC ID: C00113753
Contact: Eric Walsh
Nine Roszel Rd.   Tel: (202) 393-5100
Princeton, NJ 08540   Fax: (202) 393-5110

   Contributions to Candidates: $273,750 (2015-2016)
   Democrats: $65,500; Republicans: $208,250

     Principal Recipients

       SENATE
       AYOTTE, KELLY A (REP-NH)
       BURR, RICHARD (REP-NC)
       KIRK, MARK STEVEN (REP-IL)
       PORTMAN, ROB (REP-OH)

       HOUSE
       BRADY, KEVIN (REP-TX)
       COFFMAN, MIKE REP. (REP-CO)
       MEEHAN, PATRICK L. MR. (REP-PA)
       PAULSEN, ERIK (REP-MN)
       RYAN, PAUL D. (REP-WI)

Corporate Foundations and Giving Programs
Tyco International (us) Inc. Contributions Program
Nine Roszel Rd.   Tel: (609) 720-4200
Princeton, NJ 08540   Fax: (609) 720-4208

Public Affairs and Related Activities Personnel

At Headquarters

BROWN, Chris   Tel: (609) 720-4200
Vice President Strategy   Fax: (609) 720-4208

CLEMENTS, Scott   Tel: (609) 720-4200
President of Vertical Market Solutions and Chief Technology   Fax: (609) 720-4208
Officer

COSTELLO, Larry   Tel: (609) 720-4200
Executive Vice President and Chief Human Resources Officer   Fax: (609) 720-4208

GREWAL, CPA, CMA, Manpreet Singh   Tel: (609) 720-4200
Global Director, Financial Audits and Enterprise Risk   Fax: (609) 720-4208

NAYAR, Arun   Tel: (609) 720-4200
Executive Vice President and Chief Financial Officer   Fax: (609) 720-4208

REINSDORF, Judith A.   Tel: (609) 720-4200
Executive Vice President and General Counsel   Fax: (609) 720-4208

REPKO, John *Senior Vice President and Chief Information Officer*	Tel: Fax:	(609) 720-4200 (609) 720-4208		

REPKO, John
Senior Vice President and Chief Information Officer
Tel: (609) 720-4200
Fax: (609) 720-4208

WALSH, Eric
Lobbyist and PAC Treasurer
Tel: (609) 720-4200
Fax: (609) 720-4208

YOUNG, Brian
Senior Vice President, Global Enterprise Sales
Tel: (609) 720-4200
Fax: (609) 720-4208

At Washington Office

BENNETT, Catherine
Vice President, Public Affairs
cbennett@tyco.com
Tel: (202) 350-6906
Fax: (202) 393-5110

JONES, Arthur
Senior Director, Public Affairs
Registered Federal Lobbyist
Tel: (202) 471-3355
Fax: (202) 393-5110

PHILSON, Kelly
Director, Public Affairs
kphilson@tyco.com
Registered Federal Lobbyist
Tel: (202) 350-6917
Fax: (202) 393-5110

SHARMAN, Craig
Director, Government Affairs
Registered Federal Lobbyist
Tel: (202) 393-5100
Fax: (202) 393-5110

STEELE, John
Senior Director, State Government Affairs
jsteele@tyco.com
Tel: (202) 393-5100
Fax: (202) 393-5110

Tyco Laboratories, Inc.

See listing on page 805 under Tyco International (US), Inc.

Tyson Foods, Inc.

A processor of chicken, beef, and pork as well as flour and corn tortilla products.
www.tysonfoods.com
Annual Revenues: $40.58 billion
Employees: 124,000
Ticker: NYSE: TSN
SIC: 2015
NAICS: 311119
Industry/ies: Food And Beverage Industry
Legislative Issues: AGR; ENG; ENV; LBR; TAX; TRA; TRD

Chairman of the Board
TYSON, John H.
john.tyson@tyson.com
Tel: (479) 290-4000
Fax: (479) 751-0834

President and Chief Executive Officer
SMITH, Donnie
Tel: (479) 290-4000
Fax: (479) 751-0834

Main Headquarters
Mailing: 2200 W. Don Tyson Pkwy.
Springdale, AR 72762
Tel: (479) 290-4000
Fax: (479) 751-0834
TF: (800) 233-6332

Washington Office
Mailing: 601 Pennsylvania Ave. NW
Suite 750
Washington, DC 20004
Tel: (202) 393-3921
Fax: (202) 393-3922

Political Action Committees
Tyson Foods Inc. PAC (TYPAC)
FEC ID: C00169821
Contact: Adam Kees
P.O. Box 2020
Springdale, AR 72765
Tel: (479) 290-4000
Fax: (479) 290-4061

> **Contributions to Candidates:** $119,483 (2015-2016)
> Democrats: $24,500; Republicans: $94,983

> **Principal Recipients**

> **SENATE**
> BOOZMAN, JOHN (REP-AR)

> **HOUSE**
> WOMACK, STEVE (REP-AR)

Corporate Foundations and Giving Programs
Tyson Foods Foundation
Contact: Annetta Young
P.O. Box 2020
Springdale, AR 72764

Public Affairs and Related Activities Personnel

At Headquarters

CARPER , Hal
Executive Vice President, Strategy and New Ventures
Tel: (479) 290-4000
Fax: (479) 751-0834

COLE, Devin
President, Sales, Marketing and Chief Commercial Officer
Tel: (479) 290-4000
Fax: (479) 751-0834

COOPER, Gary
Senior Vice President and Chief Information Officer
Tel: (479) 290-4000
Fax: (479) 751-0834

HUDSON, R. Read
Vice President / Associate General Counsel / Secretary
Tel: (479) 290-4000
Fax: (479) 751-0834

KATHOL, Jon
Tel: (479) 290-4235

Vice President, Investor Relations
jon.kathol@tyson.com
Fax: (479) 751-0834

KEES, Adam
PAC Contact and Treasury Manager
Tel: (479) 290-4000
Fax: (479) 751-0834

LAWSON, Libby
Vice President, Public Relations
libby.lawson@tyson.com
Tel: (479) 290-4000
Fax: (479) 751-0834

LEATHERBY, Dennis
Executive Vice President and Chief Financial Officer
Tel: (479) 290-4000
Fax: (479) 751-0834

LILYGREN, Sara J.
Executive Vice President, Corporate Affairs
sara.lilygren@tyson.com
Registered Federal Lobbyist
Tel: (479) 290-4000
Fax: (479) 751-0834

LOCHNER, James V.
Advisor
Tel: (479) 290-4000
Fax: (479) 751-0834

MICKELSON, Gary R.
Senior Director, Public Relations
Tel: (479) 290-6111
Fax: (479) 751-0834

NICHOLSON, Ed
Director, Social Media and Community Relations
ed.nicholson@tyson.com
Tel: (479) 290-4000
Fax: (479) 751-0834

OLEKSIUK, Mary
Executive Vice President and Chief Human Resources Officer
Tel: (479) 290-4000
Fax: (479) 751-0834

SCHAFFER, III, Archie
Executive Vice President, Corporate Affairs
Registered Federal Lobbyist
Tel: (479) 290-4000
Fax: (479) 751-0834

VAN BEBBER, David L.
Executive Vice President and General Counsel
Tel: (479) 290-4000
Fax: (479) 751-0834

YOUNG, Annetta
Director, Corporate Philanthropy
charitablegiving@tyson.com
Tel: (479) 290-4813
Fax: (479) 751-0834

At Washington Office

MENOTTI, Todd
Senior Director, International Corporate Affairs
todd-menotti@tyson.com
Registered Federal Lobbyist
Tel: (202) 393-3921
Fax: (202) 393-3922

MENOTTI, Esq., David E.
Federal Lobbyist
david.menotti@pillsburylaw.com
Registered Federal Lobbyist
Tel: (202) 393-3921
Fax: (202) 393-3922

MIKA, Matt
Director, Government Relations
matt.mika@tyson.com
Registered Federal Lobbyist
Tel: (202) 393-3921
Fax: (202) 393-3922

PENRY, Charles
Vice President, Federal Government Relations
Registered Federal Lobbyist
Tel: (202) 393-3921
Fax: (202) 393-3922

VENEGAS, Nora H.
Director, Federal Governmental Relations
nora.venegas@tyson.com
Registered Federal Lobbyist
Tel: (202) 393-3921
Fax: (202) 393-3922

U.S. Bancorp

A bank holding company. Merged with Firstar Corp. in 2001.
www.usbank.com
Annual Revenues: $18.35 billion
Employees: 66,750
Ticker: NYSE: USB
Industry/ies: Banking/Finance/Investments
Legislative Issues: BAN; INT; TAX

Chairman, President and Chief Executive Officer
DAVIS, Richard K.
richard.davis@usbank.com
Tel: (651) 466-3000
Fax: (612) 303-0782

Main Headquarters
Mailing: 800 Nicollet Mall
Minneapolis, MN 55402-4302
Tel: (651) 466-3000
Fax: (612) 303-0782
TF: (800) 872-2657

Washington Office
Mailing: 950 F St. NW
Suite 750
Washington, DC 20004
Tel: (202) 442-2713

Political Action Committees
U.S. Bancorp Political Participation Program PAC
FEC ID: C00018036
Contact: Kevin MacMillan
950 F St. NW
Suite 750
Washington, DC 20004

US Bancorp Federal Political Action Committee
FEC ID: C00488882
Contact: Kevin MacMillan
950 F St. NW
Tel: (651) 466-3000

Suite 750
Washington, DC 20004
Fax: (612) 303-0782

Contributions to Candidates: $294,700 (2015-2016)
Democrats: $111,500; Republicans: $182,200; Other: $1,000

Principal Recipients

HOUSE
CROWLEY, JOSEPH (DEM-NY)
RYAN, PAUL D. (REP-WI)

Corporate Foundations and Giving Programs

U.S. Bancorp Foundation
Contact: Reba Dominski
Princeton, NJ
Tel: (651) 466-3000

Public Affairs and Related Activities Personnel

At Headquarters

BURKE, Deborah M.
Senior Vice President, Government and Community Relations
Mail Stop BC-MN-H2I0
deb.burke@usbank.com
Tel: (612) 303-0746
Fax: (612) 303-0782

CARLSON, Jennie P.
Executive Vice President, Human Resources
jennie.carlson@usbank.com
Tel: (651) 466-3000
Fax: (612) 303-0782

CECERE, Andrew
Vice Chairman and Chief Operating Officer
andrew.cecere@usbank.com
Tel: (651) 466-3000
Fax: (612) 303-0782

CHAREST, Teri L.
Vice President, Corporate Communications
teri.charest@usbank.com
Tel: (612) 303-0732
Fax: (612) 303-0735

CHOSY, James L.
Executive Vice President, General Counsel and Corporate Secretary
Tel: (651) 466-3000
Fax: (612) 303-0782

DOMINSKI, Reba
Senior Vice President of U.S. Bank Foundation and Community Relations
Tel: (651) 466-3000
Fax: (612) 303-0782

GRINER, Robert
Vice President, Federal Government Relations and Corporate Counsel
Registered Federal Lobbyist
Tel: (651) 466-3000
Fax: (612) 303-0782

QUINN, Katherine B.
Executive Vice President, Strategy and Corporate Affairs
Tel: (651) 466-3000
Fax: (612) 303-0782

ROGERS, Kathleen A.
Vice Chairman and Chief Financial Officer
Tel: (651) 466-3000
Fax: (612) 303-0782

WHITAKER, Stephen
Federal Lobbyist
Registered Federal Lobbyist
Tel: (651) 466-3000
Fax: (612) 303-0782

At Washington Office

LOWRY, Carolyn
Government Relations Assistant and PAC Coordinator
Tel: (202) 442-2713

MACMILLAN, Kevin
Managing Director, Federal Government Relations & PAC Treasurer
kevin.macmillan@usbank.com
Registered Federal Lobbyist
Tel: (202) 442-2713

U.S. Healthworks Inc.

Provides occupational medicine and urgent care services.
www.ushealthworks.com
Annual Revenues: $154.9 million
Employees: 3,600
Industry/ies: Medicine/Health Care/Mental Health
Legislative Issues: BUD; HCR; LBR; RET; WEL

Chairman of the Board, President and Chief Executive Officer
CROWLEY, Daniel D.
Tel: (661) 678-2600
Fax: (661) 678-2700

Main Headquarters
Mailing: 25124 Springfield Ct.
Suite 200
Valencia, CA 91355
Tel: (661) 678-2600
Fax: (661) 678-2700
TF: (800) 720-2432

Political Action Committees
U.S. Healthworks Inc. PAC
FEC ID: C00414706
Contact: Robert Hutchinson
25124 Springfield Ct.
Suite 200
Valencia, CA 91355

Public Affairs and Related Activities Personnel

At Headquarters

ARNDS, Brian
Vice President, Human Resources
Tel: (661) 678-2600
Fax: (661) 678-2700

COYLE, Kevin
General Counsel
Tel: (661) 678-2600
Fax: (661) 678-2700

DUNCAN, John C.
Vice President, Government Affairs
Tel: (661) 678-2600
Fax: (661) 678-2700

HUTCHINSON, Robert
Chief Finance Officer
Mail Stop Suite 250
rhutchinson@ushealthworks.com
Tel: (661) 678-2600
Fax: (661) 678-2700

MALLAS, Joseph T.
President and Chief Operating Officer
Tel: (661) 678-2600
Fax: (661) 678-2700

YU, Diane
Vice President, Marketing and Sales
Tel: (661) 678-2600
Fax: (661) 678-2700

U.S. Physical Therapy

Provides post-operative care for orthopedic-related disorders and sports-related injuries.
www.usph.com
Annual Revenues: $308.40 million
Employees: 2,200
Ticker: NASDAQ (GS): USPH
Industry/ies: Medicine/Health Care/Mental Health

Chairman of the Board
PULLINS, Jerald L.
Tel: (713) 297-7000
Fax: (713) 297-7090

President and Chief Executive Officer and Director
READING, Christopher J.
Tel: (701) 297-7000
Fax: (701) 297-7090

Main Headquarters
Mailing: 1300 W. Sam Houston Pkwy. South
Suite 300
Houston, TX 77042
Tel: (713) 297-7000
Fax: (713) 297-7090
TF: (800) 580-6285

Public Affairs and Related Activities Personnel

At Headquarters

MCAFEE, Larry W.
Executive Vice President, Chief Financial Officer and Director
lmcafee@usph.com
Tel: (701) 297-7000
Fax: (701) 297-7090

At Other Offices

GLYNN, Amy
Contact, Communications
757 Third Ave.
New York City, NY 10017
aglynn@theruthgroup.com
Tel: (646) 536-7023

Uber Technologies

Uber Technologies is a startup technology compnay that creates a mobile application that connects users with luxury car drivers for hire.
www.uber.com
Industry/ies: Automobiles See Also Motor Vehicles; Automotive Industry; Computer/Technology; Transportation
Legislative Issues: CPI; LAW; SMB; TAX; TRA; VET

Co-founder and Chief Executive Officer
KALANICK, Travis
Tel: (866) 576-1039
Fax: (877) 223-8023

Main Headquarters
Mailing: 1455 Market St., 4th Floor
Suite 8
San Francisco, CA 94103
Tel: (866) 576-1039
Fax: (877) 223-8023

Washington Office
Mailing: 1875 Connecticut Ave. NW
Washington, DC 20009

Public Affairs and Related Activities Personnel

At Headquarters

KINTZ, Justin
Director, Global Public Policy
Tel: (866) 576-1039
Fax: (877) 223-8023

YOO, Salle
General Counsel
Tel: (866) 576-1039
Fax: (877) 223-8023

At Washington Office

HAZELBAKER, Jill
Vice President, Policy & Communications

TOOZE, Colin D.
Director, Public Policy

UBS Americas

A financial services firm offering wealth management, investment banking, asset management and business banking services to clients.
www.ubs.com
Employees: 21,000
Ticker: NYSE: UBS
Industry/ies: Banking/Finance/Investments
Legislative Issues: FIN; TAX

Main Headquarters
Mailing: 1285 Avenue of the Americas
New York City, NY 10019 6111
Tel: (212) 713-2000
Fax: (212) 882-5730

Washington Office
Mailing: 1501 K St. NW
Tel: (202) 585-4000

Suite 1100
Washington, DC 20005

Fax: (202) 585-8988
TF: (800) 382-9989

Political Action Committees
UBS Americas Inc. Political Action Committee
FEC ID: C00012245
Contact: Per Dyrvik
400 Atlantic St.
Stamford, CT 06901

Tel: (203) 658-9287

Contributions to Candidates: $831,250 (2015-2016)
Democrats: $311,000; Republicans: $513,750; Other: $6,500

Principal Recipients

SENATE
SCOTT, TIMOTHY E (REP-SC)
YOUNG, TODD CHRISTOPHER (REP-IN)

HOUSE
BECERRA, XAVIER (DEM-CA)
BOUSTANY, CHARLES W. DR. JR. (REP-LA)
BUCHANAN, VERNON (REP-FL)
CLYBURN, JAMES E. (DEM-SC)
DUFFY, SEAN (REP-WI)
GARRETT, SCOTT REP. (REP-NJ)
GOWDY, TREY (REP-SC)
HENSARLING, JEB HON. (REP-TX)
HOLDING, GEORGE E MR. (REP-NC)
MCCARTHY, KEVIN (REP-CA)
MCMORRIS RODGERS, CATHY (REP-WA)
MEEHAN, PATRICK L. MR. (REP-PA)
MEEKS, GREGORY W. (DEM-NY)
MESSER, ALLEN LUCAS (REP-IN)
MOULTON, SETH (DEM-MA)
NOEM, KRISTI LYNN (REP-SD)
NUNES, DEVIN G (REP-CA)
PERLMUTTER, EDWIN G (DEM-CO)
POLIQUIN, BRUCE L (REP-ME)
REED, THOMAS W II (REP-NY)
RENACCI, JAMES B. (REP-OH)
ROYCE, ED MR. (REP-CA)
RYAN, PAUL D. (REP-WI)
SCALISE, STEVE MR. (REP-LA)
STIVERS, STEVE MR. (REP-OH)
TIBERI, PATRICK J. (REP-OH)
WAGNER, ANN L. (REP-MO)
WALDEN, GREGORY P MR. (REP-OR)

Public Affairs and Related Activities Personnel

At Headquarters

ASKINS, Marsha
Chief Communication Officer - Americas
marsha.askins@ubs.com

Tel: (212) 713-6151
Fax: (212) 882-5728

BYRNE, Karina
Head, Media Relations
karina.byrne@ubs.com

Tel: (212) 882-5692
Fax: (212) 882-5728

At Washington Office

LIEBERMAN, Shane
Federal Lobbyist
Registered Federal Lobbyist

Tel: (202) 585-4000
Fax: (202) 585-8988

NOLAN, John
Federal Lobbyist
Registered Federal Lobbyist

Tel: (202) 585-4000
Fax: (202) 585-8988

RIBBENTROP, Richard
Executive Director and Federal Lobbyist
dick.ribbentrop@ubs.com

Tel: (202) 585-8986
Fax: (202) 585-8988

ROWAN, Peter
Federal Lobbyist
peter.rowan@ubs.com

Tel: (202) 585-8986
Fax: (202) 585-8988

SAVERCOOL, John
Managing Director
john.savercool@ubs.com
Registered Federal Lobbyist

Tel: (202) 585-8987
Fax: (202) 585-8988

At Other Offices

DYRVIK, Per
Lobbyist and PAC Treasurer
400 Atlantic St.
Stamford, CT 06901
Per.Dyrvik@ubsw.com

Tel: (203) 658-9287

UCB Pharma, Inc.
A pharmaceutical research and manufacturing company.
www.ucb-group.com
Industry/ies: Medicine/Health Care/Mental Health; Pharmaceutical Industry
Legislative Issues: HCR; MMM

Chairman and Chief Executive Officer

Tel: (770) 970-8769

DOLIVEUX, Roch

Main Headquarters
Mailing: 1950 Lake Park Dr.
Smyrna, GA 30080

Tel: (770) 970-8769

Public Affairs and Related Activities Personnel

At Headquarters

ENDERLIN, Fabrice
*Executive Vice President, Corporate Human Resources,
Communication and Corporate Societal Responsibility*

Tel: (770) 970-8769

FRITZ, Patty
Vice President Government Affairs & Policy

Tel: (770) 970-8769

RICHO, Anna S.
Executive Vice President and General Counsel

Tel: (770) 970-8769

THIELGEN, Detlef
Chief Financial Officer

Tel: (770) 970-8769

ZORZOLI, Joseph
*Senior Director, Public Policy, Federal & State Government
Affairs*

Tel: (770) 970-8769

UGI Corporation
*Retail distributor of propane and natural gas and electricity focused on providing energy
distribution, transportation, marketing and storage services.*
www.ugicorp.com
Annual Revenues: $7.26 billion
Employees: 12,800
Ticker: NYSE: UGI
SIC: 4925; 1311; 1382; 1389; 2813
NAICS: 22121; 211111; 213112; 32512; 54136
Industry/ies: Utilities

Non Executive Chairman of the Board
GREENBERG, Lon R.
greenbergl@ugicorp.com

Tel: (610) 337-1000
Fax: (610) 992-3254

President and Chief Executive Officer
WALSH, John L.

Tel: (610) 337-1000
Fax: (610) 992-3254

Main Headquarters
Mailing: P.O. Box 858
Valley Forge, PA 19482

Tel: (610) 337-1000
Fax: (610) 992-3254

Political Action Committees
UGI Corporation PAC (UGI/PAC)
FEC ID: C00139667
Contact: Dhara Lalani
2525 N. 12th St., Suite 360
P.O. Box 12677
Reading, PA 19612

Contributions to Candidates: $9,000 (2015-2016)
Republicans: $9,000

Public Affairs and Related Activities Personnel

At Headquarters

BLAKE, Brenda
Coordinator, Media and Investor Relations
blakeb@ugicorp.com

Tel: (610) 337-1000
Fax: (610) 992-3254

BOWMAN, Simon
*Manager, Investor Relations and Treasury and Contact,
Media Relations*
bowmans@ugicorp.com

Tel: (610) 337-1000
Fax: (610) 992-3254

GALLAGHER, Hugh J.
Treasurer and Contact, Investor Relations

Tel: (610) 337-1000
Fax: (610) 992-3254

GAUDIOSI, Monica
Vice President, General Counsel and Secretary

Tel: (610) 337-1000
Fax: (610) 992-3254

KRICK, Robert W.
Vice President and Treasurer

Tel: (610) 337-1000
Fax: (610) 992-3259

OLIVER, Kirk R.
Chief Financial Officer

Tel: (610) 337-1000
Fax: (610) 992-3254

At Other Offices

LALANI, Dhara
PAC Treasurer
P.O. Box 13009
Reading, PA 19612

Fax: (610) 992-3259

UHS of Delaware, Inc.
*A healthcare management company. Acquired Psychiatric Solutions, Inc. It owns and operates
acute care hospitals, behavioral health centers, surgical hospitals, ambulatory surgery centers,
and radiation oncology centers.*
www.uhsinc.com
Annual Revenues: $8.35 billion
Employees: 48,700
Ticker: NYSE:UHS
SIC: 8093
Industry/ies: Medicine/Health Care/Mental Health

Legislative Issues: BUD

Chief Executive Officer and Chairman of the Board

MILLER, Alan B.

Tel: (610) 768-3300
Fax: (302) 655-5049

Main Headquarters

Mailing: 367 S. Gulph Rd.
P.O. Box 61558
King of Prussia, PA 19406

Tel: (610) 768-3300
Fax: (302) 655-5049
TF: (800) 347-7750

Political Action Committees

Universal Health Services Inc Employees' Good Government Fund
FEC ID: C00185520
Contact: Cheryl K. Ramagano
367 S. Gulph Rd.
P.O. Box 61558
King of Prussia, PA 19406

Tel: (610) 768-3300

Contributions to Candidates: $32,350 (2015-2016)
Democrats: $14,000; Republicans: $18,350

Corporate Foundations and Giving Programs

Psychiatric Solutions Contributions Program
6640 Carothers Pkwy.
Suite 500
Franklin, TN 37067

Public Affairs and Related Activities Personnel

At Headquarters

FILTON, Steve G.
Senior Vice President and Chief Financial Officer
steve.filton@uhsinc.com

Tel: (610) 768-3300
Fax: (302) 655-5049

GECKLE, Geraldine Johnson
Vice President, Human Resources
gerry.geckle@uhsinc.com

Tel: (610) 768-3300
Fax: (302) 655-5049

KLEIN, Matthew D.
Vice President and General Counsel
matthew.klein@uhsinc.com

Tel: (610) 768-3300
Fax: (302) 655-5049

MILLER, Marc D.
President

Tel: (610) 768-3300
Fax: (302) 655-5049

RAMAGANO, Cheryl K.
Vice President, Treasurer and PAC Treasurer

Tel: (610) 768-3300
Fax: (302) 655-5049

WRIGHT, Richard C.
Vice President, Development

Tel: (610) 768-3300
Fax: (302) 655-5049

ULTRA Electronics Advanced Tactical Systems

Specializes in designing, manufacturing and supporting tactical command and control systems, subsystems and products for defense and homeland security applications worldwide.
ultra-ats.com
Industry/ies: Electricity & Electronics; Energy/Electricity
Legislative Issues: BUD; DEF

RIELS, W. Greg G.

Tel: (202) 460-0199
Fax: (512) 327-8043

Main Headquarters

Mailing: 4101 Smith School Rd.
Bldg IV, Suite 100
Austin, AL 78744

Tel: (512) 327-6795
Fax: (512) 327-8043

Ultra Electronics, Prologic

A wholly owned subsidiary of Ultra Electronics, which is headquartered in the United Kingdom. Provides Information Technology (IT) solutions to many government agencies, including the Department of Defense and the Department of Energy and NASA.
www.ultra-prologic.com
Employees: 300
Industry/ies: Computer/Technology

Chairman of the Board and Director

BAUR, James F.

Tel: (703) 335-6986
Fax: (703) 335-5176

Main Headquarters

Mailing: 9400 Innovation Dr.
Manassas, VA 20110

Tel: (703) 335-6986
Fax: (703) 335-5176

Political Action Committees

Ultra Electronics Usa Group Inc
FEC ID: C00558668
Contact: Scott Meyers
107 Church Hill Rd.
Suite Gl-2
Sandy Hook, CT 06482

Contributions to Candidates: $20,500 (2015-2016)
Republicans: $20,500

Public Affairs and Related Activities Personnel

At Headquarters

BARRETT, Sophie
Contact, Media
Sophie.Barrett@ultra-prologic.com

Tel: (703) 335-2113
Fax: (703) 331-0479

At Other Offices

MEYERS, Scott
PAC Contact
107 Church Hill Rd., Suite Gl-2
Sandy Hook, CT 06482

UltraVision Security Systems, Inc.

Involved in developing ultra wideband (UWB) technologies for use in life rescue and safety systems.
www.ultravisionsecurity.com
Annual Revenues: $1.50 million
Industry/ies: Computer/Technology; Defense/Homeland Security; Electricity & Electronics; Electronics; Energy/Electricity; Government-Related; Law Enforcement/Security

Chief Executive Officer

JOHNSON, Dennis J.

Tel: (603) 685-0303
Fax: (603) 898-1840

Main Headquarters

Mailing: 12 Industrial Way
Salem, NH 03079

Tel: (603) 681-2080
Fax: (603) 898-1840

Public Affairs and Related Activities Personnel

At Headquarters

KENDALL, Angie
Contatc, Communications
akendall@dkdmarketing.com

Tel: (407) 760-7360
Fax: (603) 898-1840

LOZON, Bill
Vice President, Sales and Marketing

Tel: (603) 685-0303
Fax: (603) 898-1840

WALCZYK, Donald
Chief Financial Officer

Tel: (603) 685-0303
Fax: (603) 898-1840

UMB Financial Corporation

A financial holding company.
www.umb.com
Annual Revenues: $840.40 million
Employees: 3,592
Ticker: NASDAQ (GS): UMBF
SIC: 6021
Industry/ies: Banking/Finance/Investments

Chairman of the Board and Chief Executive Officer

KEMPER, J. Mariner

Tel: (816) 860-7000
Fax: (816) 860-7610

Main Headquarters

Mailing: P.O. Box 419226
Kansas City, MO 64141-6226

Tel: (816) 860-7000
Fax: (816) 860-7610

Public Affairs and Related Activities Personnel

At Headquarters

DESILVA, Peter J.
President and Chief Operating Officer

Tel: (816) 860-7000
Fax: (816) 860-7610

HAGEDORN, Michael D.
Vice Chairman
michael.hagedorn@umb.com

Tel: (816) 860-7000
Fax: (816) 860-7610

KLUMB, Begonya
Executive Vice President & Chief Strategy Officer

Tel: (816) 860-7906
Fax: (816) 860-5675

MAYER, Abby
Director, Investor Relations

Tel: (816) 860-1685
Fax: (816) 860-7610

MCMILLAN, Kay
Vice President and Investor Relations Consultant

Tel: (816) 860-7000
Fax: (816) 860-7610

MILLER, Heather Kemper
Executive Vice President, Sales, Marketing and Communications
heather.miller@umb.com

Tel: (816) 860-1685
Fax: (816) 860-7610

WALKER, Brian J.
Executive Vice President, Chief Financial Officer and Chief Accounting Officer

Tel: (816) 860-7000
Fax: (816) 860-7610

Unaka Company, Inc.

A holding company for diverse industries.
www.unaka.com
Annual Revenues: $45.80 million
Employees: 600
Industry/ies: Machinery/Equipment

Chief Executive Officer

AUSTIN, Jr., Robert

Tel: (800) 251-7558
Fax: (423) 639-1171

Main Headquarters

Mailing: 1500 Industrial Rd.
Greeneville, TN 37745

Tel: (423) 639-1171
Fax: (423) 639-1171
TF: (800) 251-7558

Political Action Committees

Unaka Company PAC Inc
FEC ID: C00371229
Contact: L.A. Yonz

1500 Industrial Rd.
Greeneville, TN 37743

Contributions to Candidates: $7,700 (2015-2016)
Democrats: $5,000; Republicans: $2,700

Public Affairs and Related Activities Personnel

At Headquarters

YONZ, L.A.	Tel:	(423) 639-1171
PAC Treasurer	Fax:	(423) 639-1171

Underwriters Laboratories Inc.

An product-safety testing and certification organization headquartered in Northbrook, IL.
www.ul.com
Annual Revenues: $895.63 million
Employees: 6,000
Industry/ies: Insurance Industry; Management; Manufacturers
Legislative Issues: ENG; TRD

President, Chief Executive Officer and Trustee
WILLIAMS, Keith E.	Tel:	(847) 272-8800
	Fax:	(847) 272-8129

Main Headquarters
Mailing:	333 Pfingsten Rd.	Tel:	(847) 272-8800
	Northbrook, IL 60062-2096	Fax:	(847) 272-8129
		TF:	(877) 854-3577

Washington Office
Mailing:	1850 M St. NW	Tel:	(202) 296-7840
	Suite 1000	Fax:	(202) 872-1576
	Washington, DC 20036		

Corporate Foundations and Giving Programs

UL Contributions Program
2600 N.W. Lake Rd.
Camas, WA 98607-8542

Public Affairs and Related Activities Personnel

At Headquarters

ANSCHUETZ, Christian	Tel:	(847) 272-8800
Senior Vice President and Chief Information Officer	Fax:	(847) 272-8129
BOYLE, Patrick	Tel:	(847) 272-8800
Senior Vice President and Chief Learning Officer	Fax:	(847) 272-8129
BRADY, Terry	Tel:	(847) 272-8800
Senior Vice President, Chief Legal Officer and Chief Commercial Officer	Fax:	(847) 272-8129
DRENGENBERG, John	Tel:	(847) 272-8800
Consumer Safety Director	Fax:	(847) 272-8129
GROOM, Adrian	Tel:	(847) 272-8800
Senior Vice President and Chief Human Resources Officer	Fax:	(847) 272-8129
JOHNSON, Victoria	Tel:	(847) 272-8800
Global Manager, Strategic Meetings Management	Fax:	(847) 272-8129
KOFMAN, Clyde	Tel:	(847) 272-8800
Chief Operating Officer	Fax:	(847) 272-8129
PRESS, Michelle	Tel:	(847) 664-1966
Manager, Global Marketing Communications	Fax:	(847) 272-8129
Michelle.Press@ul.com		
SALTZMAN, Michael	Tel:	(847) 272-8800
Senior Vice President and Chief Financial Officer	Fax:	(847) 272-8129
ZHOU, Weifang	Tel:	(847) 272-8800
Senior Vice President, Ventures	Fax:	(847) 272-8129

At Washington Office

KAMMER, Claire A.	Tel:	(202) 296-1435
General Manager, Global Accounts	Fax:	(202) 872-1576
claire.a.kammer@us.ul.com		
TORRES, Abelardo	Tel:	(202) 296-1435
Federal Lobbyist	Fax:	(202) 872-1576
WEEKS, Ann M.	Tel:	(202) 296-1435
Vice President, Global Government Affairs	Fax:	(202) 872-1576
Ann.Weeks@ul.com		

UNIFI, Inc.

Producer and processor of multi-filament polyester and nylon textured yarns and related raw materials. UNIFI, Inc. provides innovative, global textile solutions and unique branded yarns for customers at every level of the supply chain.
www.unifi.com
Annual Revenues: $689.61 million
Employees: 2,500
Ticker: NYSE: UFI
SIC: 2200
Industry/ies: Apparel/Textiles Industry

Chairman and Chief Executive Officer
JASPER, William L.	Tel:	(336) 294-4410
	Fax:	(336) 316-5422

Main Headquarters
Mailing:	7201 W. Friendly Ave.	Tel:	(336) 294-4410

Greensboro, NC 27410   Fax: (336) 316-5422

Political Action Committees
UNIFI, Inc. PAC
FEC ID: C00502351
Contact: Christopher Smosna
7201 W. Friendly Ave.	Tel:	(336) 294-4410
Greensboro, NC 27410	Fax:	(336) 316-5422

Contributions to Candidates: $11,000 (2015-2016)
Democrats: $2,000; Republicans: $9,000

Public Affairs and Related Activities Personnel

At Headquarters

BERRIER, Jr., R. Roger	Tel:	(336) 294-4410
President and Chief Operating Officer	Fax:	(336) 316-5422
EADDY, W. Randy	Tel:	(336) 294-4410
General Counsel and Corporate Secretary	Fax:	(336) 316-5422
HUNTER, Neil	Tel:	(336) 316-5539
Contact, Investor Relations	Fax:	(336) 316-5422
LANDAS , Rebecca	Tel:	(336) 316-5676
Coordinator, Investor Relations	Fax:	(336) 316-5422
rlandas@unifi.com		
OTTERBERG, James M.	Tel:	(336) 294-4410
Vice President and Chief Financial Officer	Fax:	(336) 316-5422
SMOSNA, Christopher	Tel:	(336) 294-4410
Vice President/Treasurer and PAC Treasurer	Fax:	(336) 316-5422

Unified Grocers

A wholesale cooperative grocery distributor. The cooperative was formed in 1922 as Certified Grocers of California.
www.unifiedgrocers.com
Annual Revenues: $3.92 billion
Employees: 3,100
SIC: 5141; 2051; 5099; 5142; 5143
Industry/ies: Food And Beverage Industry; Retail/Wholesale

Chairman of the Board
GOODSPEED, Richard E.	Tel:	(323) 264-5200
	Fax:	(323) 729-6610

President and Chief Executive Officer
LING, Jr., Robert M.	Tel:	(323) 264-5200
	Fax:	(323) 729-6610

Main Headquarters
Mailing:	5200 Sheila St.	Tel:	(323) 264-5200
	Commerce, CA 90040	Fax:	(323) 729-6610
		TF:	(800) 724-7762

Corporate Foundations and Giving Programs

Unified Grocers Contributions Program
5200 Sheila St.	Tel:	(323) 264-5200
Commerce, CA 90040	Fax:	(323) 265-4006

Public Affairs and Related Activities Personnel

At Headquarters

BODWIN, Terry Ann	Tel:	(323) 264-5200
Vice President, Chief Human Resources Officer	Fax:	(323) 729-6610
DINGSDALE, Paul	Tel:	(323) 881-4150
Director, Corporate Communications	Fax:	(323) 729-6610
KLUG, Susan M.	Tel:	(323) 264-5200
Senior Vice President and Chief Marketing Officer	Fax:	(323) 729-6610
MARTIN, Richard J.	Tel:	(323) 264-5200
Executive Vice President, Finance and Administration and Chief Financial Officer	Fax:	(323) 729-6610
NEAL, Christine	Tel:	(323) 264-5200
Senior Vice President, Finance and Treasurer	Fax:	(323) 729-6610
SAYLES, Thomas S.	Tel:	(323) 264-5200
Vice President, Government and Community Relations	Fax:	(323) 729-6610

Unified Western Grocers Inc.

See listing on page 810 under Unified Grocers

UniGroup, Inc.

A household goods and products transportation company. Unigroup originated in 1928. In 1995 Unigroup acquired Carmel,IN based Mayflower Transit.
www.unigroupinc.com
Annual Revenues: $2.2 billion
Employees: 1,800
Industry/ies: Transportation

Chairman of the Board and Chief Executive Officer
MCCOLLISTER, H. Daniel	Tel:	(636) 305-5000
	Fax:	(636) 326-1106

President
MCCLURE, Rich	Tel:	(636) 305-5000
	Fax:	(636) 326-1106

Main Headquarters
Mailing:	One Premier Dr.	Tel:	(636) 305-5000
	Fenton, MO 63026	Fax:	(636) 326-1106

TF: (800) 637-2154

Political Action Committees
UniGroup Inc. PAC
FEC ID: C00435909
Contact: Jan Robey Alonzo
One Premier Dr.
Fenton, MO 63026

Contributions to Candidates: $1,000 (2015-2016)
Republicans: $1,000

Public Affairs and Related Activities Personnel

At Headquarters

ALONZO, Jan Robey — Tel: (636) 305-5000 / Fax: (636) 326-1106
Senior Vice President, General Counsel and Compliance Officer
jan_alonzo@unigroupinc.com

BURKHARDT, Steve — Tel: (636) 305-5000 / Fax: (636) 326-1106
Senior Vice President and Chief Medical Officer, Integrated Global Marketing

MALEAR, Cathy — Tel: (636) 305-5000 / Fax: (636) 326-1106
Senior Vice President, Human Resources

SCHROEDER, Mark — Tel: (636) 305-5000 / Fax: (636) 326-1106
Chief Financial Officer

WALTER, Carl O. — Tel: (636) 349-8508 / Fax: (636) 326-1106
Vice President, Marketing and Communications

Unilever United States, Inc.
Develops, manufactures, markets home and personal care products. Products/brands include: All, Wisk, Surf, Dove, Mentadent, Degree, Pond's, Lever 2000, Suave, and Finesse.
www.unileverusa.com
Annual Revenues: $1.80 billion
Industry/ies: Chemicals & Chemical Industry; Food And Beverage Industry; Personal Care/Hygiene
Legislative Issues: AGR; CSP; ENG; TRD

Chief Executive Officer — Tel: (201) 894-7760 / Fax: (201) 871-8117
POLMAN, Paul

Main Headquarters
Mailing: 800 Sylvan Ave.
Englewood Cliffs, NJ 07632 — Tel: (201) 894-7760 / Fax: (201) 871-8117 / TF: (800) 298-5018

Washington Office
Mailing: 816 Connecticut Ave. NW
Suite 700
Washington, DC 20006-2705 — Tel: (202) 828-1010 / Fax: (202) 828-4550

Public Affairs and Related Activities Personnel

At Headquarters

BAILLIE, Douglas — Tel: (201) 894-7760 / Fax: (201) 871-8117
Chief Human Resource Officer

BERGER, Geneviève — Tel: (201) 894-7760 / Fax: (201) 871-8117
Director

HUET, Jean Marc — Tel: (201) 894-7760 / Fax: (201) 871-8117
Chief Financial Officer

KRUYTHOFF, Kees — Tel: (201) 894-7760 / Fax: (201) 871-8117
President, North America

LARSEN, Anita — Tel: (201) 894-7760 / Fax: (201) 871-8117
Director, External Communications
anita.larsen@unilever.com

MANWANI, Harish — Tel: (201) 894-7760 / Fax: (201) 871-8117
Chief Operating Officer

NICHOLS, Charles — Tel: (201) 894-7760 / Fax: (201) 871-8117
Group Controller

WEED, Keith — Tel: (201) 894-7760 / Fax: (201) 871-8117
Chief Marketing and Communication Officer

WILLIAMS, Stephen — Tel: (201) 894-7760 / Fax: (201) 871-8117
General Counsel and Chief Legal Officer

At Washington Office

BESCHER, Mark — Tel: (202) 828-1010 / Fax: (202) 828-4550
Manager, Federal Government Relations & External Affairs
Registered Federal Lobbyist

EICHMAN, Kelly — Tel: (202) 828-1010 / Fax: (202) 828-4550
Associate, Government Relations and External Affairs

LANGAN, Thomas P. — Tel: (202) 828-1010 / Fax: (202) 828-4550
Mail Stop Head, North America Government Relations & External Affairs
tom.langan@unilever.com
Registered Federal Lobbyist

MILLIE, Stefani — Tel: (202) 828-1010 / Fax: (202) 828-4550
Manager, State Government Relations and External Affairs
stefani.millie@unilever.com

Union Bank N.A.
Union Bank is a full-service commercial bank, providing financial services to businesses and individuals. Formerly known as Union Bank of California N.A.
www.unionbank.com
Annual Revenues: $3.75 billion
Employees: 11,000
Industry/ies: Banking/Finance/Investments

Chairman of the Board — Tel: (415) 765-2969 / Fax: (415) 765-2220
MORIMURA, Takashi

President and Chief Executive Officer — Tel: (415) 765-2969 / Fax: (415) 765-2220
OKA, Masashi

Main Headquarters
Mailing: 400 California St., 13th Floor
Suite 200
San Francisco, CA 94104 — Tel: (415) 765-2969 / Fax: (415) 765-2220

Corporate Foundations and Giving Programs
Union Bank of California Foundation
Contact: Carl A. Ballton
400 California St.
Sutie 200
San Francisco, CA 94104

Public Affairs and Related Activities Personnel

At Headquarters

BALLTON, Carl A. — Tel: (415) 765-2780 / Fax: (415) 765-2220
Managing Director, Deputy Group Head and Corporate Social Responsibility
carl.ballton@uboc.com

CURRAN, Joanne — Tel: (213) 326-5017 / Fax: (415) 765-2220
Senior Vice President and Contact, Public Relations
joanne.curran@uboc.com

HERNANDEZ, Randal — Tel: (415) 765-2969 / Fax: (415) 765-2220
Managing Director, Government Relations

PEEBLES-HILL, Tanya — Tel: (213) 236-5329 / Fax: (415) 765-2220
Media Contact
tanya.peebleshill@unionbank.com

RICE, Jr., John A. — Tel: (415) 765-2969 / Fax: (415) 765-2220
Investor Relations Contact
investor.relations@uboc.com

ROBINSON, Julius — Tel: (415) 765-2969 / Fax: (415) 765-2220
Managing Director, Corporate Social Responsibility For The Americas

VAN DER WERFF, Annemieke — Tel: (415) 765-2969 / Fax: (415) 765-2220
Chief Human Resources Officer

WOODS, John F. — Tel: (415) 765-2969 / Fax: (415) 765-2220
Vice Chairman & Chief Financial Officer

WOOLSEY, Jan — Tel: (415) 765-2969 / Fax: (415) 765-2220
Managing Director, Strategy and Operations

Union Pacific
A holding company for subsidiaries engaged in railroad and other transportation.
www.up.com
Annual Revenues: $23.96 billion
Employees: 48,830
Ticker: NYSE: UNP
SIC: 4011
NAICS: 482111
Industry/ies: Railroads; Transportation
Legislative Issues: BUD; CAW; ENG; ENV; LBR; RRR; TAX; TRA

Chairman of the Board — Tel: (402) 544-5000 / Fax: (402) 501-2133
KORALESKI, John J.

President and Chief Operating Officer — Tel: (402) 544-5000 / Fax: (402) 501-2133
FRITZ, Lance M.

Main Headquarters
Mailing: 1400 Douglas St.
Omaha, NE 68179 — Tel: (402) 544-5000 / Fax: (402) 501-2133 / TF: (888) 870-8777

Washington Office
Mailing: 700 13th St. NW
Suite 350
Washington, DC 20005

Political Action Committees
Union Pacific Corporation Fund for Effective Government
FEC ID: C00010470
Contact: Michael A. Rock
700 13th St. NW — Tel: (202) 662-0100
Suite 350 — Fax: (202) 662-0199
Washington, DC 20005

Contributions to Candidates: $1,678,500 (2015-2016)
Democrats: $542,500; Republicans: $1,132,000; Other: $4,000

Principal Recipients

SENATE

BARRASSO, JOHN A (REP-WY)
BENNET, MICHAEL F (DEM-CO)
BLUNT, ROY (REP-MO)
BOOKER, CORY A (DEM-NJ)
BOOZMAN, JOHN (REP-AR)
CASSIDY, WILLIAM M (REP-LA)
COCHRAN, THAD (REP-MS)
DAINES, STEVEN (REP-MT)
ERNST, JONI K (REP-IA)
GARDNER, CORY (REP-CO)
GRASSLEY, CHARLES E SENATOR (REP-IA)
INHOFE, JAMES M SEN (REP-OK)
JOHNSON, RONALD HAROLD (REP-)
KIRK, MARK STEVEN (REP-IL)
LEAHY, PATRICK J (DEM-VT)
LEE, MIKE (REP-UT)
MCCAIN, JOHN S (REP-VA)
MORAN, JERRY (REP-KS)
MURRAY, PATTY (DEM-WA)
PORTMAN, ROB (REP-OH)
SCHATZ, BRIAN (DEM-HI)
SHELBY, RICHARD C (REP-AL)
THUNE, JOHN (REP-SD)

HOUSE

ASHFORD, BRAD (DEM-NE)
BLUMENAUER, EARL (DEM-OR)
BROWN, CORRINE (DEM-FL)
CAPUANO, MICHAEL E (DEM-MA)
CLYBURN, JAMES E. (DEM-SC)
DAVIS, RODNEY L (REP-IL)
DEFAZIO, PETER A (DEM-OR)
DENHAM, JEFF (REP-CA)
DOLD, ROBERT JAMES JR (REP-IL)
DUNCAN, JOHN J REP. JR. (REP-TN)
FARENTHOLD, RANDOLPH BLAKE (REP-TX)
FORTENBERRY, JEFFREY L. HONORABLE (REP-NE)
GRANGER, KAY (REP-TX)
GRAVES, GARRET (REP-LA)
GRAVES, SAMUEL B JR 'SAM' (REP-MO)
HARDY, CRESENT (REP-NV)
HURD, WILLIAM (REP-TX)
JOHNSON, EDDIE BERNICE (DEM-TX)
LAHOOD, DARIN MCKAY (REP-IL)
LANKFORD, JAMES PAUL MR. (REP-OK)
LIPINSKI, DANIEL WILLIAM WILLIAM (DEM-IL)
MCCARTHY, KEVIN (REP-CA)
MCCAUL, MICHAEL (REP-TX)
MCGOVERN, JAMES P (DEM-MA)
MCMORRIS RODGERS, CATHY (REP-WA)
MICA, JOHN L. MR. (REP-FL)
NADLER, JERROLD L. MR. (DEM-NY)
RYAN, PAUL D. (REP-WI)
SCALISE, STEVE MR. (REP-LA)
SHUSTER, WILLIAM MR. (REP-PA)
SMITH, ADRIAN (REP-NE)
TIBERI, PATRICK J. (REP-OH)
UPTON, FREDERICK STEPHEN (REP-MI)
WALDEN, GREGORY P MR. (REP-OR)
WALTERS, MIMI (REP-CA)
YOUNG, DAVID (REP-IA)

Corporate Foundations and Giving Programs

Union Pacific Foundation
1400 Douglas St.
Omaha, NE 68179

Public Affairs and Related Activities Personnel

At Headquarters

ARBONA, Joe
General Director, Policy and Partnerships
Tel: (402) 544-5000
Fax: (402) 501-2133

BUTLER, Eric L.
Executive Vice President, Marketing and Sales
Tel: (402) 544-5000
Fax: (402) 501-2133

DAVIS, Mark
Director, Corporate Relations and Media
Tel: (402) 544-5000
Fax: (402) 501-2133

DUREN, Diane K.
Executive Vice President and Corporate Secretary
Tel: (402) 544-5000
Fax: (402) 501-2133

JONES, Mary Sanders
Vice President and Treasurer
Tel: (402) 544-6111
Fax: (402) 501-2133

KNIGHT, Robert M.
Executive Vice President and Chief Financial Officer
Tel: (402) 544-5000
Fax: (402) 501-2133

LANGE, Tom
Assistant Vice President, Corporate Communications and Contact, Media Relations
Tel: (402) 544-3560
Fax: (402) 501-2133

tomlange@up.com

SCOTT, Cameron
Executive Vice President, Operations
Tel: (402) 544-5000
Fax: (402) 501-2133

THAL, Gayla
Senior Vice President, Law and General Counsel
gaylathal@up.com
Tel: (402) 544-5000
Fax: (402) 501-2133

TURNER, Robert W.
Senior Vice President, Corporate Relations
Tel: (402) 544-5255
Fax: (402) 501-2133

VALDEZ, Lupe
Director, Public Affairs
Tel: (402) 544-5000
Fax: (402) 501-2133

At Washington Office

ANDRES, Susan Auther
Director, Washington Affairs
smandres@up.com
Registered Federal Lobbyist

BLACK, David
Registered Federal Lobbyist

BOLIN, Prentiss W.
Assistant Vice President, External Relations
pbolin@up.com
Registered Federal Lobbyist

HOUTON, Jamie
Assistant Vice President, External Relations
jhouton@up.com
Registered Federal Lobbyist

LEDDY, Elizabeth
Registered Federal Lobbyist

ROCK, Michael A.
Vice President, External Relations
marock@up.com
Registered Federal Lobbyist

Unisource Energy Corporation

An electric utility holding company.
www.uns.com
Annual Revenues: $1.51 billion
Employees: 1,977
Ticker: NYSE: UNS
SIC: 4911
Industry/ies: Utilities

President and Chief Executive Officer
HUTCHENS, David G.
Tel: (520) 571-4000
Fax: (520) 884-3602

Main Headquarters
Mailing: 88 E. Broadway Blvd.
Tucson, AZ 85702
Tel: (520) 571-4000
Fax: (520) 884-3602

Corporate Foundations and Giving Programs

Unisource Energy Corporation Contributions Program
88 E. Broadway
Tucson, AZ 85702

Public Affairs and Related Activities Personnel

At Headquarters

BARRIOS , Joseph
Contact, Media Relations
Tel: (520) 571-4000
Fax: (520) 884-3602

DION, III, Philip J.
Senior Vice President, Public Policy and Customer Solutions
Tel: (520) 571-4000
Fax: (520) 884-3602

HIXON, Todd C.
Vice President and General Counsel
Tel: (520) 571-4000
Fax: (520) 884-3602

KENNEDY, Herlinda H.
Corporate Secretary
Tel: (520) 571-4000
Fax: (520) 884-3602

KISSINGER, Karen G.
Vice President and Chief Compliance Officer
Tel: (520) 571-4000
Fax: (520) 884-3602

LARSON, Kevin P.
Senior Vice President, Chief Financial Officer and PAC Treasurer
Mail Stop HQE901, P.O. Box 711
KLarson@uns.com
Tel: (520) 571-4000
Fax: (520) 884-3602

MARINO, Frank P.
Vice President and Controller
Tel: (520) 571-4000
Fax: (520) 884-3602

NORMAN, Chris
Manager, Investor Relations
cnorman@uns.com
Tel: (520) 571-4000
Fax: (520) 884-3602

RIES, Catherine E.
Vice President, Human Resources and Information Technology
Tel: (520) 571-4000
Fax: (520) 884-3602

SALKOWSKI, Joe
Manager, Corporate Communications
jsalkowski@tucsonelectric.com
Tel: (520) 884-3625
Fax: (520) 884-3602

SMITH, Jo
Director, Regulatory Services and Corporate Communications
Tel: (520) 884-3650
Fax: (520) 884-3606

josmith@unisourceenergy.com

Unistar Nuclear Energy

A strategic joint venture between Constellation Energy (CEG) and EDF Group, that provides reactor safety, security and reliability.
www.unistarnuclear.com
Annual Revenues: $4.80 million
Employees: 16
Industry/ies: Energy/Electricity

| **President, Chief Executive Officer and Chief Nuclear Officer** | Tel: | (410) 369-1900 |
| GIBSON, Greg | Fax: | (410) 369-1911 |

Main Headquarters
Mailing:	750 E. Pratt St.	Tel:	(410) 369-1900
	14th Floor	Fax:	(410) 369-1911
	Baltimore, MD 21202-3142		

Public Affairs and Related Activities Personnel

At Headquarters

BLANDIN, Patrick	Tel:	(410) 470-4400
Senior Vice President and Chief Financial Officer	Fax:	(410) 470-5606
EIFLER, Laura	Tel:	(410) 470-7047
Contact, Media Relations	Fax:	(410) 470-5606
Laura.Eifler@unistarnuclear.com		
TURNAGE, Joseph	Tel:	(410) 470-4400
Senior Vice President, Strategy and Infrastructure	Fax:	(410) 470-5606

Unisys Corporation

Provides information technology (IT) services, software, and technology for clients worldwide.
www.unisys.com
Annual Revenues: $2.96 billion
Employees: 23,000
Ticker: NYSE: UIS
SIC: 7373
NAICS: 334111; 334119; 334112
Industry/ies: Computer/Technology; Electricity & Electronics; Electronics; Energy/Electricity
Legislative Issues: AGR; BUD; DEF; EDU; GOV; HCR; HOM; IMM; LBR; RET; TAX; TRD

| **President and Chief Executive Officer** | Tel: | (215) 986-4011 |
| ALTABEF, Peter | Fax: | (215) 986-2312 |

Main Headquarters
Mailing:	801 Lakeview Dr.	Tel:	(215) 986-4011
	Suite 100	Fax:	(215) 986-2312
	Blue Bell, PA 19422		

Washington Office
Mailing:	11720 Plaza America Dr.	Tel:	(703) 439-5000
	Tower Three	Fax:	(703) 439-5172
	Reston, VA 20190		

Political Action Committees
Unisys Corporation Employees PAC
FEC ID: C00345603
Contact: Joseph Toth
11720 Plaza America Dr.
Tower III
Washington, DC 20190

> **Contributions to Candidates:** $67,500 (2015-2016)
> Democrats: $19,500; Republicans: $48,000

Principal Recipients

HOUSE
CONNOLLY, GERALD EDWARD (DEM-VA)

Corporate Foundations and Giving Programs

Unisys Corporation Contributions Program
801 Lakeview Dr.	Tel:	(215) 986-4011
Suite 100	Fax:	(215) 986-2312
Blue Bell, PA 19422		

Public Affairs and Related Activities Personnel

At Headquarters

BASS, Brad	Tel:	(703) 439-5887
Director, Public Relations for Public Sector and U.S. Federal	Fax:	(215) 986-2312
Government and Security		
brad.bass@unisys.com		
BATTERSBY, Scott A.	Tel:	(215) 986-4011
Vice President and Treasurer	Fax:	(215) 986-2312
HAUGEN, Janet B.	Tel:	(215) 986-4011
Senior Vice President and Chief Financial Officer	Fax:	(215) 986-2312
LOESER, David	Tel:	(215) 986-4011
Senior Vice President, Worldwide Human Resources	Fax:	(215) 986-2312
RENZI, Jeff	Tel:	(215) 986-4011
Senior Vice President and President, Global Sales	Fax:	(215) 986-2312
SINGH, Inder M	Tel:	(215) 986-4011

Senior Vice President, Chief Marketing and Strategy Officer	Fax:	(215) 986-2312
SMITH, M. Lazane	Tel:	(215) 986-4011
Senior Vice President, Corporate Development	Fax:	(215) 986-2312

At Washington Office

FLEENOR, Camille	Tel:	(703) 439-5526
Vice President, Government Relations	Fax:	(703) 439-5172
HOYDYSH, Dan	Tel:	(703) 439-5000
Director, Public Policy	Fax:	(703) 439-5172
dan.hoydysh@unisys.com		
Registered Federal Lobbyist		
KENNEY, Gerald	Tel:	(703) 439-5526
Senior Vice President, General Counsel and Secretary	Fax:	(703) 439-5172
TOTH, Joseph	Tel:	(703) 439-5526
Director, Government Relations & PAC Treasurer	Fax:	(703) 439-5172
Registered Federal Lobbyist		

Unitech Composites and Structures

Unitech Composites manufacturers of composite products for aerospace, transportation, military, commercial, and industrial applications in the Pacific Northwest.
www.unitechcomp.com
Annual Revenues: $10 million
Employees: 100
SIC: 3728; 3089; 3544
NAICS: 336413; 326199; 333511
Industry/ies: Aerospace/Aviation; Architecture And Design; Automotive Industry; Construction/Construction Materials; Defense/Homeland Security; Government-Related; Transportation

| **Vice President, Business Development** | Tel: | (208) 772-0533 |
| APPLEGRATH, Don | Fax: | (208) 772-8591 |

Main Headquarters
Mailing:	P.O. Box 370	Tel:	(208) 772-0533
	10413 Aero Dr.	Fax:	(208) 772-8591
	Hayden, ID 83835-0370	TF:	(800) 775-0861

Public Affairs and Related Activities Personnel

At Headquarters

LANTZ, Johnny	Tel:	(405) 737-2676
Director, Marketing and Communications	Fax:	(208) 772-8591
Mail Stop C/O AGC Aerospace and Defense		
jlantz@agcaerospace.com		
SHUBURG, Tim	Tel:	(208) 772-0533
General Manager	Fax:	(208) 772-8591
Tim.shuburg@agcaerocomposites.com		

Unitech Composites Inc.

See listing on page 813 under Unitech Composites and Structures

United Airlines (UA)

A commercial air carrier. A wholly-owned subsidiary of United Continental Holdings. Merged with Continental Airlines in 2011.
www.united.com
Annual Revenues: $38.81 billion
Employees: 84,000
Ticker: NYSE: UAL
SIC: 4512
Industry/ies: Aerospace/Aviation; Airlines; Transportation; Travel/Tourism/Lodging
Legislative Issues: AVI; TAX; TRA

| **Chairman of the Board, President and Chief Executive Officer** | Tel: | (872) 825-4000 |
| SMISEK, Jeffery A. | Fax: | (847) 700-4899 |

Main Headquarters
| Mailing: | P.O. Box 06649 | Tel: | (872) 825-4000 |
| | Chicago, IL 60606-0649 | | |

Washington Office
Mailing:	1225 New York Ave.	
	Suite 1100	
	Washington, DC 20005	

Political Action Committees
United Airlines Political Action Committee (UAPAC)
FEC ID: C00078261
Contact: Mark R. Anderson
| P.O. Box 66100 | Tel: | (202) 296-2337 |
| Chicago, IL 60666 | Fax: | (202) 296-2873 |

Corporate Foundations and Giving Programs

United Airlines Foundation
P.O. Box 66100
Chicago, IL 60666

Public Affairs and Related Activities Personnel

At Headquarters

| BONDS, Michael P. | Tel: | (872) 825-4000 |

Executive Vice President, Human Resources and Labor Relations

FOXHALL, Nene   Tel: (872) 825-4000
Executive Vice President, Communications and Government Affairs

HART, Brett J.   Tel: (872) 825-4000
Executive Vice President, General Counsel and Corporate Secretary

HART, Gregory   Tel: (872) 825-4000
Executive Vice President and Chief Operations Officer

KAMEN, Hershel I.   Tel: (872) 825-4000
Senior Vice President Alliances, Regulatory and Policy

O'TOOLE, Thomas F.   Tel: (872) 825-4000
Senior Vice President and Marketing and Loyalty

PHILIP , Rohit   Tel: (872) 825-4000
Senior Vice President, Finance

RAINEY, John D.   Tel: (872) 825-4000
Executive Vice President and Chief Financial Officer

At Other Offices

ANDERSON, Mark R.   Fax: (847) 700-4899
Senior Vice President, Corporate and Government Affairs
P.O. Box 66100
Chicago, IL 60666

HART, Gregory   Tel: (872) 825-8610
Executive Vice President and Chief Operations Officer   Fax: (847) 700-4899
P.O. Box 66100
Chicago, IL 60666

IRELAND, Jonathan   Tel: (872) 825-8610
Managing Director, Investor Relations   Fax: (847) 700-4899
P.O. Box 66100
Chicago, IL 60666

JOHNSON, Sasha
Managing Director, Regulatory Issues and Policy
1025 Connecticut Ave. NW, Suite 1210
Washington, DC 20005

MORRISEY, Stephen J.
Senior Director, Governmental Affairs
1025 Connecticut Ave. NW, Suite 1210
Washington, DC 20005
steve.morrissey@ual.com

O'TOOLE, Thomas F.   Tel: (872) 825-8610
Senior Vice President and Marketing and Loyalty   Fax: (847) 700-4899
P.O. Box 66100
Chicago, IL 60666

PHILIP , Rohit   Tel: (872) 825-8610
Senior Vice President, Finance   Fax: (847) 700-4899
P.O. Box 66100
Chicago, IL 60666

RAINEY, John D.   Tel: (872) 825-8610
Executive Vice President and Chief Financial Officer   Fax: (847) 700-4899
P.O. Box 66100
Chicago, IL 60666

United Continental Holdings, Inc.

Airline that maintains 370 mainline jets and 270 aircraft in its regional operations. Formerly known as Continental Airlines; merged with United Airlines in 2012 and now operates as United Airlines.
www.unitedcontinentalholdings.com
Annual Revenues: $38.81 billion
Employees: 84,000
Ticker: NYSE: UAL
SIC: 4512
NAICS: 41000
Industry/ies: Aerospace/Aviation; Airlines; Transportation; Travel/Tourism/Lodging
Legislative Issues: BUD; HOM

Chairman of the Board, President and Chief Executive Officer   Tel: (202) 521-4400
SMISEK, Jeffery A.   Fax: (202) 289-1546

Main Headquarters
Mailing: 233 S. Wacker Dr.   Tel: (872) 825-4000
         P.O. Box 06649
         Chicago, IL 60606

Washington Office
Mailing: 1225 New York Ave. NW   Tel: (202) 521-4400
         Suite 1100   Fax: (202) 289-1546
         Washington, DC 20005

Public Affairs and Related Activities Personnel

At Headquarters

BONDS, Michael P.   Tel: (872) 825-4000

Executive Vice President, Human Resources and Labor Relations

COMPTON, James   Tel: (872) 825-4000
Vice Chairman and Chief Revenue Officer

FOLAND, Jeffrey T.   Tel: (872) 825-4000
Executive Vice President, Marketing, Technology and Strategy

FOXHALL, Irene   Tel: (872) 825-4000
Executive Vice President, Communications and Government Affairs

GEBO, John   Tel: (872) 825-4000
Senior Vice President Alliances, Regulatory and Policy Affairs

HART, Brett J.   Tel: (872) 825-4000
Executive Vice President, General Counsel and Secretary

HART, Gregory   Tel: (872) 825-4000
Executive Vice President and Chief Operations Officer

RAINEY , John D.   Tel: (872) 825-4000
Executive Vice President and Chief Financial Officer

At Washington Office

ANDERSON, Mark R.   Tel: (202) 521-4400
Senior Vice President, Corporate and Government Affairs   Fax: (202) 289-1546

HEPBURN, Adam   Tel: (202) 521-4400
                       Fax: (202) 289-1546

KUHLMAN, Karen   Tel: (202) 521-4400
                       Fax: (202) 289-1546

VAN DUYNE, Nancy H.   Tel: (202) 521-4400
Vice President, Congressional Affairs   Fax: (202) 289-1546

United Health Group

Formerly United HealthCare Corp. Health care management and evaluation services. Acquired Mid Atlantic Medical Services Inc. (MAMSI) (see separate listing) in February, 2004. Acquired PacifiCare Health Systems in late 2005 and Sierra Health Services in 2008.
www.unitedhealthgroup.com
Annual Revenues: $134.52 billion
Employees: 170,000
Ticker: NYSE: UNH
SIC: 6324
Industry/ies: Insurance Industry; Medicine/Health Care/Mental Health
Legislative Issues: BUD; DEF; GOV; HCR; INS; MMM; TAX; VET

Chairman of the Board   Tel: (714) 226-3530
BURKE, Richard T.   Fax: (952) 936-0044

Chief Executive Officer   Tel: (714) 226-3530
HEMSLEY, Stephen J.   Fax: (952) 936-0044

Chief Executive Officer   Tel: (202) 383-6400
HEYMAN, Stephen M.   Fax: (202) 383-6412

Main Headquarters
Mailing: P.O. Box 1459   Tel: (714) 226-3530
         Minneapolis, MN 55440-1459   Fax: (952) 936-0044
                       TF: (800) 328-5979

Washington Office
Mailing: 701 Pennsylvania Ave. NW, Suite 650
         Washington, DC 20004

Political Action Committees
United Health Group Incorporated PAC (United for Health)
FEC ID: C00274431
Contact: Susan Sherwood
9900 Bren Rd., East   Tel: (952) 936-1300
Minnetonka, MN 55343   Fax: (952) 936-1819

    Contributions to Candidates: $266,000 (2015-2016)
    Democrats: $116,000; Republicans: $150,000

Corporate Foundations and Giving Programs

United Health Foundation
Contact: Lauren Mihajlov
9900 Bren Rd. East
Minnetonka, MN 55343

UnitedHealthcare Childrens Foundation
Contact: Lauren Mihajlov
P.O. BOX 41   Tel: (952) 992-4459
Minneapolis, MN 55440-0041

Public Affairs and Related Activities Personnel

At Headquarters

NATHAN, Don   Tel: (714) 226-3530
Senior Vice President and Chief Communications Officer   Fax: (952) 936-0044

SHORT, Marianne D.   Tel: (714) 226-3530
Executive Vice President and Chief Legal Officer   Fax: (952) 936-0044

TINKER, Ann   Tel: (714) 226-3530
Manager, Lobbying Compliance Services   Fax: (952) 936-0044
ann.tinker@uhc.com

WICHMANN, David S.   Tel: (714) 226-3530

President and Chief Financial Officer — Fax: (952) 936-0044

WILSON, Ellen — Tel: (714) 226-3530
Executive Vice President, Human Capital — Fax: (952) 936-0044

At Other Offices

ALEXANDER, Cory — Tel: (202) 383-6400
Executive Vice President, External Affairs and Head, — Fax: (202) 383-6412
Government Affairs
701 Pennsylvania Ave. NW, Suite 200
Washington, DC 20004

JACOBS, Frances — Tel: (800) 328-5979
Executive Assistant and Contact, Investor Relations — Fax: (952) 936-1819
9900 Bren Rd., East
Minnetonka, MN 55343
Investor_Relations@uhc.com

JACOBY, Peter — Tel: (202) 383-6400
701 Pennsylvania Ave. NW, Suite 200 — Fax: (202) 383-6412
Washington, DC 20004

JINDAL, Sohini — Tel: (202) 383-6400
Federal Lobbyist — Fax: (202) 383-6412
701 Pennsylvania Ave. NW, Suite 200
Washington, DC 20004
Registered Federal Lobbyist

KENIRY, Daniel J. — Tel: (202) 383-6400
Vice President and Head, Federal Government Affairs — Fax: (202) 383-6412
701 Pennsylvania Ave. NW, Suite 200
Washington, DC 20004
Registered Federal Lobbyist

MIHAJLOV, Lauren — Tel: (952) 936-1300
Director, Social Responsibility Communications — Fax: (952) 936-1819
9900 Bren Rd., East
Minnetonka, MN 55343
lauren_mihajlov@uhg.com%20

PRIBLE, John M. — Tel: (202) 383-6400
701 Pennsylvania Ave. NW, Suite 200 — Fax: (202) 383-6412
Washington, DC 20004
Registered Federal Lobbyist

SHERWOOD, Susan — Tel: (952) 936-1300
PAC Treasurer — Fax: (952) 936-1819
9900 Bren Rd., East
Minnetonka, MN 55343

SMITH, Kara Vlasaty — Tel: (202) 383-6400
Federal Lobbyist — Fax: (202) 383-6412
701 Pennsylvania Ave. NW, Suite 200
Washington, DC 20004
Registered Federal Lobbyist

VERSAGGI, John — Tel: (202) 383-6400
Federal Lobbyist — Fax: (202) 383-6412
701 Pennsylvania Ave. NW, Suite 200
Washington, DC 20004
Registered Federal Lobbyist

The United Illuminating Company

An electric utility and energy services company.
www.uinet.com
Annual Revenues: $1.57 billion
Employees: 900
SIC: 4911
Industry/ies: Utilities

Chairman of the Board — Tel: (203) 499-2000
LAHEY, John L. — Fax: (203) 499-2411

President and Chief Executive Officer — Tel: (203) 499-2000
TORGERSON, James P. — Fax: (203) 499-3626

Main Headquarters
Mailing: 157 Church St. — Tel: (203) 499-2000
P.O. Box 1564 — Fax: (203) 499-2411
New Haven, CT 06506-0901 — TF: (800) 722-5584

Political Action Committees
Electric Employees Committee of The United Illuminating Company PAC
FEC ID: C00216341
Contact: Patricia C. Cosgel
157 Church St.
P.O. Box 1564
New Haven, CT 6506

   Contributions to Candidates: $4,000 (2015-2016)
   Democrats: $500; Republicans: $3,500

Corporate Foundations and Giving Programs
United Illuminating Contributions Program
Contact: Shelly Saczynski
157 Church St. — Tel: (203) 499-1000
New Haven, CT 06510 — Fax: (203) 499-4333

Public Affairs and Related Activities Personnel

At Headquarters

ALLEN, Susan E. — Tel: (203) 499-2409
Vice President, Investor Relations and Treasurer — Fax: (203) 499-2414
Mail Stop MS 1-15A
susan.allen@uinet.com

CARBONE, Albert — Tel: (203) 499-2000
Government Relations Professional — Fax: (203) 499-2411
albert.carbone@uinet.com

CORETTO, Michael A. — Tel: (203) 499-2000
Vice President, Regulatory Affairs — Fax: (203) 499-2411

COSGEL, Patricia C. — Tel: (203) 499-2000
Vice President and Treasurer — Fax: (203) 499-2411

DEBOISSIERE, Alex — Tel: (203) 499-2000
Senior Vice President, Government Relations and — Fax: (203) 499-2411
Communications

NICHOLAS, Richard J. — Tel: (203) 499-2000
Executive Vice President and Chief Financial Officer — Fax: (203) 499-2411

PIVIROTTO, Diane M. — Tel: (203) 499-2000
Senior Vice President, Human Resources, Administrative — Fax: (203) 499-2411
Services, Chief Compliance Officer and Assistant Corporate
Secretary

RANDELL, Linda L. — Tel: (203) 499-2000
Senior Vice President and General Counsel — Fax: (203) 499-2411
linda.randell@uinet.com

SACZYNSKI, Shelly — Tel: (203) 499-2000
Director, Economic and Community Development — Fax: (203) 499-2411

WEST, Jr., Michael A. — Tel: (203) 499-3858
Vice President, Corporate Communications — Fax: (203) 499-2411
michael.west@uinet.com

United Maritime Group, LLC

United Maritime Group provides marine transportation business.
www.unitedmaritimegroup.com
Annual Revenues: $323.45 million
Employees: 1,000
SIC: 4400
Industry/ies: Marine/Maritime/Shipping; Transportation

Chief Executive Officer — Tel: (813) 209-4200
GREEN, Steven — Fax: (813) 273-0248

Main Headquarters
Mailing: 601 S. Harbour Island Blvd. — Tel: (813) 209-4200
Suite 230 — Fax: (813) 273-0248
Tampa, FL 33602

Public Affairs and Related Activities Personnel

At Headquarters

COOPER, Monica — Tel: (813) 209-4200
Director, Human Resources — Fax: (813) 273-0248

United Parcel Service (UPS)

Global shipping and parcel delivery company.
www.ups.com
Annual Revenues: $58.43 billion
Employees: 237,300
Ticker: NYSE: UPS
SIC: 4210
Industry/ies: Transportation
Legislative Issues: AVI; BUD; DEF; FOR; HCR; HOM; LBR; POS; RET; TAX; TRA; TRD; TRU; VET

Chairman of the Board and Chief Executive Officer — Tel: (404) 828-6000
DAVIS, D. Scott — Fax: (404) 828-6562

Main Headquarters
Mailing: 55 Glenlake Pkwy. NE — Tel: (404) 828-6000
Atlanta, GA 30328 — TF: (800) 874-5877

Washington Office
Mailing: 316 Pennsylvania Ave. SE
Suite 300
Washington, DC 20003

Political Action Committees
United Parcel Service PAC
FEC ID: C00064766
Contact: Susan F. Ward
55 Glenlake Pkwy. NE — Tel: (202) 675-4220
Atlanta, GA 30328 — Fax: (202) 675-4230

   Contributions to Candidates: $1,453,049 (2015-2016)
   Democrats: $455,052; Republicans: $995,497; Other: $2,500

   Principal Recipients

   HOUSE
   CHAFFETZ, JASON (REP-UT)
   CROWLEY, JOSEPH (DEM-NY)
   DIAZ-BALART, MARIO (REP-FL)

HILL, JAMES FRENCH (REP-AR)
HUDSON, RICHARD L. JR. (REP-NC)
KATKO, JOHN M (REP-NY)
KINZINGER, ADAM (REP-IL)
MCCARTHY, KEVIN (REP-CA)
MCMORRIS RODGERS, CATHY (REP-WA)
MEEHAN, PATRICK L. MR. (REP-PA)
PRICE, THOMAS EDMUNDS (REP-GA)
REED, THOMAS W II (REP-NY)
ROGERS, HAROLD DALLAS (REP-KY)
SCALISE, STEVE MR. (REP-LA)
SCOTT, JAMES AUSTIN (REP-GA)
SHUSTER, WILLIAM MR. (REP-PA)
SMITH, ADRIAN (REP-NE)
VALADAO, DAVID (REP-CA)
WAGNER, ANN L. (REP-MO)
WALDEN, GREGORY P MR. (REP-OR)

Corporate Foundations and Giving Programs

The UPS Foundation
Contact: Christine M. Owens
55 Glenlake Pkwy. NE
Atlanta, GA 30328

Public Affairs and Related Activities Personnel

At Headquarters

ABNEY, David *Chief Operating Officer*	Tel:	(404) 828-6000
BLACK, Norman *Director, Global Media Services* norman.black@ups.com	Tel: Fax:	(404) 828-7593 (404) 828-6562
DOLNY, Andy *Retired Treasurer*	Tel: Fax:	(404) 828-8901 (404) 828-6562
FINLEY, Teresa M. *Senior Vice President, Global Marketing*	Tel:	(404) 828-6000
FRANCESCONI, Michael *Corporate Counsel*	Tel:	(404) 828-6000
GARDNER, Peggy *Senior Director, Global Media Relations*	Tel: Fax:	(404) 828-6051 (404) 828-6562
GERSHENHORN, Alan *Executive Vice President and Chief Commercial Officer*	Tel:	(404) 828-6000
KING, Victoria *Vice President, Public Affairs*	Tel:	(404) 828-6000
KUEHN, Kurt *Chief Financial Officer*	Tel:	(404) 828-6000
MCCLURE, Teri Plummer *Senior Vice President, Legal, Compliance and Public Affairs, General Counsel and Corporate Secretary*	Tel: Fax:	(404) 828-6000 (404) 828-6562
MCDEVITT, John *Senior Vice President, Human Resources and Labor Relations*	Tel:	(404) 828-7123
WARD, Susan F. *Vice President and PAC Treasurer*	Tel: Fax:	(404) 828-6000 (404) 828-6562

At Washington Office

GRIFFIN, Leslie
Federal Lobbyist
Registered Federal Lobbyist

PALMER, Brian
Registered Federal Lobbyist

POLICASTRO, Anne
Contact, Government Relations
Registered Federal Lobbyist

At Other Offices

ALAGNA, Mark *Manager, Public Affairs* 316 Pennsylvania Ave. SE, Suite 500 Washington, DC 20003 malagna@ups.com *Registered Federal Lobbyist*	Tel: Fax:	(202) 675-4220 (202) 675-4230
BERGMAN, Robert *Vice President, Public Affairs* 316 Pennsylvania Ave. SE, Suite 500 Washington, DC 20003 bbergman@ups.com	Tel: Fax:	(202) 675-3354 (202) 675-4230
BONILLA, Sheryl *Manager, Public Affairs* 316 Pennsylvania Ave. SE, Suite 500 Washington, DC 20003 sshelby@ups.com	Tel: Fax:	(202) 675-4220 (202) 675-4230
BRUCE, James *Vice President, Corporate Public Affairs* 316 Pennsylvania Ave. SE, Suite 500 Washington, DC 20003	Tel:	(202) 675-4220

Registered Federal Lobbyist

CLIFTON, Nicole *Vice President, Public Affairs* 316 Pennsylvania Ave. SE, Suite 500 Washington, DC 20003 nicoleclifton@ups.com *Registered Federal Lobbyist*	Tel:	(202) 675-4220
DUBOIS, Marcel *Vice President, Public Affairs* 316 Pennsylvania Ave. SE, Suite 500 Washington, DC 20003 *Registered Federal Lobbyist*	Tel: Fax:	(202) 675-4237 (202) 675-4230
EYGENSON, Serge *Policy Manager* 316 Pennsylvania Ave. SE, Suite 500 Washington, DC 20003	Tel:	(202) 675-4223
JENSEN, Thomas 316 Pennsylvania Ave. SE, Suite 500 Washington, DC 20003 *Registered Federal Lobbyist*	Tel:	(202) 675-4223
KELLISON, Keith *Vice President, Retail and Residential Operations* 316 Pennsylvania Ave. SE, Suite 500 Washington, DC 20003 *Registered Federal Lobbyist*	Tel:	(202) 675-4220
KIELY, Stephen *Manager, Public Affairs* 316 Pennsylvania Ave. SE, Suite 500 Washington, DC 20003 *Registered Federal Lobbyist*	Tel: Fax:	(202) 675-4220 (202) 675-4230
KIELY, Michael 316 Pennsylvania Ave. SE, Suite 500 Washington, DC 20003 *Registered Federal Lobbyist*	Tel:	(202) 675-4223
KINNEY, Sharen A. 316 Pennsylvania Ave. SE, Suite 500 Washington, DC 20003 sakinney@ups.com	Tel: Fax:	(202) 675-1712 (202) 675-4230
LANE, Laura *Corporate Vice President, Domestic/International Public Affairs* 316 Pennsylvania Ave. SE, Suite 500 Washington, DC 20003	Tel: Fax:	(202) 675-4220 (202) 675-4230
LEWIS, Nicholas *Vice President, Corporate Public Affairs* 316 Pennsylvania Ave. SE, Suite 500 Washington, DC 20003 nlewis@ups.com *Registered Federal Lobbyist*	Tel: Fax:	(202) 675-4222 (202) 675-4230
MEYERS, Charles Chip *Manager, Public Affairs* 316 Pennsylvania Ave. SE, Suite 500 Washington, DC 20003 cmeyers@ups.com *Registered Federal Lobbyist*	Tel: Fax:	(202) 675-4220 (202) 675-4230
PIERRE, Nicole *Vice President, Public Affairs* 316 Pennsylvania Ave. SE, Suite 500 Washington, DC 20003 npierre@ups.com *Registered Federal Lobbyist*	Tel: Fax:	(202) 675-4220 (202) 675-4230
RICHARDSON, Dana *Manager, Public Affairs* 316 Pennsylvania Ave. SE, Suite 500 Washington, DC 20003 drichardson@ups.com	Tel: Fax:	(202) 675-4220 (202) 675-4230
ROTH, Royal *Manager* 316 Pennsylvania Ave. SE, Suite 500 Washington, DC 20003 *Registered Federal Lobbyist*	Tel: Fax:	(202) 675-4220 (202) 675-4230
SMALLS, Dontai *Vice President, Corporate Public Affairs* 316 Pennsylvania Ave. SE, Suite 500 Washington, DC 20003 dsmalls@ups.com *Registered Federal Lobbyist*	Tel: Fax:	(202) 675-4220 (202) 675-4230
TAPIA-HADLEY, Zuraya 316 Pennsylvania Ave. SE, Suite 500 Washington, DC 20003 *Registered Federal Lobbyist*	Tel:	(202) 675-4223

United Refining Company

A refiner and marketer of petroleum products.
www.urc.com
Annual Revenues: $3.17 billion
Employees: 4,000
SIC: 2911
Industry/ies: Fuels See Coal, Gas, Oil, Petroleum; Natural Resources; Petroleum Industry

Chairman of the Board and Chief Executive Officer
CATSIMATIDIS, John A.
Tel: (814) 723-1500
Fax: (814) 726-4709

Main Headquarters
Mailing: 15 Bradley St.
Warren, PA 16365
Tel: (814) 723-1500
Fax: (814) 726-4709

Public Affairs and Related Activities Personnel

At Headquarters

DITKA, Ashton L.
Senior Vice President, Marketing
Tel: (814) 723-1500
Fax: (814) 726-4709

MURPHY, James E.
Chief Financial Officer
Tel: (814) 723-1500
Fax: (814) 726-4709

TURFITT, Myron L.
President and Chief Operating Officer
Tel: (814) 723-1500
Fax: (814) 726-4709

United Rentals

Provides service, quality equipment and supplies, training and assistance and information technologies. Its fleet of rental equipment includes general construction and industrial equipment and it offers them for rent to construction and industrial companies, manufacturers, utilities, municipalities, homeowners, government entities, and other customers.
www.unitedrentals.com
Annual Revenues: $5.82 billion
Employees: 12,500
Ticker: NYSE: URI
SIC: 7359
Industry/ies: Machinery/Equipment
Legislative Issues: GOV

Chairman of the Board
BRITELL, Jenne K.
Tel: (203) 622-3131
Fax: (203) 622-6080

President and Chief Executive Officer
KNEELAND, Michael J.
Tel: (203) 622-3131
Fax: (203) 622-6080

Main Headquarters
Mailing: 100 First Stamford Pl.
Suite 700
Stamford, CT 06902
Tel: (203) 622-3131
Fax: (203) 622-6080
TF: (800) 877-3687

Corporate Foundations and Giving Programs

United Rentals Contribution Program
Five Greenwich Office Park
Greenwich, CT 06831
Tel: (203) 622-3131
Fax: (203) 622-6080

Public Affairs and Related Activities Personnel

At Headquarters

BRATMAN, Fred B.
Senior Vice President, Corporate Communications and Investor Relations
Tel: (203) 618-7318
Fax: (203) 622-6080

CORSILLO, Juan P.
Senior Vice President, Sales and Marketing
Tel: (203) 622-3131
Fax: (203) 622-6080

FLANNERY, Matthew
Executive Vice President and Chief Operating Officer
Tel: (203) 622-3131
Fax: (203) 622-6080

GOTTSEGEN, Jonathan M.
Senior Vice President, General Counsel and Corporate Secretary
jgottsegen@ur.com
Tel: (203) 622-3131
Fax: (203) 622-6080

GROSS, Joli L.
Vice President, Deputy General Counsel and Assistant Corporate Secretary
Tel: (203) 622-3131
Fax: (203) 622-6080

METTEL, Kenneth B.
Senior Vice President, Strategy and Planning
Tel: (203) 622-3131
Fax: (203) 622-6080

PINTOFF, Craig A.
Senior Vice President, Human Resources
cpintoff@ur.com
Tel: (203) 622-3131
Fax: (203) 622-6080

PLUMMER, William B.
Executive Vice President and Chief Financial Officer
Tel: (203) 622-3131
Fax: (203) 622-6080

United Space Alliance LLC

A spaceflight operations company. It is equally owned by The Boeing Company and Lockheed Martin Corporation.
www.unitedspacealliance.com
Annual Revenues: $1.82 billion
Employees: 3,000
SIC: 3761; 3769
NAICS: 336414; 336419
Industry/ies: Aerospace/Aviation; Transportation

President and Chief Executive Officer
HARTWIG, Scott Q.
Tel: (281) 212-6200
Fax: (281) 212-6177

Main Headquarters
Mailing: 3700 Bay Area Blvd.
Suite HB5-10
Houston, TX 77058-1160
Tel: (281) 212-6200
Fax: (281) 212-6177

Washington Office
Mailing: 17623 Tobermory Pl.
Leesburg, VA 20175
Tel: (703) 777-0096

Corporate Foundations and Giving Programs

United Space Alliance LLC Contributions Program
1150 Gemini St.
Houston, TX 77058

Public Affairs and Related Activities Personnel

At Headquarters

CAPEL, William R.
Vice President and Chief Financial Officer
Tel: (281) 212-6200
Fax: (281) 212-6177

GOOKINS, Norman
Vice President, Human Resources and Administration
Tel: (281) 212-6200
Fax: (281) 212-6177

LEE, Sherri K.
Vice President, Human Resources, Communications and Public Relations
Tel: (281) 212-6200
Fax: (281) 212-6177

YATES, Tracy
Manager, Communications and Public Relations
Tel: (321) 861-3956
Fax: (281) 212-6177

At Washington Office

ALLEN, Margaret
Vice President, Government Affairs
Meghan.W.Allen@usa-spaceops.com
Tel: (703) 777-0093

United States Cellular Corporation

Provides wireless phone services.
www.uscellular.com
Annual Revenues: $3.99 billion
Employees: 6,500
Ticker: NYSE: USM
SIC: 4812
Industry/ies: Communications; Telecommunications/Internet/Cable
Legislative Issues: COM; TEC

Chairman of the Board
CARLSON, Jr., LeRoy T.
Tel: (773) 399-8900
Fax: (773) 399-8936

President and Chief Executive Officer
MEYERS, Kenneth R.
Tel: (773) 399-8900
Fax: (773) 399-8936

Main Headquarters
Mailing: 8410 W. Bryn Mawr Ave.
Chicago, IL 60631-3486
Tel: (773) 399-8900
Fax: (773) 399-8936
TF: (888) 944-9400

Political Action Committees
United States Cellular PAC
FEC ID: C00336057
Contact: Thomas S. Weber
8410 W. Bryn Mawr Ave.
Suite 700
Chicago, IL 60631

    Contributions to Candidates: $10,311,015 (2015-2016)
    Democrats: $40,000; Republicans: $79,000; Other: $10,192,015

        Principal Recipients
            SENATE
            THUNE, JOHN (REP-SD)
            HOUSE
            MCMORRIS RODGERS, CATHY (REP-WA)

Corporate Foundations and Giving Programs

United States Cellular Contributions Program
8410 W. Bryn Mawr Ave.
Suite 700
Chicago, IL 60631

Public Affairs and Related Activities Personnel

At Headquarters

CAMPBELL, Steven T.
Executive Vice President, Finance and Chief Financial Officer and Treasurer
Tel: (773) 399-8900
Fax: (773) 399-8936

DRAKE, Deirdre C.
Senior Vice President, Chief Human Resources Officer
Tel: (773) 399-8900
Fax: (773) 399-8936

FREY, Katie
Media Relations Specialist
katie.frey@uscellular.com
Tel: (773) 355-3275
Fax: (773) 399-8936

GOCKLEY, John C.
Vice President, Legal and Regulatory Affairs
john.gockley@uscellular.com
Tel: (773) 399-8900
Fax: (773) 399-8936

HOERSCH, Jeffrey S.
Vice President, Financial Planning and Analysis
Tel: (773) 399-8900
Fax: (773) 399-8936

JAGHER, Eric
Vice President, Business Strategy
Tel: (773) 399-8900
Fax: (773) 399-8936

MCCAHON, Jane W.
Senior Vice President, Corporate Relations
jane.mccahon@teldta.com
Tel: (312) 592-5379
Fax: (312) 630-9299

PEREZ, Edward
Senior Vice President, Sales
Tel: (773) 399-8900
Fax: (773) 399-8936

SETTIMI , Joe
Vice President, Marketing
Tel: (773) 399-8900
Fax: (773) 399-8936

SPELLMEYER, Grant B.
Vice President, Federal Affairs & Public Policy
Grant.Spellmeyer@uscellular.com
Registered Federal Lobbyist
Tel: (778) 399-4280
Fax: (773) 399-8936

WEBER, Thomas S.
Vice President, Financial Strategy and PAC Treasurer
Tel: (773) 399-8900
Fax: (773) 399-8936

US Ecology

Provides hazardous and radioactive materials management solutions to industry and government.
www.americanecology.com
Annual Revenues: $530.71 million
Employees: 1,800
Ticker: NASDAQ: ECOL
SIC: 4953
Industry/ies: Environment And Conservation; Pollution And Waste
Legislative Issues: BUD; ENV; WAS

Chairman of the Board
ROMANO, Stephen A.
Tel: (800) 590-5220
Fax: (208) 331-7900

PAC Contact, President and Chief Executive Officer
FEELER, CPA, Jeffrey R.
Tel: (208) 331-8400
Fax: (208) 331-7900

Main Headquarters
Mailing: 251 E. Front St.
          Suite 400
          Boise, ID 83702
Tel: (800) 590-5220
Fax: (208) 331-7900
TF: (800) 590-5220

Political Action Committees
US Ecology, Inc. PAC (USE PAC)
FEC ID: C00375782
Contact: Jeffrey R. Feeler CPA
251 E. Front St.
Suite 400
Boise, ID 83702
Tel: (208) 331-8400
Fax: (208) 331-7900

  Contributions to Candidates: $4,000 (2015-2016)
  Republicans: $4,000

Public Affairs and Related Activities Personnel
At Headquarters

BELL, Simon
Executive Vice President of Operations and Technology Development
Tel: (800) 590-5220
Fax: (208) 331-7900

GERRATT, Eric
Executive Vice President, Chief Financial Officer and Treasurer
Tel: (800) 590-5220
Fax: (208) 331-7900

HYSLOP, Chad
Director, Sales and Marketing
chyslop@usecology.com
Tel: (208) 319-1604
Fax: (208) 331-7900

IPSEN, Wayne
Vice President, Corporate Counsel, Compliance Officer and Secretary
Tel: (800) 590-5220
Fax: (208) 331-7900

STERK, Betsy
Director, Human Resources
Tel: (800) 590-5220
Fax: (208) 331-7900

WELLING, Steve
Executive Vice President, Sales and Marketing
Tel: (800) 590-5220
Fax: (208) 331-7900

United States Investigations Services (USIS)

Information and security services company.
www.usis.com
Annual Revenues: $750.0 million
Employees: 8,000
Industry/ies: Law Enforcement/Security
Legislative Issues: BUD; DEF; HOM; IMM

President and Chief Executive Officer
PHILLIPS, Sterling
Tel: (888) 270-8978

Main Headquarters
Mailing: 125 Lincoln Ave.
          Grove City, PA 16127

Washington Office
Mailing: 7799 Leesburg Pike
          Suite 400, South
          Falls Church, VA 22043-2413
Tel: (888) 270-8978
TF: (888) 270-8978

Public Affairs and Related Activities Personnel
At Headquarters

COLE, Andrew
Contact, Media

At Washington Office

ALTEMUS, Barbara
Government Affairs Manager
Tel: (703) 637-4883

CORREIRA, Christina
Chief Human Resources Officer
Tel: (888) 270-8978

ELIA, Adelle
Chief Ethics and Compliance Officer
Tel: (888) 270-8978

MEYER , Francis
Senior Vice President and Chief Financial Officer
Tel: (888) 270-8978

SIMMONS, Keith R.
Vice President, Deputy General Counsel
Tel: (703) 637-4883

U.S. Jails & Prisons Forum, Inc.

US Jails & Prisons Forum in Washington, DC 20032. Map & Driving Directions. US Jails & Prisons Forum is Listed Under Human Services Organizations.
Industry/ies: Law Enforcement/Security

Chief Executive Officer
JONES, Michelle
Tel: (301) 218-2176

Main Headquarters
Mailing: 513 Jennings Mill Dr.
          Bowie, MD 20721
Tel: (301) 218-2176

Public Affairs and Related Activities Personnel
At Other Offices

CLEMMONS, Luther
P.O. Box 26344
Washington, DC 20001
Tel: (301) 218-2176

HILLIARD, Kenneth
Treasurer
P.O. Box 26344
Washington, DC 20001
Tel: (301) 218-2176

United States Olympic Committee

USOC's mission is to support U.S. Olympic and Paralympic athletes in achieving sustained competitive excellence and preserve the Olympic ideals, and thereby inspire all Americans.
www.teamusa.org
Employees: 7
Industry/ies: Foreign Relations; Sports/Leisure/Entertainment
Legislative Issues: CPT; HOM; IMM; SPO; TAX; TOU

Chairman of the Board
PROBST, Larry
Tel: (719) 866-4583
Fax: (719) 632-6071

Chief Executive Officer
BLACKMUN, Scott
Tel: (719) 866-4583
Fax: (719) 632-6071

Main Headquarters
Mailing: One Olympic Plaza
          Colorado Springs, CO 80909
Tel: (719) 866-4583
Fax: (719) 632-6071
TF: (888) 222-2313

Washington Office
Mailing: 1100 H St. NW
          Suite 600
          Washington, DC 20005
Tel: (202) 466-3399
Fax: (202) 466-5068

Corporate Foundations and Giving Programs
United States Olympic Foundation
One Olympic Plaza
Colorado Springs, CO 80909
Tel: (719) 866-4583
Fax: (719) 632-6071

Public Affairs and Related Activities Personnel
At Headquarters

BAIRD, Lisa
Chief Marketing Officer
Tel: (719) 866-4583
Fax: (719) 632-6071

GLOVER , Walter
Chief Financial Officer
Tel: (719) 866-4583
Fax: (719) 632-6071

KEREK, Morane
Managing Director, Internal Audit
Tel: (719) 866-4583
Fax: (719) 632-6071

MCCLEARY, Christopher
General Counsel
Tel: (719) 866-4583
Fax: (719) 632-6071

SANDUSKY , Patrick D.
Chief Communications and Public Affairs Officer
Tel: (719) 866-4583
Fax: (719) 632-6071

SAWYER, Pam
Managing Director, Human Resources
Tel: (719) 866-4583
Fax: (719) 632-6071

At Washington Office

FILIPPONE, Desiree
Managing Director, Government Relations
Tel: (202) 466-3399
Fax: (202) 466-5068

United States Steel Corporation

A manufacturer of steel products, coke and taconite pellets. The company manufactures a wide range of value-added steel sheet and tubular products for the automotive, appliance, container, industrial machinery, construction, and oil and gas industries.
www.ussteel.com
Annual Revenues: $16.33 billion
Employees: 35,500
Ticker: NYSE: X
SIC: 5051; 5099; 8011; 3312
Industry/ies: Engineering/Mathematics; Fuels See Coal, Gas, Oil, Petroleum; Metals; Natural Resources; Petroleum Industry; Real Estate
Legislative Issues: BUD; ENV; LBR; MAN; TAX; TRA; TRD

President and Chief Executive Officer — Tel: (412) 433-1121
LONGHI, Mario — Fax: (412) 433-5733

Main Headquarters
Mailing: 600 Grant St. — Tel: (412) 433-1121
Pittsburgh, PA 15219-2800 — Fax: (412) 433-5733

Washington Office
Mailing: 901 K St. NW — Tel: (202) 783-6333
Suite 1250 — Fax: (202) 783-6309
Washington, DC 20001

Political Action Committees
United States Steel Corporation PAC
FEC ID: C00030676
Contact: Lori Ruppen
600 Grant St. — Tel: (412) 433-1121
Room 669 — Fax: (412) 433-5733
Pittsburgh, PA 15219

Contributions to Candidates: $101,000 (2015-2016)
Democrats: $52,000; Republicans: $49,000

Principal Recipients

HOUSE
KIND, RONALD JAMES (DEM-WI)
MURPHY, TIMOTHY (REP-PA)

Corporate Foundations and Giving Programs

United States Steel Foundation Inc.
Contact: Susan M. Kapusta
600 Grant St.
Pittsburgh, PA 15219

Public Affairs and Related Activities Personnel

At Headquarters

BALAWAJDER, Charles G. — Tel: (412) 433-1121
Vice President and Chief Information Officer — Fax: (412) 433-5733

BOONE, Courtney — Tel: (412) 433-6791
Manager, Public Affairs — Fax: (412) 433-5733
caboone@uss.com

BURRITT, David B. — Tel: (412) 433-1121
Executive Vice President and Chief Financial Officer — Fax: (412) 433-5733

DIPIETRO, Erin — Tel: (412) 433-6845
Manager, Executive Communications — Fax: (412) 433-5733

GARRAUX, James D. — Tel: (412) 433-1121
General Counsel and Senior Vice President, Corporate Affairs — Fax: (412) 433-5733

LESNAK, Dan — Tel: (412) 433-1184
Manager, Investor Relations — Fax: (412) 433-1167
investorrelations@uss.com

RUPPEN, Lori — Tel: (412) 433-1121
PAC Contact — Fax: (412) 433-5733

SCHERRBAUM, Jr., Joseph R. — Tel: (412) 433-1121
Vice President, Sales — Fax: (412) 433-5733

STRAUB, Terrence D. — Tel: (412) 433-1121
Senior Vice President, Public Policy and Governmental Affairs — Fax: (412) 433-5733
Registered Federal Lobbyist

SLIVER, Susan M. — Tel: (412) 433-1121
Vice President, Human Resources and Administration — Fax: (412) 433-5733

WILLIAMS, Michael S. — Tel: (412) 433-1121
Senior Vice President, Strategic Planning and Business Development — Fax: (412) 433-5733

At Washington Office

FOLSOM, Suzanne — Tel: (202) 783-6333
Chief Compliance Officer, General Counsel and Senior Vice President, Governmental Affairs — Fax: (202) 783-6309

LINDSEY, Jennifer W. — Tel: (202) 783-6333
Legislative Representative — Fax: (202) 783-6309

MCCALL, Katie R. — Tel: (202) 783-6333
Manager, Federal Government Affairs — Fax: (202) 783-6309
Registered Federal Lobbyist

SALMON, Scott R. — Tel: (202) 783-6333
General Manager, Governmental Affairs — Fax: (202) 783-6309

SHON, Debbie — Tel: (202) 783-6333
Federal Lobbyist — Fax: (202) 783-6309

SPEICE, Patrick F. — Tel: (202) 783-6333
Assistant General Counsel, Regulatory and Compliance — Fax: (202) 783-6309

YOUNG, Todd D. — Tel: (202) 783-6333
Registered Federal Lobbyist — Fax: (202) 783-6309

United States Sugar Corporation

A sugar cane and citrus grower, processor and refiner.
www.ussugar.com
Employees: 1,500
SIC: 2061
Industry/ies: Commodities; Food And Beverage Industry
Legislative Issues: AGR; TAX; TRD

Chairman of the Board — Tel: (863) 983-8121
WHITE, William S. — Fax: (863) 983-9827

President & Chief Executive Officer — Tel: (863) 983-8121
BUKER, Robert H. — Fax: (863) 983-9827

Main Headquarters
Mailing: 111 Ponce de Leon Ave. — Tel: (863) 983-8121
Clewiston, FL 33440 — Fax: (863) 983-9827

Political Action Committees
United States Sugar Corp-Employee Stock Ownership Plan PAC
FEC ID: C00234120
Contact: Elaine M. Wood
111 Ponce de Leon Ave.
Clewiston, FL 33440

Contributions to Candidates: $14,798 (2015-2016)
Democrats: $6,500; Republicans: $8,298

Public Affairs and Related Activities Personnel

At Headquarters

BERNARD, Gerard — Tel: (863) 983-8121
Senior Vice President, Chief Financial Officer — Fax: (863) 983-9827

COKER, Robert E. — Tel: (863) 902-2461
Senior Vice President, Public Affairs — Fax: (863) 983-9827

SANCHEZ, Judy C. — Tel: (863) 902-2210
Senior Director, Corporate Communications and Public Affairs — Fax: (863) 261-3167
jsanchez@ussugar.com

SHIDE, Charles F. — Tel: (863) 983-8121
Vice President, Human Resources — Fax: (863) 983-9827

WADE, Jr., Malcolm S. — Tel: (863) 983-8121
Senior Vice President Corporate Strategy and Business Development — Fax: (863) 983-9827

WOOD, Elaine M. — Tel: (863) 983-8121
PAC Contact — Fax: (863) 983-9827

United Surgical Partners International, Inc.

A provider of ambulatory surgery and short-stay medicine.
www.uspi.com
Annual Revenues: $576.67 million
Employees: 10,000
SIC: 8062
Industry/ies: Medicine/Health Care/Mental Health
Legislative Issues: HCR; MMM

Chairman of the Board — Tel: (972) 713-3500
STEEN, Donald E. — Fax: (972) 713-3550

Chief Executive Officer — Tel: (972) 713-3500
WILCOX, William H. — Fax: (972) 713-3550

Main Headquarters
Mailing: 15305 Dallas Pkwy. — Tel: (972) 713-3500
Suite 1600 — Fax: (972) 713-3550
Addison, TX 75001

Political Action Committees
United Surgical Partners International Inc. PAC
FEC ID: C00402073
Contact: J. Anthony Martin
15305 Dallas Pkwy.
Suite 1600
Addison, TX 75001

Contributions to Candidates: $44,000 (2015-2016)
Democrats: $11,500; Republicans: $32,500

Corporate Foundations and Giving Programs

United Surgical Partners International Contributions Program
15305 Dallas Pkwy.
Suite 1600
Addison, TX 75001

Public Affairs and Related Activities Personnel

At Headquarters

BLEWETT, Kristin — Tel: (972) 713-3500

Senior Vice President, Marketing and Communications	Fax: (972) 713-3550
BRODNAX, Brett P.	Tel: (972) 713-3500
President and Chief Development Officer	Fax: (972) 713-3550
CAGLE, Jason B.	Tel: (972) 713-3500
Chief Financial Officer	Fax: (972) 713-3550
JOHNSTON, Jr., Isaac N.	Tel: (972) 713-3500
Executive Vice President, Chief Financial Officer Operations and Chief Transformation Officer	Fax: (972) 713-3550
JONES, Milla	Tel: (972) 713-3575
Vice President, Communications and Government Relations	Fax: (972) 713-3550
mijones@uspi.com	
KARRMANN, Sandi	Tel: (972) 713-3500
Chief Human Resources Officer and Support Services Officer	Fax: (972) 713-3550
MARTIN, J. Anthony	Tel: (972) 713-3500
PAC Treasurer	Fax: (972) 713-3550
MOSS, Jarod T.	Tel: (972) 713-3500
Senior Vice President, Strategy	Fax: (972) 713-3550
SPENCER, Phililp A.	Tel: (972) 713-3500
Executive Vice President, Business Development	Fax: (972) 713-3550

United Technologies Corporation

United Technologies Corporation products include Carrier heating and air conditioning, Hamilton Sundstrand aerospace systems and industrial products, Otis elevators and escalators, Pratt & Whitney aircraft engines, Sikorsky helicopters, UTC Fire & Security systems and UTC Power fuel cells.
www.utc.com
Annual Revenues: $64.90 billion
Employees: 211,500
Ticker: NYSE: UTX
SIC: 3760; 3724
Industry/ies: Aerospace/Aviation; Automotive Industry; Chemicals & Chemical Industry; Communications; Defense/Homeland Security; Government-Related; Heating And Air Conditioning; Telecommunications/Internet/Cable; Transportation
Legislative Issues: AER; AGR; AVI; BUD; CPT; DEF; ENG; ENV; FIN; GOV; HOU; MAN; NAT; SCI; TAX; TRD

Chairman of the Board — Tel: (860) 728-7000
KANGAS, Edward A.

President and Chief Executive Officer — Tel: (860) 728-7000
HAYES, Gregory J.
Gregory.Hayes@utc.com

Main Headquarters
Mailing: One Financial Plaza, MS 525 — Tel: (860) 728-7000
Hartford, CT 06101

Washington Office
Mailing: 1401 Eye St. NW
Washington, DC 20005

Political Action Committees
Goodrich Corporation Political Action Committee
FEC ID: C00101725
Contact: Vanessa Heffron
2730 W. Tyvola Rd.
Four Colesium Rd.
Charlotte, NC 28217

United Technologies Corporation PAC
FEC ID: C00035683
Contact: Christopher Peace
1101 Pennsylvania Ave. NW — Tel: (202) 336-7400
Tenth Floor — Fax: (202) 336-7515
Washington, DC 20005

Contributions to Candidates: $877,625 (2015-2016)
Democrats: $306,500; Republicans: $569,125; Other: $2,000

Principal Recipients

SENATE
BLUMENTHAL, RICHARD (DEM-CT)
BLUNT, ROY (REP-MO)
MURKOWSKI, LISA (REP-AK)

HOUSE
BYRNE, BRADLEY ROBERTS (REP-AL)
SHUSTER, WILLIAM MR. (REP-PA)
WALORSKI SWIHART, JACKIE (REP-IN)

Corporate Foundations and Giving Programs
Goodrich Foundation
Contact: Kelly Chopus
2730 W. Tyvola Rd. — Tel: (704) 423-7000
Four Colesium Center
Charlotte, NC 28217

United Technologies Corporation Contributions Program
One Financial Plaza — Tel: (860) 728-7000
Hartford, CT 06101

Public Affairs and Related Activities Personnel
At Headquarters

AMATO, Elizabeth B. — Tel: (860) 728-7000
Senior Vice President, Human Resources and Organization

DUMAIS, Michael — Tel: (860) 728-7000
Senior Vice President, Strategic Planning

GILL, Charles D. — Tel: (860) 728-7000
Senior Vice President and General Counsel
Charles.Gill@utc.com

HASSETT, Neil A. — Tel: (860) 728-7000
PAC Contact

JOHRI, Akhil — Tel: (860) 728-7000
Senior Vice President and Chief Financial Officer

MORAN, John — Tel: (860) 728-7000
Director, Public Relations
john.moran@utc.com

At Other Offices

CHOPUS, Kelly — Tel: (704) 423-7000 / Fax: (704) 423-7002
Secretary, Goodrich Foundation
Four Colesium Center, 2730 W. Tyvola Rd.
Charlotte, NC 28217-4578
kelly.chopus@goodrich.com

COFFIN, Elizabeth — Tel: (202) 336-7400
Vice President, Fiscal and Trade Policy
1101 Pennsylvania Ave. NW, Tenth Floor
Washington, DC 20004
elizabeth.coffin@utc.com
Registered Federal Lobbyist

DOUGLAS, Kimberly — Tel: (202) 336-7423
Federal Lobbyist
1101 Pennsylvania Ave. NW, Tenth Floor
Washington, DC 20004
kimberly.douglas@utc.com

ELLIOTT, Elizabeth Camp — Tel: (202) 336-7406
Director, Government Relations
1101 Pennsylvania Ave. NW, Tenth Floor
Washington, DC 20004
Registered Federal Lobbyist

GALE, Jody — Tel: (202) 336-7400
Federal Lobbyist
1101 Pennsylvania Ave. NW, Tenth Floor
Washington, DC 20004

HEFFRON, Vanessa — Tel: (704) 423-7000 / Fax: (704) 423-7002
PAC Treasurer
Four Colesium Center, 2730 W. Tyvola Rd.
Charlotte, NC 28217-4578

HOLLADAY, Krister — Tel: (202) 336-7400
1101 Pennsylvania Ave. NW, Tenth Floor
Washington, DC 20004
Registered Federal Lobbyist

HOLLAND, Peter — Tel: (202) 336-7400
1101 Pennsylvania Ave. NW, Tenth Floor
Washington, DC 20004
Registered Federal Lobbyist

HOLLIDAY, Krister — Tel: (202) 336-7400
Federal Lobbyist
1101 Pennsylvania Ave. NW, Tenth Floor
Washington, DC 20004
Registered Federal Lobbyist

JIMENEZ, Cindy — Tel: (202) 336-7400
Director, Government Relations
1101 Pennsylvania Ave. NW, Tenth Floor
Washington, DC 20004
cindy.jimenez@utc.com
Registered Federal Lobbyist

JORDAN, Peter — Tel: (202) 336-7400
Director and Senior International Trade Counsel
1101 Pennsylvania Ave. NW, Tenth Floor
Washington, DC 20004
peter.jordan@utc.com
Registered Federal Lobbyist

LARSEN, Marshall O. — Tel: (704) 423-7000 / Fax: (704) 423-7002
Former Chairman, President & Chief Executive Officer of Goodrich Corporation
Four Colesium Center, 2730 W. Tyvola Rd.
Charlotte, NC 28217-4578

LASSETER, David Forrest — Tel: (202) 336-7400
Federal Lobbyist
1101 Pennsylvania Ave. NW, Tenth Floor
Washington, DC 20004
Registered Federal Lobbyist

LINNERT, Terrence G.
General Counsel
Four Colesium Center, 2730 W. Tyvola Rd.
Charlotte, NC 28217-4578
terry.linnert@goodrich.com

Tel: (704) 423-7000
Fax: (704) 423-7002

MANKE, David
Vice President, Government Business Development
1101 Pennsylvania Ave. NW, Tenth Floor
Washington, DC 20004
david.manke@utc.com

Tel: (202) 336-7400

MCBRIDE, Timothy
Senior Vice President, Government Relations
1000 Wilson Blvd., Suite 1000
Arlington, VA 22209-3901
Registered Federal Lobbyist

Tel: (703) 558-8230
Fax: (703) 558-8261

PEACE, Christopher
Director, Government Relations and PAC Contact
1101 Pennsylvania Ave. NW, Tenth Floor
Washington, DC 20004

Tel: (202) 336-7400

PYATT, Richard L.
Federal Lobbyist
1101 Pennsylvania Ave. NW, Tenth Floor
Washington, DC 20004

Tel: (202) 336-7400

RICH, Joseph
Federal Lobbyist
1101 Pennsylvania Ave. NW, Tenth Floor
Washington, DC 20004

Tel: (202) 336-7400

RISSEEUW, Hugh
Federal Lobbyist
1101 Pennsylvania Ave. NW, Tenth Floor
Washington, DC 20004

Tel: (202) 336-7400

THOMAS, Juanita
Federal Lobbyist
1101 Pennsylvania Ave. NW, Tenth Floor
Washington, DC 20004
Registered Federal Lobbyist

Tel: (202) 336-7400

THOMPSON, Allen
1101 Pennsylvania Ave. NW, Tenth Floor
Washington, DC 20004
Registered Federal Lobbyist

Tel: (202) 336-7400

THORNBLAD, Matthew
Director, Government Relations Energy and Environment
1101 Pennsylvania Ave. NW, Tenth Floor
Washington, DC 20004
Registered Federal Lobbyist

Tel: (202) 336-7400

WALSH, Susan M.
Federal Lobbyist
1101 Pennsylvania Ave. NW, Tenth Floor
Washington, DC 20004
susan.walsh@utc.com
Registered Federal Lobbyist

Tel: (202) 336-7400

WARD, Gregg
Senior Vice President, Government Relations
1101 Pennsylvania Ave. NW, Tenth Floor
Washington, DC 20004

Tel: (202) 336-7400

United Therapeutics Corporation

A biotechnology company focused on the development and commercialization of unique products to address the unmet medical needs of patients with chronic and life-threatening cardiovascular and infectious diseases and cancer.
www.unither.com
Annual Revenues: $1.33 billion
Employees: 740
Ticker: NASDAQ: UTHR
SIC: 2834
Industry/ies: Pharmaceutical Industry

Chairman of the Board and Chief Executive Officer
ROTHBLATT, JD, MBA, PhD, Martine A.
Mar@unither.com

Tel: (301) 608-9292
Fax: (301) 608-9291

President and Co-Chief Executive Officer
JEFFS, Roger

Tel: (301) 608-9292
Fax: (301) 608-9291

Main Headquarters
Mailing: 1040 Spring St.
            Silver Spring, MD 20910

Tel: (301) 608-9292
Fax: (301) 608-9291

Corporate Foundations and Giving Programs

United Therapeutics Corporation Contributions Program
1110 Spring St.
Silver Spring, MD 20910-4028

Tel: (301) 608-9292

Public Affairs and Related Activities Personnel

At Headquarters

BUNCE, Dean

Tel: (301) 608-9292

Executive Vice President, Regulatory Affairs and Compliance Services

Fax: (301) 608-9291

FISHER, Andrew
Deputy General Counsel
andy@unither.com

Tel: (301) 608-9292
Fax: (301) 608-9291

FRIEDIRCH, Alyssa
Senior Vice President, Human Resources
afriedrich@unither.com

Tel: (240) 821-1730
Fax: (301) 608-9291

MAHON, J.D., Paul A.
Executive Vice President, General Counsel & Corporate Secretary
paul@unither.com

Tel: (301) 608-9292
Fax: (301) 608-9291

United Water

Formerly known as United Water Resources.
www.unitedwater.com
Employees: 2,300
SIC: 4941
Industry/ies: Utilities

Chief Executive Officer
CAMUS, Bertrand

Tel: (201) 767-9300
Fax: (201) 767-7142

Main Headquarters
Mailing: 200 Old Hook Rd.
            Harrington Park, NJ 07640

Tel: (201) 767-9300
Fax: (201) 767-6746
TF: (877) 219-5520

Political Action Committees
United Water Inc. Federal PAC (UW PAC)
FEC ID: C00280156
Contact: Michael Algranati
200 Old Hook Rd.
Harrington Park, NJ 07640

> **Contributions to Candidates:** $22,100 (2015-2016)
> Democrats: $9,000; Republicans: $13,100

Corporate Foundations and Giving Programs

United Water Cares
200 Old Hook Rd.
Harrington Park, NJ 07640

Tel: (201) 767-9300
Fax: (201) 767-6746

United Water Foundation Giving for Good Causes
200 Old Hook Rd.
Harrington Park, NJ 07640

Tel: (201) 767-9300
Fax: (201) 767-6746

Public Affairs and Related Activities Personnel

At Headquarters

CAIRO, Patrick
Senior Vice President, Corporate Development
patrick.cairo@unitedwater.com

Tel: (201) 767-9300
Fax: (201) 767-6746

DARTIENNE, Philippe
Senior Vice President and Chief Financial Officer

Tel: (201) 767-9300
Fax: (201) 767-6746

GERBER, Robert
Senior Vice President and General Counsel

Tel: (201) 767-9300
Fax: (201) 767-2892

HENNING, Rich
Senior Vice President, Communications
Rich.Henning@UnitedWater.com

Tel: (201) 767-9300
Fax: (201) 767-7142

IACULLO, Robert J.
Exeutive Vice President

Tel: (201) 767-9300
Fax: (201) 767-6746

RIZZI, Deborah
Director, Corporate Communications
deborah.rizzi@unitedwater.com

Tel: (201) 767-9300
Fax: (201) 767-2892

STANTON, David
President, Regulated Business

Tel: (201) 767-9300
Fax: (201) 767-6746

WAUGH, Marie
Senior Vice President, Human Resources

Tel: (201) 767-9300
Fax: (201) 767-6746

At Other Offices

ALGRANATI, Michael
Vice President, Treasurer and PAC Contact
461 From Rd., Suite 400
Paramus, NJ 07652

UnitedHealthOne

An insurance company.
www.goldenrule.com
Annual Revenues: $1.18 billion
Employees: 1,000
Industry/ies: Insurance Industry

Chief Executive Officer
COLLINS, Richard A.

Tel: (317) 297-4123
Fax: (317) 298-0875

Main Headquarters
Mailing: 7440 Woodland Dr.
            Indianapolis, IN 46278

Tel: (317) 715-7111
Fax: (317) 298-0875
TF: (800) 444-8990

Public Affairs and Related Activities Personnel

At Headquarters

CARR, Patrick
Senior Vice President, Chief Financial Officer, Treasurer and Secretary
Tel: (317) 943-8000
Fax: (618) 943-8031

JACOBY, Peter G.
Senior Vice President, Government Affairs
Tel: (317) 715-7111
Fax: (317) 298-0875

LADEN, Ellen
Director, Public Relations
eladen@goldenrule.com
Tel: (317) 715-7843
Fax: (317) 298-0875

TUFFIN, Mike
Senior Vice President, Public Affairs
Tel: (317) 715-7111
Fax: (317) 298-0875

Univar USA, Inc.

Univar USA is a wholly owned subsidiary of Univar. The company distributes hundreds of chemicals, including acids, alcohols, catalysts, solvents, and flavorings. In 2007 parent company Univar Inc. acquired US distributor CHEMCENTRAL.
www.univar.com/us
Annual Revenues: $10.16 billion
Employees: 8,900
Ticker: NYSE: UNVR
SIC: 3089; 5160
NAICS: 326199
Industry/ies: Chemicals & Chemical Industry

Non-Executive Chairman of the Board
STAVROPOULOS, William S.
Tel: (425) 889-3400
Fax: (425) 889-4100

President and Chief Executive Officer
FYRWALD, J. Erik
Tel: (425) 889-3400
Fax: (425) 889-4100

Main Headquarters
Mailing: 17425 N.E. Union Hill Rd .
Redmond, WA 98052
Tel: (425) 889-3400
Fax: (425) 889-4100

Corporate Foundations and Giving Programs
Univar Foundation
P.O. Box 34325
Seattle, WA 98124-1325

Public Affairs and Related Activities Personnel

At Headquarters

JAHN, Alison
Director, Public Relations
alison.jahn@univar.com
Tel: (425) 889-3501
Fax: (425) 889-4100

LANDSMAN, Stephen N.
Executive Vice President, General Counsel
Tel: (425) 889-3400
Fax: (425) 889-4100

At Other Offices

DOHERTY, Kevin
Contact, Investor Relations
P.O. Box 34325
Seattle, WA 98124-1325
Tel: (844) 632-1060
Fax: (425) 889-4100

HILL, W. Terry
Executive Vice President, Industry Relations
P.O. Box 34325
Seattle, WA 98124-1325
Tel: (425) 889-3400
Fax: (425) 889-4100

JOHNSON, Scott
Director, Marketing and Corporate Communications
3075 Highland Pkwy., Suite 200
Downers Grove, IL 60515
scott.johnson@univarusa.com
Tel: (331) 777-6187
Fax: (331) 777-6291

LUKACH, Carl J.
Executive Vice President and Chief Financial Officer
P.O. Box 34325
Seattle, WA 98124-1325
Tel: (425) 889-3400
Fax: (425) 889-4100

Universal American Corporation

A specialty health and life insurance holding company provides health insurance and managed care products and services to Medicare and Medicaid customers.
www.universalamerican.com
Annual Revenues: $1.97 billion
Employees: 1,500
Ticker: NYSE: UAM
SIC: 6324
Industry/ies: Banking/Finance/Investments; Insurance Industry
Legislative Issues: MMM

Chairman of the Board, and Chief Executive Officer
BARASCH, Richard A.
Tel: (914) 934-5200
Fax: (914) 934-0700

Main Headquarters
Mailing: 44 S. Broadway
Suite 1200
White Plains, NY 10601
Tel: (914) 934-5200
Fax: (914) 934-0700

Washington Office
Mailing: 300 New Jersey Ave. NW
Suite 900
Washington, DC 20001

Political Action Committees
Universal American Corporation PAC
FEC ID: C00433029
Contact: P. James McAleer
44 South Broadway
Suite 1200
White Plains, NY 10601
Tel: (914) 934-5200
Fax: (914) 934-0700

Contributions to Candidates: $5,000 (2015-2016)
Democrats: $5,000

Public Affairs and Related Activities Personnel

At Headquarters

BLACK, Steven H.
Chief Administrative Officer
Tel: (914) 934-5200
Fax: (914) 934-0700

LATMAN, Linda
Contact, Investor Relations
llatman@equityny.com
Tel: (212) 836-9609
Fax: (914) 934-0700

MCALEER, P. James
Vice President, Treasure and PAC Treasurer
JMcAleer@UniversalAmerican.com
Tel: (914) 934-5200
Fax: (914) 934-0700

WAEGELEIN, CPA, Robert A.
President, Chief Financial Officer and Contact, Media Relations
rwaegelein@universalamerican.com
Tel: (914) 934-8820
Fax: (914) 934-0700

WOLK, Anthony L.
Senior Vice President, General Counsel and Secretary
Tel: (914) 934-5200
Fax: (914) 934-0700

Universal Forest Products Inc.

A manufacturer of lumber products.
www.ufpi.com
Annual Revenues: $2.94 billion
Employees: 7,000
Ticker: NASDAQ: UFPI
SIC: 2421; 2439; 2121; 2499
NAICS: 321214; 321912; 321999
Industry/ies: Forestry; Paper And Wood Products Industry

Chairman of the Board
CURRIE, William G.
Tel: (616) 364-6161
Fax: (616) 361-8302

Chief Executive Officer
MISSAD, Matthew J.
Tel: (616) 364-6161
Fax: (616) 361-8302

Main Headquarters
Mailing: 2801 E. Beltline Ave. NE
Grand Rapids, MI 49525
Tel: (616) 364-6161
Fax: (616) 361-8302
TF: (800) 598-9663

Public Affairs and Related Activities Personnel

At Headquarters

AFENDOULIS, Lynn
Director, Corporate Communications
lafendoulis@ufpi.com
Tel: (616) 364-6161
Fax: (616) 364-6919

COLE, Michael R.
Chief Financial Officer
Tel: (616) 364-6161
Fax: (616) 361-8302

DEREMO, Mark
Director, Marketing Communications
maderemo@ufpi.com
Tel: (616) 364-6161
Fax: (616) 361-8302

FOX, Chris
Product Manager and Brand Manager
Tel: (616) 364-6161
Fax: (616) 361-8302

GREENE, C. Scott
Executive Vice President, Marketing
Tel: (616) 364-6161
Fax: (616) 361-8302

TUTAS, Dave
Vice President, Legal and General Counsel
Tel: (616) 364-6161
Fax: (616) 361-8302

WEBSTER, Patrick M.
President and Chief Operating Officer
Tel: (616) 364-6161
Fax: (616) 361-8302

Universal Health Services Inc.

A hospital management company.
www.uhsinc.com
Annual Revenues: $8.35 billion
Employees: 48,700
Ticker: NYSE: UHS
SIC: 8062
Industry/ies: Medicine/Health Care/Mental Health

Chairman of the Board and Chief Executive Officer
MILLER, Alan B.
Tel: (610) 768-3300
Fax: (610) 768-3336

Main Headquarters
Mailing: 367 S. Gulph Rd.
P.O. Box 61558
King of Prussia, PA 19406
Tel: (610) 768-3300
Fax: (610) 768-3336

Political Action Committees
Universal Health Services Inc. Employees' Good Government Fund PAC

FEC ID: C00185520
Contact: Cheryl K. Ramagano
367 S. Gulph Rd.
P.O. Box 61558
King of Prussia, PA 19406

Contributions to Candidates: $60,850 (2015-2016)
Democrats: $20,500; Republicans: $40,350

Corporate Foundations and Giving Programs

Universal Health Services Inc. Contribution Program
367 S. Gulph Rd.   Tel: (610) 768-3300
P.O. Box 61558   Fax: (610) 768-3336
King of Prussia, PA 19406

Public Affairs and Related Activities Personnel

At Headquarters

FILTON, Steve G.   Tel: (610) 768-3300
Senior Vice President and Chief Financial Officer   Fax: (610) 768-3336
steve.filton@uhsinc.com

GECKLE, Geraldine Johnson   Tel: (610) 768-3300
Vice President, Human Resources   Fax: (610) 768-3336
gerry.geckle@uhsinc.com

KLEIN, Matthew D.   Tel: (610) 768-3300
Vice President and General Counsel   Fax: (610) 768-3336
matthew.klein@uhsinc.com

RAMAGANO, Cheryl K.   Tel: (610) 768-3300
Vice President and PAC Treasurer   Fax: (610) 768-3336
cheryl.ramagano@uhsinc.com

Universal Leaf Tobacco Company, Inc.

Involves in procuring and processing of flue-cured and burley leaf tobacco for manufacturers of consumer tobacco products.
www.universalcorp.com
Employees: 26,000
SIC: 5150
Industry/ies: Tobacco Industry

Chairman of the Board, President, and Chief Executive Officer   Tel: (804) 359-9311
FREEMAN, III, George C.   Fax: (804) 254-3584

Main Headquarters
Mailing: P.O. Box 25099   Tel: (804) 359-9311
     Richmond, VA 23260   Fax: (804) 254-3582

Political Action Committees
Universal Leaf Tobacco Company Inc. PAC
FEC ID: C00214072
Contact: Jennifer S Rowe
9201 Forest Hill Ave.
Stony Point II Bldg.
Richmond, VA 23235

Contributions to Candidates: $11,500 (2015-2016)
Democrats: $3,000; Republicans: $8,500

Corporate Foundations and Giving Programs

Universal Leaf Tobacco Foundation
P.O. Box 25099
Richmond, VA 23260

Public Affairs and Related Activities Personnel

At Headquarters

FORMACEK, Candace C.   Tel: (804) 359-9311
Vice President and Treasurer   Fax: (804) 254-3584

HENTSCHKE, Airton L.   Tel: (804) 359-9311
Senior Vice President and Chief Operating Officer   Fax: (804) 254-3584

MOORE, David C.   Tel: (804) 359-9311
Senior Vice President and Chief Financial Officer   Fax: (804) 254-3584

PEEBLES, Robert M   Tel: (804) 359-9311
Vice President and Controller   Fax: (804) 254-3584

WIGNER, Preston D.   Tel: (804) 359-9311
Vice President, General Counsel, and Secretary   Fax: (804) 254-3584

At Other Offices

ROWE, Jennifer S   Tel: (804) 359-9311
PAC Treasurer   Fax: (804) 254-3584
9201 Forest Hill Ave., Stony Point II Building
Richmond, VA 23235
Mail Stop Stony Point II Building

Universal Music Group

An American music corporation. Subsidiary of Paris-based media conglomerate Vivendi.
www.universalmusic.com
Employees: 1,100
SIC: 2741; 8999
NAICS: 512220; 512230
Industry/ies: Food And Beverage Industry
Legislative Issues: ART; COM; CPT; TRD

Chairman of the Board and Chief Executive Officer   Tel: (301) 865-4500
GRAINGE, Lucian

Main Headquarters
Mailing: 2220 Colorado Ave.   Tel: (310) 865-5000
     Santa Monica, CA 90404

Washington Office
Mailing: 701 Eighth St. NW   Tel: (202) 638-2568
     Suite 420   Fax: (202) 393-1846
     Washington, DC 20001

Political Action Committees
Universal Music Group PAC
FEC ID: C00392464
Contact: Cary Davidson
2220 Colorado Ave.   Tel: (202) 393-8662
Suite 420   Fax: (202) 393-1846
Santa Monica, CA 90404

Contributions to Candidates: $87,000 (2015-2016)
Democrats: $38,500; Republicans: $48,500

Public Affairs and Related Activities Personnel

At Headquarters

DAVIDSON, Cary   Tel: (310) 865-5000
PAC Contact

HARLESTON, Jeffrey   Tel: (310) 865-5000
General Counsel, Executive Vice President, Business and
Legal Affairs

KRONFELD, Andrew   Tel: (301) 865-4500
Executive Vice President, Marketing

LEVIN, Rand   Tel: (301) 865-4500
Senior Vice President, Business and Legal Affairs

MUIR, Boyd   Tel: (310) 865-5000
Chief Financial Officer and Executive Vice President

NASH, Michael   Tel: (310) 865-5000
Executive Vice President, Digital Strategy

SRIVASTAVA, Gautam   Tel: (310) 865-5000
Executive Vice President, Human Resources

TANOUS, Will   Tel: (310) 865-5000
Executive Vice President, Communications

At Washington Office

ISBELL, Amy   Tel: (202) 393-8661
Senior Vice President, Public Policy & Government Relations   Fax: (202) 393-1846
amy.isbell@umusic.com
Registered Federal Lobbyist

Univision Communications, Inc.

A Spanish-language media company.
corporate.univision.com
Annual Revenues: $363.5 million
Employees: 6,000
Industry/ies: Communications; Telecommunications/Internet/Cable
Legislative Issues: AVI; COM; FIN; MIA; TAX; TEC

President and Chief Executive Officer   Tel: (212) 455-5200
FALCO, Randy   Fax: (212) 867-6710

Main Headquarters
Mailing: 605 Third Ave.   Tel: (212) 455-5200
     12th Floor   Fax: (212) 867-6710
     New York City, NY 10158

Washington Office
Mailing: 101 Constitution Ave. NW   Tel: (202) 589-2550
     Suite 350
     Washington, DC 20001

Political Action Committees
Univision Communications, Inc. PAC
FEC ID: C00435735
Contact: Cary Davidson
3699 Wilshire Blvd.
Suite 1290
Los Angeles, CA 90010

Contributions to Candidates: $114,500 (2015-2016)
Democrats: $83,000; Republicans: $31,500

Principal Recipients

SENATE
SCHUMER, CHARLES E (DEM-NY)

Public Affairs and Related Activities Personnel

At Headquarters

ESTRADA, Ivelisse   Tel: (212) 455-5200
Senior Vice President, Corporate and Community Relations   Fax: (212) 867-6710

LLAMAS, Roberto   Tel: (212) 455-5200
   Fax: (212) 867-6710

Executive Vice President and Corporate Officer, Human Resources and Community Empowerment

LOPEZ-BALBOA, Francisco J.
Executive Vice President and Chief Financial Officer
Tel: (212) 455-5200
Fax: (212) 867-6710

MERCEDES BEEPAT, Rosemary
Vice President, Corporate and Digital Communications
rmercedes@univision.net
Tel: (212) 455-5335
Fax: (212) 867-6710

O'CONNOR , Tonia
President, Content Distribution and Corporate Business Development
Tel: (212) 455-5200
Fax: (212) 867-6710

RODRIGUEZ, Jessica
Executive Vice President and Chief Marketing Officer
Tel: (212) 455-5200
Fax: (212) 867-6710

SCHWARTZ , Jonathan
General Counsel and Executive Vice President, Government Relations
Tel: (212) 455-5200
Fax: (212) 867-6710

TALAN, Monica
Executive Vice President, Corporate Communications and Public Relations
mtalan@univision.net
Tel: (212) 455-5200
Fax: (212) 867-6710

At Washington Office

GARZA, Belinda
Vice President, Government Relations and Public Engagement
Tel: (202) 589-2550

GARZA HARTWIG, Belinda
Federal Lobbyist
Tel: (202) 589-2550

GOMEZ, Jr., Humberto
Senior Vice President, Government Relations
Registered Federal Lobbyist
Tel: (202) 589-2550

HERRERA-FLANIGAN, Jessica R.
Executive Vice President, Government Relations & Public Policy
Registered Federal Lobbyist
Tel: (202) 589-2550

JEFFRIES, Victoria Luxardo
Associate General Counsel & Vice President, Public Policy
Tel: (202) 589-2550

At Other Offices

DAVIDSON, Cary
PAC Treasurer
515 S. Figueroa St.
Los Angeles, CA 90071

Unum Group

Provider of employee benefits.
www.unum.com
Annual Revenues: $10.54 billion
Employees: 9,500
Ticker: NYSE: UNM
SIC: 6321
Industry/ies: Insurance Industry
Legislative Issues: HCR; INS

President and Chief Executive Officer
MCKENNEY, Rick
Tel: (423) 294-1011
Fax: (423) 294-3962

Main Headquarters
Mailing: One Fountain Sq.
Chattanooga, TN 37402
Tel: (423) 294-1011
Fax: (423) 294-3962
TF: (800) 718-8824

Political Action Committees
Unum Group PAC (UNUMPAC)
FEC ID: C00177436
Contact: Elizabeth H. Simon
One Fountain Square
Chattanooga, TN 37402

Contributions to Candidates: $3,318,516 (2015-2016)
Democrats: $102,500; Republicans: $103,000; Other: $3,113,016

Principal Recipients

SENATE
BOOZMAN, JOHN (REP-AR)
MURRAY, PATTY (DEM-WA)

HOUSE
NEAL, RICHARD E MR. (DEM-MA)

Corporate Foundations and Giving Programs
Unum Group Contributions Program
One Fountain Sq.
Chattanooga, TN 37402

Public Affairs and Related Activities Personnel

At Headquarters

MCGARRY, Jack
Chief Financial Officer
Tel: (423) 294-1011
Fax: (423) 294-3962

FOLEY, Joseph R.
Tel: (423) 294-1011
Fax: (423) 294-3962

Senior Vice President, Corporate Marketing and Public Relations

FORTUNE, Mary
Director, Corporate Communications
mfortune@unum.com
Tel: (423) 294-1011
Fax: (423) 294-3962

GAROFALO, Diane
Senior Vice President, Corporate Human Resources
Tel: (423) 294-1011
Fax: (423) 294-3962

GUENTHER, Mary Clarke
Director, Media Relations
mguenther@unum.com
Tel: (423) 294-1011
Fax: (423) 294-3962

IGLESIAS, Lisa
Executive Vice President and General Counsel
Tel: (423) 294-1011
Fax: (423) 294-3962

MCGUINNESS, Martin E.
Vice President, Government Affairs
Registered Federal Lobbyist
Tel: (423) 294-1011
Fax: (423) 294-3962

SABOURIN, Jim
Vice President, Corporate Communications
jsabourin@unum.com
Tel: (423) 294-6300
Fax: (423) 294-3962

SIMON, Elizabeth H.
PAC Treasurer
Tel: (423) 294-1011
Fax: (423) 294-3962

WHITE, Thomas A. H.
Senior Vice President, Investor Relations
tawhite@unumprovident.com
Tel: (423) 294-8996
Fax: (423) 294-3962

At Other Offices

COOK, Alexandra W.
Vice President, Government Affairs
2211 Congress St., Suite C469
Portland, ME 04122
Tel: (207) 575-3200

FARRELL, CFA, Breege A.
Executive Vice President and Chief Investment Officer
2211 Congress St., Suite C469
Portland, ME 04122
Tel: (207) 575-2211

MAKER, Scott T.
Senior Vice President & Chief Government Affairs Officer
2211 Congress St., Suite C469
Portland, ME 04122
smaker@unum.com
Tel: (207) 575-3200

WILLIAMS, Pieter
Senior Regulatory Counsel
2211 Congress St., Suite C469
Portland, ME 04122
Registered Federal Lobbyist
Tel: (207) 575-2211

UPC Wind Management, LLC

See listing on page 329 under First Wind Energy, LLC

See listing on page 329 under First Wind Energy, LLC

Uranium Energy Corporation

Producers of uranium energy.
www.uraniumenergy.com
Annual Revenues: $14.56 million
Employees: 61
Ticker: NYSE: UEC
SIC: 1090
Industry/ies: Energy/Electricity; Natural Resources

Chairman of the Board
LINDSAY, Alan
Tel: (361) 888-8235
Fax: (361) 888-5041

Director, President and Chief Executive Officer
ADNANI, Amir
Tel: (361) 888-8235
Fax: (361) 888-5041

Main Headquarters
Mailing: 500 N. Shoreline
Suite 800N
Corpus Christi, TX 78401
Tel: (361) 888-8235
Fax: (361) 888-5041
TF: (866) 748-1030

Public Affairs and Related Activities Personnel

At Headquarters

KATSUMATA , Mark
Chief Financial Officer
Tel: (361) 888-8235
Fax: (361) 888-5041

NICHOLSON, Bruce J.
Vice President, Corporate Development
Tel: (361) 888-8235
Fax: (361) 888-5041

NICHOLSON, Bruce
Vice president Corporate Development
Tel: (361) 888-8235
Fax: (361) 888-5041

OBARA, Pat
Vice President, Administration
Tel: (361) 888-8235
Fax: (361) 888-5041

POWELL, F. P.
Vice President, Marketing and Sales
Tel: (361) 888-8235
Fax: (361) 888-5041

SEALY, MSc, Curtis O.
Vice President, Strategic Development
Tel: (361) 888-8235
Fax: (361) 888-5041

Urban Innovations Companies, Inc.

Community building, family strengthening and community leadership.
www.urbaninnovations.com

Chairman of the Board
CONANT, Jr., Howard
hconant@urbaninnovations.com
Tel: (312) 222-0777
Fax: (312) 222-5369

President & Chief Executive Officer
HARRIS, Kirk E.
Tel: (708) 955-3015

President
SCILINGO, Mike
Tel: (312) 222-0777
Fax: (312) 222-5369

Main Headquarters
Mailing: 445 N. Wells
Suite 200
Chicago, IL 60654
Tel: (312) 222-0777
Fax: (312) 222-5369

Corporate Foundations and Giving Programs
Urban Innovations Contribution Program
Contact: Pam Gennusa
445 N. Wells
Suite 200
Chicago, IL 60654
Tel: (312) 222-0777
Fax: (312) 222-5369

Public Affairs and Related Activities Personnel

At Headquarters

GENNUSA, Pam
Vice President of Knowledge Management and Compliance
Tel: (312) 222-0777
Fax: (312) 222-5369

GOTTFRIED, Jo Anne
Vice President, Marketing
Tel: (312) 222-0777
Fax: (312) 222-5369

SISNEY, Kim
Director, Operations
Tel: (312) 222-0777
Fax: (312) 222-5369

SOLARI, John
Chief Financial Officer
Tel: (312) 222-0777
Fax: (312) 222-5369

VEARIL, Stacy
Director, Human Resources
Tel: (312) 222-0777
Fax: (312) 222-5369

Urban Lending Solutions

Provides of customized mortgage solutions.. Urban Settlement Services, LLC channged its name to Urban Lending Solutions.
www.urban-ls.com
Employees: 100
Industry/ies: Banking/Finance/Investments; Housing; Social Service/Urban Affairs

Founder and Chief Executive Officer
SANDERS, Charles Samuel
charles.sanders@urbansettlement.com
Tel: (412) 325-7046
Fax: (412) 325-7051

Main Headquarters
Mailing: 11802 Ridge Pkwy.
Suite 200
Broomfield, CO 80021
Tel: (303) 996-8900
TF: (855) 996-8900

Public Affairs and Related Activities Personnel

At Headquarters

CHITWOOD, Dan
Executive Vice President, Chief Financial Officer
Tel: (303) 996-8900

FORGAS, Mike
President
Tel: (303) 996-8900

LEWIS, T. J.
Executive Vice President, Corporate Diversity and Business Development
tjlewis@urban-ls.com
Tel: (303) 996-8900

STEVENS, Glenn H.
Executive Vice President, Human Resources and General Counsel
Tel: (303) 996-8900

At Other Offices

BETTIS, John
Senior Vice President, Communications and Marketing
1001 Liberty Ave., Suite 1050
Pittsburgh, PA 15222
jbettis@urban-ls.com
Tel: (412) 325-7046
Fax: (412) 325-7051

Urban Settlement Services, LLC

See listing on page 825 under Urban Lending Solutions

URS Corporation

The Washington division of an international engineering and construction firm. Formerly Washington Group International.
www.urscorp.com
Annual Revenues: $10.99 billion
Employees: 56,000
Ticker: NYSE: URS
SIC: 8711
Industry/ies: Construction/Construction Materials; Engineering/Mathematics; Environment And Conservation
Legislative Issues: DUD, DEF, ENO, TRA, WA

Chairman of the Board and Chief Executive Officer
KOFFEL, Martin M.
martinkoffel@urscorp.com
Tel: (415) 774-2700
Fax: (415) 398-1905

Vice President
BISHOP, Thomas W.
Tel: (415) 774-2700
Fax: (415) 398-1905

Main Headquarters
Mailing: 600 Montgomery St.
26th Floor
San Francisco, CA 94111-2728
Tel: (415) 774-2700
Fax: (415) 398-1905
TF: (877) 877-8970

Washington Office
Mailing: 2450 Crystal Dr.
Suite 500
Arlington, VA 22202
Tel: (703) 236-2700
Fax: (703) 226-1931

Corporate Foundations and Giving Programs
URS Corporation Contributions Program
600 Montgomery St.
26th Floor
San Francisco, CA 94111-2728
Tel: (415) 774-2700
Fax: (415) 398-1905

Public Affairs and Related Activities Personnel

At Headquarters

HICKS, H. Thomas
Chief Financial Officer
Tel: (415) 774-2700
Fax: (415) 398-1905

MASTERS, Joseph
Vice President, General Counsel and Secretary
Tel: (415) 774-2700
Fax: (415) 398-1905

RAMRAJ, Sreeram
Vice President, Investor Relations
investor_relations@urscorp.com
Tel: (415) 774-2700
Fax: (415) 772-8290

At Washington Office

BERNAL, Ricardo
Director, Government Affairs
ricardo.bernal@urs.com
Registered Federal Lobbyist
Tel: (703) 236-2700
Fax: (703) 236-1930

SEIPP, Dennis G.
Director, Government Affairs
Registered Federal Lobbyist
Tel: (703) 236-2747
Fax: (703) 236-1930

STINGER, Cynthia M.
Vice President, Government Affairs
cynthia_stinger@urscorp.com
Registered Federal Lobbyist
Tel: (703) 236-2740
Fax: (703) 236-1931

TYNAN, Brian M.
Registered Federal Lobbyist
Tel: (703) 236-2700
Fax: (703) 226-1931

At Other Offices

KILGANNON, Susan B.
Vice President, Corporate Communications
One Penn Plaza, Suite 610
New York City, NY 10119-0698
Sue_kilgannon@urscorp.com
Tel: (212) 330-1998
Fax: (212) 947-6975

US Borax

Borate technology, research and development.
www.borax.com
SIC: 1474
Industry/ies: Mining Industry; Natural Resources

Director, Communications and External Relations
WITMER, Deb
deb.witmer@riotinto.com
Tel: (303) 713-5000

Main Headquarters
Mailing: 8051 E. Maplewood Ave.
Building 4
Greenwood Village, CO 80111
Tel: (303) 713-5000

Public Affairs and Related Activities Personnel

At Headquarters

KEEFE, Susan
Manager, Global Public Affairs
susan.keefe@riotinto.com
Tel: (303) 713-5055
Fax: (661) 287-5495

RUSH, Brent
Manager, Government and Community Affairs
Tel: (303) 713-5055

US Foods

Provides food and related services.
www.usfoods.com
SIC: 5140
Industry/ies: Food And Beverage Industry
Legislative Issues: FOO

President and Chief Executive Officer and Director
LEDERER, John
Tel: (847) 720-8000
Fax: (847) 720-8099

Main Headquarters
Mailing: 9399 W. Higgins Rd.
Suite 500
Tel: (847) 720-8000
Fax: (847) 720-8099

Rosemont, IL 60018   TF: (877) 583-9659

Corporate Foundations and Giving Programs

US Foods Contributions Program
9399 W. Higgins Rd.
Suite 500
Rosemont, IL 60018

Public Affairs and Related Activities Personnel

At Headquarters

CALCAGNI, Michelle	Tel:	(847) 720-1652
Senior Director, Corporate Communications	Fax:	(847) 720-8099
ESLER, Dave	Tel:	(847) 720-8000
Chief Human Resources Officer	Fax:	(847) 720-8099
KHAN, Fareed	Tel:	(847) 720-8000
Chief Financial Officer	Fax:	(847) 720-8099
LECAS, Lisa	Tel:	(847) 720-8243
Director, Acting, Manager, Corporate Communications	Fax:	(847) 720-8099
LYNCH , Tom	Tel:	(847) 720-8000
Senior Vice President, National Sales	Fax:	(847) 720-8099
PRYOR, Juliette	Tel:	(847) 720-8000
Executive Vice President, General Counsel and Chief Compliance Officer	Fax:	(847) 720-8099
SCHREIBMAN, David	Tel:	(847) 720-8000
Executive Vice President, Strategy	Fax:	(847) 720-8099
SCHUETT, Stuart	Tel:	(847) 720-8000
Chief Operating Officer	Fax:	(847) 720-8099

US Magnesium, LLC

Specialized in the manufacture and supply of magnesium ingot products, magnesium recycling services, chemical by-products and energy.
www.usmagnesium.com
Annual Revenues: $39.40 million
Employees: 500
Industry/ies: Chemicals & Chemical Industry
Legislative Issues: TRD

President   Tel: (801) 532-2043
LEGGE, Mike   Fax: (801) 534-1407
mlegge@usmagnesium.com

Main Headquarters
Mailing: 238 N. 2200 West   Tel: (801) 532-2043
Salt Lake City, UT 84116-2921   Fax: (801) 534-1407

Public Affairs and Related Activities Personnel

At Headquarters

GEORGE, Paula   Tel: (801) 532-2043
Vice President, Finance and Administration   Fax: (801) 534-1407

US Oncology, Inc.

An integrated oncology company.
www.usoncology.com
Annual Revenues: $3.51 billion
Employees: 10,000
SIC: 8060; 8093
Industry/ies: Medicine/Health Care/Mental Health
Legislative Issues: MMM

Main Headquarters
Mailing: 10101 Woodloch Forest   Tel: (281) 863-1000
The Woodlands, TX 77380   Fax: (832) 348-5765
   TF: (800) 381-2637

Washington Office
Mailing: 700 13th St. NW   Tel: (202) 636-4179
Suite 525   Fax: (202) 638-7677
Washington, DC 20005

Political Action Committees
US Oncology Inc. Network Political Action Committee
FEC ID: C00339655
Contact: Ben Jones
10101 Woodloch Dr.   Tel: (281) 863-1000
The Woodlands, TX 77380   Fax: (832) 348-5765

    Contributions to Candidates: $291,600 (2015-2016)
    Democrats: $103,850; Republicans: $186,750; Other: $1,000

Principal Recipients

HOUSE
POMPEO, MICHAEL RICHARD (REP-KS)

Corporate Foundations and Giving Programs

US Oncology Foundation
10101 Woodloch Forest
The Woodlands, TX 77380

Public Affairs and Related Activities Personnel

At Headquarters

CRYE, Claire	Tel:	(281) 825-9927
Manager, Public Relations	Fax:	(832) 348-5765
claire.crye@usoncology.com		
JONES, Ben	Tel:	(281) 863-1000
Senior Director, Government Relations, Public Policy and PAC Treasurer	Fax:	(832) 348-5765
ben.jones@usoncology.com		

USA Mobility, Inc.

Formed by the merger of Metrocall Holdings Inc. and Arch Wireless Inc. A provider of wireless solutions.
www.usamobility.com
Annual Revenues: $216.09 million
Employees: 656
Ticker: NASDAQ (GS): USMO
SIC: 3679; 4812; 5065; 4813; 3663
NAICS: 513321; 513322; 334419; 33422; 51331
Industry/ies: Communications; Telecommunications/Internet/Cable

Chairman of the Board   Tel: (703) 269-6850
YUDKOFF, Royce R.

President and Chief Executive Officer   Tel: (703) 269-6850
KELLY, Vincent D.

Main Headquarters
Mailing: 6850 Versar Center   Tel: (703) 269-6850
Suite 420
Springfield, VA 22151

Political Action Committees
USA Mobility Inc. PAC
FEC ID: C00423855
Contact: Sharon Woods Keisling
6850 Versar Center
Suite 420
Springfield, VA 22151

Corporate Foundations and Giving Programs

USA Mobility Contributions Program
6850 Versar Center   Tel: (800) 611-8488
Suite 420
Springfield, VA 22151

Public Affairs and Related Activities Personnel

At Headquarters

ENDSLEY, Shawn   Tel: (703) 269-6850
Chief Financial Officer

KEISLING, Sharon Woods   Tel: (703) 269-6850
Corporate Secretary, Assistant Treasurer, and Vice President, Treasury and Operations

LOUGEE, Jr., Robert W.   Tel: (703) 269-6850
Investor Relations and Corporate Communications Contact
bob.lougee@usamobility.com

USA Synthetic Fuel Corporation

Produce low cost ultra clean energy for America.
Legislative Issues: AGR; AUT; AVI; CAW; DEF; ECN; ENG; ENV; FUE; SCI; TRA

Main Headquarters
Mailing: 1717 Pennsylvania Ave. NW   Tel: (202) 559-9303
Suite 1025
Washington, DC 20006

Public Affairs and Related Activities Personnel

At Headquarters

HARDING, Andrew   Tel: (202) 559-9303
Registered Federal Lobbyist

USAA - United Services Automobile Association

Provider of financial services and insurance products for military personnel and their dependents.
www.usaa.com
Annual Revenues: $22.10 billion
Employees: 25,000
Industry/ies: Banking/Finance/Investments; Defense/Homeland Security; Government-Related; Insurance Industry; Military/Veterans
Legislative Issues: BAN; CSP; DIS; FIN; HCR; HOM; HOU; INS; INT; TAX; TRA

Chairman of the Board   Tel: (210) 531-8722
LYLES, GEN Lester L.

President, Chief Executive Officer   Tel: (210) 531-8722
PARKER, Stuart

Main Headquarters
Mailing: 9800 Fredericksburg Rd.   Tel: (210) 531-8722
San Antonio, TX 78288   TF: (800) 531-8722

Washington Office
Mailing: 601 Pennsylvania Ave. NW   Tel: (202) 628-6442
North Tower, Suite 225   Fax: (202) 628-6537

Washington, DC 20004

Political Action Committees

United Services Automobile Association Employee PAC - USAA Employee PAC

FEC ID: C00164145

Contact: Laura M Bishop

9800 Frederickburg Rd.

San Antonio, TX 78288

Contributions to Candidates: $877,500 (2015-2016)

Democrats: $220,500; Republicans: $657,000

Principal Recipients

SENATE

CRAPO, MICHAEL D (REP-ID)

HECK, JOE (REP-NV)

JOHNSON, RONALD HAROLD (REP-)

HOUSE

BILIRAKIS, GUS M (REP-FL)

CASTRO, JOAQUIN REP. (DEM-TX)

COFFMAN, MIKE REP. (REP-CO)

COMSTOCK, BARBARA J HONORABLE (REP-VA)

DUFFY, SEAN (REP-WI)

GUTHRIE, S. BRETT HON. (REP-KY)

HIMES, JIM (DEM-CT)

HOYER, STENY HAMILTON (DEM-DC)

HURD, WILLIAM (REP-TX)

ISSA, DARRELL (REP-CA)

JOHNSON, BILL (REP-OH)

KIND, RONALD JAMES (DEM-WI)

LARSON, JOHN B (DEM-CT)

LUETKEMEYER, W BLAINE (REP-MO)

MCCARTHY, KEVIN (REP-CA)

MCMORRIS RODGERS, CATHY (REP-WA)

NUNES, DEVIN G (REP-CA)

OLSON, PETER G. (REP-TX)

PERLMUTTER, EDWIN G (DEM-CO)

POMPEO, MICHAEL RICHARD (REP-KS)

PRICE, THOMAS EDMUNDS (REP-GA)

REED, THOMAS W II (REP-NY)

ROSKAM, PETER (REP-IL)

ROSS, DENNIS ALAN (REP-FL)

ROYCE, ED MR. (REP-CA)

RYAN, PAUL D. (REP-WI)

SCHULTZ, DEBBIE WASSERMAN (DEM-FL)

SHIMKUS, JOHN M (REP-IL)

SHUSTER, WILLIAM MR. (REP-PA)

SINEMA, KYRSTEN (DEM-AZ)

SMITH, LAMAR (REP-TX)

STIVERS, STEVE MR. (REP-OH)

THORNBERRY, MAC (REP-TX)

TIBERI, PATRICK J. (REP-OH)

WAGNER, ANN L. (REP-MO)

WALDEN, GREGORY P MR. (REP-OR)

WILSON, JOE THE HON. (REP-SC)

ZELDIN, LEE M (REP-NY)

ZINKE, RYAN K (REP-MT)

Corporate Foundations and Giving Programs

USAA Educational Foundation

9800 Frederickburg Rd.   Tel: (800) 531-6196

San Antonio, TX 78288

Public Affairs and Related Activities Personnel

At Headquarters

BENNETT, Steven A.   Tel: (210) 498-2211

Executive Vice President, General Counsel and Corporate Secretary

BISHOP , Laura M   Tel: (210) 531-8722

Executive Vice President, Chief Financial Officer and Treasurer

LIEBERT , Carl   Tel: (210) 531-8722

Executive Vice President and Chief Operating Officer

MANASCO, Shon   Tel: (210) 531-8722

Executive Vice President and Chief Administrative Officer

MARTINKO, Erin   Tel: (210) 498-2211

Director, Federal Government Relations

Registered Federal Lobbyist

PEACOCK , Wayne   Tel: (210) 531-8722

Executive Vice President, Enterprise Strategy and Marketing

REID , Mark   Tel: (210) 531-8722

Executive Vice President, Human Resources

SIMMONS, Dana   Tel: (210) 531-8722

Executive Vice President, Enterprise Operations Support

STRONG, Wendi F   Tel: (210) 156 1000

Executive Vice President, Enterprise Affairs   Fax: (210) 498-9940

At Washington Office

BROUILLETTE, Dan R.   Tel: (202) 628-6442

Senior Vice President, Government and Industry Affairs   Fax: (202) 628-6537

CONKLIN, Brian C.   Tel: (202) 628-6442

Vice President   Fax: (202) 628-6537

brian.conklin@usaa.com

Registered Federal Lobbyist

KILLIN, Jessica   Tel: (202) 628-6442

Assistant Vice President, Federal Government Relations   Fax: (202) 628-6537

Registered Federal Lobbyist

MONTOYA, Rebecca   Tel: (202) 628-6442

Senior Associate, Federal Government Relations   Fax: (202) 628-6537

rebecca.montoya@usaa.com

USEC Inc. (United States Enrichment Corporation)

A global energy company. Supplies enriched uranium fuel to commercial nuclear power plants.

www.usec.com

Annual Revenues: $1.14 billion

Employees: 1,300

Ticker: NYSE: USU

SIC: 1400

Industry/ies: Energy/Electricity; Mining Industry; Natural Resources

Legislative Issues: BUD; ENG

| **Chairman of the Board** | Tel: | (301) 564-3200 |
| MELLOR, James R. | Fax: | (301) 564-3201 |

| **President and Chief Executive Officer** | Tel: | (301) 564-3200 |
| WELCH, John K. | Fax: | (301) 564-3201 |

Main Headquarters

Mailing: Two Democracy Center   Tel: (301) 564-3200

6903 Rockledge Dr.   Fax: (301) 564-3201

Bethesda, MD 20817

Washington Office

Mailing: 300 New Jersey Ave. NW   Tel: (202) 525-5556

Suite 675   Fax: (202) 525-5883

Washington, DC 20001

Political Action Committees

USEC Inc. PAC

FEC ID: C00355719

Contact: John C. Barpoulis

6903 Rockledge Dr.   Tel: (301) 564-3307

Bethesda, MD 20817   Fax: (301) 564-3490

Contributions to Candidates: $63,500 (2015-2016)

Democrats: $12,000; Republicans: $51,500

Public Affairs and Related Activities Personnel

At Headquarters

BARPOULIS, John C.   Tel: (301) 564-3200

Senior Vice President, Chief Financial Officer and PAC Treasurer   Fax: (301) 564-3201

DERRYBERRY, Jeremy   Tel: (301) 564-3392

Manager, Communications   Fax: (301) 564-3211

derryberryj@usec.com

DONALD, Jeff   Tel: (301) 564-3418

Manager, Communications   Fax: (301) 564-3201

donaldj@usec.com

DONELSON, John   Tel: (301) 564-3200

Vice President, Marketing, Sales and Power   Fax: (301) 564-3201

DUDUIT , Angie   Tel: (301) 564-3200

Public Affairs Manager   Fax: (301) 564-3201

duduitaj@usec.com

HOWE, Jim   Tel: (301) 564-3200

Registered Federal Lobbyist   Fax: (301) 564-3201

JACOBSON, Paul   Tel: (301) 564-3399

Vice President, Corporate Communications   Fax: (301) 564-3201

jacobsonp@usec.com

NEUMANN, John   Tel: (202) 742-4452

Vice President, Government Relations   Fax: (202) 742-4444

ROWLAND, Richard V.   Tel: (301) 564-3200

Vice President, Human Resources   Fax: (301) 564-3201

SABA, Peter B.   Tel: (301) 564-3200

Senior Vice President, General Counsel, Chief Compliance Officer and Corporate Secretary   Fax: (301) 564-3201

SEWELL, Philip   Tel: (301) 564-3200

Senior Vice President and Chief Development Officer   Fax: (301) 564-3201

WINGFIELD, Steve   Tel: (301) 564-3354

Director, Investor Relations   Fax: (301) 564-3237

wingfieldd@usec.com

At Washington Office

WHITE, William D.   Tel: (202) 525-5556

Executive   Fax: (202) 525-5883

USG Corporation

A building materials manufacturer.
www.usg.com
Annual Revenues: $3.78 billion
Employees: 8,900
Ticker: NYSE: USG
SIC: 3270
Industry/ies: Construction/Construction Materials
Legislative Issues: MAN

Chairman, President and Chief Executive Officer
METCALF, James S.
Tel: (312) 436-4000
Fax: (312) 436-4093

Main Headquarters
Mailing: 550 W. Adams St.
Chicago, IL 60661-3676
Tel: (312) 436-4000
Fax: (312) 436-4093
TF: (800) 874-4968

Corporate Foundations and Giving Programs
The USG Foundation
550 W. Adams St.
Chicago, IL 60661-3676
Tel: (312) 436-4000
Fax: (312) 436-4093

Public Affairs and Related Activities Personnel

At Headquarters

COOK, Brian J.
Senior Vice President, Human Resources and Communications
Tel: (312) 436-4000
Fax: (312) 436-4093

DONAHUE, John A.
Senior Director, Government Affairs
jdonahue@usg.com
Registered Federal Lobbyist
Tel: (312) 436-4006
Fax: (312) 436-4093

FERGUSON, Stanley L.
Executive Vice President, General Counsel and Secretary
Tel: (312) 436-4000
Fax: (312) 436-4093

GRIFFIN, Christopher R.
Executive Vice President and Chief Operating Officer
Tel: (312) 436-4000
Fax: (312) 436-4093

HILZINGER, Matthew F.
Executive Vice President and Chief Financial Officer
Tel: (312) 436-4000
Fax: (312) 436-4093

LOWES, D. Rick
Senior Vice President, Business Development and Operational Services
Tel: (312) 436-4000
Fax: (312) 436-4093

ROSENTHAL, Chris A.
Vice President, Compensation, Benefits and Corporate Services
Tel: (312) 436-4000
Fax: (312) 436-4093

WILLIAMS, Robert R.
Director, Corporate Communications
rwilliams@usg.com
Tel: (312) 436-4000
Fax: (312) 436-4093

USHF Communications Company, LLC

Communications Security

Main Headquarters
Mailing: 1100 S. Flower St.
Suite 3300
Los Angeles, CA 90015

Public Affairs and Related Activities Personnel

At Headquarters

BURKE, Robert E.
Vice President
Tel: (213) 896-8920

MORABITO, Paul
Member
Tel: (213) 896-8920

PRANG, Jeffrey
Tel: (213) 896-8920

USX Corp.

See listing on page 509 under Marathon Oil Corporation

Valeant Pharmaceuticals International, Inc.

A multinational, specialty pharmaceutical company that develops, manufactures and markets a range of pharmaceutical products.
www.valeant.com
Annual Revenues: $3,864 Million
Employees: 17,200
Ticker: NYSE:VRX
SIC: 2834
Industry/ies: Pharmaceutical Industry
Legislative Issues: FIN; HCR; LBR; TAX

Chairman of the Board and Chief Executive Officer
PEARSON, Michael J.
Tel: (800) 361-1448
Fax: (514) 744-6272

Main Headquarters
Mailing: 2150 St. Elzéar Blvd.
West Laval, QC 4A8
Tel: (800) 361-1448
Fax: (514) 744-6272

Public Affairs and Related Activities Personnel

At Headquarters

CHAI-ONN, Robert
Executive Vice President, General Counsel and Corporate Secretary
Tel: (800) 361-1448
Fax: (514) 744-6272

KELLEN, Dr. Ari
Executive Vice President/Company Group Chairman
Tel: (800) 361-1448
Fax: (514) 744-6272

ROSIELLO, Robert
Executive Vice President and Chief Financial Officer
Tel: (800) 361-1448
Fax: (514) 744-6272

STOLZ, Brian
Executive Vice President of Administration and Chief Human Capital Officer
Tel: (800) 361-1448
Fax: (514) 744-6272

Valero Energy Corporation

An independent refining and marketing company. A producer of environmentally clean products such as reformulated gasoline, CARB Phase II gasoline, low-sulfur diesel, and oxygenates. Acquired Ultramar Diamond Shamrock Corp. in January 2002.
www.valero.com
Annual Revenues: $82.22 billion
Employees: 10,103
Ticker: NYSE: VLO
SIC: 2911
NAICS: 324110
Industry/ies: Fuels See Coal, Gas, Oil, Petroleum; Natural Resources; Petroleum Industry
Legislative Issues: ENV; FUE; HOM; TAX

Chairman, President and Chief Executive Officer
GORDER, Joe
Tel: (210) 345-2615
Fax: (210) 345-2103

Main Headquarters
Mailing: One Valero Way
San Antonio, TX 78249
Tel: (210) 345-2000
Fax: (210) 345-2646
TF: (800) 531-7911

Washington Office
Mailing: 601 Pennsylvania Ave. NW
Suite 900
Washington, DC 20004

Political Action Committees
Valero Energy Corporation PAC
FEC ID: C00109546
Contact: Richard Johnston
One Valero Way
San Antonio, TX 78249
Tel: (210) 345-2000
Fax: (210) 345-2646

Contributions to Candidates: $345,000 (2015-2016)
Democrats: $15,000; Republicans: $330,000

Principal Recipients

SENATE
AYOTTE, KELLY A (REP-NH)
LEE, MIKE (REP-UT)

HOUSE
DESANTIS, RONALD D (REP-FL)
FLORES, BILL (REP-TX)
GRIFFITH, H MORGAN (REP-VA)
MEEHAN, PATRICK L. MR. (REP-PA)
POMPEO, MICHAEL RICHARD (REP-KS)
WALDEN, GREGORY P MR. (REP-OR)

Corporate Foundations and Giving Programs
Valero Energy Foundation
Contact: Sylvia Rodriguez
One Valero Place
San Antonio, TX 78249

Public Affairs and Related Activities Personnel

At Headquarters

FELNER, Craig
Director, Federal Governmental Affairs
craig.felner@valero.com
Registered Federal Lobbyist
Tel: (210) 370-2016
Fax: (210) 345-2646

FISHER, Eric
Vice President, Investor Relations, Market Analysis and Strategic Planning
Tel: (210) 345-2000
Fax: (210) 345-2646

GREENWOOD, Jim A.
Vice President, Governmental Affairs
jim.greenwood@valero.com
Registered Federal Lobbyist
Tel: (210) 370-2016
Fax: (210) 345-2646

JOHNSTON, Richard
PAC Contact
Tel: (210) 345-2000
Fax: (210) 345-2646

At Washington Office

PARINELLO, Chris
Manager, Federal Government Affairs
Registered Federal Lobbyist

At Other Offices

ARTHUR , Jr., Gary
Senior Vice President, Wholesale Marketing
Tel: (210) 345-2615
Fax: (210) 345-2103

P.O. Box 696000
San Antonio, TX 78269-6000

BROWNING, Jay	Tel:	(210) 345-2615
Executive Vice President and General Counsel	Fax:	(210) 345-2103

P.O. Box 696000
San Antonio, TX 78269-6000

CISKOWSKI, Mike	Tel:	(210) 345-2615
Executive Vice President and Chief Financial Officer	Fax:	(210) 345-2103

P.O. Box 696000
San Antonio, TX 78269-6000

KLUMPYAN, Julie	Tel:	(210) 345-2615
Director, Government Affairs	Fax:	(210) 345-2103

P.O. Box 696000
San Antonio, TX 78269-6000
julie.klumpyan@valero.com

QUINN, Chris	Tel:	(210) 345-2615
Vice President and Assistant Treasurer	Fax:	(210) 345-2103

P.O. Box 696000
San Antonio, TX 78269-6000

RODRIGUEZ, Sylvia	Tel:	(210) 345-2615
Manager, Community Relations	Fax:	(210) 345-2103

P.O. Box 696000
San Antonio, TX 78269-6000
sylvia.rodriguez@valero.com

THOMAS, Cheryl	Tel:	(210) 345-2615
Vice President and Chief Information Officer	Fax:	(210) 345-2103

P.O. Box 696000
San Antonio, TX 78269-6000

Valhi, Inc.

Valhi, Inc is a corporation that has operations through majority-owned subsidiaries or less than majority-owned affiliates in the chemicals, component products, and waste management businesses.
www.valhi.net
Annual Revenues: $1.47 billion
Employees: 3,012
Ticker: NYSE: VHI
SIC: 2810
Industry/ies: Chemicals & Chemical Industry; Commodities; Food And Beverage Industry; Paper And Wood Products Industry

Chairman of the Board	Tel:	(972) 233-1700
SIMMONS, Harold C.	Fax:	(972) 448-1445

President and Chief Executive Officer	Tel:	(972) 233-1700
WATSON, Steven L.	Fax:	(972) 448-1445

Main Headquarters

Mailing:	5430 LBJ Fwy.	Tel:	(972) 233-1700
	Suite 1700	Fax:	(972) 448-1445
	Dallas, TX 75240		

Public Affairs and Related Activities Personnel

At Headquarters

GRAHAM, Robert D.	Tel:	(972) 233-1700
Vice President and Assistant Secretary	Fax:	(972) 448-1445

HOLLINGSWORTH, J. Mark	Tel:	(972) 233-1700
Vice President, General Counsel and Assistant Secretary	Fax:	(972) 448-1445
markh@valhi.net		

LOUIS, A. Andrew R.	Tel:	(972) 233-1700
Secretary and Associate General Counsel	Fax:	(972) 448-1445
alouis@valhi.net		

O'BRIEN, Bobby D.	Tel:	(972) 233-1700
Vice President and Chief Financial Officer	Fax:	(972) 448-1445

Valmont Industries

Designs and manufactures mechanized poles, towers and structures for lighting, traffic, utility and communications.
www.valmont.com
Annual Revenues: $2.55 billion
Employees: 10,697
Ticker: NYSE: VMI
SIC: 3499
NAICS: 332999
Industry/ies: Communications; Construction/Construction Materials; Telecommunications/Internet/Cable
Legislative Issues: TRD

Chairman of the Board and Chief Executive Officer	Tel:	(402) 963-1000
BAY, Mogens C.	Fax:	(402) 963-1198

Main Headquarters

Mailing:	One Valmont Plaza	Tel:	(402) 963-1000
	Omaha, NE 68154-5215	Fax:	(402) 963-1198

Political Action Committees
Valmont Industries Inc (PAC)
FEC ID: C00152843

Contact: Mark Jaksich

One Valmont Plaza	Tel:	(402) 963-1000
Omaha, NE 68154	Fax:	(402) 963-1198

Public Affairs and Related Activities Personnel

At Headquarters

BROWN , Vanessa	Tel:	(402) 963-1000
Senior Vice President, Human Resources	Fax:	(402) 963-1198
vbrown@valmont.com		

DESIGIO, Brian	Tel:	(402) 963-1000
President, North America Structures	Fax:	(402) 963-1198

JAKSICH, Mark	Tel:	(402) 963-1000
Executive Vice President, Chief Financial Officer and PAC Treasurer	Fax:	(402) 963-1198

KEHOE, John A.	Tel:	(402) 963-1000
Vice President, Information Technology and Chief Information Officer	Fax:	(402) 963-1198

LAUDIN, Jeffrey S.	Tel:	(402) 963-1158
Manager, Investor Relations	Fax:	(402) 963-1198
investor_relations@valmont.com		

MASSEY, R. Andrew	Tel:	(402) 963-1000
Vice President, Legal and Compliance Officer	Fax:	(402) 963-1198

Valneva

Formerly known as Intercell USA, Inc., the company adopted its current name in 2013 through the merger of Intercell AG and Vivalis SA. A biotechnology company which develops vaccines for the prevention and treatment of infectious diseases. Acquired Iomai Corporation in 2009. A subsidiary of Intercell AG, which is headquartered in Austria.
www.valneva.com/?page = 27
Annual Revenues: $5 million
Employees: 100
SIC: 2834
Industry/ies: Pharmaceutical Industry

President and Chief Executive Officer	Tel:	(301) 556-4500
LINGELBACH, Thomas	Fax:	(301) 556-4505

Main Headquarters

Mailing:	910 Clopper Rd.	Tel:	(301) 556-4500
	Suite 160S		
	Gaithersburg, MD 20878		

Washington Office

Mailing:	22 Firstfield Rd.	Tel:	(301) 556-4500
	Gaithersburg, MD 20878	Fax:	(301) 556-4505

Public Affairs and Related Activities Personnel

At Headquarters

GOLAN, Jason	Tel:	(301) 556-4500
Vice President, Sales and Marketing		

JACOTOT, Frederic	Tel:	(301) 556-4500
Vice President, General Counsel		

JANKOWITSCH, Olivier	Tel:	(301) 556-4500
Vice President Corporate Development		

LEGROS, Frédéric	Tel:	(301) 556-4500
Vice President, Business Development		

At Washington Office

KANDERA, Reinhard	Tel:	(301) 556-4500
Chief Financial Officer	Fax:	(301) 556-4505

STROHMAIER , Gerald	Tel:	(301) 556-4500
Head, Human Resources	Fax:	(301) 556-4505
HR@intercell.com		

Value City Department Stores, Inc.

See listing on page 682 under Retail Ventures, Inc.

The Vanguard Group, Inc.

Financial advisors. A government affairs consulting firm.
www.vanguard.com
Annual Revenues: $16 Million
Employees: 13,500
Industry/ies: Banking/Finance/Investments
Legislative Issues: BUD; FIN; HOM; RET; TAX

Chairman and Chief Executive Officer	Tel:	(610) 669-6219
MCNABB, III, F. William	Fax:	(610) 669-6605

Main Headquarters

Mailing:	P.O. BOX 1101	Tel:	(610) 669-6219
	Valley Forge, PA 19482-1101	Fax:	(610) 669-6605

Washington Office

Mailing:	975 F St NW
	Suite 500
	Washington, DC 20001

Political Action Committees
Vanguard Group Committee for Responsible Government PAC

FEC ID: C00410266
Contact: Brian S. Mattes
400 Devon Park Dr.
Wayne, PA 19087

Contributions to Candidates: $240,000 (2015-2016)
Democrats: $99,000; Republicans: $141,000

Principal Recipients

HOUSE
DELANEY, JOHN K (DEM-MD)
RYAN, PAUL D. (REP-WI)

Corporate Foundations and Giving Programs

Vanguard Charitable
Contact: Benjamin R. Pierce
P.O. BOX 2600   Tel: (610) 669-6219
Valley Forge, PA 19482   Fax: (610) 669-6605

Public Affairs and Related Activities Personnel

At Headquarters

BUCKLEY, Mortimer J. (Tim)   Tel: (610) 669-6219
Managing Director and Chief Investment Officer   Fax: (610) 669-6605

COMBS, Ann L.   Tel: (610) 669-6219
Principal   Fax: (610) 669-6605
Registered Federal Lobbyist

DELAPLANE, Jr., James M.   Tel: (610) 669-6219
Principal and Head   Fax: (610) 669-6605

GOLDEN, Gerard M.   Tel: (610) 669-6219
Federal Lobbyist   Fax: (610) 669-6605
Registered Federal Lobbyist

GUBANICH, Kathleen C.   Tel: (610) 669-6219
Managing Director, Human Resources   Fax: (610) 669-6605
kathleen.gubanich@vanguard.com

MILLER, Michael S.   Tel: (610) 669-6219
Managing Director, Planning and Development   Fax: (610) 669-6605

NORRIS, James M.   Tel: (610) 669-6219
Managing Director, International Operations,   Fax: (610) 669-6605

REED , Glenn   Tel: (610) 669-6219
Managing Director, Strategy and Finance   Fax: (610) 669-6605

STAM , Heidi   Tel: (610) 669-6219
General Counsel   Fax: (610) 669-6605
heidi.stam@vanguard.com

WOERTH, John   Tel: (610) 669-6224
Principal, Communications   Fax: (610) 669-6605

At Washington Office

MATTES, Brian S.
Principal, Government Relations
Registered Federal Lobbyist

At Other Offices

FLORES, Jillien
P.O. Box 2600
Valley Forge, PA 19482
Registered Federal Lobbyist

HULA, Alex
P.O. Box 2600
Valley Forge, PA 19482

PIERCE, Benjamin R.   Tel: (888) 383-4483
President, Vanguard Charitable Endowment Program   Fax: (866) 485-9414
P.O. Box 55766
Boston, MA 02205-5766

Varian Associates

See listing on page 830 under Varian Medical Systems, Inc.

Varian Medical Systems, Inc.

The company is the manufacturer of medical devices and software for treating cancer. The company's oncology unit makes linear accelerators, simulators, and data management software, primarily for cancer radiotherapy. In early 1999, Varian Associates changed its name to Varian Medical Systems.
www.varian.com
Annual Revenues: $3.06 billion
Employees: 6,800
Ticker: NYSE: VAR
SIC: 3845
Industry/ies: Medicine/Health Care/Mental Health
Legislative Issues: BUD; ENG; HCR; MMM; TRD

Chairman of the Board   Tel: (650) 493-4000
ECKERT, R. Andrew   Fax: (650) 842-5196

President and Chief Executive Officer   Tel: (650) 493-4000
WILSON, Dow R.   Fax: (650) 842-5196

Main Headquarters
Mailing: 525 Ninth St. NW   Tel: (202) 629-3441

Suite 730
Washington, DC 20004

Political Action Committees
Varian Medical Systems PAC
FEC ID: C00450965
Contact: Zilly Maureen Tracy
525 Ninth St. NW
Suite 450
Washington, DC 20004

Contributions to Candidates: $28,500 (2015-2016)
Democrats: $9,500; Republicans: $19,000

Corporate Foundations and Giving Programs

Varian Medical Systems Foundation
Contact: Sheila Villadelgado
3100 Hansen Way   Tel: (650) 493-4000
M/S E-190
Palo Alto, CA 94304

Public Affairs and Related Activities Personnel

At Headquarters

CHANEY, Julia   Tel: (202) 629-3441
Associate, Government Affairs

EDWARDS, Allison   Tel: (202) 629-3441

MICKELSEN, Katie Beth   Tel: (202) 629-3441
Government Affairs Assistant

SHEEHY-CHAN, Julia   Tel: (202) 629-3441
International Programs Manager

TRACY, Zilly Maureen   Tel: (202) 629-3441
Federal Lobbyist and PAC Treasurer
Registered Federal Lobbyist

WALLACE, Pete   Tel: (202) 629-3441
Senior Manager, Federal Affairs
Registered Federal Lobbyist

WHITMAN, Andrew   Tel: (202) 629-3441
Vice President, Government Affairs
andrew.whitman@varian.com
Registered Federal Lobbyist

At Other Offices

FINNEY, Elisha W.   Tel: (650) 493-4000
Executive Vice President, Finance and Chief Financial Officer   Fax: (650) 842-5196
3100 Hansen Way
Palo Alto, CA 94304-1038

GINSBERG, Meryl   Tel: (650) 424-6444
Director, Public Relations   Fax: (650) 842-5196
3100 Hansen Way
Palo Alto, CA 94304-1038

KUO, John W.   Tel: (650) 493-4000
Senior Vice President, General Counsel and Corporate   Fax: (650) 842-5196
Secretary
3100 Hansen Way
Palo Alto, CA 94304-1038

MCGEE, Keelin
801 Pennsylvania Ave. NW, Suite 730
Washington, DC 20004

PALOMBA, Franco N.   Tel: (650) 493-4000
Senior Vice President, Finance and Teasurer   Fax: (650) 842-5196
3100 Hansen Way
Palo Alto, CA 94304-1038

REITHERMAN, Wendy Scott   Tel: (650) 493-4000
Senior Vice President and Chief Human Resources Officer   Fax: (650) 842-5196
3100 Hansen Way
Palo Alto, CA 94304-1038

SIAS, Spencer R.   Tel: (650) 424-5782
Vice President, Corporate Communications and Investor   Fax: (650) 842-5196
Relations
3100 Hansen Way
Palo Alto, CA 94304-1038

TRAN, Vy H.   Tel: (650) 493-4000
Vice President, Regulatory Affairs and Quality Assuranc   Fax: (650) 842-5196
3100 Hansen Way
Palo Alto, CA 94304-1038

VILLADELGADO, Sheila   Tel: (650) 493-4000
Public Relations Representative   Fax: (650) 842-5196
3100 Hansen Way
Palo Alto, CA 94304-1038
Mail Stop M/S E-190

Venator Group

See listing on page 336 under Foot Locker Inc.

Vericel Corporation

Formerly Aastrom Biosciences. A developer of autologous cell products for the repair or regeneration of human tissue.
www.vcel.com
Annual Revenues: $39.65 million
Employees: 190
Ticker: NASDAQ: VCEL
SIC: 8731; 2836; 8733; 2833
NAICS: 325411; 325414
Industry/ies: Science; Scientific Research

President and Chief Executive Officer	Tel:	(734) 418-4400
COLANGELO, Dominick	Fax:	(734) 665-0485

Main Headquarters
Mailing:	P.O. Box 376	Tel:	(734) 418-4400
	Ann Arbor, MI 48106	Fax:	(734) 665-0485
		TF:	(888) 556-0311

Public Affairs and Related Activities Personnel

At Headquarters

MICHEL, Gerard	Tel:	(734) 418-4400
Chief Financial Officer and Vice President, Corporate	Fax:	(734) 665-0485
Development		
ORLANDO, Daniel	Tel:	(734) 418-4400
Chief Operating Officer	Fax:	(734) 665-0485
RUBIN, Chad	Tel:	(734) 418-4400
Contact, Investor Relations	Fax:	(734) 665-0485
SALISBURY, David	Tel:	(212) 253-8881
Contact, Media	Fax:	(734) 665-0485
dsalisbury@berrypr.com		

Verint Systems, Inc.

Designs, manufactures and markets computer and telecommunications systems and software.On February 4, 2013 Comverse Technology, Inc. is acquired by Verint Systems Inc.
www.cmvt.com
Annual Revenues: $1.14 billion
Employees: 4,900
Ticker: NASDAQ: VRNT
SIC: 3661
Industry/ies: Computer/Technology

Chairman	Tel:	(631) 962-9600
DE MARINES, Victor A.		

Corporate Officer, President, Chief Executive Officer, and	Tel:	(631) 962-9600
Director		
BODNER, Dan		

Main Headquarters
Mailing:	330 S. Service Rd.	Tel:	(631) 962-9600
	Melville, NY 11747		

Public Affairs and Related Activities Personnel

At Headquarters

FANTE, Peter	Tel:	(631) 962-9600
Chief Legal Officer, and Chief Compliance Officer		
GINO, Hanan	Tel:	(631) 962-9600
President, Communications and Cyber Intelligence		
O'DONNELL, Jane	Tel:	(631) 962-9600
Senior Vice President, Global Human Resources		
ROBINSON, Douglas E.	Tel:	(631) 962-9600
Corporate Officer and Chief Financial Officer		
RODEN, Alan	Tel:	(631) 962-9600
Senior Vice President, Corporate Development and Investor		
Relations		
SPERLING, Meir	Tel:	(631) 962-9600
Corporate Officer and Chief Strategy Officer		

VeriSign

Provides infrastructure services for information technology used by the US government and the networked world.
www.verisigninc.com
Annual Revenues: $1.02 billion
Employees: 1,025
Ticker: NASDAQ: VRSN
SIC: 7371
Industry/ies: Computer/Technology; Science; Scientific Research
Legislative Issues: CPI; HOM

President, Chief Executive Officer and Chairman of the Board	Tel:	(703) 948-3200
BIDZOS, D. James	Fax:	(650) 961-7300

Main Headquarters
Mailing:	12061 Bluemont Way	Tel:	(703) 948-3200
	Reston, VA 20190		

Washington Office
Mailing:	21355 Ridgetop Cir.	
	Dulles, VA 20166-6503	

Public Affairs and Related Activities Personnel

At Headquarters

DRAZEK, Keith	Tel:	(703) 948-3200
INDELICARTO, Thomas	Tel:	(703) 948-3200
Senior Vice President, General Counsel and Secretary		
KANE, Patrick	Tel:	(703) 948-3200
Vice President		
Registered Federal Lobbyist		
KILGUSS , III, George	Tel:	(703) 948-3200
Senior Vice President and Chief Financial Officer		
SCHNELL , Scott	Tel:	(703) 948-3200
Senior Vice President, Marketing, Strategy and Business		
Development		
STRUBBE, Todd	Tel:	(703) 948-3200
Executive Vice President and Chief Operating Officer		
THOMAS, Gregory	Tel:	(703) 948-3200

Verisk Analytics

A provider of information on property/casualty insurance.
www.iso.com
Annual Revenues: $206.40 million
Employees: 4,000
Industry/ies: Insurance Industry

Chairman of the Board and Chief Executive Officer	Tel:	(201) 469-2000
COYNE, Frank J.	Fax:	(201) 748-1472

President and and Chief Executive Officer	Tel:	(201) 469-2000
STEPHENSON, Scott G.	Fax:	(201) 748-1472

Main Headquarters
Mailing:	545 Washington Blvd.	Tel:	(201) 469-2000
	Jersey City, NJ 07310-1686	Fax:	(201) 748-1472
		TF:	(800) 888-4476

Washington Office
Mailing:	1101 Pennsylvania Ave. NW	Tel:	(202) 756-3631
	Washington, DC 20004	Fax:	(201) 748-1472

Political Action Committees
Insurance Services Office Inc. PAC
FEC ID: C00361063
Contact: Mark V. Anquillare
545 Washington Blvd.	Tel:	(201) 469-2000
Jersey City, NJ 07310	Fax:	(201) 469-2000

Public Affairs and Related Activities Personnel

At Headquarters

ANQUILLARE, Mark V.	Tel:	(201) 469-2000
PAC Contact, Executive Vice President and Chief Financial	Fax:	(201) 748-1472
Officer		
BANFIELD, Carole J.	Tel:	(201) 469-2000
Executive Vice President, Information Services and	Fax:	(201) 748-1472
Government Relations		
HELTON, Erica	Tel:	(201) 507-9500
Contact, Media Relations	Fax:	(201) 748-1472
ehelton@mww.com		
HUSTON, Eva F	Tel:	(201) 469-2000
Senior Vice President, Treasurer, and Chief Knowledge Office	Fax:	(201) 748-1472
KENNEY, Susan	Tel:	(201) 507-9500
Contact, Media Relations	Fax:	(201) 748-1472
skenney@mww.com		
MAGATH, Mark S	Tel:	(201) 469-2000
Senior Vice President, Risk and Compliance	Fax:	(201) 748-1472
MCCARTHY, Vince	Tel:	(201) 469-2000
Senior Vice President, Corporate Development and Strategy	Fax:	(201) 748-1472
PERINI, Christopher H.	Tel:	(201) 469-2000
Vice President and Chief Marketing Officer	Fax:	(201) 748-1472
REISMAN, Marlene P	Tel:	(201) 469-2000
Vice President, Human Resources	Fax:	(201) 748-1472
THOMPSON, Kenneth E.	Tel:	(201) 469-2000
Executive Vice President, General Counsel and Corporate	Fax:	(201) 748-1472
Secretary		

Verizon Communications

A national-global voice/data/wireless/information services provider. Formed from the merger of Bell Atlantic and GTE. The company acquired MCI Inc. in January of 2006.
www22.verizon.com
Annual Revenues: $128.24 billion
Employees: 176,200
Ticker: NYSE, NASDAQ: VZ
SIC: 4813
NAICS: 511140; 513322; 513340; 514101; 512210
Industry/ies: Communications; Telecommunications/Internet/Cable
Legislative Issues: BUD; COM; CPT; DOC; HCR; INT; LAW; LBR; TAX; TEC; TRD

Chairman, Chief Executive Officer
MCADAM, Lowell C.

Main Headquarters
Mailing: P.O. Box 15124
               Albany, NY 12212-5124

Washington Office
Mailing: 1300 I St. NW
               Suite 400 West
               Washington, DC 20005

Political Action Committees
Verizon Communications Inc. Good Government Club PAC
FEC ID: C00186288
Contact: Taylor Craig
1300 Eye St. NW   Tel: (202) 515-2400
Suite 400 West   Fax: (202) 589-3750
Washington, DC 20005

Contributions to Candidates: $11,465,265 (2015-2016)
Democrats: $513,000; Republicans: $677,250; Other: $10,275,015

Principal Recipients

SENATE
BURR, RICHARD (REP-NC)
GRASSLEY, CHARLES E SENATOR (REP-IA)
SCHATZ, BRIAN (DEM-HI)
TOOMEY, PATRICK JOSEPH (REP-PA)

HOUSE
CARDENAS, TONY (DEM-CA)
GREEN, RAYMOND E. 'GENE' (DEM-TX)
HASTINGS, ALCEE L (DEM-DC)
HOYER, STENY HAMILTON (DEM-DC)
LUJAN, BEN R MR. (DEM-NM)
MATSUI, DORIS (DEM-CA)
NUNES, DEVIN G (REP-CA)
REED, THOMAS W II (REP-NY)
ROSKAM, PETER (REP-IL)
RYAN, PAUL D. (REP-WI)
SCALISE, STEVE MR. (REP-LA)
SCHRADER, KURT (DEM-OR)
SHIMKUS, JOHN M (REP-IL)

Corporate Foundations and Giving Programs

Verizon Foundation
140 West St.   Tel: (908) 559-6434
New York City, NY 10007   Fax: (908) 630-2660

Public Affairs and Related Activities Personnel

At Headquarters

ASKEW, Joseph L.
Vice President, State Government Affairs
joseph.l.askew.jr@verizon.com

BRITTINGHAM, Donald
Vice President, National Security and Public Safety Policy
donald.c. brittingham@verizon.com

CANTREL, Jr., Frank J.
Vice President, Federal Government Relations

CHESTNUTT, Roy H.
Executive Vice President and Chief Strategy Officer

CLARK, Nancy B.
Senior Vice President & Chief Marketing Officer

DAVIDSON, Peter
Senior Vice President
Registered Federal Lobbyist

DEBOSIER, Chris M.
Registered Federal Lobbyist

EDWARDS, Thomas
Vice President, State and Federal Affairs and Federal Lobbyist
tom_edwards@verizon.net
Registered Federal Lobbyist

FISHER, Robert
Vice President, Federal Government Affairs
Registered Federal Lobbyist

GERACE, James J.
Chief Communications Officer

GONZALEZ, Emilio
Executive Director, Strategic Alliances
emilio.x.gonzalez@verizon.com

HOEWING, C. Lincoln
Vice President, Internet & Technology Policy

JOHNSON, Michone
Vice President, Federal Government Relations
Registered Federal Lobbyist

KOLEGO, Jacqueline Moran

Vice President
Registered Federal Lobbyist

MACKAY, Christopher
Vice President, Federal Government Relations
Registered Federal Lobbyist

MEAD, Daniel S
Executive Vice President and President of Strategic Initiatives

MULLET, Mark S.
Vice President, Federal Government Relations
mark.s.mullet@verizon.com
Registered Federal Lobbyist

SCOTTI, Diego
Executive Vice President and Chief Marketing Officer

SENN, W. Edward
Vice President, State Government Relations
w.e.senn@verizon.com
Registered Federal Lobbyist

SHAMMO, Francis J.
Executive Vice President and Chief Financial Officer

SILLIMAN, Craig
Executive Vice President Public Policy and General Counsel

SPRINKLE, Stacey L.
Vice President, Federal Tax Policy
Registered Federal Lobbyist

STEFANSKI, Mike
Senior Vice President, Investor Relations

STRATTON, John G.
Executive Vice President and President of Operations

WHITE, Walter
Vice President, State and Local Government

ZAMORA, Marcela Urrutia
Vice President, Federal Government Relations
Registered Federal Lobbyist

At Washington Office

ANDERSON REINHARD, Courtney
Registered Federal Lobbyist

CRAIG, Taylor
Lobbyist and PAC Treasurer

LYNCH, Joshua
Registered Federal Lobbyist

MORAN, Jacqueline
Registered Federal Lobbyist

PROLAGO, Natosha
Registered Federal Lobbyist

At Other Offices

BONOMO, John J.   Tel: (212) 321-8033
Director,Media Relations   Fax: (212) 571-1897
140 West St.
New York City, NY 10007
john.j.bonomo@verizon.com

CANAL, Alberto   Tel: (908) 559-6434
Vice President, Corporate Communications   Fax: (908) 630-2651
One Verizon Way
Basking Ridge, NJ 07920
alberto.c.canal@verizon.com

DIERCKSEN, John W.   Tel: (212) 395-1000
Executive Vice President   Fax: (212) 571-1897
140 West St.
New York City, NY 10007

MILCH, Randal S.   Tel: (212) 395-2121
Executive Vice President, Strategic Policy Advisor to the   Fax: (212) 571-1897
Chair and CEO
140 West St.
New York City, NY 10007
randal.s.milch@verizon.com

REED, Marc C.   Tel: (212) 395-2121
Executive Vice President Human Resources   Fax: (212) 571-1897
140 West St.
New York City, NY 10007

THONIS, Peter   Tel: (212) 395-2355
Chief Communications Officer   Fax: (212) 571-1897
140 West St.
New York City, NY 10007
peter.thonis@verizon.com

VARETTONI, Robert A.   Tel: (908) 559-6388
Executive Director, Corporate Communications   Fax: (908) 630-2651
One Verizon Way
Basking Ridge, NJ 07920
robert.a.varettoni@verizon.com

Verizon Telematics

Verizon Communications Inc. acquired acquire Hughes Telematics, Inc. Verizon Communications Inc. delivers the next generation of vehicle information-based technologies and services
www.verizontelematics.com
Annual Revenues: $71.27 million
Employees: 400
Ticker: NYSE, Nasdaq: VZ
SIC: 3669
Industry/ies: Communications; Telecommunications/Internet/Cable

Chief Executive Officer	Tel:	(404) 573-5800
LEDDY, Jeff	Fax:	(404) 573-5827

Main Headquarters
Mailing:	2002 Summit Blvd.	Tel:	(404) 573-5800
	Suite 1800	Fax:	(404) 573-5827
	Atlanta, GA 30319		

Washington Office
Mailing: 1300 I St. NW
Washington, DC 20005

Public Affairs and Related Activities Personnel

At Headquarters

KAUFMANN, Craig	Tel:	(404) 573-5800
Senior Vice President and Treasurer	Fax:	(404) 573-5827
LEWIS, Rob	Tel:	(404) 573-5800
General Counsel & Secretary	Fax:	(404) 573-5827
LINK, Kevin	Tel:	(404) 573-5800
Senior Vice President, Public Relations	Fax:	(770) 391-6429
kevin.link@verizon.com		
TRICARICO, Rocco	Tel:	(404) 573-5800
Vice President, Sales & Marketing	Fax:	(404) 573-5827

Verizon Terremark

Terremark Worldwide is a provider of IT infrastructure services and a subsidiary of Verizon Communications Inc. (NYSE, NASDAQ:VZ).
www.terremark.com
Annual Revenues: $292.35 million
Employees: 900
Ticker: NASDAQ: TMRK
SIC: 4813
Industry/ies: Computer/Technology

Main Headquarters
Mailing:	One Biscayne Tower, Two S. Biscayne Blvd.	Tel:	(305) 961-3200
	Suite 2800	Fax:	(305) 961-8190
	Miami, FL 33131	TF:	(800) 983-7060

Washington Office
Mailing:	460 Springpark Pl.	Tel:	(703) 964-8900
	Suite 1000		
	Herndon, VA 20170		

Public Affairs and Related Activities Personnel

At Headquarters

GONZALEZ, Xavier	Tel:	(305) 961-3134
Vice President, Corporate Communications	Fax:	(305) 961-8190
RODRIGUEZ, Maria	Tel:	(305) 961-3181
Administrative Assistant	Fax:	(305) 961-8190
mrodriguez@terremark.com		

Verizon Washington, DC, Inc.

An operating company of Verizon Communications Inc.
www22.verizon.com/about/community/dc.html
Annual Revenues: $75.6 million
Employees: 1,500
SIC: 4813
Industry/ies: Communications; Telecommunications/Internet/Cable

Chairman of the Board and Chief Executive Officer	Tel:	(202) 392-9900
MCADAM, Lowell C.	Fax:	(202) 887-9195
loWell.c.mcadam@verizon.com		

President	Tel:	(202) 392-9900
ROBERTS, William R.	Fax:	(202) 887-9195

Main Headquarters
Mailing:	1300 I St. NW	Tel:	(202) 392-9900
	Suite 400, West	Fax:	(202) 887-9195
	Washington, DC 20005	TF:	(877) 447-4819

Corporate Foundations and Giving Programs

Verizon Foundation
Contact: Rose Stuckey Kirk
140 West St.	Tel:	(908) 559-6434
New York City, NY 10007	Fax:	(908) 630-2660

Public Affairs and Related Activities Personnel

At Headquarters

ARNETTE, Sandra U.	Tel:	(410) 393-7109
Manager, Public Relations	Fax:	(202) 887-9195
sandra.u.arnette@verizon.com		
CAMPBELL, Karen	Tel:	(202) 515-2534
Vice President, State Government Affairs	Fax:	(202) 887-9195
karen.i.campbell@verizon.com		
CHESTNUTT, Roy H.	Tel:	(202) 392-9900
Executive Vice President and Chief Strategy Officer	Fax:	(202) 887-9195
DOHERTY, John N.	Tel:	(202) 392-9900
Senior Vice President, Corporate Development	Fax:	(202) 887-9195
john.n.doherty@verizon.com		
GERACE, James J.	Tel:	(202) 392-9900
Chief Communications Officer	Fax:	(202) 887-9195
MILCH, Randal	Tel:	(202) 392-9900
Executive Vice President, Public Policy and General Counsel	Fax:	(202) 887-9195
randal.s.milch@verizon.com		
SHAMMO, Francis J.	Tel:	(202) 392-9900
Executive Vice President and Chief Financial Officer	Fax:	(202) 887-9195
francis.shammo@verizon.com		
SILLIMAN, Craig	Tel:	(202) 392-9900
Executive Vice President, Public Policy and General Counsel	Fax:	(202) 887-9195

At Other Offices

KIRK, Rose Stuckey
President, Verizon Foundation
Verizon Foundation, One Verizon Way, VC34W539B
Basking Ridge, NJ 07920

Verizon Wireless

Formerly Bell Atlantic Mobile, operates the 4G network and reliable 3G network. A joint venture of Verizon Communications and Vodafone.
www.verizonwireless.com
Annual Revenues: $1.00 billion
Employees: 10,000
SIC: 4812
Industry/ies: Communications; Telecommunications/Internet/Cable
Legislative Issues: HCR; TAX; TEC

Chairman and Chief Executive Officer	Tel:	(908) 607-8001
MCADAM, Lowell C.	Fax:	(908) 559-7111

Main Headquarters
Mailing:	One Verizon Way	Tel:	(908) 607-8001
	Basking Ridge, NJ 07920-1097	Fax:	(908) 559-7111
		TF:	(800) 922-0204

Washington Office
Mailing:	1300 I St. NW	Tel:	(202) 589-3781
	Suite 400 West	Fax:	(202) 589-3750
	Washington, DC 20036		

Political Action Committees

Verizon Communications Inc. Good Government Club PAC
FEC ID: C00186288
Contact: Craig Taylor
1300 Eye St. NW	Tel:	(202) 515-2400
Suite 400 West	Fax:	(202) 589-3750
Washington, DC 20005		

Contributions to Candidates: $11,465,265 (2015-2016)
Democrats: $513,000; Republicans: $677,250; Other: $10,275,015

Principal Recipients

SENATE
BURR, RICHARD (REP-NC)
GRASSLEY, CHARLES E SENATOR (REP-IA)
SCHATZ, BRIAN (DEM-HI)
TOOMEY, PATRICK JOSEPH (REP-PA)

HOUSE
CARDENAS, TONY (DEM-CA)
GREEN, RAYMOND E. 'GENE' (DEM-TX)
HASTINGS, ALCEE L (DEM-DC)
HOYER, STENY HAMILTON (DEM-DC)
LUJAN, BEN R MR. (DEM-NM)
MATSUI, DORIS (DEM-CA)
NUNES, DEVIN G (REP-CA)
REED, THOMAS W II (REP-NY)
ROSKAM, PETER (REP-IL)
RYAN, PAUL D. (REP-WI)
SCALISE, STEVE MR. (REP-LA)
SCHRADER, KURT (DEM-OR)
SHIMKUS, JOHN M (REP-IL)

Public Affairs and Related Activities Personnel

At Headquarters

CHESTNUTT, Roy H.	Tel:	(908) 607-8001
Executive Vice President and Chief Strategy Officer	Fax:	(908) 559-7111

DIXON, Ken
President, Northeast Area
Tel: (908) 607-8001
Fax: (908) 559-7111

FELIX, Christopher
President
Tel: (908) 559-7000
Fax: (908) 559-7111

GARDNER, M. Alan
Senior Vice President, Human Resources
Tel: (908) 559-7000
Fax: (908) 559-7111

GERACE, James J.
Chief Communications Officer
Tel: (908) 607-8001
Fax: (908) 559-7111

MEAD, Daniel S.
Executive Vice President and President of Strategic Initiatives
Tel: (908) 559-7000
Fax: (908) 559-7111

NEPTUNE, Torod B.
Vice President, Corporate Communications
Tel: (908) 607-8001
Fax: (908) 559-7111

PETERSEN, William B.
Vice President, General Counsel and Secretary
Tel: (908) 559-7000
Fax: (908) 559-7111

REED, Marc C.
Executive Vice President and Chief Administrative Officer
Tel: (908) 607-8001
Fax: (908) 559-7111

SCOTTI, Diego
Executive Vice President and Chief Marketing Officer
Tel: (908) 607-8001
Fax: (908) 559-7111

SHAMMO, Francis J.
Executive Vice President and Chief Financial Officer
Tel: (908) 607-8001
Fax: (908) 559-7111

SILLIMAN, Craig
Executive Vice President, Public Policy and General Counsel
Tel: (908) 607-8001
Fax: (908) 559-7111

SMALL, David
Executive Vice President and Chief Operating Officer
Tel: (908) 607-8001
Fax: (908) 559-7111

SMITH, Marquett
Vice President, Federal Government Sales
Marquett.Smith@VerizonWireless.com
Tel: (908) 559-7000
Fax: (908) 559-7111

STRATTON, John G.
Executive Vice President and President, Operations
Tel: (908) 607-8001
Fax: (908) 559-7111

At Washington Office

BRITTINGHAM, Donald
Vice President, National Security and Public Safety Policy
Tel: (202) 589-3781
Fax: (202) 589-3750

STACY, Brian
Vice President, Contact Center and Online Services (Global)
Tel: (202) 589-3781
Fax: (202) 589-3750

TAYLOR, Craig
Lobbyist and PAC Treasurer
Tel: (202) 589-3781
Fax: (202) 589-3750

Vertex Inc.

Vertex Inc. provides tax software that government agencies, tax collectors, and corporations use to process income, sales, consumer use, value-added, communications, payroll, and property taxes.
www.vertexinc.com
Employees: 700
Industry/ies: Taxation

Chairman of the Board
LUCAS, Stefanie Westphal
Tel: (610) 640-4200
Fax: (610) 640-5892

President, Chief Executive Officer and Co-Owner
WESTPHAL, Jeffrey R.
Tel: (610) 640-4200
Fax: (610) 640-5892

Main Headquarters
Mailing: 1041 Old Cassatt Rd.
Berwyn, PA 19312
Tel: (610) 640-4200
Fax: (610) 640-5892
TF: (800) 355-3500

Corporate Foundations and Giving Programs
Vertex Contributions Program
1041 Old Cassatt Rd.
Berwyn, PA 19312

Public Affairs and Related Activities Personnel

At Headquarters

BUTLER, Lisa
Chief Financial Officer
Tel: (610) 640-4200
Fax: (610) 640-5892

DESTEFANO, David
Executive Vice President
Tel: (610) 640-4200
Fax: (610) 640-5892

DYSON, Barb
Vice President, Human Resources
barb.dyson@vertexinc.com
Tel: (610) 640-4200
Fax: (610) 640-5892

ROEDE, Gretchen
Contact, Media Relations
groede@garfieldgroup.com
Tel: (610) 640-4200
Fax: (610) 640-5892

SMITH, Alex
Consultant, Government Relations
Tel: (610) 640-4200
Fax: (610) 640-5892

At Other Offices

CAYO, Carol
Director, Government Affairs
3855 Margits Ln.
Trappe, MD 21673
Tel: (410) 476-7829

Vertex Pharmaceuticals

A global biotechnology company.

www.vrtx.com
Annual Revenues: $1.18 billion
Employees: 1,830
Ticker: NASDAQ: VRTX
SIC: 2834
Industry/ies: Pharmaceutical Industry; Science; Scientific Research
Legislative Issues: BUD; CPT; HCR; MED; MMM; TAX

Chairman of the Board, President and Chief Executive Officer
LEIDEN, MD, PhD, Jeffrey
Tel: (617) 444-6100
Fax: (617) 444-6680

Main Headquarters
Mailing: 50 Northern Ave.
Boston, MA 02210
Tel: (617) 444-6100
Fax: (617) 444-6680

Washington Office
Mailing: 1050 K St. NW
Suite 1125
Washington, DC 20001

Public Affairs and Related Activities Personnel

At Headquarters

BARBER, Zachry
Senior Director, Corporate Communications
Tel: (617) 444-6100
Fax: (617) 444-6680

BEDSON, Simon
Senior Vice President and General Manager, International Commercial Operations
Tel: (617) 444-6100
Fax: (617) 444-6680

HORTON, Kenneth L.
Executive Vice President and Chief Legal Officer
Tel: (617) 444-6100
Fax: (617) 444-6680

KALMAR, Dawn
Vice President, Corporate Communications
Tel: (617) 444-6100
Fax: (617) 444-6680

MACK, Rachel
Associate Director, Government Affairs and Public Policy
Registered Federal Lobbyist
Tel: (617) 444-6100
Fax: (617) 444-6680

MACK RADOMSKI, Rachel
Registered Federal Lobbyist
Tel: (617) 444-6100
Fax: (617) 444-6680

MACKNIGHT, Rachel
Federal Lobbyist
Registered Federal Lobbyist
Tel: (617) 444-6100
Fax: (617) 444-6680

MATTOON, Michael
Associate Director, Government Affairs and Public Policy
Registered Federal Lobbyist
Tel: (617) 444-6100
Fax: (617) 444-6680

PALLADINO, G. Michael
Senior Vice President, Human Resources
Tel: (617) 444-6100
Fax: (617) 444-6680

PARTRIDGE, Michael
Vice President, Investor Relations
Tel: (617) 444-6108
Fax: (617) 444-6680

QUINN, Thomas H.
Federal Lobbyist
Tel: (617) 444-6100
Fax: (617) 444-6680

REIDY, Eustacia
Federal Lobbyist
eustacia_reidy@vrtx.com
Registered Federal Lobbyist
Tel: (617) 444-6100
Fax: (617) 444-6680

SACHDEV, Amit K.
Executive Vice President, Policy, Access and Value
amit_sachdev@vrtx.com
Registered Federal Lobbyist
Tel: (617) 444-6100
Fax: (617) 444-6680

SMITH, Ian F.
Executive Vice President and Chief Financial Officer
Tel: (617) 444-6100
Fax: (617) 444-6680

VENTIMIGLIA, Samantha
Vice President, Government Affairs & Public Policy
Registered Federal Lobbyist
Tel: (617) 444-6100
Fax: (617) 444-6680

At Washington Office

BARNES, Scott
Associate Director, Federal Government Affairs

Vestas-American Wind Technology, Inc.

A wind energy company.
www.vestas.com
Industry/ies: Energy/Electricity
Legislative Issues: BUD; ENG; TAX

Group President and Chief Executive Officer
RUNEVAD, Anders
Tel: (503) 327-2000
Fax: (503) 327-2001

Main Headquarters
Mailing: 1417 N.W. Everett St.
Portland, OR 97209
Tel: (503) 327-2000
Fax: (503) 327-2001

Public Affairs and Related Activities Personnel

At Headquarters

CHASE, Jon
Vice President, Public Affairs Americas
Joche@vestas.com
Registered Federal Lobbyist
Tel: (503) 327-2000
Fax: (503) 327-2001

FREDRIKSSON, Marika
Tel: (503) 327-2000

Executive Vice President and Chief Financial Officer	Fax:	(503) 327-2001
LECHENE, Jean-Marc	Tel:	(503) 327-2000
Executive Vice President and Chief Operating Officer	Fax:	(503) 327-2001
SENATORE, Velia	Tel:	(503) 327-2000
Contact, Media and External Relations	Fax:	(503) 327-2001
veise@vestas.com		

VF Corporation

An apparel producer.
www.vfc.com
Annual Revenues: $12.38 billion
Employees: 64,000
Ticker: NYSE: VFC
Industry/ies: Apparel/Textiles Industry; Retail/Wholesale
Legislative Issues: BUD; FOR; TAX; TRD

Chairman of the Board and Chief Executive Officer	Tel:	(336) 424-6000
WISEMAN, Eric C.	Fax:	(336) 424-7631

Main Headquarters

Mailing:	105 Corporate Center Blvd.	Tel:	(336) 424-6000
	Greensboro, NC 27408	Fax:	(336) 424-7631
		TF:	(877) 285-4152

Corporate Foundations and Giving Programs

VF Foundation

105 Corporate Center Blvd.	Tel:	(336) 424-6000
Greensboro, NC 27408	Fax:	(336) 424-6000

Public Affairs and Related Activities Personnel

At Headquarters

ALLEGA, Lance	Tel:	(336) 424-6082
Vice President, Investor Relations	Fax:	(336) 424-7631
CROSSLIN, Carole	Tel:	(336) 424-7836
Director, Corporate Communications	Fax:	(336) 424-7631
DULL, Stephen	Tel:	(336) 424-6000
Vice President, Strategy and Innovation	Fax:	(336) 424-7631
GRAHAM, Anita	Tel:	(336) 424-6000
Vice President, Global Human Resources	Fax:	(336) 424-7631
MEAGHER, Laura C.	Tel:	(336) 424-6000
Vice President, General Counsel and Secretary	Fax:	(336) 424-7631
RENDLE, Steve	Tel:	(336) 424-6000
President and Chief Operating Officer	Fax:	(336) 424-7631
ROE, Scott A.	Tel:	(336) 424-6000
Vice President and Chief Financial Officer	Fax:	(336) 424-7631
TERKELSEN, Franklin L.	Tel:	(336) 424-6000
Vice President, Business Development	Fax:	(336) 424-7631

VHA, Inc.

A nationwide network of community-owned health care systems and their physicians. Effective April 1, 2015, VHA, the national health care network of not-for-profit hospitals, and UHC, the alliance of the nation's leading academic medical centers, combined to form the largest member-owned health care company in the country. The combined organization includes Novation, the health care services company we already jointly own. The new name will be announced in January 2016.
www.vha.com
Annual Revenues: $681.00 million
Employees: 5,200
Industry/ies: Medicine/Health Care/Mental Health; Pharmaceutical Industry
Legislative Issues: HCR; MMM; TAX

President and Chief Executive Officer	Tel:	(972) 830-0000
NONOMAQUE, Curt	Fax:	(972) 830-0332

Main Headquarters

Mailing:	P.O. Box 140909	Tel:	(972) 830-0000
	Irving, TX 75014-0909	Fax:	(972) 830-0332
		TF:	(800) 750-4972

Washington Office

Mailing:	799 Ninth St. NW	Tel:	(202) 354-2640
	Suite 210	Fax:	(202) 354-2605
	Washington, DC 20001		

Political Action Committees

VHA, Inc. PAC
FEC ID: C00199497
Contact: Edward N. Goodman

901 New York Ave. NW	Tel:	(202) 721-8100
Suite 500 East	Fax:	(202) 721-8105
Washington, DC 20001		

Contributions to Candidates: $38,700 (2015-2016)
Democrats: $20,200; Republicans: $18,500

Corporate Foundations and Giving Programs

VHA Foundation

220 E. Las Colinas Blvd	Tel:	(972) 830-0122
Irving, TX 75039-5500	Fax:	(972) 830-0422

Public Affairs and Related Activities Personnel

At Headquarters

ALLEN, Pete	Tel:	(972) 830-0000
Executive Vice President, Sales and Marketing	Fax:	(972) 830-0332
BERRY, David	Tel:	(972) 830-0000
Senior Vice President and General Counsel	Fax:	(972) 830-0332
DOWNING, Scott	Tel:	(972) 830-0000
Executive Vice President and Chief Sales and Marketing Officer	Fax:	(972) 830-0332
DUNLEAVY, Christopher	Tel:	(972) 830-0000
Area Senior Vice President and Chief Financial Officer	Fax:	(972) 830-0332
JOBE, Byron	Tel:	(972) 830-0000
President, Strategic Growth, Marketing and Innovation	Fax:	(972) 830-0332
LEVY, Maxine	Tel:	(972) 830-0000
Manager, Public Relations	Fax:	(972) 830-0332
mlevy@vha.com		
PYRON, Kyle	Tel:	(972) 830-0000
Senior Vice President, Marketing and Communications	Fax:	(972) 830-0332
RENER, Anne	Tel:	(972) 830-0737
Senior Director, Corporate Communications	Fax:	(972) 830-0332
arener@vha.com		
RISK, Colleen	Tel:	(972) 830-0000
Executive Vice President, Research, Public Affairs and Human Resources	Fax:	(972) 830-0332
crisk@vha.com		

At Washington Office

GOODMAN, Edward N.	Tel:	(202) 354-2607
Vice President, Public Policy	Fax:	(202) 354-2605
KRILOW, Shoshana	Tel:	(202) 354-2640
Registered Federal Lobbyist	Fax:	(202) 354-2605
PERRIN, Cidette S.	Tel:	(202) 354-2608
Senior Director, Government Relations	Fax:	(202) 354-2605
cperrin@vha.com		
RIXEN, Steven	Tel:	(202) 354-2611
Strategic Policy and Communications Consultant	Fax:	(202) 354-2605
Registered Federal Lobbyist		

VHB Engineering Surveying and Landscape Architecture P.C.

Appera on website as Vanasse Hangen Brustlin, Inc. Provides multidisciplinary planning, design, engineering, and consulting.
www.vhb.com
Employees: 850
Legislative Issues: ENG

Chief Executive Officer	Tel:	(631) 234-3444
BRUSTLIN, Bob	Fax:	(631) 234-3477

Main Headquarters

Mailing:	100 Motor Pkwy.	Tel:	(631) 787-3400
	Suite 135	Fax:	(631) 813-2545
	Hauppauge, NY 11788		

Public Affairs and Related Activities Personnel

At Headquarters

BOZADJIAN, Becky	Tel:	(631) 787-3400
Vice President, Marketing	Fax:	(631) 813-2545
CARRAGHER, Michael J	Tel:	(631) 787-3400
President	Fax:	(631) 813-2545
CRANNELL, Cathy	Tel:	(631) 234-3444
Risk Administrator	Fax:	(631) 234-3477
ccrannell@vhb.com		
DUBINSKY, Robert M	Tel:	(631) 787-3400
Senior Vice President, Corporate Resources	Fax:	(631) 813-2545
GREGOIRE, Khristopher M	Tel:	(631) 787-3400
Vice President, General Counsel	Fax:	(631) 813-2545
JACKSON, John B	Tel:	(631) 787-3400
Executive Vice President, Chief Financial Officer	Fax:	(631) 813-2545
KOCUR, Keri	Tel:	(631) 787-3400
Senior Vice President, Human Resources	Fax:	(631) 813-2545
MANNING, David	Tel:	(631) 234-3444
Senior Vice President and Energy Practice Leader	Fax:	(631) 234-3477
Registered Federal Lobbyist		
ROACHE, William J	Tel:	(631) 787-3400
Executive Vice President, Chief Strategic Officer	Fax:	(631) 813-2545
WALSH, PE, Kevin	Tel:	(631) 234-3444
Managing Director	Fax:	(631) 234-3477
kevinwalsh@vhb.com		

Viacom Inc.

A global entertainment content companies, with brands in focused demographics, offering programming and content for television, motion pictures and digital platforms. Viacom's

brands include MTV Networks (MTV, VH1, Nickelodeon, Nick at Nite, Comedy Central, CMT:Country Music Television, Spike TV, TV Land, Logo and more than 120 networks around the world), BET Networks, Paramount Pictures, Paramount Home Entertainment, and DreamWorks.
www.viacom.com
Annual Revenues: $13.83 billion
Employees: 9,900
Ticker: NYSE: VIA
SIC: 2731; 4833; 4841; 7812
NAICS: 513210; 511130; 512110; 513120
Industry/ies: Communications; Media/Mass Communication
Legislative Issues: ADV; COM; CPT; HOM; IMM; TAX; TEC; TRD

Executive Chairman of the Board and Founder	Tel:	(212) 258-6000
REDSTONE, Sumner M.	Fax:	(212) 258-6464

sumner.redstone@viacom.com

President and Chief Executive Officer	Tel:	(212) 258-6000
DAUMAN, Philippe P.	Fax:	(212) 258-6464

philippe.dauman@viacom.com

Main Headquarters
Mailing:	1515 Broadway	Tel:	(212) 258-6000
	New York City, NY 10036	Fax:	(212) 258-6464
		TF:	(800) 516-4399

Washington Office
Mailing:	1275 Pennsylvania Ave. NW	Tel:	(202) 785-7300
	Suite 710	Fax:	(202) 785-6360
	Washington, DC 20005		

Political Action Committees
Viacom International Inc. PAC
FEC ID: C00167759
Contact: Dede Lea
1501 M St. NW, Suite 1100	Tel:	(202) 785-7300
Washington, DC 20005	Fax:	(202) 785-6360

Contributions to Candidates: $221,800 (2015-2016)
Democrats: $89,000; Republicans: $131,300; Other: $1,500

Corporate Foundations and Giving Programs
Viacom Inc. Contribution Program
1515 Broadway	Tel:	(212) 258-6000
New York City, NY 10036	Fax:	(212) 258-6464

Public Affairs and Related Activities Personnel
At Headquarters

BARGE, James	Tel:	(212) 258-6000
Controller	Fax:	(212) 258-6464
BOMBASSEI, James	Tel:	(212) 258-6377
Senior Vice President, Investor Relations	Fax:	(212) 258-6464

james.bombassei@viacom.com

DAVIS, Wade	Tel:	(212) 258-6000
Chief Financial Officer and Executive Vice President, Strategy and Corporate Development	Fax:	(212) 258-6464
DOOLEY, Thomas E.	Tel:	(212) 258-6000
Chief Operating Officer	Fax:	(212) 258-6464
FOLTA, Carl D.	Tel:	(212) 258-6352
Executive Vice President, Corporate Communications	Fax:	(212) 258-6464

carl.folta@viacom.com

FRICKLAS, Michael D.	Tel:	(212) 258-6000
Executive Vice President, General Counsel and Secretary	Fax:	(212) 258-6464
MILLS, Scott M.	Tel:	(212) 258-6000
Executive Vice President and Chief Administrative Officer	Fax:	(212) 258-6464

At Washington Office

DANSKY, Stacey	Tel:	(202) 785-7300
Vice President, Government Relations	Fax:	(202) 785-6360
Registered Federal Lobbyist		
KEITH, Murphy	Tel:	(202) 785-7300
Registered Federal Lobbyist	Fax:	(202) 785-6360
LEA, Dede	Tel:	(202) 785-0777
Executive Vice President, Government Affairs and PAC Treasurer	Fax:	(202) 785-6360
Registered Federal Lobbyist		
MURPHY, Keith	Tel:	(202) 785-7300
Registered Federal Lobbyist	Fax:	(202) 785-6360
MURPHY, Keith R.	Tel:	(202) 785-6347
Senior Vice President, Government Relations	Fax:	(202) 785-6360

keith.murphy@viacom.com
Registered Federal Lobbyist

SCHUEMANN, Hollyn Kidd	Tel:	(202) 785-6352
Vice President, Government Relations	Fax:	(202) 785-6360

hollyn.schuemann@viacom.com
Registered Federal Lobbyist

Viad Corporation

An event marketing and payment service company.

www.viad.com
Annual Revenues: $1.04 billion
Employees: 3,810
Ticker: NYSE: VVI
SIC: 7389
Industry/ies: Advertising And Marketing; Conventions/Trade Shows/Exhibits

Chairman of the Board	Tel:	(602) 207-1000
DOZER, Richard H.		

President and Chief Executive Officer	Tel:	(602) 207-1000
MOSTER, Steven W.		

Main Headquarters
Mailing:	1850 N. Central Ave.	Tel:	(602) 207-1000
	Suite 1900		
	Phoenix, AZ 85004-4565		

Political Action Committees
Viad Corp Good Government Project
FEC ID: C00097238
Contact: Deborah J. DePaoli
1850 N. Central Ave.
Suite 1900
Phoenix, AZ 85004-4565

Public Affairs and Related Activities Personnel
At Headquarters

DEPAOLI, Deborah J.	Tel:	(602) 207-1000
General Counsel, Secretary and PAC Treasurer		
DIAZ, Joe	Tel:	(602) 889-9660
Contact, Investor Relations		

diaz@lythampartners.com

INGERSOLL, Ellen M.	Tel:	(602) 207-1000
Chief Financial Officer		
KUCZYNSKI, Thomas M.	Tel:	(602) 207-1000
Chief Corporate Development and Strategy Officer		
LONG, Carrie	Tel:	(602) 207-2681
Executive Director, Finance and Investor Relations		

ViaGen Inc.

ViaGen was founded in January 2002 to provide commercial bovine, equine, and porcine gene banking, cloning, and genomics services.
www.viagen.com
Employees: 50
Industry/ies: Animals; Science; Scientific Research

President	Tel:	(512) 401-5900
RUSSELL, Blake	Fax:	(512) 401-5919

Main Headquarters
Mailing:	715 Discovery Blvd.	Tel:	(512) 401-5900
	Suite 140	Fax:	(512) 401-5919
	Cedar Park, TX 78613	TF:	(888) 884-2436

Public Affairs and Related Activities Personnel
At Headquarters

ASTON, Lauren	Tel:	(512) 986-7830
Office Manager and Contact, Accounting Services	Fax:	(512) 401-5919

lauren.aston@viagen.com

BROEK, Diane	Tel:	(512) 401-5900
Manager, Marketing	Fax:	(512) 401-5919
SCHMIDT, Scott	Tel:	(512) 401-5900
Chief Financial Officer	Fax:	(512) 401-5919

Viasat, Inc.

High-tech co. designs and manufactures communications and networking equipment.
www.viasat.com
Annual Revenues: $1.42 billion
Employees: 3,800
Ticker: NasdaqGS: VSAT
SIC: 3663
Industry/ies: Aerospace/Aviation; Transportation
Legislative Issues: DEF; TEC

Chairman of the Board and Chief Executive Officer	Tel:	(760) 476-2200
DANKBERG, Mark D.	Fax:	(760) 929-3941

Main Headquarters
Mailing:	6155 El Camino Real	Tel:	(760) 476-2200
	Carlsbad, CA 92009	Fax:	(760) 929-3941

Washington Office
Mailing:	901 K St. NW, 4th Floor	
	Washington, DC 20001	

Public Affairs and Related Activities Personnel
At Headquarters

BALDRIDGE, Richard A.	Tel:	(760) 476-2200
President and Chief Operating Officer	Fax:	(760) 929-3941

DIRKS, Bruce   Tel: (760) 476-2200
Senior Vice President, Treasury and Corporate Development   Fax: (760) 929-3941

DUFFY, Shawn   Tel: (760) 476-2200
Senior Vice President, Chief Financial Officer   Fax: (760) 929-3941

ESTES, H. Stephen   Tel: (760) 476-2200
Vice President, General Manager, Enterprise Services   Fax: (760) 929-3941

JOHANSON, Karen   Tel: (760) 476-2200
Paralegal   Fax: (760) 929-3941

LIPPERT, Keven K.   Tel: (760) 476-2200
Executive Vice President, General Counsel and Secretary   Fax: (760) 929-3941

PETERMAN, Ken   Tel: (760) 476-2200
Senior Vice President, Government Systems   Fax: (760) 929-3941

RAPELYEA, Michael   Tel: (760) 476-2200
Director, Government Affairs   Fax: (760) 929-3941

At Other Offices

GONZALEZ, John A.   Tel: (703) 250-8602
Director, Congressional Affairs
6700 Tempo Ln.
Fairfax, VA 22039
john.gonzalez@viasat.com

Viavi Solutions

Manufactures, designs and markets electrical machinery and components.
www.jdsu.com
Annual Revenues: $1.73 billion
Employees: 5,100
Ticker: NASDAQ: JDSU
SIC: 3674; 3699; 3229; 3357; 3663
NAICS: 334413; 335999; 327212; 335921
Industry/ies: Electricity & Electronics; Electronics; Energy/Electricity;
Machinery/Equipment

Chairman of the Board   Tel: (408) 546-5000
BELLUZZO, Richard E.   Fax: (408) 546-4300

President and Chief Executive Officer   Tel: (408) 546-5000
WAECHTER, Thomas   Fax: (408) 546-4300

Main Headquarters
Mailing: 430 N. McCarthy Blvd.   Tel: (408) 546-5000
Milpitas, CA 95035   Fax: (408) 546-4300
   TF: (800) 498-5378

Corporate Foundations and Giving Programs

JDS Uniphase Corporation Contributions Program
430 N. McCarthy Blvd.
Milpitas, CA 95035

Public Affairs and Related Activities Personnel

At Headquarters

BILODEAU , Noel   Tel: (408) 546-4567
Director, Corporate Communications   Fax: (408) 546-4300
noel.bilodeau@jdsu.com

HOOPER, Brett   Tel: (408) 546-5000
Senior Vice President, Human Resources   Fax: (408) 546-4300

JACKSON, Rex   Tel: (408) 546-5000
Executive Vice President and Chief Financial Officer   Fax: (408) 546-4300

KAPLAN, Martin A.   Tel: (408) 546-5000
Governance Committee Chair   Fax: (408) 954-0760

LOWE, Alan   Tel: (408) 546-5000
Contact, Communications and Commercial Optical Products   Fax: (408) 546-4300
Business Segment

MCNAB, Paul   Tel: (408) 546-5000
Executive Vice President, Chief Marketing and Strategy   Fax: (408) 546-4300
Officer

MONROE, Jim   Tel: (240) 404-1922
Vice President, Corporate Marketing and Communications   Fax: (408) 546-4300
jim.monroe@jdsu.com

ONG, Bill   Tel: (408) 546-4521
Senior Director, Finance and Investor Relations Contact   Fax: (408) 546-4300
bill.ong@jdsu.com

TYLOR, Bernie   Tel: (240) 404-1913
Senior Manager, Public Relations   Fax: (408) 546-4300
bernie.tylor@jdsu.com

VILF Consultants, LLC

A government affairs consulting firm.
Industry/ies: Banking/Finance/Investments

Main Headquarters
Mailing: 6501 Red Hook Plaza   Tel: (203) 637-3839
Suite 201
St. Thomas, VI 00802

Public Affairs and Related Activities Personnel

At Headquarters

FREYER, Carl   Tel: (203) 637-3839
Registered Federal Lobbyist

GATES, Richard   Tel: (203) 637-3839
Director
rgates7@gmail.com
Registered Federal Lobbyist

Virent Energy Systems, Inc.

Engages in the development and commercialization of biorefinery solutions for the production of fungible biofuels. It converts soluble biomass-derived sugars into products molecularly identical to those made with petroleum, including gasoline, diesel, jet fuel, and chemicals used for plastics and fibers.
www.virent.com
Employees: 80
Industry/ies: Energy/Electricity

Chairman, President and Chief Executive Officer   Tel: (608) 663-0228
EDWARDS, Lee   Fax: (608) 663-1630

Main Headquarters
Mailing: 3571 Anderson St.   Tel: (608) 663-0228
Madison, WI 53704   Fax: (608) 663-1630

Public Affairs and Related Activities Personnel

At Headquarters

GIESEN, Cari   Tel: (608) 237-8615
Administrative Manager   Fax: (608) 663-1630

HITCHCOCK, David   Tel: (608) 237-8615
Vice President, Government Relations   Fax: (608) 663-1630

KETTNER , David   Tel: (608) 663-0228
Vice President, Legal Affairs   Fax: (608) 663-1630

LIOTTA, Frank   Tel: (608) 663-0228
Director, Business Development   Fax: (608) 663-1630

MOORE , Jeff   Tel: (608) 663-0228
Chief Operating Officer   Fax: (608) 663-1630

MOYNIHAN, Lori   Tel: (608) 663-0228
Director, Human Resources   Fax: (608) 663-1630

NORRIS, Shelly   Tel: (608) 210-3365
Executive Administrative Specialist   Fax: (608) 663-1630
shelly_norris@virent.com

SMITH, Ned   Tel: (608) 663-0228
   Fax: (608) 663-1630

WHITE, Jeff   Tel: (608) 663-0228
Chief Financial Officer   Fax: (608) 663-1630

Virginia Tech Foundation, Inc.

Foundation
Industry/ies: Communications

Chief Executive Officer and secretary-treasurer   Tel: (540) 231-2861
DOOLEY, John E.

Main Headquarters
Mailing: 902 Prices Fork Rd.   Tel: (540) 231-2861
Suite 4500
Blacksburg, VA 24061

Public Affairs and Related Activities Personnel

At Headquarters

MITCHELL, Terri   Tel: (540) 231-2861
Assistant Vice President, Administration and Controller

CUSIMANO, John   Tel: (540) 231-2861
Assistant Vice President, Finance and University Treasurer

SULLIVAN, Kevin   Tel: (540) 231-2861
Assistant Vice President, Administration and General Counsel

Viropharma Incorporated

Biopharmaceutical company.
www.viropharma.com
Annual Revenues: $399.28 million
Employees: 410
Ticker: NASDAQ: VPHM
SIC: 2834
Industry/ies: Pharmaceutical Industry

President, Chief Executive Officer and Chairman of the Board   Tel: (610) 458-7300
MILANO , Vincent J.   Fax: (610) 458-7380

Main Headquarters
Mailing: 730 Stockton Dr.   Tel: (610) 458-7300
Exton, PA 19341   Fax: (610) 458-7380
   TF: (888) 651-0201

Political Action Committees
Viropharma Incorporated PAC (VIRCPAC)
FEC ID: C00542225
Contact: John Greissing

730 Stockton Dr.
Exton, PA 19341

Public Affairs and Related Activities Personnel

At Headquarters

BROADBELT, Kristina	Tel:	(610) 321-2358
Contact, Public Relations and Advocacy	Fax:	(610) 458-7380
DOYLE, Thomas F.	Tel:	(610) 458-7300
Vice President, Strategic Initiatives	Fax:	(610) 458-7380
FLETCHER, Robert C.	Tel:	(610) 458-7300
Vice President, Business Development and Project Management	Fax:	(610) 458-7380
PIETRUSKO , Robert G.	Tel:	(610) 458-7300
Vice President, Global Regulatory Affairs and Quality	Fax:	(610) 458-7380
ROWLAND, Jr., Charles A.	Tel:	(610) 458-7300
Vice President, Chief Financial Officer	Fax:	(610) 458-7380
WOLF , J. Peter	Tel:	(610) 458-7300
Vice President, General Counsel and Secretary	Fax:	(610) 458-7380

VISA U.S.A., Inc.

VISA U.S.A., Inc.is a credit and debit card payment network.
www.usa.visa.com
Annual Revenues: $13.18 billion
Employees: 9,500
Ticker: NYSE: V
SIC: 7389
Industry/ies: Banking/Finance/Investments
Legislative Issues: BAN; BUD; CPT; FIN; HCR; HOM; LAW; SCI; TAX; TRD

Independent Chair, Former Vice Chairman and Chief Financial Officer	Tel:	(650) 432-3200
	Fax:	(650) 432-3631
MATSCHULLAT, Robert W.		

Chief Executive Officer	Tel:	(650) 432-3200
SCHARF, Charles W.	Fax:	(650) 432-3631

Main Headquarters

Mailing:	P.O. Box 8999	Tel:	(415) 932-2100
	San Francisco, CA 94128-8999	TF:	(800) 847-2911

Washington Office

Mailing:	325 Seventh St. NW	Tel:	(202) 419-4100
	Suite 800	Fax:	(202) 862-5498
	Washington, DC 20004		

Corporate Foundations and Giving Programs

VISA U.S.A. Contribution Program
P.O. Box 8999
San Francisco, CA 94128-8999

Public Affairs and Related Activities Personnel

At Washington Office

BRADSHAW, Pace	Tel:	(202) 419-4100
Deputy Head, U.S. Government Relations	Fax:	(202) 862-5498
Registered Federal Lobbyist		
DUMONT MERCHAK, Sarah	Tel:	(202) 419-4121
Vice President, Global Government Relations and Lobbyist	Fax:	(650) 554-4826
sdumont@visa.com		
FOX, Todd	Tel:	(202) 419-4100
Senior Director, Global Government Relations and Federal Lobbyist	Fax:	(202) 862-5498
HOLSHOUSER, Carl	Tel:	(202) 419-4100
Head, Government Relations	Fax:	(202) 862-5498
Registered Federal Lobbyist		
KENYON, Nicole	Tel:	(202) 419-4100
Senior Director	Fax:	(202) 862-5498
KUTLER, Alison L.	Tel:	(202) 419-4100
Head of Government Policy, Americas	Fax:	(202) 862-5498
SLATER, Amanda	Tel:	(202) 419-4100
Senior Director, Government Relations	Fax:	(202) 862-5498
Registered Federal Lobbyist		
SMITH, W. Lamar	Tel:	(202) 296-9230
Senior Vice President, Government Relations	Fax:	(202) 862-5498
Registered Federal Lobbyist		
THOMSON, III, III, Robert B.	Tel:	(202) 419-4100
Head, U.S. Government Relations	Fax:	(202) 862-5498
Registered Federal Lobbyist		

At Other Offices

CARSKY, John	Tel:	(650) 432-3200
Global Head, Investor Relations	Fax:	(650) 432-3631
900 Metro Center Blvd.		
Foster City, CA 94404-2172		
HYDE-DUNN, Victoria	Tel:	(650) 432-7644
Director, Investor Relations	Fax:	(650) 432-3631
900 Metro Center Blvd.		

Foster City, CA 94404-2172
ir@visa.com

JAQUES, Carleigh	Tel:	(650) 432-3200
Senior Vice President, Global Head, Corporate Strategy, Corporate Development and M&A	Fax:	(650) 432-3631
900 Metro Center Blvd.		
Foster City, CA 94404-2172		
MCCARTHY, Jim	Tel:	(650) 432-3200
Global Head, Innovation & Strategic Partnerships	Fax:	(650) 432-3631
900 Metro Center Blvd.		
Foster City, CA 94404-2172		
MCINERNEY, Ryan	Tel:	(650) 432-3200
President	Fax:	(650) 432-3631
900 Metro Center Blvd.		
Foster City, CA 94404-2172		
PIRES, Amanda	Tel:	(650) 445-8169
Vice President, Global Corporate Communications	Fax:	(650) 432-3631
900 Metro Center Blvd.		
Foster City, CA 94404-2172		
apires@visa.com		
PRABHU, Vasant M.	Tel:	(650) 432-3200
Executive Vice President and Chief Financial Officer	Fax:	(650) 432-3631
900 Metro Center Blvd.		
Foster City, CA 94404-2172		
ROSS, Michael	Tel:	(650) 432-3200
Global Head, Human Resources	Fax:	(650) 432-3631
900 Metro Center Blvd.		
Foster City, CA 94404-2172		
TULLIER , Kelly Mahon	Tel:	(650) 432-3200
Executive Vice President, General Counsel and Corporate Secretary	Fax:	(650) 432-3631
900 Metro Center Blvd.		
Foster City, CA 94404-2172		

Vishay Intertechnologies, Inc.

A global manufacturer and supplier of discrete semiconductors and passive components.
www.vishay.com
Annual Revenues: $2.28 billion
Employees: 22,400
Ticker: NYSE: VSH
SIC: 3670
Industry/ies: Electricity & Electronics; Electronics; Energy/Electricity

Executive Chairman of the Board and Chief Business Development Officer	Tel:	(610) 644-1300
	Fax:	(610) 296-0657
ZANDMAN, Marc		
President and Chief Executive Officer	Tel:	(610) 644-1300
PAUL, Dr. Gerald	Fax:	(610) 296-0657

Main Headquarters

Mailing:	63 Lancaster Ave.	Tel:	(610) 644-1300
	Malvern, PA 19355-2143	Fax:	(610) 889-9349

Public Affairs and Related Activities Personnel

At Headquarters

GEBHARDT, Werner	Tel:	(610) 644-1300
Executive Vice President, Global Human Resources	Fax:	(610) 889-9349
HENRICI, Peter G.	Tel:	(610) 644-1300
Senior Vice President, Corporate Communications and Corporate Secretary and Investor Relations Contact	Fax:	(610) 296-0657
LIPCAMAN, Lori	Tel:	(610) 644-1300
Executive Vice President and Chief Financial Officer	Fax:	(610) 296-0657
MCCONNELL , David E.	Tel:	(610) 644-1300
Vice President, Corporate Treasurer and Risk Management	Fax:	(610) 889-9349
O'SULLIVAN, Michael	Tel:	(610) 644-1300
Senior Vice President and Corporate General Counsel	Fax:	(610) 889-9349
POST, Andrew	Tel:	(610) 251-5287
Manager, Global Communications	Fax:	(610) 889-9349
TATE, Brenda R.	Tel:	(610) 644-1300
Contact, Corporate Investor Relations	Fax:	(610) 889-9349
Brenda.Tate@vishay.com		
VALLETTA, David	Tel:	(610) 644-1300
Executive Vice President, Worldwide Sales	Fax:	(610) 889-9349
WUNDERLICH, Dieter	Tel:	(610) 644-1300
Executive Vice President and Chief Operating Officer	Fax:	(610) 296-0657

Vision Service Plan

Offers affordable, quality eye care plans.
www.vsp.com
Industry/ies: Insurance Industry; Medicine/Health Care/Mental Health
Legislative Issues: HCR; TAX

Chairman of the Board	Tel:	(916) 851-5000
THOMAS, Stuart	Fax:	(916) 851-4858

| **President and Chief Executive Officer** | Tel: | (916) 851-5000 |
| LYNCH, Rob | Fax: | (916) 851-4858 |

| **President** | Tel: | (916) 851-5000 |
| MCGRANN, Jim | Fax: | (916) 851-4858 |

Main Headquarters

Mailing:	3333 Quality Dr.	Tel:	(916) 851-5000
	Rancho Cordova, CA 95670	Fax:	(916) 851-4858
		TF:	(888) 867-8867

Public Affairs and Related Activities Personnel

At Headquarters

| BALL , Donald J. | Tel: | (916) 851-5000 |
| *Chief Financial Officer* | Fax: | (916) 851-4858 |

MCNEIL, Pat	Tel:	(916) 851-4287
Corporate Communications Director	Fax:	(916) 851-4858
PatrMc@vsp.com		

SWAMIDOSS, Cecil	Tel:	(202) 239-3788
Director, Government Affairs & Senior Counsel	Fax:	(916) 851-4858
Registered Federal Lobbyist		

VITAS Healthcare Corporation

The company tends to terminally ill patients in their homes, its own inpatient hospice facilities, and nursing homes and hospitals.
www.vitas.com
Employees: 9,000
SIC: 8000
Industry/ies: Medicine/Health Care/Mental Health
Legislative Issues: HCR

| **Chairman of the Board** | Tel: | (305) 374-4143 |
| MCNAMARA, Kevin | Fax: | (305) 350-6797 |

Chief Executive Officer	Tel:	(305) 374-4143
O'TOOLE, Timothy	Fax:	(305) 350-6797
tim.otoole@vitas.com		

Main Headquarters

Mailing:	201 S. Biscayne Blvd.	Tel:	(305) 374-4143
	Suite 400	Fax:	(305) 350-6797
	Miami, FL 33131	TF:	(866) 418-4827

Washington Office

Mailing:	3803 Porter St. NW	Tel:	(202) 248-9669
	Suite 302	Fax:	(202) 638-2457
	Washington, DC 20016		

Corporate Foundations and Giving Programs

VITAS Hospice Charitable Fund
Contact: Jim Fife

5430 NW 33rd Ave.	Tel:	(954) 777-2447
Suite 106	Fax:	(954) 777-2447
Ft Lauderdale, FL 33309		

Public Affairs and Related Activities Personnel

At Headquarters

| DALLOB, Naomi C. | Tel: | (305) 374-4143 |
| *Executive Vice President and General Counsel* | Fax: | (305) 350-6797 |

FIFE, Jim	Tel:	(305) 374-4143
President	Fax:	(305) 350-6797
richard@vitascharityfund.org		

GADDY, II, Donald W.	Tel:	(305) 374-4143
Senior Vice President, Market Development and Sales	Fax:	(305) 350-6797
donald.gaddy@vitas.com		

HART, Vicki	Tel:	(305) 374-4143
Contact, Government Relations	Fax:	(305) 350-6797
Registered Federal Lobbyist		

| LANDMEIER, Drew | Tel: | (305) 374-4143 |
| *Senior Vice President and Chief Marketing Officer* | Fax: | (305) 350-6797 |

| MILLER, Bob | Tel: | (305) 374-4143 |
| *Senior Vice President, Operations* | Fax: | (305) 350-6797 |

MISTRY, Kalpana	Tel:	(305) 374-4143
Chief Administrative Officer and Executive Vice President	Fax:	(305) 350-6797
kal.mistry@vitas.com		

SARGENT, Mary Jane	Tel:	(305) 374-4143
Contact, Government Relations	Fax:	(305) 350-6797
Registered Federal Lobbyist		

| TRACEY, Bert | Tel: | (305) 374-4143 |
| *Senior Vice President and Chief Accounting Officer* | Fax: | (305) 350-6797 |

| WESTER, David | Tel: | (305) 374-4143 |
| *President and Chief Financial Officer* | Fax: | (305) 350-6797 |

| WESTFALL, Nick | Tel: | (305) 374-4143 |
| *Chief Operating Officer and Executive Vice President* | Fax: | (305) 350-6797 |

At Washington Office

| RAMTHUN, Sue | Tel: | (202) 248-9669 |
| *Federal Lobbyist* | Fax: | (202) 638-2457 |

Registered Federal Lobbyist

Volcanic Repeating Arms Company
See listing on page 726 under Smith and Wesson Holding Company

Volkswagen Group of America
The company sells Volkswagen and AUDI cars through about 800 dealerships in the US. Volkswagen Group of America also handles other VW brands, including Bentley, Bugatti, and Lamborghini, in North America. In addition, it offers leasing and financing through its subsidiary VW Credit (VCI).
www.volkswagengroupamerica.com
Annual Revenues: $17.92 billion
Employees: 2,000
SIC: 6189
Industry/ies: Automotive Industry; Transportation
Legislative Issues: ENV; TRA; TRD

| **President and Chief Executive Officer** | Tel: | (248) 754-5000 |
| HORN, Michael | Fax: | (703) 364-7076 |

Main Headquarters

| Mailing: | 2200 Ferdinand Porsche Dr. | Tel: | (248) 754-5000 |
| | Herndon, VA 20171 | Fax: | (703) 364-7076 |

Corporate Foundations and Giving Programs

Volkswagen Group of America Contribution Program

| 2200 Ferdinand Porsche Dr. | Tel: | (703) 364-7000 |
| Herndon, VA 20171 | | |

Public Affairs and Related Activities Personnel

At Headquarters

| GEORGES, Christophe | Tel: | (248) 754-5000 |
| *Chief Operating Officer* | Fax: | (703) 364-7076 |

KREBS, Carsten	Tel:	(703) 364-7165
Director, Corporate Communications	Fax:	(703) 364-7076
carsten.krebs@vw.com		

SCHNEIDER, Anna-Maria	Tel:	(703) 364-7000
Vice President, Industry-Government Relations	Fax:	(703) 364-7076
Registered Federal Lobbyist		

STERTZ, Bradley	Tel:	(703) 364-7440
Manager, Corporate Communications	Fax:	(703) 364-7076
brad.stertz@audi.com		

At Other Offices

SCHERELIS, Guenther	Tel:	(423) 582-5415
General Manager, Communications		
8001 Volkswagen Dr.		
Chattanooga, TN 37416		
guenther.scherelis@vw.com		

WILSON, Scott	Tel:	(423) 582-5416
Head, Communications		
8001 Volkswagen Dr.		
Chattanooga, TN 37416		
scott.wilson@vw.com		

Volvo Car Corporation

Automobile Manufacturer.
www.volvocars.com
Industry/ies: Automotive Industry; Transportation
Legislative Issues: AUT

Main Headquarters

Mailing:	One Volvo Dr.	Tel:	(800) 458-1552
	P.O. Box 914	TF:	(800) 458-1552
	Rockleigh, NJ 07647		

Washington Office

Mailing:	2900 K St. NW		
	Suite 502		
	Washington, DC 20007		

Public Affairs and Related Activities Personnel

At Headquarters

| SHAW, Dean | Tel: | (800) 458-1552 |
| *Vice President, Corporate Communications* | | |

YEHL, Katherine	Tel:	(800) 458-1552
Director, Government Affairs		
Registered Federal Lobbyist		

Volvo Group North America, Inc.

Volvo Group North America, Inc., based in Greensboro, North Carolina, is the U.S. subsidiary of Volvo AB, headquartered in Gothenburg, Sweden. Operates in the transportation and equipment industries - trucks, buses, construction equipment, marine and industrial power, and aerospace engines and components.
www.volvogroup.com/group/global/en-gb/volvo
Annual Revenues: $383.20 million
Employees: 15,000
Industry/ies: Automotive Industry; Transportation

Legislative Issues: BUD; ENV; TAX; TRA; TRD

President and Chief Executive Officer
PERSSON, Olof

Tel:	(336) 393-2000
Fax:	(336) 393-2277

Main Headquarters
Mailing: 7900 National Service Rd.
P.O. Box 26115
Greensboro, NC 27402-6115

Tel:	(336) 393-2000
Fax:	(336) 393-2277

Washington Office
Mailing: 2900 K St. NW
South Building, Suite 401
Washington, DC 20007

Tel: (202) 536-1553

Corporate Foundations and Giving Programs

Volvo Group North America Contributions Program
7900 National Service Rd.
P.O. Box 26115
Greensboro, NC 27402-6115

Tel:	(336) 393-2000
Fax:	(336) 393-2277

Public Affairs and Related Activities Personnel

At Headquarters

CRAWFORD, Robin
Executive Director, Corporate Affairs
robin.crawford@volvo.com

Tel:	(336) 393-2393
Fax:	(336) 393-2900

HARTWELL, John
Vice President, Investor Relations
john.hartwell@volvo.com

Tel:	(212) 418-7432
Fax:	(336) 393-2277

MIES, John
Vice President, Communications
john.mies@volvo.com
Registered Federal Lobbyist

Tel:	(336) 393-4300
Fax:	(336) 393-2277

At Washington Office

BOBEK, Kelly R.
Director, Government Relations
Registered Federal Lobbyist

Tel: (202) 536-1553

FENTON, Dawn
Director, Federal Government Relations

Tel: (202) 536-1553

KLEIN, Kevin

Tel: (202) 536-1553

MICELI, John
Registered Federal Lobbyist

Tel: (202) 536-1553

MILLER, Jonathan
Vice President, Government Relations
jonathan.miller@volvo.com
Registered Federal Lobbyist

Tel: (202) 536-1555

YEHL, Katherine
Director, Government Affairs, North America
kyehl@volvocars.com
Registered Federal Lobbyist

Tel: (202) 536-1553

Volvo Technology of America

Suppliers of commercial transport.
www.volvo.com
Employees: 15,000
Industry/ies: Automotive Industry; Transportation

Chairman of the Board
SVANBERG, Carl-Henric

Tel: (336) 393-2647

President and Chief Executive Officer
PERSSON, Olof

Tel: (336) 393-2647

Main Headquarters
Mailing: 7825 National Service Rd.
Greensboro, NC 27409

Tel:	(336) 393-2647
TF:	(877) 865-8623

Washington Office
Mailing: 2900 K St. NW
House of Sweden
Washington, DC 20007

Public Affairs and Related Activities Personnel

At Headquarters

CARLANDER, Magnus
Executive Vice President, Corporate Process and Information Technology

Tel: (336) 393-2647

DEEDY, Conal
Manager, Product Marketing
conal.deedy@volvo.com

Tel: (336) 393-2647

FALK, Karin
Executive Vice President, Corporate Strategy

Tel: (336) 393-2647

FRÄNDBERG, Sofia
Executive Vice President, Corporate Legal and Compliance and General Counsel

Tel: (336) 393-2647

GUSTAVSSON, Niklas
Executive Vice President, Public and Environmental Affairs

Tel: (336) 393-2647

HARTWELL, John

Tel: (201) 252-8844

Contact, Investor Relations

KARLSSON, Håkan
Executive Vice President, Business

Tel: (336) 393-2647

MIES, John
Vice President, Communications
johnmies@volvo.com

Tel: (336) 393-4300

OSBERG, Anders
Chief Financial Officer and Executive Vice President, Corporate Finance and Control

Tel: (336) 393-2647

RENARD, Kerstin
Executive Vice President, Corporate Human Resources

Tel: (336) 393-2647

WEISSBURG, Martin
Executive Vice President, Financial Services

Tel: (336) 393-2647

WIKFORSS, Mårten
Executive Vice President, Corporate Communication

Tel: (336) 393-2647

Vonage Holdings Corporation

Provides communications services that connect individuals through cloud-connected devices worldwide.
www.vonage.com
Annual Revenues: $902.17 million
Employees: 1,752
Ticker: NYSE: VG
Industry/ies: Communications; Computer/Technology; Telecommunications/Internet/Cable
Legislative Issues: TEC

Chairman of the Board and Director
CITRON, Jeffrey Adam

Tel:	(848) 248-1809
Fax:	(732) 834-0189

Chief Executive Officer
MASAREK, Alan

Tel:	(732) 528-2600
Fax:	(732) 834-0189

Main Headquarters
Mailing: 23 Main St.
Holmdel, NJ 07733

Tel:	(732) 528-2600
Fax:	(732) 834-0189

Public Affairs and Related Activities Personnel

At Headquarters

GILVAR, Ted
Chief Marketing Officer

Tel:	(732) 528-2600
Fax:	(732) 834-0189

PEARSON, David
Chief Financial Officer and Treasurer

Tel:	(848) 248-1809
Fax:	(732) 834-0189

QUACKENBUSH, Sue
Chief Human Resources Officer

Tel:	(732) 528-2600
Fax:	(732) 834-0189

REDLING, Joe
Chief Operating Officer

Tel:	(732) 528-2600
Fax:	(732) 834-0189

ROGERS, Kurt
Chief Legal Officer

Tel:	(848) 248-1809
Fax:	(732) 834-0189

Voya

See listing on page 840 under Voya Financial, Inc.

Voya Financial, Inc.

A financial services provider. Subsidiaries include ING Equitable Life and ING Life of Georgia. Acquired ReliaStar Financial Corp., AETNA Financial Services and AETNA Internat'l in 2000. On path to rebrand to become "Voya Financial" starting in 2014.
www.voya.com
Annual Revenues: $11.03 billion
Employees: 6,500
Ticker: NYSE: VOYA
SIC: 6311
Industry/ies: Insurance Industry
Legislative Issues: FIN; INS; RET; TAX

Chairman of the Board and Chief Executive Officer
MARTIN, Rodney O.

Tel: (212) 309-8200

Main Headquarters
Mailing: 230 Park Ave.
New York City, NY 10169

Tel: (212) 309-8200

Washington Office
Mailing: 901 K St. NW
Suite 220
Washington, DC 20001

Political Action Committees
Voya Financial, Inc., PAC (Voya Financial PAC)
FEC ID: C00184028
Contact: Elizabeth Byrne
230 Park Ave.
Legal P-Three
New York City, NY 10169

Contributions to Candidates: $4,270,516 (2015-2016)
Democrats: $71,000; Republicans: $87,500; Other: $4,112,016

Corporate Foundations and Giving Programs

Voya Foundation
Contact: Amy Springsteel
230 Park Ave.
New York City, NY 10169

Public Affairs and Related Activities Personnel

At Headquarters

ARITA, CFA, Darin	Tel:	(212) 309-8999
Senior Vice President, Investor Relations		
BYRNE, Elizabeth	Tel:	(212) 309-8200
PAC Treasurer		
elizabeth.byrne@us.ing.com		
HEALY, Bridget M.	Tel:	(212) 309-8200
Chief Legal Officer		
SILVA, Kevin D.	Tel:	(212) 309-8200
Executive Vice President and Chief Human Resources Officer		
SPRINGSTEEL, Amy	Tel:	(212) 309-8200
Director, Corporate Responsibility		
STEENBERGEN, Ewout	Tel:	(212) 309-8200
Executive Vice President and Chief Financial Officer		

At Washington Office

CASSIDY, Sean M.	Tel:	(202) 383-1771
Vice President, Federal Government Affairs		
sean.cassidy@voya.com		
Registered Federal Lobbyist		

At Other Offices

KAPLAN, Robert	Tel:	(770) 980-5100
Vice President and National Training Consultant	Fax:	(770) 850-7650
5780 Powers Ferry Rd. NW, Legal P-3		
Atlanta, GA 30327		
robert.kaplan@us.ing.com		
LINS, Gerry	Tel:	(770) 980-5100
General Counsel	Fax:	(770) 850-7650
5780 Powers Ferry Rd. NW, Legal P-3		
Atlanta, GA 30327		

VT iDirect

See listing on page 423 under iDirect Technologies, Inc.

Vulcan Materials Company

A producer of construction aggregates, asphalt mix, concrete and cement.
www.vulcanmaterials.com
Annual Revenues: $3.55 billion
Employees: 7,187
Ticker: NYSE: VMC
SIC: 1400
Industry/ies: Chemicals & Chemical Industry; Construction/Construction Materials
Legislative Issues: FIN; ROD; TRA

Chairman of the Board, President and Chief Executive Officer	Tel:	(205) 298-3000
HILL, J. Thomas	Fax:	(205) 298-2960

Main Headquarters

Mailing:	1200 Urban Center Dr.	Tel:	(205) 298-3000
	P.O. Box 385014	Fax:	(205) 298-2960
	Birmingham, AL 35242-5014		

Political Action Committees

Vulcan Materials Company PAC
FEC ID: C00116020
Contact: Carol Maxwell

P.O. BOX 385014	Tel:	(205) 298-3000
Birmingham, AL 35238	Fax:	(205) 298-3000

Contributions to Candidates: $40,200 (2015-2016)
Democrats: $7,250; Republicans: $32,950

Principal Recipients

HOUSE
ADERHOLT, ROBERT BROWN (REP-AL)

Corporate Foundations and Giving Programs

Vulcan Materials Company Foundation
Contact: David Donaldson

1200 Urban Center Dr.	Tel:	(205) 298-3222
P.O. Box 385014	Fax:	(205) 298-2960
Birmingham, AL 35242-5014		

Public Affairs and Related Activities Personnel

At Headquarters

DONALDSON, David	Tel:	(205) 298-3220
Media Contact, Vice President, Governmental and	Fax:	(205) 298-2960
Community Relations		
HOUSTON, J. Wayne	Tel:	(205) 298-3000
Senior Vice President, Human Resources	Fax:	(205) 298-2960
MAXWELL, Carol	Tel:	(205) 298-3000

PAC Contact, Secretary and Treasurer, Foundation	Fax:	(205) 298-2960
giving@vmcmail.com		
MCPHERSON, John R.	Tel:	(205) 298-3000
Executive Vice President, Chief Financial and Strategy Officer	Fax:	(205) 298-2960
MILLS, Michael R.	Tel:	(205) 298-3000
Chief Administrative Officer	Fax:	(205) 298-2960
PERKINS, Jr., Jerry F.	Tel:	(205) 298-3000
General Counsel and Secretary	Fax:	(205) 298-2960
WARREN, Mark	Tel:	(205) 298-3220
Director, Investor Relations and Media Contact	Fax:	(205) 298-2960

W.H. Brady Company

See listing on page 141 under Brady Corporation

Wackenhut Corporation

See listing on page 346 under G4S Secure Solutions (USA) Inc.

Wakefern Food Corporation

A supermarket cooperative.
wakefern.shoprite.com
Industry/ies: Food And Beverage Industry
Legislative Issues: FOO

Chairman of the Board and Chief Executive Officer	Tel:	(908) 527-3300
COLALILLO, Joseph	Fax:	(908) 527-3397

Main Headquarters

Mailing:	5000 Riverside Dr.	Tel:	(908) 527-3300
	Keasbey, NJ 08832	Fax:	(908) 527-3397

Political Action Committees

Wakefern Food Corporation PAC
FEC ID: C00489005
Contact: Douglas Wille
33 Northfield Ave.
Edison, 8818

Contributions to Candidates: $98,500 (2015-2016)
Democrats: $31,500; Republicans: $67,000

Corporate Foundations and Giving Programs

Wakefern Contributions Program
5000 Riverside Dr.
Keasbey, NJ 08832

Public Affairs and Related Activities Personnel

At Headquarters

BERGER, Allison	Tel:	(908) 527-3300
General Counsel and Chief Compliance Officer	Fax:	(908) 527-3397
BURKE, Ann Marie	Tel:	(908) 527-3300
Vice President, Human Resources	Fax:	(908) 527-3397
CROMBIE , Bill	Tel:	(908) 527-3300
Vice President, Strategic Development and Member Relations	Fax:	(908) 527-3397
MELETA , Karen	Tel:	(908) 527-3300
Vice President, Consumer and Corporate Communications	Fax:	(908) 527-3397
REAGAN , Jeff	Tel:	(908) 527-3300
Senior Vice President, Marketing	Fax:	(908) 527-3397

At Other Offices

MOTTESE, Lorelei	Tel:	(732) 906-5153
Director, Government Relations		
P.O. Box 506, 600 York St.		
Elizabeth, NJ 07207		
lorelei.mottese@wakefern.com		
Registered Federal Lobbyist		
WILLE, Douglas		
PAC Contact and Chief Financial Officer		
33 Northfield Ave.		
Edison, NJ 08818		

Walgreen Company

A member of the Public Affairs Council. A retail drug store chain.
www.walgreens.com
Annual Revenues: $74.19 billion
Employees: 173,000
Ticker: NYSE: WAG
SIC: 5912; 4225; 5099; 5812
Industry/ies: Pharmaceutical Industry; Retail/Wholesale
Legislative Issues: ALC; HCR; LBR; PHA; TAX; VET

Chairman of the Board	Tel:	(847) 914-2500
SKINNER , James A.	Fax:	(847) 914-2804
Executive Vice Chairman and Acting Chief Executive Officer	Tel:	(847) 914-2500
PESSINA, Stefano	Fax:	(847) 914-2804

Main Headquarters

Mailing:	104 Wilmot Rd., MS 1459	Tel:	(847) 914-2500
	Suite L390	Fax:	(847) 914-2804
	Deerfield, IL 60015	TF:	(800) 925-4733

Washington Office

Mailing: 1399 New York Ave. NW   Tel: (202) 393-0414
         Suite 725
         Washington, DC 20005

Political Action Committees

Walgreen Co PAC
FEC ID: C00160770
Contact: Joel Baise
104 Wilmot Rd.
Deerfield, IL 60015

> **Contributions to Candidates:** $253,500 (2015-2016)
> Democrats: $107,500; Republicans: $144,500; Other: $1,500

> ### Principal Recipients
>
> #### HOUSE
> DOLD, ROBERT JAMES JR (REP-IL)
> MCCARTHY, KEVIN (REP-CA)

Corporate Foundations and Giving Programs

Walgreen Corporate Contributions Program
Contact: John F. Gremer
104 Wilmot Rd.   Tel: (847) 315-2856
Deerfield, IL 60015   Fax: (847) 315-4417

Public Affairs and Related Activities Personnel

At Headquarters

BAISE, Joel   Tel: (847) 914-2500
Director, Government Relations   Fax: (847) 914-2804
Mail Stop 104 Wilmot Rd., Suite 459
joel.baise@walgreens.com

CHAWLA, Sona   Tel: (847) 914-2500
President, Digital & Chief Marketing Officer   Fax: (847) 914-2804

FAIRWEATHER, George   Tel: (847) 914-2500
Executive Vice President and Global Chief Financial Officer   Fax: (847) 914-2804

FLUEGEL, Brad   Tel: (847) 914-2500
Chief Strategy Officer   Fax: (847) 914-2804

GREMER, John F.   Tel: (847) 914-2500
Director, Community Affairs   Fax: (847) 914-2804

HANS, CFA, Rick J.   Tel: (847) 914-2385
Divisional Vice President, Investor Relations and Finance   Fax: (847) 914-2804
investor.relations@walgreens.com

PAGNI, Marco   Tel: (847) 914-2500
Executive Vice President, Global Chief Legal and   Fax: (847) 914-2804
Administrative Officer

REED, Jan Stern   Tel: (847) 914-2500
Senior Vice President, General Counsel and Corporate   Fax: (847) 914-2804
Secretary

WAGNER, Mark A.   Tel: (847) 914-2500
President, Operations & Community Management   Fax: (847) 914-2804

WILSON-THOMPSON, Kathleen   Tel: (847) 914-2500
Senior Vice President and Chief Human Resources Officer   Fax: (847) 914-2804
kathleen.wilson-thompson@walgreens.com

At Washington Office

GARZA, Debbie   Tel: (202) 393-0414
Divisional Vice President, Government & Community
Relations
debbie.garza@walgreens.com
Registered Federal Lobbyist

JACKSON, Alethia   Tel: (202) 393-0414
Director, Federal Government Relations
Registered Federal Lobbyist

KALETA, Ed   Tel: (202) 393-0414
Senior Director, Government Relations
Registered Federal Lobbyist

TROLLER, Katharine   Tel: (202) 393-0414
Registered Federal Lobbyist

UA, Mai Lee   Tel: (202) 393-0414
Senior Manager, Public & External Relations

Wal-Mart Stores, Inc.

A discount retail stores chain.
corporate.walmart.com
Annual Revenues: $485.52 billion
Employees: 2,200,000
Ticker: NYSE: WMT
SIC: 5331
Industry/ies: Retail/Wholesale
Legislative Issues: AGR; CHM; CPT; CSP; DEF; ENV; FIN; FOO; FOR; GOV; HCR;
HOM; INS; LBR; MAN; PHA; SMB; TAX; TRD

Chairman of the Board   Tel: (479) 273-4000
WALTON, Robson S.   Fax: (479) 277-1830

President and Chief Executive Officer, Wal-Mart Stores, Inc   Tel: (479) 273-4000
MCMILLON, Doug   Fax: (479) 277-1830

Main Headquarters

Mailing: 702 S.W. Eighth St.   Tel: (479) 273-4000
         Bentonville, AR 72716-8611   Fax: (479) 277-1830

Washington Office

Mailing: 701 Eighth St. NW   Tel: (202) 434-0717
         Suite 200   Fax: (202) 737-6069
         Washington, DC 20001

Political Action Committees

Wal-Mart Stores Inc. PAC for Responsible Government
FEC ID: C00093054
Contact: Lee R. Culpepper
702 S.W. Eighth St.
Terrell Bldg.
Bentonville, AR 72716

> **Contributions to Candidates:** $745,625 (2015-2016)
> Democrats: $301,000; Republicans: $444,625

> ### Principal Recipients
>
> #### SENATE
> SCHUMER, CHARLES E (DEM-NY)
>
> #### HOUSE
> RYAN, PAUL D. (REP-WI)
> WOMACK, STEVE (REP-AR)

Corporate Foundations and Giving Programs

Wal-Mart Foundation
Contact: Margaret A. McKenna
702 S.W. Eighth St.   Tel: (479) 273-4000
Bentonville, AZ 72716-8611   Fax: (479) 277-1830

Public Affairs and Related Activities Personnel

At Headquarters

(WANG) REED, Theresa Federal Lobbyist   Tel: (479) 273-4000
Registered Federal Lobbyist   Fax: (479) 277-1830

BAILEY, James   Tel: (479) 273-4000
Contact, Government Relations   Fax: (479) 277-1830
Registered Federal Lobbyist

BRESETT, Sean   Tel: (479) 273-4000
Senior Director, Political Programs   Fax: (479) 277-1830
Registered Federal Lobbyist

CHAMBERS, Susan M.
Executive Vice President, People Division

CULPEPPER, Lee R.   Tel: (479) 273-4000
PAC Treasurer   Fax: (479) 277-1830
lee.culpepper@wal-mart.com

DE ARMAS, Mario   Tel: (479) 273-4000
Senior Director, Government Relations   Fax: (479) 277-1830

FORD , Rollin L.   Tel: (479) 273-4000
Executive Vice President, Chief Administrative Officer   Fax: (479) 277-1830

GEARHART, Jeffrey J.   Tel: (479) 273-4000
Executive Vice President, Global Governance and Corporate   Fax: (479) 277-1830
Secretary

HARRIS, Bruce   Tel: (479) 273-4000
Federal Lobbyist   Fax: (479) 277-1830
Registered Federal Lobbyist

HEMPHILL, Adam   Tel: (202) 434-0715
Federal Government Relations Manager   Fax: (202) 737-6069
Registered Federal Lobbyist

HOLLEY, Jr., Charles M.   Tel: (479) 273-4000
Executive Vice President and Chief Financial Officer   Fax: (479) 277-1830

JANA, Barresi   Tel: (479) 273-4000
Registered Federal Lobbyist   Fax: (479) 277-1830

JORGENSEN, Jay   Tel: (479) 273-4000
Executive Vice President, Global Chief Ethics and   Fax: (479) 277-1830
Compliance Officer

QUINN, Stephen F.   Tel: (479) 273-4000
Executive Vice President, Chief Marketing Officer   Fax: (479) 277-1830

ROBERTS, Karen   Tel: (479) 273-4000
Executive Vice President and General Counsel, Wal-Mart   Fax: (479) 277-1830
Stores, Inc.

ROBITAILLE, Lauren   Tel: (479) 273-4000
Federal Lobbyist   Fax: (479) 277-1830
Registered Federal Lobbyist

ROGERS, Sarah   Tel: (479) 273-4000
Federal Lobbyist   Fax: (479) 277-1830
Registered Federal Lobbyist

SCHUMACHER, Carol   Tel: (479) 277-1498
Vice President, Investor Relations   Fax: (479) 277-1830

THORN, Sarah   Tel: (202) 434-0999

Senior Director, Corporate Affairs	Fax:	(202) 737-6069
Registered Federal Lobbyist		
WANG, Theresa	Tel:	(479) 273-4000
Contact, Government Relations	Fax:	(479) 277-1830
Registered Federal Lobbyist		
ZAPIEN, Ivan	Tel:	(202) 434-0999
Vice President, Federal Government Relations	Fax:	(202) 737-6069

At Washington Office

BARRESI, Jana	Tel:	(202) 434-0717
Director, Federal Government Relations	Fax:	(202) 737-6069
Registered Federal Lobbyist		
BARTLETT, Dan	Tel:	(202) 434-0717
Executive Vice President, Corporate Affairs	Fax:	(202) 737-6069
BEATTY, Sarah E.	Tel:	(202) 434-0999
Director, Federal Government Relations	Fax:	(202) 737-6069
Registered Federal Lobbyist		
BEEHLER, Angela	Tel:	(202) 434-0715
Federal Lobbyist	Fax:	(202) 737-6069
angie.beehler@wal-mart.com		
Registered Federal Lobbyist		
BESANCENEY, Brian	Tel:	(202) 434-0717
Chief Communication Officer	Fax:	(202) 737-6069
BRYANT, Daniel J.	Tel:	(202) 434-0717
Senior Vice President, Global Public Policy & Government	Fax:	(202) 737-6069
Affairs		
FERNANDEZ, Micaela	Tel:	(202) 434-0717
Director, Federal Government Relations	Fax:	(202) 737-6069
Registered Federal Lobbyist		
HILL, Jason J.	Tel:	(202) 737-6049
Director, U.S. Federal Government Relations	Fax:	(202) 737-6069
Registered Federal Lobbyist		
HOFMANN, Angela Marshall	Tel:	(202) 737-6049
Senior Director, International Trade	Fax:	(202) 737-6069
Registered Federal Lobbyist		
MITCHELL, Chad	Tel:	(202) 434-0999
Director, Digital Outreach and Advocacy	Fax:	(202) 737-6069
SU, Szu-Nien	Tel:	(202) 434-0717
Director, International Government Affairs	Fax:	(202) 737-6069

Walsh Capitol Consulting LLC

Consulting and government relations.
www.walshcap.com
Legislative Issues: FOO; HCR; LAW; MAN; SMB

Main Headquarters

Mailing: 124 South St.	Tel:	(202) 834-3441
Annapolis, MD 21401		

Public Affairs and Related Activities Personnel

At Headquarters

WALSH, Mary Anne	Tel:	(202) 834-3441
MaryAnne@walshcap.com		
Registered Federal Lobbyist		

Warner Music Group

A publicly-traded music company that comprises an array of businesses. Engaged in the recorded music business (including artist services) and the music publishing business.
www.wmg.com
Annual Revenues: $2.98 billion
Employees: 3,700
Ticker: NYSE: WMG
SIC: 7900
Industry/ies: Sports/Leisure/Entertainment

Chief Executive Officer	Tel:	(212) 275-2000
COOPER, Stephen F.	Fax:	(212) 757-3985

Main Headquarters

Mailing: 1633 Broadway	Tel:	(212) 275-2000
New York City, NY 10019	Fax:	(212) 757-3985

Washington Office

Mailing: 1025 F St. NW	Tel:	(202) 857-9645
Washington, DC 20004		

Public Affairs and Related Activities Personnel

At Headquarters

LEVIN, Eric	Tel:	(212) 275-2000
Executive Vice President and Chief Financial Officer	Fax:	(212) 757-3985
OSHEROVA, Maria	Tel:	(212) 275-2000
Executive Vice President, Human Resources	Fax:	(212) 757-3985
ROBERTS, Brian	Tel:	(212) 275-2000
Executive Vice President, Corporate Strategy & Operations	Fax:	(212) 757-3985
ROBINSON, Paul M.	Tel:	(212) 275-2000

Executive Vice President and General Counsel	Fax:	(212) 757-3985
STEVENS, James	Tel:	(212) 275-2000
Senior Vice President, Communications & Marketing	Fax:	(212) 757-3985
WIESENTHAL, Rob	Tel:	(212) 275-2000
Chief Operating Officer	Fax:	(212) 757-3985

Washington Federal Savings

The savings and loan subsidiary of Washington Federal Inc.
www.washingtonfederal.com
Employees: 1,909
SIC: 6035
Industry/ies: Banking/Finance/Investments

Chairman of the Board, President and Chief Executive Officer	Tel:	(206) 624-7930
WHITEHEAD, Roy M.	Fax:	(206) 624-2334

Main Headquarters

Mailing: 425 Pike St.	Tel:	(206) 624-7930
Seattle, WA 98101	Fax:	(206) 654-9420
	TF:	(800) 324-9375

Political Action Committees

Washington Federal Savings and Loan Association PAC
FEC ID: C00257527
Contact: Robert C. Zirk

425 Pike St.	Tel:	(206) 624-7930
Seattle, WA 98101-4062	Fax:	(206) 624-2334

    Contributions to Candidates: $500 (2015-2016)
    Democrats: $500

Corporate Foundations and Giving Programs

Washington Federal Foundation
425 Pike St.
Seattle, WA 98101

Public Affairs and Related Activities Personnel

At Headquarters

BEARDALL, Brent	Tel:	(206) 624-7930
Executive Vice President, Chief Banking Officer	Fax:	(206) 624-2334
BROWER, Linda	Tel:	(206) 624-7930
Executive Vice President, Human Resources and Deposit	Fax:	(206) 654-9420
Operations		
COOPER, Catherine E.	Tel:	(206) 777-8246
Senior Vice President, Marketing and Communications	Fax:	(206) 624-2334
HEDLUND, Edwin	Tel:	(206) 624-7930
Executive Vice President and Corporate Secretary	Fax:	(206) 654-9420
KASANDERS, Tom	Tel:	(206) 624-7930
Executive Vice President, Business Banking	Fax:	(206) 654-9420
ZIRK, Robert C.	Tel:	(206) 624-7930
Vice President, Internal Controls, Taxes and PAC Treasurer	Fax:	(206) 624-2334

Washington Gas

A member of the Public Affairs Council. A natural gas utility company that is a subsidiary of WGL Holdings, Inc.
www.washgas.com
Annual Revenues: $1.32 billion
Employees: 1,400
SIC: 4924
Industry/ies: Energy/Electricity; Natural Resources; Utilities
Legislative Issues: BUD; ENG

Chairman of the Board and Chief Executive Officer	Tel:	(703) 750-1400
MCCALLISTER, Terry D.	Fax:	(703) 750-4574
tmccallister@washgas.com		

Main Headquarters

Mailing: 101 Constitution Ave. NW	Tel:	(703) 750-1400
Washington, DC 20080	TF:	(800) 752-7520

Political Action Committees

Washington Gas Light Company PAC
FEC ID: C00102152
Contact: David Mason

101 Constitution Ave. NW	Tel:	(202) 624-6033
Third Floor		
Washington, DC 20001		

    Contributions to Candidates: $29,200 (2015-2016)
    Democrats: $28,200; Republicans: $1,000

Corporate Foundations and Giving Programs

Washington Area Fuel Fund
Contact: Kelly Gibson

101 Constitution Ave. NW	Tel:	(202) 624-6042
Third Floor	Fax:	(202) 624-6042
Washington, DC 20080		

Washington Gas Corporate Giving Program
Contact: Tracye Funn

101 Constitution Ave. NW	Tel:	(202) 750-2000
Washington, DC 20080	Fax:	(703) 750-4574

Public Affairs and Related Activities Personnel

At Headquarters

AMMANN, Jr., Vincent L.
Senior Vice President and Chief Financial Officer
Tel: (703) 750-1400
Fax: (703) 750-4574

CHANDRA, Gautam
Senior Vice President, Strategy, Business Development and Non-Utility Operations
gchandra@washgas.com
Tel: (703) 750-1400
Fax: (703) 750-4574

CHAPMAN, Adrian P.
President and Chief Operating Officer
Tel: (703) 750-1400

DENNIS, Robert L.
Director, Investor Relations
robertdennis@washgas.com
Tel: (202) 624-6129
Fax: (202) 624-6221

FUNN, Tracye
Manager, Regional Public Policy
Mail Stop Third Floor
tfunn@washgas.com
Tel: (703) 750-1400
Fax: (703) 750-4574

GUTERMUTH, Luanne S.
Senior Vice President, Shared Services and Chief Human Resources Officer
lgutermuth@washgas.com
Tel: (703) 750-1400

HOPE, Doreen C.
Manager
dhope@washgas.com
Registered Federal Lobbyist
Tel: (202) 624-6033
Fax: (202) 624-6221

MASON, David
PAC Treasurer
Mail Stop Third Floor
Tel: (703) 750-1400

MCGEARY, Scott
Federal Lobbyist
Registered Federal Lobbyist
Tel: (703) 750-1400

RODRIGUEZ, Ruben E.
Director, Corporate Communications
rrodriguez@washgas.com
Tel: (202) 624-6334
Fax: (202) 624-6221

SIMS, Roberta Willis
Vice President, Regulatory Affairs and Energy Acquisition
Tel: (202) 624-6620
Fax: (202) 624-6221

STAEBLER, Douglas A.
Senior Vice President, Utility Operations
Tel: (703) 750-1400

THORNTON, Leslie T.
Senior Vice President, General Counsel and Corporate Secretary
Tel: (703) 750-1400

The Washington Post Company

A diversified media company. Principal operations include newspaper and magazine publishing, broadcasting, cable television systems, electronic information, test preparation, and education and career services. On November 18/2013, the Company was renamed Graham Holdings Company, effective on November 29/2013.
www.ghco.com
Annual Revenues: $4.06 billion
Employees: 18,000
Ticker: NYSE: GHC
SIC: 2711; 2791
Industry/ies: Communications; Media/Mass Communication

Chairman of the Board and Chief Executive Officer
GRAHAM, Donald E.
Tel: (202) 334-6000
Fax: (202) 334-4536

Main Headquarters
Mailing: 1300 N 17th St.
17th Floor
Arlington, VA 22209
Tel: (703) 345-6300

Washington Office
Mailing: 1150 15th St. NW
Washington, DC 20071
Tel: (202) 334-6000
Fax: (202) 334-4536

Corporate Foundations and Giving Programs
The Philip L. Graham Fund
Contact: Eileen F. Daly
1150 15th St. NW
Washington, DC 20071
Tel: (202) 334-6000
Fax: (202) 334-4536

Public Affairs and Related Activities Personnel

At Headquarters

DEMETER, Denise
Vice President and Chief Human Resources Officer
Tel: (703) 345-6300

MADDREY, Nicole M.
Senior Vice President, General Counsel and Secretary
Tel: (703) 345-6300

MAYFIELD, Pinkie Dent
Vice President–Corporate Affairs and Special Assistant to the Chairman
Pinkie.Mayfield@ghco.com
Tel: (703) 345-6450

O'SHAUGHNESSY, Timothy J.
President
Tel: (703) 345-6300

At Washington Office

CALDERON, Rima
Vice President, Communications and External Relations
Rima.Calderon@ghco.com
Tel: (202) 334-6617
Fax: (202) 334-4536

CORATTI, Kris
Director, Public Relations and Communications
Tel: (202) 334-6000
Fax: (202) 334-4536

DALY, Eileen F.
President, Philip L. Graham Fund
Tel: (202) 334-6000
Fax: (202) 334-4536

DILLON, Veronica
Senior Vice President, General Counsel and Corporate Secretary
Tel: (202) 334-4697
Fax: (202) 334-4536

JONES, Hal S.
Senior Vice President, Finance and Chief Financial Officer
Tel: (202) 334-6000
Fax: (202) 334-4536

MCDANIEL, Ann L.
Senior Vice President & Media Relations
Tel: (202) 334-6000
Fax: (202) 334-4536

ROSBERG, Gerald M.
Senior Vice President, Planning and Development
Tel: (202) 334-6000
Fax: (202) 334-4536

Waste Management, Inc.

Formerly known as WMX Technologies, Inc. An international environmental services and waste management company.
www.wm.com
Annual Revenues: $13.10 billion
Employees: 40,600
Ticker: NYSE: WM
SIC: 4953
NAICS: 333319
Industry/ies: Environment And Conservation; Pollution And Waste
Legislative Issues: ENV; GOV; TAX; TRA; WAS

Non-Executive Chairman of the Board
REUM, W. Robert
Tel: (713) 512-6200

President and Chief Executive Officer
STEINER, David P.
david.steiner@wm.com
Tel: (713) 512-6200

Main Headquarters
Mailing: 1001 Fannin
Suite 4000
Houston, TX 77002
Tel: (713) 512-6200

Washington Office
Mailing: 701 Pennsylvania Ave. NW
Suite 590
Washington, DC 20004
Tel: (202) 639-1225
Fax: (202) 628-0400

Political Action Committees
Waste Management Inc. Employees Better Government Fund PAC
FEC ID: C00119008
Contact: James C. Fish Jr.
701 Pennsylvania Ave. NW, Suite 590
Washington, DC 20004
Tel: (202) 628-3500
Fax: (202) 628-0400

Contributions to Candidates: $21,250 (2015-2016)
Democrats: $12,250; Republicans: $9,000

Corporate Foundations and Giving Programs
Waste Management Inc. Contributions Program
1001 Fannin St.
Houston, TX 77002
Tel: (713) 512-6200
Fax: (713) 512-6299

Public Affairs and Related Activities Personnel

At Headquarters

CALDWELL, Barry H.
Senior Vice President Corporate Affairs and Chief Legal Officer
bcaldwell@wm.com
Tel: (713) 512-6200

MALANGONE, Kathy
Senior Director, Marketing Communications
kathy.malangone@mhfi.com
Tel: (212) 904-4376

POPE, John C.
Chairman, PFI Group
Tel: (713) 512-6200

SCHWARTZ, Mark
Senior Vice President, Human Resources
Tel: (713) 512-6200

SKOUTELAS, John S.
Vice President and Group General Counsel
JSkoutelas@wm.com
Tel: (713) 512-6200

TREVATHAN, James E.
Executive Vice President and Chief Operating Officer
Tel: (713) 512-6200

At Washington Office

BRIGGUM, Sue M.
Vice President, Federal Public Affairs
sbriggum@wm.com
Tel: (202) 628-3500

EISENBUD, Robert
Vice President, Federal Public Affairs
Registered Federal Lobbyist
Tel: (202) 639-1225
Fax: (202) 628-0400

FISH, Jr., James C.
PAC Treasurer, Executive Vice President and Chief Financial Officer
Tel: (202) 639-1225
Fax: (202) 628-0400

KARDELL, Lisa R.
Director, Public Affairs
lkardell@wm.com
Tel: (202) 639-1225
Fax: (202) 628-0400

KELLY, Kerry
Director, Federal Public and Regulatory Affairs
kkelly5@wm.com
Registered Federal Lobbyist
Tel: (202) 628-3500

Watco Companies, Inc.
Transporation: serving freight rail, switching, mechanical, and transload/intermodal needs.
www.watcocompanies.com
Industry/ies: Railroads; Transportation

Chief Executive Officer
WEBB, Rick
rwebb@watcocompanies.com
Tel: (620) 231-2230
Fax: (620) 231-0812

Main Headquarters
Mailing: 1890 E. Johnson St.
Madison, WI 53704
Tel: (414) 438-8820
Fax: (608) 243-9225

Public Affairs and Related Activities Personnel

At Other Offices

BADEN, Rick
President and Interim Chief Financial Officer
315 W. 3rd St.
Pittsburg, KS 66762
rbaden@watcocompanies.com
Tel: (620) 231-2230
Fax: (620) 231-0812

BLAZER, Mark
Senior Vice President, Strategic Development
1900 N. Main, Suite 14
Helena, MT 59601
mblazer@watcocompanies.com
Tel: (406) 495-1096
Fax: (406) 495-1098

LOEB, Stefan
Executive Vice President, Chief Marketing Officer
315 W. 3rd St.
Pittsburg, KS 66762
sloeb@watcocompanies.com
Tel: (620) 231-2230
Fax: (620) 231-0812

PETERSON, Rachael
Senior Vice President, Human Resources
315 W. 3rd St.
Pittsburg, KS 66762
Tel: (620) 231-2230
Fax: (620) 231-0812

RICHEY, Craig
Executive Vice President, General Counsel
315 W. 3rd St.
Pittsburg, KS 66762
crichey@watcocompanies.com
Tel: (620) 231-2230
Fax: (620) 231-0812

SMITH, Dan
Executive Vice President, Chief Operating Officer
315 W. 3rd St.
Pittsburg, KS 66762
dsmith@watcocompanies.com
Tel: (620) 231-2230
Fax: (620) 231-0812

VAN SCHAICK, Jeff
Assistant Vice President, Government Affairs
900 S. Byers Ave.
Oklahoma City, OK 73129
jvanschaick@watcocompanies.com

VANBECELAERE, Tracie
Director, Communications
315 W. 3rd St.
Pittsburg, KS 66762
tvan@watcocompanies.com
Tel: (620) 231-2230
Fax: (620) 231-0812

Wausau Insurance Companies
See listing on page 489 under Liberty Mutual Middle Market

Wawa, Inc.
Specialized convenience stores.
www.wawa.com
Employees: 16,400
SIC: 2026
NAICS: 311511
Industry/ies: Food And Beverage Industry; Retail/Wholesale

Chairman of the Board, Director, Government Relations and Sustainability
WOOD, Jr., Richard D.
Tel: (610) 358-8000
Fax: (610) 358-8878

President and Chief Executive Officer
GHEYSENS, Chris
Tel: (610) 358-8000
Fax: (610) 358-8878

Main Headquarters
Mailing: Red Roof
260 W. Baltimore Pke.
Tel: (610) 358-8000
Fax: (610) 358-8878

Wawa, PA 19063
TF: (800) 444-9272

Political Action Committees
Wawa Inc. PAC
FEC ID: C00148510
Contact: John Nihill
C/O Elko & Associates Ltd.
Two W. Baltimore Pke. Suite 210
Media, PA 19063
Contributions to Candidates: $28,450 (2015-2016)
Democrats: $9,450; Republicans: $19,000

Corporate Foundations and Giving Programs
Wawa Inc. Contributions Program
Contact: Lori Bruce
Red Roof
260 W. Baltimore Pke.
Wawa, PA 19063
Tel: (610) 358-8039
Fax: (610) 358-8878

Public Affairs and Related Activities Personnel

At Headquarters

BRUCE, Lori
Manager, Culture and Communications
lori.a.bruce@wawa.com
Tel: (610) 358-8039
Fax: (610) 358-8878

STOECKEL, Howard B.
Vice Chairman
Tel: (610) 358-8000
Fax: (610) 358-8878

At Other Offices

NIHILL, John
PAC Treasurer
C/o Elko & Associates, Ltd, Two W. Baltimore Ave., Suite 210
Media, PA 19063

We Energies
A member of the Public Affairs Council. A natural gas distribution utility that is a subsidiary of Wisconsin Energy Corporation (see separate listing).
www.we-energies.com
Annual Revenues: $4.33 billion
Employees: 4,504
SIC: 4922
Industry/ies: Energy/Electricity; Natural Resources; Utilities
Legislative Issues: ENG

Chairman of the Board, President and Chief Executive Officer
KLAPPA, Gale E.
gale.klappa@we-energies.com
Tel: (414) 221-2345
Fax: (414) 221-3213

Main Headquarters
Mailing: P.O.Box 2046
Milwaukee, WI 53201-2046
Tel: (414) 221-2345
Fax: (414) 221-3213
TF: (800) 714-7777

Washington Office
Mailing: 122 C St. NW
Suite 840
Washington, DC 20001

Corporate Foundations and Giving Programs
We Energies Foundation
Contact: Thelma Sias
P.O.Box 2046
Milwaukee, WI 53201-2046
Tel: (414) 221-2345
Fax: (414) 221-3213

Public Affairs and Related Activities Personnel

At Headquarters

DEMASTERS, Darnell K.
Vice President, Federal Government Affairs
darnell.demasters@we-energies.com
Tel: (414) 221-2345
Fax: (414) 221-3213

GARVIN, Robert M.
Senior Vice President, External Affairs
Tel: (414) 221-2345
Fax: (414) 221-3213

KEYES, J. Patrick
Executive Vice President and Chief Financial Officer
Tel: (414) 221-2345
Fax: (414) 221-3213

MANTHEY, Brian
Manager, Media Relations
brian.manthey@we-energies.com
Tel: (414) 221-4444
Fax: (414) 221-3213

MARTIN, Susan H.
Executive Vice President, General Counsel and Corporate Secretary
Tel: (414) 221-2345
Fax: (414) 221-3213

MCNULTY, Barry
Director, Corporate Communications
barry.mcnulty@we-energies.com
Tel: (414) 221-2345
Fax: (414) 221-3213

SHAFER, Joan M.
Executive Vice President, Human Resources and Organizational Effectiveness
Tel: (414) 221-2345
Fax: (414) 221-3213

SIAS, Thelma
Vice President, Local Affairs
thelma.sias@we-energies.com
Tel: (414) 221-2345
Fax: (414) 221-3213

STRAKA, M. Beth
Senior Vice President, Communications and Investor Relations
Tel: (414) 221-2345
Fax: (414) 221-3213

At Washington Office

GREY, Eric
Manager, Federal Government Affairs

Weatherford International

Provides gas and oil field services.
www.weatherford.com
Annual Revenues: $8.22 billion
Employees: 39,500
Ticker: NYSE: WFT
SIC: 1381; 3533
NAICS: 333132
Industry/ies: Fuels See Coal, Gas, Oil, Petroleum; Machinery/Equipment; Natural Resources; Petroleum Industry
Legislative Issues: ENG; FUE; TAX

Chairman of the Board, President, and Chief Executive Officer
DUROC-DANNER, Bernard J.
Tel: (713) 693-4000
Fax: (713) 693-4323

Main Headquarters
Mailing: 2000 St. James Pl.
Houston, TX 77056
Tel: (713) 693-4000
Fax: (713) 693-4323
TF: (800) 257-3826

Political Action Committees
Weatherford US LP PAC aka Weatherford PAC
FEC ID: C00435503
Contact: Dianne Ralston
2000 St. James Pl.
Houston, TX 77056

Public Affairs and Related Activities Personnel

At Headquarters

DAVID-GREEN, Karen
Vice President, Investor Relations
Tel: (713) 836-7430
Fax: (713) 693-4323

FULGHAM, Steve
Vice President, Operations and Chief Business Development Officer
Tel: (713) 693-4000
Fax: (713) 693-4323

HUGHES, Kelley
Manager, Corporate Communications
Kelley.hughes@weatherford.com
Tel: (713) 836-4193
Fax: (713) 693-4323

RALSTON, Dianne
PAC Contact
Tel: (713) 693-4000
Fax: (713) 693-4323

Weber Shandwick

A public relations and communications management company.
www.webershandwick.com
Employees: 600

Chairman of the Board
LESLIE, Jack
jleslie@webershandwick.com
Tel: (212) 445-8000
Fax: (212) 445-8001

Chief Executive Officer
POLANSKY, Andy
Tel: (212) 445-8000
Fax: (212) 445-8001

Main Headquarters
Mailing: 919 Third Ave.
New York City, NY 10022
Tel: (212) 445-8000
Fax: (212) 445-8001

Washington Office
Mailing: 733 Tenth St. NW
Washington, DC 20001
Tel: (202) 383-9700
Fax: (202) 383-0079

Corporate Foundations and Giving Programs
Weber Shandwick Contributions Program
919 Third Ave.
New York City, NY 10022
Tel: (212) 445-8000
Fax: (212) 445-8001

Public Affairs and Related Activities Personnel

At Headquarters

GIUDA, Michelle Selesky
Senior Vice President, Global Corporate Communications
Tel: (212) 445-8000
Fax: (212) 445-8001

GOLD, Abby
Chief Human Resources Officer
agold@webershandwick.com
Tel: (212) 445-8000
Fax: (212) 445-8001

GOODWIN, Nicholas Reid
Director
ngoodwin@webershandwick.com
Tel: (212) 445-8000
Fax: (212) 445-8001

HEIMANN, Gail
President
Tel: (212) 445-8000
Fax: (212) 445-8001

KERRIGAN, Ken
Executive Vice President, Corporate Practice
Tel: (212) 445-8000
Fax: (212) 445-8001

OKUNAK, Frank
Chief Operating Officer
fokunak@webershandwick.com
Tel: (212) 445-8000
Fax: (212) 445-8001

At Washington Office

FRIEDMAN, Sara Y.
Senior Account Executive
Tel: (202) 383-9700
Fax: (202) 383-0079

MESZAROS, James A.
Executive Vice President and Head, International Public Affairs
jmeszaros@webershandwick.com
Tel: (310) 854-8200
Fax: (310) 854-8201

MORGAN, Lance I.
Chief Communications Strategist
lmorgan@webershandwick.com
Tel: (202) 383-9700
Fax: (202) 383-0079

At Other Offices

AZARLOZA, Armando
Executive Vice President and Press Secretary, Communications
8687 Melrose Ave., Seventh Floor
Los Angeles, CA 90069
Tel: (310) 854-8200
Fax: (310) 854-8201

WebMD Corporation

A web-based healthcare information company.
www.webmd.com
Annual Revenues: $475.68 million
Employees: 1,700
Ticker: NASDAQ: WBMD
Industry/ies: Communications; Computer/Technology; Medicine/Health Care/ Mental Health; Telecommunications/Internet/Cable
Legislative Issues: BUD; HCR

Chairman of the Board
WYGOD, Martin J.
Tel: (212) 624-3700

Chief Executive Officer
SCHLANGER, David J.
Tel: (212) 624-3700

Main Headquarters
Mailing: 111 Eighth Ave.
Seventh Floor
New York City, NY 10011
Tel: (212) 624-3700

Public Affairs and Related Activities Personnel

At Headquarters

ANEVSKI, Peter
Chief Financial Officer
Tel: (212) 624-3700

DUBLIN, Adam
Senior Vice President, Strategy and Analytics
Tel: (212) 624-3700

GLICK, Michael B.
Executive Vice President, Co-General Counsel
Tel: (212) 624-3700

TOURJEE, Kathleen
Vice President, Human Resources
KTourjee@webmd.net
Tel: (212) 624-3700

Webster-Hoff

Webster-Hoff's manufacturing excellence starts with its experienced engineers working as a team, monitoring every aspect of a P/M project.
www.webster-hoff.com
Annual Revenues: $6.20 million
Employees: 52
SIC: 3499
Industry/ies: Metals

Chairman of the Board
WEBSTER, Judy
Tel: (630) 858-8030
Fax: (630) 858-4993

President and Chief Executive Officer
WEBSTER, Bryan
bwebster@webster-hoff.com
Tel: (630) 858-8030
Fax: (630) 858-4993

Main Headquarters
Mailing: 704 E. Fullerton
Glendale Heights, IL 60139
Tel: (630) 858-8030
Fax: (630) 858-4993
TF: (877) 622-6402

Public Affairs and Related Activities Personnel

At Headquarters

D'ALESANDRO, Marge
Manager, Human Resources
Tel: (630) 858-8030
Fax: (630) 858-4993

GANDHI, Sonal
Manager, Financial Services
Tel: (630) 858-8030
Fax: (630) 858-4993

Weight Watchers International, Inc.

Provides consumers with a weight loss diet plan.
www.weightwatchers.com
Annual Revenues: $1.15 billion
Employees: 19,000
Ticker: NYSE: WTW
SIC: 7200
Industry/ies: Nutrition; Personal Care/Hygiene
Legislative Issues: HCR

Main Headquarters
Mailing: 675 Ave. of the Americas | Tel: (212) 589-2700
Sixth Floor | Fax: (212) 589-2601
New York City, NY 10010 | TF: (800) 828-9675

Corporate Foundations and Giving Programs

Weight Watchers Foundation
11th Madison Ave. | Tel: (212) 589-2700
17th Floor | Fax: (212) 589-2601
New York City, NY 10010

Public Affairs and Related Activities Personnel

At Headquarters

COLOSI, Michael F. | Tel: (212) 589-2700
General Counsel and Secretary | Fax: (212) 589-2601

HOTCHKIN, Nicholas P. | Tel: (212) 589-2700
Chief Financial Officer | Fax: (212) 589-2601

Welch Allyn, Inc.

A privately-held manufacturer of medical diagnostic equipment and therapeutic devices, cardiac defibrillators, patient monitoring systems, and miniature precision lamps.
www.welchallyn.com
SIC: 3641; 3845
NAICS: 335110; 334510
Industry/ies: Medicine/Health Care/Mental Health; Pharmaceutical Industry

Co-Chairman of the Board | Tel: (315) 685-4245
ALLYN, Eric | Fax: (315) 685-4091

President and Chief Executive Officer | Tel: (315) 685-4245
MEYER, Steve | Fax: (315) 685-4091

Main Headquarters
Mailing: 4341 State Street Rd., P.O. Box 220 | Tel: (315) 685-4245
P.O. Box 220 | Fax: (315) 685-4091
Skaneateles, NY 13152 | TF: (800) 535-6663

Political Action Committees
Welch Allyn Inc. Federal PAC
FEC ID: C00363150
Contact: Sarah Cates
4341 State Street Rd.
P.O. Box 220
Skaneateles Falls, NY 13153

> **Contributions to Candidates:** $4,500 (2015-2016)
> Democrats: $2,500; Republicans: $2,000

Corporate Foundations and Giving Programs

Welch Allyn Contributions Program
4341 State Street Rd.
P.O. Box 220
Skaneateles Falls, NY 13153

Public Affairs and Related Activities Personnel

At Headquarters

ARNOLD, Jamie | Tel: (315) 685-4599
Public Relations and Internal Communications Manager | Fax: (315) 685-4091
jamie.arnold@welchallyn.com

BLACKORBY, Julie | Tel: (800) 535-6663
Federal Lobbyist | Fax: (315) 685-3361

CATES, Sarah | Tel: (315) 685-4245
PAC Treasurer | Fax: (315) 685-3361

FISHER, Dan | Tel: (315) 685-4245
Executive Vice President, Human Resources and | Fax: (315) 685-4091
Organization Leadership

GODDARD, Janie | Tel: (315) 685-4245
Executive Vice President, Strategic Business Units and | Fax: (315) 685-4091
Marketing

HENNIGAN, Joseph | Tel: (315) 685-4245
Executive Vice President and Chief Operating Officer | Fax: (315) 685-4091

KOHLER, Adriana | Tel: (800) 535-6663
Federal Lobbyist | Fax: (315) 685-3361

PORTER, Gregory | Tel: (315) 685-4245
Executive Vice President, General Counsel | Fax: (315) 685-4091

SODERBERG , Jon | Tel: (315) 685-4245
Executive Vice President, Corporate Development | Fax: (315) 685-3361

Welch's Foods, Inc.

Welch's Foods, Inc. is a food processing company based in Massachusetts in the U.S. The products of the company include grape juice and soda.
www.welchs.com
Annual Revenues: $640.93 million
Employees: 1,300
SIC: 2033; 2037; 2087
NAICS: 311421; 311411
Industry/ies: Food And Beverage Industry
Legislative Issues: AGR; BEV; FOO

Chairman of the Board | Tel: (978) 371-1000
FALCONE, Joseph | Fax: (978) 371-3879

President and Chief Executive Officer | Tel: (978) 371-1000
IRWIN, Brad | Fax: (978) 371-3879

Main Headquarters
Mailing: 300 Baker Ave. | Tel: (978) 371-1000
Suite 101 | Fax: (978) 371-3879
Concord, MA 01742

Public Affairs and Related Activities Personnel

At Headquarters

MITCHELL, Karen | Tel: (978) 371-3765
Director, Marketing | Fax: (978) 371-3879
kmitchell@welchs.com

PERDA, Michael J. | Tel: (978) 371-1000
Chief Financial Officer | Fax: (978) 371-3879

ZEIGLER, Michelle | Tel: (215) 928-2352
Contact, Media Relations | Fax: (978) 371-3879
michelle.zeigler@toniclc.com

Wellmark

Wellmark is a large scale, post industrial, plastic-waste recycler offering the most professional and reliable recycling services.
www.wellmark.com
Annual Revenues: $88.90 million
Employees: 2,000
Industry/ies: Insurance Industry; Medicine/Health Care/Mental Health

Chairman and Chief Executive Officer | Tel: (515) 245-4500
FORSYTH, John D. | Fax: (515) 248-5617

Main Headquarters
Mailing: 1331 Grand Ave. | Tel: (515) 245-4500
PO Box 9232 | Fax: (515) 248-5617
Des Moines, IA 50306-9232

Political Action Committees
Wellmark, Inc. PAC (WELLPAC)
FEC ID: C00342022
Contact: Cory Harris
1331 Grand Ave. | Tel: (515) 245-5139
Station 5W570 | Fax: (515) 248-5617
Des Moines, IA 50309

> **Contributions to Candidates:** $19,000 (2015-2016)
> Republicans: $19,000

Corporate Foundations and Giving Programs

The Wellmark Foundation
Contact: Matt McGarvey
636 Grand Ave. | Tel: (515) 245-4819
Ruan Center, Station 150 | Fax: (515) 245-4819
Des Moines, IA 50309

Public Affairs and Related Activities Personnel

At Headquarters

BROWN, David | Tel: (515) 245-4500
Executive Vice President, Chief Financial Officer and | Fax: (515) 248-5617
Treasurer

CROWLEY, Mike | Tel: (515) 245-4500
Vice President, Finance and Controller | Fax: (515) 248-5617

GERRISH, Mike | Tel: (515) 245-4500
Vice President, Marketing | Fax: (515) 248-5617

HARRIS, Cory | Tel: (515) 245-4500
Senior Vice President and General CounselPAC Treasurer | Fax: (515) 248-5617

JACKSON, Laura | Tel: (515) 245-4500
Executive Vice President, Health Care Innovation and | Fax: (515) 248-5617
Business Development

LICKTEIG, M. Michelle | Tel: (515) 245-4500
Assistant General Counsel | Fax: (515) 248-5617

MCTAGGART, Sean | Tel: (515) 245-4500
Vice President, Sales | Fax: (515) 248-5617

PALMER, Elaine M | Tel: (515) 245-4500
Vice President, Operations | Fax: (515) 248-5617

STORK, Frank | Tel: (515) 245-4500
Vice President and Senior Counsel, Regulatory and | Fax: (515) 248-5617
Government Affairs
storkfj@wellmark.com

At Other Offices

CHICKERING, Marcelle J. | Tel: (515) 245-4500
Executive Vice President, Human Resources | Fax: (515) 248-5617
636 Grand Ave., Ruan Center, Station 13
Des Moines, IA 50309

GRIFFIN, Janet | Tel: (515) 245-5139
| Fax: (515) 248-5617

Vice President, Public Policy, Board Secretary and PAC Treasurer
636 Grand Ave., Ruan Center, Station 13
Des Moines, IA 50309

KNIGHT, Angela	Tel:	(515) 245-4931
Consultant, Public Relations	Fax:	(515) 245-4500

636 Grand Ave., Ruan Center, Station 13
Des Moines, IA 50309
KnightA@wellmark.com

MCGARVEY, Matt	Tel:	(515) 245-4819
Director, Foundation	Fax:	(515) 245-4925

636 Grand Ave., Ruan Center, Station 13
Des Moines, IA 50309
mcgarveym@wellmark.com

Wells Fargo & Company

A residential mortgage lender in the US. Acquired Wachovia in early October 2008.
www.wellsfargo.com
Annual Revenues: $83.32 billion
Employees: 266,000
Ticker: NYSE: WFC
SIC: 6021
Industry/ies: Banking/Finance/Investments
Legislative Issues: AGR; BAN; BNK; FIN; HOU; INS; SMB; TAX

Chairman of the Board, President and Chief Executive Officer	Tel:	(415) 396-2619
STUMPF, John G.	Fax:	(626) 312-3015

John.G.Stumpf@wellsfargo.com

Main Headquarters
Mailing:	420 Montgomery St.	Tel:	(415) 371-6521
	3123015	Fax:	(626) 312-3015
	San Francisco, CA 94104	TF:	(866) 876-5865

Washington Office
Mailing: 1750 H St. NW
Fifth Floor
Washington, DC 20006

Political Action Committees
Wells Fargo and Company Employee PAC
FEC ID: C00034595
Sixth and Marquette
MAC N9305-084
Minneapolis, MN 55479

Contributions to Candidates: $721,700 (2015-2016)
Democrats: $240,700; Republicans: $481,000

Principal Recipients

SENATE
BOOZMAN, JOHN (REP-AR)
BURR, RICHARD (REP-NC)
KIRK, MARK STEVEN (REP-IL)
MURPHY, PATRICK E (DEM-FL)
MURRAY, PATTY (DEM-WA)

HOUSE
BECERRA, XAVIER (DEM-CA)
BOEHNER, JOHN A. (REP-OH)
LUCAS, FRANK D. (REP-OK)
ROYCE, ED MR. (REP-CA)
RYAN, PAUL D. (REP-WI)
SCALISE, STEVE MR. (REP-LA)
SESSIONS, PETE MR. (REP-TX)

Corporate Foundations and Giving Programs
Wells Fargo Housing Foundation
Wells Fargo Center	Tel:	(612) 667-5131
90 S. Seventh St., N9305-084
Minneapolis, MN 55402

Public Affairs and Related Activities Personnel
At Headquarters

CALLAHAN, Patricia R.	Tel:	(415) 371-6521
Senior Executive Vice President and Chief Administrative Officer	Fax:	(626) 312-3015
HANLON, Tim	Tel:	(415) 396-3567
Senior Vice President, Wells Fargo Foundation	Fax:	(626) 312-3015
Mail Stop M/S A011 2-073
HARDISON, Hope	Tel:	(415) 371-6521
Executive Vice President, Human Resources	Fax:	(626) 312-3015
LEVY, Richard D.	Tel:	(415) 371-6521
Executive Vice President, Controller	Fax:	(626) 312-3015
LIN, Eileen	Tel:	(571) 314-4660
Media Contact	Fax:	(626) 312-3015
Eileen.Lin@unitedway.org
MODJTABAI, Avid	Tel:	(415) 396-3612
Senior Executive Vice President, Consumer Lending	Fax:	(626) 312-3015
Avid.Modjtabai@wellsfargo.com

ROBY, Carolyn	Tel:	(415) 371-6521
Vice President, Wells Fargo Foundation Minnesota	Fax:	(626) 312-3015
Carolyn.H.Roby@wellsfargo.com
SHREWSBERRY, John	Tel:	(415) 371-6521
Senior Executive Vice President, Chief Financial Officer	Fax:	(626) 312-3015
SLOAN, Timothy J.	Tel:	(415) 371-6521
Senior Executive Vice President	Fax:	(626) 312-3015
STROTHER, James M.	Tel:	(415) 371-6521
Senior Executive Vice President, General Counsel Legal Group	Fax:	(626) 312-3015
SURIS, Oscar	Tel:	(415) 396-3300
Executive Vice President and Head, Corporate Communications	Fax:	(626) 312-3015
oscar.suris@wellsfargo.com

At Washington Office

CHEN, John S.
Board Member
DUNN, Hon. Jennifer
Senior Vice President, Government & Community Relations Communications
MCCINNIS, Ellen
Senior Vice President, Twin Cities Local Government Relations
REYNOSO, Erika
Assistant Vice President, Communications
ROSS, Dasha
Media Contact
Dasha.ross@wellsfargo.com
WONG, Johnny
Corporate Communications

At Other Offices

ADU, Sanders	Tel:	(612) 667-9917
Director, Federal Government Relations		
Wells Fargo Center, 90 S. Seventh St.
Minneapolis, MN 55402
Registered Federal Lobbyist
| ARCHER, Daniel | Tel: | (612) 667-9917 |
| *Director, Federal Government Relations* | | |
Wells Fargo Center, 90 S. Seventh St.
Minneapolis, MN 55402
daniel.m.archer@wellsfargo.com
Registered Federal Lobbyist
| DE LA VEGA, Robert | Tel: | (612) 667-5051 |
| *Director, State Government Relations* | | |
301 S. College St.
Charlotte, NC 28288
EOLOFF, Anita B.
Senior Director, Federal Government Relations & PAC Contact
Sixth and Marquette
Minneapolis, MN 55479
anita.b.eoloff@wellsfargo.com
Registered Federal Lobbyist
RONQUILLO, Kim
Executive Assistant
P.O. BOX 1081
Alburquerque, NM 87103
| ROSELLO, Christopher | Tel: | (612) 667-9917 |
| *Federal Lobbyist* | | |
Wells Fargo Center, 90 S. Seventh St.
Minneapolis, MN 55402
Registered Federal Lobbyist
| SEYFERT, Christy | Tel: | (612) 667-9917 |
| *Federal Lobbyist* | | |
Wells Fargo Center, 90 S. Seventh St.
Minneapolis, MN 55402
| SIMMONS, Margaret | Tel: | (612) 667-9917 |
| *Federal Lobbyist* | | |
Wells Fargo Center, 90 S. Seventh St.
Minneapolis, MN 55402
Registered Federal Lobbyist
| SLOCUM, Julie | Tel: | (612) 667-9917 |
| *Director, Federal Government Relations* | | |
Wells Fargo Center, 90 S. Seventh St.
Minneapolis, MN 55402
Registered Federal Lobbyist
| VICKERS, Linda | Tel: | (612) 667-9917 |
| *Fedaral Lobbyist* | | |
Wells Fargo Center, 90 S. Seventh St.
Minneapolis, MN 55402

Wendy's International, Inc.

Wendy's is a quick-service hamburger company and offers made-to-order burgers and fries as well as such alternative menu items as baked potatoes, chili, and salads.
www.wendys.com
Annual Revenues: $2.06 billion
Employees: 31,200
Ticker: NASDAQ: WEN
Industry/ies: Food And Beverage Industry
Legislative Issues: ENG; LBR; TAX

Chairman of the Board   Tel: (614) 764-3100
PELTZ, Nelson   Fax: (614) 764-3330

President and Chief Executive Officer   Tel: (614) 764-3100
BROLICK, Emil J.   Fax: (614) 764-3330

Main Headquarters
Mailing: One Dave Thomas Blvd.   Tel: (614) 764-3100
Dublin, OH 43017   Fax: (614) 764-3330
  TF: (888) 624-8140

Corporate Foundations and Giving Programs

Wendy's International, Inc. Contributions Program
One Dave Thomas Blvd.   Tel: (614) 764-3100
Dublin, OH 43017   Fax: (614) 764-3100

Public Affairs and Related Activities Personnel

At Headquarters

BERTINI, Bob   Tel: (614) 764-3327
Senior Director, Internal Communications   Fax: (614) 764-3330
bob.bertini@wendys.com

ESPOSITO, Liliana M.   Tel: (614) 764-3100
Chief Communications Officer   Fax: (614) 764-3330

FRISSORA, David   Tel: (614) 764-3100
Director, Government Relations and Corporate Affairs   Fax: (614) 764-3330

PENEGOR, Todd A.   Tel: (614) 764-3100
Senior Vice President and Chief Financial Officer   Fax: (614) 764-3330

POPLAR, David D.   Tel: (614) 764-3311
Vice President, Investor Relations   Fax: (614) 764-3330
david.poplar@wendys.com

SOLANO, Brandon L.   Tel: (614) 764-3100
Chief Marketing Officer   Fax: (614) 764-3330

TOOP, R. Scott   Tel: (614) 764-3100
Senior Vice President, General Counsel and Secretary   Fax: (614) 764-3330
scott.toop@wendys.com

WEISBERG, Scott A.   Tel: (614) 764-3100
Chief People Officer   Fax: (614) 764-3330

WRIGHT, Robert D.   Tel: (614) 764-3100
Executive Vice President and Chief Operations Officer   Fax: (614) 764-3330

Westar Energy, Inc.

An electric utility. Formed by the merger of Kansas Power & Light and Kansas Gas & Electric in 1992.
www.westarenergy.com
Annual Revenues: $2.44 billion
Employees: 2,330
Ticker: NYSE: WR
SIC: 4931
Industry/ies: Energy/Electricity
Legislative Issues: COM; ENG; TAX

Chairman of the Board   Tel: (785) 575-6300
CHANDLER, IV, Charles Q.   Fax: (785) 575-8182

President and Chief Executive Officer   Tel: (785) 575-6300
RUELLE, Mark A.   Fax: (785) 575-1796

Main Headquarters
Mailing: P. O. Box 889   Tel: (785) 575-6300
Topeka, KS 66601-0889   Fax: (785) 575-1796
  TF: (800) 401-5666

Political Action Committees
Westar Energy Employees PAC
FEC ID: C00390989
Contact: Angela Cool
818 S. Kansas Ave.
P.O. Box 889
Topeka, KS 66601

Contributions to Candidates: $12,000 (2015-2016)
Republicans: $12,000

Corporate Foundations and Giving Programs
Westar Energy Foundation
Contact: Terry Wilson
P.O. Box 758000   Tel: (785) 575-8097
Topeka, KS 66675   Fax: (785) 575-1796

Public Affairs and Related Activities Personnel

At Headquarters

BANNING, Jerl   Tel: (785) 575-6300
Senior Vice President, Operations Support and Administration   Fax: (785) 575-1796

BRIDSON, John   Tel: (785) 575-6300
Senior Vice President, Generation and Marketing   Fax: (785) 575-1796

COLE, ABC, Michel' Philipp   Tel: (785) 575-6300
Vice President, Corporate Communications and Public Affairs   Fax: (785) 575-1796

GREENWOOD, Greg A.   Tel: (785) 575-6300
Senior Vice President, Strategy   Fax: (785) 575-1796

IRICK, Larry   Tel: (785) 575-6300
Vice President, General Counsel and Corporate Secretary   Fax: (785) 575-1796

MARTIN, Jeffrey   Tel: (785) 575-6300
Vice President, Regulatory Affairs   Fax: (785) 575-1796

PENZIG, Gina   Tel: (785) 575-6300
Manager, Media Relations   Fax: (785) 575-1796
gina.penzig@WestarEnergy.com

ROW, Erin La   Tel: (785) 575-6060
Senior Communications Representative   Fax: (785) 575-1796
Erin.m.la.row@WestarEnergy.com

SCHREIBER, Mark   Tel: (785) 575-6300
Vice President, Government Affairs   Fax: (785) 575-1796

SHERMAN, Don   Tel: (785) 575-6300
Vice President, Community Relations and Strategic Partnerships   Fax: (785) 575-1796

SOMMA, Tony   Tel: (785) 575-6300
Senior Vice President, Chief Financial Officer and Treasurer   Fax: (785) 575-1796

VANDEVELDE, Cody   Tel: (785) 575-6300
Director, Investor Relations   Fax: (785) 575-1796
ir@westarenergy.com

WILSON, Cindy   Tel: (785) 575-6300
Executive Director, Corporate Compliance and Internal Audit   Fax: (785) 575-1796

At Other Offices

COOL, Angela   Tel: (785) 575-6300
PAC Treasurer   Fax: (785) 575-1796
818 S. Kansas Ave.
Topeka, KS 66612

Western Refining, Inc.

An oil refiner company, operates primarily in the Southwestern and Mid-Atlantic regions of the United States.
www.wnr.com
Annual Revenues: $13.75 billion
Employees: 5,700
Ticker: NYSE: WNR
SIC: 2911
Industry/ies: Fuels See Coal, Gas, Oil, Petroleum; Natural Resources; Petroleum Industry

Chairman of the Board   Tel: (915) 534-1400
FOSTER, Paul L.
paul.foster@wnr.com

President and Chief Executive Officer   Tel: (915) 534-1400
STEVENS, Jeff A.

Main Headquarters
Mailing: 123 W. Mills Ave.   Tel: (915) 534-1400
El Paso, TX 79901

Public Affairs and Related Activities Personnel

At Headquarters

BARFIELD, Lowry   Tel: (915) 534-1400
Senior Vice President, Legal, General Counsel and Secretary
lowry.barfield@wnr.com

BEYERSDORFER, Jeffrey S.   Tel: (602) 286-1530
Senior Vice President, Treasurer and Director, Investor Relations

DALKE, Gary R.   Tel: (915) 534-1400
Chief Financial Officer

HANSON, Gary   Tel: (602) 286-1777
Contact, Media Relations

JEWELL, William R.   Tel: (915) 534-1400
Chief Accounting Officer

SMITH, Mark J.   Tel: (915) 534-1400
President, Refining and Marketing

WEAVER, Scott D.   Tel: (915) 534-1400
Vice President, Assistant Treasurer and Assistant Secretary

Western Resources Inc
See listing on page 849 under Westar Energy, Inc.

The Western Union Company

A worldwide money transferring service, which promotes global economic opportunity and growth by bridging gaps in the financial services sector. Their growing product portfolio includes business solutions, consumer-to-consumer money transfer, bill-payment services and stored-value options such as prepaid cards.
www.westernunion.com
Annual Revenues: $5.58 billion
Employees: 10,000
Ticker: NYSE: WU
SIC: 7389
Industry/ies: Banking/Finance/Investments
Legislative Issues: BAN; CSP; FIN; HOM; IMM

Chairman of the Board
GREENBERG, Jack M.

Tel: (720) 332-1000
Fax: (720) 332-4753

President, Chief Executive Officer and Director
ERSEK, Hikmet
Hikmet.ersek@westernunion.com

Tel: (720) 332-1000
Fax: (720) 332-4753

Main Headquarters
Mailing: 12500 E. Belford Ave.
Englewood, CO 80112

Tel: (720) 332-1000
Fax: (720) 332-4753
TF: (866) 405-5012

Political Action Committees
Western Union Company PAC
FEC ID: C00429050
Contact: Tim Daly
125000 E. Belford Ave.
Englewood, CO 80112

Tel: (720) 332-1000
Fax: (720) 332-4753

Contributions to Candidates: $15,000 (2015-2016)
Democrats: $10,000; Republicans: $5,000

Corporate Foundations and Giving Programs
The Western Union Foundation
Contact: Luella Chavez D'Angelo
125000 E. Belford Ave.
Englewood, CO 80112

Tel: (720) 332-4764
Fax: (720) 332-4753

Public Affairs and Related Activities Personnel

At Headquarters

AGRAWAL, Raj
Executive Vice President, Interim Chief Financial Officer

Tel: (720) 332-1000
Fax: (720) 332-4753

ALMEIDA, Odilon
President, Americas

Tel: (720) 332-1000
Fax: (720) 332-4753

CIPRIANO, meredith M.
Senior Manager, Government Relations

Tel: (720) 332-1000
Fax: (720) 332-4753

D'ANGELO, Luella Chavez
Chief Communications Officer and President, The Western Union Foundation
luella.dangelo@westernunion.com

Tel: (720) 332-1000
Fax: (720) 332-4753

DALY, Tim
Lobbyist & PAC Treasurer
tim.daly@westernunion.com
Registered Federal Lobbyist

Tel: (720) 332-1000
Fax: (720) 332-4753

DYE, John R.
Executive Vice President, General Counsel and Secretary

Tel: (720) 332-1000
Fax: (720) 332-4753

KELLY, Kristen
Director, Global Corporate Communications & Social Media
kristen.kelly@westernunion.com

Tel: (720) 332-1000
Fax: (720) 332-4753

PEVO, Jillian M.
Registered Federal Lobbyist

Tel: (720) 332-1000
Fax: (720) 332-4753

SALOP, Michael
Senior Vice President, Investor Relations

Tel: (720) 332-1000
Fax: (720) 332-4753

SCOTT, Diane
Executive Vice President and Chief Marketing Officer

Tel: (720) 332-1000
Fax: (720) 332-4753

THOMPSON, John David
Executive Vice President, Global Operations and Technology, Chief Information Officer

Tel: (720) 332-1000
Fax: (720) 332-4753

WILLIAMS, Richard
Executive Vice President & Chief Human Resources Officer

Tel: (720) 332-1000
Fax: (720) 332-4753

Westinghouse Electric Company

A supplier of techology-based products and services for the commercial nuclear power industry worldwide. A BNFL Group company.
www.westinghousenuclear.com
Annual Revenues: $988.10 million
Employees: 7,000
SIC: 4833
Industry/ies: Energy/Electricity
Legislative Issues: BUD; ENG; ENV; TRD

President and Chief Executive Officer
RODERICK, Danny

Tel: (412) 374-4111
Fax: (412) 374-3272

Main Headquarters
Mailing: 1000 Westinghouse Dr.
Cranberry Township, PA 16066

Tel: (412) 374-2020
Fax: (412) 374-3272

Washington Office
Mailing: 900 19th St. NW
Suite 350
Washington, DC 20006

Tel: (202) 945-6401
Fax: (202) 945-6404

Political Action Committees
Westinghouse Electric Company PAC
FEC ID: C00346361
Contact: Penny E. Smith
900 19th St. NW
Suite 350
Washington, DC 20006

Tel: (202) 945-6401
Fax: (202) 945-6404

Contributions to Candidates: $89,000 (2015-2016)
Democrats: $20,000; Republicans: $69,000

Corporate Foundations and Giving Programs
Westinghouse Electric Company Contributions Program
Contact: Tracey Rapali
1000 Westinghouse Dr.
Suite 170
Cranberry Township, PA 16066

Public Affairs and Related Activities Personnel

At Headquarters

FISCHETTI, Karen
Consultant, Communications
fisch1ks@westinghouse.com

Tel: (412) 374-3373
Fax: (412) 374-3244

GABBIANELLI, Rick
Senior Vice President, Global Strategy and Operations Support

Tel: (412) 374-4111
Fax: (412) 374-3272

GILBERT, H. Vaughn
Manager, Public Relations and Advertising
gilberthv@westinhouse.com

Tel: (412) 374-3896
Fax: (412) 374-3272

HAGAN, Cassie
Senior vice president, Communications

Tel: (412) 374-2020
Fax: (412) 374-3272

HUDOK, Ron
Manager, NPP Communications
hudokrm@westinghouse.com

Tel: (412) 374-2613
Fax: (724) 940-8518

MARANO, Mark
President, Americas

Tel: (412) 374-2020
Fax: (412) 374-3272

MCALLISTER, Eric
Senior Vice President, Human Resources

Tel: (412) 374-2020
Fax: (412) 374-3272

MILLER, Angus
Senior Communications Specialist

Tel: (412) 374-2020
Fax: (412) 374-3272

RAPALI, Tracey
Communications Consultant, Charitable Giving and Community Outreach
rapalit@westinghousenuclear.com

Tel: (412) 374-4111
Fax: (412) 374-3272

SAKAMOTO, Ichiro
Senior Vice President and Chief Financial Officer

Tel: (412) 374-2020
Fax: (412) 374-3272

SWEENEY, Mike
Senior Vice President and General Counsel Legal and Contracts

Tel: (412) 374-4111
Fax: (412) 374-3272

TAKAHASHI, Tsutomu
Senior Vice President & Chief Financial Officer

Tel: (412) 374-4111
Fax: (412) 374-3272

At Washington Office

LOPATTO, Jeanne T.
Vice President, Government & International Affairs
lopattjt@westinghouse.com
Registered Federal Lobbyist

Tel: (202) 945-6410
Fax: (202) 945-6404

SMITH, Penny E.
PAC Treasurer

Tel: (202) 945-6410
Fax: (202) 945-6404

YOST, Chip
Registered Federal Lobbyist

Tel: (202) 945-6401
Fax: (202) 945-6404

Westmoreland Coal Company

A coal company which through its subsidiaries, operates as an energy company. The company engages in the production and sale of sub-bituminous coal and lignite to plants that generate electricity.
www.westmoreland.com
Employees: 3,440
Ticker: NASDAQ: WLB
SIC: 1221
Industry/ies: Natural Resources
Legislative Issues: IND; NAT; RET; TAX

Chief Executive Officer
PAPRZYCKI, Kevin A.

Tel: (719) 442-2600
Fax: (719) 219-2594

Main Headquarters
Mailing: 9540 S. Maroon Cir.
Suite 200
Englewood, CO 80112

Tel: (303) 922-6463
Fax: (719) 219-2594
TF: (855) 922-6463

Political Action Committees
Westmoreland Coal Company Political Action Committee

FEC ID: C00246686
Contact: Michael H. Santistevan
Two N.Cascade Ave.
Third Floor
Colorado Springs, CO 80903

Public Affairs and Related Activities Personnel

At Headquarters

BARR, Jonathan	Tel:	(720) 354-4467
Vice President, Sales and Power	Fax:	(719) 219-2594
sales@westmoreland.com		
GRAFTON, Jennifer S.	Tel:	(720) 354-4476
Senior Vice President, Chief Administrative Officer and	Fax:	(719) 219-2594
Secretary		
HAUCK, Mary A.	Tel:	(719) 442-2600
Vice President, Human Resources and Administration	Fax:	(719) 219-2594
SANTISTEVAN, Michael H.	Tel:	(719) 442-2600
PAC Treasurer	Fax:	(719) 219-2594
STANLEY-MADDOCKS, Lynette J.	Tel:	(303) 922-6463
General Counsel and Assistant Secretary	Fax:	(719) 219-2594
VEENSTRA, Jason W.	Tel:	(303) 922-6463
Chief Financial Officer and Treasurer	Fax:	(719) 219-2594

WestRock Company
Manufacturing

Main Headquarters
Mailing: 1101 17th St. NW
Suite 1005
Washington, DC 20036

Public Affairs and Related Activities Personnel

At Headquarters

STODDARD, Alexander H.

Weyerhaeuser Company
Develops forest products. The Company's wood products are used to build homes, where families are sheltered and raised. Their cellulose fibers are used to make diapers and other hygiene products that keep people clean and healthy. We innovate to use trees in products you may not expect, such as fabric, plastics and energy.
www.weyerhaeuser.com
Annual Revenues: $7.39 billion
Employees: 12,800
Ticker: NYSE: WY
SIC: 6798
Industry/ies: Paper And Wood Products Industry
Legislative Issues: AGR; CAW; ENG; IMM; NAT; TAX; TRA; TRD

Chairman of the Board	Tel:	(253) 924-2754
WILLIAMSON, Charles R.		

President and Chief Executive Officer	Tel:	(253) 924-2754
SIMONS, Doyle R.		

Main Headquarters
Mailing:	P.O. Box 9777	Tel:	(253) 924-2754
	CH 3D21	TF:	(800) 525-5440
	Federal Way, WA 98063-9777		

Washington Office
Mailing:	400 N. Capitol St. NW	Tel:	(202) 293-7222
	Suite 490	Fax:	(202) 293-2955
	Washington, DC 20001		

Political Action Committees
Plum Creek Timber Company, Inc. PAC
FEC ID: C00255224
Contact: Kathleen Sims
601 Union St.
Suite 3100
Seattle, WA 98101

> **Contributions to Candidates:** $66,750 (2015-2016)
> Democrats: $24,750; Republicans: $42,000

Weyerhaeuser Company PAC
FEC ID: C00007948
Contact: Kristen Sawin
P.O. Box 9777
CH-3D21
Federal Way, WA 98063

> **Contributions to Candidates:** $216,500 (2015-2016)
> Democrats: $79,000; Republicans: $137,500

> **Principal Recipients**
> **HOUSE**
> HERRERA BEUTLER, JAIME (REP-WA)

Corporate Foundations and Giving Programs
Plum Creek Foundation
Contact: Kirsten Smith

999 Third Ave.
Suite 4300
Seattle, WA 98104
Weyerhaeuser Company Foundation
33663 Weyerhaeuser Way South	Tel:	(253) 924-2345
Federal Way, WA 98003	Fax:	(253) 924-2685
	TF:	(800) 525-5440

Public Affairs and Related Activities Personnel

At Headquarters

BEDIENT, Patricia	Tel:	(253) 924-2345
Executive Vice President and Chief Financial Officer	Fax:	(253) 924-2685
CHAVEZ, Anthony	Tel:	(253) 924-7148
Manager, Government and Community Relations		
anthony.chavez@weyerhaeuser.com		
LOEB, Locke	Tel:	(253) 924-2754
Registered Federal Lobbyist		
MERLE, Denise M.	Tel:	(253) 924-2754
Senior Vice President, Human Resources		
SEATON, Elizabeth W.	Tel:	(253) 924-2345
Vice President, Strategic Planning		
STOCKFISH, Devin W.	Tel:	(253) 924-2754
Senior Vice President, General Counsel and Secretary		

At Washington Office

CHAPMAN, Richard	Tel:	(202) 293-7222
Public Relations and Communications	Fax:	(202) 293-2955
HOWELL, Andrea	Tel:	(202) 293-7222
Manager, Federal Government Affairs	Fax:	(202) 293-2955
andrea.howell@weyerhaeuser.com		
Registered Federal Lobbyist		
JIRSA, Robert J.	Tel:	(202) 293-7222
Vice President, Government Affairs	Fax:	(202) 293-2955
Mail Stop Suite 4300		
bob.jirsa@plumcreek.com		
MILLER, Fred	Tel:	(253) 924-2345
Manager, Political Affairs	Fax:	(202) 293-2955
frederick.miller@weyerhaeuser.com		
MURPHY, Hon. Scott	Tel:	(202) 293-7222
Federal anad International Affairs	Fax:	(202) 293-2955
Registered Federal Lobbyist		
PUNKE, Timothy E.	Tel:	(202) 293-7222
Senior Vice President, Corporate Affairs	Fax:	(202) 293-2955
SAWIN, Kristen	Tel:	(202) 293-7222
Vice President, Corporate Affairs & Public Policy	Fax:	(202) 293-2955
Registered Federal Lobbyist		
SIMS, Kathleen	Tel:	(202) 293-7222
Vice President, Government Relations & PAC Contact	Fax:	(202) 293-2955
STRING, Marik	Tel:	(202) 293-7222
Federal Lobbyist	Fax:	(202) 293-2955
Registered Federal Lobbyist		
SUM, Jay	Tel:	(202) 293-7222
Environmental Manager	Fax:	(202) 293-2955

At Other Offices

BROWN, Shari	Tel:	(859) 485-1110
Director, New Products & Technical Solutions		
380 Shorland Dr.		
Detroit, KY 41094		
CUSHMAN, Nancy	Tel:	(859) 485-1110
PAC Treasurer		
380 Shorland Dr.		
Detroit, KY 41094		

Wheeling Pittsburgh Steel Corporation
See listing on page 715 under Severstal North America

Whirlpool Corporation
A global home appliance industry.
www.whirlpoolcorp.com
Annual Revenues: $20.66 billion
Employees: 97,000
Ticker: NYSE: WHR
SIC: 3639; 3589; 5099
NAICS: 335228; 333319; 42199
Industry/ies: Electricity & Electronics; Electronics; Energy/Electricity; Furniture/Home Furnishings; Machinery/Equipment
Legislative Issues: CHM; ENG; MAN; RET; TAR; TAX; TRD

Chairman of the Board and Chief Executive Officer	Tel:	(269) 923-5000
FETTIG, Jeff M.	Fax:	(269) 923-3722
Jeff.Fettig@whirlpool.com		

Main Headquarters
Mailing:	2000 N. M-63	Tel:	(269) 923-5000

Benton Harbor, MI 49022-2692   Fax: (269) 923-3525

Washington Office

Mailing: 701 Pennsylvania Ave. NW   Tel: (202) 639-9420
            Suite 750   Fax: (202) 639-9421
            Washington, DC 20004

Political Action Committees

Whirlpool Corporation PAC
FEC ID: C00039040
Contact: Jason S. Eberstein
701 Pennsylvania Ave. NW   Tel: (202) 639-9420
Suite 750   Fax: (202) 639-9421
Washington, DC 20004

    Contributions to Candidates: $77,000 (2015-2016)
    Democrats: $12,500; Republicans: $64,500

Principal Recipients

HOUSE

UPTON, FREDERICK STEPHEN (REP-MI)

Corporate Foundations and Giving Programs

Whirlpool Foundation
Contact: Candy Garman
Administrative Center   Tel: (269) 923-5000
2000 N. M-63   Fax: (269) 923-3722
Benton Harbor, MI 49022

Public Affairs and Related Activities Personnel

At Headquarters

BINKLEY, David A.   Tel: (269) 923-5000
Senior Vice President, Global Human Resources Fax: (269) 923-3722
david_a_binkley@whirlpool.com

BITZER , Marc   Tel: (269) 923-5000
President and Chief Operating Officer   Fax: (269) 923-3525

GARMAN, Candy   Tel: (269) 923-5580
Manager, Foundation   Fax: (269) 925-0154

HEWITT, Kirsten   Tel: (269) 923-5000
Senior Vice President, Corporate Affairs and General Counsel   Fax: (269) 923-3722

TEAGUE, Monica   Tel: (269) 923-7405
Senior Manager, Public Relations and Brand Experience   Fax: (269) 923-3722
monica.teague@whirlpool.com

VENTURELLI, Larry   Tel: (269) 923-5000
Executive Vice President and Chief Financial Officer   Fax: (269) 923-3722
Larry.Venturelli@whirlpool.com

At Washington Office

BOVIM, Sarah H.   Tel: (202) 639-9420
Corporate Director, Government Relations   Fax: (202) 639-9421
sarah_bovim@whirlpool.com
Registered Federal Lobbyist

CATANIA, Jr., Thomas F.   Tel: (202) 639-9420
Vice President, Government Affairs   Fax: (202) 639-9421
thomas_f_catania@whirlpool.com
Registered Federal Lobbyist

EBERSTEIN, Jason S.   Tel: (202) 639-9420
Deputy Director, Government Relations   Fax: (202) 639-9421
Registered Federal Lobbyist

HARMS, Luke M.   Tel: (202) 639-9420
Senior Manager, Government Relations   Fax: (202) 639-9421
luke_m_harms@whirlpool.com
Registered Federal Lobbyist

MCKAY, Sean Christopher   Tel: (202) 639-9420
Senior Specialist, Government Relations   Fax: (202) 639-9421
sean_mackay@whirlpool.com
Registered Federal Lobbyist

Whole Foods Market Inc.

A natural and organic foods retailer.
www.wholefoodsmarket.com
Annual Revenues: $15.38 billion
Employees: 61,700
Ticker: NASDAQ; WFM
SIC: 5411
Industry/ies: Food And Beverage Industry

Chairman of the Board   Tel: (512) 477-4455
ELSTROTT, Dr. John B.   Fax: (512) 482-7000

Co-Chief Executive Officer   Tel: (512) 477-4455
ROBB, Walter   Fax: (512) 482-7000

Co-Chief Executive Officer and Co-Founder   Tel: (512) 477-4455
MACKEY, John   Fax: (512) 482-7000

Main Headquarters

Mailing: 550 Bowie St.   Tel: (512) 477-4455
            Austin, TX 78703-4644   Fax: (512) 482-7000

Corporate Foundations and Giving Programs

The Whole Planet Foundation
Contact: Philip Sansone
550 Bowie St.   Tel: (512) 477-4455
Austin, TX 78703-4644   Fax: (512) 476-5704

Public Affairs and Related Activities Personnel

At Headquarters

BURKHART, Liz   Tel: (512) 284-1836
Senior Global Media Relations Specialist   Fax: (512) 482-7000
Liz.Burkhart@wholefoods.com

FLANAGAN, Glenda Jane   Tel: (512) 477-4455
Executive Vice President and Chief Financial Officer   Fax: (512) 482-7000

GALLO, A.C.   Tel: (512) 477-4455
President and Chief Operating Officer   Fax: (512) 482-7000

LANG, Roberta   Tel: (512) 477-4455
General Counsel, Global Vice President, Chief Legal Officer   Fax: (512) 482-7000
and Corporate Secretary
roberta.lang@wholefoods.com

LANNON, David   Tel: (512) 477-4455
Executive Vice President, Operations   Fax: (512) 482-7000

MCCANN, Cindy   Tel: (512) 542-0204
Global Vice President, Investor Relations   Fax: (512) 482-7000

SANSONE, Philip   Tel: (512) 477-4455
President and Executive Director, Foundation Fax: (512) 476-5704

SUD, Jim   Tel: (512) 477-4455
Executive Vice President, Growth and Business Development   Fax: (512) 482-7000

WITTENBERG, Margaret   Tel: (512) 477-4455
Global Vice President, Quality Standards and Public Affairs   Fax: (512) 482-7000
margaret.wittenberg@wholefoods.com

Wildfire Protection Systems, LLC

Maker of wildfire supression systems for residences and commercial properties.
www.wildfireprotectionsystems.com
Industry/ies: Disaster

Main Headquarters

Mailing: 1627 Sarazen Dr.   Tel: (219) 728-6313
            Chesterton, IN 46304

Public Affairs and Related Activities Personnel

At Headquarters

FINNEY, Stephen   Tel: (219) 728-6313
Registered Federal Lobbyist

The Williams Companies, Inc.

A gas pipeline, energy services, and communications company based in Tulsa, Okla.
co.williams.com
Annual Revenues: $7.60 billion
Employees: 6,742
Ticker: NYSE: WMB
SIC: 4922
Industry/ies: Energy/Electricity; Fuels See Coal, Gas, Oil, Petroleum; Natural Resources; Petroleum Industry
Legislative Issues: FUE; NAT; TAX; TRA

Chairman of the Board   Tel: (918) 573-2000
MACINNIS, Frank T.   Fax: (918) 573-6714

President and Chief Executive Officer   Tel: (918) 573-2000
ARMSTRONG, Alan S.   Fax: (918) 573-6714

Main Headquarters

Mailing: One Williams Center   Tel: (918) 573-2000
            Tulsa, OK 74172   Fax: (918) 573-6714
                                                TF: (800) 945-5426

Washington Office

Mailing: 1627 Eye St. NW   Tel: (202) 833-8994
            Suite 900   Fax: (202) 835-0707
            Washington, DC 20006

Political Action Committees

Williams Companies, Inc. PAC, The
FEC ID: C00040394
Contact: William Gault
1627 I St. NW
Suite 900
Washington, DC 20006

    Contributions to Candidates: $314,500 (2015-2016)
    Democrats: $25,500; Republicans: $289,000

Corporate Foundations and Giving Programs

The Williams Companies, Inc. Contributions Program
One Williams Center   Tel: (918) 573-2000
Tulsa, OK 74142   Fax: (918) 573-6714

Public Affairs and Related Activities Personnel

At Headquarters

BILLINGS, Frank E.   Tel: (918) 573-2000
Senior Vice President, Corporate Strategic Development   Fax: (918) 573-6714

CHAPPEL, Donald R.   Tel: (918) 573-2000
Senior Vice President and Chief Financial Officer   Fax: (918) 573-6714

EWING, Robyn L.   Tel: (918) 573-2000
Senior Vice President, Strategic Services and Administration   Fax: (918) 573-6714
and Chief Administrative Officer

GAULT, William   Tel: (918) 573-2000
PAC Contact, Government Affairs   Fax: (918) 573-6714

GENTZ, Julie   Tel: (918) 573-3053
Manager, External Communications   Fax: (918) 573-6714
julie.gentz@williams.com

ISBELL, Keith   Tel: (918) 573-2000
Senior Communications Specialist   Fax: (918) 573-6714

MILLER, Sarah C.   Tel: (918) 573-2000
Interim Senior Vice President & General Counsel   Fax: (918) 573-6714

NEASON, Judith L.   Tel: (918) 573-2000
Federal Lobbyists   Fax: (918) 573-6714
Registered Federal Lobbyist

PORTER, John D.   Tel: (918) 573-0797
Director, Investor Relations, Enterprise Planning and   Fax: (918) 573-6714
Analysis

RAINEY, Craig L.   Tel: (918) 573-2000
Senior Vice President and General Counsel   Fax: (918) 573-6714
craig.rainey@williams.com

At Washington Office

JACKSON, Glenn F.   Tel: (202) 833-8994
Director, Government Affairs   Fax: (202) 835-0707

Williams Sonoma, Inc.

Multi-channel specialty retailer of home products. It operates in two segments, Direct-to-Customer and Retail
www.williams-sonomainc.com
Annual Revenues: $5.04 billion
Employees: 11,600
Ticker: NYSE: WSM
SIC: 5700
Industry/ies: Apparel/Textiles Industry; Furniture; Furniture/Home Furnishings; Housewares; Textiles

Chairman of the Board   Tel: (415) 421-7900
BELLAMY, Adrian

Director, President and Chief Executive Officer   Tel: (415) 421-7900
ALBER, Laura J.

Main Headquarters
Mailing: 3250 Van Ness Ave.   Tel: (415) 421-7900
     San Francisco, CA 94109

Corporate Foundations and Giving Programs
Williams Sonoma Contributions Program
3250 Van Ness Ave.
San Francisco, CA 94109

Public Affairs and Related Activities Personnel

At Headquarters

CONNOLLY, Patrick J.   Tel: (415) 421-7900
Director, Executive Vice President and Chief Strategy and
Business Development Officer

HAYES, Janet   Tel: (415) 421-7900
President

KING, David   Tel: (415) 421-7900
General Counsel and Senior Vice President

LEWIS, Linda   Tel: (415) 421-7900
Chief Talent Officer and Executive Vice President

MILLER, Dean A.   Tel: (415) 421-7900
Executive Vice President and Chief Operating Officer

WHALEN, Julie   Tel: (415) 421-7900
Executive Vice President and Chief Financial Officer

Windstream Communications

Telecommunications service provider.
www.windstream.com
Annual Revenues: $5.72 billion
Employees: 12,326
Ticker: NASDAQ: WIN
SIC: 4813
Industry/ies: Communications; Telecommunications/Internet/Cable
Legislative Issues: BUD; CPT; TAX; TEC

Chairman of the Board   Tel: (877) 759-9020
HINSON , Jeffrey T.

President and Chief Executive Officer   Tel: (501) 748-7000
THOMAS, Tony

Main Headquarters
Mailing: 4001 Rodney Parham Rd.   Tel: (877) 759-9020
     Little Rock, AR 72212   TF: (866) 445-5882

Washington Office
Mailing: 1101 17th St. NW   Tel: (202) 223-7665
     Suite 802
     Washington, DC 20036

Political Action Committees
Windstream Corporation PAC
FEC ID: C00425975
Contact: Christie Grumbos
4001 Rodney Parham Rd.   Tel: (501) 748-7000
Little Rock, AR 72212

   Contributions to Candidates: $139,500 (2015-2016)
   Democrats: $57,500; Republicans: $81,000; Other: $1,000

Public Affairs and Related Activities Personnel

At Headquarters

AVERY, David   Tel: (501) 748-5876
Vice President, Corporate Communications
david.avery@windstream.com

DEMENT, Matt   Tel: (877) 759-9020
Senior Vice President, Strategy, Corporate Development and
Financial Planning and Analysis

EINHORN, Eric   Tel: (202) 997-9387
Senior Vice President, Government Affairs
eric.n.einhorn@windstream.com
Registered Federal Lobbyist

FARIS, Mark   Tel: (877) 759-9020
Executive Vice President, Network Deployment and
Management

FLETCHER, John   Tel: (501) 748-7000
Executive Vice President, Chief Human Resources Officer and
General Counsel

GRUMBOS, Christie   Tel: (877) 759-9020
Senior Vice President, Treasurer and PAC Treasurer

GUNDERMAN, Bob   Tel: (877) 759-9020
Chief Financial Officer

HAWKINS, Rodney   Tel: (877) 759-9020
Vice President, Internal Audit and Chief Compliance Officer

LAPERCH, William G.   Tel: (501) 748-7000
Board Member

MOODY, Kristi   Tel: (877) 759-9020
Senior Vice President and Corporate Secretary

PERKINS, Don   Tel: (877) 759-9020
Vice President, Product Marketing

REDMOND, David   Tel: (877) 759-9020
President, Consumer Services

TEAGUE, Micheal   Tel: (877) 759-9020
Media Contact
michael.teague@windstream.com

WORKS, David   Tel: (877) 759-9020
President, Enterprise

At Washington Office

HIGHFILL, Clinton A.   Tel: (202) 223-7665
Senior Legislative Counsel
Clinton.Highfill@windstream.com
Registered Federal Lobbyist

Winn-Dixie Stores

A supermarket chain.
www.winndixie.com
Annual Revenues: $6.88 billion
Employees: 20,680
Ticker: NASDAQ: WINN
SIC: 5411
Industry/ies: Food And Beverage Industry; Retail/Wholesale

President and Chief Executive Officer
MCLEOD, Ian

Main Headquarters
Mailing: 5050 EDGEWOOD Ct.   Tel: (904) 783-5000
     Suite 200   Fax: (904) 370-7224
     Jacksonville Beach, FL 32254   TF: (800) 967-9105

Political Action Committees
WIN-PAC of Winn-Dixie Stores, Inc.
FEC ID: C00033092
Contact: Jeffrey Gleason
5050 Edgewood Ct.   Tel: (904) 783-5000
Jacksonville Beach, FL 32254   Fax: (904) 783-5294

Corporate Foundations and Giving Programs

Winn-Dixie Stores Foundation
5050 Edgewood Ct.
Jacksonville Beach, FL 32254

Tel: (904) 783-5000
Fax: (904) 783-7224

Public Affairs and Related Activities Personnel

At Headquarters

GLEASON, Jeffrey
PAC Treasurer

Tel: (904) 783-5000
Fax: (904) 783-5294

Wipro Technologies Inc.

A provider of integrated business, technology, consulting, testing and process solutions on a global delivery platform.
www.wipro.com
Industry/ies: Computer/Technology

Main Headquarters
Mailing: Two Tower Center Blvd.
Suite 2200
E. Brunswick, NJ 08816

Tel: (732) 509-1500
Fax: (732) 514-0860

Washington Office
Mailing: 601 13th St. NW
11th Floor
Washington, DC 20005

Tel: (202) 534-1795

Public Affairs and Related Activities Personnel

At Washington Office

CARTER-MAGUIRE, Melanie
Vice President and Head, Government Relations

Tel: (202) 534-1795

Wisconsin Energy Corporation

An electric, natural gas, and steam utility.
www.wisconsinenergy.com
Annual Revenues: $4.69 billion
Employees: 4,248
Ticker: NYSE: WEC
SIC: 4931
Industry/ies: Energy/Electricity; Utilities
Legislative Issues: BUD; CAW; COM; ENG; ENV; LBR; TAX; TRA; UTI

Chairman of the Board, President, and Chief Executive Officer
KLAPPA, Gale E.

Tel: (414) 221-2345
Fax: (414) 221-2554

Main Headquarters
Mailing: P.O. Box 1331
Milwaukee, WI 53201

Tel: (414) 221-2345
Fax: (414) 221-2554

Washington Office
Mailing: 122 C St. NW
Suite 840
Washington, DC 20001

Tel: (202) 662-4340
Fax: (202) 662-4359

Corporate Foundations and Giving Programs

Wisconsin Energy Foundation
Contact: Patricia L. McNew
231 W. Michigan St.
Room P409A
Milwaukee, WI 53203

Public Affairs and Related Activities Personnel

At Headquarters

HENDERSON, CFA, Colleen F.
Manager, Strategic Planning and Investor Relations
colleen.henderson@wisconsinenergy.com

Tel: (414) 221-2592
Fax: (414) 221-2554

KEYES, J. Patrick
Executive Vice President and Chief Financial Officer

Tel: (414) 221-2345
Fax: (414) 221-2554

MARTIN, Susan H.
Executive Vice President, General Counsel and Corporate Secretary

Tel: (414) 221-2345
Fax: (414) 221-2554

At Washington Office

DEMASTERS, Darnell K.
Vice President, Federal Policy
darnell.demasters@we-energies.com
Registered Federal Lobbyist

Tel: (202) 662-4340
Fax: (202) 662-4359

GARVIN, Robert M.
Senior Vice President, External Affairs
robert.garvin@wisconsinenergy.com

Tel: (202) 662-4340
Fax: (202) 662-4359

SCOTT, Tiffany
Registered Federal Lobbyist

Tel: (202) 662-4340
Fax: (202) 662-4359

At Other Offices

MCNEW, Patricia L.
Foundation Administrator
231 W. Michigan St.
Milwaukee, WI 53203
patti.mcnew@we-energies.com

Tel: (414) 221-2107
Fax: (414) 221-2412

Wisconsin Public Service Corporation

Mission is to Provide Customers with the Best Value in Energy and Related Services.

www.wisconsinpublicservice.com
SIC: 4931
Industry/ies: Energy/Electricity

President
SCHROCK, Charles

Tel: (920) 433-5522

Main Headquarters
Mailing: P.O. Box 19003
Green Bay, WI 54307-9003

Tel: (920) 433-5522
TF: (800) 450-7260

Corporate Foundations and Giving Programs

Wisconsin Public Service Foundation
Contact: Lynn Kroll
P.O. Box 19001
Green Bay, WI 54307

Tel: (920) 655-1949
Fax: (920) 433-1693

Public Affairs and Related Activities Personnel

At Headquarters

ANTONNEAU, Ron
Director, Government Affairs
RRAntonneau@wisconsinpublicservice.com

Tel: (920) 433-5522

KROLL, Lynn
Leader, Community Relations
lmkroll@wisconsinpublicservice.com

Tel: (920) 617-5160

LEMKE, Karmen
Manager, Community Relations and Contributions
KMLemke@wisconsinpublicservice.com

Tel: (920) 433-1433

PRUNTY, Lisa
Manager, Public Relations
lprunty@integrysgroup.com

Tel: (920) 433-1533

STEFFEN, Todd
Senior Public Relations Specialist
Mail Stop A2
tjsteffen@integrysgroup.com

Tel: (920) 433-1617

Wm. Wrigley Jr. Company

Wrigley operates as a subsidiary of Mars and was founded in 1911. The company's products include Big Red, Doublemint, Spearmint, Eclipse, Extra, and Juicy Fruit, as well as novelty gums (Hubba Bubba and other kid-friendly chews). Wrigley also offers non-gum items, including breath mints Altoids and Velamints and candies Creme Savers and Life Savers.
www.wrigley.com
Employees: 17,000
Ticker: NYSE: WWY
SIC: 2060; 2067
Industry/ies: Food And Beverage Industry

Chairman of the Board
WRIGLEY, Jr., William

Tel: (312) 644-2121
Fax: (312) 644-0353

President
RADVAN, Martin

Tel: (312) 644-2121
Fax: (312) 644-0353

Main Headquarters
Mailing: 410 N. Michigan Ave.
Chicago, IL 60610

Tel: (312) 644-2121
Fax: (312) 644-0353
TF: (800) 974-4539

Corporate Foundations and Giving Programs

Wm. Wrigley Jr. Company Foundation
Contact: Maureen Jones
410 N. Michigan Ave.
Chicago, IL 60611

Tel: (312) 644-2121
Fax: (312) 644-0015
TF: (800) 974-4539

Public Affairs and Related Activities Personnel

At Headquarters

GAMORAN, Reuben
Chief Financial Officer and Executive Vice President

Tel: (312) 644-2121
Fax: (312) 644-0353

JONES, Maureen
Manager and Executive Director of the Wrigley Company Foundation
maureen.jones@wrigley.com

Tel: (312) 794-7126
Fax: (312) 644-0353

LUTH , Jennifer Jackson
Senior Manager, North American Corporate Affairs
jennifer.jacksonluth@wrigley.com

Tel: (312) 645-8876
Fax: (312) 644-0353

PHAROAH, Andy
Media Contact and Vice President, Corporate Affairs, Sustainability and Strategy
andy.pharoah@wrigley.com

Tel: (312) 645-3696
Fax: (312) 644-0353

WorldSpace Corporation

Satellite communications company.
www.world-space.com
Annual Revenues: $13.44 million
Employees: 500
Ticker: NASDAQ: WRSP
Industry/ies: Aerospace/Aviation; Communications; Telecommunications/Internet/Cable; Transportation

President and Chief Executive Officer
SAMARA, Noah A.

Tel: (301) 960-1200
Fax: (301) 960-2200

Main Headquarters
Mailing: 8515 Georgia Ave.
Silver Spring, MD 20910

Tel: (301) 960-1233
Fax: (202) 861-6407

Public Affairs and Related Activities Personnel

At Headquarters

FRICKEL, Donald J.
Executive Vice President, General Counsel and Secretary

Tel: (301) 960-1233
Fax: (202) 861-6407

GANESAN, Sridhar
Executive Vice President and Chief Financial Officer

Tel: (301) 960-1233
Fax: (202) 861-6407

Worthington Industries

A steel processor and manufacturer of metal related products.
www.worthingtonindustries.com
Annual Revenues: $3.43 billion
Employees: 10,000
Ticker: NYSE: WOR
SIC: 3310; 2542; 3441
NAICS: 337215; 332312
Industry/ies: Metals

Chairman of the Board and Chief Executive Officer
MCCONNELL, John P.

Tel: (614) 438-3210
Fax: (614) 438-3136

Main Headquarters
Mailing: 200 Old Wilson Bridge Rd.
Columbus, OH 43085

Tel: (614) 438-3210
Fax: (614) 438-7948

Political Action Committees
Worthington Industries PAC
FEC ID: C00397554
Contact: Cathy Lyttle
200 Old Wilson Bridge Rd.
Columbus, OH 43085

Tel: (614) 438-3210
Fax: (614) 840-4150

> **Contributions to Candidates:** $11,500 (2015-2016)
> Democrats: $1,000; Republicans: $10,500

Corporate Foundations and Giving Programs
Worthington Industries Foundation
Contact: Cathy Lyttle
200 Old Wilson Bridge Rd.
Columbus, OH 43085

Tel: (614) 438-3077
Fax: (614) 840-4150

Public Affairs and Related Activities Personnel

At Headquarters

BRINKMAN, Dale T.
Vice President, Administration, General Counsel, and Secretary
dale.brinkman@worthingtonindustries

Tel: (614) 438-3210
Fax: (614) 840-4150

DYER , Terry M.
Vice President, Human Resources

Tel: (614) 438-3210
Fax: (614) 438-7948

HIGGINBOTHAM, Sonya L.
Director, Corporate Communications
slhiggin@WorthingtonIndustries.com

Tel: (614) 438-7391
Fax: (614) 438-7948

LOCKARD, Matthew
Vice President, Finance and Strategy

Tel: (614) 438-3210
Fax: (614) 438-7948

LYTTLE, Cathy
Vice President, Corporate Communications and Investor Relations
cmlyttle@worthingtonindustries.com

Tel: (614) 438-3077
Fax: (614) 840-4150

ROSE, Andy
Vice President and Chief Financial Officer

Tel: (614) 438-3210
Fax: (614) 438-7948

RUSSELL, Mark A.
President and Chief Operating Officer

Tel: (614) 438-3210
Fax: (614) 438-7948

SCHLABIG, Matt
Chief Information Officer

Tel: (614) 438-3210
Fax: (614) 438-7948

STOE, George P.
Director, International Business Development

Tel: (614) 438-3210
Fax: (614) 438-7948

WPX Energy Inc

An independent natural gas, natural gas liquids and oil from non-conventional resources company.
www.wpxenergy.com
Annual Revenues: $1.31 billion
Employees: 1,040
Ticker: NYSE: WPX
SIC: 1311
Legislative Issues: ENG; FUE; NAT; RES

Chairman
LOWRIE, William G.

Tel: (855) 979-2012

President and Chief Executive Officer
MUNCRIEF, Richard L.

Tel: (855) 979-2012

Main Headquarters

Mailing: 801 Pennsylvania Ave. NW
Suite 315
Washington, DC 20004

Tel: (202) 347-6103

Corporate Foundations and Giving Programs

WPX Energy Contribution Programme
Contact: Sarah Walker
One Williams Center
Tulsa, OK 74172

Tel: (539) 573-5631

Public Affairs and Related Activities Personnel

At Headquarters

GASPAR, Clay
Senior Vice President, Chief Operating Officer

Tel: (202) 347-6103

GUDERIAN, Bryan
Senior Vice President, Business Development

Tel: (202) 347-6103

ROTH, Pam
PAC Treasurer
Registered Federal Lobbyist

Tel: (202) 347-6103

At Other Offices

BEAVER, Trent
Manager, Legal Business Services
3500 One Williams Center, MD 38
Tulsa, OK 74172

Tel: (855) 979-2012

CAMERON, Dennis C.
Senior Vice President and General Counsel
3500 One Williams Center, MD 38
Tulsa, OK 74172

Tel: (855) 979-2012

FISER, Michael R.
Senior Vice President, Marketing
3500 One Williams Center, MD 38
Tulsa, OK 74172

Tel: (855) 979-2012

FLAKNE, Amy
Senior Counsel
3500 One Williams Center, MD 38
Tulsa, OK 74172

Tel: (855) 979-2012

MACLEOD, Marcia M.
Senior Vice President, Human Resources and Administration
3500 One Williams Center, MD 38
Tulsa, OK 74172

Tel: (855) 979-2012

ROTH, Pam
PAC Treasurer
1001 17th St., Suite 1200
Denver, CO 80202
Registered Federal Lobbyist

SULLIVAN, David
Manager, Investor Relations
3500 One Williams Center, MD 38
Tulsa, OK 74172
WPXInvestorRelations@WPXEnergy.com

Tel: (539) 573-9360

VANN, J. Kevin
Senior Vice President and Chief Financial Officer
3500 One Williams Center, MD 38
Tulsa, OK 74172

Tel: (855) 979-2012

WALKER, Sarah
Manager, Community Affairs and Administration Services
3500 One Williams Center, MD 38
Tulsa, OK 74172

Tel: (539) 573-5631

W. R. Grace & Company

Produces and sells specialty chemicals and materials worldwide.
www.grace.com
Annual Revenues: $3.22 billion
Employees: 6,500
Ticker: NYSE: GRA
SIC: 2819; 2869
Industry/ies: Chemicals & Chemical Industry
Legislative Issues: ENV

Chairman of the Board and Chief Executive Officer
FESTA, Alfred E.

Tel: (410) 531-4000
Fax: (410) 531-4367

Main Headquarters
Mailing: 7500 Grace Dr.
Columbia, MD 21044

Tel: (410) 531-4000
Fax: (410) 531-4367

Corporate Foundations and Giving Programs

Grace Foundation Inc.
Contact: Shirley Hewitt
7500 Grace Dr.
Columbia, MD 21044

Tel: (410) 531-4000

Public Affairs and Related Activities Personnel

At Headquarters

BADMINGTON, Rich R.
Vice President, Global Communications, Media Relations

Tel: (410) 531-4370
Fax: (410) 531-4367

rich.badmington@grace.com.

BROWN, Elizabeth
Vice President and Chief Human Resources Officer
Tel: (410) 531-4000
Fax: (410) 531-4367

COLE, Keith
Vice President, Government Relations & Environment, Health, & Safety
Tel: (410) 531-4000
Fax: (410) 531-4367

CORCORAN, William M.
Vice President, Public and Regulatory Affairs
Tel: (410) 531-4000
Fax: (410) 531-4367

FORCE, Hudson La
Senior Vice President and Chief Financial Officer
Tel: (410) 531-4000
Fax: (410) 531-4367

HEWITT, Shirley
Executive Assistant to Vice President, Government Relations
Tel: (410) 531-4000
Fax: (410) 531-4367

JONES, Mike
Director, Global Branding
Tel: (410) 531-8228
Fax: (410) 531-4367

KUCHINSKY, Dori Anne
Assistant General Counsel, Litigation and Global Privacy
Tel: (410) 531-4000
Fax: (410) 531-4367

POLING, Gregory E.
President and Chief Operating Officer
Tel: (410) 531-4000
Fax: (410) 531-4367

SHELNITZ, Mark A.
Vice President, General Counsel and Secretary
mark.shelnitz@grace.com
Tel: (410) 531-4000
Fax: (410) 531-4367

SUTHERLAND, Mark
Vice President, Investor Relations
mark.sutherland@grace.com
Tel: (410) 531-4590
Fax: (410) 531-4367

WSFS Financial Corporation

A financial services holding company.
www.wsfsbank.com
Annual Revenues: $228.55 million
Employees: 857
Ticker: NASDAQ: WSFS
SIC: 6021
Industry/ies: Banking/Finance/Investments

Chairman of the Board
SCHOENHALS, Marvin N.
mschoenhals@wsfsbank.com
Tel: (302) 792-6000
Fax: (302) 571-6842

President and Chief Executive Officer
TURNER, Mark A.
Tel: (302) 792-6000
Fax: (302) 571-6842

Main Headquarters
Mailing: 500 Delaware Ave.
        Wilmington, DE 19801
Tel: (302) 792-6000
Fax: (302) 571-6842
TF: (888) 973-7226

Political Action Committees
WSFS Financial Corporation PAC
FEC ID: C00380816
Contact: Charles Mosher
500 Delaware Ave.
Wilmington, DE 19801

Corporate Foundations and Giving Programs
WSFS Community Relations Program
500 Delaware Ave.
Wilmington, DE 19801
Tel: (302) 792-6000
Fax: (302) 571-5842
TF: (888) 973-7226

Public Affairs and Related Activities Personnel

At Headquarters

EDDENS, Peggy H.
Executive Vice President and Chief Human Capital Officer
Tel: (302) 792-6000
Fax: (302) 571-6842

HEIST, Stephanie
Vice President, Marketing
sheist@wsfsbank.com
Tel: (302) 571-5259
Fax: (302) 571-6842

KLEIN, Cortney
Associate Vice President, Marketing
cklein@wsfsbank.com
Tel: (302) 571-5253
Fax: (302) 571-6842

LEVENSON, Rodger
Executive Vice President and Chief Financial Officer
Tel: (302) 792-6000
Fax: (302) 571-6842

MOSHER, Charles
PAC Contact
Tel: (302) 792-6000
Fax: (302) 571-6842

SELLERS, Beth
Contact, Investor Relations and Media Relations
bsellers@wsfsbank.com
Tel: (302) 571-7264
Fax: (302) 571-6842

Wyndham Worldwide Corporation

Offers individual consumers and business customers an array of hospitality products and services as well as various accommodation alternatives and price ranges through its brands.
www.wyndhamworldwide.com
Annual Revenues: $5.58 billion
Employees: 37,700
Ticker: NYSE: WYN
SIC: 7011
Industry/ies: Travel/Tourism/Lodging

Legislative Issues: LBR

Chairman of the Board and Chief Executive Officer
HOLMES, Stephen P.
Tel: (973) 753-6000
Fax: (973) 753-7537

Main Headquarters
Mailing: 22 Sylvan Way
        Parsippany, NJ 07054
Tel: (973) 753-6000
Fax: (973) 753-7537

Political Action Committees
Wyndham Worldwide Corporation PAC (Wyndham PAC)
FEC ID: C00424374
Contact: Nicola Rossi
22 Sylvan Way
Parsippany, NJ 07054
Tel: (973) 496-8900
Fax: (973) 496-7658

   Contributions to Candidates: $14,000 (2015-2016)
   Democrats: $1,000; Republicans: $13,000

Corporate Foundations and Giving Programs
Wyndham Worldwide Corporation Contributions Program
22 Sylvan Way
Parsippany, NJ 07054
Tel: (973) 753-6000
Fax: (973) 753-7537

Public Affairs and Related Activities Personnel

At Headquarters

AYALA , Nadeen A.
Senior Vice President, Communications
Nadeen.Ayala@wyn.com
Tel: (973) 753-6590
Fax: (973) 753-7537

CONFORTI, Thomas G.
Executive Vice President, Chief Financial Officer
thomas.conforti@wyndhamworldwide.com
Tel: (973) 753-6000
Fax: (973) 753-7537

FALVEY, Mary R.
Executive Vice President, Chief Human Resources Officer
mary.falvey@wyndhamworldwide.com
Tel: (973) 753-6000
Fax: (973) 753-7537

HAPPER, Margo C.
Senior Vice President, Investor Relations
margo.happer@wyndhamworldwide.com
Tel: (973) 753-5500
Fax: (973) 753-7537

MCLESTER, Scott G.
Executive Vice President and General Counsel
Tel: (973) 496-8900
Fax: (973) 753-7537

ROSSI, Nicola
Senior Vice President and Chief Accounting Officer
Tel: (973) 496-8900
Fax: (973) 753-7537

Xcel Energy, Inc.

Formed by the merger of New Century Energies and Northern States Power Company in 2000. Engaged in the generation, purchase, transmission, distribution, and sale of electricity.
www.xcelenergy.com
Annual Revenues: $10.83 billion
Employees: 11,601
Ticker: NYSE: XEL
SIC: 4911
NAICS: 221119
Industry/ies: Energy/Electricity; Utilities
Legislative Issues: BUD; ENG; ENV; HOM; RET; TAX; TRA; UTI

Chairman of the Board, President and Chief Executive Officer
FOWKE, III, Benjamin G. S.
benjamin.g.fowke@xcelenergy.com
Tel: (612) 330-5500
Fax: (800) 895-2895

Main Headquarters
Mailing: P.O. Box 9477
        Minneapolis, MN 55484-9477
Tel: (612) 330-5500
Fax: (800) 895-2895
TF: (800) 895-4999

Washington Office
Mailing: 701 Pennsylvania Ave. NW
        Suite 250
        Washington, DC 20004
Tel: (202) 783-3598

Political Action Committees
Xcel Energy Employee PAC (XPAC)
FEC ID: C00107771
Contact: Julia Evans
1800 Larimer St.
Suite 1600
Denver, CO 80202
Tel: (303) 571-7511
Fax: (303) 294-9120

   Contributions to Candidates: $170,800 (2015-2016)
   Democrats: $44,500; Republicans: $126,300

Corporate Foundations and Giving Programs
Xcel Energy Foundation
Contact: Benjamin G. S. Fowke III
1225 17th St.
Suite 900
Denver, CO 80202
Tel: (303) 571-7511
Fax: (303) 294-8120

Public Affairs and Related Activities Personnel

At Headquarters

ABEL, Brian Van
Vice President and Treasurer
Tel: (612) 330-5500
Fax: (800) 895-2895

FRENZEL, Robert (Bob)
Tel: (612) 330-5500

Executive Vice President and Chief Financial Officer	Fax:	(800) 895-2895

JOHNSON, Paul A.
Vice President, Investor Relations and Business Development
Paul.A.Johnson@xcelenergy.com
Tel: (612) 215-4535
Fax: (800) 895-2895

LOVATO, Monique L.
Director, XCEL Energy Foundation
monique.l.lovato@xcelenergy.com
Tel: (612) 330-5500
Fax: (800) 895-2895

POFERL, Judy M.
Senior Vice President, Corporate Secretary and Executive Services
Tel: (612) 330-5500
Fax: (800) 895-2895

WILENSKY, Scott
Senior Vice President and General Counsel
Tel: (612) 330-5500
Fax: (800) 895-2895

At Other Offices

BRAVO, Summer
325 Seventh St. NW, Suite 550
Washington, DC 20004
Registered Federal Lobbyist
Tel: (202) 661-4490

DOERN, Martin
325 Seventh St. NW, Suite 550
Washington, DC 20004
Registered Federal Lobbyist
Tel: (202) 661-4490

EVANS, Julia
Manager, Performance and Planning, Lobbyist and PAC Treasurer
1800 Larimer St., Suite 1600
Denver, CO 80202
Mail Stop Suite 1600
Tel: (303) 571-7068
Fax: (303) 294-8120

HUDSON, David
President
1800 Larimer St., Suite 1600
Denver, CO 80202
David.Hudson@xcelenergy.com
Tel: (303) 571-7068
Fax: (303) 294-8120

PLEVNIAK, Stephen L.
Manager, Federal Government Affairs
325 Seventh St. NW, Suite 550
Washington, DC 20004
L.Plevniak@xcelenergy.com
Registered Federal Lobbyist
Tel: (202) 661-4490

WOZNIAK, Jennifer
Director, Strategic Communications
1800 Larimer St., Suite 1600
Denver, CO 80202
jennifer.b.wozniak@xcelenergy.com
Tel: (303) 294-2232
Fax: (303) 294-8120

Xerox Corporation

A designer, engineer, developer, manufacturer, marketer and servicer of document processing products and systems.
www.xerox.com
Annual Revenues: $17.86 billion
Employees: 135,300
Ticker: NYSE: XRX
SIC: 7389
Industry/ies: Electricity & Electronics; Electronics; Energy/Electricity; Machinery/Equipment
Legislative Issues: AGR; FIN; HCR; LBR; RET; TAR; TAX; TEC; TRD

Chairman of the Board and Chief Executive Officer
BURNS, Ursula M.
Tel: (203) 968-3000
Fax: (203) 968-3218

Main Headquarters
Mailing: 45 Glover Ave.
P.O. Box 4505
Norwalk, CT 06856-4505
Tel: (203) 968-3000
Fax: (203) 968-3218
TF: (800) 334-6200

Washington Office
Mailing: 1800 M St. Northwest
North Tower, 5th Floor
Washington, DC 20036
Tel: (202) 414-1200

Political Action Committees
Xerox Corporation Political Action Committee (X-PAC)
FEC ID: C00207258
Contact: Michele L. Cahn
1800 M St. NW
North Tower, Suite 700
Washington, DC 20036
Tel: (202) 414-1200
Fax: (202) 414-1217

> **Contributions to Candidates:** $29,000 (2015-2016)
> Democrats: $12,000; Republicans: $17,000

Corporate Foundations and Giving Programs
Xerox Foundation
Contact: Mark Conlin
45 Glover Ave.
P.O. Box 4505
Norwalk, CT 06856-10
Tel: (203) 968-3333
Fax: (203) 968-4312

Public Affairs and Related Activities Personnel

At Headquarters

COLLINS, Sean Collins
Corporate Public Relations Contact
sean.collins2@xerox.com
Tel: (310) 497-9205
Fax: (203) 968-3218

CONLIN, Mark
President, Xerox Foundation
mark.conlin@xerox.com
Tel: (203) 968-3333
Fax: (203) 968-4312

FORD, Darrell L.
Corporate Senior Vice President, Chief Human Resources Officer
Tel: (203) 968-3000
Fax: (203) 968-3218

KENNEDY, John
Corporate Vice President and Chief Marketing Officer
Tel: (203) 968-3000
Fax: (203) 968-3218

LIU, Don H.
Corporate Senior Vice President, General Counsel and Secretary
Don.Liu@xerox.com
Tel: (203) 968-3000
Fax: (203) 968-3944

MAATY, Yehia
Corporate Vice President President, Developing Markets Operations
Tel: (203) 968-3000
Fax: (203) 968-3218

PHILIP, Rohit
Corporate Vice President XLN and Treasurer
Tel: (203) 968-3000
Fax: (203) 968-3218

VARON, Leslie F.
Corporate Vice President, Interim Chief Financial Officer and Vice President, Investor Relations
Tel: (203) 968-3000
Fax: (203) 968-3218

At Washington Office

CAHN, Michele L.
Vice President, Global Government Affairs
michele.cahn@xerox.com
Registered Federal Lobbyist
Tel: (202) 414-1200

EGEE, Edwin W.
Federal Lobbyist and Manager, Government Affairs
Registered Federal Lobbyist
Tel: (202) 414-1200

HENNING, Stephanie
Manager, International Government Relations
Tel: (202) 414-1200

IGBOKWE, Olivia
Registered Federal Lobbyist
Tel: (202) 414-1200

REISER, Martin
Manager, Government Policy
Registered Federal Lobbyist
Tel: (202) 414-1200

ROGERS, Alec
Federal Lobbyist and Manager, Government Policy
Alec.Rogers@xerox.com
Registered Federal Lobbyist
Tel: (202) 414-1200

SCHAEFER, Stephen
Federal Lobbyist
Registered Federal Lobbyist
Tel: (202) 414-1200

At Other Offices

FIRESTONE, James A.
Corporate Executive Vice President President, Corporate Strategy
100 S. Clinton Ave.
Rochester, NY 14604-1801
Tel: (585) 422-5721
Fax: (585) 423-4272

LANGSENKAMP, Carl
Director, Global Public Relations
100 S. Clinton Ave.
Rochester, NY 14604-1801
Mail Stop XRX2-004
Carl.Langsenkamp@xerox.com
Tel: (585) 423-5782
Fax: (585) 423-4272

NESBITT, Elissa
Manager, Community Relations
100 S. Clinton Ave.
Rochester, NY 14604-1801
elissa.nesbitt@xerox.com
Tel: (585) 423-3591
Fax: (585) 423-4272

Xilinx

A supplier of field-programmable gate arrays (FPGAs) and complex programmable logic devices (CPLDs).
www.xilinx.com
Annual Revenues: $2.38 billion
Employees: 3,500
Ticker: NASDAQ: XLNX
SIC: 3679; 3674
Industry/ies: Banking/Finance/Investments

Chairman of the Board
GIANOS, Philip T.
Tel: (408) 559-7778
Fax: (408) 559-7114

President and Chief Executive Officer
GAVRIELOV, Moshe
Tel: (408) 559-7778
Fax: (408) 559-7114

Main Headquarters
Mailing: 2100 Logic Dr.
San Jose, CA 95124-3400
Tel: (408) 559-7778
Fax: (408) 559-7114

		TF:	(800) 255-7778

Corporate Foundations and Giving Programs

Xilinx Contributions Program
2100 Logic Dr.
San Jose, CA 95124

Tel:	(408) 559-7778
Fax:	(408) 559-7778

Public Affairs and Related Activities Personnel

At Headquarters

GIANELLI, Silvia E.
Director, Integrated Marketing
silvia.gianelli@xilinx.com

Tel:	(408) 626-4328
Fax:	(408) 559-7114

GLASER, Steve
Senior Vice President, Corporate Strategy and Marketing Group

Tel:	(408) 559-7778
Fax:	(408) 559-7114

HOVER-SMOOT, Scott
Corporate Vice President, General Counsel and Secretary

Tel:	(408) 559-7778
Fax:	(408) 559-7114

MEYER, Marilyn Stiborek
Senior Vice President, Human Resources

Tel:	(408) 559-7778
Fax:	(408) 559-7114

OLSON, Jon
Executive Vice President and Chief Financial Officer

Tel:	(408) 559-7778
Fax:	(408) 559-7114

OWEN, Lori
Director, Investor Relations
ir@xilinx.com

Tel:	(408) 879-6911
Fax:	(408) 371-2942

RANGASAYEE, Krishna
Senior Vice President and General Manager, Global Sales and Markets

Tel:	(408) 559-7778
Fax:	(408) 559-7114

XO Communications

Formerly named Nextlink. A provider of communications services.
www.xo.com
Employees: 3,600
SIC: 4813
Industry/ies: Communications; Telecommunications/Internet/Cable
Legislative Issues: TEC

Chief Executive Officer
ANCELL, Chris

Tel:	(703) 547-2000
Fax:	(703) 547-2881

Main Headquarters

Mailing: 13865 Sunrise Valley Dr.
Herndon, VA 20171

Tel:	(703) 547-2000
Fax:	(703) 547-2881
TF:	(800) 421-3872

Political Action Committees

XO Communications PAC
FEC ID: C00342238
13865 Sunrise Valley Dr.
Herndon, VA 20171

Tel:	(703) 547-2000
Fax:	(703) 547-2881

Contributions to Candidates: $11,132,015 (2015-2016)
Democrats: $64,000; Republicans: $46,000; Other: $11,022,015

Principal Recipients

HOUSE
MATSUI, DORIS (DEM-CA)

Public Affairs and Related Activities Personnel

At Headquarters

DRAGISICH, Dominic
Chief Financial Officer

Tel:	(703) 547-2000
Fax:	(703) 547-2881

FARMER, David
Contact, Media Relations
david.g.farmer@xo.com

Tel:	(703) 547-2219
Fax:	(703) 547-2881

HAGHIGHI, Navid
Executive Vice President, General Counsel and Secretary

Tel:	(703) 547-2000
Fax:	(703) 547-2881

HEINZ, Jake
Senior Vice President, Marketing and Product

Tel:	(703) 547-2000
Fax:	(703) 547-2881

JUNG, Kristi
Vice President, Treasurer, Lobbyist and PAC Treasurer

Tel:	(703) 547-2000
Fax:	(703) 547-2881

LUCERO, Amador
Chief Operating Officer

Tel:	(703) 547-2000
Fax:	(703) 547-2881

SCHAFFER, Maureen
Vice President, Human Resources

Tel:	(703) 547-2000
Fax:	(703) 547-2881

THOMPSON, Patrick
Director, Legislative Affairs
Patrick.Thompson@xo.com
Registered Federal Lobbyist

Tel:	(703) 547-2214
Fax:	(703) 547-2881

YOUNGERS, Lisa R.
Vice. President, Federal Affairs
lisa.r.youngers@xo.com

Tel:	(703) 547-2356
Fax:	(703) 547-2881

XOMA, LLC

A manufacturer of recombinant proteins and peptides, in partnership with big pharmas.
www.xoma.com
Annual Revenues: $18.11 million

Employees: 181
Ticker: NASDAQ: XOMA
Industry/ies: Pharmaceutical Industry

Chairman of the Board and Lead Independent Director
NESS , W. Denman Van

Tel:	(510) 204-7200
Fax:	(302) 655-5049

Chief Executive Officer
VARIAN, John

Tel:	(510) 204-7200
Fax:	(302) 655-5049

Main Headquarters

Mailing: 2910 Seventh St.
Berkeley, CA 94710

Tel:	(510) 204-7200
Fax:	(302) 655-5049

Public Affairs and Related Activities Personnel

At Headquarters

BARRETO, Ashleigh
Contact, Investor Relations
barreto@xoma.com

Tel:	(510) 204-7200
Fax:	(302) 655-5049

BURNS, Tom
Vice President, Finance and Chief Financial Officer

Tel:	(510) 204-7200
Fax:	(302) 655-5049

CAFARO, Dan
Vice President Regulatory Affairs and Compliance
cafaro@xoma.com

Tel:	(510) 204-7456
Fax:	(302) 655-5049

NEAL, Jim
Vice President, Business Development

Tel:	(510) 204-7200
Fax:	(302) 655-5049

RADA, Beth
Senior Director, Government Affairs

Tel:	(510) 204-7456
Fax:	(302) 655-5049

SCANNON, Pat
Founder / Executive Vice President / Chief Scientific Officer
scannon@xoma.com

Tel:	(510) 204-7456
Fax:	(302) 655-5049

WELLS, Charles C.
Vice President, Human Resources and Information Technology

Tel:	(510) 204-7200
Fax:	(302) 655-5049

Yahoo! Inc.

An internet communications company headquartered in Sunnyvale, CA.
info.yahoo.com
Annual Revenues: $4.71 billion
Employees: 12,500
Ticker: NASDAQ: YHOO
SIC: 7373
Industry/ies: Computer/Technology
Legislative Issues: ADV; CPI; CPT; CSP; FOR; HOM; IMM; INT; TAX; TEC; TRD

Chairman of the Board
WEBB, Jr., Maynard

Tel:	(408) 349-3300
Fax:	(408) 349-3301

Chief Executive Officer, President and Director
MAYER, Marissa

Tel:	(408) 349-3300
Fax:	(408) 349-3301

Main Headquarters

Mailing: 701 First Ave.
Sunnyvale, CA 94089-0703

Tel:	(408) 349-3300
Fax:	(408) 349-3301

Washington Office

Mailing: 101 Constitution Ave. NW
Suite 800 West
Washington, DC 20001

Tel:	(202) 777-1050
Fax:	(202) 777-1051

Political Action Committees

Yahoo! Inc. PAC
FEC ID: C00380535
Contact: Margaret Stewart Nagle
101 Constitution Ave. NW
Suite 800 West
Washington, DC 20001

Tel:	(202) 777-1050
Fax:	(202) 777-1051

Contributions to Candidates: $119,600 (2015-2016)
Democrats: $59,500; Republicans: $60,100

Public Affairs and Related Activities Personnel

At Headquarters

ARMSTRONG, Lauren
Manager, Corporate Communications

Tel:	(408) 349-3300
Fax:	(408) 349-3301

BELL, Ron
General Counsel and Secretary

Tel:	(408) 349-3300
Fax:	(408) 349-3301

BERG, Mara
Associate, Public Relations

Tel:	(408) 349-3300
Fax:	(408) 349-3301

GOLDMAN, Ken
Chief Financial Officer

Tel:	(408) 349-3300
Fax:	(408) 349-3301

HUH, Joon
Vice President, Finance and Investor Relations
investorrelations@yahoo-inc.com

Tel:	(408) 349-3382
Fax:	(408) 349-3301

POWER, Bryan
Senior Vice President, Human Resources

Tel:	(408) 349-3300
Fax:	(408) 349-3301

SAVITT, Kathy
Chief Marketing Officer and Head, Media Relations

Tel:	(408) 349-3300
Fax:	(408) 349-3301

At Washington Office

ALEXANDER, Nick
Federal Lobbyist
Registered Federal Lobbyist
Tel: (202) 777-1050
Fax: (202) 777-1051

ASHWORTH, Bill
Senior Director, State Government Affairs
billashw@yahoo-inc.com
Tel: (202) 777-1050
Fax: (202) 777-1051

BOYD, April
Head, Global Public Policy
Tel: (202) 777-1050
Fax: (202) 777-1051

GRAHAM, Leah Harrelson
Registered Federal Lobbyist
Tel: (202) 777-1050
Fax: (202) 777-1051

HARRELSON, Leah
Manager, Government Affairs
Registered Federal Lobbyist
Tel: (202) 777-1050
Fax: (202) 777-1051

MAWAKANA, Tekedra
Deputy General Counsel & Vice President, Global Public Policy
Tel: (202) 777-1050
Fax: (202) 777-1051

MORTIER, Nicole
Director, Federal Government Affairs
Registered Federal Lobbyist
Tel: (202) 777-1050
Fax: (202) 777-1051

NAGLE, Margaret Stewart
Head, U.S. Government Affairs
margaretstewart91@yahoo.com
Registered Federal Lobbyist
Tel: (202) 777-1050
Fax: (202) 777-1051

Yale-New Haven Health Services Corporation

A provider of healthcare support services.
yalenewhavenhealth.org
Industry/ies: Medicine/Health Care/Mental Health
Legislative Issues: DIS; HCR

President and Chief Executive Officer
BORGSTROM, Marna P.

Main Headquarters
Mailing: 789 Howard Ave.
New Haven, CT 06519

Public Affairs and Related Activities Personnel

At Headquarters
CAPOZZALO, Gayle L.
Executive Vice President, Strategy and System Development

MYATT, Kevin
Senior Vice President, Human Resources

O'CONNOR, Christopher M
Executive Vice President and Chief Operating Officer

STATEN, James M.
Executive Vice President, Corporate and Financial Services

Yelp

Yelp, inc. is an international company which operates an online review and local business search site.
Industry/ies: Computer/Technology; Food And Beverage Industry; Food Industry; Resturants/Catering/Food
Legislative Issues: CIV; CPI; LBR

Main Headquarters
Mailing: 140 New Montgomery St.
San Francisco, CA 94105

Political Action Committees
Yelp, Inc. PAC
FEC ID:
Contact: Joel Edelmann
140 New Montgomery St.
Floor 9
San Francisco, 94105

Public Affairs and Related Activities Personnel

At Headquarters
CRENSHAW, Laurent
Lobbyist
Tel: (415) 908-3801

EDELMANN, Joel
PAC Contact
Tel: (415) 908-3801

YGOMI, LLC

An international technology services company, headquartered in Oak Brook, IL with an office in Washington, DC, operating through five information and communications subsidiaries: ArrayComm, Connexis, SEI, Verety, and VSI.
www.ygomi.com
Annual Revenues: $2.10 million
Industry/ies: Computer/Technology

Chairman of the Board
SHIELDS, Russell
Tel: (701) 293-2650
Fax: (701) 235-0257

Main Headquarters
Mailing: 701 DeMers Ave.
Tel: (701) 335-2730

Third Floor
Grand Forks, ND 58201

Washington Office
Mailing: 601 Pennsylvania Ave. NW
Suite 900, South Bldg.
Washington, DC 20004
Tel: (202) 680-2430

Public Affairs and Related Activities Personnel

At Headquarters
GOMI, Yuka
President
yuka@ygomi.com
Tel: (701) 235-0257

SCIALOM, Errol
Chief Financial Officer

At Washington Office
WATERHOUSE, Desmarie M.
Director, Government Affairs
Tel: (202) 680-2430

York International Corporation

Heating, ventilation, air conditioning and refrigeration (HVAC&R) supplier. Acquired by Johnson Controls Company in December 2005.
www.york.com
Annual Revenues: $1.1 billion
SIC: 3585; 5075
NAICS: 333415; 42173
Industry/ies: Heating And Air Conditioning

Chairman and Chief Executive Officer
BARTH, John M.
Tel: (717) 771-7890
Fax: (717) 771-7381

Chairman of the Board
MCDONOUGH, Gerald
Tel: (717) 771-7890
Fax: (717) 771-7381

Main Headquarters
Mailing: P.O. Box 1592
York, PA 17405
Tel: (717) 771-7890
Fax: (717) 771-7381
TF: (877) 967-5768

Corporate Foundations and Giving Programs
York International Corporate Contributions Program
P.O. Box 1592
York, PA 17405
Tel: (717) 771-7890
Fax: (717) 771-7381
TF: (877) 967-5768

Yorktown Group LLC

Public policy consulting.
www.yorktownmanagementconsulting.com
Industry/ies: Consultants

Management Consultant, President and Owner
ALGER, Christopher
wcalger@gmail.com
Tel: (412) 721-8954
Fax: (724) 942-6944

Main Headquarters
Mailing: Yorktown Rd.
Suite 119
McMurray, PA 15317
Tel: (412) 721-8954
Fax: (724) 942-6944

Washington Office
Mailing: 1701 Pennsylvania Ave. NW
Suite 300
Washington, DC 20006

Public Affairs and Related Activities Personnel

At Washington Office
ABEGG, Heidi K.
Tel: (202) 494-0202

WOOTTON, James M.
jwootton@nationscourt.com
Registered Federal Lobbyist
Tel: (202) 494-0202

Yukon-Kuskokwim Health Corporation

YKHC is a Tribal Organization. A comprehensive health care delivery system for 58 rural communities in southwest Alaska including community clinics, sub regional clinics, a regional hospital, dental services, mental health services, substance abuse counseling and treatment, health promotion and disease prevention programs, and environmental health services.
www.ykhc.org
Employees: 1,600
Industry/ies: Medicine/Health Care/Mental Health
Legislative Issues: BUD; IND

Chairman of the Board
TWITCHELL, Jr., Esai
Tel: (907) 543-6000

President and Chief Executive Officer
WINKELMAN, Dan
Tel: (907) 543-6000

Main Headquarters
Mailing: P.O. Box 528
Bethel, AK 99559
Tel: (907) 543-6000
TF: (800) 478-3321

Public Affairs and Related Activities Personnel

At Headquarters

BACH, Donna — Tel: (907) 543-6037
Director, Public Relations
Donna_Bach@ykhc.org

TOMPKINS, Tommy — Tel: (907) 543-6000
Chief Financial Officer

TRENIER, Darlene — Tel: (907) 543-6000
Vice President, Workforce Development

Yum! Brands

A restaurant company. Formerly known as Tricon Global Restaurants.
www.yum.com
Annual Revenues: $13.10 billion
Employees: 505,000
Ticker: NYSE: YUM
SIC: 5812
Industry/ies: Food And Beverage Industry
Legislative Issues: ENG; FIN; FOO; HCR; LBR; TAX; TRD

Chairman of the Board and Chief Executive Officer — Tel: (502) 874-8300
NOVAK, David C. — Fax: (502) 874-2410
David.novak@yum.com

Main Headquarters
Mailing: 1900 Colonel Sanders Ln. — Tel: (502) 874-8300
Louisville, KY 40213 — Fax: (502) 874-2410

Political Action Committees
Yum! Brands Inc. Good Government Fund PAC
FEC ID: C00329474
Contact: D. Brett Hale
1441 Gardiner Ln. — Tel: (502) 874-8300
Third Floor, Mail Stop L2230 — Fax: (502) 874-8790
Louisville, KY 40213

    Contributions to Candidates: $47,250 (2015-2016)
    Democrats: $1,000; Republicans: $46,250

Corporate Foundations and Giving Programs
Yum! Brands Foundation
1441 Gardiner Ln. — Tel: (502) 874-8300
Louisville, KY 40213 — Fax: (502) 874-8790

Public Affairs and Related Activities Personnel

At Headquarters

BLUM, Jonathan D. — Tel: (502) 874-8300
Senior Vice President, Chief Public Affairs Officer and Global — Fax: (502) 874-2410
Nutrition Officer

BYERLEIN, Anne P. — Tel: (502) 874-8300
Chief People Officer — Fax: (502) 874-2410
anne.byerlein@yum.com

FERGUSON, Virginia — Tel: (502) 874-8200
Director, Public Relations — Fax: (502) 874-2410

GRENFELL, Elizabeth — Tel: (502) 874-8300
Director, Investor Relations — Fax: (502) 874-2410

LATHROP, Matthew — Tel: (502) 874-8300
Director, Government and Community Affairs — Fax: (502) 874-2410
Registered Federal Lobbyist

SCHMITT, Steve — Tel: (502) 874-8300
Vice President Investor Relations and Corporate Strategy — Fax: (502) 874-2410

At Other Offices

CAMPBELL, Christian L. — Tel: (502) 874-8300
Senior Vice President, General Counsel, Secretary and Chief — Fax: (502) 874-8790
Franchise Policy Officer
1441 Gardiner Ln.
Louisville, KY 40213

HALE, D. Brett — Tel: (502) 874-8300
Vice President, Government Affairs — Fax: (502) 874-8790
1441 Gardiner Ln.
Louisville, KY 40213
Registered Federal Lobbyist

SHERWOOD, Amy — Tel: (502) 874-8200
Vice President, Public Relations — Fax: (502) 874-8790
1441 Gardiner Ln.
Louisville, KY 40213

Zachry Holdings

A builder and maintainer of facilities in power, cement and nuclear sectors.
www.zhi.com
Employees: 11,500
SIC: 1629; 1622; 1611; 1542; 1541
NAICS: 237990; 237310; 236220; 236210
Industry/ies: Construction/Construction Materials
Legislative Issues: ENV; IMM; TAX; UTI

Chairman of the Board and Chief Executive Officer — Tel: (210) 588-5000
ZACHRY, John B. — Fax: (210) 475-8060

Main Headquarters
Mailing: 527 Logwood Ave. — Tel: (210) 588-5000
San Antonio, TX 78221 — Fax: (210) 475-8060

Political Action Committees
Continuum Fund Of Zachry Holdings Inc PAC
FEC ID: C00471565
Contact: Glenn Kloos
527 Logwood Ave.
San Antonio, TX 78221

    Contributions to Candidates: $54,000 (2015-2016)
    Democrats: $6,000; Republicans: $48,000

Corporate Foundations and Giving Programs
Zachry Contributions Program
527 Logwood Ave.
San Antonio, TX 78221

Public Affairs and Related Activities Personnel

At Headquarters

DUFFY, Scott — Tel: (210) 588-5000
Senior Vice President, Enterprise Strategic Development — Fax: (210) 475-8060

GOFF, Colleen Mullen — Tel: (210) 588-5000
Vice President, General Counsel — Fax: (210) 475-8060

KLOOS, Glenn — Tel: (210) 588-5000
PAC Treasurer — Fax: (210) 475-8060

LOZANO, Joe J. — Tel: (210) 588-5000
Executive Vice President, Accounting and Administration — Fax: (210) 475-8060

MALLAISE, Tammy — Tel: (210) 588-5000
Vice President, Employee Relations — Fax: (210) 475-8060

MANNING, Keith D. — Tel: (210) 588-5000
Executive Vice President, Enterprise Strategic Development — Fax: (210) 475-8060

MCDONALD, D. Kirk — Tel: (210) 588-5000
Executive Vice President, Finance — Fax: (210) 475-8060

PARK, Randy — Tel: (210) 588-5000
Senior Vice President, Employee Relations — Fax: (210) 475-8060

SCHWAB, David — Tel: (210) 588-5000
Senior Vice President, General Counsel and Secretary — Fax: (210) 475-8060

Zalicus Inc.

Zalicus Inc. discovers and develops novel treatments for patients suffering from pain and immuno-inflammatory diseases.
www.zalicus.com
Annual Revenues: $13.90 million
Employees: 36
Ticker: NASDAQ: ZLCS
SIC: 2834
Industry/ies: Science; Scientific Research

Chairman of the Board — Tel: (617) 301-7000
HAYDU, Frank — Fax: (617) 301-7010

President and Chief Executive Officer — Tel: (617) 301-7000
CORRIGAN, MD, Mark H.N. — Fax: (617) 301-7010

Main Headquarters
Mailing: 245 First St. — Tel: (617) 301-7000
Third Floor — Fax: (617) 301-7010
Cambridge, MA 02142

Corporate Foundations and Giving Programs
Zalicus Contributions Program
245 First St.
Third Floor — Tel: (617) 301-7000
Cambridge, MA 02142 — Fax: (617) 301-7010

Public Affairs and Related Activities Personnel

At Headquarters

COLE, Esq., Jason F. — Tel: (617) 301-7000
Executive Vice President, Corporate Development, General — Fax: (617) 301-7010
Counsel and Secretary

NUGENT, Gina — Tel: (857) 753-6562
Vice President, Corporate Communications and Investor — Fax: (617) 301-7010
Relations
gnugent@combinatorx.com

RENZ, Justin — Tel: (617) 301-7575
Executive Vice President, Chief Financial Officer and — Fax: (617) 301-7010
Treasurer
JRenz@zalicus.com

Zebra Imaging, Inc.

A company that makes digitally-mastered, full color holographic images that can be scaled to any size.
www.zebraimaging.com
Industry/ies: Architecture And Design
Legislative Issues: BUD; DEF; FOR; HOM

Chairman of the Board — Tel: (512) 251-5100

WARGO, Albert E.
President and Chief Executive Officer   Tel: (512) 251-5100
SCULLION, Chuck

Main Headquarters
Mailing: 9802 Metric Blvd.   Tel: (512) 251-5100
            Suite 300   TF: (888) 772-4062
            Austin, TX 78758-5455

Public Affairs and Related Activities Personnel

At Headquarters

ANDERSON, Robert G   Tel: (512) 251-5100
Chief Financial Officer & Secretary
banderson@zebraimaging.com

DANNENBRINK, Stacey   Tel: (512) 251-5100
Controller

GARDNER, James   Tel: (512) 251-5100
Vice President, Defense Programs

HILL, Brian G.   Tel: (512) 251-5100
Chief Operating Officer

Zebra Technologies Corporation

Designs, manufactures, and sells various printers and related products.
www.zebra.com
Annual Revenues: $3.61 billion
Employees: 7,000
Ticker: NASDAQ: ZBRA
SIC: 3560
Industry/ies: Printing Industry
Legislative Issues: CPI; CPT; CSP; DEF; GOV; HCR; HOM; IMM; INT; MMM; SCI;
TEC; TRA; TRD; VET

Chairman of the Board   Tel: (847) 634-6700
SMITH, Michael A.   Fax: (847) 913-8766

Chief Executive Officer   Tel: (847) 634-6700
GUSTAFSSON, Anders   Fax: (847) 913-8766

Main Headquarters
Mailing: Three Overlook Point   Tel: (847) 634-6700
            Lincolnshire, IL 60069   Fax: (847) 913-8766
                                                    TF: (866) 230-9494

Corporate Foundations and Giving Programs

Zebra Technologies Corporation Contributions Program
475 Half Day Rd.
Suite 500
Lincolnshire, IL 60069

Public Affairs and Related Activities Personnel

At Headquarters

ABELSON, Bill   Tel: (917) 952-2551
Contact, Media   Fax: (847) 913-8766
Bill.abelson@zebra.com

CHO, Michael   Tel: (847) 634-6700
Senior Vice President, Corporate Development   Fax: (847) 913-8766

FLAHERTY, Patrick   Tel: (847) 793-5592
Manager, Investor Relations   Fax: (847) 913-8766
pflaherty@zebra.com

FOX, CFA, Douglas A.   Tel: (847) 793-6735
Vice President, Investor Relations and Treasurer   Fax: (847) 913-8766
dfox@zebra.com

HEEL, Joachim   Tel: (847) 634-6700
Senior Vice President, Global Sales   Fax: (847) 913-8766

KAPUT, Jim L.   Tel: (847) 634-6700
Senior Vice President, General Counsel and Secretary Fax: (847) 913-8766

KNEISLER, Stephanie   Tel: (847) 634-6700
Manager, Executive Business Communications   Fax: (847) 913-8766
skneisler@zebra.com

LARIMER, Juliann S.   Tel: (847) 634-6700
Vice President and General Manager   Fax: (847) 913-8766

LINDROTH, Dean   Tel: (847) 634-6700
Vice President, Finance   Fax: (847) 913-8766
pflaherty@zebra.com

SCHMITZ, Jeff   Tel: (847) 634-6700
Chief Marketing Officer   Fax: (847) 913-8766

SMILEY, Michael C.   Tel: (847) 634-6700
Chief Financial Officer and Treasurer   Fax: (847) 913-8766

TERZICH, Michael H.   Tel: (847) 634-6700
Chief Administrative Officer   Fax: (847) 913-8766

Zenith Electronics Corporation

Manufacturer of home electronics.
www.zenith.com
Employees: 1,000

SIC: 3651
Industry/ies: Electricity & Electronics; Electronics; Energy/Electricity
Legislative Issues: ENV; MAN; TEC

Main Headquarters
Mailing: 2000 Millbrook Dr.   Tel: (847) 941-8000
            Lincolnshire, IL 60069   Fax: (847) 941-8200
                                                    TF: (877) 993-6484

Public Affairs and Related Activities Personnel

At Headquarters

LEWIS, Richard   Tel: (847) 941-8000
Senior Vice President and Contact, Business Development Fax: (847) 941-8200
richard.lewis@zenith.com

TAYLOR, John   Tel: (847) 941-8181
Contact, Media Relations   Fax: (847) 941-8200
john.taylor@zenith.com

Zephyr Photonics

An optoelectronics research and development company. It has developed innovative and
advanced photonic solutions for government agencies, communication companies, and defense
prime contractors.
www.zephyrphotonics.com
Annual Revenues: $1.60 million
Employees: 30
Industry/ies: Electricity & Electronics; Electronics; Energy/Electricity

Chairman of the Board   Tel: (775) 588-4176
KAPPES, Stephen R.   Fax: (775) 588-1348

President and Chief Technology Officer   Tel: (775) 588-4176
LOUDERBACK, PhD, Dr. Duane   Fax: (775) 588-1348

Main Headquarters
Mailing: 215 Elks Point Rd.   Tel: (775) 588-4176
            P.O. Box 10779   Fax: (775) 588-1348
            Zephyr Cove, NV 89448

Public Affairs and Related Activities Personnel

At Headquarters

MANNING, Chris   Tel: (775) 588-4176
Corporate Controller   Fax: (775) 588-1348

MCALLISTER, Tim   Tel: (707) 529-4694
Vice President, Business Development   Fax: (775) 588-1348
sales@zephyrphotonics.com

O'LEARY, Scott   Tel: (775) 588-4176
Chief Operating Officer   Fax: (775) 588-1348

THOMAS, Terry   Tel: (408) 646-7770
Executive Vice President, Business Development   Fax: (775) 588-1348

WILSON, Kevin   Tel: (513) 898-1008
Contact, Media Relations   Fax: (775) 588-1348
kevin@wilsonpr.com

ZF TRW

An automotive supplier. In 2015, TRW Automotive was acquired by global automobile
supplier ZF Friedrichshafen AG. ZF TRW is now a division of the parent company. It is a
developer and producer of active and passive safety systems and serves all major vehicle
manufacturers worldwide.
www.trw.com
Annual Revenues: $17.54 billion
Employees: 78,900
Ticker: NYSE: TRW
SIC: 3714
Industry/ies: Automotive Industry; Transportation
Legislative Issues: AUT

Chairman of ZF TRW   Tel: (734) 855-2600
KLEINER, Dr. Franz   Fax: (734) 855-3345

President and Chief Executive Officer   Tel: (734) 855-2600
PLANT, John C.   Fax: (734) 855-3345
John.plant@trw.com

Main Headquarters
Mailing: 12001 Tech Center Dr.   Tel: (734) 855-2600
            Livonia, MI 48150   Fax: (734) 855-3345

Political Action Committees
TRW Automotive Inc. Good Government Fund (TRW Good Government Fund)
PAC
FEC ID: C00025536
Contact: Robin Walker-Lee
12001 Tech Center Dr.   Tel: (734) 855-2600
Livonia, MI 48150   Fax: (734) 855-2999

Public Affairs and Related Activities Personnel

At Headquarters

CANTIE, Joseph S   Tel: (734) 855-2600
Executive Vice President and Chief Financial Officer Fax: (734) 855-3345

LAKE, Peter J.   Tel: (734) 855-2600
Executive Vice President, Sales and Business Development   Fax: (734) 855-3345

MARCHUK, Neil E.   Tel: (734) 855-2600
Executive Vice President, Human Resources, Information   Fax: (734) 855-3345
Technology, Legal, Compliance & Governance, Health, Safety
& Environment, and Facilities

OLNEY, Patrick   Tel: (734) 855-2600
Executive Vice President and Chief Operating Officer   Fax: (734) 855-3345

WALKER-LEE, Robin   Tel: (734) 855-2600
Executive Vice President, General Counsel and Secretary and   Fax: (734) 855-3345
PAC Treasurer

WILKERSON, John   Tel: (734) 855-3864
Senior Communications Manager   Fax: (734) 855-2450
john.wilkerson@trw.com

Zimmer Biomet

Musculoskeletal health care and innovative and personalized joint-replacement technologies.
www.zimmer.com
Annual Revenues: $4.65 billion
Employees: 9,500
Ticker: NYSE: ZMH
SIC: 3842
Industry/ies: Medicine/Health Care/Mental Health
Legislative Issues: BUD; HCR; MMM; TAX; TRD

Chairman of the Board   Tel: (800) 613-6131
GLASSCOCK, Larry C.   Fax: (574) 371-8755

President and Chief Executive Officer   Tel: (574) 267-6639
BINDER, Jeffrey R.   Fax: (574) 267-8137

President and Chief Executive Officer   Tel: (800) 613-6131
DVORAK, David C.   Fax: (574) 371-8755

Main Headquarters
Mailing: P.O. Box 708   Tel: (800) 613-6131
     1800 W. Center St.   Fax: (574) 371-8755
     Warsaw, IN 46581-0708   TF: (800) 348-2759

Washington Office
Mailing: 801 Pennsylvania Ave. NW
     Suite 330
     Washington, DC 20004

Political Action Committees
Zimmer Inc Better Government Committee (Federal)
FEC ID: C00399386
Contact: Christopher A. Cerone
P.O. Box 708
1800 W. Center St.
Warsaw, IN 46581-0708

   Contributions to Candidates: $66,500 (2015-2016)
   Democrats: $7,000; Republicans: $59,500

Corporate Foundations and Giving Programs
Biomet Foundation
56 E. Bell Dr.   Tel: (574) 267-6639
P.O. Box 587
Warsaw, IN 46581

Zimmer Contributions Program
P.O. Box 708
1800 W. Center St.
Warsaw, IN 46581-0708

Public Affairs and Related Activities Personnel

At Headquarters

CERONE, Christopher A.   Tel: (800) 613-6131
Vice President, Global Government Affairs and PAC Treasurer   Fax: (574) 371-8755
Mail Stop 345 E. Main St.
chris.cerone@zimmer.com
Registered Federal Lobbyist

CRINES, James T.   Tel: (800) 613-6131
Executive Vice President, Finance and Chief Financial Officer   Fax: (574) 371-8755

CUCOLO, Joseph A.   Tel: (800) 613-6131
President, Americas Sales   Fax: (574) 371-8755

DAVIS, Derek   Tel: (800) 613-6131
Vice President, Finance and Corporate Controller and Chief   Fax: (574) 371-8755
Accounting Officer

FISHER, William P.   Tel: (800) 613-6131
Senior Vice President, Global Human Resources   Fax: (574) 371-8755

GILL, Jim   Tel: (574) 371-1984
Contact, Media   Fax: (574) 371-8755
james.gill@zimmer.com

HWANG, Nathaniel H.   Tel: (800) 613-6131
Compliance Officer and Senior Healthcare Counsel   Fax: (574) 371-8755

MARSHALL, Jr., CFA, Robert J.   Tel: (800) 613-6131
Vice President, Investor Relations and Treasurer   Fax: (574) 371-8755

NYAKAKO, Emmanuel   Tel: (800) 613-6131
Senior Vice President, Global Quality and Regulatory Affairs   Fax: (574) 371-8755

PHIPPS, Chad F.   Tel: (800) 613-6131
Senior Vice President, General Counsel and Secretary   Fax: (574) 371-8755

STAIR , Richard C.   Tel: (800) 613-6131
Senior Vice President, Global Operations and Logistics   Fax: (574) 371-8755

At Washington Office

TULL, Whitney
Federal Lobbyist
Registered Federal Lobbyist

At Other Offices

BARNEY, Robin T.   Tel: (574) 267-6639
Senior Vice President, Worldwide Operations   Fax: (574) 267-8137
56 E. Bell Dr., P.O. Box 587
Warsaw, IN 46581-0587

FLORIN, Daniel P.   Tel: (574) 267-6639
Senior Vice President and Chief Financial Officer   Fax: (574) 267-8137
56 E. Bell Dr., P.O. Box 587
Warsaw, IN 46581-0587

GOSLEE, Barbara   Tel: (574) 372-1514
Director, Corporate Communications   Fax: (574) 267-8137
56 E. Bell Dr., P.O. Box 587
Warsaw, IN 46581-0587

GRANDON, Jonathan M.   Tel: (574) 267-6639
Senior Vice President and General Counsel   Fax: (574) 267-8137
56 E. Bell Dr., P.O. Box 587
Warsaw, IN 46581-0587

KLEOPFER, Stuart G.   Tel: (574) 267-6639
President   Fax: (574) 267-8137
56 E. Bell Dr., P.O. Box 587
Warsaw, IN 46581-0587

KOLTER, William C.   Tel: (574) 372-1932
Corporate Vice President, Government Affairs   Fax: (574) 267-8137
56 E. Bell Dr., P.O. Box 587
Warsaw, IN 46581-0587
bill.Kolter@Biomet.com

PLUMLEE, Millard P.   Tel: (574) 267-6639
Associate General Counsel, Biomet, Inc.   Fax: (574) 267-8137
56 E. Bell Dr., P.O. Box 587
Warsaw, IN 46581-0587

TAYLOR, Peggy   Tel: (574) 267-6639
Senior Vice President, Human Resources   Fax: (574) 267-8137
56 E. Bell Dr., P.O. Box 587
Warsaw, IN 46581-0587
Peggy.Taylor@biomet.com

Zions Bancorporation

A financial services company consisting of a collection of banks in growth markets.
www.zionsbancorporation.com
Annual Revenues: $2.04 billion
Employees: 10,092
Ticker: NASDAQ: ZION
SIC: 6021
Industry/ies: Banking/Finance/Investments
Legislative Issues: BAN; SMB

Chairman of the Board and Chief Executive Officer   Tel: (801) 524-4787
SIMMONS, Harris H.   Fax: (801) 524-4805

Main Headquarters
Mailing: One S. Main St.   Tel: (801) 524-4787
     Salt Lake City, UT 84133-1109   Fax: (801) 524-4805
        TF: (800) 974-8800

Political Action Committees
Zions Bancorporation PAC
FEC ID: C00275230
Contact: Steven Earley
180 North University Ave
STE 300
Provo, UT 84601

   Contributions to Candidates: $29,700 (2015-2016)
   Democrats: $2,500; Republicans: $27,200

Public Affairs and Related Activities Personnel

At Headquarters

ABBOTT, James R.   Tel: (801) 844-7637
Senior Vice President, Investor Relations and External   Fax: (801) 524-4805
Communications
james.abbott@zionsbancorp

BURDISS, Paul E.   Tel: (801) 524-4787
Chief Financial Officer   Fax: (801) 524-4805

JAMES, Dianne R.   Tel: (801) 524-4787
Executive Vice President, Chief Human Resources   Fax: (801) 524-4805

LAURSEN, Thomas E.
Executive Vice President and General Counsel
Tel: (801) 524-4787
Fax: (801) 524-4805

LEE, Alvin
Senior Vice President, Corporate Development
Tel: (801) 524-4787
Fax: (801) 524-4805

MCLEAN, Scott J.
President and Chief Operating Officer
Tel: (801) 524-4787
Fax: (801) 524-4805

MERRITT, Norman W.
Executive Vice President and Director, Corporate Compliance
Tel: (801) 524-4787
Fax: (801) 524-4805

SCHREIBER, Edward P.
Executive Vice President, Chief Risk Officer
Tel: (801) 524-4787
Fax: (801) 524-4805

At Other Offices

EARLEY, Steven
PAC Treasurer
7730 Union Park Ave., Suite 350
Midvale, UT 84047

Zippo Manufacturing Company

A manufacturer of lighters.
www.zippo.com
Annual Revenues: $59.40 million
Employees: 1,000
SIC: 2499; 3421; 3423; 3634
NAICS: 332212; 321999; 332211; 339999
Industry/ies: Computer/Technology; Electricity & Electronics; Electronics; Energy/Electricity
Legislative Issues: CSP

Owner and Chairman of the Board
DUKE, George
Tel: (814) 368-2700

President and Chief Executive Officer
BOOTH, Gregory W.
Tel: (814) 368-2700

Main Headquarters
Mailing: 33 Barbour St.
Bradford, PA 16701
Tel: (814) 368-2700

Public Affairs and Related Activities Personnel

At Headquarters

ERRERA, Peggy
Manager, Corporate Communications
Tel: (814) 368-2786

GRANDY, Patrick
Manager, Marketing Communications
Tel: (814) 368-2700

PAUP, Mark
Vice President, Sales and Marketing
Tel: (814) 368-2700

RUPE, Richard
Chief Financial Officer
Tel: (814) 368-2700

ZLB Behring

See listing on page 233 under CSL Behring LLC

ZTE Corporation

A telecommunications company.
wwwen.zte.com.cn
Annual Revenues: $15.41 billion
Employees: 84,622
Ticker: OTC: ZTCOF
Industry/ies: Communications; Telecommunications/Internet/Cable
Legislative Issues: TEC; TRD

Main Headquarters
Mailing: 2425 N. Central Expwy.
Suite 600
Richardson, VA 75080
Tel: (972) 671-8885

Washington Office
Mailing: 607 Herndon Pkwy.
Suite 101
Herndon, VA 20170
Tel: (703) 956-6412

Public Affairs and Related Activities Personnel

At Washington Office

RUFFO, Peter
Director, Government Relations
Registered Federal Lobbyist
Tel: (703) 956-6412

Zurich North America

A provider of commercial property/casualty insurance.
www.zurichna.com
Annual Revenues: $5.32 million
Employees: 25
Industry/ies: Insurance Industry
Legislative Issues: AGR; ENG; FIN; GOV; INS; LBR; TAX; TRA; TRD

Chief Executive Officer
FOLEY, Mike
Tel: (847) 605-6000
Fax: (017) 005 0100

Main Headquarters

Mailing: 1400 American Ln.
Schaumburg, IL 60196
Tel: (800) 987-3373
Fax: (877) 962-2567
TF: (800) 382-2150

Washington Office
Mailing: 1201 F St. NW
Suite 950
Washington, DC 20004
Tel: (917) 534-4536

Political Action Committees
Zurich Holding Company of American Inc. Committee for Good Government (Z-PAC)
FEC ID: C00235036
Contact: MCCROCKLIN THOMAS C
1201 F St. NW
Suite 250
Washington, DC 20004
Tel: (202) 585-3100

> **Contributions to Candidates:** $92,000 (2015-2016)
> Democrats: $41,500; Republicans: $50,500

Corporate Foundations and Giving Programs
Zurich North America Contributions Program
Contact: Jillian Walsh
1400 American Ln.
Schaumburg, IL 60196
Tel: (847) 605-6000
Fax: (847) 605-6000

Public Affairs and Related Activities Personnel

At Headquarters

HOCH, Dalynn
Chief Financial Officer
Tel: (847) 605-6000
Fax: (847) 605-6403

KERRIGAN, Jr., Dennis F.
Chief Legal Officer
Tel: (847) 605-6000
Fax: (847) 605-6403

LITTLE, Brian
Head, Human Resources
Tel: (847) 605-6000
Fax: (847) 605-6403

NOWACKI, Jennifer
Director, Media & Public Relations
jennifer.nowacki@zurichna.com
Tel: (847) 605-6000
Fax: (847) 605-6403

SCHNEIDER, Jennifer
Director, Media Relations
jennifer.schneider@zurichna.com
Tel: (847) 605-6511
Fax: (877) 962-2567

WALSH, Jillian
Head of Community
jillian.walsh@zurichna.com
Tel: (847) 762-7647
Fax: (847) 605-6403

At Washington Office

KEVELIGHAN, Sean
Tel: (917) 534-4536

MCCROCKLIN, Thomas
Vice President & Head, Federal Affairs
Registered Federal Lobbyist
Tel: (917) 534-4536

MORAN, Michael
Assistant Vice President, Government Affairs
Registered Federal Lobbyist
Tel: (917) 534-4536

SEPANIK, Damian
Chief Compliance Officer
Tel: (917) 534-4536

SHEIOWITZ, Gregg
Assistant Vice President
Registered Federal Lobbyist
Tel: (917) 534-4536

THOMAS C, MCCROCKLIN
PAC Treasurer
Tel: (917) 534-4536

TRUMBULL, Will
Communication and Political Director, Federal Affairs
william.trumbull@zurichna.com
Registered Federal Lobbyist
Tel: (202) 585-3155

Industry Index

Every company in this book has been coded under subject headings that best describe the nature of the company's principal business activity.

Baseball

Beer/Brewers

Beverage Industry

Biology

Boating

Business

Computer/Technology

Computers & Databases

Conservation

Construction/Construction Materials

Disabilities

Disaster

Drug And Alcohol Abuse

Economics And Economic Development

Education

Electricity & Electronics

Electronics

Employees & Employment

Energy

Energy/Electricity

Investments/Securities Industry

Jewelry & Gems

Law Enforcement/Security

Law/Law Firms

Liquor

Machinery/Equipment

Management

Manufacturers

Marine/Maritime/Shipping

Metals

Military/Veterans

Minerals

Mining Industry

Minorities

Museums

Music See Also Bands

Native American

Natural Resources

Nonprofit

Nursing

Nutrition

Packaging

Paper And Wood Products Industry

Performing Arts/Music

Personal Care/Hygiene

Petroleum Industry

Retailers See Also Merchandising

Rubber Industry

Science

Scientific Research

Security

Shipping Industry

Small Business

Social Service/Urban Affairs

Sports See Also Specific Sport

Telephones

Testing

Textiles

Tobacco Industry

Trade (Foreign And Domestic)

Transportation

Travel/Tourism/Lodging

Trucking Industry

Utilities

Waste

Geographic Index

All companies are listed here according to the location of their headquarters offices.

The listings in this index are arranged as follows:

- alphabetically by state
- alphabetically by city within state
- alphabetically by company name within city within state

Florida

Alachua

Belleview

Boca Raton

Bradenton

Cape Canaveral

Clearwater

Clewiston

Coral Gables

Daytona Beach

Deerfield Beach

Minnesota

New Hampshire

New Jersey

North Carolina